MAJOR 20th- CENTURY WRITERS

MAJOR 20th-CENTURY WRITERS

A Selection of Sketches from
Contemporary Authors

Contains more than one thousand entries on the most widely studied twentieth-century writers, all originally written or updated for this set.

First Edition

Bryan Ryan, Editor

Volume 2: E–K

Gale Research Inc. · DETROIT · LONDON

STAFF

Bryan Ryan, **Editor**

Marilyn K. Basel, Barbara Carlisle Bigelow, Christa Brelin, Carol Lynn DeKane, Janice E. Drane,
Kevin S. Hile, Thomas Kozikowski, Sharon Malinowski, Emily J. McMurray,
Michael E. Mueller, Kenneth R. Shepherd, Les Stone, Diane Telgen,
Polly A. Vedder, and Thomas Wiloch, **Associate Editors**

Marian Gonsior, Katherine Huebl, James F. Kamp, Margaret Mazurkiewicz,
Jani Prescott, and Neil R. Schlager, **Assistant Editors**

Anne Janette Johnson, Donna Olendorf, and Curtis Skinner, **Contributing Sketchwriters**

Hal May, **Senior Editor,** *Contemporary Authors*

Mary Rose Bonk, **Research Supervisor, Biography Division**

Jane Cousins, Andrew Guy Malonis, and Norma Sawaya, **Editorial Associates**

Reginald A. Carlton, Shirley Gates, Sharon McGilvray,
Diane Linda Sevigny, and Tracey Head Turbett, **Editorial Assistants**

Mary Beth Trimper, **Production Manager**
Evi Seoud, **Assistant Production Manager**

Arthur Chartow, **Art Director**
Kathleen A. Mouzakis, **Graphic Designer**
C. J. Jonik, **Keyliner**

∞™ This book is printed on acid-free paper that meets the minimum requirements of American National Standard for Information Sciences Permanence Paper for Printed Library Materials, ANSI Z39.48-1984.

♻ This book is printed on recycled paper that meets Environmental Protection Agency standards.

Library of Congress Catalog Card Number: 90-84380
ISBN 0-8103-7766-7 (Set)
ISBN 0-8103-7913-9 (Volume 2)

Printed in the United States of America.

Published simultaneously in the United Kingdom
by Gale Research International Limited
(An affiliated company of Gale Research Inc.)

CONTENTS

INTRODUCTION

An Important Information Source on 20th-Century Literature and Culture

Major 20th-Century Writers provides students, educators, librarians, researchers, and general readers with an affordable and comprehensive source of biographical and bibliographical information on more than 1,000 of the most influential authors of our time. Of primary focus are novelists, short story writers, poets, and dramatists from the United States and the United Kingdom, but prominent writers from over sixty other nations have also been included. Important figures from beyond the literary realm, nonfiction writers who have influenced twentieth-century thought, are also found here.

The vast majority of the entries in *Major 20th-Century Writers* were selected from Gale's acclaimed *Contemporary Authors* series and completely updated for this publication. About 40 sketches on important authors not already in *CA* were written especially for this four-volume set to furnish readers with the most comprehensive coverage possible. These newly written entries will also appear in future volumes of *Contemporary Authors*.

International Advisory Board

Before preparing *Major 20th-Century Writers*, the editors of *Contemporary Authors* conducted a telephone survey of librarians and mailed a print survey to more than four thousand libraries to help determine the kind of reference tool libraries wanted. Once it was clear that a comprehensive, yet affordable source of information on the best 20th-century writers was needed to serve small and medium-sized libraries, a wide range of resources was consulted: national surveys of books taught in American high schools and universities; British secondary school syllabi; reference works such as the *New York Public Library Desk Reference, Reading Lists for College-Bound Students: The Books Most Recommended by America's Top Colleges, The List of Books,* E. D. Hirsch's *Cultural Literacy,* and volumes in Gale's Literary Criticism series and *Dictionary of Literary Biography.*

A preliminary list of authors drawn from these sources was then sent to an advisory board of librarians and teaching professionals in both the United States and Great Britain. The recommendations made by these advisors helped define the scope of the project and the final list of authors to be included in the four-volume set. Stephen T. Willis, Social Sciences Librarian at the Manchester Central Library in Manchester, England, focused on the literary and nonliterary writers of most interest to British school libraries and public libraries, with special consideration for those authors who are relevant to the GCSE and A-level public examinations. Jacqueline G. Morris of the Indiana Department of Education provided input from an American secondary school perspective; Tim LaBorie of St. Joseph University in Philadelphia and Rev. John P. Schlegel, S.J., the Executive and Academic Vice President of John Carroll University in Cleveland, reviewed the list with college students in mind.

Broad Coverage in a Single Source

Built upon these suggestions, *Major 20th-Century Writers* provides single-source coverage of the most influential writers of our time, including:

- *Novelists and short story writers*: James Baldwin, Saul Bellow, Willa Cather, James Joyce, Franz Kafka, Thomas Mann, Flannery O'Connor, George Orwell, Eudora Welty, and Edith Wharton.

- *Dramatists*: Samuel Beckett, Bertolt Brecht, Eugene O'Neill, and Tennessee Williams.

- *Poets*: W. H. Auden, T. S. Eliot, Robert Frost, Ezra Pound, and William Butler Yeats.

- *Contemporary literary figures*: Chinua Achebe, Don DeLillo, Gabriel Garcia Marquez, Nadine Gordimer, Guenter Grass, John Irving, Toni Morrison, V. S. Naipaul, Joyce Carol Oates, and Thomas Pynchon.

- *Genre writers*: Isaac Asimov, Agatha Christie, Tom Clancy, Stephen King, Louis L'Amour, John le Carre, Ursula K. Le Guin, Danielle Steel, and J. R. R. Tolkien.

- *20th-Century thinkers*: Hannah Arendt, Bruno Bettelheim, Joseph Campbell, Albert Einstein, Sigmund Freud, Mohandas Gandhi, Margaret Mead, Jean Piaget, Bertrand Russell, and Jean-Paul Sartre.

Easy Access to Information

Both the newly written and the completely updated entries in *Major 20th-Century Writers* provide in-depth information in a format designed for ease of use. Individual paragraphs within each entry, labeled with descriptive rubrics, ensure that a reader seeking specific information can quickly focus on the pertinent portion of an entry.

A typical entry in *Major 20th-Century Writers* contains the following, clearly labeled information sections:

- *PERSONAL:* dates and places of birth and death; parents' names and occupations; name(s) of spouse(s), date(s) of marriage(s); names of children; colleges attended and degrees earned; political and religious affiliation when known.

- *ADDRESSES:* complete home, office, and agent's addresses.

- *CAREER:* name of employer, position, and dates for each career post; résumé of other vocational achievements; military service.

- *MEMBER:* memberships and offices held in professional and civic organizations.

- *AWARDS, HONORS:* literary and professional awards received and dates.

- *WRITINGS:* title-by-title chronological bibliography of books written and edited, listed by genre when known; list of other notable publications, such as plays, screenplays, and periodical contributions.

- *WORK IN PROGRESS:* description of projects in progress.

- *SIDELIGHTS:* a biographical portrait of the author's development; information about the critical reception of the author's works; revealing comments, often by the author, on personal interests, aspirations, motivations, and thoughts on writing.

- *BIOGRAPHICAL/CRITICAL SOURCES:* books, feature articles, and reviews in which the writer's work has been treated.

Nationality Index Reveals International Scope

Authors included in *Major 20th-Century Writers* appear alphabetically in an index organized by country of birth and/or citizenship. More than 60 nations are represented, reflecting the international scope of this set.

Genre/Subject Index Indicates Range of Writers' Works

The written works composed by the authors collected in this four-volume set represent not only literary novels, short stories, plays, and poems, but also over 25 other genres and subject areas of fiction and nonfiction.

Acknowledgments

The editor wishes to thank: Barbara Carlisle Bigelow for her editorial assistance; Kenneth R. Shepherd for his technical assistance; and James G. Lesniak and Susan M. Trosky, editors of the *Contemporary Authors* series, for their cooperation and assistance, and for that of their staffs.

Comments Are Appreciated

Major 20th-Century Writers is intended to serve as a useful reference tool for a wide audience, so your comments about this work are encouraged. Suggestions of authors to include in future editions of *Major 20th-Century Writers* are also welcome. Send comments and suggestions to: The Editor, *Major 20th-Century Writers*, Gale Research Inc., 835 Penobscot Bldg., Detroit, MI 48226-4094. Or, call toll-free at 1-800-347-GALE.

MAJOR 20th-CENTURY WRITERS

VOLUME 1: A-D

Abe, Kobo 1924-
Abrahams, Peter 1919-
Achebe, Chinua 1930-
Adamov, Arthur 1908-1970
Adams, Alice 1926-
Adams, Richard 1920-
Adamson, Joy 1910-1980
Adler, Mortimer J. 1902-
Adler, Renata 1938-
Agnon, S. Y. 1888-1970
Aiken, Conrad 1889-1973
Aiken, Joan 1924-
Aitmatov, Chingiz 1928-
Akhmatova, Anna 1888-1966
Albee, Edward 1928-
Alcayaga, Lucila Godoy
  See Godoy Alcayaga, Lucila
Aldiss, Brian W. 1925-
Aleixandre, Vicente 1898-1984
Alexander, Lloyd 1924-
Algren, Nelson 1909-1981
Allen, Woody 1935-
Allende, Isabel 1942-
Allingham, Margery 1904-1966
Alther, Lisa 1944-
Amado, Jorge 1912-
Ambler, Eric 1909-
Amichai, Yehuda 1924-
Amis, Kingsley 1922-
Ammons, A. R. 1926-
Anand, Mulk Raj 1905-
Anaya, Rudolfo A. 1937-
Andersch, Alfred 1914-1980
Anderson, Poul 1926-
Anderson, Sherwood 1876-1941
Andrews, V. C. ?-1986
Andric, Ivo 1892-1975
Angelou, Maya 1928-
Anouilh, Jean 1910-1987
Anthony, Piers 1934-
Antschel, Paul 1920-1970
Aragon, Louis 1897-1982
Arden, John 1930-
Arendt, Hannah 1906-1975
Armah, Ayi Kwei 1939-
Arnow, Harriette Simpson 1908-
  1986
Ashbery, John 1927-
Ashton-Warner, Sylvia 1908-1984
Asimov, Isaac 1920-

Asturias, Miguel Angel 1899-1974
Atwood, Margaret 1939-
Auchincloss, Louis 1917-
Auden, W. H. 1907-1973
Avison, Margaret 1918-
Ayckbourn, Alan 1939-
Azuela, Mariano 1873-1952
Bach, Richard 1936-
Bachman, Richard
  See King, Stephen
Bainbridge, Beryl 1933-
Baker, Russell 1925-
Baldwin, James 1924-1987
Ballard, J. G. 1930-
Bambara, Toni Cade 1939-
Baraka, Amiri 1934-
Barker, Clive 1952-
Barker, George Granville 1913-
Barnes, Djuna 1892-1982
Barnes, Peter 1931-
Barth, John 1930-
Barthelme, Donald 1931-1989
Barthes, Roland 1915-1980
Bashevis, Isaac
  See Singer, Isaac Bashevis
Bassani, Giorgio 1916-
Bates, H. E. 1905-1974
Baum, L. Frank 1856-1919
Baumbach, Jonathan 1933-
Beattie, Ann 1947-
Beauvoir, Simone de 1908-1986
Beckett, Samuel 1906-1989
Behan, Brendan 1923-1964
Bell, Clive 1881-1964
Bell, Marvin 1937-
Bellow, Saul 1915-
Benavente, Jacinto 1866-1954
Benchley, Peter 1940-
Bennett, Alan 1934-
Berger, Thomas 1924-
Berne, Eric 1910-1970
Bernhard, Thomas 1931-1989
Berryman, John 1914-1972
Bester, Alfred 1913-1987
Beti, Mongo
  See Biyidi, Alexandre
Betjeman, John 1906-1984
Bettelheim, Bruno 1903-1990
Bioy Casares, Adolfo 1914-
Birney, Earle 1904-

Bishop, Elizabeth 1911-1979
bissett, bill 1939-
Biyidi, Alexandre 1932-
Blackwood, Caroline 1931-
Blair, Eric 1903-1950
Blais, Marie-Claire 1939-
Blasco Ibanez, Vicente 1867-1928
Blish, James 1921-1975
Blixen, Karen 1885-1962
Blount, Roy, Jr. 1941-
Blume, Judy 1938-
Blunden, Edmund 1896-1974
Bly, Robert 1926-
Bodet, Jaime Torres
  See Torres Bodet, Jaime
Boell, Heinrich 1917-1985
Bogan, Louise 1897-1970
Boll, Heinrich
  See Boell, Heinrich
Bolt, Robert 1924-
Bombeck, Erma 1927-
Bond, Edward 1934-
Bonnefoy, Yves 1923-
Bontemps, Arna 1902-1973
Borges, Jorge Luis 1899-1986
Bova, Ben 1932-
Bowen, Elizabeth 1899-1973
Bowles, Paul 1910-
Boyle, Kay 1902-
Bradbury, Malcolm 1932-
Bradbury, Ray 1920-
Bradford, Barbara Taylor 1933-
Bradley, Marion Zimmer 1930-
Braine, John 1922-1986
Brautigan, Richard 1935-1984
Brecht, Bertolt 1898-1956
Brenton, Howard 1942-
Breslin, James 1930-
Breslin, Jimmy
  See Breslin, James
Breton, Andre 1896-1966
Brink, Andre 1935-
Brittain, Vera 1893(?)-1970
Brodsky, Iosif Alexandrovich 1940-
Brodsky, Joseph
  See Brodsky, Iosif Alexandrovich
Brook, Peter 1925-
Brooke, Rupert 1887-1915
Brookner, Anita 1938-
Brooks, Cleanth 1906-

Brooks, Gwendolyn 1917-
Brophy, Brigid 1929-
Brother Antoninus
    See Everson, William
Brown, Dee 1908-
Brown, George Mackay 1921-
Brown, Rita Mae 1944-
Brown, Sterling Allen 1901-1989
Brownmiller, Susan 1935-
Brunner, John 1934-
Buber, Martin 1878-1965
Buchwald, Art 1925-
Buck, Pearl S. 1892-1973
Buckley, William F., Jr. 1925-
Buechner, Frederick 1926-
Buero Vallejo, Antonio 1916-
Bukowski, Charles 1920-
Bullins, Ed 1935-
Bultmann, Rudolf Karl 1884-1976
Burgess, Anthony
    See Wilson, John Burgess
Burke, Kenneth 1897-
Burroughs, Edgar Rice 1875-1950
Burroughs, William S. 1914-
Bustos Domecq, H.
    See Bioy Casares, Adolfo
    and Borges, Jorge Luis
Butler, Octavia E. 1947-
Butor, Michel 1926-
Byars, Betsy 1928-
Byatt, A. S. 1936-
Cabrera Infante, G. 1929-
Cade, Toni
    See Bambara, Toni Cade
Cain, Guillermo
    See Cabrera Infante, G.
Cain, James M. 1892-1977
Calder, Nigel 1931-
Caldicott, Helen 1938-
Caldwell, Erskine 1903-1987
Calisher, Hortense 1911-
Callaghan, Morley Edward 1903-
    1990
Calvino, Italo 1923-1985
Cameron, Eleanor 1912-
Campbell, John W. 1910-1971
Campbell, Joseph 1904-1987
Camus, Albert 1913-1960
Canetti, Elias 1905-
Capote, Truman 1924-1984
Card, Orson Scott 1951-
Cardenal, Ernesto 1925-
Carey, Peter 1943-
Carr, John Dickson 1906-1977
Carruth, Hayden 1921-
Carson, Rachel Louise 1907-1964
Carter, Angela 1940-
Carter, James Earl, Jr. 1924-
Carter, Jimmy
    See Carter, James Earl, Jr.
Cartland, Barbara 1901-

Carver, Raymond 1938-1988
Casares, Adolfo Bioy
    See Bioy Casares, Adolfo
Castaneda, Carlos 1931(?)-
Cather, Willa
    See Cather, Willa Sibert
Cather, Willa Sibert 1873-1947
Causley, Charles 1917-
Cela, Camilo Jose 1916-
Celan, Paul
    See Antschel, Paul
Celine, Louis-Ferdinand
    See Destouches, Louis-Ferdinand
Cendrars, Blaise
    See Sauser-Hall, Frederic
Cesaire, Aime 1913-
Chandler, Raymond 1888-1959
Char, Rene 1907-1988
Charyn, Jerome 1937-
Cheever, John 1912-1982
Chesnutt, Charles W. 1858-1932
Chesterton, G. K. 1874-1936
Ch'ien Chung-shu 1910-
Childress, Alice 1920-
Chomsky, Noam 1928-
Christie, Agatha 1890-1976
Churchill, Caryl 1938-
Churchill, Winston 1874-1965
Ciardi, John 1916-1986
Cixous, Helene 1937-
Clancy, Thomas L., Jr. 1947-
Clancy, Tom
    See Clancy, Thomas L., Jr.
Clark, Kenneth 1903-1983
Clark, Mary Higgins 1929-
Clarke, Arthur C. 1917-
Clavell, James 1925-
Cleary, Beverly 1916-
Cleese, John 1939-
Clifton, Lucille 1936-
Clutha, Janet Paterson Frame 1924-
Cocteau, Jean 1889-1963
Coetzee, J. M. 1940-
Cohen, Leonard 1934-
Colegate, Isabel 1931-
Colette 1873-1954
Colum, Padraic 1881-1972
Colwin, Laurie 1944-
Commager, Henry Steele 1902-
Commoner, Barry 1917-
Compton-Burnett, I. 1884(?)-1969
Condon, Richard 1915-
Connell, Evan S., Jr. 1924-
Connolly, Cyril 1903-1974
Conrad, Joseph 1857-1924
Conran, Shirley 1932-
Conroy, Pat 1945-
Cookson, Catherine 1906-
Coover, Robert 1932-
Cormier, Robert 1925-
Cornwell, David 1931-

Corso, Gregory 1930-
Cortazar, Julio 1914-1984
Cousins, Norman 1915-
Cousteau, Jacques-Yves 1910-
Coward, Noel 1899-1973
Cowley, Malcolm 1898-1989
Cox, William Trevor 1928-
Cozzens, James Gould 1903-1978
Crane, Hart 1899-1932
Creasey, John 1908-1973
Creeley, Robert 1926-
Crews, Harry 1935-
Crichton, Michael 1942-
Cullen, Countee 1903-1946
Cummings, E. E. 1894-1962
Dahl, Roald 1916-
Dahlberg, Edward 1900-1977
Dailey, Janet 1944-
Daly, Mary 1928-
Dannay, Frederic 1905-1982
Dario, Ruben 1867-1916
Davie, Donald 1922-
Davies, Robertson 1913-
Day Lewis, C. 1904-1972
de Beauvoir, Simone
    See Beauvoir, Simone de
de Bono, Edward 1933-
de Filippo, Eduardo 1900-1984
Deighton, Len
    See Deighton, Leonard Cyril
Deighton, Leonard Cyril 1929-
Delaney, Shelagh 1939-
Delany, Samuel R. 1942-
Delibes, Miguel
    See Delibes Setien, Miguel
Delibes Setien, Miguel 1920-
DeLillo, Don 1936-
Deloria, Vine, Jr. 1933-
del Rey, Lester 1915-
de Man, Paul 1919-1983
de Montherlant, Henry
    See Montherlant, Henry de
Dennis, Nigel 1912-
Desai, Anita 1937-
Destouches, Louis-
    Ferdinand 1894-1961
De Vries, Peter 1910-
Dexter, Pete 1943-
Dick, Philip K. 1928-1982
Dickey, James 1923-
Dickson, Carter
    See Carr, John Dickson
Didion, Joan 1934-
Dillard, Annie 1945-
Dinesen, Isak
    See Blixen, Karen
Diop, Birago 1906-1989
Disch, Thomas M. 1940-
Doctorow, E. L. 1931-
Donleavy, J. P. 1926-
Donoso, Jose 1924-

Doolittle, Hilda 1886-1961
Dos Passos, John 1896-1970
Doyle, Arthur Conan 1859-1930
Drabble, Margaret 1939-
Dreiser, Theodore 1871-1945
Du Bois, W. E. B. 1868-1963
Duerrenmatt, Friedrich 1921-
Duffy, Maureen 1933-
Duhamel, Georges 1884-1966

du Maurier, Daphne 1907-1989
Dunbar, Alice
    See Nelson, Alice Ruth Moore
    Dunbar
Dunbar-Nelson, Alice
    See Nelson, Alice Ruth Moore
    Dunbar
Duncan, Robert 1919-1988

Dunn, Douglas 1942-
Durant, Will 1885-1981
Duras, Marguerite 1914-
Durrell, Gerald 1925-
Durrell, Lawrence 1912-
Durrenmatt, Friedrich
    See Duerrenmatt, Friedrich
Dworkin, Andrea 1946-

VOLUME 2: E-K

Eagleton, Terence 1943-
Eagleton, Terry
    See Eagleton, Terence
Eberhart, Richard 1904-
Echegaray, Jose 1832-1916
Eco, Umberto 1932-
Edgar, David 1948-
Ehrenreich, Barbara 1941-
Einstein, Albert 1879-1955
Ekwensi, Cyprian 1921-
Eliade, Mircea 1907-1986
Eliot, T. S. 1888-1965
Elkin, Stanley L. 1930-
Ellin, Stanley 1916-1986
Ellison, Harlan 1934-
Ellison, Ralph 1914-
Ellmann, Richard 1918-1987
Elytis, Odysseus 1911-
Emecheta, Buchi 1944-
Empson, William 1906-1984
Endo, Shusaku 1923-
Erdrich, Louise 1954-
Erikson, Erik H. 1902-
Esslin, Martin 1918-
Estleman, Loren D. 1952-
Everson, William 1912-
Ewart, Gavin 1916-
Fallaci, Oriana 1930-
Farmer, Philip Jose 1918-
Farrell, J. G. 1935-1979
Farrell, James T. 1904-1979
Faulkner, William 1897-1962
Feiffer, Jules 1929-
Feinstein, Elaine 1930-
Ferber, Edna 1887-1968
Ferlinghetti, Lawrence 1919(?)-
Fermor, Patrick Leigh
    See Leigh Fermor, Patrick
Feynman, Richard Phillips 1918-
    1988
Fiedler, Leslie A. 1917-
Filippo, Eduardo de
    See de Filippo, Eduardo
Fitzgerald, F. Scott 1896-1940
Flanagan, Thomas 1923-
Fleming, Ian 1908-1964
Fo, Dario 1926-
Follett, Ken 1949-
Ford, Ford Madox 1873-1939

Fornes, Maria Irene 1930-
Forster, E. M. 1879-1970
Forsyth, Frederick 1938-
Fossey, Dian 1932-1985
Foucault, Michel 1926-1984
Fowles, John 1926-
Fox, Paula 1923-
Frame, Janet
    See Clutha, Janet Paterson
    Frame
France, Anatole
    See Thibault, Jacques Anatole
    Francois
Francis, Dick 1920-
Frank, Anne 1929-1945
Fraser, Antonia 1932-
Frayn, Michael 1933-
French, Marilyn 1929-
Freud, Anna 1895-1982
Freud, Sigmund 1856-1939
Friday, Nancy 1937-
Friedan, Betty 1921-
Friedman, Milton 1912-
Friel, Brian 1929-
Frisch, Max 1911-
Fromm, Erich 1900-1980
Frost, Robert 1874-1963
Fry, Christopher 1907-
Frye, Northrop 1912-
Fuentes, Carlos 1928-
Fugard, Athol 1932-
Fuller, Buckminster
    See Fuller, R. Buckminster
Fuller, Charles 1939-
Fuller, R. Buckminster 1895-1983
Fussell, Paul 1924-
Gaddis, William 1922-
Gaines, Ernest J. 1933-
Galbraith, John Kenneth 1908-
Gallant, Mavis 1922-
Gallegos, Romulo 1884-1969
Gandhi, Mahatma
    See Gandhi, Mohandas Karam-
    chand
Gandhi, Mohandas Karamchand
    1869-1948
Garcia Lorca, Federico 1898-1936
Garcia Marquez, Gabriel 1928-
Gardam, Jane 1928-

Gardner, Erle Stanley 1889-1970
Gardner, John 1926-
Gardner, John, Jr. 1933-1982
Garner, Alan 1934-
Gascoyne, David 1916-
Gass, William H. 1924-
Gasset, Jose Ortega y
    See Ortega y Gasset, Jose
Geisel, Theodor Seuss 1904-
Genet, Jean 1910-1986
Gide, Andre 1869-1951
Gilbert, Sandra M. 1936-
Gilchrist, Ellen 1935-
Gill, Brendan 1914-
Ginsberg, Allen 1926-
Ginzburg, Natalia 1916-
Giono, Jean 1895-1970
Giovanni, Nikki 1943-
Godoy Alcayaga, Lucila 1889-1957
Godwin, Gail 1937-
Golding, William 1911-
Goodall, Jane 1934-
Goodman, Paul 1911-1972
Gorbachev, Mikhail 1931-
Gordimer, Nadine 1923-
Gordon, Caroline 1895-1981
Gordon, Mary 1949-
Gordone, Charles 1925-
Gould, Lois
Gould, Stephen Jay 1941-
Gouldner, Alvin W. 1920-1980
Goytisolo, Juan 1931-
Grass, Guenter 1927-
Grau, Shirley Ann 1929-
Graves, Robert 1895-1985
Gray, Alasdair 1934-
Gray, Francine du Plessix 1930-
Gray, Simon 1936-
Greeley, Andrew M. 1928-
Green, Julien 1900-
Greene, Graham 1904-
Greer, Germaine 1939-
Grey, Zane 1872-1939
Grieve, C. M. 1892-1978
Grigson, Geoffrey 1905-1985
Grimes, Martha
Grizzard, Lewis 1946-
Grossman, Vasily 1905-1964
Guare, John 1938-

Gubar, Susan 1944-
Guest, Judith 1936-
Guiraldes, Ricardo 1886-1927
Gunn, Thom 1929-
H. D.
    See Doolittle, Hilda
Hailey, Arthur 1920-
Haley, Alex 1921-
Hall, Willis 1929-
Hamilton, Virginia 1936-
Hammett, Dashiell 1894-1961
Hampton, Christopher 1946-
Hamsun, Knut
    See Pedersen, Knut
Handke, Peter 1942-
Hanley, James 1901-1985
Hannah, Barry 1942-
Hansberry, Lorraine 1930-1965
Hardwick, Elizabeth 1916-
Hardy, Thomas 1840-1928
Hare, David 1947-
Harris, Wilson 1921-
Harrison, Tony 1937-
Hartley, L. P. 1895-1972
Hasek, Jaroslav 1883-1923
Havel, Vaclav 1936-
Hawkes, John 1925-
Hayden, Robert E. 1913-1980
Hayek, F. A. 1899-
Hazzard, Shirley 1931-
Head, Bessie 1937-1986
Heaney, Seamus 1939-
Hearne, John 1926-
Heath, Roy A. K. 1926-
Hebert, Anne 1916-
Heidegger, Martin 1889-1976
Heinlein, Robert A. 1907-1988
Heller, Joseph 1923-
Hellman, Lillian 1906-1984
Helprin, Mark 1947-
Hemingway, Ernest 1899-1961
Henley, Beth
    See Henley, Elizabeth Becker
Henley, Elizabeth Becker 1952-
Henri, Adrian 1932-
Henry, O.
    See Porter, William Sydney
Herbert, Frank 1920-1986
Herbert, Zbigniew 1924-
Herr, Michael 1940(?)-
Hersey, John 1914-
Hesse, Hermann 1877-1962
Heyer, Georgette 1902-1974
Heyerdahl, Thor 1914-
Higgins, George V. 1939-
Higgins, Jack
    See Patterson, Harry
Highsmith, Patricia 1921-
Hill, Geoffrey 1932-
Hill, Susan 1942-
Himes, Chester 1909-1984

Hinton, S. E. 1950-
Hiraoka, Kimitake 1925-1970
Hirsch, E. D., Jr. 1928-
Hite, Shere 1942-
Hoban, Russell 1925-
Hochhuth, Rolf 1931-
Hochwaelder, Fritz 1911-1986
Hoffman, Abbie 1936-1989
Hoffman, Alice 1952-
Hofstadter, Douglas R. 1945-
Holroyd, Michael 1935-
Hope, A. D. 1907-
Horgan, Paul 1903-
Housman, A. E. 1859-1936
Howard, Maureen 1930-
Howe, Irving 1920-
Hoyle, Fred 1915-
Hughes, Langston 1902-1967
Hughes, Richard 1900-1976
Hughes, Ted 1930-
Hunter, Evan 1926-
Hurston, Zora Neale 1903-1960
Huxley, Aldous 1894-1963
Huxley, Julian 1887-1975
Ibanez, Vicente Blasco
    See Blasco Ibanez, Vicente
Illich, Ivan 1926-
Infante, G. Cabrera
    See Cabrera Infante, G.
Inge, William Motter 1913-1973
Innes, Michael
    See Stewart, J.I.M.
Ionesco, Eugene 1912-
Irving, John 1942-
Isaacs, Susan 1943-
Isherwood, Christopher 1904-1986
Ishiguro, Kazuo 1954-
Jacobson, Dan 1929-
Jaffe, Rona 1932-
Jakes, John 1932-
James, C. L. R. 1901-1989
James, Clive 1939-
James, Henry 1843-1916
James, P. D.
    See White, Phyllis Dorothy
    James
Jarrell, Randall 1914-1965
Jeffers, Robinson 1887-1962
Jennings, Elizabeth 1926-
Jhabvala, Ruth Prawer 1927-
Jimenez, Juan Ramon 1881-1958
Johnson, Diane 1934-
Johnson, James Weldon 1871-1938
Johnson, Pamela Hansford 1912-
    1981
Johnson, Uwe 1934-1984
Jones, David 1895-1974
Jones, Gayl 1949-
Jones, James 1921-1977
Jones, LeRoi
    See Baraka, Amiri

Jones, Mervyn 1922-
Jong, Erica 1942-
Jordan, June 1936-
Joyce, James 1882-1941
Jung, C. G. 1875-1961
Kafka, Franz 1883-1924
Kammen, Michael G. 1936-
Karnow, Stanley 1925-
Kavan, Anna 1901-1968
Kavanagh, Patrick 1904-1967
Kaye, M. M. 1909-
Kazakov, Yuri Pavlovich 1927-
Kazantzakis, Nikos 1883(?)-1957
Keating, H. R. F. 1926-
Keillor, Garrison
    See Keillor, Gary
Keillor, Gary 1942-
Keller, Helen 1880-1968
Keneally, Thomas 1935-
Kennedy, John Fitzgerald 1917-
1963
Kennedy, William 1928-
Kenyatta, Jomo 1891(?)-1978
Kerouac, Jack
    See Kerouac, Jean-Louis Lebrid
de
Kerouac, Jean-Louis Lebrid de
1922-1969
Kerr, M. E.
    See Meaker, Marijane
Kesey, Ken 1935-
Kidder, Tracy 1945-
Kienzle, William X. 1928-
King, Francis 1923-
King, Larry L. 1929-
King, Martin Luther, Jr. 1929-
1968
King, Stephen 1947-
Kingston, Maxine Hong 1940-
Kinnell, Galway 1927-
Kinsella, Thomas 1928-
Kinsella, W. P. 1935-
Kipling, Rudyard 1865-1936
Kirk, Russell 1918-
Kis, Danilo 1935-
Kissinger, Henry A. 1923-
Knowles, John 1926-
Koestler, Arthur 1905-1983
Konigsburg, E. L. 1930-
Konwicki, Tadeusz 1926-
Koontz, Dean R. 1945-
Kopit, Arthur 1937-
Kosinski, Jerzy 1933-
Krantz, Judith 1927-
Kroetsch, Robert 1927-
Kueng, Hans 1928-
Kumin, Maxine 1925-
Kundera, Milan 1929-
Kung, Hans
    See Kueng, Hans
Kunitz, Stanley 1905-

VOLUME 3: L-Q

Lagerkvist, Paer 1891-1974
La Guma, Alex 1925-1985
Laing, R. D. 1927-1989
Lamming, George 1927-
L'Amour, Louis 1908-1988
Langer, Susanne K. 1895-1985
Lardner, Ring
  See Lardner, Ring W.
Lardner, Ring W. 1885-1933
Larkin, Philip 1922-1985
Lasch, Christopher 1932-
Laurence, Margaret 1926-1987
Lavin, Mary 1912-
Lawrence, D. H. 1885-1930
Laye, Camara 1928-1980
Layton, Irving 1912-
Leakey, Louis S. B. 1903-1972
Leary, Timothy 1920-
Leavis, F. R. 1895-1978
Lebowitz, Fran 1951(?)-
le Carre, John
  See Cornwell, David
Lee, Harper 1926-
Lee, Laurie 1914-
Leger, Alexis Saint-Leger 1887-1975
Le Guin, Ursula K. 1929-
Leiber, Fritz 1910-
Leigh Fermor, Patrick 1915-
Lem, Stanislaw 1921-
L'Engle, Madeleine 1918-
Leonard, Elmore 1925-
Leonov, Leonid 1899-
Lessing, Doris 1919-
Levertov, Denise 1923-
Levi, Primo 1919-1987
Levin, Ira 1929-
Levi-Strauss, Claude 1908-
Lewis, C. S. 1898-1963
Lewis, Norman 1918-
Lewis, Sinclair 1885-1951
Lindbergh, Anne Morrow 1906-
Lippmann, Walter 1889-1974
Little, Malcolm 1925-1965
Lively, Penelope 1933-
Livesay, Dorothy 1909-
Llosa, Mario Vargas
  See Vargas Llosa, Mario
Lodge, David 1935-
London, Jack
  See London, John Griffith
London, John Griffith 1876-1916
Lopez, Barry Holstun 1945-
Lorca, Federico Garcia
  See Garcia Lorca, Federico
Lorde, Audre 1934-
Lorenz, Konrad Zacharias 1903-
Lovecraft, H. P. 1890-1937
Lovelace, Earl 1935-

Lovesey, Peter 1936-
Lowell, Robert 1917-1977
Lowry, Malcolm 1909-1957
Luce, Henry R. 1898-1967
Ludlum, Robert 1927-
Lukacs, George
  See Lukacs, Gyorgy
Lukacs, Gyorgy 1885-1971
Lukas, J. Anthony 1933-
Luria, Alexander R. 1902-1977
Lurie, Alison 1926-
MacBeth, George 1932-
MacDiarmid, Hugh
  See Grieve, C. M.
MacDonald, John D. 1916-1986
Macdonald, Ross
  See Millar, Kenneth
MacInnes, Colin 1914-1976
MacInnes, Helen 1907-1985
MacLean, Alistair 1922(?)-1987
MacLeish, Archibald 1892-1982
MacLennan, Hugh 1907-
MacNeice, Louis 1907-1963
Madden, David 1933-
Mahfouz, Naguib 1911(?)-
Mahfuz, Najib
  See Mahfouz, Naguib
Mailer, Norman 1923-
Mais, Roger 1905-1955
Malamud, Bernard 1914-1986
Malcolm X
  See Little, Malcolm
Malraux, Andre 1901-1976
Mamet, David 1947-
Manchester, William 1922-
Mann, Thomas 1875-1955
Manning, Olivia 1915-1980
Mao Tse-tung 1893-1976
Marcel, Gabriel Honore 1889-1973
Marsh, Ngaio 1899-1982
Marshall, Paule 1929-
Martin, Steve 1945-
Masefield, John 1878-1967
Maslow, Abraham H. 1908-1970
Mason, Bobbie Ann 1940-
Masters, Edgar Lee 1868-1950
Matthews, Patricia 1927-
Matthiessen, Peter 1927-
Matute, Ana Maria 1925-
Maugham, W. Somerset
  See Maugham, William Somerset
Maugham, William Somerset 1874-1965
Mauriac, Francois 1885-1970
Maurois, Andre 1885-1967
Maxwell, Gavin 1914-1969
McBain, Ed
  See Hunter, Evan
McCaffrey, Anne 1926-

McCarthy, Mary 1912-1989
McCullers, Carson 1917-1967
McCullough, Colleen 1938(?)-
McEwan, Ian 1948-
McGahern, John 1934-
McGrath, Thomas 1916-
McGuane, Thomas 1939-
McIntyre, Vonda N. 1948-
McKay, Claude
  See McKay, Festus Claudius
McKay, Festus Claudius 1889-1948
McKillip, Patricia A. 1948-
McLuhan, Marshall 1911-1980
McMurtry, Larry 1936-
McPhee, John 1931-
McPherson, James Alan 1943-
McPherson, James M. 1936-
Mead, Margaret 1901-1978
Meaker, Marijane 1927-
Mehta, Ved 1934-
Mencken, H. L. 1880-1956
Menninger, Karl 1893-1990
Mercer, David 1928-1980
Merril, Judith 1923-
Merrill, James 1926-
Merton, Thomas 1915-1968
Merwin, W. S. 1927-
Michaels, Leonard 1933-
Michener, James A. 1907(?)-
Millar, Kenneth 1915-1983
Millay, Edna St. Vincent 1892-1950
Miller, Arthur 1915-
Miller, Henry 1891-1980
Millett, Kate 1934-
Milligan, Spike
  See Milligan, Terence Alan
Milligan, Terence Alan 1918-
Milne, A. A. 1882-1956
Milner, Ron 1938-
Milosz, Czeslaw 1911-
Mishima, Yukio
  See Hiraoka, Kimitake
Mistral, Gabriela
  See Godoy Alcayaga, Lucila
Mitchell, Margaret 1900-1949
Mo, Timothy 1950(?)-
Momaday, N. Scott 1934-
Montague, John 1929-
Montale, Eugenio 1896-1981
Montherlant, Henry de 1896-1972
Moorcock, Michael 1939-
Moore, Brian 1921-
Moore, Marianne 1887-1972
Morante, Elsa 1918-1985
Moravia, Alberto
  See Pincherle, Alberto
Morgan, Robin 1941-
Morris, Desmond 1928-

Morris, James
    See Morris, Jan
Morris, Jan 1926-
Morris, Wright 1910-
Morrison, Toni 1931-
Mortimer, John 1923-
Mowat, Farley 1921-
Mrozek, Slawomir 1930-
Muggeridge, Malcolm 1903-
Mukherjee, Bharati 1940-
Munro, Alice 1931-
Munro, H. H. 1870-1916
Murdoch, Iris 1919-
Nabokov, Vladimir 1899-1977
Naipaul, Shiva 1945-1985
Naipaul, V. S. 1932-
Narayan, R. K. 1906-
Nash, Ogden 1902-1971
Naughton, Bill 1910-
Naylor, Gloria 1950-
Nehru, Jawaharlal 1889-1964
Nelson, Alice Ruth Moore Dunbar
    1875-1935
Nemerov, Howard 1920-
Neruda, Pablo 1904-1973
Newby, P. H. 1918-
Ngugi, James T.
    See Ngugi wa Thiong'o
Ngugi wa Thiong'o 1938-
Nichols, Peter 1927-
Nin, Anais 1903-1977
Niven, Larry
    See Niven, Laurence Van Cott
Niven, Laurence Van Cott 1938-
Nixon, Richard M. 1913-
Norton, Andre 1912-
Nye, Robert 1939-
Oates, Joyce Carol 1938-
O'Brien, Edna 1936-
O'Casey, Sean 1880-1964
O'Cathasaigh, Sean
    See O'Casey, Sean
O'Connor, Flannery 1925-1964
Odets, Clifford 1906-1963
Oe, Kenzaburo 1935-
O'Faolain, Julia 1932-
O'Faolain, Sean 1900-
O'Flaherty, Liam 1896-1984
O'Hara, Frank 1926-1966
O'Hara, John 1905-1970

Okigbo, Christopher 1932-1967
Olsen, Tillie 1913-
Olson, Charles 1910-1970
O'Neill, Eugene 1888-1953
Onetti, Juan Carlos 1909-
Oppenheimer, J. Robert 1904-1967
Ortega y Gasset, Jose 1883-1955
Orton, Joe
    See Orton, John Kingsley
Orton, John Kingsley 1933-1967
Orwell, George
    See Blair, Eric
Osborne, John 1929-
Ousmane, Sembene 1923-
Oz, Amos 1939-
Ozick, Cynthia 1928-
Page, P. K. 1916-
Pagnol, Marcel 1895-1974
Paley, Grace 1922-
Panova, Vera 1905-1973
Pargeter, Edith Mary 1913-
Parker, Dorothy 1893-1967
Parker, Robert B. 1932-
Parra, Nicanor 1914-
Parsons, Talcott 1902-1979
Pasolini, Pier Paolo 1922-1975
Pasternak, Boris 1890-1960
Patchen, Kenneth 1911-1972
Paterson, Katherine 1932-
Paton, Alan 1903-1988
Patterson, Harry 1929-
Pauling, Linus 1901-
Paz, Octavio 1914-
p'Bitek, Okot 1931-1982
Peake, Mervyn 1911-1968
Peale, Norman Vincent 1898-
Pearson, Andrew Russell 1897-
    1969
Pearson, Drew
    See Pearson, Andrew Russell
Pedersen, Knut 1859-1952
Percy, Walker 1916-1990
Perelman, S. J. 1904-1979
Perse, Saint-John
    See Leger, Alexis Saint-Leger
Peters, Ellis
    See Pargeter, Edith Mary
Petry, Ann 1908-
Pevsner, Nikolaus 1902-1983

Phillips, Jayne Anne 1952-
Piaget, Jean 1896-1980
Piercy, Marge 1936-
Pilcher, Rosamunde 1924-
Pincherle, Alberto 1907-
Pinter, Harold 1930-
Pirsig, Robert M. 1928-
Plante, David 1940-
Plath, Sylvia 1932-1963
Plimpton, George 1927-
Plomer, William Charles Franklin
    1903-1973
Plowman, Piers
    See Kavanagh, Patrick
Pohl, Frederik 1919-
Pollitt, Katha 1949-
Popper, Karl R. 1902-
Porter, Katherine Anne 1890-1980
Porter, William Sydney 1862-1910
Potok, Chaim 1929-
Potter, Dennis 1935-
Potter, Stephen 1900-1969
Pound, Ezra 1885-1972
Powell, Anthony 1905-
Powers, J. F. 1917-
Powys, John Cowper 1872-1963
Prevert, Jacques 1900-1977
Prichard, Katharine Susannah
    1883-1969
Priestley, J. B. 1894-1984
Pritchett, V. S. 1900-
Proust, Marcel 1871-1922
Puig, Manuel 1932-1990
Purdy, James 1923-
Puzo, Mario 1920-
Pym, Barbara 1913-1980
Pynchon, Thomas 1937-
Python, Monty
    See Cleese, John
Qian Zhongshu
    See Ch'ien Chung-shu
Quasimodo, Salvatore 1901-1968
Queen, Ellery
    See Dannay, Frederic
    and Sturgeon, Theodore
    and Vance, John Holbrook
Queneau, Raymond 1903-1976
Quiroga, Horacio 1878-1937
Quoirez, Francoise 1935-

VOLUME 4: R-Z

Raine, Kathleen 1908-
Rand, Ayn 1905-1982
Ransom, John Crowe 1888-1974
Rao, Raja 1909-
Rattigan, Terence 1911-1977
Ravitch, Diane 1938-
Reed, Ishmael 1938-
Remarque, Erich Maria 1898-1970

Rendell, Ruth 1930-
Rexroth, Kenneth 1905-1982
Rhys, Jean 1894-1979
Rice, Elmer 1892-1967
Rich, Adrienne 1929-
Richler, Mordecai 1931-
Richter, Conrad 1890-1968
Rilke, Rainer Maria 1875-1926

Ritsos, Giannes
    See Ritsos, Yannis
Ritsos, Yannis 1909-
Robbe-Grillet, Alain 1922-
Robbins, Harold 1916-
Robbins, Thomas Eugene 1936-
Robbins, Tom
    See Robbins, Thomas Eugene

Robinson, Edwin Arlington 1869–1935

Robinson, Joan 1903–1983

Rodd, Kylie Tennant 1912–1988

Roethke, Theodore 1908–1963

Rogers, Carl R. 1902–1987

Rogers, Rosemary 1932–

Romains, Jules 1885–1972

Rooney, Andrew A. 1919–

Rooney, Andy
    See Rooney, Andrew A.

Rossner, Judith 1935–

Rostand, Edmond 1868–1918

Roth, Henry 1906–

Roth, Philip 1933–

Roy, Gabrielle 1909–1983

Rozewicz, Tadeusz 1921–

Rubens, Bernice 1923–

Rukeyser, Muriel 1913–1980

Rulfo, Juan 1918–1986

Rushdie, Salman 1947–

Russ, Joanna 1937–

Russell, Bertrand 1872–1970

Sabato, Ernesto 1911–

Saberhagen, Fred 1930–

Sacks, Oliver 1933–

Sackville-West, V. 1892–1962

Sagan, Carl 1934–

Sagan, Francoise
    See Quoirez, Francoise

Saint-Exupery, Antoine de 1900–1944

Saki
    See Munro, H. H.

Salinger, J. D. 1919–

Salisbury, Harrison E. 1908–

Sanchez, Sonia 1934–

Sandburg, Carl 1878–1967

Sanders, Lawrence 1920–

Sandoz, Mari 1896–1966

Sansom, William 1912–1976

Santmyer, Helen Hooven 1895–1986

Saroyan, William 1908–1981

Sarraute, Nathalie 1900–

Sarton, May 1912–

Sartre, Jean-Paul 1905–1980

Sassoon, Siegfried 1886–1967

Sauser-Hall, Frederic 1887–1961

Sayers, Dorothy L. 1893–1957

Schaeffer, Susan Fromberg 1941–

Schlafly, Phyllis 1924–

Schlesinger, Arthur M., Jr. 1917–

Schmitz, Aron Hector 1861–1928

Schwartz, Delmore 1913–1966

Sciascia, Leonardo 1921–1989

Scott, Paul 1920–1978

Seferiades, Giorgos Stylianou 1900–1971

Seferis, George
    See Seferiades, Giorgos Stylianou

Segal, Erich 1937–

Seifert, Jaroslav 1901–1986

Selvon, Samuel 1923–

Sendak, Maurice 1928–

Sender, Ramon 1902–1982

Senghor, Leopold Sedar 1906–

Sepheriades, Georgios
    See Seferiades, Giorgos Stylianou

Setien, Miguel Delibes
    See Delibes Setien, Miguel

Seuss, Dr.
    See Geisel, Theodor Seuss

Sexton, Anne 1928–1974

Shaffer, Peter 1926–

Shange, Ntozake 1948–

Shapiro, Karl 1913–

Shaw, George Bernard 1856–1950

Shaw, Irwin 1913–1984

Sheed, Wilfrid 1930–

Sheehy, Gail 1936(?)–

Sheen, Fulton J. 1895–1979

Sheldon, Alice Hastings Bradley 1915–1987

Sheldon, Sidney 1917–

Shepard, Sam 1943–

Shirer, William L. 1904–

Sholokhov, Mikhail 1905–1984

Siddons, Anne Rivers 1936–

Sillanpaa, Frans Eemil 1888–1964

Sillitoe, Alan 1928–

Silone, Ignazio 1900–1978

Silverberg, Robert 1935–

Simak, Clifford D. 1904–1988

Simenon, Georges 1903–1989

Simon, Claude 1913–

Simon, Kate 1912–1990

Simon, Neil 1927–

Simpson, Dorothy 1933–

Simpson, George Gaylord 1902–1984

Simpson, Harriette
    See Arnow, Harriette Simpson

Simpson, Louis 1923–

Sinclair, Andrew 1935–

Sinclair, Upton 1878–1968

Singer, Isaac Bashevis 1904–

Sitwell, Dame Edith 1887–1964

Skinner, B. F. 1904–1990

Skvorecky, Josef 1924–

Smith, Florence Margaret 1902–1971

Smith, Stevie
    See Smith, Florence Margaret

Smith, Wilbur 1933–

Snodgrass, William D. 1926–

Snow, C. P. 1905–1980

Solzhenitsyn, Aleksandr I. 1918–

Sontag, Susan 1933–

Soyinka, Wole 1934–

Spark, Muriel 1918–

Spencer, Elizabeth 1921–

Spender, Stephen 1909–

Spillane, Frank Morrison 1918–

Spillane, Mickey
    See Spillane, Frank Morrison

Spock, Benjamin 1903–

Stafford, Jean 1915–1979

Stead, Christina 1902–1983

Steel, Danielle 1947–

Stegner, Wallace 1909–

Stein, Gertrude 1874–1946

Steinbeck, John 1902–1968

Steinem, Gloria 1934–

Steiner, George 1929–

Stevens, Wallace 1879–1955

Stevenson, Anne 1933–

Stewart, J. I. M. 1906–

Stone, Irving 1903–1989

Stone, Robert 1937–

Stoppard, Tom 1937–

Storey, David 1933–

Stow, Randolph 1935–

Straub, Peter 1943–

Sturgeon, Theodore 1918–1985

Styron, William 1925–

Susann, Jacqueline 1921–1974

Suzuki, D. T.
    See Suzuki, Daisetz Teitaro

Suzuki, Daisetz Teitaro 1870–1966

Svevo, Italo
    See Schmitz, Aron Hector

Swenson, May 1919–1989

Symons, Julian 1912–

Tagore, Rabindranath 1861–1941

Talese, Gay 1932–

Tate, Allen 1899–1979

Taylor, A. J. P. 1906–

Taylor, Elizabeth 1912–1975

Taylor, Peter 1917–

Taylor, Telford 1908–

Teller, Edward 1908–

Tennant, Kylie
    See Rodd, Kylie Tennant

Terkel, Louis 1912–

Terkel, Studs
    See Terkel, Louis

Theroux, Paul 1941–

Thibault, Jacques Anatole Francois 1844–1924

Thomas, Audrey 1935–

Thomas, D. M. 1935–

Thomas, Dylan 1914–1953

Thomas, Joyce Carol 1938–

Thomas, Lewis 1913–

Thomas, R. S. 1913–

Thompson, Hunter S. 1939–

Thurber, James 1894–1961

Tillich, Paul 1886–1965

Tiptree, James, Jr.
    See Sheldon, Alice Hastings Bradley

Toffler, Alvin 1928-
Toland, John 1912-
Tolkien, J. R. R. 1892-1973
Toomer, Jean 1894-1967
Torres Bodet, Jaime 1902-1974
Torsvan, Ben Traven
    See Traven, B.
Tournier, Michel 1924-
Townsend, Sue 1946-
Traven, B. ?-1969
Tremblay, Michel 1942-
Trevor, William
    See Cox, William Trevor
Trifonov, Yuri 1925-1981
Trillin, Calvin 1935-
Trilling, Diane 1905-
Trilling, Lionel 1905-1975
Troyat, Henri 1911-
Truman, Margaret 1924-
Tryon, Thomas 1926-
Tsvetaeva, Marina 1892-1941
Tuchman, Barbara W. 1912-1989
Tutuola, Amos 1920-
Tyler, Anne 1941-
Tynan, Kenneth 1927-1980
Uchida, Yoshiko 1921-
Unamuno, Miguel de 1864-1936
Undset, Sigrid 1882-1949
Updike, John 1932-
Uris, Leon 1924-
Valery, Paul 1871-1945
Vallejo, Antonio Buero
    See Buero Vallejo, Antonio
Vance, Jack
    See Vance, John Holbrook
Vance, John Holbrook 1916-
Van Doren, Mark 1894-1972
van Lawick-Goodall, Jane
    See Goodall, Jane
Vargas Llosa, Mario 1936-
Vendler, Helen 1933-
Vidal, Gore 1925-
Vine, Barbara
    See Rendell, Ruth
Voinovich, Vladimir 1932-

von Hayek, Friedrich August
    See Hayek, F. A.
Vonnegut, Kurt, Jr. 1922-
Voznesensky, Andrei 1933-
Wain, John 1925-
Walcott, Derek 1930-
Walker, Alice 1944-
Walker, Margaret 1915-
Wallace, Irving 1916-1990
Wallant, Edward Lewis 1926-1962
Wambaugh, Joseph 1937-
Warner, Sylvia Ashton
    See Ashton-Warner, Sylvia
Warner, Sylvia Townsend 1893-
    1978
Warren, Robert Penn 1905-1989
Waruk, Kona
    See Harris, Wilson
Waterhouse, Keith 1929-
Waugh, Evelyn 1903-1966
Wedgwood, C. V. 1910-
Weinstein, Nathan
    See West, Nathanael
Weldon, Fay 1933(?)-
Wells, H. G. 1866-1946
Welty, Eudora 1909-
Wesker, Arnold 1932-
Wesley, Mary 1912-
West, Jessamyn 1902-1984
West, Morris L. 1916-
West, Nathanael 1903-1940
West, Rebecca 1892-1983
Wharton, Edith 1862-1937
Wheatley, Dennis 1897-1977
White, E. B. 1899-1985
White, Edmund 1940-
White, Patrick 1912-
White, Phyllis Dorothy James 1920-
White, Theodore H. 1915-1986
Wiesel, Elie 1928-
Wilbur, Richard 1921-
Wilder, Thornton 1897-1975
Wilhelm, Kate
    See Wilhelm, Katie Gertrude

Wilhelm, Katie Gertrude 1928-
Will, George F. 1941-
Willard, Nancy 1936-
Williams, Emlyn 1905-1987
Williams, Raymond 1921-1988
Williams, Tennessee 1911-1983
Williams, William Carlos 1883-
    1963
Williamson, Henry 1895-1977
Willingham, Calder 1922-
Wilson, Angus 1913-
Wilson, August 1945-
Wilson, Colin 1931-
Wilson, Edmund 1895-1972
Wilson, Edward O. 1929-
Wilson, Ethel Davis 1888(?)-1980
Wilson, John Burgess 1917-
Wilson, Robert M. 1944-
Winters, Yvor 1900-1968
Wodehouse, P. G. 1881-1975
Wolf, Christa 1929-
Wolfe, Thomas 1900-1938
Wolfe, Thomas Kennerly, Jr. 1931-
Wolfe, Tom
    See Wolfe, Thomas Kennerly, Jr.
Woodiwiss, Kathleen E. 1939-
Woodward, Bob
    See Woodward, Robert Upshur
Woodward, Robert Upshur 1943-
Woolf, Virginia 1882-1941
Wouk, Herman 1915-
Wright, Charles 1935-
Wright, James 1927-1980
Wright, Judith 1915-
Wright, Richard 1908-1960
Yeats, William Butler 1865-1939
Yerby, Frank G. 1916-
Yevtushenko, Yevgeny 1933-
Yezierska, Anzia 1885(?)-1970
Yglesias, Helen 1915-
Yourcenar, Marguerite 1903-1987
Zelazny, Roger 1937-
Zindel, Paul 1936-
Zukofsky, Louis 1904-1978

MAJOR ♦
20th- ♦
CENTURY ♦
WRITERS ♦

Volume 2: E-K

E

EAGLETON, Terence (Francis) 1943-
(Terry Eagleton)

PERSONAL: Born February 22, 1943, in Salford, England. *Education:* Trinity College, Cambridge, B.A., 1964; Jesus College, Cambridge, Ph.D., 1968.

ADDRESSES: Home and office—Wadham College, Oxford University, Oxford, England.

CAREER: Cambridge University, Jesus College, Cambridge, England, fellow, 1964-69; Oxford University, Wadham College, Oxford, England, fellow and tutor in poetry, 1969—. Selector for Poetry Book Society, 1969-71; judge, Sinclair Fiction Prize, 1985.

MEMBER: Society for the Study of Narrative Literature (president).

WRITINGS:

The New Left Church (essays), Helicon, 1966.
Shakespeare and Society: Critical Studies in Shakespearean Drama, Schocken, 1967.

UNDER NAME TERRY EAGLETON

(Editor) *Directions: Pointers for the Post-Conciliar Church* (essays), Sheed, 1968.
(Editor with Brian Wicker) *From Culture to Revolution: The Slant Symposium, 1967* (essays), Sheed, 1968.
The Body as Language: Outline of a "New Left" Theology, Sheed, 1970.
Exiles and Emigres: Studies in Modern Literature, Schocken, 1970.
Myths of Power: A Marxist Study of the Brontes, Barnes & Noble, 1975.
Marxism and Literary Criticism, University of California Press, 1976.
Criticism and Ideology: A Study in Marxist Literary Theory, Verso, 1976, Schocken, 1978.
Walter Benjamin; or, Towards a Revolutionary Criticism, Schocken, 1981.
The Rape of Clarissa: Writing, Sexuality and Class Struggle in Samuel Richardson, University of Minnesota Press, 1982.
Literary Theory: An Introduction, University of Minnesota Press, 1983.

The Function of Criticism: From the Spectator to Post-Structuralism, Verso, 1984.
(Editor) Laura Brown, *Alexander Pope,* Basil Blackwell, 1985.
(Editor) James Kavanaugh, *Emily Bronte,* Basil Blackwell, 1985.
(Editor) Stan Smith, *W. H. Auden,* Basil Blackwell, 1985.
William Shakespeare, Basil Blackwell, 1986.
Against the Grain: Selected Essays, 1975-1985, Verso, 1986.
Saints and Scholars (novel), Verso, 1987.
(Editor) *Raymond Williams: A Critical Reader,* Northeastern University Press, 1989.
Saint Oscar (play), first produced in London, 1990.

OTHER

Contributor to *Slant, Times Literary Supplement, Stand, Commonweal,* and other periodicals. Poetry reviewer, *Stand,* 1968—.

SIDELIGHTS: Terry Eagleton is "widely regarded as the foremost young Marxist literary thinker in England," writes a *Washington Post Book World* contributor. Concerned with the ideologies found in literature, Eagleton examines the role of Marxism in discerning these ideologies. "Always alert to the underside or reversible lining of any intellectual model, Eagleton tracks the cross-currents and strategies of literary criticism with a uniquely agile understanding," states Chris Baldick in the *Times Literary Supplement.* Eagleton's books have not only clarified arcane critical theories of literature for the novice but have also posed provocative questions to the specialists. His polemical expositions in literary theory have generated a spirited critical response, and even those opposed to his stance speak readily about his "accessible" and persuasive prose. "Unlike too many other theorists, Marxist or otherwise," says Steven G. Kellman in *Modern Fiction Studies,* "Eagleton writes with grace, clarity, and force." In *Thought,* Walter Kendrick points also to Eagleton's "sprightly style and . . . lively sense of humor, rare commodities in his field."

Eagleton's brief but concise *Marxism and Literary Criticism* discusses the author of a work as producer, as well as the relationships between literature and history, form and content, and the writer and commitment. As George Woodcock observes in the *Sewanee Review,* Eagleton perceives Marxist criticism to be "part of a larger body of theoretical analysis that aims to understand *ideologies*—the ideas, values and feelings by which men experience their societies at various times. And certain of those ideas, values and feelings are available to us only in literature."

Woodcock praises Eagleton's clear and vigorous writing, adding that he is "brisk and specific, and tells us a great deal . . . about the more important continental European Marxist critics, their books, and their theories." Peter Conrad, however, sees a need for more textual examples in *Marxism and Literary Criticism,* and he refers to it in the *Spectator* as "a case of theory talking about itself." Michael Wilding similarly finds the book "academic and self-referential," suggesting in *Modern Language Review* that Eagleton approaches Marxist literary criticism "as a subject, rather than as an instrument for revealing other subjects." Nevertheless, noting that the book avoids "pseudo-philosophical jargon," R. Berg-Pan maintains in *World Literature Today* that Eagleton "introduces the neophyte to a very complex set of problems with ease and great skill." Moreover, Woodcock says that Eagleton is "one of the few Marxist theoreticians willing to see Marxism itself not as a self-sufficient doctrine but as part of a spectrum of related doctrines."

According to Jonathan Culler in *Poetics Today,* Eagleton's academic best-seller, *Literary Theory: An Introduction,* is a "vigorous articulation of what has become a common theme today in the realm of critical theory: the call for criticism and for literary theory to assume a relationship to history, both by confronting the question of their insertion in social and political history and by taking account of their own history." As John Lucas notes in a *Times Literary Supplement* review of *Against the Grain: Selected Essays, 1975-1985,* Eagleton is "one of a number of critics and theorists on the left who have necessarily drawn attention to improper or at least ideologically-based privileging of certain authors and texts." In *Literary Theory,* Eagleton begins with the observation that "literary criticism is by nature a political act, even (or especially) when it eschews direct political engagement," writes Kendrick, and in this volume, Eagleton connects each school of literary study with the ideology of its particular time and place.

Literary Theory is a "remarkable and important book," writes Charles Sugnet in *American Book Review,* adding that it "does what a good introduction should do—it synthesizes tendencies already in the air and makes them widely accessible in clear prose." Culler believes it to be Eagleton's "best work: provocative, efficient, and for the most part well-informed." Praising the stylistic grace and precision with which Eagleton distills complex theories of literature, critics especially address the book's provocative premise. "A Marxist with wit, Terry Eagleton is magisterial in his deployment of a wide range of ideas, but rarely dispassionate . . . ," says Kellman. "After patient scrutiny of the writings of numerous contemporary critics, Eagleton confesses that he has not come to praise theory but to bury it."

"Under cover of writing a primer on current literary criticism," writes Sugnet, ". . . Eagleton dissolves his own field of inquiry by arguing that there is no such thing as 'literature,' and therefore no 'literary theory.'" As Lennard J. Davis explains in *Nation,* "Literature and the cult of the literary are ideologies that exalt high cultural artifacts like novels, poems and plays over other forms of writing and representation." Eagleton would prefer to replace literature, as it is presently being studied, with the more encompassing discipline of rhetoric as it was practiced from Greek and Roman times until the eighteenth century. "Literature would be, of course, only a branch of this study," summarizes Kendrick. "It would share the field with polemics, journalism, and even the labels on beer cans. . . . A rhetorical approach to literary texts would at least acknowledge one important fact about them that all current critical methodologies tend to ignore: that they are modes of persuasion, designed to elicit some response, even if only complacency, in their readers."

That response, like the text which provokes it, must be political in the widest sense."

David Forgacs questions Eagleton's proposal of subsuming literature into a wider study and wonders in *Poetics Today,* "Who is going to supply the methodologies and the courses, and with what claims to expertise in the field." Among other criticisms, Denis Donoghue in the *New York Review of Books* faults Eagleton for failing to adequately define "history" or how it "proves invulnerable to the irony he so relentlessly directs against other ultimate categories." But in *South Atlantic Quarterly,* Wallace Jackson thinks that Eagleton "de-mythologizes the high-cultural pretensions of literary study in the university, recognizes that in fact such study underwrites the practices of state capitalism, and effectively nullifies whatever radical power literature may have as an instrument of social criticism and social change." Kendrick notes in the *New York Times Book Review* that while *Literary Theory* is intended for a nonacademic audience, "academics will be unable to ignore it. . . . Eagleton's expositions render even the most jargon-ridden of contemporary theories accessible to the ordinary educated person, and the questions posed by *Literary Theory* will have to be answered, either by the theoreticians themselves or by those who validate them by accepting their authority." Kellman, who believes that Eagleton successfully assimilates "a motley crowd of structuralists, feminists, hermeneuticians, psychoanalysts, and deconstructionists to his argument that there are no innocent readings, that every literary experience is shaped by ideology," recommends that it "ought to be read with the same blend of enthusiasm and wariness with which it was written, but it ought to be read by anyone concerned with contemporary theory."

Eagleton's *The Function of Criticism: From the Spectator to Post-Structuralism* augments *Literary Theory* in that it traces the history of English literary criticism "from its earliest recognizable appearance around the turn of the eighteenth century to its present institutionalized form," writes Kendrick in the *Voice Literary Supplement.* It is a "polemical history, not of criticism as such," observes Patrick Parrinder in the *London Review of Books,* "but of the 'critical institution' within which it acquired what Eagleton recognises as social significance." And David Montrose points out in the *New Statesman* that Eagleton "seeks to 'recall criticism to its traditional role'—engagement in cultural politics—from what he considers a position of crisis, where it is narrowly preoccupied with literary texts and estranged from social life through confinement to Academe and 'the literary industry.'" "But the heart of this book," says Christopher Norris in *British Book News,* "is clearly to be found in Eagleton's use of the 'public sphere' as a concept to articulate and clarify the relation between criticism and ideology."

Citing Eagleton's greatest strength as "his tenacity in pursuing a contradiction through its every shifting guise and permutation," Baldick adds: "Of all living Marxist critics, he is most emphatically the dialectician . . . and it is the resulting stress upon contradiction which ensures that his historical placings of writers highlight rather than erase their particular features." Norris suggests, however, that at times the polemics are too forceful and reduce his opponents to "so many shadowy figures in a dance-like routine of ingenious argumentation." But understanding the book to concern "all that is wrong with professionalism," Gary Wihl indicates in *South Atlantic Quarterly* that it "enables us to keep in mind its overriding revolutionary point; it attempts to draw us out of our narrowly sanctifying view of literary history and reminds us of our predicament as critics." Baldick believes that in the "urgency and integrity of this view, Terry Eagleton has marked out a position which further discussions of the state of criticism will have to address if they are to take their historical bearings."

Norris concludes in *Southern Humanities Review* that "Eagleton is a stylist of great resource whose arguments derive much of their power from the presently embattled situation of literary theory." And Parrinder suggests that while "one does not go to Eagleton's works for true judgment, by and large, and it is hard to know what contribution he has made to the emancipation of the masses," he nonetheless maintains that "Eagleton remains one of the most spectacular orators in the park, and English criticism would be a good deal less entertaining without his pamphlets."

AVOCATIONAL INTERESTS: Poetry, theatre.

BIOGRAPHICAL/CRITICAL SOURCES:

PERIODICALS

American Book Review, May-June, 1985.
British Book News, February, 1985.
Commentary, March, 1984.
London Review of Books, February 7, 1985.
Modern Fiction Studies, summer, 1984.
Modern Language Review, January, 1979, April, 1985.
Nation, December 24, 1983, January 21, 1984.
New Republic, November 10, 1986.
New Statesman, June 3, 1983, October 5, 1984.
New York Review of Books, July 21, 1983, December 8, 1983, November 6, 1986.
New York Times, April 18, 1986.
New York Times Book Review, September 4, 1983.
Poetics Today, Volume 5, number 1, 1984, Volume 5, number 2, 1985, Volume 7, number 1, 1986.
Sewanee Review, fall, 1978.
South Atlantic Quarterly, summer, 1985, spring, 1986.
Southern Humanities Review, summer, 1985.
Spectator, August 21, 1976.
Thought, December, 1984.
Times Literary Supplement, July 13, 1967, January 23, 1969, August 14, 1970, October 23, 1970, May 20, 1977, November 12, 1982, February 4, 1983, June 10, 1983, November 23, 1984, July 4, 1986.
Voice Literary Supplement, June, 1983, March, 1985.
Washington Post Book World, October 2, 1983.
World Literature Today, winter, 1977.

*   *   *

EAGLETON, Terry
 See EAGLETON, Terence (Francis)

*   *   *

EAST, Michael
 See WEST, Morris L(anglo)

*   *   *

EBERHART, Richard (Ghormley) 1904-

PERSONAL: Born April 5, 1904, in Austin, Minn.; son of Alpha La Rue and Lena (Lowenstein) Eberhart; married Helen Elizabeth Butcher, 1941; children: Richard, Gretchen. *Education:* Attended University of Minnesota, 1922-23; Dartmouth College, B.A., 1926; St. John's College, Cambridge, B.A., 1929, M.A.,

1933; Harvard University, additional study, 1932-33. *Politics:* Democrat. *Religion:* Episcopal.

ADDRESSES: Office—Department of English, Dartmouth College, Hanover, N.H. 03755.

CAREER: Private tutor to son of King Prajadhipok of Siam, 1930-31; St. Mark's School, Southboro, Mass., master in English, 1933-41; Cambridge School, Kendal Green, Mass., English teacher, 1941-42; Butcher Polish Co., Boston, Mass., assistant manager to vice-president, 1946-52, honorary vice-president and member of board of directors; University of Washington, Seattle, poet-in-residence, 1952-53; University of Connecticut, Storrs, professor of English, 1953-54; Wheaton College, Norton, Mass., professor of English and poet-in-residence, 1954-55; Princeton University, Princeton, N.J., Christian Gauss Lecturer and resident fellow, 1955-56; Dartmouth College, Hanover, N.H., professor of English and poet-in-residence, 1956-68, Class of 1925 professor, 1968-71, professor emeritus, 1970—. Elliston Lecturer, University of Cincinnati, 1961. Visiting professor, University of Washington, Seattle, 1952-53, 1967, and 1972, Wheaton College, 1954-55, and University of Florida, 1974-86; adjunct professor, Columbia University, spring, 1975; regents professor, University of California, Davis, fall, 1975. Phi Beta Kappa poet at Tufts University, 1941, Brown University, 1957, Swarthmore College, 1963, Trinity College, 1963, College of William and Mary, 1963, University of New Hampshire, 1964, and Harvard University, 1967. Yaddo Corp., member, 1955—, director, 1964. Founder and president, The Poets' Theatre, Inc., 1950. Member of advisory committee on the arts, John F. Kennedy Memorial Theatre, 1959—. Library of Congress, Washington, D.C., consultant in poetry, 1959-61, honorary consultant in American letters, 1963-69. *Military service:* U.S. Naval Reserve, 1942-46; became lieutenant commander.

MEMBER: Poetry Society of America (honorary president, 1972—), Academy of American Poets (fellow), American Academy and Institute of Arts and Letters, American Academy of Arts and Sciences, Phi Beta Kappa, Century Club (New York), Signet Club, Bucks Harbor Yacht Club (Maine).

AWARDS, HONORS: Harriet Monroe Memorial Prize, 1950; New England Poetry Club award, 1950; Shelley Memorial Award, 1952; Harriet Monroe Poetry Award, 1955; National Institute of Arts and Letters grant in literature, 1955; Bollingen Prize in Poetry (shared with John Hall Wheelock), Yale University, 1962, for highest achievement in field of American poetry; Pulitzer Prize, 1966, for *Selected Poems, 1930-1965;* Academy of American Poets fellowship, 1969; National Book Award, 1977, for *Collected Poems, 1930-1976;* received President's Medallion, University of Florida, 1977; appointed Poet Laureate of the state of New Hampshire, 1979; Rhode Island governor proclaimed a "Richard Eberhart Day" in July, 1982; Sarah Josepha Hall Award, 1982; honorary degrees from Dartmouth College, Skidmore College, College of Wooster, Colgate University, and St. Lawrence University.

WRITINGS:

POETRY

A Bravery of Earth, J. Cape, 1930, Cape & Smith, 1931.
Reading the Spirit, Chatto & Windus, 1936, Oxford University Press, 1937.
Song and Idea, Chatto & Windus, 1940, Oxford University Press, 1947.
Poems, New and Selected, New Directions, 1944.
Burr Oaks, Oxford University Press, 1947.
Brotherhood of Men, Banyan Press, 1949.

An Herb Basket, Cummington Press, 1950.

Selected Poems, Oxford University Press, 1951.

Undercliff Poems, 1946-1953, Chatto & Windus, 1953, Oxford University Press, 1954.

Great Praises, Oxford University Press, 1957.

The Oak: A Poem, Pine Tree Press, 1957.

Collected Poems, 1930-1960, Oxford University Press, 1960.

The Quarry: New Poems, Oxford University Press, 1964.

The Vastness and Indifference of the World, Ferguson Press, 1965.

Fishing for Snakes, privately printed, 1965.

Selected Poems, 1930-1965, New Directions, 1965.

Thirty One Sonnets, Eakins, 1967.

Shifts of Being: Poems, Oxford University Press, 1968.

The Achievement of Richard Eberhart: A Comprehensive Selection of His Poems, edited by Bernard F. Engle, Scott, Foresman, 1968.

Three Poems, Pym Randall Press, 1968.

Fields of Grace, Oxford University Press, 1972.

Collected Poems, 1930-1976, Oxford University Press, 1976, revised edition published as *Collected Poems, 1930-1986,* 1988.

Poems to Poets, Penmaen Press, 1976.

Survivors, Boa Editions, 1979.

Ways of Light, Oxford University Press, 1980.

Chocorua, Nadja, 1980.

Florida Poems, Konglomerati Press, 1983.

The Long Reach: New and Uncollected Poems, 1948-1984, New Directions, 1984.

Maine Poems, Oxford University Press, 1989.

Poetry represented in many anthologies, including *Moment of Poetry,* Johns Hopkins Press, 1962. Contributor of poetry and reviews to journals in United States and other countries.

PLAYS

Collected Verse Plays (contains "The Apparition," first produced in Cambridge, Mass., 1951; "The Visionary Farms," first produced in Cambridge, Mass., 1952; "Triptych," first produced in Chicago, 1955; "The Mad Musician, and Devils and Angels," first produced in Cambridge, Mass., 1962), University of North Carolina Press, 1962.

(Adapter of play) "The Bride From Mantua," first produced in Hanover, New Hampshire, 1964.

OTHER

(Contributor) Michael Roberts, editor, *New Signatures,* Hogarth Press, 1932.

(Editor with Selden Rodman) *War and the Poet,* Devin-Adair, 1945, reprinted, Greenwood Press, 1974.

(Editor) "Dartmouth Poems" series, twelve volumes, Dartmouth Publications, 1958-59, 1962-71.

(Contributor) Manuel A. Viray, editor, *After This Exile,* Phoenix House, 1965.

Of Poetry and Poets (criticism), University of Illinois Press, 1979.

Also author of *Dream Journey of the Head and Heart,* 1962; author and compiler, with Allen Ginsberg, of *To Eberhart From Ginsberg,* Penmaen Press, 1976.

WORK IN PROGRESS: Two books.

SIDELIGHTS: Richard Eberhart is considered by many critics and readers to be one of the major lyric poets of this century. As Ralph J. Mills explains in his book *Richard Eberhart,* "Eberhart explores the possibilities of a personal lyricism enclosing a broad spectrum of human experience and boldly testing the forms and language for articulating what imagination gives and intuition seizes. Dispensing for the most part with the device of the personal persona or fictional speaker . . . and lacking an inclination to commit himself to systematic frameworks of ideas to build private mythologies to support the imaginative interpretation of experience, [Eberhart] . . . openly engage[s] the material of [his] work in fresh, dramatic, and often original ways."

Acknowledging Eberhart's special ability as a lyric poet, Jean Garrigue writes in the *New York Times Book Review* that Eberhart is "essentially a visionary for whom the sensory world is wonderfully vivid, his art from the beginning has been based upon the marriage of the abstract with the passionate and immediate. But it is a poetry of conflict, for his sensory world is usually haunted by some great ghost of its original maker. Or by powers or mysteries that ultimately rule us. This largeness and darkness of reference is essential for his airiness of style when he is airy, his delicacy, his gusto and his elan. And all this is set to a surge of sound, a metered and yet roughened beat."

However, some critics find a possible flaw with this style of writing; the author may be too dependent on inspiration. As a reviewer for the *New York Times Book Review* writes: "He is a poet of fine senses and, being also a poet of visionary intensity, he is dependent on the bolt out of the blue. When he is not sufficiently enthralled, he falls back on his second-best language or that kind of self-created diction where he is talking more than making. He is best when he is complexly sensuous or opaque and compact."

Still, it appears that the majority of critics feel his visionary intensity is what makes Eberhart the poetic genius he is today. Peter Thorsley, Jr., feels strongly that "one may sometimes question the felicity of the expression, but one is never tempted to question the validity of the experience."

While many of Eberhart's poems are examples of what he terms "the rational use of the intellect," and not what the *New York Times Book Review* called "a bolt out of the blue," he wrote in *Poets on Poetry* that he admires "Plato's idea in the Ion when he says, 'For the poet is a light and winged and holy thing, and there is no inventional in him until he has been inspired and is out of his senses, and the mind is no longer in him: when he has not attained to this state, he is powerless and is unable to utter his oracles.' I respect this theory of inspiration because it is beyond and above conscious will. A poem composed as the reception of a 'gift of the gods' would seem to be of a higher origin and nature than a poem composed by taking thought and then by taking care."

Eberhart expanded this thought when he wrote to *CA* in 1980: "Consciousness is still a vast reservoir of spirit which we only partially perceive. If we could see or feel beyond the human condition, is it possible to think that we could feel or think the unthinkable? The Greeks had aspiration to ideas of immortality. We twentieth-century Americans live closer to materialism than to idealism, so we are more nearly measurers, like Aristotle, than dreamers of immortal types, like Plato. I am on Plato's side rather than on Aristotle's. However, our highest imaginations are ungraspable and we are constantly thrown back into the here and now, into materialistic reality. I think that poetry is allied to religion and to music. It helps us to live because it expresses our limitations, our mortality, while exciting us to a beyond which may or not be there; therefore death poems can be written in fullness of spirit, inviting contemplation of ultimate mysteries. Death poems are as good as life poems because they are also life poems, written in flesh and blood. Poetry embraces the moment as it flies."

MEDIA ADAPTATIONS: Eberhart has recorded his poems on long-playing records for the Library of Congress series, "Twentieth Century Poetry in English," and for the "Yale Series of Recorded Poets"; works are also available on audio cassettes. Eberhart has also been the subject of documentary films: one directed by Samuel Mandelbaum, for Tri-Prix in 1972, and others directed by Irving Broughton, for University of Washington in 1974 and 1986 and by Stephen Robitaille, for University of Florida, Gainesville, in 1987.

AVOCATIONAL INTERESTS: Swimming, sailing.

BIOGRAPHICAL/CRITICAL SOURCES:

BOOKS

Concise Dictionary of American Literary Biography: The New Consciousness, 1941-1968, Gale, 1987.
Contemporary Literary Criticism, Gale, Volume 3, 1975, Volume 11, 1979, Volume 56, 1989.
Dictionary of Literary Biography, Volume 48: *American Poets, 1880-1945, Second Series,* Gale, 1986.
Dillard, R. H. W., George Garrett, and John Rees Moore, editors, *The Sounder Few,* University of Georgia Press, 1971.
Engle, Bernard F., *Richard Eberhart,* Twayne, 1972.
Mills, Ralph J., Jr., *Richard Eberhart,* University of Minnesota Press, 1966.
Nemerov, Howard, editor, *Poets on Poetry,* Basic Books, 1966.
Roache, Joel, *Richard Eberhart: The Achievement of an American Poet,* Oxford University Press, 1971.
Thorsley, Peter L., Jr., *Poets in Progress,* Northwestern University Press, 1967.

PERIODICALS

Book Week, August 2, 1964.
Christian Science Monitor, December 22, 1960, July 23, 1968.
Commonweal, December 30, 1960, May 14, 1971.
Forum, spring, 1969.
Nation, January 21, 1961, August 10, 1964.
New Republic, November 20, 1976.
New Statesman, October 15, 1960, September 25, 1964.
New York Herald Tribune, December 4, 1960.
New York Times Book Review, November 22, 1953, January 8, 1961, September 6, 1964, January 12, 1969, January 1, 1978, July 8, 1979.
Northwestern University Tri-Quarterly, winter, 1960.
Parnassus, spring/summer, 1973.
Poetry, December, 1942, January, 1949, October, 1957, February, 1970.
Publishers Weekly, April 29, 1968, February 12, 1979.
Saturday Review, February 11, 1961, December 6, 1962, March 6, 1971.
Southern Review, October, 1977.
Spectator, September 30, 1960.
Times Literary Supplement, October 29, 1964, June 23, 1989.
Virginia Quarterly Review, winter, 1965.
Yale Review, March, 1961.

*   *   *

ECHEGARAY (y EIZAGUIRRE), Jose (Maria Waldo) 1832-1916
(Jorge Hayaseca y Eizaguirre)

PERSONAL: Born in 1832 in Madrid, Spain; died in 1916 in Madrid, Spain.

CAREER: Spanish mathematician, engineer, statesman, and playwright. Worked as a professor of hydraulics, School of Civil Engineering, Madrid, Spain; held several government posts during the Spanish revolutionary period, 1868-1874; lived briefly as an exile in Paris, France; returned to Spain in 1874. Former Minister of Finance for Spain; founder of the Bank of Spain.

AWARDS, HONORS: Elected to Royal Spanish Academy, 1894; recipient, with Frederic Mistral, of the Nobel Prize for literature, 1904.

WRITINGS:

PLAYS

(Under pseudonym Jorge Hayaseca y Eizaguirre) *El libro talonario* (also see below; one-act), [Spain], 1874, 3rd edition, Jose Rodriguez (Madrid), 1881, microcard edition, Falls City Press (Louisville, Ky.), 1968.
La esposa del vengador (also see below; three-act; title means "The Wife of the Avenger"), Jose Rodriguez, 1874.
En el puno de la espada (also see below; three-act), [Madrid], 1875, 3rd edition, Jose Rodriguez, 1876, microcard edition, Falls City Microcards (Louisville, Ky.), 1960.
O locura o santidad (also see below; three-act; title means "Folly or Saintliness"; first produced at Teatro Espanol, January 22, 1877), Imprento de J. M. Ducazcal (Madrid), 1877, translation by Ruth Lansing published as *Madman or Saint,* R. G. Badger (Boston), 1912.
El gladiator de Ravena: Imitacion de las ultimas escenas de la tragedia alemana de Federico Halm (Munch de Bellinghaussen), T. Fortanet (Madrid), 1877, microcard edition, Falls City Press, 1968.
Como empieza y come acaba (three-act), T. Fortanet, 1877, microcard edition, Falls City Press, 1968.
Ni la paciencia de Job (three-act), Jose Rodriguez, 1879, microcard edition, Falls City Microcards, 1959.
Mar sin orillas (three-act), Jose Rodriguez, 1880, microcard edition, Falls City Microcards, 1960.
La muerte en los labios (also see below; three-act; first produced at Teatro Espanol, November 30, 1880), Jose Rodriguez, 1880, 9th edition, Sucesores de Rodriguez y Odriozola, 1897, microcard edition, Falls City Microcards, 1959.
El gran galeoto (also see below; three-act; produced in the United States as *The World and His Wife;* produced in England as *Calumny*), [Spain], 1881, edited with introduction, notes, and vocabulary by Aurelio M. Espinosa, C. A. Koehler & Co. (Boston), 1903, translation by Hannah Lynch published as *The Great Galeoto: A Play in Three Acts,* introduction by Elizabeth R. Hunt, Doubleday, 1914, new and revised edition, Knopf, 1918, reprinted, Las Americas (New York), 1964.
Haroldo el Normado (three-act), Jose Rodriguez, 1881, microcard edition, Falls City Press, 1970.
Conflicto entre dos deberes (three-act), Cosme Rodriguez (Madrid), 1883, microcard edition, Falls City Press, 1968.
Correr en pos de un ideal (three-act), Cosme Rodriguez, 1883, microcard edition, Falls City Press, 1968.
En el pilar y en la cruz (three-act), Cosme Rodriguez, 1883, microcard edition, Falls City Press, 1968.
Un milagro en Egipto (three-act), Cosme Rodriguez, 1883, microcard edition, Falls City Press, 1968.
La peste de Otranto (three-act), Jose Rodriguez, 1884, microcard edition, Falls City Microcards, 1960.
Piensa mal . . . ¿y acertaras? (also see below), first produced in Spain, February 5, 1884.
Obras dramaticas escogidas (contains *La esposa del vengador, En el puno de la espada, O locura o santidad, En el seno de la*

muerte, La muerte en los labios, and *El gran galeoto*), 12 volumes, Imprento de Tello (Madrid), 1884-1905.

Mancha que limpia (also see below; four-act), [Spain], 1885, Jose Rodriguez, 1895, microcard edition, Falls City Press, 1968.

Vida alegre y muerte triste (three-act), Jose Rodriguez, 1885.

Dos fanatismos (three-act), Jose Rodriguez, 1887, reprinted on microcards, Falls City Microcards, 1959.

Manantial que no se agota (three-act), Jose Rodriguez, 1889, microcard edition, Fall City Press, 1968.

Los rigidos (three-act), Jose Rodriguez, 1889, microcard edition, Falls City Press, 1970.

Siempre en ridiculo, [Spain], 1890, translation by T. Walter Gilkyson published as *Always Ridiculous: A Drama in Three Acts,* R. G. Badger, 1916.

Un critico incipiente: Capricho en tres actos y en prosa sobre critica dramatica, Jose Rodriguez, 1891, microcard edition, Falls City Microcards, 1960.

Irene de Otranto (three-act opera), music by Emilio Serrano, Jose Rodriguez, 1891, microcard edition, Falls City Press, 1968.

El hijo de Don Juan, [Spain], 1892, translation by James Graham published as *The Son of Don Juan: An Original Drama in Three Acts; Inspired by the Reading of Ibsen's Work Entitled "Gengangere,"* Roberts Brothers (Boston), 1895, reprinted, Little, Brown, 1918.

Mariana: An Original Drama in Three Acts and an Epilogue, [Spain], 1892, translated by Graham, Roberts Brothers, 1895.

A la orilla del mar (three-act; first performed in Spain at Teatro de la Comedia, December 12, 1893), R. Velasco, 1903.

The Great Galeoto; Folly or Saintliness: Two Plays, translated by Hannay Lynch, L. Wolffe & Co. (Boston), 1895, reprinted, Fertig, 1989.

El estigma (three-act), E. Odriozola (Madrid), 1896.

El prologo de un drama (also see below; one-act), E. Odriozola, 1896, microcard edition, Falls City Press, 1970.

El poder de la impotencia (three-act), Jose Rodriguez, 1897, edited with introduction, notes, and vocabulary by Aurelio M. Espinosa, Schoenhof (Boston), 1906.

La duda (also see below), [Spain], 1898.

El loco dios (four-act; title means "The Insane Gods"), [Spain], 1900, translation by Hunt published in *Poet Lore* as *The Madman Divine (El loco dios),* 1908.

Sic vos non vobis; o, La ultima limosna (also see below; three-act), R. Velasco (Madrid), 1905, microcard edition, Falls City Press, 1970.

A fuerza de arrastrarse (also see below), [Spain], 1905.

Silencio de muerte (three-act), R. Velasco, 1906, microcard edition, Falls City Press, 1970.

El preferido y los cenicientos, [Spain], 1908.

Tierra baja (three-act), R. Velasco, 1909, microcard edition, Falls City Press, 1968.

El primer acto de un drama (continuation of *El prologo de un drama*), R. Velasco, 1914, microcard edition, Falls City Press, 1970.

La rencorosa (three-act), R. Velasco, 1915, microcard edition, Falls City Press, 1970.

Lo sublime en lo vulgar (three-act), R. Velasco, 1918, microcard edition, Falls City Press, 1970.

Teatro escogido (contains *El libro talonario, La ultima noche, En el puno de la espada, O locura o santidad, En el seno de la muerte, La muerte en los labios, El gran galeoto, Piensa mal . . . ¿y acertaras?, De mala raza, Sic vos non vobis: o, La ultima limosna, Mancha que limpia, La duda,* and *A fuerza de arrastrase*), introduction by Amando Lazaro Ros, Aguilar (Madrid), 1955.

Also author of *La realidad y el delirio.*

OTHER

Teoria matematica de la luz, Imprenta de la Viuda de Agualo (Madrid), 1871.

Disertaciones matematicas sobre la cuadratura del circulo, el metodo de Wantzel, y la division de la circunferencia en partes iguales (mathematics), Imprento de la Viuda e Hijo de D. E. Aguado (Madrid), 1887.

Algunas reflexiones generales sobre la critica y el arte literario [Spain], 1894.

Discursos leidos ante la Real Academia Espanola (lectures), Imprenta de los Hijos de J. A. Garcia (Madrid), 1894.

Discurso leido en la Universidad central en la solemne inauguracion del curso academico de 1905 a 1906 (mathematical physics), Colonial (Madrid), 1905.

Cuentos (short stories), [Spain], 1912.

(Translator of Spanish text) Angel Guimera, *Marta of the Lowlands (Terra baixa)* (also see below), English text translation by Wallace Gillpatrick, introduction by John Garrett Underhill, Doubleday, 1914.

Recuerdos (autobiography), three volumes, Ruiz Hermanos (Madrid), 1917.

(Translator) Guimera, *Tierra baja* (three-act play; translation of *Terra baixa*), illustrated by Mauricio de Vassal, Orbis (Barcelona), 1930.

SIDELIGHTS: Regarded as an important link in the history of Spanish drama, the plays of Jose Echegaray recall the romantic style of the nineteenth century, while also foreshadowing the socially conscious plays of the twentieth. Writing both romantic and naturalistic plays, the author drew large audiences during the three decades that followed his first popular work, *La esposa del vengador* ("The Wife of the Avenger"). Critics, however, felt that Echegaray's romances were too melodramatic and that his naturalistic plays were too contrived and suffered from lack of characterization. Consequently, some reviewers objected to the Nobel Prize committee's decision to honor the playwright in 1904. Frank W. Chandler summarized Echegaray this way in his *Modern Continental Playwrights:* Echegaray "delights to portray high-strung characters, intense hysterical souls, driven by passion or idea. He shows the individual struggling with himself or against social institutions. He loves the moral, the heroic, the perfervid. He is a natural rhetorician, less poetic than theatric. At his worst, Echegaray sinks to the level of extravagant melodrama; at his best, he rises to the heights with such original creations as *Folly or Saintliness* and *The Great Galeoto.*"

Part of Echegaray's success, according to Nora Archibald Smith in *Poet Lore,* may be attributed to his entering "upon the dramatic arena at a critical time, when the political disorder and disturbance which followed the revolution of 1868 were paralleled by similar disorder and disturbance upon the stage." Spanish drama had begun to seek its own individuality after a period when it followed the style of the French classicists and needed a playwright to spearhead this change. Echegaray's first works, such as *La esposa del vengador,* were romances in the same vein as *Romeo and Juliet.* Later, with the rise in popularity of dramas about social issues, the playwright also began to address this concern; but "he did so without in any way forsaking the Romantic tradition," noted E. Allison Peers in his *A History of the Romantic Movement in Spain.*

A major influence of Echegaray's social dramas was Norwegian playwright Henrik Ibsen, a point that was readily acknowledged by Echegaray and even noted directly in his play *The Son of Don Juan: An Original Drama in Three Acts; Inspired by the Readings* of Ibsen's Work Entitled "Gengangere." But although both *The Son of Don Juan* and Ibsen's "Gengangere" ("Ghosts") are studies of a character's decline into madness and contain other similarities in plot and dialogue, a number of critics argued that they are indeed completely different works. Bernard Shaw pointed out in a *Saturday Review* article that the cause of insanity in Ibsen's play is due to outside pressures of society beyond the protagonist's control, while in *The Son of Don Juan* Echegaray places all the blame on the main character himself. "Indeed," noted Shaw, "had Echegaray adapted Ibsen's moral to the conditions of domestic life and public opinion in Spain, the process would have destroyed all the superficial resemblances to 'Ghosts' which has led some critics hastily to describe Echegaray's play as a wholesale plagiarism."

Other Echegaray plays, such as *El loco dios* ("The Insane Gods"), also reveal the playwright's debt to Ibsen. As *Sewanee Review* contributor Ruth Lee Kennedy warned, however, not all resemblances in the author's plays are attributable to Ibsen's influence. In Echegaray's *Piensa mal . . . ¿y acertaras?,* for example, the "symbolic story of a wounded bird . . . immediately recalls the use of the wild duck in Ibsen's drama of that name." But *Piensa mal* was staged in early 1884, three years before Echegaray could have read Ibsen's *The Wild Duck.*

Besides *The Son of Don Juan,* other well-known Echegaray plays include *O locura o santidad* ("Folly or Saintiness") and *El gran galeoto* ("The Great Galeoto"), which are "undoubtedly two of Echegaray's best," in *Academy* critic Wentworth Webster's opinion. Both plays are about the destructive powers of public opinion. In *The Great Galeoto,* the author begins with the story of Francesca and Paolo from Dante's *Inferno,* and adds a twist in which the couple's pure love is destroyed by slanderous rumors. In a similar manner, Lorenzo, the protagonist in "Folly or Saintliness" is declared insane by those who cannot understand his high moral principles. Critics like Webster considered the first acts in "Folly or Saintliness" "excellent," but the critic felt the story's resolution suffers when Lorenzo's fate is decided by the destruction of an important document that would vindicate him. "And thus, instead of the solution of the moral problem being laid before us, we have only the more commonplace result, that the world's sentence . . . on a man's sanity may depend on a mere accident."

When considering the lasting relevance of Echegaray's plays, some critics regarded his works as dated. Others, though, took more into consideration the time period in which he wrote. "To get any evaluation of the works of the Spaniard," remarked Kennedy, "his drama should be compared with what was being written in England, France, Italy, and Germany from 1874 to 1884. . . . [By] 1881 Echegaray had written both *O locura o santidad* and *El gran galeoto,* dramas that certainly, from the standpoint of technique, bear comparison with anything written during that decade." Echegaray "is usually classified as a neo-romanticist," Wilma Newberry summarized in *PMLA,* "he is accused of being too melodramatic . . . [and] is called anachronistic and is criticised for blocking the Spanish realist movement." But, Newberry proposed, "Echegaray's true position in the procession of dramatists who have made important contributions to the history of ideas should be reevaluated. Although some aspects of his work may seem anachronistic at the end of the nineteenth century, in many ways he looks forward to the twentieth century, while often drawing inspiration from the great literature of the past."

BIOGRAPHICAL/CRITICAL SOURCES:

BOOKS

Chandler, Frank W., *Modern Continental Playwrights,* Harper, 1931.
Echegaray, Jose, *The Great Galeoto: A Play in Three Acts,* Doubleday, 1914.
Echegaray, Jose, *The Son of Don Juan: An Original Drama in Three Acts; Inspired by the Reading of Ibsen's Work Entitled "Gengangere,"* Little, Brown, 1918.
Jameson, Storm, *Modern Drama in Europe,* Collins, 1920.
Peers, E. Allison, *A History of the Romantic Movement in Spain,* Volume 2, Cambridge University Press, 1940.
Shaw, Donald L., *The Nineteenth Century,* Barnes & Noble, 1972.
Twentieth Century Literary Criticism, Volume 4, Gale, 1981.

PERIODICALS

Academy, November 2, 1895.
PMLA, March, 1966.
Poet Lore, May-June, 1909.
Saturday Review, April 27, 1895, June 1, 1901.
Sewanee Review, October-December, 1926.

—*Sketch by Kevin S. Hile*

*   *   *

ECHO

See PROUST, (Valentin-Louis-George-Eugene-)Marcel

*   *   *

ECO, Umberto 1932-

PERSONAL: Born January 5, 1932, in Alessandria, Italy; son of Giulio and Giovanna (Bisio) Eco; married Renate Ramge (a teacher) September 24, 1962; children: Stefano, Carlotta. *Education:* University of Turin, Ph.D., 1954.

ADDRESSES: Home—Via Melzi d'Eril 23, 20154 Milano, Italy. *Office*—Universita di Bologna, Via Toffano 2, Bologna, Italy.

CAREER: RAI (Italian Radio-Television), Milan, Italy, editor for cultural programs, 1954-59; University of Turin, Turin, Italy, assistant lecturer, 1956-63, lecturer in aesthetics, 1963-64; University of Milan, Milan, lecturer on faculty of architecture, 1964-65; University of Florence, Florence, Italy, professor of visual communications, 1966-69; Milan Polytechnic, Milan, professor of semiotics, 1969-71; University of Bologna, Bologna, Italy, associate professor, 1971-75, professor of semiotics, 1975—. Visiting professor, New York University, 1969, 1976, Northwestern University, 1972, University of California, San Diego, 1975, Yale University, 1977, 1980, 1981, and Columbia University, 1978. Lecturer on semiotics at various institutions throughout the world, including University of Antwerp, Ecole Pratique des Hautes Etudes, University of London, Nobel Foundation, University of Warsaw, University of Budapest, University of Toronto, Murdoch University—Perth, and Amherst College. Member of the Council for the United States and Italy. *Military service:* Italian Army, 1958-59.

MEMBER: International Association for Semiotic Studies (secretary-general, 1972-79, vice-president, 1979—), James Joyce Foundation (honorary trustee).

AWARDS, HONORS: Premio Strega and Premio Anghiari, both 1981, both for *Il nome della rosa;* named honorary citizen of

Monte Cerignone, Italy, 1982; Prix Medicis for best foreign novel, 1982, for French version of *Il nome della rosa;* *Los Angeles Times* fiction prize nomination, 1983, and best fiction book award from Association of Logos Bookstores, both for *The Name of the Rose;* McLuhan Teleglobe Canada Award from UNESCO's Canadian Commission, 1985, for achievement in communications; honorary degrees from Catholic University, Leuven, 1985, Odense University, 1986, Loyola University, Chicago, 1987, State University of New York at Stony Brook, 1987, Royal College of Arts, London, 1987, and Brown University, 1988.

WRITINGS:

IN ITALIAN

Filosofi in liberta, Taylor (Turin), 1958, 2nd edition, 1959.

(Contributor) *Momenti e problema di storia dell'estetica,* Marzorati, 1959.

Opera aperta: Forma e indeterminazione nelle poetiche contemporanee (includes *Le poetiche di Joyce;* also see below), Bompiani, 1962, revised edition, 1972, translation by Anna Cancogni published as *The Open Work,* Harvard University Press, 1989.

Diario minimo, Mondadori, 1963, 2nd revised edition, 1976.

Apocalittici e integrati: Comunicazioni di massa e teoria della cultura di massa, Bompiani, 1964, revised edition, 1977.

Le poetiche di Joyce, Bompiani, 1965, 2nd edition published as *Le poetiche di Joyce dalla "Summa" al "Finnegans Wake,"* 1966.

Appunti per una semiologia delle comunicazioni visive (also see below), Bompiani, 1967.

(Author of introduction) Mimmo Castellano, *Noi vivi,* Dedalo Libri, 1967.

La struttura assente (includes *Appunti per una semiologia delle comunicazioni visive*), Bompiani, 1968, revised edition, 1983.

La definizione dell'arte (title means "The Definition of Art"), U. Mursia, 1968.

(Editor) *L'uomo e l'arte,* Volume 1: *L'arte come mestiere,* Bompiani, 1969.

(Editor with Remo Faccani) *I sistemi di segni e lo strutturalismo sovietico,* Bompiani, 1969, 2nd edition published as *Semiotica della letteratura in URSS,* 1974.

(Editor) *Socialismo y consolacion: Reflexiones en torno a "Los misterios de Paris" de Eugene Sue,* Tusquets, 1970, 2nd edition, 1974.

Le forme del contenuto, Bompiani, 1971.

(Editor with Cesare Sughi) *Cent'anni dopo: Il ritorno dell'intreccio,* Bompiani, 1971.

Il segno, Isedi, 1971, 2nd edition, Mondadori.

(Editor with M. Bonazzi) *I pampini bugiardi,* Guaraldi, 1972.

(Editor) *Estetica e teoria dell'informazione,* Bompiani, 1972.

(Contributor) *Documenti su il nuovo medioevo,* Bompiani, 1973.

(Editor) *Eugenio Carmi: Una pittura de paesaggio?,* G. Prearo, 1973.

Il costume di casa: Evidenze e misteri dell'ideologia italiano, Bompiani, 1973.

Beato di Liebana: Miniature del Beato de Fernando I y Sancha, F. M. Ricci, 1973.

Il superuomo di massa: Studi sul romanzo popolare, Cooperativa Scrittori, 1976, revised edition, Bompiani, 1978.

(Co-editor) *Storia di una rivoluzione mai esistita l'esperimento Vaduz,* Servizio Opinioni, RAI, 1976.

Dalla periferia dell'Impero, Bompiani, 1976.

Come si fa una tesi di laurea, Bompiani, 1977.

Lector in fabula: La cooperazione interpretative nei testi narrativa (also see below), Bompiani, 1979.

(Contributor) *Carolina Invernizio, Matilde Serao, Liala,* La Nuova Italia, 1979.

(Contributor) *Convegno su realta e ideologie dell'informazione,* Milan, 1978, Il Saggiatore, 1979.

(With others) *Perche continuiamo a fare e a insegnare arte?,* Cappelli, 1979.

Sette anni di desiderio, Bompiani, 1983.

Sugli specchi e altri saggi, Bompiani, 1985.

IN ENGLISH TRANSLATION

Il problema estetico in San Tommaso, Edizioni di Filosofia, 1956, 2nd edition published as *Il problema estetico in Tommaso d'Aquino,* Bompiani, 1970, translation by Hugh Bredin published as *The Aesthetics of Thomas Aquinas,* Harvard University Press, 1988.

(Editor with G. Zorzoli) *Storia figurata delle invenzioni: Dalla selce scheggiata al volo spaziali,* Bompiani, 1961, translation by Anthony Lawrence published as *The Picture History of Inventions From Plough to Polaris,* Macmillan, 1963, 2nd Italian edition, Bompiani, 1968.

(Editor with Oreste del Buono) *Il caso Bond,* Bompiani, 1965, translation by R. Downie published as *The Bond Affair,* Macdonald, 1966.

(Editor with Jean Chesneaux and Gino Nebiolo) *I fumetti di Mao,* Laterza, 1971, translation by Frances Frenaye published as *The People's Comic Book: Red Women's Detachment, Hot on the Trail, and Other Chinese Comics,* Anchor Press, 1973.

Il nome della rosa, Bompiani, 1980, translation by William Weaver published as *The Name of the Rose,* Harcourt, 1983.

Postscript to "The Name of the Rose" (originally published in Italian), translation by Weaver, Harcourt, 1984.

Art and Beauty in the Middle Ages (originally published in Italian), translation by Bredin, Yale University Press, 1986.

Travels in Hyper Reality (originally published in Italian), edited by Helen Wolff and Kurt Wolff, translation by Weaver, Harcourt, 1986.

Il pendolo di Foucault (novel), Bompiani, 1988, translation by Weaver published as *Foucault's Pendulum,* Harcourt, 1989.

The Aesthetics of Chaosmos: The Middle Ages of James Joyce (originally published in Italian), translation by Ellen Esrock, Harvard University Press, 1989.

The Bomb and the General (juvenile; originally published in Italian), translation by Weaver, illustrations by Eugenio Carmi, Harcourt, 1989.

IN ENGLISH

A Theory of Semiotics, Indiana University Press, 1976, translation from original English manuscript published as *Trattato di semiotica generale,* Bompiani, 1975.

The Role of the Reader: Explorations in the Semiotics of Texts, Indiana University Press, 1979, revised Italian edition published as *Lector in fabula: La cooperazione interpretative nei testi narrativa,* Bompiani, 1979.

Semiotics and the Philosophy of Language, Indiana University Press, 1984.

(Editor with Thomas A. Sebeok) *Sign of the Three: Dupin, Holmes, Peirce,* Indiana University Press, 1984.

(Editor with others) *Meaning and Mental Representations,* Indiana University Press, 1988.

The Three Astronauts (for children), Harcourt, 1989.

(Editor with Costantino Marmo) *On the Medieval Theory of Signs,* John Benjamins, 1989.

OTHER

Many of Umberto Eco's books have been translated into foreign languages, including German, French, and Spanish. Contributor to numerous encyclopedias, including *Enciclopedia Filosofica* and *Encyclopedic Dictionary of Semiotics.* Also contributor to proceedings of the First Congress of the International Association for Semiotic Studies. Columnist for *Il giorno, La stampa, Corriere della Sera,* and other newspapers and magazines. Contributor of essays and reviews to numerous periodicals, including *Espresso, Corriere della Sera, Times Literary Supplement, Revue Internationale de Sciences Sociales,* and *Nouvelle Revue Francaise.* Member of editorial board, *Semiotica, Poetics Today, Degres, Structuralist Review, Text, Communication, Problemi dell'informazione,* and *Alfabeta;* nonfiction senior editor, Casa Editrice Bompiani, Milan, 1959-75; editor, *VS-Semiotic Studies.*

SIDELIGHTS: No one expected *The Name of the Rose* to become an internationally acclaimed best-seller, least of all Umberto Eco, the man who wrote the book. A respected Italian scholar, Eco had built his literary reputation on specialized academic writing about semiotics—the study of how cultures communicate through signs. Not only was *The Name of the Rose* his first novel, it was also a complex creation, long on philosophy and short on sex—definitely not blockbuster material, especially not in Italy where the market for books is small. Eco himself considered the initial press run of 15,000 copies excessive, according to the London *Times.* That was in 1980. By 1983 *The Name of the Rose* had been translated into more than twenty languages, won several of Europe's most prestigious literary prizes, and sold millions of hardback copies worldwide. Today the novel is considered a publishing phenomenon, and people in the book business are still asking themselves why.

Some experts attribute its success to the current interest in fantasy literature. "For all its historical accuracy, *The Name of the Rose* has the charm of an invented world," Drenka Willen, Eco's editor at Harcourt Brace Jovanovich, told *Newsweek.* Others chalk it up to snob appeal. "Every year there is one great *unread* best-seller. A lot of people who will buy the book will never read it," Howard Kaminsky, president of Warner Books, suggests in that same *Newsweek* article.

But perhaps the most plausible explanation is the one offered by Franco Ferrucci in the *New York Times Book Review:* "The answer may lie in the fact that Mr. Eco is the unacknowledged leader of contemporary Italian culture, a man whose academic and ideological prestige has grown steadily through years of dazzling and solid work." In addition to semiotics—a field that he almost singlehandedly legitimatized—Eco is an expert on logic, literature, aesthetics, and history. In fact, in Eco's opinion, the science of semiotics embraces not only these, but all aspects of culture. Academics have been reading Eco's hypotheses for years in specialized texts such as *A Theory of Semiotics* and *The Role of the Reader: Explorations in the Semiotics of Texts.* While these works are unintelligible to the public at large, some of Eco's concepts have begun to filter down. "Only a specialist or a panicky grad student would read a book called *A Theory of Semiotics,*" Walter Kendrick observes, "but a general reader might well pick up a semiotic novel if it promised to give the gist of the matter without bogging down in jargon. For most readers," Kendrick continues in the *Village Voice Literary Supplement,* "*The Name of the Rose* is worth reading as a sugarcoated version of that otherwise unpalatable subject."

On one level *The Name of the Rose* is a murder mystery in which a number Catholic monks are inexplicably killed. The setting is an ancient monastery in northern Italy, the year is 1327, and the air is rife with evil. Dissention among rival factions of the Franciscan order threatens to tear the church apart, and each side is preparing for a showdown. On one side stand the Spiritualists and the emperor Louis IV who endorse evangelical poverty; on the other, the corrupt Pope John XXII and the monks who believe that the vow of poverty will rob the church of earthly wealth and power. In an effort to avoid a confrontation, both sides agree to meet at the monastery—a Benedictine abbey that is considered neutral ground. To this meeting come William of Baskerville, an English Franciscan empowered to represent the emperor, and Adso, William's disciple and scribe. Before the council can convene, however, the body of a young monk is discovered at the bottom of a cliff, and William, a master logician in the tradition of Sherlock Holmes, is recruited to solve the crime, assisted by Adso, in Watson's role. As the murders proliferate in seeming fulfillment of an apocalyptic prophecy, the sleuths engage in passionate debates about the meaning of scriptures. These theological digressions, which are grounded in fact and frequently studded with Latin quotations, lend a historical dimension to the book. What's more, the evidence that William and Adso pursue involves secret symbols and coded manuscripts—in other words, semiotics.

Nowhere is the importance of decoding symbols more apparent than in the library—an intricate labyrinth that houses all types of books, including volumes on pagan rituals and black magic. The secret of the maze is known to only a few, among them the master librarian whose job it is to safeguard the collection and supervise the circulation of appropriate volumes. William suspects that the murders relate to a forbidden book—a rare work with "the power of a thousand scorpions"—that some of the more curious monks have been trying to obtain. "What the temptation of adultery is for laymen and the yearning for riches is for secular ecclesiastics, the seduction of knowledge is for monks," William explains to Adso. "Why should they not have risked death to satisfy a curiosity of their minds, or have killed to prevent someone from appropriating a jealously guarded secret of their own?"

After being put off the track by a number of red herrings, William finally locates the prohibited book and the "Anti-Christ" who has committed the murders. To reveal the culprit would spoil the story, but it can be reported that the volume in question turns out to be the "lost" second volume of Aristotle's *Poetics,* which extols comedy as a force for good. This the murderer could not stand. As Gerard Reedy explains in his *America* review, the killer "fears that this authoritative explication of comic genres will undermine the seriousness of truth." Believing that Christ never laughed, the murderer cannot abide the laughter of others. He "did a diabolical thing because he loved his truth so lewdly that he dared anything in order to destroy falsehood," William explains to Adso, adding: "Perhaps the mission of those who love mankind is to make people laugh at the truth, *to make truth laugh,* because the only truth lies in learning to free ourselves from insane passion for the truth."

This statement appears to reflect Eco's attitude as well as William's. "It is almost too obvious that William is Mr. Eco himself," Franco Ferrucci points out in the *New York Times Book Review.* Writing in the *Village Voice Literary Supplement* Walter Kendrick explains the connection between William's philosophy and modern semiotics: "Throughout the book, the naive realism of Adso, the narrator, bumps heads with the nominalism of William, his mentor. Realism and nominalism were schools of medieval philosophy. . . . But the two positions correspond rather well to the common sense of a modern reader and the apparent nihilism of a semiotician. . . . Baldly stated, realism maintains that the names of things are directly attached to the essence of what they denote, that universals are 'realer' than particulars. Nominalism attributes no reality to names; they are merely human ways of organizing a world that would otherwise be unmanageable."

Some medievalists have suggested that this is a distinctly modern point of view, out of place in William's world. His comment upon finally solving the case is revealing. "I behaved stubbornly," he tells Adso, "pursuing a semblance of order, when I should have known well there is no order in the universe." Kendrick points out that "such an idea goes far beyond all the heresies for which fourteenth-century people were burned at the stake; not only shouldn't William have known it, he wouldn't have thought it for another 600 years." While acknowledging the inaccuracy, Walter Goodman excuses it in the name of poetic license. "In this novel," he writes in the *New York Times,* "imagination carries the day. William of Baskerville may be an anachronism, but Mr. Eco wants us to know that his rationality, tolerance and compassion would have added light to what used to be known as the Dark Ages." In a letter to *CA,* Eco contests these criticisms. "Many medievalists say that I am correctly mirroring the most advanced ideas of the fourteenth century," he writes, adding that the novel has prompted several articles in academic journals as well as a symposium at the University of Louvain.

If William speaks for reason, Adso—the young novice who, in his old age, will relate the story—represents the voice of faith. Ferrucci believes that Adso reflects the author's second side: "The Eco who writes *The Name of the Rose* is Adso: a voice young and old at the same time, speaking from nostalgia for love and passion. William shapes the story with his insight; Adso gives it his own pathos. He will never think, as William does, that 'books are not made to be believed but to be subjected to inquiry'; Adso writes to be believed."

Another way Eco's novel can be interpreted is as a parable of modern life. The vehement struggle between church and state mirrors much of recent Italian history with its "debates over the role of the left and the accompanying explosion of terrorist violence," writes Sari Gilbert in the *Washington Post.* Eco acknowledges the influence that former Italian premier Aldo Moro's 1978 kidnapping and death had on his story, telling Gilbert that it "gave us all a sense of impotence," but he also warned that the book was not simply a *roman a clef.* "Instead," he told Herbert Mitgang in a *New York Times Book Review* article, "I hope readers see the roots, that everything that existed then—from banks and the inflationary spiral to the burning of libraries—exists today. We are always approaching the time of the anti-Christ. In the nuclear age, we are never far from the Dark Ages."

As with his first novel, Eco's second novel was an international best-seller. Published in 1989 in English as *Foucault's Pendulum,* the book is similar to *The Name of the Rose* in that it is a semiotic murder mystery wrapped in several layers of meaning. The plot revolves around Casaubon the narrator and two Milan editors who break up the monotony of reviewing manuscripts on the occult by combining information from all of them into one computer program called the Plan. Initially conceived as a joke, the Plan connects the Knights Templar—a medieval papal order who fought in the Crusades—with other occult groups throughout history. The program produces a map indicating the geographical point at which the powers of the earth can be controlled. That point is in Paris, France, at Foucault's Pendulum. When occult groups including Satanists get wind of the Plan, they go so far as to kill one of the editors in their quest to gain control of the earth. While this is the basic plot, readers who

move through it will also encounter William Shakespeare, Rene Descartes, Tom and Jerry, Karl Marx, Rhett Butler and Scarlett O'hara, Sam Spade, Frederick the Great of Prussia, Nazis, Rosicrucians, and Jesuits. Eco orchestrates all of these and other diverse characters and groups into his multilayered semiotic story.

Some of the interpretations of the book critics have suggested include reading it as nothing more than an elaborate joke, as an exploration of the ambiguity between text as reality and reality as text, and as a warning that harm comes to those who seek knowledge through bad logic and faulty reasoning. Given this range of interpretation and Eco's interest in semiotics, *Foucault's Pendulum* is probably best described as a book about many things, including the act of interpretation itself.

Foucault's Pendulum generated a broad range of commentary. Some critics faulted the book for digressing too often into scholarly minutia, and others felt Eco had only mixed success in relating the different levels of his tale. Several reviewers, however, praised *Foucault's Pendulum.* Comparing the work to his first novel, Herbert Mitgang, for example, said in the *New York Times* that the book "is a quest novel that is deeper and richer than 'The Name of the Rose.' It's a brilliant piece of research and writing—experimental and funny, literary and philosophical—that bravely ignores the conventional expectations of the reader." Eco offered his own opinion of his novel in *Time:* "This was a book conceived to irritate the reader. I knew it would provoke ambiguous, nonhomogeneous responses because it was a book conceived to point up some contradictions."

In 1979—before the publication of his two best-selling novels—Eco told *CA:* "I think the duty of a scholar is not only to do scientific research but also to communicate with people through various media about the most important issues of social life from the point of view of his own discipline."

MEDIA ADAPTATIONS: Jean-Jacques Annaud directed a 1986 film adaptation of Eco's novel, *The Name of the Rose;* the movie starred Sean Connery as William of Baskerville.

BIOGRAPHICAL/CRITICAL SOURCES:

BOOKS

Bestsellers 90, Issue 2, Gale, 1990.
Contemporary Literary Criticism, Volume 28, Gale, 1984.
Eco, Umberto, *The Name of the Rose,* translation by William Weaver, Harcourt, 1983.

PERIODICALS

America, August 3, 1983.
American Anthropologist, September, 1978.
Art Journal, winter, 1976-77.
Atlantic, November, 1989.
Corriere della Sera, June 1, 1981.
Harper's, August, 1983.
International Philosophical Quarterly, June, 1980.
Journal of Communication, autumn, 1976.
Language, Volume 53, number 3, 1977.
Language in Society, April, 1977.
Los Angeles Times, November 9, 1989.
Maclean's, July 18, 1983.
Merkur, Volume 37, number 1, 1983.
New Republic, September 5, 1983.
Newsweek, July 4, 1983, September 26, 1983, September 29, 1986, November 13, 1989.
New York Review of Books, July 21, 1983.
New York Times, June 4, 1983, December 13, 1988, October 11, 1989.

New York Times Book Review, June 5, 1983, July 17, 1983, October 15, 1989.

People, August 29, 1983.

Quaderni Medievali, June 1, 1981.

Time, June 13, 1983, March 6, 1989.

Times (London), September 29, 1983, November 3, 1983.

Times Literary Supplement, July 8, 1977, March 3, 1989.

Village Voice Literary Supplement, October, 1983, November, 1989.

Wall Street Journal, June 20, 1983, November 14, 1989.

Washington Post, October 9, 1983, November 26, 1989.

Washington Post Book World, October 29, 1989.

*   *   *

EDGAR, David 1948-

PERSONAL: Born February 26, 1948, in Birmingham, Warwickshire, England; son of Barrie (a television producer) and Joan (Burman) Edgar. *Education:* Manchester University, B.A. (with honors), 1969. *Politics:* Socialist. *Religion:* None. *Avocational interests:* Cooking.

ADDRESSES: Home—Birmingham, England. *Agent*—Michael Imison, 28 Almeida St., London N1 1TD, England.

CAREER: Playwright. Bradford *Telegraph and Argus,* reporter, 1969-72; Leeds Polytechnic, fellow in creative writing, 1972-74; Birmingham Repertory Theatre, resident playwright, 1974-75; Birmingham University, lecturer in play writing, 1974-78, honorary fellow in play writing, 1988—; Royal Shakespeare Company, literary adviser, 1984-88.

MEMBER: Association of Cinematograph, Television and Allied Technicians, Writers' Guild, Theatre Writers' Union.

AWARDS, HONORS: United Kingdom/United States Bicentennial Arts fellow, 1978-79; John Whiting Award, Arts Council of Great Britain, for "Destiny"; Society of West End Theatres award for best play, Antoinette Perry Award ("Tony"), and New York Drama Critics Circle award for best play, all 1982, for "The Life and Adventures of Nicholas Nickleby"; Emmy Award nomination, Academy of Television Arts and Sciences, 1983, for television production of "The Life and Adventures of Nicholas Nickleby"; "Maydays" was named best new play by a number of periodicals, including *Plays and Players, Punch, The Stage,* and *Daily Express.*

WRITINGS:

PLAYS

"Two Kinds of Angel" (one-act), first produced in Bradford, England, at Bradford University Theatre, July, 1970; produced in London, England, at Basement Theatre, February, 1971.

"A Truer Shade of Blue," first produced in Bradford at Bradford University Theatre, August, 1970.

"Bloody Rosa," first produced in Bradford at Bradford University Theatre, September, 1970; produced in Edinburgh, Scotland, at Edinburgh Festival, August, 1971.

"Still Life: Man in Bed," first produced in Edinburgh at Pool Theatre, May, 1971; produced in London at Little Theatre, July, 1972.

"Acid," first produced in Bradford at Bradford University Theatre, July, 1971; produced in Edinburgh at Edinburgh Festival, August, 1971.

"The National Interest" (one-act), produced by General Will (theatre company), August, 1971.

"Conversation in Paradise," first produced in Edinburgh at Edinburgh University Theatre, October, 1971.

"Tedderella," first produced in Edinburgh at Pool Theatre, December, 1971; produced in London at Bush Theatre, January 10, 1973.

"The Rupert Show" (one-act), first produced in Bradford at Bradford University Theatre; produced by General Will, January, 1972.

"The End," first produced in Bradford at Bradford University Theatre, March, 1972.

"Rent; or, Caught in the Act," produced by General Will, May, 1972; produced in London at Unity Theatre, June, 1972.

"Excuses, Excuses" (two-act), first produced in Coventry, England, at Belgrade Theatre, May, 1972; produced in London at Open Space Theatre, July, 1973; produced as "Fired" by Second City Theatre Co., January, 1975.

"State of Emergency" (one-act), first produced by General Will, August, 1972; produced in London at Royal Court Theatre Upstairs, November 7, 1972.

(With Tony Bicat, Howard Brenton, Brian Clark, Francis Fichs, David Hare, and Snoo Wilson) "England's Ireland," first produced in Amsterdam, Netherlands, at Mickery Theatre, September, 1972; produced in London at Round House Theatre, October 2, 1972.

"Road to Hanoi," first produced by Paradise Foundry (theatre company), October, 1972.

"Not with a Bang But a Whimper," first produced in Leeds, England, at Leeds Polytechnic Theatre, November, 1972.

"Death Story," first produced in Birmingham, England, at Birmingham Repertory Studio Theatre, November, 1972; produced in New York by Manhattan Theatre Club, March, 1975.

(With Brenton) "A Fart for Europe" (one-act); produced in London at Royal Court Theatre Upstairs, January 18, 1973.

(With others) "Up Spaghetti Junction," first produced in Birmingham at Birmingham Repertory Studio Theatre, February, 1973.

"Gangsters" (also see below), produced in London at Soho Polytechnic Lunchtime Theatre, February 13, 1973.

"Baby Love" (one-act; also see below), first produced in Leeds at Leeds Playhouse, March 16, 1973; produced in London at Soho Polytechnic Lunchtime Theatre, May 28, 1973.

"Liberated Zone," produced in Bingley, England, at Bingley College of Education, June, 1973.

"The Case of the Workers' Plane" (two-act), produced in Bristol, England, at Bristol New Vic, June, 1973; revised play produced as "Concorde Cabaret" (also see below), by Avon Touring Co., January, 1975.

"Operation Iskra" (three-act); produced by Paradise Foundry, September 4, 1973.

"The Eagle Has Landed" (also see below), produced in Liverpool, England, at Liverpool University, November, 1973.

"The Dunkirk Spirit," produced by General Will, January, 1974.

Dick Deterred (two-act; produced in London at Bush Theatre, February 25, 1974; produced in New York at Redfield Theatre, January, 1983), Monthly Review Press, 1974.

"The All-Singing All-Talking Golden Oldie Rock Revival Ho Chi Minh Peace Love and Revolution Show," produced in Bingley at Bingley College of Education, March, 1974.

"Man Only Dines," produced in Leeds at Leeds Polytechnic Theatre, June, 1974.

O Fair Jerusalem (produced in Birmingham at Birmingham Repertory Studio Theatre, May, 1975), Methuen, 1987.

"Summer Sports," first produced in Birmingham by Birmingham Arts Lab, July, 1975; produced in London at Bankside Globe Theatre, August 7, 1975; produced as "Blood Sports" at Bush Theatre, June 28, 1976.

"The National Theatre," produced in London at Open Space Theatre, October 14, 1975.

"Events Following the Closure of a Motorcycle Factory," produced in Birmingham at Birmingham Repertory Studio Theatre, February, 1976.

Saigon Rose (also see below; produced in Edinburgh at Traverse Theatre, July, 1976; produced in New York at Westside Mainstage, November, 1982), Methuen, 1987.

Destiny (also see below; first produced in Stratford, England, at Other Place, September 22, 1976; produced on the West End at Aldwych Theatre, May 12, 1977), Eyre Methuen, 1976.

(Adapter) "Welcome to Dallas, J. C." (based on a play by Alfred Jarry), produced in London, 1976.

"The Perils of Bardfrod," produced in Bradford at Theatre in the Mill, Bradford University, November, 1976.

Wreckers (first produced in Exeter, England, by 7:84 Theatre Co., February 10, 1977; produced in London at Half Moon Theatre, April 19, 1977), Eyre Methuen, 1977.

Our Own People (first produced by Pirate Jenny [theatre company], November, 1977; produced in London at Royal Court Theatre, January 9, 1978), Eyre Methuen, 1987.

Ball Boys, Pluto Press, 1978.

(Adapter) *The Jail Diary of Albie Sachs* (also see below; produced in London at Warehouse Theatre, June 16, 1978; produced in New York by Manhattan Theatre Club, November, 1979), Collings, 1978.

(Adapter) *Mary Barnes* (first produced in Birmingham at Birmingham Repertory Studio Theatre, August 31, 1978; produced in London at Royal Court Theatre, January 10, 1979; produced in New York at New York Theatre Studio, July, 1983), Eyre Methuen, 1979.

(With Susan Todd) *Teendreams* (produced in Bristol at Vandyck Theatre, January 26, 1979; revised version produced at Bristol University, March, 1987), Eyre Methuen, 1979.

(Adapter) *The Life and Adventures of Nicholas Nickleby* (also see below; based on the Charles Dickens novel; first produced on the West End by Royal Shakespeare Co. at Aldwych Theatre, June 21, 1980; produced on Broadway at Plymouth Theatre, October 5, 1981), Dramatists Play Service, 1982.

Maydays (produced in London at Barbican Theatre, 1983), Eyre Methuen, 1983.

Entertaining Strangers: A Play for Dorchester (produced in Dorchester, England, 1985; revised version produced in London, 1987), Methuen, 1985.

That Summer (produced in London, 1987), Methuen, 1987.

Plays 1, Methuen, 1987.

TELEVISION SCRIPTS

"The Eagle Has Landed" (based on play of the same title), Granada Television, 1973.

"Sanctuary" (based on the author's play "Gangsters"), Scottish Television, 1973.

"I Know What I Meant," Granada Television, 1974.

"Baby Love" (based on play of the same title), British Broadcasting Corp. (BBC), 1974.

"Concorde Cabaret" (based on play of the same title), Harlech Television, 1975.

(With Robert Muller and Hugh Whitemore) "Censors," BBC, 1975.

"The Midas Touch," BBC, 1975.

"Destiny" (based on play of the same title), BBC, 1978.

"The Jail Diary of Albie Sachs" (based on play of the same title), BBC, 1980.

"The Life and Adventures of Nicholas Nickleby" (based on play of the same title), Channel Four, 1982, syndicated in America by Mobil Showcase Theatre, 1983.

OTHER

"Ecclesiastes" (radio play), BBC Radio 4, 1977.

"Saigon Rose" (radio play; based on play of the same title), BBC Radio 3, 1979.

"Lady Jane" (screenplay), Paramount, 1986.

The Second Time as Farce: Reflections on the Drama of Mean Times, Lawrence & Wishart, 1988.

Contributor to books and periodicals.

SIDELIGHTS: Best known for adapting Charles Dickens's book *The Life and Adventures of Nicholas Nickleby* into the highly-publicized theatre event of the 1980-81 season, David Edgar is also notable as one of the most outspoken—and prolific—playwrights of Britain's New Left. Since 1970, when "Two Kinds of Angel" premiered, Edgar has seen more than forty of his plays and musicals successfully staged.

Most of Edgar's early work reflected his interest in the "agit-prop" (extremely liberal) politics of Britain's counterculture; throughout his career, his dramatic style has often drawn from the encompassing, audience-involving mode popularized by Bertolt Brecht. One scene from "The Jail Diary of Albie Sachs," for instance, calls for the audience to join the political-prisoner title character in remaining absolutely quiet for two minutes. This gesture "actually conveys the nature of prison solitude," says Michael Billington in the *New York Times.* "The relief with which the audience shuffles and coughs at the end of that period says a lot about the torture of confinement."

The theme of imprisonment is also explored in Edgar's adaptation "Mary Barnes," the true story of a woman's harrowing treatment for schizophrenia at an East London "therapy community." The play, according to Stanley Weintraub in his *Dictionary of Literary Biography* article, examines "not only what constitutes madness by societal standards but also whether or not society is guilty of complicity in the maladjustment of a talented human being, whether or not the mind's potential is wasted in order to seize easy solutions for controlling a 'mad' person, and whether or not one can even talk of sanity in a less-than-sane society."

In a lighter vein, the playwright created a musical farce, "Dick Deterred," which compares the administration of U.S. President Richard Nixon to the court of the corrupt King Richard III. This work features such characters as H. R. (Bob) Buckingham, the king's chief of staff, and Eugene McClarence, "duke and Senator from Minnesota, [who] is done in by Richard, Mayor of Chicago," as Richard F. Shepard writes in a *New York Times* review. With another comedy, "Rent; or, Caught in the Act," Edgar prefigured his success with "Nicholas Nickleby" by giving his characters Dickensian names like Mr. Devious (of the legal firm of Devious, Devious, and Downright Dishonest) and Honest Tom Hard-Done-By, the corruptible hero of the piece. "State of Emergency" and "Operation Iskra" constitute two more titles of what Weintraub calls the author's "agitprop cartoons."

Running eight and one half hours, Edgar's "Nicholas Nickleby" set transatlantic records as the longest play ever produced and, in New York, for the highest theatre ticket price ever legally set.

While many objected to the one-hundred-dollar price for the two evenings of entertainment (hardier playgoers could opt to see the entire show in one day), *Time* magazine critic Richard Corliss points out that at twenty cents per minute, "Nicholas Nickleby" was one of Broadway's biggest bargains. In adapting Dickens's book, Edgar observes to Corliss, the author faced "a twofold challenge: to convert a rambling, complexly plotted novel into a play in a few months, and to respond to ideas from the two directors [Trevor Nunn and John Caird], from Designer John Napier, from Composer Stephen Oliver and all those actors." The challenge was met with overwhelming success: "Nicholas Nickleby" went on to win several theatre awards in both artistic and technical categories. The production also captured praise such as that of Bernard Levin in the *Times,* who describes the event as "a celebration of love and justice that is true to the spirit of Dickens's belief that those are the fulcrums on which the universe is moved, and the consequence is that we come out not merely delighted but strengthened, not just entertained but uplifted, not only affected but changed."

Edgar told *CA:* "The aim of my work is to create a theatre of public life, as a counter to the domestic drama which dominates theatre and television on both sides of the Atlantic. I have become interested in adaptation of historical and contemporary works in pursuit of this aim."

BIOGRAPHICAL/CRITICAL SOURCES:

BOOKS

Contemporary Literary Criticism, Volume 42, Gale, 1987.
Dictionary of Literary Biography, Volume 13: *British Dramatists since World War II,* Gale, 1982.
Hayman, Ronald, *British Theatre since 1955,* Oxford University Press, 1979.
Itzin, Catherine, *Stages in the Revolution,* Eyre Methuen, 1980.
Swain, Elizabeth, *David Edgar: Playwright and Politician,* Peter Lang, 1986.
Trussler, Simon, editor, *New Theatre: Voices of the Seventies,* Eyre Methuen, 1981.

PERIODICALS

Los Angeles Times, October 23, 1985, February 7, 1986.
Newsweek, October 12, 1981.
New York Times, March 18, 1979, March 6, 1980, October 5, 1981, January 10, 1982, November 30, 1982, January 24, 1983, February 7, 1986, February 23, 1986, July 29, 1986, August 25, 1986, November 19, 1987, January 17, 1988.
Time, October 5, 1981, February 24, 1986, July 14, 1986.
Times (London), July 8, 1980, October 22, 1983, October 14, 1987.

*   *   *

EDMONDSON, Wallace
See ELLISON, Harlan

*   *   *

EDWARDS, Eli
See McKAY, Festus Claudius

*   *   *

EHRENREICH, Barbara 1941-

PERSONAL: Born August 26, 1941, in Butte, Mont.; daughter of Ben Howes and Isabelle Oxley (Isely) Alexander; married John Ehrenreich, August 6, 1966 (marriage ended); married second husband, Gary Stevenson, December 10, 1983; children: (first marriage) Rosa, Benjamin. *Education:* Reed College, B.A., 1963; Rockefeller University, Ph.D., 1968. *Politics:* "Socialist and feminist." *Religion:* None.

ADDRESSES: Home—9 Devine Ave., Syosset, N.Y. 11791.

CAREER: Health Policy Advisory Center, New York City, staff member, 1969-71; State University of New York College at Old Westbury, assistant professor of health sciences, 1971-74; writer, 1974—. Associate fellow, New York Institute for the Humanities, 1980-; fellow, Institute for Policy Studies, 1982—. Cochairperson, Democratic Socialists of America, 1983—.

AWARDS, HONORS: National Magazine award, 1980; Ford Foundation for Humanistic Perspectives on Contemporary Issues, 1981; Guggenheim fellow, 1987.

WRITINGS:

(With husband, John Ehrenreich) *Long March, Short Spring: The Student Uprising at Home and Abroad,* Monthly Review Press, 1969.
(With J. Ehrenreich) *The American Health Empire: Power, Profits, and Politics, a Report from the Health Policy Advisory Center,* Random House, 1970.
(With Deirdre English) *Witches, Midwives, and Nurses,* Feminist Press, 1972.
(With English) *Complaints and Disorders: The Sexual Politics of Sickness,* Feminist Press, 1973.
(With English) *For Her Own Good: One Hundred Fifty Years of the Experts' Advice to Women,* Doubleday, 1978.
The Hearts of Men: American Dreams and the Flight from Commitment, Doubleday, 1983.
(With Elizabeth Hess and Gloria Jacobs) *Re-making Love: The Feminization of Sex,* Anchor Press/Doubleday, 1986.
(With Fred Block, Richard Cloward, and Frances Fox Piven) *The Mean Season: An Attack on the Welfare State,* Pantheon, 1987.
Fear of Falling: The Inner Life of the Middle Class, Pantheon Books, 1989.
The Worst Years of Our Lives: Irreverent Notes from a Decade of Greed, Pantheon Books, 1990.

Also author, with Annette Fuentes, of the pamphlet *Women in the Global Factory,* South End Press, 1983. Contributor to magazines, including *Radical America, Nation, Esquire, Vogue, New Republic,* and the *New York Times Magazine.* Contributing editor, *Ms.,* 1981—, and *Mother Jones,* 1988—.

SIDELIGHTS: Outspoken feminist and socialist party leader, Barbara Ehrenreich crusades for social justice in her books. While working for the Health Policy Advisory Center, she published a scathing critique of the American health "empire," exposing its inefficiency, inhumanity, and self-serving policies. Then, turning from the population in general to women in particular, Ehrenreich and her co-author Deirdre English unveiled the male domination of the female health care system in *Complaints and Disorders: The Sexual Politics of Sickness* and *For Her Own Good: One Hundred Fifty Years of the Experts' Advice to Women.* In her most controversial book to date, *The Hearts of Men: American Dreams and the Flight from Commitment,* Ehrenreich takes on the whole male establishment, challenging the assumption that feminism is at the root of America's domestic upheaval.

Describing *The Hearts of Men* as a study of "the ideology that shaped the breadwinner ethic," Ehrenreich surveys the three decades between the 1950s and the 1980s, showing how male commitment to home and family collapsed during this time. "The result," according to *New York Times* contributor Eva Hoffman, "is an original work of cultural iconography that supplements—and often stands on its head—much of the analysis of the relations between the sexes that has become the accepted wisdom of recent years." Ehrenreich's interpretation of the evidence led her to the surprising conclusion that anti-feminism evolved not in response to feminism—but to men's abdication of their breadwinner role.

The seeds of male revolt were planted as far back as the 1950s, according to Ehrenreich, when what she calls "the gray flannel dissidents" began to balk at their myriad responsibilities. "The gray flannel nightmare of the commuter train and the constant pressure to support a houseful of consumers caused many men to want to run away from it all," Carol Cleaver writes in the *New Leader*. What held these men in check, says Ehrenreich, was the fear that, as bachelors, they would be associated with homosexuality. Hugh Hefner banished that stigma with the publication of *Playboy,* a magazine whose name alone "defied the convention of hard-won maturity," Ehrenreich says in her book. "The magazine's real message was not eroticism, but escape . . . from the bondage of breadwinning. Sex—or Hefner's Pepsi-clean version of it—was there to legitimize what was truly subversive about *Playboy*. In every issue, every month, there was a Playmate to prove that a playboy didn't have to be a husband to be a man." Around this time, another more openly rebellious group called the Beats came into ascendancy. Rejecting both marriage and job for the glory of the road, Beats like Jack Kerouac embodied a freewheeling lifestyle that appealed to many men, Ehrenreich maintains.

Neither separately nor in conjunction with one another did these dissident groups possess the power to lure large numbers of male breadwinners from their traditional roles. To allow them "comfortable entree into a full-scale male revolt . . . would take the blessing of those high priests of normalcy, psychologists and doctors," writes Judith Levine in the *Village Voice*. "The *deus ex medica*—the 'scientific' justification for a male revolt—was coronary heart disease. The exertion of breadwinning, Ehrenreich writes in the most original section of her book, was allegedly, literally attacking the hearts of men.

In the decades that followed, men's increasing "flight from commitment" was sanctioned by pop psychologists and other affiliates of the Human Potential Movement, who banished guilt and encouraged people to "do their own thing." Unfortunately for women, Ehrenreich concludes that men abandoned the breadwinner role "without overcoming the sexist attitudes that role has perpetuated: on the one hand, the expectation of female nurturance and submissive service as a matter of right; on the other hand a misogynist contempt for women as 'parasites' and entrappers of men." In response to male abdication, women increasingly adopted one of two philosophies: they became feminists, committed to achieving economic and social parity with men, or they became anti-feminists, who tried to keep men at home by binding themselves ever more tightly to them.

Despite such efforts, Ehrenreich concludes that women have not fared well, but instead have found themselves increasingly on their own "in a society that never intended to admit us as independent persons, much less as breadwinners for others."

Widely reviewed in both magazines and newspapers, *The Hearts of Men* was hailed for its provocative insights—even as individual sections of the study were soundly criticized. In her *Village Voice* review, for instance, Judith Levine is both appreciative of the work and skeptical of its conclusions: "Barbara Ehren-

reich—one of the finest feminist-socialist writers around—has written a witty, intelligent book based on intriguing source material. *The Hearts of Men* says something that needs saying: men have not simply reacted to feminism—skulking away from women and children, hurt, humiliated, feeling cheated of their legal and emotional rights. Men, as Ehrenreich observes, have, as always, done what they want to do. . . . I applaud her on-the-mark readings of *Playboy,* medical dogma, and men's liberation; her insistence that the wage system punishes women and children when families disintegrate; her mordant yet uncynical voice. . . . But I believe *The Hearts of Men* is wrong. When she claims that the glue of families is male volition and the breadwinner ideology—and that a change in that ideology caused the breakup of the family—I am doubtful. The ideology supporting men's abdication of family commitment is not new. It has coexisted belligerently with the breadwinner ethic throughout American history."

Similarly, in a *New York Times Book Review* article, Carol Tarvis describes *The Hearts of Men* as "a pleasure to read, entertaining and imaginative," but goes on to say that "Ehrenreich's analysis falters in its confusion of causes and effects. She continually implies a sequence (first came concerted pressures upon men to conform, then male protest, then scientific legitimation of male protest) when her own evidence shows simultaneity. . . . Further, to suggest that feminism came after the male revolt is to mix what people say with what they do. . . . In arguing that male protest preceded female protest, Miss Ehrenreich succumbs to an unhelpful, unanswerable 'Who started this?' spiral."

While *New York Times* contributor Eva Hoffman echoes Tarvis's concern about the confusion of causes and effects, she points out that "by her own admission, Miss Ehrenreich is more interested in cultural imagery and ideas than in sociological proof; and to this reader, her narrative makes good, if sometimes unexpected sense." *Los Angeles Times* reviewer Lois Timnick reaches a similar conclusion: "One may take issue with her cause-and-effect pairings, her prescription for cure . . . and her rather gloomy view of the '80s. . . . But Ehrenreich needs especially to be read by those who fear that 'women's libbers' will wrest away the values she shows men tossed out long ago, or who still cling to the notion that we could, if we wanted, go back to the mythical 'Ozzie and Harriet' days."

In the 1986 *Re-making Love: The Feminization of Sex,* co-authored with Elizabeth Hess and Gloria Jacobs, Ehrenreich reports and applauds the freer attitudes towards sex that women adopted in the 1970s and 1980s. The authors assert that women have gained the ability to enjoy sex just for the sake of pleasure, separating it from idealistic notions of love and romance. In her review of *Re-making Love* for the *Chicago Tribune,* Joan Beck noted that the book "is an important summing up of what has happened to women and sex in the last two decades and [that it] shows why the sex revolution requires re-evaluation." Beck, however, argued that the authors ignore the "millions of walking wounded"—those affected by sexually transmitted diseases, unwanted pregnancy, or lack of lasting relationships. *Washington Post Book World* contributor Anthony Astrachan also expressed a wish for a deeper analysis, but nevertheless found *Re-making Love* "full of sharp and sometimes surprising insights that come from looking mass culture full in the face."

Ehrenreich's next work to attract critical notice, *Fear of Falling: The Inner Life of the Middle Class,* examines the American middle class and its attitudes towards people of the working and poorer classes. Jonathan Yardley wrote in the *Washington Post* that what Ehrenreich actually focuses on is a class "composed of articulate, influential people. . . . in fact what most of us think of as the upper-middle class." According to Ehrenreich this group perceives itself as threatened, is most concerned with self-preservation, and has isolated itself—feeling little obligation to work for the betterment of society. This attitude, Ehrenreich maintains, is occurring at a time when the disparity in income between classes has reached the greatest point since World War II and has become "almost as perilously skewed as that of India," Joseph Coates quoted *Fear of Falling* in *Tribune Books.*

Globe and Mail contributor Maggie Helwig, though praising the book as "witty, clever, [and] perceptive," described as unrealistic Ehrenreich's hope for a future when everyone could belong to the professional middle class and hold fulfilling jobs. Similarly, David Rieff remarked in the *Los Angeles Times Book Review* that Ehrenreich's proposed solutions to class polarization are overly optimistic and tend to romanticize the nature of work. "Nonetheless," Rieff concluded, " 'Fear of Falling' is a major accomplishment, a breath of fresh thinking about a subject that very few writers have known how to think about at all." The book elicited even higher praise from Coates, who deemed it "a brilliant social analysis and intellectual history, quite possibly the best on this subject since Tocqueville's."

BIOGRAPHICAL/CRITICAL SOURCES:

BOOKS

Ehrenreich, Barbara, *Fear of Falling: The Inner Life of the Middle Class,* Pantheon, 1989.
Ehrenreich, Barbara, *The Hearts of Men: American Dreams and the Flight from Commitment,* Doubleday, 1983.

PERIODICALS

Chicago Tribune, September 25, 1986.
Globe and Mail (Toronto), August 26, 1986.
Los Angeles Times, July 24, 1983.
Los Angeles Times Book Review, August 20, 1989.
Nation, December 24, 1983.
New Leader, July 11, 1983.
New Republic, July 11, 1983.
New York Review of Books, July 1, 1971.
New York Times, January 20, 1971, August 16, 1983.
New York Times Book Review, March 7, 1971, June 5, 1983, August 6, 1989.
Times Literary Supplement, July 22, 1977.
Tribune Books, November 8, 1987, September 24, 1989.
Village Voice, February 5, 1979, August 23, 1983.
Washington Post, August 23, 1989.
Washington Post Book World, August 19, 1979, July 24, 1983, November 9, 1986.

*   *   *

EINSTEIN, Albert 1879-1955

PERSONAL: Born March 14, 1879, in Ulm, Germany (now West Germany); naturalized Swiss citizen, 1901; immigrated to United States, 1933, naturalized citizen, 1940; died of a ruptured aorta, April 18, 1955, in Princeton, NJ; son of Hermann and Pauline (Koch) Einstein; married Mileva Maric, 1903 (divorced, 1919); married cousin, Elsa Einstein Lowenthal, 1919 (died, 1936); children: (first marriage) Hans Albert, Edward. *Education:* Graduated from Swiss Federal Institute of Technology, c. 1900; University of Zurich, Ph.D., 1905. *Avocational interests:* Playing the violin, sailing.

ADDRESSES: Home—112 Mercer St., Princeton, NJ.

CAREER: Theoretical physicist, peace activist, and writer. Teacher at Winterthur Technical School, 1901; Swiss Patent Office, Bern, Switzerland, technical assistant, 1902-09; University of Bern, Bern, lecturer, 1908-09; University of Zurich, Zurich, Switzerland, associate professor of physics, 1909-11; German University, Prague, Czechoslovakia, professor of physics, 1911-12; Swiss Federal Institute of Technology, Zurich, professor of physics, 1912-14; University of Berlin, Berlin, Germany, professor of physics, 1914-c. 1932; Kaiser Wilhelm Institute for Physics, Berlin, director, 1914-c. 1932; Institute for Advanced Study, Princeton, NJ, professor of theoretical physics, 1933-45, life member, 1933-55. Herbert Spencer Lecturer at Oxford University, 1933. Participated in World Government Movement.

MEMBER: Prussian Academy of Sciences, Royal Society (fellow), French Academy of Sciences (fellow).

AWARDS, HONORS: Nobel Prize in Physics, 1921; named first honorary citizen of Tel Aviv, 1923; Copley Medal, Royal Society of London, 1925; Gold Medal, Royal Astronomical Society, London, 1926; Franklin Institute Medal, 1935; offered presidency of Israel, 1952 (declined); received honorary degrees from Universities of Geneva, Zurich, Rostock, Madrid, Brussels, Buenos Aires, Paris, London, Glasgow, Leeds, and Manchester, and Cambridge, Oxford, Harvard, Princeton, New York State, and Yeshiva Universities.

WRITINGS:

PHYSICS

Eine neue Bestimmung der Molekueldimensionen, K. J. Wyss (Bern), 1905.
(With Marcel Grossman) *Entwurf einer verallgemeinerten Relativitaetstheorie und eine Theorie der Gravitation,* Teubner (Leipzig), 1913.
Die Grundlage der allgemeinen Relativitaetstheorie, J. A. Barth (Leipzig), 1916 (also see below).
Ueber die spezielle und allgemeine Relativitaetstheorie, gemeinverstaendlich, F. Vieweg (Braunschweig), 1917, translation by Robert W. Lawson published as *Relativity: The Special and General Theory,* Holt, 1920, 17th edition, Crown, 1961.
(With H. Minkowski) *The Principle of Relativity* (includes *Die Grundlage der allgemeinen Relativitaetstheorie*), translated by M. N. Saha and S. N. Bose, introduction by P. C. Mahalanobis, University of Calcutta, 1920.
Aether und Relativitaetstheorie, J. Springer (Berlin), 1920 (also see below).
Geometrie und Erfahrung, J. Springer, 1921 (also see below).
Sidelights on Relativity (contains translations by G. B. Jeffery and W. Perrett of *Aether und Relativitaetstheorie* and *Geometrie und Erfahrung*), Methuen, 1922, Dutton, 1923.
The Meaning of Relativity: Four Lectures Delivered at Princeton University, translated by Edwin Plimpton Adams, Methuen, 1922, Princeton University Press, 1923, 5th edition, 1955, revised edition, Methuen, 1956.
Untersuchjungen ueber die Theorie der Brownschen Bewegung, Akademische Verlagsgesellschaft (Leipzig), 1922, translation by A. D. Cowper published as *Investigations on the Theory of the Brownian Movement,* edited with notes by R. Furth, Methuen, 1926, Dover, 1956.
On the Method of Theoretical Physics, Oxford University Press, 1933 (also see below).
The Origins of the General Theory of Relativity, Jackson, Wylie (Glasgow), 1933 (also see below).
(With Leopold Infeld) *The Evolution of Physics: The Growth of Ideas From Early Concepts to Relativity and Quanta,* Simon & Schuster, 1938, new edition, 1967.

Grundzuge der Relativitaetstheorie, F. Vieweg, 1956.
(With Erwin Schroedinger, Max Planck, and H. A. Lorentz) *Letters on Wave Mechanics: Schroedinger, Planck, Einstein, Lorentz,* edited by K. Przibram, translated by Martin J. Klein, Philosophical Library, 1967.

Also author of *The Unitary Field Theory,* 1929, and *Builders of the Universe,* 1932.

OTHER

About Zionism (speeches and letters), translated and edited with an introduction by Leon Simon, Soncino Press, 1930, Macmillan, 1931.
Cosmic Religion, Covici-Friede (New York), 1931.
(With others) *Living Philosophies,* Simon & Schuster, 1931, reprinted, AMS Press, 1979.
The Fight Against War, edited by Alfred Lief, John Day Company (New York), 1933.
(With Sigmund Freud) *Why War?,* International Institute of Intellectual Cooperation, League of Nations, 1933.
Mein Weltbild (essays; also see below), Querido Verlag (Amsterdam), 1934, translation by Alan Harris published as *The World As I See It* (includes *On the Method of Theoretical Physics* and *The Origins of the General Theory of Relativity*), Covici-Friede, 1934, abridged edition, Philosophical Library, 1949.
Test Case for Humanity, Jewish Agency for Palestine (London), 1944.
(With Eric Kahler) *The Arabs and Palestine,* Christian Council on Palestine and American Palestine Committee (New York), 1944.
(With others) *Albert Einstein: Philosopher-Scientist,* edited by Paul Arthur Schilpp, Library of Living Philosophers (Evanston, Ill.), 1949 (also see below).
Essays in Humanism, Philosophical Library, 1950, reprinted, 1983.
Out of My Later Years (essays), Philosophical Library, 1950, revised edition, Greenwood Press, 1970.
Ideas and Opinions (based on *Mein Weltbild*), edited by Carl Seelig, Crown, 1954.
Essays in Science (selected essays from *Mein Weltbild*), Philosophical Library, 1955.
Lettres a Maurice Solovine, Gauthier-Villars (Paris), 1956, translation published as *Letters to Solovine,* introduction by Maurice Solovine, Philosophical Library, 1987.
Einstein on Peace, edited by Otto Nathan and Heinz Norden, preface by Bertrand Russell, Simon & Schuster, 1960.
(With Arnold Sommerfeld) *Briefwechsel: 60 Briefe aus dem goldenen Zeitalter der modernen Physik,* Schwabe (Stuttgart), 1968.
(With Max and Hedwig Born) *Briefwechsel, 1916-1955,* Nymphenburger Verlagshandlung (Munich), 1969, translation by Irene Born published as *The Born-Einstein Letters: Correspondence Between Albert Einstein and Max and Hedwig Born From 1916 to 1955,* Walker, 1971.
Albert Einstein, the Human Side: New Glimpses From His Archives, selected and edited by Helen Dukas and Banesh Hoffmann, Princeton University Press, 1979.
Autobiographical Notes (first published in *Albert Einstein: Philosopher-Scientist*), translated and edited by Paul Arthur Schilpp, Open Court, 1979.
Einstein: A Centenary Volume, edited by A. P. French, Harvard University Press, 1979.
(With Elie Cartan) *Elie Cartan-Albert Einstein: Letters on Absolute Parallelism, 1929-1932,* translated by Jules Leroy and Jim Ritter, edited by Robert Debever, Princeton University Press, 1979.
Some Strangeness in the Proportion: A Centennial Symposium to Celebrate the Achievements of Albert Einstein, edited by Harry Woolf, Addison-Wesley, Advanced Book Program, 1980.
The Collected Papers of Albert Einstein, Volume 1: *The Early Years, 1879-1901,* edited by John Stachel, Princeton University Press, 1987.

SIDELIGHTS: Albert Einstein is generally considered the greatest scientist of the twentieth century. Creator of the theory of relativity and recipient of a Nobel Prize, the theoretical physicist is acclaimed for revolutionizing the world's understanding of space, time, and matter. Einstein is also revered for his longtime commitment to pacifism, but it is for his pioneering research on laws governing the physical universe that he will be most remembered. According to historians, Einstein's achievements in physics place him among the ranks of scientists Archimedes, Galileo Galilei, and Isaac Newton.

Born to Jewish parents in Ulm, Germany, Einstein grew up in Munich, where his father operated a small electrochemical plant. A rebellious student, he resisted the stringent discipline of German schools and instead indulged in independent readings of philosophy, math, and science. When his father's business failed in 1895, the family moved to Milan, leaving Einstein behind to finish his education. The student, though, soon quit school to join his family in Italy. Enjoying there a short period of unstructured learning, Einstein taught himself calculus and higher scientific principles. Despite his advanced intelligence, he failed an entrance examination to the Swiss Federal Institute of Technology in Zurich. Dedicating the following year to preparation, Einstein retook the examination and earned acceptance in 1896. At the Institute he studied physics and mathematics, graduating in 1901 and becoming a Swiss citizen.

Einstein significantly nurtured his profound understanding of science while working at the Swiss Patent Office in Bern as a technical assistant. Relishing the job's relatively undemanding work, he was able to concentrate on his own theoretical scientific investigations. Einstein described such subjects as capillarity, intermolecular forces, and applications of statistical thermodynamics in a number of papers, one of which was accepted in 1905 as a doctoral dissertation at the University of Zurich. Other papers produced that same year would distinguish him as a preeminent thinker among scientists of his day.

One significant document of this time illustrates Einstein's theory concerning Brownian motion, the random movement of particles suspended in liquid. By observing liquid under a microscope, Einstein determined that the particle motion was caused by collisions with unseen molecules, thus verifying for the first time the existence of molecules. Another major paper published in 1905 described Einstein's revolutionary research into light, which he determined was dualistic in its ability to exist as either a wave or a particle. Theorizing that light energy travels in discrete packets of photons, or quanta, Einstein helped shape the modern quantum theory of light and furthered research on the nature of matter and the molecular process.

While these discoveries significantly advanced the science of physics, they are considered minor when compared to Einstein's major proposal of 1905, his theory of special relativity. Discarding the existing concept that time and space are absolute, the theory proposes that time and space vary with circumstances and can only be measured relative to two systems or frames of reference. Mind-bending postulates of this discovery theorize that time slows down for a moving body, nothing can travel faster than light, and all objects become more massive as they seem to travel faster.

Following the publication of his findings, Einstein received substantial academic attention. He worked as a professor of physics at universities in Zurich and Czechoslovakia before returning to Germany in 1914 to become a professor at the University of Berlin and director of the Kaiser Wilhelm Institute for Physics. Despite his opposition to the German cause during World War I at this time—adopting instead a stance of pacifism—Einstein restored his German citizenship and was elected a member of the prestigious Prussian Academy of Sciences. This secure professional stature allowed the physicist to devote time and money toward scientific research.

In 1915 Einstein produced significant discoveries that expanded his 1905 theory of special relativity. In what he termed the general theory of relativity, Einstein, upon observing the behavior of light as it reacts to gravitational forces in the universe, was able to postulate that energy and mass interact in a four-dimensional continuum called space-time. Summed up in the now well-known equation "energy equals mass times the speed of light squared," this theory, according to John Maddox writing in the *Washington Post Book World,* "provided for the first time a way of calculating how the universe behaves." Additional related discoveries by Einstein include his theory of an expanding universe, in which the physicist reconciled seemingly conflicting notions of finite mass and infinite space. His findings were published in such books as *The Principle of Relativity, Sidelights on Relativity,* and *The Meaning of Relativity.*

Einstein's brilliant scientific findings earned him the 1921 Nobel Prize in Physics, among other prestigious prizes. Although he had attained worldwide admiration, he came under increasing attack in Germany for his continued commitment to pacifism and for his scientific theories that conflicted with those of other prominent German scientists. Einstein nevertheless persisted in his independent studies of physics and continued to espouse pacifist causes, including supporting the peace efforts of the League of Nations and becoming a spokesperson for Zionist issues. Eventually, though, he was unable to reconcile his humanitarianism with the rising fascist ideals and militant nationalism permeating German culture; Einstein left his country, and, in so doing, avoided the 1933 rise to power of Nazi leader Adolf Hitler.

Einstein settled permanently in Princeton, New Jersey, where he became a professor of theoretical physics at the Institute for Advanced Study. While he continued intense scientific investigations, he remained active in propagating pacifist ideals, producing such books as *The Fight Against War* and, with German psychologist Sigmund Freud, *Why War?* At the onset of World War II, however, Einstein realized the importance of thwarting German expansion and, reluctantly concluding that U.S. military superiority was essential, appealed to President Franklin D. Roosevelt to step up nuclear fission research. The scientist, though, played no role in subsequent developments of the atomic bomb and was ultimately horrified by the United States's atomic bombing of Japan during the closing months of World War II. He consequently renewed his pacifist position, arduously campaigning for the abolition of war and controlled development of nuclear arms in order to ensure the survival of humanity.

Following World War II, Einstein produced a number of books reflecting his firm commitment to world peace, including *Essays in Humanism* and *Ideas and Opinions.* While his later years seem to have been dominated by political activism, Einstein remained dedicated to furthering his understanding of the universe through science. "Equations are more important to me," the scientist was quoted by Stephen W. Hawking in *A Brief History of Time.* "Politics is for the present, but an equation is something for eternity." Einstein spent the final thirty years of his life in pursuit of what he called a grand unified theory of physics. Striving to develop a model of nature that would express the properties of matter and energy in a single formula, Einstein was ultimately unsuccessful. He died in 1955 at the age of seventy-six. When once asked what motivated his relentless quest for scientific truth, Einstein, as quoted by Ronald W. Clark in *Einstein: The Life and Times,* replied: "The important thing is not to stop questioning. . . . Curiosity has its own reason for existence. One cannot help but be in awe when [one] contemplates the mysteries of eternity, of life, of the marvelous structure of reality. It is enough if one tries merely to comprehend a little of this mystery each day. Never lose a holy curiosity."

BIOGRAPHICAL/CRITICAL SOURCES:

BOOKS

Barnett, Lincoln, *The World and Dr. Einstein,* Bantam, 1968.
Bernstein, Jeremy, *Einstein,* Penguin, 1975.
Born, Max, *Einstein's Theory of Relativity,* Dover, 1962.
Clark, Ronald W., *Einstein: The Life and Times,* World Publishing Company, 1971.
Cuny, Hilaire, *Albert Einstein: The Man and His Theories,* translated by Mervyn Savill, Souvenir Press, 1963.
Einstein, Albert, *Essays in Humanism,* Philosophical Library, 1950, reprinted, 1983.
Einstein, Albert, *Einstein on Peace,* edited by Otto Nathan and Heinz Norden, Simon & Schuster, 1960.
Fine, Arthur, *The Shaky Game: Einstein, Realism, and the Quantum Theory,* University of Chicago Press, 1986.
Frank, Philipp, *Einstein: His Life and Times,* Knopf, 1953.
Friedman, Alan J. and Carol C. Donley, *Einstein as Myth and Muse,* Cambridge University Press, 1985.
Goldsmith, Maurice and other editors, *Einstein: The First Hundred Years,* Pergamon Press, 1980.
Hamilton, Peter N., *Albert Einstein,* Judson, 1973.
Hawking, Stephen W., *A Brief History of Time: From the Big Bang to Black Holes,* Bantam, 1988.
Hermanns, William, *Einstein and the Poet: In Search of the Cosmic Man,* Branden Press, 1983.
Infeld, Leopold, *Albert Einstein: His Work and Its Influence on Our World,* Scribner, 1950.
Pais, Abraham, *Subtle Is the Lord: The Science and Life of Albert Einstein,* Oxford University Press, 1982.
Parker, Barry, *Einstein's Dream: The Search for a Unified Theory of the Universe,* Plenum, 1986.
Paul, Iain, *Science, Theology and Einstein,* Oxford University Press, 1982.
Pyenson, Lewis, *The Young Einstein: The Advent of Relativity,* Adam Hilger, 1985.
Whitrow, G. J., editor, *Einstein: The Man and His Achievement,* Dover, 1973.

PERIODICALS

New York Times, April 19, 1955.
New York Times Book Review, September 27, 1987.
Science Digest, February, 1979.
Time, February 19, 1979.
Times Literary Supplement, January 15, 1970.
Washington Post, March 8, 1990.

Washington Post Book World, March 25, 1979.

* * *

EKWENSI, C. O. D.
See EKWENSI, Cyprian (Odiatu Duaka)

* * *

EKWENSI, Cyprian (Odiatu Duaka) 1921-
(C. O. D. Ekwensi)

PERSONAL: Born September 26, 1921, in Minna, Nigeria; son of Ogbuefi David Duaka and Uso Agnes Ekwensi; married Eunice Anyiwo; children: five. *Education:* Attended Achimota College, Ghana, and Ibadan University; received B.A.; further study at Chelsea School of Pharmacy, London, and University of Iowa, Iowa City.

ADDRESSES: Home—12 Hillview, Independence Layout, P.O. Box 317, Enugu, Nigeria.

CAREER: Novelist and writer of short stories and stories for children. Igbodi College, Lagos, Nigeria, lecturer in biology, chemistry, and English, 1947-49; School of Pharmacy, Lagos, lecturer in pharmacognosy and pharmaceutics, 1949-56; pharmacist superintendent for Nigerian Medical Services, 1956-57; head of features, Nigerian Broadcasting Corp., 1957-61; Federal Ministry of Information, Lagos, director of information, 1961-66; chairman of Bureau for External Publicity during Biafran secession, 1967-69, and director of an independent Biafran radio station; chemist for a plastics firm in Enugu, Nigeria; managing director of Star Printing & Publishing Co. (publishers of *Daily Star*), 1975-79; managing director of Niger Eagle Publishing Co., 1980-81; managing director of Ivory Trumpet Publishing Co., 1981-83. Owner of East Niger Chemists and East Niger Trading Company. Chairman of East Central State Library Board, 1972-75, and Hospitals Management Board, 1986. Newspaper consultant to *Weekly Trumpet* and *Daily News* of Anambra State and to *Weekly Eagle* of Imo State, 1980-83; consultant on information to the executive office of the president; consultant to Federal Ministry of Information; public relations consultant.

MEMBER: P.E.N., Society of Nigerian Authors, Pharmaceutical Society of Great Britain, Institute of Public Relations (London), Institute of Public Relations (Nigeria; fellow).

AWARDS, HONORS: Dag Hammarskjold International Prize for Literary Merit, 1969.

WRITINGS:

(Under name C. O. D. Ekwensi) *When Love Whispers* (novella), Tabansi Bookshop (Onitsha, Nigeria), 1947.
People of the City (novel), Andrew Dakers, 1954, Northwestern University Press, 1967, revised edition, Fawcett, 1969.
Jagua Nana (novel), Hutchinson, 1961, Fawcett, 1969, Heinemann, 1975.
Burning Grass (novel), Heinemann, 1962.
Beautiful Feathers (novel), Hutchinson, 1963.
The Rainmaker and Other Stories (short story collection), African Universities Press, 1965.
Lokotown and Other Stories (short story collection), Heinemann, 1966.
Iska, Hutchinson, 1966.
The Restless City and Christmas Gold, Heinemann, 1975.
Survive the Peace, Heinemann, 1976.

(Editor) *Festac Anthology of Nigerian Writing,* Festac, 1977.
Divided We Stand (novel), Fourth Dimension Publishers, 1980.
Motherless Baby (novella), Fourth Dimension Publishers, 1980.

Also author of *Jagua Nana's Daughter,* 1986, *For a Roll of Parchment,* 1987, and *Behind the Convent Wall,* 1987.

FOR YOUNG PEOPLE

(Under name C. O. D. Ekwensi) *Ikolo the Wrestler and Other Ibo Tales,* Thomas Nelson, 1947.
(Under name C. O. D. Ekwensi) *The Leopard's Claw,* Thomas Nelson, 1950.
The Drummer Boy, Cambridge University Press, 1960.
The Passport of Mallam Ilia, Cambridge University Press, 1960.
An African Night's Entertainment (folklore), African Universities Press, 1962.
Yaba Roundabout Murder (short novel), Tortoise Series Books (Lagos, Nigeria), 1962.
The Great Elephant-Bird, Thomas Nelson, 1965.
Juju Rock, African Universities Press, 1966.
The Boa Suitor, Thomas Nelson, 1966.
Trouble in Form Six, Cambridge University Press, 1966.
Coal Camp Boy, Longman, 1971.
Samankwe in the Strange Forest, Longman, 1973.
The Rainbow Tinted Scarf and Other Stories (collection), Evans Africa Library, 1975.
Samankwe and the Highway Robbers, Evans Africa Library, 1975.

OTHER

Writer of plays and scripts for BBC radio and television, Radio Nigeria, and other communication outlets. Contributor of stories, articles, and reviews to magazines and newspapers in Nigeria and England, including *West African Review,* London *Times, Black Orpheus, Flamingo,* and *Sunday Post.*

SIDELIGHTS: Reviewing Cyprian Ekwensi's *Beautiful Feathers* in *Critique: Studies in Modern Fiction,* John F. Povey writes: "The very practice of writing, the developing professionalism of his work, makes us find in Ekwensi a new and perhaps important phenomenon in African writing. By constant productivity, his style is becoming purged of its derivative excess and his plots begin to take on a less picaresque structure. Ekwensi is interesting because he is concerned with the present, with the violence of the new Lagos slums, the dishonesty of the new native politicians. Other Nigerian novelists have sought their material from the past, the history of missionaries and British administration as in Chinua Achebe's books, the schoolboy memoirs of Onuora Nzekwu. Ekwensi faces the difficult task of catching the present tone of Africa, changing at a speed that frighteningly destroys the old certainties. In describing this world, Ekwensi has gradually become a significant writer."

Ekwensi states that his life in government and quasi-government organizations like the Nigerian Broadcasting Corporation has prevented him from expressing any strong political opinions, but adds, "I am as much a nationalist as the heckler standing on the soap-box, with the added advantage of objectivity." During the late 1960s Biafran war, during which the eastern region of Biafra seceded temporarily from the rest of Nigeria, Ekwensi visited the United States more than once to help raise money for Biafra and to purchase radio equipment for the independent Biafran radio station of which he was director. He has also traveled in western Europe.

Several of Ekwensi's novels have been translated into other languages, including Russian, Italian, German, Serbo-Croatian,

Danish, and French. His novellas have been used primarily in schools as supplementary readers.

AVOCATIONAL INTERESTS: Hunting game, swimming, photography, motoring, and weightlifting.

BIOGRAPHICAL/CRITICAL SOURCES:

BOOKS

Contemporary Literary Criticism, Volume 4, Gale, 1975.
Tucker, Martin, *Africa in Modern Literature: A Survey of Contemporary Writing in English,* Ungar, 1967.

PERIODICALS

Books Abroad, autumn, 1967.
Critique: Studies in Modern Fiction, October, 1965.
Times Literary Supplement, June 4, 1964.

*   *   *

ELIADE, Mircea   1907-1986

PERSONAL: Born March 9, 1907, in Bucharest, Romania; came to United States, 1956; died April 22, 1986, in Chicago, Ill.; son of Gheorghe and Ioana (Stonescu) Eliade; married Nina Mares, 1935 (some sources say 1933; died in Portugal during World War II); married Georgette Christinel Cottescu, January 9, 1950; children: Adalgiza Tattaresco, a stepdaughter. *Education:* University of Bucharest, M.A., 1928, Ph.D., 1933; graduate study at University of Calcutta, 1928-32.

ADDRESSES: Office—Swift Hall, University of Chicago, 1025-35 East 58th St., Chicago, Ill. 60637.

CAREER: University of Bucharest, Bucharest, Romania, assistant professor of philosophy, 1933-39; Romanian legation, cultural attache in London, England, 1940-41, cultural adviser in Lisbon, Portugal, 1941-45; University of Paris, Sorbonne, Paris, France, visiting professor of history of religion, 1946-48; lecturer at universities in Rome, Lund, Marburg, Munich, Frankfurt, Uppsala, Strasbourg, and Padua, 1948-56; University of Chicago, Chicago, Ill., Haskell Lecturer, 1956, professor of history of religions, 1957-62, Sewell L. Avery Distinguished Service Professor, beginning in 1962, professor emeritus until 1985.

MEMBER: American Academy of Arts and Sciences, American Society for Study of Religion (president, 1963-67), British Academy, Centre Roumain de Recherches (Paris; president, 1950-55), Societe Asiatique, Romanian Writers Society (secretary, 1939), Frobenius Institut, Acadmemie Royale de Belgique, Osterreichische Akademie der Wissenschaften.

AWARDS, HONORS: Honorary doctorates from Yale University, 1966, Universidad Nacional de la Plata, 1969, Universidad del Salvador, 1969, Ripon College, 1969, Loyola University, 1970, Boston College, 1971, La Salle College, 1972, Oberlin College, 1972, University of Lancaster, 1975, and Sorbonne, University of Paris, 1976.

WRITINGS:

IN ENGLISH

Metallurgy, Magic, and Alchemy, Geunther, 1938.
Traite d'histoire des religions, Payot, 1948, translation by Rosemary Sheed published as *Patterns in Comparative Religion,* Sheed, 1958, new French edition, Payot, 1964, reprinted, 1974.
Le Mythe de l'eternel retour; Archetypes et repetition, Gallimard, 1949, translation by Willard R. Trask published as *The Myth of the Eternal Return; or, Cosmos and History,* Pantheon, 1954, published as *Cosmos and History,* Pantheon, 1955, published as *Cosmos and History: The Myth of the Eternal Return,* Harper, 1959, reprinted version edited by Robin W. Winks, Garland Publishing, 1985, original Trask edition reprinted, Princeton University Press, 1987.
Le Chamanisme et les techniques archaiques de l'extase, Payot, 1951, translation by Trask published as *Shamanism: Archaic Techniques of Ecstasy,* Pantheon, 1964, 2nd French edition, Payot, 1968, 2nd English edition, Princeton University Press, 1970.
Images et symboles: Essais sur le symbolisme magicoreligieux, Gallimard, 1952, translation by Philip Mairet published as *Images and Symbols: Studies in Religious Symbolism,* Harvill Press, 1961.
Le Yoga: Immortalitie et liberte, Payot, 1954, translation by Trask published as *Yoga: Immortality and Freedom,* Pantheon, 1958, 2nd edition with corrections and notes, Princeton University Press, 1969.
Forgerons et alchemistes, Flammarion, 1956, translation by Stephen Corrin published as *The Forge and the Crucible,* Harper, 1962, 2nd edition, University of Chicago Press, 1978.
Das Heilige und das profane: Vom Wesen des religiosen, Rowohlt, 1957, translation by Trask published as *The Sacred and the Profane: The Nature of Religion,* Harcourt, 1959, reprinted, 1968.
Mythes, reves, et mysteres, Gallimard, 1957, reprinted in two volumes, 1972, translation by Mairet published as *Myths, Dreams, and Mysteries: The Encounter between Contemporary Faiths and Archaic Realities,* Harvill Press, 1960, reprinted, Harper, 1987.
Birth and Rebirth: The Religious Meaning of Initiation in Human Culture, translated by Trask, Harper, 1958, published as *Rites and Symbols of Initiation: The Mysteries of Birth and Rebirth,* 1965.
(Editor with Joseph M. Kitagawa) *The History of Religions: Essays in Methodology,* University of Chicago Press, 1959, reprinted, 1973.
Patanjali et le yoga, Editions du Seuil, 1962, translation by Charles Lam Markmann published as *Patanjali and Yoga,* Funk, 1969, Schocken, 1975.
Mephistopheles et l'androgyne, Gallimard, 1962, translation by J. M. Cohen published as *Mephistopheles and the Androgyne: Studies in Religious Myth and Symbol,* Sheed, 1965, published in England as *The Two and the One,* Harvill Press, 1965, reprinted, University of Chicago Press, 1979.
Myth and Reality, translated by Trask, Harper, 1963.
(Editor) *From Primitives to Zen: A Thematic Sourcebook of the History of Religions,* Collins, 1967, reprinted in four parts, Part 1: *Gods, Goddesses, and Myths of Creation,* Part 2: *Man and the Sacred,* Part 3: *Death, Afterlife, and Eschatology,* Part 4: *From Medicine Man to Muhammad,* Harper, 1974.
(Editor with Kitagawa and Charles H. Long, and contributor) *The History of Religions: Essays on the Problem of Understanding,* University of Chicago Press, 1967.
Pe Strada Mantuleasa (title means "On Mantuleasa Street"), Caitele Inorugului, 1968, translation by Stevenson published as *The Old Man and the Bureaucrats,* University of Notre Dame Press, 1979.
The Quest: History and Meaning in Religion, University of Chicago Press, 1969, reprinted, 1984.
(With Mihai Niculescu) *Fantastic Tales,* translated and edited by Eric Tappe, Dillon's University Bookstore, 1969.
De Zalmoxis a Gengis Khan: Etudes comparatives sur les religions et le folklore de la Dacie et de l'Europe orientale, Payot,

1970, translation by Trask published as *Zalmoxis, the Van-ishing God: Comparative Studies in the Religions and Folk-lore of Dacia and Eastern Europe,* University of Chicago Press, 1972, reprinted, 1986.

Two Tales of the Occult, translation from the Rumanian by William Ames Coates, Herder & Herder, 1970, published as *Two Strange Tales,* Shambhala Publications, 1986.

Religions australiennes (two volumes; translation of lectures originally given in English), translation by L. Jospin, Payot, 1972, published as *Australian Religions: An Introduction,* Cornell University Press, 1973.

Fragments d'un journal, translation from the Rumanian by Luc Badesco, Gallimard, 1973, translation by Fred H. Johnson, Jr., published as *No Souvenirs: Journal, 1957-1969,* Harper, 1977.

Myths, Rites and Symbols: A Mircea Eliade Reader, edited by Wendell C. Beane and William G. Doty, Harper, 1976.

Occultism, Witchcraft, and Cultural Fashions: Essays in Comparative Religions, University of Chicago Press, 1976.

Histoire des croyances et des idees religieuses, Payot, Volume 1: *De l'age de la Pierre aux mysteres d'Eleusis,* 1976, Volume 2: *De Gautama Bouddha au triomphe du christianisme,* 1978, Volume 3: *De Mahomet a l'age des reformes,* 1983, published as *A History of Religious Ideas,* University of Chicago Press, Volume 1: *From the Stone Age to the Eleusinian Mysteries,* translation from French by Trask, 1979, Volume 2: *From Gautama Buddha to the Triumph of Christianity,* translation from French by Trask, 1982, Volume 3: *From Muhammed to the Age of Reforms,* translation by Alf Hilte-beiten and Diane Apostolos-Cappadona, 1985.

La foret interdite (novel; title means "The Forbidden Forest"), translation by MacLinscott Ricketts amd Mary P. Stevenson, University of Notre Dame Press, 1978.

L'Epreuve du labyrinthe: Entretien avec Claude-Henri Rocquet, Belfond (Paris), 1978, translation from the French by Derek Coltman published as *Ordeal by Labyrinth: Conversations with Claude-Henri Rocquet, with an Essay on Brancusi and Mythology,* University of Chicago Press, 1982.

(Editor with David Tracy) *What Is Religion?: An Inquiry for Christian Theology,* T. & T. Clarke, 1980.

Aminitiri: I. Mansarda (title means "An Autobiography: I. The Attic"), Editura Destin, 1966, translation from the Rumanian by Ricketts published as *Autobiography,* Volume I: *Journey East, Journey West: 1907-1937,* Harper, 1981, and Volume 2: *1937-1960, Exile's Odyssey,* University of Chicago Press, 1988.

Tales of the Sacred and the Supernatural, Westminster Press, 1981.

Imagination and Meaning, Seabury Press, 1982.

The Quest: History and Meaning in Religion, University of Chicago Press, 1984.

Symbolism, the Sacred, and the Arts, edited by D. Apostolos-Cappadona, Crossroad Publishing, 1985.

(Editor) *Encyclopedia of Religion,* sixteen volumes, Macmillan, 1986.

Youth without Youth and Other Novellas, edited by Matei Ca-linescu, translated by Ricketts, Ohio State University Press, 1988.

OTHER

Isabel si Apele Diavolului (novel; title means "Isabel and the Devil's Waters"), Editura Nationala-Ciornei (Bucharest), 1930.

Intr'o Manastire din Hamalaya (title means "In a Himalayan Monastery"), Editura Cartea Romaneasca, 1932.

Soliliquii (aphorisms; title means "Soliloquies"), Editura Cartea ce Semne, 1932.

Maitreyi (novel), Editura Nationala-Ciornei, 1933.

India (autobiographical novel), Editura Cugetarea, 1934.

Lumina ce se stinge (title means "The Light that Fails"), Editura Cartea Romaneasca, 1934.

Alchimia Asiatica (title means "Asiatic Alchemy"), Editura Cultura Porporului, 1934.

Oceanographie (essays), Editura Cultura Porporului, 1934.

(Translator) T. E. Lawrence, *Revolt in the Desert,* two volumes, Editura Fundatia Regala pentru Literatura si Arta, 1934.

Intoarcerea din Rai (novel; also see below; first part of trilogy; title means "The Return from Paradise"), Editura Nationala-Ciornei, 1934-54.

Huliganii (novels; two-volume sequel to *Intoarcerea din Rai;* title means "The Hooligans"), Editura Nationala-Ciornei, 1935.

Santier (autobiographical novel; title means "Work in Progress"), Editura Cugetarea, 1935.

Yoga: Essai sur les origines de la mystique indienne (title means "Yoga: Essays on the Origins of Indian Mystic Techniques"), Librairie Orientaliste Geunther (Paris), 1936.

(Editor) Nae Ionescu, *Roza Vanturilor,* Cultura Nationala, 1936.

Domnisoara Christina (novel; title means "Mademoiselle Christina"), Editura Cultura Nationala, 1936.

Sarpele (novel; title means "The Serpent"), Editura Nationala-Ciornei, 1937.

(Editor) *Scrieri Literare, Morlae si Politice de B. P. Hasdeu,* two volumes, Editura Fundatia Regala pentru Literatura si Arta, 1937.

Cosmologie si Alchimie Babiloniana (title means "Babylonian Cosmology and Alchemy"), Editura Vremea, 1937.

Nunta in Cer (novel; title means "Marriage in Heaven"), Editura Cugetarea, 1938.

Mitul Reintegrarii (title means "The Myth of Reintegration"), Editura Vremea, 1938.

Fragmentarium (essays), Editura Vremea, 1939.

(Translator) Pearl S. Buck, *Fighting Angel,* Editura Fundatia Regala pentru Literatura si Arta, 1939.

Secretul Doctoru lui Honigberger (title means "The Secret of Dr. Honigberger"; also see below), Editura Socec, 1940.

Salaza si Revolutia in Portugalia (title means "Salazar and the Revolution in Portugal"), Editura Gorjan, 1942.

Commentarii la Legenda Mesterlui Manole (title means "Commentaries on the Legend of Master Manole"), Editura Publicom, 1943.

Insula lui Euthanasius (title means "The Island of Euthanasius"), Editura Fundatia Regala pentru Literatura si Arta, 1943.

Os Romenos, Latinos do Oriente (title means "The Romanians, Latins of the East"), Livraria Classica Editora, 1943.

Techniques du Yoga (title means "Techniques of Yoga"), Gallimard, 1948, new edition in three volumes, 1975.

Iphigenia (a play), Editura Cartea Pribegiei, 1951.

Minuit a Serampore [suivi de] *Le Secret du Docteur Honigberger* (title means "Midnight at Seramapore" and "The Secret of Dr. Honigberger"), translated from the Rumanian by Albert Marie Schmidt, Stock, 1956.

Nuvele (novellas; includes "La Tiganci," "O fotografie veche de 14 ani," "Ghicitor in pietre," "Un om mare," "Feta capitanului," and "Douasprezece mil de capete de vite"), Editura Destin, 1963.

Aspects du mythe, Gallimard, 1963.

(With others) *Temoignages sur Brancusi,* Arted (Paris), 1967.

La Tiganci si Alte Povestiri, cu un Studiu Introductiv de Sorin Alexandrescu (title means "At the Gypsies and Other Short Stories"), Editura pentru Literatura (Bucharest), 1969.

Die Pelerine (title means "The Cape"), Suhrkamp (Frankfurt), 1970.

In Curte la Dionis, Caitele Inorogului, 1977.

La Colonne sans fin, translation by Florence M. Hetzler, University Press of America, 1984.

Briser le toit de la maison: La Creativite et ses symbols, Gallimard, 1986.

Autobiography, Volume 2: *1937-1960, Exile's Odyssey,* University of Chicago Press, 1988.

Also author of some twenty volumes published in Rumanian, 1933-45. Contributor to many books about religions and religious history, including Joseph Campbell's *Man and Time,* Pantheon, 1957, and *Man and Transformation,* Pantheon, 1964. Founder and editor, *Zalmoxis* (an international journal for history of religions), 1938-42; founder and senior editor, *History of Religions,* 1961-1986. Contributor to journals in his field.

SIDELIGHTS: Romanian novelist and religious historian Mircea Eliade sought a place among the intellectuals of his homeland "who thought of themselves as provincial outposts on the confines of European culture," encyclopedists who "often found a kind of over-compensation in . . . a thirst for universalism, in prodigies of (disorderly) knowledge, and in resorting to an aesthetic management of their material," reports *Times Literary Supplement* contributor Virgil Nemoianu. The reviewer adds that a survey of Eliade's numerous works in a variety of languages reveals "how the mixture of encyclopedic and aesthetic impulses . . . shaped his entire career."

Eliade was a voracious reader and a life-long student. At first fascinated with natural science, he collected rocks, plants and insects and set up a small chemistry lab in his family's home, filling notebooks with his observations. More than one hundred articles he wrote were published before he turned twenty. By the time he entered the University of Bucharest, his interests turned to the study of metaphysics and mystical experience. His enthusiasm for the study of primitive and Eastern religions led him to Rome, Geneva, and eventually India, where he became the avid student of Surendranath Dasgupta, a religious historian from whom he learned Yoga. The influence of this religious discipline on his understanding of religious experience appears throughout his writings. Of *Images and Symbols: Studies in Religious Symbolism,* for example, *Hibbert Journal* contributor S. G. F. Brandon remarked that it is "characterized by his . . . implied conviction that the praxis of Yoga is the way par excellence to a proper apprehension of reality."

Writing in the *New York Times Book Review,* Gerald Sykes recognized Eliade as "a scientist-artist who [wrote] not only works of scholarship but novels of admirable intensity." The novels reflect his understanding of world cultures, and their themes parallel his findings "as a historian of religions," George Uscatescu writes in *Myths and Symbols: Studies in Honor of Mircea Eliade,* edited by Joseph M. Kitagawa and Charles H. Long. Spiritual crisis is the "central problem" in Eliade's "great novel *Foret Interdite,*" a seven-hundred-page work that shows its author "at the fullest unfolding of his epic faculties and establishes for the reader a problematical situation of great literary authenticity and verisimilitude," Uscatescu remarked. Critics praised the novelist for his craftsmanship as much as for his subject matter, Uscatescu notes: "The first long novels, *Isabel si Apele Diavolului* (1930) and *Maitreyi* (1933), draw their inspiration from Indian themes of a strong erotic character and reveal in the hands of a new author both a solid technique and understanding which assures significant success to the works."

Eliade is best known in the United States for his critical and philosophical works on Indian religions, Asiatic alchemy, and mythical thought. However, he felt that his well-received novels—in particular, *La Foret Interdite (The Forbidden Forest)*—more competently conveyed the experience of the power of myth. He continued writing in both forms because he believed that history, philosophy, and fiction are complementary as instruments of expression. Both his fiction and non-fiction are united by their focus on problems which obsessed him from his youth, including the history of religions, the structure of myths, and religious symbolism.

Eliade identified two stances toward reality: the religious stance, in which man and the world are perceived as sacred, inhabited by powers and meanings beyond the mundane; and the profane, in which man denies the existence of the sacred. Eliade cited Rudolph Otto's book *Das Heilige* (title means "The Sacred") for his definition of the sacred as "something 'wholly other'. . . . Confronted with it, man senses his profound nothingness, feels that he is only a creature." This statement in *The Sacred and the Profane* precedes Eliade's observation that man knows the sacred exists only after something from beyond nature reveals itself to man. The history of religions, therefore, can be seen as a series of "manifestations of sacred realities," encounters with "something of a wholly different order, a reality that does not belong to our world, in objects that are an integral part of our natural 'profane' world," he wrote.

The difference between religious and nonreligious man, Eliade observed in *The Sacred and the Profane,* is that "the nonreligious man refuses transcendence. . . . In other words, he accepts no model for humanity outside the human condition," and "desacralizes himself and the world." Yet beyond that, the tragedy of modern nonreligious man is that his "camouflaged myths and degenerated rituals" show that he can never completely desacralize himself and should not try: "Do what he will he is an inheritor. He cannot utterly abolish his past, since he is himself the product of his past. . . . He continues to be haunted by the realities that he has refused and denied. To acquire a world of his own, he has desacralized the world in which his ancestors lived; but to do so he has been obliged to adopt the opposite of an earlier type of behavior, and that behavior is still emotionally present to him, in one form or another, ready to be reactualized in his deepest being."

Eliade contended it is worthwhile to examine the nature of religious experience because it occurs in every culture. To understand religious man, "to understand his spiritual universe, is, in sum, to advance our general knowledge of man," he claimed in *The Sacred and the Profane.* Eliade criticized early ethnologists and philologists for taking an outsider's approach to religious experience. Eliade insisted the historian of religions needs to empathize, if not to participate, with those who claim to encounter the sacred. In *The Sacred and the Profane,* Eliade stated, "There is no other way of understanding a foreign mental universe than to place oneself *inside* it, at its very center, in order to progress from there to all the values that it possesses." Furthermore, for the historian of religions, scientific study means dealing with religious facts, man's experiences of time and space.

Central to the patterns of Eliade's thought on the history of religions are sacred time and space, problems to which he has returned frequently and about which he has contributed much significant research. As he explains in *The Myth of the Eternal Return; or, Cosmos and History,* some cultures view time as history, as a one-way progression from the irretrievable past into the unknown future. Others view time as cosmos, an infinitely repeatable cycle reactivated by ceremonies preserved in myths. Men who perceive time as cyclical periodically abolish history by re-enacting the conquering of chaos and the creation of the world; actions in the present acquire meaning from their similarity to "first things," encounters with the sacred at the beginning of time. Man trapped in history, however, lives in terror, unable to extract himself from meaningless events. In Christian man, Eliade sees components of both views: "Christianity translates the periodic regeneration of the world into a regeneration of the human individual. But for him who shares in this eternal *nunc* of the reign of God, history ceases as totally as it does for the man of the archaic cultures, who abolishes it periodically."

Substantial sections of *The Myth of the Eternal Return, The Sacred and the Profane,* and *Patterns in Comparative Religion* discuss religious man's concepts of sacred space. Any place where "*something* that does not belong to this world has manifested itself " becomes a symbolic foundation of the world, "a fixed point . . . in the chaos," a central point from which religious man draws his orientation to time and space, Eliade writes in *The Sacred and the Profane.* Thus certain landmarks and buildings become, for religious man, gateways to continued communication with the sacred. These three books, particularly *The Myth of the Eternal Return,* provide a wealth of supporting examples from cultures in all nations and time periods.

Critics were consistently impressed by Eliade's encyclopedic mode, but were not uncritical of the role that his personal beliefs played in his studies. "Too great a respect for the intimations of Indian thought (great though its achievement is) can be misleading," Brandon stated. Eliade's "apparent assumption of social evolution" was "a hindrance to acceptance by non-religious scholars," reported Dorothy Libby in *American Anthropology.* T. J. J. Altizer, writing in the *Journal of Religion,* commented that generally speaking, "One expects from Eliade an argument that is clear, precise, comprehensive, and fully documented." However, he adds, when Eliade equates religious man with primitive man, this "romantic" view makes it difficult for him to discuss modern-day religious experience. Apart from this, Altizer calls Eliade a master of the art of describing religions without proposing questionable explanations or claims about their origins.

Eliade's studies of religious experience gave him a permanent place in the history of religious thought. "On the plane of international academic life, Eliade became a kind of prophet of the trans-historical," or timeless common ground shared by members of many cultures, explains Ivan Strenski in the *Los Angeles Times Book Review.* Before he entered the American academic community as a professor at the University of Chicago, the study of religions consisted of pitting belief systems against each other—a process which fell outside the perameters set by the law of separation of church and state in the United States. Eliade saw in the history of religious man a desire for contact with the sacred that transcended cultural boundaries. This new approach helped to establish the study of religion as an academic discipline in American schools. "A true cultural revolutionary to the end, Eliade challenged the whole secular bourgeois world's comforting belief in the adequacy of its own works of science, politics, and economics," Strenski relates. Robert S. Ellwood, Jr. remarks in the *New York Times Book Review,* "Only a few in his often arcane discipline have equaled his broad impact on his age. With C. G. Jung and Joseph Campbell, Mircea Eliade helped create the midcentury vogue for myth and ritual popularized by critics, dramatists and assorted spiritual seekers."

All but Eliade's earliest works are still in print, and many have been translated into more than a dozen languages. Reviewers repeatedly call for more English translations of the Romanian scholar's works. Considering these facts and Eliade's impact on the American academic community, Sykes concluded, "The work of this important scholar gains yearly in effect."

BIOGRAPHICAL/CRITICAL SOURCES:

BOOKS

Allen, Douglas, *Structure and Creativity in Religion: Hermeneutics in Mircea Eliade's Phenomenology and New Directions,* Mouton, 1978.
Allen, Douglas and Dennis Doeing, *Mircea Eliade: An Annotated Bibliography,* Garland Press, 1980.
Altizer, Thomas J. J., *Mircea Eliade and the Dialectic of the Sacred,* Westminster Press, 1963.
Apostolos-Cappadona, Diane, editor, *Symbolism, the Sacred, and the Arts,* Crossroad Publishing, 1985.
Carrasco, David and Jane Swanberg, editors, *Waiting for the Dawn: Mircea Eliade in Perspective,* Westview Press, 1985.
Contemporary Literary Criticism, Volume 19, Gale 1981.
Dudley, G., *Religion on Trial: Mircea Eliade and His Critics,* Temple University Press, 1977.
Eliade, Mircea, *The Sacred and the Profane: The Nature of Religion,* Harper, 1961.
Eliade, Mircea, *Two Tales of the Occult,* Herder, 1970.
Eliade, Mircea, *The Myth of the Eternal Return; or, Cosmos and History,* Princeton University Press, 1974.
Eliade, Mircea, *Autobiography,* Volume 1: *1907-1937, Journey East, Journey West,* Harper, 1981, Volume 2: *1937-1960, Exile's Odyssey,* University of Chicago Press, 1989.
Encyclopedia of Occultism and Parapsychology, 2nd edition, Gale, 1985.
Girardot, Norman and MacLinscott Ricketts, editors, *Imagination and Meaning: The Scholarly and Literary Worlds of Mircea Eliade,* Seabury, 1982.
Kitagawa, Joseph M. and Charles H. Long, editors, *Myths and Symbols: Studies in Honor of Mircea Eliade,* University of Chicago Press, 1969.
Silabu, John A., *"Homo Religiosus" in Mircea Eliade: An Anthropological Evaluation,* Brill, 1976.

PERIODICALS

America, March 10, 1979.
American Anthropologist, August, 1959.
Books Abroad, Volume 49, number 1, 1975.
Encounter, March, 1980.
Hibbert Journal, October, 1961.
Journal of Asian Studies, Volume 30, number 3, 1971.
Journal of Bible and Religion, July, 1965.
Journal of Religion, April, 1960, January 1, 1961, April, 1972, October, 1986.
Listener, Volume 99, number 2543, January 19, 1978.
Los Angeles Times Book Review, December 22, 1985, January 22, 1989.
New Statesman, December 17, 1960, October 16, 1964.
Newsweek, July 15, 1985.
New York Review of Books, October 20, 1966.
New York Times Book Review, July 12, 1964, August 11, 1974, April 15, 1979, November 22, 1981.
Religion in Life, spring, 1967.
Religion: Journal of Religion and Religions, spring, 1973.
Religious Studies, 1972, 1974.
Time, February 11, 1966, October 26, 1981.

Times Literary Supplement, November 11, 1960, October 13, 1978, April 2, 1982, September 26, 1986.
Tribune Books (Chicago), October 9, 1988.
Union Seminary Quarterly Review, winter, 1970, summer, 1970.
World Literature Today, Volume 51, number 3, 1977, Volume 52, number 4, 1978, Volume 54, number 1, 1980.

OBITUARIES:

BOOKS

Encyclopedia of Occultism and Parapsychology, 2nd edition, Gale, 1984.

PERIODICALS

Chicago Tribune, April 24, 1986.
Los Angeles Times, April 26, 1986.
National Review, June 6, 1986.
New York Times, April 23, 1986.
Time, May 5, 1986.
Times (London), April 29, 1986.

—Sketch by Marilyn K. Basel

*   *   *

ELIOT, Dan
   See SILVERBERG, Robert

*   *   *

ELIOT, T(homas) S(tearns) 1888-1965
(Charles Augustus Conybeare, Reverend Charles James Grimble, Gus Krutzch, Muriel A. Schwartz, J. A. D. Spence, Helen B. Trundlett)

PERSONAL: Born September 26, 1888, in St. Louis, Mo.; moved to England, 1914, naturalized British subject, 1927; died January 4, 1965, in London, England; buried in Westminster Abbey; son of Henry Ware (president of Hydraulic Press Brick Co.) and Charlotte Chauncey (a teacher, social worker and writer; maiden name Stearns) Eliot; married Vivienne Haigh Haigh-Wood (a dancer), January, 1915 (divorced c. 1930; died, 1947); married (Esme) Valerie Fletcher (his private secretary before their marriage), 1957; children: none. *Education:* Attended Smith Academy (of Washington University), St. Louis, 1898-1905; Milton Academy, Milton, Mass., graduated, 1906; Harvard University, B.A. (philosophy), 1909, M.A. (philosophy), 1910, graduate study, 1911-14 (his doctoral dissertation "Experience and the Objects of Knowledge in the Philosophy of F. H. Bradley," was accepted in 1916 but never presented for the degree; the dissertation was published in 1964 as *Knowledge and Experience in Philosophy of F. H. Bradley*); attended University of Paris (Sorbonne), 1910-11; studied in Munich, 1914; read philosophy at Merton, Oxford, 1914-15; also studied under Edward Kennard Rand, Irving Babbitt, and Alain Fournier, and attended courses given by Henri Bergson. *Politics:* Conservative ("royalist"). *Religion:* Church of England (Anglo-Catholic wing; confirmed, 1927; served as vestryman in a London church). (In his 1028 essay "For Lancelot Andrewes," Eliot called himself a "classicist," "royalist," and "Anglican." Later, in *After Strange Gods,* he regretted that declaration as "injudicious.")

ADDRESSES: Home—London, England. *Office*—Faber & Faber Ltd., 24 Russell Sq., London .W.C.1, England.

CAREER: Harvard University, Cambridge, Mass., assistant in philosophy department, 1913-14; teacher of French, Latin,

mathematics, drawing, geography, and history at High Wycombe Grammar School, London, then at Highgate School, London, 1915-17; Lloyds Bank Ltd., London, clerk in the Colonial and Foreign Department, 1917-25; *The Egoist,* London, assistant editor, 1917-19; founder of the *Criterion* (literary quarterly), London, 1922, and editor, 1922-39 (ceased publication, at Eliot's decision, in 1939 because of the war and paper shortage); Faber and Gwyer Ltd. (publishers), later Faber & Faber Ltd., London, literary editor and member of the advisory hoard, 1925-65. Clark Lecturer at Trinity College, Cambridge, 1926; Charles Eliot Norton Professor of Poetry at Harvard University, six months, 1932-33; Page-Barbour Lecturer at University of Virginia, 1933; resident at Institute for Advanced Study at Princeton, 1948; Theodore Spencer Memorial Lecturer at Harvard University, 1950; lecturer at University of Chicago during the fifties; lecturer at Library of Congress, at University of Texas, at University of Minnesota, and before many other groups. President of London Library, 1952-65. *Military service:* None; was rejected by the U.S. Navy, 1918, because of poor health.

MEMBER: Classical Association (president, 1941), Virgil Society (president, 1943), Books Across the Sea (president, 1943-46), American Academy of Arts and Sciences (honorary member), Accademia dei Lincei (Rome; foreign member), Bayerische Akademie der Schoenen Kuenste (Munich; foreign member), Athenaeum, Garrick Club, Oxford and Cambridge Club.

AWARDS, HONORS: Sheldon Travelling Fellowship for study in Munich, 1914; Dial award ($2,000), 1922, for *The Waste Land;* Nobel Prize for Literature, 1948; Order of Merit, 1948; Commander, Ordre des Arts et des Lettres; Officier de la Legion d'Honneur; New York Drama Critics Circle Award, 1950, for *The Cocktail Party* as best foreign play; Hanseatic Goethe Prize of Hamburg University, 1954; Dante Gold Medal (Florence), 1956; Ordre pour le Merite (West Germany), 1959; Emerson-Thoreau Medal of the American Academy of Arts and Sciences, 1959; honorary fellow of Merton College, Oxford, and of Magdalene College, Cambridge; honorary citizen of Dallas, Tex.; honorary deputy sheriff of Dallas County, Tex.; Campion Medal of the Catholic Book Club, 1963, for "long and distinguished service to Christian letters"; received President Johnson's award for distinguished contribution to American literature and public life. Honorary degrees: Litt.D., Columbia University, 1933, Cambridge University, 1938, University of Bristol, 1938, University of Leeds, 1939, Harvard University 1947, Yale University, 1947, Princeton University, 1947, Washington University, 1953, University of Rome, 1958, University of Sheffield, 1959; LL.D., University of Edinburgh, 1937, St. Andrews' University, 1953; D.Litt., Oxford University, 1948, University of London, 1950; D.Philos., University of Munich, 1959; D. es L., University of Paris, 1959, Universite d'Aix-Marseille, 1959, University of Rennet, 1959.

WRITINGS:

POETRY

Prufrock, and Other Observations (contains 11 poems and a prose piece, "Hysteria"; the title poem, "The Love Song of J. Alfred Prufrock," was first published in *Poetry,* June, 1915; five other poems were originally published in *Catholic Anthology,* edited by Ezra Pound, 1915), The Egoist (London), 1917.
Poems by T. S. Eliot, Hogarth, 1919.
Ara Vos Prec (includes *Poems by T. S. Eliot,* above), Ovid Press (London), 1920, published in America as *Poems,* Knopf, 1920.

The Waste Land (first published in *Criterion,* first issue, October, 1922), Boni & Liveright, 1922.

Poems, 1909-1925 (contains all works cited above and "The Hollow Men"; earlier drafts and sections of "The Hollow Men" appeared in *Chapbook, Commerce, Criterion,* and *Dial,* 1924-25), Faber, 1925.

Journey of the Magi (one of the "Ariel Poems"), Faber, 1927.

Animula (one of the "Ariel Poems"), Faber, 1929.

Ash-Wednesday (first 3 parts originally published in French, American, and English magazines, respectively; Part 2, first published as "Salutation" in *Saturday Review of Literature,* was intended as another "Ariel Poem" and as a compliment to *Journey of the Magi;* the publisher also intended to issue this part separately as a Christmas card), Putnam, 1930.

Marina (one of the "Ariel Poems"), Faber, 1930.

Triumphal March, Faber, 1931.

The Waste Land, and Other Poems, Harcourt, 1934.

Words for Music, [Bryn Mawr], 1935.

Collected Poems, 1909-1935, Harcourt, 1936.

A Song for Simeon (written in the 1920's; one of the "Ariel Poems"), Faber, 1938.

(With Geoffrey Faber, Frank Morley, and John Hayward) *Noctes Binanianae* (limited edition of 25 copies for the authors and friends; never reprinted), privately printed (London), 1939.

Old Possum's Book of Practical Cats, Harcourt, 1939.

East Coker, Faber, 1940.

Burnt Norton, Faber, 1941.

The Dry Salvages, Faber, 1941.

Later Poems, 1925-1935, Faber 1941.

Little Gidding, Faber, 1942.

Four Quartets (consists of *Burnt Norton, East Coker, The Dry Salvages,* and *Little Gidding*), Harcourt, 1943.

A Practical Possum, Harvard Printing Office, 1947.

Selected Poems, Penguin, 1948, Harcourt, 1967.

The Undergraduate Poems, Harvard Advocate (unauthorized reprint of poems originally published in the *Advocate*), 1949.

Poems Written in Early Youth, privately printed by Bonniers (Stockholm), 1950, new edition prepared by Valerie Eliot and John Hayward, Farrar, Straus, 1967.

The Cultivation of Christmas Trees (one of the "Ariel Poems"), Faber, 1954, Farrar, Straus, 1956.

Collected Poems, 1909-1962, Harcourt, 1963.

The Waste Land: A Facsimile of the Original Drafts, Including the Annotations of Ezra Pound, edited and with introduction by Valerie Eliot, Harcourt, 1971.

Poetry also represented in anthologies.

PLAYS

Fragment of a Prologue, [London], 1926.

Fragment of the Agon, [London], 1927.

Sweeney Agonistes: Fragments of an Aristophanic Melodrama (provisionally titled "Wanna Go Home, Baby?" during composition; consists of two fragments cited above; first produced in New York at Cherry Lane Theater, March 2, 1952), Faber, 1932.

The Rock: A Pageant Play (a revue with scenario by E. Martin Browne and music by Martin Shaw; first produced in London at Sadler Wells Theatre, May 9, 1934), Faber, 1934.

Murder in the Cathedral (provisionally titled "Fear in the Way" during composition; first produced in an abbreviated form for the Canterbury Festival in the Chapter House of Canterbury Cathedral, June, 1935; produced in London at Mercury Theatre, November 1, 1935; first produced in America at Yale University, January, 1936; first produced in New York at Manhattan Theater, March 20, 1936), Harcourt, 1935.

The Family Reunion (often cited as a rewriting of the unfinished *Sweeney Agonistes;* first produced in London at Westminster Theatre, March 21, 1939; produced in New York at Phoenix Theater, October 20, 1958), Harcourt, 1939.

The Cocktail Party (provisionally titled "One-Eyed Riley" during composition; first produced for the Edinburgh Festival, Scotland, August, 1949; produced in New York at Henry Miller's Theater, January 21, 1950), Harcourt, 1950.

The Confidential Clerk (first produced for the Edinburgh Festival, August, 1953; produced in London at Lyric Theatre, September 16, 1953; produced in New York at Morosco Theater, February 11, 1954), Harcourt, 1954.

The Elder Statesman (first produced for the Edinburgh Festival, August, 1958; produced in London at Cambridge Theatre, September 25, 1958), Farrar, Straus, 1959.

Collected Plays, Faber, 1962.

Plays also represented in anthologies.

PROSE

Ezra Pound: His Metric and Poetry (published anonymously) Knopf, 1917.

The Sacred Wood (essays on poetry and criticism), Methuen, 1920, 7th edition, 1950, Barnes & Noble, 1960.

Homage to John Dryden (three essays on 17th-century poetry), L. and V. Woolf at Hogarth Press, 1924, Doubleday, 1928.

Shakespeare and the Stoicism of Seneca (an address), Oxford University Press, for the Shakespeare Association, 1927.

For Lancelot Andrewes: Essays on Style and Order, Faber, 1928, Doubleday, 1929.

Thoughts After Lambeth, (a criticism of the *Report* of the Lambeth Conference, 1930), Faber, 1931.

Charles Whibley: A Memoir, Oxford University Press, for the English Association, 1931.

Selected Essays, 1917-1932, Harcourt, 1932, 2nd edition published as *Selected Essays,* Harcourt, 1950, 3rd edition, Faber, 1951.

John Dryden, the Poet, the Dramatist, the Critic (three essays), T. & Elsa Holiday (New York), 1932.

The Use of Poetry and the Use of Criticism: Studies in the Relation of Criticism to Poetry in England (the Charles Eliot Norton lectures), Harvard University Press, 1933, 2nd edition, Faber, 1964.

Elizabethan Essays (includes *Shakespeare and the Stoicism of Seneca*), Faber, 1934, Haskell House, 1964.

After Strange Gods: A Primer of Modern Heresy (the Page-Barbour lectures), Harcourt, 1934.

Essays, Ancient and Modern (first published in part as *For Lancelot Andrewes*), Harcourt, 1936.

The Idea of a Christian Society (three lectures), Faber, 1939, Harcourt, 1940.

Christianity and Culture (contains *The Idea of a Christian Society* and *Notes Towards the Definition of Culture*), Harcourt, 1940.

Points of View (selected criticism), edited by John Hayward, Faber, 1941.

The Classics and the Man of Letters (an address), Oxford University Press, 1942.

The Music of Poetry (lecture), Jackson (Glasgow), 1942.

Reunion by Destruction: Reflections on a Scheme for Church Union in South India (an address), Pax House (London), 1943.

What Is a Classic? (an address), Faber, 1945.

Die Einheit der europaischen Kultur, Carl Havel, 1946.

On Poetry, [Concord], 1947.

A Sermon, [Cambridge], 1948.

From Poe to Valery (first published in *Hudson Review,* 1948), privately printed for friends by Harcourt, 1948.

Milton (lecture), Cumberlege (London), 1948.

Notes Towards the Definition of Culture (seven essays; a few copies erroneously stamped *Notes Towards a Definition of Culture*), Harcourt, 1949.

The Aims of Poetic Drama, Galleon, 1949.

The Value and Use of Cathedrals in England Today, [Chichester], 195?.

Poetry by T. S. Eliot: An NBC Radio Discussion, [Chicago], 1950.

Poetry and Drama (the Theodore Spencer lecture), Harvard University Press, 1951.

American Literature and the American Language (an address and an appendix entitled "The Eliot Family and St. Louis," the latter prepared by the English Department at Washington University), Washington University Press, 1953.

The Three Voices of Poetry (lecture), Cambridge University Press, for the National Book League, 1953, Cambridge University Press (New York), 1954.

Selected Prose, edited by John Hayward, Penguin, 1953.

Religious Drama, House of Books (New York), 1954.

The Literature of Politics (lecture), foreword by Sir Anthony Eden, Conservative Political Centre, 1955.

The Frontiers of Criticism (lecture), University of Minnesota, 1956.

Essays on Elizabethan Drama (contains nine of the eleven essays originally published as *Elizabethan Essays*), Harcourt, 1956.

On Poetry and Poets (essays), Farrar, Straus, 1957.

Essays on Poetry and Criticism, introduction and notes in Japanese by Kazumi Yano, Shohakusha (Tokyo), 1959.

William Collin Brooks (an address), The Statist (London), 1959.

Geoffrey Faber, 1889-1961, Faber, 1961.

George Herbert, Longmans, Green, for the British Council and the National Book League, 1962.

Elizabethan Dramatists, Faber, 1963.

Knowledge and Experience in the Philosophy of F. H. Bradley (doctoral dissertation), Farrar, Straus, 1964.

To Criticize the Critic, and Other Writings (contains *From Poe to Valery; American Literature and the American Language; The Literature of Politics; The Classics and the Man of Letters; Ezra Pound, His Metric and Poetry*; and new essays), Farrar, Straus, 1965.

Prose also represented in anthologies.

OMNIBUS VOLUMES

The Complete Poems and Plays, 1909-1950, Harcourt, 1952.

CONTRIBUTOR

"A Dialogue on Poetic Drama," in *Of Dramatic Poesie* (edition of an essay by John Dryden), Etchells & Macdonald (London), 1928.

"The Place of Pater," in *The Eighteen-Eighties: Essays by Fellows of the Royal Society of Literature* (Eliot did not, however, hold the title F.R.S.L.), edited by Walter de la Mare, [Cambridge], 1930.

"Donne in Our Time," in *A Garland for John Donne,* edited by Theodore Spencer, Harvard University Press, 1931.

"Religion and Literature," in *The Faith That Illuminates,* edited by V. A. Demant, Centenary (London), 1935.

"Byron," in *From Anne to Victoria: Essays by Various Hands,* edited by Bonamy Dobree, Cassell, 1937.

(Author of text) *Britain at War* (pictorial essay), Museum of Modern Art (New York), 1941.

"Henry James," in *The Shock of Recognition,* edited by Edmund Wilson, Doubleday, 1943, reprinted as "On Henry James," in *The Question of Henry James,* edited by F. W. Dupee, Wingate, 1947.

Peter Russell, editor, *Examination of Ezra Pound,* New Directions, 1950 (published in England as *Ezra Pound: A Collection of Essays,* Nevill, 1950).

"Andrew Marvell," in *Gedichte* (an edition of Marvell's poems), Karl H. Henssel Verlag, 1962.

"George Herbert," in *British Writers and Their Work* (periodical), number 4, University of Nebraska Press, 1964.

AUTHOR OF INTRODUCTION

Charlotte Chauncey Eliot, *Savonarola* (dramatic poem), R. Cobden Sanderson, 1926.

Seneca His Tenne Tragedies, Knopf, 1927, introduction reprinted as "Seneca in Elizabethan Translation," in *Eliot's Selected Essays.*

Wilkie Collins, *The Moonstone* (novel), Oxford University Press, 1928.

James B. Connolly, *Fishermen of the Banks,* Faber, 1928.

Edgar Ansel Mowrer, *This American World,* Faber, 1928.

Ezra Pound, *Selected Poems,* Faber, 1928.

Samuel Johnson, *London, a Poem [and] The Vanity of Human Wishes,* Etchells & Macdonald, 1930, introduction reprinted as "Johnson's *London* and *The Vanity of Human Wishes,*" in *English Critical Essays: Twentieth Century,* edited by Phyllis M. Jones, Oxford University Press, 1933.

G. Wilson Knight, *The Wheel of Fire: Essays in Interpretation of Shakespeare's Sombre Tragedies,* Oxford University Press, 1930.

Charles Baudelaire, *Intimate Journals,* translated by Christopher Isherwood, Random House, 1930, introduction reprinted as "Baudelaire," in *Eliot's Selected Essays.*

Pascal's Pensees, translated by W. F. Trotter, Dutton, 1931, introduction reprinted as "The Pensees of Pascal," in *Eliot's Selected Essays.*

Marianne Moore, *Selected Poems,* Macmillan, 1935.

Poems of Tennyson, Nelson, 1936, introduction reprinted as "In Memoriam," in *Eliot's Selected Essays.*

Djuna Barnes, *Nightwood* (novel), Harcourt, 1937, 2nd edition, Faber, 1950.

(And compiler) *A Choice of Kipling's Verse,* Faber, 1941.

Charles-Louis Philippe, *Bubu of Montparnasse,* English translation by Laurence Vail and others, 2nd edition (not associated with first edition), Avalon, 1945.

Simone Weil, *The Need for Roots,* Putnam, 1952.

Literary Essays of Ezra Pound, New Directions, 1954.

Opada bhul (Oriya translation of some of Eliot's poems), P. C. Das, c. 1957.

Stanislaus Joyce, *My Brother's Keeper,* edited by Richard Ellmann, Viking, 1958.

Paul Valery, *The Art of Poetry,* translated by Denise Folliot, Pantheon, 1958.

Ezra Pound Kabita (Oriya translation of Pound's *Selected Poems*), translated by Jnanindra Barma, P. C. Das, 1958.

Hugo von Hofmannsthal, *Poems and Verse Plays,* edited by Michael Hamburger, Pantheon, 1961.

David Jones, *In Parenthesis* (novel), Viking, 1961.

John Davidson: A Selection of His Poems, edited by Maurice Lindsay, Hutchinson, 1961.

(Editor and author of introduction) *Introducing James Joyce* (selected prose), Faber, 1962.

Also author, between 1930 and 1941, of introductions to books of poems by Harry Crosby and Abraham Cowley; author, prior to 1952, of introduction to an edition of Mark Twain's *The Adventures of Huckleberry Finn.*

OTHER

(Translator) St. John Perse (pseudonym of Alexis Saint-Leger Leger) *Anabasis* (poem; published in a bilingual edition with the original French), Faber, 1930, revised edition, Harcourt, 1949.
(With George Hoellering) "Murder in the Cathedral" (screenplay based on Eliot's play), Harcourt, 1952.
The Letters of T. S. Eliot, Volume 1: *1898-1922,* Harcourt, 1988.

Also lyricist for songs "For An Old Man," [New York], 1951, and "The Greater Light," [London], released in 1956, with music by David Diamond and Martine Shaw. A complete run of Eliot's periodical, *Criterion* (1922-1939), was published by Barnes & Noble, 1967. Also author under pseudonyms Charles Augustus Conybeare, Reverend Charles James Grimble, Gus Krutzch, Muriel A. Schwartz, J. A. D. Spence, and Helen B. Trundlett. Editor of the *Harvard Advocate,* 1909-1910. Member of the editorial boards of *New English Weekly, Inventario, Christian News-Letter,* and other periodicals. Contributor to periodicals.

SIDELIGHTS: When T. S. Eliot died, wrote Robert Giroux, "the world became a lesser place." Certainly the most imposing poet of his time, Eliot was revered by Igor Stravinsky "not only as a great sorcerer of words but as the very key keeper of the language." For Alfred Kazin he was "the *mana* known as 'T. S. Eliot,' the model poet of our time, the most cited poet and incarnation of literary correctness in the English-speaking world." Northrup Frye simply states: "A thorough knowledge of Eliot is compulsory for anyone interested in contemporary literature. Whether he is liked or disliked is of no importance, but he must be read."

In 1945 Eliot wrote: "A poet must take as his material his own language as it is actually spoken around him." Correlatively, the duty of the poet, as Eliot emphasized in a 1943 lecture, "is only indirectly to the people: his direct duty is to his language, first to preserve, and second to extend and improve." Thus he dismisses the so-called "social function" of poetry. The only "method," Eliot once wrote, is "to be very intelligent." As a result, his poetry "has all the advantages of a highly critical habit of mind," writes A. Alvarez; "there is a coolness in the midst of involvement; he uses texts exactly for his own purpose; he is not carried away. Hence the completeness and inviolability of the poems. What he does in them can be taken no further. . . . [One gets] the impression that anything he turned his attention to he would perform with equal distinction." Alvarez believes that "the strength of Eliot's intelligence lies in its training; it is the product of a perfectly orthodox academic education." But Jacques Maritain once told Marshall McLuhan that "Eliot knows so much philosophy and theology that I do not see how he can write poetry at all." Eliot, however, never recognized a conflict between academic and creative pursuits.

Of his early work, Eliot has said: "The form in which I began to write, in 1908 or 1909, was directly drawn from the study of Laforgue together with the later Elizabethan drama; and I do not know anyone who started from exactly that point." Elsewhere he said: "The kind of poetry that I needed, to teach me the use of my own voice, did not exist in English at all; it was only found in French," and Leonard Unger concludes that, "insofar as Eliot started from an *exact point,* it was exclusively and emphatically

the poetry of Laforgue." To a lesser extent, he was influenced by other Symbolists, by the metaphysical poets, by Donne, Dryden, and Dante. "His appreciation of Shakespeare," writes Sir Herbert Read, "was subject to his moral or religious scruples." With Samuel Johnson, whom, according to Sir Herbert, Eliot "honoured above all other English writers," he shared "a faith in God and the fear of death."

In *After Strange Gods* Eliot wrote: "I should say that in one's prose reflections one may be legitimately occupied with ideals, whereas in the writing of verse one can deal only with actuality." From this Cleanth Brooks elaborates: "Poetry is the medium *par excellence* for rendering a total situation—for letting us know what it feels like to take a particular action or hold a particular belief or simply to look at something with imaginative sympathy." Brook's explains that it is Eliot's notion that the poet is thus "committed 'to turn the unpoetical into poetry' [and to fuse] 'the matter-of-fact and the fantastic.' " But the meaning of "reality," for Eliot, is especial, existing always "at the edge of nothingness," where, as B. Rajan writes, "the birth of meaning . . . takes place in a manner both creative and ancient. Poetry cannot report the event; it must *be* the event, lived through in a form that can speak about itself while remaining wholly itself. This is a feat at least as difficult as it sounds, and if the poem succeeds in it, it is because, however much it remembers previous deaths by drowning, it creates its own life against its own thrust of questioning."

"In effect," writes Herbert Howarth, "Eliot demonstrated that a poet's business is not just reporting feeling, but extending feeling, and creating a shape to convey it." Eliot's poetry, then, is a process of "living by thought," says Rajan, "of seeking to find peace 'through a satisfaction of the whole being.' It is singular in its realization of passion through intelligence. It is driven by a scepticism which resolutely asks the question but refuses to stop short at it, by a sensibility sharply aware of 'the disorder, the futility, the meaninglessness, the mystery of life and suffering.' If it attains a world of belief or a conviction of order, that conviction is won against the attacking strength of doubt and remains always subject to its corrosive power. Not all of us share Eliot's faith. But all of us can accept the poetry because nearly every line of it was written while looking into the eyes of the demon."

In 1921 Conrad Aiken, although a life-long friend and admirer of Eliot, not only could not share Eliot's faith, but further questioned the validity of the poetry as poetry. "His sense of the definite is intermittent," Aiken wrote; "it abandons him often at the most critical moment, and in consequence Mr. Eliot himself is forever abandoning *us* on the very doorstep of the illuminating. One has again and again the feeling that he is working, as it were, too close to the object. . . . He passes quickly from one detail of analysis to another; he is aggressively aware that he is 'thinking,' his brow is knit; but he appears to believe that mere fineness of detail will constitute, in the sequence of his comments, a direction. What happens is that he achieves a kind of filigree without pattern."

But Alvarez, who calls Eliot "a supreme interpreter of meditated experience," provides perhaps the most lucid analysis of Eliot's "method." "The moments of greatest intensity have, as Eliot presents them, a certain obliqueness, an allusiveness, a controlling detachment," writes Alvarez. "It is a poetry apart. . . . He is, in some ways, a meditative poet. But this does not mean a poet who deals in abstractions; Eliot's meditations are meditations on experience, in which the abstractions belong as much as the images; they are all a part of his particular cast of mind, the meaning he gives to past experience. But Eliot is, I think, a relatively indifferent, or uninterested, observer of the phenomenal world. . . . His direct affirmations are always summings-up of this style, concentrations for which the rest of his verse appears as so many hints."

Aiken's "filigree without pattern" may then be seen as Unger's "magic lantern," which throws "the nerves in patterns on a screen." Citing "Prufrock," Unger compares Eliot's poetry to a series of slides. "Each slide is an isolated, fragmentary image, producing its own effect, including suggestions of some larger action or situation of which it is but an arrested moment." Richard Poirier explains that these "procedural hesitancies," as a characteristic of form, "have the total effect of enormous stamina; [Eliot's] reluctance of self-assertion, by acknowledging all the possibilities open to it, emerges as an ever dangerously controlled strength." Poirier continues: "In Eliot the form is shaped by creative and de-creative movements: each movement is in itself usually very tentative, and yet each achieves by cumulative interaction a firmness that supports the other. The result is an extraordinary fusion of diffidence and dogmatism." And it is by this fusion that "the poet's experiences," says Frye, "are shaped into a unity which takes its place in a literary tradition." By being assimilated into a tradition (of which Eliot was always sharply aware), then, genuine poetry does contribute, as G. Wilson Knight notes, "to the health of a culture," in that it "tells us the truth about ourselves in our present situation . . . is capable of dealing with the present world, [and] does not have to leave out the boredom and the horror of our world in order to discern its true glory." And it is just here, by creating such a poetry, that Eliot made his greatest gift to poetry. "No poet has been so deeply honest," says Knight, and A. R. Scott-James adds: "He excels by introducing us to our own generation." McLuhan summarizes: "To purify the 'dialect of the tribe' and to open the doors of perception by discovering a host of new poetic themes and rhythms was the especial achievement of T. S. Eliot. He gave us back our language enlivened and refreshed by new contacts with many other tongues."

Certainly one of the most important ways in which Eliot fulfilled his self-imposed duty to his own voice was by using the materials of the city for building his poetry. Potter Woodbery writes that "the modern poet, as Eliot himself on occasions has pointed out, finds himself faced with the task of revitalizing a language that has gone dead, of seeking out genuine but novel avenues of expression so that a sharpness of impact can once again be felt in English poetry. . . . The fresh vitality that the materials of the city give to these modern metaphors and similes makes them unusually arresting with the result that one finds himself drawn into a fuller and closer examination of their poetic meaning rather than gliding over them as is the tendency in the case of the more traditional 'poetic' figures." The city, for Eliot, further serves as "the one great artifact of secularized Enlightenment man"; it stands as a "monument to humanity and testifies to the absence of God in the modern world." But, as Woodbery quickly adds, "because the city presents itself throughout his poetry in a consistently dark light, one should not infer on Eliot's part a naive primitivistic longing for a restoration of the non-urban modes of life characteristic of the preindustrial world. Eliot's indictment of the present age is spiritual rather than sociological." Similarly Eliot believes that the primary value of religion, for mankind, lies "in the quality of its worldliness," in the context of a social institution (although Stephen Spender reports that Eliot once told him that religion "is a less effective escape than that used by thousands who 'escape by reading novels, looking at films, or best of all, by driving very fast on land or in air, which

makes even dreams unnecessary.' ") Religion is most effective as a device, then, but cannot even work as well as other devices.

Frye writes: "The particular continuum into which an individual is born, Eliot calls his culture or tradition. By culture Eliot means 'that which makes life worth living': one's total way of life, including art and education, but also cooking and sports. By tradition, also, Eliot means both a conscious and an unconscious life in a social continuum. . . . He speaks of culture metaphorically as the 'incarnation' of a religion, the human manifestation of a superhuman reality. A culture's religion 'should mean for the individual and for the group something toward which they strive, not merely something which they possess.' " (It is tangentially interesting to apply Eliot's definition of culture as a continuum—in which the upper class possesses not more culture, but a more conscious culture—to his own readership. His popular reputation, Frye writes, "was that of an erudite highbrow. But such a reputation would be contradictory to Eliot's view of the 'elite' as responsible for articulating the unconscious culture of their societies. Eliot would like, he says, an audience that could neither read nor write." As Geoffrey Dearmer adds sympathetically, "poor Eliot has become a subject for university schools and a burden on those in pursuit of degrees when all that he asked of readers was to be read with enjoyment.") "All views of life that Eliot would call serious or mature," Frye concludes, "distinguish between two selves in man: the selfish and the self-respecting. These are not only distinguishable but opposed, and in Christianity the opposition is total, as for it the selfish self is to be annihilated, and the other is the immortal soul one is trying to save. Theories of conduct exalting the freedom of the personality or character without making this distinction are disastrous."

Like Emerson, then, Eliot recognized the duality of man's soul "struggling," as Kazin writes, "for its own salvation"—and the world, "meaning everything outside the soul's anxious efforts," and that this duality is more "real" than society. Just as Eliot never accepted the statement that *The Waste Land* represented "the disillusionment of a generation," Braybrooke submits, he would never admit that his use of broken images "meant a separation from belief, since for him doubts and certainties represented varieties of belief." As Knight astutely points out, the "wonderful lyric in *East Coker* [beginning] 'The wounded surgeon plies the steel' [is] surely the grimmest statement on the Christian world-view ever penned by a devotee [and] offers a universe so riddled with negations and agonies that we must go to the anti-Christian polemics of Nietzsche—which its cutting phraseology recalls—for an analogy." But as always, Eliot is applying to the city and to the institutions of men his own peculiar vision in order to make a poetry which he in turn uses to test the validity of poetry. There is no deceit; from the outset he tells us that he will take us through half-deserted streets "that follow like a tedious argument / Of insidious intent / To lead you to an overwhelming question." Eliot presents us with a pattern which, as Frank Kermode writes in his discussion of *The Waste Land,* "suggests a commitment, a religion; and the poet retreats to it. But the poem is a great poem because it will not force us to follow him. It makes us wiser without committing us. . . . It joins the mix of our own minds but it does not tell us what to believe. . . . The poem resists an imposed order; it is a part of its greatness that it can do so."

Scott-James, in his analysis of the poetry, is able to tell us what is not to be found in Eliot. "There is no joy, no exultation, not even pleasure except the pleasure which is shown as spurious. There is no portrayal of common emotions, except when they are depraved, or silly. All the things which common men think of as practical and desirable vanish into insignificance under his vision." And Wallace Fowlie tells us what can be discovered there: "More fervently than any other poet of the twentieth century, Eliot has sung of the permanence of time, the experience of one time which is all time. He sings of it when he speaks of the flower that fades, of the sea that seems eternal, of the rock in the sea, and of the prayer of the Annunciation. . . . In such [passages] the poet reveals his true mission, that of transmuting his intimate emotions, his personal anguish, into a strange and impersonal work. In this way, the poet becomes aware of his presence in the world, where his major victory is the imposing of his presence as a man by means of his lucidity and his creative power."

Eliot told Donald Hall in 1959 that he considered *The Four Quartets* to be his best work; "and," he added, "I'd like to feel that they get better as they go on. The second is better than the first, the third is better than the second, and the fourth is the best of all. At any rate, that's the way I flatter myself." Neville Braybrooke writes: "It is . . . generally agreed . . . that in his *Four Quartets* [Eliot] attempted . . . to achieve a poetry so transparent that in concentrating on it attention would not fall so much on the words, but on the words pointed to. And in his rigorous stripping away of the poetic, such a pure poetry is sustained." Further, Eliot shaped the *Quartets* into a gyre, and, by imposing such a form, directed us to see the work as a totality in which each part contributes to and is enhanced by the process of synthesis.

Although many critics have commented on the cyclical nature of the *Four Quartets,* Frye has actually diagrammed these poems. "Draw a horizontal line on a page," he says, "then a vertical line of the same length cutting it in two and forming a cross, then a circle of which these lines are diameters, then a smaller circle inside with the same centre. The horizontal line is clock time, the Heraclitean flux, the river into which no one steps twice. The vertical line is the presence of God descending into time, and crossing it at the Incarnation, forming the 'still point of the turning world.' The top and bottom of the vertical line represent the goals of the way up and the way down, though we cannot show that they are the same point in two dimensions. The top and bottom halves of the larger circle are the visions of plenitude and of vacancy respectively; the top and bottom halves of the smaller circle are the world of the rose-garden and (not unnaturally for an inner circle) of the subway, innocence and experience. . . . What lies below experience is ascesis or dark night. There is thus no hell in *Four Quartets,* which belong entirely to the purgatorial vision." "The archetype of this cycle is the Bible," he continues, "which begins with the story of man in a garden." So in Eliot we begin and end at the same point, "with the Word as the circumference of reality, containing within itself time, space, and poetry viewed in the light of the conception of poetry as a living whole of all the poetry that has ever been written." All this to say, as Alvarez writes, that "the triumphant achievement of the *Four Quartets* is in the peculiar wholeness and isolation of their poetic world. . . . Eliot has always worked obliquely, by suggestion and by his penetrating personal rhythms. His power is in his sureness and mastery of subject and expression. And this sense of inviolable purpose seems to remove his verse from the ordinary realm of human interchange. He has created a world of formal perfection. It lacks the dimension of human error."

Carol H. Smith writes: "Just as a religious interpretation of existence was needed to order the world of nature and of man, so art, [Eliot] felt, required a form which could impose order and meaning on experience. The form which Eliot came to see as the most perfectly ordered and most complete as a microcosmic creation of experience was drama." In the *Aims of Poetic Drama* Eliot wrote: "What I should like to do is this: that the people on the stage should seem to the audience so like themselves that they would find themselves thinking: 'I could talk in poetry too!' Then they are not transported into an unaccustomed, artificial world; but their ordinary, sordid world is suddenly illuminated and transfigured. And if poetry cannot do that for people, it is merely superfluous decoration." But for many, accustomed to the conventions of modern theater, Eliot was not a successful dramatist. As Miss Smith writes: "The plays of T. S. Eliot are more likely to baffle than to inspire. Not only do Eliot's plays refuse to conform to today's dramatic modes but each play is theatrically different from the others." And John Gross explains that, "having arrived in the *Quartets* at a state of mind so specialised as to be barely communicable, Eliot went on to devote what remained of his energy to the most unashamedly public of poetic activities, writing for the theater. Was it a mistake? In all probability, yes. Certainly at his death Eliot's standing as a poet was secure, while his reputation as a dramatist was in the trough of the wave." But, says Knight, "how much more illuminating is Eliot's failure than the successes of lesser poets!"

That Eliot's intentions as a playwright were serious can hardly be questioned. Miss Smith writes: "Eliot's interest in drama dates back to the beginnings of his career. His critical essays on Elizabethan and Jacobean dramatists, his use of the dramatic monologue in some of his best-known early poems . . . and the dramatic contrasts of episodes in *The Waste Land* all testify to what Edmund Wilson called 'the dramatic character of his imagination.' " Eliot himself told Donald Hall that, in writing *The Confidential Clerk,* he "wanted to get to learn the technique of the theater so well that I could then forget about it. I always feel it's not wise to violate rules until you know how to observe them." As a result of his conscientiousness, he said, the play "was so well constructed in some ways that people thought it was just meant to be a farce." He told Lawrence Durrell: "If I am writing a play I think I am better concerned with becoming conscious of how to do it rather than in becoming conscious of what I am trying to do." But Eliot later told Hall: "In 1939, if there hadn't been a war, I would probably have tried to write another play. And I think it's a very good thing I didn't have the opportunity. From my personal point of view, the one good thing the war did was to prevent me from writing another play too soon."

"Eliot's desire," writes Miss Smith, "was for a dramatic form which would make drama conform to the criterion of all art: the harmonious relationship of the parts to the whole." And, she continues, "Eliot's ideal of dramatic form was a work which would re-create in its theme, its form and its language the harmony which explained the untidy surface of life. The dramatist's mission was thus both artistic and religious, and it was envisioned as a process of transformation." In 1949, Eliot wrote in a letter to Lawrence Durrell: "We have got to make plays in which the mental movements cannot find physical equivalents. But when one comes to the big moment (and if we can't get it we can't do drama) there must be some simple fundamental emotion (expressed, of course, in deathless verse) which *everybody* can understand."

Eliot chose *poetic* drama, as McLuhan explains, because it is within this kind of play that "the participation of the audience in the action is achieved both poetically and liturgically. It was Eliot's discovery that prose drama isolates the audience from the action of the play. Poetic drama that makes a skillful use of contemporary idiom can be a means of involving the audience centrally in the action once more." He labored to "maintain the supremacy of reason" in the plays, and succeeded, Howarth writes, in that "his audience feels the constant presence of an ordering intelligence." It is, however, the very erudition governing the writing that is frequently cited as the major dramatic flaw in the plays. For centuries drama has depended upon the Dionysian properties which Eliot's dramatic theories reject in favor of "reason." Frederick Lumley writes: "Eliot was a conservative, too consciously a critic to wander an inch from the theories of drama he so carefully propounded beforehand. The best criticism of Eliot's plays has been written by Eliot himself, and few theoreticians have proved their views so convincingly in practice. Eliot, a great poet, became both master and pupil of dramatic theory, yet however important his plays were, he was never to write a *chef-d'oeuvre*. His best play, *Murder in the Cathedral,* is noble in its theme and treatment, but lacks the natural abundance of creative genius. His cold, austere intellectuality is apparent in all his plays, and the more his plays have moved from spiritual to secular, the more onerous this has become in making his plays acceptable." But perhaps the statement most frequently trotted out by those unsympathetic to Eliot as dramatist is simply that he wrote verse plays that were social caricatures. Miss Gardner answers thus: "I cannot take very seriously a criticism that assumes that what is temporarily unfashionable is permanently out-of-date. The tradition of social comedy which Eliot took up is a very tough tradition. At the moment these plays are dated, but as they recede into history their social verisimilitude will be as much a source of strength as is the social truth of Restoration Comedy."

Eliot himself believed that *The Family Reunion,* at least poetically, was the best of all his plays. Helen Gardner, among several others, believes that *The Cocktail Party* and *The Confidential Clerk* are his finest. Miss Gardner says of these plays: "No other plays of our generation present with equal force, sympathy, wisdom, and wit the classic subject of comedy: our almost, but mercifully not wholly, unlimited powers of self-deception, and the shocks and surprises that life gives to our poses and pretences." But history will almost certainly endow *Murder in the Cathedral* with the longest life and the greatest fame. John Gross notes: "Whether or not *Murder in the Cathedral* augments our ability to live, it is certainly a remarkable piece of work. It is Eliot's one indubitable theatrical triumph, and the one English addition to the classic repertoire since Shaw."

Stephen Spender has said of Eliot: "He was more inimitable than any other modern poet . . . yet more could be learned from his theory and practice than from any other writer. This man who seemed so unapproachable was the most approached by younger poets—and the most helpful to them—of any poet of his generation," except for Ezra Pound. Certainly it was because he was willing to explicate, and thus to share, the principles by which he worked and lived that he became a great critic. Carlo Linati, one of the first in Italy to write about Eliot, found his poetry "irrational, incomprehensible." But, he added, "because Eliot is first of all a critic, literary criticism is the field in which his personality has found its full expression." Mario Praz notes that, "in the *Partisan Review* for February, 1949, when Eliot's career was nearly concluded, Delmore Schwartz expressed this opinion: 'When we think of the character of literary dictators in the past, it is easy to see that since 1922, at least, Eliot has occupied a position in the English-speaking world analogous to that occupied by Ben Jonson, Dryden, Pope, Samuel Johnson, Coleridge, and Matthew Arnold. It is noticeable that each of these dictators has been a critic as well as a poet, and we may infer from this the fact that it is necessary for them to practice both poetry and criticism.' And the eminent historian of criticism Rene Wellek wrote in The *Sewanee Review* for July, 1956: 'T. S. Eliot is by far the most important critic of the twentieth century in the English-speaking world.' "

Grant T. Webster states that "it is an error in tone and taste to treat [Eliot] as a systematic thinker, as a builder of a critical system" because Eliot himself, dividing criticism into "essays of generalization" and "appreciations of individual authors," came to abandon the former in favor of the latter which, he said, "seem to me to have the best chance of retaining some value for future readers." Praz writes: "Eliot . . ., with a typical Anglo-Saxon shyness, has waived any claim to systematic philosophical thought, in statements like the following: 'I have no general theory of my own. . . . The extreme of theorizing about the nature of poetry, the essence of poetry if there is any, belongs to the study of aesthetics and is no concern of the poet or of a critic with my limited qualifications.'"

Eliot's concern for the lasting value of his (or any) criticism is paralleled by his own awareness of those who preceded him. As John Paul Pritchard explains: "Eliot required that for the understanding of any living artist he be set for contrast and comparison among those dead artists" before him; and "the poet's contribution is not that in which he differs from tradition, but that part of his work most in harmony with the dead poets who preceded him. From these premises Eliot concluded that the poet's work must be judged by standards from the past." And since, as Poirier suggests, he "chooses to devalue literature in the interests of the pre-eminent values of language," Eliot is again led to a poetry which primarily serves the language as it has been invested with life *by tradition.* But, Praz points out, "the critic's task should be to see literature '*not* as consecrated by time, but to see it beyond time; to see the best work of our time and the best work of twenty-five hundred years ago with the same eyes.' " In other words, the poetry itself "does not matter" for Eliot in this sense; as he told Durrell, the "prose sense comes first, and . . . poetry is merely prose developed by a knowledge of aeronautics."

Eliot's type of criticism, writes Praz, "in his own words, is meant to be an integration of scholarly criticism. In *The Music of Poetry* he said that his method was that of a poet 'always trying to defend the kind of poetry he is writing.' " Since Eliot wanted to write poetry "with the greatest economy of words, and with the greatest austerity in the use of metaphor, simile, verbal beauty, and elegance," he turned to Dante, whose language, says Praz, "is the perfection of a common language." Also, Praz continues, "what Eliot [saw] in Dante—who is almost the sole poet for whom he [had] kept up a constant cult—is more the fruit of a poet's sensibility than of a critical evaluation. He [saw] in Dante clear visual images [and] a concise and luminous language." Thus, in establishing criteria for his own poetry, Eliot formalized critical "theories" useful to his own thinking. The resultant eclecticism is, according to Austin Warren, a theory of poetry which "falls neither into didacticism nor into its opposite heresies, imagism and echolalia. The real 'purity' of poetry—to speak in terms at once paradoxical and generic—is to be constantly and richly impure: neither philosophy, nor psychology, nor imagery, nor music alone, but a significant tension between all of them."

Certainly among the most celebrated of Eliot's critical statements are his terms "objective correlative" and "dissociation of sensibility." The former, Praz explains, is Eliot's term for "a set of objects, a situation, a chain of events which shall be the formula of that *particular* emotion," which is to be expressed "in the form of art." The latter term, writes Pritchard, was used by Eliot "to indicate [an] inability to 'devour any kind of experience.' " Frank Kermode defines Eliot's "dissociation of sensibility" as "an historical theory to explain the dearth of objective correlatives in a time when the artist, alienated from his environment . . . is working at the beginning of a dark age 'under conditions that seem unpropitious,' in an everworsening climate of imagination.''

Regardless of his imposing stature as a literary critic, Eliot, in his later years, seemed to re-examine his earlier statements with mistrust. Eliot told Donald Hall in 1959 that, ''as one gets older, one is not quite confident in one's ability to distinguish new genius among younger men.'' Perhaps the same diminishing confidence in his critical ability led to the various recantations (most notable in his Milton criticism) which characterized much of his later work. I. A. Richards writes: ''Gentleness and justness, these are the marks of his later criticism, with its elaborate measures taken to repair any injustices—to Milton, to Shelley, to Coleridge, or to _meaning_ or to _interpretation_ or even to _education_— that his earlier pronouncements seemed to him to have committed. I doubt if another critic can be found so ready to amend what he had come to consider his own former aberrations.'' (Conrad Aiken recently quoted from a very early letter in which Eliot called Ezra Pound's poetry ''touchingly incompetent.'' When Hall asked him about this evaluation Eliot replied, ''Hah! That was a bit brash, wasn't it?'') Richards continues: ''These reversals and recantations strike me as springing from an everdeepening scepticism, a questioning of the very roots of critical pretensions. It is as though, in the course of acquiring the tremendous authority that the editor of _The Criterion_ came to enjoy, TSE had learned too much about the game of opinion-forming and had become alarmed and indeed irked by the weight his judgments were being accorded. He was no longer amused by the reverence with which they were received.''

In his excellent summary of Eliot's critical stance, Alvarez writes: ''Our interest and standards in literature are Eliot's creation. And of course this is something more profound than the enthusiasm aroused by a few well-timed articles. His critical pronouncements were made valid by his poetry. So he did more than change the standards of critical judgment; he altered the whole mode of expression in order to make room for his originality.''

To draw a portrait of Eliot the man, Neville Braybrooke writes, one must follow hints with guesses; ''and this is precisely what Eliot would have liked, because it is a method in which surprises will frequently recur.'' For instance, Braybrooke continues, one might be shocked to learn that the author of _The Idea of a Christian Society_ loved ''whoopie cushions and joke cigars. But no man can always stay at the sublime heights, and if, paradoxically enough, some of the more conservative elements in his family were baffled by the sublime heights that he reached in his work, then at least they would have understood his practical joker side.'' One might also be surprised to learn that the greatest man of letters of his time was devoted to Sherlock Holmes. Durrell writes: ''At the mention of the name he lit up like a torch. He, it seemed, was a tremendous fan of Holmes and could quote at length from the saga. 'I flatter myself,' he said—and this is the nearest to an immodesty that I had ever heard him go—'that I know the names of everyone, even the smallest character.' Two minutes afterward he found he could not recall the name of one of Doyle's puppets. His annoyance was comical. He struck his knee with irritation and concentrated. It would not come. Then he burst out laughing at himself.'' Allen Tate reports fondly that Eliot's laugh ''was never hearty; it was something between a chuckle and a giggle.''

The Eliot family motto is _Tace et fac,_ and it has been said that he ''worked assiduously'' and ''grew silently.'' Sir Herbert Read describes him as ''a serious but not necessarily a solemn man, a

severe man never lacking in kindness and sympathy, a profound man (profoundly learned, profoundly poetic, profoundly spiritual). And yet to outward appearance a correct man, a conventional man, an infinitely polite man—in brief, a gentleman.'' Richard Poirier writes: ''Eliot as a projection of his _oeuvres_ has a form distinctly unlike the form of any of his poems. He is infrangible, while his poems are fragmentary and seemingly irresolute about their fragmentariness. His poetry is about the difficulty of conceiving anything. Never merely expressive of ideas already successfully shaped in the mind, his poems enact the mind's effort even to form an idea. Yet he thrives upon some inward assurance, mysterious and not always accessible, that cannot be translated into programmatic thinking or into daytime sense.'' And Stephen Spender summarizes: ''Religiously, poetically and intellectually, this very private man kept open house. . . . Yet in spite of all this, he was sly, ironic, a bit cagey, a bit calculating perhaps, the Eliot whom Ezra Pound called 'old Possum.' ''

One can read the reminiscences of his friends and guess at personal things about ''Tom'' Eliot (although he would be highly pleased, one is sure, to be able to invalidate our conclusions). Spender, for instance, writes: ''[Eliot's] first wife, who had been a dancer . . ., was gay, talkative, a chatter-box. She wanted to enjoy life, found Eliot inhibiting and inhibited, yet worshipped him. . . . There was a time when the Eliots separated, and Eliot lived by himself, wore a monocle, was known to the neighbours as Captain Eliot.'' Aldous Huxley once told Robert Craft that ''the marriage in _The Cocktail Party_ was inspired—if that is the word—by Tom's own [first] marriage. His wife, Vivienne, was an ether addict, you know, and the house smelled like a hospital. All that dust and despair in Eliot's poetry is to be traced to this fact.'' Derek Stanford, too, has done some conjecturing about the subjectivity of Eliot's work. Citing the well-known lines, ''Go, said the bird, for the leaves were full of children, / Hidden excitedly, containing laughter. / Go, go, go, said the bird: human kind / Cannot bear very much reality,'' Stanford writes: ''This is as near to confession as Eliot need ever come. _The Four Quartets_ are deeply concerned with first and last things, with archetypal experience and states: birth, pro-creation, death, judgment, salvation, damnation; and if I read this passage aright it originates in Eliot's loss and need of domestic life before his second marriage.'' But, as Stanford later points out, the origin doesn't really matter.

Of course Eliot himself has told us (''no,'' says Stravinsky, ''Eliot never 'told,' he imparted'') something about his life, his work, and the circumstances of the former as they are manifested in the latter. He told Hall that he began to write poetry when he was about fourteen years old, ''under the inspiration of Fitzgerald's _Omar Khayyam,_ [and I wrote] a number of very gloomy and atheistical and despairing quatrains in the same style, which fortunately I suppressed completely—so completely that they don't exist.'' When George Seferis asked him how he wrote _The Waste Land,_ Eliot answered: ''I'd been sick and the doctors recommended rest. I went to Mar-gate (he smiled), in November. There I wrote the first part. Then I went to Switzerland on vacation and finished the poem. It was double its present length. I sent it to Pound; he cut out half of it.'' (The half which Pound excised and which was thought for many years to be lost or destroyed was found recently and has been on display at the New York Public Library.) (Leonard Unger adds that Pound the mentor also ''persuaded Eliot not to use as epigraph a quotation from Conrad's _Heart of Darkness,_ not to use 'Gerontion' as a prelude to _The Waste Land,_ [and] to retain the section called 'Death by Water' [which is Eliot's translation of his own French verses in 'Dans le Restaurant']." When the resultant poem appeared, "the first issue of *Time* [March 3, 1923] reported the rumor that *The Waste Land* was written as a hoax.") Eliot also told Hall: "Whether I write or type, composition of any length, a play for example, means for me regular hours, say ten to one. I found that three hours a day is about all I can do of actual composing." He told Durrell that "a poet must be deliberately lazy. One should write as little as one possibly can. I always try to make the whole business seem as unimportant as I can." Durrell once tried to persuade Eliot to go to Greece, but Eliot said that he "preferred gloomy places to write in." When Hall asked him if "the optimal career for a poet would involve no work at all but writing and reading," Eliot said, "No, . . . it is very dangerous to give an optimal career for everybody. . . . I feel quite sure that if I'd started by having independent means, if I hadn't had to bother about earning a living and could have given all my time to poetry, it would have had a deadening influence on me."

Eliot has said that his poetry "has obviously more in common with my distinguished contemporaries in America than with anything written in my generation in England. That I'm sure of." He admits that, in his own youth, he had very little sense of the literary times, that he felt no dominating presence of an older poet as one now feels the immediate influence of Eliot, Pound, and Stevens. "I think it was rather an advantage not having any living poets in England or America in whom one took any particular interest," he told Hall. "I don't know what it would be like, but I think it would be a rather troublesome distraction to have such a lot of dominating presences . . . about. Fortunately we weren't bothered by each other. . . . There was Yeats, but it was the early Yeats. It was too much Celtic twilight for me. There was really nothing except the people of the 90's who had all died of drink or suicide or one thing or another."

Today, as always, critical evaluations include sincere dislike of Eliot's work. In 1963 John Frederick Nims observed that Eliot "woos the lugubrious," that his poems "are a bore, obtruding and exhorting, buttonholing us with 'Redeem the time' and so forth." Though Nims concedes that Eliot "outranks . . . just about all [contemporary poets]," he is concerned because Eliot does not readily enchant the reader, and because his poetry tends to translate easily. The sterility, inaction, detachment, and despair which dominate Eliot's poetry are, in the opinion of several critics, epitomized in V.S. Pritchett's description of Eliot as "a trim anti-Bohemian with black bowler and umbrella . . . ushering us to our seats in hell." But for most, Eliot was, at the time of his death, the most imposing literary figure in the world. As early as 1917 Eliot declared: "The existing order is complete before the new work arrives; for order to persist after the supervention of novelty, the *whole* existing order must be, if ever so slightly, altered." Stephen Spender writes: "I think it can now be said that the novelties he introduced—none more striking than the reappearance of *ideas* in poetry—have been assimilated and become part of that marvelous order, now slightly altered, of imperishable works in English." Frank Kermode adds: "Eliot certainly has the marks of a modern kind of greatness, those beneficial intuitions of irregularity and chaos, the truth of the foul rag-and-bone shop. Yet we remember him as celebrating order. Over the years be explored the implications of his attitudes to order, and it is doubtful whether many people capable of understanding him now have much sympathy with his views. Hit greatness will rest on the fruitful recognition of disorder, though the theories will have their interest as theories held by a great man." And Scott-James has said that Eliot "brought into poetry something which in this generation was needed: a language spare, sinewy, modern; a fresh and springy metrical form;

thought that was adult; and an imagination aware of what is bewildering and terrifying in modern life and in all life. He has done more than any other [contemporary] English poet to make this age conscious of itself, and, in being conscious, apprehensive."

Eliot himself once said: "One seems to become a myth, a fabulous creature that doesn't exist. One doesn't feel any different. It isn't that you get bigger to fit the world, the world gets smaller to fit you. You remain exactly the same. Obscurity in writing is confused with novelty." But as Eliot's reputation grew, his poetry became increasingly more private. He never attempted to "redeem mankind"; but he did give to his age, as John Gross writes, "an idiom and a mythology." In 1948 his contribution was justly recognized. Harvey Breit tells us that, "when the official cable from the Nobel Prize Committee in Stockholm reached him, he was immensely pleased. There must have been, it was suggested, some ironic satisfaction as well: . . . in the Forties, the recipient of the highest formal literary honor; in the Twenties, Mr. Eliot had been almost universally considered decadent, obscure and a passing fashion. 'It amuses me,' he said without amusement. ('Shall I say it just that way—gently?' [Breit] asked. 'Say it just that way—gently,' he agreed, 'for I don't wish to ridicule anyone.')"

It has been said that Eliot never lost his charm. Analyses of the poetry, the plays, the criticism, will be added for years to come to the many shelves of existing Eliot criticism. Readers will continue to guess about what the man "was really like." But perhaps Frank Morley made the most appropriate statement of all when he related that, while he listened to the funeral service at Westminster Abbey, he was "thinking of Eliot as a man who had very unusual powers of trespass into different hearts."

A memorial service for Eliot at Westminster Abbey, February 4, 1965, was published as *Order of Service in Memory of Thomas Stearns Eliot,* Hove Shirley Press (London), 1965. On June 14, 1965, a program entitled "Homage to T. S. Eliot" was presented at the Globe Theatre in London. To the program Igor Stravinsky contributed "Introitus," a new choral work written in Eliot's memory, and Henry Moore a huge sculpture entitled "The Archer." Andrei Voznesensky, Peter O'Toole, Laurence Olivier, and Paul Scofield recited. Poems read during the program were selected by W.H. Auden, and Cleanth Brooks contributed a brief narration.

Eliot's works have been translated into at least twenty-two languages. Harvard University has recorded his readings of "The Hollow Men," "Gerontion," "The Love Song of J. Alfred Prufrock," "Journey of the Magi," "A Song for Simeon, Triumphal March," "Difficulties of a Statesman," "Fragment of an Agon," and "Four Quartets." Eliot's readings of "The Waste Land," "Landscapes I and II," and "Sweeney Among the Nightingales" have been recorded by the Library of Congress.

MEDIA ADAPTATIONS: "The Hollow Men" was set for baritone solo, male voice chorus, and orchestra, published by Oxford University Press, 1951; Stravinsky set sections of "Little Gidding" to music; *Murder in the Cathedral* was filmed in 1952, and Eliot wrote some new lines for the script and himself read the part of The Fourth Tempter, who is never seen on the screen; The Old Vic issued a recording of *Murder in the Cathedral* in 1953; "Sweeney Agonistes" was adapted into a jazz musical by John Dankworth for "Homage to T. S. Eliot"; *Old Possum's Book of Practical Cats* was adapted as the stage musical "Cats," 1981.

BIOGRAPHICAL/CRITICAL SOURCES:

BOOKS

Ackroyd, Peter, *T. S. Eliot: A Life,* Simon & Schuster, 1984.

Aiken, Conrad, *A Reviewer's ABC,* World Publishing, 1958.

Alvarez, A., *Stewards of Excellence,* Scribner, 1958.

Baybrooke, Neville, editor, *T.S. Eliot: A Symposium for His Seventieth Birthday,* Farrar, Straus, 1958.

Braybrooke, Neville, *T. S. Eliot,* Eerdmans, 1967.

Bogard, Travis, and William I. Oliver, editors, *Modern Drama: Essays in Criticism,* Oxford University Press, 1965.

Bradbrook, Muriel, *T. S. Eliot,* revised edition, Longmans, Green, 1963.

Breit, Harvey, *The Writer Observed,* World Publishing, 1956.

Browne, E. Martin, *The Making of T. S. Eliot's Plays,* Cambridge University Press, 1969.

Concise Dictionary of American Literary Biography: The New Maturity, 1929-1941, Gale, 1989.

Contemporary Literary Criticism, Gale, Volume 1, 1973, Volume 2, 1974, Volume 3, 1975, Volume 6, 1976, Volume 9, 1978, Volume 10, 1979, Volume 13, 1980, Volume 15, 1980, Volume 24, 1983, Volume 34, 1985, Volume 41, 1987, Volume 55, 1989.

Dictionary of Literary Biography, Gale, Volume 7: *Twentieth-Century American Dramatists,* 1981, Volume 10: *Modern British Dramatists, 1940-1945,* 1982, Volume 45: *American Poets, 1880-1945, First Series,* 1986, Volume 63: *Modern American Criticism, 1920-1955,* 1988.

Donoghue, Denis, *Modern British and American Verse Drama,* Princeton University Press, 1959.

Frye, Northrup, *T. S. Eliot,* Oliver & Boyd, 1963.

Gardner, Helen, *The Art of T. S. Eliot,* Dutton, 1959.

Gordon, Lyndall, *Eliot's Early Years,* Oxford University Press, 1977.

Gordon, Lyndall, *Eliot's New Life,* Farrar, Straus, 1988.

Headings, Philip R., *T. S. Eliot,* Twayne, 1964.

Howarth, Herbert, *Notes on Some Figures Behind T. S. Eliot,* Houghton, 1964.

Howe, Irving, editor, *Modern Literary Criticism,* Beacon, 1958.

Hyman, Stanley Edgar, editor, *The Critical Performance,* Vintage, 1956.

Jones, Genesius, *Approach to the Purpose: A Study of the Poetry of T. S. Eliot,* Hodder & Stoughton, 1964.

Lumley, Frederick, *New Trends in 20th Century Drama,* Oxford University Press, 1967.

Matthiessen, F. O., *The Achievement of T.S. Eliot,* revised edition, Oxford University Press, 1947.

Pritchard, John Paul, *Criticism in America,* University of Oklahoma Press, 1956.

Rexroth, Kenneth, *Assays,* New Directions, 1961.

Scott-James, R. A., *Fifty Years of English Literature, 1900-1950,* Longmans, Green, 1951.

Tate, Allen, editor, *T. S. Eliot: The Man and His Work,* Dell, 1966.

Tynan, Kenneth, *Curtains,* Atheneum, 1961.

Unger, Leonard, editor, *T.S. Eliot: A Selected Critique,* Rinehart, 1948.

Unger, Leonard, *T. S. Eliot,* University of Minnesota Press, 1961.

Untermeyer, Louis, *Lives of the Poets,* Simon & Schuster, 1959.

Weales, Gerald, *Religion in Modern English Drama,* University of Pennsylvania Press, 1961.

PERIODICALS

American Literature, January, 1962.

American Quarterly, summer, 1961.

Arizona Quarterly, spring, 1966.

Atlantic Monthly, May, 1965.

Book Week, February 13, 1966.

Canadian Forum, February, 1965.

Contemporary Literature, winter, 1968.

Criticism, fall, 1966, winter, 1967.

Drama, summer, 1967.

Encounter, March, 1965, April, 1965, November, 1965.

Esquire, August, 1965.

Listener, June 25, 1967.

Nation, October 3, 1966.

New York Review of Books, March 3, 1966.

New Leader, November 6, 1967.

New Republic, May 20, 1967.

New Statesman, October 11, 1963, March 13 1964.

New York Times, January 5, 1965, June 14, 1965, August 22, 1989.

New York Times Book Review, November 19, 1967.

New York Times Magazine, September 21, 1958.

Observer, June 11, 1967.

Paris Review, spring-summer, 1959.

Partisan Review, spring, 1966.

Publishers Weekly, December 10, 1962.

Quarterly Review of Literature, numbers 1-2 (double issue), 1967.

Saturday Review, September 13, 1958, October 19, 1963, February 8, 1964.

Sewanee Review, winter, 1962, spring, 1967.

Southwest Review, summer, 1965.

Times Educational Supplement, September 26, 1958.

Times (London), September 29, 1958.

Times Literary Supplement, June 1, 1967.

Virginia Quarterly Review, autumn, 1967.*

*   *   *

ELKIN, Stanley L(awrence) 1930-

PERSONAL: Born May 11, 1930, in New York, N.Y.; son of Philip (a salesman) and Zelda (Feldman) Elkin; married Joan Marion Jacobson, February 1, 1953; children: Philip Aaron, Bernard Edward, Molly Ann. *Education:* University of Illinois, A.B., 1952, M.A., 1953, Ph.D., 1961. *Religion:* Jewish.

ADDRESSES: Home—225 Westgate, University City, Mo. 63130. *Office*—Department of English, Washington University, St. Louis, Mo. 63130. *Agent*—Georges Borchardt, Inc., 136 East 57th St., New York, N.Y. 10022.

CAREER: Washington University, St. Louis, Mo., instructor, 1960-62, assistant professor, 1962-66, associate professor, 1966-69, professor of English, 1969—. Visiting professor at Smith College, 1964-65, University of California, Santa Barbara, 1967, University of Wisconsin-Milwaukee, 1969, University of Iowa, 1974, Yale University, 1975, and Boston University, 1976. *Military service:* U.S. Army, 1955-57.

MEMBER: Modern Language Association of America, American Academy and Institute of Arts and Letters.

AWARDS, HONORS: Longview Foundation Award, 1962; Paris Review humor prize, 1964; Guggenheim fellow, 1966-67; Rockefeller Foundation grant, 1968-69; National Endowment for the Arts and Humanities grant, 1972; American Academy of Arts and Letters award, 1974; Richard and Hinda Rosenthal Award, 1980; Sewanee Review prize, 1981, for *Stanley Elkin's Greatest Hits;* National Book Critics Circle Award, 1982, for

George Mills; Brandeis University Creative Arts Award, 1986; L.H.D., 1986, Washington University. Has been nominated twice for the National Book Award.

WRITINGS:

Boswell: A Modern Comedy (novel), Random House, 1964, reprinted, Warner Books, 1980.

Criers and Kibitzers, Kibitzers and Criers (stories), Random House, 1966, reprinted, Warner Books, 1980.

A Bad Man (novel), Random House, 1967, reprinted, Warner Books, 1980.

The Dick Gibson Show (novel), Random House, 1971.

The Making of Ashenden (novella; also see below), Covent Garden Press, 1972.

Searches and Seizures (contains "The Bailbondsman," "The Making of Ashenden," and "The Condominium"), Random House, 1973 (published in England as *Eligible Men: Three Short Novels,* Gollancz, 1974), published as *Alex and the Gypsy: Three Short Novels,* Penguin, 1977.

The Franchiser (novel), Farrar, Straus, 1976.

The Living End (contains three contiguous novellas, "The Conventional Wisdom," "The Bottom Line," and "The State of the Art," which first appeared, in slightly different form, respectively in *American Review, Antaeus,* and *TriQuarterly*), Dutton, 1979.

Stanley Elkin's Greatest Hits, foreword by Robert Coover, Dutton, 1980.

(Editor with Shannon Ravenel and author of introduction) *The Best American Short Stories, 1980,* Houghton, 1980.

The First George Mills (novel), Pressworks, 1981.

George Mills, Dutton, 1982.

Early Elkin, Bamberger, 1985.

The Magic Kingdom, Dutton, 1985.

The Rabbi of Lud, Scribner, 1987.

The Six-Year Old Man, Bamberger, 1987.

Also author of film scenario "The Six-Year-Old Man," published in *Esquire,* December, 1968, and contributor of dialogue to "Demon Seed," 1977. Stories appear in *The Best American Short Stories,* Houghton, 1962, 1963, 1965, and 1978. Contributor to *Epoch, Views, Accent, Esquire, American Review, Antaeus, TriQuarterly, Perspective, Chicago Review, Journal of English and Germanic Philology, Southwest Review, Paris Review, Harper's, Oui,* and *Saturday Evening Post.*

SIDELIGHTS: " 'What happens next?' is a question one doesn't usually ask in Stanley Elkin's [works]," writes Christopher Lehmann-Haupt of the *New York Times.* "Plot is not really Mr. Elkin's game. His fiction runs on language, on parody, on comic fantasies and routines. Give him conventional wisdom and he will twist it into tomfoolery. . . . Give [him] cliche and jargon and he will fashion of it a kind of poetry." Long recognized and praised for his extraordinary linguistic vitality and comic inventiveness, Elkin, though he dislikes these terms, has been described as a "stand-up literary comedian" and a "black humorist" who invites us to laugh at the painful absurdities, frustrations, and disappointments of life. His books "aren't precisely satires," according to Bruce Allen in the *Chicago Tribune Book World,* but rather are "unillusioned yet affectionate commemorations of rascally energy and ingenuity." Ironically, in the view of some critics, Elkin's strength has often been his weakness as well, for he is sometimes criticized for carrying his high-energy rhetoric and comic monologues to extremes. Nonetheless, Josh Greenfeld, who considers Elkin "at once a bright satirist, a bleak absurdist, and a deadly moralist," declares in the *New York*

Times Book Review, "I know of no serious funny writer in this country who can match him."

Searches and Seizures, a collection of three novellas, "should provide the uninitiated with an ideal introduction to [Elkin's] art even as it confirms addicts like me in our belief that no American novelist tells us more about where we are and what we're doing to ourselves," claims Thomas R. Edwards in the *New York Times Book Review.* "This is an art that takes time—his scenes are comic turns that build cunningly toward climax in deflative bathos, and in the novels there's an inclination toward the episodic, the compulsive storyteller's looseness about connections and logic. [The first novella,] 'The Bailbondsman,' . . . is just about perfectly scaled to Elkin's imagination; we have a tight focus, one day in the life of an aging Cincinnati bondsman of Phoenician descent, which nevertheless accommodates an astonishing thickness of texture, a weaving of events and psychic motifs that is as disturbing as it is funny."

The other two stories in *Searches and Seizures* are "The Making of Ashenden" and "The Condominium." The former is, in the words of Clancy Sigal in the *New Republic,* "a fantasy satirizing Brewster Ashenden, an idle wastrel in love with Jane Loes Lipton, a kind of Baby Jane Holzer with a Schweitzerian yen to do good. The 'shocking' climax, within the dream landscape of a rich Englishman's private zoo, has Brewster interminably screwing a bear." The man-bear sex scene "is vigorous, raunchy, painful, smelly—and downright *touching*," exclaims Allen in the *Hudson Review,* and it forces Brewster, humbly and hilariously, to admit his animal nature.

"The Condominium" is a tale about a graduate student who inherits his father's Chicago condominium and "then gets fatally drawn into the numbing quality of its community life," notes Lehmann-Haupt. Though the pieces of these stories seem to be always "flying apart," Lehmann-Haupt concludes: "In some subtle way that defies all equations—metaphorical, symbolical, allegorical, or otherwise—everything connects with everything else. And tells us in a way that lies just beyond explanation, in crazy poetic searches and seizures, much about loneliness, sex, and mortality."

According to Michael Wood in the *New York Review of Books,* "the real subject of the three short novels contained in *Searches and Seizures* is a complicated invention of character by means of snowballing language. The writer invents characters who invent themselves as they talk and thereby invent him, the writer." The protagonist of "The Bailbondsman," for example, introduces himself as "Alexander Main the Bailbondsman. I go surety. . . . My conditions classic and my terms terminal. Listen, I haven't much law—though what I have is on my side, binding as clay, advantage to the house—but am as at home in replevin, debenture, and gage as someone on his own toilet seat with the door closed and the house empty." "The motive force of Elkin's writing," says William Plummer in the *New Republic,* "is the 'conventional wisdom' itself. His aggressive, high energy rhetoric comes into being under the pressure of cliche, which is not to suggest that his metier is either satire or camp. Rather, he seems to share with Emerson the vaguely platonic idea that the hackneyed is 'fossile poetry'—the Truth in tatters, in its fallen condition."

Edwards claims the first story "shows that an art founded on aggression, on assaults against the reader's habits of association and sense of good manners, can be both wrenchingly funny and oddly moving." Plummer concurs, calling "The Bailbondsman" "one of the great works in the language—right up there, perhaps, with [Faulkner's] 'The Bear' and [Melville's] 'Bartleby.' " He adds, however, one qualification: "But you must grant Elkin his premises. He has no interest in 'the arduous, numbing connections' in plot or even structure. He's not anti-story, . . . but rather has an insatiable 'sweet tooth for instance,' which he treats with gags, interpolated tales, catalogues and assorted pieces. Like *Tristram Shandy,* he believes in progress by digression."

But Sigal, also writing in the *New Republic,* will not grant Elkin's premises: "Elkin's monologues, at which he excels, are the alienated patter of a brilliant, but turned off, standup literary comic. I'm very suspicious of it in large doses." Moreover, L. J. Davis charges in the *Washington Post Book World* that Elkin's focus on language weakens the characterization. "Elkin's characters," declares Davis, "are artifacts, superbly sculptured statuary adorned with rich garlands of prose. Sedentary, separate from us, their gestures frozen, they are meant to be observed but not experienced, admired but not touched. The strength of the writing imbues them with a kind of static life, but it does not bestow upon them either an autonomous vitality or a poignant humanity. They exist to prove a point. The way in which they are written about is more important than the way they react to their surroundings, and they are trundled from place to place like demonstration models, more for the purpose of description than for faltering and imperfect reasons of their own. In a way, the prose itself becomes a hero."

Far from seeing Elkin's characters as passive instruments, however, Jonathan Raban argues in *Encounter* that the heroes in *Searches and Seizures* are tragic, in the classical sense: "They build up glittering verbal palaces around themselves, in cascading rhetorical monologues, in dreams, in deep wordy caverns of introspection. Their worlds are perfected right down to the final bauble on the last minaret. Then the crunch comes. They discover that no one else is living there but them. The brilliant talker is the proprietor and sole inhabitant of his universe, and he might as well be adrift in outer space. His fatal proficiency in language has taken him clean out of the world of other people. This is the central theme."

The Dick Gibson Show, Elkin's third novel, "contains enough comic material for a dozen nightclub acts," notes R. Z. Sheppard in *Time,* "yet it is considerably more than an entertainment." Joseph McElroy claims in the *New York Times Book Review* that this "absolutely American compendium . . . may turn out to be our classic about radio." The hero of the book is a disc jockey who has worked for dozens of small-town radio stations across the country. "As the perpetual apprentice, whetting his skills and adopting names and accents to suit geography," says Sheppard, "he evolves into part of American folklore. As Dick Gibson, the paradox of his truest identity is that he is from Nowhere, U.S.A."

A radio talk-show host, Gibson is the principal listener for a bizarre cast of callers: Norman, the "caveman from Africa," whose linguistic equivalent for "chief" is "Aluminum Siding Salesman"; a rich orphaned boy—his skydiving parents accidentally parachuted into a zoo's tiger den—who has fears of being adopted for his money; a woman who wants to trade a bow and arrow, and in exchange will accept nothing but used puppets. Sheppard surmises that Gibson is "a McLuhan obfuscation made flesh—a benevolent witch doctor in an electronic village of the lonely, the sick, and the screwed up." McElroy concurs, arguing that Elkin "unites manic narrative and satiric wit to ensure that we know Dick Gibson [as] . . . receiver of an America whose invisibility speaks live into the great gap of doubt inside him, itinerant listener in this big-hearted country where it's so hard to get anyone to listen."

Lehmann-Haupt, however, believes that while it could be argued that Dick Gibson is "the sound of American silence, . . . this is forcing things somewhat. . . . The bittersweet and seriocomic truth is that Stanley Elkin is [merely] stringing routines together. . . . Which is not to say that I didn't love passages like 'the wide laps beneath her nurse's white uniform with its bas-relief of girdle and garter like landmarks under a light snow.' Or that I didn't sink to my knees from laughing time and again. It's just that after a while one gets tired, can predict the patterns, begins to look for more than gags, and can't really find much."

But Geoffrey Wolff of *Newsweek* finds that the novel's loose structure is patterned after that of radio itself. Acknowledging that the book "flies straight in the teeth of fiction's decorums," Wolff concludes that Elkin "insists on his freedom, radio's freedom to wander, and seems to accept radio's risk, the risk that the audience's attention will wander." McElroy, too, is convinced that Elkin's digressions enhance the thematic concerns of the novel: "Far from seeming prolix, Mr. Elkin's expansiveness—notably in the lunatic monologues of one horrendous talk-show night fourteen years after [World War II]—proves a rich and anxious means of further surrounding his theme."

John Leonard, writing in *Saturday Review,* considers *The Franchiser* to be the closest of Elkin's novels to *The Dick Gibson Show;* he also deems it Elkin's best. "It is a brilliant conceit—the franchising of America on the prime interest rate; manifest destiny on credit," states Leonard. "It is also considerably more than a conceit. It is a frenzied parable, rather as though the Wandering Jew and Willy Loman had gotten together on a vaudeville act. Who, after all, is displaced by the franchise? Ben Flesh, [the protagonist,] knows: 'Kiss off the neighborhood grocers and corner druggists and little shoemakers.' Kiss off, in other words, ethnicity, roots. Assimilate. Homogenize. What's in the melting pot? Campbell's soup, Kraft cheese, Kool-Aid. . . . The immigrants who shortened their names, the Jews who changed them, the slaves who borrowed new ones from their masters, were consequently diminished. They tailored who they were to the specifications of a culture that wanted someone else, insofar as the culture knew anything at all about what it wanted."

Despite Leonard's explication and the fact that his assessment is shared by other reviewers, some critics fault the book for its digressiveness—a common flaw in Elkin's novels according to Lehmann-Haupt, Robert Towers, and John Irving. Towers says in the *New York Times Book Review:* "While he can invent wonderful scenes full of madness and power, Elkin seems unable to create a sustaining comic action or plot that could energize the book as a whole and carry the reader past those sections where invention flags or becomes strained. Without the onward momentum of plot—no matter how zany—we are left with bits, pieces and even large chunks that tend to cancel each other out and turn the book into a kind of morass. . . . The need is especially felt in a book as long as *The Franchiser,* where the potentials of situation, character, and theme—very rich potentials—are never fully mobilized into a truly memorable novel." Novelist Irving, also writing in the *New York Times Book Review,* declares that the "rap against Elkin is that he's too funny, and too fancy with his prose, for his own good. . . . It is brilliant comedy, but occasionally stagnant: the narrative flow is interrupted by Elkin's forays into some of the best prose-writing in English today; it is extraordinary writing, but it smacks at times of showing off—and it is digressive. Despite the shimmering language, the effect is one of density; I know too many readers who say they admire Stanley Elkin as a writer, but they haven't finished a single Elkin novel."

Anthony Heilbut, however, maintains that as in *Searches and Seizures* and *The Dick Gibson Show,* Elkin's "stylistic pyrotechnics" clearly have a thematic function: "The novel's bravado is to set itself against cultural illiteracy of the untellable in all its forms; when the untellable is the truly monstrous disease of multiple sclerosis, [with which Elkin himself is afflicted,] Elkin's verbal triumph is very moving. It may not be an insight into our public mess, but when Ben Flesh observes that his multiple sclerosis is 'always incurable but only generally fatal' his grammatical trickery is literally lifesaving." Wood of the *New York Review of Books* shares Heilbut's belief. He writes that jokes and "gags for Elkin seem to represent some sort of hold on randomness, serve both to clarify and to stave off the dizzying sense that nothing has to happen the way it does, and they afford Elkin and his heroes a recurring, cheerfully defeated stance."

The Living End is, in the opinion of many critics, Elkin's best work. Irving, for example, calls it a "narrative marvel [with] a plot and such a fast pace that a veteran Elkin reader may wonder about the places where he lost interest, or lost his way, in reading Elkin before." The book consists of three contiguous novellas, "The Conventional Wisdom," "The Bottom Line," and "The State of the Art," which provide the kind of conventional, "beginning-middle-end," structure often lacking in Elkin's other novels. The titles of the novellas also reflect Elkin's characteristic attention to cliche, according to Harold Robbins in the *Washington Post Book World.* Echoing Plummer's comment on *Searches and Seizures,* Robbins points out that Elkin "knows that cliches are the substance of our lives, the coinage of human intercourse, the ways and means that hold our messy selves and sprawling nation intact. To exploit their vigor and set them forth with unexpected force has been the basis of his success as a novelist; no writer has maneuvered life's shoddy stock-in-trade into more brilliantly funny forms."

In addition to the strenuous language and the book's structural balance, "in T*he Living End* Elkin has finally found a subject worthy of him," writes Geoffrey Stokes in the *Village Voice.* "No more does he diddle with the surrogates, no more leave us wiping the laughter from our eyes and wondering if we really care quite all that much about One-Hour Martinizing. This time, Elkin goes directly for the big one: God, He Who, etc." *Time*'s Sheppard believes that with *The Living End* "Elkin must finally be recognized as the grownup's Kurt Vonnegut, the Woody Allen for those who prefer their love, death, and cosmic quarrels with true bite and sting."

With a vision that is sometimes blasphemous, the book begins with Ellerbee, a Minneapolis liquor-store owner and "the nicest of guys," notes Sheppard, who goes to Heaven after being gunned down behind the counter during a robbery. His surprise at Heaven's unsurprising sights, sounds, and smells—pearly gates, angels with harps, ambrosia, manna, and a choir that sings "Oh dem golden slippers"—however, turns to shock when St. Peter tells him, "beatifically," to go to Hell. The "ultimate ghetto," Hell also gives Ellerbee a sense of *deja vu,* with the devils' horns and pitchforks, and the sinners raping and mugging each other endlessly and pointlessly; moreover, there is cancer, angina, indigestion, headache, toothache, earache, and a painful, third-degree burning itch everywhere. "What Ellerbee discovers," declares Irving, "is that everything [about the afterlife] is true. . . . It's like life itself, of course, but so keenly exaggerated that Elkin manages to make the pain more painful, and the comedy more comic."

After several years God visits Hell, and Ellerbee asks why he, a good man, has been condemned. A mean-spirited and petty God charges him with selling the demon rum, keeping his store open on the Sabbath, uttering an occasional oath, having impure thoughts, and failing to honor his parents, even though he was orphaned as an infant. Sheppard infers that Ellerbee "ignored what Elkin labels 'the conventional wisdom.' The corollary: in a cosmos ruled by an unforgiving stickler, 'one can never have too much virtue.' "

Jeffrey Burke points out in *Harper's* that Elkin "founds his irreverence on the truths of contemporary religion, that is, on the myriad inconsistencies, cliches, superstitions, and insanities derived from centuries of creative theology," but claims that Elkin's purpose lies beyond satire. Robbins explains: "Unlike others of his generation, . . . Elkin does not identify with the laughter of the gods, he does not dissociate himself from the human spectacle by taking out a franchise on the cosmic joke. Hard and unyielding as his comic vision becomes, Elkin's laughter is remission and reprieve, a gesture of willingness to join the human mess, to side with the damned, to laugh in momentary grace at whatever makes life Hell."

The remainder of the story leads up to the Day of Judgment, when God appears before the Heavenly Host to reveal that the purpose of creation was theatrical, though He never found His audience: "Goodness? Is that what you think? . . . Were you born yesterday? You've been in the world. Is that how you explain trial and error, history by increment, God's long Slap and Tickle, His Indian-gift wrath? *Goodness?* No. It was Art! It was always Art. I work by the contrasts and metrics, by beats and the silences. It was all Art. *Because it makes a better story is why.*" "Precisely because it's God talking," surmises Stokes, "the question of why He does what He does is genuinely important—especially when it turns out that Elkin is ultimately addressing the obligations of all creators. And suddenly—when the eternally-disfigured Christ learns that his suffering occurred solely because God thought it would make a better story—the laughter stops, and the very funny, very serious Elkin goes deeper than he's ever gone before. *The Living End* makes it at once possible to forgive God, and unnecessary to forgive Stanley Elkin."

MEDIA ADAPTATIONS: Of his novellas, "The Bailbondsman" was filmed as "Alex and the Gypsy." The film rights to *Boswell* and *A Bad Man* have been purchased; and *The Living End* and *The Franchiser* have been optioned.

BIOGRAPHICAL/CRITICAL SOURCES:

BOOKS

Bargen, Doris G., *The Fiction of Stanley Elkin,* Lang, 1980.
Contemporary Literary Criticism, Gale, Volume 4, 1975, Volume 6, 1976, Volume 9, 1978, Volume 14, 1980, Volume 27, 1984, Volume 51, 1989.
Dictionary of Literary Biography, Gale, Volume 2: *American Novelists since World War II,* 1978, Volume 28: *Twentieth-Century American-Jewish Fiction Writers,* 1984.
Dictionary of Literary Biography Yearbook: 1980, Gale, 1981.
Elkin, Stanley, *The Dick Gibson Show,* Random House, 1971.
Elkin, Stanley, *Searches and Seizures,* Random House, 1973.
Elkin, Stanley, *The Living End,* Dutton, 1979.
Guttman, Allan, *The Jewish Writer in America: Assimilation and the Crisis of Identity,* Oxford University Press, 1971.
Lebowitz, Naomi, *Humanism and the Absurd in the Modern Novel,* Northwestern University Press, 1971.
Olderman, Raymond M., *Beyond the Waste Land: A Study of the American Novel in the 1960s,* Yale University Press, 1972.

Tanner, Tony, *City of Words,* J. Cape, 1971.

PERIODICALS

Books and Bookmen, May, 1968.
Book Week, June 21, 1964.
Chicago Tribune, April 21, 1985, November 4, 1987.
Chicago Tribune Book World, July 8, 1979.
Choice, October, 1966.
Christian Science Monitor, May 12, 1966.
Commonweal, December 8, 1967.
Contemporary Literature, spring, 1975.
Critique, Volume XXI, number 2, 1979.
Detroit Free Press, February 27, 1983.
Encounter, February, 1975.
Esquire, November, 1980.
Harper's, July, 1979, November, 1982.
Hudson Review, spring, 1974.
Library Journal, January 15, 1966.
Life, October 27, 1967.
Listener, March 28, 1968.
Los Angeles Times, October 28, 1987.
Los Angeles Times Book Review, July 15, 1979, October 31, 1982, March 24, 1985.
Nation, November 27, 1967, August 28, 1976.
New Leader, December 4, 1967.
New Republic, November 24, 1973, March 23, 1974, June 12, 1976, June 23, 1979.
Newsweek, April 19, 1971, June 18, 1979, October 25, 1982.
New York, June 18, 1979.
New Yorker, February 24, 1968.
New York Review of Books, February 3, 1966, January 18, 1967, March 21, 1974, August 5, 1976, August 16, 1979.
New York Times, February 17, 1971, October 9, 1973, May 21, 1976, May 25, 1979, October 20, 1982, March 18, 1985, October 29, 1987.
New York Times Book Review, July 12, 1964, January 23, 1966, October 15, 1967, February 21, 1971, October 21, 1973, June 13, 1976, June 10, 1979, October 31, 1982, March 24, 1985, May 18, 1986, November 8, 1987, January 29, 1989.
Paris Review, summer, 1976.
Publishers Weekly, October 22, 1973, May 29, 1985.
Punch, March 27, 1968, January 1, 1969.
Saturday Review, August 15, 1964, January 15, 1966, November 18, 1967, May 29, 1976.
Studies in Short Fiction, fall, 1974.
Time, October 27, 1967, March 1, 1971, October 29, 1973, May 24, 1976, June 4, 1979, November 10, 1980.
Times Literary Supplement, October 22, 1964, August 27, 1971, January 18, 1980.
TriQuarterly, spring, 1975.
Village Voice, August 20, 1979.
Washington Post Book World, October 22, 1967, October 29, 1967, March 7, 1971, October 28, 1973, June 13, 1976, January 7, 1979, July 1, 1979, October 10, 1982, April 14, 1985, November 29, 1987.

* * *

ELLIN, Stanley (Bernard) 1916-1986

PERSONAL: Born October 6, 1916, in Brooklyn, N.Y.; died of heart attack, July 31, 1986, in Brooklyn; son of Louis and Rose (Mandel) Ellin; married Jeanne Michael (a free-lance editor), 1937; children: Susan. *Education:* Brooklyn College (now Brooklyn College of the City University of New York), B.A., 1936.

ADDRESSES: Agent—Curtis Brown Ltd., 10 Astor Place, New York, N.Y. 10003.

CAREER: Writer. Until World War II, worked as a "push-manager" for a newspaper distributor, taught at a junior college, managed a dairy farm, and was a steelworker. *Military service:* U.S. Army, one year.

MEMBER: PEN American Center, Mystery Writers of America (former president), Crime Writers Association (England).

AWARDS, HONORS: Ellery Queen Awards for best story of the year, 1948, for "The Specialty of the House," 1949, for "The Cat's Paw," 1950, for "Orderly World of Mr. Appleby," 1951, for "Fool's Mate," 1952, for "Best of Everything," 1953, for "The Betrayers," 1954, for "The House Party," 1955, for "Moment of Decision," 1956, for "The Blessington Method," and 1957, for "Faith of Aaron Memfee"; Edgar Allan Poe Awards, Mystery Writers of America, 1954, for "The Blessington Method," 1956 for "The House Party," and 1958, for *The Eighth Circle;* short story "The Day of the Bullet" included in *Best American Short Stories,* Foley, 1960; Grand Prix de Litterature Policiere (France), 1975, for *Mirror, Mirror on the Wall;* Grand Master Award, Mystery Writers of America, 1981, for lifetime writing accomplishment.

WRITINGS:

NOVELS

Dreadful Summit: A Novel of Suspense, Simon & Schuster, 1948, published as *The Big Night: A Novel of Suspense* (also see below), New American Library, 1966, reprinted under original title, Countryman Press, 1981.
The Key to Nicholas Street, Simon & Schuster, 1952, published with new introduction, Garland, 1983.
The Eighth Circle, Random House, 1958, published with new introduction by Otto Penzler, Gregg Press, 1979.
The Winter after This Summer, Random House, 1960.
The Panama Portrait, Random House, 1962, reprinted, Foul Play Press, 1981.
House of Cards, Random House, 1967.
The Valentine Estate, Random House, 1968.
The Bind, Random House, 1970 (published in England as *The Man from Nowhere,* Cape, 1970.
Mirror, Mirror on the Wall, Random House, 1972.
Stronghold, Random House, 1974.
The Luxembourg Run, Random House, 1977.
Star Light, Star Bright, Random House, 1979.
The Dark Fantastic, Mysterious Press, 1983.
Very Old Money (Book-of-the-Month Club selection), Arbor House, 1985.

SHORT STORIES

Mystery Stories, Simon & Schuster, 1956, published as *Quiet Horror,* Dell, 1959, and as *The Specialty of the House, and Other Stories,* Penguin, 1968.
The Blessington Method, and Other Strange Tales, Random House, 1964.
Kindly Dig Your Grave and Other Wicked Stories, edited by Ellery Queen, Random House, 1975.
The Specialty of the House and Other Stories: The Complete Mystery Tales, 1948-1978, Mysterious Press, 1979.

SHORT STORIES REPRESENTED IN ANTHOLOGIES

David C. Cooke, editor, *Best Detective Stories of the Year, 1950,* Dutton, 1950.

Cooke, editor, *Best Detective Stories of the Year, 1951,* Dutton, 1951.

Cooke, editor, *Best Detective Stories of the Year, 1956,* Dutton, 1956.

Alfred Hitchcock, editor, *Alfred Hitchcock Presents Stories They Wouldn't Let Me Do on TV,* Simon & Schuster, 1957.

Martha Foley and David Burnett, editors, *The Best American Short Stories, 1960,* Houghton, 1960.

Leonora Hornblow and Bennett Cerf, editors, *Bennett Cerf's Take Along Treasury,* Doubleday, 1963.

Elizabeth Lee, editor, *Murder Mixture: An Anthology of Crime Stories,* Elek, 1963.

Howard Haycraft and John Beecroft, editors, *Three Times Three: Mystery Omnibus,* Doubleday, 1964.

Dorothy Parker and Frederick B. Shroyer, editors, *Short Story: A Thematic Anthology,* Scribner, 1965.

Basil Davenport, editor, *13 Ways to Kill a Man: An Anthology,* Dodd, 1965.

Joan Kahn, editor, *The Edge of the Chair,* Harper, 1967.

Ross Macdonald, editor, *Great Stories of Suspense,* Knopf, 1974.

Arthur Liebman, compiler, *Tales of Horror and the Supernatural: The Occult in Literature,* Richards Rosen Press, 1975.

Otto Penzler, editor, *Whodunit? Houdini?: Thirteen Tales of Magic, Murder, Mystery,* Harper, 1976.

John Ball, editor, *Cop Cade,* Doubleday for the Crime Club, 1978.

Helen Hoke, editor, *Terrors, Torments and Traumas: An Anthology,* Nelson, 1978.

Charles G. Waugh, Martin Harry Greenburg, and Joseph Olander, editors, *Mysterious Visions: Great Science Fiction by Masters of the Mystery,* St. Martin's, 1979.

Hoke, editor, *Terrors, Terrors, Terrors,* illustrations by Bill Prosser, F. Watts, 1979.

Eric Potter, editor, *A Harvest of Horrors,* illustrations by Hank Blaustein, Vanguard, 1980.

Carol-Lynn Roessel Waugh, Greenburg, and Isaac Asimov, editors, *The Twelve Crimes of Christmas,* Avon Books, 1981.

Bill Pronzini, Barry N. Maltzburg, and Greenburg, editors, *The Arbor House Treasury of Mystery and Suspense,* Arbor House, 1981.

Great Short Tales of Mystery and Terror, illustrations by Leo and Diane Dillon, Readers Digest, 1982.

Thomas Godfrey, editor, *Murder for Christmas,* illustrations by Gahan Wilson, Mysterious Press, 1982.

Josh Pachter, editor, *Top Crime: The Authors' Choice; Selected and Introduced by the Authors Themselves,* St. Martin's, 1983.

Barry Woelfel, editor, *Through Glass Darkly: 13 Tales of Wine and Crime,* Beaufort Books, 1984.

Edward D. Hoch, editor, *The Year's Best Mystery and Suspense Stories, 1984,* Walker & Co., 1984.

Julian Symonds, editor, *The Penguin Classic Crime Omnibus,* Penguin Books, 1984.

Hugh Hood and Peter O'Brien, editors, *Fatal Recurrences: New Fiction in English from Montreal,* Vehicule Press, 1984.

Marcia Muller and Pronzini, editors, *The Wickedest Show on Earth: A Carnival of Circus Suspense,* Morrow, 1985.

Francis M. Nevins, Jr., and Greenburg, editors, *Hitchcock in Prime Time,* Avon Books, 1985.

Marvin Kaye and Saralee Kaye, compilers, *Masterpieces of Terror and the Supernatural: A Treasury of Spellbinding Tales Old and New,* Doubleday, 1985.

Pronzini and Muller, editors, *The Deadly Arts,* Arbor House, 1985.

Scott Walker, editor, *Buying Time: An Anthology Celebrating 20 Years of the Literature Program of the National Endowment for the Arts,* introduction by Ralph Ellison, Graywolf Press, 1985.

Daniel Halpern, editor, *The Art of the Tale: An International Anthology of Short Stories, 1945-1985,* Viking, 1986.

SHORT STORIES REPRESENTED IN "ELLERY QUEEN" ANTHOLOGIES

Queen's Awards, 1948 (3rd annual), Little, 1948.
Queen's Awards, 1949 (4th annual), Little, 1949.
Queen's Awards (5th annual), Little, 1950.
Queen's Awards (6th annual), Little, 1951.
Queen's Awards (7th annual), Little, 1952.
Queen's Awards (8th annual), Little, 1953.
Ellery Queen's Awards (9th annual), Little, 1954.
... Awards (10th annual), Simon & Schuster, 1955.
... Awards (11th annual), Simon & Schuster, 1956.
... Awards (12th annual), Simon & Schuster, 1957.
... Annual (13th annual), Simon & Schuster, 1958.
... Mystery Annual (14th annual), Random House, 1959.
... Mystery Annual (15th annual), Random House, 1960.
... Mystery Annual (16th annual), Random House, 1961.
Anthony Boucher, editor, *The Quintessence of Queen: Best Prize Stories from Twelve Years of Ellery Queen's Mystery Magazine,* Random House, 1962.
To Be Read before Midnight (17th annual), Random House, 1962.
Ellery Queen's Mystery Mix (18th annual), Random House, 1963.
... Double Dozen (19th annual), Random House, 1964.
... 20th Anniversary Annual (20th annual), Random House, 1965.
... Crime Carousel (21st annual), New American Library, 1966.
... All-Star Lineup (22nd annual), New American Library, 1967.
... Mystery Parade (23rd annual), New American Library, 1968.
... Murder Menu (24th annual), World Publishing, 1969.
... Grand Slam (25th annual), World Publishing, 1970.
... The Golden 13: 13 First Prize Winners from Ellery Queen Mystery Magazine, World Publishing, 1970.
... Headliners (26th annual), World Publishing, 1971.
... Mystery Bag (27th annual), World Publishing, 1972.
... Crookbook (28th annual), Random House, 1974.
... Murdercade (29th annual), Random House, 1975.
... Magicians of Mystery, Davis Publications, 1976.
Searches and Seizures (31st annual), Davis Publications, 1977.
Ellery Queen's A Multitude of Sins (32nd annual), Davis Publications, 1978.
... Scenes of the Crime (33rd annual), Davis Publications/Dial Press, 1979.
... Circumstantial Evidence (34th annual), Davis Publications/Dial Press, 1980.
... Crime Cruise Round the World (35th annual), Davis Publications/Dial Press, 1981.
Ellery Queen and Eleanor Sullivan, editors, *... Book of First Appearances,* Davis Publications/Dial Press, 1982.
Queen and Sullivan, editors, *... Lost Ladies,* Dial Press/Davis Publications, 1983.
Sullivan, editor, *... Lost Men,* Dial Press/Davis Publications, 1983.
Sullivan and Karen A. Prince, editors, *... Memorable Characters,* Dial Press/Davis Publications, 1984.

SHORT STORIES REPRESENTED IN "MYSTERY WRITERS OF AMERICA" ANTHOLOGIES

Maiden Murders, Harper, 1952.

George Hamilton Coxe, editor, *Butcher, Baker, Murder-maker,* Knopf, 1954.

Dorothy Salisbury Davis, editor, *A Choice of Murders,* Scribner, 1958.

Rex Stout, editor, *For Tomorrow We Die,* Macdonald & Co., 1958.

David Alexander, editor, *Tales for a Rainy Night,* Holt, 1961.

Cream of the Crime, Holt, 1962.

Thomas B. Dewey, editor, *Sleuths and Consequences,* Simon & Schuster, 1966.

Robert L. Fish, editor, *With Malice toward All,* Putnam, 1968.

Lucy Freeman, editor, *Killers of the Mind,* Random House, 1974.

Fish, editor, *Every Crime in the Book,* Putnam, 1975.

Arthur Maling, *When Last Seen,* Harper, 1977.

Joe Gores and Pronzini, editors, *Tricks and Treats,* Doubleday for the Crime Club, 1976.

Michele Slung, editor, *Women's Wiles,* Harcourt, 1979.

Pronzini, editor, *The Edgar Winners,* Random House, 1980.

Lawrence Treat, editor, *A Special Kind of Crime,* Doubleday for the Crime Club, 1982.

Brian Garfield, editor, *The Crime of My Life,* Walker & Co., 1984.

OTHER

(With Joseph Losey) "The Big Night" (screenplay; based on Ellin's novel *Dreadful Summit: A Novel of Suspense,* also published as *The Big Night: A Novel of Suspense*), United Artists, 1951.

Also author of *The Other Side of the Wall.* Contributor of chapter on crime writing to *Writers Handbook.* Also contributor of short stories to periodicals, including *Ellery Queen's Mystery Magazine,* and of nonfiction to *Writer.* Ellin's manuscripts are collected at Boston University's Mugar Memorial Library.

SIDELIGHTS: Stanley Ellin received numerous awards for excellence in mystery writing, including the prestigious Grand Master Award from the Mystery Writers of America for lifetime writing accomplishment. Widely considered a master who transcended the bounds of his genre, Ellin was most highly regarded for his short stories; however, his novels were also well received. Several of his stories and novels have been adapted for television or motion pictures, testifying to the visual immediacy of Ellin's writing as well. "From his earliest days," wrote a London *Times* contributor, "it was apparent to reviewers that a talent capable of raising that much-abused genre, the thriller, to the level of, at least, minor art, had made its appearance."

Asked by Matthew J. Bruccoli in *Conversations with Writers II* why he became a mystery writer, Ellin recalled that after reading Dashiell Hammett and Graham Greene, he found himself "gravitating more or less toward the idea of a crime being the most dramatic thing you could write about," but thought he had been "hijacked into the mystery field." Launching his career in 1948 with a much anthologized classic short story about cannibalism entitled "The Specialty of the House," Ellin also published his first novel, *Dreadful Summit: A Novel of Suspense,* a psychological study about a youth who seeks to avenge the humiliation that his father suffered by murdering the man responsible. Ellin told Bruccoli that he considered the book a straight novel, but the publisher believed that its "emphasis on crime made it a novel in the mystery field." Ellin added that because the publisher felt its "particular treatment didn't put it squarely in the field . . . a new category was created . . . 'suspense specials.'" Financially compelled to publish his first novel within the mystery genre, Ellin remarked to Bruccoli: "I have all along, by the way,

been uneasily balanced between the genre and the straight novel."

Praised for an essential veracity in his work, Ellin was especially credited for his ability to realistically render a sense of time and place. Ellin told Bruccoli that he regarded the mystery novel as a sociological document: "They mark—I hit on this long ago—their times very clearly, as Holmes and his people marked London at that period. You had in the twenties Hammett coming along—the cynical era . . . and Chandler picking that up. You had Mickey Spillane coming along at the McCarthy time, because Spillane's Mike Hammer was the quintessential McCarthy hero: the 'I-am-the-judge-jury-and-executioner' thing was implicit in that time. And during the nadir of the Cold War Bond came along, but Bond had to be transformed as social events were transformed. . . . So that there is always a picture of the time and place." The sense of authenticity in Ellin's own work resulted from thorough research. "I also enjoy, and I think readers enjoy, novels which are set in what to a local person is an exotic place," he told Bruccoli, adding that while travelling in Europe, he and his wife Jeanne, who was also his editor, would "settle down in a city and every day simply walk in the city, live the city." His wife would make extensive notes during their travels while Ellin would be "enjoying the local television, whatever language," absorbing the atmosphere and "enjoying the experience." Ellin remarked to Bruccoli, "It's only when bit by bit as I go along, usually near the end of a trip, that pieces start falling together—that I become acutely aware that I now have the makings of my story material."

According to Edwin McDowell in the *New York Times,* Otto Penzler, owner and publisher of the Mysterious Press, said of Ellin, "He was probably the most highly rated among his peers of any mystery writer I know." Noting that Ellin's work has been translated into twenty-two languages, Penzler added that in some European countries, Ellin is considered "a major literary figure." Despite his established reputation, though, Ellin experienced great difficulty in finding a publisher for his *The Dark Fantastic,* a novel about a retired white, and once liberal, professor who is dying from cancer and whose mind has slipped into insanity. Espousing bigotry, he also harbors a suicidal plot to blow up the Brooklyn apartment house in which he was born, thereby killing its black inhabitants as well as himself. Publishers were apparently reluctant to publish the novel because of the racist tenor of some of its segments: "No fewer than 10 commercial presses rejected the manuscript," wrote David Lehmann in *Newsweek,* "evidently underestimating the ability of readers to distinguish the author from the hate-riddled Kirwan." In the *Washington Post Book World,* Michele Slung discussed Ellin's reaction: "'You'd have to read the book with an astigmatic eye in order to come out thinking I'm a racist,' Ellin says, with a flicker of bitterness at the lack of understanding he ran into." According to Anthony Olcott's report of the controversy in the *Chicago Tribune Book World,* Ellin admitted: "I knew I was taking some risks when I did the book, but I never expected rejection."

Once published, though, *The Dark Fantastic* was favorably received. For instance, in the *Los Angeles Times Book Review,* Charles Champlin wrote that the novel "has all the requisites of the successful thriller: The characters are vivid, the dialogue has the authentic ring of silver dollars on marble, the scenes are remarkably envisionable (no wonder Ellin's work has been so often seized for film), the suspense escalates with what can be called a terrible efficiency." Ellin's hate-consumed character is balanced by the characterization of the white detective who falls in love with a black resident of the apartment building; and, according to Olcott: "Their courtship is a masterpiece of erotic, racial and social tension, as the two lurch toward what Ellin sees as the only possible hope for racial harmony, a one-to-one relationship between human beings." Calling it "a book by one of the truth-tellers," H. R. F. Keating added in the London *Times:* "The nasty equally with the good are depicted so you believe this is what such people are like through and through."

Ellin's last book, *Very Old Money,* "falls somewhere between a mystery and a serious work of fiction," Jonathan Yardley commented in the *Washington Post Book World,* adding that Ellin managed to achieve that "difficult balance" with "ease and aplomb." The novel is about a couple of unemployed teachers who become domestic servants in the Manhattan mansion of an elderly wealthy recluse. Although T. J. Binyon suggested in the *Times Literary Supplement* that *Very Old Money* is a "disappointing successor to the author's previous books," Yardley concluded that "it is intelligent, good-humored, thoughtful and sophisticated: adult entertainment, in the best sense of both words." A *New Yorker* contributor praised Ellin's "special ability to create an almost imperceptible spiral of suspense." However, Yardley maintained that the suspense was "incidental to the setting and the characters he creates. At this more serious work Ellin . . . is most accomplished." Although Ellin's work is often characterized by inventive plotting, in the *New York Times Book Review,* Melik Kaylin found that the plot of *Very Old Money* "lacks suspense" and that Ellin "strays too far from the exigencies of the genre in pursuit of a moral, which is that very old money is corrupt and alluring." Ellin did not believe that a work should revolve around plot, though: "I always have the feeling in all mystery writing that you must have a sound and valid plot, and that is the skeleton," Ellin told Bruccoli. "But as you build and as you work, the skeleton should properly and will properly sort of disappear."

Describing Ellin's books as "densely woven and subtly timed adventures," the London *Times* contributor indicated that "both his prose and his play of mind were things of elegance." Ellin wrote six hours a day, six days a week, and a novel would take him fourteen or sixteen months to complete; but he acknowledged to Bruccoli that his method of writing was "atrocious" and "damaging to productivity" because he was unable to abandon a page until it was in its final form: "It's a compulsion. . . . I find that when I try to just gallop ahead, I am frozen with the thought that there's something wrong on that preceding page and I will work and rework it at length, until I am as satisfied as I can be with it." He found, however, that the method did have its advantages: "When I read my own stuff back, I find that each page has a tension in manuscript, and if they all interlock properly they create tension throughout a book."

MEDIA ADAPTATIONS: Several of Ellin's stories have been adapted for television and broadcast on "Alfred Hitchcock Presents," including "Specialty of the House," featuring Robert Morely, in 1959; *The Key to Nicholas Street* was made into a film starring Jean-Paul Belmondo, released in France, 1959, as "Leda," and in 1961 as "Web of Passion"; Ellin's story "The Best of Everything" provided the basis for the film "Nothing but the Best," starring Alan Bates, produced by Royal and released in Britain, 1964; *House of Cards* was made into a film of the same title by Universal, 1968, starring Orson Welles and George Peppard; "Sunburn," a 1979 film by Paramount starring Farrah Fawcett, Charles Grodin, Art Carney, and Joan Collins, was based on Ellin's novel *The Bind.*

BIOGRAPHICAL/CRITICAL SOURCES:

BOOKS

Conversations with Writers II, Gale, 1978.

PERIODICALS

Books and Bookmen, June, 1971.
Chicago Tribune Book World, December 18, 1983.
Los Angeles Times Book Review, June 22, 1980, July 10, 1983, February 1, 1985.
National Observer, March 20, 1967, November 11, 1968.
New Republic, May 30, 1981.
Newsweek, July 11, 1983.
New Yorker, April 9, 1979, April 8, 1985.
New York Times, August 8, 1970, November 15, 1977, August 1, 1986.
New York Times Book Review, February 26, 1967, July 12, 1970, September 24, 1972, October 16, 1977, April 8, 1979, May 6, 1979, April 5, 1981, September 11, 1983, March 17, 1985.
Punch, November 16, 1983, August 21, 1985.
Saturday Review, August 1, 1970, August 26, 1972, March, 1985.
Spectator, June 23, 1973, April 8, 1978, February 11, 1984.
Time, September 18, 1972.
Times (London), December 8, 1983, August 4, 1986.
Times Literary Supplement, June 29, 1967, October 18, 1985.
Washington Post Book World, March 18, 1979, July 20, 1980, April 19, 1981, June 5, 1983, February 17, 1985.

OBITUARIES:

PERIODICALS

AB Bookman's Weekly, September 8, 1986.
Detroit Free Press, August 1, 1986.
Globe and Mail (Toronto), August 2, 1986.
Newsweek, August 11, 1986.
New York Times, August 1, 1986.
Publishers Weekly, August 15, 1986.
Rochester Times-Union, August 1, 1986.
Time, August 11, 1986.
Times (London), August 4, 1986.
Washington Post, August 2, 1986.
Writer, November, 1986.

*   *   *

ELLIOTT, Don
  See SILVERBERG, Robert

*   *   *

ELLIS, Landon
  See ELLISON, Harlan

*   *   *

ELLISON, Harlan 1934-
(Lee Archer, Robert Courtney, E. K. Jarvis, Ivar Jorgensen, and Clyde Mitchell, house pseudonyms; Sley Harson and Ellis Robertson, joint pseudonyms; Phil "Cheech" Beldone, C. Bird, Cordwainer Bird, Jay Charby, Price Curtis, Wallace Edmondson, Landon Ellis, Ellis Hart, Al[an] Maddern, Paul Merchant, Nabrah Nosille, Bert Parker, Jay Solo, and Derry Tiger)

PERSONAL: Born May 27, 1934, in Cleveland, Ohio; son of Louis Laverne (a dentist and jeweler) and Serita (Rosenthal) Ellison; married Charlotte B. Stein, February 19, 1956 (divorced, 1960); married Billie Joyce Sanders, November 13, 1960 (divorced, 1963); married Lory Pastick Patrick, January 30, 1966 (divorced, 1966); married Lori Horowitz, June 5, 1976 (divorced, 1977); married Susan Toth, 1986. *Education:* Attended Ohio State University, 1953-54.

ADDRESSES: Home—3484 Coy Dr., Sherman Oaks, Calif. 91403. *Agent*—Robert P. Mills, Ltd., 156 East 52nd St., New York, N.Y. 10022.

CAREER: Free-lance writer, 1954—. Editor, *Rogue* (magazine), 1959-60; founder and editor, Regency Books, 1961-62. Editorial commentator, Canadian Broadcasting Co., 1972-78; president of Kilimanjaro Corp, 1979—. Creator of weekly television series, including "The Starlost," 1973, "Brillo," with Ben Bova, American Broadcasting Companies, Inc., 1974, and "The Dark Forces," with Larry Brody, Columbia Broadcasting System, Inc., 1986; creative consultant and director of television series, including "The Twilight Zone"; actor. Has lectured at universities, including Michigan State University, University of California, and New York University. *Military service:* U.S. Army, 1957-59.

MEMBER: Science Fiction Writers of America (vice-president, 1965-66), Writers Guild of America, West (former member of board of directors), Cleveland Science Fiction Society (founder).

AWARDS, HONORS: Writers Guild of America Award, 1965, for "Outer Limits" television series episode, "Demon with a Glass Hand," 1967, for "Star Trek" television series episode, "City on the Edge of Forever," and 1973, for "The Starlost"; Nebula Award from Science Fiction Writers of America, for best short story, 1965, for " 'Repent, Harlequin!' Said the Ticktockman," and 1977, for "Jeffty Is Five," and for best novella, 1969, for "A Boy and His Dog"; Hugo Award from World Science Fiction Convention, for best short fiction, 1965, for " 'Repent, Harlequin!' Said the Ticktockman" for best short story, 1967, for "I Have No Mouth, and I Must Scream," 1968, for "The Beast That Shouted Love at the Heart of the World," and 1977, for "Jeffty Is Five," for best dramatic presentation, 1967, for "Star Trek" television series episode, "City on the Edge of Forever," and 1975, for "A Boy and His Dog," for best novelette, 1973, for "The Deathbird," 1974, for "Adrift, Just Off the Islets of Langerhans," and 1986, for "Palladin of the Lost Hour"; special plaque from the World Science Fiction Convention, 1968, for *Dangerous Visions,* and 1972, for *Again, Dangerous Visions;* Nova Award, 1968, for most outstanding contribution to the field of science fiction; Edgar Allan Poe Award from Mystery Writers of America, 1973, for "The Whimper of Whipped Dogs"; Jupiter Award from Instructors of Science Fiction in Higher Education, for best novelette, 1973, for "The Deathbird," and for best short story, 1977, for "Jeffty Is Five"; Locus Award from *Locus* (magazine), for best short fiction, 1970, for "The Region Between," 1972, for "Basilisk," 1973, for "The Deathbird," 1975, for "Croatoan," and 1977, for "Jeffty Is Five," for best original anthology, 1972, for *Again, Dangerous Visions,* and 1986, for *Medea: Harlan's World,* for best novelette, 1974, for "Adrift, Just Off the Islets of Langerhans," and 1982, for "Dijnn, No Chaser," and for best nonfiction, 1986, for *Sleepless Nights in the Procrustean Bed.*

WRITINGS:

The Glass Teat: Essays of Opinion on the Subject of Television, Ace Books, 1970.
The Other Glass Teat: Further Essays of Opinion on Television, Pyramid Publications, 1975.

(Contributor) Roger Elwood, editor, *Six Science Fiction Plays,* Pocket Books, 1976.
(Contributor) Jack Dann and George Zebrowski, editors, *Faster than Light,* Harper, 1976.
The Book of Ellison, edited by Andrew Porter, Algol Press, 1978.
Sleepless Nights in the Procrustean Bed (essays), Borgo, 1984.
An Edge in My Voice (essays), Donning, 1985.
Harlan Ellison's Watching, Underwood-Miller, 1989.

NOVELS

Rumble, Pyramid Publications, 1958, published as *Web of the City,* 1975.
The Man with Nine Lives [and] *A Touch of Infinity,* Ace Books, 1960.
Memos from Purgatory: Two Journeys of Our Times, Regency Books, 1961.
Rockabilly, Fawcett, 1961, published as *Spider Kiss,* Pyramid Publications, 1975.
Demon with a Glass Hand (based on television script), Doubleday, 1967.
From the Land of Fear, Belmont, 1967.
Kill Machine, Belmont, 1967.
Doomsman (bound with *Telepower* by Lee Hoffman), Belmont, 1967, reprinted (bound with *The Thief of Thoth* by Lin Carter), Belmont, 1972.
(With Edward Bryant) *Phoenix without Ashes,* Fawcett, 1975.
All the Lies That Are My Life, Underwood-Miller, 1980.

SHORT STORY COLLECTIONS

The Deadly Streets, Ace Books, 1958, reprinted, Pyramid Publications, 1975.
The Juvies, Ace Books, 1961.
Gentleman Junkie, and Other Stories of the Hung-Up Generation, Regency Books, 1961.
Ellison Wonderland, Paperback Library, 1962, published as *Earthman, Go Home,* 1964.
Paingod, and Other Delusions, Pyramid Publications, 1965.
I Have No Mouth and I Must Scream, Pyramid Publications, 1967.
Perhaps Impossible, Pyramid Publications, 1967.
Love Ain't Nothing But Sex Misspelled, Trident, 1968.
The Beast That Shouted Love at the Heart of the World, Avon, 1969.
Over the Edge: Stories from Somewhere Else, Belmont, 1970.
Alone against Tomorrow: Stories of Alienation in Speculative Fiction, Macmillan, 1971, abridged edition published in England as *All the Sounds of Fear,* Panther, 1973, and *The Time of the Eye,* Panther, 1974.
(With others) *Partners in Wonder,* Walker & Co., 1971.
Approaching Oblivion: Road Signs on the Treadmill toward Tomorrow, Walker & Co., 1974.
Deathbird Stories: A Pantheon of Modern Gods, Harper, 1975.
No Doors, No Windows, Pyramid Publications, 1975.
Strange Wine: Fifteen New Stories from the Nightside of the World, Harper, 1978.
The Illustrated Harlan Ellison, edited by Byron Preiss, Baronet, 1978.
The Fantasies of Harlan Ellison, Gregg, 1979.
Shatterday, Houghton, 1980.
Stalking the Nightmare, Phantasia, 1982.
Angry Candy, Houghton, 1989.

EDITOR

Dangerous Visions: 33 Original Stories, Doubleday, 1967, published in three volumes, Berkley, 1969.

Gerald Kersh, *Nightshade and Damnations,* Fawcett, 1968.

Again, Dangerous Visions: 46 Original Stories, Doubleday, 1972.

James Sutherland, *Stormtrack,* Pyramid Publications, 1974.

Terry Carr, *The Light at the End of the Universe,* Pyramid Publications, 1976.

Bruce Sterling, *Involution Ocean,* Pyramid Publications, 1977.

The Last Dangerous Visions, Berkley, 1981.

Medea: Harlan's World, Bantam, 1985.

Also author of *Night and the Enemy,* Comico Comic Co., 1987; author of motion picture script, "The Oscar," Embassy, 1966, and of television scripts for "Star Trek," "Outer Limits," "Voyage to the Bottom of the Sea," "The Man from UNCLE," "Cimarron Strip," "Burke's Law," "The Flying Nun," "Route 66," "The Alfred Hitchcock Hour," "Logan's Run," and other series.

Former author of columns "The Glass Teat" and "Harlan Ellison Hornbook," *Los Angeles Free Press.* Contributor of over nine hundred short stories, some under pseudonyms, to numerous publications, including *Magazine of Fantasy and Science Fiction, Ariel, Twilight Zone,* and *Galaxy;* publisher of magazine *Dimensions.*

SIDELIGHTS: Described by J. G. Ballard as "an aggressive and restless extrovert who conducts his life at a shout and his fiction at a scream," Harlan Ellison is a writer of what he very particularly describes as "magic realism."

Ellison began his writing career in the middle l950s after being dismissed from college over a disagreement with a writing teacher who told Ellison that he had no talent. Ellison moved to New York City to become a free-lance writer and in his first two years as a writer sold some 150 short stories to magazines in every genre from crime fact to science fiction.

It was the science fiction genre that most appreciated Ellison's talent—much to Ellison's benefit and chagrin. He quickly established himself as a major figure in the field and has won a number of its major awards. But he has also been labeled a "science fiction writer," something that upsets him. Despite his work in television, his fiction in other genres, and his nonfiction works, Ellison is still plagued with the science fiction label. "Once you get yourself typed," Ellison told Michael E. Stamm of *Fantasy Newsletter,* "you're fad forever." "I've long ago ceased to write anything even remotely resembling science fiction," he told Alice K. Turner of *Publishers Weekly,* "if indeed I ever really did write it." Joseph McLellan of the *Washington Post* maintains that "the categories are too small to describe Harlan Ellison. Lyric poet, satirist, explorer of odd psychological corners, moralist, one-line comedian, purveyor of pure horror and of black comedy; he is all these and more." Ellison prefers to call his writing "magic realism," a term he says can be applied to the work of many other writers, including Kurt Vonnegut and John Barth.

In 1967, Ellison decided to edit a collection of "magic realism" stories as a means of better defining the term and distinguishing it from science fiction. The result was *Dangerous Visions.* Specifically designed to include those stories too controversial or experimental (or too well written) to appear in the popular magazines, *Dangerous Visions* broke new ground in both theme and style. "[*Dangerous Visions*] was intended to shake things up," Ellison wrote in his introduction to the book. "It was conceived out of a need for new horizons, new forms, new styles, new challenges in the literature of our times."

Critical reaction to the book was largely favorable. "You should buy this book immediately," Algis Budrys urged his readers. "There has never been a collection like this before," James Blish, under his pseudonym William Atheling, Jr., wrote in *Amazing Stories.* "It will entertain, infuriate, and reward you for years." Damon Knight, writing in the *Saturday Review,* called it "a gigantic, shapeless, exuberant, and startling collection [of] vital, meaningful stories." Of the thirty-three stories in *Dangerous Visions,* seven became winners of either the Hugo or Nebula Award while another thirteen stories were nominees. The collection received a special plaque from the World Science Fiction Convention.

Again, Dangerous Visions, Ellison's sequel to *Dangerous Visions,* met with the same success as its predecessor. J. B. Post of *Library Journal* predicted that *Again, Dangerous Visions* "will become a historically important book." W. E. McNelly of *America* claimed that the collection was "so experimental in design, concept, and execution that this one volume may well place science fiction in the very heart of mainstream literature."

Both *Dangerous Visions* and *Again, Dangerous Visions* employ a unique format. Each story is preceded by a short introduction by Ellison, who speaks about the author and why the story was chosen for the collection, and is followed by an afterword from the author, who describes how the story came to be written. The format serves to personalize each story and to highlight its place in the collection. Theodore Sturgeon, writing in the *National Review,* describes Ellison's introductions to the stories as a "one-man isometrics course [that] will stretch your laughmuscles, your retch-muscles, your indignation-, wonder-, delight-, mad-, appall-, admiration-, and disbelief-muscles, and strongly affect your blood-pressure thing. You may have perceived that I have not used the word 'dull.' [Ellison] might numb you, but you will not be bored."

Similar remarks have been made by other critics about Ellison's fiction. Blish (again writing under the pseudonym William Atheling, Jr.) notes in his book *More Issues at Hand* that Ellison is "a born writer, almost entirely without taste or control but with so much fire, originality and drive, as well as compassion, that he makes the conventional virtues of the artist seem almost irrelevant." Gerald Jonas of the *New York Times Book Review* claims that Ellison "has always specialized in excess [and the story] 'The Deathbird' is a compendium of every trick Ellison has ever pulled, every artistic sin he has ever committed; I found it genuinely moving." In *The Universe Makers,* Donald A. Wollheim calls Ellison "a unique sort of genius who can lead where others can never successfully follow, who can hold an audience enthralled yet never gain a convert, [and] who can insult and have only the stupid offended." In his book-length study, *Harlan Ellison: Unrepentant Harlequin,* George Edgar Slusser calls Ellison "a tireless experimenter with forms and techniques" and concludes that he "has produced some of the finest, most provocative fantasy in America today." George Martin writes in the *Washington Post Book World* that Ellison "is one of the great living American short story writers."

Ellison's short story "'Repent, Harlequin!' Said the Ticktockman" is one of the ten most reprinted stories in the English language. "A Boy and His Dog" has been filmed.

Ellison told *CA:* "It is a love/hate relationship that I have with the human race. I am an elitist, and I feel that my responsibility is to drag the human race along with me—that I will never pander to, or speak down to, or play the safe game. Because my immortal soul will be lost."

BIOGRAPHICAL/CRITICAL SOURCES:

BOOKS

Atheling, Jr., William, *More Issues at Hand,* Advent, 1970.

Contemporary Literary Criticism, Gale, Volume 1, 1973, Volume 13, 1980, Volume 42, 1987.

Dictionary of Literary Biography, Volume 8: *Twentieth-Century American Science Fiction Writers,* Gale, 1981.

Platt, Charles, *The Dream Makers: The Uncommon People Who Write Science Fiction,* Berkley, 1980.

Porter, Andrew, editor, *The Book of Ellison,* Algol Press, 1978.

Slusser, George Edgar, *Harlan Ellison: Unrepentant Harlequin,* Borgo, 1977.

Swigart, Leslie Kay, *Harlan Ellison: A Bibliographical Checklist,* Williams Publishing (Dallas), 1973.

Walker, Paul, *Speaking of Science Fiction: The Paul Walker Interviews,* Luna, 1978.

Wollheim, Donald A., *The Universe Makers,* Harper, 1971.

PERIODICALS

America, June 10, 1972.

Analog, September, 1960, December, 1962, May, 1968, June, 1968, August, 1970, April, 1973.

Chicago Tribune, September 24, 1961, June 2, 1985, January 17, 1989.

Esquire, January, 1962.

Extrapolation, May, 1977, winter, 1979.

Fantasy Newsletter, April, 1981.

Galaxy, April, 1968, May, 1972.

Library Journal, April 15, 1972.

Los Angeles Times, September 20, 1988.

Luna Monthly, May, 1970, July, 1970, May/June, 1971, June, 1972, September, 1972.

Magazine of Fantasy and Science Fiction, January, 1968, November, 1971, September, 1972, October, 1975, July, 1977.

Manchester Guardian, July 4, 1963.

National Review, July 12, 1966, May 7, 1968.

New Statesman, March 25, 1977.

New York Times Book Review, October 26, 1958, June 30, 1960, August 20, 1961, June 30, 1968, September 3, 1972, March 23, 1975, April 1, 1979, September 17, 1989.

Publishers Weekly, February 10, 1975.

Renaissance, summer, 1972.

Saturday Review, December 30, 1967.

Science Fiction Review, January, 1971, September/October, 1978.

Spectator, January, 1971.

Times Literary Supplement, April 16, 1971, January 14, 1977.

Variety, July 8, 1970, March 17, 1971.

Washington Post, August 3, 1978.

Washington Post Book World, January 25, 1981, December 26, 1982, July 30, 1985.

Worlds of If, July, 1960, September/October, 1971.

*   *   *

ELLISON, Ralph (Waldo) 1914-

PERSONAL: Born March 1, 1914, in Oklahoma City, Okla.; son of Lewis Alfred (a construction worker and tradesman) and Ida (Millsap) Ellison; married Fanny McConnell, July, 1946. *Education:* Attended Tuskegee Institute, 1933-36. *Avocational interests:* Jazz and classical music, photography, electronics, furniture-making, bird-watching, gardening.

ADDRESSES: Home and office—730 Riverside Dr., New York, N.Y. 10031; and Plainfield, Mass. *Agent*—Owen Laster, William Morris Agency, 1350 Ave. of the Americas, New York, N.Y. 10019.

CAREER: Writer, 1937—; worked as a researcher and writer on Federal Writers' Project in New York City, 1938-42; edited

Negro Quarterly, 1942; lecture tour in Germany, 1954; lecturer at Salzburg Seminar, Austria, fall, 1954; U.S. Information Agency, tour of Italian cities, 1956; Bard College, Annandale-on-Hudson, N.Y., instructor in Russian and American literature, 1958-61; New York University, New York City, Albert Schweitzer Professor in Humanities, 1970-79, professor emeritus, 1979—. Alexander White Visiting Professor, University of Chicago, 1961; visiting professor of writing, Rutgers University, 1962-64; visiting fellow in American studies, Yale University, 1966. Gertrude Whittall Lecturer, Library of Congress, January, 1964; delivered Ewing Lectures at University of California, Los Angeles, April, 1964. Lecturer in American Negro culture, folklore, and creative writing at other colleges and universities throughout the United States, including Columbia University, Fisk University, Princeton University, Antioch University, and Bennington College.

Member of Carnegie Commission on Educational Television, 1966-67; honorary consultant in American letters, Library of Congress, 1966-72. Trustee, Colonial Williamsburg Foundation, John F. Kennedy Center for the Performing Arts, 1967-77, Educational Broadcasting Corp., 1968-69, New School for Social Research, 1969-83, Bennington College, 1970-75, and Museum of the City of New York, 1970-86. Charter member of National Council of the Arts, 1965-67, and of National Advisory Council, Hampshire College. *Military service:* U.S. Merchant Marine, World War II.

MEMBER: PEN (vice-president, 1964), Authors Guild, Authors League of America, American Academy and Institute of Arts and Letters, Institute of Jazz Studies (member of board of advisors), Century Association (resident member).

AWARDS, HONORS: Rosenwald grant, 1945; National Book Award and National Newspaper Publishers' Russwurm Award, both 1953, both for *Invisible Man;* Certificate of Award, *Chicago Defender,* 1953; Rockefeller Foundation award, 1954; Prix de Rome fellowships, American Academy of Arts and Letters, 1955 and 1956; *Invisible Man* selected as the most distinguished postwar American novel and Ellison as the sixth most influential novelist by *New York Herald Tribune Book Week* poll of two hundred authors, editors, and critics, 1965; recipient of award honoring well-known Oklahomans in the arts from governor of Oklahoma, 1966; Medal of Freedom, 1969; Chevalier de l'Ordre des Arts et Lettres (France), 1970; Ralph Ellison Public Library, Oklahoma City, named in his honor, 1975; National Medal of Arts, 1985, for *Invisible Man* and for his teaching at numerous universities. Honorary doctorates from Tuskegee Institute, 1963, Rutgers University, 1966, Grinnell College, 1967, University of Michigan, 1967, Williams College, 1970, Long Island University, 1971, Adelphi University, 1971, College of William and Mary, 1972, Harvard University, 1974, Wake Forest College, 1974, University of Maryland, 1974, Bard College, 1978, Wesleyan University, 1980, and Brown University, 1980.

WRITINGS:

Invisible Man (novel), Random House, 1952, published as a limited edition with illustrations by Steven H. Stroud, Franklin Library, 1980, original edition reprinted with new introduction by author as special thirtieth-anniversary edition, Random House, 1982.

(Contributor) Granville Hicks, editor, *The Living Novel: A Symposium,* Macmillan, 1957.

(Author of introduction) Stephen Crane, *The Red Badge of Courage and Four Great Stories,* Dell, 1960.

Shadow and Act (essays), Random House, 1964.

(With Karl Shapiro) *The Writer's Experience* (lectures; includes "Hidden Names and Complex Fate: A Writer's Experience in the U.S.," by Ellison, and "American Poet?," by Shapiro), Gertrude Clarke Whittall Poetry and Literature Fund for Library of Congress, 1964.

(Contributor) *Education of the Deprived and Segregated* (report of seminar on education for culturally-different youth, Dedham, Mass., September 3-15, 1963), Bank Street College of Education, 1965.

(Contributor) Robert Penn Warren, *Who Speaks for the Negro?*, Random House, 1965.

(With Whitney M. Young and Herbert Gnas) *The City in Crisis*, introduction by Bayard Rustin, A. Philip Randolph Educational Fund, 1968.

(Author of introduction) Romare Bearden, *Paintings and Projections* (catalogue of exhibition, November 25-December 22, 1968), State University of New York at Albany, 1968.

(Contributor) James MacGregor Burns, editor, *To Heal and to Build: The Programs of Lyndon B. Johnson*, prologue by Howard K. Smith, epilogue by Eric Hoffer, McGraw, 1968.

(Author of foreword) Leon Forrest, *There Is a Tree More Ancient than Eden*, Random House, 1973.

(Contributor) Bernard Schwartz, editor, *American Law: The Third Century, the Law Bicentennial Volume*, F. B. Rothman for New York University School of Law, 1976.

Going to the Territory (essays), Random House, 1986.

RECORDINGS

"Ralph Ellison: An Interview with the Author of Invisible Man" (sound recording), Center for Cassette Studies, 1974.

(With William Styron and James Baldwin) "Is the Novel Dead?: Ellison, Styron and Baldwin on Contemporary Fiction" (sound recording), Center for Cassette Studies, 1974.

OTHER

Contributor to numerous anthologies and to *Proceedings, American Academy of Arts and Letters and the National Institute of Arts and Letters*, second series, 1965 and 1967. Also contributor of short fiction, critical essays, articles, and reviews to numerous journals and periodicals, including *American Scholar, Contemporary Literature, Iowa Review, New York Review of Books, New York Times Book Review, Noble Savage, Partisan Review, Quarterly Review of Literature, Reporter, Time*, and *Washington Post Book World*. Contributing editor, *Noble Savage*, 1960, and member of editorial board of *American Scholar*, 1966-69.

WORK IN PROGRESS: A second novel.

SIDELIGHTS: Growing up in Oklahoma, a "frontier" state that "had no tradition of slavery" and where "relationships between the races were more fluid and thus more human than in the old slave states," Ralph Ellison became conscious of his obligation "to explore the full range of American Negro humanity and to affirm those qualities which are of value beyond any question of segregation, economics or previous condition of servitude." This sense of obligation, articulated in his 1964 collection of critical and biographical essays, *Shadow and Act*, led to his staunch refusal to limit his artistic vision to the "uneasy sanctuary of race" and committed him instead to a literature that explores and affirms the complex, often contradictory frontier of an identity at once black and American and universally human. For Ellison, whom John F. Callahan in a *Chant of Saints: A Gathering of Afro-American Literature, Art, and Scholarship* essay calls a "moral historian," the act of writing is fraught with both great possibility and grave responsibility; as Ellison asserts, writing "offers me the possibility of contributing not only to the growth

of the literature but to the shaping of the culture as I should like it to be. The American novel is in this sense a conquest of the frontier; as it describes our experience, it creates it."

For Ellison, then, the task of the novelist is a moral and political one. In his preface to the thirtieth anniversary edition of *Invisible Man*, Ellison argues that the serious novel, like the best politics, "is a thrust toward a human ideal." Even when the ideal is not realized in the actual, he declares, "there is still available that fictional vision of an ideal democracy in which the actual combines with the ideal and gives us representations of a state of things in which the highly placed and the lowly, the black and the white, the Northerner and the Southerner, the native-born and the immigrant are combined to tell us of transcendent truths and possibilities such as those discovered when Mark Twain set Huck and Jim afloat on the raft." Ellison sees the novel as a "raft of hope" that may help readers stay above water as they try "to negotiate the snags and whirlpools that mark our nation's vacillating course toward and away from the democratic ideal."

This vision of pluralism and possibility as the basic definition of self and serious fiction has its roots in Ellison's personal history, a history marked by vacillations between the ideal and the real. He recalls in *Shadow and Act* that, as teenagers, he and his friends saw themselves as "Renaissance Men" unlimited by any sense of racial inferiority and determined to be recipients of the American Dream, to witness the ideal become the real. Ellison recounts two "accidents" that contributed to his sense of self as something beyond the external definition of race. The first occurred while he lived in a white, middleclass neighborhood where his mother worked as a building custodian. He became friends with a young white boy, a friendship based not on the "race question as such" but rather on their mutual loneliness and interest in radios. The other contact with "that world beyond the Negro community" came as his mother brought home discarded copies of magazines such as *Vanity Fair* and *Literary Digest* and old recordings of operas. Ellison remembers that these books and music "spoke to me of a life which was broader" and which "I could some day make my own."

This sense of a world beyond his but to which he would ultimately belong translated itself into his sense of the world that was his and to which he did belong. He was profoundly aware of the richness, vitality, and variety in his black community; he was aware, also, that the affirmative reality of black life was something he never found in the books he read, was never taught in the schools he attended. Ellison had experienced the nonverbal articulation of these qualities in the jazz and blues that were so much a part of his upbringing. In particular he recalls, in *Shadow and Act*, Jimmy Rushing, the blues singer who "represented, gave voice to, something which was very affirming of Negro life, feelings which you couldn't really put into words." But recording and preserving the value of black life only in this medium did not satisfy Ellison; he was haunted, he admits, by a need "for other forms of transcendence and identification which I could only associate with classical music." As he explains, "I was taken very early with a passion to link together all I loved within the Negro community and all those things I felt in the world which lay beyond." This passion to join separate worlds and disparate selves into a unity of being infuses the content and style of *Invisible Man* and lies at the heart of Ellison's theory of fiction.

Early in his career, however, Ellison conceived of his vocation as a musician, as a composer of symphonies. When he entered Alabama's Tuskegee Institute in 1933 he enrolled as a music major; he wonders in *Shadow and Act* if he did so because, given his background, it was the only art "that seemed to offer some possibility for self-definition." The act of writing soon presented itself as an art through which he could link the disparate worlds he cherished, could verbally record and create the "affirmation of Negro life" he knew was so intrinsic a part of the universally human. To move beyond the old definitions that separated jazz from classical music, vernacular from literary language, the folk from the mythic, he would have to discover a prose style that could equal the integrative imagination of the "Renaissance Man."

Shadow and Act records that during 1935, his second year at Tuskegee, Ellison began his "conscious education in literature." Reading Emily Bronte's *Wuthering Heights* and Thomas Hardy's *Jude the Obscure* produced in him "an agony of unexpressible emotion," but T. S. Eliot's *The Waste Land* absolutely seized his imagination. He admits: "I was intrigued by its power to move me while eluding my understanding. Somehow its rhythms were often closer to those of jazz than were those of the Negro poets, and even though I could not understand then, its range of allusion was as mixed and varied as that of Louis Armstrong." Determined to understand the "hidden system of organization" that eluded him, Ellison began to explore the sources that Eliot had identified in the footnotes to the poem. This reading in ancient mythology, history, literature, and folklore led, in turn, to his reading of such twentieth-century writers as Ezra Pound, Ernest Hemingway, and Gertrude Stein, who led him back to the nineteenth-century authors Herman Melville and Mark Twain. The more Ellison read in literature and the sources of literature, the more he found that the details of his own history were "transformed." Local customs took on a "more universal meaning"; he became aware of the universal in the specific. His experience with *The Waste Land,* which forced him to wonder why he "had never read anything of equal intensity and sensibility by an American Negro writer," was his introduction to the universal power of the folk tradition as the foundation of literature.

During this same year, Ellison took a sociology course, an experience he describes in *Shadow and Act* as "humiliating." Presenting a reductive, unrealistic portrait of the American black as the "lady of the races," this sociological view denied the complex richness of black life that Ellison had so often experienced. In *The Craft of Ralph Ellison* Robert G. O'Meally argues that this encounter with a limited and limiting definition of blacks created in Ellison "an accelerated sense of urgency" to learn more about black culture and to find an artistic form to capture the vital reality of the black community that he had heard in the blues sessions, in the barbershops, and in the stories and jokes he had heard from some classmates as they returned from seasonal work in the cotton fields. Ironically, an accident intervened that propelled him on this course. Because of a mix-up about his scholarship, Ellison found himself without the money to return to Tuskegee. He went instead to New York, enacting the prototypical journey North, confident that he would return to Tuskegee after he had earned enough money.

Because Ellison did not get a job that paid him enough to save money for tuition, he stayed in New York, working and studying composition until his mother died in Dayton, Ohio. After his return to Dayton, he and his brother supported themselves by hunting. Though Ellison had hunted for years, he did not know how to wing-shoot; it was from Hemingway's fiction that he learned this process. Ellison studied Hemingway to learn writing techniques; from the older writer he also learned a lesson in descriptive accuracy and power, in the close relationship between fiction and reality. Like his narrator in *Invisible Man,* Ellison did not return to college; instead he began his long apprenticeship as a writer, his long and often difficult journey toward self-definition.

Ellison's early days in New York, before his return to Dayton, provided him with experiences that would later translate themselves into his theory of fiction. Two days after his arrival in "deceptively 'free' Harlem," he met black poet Langston Hughes who introduced him to the works of Andre Malraux, a French writer defined as Marxist. Though attracted to Marxism, Ellison sensed in Malraux something beyond a simplistic political sense of the human condition. Says Ellison: Malraux "was the artist-revolutionary rather than a politician when he wrote *Man's Fate,* and the book lives not because of a political position embraced at the time, but because of its larger concern with the tragic struggle of humanity." Ellison began to form his definition of the artist as a revolutionary concerned less with local injustice than with the timelessly tragic.

Ellison's view of art was furthered after he met black novelist Richard Wright. Wright urged him to read Joseph Conrad, Henry James, James Joyce, and Feodor Dostoevsky and invited Ellison to contribute a review essay and then a short story to the magazine he was editing. Wright was then in the process of writing *Native Son,* much of which Ellison read, he declares in *Shadow and Act,* "as it came out of the typewriter." Though awed by the process of writing and aware of the achievement of the novel, Ellison, who had just read Malraux, began to form his objections to the "sociological," deterministic ideology which informed the portrait of the work's protagonist, Bigger Thomas. In *Shadow and Act,* which Arthur P. Davis in *From the Dark Tower: Afro-American Writers, 1900 to 1960* accurately describes as partly an apologia pro vita sua (a defense of his life), Ellison articulates the basis of his objection: "I, for instance, found it disturbing that Bigger Thomas had none of the finer qualities of Richard Wright, none of the imagination, none of the sense of poetry, none of the gaiety." Ellison thus refutes the depiction of the black individual as an inarticulate victim whose life is one only of despair, anger, and pain. He insists that art must capture instead the complex reality, the pain and the pleasure of black existence, thereby challenging the definition of the black person as something less than fully human. Such a vision of art, which is at the heart of *Invisible Man,* became the focal point of an extended debate between Ellison and Irving Howe, who in a 1963 *Dissent* article accused Ellison of disloyalty to Wright in particular and to "protest fiction" in general.

From 1938 to 1944, Ellison published a number of short stories and contributed essays to journals such as the communist *New Masses.* As with most of Ellison's work, these stories have provoked disparate readings. In an essay in *Black World,* Ernest Kaiser calls the earliest stories and the essays in *New Masses* "the healthiest" of Ellison's career. The critic praises the economic theories that inform the early fiction, and he finds Ellison's language pure, emotional, and effective. Lamenting a change he attributes to Ellison's concern with literary technique, Kaiser charges the later stories, essays, and novel with being no longer concerned with people's problems and with being "unemotional."

Other critics, like Marcus Klein in *After Alienation: American Novels in Mid-Century,* see the early work as a progressive preparation for Ellison's mature fiction and theory. In the earliest of these stories, "Slick Gonna Learn," Ellison draws a character shaped largely by an ideological, naturalistic conception of existence, the very type of character he later repudiated. From this imitation of proletarian fiction, Ellison's work moves towards psychological and finally metaphysical explorations of the human condition. His characters thus are freed from restrictive definitions as Ellison develops a voice that is his own, Klein maintains.

In the two latest stories of the 1938-1944 period, "Flying Home" and "King of the Bingo Game," Ellison creates characters congruent with his sense of pluralism and possibility and does so in a narrative style that begins to approach the complexity of *Invisible Man.* As Arthur P. Davis notes, in "Flying Home" Ellison combines realism, folk story, symbolism, and a touch of surrealism to present his protagonist, Todd. In a fictional world composed of myriad levels of the mythic and the folk, the classical and the modern, Todd fights to free himself of imposed definitions. However, it is in "King of the Bingo Game," published just before he began *Invisible Man,* that Ellison's growth is most evident.

As in "Flying Home," the writer experiments in "King of the Bingo Game" with integrating sources and techniques. As in all of Ellison's early stories, the protagonist is a young black man fighting for his freedom against forces and people that attempt to deny it. In "King of the Bingo Game," O'Meally argues, "the struggle is seen in its most abstracted form." This abstraction results from the "dreamlike shifts of time and levels of consciousness" that dominate the surrealistic story and also from the fact that "the King is Ellison's first character to sense the frightening absurdity of everyday American life." In an epiphany which frees him from illusion and which places him, even if for only a moment, in control, the King realizes "that his battle for freedom and identity must be waged not against individuals or even groups, but against no less than history and fate," O'Meally declares. The parameters of the fight for freedom and identity have been broadened. Ellison sees his black hero as one who wages the oldest and most universal battle in human history: the fight for freedom to be timelessly human, to engage in the "tragic struggle of humanity," as the writer asserts in *Shadow and Act.* The King achieves awareness for a moment; the *Invisible Man* not only becomes aware but is able to articulate fully the struggle. As Ellison notes in his preface to the anniversary edition of the novel, too often characters have been "figures caught up in the most intense forms of social struggle, subject to the most extreme forms of the human predicament but yet seldom able to articulate the issues which tortured them." The *Invisible Man* is endowed with eloquence; he is Ellison's radical experiment with a fiction that insists upon the full range and humanity of the black character.

Ellison began *Invisible Man* in 1945. Although he was at work on a never-completed war novel at the time, Ellison recalls in his 1982 preface that he could not ignore the "taunting, disembodied voice" he heard beckoning him to write *Invisible Man.* Published in 1952 after a seven-year creative struggle, and awarded the National Book Award in 1953, *Invisible Man* received critical acclaim. Although some early reviewers were puzzled or disappointed by the experimental narrative techniques, most now agree that these techniques give the work its lasting force and account for Ellison's influence on later fiction. The novel is a veritable fugue of cultural fragments, blended and counterpointed in a uniquely Ellisonian composition. Echoes of Homer, Joyce, Eliot, and Hemingway join forces with the sounds of spirituals, blues, jazz, and nursery rhymes. The *Invisible Man* is as haunted by Louis Armstrong's "What did I do / To be so black / And blue?" as he is by Hemingway's bullfight scenes and his matadors' grace under pressure. The linking together of these disparate cultural elements is what allows the *Invisible Man* to draw the portrait of his inner face that is the way out of his wasteland.

In the work, Ellison clearly employs the traditional motif of the *Bildungsroman,* or novel of education: the Invisible Man moves from innocence to experience, from darkness to light, from blindness to sight. Complicating this linear journey, however, is the narrative frame provided by the Prologue and Epilogue which the narrator composes after the completion of his aboveground educational journey. Yet readers begin with the Prologue, written in his underground chamber on the "border area" of Harlem where he is waging a guerrilla war against the Monopolated Light & Power Company by invisibly draining their power. At first denied the story of his discovery, readers must be initiated through the act of re-experiencing the events that led them and the narrator to this hole. Armed with some suggestive hints and symbols, readers then start the journey toward a revisioning of the Invisible Man, America, and themselves.

The journey is a deliberate baptism by fire. From the Battle Royal where the Invisible Man swallows his own blood in the name of opportunity; to the madness of The Golden Day; to the protagonist's anguished expulsion from the College; to the horror of his lobotomy; to his dehumanization by the Brotherhood; to his jubilant discovery of the unseen people of Harlem; to the nightmare that is Ras and the riots; and finally to the descent underground and the ritualistic burning of the contents of his briefcase, readers are made to participate in the plot because they, finally, are a part of it. The novel is about plots: the plots against the Invisible Man by Bledsoe and the Brotherhood; the conspiracy against himself that is the inevitable result of his illusions; the plot of the American ideal that keeps him dodging the forces of the actual; the plot of the reader against the writer; and the plot, ultimately, against every human being by life itself. The multiplicity of plot is part of the brilliance of the novel. Like the Invisible Man, readers are duped, time and time again, resisting the reality before them. And like him, they undergo a series of deaths and rebirths in their narrative journey. They are cast out of the realism of the college scenes into the surrealistic void of the riots, wondering what they did to be, if not always black, at least so blue. They are made to feel, in the words of the novel, every "itch, taunt, laugh, cry, scar, ache, rage or pain of it." And readers come to know that they—and the Invisible Man—share the responsibility for all of it.

In the Prologue and Epilogue the Invisible Man is the conscious, reflexive artist, recording his perceptions of self and other as he articulates the meaning of the journey and the descent. In the Epilogue he lets readers understand more clearly the preparatory hints and symbols he offered in the Prologue. He articulates his understanding of the old woman's words when she told him that freedom lay not in hating but in loving and in "knowing how to say" what is in one's head. Here too he unveils his insight into his grandfather, an ex-slave who "never had any doubts about his humanity" and who accepted the principle of America "in all its human and absurd diversity." As the Invisible Man records his journey through the underground America, he asserts a vision of America as it should be. He becomes the nation's moral conscience, embodying its greatest failure and its highest possibility. He reclaims his full humanity and freedom by accepting the world as a "concrete, ornery, vile and sublimely wonderful" reflection of the perceptive self.

The act of writing, of ordering and defining the self, is what gives the Invisible Man freedom and what allows him to manage the absurdity and chaos of everyday life. Writing frees the self from imposed definitions, from the straitjacket of all that would limit the productive possibilities of the self. Echoing the pluralism of the novel's form, the Invisible Man insists on the freedom to be ambivalent, to love and to hate, to denounce and to defend the America he inherits. Ellison himself is well-acquainted with the ambivalence of his American heritage; nowhere is it more evident than in his name. Named after the nineteenth-century essayist and poet Ralph Waldo Emerson, whom Ellison's father admired, the name has created for Ellison embarrassment, confusion, and a desire to be the American writer his namesake called for. And Ellison places such emphasis on his unnamed yet self-named narrator's breaking the shackles of restrictive definitions, of what others call reality or right, he also frees himself, as Robert B. Stepto in *From Behind the Veil: A Study of Afro-American Narrative* argues, from the strictures of the traditional slave narratives of Frederick Douglas and W. E. B. DuBois. By consciously invoking this form but then not bringing the motif of "ascent and immersion" to its traditional completion, Ellison revoices the form, makes it his own, and steps outside it.

This stepping outside of traditional form, however, can be a dangerous act. In *Invisible Man,* Tod Clifton steps outside the historically powerful Brotherhood and is shot for "resisting reality." At the other extreme, Rinehart steps outside all definitions and becomes the embodiment of chaos. In *City of Words: American Fiction, 1950-1970* Tony Tanner notes that Ellison presents an overriding preoccupation of postmodern fiction: the fear of a rigid pattern that would limit all freedom of self, coupled with the fear of no pattern, of a chaotic void that would render illusory all sense of self. The Invisible Man is well aware of form and formlessness. As he says, "Without light I am not only invisible but formless as well; and to be unaware of one's form is to live a death." But step outside, or underneath, the Invisible Man does, although he would be the first to admit that he has had to be hit over the head to do it. Ellison, too, steps outside in his creation of the form of Invisible Man; he also steps inside the history of great literature that refuses to diminish the complexity of human identity and the search for the self.

The search for identity, which Ellison says in *Shadow and Act* is "the American theme," is the heart of the novel and the center of many critical debates over it. At novel's end, the journey is not complete; the Invisible Man must emerge from his hole and test the sense of self formed in hibernation. As he journeys toward this goal, toward the emergence of a sense of self that is at once black and American and universally human, questions recur: In his quest for pluralism, does he sacrifice his blackness? In his devotion to an imaginative rendering of self, does he lose his socially active self?

In her 1979 *PMLA* essay, Susan Blake argues that Ellison's insistence that black experience be ritualized as part of the larger human experience results in a denial of the unique social reality of black life. Because Ellison so thoroughly adapts black folklore into the Western tradition, Blake finds that the definition of black life becomes "not black but white"; it "exchanges the self-definition of the folk for the definition of the masters." Thorpe Butler, in a 1984 *College Language Association Journal* essay, defends Ellison against Blake's criticism. He declares that Ellison's depiction of specific black experience as part of the universal does not "diminish the unique richness and anguish" of that experience and does not "diminish the force of Ellison's protest against the blind, cruel dehumanization of black Americans by white society." This debate extends arguments that have appeared since the publication of the novel. Underlying these controversies is the old, uneasy argument about the relationship of art and politics, of literary practice and social commitment.

Ellison's sensitivity to this issue is painfully clear. He repeatedly defends his view, here voiced in *Shadow and Act,* that "protest is an element of all art, though it does not necessarily take the form of speaking for a political or social program." In a 1970 *Time* essay, Ellison defines further his particular definition of protest, of the "soul" of his art and his people: "An expression of American diversity within unity, of blackness with whiteness, soul announces the presence of a creative struggle against the realities of existence." Insisting in *Shadow and Act* that the novelist is a "manipulator and depictor of moral problems," Ellison claims that as novelist he does not try to escape the reality of black pain. He frequently reminds readers that he knows well the pain and anger that come with being black; his mother was arrested for violating Jim Crow housing laws, and in Alabama he was subjected daily to the outrageous policies of segregation. But for Ellison there needs to be more than even an eloquent depiction of this part of reality; he needs, as he says in Shadow and Act, "to transform these elements into art . . . to transcend, as the blues transcend the painful conditions with which they deal." In *Invisible Man* he declares that Louis Armstrong "made poetry out of being invisible." Social reality may place the creator in the underground, render him invisible, but his art leads him out of the hole, eloquent, visible, and empowered by the very people who put him there.

Although the search for identity is the major theme of *Invisible Man,* other aspects of the novel receive a great deal of critical attention. Among them, as Joanne Giza notes in her essay in *Black American Writers: Bibliographical Essays,* are literary debts and analogies; comic elements; the metaphor of vision; use of the blues; and folkloric elements. Although all of these concerns are part of the larger issue of identity, Ellison's use of blues and folklore has been singled out as a major contribution to contemporary literature and culture. Since the publication of *Invisible Man,* scores of articles have appeared on these two topics, a fact which in turn has led to a rediscovery, a revisioning of the importance of blues and folklore to American literature and culture in general.

Much of Ellison's groundbreaking work is presented in *Shadow and Act.* Published in 1964, this collection of essays, says Ellison, is "concerned with three general themes: with literature and folklore, with Negro musical expression—especially jazz and the blues—and with the complex relationship between the Negro American subculture and North American culture as a whole." This volume has been hailed as one of the most profound pieces of cultural criticism of the century. Writing in *Commentary,* Robert Penn Warren praises the astuteness of Ellison's perceptions; in *New Leader,* Stanley Edgar Hyman proclaims Ellison "the profoundest cultural critic we have." In the *New York Review of Books,* R. W. B. Lewis explores Ellison's study of black music as a form of power and finds that "Ellison is not only a self-identifier but the source of self-definition in others."

Published in 1986, *Going to the Territory* is a second collection of essays reprising many of the subjects and concerns treated in *Shadow and Act*—literature, art, music, the relationships of black and white cultures, fragments of autobiography, tributes to such noted black Americans as Richard Wright, Duke Ellington, and painter Romare Beardon. With the exception of "An Extravagance of Laughter," a lengthy examination of Ellison's response to Jack Kirkland's dramatization of Erskine Caldwell's novel *Tobacco Road,* the essays in *Going to the Territory* are reprints of previously published articles or speeches, most of them dating from the 1960s. While it conveniently gathers this material, the volume provides few new insights into the direction Ellison's work may take.

Ellison's influence as both novelist and critic, as artist and cultural historian, is enormous. Whether in agreement with or reaction against, writers respond passionately to his work. In special issues of *Black World* and *College Language Association Journal* devoted to Ellison, strident attacks appear alongside equally spirited accolades. Perhaps another measure of Ellison's stature and achievement is his readers' vigil for his long-awaited second novel. Although Ellison often refuses to answer questions about the work-in-progress, there is enough evidence to suggest that the manuscript is very large, that all or part of it was destroyed in a fire and is being rewritten, and that its creation has been a long and painful task. Most readers wait expectantly, believing that Ellison, who has said in *Shadow and Act* that he "failed of eloquence" in *Invisible Man,* is waiting until his second novel equals his imaginative vision of the American novel as conquerer of the frontier, equals the Emersonian call for a literature to release all people from the bonds of oppression.

Eight excerpts from this novel-in-progress have been published in journals such as *Quarterly Review of Literature, Massachusetts Review,* and *Noble Savage.* Set in the South in the years spanning the Jazz Age to the Civil Rights movement these fragments seem an attempt to recreate modern American history and identity. The major characters are the Reverend Hickman, a one-time jazz musician, and Bliss, the light-skinned boy whom he adopts and who later passes into white society and becomes Senator Sunraider, an advocate of white supremacy. As O'Meally notes in *The Craft of Ralph Ellison,* the major difference between Bliss and Ellison's earlier young protagonists is that despite some harsh collisions with reality, Bliss refuses to divest himself of his illusions and accept his personal history. Says O'Meally: "Moreover, it is a renunciation of the blackness of American experience and culture, a refusal to accept the American past in all its complexity."

Like *Invisible Man,* this novel promises to be a broad and searching inquiry into identity, ideologies, culture, and history. The narrative form is similar as well; here, too, is the blending of popular and classical myth, of contradictory cultural memories, of an intricate pattern of images of birth, death, and rebirth. In *Shadow and Act* Ellison describes the novel's form as "a realism extended beyond realism" in which he explores again the multifaceted meanings of the folk as the basis of all literature and culture. What the ultimate form of the novel will be—if, indeed, these excerpts are to be part of one novel—remains hidden. But the pieces seize the reader's imagination even if they deny systematic analysis.

One thing does seem certain about these stories. In them Bliss becomes a traitor to his own race, loses his hold on those things of transforming, affirmative value. Hickman, on the other hand, accepts and celebrates his heritage, his belief in the timeless value of his history. As O'Meally writes in his book-length study of Ellison, Hickman "holds fast to personal and political goals and values." Ellison, too, holds fast to his values in the often chaotic and chameleon world of art and politics. The tone of these excerpts is primarily tragicomic, a mode well-suited to Ellison's definition of life. As he says in *Shadow and Act,* "I think that the mixture of the marvelous and the terrible is a basic condition of human life and that the persistence of human ideals represents the marvelous pulling itself up out of the chaos of the universe." Elsewhere in the book, Ellison argues that "true novels, even when most pessimistic and bitter, arise out of an impulse to celebrate human life." As *Invisible Man* before and the Hickman novel yet to come, they celebrate the "human and absurd" commixture of American life.

BIOGRAPHICAL/CRITICAL SOURCES:

BOOKS

Allen, Walter Ernest, *The Modern Novel in Britain and the United States,* Dutton, 1964.

Alvarez, A., editor, *Under Pressure: The Writer in Society; Eastern Europe and the U.S.A.,* Penguin, 1965.

Baker, Houston, A., Jr., *Long Black Song: Essays in Black American Literature and Culture,* University Press of Virginia, 1972.

Baumbach, Jonathan, *The Landscape of Nightmare: Studies in the Contemporary American Novel,* New York University Press, 1965.

Benston, Kimberly W., editor, *Speaking for You: The Vision of Ralph Ellison,* Howard University Press, 1987.

Bigsby, C. W. E., editor, *The Black American Writer,* Volume 1, Everett Edwards, 1969.

Bloom, Harold, editor, *Ralph Ellison: Modern Critical Views,* Chelsea Publishing, 1986.

Bone, Robert, *The Negro Novel in America,* Yale University Press, revised edition, 1965.

Breit, Harvey, *The Writer Observed,* World Publishing, 1956.

Callahan, John F., *In the African-American Grain: The Pursuit of Voice in Twentieth-Century Black Fiction,* University of Illinois Press, 1988.

Concise Dictionary of American Literary Biography: The New Consciousness, 1941-1948, Gale, 1987.

Contemporary Fiction in America and England, 1950-1970, Gale, 1976.

Contemporary Literary Criticism, Gale, Volume 1, 1973, Volume 3, 1975, Volume 11, 1979.

Cooke, Michael, *Afro-American Literature in the Twentieth Century: The Achievement of Intimacy,* Yale University Press, 1984.

Covo, Jacqueline, *The Blinking Eye: Ralph Waldo Ellison and His American, French, German, and Italian Critics, 1952-1971: Bibliographic Essays and a Checklist,* Scarecrow, 1974.

Davis, Arthur P., *From the Dark Tower: Afro-American Writers (1900 to 1960),* Howard University Press, 1974.

Davis, Charles T., *Black Is the Color of the Cosmos: Essays on Afro-American Literature and Culture, 1942-1981,* edited by Henry Louis Gates, Jr., Garland, 1982.

Dictionary of Literary Biography, Volume 2: *American Novelists since World War II,* Gale, 1978.

Dietze, Rudolf F., *Ralph Ellison: The Genius of an Artist,* Carl (Nuremburg), 1982.

Ellison, Ralph, *Shadow and Act,* Random House, 1964.

Fabre, Michael, editor, *Delta Number 18: Ralph Ellison,* University Paul Valery (Paris), 1984.

Fischer-Homung, Dorothea, *Folklore and Myth in Ralph Ellison's Early Works,* Hochschul (Stuttgart), 1979.

Fisher, Dexter, and Robert B. Stepto, editors, *Afro-American Literature: The Reconstruction of Instruction,* Modern Language Association of America, 1979.

Gayle, Addison, Jr., editor, *Black Expression: Essays by and about Americans in the Creative Arts,* Weybright & Talley, 1969.

Gayle, Addison, Jr., compiler, *The Black Aesthetic,* Doubleday, 1971.

Gayle, Addison, Jr., *The Way of the New World: The Black Novel in America,* Anchor Press, 1975.

Gibson, Donald B., compiler, *Five Black Writers: Essays on Wright, Ellison, Baldwin, Hughes, and Le Roi Jones,* New York University Press, 1970.

Gottesman, Ronald, editor, *Studies in Invisible Man,* Merrill, 1971.
Graham, John, *The Writer's Voice: Conversations with Contemporary Writers,* edited by George Garrett, Morrow, 1973.
Gross, Seymour L., and John Edward Hardy, editors, *Images of the Negro in American Literature,* University of Chicago Press, 1966.
Harper, Michael S., and R. B. Stepto, editors, *Chant of Saints: A Gathering of Afro-American Literature, Art, and Scholarship,* University of Illinois Press, 1979.
Henderson, Bill, editor, *The Pushcart Prize, III: Best of the Small Presses,* Avon, 1979.
Hersey, John, editor, *Ralph Ellison: A Collection of Critical Essays,* Prentice-Hall, 1974.
Hill, Herbert, editor, *Anger and Beyond: The Negro Writer in the United States,* Harper, 1966.
Inge, M. Thomas, and others, editors, *Black American Writers: Bibliographical Essays, Volume 2: Richard Wright, Ralph Ellison, James Baldwin, and Amiri Baraka,* St. Martin's, 1978.
Kazin, Alfred, *Bright Book of Life: American Novelists and Storytellers from Hemingway to Mailer,* Atlantic/Little, Brown, 1973.
Klein, Marcus, *After Alienation: American Novels in Mid-Century,* World Publishing, 1964.
Kostelanetz, R., *On Contemporary Literature: An Anthology of Critical Essays on the Major Movements and Writers of Contemporary Literature,* Avon, 1964.
Margolies, Edward, *Native Sons: A Critical Study of Twentieth-Century Negro American Authors,* Lippincott, 1968.
O'Brien, John, *Interviews with Black Writers,* Liveright, 1973.
O'Meally, Robert G., *The Craft of Ralph Ellison,* Harvard University Press, 1980.
Ottley, Roi, William J. Weatherby, and others, editors, *The Negro in New York: An Informal Social History,* New York Public Library, 1967.
Plimpton, George, editor, *Writers at Work: The Paris Review Interviews,* second series, Viking, 1963.
Reilly, John M., editor, *Twentieth-Century Interpretations of Invisible Man: A Collection of Critical Essays,* Prentice-Hall, 1970.
Stepto, R. B., *From Behind the Veil: A Study of Afro-American Narrative,* University of Illinois Press, 1979.
Tanner, Tony, *City of Words: American Fiction, 1950-1970,* Harper, 1971.
Trimmer, Joseph F., editor, *A Casebook on Ralph Ellison's Invisible Man,* Crowell, 1972.
Waldmeir, Joseph J., editor, *Recent American Fiction: Some Critical Views,* Houghton, 1963.
Warren, Robert Penn, *Who Speaks for the Negro?,* Random House, 1965.
The Writer as Independent Spirit, [New York], 1968.

PERIODICALS

American Quarterly, March, 1972.
American Scholar, autumn, 1955.
Atlantic, July, 1952, December, 1970, August, 1986.
Barat Review, January, 1968.
Black Academy Review, winter, 1970.
Black American Literature Forum, summer, 1978.
Black Books Bulletin, winter, 1972.
Black Creation, summer, 1970.
Black World, December, 1970 (special Ellison issue).
Book Week, October 25, 1964.
Boundary 2, winter, 1978.

Brown Alumni Monthly, November, 1979.
Carleton Miscellany, winter, 1980 (special Ellison issue).
Chicago Review, Volume 19, number 2, 1967.
Chicago Tribune Book World, August 10, 1986.
College Language Association Journal, December, 1963, June, 1967, March, 1970 (special Ellison issue), September, 1971, December, 1971, December, 1972, June, 1973, March, 1974, September, 1976, September, 1977, Number 25, 1982, Number 27, 1984.
Commentary, November, 1953, Number 39, 1965.
Commonweal, May 2, 1952.
Crisis, March, 1953, March, 1970.
Critique, Number 2, 1968.
Daedalus, winter, 1968.
Daily Oklahoman, August 23, 1953.
December, winter, 1961.
English Journal, September, 1969, May, 1973, November, 1984.
'48 Magazine of the Year, May, 1948.
Grackle, Volume 4, 1977-78.
Harper's, October, 1959, March, 1967, July, 1967.
Journal of Black Studies, Number 7, 1976.
Los Angeles Times, August 8, 1986.
Massachusetts Review, autumn, 1967, autumn, 1977.
Modern Fiction Studies, winter, 1969-70.
Motive, April, 1966.
Muhammad Speaks, September, 1972, December, 1972.
Nation, May 10, 1952, September 9, 1964, November 9, 1964, September 20, 1965.
Negro American Literature Forum, July, 1970, summer, 1973, Number 9, 1975, spring, 1977.
Negro Digest, May, 1964, August, 1967.
Negro History Bulletin, May, 1953, October, 1953.
New Criterion, September, 1983.
New Leader, October 26, 1964.
New Republic, November 14, 1964, August 4, 1986.
Newsday, October, 1967.
Newsweek, August 12, 1963, October 26, 1964.
New Yorker, May 31, 1952, November 22, 1976.
New York Herald Tribune Book Review, April 13, 1952.
New York Review of Books, January 28, 1964, January 28, 1965.
New York Times, April 13, 1952, April 24, 1985.
New York Times Book Review, April 13, 1952, May 4, 1952, October 25, 1964, January 24, 1982, August 3, 1986.
New York Times Magazine, November 20, 1966.
Paris Review, spring, 1955, spring/summer, 1957.
Partisan Review, Number 25, 1958.
Phoenix, fall, 1961.
Phylon, winter, 1960, spring, 1970, spring, 1973, summer, 1973, summer, 1977.
PMLA, January, 1979.
Renascence, spring, 1974, winter, 1978.
Saturday Review, April 12, 1952, March 14, 1953, December 11, 1954, January 1, 1955, April 26, 1958, May 17, 1958, July 12, 1958, September 27, 1958, July 28, 1962, October 24, 1964.
Shenandoah, summer, 1969.
Smith Alumni Quarterly, July, 1964.
Southern Humanities Review, winter, 1970.
Southern Literary Journal, spring, 1969.
Southern Review, fall, 1974, summer, 1985.
Studies in American Fiction, spring, 1973.
Studies in Black Literature, autumn, 1971, autumn, 1972, spring, 1973, spring, 1975, spring, 1976, winter, 1976.
Tamarack Review, October, 1963, summer, 1964.

Time, April 14, 1952, February 9, 1959, February 1, 1963, April 6, 1970.
Times Literary Supplement, January 18, 1968.
Village Voice, November 19, 1964.
Washington Post, August 19-21, 1973, April 21, 1982, February 9, 1983, March 30, 1983, July 23, 1986.
Washington Post Book World, May 17, 1987.
Wisconsin Studies in Literature, winter, 1960, summer, 1966.
Y-Bird Reader, autumn, 1977.

*   *   *

ELLMANN, Richard (David) 1918-1987

PERSONAL: Born March 15, 1918, in Highland Park, Mich.; died May 13, 1987 of pneumonia brought on by amyotrophic lateral sclerosis (Lou Gherig's disease) in Oxford, England; son of James I. (a lawyer) and Jeanette (Barsook) Ellmann; married Mary Donahue (a writer), August 12, 1949; children: Stephen, Maud, Lucy. *Education:* Yale University, B.A., 1939, M.A., 1941, Ph.D., 1947; Trinity College, Dublin, B.Litt., 1947.

ADDRESSES: Home—39 St. Giles, Oxford OX1 3LW, England.

CAREER: Harvard University, Cambridge, Mass., instructor, 1942-43, 1947-48, Briggs-Copeland Assistant Professor of English Composition, 1948-51; Northwestern University, Evanston, Ill., professor of English, 1951-63, Franklin Bliss Snyder Professor, 1963-68; Yale University, New Haven, Conn., professor of English, 1968-70; Oxford University, Oxford, England, Goldsmiths' Professor of English Literature, 1970-1984, New College, fellow, 1970-84, honorary fellow, 1984-87; Wolfson College, extraordinary fellow, 1984-87. Frederick Ives Carpenter Visiting Professor, University of Chicago, 1959, 1967, and 1975-77; Emory University, visiting professor, 1978-81, Woodruff Professor of English, 1982-87. Member of United States/United Kingdom Educational Commission, 1970-85. Consultant to "The World of James Joyce," Public Broadcasting Service, 1983. *Military service:* U.S. Navy and Office of Strategic Services, 1943-46.

MEMBER: British Academy (fellow), Modern Language Association of America (chairman of English Institute, 1961-62; member of executive council, 1961-65), English Institute (chairman, 1961-62), Royal Society of Literature (fellow), American Academy and Institute of Arts and Letters (fellow), American Academy and Institute of Arts and Letters (fellow), Phi Beta Kappa, Chi Delta Theta, Signet.

AWARDS, HONORS: Rockefeller Foundation fellow in humanities, 1946-47; Guggenheim fellow, 1950, 1957-58, and 1970; grants from American Philosophical Society and Modern Language Association of America, 1953; *Kenyon Review* fellowship in criticism, 1955-56; School of Letters fellow, Indiana University, 1956 and 1960, senior fellow, 1966-72; National Book Award for nonfiction, Friends of Literature Award in biography, Thormond Monson Award from Society of Midland Authors, and Carey-Thomas Award for creative book publishing to Oxford University Press, all for *James Joyce,* 1960, and Duff Cooper Prize and James Tair Black Prize for new and revised edition, 1982; George Polk Memorial Award, 1970, for *The Artist As Critic: Critical Writings of Oscar Wilde;* M.A., Oxford University, 1970; D.Litt. from National University of Ireland, 1975, Emory University, 1979, and Northwestern University, 1980; National Endowment for the Humanities research grant, 1977; Ph.D., University of Gothenburg (Sweden), 1978; D.H.L. from Boston College and University of Rochester, both 1979; Pulitzer

Prize for best biography, National Book Critics Circle Award for best biography/autobiography, both 1989, both for *Oscar Wilde.*

WRITINGS:

Yeats: The Man and the Masks, Macmillan, 1948, reprinted, Norton, 1978, corrected edition with new preface, Oxford University Press, 1979.
The Identity of Yeats, Oxford University Press, 1954, 2nd edition, 1964, reprinted, 1985.
James Joyce, Oxford University Press, 1959, new and revised edition with corrections, 1982.
Edwardians and Late Victorians, Columbia University Press, 1960.
(With E. D. H. Johnson and Alfred L. Bush) *Wilde and the Nineties: An Essay and an Exhibition,* edited by Charles Ryskamp, Princeton University Library, 1966.
Eminent Domain: Yeats among Wilde, Joyce, Pound, Eliot, and Auden, Oxford University Press, 1967.
Ulysses on the Liffey, Oxford University Press, 1972, corrected edition, Faber and Faber, 1984.
Golden Codgers: Biographical Speculations, Oxford University Press, 1973.
(With John Espey) *Oscar Wilde: Two Approaches* (papers read at a Clark Library Seminar, April 17, 1976), Williams Andrews Clark Memorial Library, 1977.
The Consciousness of Joyce, Oxford University Press, 1977.
Four Dubliners: Wilde, Yeats, Joyce, and Beckett, U.S. Government Printing Office, 1986.
Oscar Wilde, Hamish Hamilton, 1987, Knopf, 1988.
a long the riverrun: Selected Essays, Knopf, 1989.

EDITOR

(And translator, and author of introduction) Henri Michaux, *Selected Writings,* Routledge & Kegan Paul, 1952.
Stanislaus Joyce, *My Brother's Keeper: James Joyce's Early Years,* Viking, 1958.
(With others) *English Masterpieces,* 2nd edition, two volumes, Prentice-Hall, 1958.
Arthur Symons, *The Symbolist Movement in Literature,* Dutton, 1958.
(With Ellsworth Mason) *The Critical Writings of James Joyce,* Faber and Faber, 1959, reprinted, 1979.
(With Charles Feidelson, Jr.) *The Modern Tradition: Backgrounds of Modern Literature,* Oxford University Press, 1965.
James Joyce, *Letters of James Joyce,* Volumes 2-3, Viking, 1966.
(Of corrected holograph) James Joyce, *A Portrait of the Artist As a Young Man,* drawings by Robin Jacques, Cape, 1968.
Oscar Wilde, *The Artist As Critic: Critical Writings of Oscar Wilde,* Random House, 1969.
Oscar Wilde: A Collection of Critical Essays, Prentice-Hall, 1969.
(With Robert O'Clair) *The Norton Anthology of Modern Poetry,* Norton, 1973.
James Joyce, *Selected Letters of James Joyce,* Viking, 1975.
(With O'Clair) *Modern Poems: An Introduction to Poetry,* Norton, 1976.
The New Oxford Book of American Verse, Oxford University Press, 1976.
(And author of introduction) Oscar Wilde, *The Picture of Dorian Gray and Other Writings,* Bantam, 1982.

OTHER

(Contributor of "A Chronology on the Life of James Joyce") James Joyce, *Letters,* Volume 1, edited by Stuart Gilbert, Viking, 1957.

Ulysses the Divine Nobody (monograph), Yale University Press, 1957, reprinted, 1981.

Joyce in Love (monograph), Cornell University Library, 1959.

(Contributor of "Overtures to Wilde's Salome") *Twentieth Anniversary, 1968,* Indiana University School of Letters, 1968.

(Author of introduction and notes) James Joyce, *Giacomo Joyce,* Faber, 1968, reprinted, 1984.

(Contributor of "Ulysses: A Short History") James Joyce, *Ulysses,* Penguin, 1969.

James Joyce's Tower (monograph), Eastern Regional Tourism Organisation (Dublin), 1969.

Literary Biography (monograph; inaugural lecture, University of Oxford, May 4, 1971), Clarendon Press, 1971.

The Poetry of Yeats (phono tape), BFA Educational Media, 1974.

James Joyce's Hundredth Birthday, Side and Front Views (monograph), Library of Congress, 1982.

Oscar Wilde at Oxford (monograph), Library of Congress, 1984.

(Author of introduction) Michael Moscato and Leslie LeBlanc, *The United States of America vs. One Book Entitled Ulysses by James Joyce; Documents and Commentary: 50-Year Retrospective,* University Publications of America, 1984.

Henry James among the Aesthetes (lectures), Longwood Publishing Group, 1985.

W. B. Yeats' Second Puberty (monograph), Library of Congress, 1985.

Samuel Beckett, Nayman of Noland (monograph), Library of Congress, 1986.

Also author of monographs *Wallace Stevens' Ice-Cream,* 1957, and *The Background of Joyce's The Dead,* 1958.

SIDELIGHTS: Renowned biographer, literary critic, and educator, Richard Ellmann held professorial posts at such universities as Harvard, Northwestern, and Yale before becoming the first American to teach English literature at Oxford University, a position he held for many years. Ellmann devoted most of his distinguished academic career to the study of the Irish literary renaissance. "It is difficult to think of the great writers of Irish literature—W. B. Yeats, James Joyce, or Oscar Wilde—without thinking of Ellmann," remarked Steven Serafin in a *Dictionary of Literary Biography Yearbook, 1987* essay. Ellmann's scholarship on Yeats remains a standard reference, and he is widely acknowledged as having been the foremost authority on Joyce. His much heralded, National Book Award-winning biography *James Joyce,* not only represents the definitive work on the artist but, in the opinion of many, casts its shadow as the best literary biography ever written. Referring to him as "an extraordinary individual of rare and exceptional talent," Serafin believed that "Ellmann essentially redefined the art of biography." And in a *Times Literary Supplement* review of Ellmann's Pulitzer Prize-winning final work, the biography *Oscar Wilde,* Gore Vidal deemed him "our time's best academic biographer."

Ellmann's scholarship sought the literary influences upon and connections among writers and their work. Calling Ellmann "particularly sensitive to the impingement of one talent upon another," Denis Donoghue added in a *New York Times Book Review* essay about *Eminent Domain: Yeats among Wilde, Joyce, Pound, Eliot, and Auden:* "As critics we look for corresponding moments in the work, moments of representative force and definition. Mr. Ellmann is a keen student of these epiphanies in life and art. He finds them more often than not in the pressure of one mind upon another, and he delights in these occasions." In Ellmann's *Eminent Domain,* "Yeats's greatness as a poet is seen as illustrated by his gift for expropriating or confiscating, from youth to age, ideas or tactics from other writers," stated a *Times Literary Supplement* contributor.

Ellmann, whose work on Yeats "set the tone of much subsequent criticism," stated Kevin Sullivan in a *Nation* review of *Eminent Domain,* believed that as "a young poet in search of an aesthetic," Yeats was significantly indebted to Wilde, whose "professional reputation rested . . . on his skill as a talker before all else." Yeats "pillaged freely" of this talk during their London meetings and believed that "Wilde's dazzling conversation was an aristocratic counterpart to the oral culture that had persisted among the Irish peasantry at home," explained Sullivan. "But what really attracted him was Wilde's easy assumption of the superiority of imagination to reason and intellect, and the corollary that followed almost at once upon that assumption—the primacy and autonomy of art." And about the relationship between Yeats and Joyce, the *Times Literary Supplement* contributor noted that while "Joyce's attitude to Yeats was that of a rebel in the Irish literary movement," according to Sullivan, Ellmann believed that "Joyce turned from verse to prose out of an awareness of Yeats's unchallengeable mastery as a poet." Praised by Sullivan for describing "a wide and graceful arc that encompasses many of the major developments in English poetry during a full half-century," *Eminent Domain* was labeled "lucid, perceptive, urbane, in itself a graceful occasion" by Donoghue.

James Joyce, Ellmann's masterwork, was hailed with critical superlatives. "This immensely detailed, massive, completely detached and objective, yet loving biography, translates James Joyce's books back into his life," wrote Stephen Spender in the *New York Times.* "Here is the definitive work," assessed Dwight Macdonald in *New Yorker,* "and I hope it will become a model for future scholarly biographies." And according to Mark Schorer in the *San Francisco Chronicle,* "This is not only the most important book that we have had on James Joyce until now (and the only reliable biography), it is also, almost certainly, one of the great literary biographies of this century, a book that will last for years, probably for generations." A few critics, however, faulted the biography for the enormity of its detail. A *Times Literary Supplement* contributor, for example, contended that "much of the difficulty with Mr. Ellmann's book is in seeing the wood for the trees." But in the *Saturday Review,* Stuart Gilbert echoed the widely shared critical recognition that Ellmann performed commendably, calling *James Joyce* "a masterpiece of scholarly objectivity and exact research, in which the facts are marshaled and set forth with fine lucidity, and the imposing mass of detail never clogs the analysis."

In 1982, more than twenty years after the publication of *James Joyce,* Ellmann marked the centennial year of Joyce's birth with a new and revised edition of his biography. Having had access to Joyce's private library and other previously unavailable material, Ellmann was able to define the influences upon Joyce's art, especially *Ulysses.* "Ellmann's task was a dual one," wrote Thomas Flanagan in the *Washington Post Book World.* "He recreated for the reader what had become one of the exemplary lives of modern literature, conveying its color and its textures, its characterizing movements and stances, by the adroit but unobtrusive deployment of many thousands of details." The *New York Time's* Christopher Lehmann-Haupt, who felt that this minutely detailed new material was "entirely appropriate and desirable, considering the obsessive sort of attachment that Joyce's art inspires," remarked: "And the effect of this experience is fairly stunning, not alone because of the remarkable wealth of details that the author has gathered up and artfully pieced together. What also strikes the reader is the number of those details that wound up in Joyce's fiction, or, to put it the other way around, the degree to which Joyce's art was grounded in actuality."

Although *Newsweek*'s Peter S. Prescott regarded it "a pleasure to salute this masterly book as it marches past again," critics such as Hugh Kenner in the *Times Literary Supplement* acknowledged the book's achievement while pondering its veracity. Kenner suggested that because much of Ellmann's data was based upon interviews with those who claimed a link to Joyce, it was essentially unreliable, citing in particular Ellmann's use of "Irish Fact, definable as anything you get told in Ireland, where you get told a great deal." Kenner further maintained: " 'Definitive' in 1959, was a word that got thrown around rather thoughtlessly by reviewers stunned beneath an avalanche of new information. But there can be no 'definitive' biography. Biography is a narrative form: that means, a mode of fiction. Many narratives can be woven from the same threads. Biography incorporates 'facts', having judged their credibility. Its criteria for judgment include assessment of sources . . . and, pervasively, assessment of one's man." Moreover, Kenner also questioned whether Ellmann's detachment from his subject was sufficient: "Tone is a delicate matter; we don't want a hagiography. We'd like, though, to feel the presence of the mind that made the life worth writing and makes it worth reading." Conversely, Flanagan concluded that it was "because of the unsparing scrupulousness of his own methods," that Ellmann wrote "the kind of book which has become unhappily rare—a work of exacting scholarship which is also a humane and liberating document. Joyce found the proper biographer, and there can be no higher praise." John Stallworthy concurred in the *Times Literary Supplement*, "Speaking with his master's voice, his master's elegance, and his master's wit, Ellmann has produced a biography worth its place on the shelf beside *Dubliners, Ulysses,* and *Finnegans Wake.*"

James Joyce marked a turning point for Ellmann, even though he was encouraged by its critical reception, said Serafin: "Shortly after its publication he ruminated about the future of his career: 'There really aren't any other modern writers that measure up to Yeats or Joyce. I can't think of anyone else I'd want to work on the way I've worked on them.' " Vidal suggested that "since Ellmann had already written magisterial works on two of the four [subjects of his essays, *Four Dubliners: Wilde, Yeats, Joyce, and Beckett*], symmetry and sympathy plainly drew him to a third." Ellmann spent the last twenty years of his life working on *Oscar Wilde*. Suffering from Lou Gherig's disease, "during the last weeks of his life, with the help of small machines on which he typed out messages that were then printed on a screen or on paper, he made final revisions on his long-awaited biography," reported Walter Goodman in the *New York Times*.

"While the literary world will continue to mourn his passing, we must all be grateful that he lived long enough to complete his magnificent life of Oscar Wilde . . . ," wrote Robert E. Kuehn in *Tribune Books*. "Like his earlier life of James Joyce, this book is biography on the grand scale: learned, expansive, judicious, magnanimous, and written with care and panache." Ellmann perceived Wilde, said Michael Dirda of the *Washington Post Book World*, "chiefly as a fearless artist and social critic who, like a kamikaze pilot, used himself as the bomb to explode the bourgeois values, pretentions and hypocrisies of late Victorian society." Likening Wilde's fate to that of "a hero of classic tragedy [who] plummeted from the heights of fame to utter ruin," Dirda pointed out that although Wilde has been the subject of several biographies, "they cannot compete with this capacious, deeply sympathetic and vastly entertaining new life of Richard Ellmann."

"There's no question that *Oscar Wilde* is brilliant," declared Walter Kendrick in the *Voice Literary Supplement;* "its posthumous publication splendidly caps Ellmann's career and, like his *James Joyce,* it belongs on the short shelf of biographies correctly labeled definitive." Although praising Ellmann as "a masterful biographer," Elspeth Cameron continued in the Toronto *Globe and Mail* that "no biography is definitive, and this one is not without its flaws. Ellmann's intellectual grasp of Wilde is firmer than his comprehension of Wilde's emotional life." However, Kuehn found that "when it comes to interpretation, the psychological patterns he traces tend to be all the more persuasive for his refusal to overstate the case." Declaring that "Oscar Wilde is not easily led," Richard Eder acknowledged in the *Los Angeles Times Book Review* that "Ellmann does everything a biographer could do, and some things that few biographers have the courage and talent to do. He refuses to net the butterfly Wilde; he flies with him instead."

Regarding Ellmann as "unusually intelligent, a quality seldom found in academe or, indeed, on Parnassus itself," Vidal felt that Wilde did "not quite suit his schema or his talent." Wilde does not require "explication or interpretation," assessed Vidal. "He needs only to be read, or listened to." Noting that "Wilde provides little occasion for Ellmann's formidable critical apparatus," Vidal added that "where Ellmann showed us new ways of looking at Yeats and, above all, at Joyce, he can do nothing more with Wilde than fit him into a historical context and tell, yet again, the profane story so well known to those who read." Concluding, however, that "nobody could do better than Ellmann," Eder questioned how does one "deliver up a figure who lived and wrote under such polymorphous signs of evasion?"

In Serafin's estimation, Ellmann's *Oscar Wilde* has "rekindled interest in both the subject and the biographer. Virtually assured a permanent position in the history of literary biography, Ellmann has given new and sustained meaning to an ancient art." Serafin also credited Ellmann with "establishing a standard of excellence in the art of contemporary life writing" by fulfilling " 'the ideal of sympathetic intuition' in re-creating and virtually reliving the lives of his subjects." As Seamus Heaney observed in *Atlantic*, "There is an overall sense of Wilde's being tolerantly supervised by an intelligence at once vigilant and dignified." Remarking that "Joyce as well as his Irish compatriot Oscar Wilde might have agonized less in knowing Ellmann would write the story of his life," Serafin recalled: "It was Wilde who professed every great man has his disciples, and it is usually Judas who writes the biography. Surely no Judas, Ellmann would neither deceive nor deny."

"He loved language as he loved life," said Serafin, "and never failed in his work, as Anthony Burgess would astutely observe, 'to stimulate, instruct, amuse, and, for this writer, reawaken a sleeping belief in the glory of making literature.' " Critics and colleagues alike unanimously admired Ellmann's intelligence as well as his humility. "He carries much learning with lightness and illumination," wrote Stephen Spender in a *New York Review of Books* piece on Ellmann's book of essays, *Golden Codgers: Biographical Speculations*. And in the *Chicago Sun Times*, Bob Hergath observed: "The nice thing about Ellmann, for all his scholarship and erudition, he was a regular guy. He had a terrific sense of humor." Referring to Ellmann's "notable sense of humor and a donnishly droll way with a punchline," Goodman remarked that "his wit remained intact throughout his illness; with speech difficult, he typed out jokes and repartee with visitors." As his brother, William Ellmann, is quoted in the *Detroit Free Press,* "Dick Ellmann was a literary giant whose first question might be, 'How are the Tigers doing?' "

BIOGRAPHICAL/CRITICAL SOURCES:

BOOKS

Bestsellers 89, Issue 2, Gale, 1989.
Contemporary Literary Criticism, Volume 50, Gale, 1988.
Dictionary of Biography Yearbook, 1987, Gale, 1988.

PERIODICALS

Antioch Review, spring, 1972, winter, 1978.
Chicago Sun Times, May 15, 1987.
Contemporary Literature, winter, 1969.
Detroit Free Press, May 14, 1987.
Globe and Mail (Toronto), December 26, 1987.
Guardian, October 30, 1959.
Hudson Review, spring, 1968.
Los Angeles Times, May 16, 1987.
Los Angeles Times Book Review, November 14, 1982, February 14, 1988.
Maclean's, December 21, 1987.
Nation, October 17, 1959, November 13, 1967, June 23, 1969, June 19, 1972, November 20, 1982, February 13, 1988.
New Republic, June 3, 1972, February 15, 1988.
Newsweek, September 27, 1982.
New Yorker, December 12, 1959, March 21, 1988.
New York Review of Books, August 26, 1965, October 18, 1973, September 19, 1974, October 13, 1977, February 18, 1988.
New York Times, October 25, 1959, January 1, 1968, October 25, 1969, November 25, 1969, May 17, 1972, December 15, 1975, June 1, 1977, September 21, 1982, May 14, 1987.
New York Times Book Review, December 10, 1967, January 21, 1968, May 14, 1972, June 19, 1977, April 19, 1981, February 21, 1988.
San Francisco Chronicle, November 1, 1959.
Saturday Review, October 24, 1959, May 24, 1969, March 28, 1970, May 13, 1972.
Sewanee Review, winter, 1969.
South Atlantic Quarterly, winter, 1968, winter, 1973, summer, 1978.
Spectator, November 13, 1959, February 12, 1977, October 23, 1982.
Time, January 4, 1988.
Times (London), November 20, 1959, January 5, 1967, July 25, 1968, March 17, 1972, February 18, 1977, October 8, 1987.
Times Literary Supplement, December 30, 1965, July 25, 1968, April 2, 1970, March 17, 1972, October 26, 1973, January 24, 1975, December 17, 1982, March 23, 1984, November 14, 1986, October 2-8, 1987.
Tribune Books (Chicago), February 7, 1988.
Virginia Quarterly Review, spring, 1968.
Washington Post Book World, May 21, 1972, March 29, 1981, October 31, 1982, October 30, 1983, January 24, 1988, March 26, 1989.
World Literature Today, winter, 1979, summer, 1983.

OBITUARIES:

PERIODICALS

Chicago Sun Times, May 15, 1987.
Cincinnati Post, May 14, 1987.
Detroit Free Press, May 14, 1987.
International Herald Tribune, May 16-17, 1987.
Long Island Newsday, May 15, 1987.
Los Angeles Times, May 16, 1987.
Newsweek, May 25, 1987.
New York Times, May 14, 1987.
Time, May 25, 1987.

Times (London), May 15, 1987.

*   *   *

EL-SHABAZZ, El-Hajj Malik
See LITTLE, Malcolm

*   *   *

ELYTIS, Odysseus 1911-

PERSONAL: Original name, Odysseus Alepoudelis; born November 2, 1911, in Heraklion, Crete, Greece. *Education:* Attended University of Athens, 1930-35, and Sorbonne, University of Paris, 1948-52.

ADDRESSES: Home—23 Skoufa St., Athens, Greece.

CAREER: Writer. Hellenic National Broadcasting Institution, Athens, Greece, broadcasting and program director, 1945-46 and 1953-54; art and literary critic for *Kathimerini* (newspaper) in Greece, 1946-48. Adviser to Art Theatre, 1955-56, and to Greek National Theatre, 1965-68; represented Greece at Second International Gathering of Modern Painters, in Geneva, Switzerland, 1948, and at Congress of International Association of Art Critics, in Paris, France, 1949; president of governing board of Greek Ballet, 1956-58. *Military service:* First Army Corps, 1940-41; served in Albania; became second lieutenant.

MEMBER: International Union of Art Critics, Societe Europeenne de Culture.

AWARDS, HONORS: National Poetry Prize and National Book Award, both 1960, both for *To axion esti;* Order of the Phoenix, 1965; Nobel Prize for literature, 1979; Benson Silver Medal, c. 1982; honorary degrees.

WRITINGS:

POETRY IN ENGLISH TRANSLATION

To axion esti (title means "Worthy It Is"), Ikaros, 1959, translation by Edmund Keeley and George Savidis published as *The Axion Esti of Odysseus Elytis,* University of Pittsburgh Press, 1974.
O ilios o iliatoras, Ikaros, 1971, translation by Kimon Friar published as *The Sovereign Sun: Selected Poems,* Temple University Press, 1974.
What I Love: Selected Poems of Odysseus Elytis, translated by Olga Broumas, Copper Canyon, 1978.
Maria Nefeli: Skiniko piima (title means "Maria the Cloud: Dramatic Poem"), [Athens, Greece], 1978, 3rd edition published as *Maria Nefeli,* 1979, translation by Athan Anagnostopoulos published as *Maria Nephele,* Houghton, 1981.

Work represented in anthologies, including *Six Poets of Modern Greece,* edited and translated by Edmund Keeley and Philip Sherrard, Knopf, 1961; and *Modern Greek Poetry: From Cavafis to Elytis,* edited by Kimon Friar, Simon & Schuster, 1973.

OTHER

Prosanatolizmi (title means "Orientations"), first published in *Makedhonikes Imeres,* 1936, published under same title, Pirsos, 1939.
Ilios o protos, mazi me tis parallayies pano se mian ahtidha (title means "Sun the First, Together With Variations on a Sunbeam"), O Glaros, 1943.
Iroiko kai penthimo asma ghia ton hameno anthypolohagho tis Alvanias (title means "A Heroic and Elegiac Song of the

Lost Second Lieutenant of the Albanian Campaign"), first published in *Tetradhio,* August-September, 1945, published under same title, Ikaros, 1962.

"I kalosini stis likopories" (title means "Kindness in the Wolf-passes"), published in *Tetradhio,* December, 1946.

Hexe kai mia typheis gia ton ourano (title means "Six and One Regrets for the Sky"), Ikaros, 1960.

"Alvaniadha. Piima yia dhio phones. Meros proto." (title means "Albaniad. Poems for Two Voices. First Part."), published in *Panspoudhastiki,* December 25, 1962.

Ho helios ho protos, Ikaros, 1963.

To fotodhendro ke dhekati tetarti omorfia (title means "The Light Tree and the Fourteenth Beauty"), Ikaros, 1971.

Thanatos ke anastasis tou Konstandinou Paleologhou (title means "Death and Resurrection of Constandinos Paleologhos"), Duo d'Art, 1971.

Ta ro tou erota (title means "The Ro of Eros"), Asterias, 1972.

To monograma (title means "The Monogram"), first published in *L'Oiseau,* 1971, published under same title, Ikaros, 1972.

Ho zographos Theophilos (art criticism, title means "The Painter Theophilos"), Asterias, 1973.

O fillomandis (title means "The Leaf Diviner"), Asterias, 1973.

Anihta hartia (essays, title means "Open Book"), Asterias, 1974.

Ta eterothali (title means "The Stepchildren"), Ikaros, 1974.

I mayia tou papadhiamandhi (essays), Ermias, 1978.

Also author of works with titles that mean "Journal of an Unforeseen April," Ipsilon, 1984, and "The Little Navigator," Ikaros, 1985. Translator of works with titles that mean "Saphfo" (poems by Saphfo), Ikaros, 1984, and "The Apocalypse of John" (from the Bible), Ipsilon, 1985.

SIDELIGHTS: Odysseus Elytis was relatively unknown outside his native Greece when he was awarded the Nobel Prize for literature in 1979. Although the Swedish Academy of Letters has in recent years bestowed the honor upon other previously little-known writers—notably Eugenio Montale, Vicente Aleixandre, and Harry Martison—their choice of Elytis came as a surprise nonetheless. The academy declared in its presentation that his poetry "depicts with sensual strength and intellectual clear-sightedness modem man's struggle for freedom and creativeness. . . . [In] its combination of fresh, sensuous flexibility and strictly disciplined implacability in the face of all compulsion, Elytis' poetry gives shape to its distinctiveness, which is not only very personal but also represents the traditions of the Greek people."

To be a Greek and a part of its twenty-five-century-old literary tradition is to Elytis a matter of great pride. His words upon acceptance of the Nobel Prize give evidence of this deep regard for his people and country: "I would like to believe that with this year's decision, the Swedish Academy wants to honor in me Greek poetry in its entirety. I would like to think it also wants to draw the attention of the world to a tradition that has gone on since the time of Homer, in the embrace of Western civilization."

Elytis was born Odysseus Alepoudelis in the city of Heraklion on the island of Crete. To avoid any association to his wealthy family of soap manufacturers, he later changed his surname to reflect those things he most treasured. Frank J. Prial of the *New York Times* explained that the poet's pseudonymous name is actually "a composite made up of elements of Ellas, the Greek word for Greece; elpidha, the word for hope; eleftheria, the word for freedom, and Eleni, the name of a figure that, in Greek mythology, personifies beauty and sensuality."

Elytis first became interested in poetry around the age of seventeen. At the same time he discovered surrealism, a school of thought just emerging in France. He soon became absorbed in the literature and teachings of the surrealists and worked to incorporate aspects of this new school into the centuries-old Greek literary tradition. Elytis has since explained the motivations behind his embracing of the French ideals: "Many facets of surrealism I cannot accept, such as its paradoxical side, its championing of automatic writing; but after all, it was the only school of poetry—and, I believe, the last in Europe—which aimed at spiritual health and reacted against the rationalist currents which had filled most Western minds. Since surrealism had destroyed this rationalism like a hurricane, it had cleared the ground in front of us enabling us to link ourselves physiologically with our soil and to regard Greek reality without the prejudices that have reigned since the Renaissance."

Thus, Elytis adapted only selected principles of surrealism to his Greek reality. Free association of ideas, a concept he often made use of, allowed him to portray objects in their "reality" but also in their "surreality." This is shown in various poems, as when a young girl is transformed into a fruit, a landscape becomes a human body, and the mood of a morning takes on the form of a tree. "I have always been preoccupied with finding the analogies between nature and language in the realm of imagination, a realm to which surrealists also gave much importance, and rightly so," claims Elytis. "Everything depends on imagination, that is, on the way a poet sees the same phenomenon as you do, yet differently from you."

Prosanatolizmi ("Orientations"), published in 1936, was Elytis's first volume of poetry. Filled with images of light and purity, the work earned for its author the title of the "sun-drinking poet." Edmund Keeley, a frequent translator of Elytis's work, observed that these "first poems offered a surrealism that had a distinctly personal tone and a specific local habitation. The tone was lyrical, humorous, fanciful, everything that is young." In a review of a later work, *The Sovereign Sun,* a writer for the *Virginia Quarterly Review* echoed Keeley's eloquent praise: "An intuitive poet, who rejects pessimism and engages in his surrealistic images the harsh realities of life, Elytis is a voice of hope and naked vigor. There is light and warmth, an awakening to self, body, and spirit, in Elytis."

The poet, however, bridles at such descriptions of his work. He has suggested that "my theory of analogies may account in part for my having been frequently called a poet of joy and optimism. This is fundamentally wrong. I believe that poetry on a certain level of accomplishment is neither optimistic nor pessimistic. It represents rather a third state of the spirit where opposites cease to exist. There are no more opposites beyond a certain level of elevation. Such poetry is like nature itself, which is neither good nor bad, beautiful nor ugly; it simply *is.* Such poetry is no longer subject to habitual everyday distinctions."

With the advent of the second world war Elytis interrupted his literary activities to fight with the First Army Corps in Albania against the fascists of Benito Mussolini. His impressions of this brutal period of his life were later recorded in the long poem *Iroiko kai penthimo asma ghia ton maneno anthypolohagho tis Alvanias* ("A Heroic and Elegiac Song of the Lost Second Lieutenant of the Albanian Campaign"). Regarded as one of the most touchingly human and poignant works inspired by the war, the poem has since become one of the writer's best-loved works.

Elytis's next work, *To axion esti* ("Worthy It Is"), came after a period of more than ten years of silence. Widely held to be his *chef d'oeuvre,* it is a poetic cycle of alternating prose and verse patterned after the ancient Byzantine liturgy. As in his other writings, Elytis depicts the Greek reality through an intensely personal tone. Keeley, the translator of the volume into English, suggested that *To axion esti* "can perhaps be taken best as a kind of spiritual autobiography that attempts to dramatize the national and philosophical extensions of the poet's personal sensibility. Elytis's strategy in this work . . . is to present an image of the contemporary Greek consciousness through the developing of a persona that is at once the poet himself and the voice of his country."

After the overwhelming success of *To axion esti,* questions were raised regarding what new direction Elytis would pursue and whether it would be possible to surpass his masterpiece. When *Maria Nefeli* was first published in 1978, it met with a curious yet hesitant public. M. Byron Raizis related in *World Literature Today* that "some academicians and critics of the older generations still [wanted] to cling to the concept of the 'sun-drinking' Elytis of the Aegean spume and breeze and of the monumental *Axion Esti,* so they [approached] *Maria Nefeli* with cautious hesitation as an experimental and not-so-attractive creation of rather ephemeral value."

The reason behind the uncertainty many Elytis devotees felt toward this new work stemmed from its radically different presentation. Whereas his earlier poems dealt with the almost timeless expression of the Greek reality, "rooted in my own experience, yet . . . not directly [transcribing] actual events," he once stated, *Maria Nefeli* is based on a young woman he actually met. Different from the women who graced his early work, the woman in Elytis's poem has changed to reflect the troubled times in which she lives. "This Maria then is the newest manifestation of the eternal female," noted Raizis, "the most recent mutation of the female principle which, in the form of Maria, Helen and other more traditional figures, had haunted the quasi-idyllic and erotic poems of [Elytis's youth]." Raizis explained further that Maria is the "attractive, liberated, restless or even blase representative of today's young woman. . . . This urban Nefeli is the offspring, not the sibling, of the women of Elytis's youth. Her setting is the polluted city, not the open country and its islands of purity and fresh air."

The poem consists of the juxtaposed statements of Maria Nefeli, who represents the ideals of today's emerging woman, and Antifonitis, or the Responder, who stands for more traditional views. Through Maria, the Responder is confronted with issues which, though he would like to ignore them, he is forced to come to terms with. Rather than flat, lifeless characters who expound stale and stereotyped maxims, however, "both are sophisticated and complex urbanites who express themselves in a wide range of styles, moods, idioms and stanzaic forms," maintained Raizis.

Despite the initial reservations voiced by some critics, *Maria Nefeli* has come to be regarded as the summa of Elytis's later writings. Gini Politi, for example, announced: "I believe that *Maria Nefeli* is one of the most significant poems of our times, and the response to the agony it includes *is written;* this way it saves for the time being the language of poetry and of humaneness." Kostas Stamatiou, moreover, expressed a common reaction to the work: "After the surprise of a first reading, gradually the careful student discovers beneath the surface the constants of the great poet: faith in surrealism, fundamental humanism, passages of pure lyricism."

In an interview with Ivar Ivask for *Books Abroad,* Elytis summarized his life's work: "I consider poetry a source of innocence full of revolutionary forces. It is my mission to direct these forces against a world my conscience cannot accept, precisely so as to bring that world through continual metamorphoses more in harmony with my dreams. I am referring here to a contemporary kind of magic whose mechanism leads to the discovery of our true reality. It is for this reason that I believe, to the point of idealism, that I am moving in a direction which has never been attempted until now. In the hope of obtaining a freedom from all constraint and the justice which could be identified with absolute light, I am an idolater who, without wanting to do so, arrives at Christian sainthood."

BIOGRAPHICAL/CRITICAL SOURCES:

BOOKS

Contemporary Literary Criticism, Gale, Volume 15, 1980, Volume 49, 1988.
Odysseus Elytis: Analogies of Light, University of Oklahoma Press, 1980.

PERIODICALS

Books Abroad, spring, 1971, autumn, 1975.
Chicago Tribune, October 19, 1979.
Hudson Review, winter, 1975-76.
New York Times, October 19, 1979.
New York Times Book Review, February 7, 1982.
Publishers Weekly, October 29, 1979.
Times Literary Supplement, October 9, 1981.
Virginia Quarterly Review, spring, 1975.
Washington Post, October 19, 1979.
World Literature Today, spring, 1980.

*   *   *

EMECHETA, (Florence Onye) Buchi 1944-

PERSONAL: Born July 21, 1944, in Yaba, Lagos, Nigeria; daughter of Jeremy Nwabudike (a railway worker and molder) and Alice Ogbanje (Okwuekwu) Emecheta; married Sylvester Onwordi, 1960 (separated, 1966); children: Florence, Sylvester, Jake, Christy, Alice. *Education:* University of London, B.Sc. (with honors), 1972. *Religion:* Anglican. *Avocational interests:* Gardening, attending the theatre, listening to music, reading.

ADDRESSES: Home—7 Briston Grove, Crouch End, London N8 9EX, England.

CAREER: British Museum, London, England, library officer, 1965-69; Inner London Education Authority, London, youth worker and sociologist, 1969-76; community worker, Camden, NJ, 1976-78. Writer and lecturer, 1972—. Visiting professor at several universities throughout the United States, including Pennsylvania State University, University of California, Los Angeles, and University of Illinois at Urbana-Champaign, 1979; senior resident fellow and visiting professor of English, University of Calabar, Nigeria, 1980-81; lecturer, Yale University, 1982, London University, 1982—; fellow, London University, 1986. Proprietor, Ogwugwu Afor Publishing Company, 1982-83. Member of Home Secretary's Advisory Council on Race, 1979—, and of Arts Council of Great Britain, 1982-83.

AWARDS, HONORS: Jock Campbell Award for literature by new or unregarded talent from Africa or the Caribbean, *New Statesman,* 1978; selected as the Best Black British Writer, 1978, and one of the Best British Young Writers, 1983.

WRITINGS:

In the Ditch, Barrie & Jenkins, 1972.
Second-Class Citizen (novel), Allison & Busby, 1974, Braziller, 1975.

The Bride Price: A Novel (paperback published as *The Bride Price: Young Ibo Girl's Love; Conflict of Family and Tradition*), Braziller, 1976.

The Slave Girl: A Novel, Braziller, 1977.

The Joys of Motherhood: A Novel, Braziller, 1979.

Destination Biafra: A Novel, Schocken, 1982.

Naira Power (novelette directed principally to Nigerian readers), Macmillan (London), 1982.

Double Yoke (novel), Schocken, 1982.

The Rape of Shavi (novel), Ogwugwu Afor, 1983, Braziller, 1985.

Adah's Story: A Novel, Allison & Busby, 1983.

Head above Water (autobiography), Ogwugwu Afor, 1984, Collins, 1986.

A Kind of Marriage (novelette), Macmillan, 1987.

The Family (novel), Braziller, 1990.

Gwendolen (novel), Collins, 1990.

JUVENILE

Titch the Cat (based on story by daughter, Alice Emecheta), Allison & Busby, 1979.

Nowhere to Play (based on story by daughter, Christy Emecheta), Schocken, 1980.

The Moonlight Bride, Oxford University Press in association with University Press, 1981.

The Wrestling Match, Oxford University Press in association with University Press, 1981, Braziller, 1983.

Family Bargain (publication for schools), British Broadcasting Corp., 1987.

OTHER

(Author of introduction and commentary) Maggie Murray, *Our Own Freedom* (book of photographs), Sheba Feminist (London), 1981.

A Kind of Marriage (teleplay; produced by BBC-TV), Macmillan (London), 1987.

Also author of teleplays "Tanya, a Black Woman," produced by BBC-TV, and "The Juju Landlord." Contributor to journals, including *New Statesman, Times Literary Supplement,* and *Guardian.*

SIDELIGHTS: Although Buchi Emecheta has resided in London since 1962, she is "Nigeria's best-known female writer," comments John Updike in the *New Yorker.* "Indeed, few writers of her sex . . . have arisen in any part of tropical Africa." Emecheta enjoys much popularity in Great Britain, and she has gathered an appreciative audience on this side of the Atlantic as well. Although Emecheta has written children's books and teleplays, she is best known for her historical novels set in Nigeria, both before and after independence. Concerned with the clash of cultures and the impact of Western values upon agrarian traditions and customs, Emecheta's work is strongly autobiographical; and, as Updike observes, much of it is especially concerned with "the situation of women in a society where their role, though crucial, was firmly subordinate and where the forces of potential liberation have arrived with bewildering speed."

Born to Ibo parents in Yaba, a small village near Lagos, Nigeria, Emecheta indicates that the Ibos "don't want you to lose contact with your culture," writes Rosemary Bray in the *Voice Literary Supplement.* Bray explains that the oldest woman in the house plays an important role in that she is the "big mother" to the entire family. In Emecheta's family, her father's sister assumed this role, says Bray: " 'She was very old and almost blind,' Buchi recalls, 'And she would gather the young children around her after dinner and tell stories to us.' " The stories the children heard

were about their origins and ancestors; and, according to Bray, Emecheta recalls: "I thought to myself 'No life could be more important than this.' So when people asked me what I wanted to do when I grew up I told them I wanted to be a storyteller—which is what I'm doing now."

Orphaned as a young child, Emecheta lived with foster parents who mistreated her. She attended a missionary high school for girls on a scholarship until she was sixteen, and then wed a man to whom she had been betrothed since the age of eleven. A mother at seventeen, she had two sons and three daughters by the time she was twenty-two. After the birth of her second child, Emecheta followed her husband to London, where she endured poor living conditions, including one-room apartments without heat or hot water, to help finance his education. "The culture shock of London was great," notes Bray, "but even more distressing was her husband's physical abuse and his constant resistance to her attempts at independence." The marriage ended when he read and then burned the manuscript of her first book. Supporting herself and five children on public assistance and by scrubbing floors, Emecheta continued to write in the mornings before her children arose, and also managed to earn an honors degree in sociology. *In the Ditch,* her first book, originally appeared as a series of columns in the *New Statesman.* Written in the form of a diary, it "is based on her own failed marriage and her experiences on the dole in London trying to rear alone her many children," state Charlotte and David Bruner in *World Literature Today.* Called a "sad, sonorous, occasionally hilarious . . . extraordinary first novel," by Adrianne Blue of the *Washington Post Book World,* it details her impoverished existence in a foreign land, as well as her experience with racism, and "illuminates the similarities and differences between cultures and attitudes," remarks a *Times Literary Supplement* contributor, who thinks it merits "special attention."

Similarly autobiographical, Emecheta's second novel, *Second-Class Citizen,* "recounts her early marriage years, when she was trying to support her student-husband—a man indifferent to his own studies and later indifferent to her job searches, her childbearing, and her resistance to poverty," observe the Bruners. The novel is about a young, resolute and resourceful Nigerian girl who, despite traditional tribal domination of females, manages to continue her own education; she marries a student and follows him to London, where he becomes abusive toward her. "Emecheta said people find it hard to believe that she has not exaggerated the truth in this autobiographical novel," reports Nancy Topping Bazin in *Black Scholar.* "The grimness of what is described does indeed make it painful to read." Called a "brave and angry book" by Marigold Johnson in the *Times Literary Supplement,* Emecheta's story, however, "is not accompanied by a misanthropic whine," notes Martin Levin in the *New York Times Book Review.* Alice Walker, who thinks it is "one of the most informative books about contemporary African life" that she has read, observes in *Ms.* that "it raises fundamental questions about how creative and prosaic life is to be lived and to what purpose."

"Emecheta's women do not simply lie down and die," observes Bray. "Always there is resistance, a challenge to fate, a need to renegotiate the terms of the uneasy peace that exists between them and accepted traditions." Bray adds that "Emecheta's women know, too, that between the rock of African traditions and the hard place of encroaching Western values, it is the women who will be caught." Concerned with the clash of cultures, in *The Bride Price: A Novel,* Emecheta tells the story of a young Nigerian girl "whose life is complicated by traditional attitudes toward women," writes Richard Cima in *Library Journal.* The young girl's father dies when she is thirteen; and, with her brother and mother, she becomes the property of her father's ambitious brother. She is permitted to remain in school only because it will increase her value as a potential wife. However, she falls in love with her teacher, a descendant of slaves; and because of familial objections, they elope, thereby depriving her uncle of the "bride price." When she dies in childbirth, she fulfills the superstition that a woman would not survive the birth of her first child if her bride price had not been paid; and Susannah Clapp maintains in the *Times Literary Supplement,* that the quality of the novel "depends less on plot or characterization than on the information conveyed about a set of customs and the ideas which underlay them." Calling it "a captivating Nigerian novel lovingly but unsentimentally written, about the survival of ancient marriage customs in modern Nigeria," Valerie Cunningham adds in *New Statesman* that this book "proves Buchi Emecheta to be a considerable writer."

Emecheta's *Slave Girl: A Novel* is about "a poor, gently raised Ibo girl who is sold into slavery to a rich African marketwoman by a feckless brother at the turn of the century," writes a *New Yorker* contributor. Educated by missionaries, she joins the new church where she meets the man she eventually marries. In *Library Journal,* Cima thinks that the book provides an "interesting picture of Christianity's impact on traditional Ibo society." Perceiving parallels between marriage and slavery, Emecheta explores the issue of "freedom within marriage in a society where slavery is supposed to have been abolished," writes Cunningham in the *New Statesman,* adding that the book indicts both "pagan and Christian inhumanity to women." And although a contributor to *World Literature Today* suggests that the "historical and anthropological background" in the novel tends to destroy its "emotional complex," another contributor to the same journal believes that the sociological detail has been "unobtrusively woven into" it and that *The Slave Girl* represents Emecheta's "most accomplished work so far. It is coherent, compact and convincing."

"Emecheta's voice has been welcomed by many as helping to redress the somewhat one-sided picture of African women that has been delineated by male writers," according to *A New Reader's Guide to African Literature.* Writing in *African Literature Today,* Eustace Palmer indicates that "the African novel has until recently been remarkable for the absense of what might be called the feminine point of view." Because of the relatively few female African novelists, "the presentation of women in the African novel has been left almost entirely to male voices . . . and their interest in African womanhood . . . has had to take second place to numerous other concerns," continues Palmer. "These male novelists, who have presented the African woman largely within the traditional milieu, have generally communicated a picture of a male-dominated and male-oriented society, and the satisfaction of the women with this state of things has been . . . completely taken for granted." Palmer adds that the emergence of Emecheta and other "accomplished female African novelists . . . seriously challenges all these cosy assumptions. The picture of the cheerful contented female complacently accepting her lot is replaced by that of a woman who is powerfully aware of the unfairness of the system and who longs to be fulfilled in her self, to be a full human being, not merely somebody else's appendage." For instance, Palmer notes that *The Joys of Motherhood: A Novel* "presents essentially the same picture of traditional society . . . but the difference lies in the prominence in Emecheta's novel of the female point of view registering its disgust at male chauvinism and its dissatisfaction with what it considers an unfair and oppressive system."

The Joys of Motherhood is about a woman "who marries but is sent home in disgrace because she fails to bear a child quickly enough," writes Bazin. "She then is sent to the city by her father to marry a man she has never seen. She is horrified when she meets this second husband because she finds him ugly, but she sees no alternative to staying with him. Poverty and repeated pregnancies wear her down; the pressure to bear male children forces her to bear child after child since the girls she has do not count." Palmer observes that "clearly, the man is the standard and the point of reference in this society. It is significant that the chorus of countrymen say, not that a woman without a child is a failed woman, but that a woman without a child *for her husband* is a failed woman." Bazin observes that in Emecheta's novels, "a woman must accept the double standard of sexual freedom: it permits polygamy and infidelity for both Christian and non-Christian men but only monogamy for women. These books reveal the extent to which the African woman's oppression is engrained in the African mores."

Acknowledging that "the issue of polygamy in Africa remains a controversial one," Palmer states that what Emecheta stresses in *The Joys of Motherhood* is "the resulting dominance, especially sexual, of the male, and the relegation of the female into subservience, domesticity and motherhood." Nonetheless, despite Emecheta's "angry glare," says Palmer, one can "glean from the novel the economic and social reasons that must have given rise to polygamy. . . . But the author concentrates on the misery and deprivation polygamy can bring." Palmer praises Emecheta's insightful psychological probing of her characters' thoughts: "Scarcely any other African novelist has succeeded in probing the female mind and displaying the female personality with such precision." Blue likewise suggests that Emecheta "tells this story in a plain style, denuding it of exoticism, displaying an impressive, embracing compassion." Calling it a "graceful, touching, ironically titled tale that bears a plain feminist message," Updike adds that "in this compassionate but slightly distanced and stylized story of a life that comes to seem wasted, [Emecheta] sings a dirge for more than African pieties. The lives within 'The Joys of Motherhood' might be, transposed into a different cultural key, those of our own rural ancestors."

Emecheta's "works reveal a great deal about the lives of African women and about the development of feminist perspectives," observes Bazin, explaining that one moves beyond an initial perspective of "personal experience," to perceive "social or communal" oppression. This second perspective "demands an analysis of the causes of oppression within the social mores and the patriarchal power structure," adds Bazin. Finding both perspectives in Emecheta's work, Bazin thinks that through her descriptions of "what it is like to be female in patriarchal African cultures," the author provides a voice for "millions of black African women." Although her feminist perspective is anchored in her own personal life, says Bazin, Emecheta "grew to understand how son preference, bride price, polygamy, menstrual taboos, . . . wife beating, early marriages, early and unlimited pregnancies, arranged marriages, and male dominance in the home functioned to keep women powerless." The Bruners write that "obviously Emecheta is concerned about the plight of women, today and yesterday, in both technological and traditional societies, though she rejects a feminist label." Emecheta told the Bruners: "The main themes of my novels are African society and family; the historical, social, and political life in Africa as seen by a woman through events. I always try to show that the African male is oppressed and he too oppresses the African women. . . . I have not committed myself to the cause of African women only. I write about Africa as a whole."

Emecheta's *Destination Biafra: A Novel* is a story of the "history of Nigeria from the eve of independence to the collapse of the Biafran secessionist movement," writes Robert L. Berner in *World Literature Today.* The novel has generated a mixed critical response, though. In the *Times Literary Supplement,* Chinweizu feels that it "does not convey the feel of the experience that was Biafra. All it does is leave one wondering why it falls so devastatingly below the quality of Buchi Emecheta's previous works." Noting, however, that Emecheta's publisher reduced the manuscript by half, Berner suggests that "this may account for what often seems a rather elliptical narrative and for the frequently clumsy prose which too often blunts the novel's satiric edge." Finding the novel "different from any of her others . . . larger and more substantive," the Bruners state: "Here she presents neither the life story of a single character nor the delineation of one facet of a culture but the whole perplexing canvas of people from diverse ethnic groups, belief systems, levels of society all caught in a disastrous civil war." Moreover, the Bruners feel that the "very objectivity of her reporting and her impartiality in recounting atrocities committed by all sides, military and civilian, have even greater impact because her motivation is not sadistic."

The Rape of Shavi represents somewhat of a departure in that "Emecheta attempts one of the most difficult of tasks: that of integrating the requirements of contemporary, realistic fiction with the narrative traditions of myth and folklore," writes Somtow Sucharitkul in the *Washington Post Book World.* Roy Kerridge describes the novel's plot in the *Times Literary Supplement:* "A plane crashes among strange tribespeople, white aviators are made welcome by the local king, they find precious stones, repair their plane and escape just as they are going to be forcibly married to native girls. The king's son and heir stows away and has adventures of his own in England." Called a "wise and haunting tale" by a *New Yorker* contributor, *The Rape of Shavi* "recounts the ruination of this small African society by voracious white interlopers," says Richard Eder in the *Los Angeles Times.* A few critics suggest that in *The Rape of Shavi,* Emecheta's masterful portrayal of her Shavian community is not matched by her depiction of the foreigners. Eder, for instance, calls it a "lopsided fable," and declares: "It is not that the Shavians are noble and the whites monstrous; that is what fables are for. It is that the Shavians are finely drawn and the Westerners very clumsily. It is a duet between a flute and a kitchen drain." However, Sucharitkul thinks that portraying the Shavians as "complex individuals" and the Westerners as "two dimensional, mythic types" presents a refreshing, seldom expressed, and "particularly welcome" point of view.

Although in the *New York Times* Michiko Kakutani calls *The Rape of Shavi* "an allegorical tale, filled with ponderous morals about the evils of imperialism and tired aphorisms about nature and civilization," Sucharitkul believes that "the central thesis of [the novel] is brilliantly, relentlessly argued, and Emecheta's characters and societies are depicted with a bittersweet, sometimes painful honesty." The critic also praises Emecheta's "persuasive" prose: "It is prose that appears unusually simple at first, for it is full of the kind of rhythms and sentence structures more often found in folk tales than in contemporary novels. Indeed, in electing to tell her multilayered and often very contemporary story within a highly mythic narrative framework, the author walks a fine line between the pitfalls of preciosity and pretentiousness. By and large, the tightrope act is a success."

"Emecheta has reaffirmed her dedication to be a full-time writer," say the Bruners. "Her culture and her education at first were obstacles to her literary inclination. She had to struggle against precedent, against reluctant publishers, and later against male-dominated audiences and readership." Her fiction is intensely autobiographical, drawing on the difficulties she has both witnessed and experienced as a woman, and most especially as a Nigerian woman. Indicating that in Nigeria, however, "Emecheta is a prophet without honor," Bray adds that "she is frustrated at not being able to reach women—the audience she desires most. She feels a sense of isolation as she attempts to stake out the middle ground between the old and the new." Remarking that "in her art as well as in her life, Buchi Emecheta offers another alternative," Bray quotes the author: "What I am trying to do is get our profession back. Women are born storytellers. We keep the history. We are the true conservatives—we conserve things and we never forget. What I do is not clever or unusual. It is what my aunt and my grandmother did, and their mothers before them."

BIOGRAPHICAL/CRITICAL SOURCES:

BOOKS

Contemporary Literary Criticism, Gale, Volume 14, 1980, Volume 28, 1984.

Zell, Hans M., and others, *A New Reader's Guide to African Literature,* 2nd revised and expanded edition, Holmes & Meier, 1983.

PERIODICALS

African Literature Today, Number 3, 1983.
Atlantic, May, 1976.
Black Scholar, November/December, 1985, March/April, 1986.
Library Journal, September 1, 1975, April 1, 1976, January 15, 1978, May 1, 1979.
Listener, July 19, 1979.
Los Angeles Times, October 16, 1983, March 6, 1985, January 16, 1990.
Ms., January, 1976, July, 1984, March, 1985.
New Statesman, June 25, 1976, October 14, 1977, June 2, 1978, April 27, 1979.
New Yorker, May 17, 1976, January 9, 1978, July 2, 1979, April 23, 1984, April 22, 1985.
New York Times, February 23, 1985, June 2, 1990.
New York Times Book Review, September 14, 1975, November 11, 1979, January 27, 1980, February 27, 1983, May 5, 1985, April 29, 1990.
Times Literary Supplement, August 11, 1972, January 31, 1975, June 11, 1976, February 26, 1982, February 3, 1984, February 27, 1987, April 20, 1990.
Voice Literary Supplement, June, 1982.
Washington Post Book World, May 13, 1979, April 12, 1981, September 5, 1982, September 25, 1983, March 30, 1985.
World Literature Today, spring, 1977, summer, 1977, spring, 1978, winter, 1979, spring, 1980, winter, 1983, autumn, 1984, winter, 1985.

*   *   *

EMPSON, William   1906-1984

PERSONAL: Born September 27, 1906, in Yokefleet, Howden, East Yorkshire, England; died April 15, 1984, in London, England; son of A. R. and Laura (Micklethwait) Empson; married Hester Henrietta Crouse, 1941; children: William Hendrick Mogador, Jacobus Arthur Calais. *Education:* Winchester College, 1920-25; Magdalen College, Cambridge, B.A., 1929, M.A., 1935.

ADDRESSES: Home—Studio House, 1 Hampstead Hill Gardens, London N.W. 3, England.

CAREER: Bunrika Daigaku, Tokyo, Japan, chair of English literature, 1931-34; Peking National University (then part of South-Western Combined Universities), Peking, China, professor of English literature, 1937-39; British Broadcasting Co., London, England, editor in monitoring department, 1940-41, Chinese editor, 1941-46; Peking National University, Peking, China, professor of English, 1947-52; Sheffield University, Sheffield, England, professor of English literature, 1953-1971, became professor emeritus. Visiting fellow, Kenyon College, Gambier, Ohio, summers, 1948, 1950, and 1954; visiting professor, University of Toronto, 1973-74, and Pennsylvania State University, University Park, 1974-75.

AWARDS, HONORS: Ingram Merrill Foundation Award for Literature, 1968; D.Litt., from University of East Anglia, Norwich, 1968, University of Bristol, 1971, and University of Sheffield, 1974; knighted, 1979.

WRITINGS:

Letter IV (poems), privately printed, 1929.
Seven Types of Ambiguity: A Study of its Effects on English Verse (criticism), Chatto & Windus, 1930, revised edition, 1947, Meridan, 1957.
Poems, privately printed, 1934, Chatto & Windus, 1935.
Some Versions of Pastoral, Chatto & Windus, 1935, New Directions, 1950, published as *English Pastoral Poetry,* Norton, 1938, reprinted, Books for Libraries, 1972.
(Editor and translator from technical into basic English) John Haldane, *Outlook of Science,* Routledge & Kegan Paul, 1935.
(Editor and translator from technical into basic English) Haldane, *Science and Well-Being,* Routledge & Kegan Paul, 1935.
(With George Garrett) *Shakespeare Survey,* Brendin Publishing Co., 1937.
The Gathering Storm (poems), Faber, 1940.
Collected Poems of William Empson, Harcourt, 1949, enlarged edition, 1961.
The Structure of Complex Words, New Directions, 1951, 3rd edition, Rowman, 1979.
(Contributor) Derek Hudson, *English Critical Essays: Twentieth Century, Second Series,* Oxford University Press, 1958.
Milton's God, Chatto & Windus, 1961, New Directions, 1962, enlarged edition, Cambridge University Press, 1981.
(Author of introduction) John R. Harrison, *The Reactionaries: Yeats, Lewis, Pound, Eliot, Lawrence,* Schocken, 1967.
(Editor) *Shakespeare's Poems,* New American Library, 1969.
(Editor with David Pirie) *Coleridge's Verse: A Selection,* Faber, 1972, Schocken, 1973.
Using Biography (criticism), Harvard University Press, 1984.
Essays on William Shakespeare, edited by Pirie, Cambridge University Press, 1986.
The Royal Beasts and Other Works, edited by John Haffenden, Chatto & Windus, 1986.
Argufying, edited by Haffenden, Chatto & Windus, 1988.
Faustus and the Censor, edited by John Henry Jones, 1988.

SIDELIGHTS: Sir William Empson, professor of English literature at Sheffield University for nearly twenty years, "revolutionized our ways of reading a poem," notes a London *Times* writer. The school of literary criticism known as New Criticism gained important support from Empson's *Seven Types of Ambiguity: A Study of Its Effects on English Verse.* This work, together with his other published essays, has become "part of the furniture of any good English or American critic's mind," G. S. Fraser remarks in *Great Writers of the English Language: Poets.* Empson will also be remembered for "the peculiar, utterly original and startling tenor of his works," says the *Times* writer. Radically different from the romantic poetry produced by Dylan Thomas and Empson's other peers, Empson's poetry employed a more objective, nonsentimental language that reflected his competence as a mathematician and his reverence for science. The *Times* article relates that his first collection, *Poems,* "made an immediate deserved and explosive impact such as the literary scene in Britain knows only two or three times in a century."

John Gross of the *New York Times Book Review* relates, "An essentially positive critic, [Empson] had the gift of being able to show you qualities in a work you would never have seen without him, and the even more important gift of enlarging your imagination, encouraging you to go on looking for yourself." This new approach to poetry appreciation centered on the reader's close attention to the properties of poetic language opened up a new field of literary criticism—a remarkable accomplishment, considering that Empson did so without proposing to alter previous methods of criticism; neither did he revise the standards by which literature is traditionally judged, nor did he invent new ways to reclassify well-known works of literature, Hugh Kenner points out in *Gnomon: Essays on Contemporary Literature.* Empson's explanations of how meaning is carried in poetic language have made poetry accessible to hundreds of readers, Kenner observes.

Perhaps most helpful to erstwhile readers of poetry is Empson's first book-length work of criticism, *Seven Types of Ambiguity.* In general usage, a word or reference is deemed ambiguous if it has more than one possible meaning. In *Seven Types,* Empson wrote, "I propose to use the word in an extended sense, and shall think relevant to my subject any verbal nuance, however slight, which gives room for alternative reactions to the same piece of language." Empson's seven types are briefly defined in the table of contents: "First-type ambiguities arise when a detail is effective in several ways at once. . . . In second-type ambiguities two or more alternative meanings are fully resolved into one. . . . The condition for the third type ambiguity is that two apparently unconnected meanings are given simultaneously. . . . In the fourth type the alternative meanings combine to make clear a complicated state of mind in the author. . . . The fifth type is a fortunate confusion, as when the author is discovering his idea in the act of writing . . . or not holding it in mind all at once. . . . In the sixth type what is said is contradictory or irrelevant and the reader is forced to invent interpretations. . . . The seventh type is that of full contradiction, marking a division in the author's mind."

Ambiguity impedes communication when it results from the writer's indecision, Empson wrote in *Seven Types:* "It is not to be respected in so far as it is due to weakness or thinness of thought, obscures the matter at hand unnecessarily . . . or when the interest of the passage is not focussed upon it, so that it is merely an opportunism in the handling of the material, if the reader will not understand the ideas which are being shuffled, and will be given a general impression of incoherence." However, the protean properties of words—their ability to carry multiple meanings in a variety of ways—are a major component of poetic language, and being aware of how this facet of language operates is one of the pleasures of poetry, said Empson. "*Seven Types* is primarily an exercise intended to help the reader who has already felt the pleasure understand the nature of his response," a *Contemporary Literary Critics* contributor suggests.

"Some of Empson's early critics felt that he had simply written himself a license to search for multiple meanings with no awareness of the controlling context in which the local ambiguity appears," reports the same contributor. On the contrary, Empson guides critics to consider "purpose, context and person" in addition to "the critical principles of the author and of the public he is writing for" when explicating meaning. *Hudson Review* contributor Roger Sale believes that the book has been too harshly judged in many reviews. He writes, "Most discussions have picked on its least interesting aspects, its use of the word 'ambiguity' and its ranging of the 'types' along a scale of 'advancing logical disorder.' But these matters are really minor. . . . The book, [Empson] says, is not philosophical but literary, and its aim is to examine lines Empson finds beautiful and haunting. . . . But in at least fifteen places Empson shows that the aim of analysis is not so much understanding lines as uncovering whole tracts of the mind, and the book is studded with the right things said about a poet or an historical period." In fact, concludes Robert M. Adams in the *New York Review of Books,* "Already certain passages of Empsonian exegesis . . . have attained classic status, so that the text can't be intelligently considered without them. . . . I think he had, though in lesser measure, Dr. Johnson's extraordinary gift for laying his finger on crucial literary moments; and that alone is likely to ensure him a measure of permanence."

Some Versions of Pastoral addresses the modern propensity to express nostalgia for idyllic world views that belong to the past. According to Empson, pastoral literature implied "a beautiful relation between rich and poor [and made] . . . simple people express strong feelings . . . in learned and fashionable language (so that you wrote about the best subject in the best way)." Empson maintains that contemporary expressions of the pastoral are for the most part pretenses: "in pastoral you take a limited life and pretend it is the full and normal one." Writing in *Modern Heroism: Essays on D. H. Lawrence, William Empson, and J. R. R. Tolkien,* Sale contends that by examining a series of leader/heroes from the sixteenth century forward, Empson means to say that the moieties that used to bind leaders to their people no longer exist—in Sales's words, "the people have become a mob and the hero painfully alienated"—and that, therefore, the role of hero or Christ-figure is not attainable.

Sale believes that *Some Versions of Pastoral* is Empson's best book, although it too has been misjudged as a literary work and misused as a critical tool. Sale notes that "in [this book] he can move from the work at hand to his vision with almost no shoving of the evidence, so even though his prose and organization may seem difficult on first reading, he turns with almost indescribable grace from the smallest particular to the largest generalization and then back to various middle grounds. When one becomes used to the book and begins to hear the massive chords of its orchestrations supporting even the most irrelevant aside, the effect is one only the greatest books can produce—it envelopes and controls such large areas of the imagination that for a while one is willing to admit it is the only book ever written. As a modern work of persuasion it is unrivaled."

Milton's God is "a diatribe against Christianity which Empson feels has had a monopoly on torture-worship, sexual repression and hypocrisy," the *Contemporary Literary Critics* essayist relates. Milton's God, Empson maintains, seems to want to set aside the cruelty of his absolute rule, and "has cut out of Christianity both the torture-horror and the sex-horror, and after that the monster seems almost decent." Questioning Milton's orthodoxy on these grounds, Empson presents Milton as a humanist—a view that raised a "furor" among the "entrenched Miltonic establishment," says Adams. It was, he says, the eccentric

professor's "last raid on the academic chicken coop" before his retirement from the University of Sheffield in 1971.

Empson's own humanism accounts in part for his open-minded approach to the topic of meaning in literature. Kenner notes: " 'The object of life, after all,' [Empson] tells us late in *Ambiguity,* 'is not to understand things, but to maintain one's defenses and equilibrium and live as well as one can; it is not only maiden aunts who are placed like this.' " In *Milton's God,* he declared his agreement with philosopher Jeremy Bentham "that the satisfaction of any impulse is in itself an elementary good, and that the practical ethical question is how to satisfy the greatest number." Empson's poetry and criticism are the natural extensions of his views. Empson offers "not a theory of literature or a single method of analysis but a model of how to read with pleasure and knowledge," notes *New Statesman* reviewer Jon Cook. In *Using Biography,* for example, he demonstrates how familiarity with an author's life helps the critic to empathize with the author, allowing the critic to apply corresponding personal experiences to see into an author's intentions. The resulting insights on Andrew Marvell and W. B. Yeats, says James Fenton in the London *Times,* owe more to Empson's speculations and free associations than to systematic analysis of biographical detail. According to Cook, Empson makes it clear that it is far worse to succumb to "the critical habit of pressing literary works into the service of authoritarian and repressive ideologies, all this, of course, under the comforting guise that to receive authority in this way does us good."

Although Empson is best known for his criticism, *Preliminary Essays* author John Wain writes: "It may well be that criticism will be read and remembered while poetry is forgotten, for criticism breeds fresh criticism more easily than poetry breeds fresh poetry; but in Empson's case it would be a pity if he were known simply as the 'ambiguity' man, and not as a poet." A. Alvarez writes in *Stewards of Excellence,* "The poetry of William Empson has been more used [as a model] than that of any other English poet of our time." As the upheavals of World War II threatened to render romanticism and pastoralism obsolete, poets were challenged to find language and forms equal to the age. "Empson's verse was read with an overwhelming sense of relief after the brash and embarrassed incoherence of wartime and post-war poetry," notes Alvarez, who elaborates, "there is something in his work which encourages other writers to use it for their own ends. It has, I think, an *essential* objectivity. . . . In the later poems what goes in as strong personal feeling comes out as something more general; whilst in the earlier work all the personal energy goes into a particularly impersonal business."

In addition, Empson's best verses "have a quality of mystery and incantation which runs quite counter to his professed rationalism," notes Robert Nye in the London *Times.* The poems, says a writer for the London *Times,* were perceived by some critics to be like "exercises: ingenious, resembling staggeringly clever crossword puzzles, abstruse, riddling—in a word, over-intellectual. But as Edwin Muir and other shrewder readers noted, their real keynote was passion. They represent, as Empson put it in one of the most famous of them, a style learned from a despair. The subject matter of the great ones . . . is the nature of sexual passion and the nature of political passion." Writers found in Empson's verse the balance between intense emotion and detachment that seemed appropriate to describe life in the contemporary world.

Alvarez believes that Empson's poetry depends on his control over a large range of ideas: "[Empson] is less interested in saying his own say than in the agility and skill and variety with which he juggles his ideas. So it is a personal poem only at a remove: the subject is impersonal; the involvement is all his effort to make as much as he can out of the subject, and in the accomplishment with which he relates his manifold themes so elegantly together. Empson's, in short, is a poetry of wit in the most traditional sense. . . . And, like most wit, the pleasure it gives is largely in the immaculate performance, which is a rare pleasure but a limited one."

In tracing the development of Empson's poetry, Alvarez says of the early poems: "In his sardonic way, Empson made his polish and inventiveness seem like a personal claim for sanity, as though he saw everything in a fourth and horrifying dimension but was too well-mannered to say so. Hence the wry despair and vigorous stylishness seemed not at all contradictory." He notes that "It is as a stylist of poetry and ideas that, I think, Empson is most important. He took over all [T. S.] Eliot's hints about what was most significant in the English tradition, and he put them into practice without any of the techniques Eliot had derived from the French and Italians. And so his poetry shows powerfully and with great purity the perennial vitality of the English tradition; and in showing this it also expresses the vitality and excitement of the extraordinarily creative moment when Empson began writing."

BIOGRAPHICAL/CRITICAL SOURCES:

BOOKS

Alvarez, A., *Stewards of Excellence,* Scribner, 1958.
Contemporary Literary Criticism, Gale, Volume 3, 1975, Volume 8, 1981, Volume 19, 1981, Volume 33, 1985, Volume 34, 1985.
Contemporary Literary Critics, St. James, 1977.
Crane, R. S., *Critics and Critics: Ancient and Modern,* University of Chicago Press, 1952.
Dictionary of Literary Biography, Volume 20: *British Poets, 1914-1945,* Gale, 1983.
Gill, Roma, editor, *William Empson: The Man and His Work,* Routledge & Kegan Paul, 1974.
Hamilton, Ian, editor, *The Modern Poet: Essays from "The Review",* MacDonald, 1968.
Hyman, Stanley Edgar, *The Armed Vision: A Study in the Methods of Modern Literary Criticism,* Knopf, 1948, revised edition, 1955.
Kenner, Hugh, *Gnomon: Essays in Contemporary Literature,* McDowell, 1958.
Makers of Modern Culture, Facts on File, 1981.
Norris, Christopher, *William Empson and the Philosophy of Literary Criticism,* Athlone Press, 1978.
Sale, Roger, *Modern Heroism: Essays on D. H. Lawrence, William Empson, and J. R. R. Tolkien,* University of California Press, 1973.
Untermeyer, Louis, *Lives of the Poets,* Simon & Schuster, 1959.
Vinson, James, editor, *Great Writers of the English Language: Poets,* St. Martins, 1979.
Wain, John, *Preliminary Essays,* Macmillan (London), 1957.
William Empson: The Man and His Work, Routledge & Kegan Paul, 1974.
Wills, J. H., *William Empson,* Columbia University Press, 1969.

PERIODICALS

Criticism, fall, 1966.
Hudson Review, spring, 1952, autumn, 1966.
Nation, June 16, 1962.
New Statesman, October 12, 1984.
New York Review of Books, April 11, 1985.

New York Times Book Review, May 20, 1984.
Observer, September 30, 1984.
Scrutiny, Volume 2, number 3, December, 1933.
Southern Review, autumn, 1938.
Time, April 18, 1949, August 10, 1962.
Times (London), October 25, 1984, February 8, 1985, November 13, 1986.
Times Literary Supplement, November 14, 1986, January 1, 1988, February 26, 1988.
Washington Post Book World, May 19, 1985.
Yale Review, June, 1962.

OBITUARIES:

PERIODICALS

Chicago Tribune, April 18, 1984.
Times (London), April 16, 1984, February 28, 1985.
Times Literary Supplement, November 14, 1986, January 1, 1988, February 26, 1988.
Washington Post, April 17, 1984.
Washington Post Book World, May 19, 1985.

—*Sketch by Marilyn K. Basel*

*   *   *

ENDO, Shusaku 1923-

PERSONAL: Born March 27, 1923, in Tokyo, Japan; son of Tsunehisa and Iku (Takei) Endo; married Junko Okada, September 3, 1955; children: Ryunosuke (son). *Education:* Keio University, Tokyo, B.A., 1949; Lyon University, Lyon, France, student in French literature, 1950-53. *Religion:* Roman Catholic.

ADDRESSES: c/o Japanese P.E.N. Club Room, 265 Syuwa Residential Hotel, 9-1-7 Akasaka Minato-ku, Tokyo, Japan.

MEMBER: International P.E.N. (president of Japanese Centre, 1969), Association of Japanese Writers (member of executive committee, 1966).

AWARDS, HONORS: Akutagawa prize (Japan), 1955, for *Shiroihito;* Tanizaki prize (Japan), 1967, and Gru de Oficial da Ordem do Infante dom Henrique (Portugal), 1968, both for *Chinmoku;* Sanct Silvestri, awarded by Pope Paul VI, 1970.

WRITINGS:

IN ENGLISH TRANSLATION

Umi to Dokuyaku (novel), Bungeishunju, 1958, translation by M. Gallagher published as *The Sea and Poison,* P. Owen, 1971, Taplinger, 1980.
Kazan (novel), [Japan], 1959, translation by Richard A. Schuchert published as *Volcano,* P. Owen, 1978, Taplinger, 1980.
Obaka-san, [Japan], 1959, translation by Francis Mathy published as *Wonderful Fool,* Harper, 1983.
Chinmoku (novel), Shinkosha, 1966, translation by William Johnston published as *Silence,* P. Owen, 1969, Taplinger, 1979.
Ougon no Ku (play), Shinkosha, 1969, translation by Mathy published as *The Golden Country,* Tuttle (Tokyo), 1970.
Iesu no shogai, [Japan], 1973, translation by Schuchert published as *A Life of Jesus,* Paulist Press, 1978.
Kuchibue o fuku toki (novel), [Japan], 1974, translation by Van C. Gessel published as *When I Whistle,* Taplinger, 1979.
Juichi no iro-garasu (short stories), [Japan], 1979, translation published as *Stained Glass Elegies,* Dodd, 1985.
Samauri (novel), [Japan], 1980, translation by Gessel published as *The Samauri,* Harper, 1982.
Scandal, translated by Gessel, Dodd, 1988.

Foreign Studies, translated by Mark Williams, P. Owen, 1989.

IN JAPANESE

Shiroihito (novel), Kodansha, 1955.
Seisho no Naka no Joseitachi (essays; title means "Women in the Bible"), Shinchosha, 1968.
Bara no Yakat (play), Shinchosha, 1969.
Yumoa shosetsu shu (short stories), Kodansha, 1974.
France no daigakusei (essays on travel in France), Kadokawashoten, 1974.
Seisho no naka no joseitachi (essays), Kodansha, 1975.
Kitsunegata tanukigata (short stories), Kodansha, 1976.
Watashi ga suteta onna, Kodansha, 1976.
Yukiaru kotoba (essays), Shinchosha, 1976.
Nihonjin wa Kirisuto kyo o shinjirareru ka, Shogakukan, 1977.
Kare no ikikata, Shinchosha, 1978.
Kirisuto no tanjo, Shinchosha, 1978.
Ningen no naka no X (essays), Chuokoronsha, 1978.
Rakuten taisho, Kodansha, 1978.
Ju to jujika (biography of Pedro Cassini), Shuokoronsha, 1979.
Marie Antoinette (fiction), Asahi shinbunsha, 1979.
Chichioya, Shinchosha, 1980.
Kekkonron, Shufunotomosha, 1980.
Sakka no nikki (diary excerpts), Toju-sha, 1980.
Endo Shusaku ni yoru Endo Shusaku, Seidosha, 1980.
Meiga Iesu junrei, Bungei Shunju, 1981.
Onna no issho (fiction), Asahi Shinbunsha, 1982.
Endo Shusaku to Knagaeru, PHP Kekyujo, 1982.
Fuyu no yasashisa, Bunka Shuppakyoku, 1982.

Also author of *Watakusi no Iesu,* 1976, *Usaba kagero nikki,* 1978, *Shinran,* 1979, *Tenshi,* 1980, *Ai to jinsei o meguru danso,* 1981, and *Okuku e no michi,* 1981. Author of essay collection with title meaning "Spring Comes Riding in on a Horse-drawn Carriage," 1989.

SIDELIGHTS: Of all leading modern Japanese novelists, Shusaku Endo is considered by many critics to be the one whose novels are easiest for Western readers to grasp. His Roman Catholic upbringing is often cited as the key to his accessibility, for it has given him a philosophical background shaped by Western traditions rather than those of the East. Christianity is a rarity in Japan, where two sects of Buddhism predominate. As Garry Wills explains in the *New York Review of Books,* "Christ is not only challenging but embarrassing [to the Japanese] because he has absolutely no 'face'. . . . He will let anyone spit on him. How can the Japanese ever honor such a disreputable figure?" While strongly committed to his adopted religion, Endo has often described the sense of alienation felt by a Christian in Japan. Most of his novels translated into English address the clash of Eastern and Western morals and philosophy, as well as illustrate the difficulty and unlikelihood of Christianity's establishment in Japan.

John Updike writes in the *New Yorker* that Endo's first novel in English translation, *Silence,* is "a remarkable work, a somber, delicate, and startlingly empathetic study of a young Portuguese missionary during the relentless persecution of the Japanese Christians in the early seventeenth century." The young missionary, Rodrigues, travels to Japan to investigate rumors that his former teacher, Ferreira, has not only converted to Buddhism, but is even participating in the persecution of Christians. Updike notes, "One can only marvel at the unobtrusive, persuasive effort of imagination that enables a modern Japanese to take up a viewpoint from which Japan is at the outer limit of the world."

Rodrigues is captured soon after his clandestine entry into Japan, and is handed over to the same jailer who effected Ferreira's conversion. Rodrigues is never physically harmed but is forced to watch the sufferings of native converts while repeatedly being told that his public denouncement of Christ is the only thing that will save them. At first he resists, anticipating a glorious martyrdom for himself, but eventually a vision of Christ convinces him of the selfishness of this goal. He apostatizes, hoping to save at least a few of the Japanese converts by his example. This "beautifully simple plot," writes Updike, "harrowingly dramatizes immense theological issues."

Endo seeks to illustrate Japan's hostility toward a Christ figure in another of his translated novels, *Wonderful Fool.* Set in modern times, this story centers on a Frenchman, Gaston Bonaparte. Gaston is a priest who longs to work with missionaries in Japan; after being defrocked, he travels there alone to act as a lay missionary. Completely trusting, pure-hearted, and incapable of harming anyone, Gaston is seen only as a bumbling fool by the Japanese. At their hands he is "scorned, deceived, threatened, beaten and finally drowned in a swamp," reports *Books Abroad* contributor Kinya Tsuruta. "In the end, however, his total faith transforms all the Japanese, not excluding even a hardened criminal. Thus, the simple Frenchman has successfully sowed a seed of good will in the corrupting mud swamp, Endo's favorite metaphor for non-Christian Japan."

Wonderful Fool is seen by some reviewers as Endo's condemnation of his country's values. "What shocks him . . . ," notes a *Times Literary Supplement* contributor, "is the spiritual emptiness of what he calls 'mud-swamp Japan,' an emptiness heightened by the absence of any appropriate sense of sin. . . . [But] is it not, perhaps, too self-righteous to ask whether Japan needs the sense of sin which the author would have it assume?" Addressing this issue in a *New Republic* review, Mary Jo Salter believes that "ultimately it is the novelist's humor—slapstick, corny, irreverent—that permits him to moralize so openly."

Louis Allen concurs in the *Listener* that Endo "is one of Japan's major comic writers." Praising the author's versatility, he continues, "In *When I Whistle,* he explores yet another vein, a plain realism behind which lingers a discreet but clear symbolism." *When I Whistle* tells two parallel stories, Ozu's and his son, Eiichi's. Ozu is an unsuccessful businessman who thinks nostalgically of his childhood in pre-war Japan and his youthful romance with the lovely Aiko. Eiichi is a coldly ambitious surgeon who "despises his father—and his father's generation—as sentimentally humanist," explains Allen. The parallel stories merge when Eiichi, in the hopes of furthering his career, decides to use experimental drugs on a terminal cancer patient—Ozu's former sweetheart, Aiko.

Like *Wonderful Fool, When I Whistle* presents "an unflattering version of postwar Japan," notes Allen. But while *Wonderful Fool* is marked by its humor, "sadness is the keynote [of *When I Whistle*], and its symbol the changed Aiko: a delicate beauty, unhoused and brought to penury by war, and ultimately devoured by a disease which is merely a pretext for experiment by the new, predatory generation of young Japan." *When I Whistle* differs from many of Endo's novels in its lack of an overtly Christian theme, but here as in all his fiction, believes *New York Times Book Review* contributor Anthony Thwaite, "what interests Mr. Endo—to the point of obsession—are the concerns of both the sacred and secular realms: moral choice, moral responsibility. . . . 'When I Whistle' is a seductively readable—and painful—account of these issues."

Endo returns to the historical setting of *Silence*—the seventeenth century—with *The Samauri*. This work has proved to be his most popular in Japan, and like *Silence,* it is based on historical fact. Whereas *Silence* gave readers a Portuguese missionary traveling to Japan, *The Samauri* tells of a Japanese warrior journeying to Mexico, Spain, and finally the Vatican. The samauri, Hasekura, is an unwitting pawn in his shogun's complex scheme to open trade routes to the West. Instructed to feign conversion to Christianity if it will help his cause, Hasekura does so out of loyalty to the shogun, although he actually finds Christ a repulsive figure. Unfortunately, by the time he returns to Japan five years later, political policy has been reversed, and he is treated as a state enemy for his "conversion." Finally, through his own suffering, Hasekura comes to identify with Jesus and becomes a true Christian.

Geoffry O'Brien in his *Village Voice* review judges *The Samauri* to be Endo's most successful novel, giving particular praise to its engrossing storyline and to Endo's "tremendously lyrical sensory imagination." *Washington Post Book World* reviewer Noel Perrin agrees that *The Samauri* functions well as an adventure story but maintains that "Endo has done far more than write a historical novel about an early and odd encounter between East and West. Taking the history of Hasekuru's embassy as a mere base, he has written a really quite profound religious novel. . . . It is calm and understated and brilliantly told. Simple on the surface, complex underneath. Something like a fable from an old tapestry. . . . If you're interested in how East and West really met, forget Kipling. Read Endo."

A subsequent translated work that achieved widespread attention is Endo's 1988 *Scandal.* Set in present-day Japan, the book focuses on sixty-five-year-old Sugaro, a distinguished Japanese novelist whose writings, while consistently exploring the darker side of human nature, avoid discussion of sex, a topic Sugaro finds seamy and undignified. One evening, while attending an awards ceremony in his honor, Sugaro is confronted by a drunken stranger, a woman who claims she knows him from Tokyo's red-light district and tells him that his portrait is hanging in a gallery in the disreputable neighborhood. Puzzled and embarrassed by the woman's accusations, Sugaro momentarily ignores the incident and attempts to resume a life of tranquil retirement with his wife. His placid existence soon crumbles, though, when Sugaro, compelled to search out his shadowy doppleganger, becomes submerged in a sordid, promiscuous world of danger and sadomasochism.

Scandal summoned favorable critical reaction. Describing it as "a book about perversion" in the *Los Angeles Times Book Review,* Tomas Cahill writes that *Scandal* is "stark, spare, and compulsively readable." The reviewer continues that in the novel, "we are admitted to the arcana of human corruption. Amid the writhing and the stench we are brought to acknowledge the depths of our own depravity." Likewise, John Gross in the *New York Times* declares: "Mr. Endo is intent on exploring darker mysteries . . .: the erotic allure of cruelty, and the incalculable role played in human affairs by a perverse devouring rage." Gross concludes that while the novel is quite somber, *Scandal* "is extremely gripping."

The next of Endo's works to appear in English translation is *Foreign Studies.* In this collection of three short works of fiction that were published in Japan during the 1960s, Endo returns to the topic of Christianity. Based on the author's experiences when he studied in France during the 1950s, *Foreign Studies* is, according to Endo in an interview with Euan Cameron in the London *Times,* "a work of my youth." In the main narrative, Japanese student Tanaka travels to France to study the Marquis de Sade. Once there, he observes the vast cultural and religious differences between the East and West and, finding these differences insurmountable, suffers emotional and physical pain.

Discussing the author's purpose in writing *Foreign Studies,* Cameron writes, "Endo sees it as his duty to make Christianity comprehensible to the Eastern mind." In the introduction to the book, Endo declares that communication between opposing East and West sensibilities is possible and that in fact the two cultures "hold much in common at the unconscious level." Endo concluded by telling Cameron: "Twenty-five years ago . . . the West was far less interested in Japan and the East. Christianity looked on Buddhism as a religion that was faulty. Today Christianity tries to communicate with Buddhism and vice versa and that is why I feel confident that we can reach each other."

BIOGRAPHICAL/CRITICAL SOURCES:

BOOKS

Contemporary Literary Criticism, Gale, Volume VII, 1977, Volume XIV, 1980, Volume XIX, 1981, Volume LIV, 1989.
Endo, Shusaku, *Foreign Studies,* translated by Mark Williams, P. Owen, 1989.
Rimer, J. Thomas, *Modern Japanese Fiction and Its Traditions: An Introduction,* Princeton University Press, 1978.

PERIODICALS

America, June 21, 1980, February 2, 1985.
Antioch Review, winter, 1983.
Best Sellers, November, 1980.
Books Abroad, spring, 1975.
Chicago Tribune Book World, October 7, 1979.
Christian Century, September 21, 1966.
Commonweal, November 4, 1966.
Contemporary Review, April, 1978.
Critic, July 15, 1979.
Globe and Mail (Toronto), May 21, 1988.
Listener, May 20, 1976, April 12, 1979.
London Magazine, April/May, 1974.
Los Angeles Times, November 13, 1980, December 1, 1983.
Los Angeles Times Book Review, December 5, 1982, November 13, 1988.
New Republic, December 26, 1983.
New Statesman, May 7, 1976, April 13, 1979.
Newsweek, December 19, 1983.
New Yorker, January 14, 1980.
New York Review of Books, February 19, 1981, November 4, 1982.
New York Times, August 5, 1988.
New York Times Book Review, January 13, 1980, June 1, 1980, December 26, 1982, November 13, 1983, July 21, 1985, August 28, 1988.
Saturday Review, July 21, 1979.
Spectator, May 1, 1976, April 14, 1979, May 15, 1982.
Times (London), April 18, 1985, May 13, 1989, May 18, 1989.
Times Literary Supplement, July 14, 1972, January 25, 1974, May 5, 1978, May 21, 1982, October 26, 1984, April 29, 1988, April 28, 1989.
Village Voice, November 16, 1982.
Washington Post Book World, September 2, 1979, October 12, 1980, October 24, 1982, June 23, 1985.
World Literature Today, summer, 1979, winter, 1984.

EPSILON
See BETJEMAN, John

*　　　*　　　*

ERDRICH, Louise 1954-
(Milou North, a joint pseudonym)

PERSONAL: Born July 6, 1954, in Little Falls, Minn.; daughter of Ralph (a teacher with the Bureau of Indian Affairs) and Rita (an employee of the Bureau of Indian Affairs; maiden name, Gourneau) Erdrich; married Michael Dorris (a professor and writer); children: Abel, Jeffrey, Madeline, Persia. *Education:* Dartmouth College, B.A., 1976; Johns Hopkins University, M.A., 1977.

ADDRESSES: Home—Cornish, N.H. *Agent*—Michael Dorris, 307 Bartlett, Dartmouth College, Hanover, N.H. 03755.

CAREER: Writer.

AWARDS, HONORS: Nelson Algren Award from *Chicago* magazine, 1982, for story "The World's Greatest Fishermen"; National Book Critics Circle Award, 1984, and Book Prize from *Los Angeles Times,* 1985, both for *Love Medicine;* nomination for National Book Critics Circle Award, 1986, for *The Beet Queen;* O. Henry Joint Prize, 1987, for "Fleur."

WRITINGS:

Jacklight (poems), Holt, 1984.
Love Medicine (novel), Holt, 1984.
The Beet Queen (novel), Holt, 1986.
(Author of introduction) Michael Dorris, *The Broken Cord* (nonfiction), Harper, 1987.
Tracks (novel), Holt, 1988.

Work represented in anthologies, including *Best American Short Stories,* 1981-83. Contributor—sometimes with husband, Michael Dorris, under joint pseudonym Milou North—to magazines, including *Chicago, North American Review, Frontiers,* and *Atlantic Monthly.*

WORK IN PROGRESS: A fourth novel about American Indians; with husband, Michael Dorris, *The Crown of Columbus,* a novel about Christopher Columbus.

SIDELIGHTS: Louise Erdrich has received acclaim for *Love Medicine, The Beet Queen,* and *Tracks,* her series of novels about American Indians. In *Love Medicine,* Erdrich relies on as many as seven narrators in introducing the series' various Cherokee characters. This novel, which earned both the 1984 National Book Critics Circle Award and the 1985 Book Prize of the *Los Angeles Times,* was followed by *The Beet Queen,* a compelling account of abandoned siblings and their struggle for survival. *Tracks,* the third installment of the series, realized best-seller status in the autumn of 1988. In the novel Erdrich writes about romantic intrigues among members of a tribe facing disease and poverty in the early decades of the twentieth century. "*Tracks* is the latest chapter in Erdrich's lustrous cycle of scrupulous listening," wrote Katherine Dieckmann in the *Voice Literary Supplementary.* "Trust that the journey will continue to be well worth accompanying." A fourth and concluding volume is forthcoming.

Erdrich told *CA:* "My father used to give me a nickel for every story I wrote, and my mother wove strips of construction paper together and stapled them into book covers. So at an early age I felt myself to be a published author earning substantial royalties. Mine were wonderful parents; they got me excited about reading and writing in a lasting way."

BIOGRAPHICAL/CRITICAL SOURCES:

BOOKS

Bestsellers, Issue 1, Gale, 1989.
Contemporary Literary Criticism, Gale, Volume 39, 1986, Volume 54, 1989.

PERIODICALS

New York Times, August 24, 1988.
New York Times Book Review, October 2, 1988.
Time, September 12, 1988.
Times (London), October 27, 1988.
Voice Literary Supplement, October, 1988.

*　　　*　　　*

ERIKSON, Erik H(omburger) 1902-

PERSONAL: Born June 15, 1902, in Frankfurt-am-Main, Germany; came to U.S., 1933, naturalized citizen, 1939; son of Danish parents; after mother's second marriage used stepfather's surname Homburger until his naturalization; married Joan Mowat Serson, April 1, 1930; children: Kai T., Jon M., Sue (Mrs. Harland G. Bloland). *Education:* Graduated from the Vienna Psychoanalytic Institute in 1933; received certificate from the Maria Montessori School; studied under Anna Freud; also studied at Harvard University Psychological Clinic.

ADDRESSES: Home—1705 Centro West, Tiburon, Calif. 94920.

CAREER: Practicing psychoanalyst, beginning in 1933. Training psychoanalyst, 1942. Teacher and researcher at Harvard University, School of Medicine, Department of Neuropsychiatry, Cambridge, Mass., 1934-35, Yale University, School of Medicine, New Haven, Conn., 1936-39, University of California, Berkeley, and San Francisco, 1939-51, San Francisco Psychoanalytic Institute, San Francisco, Calif., and Menninger Foundation, Topeka, Kan., 1944-50; Austen Riggs Center, Stockbridge, Mass., senior staff member, 1951-60; visiting professor, 1951-60, Western Psychiatric Institute, Pittsburgh, Pa., Massachusetts Institute of Technology, Boston, Mass., and University of Pittsburgh, School of Medicine, Pittsburgh; Harvard University, professor of human development and lecturer on psychiatry, 1969-70, professor emeritus, 1970—. Trustee of Radcliffe College, Cambridge.

MEMBER: American Psychological Association (fellow), American Psychoanalytic Association (life member), American Academy of Arts and Science, National Academy of Education, Cambridge Scientific Club, Signet Society, Phi Beta Kappa.

AWARDS, HONORS: Harvard University, M.S., 1960, LL.D., 1978; University of California, LL.D., 1968; Loyola University, Sc.D., 1970; National Book Award for philosophy and religion, and Pulitzer Prize, both 1970, both for *Gandhi's Truth;* Yale University, Soc.Sc.D., 1971; Brown University, LL.D., 1972; National Association for Mental Health research award, and Aldrich Award from American Academy of Pediatrics, both 1974; Golden Bagel award from Mt. Zion Hospital, San Francisco, Calif., 1976; Lund University, Fil.Dr.H.C., 1980.

WRITINGS:

Observations on the Yurok: Childhood and World Image, University of California Press, 1943.
Childhood and Society, Norton, 1950, revised edition, 1963.
Young Man Luther: A Study in Psychoanalysis and History, Norton, 1958.

Identity and the Life Cycle, International Universities Press, 1959. (Editor) *Youth: Change and Challenge,* Basic Books, 1963, published as *The Challenge of Youth,* Doubleday, 1963.

Insight and Responsibility: Lectures on the Ethical Implications of Psychoanalytic Insight, Norton, 1964.

Identity: Youth and Crisis, Norton, 1968.

Gandhi's Truth: On the Origins of Militant Nonviolence, Norton, 1969.

(With Huey P. Newton) *In Search of Common Ground,* edited by Kai T. Erikson, Norton, 1973.

Dimensions of a New Identity: The 1973 Jefferson Lectures, Norton, 1974. *Life History and the Historical Moment,* Norton, 1975.

Toys and Reasons: Stages in the Ritualizations of Experience, Norton, 1976.

Identity and the Life Cycle: A Reissue, Norton, 1980.

The Life Cycle Completed: A Review, Norton, 1982.

(With Joan M. Erikson and Helen Q. Kivnick) *Vital Involvement in Old Age: The Experience of Old Age in Our Time,* Norton, 1986.

A Way of Looking at Things: Selected Papers From 1930 to 1980, edited by Stephen Schlein, Norton, 1987.

CONTRIBUTOR

P. G. Davis, editor, *The Cyclopedia of Medicine,* Volume XII, Davis, 1940.

R. C. Barker and others, *Child Behavior and Development,* McGraw, 1943.

O. Fenichel and others, editors, *The Psychoanalytic Study of the Child,* Volume I, International Universities Press, 1945.

Phyllis Greenacre and others, editors, *The Psychoanalytic Study of the Child,* Volume II, International Universities Press, 1946.

M. J. E. Seen, editor, *Symposium on the Healthy Personality,* Josiah Macy, Jr. Foundation, 1950.

C. J. Friedrich, editor, *Totalitarianism,* Harvard University Press, 1954. Clara Thompson, *An Outline of Psychoanalysis,* Random House, 1955.

Helen Witmer and Ruth Kotinsky, editors, *New Perspectives for Research in Juvenile Delinquency,* U.S. Department of Health, Education, and Welfare, 1956.

B. Schaffner, editor, *Group Processes,* Josiah Macy, Jr. Foundation, 1956. J. M. Tanner and B. Inhelder, editors, *Discussions on Child Development,* International Universities Press, Volume III, 1958, Volume IV, 1960.

Daniel H. Funkenstein, editor, *The Student and Mental Health,* World Federation of Mental Health and International Association of Universities, 1959.

Psychological Issues, Volume I, International Universities Press, 1959. (Author of introduction) Blaine and McArthur, *Emotional Problems of the Student,* Crofts, 1961.

Sir Julian Huxley, editor, *The Humanist Frame,* Harper, 1961.

(And editor) *Adulthood: Essays,* Norton, 1978.

SIDELIGHTS: David Elkind calls Erik H. Erikson "the most widely known and read psychoanalyst in America today." He adds: "like the other giants of psychology, Freud and Piaget, Erikson is not an experimentalist but rather a gifted and sensitive observer and classifier of human behavior and experience. Like Freud, Erikson knows how to use his own psyche as a delicate register of what is universal in man and of what is particular to himself. And, like Piaget, Erikson has been concerned with epigenesis, with the emergent phenomena in human growth. In Erikson's case, this has amounted to a concern with how new feelings, attitudes, and orientations arise in the course of personality development, and how these new features fit within the continuous pattern that is the human life cycle."

Reviewing Erikson's Pulitzer Prize-winning biography, *Gandhi's Truth,* Christopher Lasch writes that this book "even more brilliantly than its predecessor, *Young Man Luther,* shows that psychoanalytic theory, in the hands of an interpreter both resourceful and wise, can immeasurably enrich the study of 'great lives' and of much else besides. With these books Erikson has single-handedly rescued psychoanalytic biography from neglect and disrepute." Elizabeth Hardwick states that "*Gandhi's Truth* opens up for our enlightenment so many thoughts about Gandhi that one almost loses sight of the peculiar, tranquil contribution of Erikson's own temperament upon that of his subject. There is a sort of hidden fullness and richness in this work—hidden in the discreet, rather genteel style, in the mood always courteous and forever wondering. Erikson's mind is free of the temptation to dramatize in a journalistic way and to schematize in the way of his profession, psychoanalysis." Geoffrey Gorer agrees: "In his earlier writings Erik Erikson showed himself to be one of the most insightful and innovative writers on psychoanalytical themes, above all in his work with young children and adolescents. More recently he has shown his awareness of the relevance of cultural differences in the interpretation of the behaviour of members of different societies and in *Young Man Luther,* of the importance of historical context." However, he then adds that "these critical and analytical faculties are almost entirely replaced by a pious uncritical acceptance of the whole myth about Gandhi as a modern saint who, with his unparalleled insight and skills, single-handedly mobilised the whole Indian population and enabled them to throw out the wicked British Empire."

BIOGRAPHICAL/CRITICAL SOURCES:

BOOKS

Maier, Henry W., *Three Theories of Child Development,* Harper, 1965.

PERIODICALS

American Scholar, summer, 1965.
American Sociological Review, December, 1960.
Antioch Review, winter, 1969-70.
Canadian Forum, February, 1970.
Chicago Tribune, December 17, 1986, June 29, 1987.
Christian Century, April 17, 1968, April 8, 1970.
Commonweal, March 13, 1970.
Los Angeles Times Book Review, February 1, 1987.
Nation, June 3, 1968, November 22, 1969.
New Leader, April 8, 1968.
New Republic, October 18, 1969.
New Statesman, January 17, 1969.
Newsweek, August 10, 1964, August 18, 1969, December 21, 1970.
New York Herald Tribune Book Review, November 16, 1958.
New York Times, June 14, 1988.
New York Times Book Review, November 19, 1950, March 31, 1968, September 14, 1969, April 5, 1987.
Observer Review, January 4, 1970.
Saturday Review, January 16, 1971.
Time, November 30, 1970.
Times Literary Supplement, September 9, 1983, February 26, 1988.
Village Voice, November 20, 1969.
Vogue, December, 1969.
Washington Post, June 29, 1968.
Washington Post Book World, November 9, 1986, June 14, 1987.

ESSLIN, Martin (Julius) 1918-

PERSONAL: Born June 8, 1918, in Budapest, Hungary; came to Great Britain, 1939; naturalized British citizen, 1947; son of Paul (a journalist) and Charlotte (Schiffer) Pereszlenyi; married Renate Gerstenberg, 1947; children: one daughter. *Education:* Attended University of Vienna, 1936-38; received degree from Reinhardt Seminar of Dramatic Art, Vienna, 1938.

ADDRESSES: Home—66 Loudoun Rd., London NW8, England; and Ballader's Plat, Winchelsea, Sussex, England. *Office*—Department of Drama, Stanford University, Stanford, Calif. 94305. *Agent*—Curtis Brown Ltd., 162-168 Regent St., London W1R 5TB, England.

CAREER: British Broadcasting Corp. (BBC), London, England, director and writer on theatre, 1940-77, producer and scriptwriter for European services, 1941-55, became assistant head of European productions, 1955, became assistant head of drama (sound), 1961, head of drama (radio), 1963-77; Stanford University, Stanford, California, professor of drama, 1977—. Visiting professor of theatre at Florida State University, 1969-76.

MEMBER: Arts Council of Great Britain (member of drama panel), Garrick Club.

AWARDS, HONORS: Title of Professor by president of Austria, 1967; member of the Order of the British Empire, 1972; D.Litt., Kenyon College, 1978.

WRITINGS:

Brecht: A Choice of Evils; A Critical Study of the Man, His Work, and His Opinions, Eyre & Spottiswoode, 1959, published as *Brecht: The Man and His Work,* Doubleday, 1960, 4th revised edition, Methuen, 1984.
The Theatre of the Absurd, Doubleday, 1961, third revised edition, Penguin, 1983.
(Editor with others) *Sinn oder Unsinn? Das Groteske im Modernen Drama,* Basilius, 1962.
(Editor) *Samuel Beckett: A Collection of Critical Essays,* Prentice-Hall, 1965.
(Editor) *Absurd Drama,* Penguin (London), 1965.
Harold Pinter, Friedrich Verlag, 1967.
(Editor and author of introduction) *The Genius of the German Theater,* New American Library, 1968.
Bertolt Brecht, Columbia University Press, 1969.
Reflections: Essays on Modern Theatre, Doubleday, 1969 (published in England as *Brief Chronicles: Essays on Modern Theatre,* Maurice Temple Smith, 1970).
(Editor) *The New Theatre of Europe,* Volume IV, Dell, 1970.
The Peopled Wound: The Work of Harold Pinter, Doubleday, 1970, revised edition published as *Pinter: A Study of His Plays,* Methuen, 1973, 4th revised edition, 1982.
An Anatomy of Drama, T. Smith, 1976, Hill & Wang, 1977.
Artaud, J. Calder, 1976, Penguin, 1977.
(Editor and author of introduction) *The Encyclopedia of World Theater,* Scribner, 1977 (published in England as *The Illustrated Encyclopaedia of World Theatre,* Thames & Hudson, 1977).
Mediations: Essays on Brecht, Beckett, and the Media, Louisiana University Press, 1980.
The Age of Television, Stanford, 1981.
(Author of introduction) Jan Kott, *The Theater of Essence and Other Essays,* Northwestern University Press, 1984.
The Field of Drama, Methuen, 1987.

Contributor of reviews and essays on theatre to numerous periodicals. Advisory editor of *Drama Review;* drama editor of *Kenyon Review.*

SIDELIGHTS: Martin Esslin has been a prominent, and sometimes controversial, critic of contemporary theatre. Besides volumes on individual playwrights such as Bertolt Brecht, Antonin Artaud, and Harold Pinter, he has written and edited numerous other books on theatre, most notably *The Theatre of the Absurd.*

The Theatre of the Absurd is considered a major study of the school of avant-garde dramatists who emerged in the late 1950s and early 1960s. Such playwrights as Samuel Beckett, Jean Genet, and Eugene Ionesco had bewildered many critics and audiences who found no recognizable plot, theme, characterization, or any other "typical" elements of drama in their work. Instead, in Esslin's words, viewers saw an expression "of the senselessness of the human condition and the inadequacy of the rational approach by the open abandonment of rational devices and discursive thought." To better comprehend these works, then, a new set of judgments had to be used, those which Esslin sought to define and clarify in his book.

One of Esslin's major theses expressed in *The Theatre of the Absurd* held that these plays, often dismissed as "nonsense or mystification, *have* something to say and *can* be understood." Essentially, he said, the theatre of the absurd reflected the absurdity of human life not by argument or theory, but by actually presenting the experience; it strove for "an integration between the subject matter and the form." Esslin cited changing critical response to Beckett's *Waiting for Godot* as evidence that audiences have come to look past their preconceived notions of what a play should be: While the 1955 premier of *Godot* met with "a wide measure of incomprehension," its 1964 London revival was criticized for having "one great fault: its meaning and symbolism were a little too obvious."

Another playwright whose avant-garde style warrants Esslin's attention is Pinter. With such plays as *The Caretaker* and *The Birthday Party,* Pinter creates a stage where domination and self-doubt boil together into a hazy neo-reality. In Esslin's study *The Peopled Wound: The Work of Harold Pinter,* the author "has moved in on Pinter as remorselessly as one Pinter character moves in on another Pinter character," according to *New York Review of Books* critic Nigel Dennis. And while Dennis doesn't claim to agree with Esslin's assessments of Pinter's work, the reviewer notes that among Pinter scholars, Esslin is "the kindest and gentlest." *New York Times Book Review* writer Richard Gilman expresses similar mixed feelings, remarking that Esslin is a critic "whose usefulness lies less in original thinking or insightfulness than in lucid exposition, the kind of critic who possesses thoroughness in place of brilliance, breadth instead of depth." While citing Esslin's tendency to "encircle the [Pinter] plays with [descriptive] terminology and his narrow experience of them as sensuous, independent, unprogrammatic works," Gilman also finds that "at his best . . . Esslin is able to offer some helpful illustrations of how Pinter's dialogue achieves its effects and some minor illumination of the way he departs from traditional dramaturgy." And in a *Times Literary Supplement* critic's opinion, *The Peopled Wound* (published in a revised edition as *Pinter: A Study of His Plays*) "holds its place as the most straightforwardly useful account of Pinter's work to date."

With such works as *Brief Chronicles, Mediations: Essays on Brecht, Beckett, and the Media,* and *The Field of Drama,* Esslin draws the usual mixed critical reaction. All three books contain the author's thoughts on the direction of modern drama in its many manifestations. "In *Brief Chronicles* the best pieces are those in which [Esslin] focuses on a play, a playwright or a performance," says another *Times Literary Supplement* critic. "He provides, for example, a fine structural analysis of Ibsen's *Hedda Gabler*. Another excellent piece deals with three plays by Edward Bond: The remarks on *Early Morning* are a first-rate exposition of that mordant piece." And while London *Times* writer Peter Ackroyd acknowledges that some of Esslin's views are controversial, he says of *The Field of Drama:* "It is not necessary to agree with this book in order to be impressed by it. It is engagingly written, elegantly argued, and filled with those genuine perceptions which spring from what might be described as cross-cultural magnanimity."

AVOCATIONAL INTERESTS: Reading, book-collecting.

BIOGRAPHICAL/CRITICAL SOURCES:

BOOKS

Esslin, Martin, *The Theatre of the Absurd,* Doubleday, 1961, 3rd revised edition, Penguin, 1983.

PERIODICALS

Books and Bookmen, January, 1977, March, 1978.
Drama Review, winter, 1970, spring, 1974.
Economist, October 23, 1976.
New York Review of Books, December 17, 1970, June 3, 1971.
New York Times, December 14, 1984.
New York Times Book Review, January 23, 1966, September 13, 1970, July 17, 1977.
Times (London), July 2, 1987.
Times Literary Supplement, July 23, 1970, July 6, 1973, December 17, 1976, April 10, 1981.
World Literature Today, summer, 1978, winter, 1982.

*   *   *

ESTLEMAN, Loren D. 1952-

PERSONAL: Born September 15, 1952, in Ann Arbor, Mich.; son of Leauvett Charles (a truck driver) and Louise (a postal clerk; maiden name, Milankovich) Estleman; married Carole Ann Ashley (a marketing and public relations specialist), September 5, 1987. *Education:* Eastern Michigan University, B.A., 1974.

ADDRESSES: Home—Whitmore Lake, Mich. *Agent*—Barbara Puechner, Ray Peekner Literary Agency, 3418 Shelton Ave., Bethlehem, Pa. 18017.

CAREER: Writer. *Michigan Fed,* Ann Arbor, Mich., cartoonist, 1967-70; *Ypsilanti Press,* Ypsilanti, Mich., reporter, 1973; *Community Foto-News,* Pinckney, Mich., editor in chief, 1975-76; *Ann Arbor News,* Ann Arbor, special writer, 1976-77; *Dexter Leader,* Dexter, Mich., staff writer, 1977-80. Has been an instructor for Friends of the Dexter Library, and a guest lecturer at colleges.

MEMBER: Western Writers of America, Private Eye Writers of America.

AWARDS, HONORS: American Book Award nomination, 1980, for *The High Rocks; Motor City Blue* named most notable book of 1980 by *New York Times Book Review;* Golden Spur Award for best western historical novel, Western Writers of America, 1982, for *Aces & Eights; The Midnight Man* was named most notable book of 1982 by *New York Times Book Review;* Shamus Award nomination for best private eye novel, Private Eye Writers of America, 1984, for *The Glass Highway;* Pulitzer Prize in Letters nomination, 1984, for *This Old Bill;* Shamus

Awards, Private Eye Writers of America, for *Sugartown,* and for short story "Eight Mile and Dequindre," both 1985; Golden Spur Award for best western short story, Western Writers of America, 1986, for "The Bandit"; Michigan Arts Foundation Award for Literature, 1986.

WRITINGS:

The Oklahoma Punk (crime novel), Major Books (Canoga Park, Calif.), 1976.
Sherlock Holmes vs. Dracula; or, The Adventure of the Sanguinary Count (mystery-horror novel), Doubleday, 1978.
Dr. Jekyll and Mr. Holmes (mystery-horror novel), Doubleday, 1979.
The Wister Trace: Classic Novels of the American Frontier (criticism), Jameson Books, 1987.
Red Highway (novel), PaperJacks, 1988.
Peeper (mystery novel), Bantam, 1989.
The Best Western Stories of Loren D. Estleman, edited by Bill Pronzini and Martin H. Greenberg, Ohio University Press, 1989.

"AMOS WALKER" MYSTERY SERIES

Motor City Blue, Houghton, 1980.
Angel Eyes, Houghton, 1981.
The Midnight Man, Houghton, 1982.
The Glass Highway, Houghton, 1983.
Sugartown, Houghton, 1984.
Every Brilliant Eye, Houghton, 1986.
Lady Yesterday, Houghton, 1987.
Downriver, Houghton, 1988.
General Murders (short story collection), Houghton, 1988.
Silent Thunder, Houghton, 1989.

"PETER MACKLIN" MYSTERY SERIES

Kill Zone, Mysterious Press, 1984.
Roses Are Dead, Mysterious Press, 1985.
Any Man's Death, Mysterious Press, 1986.

WESTERN NOVELS

The Hider, Doubleday, 1978.
Aces & Eights (first book in historical western trilogy), Doubleday, 1981.
The Wolfer, Pocket Books, 1981.
Mister St. John, Doubleday, 1983.
This Old Bill (second book in historical western trilogy), Doubleday, 1984.
Gun Man, Doubleday, 1985.
Bloody Season, Bantam, 1988.
Western Story, Doubleday, 1989.

"PAGE MURDOCK" WESTERN SERIES

The High Rocks, Doubleday, 1979.
Stamping Ground, Doubleday, 1980.
Murdock's Law, Doubleday, 1982.
The Stranglers, Doubleday, 1984.

OTHER

(Contributor) Robert J. Randisi, editor, *The Eyes Have It: The First Private Eye Writers of America Anthology,* Mysterious Press, 1984.
(Contributor) Edward D. Hoch, editor, *The Year's Best Mystery and Suspense Stories, 1986,* Walker & Co., 1986.

Contributor to periodicals, including *Alfred Hitchcock's Mystery Magazine, Baker Street Journal, Fiction Writers Magazine, A Matter of Crime, Mystery, New Black Mask, Pulpsmith,*

Roundup, Saint Magazine, TV Guide, Writer, and *Writer's Digest.*

WORK IN PROGRESS: A novel about George Armstrong Custer to complete the historical western trilogy; historical trilogy of city of Detroit from Prohibition to the present.

SIDELIGHTS: Loren D. Estleman, the prolific author of what James Kindall describes in *Detroit* as "hard-bitten mysteries, a herd of reality-edged westerns and an occasional fantasy or two," is perhaps best known for his series of hard-boiled mysteries that unravel in an authentically evoked Detroit. "A country boy who has always lived outside of Detroit, he writes with convincing realism about inner city environments," states Kindall, adding that "probably no other area pensmith can lay as convincing a claim to the title of Detroit's private eye writer as Estleman." Had it not been for the success of fellow Detroiter and mystery writer Elmore Leonard, pronounces William A. Henry in *Time,* "Estleman would doubtless be known as the poet of Motor City."

Trained as a journalist, Estleman researches his work thoroughly and draws deeply from his experience as a reporter who covered the police beat of a small-town newspaper: He "killed a lot of time . . . just listening to cops," notes Beauford Cranford in a *Detroit News* interview with the author; and according to Kindall, he "sometimes rode with police and held shotgun during arrests." Kindall proposes that Estleman's "affection for the street life which permeates his detective books" can be attributed partially to the stories he heard as a child from his family: "His mother nearly married a member of Detroit's Purple Gang and his father told tales of his rowdy but harmless past. Only in later years after talking to his Austrian-born grandmother, a professional cook who took hotel jobs across the country, did he find out her roving was because of an insatiable thirst for gambling, he says. And one of her casino acquaintances was Al Capone."

For Estleman, writing is an avowed compulsion: "Can't not write," he admits to Kindall. Devoting six hours a day, seven days a week to his craft, he tries to produce five pages of manuscript daily. "Clarity distinguishes Estleman's writing," declares Bob McKelvey in the *Detroit Free Press.* "Just what you'd expect from a guy who sneers at murky, avant-garde authors who go in for what Estleman calls 'ropy subjunctives and diarrhetic stream-of-consciousness.'" Estleman concurs with *CA* interviewer Jean W. Ross that his style, which he characterizes in *Twentieth-Century Western Writers* as "highly visual," has been influenced by television and motion pictures. Critics commend the clarity, good dialogue, and cinematic framing that hallmark Estleman's writing and frequently compare him to his predecessors in the genre, Dashiell Hammett and Raymond Chandler. However, Estleman is "a genre writer with ambitious intent," discerns Cranford, to whom Estleman explains: "I'm trying to delve into crime as a metaphor for society. One of the reasons crime novels are so popular now is that crime isn't something that always happens to the other guy any more. Everybody has been touched by crime, and you can't turn on the television without hearing about it. So more and more, crime and law and cops and robbers tend to become a metaphor for the way we live. Crime is probably our basic conflict."

Estleman has crafted an increasingly popular series of mysteries around the character of Amos Walker, a witty and rugged Detroit private investigator who recalls Chandler's Philip Marlowe and Hammett's Sam Spade. Considered "one of the best the hard-boiled field has to offer" by Kathleen Maio in *Wilson Library Bulletin,* "Walker is the very model of a Hammett-Chandler descendant," observes the *New York Times Book Review*'s Newgate Callendar. "He is a big man, very macho, who talks tough and is tough. He hates hypocrisy, phonies and crooks. He pretends to cynicism but is a teddy bear underneath it all. He is lonely, though women swarm all over him." Conceding to Ross that the character represents his "alter ego," Estleman once refused a six-figure offer from a major film company for exclusive rights to Walker, explaining to Kindall: "Twenty years from now, the money would be spent and I'd be watching the umpteenth movie with Chevy Chase or Kurt Russell playing Amos with the setting in Vegas or L.A. and blow my brains out."

Amos Walker "deals with sleaze from top to bottom—Motor City dregs, cop killers and drug dealers," remarks Andrew Postman in *Publishers Weekly,* and reviewers admire the storytelling skills of his creator. Walker made his debut searching the pornographic underworld of Detroit for the female ward of an aging ex-gangster in *Motor City Blue,* a novel that Kristiana Gregory appraises in the *Los Angeles Times Book Review* as "a dark gem of a mystery." About *Angel Eyes,* in which a dancer who anticipates her own disappearance hires Walker to search for her, the *New Republic*'s Robin W. Winks believes that "Estleman handles the English language with real imagination . . . so that one keeps reading for the sheer joy of seeing the phrases fall into place." In *Midnight Man,* which Callendar describes as "tough, side-of-the-mouth stuff, well written, positively guaranteed to keep you awake," Walker encounters a contemporary bounty hunter in his pursuit of three cop killers; and writing about *The Glass Highway,* in which Walker is hired to locate the missing son of a television anchor and must contend with a rampaging professional killer, Callendar believes that Estleman "remains among the top echelon of American private-eye specialists."

Although critics generally enjoy Estleman's narrative skill, plots, dialogue, and well-drawn characters, they are especially fond of his realistic portraits of the Motor City. Estleman and his private-eye character "share a unique view" of the city of Detroit, observes Kindall: "The things I like about Detroit are everything the mayor hates," states Estleman. "I love the warehouse district, for instance; that's Detroit to me . . . I like the character of a city that grew up without anybody's help." According to Jean M. White in a *Washington Post Book World* review of *Angel Eyes:* "Estleman knows the seamy underworld of Detroit's mean streets. He has a nice touch for its characters and language. His knife-sharp prose matches the hurtling pace of the action." Bill Ott suggests in *Booklist* that "Detroit becomes more than merely a setting" in Estleman's Shamus Award-winning *Sugartown,* in which an elderly Polish immigrant hires Walker to find her grandson who has been missing for nineteen years: "As the city's neighborhoods fall prey to the wrecker's ball, the dreams and even the very histories of its residents become part of the rubble." Maio believes that "Estleman writes so well of the threadworn respectability of working people stranded on the edge of an urban wasteland. His vivid and merciless descriptions of the revitalized Detroit root his complex story in reality."

As "one of the major current practitioners of the tough-guy private-eye novel," proclaims Callendar, Estleman is "at his best" in *Downriver,* a novel in which Walker investigates the claim of an intimidating black ex-convict that he was framed for the murder that sent him to prison for twenty years. "The dialogue is crackling, the writing is unpadded," Callendar continues, "and one can smell and even taste the city of Detroit." In a *Chicago Tribune Books* review of the novel, Kevin Moore considers Estleman a "polished craftsman," commending especially his "sharp, cleanly defined writing." Reviewing *Every Brilliant Eye,* in which Walker searches for a vanished friend, Callendar thinks that there exists "a kind of poetry in his snapshots of the underside of a city with which he so clearly has a love-hate relationship." Despite praise for the novel itself, Marcel Berlins adds in the London *Times* that he nonetheless wishes "Walker would move elsewhere." Resolved, according to Kindall, to continue the series until "it begins to be [like] pulling boxcars to write another one," Estleman intends to keep Walker in Detroit, remarking to Cranford: "If L.A. was where the American dream went wrong, then Detroit is where it bellied up dead. But there's still a nobility to Detroit, a certain kind of grittiness among people who can live here from day to day that may not be so true for L.A."

Although some reviewers fault Estleman's tough-guy fiction for occasional cliched conventionality, most find his Walker novels especially well-written and riveting. Henry, for instance, faults Estleman for generally resolving his plots "unsatisfyingly" through withheld information, but nevertheless believes that Estleman's "ear for diverse patois seems impeccable, and so does the inner mechanism that tells him when an unlikely escape can be plausible." Estleman's vibrant renderings of Detroit's jazz world also elicit a favorable critical response. For example, in a *Washington Post Book World* review of *Lady Yesterday,* in which Walker helps an ex-prostitute hunt for her missing father, Alan Ryan praises the novel's "great narrative and dialogue," adding: "All of this is good. I'm caught up in the story, but best of all is the way Estleman writes about jazz, the sound of it, the smoky clubs it lives in and the musicians who play it. . . . Well done. I like Estleman." And although Kindall regards Estleman as "one of those rare people who can write about deadly things in poetic terms," he perceives that a few critics have difficulty determining "who's zoomin' who," especially since Walker himself seems to border on parody rather than a realistic portrayal. "There are some critics out there who don't know what I'm doing," Estleman responds. "Some don't know if I'm parodying the form, if I'm being serious or what. The only answer to that is I'm doing both."

In another series of mysteries, Estleman slants the perspective to that of a criminal, Peter Macklin, who also free-lances out of Detroit. "Macklin is the result of my wanting to do an in-depth study of a professional killer," Estleman tells McKelvey. "It presents a challenge to keep a character sympathetic who never has anything we would call morals." Kindall suggests that "although a killer, he always seems to end up facing opponents even lower on the evolutionary scale, which shades him into the quasi-hero side." However, in a review of *Kill Zone,* the first novel in the Macklin series, Callendar feels that "not even Mr. Estleman's considerable skill can hide the falsity of his thesis" that even hired killers can be admirable characters. The plot of the novel concerns the seizure of a Detroit riverboat by terrorists who hold hundreds of passengers hostage, attracting other professional killers from organized crime and a governmental agency as well—a plot that a *Publishers Weekly* contributor finds "confusing and glutted with a plethora of minor characters who detract from the story's credibility." And although Peter L. Robertson detects an implausibility of plot in the second of the series' novels, *Roses Are Dead,* in which Macklin tries to determine who and why someone has contracted to kill him, he says in *Booklist* that the novel is "a guaranteed page-turner that features an intoxicating rush of brutal events and a fascinating anti-hero in Macklin." Describing the action of *Any Man's Death,* in which Macklin is hired to guard the life of a television evangelist and is caught in the struggle between rival mob families for control of a proposed casino gambling industry in Detroit, Wes Lukowsky suggests in *Booklist* that Estleman "has created a surprisingly credible and evolving protagonist." And as a *Time* con-

tributor remarks: "For urban edge and macho color . . . nobody tops Loren D. Estleman."

Estleman explains to Kindall that the hard-boiled mystery genre is particularly popular in this country because "America has always tended to revere the revolutionary types . . . who are not allied with any official organization . . . someone who lives pretty much according to his own rules." Estleman's work enjoys popularity in several other countries as well, though, including West Germany, Holland, Great Britain, Spain, and Japan, where his Detroit-based mysteries are enthusiastically received, notes Kindall. "Genre fiction is just American literature," Estleman tells Cranford, adding that "mysteries and westerns are our contribution to world literature." He further suggests to Ross that "private-eye fiction is the modern counterpart of the western story" because its solitary hero, when confronted with dreadful odds, must depend solely on his own "wits and personal sense of integrity." Estleman alternates between writing mysteries and westerns to keep the ideas fresh, he tells Ross, dubbing it "literary crop rotation."

The Hider, a novel about the last buffalo hunt in America, was Estleman's first western novel and was purchased immediately—a rarity in the genre. He has since written several other successful western novels plus a critical analysis of western fiction itself, *The Wister Trace: Classic Novels of the American Frontier;* and several of his books about the American West have earned critical distinction. *The High Rocks,* for instance, which is set in the mountains of Montana and relates the story of a man's battle with the Indians who murdered his parents, was nominated for an American Book Award. And the first two books of his proposed historical western trilogy have also earned honors: *Aces & Eights,* about the murder of Wild Bill Hickok, was awarded the Golden Spur; and *This Old Bill,* a fable based on the life of William Frederick "Buffalo Bill" Cody, was nominated for a Pulitzer Prize.

In the *Los Angeles Times Book Review,* David Dary discusses Estleman's *Bloody Season,* an extensively researched historical novel about the gunfight at the O.K. Corral: "The author's search for objectivity and truth, combined with his skill as a fine writer, have created a new vision of what happened in Tombstone . . . , and he avoids the hackneyed style that clutters the pages of too many Westerns." Dary concludes that although it is a fictional account, the novel "probably comes closer to the truth" than anything else published on the subject. In *Twentieth-Century Western Writers,* Bill Crider observes: "All of Estleman's books appear solidly researched, and each ends in a way which ties all the story threads together in an effective pseudo-historical manner, giving each an air of reality and credibility."

Estleman once wrote *CA:* "The three writers whose works have had the most profound influence on my writing are all dead, which should prove some indication of my opinion of most writers who have since arisen. Edgar Allan Poe, Jack London, and Raymond Chandler have impressed me since childhood with their lyrical, poetical approach to action and adventure. The literature of violence is purely an American development and only the English language, that most elusive, infinitely fascinating of tongues, fulfills all the requirements for its proper expression. The icy deliberation of the murderer in Poe's 'A Cask of Amontillado,' the tortured psyche of the brutal Wolf Larsen in London's *The Sea Wolf,* and the parade of grotesques that march through all of Chandler's best works are products of the American experience beside which the elements of the great fiction of Europe seem tame as a houseplant. That there is a prejudice in literary circles against these three masters is evidence of how far we still have to go to cast off the shackles forged by those potentially great writers who accepted the restrictions of Victorian society during literature's so-called Golden Age. Shakespeare was aware of the importance of violence in human nature, as were Homer and Dostoevski, but today's civilization prefers to forget that it even exists.

"All of this may sound strange coming from the author of *Sherlock Holmes vs. Dracula.* Indeed, one or two reviewers commented upon a rather bloody scene in that book and said that Conan Doyle would have been repelled by it. If they'd taken the trouble to read one or two of the original Holmes adventures, they'd have recognized his debt to Poe and his own 'morbid' fascination with brutality and the grotesque.

"I've never killed anyone off the written page. I am, however, a hunter, and I doubt that I'm being original in saying that people and animals die similarly. I'm a good boxer, a fair wrestler, and with a name like Loren I saw my share of schoolyard fights. Although I hardly appreciated it then, those tussles have come in handy every time I've sat down to write a fight scene. Since we have no memory of pain, though, I've occasionally had to remind myself of certain sensations, which has entailed slugging myself in the jaw while seated at the typewriter. Writing was never more painful than this."

MEDIA ADAPTATIONS: The Amos Walker mysteries *Motor City Blue, Angel Eyes, The Midnight Man, Sugartown, The Glass Highway,* and *Every Brilliant Eye* were recorded on audio cassettes in unabridged readings by David Regal for Brilliance Corp. (Grand Haven, Mich.) in 1988. *Sherlock Holmes vs. Dracula* was broadcast by the British Broadcasting Corporation. One of Estleman's western novels has been optioned by a California film company.

BIOGRAPHICAL/CRITICAL SOURCES:

BOOKS

Contemporary Literary Criticism, Volume 48, Gale, 1988.
Twentieth-Century Crime and Mystery Writers, 2nd edition, St. Martin's, 1985.
Twentieth-Century Western Writers, Gale, 1982.

PERIODICALS

Ann Arbor News, September 24, 1978.
Ann Arbor Observer, July, 1978.
Booklist, November 15, 1984, September 1, 1985, October 15, 1986.
Chicago Tribune Book World, January 18, 1981, August 10, 1986.
Detroit, March 8, 1987.
Detroit Free Press, September 26, 1984.
Detroit News, May 18, 1979, August 21, 1983.
Eastern Echo, September 8, 1978.
Los Angeles Times Book Review, August 21, 1983, January 19, 1986, January 24, 1988.
New Black Mask, Number 4, 1986.
New Republic, November 25, 1981.
New York Times Book Review, November 11, 1979, October 26, 1980, November 1, 1981, August 22, 1982, August 14, 1983, October 23, 1983, December 2, 1984, December 23, 1984, March 24, 1985, November 24, 1985, April 20, 1986, October 26, 1986, March 6, 1988, January 29, 1989, October 15, 1989.
Publishers Weekly, August 23, 1985, January 22, 1988.
Time, July 31, 1978, December 22, 1986, August 17, 1987, February 1, 1988.

Times (London), November 20, 1986, November 29, 1986, December 31, 1987.
Times Literary Supplement, March 14, 1986, April 10, 1987.
Tribune Books (Chicago), January 31, 1988.
Village Voice, February 24, 1987.
Washington Post Book World, October 18, 1981, May 17, 1987.
Wilson Library Bulletin, March, 1985.

*   *   *

EVERSON, William (Oliver)   1912-
(Brother Antoninus)

PERSONAL: Surname rhymes with "weaver's son"; born September 10, 1912, in Sacramento, Calif.; son of Louis Waldemar (a bandmaster, composer, and printer) and Francelia Maria (Herber) Everson: married Edwa Poulson, 1938 (divorced); married Mary Fabilli (a writer and artist), 1947 (separated, 1949); married Susanna Rickson, December 13, 1969; children: (third marriage) Jude (stepson). *Education:* Attended Fresno State College (now California State College), 1931, 1934-35. *Religion:* Roman Catholic.

ADDRESSES: Home—705 Big Creek Rd., Davenport, Calif. 95017.

CAREER: Roman Catholic monk in Dominican order, 1951-69, name in religion, Brother Antoninus; poet. Cannery worker and laborer for Civilian Conservation Corps, 1932-33; worked as a farmer in the mid-1930s; co-founder, Untide Press, Waldport, Ore., c. 1944; after war joined anarchopacifist group of poets surrounding Kenneth Rexroth in San Francisco; active in Catholic Worker Movement in the slums of Oakland, Calif., 1950-51; has given numerous poetry readings across the United States and Europe, 1957—; master printer, Lime Kiln Press, 1971-81; poet-in-residence, University of California, Santa Cruz, 1971-81. *Wartime service:* Conscientious objector working in forestry service at Camp Angel and Cascade Locks, Oregon, 1943-46.

AWARDS, HONORS: Guggenheim fellowship, 1949; California Silver Medal, Commonwealth Club, 1968, for *The Rose of Solitude; Granite and Cyprus* was included in Joseph Blumenthal's 1975 exhibition "The Printed Book in America," as one of the seventy best-printed books in American history; Shelley Memorial Award and Book of the Year Award, Conference on Christianity and Literature, 1978, for *The Veritable Years, 1949-1966;* Pulitzer Prize nomination for *The Crooked Lines of God;* National Endowment for the Arts grant, 1981.

WRITINGS:

POETRY

These Are the Ravens, Greater West, 1935.
San Joaquin, Ward Ritchie, 1939.
The Masculine Dead: Poems 1938-1940, J. A. Decker, 1942.
X War Elegies, 3rd edition, Untide, 1943, new edition published as *War Elegies,* 1944.
The Waldport Poems, Untide, 1944.
The Residual Years: Poems, 1940-41, Untide, 1944, published with additional poems as *The Residual Years,* New Directions, 1948, enlarged edition, with an introduction by Kenneth Rexroth, published as *The Residual Years: Poems, 1934-48—The Pre-Catholic Poetry of Brother Antoninus,* New Directions, 1968.
Poems MCMXLII, Untide, 1945.
A Privacy of Speech: Ten Poems in Sequence, Equinox, 1949.
Triptych for the Living (with prints by Mary Fabilli), Seraphim, 1951.

There Will Be Harvest, Albion Press, 1961.

The Year's Declension, Albion Press, 1961.

Single Source: The Early Poems of William Everson, 1934-1940 (introduction by Robert Duncan), Oyez, 1966.

The Blowing of the Seed, Henry W. Wenning, 1966.

In the Fictive Wish, Oyez, 1967.

Poems of Nineteen Forty Seven, Black Rock Press, 1968.

Tendril in the Mesh, Cayucos Books, 1973.

Black Hills, Didymus Press, 1973.

Man-Fate: The Swan-Song of Brother Antoninus, New Directions, 1974.

River-Root: A Syzygy for the Bicentennial of These States, Oyez, 1976.

Missa Defunctorum, Lime Kiln Press, 1976.

The Mate-Flight of Eagles, Blue Oak Press, 1977.

Blackbird Sundown, Lord John Press, 1978.

Rattlesnake August, Santa Susana Press, 1978.

The Veritable Years: Poems 1949-1966, Black Sparrow Press, 1978.

Cutting the Firebreak, Kingfisher Press, 1978.

Blame It on the Jet Stream!, Lime Kiln Press, 1978.

The Masks of Drought, Black Sparrow Press, 1979.

Renegade Christmas, Lord John, 1984.

Also author of *In Media Res,* 1984.

POETRY; UNDER NAME BROTHER ANTONINUS

At the Edge, Albertus Magnus, 1958.

A Fragment for the Birth of God, Albertus Magnus, 1958.

An Age Insurgent, Blackfriars, 1959.

The Crooked Lines of God: Poems, 1949-1954, University of Detroit Press, 1959, 2nd edition, 1960, 3rd edition, 1962.

The Hazards of Holiness: Poems, 1957-1960, Doubleday, 1962.

The Poet Is Dead: A Memorial for Robinson Jeffers, Auerhahn, 1964.

The Rose of Solitude, Oyez, 1964, published with additional poems, Doubleday, 1967.

The Vision of Felicity, Lowell House, 1967.

The Achievement of Brother Antoninus (selection of poems, an introduction by William E. Stafford), Scott, Foresman, 1967.

A Canticle to the Waterbirds, Eizo, 1968.

The Springing of the Blade, Black Rock Press, 1968.

The City Does Not Die, Oyez, 1969.

The Last Crusade Oyez, 1969.

Who Is She That Looketh Forth as the Morning?, Capricorn Press, 1972.

EDITOR

(Under name Brother Antoninus) *Robinson Jeffers: Fragments of an Older Fury,* Oyez, 1968.

Robinson Jeffers, *Cawdor and Medea,* New Directions, 1970.

Jeffers, *Californians,* Cayucos, 1971.

Jeffers, *The Alpine Christ,* Cayucos, 1973.

Jeffers, *Tragedy Has Obligations,* Lime Kiln Press, 1973.

Jeffers, *Brides of the South Wind,* Cayucos, 1974.

Jeffers, *Granite and Cypress,* Lime Kiln Press, 1975.

Jeffers, *The Double Axe and Other Poems,* Liveright, 1977.

SOUND RECORDINGS

(Under name Brother Antoninus) "The Savagery of Love: Brother Antoninus Reads His Poetry," Caedmon, 1968.

"Poetry of Earth" (selections from Everson's and Robinson Jeffers's poetry), Big Sur Recordings, 1970.

"Robinson Jeffers" (lecture; cassette tape), Everett/Edwards, 1972.

OTHER

(Under name Brother Antoninus) *Novum Psaltertum Pii xii* (liturgy and ritual; unfinished folio edition), [Los Angeles], 1955.

(With Brother Kurt) *Friar among Savages: Father Luis Cancer,* Benzinger, 1958.

(Author of text) *The Dominican Brother, Province of the West,* Dominican Vocation Office, 1965.

(With J. Burns) *If I Speak Truth: An Inter View-ing with Brother Antoninus,* Goliards Press, 1968.

Archetype West: The Pacific Coast as a Literary Region (criticism), Oyez, 1976.

Lee Bartlett, editor, *Earth Poetry: Selected Essays and Interviews, 1950-1977,* Oyez, 1980.

Birth of a Poet: The Santa Cruz Meditations, edited by Lee Bartlett, Black Sparrow Press, 1982.

The Excesses of God: Robinson Jeffers as a Religious Figure, Stanford University Press, 1988.

Also author of *On Writing the Waterbirds: Collected Forewords and Afterwords,* 1988. Contributor, sometimes under name Brother Antoninus, to periodicals, including *Ramparts* and *Evergreen Review.*

SIDELIGHTS: Though William Everson had established himself as a respected regional poet many years before the Beat movement of the 1950s came into being, he first came to national attention when he was identified as a member of that group. A deeply serious and religious writer, Everson spent eighteen years as a Dominican monk, and published many of his works under his name in religion, Brother Antoninus. He has been variously classified as a nature poet, an erotic poet, and a religious poet, but, contends *Dictionary of Literary Biography* contributor James A. Powell, "above all else, Everson is an autobiographical, even a confessional poet. Throughout his career . . . he has made his personal life the predominant subject of his poetry."

Everson credits his first exposure to the poetry of Robinson Jeffers as revealing to him his own poetic vocation. "It was an intellectual awakening and a religious conversion in one. . . . Jeffers showed me God," Powell quotes him. So powerful was the experience that Everson was inspired to immediately drop his university studies, plant a vineyard, and begin writing his own verse. His early work focused on farming, the change of seasons, and a theme that would endure throughout his entire writing career, his love of the California landscape. His first collections, *These Are the Ravens, San Joaquin,* and *The Masculine Dead* brought him enthusiastic—though not widespread—acclaim, along with the classification of nature poet. Donna Nance points out in her *Dictionary of Literary Biography* essay that in retrospect it is obvious that this is "too narrow a characterization of Everson's early work. For the poems are neither pastoral nor idyllic in the general manner of nature poetry, but rather infused with a somber awareness of the violence inherent in the natural world—and by extension, in man's collective nature." Nance suggests that the predominant theme of Everson's early poetry is actually "the problem of violence and man's susceptibility to it."

Man's struggle with violence suddenly became a very timely theme as the United States entered World War II. Everson chose conscientious objector status and was sent to work at lumber camps in the Northwest. The poetry he wrote while stationed there reflected the dilemmas he faced as a pacifist in a society at war. Much of the verse Everson wrote at this time would later be collected in *The Residual Years,* including his long poem "Chronicle of Division." This multi-part poem details the disintegration of the author's first marriage due to the long separation required by his wartime service. Nance calls "Chronicle of Division" "a stylistic victory for Everson as he recreates, in language forceful yet graceful, the frustration, loneliness, and betrayal of faith that he experienced" during this break-up. These poems were enthusiastically received among pacifists and those already familiar with Everson, but did little to advance his reputation further.

When released from Civilian Public Service in June, 1946, Everson moved to Sebastapol, California, where he met poet and artist Mary Fabilli. Their love provided the inspiration for Everson's next work, *The Blowing of the Seed*. In November the couple moved to Berkeley, where they were quickly accepted into the circle of poets surrounding Kenneth Rexroth in San Francisco; they married the following year. It was also in 1947 that Everson first received widespread critical attention, spurred by New Direction's reprinting of *The Residual Years*, complete with these controversial dust jacket notes by Kenneth Rexroth: "This kind of poetry may outrage academic circles where an emasculated and hallucinated imitation of John Donne is still considered chic; but others, who have been waiting for modern poetry to stop clearing its throat and stammering, should be delighted." In Nance's estimation, "the statement amounted to a literary throwing down of the gauntlet. At once defensive and aggressive, it challenged contemporary academic critics to accept Everson on his own terms—terms that in their insistence on the primacy of personal statement, Rexroth was later to argue, represented 'a different definition of poetic integrity' " than that generally agreed upon by the academic critics of the 1950s.

Nance reports that many critics did respond favorably to "the obvious sincerity of Everson's quest for value and certainty in an uncertain and frequently violent world." Although some reviewers voiced complaints about Everson's excessive personalism and his sometimes obscure syntax, most awarded him "praise for his forceful language and for the rhythm . . . of his verse." From 1947 onwards, Everson could be considered a poet of national standing.

Everson's life and work underwent radical changes in the next few years as a result of a profound religious experience. Mary Fabilli was a lapsed Catholic in the process of returning to the church. Everson, who had been raised a Christian Scientist but by his teen years had declared himself an agnostic—sometimes accompanied his wife to Mass. On Christmas Eve, 1948, he had an intense religious experience while in church; by July of the following year, Everson had completed his course of religious instruction and been baptized. Ironically, however, because he and Fabilli had both been previously married and divorced, the Roman Catholic church did not recognize their union as valid. Accordingly, they separated. After working for a year at the Catholic Worker House in the slums of Oakland, California, Everson entered the Dominican order as a monk, taking the name Brother Antoninus.

James A. Powell believes that "the poetry Everson composed during the first five years following his conversion . . . represents very possibly his best work." Most of this verse was later collected in *The Crooked Lines of God* and *The Veritable Years*. Turning to the narrative style favored by Robinson Jeffers, "Everson rewrote many famous Bible stories and Christian legends. Remaining true to one of his most constant themes—his love of the California landscape—he set these stories not in Palestine, but in California." In using Jeffers's techniques, Powell assesses, Everson not only lives up to the standard set by the older poet, he actually "bests his master." Besides being "consistently powerful in its utterance," this poetry is "striking both for

its departures from and for its continuities with his previous practice. . . . The intense demands on his poetic craft [Everson] must have felt as he returned to confront Jeffers on the master's own ground, the necessary encounter with the simple concision good narrative requires, the inspiration he drew from the stories themselves, the personal (and revelatory) significance they had taken on for him, and the respect for their simplicities his reverence for them exacted—all coincided to produce verse of a graceful tension, a fervent constraint, an earnest, highly-wrought yet subdued music. These are poems of quite remarkable force," concludes Powell.

Such enthusiasm was not universal, however. While acknowledging that "Everson . . . wrote some of the first poetry I ever truthfully liked," James Dickey recalls in his book *Babel to Byzantium* that on reading *The Veritable Years* he was unfavorably "struck by the author's humorless, even owlish striving after self-knowledge and certainty, his intense and bitter inadequacy and frustration." Dickey goes on to characterize *The Crooked Lines of God* as "page after page of not-very-good, learned dry sermonizing which in several places leans toward an attitude which I cannot help believing is somewhat self-righteous and even self-congratulatory. . . . What Brother Antoninus offers, instead of the 'vision' he speaks of, is a sober, unimaginative forthrightness and a nagging insistence that he is right and you are, no matter what *else* you may believe, wrong. What I find peculiarly disagreeable in Brother Antoninus's work is his basic dislike of people and of sex, and this seems to me to be based at least as much on secular reasons as on religious."

Kenneth Rexroth's appraisal of *The Crooked Lines of God* differs sharply from Dickey's. Always a staunch supporter of Everson, he calls it in his book *Assays* "a collection of poems of stunning impact, utterly unlike anything else being written nowadays." Like Powell, he judges Everson superior even to Jeffers, writing, "As far as his verse is concerned, Brother Antoninus is more or less a disciple of Robinson Jeffers, but I think he has made a harder and more honest instrument of it than his master."

During the mid-fifties, Everson's literary output dropped considerably. The demands of monastic life were partly responsible, but a fuller explanation for this dry period lies in the conflict Everson was then experiencing between his poetic and religious vocations. He finally broke through his writer's block in 1957 with "River-Root," a thirty-page poem which, due to its explicit eroticism, was not published until 1976. Powell describes the poem: "Bathing all nature in an aura of universal phallicism, 'River-Root' not only presents in close, loving and extensive physical detail the lengthy and inventive coupling of its properly married, Catholic, and procreatively minded central characters but also attempts to link their love-making on the one hand to a universal natural eroticism and, on the other, through the poem's depiction of sexual intercourse as a mode of contemplation, to God. . . . The poem . . . bespeaks the psychic trouble the requirement of celibacy would arouse in Everson throughout his monastic career."

It was also in 1957 that Kenneth Rexroth's now-famous "San Francisco Letter" appeared in the *Evergreen Review*. In it, Rexroth announced the importance of the San Francisco Renaissance poets (who would come to be known as "the Beats") to the literary world, including Everson among them. Following the publication of the letter, Everson received substantial attention nationwide, not only from those in the literary world, but from the popular press as well. The apparent incongruity of a Catholic monk being identified with the supposedly hedonistic, amoral, Beat movement delighted reporters, who promptly tagged Everson "the Beat friar." Suddenly he was in great demand for poetry readings across the country and in Europe; he continued to devote considerable time to these until the late 1960s.

Throughout the late fifties and the sixties, Everson's poetry continued to suggest a difficult struggle taking place within him. Most of the works collected in *The Hazards of Holiness* "seem to represent moments of crisis in Everson's spiritual autobiography," notes Powell. While many of them are quite explicitly erotic, others tell of a quest for celibacy without torment. *The Rose of Solitude,* published in 1960, depicts Everson's long, platonic—but sometimes tortured with passion—relationship with a woman named Rose Tunnland.

The poet's language had always been notably rich, but became even more so at this point in his career. This development displeased critic William Dickey, who complains in the *Hudson Review:* "The language of this book [*The Rose of Solitude*] is, like its substance, overblown. Antoninus makes a simple equation between suffering and unintelligibility: the greater the pain, the more tortured the syntax. In pursuit of this relationship he arrives at distortions which can best be called grotesque." Yet Samuel Charters disagrees sharply in his *Some Poems/Poets: Studies in American Underground Poetry since 1945:* "Antoninus, in a period when the poetic idiom has become dry and understated, has an almost seventeenth century richness of language and expression. . . . Antoninus's language is so intense, so vivid, that the poems can almost be read in clusters of words and phrases."

William Everson took the first vows of priesthood in 1964; in 1965, he met Susanna Rickson and began to compose a long poem to her. On December 7, 1969, he gave the first public reading of this poem, entitled "Tendril in the Mesh." As he concluded the reading, he threw off his monk's habit and left the stage, announcing his intention to return to secular life. One week later, he and Susanna Rickson were married. "Tendril in the Mesh" and other poems written in 1970 and 1971 were printed in what Powell deems one of Everson's "best volumes, as well as one of his richest," *Man-Fate: The Swan Song of Brother Antoninus.* Most of the book explains the poet's passion for his new wife and how it led him to renounce his vows; the remaining verse expresses the difficulties encountered in his adjustment to a secular way of living.

Since leaving the monastery, Everson has turned his energies toward critical writing, printing, teaching, and editing the works of Robinson Jeffers. While the body of his work has expressed a sharp conflict between body and spirit, his most recent writings, collected in *The Masks of Drought,* bespeak a "reconciliation with the world of nature and his own place in it," notes Powell. As always, the poems are autobiographical, concerning the poet's relations with his wife, his advancing age, and his continuing love of the land. Remarking on Everson's dedication to intensely personal themes, Kenneth Rexroth writes in his introduction to *The Residual Years:* "Everson has been accused of self-dramatization. Justly. All of his poetry, that under the name of Brother Antoninus, too, is concerned with the drama of his own self, rising and falling along the sine curve of life, from comedy to tragedy and back again, never quite going under, never quite escaping for good into transcendence. . . . Everything is larger than life with a terrible beauty and pain. Life isn't like that to some people and to them these poems will seem too strong a wine. But of course life is like that."

BIOGRAPHICAL/CRITICAL SOURCES:

BOOKS

Bartlett, Lee, editor, *Benchmark and Blaze: The Emergence of William Everson,* Scarecrow, 1979.
Bartlett, Lee, and Allan Campo, *William Everson: A Descriptive Bibliography,* Scarecrow, 1977.
Bartlett, Lee, and others, *William Everson: Poet from the San Joaquin,* Blue Oak Press, 1978.
Charters, Samuel, *Some Poems/Poets: Studies in American Underground Poetry since 1945,* Oyez, 1971.
Contemporary Literary Criticism, Gale, Volume 1, 1973, Volume 5, 1976, Volume 14, 1980.
Dickey, James, *Babel to Byzantium,* Farrar, Straus, 1956.
Dictionary of Literary Biography, Gale, Volume 5: *American Poets since World War II,* 1980, Volume 16: *The Beats: Literary Bohemians in Postwar America,* 1983.
Everson, William, *The Residual Years: Poems, 1934-1938—The Pre-Catholic Poetry of Brother Antoninus,* New Directions, 1968.
Everson, William, and J. Burns, *If I Speak Truth: An Inter Viewing with Brother Antoninus,* Goliards Press, 1968.
Kherdian, David, *Six Poets of the San Francisco Renaissance: Portraits and Checklists,* Giliga, 1967.
Meltzer, David, editor, *The San Francisco Poets,* Ballantine, 1971, published as *Golden Gate: Interview with Five San Francisco Poets,* Wingbow Press, 1976.
Rexroth, Kenneth, *Assays,* New Directions, 1961.

PERIODICALS

Atlantic, December, 1963.
Choice, June, 1969, September, 1977.
Commonweal, October 19, 1962, December 20, 1968, May 9, 1975.
Hudson Review, winter, 1967-68, spring, 1979.
Los Angeles Times, March 18, 1980.
Minnesota Review, spring, 1979.
National Observer, July 10, 1967.
New York Times Book Review, September 9, 1962, October 8, 1967.
Poetry, April, 1963, autumn, 1968, December, 1969.
Prairie Schooner, spring, 1970.
Virginia Quarterly Review, winter, 1968.
Western American Literature, May, 1977.

*   *   *

EWART, Gavin (Buchanan) 1916-

PERSONAL: Born in 1916 in London, England; son of George Arthur (a surgeon) and Dorothy (Turner) Ewart; married Margo Bennett (a school secretary), March 24, 1956; children: Jane Susan, Julian Robert. *Education:* Attended Christ's College, Cambridge, 1934-37. *Politics:* Labour. *Religion:* None.

ADDRESSES: Home—57 Kenilworth Court, Lower Richmond Rd., London SW 15, England.

CAREER: Assistant in book review department, British Council, 1946-52; advertising copywriter, 1952-71; free-lance writer, 1971—. *Military service:* British Army, Royal Artillery, 1940-46; became captain.

MEMBER: Royal Society of Literature (fellow), Poetry Society (chairperson, 1978-79), Society of Authors, Performing Rights Society.

AWARDS, HONORS: Cholmondeley Award, 1971, for achievement as a poet; travel scholarship from Royal Society of Literature, 1978.

WRITINGS:

POETRY

Poems and Songs, Fortune Press, 1939.
Londoners, Heinemann, 1964.
Throwaway Lines, Keepsake Press, 1964.
Two Children, Keepsake Press, 1966.
Pleasures of the Flesh, Alan Ross, 1966.
The Deceptive Grin of the Gravel Porters, London Magazine Editions, 1968.
Twelve Apostles, Ulsterman Publications, 1970.
The Gavin Ewart Show, Trigram Press, 1971.
Venus, Poem-of-the-Month Club, 1972.
The Select Party, Keepsake Press, 1972.
Alphabet Soup, Sycamore Press, 1972.
By My Guest!, Trigram Press, 1975.
An Imaginary Love Affair, Ulsterman Publications, 1975.
(With Zulfikar Ghose and B. S. Johnson) *Penguin Modern Poets 25,* Penguin, 1975.
A Question Partly Answered, Sceptre Press, 1976.
No Fool Like an Old Fool, Gollancz, 1976.
Or Where a Young Penguin Lies Screaming, Gollancz, 1977.
All My Little Ones, Anvil Press, 1978.
The Collected Ewart, 1933-1980, Hutchinson, 1980.
The New Ewart: Poems, 1980-1982, Hutchinson, 1982.
More Little Ones, Anvil Press, 1982.
Capital Letters, Sycamore Press, 1983.
Festival Nights, Other Branch Readings, 1984.
The Ewart Quarto, Hutchinson, 1984.
The Young Pobble's Guide to His Toes, Hutchinson, 1985.
Useful Information about Animals, Century/Hutchinson, 1986.
The Gavin Ewart Show: Selected Poems, 1939-1985, Bits Press, 1986.
The Complete Little Ones, Hutchinson, 1986.
The Learned Hippopotamus, Hutchinson, 1987.
Late Pickings, Hutchinson, 1987.
Selected Poems, 1933-1988, New Directions, 1988.
Penultimate Poems, 1989.

Work is also represented in James Laughlin's *New Directions* anthologies.

EDITOR

Forty Years On: An Anthology of School Songs, Sidgwick & Jackson, 1964.
The Batsford Book of Children's Verse, Batsford, 1976.
New Poems 1977-78: A P.E.N. Anthology of Contemporary Poetry, Hutchinson, 1977.
The Batsford Book of Light Verse for Children, Batsford, 1978.
The Penguin Book of Light Verse, Penguin, 1980.
Other People's Clerihews, Oxford University Press, 1983.

OTHER

(Author of introduction) E. C. Bentley, *The Complete Clerihews of E. Clerihew Bentley,* Oxford University Press, 1981.

WORK IN PROGRESS: Literary Landmarks, a book of short satirical poems on "literary" subjects.

SIDELIGHTS: "One of the few bright features about poetry in the late 1970s is that Gavin Ewart is growing old disgracefully," wrote Anthony Thwaite in a 1978 *Times Literary Supplement* review. "He grows more prolific, wider-ranging, funnier and more scabrous as the years go by." The books of light verse Ewart has published in the 1980s—and their increasing acceptance as legitimate poetry—suggest that Thwaite's observation still applies. Reviewers find the recent flowering of this British satirist all the more remarkable because his poetic voice was silent for twenty-five years.

First published nationally at the precocious age of seventeen, Ewart had a poetry book, *Poems and Songs,* to his credit by the time he was twenty-three. T. S. Eliot, Ezra Pound, and Ronald Bottrall are all acknowledged influences in this early verse, with W. H. Auden making his presence felt later on. But just as he was establishing his own poetic voice, Ewart found his writing interrupted by the outbreak of war. "I found it very hard to write during World War II, when I was on active service in North Africa and Italy," Ewart told *CA.* And when the war was over, he pursued a different path, first becoming an assistant in the book review department of the British Council and then an advertising copywriter for eighteen years. He didn't pursue his old vocation until, as he told *CA,* "Alan Ross, editor of *London Magazine,* encouraged me to begin writing poetry again in 1959." Following what the *Times Literary Supplement* has described as his "remarkable poetic rebirth in the early 1960s," Ewart has produced an uninterrupted stream of light-hearted verse that is known for its irreverence, sexual content, and effortless technical skill.

An acknowledged master of forms who can mimic almost any style of writing, Ewart has depth as well as breadth, as a *Times Literary Supplement* reviewer explains: "What makes him different is that he isn't content with satirical pastiche or parody. He has a strong, gamey talent of his own, much concerned with the disputed territory that lies between things-as-they-are, things-as-they-might-be, and things-as-people-say-they-are." For instance, in "The Gentle Sex," which recounts how a group of Ulster Defence Association women beat a political opponent to death in Belfast, Northern Ireland, Ewart employs a metric form that Gerald Manley Hopkins used. "On the face of it what could be less apt than to tell this bleak story in the stanza form of 'The Wreck of the Deutschland'?" asks Anthony Thwaite. "But this is very precisely what Ewart does; and in the process one feels the ghostly presence of Hopkins's nuns behind the brutally vicious tale."

While Ewart's subtle literary allusions may be lost on unknowing readers, there is no mistaking his preoccupation with sex, which frequently serves as a springboard for larger concerns. "Starting off from sex, often in one of its unhappier forms, Ewart comments on ambition, middle age, life in the suburbs, the boredom of wives, office politics, children, history, etc.," writes Peter Porter in *London Magazine.* One of Ewart's earliest successes was a take-off on the Lewis Carroll classic, irreverently titled "Phallus in Wonderland," and he seems to have become even less inhibited with advancing age. In the opening poem of his more recent *Pleasures of the Flesh,* for instance, Ewart embraces his lusts joyfully: "A small talent, like a small penis, / Should not be hidden lightly under a bushel, / But shine in use, or exhibitionism. / Otherwise how should one know it was there?"

With the appearance of *Pleasures of the Flesh,* "it becomes clear how perfectly Ewart's creative life has conformed to the butterfly system," notes *Times Literary Supplement* contributor Russell Davies. "An active and noticeable caterpillar in youth, and twenty years a chrysalis, he struggles out stickily in *Londoners* and bursts forth, at last, into a gaudy maturity with *Pleasures.*" In his *London Magazine* review of this volume, Porter expresses a similar view: "*Pleasures of the Flesh* establishes Ewart as an important poet . . . with something to say to us directly. The gestation which followed that early promise was a long one, but the results have been worth waiting for."

Davies believes that since the early 1970s Ewart has been "the star of his own production. The very title of *The Gavin Ewart Show* proclaims it. In a curious way, he has become the sort of poet whom one 'follows,' as one might an actor or a sportsman or a singer. Ewart never produces a tight, interlocking performance at book length, but nor do singers with their 'albums'; yet there are always one or two songs you play over and over. To have established this kind of career at all is a very considerable achievement." When reading *The Gavin Ewart Show,* David Howarth suggests in his *Phoenix* review that rather than approaching the volume academically, it's "much better to take Ewart's advice: 'Slup me rough and homely and I'll taste fine.'"

BIOGRAPHICAL/CRITICAL SOURCES:

BOOKS

Contemporary Literary Criticism, Gale, Volume 13, 1980, Volume 46, 1988.
Dictionary of Literary Biography, Volume 40: *Poets of Great Britain and Ireland since 1960,* Gale, 1985.

Ewart, Gavin, *Pleasures of the Flesh,* Alan Ross, 1966.

PERIODICALS

London Magazine, May, 1966.
New York Times Book Review, August 17, 1986.
Phoenix, July, 1973.
Times (London), April 25, 1985.
Times Literary Supplement, October 30, 1969, April 21, 1972, March 19, 1976, December 10, 1976, April 14, 1978, July 11, 1980, January 9, 1981, July 30, 1982, May 27, 1983, November 11, 1983, September 20, 1985, February 13, 1987, November 3, 1989.

*   *   *

EWING, Frederick R.
    See STURGEON, Theodore (Hamilton)

*   *   *

EYNHARDT, Guillermo
    See QUIROGA, Horacio (Sylvestre)

F

FAIR, A. A.
See GARDNER, Erle Stanley

* * *

FALLACI, Oriana 1930-

PERSONAL: Born June 29, 1930, in Florence, Italy; daughter of Edoardo (a cabinet maker and politician) and Tosca (Cantini) Fallaci; lived with Alexandros Panagoulis (a political activist; died May 1, 1976). *Education:* Attended University of Florence. *Politics:* Liberal. *Religion:* "None."

ADDRESSES: c/o Rizzoli Editore Corp., 712 Fifth Ave., New York, N.Y. 10019.

CAREER: Writer. Special correspondent for Europe (Italian magazine) since 1950s; formerly reporter for *Epoca* (Italian magazine). Has interviewed internationally known figures, including Nguyen Cao Ky, Yasir Arafat, the Shah of Iran, Henry Kissinger, Walter Cronkite, Indira Gandhi, Golda Meir, Nguyen Van Thieu, Zulfikar Ali Bhutto, Willy Brandt, the Aytollah Khomeini, and Mu'ammar Muhammad al-Gaddafi.

AWARDS, HONORS: Has twice received St. Vincent prize journalism; Bancarella Prize, 1971 for *Nothing, and So Be It;* Doctorate in Letters honoris causa from Columbia College (Chicago); Viareggio Prize for *Un uomo: Romanzo.*

WRITINGS:

I sette peccati di Hollywood (title means "The Seven Sins of Hollywood"), preface by Orson Welles, Longanesi (Milan), 1958.
Il sesso inutile: Viaggio intorno all donna, Rizzoli (Milan), 1961, translation by Pamela Swinglehurst published as *The Useless Sex,* Horizon Press, 1964.
Penelope alla guerra (novel), Kizzoli, 1962, translation by Swinglehurst published as *Penelope at War,* Joseph, 1966.
Gli antipatici, Rizzoli, 1963, translation by Swinglehurst published in England as *Limelighters,* Joseph, 1967, published as *The Egotists: Sixteen Surprising Interviews,* Regnery, 1968.
Se il sole muore, Rizzoli, 1965, translation by Swinglehurst published as *If the Sun Dies,* Atheneum, 1966.
Niente a cosi sia, Rizzoli, 1969, translation by Isabel Quigly published as *Nothing, and So Be It,* Doubleday, 1972 (published in England as *Nothing and Amen,* M. Joseph, 1972).

Quel giorno sulla Luna, Rizzoli, 1970.
Intervista con la Storia Rizzoli, 1974, translation by John Shepley published as *Interview with History,* Liveright, 1976.
Lettera a un bambino mai nato, Rizzoli, 1975, translation by Shepley published as *Letter to a Child Never Born,* Simon & Schuster, 1976.
Un uomo: Romanzo (novel), Rizzoli, 1979, translation by William Weaver published as *A Man,* Simon & Schuster, 1980.

Contributor of numerous articles to periodicals throughout the world, including *New Republic, New York Times Magazine, Life, La Nouvelle Observateur, Washington Post, Der Stern,* and *Corriere della Sera.*

SIDELIGHTS: Though she has written novels and memoirs, Italian author Oriana Fallaci remains best known as a hard hitting political interviewer, or, as Elizabeth Mehren puts it in the *Los Angeles Times,* "the journalist to whom virtually no world figure would say no." Her subjects include Henry Kissinger, Willy Brandt, the Ayatollah Khomeini, and the late Pakistani leader Zulfikar Ali Bhutto, from whom she extracted such criticism of India's Indira Gandhi that a 1972 peace treaty between the two countries almost went unsigned. Already as famous as many of the figures she interviews, Fallaci is a freethinker passionately committed to her craft. "I do not feel myself to be, nor will I ever succeed in feeling like, a cold recorder of what I see and hear," she writes in the preface to *Interview with History.* "On every professional experience I leave shreds of my heart and soul; and I participate in what I see or hear as though the matter concerned me personally and were one on which I ought to take a stand (in fact I always take one, based on a specific moral choice)."

While Fallaci's morality has seldom been questioned, her interviewing techniques are highly controversial. According to *New York Times Book Review* contributor Francine du Plessix Gray, Fallaci combines "the psychological insight of a great novelist and the irreverence of a bratty quiz kid." Known for her abrasive interviewing tactics, Fallaci often goads her subjects into revelations. "Let's talk about war," she challenged Henry Kissinger in their 1972 interview. "You're not a pacifist, are you?" When a subject refuses to cooperate, he becomes "a bastard, a fascist, an idiot," notes *Esquire* contributor David Sanford.

Fallaci denies her reputation as a brutal interrogator, insisting instead that she merely frames the questions other reporters lack the courage to ask. Where others seek objectivity, Fallaci prefers an approach that she calls "correct" and "honest." Each interview, "is a portrait of myself," she told *Time* contributor Jordan Bonfante. "They are a strange mixture of my ideas, my temperament, my patience, all of these driving the questions."

Although Ted Morgan complains in the *Washington Post* that Fallaci "wants to be more than a brilliant interviewer, she wants to be an avenging angel," Fallaci defends her unique approach on the grounds that she is not simply a journalist but a historian as well. She told Bonfante: "A journalist lives history in the best of ways, that is in the moment that history takes place. He lives history, he touches history with his hands, looks at it with his eyes, he listens to it with his ears." To Jonathan Cott in a *Rolling Stone* interview, she explained: "I am the judge. I am the one who decides. Listen: if I am a painter and I do your portrait, have I or haven't I the right to paint you as I want?"

Fallaci's commitment to self-expression began at an early age. She told *CA* that she remembers writing "short naive stories" at age nine. "Yet," she continues, "I really started writing at sixteen when I became a reporter in Florence. I got into journalism to become a writer." When asked what circumstances had been important to her career, Fallaci said, "first of all, the fact of belonging to a liberal and politically engaged family. Also, the fact of having lived—though as a child—the heroic days of the Resistance in Italy through a father who was a leader of it. Then, the fact of being a Florentine. That is, the result of a certain civilization and culture. However, I sometimes wonder if the most motivating factor has not been the fact of being born a woman and poor. When you are a woman, you have to fight more. Consequently, to see more and to think more and to be more creative. The same, when you were born poor. Survival is a great pusher."

Fallaci told *CA* that the purpose behind her writing is "to tell a story with meaning. Certainly not money. I never wrote for money. I could never write for money—which means by order or for an engagement with a publisher." Instead, the motivating factor of each of her books is "a great emotion, both a psychological or political and [an] intellectual emotion. Think of *Nothing, and So Be It,* the book on Vietnam. For me, it is not even a book on Vietnam, it is a book on the war. (I am obsessed by the uselessness and the stupidity and the cruelty and the folly of the war.) *Letter to a Child Never Born* (which was not written for the issue of abortion as it has been said so often and so gratuitously) was born out of the loss of a child. *A Man* was written out of the death of my companion Alekos Panagoulis and the grief for such loss. However, one should notice that the leitmotiv of all my books is the theme of death. These three books always speak of death or refer to death, my hate for death, my fight against death. . . . Freedom is only one of the many other elements. What really pushes me to write is my obsession with death."

Her work habits are Spartan. "I start working early in the morning (eight or eight-thirty a.m.) and go on until six p.m. or seven p.m. without interruption," she told *CA*. "That is, without eating and without resting. I smoke more than usual, which means, around fifty cigarettes a day. I sleep badly in the night. I don't see anybody. I don't answer the telephone. I don't go anywhere. I ignore the Sundays, the holidays, the Christmases, the New Year's Eves. I get hysterical, in other words, and unhappy and unsatisfied and guilty if I don't produce much. By the way, I am a very slow writer. And I rewrite obsessively. So I get ill and ugly, and lose weight and get wrinkles."

Fallaci finds the current literary scene, "rich, even too rich. How much substance under such richness, who knows? Only time can give such measurement. A writer needs time to be tested in his/her value. Having success in life means nothing. Success in life has too much to do with fashion, publicity, and so on. A writer stays a writer after his death or many years after his/her books were published. Also, a writer is a writer when his work goes beyond the limits and frontiers of the language he/she writes in. Because a writer must be universal, timeless, and spaceless."

In *A Man,* Fallaci attempts to immortalize the martyred poet and Greek resistance leader Alekos Panagoulis, the great love of her life. Though she calls the book a novel, *A Man* recounts the real story of Panagoulis's fight for Greece's freedom—a fight he continued until his death. In 1967, Panagoulis attempted to assassinate the fascist Greek dictator Georgios Papadopoulos by planting a series of bombs along the roads he traveled each day. The plan failed, and Panagoulis was captured and imprisoned almost immediately. During the next five years, the revolutionary was subjected to physical abuse as well as psychological torture in an effort to break his spirit and will. Despite the inhuman treatment, Panagoulis refused to succumb, and his repeated escape attempts and uncompromising rebelliousness finally led him to be isolated in a specially constructed cell, not much larger than a double bed, with no windows and only three paces' worth of standing room. He remained there until he was freed under a general amnesty in 1973. Two days after his release, Panagoulis was interviewed by Fallaci, and, firmly convinced that their meeting was an act of fate, the two became lovers within a few weeks.

For the next three years, Fallaci and Panagoulis shared a tempestuous relationship. According to Marcia Seligson in the *Los Angeles Times,* "he told her: 'I don't want a woman to be happy with. The world is full of women you can be happy with. . . . And I want a companion. A companion who will be my comrade, friend, accomplice, brother. I'm a man in battle. I always will be.' She became all those things, surrendering her own full and independent life to follow this difficult, maddening, towering man. She lived an emotional pendulum of anguish/bliss; there was no serenity, no future, only thrills and chills." Panagoulis was killed by political enemies in an ambush made to look like an auto accident in 1976. Within months of his death, Fallaci began work on the book she would dedicate to him, and, in 1979, published what she considers her most important work, *A Man.*

Critical reaction to the book runs the gamut from praise to disdain. Supporters, such as Seligson, hail *A Man* as "a work of passion, courage, candor and exquisite skill." *Saturday Review* contributor Julie Stone Peters describes it as "a majestic and soul-stirring narration," maintaining that Fallaci "has learned from her interviews how to control the novel." Peter Brunette believes that her ideas transcend "the 'merely' political: Fallaci places her subject in the most deeply Greek context of all, that of ancient tragedy, as she marvelously adduces one resonant mythic parallel after another on the way to her lover's final submission to his tragic fate," he writes in the *New Republic.*

Others eschew her approach. "Throughout this catalogue of misery, Fallaci never makes the right choice," notes a *Time* reviewer. "When the account needs historical analysis, she offers tantrums; when suffering cries out for a tragic spirit, she substitutes bathos." Vivian Gomick compares it to "an old fashioned dish of hearty melodrama being offered as though it were the cuisine of tragedy."

None of which matters much to Oriana Fallaci, who doesn't keep reviews of her books and told *CA,* "I do not respect reviewers. They are almost always failed writers, consequently envious and jealous of those who write. I find their profession kind of despicable, because it is so unfair and stupid to snap judgments in a little article after the work of years. I think that the real reviewers are the readers. I care very much for the letters of my readers. I receive them from all over the world, and they always say much more intelligent things than those written by the 'reviewers.'

"There are a couple of incisive reviews from my readers that I could quote. One came from a poor worker, a forty-year-old carpenter from Florence, after reading *Letter To a Child Never Born.* It said: 'I read your book three times. You know why? Because it said the same things I always thought about life. Though I did not know that I was thinking them.' Another one came from a fifty-year-old concierge of Milan: 'Your books have taught us courage.' Another one from a student of Shanghai: 'I learnt from you the meaning of the word freedom.' "

Through her books, Fallaci says she hopes "to die a little less when I die. To leave the children I did not have. . . . To make people think a little more, outside the dogmas that this society has nourished us with through centuries. To give stories and ideas that help people to see better, to think better, to know a little more. Then what? Writing is my way of expression. Therefore, a need."

Her advice to aspiring writers is "not to be in a hurry to publish. And to rewrite, to rewrite, to rewrite." Though she has respect for the work of many contemporary writers, Fallaci admits "all my direct encounters with the contemporary writers I admire or still admire professionally, ended in bitterness. I mean, I found out that as persons they were not as admirable and respectable as they were as writers. And I am incapable of dividing the judgment between the writer and the private person."

Most of Fallaci's books have been translated from Italian into numerous other languages, including French, Spanish, German, Swedish, Dutch, Croatian, and Greek.

BIOGRAPHICAL/CRITICAL SOURCES:

BOOKS

Contemporary Literary Criticism, Volume 11, Gale, 1979.
Fallaci, Oriana, *Interview With History,* Liveright, 1976.
Fallaci, Oriana, *A Man,* Simon & Schuster, 1980.

PERIODICALS

Chicago Tribune Book World, November 30, 1980.
Esquire, November, 1968, June, 1975.
Harper's, November, 1980.
Life, February 21, 1969.
Los Angeles Times, November, 1980, December 2, 1980.
New Republic, November 22, 1980.
New York, May 22, 1978.
New Yorker, February 21, 1977.
New York Times, January 25, 1973, November 3, 1980.
New York Times Book Review, February 5, 1967, February 13, 1977, November 23, 1980.
People, March 14, 1977.
Publishers Weekly, November 7, 1980.
Rolling Stone, June 17, 1976.
Saturday Review, March 18, 1972, November, 1980.
Times Literary Supplement, August 11, 1972, May 22, 1981.
Time, October 20, January 19, 1981.
Washington Post, February 23, 1972, March 13, 1972, May 18, 1976.
Washington Post Book World, February 13, 1977, November 30, 1980.

FALLON, Martin
See PATTERSON, Harry

*   *   *

FARIGOULE, Louis
See ROMAINS, Jules

*   *   *

FARMER, Philip Jose   1918-
(Kilgore Trout, John H. Watson)

PERSONAL: Born January 26, 1918, in North Terre Haute, Ind.; son of George (a civil and electrical engineer) and Lucile Theodora (Jackson) Farmer; married Elizabeth Virginia Andre, May 10, 1941; children: Philip Laird, Kristen. *Education:* Attended University of Missouri, 1936-37, 1942; Bradley University, B.A., 1950; Arizona State University, graduate study, 1961-62.

ADDRESSES: Home—5617 North Fairmont Dr., Peoria, Ill. 61614. *Agent*—Ted Clark, Scott Meredith Literary Agency, 845 Third Ave., New York, N.Y. 10022.

CAREER: Worked at various jobs, 1936-56, with some periods as full-time writer; General Electric, Syracuse, N.Y., technical writer, 1956-58; Motorola, Scottsdale, Ariz., technical writer, 1958-65; technical writer for MacDonnel-Douglas, 1967-69; free-lance writer, 1965-67, 1969—. *Military service:* U.S. Army Air Forces, 1942-43; aviation cadet.

MEMBER: Society of Technical Writers and Editors, Burroughs Bibliophiles, American Association for the Advancement of Science, Lambda Chi Alpha.

AWARDS, HONORS: Hugo Award, World Science Fiction Convention, 1952, as the best new writer in the science fiction field, 1967, for best novella, "Riders of the Purple Wage," and 1971, for best novel, *To Your Scattered Bodies Go;* guest of honor at 26th World Science Fiction Convention, 1968, and at other science fiction conventions.

WRITINGS:

The Green Odyssey, Ballantine, 1957, reprinted, Gregg Press, 1978.
Strange Relations, Ballantine, 1960, reprinted, Avon, 1978.
Flesh, Beacon, 1960.
A Woman a Day, Beacon, 1960, published as *The Day of Timestop,* Lancer Books, 1968 (published in England as *Timestop!,* Quartet, 1973).
The Lovers, Ballantine, 1961, reprinted, 1979.
The Alley God, Ballantine, 1962.
Fire and the Night, Regency, 1962.
Cache from Outer Space [and] *The Celestial Blueprint, and Other Stories,* Ace, 1962.
Tongues of the Moon, Pyramid Publications, 1964.
Inside Outside, Ballantine, 1964, reprinted, Berkley, 1979.
Dare, Ballantine, 1965.
The Maker of Universes, Ace, 1965.
The Gates of Creation, Ace, 1966.
The Gate of Time, Belmont Books, 1966, expanded edition published as *Two Hawks from Earth,* Ace, 1979.
Night of Light, Berkley, 1966, reprinted, Berkley, 1983.
The Image of the Beast; An Exorcism: Ritual One (also see below), Essex House, 1968.
Blown, Or Sketches among the Ruins of My Mind; An Exorcism: Ritual Two (also see below), Essex House, 1969.

A Feast Unknown: Volume IX of the Memoirs of Lord Grandrith, Essex House, 1969.

Lord of the Trees: Volume X of the Memoirs of Lord Grandrith (also see below), Ace, 1970.

The Mad Goblin (also see below), Ace 1970.

Lord Tyger, Doubleday, 1970.

Love Song, Brandon House, 1970.

The Stone God Awakens, Ace, 1970.

Down in the Black Gang, and Other Stories, Doubleday, 1971.

The Wind Whales of Ishmael, Ace, 1971.

Tarzan Alive: A Definitive Biography of Lord Greystoke, Doubleday, 1972.

Time's Last Gift, Ballantine, 1972.

The Book of Philip Jose Farmer, or The Wares of Simple Simon's Custard Pie and Space Man, Daw Books, 1973.

Doc Savage: His Apocalyptic Life, Doubleday, 1973.

The Other Log of Phileas Fogg, Daw Books, 1973, reprinted, Tor, 1988.

Traitor to the Living, Ballantine, 1973.

Hadon of Ancient Opar, Daw Books, 1974.

(Compiler) *Mother Was a Lovely Beast: A Feral Man Anthology—Fiction and Fact about Humans Raised by Animals,* Chilton, 1974.

(Editor under name Philip Jose Farmer; author under pseudonym John H. Watson) *The Adventure of the Peerless Peer,* Aspen Press, 1974.

(Under pseudonym Kilgore Trout) *Venus on the Half-Shell,* Dell, 1975.

Flight to Opar, Daw Books, 1976.

(With J. H. Rosny) *Ironcastle,* Daw Books, 1978.

Dark is the Sun, Ballantine, 1979.

Riverworld and Other Stories, Berkley, 1979.

Image of the Beast (contains *Image of the Beast and Blown*), Playboy Press, 1979.

Jesus on Mars, Pinnacle Books, 1979.

Lord of the Trees [and] *The Mad Goblin,* Ace, 1980.

Riverworld War: The Suppressed Fiction of Philip Jose Farmer, Ellis Press, 1980.

River of Eternity, Phantasia Press, 1981.

A Barnstormer in Oz, Berkley, 1982.

The Grand Adventure, Berkley, 1984.

The Classic Philip Jose Farmer, Robson, 1985.

The Cache, Tor, 1986.

Father to the Stars, Tor, 1988.

Stations of the Nightmare, Tor, 1988.

"WORLD OF TIERS" SERIES

The Maker of Universes, Ace, 1965, revised edition, Phantasia Press, 1980.

The Gates of Creation, Ace, 1966.

A Private Cosmos, Ace, 1968.

Behind the Walls of Terra, Ace, 1970.

The Lavalite World, Ace, 1977.

The World of Tiers (contains *The Maker of Universes, The Gates of Creation, A Private Cosmos, Behind the Walls of Terra,* and *The Lavalite World;* Science Fiction Book Club selection), two volumes, Thomas Nelson-Doubleday, 1980.

"RIVERWORLD" SERIES

To Your Scattered Bodies Go, Putnam, 1971.

The Fabulous Riverboat, Putnam, 1971.

The Dark Design, Berkley, 1977.

The Magic Labyrinth, Berkley, 1980.

Gods of the Riverworld, Putnam, 1983.

Philip Jose Farmer: The Complete Riverworld Novels, five volumes, Berkley, 1982.

"DAYWORLD" SERIES

Dayworld, Granada, 1985.

Dayworld Rebel, Putnam, 1987.

OTHER

Work appears in anthologies. Contributor to *Visual Encyclopedia of Science Fiction.* Contributor of short stories to *Magazine of Fantasy and Science Fiction, Startling Stories, Adventure,* and other magazines.

SIDELIGHTS: Philip Jose Farmer's science fiction novels, Donald A. Wollheim believes, are a "veritable fireworks of new concepts in biology and fantasy lands." One of Farmer's most noted innovations was his introduction of sex to the science fiction field. Sex became, Wollheim notes in *The Universe Makers,* "a legitimate subject of science fiction extrapolation." The introduction occurred in Farmer's novel *The Lovers,* first published in 1952 as a magazine story. In it, a human being has sexual intercourse with an alien. Both the sex act itself and the fact that it involved an alien being triggered off a controversy within science fiction circles. Despite the initial reaction, the story stands as a historically important work in the field.

Farmer's talent for new concepts is given full rein in his "Riverworld" series, which Roland Green of *Booklist* calls "one of the largest, most ambitious, and least conventional works of modern science fiction." The tetralogy concerns the planet Riverworld, a single, million-miled river valley into which the entire human race is reincarnated at the same time. A few of the reborn humans, including such diverse characters as Mark Twain, Cyrano de Bergerac, and Hermann Goering, search for the headwaters of the River in the hope that it may hold the answer to their reincarnation.

Farmer began the "Riverworld" series in 1952 when he entered a writing contest sponsored by two publishing companies. Farmer won the contest with his first Riverworld novel but, before he collected his $4,000 prize money, one of the publishers went bankrupt, taking his prize money with it. Worse, Farmer lost the rights to his book for many years.

It wasn't until the late 1960s that Farmer revived the Riverworld idea. He wrote a series of novelettes for magazine publication that contained "very little of the original novel, aside from the basic concept," as Farmer states in *Dream Makers.* When these novelettes were published together as a novel, the result was the Hugo Award-winning *To Your Scattered Bodies Go,* and the "Riverworld" series was on its way. As Peter Stoler of *Time* writes, "the auspicious opening [of the series] was a difficult act to follow, and many Farmerites wondered whether the Riverworld was wide enough to sustain a projected tetralogy. The author's next works allayed all fears."

Farmer's characters build a paddle wheel boat, several blimps, and even an air force of small planes in their quest for the headwaters of the River. Besides fighting among themselves and against hostile peoples they must voyage past during their journey, the explorers must be on guard against agents of the Ethicals, the mysterious creators of Riverworld, who are secretly in their midst. In the course of this adventure, many theological, political, and cultural questions are raised and discussed by historical figures from widely different times and cultures. Stoler concludes that "Farmer offers his audience a wide-screen adventure that never fails to provoke, amuse, and educate."

Further examples of Farmer's innovative concepts are found in the "World of Tiers" series, which concerns a highly advanced race of men who, through the use of technology, create entire self-contained universes governed by arbitrary natural laws. Although other writers have examined man's evolution and technological development, Farmer makes, Wollheim states, "the implication that God Himself might be just another mortal playing at scientific games."

In other books, such as *The Adventure of the Peerless Peer* and *Tarzan Alive,* Farmer plays tongue-in-cheek games using famous literary characters. In *The Peerless Peer,* he writes a new Sherlock Holmes adventure under the pseudonym of Holmes's assistant, John H. Watson. *Tarzan Alive* is a thorough biography of the "real" Tarzan that answers questions, a reviewer for the *New York Times* holds, that "have been plaguing practically nobody at all for many years now. . . . Rarely has so much been written so obscurely about so little." He concludes that Farmer is "some kind of a genius of Dada."

Under the pseudonym Kilgore Trout, Farmer wrote *Venus on the Half-Shell,* a parody of Kurt Vonnegut. Trout, a character in several of Vonnegut's novels, is a science fiction writer who has authored hundreds of books, all of them unfortunately published by pornography houses who marketed them under rather non-SF titles. "I thought people would flip their minds," Farmer explains in *Dream Makers,* "if they saw a book by Trout, a supposedly fictional character, on the stands. Also, I did it as a tribute, the highest, to an author whom I loved and admired at that time. And I identify with Trout." Farmer's parody was so well done that several critics assumed Vonnegut had written the book. "Who is Kilgore Trout?," Walton R. Collins of the *National Observer* asks. "The odds are good that he is Vonnegut. . . . You can't read a dozen pages anywhere in *Venus* without becoming morally certain you're reading Vonnegut. The style is unmistakable."

Speaking of his many novels, Farmer states in *Dream Makers:* "I can see where I could have done better. I can see innumerable cases. But it's no good to go back and rewrite them, because if you did you'd lose a certain primitive vigor that they have. The thing to do is to go on and write new stuff."

The Philip Jose Farmer Society, an organization for enthusiasts and collectors of Farmer's work, was founded in 1978.

BIOGRAPHICAL/CRITICAL SOURCES:

BOOKS

Brizzi, Mary, *The Reader's Guide to Philip Jose Farmer,* Starmont, 1980.
Clareson, Thomas D., editor, *Voices for the Future,* Volume 2, Bowling Green University Popular Press, 1979.
Contemporary Literary Criticism, Gale, Volume 1, 1973, Volume 19, 1981.
Dictionary of Literary Biography, Gale, Volume 8: *Twentieth-Century American Science-Fiction Writers,* 1981.
Knapp, Lawrence J., *The First Editions of Philip Jose Farmer, Science Fiction Bibliographies 2,* David G. Turner, 1976.
Moskowitz, Sam, *Seekers of Tomorrow: Masters of Modern Science Fiction,* Hyperion, 1974.
Platt, Charles, *Dream Makers: The Uncommon People Who Write Science Fiction,* Berkley, 1980.
Wollheim, Donald A., *The Universe Makers,* Harper, 1971.

PERIODICALS

Amazing Science Fiction, October, 1961.
Analog, December, 1977, July, 1978, December, 1980.
Booklist, October 1, 1977, July 15, 1980.
Books and Bookmen, December, 1966.
Extrapolation, May, 1976, December, 1976, May, 1977.
Galaxy, January, 1958.
Magazine of Fantasy and Science Fiction, October, 1953, July, 1962, September, 1965, May, 1967, February, 1978.
National Observer, May 17, 1975.
National Review, April 14, 1972.
New York Times, April 22, 1972.
Observer, December 21, 1969, August 8, 1976.
Science Fiction Collector, September, 1977.
Science Fiction Review, August, 1975, November, 1977, February, 1978.
Science Fiction Studies, Volume 1, 1973, Volume 4, 1977.
Spectator, August 4, 1973.
Time, July 28, 1980.
Times Literary Supplement, January 8, 1970, April 12, 1974.
Village Voice, June 13, 1974.
Xenophile, September-October, 1977, September-October, 1979.

*   *   *

FARRELL, J(ames) G(ordon)   1935-1979

PERSONAL: Born January 23, 1935, in Liverpool, England; drowned after being swept out to sea while fishing, August 14, 1979, in Bantry Bay, Ireland. *Education:* Brasenose College, Oxford, B.A., 1960.

CAREER: Writer.

AWARDS, HONORS: Harkness Fellowship for residence in United States, 1966-68; Arts Council Award, 1970; Faber Memorial Prize, 1970, for *Troubles;* Booker Literary Prize, 1973, for *The Siege of Krishnapur.*

WRITINGS:

NOVELS

A Man from Elsewhere, Hutchinson, 1963.
The Lung, Hutchinson, 1965.
A Girl in the Head, J. Cape, 1967, Harper, 1969.
Troubles, J. Cape, 1970, Knopf, 1971.
The Siege of Krishnapur, Weidenfeld & Nicolson, 1973, Harcourt, 1974.
The Singapore Grip, Knopf, 1979.
The Hill Station: An Unfinished Novel [and] *An Indian Diary,* edited by John Spurling, Weidenfeld & Nicolson, 1981.

SIDELIGHTS: James Farrell's *Siege of Krishnapur* is set in India during the 1857 Sepoy Rebellion. Critic Walter Clemons noted that the novel "begins as a comedy of Victorian conventions and imperial pride. It accelerates into a terrific narration of action as the prolonged siege tests the inmates of Krishnapur with cholera, stench, despair and religious mania. Before it ends, steep clefts have opened in the assumptions of progress and civilized order." Clemons concluded his enthusiastic review by stating that the book "is a work of wit, lively historical reconstruction and imaginative intensity. Farrell is an original, and I only mean to chart rough points of reference by suggesting that his book combines the pleasures of *The Reason Why,* Cecil Woodham-Smith's astringent study of the Charge of the Light Brigade, and Richard Hughes's classic *A High Wind in Jamaica.*"

Melvin Maddocks wrote: "Novelist Farrell takes his Englishmen out of a quaint hunting print and frames them in a painting by Hieronymus Bosch. The once happy few, besieged in the compound at Krishnapur for three months, come to resemble the natives they had so exquisitely ignored. . . . Farrell can write with a fury to match his theme," Maddocks continued. "As spectacle, *The Siege of Krishnapur* has the blaze and the agony of a scenario for hell. But as moral commentary, it is overcalculated—and its ironies unsuitably neat."

L. E. Sissman commented that "Farrell's interesting and entertaining novel is merely the rather early effort of a writer who has not yet hit his stride." He criticized Farrell for attempting to cover too much ground ("its audacious idea . . . promises more than it is able to deliver") with a plot "which is sort of pat, [and] is strung out on a series of carefully staged set pieces." But, Sissman added: "When Mr. Farrell is not caught up in an understandable desire to poke fun at his characters and their orotund respectabilities, he can be both direct and affecting; then even his ordinary diction comes to life."

BIOGRAPHICAL/CRITICAL SOURCES:

BOOKS

Contemporary Literary Criticism, Volume 6, Gale, 1976.
Dictionary of Literary Biography, Volume 14: *British Novelists since 1960,* Gale, 1982.

PERIODICALS

Newsweek, October 21, 1974.
New Yorker, November 25, 1974.
Time, September 30, 1974.
Washington Post, May 5, 1979.

OBITUARIES:

PERIODICALS

AB Bookman's Weekly, October 8, 1979.
Chicago Tribune, August 15, 1979.
New York Times, August 15, 1979.
Publishers Weekly, September 3, 1979.

*   *   *

FARRELL, James T(homas) 1904-1979
(Jonathan Titulescu Fogarty, Esq.)

PERSONAL: Born February 27, 1904, in Chicago, Ill.; died of a heart attack, August 22, 1979, in New York, N.Y.; son of James Francis and Mary (Daly) Farrell; married Dorothy Patricia Butler, 1931 (divorced); married Hortense Alden (divorced September, 1955); remarried Dorothy Butler Farrell, September, 1955 (separated, 1958); children: (with second wife) Kevin. *Education:* Attended night classes at De Paul University, one semester, 1924-25; attended University of Chicago, eight quarters, until 1929; attended New York University, one semester.

ADDRESSES: Home—310 East 44th St., New York, N.Y.

CAREER: Writer. Worked wrapping shoes in a chain store in Chicago, Ill.; as a clerk for the American Railway Express Co. in Chicago; a filling-station attendant; a cigar store clerk in New York City; an advertising salesman for Donnelly's *Red Book* in Queens, New York; in an undertaking parlor in Chicago; as a campus reporter for the *Chicago Herald Examiner;* and, for two weeks, as a scenario writer in Hollywood, Calif. Served as chairman of the national board, Workers Defense League, New York City, and as a member of the Spanish Refugee Aid Committee.

MEMBER: National Institute of Arts and Letters, Authors League of America, American Civil Liberties Union, Overseas Press Club.

AWARDS, HONORS: Guggenheim fellowship for creative writing, 1936; Book-of-the-Month Club prize, 1937, for *Studs Lonigan: A Trilogy;* Messing Award, St. Louis University Library Association; honorary degrees from Miami University, Oxford University, Ohio State University, Columbia University, University of Chicago, and Glassboro State College.

WRITINGS:

Young Lonigan: A Boyhood in Chicago Streets (also see below), Vanguard, 1932, reprinted with new introduction, World Publishing, 1943, published as *Young Lonigan: The Studs Lonigan Story,* Avon, 1972.
Gas-House McGinty, Vanguard, 1933.
Calico Shoes, and Other Stories (also see below), Vanguard, 1934 (published in England as *Seventeen, and Other Stories,* Panther, 1959).
The Young Manhood of Studs Lonigan (also see below), Vanguard, 1934, reprinted with new introduction, World Publishing, 1944, reprinted, Avon, 1973.
Judgment Day, Vanguard, 1935, reprinted with new introduction, World Publishing, 1945, reprinted, Avon, 1973.
Studs Lonigan: A Trilogy (contains *Young Lonigan, The Young Manhood of Studs Lonigan,* and *Judgment Day*), Vanguard, 1935, reprinted with new introduction, Modern Library, 1938, published with an introduction and a new epilogue by the author, Vanguard, 1978.
Guillotine Party, and Other Stories (also see below), Vanguard, 1935.
A World I Never Made, Vanguard, 1936, reprinted with new introduction, World Publishing, 1947.
A Note on Literary Criticism, Vanguard, 1937.
Fellow Countrymen: Collected Stories, Vanguard, 1937.
Can All This Grandeur Perish?, and Other Stories (also see below), Vanguard, 1937.
The Short Stories of James T. Farrell (contains *Calico Shoes, and Other Stories, Guillotine Party, and Other Stories,* and *Can All This Grandeur Perish?, and Other Stories*), Vanguard, 1937.
No Star Is Lost, Vanguard, 1938, reprinted with new introduction, World Publishing, 1947, reprinted, Popular Library, 1961.
Father and Son, Vanguard, 1940, reprinted with new introduction, World Publishing, 1947 (published in England as *Father and His Son,* Routledge & Kegan Paul, 1943).
Ellen Rogers, Vanguard, 1941.
Short Stories, Blue Ribbon Books, 1941.
$1000 a Week, and Other Stories (also see below), Vanguard, 1942.
My Days of Anger, Vanguard, 1943, reprinted with new introduction, World Publishing, 1947.
Fifteen Selected Stories, Avon, 1943.
To Whom It May Concern, and Other Stories, Vanguard, 1944 (also see below), published as *More Stories,* Sun Dial Press, 1946.
Twelve Great Stories, Avon, 1945.
The League of Frightened Philistines, and Other Papers, Vanguard, 1945.
When Boyhood Dreams Come True, Vanguard, 1946, published as *Further Short Stories,* Sun Dial Press, 1948.
More Fellow Countrymen, Routledge & Kegan Paul, 1946.
Bernard Clare, Vanguard, 1946, published as *Bernard Carr,* New American Library, 1952.
The Fate of Writing in America, New Directions, 1946.
The Life Adventurous, and Other Stories (also see below), Vanguard, 1947.

Literature and Morality, Vanguard, 1947.

A Hell of a Good Time, and Other Stories, Avon, 1947.

Yesterday's Love, and Eleven Other Stories, Avon, 1948.

The Road Between, Vanguard, 1949.

A Misunderstanding, House of Books, 1949.

An American Dream Girl, and Other Stories, Vanguard, 1950.

(Under pseudonym Jonathan Titulescu Fogarty, Esq.) *The Name Is Fogarty: Private Papers on Public Matters,* Vanguard, 1950.

This Man and This Woman, Vanguard, 1951.

(Contributor of "The Frontier and James Whitcomb Riley") *Poet of the People,* Indiana University Press, 1951.

Yet Other Waters, Vanguard, 1952.

The Face of Time, Vanguard, 1953.

Reflections at Fifty, and Other Essays, Vanguard, 1954.

French Girls Are Vicious, and Other Stories, Vanguard, 1955.

(Author of introduction) Theodore Dreiser, *Best Short Stories,* World Publishing, 1956.

An Omnibus of Short Stories (contains *$1000 a Week, and Other Stories, To Whom It May Concern, and Other Stories,* and *The Life Adventurous, and Other Stories*), Vanguard, 1956.

My Baseball Diary, A. S. Bames, 1957.

A Dangerous Woman, and Other Stories, Vanguard, 1957.

Saturday Night, and Other Stories, Hamish Hamilton, 1958.

It Has Come to Pass, T. Herzl Press, 1958.

(Editor) H. L. Mencken, *Prejudices,* Vintage, 1958.

The Girl at the Sphinx (collection of short stories previously published by Vanguard), Hamish Hamilton, 1959.

(With others) *Dialogue on John Dewey,* edited by Corliss Lamont and Mary Redmer, Horizon, 1959.

Boarding House Blues, Paperback Library, 1961.

Side Street, and Other Stories, Paperback Library, 1961.

Sound of a City (short stories), Paperback Library, 1962.

The Silence of History (first of a projected 29-volume series), Doubleday, 1963.

Selected Essays, edited by Luna Wolf, McGraw, 1964.

What Time Collects, Doubleday, 1964.

The Collected Poems of James T. Farrell, Fleet, 1965.

Lonely for the Future, Doubleday, 1966.

When Time Was Born (prose poem), The Smith, 1966.

The Letters to Theodore Dreiser, The Smith, 1966.

New Year's Eve, 1929, The Smith, 1967.

A Brand New Life (novel), Doubleday, 1968.

Childhood Is Not Forever, Doubleday, 1969.

Judith (also see below), Duane Schneider Press, 1969.

Invisible Swords, Doubleday, 1971.

(Contributor) Ray Boxer and Harry Smith, editors, *The Smith-Fourteen,* The Smith, 1972.

Judith, and Other Stories, Doubleday, 1973.

The Dunne Family, Doubleday, 1976.

Literary Essays, 1954-1974, edited by Jack Alan Robbins, Kennikat Press, 1976.

Olive and Maryanne, Stonehill Publishing, 1977.

The Death of Nora Ryan, Doubleday, 1978.

Eight Short Stories and Sketches, Arts End, 1981.

Also author of *Tommy Gallagher's Crusade,* 1939, and *Sam Holman;* editor of *A Dreiser Reader,* 1962. Contributor to magazines and to the Asian press.

SIDELIGHTS: In 1941, Joseph Warren Beach described James T. Farrell's writing as "perhaps the plainest, soberest, most straightforward of any living novelist," thus citing the basis of both the criticism and praise of Farrell's work. Farrell is most often recognized as a naturalistic writer, a school to which he adhered even during the 1930s when symbolism was increasingly popular. In *Reflections at Fifty,* Farrell wrote: "I have been called a naturalist and I have never denied it. However, my own conception of naturalism is not that which is usually attributed to me. By naturalism I mean that whatever happens in this world must ultimately be explainable in terms of events in this world, in terms of natural origins rather than of extranatural or supernatural origins." In *The Modern Novel in Britain and the United States,* Walter Allen wrote: "James T. Farrell, for all his indebtedness to Joyce, began as a naturalist and has remained one, unrepentant and defiant. He is the true heir of Dreiser. If he lacks Dreiser's tragic sense, he has an icily relentless passion that transforms his best work into a formidable indictment of society."

In *American Fiction, 1920-1940,* Beach wrote: "Farrell's type of naturalism is not a kind to appeal to the common run of readers. It has little to offer those who go to fiction for light entertainment, the glamour of the stage, or the gratification of their bent for wishful thinking. There is no reason why the squeamish or tender-minded should put themselves through the ordeal of trying to like his work. But there will always be a sufficient number of those whom life and thought have ripened and disciplined, who have a taste for truth, however unvarnished, provided it be honestly viewed, deeply pondered, and imaginatively rendered. For many such it may well turn out that James T. Farrell is the most significant of American novelists writing in 1940."

Farrell's ambition and direction as a writer, as well as his thematic material, sprang directly from his own youth in Chicago's South Side. Blanche Housman Gelfant noted in *The American City Novel* that, although the South Side was a slum, without variety, beauty, or surprise, "it provided Farrell with the substance of his art and his purpose as a city novelist. . . . Few city writers are as much the insider as he; and of the writers who have the same kind of inmost knowledge of manners, none has exploited his material to such powerful effect." Beach added: "His literary performance is determined by his pity and loathing for all that was mean, ugly, and spiritually poverty stricken in the mores and culture to which he was born. All his work is a representation, patient, sober, feeling, tireless, pitiless, of a way of living and a state of mind which he abhors, and from which he has taken flight as one flees from the City of Destruction."

Beach contended that "the main theme of all this writing is a state of mind widely diffused in the world [Farrell] knows best—a social state of mind highly unfavorable to the production of full and happy lives, to beauty of thought and sentiment or any of those spiritual values that characterize human civilization at its best." The state of mind is the product of the environment; the environment, in turn, is "defined in its effect upon the inner man," wrote Gelfant. The development of the individual is thus shown as a cumulative process of assimilating these environmental influences. Gelfant noted that Farrell once said: "The conditions of American life create alienated and truncated personalities" because the individual is forced to rely on himself in the face of chaos and "his inner experience becomes one of loneliness, alienation, and unfulfillment." It was Farrell's purpose, according to Gelfant, to utilize the novel to "establish communication between people who in real life had become lost in their private inner worlds and were no longer able to reach out towards each other." And although "the emotional drive behind Farrell's art was anger," he proceeded by objectively considering those problems which are characteristically rooted in emotional involvement. His method was to develop a cinematic sequence of self-contained episodes (each "significant as a revelation of individual character, as well as of a total way of life," noted Gelfant) that would best portray the lack of orientation and the fragmented nature of life in the South Side.

Beach said of the novels: "These are linguistic documents, as they are social documents, of high seriousness and value, but not slavishly photographic. Farrell is obviously more concerned with the spirit than the letter of truth. The documentation is really prodigious, but it did not require the author's going beyond the limits of experience and memory. [Scenes] spring like geysers from the seething burdened depths of the author's being. The appeal is first to the imagination, and only in retrospect to the mind and conscience. In so far as anything is lacking it is some principle of relief." Gelfant stated: "And in the vision of life projected in Farrell's novels this lack of relief is an essential and fundamental quality." Without this relief the world created by Farrell becomes a dynamic oppressive force with which the individual must unsuccessfully contend. Gelfant summarized: "Although Farrell's style has been severely criticized, it is an effective medium through which milieu and character come to life. As a city novelist, Farrell was keenly aware of the inappropriateness of a lyrical manner to the materials of everyday urban life. He adopted the language of his characters as his aesthetic medium, and his versatility as a stylist is revealed in the variety of distinctive speech patterns he recreated."

During the 1930s, Farrell decided that certain literary critics were "perpetrating error and should be exposed before they could do further damage," noted Walter B. Rideout in *The Radical Novel in the United States, 1900-1954.* In 1936 Farrell published *A Note on Literary Criticism,* which, according to Rideout, was the "only extended discussion of Marxist aesthetics written from a Marxist standpoint in the United States during the thirties." Rideout contended that "the book constitutes a simultaneous attack and defense. The attack is directed against both 'revolutionary sentimentalism,' as represented by [Michael] Gold, and 'mechanical Marxism,' as represented by [Granville] Hicks. Since each of these two 'Leftist' tendencies in literary criticism has, in its extreme emphasis on the functional ('use-value') aspect of literature, ignored the aesthetic aspect, they have together, Farrell argued, kept Marxist criticism weak, because they substitute measurement for judgment. Hence, the critic's task, which is ultimately one of judgment, of evaluation, has been avoided." Rideout added later: "If Farrell's own statement of the critic's function is not strikingly original, if his dissection of the deficiencies of proletarian literature and criticism is, stylistically speaking, performed as much with a meat ax as with a scalpel, still the dissection itself was a thorough one." Farrell, in fact, aroused so much critical feeling with this work that *The New Masses* summarized his comments, and those of his supporters, with the arguments of his opponents under the heading "The Farrell Controversy."

Rideout believed that Farrell was prompted, to some extent, to write the criticism by the demands of "several extremist reviewers [who] had called for the display of more 'class-consciousness' in the un-class-conscious characters of whom he wrote." But Farrell also believed that critics were essentially redefining literature as a socially effective instrument. Gelfant wrote: "Farrell's definition of literature as an 'instrument of social control,' makes clear his belief that fiction could not be directly a 'means of solving problems' within society. Rather it was 'a means of helping people to discover more about themselves and about the condition of life about them.' As literature brought the reader to a sharper awareness, it was . . . instrumental in social reform, for it is awareness that produces the pressing sense of concern that moves man finally to act. In order to make the reader more sensitive to his world, literature must exploit fully its aesthetic poten-

tialities." And in 1967 Farrell told the *New York Times:* "I don't think literature should include partisan thinking. I don't believe in things like political commitment in novels." He admitted that he had been in "political campaigns of all kinds" though, and he once bought Russian Communist leader Leon Trotsky a typewriter. "Why? Because he needed it."

Farrell's was not a simple separation of art from propaganda, however. Gelfant noted: "He distinguished between the two by defining literature as a form of revelation, and propaganda as a form of political action. The implicit assumption underlying Farrell's theory is that knowledge will make us free. Whatever the artist has to add to our experience and understanding of the world about us, of any part of it, can be of social consequences."

Many critics believed that Farrell's Studs Lonigan trilogy was extremely successful as a work of "social consequence." Rideout contended that Farrell was the only writer who succeeded in chronicling "with great zest and passion the slow downward spiral of what [was then] considered both a dull and ideologically unimportant class. [Farrell succeeded] because setting down the minutely detailed degradation of Studs Lonigan represented for [Farrell] an angry act of catharsis." Rideout believed that the Studs Lonigan trilogy is one of the "most durable achievements of the radical novel of the thirties."

Farrell's later work, however, received less critical acclaim. James R. Frakes wrote of *Lonely for the Future:* "At this late date Farrell's style reads like vicious self-parody. In this world of human wrecks and pointless waste, James T. Farrell continues to chronicle his bleak Chicago inferno like a bleeding Virgil." Although the *Time* reviewer called Farrell "the most heroic figure in modern American letters," he wrote in his review of *When Time Was Born:* "Farrell calls his latest literary enterprise a prose poem. It is neither prose nor poem, but it appears to be an attempt to rewrite the first chapters of the Book of Genesis. The first sentence blithers and blathers and blunders along for five pages and 1,390 words. Reading it can only be likened to the experience of a man who, having lost an election bet, has undertaken to eat a pad of Brillo and is wondering which is the more unpalatable—the steel-wool structure or the pink soapy filling." But Beach summarized: "The best single test for a writer of fiction is the creation of characters that live in the imagination. Farrell has brought to life an unusual number of such living characters. Studs Lonigan, Jim O'Neill, Al O'Flaherty, Aunt Margaret, and grandmother O'Flaherty are among the memorable people in English fiction."

To comment on his life's work, Farrell borrowed a line from Yeats: "I, too," said Farrell, "spit into the face of time, even though I am aware that this is merely a symbolic expression of a mood: Time slowly transfigures me. . . . Joy and sadness, growth and decay, life and death are all part of the transfiguration of time. To look into the Face of Time, and to master its threat to us—this is one of the basic themes and purposes of art and literature."

Farrell told *CA* that his works have been translated into about 25 languages. A Farrell archive is maintained at the University of Pennsylvania.

MEDIA ADAPTATIONS: "Studs Lonigan" was filmed by United Artists in 1960.

AVOCATIONAL INTERESTS: Baseball.

BIOGRAPHICAL/CRITICAL SOURCES:

BOOKS

Allen, Walter, *The Modern Novel in Britain and the United States,* Dutton, 1965.
Beach, Joseph Warren, *American Fiction, 1920-1940,* Macmillan, 1941.
Branch, Edgar Marquess, *A Bibliography of James T. Farrell's Writings, 1921-1957,* University of Pennsylvania Press, 1959.
Branch, Edgar Marquess, *James T. Farrell,* University of Minnesota Press, 1963.
Contemporary Literary Criticism, Gale, Volume 1, 1973, Volume 4, 1975, Volume 8, 1978, Volume 11, 1979.
Conversations With Writers, Volume 2, Gale, 1978.
Dictionary of Literary Biography, Gale, Volume 4: *American Writers in Paris, 1920-1939,* 1980, Volume 9: *American Novelists, 1910-1945,* 1981.
Dictionary of Literary Biography Documentary Series, Volume 2, Gale, 1982.
Farrell, James T., *Reflections at Fifty, and Other Essays,* Vanguard, 1954.
Gelfant, Blanche Housman, *The American City Novel,* University of Oklahoma Press, 1954.
Kazin, Alfred, *On Native Grounds,* Harcourt, 1942.
Rideout, Walter B., *The Radical Novel in the United States, 1900-1954,* Harvard University Press, 1956.
Walcutt, Charles Child, editor, *Seven Novelists in the American Naturalist Tradition,* University of Minnesota Press, 1974.
Wald, A. M., *James T. Farrell,* New York University Press, 1978.

PERIODICALS

American Book Collector, May, 1967.
American Quarterly, winter, 1977.
Best Sellers, May 15, 1971.
Esquire, December, 1962.
Harper's, October, 1954.
Literary Times, April, 1965.
Nation, June 3, 1968, October 16, 1976.
National Observer, June 29, 1964.
New Yorker, March 18, 1974.
New York Herald Tribune Book Week, February 27, 1966.
New York Times, December 3, 1967.
New York Times Book Review, August 12, 1962, January 7, 1968, July 14, 1968, January 19, 1969, November 25, 1973, September 16, 1979.
People, March 12, 1979.
Prairie Schooner, spring, 1967.
Saturday Review, June 20, 1964.
Time, May 27, 1966.
Twentieth Century Literature, February, 1976.
Washington Post, September 11, 1968.

OBITUARIES:

PERIODICALS

Chicago Tribune, August 23, 1979, August 28, 1979.
Detroit News, August 26, 1979.
New Republic, October 6, 1979.
Newsweek, September 3, 1979.
New York Times, August 23, 1979.
Time, September 3, 1979.
Washington Post, August, 23, 1979.

FARREN, Richard M.
See BETJEMAN, John

*   *   *

FAULKNER, William (Cuthbert) 1897-1962

PERSONAL: Surname originally Falkner, later changed to Faulkner; born September 25, 1897, in New Albany, Miss.; died July 6, 1962, in Byhalia, Miss.; son of Murry Cuthbert (a railroad worker, owner of a cottonseed oil and ice plant, livery stable operator, hardware store employee, secretary and business manager at University of Mississippi) and Maud (Butler) Falkner; married Lida Estelle Oldham Franklin, June 20, 1929; children: Alabama (died, 1931), Jill (Mrs. Paul Dilwyn Summers, Jr.); (step-children) Victoria, Malcolm Argyle. *Education:* Attended University of Mississippi, 1919-20.

ADDRESSES: Home—Rowan Oak, Oxford, Miss.

CAREER: First National Bank, Oxford, Miss., clerk, 1916; Winchester Repeating Arms Co., New Haven, Conn., ledger clerk, 1918; Lord & Taylor, New York, N.Y., bookstore clerk, 1921; University of Mississippi, Oxford, postmaster, 1921-24; worked as roof painter, carpenter, and paper hanger, New Orleans, La., 1925; deckhand on Genoa-bound freighter, 1925; full-time writer, 1925-62. Coal shoveler at Oxford Power Plant, 1929. Screenwriter for Metro-Goldwyn-Mayer, 1932-33, and for Warner Bros., 1942-45, 1951, 1953, and 1954. Chairman of Writer's Group People-to-People Program, 1956-57. Writer in residence, University of Virginia, 1957-62. *Military service:* British Royal Air Force, cadet pilot, 1918; became honorary second lieutenant.

MEMBER: American Academy of Arts and Letters, Sigma Alpha Epsilon.

AWARDS, HONORS: Elected to National Institute of Arts and Letters, 1939; O. Henry Memorial Short Story Awards, 1939, 1940, and 1949; elected to American Academy of Arts and Letters, 1948; Nobel Prize for Literature, 1949; William Dean Howells Medal, American Academy of Arts and Letters, 1950; National Book Award, 1951, for *Collected Stories;* Legion of Honor of Republic of France, 1951; National Book Award and Pulitzer Prize, both 1955, both for *A Fable;* Silver Medal of the Greek Academy, 1957; gold medal for fiction, National Institute of Arts and Letters, 1962.

WRITINGS:

POETRY

Vision in Spring, privately printed [Mississippi], 1921.
The Marble Faun (also see below), Four Seas (Boston), 1924.
This Earth, a Poem, drawings by Albert Heckman, Equinox, 1932.
A Green Bough (contains *The Marble Faun*), H. Smith and R. Haas, 1933, published as *The Marble Faun* [and] *A Green Bough,* Random House, 1965.
Mississippi Poems (also see below), limited edition with introduction by Joseph Blotner and afterword by Luis Daniel Brodsky, Yoknapatawpha Press (Oxford, Mississippi), 1979.
Helen, a Courtship [and] *Mississippi Poems,* introductory essays by Carvel Collins and Joseph Blotner, Tulane University and Yoknapatawpha Press, 1981.

NOVELS

Soldiers' Pay, Boni & Liveright, 1926, published with author's speech of acceptance of Nobel Prize, New American Library of World Literature, 1959.
Mosquitoes, Boni and Liveright, 1927.

Sartoris (abridged version of *Flags in the Dust;* also see below), Harcourt, 1929.

The Sound and the Fury, J. Cape & H. Smith, 1929.

As I Lay Dying, J. Cape & H. Smith, 1930, new and corrected edition, Random House, 1964.

Sanctuary, J. Cape & H. Smith, 1931, published as *Sanctuary: The Original Text,* edited with afterword and notes by Noel Polk, Random House, 1981.

Light in August, H. Smith and R. Haas, 1932.

Pylon, H. Smith and R. Haas, 1935.

Absalom, Absalom!, Random House, 1936, casebook edition edited by Elisabeth Muhlenfeld published as *William Faulkner's Absalom, Absalom!,* Garland Publishing, 1984.

The Unvanquished, drawings by Edward Shenton, Random House, 1938.

The Wild Palms, Random House, 1939.

The Hamlet (first book in the "Snopes Trilogy"; also see below), Random House, 1940.

Intruder in the Dust, Random House, 1948.

Requiem for a Nun, Random House, 1951.

A Fable, Random House, 1954.

The Town (second book of the "Snopes Trilogy"; also see below), Random House, 1957.

The Long Hot Summer: A Dramatic Book from the Four-Book Novel; The Hamlet, New American Library, 1958.

The Mansion (third book in the "Snopes Trilogy"; also see below), Random House, 1959.

The Reivers, a Reminiscence, Random House, 1962 (condensation published as *Hell Creek Crossing,* illustrations by Noel Sickles, Reader's Digest Association, 1963), New American Library, 1969.

Snopes: A Trilogy, Volume 1: *The Hamlet,* Volume 2: *The Town,* Volume 3: *The Mansion,* Random House, 1965.

Flags in the Dust (unabridged version of *Sartoris*), edited with an introduction by Douglas Day, Random House, 1973.

Mayday, University of Notre Dame Press, 1976.

SHORT FICTION

These Thirteen (also see below; contains "Victory," "Ad Astra," "All the Dead Pilots," "Crevasse," "Red Leaves", "A Rose for Emily," "A Justice," "Hair," "That Evening Sun," "Dry September," "Mistral," "Divorce in Naples," and "Carcassonne"), J. Cape & H. Smith, 1931.

Doctor Martino, and Other Stories (also see below), H. Smith and R. Haas, 1934.

Go Down, Moses, and Other Stories (also see below), Random House, 1942 (also published in a limited edition), published as *Go Down, Moses,* Vintage, 1973.

Three Famous Short Novels (contains "Spotted Horses," "Old Man," and "The Bear"), Random House, 1942, published as *Three Famous Short Novels: Spotted Horses; Old Man; The Bear,* Vintage, 1978.

Knight's Gambit, Random House, 1949 (published in England as *Knight's Gambit: Six Stories,* Chatto & Windus, 1960).

Collected Stories, Random House, 1950, published as *Collected Stories of William Faulkner,* Vintage, 1977 (published in England as *Collected Short Stories,* Volume 1: *Uncle Willy and Other Stories,* Volume 2: *These Thirteen,* Volume 3: *Dr. Martino and Other Stories,* Chatto & Windus, 1958, reprinted, 1978).

Mirrors of Chartres Streets (includes sketches), introduction by William Van O'Connor, illustrations by Mary Demopoulous, Faulkner Studies (Minneapolis), 1953.

Big Woods (contains "The Bear," "The Old People," "A Bear Hunt," and "Race at Morning"), drawings by Edward Shenton, Random House, 1955.

Jealousy, and Episode (originally published in New Orleans *Times-Picayune,* 1925), limited edition, Faulkner Studies (Minneapolis), 1955.

Uncle Willy, and Other Stories, Chatto & Windus, 1958.

Selected Short Stories, Modern Library, 1961.

Bear, Man, and God: Seven Approaches to William Faulkner's "The Bear" (contains "The Bear," "Delta Autumn," and selections from other works), edited by Francis Lee Utley, Lynn Z. Bloom, and Arthur F. Kinney, Random House, 1964.

The Wishing Tree (children's fiction), with illustrations by Don Bolognese, Random House, 1964.

The Tall Men, and Other Stories, edited with notes by K. Sakai, Apollonsha (Kyoto), 1965.

A Rose for Emily, edited by M. Thomas Inge, Merrill, 1970.

Fairchild's Story, limited edition, Warren Editions (London), 1976.

Uncollected Stories of William Faulkner, edited by Joseph Blotner, Random House, 1979.

Short fiction anthologized in *Post Stories, 1957* ("The Waifs"), Random House, 1980.

SCREENPLAYS

"Today We Live," Metro-Goldwyn-Mayer, 1933.

(With Joel Sayre) *The Road to Glory* (Twentieth Century-Fox, 1936), with afterword by George Garrett, Southern Illinois University Press, 1981.

(With Nunnally Johnson) "Banjo on My Knee," Twentieth Century-Fox, 1936.

(With Sam Hellman, Lamar Trotti, and Gladys Lehman) "Slave Ship," Twentieth Century-Fox, 1937.

(With Sayre, Fred Guiol, and Ben Hecht) "Gunga Din," 1939.

(With Jean Renoir) "The Southerner," Universal, 1945.

(With Jules Furthman) *To Have and Have Not* (Warner Bros., 1945), based on novel by Ernest Hemingway, edited with introduction by Bruce F. Kawin, University of Wisconsin Press, 1980.

(With Leigh Brackett and Jules Furthman) "The Big Sleep," Warner Bros., 1946.

(With Harry Kurnitz and Harold Jack Bloom) "Land of the Pharoahs," Warner Bros., 1955.

Faulkner's MGM Screenplays, University of Tennessee Press, 1982.

OTHER

"Marionettes" (one-act play) first produced at University of Mississippi, March 4, 1921; published as *The Marionettes,* limited edition, Bibliographical Society, University of Virginia, 1975, published as *The Marionettes: A Play in One Act,* Yoknapatawpha Press (Oxford, Miss.), 1978.

Sherwood Anderson and Other Famous Creoles: A Gallery of Contemporary New Orleans, drawings by William Spratling, Pelican Bookshop Press, 1926.

Idyll in the Desert, limited edition, Random House, 1931.

Miss Zilphia Gant, limited edition, Book Club of Texas, 1932.

Salmagundi (contains poem by Ernest M. Hemingway), limited edition, Casanova Press (Milwaukee), 1932.

The Portable Faulkner, edited by Malcolm Cowley, Viking, 1946, revised and expanded edition, 1967 (published in England as *The Essential Faulkner,* Chatto & Windus, 1967).

Notes on a Horsethief, illustrations by Elizabeth Calvert, Levee Press (Greenville, Miss.), 1950.

William Faulkner's Speech of Acceptance upon the Award of the Nobel Prize for Literature, Delivered in Stockholm on the Tenth of December, 1950, [New York], 1951.

(And author of foreword) *The Faulkner Reader: Selections from the Works of William Faulkner,* Random House, 1954.

Faulkner's County: Tales of Yoknapatawpha County, Chatto & Windus, 1955.

Faulkner on Truth and Freedom: Excerpts from Tape Recordings of Remarks Made by William Faulkner during His Recent Manila Visit, Philippine Writer's Association (Manila), 1956, reprinted, 1978.

Faulkner at Nagano, edited by Robert A. Jelliffe, Kenkyusha (Tokyo), 1956.

New Orleans Sketches, introduction by Carvel Collins, Rutgers University Press, 1958.

Faulkner in the University: Class Conferences at the University of Virginia, 1957-1958 (interviews and conversations), edited by Frederick L. Gwynn and Joseph Blotner, University Press of Virginia, 1959.

William Faulkner: Early Prose and Poetry, compiled and introduced by Carvel Collins, Little, Brown, 1962.

Faulkner's University of Mississippi Pieces, compiled and introduced by Carvel Collins, Kenkyusha (Tokyo), 1962.

William Faulkner's Library: A Catalogue, compiled with an introduction by Joseph Blotner, University Press of Virginia, 1964.

Faulkner at West Point (interviews), edited by Joseph L. Fant III and Robert Ashley, Random House, 1964.

The Faulkner-Cowley File: Letters and Memories, 1944-1962, edited by Cowley, Viking, 1966.

Essays, Speeches and Public Letters, edited by James B. Merriwether, Random House, 1966.

The Best of Faulkner, Chosen by the Author, special edition, World Books Society, 1967.

Man, introduction by Bernard H. Porter, limited edition, [Rockland, Me.], 1969.

Faulkner's University Pieces, compiled with an introduction by Carvel Collins, Folcroft Press, 1970.

Selected Letters of William Faulkner, edited by Joseph Blotner, limited edition, Franklin Library, 1976, Random House, 1977.

Also author of *Faulkner on Love: A Letter to Marjorie Lyons,* limited edition edited by Richard Lyons, Merrykit Press (Fargo, N.D.), 1974; and *Faulkner's Ode to the Louver, Speech at Teatro Municipal, Caracas, 1961,* edited by James B. Merriwether, State College of Mississippi, 1979. Featured on sound recordings: *William Faulkner Reads Selections from His Novel: The Sound and the Fury—Dilsey,* Listening Library, 1976; *William Faulkner Reads a Selection from His Novel: Light in August,* Listening Library, 1979. Also contributor of poems, short stories, and articles to magazines and newspapers, including *New Orleans Times-Picayune, New Republic, Saturday Evening Post, Scribner's,* and *Sports Illustrated.*

SIDELIGHTS: William Faulkner is considered one of America's greatest twentieth-century novelists. He spent most of his literary career in the South, which both inspired and informed his fiction. Many critics have expressed amazement that Faulkner, in many ways such an isolated and provincial artist, was able to produce such impressive, universal work. Perhaps John W. Aldridge put it best when he wrote, "Working alone down there in that seemingly impenetrable cultural wilderness of the sovereignly backward state of Mississippi, he managed to make a clearing for his mind and a garden for his art, one which he culti-

vated so lovingly and well that it has come in our day to feed the imagination of literate men throughout the civilized world."

Most of the biographical facts about Faulkner have been thoroughly documented. He was born into a genteel Southern family that had played a significant part in the history of Mississippi. His great-grandfather, William Clark Falkner, was a colorful figure who had built railroads, served in the Confederate Army, and written a popular novel, *The White Rose of Memphis.* An indifferent student, Faulkner dropped out of Oxford High School in 1915 and then worked for a time as a clerk in his grandfather's bank. During this period he wrote bad imitative verse and contributed drawings to the University of Mississippi's yearbook, *Ole Miss.* When the United States declared war on Germany, Faulkner tried to enlist but was rejected because of his small stature.

Instead of going to war, Faulkner went to New Haven, Connecticut, to visit his friend Phil Stone, then a student at Yale. Stone had recognized Faulkner's talent early on and had encouraged his literary bent. The two men read and discussed Balzac and the French Symbolist poets. Although some critics have pointed to Stone as the determining factor in Faulkner's success, Michael Millgate theorized that the "apparent passivity of the younger man [Faulkner], his willingness to accept the position of listener, learner, recipient, and protege, undoubtedly led Stone to exaggerate in his own mind, and in public and private statements, the real extent of his influence. . . . Inevitably, Faulkner grew beyond Stone." At this time, however, Stone and Faulkner were still close friends. With Stone's help, Faulkner hatched a scheme to get admitted into the Royal Canadian Air Force. By affecting a British accent and forging letters of recommendation from nonexistent Englishmen, Faulkner was accepted into the RAF.

The war ended before Faulkner saw combat duty. He returned to his hometown, where he intermittently attended Ole Miss as a special student. His dandified appearance and lack of a stable job led townspeople to dub him "Count No' Count." On August 6, 1919, he surprised them when his first poem, "L'Apres-midi d'un faune," was published in *New Republic;* later in the same year the *Mississippian* published one of his short stories, "Landing in Luck." After Faulkner dropped out of Ole Miss, he went to New York City at the invitation of Stark Young, a Mississippi novelist and drama critic. While he was there, Faulkner worked for Elizabeth Prall as a bookstore clerk.

Back at Oxford, Faulkner was hired as university postmaster, but his mind was rarely on his duties. Before putting magazines into the proper subscriber's post office box, he read through the issues. He brought his writing to the post office with him and became so immersed in what he was doing that he ignored patrons. Eventually his laxness came to the attention of the postal inspector, and he resigned rather than be fired. Faulkner remarked that he quit the job because he "didn't want to be at the beck and call of every son-of-a-bitch with the price of a two-cent stamp."

His career in the postal service over, Faulkner called on Elizabeth Prall in New Orleans. She was now married to novelist Sherwood Anderson, and the two men struck up a friendship. The association with Anderson helped Faulkner realize that his true metier was not poetry but the novel. Faulkner's first book, *The Marble Faun,* a collection of verse, was published after he arrived in New Orleans in 1924. Sales were so poor that most of the five hundred copies were sold to a bookstore for a mere ten cents a volume. Acting upon Anderson's advice, Faulkner wrote a novel and set it in the South. Anderson told Faulkner he would recommend the book, entitled *Soldiers' Pay,* to a publisher as long as he didn't have to read it. Although the two men were very close for several months, a rift developed between them. Millgate postulated that "Faulkner's early realisation that Anderson's way was not to be his way must always have been a source of strain in their relationship." During this period in New Orleans, Faulkner also contributed short stories and sketches to the *Times-Picayune.*

In 1925, Faulkner joined the American literary expatriates and went to Europe. He did not remain there long, however, and after a brief stay in New Orleans, he returned to Oxford, where he finally settled down. While he had been in Europe, *Soldiers' Pay* had appeared on the bookstands. It attracted some favorable notices but was not a commercial success. Years later, Robert Penn Warren, also a Southern writer, remembered his own reactions when he first read *Soldiers' Pay* in the spring of 1929: "As a novel, *Soldiers' Pay* is no better than it should be, but it made a profound and undefinable impression on me." *Mosquitoes,* a mildly satirical novel on literary life in New Orleans, came out in 1927. Faulkner then penned *Flags in the Dust,* the first of his novels to be set in Yoknapatawpha County.

Early in 1928 *Flags in the Dust* was being shuffled from one publisher to another without success, and Faulkner had grown disgusted with the entire publication process. Abruptly, he decided to stop worrying about whether or not others liked his manuscripts. "One day I seemed to shut a door," he recalled, "between me and all publishers' addresses and book lists. I said to myself, Now I can write. Now I can make myself a vase like that which the old Roman kept at his bedside and wore the rim slowly away with kissing it. So I, who never had a sister and was fated to lose my daughter in infancy, set out to make myself a beautiful and tragic little girl." The story that Faulkner sat down to write was, of course, *The Sound and the Fury,* and "the beautiful and tragic little girl" was Caddy Compson. It was *The Sound and the Fury* that helped Faulkner establish a solid reputation among critics. Stirred by Faulkner's novel, Lyle Saxon wrote, "I believe simply and sincerely this is a great book." A reviewer for the Boston Evening Transcript called *The Sound and the Fury* a novel "worthy of the attention of a Euripides."

When writing his next novel, *As I Lay Dying,* Faulkner did not experience the same rapture he had felt when he was working on *The Sound and the Fury. As I Lay Dying* was written in a six-week period while Faulkner was working the night shift at a powerhouse. The constant humming noise of a dynamo serenaded him while he wrote his famous tour de force on the nature of being. By the time *As I Lay Dying* came out in 1930, John Bassett observed that "Faulkner's name, if not a household word, was at least known to many critics and reviewers, who spoke of him no longer as a neophyte, or a new voice in fiction, but as one either continuing his development in fruitful ways or floundering after several attempts, in either case as a writer known to the literary world."

Faulkner was not recognized by the general public until *Sanctuary,* one of his most violent and shocking novels, appeared in 1931. When he wrote *Sanctuary,* Faulkner later admitted, he had one purpose in mind: to make money. By this time he had a family to support, and out of desperation he concocted a book he thought would sell to the masses. Faulkner was ashamed when he saw the printer's galleys of the book and extensively rewrote his potboiler so that it would have a more serious intent. The scandalous subject matter of *Sanctuary* appealed to the reading public, and it sold well. For a brief time Faulkner became a minor celebrity, but the rest of the decade did not go as well. Many reviewers had favorable comments to make about *Sanctuary*—Andre Malraux declared it "marks the intrusion of Greek

tragedy into the detective story"—but in the view of others, the novel proved that Faulkner was merely a purveyor of the monstrous, the gory, and the obscene, and they judged his subsequent books in the same light. Faulkner was also a victim of the times. The Depression caused book sales in general to plummet, but his novels were particularly unpopular because they were not in keeping with the nation's mood. Warren speculated that critics and the public became disenchanted with Faulkner because his books offered no practical solutions to the pressing problems of the day—feeding the hungry and providing jobs for the millions of unemployed. Some readers were offended by Faulkner's novels because they were not written in the optimistic spirit of the New Deal, while still others discerned fascist tendencies in his work.

During the 1930s and 1940s Faulkner wrote many of his finest books, including *Light in August, Absalom, Absalom!, The Wild Palms, The Hamlet,* and *Go Down, Moses.* They brought in very little revenue, however, and he was forced to work in Hollywood as a screenwriter. Faulkner worked on and off in Hollywood for a number of years, but he was never happy there. He fled from the movie capital as soon as he had amassed enough money to pay his bills.

It should not be assumed that Faulkner was completely unappreciated during this time period. Bassett pointed out that the majority of reviews were positive, and that between 1939 and 1942 several important examinations of Faulkner appeared in literary journals and in literary histories. Although hardly noticed by the public, Faulkner was esteemed by many of his fellow writers. His work had also attracted a substantial following in France. Maurice Coindreau translated several of Faulkner's novels and short stories into French, and his fiction received perceptive treatment from such critics as Andre Malraux, Maurice LeBreton, Jean Pouillon, and Jean-Paul Sartre.

Despite Faulkner's stature in literary circles at home and abroad, in the 1940s his books gradually began dropping out of print, partly because of lack of popular interest, partly because of the war effort. By 1945 all seventeen of his books were out of print. In 1946 the publication of *The Portable Faulkner,* edited by Malcolm Cowley, created a resurgence of interest in Faulkner. Cowley's introduction to the volume, with its emphasis on the Southern legend that Faulkner had created in his works, served as a springboard for future critics. "Faulkner performed a labor of imagination that has not been equaled in our time, and a double labor," Cowley asserted. "First, to invent a Mississippi county that was like a mythical kingdom, but was complete and living in all its details; second, to make his story of Yoknapatawpha County stand as a parable or legend of all the Deep South."

Fifteen of Faulkner's novels and many of his short stories are set in Yoknapatawpha County, which bears a close resemblance to the region in northern Mississippi where Faulkner spent most of his life. Faulkner defined Yoknapatawpha as an "Indian word meaning water runs slow through flat land." The county is bounded by the Tallahatchie River on the north and by the Yoknapatawpha River on the south. Jefferson, the county seat, is modeled after Oxford. Up the road a piece is Frenchman's Bend, a poverty-stricken village. Scattered throughout the countryside are ramshackle plantation houses, farmhouses, and the hovels of tenant farmers. Depicted in both the past and the present, Yoknapatawpha is populated with a vast spectrum of people—the Indians who originally inhabited the land, the aristocrats, those ambitious men who fought their way into the landed gentry, yeoman farmers, poor whites, blacks, carpetbaggers, and bushwhackers. Faulkner was proud of the kingdom he had erected in his imagination. On a map of Yoknapatawpha County he prepared for the first edition of *Absalom, Absalom!*, he wrote, "William Faulkner, Sole Owner & Proprietor."

Although there are some inconsistencies in the Yoknapatawpha novels and although the books are certainly not arranged in a neat chronological order, the saga does have unity. Millgate called this unity "a unity of inspiration, of a single irradiating tragi-comic vision." In order to appreciate Faulkner's vision fully, one must read the entire saga, which Yardley described as "a tapestry of incomparable intricacy, past and present woven together in a design that can be comprehended through one book but that gains astonishing richness when seen as a whole." The greatness of Faulkner's design led critics to recognize that he was not just a provincial writer. Like the works of such famous regional authors as Robert Frost, Thomas Hardy, and William Butler Yeats, Faulkner's novels have a universal appeal. Faulkner created, Arthur Edelstein remarked, a "hallucinated version of the Deep South which has escaped its local origins to become a region of the modern consciousness."

Those who investigated the Yoknapatawpha legend began exploring other aspects of Faulkner's fiction. Warren Beck observed that Faulkner's reiteration of certain words and his habit of piling one adjective upon another sometimes help to create a mood or to accentuate a particular character trait. For examples, Beck turned to *Absalom, Absalom!* In that novel, Miss Rosa's persistent use of the word "demon" indicates her crazed obsession, while the description of the "long still hot weary dead September afternoon" when Quentin hears Miss Rosa's story emphasizes not only the muggy weather but also the spiritual malaise of the characters. Joseph Blotner noted that sometimes Faulkner followed James Joyce's lead and "would omit all punctuation to denote the flowing stream of consciousness." This technique was used in Benjy's and Quentin's sections in *The Sound and the Fury.* As for Faulkner's vague pronoun references, Helen Swink surmised that he used them because he wanted to adapt the art of the oral storyteller to the written page. In attempting to sound like he was spinning yarns aloud, Faulkner used vague pronoun references because this is a characteristic of oral speech.

Most often, Faulkner's style is keyed to his themes. One of Faulkner's chief thematic preoccupations is the past, and this theme is also reflected in his form. In a famous analogy, Jean-Paul Sartre compared the Faulknerian character's point of view to that "of a passenger looking backward from a speeding car, who sees, flowing away from him, the landscape he is traversing. For him the future is not in view, the present is too blurred to make out, and he can see clearly only the past as it streams away before his obsessed and backward-looking gaze." Faulkner's pages are filled with characters who are fettered to the past. Millgate pointed out that in *The Sound and the Fury* the suicidal Quentin Compson searches "for a means of arresting time at a moment of achieved perfection, a moment when he and Caddy could be eternally together in the simplicity of their childhood relationship." The Reverend Gail Hightower in *Light in August* is also locked in the past, endlessly reliving the glory of his grandfather's cavalry charge. Robert Hemenway believed that in *As I Lay Dying* Faulkner is showing "that the South, like the Bundrens, must bury the past; that it cannot remain true—without courting tragedy or absurdity—to the promises given to dead ancestors or to the illusions of former glory." In "A Rose for Emily," Emily Grierson's embracing of her dead lover becomes a gruesome symbol of what happens when one clings to the past.

The stylistic methods most closely associated with Faulkner's treatment of the past are his use of long sentences, flashbacks, and multiple viewpoints. Aiken suggested that Faulkner utilizes complicated sentence structures because he wants "a medium without stops or pauses, a medium which is always *of the moment,* and of which the passage from moment to moment is as fluid and undetectable as in the life itself which he is purporting to give." Swink posited that the confusing sentences that withhold meaning from the reader "intensify the emotional experience," while Millgate claimed that these sentences enable Faulkner "to hold a single moment in suspension while its full complexity is explored." The flashbacks are even more clearly related to Faulkner's interest in the past. Edward Murray pointed out that in *Light in August* the minds of Joe Christmas, Gail Hightower, Joanna Burden, and Lena Grove frequently revert back to the past, but "the flashbacks are not there merely to supply expository material for the actions in the present that need further explanation. Since the past is Faulkner's subject—or a large part of it—the flashbacks are not simply 'functional': they are thematically necessary."

By telling a story from several points of view, Faulkner adds a further dimension to his concept of time. The past is part of the present; thus, it is subject to re-evaluation and re-interpretation. Faulkner's view of time as a continuum has certain moral implications, Millgate explained: "The all important point consisted in the idea that there could be no such thing as 'was': since time constituted a continuum the chain of cause and effect could never be broken, and every human action must continue to reverberate, however faintly, into infinity. Hence the all-importance of conduct, of personal responsibility for all one's actions." This belief partially accounts for Faulkner's frequent allusions to the Bible. "Faulkner's true domain is that of the eternal myths, particularly those popularized by the Bible," Maurice Coindreau observed. "The themes that he prefers, his favorite images and metaphors, are those which ornament the fabric of the Old Testament." Like the writers of the Old Testament, Faulkner believes that the sins of the fathers are visited upon their children. Many of his characters are plagued by guilt, precipitated by their own sins as well as by the actions of their forefathers, who had callously shoved aside the Indians, enslaved the blacks, and laid waste the land.

Perhaps the greatest moral burden borne by Southerners was slavery. Much of Faulkner's fiction shows the evil that results from the failure to recognize the humanity of black people. Certainly many of the slave owners he depicts are cruel to their human property. In *Go Down, Moses,* Carothers McCaslin seduces Eunice, one of his Negroes. Years later he seduces the daughter who resulted from that union, thus driving Eunice to suicide. One of the reasons that Thomas Sutpen's grand design fails in *Absalom, Absalom!* is his acceptance of racism. When Sutpen leaves Haiti to found a dynasty in Mississippi, he abandons his black wife and infant son because their color would not be acceptable to Southerners. That deed comes back to haunt Sutpen and the children from his second marriage, Judith and Henry. Sutpen's mulatto son shows up and wants to marry Judith. As horrified by the thought of miscegenation as he is by the possibility of incest, Henry guns down his half brother. This is only one incident in *Absalom, Absalom!* that demonstrates, as John V. Hagopian pointed out, how "the novel as a whole clearly repudiates Southern racism."

Men do not only exploit one another, Faulkner points out; they also exploit the earth. Cleanth Brooks noted that "Faulkner seems to accept the Christian doctrine of original sin. Men are condemned to prey upon nature. The only question is whether in doing so they will exercise some kind of restraint and love the nature that they are forced to use, or whether they will exploit nature methodically and ruthlessly, in a kind of rape."

Another important aspect of Faulkner's fiction is love between family members. Cowley observed that Faulkner's books "have what is rare in the novels of our time, a warmth of family affection, brother for brother and sister, the father for his children—a love so warm and proud that it tries to shut out the rest of the world." But family life has eroded in Faulkner's fiction, at least partially because society is debilitated. "Faulkner's recurrent dramatization of the decay of families," Philip Momberger reflected, "e.g., the deterioration of the Compson, Sutpen, and Sartoris lines—is an expression in the domestic sphere of a more general, public disintegration: the collapse of the ideal of 'human family' in the modern world and the resulting deracination of the individual." Momberger went on to say that the social ideal that underpins Faulkner's work is "a state of communal wholeness within which, as within a coherent and loving family, the individual's identity would be defined, recognized, and sustained."

Although a person's ties to the community are important, Faulkner suggests that men must never let the community become the sole arbiter of their values. Brooks stated that the "community is at once the field for man's action and the norm by which his action is judged and regulated" and further indicated that Faulkner's "fiction also reveals keen awareness of the perils risked by the individual who attempts to run counter to the community. The divergent individual may invite martyrdom; he certainly risks fanaticism and madness." For examples of divergent individuals, Brooks turned to *Light in August*. In that novel, many of the characters are social outcasts—Joe Christmas because of his suspected Negro blood, Joanna Burden because of her abolitionist background, Gail Hightower because he does not conform to the conventional behavior of a minister, Percy Grimm because he did not serve in World War I.

Established religion also comes under close scrutiny in Faulkner's fiction, and his characters are often deeply disturbed by the rigid attitudes of the church-going populace. In *Sanctuary*, Horace Benbow is taken aback when the Christian community refuses to help a man who is falsely accused of murder. Waggoner declared that in that novel "Southern fundamentalist Protestantism is pictured as selfrighteous moralism." Calvinist righteousness is also attacked in *Light in August*, where Hightower comes to realize that rigid religious attitudes encourage people to crucify themselves and others. One of the people they feel compelled to crucify is Joe Christmas, who is clearly an outcast in the community. The major significance in Christmas's name, O'Connor noted, "is the irony of Joe Christmas' being pursued and harassed throughout his life by voices of Christian righteousness."

Allied with the theme of the individual running counter to the community and its values is the theme of a young boy's initiation into manhood. This initiation process usually involves some ritualistic gesture or task that a youth must perform in order to achieve knowledge and manhood, and a choice, as Brooks observed, "between a boy's ties with his community—his almost fierce identification with it—and his revulsion from what the community seems committed to do." After he kills his first deer, Ike McCaslin is initiated into manhood by Sam Fathers, who anoints his forehead with the deer's blood. This initiation process is the first step in Ike's decision to eschew the values of society. *The Unvanquished* consists of a series of short stories recounting the growth of Bayard Sartoris. In the final story, Bayard refuses to avenge the death of his father. By so doing, he defies the community, for the townspeople think vengeance is honorable. Chick

Mallison in *Intruder in the Dust* is another sensitive adolescent who is forced to choose between the community's standards and what his heart tells him is right. Faulkner's last novel, *The Reivers, a Reminiscence,* also deals with a young boy's initiation into manhood. When he runs away to Memphis with Boon Hogganbeck and Ned McCaslin, Lucius Priest is forced to grow up.

M.E. Bradford pointed out that the thematic corollary to Faulkner's consideration of a young man's coming into his majority is the question of pride, "or pride's proper role in the formation of good character and of its necessary limitation in contingency. The gentleman, the exemplar of ordinate pride and enactor of a providentially assigned place, sums up in his person the possibility of a civil and religiously grounded social order. In him either presumption or passivity is communal and spiritual disaster." Closely linked to pride is the Faulknerian concept of honor, the need for a man to prove himself. In Faulkner's novels, exaggerated notions of honor lead to trouble. Quentin Compson's fanatic defense of his sister's honor is narcissistic; his "insistence upon honor and dignity have become extreme, forms of self love," O'Connor noted. In *As I Lay Dying,* the Bundren family's attempt to honor Addie's dying wish is ludicrous, yet Brooks pointed out that Cash and Jewel "exhibit true heroism—Cash in his suffering, Jewel in his brave actions." The scruple of honor is also of great significance in *The Hamlet*. After Eula Varner becomes pregnant, her honor is ironically preserved when her father pays Flem Snopes to marry her. Even Mink Snopes has a warped sense of honor that compels him to kill Zack Houston. But Mink discovers that his cousin Flem is so devoid of honor that he won't even help Mink when he is arrested. Mink evens this score in a later novel, *The Mansion*. When he is released from prison, Mink kills Flem for the sake of honor.

When Faulkner's characters are initiated into manhood, they lose their innocence and are forced to face reality. The world they discover is one in which good and evil are intermingled. The "Snopes Trilogy," Stanley Edgar Hyman claimed, that is "Faulkner's fullest exploration of natural evil." In *The Hamlet,* the heartless Flem Snopes is pitted against V. K. Ratliff, an itinerant sewing machine salesman. Flem is almost the perfect embodiment of evil, whereas Ratliff, John Lewis Longley demonstrated, is a man "who is willing to actively commit himself against evil, but more important, to form actions of positive good." Although Flem is depicted as the incarnation of evil in *The Hamlet*, commentators have noted that he is portrayed more sympathetically in the succeeding two books in the trilogy. This treatment is in keeping with Faulkner's view of the nature of man. "I think that you really can't say that any man is good or bad. I grant you there are some exceptions, but man is the victim of himself or his fellows, or his own nature, or his environment, but no man is good or bad either. He tries to do the best he can within his rights," the novelist once said.

From today's perspective, it is difficult to understand the outcry that arose when Faulkner was awarded the Nobel Prize in 1949. The preponderance of criticism has shown that his concerns are ultimately moral, but at that time many readers still considered Faulkner a naturalistic monster. Reflecting the views of many other small-town newspapers, the editor of the *North Mississippi Herald* declared that Faulkner was a member of the "privy school of literature." Even the *New York Times* expressed the fear that the rest of the world might consider Yoknapatawpha County an accurate depiction of life in America. Faulkner's reply to those who accused him of promoting immorality was contained in his acceptance speech. He explained that it is the writer's duty and privilege "to help man endure by lifting his heart, by reminding him of the courage and honor and hope and pride and compassion and pity and sacrifice which have been the glory of his past. The poet's voice need not merely be the record of man, it can be one of the props, the pillars, to help him endure and prevail."

Faulkner's stirring acceptance speech caused many to change their opinion of him overnight. Suddenly he became a moral hero. As Herman Spivey pointed out, the truth is that Faulkner's outlook had undergone no dramatic change; from the beginning of his writing career he had concerned himself with "the old verities and truths of the heart, the old universal truths lacking which any story is ephemeral and doomed." Faulkner's later books became didactic, however, often seeming to be mere echoes of his Nobel Prize acceptance speech. Spivey contended that in Faulkner's later novels "there is a major and regrettable shift from mythic and symbolic and implicit communication to allegorical and explicit communication." In *A Fable,* which Faulkner hoped would be his masterpiece, allegory is used to convey a moral message. Few critics were happy with the book's general and abstract statements. Brendan Gill called *A Fable* "a calamity," while Charles Rolo termed it "a heroically ambitious failure."

Though Faulkner occasionally failed greatly, he usually succeeded mightily. Whatever the faults of his later books, few would dispute the general excellence of his canon. Even Faulkner seemed overwhelmed by his achievement. Toward the end of his life, he wrote to a friend: "And now I realize for the first time what an amazing gift I had: uneducated in every formal sense, without even very literate, let alone literary, companions, yet to have made the things I made. I don't know where it came from. I don't know why God or gods or whoever it was, elected me to be the vessel. Believe me, this is not humility, false modesty: it is simply amazement."

Each of Faulkner's novels has been translated into at least one other language, and several have been translated into as many as thirteen languages.

AVOCATIONAL INTERESTS: Aviation, raising and training horses, hunting, sailing.

MEDIA ADAPTATIONS: The following novels by Faulkner have been adapted for movies: "Intruder in the Dust," Metro-Goldwyn-Mayer, 1949; "Tarnished Angels" (based on *Pylon*), Universal, 1957; "The Long Hot Summer" (based on *The Hamlet*), Twentieth Century-Fox, 1958; "The Sound and the Fury," Twentieth Century-Fox, 1959; "Sanctuary" (also includes parts of *Requiem for a Nun*), Twentieth Century-Fox, 1961; "The Reivers," Cinema Center Films, 1969. *The Sound and the Fury* was adapted for television in 1955, and several of Faulkner's short stories have been adapted for television, including "An Error in Chemistry" and "The Brooch."

BIOGRAPHICAL/CRITICAL SOURCES:

BOOKS

Aldridge, John W., *The Devil in the Fire,* Harper's Magazine Press, 1972.

Backman, Melvin, *Faulkner, The Major Years: A Critical Study,* Indiana University Press, 1966.

Beck, Warren, *Man in Motion: Faulkner's Trilogy,* University of Wisconsin Press, 1961.

Beck, *Faulkner,* University of Wisconsin Press, 1976.

Blotner, Joseph L., *Faulkner: A Biography,* two volumes, Random House, 1974.

Blotner, editor, *Selected Letters of William Faulkner,* Random House, 1977.

Brooks, Cleanth, *The Yoknapatawpha Country,* Yale University Press, 1963.

Brooks, *Toward Yoknapatawpha and Beyond,* Yale University Press, 1978.

Campbell, Harry M., and Reuel M. Foster, *William Faulkner: A Critical Appraisal,* University of Oklahoma Press, 1951, reprinted, Cooper Square, 1971.

Concise Dictionary of Literary Biography: The Age of Maturity, 1929-1941, Gale, 1989.

Contemporary Literary Criticism, Gale, Volume 1, 1973, Volume 3, 1975, Volume 6, 1976, Volume 8, 1978, Volume 9, 1978, Volume 11, 1979, Volume 14, 1980, Volume 18, 1981, Volume 28, 1984, Volume 52, 1989.

Cowley, Malcolm, editor, *The Faulkner-Cowley File: Letters and Memories,* Viking, 1966.

Cowley, *The Second Flowering: Works and Days of the Lost Generation,* Viking, 1973.

Dictionary of Literary Biography, Gale, Volume 9: *American Novelists, 1910-1945,* 1981, Volume 11: *American Humorists, 1800-1950,* 1982, Volume 44: *American Screenwriters, Second Series,* 1986.

Dictionary of Literary Biography Documentary Series, Volume 2, Gale, 1982.

Dictionary of Literary Biography Yearbook 1986, Gale, 1987.

Faulkner, John, *My Brother Bill: An Affectionate Reminiscence,* Trident, 1963.

Faulkner, William, *Faulkner at West Point,* edited by Joseph L. Fant and Robert Ashley, Random House, 1964.

Gold, Joseph, *William Faulkner: A Study in Humanism from Metaphor to Discourse,* University of Oklahoma Press, 1966.

Hoffman, Frederick J., and Olga W. Vickery, editors, *William Faulkner: Two Decades of Criticism,* Michigan State University Press, 1951.

Hoffman and Vickery, editors, *William Faulkner: Three Decades of Criticism,* Michigan State University Press, 1960.

Hoffman, *William Faulkner,* Twayne, 1961.

Howe, Irving, *William Faulkner: A Critical Study,* Random House, 1952.

Hyman, Stanley Edgar, *Standards: A Chronicle of Books for Our Time,* Horizon Press, 1966.

Merriwether, James B., *The Literary Career of William Faulkner: A Bibliographical Study,* Princeton University Press, 1961.

Merriwether, and Michael Millgate, *Lion in the Garden: Interviews with William Faulkner,* Random House, 1968.

Millgate, *The Achievement of William Faulkner,* Random House, 1966.

Miner, Ward L., *The World of William Faulkner,* Duke University Press, 1952.

Slatoff, Walter J., *Quest for Failure: A Study of William Faulkner,* Cornell University Press, 1960.

Vickery, *The Novels of William Faulkner: A Critical Interpretation,* Louisiana State University Press, 1959, revised edition, 1964.

Vogel, Dan, *The Three Masks of American Tragedy,* Louisiana State University Press, 1974.

Volpe, Edmond, *Reader's Guide to William Faulkner,* Farrar, Straus, 1964.

Wagner, Linda Welshimer, *William Faulkner: Four Decades of Criticism,* Michigan State University Press, 1973.

Warren, Robert Penn, editor, *Faulkner: A Collection of Critical Essays,* Prentice-Hall, 1967.

PERIODICALS

American Literature, May, 1973.

Georgia Review, summer, 1972.
Journal of Popular Culture, summer, 1973.
Modern Fiction Studies, summer, 1973, winter, 1973-74, summer, 1975.
New Republic, September 8, 1973.
Sewanee Review, winter, 1970, autumn, 1971.
Southern Review, summer, 1968, autumn, 1972.
Studies in Short Fiction, summer, 1974.
Twentieth Century Literature, July, 1973.

*   *   *

FECAMPS, Elise
See CREASEY, John

*   *   *

FEIFFER, Jules (Ralph) 1929-

PERSONAL: Born January 26, 1929, in Bronx, N.Y.; son of David (held a variety of positions, including dental technician and salesman) and Rhoda (a fashion designer; maiden name, Davis) Feiffer; married Judith Sheftel (a production executive with Warner Bros.), September 17, 1961 (divorced); married Jennifer Allen (a journalist); children: (first marriage) Kate; (second marriage) one daughter. *Education:* Attended Art Students League, New York, N.Y., 1946, and Pratt Institute, 1947-48 and 1949-51.

ADDRESSES: Home—325 West End Ave., New York, N.Y. 10023. *Office*—c/o Universal Press Syndicate, 4400 Johnson Dr., Fairway, Kan. 66205.

CAREER: Assistant to cartoonist Will Eisner, 1946-51, and ghostwriter for Eisner's comic book "The Spirit," 1949-51; author of syndicated cartoon strip, "Clifford," 1949-51; held a variety of positions in the art field, 1953-56, including producer of slide films, writer for Columbia Broadcasting System, Inc.'s "Terry Toons," and designer of booklets for an art firm; author of cartoon strip (originally entitled "Sick, Sick, Sick," later changed to "Feiffer"), published in *Village Voice,* 1956—, published weekly in London *Observer,* 1958-66, and 1972-82, and regularly in *Playboy,* 1959—; syndicated cartoonist, 1959—. Faculty member, Yale Drama School, 1973-74. *Military service:* U.S. Army, Signal Corps, 1951-53; worked in cartoon animation unit.

MEMBER: Authors League of America, Dramatists Guild (member of council), PEN, Writers Guild of America, East.

AWARDS, HONORS: Special George Polk Memorial Award, 1962; named most promising playwright of 1966-67 season by New York drama critics, London Theatre Critics Award, 1967, Outer Circle Critics Award, 1969, and Obie Award of *Village Voice,* 1969, all for "Little Murders"; Outer Circle Critics Award, 1970, for "The White House Murder Case"; Pulitzer Prize, 1986, for editorial cartooning.

WRITINGS:

CARTOON BOOKS

Sick, Sick, Sick, McGraw, 1958, published with introduction by Kenneth Tynan, Collins, 1959.
Passionella, and Other Stories (also see below), McGraw, 1959.
Boy, Girl, Boy, Girl, Random House, 1961.
Feiffer's Album, Random House, 1963.
The Penguin Feiffer, Penguin, 1966.
Feiffer's Marriage Manual, Random House, 1967.
Feiffer on Civil Rights, Anti-Defamation League of B'nai B'rith, 1967.

Pictures at a Prosecution: Drawings and Text from the Chicago Conspiracy Trial, Grove, 1971.
Feiffer on Nixon: The Cartoon Presidency, Random House, 1974.
(With Israel Horovitz) *VD Blues,* Avon, 1974.
Tantrum: A Novel in Cartoons, Knopf, 1979.
Jules Feiffer's America: From Eisenhower to Reagan, edited by Steve Heller, Knopf, 1982.
Marriage Is an Invasion of Privacy and Other Dangerous Views, Andrews & McMeel, 1984.
Feiffer's Children, Andrews & McMeel, 1986.
Ronald Reagan in Movie America: A Jules Feiffer Production, Andrews & McMeel, 1988.

PUBLISHED PLAYS

The Explainers (satirical review; produced in Chicago, Ill., at Playwright's Cabaret Theatre, May 9, 1961), McGraw, 1960.
Crawling Arnold (one-act; first produced in Spoleto, Italy, at Festival of Two Worlds, June 28, 1961; first produced in United States in Cambridge, Mass., at Poets' Theatre, 1961), Dramatists Play Service, 1963.
Hold Me! (first produced Off-Broadway at American Place Theatre, January, 1977), Random House, 1963.
The Unexpurgated Memoirs of Bernard Mergendeiler (one-act; first produced in Los Angeles, Calif., at Mark Taper Forum, October 9, 1967), Random House, 1965.
Little Murders (two-act comedy; first produced on Broadway at Broadhurst Theatre, April 25, 1967; first American play produced on the West End by Royal Shakespeare Co. at Aldwych Theatre, 1967; also see below), Random House, 1968, reprinted, Penguin, 1983.
(Contributor) "Dick and Jane" (one-act; produced in New York City at Eden Theatre as part of "Oh! Calcutta!," devised by Tynan, June 17, 1969; also see below), published in *Oh! Calcutta!,* edited by Tynan, Grove, 1969.
Feiffer's People: Sketches and Observations (produced as "Feiffer's People" in Edinburgh, Scotland, at International Festival of Music and Drama, August, 1968), Dramatists Play Service, 1969.
The White House Murder Case: A Play in Two Acts [and] *Dick and Jane: A One-Act Play* ("The White House Murder Case" first produced Off-Broadway at Circle in the Square Downtown, February 18, 1970), Grove, 1970.
Knock Knock (first produced Off-Off-Broadway at Circle Repertory Theatre, January 18, 1976), Hill & Wang, 1976.
Elliot Loves (first produced on Broadway at Promenade Theater, 1989), Grove, 1989.

UNPUBLISHED PLAYS

"The World of Jules Feiffer," produced in New Jersey at Hunterdon Hills Playhouse, 1962.
"God Bless," first produced in New Haven, Conn., at Yale School of Drama, October 10, 1968; produced on the West End by Royal Shakespeare Co. at Aldwych Theatre, 1968.
"Munro" (adapted by Feiffer from story in *Passionella, and Other Stories*), first produced in Brooklyn, N.Y., in Prospect Park, August 15, 1971.
(With others) "Watergate Classics," first produced at Yale School of Drama, November 16, 1973.
"Grownups," first produced in Cambridge, Mass., at Loeb Drama Center, June, 1981; produced on Broadway at Lyceum Theater, December, 1981.
"A Think Piece," first produced Off-Off-Broadway at Circle Repertory Theatre, 1982.

"Carnal Knowledge" (revised version of play of same title originally written c. 1970; also see below), first produced in
Houston, Tex., at Stages Repertory Theater, spring, 1988.

Also author of "Interview" and "You Should Have Caught Me
at the White House," both c. 1962.

SCREENPLAYS

"Munro" (animated cartoon; adapted by Feiffer from story in
Passionella, and Other Stories), Rembrandt Films, 1961.
"Carnal Knowledge" (adapted from Feiffer's unpublished, un-
produced play of same title written c. 1970), Avco Embassy,
1971.
"Little Murders" (adapted by author from play of same title),
Twentieth Century-Fox, 1971.
"Popeye," Paramount/Walt Disney Productions, 1980.

Also author of unproduced screenplays, "Little Brucie," "Bernard and Huey," and "I Want to Go Home."

OTHER

(Illustrator) Robert Mines, *My Mind Went All to Pieces,* Dial,
1959.
(Illustrator) Norton Juster, *The Phantom Tollbooth,* Random
House, 1961.
Harry, the Rat with Women (novel), McGraw, 1963.
(Editor and annotator) *The Great Comic Book Heroes,* Dial,
1965.
"Silverlips" (teleplay), Public Broadcasting Service, 1972.
(With Herb Gardner, Peter Stone, and Neil Simon) "Happy
Endings" (teleplay), American Broadcasting Companies,
1975.
Akroyd (novel), Simon & Schuster, 1977.
(Author of introduction) Rick Marshall, editor, *The Complete
E. C. Segar Popeye,* Fantagraphics (Stamford, Conn.), 1984.

WORK IN PROGRESS: Feiffer's screenplay, "I Want to Go
Home," is being made into a film directed by Alain Resnais.

SIDELIGHTS: On learning that *Hudson Review* contributor
John Simon describes Jules Feiffer's play "Little Murders" as
"bloody-minded," and makes reference to its "grotesque horror"
and "hideous reality," those who only know Feiffer as a cartoonist and not as a playwright might be more than a little surprised.
Such brutal words are unexpected when used to characterize the
work of a cartoonist—whom we might imagine would only want
to make us laugh—but, then, Feiffer comes to his work as a playwright from the perspective of someone, as Clive Barnes points
out in the *New York Times,* who despite his profession "never
makes jokes." Instead of looking for a laugh, Barnes observes,
Feiffer "muses on urban man, the cesspool of urban man's mind,
the beauty of his neurosis, and the inevitability of his wilting disappointment." The laughter Feiffer seeks centers on our willingness to find humor in some of life's darkest moments.

Feiffer reveals the origins of his somewhat black humor in a
Washington Post interview with Henry Allen: "Back then [in the
fifties], comedy was still working in a tradition that came out of
World War I. . . . Comedy was mired in insults and gags. It
was Bob Hope and Bing Cosby, Burns and Allen, Ozzie and Harriet. There was no such thing as comedy about relationships,
nothing about the newly urban and collegiate Americans. What
I was interested in was using humor as a reflection of one's own
confusion, ambivalence and dilemma, dealing with sexual life as
one knew it to be." The *Chicago Tribune*'s Connie Lauerman
notes that because his cartoons dealt with the social reality of the
day, Feiffer became "the original satirist-spokesman for the
urban, middle-class, newly educated, going-through-analysis,

post World War II generation." His cartoons presented a mixture of social commentary and political satire previously reserved for—and seen there only in fleeting glimpses—the editorial page of the newspaper.

From the very beginning of his career Feiffer avoided the silliness expected of a non-political cartoonist and created what
Barnes calls "the magically peculiar and peculiarly magical
world of Feiffer: a world full of the perils of rejection, the dangers of acceptance, the wild and perpetual struggles of ego for
id, the dire discomfort of parenthood, [and] the unceasing wars
between men and women." His characters include people who
are odd enough to be humorous but who at the same time can
elicit a painful, empathetic response from his readers: Passionella, who achieves movie stardom because she has the world's
largest breasts; Bernard Mergeneiler, known for his romantic
failures; and an inventor who creates a "Lonely Machine" that
makes light conversation and delivers sympathetic remarks
whenever necessary.

Feiffer's concerns as a cartoonist have followed him to the stage,
as the *New York Times*'s Michiko Kakutani observes: "Clearly
those cartoons . . . share with 'Grown Ups' and his earlier plays
certain recognizable themes and preoccupations. The interest in
adult responsibilities and the difficulty of 'growing up,' for instance, first surfaced in Mr. Feiffer's early cartoons about
Munro, a 4-year-old boy who finds himself drafted into the
Army; and it was developed further in such works as 'Tantrum,'
the story of a husband and father who reverts to being a 2-year
old." In the *Chicago Tribune,* Richard Christiansen notes that
"Hold Me!" is filled with "humorous Jules Feiffer sketches that
deal with the . . . cartoonist's constant themes of anxiety, depression, rejection, disappointment, and other light matters."

Some critics fault Feiffer's plays for being too dependent on his
cartoons for inspiration. In the *Village Voice* Carll Tucker, for
example, comments: "Feiffer's genius as a cartoonist is for dramatic moments—establishing and comically concluding a situation in eight still frames. His characters have personality only for
the purpose of making a point: They do not have, as breathing
dramatic characters must, the freedom to develop, to grow away
from their status as idea-bearers." A similar criticism is leveled
by the *New York Times*'s Frank Rich, who writes: "As yet more
cartoonist than dramatist, Mr. Feiffer presents his most inspired
riffs as set pieces, often monologues."

Other critics voice their approval for what they see as the influence of Feiffer's cartoons on his work for the theater. In Alan
Rich's *New York* review of Feiffer's play, "Knock Knock," for
example, the critic notes: "What gives ['Knock Knock'] its
humor—and a great deal of it is screamingly funny—is the incredible accuracy of [Feiffer's] language, and his use of it to paint
the urban neurosis in exact colors. This we know from his cartoons, and we learn it anew from this endearing, congenial theater piece." Other commentators on New York's theatrical
scene, such as *Dictionary of Literary Biography* contributor
Thomas Edward Ruddick, are able to separate Feiffer's dramatic
work from his other creative efforts. "Feiffer's plays show considerable complexity of plot, character, and idea, and command
attention," Ruddock asserts, "not dependent upon Feiffer's
other achievements. His plays, independently, constitute a noteworthy body of work."

Feiffer, undaunted by negative criticism, continues to write
plays, as well as novels, screenplays, and cartoons. "It bothers
him not," observes Jay Sharbutt in the *Los Angeles Times,* "that
his plays tend to demand a lot from an audience." As Feiffer remarked to Sharbutt: "I found that when a play didn't ask of me

anything but to love it, I almost never loved it. But when a play attacked me, confused me, made me wonder about myself and my attitudes, I found that, in the end, most entertaining and most edifying. . . . And that was the kind of theater I was hoping that I could learn to write."

MEDIA ADAPTATIONS: "The Feiffer Film," based on Feiffer's cartoons, was released in 1965; *Harry, the Rat with Women* was made into a play and produced at Detroit Institute of Arts, 1966; *Passionella, and Other Stories* was adapted by Jerry Bock and Seldon Harnick into "Passionella," a one-act musical produced on Broadway as part of "The Apple Tree," 1967; *Jules Feiffer's America: From Eisenhower to Reagan* was adapted by Russell Vandenbroucke into a play entitled "Feiffer's America"; "What Are We Saying?," a parody on Feiffer's cartoons, was produced in Rome.

BIOGRAPHICAL/CRITICAL SOURCES:

BOOKS

Contemporary Literary Criticism, Gale, Volume 2, 1974, Volume 8, 1978.
Dictionary of Literary Biography, Gale, Volume 7: *Twentieth-Century American Dramatists,* 1981, Volume 44: *American Screenwriters, Second Series,* 1986.

PERIODICALS

Chicago Tribune, June 29, 1979, November 2, 1982.
Hudson Review, summer, 1967.
Los Angeles Times, November 13, 1988.
New York, February 2, 1976.
New York Times, January 21, 1977, December 15, 1981, May 7, 1987.
New York Times Magazine, May 16, 1976.
Village Voice, February 2, 1976.
Washington Post, August 17, 1979.

*　　*　　*

FEIGE, Hermann Albert Otto Maximilian
See TRAVEN, B.

*　　*　　*

FEINSTEIN, Elaine 1930-

PERSONAL: Born October 24, 1930, in Bootle, England; daughter of Isidore and Fay (Compton) Cooklin; married Arnold Feinstein (an immunologist), July 22, 1957; children: Adam, Martin, Joel. *Education:* Cambridge University, B.A., 1952, M.A., 1955.

ADDRESSES: Agent—Gill Coleridge, Anthony Sheil Associates, Ltd., 2-3 Morwell St., London WC1B 3AR, England.

CAREER: Cambridge University Press, London, England, editorial staff member, 1960-62; Bishop's Stortford Training College, Hertfordshire, England, lecturer in English, 1963-66; University of Essex, Wivenhoe, England, assistant lecturer in literature, 1967-70; full-time writer, 1971—. Has also worked as a journalist.

MEMBER: Poetry Society, Eastern Arts Association.

AWARDS, HONORS: Arts Council grants, 1970, 1977; Daisy Miller Award, 1971, for fiction; F.R.S.L.

WRITINGS:

POETRY

In a Green Eye, Goliard Press, 1966.

The Magic Apple Tree, Hutchinson, 1971.
At the Edge, Sceptre Press, 1972.
The Celebrants and Other Poems, Hutchinson, 1973.
Some Unease and Angels, Green River Press, 1977, 2nd edition, Hutchinson, 1982.
The Feast of Euridice, Faber, 1981.
Badlands, Hutchinson, 1986.

FICTION

The Circle (novel), Hutchinson, 1970.
The Amberstone Exit (novel), Hutchinson, 1972.
Matters of Chance (short stories), Covent Garden Press, 1972.
The Glass Alembic (novel), Hutchinson, 1973, published as *The Crystal Garden* (novel), Dutton, 1974.
The Children of the Rose (novel), Hutchinson, 1974.
The Ecstasy of Dr. Miriam Garner (novel), Hutchinson, 1976.
The Shadow Master (novel), Hutchinson, 1977, Simon & Schuster, 1978.
The Silent Areas (short stories), Hutchinson, 1980.
The Survivors (novel), Hutchinson, 1982.
The Border (novel), Hutchinson, 1984.
Mother's Girl (novel), Dutton, 1988.

OTHER

(Editor) *Selected Poems of John Clare,* University Tutorial Press, 1968.
The Selected Poems of Marina Tsvetayeva, Oxford University Press, 1971, reprinted, Dutton, 1987.
"Breath" (teleplay), British Broadcasting Corporation (BBC), 1975.
(Translator) *Three Russian Poets: Margarita Aliger, Yunna Moritz & Bella Akhmadulina,* Carcanet Press, 1979.
(Editor with Fay Weldon) *New Stories,* Arts Council of Great Britain, 1979.
"Echoes" (radio play), 1980.
"Lunch" (teleplay), 1981.
"Lear's Daughters" (play), first produced in London at Battersea Arts Centre, September 27, 1982.
"The Diary of a Country Gentlewoman" (teleplay; twelve-part series), ITV, 1984.
Bessie Smith (biography; Lives of Modern Women Series), Viking, 1986.
A Captive Lion: The Life of Marina Tsvetayeva, Dutton, 1987.
(Translator with Antonina W. Bouis) Nika Turbina, *First Draft,* Marion Boyars, 1988.

Also author of essays and reviews for periodicals, including *Times Literary Supplement.*

SIDELIGHTS: Elaine Feinstein is an English writer whose works include poetry, fiction, plays, and translations of several well-known Russian poets. Such diversity of interest and talent is relatively rare, but according to Michael Schmidt in the *Times Literary Supplement,* all of Feinstein's disparate writings "are very much one voice." The granddaughter of Jews who fled persecution in Tsarist Russia, Feinstein retains a strong preoccupation with her background and upbringing; this fascination with her Eastern European origins informs both her poetry and most of her novels. *Dictionary of Literary Biography* contributor Peter Conradi calls Feinstein "a writer who has made fragmentation and deracination her special topics" and adds that she "has developed a language of formidable efficiency for evoking each, and for searching for authentication in the teeth of each. If her earliest books defamiliarized the ordinary world and the domestic self, her later books appropriately domesticated the exotic." *New Yorker* essayist George Steiner likewise notes that a "pulse of narrative and of dramatic voice is vivid in [Feinstein's] verse," and in the *New Statesman,* Peter Buckman calls the author "a discovery, a writer of limitless simplicity and mistress of a musical prose that can apparently find rhythm anywhere."

Feinstein was born in Bootle, Lancashire and brought up in the industrial town of Leicester in the English Midlands. Her father owned a factory, but his success with it fluctuated wildly. Although her family was never destitute, Feinstein did know some genteel poverty in her childhood. An only child, she was raised to respect religion, but it was only after the Second World War that she came to realize just what being Jewish meant. Feinstein told the *Contemporary Authors Autobiography Series* that her childhood sense of security "was exploded, once and for all, at the war's end, when I read what exactly had been done to so many children, as young as I was, in the hell of Hitler's camps. You could say that in that year I became Jewish for the first time. That is not something I regret. But no doubt the knowledge of human cruelty damaged me. For a very long time afterwards, I could feel no ordinary human emotion without testing it against that imagined experience, and either suspecting it or dismissing it." Conradi puts it another way. After the war, he writes, Feinstein came "to an understanding of the degree to which being Jewish could mean to suffer and live in danger."

Feinstein was educated with a grant provided by the Butler Education Act of 1944, receiving both her Bachelor's and Master's degrees from Cambridge University. In 1957, two years after leaving Cambridge, she married Arnold Feinstein, an immunologist. For several years thereafter she devoted herself to rearing three sons, but she was also able to work as an editor for Cambridge University Press and as a part-time English lecturer at several colleges. Her first volume of poetry, *In a Green Eye,* was published in 1966. According to Deborah Mitchell in the *Dictionary of Literary Biography,* the book "already shows an unassuming sureness of diction and imagery. . . . The poems are simple and generously affectionate—she is always anxious to do justice to whomever she is 'portraying' as well as to express her own relationship with the individual. There is also an unsentimental recognition that, in human relationships, people are tied to one another, pushing and pulling toward and away from one another in mutual dependency."

For a time in the late 1960s Feinstein joined a poetry group in an effort to gain more contact with her poetic voice. The group helped her to do that, primarily because she came to disagree with its insistence on "Englishness" as a motivating characteristic. Conradi suggests that members of the group "wished to de-Europeanize themselves, to make a cult of and to explore the history of their particular Englishness. This helped [Feinstein] define herself against any such cult, as a person who had never definitely 'settled' in England, and whose roots, if she had them and was not nomadic, were certainly not to be discovered in a nationalist version of 'Little England.' " Thereafter Feinstein's work began to explore her ancestry and heritage as well as the horrors inflicted on modern Jews. Her poetry was especially influenced by the verse of Marina Tsvetayeva, a Russian author of the early twentieth century.

Feinstein told *CA:* "I began to write poetry in the '60's very *consciously* influenced by American poets; at a time when the use of line, and spacing, to indicate the movement of poetry, was much less fashionable than it is now among young British poets. It was my translations from the Russian of Marina Tsvetayeva, however, that gave me my true voice, or at least made me attend to a strength and forward push, *against* and *within* a formal structure, that I could have only learnt from Tsvetayeva herself.

In the wholeness of her self exposure, she opened a whole world of experience. Without her, I should never have written novels, still less plays."

Feinstein's early novels "came out of domestic and personal experience whose woes and wonders they to some degree make lyrical," to quote Conradi. A favorite early theme with Feinstein is a woman's search for identity within and outside of familial relationships. In the *Times Literary Supplement,* D. M. Thomas observes that Feinstein wants to show "that women's dreams are common and commonplace, because of their depressed lives." Both *The Circle* and *The Amberstone Exit* feature young women so mired in domestic or family responsibilities that they cannot fully explore themselves. Mitchell contends that Feinstein's early work, "concerned with the world of personal emotion and relationships and with the domestic environment, is remarkable for its economy, its stringent emotional honesty, and tough ironic humor, as well as an intensity and richness of metaphor unusual with this sort of subject matter." Most critics agree, however, that the death of Feinstein's parents in 1973 marks the author's movement into new thematic territory. Conradi states: "It was about this time that [Feinstein] began to enquire into Jewish history more systematically and enlarge her reading. A wish to make her characters more securely substantial also entered into this investigation; the result was not merely more substantial characterization, but also more satisfying mythmaking." To quote *Times Literary Supplement* correspondent Susannah Clapp, Feinstein's characters began to be "not just incidentally irritated or pleased by their dreams and memories, but changed and controlled by them. . . . Some of [her] most persuasive writing . . . describes people in the grip of flashback or nightmare."

Mitchell writes: "In a complex process Feinstein has combined traditional myths with myths she has created out of themes that arose originally from direct reactions to her personal experience and that have been gradually clarified and set into a broader historical perspective." In works such as *The Shadow Master, The Ecstasy of Dr. Miriam Garner,* and *The Border,* Feinstein leaves not only the boundaries of England but the constraints of realism; characters confront the drama of Jewish history, and one way or another it begins to control their lives. Lorna Sage describes Feinstein's intentions in the *Times Literary Supplement:* "Elaine Feinstein has long been obsessed with the persistence of the past in her characters' lives," Sage declares. "The last war, the holocaust, the webs of violence, fanaticism, exile and betrayal that make up recent history (especially Jewish history) reach out to reclaim her cosmopolitan, clever, 'free' people again and again." Conradi observes that in many of Feinstein's novels "someone falls dangerously ill, sick beyond the reach even of modern pharmacy, and it is often the past which can be said figuratively to have sickened them, and which has returned to get them." In *New Statesman,* Clapp contends that this obsession with the past is represented by ghostly visitations. "Now the spectres have been unleashed," Clapp concludes, "and, though it's not easy to give whole-hearted assent to their original necessity, the open acknowledgment of their presence brings remarkable release."

One of Feinstein's best known novels is *The Survivors,* a multi-generational story of two Jewish families who flee Odessa for turn-of-the-century Liverpool. In the *Times Literary Supplement,* Peter Lewis describes the families: "The Gordons are extremely well-to-do and middle-class, and have been assimilated to a considerable extent into English social life. The Katz family is working class, belongs to the Liverpool equivalent of a ghetto (within a slum area), and is orthodox in religion." The tale revolves around a marriage between the Gordon and Katz families, and the subsequent offspring of that union. Lewis notes a good probability that Feinstein "has transmuted her family and personal history into fiction in *The Survivors,* which is full of insights into the changing patterns of Jewish life during this century." *Listener* contributor John Mellors finds more to praise than just the novel's story, however. "It is the poet's precision and verbal fastidiousness which make *The Survivors* far more than just another family chronicle," Mellors writes. Neil Philip offers a similar opinion in *British Book News. The Survivors,* concludes Philip, "is an exceptional novel: intimate, engrossing, economical, yet covering sixty years, two world wars and immense social change. It is Elaine Feinstein's remarkably sure grip on her material which enables her to treat such large themes, to encompass three generations, to manage such a large cast, without losing sight of the personal, the individual, the sense of the minute as well as the year. . . . Fiction as rich and rewarding as this is rare."

Her novels and short stories may attract a wider readership, but Feinstein is also respected in British literary circles for her poetry. In *Spectator,* Emma Tennant calls the author "a powerful poet, whose power lies in the disarming combination of openness and sibylline cunning, a fearless and honest eye on the modern world, the smallest domestic detail, the nerve-bare feelings of people lashed together in marriage, parental and filial relationships—and then, suddenly, like a buried sketch emerging from under an accepted picture and proving to be of a totally different subject, terrifying, uneasy, evoking the old spells that push us this way and that in our lives of resisted superstitions." Tennant adds that the works "have lives of their own, they are very delicately observed. And, in poems which can seem at first spare and slight, there is a powerful undertow of sane love." Mitchell expresses a similar opinion. "The poems come from a familiar world but there is nothing cozy or reassuringly safe about Feinstein's domesticity," Mitchell writes. ". . . [Feinstein's] poems are faithful to the actual experience described . . . but she is less interested, finally, in realism for its own sake than in the 'making strange' of familiar experience to enable the reader to recognize its importance once more." Schmidt discusses Feinstein's style, noting that her language "evokes a memory, thought or perception in just the way it came to consciousness—brokenly, or in a pondered fashion, or suddenly in a flash. This is not language miming experience, but miming rather the process by which experience is registered and understood. Thus the freshness of her writing, the occasional obscurities, and the sense that despite the apparent self-consciousness of style, she is paradoxically the least artificial, the least *literary* of writers. The poems are composed . . . not to *be* poems but to witness accurately to how she experiences."

Feinstein's interest in the poet Tsvetayeva, who she calls "my teacher of courage," has continued for more than twenty years. Feinstein has not only translated Tsvetayeva's poetry, she has also written a biography entitled *A Captive Lion: The Life of Marina Tsvetayeva.* In a *Spectator* review, Peter Levi contends that the work "as it now stands is like the ultimate Tsvetayeva poem, a painful extension of the painful life, with its final focus on a nail used for tethering horses from which she hung herself. It is not the kind of truth one enjoys hearing." Most critics have praised Feinstein's translations from the Russian—a difficult undertaking given the disparities between the two languages. Levi observes that some of the resultant works "are magnificent poems that do not look like translations at all, they are so good." *Spectator* correspondent Emma Fisher writes: "The thought, the feeling, even the wit, [Feinstein] transfers into plain but intense

English, sometimes using rhyme, assonance and regular metres, but often preferring to let the words make their own awkward, blatant shapes on the page." According to Ellendea Proffer in the *New York Times Book Review,* readers "can only be grateful for her work in bringing this difficult poet [Tsvetayeva] into English, and certainly it can be said that these are the best translations available."

Conradi feels that Feinstein's "impressive progress as a novelist can be seen . . . as an emancipation of prose from a provincial sense of its limits," a discovery the author gleaned from her work on Tsvetayeva. Conradi adds that Feinstein "wants to write novels which *move* her readers, as the great novels of the past have done, and to involve them in the fate of her characters so that they will care about what happens to them." Addressing herself to Feinstein's poetic contributions, Mitchell writes: "The mature achievement of her verse has been recognized by a small number of diverse critics, [although] . . . the very individuality which is so refreshing in her work, as well as its diversity, has puzzled a sometimes parochial English reading public." Nevertheless, concludes Mitchell, Feinstein is "something of a rarity among writers—equally at home in verse and fiction, being too well aware of the distinct qualities of each form to make one an adjunct of the other. The cross-fertilization between narrative and lyric means that she is continually developing new and enriching approaches to writing poetry." Schmidt declares that as she enters her third decade as a professional writer, Feinstein has become the creator of "a richly *moral* art" that "eschews facile effect, focuses on its subject, not its audience." In Peter Lewis's opinion, Feinstein "is well on the way to being a writer of infinite variety."

BIOGRAPHICAL/CRITICAL SOURCES:

BOOKS

Contemporary Authors Autobiography Series, Volume 1, Gale, 1984.
Contemporary Literary Criticism, Volume 36, Gale, 1986.
Dictionary of Literary Biography, Gale, Volume 14: *British Novelists since 1960,* 1983, Volume 40: *Poets of Great Britain and Ireland since 1960,* 1985.
Schmidt, Michael and Grevel Lindop, editors, *British Poetry since 1960,* Carcanet Press, 1972.
Schmidt, Michael and Peter Jones, editors, *British Poetry since 1970,* Carcanet Press, 1980.

PERIODICALS

Books, October, 1970.
British Book News, July, 1982.
Chicago Tribune Book World, December 29, 1985.
Contemporary Review, January, 1979.
Encounter, September-October, 1984.
Globe and Mail (Toronto), March 15, 1986.
Harper's, June, 1974.
Listener, August 20, 1970, November 28, 1974, September 28, 1978, March 11, 1982.
Literary Review, April, 1982.
London Review of Books, July 5-19, 1984.
Los Angeles Times, June 6, 1985.
Los Angeles Times Book Review, December 11, 1988.
Nation, June 25, 1988.
New Statesman, August 21, 1970, May 7, 1971, August 4, 1972, April 11, 1975, June 4, 1976.
New Yorker, June 3, 1974, April 29, 1985.
New York Review of Books, October 8, 1987.
New York Times, February 25, 1974, August 21, 1987.

New York Times Book Review, May 19, 1974, November 4, 1979, September 27, 1987.

Observer, August 16, 1970, August 20, 1972, May 27, 1973, April 20, 1975.

Spectator, June 5, 1976, September 24, 1977, September 23, 1978, June 16, 1979, February 9, 1980, March 7, 1987.

Times (London), November 9, 1985, April 2, 1987, January 21, 1988.

Times Literary Supplement, August 28, 1970, August 11, 1972, June 29, 1973, December 7, 1973, April 25, 1975, June 4, 1976, February 3, 1978, October 6, 1978, January 18, 1980, February 22, 1980, February 26, 1982, June 8, 1984, July 17, 1987, July 31, 1987, January 22, 1988.

Village Voice, May 27, 1986.

—Sketch by Anne Janette Johnson

*   *   *

FERBER, Edna   1887-1968

PERSONAL: Born August 15, 1887, in Kalamazoo, Mich.; died of cancer, April 16, 1968, in New York, N.Y.; daughter of Jacob Charles (Hungarian-born small businessman) and Julia (Newmann) Ferber. *Education:* Graduated from Ryan High School, Appleton, Wis.

CAREER: Novelist, short story writer, playwright. At seventeen, began working as a full-time reporter for *Appleton Daily Crescent,* Appleton, Wis.; later worked as a writer and reporter for *Milwaukee Journal. Wartime service:* During World War II, served in civilian capacity as war correspondent for U.S. Army Air Forces.

MEMBER: National Institute of Arts and Letters, Authors League of America, Authors Guild, Dramatists Guild.

AWARDS, HONORS: Pulitzer Prize for Fiction, 1924, for *So Big;* Litt.D., Columbia University and Adelphi College.

WRITINGS:

NOVELS

Dawn O'Hara, the Girl Who Laughed, Stokes, 1911.
Fanny Herself, Stokes, 1917.
The Girls, Doubleday, 1921.
So Big, Doubleday, 1924.
Show Boat, Doubleday, 1926.
Cimarron, Doubleday, 1930, revised edition, Grosset, 1942, new edition by Frederick H. Law, Globe, 1954.
American Beauty, Doubleday, 1931.
Come and Get It, Doubleday, 1935.
Nobody's In Town (two novellas, including "Trees Die at the Top"), Doubleday, 1938.
Saratoga Trunk, Doubleday, 1941.
Great Son, Doubleday, 1945.
Giant, Doubleday, 1952.
Ice Palace, Doubleday, 1958.

SHORT STORIES

Buttered Side Down, Stokes, 1912.
Roast Beef, Medium: The Business Adventures of Emma McChesney, Stokes, 1913.
Personality Plus: Some Experiences of Emma McChesney and Her Son, Jock, Stokes, 1914.
Emma McChesney & Co., Stokes, 1915.
Cheerful, by Request, Doubleday, 1918.
Half Portions, Doubleday, 1920.

Gigolo (includes "Old Man Minick"; also see below), Doubleday, 1922.
Mother Knows Best: A Fiction Book, Doubleday, 1927.
They Brought Their Women: A Book of Short Stories, Doubleday, 1933.
No Room at the Inn, Doubleday, 1941.
One Basket: Thirty-One Short Stories, Simon & Shuster, 1947.

PLAYS

(With George V. Hobart) "Our Mrs. McChesney," first produced in New York at Lyceum Theater, October 19, 1915.
(With George S. Kaufman) "Minick" (dramatization of her short story, "Old Man Minick"; also see below), first produced in New York at Booth Theater, September 24, 1924.
The Eldest: A Drama of American Life, Appleton, 1925.
(With Kaufman) *The Royal Family* (first produced in New York at Selwyn Theater, December 28, 1927; produced as television play, 1954), Doubleday, 1928.
(With Kaufman) *Dinner at Eight* (first produced on Broadway at Music Box Theater, October 22, 1932), Doubleday, 1932.
(With Kaufman) *Stage Door* (first produced on Broadway at Music Box Theater, October 22, 1936), Doubleday, 1936.
(With Kaufman) *The Land Is Bright* (first produced on Broadway at Music Box Theater, October 28, 1941), Doubleday, 1941.
(With Kaufman) *Bravo!* (first produced in New York at Lyceum Theater, November 11, 1948), Dramatists Play Service, 1949.

OTHER

(Author of filmscript) "A Gay Old Dog," Pathe Exchange, 1919.
(With Newman Levy) *$1200 a Year,* Doubleday, 1920.
(Contributor) *My Story That I Like Best,* International Magazine Co., 1924.
Old Man Minick [and] *Minick* (the story and the play; the latter with Kaufman), Doubleday, 1924.
(With Kaufman, author of filmscript) "Welcome Home," Paramount, 1925.
A Peculiar Treasure (autobiography), Doubleday, 1939.
Your Town, World, 1948.
Show Boat, So Big, [and] *Cimarron: Three Living Novels of American Life,* Doubleday, 1962.
A Kind of Magic (autobiography; sequel to *A Peculiar Treasure*), Doubleday, 1963.

WORK IN PROGRESS: At the time of her death, Miss Ferber was collecting material for a book on American Indians but, according to *Variety,* "it is not believed that anything was actually written."

SIDELIGHTS: Edna Ferber loved America and all of her stories in many ways depict a passing American way of life. Along with her great love for America, Edna Ferber greatly admired the characters she portrayed. These characters, drawn from the Midwestern lower middle and middle classes, exemplify the American ideal for her. (She always found the conversation of a truck driver more vigorous and stimulating that the conversation of a Cadillac owner.) When Edna Ferber died at the age of 82, the *New York Times* stated: "Miss Ferber was a dramatic writer with a keen eye for a story, a wholesome respect for the color and harmony of words and a precise ability at portraiture. She [owed] much of this to early journalistic training as a reporter. . . . Reporting, she maintained, developed in her a super-camera eye, a sense of the dramatic and a 'vast storehouse of practical and psychological knowledge' that proved invaluable in her creative writing. . . . Like all good reporters, Miss Ferber was indefatigably curious. The ideas for many of her novels came from snatches of conversation that piqued her interest." She attributed her success to her ability to project herself into any environment. Whatever captured her fancy she could easily write about. Although her books were not profound, they were vivid representations and as a result afford pleasurable reading. (Many of her books and stories are required reading in schools.)

Miss Ferber continued writing about the United States for four decades. Even though her father, a Hungarian Jew, was an unsuccessful storekeeper and she was forced to work instead of attending college where she wanted to study drama, she learned to write "smoothly and brightly, with . . . so wide-awake a style and so clever a selection of detail," Louis Kronenberger perceived. Her enthusiasm made her books especially enjoyable reading for young people. Though a *Dial* reviewer was critical of Edna Ferber—her "talents go to polishing the bright pebbles of life, rather than to touching the bedrock of reality"—this comment may as well be taken as a compliment to her talent. Edna Ferber gave us a fragment of life important to her. Her "sentimentality" was typical of an era we may never see again. William Allen White believed that "the historian will find no better picture of America in the first three decades of this century than Edna Ferber has drawn."

Critics of the twenties and thirties did not hesitate to call her the greatest American woman novelist of her day. *So Big,* her Pulitzer Prize-winning novel of 1924, is the story of Selina Peake Dejong who is left penniless when her gambler father dies of a bullet wound. "Selina's victory in the novel is [Miss] Ferber's extended homily on the gospel of rugged individualism," W. T. Stuckey concluded. She continued writing with the "escapist" technique in *Showboat,* living in James Adams' Floating Theater for two months to get the right atmosphere; in 1924, she dramatized her own personal doubts in *Cimarron* (she had been fired by a new city editor after working on the paper for a year and a half). Her eleventh novel, *Giant,* was, according to the author, "not only a story of Texas today but, I hope, Texas tomorrow." Her last novel, *Ice Palace,* which concerns Alaska, "was given much credit for the admission of the territory," noted William Rutledge III.

In later years, Miss Ferber often helped young writers and used her leisure time for travel (in her youth, she wrote more than 1,000 words a day, 350 days a year). Her own philosophy continues to help the talented young writers in whom she was so interested: "Life," she said, "can't ever really defeat a writer who is in love with writing, for life itself is a writer's lover until death-fascinating, cruel, lavish, warm, cold, treacherous, constant; the more varied the moods the richer the experience."

MEDIA ADAPTATIONS: The following films were based on Miss Ferber's work: "Our Mrs. McChesney," Metro, 1918; "No Woman Knows" (based on Fanny Herself), Universal, 1921; "Classified" (based on her short story of the same title), Corinne Griffith Productions, 1925; "Gigolo," Cinema Corporation of America, 1926; "Mother Knows Best," Fox, 1928; "The Home Girl" (based on a short story), Paramount, 1928; "Show Boat," Universal, 1929, remade by Universal, 1936, and M-G-M, 1951; "The Royal Family of Broadway" (based on the play "The Royal Family," by Miss Ferber and Kaufman), Paramount, 1930; "Cimarron," RKO, 1931, remade by M-G-M, 1960; "The Expert" (based on her short story, "Old Man Minick"), Warner Bros., 1932; "So Big," Warner Bros., 1932, remade by Warner Bros., 1953; "Dinner at Eight" (based on play written with Kaufman), M-G-M, 1933; "Come and Get It," United Artists,

1936; "Stage Door," RKO, 1937; "No Place to Go" (based on the play, "Minick," by Miss Ferber and Kaufman), Warner Bros., 1939; "Saratoga Trunk," Warner Bros., 1945; "Giant," Warner Bros., 1956; "Ice Palace," Warner Bros., 1960. *Show Boat* was adapted for the stage with music by Jerome Kern, and was first produced in New York at Ziegfeld Theater, December 27, 1927. *Saratoga Trunk* was adapted for a musical, "Saratoga," with a libretto by Harold Arlen; it was first produced on Broadway at Winter Garden Theater, December 7, 1959.

BIOGRAPHICAL/CRITICAL SOURCES:

BOOKS

Authors in the News, Volume 1, Gale, 1976.
Contemporary Literary Criticism, Volume 18, Gale, 1981.
Cournos, John, and Sybil Norton (pseudonym of H. S. N. K. Cournos), *Famous American Modern Novelists,* Dodd, 1952.
Dickinson, R., *Edna Ferber,* Doubleday, 1925.
Dictionary of Literary Biography, Gale, Volume 9: *American Novelists, 1910-1945,* 1981, Volume 28: *Twentieth-Century American-Jewish Fiction Writers,* 1984.
Dodd, Loring Holmes, *Celebrities at Our Hearthside,* Dresser, 1959.
Van Gelder, Robert, *Writers and Writing,* Scribner, 1946.
Witham, W. Tasker, *Panorama of American Literature,* Doubleday, 1947.

PERIODICALS

Atlantic, November, 1912, December 1941.
Atlantic Bookshelf, December, 1931.
Chicago Sunday Tribune Book Review, March 30, 1958.
Christian Science Monitor, March 27, 1958.
Dial, November 20, 1950.
Literary Journal, November 1, 1941.
Literary Review, October 28, 1922, August 21, 1926.
Nation, April 23, 1930.
New Republic, April 30, 1930.
New Yorker, February 4, 1939.
New York Times Book Review, August 22, 1926, April 17, 1927, March 23, 1930, May 14, 1933, April 17, 1968.
New York World, March 20, 1930.
Saturday Review, October 17, 1931, September 27, 1952, March 29, 1958.
Springfield Republican, March 2, 1924.
Times (London), April 17, 1968.
United States Quarterly Booklist, September, 1947.
Variety, April 24, 1968.

OBITUARIES:

PERIODICALS

Newsweek, April 29, 1968.
New York Times, April 17, 1968.
Publishers Weekly, April 29, 1968.
Time, April 26, 1968.
Times (London), April 17, 1968.
Washington Post, April 17, 1968.

*　　*　　*

FERGUSON, Helen
See KAVAN, Anna

FERLING, Lawrence
See FERLINGHETTI, Lawrence (Monsanto)

* * *

FERLINGHETTI, Lawrence (Monsanto) 1919(?)-
(Lawrence Ferling)

PERSONAL: Born Lawrence Ferling; restored original family name, 1954; born March 24, c. 1919, in Yonkers, N.Y.; son of Charles S. (an auctioneer) and Clemency (Monsanto) Ferling; married Selden Kirby-Smith, April, 1951 (divorced); children: Julie, Lorenzo. *Education:* University of North Carolina, A.B.; Columbia University, M.A., 1948; Sorbonne, University of Paris, Doctorat de l'Universite (with honors), 1951. *Politics:* "Now an enemy of the State." *Religion:* "Catholique manque."

ADDRESSES: Home—San Francisco, Calif. *Office*—City Lights Books, 261 Columbus Ave., San Francisco, Calif. 94133.

CAREER: Poet, playwright, editor, and painter; worked for *Time* magazine after World War II; taught French in an adult education program in San Francisco, Calif., 1951-53; City Lights Pocket Bookshop (now City Lights Books), San Francisco, co-owner, 1953—, founder and editor of City Lights Books (publishing house), 1955—. Participated with Allen Ginsberg in numerous international literary conferences. *Military service:* U.S. Naval Reserve, 1941-45; became lieutenant commander; was command officer during Normandy invasion.

AWARDS, HONORS: Silver Medal for poetry from Commonwealth Club of California, 1986, for *Over All the Obscene Boundaries.*

WRITINGS:

(Translator) Jacques Prevert, *Selections From Paroles,* City Lights, 1958.
Her (novel), New Directions, 1960.
Howl of the Censor (trial proceedings), edited by J. W. Ehrlich, Nourse Publishing, 1961, reprinted, Greenwood Press, 1976.
(With Jack Spicer) *Dear Ferlinghetti,* White Rabbit Press, 1962.
The Mexican Night: Travel Journal, New Directions, 1970.
Northwest Ecolog, City Lights, 1978.
(With Nancy J. Peters) *Literary San Francisco: A Pictorial History From the Beginning to the Present,* Harper, 1980.
The Populist Manifestos, Grey Fox Press, 1983.
Seven Days in Nicaragua Libre (journal), City Lights, 1985.
Leaves of Life: Fifty Drawings From the Model, City Lights, 1985.
Love in the Days of Rage (novel), Dutton, 1988.

POETRY

Pictures of the Gone World, City Lights, 1955, reprinted, Kraus Reprint, 1973.
Tentative Description of a Dinner Given to Promote the Impeachment of President Eisenhower, Golden Mountain Press, 1958.
A Coney Island of the Mind, New Directions, 1958.
Berlin, Golden Mountain Press, 1961.
One Thousand Fearful Words for Fidel Castro, City Lights, 1961.
Starting From San Francisco, with recording of poems, New Directions, 1961, revised edition without recording, 1967.
(With Gregory Corso and Allen Ginsberg) *Penguin Modern Poets 5,* Penguin, 1963.
Thoughts of a Concerto of Telemann, Four Seasons Foundation, 1963.
Where Is Vietnam?, City Lights, 1965.

To F—- Is to Love Again, Kyrie Eleison Kerista; or, The Situation in the West, Followed by a Holy Proposal, F—- You Press, 1965.
Christ Climbed Down, Syracuse University, 1965.
An Eye On the World: Selected Poems, MacGibbon & Kee, 1967.
Moscow in the Wilderness, Segovia in the Snow, Beach Books, 1967.
After the Cries of the Birds, Dave Haselwood Books, 1967.
Fuclock, Fire Publications, 1968.
The Secret Meaning of Things, New Directions, 1969.
Tyrannus Nix?, New Directions, 1969.
Back Roads to Far Places, New Directions, 1971.
Love Is No Stone on the Moon, ARIF Press, 1971.
The Illustrated Wilfred Funk, City Lights, 1971.
Open Eye, Open Heart, New Directions, 1973.
Who Are We Now?, City Lights, 1976.
Landscapes of Living and Dying, New Directions, 1979.
A Trip to Italy and France, New Directions, 1980.
Endless Life: Selected Poems, New Directions, 1984.
Over All the Obscene Boundaries: European Poems and Transitions, New Directions, 1985.

PLAYS

Unfair Arguments with Existence: Seven Plays for a New Theatre (contains "The Soldiers of No Country" [first produced in London, 1969], "Three Thousand Red Ants" [first produced in New York City, 1970; also see below], "The Alligation" [first produced in San Francisco, 1962; also see below], "The Victims of Amnesia" [first produced in New York City, 1970; also see below], "Motherlode," "The Customs Collector in Baggy Pants" [first produced in New York City, 1964], and "The Nose of Sisyphus"), New Directions, 1963.
Routines (contains thirteen short plays, including "The Jig Is Up," "His Head," "Ha-Ha," and "Non-Objection"), New Directions, 1964.
"3 by Ferlinghetti: Three Thousand Red Ants, The Alligation, [and] The Victims of Amnesia," first produced in New York City, 1970.

EDITOR

Beautitude Anthology, City Lights, 1960.
Pablo Picasso, *Hunk of Skin,* City Lights, 1969.
Charles Upton, *Panic Grass,* City Lights, 1969.
City Lights Anthology, City Lights, 1974.

AUTHOR OF INTRODUCTION

Diane Di Prima, *This Kind of Bird Flies Backward,* Totem Press, 1958.
Michael McClure, *Meat Science Essays,* City Lights, 1963.
Bob Kaufmann, *Solitudes,* Union General d'Editions (Paris), 1966.
Ray Bremser, *Angel,* Tompkins Square Press, 1967.
Tom Picard, *High on the Walls,* Fulcrum, 1967.

CONTRIBUTOR

New Directions in Prose and Poetry 16, New Directions, 1957.
Ralph J. Gleason, editor, *Jam Session: An Anthology of Jazz,* Putnam, 1958.
Seymour Krim, editor, *The Beats,* Fawcett, 1960.
Elias Wilentz, *The Beat Scene,* Corinth, 1960.
Donald M. Allen, editor, *The New American Poetry: 1945-1960,* Grove, 1960.
Alain Bosquet, editor and translator, *Trente-cinq Jeunes Poetes americains,* Gallimard, 1960.

Lyle E. Linville, editor, *Tiger,* Linville-Hansen Associates, 1961.

Ursule Spier Erickson and Robert Pearsall, editors, *The Californians,* Hesperian House, 1961.

Thomas Parkinson, editor, *A Casebook on the Beat,* Crowell, 1961.

Gregory Corso and Walter Hollerer, editors, *Junge Amerikanische Lyrik,* Carl Hanser (Munich), 1961.

Gene Baro, editor, *Beat Poets,* Vista Books (London), 1961.

J. Laughlin, editor, *New Directions in Prose and Poetry 17,* New Directions, 1961.

Markku Lahtela and Anselm Hollo, translators, *Idan Ja Lannen Runot,* Weilin & Goos (Helsinki), 1962.

Poetry Festival, Poetry Center, San Francisco State College, 1962.

Nuestra Decada, Universidad Nacional Autonoma de Mexico, 1964.

Laughlin, editor, *New Directions in Prose and Poetry 18,* New Directions, 1964.

Paris Leary and Robert Kelly, editors, *A Controversy of Poets,* Doubleday, 1965.

Chad Walsh, editor, *Garlands for Christmas,* Macmillan, 1965.

Louis Dudek, editor, *Poetry of Our Time,* Macmillan (Toronto), 1965.

(Contributor of translation) Willis Barnstone, editor, *Modern European Poetry,* Bantam, 1966.

Harriet W. Sheridan, *Structure and Style,* Harcourt, 1966.

Walter Lowenfels, editor, *Where Is Vietnam?,* Doubleday, 1967.

Contributor to numerous publications, including *San Francisco Chronicle, Nation, Evergreen Review, Liberation, Chicago Review, Transatlantic Review,* and *New Statesman.* Editor, *Journal for the Protection of All Beings, Interim Pad,* and *City Lights Journal.*

RECORDINGS

(With Kenneth Rexroth) "Poetry Readings in 'The Cellar'," focused, Fantasy, 1958.

"Tentative Description of a Dinner to Impeach President Eisenhower, and Other Poems," Fantasy, 1959.

"Tyrannus Nix? and Assassination Raga," Fantasy, 1971.

(With Corso and Ginsberg) "The World's Greatest Poets 1," CMS, 1971.

Also author of narration for film "Have You Sold Your Dozen Roses?," California School of Fine Arts Film Workshop, 1957.

SIDELIGHTS: Lawrence Ferlinghetti was a prominent figure in the Beat poetry movement of the 1950s, a movement whose primary purpose was to bring poetry back to the people. Often concerned with political or social issues, Beat poetry was written in a common language owing more to the patterns of ordinary speech than to traditional poetic structures. Many literary critics greeted the movement with stiff resistance. As Peter Collier notes, however, the Beat poets have won "a grudging respect even from the literary elite, whose definitions of the world, of art and the artist's role, they originally set out to dispute. Beginning as renegades, they have had a considerable impact on their times. They have made poetry public, and made it vital." Ferlinghetti's City Lights Bookstore served as a meeting place for Beat writers while his press published and promoted Beat writings. His publication of Allen Ginsberg's poetry collection *Howl* in 1956 led to Ferlinghetti's arrest on obscenity charges. The subsequent trial, during which he was acquitted of the charges in a landmark decision, drew national attention to the Beat movement.

Ferlinghetti's own poetry has been both praised and condemned. M. I. Rosenthal writes in the *Nation* that Ferlinghetti is "a deft, rapid-paced, whirling performer. He has a wonderful eye for meaning in the commonplace." Kathleen Wiegner notes in the *American Poetry Review* that "what is always delightful about Ferlinghetti is the good time he has at what is often a deadly serious business—telling people what is good for them." Noting that Ferlinghetti has been grouped with other Beat poets and criticized accordingly, Crale D. Hopkins writes: "His poetry cannot be dismissed either as protest polemic or as incoherently personalized lyric. His craftsmanship, thematics, and awareness of the tradition justify a further consideration." On the more negative side, Vernon Young describes Ferlinghetti as "one of those spiritual panhandlers bred of our age who has been *infected* by poetry." Jonathan Williams thinks Ferlinghetti's poetry is "real jivy, real groovy, all that—but ultimately kind of stupid." Nevertheless, F. Moramarco of *World Literature Today* describes Ferlinghetti as "one of America's most popular poets."

Although his poetry is best known, Ferlinghetti's first novel *Her* has been well received. Described by the author as "a surreal semi-autobiographical blackbook of a semi-mad period of my life," the book deals with a young man's search for his identity. Pierre Lepape calls it "a masterpiece of the young American novel." Vincent McHugh of the *San Francisco Chronicle* considers *Her* "the most important American prose work I've seen in the last 20 years and decidedly one of the pleasantest." Ferlinghetti wrote a second novel—*Love in the Days of Rage*—in 1988. Focusing on the romance between an American artist and a radical banker and taking place in 1968, the novel received mixed reviews.

A less favorable response has greeted Ferlinghetti's dramatic work. Writing in the *New York Times* of the three-play performance "Three by Ferlinghetti," Clive Barnes states: "Lawrence Ferlinghetti is a poet for whom I have considerable respect. But as a playwright he does not, so far, even begin to make dramatic sense or theatrical logic." Speaking of the same work, John Simon comments in *New York* that "Ferlinghetti tends to be unfocused, diffuse (quite an achievement, considering the brevity of the pieces), [and] bereft of a genuine dramatic impulse and pulsation." On a more positive note, the reviewer for *Cue* concludes that "the most impressive thing about [the three plays] is the intensity of their themes and the depth of Ferlinghetti's commitment to the gut-issue of man's destruction of man."

In all of his work, Ferlinghetti has displayed a continuing concern with political expression. His poetry often addresses political subjects, as in *Where Is Vietnam?* and *Tyrannus Nix?,* while the work he publishes through City Lights Books often exhibits both literary and political concerns.

As a publisher, Ferlinghetti is particularly sensitive to matters of government censorship. He holds that government grants to writers constitute a subtle form of control. Speaking to Ben Pleasants of the *Los Angeles Times,* Ferlinghetti declares: "Officially, [writers receiving grants] can say anything they want and still get the grant. Nevertheless, there's an . . . influence at work, unspoken, that says, 'Don't Bite the Hand That Feeds You.'" Comparing censorship in other countries to that in the United States, Ferlinghetti believes there is "very real censorship in Russia. . . . There's no comparison between the U.S. and Russia. Here it's more innocuous, it's a self-imposed censorship, really an *abdication* of freedom of speech."

Ferlinghetti is well aware of his position as social-dissident-turned-successful-publisher. "Herbert Marcuse once noted," he tells Pleasants, "the enormous capacity of society to ingest its own most dissident elements. As soon as you become a successful dissident you get on TV and you're writing books for publishers and living in a beach community in Los Angeles. . . . It happens to everyone successful within the system. I'm ingested myself."

MEDIA ADAPTATIONS: Ferlinghetti's poem "Autobiography" was choreographed by Sophie Maslow in 1964. "A Coney Island of the Mind" was adapted for the stage by Steven Kyle Kent, Charles R. Blaker, and Carol Brown and produced at the Edinburgh Festival in Scotland in 1966. Another adaptation of the poem was presented by Ted Post on the television program "Second Experiment in Television" in 1967.

BIOGRAPHICAL/CRITICAL SOURCES:

BOOKS

Allen, David M., editor, *The New American Poetry: 1945-1960,* Grove, 1960.
Charters, Samuel, *Some Poems/Poets: Studies in American Underground Poetry Since 1945,* Oyez, 1971.
Cherkovski, Neeli, *Ferlinghetti: A Biography,* Doubleday, 1979.
Cohn, Ruby, *Dialogue in American Drama,* Indiana University Press, 1971.
Concise Dictionary of American Literary Biography: The New Consciousness, 1941-1968, Gale, 1987.
Contemporary Literary Criticism, Gale, Volume 2, 1974, Volume 6, 1976, Volume 10, 1979, Volume 27, 1984.
Dictionary of Literary Biography, Volume 16: *The Beats: Literary Bohemians in Postwar America,* Gale, 1983.
Kherdian, David, *Six Poets of the San Francisco Renaissance: Portraits and Checklists,* Giligia Press, 1967.
Rexroth, Kenneth, *Assays,* New Directions, 1961.

PERIODICALS

America, August 20, 1977.
American Poetry Review, September/October, 1977.
Books and Bookmen, November, 1967.
Carleton Miscellany, spring, 1965.
Chicago Tribune, May 19, 1986, September 13, 1988.
Chicago Tribune Book World, February 28, 1982.
Cite, October 3, 1970.
Commentary, December, 1957.
Commonweal, February 3, 1961.
Critique: Studies in Modern Fiction, Volume XIX, number 3, 1978.
Italian Americana, autumn, 1974.
Liberation, June, 1959.
Library Journal, November 15, 1960.
Life, September 9, 1957.
Listener, February 1, 1968.
Los Angeles Times, July 20, 1969, March 18, 1980.
Los Angeles Times Book Review, August 24, 1980, October 19, 1980, March 24, 1985.
Midwest Quarterly, autumn, 1974.
Minnesota Review, July, 1961.
Nation, October 11, 1958.
New Republic, February 22, 1975.
New Statesman, April 14, 1967.
New York, October 5, 1970.
New York Times, April 14, 1960, April 15, 1960, April 16, 1960, April 17, 1960, February 6, 1967, February 27, 1967, September 13, 1970.
New York Times Book Review, September 2, 1956, September 7, 1958, April 29, 1962, July 21, 1968, September 8, 1968, September 21, 1980, November 1, 1981.
Observer, November 1, 1959, April 9, 1967.
Parnassus: Poetry in Review, spring/summer, 1974.

Poetry, November, 1958, July, 1964, May, 1966.
Prairie Schooner, fall, 1974, summer, 1978.
Punch, April 19, 1967.
Ramparts, March, 1968.
Reporter, December 12, 1957.
San Francisco Bay Guardian, October 6, 1977.
San Francisco Chronicle, March 5, 1961.
San Francisco Oracle, February, 1967.
San Francisco Review of Books, September, 1977.
Saturday Review, October 5, 1957, September 4, 1965.
Sewanee Review, fall, 1974.
Sunday Times (London), June 20, 1965.
Times (London), October 27, 1988.
Times Literary Supplement, April 27, 1967, November 25, 1988.
Virginia Quarterly Review, autumn, 1969, spring, 1974.
Washington Post Book World, August 2, 1981.
Wilson Library Bulletin, June, 1958.
Wisconsin Studies in Contemporary Literature, summer, 1967.
World Literature Today, summer, 1977.

* * *

FERMOR, Patrick Leigh
See LEIGH FERMOR, Patrick (Michael)

* * *

FEYNMAN, R. P.
See FEYNMAN, Richard Phillips

* * *

FEYNMAN, Richard
See FEYNMAN, Richard Phillips

* * *

FEYNMAN, Richard P.
See FEYNMAN, Richard Phillips

* * *

FEYNMAN, Richard Phillips   1918-1988
(R. P. Feynman, Richard Feynman, Richard P. Feynman)

PERSONAL: Surname is pronounced "*Fine*-man"; born May 11, 1918, in New York, N.Y.; died of abdominal cancer, February 15, 1988, in Los Angeles, Calif.; son of Melville Arthur (a sales manager) and Lucille (a homemaker; maiden name, Phillips) Feynman; married Arlene H. Greenbaum, 1941 (deceased), married Mary Lou Bell (divorced), married Gweneth Howarth, 1960; children: (third marriage) Carl, Michelle. *Education:* Massachusetts Institute of Technology, B.S. (with honors), 1939; Princeton University, Ph.D., 1942. *Religion:* Atheist.

ADDRESSES: Home—2475 Boulder Rd., Altadena, Calif. 91001. *Office*—Department of Physics, California Institute of Technology, Pasadena, Calif. 91125.

CAREER: Frankfort Arsenal, Philadelphia, Pa., scientist, 1939-42; Atomic Bomb Project (also known as the Manhattan Project), Princeton, N.J., staff member, 1942-43, Los Alamos, N.M., group leader, 1943-46; Cornell University, Ithaca, N.Y., associate professor of theoretical physics, 1946-50; teacher in Brazil, 1950-51; California Institute of Technology, Pasadena,

Calif., Tolman Professor of theoretical physics, 1951-88. Public lecturer; served on California State Curriculum Commission in the 1960s, and on presidential commission investigating the 1986 space shuttle *Challenger* explosion; writer.

MEMBER: American Association for the Advancement of Science, American Physical Society, National Academy of Sciences, Royal Society of London (fellow; foreign member), Brazilian Academy of Sciences.

AWARDS, HONORS: Einstein Award, 1954; shared Nobel Prize for Physics from Nobel Foundation, 1965, for "fundamental work in quantum electrodynamics"; Oersted Medal, 1972; Niels Bohr International Gold Medal, 1973.

WRITINGS:

(Under name R. P. Feynman) *The Theory of Fundamental Processes: A Lecture Note Volume,* W. A. Benjamin, 1961.
Quantum Electrodynamics (lectures), W. A. Benjamin, 1961.
(With Robert B. Leighton and Matthew Sands, under name Richard P. Feynman) *The Feynman Lectures on Physics* (includes *The Electromagnetic Field* and *Quantum Mechanics*), three volumes, Addison-Wesley, 1963-65.
(Under name Richard Feynman) *The Character of Physical Law* (the Messenger lectures, Cornell University, 1964), MIT Press, 1965.
(With A. R. Hibbs, under name R. P. Feynman) *Quantum Mechanics and Path Integrals,* McGraw, 1965.
(Under name R. P. Feynman) *Photon-Hadron Interactions,* W. A. Benjamin, 1972.
(Under name R. P. Feynman) *Statistical Mechanics* (lectures), edited by Jacob Shaham, W. A. Benjamin, 1972.
(Contributor, under name R. P. Feynman) *Hawaii Topical Conference in Particle Physics, 5th, University of Hawaii, 1973,* University of Hawaii Press, 1974.
QED: The Strange Theory of Light and Matter (lectures, speeches, and essays), Princeton University Press, 1985.
(With Ralph Leighton, under name Richard P. Feynman) *"Surely You're Joking, Mr. Feynman!": Adventures of a Curious Character* (memoirs), edited by Edward Hutchings, Norton, 1985.
(With Steven Weinberg, under name Richard P. Feynman) *Elementary Particles and the Laws of Physics: The 1986 Dirac Memorial Lecture,* compiled by Richard MacKenzie and Paul Doust, Cambridge University Press, 1987.
(With Ralph Leighton, under name Richard P. Feynman) *"What Do You Care What Other People Think?": Further Adventures of a Curious Character* (memoirs), Norton, 1988.

Also author of "Personal Observations on the Reliability of the Shuttle," an appendix to the report of the commission investigating the 1986 space shuttle *Challenger* disaster. Contributor of articles to scientific journals.

SIDELIGHTS: Richard Phillips Feynman was "arguably the most brilliant, iconoclastic and influential of the postwar generation of theoretical physicists," stated James Gleick in a *New York Times* article. Feynman assisted in the development of the atomic bomb and eventually shared the Noble Prize for physics for his work in quantum electrodynamic theory. He served as Tolman Professor of theoretical physics at California Institute of Technology, where he classified subatomic particles and postulated the existence of a nuclear particle—the "quark"—as the smallest unit of matter. Feynman was revered for his teaching ability as well as for his scholarship, and his lecture transcriptions are considered classic texts in the discipline. In the 1980s,

he wrote two best-selling memoirs and served on the commission investigating the explosion of the space shuttle *Challenger.* Feynman may be most remembered, however, for the ingenuity he used in solving scientific problems: often flamboyant and always an individualist, he became known for his ability to view difficult conceptual problems from radically new perspectives. Said Feynman's colleague Sidney D. Drell in the *New York Times:* "He [was] the most creative theoretical physicist of his time and a true genius. He has touched with his unique creativity just about every field of physics."

Feynman, son of a sales manager for a uniform company, was born in New York City and grew up in the Queens community of Far Rockaway. Feynman later credited his father for instilling in him a love for nature and the desire to investigate it in all its forms. "My father taught me continuity and harmony in the world. He didn't know anything exactly, whether the insect had eight legs or a hundred legs, but he understood everything. And I was interested because there was always this kick at the end—a revelation of how wonderful nature really is," he told Lee Edson in the *New York Times Magazine.* As a toddler, Feynman began studying math, a subject for which he showed immense talent and which he came to regard as nature's language. By the time he finished high school, he had taught himself calculus.

After receiving his bachelor's degree from Massachusetts Institute of Technology in 1939, Feynman entered Princeton University for postgraduate study in physics. He was excused from military service during World War II because he failed the army psychiatric exam by responding to the question "How much do you value your life?" with the answer "64." Instead, while attending graduate school, he accepted a job at Philadelphia's Frankfort Arsenal, assisting in the development of a computer that would direct artillery. When he received his doctorate in 1942, he was invited to join the Manhattan Project, the American effort to produce the atomic bomb. Collaborating in Los Alamos, New Mexico, with such leading twentieth-century physicists as Robert Oppenheimer and Enrico Fermi, Feynman conceived the formula for nuclear weapon energy yield prediction—a mathematical calculation that is still classified information—and led the scientists in efforts to computerize the cumbersome calculations required in their work. Feynman also counted himself among the physicists who witnessed the first atomic bomb detonation.

Feynman's Los Alamos experience earned him an associate professorship of theoretical physics at Cornell University following World War II. There he began investigating certain functional problems in quantum electrodynamics, a field that studies the interaction of subatomic particles. Although physicists accepted the validity of quantum electrodynamic theory, they encountered increasing difficulty using its existing formulations to explain, predict, or quantify phenomena observed in the laboratory. In his characteristically imaginative manner, Feynman developed practical diagrams of particle interactions that simplified analyses and made possible more accurate predictions and calculations concerning particle behavior. "Feynman diagrams," as they came to be known, depicted particle movement probabilities using squiggly lines and arrows. These simple representations essentially reconceptualized quantum physics, and scientists found a wide variety of other applications for the diagrams. For his achievement, Feynman shared the 1965 Nobel Prize.

In 1951, after teaching for a year in Brazil, Feynman became professor at California Institute of Technology, where he developed theories accounting for the behavior of low-temperature helium and conducted research on radioactivity. He spent the late 1950s and the 1960s investigating the composition of the atom's nucleus with fellow Cal Tech physicist Murray Gell-Mann. The scientists hypothesized that protons, particles that form the nucleus, are themselves made up of particles—believed to be the smallest units of matter—called "partons" or "quarks." This theory, like many of Feynman's other accomplishments, has become fundamental to quantum physics.

Feynman's intellect was matched by his unpretentiousness and his sense of humor. He was gifted in his ability to explain physics phenomena in enlightening, accessible, and entertaining lectures. During one public lecture, for example, Feynman described a subatomic particle as "almost, but not quite, totally useless—take your son-in-law as a model." Of Feynman's style an anonymous friend wrote in a *Scientific American* tribute that the professor "was patently not struck in the prewar mold of most young academics. He had the flowing, expressive postures of a dancer, the quick speech we thought of as Broadway, the pat phrases of the hustler and the conversational energy of a finger snapper." Gleick likewise asserted that "Feynman developed a . . . style that kept him at the center of attention, the impossible combination of theoretical physicist and circus barker, all body motion and sound effects."

Feynman's lectures are gathered in such volumes as *The Theory of Fundamental Processes, Quantum Electrodynamics, Statistical Mechanics,* and the three-volume *Feynman Lectures on Physics,* which has become required reading in physics classrooms both in the United States and the Soviet Union. Writing in the *New York Times Book Review,* K. C. Cole recommended *The Feynman Lectures on Physics* as "well worth going through even for those who will skip 90 percent of the often difficult text." Feynman's *Elementary Particles and the Laws of Physics,* a 1986 lecture dedicated to British physicist P. A. M. Dirac, was deemed in a *Scientific American* article "a *tour de force* of exposition," and John Roche, in his *Times Literary Supplement* review of *QED: The Strange Theory of Light and Matter,* proclaimed Feynman the "acknowledged master of clear explanation in physics, . . . eminently luminous, humorous and reasonable."

Feynman received widespread publicity in 1985 when he published the first of two best-selling personal memoirs. In *"Surely You're Joking, Mr. Feynman!": Adventures of a Curious Character* Feynman discussed his involvement at Los Alamos, where, in addition to his scientific achievements, he became known as "Feynman the Safecracker" for his exploits in outwitting the facility's strict security systems. As told to Feynman's longtime friend, writer Ralph Leighton, the book also contains Feynman's anecdotes about playing the bongo drums in a Brazilian samba band, gambling in Las Vegas, picking up women in bars, flunking the Army psychiatric exam, and winning the Nobel Prize. The memoir drew favorable criticism, with some reviewers commenting on the contrast between the importance of Feynman's achievements and the often irreverent attitudes emerging from the book. Cole, for instance, in his *New York Times Book Review* critique of *"Surely You're Joking, Mr. Feynman!",* asserted that "while the man presented in this book may look distressingly like a cartoon caricature of a great man, . . . Feynman is a storyteller in the tradition of Mark Twain. He proves once again that it is possible to laugh out loud and scratch your head at the same time. He is a master at summing up a complex situation in a few well-chosen words."

Feynman claimed more attention after he was named to the commission formed by then President Ronald Reagan to investigate the January, 1986, space shuttle *Challenger* explosion, in which seven crew members were killed. Known in the scientific community for questioning established attitudes and procedures, Feynman's outspoken opinions and unorthodox methods of inquiry reportedly annoyed some of his fellow commissioners. Suspecting that the blame for the accident lay as much with National Aeronautics and Space Administration (NASA) bureaucracy as with the shuttle's design, Feynman conducted independent interviews with NASA managers and low-level technicians and engineers. He also aggressively questioned NASA witnesses at the hearings and refused to let political considerations prevent him from uncovering the disaster's true causes. At perhaps the climax of the televised hearings, the scientist astounded his audience by cooling—in his glass of ice water—a sample of the rubber used in the shuttle's critical rocket booster seals. Squeezing the cold rubber with a clamp and noting that the material was not resilient enough to function safely in the near-freezing temperatures prevalent at the shuttle's launch, Feynman demonstrated in his simple experiment both the cause of the tragedy and the inefficiency of the NASA bureaucracy. Feynman refused to sign the commission's formal report until he was satisfied that it portrayed the facts truthfully. In addition, he wrote "Personal Observations on the Reliability of the Shuttle"—his own appendix to the report, in which he faulted NASA management for ignoring warning signals and underestimating risks inherent in space shuttle flight.

During his service on the commission Feynman was battling abdominal cancer. The Nobel laureate died in February of 1988, after completing his second book of reminiscences. *"What Do You Care What Other People Think?": Further Adventures of a Curious Character* appeared less than a year after Feynman's death. The volume includes a lecture, correspondence, and several essays, also in the conversational style of *"Surely You're Joking, Mr. Feynman!",* on subjects ranging from Feynman's first marriage (which ended with his wife's death from Hodgkin's disease while Feynman was working at Los Alamos), to his ideas about the role of science in mankind's future. The memoir's longest section, titled "Mr. Feynman Goes to Washington," details the physicist's activity on the space shuttle *Challenger* investigation, describes his strategies for determining the cause of the accident, and states candidly his opinions about the problems in the space program.

Reviewers found a more solemn portrait of Feynman in *"What Do You Care What Other People Think?"* "These reminiscences present the cocky hero in greater depth," observed Feynman's former Caltech colleague Bettyann Kevles in the *Los Angeles Times Book Review,* who also noted that *"What Do You Care What Other People Think?"* is "a gentler book, and for those interested in the man, a more substantial one." James Gleick, in the *New York Times Book Review,* expressed a similar opinion, remarking that "the assortment lacks the natural, easy flow of its predecessor. Yet in many ways, the new book gives a far more somber and realistic picture of Feynman: not just a bongo-playing, skirt-chasing, joke-telling prankster, but a man, always in earnest and sometimes troubled, who thought more deeply than most about the power and limitations of science."

Feynman was perhaps the best-known twentieth-century physicist since Albert Einstein. His achievements extended beyond the laboratory to the classroom, the government, and mankind in general, to which he felt all scientists owed an allegiance. "It is our responsibility as scientists, knowing the great progress which . . . is the fruit of freedom of thought," Feynman wrote in *"What Do You Care What Other People Think?",* "to proclaim the value of this freedom; to teach how doubt is not to be feared but welcomed and discussed; and to demand this freedom as our duty to all coming generations."

AVOCATIONAL INTERESTS: Mayan hieroglyphics, playing bongo drums, drawing.

BIOGRAPHICAL/CRITICAL SOURCES:

BOOKS

Feynman, Richard P. and Ralph Leighton, *"Surely You're Joking, Mr. Feynman!": Adventures of a Curious Character,* Norton, 1985.

Feynman, Richard P. and Ralph Leighton, *"What Do You Care What Other People Think?": Further Adventures of a Curious Character,* Norton, 1988.

PERIODICALS

Chicago Tribune, November 30, 1988.
Los Angeles Times, February 24, 1985, November 13, 1988, February 4, 1989.
Nature, November 3, 1988.
New York Times Book Review, January 27, 1985, November 13, 1988.
New York Times Magazine, October 8, 1967.
People, July 22, 1985.
Time, January 7, 1985.
Washington Post Book World, January 12, 1989.

OBITUARIES:

PERIODICALS

Economist, February 20, 1988.
New Yorker, March 14, 1988.
New York Times, February 17, 1988.
Scientific American, June, 1988.
Time, February 29, 1988.

*   *   *

FIEDLER, Leslie A(aron) 1917-

PERSONAL: Born March 8, 1917, in Newark, N.J.; son of Jacob J. (a pharmacist) and Lillian (Rosenstrauch) Fiedler; married Margaret Ann Shipley, October 6, 1939 (divorced, 1972); married Sally Andersen, February, 1973; children: (first marriage) Kurt, Eric, Michael, Deborah, Jenny, Miriam; (second marriage; stepchildren) Soren Andersen, Eric Andersen. *Education:* New York University, B.A., 1938; University of Wisconsin, M.A., 1939, Ph.D., 1941; Harvard University, postdoctoral study, 1946-47. *Religion:* Jewish.

ADDRESSES: Home—154 Morris Ave., Buffalo, N.Y. 14214. *Office*—Department of English, State University of New York at Buffalo, Buffalo, N.Y. 14260.

CAREER: Montana State University, Missoula, assistant professor, 1941-48, associate professor, 1948-52, professor of English, 1954-64, department chairman and director of humanities courses, 1954-56; State University of New York at Buffalo, professor of English, 1964-72, Samuel L. Clemens Professor of Literature, 1972—. Fulbright fellow and lecturer, universities of Rome and Bologna (Italy), 1951-53, and University of Athens (Greece), 1961-62; junior fellow, School of Letters, Indiana University, 1953; resident fellow in creative writing and Gauss Lecturer, Princeton University, 1956-57; associate fellow, Calhoun College, Yale University, 1969. Visiting professor, University of Sussex (England), 1967-68, and University of Vincennes (France), 1971. Summer professor at New York University, Columbia University, University of Vermont, and Indiana University. Lecturer. National Book Awards judge, 1956 and 1972.

Military service: U.S. Naval Reserve, 1942-46; Japanese interpreter; became lieutenant junior grade.

MEMBER: American Association of University Professors, Modern Language Association of America, English Institute, Dante Society of America, P.E.N., Phi Beta Kappa.

AWARDS, HONORS: Rockefeller fellow, Harvard University, 1946-47; Furioso poetry prize, 1951; *Kenyon Review* fellow in literary criticism, 1956-57; National Institute of Arts and Letters prize for excellence in creative writing, 1957; American Council of Learned Societies grants-in-aid, 1960 and 1961; Guggenheim fellow, 1970-71.

WRITINGS:

CRITICISM

An End to Innocence: Essays on Culture and Politics, Beacon Press, 1955, reprinted, Stein & Day, 1973.
The Jew in the American Novel, Herzl Press, 1959, second edition, 1966.
Love and Death in the American Novel, Criterion, 1960, revised edition, Stein & Day, 1966.
No! In Thunder: Essays on Myth and Literature, Beacon Press, 1960, reprinted, 1973.
The Riddle of Shakespeare's Sonnets, Basic Books, 1962.
Waiting for the End, Stein & Day, 1964 (published in England as *Waiting for the End: The American Literary Scene from Hemingway to Baldwin,* J. Cape, 1965).
The Return of the Vanishing American, Stein & Day, 1968.
Collected Essays (includes *An End to Innocence* [also see above], *The Jew in the American Novel* [also see above], *No! In Thunder* [also see above], *Unfinished Business* [also see below], *To the Gentiles* [also see below], and *Cross the Border, Close the Gap* [also see below]), two volumes, Stein & Day, 1971.
The Stranger in Shakespeare, Stein & Day, 1972.
Unfinished Business, Stein & Day, 1972.
To the Gentiles, Stein & Day, 1972.
Cross the Border, Close the Gap, Stein & Day, 1972.
A Fiedler Reader, Stein Day, 1977.
Freaks: Myths and Images of the Secret Self, Simon & Schuster, 1978.
The Inadvertent Epic: From Uncle Tom's Cabin to Roots, Simon & Schuster, 1980.
Olaf Stapledon, Oxford University Press, 1982.
What Was Literature? Class Culture and Mass Society, Simon & Schuster, 1982.

NOVELS

The Second Stone: A Love Story, Stein & Day, 1963.
Back to China, Stein & Day, 1965.
The Messengers Will Come No More, Stein & Day, 1974.

SHORT STORIES

Pull Down Vanity and Other Stories, Lippincott, 1962.
The Last Jew in America, Stein & Day, 1966.
Nude Croquet and Other Stories, Stein & Day, 1969.

EDITOR

The Art of the Essay, Crowell, 1958, revised edition, 1969.
(And author of introduction) *Walt Whitman: Selections from "Leaves of Grass,"* Dell, 1959.
(With Jacob Vinocur) *The Continuing Debate: Essays on Education,* St. Martin's, 1965.

(With Arthur Zeiger) *A Critical Anthology of American Literature,* Volume I: *O Brave New World: American Literature From 1600 to 1840,* Dell, 1968.

(With J. W. Field) *Bernard Malamud and the Critics,* New York University Press, 1970.

In Dreams Awake: A Historical-Critical Anthology of Science Fiction, Dell, 1976.

English Literature: Opening Up the Canon, Johns Hopkins Press, 1981.

Advisory editor, *Ramparts* and *Studies in Black Literature;* advisory editor in English, St. Martin's Press.

OTHER

(Author of introduction) Robert Louis Stevenson, *Master of Ballantrae,* Rinehart, 1954.

(Contributor) Milton Hindus, editor, *Leaves of Grass One Hundred Years After,* Stanford University Press, 1955.

(With others) *Negro and Jew: Encounter in America,* [New York], 1956.

(Contributor) Fred Eychaner, editor, *Reflections on Rebellion: The 1965 Northwestern Student Symposium,* [Evanston], 1965.

(Author of afterword) Samuel Langhorne Clemens, *The Innocents Abroad,* New American Library, 1966.

Being Busted, Stein & Day, 1969.

(Contributor) Arthur A. Cohen, compiler, *Arguments and Doctrines: A Reader of Jewish Thinking in the Aftermath of the Holocaust,* Harper, 1970.

Fiedler on the Roof: Epistle to the Apostles, Scarborough House, 1987.

Regular columnist for *American Judaism.* Contributor to periodicals, including *Kenyon Review, Partisan Review, Poetry, Commentary, New Republic,* and *Encounter.*

WORK IN PROGRESS: Editing further volumes of *A Critical Anthology of American Literature;* a book of poems.

SIDELIGHTS: In his major critical work *Love and Death in the American Novel,* Leslie A. Fiedler examines American and European novels and claims that the principal difference lies in the way the themes of death and adult sexuality are treated. He believes that American novelists are not only obsessed with death but also are incapable of portraying adult heterosexual relationships. He writes, "American authors have shied away from permitting in their fiction the presence of any full-fledged mature women, giving us instead monsters of virtue or bitchery, symbols of the rejection or fear of sexuality."

Statements such as this one have divided Fiedler's audience into those who find him provocative and those who find him provoking. This polarity is apparent in the critical evaluation of *Love and Death in the American Novel.* In the *Spectator* Kingsley Amis praises the book as "witty, exasperating, energetic, penetrating" while in the *Guardian* Donald Davie declares it "a sustained fouling of the American nest." Granville Hicks, writing in the *Saturday Review,* describes the book as "a serious and impressively well-informed attempt to look at American fiction in a new way." On the other hand, a *Times Literary Supplement* reviewer believes that the book offers "under the guise of criticism . . . a spiritual autobiography: a confession of the impact upon [Fiedler] of 'the American Experience.' "

No! In Thunder received similar critical response. "There is something here to offend almost everyone," contends *Catholic World*'s S. P. Ryan. "Much of [the book] seems close to angry raving; but there are passages of sheer brilliance." *New York*

Herald Tribune's Perry Miller calls the book "a set of lively, witty, stimulating pieces" which have been marred by Fiedler's feeling "obliged . . . to make himself offensive to somebody or other." A *Kirkus* reviewer sums up the general opinion of *No! In Thunder:* "Fiedler's critical theories have generated a great deal of partisanship and no doubt this collection will prove as continuingly provocative and/or provoking."

Some critics, such as *New York Herald Tribune Book Review*'s Willard Thorp, comment on Fiedler's psychological/sociological approach to literature: "The reader who has not before encountered Mr. Fiedler at work may be in for a shock. . . . To him novels are documents from which the secret cultural history of America can be read." Amis agrees with Fiedler's approach and finds that the use of "the American novel as a couch-monologue wherewith to analyse the American psyche is a valid enterprise." A *Time* critic, however, remarks that while Fiedler's "nonstop psychologizing is at times brilliant and rarely a bore, the head shrinker's touch is a trifle grotesque."

In *Commonweal,* Bernard Murchland and Richard Gilman discuss Fiedler's style. Murchland states, "Fiedler is a frustrating critic in the sense that he is more adept than most at stirring his readers to ready disagreement." Gilman concurs: "Fiedler's Freudian orientation and strong-arm tactics [are] unfailingly evocative and illuminating. You'll quarrel with him on every page, but that new light is there."

"It would be greatly oversimplifying the issue, however, to believe that Fiedler is simply playing the role of the American critics' bad boy," Charles R. Larson states in *Literary Review.* Larson cites Fiedler's 1967 run in with the law and the resultant book, *Being Busted,* as examples of how sensitive Fiedler can be. In *Being Busted,* Fiedler writes about his experience at the State University of New York at Buffalo where he was a faculty adviser to a student group working to legalize marijuana. The police raided Fiedler's house and arrested him on charges of "maintaining premises where marijuana was used." At his trial, Fiedler was found guilty as charged and sentenced to six months in jail. The sentence was later reversed by the Court of Appeals of the State of New York, which found that Fiedler "had never been convicted of a crime, or charged with a crime."

Later summations of Fiedler's work generally accept his eccentricities and acknowledge his contribution to the field of literary criticism. "By now the objections to Fiedler's procedures are virtually standardized," remarks Thomas R. Edwards in the *Partisan Review.* "He can be careless about little accuracies . . . and silly with his analogies . . . and his habit of melodramatizing history will not be to everyone's taste. . . . Fiedler is an incorrigible rascal, and to forbid him his tricks would deprive us of the often brilliant insights he has up his sleeve."

In an article for the *Literary Review,* Larson describes Fiedler's method as "a frontal attack based on shock, entertainment . . . and the destruction of shibboleths and prejudices. . . . [His] criticism remains for the most part highly readable and almost uniformly fresh." Larson also believes that many critics have misunderstood Fiedler simply because they have insisted on taking him at face value: "Fiedler's work so frequently approaches the superlative that one would think that by now the critics would be catching on."

New Republic critic Jonathan Yardley observes that Fiedler, being middle-aged with a substantial body of publications, "can no longer lay claim to the title of *enfant terrible* of American letters." As the dust jacket of Fiedler's novel *The Messengers Will Come No More* notes, *Love and Death in the American Novel* "is now being taught by the same people who were originally outraged by it." Yardley comments, "Even if he has moved perilously close to membership in the literary establishment Fiedler has shown little evidence of losing his refreshing talent for slaying dragons and tilting at windmills, his instinct for the jugular and the provocative."

BIOGRAPHICAL/CRITICAL SOURCES:

BOOKS

Amis, Kingsley, *What Became of Jane Austen? and Other Questions,* J. Cape, 1970, Harcourt, 1971.
Contemporary Literary Criticism, Gale, Volume 4, 1975, Volume 13, 1980, Volume 24, 1983.
Dictionary of Literary Biography, Gale, Volume 28: *Twentieth-Century American Jewish Fiction Writers,* 1984, Volume 67: *Modern American Critics Since 1955,* 1988.
Fiedler, Leslie A., *Love and Death in the American Novel,* Stein & Day, 1966.

PERIODICALS

Catholic World, December, 1960.
Commonweal, December 9, 1960, January 6, 1967.
Georgia Review, fall, 1980.
Guardian, January 13, 1961.
Harper's, January, 1970, February, 1978.
Kirkus, January 15, 1960, September 15, 1960.
Literary Review, fall, 1970.
Los Angeles Times Book Review, November 31, 1982.
Nation, August 15, 1959, September 22, 1969.
New Republic, December 5, 1960, May 22, 1965, November 9, 1974.
Newsweek, August 2, 1971, January 9, 1984.
New York Herald Tribune, January 1, 1961.
New York Herald Tribune Book Review, April 10, 1960.
New York Review of Books, April 10, 1969.
New York Times, April 9, 1988.
Partisan Review, fall, 1968.
Saturday Review, July 2, 1960.
Spectator, January 13, 1961.
Time, April 18, 1960.
Times Literary Supplement, March 17, 1961, October 15, 1982, October 23, 1983.
U.S. Quarterly Book Review, September, 1955.
Village Voice, December 25, 1969.
Village Voice Literary Supplement, November, 1982.
Virginia Quarterly Review, spring, 1978.
Washington Post Book World, November 14, 1982.

*   *   *

FILIPPO, Eduardo de
See de FILIPPO, Eduardo

*   *   *

FINK, William
See MENCKEN, H(enry) L(ouis)

*   *   *

FITCH, Clarke
See SINCLAIR, Upton (Beall)

FITCH, John IV
See CORMIER, Robert (Edmund)

*   *   *

FITZGERALD, Captain Hugh
See BAUM, L(yman) Frank

*   *   *

FITZGERALD, F(rancis) Scott (Key)   1896-1940

PERSONAL: Born September 24, 1896, in St. Paul, Minn.; died of a heart attack, December 21, 1940, in Hollywood, Calif.; buried in Rockville Union Cemetery, Rockville, Md.; reburied near his parents in St. Mary's Cemetery, Rockville, Md., in 1975; son of Edward (in business) and Mary (an heiress; maiden name, McQuillan) Fitzgerald; married Zelda Sayre (an artist, dancer, and writer), April 3, 1920 (died March 10, 1948); children: Frances Scott Fitzgerald Smith (formerly Mrs. Samuel J. Lanahan). *Education:* Attended Princeton University, 1913-17. *Religion:* Catholic.

CAREER: Novelist, poet, playwright, screenwriter, and author of short stories. Worked briefly as a copywriter at Barron Collier Advertising Agency in New York, 1919; worked sporadically as a screenwriter at motion picture studios in Los Angeles, Calif., including Metro-Goldwyn-Mayer and United Artists, 1927-40, contributing to film scripts such as "Winter Carnival," "The Women," and "Gone With the Wind," all 1939. *Military service:* U.S. Army, 1917-19; became second lieutenant.

WRITINGS:

NOVELS

This Side of Paradise, Scribner, 1920, reprinted, 1971.
The Beautiful and Damned (first published serially in *Metropolitan Magazine,* September, 1921-March, 1922), revised edition of original text, Scribner, 1922, reprinted, Collier Books, 1982.
The Great Gatsby, Scribner, 1925, reprinted, 1981, Chelsea House, 1986.
Tender Is the Night: A Romance, decorations by Edward Shenton, Scribner, 1934, new edition with Fitzgerald's final revisions, preface by Malcolm Cowley, 1951, reprinted, 1970, revised from original text as *Tender Is the Night,* Scribner, 1960, reprinted, Collier Books, 1986; revised edition published in England as *Tender Is the Night,* with Fitzgerald's final revisions, preface by Cowley, Grey Walls Press, 1953, reprinted, 1970.
The Last Tycoon, first published as *The Last Tycoon: An Unfinished Novel, Together With "The Great Gatsby" and Selected Stories* (includes "Notes for *The Last Tycoon*"), with additional notes by Fitzgerald, foreword by Edmund Wilson, Scribner, 1941, reprinted, 1977, published as *The Last Tycoon: An Unfinished Novel,* with notes by Fitzgerald, foreword by Wilson, Scribner, 1958, reprinted as *The Last Tycoon,* 1983; published in England as *The Last Tycoon: An Unfinished Novel,* Grey Walls Press, 1949, as *The Last Tycoon,* Penguin, 1960, 1977, reprinted with notes by Fitzgerald, foreword by Wilson, 1965, 1974.

SHORT STORIES

Flappers and Philosophers (includes "The Offshore Pirate," "The Ice Palace," "Head and Shoulders," and "Bernice Bobs Her

Hair"), Scribner, 1920, reprinted, with introduction by Arthur Mizener, 1959, 1972.

Tales of the Jazz Age (contains "The Camel's Back," "May Day," and "The Diamond as Big as the Ritz"), Scribner, 1922, revised as *Six Tales of the Jazz Age, and Other Stories,* introduction by Frances Fitzgerald Lanahan, Scribner, 1960, reprinted, 1968.

All the Sad Young Men (includes "The Rich Boy," "Winter Dreams," and "Absolution"), Scribner, 1926.

Taps at Reveille (includes "Crazy Sunday" and "Babylon Revisited"), Scribner, 1935, reprinted, 1976.

The Pat Hobby Stories, introduction by Arnold Gingrich, Scribner, 1962, reprinted, 1970, Penguin, 1974.

The Basil and Josephine Stories (includes "The Scandal Detectives"), edited with an introduction by Jackson R. Bryer and John Kuehl, Scribner, 1973, reprinted, 1985.

(With wife, Zelda Fitzgerald) *Bits of Paradise: Twenty-one Uncollected Stories by F. Scott and Zelda Fitzgerald,* selected by Matthew J. Bruccoli, with the assistance of Scottie Fitzgerald Smith, Scribner, 1973.

The Price Was High: The Last Uncollected Stories of F. Scott Fitzgerald (contains "Myra Meets His Family" and "The Pusher-in-the-Face"), edited by Bruccoli, Harcourt, 1979.

PLAYS

(And lyricist) "Fie! Fie! Fi-Fi!" (two-act musical comedy; first produced in Princeton, N.J., at Princeton University, December 19, 1914), published in pamphlet form for distribution at performances (extent of Fitzgerald's authorship disputed in some sources [also see below]).

(And lyricist) "The Evil Eye" (two-act musical comedy; first produced at Princeton University, December 18, 1915), published in pamphlet form for performances (extent of Fitzgerald's authorship disputed in some sources [also see below]).

(And lyricist) "Safety First" (two-act musical comedy; first produced at Princeton University, December 15, 1916), published in pamphlet form for performances (extent of Fitzgerald's authorship disputed in some sources [also see below]).

The Vegetable; or, From President to Postman (first produced at Apollo Theatre, Atlantic City, November 19, 1923), Scribner, 1923, reprinted, August M. Kelley, 1972, revised and enlarged edition, with previously unpublished scenes and corrections, introduction by Charles Scribner III, Scribner, 1976.

F. Scott Fitzgerald's St. Paul Plays, 1911-1914, edited with an introduction by Alan Margolies, Princeton University Library, 1978.

CORRESPONDENCE

The Letters of F. Scott Fitzgerald, edited by Andrew Turnbull, Scribner, 1963, reprinted, 1981.

Scott Fitzgerald: Letters to His Daughter, edited by Turnbull, introduction by Frances Fitzgerald Lanahan, Scribner, 1965.

Dear Scott, Dear Max: The Fitzgerald-Perkins Correspondence, edited by Kuehl and Bryer, Scribner, 1971, reprinted, 1973.

As Ever, Scott Fitz—: Letters Between F. Scott Fitzgerald and His Literary Agent, Harold Ober, 1919-1940, edited by Bruccoli, with Jennifer McCabe Atkinson, foreword by Scottie Fitzgerald Smith, Lippincott, 1972.

Correspondence of F. Scott Fitzgerald, edited by Bruccoli and Margaret M. Duggan, with Susan Walker, Random House, 1980.

COLLECTIONS

The Crack-Up: With Other Uncollected Pieces, Note-Books, and Unpublished Letters (includes "The Crack-Up," "Handle With Care," and "Early Success"), edited by Edmund Wilson, J. Laughlin, 1945, reprinted, 1964; published in England as *The Crack-Up, With Other Pieces and Stories,* Penguin, 1965, reprinted, 1974.

The Portable F. Scott Fitzgerald (includes novels and short stories), selected by Dorothy Parker, introduction by John O'Hara, Viking, 1945, reprinted as *The Indispensable F. Scott Fitzgerald,* Book Society, 1949, 1951.

The Diamond as Big as the Ritz, and Other Stories, first published in limited edition, with an introduction by Louis Untermeyer, for the U.S. Armed Services, 1946, Penguin, 1962, reprinted, 1965.

The Stories of F. Scott Fitzgerald: A Selection of Twenty-eight Stories (includes "Three Hours Between Planes"), introduction by Malcolm Cowley, Scribner, 1951, reprinted, 1984.

Three Novels: The Great Gatsby, With an Introduction by Malcolm Cowley. Tender Is the Night, With the Author's Final Revisions; Edited by Malcolm Cowley. The Last Tycoon, an Unfinished Novel; Edited by Edmund Wilson, Scribner, 1953, reprinted, 1956.

Afternoon of an Author: A Selection of Uncollected Stories and Essays (includes "How to Live on $36,000 a Year"), introduction and notes by Mizener, Princeton University Library, 1957, Scribner, 1958, reprinted, 1981.

The Bodley Head Scott Fitzgerald, six volumes, introduction by J. B. Priestley, Bodley Head, 1958-63.

Babylon Revisited, and Other Stories, Scribner, 1960, reprinted, 1971.

The Stories of F. Scott Fitzgerald, five volumes, Penguin, 1962-68.

The Fitzgerald Reader, edited by Mizener, Scribner, 1963, reprinted, Macmillan, 1978.

The Apprentice Fiction of F. Scott Fitzgerald, edited with an introduction by Kuehl, Rutgers University Press, 1965, reprinted, 1974.

F. Scott Fitzgerald in His Own Time: A Miscellany, edited by Bruccoli and Bryer, Kent State University Press, 1971, reprinted, Popular Library, 1974.

OTHER

"Let's Go Out and Play" (radio script), first broadcast in New York City on WABC-Radio (CBS), October 3, 1935.

(With Edward E. Paramore, Jr.) "Three Comrades" (screenplay; based on English translation of novel of the same title by Erich Maria Remarque), Metro-Goldwyn-Mayer, 1938 (also see below).

Thoughtbook of Francis Scott Fitzgerald, With an Introduction by John R. Kuehl, Princeton University Library, 1965.

F. Scott Fitzgerald's Ledger: A Facsimile, introduction by Bruccoli, NCR/Microcard Editions, 1972.

The Great Gatsby: A Facsimile, edited with an introduction by Bruccoli, Microcard Editions Books, 1973.

F. Scott Fitzgerald's Screenplay for "Three Comrades," by Erich Maria Remarque (includes original version by Fitzgerald alone), edited with afterword by Bruccoli, Southern Illinois University Press, 1978.

The Notebooks of F. Scott Fitzgerald, edited by Bruccoli, Harcourt/Bruccoli Clark, 1978, reprinted, Harcourt, 1980.

F. Scott Fitzgerald: Triangle Club Songs (cassette recording; songs from three plays produced at Princeton University), performed by After-Dinner Opera Co. of New York, Bruccoli Clark, 1979.

Poems, 1911-1940, edited by Bruccoli, foreword by James Dickey, Bruccoli Clark, 1981.

F. Scott Fitzgerald on Writing, edited by Larry W. Phillips, Scribner, 1985.

Author of "The Count of Darkness," "The Passionate Eskimo," and numerous other fiction works.

Author of unproduced screenplays, such as "Red-Headed Woman" and "Lipstick." Contributor to film scripts, among them "A Yank at Oxford," 1937; "Infidelity" and "Madame Curie," both 1938; "Winter Carnival," "The Women," and "Gone With the Wind," all 1939; and "Cosmopolitan," 1940.

Author of book reviews, introductions, and forewords. Contributor to periodicals and popular magazines, including *Saturday Evening Post, Esquire, Metropolitan Magazine, Smart Set, American Mercury, Nassau Literary Magazine, New Yorker, Scribner's Magazine, Motor, Bookman, Woman's Home Companion, New Republic, McCall's, Red Book, Collier's,* and *Hearst's International.*

Work represented in hundreds of anthologies, such as *Innocent Merriment: An Anthology of Light Verse,* McGraw, 1942; *Fifty Best American Short Stories, 1915-1965,* Houghton, 1965; *The Age of Anxiety: Modern American Stories,* Allyn & Bacon, 1972; and *The Short Story: An Introductory Anthology,* 2nd edition, Little, Brown, 1975.

SIDELIGHTS: Beginning early in his life, F. Scott Fitzgerald strove to become a great writer. In a 1944 essay, "Thoughts on Being Bibliographed," Edmund Wilson wrote that Fitzgerald told him soon after college, "I want to be one of the greatest writers who have ever lived, don't you?" Although today most college-level American literature survey courses usually include at least one of his works, during Fitzgerald's lifetime he was regarded mainly as a portrayer of the 1920s Jazz Age and of flaming youth, but not as one of this country's most important writers. And while close to fifty thousand copies of his first novel, *This Side of Paradise,* were printed in 1920 and 1921, he was never a best-selling novelist. Fewer than twenty-nine thousand copies of *The Great Gatsby* and some fifteen thousand copies of *Tender Is the Night* were published in the United States during Fitzgerald's lifetime. By the time of his death in 1940, very few copies of his books were being sold, and he was earning his living as a free-lance film writer. Since then, however, Fitzgerald's popularity has increased dramatically.

Even at an early age, F. Scott Fitzgerald exhibited talent. At St. Paul Academy, he wrote stories for the school magazine and participated in dramatics. According to Andrew Turnbull in his biography *Scott Fitzgerald,* C. N. B. Wheeler—one of Fitzgerald's teachers at St. Paul Academy—said years later: "I helped him by encouraging his urge to write adventures. It was also his best work, he did not shine in his other subjects. He was inventive in all playlets we had and marked his course by his pieces for delivery before the school. . . . I imagined he would become an actor of the variety type, but he didn't. . . . It was his pride in his literary work that put him in his real bent."

From 1911 to 1913, Fitzgerald attended the Newman School in Hackensack, New Jersey, where he continued to write for various school publications. There he fell under the influence of Father Sigourney Fay, who was to be fictionalized as Monsignor Darcy in Fitzgerald's first novel, *This Side of Paradise.* In *Some Sort of Epic Grandeur,* Matthew J. Bruccoli explained that "Fay soon became Scott's surrogate father." Fay introduced Fitzgerald to Anglo-Irish writer Shane Leslie who, Fitzgerald later wrote in a review-essay titled "Homage to the Victorians"

(1922), "came into my life as the most romantic figure I had ever known."

Fitzgerald wrote a play each summer from 1911 to 1914 for a St. Paul amateur group, the Elizabethan Dramatic Club, made up of youngsters in his neighborhood who performed for St. Paul charities. The director of the group, Elizabeth Magoffin, was another who recognized the youthful Fitzgerald's talent when, according to Alan Margolies in his introduction to *F. Scott Fitzgerald's St. Paul Plays, 1911-1914,* she inscribed a photograph to him: "He had that Spark—Magnetic Mark—."

At this time Fitzgerald had other interests as well. He played on the Newman School football team, and when he was admitted to Princeton University in 1913, one of his first acts, as recorded in the 1974 scrapbook volume, *The Romantic Egoists,* was to wire his mother: "ADMITTED SEND FOOTBALL PADS AND SHOES IMMEDIATELY PLEASE WAIT TRUNK." But there were better and heavier candidates for the team, and he soon devoted most of his time to writing short stories, poems, plays, book reviews, and even jokes for the *Nassau Literary Magazine* and the humor magazine *Princeton Tiger.* For Princeton's Triangle Club, he wrote the lyrics and conceived the plot for the 1914 to 1915 show "Fie! Fie! Fi-Fi!," the lyrics for the 1915 to 1916 show "The Evil Eye," and the lyrics for the 1916 to 1917 show "Safety First." These extracurricular activities impinged on his classroom work, however, and in January, 1916, Fitzgerald withdrew from Princeton because of low grades. He returned the following school year but never graduated. World War I intervened; he applied for a U.S. Army commission, and in October, 1917, he was appointed second lieutenant.

Fitzgerald's army career was a disappointment to him. He never served overseas and, as he later declared in "Early Success" (1937), spent two of his fifteen months' service as "the army's worst aide-de-camp." And yet, during this period he completed a draft of a novel, "The Romantic Egotist." In a January 10, 1918, letter, reprinted in *The Letters of F. Scott Fitzgerald,* he told Edmund Wilson that the work was the story of a young man's boyhood "from the San Francisco fire thru school, Princeton, to the end, where at twenty-one he writes his autobiography at the Princeton aviation school." Although the publishing house Charles Scribner's Sons did not accept his manuscript, he was encouraged to rewrite and resubmit it. Further, while stationed at Camp Sheridan near Montgomery, Alabama, he met and soon fell in love with the eighteen-year-old Zelda Sayre, daughter of Minnie Machen Sayre and Judge Anthony Dickinson Sayre of the Alabama Supreme Court.

Fitzgerald was discharged from the army in 1919 and subsequently worked for a short while at a New York advertising agency. Eventually he returned to St. Paul where he rewrote his novel, retitling it *This Side of Paradise.* In the letter of acceptance, collected in *Dear Scott, Dear Max,* Scribner editor Maxwell Perkins wrote Fitzgerald, "We are all for publishing your book. . . . I think you have improved it enormously. . . . It abounds in energy and life."

On publication *This Side of Paradise* was greeted enthusiastically. Harry Hansen wrote in the *Chicago Daily News* for March 31, 1920: "It is one of the few American novels extant. . . . Fitzgerald has taken a real American type—the male flapper of our best colleges—and written him down with startling verisimilitude. He has taken a slice of American life, part of the pie-crust. Only a man on the inside could have done it." And critic H. L. Mencken in the August, 1920, *Smart Set* found the work "a truly amazing first novel—original in structure, extremely sophisticated in manner, and adorned with a brilliancy that is as rare in

American writing as honesty is in American statecraft." Today, while one can understand the reaction at the time, *This Side of Paradise* is not considered one of Fitzgerald's best works. Bruccoli noted in *Some Sort of Epic Grandeur:* "Although *This Side of Paradise* now seems naive after sixty years, it was received in 1920 as an iconoclastic social document—even as a testament of revolt." Bruccoli went on to point out that what "was regarded as an experimental or innovative narrative because of the mixture of styles and the inclusion of plays and verse" was actually the result of "the circumstance that Fitzgerald did not yet know how to structure a novel."

And yet, despite these flaws and others, the novel is still read and enjoyed. Turnbull declared, "As a picture of American college life it has never been surpassed." And one can still sense the vitality in this tale of young Amory Blaine's initiation into life and his final awareness of himself. Of post-World War I youth, Fitzgerald wrote at the conclusion of *This Side of Paradise:* "Here was a new generation, shouting the old cries, learning the old creeds, through a revery of long days and nights; destined finally to go out into that dirty gray turmoil to follow love and pride; a new generation dedicated more than the last to the fear of poverty and the worship of success; grown up to find all Gods dead, all wars fought, all faiths in man shaken." Amory Blaine feels sorry for his generation but not for himself. Ready to encounter the world, but hoping not to repeat the mistakes of the past, he cries out: "I know myself . . . but that is all."

This Side of Paradise was published on March 26, 1920, and Fitzgerald married Zelda Sayre the following week, on April 3. Meanwhile, he was publishing short stories, and in September, 1920, his first collection, *Flappers and Philosophers,* appeared. While Fitzgerald admitted that most of his short stories were written much more quickly and carelessly than his novels, many hold up well today. Of this first collection, two stories are probably most memorable: "The Ice Palace," the story of a Southern girl who finds herself unable to adjust to the cold North of her fiance and, after being trapped in an ice palace, returns home; and "Bernice Bobs Her Hair," about another young girl who gives in to the dares of her cousin and others and bobs her hair. While some of the critics praised the collection, for the most part the reviews reflected a feeling that the book was not up to the level of *This Side of Paradise.* William Huse, for example, in the September 24, 1920, *Chicago Evening Post* lamented that the book was "scarcely as satisfying," and Mencken in the December, 1920, *Smart Set* deemed it "a collection that shows both the very good and the very bad."

In March, 1922, Fitzgerald's next major work, *The Beautiful and Damned,* was published. This second novel, Fitzgerald's story of the disintegration of the lives of the once young and glamorous Anthony and Gloria Patch, was a much more carefully constructed novel than *This Side of Paradise.* Many of the book's reviewers, however, were disappointed. Louise Maunsell Field in the March 5, 1922, *New York Times Book Review,* for example, began her assessment by stating, "It would not be easy to find a more thoroughly depressing book than this new novel by F. Scott Fitzgerald." On the other hand, Mencken asserted in the *Smart Set* for April, 1922: "There are a hundred signs in it of serious purpose and unquestionable skill." Further, he compared it with Fitzgerald's previous novel and stated that Fitzgerald had "tried something much more difficult, and if the result is not a complete success, it is nevertheless near enough to success to be worthy of respect."

Then in September, 1922, Fitzgerald's second collection of short stories, *Tales of the Jazz Age*—which included the well-known

fantasy "The Diamond as Big as the Ritz" as well as "May Day," a powerful tale of post-World War I days in New York City—was published. Much of the remainder, however, was not at all representative of Fitzgerald at his best. Jackson R. Bryer related in *Scott Fitzgerald: The Critical Reception* that the reviewers of the time "were, for the most part, charmed by its table of contents—in which the author humorously described each story and its genesis—but they found the collection itself uneven, although many applauded Fitzgerald's apparent shift away from stories about flappers into what he himself called his 'second manner.' " And Bruccoli in *Some Sort of Epic Grandeur* assessed: "Despite the inclusion of two major stories, 'May Day' and 'Diamond,' the collection was a grab bag; Fitzgerald did not have enough good material for a volume and padded it with pieces that had been left out of *Flappers and Philosophers.*"

During this era Fitzgerald had been devoting much time to a play, "The Vegetable." In an August, 1922, letter reprinted in *The Letters of F. Scott Fitzgerald,* he told Perkins of his hopes for it and for his financial future: "It is, I think, the best American comedy to date and undoubtedly the best thing I have ever written. . . . After my play is produced I'll be rich forever and never have to bother you again." In a letter later published in *Letters on Literature and Politics,* Edmund Wilson agreed with Fitzgerald's preproduction assessment: "I think it is one of the best things you ever wrote," he declared of an early draft. Unfortunately, the audiences and critics did not agree, and the play closed without reaching Broadway. Fitzgerald wrote the obituary for the play a year later when he referred to its failure and punned on the name of the play's main character, postman Jerry Frost: "It was a colossal frost," he wrote in "How to Live on $36,000 a Year" (1924). "People left their seats and walked out, people rustled their programs and talked audibly in bored impatient whispers." As a result of this failure, Fitzgerald, who maintained his high standard of living by continually borrowing money from Scribner as well as from his literary agent, Harold Ober, against the sale of future writing, was even further in debt. Thus he wrote and sold ten short stories between late 1923 and March, 1924, both to alleviate his financial situation and to permit him to devote time to his next novel.

Fitzgerald had started thinking about this next major work as early as the summer of 1922 when he wrote to Perkins, as reported in *Dear Scott, Dear Max,* that "its locale will be the middle west and New York of 1885 I think." The following month, in a letter printed in *Correspondence of F. Scott Fitzgerald,* he told Perkins of his goal: "I want to write something *new*—something extraordinary and beautiful and simple & intricately patterned." But although Fitzgerald did devote some time to the novel in 1923, it wasn't until April, 1924, that he began seriously to work on it. That same month, the Fitzgerald family traveled to the Riviera where he completed the novel. Its title, *The Great Gatsby,* was not Fitzgerald's final choice; in March, 1925, he asked Perkins to change it to *Under the Red White and Blue,* but the publication date's imminence made the request impossible to carry out.

The Great Gatsby was a great advance over Fitzgerald's two earlier novels. The intricate pattern he mentioned to Perkins reveals itself in the book's time span from spring to fall of one year with the climax, the reunion between Jay Gatsby and Daisy Buchanan, taking place exactly in the center of the novel. And yet, as it moves forward in time, it also moves backward, as Fitzgerald makes the reader aware of events in Jay Gatsby's past. In addition, *The Great Gatsby* also marked progress in Fitzgerald's method of narration. In the novel all information is filtered through the narrator, Nick Carraway. To assist Nick, Fitzgerald employed in the character of Jordan Baker a device that writer Henry James had popularized—that of a confidante, a person whose major purpose is to bring information to the narrator. Sometimes, information in the novel is filtered through several people, a device previously used by writer Joseph Conrad. As a result of this technique, the reader does not know what is true and what isn't in the novel's tale of love and murder.

Fitzgerald's plot was equal to his method of storytelling. His story of the vulgar and yet romantic Jay Gatsby who attempts, through illicit means, to rewin the hand of the now married Daisy Buchanan, however, was only part of his story. Rich versus poor, old rich versus new rich, East versus West, and America when it was still new versus more recent times were just some of the novel's issues. Of Tom and Daisy Buchanan, representatives of the old rich, Fitzgerald wrote: "They were careless people, Tom and Daisy—they smashed up things and creatures and then retreated back into their money or their vast carelessness, or whatever it was that kept them together, and let other people clean up the mess they had made." But contrasting with the Buchanans and the evil East is the still innocent West with what Nick Carraway identified as its "thrilling returning trains of my youth, and the street lamps and sleigh bells in the frosty dark and the shadows of holly wreaths thrown by lighted windows on the snow." And contrasting with both of these symbols is the virgin past of the United States when the "vanished trees, the trees that had made way for Gatsby's house, had once pandered in whispers to the last and greatest of all human dreams."

While a few reviewers criticized the work (the headline in the April 12, 1925, *New York World* was "F. Scott Fitzgerald's Latest a Dud"), most recognized the advance in Fitzgerald's art. Fanny Butcher in the April 18, 1925, *Chicago Daily Tribune,* for example, wrote, " 'The Great Gatsby' proves that Scott Fitzgerald is going to be a writer, and not just a man of one book." And Gilbert Seldes went even further when he wrote in *Dial* for August, 1925: "Fitzgerald has more than matured; he has mastered his talents and gone soaring in a beautiful flight, leaving behind him everything dubious and tricky in his earlier work, and leaving even farther behind all the men of his own generation and most of his elders." Many of Fitzgerald's peers agreed. Writer T. S. Eliot, in a letter to Fitzgerald that was later published in *The Crack-Up,* called the novel "the first step that American fiction has taken since Henry James."

After the completion of *The Great Gatsby* in 1925, Fitzgerald began his fourth novel. Completion, however, took some nine years of noncontinuous work with at least three major plot changes and many other revisions. During this period Fitzgerald's alcohol abuse worsened, while Zelda Fitzgerald's increasingly apparent mental illness eventually necessitated, starting in 1930, periods of hospitalization. Further, Fitzgerald was falling more and more into debt. All of these factors negatively affected his writing.

Nonetheless, in February, 1926, Fitzgerald's third collection of short stories, *All the Sad Young Men,* appeared. This volume included three of Fitzgerald's best and most popular stories, "Winter Dreams," originally published in the December, 1922, *Metropolitan Magazine;* "Absolution," published in *American Mercury* for June, 1924; and "The Rich Boy," published in January and February, 1926, issues of *Red Book* magazine. Critical reaction to *All the Sad Young Men* was far more favorable than that attracted by Fitzgerald's earlier short story collections. A reviewer in the May, 1926, *Bookman,* for example, wrote: "As F. Scott Fitzgerald continues to publish books, it becomes apparent that he is head and shoulders better than any writer of his generation.

'All the Sad Young Men' contains several stories of compelling fineness, along with more conventional pieces of story telling that are sufficiently amusing with the old Fitzgerald talent."

In December, 1926, the Fitzgeralds returned to the United States, eventually living for a year in "Ellerslie," near Wilmington, Delaware. In January, 1927, Fitzgerald worked for two months in Hollywood on "Lipstick," a treatment for a silent film with a college setting for actress Constance Talmadge; but the treatment was judged unsatisfactory and the movie was never made. While in Hollywood, however, Fitzgerald met Metro-Goldwyn-Mayer (MGM) producer Irving Thalberg, who later served as the primary model for the hero of *The Last Tycoon*—Fitzgerald's final but unfinished novel. Also during this period he wrote, among other short stories, a series of eight tales based on his childhood in St. Paul, the adventures of young Basil Duke Lee. These were published in the *Saturday Evening Post,* beginning with "The Scandal Detectives" on April 28, 1928.

In April, 1934, Scribner published Fitzgerald's fourth novel, *Tender Is the Night,* the story of the deterioration of psychiatrist Richard Diver, who falls in love with and marries his patient Nicole Warren. Utilizing an international setting, the novel also reflects destructive impulses implicit in the United States. The wealthy Nicole, Fitzgerald wrote, "was the product of much ingenuity and toil. For her sake trains began their run at Chicago and traversed the round belly of the continent to California; chicle factories fumed and link belts grew link by link in factories; men mixed toothpaste in vats and drew mouthwash out of copper hogsheads; girls canned tomatoes quickly in August or worked rudely at the Five-and-Tens on Christmas Eve; half-breed Indians toiled on Brazilian coffee plantations and dreamers were muscled out of patent rights in new tractors."

Milton R. Stern in *The Golden Moment: The Novels of F. Scott Fitzgerald* noted that in this fourth novel Fitzgerald was continuing themes that he had touched on in his first two novels and had expressed even more clearly in *The Great Gatsby.* In *Tender Is the Night,* according to Stern, "the corrupt new world of soulless wealth becomes identified with the new America as the new America spreads over the world, is internationalized, and loses its old unique identity." Here, "the destroyed, old world of our Gatsby-youth, Dick Diver's lost 'safe, beautiful world' of promise, hope, passion, charm, virtues, and graces, is identified with an older America that is forever buried, as with Dick, we say goodbye to all our fathers."

In form, however, *Tender Is the Night* differs greatly from *The Great Gatsby.* Fitzgerald wrote in a letter to John Peale Bishop later published in *The Letters of F. Scott Fitzgerald:* "The intention in the two books was entirely different. . . . *Gatsby* was shooting at something like [William Makepeace Thackeray's] *Henry Esmond* while [*Tender Is the Night*] was shooting at something like [Thackeray's] *Vanity Fair.* The dramatic novel has canons quite different from the philosophical, now called psychological, novel. One is a kind of *tour de force* and the other a confession of faith. It would be like comparing a sonnet sequence with an epic."

Fitzgerald received many letters from friends praising *Tender Is the Night.* Turnbull reported that Bishop, for example, wrote, "You have shown us what we have waited so long and impatiently to see, that you are a true, a beautiful and a tragic novelist." And some reviewers, such as Gilbert Seldes in the April 12, 1934, *New York Evening Journal* who said that Fitzgerald had "written the great novel," praised it too. But the majority of the critics were disappointed. William Troy, writing in the *Nation* for May 9, 1934, contended that Fitzgerald was merely repeating his earlier work, claiming, "Dick Diver turns out to be Jay Gatsby all over again. . . . And the repetition of the pattern turns out to be merely depressing." Others criticized the novel's structure. James Gray in the April 12, 1934, *St. Paul Dispatch* deemed *Tender Is the Night* a "big, sprawling, undisciplined, badly coordinated book."

In 1938 Fitzgerald suggested a revised edition of *Tender Is the Night.* "It's great fault is that the *true* beginning—the young psychiatrist in Switzerland—is tucked away in the middle of the book," he wrote Perkins in a letter later published in *Dear Scott, Dear Max.* "If pages 151-212 were taken from their present place and put at the start," Fitzgerald argued, "the improvement in appeal would be enormous." He revised his own copy by tearing out these pages and placing them at the beginning as well as making other changes. In the front of this copy, as noted in Bruccoli's *Some Sort of Epic Grandeur,* Fitzgerald wrote: "This is the *final version* of the book as I would like it." In 1951 Scribner published this revised version edited by Malcolm Cowley, but today the 1934 version is considered the standard text. As Bruccoli noted: "Whatever its flaws, the 1934 version has been vindicated by reader preference."

Critical reaction to *Tender Is the Night* has also reversed itself, especially since Fitzgerald's death, thus vindicating a 1935 statement by Ernest Hemingway; as reported in *Dear Scott, Dear Max,* Hemingway had written Perkins, "A strange thing is that in retrospect his *Tender Is the Night* gets better and better." One recent explanation for the original disappointing reception has been suggested by Bryer in *F. Scott Fitzgerald: The Critical Reception:* "The world that greeted *Tender Is the Night* on April 12, 1934, was far different from that of 1920 or 1925. Readers who had been charmed earlier by the excesses and harmless eccentricities of Fitzgerald's young people were now living through the deprivations caused by a depression. Their responses to a novel about wealthy expatriates cavorting on the Riviera were, predictably, varied, more so than to any other Fitzgerald book."

Very few publications reviewed Fitzgerald's last collection of short stories, *Taps at Reveille,* which appeared in 1935. Bryer viewed this lack of critical response as "a further indication that readers and critics were no longer interested in his Jazz Age subject matter." Bryer continued: "The silence of the reviewers implied that their minds were made up—they had either forgotten or dismissed Fitzgerald."

During the mid-1930s Fitzgerald published little. He was drinking heavily at times, and his health continued to deteriorate. Furthermore, his debts increased. He was unable to sell *Tender Is the Night* to Hollywood, and his short stories were no longer commanding the large fees of the past. Among those that were published during this period were a series of stories for *Red Book* magazine in 1934 and 1935 about a medieval hero modeled after Ernest Hemingway. Fitzgerald's plan was eventually to combine them into a book, but their quality was far below that of his usual work, and the final episode was published only after his death.

Between February, 1935, and July, 1937, Fitzgerald, when not living in Baltimore, divided his time between Tryon, Asheville, and Hendersonville, North Carolina. "One harassed and despairing night I packed a brief case," he wrote of his flight to Tryon in "Handle With Care" (1936), "and went off a thousand miles to think it over. I took a dollar room in a drab little town where I knew no one and sunk all the money I had with me in a stock of potted meat, crackers and apples." He treated this difficult period in three confessional essays published in *Esquire* in 1936. In the first, "The Crack-Up," he compared himself to an old plate that suddenly cracks. He wrote: "I began to realize that

for two years my life had been a drawing on resources that I did not possess, that I had been mortgaging myself physically and spiritually up to the hilt."

By mid-1937 Fitzgerald's health had improved somewhat and he was able to curb his drinking. To help pay debts and defray new expenses he went to Hollywood in July, 1937, to work as a scriptwriter, spending the first eighteen months at Metro-Goldwyn-Mayer and then working at other studios as a free-lancer. Shortly after his arrival in Hollywood, Fitzgerald met film columnist Sheilah Graham and soon began a relationship with her that was to last, though somewhat stormily at times because of his drinking, until the novelist's death.

During this final Hollywood period Fitzgerald worked on some fourteen films, including two weeks on "Gone With the Wind." However, his only screen credit, shared with Edward E. Paramore, Jr., was for MGM's "Three Comrades." In addition he was taking notes on this Hollywood experience for his final novel, *The Last Tycoon.* As work opportunities dwindled, he began writing a series of brief humorous stories for *Esquire* about a hack film writer named Pat Hobby. More importantly, he was able to devote more time to the novel despite tenuous health and discouragement at times. "I am a forgotten man," he wrote his wife in March, 1940, in a letter later printed in *The Letters of F. Scott Fitzgerald;* "*Gatsby* had to be taken out of the Modern Library because it didn't sell, which was a blow." And Fitzgerald's last royalty statement in August, 1940, reported that his publishers had sold only forty copies of all of his books for a total royalty of $13.13.

But he was working diligently. "My room is covered with charts like it used to be for *Tender Is the Night,* telling the different movements of the characters and their histories," he wrote to his wife in October. "However," he continued, "this one is to be short, as I originally planned it two years ago, and more on the order of *Gatsby.*"

In this final novel Fitzgerald portrayed the Hollywood of the 1930s, with special emphasis on the studio system and its need for a strong leader, embodied in the character Monroe Stahr. Stahr is fashioned in the tradition of the great leaders who have contributed to the success of the United States despite flaws in their natures. Stahr displays great sensitivity in his relationship with Kathleen, the young woman with whom he falls in love, and with the many employees in his studio, especially (as suggested by Edmund Wilson in his synopsis of the unfinished ending based on Fitzgerald's notes, outlines, and other information) when he sides with them in a wage fight with stockholders. But eventually, as conceived but not carried out by Fitzgerald, Stahr was to have a falling out with his partner, Brady, and, fearing that the latter would murder him, was to arrange with a gangster to have Brady murdered. The novel, however, was never finished. On December 21, 1940, at the age of forty-four, Fitzgerald died suddenly of a heart attack.

Ten months later Scribner published Wilson's edition of what Fitzgerald had completed of *The Last Tycoon:* five chapters and a fraction of a sixth, some of the notes, and Fitzgerald's plan for the novel. Not only were the reviewers in full agreement as to the worth of the volume, but many also used the occasion to praise Fitzgerald's entire body of work. Clifton Fadiman in the November 15, 1941, *New Yorker* stated, for example, "that Fitzgerald was on the point of becoming a major novelist." And J. Donald Adams on the front page of the *New York Times Book Review* for November 9, 1941, said that *The Last Tycoon* "would have been Fitzgerald's best novel." Poet Stephen Vincent Benet concluded in the December 6, 1941, *Saturday Review of Litera-*

ture: "You can take off your hats, gentlemen, and I think perhaps you had better. This is not a legend, this is a reputation—and, seen in perspective, it may well be one of the most secure reputations of our time."

Fitzgerald's works have been translated into thirty-five languages and, according to Scribner, his books sell at some half a million copies per year.

MEDIA ADAPTATIONS: Writings adapted for film include "Head and Shoulders," adapted as "The Chorus Girl's Romance," Metro Pictures, 1920; "Myra Meets His Family," adapted as "The Husband Hunter," Fox Film Corp., 1920; "The Offshore Pirate," Metro Pictures, 1921; *The Beautiful and Damned,* Warner Bros., 1922; "The Camel's Back," adapted as "Conductor 1492," Warner Bros., 1924; *The Great Gatsby,* Players-Lasky-Paramount, 1926, Paramount, 1949 and 1974; "The Pusher-in-the-Face," adapted as a movie short, Paramount, 1929; "Babylon Revisited," adapted as "The Last Time I Saw Paris," Metro-Goldwyn-Mayer, 1954; *Tender Is the Night,* Twentieth Century-Fox, 1962; and *The Last Tycoon,* Paramount, 1976. The 1924 Film Guild movie "Grit" was based on an original story by Fitzgerald.

Works adapted for stage include *The Great Gatsby,* first produced in New York City at the Ambassador Theatre, February 2, 1926, and produced as a ballet by the Pittsburgh Ballet Theater at State University of New York, State University College at Purchase, N.Y., March 31, 1989; "Three Hours Between Planes," adapted as a one-act play, 1958; and *This Side of Paradise,* adapted as an Off-Broadway play, 1962.

Some of Fitzgerald's writings were also adapted for radio and television.

BIOGRAPHICAL/CRITICAL SOURCES:

BOOKS

Allen, Joan, *Candles and Carnival Lights,* New York University Press, 1978.
Bruccoli, Matthew J., *The Composition of "Tender Is the Night": A Study of the Manuscripts,* University of Pittsburgh Press, 1963.
Bruccoli, editor, *Fitzgerald Newsletter: No. 1-40, Spring, 1958-Winter, 1968,* reprinted, NCR/Microcard Editions, 1969.
Bruccoli, *F. Scott Fitzgerald: A Descriptive Bibliography,* University of Pittsburgh Press, 1972, supplement, 1980.
Bruccoli, *"The Last of the Novelists": F. Scott Fitzgerald and "The Last Tycoon,"* Southern Illinois University Press, 1977.
Bruccoli, *Scott and Ernest: The Authority of Failure and the Authority of Success,* Random House, 1978.
Bruccoli, *Some Sort of Epic Grandeur: The Life of F. Scott Fitzgerald,* Harcourt, 1981.
Bruccoli and Jackson R. Bryer, editors, *F. Scott Fitzgerald in His Own Time: A Miscellany,* Kent State University Press, 1971.
Bruccoli and Margaret Duggan, editors, *Correspondence of F. Scott Fitzgerald,* Random House, 1980.
Bruccoli, Scottie Fitzgerald Smith, and Joan P. Kerr, editors, *The Romantic Egoists: Scott and Zelda Fitzgerald,* Scribner, 1974.
Bruccoli and others, editors, *Fitzgerald/Hemingway Annual,* NCR/Microcard Editions Books/Information Handling Services, 1969-76, Gale, 1977-79.
Bryer, Jackson R., editor, *F. Scott Fitzgerald: The Critical Reception,* Burt Franklin, 1978.
Bryer, *The Short Stories of F. Scott Fitzgerald: New Approaches to Criticism,* University of Wisconsin Press, 1982.
Bryer, *The Critical Reputation of F. Scott Fitzgerald: A Bibliographical Study,* supplement, Archon Books, 1984.
Concise Dictionary of American Literary Biography: The Twenties, 1917-1929, Gale, 1989.
Cowley, Malcolm and Robert Cowley, editors, *Fitzgerald and the Jazz Age,* Scribner, 1966.
Dictionary of Literary Biography, Gale, Volume 4: *American Writers in Paris, 1920-1939,* 1980, Volume 9: *American Novelists, 1910-1945,* 1981.
Dictionary of Literary Biography Documentary Series, Volume 1, Gale, 1982.
Dictionary of Literary Biography Yearbook: 1981, Gale, 1982.
Donaldson, Scott, *Fool for Love: F. Scott Fitzgerald,* Congdon & Weed, 1983.
Donaldson, editor, *Critical Essays on F. Scott Fitzgerald's "The Great Gatsby,"* G. K. Hall, 1984.
Eble, Kenneth, *F. Scott Fitzgerald,* Twayne, 1963, revised edition, G. K. Hall, 1977.
Fitzgerald, F. Scott, *This Side of Paradise,* Scribner, 1920.
Fitzgerald, *Tender Is the Night: A Romance,* Scribner, 1934.
Fitzgerald, *The Crack-Up: With Other Uncollected Pieces, Note-Books, and Unpublished Letters,* edited by Edmund Wilson, J. Laughlin, 1945.
Fitzgerald, *The Great Gatsby,* Scribner, 1953.
Graham, Sheilah, *The Rest of the Story,* Coward-McCann, 1964.
Graham, *College of One,* Viking, 1967.
Graham and Gerold Frank, *Beloved Infidel,* Holt, 1958.
Hemingway, Ernest, *A Moveable Feast,* Scribner, 1964.
Higgins, John A., *F. Scott Fitzgerald: A Study of the Stories,* St. John's University Press, 1971.
Hoffman, Frederick J., editor, *"The Great Gatsby": A Critical Study,* Scribner, 1962.
Kazin, Alfred, editor, *F. Scott Fitzgerald: The Man and His Work,* World Publishing Co., 1951.
Kuehl, John and Jackson R. Bryer, editors, *Dear Scott, Dear Max: The Fitzgerald-Perkins Correspondence,* Scribner, 1971.
Lehan, Richard D., *F. Scott Fitzgerald and the Craft of Fiction,* Southern Illinois University Press, 1966.
Le Vot, Andre, *F. Scott Fitzgerald: A Biography,* translation by William Byron, Doubleday, 1983.
Margolies, Alan, editor and author of introduction, *F. Scott Fitzgerald's St. Paul Plays, 1911-1914,* Princeton University Library, 1978.
Milford, Nancy, *Zelda: A Biography,* Harper, 1970.
Miller, James E., *F. Scott Fitzgerald: His Art and His Technique,* New York University Press, 1964.
Mizener, Arthur, editor, *F. Scott Fitzgerald: A Collection of Critical Essays,* Prentice-Hall, 1963.
Mizener, *The Far Side of Paradise,* 2nd edition, Houghton, 1965.
Perosa, Sergio, *The Art of F. Scott Fitzgerald,* University of Michigan Press, 1965.
Ring, Frances Kroll, *Against the Current: As I Remember F. Scott Fitzgerald,* Creative Arts Book Co., 1985.
Sklar, Robert, *F. Scott Fitzgerald: The Last Laocoon,* Oxford University Press, 1967.
Stern, Milton R., *The Golden Moment: The Novels of F. Scott Fitzgerald,* University of Illinois Press, 1970.
Tompkins, Calvin, *Living Well Is the Best Revenge,* Viking, 1971.
Turnbull, Andrew, *Scott Fitzgerald: A Biography,* Scribner, 1962.
Turnbull, editor, *The Letters of F. Scott Fitzgerald,* Scribner, 1963.
Twentieth-Century Literary Criticism, Gale, Volume 1, 1978, Volume 6, 1982, Volume 14, 1984, Volume 28, 1988.

Way, Brian, *F. Scott Fitzgerald and the Art of Social Criticism,* St. Martin's, 1980.
Wilson, Edmund, editor, *"The Last Tycoon": An Unfinished Novel,* Scribner, 1941.
Wilson, *Letters on Literature and Politics, 1912-1972,* edited by Elena Wilson, introduction by Daniel Aaron, foreword by Leon Edel, Farrar, Straus, 1977.

PERIODICALS

American Cavalcade, October, 1937.
Bookman, May, 1926.
Chicago Daily News, March 31, 1920.
Chicago Daily Tribune, April 18, 1925.
Chicago Evening Post, September 24, 1920.
Dial, August, 1925.
Esquire, February, 1936, April, 1936, August, 1936.
Nation, May 9, 1934.
New Yorker, November 15, 1941.
New York Evening Journal, April 12, 1934.
New York Times, April 4, 1989.
New York Times Book Review, March 5, 1922, November 9, 1941.
New York Tribune, May 7, 1922.
New York World, April 12, 1925.
Princeton University Library Chronicle, Number 5, 1944.
Saturday Evening Post, April 5, 1924.
Saturday Review of Literature, December 6, 1940.
Smart Set, August, 1920, December, 1920, April, 1922.
St. Paul Dispatch, April 12, 1934.
Washington Post, September 25, 1989.

*   *   *

FLANAGAN, Thomas (James Bonner) 1923-

PERSONAL: Born November 5, 1923, in Greenwich, Conn.; son of Owen de Sales and Mary Helen (Bonner) Flanagan; married Jean Parker, June 10, 1949; children: Ellen Treacy, Caitlin Honor. *Education:* Amherst, B. A., 1945; Columbia University, M.A., 1949, Ph.D., 1958.

ADDRESSES: Home—Long Island, N.Y. *Office*—Department of English, State University of New York at Stony Brook, Stony Brook, N.Y. 11794. *Agent*—Wallace & Sheil Agency, Inc., 77 East 70th St., New York, N.Y. 10021.

CAREER: Columbia University, New York, N.Y., instructor, 1949-52, assistant professor, 1952-59; University of California, Berkeley, assistant professor, 1960-67, associate professor, 1967-73, professor of English literature, 1973-78, chairman of department, 1973-76; State University of New York at Stony Brook, professor of English literature, 1978—. *Military service:* U.S. Naval Reserve, 1942-44, served in the Pacific.

MEMBER: International Association for Study of Anglo-Irish Literature (member of board of governors, 1970—), American Committee for Irish Studies, Modern Language Association of America.

AWARDS, HONORS: "The Fine Italian Hand" selected best first story of 1948, and "The Cold Winds of Adesta" selected best short short story of 1951, both by *Ellery Queen's Mystery Magazine;* grant-in-aid from American Council of Learned Societies, 1962; Guggenheim fellowship, 1962-63; National Book Critics Circle Award for fiction, 1979, for *The Year of the French.*

WRITINGS:

The Irish Novelists, 1800-1850 (nonfiction), Columbia University Press, 1959.
The Year of the French (novel; Book-of-the-Month Club selection), Holt, 1979.
The Tenants of Time, Dutton, 1987.

Also author of short stories, including "The Cold Winds of Adesta," "The Point of Honor," "The Lion's Mane," "This Will Do Nicely," "The Customs of the Country," "Suppose You Were on the Jury," and "The Fine Italian Hand." Contributor of essays, stories, and literary criticism to periodicals, including *Kenyon Review, Irish University Review, Victorian Studies, Ellery Queen's Mystery Magazine,* and *Hibernia.* Member of advisory board of *Irish University Review,* 1969—; member of editorial board of *Critical Inquiry,* 1974.

SIDELIGHTS: Thomas Flanagan's highly praised first novel, *The Year of the French,* received the National Book Critics Circle Award for fiction in 1979. "It is certainly the finest historical novel by an American to appear in more than a decade," reported Julian Moynahan in the *Chicago Tribune Book World.* The novel, which some reviewers have compared with Leo Tolstoy's *War and Peace,* depicts Ireland's ill-fated uprising against British rule in 1798. The rebellion was precipitated by the eviction of impoverished tenant farmers from their homes in Ireland's County Mayo by their absentee landlord, Lord Glenthorne, who planned to allocate additional profits to be had from raising cattle on the land to his favorite charitable causes.

The French became involved when Napoleon Bonaparte, in an attempt to divert Britain's attention from his own campaign against the British in Egypt, sent an expeditionary force of one thousand men to County Mayo in support of the rebel troops there. Although their initial engagements against the British militia in the summer of 1798 met with great success, the insurgents were soon overwhelmed by a superior force led by Lord Cornwallis. The French surrendered and were sent home, but the Irish, who were viewed as traitors, were brutally slaughtered. "There was much heroism, some brilliance and a great deal of treachery and savagery on all sides," noted *Listener*'s John Naughton. The memory of that violent year when thirty thousand people were killed in Ireland still lingers in Mayo, for, according to Flanagan, people there "still refer to 1798 as 'the year of the French.' "

"In his prodigious first novel," wrote a *Time* reporter, "Thomas Flanagan grants this historic episode a new and panoramic life." Using a part-documentary, part-narrative style, Flanagan tells the story of the rebellion from the perspectives of a variety of characters, including loyalists, rebels, soldiers, and interested bystanders. "By admitting every shade of political opinion," commented an *Encounter* critic, the author "builds a rich, intelligent and exciting fiction." The novel "is violent and provocative, and overflowing with local color," added *Books and Bookmen*'s Joanna Richardson. Naughton agreed, praising Flanagan's "mastery of the historical material, his ear for Irish dialogue, his knowledge of the topography of Mayo and his stylistic mimicry." "Flanagan attempts nothing less than a re-creation of eighteenth-century Ireland, with its small Protestant world of property and the 'multitudinous Papist world of want,' " said Hubert de Santana in *Maclean's.* "The result," summarized de Santana, "is a work of scholarship and imagination."

Flanagan's focus, though, is on the timelessness of the Irish situation, according to a *New Yorker* critic who noted that the author's "concern is the way this episode fitted an age-old pattern:

it was not the first time that Ireland had attempted to behave like a nation but found herself bogged down in her own fanaticism and sloth." Moreover, as Naughton pointed out, Flanagan's "evocation of the cruel, confused, ambiguous, contradictory, impassioned, poisoned atmosphere of late eighteenth-century Ireland remains one of Northern Ireland today." An *Encounter* critic agreed, observing that "Flanagan has an unerring sense of the parallels between the political situation in 1798 and the events in Ulster over the last ten years." At the same time, noted Moynahan, "as [Flanagan] masterfully traces the full course of this most brutal and eccentric military campaign, [he] avoids partisan myths while deploying his ironies, wryly, compassionately, authoritatively." The author intends, said *Newsweek*'s Peter S. Prescott, "to convince us of the inevitability of this useless confrontation, to expose for our sympathetic consideration the roots of this hatred, this despair, this fanaticism that spurs honorable or ignorant men to throw away their lives without hope of anything gained." "Flanagan's book cries out for justice, but never ceases to be gentlemanly about it and never raises its voice," said *Chicago Tribune Book World* reviewer David O'Connell. As a result, wrote *National Review*'s Thomas Bridges, *The Year of the French* is one of the few works on Ireland's past that do[es] not add fuel to the current fire in the North."

Flanagan told *CA* that the complexities of the Rebellion of 1798 are reflected in his book *The Year of the French:* "There were those who supported the rebellion; those who would have supported the rebellion if they had thought it would work, but who didn't think it would work; and those who had divided feelings about it. One of the reasons there are so many narrators in *Year* is that I tried to create a kind of mosaic of feelings about the uprising. I think that if I had to pick sides between the nationalists and the loyalists, my side would be the nationalist side."

Flanagan's second historical novel, *The Tenants of Time*, focuses on the Fenian uprising of 1867 (efforts by a clandestine revolutionary society to achieve Irish independence from England) and the late nineteenth-century rise and fall of Irish nationalist leader Charles Stewart Parnell.

BIOGRAPHICAL/CRITICAL SOURCES:

BOOKS

Contemporary Literary Criticism, Gale, Volume 25, 1983, Volume 52, 1989.
Dictionary of Literary Biography Yearbook: 1980, Gale, 1981.

PERIODICALS

Atlantic Monthly, June, 1979.
Books and Bookmen, September, 1979.
Canadian Forum, June, 1979.
Chicago Tribune Book World, May 13, 1979.
Christian Science Monitor, May 14, 1979.
Encounter, January, 1980.
Irish Times, August 28, 1988.
Listener, August 9, 1979.
Los Angeles Times Book Review, December 13, 1987, February 14, 1988.
Maclean's, September 10, 1979.
National Review, February 8, 1980.
Newsweek, May 14, 1979.
New Yorker, June 11, 1979.
New York Review of Books, June 14, 1979.
New York Times, May 8, 1979, December 28, 1987, January 18, 1988.
New York Times Book Review, December 20, 1959, May 13, 1979, January 3, 1988.

Publishers Weekly, May 14, 1979.
Time, July 9, 1979, January 11, 1988.
Times Literary Supplement, March 18, 1960.
Tribune Books (Chicago), January 10, 1988.
Washington Post, February 10, 1988.
Washington Post Book World, January 24, 1988.
West Coast Review of Books, May, 1979.

* * *

FLEMING, Ian (Lancaster) 1908-1964 (Atticus)

PERSONAL: Born May 28, 1908, in London, England; died August 12, 1964; son of Valentine (a major and a Conservative member of the British Parliament) and Evelyn Beatrice (Ste. Crois Rose) Fleming; younger brother of Peter Fleming, also an author; married Anne Geraldine Charteris (formerly Lady Rothermere), March 24, 1952; children: Caspar. *Education:* Attended Eton, Royal Military Academy at Sandhurst, University of Munich, and University of Geneva.

ADDRESSES: Home—16 Victoria Sq., London S.W.1, England; also maintained a home in Jamaica, and a flat on Pegwell Bay, Sandwich, Kent, England.

CAREER: Writer. Moscow correspondent for Reuters Ltd., London, England, 1929-33; associated with Cull & Co. (merchant bankers), London, 1933-35; stockbroker with Rowe & Pitman, London, 1935-39; returned to Moscow, 1939, officially as a reporter for the *Times,* London, unofficially as a representative of the Foreign Office; Kemsley (later Thomson) Newspapers, foreign manager, 1945-59; publisher of *The Book Collector,* 1949-64. *Military service:* Royal Naval Volunteer Reserve, 1939-45; lieutenant; did secret service work as a personal assistant to the director of Naval Intelligence.

MEMBER: Turf Club, Broodle's Club, Portland Club (all London).

AWARDS, HONORS: Young Readers' Choice award, 1967, for *Chitty-Chitty-Bang-Bang.*

WRITINGS:

FICTION

Casino Royale, J. Cape, 1953, Macmillan, 1954, published in paperback as *You Asked for It,* Popular Library, 1955.
Live and Let Die, J. Cape, 1954, Macmillan, 1955.
Moonraker, Macmillan, 1955, published in paperback as *Too Hot to Handle,* Perma Books, 1957.
Diamonds are Forever, Macmillan, 1956.
The Diamond Smugglers, J. Cape, 1957, Macmillan, 1958.
From Russia, With Love, Macmillan, 1957.
Doctor No, Macmillan, 1958.
Goldfinger, Macmillan, 1959.
For Your Eyes Only: Five Secret Exploits of James Bond, Viking, 1960.
Gilt-Edged Bonds (omnibus volume), introduction by Paul Gallico, Macmillan, 1961.
Thunderball, Viking, 1961.
The Spy Who Loved Me, Viking, 1962.
On Her Majesty's Secret Service, New American Library 1963.
You Only Live Twice, New American Library, 1964.
Bonded Fleming: A James Bond Omnibus, Viking, 1965.
The Man With the Golden Gun, New American Library, 1965.
More Gilt-Edged Bonds (omnibus volume), Macmillan, 1965.

Octopussy: The Last Great Adventures of James Bond 007, New American Library, 1967, published with an additional story, Signet, 1967.

OTHER

Thrilling Cities (thirteen essays), J. Cape, 1963, New American Library, 1964.
Chitty-Chitty-Bang-Bang (juvenile), Random, 1964.
Ian Fleming Introduces Jamaica (nonfiction), edited by Morris Cargill, Hawthorn, 1966.

Columnist, under pseudonym Atticus, for the *Sunday Times,* London, during the 1950s. Contributor to *Horizon, Spectator,* and other magazines.

SIDELIGHTS: The success of Ian Fleming's espionage adventure tales about the fictional James Bond has been astounding, both in the English versions and in translations, even though Fleming called his works "trivial piffle." Malcolm Muggeridge inimitably described the books' popularity thus: "Fleming's squalid aspirations and dream fantasies happened to coincide with a whole generation's. He touched a nerve. The inglorious appetites for speed at the touch of a foot on the accelerator and for sex at the touch of a hand on the flesh, found expression in his books. We live in the Century of the Common Bond, and Fleming created him." William Plomer has another view of the stories: "They are brilliant, romantic fairy-tales in which a dragon-slaying maiden-rescuing hero wins battle after battle against devilish forces of destruction, and yet is indestructible himself: an ancient kind of myth skillfully re-created in a modern idiom. They are, like life, sexy and violent, but I have never thought them corrupting. Compared with some of the nasty stuff that gets into print, they have a sort of boyish innocence." For whatever reasons, people continue to read him. Even John F. Kennedy was an avid fan of Bond adventures. It was he, in fact, who boosted Fleming's reputation and sales in America. Sarel Eimerl notes one difference between Fleming's stories and most espionage novels, a difference which may account for part of this success. Fleming, who had worked with British Intelligence had, or gave the impression of having, "the inside dope." He sounded authentic. In an introduction to *From Russia, With Love* Fleming wrote that "a great deal of the background to this story is accurate. SMERSH . . . exists and remains today the most secret department of the Soviet government."

Fleming and Bond often became confused in the public mind. John Pearson described Fleming as a modern-day Lord Byron, "tall, saturnine, hollow-cheeked, his face lopsided with its magnificently broken nose, his brow half-covered by that thoughtful comma of black hair which he was to pass on to his hero." Albert Goldman adds: "The fact is that Fleming succeeded because he distilled honestly, even lovingly, the essence of his own narcissistic temperament. What he offers his readers is the beguiling modern dream of a life of total self-sufficiency and sophisticated self-indulgence." Plomer disagrees with such analyses: "There may be something Flemingish about Bond, but I didn't see much of Bond in Fleming, who was more perturbable. Let us admit, as Fleming himself did, that Bond and his adventures are something of an adolescent fantasy," or as Fleming later said, "a highly romanticized version of anybody." Fleming, who named his principal character after the ornithologist who wrote *Birds of the West Indies,* considered Bond to be "an extremely dull, uninteresting man to whom things happened," and in the end tired of him, calling him "a cardboard dummy," and seriously considered killing him off. A *Times Literary Supplement* writer nonetheless believes that Fleming and his character were undoubtedly related: "We are left with the image of a rather sad, middle-aged

Mitty threatened with heart trouble, steering his Thunderbird through the London streets with decent care, brooding on his lucrative fantasies. Yet he had to have his material. He had to make a show of living dangerously. He had to keep up with James Bond, and Bond killed him in the end."

Bond's genesis occurred during World War II, when, as Plomer reports, Fleming came to him "with a diffidence that came surprisingly from so buoyant a man, [and] said he had a wish to write a thriller. . . . I at once made it . . . plain how strongly I believed in his ability to write such a book, and in its probable originality. 'But,' I said, 'it's no good writing just *one.* With that sort of book, you must become regular in your habits. You must hit the nail again and again with the same hammer until it's driven into the thick head of your potential public." Muggeridge, who recalls discussing Fleming's writing with him when he was at work on *Casino Royale,* remembers that Fleming "was insistent that he had no 'literary' aspiration at all, and that his only purpose was to make money and provide entertainment." By the time he died, Fleming reportedly had made 2.8 million dollars from his books alone. (The series is being continued by Kingsley Amis, under the pseudonym Robert Markham.)

MEDIA ADAPTATIONS: Many of Fleming's James Bond books have been filmed, usually with Sean Connery, Roger Moore, or Timothy Dalton playing the lead; in addition, *Chitty-Chitty-Bang-Bang* was adapted into a musical and into a film starring Dick Van Dyke.

AVOCATIONAL INTERESTS: Swimming, gambling, and golf.

BIOGRAPHICAL/CRITICAL SOURCES:

BOOKS

Amis, Kingsley, *The James Bond Dossier,* New American Library, 1965.
Boyd, Ann S., *The Devil With James Bond!,* John Knox, 1966.
Gant, Richard, *Ian Fleming: The Man With the Golden Pen,* Mayflower, 1966.
Pearson, John, *The Life of Ian Fleming,* McGraw, 1966.
Zeiger, Henry A., *Ian Fleming: The Spy Who Came in With the Gold,* Duell, Sloan & Pearce, 1965.

PERIODICALS

Commentary, July, 1968.
Critic, October-November, 1965.
Encounter, January, 1965.
Life, August 10, 1962
New Yorker, April 21, 1962.
New York Times, February 16, 1967, April 25, 1967.
New York Times Book Review, July 4, 1961, November 5, 1961, April 1, 1962, December 11, 1966.
Playboy Interviews, Playboy Press, 1967.
Publishers Weekly, August 24, 1964.
Reporter, July 13, 1967.
Times Literary Supplement, October 27, 1966.

*   *   *

FLEUR, Paul
  See POHL, Frederik

*   *   *

FLYING OFFICER X
  See BATES, H(erbert) E(rnest)

FO, Dario 1926-

PERSONAL: Born March 24, 1926, in San Giano, Lombardy, Italy; son of Felice (a railroad stationmaster) and Pina (Rota) Fo; married Franca Rame (a playwright and actress), June, 1954; children: three. *Education:* Attended Accademia di Belle Arti, Milan.

ADDRESSES: Home—Milan, Italy. *Agent*—Maria Nadotti, 349 East 51st St., New York, N.Y. 10022.

CAREER: Playwright, director, actor, and theatrical company leader. Has written more than forty plays, many of which have been translated and performed in more than thirty countries, beginning in 1953; performs plays in Italy, Europe, and the United States, and runs classes and workshops for actors, 1970s—. Worked as a member of small theatrical group, headed by Franco Parenti, performing semi-improvised sketches for radio before local audiences, 1950; wrote and performed comic monologues for his own radio program, *Poer nano* ("Poor Dwarf"), broadcast by the Italian national radio network RAI, 1951; formed revue company, *I Dritti* ("The Stand-Ups"), with Giustino Durano and Parenti, 1953; screenwriter in Rome, 1956-58; formed improvisational troupe *Compagnia Fo-Rame,* with wife, Franca Rame, 1958; named artistic director of Italian state television network's weekly musical revue, *Chi l'ha visto?* ("Who's Seen It?"), and writer and performer of sketches for variety show *Canzonissima* ("Really Big Song"), 1959; formed theater cooperatives *Nuova Scena,* with Rame, 1968, and *La Comune,* 1970.

AWARDS, HONORS: Premio Sonning, University of Denmark, 1981; Premio Eduardo da Taormina Arte, 1986; "V Premio Nazionale contro la violenza e la camorra," Associazione M. Torre, 1986; special Obie (Off-Broadway) Award, *Village Voice,* 1987.

WRITINGS:

PLAYS PUBLISHED IN ITALIAN

Teatro comico, Garzanti, 1962.

Le commedie, Einaudi, 1966, enlarged edition published as *Le commedie di Dario Fo,* 6 volumes, Einaudi, 1974, reprinted, 1984.

Mistero buffo (title means "The Comic Mystery"; first produced in Milan, Italy, 1969; produced on Broadway, 1986), Bertani, 1973, revised edition, 1974.

Vorrei morire anche stasera se dovessi pensare che no e servito a niente, E.D.B., 1970.

Morte e resurrezione di un pupazzo, Sapere Edizioni, 1971.

Ordine per Dio.ooo.ooo.ooo, Bertani, 1972.

Pum, pum! Chi e? La polizia! (title means "Knock, Knock! Who's There? Police!"), Bertani, 1972.

Tutti uniti! Tutti insieme! Ma scusa quello non e il padrone? (title means "United We Stand! All Together Now! Oops, Isn't That the Boss?"), Bertani, 1972.

Guerra di popolo in Cile (title means "The People's War in Chile"), Bertani, 1973.

Ballate e canzoni (title means "Ballads and Songs"), introduction by Lanfranco Binni, Bertani, 1974, reprinted, Newton Compton, 1976.

La guillarata, Bertani, 1975.

Il Fanfani rapito, Bertani, 1975.

La marijuana della mamma e la piu bella, Bertani, 1976.

La signora e da buttare (title means "The Old Girl's for the Scrapheap"), Einuadi, 1976.

Il teatro politico, G. Mazzotta, 1977.

(And director) *La storia di un soldato,* (adapted from "L'Historie du Soldat" by Igor Stravinsky; first produced in Milan,

1979), photographs by Silvia Lelli Masotti, commentary by Ugo Volli, Electa, 1979.

Storia vera di Piero d'Angera: Che alla crociata non c'era (first produced in Genova, Italy, 1984), La Comune, 1981.

PLAYS PUBLISHED IN ENGLISH TRANSLATION

Morte accidentale di un anarchico (first produced in Milan, 1970), Einaudi, 1974, translation by Gavin Richards published as *Accidental Death of an Anarchist* (adaptation by Richard Nelson produced on Broadway, 1984), Pluto Press, 1980.

Non si paga, non si paga (first produced in Milan, 1974), La Comune, 1974, translation by Lino Pertite published as *We Can't Pay? We Won't Pay!,* adapted by Bill Colvill and Robert Walker, Pluto Press, 1978, reprinted as *Can't Pay? Won't Pay!,* 1982, North American version by R. G. Davis published as *We Won't Pay! We Won't Pay!,* Samuel French, 1984.

(With wife, Franca Rame) *Tutta casa, letto e chiesa* (title means "All House, Bed, and Church"), Bertani, 1978, translation published as *Orgasmo Adulto Escapes From the Zoo,* adapted by Estelle Parsons, Broadway Play Publishing, 1985.

"La Storia della tigre e altre storie," produced in Italy, 1979, translation published as *The Tale of a Tiger,* Theatretexts, 1984.

"Clacson, trombette e pernacchi," first produced in Milan, 1981, translation by R. C. McAvoy and A. H. Giugni published as *Car Horns, Trumpets and Raspberries* (produced in New Haven, CT, as "About Face," 1981), Pluto Press, 1981, reprinted, 1984.

(With Rame) "Tutta casa . . . ," produced in 1982, translation by Margaret Kunzle and Stuart Hood published as *Female Parts: One Woman Plays* (produced in London, 1982), adapted by Olwen Wymark, Pluto Press, 1981.

(With Rame) "Coppia aperta, quasi spalancata," produced in Milano, 1986, translation published as *The Open Couple—Wide Open Even,* Theatretexts, 1984.

One Was Nude and One Wore Tails, Theatretexts, 1985.

UNPUBLISHED PLAYS

"Il dito nell'occhio" (title means "A Finger in the Eye"), first produced in Milan, 1953.

"I sani da legare" (title means "A Madhouse for the Sane"), first produced in Milan, 1954.

"Ladri, manachini e donne nude" (title means "Thieves, Dummies, and Naked Women"), first produced in Milan, 1958.

"Comica Finale," first produced in Torino, Italy, 1958.

"Gli arcangeli non giocano a Flipper" (title means "Archangels Don't Play Pinball"), first produced in Milan, 1959, produced in Cambridge, MA, 1987.

"Aveva due pistole con gli occhi bianchi e neri" (title means "He Had Two Pistols With White and Black Eyes"), first produced in Milan, 1960.

"Chi ruba un piede e fortunato in amore," first produced in Milan, 1961.

"Isabella, tre caravelle, e un cacciaballe" (title means "Isabella, Three Ships, and a Con Man"), first produced in Milan, 1963.

"Settimo: ruba un po' meno" (title means "Seventh Commandment: Thou Shalt Steal a Bit Less"), first produced in Milan, 1964.

"La copla e sempre del Diavolo" (title means "Always Blame the Devil"), first produced in Milan, 1965.

"Grande pantomima con bandiere e pupazzi piccoli e medi" (title means "Grand Pantomime With Flags and Small and Medium-Sized Puppets"), first produced in Milan, 1968.

"Fedayn," first produced in Italy, 1971.

(Adapter) "L'Opera dello Sghignazzo" (from "The Beggar's Opera" by John Gay), first produced in Torino, Italy, 1982.

"Il fabulazzo osceno" (title means "The Obscene Fable"), first produced in Italy, 1982.

"Quasi per caso una donna: Elisabetta" (title means "A Woman Almost by Chance: Elizabeth"), first produced in Italy, 1984.

"Hellequin, Arlekin, Arlechino," first produced in Italy, 1986.

(Adaptor) "Il Barbiere di Siviglia" (from the opera by G. Rossini), first produced in Amsterdam, 1986.

Also author of numerous other plays, including "La vera storia di Piero d'Angera, che alla Crociata non c'era," 1960, "L'operaio conosce 300 parole, il padrone 1000, per questo lui e il padrone," c. 1970, "Legami pure, che tanto io spacco tutto lo stesso," c. 1970, "Ci ragiono e canto No 3," 1973, (with Rame) "Parliamo di donne" (title means "Let's Talk about Women"), c. 1976, "La tragedia di Aldo Moro," 1979, "Dio li fa e poi li accoppa," and "Lisistrata romana," both 1983, "Arlecchino," and "Diario di Eva," both 1985, and "Il Braccoto," and "Il Papa e la Strega," both 1989. Other stage credits include *Patapunfete,* for the clown duo I Colombaioni, 1983.

OTHER

Manuale minimo dell'attore (title means "Basic Handbook for the Actor"), Einuadi, 1987.

(With Rame) *Theatre Workshops,* Applause Theatre, 1987.

Also author of screenplay "Lo svitato," 1956; author of radio play "Trasmissione Forzata," RAI 3, 1988. Has adapted many of his plays for television and radio.

SIDELIGHTS: Playwright, director, and actor Dario Fo is one of the most controversial figures in the world of Italian theater. Through his avant-garde comedic stage productions—which have been likened in spirit to the works of such diverse artists as German playwright and poet Bertolt Brecht and American comedians Sid Caesar, Lucille Ball, and the Marx Brothers—Fo reacts against injustice, discredits symbols of authority, and espouses a progressive left-wing political theory. Although his works were banned and censored in both Europe and the United States for years, by the mid-1980s Fo gained prominence as one of the most widely produced contemporary Italian playwrights outside of his native country.

The characters, themes, and situations in Fo's plays were inspired by the elements of *commedia dell'arte,* the professional improvised comedy of the sixteenth and seventeenth centuries that featured masked actors and clowns portraying stock characters. In an article for *American Theatre* by Ron Jenkins, Fo referred to his crude, bawdy, and often bitingly satiric conception of the clown as a symbol of universal human desires: "the hunger for dignity, the hunger for power, and the hunger for justice." He went on to call his resurrected comedic vision "what Harlequin was before he was castrated."

Fo began refining his animated method of storytelling as a child, listening to the tales told by the locals in San Giano, the small fishing village in northern Italy where he was born. After leaving Milan's Academy of Fine Arts without earning a degree, Fo wrote and performed with several improvisational theatrical groups. He first earned acclaim as a playwright in 1953 with "Il dito nell'occhio" ("A Finger in the Eye"), a socially satiric production that presented Marxist ideas against a circus-like background. His 1954 attack on the Italian government in "I sani de legare" ("A Madhouse for the Sane"), in which Fo labeled several government officials fascist sympathizers, resulted in the cutting of some material from the original script and the mandated presence of state inspectors at each performance of the play to insure that the country's strict libel laws were not violated.

Following a brief stint as a screenwriter in Rome, Fo, together with his wife, actress Franca Rame, returned to the theater and produced a more generalized, less explicitly political brand of social satire. Widely regarded as his best work during this phase of his career, "Gli arcangeli non giocano a Flipper" ("Archangels Don't Play Pinball") was the first of Fo's plays to be staged outside of Italy. As quoted by Irving Wardle in the London *Times,* the heroic clown in "Archangels" voices the playwright's basic contention, stating, "My quarrel is with those who organize our dreams."

In 1968 Fo and Rame rejected the legitimate theater as an arm of the bourgeoisie and, backed by the Italian Communist party, they formed Nuova Scena, a noncommercial theater group designed to entertain and inform the working class. The plays produced by this company centered on political issues and grew increasingly radical in tone. The communist government withdrew its support from Nuova Scena after the staging of "Grande pantomima con bandiere e pupazzi piccoli e medi" ("Grand Pantomime With Flags and Small and Medium-Sized Puppets"), a satire of Italy's political history in the wake of World War II. The highly symbolic play depicts the birth of capitalism (portrayed by a beautiful woman) from fascism (a huge monster puppet) and the subsequent seduction of communism by capitalism. Through the play Fo demonstrated his disenchantment with the authoritative, antirevolutionary policies of the Italian Communist party, allowing communism to succumb to capitalism's enticement.

Steeped in an atmosphere of political and social unrest, the 1960s proved to be a decade of increased popularity for Fo, providing him with new material and a receptive audience. He first performed "Mistero buffo," generally considered his greatest and most controversial play, in 1969. An improvised production based on a constantly changing script, the play is a decidedly irreverent retelling of the gospels that indicts landowners, government, and, in particular, the Catholic church as public oppressors. Fo based the show's format on that of the medieval mystery plays originally parodied by *giullari,* strolling minstrel street performers of the Middle Ages. "Mistero buffo" was written in Italian as a series of sketches for a single actor—Fo—to perform on an empty stage. The playwright introduces each segment of the work with an informal prologue to establish a rapport with his audience. He links together the satiric religious narratives, portraying up to a dozen characters at a time by himself. The sketches include a reenactment of Lazarus's resurrection, complete with opportunists who pick the pockets of the awestruck witnesses; the tale of a contented cripple's efforts to avoid being cured by Jesus; an account of the wedding feast at Cana as told by a drunkard; and an especially dark portrait of the corrupt Pope Boniface VIII.

Jenkins considered Fo's black humor and "sense of moral indignation" most effectively illuminated in a fable from "Mistero buffo" titled "The Birth of the Giullare," which explains how the minstrel received his narrative gift. A former peasant, the *giullare* had been humiliated and victimized by corrupt politicians, priests, and landowners. In his despair, he decides to kill himself but is interrupted by a man asking for water. The man is Jesus

Christ, who, in kissing the peasant's lips gives him the facility to mesmerize an audience—and deflate the very authorities that had oppressed him—with his words. Jenkins remarked, "Fo performs the moment of the miracle with an exhilarating sense of musicality. . . . The triumph of freedom over tyranny is palpable in [his] every sound and movement."

According to Charles C. Mann in *Atlantic Monthly,* Fo took pleasure in the Vatican's description of the play, which was taped and broadcast on television in 1977, as "the most blasphemous" program ever televised. "Mistero buffo" was nevertheless a critical and popular success throughout Europe. The staging of the play in London in 1983 singlehandedly saved from bankruptcy the financially ailing theater in which it was performed. Despite the reception of his masterpiece abroad, Fo was unable to perform the play in the United States until 1986 when he and Rame were finally granted permission to enter the country. The couple had been denied visas in 1980 and 1984 because of their alleged involvement in fund-raising activities for an Italian terrorist organization. Fo and his wife dismissed the accusation and maintained their innocence. Through the efforts of civil libertarian and cultural groups in Europe and the United States, Fo and Rame ultimately received visas, and "Mistero buffo" opened in New York in the spring of 1986. Jenkins termed the play "a brilliant one-man version of biblical legends and church history" whose comedy "echo[es] the rhythms of revolt."

Fo's penchant for justice prompted him to compose the absurdist play "Morte accidentale di un anarchico" ("Accidental Death of an Anarchist") in response to the untimely death of anarchist railway man Giuseppi Pinelli in late 1969. Pinelli's death was apparently connected to efforts by right-wing extremists in Italy's military and secret service agencies to discredit the Italian Communist party by staging a series of seemingly leftist-engineered bombings. The railway worker was implicated in the worst of these bombings, the 1969 massacre at Milan's Agricultural Bank. While being held for interrogation, Pinelli fell—it was later shown that he was pushed—from the fourth-floor window of Milan's police headquarters.

In "Accidental Death" Fo introduces a stock medieval character, the maniac, into the investigation of the bombing to illuminate the truth. Fo commented in *American Theatre,* "When I injected absurdity into the situation, the lies became apparent. The maniac plays the role of the judge, taking the logic of the authorities to their absurd extremes," thus demonstrating that Pinelli's death could not have occurred in the way the police had described. John Lahr reported in the *Los Angeles Times* that because of their part in the exposure of the police cover-up, Fo was assaulted and jailed and Rame kidnapped and beaten in the first few years that the play was staged.

"Accidental Death of an Anarchist" was a smash hit in Italy, playing to huge crowds for more than four years. When officials pressured a theater in Bologna to halt plans for production, the play was alternatively staged in a sports stadium for an audience of more than six thousand people. After receiving rave reviews throughout Europe—Lahr, writing in *New Society,* called the show "loud, vulgar, kinetic, scurrilous, smart, [and] sensational. . . . Everything theatre should be"—and enjoying a thirty-month run in London, "Accidental Death" opened in the United States in 1984, only to close a short time later.

Because Fo's plays are often either loosely translated or performed in Italian and center on historical, political, and social events that bear more significance for audiences in Italy than in the States, American versions of the playwright's works are frequently considered less dazzling than their Italian counterparts.

In an article for the *New York Times* Mel Gussow pointed out that "dealing with topical Italian materials in colloquial Italian language . . . presents problems for adapters and directors." For instance, a few critics found the presence of a translator on stage during "Mistero buffo" mildly distracting. And many reviewers agreed that the English translation of "Accidental Death" lacked the power of the Italian production. Frank Rich insisted in the *New York Times* that adapter Richard Nelson's introduction of timely American puns into the "Accidental Death" script "wreck[ed] the play's farcical structure and jolt[ed] both audience and cast out of its intended grip."

Fo's 1978 collaboration with Rame, "Tutta casa, letto e chiesa," produced in the United States as "Orgasmo Adulto Escapes From the Zoo," also "may have lost some of its punch crossing the Atlantic," asserted David Richards in the *Washington Post.* A cycle of short sketches written for a single female player, "Orgasmo" focuses on women's status in a patriarchal society. Richards felt that, to an American audience in the mid-1980s (when the play was produced in the United States), "the women in 'Orgasmo' seem to be fighting battles that have long been conceded on these shores." Still, if not timely, the performances were judged favorably for their zest and honesty in portraying Italian sexism.

Gussow noted, "For Mr. Fo, there are no sacred cows, least of all himself or his native country," and concluded that Fo's social commentary is more "relevant" than "subversive." Commenting on the underlying philosophy that shapes and informs his works, Fo asserted in *American Theatre,* "My plays are provocations, like catalysts in a chemical solution. . . . I just put some drops of absurdity in this calm and tranquil liquid, which is society, and the reactions reveal things that were hidden before the absurdity brought them out into the open."

BIOGRAPHICAL/CRITICAL SOURCES:

BOOKS

Artese, Erminia, *Dario Fo parla di Dario Fo,* Lerici, 1977.
Contemporary Literary Criticism, Volume 32, Gale, 1985.
Current Biography, H. W. Wilson, 1986.
McAvoy, R. C., editor, *Fo Dario and Franca Rame: The Theatre Workshops at Riverside Studios,* Red Notes, 1983.
Mitchell, Tony, *Dario Fo: People's Court Jester,* Methuen, 1984.

PERIODICALS

American Theatre, June, 1986.
Atlantic Monthly, September, 1985.
Los Angeles Times, January 16, 1983, January 21, 1983.
New Society, March 13, 1980.
New York Times, December 18, 1980, April 17, 1983, August 5, 1983, August 14, 1983, August 27, 1983, February 15, 1984, October 31, 1984, November 16, 1984, May 29, 1986, May 30, 1986, May 9, 1987, November 27, 1987.
Times (London), November 17, 1984, September 22, 1986, September 25, 1986.
Times Literary Supplement, December 18, 1987.
Washington Post, August 27, 1983, November 17, 1984, January 17, 1985, June 12, 1986.

*　　　*　　　*

FOGARTY, Jonathan Titulescu, Esq.
See FARRELL, James T(homas)

FOLLETT, Ken(neth Martin) 1949-
(Martin Martinsen, Symon Myles, Bernard L. Ross, Zachary Stone)

PERSONAL: Born June 5, 1949, in Cardiff, Wales; son of Martin D. (a lecturer) and Lavinia C. (Evans) Follett; married Mary Emma Ruth Elson, January 5, 1968; children: Emanuele, Marie-Claire. *Education:* University College, London, B A., 1970. *Religion:* Atheist.

ADDRESSES: Home—Surrey, England. *Agent*—Writers House, Inc., 21 West 26th St., New York, N.Y. 10010.

CAREER: Rock music columnist at *South Wales Echo,* 1970-73; *Evening News,* London, England, reporter, 1973-74; Everest Books Ltd., London, editorial director, 1974-76, deputy managing director, 1976-77; full-time writer, 1977—.

AWARDS, HONORS: Edgar Award, Mystery Writers of America, 1978, for *Eye of the Needle.*

WRITINGS:

NOVELS

The Shakeout, Harwood-Smart, 1975.
The Bear Raid, Harwood-Smart, 1976.
The Secret of Kellerman's Studio, Abelard, 1976.
Eye of the Needle (Literary Guild selection), Arbor House, 1978 (published in England as *Storm Island,* Macdonald & Jane's, 1978).
Triple, Arbor House, 1979.
The Key to Rebecca, Morrow, 1980.
The Man from St. Petersburg, Morrow, 1982.
Lie Down with Lions, Hamilton, 1985, Morrow, 1986.
The Pillars of the Earth, Morrow, 1989.

NONFICTION

(With Rene Louis Maurice) *The Heist of the Century* (nonfiction), Fontana Books (London), 1978, published as *The Gentlemen of 16 July,* Arbor House, 1980.
On Wings of Eagles (nonfiction), Morrow, 1983.

UNDER PSEUDONYM MARTIN MARTINSEN

The Power Twins and the Worm Puzzle, Abelard, 1976.

UNDER PSEUDONYM SYMON MYLES

The Big Needle, Everest Books, 1974, published as *The Big Apple,* Kensington, 1975.
The Big Black, Everest Books, 1974.
The Big Hit, Everest Books, 1975.

UNDER PSEUDONYM BERNARD L. ROSS

Amok: King of Legend, Futura, 1976.
Capricorn One, Futura, 1978.

UNDER PSEUDONYM ZACHARY STONE

The Modigliani Scandal, Collins (London), 1976.
Paper Money, Collins, 1977.

OTHER

Also author of film scripts, "Fringe Banking," for British Broadcasting Corp., 1978, and "A Football Star," with John Sealey, 1979. Contributor to *New Statesman* and *Writer.*

MEDIA ADAPTATIONS: Eye of the Needle was adapted for the screen by Stanley Mann. The 1981 United Artists film was directed by Richard Marquand and starred Donald Sutherland and Kate Nelligan. *The Key to Rebecca* was filmed as an Operation Prime Time television miniseries in April, 1985.

SIDELIGHTS: Ken Follett has been hailed as "the most popular and most interesting writer of spy thrillers to appear since the generation of Le Carre, Forsyth, Ian Fleming, and Len Deighton" by Michael Adams in the *Dictionary of Literary Biography.* Follett began writing novels while working as a reporter for the London *Evening News.* Shortly after the birth of his daughter and the purchase of a new home, his car broke down, and the twenty-four-year-old Follett found himself unable to pay the repair bill. Since a fellow reporter had just made some fast money writing a mystery novel, Follett was inspired to try his hand at fiction. The result, *The Big Needle,* a novel about drug dealers, sold well enough for him to get his car fixed but could not be considered a great success, either commercially or artistically. Convinced that he could do better, Follett joined the staff of Everest Books, a small London publishing house, intending to educate himself in the business end of book publishing—to learn, in effect, how best-sellers are made.

Although Follett never intended to remain in the publishing field, he nevertheless did quite well at Everest Books, becoming deputy managing director by the end of his three-year tenure with the firm. Before resigning in 1977 to become a full-time writer, he had produced nine more novels, all thrillers, most written under pseudonyms. None of these books became very well known, but each earned him around $5,000, and each contributed to his literary education. As he explained to Barbara Isenberg of the *Los Angeles Times,* he learned to write good books "by writing mediocre ones and wondering what was wrong with them."

This methodical perfecting of his craft eventually resulted in *Eye of the Needle,* Follett's first best-seller and the novel for which he is still best known. The book began its life at a sales conference held by Futura Publications, a company that distributed titles published by Everest Books. At the conference, Anthony Cheetham, Futura's managing director, suggested that Follett write a World War II adventure novel. That night he went out on the town with some other publishing executives, and the following morning—without having gotten any sleep—he wrote a three-paragraph plot synopsis for the book. He gave it to Cheetham, who promptly lost it. Fortunately, says Follett, he remembered the story when he sobered up and was able to begin work. Three months later, *Eye of the Needle* was finished, and shortly after that it reached the best-seller lists, eventually selling over ten million copies worldwide.

The book tells the story of Die Nadel ("The Needle"), a paranoic German superspy, planted in London before the start of World War II, whose code name is derived from his favorite method of disposing of enemies: a stiletto. Die Nadel, referred to throughout the book as "Faber," one of his aliases, learns of the complicated Allied plan to convince the Germans that the D-Day invasion will take place at Calais rather than Normandy, the actual site of the European landing. Carrying photographic evidence of the elaborate hoax—pictures of dummy aircraft, plywood tanks, and fake troop encampments—Faber, with British Intelligence agents in close pursuit, makes his way north to the coast of Scotland, where he is scheduled to be picked up by a German submarine. En route to the rendezvous, however, he is caught in a gale and shipwrecked on Storm Island, a rocky outcropping in the North Sea, whose only inhabitants are Lucy and David Rose, their infant son, and an old shepherd. In the course of the action, Faber has a torrid love affair with Lucy, then kills her husband and the shepherd, leaving the success of the Allied invasion in the hands of the young housewife. Fortunately, she discovers Faber's true identity before he can meet the submarine and, in a superhuman display of heroism, prevents him from fulfilling his mission.

Many critics have expressed appreciation for the novel's finely-crafted plot. Michael Wood, in a *Saturday Review* article, compares this book to Frederick Forsyth's classic *The Day of the Jackal*, noting that in both thrillers "a double narrative focuses on the pursuer and the pursued, with the suspense extremely well sustained." And *New York Times Book Review* writer Richard Freedman states that Follett "has put together a thriller that really thrills, on both the visceral and intellectual levels." But a *Time* reviewer, while agreeing that the plotting is "crisp," emphasizes that "it does not get in the way of [Follett's] people—nicely crafted, three-dimensional figures who linger in the memory long after the circumstances blur." Roderick MacLeish, writing in the *Washington Post Book World*, explains that "Follett brings The Needle slowly to life, developing and complicating him with a skilful leisure that reminds you of Wilkie Collins' gradual character development of Count Fosco, the villain of the master-thriller, *The Woman in White*. If we never develop fondness for The Needle, we eventually see him as a whole man. He is like us and—if anything—that makes him more sinister." Wood feels that Follett has given him a personality that sets him apart from the spies that typically populate thrillers: Faber "throws up every time he kills someone and has an absurd and moving dream in which he is caught shifting his verbs to the end of his sentences [where they appear in the German language] and wearing socks with swastikas on them. He loves his country but has no respect for the Nazis. He is a man of charm, ingenuity, and endurance. He has a sense of humor. . . . We don't have to like this spy, only recognize him when we meet him outside the pages of this thriller. And we shall do this a little more easily because of Ken Follett's perceptive and sympathetic sketch of The Needle." Concludes MacLeish: "This is, quite simply, the best spy novel to come out of England in years."

"Ken Follett's forte," writes Robert Lekachman in the *Nation*, "is the variation upon history." Historical fact, the Allied plot to disguise the Normandy invasion site, was the inspiration for *Eye of the Needle*, while his second best-seller, *Triple*, was based on a news item that appeared in the late sixties, "one of the most bizarre episodes in nuclear history," according to *Time* writer Michael Demarest. This was a series of events involving the 1968 disappearance at sea—in the Mediterranean—of two hundred tons of uranium ore, enough to build thirty atomic bombs. The affair received a great deal of publicity due to the efforts of a team of British journalists, and, although nothing was ever proven and the ore never found, it was generally assumed that the Israelis, who had been unsuccessful in their efforts to purchase uranium, were behind the theft. Demarest says that Follett seized this news item and "processed it into one of the liveliest thrillers of the year."

Follett's explanation for the mysterious disappearance is related by Anatole Broyard of the *New York Times:* "It is 1968, and Israeli intelligence has learned that Egypt, with Soviet aid, is about to develop atomic bombs. . . . Because oil is the name of the game, no one is willing to sell Israel the necessary uranium to build its own atomic bomb. The only solution is to steal it. And it must be stolen in complete secrecy, or Israel's allies . . . will interfere with its desperate attempts at self-defense." The action in *Triple* involves the intelligence agencies of three countries, the Soviet KGB, Egypt's General Intelligence, and the Mossad of Israel, as well as Arab terrorists and the Mafia. Demarest finds that "Follett is a master of crafty ploy and credible detail, rang-

ing effortlessly from an Israeli kibbutz to the intricacies of Euratom [the European atomic energy watchdog agency] and the shipping world."

Lisa Derman, in her *New Republic* review, states that there are "no secrets and few surprises" in *Triple*. As in *Eye of the Needle*, readers have a pretty good idea of what will happen in the end. At the conclusion of the earlier book, the spy will fail, or else Germany would have won the war; at the end of *Triple*, Israel will possess the uranium, or (in accordance with Follett's explanation) it would since have been destroyed by Egypt's atomic weapons. Still, Derman maintains, Follet is skilled at keeping the tension high. He "has taken one convention of the spy novel—spy accomplishes dangerous mission, barely avoiding treacherous counter-agents—and turned it inside-out." In the book, Israeli agent Nat Dickstein is uncovered by his enemies, his plans are known, and he is constantly followed by the Russians and the Egyptians. "So the tension in the well-constructed thriller," writes Derman, "stems solely from Nat keeping one step ahead of his opponents. His mission includes several topics of current interest, and is complicated enough to keep one wondering how it ever could be concluded successfully."

This lack of a surprise ending is also a feature of Follett's next best-seller, *The Key to Rebecca*, another World War II adventure. No matter that readers know who won the war, says *Newsweek*'s Allan J. Mayer, for "good thrillers are like elegant geometrical proofs: their drama lies not in their ultimate outcome but in their method. Though we know that the good guys will eventually triumph, we don't know how; a good thriller should keep us guessing until the last page. Ken Follett did just that in 'Triple' and 'Eye of the Needle.' He did it again in 'The Key to Rebecca.' " The setting is the Middle East, with Rommel's tanks pushing across the desert toward Cairo and Alexandria, meeting unsteady British resistance. A group of Egyptian army officers, among them young Captain Anwar el-Sadat, are very much interested in seeing the British driven out of Egypt and would like to help Rommel. But if they don't help him soon, he will defeat the British on his own, and their country will be treated as conquered territory rather than as an independent ally. The key to their plan is a ruthless, efficient German spy who has been operating in Cairo, transmitting intelligence reports in a code based on Daphne du Maurier's 1938 novel *Rebecca*. (Again Follett makes use of historical fact: A real German spy, John Eppler, was reported to have used a code based on the du Maurier novel.) The Eyptians would like to get their hands on the code, and the spy's radio transmitter, and use it to contact the Germans. Of course the British, too, are after the German spy, and in the course of the novel Follett introduces such characters as a British intelligence agent who is experienced but unsure of himself, an Egyptian Jewish woman who, hoping to immigrate to Palestine, helps the British agent, and an Egyptian belly dancer who works with the German spy.

"Against this background," writes Joseph McLellan in the *Washington Post Book World*, Follett "has woven an intricate story of violence, intrigue and exotic passions." *The Key to Rebecca*, he continues, "is a novel primarily in the post-Helen MacInnes school, rather than the post-Ian Fleming school that has set the trend for a decade or more. . . . Its characters and action are, on the whole, slower-moving, less chrome-hard and glittery, not quite so eccentric or one-dimensional." *Time*'s Michael Demarest believes "Follett's true strength remains an acute sense of geographical place, and the age-old knowledge that character is action. In *Rebecca* as in *Needle* and *Triple*, he brilliantly reproduces a distant terrain, complete with sounds and smells and tribal rites." And Tom Nolan, in a *Los Angeles Times Book Re-*

view article, writes: "Follett plays his story out expertly, building suspense with a steady hand, creating three-dimensional characters who induce sympathy, fear and fascination. With seemingly effortless economy, the author sketches vivid pictures of wartime Egypt." Concludes Nolan: "From opening sentence . . . to gripping climax, . . . [*The Key to Rebecca*] delivers the sure-fire blend of suspense and detail readers have come to expect" from the author.

Follett steps even farther back in history with *The Man from St. Petersburg,* which is set in pre-World War I London. The Germans are preparing for war, and England would like to negotiate a treaty with Russia, thus insuring a second front for Germany when the inevitable conflict begins. Luckily, Russian Prince Orlov is nephew to both Czar Nicholas II and the British Earl of Walden, who was like a father to the young prince during his days as a student at Oxford. It is logical, therefore, for First Lord of the Admiralty Winston Churchill to call upon his good friend the earl to represent England in the treaty negotiations and to act as host for the prince during his stay in London. In the meantime, the Russians are experiencing some political unrest at home, and thus is introduced "The Man from St. Petersburg," a Russian terrorist whose assignment it is to assassinate Orlov before the negotiations can be completed.

In the *Washington Post Book World,* Roderick MacLeish calls Follett "a master of appropriate settings," reporting that in *The Man from St. Petersburg* the author "evokes a world of masters, servants, kings and suffragettes, Hogarthian cockneys and Irish immigrants, of London's unique juxtapositions of privilege's light and poverty's squalid darkness." And while the richness of the book's setting, and its intricate plot, are mentioned by a number of critics, it is once again characterization for which Follett receives the most praise. *Times Literary Supplement* reviewer T. J. Binyon describes the main character, the terrorist, as "a fiercely independent loner, sexually irresistible, who bends women to his will and uses them to further his plans." Binyon points out that the action throughout the book "takes second place to emotional and sexual entanglements, to complicated relations between husband and wife, lover and mistress, father and daughter." Stanley Ellin, in a *New York Times Book Review* piece, states that the ultimate success of the novel "stems from the way events seem to evolve from the interplay between characters," concluding that *The Man from St. Petersburg* "goes down with the ease and impact of a well-prepared martini."

Adams relates some of the reasons for Ken Follett's extraordinary success as a thriller novelist, explaining that in his "exciting, intelligent, generally well-written . . . thrillers, not only are the major characters well developed, but the minor characters are given attention as well. The reader is always able to understand all the characters' political, social, economic, and sexual motives. Follett makes certain that even his villains have sympathetic sides. . . . Moreover, Follett, as a calculating surveyor of the mass market, also realizes that while loyal spy-novel readership is predominantly male, female readers are needed, as they always have been, to insure best-sellers. As a result, his heroines are realistically portrayed women who have led fairly ordinary lives but who are capable of heroics when needed. (The heroine saves the day in each of the novels.) He also reveals a thorough understanding not only of the history and techniques of espionage but of the intertwining complexities of twentieth-century world politics. Equally important is the skill of his plotting. While spy fiction is frequently complex and bewildering to the reader, Follett's work is consistently clear and easy to follow."

In 1989, Follett made a break with thriller fiction to write a massive historical novel set in 12th century England, *The Pillars of the Earth.* Concerned with the four-decades-long construction of a cathedral, the story follows the efforts of Prior Philip and his master mason Tom Builder to complete the building and keep it from falling into the hands of a rival bishop. Critical reaction to the novel was mixed, primarily because it was such an unexpected departure for Follett. Gary Jennings in the *Washington Post Book World,* for example, finds that "the legions of fanciers of Ken Follett's spy novels will likely be dismayed by his having turned now to historical fiction." Yet, Margaret Flanagan of *Booklist* calls *The Pillars of the Earth* "a towering triumph of romance, rivalry, and spectacle from a major talent." And Margaret Cannon of the Toronto *Globe and Mail,* while acknowledging the book's tendency toward overwriting, admits that "the period is so good and the cathedrals so marvelous that one keeps reading anyway."

Being one of the best-selling novelists of his generation, Follett often has to deal with the label "popular writer." Unlike many of his contemporaries, however, he does not object. He considers himself a craftsman rather than an artist and thus takes no artistic offense when some critics use the term "popular" as an insult. Follett takes great pride in his craft and is happy with the work he has done, while still seeking constantly to improve. He told *Washington Post* writer Paul Hendrickson: "[I] compare myself to the great classical writers. Why compare yourself to John le Carre when you might just as well compare yourself to, say, Jane Austen? I compare myself all the time with great English writers like Dickens and Thomas Hardy and George Eliot—and wonder why I can't do better." In the end, he sees no reason to apologize for selling millions of books: "I think I'm one of the best in the world at what I do." And as a *New Yorker* critic, who compares Follett to Somerset Maugham, points out, "it is the entertainers rather than the 'serious' writers who best provide us with the details of daily living."

BIOGRAPHICAL/CRITICAL SOURCES:

BOOKS

Contemporary Literary Criticism, Volume 18, Gale, 1981.
Dictionary of Literary Biography, Volume 87: *British Mystery and Thriller Writers since 1940,* first series, Gale, 1989.
Dictionary of Literary Biography Yearbook: 1981, Gale, 1982.

PERIODICALS

Booklist, June 15, 1989.
Chicago Tribune, October 14, 1983.
Chicago Tribune Book World, October 5, 1980.
Detroit Free Press, September 10, 1989.
Globe and Mail (Toronto), September 2, 1989.
Library Journal, July, 1989.
Los Angeles Times, October 1, 1980.
Los Angeles Times Book Review, October 7, 1979, September 28, 1980, May 30, 1982, September 11, 1983.
New Statesman, April 10, 1987.
Newsweek, August 7, 1978, September 29, 1980.
New Yorker, August 21, 1978, August 16, 1982.
New York Times, May 12, 1978, October 3, 1979.
New York Times Book Review, July 16, 1978, September 21, 1980, May 9, 1982.
People, September 25, 1978.
Publishers Weekly, January 17, 1986, June 30, 1989, July 21, 1989.
Saturday Review, August, 1978.

Time, October 30, 1978, November 5, 1979, September 29, 1980, May 3, 1982.

Times Literary Supplement, December 26, 1980, June 4, 1982.

Washington Post, October 11, 1979, September 15, 1980, September 7, 1983, September 21, 1983.

Washington Post Book World, April 25, 1982, August 20, 1989.

Writer, June, 1979.

*   *   *

FORD, Ford Madox   1873-1939
(Ford Madox Hueffer; pseudonyms: Daniel Chaucer, Fenil Haig)

PERSONAL: Birth name Ford Hermann Madox Hueffer; name legally changed, 1919; born December 17, 1873, in Merton, Surrey, England; died of heart failure June 26, 1939, in Deauville, France; son of Francis (formerly Franz; an author and music critic for the London *Times*) and Catherine Madox (an artist; maiden name, Brown) Hueffer; married Elsie Martindale, May 17, 1894 (separated, 1909); children: Christina, Katherine; (with Stella Bowen) Esther Julia. *Education:* Educated at schools in England. *Religion:* Roman Catholic.

CAREER: Novelist, poet, critic, and editor. Founder and editor, 1908-10, *English Review;* founder and editor, *transatlantic review,* Paris, France, 1924; writer and critic in residence, Olivet College, Olivet, Mich., 1937. *Military service:* British Army, World War I, beginning 1915; transportation officer.

AWARDS, HONORS: Doctor of Literature, Olivet College, 1938.

WRITINGS:

FICTION; UNDER NAME FORD MADOX HUEFFER

The Brown Owl: A Fairy Story (for children), Stokes, 1891.

The Feather (for children), frontispiece by grandfather, Ford Madox Brown, Cassell, 1892.

The Shifting of the Fire, Putnam, 1892.

The Queen Who Flew: A Fairy Tale (for children), Bliss, Sands & Foster, 1894.

(With Joseph Conrad) *The Inheritors: An Extravagant Story,* McClure, Phillips, 1901.

(With Conrad) *Romance: A Novel,* Smith, Elder, 1903, McClure, Phillips, 1904.

The Benefactor: A Tale of a Small Circle, Brown, Langham, 1905.

Christina's Fairy Book (for children), Alston Rivers, 1906.

The Fifth Queen: And How She Came to Court (first novel in "Fifth Queen" trilogy; also see below), Alston Rivers, 1906.

Privy Seal: His Last Venture (second novel in "Fifth Queen" trilogy; also see below), Alston Rivers, 1907.

An English Girl: A Romance, Methuen, 1907.

The Fifth Queen Crowned: A Romance (third novel in "Fifth Queen" trilogy; also see below), E. Nash, 1908.

Mr. Apollo: A Just Possible Story, Methuen, 1908.

The "Half Moon": A Romance of the Old World and the New, Doubleday, Page, 1909.

A Call: The Tale of Two Passions, Chatto & Windus, 1910.

The Portrait, Methuen, 1910.

Ladies Whose Bright Eyes: A Romance, Constable, 1911, Doubleday, 1912, revised edition published under name Ford Madox Ford, Lippincott, 1935.

The Panel: A Sheer Comedy, Constable, 1912, revised and expanded version published as *Ring for Nancy: A Sheer Comedy,* Bobbs-Merrill, 1913.

Mr. Fleight, Latimer, 1913.

The Young Lovell: A Romance, Chatto & Windus, 1913.

The Good Soldier: A Tale of Passion (novel), John Lane, 1915, reprinted under name Ford Madox Ford, Vintage, 1989.

(With Conrad) *The Nature of a Crime* (novel), Duckworth, 1923, Doubleday, Page, 1924.

FICTION; UNDER NAME FORD MADOX FORD

The Marsden Case: A Romance, Duckworth, 1923.

Some Do Not . . . (first novel in tetralogy; also see below), Seltzer, 1924.

No More Parades (second novel in tetralogy; also see below), A. & C. Boni, 1925.

A Man Could Stand Up (third novel in tetralogy; also see below), A. & C. Boni, 1926.

The Last Post (fourth novel in tetralogy; also see below), A. & C. Boni, 1928.

A Little Less Than Gods: A Romance, Viking, 1928.

No Enemy: A Tale of Reconstruction, Macaulay, 1929.

When the Wicked Man, Liveright, 1931.

The Rash Act, Long & Smith, 1933.

Henry for Hugh (sequel to *The Rash Act*), Lippincott, 1934.

Vive le Roy, Lippincott, 1936.

Parade's End (contains *Some Do Not . . . , No More Parades, A Man Could Stand Up,* and *The Last Post*), Knopf, 1950, revised edition, 1961.

The Fifth Queen (contains *The Fifth Queen, Privy Seal,* and *The Fifth Queen Crowned*), Ecco Press, 1980.

MEMOIRS

(Under name Ford Madox Hueffer) *Memories and Impressions: A Study in Atmospheres,* Harper, 1911 (published in England as *Ancient Lights and Certain New Reflections, Being the Memories of a Young Man,* Chapman & Hall, 1911).

(Under name Ford Madox Hueffer) *Thus to Revisit: Some Reminiscences of Ford Madox Hueffer,* Chapman & Hall, 1921.

Joseph Conrad: A Personal Remembrance, Little, Brown, 1924.

Return to Yesterday: Reminiscences 1894-1914, Gollancz, 1931, Liveright, 1932.

It Was the Nightingale, Lippincott, 1933.

Portraits from Life: Memories and Criticisms, Houghton, 1937 (published in England as *Mightier Than the Sword: Memories and Criticisms,* Allen & Unwin, 1938).

UNDER NAME FORD MADOX HUEFFER

Ford Madox Brown: A Record of His Life and Work (biography), Longmans, Green, 1896.

The Cinque Ports: A Historical and Descriptive Record, Blackwood, 1900.

Poems for Pictures and for Notes of Music, Macqueen, 1900.

Rossetti: A Critical Essay on His Art, Dutton, 1902.

The Face of the Night: A Second Series of Poems for Pictures, Macqueen, 1904.

The Soul of London: A Survey of a Modern City (also see below), Alston Rivers, 1905.

Hans Holbein, the Younger: A Critical Monograph, Dutton, 1905.

The Heart of the Country: A Survey of a Modern Land (also see below), Alston Rivers, 1906.

The Pre-Raphaelite Brotherhood: A Critical Monograph, Dutton, 1907.

The Spirit of the People: An Analysis of the English Mind (also see below), Alston Rivers, 1907.

From Inland and Other Poems, Alston Rivers, 1907.

England and the English: An Interpretation (contains *The Soul of London, The Heart of the Country,* and *The Spirit of the People*), McClure, Phillips, 1907.
Songs from London, Elkin Mathews, 1910.
The Critical Attitude (essays), Duckworth, 1911.
High Germany: Eleven Sets of Verse, Duckworth, 1911.
Henry James: A Critical Study, Secker, 1913, A. & C. Boni, 1915.
Collected Poems, Goschen, 1913.
Antwerp (poem), Poetry Bookshop, 1914.
Between St. Dennis and St. George: A Sketch of Three Civilizations, Hodder & Stoughton, 1915.
When Blood Is Their Argument: An Analysis of Prussian Culture, Hodder & Stoughton, 1915.
(With Violet Hunt) *Zeppelin Nights: A London Entertainment,* John Lane, 1916.
(Translator) Pierre Loti, *The Trail of the Barbarians,* Longmans, 1917.
On Heaven, and Poems Written on Active Service, John Lane, 1918.
A House: Modern Morality Play, Monthly Chapbook, Number 21, 1921.

OTHER

(Under pseudonym Fenil Haig) *The Questions at the Well: With Sundry Other Verses for Notes of Music,* Digby, Long, 1893.
(Under pseudonym Daniel Chaucer) *The Simple Life Limited* (novel), John Lane, 1911.
(Under pseudonym Daniel Chaucer) *The New Humpty-Dumpty* (novel), John Lane, 1912.
Women and Men, Three Mountains Press (Paris), 1923.
Mister Bosphorus and the Muses; or, A Short History of Poetry in Britain: Variety Entertainment in Four Acts, Duckworth, 1923.
A Mirror to France, A. & C. Boni, 1926.
New Poems, W. E. Rudge, 1927.
New York Essays, W. E. Rudge, 1927.
New York Is Not America: Being a Mirror to the States, A. &. C. Boni, 1927.
The English Novel, from the Earliest Days to the Death of Joseph Conrad (criticism), Lippincott, 1929.
Provence: From Minstrels to the Machine (travel), drawings by Janice Biala, Lippincott, 1935.
Collected Poems, Oxford University Press, 1936.
Great Trade Route (travel), drawings by Biala, Oxford University Press, 1937.
The March of Literature, from Confucius' Day to Our Own, Dial, 1938 (published in England as *The March of Literature from Confucius to Modern Times,* Allen & Unwin, 1939).
The Bodley Head Ford Madox Ford (collected works), Bodley Head, Volumes 1-4, edited by Graham Greene, 1962, Volume 5, edited by Michael Killigrew, 1971.
Critical Writings of Ford Madox Ford, edited by Frank McShane, University of Nebraska Press, 1964.
Letters of Ford Madox Ford, edited by Richard M. Ludwig, Princeton University Press, 1965.
Buckshee (poems), Pym-Randall Press, 1966.
(With Ezra Pound) *Pound-Ford: The Story of a Literary Friendship* (letters), edited by Brita L. Seyersted, New Directions, 1982.
The Ford Madox Ford Reader (collected works), edited by Sondra Stang, foreword by Greene, Ecco Press, 1986.
A History of Our Own Times, edited by Stang and Solon Beinfeld, Indiana University Press, 1988.

SIDELIGHTS: "Though a controversial writer and often an easy target for critics because of his literary and personal ex-

cesses, Ford Madox Ford played a key role in the development of modern literature," Richard F. Peterson maintained in a *Dictionary of Literary Biography* essay. A prolific writer of novels, memoirs, nonfiction, and criticism, Ford also introduced and supported the efforts of such writers as D. H. Lawrence, Ezra Pound, and James Joyce through his editing of two progressive periodicals, the *English Review* and *transatlantic review.* He "firmly believed that he had played a major role in shaping the most important literary movement of the modern age, a movement he termed impressionism," Peterson continued. In works such as *The Good Soldier* and the *Parade's End* tetralogy, Ford developed his impressionistic techniques of time shift and point of view into complex narratives that arrived at subtle human truths through seemingly simple incidents and details. "He succeed[ed], more often than not, in his ingenious system of getting at the inside of things by looking intensely at the surface alone," V. S. Pritchett commented in *The Working Novelist.*

Despite his numerous accomplishments, Ford was "a man who has been in the thick of every literary fray and yet [has been] ignored by the literary historians, a man whose individual books have, as they appeared, been greeted as unusual achievements but whose work as a whole has made little impression on the contemporary mind," *Bookman* contributor Granville Hicks summarized. Ford's lack of acceptance during his lifetime was "no accident at all," Grover Smith claimed in his study *Ford Madox Ford,* attributing Ford's problems to a combination of his tendency to embellish his past to promote himself, his romantic affairs, which he carried on despite never obtaining a divorce, and his forthright and unconventional opinions about literature. Ezra Pound, who praised Ford in *Pavannes and Divisions* as "the best critic in England," reported in his 1914 essay that "what [Ford] says today the press, the reviewers, who hate him and who disparage his books, will say in about nine years' time, or possibly sooner. . . . And the general public will have little or none of him because he does not put on pontifical robes, because he does not take up the megaphone of some known and accepted pose, and because he makes enemies among the stupid by his rather engaging frankness."

Ford's memoirs in particular exhibited the dual nature that aggravated his critics and delighted his supporters. *Joseph Conrad: A Personal Remembrance,* Ford's account of his relationship with the famous novelist, was faulted for its inaccuracies, and Conrad's widow publicly denounced it as pandering to Ford's vanity at her husband's expense. But "in its peculiar way, [*Joseph Conrad*] is quite a clever production," noted *Nation and Athenaeum* reviewer E. Garnett, "and does, with all its exaggerations and distortions of facts, contain many interesting picturesque impressions of Conrad as he 'revealed himself' to his collaborator." American critic H. L. Mencken similarly observed that while Ford was prone to exaggeration, "what he says, even when he is most impudent, always has a well-greased reasonableness," he wrote in the *American Mercury.* "He depicts a Conrad who is always plausible, and sometimes overwhelmingly convincing. The man emerges from behind his smoky monocle, and begins to take on the color and heat of life." The critic concluded that Ford's book "is affected and irritating, but full of valuable information."

The embellishments in Ford's literary reminiscences could be attributed to his attempt "to recreate the literary past and his relationships with the great novelists who had shared his vision of literature," Peterson explained. *Return to Yesterday,* for instance, "should be considered as an impressionist picture and not as a record," a *Spectator* reviewer proposed. Because of Ford's imaginative nature, "what might have occurred is as vivid to him as what actually did; and in an account of what might have occurred he will etch in details which really make the value of his book. And the reason is this," the critic continued: "Mr. Ford, as a novelist, knows the supreme importance of details: 'atmosphere.' " The memoir "is a series of impressions, confessedly careless of factual accuracy, but designed to convey the color and feeling and purpose of the period," Isabel Paterson likewise stated in *Books.* For these "penetrating accounts" of his literary contemporaries at work, "what counts is Ford's role as witness, middleman, and impresario," *New Yorker* contributor George Steiner concluded, adding "it is difficult to separate his animating presence from the essential tone of modern English and American literature."

His efforts as chronicler and editor of a literary age notwithstanding, Ford wrote several renowned fictions that are acknowledged as his greatest contributions. One of his earlier works, *The Fifth Queen* trilogy (consisting of *The Fifth Queen, Privy Seal,* and *The Fifth Queen Crowned*), exhibits qualities that distinguish his later masterpieces. Set in the court of Henry VIII, the trilogy follows the efforts of Katherine Howard—the fifth of Henry's wives—to neutralize the immoral and corrupt influences of her husband's advisors. As with his literary memoirs, the strong point of Ford's historical trilogy is his construction of atmosphere and detail; London *Times* reviewer Anne Barnes, for instance, noted that "the story is built up through a mass of impressions" and likened the book's descriptions to "a film [Ford] sees in his own mind." As Arthur Mizener recounted in *The Saddest Story: A Biography of Ford Madox Ford,* "the remarkable moments of Ford's *Fifth Queen* trilogy are its dazzling historical scenes. . . . These scenes are dazzling reconstructions, paintings in the tradition of [Ford's grandfather, painter] Ford Madox Brown," the biographer added, and the work's "pageantry" reveals "the complex political purposes that cause these events, and the scenes of plotting and planning that bring them about."

While *The Fifth Queen* treated the traditional subjects of historical fiction, it was also a precursor to Ford's later, more impressionistic work. "No doubt *The Fifth Queen* is too close to the eye in a cinematic way to have the spacious historical sense of a great historical novel," Pritchett commented, ". . .but it makes most of our historical fiction up to 1914 look like the work of interior decorators." Hicks elaborated on the nature of the trilogy: "The author's interest [in the series] is centered in the presentation of states of mind and the rendering of sequences that are largely psychological. Lacking the animation, the pageantry and the simplicity of the true romance, [the books] derive their interest almost altogether from virtues not ordinarily discoverable in works of their kind." The critic added that "what Ford was clearly working toward was the psychological novel." In the character of Henry VIII, Mizener suggested, Ford not only "produced what is in some ways his subtlest dramatization" of the divided hero, a character common in his works, but also "produced a believable character who is almost as radically mixed in his impulses as Ford himself was." "It is a virtuoso performance—the first of Ford's great shows—and closes out the historical novel like an emptied account," William Gass noted in his essay from *The Presence of Ford Madox Ford,* calling *The Fifth Queen* "the door through which [the English] novel passed to become modern."

While Ford wrote over thirty novels, it is *The Good Soldier* that "stands out as a masterpiece of modern fiction," Peterson claimed, calling it "a masterstroke of impressionistic fiction that ranks with [other modern classics] in its perfect balance of point of view, character, and theme." "*The Good Soldier* is 'A Tale of Passion,' " Samuel Hynes related in the *Sewanee Review,* "a story of seduction, adultery, and suicide told by a deceived husband." For several years, American John Dowell and his wife Florence have sustained a friendly relationship with Edward and Leonora Ashburnham, a British couple they met at a European spa. Dowell, who narrates the story, makes clear his admiration for Edward Ashburnham's gentlemanly virtues, even though, as the reader learns, the former soldier indulged in several affairs, including one with Dowell's wife that led to her suicide. "These are melodramatic materials," maintained Hynes; "yet the novel is not a melodrama, because the action of which it is an imitation is not the sequence of passionate gestures which in another novel we would call the plot, but rather the action of the narrator's mind as it gropes for the meaning, the reality of what has occurred."

This emphasis on the "meaning" of Dowell's account is due to Ford's innovative use of time shift; instead of recounting the story in a linear manner, Dowell reconstructs the events in bits and pieces, returning to add new interpretations to previous perceptions. As Hynes explained: "Dowell tells his story as a puzzled man thinks—not in chronological order, but compulsively, going over the ground in circles, returning to crucial points, like someone looking for a lost object in a dim light. What he is looking for is the meaning of his experience." "As the poet fits together images taken from widely-different areas of knowledge and feeling to make a poem," Robie Macauley detailed in the *Kenyon Review,* so Ford "ranges over the whole field of memory, selecting events or sequences of events from all the tenses of memory . . . and fits them together so that they will supplement and comment on each other as images in a poem do." Although Ford deliberately manipulated the sequence of Dowell's revelations, Hicks contended, "you cannot find a phrase that is misleading nor can you discover any withholding of facts that the narrator could justly be expected to give. On the other hand," the critic continued, "you discover in the early chapters references and allusions that carefully prepare the reader for his final impression. It comes close to being a flawless book, remarkable for its sustained inventiveness and its sound, unfaltering progress." The result is a narrative that many critics have compared to a "hall of mirrors" containing an endless number of reflections.

Complementing Ford's use of time shift in *The Good Soldier* is Dowell's narrative point of view, which adds another dimension of irony to the novel. As Dowell continues to reconsider the events of his narrative, he creates an ironic contrast between his present and past interpretations. As Mizener stated: "The ironic wit of *The Good Soldier*'s style depends . . . on a discrepancy between Dowell's attitude as a participant in the events and Dowell's attitude as a narrator of them. All the perception, the tolerance, the humility that recognizes the limitations of its own understanding; all the poetic wit of the book's figures of speech; all the powerful ironies of the narration; all these things are Dowell's." "In choosing for the narrator a dull and unemotional man who fumbles his way through a tale of passion which leads to death and madness," Pritchett asserted, "Ford has found someone who will perfectly put together the case of the [passionate] heart versus conventional society, for he is a mild American Quaker perpetually astonished by Catholic puritanism. Meanwhile," the critic added, "his own do-gooding wife is, unknown to him, a destroyer and nymphomaniac." Further, wrote Mizener, Edward Ashburnham's gentlemanly behavior contains its own contradictions, for the novel "includes a judgment of the world in which Edward Ashburnham has to exist and an ironic awareness of the impossibility of Edward's conduct in that world."

This conflict in *The Good Soldier* between the ideal of being a gentleman in the rural tradition and the reality of modern industrial life was one of Ford's most common themes. As John A. Meixner related in *Ford Madox Ford's Novels: A Critical Study:* "In *The Good Soldier,* a book which dramatizes the emotional meaning of this change in the life of modern man, Ford's great theme . . . finds its quintessential rendering." "Ford has taken the most common materials and used them artistically," Macauley maintained: "he has employed the wandering style of narration and used it for a series of brilliant *progressions d'effet;* he has used a commonplace vocabulary sensitively and precisely, making it sound fresh; he has taken the threadbare plot of unhappy marriage—even the 'triangle'—and given it such new life and meaning that it becomes a passionate and universal story." As a result, Meixner concluded, *The Good Soldier* is "one of the literary triumphs of the twentieth century—a creation of the very highest art which must also be ranked among the more powerful novels that have been written."

While *The Good Soldier* stands out among Ford's many novels and thus "might be the lucky try of a gifted and fortunate minor novelist," Macauley suggested, "it isn't. It isn't, because of the evidence of the . . . Tietjens series [*Parade's End*]." The four novels comprising *Parade's End* create "the terrifying story of a good man tortured, pursued, driven into revolt, and ruined as far as the world is concerned by the clever devices of a jealous and lying wife," Graham Greene described in his *Collected Essays,* adding that the series, set in World War I England, is an "appalling examination of how private malice goes on during public disaster." Christopher Tietjens is caught in a loveless marriage with his wife, Sylvia, who undermines and betrays him at every turn; Tietjens remains faithful but enters into military service in order to escape her. *The Good Soldier,* "Ford's best-written book, probes into the secret heart of the Fordian hero and discovers a conflict that ends in suicide," Peterson remarked. "*Parade's End,* however, portrays with a broad stroke the social struggle of that same hero who tries to make his separate peace with the world that no longer honors his Tory values."

Many critics have observed that *Parade's End* contains Ford's most convincing rendition of his theme of the virtuous gentleman ruined by modern society. Frank MacShane, for example, reported in the *New Republic* that this theme is "more clearly defined and more satisfactorily projected in *Parade's End*" than in his other works. Tietjens's "chivalric behavior, his complete honesty, his willingness always to turn the other cheek—all these qualities so enrage his fellows that he meets disaster . . . in a world run on the principles of dog-eat-dog," the critic added. In the Tietjens tetralogy, Marlene Griffith proposed in a *Modern Fiction Studies* article, Ford "had . . . to show an individual coming to grips with the new dichotomy of private man and social man, and at the same time to show how the social and private worlds relate. It is a remarkable accomplishment that Ford was able to resolve this complex task."

Parade's End is Ford's "most wide-ranging and serious judgment of the failure of the modern world to sustain the essential truths and traditions that most define culture and civilization," Peterson stated, and the optimum setting for this theme is "the critical years surrounding World War I when the values of Western civilization changed so dramatically." A *Saturday Review* critic, among others, found the tetralogy's war sequences most convincing, commenting that they "easily surpass everything else that has yet been written in English about the physical cir-

cumstances and moral atmosphere of the [First World] War." Ford's descriptions of war, however, are not graphic but rather ironic; "there is not a great deal of mud, blood, tears, and death, but what there is is awful—and it is not merely awful, but hideously silly," Kenneth Rexroth claimed in the *Saturday Review*. "No book has ever revealed more starkly the senselessness of the disasters of war, nor shown up with sharper X-ray vision, under the torn flesh of war, the hidden, all-corrupting sickness of the vindictive world of peace-behind-the-lines." "We catch the true Fordian note from the start," Ambrose Gordon, Jr., noted in *Sewanee Review,* for "the prose is the quietest and suavest imaginable." In the tetralogy's second volume, *No More Parades,* the critic concluded, "we are given a glimpse of [war's] violence in a matrix of quietness, of intimacy being violated by more than sound."

Ford also employed his impressionistic techniques in the execution of *Parade's End*. As Paterson declared in *New York Herald Tribune Books,* in *Parade's End* "Ford has employed very brilliantly the modern structure of the novel, in which the events are linked together, not chronologically, but by their realization or recurrence in the consciousness and memory of the various principal persons involved." "There is no general narrative," Gordon said: "we are always locked up in a particular scene, but the scene in turn is locked up in a particular mind." The result, L. P. Hartley asserted in the *Saturday Review,* is a "*tour-de-force* . . . [which] moves with the *tempi* of life, sometimes tediously slow, sometimes at break-neck speed." Some critics, however, faulted Ford for emphasizing technique over substance in parts of the tetralogy, protesting that the time shift made *Parade's End* exceedingly difficult to read at times. "The very sharpness of impression prevents a flow," contended Gordon, "especially since anything like ordinary chronological continuity is avoided by Ford." But, the critic suggested, "life does not narrate; it impresses itself upon our minds and senses; and that is what Ford sought through his brand of impressionism."

"Rereading *Parade's End* is a practically unique reminder of a novelist's resources when he is both superbly intelligent and saturated with the lives he is imagining," Roger Sale argued in the *Hudson Review*. Due to Ford's technique, Paterson proposed, "Christopher Tietjens emerges as the most vital and fully realized character in post-war fiction. . . . He is entirely human and quite unlike anybody else; which is the peculiarity of all human beings and the touchstone of character creation." Although the tetralogy garnered generally good reviews upon publication of the separate volumes, it was largely overlooked by critics until it appeared as one volume in 1950. "This novel, so curiously neglected for a quarter of a century, now emerges as one of the few real masterpieces of fiction that have been produced during our era," Lloyd Morris maintained in a *New York Herald Tribune Book Review* article. Caroline Gordon of the *New York Times* similarly deplored the lack of critical attention on the book, stating: "It is becoming apparent that when he wrote [the Tietjens novels] Ford was writing history, as any novelist is writing history when he records faithfully the happenings of his times." "Ford Madox Ford was so magnificently able a novelist," J. H. Jackson similarly commented in the *San Francisco Chronicle,* "so fine a technician and craftsman, that anyone with a serious interest in fiction cannot afford to miss him."

"There is no other living writer whose work is more generally effective than Mr. Ford Madox Ford's," Charles Williams wrote in a 1938 *Time & Tide* article. In *Parade's End,* for example, "the quietness and the accuracy [of his narrative] were so extreme that the voice seemed to come from under one's own skin; if the experiences of those books were not one's own, yet the nightmare of them was." "As a story-teller Ford recognised life when he saw complication and chance," Pritchett summarized, explaining the author's fondness for exploring incongruities. As C. H. Sisson elaborated in *The Presence of Ford Madox Ford*: "The surface of Ford's writing is wavering, offering sometimes sharp, definite sketches and assertions which are inconsistent with one another; yet one carries away from his work the impression of a truthfulness hidden somewhere in this unstable mass. At the center, wherever it is, there is a passionate and painful care for good writing." "If [Ford] neither was nor thought himself the greatest writer of his time, he was nonetheless a superbly talented man," Mizener declared. "It is almost literally true that he could . . . write anything and write it well. He wrote poetry that anticipates—in style if not feeling—some of the essential qualities of twentieth-century poetry. He was, at moments, a fine novelist and . . . even more frequently he was a very good novelist who wrote half-a-dozen period books that will stand comparison with the work of contemporaries . . . and several clever experimental novels." "Ford is now generally perceived as a legitimate member of an exclusive company of artists who shaped modern literature because of their belief in the autonomy of the artist and the primacy of literature in defining the values of civilization," Peterson remarked. Ford's achievements both as an author and in discovering and supporting the writing of others, concluded the critic, entitle him "to be regarded as one of the main architects of modern literature."

BIOGRAPHICAL/CRITICAL SOURCES:

BOOKS

Cassell, Richard A., *Ford Madox Ford: A Study of His Novels*, Johns Hopkins Press, 1961.
Dictionary of Literary Biography, Volume 34: *British Novelists, 1890-1929: Traditionalists*, Gale, 1985.
Ford, Ford Madox, *Joseph Conrad: A Personal Remembrance*, Little, Brown, 1924.
Ford, Ford Madox, *Return to Yesterday: Reminiscences 1894-1914*, Gollancz, 1931, Liveright, 1932.
Greene, Graham, *Collected Essays*, Viking, 1969.
Harvey, David Dow, *Ford Madox Ford, 1873-1939: A Bibliography of Works and Criticism*, Princeton University Press, 1962.
Hoffman, Charles G., *Ford Madox Ford*, Twayne, 1967.
MacShane, Frank, *The Life and Work of Ford Madox Ford*, Horizon Press, 1965.
MacShane, Frank, editor, *Ford Madox Ford: The Critical Heritage*, Routledge & Kegan Paul, 1972.
Meixner, John A., *Ford Madox Ford's Novels: A Critical Study*, University of Minnesota Press, 1962.
Mizener, Arthur, *The Saddest Story: A Biography of Ford Madox Ford*, World Publishing, 1971.
Pound, Ezra, *Pavannes and Divisions*, Knopf, 1918.
Pritchett, V. S., *The Working Novelist*, Chatto & Windus, 1965.
Smith, Grover, *Ford Madox Ford*, Columbia University Press, 1972.
Snitow, Ann Barr, *Ford Madox Ford and the Voice of Uncertainty*, Louisiana State University Press, 1984.
Stang, Sondra J., editor, *The Presence of Ford Madox Ford: A Memorial Volume of Essays, Poems, and Memoirs*, University of Pennsylvania Press, 1981.
Twentieth-Century Literary Criticism, Gale, Volume 1, 1978, Volume 15, 1985.

PERIODICALS

American Mercury, April, 1925.
Bookman, December, 1930.

Books, January 17, 1932.
Hudson Review, autumn, 1971.
Kenyon Review, spring, 1949.
Modern Fiction Studies (special Ford issue), spring, 1963.
Nation, July 30, 1949.
Nation and Athenaeum, December 6, 1924.
New Republic, April 4, 1955.
New Yorker, February 12, 1972.
New York Herald Tribune Book Review, October 1, 1950.
New York Herald Tribune Books, October 17, 1926.
New York Times, September 17, 1950.
San Francisco Chronicle, September 24, 1950.
Saturday Review, February 18, 1928, May 16, 1964, September 4, 1965, March 16, 1968.
Sewanee Review, spring, 1961, summer, 1962.
Spectator, November 21, 1931.
Time & Tide, March 12, 1938.
Times (London), September 8, 1984.
Times Literary Supplement, June 14, 1985.
Vogue, July, 1971.

OBITUARIES:

PERIODICALS

Newsweek, July 3, 1939.
Saturday Review, July 1, 1939.
Time, July 3, 1939.

—*Sketch by Diane Telgen*

*   *   *

FORD, Webster
   See MASTERS, Edgar Lee

*   *   *

FOREZ
   See MAURIAC, Francois (Charles)

*   *   *

FORNES, Maria Irene   1930-

PERSONAL: Born May 14, 1930, in Havana, Cuba; immigrated to the United States, 1945; naturalized U.S. citizen, 1951; daughter of Carlos Luis (a public servant) and Carmen Hismenia (Collado) Fornes. *Education:* Attended public schools in Havana, Cuba. *Politics:* Democrat. *Religion:* Catholic.

ADDRESSES: Home—One Sheridan Sq., New York, N.Y. 10014. *Agent*—Helen Merrill, 435 West 23rd St. #1A, New York, N.Y. 10011.

CAREER: Playwright, 1960—. Painter in Europe, 1954-57; textile designer in New York City, 1957-60. Director of her plays, including "Tango Palance," "The Successful Life of 3," "The Annunciation," "Molly's Dream," "Aurora," "Cap-a-Pie," "Fefu and Her Friends," "Washing," "Eyes on the Harem," "Evelyn Brown (A Diary)," "Life Is Dream," "A Visit," "The Danube," "Abingdon Square," "Sarita," "Mud," "Cold Air," "The Conduct of Life," "A Matter of Faith," and "Lovers and Keepers." Founding member and president, New York Theatre Strategy, 1973-78. Teacher with Theatre for the New City, New York City, 1972-73, Padua Hills Festival, Claremont, Calif., 1978—, INTAR (International Arts Relations), New York City,

1981—, and at numerous universities and theatre festivals in the United States.

MEMBER: Dramatists Guild, ASCAP, League of Professional Theatre Women, Society of Stage Directors and Choreographers.

AWARDS, HONORS: John Hay Whitney Foundation fellowship, 1961; Centro Mexicano de Escritores fellowship, 1962; Obie Award (Off-Broadway theatre award) for distinguished playwriting (and direction), 1965, for "Promenade" and "The Successful Life of 3," 1977, for "Fefu and Her Friends," 1984, for "The Danube," "Mud," and "Sarita," and 1988, for "Abingdon Square"; Yale University fellowships, 1967, 1968; Cintas Foundation fellowship, 1967; Boston University-Tanglewood fellowship, 1968; Rockefeller Foundation grants, 1971, 1984; Guggenheim fellowship, 1972; Creative Artist Public Service grants, 1972, 1975; National Endowment for the Arts grants, 1974, 1984; Obie Award for distinguished direction, 1979, for "Eyes on the Harem"; Obie Award for sustained achievement, 1982; Obie Award for best new play, 1985, for "The Conduct of Life"; American Academy and Institute of Arts and Letters Award in Literature, 1985; Playwrights U.S.A. Award, 1986, for translation of "Cold Air."

WRITINGS:

PLAYS

"The Widow" (published as "La Viuda" in *Cuatro Autores Cubanos*), Casa de las Americas (Havana), 1961.

"There! You Died" (also see below) first produced in San Francisco at Actor's Workshop, November 19, 1963; title changed to "Tango Palace" (also see below), first produced on double bill with "The Successful Life of 3" in Minneapolis at Firehouse Theatre, January 22, 1965; produced in New York City at Theatre Genesis, 1973.

"The Successful Life of 3" (also see below), first produced on double bill with "Tango Palace" at Firehouse Theatre, January 22, 1965; produced Off-Broadway at Sheridan Square Playhouse Theatre, March 15, 1965.

"Promenade" (musical; also see below), music by Al Carmines, first produced Off-Off-Broadway at Judson Poets' Theatre, April 9, 1965; produced Off-Broadway at Promenade Theatre, June 4, 1969.

The Office (first produced on Broadway at Henry Miller's Theatre, April 21, 1966 [preview performances; never officially opened]), Establishment Theatre Co., 1965.

"A Vietnamese Wedding" (also see below), first produced in New York City at Washington Square Methodist Church, February 4, 1967; produced Off-Broadway at La Mama Experimental Theatre, April 12, 1969.

"The Annunciation," first produced on double bill with "The Successful Life of 3" at Judson Poets' Theater, May, 1967.

"Dr. Kheal" (also see below), first produced at Judson Poets' Theater, April 3, 1968; produced in London, 1969.

"The Red Burning Light: or Mission XQ3" (also see below), first produced in Zurich, Switzerland, for Open Theatre European Tour, June 19, 1968; produced at La Mama Experimental Theatre, April 12, 1969.

"Molly's Dream" (also see below), music by Cosmos Savage, first produced Off-Off-Broadway at New York Theatre Strategy, 1968.

Promenade and Other Plays (includes "Tango Palace," "The Successful Life of 3," "Promenade," "A Vietnamese Wedding," "Dr. Kheal," "The Red Burning Light: or Mission XQ3," and "Molly's Dream"), Winter House, 1971, reprinted, PAJ Publications, 1987.

"The Curse of the Langston House," first produced in Cincinnati at Playhouse in the Park, October, 1972.

"Aurora," first produced at New York Theatre Strategy, 1974.

"Cap-a-Pie," music by Jose Raul Bernardo, first produced Off-Off-Broadway at INTAR (International Arts Relations), May, 1975.

"Washing," first produced Off-Off-Broadway at the Theatre for the New City, November 11, 1976.

"Lolita in the Garden," first produced at INTAR, 1977.

"Fefu and Her Friends," first produced at New York Theatre Strategy, May 5, 1977; produced Off-Broadway at the American Place Theater, January 6, 1978; published in *Wordplays 1*, PAJ Publications, 1981.

"In Service," first produced in Claremont, Calif., at the Padua Hills Festival, 1978.

"Eyes on the Harem," first produced at INTAR, April 23, 1979.

"Evelyn Brown (A Diary)," first produced at Theatre for the New City, April 3, 1980.

(Adaptor) Federico Garcia Lorca, "Blood Wedding," produced at INTAR, May 15, 1980.

(Adaptor) Pedro Calderon de la Barca, "Life Is Dream," produced at INTAR, May 28, 1981.

"A Visit," first produced at the Padua Hills Festival, 1981; produced at Theatre for the New City, December 24, 1981.

"The Danube" (also see below), first produced at the Padua Hills Festival, 1982; produced at Theatre for the New City, February 17, 1983; produced at the American Place Theater, March 11, 1984.

"Mud" (also see below), first produced at the Padua Hills Festival, 1983; produced at Theatre for the New City, November 10, 1983.

"Sarita" (musical; also see below), music by Leon Odenz, first produced at INTAR, January 18, 1984.

"No Time," first produced at the Padua Hills Festival, 1984.

"The Conduct of Life" (also see below), first produced at Theatre for the New City, February 21, 1985.

(Adaptor and translator) Virgilio Pinera, *Cold Air* (produced at INTAR, March 27, 1985), Theatre Communications Group, 1985.

Maria Irene Fornes: Plays (includes "Mud," "The Danube," "Sarita," and "The Conduct of Life"), preface by Susan Sontag, PAJ Publications, 1986.

"A Matter of Faith," first produced at Theatre for the New City, March 6, 1986.

Lovers and Keepers (three one-act musicals; first produced at INTAR, April 4, 1986), music by Tito Puente and Fernando Rivas, Theatre Communications Group, 1987.

"Drowning" (one-act; adapted from Anton Chekhov's story of the same title; produced with six other one-act plays under collective title "Orchards"), first produced Off-Broadway at Lucille Lortel Theater, April 22, 1986; published in *Orchards*, Knopf, 1986.

"Art," first produced at Theatre for the New City, 1986.

"The Mothers" (also see below), first produced at the Padua Hills Festival, 1986.

"Abingdon Square," first produced the American Place Theater, October, 1987.

(Adaptor) Chekhov, "Uncle Vanya," produced Off-Broadway at the Classic Stage Company, December, 1987.

"Hunger" (also see below), first produced Off-Off-Broadway by En Garde Productions, 1989.

"And What of the Night" (includes "Hunger," "Springtime," "Lust," and "Charlie" [previously "The Mothers"]), first produced in Milwaukee, Wis., at Milwaukee Repertory, 1989.

Also author of "The Anatomy of Inspiration."

SIDELIGHTS: "One would almost think," writes the *Chicago Tribune*'s Sid Smith, that playwright and director Maria Irene Fornes "was a hot young New York experimentalist—indeed, in a sense, she is and always will be. Her work spans decades, but she endures as a refreshing influence." Smith comments that although Fornes has won six "Obie" awards for her plays Off-Broadway, she is "one of the art form's most cherished secrets. Ask playgoers about her, and they are apt to answer with a blank look. Mention Fornes to those who work in the theater, and their faces light up." As Wynn Handman of the American Place Theatre told *New York*'s Ross Wetzsteon, "She's clearly among the top five playwrights in America today. [But] playwrights like Irene, whose work haunts and resonates rather than spelling everything out, almost never receive immediate recognition." Although they frequently deal with human and even "political" issues, "Fornes's plays are whimsical, gentle and bittersweet, and informed with her individualistic intelligence," states Bonnie Marranca in *American Playwrights: A Critical Survey.* "Virtually all of them have a characteristic delicacy, lightness of spirit, and economy of style. Fornes has always been interested in the emotional lives of her characters, so human relationships play a significant part in the plays." The critic adds that Fornes "apparently likes her characters, and often depicts them as innocent, pure spirits afloat in a corrupt world which is almost absurd rather than realistic. . . . Political consciousness is present in a refined way."

It is not Fornes's subjects, however, that make her work unconventional; as the playwright told Kathleen Betsko and Rachel Koenig in *Interviews with Contemporary Women Playwrights,* "I realized that what makes my plays unacceptable to people is the form more than the content. My content is usually not outrageous. . . . What makes people vicious must be the form." This form is influenced by diverse factors, "neither theatre nor literature but certain styles of painting and the movies," notes Susan Sontag in her preface to *Maria Irene Fornes: Plays.* "But unlike similarly influenced New York dramatists, her work did not eventually become parasitic on literature (or opera, or movies). It was never a revolt against theatre, or a theatre recycling fantasies encoded in other genres." The critic continues by remarking that "Fornes is neither literary nor anti-literary. These are not cerebral exercises or puzzles but the real questions."

Fornes's first major critical success was "Promenade," a musical which debuted in 1965 and contributed to her first Obie Award. "The play mixes wit and compassion, humor and tenderness, zaniness and social satire as prisoners named 105 and 106 journey from prison out into the world and back again," describes Phyllis Mael in a *Dictionary of Literary Biography* essay. While much of the play's action concerns the comic conflict between the prisoners and the rich and powerful people they meet, it is Fornes's lyrics that "comment on unrequited love, the abuse of power, the injustice of those who are supposed to uphold the law, and the illogical and random nature of life," adds Mael. "In a work that is really more a choreographed oratorio than a conventional musical," comments Stephen Holden in the *New York Times,* "the music and language are reduced to artful basics, as in the Virgil Thomson-Gertrude Stein operas." Because of this lack of conventional plot, "there may be those who will question the slightness of the story line," maintains *New York Times* critic Clive Barnes, "but there will be more, many, many more who will glory in the show's dexterity, wit and compassion. Miss Fornes's lyrics, like her book, seem to have a sweetly irrelevant relevance." Marranca similarly observes that "*Promenade* has the joie de vivre, the disregard for external logic and spatial conven-

tion, the crazy-quilt characters that one associates with the plays of Gertrude Stein. . . . The satire seems almost effortless because the playwright's touch is so playful and laid back. Yet Fornes makes her point, and there's no confusion as to whose side she is on in this comedy of manners." As Barnes concludes in his review: "One definition of 'Promenade' might be that it is a protest musical for people too sophisticated to protest."

"Fefu and Her Friends," Fornes's next major success, ventures even farther into new dramatic forms. Set in one house where eight women are meeting, "the play has no plot in the conventional sense, and the characters are presented as fragments," remarks Marranca. "Though there is much about them that Fornes keeps hidden, the play—seeming at first like realism—is purposely set in the realm of the mysterious and abstract. By setting the play in a home, and then offering a narrative that subverts realistic conventions, Fornes plays ironically with domestic space, and the notion of domestic drama." The playwright presents a further innovation by having the audience separate and move out of the main theatre to view four separate scenes in different areas of the house. "[But] the conceit is more than just a gimmick," writes David Richards in the *Washington Post.* "Fornes, you see, is literally asking her audience to 'track down' her characters. . . . Theater-goers are being transformed into sleuths." The result of this fragmentation, claims Richard Eder in the *New York Times,* is that " 'Fefu' is the dramatic equivalent of a collection of poems. Each conversation, each brief scene tries to capture an aspect of the central, anguished vision."

This reformation of traditional staging has disturbed some critics, however. Walter Kerr believes that there is too much emphasis on the structure of the play; he states in the *New York Times* that while "everyone finally gets to see every scene, though not in the same sequence . . . this does not matter for the play is not going anywhere; *you* are." The critic also comments that "if I lasted as long as I did, it was because I kept hoping during my constant journeyings that I *might* find a play in the very next room." But others, such as *Washington Post* contributor Lloyd Grove, find that this complicated staging is effective: "You're close enough to touch the characters in action, and suddenly on intimate-enough terms with them to grasp what they're about." Mael similarly believes that "these close-ups (another example of Fornes's use of cinematic style) enable members of the audience to experience the women's relationship in a more intimate manner than would be possible on a proscenium stage." And Richards feels that "the strength of this production is that it has you thinking, 'If only I could look into one more room, catch one more exchange, come back a minute later.' In short, it lures you into a labyrinth of the mind." *Fefu and Her Friends* has the delicacy of tone and economical style of Fornes's earlier plays," concludes Marranca. "[But] what makes this play stand apart—and ahead—of the others is, more than the inclusiveness of the experiment in text and performance, the embodiment of a deeply personal vision."

"Ever since *Fefu and Her Friends* Maria Irene Fornes has been writing the finest realistic plays in this country," asserts Marranca in *Performing Arts Journal.* "In fact, one could say that *Fefu* and the plays that followed it . . . have paved the way for a new language of dramatic realism, and a way of directing it." The critic explains: "Fornes brings a much needed intimacy to drama, and her economy of approach suggests another vision of theatricality, more stylized for its lack of exhibitionism." Calling Fornes "America's truest poet of the theatre," a *Village Voice* critic observes that in 1985 Obie-winner "The Conduct of Life," the author "takes on a subject so close to the bones of our times you'd think it unapproachable." "The Conduct of Life" follows the family life of a torturer who works for a fascist Latin American government. Although "we don't think of the fascist classes in Latin America bothering with disgust or introspection or moral concern," remarks Paul Berman in the *Nation,* ". . . of course they do, and no doubt they ask [questions] much the way Fornes shows this officer's unhappy wife asking in *The Conduct of Life,* with agonies of soul and eventually with a gun. And what is this, by the way, if not the spirit of our time?"

In presenting the internal and external conflicts of these characters, Fornes uses "a dozen or so vignettes, some lasting only a moment or two, that are punctuated by lighting that fades slowly," describes Herbert Mitgang of the *New York Times.* The critic adds that "these theatrical punctuation marks are the equivalent of the ellipses that some poets and novelists use, and abuse, to tell the reader: At this point it's time to think about the wisdom of what is being said." Thus "the play conjures a lot of tension, mostly by keeping the scenes tight and disciplined and unsettlingly short," states Berman. "The dialogue and staging seem almost to have been cropped too close . . . [but] sometimes the cropping pares away everything but the musing of a single voice, and these monologues are the most effective aspect of all." Although he finds some faults with the play, Berman concludes that "*The Conduct of Life* is incomparably more serious than any of the new plays on Broadway and will surely stand out in memory as a bright spot of the season." And another *Village Voice* critic presents a comparable assessment, calling Fornes's work "as important and as entertaining as any you're likely to see this year."

"Fornes's work goes to the core of character," writes Marranca. "Instead of the usual situation in which a character uses dialogue or action to explain what he or she is doing and why, her characters exist in the world by their very act of trying to understand it. In other words, it is the characters themselves who appear to be thinking, not the author having thought." Sontag also praises the playwright, commenting that "Fornes's work has always been intelligent, often funny, never vulgar or cynical; both delicate and visceral. Now it is something more. . . . The plays have always been about wisdom: what it means to be wise. They are getting wiser." "Working for more than [thirty] years in Off-Broadway's unheralded spaces," declares Marranca, "Fornes is an exemplary artist who through her writing and teaching has created a life in the theatre away from the crass hype that attends so many lesser beings. How has she managed that rare accomplishment in this country's theatre—a career?" Explains the critic: "What is admirable about Fornes is that she is one of the last real bohemians among the writers who came to prominence in the sixties. She never changed to fit her style to fashion. She has simply been writing, experimenting, thinking. Writers still have to catch up to her." The critic concludes that "if there were a dozen writers in our theatre with Fornes's wisdom and graciousness it would be enough for a country, and yet even one of her is sometimes all that is needed to feel the worth of the enormous effort it takes to live a life in the American theatre."

A manuscript collection of Fornes's work is located at the Lincoln Center Library of the Performing Arts in New York City.

BIOGRAPHICAL/CRITICAL SOURCES:

BOOKS

Betsko, Kathleen and Rachel Koenig, *Interviews with Contemporary Women Playwrights,* Beech Tree Books, 1987.
Contemporary Literary Criticism, Volume 39, Gale, 1986.
Dictionary of Literary Biography, Volume 7: *Twentieth-Century American Dramatists,* Gale, 1981.

Fornes, Maria Irene, *Maria Irene Fornes: Plays,* PAJ Publications, 1986.
Marranca, Bonnie and Gautam Dasgupta, *American Playwrights: A Critical Survey,* Volume 1, Drama Books Specialists, 1981.

PERIODICALS

Chicago Tribune, June 14, 1969, February 8, 1988.
Hispanic, July, 1988.
Los Angeles Times, July 9, 1987.
Nation, April 6, 1985.
Newsweek, June 4, 1969.
New York, June 23, 1969, March 18, 1985.
New York Times, April 17, 1968, June 5, 1969, June 6, 1969, February 22, 1972, January 14, 1978, January 22, 1978, April 25, 1979, December 30, 1981, October 25, 1983, March 13, 1984, March 20, 1985, April 17, 1986, April 23, 1986, October 17, 1987, December 15, 1987.
Performing Arts Journal, Number 1, 1984.
Village Voice, April 21, 1966, April 17, 1969, March 19, 1985, March 26, 1985.
Washington Post, July 9, 1983, July 15, 1983.

—*Sketch by Diane Telgen*

*   *   *

FORSTER, E(dward) M(organ)   1879-1970

PERSONAL: Born January 1, 1879, in London, England; died in 1970; son of Edward Morgan Llewellyn and Alice Clara (Whichelo) Forster. *Education:* King's College, Cambridge, B.A. (second-class honors in classics), 1900, B.A. (second-class honors in history), 1901, M.A., 1910.

ADDRESSES: Home—King's College, Cambridge University, Cambridge, England.

CAREER: Lived in Greece and Italy after leaving Cambridge in 1901, remaining abroad until 1907, except for a brief visit to England in 1902; lectured at Working Men's College, London, for a period beginning in 1907; made first trip to India in 1912; Red Cross volunteer in Alexandria, 1915-19; returned to England after the war where he was literary editor of the Labor Party's *Daily Herald* for a time, and contributed reviews to journals including *Nation* and *New Statesman;* served as private secretary to the Maharajah of Dewas State Senior, 1921; lived in England, writing and lecturing, 1921-70. Gave annual Clark Lectures at Cambridge University, 1927, Rede Lecturer, 1941, W. P. Ker Lecturer, 1944; made lecture tour of United States in 1947. Member of general advisory council, British Broadcasting Corp., and writer of numerous broadcasts; was a vice-president of the London Library.

MEMBER: American Academy of Arts and Letters (honorary corresponding member), Bavarian Academy of Fine Arts (honorary corresponding member), Cambridge Humanists (president), Reform Club.

AWARDS, HONORS: James Tait Black Memorial Prize, and Prix Femina Vie Heureuse, both 1925, both for *A Passage to India;* LL.D., University of Aberdeen, 1931; Benson Medal, Royal Society of Literature, 1937; honorary fellow, King's College, Cambridge, 1946; Litt.D., University of Liverpool, 1947, Hamilton College, 1949, Cambridge University, 1950, University of Nottingham, 1951, University of Manchester, 1954, Leiden University, 1954, and University of Leicester, 1958; Tukojimo III Gold Medal; Companion of Honour, 1953; Companion of Royal Society of Literature; Order of Merit, 1969.

WRITINGS:

Where Angels Fear to Tread (novel), Blackwood, 1905, Knopf, 1920, recent edition, Holmes & Meier, 1978.

The Longest Journey (novel), Blackwood, 1907, Knopf, 1922, recent edition, Holmes & Meier, 1985.

A Room With a View (novel), Edward Arnold, 1908, Putnam, 1911, recent edition, Random House, 1989.

Howard's End (novel), Putnam, 1910, recent edition, Random House, 1989.

The Celestial Omnibus, and Other Stories, Sidgwick & Jackson, 1911, Knopf, 1923, recent edition, Random House, 1976.

The Story of the Siren (short story), Hogarth Press, 1920.

The Government of Egypt (history), Labour Research Department, 1921.

Alexandria: A History and a Guide, W. Morris, 1922, 3rd edition, Doubleday-Anchor, 1961, recent edition, Oxford University Press, 1986.

Pharos and Pharillon (history), Knopf, 1923, 3rd edition, Hogarth Press, 1943.

A Passage to India (novel), Harcourt, 1924, recent edition, Holmes & Meier, 1979.

Anonymity: An Enquiry, V. Woolf, 1925.

Aspects of the Novel (Clark Lecture, 1927), Harcourt, 1927, recent edition, Holmes & Meier, 1978.

The Eternal Moment, and Other Stories, Harcourt, 1928, reprinted, 1970.

A Letter to Madan Blanchard (belles lettres), Hogarth Press, 1931, Harcourt, 1932.

Goldsworthy Lowes Dickinson (biography), Harcourt, 1934, new edition, Edward Arnold, 1945, recent edition, Holmes & Meier, 1978.

Abinger Harvest (essays), Harcourt, 1936, reprinted, 1966.

What I Believe (political), Hogarth Press, 1939.

Nordic Twilight (political), Macmillan, 1940.

England's Pleasant Land (pageant play), Hogarth Press, 1940.

Virginia Woolf (criticism; Rede Lecture, 1941) Harcourt, 1942.

The Development of English Prose Between 1918 and 1939 (criticism; W. P. Ker Lecture, 1944), Jackson & Co. (Glasgow), 1945.

The Collected Tales of E. M. Forster (previously published as *The Celestial Omnibus* and *The Eternal Moment*), Knopf, 1947 (published in England as *Collected Short Stories of E. M. Forster,* Sidgwick & Jackson, 1948). (Author of libretto with Eric Crozier) *Billy Budd* (based on the novel by Herman Melville; music by Benjamin Britten), Boosey & Hawkes, 1951, revised edition, 1961.

Two Cheers for Democracy (essays), Edward Arnold, 1951.

Desmond MacCarthy, Mill House Press, 1952.

The Hill of Devi, Harcourt, 1953 (published in England as *The Hill of Devi: Being Letters from Dewas State Senior,* Edward Arnold, 1953; also see below).

Battersea Rise (first chapter of *Marianne Thornton*), Harcourt, 1955.

Marianne Thornton: A Domestic Biography, 1797-1887, Harcourt, 1956.

E. M. Forster: Selected Writings, edited by G. B. Parker, Heinemann Educational, 1968.

Albergo Empedocle and Other Writings (previously unpublished material, written 1900-15), edited by George H. Thomson, Liveright, 1971.

Maurice (novel), Norton, 1971, reprinted, 1987.

The Life to Come and Other Stories, Norton, 1973.

The Hill of Devi and Other Indian Writings (includes *The Hill of Devi*), edited by Oliver Stallybrass, Holmes & Meier, 1983.

Selected Letters of E. M. Forster, edited by Mary Lago and P. N. Furbank, Harvard University Press, Volume 1: *1879-1920,* 1983, Volume 2: *1921-1970,* 1984.

Commonplace Book, edited by Philip Gardner, Stanford University Press, 1985.

Original Letters From India, Hogarth Press, 1986.

The New Collected Short Stories by E. M. Forster, Sidgwick & Jackson, 1987.

Also author of *Reading as Usual* (criticism), 1939. Author of unfinished novel, "Arctic Summer," published in *Tribute to Benjamin Britten on His Fiftieth Birthday,* edited by Anthony Gishford, Faber, 1963. Author of plays, "The Heart of Bosnia," 1911, and "The Abinger Pageant," 1934, and script for film, "Diary for Timothy."

CONTRIBUTOR

Arnold W. Lawrence, editor, *T. E. Lawrence by His Friends,* J. Cape, 1937.

Hermon Ould, editor, *Writers in Freedom,* Hutchinson, 1942.

George Orwell, editor, *Talking to India,* Allen & Unwin, 1943.

Peter Grimes: Essays, John Lane, for the governors of Sadler's Wells Foundation, 1945.

Hermon Ould, editor, *Freedom of Expression: A Symposium,* Hutchinson, 1945.

S. Radhakrishnan, *Mahatma Gandhi: Essays and Reflections on His Life and Work,* 2nd edition, Allen & Unwin, 1949.

Hermon Ould: A Tribute, [London], 1952.

The Fearful Choice: A Debate on Nuclear Policy, conducted by Philip Toynbee, Wayne State University Press, 1959.

Also contributor to *Aspects of England,* 1935, and *Britain and the Beast,* 1937.

AUTHOR OF INTRODUCTION

(And notes) Virgil, *The Aeneid,* translated by E. Fairfax Taylor, Dent, 1906.

(And notes) Eliza Fay, *Original Letters from India, 1799-1815,* Harcourt, 1925.

Constance Sitwell, *Flowers and Elephants,* J. Cape, 1927.

George Crabbe, Jr., *The Life of George Crabbe,* Oxford University Press, 1932.

Maurice O'Sullivan, *Twenty Years A-Growing,* Chatto & Windus, 1933.

Mulk Raj Anand, *Untouchable,* Wishart, 1935.

Alec Craig, *The Banned Books of England,* Allen & Unwin, 1937.

K. R. Srinivasa Iyengar, *Literature and Authorship in India,* Allen & Unwin, 1943.

Goldsworthy Lowes Dickinson, *Letters from John Chinaman and Other Essays,* Allen & Unwin, 1946.

Huthi Singh, *Maura,* Longmans, Green, 1951.

Zeenuth Futehally, *Zohra,* Hind Kitabs (Bombay), 1951.

Peter Townsend, editor, *Cambridge Anthology,* Hogarth Press, 1952.

Forrest Reid, *Tom Barber,* Pantheon, 1955.

Dickinson, *The Greek View of Life,* University of Michigan Press, 1958.

D. Windham, *The Warm Country,* Hart-Davis, 1960.

Guiseppe Tomasi di Lampedusa, *Two Stories and a Memory,* translated by A. Colquhoun, Pantheon, 1962.

Frank Sargeson, *Collected Stories,* MacGibbon & Kee, 1965.

OTHER

Author of notes for various books, including William Golding's, *Lord of the Flies,* Coward, 1955. Work is represented in collections, including *The Challenge of Our Time,* Percival Marshall, 1948, and *Fairy Tales for Computers,* Eakins Press, 1969.

Contributor to journals and periodicals, including *Listener, Independent Review, Observer, New Statesman, Nation, Albany Review, Open Window, Athenaeum, Egyptian Mail,* and *Horizon.*

SIDELIGHTS: E. M. Forster's talent is now labeled "genius" as a matter of course—Graham Greene called it "the gentle genius"; another critic once wrote: "So erratically and spasmodically has he worked that one cannot think of his genius as in course of development; it comes and goes, apparently as it wills."

His production of novels was sparse—he had published five by 1924, and the sixth, *Maurice,* was issued posthumously after a hiatus of almost fifty years. Yet what Rose Macaulay concluded of Forster's position before his death in 1970 was undoubtedly true: "If you asked a selection of educated English readers of fiction to pick out our most distinguished living novelist, nine out of ten, I should say, would answer E. M. Forster."

It was once said that "his reputation goes up with every book he doesn't write." Morton Dauwen Zabel wrote that Forster had "no stylistic followers and perhaps few disciples in thought, yet if one were fixing the provenance of Auden's generation, Forster's name—whatever the claim of James, Lawrence, or Eliot—would suggest the most accurate combination of critical and temperamental forces, the only one stamped by the peculiarly English skeptical sensibility that survived the war with sanity. . . ."

Though his novels were early established as classics, Forster never enjoyed tremendous popular success. Zabel commented that during his lifetime Forster "practiced the difficult strategy of writing little but making it count for much. . . ." His writings are concerned with the complexity of human nature. What he called the "Primal Curse" is not the knowledge of good and evil, but the knowledge of good-and-evil in its inextricable and unknowable complexity. Such a complex relationship cannot be explained by dogma. In 1939, Forster wrote: "I do not believe in Belief. Faith, to my mind, is a stiffening process, a sort of mental starch, which ought to be applied as sparingly as possible. I dislike the stuff. . . . My law givers are Erasmus and Montaigne, not Moses and St. Paul. My temple stands not upon Mount Moriah, but in that Elysian Field where even the immoral are admitted. My motto is: 'Lord, I disbelieve—help thou my unbelief.' "

Another time Forster wrote: "Truth, being alive, is not halfway between anything." Seeking the wholeness of truth he searched for a "synthesis of matter and essence, of civilization with its inhibitions and nature with its crude energy," wrote Zabel. "And like Andre Gide, whom he respected, he is one of the 'free minds'. . . . He too makes it his task to transmit not 'life's greatness,' which he has called 'a Nineteenth Century perquisite, a Goethean job,' but 'life's complexity, and the delight, the difficulty, the duty of registering that complexity and conveying it.' "

In 1941, at a time when such tenets were losing influence, he proclaimed his support of art for art's sake. He wrote: "The work of art stands by itself, and nothing else does. It achieves something which has often been promised by society but always delusively. Ancient Athens made a mess—but the Antigone stands up. Renaissance Rome made a mess—but the ceiling of the Sistine got painted; Louis XIV made a mess—but there was Phedre; Louis XV continued it, but Voltaire got his letters written."

Forster's style is meticulous. Macaulay writes that "his presentment of people . . . is most delicately exact. Tones of speech, for instance. He is perhaps the only novelist, apart from Jane Austen, none of whose characters could, when speaking, be confused with any others in the book. And this without any of the obvious tricks and slogans which those whom he calls 'flat' characters in fiction fly like identifying flags."

Austin Warren, however, observed certain shortcomings: "Neither at wholeness nor at steadiness do his novels completely succeed. There are wide and deep *lacunae*: except for the Basts [in *Howard's End*], there are no poor. From poverty, hunger, lust, and hate, his people are exempt. Love between the sexes, though recognized with sympathy, is never explored and is central to none of his novels. Except in *A Passage to India,* the individual is not portrayed in relation to society. . . ."

Forster told his *Paris Review* interviewers that he wrote only under inspiration, but that the act of writing inspired him. His childhood was very literary—"I was the author of a number of works between the ages of six and ten," he recalled. He thought highly of his own works and read them often. ("I go gently over the bits I think are bad.") He also said: "I have always found writing pleasant, and don't understand what people mean by 'throes of creation.' I've enjoyed it, but believe that in some ways it is good. Whether it will last, I have no idea."

MEDIA ADAPTATIONS: "A Passage to E. M. Forster," a play based on his works, was compiled by William Roerick and Thomas Coley, and produced in New York, N.Y. at Theatre de Lys in October, 1970. *A Room With a View* was adapted as a play by Stephen Tait and Kenneth Allott, produced in Cambridge, February, 1950, and published by Edward Arnold, 1951; it was adapted for film by Merchant-Ivory Productions and released by Cinecom in 1986. *A Passage to India* was adapted for the stage by Santha Rama Rau, and published by Edward Arnold, 1960; it was produced in London in 1960 and on Broadway in 1962; the television adaptation by John Maynard was produced by the BBC, and broadcast by NET in 1968; it was adapted into a film, directed by David Lean, and released by Columbia Pictures in 1984. *Where Angels Fear to Tread* was adapted as a play by Elizabeth Hart, S. French, 1963. *Howard's End* was adapted for stage by Lance Sieveking and Richard Cottrell and produced in London in 1967; the BBC production, adapted by Pauline Macaulay, was broadcast in 1970. *Maurice* was adapted into a film by Merchant-Ivory Productions and released by Cinecom in 1987.

AVOCATIONAL INTERESTS: Forster was greatly interested in music and is said to have been an accomplished amateur pianist.

BIOGRAPHICAL/CRITICAL SOURCES:

BOOKS

Beer, J. B., *The Achievement of E. M. Forster,* Barnes & Noble, 1963.
Borrello, Alfred, *An E. M. Forster Dictionary,* Scarecrow, 1971.
Borrello, Alfred, *An E. M. Forster Glossary,* Scarecrow, 1972.
Bradbury, Malcolm, editor, *Forster,* Prentice-Hall, 1966.
Brander, Laurence, *E. M. Forster,* Hart-Davis, 1968.
Contemporary Literary Criticism, Gale, Volume 1, 1973, Volume 2, 1974, Volume 3, 1975, Volume 4, 1975, Volume 9, 1978, Volume 10, 1979, Volume 13, 1980, Volume 15, 1980, Volume 22, 1982, Volume 45, 1987.
Cowley, Malcolm, editor, *Writers at Work: The Paris Review Interviews,* First Series, 1958.
Crews, F. C., *E. M. Forster: The Perils of Humanism,* Princeton University Press, 1962.

Dictionary of Literary Biography, Volume 34: *British Novelists, 1890-1929: Traditionalists,* Gale, 1985.

Godfrey, Denis, *Forster's Other Kingdom,* Barnes & Noble, 1968.

Gowda, H. H. Anniah, *A Garland for E. M. Forster,* Literary Half-Yearly, 1969.

Gransden, Karl Watts, *E. M. Forster,* Grove, 1962, revised edition, Oliver & Boyd, 1970.

Johnstone, J. K., *The Bloomsbury Group,* Noonday, 1954.

Kelvin, Norman, *E. M. Forster,* Southern Illinois University Press, 1967. Levine, June P., *Creation and Criticism: A Passage to India,* University of Nebraska Press, 1971.

Macaulay, Rose, *Writings of E. M. Forster,* Harcourt, 1938, new edition, Barnes & Noble, 1970.

McConkey, James, *The Novels of E. M. Forster,* Archon Books, 1971.

Natwar-Singh, K., editor, *E. M. Forster: A Tribute,* Harcourt, 1964.

Oliver, H. J., *The Art of E. M. Forster,* Cambridge University Press, 1960.

Rose, Martial, *E. M. Forster,* Arco, 1971.

Rutherford, Andrew, *Twentieth Century Interpretations of A Passage to India,* Prentice-Hall, 1970.

Schorer, Mark, editor, *Modern British Fiction,* Oxford University Press, 1961.

Shahane, Vasant Anant, editor, *Perspectives on E. M. Forster's A Passage to India,* Barnes & Noble, 1968.

Shusterman, David, *The Quest for Certitude in E. M. Forster's Fiction,* Indiana University Press, 1965.

Stallybrass, Oliver, editor, *Aspects of E. M. Forster,* Harcourt, 1969.

Stone, Wilfred, *The Cave and the Mountain,* Oxford University Press, 1966.

Swinnerton, Frank, *The Georgian Literary Scene,* Dent, 1938, revised edition, 1951.

Thomson, George H., *The Fiction of E. M. Forster,* Wayne State University Press, 1967.

Trilling, Lionel, *E. M. Forster,* New Directions, 1943, 2nd revised edition, 1965.

Warren, Austin, *Rage for Order,* University of Michigan Press, 1948.

Zabel, Morton Dauwen, *Craft and Character,* Viking, 1957.

PERIODICALS

Books and Bookmen, August, 1970.
Chicago Tribune, April 9, 1986, April 1, 1987.
Christian Century, July 22, 1970.
Criterion, October, 1934.
Dublin Review, 1946.
Encounter, Volume 9, 1957.
Forum, December, 1927.
Globe and Mail (Toronto), January 14, 1984, March 8, 1986.
Listener, July 9, 1970.
Los Angeles Times, March 31, 1987, October 1, 1987, November 22, 1987.
Los Angeles Times Book Review, August 3, 1986.
Mademoiselle, June, 1964.
Nation, June 29, 1970, November 29, 1971.
New Republic, October 5, 1949, January 1, 1964.
Newsweek, June 22, 1970, September 21, 1987.
New Yorker, September, 1959.
New York Times, December 18, 1985, March 7, 1986, May 30, 1986, September 13, 1987, September 18, 1987, October 4, 1987.

New York Times Book Review, December 29, 1968, January 8, 1984.
Scrutiny, September, 1938.
Theology, April, 1940.
Times (London), February 4, 1982, December 29, 1983, March 14, 1987.
Times Literary Supplement, June 22, 1962, April 16, 1982, April 5, 1985, May 24, 1985.
Vogue, January 1, 1965.
Washington Post, October 2, 1987.
Washington Post Book World, January 1, 1984.
Yale Review, June, 1944.

OBITUARIES:

PERIODICALS

Christian Science Monitor, June 18, 1970.
Listener, June 18, 1970.
New Statesman, June 12, 1970.
New York Review of Books, July 23, 1970.
New York Times, June 8, 1970.
Observer, June 14, 1970.
Time, June 22, 1970.
Washington Post, June 8, 1970.

*   *   *

FORSYTH, Frederick   1938-

PERSONAL: Born in 1938 in Ashford, Kent, England; married Carole ("Carrie"), September, 1973; children: Frederick Stuart, Shane Richard.

ADDRESSES: Home—St. John's Wood, London, England. *Office*—c/o Hutchinson Publishing Group, 62-65 Chandos Pl., London WC2N 4NW, England.

CAREER: Novelist. *Eastern Daily Press,* Norwich, England, reporter, 1958-61; reporter for Reuters News Agency in London, Paris, and East Berlin, 1961-65; British Broadcasting Corp. (BBC), London, England, reporter, 1965-67, assistant diplomatic correspondent, 1967-68; free-lance journalist in Nigeria, 1968-70. *Military service:* Royal Air Force, pilot, 1956-58.

AWARDS, HONORS: Edgar Award from the Mystery Writers of America, 1972, for *The Odessa File.*

WRITINGS:

The Biafra Story, Penguin, 1969, revised edition published as *The Making of an African Legend: The Biafra Story,* 1977.
The Day of the Jackal (novel), Viking, 1971.
The Odessa File (novel), Viking, 1972.
The Dogs of War (novel), Viking, 1974.
The Shepherd (novel), Hutchinson, 1975, Viking, 1976.
The Devil's Alternative (novel), Hutchinson, 1979, Viking, 1980.
Forsyth's Three (contains *The Day of the Jackal, The Odessa File,* and *The Dogs of War*), Viking, 1980, published as *Three Complete Novels/Frederick Forsyth,* Avenel Books, 1981.
(Contributor) *Visitor's Book: Short Stories of Their New Homeland by Famous Authors Now Living in Ireland,* Arrow Books, 1982.
Emeka, Spectrum Books, 1982.
No Comebacks: Collected Short Stories, Viking, 1982.
The Fourth Protocol (novel), Viking, 1984.
The Negotiator (novel; Book-of-the-Month Club selection), Bantam, 1989.

Also author of "The Soldiers," a documentary for BBC. Contributor of articles to newspapers and magazines, including *Playboy.*

MEDIA ADAPTATIONS: The Day of the Jackal was filmed by Universal in 1973; *The Odessa File* was filmed by Columbia in 1974; *The Dogs of War* was filmed by United Artists in 1981; *The Fourth Protocol* was filmed by Lorimar in 1987. The Mobil Showcase Network filmed two of Forsyth's short stories under the title "Two by Forsyth" in 1984.

SIDELIGHTS: Frederick Forsyth's suspense thrillers have sold over 30 million copies around the world. Marked by a blend of fact and fiction, and by a journalistic writing style that makes his stories easily believable, Forsyth's novels have focused on such international intrigues as an assassination plot against French President Charles de Gaulle, the infiltration of a secret group of former Nazis, a mercenary assault on a small African nation, and a plot to install a Marxist Prime Minister in England. According to Martin Morse Wooster in the *Wall Street Journal,* Forsyth is "one of the world's best thriller writers."

With a story inspired by actual events—an attempt to assassinate French President Charles de Gaulle—Forsyth created his first best-seller, the highly successful *The Day of the Jackal.* According to the *Washington Post,* Forsyth's story was so convincing that it actually caused French newspapers to send out their reporters to check on some episodes in the book. The book's realism depends on its strict attention to factual detail; to write the novel, Forsyth consulted with a professional assassin, a passport forger, and an underground armorer. He also relied on his experiences as a Reuters correspondent in Paris.

In addition to the novel's exacting realism, *The Day of the Jackal* features a meticulous and cold professional assassin who drew positive response from many critics and readers. According to Stanley Elkin of the *New York Times Book Review,* "So plausible has Mr. Forsyth made his implausible villain, a professional assassin whose business card might well read 'Presidents and Premiers My Specialty,' and so excitingly does he lead him on his murderous mission against impossible odds, that even saintly readers will be hard put not to cheer this particular villain along his devious way." Forsyth, however, noted that he thought this positive response to his villain occurred largely in the United States where "there is this American trait of admiring efficiency, and the Jackal is efficient in his job."

Another aspect to the novel's success, according to a *Times Literary Supplement* reviewer "is that real people move in and out of the plot. . . . The technique is not new, but Mr. Forsyth handles it with a mature confidence remarkable in a first novel, and reinforces the general aura of plausibility with a fanatical attention to what one might call the logistic details." Similarly, Forsyth strengthened the believability of his story by opening the novel with a factual account of De Gaulle signing the document that gave Algeria its independence. Following were the reactions of angry right-wing French colonists who were forced to leave the former territory, and the subsequent futile attempt on De Gaulle's life by a member of the Secret Army Organization (O.A.S.). Then Forsyth proceeded to include his own fictional account of another assassination attempt, and "did it with such verissimilitude that the reader is almost persuaded he is following the reconstruction of an actual event."

The Odessa File was Forsyth's second best-seller, again displaying the author's knack for mixing real-life events with fictional situations. In the novel, a German reporter attempts to track down a fugitive Nazi war criminal by infiltrating Odessa, the un-derground organization that shields him. His efforts stir violence among the Nazi underground as well as their Jewish opponents. To assure the book's realism, Forsyth reportedly interviewed Nazi hunter Simon Wisenthal, and included as a character in his novel the former S.S. captain Eduard Roschmann, who is said to be living in South America now. Some critics fault the novel for its subject matter. Michael Crichton in *Saturday Review* finds the "use of real background in this instance often seems exploitative in a disagreeable way." Yet, the Mystery Writers of America granted the book their Edgar Award for best novel of the year.

The Dogs of War, which was supposedly based on Forsyth's experiences as a correspondent during the Nigerian civil war, proved to be his most controversial book. In an article in the London *Times,* Forsyth was accused of financing an attempted coup in Equatorial Guinea which would have ousted President Francisco Marcias Nguema. He was said to have paid out two-hundred-thousand dollars in ammunition, supplies, and salaries for mercenaries. The attempt failed when the weapons could not be delivered and when Spanish authorities became suspicious and investigated. Forsyth at first denied the story, saying it was "a load of old codswallop." His former literary agent, Bryan Hunt, dismissed the allegations by implying that Forsyth was too cheap to finance such an operation. "To imagine Freddie giving anyone 10 pence would be amusing," remarked Hunt. Later, Forsyth admitted he needed some inside information about the logistics of starting a coup, and did not intend for an actual overthrow to occur.

The Dogs of War is perhaps Forsyth's least effective work. Donald Goddard of the *New York Times Book Review* observed that it "falls as far below 'Odessa' in its craftsmanship as 'Odessa' fell short of *The Day of the Jackal.*" He also stated that the book "as a whole is informed with a kind of post-imperial condescension toward the black man that shows through not only in the bland assumption that five Europeans and six trusty native gunbearers are enough to deal with the mad dictator's palace guard of 40 to 60 elite troops and a back-up army of 400 men, but also in some openly patronizing references to the Africans' fear of fighting in the dark and their 'annoying habit' of shutting their eyes when firing automatic weapons." In a review of *The Dogs of War,* an *Atlantic* critic writes: "Forsyth gives little attention to characterization, preferring the chess master approach—that is, his people are defined by their movements on the board. The result of this style of doing things is a story in which no person arouses real sympathy on the readers' part, nor even the continuing interest based on solid dislike."

Forsyth has also been accused of showing sympathy for mercenaries in his book. To these accusations, he was quoted in the *Washington Post* as saying: "I don't have any affinity for mercenaries. They're just more interesting than most blokes, than streetsweepers or bartenders." Forsyth also stated that he intensely dislikes sweeping generalizations about mercenaries. He pointed out that European governments and African dictators had killed more people (in the millions) than the reported 40,000 deaths at the hands of mercenaries in the whole of Africa. Forsyth qualified his statements further: "That's not an affinity with mercenaries though. It's a rejection of the hypocrisy of respectable society with its set-piece attitudes that can justify killing a million children by starvation in Biafra but can object vociferously to four or five mercenaries."

With *The Fourth Protocol,* Forsyth turned to superpower conflict and a Soviet plot to detonate a small atomic device in a U.S. airbase in England. Set off a few days before a national election, the explosion will be seen as an American blunder and help push a leftist, antinuclear Labour Party into power. Critical reaction was generally favorable. One of "the pitfalls of a thriller," writes Peter Maas in the *New York Times Book Review*, "is that the wind-up more often than not doesn't live up to the promise. But in this regard Mr. Forsyth cannot be faulted. His last chapter and an epilogue contain a neat series of switches, surprises and ironies. It's as though he could hardly wait to get through to the end of this novel to show off his bag of tricks." "Forsyth," Roderick MacLeish comments in the *Washington Post Book World*, "has become a well-rounded novelist. *The Fourth Protocol* is his best book so far."

Forsyth again turned to superpower conflict in *The Negotiator*. An oil shortage threatens both the West and the Soviet Bloc, inspiring a number of plots against the Arab nations and against any reconciliation between the superpowers. When a right-wing cabal kidnaps the president's son, ace negotiator Quinn is called in to make a deal. Although deploring the novel's over-abundance of detail, the *Publishers Weekly* critic finds that "by far the best parts are the negotiations for the ransoming of the president's son, which generate real tension." But, according to Harry Anderson in *Newsweek, The Negotiator* is "a comparative rarity: a completely satisfying thriller."

Speaking to Wayne Warga of the *Los Angeles Times*, Forsyth reveals that his writing has been "accused of having no style. That's fair. It's journalism. Nice short sentences, clean-cut plot. Does the fact I worked 12 years as a journalist help? Help? It's absolutely indispensable! In both the research and the way I write. Unashamedly and, yes, commercially." Asked if he wants to write something other than thrillers, Forsyth tells Henry Allen of the *Washington Post:* "Horses for courses. It's an English expression, meaning that some horses are good for one thing, some are good for another. You run your stayers on heavy ground and you run flyers on light ground. I do what I do best, which is writing thrillers."

BIOGRAPHICAL/CRITICAL SOURCES:

BOOKS

Contemporary Literary Criticism, Gale, Volume 2, 1974, Volume 5, 1976, Volume 36, 1986.
Dictionary of Literary Biography, Volume 87: *British Mystery and Thriller Writers since 1940, First Series,* Gale, 1989.

PERIODICALS

Armchair Detective, May, 1974, winter, 1985.
Atlantic, December, 1972, August, 1974.
Book and Magazine Collector, June, 1989.
Chicago Tribune, June 14, 1989.
Listener, June 17, 1971, September 28, 1972.
Los Angeles Times, March 19, 1980.
Newsweek, May 1, 1978, April 24, 1989.
New York Times, October 24, 1972, April 18, 1978.
New York Times Book Review, August 15, 1971, December 5, 1971, November 5, 1972, July 14, 1974, October 16, 1977, September 2, 1984.
Observer, June 13, 1971, September 24, 1972, September 22, 1974.
People, October 22, 1984.
Publishers Weekly, August 9, 1971, September 30, 1974, March 17, 1989.
Saturday Review, September 9, 1972.
Times (London), August 22, 1982.
Times Literary Supplement, July 2, 1971, October 25, 1974, December 19, 1975.

Wall Street Journal, April 12, 1989, April 18, 1989.
Washington Post, August 19, 1971, September 26, 1971, December 12, 1978, February 1, 1981.
Washington Post Book World, August 26, 1984.
World Press Review, March, 1980, May, 1987.

*   *   *

FOSSEY, Dian   1932-1985

PERSONAL: Born January 16, 1932, in San Francisco, Calif.; murdered December 24, 1985 (some sources say December 26 or 27), in Ruhengeri, Rwanda. *Education:* San Jose State College (now University) B.A., 1954; Cambridge University, Ph.D., 1976.

ADDRESSES: Home and office—Karisoke Research Centre, B.P. 105 Ruhengeri, Rwanda, Africa. *Agent*—Russell & Volkening, Inc., 551 Fifth Ave., New York, N.Y. 10176.

CAREER: Occupational therapist in Kentucky, 1955-66; Karisoke Research Centre, Ruhengeri, Rwanda, scientific director, 1967-80 and 1983, project coordinator, 1980-83. Affiliated with National Geographic Society television specials and with television program "Wild Kingdom." President of Digit Fund, Ithaca, N.Y., 1978. Visiting associate professor at Cornell University, 1980-82.

AWARDS, HONORS: Franklin Burt Award from National Geographic Society, 1973, for outstanding research; Joseph Wood Krutch Medal from Humane Society of the United States, 1984, for outstanding conservation work.

WRITINGS:

Gorillas in the Mist (nonfiction), Houghton, 1983, also published as *Gorillas in the Mist: A Remarkable Woman's Thirteen Year Adventure in Remote African Rain Forests with the Greatest of the Great Apes,* 1983, film edition published as *Gorillas in the Mist: Official Movie Tie-In,* 1988.

CONTRIBUTOR

The Marvels of Animal Behaviour, National Geographic Society, 1972.
T. H. Clutton-Brock, editor, *Primate Ecology: Studies of Feeding and Ranging Behaviour in Lemurs, Monkeys, and Apes,* Academic Press (London), 1977.
D. A. Hamburg and E. R. McCown, editors, *The Great Apes,* Benjamin-Cummings, 1979.
C. E. Graham, editor, *Reproductive Biology of the Great Apes,* Academic Press (New York), 1980.
Glenn Hausfater and Sarah B. Hardy, editors, *Infanticide: Comparative and Evolutionary Perspectives,* Aldine, 1984.

Also contributor of articles to magazines, including *Nature, Journal of Reproduction and Fertility Supplement, African Journal of Ecology, Journal of Zoology, Bulletin Agricole du Rwanda, National Geographic, Animal Behavior, National Geographic Society Research Report, L. S. B. Leakey Foundation News, Africana, Living Bird Quarterly, American Journal of Primatology Supplement, Stern, Anthroquest, Animal Keepers' Forum, Omni, Terra, Science Digest,* and *Boston Globe Magazine.*

MEDIA ADAPTATIONS: Gorillas in the Mist was released under the same title by Warner Bros. and Universal Pictures in 1988. The film was written by Anna Hamilton Phelan, directed by Michael Apted, and starred Sigourney Weaver as Dian Fossey.

WORK IN PROGRESS: Scientific articles on ongoing gorilla research; running antipoacher patrols sponsored by the Digit

Fund, seven days a week, with reports available to the fund's contributors; administration of the Karisoke Research Centre and research assistants, with monthly reports available to sponsors.

SIDELIGHTS: Dian Fossey had always been fascinated by Africa. She first vacationed there in 1963 to visit anthropologist Louis B. Leakey's archaeological excavation in Tanzania. While in the Olduvai Gorge, Leakey's team discovered an important fossil, which Fossey ran down a hillside to see—cracking her ankle in the process, then vomiting all over the fossil from pain. Despite this embarrassing first meeting, Fossey impressed Leakey with both her enthusiasm for Africa and her interest in wild animals, so three years later he asked her to become one of his "ape girls." The famous anthropologist believed that women—being more patient—were better equipped than men to observe and record animal behavior. Earlier he recruited Jane Goodall to study chimpanzees, and in December of 1966 he invited Fossey to research mountain gorillas. Leakey decided on Fossey after she had her healthy appendix removed. He once told her that if she truly desired to research in Africa she should have the organ excised; shortly after the surgery, however, she received a note from the anthropologist explaining that his remark was just to test her determination.

Once situated in Africa, Fossey felt herself one of the most fortunate people in the world. She began her work in the Republic of the Congo (now Zaire), which fell under civil war six months after her arrival. Officials placed Fossey under "protective arrest," but she escaped to Rwanda with two chickens, an old Land Rover, and a pistol hidden in a box of Kleenex. Shortly thereafter she established a new camp, the Karisoke Research Center, between two extinct volcanoes of the Virunga Mountains in Rwanda. Over a seventeen-year span of time, the facility grew to eight cabins from the austere beginning of only two tents, and Fossey became an acknowledged authority on the mountain gorilla and a champion for their preservation. Gene Lyons, writing in *Newsweek,* called her "the world's leading expert on these animals," and Katherine Bouton noted in the *New York Times Book Review* that Fossey "has found out more about gorillas than the century's worth of zoologists who preceded her."

Fossey recorded her study of the creatures in the autobiographical adventure *Gorillas in the Mist.* Reviewer David Graber wrote in the *Los Angeles Times Book Review* that Fossey "designed this book with one purpose foremost: understanding, conservation and survival of her study subjects." Fossey included scientific studies—such as autopsy reports, kinship studies, dung analyses, and spectrographic charts—along with her personal accounts, leading Bouton to comment that the "research is invaluable (the book will no doubt prove to be definitive on gorilla behavior), her dedication unremitting, her subject matter of unquestionable ecological importance."

Critics, including the one from the *New York Times Book Review,* claimed that Fossey disproved "King Kong Mythology" in *Gorillas in the Mist.* According to Bouton, the scientist portrayed the animals as "a less complicated version of ourselves" rather than as terrible monsters. Lyons also commented that Fossey "treats the apes with a dignity and a respect that makes her book a classic of its kind." In the book, Fossey explained that mountain gorillas, first discovered in 1902, now inhabit a narrow strip of land surrounded by six extinct volcanoes—on a mountain preserve in parts of Zaire, Uganda, and Rwanda. She found the mountain gorillas there to be amiable, family-oriented individuals. In fact, she regarded them as gentle vegetarians who enjoy being tickled and who purr when contented. She realized that

they are curious, too. For example, Fossey once decided to climb a tree to observe a group of gorillas from a higher vantage point. She attempted unsuccessfully to reach the upper branches, finally settling—after much noise and struggle—on a lower limb. As she did so, she saw the gorillas observing her "like front-row spectators at a side show."

Fossey also noticed strong kinship bonds among gorillas. She recorded that they live in stable family units consisting of approximately twenty members led by a dominant male, which she called the "silverback." She also discovered that, though basically pacifists, gorillas would fight if a young family member was threatened, for its first instinct was to protect its family, especially the babies. Fossey documented cases in which poachers killed a dozen adult apes to capture one infant, and she witnessed silverbacks disengaging other gorillas from snares and traps.

Furthermore, Fossey recognized that gorillas have individual personalities and identifiable facial characteristics; for instance, she learned that no two gorillas have the same shaped nose. Reviewers of *Gorillas in the Mist* quickly acknowledged that Fossey perceived unique personalities for the apes she observed. Graber wrote that "among Fossey's gorillas, one recognizes the snob, the hedonist, the thoughtful brooder, the lordly patriarch, the mama's boy." He conceded that the researcher "has been criticized [by others] for excessively personifying animals," but he added that he saw "no evidence that affection has clouded objectivity." R. Z. Sheppard concurred in *Time,* stating: "Fossey firmly establishes these animals in the world where they belong. She may give them cute names like Puck, Pantsy and Macho, but she maintains her scientific distance." Yet Fossey also chronicled the gorilla's darker side by including instances of infanticide and cannibalism.

Fossey cautioned in *Gorillas in the Mist* that the apes might be near extinction. She maintained that the gorilla population halved between 1960 and 1980, and she estimated that only two hundred and forty of them remain alive. Above all, Fossey feared that the mountain gorilla might be "doomed to extinction in the same century in which it had been discovered."

Fossey battled natives, government officials, game park wardens, and poachers to prevent the gorilla's extinction. Her first opposition came from poverty-stricken farmers who encroached upon the apes' forest territory to convert it into farmland. The population of Rwanda alone is expected to double by the year 2000, so natives view the gorilla preserve as a new source of farmland and pasture. Local government officials also perceive gorilla territory as a new agricultural frontier; thus officials would not always cooperate with Fossey's conservation efforts. Some reviewers criticized Fossey for arguing with the African governments, but Graber disagreed. He remembered that Fossey kept the gorillas and their environment alive. "Without life," he maintained, "good relations are moot."

Park wardens, too, presented an obstacle to Fossey's preservation efforts. For example, a park warden sold two young gorillas to a German zoo, but to capture them he and his staff killed eighteen adult gorillas. The captives were near death, so the warden brought them to Fossey for medical care. When one of the infants, Coco, was first released from its traveling box into a cabin at camp, it climbed onto a bench to look through a window and cried upon seeing the mountain forest from which she had been seized. Park officials nevertheless honored their contract and sent Coco and the other ape to the zoo, where they died a few years later.

Park wardens also neglected to enforce antipoaching laws effectively, so Fossey organized the first patrols against poachers pursuing gorillas for zoos and for trophies. To illustrate the damage incurred by poachers, she included in *Gorillas in the Mist* a photograph of a headless, handless gorilla corpse mutilated by poachers, and she told the story of a three-year old gorilla who apparently died of extreme remorse after poachers killed three of the family members that were protecting him.

Thus critics, particularly Bouton and Graber, lauded *Gorillas in the Mist* for preserving a creature that is quickly approaching extinction. Bouton labeled the book "a monument to scientific devotion" as well as a tribute to the apes. "Should the mountain gorillas become extinct—should we suffer that death in our small primate family—they will live on in this book," she said. "We can only be grateful to Dian Fossey for having gotten there in time."

Fossey once told *CA:* "In late August, 1983, on a gloomy, overcast day, I was sitting in my cabin at camp typing some field notes when a porter came to the door with an envelope someone at the base of the mountain had given him to carry up to me. The envelope contained the first visible evidence I had received of the actual release of my book to 'the world'—R. Z. Sheppard's review in *Time.* Incredulously I read Mr. Sheppard's kind words and gazed long and hard at the article's accompanying illustration, a photograph of Macho and Kweli, a mother and an infant who had been shot and killed by poachers five years previously. It was inconceivable to me that these gorillas, among others, with whom I had lived for so many years, would now become known to the public. My biggest concern—*have I done them justice?*—was greatly allayed by Mr. Sheppard's sensitive and commendatory review.

"On that secluded and misty day, I folded up the page that had been torn out of *Time,* tucked it into my pocket, and went for a long walk in the forest to pay silent tribute to the gorillas, particularly those who live only as memories, and also to R. Z. Sheppard for sharing his genuine appreciation of the dignity and worth of the species."

On December 27, 1985, Dian Fossey's body was found in her home at the Karisoke Research Center. She had been hacked to death by a panga-knife, a machete-like African weapon. Soon after the brutal murder, Rwandan authorities suspected Wayne Richard McGuire, Fossey's assistant and at the time a doctoral candidate at the University of Oklahoma, of the crime. The Rwandan prosecutor's office, reported a *Los Angeles Times* writer, believed that the motive was that "McGuire wanted to acquire the manuscript of a book Fossey was writing . . . [that] was to have been a sequel to her 1983 work, 'Gorillas in the Mist.'" Authorities there also claimed that McGuire enlisted the help of four or five of Fossey's Rwandan employees to help him kill the researcher. But many people were skeptical of this explanation for several reasons: Fossey already permitted McGuire to have free access to her research papers; McGuire made no attempt to leave the camp for seven months after the murder; and he knew only a few words of the native French and Swahili languages, making it impossible for him to have conspired effectively with any of Fossey's employees.

Another theory about the murder is that Fossey was slain by poachers who had become enraged by the scientist's interference in their illegal trade. But there is yet another possibility. According to a *People* article written by Montgomery Brower and reported by Maryanne Vollers, Fossey had taken a *sumu*—a magic charm that some Rwandans believed would protect the bearer from harm—from a poacher she had detained not long before

her death. The man "may have engaged assassins to break into Fossey's cabin, kill her and retrieve the *sumu* packets," theorized Fossey's friend, Ian Redmond. Thus far, however, the tragic death of Dian Fossey is still cloaked in mystery. McGuire remains in the United States, though a Rwandan jury tried him in absentia and found him guilty of murder after forty minutes of deliberation and without an argument for the defense. The United States has no extradition treaty with Rwanda, and no effort has been made by the African authorities to enforce an international arrest warrant.

Fossey was buried by her camp in a cemetery that is also the final resting place of her beloved gorillas. Her grave marker is inscribed only with her Rwandan name—Nyiramacibili, "the lady who lives alone in the forest."

BIOGRAPHICAL/CRITICAL SOURCES:

BOOKS

Fossey, Dian, *Gorillas in the Mist,* Houghton, 1983.
Mowat, Farley, *Woman in the Mists: The Story of Dian Fossey and the Mountain Gorillas of Africa,* Warner Books, 1987.

PERIODICALS

Life, November, 1986.
Los Angeles Times, December 5, 1986, December 19, 1986, September 16, 1988.
Los Angeles Times Book Review, October 16, 1983.
Newsweek, August 29, 1983.
New York Times, September 23, 1988.
New York Times Book Review, September 4, 1983.
Time, August 15, 1983, September 1, 1986.
Washington Post, September 30, 1983, August 22, 1986.

OBITUARIES:

PERIODICALS

Chicago Tribune, December 30, 1985.
Los Angeles Times, December 29, 1985.
New Yorker, January 27, 1986.
New York Times, December 29, 1985, January 2, 1986.
Omni, May, 1986.
People, February 17, 1986.
Science 86, April, 1986.

*   *   *

FOUCAULT, Michel   1926-1984

PERSONAL: Born October 15, 1926, in Poitiers, France; died of neurological disorder, June 25, 1984, in Paris, France; son of Paul (a doctor) and Anne (Malapert) Foucault. *Education:* Attended Ecole Normale Superieure; Sorbonne, University of Paris, licence, 1948 and 1950, diploma, 1952.

ADDRESSES: Home—285 rue de Vaugirard, 75015 Paris, France.

CAREER: Writer. Worked as teacher of philosophy and French literature at University of Lill, University of Uppsala, University of Warsaw, University of Hamburg, University of Clermont-Ferrand, University of Sao Paulo, and University of Tunis, 1960-68; University of Paris, Vincennes, France, professor, 1968-70; chairman of history of systems of thought at College de France, 1970—84.

AWARDS, HONORS: Medal from Center of Scientific Research (France), 1961, for *Madness and Civilization.*

WRITINGS:

Folie et deraison: Histoire de la fo lie a l'age classique, Plon, 1961, abridged edition, Union Generale, 1964, translation by Richard Howard published as *Madness and Civilization: A History of Insanity in the Age of Reason,* Pantheon, 1965.

Maladie mentale et psychologie, Presses Universitaires de France, 1962, translation by Alan Sheridan published as *Mental Illness and Psychology,* Harper, 1976.

Naissance de la clinique: Une Archeologie du regard medical, Presses Universitaires de France, 1963, translation by A. M. Sheridan Smith published as *The Birth of the Clinic: An Archaeology of Medical Perception,* Pantheon, 1973.

Raymond Roussel, Gallimard, 1963, translation published as *Death and the Labyrinth: The World of Raymond Roussel,* Doubleday, 1986.

Les Mots el les choses: Une Archeologie des sciences humanes, Gallimard, 1966, translation published as *The Order of Things: An Archaeology of the Human Sciences,* Pantheon, 1971.

L'Archeologie du savoir, Gallimard, 1969, translation by Smith published as *The Archaeology of Knowledge* (includes "The Discourse on Language"; also see below), Pantheon, 1972.

L'Ordre du discours, Gallimard, 1971 (translation by Smith published in *The Archaeology of Knowledge* as "The Discourse on Language"; also see above).

(Editor) *Moi, Pierre Riviere, ayant egorge ma mere, ma soeur et mon frere* [France], 1973, translation by Frank Jellinek published as *I, Pierre Riviere, Having Slaughtered My Mother, My Sister, and My Brother . . .: A Case of Parricide in the 19th Century,* Pantheon, 1975.

Ceci n'est pas une pipe: Deux Lettres et quatre dessins de Rene Magritte, Fata Morgana, 1973, translation by James Harkness published as *This Is Not a Pipe: Illustrations and Letters by Rene Magritte,* University of California Press, 1983.

Surveiller et punir: Naissance de la prison, Gallimard, 1975, translation by Sheridan published as *Discipline and Punish: The Birth of the Prison,* Pantheon, 1977.

Histoire de la sexualite, Gallimard, Volume 1: *La Volonte de saviour* (title means "The Will to Know"; translation by Robert Hurley published as *The History of Sexuality,* Pantheon, 1978), 1976; Volume 2: *L'Usage of des Plaisirs* (translation by Hurley published as *The Use of Pleasure,* Pantheon, 1985), 1984; Volume 3: *Souci de Soi* (translation by Hurley published as *The Care of the Self,* Pantheon, 1987), 1984.

Language, Counter-Memory, Practice: Selected Essays and Interviews, edited by Donald F. Bouchard, translated by Bouchard and Sherry Simon, Cornell University Press, 1977.

(Author of introduction) *Herculine Barbin: Being the Recently Discovered Memoirs of a Nineteenth-Century French Hermaphrodite,* translation by Richard McDougall, Pantheon, 1980.

Power/Knowledge: Selected Interviews and Other Writings, 1972-1977, Pantheon, 1981.

The Foucault Reader, edited by Paul Rabinow, Pantheon, 1984.

(With Ludwig Binswanger) *Dream and Existence,* edited by Keith Hoeller, translation from French and German by Forrest Williams and Jacob Needleman, Rev. Exist. Psych., 1986.

(With Maurice Blanchot) *Foucault-Blanchot,* translation by Jeffrey Mehlman and Brian Massumi, Zone Books, 1987.

Politics, Philosophy, Culture: Interviews and Other Writings, 1977-1984, edited by Lawrence D. Kritzman, introduction by Alan Sheridan, Routledge, 1988.

Director of *Zone des tempetes,* 1973-84. Contributor to periodicals, including *Critique.*

SIDELIGHTS: In the *New York Times Book Review,* Peter Cawes wrote, "Michel Foucault is one of a handful of French thinkers who have . . . given an entirely new direction to theoretical work in the so-called 'human sciences,' the study of language, literature, psychiatry, intellectual history and the like." But according to Frank Kerrrtode, Foucault is not "writing history of ideas, or indeed history of anything. Unlike historians, he seeks not origin, continuities, and explanations which will fill in documentary breaches of continuity, but rather 'an epistemological space specific to a particular period.' He attempts to uncover the *unconscious* of knowledge."

D. W. Harding explained Foucault's disdain for the history of knowledge: "Foucault believes that our own current intellectual life and systems of scientific thought are built on assumptions profoundly taken for granted and normally not exposed to conscious inspection, and yet likely in time . . . to be discarded." *Nation's* Bruce Jackson agreed. "Foucault is one of the few social analysts whose work regularly unfits readers to continue looking at things or ideas or institutions in the same way," he wrote. "His archaeologies uncover architectures that make sensible order of what previously seemed sloppiness or incompetence or foolishness or malevolence."

Sherry Turkle characterized Foucault's method as "constructive," though a more apt definition might be "reconstructive." As Jackson noted, "Foucault works to uncover, to unearth." Similarly, Cawes wrote in *New Republic,* "The archaeologist, finding a coin here, a pot there, reconstructs cities and civilizations. Foucault, turning over words with immense scholarship and erudition, reconstructs a group of intellectual activities collectively called in French the *sciences humaines. . . .*"

Foucault introduced his archaeological method in *The Order of Things,* in which he presents the idea that "in any given culture and at any given moment there is only one *episteme* [a system of instinctual knowledge] that defines the conditions of possibility of all knowledge." Foucault then attempts "to dig up and display the 'archaeological' form or forms which would be common to all mental activity," and he traces these forms throughout historic cultures.

In *The Order of Things,* Foucault also presented his concept of "the disappearance of man." He explains that "there was no epistemological consciousness of man" before the eighteenth century. According to Foucault, only upon the advent of biology, economics, and philology did man appear "as an object of knowledge and as a subject that knows." He then describes the twentieth century as the "death of man." Foucault attributes man's decline to objectivity, which eliminates the necessity of making man the focus of history.

Foucault addressed his archaeological methods in *The Archaeology of Knowledge.* Cawes described the book as "an attempt to decide just what it is about certain utterances or inscriptions—real objects in a real world which leave traces behind to be discovered, classified and related to one another—that qualifies them as 'statements' . . . belonging to various bodies of knowledge." The English-language edition of *The Archaeology of Knowledge* included "The Discourse on Language," an investigation into the ways in which society manipulates language for purposes of politics and power. Cawes described Foucault's perception of language as "a net *thrown over* the world: it criticized, classified, analyzed. . . ."

During the 1970s Foucault shifted his emphasis from the archaeological method to a genealogical method. Whereas the former consisted of unearthing scholarly minutia from the past to understand the types of knowledge possible during a given time period, the genealogical method sought to understand how power structures shaped and changed the boundaries of "truth." Donald F. Bouchard discusses Foucault's conception of genealogy and truth in *Thinkers of the Twentieth Century:* "The classic philosophical question, 'What is the surest path to the Truth?' has been refashioned . . . into a new basis for historical interrogation: 'what is the hazardous career that Truth has followed?'—the question of genealogy for which the will to truth, in Western culture, is the most deeply enmeshed historical phenomenon. In Foucault's works, truth is no longer an unchanging, universal essence, but the perpetual object of appropriation, domination."

Foucault employed his genealogical approach in *Discipline and Punish,* published in French in 1975 and English in 1977. The work provides a history of how society has approached crime and punishment over the years. In *New Republic,* Frank McConnell noted that *Discipline and Punish,* rather than merely tracing the evolution of penal institutions, presents the argument "that the invention of the prison is the crucial, inclusive image for all those modes of brutalization, in industry, in education, in the very fabric of citizenship, which defines the modern era of humanistic tyranny, the totalitarianism of the norm."

Foucault also followed the genealogical approach in the first volume of his last work, *The History of Sexuality,* a proposed series of six volumes of which Foucault completed three and most of the fourth before his death in 1984. But, as Michael Ignatieff observed in the *Times Literary Supplement,* volumes two and three "will surprise readers expecting Foucault to continue his genealogy of modern reason. Indeed, in the interval between the publication of the first volume . . . in 1976 and the appearance of these two further volumes eight years later, the axis of his work shifted so radically that the continuity of the whole project must be put in doubt." Ignatieff remarked that Foucault's new scope expanded to include the history of "Western reason itself since the dawn of Greek philosophy."

The focus of *The History of Sexuality* is on how the self has variously perceived itself through its views on human sexuality. The first volume introduces the series and, in Turkle's words, "challenges standard interpretations of modern sexual history as a history of repression." Volume two, translated into English as *The Use of Pleasure,* examines the sexual questions and moral problems that the ancient Greeks pondered, and volume three, translated as *The Care of the Self,* centers on the Christian influence on the Romans regarding issues of marriage and procreation. In Foucault's estimation the Romans represent a transitional group between the ancient Greeks—who regularly practiced homosexuality and who did not equate sexual practice with sin—and the Christian Europeans, whose concept of sin caused them to approach sexuality with considerable anxiety. Ignatieff concluded, "Because the *History of Sexuality* will remain unfinished, the history [of] modern asceticism we are offered is only a sketchy outline. . . . [Foucault's history] begins, now, not with the confinement of the insane, the criminal and the sick in the seventeenth century, but with that sense of sin and that sense of desire which date back to the meeting between the pagan and Christian languages of the self."

Foucault's work has met with resistance, much of which stems from his manner of presentation. He has been accused of writing "obliquely" and "rhetorically," and Paul Robinson called him "one of those authors who write with their ears, not with their heads." Christopher Lasch declared, "His writing is difficult, the argument hard to follow, the arrangement of chapters seemingly arbitrary and the whole very difficult to summarize." Cawes described Foucault as "never a man to use one word where five will do, or to say straightforwardly what can be said obliquely." Similarly, Robinson contended, "What he tries to create, above all else, is a certain tone—highfalutin, patronizing . . . and, whenever the argument threatens to run thin, opaque."

Turkle defended Foucault's style as the French method of putting "poetry into science." She declared, "In order to put into question assumptions deeply embedded in our ordinary language, one has to use language in extraordinary ways." Harding summarized: "Foucault has the dreadful gift . . . of diffusing his meaning very thinly throughout an immense verbal spate, no part of which is quite empty of meaning, redundant, or merely repetitive. But behind all the abstract jargon and intimidating erudition there is undoubtedly an alert and sensitive mind which can ignore the familiar surfaces of established intellectual codes and ask new questions."

BIOGRAPHICAL/CRITICAL SOURCES:

BOOKS

Clark, Michael, *Michel Foucault: An Annotated Bibliography; A Tool Kit for a New Age,* Garland, 1983.
Hoy, David Couzens, editor, *Foucault: A Critical Reader,* Blackwell, 1986.
Sheridan, Alan, *Michel Foucault: The Will to Truth,* Tavistock, 1980.
Thinkers of the Twentieth Century, Gale, 1987.

PERIODICALS

Commonweal, May 12, 1978.
Esquire, July, 1975.
Globe and Mail (Toronto), June 7, 1986.
Horizon, autumn, 1969.
Los Angeles Times Book Review, November 24, 1985.
Nation, July 5, 1971, January 26, 1974, March 4, 1978, January 27, 1979.
New Republic, March 27, 1971, November 10, 1973, April 1, 1978, October 28, 1978.
New Yorker, January 29, 1979, July 16, 1979.
New York Review of Books, August 12, 1971, May 17, 1973, January 22, 1976.
New York Times Book Review, October 22, 1972, February 24, 1974, December 7, 1975, February 19, 1978, January 14, 1979, February 25, 1979, November 25, 1979, January 27, 1980, June 12, 1980, January 18, 1987.
Spectator, October 9, 1971.
Times Literary Supplement, June 9, 1972, February 1, 1974, June 16, 1978, April 27, 1984, September 28, 1984.
Washington Post Book World, January 7, 1979, March 15, 1981, January 5, 1986.

OBITUARIES:

PERIODICALS

Chicago Tribune, June 27, 1984.
Newsweek, July 9, 1984.
Time, July 9, 1984.
Times (London), June 27, 1984.
Washington Post, June 27, 1984.

FOWLES, John 1926-

PERSONAL: Born March 31, 1926, in Essex, England; son of Robert and Gladys (Richards) Fowles; married Elizabeth Whitton, April 2, 1954. *Education:* Oxford University, B.A. (with honours in French), 1950.

ADDRESSES: Home—Lyme Regis, Dorset, England. *Agent*—Anthony Sheil Associates Ltd., 2/3 Morwell St., London WC1B 3AR, England.

CAREER: Novelist, short story writer, translator, essayist, and poet. Once taught in France and in Greece; was head of English department at a London college. *Military service:* Royal Marines; became lieutenant.

AWARDS, HONORS: Silver Pen Award from English Centre of International PEN, 1970; W. H. Smith Literary Award, 1970, for *The French Lieutenant's Woman;* Christopher Award, 1982, for *The Tree;* D.Litt., University of Exeter, 1983.

WRITINGS:

The Collector (novel), Little, Brown, 1963.
The Aristos: A Self-Portrait in Ideas, Little, Brown, 1964, revised edition with preface, J. Cape, 1968, revised edition with extended preface, Little, Brown, 1970, 2nd revised edition published as *The Aristos,* J. Cape, 1980.
The Magus (novel; also see below), Little, Brown, 1966, revised edition, 1978.
The French Lieutenant's Woman (novel; also see below), Little, Brown, 1969.
"The Magus" (screenplay, based on Fowles's novel of the same title), Twentieth Century-Fox, 1969.
(Author of introduction, glossary, and appendix) Sabine Baring-Gould, *Mehalah: A Story of the Salt Marshes,* Chatto & Windus, 1969.
Poems, Ecco Press, 1973.
The Ebony Tower (collection of short fiction), Little, Brown, 1974.
Shipwreck, illustrated with photographs by the Gibsons of Scilly, J. Cape, 1974, Little, Brown, 1975.
(Adaptor and translator) *Cinderella,* Little, Brown, 1976.
(Translator) Clairie de Dufort, *Ourika,* W. Thomas Taylor, 1977.
Daniel Martin (novel), Little, Brown, 1977.
Islands, illustrated with photographs by Fay Godwin, Little, Brown, 1978.
The Tree, illustrated with photographs by Frank Hoorat, Aurum Press, 1979, Little, Brown, 1980.
The Enigma of Stonehenge, illustrated with photographs by Barry Brickoff, Summit Books, 1980.
(Author of foreword) Harold Pinter, *The French Lieutenant's Woman: A Screenplay* (based on Fowles's novel of the same title), Little, Brown, 1981.
(Editor) John Aubrey, *Monumenta Brittanica,* Little, Brown, 1982.
Mantissa (novel), Little, Brown, 1982.
A Maggot (novel), Little, Brown, 1985.
(Editor and author of introduction) *Thomas Hardy's England,* Little, Brown, 1985.

Contributor to books and anthologies, including *Afterwords: Novelists on Their Novels,* 1969, and *Britain: A World by Itself: Reflections on the Landscape by Eminent British Writers,* 1984; author of forewords and introductions to several books.

SIDELIGHTS: A drive for freedom dominates John Fowles's career, leading him to investigate it in his themes and to search for it in his own writing. Not only does Fowles refuse to be put into a "cage labelled 'novelist,' " as he says in the 1970 edition of *The Aristos: A Self-Portrait in Ideas,* he also rejects any label limiting him to a particular kind of novel. Fowles's ambition might be, in fact, to write every possible kind of novel before he concludes his career as a writer. This apparent desire explains why each of his new works disappoints some of the people he pleased with his previous books. A characteristic response of disappointment is that of critic Kerry McSweeney who complains in *Critical Quarterly* that Fowles is "more an unfolding than a growing artist." Such a complaint does not recognize the value Fowles places on his own themes of freedom.

A review of Fowles's career helps explain why some readers find him perplexing. Those who enjoyed *The Collector,* Fowles's first novel, as a thriller with a little something added to make it intellectually significant, were puzzled when *The Magus* departed from *The Collector*'s pattern. *The Magus* spread to the length of an "apprentice novel," a form which, like Charles Dickens's *Great Expectations,* usually follows the chronology of a youth's development and is therefore expected to sprawl, unlike the thriller with its tight, compact form. Although Fowles set *The French Lieutenant's Woman* in the 1860s, he clearly did not wish it first to strike the public as an historical novel and then come to be seen as "something more"; instead, the book overtly guides readers into Fowles's method of transforming and recreating established forms for a new era. *The Ebony Tower,* as a book of short works connected thematically to each other and to earlier books, is unusual enough not to challenge this perception. Reissuing *The Magus* was unexpected, but in a new way; it led to comments like those of James Baker, who claims in the Fowles special number of the *Journal of Modern Literature* that the author "has interfered in our critics' work" by revealing matter which "we had not discovered for ourselves."

Furthermore, apparently more concerned about not repeating himself than about avoiding the footsteps of earlier novelists, Fowles wrote *Daniel Martin* in yet another form, the high modernist realistic novel, a form in which the novelist strives to depict psychological reality by such tactics as time shifts, changes in mode and point of view, and stream of consciousness. The form is at least as old as James Joyce, who used it in the early part of this century, and Fowles did nothing in this novel to transform it. And then *Mantissa* again confounds all expectation; a pure allegory set inside a character's head, the work debates contemporary literary theory, dramatizes the conflict between the artist and his inspiration, and emerges as a comedy to boot. As Ian Gotts says in his *Critique: Studies in Modern Fiction* essay, "The appearance of *Mantissa* seems wickedly calculated to frustrate further the efforts of those endeavoring to reach an understanding of Fowles' achievement." Gotts's statement clearly can be applied to the novelist's entire canon.

The driving force for Fowles's constant variation can be found in his central theme: freedom, the question of whether a human being can act independently from the psychological and social pressures of the environment. While this is not his only theme, he says in *The Aristos,* his nonfiction manifesto, that the very "terms of existence encourage us to change, to evolve" if we are to be free; and thus the theme provides a unifying thread.

Fowles's first published work, *The Collector,* is a novel about freedom. Fred Clegg, a lower-class clerk who has won a fortune in a football pool, buys an isolated house and rigs up a basement room as a secret cell for Miranda, a twenty-year-old, upper-middle-class scholarship art student, whom Clegg kidnaps. His depriving Miranda of her freedom instantly highlights freedom's value. All the action of the novel consists of the working out of two lines of freedom, both based on Miranda's response to Clegg's imposition of his illegitimate authority over her. One line is Miranda's tentative, temporary, or pretended acceptance of the imposed authority that wins her small degrees of freedom within the limited boundaries that Clegg will permit. Miranda secures the right to have occasional gulps of fresh air, a sight of the outside at night, a bath now and then, art books, materials for drawing or painting, even the right to try to educate Clegg, to win him over to her way of thinking to persuade him voluntarily to surrender his imposed power over her.

The second line of action consists of Miranda's successive attempts to escape Clegg's control altogether, a struggle that takes on societal and universal human dimensions. The societal dimension is not a struggle between the lower and upper classes; it is, instead, the conflict between the New People and the Few. The New People, of whom Clegg is representative, are the former working class, now equipped with at least a modicum of money and able simultaneously to envy the upper class and ape its attitudes and values. They form a living parody that condemns what it imitates; mimicking the essentials of the upper class but failing to acquire its veneer of manners, furnishings, and accent, they reveal the truth at the heart of the upper-class life style. These New People conflict with the Few—Miranda's group—who stand for creativity, for reaching some level of fulfillment of human potential. Ultimately, the Few try to achieve, in a stifling society, that modicum of free will that is possible if one keeps oneself open. Though already in incipient rebellion against the deadness of her parents' life and marriage, Miranda gets most of her articulation of these points from an older artist named George Patson, a man with whom she is contemplating an affair or possibly even marriage, a marriage that she conceives as different in every way from her parents' upper-class union.

While the imprisonment of a young woman in a locked, windowless room dramatizes lost freedom in *The Collector,* Fowles deals with the issue more subtly and ironically in *The Magus,* a novel on which he had been working for years before interrupting himself to write *The Collector.* Nicholas, the novel's main character who shares the author's Oxford University background, must learn that freedom in a world of psychological and societal influences requires self-knowledge. Although Nicholas has embraced the concepts of existentialism precisely because of their emphasis on the possibility of knowing one's self and acting authentically upon such knowledge, Fowles demonstrates how the character uses them as an almost ironclad defense against self-knowledge. Even his first-person account reveals this flaw; at Oxford student meetings, Nicholas argues with his friends "about being and nothingness and called a certain kind of inconsequential behavior 'existentialist.' Less enlightened people would have called it capricious or just plain selfish." As Peter Wolfe says in *John Fowles: Magus and Moralist,* Nicholas, "unable to protest effectively, . . . compensates by preying sexually on young women." In his selfish affairs with women he verbally "lied very little . . . always careful to make sure that the current victim knew, before she took her clothes off, the difference between coupling and marrying." However, he always hints strongly of love or a loving nature by his nonverbal behavior causing "a certain kind of girl" to fall for him, in a situation that has his escape built in. Nicholas becomes more than usually involved with a woman named Alison, partly because she can teach him sexually but mainly because her innate honesty and ability to cut through to the truth challenge Nicholas's elaborate system of self-delusion.

Frightened by his deepening relationship with Alison and attracted by the adventure of a new setting, Nicholas accepts a job on an isolated Greek island, at an English-style boarding school like that in which Fowles had taught; on the island, Nicholas meets a man named Maurice Conchis, the owner of a villa nicknamed "the waiting room." On his numerous visits to the villa Nicholas encounters "the godgame"—a series of stories told to Nicholas by Conchis of staged events purporting to be supernatural and even of relationships with people whose real identity and motives Nicholas strives to discover. Because Nicholas has left Alison for the godgame, news of her suicide propels him deeply into the experience. The purpose of the godgame—with its intricate parallels to mythology, literature and the Tarot deck of fortune-telling—never becomes completely clear; but its apparent function is to dramatize to Nicholas that reality is chaotic, unpredictable, and hence ultimately unknowable. The godgame's thesis might be that most people spend their lives as if in a waiting room, but a few are selected by hazard—which means more than mere chance—to be elect, that is, to experience the godgame, leading them to better self-knowledge. Hazard, then, is the principle by which an essentially chaotic universe operates.

Twelve years after the first publication of *The Magus,* Fowles's revision appeared. In its foreword, he summarizes his reasons for rewriting the novel: to smooth out aspects that reveal it as the place where "a tyro taught himself to write novels," to correct his past "failure of nerve" by making the sexual content more explicit in two scenes, and to correct the novel's ending.

The French Lieutenant's Woman, which again addresses the issues of freedom starkly dramatized in *The Collector* and more complexly developed in *The Magus,* introduces three new dimensions. While Fowles again depicts characters struggling for physical and psychic liberation, he adds the novel's first new dimension by placing them in the restrictive atmosphere of Victorian England. The second arises from his desire to see his characters freed, not only from society but also from his own control of them as author; in this dimension, the composing process becomes part of the novel's subject. And in a third dimension, Fowles liberates even himself from limitations of the novel form; he devises three separate endings for the novel, making the reader his implied consultant on the creation of the book. The multiple possibilities opened by these tactics reinforce the theme of freedom.

The first dimension the struggle of characters to free themselves from their society centers on Sarah Woodruff, who must deal with the emotional and physical consequences of her unique rebellion. Charles Smithson, the novel's major male figure, learns only through his relationship to Sarah that he too can be free. Fascinated when he first observes Sarah staring intensely out to sea, Charles discovers that she frequently confronts seascapes in this unusual fashion and that she suffers from episodes of severe depression. Her behavior, which suggests her desire for freedom from social restraints, is analyzed through a sequence of assumptions that increasingly allows both Charles and the reader to penetrate more deeply into her mystery.

Charles hears the first assumptions about Sarah's behavior from his fiancée, Ernestina. She repeats gossip that Sarah, a poor governess, had given herself to a man named Varguennes, the French Lieutenant of the title. Ernestina says that Sarah had fallen in love with the man and believed that he loved her, that she had compromised herself with him, and that her strange behavior derived from "madness," an inability to accept that the man had betrayed and abandoned her.

More in line with Fowles's interest in freedom, however, Sarah introduces a second assumption about her motives; she tells Charles that she has not been deceived, finally, by Varguennes;

she gave herself to this man whom she knew did not love her because she wished people to know "that I have suffered, and suffer, as others suffer in every town and village in this land." Sarah implies that her pain arises not from breaking Victorian society's rules but from having for so long followed them. Her "sin" has been an attempt to deal with the severely limited scope allowed by her society, and more importantly, to strike out for greater individual freedom by putting herself "beyond the pale." Because of her action, "I have a freedom," she says, that other women "cannot understand." Her desperate act, she now realizes, has saved her from the certain suicide that she would have faced had she returned unchanged to her obscurity. And when Sarah and Charles make love, Sarah tells him that he has given her the strength to live, in her knowing that he has loved her and that he might have married her but for their world's artificial and absurd prohibitions. However, this very lovemaking disproves all of Charles's assumptions about her motivation and leads the reader, though not Charles, to a third possibility.

Charles discovers when they make love that Sarah is a virgin, which reveals that she has lied to him. Searching for a new explanation, Charles fears that she is simply evil or truly mad, and he departs in anger. Later, Charles reinterprets Sarah's motives: she has been trying to awaken him to the depth of his love for her and to test him. Charles's idea of Sarah's test reaches only part of the truth; more central is the reader's assumption—a partial, questioning assumption about—the mystery of Sarah's behavior: her standing by the sea was *itself* her act of breaking with Victorian society. Not a derivative action resulting from unnarrated events, not a symbol of the freedom to be gained by turning one's back on society, it was the literal act of freedom itself.

In Sarah's mystery lies her attractiveness—to Charles, to the author, and to the reader—and here also lies her freedom from her creator. For if Fowles gives us a definite, final explanation of her motives, he destroys her mystery; she can remain fascinating to the reader only while she remains free of such final delineation. In the novel's second dimension, the metafictional, Fowles insures Sarah's freedom by not revealing *all* about her, by leaving the reader to puzzle over her character only partially emerged from the dark.

By giving characters their freedom, Fowles also liberates himself from the tyranny of the rigid plan; but there remains a more basic limitation of fiction, and from this Fowles frees himself by means of his multiple endings: "The novelist is still a god," Fowles says in this novel, "since he creates (and not even the most aleatory avant-garde modern novel has managed to extirpate its author completely); what has changed is that we are no longer the gods of the Victorian image, omniscient and decreeing; but in the new theological image, with freedom our first principle, not authority." Aleatory means "of uncertain outcome," and its definition in regard to music reveals an important insight: "Using or consisting of sound sequences played at random or arrived at by chance, as by throwing dice." A distinction contained in this definition is crucial: playing notes at random when the spirit moves is not really a chance process but an unconscious one, while playing notes dictated by the throwing of dice is strictly random. In ordering his multiple endings, Fowles claims to have chosen by the truly aleatory method of a coin flip. The novel's third dimension of freedom thus can be labeled "the aleatory."

The novel's first ending comes when Charles decides to go through with his marriage to Ernestina and to put Sarah out of his life. Fowles declares that Charles embraces Ernestina and that they live together ever after, though not happily. Soon, how-

ever, the author admits that what he has been narrating is not what has happened but an embellished version of what Charles has imagined might have happened. And instead, Charles visits Sarah for their first lovemaking.

The relationship between Sarah and Charles provides yet two more possible conclusions for the novel. Complications of the plot soon separate the lovers, but finding Sarah after a three-year search, Charles angrily confronts her with her disappearance. In one coin-flip ending, Charles begins to leave, but she blocks his path to the door and insists he wait a minute, in which a maid carries a small child into the room; Charles realizes that she is his daughter; and subsequent conversation leads to a reconciliation between Sarah and Charles. In another ending, Sarah does not block Charles's path but simply plucks at his sleeve from behind. Consequently he leaves, catching a meaningless glimpse of a maid holding a little girl in her arms as he departs.

These multiple endings merge the three dimensions of freedom in the novel into a single theme. In terms of the characters's freedom from society, Sarah's long wait puts her in a position of choosing whether or not to marry Charles and thereby gives her an independence she would not have had in an immediate marriage to him. Consequently, the equally valid endings to their story reinforce Sarah's victory not only over the restrictions of the life of a poor governess but also over those of a Victorian marriage, even one to Charles. Further, since Fowles uses the dual endings to decline to "fix the fight" between Charles's desires and Sarah's, the endings preserve the characters's freedom from the author. Finally, the multiple endings free Fowles, the author, from the limitations imposed by the form of the novel. He need not take one fork or another; he chooses both—or all. The merging of the three dimensions of freedom into a single theme thus radiates implications for the possibilities of freedom, as no single-track ending would have done, setting up the possibility of further variations on the theme in his next work.

Fowles says in his personal note set in the middle of *The Ebony Tower* that he "meant to suggest variations on both certain themes in previous books of mine and in methods of narrative presentation." Themes and narrative methods combine to weave an intricate pattern of connection, not only with earlier works but among the novella, the translation of a Celtic medieval romance, and the three short stories that make up this collection. In "The Ebony Tower," the novella that gives the book its name, protagonist David Williams visits an old master artist to interview him for a book. David, himself an artist, prepares himself for a harrowing encounter because the crusty "old man" has a well-known aversion to abstract art, David's specialty. At the manor David meets Diana, a young art student who has become the elder artist's assistant. She is unhappy with her life but unable to leave because of a trapped feeling of obligation to her employer and because of the spell that his isolated manor casts over her.

When she turns to David as a possible lover and mentor, variations on Fowles's earlier subjects and themes abound. *The Collector* shows a young woman art student—bound though physically rather than psychologically—to a country estate and to a man who needs her. While Diana receives many more benefits than the heroine of *The Collector,* each young woman looks for comfort in thoughts of an established painter who is young enough to have a true man-woman relationship with her. David's position as a young man entering the domain of an old master, where he meets a young woman who might be available to him, parallels Nicholas's situation at Conchis's villa in *The Magus;* and both Nicholas and David have ties to another woman in their previous lives: Nicholas to Alison, David to his wife, Beth, with whom he has several children. His choice between a conventional situation and an exciting new woman who has problems that he could help solve parallels, as well, the choice faced by Charles in *The French Lieutenant's Woman.* The net effect of Fowles's veiled allusions is to reveal, as Carol Barnum says in *Texas Studies in Literature and Language,* that "Fowles's view of life is not one of despair."

When David hints that he and Diana might live together, she accepts a passionate kiss from him and returns it; he hesitates, and she decides against the affair, remaining adamant when he suggests that they might just sleep together this one night, even though it will solve nothing. As a variation on the freedom themes in earlier books, the situation projects contradictory implications. Fowles could be presenting David as a Charles who is too timid to break free of Ernestina or, in contrast, as a Nicholas wise enough to see that loyalty to an Alison takes precedence over an adventure with a mysterious island girl.

The other works in the book possibly throw light on the novella's conclusion. "Eliduc," a translated Celtic romance, tells the story of a knight who falls in love with a young woman and whose supernaturally understanding wife smoothes his path to marriage to the new woman. Here the likely message is the contrast between Eliduc's wife's reaction and any possible response that Beth, David's wife, might have. Another story, "The Cloud" depicts Paul who rejects a sexual advance by his wife's sister out of loyalty to his wife. The sister is in even deeper trouble than Diana, but her probable suicide at the end is made likely not so much by Paul's hesitation as by her sexual encounter with another character, a man who immediately abandons her after the act to return to his girlfriend. The story's reflection on "The Ebony Tower" would be that David can help Diana by making a commitment to her but only at the expense of Beth and his children; he can leave Diana about as he found her by limiting himself to expressions of regard and friendly advice; or he can hurt her, and probably himself and Beth as well, by sleeping with Diana for a single night. Linking "The Ebony Tower" with the two short stories about the emotional sterility of misspent lives, *The Ebony Tower,* like *The Magus,* takes the reader back to his starting point, the nature of which he can now partly recognize and appreciate for the first time.

David's decision contrasts with that of the central character in *Daniel Martin,* where Fowles tells the story of a man repairing a life damaged by his misuse of privileges that should have permitted him real freedom, a life spent in search of pleasure and success. In his repair, Daniel gives up an affluent but souldraining career as a Hollywood scriptwriter, breaks with his young mistress Jenny, and reconciles with Jane, the woman he should have married years before. Through the many fragmenting time shifts associated with high modernist novels, the reader watches as Daniel returns to write a novel in his boyhood farmhouse, modeled partly upon the one Fowles lived in as a child and partly upon the one in which he now lives and writes. Daniel encounters a problem while drawing the theme for the novel from his own life: the intellectual climate influences one toward a pessimistic outlook, suffused by the emotion of T. S. Eliot's *The Waste Land;* but his own experience has been mostly pampered and pleasing, at least on the surface. "It had become offensive, in an intellectually privileged caste," says Daniel, "to suggest that anything might turn out well in this world. Even when things—largely because of privilege—did in private actually turn out well, one dared not say so artistically." Freedom makes one aware of and emotionally sensitive to the ills of this world, but it simultaneously propels one toward the deep satisfactions of

fulfilling, gratifying, often creative work and makes possible authentic relationships. "In short," Daniel "felt himself, both artistically and really, in the age-old humanist trap: of being allowed (as by some unearned privilege) to enjoy life too much to make a convincing case for any real despair or dissatisfaction."

Since much of what Daniel discovers about himself and his novel also applies to Fowles's novel, *Daniel Martin,* the protagonist's decision to free himself from cultural commands to write pessimistically opens new possibilities: "To hell with cultural fashion; to hell with elitist guilt; to hell with existentialist nausea; and above all, to hell with the imagined that does not say, not only in, but behind the images, the real." This statement apparently reacts against the theme that T. S. Eliot brought to a head in *The Waste Land.* And yet Daniel's decision need not be seen as a complete rejection of Eliot's world view; it could be merely a more encompassing reaction.

When Jane and Daniel lie in bed together for what they think will be the last time, they hear a dog barking: "The wretched dog began barking again somewhere outside, and he thought once more of T. S. Eliot: *oh keep the dog far hence . . .* but couldn't stop to remember how it went on." The next day, when they see the mother dog risk her life to save her pups, the dog's courage inspires Jane to stop running from Daniel's attempt to remake their lives. Their realization that they are free to escape the trap—creating the happy ending—should not have been a surprise had Daniel completed the Eliot quotation. The entire line reads: "O keep the Dog far hence, that's *friend* to men." The waste land may be a dominant symbol for the modern world, but Eliot's poem contains images of the solution as well as of the problem. As Daniel and his creator strive for the "whole sight" caught in the novel's epigraph, *Daniel Martin* accepts the negatives related to freedom—the consequences of failing to attain it, the malaise of misusing it, and the price paid to achieve it— without forgetting the positive potential of freedom, issues with which Fowles deals allegorically in his next major work.

If *Mantissa* is not a pure allegory of the novelist's psychic process, its characters at least have semi-allegorical status; the book is an allegory transformed, in Fowlesian fashion, into a unique personal form. Set entirely inside a skull, the novel embodies a madcap, comic commentary on the creative process and a hilarious debate over the artist's position in the world. *Mantissa* is the novelist's reply to a world that contains both punk rockers and deconstructionist critics. The former look on the literary brand of creativity as square, while the latter reduce the author's role in creating the text to an inconsequentiality. The word "mantissa" in its obsolete sense means an addition of comparatively small importance, especially to a literary effort or discourse; in its modern sense the mantissa is the decimal point in a mathematical logarithm.

The older definition expresses the insignificant role in which the world and contemporary critical theory cast the author; but it also implies that this novel is a light, comic addition to Fowles's effort, of little importance compared to his major novels. In its mathematical definition, the title may suggest Fowles's regret at the increasing transfer of creative energy from art to rational, pseudo-scientific theorizing about art. There may be a subtle irony in Fowles's choice of title; the decimal looks small compared to the numerals in a logarithm, but its position gives it complete leverage over the meaning of the expression.

Fowles establishes the novel's ostensible setting as a hospital room, but the domed shape and bumpy gray padding reveal the room to be the inside of a skull lined with the gray matter of the human brain. Miles Green, a novelist being treated for amnesia, stares uncomprehendingly at a nurse's cradling arms; she shows him a manuscript the way a maternity-ward nurse shows a baby to a mother who was unconscious during its birth. When the nurse reads the opening few words, the "baby" turns out to be *Mantissa,* the writing of which the author, in line with deconstructionist theories that assign him little or no importance, has forgotten. By carrying these critical theories to their logical conclusion and showing that the result is absurd, Fowles refutes the theories. This type of argument, called *reductio ad absurdum,* forms the ironic essence of *Mantissa.* "In *Mantissa,*" says H. W. Fawkner in *The Timescapes of John Fowles,* "Fowles makes fun of the notion that the text writes itself, that the author is nonauthor."

Miles quickly recovers his memory of the text, with the hint that his lack of memory has been a fraud all along. But Miles has a deeper form of amnesia; he has forgotten all of his "frivolous," feminine, sexual, creative aspects and retains only his sense of his social self, his logic, and his masculine vanity. Thinking he is cured, Miles sees the alienated aspects of himself as another person, a woman who appears under a number of masks: as Dr. Delfie, the neuropsychologist who tries to treat him; as the Muse Erato; as a punk rock girl; as a Japanese pleasure girl. Having retained rationality in himself, Miles experiences Erato as a rather brainless, sexually attractive (and active) young woman whom he can treat like a street prostitute. However, he finds that he cannot walk out on Erato as he could on a girl in an ordinary room. He cannot escape from his own mind; Erato and Miles are part of one person.

Because recovering from this deeper amnesia would require the reuniting of these split-off parts, the closest parody of creative wholeness that Erato and Miles can manage is sexual union. At the height of their ecstasy the walls of the hospital room become transparent and any passerby can look in, a symbol for the reader's looking into the author's head by reading his work and seeing the moment when the author's "presentation self" is grappling with his "inspiration"—as private, and perhaps as sexual, a moment as the mutual orgasm of Miles and Erato. The huge number of erotic positions that Miles and Erato say they have tried represents the infinite narrative courses the author can choose, the terrifying freedom of choice among the possibilities that face him on the blank page; it is a freedom from which any author flinches even while he or she cherishes it, as Fawkner has shown. That Erato ultimately wins both the moral and physical battles over Miles, demonstrates the supreme freedom of the creative mind to manifest itself on the printed page. When Miles discovers that Erato was the writer of *The Odyssey,* a work he can never match, he concedes her complete moral ascendancy; and despite his claim that he is cured of amnesia, Erato simply knocks him out with a punch to the jaw, resumes her shape as Dr. Delfie, and continues her treatment of him. The reader finds it hard to believe that she will not continue in command.

Fowles's drive for freedom enters a new phase in *A Maggot:* a testing phase. As in the story "An Enigma" in *The Ebony Tower,* Fowles explores the disappearance in *A Maggot* of an important personage, this time an eighteenth-century duke's younger son rather than a member of the contemporary Parliament. The novel's main female character is Rebecca, known as Fanny in the brothel where she worked. Two men interrogate Rebecca, both claiming the duke's authority and threatening to harm her if she lies. They receive two different tales, the first a tale of magic and witchcraft, and the second even more mystifying. Rebecca claims the events are religious revelations that have led her to repent and join a strict dissenting Protestant sect. The second interrogator, a lawyer for the duke, believes that Rebecca has been cleverly deceived; and Fowles invites the reader to suspect that her tale reveals either space travelers or time travelers, although the science-fiction explanation is by no means the only possibility.

Interpretation of the novel and its characters depends on recognizing the importance of the twins and other family relationships with which the novel resonates. His Lordship, the only name given the disappeared man, has a strained relationship with his father, but to a deaf mute servant he is a "milk-brother": the two were born in the same hour and nursed by the same woman. Their wordless but profound communication contrasts with the total breakdown of communication between father and son. His Lordship and his twin-servant, Dick, seem to be broken halves of one person, Dick being all seething emotion and sexual capacity, His Lordship all dry intellect and impotence.

Family relationships also compound the central episode of Rebecca's tale, which occurs on the strange vehicle that she calls "the Maggot"; there, a television film that His Lordship shows Rebecca depicts three women of varying ages merging together: mother, sister, and daughter (or grandmother, mother, and wife) become one body. Soon the same thing happens with three males: grandfather, father, and husband (or father, brother, and son) become one. Then, Rebecca sees a panorama of Arcadian peace and beauty change suddenly into one of carnage and war. A child runs from a house that soldiers have set on fire; and Rebecca watches the child burn to death. The experience causes her to repent and join a Quaker splinter group. She had previously been barren, but a child conceived with Dick grows up to be Ann Lee, founder of the American community of Shakers, a religious group that grew to prominence in the United States in the early nineteenth century.

In his introduction to *Poems* Fowles explains that he has always found the writing of poetry "an enormous relief from the constant play-acting of fiction. I never pick up a book of poems without thinking . . . I shall know the writer better at the end of it." And indeed, his own poems directly state some of the elements reflected and transformed in his novels: his love of Greece; his doubt about the value of academic creative-writing seminars; his compassion for the urban man, especially the executive; and his pain for a civilization enslaved to machine thinking—and proud of its slavery. All his poems directly reveal these aspects of Fowles's self, a self that is present in his novels but detectable only through the reader's inference.

Fowles's wish to express the whole self—not only the creative self of the novels and poems but also the thinking self—has produced a substantial body of miscellaneous work, including many articles and essays and a series of books, collaborations, and forewords to books. The most substantial and significant of these are *The Aristos* and *The Tree. The Aristos,* taken from the Greek work meaning "the best for a given situation," expresses in dogmatic form ideas that Fowles's novels have embodied. "My chief concern, in *The Aristos,*" the author says in his 1968 preface, "is to preserve the freedom of the individual against those pressures-to-conform that threaten our century." In apparent (but only apparent) contrast, *The Tree* purports to be a mere autobiographical ramble, relating how trees and the woods have been important to him; but he soon clarifies how trees form a perfect metaphor for his idea of his art and its relationship to society. Again, the concept of freedom supplies the linking idea: "There are freedoms in the woods that our ancestors perhaps realized more fully than we do. I used this wood, and even this one particular dell, in *The French Lieutenant's Woman,* for scenes that it seemed to me, in a story of self-liberation, could have no other setting. This is the main reason I see trees, the wood, as the best analogue of prose fiction. All novels are also, in some way, exercises in attaining freedom—even when, at an extreme, they deny the possibility of its existence." Clearly, when Fowles speaks of freedom he affirms its possibility, even while powerfully depicting all of freedom's enemies.

John Fowles's refusal to limit himself opens his work to much of life; he sifts elements of culture, art, and historical experience into such familiar structures as the thriller, the adolescent-learning novel, the historical novel, the book of short fiction, the mainstream modernist novel, the allegory. He always recreates and makes these forms his own, mixing his insight about human beings and life into the transformed structures. Literature and myth enter through the many allusions that he makes central to the movement of the novels. History emerges most noticeably in *The Magus* and *The French Lieutenant's Woman.* Art receives extensive attention in *The Magus* as well as in *The Collector* and *The Ebony Tower.* Fowles also works hard to open his own creative processes to the reader, especially in *The French Lieutenant's Woman* and *Mantissa.* Finally, while all of Fowles's novels make significant social comment and provide insights into human character the way good novels must, his variety of forms opens continual opportunities for new possibilities. Such diversity, although presenting the reader with difficulties of adjustment from novel to novel, surely supplies evidence that Fowles pushes ahead, activated by his own major theme: the drive for freedom.

MEDIA ADAPTATIONS: The Collector was adapted for film by Columbia Pictures in 1965, starring Terence Stamp and Samantha Eggar, and was adapted for the stage and produced in London at the King's Head Theatre in 1971; *The French Lieutenant's Woman,* starring Meryl Streep and Jeremy Irons, was produced by United Artists in 1981.

BIOGRAPHICAL/CRITICAL SOURCES:

BOOKS

Alter, Robert, *Partial Magic: The Novel as a Self-Conscious Genre,* University of California Press, 1975.

Bergonzi, Bernard, *The Situation of the Novel,* University of Pittsburgh Press, 1970.

Bradbury, Malcolm, *Possibilities: Essays on the State of the Novel,* Oxford University Press, 1973.

Conradi, Peter, *John Fowles,* Methuen, 1982.

Contemporary Fiction in America and England, 1950-1970, Gale, 1976.

Contemporary Literary Criticism, Gale, Volume 1, 1973, Volume 2, 1974, Volume 3, 1975, Volume 4, 1975, Volume 6, 1976, Volume 9, 1978, Volume 10, 1979, Volume 15, 1980, Volume 33, 1985.

Dictionary of Literary Biography, Volume 14: *British Novelists since 1960,* Gale, 1983.

Fawkner, H. W., *The Timescapes of John Fowles,* Fairleigh Dickinson University Press, 1984.

Fowles, John, *The Collector,* Little, Brown, 1963.

Fowles, John, *The Aristos: A Self-Portrait in Ideas,* Little, Brown, 1964, revised edition with preface, J. Cape, 1968, revised edition with extended preface, Little, Brown, 1970, 2nd revised edition published as *Aristos,* J. Cape, 1980.

Fowles, John, *The Magus,* Little, Brown, 1966, revised edition, 1978.

Fowles, John, *The French Lieutenant's Woman,* Little, Brown, 1969.

Fowles, John, *Poems,* Ecco Press, 1973.

Fowles, John, *The Ebony Tower,* Little, Brown, 1974.

Fowles, John, *Daniel Martin,* Little, Brown, 1977.

Fowles, John, *The Tree,* Aurum Press, 1979, Little, Brown, 1980.

Fowles, John, *Mantissa,* Little, Brown, 1982.

Fowles, John, *A Maggot,* Little, Brown, 1985.

Hayman, Ronald, *The Novel Today, 1967-75,* Longman, 1976.

Higdon, David L., *Time and English Fiction,* Macmillan, 1977.

Huffaker, Robert, *John Fowles,* Twayne, 1980.

Karl, Frederick R., *A Reader's Guide to the Contemporary English Novel,* Farrar, Straus, 1972.

Kennedy, Alan, *The Protean Self: Dramatic Action in Contemporary Fiction,* Columbia University Press, 1974.

Lodge, David, *Working with Structuralism,* Routledge & Kegan Paul, 1981.

Morris, Robert, editor, *Old Lines, New Forces: Essays on the Contemporary British Novel, 1960-1970,* Associated University Presses, 1976.

Newquist, Roy, editor, *Counterpoint,* Rand McNally, 1964.

Olshen, Barry, *John Fowles,* Ungar, 1978.

Olshen, Barry, and Toni Olshen, *John Fowles: A Reference Guide,* G. K. Hall, 1980.

Palmer, William J., *The Fiction of John Fowles: Tradition, Art, and the Loneliness of Selfhood,* University of Missouri Press, 1974.

Runyon, Randolph, *Fowles/Irving/Barthes: Canonical Variations on an Apocryphal Theme,* Ohio State University Press, 1981.

Scholes, Robert, *Structuralism in Literature: An Introduction,* Yale University Press, 1974.

Scholes, Robert, *Fabulation and Meta-Fiction,* University of Illinois Press, 1979.

Shaffer, E. S., editor, *Comparative Literature: A Yearbook,* Cambridge University Press, 1980.

Wolfe, Peter, *John Fowles: Magus and Moralist,* Bucknell, 1976, revised edition, 1979.

Woodcock, Bruce, *Male Mythologies: John Fowles and Masculinity,* Barnes & Noble, 1984.

PERIODICALS

American Imago, summer, 1972.

Antioch Review, winter, 1969-70.

Ariel, July, 1982.

Best Sellers, November 15, 1969.

Boston Review, February, 1983.

Chicago Tribune, October 29, 1986.

Chicago Tribune Book World, November 2, 1969, August 29, 1982, July 7, 1985.

Christian Century, January 22, 1969.

Christian Science Monitor, December 17, 1969.

Contemporary Literature, winter, 1974, summer, 1975, spring, 1976, fall, 1976.

Contemporary Literature Studies, Volume 17, 1980.

Critical Quarterly, winter, 1973, spring, 1982.

Critique: Studies in Modern Fiction, Volume 20, summer, 1968, Volume 23, number 3, 1972, Volume 31, number 2, 1979.

Detroit Free Press, May 28, 1969.

Encounter, August, 1970, January, 1978.

English Studies in Canada, Volume 3, fall, 1977.

Genre, spring, 1981.

Globe & Mail (Toronto), September 14, 1985, September 21, 1985.

Harper's, July, 1968.

Hollins Critic, December, 1969.

Hudson Review, summer, 1966.

Journal of Modern Literature, April, 1976, Volume 8, number 2, 1980-81.

Journal of Narrative Technique, May, 1973, September, 1973, fall, 1980.

Journal of Popular Culture, fall, 1972, spring, 1976.

Library Journal, January 15, 1965.

Life, May 29, 1970.

Listener, October 31, 1974, October 7, 1982.

London Magazine, March, 1971, March, 1975.

Los Angeles Times, March 16, 1980, November 30, 1980, September 29, 1982.

Los Angeles Times Book Review, July 21, 1985, September 15, 1985, November 6, 1985, September 21, 1986.

Michigan Quarterly Review, spring, 1978.

Modern British Literature, fall, 1978.

Modern Fiction Studies, spring, 1985.

Nation, December 15, 1969, September 13, 1975.

National Observer, January 24, 1966, January 12, 1970.

National Review, December 2, 1969, January 17, 1975.

New Leader, January 5, 1970.

New Literary History, spring, 1973.

New Republic, October 18, 1982, October 7, 1985.

New Review, October, 1974, November, 1977.

New Statesman, June 21, 1963, July 2, 1965, October 11, 1974, November 28, 1986.

Newsweek, November 25, 1974, October 7, 1985.

New York Herald Tribune Book Review, July 28, 1963.

New York Review of Books, December 8, 1977, December 5, 1985.

New York Times, November 10, 1969, September 13, 1977, August 31, 1982, October 5, 1982, September 2, 1985.

New York Times Book Review, January 28, 1963, July 28, 1963, January 9, 1966, November 9, 1969, November 10, 1974, September 25, 1977, November 13, 1977, March 19, 1978, March 30, 1980, August 29, 1982, September 8, 1985, October 5, 1986.

Notes on Contemporary Literature, March, 1971, November, 1982.

Publishers Weekly, September 30, 1963.

Rocky Mountain Review of Language and Literature, spring, 1975.

Saturday Review, July 27, 1963, October 1, 1977.

Southern Review, winter, 1973.

Spectator, June 14, 1970, November 16, 1974, September 21, 1985.

Sports Illustrated, December, 1970.

Stand, Volume 16, number 3, 1975.

Stockholm Studies in English, Volume 46, 1978.

Studies in Humanities, December, 1978.

Studies in Short Fiction, winter, 1983.

Texas Studies in Literature and Language, spring, 1982.

Time, November 20, 1964, January 14, 1966, December 2, 1974, September 27, 1982, September 9, 1985.

Times (London), April 22, 1985, September 19, 1985.

Times Literary Supplement, May 17, 1963, June 12, 1969, December 6, 1974, April 17, 1981, October 8, 1982, September 20, 1985.

Twentieth Century Literature, Volume 19, 1973, Volume 28, 1982.

Victorian Studies, March, 1972.

Village Voice, September 12, 1977, February 20, 1978.

Village Voice Literary Supplement, September, 1982.

Virginia Quarterly Review, spring, 1970.

Washington Post, December 11, 1974.

Washington Post Book World, November 23, 1980, February 14, 1982, September 19, 1982, September 8, 1985, December 8, 1985, September 14, 1986.

West Coast Review, October, 1975.

World Literature Today, summer, 1986.

Yale Review, spring, 1970.

*　　　*　　　*

FOX, Paula 1923-

PERSONAL: Born April 22, 1923, in New York, NY; daughter of Paul Hervey (a writer) and Elsie (de Sola) Fox; married Richard Sigerson in 1948 (divorced, 1954); married Martin Greenberg, June 9, 1962; children: (first marriage) Adam, Gabriel. *Education:* Attended Columbia University, 1955-58.

ADDRESSES: Home—Brooklyn, NY. *Agent*—Robert Lescher, 155 East 71st St., New York, NY 10021.

CAREER: Author. Worked in Europe for a year as a reporter for a news agency. University of Pennsylvania, Philadelphia, professor of English literature, beginning 1963.

MEMBER: P.E.N., Authors League of America, Authors Guild.

AWARDS, HONORS: Finalist in National Book Award children's book category, 1971, for *Blowfish Live in the Sea;* National Institute of Arts and Letters Award, 1972; Guggenheim fellow, 1972; Newbery Medal, 1974, for *The Slave Dancer;* Hans Christian Andersen Medal, 1978; National Book Award nomination, 1979, for *The Little Swineherd and Other Tales;* American Book Award, 1983, for *A Place Apart;* Christopher Award and Newbery Honor Book, both 1985, for *One-Eyed Cat;* fiction citation, Brandeis University, 1984; *Boston Globe*/Horn Book Award for fiction and Newbery Honor Book, 1989, for *The Village by the Sea.*

WRITINGS:

FOR CHILDREN

Maurice's Room, illustrated by Ingrid Fetz, Macmillan, 1966.

A Likely Place, illustrated by Edward Ardizzone, Macmillan, 1967.

How Many Miles to Babylon?, illustrated by Paul Giovanopoulos, David White, 1967.

The Stone-Faced Boy, illustrated by Donald A. Mackay, Bradbury, 1968.

Dear Prosper, illustrated by Steve McLachlin, David White, 1968.

Portrait of Ivan, illustrated by Saul Lambert, Bradbury, 1969.

The King's Falcon, illustrated by Eros Keith, Bradbury, 1969.

Hungry Fred, illustrated by Rosemary Wells, Bradbury, 1969.

Blowfish Live in the Sea, Bradbury, 1970.

Good Ethan, illustrated by Arnold Lobel, Bradbury, 1973.

The Slave Dancer, illustrated by Keith, Bradbury, 1973.

The Little Swineherd and Other Tales, Dutton, 1978.

A Place Apart, Farrar, Straus, 1980.

One-Eyed Cat, Bradbury, 1984.

The Moonlight Man, Bradbury, 1986.

Lily and the Lost Boy, Orchard Books, 1987, published in England as *The Lost Boy,* Dent, 1988.

The Village by the Sea, Orchard Books, 1988.

ADULT NOVELS

Poor George, Harcourt, 1967.

Desperate Characters, Harcourt, 1970, reprinted with an afterword by Irving Howe, Nonpareil, 1980.

The Western Coast, Harcourt, 1972.
The Widow's Children, Dutton, 1976.
A Servant's Tale, North Point Press, 1984.
The God of Nightmares, North Point Press, 1990.

SIDELIGHTS: Paula Fox "is not a writer who could be content to mine a single narrow seam," according to John Rowe Townsend in *A Sounding of Storytellers: New and Revised Essays on Contemporary Writers for Children.* Fox is the author of novels for both children and adults, and although she is better known for her award-winning children's books, she has also been described by *Nation* contributor Blair T. Birmelin as "one of our most intelligent (and least appreciated) contemporary novelists." Fox's success in both genres is attributable, perhaps, to the fact that "she does not claim to understand what constitutes the difference between them," explains Townsend in *A Sense of Story: Essays on Contemporary Writers for Children.* "Like many other writers, she raises the question 'For whom?', and as with many other writers I can find no answer except 'For whom it may concern'." Fox herself comments in *A Sense of Story,* "I never think I'm writing for children, when I work. A story does not start *for* anyone, nor an idea, nor a feeling of an idea; but starts more for oneself."

Fox's juvenile novels have a complexity and sincerity that make them popular with readers and critics alike. As Anne Tyler comments in the *New York Times Book Review:* "In Paula Fox's twenty-odd years of writing for children, she has distinguished herself as a teller of mingled tales. Let other authors underestimate their young readers' intelligence however they will, creating entirely villainous villains and entirely heroic heroes—but Miss Fox trusts that even children know life is a complex, inconclusive, intriguingly gray-toned affair." Alice Bach states a similar opinion in a *Horn Book* essay: "Fox expresses her respect for children by never diminishing the events of their lives nor sentimentalizing their responses. Her novels written for children resound with the integrity and conviction of her novels for adults."

Fox's novels for children cover a wide range of subjects, including parental conflict, alcoholism, and death. Frequently, her young protagonists undertake a journey that is symbolic of emotional development. In *Blowfish Live in the Sea,* for example, nineteen-year-old Ben travels from New York to Boston to see his estranged father after a twelve-year absence. Although the novel is primarily concerned with Ben, it is told from the viewpoint of his adoring stepsister Carrie, who accompanies him to Boston. Carrie is upset when Ben withdraws from the family, communicating only by inscribing on every available surface "Blowfish live in the sea." This compulsion, the story later reveals, is the result of a lie his father once told him.

The importance of Ben and Carrie's journey to Boston, explains a *Horn Book* reviewer, is that "each step . . . relays something further in their tenuous gropings towards an understanding of themselves and of others." Carrie realizes that for Ben, who has been restrained by "the conventional atmosphere of their home, the disreputable [father] represents both escape and the renewal of a bond," notes Zena Sutherland in *Saturday Review.* Ben's understanding entails forgiving his father and deciding to stay with him to help him with his latest money-making venture: renovating a seedy motel. Observes Townsend in *A Sounding of Storytellers:* "We leave Ben starting on the carpentry, keeping his father off the drink; we don't know how long it will last, but we know it is something positive for Ben at last and will be the making of him."

In *The Slave Dancer,* one of Fox's most controversial children's novels, a New Orleans boy is kidnapped and placed on a slave ship bound for West Africa. The boy, Jessie Bollier, is chosen for his ability to play the fife; his task aboard ship is to "dance" the slaves so they can exercise their cramped limbs. The book was awarded the Newbery Medal in 1974 and was subsequently criticized by some reviewers for reasons that range from the dehumanizing portrayal of the slaves to the author's emphasis on the role the Africans themselves played in the slave trade. Binnie Tate, for example, comments in *Interracial Books for Children:* "Through the characters' words, [Fox] excuses the captors and places the blame for the slaves' captivity on Africans themselves. The author slowly and systematically excuses almost all the whites in the story for their participation in the slave venture and by innuendo places the blame elsewhere." Another *Interracial Books for Children* contributor, Albert V. Schwartz, observes that the slaves are depicted "as a passive, faceless mass to show their oppression." He adds that while "the device is effective sometimes in creating pity and sentimentality, . . . it is still dehumanizing, and that is a major flaw."

Other reviewers, however, view *The Slave Dancer* as a fair and humane treatment of a sensitive subject. In a *Horn Book* essay, Alice Bach calls the book "one of the finest examples of a writer's control over her material. . . . With an underplayed but implicit sense of rage, Paula Fox exposes the men who dealt in selling human beings." *The Slave Dancer,* concludes Kevin Crossley-Holland in the *New Statesman,* is "a novel of great moral integrity. . . . From start to finish Miss Fox tells her story quietly and economically; she is candid but she never wallows."

Another of Fox's award-winning children's novels is *A Place Apart,* a book that "depends on subtleties of characterisation . . . rather than on an arresting plot," according to *New Statesman* contributor Patricia Craig. The novel concerns Victoria Finch, a thirteen-year-old girl whose comfort and security are shaken when her father dies suddenly. His death leaves Victoria and her mother in financial difficulty, and they are forced to move from their Boston home to a smaller one in the suburbs.

Victoria's grief, writes *Washington Post Book World* contributor Katherine Paterson, "is the bass accompaniment to the story. Sometimes it swells, taking over the narrative, the rest of the time it subsides into a dark, rhythmic background against which the main story is played." Victoria must also come to terms with her infatuation with Hugh, a manipulative boy who "exerts . . . a power over her spirit," according to Paterson. This relationship compels Victoria "to explore the difficult terrain between the desire for closeness and the tendency to 'make ourselves a place apart,' " observes Jean Strouse in *Newsweek.*

Although *A Place Apart* belongs to the popular genre of books about troubled adolescents, Paterson notes that Victoria is "a real person, bearing very little resemblance to the breezy kid narrators who people most young adult fiction." Similarly, Anne Tyler writes in the *New York Times Book Review* that *A Place Apart* is "a story without gimmicks or exaggerations. [Fox] writes a honed prose, avoiding all traces of a gee-whillikers tone, and her language is simple and direct." Tyler concludes, " 'A Place Apart' is a book apart—quiet-voiced, believable and often very moving."

Fox's adult novels are "concerned with the cataclysmic moments of private lives, and the quiet desperation of ordinary people," writes Linda Simon in *Commonweal.* Her characters, observes Darryl Pinckney in the *New York Review of Books,* "are oddballs, restless without being rebellious. . . . They miss crucial pieces of the puzzle and yet are not altogether blameless for the shabby luck that awaits them behind every wrong door."

In her second adult novel, *Desperate Characters,* for instance, Fox portrays Sophie and Otto Bentwood, a childless couple in their mid-forties "facing the abstract menace of a world perhaps they helped through inadvertence to create," writes John Leonard in the *New York Times.* The Bentwoods live in a renovated Brooklyn townhouse amid the squalor of a slum. Their home is so close to the poor neighborhood that they can feel "the hatred that drives toward them from the slum streets crowding close against the end wall of their elegant little backyard," writes a *New Yorker* reviewer.

While the Bentwoods' marriage is described by *New York Times Book Review* contributor Peter Rowley as "if not dead, at best warring," they are content with their orderly, comfortable lives. As the novel progresses, however, their security is gradually encroached upon. "Sophie and Otto . . . are slowly revealed to be menaced by forces . . . giving off a growl of danger all the more ominous for being so essentially nameless and faceless and vague," observes Pearl K. Bell in the *New Leader.* These menacing forces—"the symptoms of modern desperation" according to a *Newsweek* critic—include the vandalization of the Bentwoods' summer home and Sophie's being bitten by a stray cat that she is trying to befriend.

Desperate Characters, writes Thomas Lask in the *New York Times,* proves "that it is impossible to build an oasis of greenery in a sea of misery." Similarly, a *Newsweek* critic comments that the novel "takes as axiomatic that life in the city is almost intolerable. Not because the streets are dirty, but because some craziness is epidemic behind the locked doors." Concludes Bell: "*Desperate Characters* is a small masterpiece, a revelation of contemporary New York middle-class life that grasps the mind of the reader with the subtle clarity of metaphor and the alarmed tenacity of nightmare."

In her fourth adult novel, *The Widow's Children,* Fox again chronicles the desperation and confusion of modern life. In observation of the classical unities, the novel takes place in and around New York City within a period of twenty-four hours. *The Widow's Children* centers on the Maldonada family, whom *Saturday Review* contributor Lynne Sharon Schwartz describes as "a portent of imminent social breakdown." The matriarch of the family, Alma, is despised by her three children and a grandchild for raising them in poverty and disorder. They are all emotionally scarred in some way from their childhood, particularly Laura, an abrasive, selfish woman. When Laura is informed of Alma's death on the eve of a family party she is hosting, she withholds the information from her siblings and daughter until the end of the night. "This concealed event," writes Peter S. Prescott in *Newsweek,* "charges the evening with electricity."

Though the Maldonadas blame Alma for their emotionlessness, Christopher Lehmann-Haupt comments in the *New York Times* that "there is no simple way to account for the striking ambivalence of the characters' feelings for one another, the extraordinary degree to which they oscillate between affection and hatred without ever quite arriving at either." Their ambivalence and unhappiness makes the Maldonadas seem more like automatons than vital characters, according to several reviewers. "It is the fictionist's old problem of how to show deadness without making the book itself dead," writes Norma Rosen in the *New York Times Book Review.* "Only Laura, eaten with demented rage, throws off enough sparks to stir the air." Expressing a similar opinion, a *New Yorker* critic observes that Fox "has battened down each character so tightly in his or her misery that they all seem like dead souls—almost beyond comprehension or curiosity."

While reviewers laud Fox's polished prose and technical expertise, they also suggest that in her quest for artistic perfection she may alienate the reader from *The Widow's Children. Washington Post Book World* contributor William McPherson, for instance, writes: "It is quite possible to admire Paula Fox's style and to appreciate her talent without feeling much more affection for this novel than its characters feel for one another or for themselves, which is very little indeed." Prescott comments that "most readers of novels want to be entertained, not subjected to art. For them, art without entertainment is difficulty." Comparing Fox to a cave explorer, Prescott writes that her searchlight "makes pleasing patterns, but there's not much room for an audience. . . . Fox's brilliance has a masochistic aspect: I will do this so well, she seems to say, that you will hardly be able to read it." While *New Republic* contributor Edith Milton concurs that *The Widow's Children* is "sometimes unpleasant to read," she adds that "it is also the most elegant exploration I have read of the chaos of modern life, and of the inertia and deprivations on which that chaos rests."

BIOGRAPHICAL/CRITICAL SOURCES:

BOOKS

Children's Literature Review, Volume 1, Gale, 1976.
Contemporary Literary Criticism, Gale, Volume 2, 1974, Volume 8, 1978.
Dictionary of Literary Biography, Volume 52: *American Writers for Children since 1960: Fiction,* Gale, 1986.
Townsend, John Rowe, *A Sense of Story: Essays on Contemporary Writers for Children,* Lippincott, 1971, revised and enlarged edition published as *A Sounding of Storytellers: New and Revised Essays on Contemporary Writers for Children,* 1979.

PERIODICALS

Commonweal, January 11, 1985.
Horn Book, December, 1970, October, 1977.
Interracial Books for Children, Volume 5, number 5, 1974.
Los Angeles Times, November 21, 1987.
Ms., October, 1984.
Nation, November 3, 1984.
New Leader, February 2, 1970.
New Republic, January 15, 1977.
New Statesman, November 8, 1974, December 4, 1981.
Newsweek, March 16, 1970, September 27, 1976, December 1, 1980.
New Yorker, February 7, 1970, November 1, 1976.
New York Review of Books, October 5, 1972, October 28, 1976, June 27, 1985.
New York Times, February 10, 1970, September 22, 1972, September 16, 1976.
New York Times Book Review, February 1, 1970, October 8, 1972, October 3, 1976, November 9, 1980, July 12, 1981, November 11, 1984, November 18, 1984, July 8, 1990.
Publishers Weekly, April 6, 1990.
Saturday Review, January 23, 1971, October 16, 1976.
Time, October 4, 1976.
Times Literary Supplement, February 21, 1986, November 28, 1986.
Washington Post, June 7, 1990.
Washington Post Book World, October 31, 1976, February 8, 1981, September 23, 1984.

FRAME, Janet
    See CLUTHA, Janet Paterson Frame

                    *   *   *

FRANCE, Anatole
    See THIBAULT, Jacques Anatole Francois

                    *   *   *

FRANCIS, Dick   1920-

PERSONAL: Born October 31, 1920, in Tenby, Wales; son of George Vincent and Molly (Thomas) Francis; married Mary Brenchley, June 21, 1947; children: Merrick, Felix. *Education:* Attended Maidenhead County School.

ADDRESSES: Home—5100 North Ocean Blvd., #609, Fort Lauderdale, Fla. 33308.

CAREER: Amateur steeplechase rider, 1946-48; professional steeplechase jockey, 1948-57; *Sunday Express,* London, England, racing correspondent, 1957-73; writer. Exercises racehorses in winter; judges hunters at horse shows in summer. *Military service:* Royal Air Force, 1940-46; became flying officer (pilot).

MEMBER: Crime Writers Association.

AWARDS, HONORS: Steeplechase jockey championship, 1954; Silver Dagger Award from Crime Writers Association, 1965, for *For Kicks;* Edgar Allan Poe Award from Mystery Writers of America, 1969, for *Forfeit,* and 1980, for *Whip Hand;* Gold Dagger Award from Crime Writers Association, 1980, for *Whip Hand;* Order of the British Empire, 1984.

WRITINGS:

MYSTERY NOVELS, EXCEPT AS INDICATED

The Sport of Queens (racing autobiography), M. Joseph, 1957, reprinted, Warner, 1986.
Dead Cert, Holt, 1962.
Nerve, Harper, 1964.
For Kicks, Harper, 1965.
Odds Against, M. Joseph, 1965, Harper, 1966.
(Compiler with John Welcome) *Best Racing and Chasing Stories* (anthology), Faber, 1966.
Flying Finish, M. Joseph, 1966, Harper, 1967.
Blood Sport, Harper, 1967.
Forfeit, Harper, 1968.
Enquiry, Harper, 1969.
Rat Race, Harper, 1970.
Bonecrack, Harper, 1971.
Smokescreen, Harper, 1972.
Slayride, Harper, 1973.
Knock Down, Harper, 1974.
High Stake, Harper, 1975.
In the Frame, Harper, 1976.
Risk, Harper, 1977.
Trial Run, Harper, 1978.
Whip Hand, Harper, 1979.
Reflex, M. Joseph, 1980, Putnam, 1981.
Twice Shy, M. Joseph, 1981, Putnam, 1982.
Banker, M. Joseph, 1982, Putnam, 1983.
The Danger, M. Joseph, 1983, Putnam, 1984.
Proof, M. Joseph, 1984, Putnam, 1985.
Break In, M. Joseph, 1985, Putnam, 1986.
A Jockey's Life: The Biography of Lester Piggott, Putnam, 1986 (published in England as *Lester, the Official Biography,* M. Joseph, 1986).

Bolt, M. Joseph, 1986, Putnam, 1987.
Hot Money, M. Joseph, 1987, Putnam, 1988.
The Edge, M. Joseph, 1988, Putnam, 1989.
Straight, Putnam, 1989.
Longshot, Putnam, 1990.

Contributor to *Horseman's Year, In Praise of Hunting, Stud and Stable,* and other magazines.

SIDELIGHTS: When steeplejockey Dick Francis retired from horseracing at age thirty-six, he speculated in his autobiography that he would be remembered as "the man who didn't win the National," England's prestigious Grand National steeplechase. If he hadn't turned to fiction, his prediction might have been correct, but with the publication of his first novel, *Dead Cert,* in 1962, Francis launched a second career that was even more successful than his first: he became a mystery writer.

Since that time, Francis has averaged a thriller a year, astounding critics with the fecundity of his imagination and garnering awards such as Britain's Silver Dagger (in 1965 for *For Kicks*) and two Edgars (for *Forfeit* in 1969 and *Whip Hand* in 1980). Since most of his books concern horses, racing still figures in his life, and his affinity for the racetrack actually enhances his prose, according to Julian Symons, who writes in the *New York Times Book Review* that "what comes most naturally to [Francis] is also what he does best—writing about the thrills, spills and chills of horse racing."

Before he began writing, Francis experienced one of racing's most publicized "spills" firsthand. In 1956, when he was already a veteran jockey, Francis had the privilege of riding Devon Loch—the Queen Mother's horse—in the annual Grand National. Fifty yards from the finish line, with the race virtually won, the horse inexplicably faltered. Later examination revealed no physical injury and no clue was ever found. "I still don't have the answer," Francis told Pete Axthelm of *Newsweek.* "Maybe he was shocked by the noise of 250,000 people screaming because the royal family's horse was winning. But the fact is that with nothing wrong with him, ten strides from the winning post he fell. The other fact is," he added, "if that mystery hadn't happened, I might never have written all these other ones."

Though each of his novels deals with what many consider a specialized subject, Francis's books have broad appeal. One explanation, offered by Judith Rascoe in the *Christian Science Monitor,* is that "you needn't know or care anything about racing to be his devoted reader." And, writing in the *New York Times,* book reviewer John Leonard agrees: "Not to read Dick Francis because you don't like horses is like not reading Dostoyevsky because you don't like God. Race tracks and God are subcultures. A writer has to have a subculture to stand upon."

Francis's ability to make this subculture come alive for his reader—to create what Rascoe calls "a background of almost Dickensian realism for his stories"—is what sets him apart from other mystery writers. "In particular," observes Charles Champlin in the *Los Angeles Times,* "his rider's view of the strains and spills, disappointments and exultations of the steeplechase is breathtaking, a far cry from the languid armchair detecting of other crime solvers." Writing in the *London Magazine,* John Welcome expresses similar admiration, praising especially Francis's ability to infuse his races with a significance that extends beyond the Jockey Club milieu: "One can hear the smash of birch, the creak of leather and the rattle of whips. The sweat, the strain, the tears, tragedies and occasional triumphs of the racing game are all there, as well as its seductive beauty. In this—as in much else—no other racing novelist can touch him. He has made racing into a microcosm of the contemporary world.''

While critics initially speculated that Francis's specialized knowledge would provide only limited fictional opportunities, most have since changed their minds. "It is fascinating to see how many completely fresh and unexpected plots he can concoct about horses," marvels Anthony Boucher in the *New York Times Book Review.* Philip Pelham takes this approbation one step further, writing in *London Magazine* that "Francis improves with every book as both a writer of brisk, lucid prose and as a concocter of ingenious and intricately worked-out plots." His racetrack thrillers deal with such varied storylines as crooks transporting horses by air (*Flying Finish*), stolen stallions (*Blood Sport*), and a jockey who has vanished in Norway (*Slayride*). To further preserve the freshness of his fiction, Francis creates a new protagonist for each novel and often develops subplots around fields unrelated to racing. "His books," notes Axthelm, "take him and his readers on global explorations as well as into crash courses in ventures like aviation, gold mining and, in *Reflex,* amateur photography."

Notwithstanding such variations in plot and theme, Francis is known as a formula writer whose novels, while well-written, are ultimately predictable. In all the Francis novels, writes John Welcome, "the hard-done-by chap [is] blindly at grips with an unknown evil, the threads of which he gradually unravels. Frequently—perhaps too frequently—he is subjected to physical torture described in some detail. His heroes are hard men used to injury and pain and they learn to dish it out as once they had to learn to take it. Racing has made them stoics."

Barry Bauska, writing in the *Armchair Detective,* offers a more detailed version of the "typical" Francis thriller: "At the outset something has happened that looks wrong (a jockey is set down by a board of inquiry that seemed predetermined to find him guilty; a horse falls going over a final hurdle it had seemed to clear; horses perfectly ready to win consistently fail to do so). The narrator protagonist (usually not a detective, but always inherently curious) begins to poke around to try to discover what has occurred. In so doing he inevitably pokes too hard and strikes a hornets' nest. The rest of the novel then centers on a critical struggle between the searcher-after-truth and the mysterious agent of evil, whose villainy had upset things in the first place."

While a number of Francis's books include a love story, a much more pressing theme, according to Pete Axthelm, is that of pain. "Again and again," he writes in *Newsweek,* the author's "villains probe the most terrifying physical or psychic weakness in his heroes. A lifetime's most treasured mementos are destroyed by mindless hired thugs; an already crippled hand is brutally smashed until it must be amputated. The deaths in Francis novels usually occur 'off-camera.' The tortures are more intimate affairs, with the reader forced to watch at shudderingly close range."

The prevalence of such violence, coupled with Francis's tendency to paint the relationship between hero and villain as a confrontation between good and evil, makes some reviewers uneasy. In his *Times Literary Supplement* review of *Risk,* for example, Alex de Jong comments that "characterization is sometimes thin and stylized, especially the villains, out to inflict pain upon the accountant who has uncovered their villainy, crooked businessmen and trainers, all a little too well dressed, florid and unexpectedly brutal bullies, created with a faint hint of paranoia." Francis, however, justifies the punishment he metes out to his characters as something his fans have come to expect. "Some-

how the readers like to read about it," he told Judy Klemesrud in the *New York Times Book Review.* "But I don't subject them to anything I wouldn't put up with myself. This old body has been knocked around quite a bit."

While the violence of his early novels is largely external, his later novels emphasize more internal stress, according to critics who believe that this shift has added a new dimension to Francis's work. *London Magazine*'s John Welcome, for instance, comments that in *Reflex,* a 1980 publication, Francis's lessened emphasis on brutality has enabled him to "flesh out his characters. The portrait of Philip More, the mediocre jockey nearing the end of his career, is created with real insight; as is the interpretation of his relations with the horses he rides." And, writing in the *Armchair Detective,* Barry Bauska expresses a similar view: "In recent years, though the plots may run along similar lines, Francis' focus has been increasingly directed at the protagonist himself, and at considering what goes into the making not so much of a 'hero' as of a good man. This line seems plainly the direction of Francis' future development as a novelist. In such works survival is still a key concept—everyone lives on a precipice—but it is no longer the ability/capacity to endure the villain's tortures, but rather the strength to prevail over one's own self doubts and private fears. Surely it is not mere coincidence that as a focus of tension physical pain is being supplanted by psychological strains as Mr. Francis himself grows farther and farther away from his riding days. The result of course is that Dick Francis is becoming less a writer of thrillers and more a creator of literature."

MEDIA ADAPTATIONS: Dead Cert was filmed by United Artists in 1973; *Odds Against* was the basis for a 1979 Yorkshire Television series called "The Racing Game."

AVOCATIONAL INTERESTS: Boating, fox hunting, tennis.

BIOGRAPHICAL/CRITICAL SOURCES:

BOOKS

Bestsellers 89, Issue 3, Gale, 1989.
Contemporary Literary Criticism, Gale, Volume 2, 1974, Volume 22, 1982, Volume 42, 1987.
Francis, Dick, *The Sport of Queens,* M. Joseph, 1957.

PERIODICALS

Armchair Detective, July, 1978.
Christian Science Monitor, July 17, 1969.
Family Circle, July, 1970.
Globe and Mail (Toronto), November 16, 1985, August 12, 1989.
London Magazine, February-March, 1975, March, 1980, February-March, 1981.
Los Angeles Times, March 27, 1981, April 9, 1982, September 12, 1984.
Newsweek, April 6, 1981.
New Yorker, March 15, 1969.
New York Times, March 6, 1969, April 7, 1971, March 20, 1981, December 18, 1989.
New York Times Book Review, March 21, 1965, March 10, 1968, March 16, 1969, June 8, 1969, July 26, 1970, May 21, 1972, July 27, 1975, September 28, 1975, June 13, 1976, July 10, 1977, May 20, 1979, June 1, 1980, March 29, 1981, April 25, 1982, February 12, 1989.
New York Times Magazine, March 25, 1984.
Time, March 11, 1974, July 14, 1975, May 31, 1976, July 7, 1978, May 11, 1981.
Times (London), December 18, 1986.

Times Literary Supplement, October 28, 1977, October 10, 1980,
    December 10, 1982.
U.S. News and World Report, March 28, 1988.
Washington Post, October 3, 1986.
Washington Post Book World, April 30, 1972, February 18, 1973,
    April 19, 1980, April 18, 1982, March 27, 1983, February
    21, 1988, February 5, 1989.

*   *   *

FRANK, Anne(lies Marie) 1929-1945

PERSONAL: Born June 12, 1929, in Frankfort on the Main,
Germany (now West Germany); died of typhoid fever and malnutrition in March, 1945, in the Bergen-Belsen concentration
camp near Belgen, Germany (now West Germany); daughter of
Otto (banker and business owner) and Edith Frank.

ADDRESSES: 263 Prinsengracht, Amsterdam, Netherlands.

WRITINGS:

Het achterhuis (diary; foreword by Annie Romein-Verschoor),
    Contact (Amsterdam), 1947, translation from Dutch by B.
    M. Mooyaart-Doubleday published as *Diary of a Young
    Girl,* introduction by Eleanor Roosevelt, Doubleday, 1952;
    with new preface by George Stevens, Pocket Books, 1958;
    published as *Anne Frank: The Diary of a Young Girl,* Wash-
    ington Square Press, 1963; published as *The Diary of Anne
    Frank,* foreword by Storm Jameson, illustrations by Elisa-
    beth Trimby, Heron Books, 1973; published as *The Diary
    of Anne Frank: The Critical Edition,* edited by David
    Barnouw and Gerrold van der Stroom, translated by Ar-
    nold J. Pomerans and B. M. Mooyaart-Doubleday, intro-
    duction by Harry Paape, Gerrold van der Stroom, and
    David Barnouw, Doubleday, 1989.
The Works of Anne Frank, introduction by Ann Birstein and Al-
    fred Kazin, Doubleday, 1959 (also see below).
*Tales From the House Behind: Fables, Personal Reminiscences,
    and Short Stories,* translation from original Dutch manu-
    script, *Verhalen rondom het achterhuis,* by H. H. B. Mos-
    berg and Michel Mok, World's Work, 1962; with drawings
    by Peter Spier, Pan Books, 1965 (also see below).
Anne Frank's Tales From the Secret Annex, with translations
    from original manuscript, *Verhaaltjes en gebeurtenissen uit
    het Achterhuis,* by Ralph Manheim and Michel Mok,
    Doubleday, 1983 (portions previously published in *The
    Works of Anne Frank* and *Tales From the House Behind*).

The diary has been translated into many languages, including
German, French, Italian, Spanish, Russian, and Polish.

MEDIA ADAPTATIONS: Frances Goodrich and Albert Hackett adapted *Anne Frank: Diary of a Young Girl* for a two-act
stage play titled *Diary of Anne Frank,* first produced in New
York, 1955, and published with a foreword by Brooks Atkinson,
Random House, 1956. The diary was also adapted for the film
The Diary of Anne Frank, released by Twentieth Century-Fox,
1959, and a television movie of the same name, starring Melissa
Gilbert, 1980. Selections of the diary were read by Julie Harris
for a recording by Spoken Arts, 1974, and by Claire Bloom for
a recording by Caedmon, 1977.

SIDELIGHTS: Anne Frank, a victim of the Holocaust during
World War II, became known throughout the world through her
eloquent diary, describing the two years she and seven others hid
from Nazis in an attic above her father's business office in Amsterdam. In the diary Anne relates the fear of being discovered
and the aggravations of life in hiding as well as the feelings and
experiences of adolescence that are recognized by people everywhere. Anne received the first notebook as a present from her
parents on her thirteenth birthday in 1942, about a month before
the family went into hiding. She wrote in the diary until the discovery of the hiding place in August, 1944. Anne's father, Otto
Frank, the only one of them to survive the concentration camps
to which they were sent, agreed to publish the diary in 1946.

Since then, Anne has been for many people a source of inspiration, a model of courage, and a symbol of the persecution, tragic
suffering, and loss of life inflicted by the Nazis. Meyer Levin declared in the *New York Times Book Review,* "Because the diary
was not written in retrospect, it contains the trembling life of
every moment—Anne Frank's voice becomes the voice of six
million vanished Jewish souls." This is not because there were
no other journals found from that time. Upon reading a copy of
Anne's diary in 1946, Jan Romein declared in the Dutch newspaper *Het Parool:* "The Government Institute for War Documentation is in possession of about two hundred similar diaries, but
it would amaze me if there was *one* among them as pure, as intelligent, and yet as human as [Anne's]."

The Franks moved from Frankfort, Germany—where Anne was
born—to Amsterdam in 1933 after Germany ruled that Jewish
and German children had to attend segregated schools. In July,
1942, after Anne's sister Margot received notice to report to the
Dutch Nazi organization, the Franks immediately went into hiding in the "Secret Annex," as Anne dubbed the attic of the Amsterdam warehouse. Soon after, Mr. and Mrs. Frank and their
two girls welcomed Mr. and Mrs. Van Daan (pseudonymous
names used by Anne) and their son Peter into their rooms, and
lastly Mr. Dussel, an elderly dentist. In an entry about her family's flight into hiding, Anne wrote that the diary was the first
thing she packed. It meant a great deal to her; she viewed the
diary as a personal friend and confidant, as she remarked June
20, 1942, in a reflection about the diary itself: "I haven't written
for a few days, because I wanted first of all to think about my
diary. It's an odd idea for someone like me to keep a diary; not
only because I have never done so before, but because it seems
to me that neither I—nor for that matter anyone else—will be
interested in the unbosomings of a thirteen-year-old schoolgirl.
Still, what does that matter? I want to write, but more than that,
I want to bring out all kinds of things that lie buried deep in my
heart. . . . [T]here is no doubt that paper is patient and as I
don't intend to show this . . . 'diary' to anyone, unless I find a
real friend, boy or girl, probably nobody cares. And now I come
to the root of the matter, the reason for my starting a diary; it
is that I have no such real friend. . . . [I]t's the same with all
my friends, just fun and joking, nothing more. I can never bring
myself to talk of anything outside the common round. . . .
Hence, this diary. . . . I don't want to set down a series of bald
facts in a diary as most people do, but I want this diary itself to
be my friend, and I shall call my friend Kitty."

"What child of 13 hasn't had these feelings, and resolved to confide in a diary?" wrote Levin. Apart from interest in the diary
for its historical value and for the extreme circumstances under
which it was written, some have admired the diary for its accurate, revealing portrait of adolescence. "She described life in the
'Annex' with all its inevitable tensions and quarrels," wrote L.
De Jong in *A Tribute to Anne Frank.* "But she created first and
foremost a wonderfully delicate record of adolescence, sketching
with complete honesty a young girl's feelings, her longings and
loneliness."

At the age of thirteen, when Anne began the diary, she was struggling with the problems of growing up. Lively and vivacious, she

was chastised at school—and later in the annex—for her incessant chattering. In the annex she was forced to whisper throughout the day. It was a great trial for Anne, who wrote on October 1, 1942, "We are as quiet as mice. Who, three months ago, would ever have guessed that quicksilver Anne would have to sit still for hours—and, what's more—could?" After a year of this silence, combined with confinement indoors, she expressed her feelings of depression, writing on October 29, 1943, "The atmosphere is so oppressive, and sleepy and as heavy as lead. You don't hear a single bird singing outside, and a deadly close silence hangs everywhere, catching hold of me as if it will drag me down deep into an underworld. . . . I wander from one room to another, downstairs and up again, feeling like a songbird whose wings have been clipped and who is hurling himself in utter darkness against the bars of his cage."

The eight people lived in constant fear of being discovered. Their concerns were heightened by seeing and hearing about other Jews who were rounded up in Amsterdam, and by burglars at the warehouse who threatened to find them accidentally. These fears, in addition to the stress of close confinement, resulted in great tension and many quarrels. Anne could be headstrong, opinionated, and critical—especially of her mother. Generally cheerful and optimistic, she adored her father and attempted to get along with the others, but she was sensitive to criticism, explaining in her diary that no one criticized her more than she herself. The diary thus traces her development from an outgoing, popular child to an introspective, idealistic young woman. Her entry on July 11, 1943, illustrates her developing tact: "I do really see that I get on better by shamming a bit, instead of my old habit of telling everyone exactly what I think." Anne herself described the two sides of her personality in her final entry: "I have, as it were, a dual personality. One half embodies my exuberant cheerfulness, making fun of everything, my high-spiritedness, and above all, the way I take everything lightly. . . . This side is usually lying in wait and pushes away the other, which is much better, deeper and purer."

It is this introspection and ability to express her various moods that distinguishes her diary, Pommer noted: "Any diary of a young girl who hid in Amsterdam during the Nazi occupation, who described her first protracted love affair, and who was a person of breeding, humor, religious sensitivity, and courage might well interest us. But Anne had one further trait of the utmost importance for her own maturity and for what she wrote: an unusual ability for self-analysis. She knew she had moods, and she could write eloquently about them—about loneliness for example. But she could also step outside her moods in order to evaluate them."

Her friend Lies Goslar later attributed Anne's rapid maturity to the many hours of quiet reflection encouraged by hiding, the severity of her situation, and her tender relationship with Peter Van Daan. A former teacher expressed surprise at the transformation in her character and writing because Anne had not been an exceptional student. Even Anne's father admitted "I never knew my little Anna was so deep." She meditated on religion, developed a strong sense of morality, and deliberately set about improving her own character. On July 15, 1944, she wrote: "It's really a wonder that I haven't dropped all my ideals, because they seem so absurd and impossible to carry out. . . . I simply can't build up my hopes on a foundation consisting of confusion, misery and death. I see the world gradually being turned into a wilderness, I hear the ever approaching thunder, which will destroy us too, I can feel the sufferings of millions and yet, if I look up into the heavens, I think that it will all come right, that this cruelty too will end, and that peace and tranquility will return

again. . . . In the meantime, I must uphold my ideals, for perhaps the time will come when I shall be able to carry them out." She vowed to make a difference, writing on April 6, 1944: "I know what I want, I have a goal, an opinion, I have a religion and love. . . . I know that I'm a woman, a woman with inward strength and plenty of courage. If God lets me live . . . I shall not remain insignificant, I shall work in the world and for mankind!"

During the course of writing the diary, Anne became certain she wanted to be a writer. She envisioned a novel based on her diary. Additionally she wrote stories, later collected in *The Works of Anne Frank* and *Tales From the House Behind.* According to *New York Times Book Review* critic Frederick Morton, the stories "show that Anne followed instinctively the best of all platitudes: Write whereof you know. Not even her little fairy tales are easy escapes into make-believe, but rather pointed allegories of reality—the two elves who are imprisoned together to learn tolerance; or Blurry the Baby who runs away from home to find the great, free, open world, and never does. . . . Still none of these . . ., not even a charming little morality tale like 'The Wise Old Dwarf,' has the power of any single entry in the diary."

The diary ends August 1, 1944, three days before the group was arrested and sent to the concentration camp at Auschwitz, Poland. They were separated, and Margot and Anne were later transferred to Bergen-Belsen. According to a survivor who knew her at the concentration camp, Anne never lost her courage, deep sensitivity, or ability to feel. An excerpt of Ernst Schnabel's *Anne Frank: A Portrait in Courage,* reprinted in *A Tribute to Anne Frank,* states that "Anne was the youngest in her group, but nevertheless she was the leader of it. She also distributed the bread in the barracks, and she did it so well and fairly that there was none of the usual grumbling. . . . Here is another example. We were always thirsty. . . . And once, when I was so far gone that I almost died because there was nothing to drink, Anne suddenly came to me with a cup of coffee. To this day I don't know where she got it." The woman continued: "She, too, was the one who saw to the last what was going on all around us. . . . we were beyond feelings. . . . Something protected us, kept us from seeing. But Anne had no such protection, to the last. I can still see her standing at the door and looking down the camp street as a herd of naked gypsy girls was driven by, to the crematory, and Anne watched them going and cried. And she cried also when we marched past the Hungarian children who had already been waiting half a day in the rain in front of the gas chambers, because it was not yet their turn. And Anne nudged me and said: 'Look, look. Their eyes. . . .'"

Both Anne and Margot died of typhoid fever at Bergen-Belsen in March, 1945. Their mother had died earlier at Auschwitz. Otto Frank, liberated from Auschwitz by Russian troops in 1945, returned to Amsterdam. He already knew of his wife's death, but he had hope that Margot and Anne were alive. He soon received a letter informing him of their deaths. It was then that Miep Gies, who had worked for Mr. Frank as a secretary and helped hide the family, gave Anne's writings to him. Gies had discovered the diaries strewn on the floor after the Franks' arrest, and she kept the writings at her home but did not read them. It took Anne's father several weeks to read the diary, as he could only bear to read a little at a time. Urged by friends, he published an edited version of the diary, deleting a number of passages he thought too personal.

Mr. Frank, who received numerous letters in response to the diary, cautioned in the preface to *A Tribute to Anne Frank,* "However touching and sincere the expressions of sympathy I receive may be, I always reply that it is not enough to think of Anne with pity or admiration. Her diary should be a source of inspiration toward the realization of the ideals and hopes she expressed in it."

The Anne Frank Foundation has preserved the Franks' hiding place in Amsterdam, and schools in several countries, as well as a village at Wuppertal, West Germany, have been named for Anne.

BIOGRAPHICAL/CRITICAL SOURCES:

BOOKS

Bettelheim, Bruno, *Surviving and Other Essays,* Knopf, 1979.
Berryman, John, *The Freedom of the Poet,* Farrar, Straus, 1976.
Ehrenberg, Ilya, *Chekhov, Stendhal, and Other Essays,* translated by Tatiana Shebunia and Yvonne Kapp, Knopf, 1963.
Dunaway, Philip, and Evans, Melvin, editors, *Treasury of the World's Great Diaries,* Doubleday, 1957.
Encyclopedia of the Third Reich, McGraw, 1976.
Fradin, Dennis B., *Remarkable Children: Twenty Who Made History,* Little, Brown, 1987.
Frank, Anne, *The Diary of a Young Girl,* Doubleday, 1967.
Gies, Miep, and Alison Leslie Gold, *Anne Frank Remembered: The Story of the Woman Who Helped to Hide the Franks,* Simon & Schuster, 1987.
Goodrich, Frances, and Albert Hackett, *Diary of Anne Frank,* Random House, 1956.
Her Way: Biographies of Women for Young People, American Library Association, 1976.
The Reader's Encyclopedia, 2nd edition, Crowell, 1965.
Schnabel, Ernst, *Anne Frank: A Portrait in Courage,* translated from German by Richard and Clara Winston, Harcourt, 1958 (published in England as *Footsteps of Anne Frank,* Longmans, 1959).
Steenmeijer, Anna G., editor, in collaboration with Otto Frank and Henri van Praag, *A Tribute to Anne Frank,* Doubleday, 1970.
Twentieth-Century Writing: A Reader's Guide to Contemporary Literature, Transatlantic, 1969.
Tridenti, Lina, *Anne Frank,* translated by Stephen Thorne, Silver Burdett, 1985.

PERIODICALS

Christian Century, May 6, 1959.
Commonweal, October 31, 1958.
Ladies' Home Journal, September, 1967.
Life, August 18, 1958.
Los Angeles Times, April 13, 1984.
McCall's, July, 1958.
New Statesman and Nation, May 17, 1952.
Newsweek, June 25, 1979.
New York Times Book Review, June 15, 1952, September 20, 1959, May 10, 1987, July 2, 1989.
New York Times Magazine, April 21, 1957.
People, September 16, 1984.
Saturday Review, July 19, 1952.
Time, June 16, 1952, February 17, 1958, January 30, 1984.

—*Sketch by Katherine Huebl*

*   *   *

FRANKLIN, Benjamin
See HASEK, Jaroslav (Matej Frantisek)

FRASER, Antonia (Pakenham) 1932-
(Antonia Pakenham)

PERSONAL: Born August 27, 1932, in London, England; daughter of Francis Aungier (a college professor, writer and politician; became 7th Earl of Longford, 1961) and Elizabeth (a writer; maiden name, Harman) Pakenham; married Hugh Charles Patrick Joseph Fraser (Member of Parliament; died, 1984), September 25, 1956 (marriage ended, 1977); married Harold Pinter (a playwright), November 27, 1980; children: (first marriage) Rebecca, Flora, Benjamin, Natasha, Damian, Orlando. *Education:* Oxford University, B.A., 1953; received M.A.

ADDRESSES: Agent—Curtis Brown Ltd., 162-168 Regent St., London W1R 5TA, England.

CAREER: Writer. Also worked as broadcaster and lecturer; panelist on British Broadcasting Corp.'s "My Word!" radio program. Member of Arts Council, 1970-71, English PEN Committee, 1978—.

MEMBER: Society of Authors (chairman, 1974-75), Crimewriters Association (vice-chairman, 1984; chairman, 1985-86).

AWARDS, HONORS: James Tait Black Prize for biography, 1969, for *Mary, Queen of Scots;* Woltsor Prize for history, 1984, for *The Weaker Vessel.*

WRITINGS:

HISTORY

Dolls, Putnam, 1963.
A History of Toys, Delacorte, 1966, new edition, Springer Books, 1972.
Mary, Queen of Scots (biography), Delacorte, 1969.
Cromwell, the Lord Protector (biography), Knopf, 1973 (published in England as *Cromwell, Our Chief of Men,* Weidenfeld & Nicolson, 1973).
King James VI of Scotland, I of England (biography), Weidenfeld & Nicolson, 1974, Knopf, 1975.
Royal Charles (biography), Knopf, 1979.
The Weaker Vessel: Woman's Lot in Seventeenth Century England, Knopf, 1984.
The Warrior Queens, Knopf, 1988 (published in England as *Boadicea's Chariot: The Warrior Queens,* Weidenfeld & Nicolson, 1988).

MYSTERIES

Quiet as a Nun, Viking, 1977.
The Wild Island: A Mystery, Norton, 1978.
(Contributor) Hilary Watson, editor *Winter's Crimes 10,* Macmillan, 1978.
(Contributor) Herbert Van Thal, editor, *The Fourth Bedside Book of Great Detective Stories,* Barker, 1979.
A Splash of Red, Norton, 1981.
Cool Repentance, Norton, 1982.
(Contributor) George Hardinge, editor, *Winter's Crimes 15,* St. Martin's Press, 1983.
(Contributor) Herbert Harris, editor, *John Creasey's Crime Collection 1983,* Gollancz, 1983.
Oxford Blood, Norton, 1985.
Jemima Shore's First Case and Other Stories, Methuen, 1986.
Your Royal Hostage, Atheneum, 1988.

Also author of scripts for television series "Jemima Shore Investigates," 1983.

EDITOR

The Lives of the Kings and Queens of England, Knopf, 1975.

Scottish Love Poems: A Personal Anthology, Canongate, 1975, Viking, 1976.

Love Letters: An Anthology, Weidenfeld & Nicolson, 1976, Knopf, 1977.

Heroes and Heroines, Weidenfeld & Nicolson, 1980.

Mary, Queen of Scots: An Anthology of Poetry, Eyre Methuen, 1981.

Oxford and Oxfordshire in Verse, Secker & Warburg, 1982.

Love Letters: An Illustrated Anthology, Contemporary Books, 1989.

OTHER

(Under name Antonia Pakenham) *King Arthur and the Knights of the Round Table* (juvenile), Weidenfeld & Nicolson, 1954, Knopf, 1970.

(Translator under name Antonia Pakenham) Jean Monsterleet, *Martyrs in China,* Longman, 1956.

(Under name Antonia Pakenham) *Robin Hood* (juvenile), Weidenfeld & Nicolson, 1957, Knopf, 1971.

(Translator under name Antonia Pakenham) *Dior by Dior: The Autobiography of Christian Dior,* Weidenfeld & Nicolson, 1957.

"Mary, Queen of Scots" (phonodisc), National Portrait Gallery, 1971.

(With Gordon Donaldson) "Sixteenth-Century Scotland" (phonotape), Holt Information Systems, 1972.

Also author of radio plays "On the Battlements," 1975, "The Heroine," 1976, and "Penelope," 1976; author of television play "Charades," 1977. General editor, "Kings and Queens of England" series, Weidenfeld & Nicolson.

SIDELIGHTS: Antonia Fraser, writes Edie Gibson in the *Chicago Tribune,* "has won many accolades for her meticulous research and attention to detail . . . [and] is also credited with bringing a lively narrative style to historical writing, capturing readers who typically shun such scholarly endeavors." Beginning with *Mary, Queen of Scots,* Fraser has chronicled the lives of such historical figures as Oliver Cromwell, James I, and Charles I. In *The Weaker Vessel* and *The Warrior Queens,* she has examined the place of women in seventeenth-century England and in leadership roles in wartime throughout history. She has also written a series of very popular mystery novels featuring Jemima Shore, an investigative television reporter.

Mary, Queen of Scots was Fraser's first biography, and set the standard for her historical writing: intensive research, vivid character portraits, and sound scholarship that nonetheless was presented in a manner that appealed to a wide audience. Jean Stafford, writing in *Book World,* said that Fraser "brings to this immense biography a vivid sense of the mores of the sixteenth century, so lucid a manner of presenting history that she succeeds in almost completely clarifying the muddied maelstrom in which Europe and the British Isles were thrashing and trumpeting, and a narrative dexterity that makes her sad tale seem told for the first time." "Mary emerges neither as a Jezebel nor as a saint," declared a reviewer for *Time* magazine, "but as a high-spirited woman who was brave, rather romantic, and not very bright." "Satisfying to scholars," maintained a *Times Literary Supplement* critic, "the book is eminently one for the general reader, its style both spirited and graceful." *Mary, Queen of Scots* proved popular with readers and won the prestigious James Tait Black award for historical writing in 1969.

Although Fraser's early works are justly celebrated for their intense research and vivid portraiture, several reviewers point out that Fraser practices strict biography—examining the life of a single person—rather than biographical history—examining a person's life in order to discover something about the age in which that person lived. In *Cromwell, the Lord Protector, King James VI of Scotland, I of England,* and *Royal Charles,* Fraser again explores the stories of historic people, "bringing them," according to Peter Stansky in the *New York Times Book Review,* "so vividly to life that the history of the age in which they play so arresting a part tends to lose itself in the background." Reviewing *Royal Charles,* Stansky draws a distinction between pure biography and historical biography: "Unlike, for example, Barbara Tuchman, who sees biography as a 'Prism of History,' and admits to using it 'less for the sake of the individual subject than as a vehicle for exhibiting an age,' Lady Antonia is wholeheartedly committed to the life of the individual subject."

Fraser changed her strict biographical approach in her 1984 award-winning study *The Weaker Vessel: Woman's Lot in Seventeenth-Century England.* Rather than focusing on a single character as her earlier biographies had done, *The Weaker Vessel* looks at the many roles of women in the 1600s, with special emphasis on "marriage, birth, widowhood, divorce, prostitution, the stage, business, and so forth," says Brigitte Weeks in the *Washington Post.* "Each chapter is a maze of interconnected life stories of women, almost always pregnant, ending all too often in sudden death, mostly in childbirth." During the English Civil War, Fraser explains, women were given positions of responsibility. The author cites examples of women who held custody of castles, who led troops into battle, who wrote treatises and presented petitions to Parliament. After the war, however, their newly-won liberties were taken away, leaving them in much the same position as they were in the previous century. "One of the lies about historical progress," declares Peter S. Prescott in *Newsweek,* "is that it hunches inexorably along its way. In fact, progress is cyclical; it jumps sporadically, only to be set back again."

The Warrior Queens, another topical survey of women's history, grew out of the research Fraser did for *The Weaker Vessel.* In it, she looks at the phenomenon of women who lead their countries in wartime, and sometimes into battle—women ranging from the Egyptian queen Cleopatra, the British tribal leader Boadicea, and Zenobia, the third-century Queen of the desert city of Palmyra, all of whom led forces against the Roman Empire, to modern-day leaders such as Israel's Golda Meir and Great Britain's Margaret Thatcher. "Seeking explanations for these women's rise to power and their enormous personal magnetism," writes Barbara Benton in *MHQ: The Quarterly Journal of Military History,* "she attempts to isolate common themes in their stories."

Fraser categorizes the patterns of behavior that these women use to hold their power. Victoria Glendenning enumerates them in the London *Times:* "the Appendance Syndrome, according to which the Warrior Queen justifies herself by stressing her connection with a famous father or husband, or fights allegedly on behalf of her son; the Shame Syndrome, otherwise the Betterman Syndrome, which means she shows up the chaps by being braver than they are; the Tomboy Syndrome, which implies that she never played with dolls when she was a little girl; and the Only-a-Weak-Woman Syndrome, when she puts on a sudden show of weakness or modesty for strategic purposes." She also separates them into models of virtue or monsters of lust (which she terms the "Voracity Syndrome"). In the end, concludes Margaret Atwood in the *Los Angeles Times Book Review,* Fraser shows that "public women are put through different tests of nerve, attract different kinds of criticism, and are subject to different sorts of mythologizing than are men, and 'The Warrior Queens' indicates what kinds."

Fraser also expresses her interest in women's studies in her fiction. "Despite the fact that she was able to bring a personal style to the writing of history," declares Rosemary Herbert in a *Publishers Weekly* interview with the author, "in the mid-'70s Fraser 'felt that there was something in myself that history didn't express.' She gave in to the impulse to write fiction and created the TV commentator/sleuth Jemima Shore, a stylish, liberated woman who shares some of the author's characteristics." P. D. James, herself a well-known mystery writer, greeted the investigator's debut in *Quiet as a Nun* with pleasure, saying that the story "is written with humour and sympathy and has a heroine of whom, happily, it is promised that we shall know more."

In some ways, reviewers feel, Fraser transcends the detective genre, thanks to her carefully described backgrounds. Margaret Cannon, writing in the Toronto *Globe and Mail,* sees much fascination—not in the crimes themselves, which are comparatively civilized (Fraser states in *Twentieth-Century Crime and Mystery Writers* that she "has a horror of blood dripping from the page," and adds, "my books are therefore aimed at readers who feel likewise")—but in the details that Fraser provides about the upper class settings through which Shore moves, circles in which Fraser herself travels. For instance, T. J. Binyon points out in the *Times Literary Supplement* that *Cool Repentence,* parodies theater personalities familiar to Fraser through her husband Harold Pinter. *Your Royal Hostage,* a recent Shore outing, takes place against the backdrop of a royal wedding, listing the problems encountered in trying to televise the event—problems Fraser faced herself when she covered the wedding of the Prince of Wales.

Critics agree that Fraser's detective stories are worthy followers of a long heritage of British detective writing. Beverly Lyon Clark writes in the *New York Times Book Review* that *Oxford Blood* is "in the tradition of the British whodunit, especially that of the Tea Cake and Country House mystery—or, in this case, the Champagne and Maserati sort. . . . Antonia Fraser is not quite Dorothy Sayers, not quite P. D. James. But she does have a seductive style." Shore believes, says Cannon, that "there's nothing in the detective code of ethics that says you have to dress badly, get married or pass up an interesting one-night stand. It's a long way from St. Mary Mead, but I somehow think that [Agatha Christie's detective] Miss Marple, shrewd student of human nature that she was, would approve."

BIOGRAPHICAL/CRITICAL SOURCES:

BOOKS

Authors in the News, Volume 2, Gale, 1976.
Twentieth-Century Crime and Mystery Writers, St. James Press/St. Martin's, 1983.

PERIODICALS

Book World, November 16, 1969.
Chicago Tribune, March 16, 1988.
Chicago Tribune Book World, September 30, 1984.
Christian Science Monitor, December 7, 1979.
Globe and Mail (Toronto), August 25, 1984.
Los Angeles Times, September 25, 1980.
Los Angeles Times Book Review, September 23, 1984, April 2, 1989.
MHQ: The Quarterly Journal of Military History, autumn, 1989.

Newsweek, September 10, 1984.
New York Times, November 13, 1979, November 14, 1984.
New York Times Book Review, November 18, 1984, April 2, 1989.
Publishers Weekly, June 19, 1987.
Time, October 17, 1969, September 17, 1984.
Times (London), May 3, 1984, October 7, 1988, October 15, 1988.
Times Literary Supplement, July 3, 1969, May 27, 1977, June 8, 1984, November 11-17, 1988.
Tribune Books (Chicago), April 2, 1989.
Washington Post, October 7, 1984.
Washington Post Book World, March 12, 1989.
WB, May/June, 1989.

—*Sketch by Kenneth R. Shepherd*

*   *   *

FRASER, Jane
See PILCHER, Rosamunde

*   *   *

FRAYN, Michael   1933-

PERSONAL: Born September 8, 1933, in London, England; son of Thomas Allen (a manufacturer's representative) and Violet Alice (Lawson) Frayn; married Gillian Palmer (a social worker), February 18, 1960 (divorced, 1989); children: three daughters. *Education:* Emmanuel College, Cambridge University, B.A., 1957.

ADDRESSES: Agent—Elaine Green Ltd., 31 Newington Green, London N16, England.

CAREER: Novelist and playwright. *Guardian,* Manchester, England, general-assignment reporter, 1957-59, "Miscellany" columnist, 1959-62; *Observer,* London, England, columnist, 1962-68. Contributor to weekly comedy series, "Beyond a Joke," British Broadcasting Corp., 1972; has made regular appearances on Granada Television's "What the Papers Say." *Military service:* British Army, 1952-54.

MEMBER: Royal Society of Literature.

AWARDS, HONORS: Somerset Maugham Award, 1966, for *The Tin Men;* Hawthornden Prize, 1967, for *The Russian Interpreter;* National Press Club Award for distinguished reporting, International Publishing Corporation, 1970, for series of *Observer* articles on Cuba; Best Comedy of the Year award, *Evening Standard,* 1975, for "Alphabetical Order," 1982, for "Noises Off," and 1984, for "Benefactors"; Society of West End Theatre Award for best comedy of the year, 1976, for "Donkeys' Years," 1982, for "Noises Off," and 1984, for "Benefactors"; American Theatre Wing's Antoinette Perry ("Tony") Award nomination for best play, 1984, Laurence Olivier Award for best play, 1984, *Plays and Players* award for best new play, 1986, and New York Drama Critics Circle award for best new foreign play, 1986, all for "Benefactors."

WRITINGS:

The Day of the Dog (selections from his *Guardian* column), illustrations by Timothy Birdsall, Collins, 1962, Doubleday, 1963.
(Editor) John Bingham Morton, *The Best of Beachcomber,* Heinemann, 1963.
(Contributor) Michael Sissons and Philip French, *Age of Austerity,* Hodder & Stoughton, 1963.

The Book of the Fub (selections from his *Guardian* column), Collins, 1963, published as *Never Put off to Gomorrah,* Pantheon, 1964.

(Editor with Bamber Gascoigne) *Timothy: The Drawings and Cartoons of Timothy Birdsall,* M. Joseph, 1964.

On the Outskirts, Collins, 1964.

At Bay in Gear Street (selections from his *Observer* column), Fontana, 1967.

Constructions (philosophy), Wildwood House, 1974.

The Original Michael Frayn: Satirical Essays, Salamander Press (Edinburgh), 1983.

NOVELS

The Tin Men, Collins, 1965, Little, Brown, 1966.

The Russian Interpreter, Viking, 1966.

Towards the End of the Morning, Collins, 1967, reprinted, 1985, published as *Against Entropy,* Viking, 1967.

A Very Private Life, Viking, 1968.

Sweet Dreams, Collins, 1973, Viking, 1974.

The Trick of It, Viking, 1989.

PLAYS

(With John Edwards) "Zounds!" (musical comedy), first produced in Cambridge, England, May, 1957.

The Two of Us: Four One-Act Plays for Two Players (contains "Black and Silver," "The New Quixote," "Mr. Foot," and "Chinamen"; first produced on West End at Garrick Theatre, July 30, 1970), Fontana, 1970.

The Sandboy (first produced in London at Greenwich Theatre, September 16, 1971), Fontana, 1971.

"Alphabetical Order" (also see below), first produced in London at Hampstead Theatre Club, March 11, 1975; transferred to May Fair Theatre on West End, April 8, 1975; produced in New Haven, Conn., at Long Wharf Theatre, October 14, 1976.

Donkeys' Years: A Play (first produced on West End at Globe Theatre, July 15, 1976; produced Off-Off Broadway at New Theatre of Brooklyn, March, 1987; also see below), French, 1977.

Clouds (first produced in London at Hampstead Theatre Club, August 16, 1976; produced on West End at Duke of York's Theatre, November 1, 1978; also see below), French, 1977.

Alphabetical Order [and] *Donkeys' Years,* Methuen, 1977.

Liberty Hall (first produced in London at Greenwich Theatre, January 24, 1980), Methuen, 1977.

Make and Break (first produced in Hammersmith, England, at Lyric Theatre, March 18, 1980; transferred to Haymarket Theatre Royal on West End, April 24, 1980; produced in Washington, D.C., at John F. Kennedy Center for the Performing Arts, 1982; also see below), Methuen, 1980.

Noises Off: A Play in Three Acts (first produced in Hammersmith at Lyric Theatre, February 11, 1982; transferred to Savoy Theatre on West End, March 31, 1982; produced in Washington, D.C., at Eisenhower Theater, November, 1983; produced on Broadway at Brooks Atkinson Theatre, December, 1983; also see below), Methuen, 1982, acting edition, French, 1982.

Benefactors: A Play in Two Acts (first produced on West End at Vaudeville Theatre, April, 1984; produced on Broadway at Brooks Atkinson Theatre, December 22, 1985), Methuen, 1984.

Plays: One (contains "Alphabetical Order," "Donkeys' Years," "Clouds," "Make and Break," and "Noises Off "), Methuen, 1985.

Balmoral: Methuen Modern Play, Routledge Chapman & Hall, 1988.

TRANSLATOR FROM THE RUSSIAN, AND ADAPTER

(And author of introduction) Anton Chekhov, *The Cherry Orchard: A Comedy in Four Acts* (first produced on West End at National Theatre, 1978), Methuen, 1978.

(And author of introduction) Leo Tolstoy, *The Fruits of Enlightenment: A Comedy in Four Acts* (first produced on West End at National Theatre, 1979), Methuen, 1979.

(And author of introduction) *Three Sisters: A Drama in Four Acts* (first produced in Manchester, England, at Royal Exchange Theatre, 1985), Methuen, 1983.

Chekhov, *Wild Honey: The Untitled Play* (unofficially known as "Platonov"; first produced on West End at National Theatre, 1984; produced in New York at Virginia Theatre, December 18, 1986), Methuen, 1984.

(And author of introduction) Chekhov, *The Seagull* (first produced in Hammersmith at the Lyric Theatre, 1986), Methuen, 1986.

Chekhov, *Uncle Vanya,* Methuen, 1987.

Chekhov, "The Sneeze" (short stories and sketches), first produced on West End at Aldwych Theatre, November, 1988.

OTHER

"Jamie, On a Flying Visit" (teleplay), British Broadcasting Corp. (BBC-TV), January, 1968.

"One Pair of Eyes" (documentary film), BBC-TV, 1968.

"Birthday" (teleplay), BBC-TV, 1969.

"Laurence Stern Lived Here" (documentary film), BBC-TV, 1973.

"Making Faces" (comedy broadcast in six parts), BBC-TV, September 25-October 30, 1975.

"Imagine a City Called Berlin" (documentary film), BBC-TV, 1975.

"Vienna: The Mask of Gold" (documentary film), BBC-TV, 1977.

"Three Streets in the Country" (documentary film), BBC-TV, 1979.

"The Long Straight," BBC-TV, 1980.

(With others) *Great Railway Journeys of the World* (based on film broadcast by BBC-TV; contains Frayn's segment on Australia), BBC, 1981, Dutton, 1982.

Clockwise: A Screenplay (produced and released by Universal, 1986), Methuen, 1986.

Also contributor to periodicals, including the *New York Times Book Review.*

SIDELIGHTS: Though best known in the United States as the playwright behind the hit stage farce "Noises Off," Briton Michael Frayn has actually produced a wide variety of writing. His beginnings as a columnist and critic for two newspapers, the Manchester *Guardian* and the London *Observer,* led to a number of published collections. Frayn's novels, including *The Tin Men* and *The Russian Interpreter,* have garnered praise for both their humor and their insights into complicated modern times. Among his other plays, Frayn's translations of Anton Chekhov's classics draw particular attention. And more recently, the writer has ventured into cinema, with a produced screenplay, "Clockwise."

A native Londoner, "Frayn believes his sense of humor began to develop during his years at Kingston Grammar School where, to the delight of his classmates, he practiced the 'techniques of mockery' on his teachers," reports Mark Fritz in the *Dictionary of Literary Biography.* "Referring to this early practice of making jokes at the expense of others, Frayn says, 'I sometimes wonder if this isn't an embarrassingly exact paradigm of much that I've done since.' " Frayn established himself as a keen social satirist on two newspapers, the *Guardian* and *Observer*. For the former, as Frayn saw it, "his job with [the column] Miscellany was to write cool, witty interviews with significant film directors passing through, but there were never enough film directors so he started making up humorous paragraphs to fill," as Terry Coleman writes in the *Guardian*. Malcolm Page explains in the *Dictionary of Literary Biography* that Frayn "invented for the column the Don't Know Party and such characters as the trendy Bishop of [Twicester]; Rollo Swavely, a public relations consultant; and the ambitious suburban couple, [Christopher and Lavinia Crumble]."

Comparing Frayn's "wit, sophistication, and imagination" to "that of American humorist S. J. Perelman," Fritz declares that Frayne's "satire is sharper." That sense of satire, along with an emerging seriousness, carried the author to his first novel, *The Tin Men*. The story, about the suitability of computers to take over the burden of human dullness, won the Somerset Maugham Award for fiction in 1963. A year later, Frayn produced *The Russian Interpreter*, "a spy story which deals more with the deceit between individuals than between nations," according to Fritz. That novel took the Hawthornden Prize.

Two more Frayn novels earned critical admiration. *A Very Private Life*, written in the future tense, "explains how life has grown more private, first through physical privacy, then through the development of drugs to cope with anger and uncertainty," writes Page. To *Spectator* reviewer Maurice Capitanchik, "Frayn, in his parable of the horrific future, does not escape the impress which [George] Orwell and [Aldous] Huxley have made upon the genre, nor does he really go beyond the area of authoritarian oppression so brilliantly illumined by [Franz] Kafka, but he does something else both valuable and unique: he shows that his 'Brave New World' is really our cowardly old world, if we did but, shudderingly, know it, in a prose which is often beautiful and, almost, poetry." And in *Sweet Dreams*, the novel Frayn considers his best to date, a young architect dies and goes to a distinctly familiar sort of English heaven, "a terribly decent place, really, where one's pleasantest dreams come true and one's most honest longings are fulfilled," as *Washington Post Book World* critic L. J. Davis describes. Caught in a permanent fantasy world, Howard, the architect, "immediately joins the small, intimate, and brilliantly unorthodox architectural firm he'd always yearned for," Davis continues. After redesigning the Matterhorn, engaging in a dramatic love affair, and realizing other superlative encounters, Howard "sells out to the movies, purges himself with a spell of rustic simplicity, rallies the best minds of his generation by means of letters to The Times, meets God . . . and eventually winds up, crinkle-eyed and aging, as prime minister. It is all rather poignant," says Davis.

Frayn's dramatic work began with a number of television plays. His prior theatrical background included a sojourn with the Cambridge Footlights revue, and a walk-on in a production of Nikolai Gogol's "The Inspector General"—a disaster that prefigured the backstage slapstick of "Noises Off." "I pulled instead of pushed at the door, it jammed in the frame, and there was no other way off," the writer tells Benedict Nightingale for a *New York Times Magazine* profile. "So I waited for what seemed like many, many hours while stagehands fought with crowbars on the other side and the audience started to slow-handclap. I've never been on the stage since."

Frayn has, however, brought to the stage many critically acclaimed productions. Among his stage plays, "Alphabetical Order" and "Donkeys' Years" earned plaudits, profits, and some measure of reputation for their author. In "Alphabetical Order," the happy disarray of a newspaper's research department—the "morgue"—is changed forever when a hyperefficient young woman joins the staff. "By the second act she has transformed [the morgue] into a model of order and efficiency. But somehow the humanness is gone," notes Fritz. "The young woman then proceeds to reorganize the personal lives of the other characters as well. She is not a total villain, however. In a way, the newspaper staff needs her: without a strong-willed person to manipulate them, weak-willed people often stagnate. At the heart of the play is the question: which is better, order or chaos?" The successful "Donkeys' Years" focuses upon a group of university graduates reunited twenty years later, only to revert to their adolescent roles and conflicts. Voted the best comedy of 1982 by London's West End Theatre Society, the play was dubbed by Stephen Holden in the *New York Times*, a "well-made farce that roundly twits English propriety."

Frayn's 1980 production "Make and Break," a comedy-drama about a salesman whose aggressive talent for business overshadows his humanity, played to capacity audiences in London, but premiered in the United States to mixed reviews. Finding the play "wretchedly constructed," *Drama* critic Harold Hobson, for instance, was also disappointed in its "old-fashioned . . . views of women." But more favorable notices came from other reviewers, including *Observer* contributor Michael Ratcliffe, who considered the production Frayn's "best play to date." Describing it as "an excessively neat, neoclassical sort of piece which draws on only a fraction of his imaginative range," the critic pointed out that the only "real problem with the play is simply that the men remain shadows and only the women come to life."

Although many renowned comedies and dramas have used the play-within-a-play format in the past—it is a device that predates Shakespeare—perhaps no self-referential play has been so widely received in this generation as "Noises Off," a no-holds-barred slapstick farce. Using the kind of manic entrances and mistaken identities reminiscent of the French master Georges Feydeau, "Noises Off " invites the audience to witness the turmoil behind a touring company of has-beens and never-weres as they attempt to perform a typically English sex farce called "Nothing On." Referring to the production as "a show that gave ineptitude a good name," *Insight* writer Sheryl Flatow indicates that "Noises Off " was criticized by some as nothing more than a relentless, if effective, laugh-getting machine. The charge of being too funny, however, is not the sort of criticism that repels audiences, and "Noises Off " enjoyed a long run on the West End and Broadway.

"The fun begins even before the curtain goes up," Frank Rich reports in his *New York Times* review of Frayn's comedy. "In the Playbill, we find a program-within-the-program. . . . Among other things, we learn that the author of 'Nothing On' is a former 'unsuccessful gents hosiery wholesaler' whose previous farce 'Socks before Marriage' ran for nine years." When the curtain does rise, Rich continues, "it reveals a hideous set . . . that could well serve all those sex farces . . . that do run for nine years." As the story opens, the "Nothing On" cast and crew are blundering through their final rehearsal; importantly, everyone establishes his onstage and offstage identities. Remarks Rich: "As the run-through is mostly devoted to setting up what follows, it's also the only sporadically mirthless stretch of Mr. Frayn's play: We're asked to study every ridiculous line and awful performance in 'Nothing On' to appreciate the varied replays yet to come. Still, the lags are justified by the payoff: Having painstakingly built his house of cards in Act I, the author brings it crashing down with exponentially accelerating hilarity in Acts II and III."

While the backstage romances simmer, the troupe systematically skewers whatever appeal the cheesy "Nothing On" should have provided. Even the props get involved: by Act II, a plate of sardines is as important an element to the play as any of the actors. By this time, "Frayn's true inspiration strikes," in the words of *Washington Post* reviewer David Richards. "The company is a month into its tour and the set has been turned around, so that we are viewing 'Nothing On' from backstage. The innocent little romances in Act I have turned lethal and, while the actors are still vaguely mindful of their cues, they are more mindful of wreaking vengeance upon one another. . . . An ax is wielded murderously, a skirt is torn off, toes are stomped on, shoelaces are tied together, bone-crunching tumbles are taken, bouquets are shredded, a cactus is sat upon and, of course, the ingenue's damned [contact] lens pops out again!" Although Richards remarks that the play "lost" him "about the time 'Nothing On' orbited into outer space," he adds, that "up to the last quarter hour, Frayn maintains contact with reality, however exaggerated, but finally the connection just snaps and what has been incisively silly turns just plain silly. Elsewhere, though, there is such an abundance of invention and such an astute knotting of misunderstanding and mishap that it would be ungrateful to carp."

"Noises Off" established Frayn in America as a farceur, on the order of Feydeau and Ben Travers. To that end, the author tells *Los Angeles Times* reporter Barbara Isenberg that farce is serious business. Its most important element, he says, is "the losing of power for coherent thought under the pressure of events. What characters in farce do traditionally is try to recover some disaster that occurred, by a course of behavior that is so ill-judged that it makes it worse. In traditional farce, people are caught in a compromising situation, try to explain it with a lie and, when they get caught, have then to explain both the original situation *and* the lie. And, when they're caught in that lie, they have to have another one."

Frayn's first produced screenplay, "Clockwise," closely resembles "Noises Off" in its wild construction. Like the play, the film takes a simple premise and lets circumstances run amok. In "Clockwise," protagonist Brian Stimpson, a small-town headmaster and a man obsessed with punctuality, wins Headmaster of the Year honors and must travel by train to a distant city to deliver his acceptance speech. Inevitably, Brian catches the wrong train, and the thought that he may arrive late drives him to desperate means. By the film's end, he has stolen a car, invaded a monastery, robbed a man of his suit, and set two squadrons of police on his trail. "It isn't the film's idea of taking a prim, controlled character and letting him become increasingly unhinged that makes 'Clockwise' so enjoyable; it's the expertise with which Mr. Frayn's screenplay sets the wheels in motion and keeps them going," according to Janet Maslin's *New York Times* critique. Noting that "Clockwise" is "far from perfect—it has long sleepy stretches and some pretty obvious farce situations," *Washington Post* critic Paul Attanasio nonetheless adds, "but at its best, here is a comedy unusual in its layered complexity, in the way Frayn has worked everything out. 'Gonna take a bit o' sortin' out, this one,' says one of the pursuing bobbies. The joke, of course, is in the understatement. And rarely has the 'sortin' out' been so much fun."

Departing from farce, Frayn has written the stage work "Benefactors" as an acerbic look at a 1960s couple wrestling with their ideals as they try to cope with their troubled neighbors, a couple caught in a failing marriage. Frank Rich, who so enjoyed "Noises Off," saw a production of "Benefactors" and told the *New York Times*, "It's hard to fathom that these two works were written by the same man. Like 'Noises Off,' 'Benefactors' is ingeniously constructed and has been directed with split-second precision . . . but there all similarities end. Mr. Frayn's new play is a bleak, icy, microcosmic exploration of such serious matters as the nature of good and evil, the price of political and psychological change and the relationship of individuals to the social state. Though 'Benefactors' evokes Chekhov, 'Othello' and 'The Master Builder' along its way, it is an original, not to mention demanding, achievement that is well beyond the ambitions of most contemporary dramatists." Likewise, Mel Gussow of the same newspaper finds strong ties between Chekhov and Frayn: "Thematically, . . . the work remains [close] to Chekhov; through a closely observed, often comic family situation we see the self-defeating aspects of misguided social action."

Fluent in Russian, Frayn served with the British Army in 1952 and was sent to Cambridge, where he trained as an interpreter and used the opportunity to hone his "passion that started in late adolescence for things Soviet," as *New York Times Magazine* writer Benedict Nightingale puts it. From his early days, Frayn has emulated the Russian writer Anton Chekhov; and references to Chekhov are more than apt to describe Frayn also. After working on English versions of Chekhov's classics "The Cherry Orchard," "Three Sisters" and "The Seagull," Frayn embarked on a more unusual project—reworking for the stage "an unwieldy, six-hour play discovered in 1920 with its title page missing," writes Flatow. "The work is usually called 'Platonov,' after its leading character, a roguish teacher who is the object of affection of every woman in town." Flatow finds Frayn's version, "Wild Honey," to be "very much a collaboration," and offers the author's own remarks about the difficulty separating his own work from Chekhov's: "It's hard to say how much is mine and how much is his. As I wrote in the introduction to the play, I thought the only thing to do was treat it as if it were a rough draft of one of my own plays and proceed from there. If that meant giving one character's speech to another or rewriting dialogue or adding my own speeches, fine—anything to make a better second draft."

Scholars have noted that the original manuscript was left largely to the archives because when he was thought to have written the work—in his late teens or early twenties—Chekhov had hardly made his reputation as a creative artist. According to Rich in his *New York Times* column, " 'Wild Honey' isn't the only distillation of ['Platonov'], but it may be the most economical and witty. Even Mr. Frayn, a master of theatrical construction . . . and Chekhovian nuance . . . , cannot turn a journeyman's work into the masterpiece it sometimes prefigures ('The Cherry Orchard'). Yet the adapter has achieved his goal, as stated in his published introduction, of making 'a text for production' rather than 'an academic contribution or a pious tribute.' " As Rich goes on, "Let academics have fun detailing, applauding or deploring the transpositions, telescopings, elisions and outright alterations Mr. Frayn has made in the original work. What's fascinating about 'Wild Honey' is how elegantly the embryonic Chekhovian cartography pops into relief."

"Although one cannot say that Michael Frayn's plays revolutionized the British stage during [our era], they certainly helped to enliven it," concludes Fritz. "Frayn contributed a string of lively, witty comedies with some serious philosophical questions lurking beneath the surfaces. Like many other playwrights of [the 1970s and 1980s,] Frayn experimented with dramatic structures borrowed from film and television—perhaps an attempt to find new methods of expression." And in Malcolm Page's opinion, the playwright "has such gifts for humor that his reputation is for comedy; however, he may be disappointed that the more solemn implications have yet to be perceived. His future may be in less comic theatre, as he continues to focus mainly on people of his age, class, and education."

BIOGRAPHICAL/CRITICAL SOURCES:

BOOKS

Contemporary Literary Criticism, Gale, Volume 3, 1975, Volume 7, 1977, Volume 31, 1985, Volume 47, 1988.
Dictionary of Literary Biography, Gale, Volume 13: *British Dramatists since World War II,* 1982, Volume 14: *British Novelists since 1960,* 1983.

PERIODICALS

Chicago Tribune, November, 1988.
Drama, summer, 1975, July, 1980.
Guardian (Manchester, England), October 1, 1968, March 11, 1975.
Horizon, January/February, 1986.
Insight, February 3, 1986.
Listener, January 21, 1965, January 15, 1966, March 20, 1975.
Los Angeles Times, October 30, 1984, February 3, 1985, February 12, 1985, October 10, 1986, July 20, 1987.
New Statesman, October 4, 1968, November 1, 1974.
Newsweek, February 18, 1974, January 20, 1986.
New York Times, September 11, 1970, June 13, 1971, June 3, 1979, December 12, 1983, July 23, 1984, January 28, 1985, December 23, 1985, January 5, 1986, March 19, 1986, September 4, 1986, October 10, 1986, December 14, 1986, December 19, 1986, March 12, 1987.
New York Times Book Review, September 15, 1968.
New York Times Magazine, December 8, 1985.
Observer (London), June 11, 1967, July 18, 1976, April 27, 1980, April 4, 1984.
Plays and Players, September, 1970, March, 1982, December, 1984.
Saturday Review, January 15, 1966.
Spectator, November 23, 1962, October 4, 1968, December 10, 1983.
Sunday Times (London), January 27, 1980.
Time, September 27, 1968, July 12, 1982.
Times (London), February 25, 1982, February 15, 1983, April 6, 1984, March 14, 1986, November 10, 1986.
Times Literary Supplement, February 1, 1980, March 5, 1982, September 22-28, 1989.
Washington Post, October 16, 1983, October 27, 1983, December 24, 1985, October 25, 1986.
Washington Post Book World, January 10, 1974.

—*Sketch by Susan Salter*

*   *   *

FRAZER, Robert Caine
See CREASEY, John

*   *   *

FREE
See HOFFMAN, Abbie

FREED, Barry
See HOFFMAN, Abbie

*   *   *

FRENCH, Marilyn   1929-
(Mara Solwoska)

PERSONAL: Born November 21, 1929, in New York, N.Y.; daughter of E. Charles and Isabel (Hazz) Edwards; married Robert M. French, Jr. (a lawyer), June 4, 1950 (divorced, 1967); children: Jamie, Robert M. III. *Education:* Hofstra College (now University), B.A., 1951, M.A., 1964; Harvard University, Ph.D., 1972.

ADDRESSES: Home—New York, N.Y. *Agent*—Charlotte Sheedy Literary Agency, 145 West 86th St., New York, N.Y. 10024.

CAREER: Writer and lecturer. Hofstra University, Hempstead, N.Y., instructor in English, 1964-68; College of the Holy Cross, Worcester, Mass., assistant professor of English, 1972-76; Harvard University, Cambridge, Mass., Mellon fellow in English, 1976-77. Artist-in-residence at Aspen Institute for Humanistic Study, 1972.

MEMBER: Modern Language Association of America, Society for Values in Higher Education, Virginia Woolf Society, James Joyce Society, Phi Beta Kappa.

WRITINGS:

The Book as World: James Joyce's "Ulysses," Harvard University Press, 1976.
The Women's Room (novel), Summit Books, 1977.
The Bleeding Heart (novel; Book-of-the-Month Club alternate selection), Summit Books, 1980.
Shakespeare's Division of Experience, Summit Books, 1981.
(Author of introduction) Edith Wharton, *House of Mirth,* Jove Books, 1981.
(Author of introduction) Wharton, *Summer,* Jove Books, 1981.
Beyond Power: On Women, Men, and Morals (essays), Summit Books, 1986.
Her Mother's Daughter (novel), Summit Books, 1987.

Also author of two unpublished novels. Contributor of articles and stories, sometimes under pseudonym Mara Solwoska, to journals, including *Soundings* and *Ohio Review.*

SIDELIGHTS: Novelist, educator, and literary scholar Marilyn French is perhaps best known for the cogent, feminist aspect of her work. "My goal in life," she asserts in an *Inside Books* interview with Ray Bennett, "is to change the entire social and economic structure of western civilization, to make it a feminist world." Noting that "feminism isn't a question of what kind of genitals you possess," she explains: "It's a kind of moral view. It's what you think with your head and feel with your heart." French, whose own feminism has been heightened by her life experience, was married with children before she read Simone de Beauvoir's *The Second Sex,* a book thematically concerned with the importance of women not living through men. Considered by many to be the first text of the current feminist movement, the book greatly impressed and influenced her, especially "the sections on women writers who kept postponing doing their literary work," French told *CA.* Soon thereafter she began to write short stories that expressed her own feelings and frustrations. Divorced in 1967, she earned a doctorate from Harvard through fellowships, and then launched an impressive academic career marked by the publication of her thesis, *The Book as World:*

James Joyce's "*Ulysses.*" In 1977, her explosive and provocative first novel, *The Women's Room,* not only granted her the financial freedom to pursue writing full-time but has, itself, become a major novel of the women's movement. And although critics respond to her work by frequently focusing on its polemics—praising in the nonfiction what they challenge in the fiction—her many readers indentify with and admire what French has to say.

"I wanted to tell the story of what it is like to be a woman in our country in the middle of the twentieth century," French explained to a *New York Times* interviewer about *The Women's Room.* Calling it "a collective biography of a large group of American citizens," Anne Tyler describes the novel's characters in the *New York Times Book Review:* "Expectant in the 40's, submissive in the 50's, enraged in the 60's, they have arrived in the 70's independent but somehow unstrung, not yet fully composed after all they've been through." The novel is about Mira, a submissive and repressed young woman whose conventional childhood prepares her for a traditional marriage, which ends suddenly in divorce and leaves her liberated but alone. "The tone of the book is rather turgid, but exalted, almost religious," says Anne Duchene in the *Times Literary Supplement,* "a huge jeremiad for a new kind of Fall, a whole new experience of pain and loss."

Writing about *The Women's Room* in the *Washington Post Book Review,* Brigitte Weeks contends that "the novel's basic thesis—that there is little or no foreseeable future for coexistence between men and women—is powerfully stated, but still invokes a lonely chaos repellent to most readers." Uncomfortable with what she perceives as the woman-as-victim perspective in *The Women's Room,* Sara Sanborn elaborates in *Ms.,* "My main objection is not that French writes about the sufferings of women; so have the best women writers. But the women of, say, George Eliot or Virginia Woolf, hampered as they are, live in the world of choice and consequence. They are implicated in their own fates, which gives them both interest and stature. The characters in this book glory in the condition which some men have ascribed to women: they are not responsible." In her interview with *People* magazine's Gail Jennes, French states: "Books, movies, TV teach us false images of ourselves. We learn to expect fairy-tale lives. Ordinary women's daily lives—unlike men's—have not been the stuff of literature. I wanted to legitimate it and I purposely chose the most ordinary lives [for the characters in the novel]—not the worst cases. . . . I wanted to break the mold of conventional women's novels." However, in the *New York Times Book Review,* Rosellen Brown notes that the novel "declared the independence of one victimized wife after another."

"French wonders not only if male-female love is *possible,* but whether it's *ethical* in the contemporary context," writes Lindsy Van Gelder in a *Ms.* review of French's second novel, *The Bleeding Heart.* "How, in other words, does one reconcile one's hard-won feminist insights about the way the System works with one's longing to open one's heart completely to a man who, at the very least, benefits from an oppressive System buttressed, in part, by women's emotional vulnerability?" *The Bleeding Heart* centers on Dolores, a liberated professor of Renaissance literature on leave researching a new book at Oxford, when she meets Victor, an unhappily married father of four in England on business. Compromising her feminist principles by engaging in an impassioned but frustratingly combative affair with him, Dolores ultimately realizes that she cannot live with him without descending into predictably prescribed roles. Commenting in *Newsweek* that "French makes her point and touches lots of raw contemporary nerves," Jean Strouse queries, "What happens when nobody wants to be the wife?" According to Brown, *The Bleeding Heart*

represents "an admirably honest admission of the human complications that arise after a few years of lonely integrity: What now? Must one wait for love until the world of power changes hands? Is there a difference between accommodation and compromise among lovers? Accommodation and surrender? How to spell out the terms of a partial affirmation?"

In the *Village Voice,* Laurie Stone observes that the political thesis of *The Bleeding Heart* is: "Although a feminist may love a man, she will ultimately have to reject him, since men axiomatically live by values inimical to women." Describing it as "a novel of love and despair in the seeming ruins of post-'60s angst and the ill-defined emotional territory of the '70s," Thomas Sanchez suggests in the *Los Angeles Times Book Review,* however, that "this is less a novel of people and their fierce concerns for survival than a melodrama of symbols clothed in philosophical and political garb." Furthermore, Sanchez calls the novel "maddening" in the sense that "French has mistaken politics for prose." But according to R. Z. Sheppard in *Time,* French softens the militancy in this novel: "Her soul on ice, Marilyn French sounded like a feminist Eldridge Cleaver [in *The Women's Room*]. *The Bleeding Heart* suggests a slight thaw. Its core is a seemingly endless and inconclusive dialogue—SALT talks in the gender wars." And *Nation* contributor Andrea Freud Loewenstein suggests that although *The Bleeding Heart* is "a depressed and depressing book," it is "not a destructive one." In the words of Alice Hoffman in the *New York Times Book Review,* "French continues to write about the inner lives of women with insight and intimacy. What she's given us this time is a page-turner with a heart."

A criticism frequently leveled at French is that "her novels suffer from a knee-jerk feminist stereotype in which all men are at worst, brutal and, at best, insensitive," notes Susan Wood in the *Washington Post Book World.* Astonished at the bitterness and anger that French expresses in *The Women's Room* and *The Bleeding Heart,* critics often object to the anti-male stance in her fiction. For example, Libby Purves writes in the London *Times* that *The Women's Room* is "a prolonged—largely autobiographical—yell of fury at the perversity of the male sex. . . . The men in the novel are drawn as malevolent stick figures, at best appallingly dull and at worst monsters." And referring in the *Chicago Tribune Book World* to a "persistently belligerent anti-male bias" in *The Bleeding Heart,* Alice Adams feels this one-sided characterization only serves to disenfranchise many readers who might otherwise read and learn from French's literature. Richard Phillips writes in the *Chicago Tribune* that "to read one of her novels . . . means wincing through hundreds of pages of professed revulsion over the male species of human kind. Man means power, control, rage. Even the nice guys finish last. Men are bastards. Women suffer. It is a message written with all the subtlety of a sledgehammer, but one that, French argues, is only a mirror reflection of what men themselves are taught from birth: Contempt for women." But, as French explains to Phillips: "Contempt for women is not an accident, it is not a by-product of our culture. It is the heart. The culture is founded on it. It is the essential central core; without it, the culture would fall apart."

"Just as feminists have identified and denounced misogyny in books written by men, it behooves us all to arraign those books which exude a destructive hatred of men," opines Suzanne Fields in the *Detroit News.* "Such feelings can infect and calcify in dangerous ways. To intersperse torrid sex scenes with tirades against men for the imagined crime of being men merely allows villains and victims to exchange places. The rules of the game, weighted as they are to create those villains and victims, go unchallenged."

However, to those critics who charge that French portrays male characters as "stick figures," "empty men," and "cardboard villains," and to readers who do not realize her purpose in creating one-sided male characters, French responds in the *New York Times*: "That infuriates me. Every time I see that I see orange. The men are there as the women see them and feel them—impediments in women's lives. That's the focus. . . . Aristotle managed to build a whole society without mentioning women once. Did anyone ever say: 'Are there women in (Joseph Conrad's) Nigger of the Narcissus?' "

Praising French's skill in eliciting response from her readers, Weeks declares that "as a polemic [*The Women's Room*] is brilliant, forcing the reader to accept the reactions of the women as the only possible ones." Noting that "the reader, a willing victim, becomes enmeshed in mixed feelings," Weeks observes that the novel "forces confrontations on the reader mercilessly." Although Weeks acknowledges the novel's flaws, she concludes, "*The Women's Room* is a wonderful novel, full of life and passions that ring true as crystal. Its fierceness, its relentless refusal to compromise are as stirring as a marching song." Yet, as Van Gelder points out in *Ms.*, despite the fact that it "is a book whose message is 'the lesson all women learn: men are the ultimate enemy,' " men do not seem to be "especially threatened by the book"; those who choose to read it probably have some degree of commitment to feminism in the first place. "The best compliment I can pay it is that I kept forgetting that it was fiction," remarks the *New York Times*' Christopher Lehmann-Haupt. "It seized me by my preconceptions and I kept struggling and arguing with its premises. Men can't be that bad, I kept wanting to shout at the narrator. There must be room for accommodation between the sexes that you've somehow overlooked. And the damnable thing is, she's right."

"Many women will recognize the world French has given us," remarks Wood. If not explicitly autobiographical, French's fiction seems at least validated by her own life experience. And when asked why she continues "to deal with men, especially if her own novels are not autobiographical, as she insists" French told Phillips that "whatever my inclinations were, and however I lead my life, I would still be writing about women and men, because women and men live on this Earth. And I assume that the Earth is going to go on being peopled." Despite mixed critical reviews, reader response to her work has been tremendous. Countless women readers have written to French to say that what she wrote in *The Women's Room*, for example, is their truth; and as French relates to Jennes, "There is nothing in [*The Women's Room*] I've not felt." Noting that the novel "speaks from the heart to women everywhere," a *Publishers Weekly* reviewer writes: "It is as if French had been taking notes for twenty years. Her dialogue, her characterizations, her knowledge of the changing relationships, sexual and otherwise, between men and women in a complex world of shifting values, are all extraordinary. It is, French says, women who best support women in crisis times." According to *Publishers Weekly*'s Barbara Bannon, it is this "genuine sympathy for other women caught in life situations, trivial or deadly serious, for which they were never prepared that made Marilyn French's first novel, *The Women's Room*, such a breakthrough bestseller in hardcover and paperback."

Suggesting still another reason for French's popularity, Bannon observes that "in both of French's novels women's commitment to raising children as one of the most important elements in their lives is clearly recognized and accepted as fact, and it is her understanding of this, her refusal to look down on such a traditional women's role, that makes her novels accessible to many women who might not relate to a more formalized 'feminist' position." As she tells Angela Brooks in the London *Times*, "I don't care whether it's a popular message or not. You can't have it all." In an interview for the *Chicago Tribune*, French relates to Beth Austin: "Women of my generation risked everything. We left our husbands, which meant that we had no money. And we had the kids, and we didn't have jobs. We were facing, and many of us entered, poverty. Some of us are still in that poverty, some of us are not." In the *New York Times*, French remarks to Nan Robertson: "Men believe men are central to women's lives and they're not even when they become economically central, even psychologically, when we have to please them. Children are the center of a woman's life. Work is always central. When you have children, they become your work, your opus."

In *Her Mother's Daughter*, a forgiving look at motherhood, French writes about the maternal legacy bequeathed to daughters by examining four generations of an immigrant family through the experiences of its women. Anastasia, the narrator, attempts to overcome several generations of wrongs by living like a man, sexually free and artistically and commercially successful. Her success, however, is juxtaposed with the hardships and sufferings endured by the women before her, and her emancipation, according to Anne Summers in the *Times Literary Supplement*, "is shown to be more illusory than real; despite every conceivable change in outward forms, it is the older women's experience which imprints itself on her inner life." Reviewing the novel in *Tribune Books*, Beverly Fields indicates that the novel "elaborates a theme that runs more or less quietly through her first two books: the ways in which female submission to male society, with its accompanying suppression of rage, is passed like contagion from mother to daughter." Marie Olesen Urbanski observes in the *Los Angeles Times Book Review* that "the more educated or liberated the mother is, the more pervasive is her sense of a guilt from which there is no absolution. . . . 'Her Mother's Daughter' celebrates mothers. It depicts the high price mothers pay for children who say they do not want, but who must have their sacrifices. . . . Has Mother's Day come at last?"

French's nonfiction seeks the origins of male dominance in society. In *Shakespeare's Division of Experience*, for example, she posits that the female's capacity to bear children has historically aligned her with nature and, consequently, under man's compulsion to exercise power over it. In the *New York Times Book Review*, Geoffrey H. Hartman describes the subject of the book as "the relationship between political power and the 'division' of experience according to gender principles. It is a division that has proved disastrous for both sexes, she writes: To the male is attributed the ability to kill; to the female the ability to give birth; and around these extremes there cluster 'masculine' and 'feminine' qualities, embodied in types or roles that reinforce a schizoid culture and produce all sorts of fatal contradictions." Calling it "the finest piece of feminist criticism we have yet had," Laurence Lerner notes in the *Times Literary Supplement* that "her concern is not merely with Shakespeare." Recognizing that "she believes the identification of moral qualities with genders impoverishes and endangers our society," Lerner adds that French thinks "every human experience should be reintegrated." Lerner continues that "whereas for Shakespeare the greatest threat may have lain in nature, it now lies in control; she therefore confesses an animus against 'the almost total dedication to masculine values that characterizes our culture.' "

Remarking that "French is intelligent, nothing if not ingenious, and obviously sincere," Anne Barton suggests in the *New York Review of Books* about *Shakespeare's Division of Experience* that "there is something very limiting, however, about the assumption upon which all her arguments are based." For example, Barton continues, "Although she does grudgingly admit from time to time that rationality, self-control, individualism, and 'permanencies' may have some little value, she is distrustful of 'civilization,' and of the life of the mind. She also leaves a major contradiction in her position unexplored. On the one hand, she indignantly denies that women are any 'closer to nature' than men. . . . On the other hand, it is not clear that the qualities she values, and according to which she would like to see live lived by both sexes, are all—in her terms—feminine." According to S. Schoenbaum in the *Washington Post Book World,* "She accepts what is after all common knowledge: that the gender principles aren't gender-specific—biological males can accommodate feminine values, and females aren't exempt from masculine power struggles. And, along with overlap, there exists the possibility for synthesis."

Beyond Power: On Women, Men, and Morals, writes Lawrence Stone in the *New York Times Book Review,* "is a passionate polemic about the way men have treated women over the past several millenniums." And according to Paul Robinson in the *Washington Post Book World,* "Nothing in her previous books, however, prepares one for the intellectual range and scholarly energy of *Beyond Power,* which is nothing less than a history of the world (from the cavewomen to the Sandinistas) seen through the critical prism of contemporary feminism." Mary Warnock explains in the *Times Literary Supplement* that French's "general thesis is that men, who have hitherto governed the world, have always sought power above all else, and, in the interests of power, have invented the system of patriarchy which dominates all Western art, philosophy, religion and education. Above all it now dominates industry and politics."

Recognizing the veracity of French's claims in the book, Stone states: "The history of the treatment of women by men in the last 2,500 years of Western civilization is truly awful. One therefore has to sympathize with her passionate indignation and admire the singleminded zeal with which she has pursued her theory through the millenniums." Nevertheless, Stone finds the book flawed. For instance, pointing to the "relentless cruelty and selfishness" that anthropologists have discovered in some of the primitive peoples that French has perceived as utopian, Stone comments: "French's attempt to resuscitate the noble savage in feminist drag is not convincing. Moreover, worship of a female does not do much to affect the lot of women one way or the other." Observing that "she is a formidable woman to argue with," Purves wonders whether the patriarchal system, whether "strife, competition, rivalry, the concentration of power and even war itself," is not responsible for even a few benefits to the world; but French responds by explaining, "We are always told this. That commercial links and inventions and knowledge of other nations come from war; but who is to say that these things wouldn't have happened anyway? There is no way we can know how the world would have been without men's domination." Calling it "a brilliant study of power and control showing how those two related systems have affected the lives of men and women throughout human history," though, Richard Rhodes concludes in the *Chicago Tribune Book World* that "it ranks high among the most important books of the decade."

Because of the types of books French writes as well as the reaction that they frequently generate, many "people think I cause divorces because women are reading my books," French tells Phillips. "A lot of men like to think that it's all me, that it is all my doing. They don't understand where women are coming from-because they don't listen to women, ever." Pointing out that the sex war is still raging, French adds: "Of course, it's dis-

guised. We love each other. We go to bed with each other. We flirt with each other. But underneath all this is the ancient history of male supremacy over females." Phillips observes, though, that "French seems neither concerned nor likely to moderate her vilification of men simply to heal the wounds of ostracism. Mankind is the enemy, after all, and French cannot give up an inch in her crusade against male supremacy. Never."

Suggesting that whatever hope there is for the future rests with those "young men who are different [from their fathers], who take responsibility for their children," French indicates to Austin that "the cultural myth for men is, first of all, that if they are real men they are alone. They are not bound into the female sphere, which is the sphere of the domestic." French sympathizes with the male, though, and believes that they, too, suffer from a patriarchal society. "You see most men are living a lie," French tells Purves. "Any human being is living a lie who pretends to be in control, even of themselves. I find it ironic that the sex which cannot control its sex organ is the one that considers itself fit to control the world. Most women who do gain power now only fall prey to the same delusion." French adds that "women who have totally accepted the male world" suffer the same "alienation, loneliness, sterility." And as she declares in an interview with Grace Glueck in the *New York Times Book Review,* "I don't want women to be like men. Women still are full of the old, traditional female virtues. . . . They create the felicities of life. These things are important, *essential,* and I don't want women to give them up. I want men to learn them. I want to feminize the world."

AVOCATIONAL INTERESTS: Amateur musician; parties, cooking, travel.

MEDIA ADAPTATIONS: The Women's Room was produced a television movie in 1980.

BIOGRAPHICAL/CRITICAL SOURCES:

BOOKS

Contemporary Literary Criticism, Gale, Volume 10, 1979, Volume 18, 1981.

PERIODICALS

Chicago Tribune, May 4, 1980, February 7, 1988.
Chicago Tribune Book World, March 9, 1980, June 23, 1985.
Detroit News, April 20, 1980.
Library Journal, November 15, 1977.
Los Angeles Times Book Review, May 4, 1980, April 19, 1981, August 25, 1985, October 18, 1987.
Ms., January, 1978, April, 1979, May, 1980.
Nation, January 30, 1988.
Newsweek, March 17, 1980.
New York Review of Books, June 11, 1981.
New York Times, October 27, 1977, March 10, 1980, March 16, 1981.
New York Times Book Review, October 16, 1977, November 11, 1977, March 16, 1980, March 22, 1981, June 12, 1983, June 23, 1985, October 25, 1987.
People, February 20, 1978.
Publishers Weekly, August 29, 1977, August 21, 1978, March 7, 1980.
Time, March 17, 1980, July 29, 1985.
Times (London), March 18, 1982, January 22, 1986, October 15, 1987, October 19, 1987.
Times Literary Supplement, February 18, 1977, April 21, 1978, May 9, 1980, June 4, 1982, January 24, 1986, October 23, 1987.

Tribune Books, October 11, 1987.
Village Voice, March 24, 1980.
Virginia Quarterly Review, Volume 54, number 2, 1978.
Washington Post, May 7, 1980.
Washington Post Book World, October 9, 1977, March 9, 1980, March 8, 1981, June 2, 1985, October 18, 1987.

—*Sketch by Sharon Malinowski*

* * *

FRENCH, Paul
See ASIMOV, Isaac

* * *

FREUD, Anna 1895-1982

PERSONAL: Born December 3, 1895, in Vienna, Austria; immigrated to England, 1938; naturalized British citizen; died October 8, 1982, in London, England; daughter of Sigmund (a psychoanalyst) and Martha (Bemays) Freud. *Education:* Attended Cottage Lyceum, Vienna, Austria.

ADDRESSES: Home—20 Maresfield Gardens, London NW3 5SX, England. *Agent*—Mark Paterson, 11/12 West Stockwell St,, Colchester CO1 1HN, England. *Office*—Hampstead Clinic, 21 Maresfield Gardens, London NW3 55H, England.

CAREER: Elementary school teacher in Vienna, Austria; Jackson Nursery, Vienna, founder and director, 1937-38; in private psychoanalytic practice in London, England, 1938-82; Hampstead Nurseries, London, co-founder and director, 1940-45; Hampstead Child Therapy Course and Clinic, London, co-founder and director, 1947-82. Vienna Training Institute, secretary, beginning in 1925; member of London Institute of Psychoanalysis, 1938-82. Lecturer on children's rights.

MEMBER: Vienna Psychoanalytic Society (chairman, 1925-38), International Psychoanalytic Association (vice president, 1938-82), British Psychoanalytic Society.

AWARDS, HONORS: LL.D. from Clark University, 1950, University of Sheffield, 1966; Sc.D. from Jefferson Medical College, 1964, University Chicago, 1966, Yale University, 1968, Columbia University, 1978, Harvard University, 1980; honorary M.D. from Vienna University, 1972; D.Phil. from J. W. Goethe University, 1981. Dolly Madison Award, 1965; Commander of the Order of the British Empire, 1967; grand decoration of honor in gold (Austria), 1975; honorary fellow of the Royal Society of Medicine, 1978.

WRITINGS:

IN ENGLISH

(With Dorothy Burlingham) *Young Children in War-Time in a Residential War Nursery,* Allen & Unwin, 1942, University Microfilms, 1975.
(With Burlingham) *War and Children,* Medical War Books, 1943, Greenwood Press, 1973.
(With Burlingham) *Infants Without Families: The Case for and Against Residential Nurseries* (also see below), Allen & Unwin, 1943, International Universities Press, 1944, reprinted, 1962.
(With Thesi Bergmann) *Children in the Hospital,* International Universities Press, 1966.
(Contributor) Franz Alexander, editor, *Psychoanalytic Pioneers,* Basic Books, 1966.
Difficulties in the Path of Psychoanalysis: A Confrontation of Past With Present Viewpoints, International Universities Press, 1969.

(With Joseph Goldstein and Albert J. Solnit) *Beyond the Best Interests of the Child,* Free Press, 1973, revised edition, 1979.
(Author of foreword) *Studies in Child Psychoanalysis: Pure and Applied,* Yale University Press, 1975.
(Contributor) Ruch S. Eissler and others, editors, *Psychoanalytic Assessment; the Diagnostic Profile: An Anthology of the Psychoanalytic Study of the Child,* Yale University Press, 1977.
(With Goldstein and Solnit) *Before the Best Interests of the Child,* Free Press, 1979.
(With Joseph Sandler, Hansi Kennedy, and Robert L. Tyson) *The Technique of Child Psychoanalysis: Discussions With Anna Freud,* Harvard University Press, 1980.
(With Sandler) *The Analysis of Defense: The Ego and the Mechanisms of Defense Revisited,* International Universities Press, 1985.
(With Joseph Epstein, Sonja Goldstein, and Solnit) *In the Best Interest of the Child,* Free Press, 1986.

IN ENGLISH TRANSLATION

Einfuehrung in die Technik der Kinderanalyse, Internationaler Psychoanalytischer Verlag, 1927, translation by L. Pierce Clark published as *Introduction to the Technique of Child Analysis,* Nervous and Mental Disease Publishing Co., 1928, Amo, 1975.
Einfuehrung in die Psychoanalyse fuer Paedagogen, [Germany], translation by Barbara Low published in England as *Introduction to Psychoanalysis for Teachers: Four Lectures by Anna Freud,* Allen & Unwin, 1931, published in the United States as *Psychoanalysis for Teachers and Parents: Introductory Lectures by Anna Freud,* Emerson Books, 1935, Norton, 1979.
Das Ich und die Abwehrmechanismen (also see below), Internationaler Psychoanalytischer Verlag, 1936, translation by Cecil Baines published in England as *The Ego and the Mechanisms of Defense,* Hogarth, 1937, published in the United States by International Universities Press, 1946, revised edition, 1967.
The Psychoanalytical Treatment of Children: Technical Lectures and Essays, translation by Nancy Procter-Gregg, Imago, 1946, International Universities Press, 1959.

COLLECTED WORKS

The Writings of Anna Freud, International Universities Press, Volume 1: *Introduction to Psychoanalysis: Lectures for Child Analysts and Teachers, 1922-1935,* 1974, Volume 2: *The Ego and the Mechanisms of Defense,* 1967, Volume 3: (with Burlingham) *Infants Without Families: Reports on the Hampstead Nurseries,* 1973, Volume 4: *Indications for Child Analysis, and Other Papers, 1945-1956,* 1968, Volume 5: *Research at the Hampstead Child Therapy Clinic, and Other Papers, 1956-1965,* 1969, Volume 6: *Normality and Pathology in Childhood: Assessments of Development,* 1965, Volume 7: *Problems of Psychoanalytic Training, Diagnosis, and the Technique of Therapy, 1966-1970,* 1971, Volume 8: *Psychoanalytic Psychology of Normal Development, 1970-1980,* 1981.

OTHER

(Translator from English) Israel Levine, *Das Unbewusste* (title means "The Unconscious"), [Leipzig], 1926.
(Co-editor) Sigmund Freud, *Gesammelte Werke: Chronologisch Geordnet,* multivolume work, Imago, 1940-52, published as *The Standard Edition of the Complete Psychological Works of Sigmund Freud,* Hogarth, 1953-74, Norton, 1976.

(Co-editor) S. Freud, *The Origins of Psychoanalysis: Letters to Wilhelm Fliess, Drafts and Notes, 1887-1902,* translation by Eric Mosbacher and James Strachey, Imago, 1954.

(Co-editor) S. Freud, *The Psychopathology of Everyday Life,* Benn, 1966.

Also co-editor of *The Collected Papers of Sigmund Freud,* five volumes, Basic Books. Also editor of *Psychoanalytic Study of the Child* (annual), Hogarth.

SIDELIGHTS: When Sigmund Freud—the father of psychoanalysis—died in 1939, his daughter Anna assumed the role of guardian and defender of psychoanalytic tradition. "With a firm grasp of her father's work, she was the accepted explicator of his texts and was listened to accordingly," commented the *New York Times.* Her own contributions to the field were considerable; she was particularly noted for her theory of child psychoanalysis. Because she preferred discussing her father's and her own work to sharing the details of her personal life, relatively little is known about her early years in Vienna. It is known that she was psychoanalyzed by her father, that she became a psychoanalyst herself when she was in her late twenties, and that, following the Nazi invasion of Austria in 1938, she fled with her family to London, where she remained until her death in 1982.

At the start of her career, Freud worked with adults, but she soon became interested in children. She met regularly with other analysts who shared her interests to discuss theories about the mental life of children. She was "one of the first to take the technique of psychoanalysis and apply it to the treatment of neurotic children," wrote Robert Sussman Stewart in the *New York Times Book Review.* "By interpreting the clues . . . children gave—in dreams, daydreams, paintings, imaginative play—she slowly made her way to their dark and shadowy inner worlds."

Prior to Freud's work in child analysis, the accepted knowledge on the mental life of the child had been gathered "almost exclusively from the 'reconstructions' of adults," Stewart explained. Through his work with middle-aged patients Sigmund Freud had developed his theory of "early psychosexual stages—the oral phase that begins at birth, the subsequent anal, phallic, and latency periods, ending in adolescence with the onset of puberty." With her own work, Anna Freud was able to prove one of her father's most basic hypotheses. By directly observing children as they developed and by "applying psychoanalysis to the treatment of disturbed children, Anna Freud and her co-workers provided the empirical evidence long needed to verify the extrapolations from previous adult case histories," Stewart wrote.

As had happened in the field of psychoanalysis, the earliest findings in the field of child psychoanalysis came from the study of disturbed patients. These findings, noted Stewart, "shed as much light on normality as on pathology" and also caused Anna Freud's detractors to accuse her of seeing every child as sick and in need of treatment. However, Stewart contended, Anna Freud continually "urged parents *against* analytic treatment for their children where a problem is not well-enough defined, or where the disturbance seems more likely to be a developmental one . . . and therefore transitory."

According to the *New York Times,* Anna Freud questioned the old assumption that children were "arbitrarily motivated and that discipline was the surest path to healthy development." She hoped, wrote Stewart, "somehow to create a new climate, new attitudes toward upbringing." Through her many writings, including *Introduction to the Technique of Child Analysis and Psychoanalysis for Teachers and Parents,* she "described the child's 'fluid' psychological nature, his swings in mood, his tendency to

make strides in one direction and then, suddenly, to fall back in another. . . . She tried to get across the idea that these alterations in growth were within the boundaries of the normal." Freud tried to make it clear that she was not arguing for total permissiveness in child-rearing, but rather for a happy medium between restraint and punishment. She urged teachers and parents alike to "allow each stage in the child's life the right proportion of instinct gratification and instinct restriction."

Freud's efforts to define normal child development led her to focus on the ego. She was, wrote David Ingleby in the *Times Literary Supplement,* "concerned with the [ego's] integrative, conflict-resolving capacities." Child analysis, she argued, was the sole means by which the ego's adaptive functions could be properly investigated, since "the past recalled by adult patients contains only unresolved conflicts—never resolved ones." According to Stewart, the ego's struggles can best be observed in children: "Caught between instinctual pressures from within and harsh demands without, [the child's ego] remains intact by seeking out for its use a variety of mechanisms of defense." Freud's studies of ego functions led to the 1936 publication of her best-known and most highly regarded work, *The Ego and the Mechanisms of Defense,* in which she classified the ego's operations. By illustrating how the total personality is structured, that work "opened up," said Stewart, "a whole series of innovations in psychoanalytic technique."

Another of Freud's more significant accomplishments was the residential nursery she established in London during World War II. The Hampstead Nurseries, partially funded by an American welfare organization, provided a home for what Freud called war orphans—children whose parents had died and children who had been separated from their families during the war. In return for financial assistance, the welfare organization requested monthly written progress reports on the children housed at the Hampstead Nurseries. The reports, written by Freud and her colleague Dorothy Burlingham, were published in *Infants Without Families: Reports on the Hampstead Nurseries,* which constitutes the third volume of Anna Freud's collected writings.

In her review of that volume for the *Times Literary Supplement,* Rosemary Dinnage commented that "The Hampstead Nurseries' reports are unique, not only because . . . no similar month-by-month account has been published of the progress of a residential Home and its children, but also because of the curious poignancy of the situation that they describe: a group, mainly, of uprooted Jewish refugees, caring for a younger generation of war victims, . . . beneficiaries of the Freud family's flight to this country in 1938." Dinnage also pointed out that the reports are of value to both lay and professional readers for their descriptions of child development. "The conditions under which these reports were written," she noted, "provided an exceptional opportunity to study children's attitudes to danger, fear, and loss, and even to fundamental problems of evil and pain." Of the children who inhabited the nurseries, Dinnage observed: "the vocabulary of war comes naturally to them—'I want him bombed,' says an irritable child of an unwelcome visitor. . . . Their games, with the usual nursery props pressed into service as planes, shelters, and ambulances instead of trains or kitchens, mimic the world around them, either in straightforward imitation or in urgent attempts to reverse the irreversible: as in the case of a boy, orphaned in a raid, who incessantly bombed toy houses and built them up again."

In *Infants Without Families* Freud's many examples illustrate her belief that children require the presence of their parents to help them withstand calamities. "It is when calamity involves separation, especially from loved adults who have sometimes [in infantile fantasies] been wished out of the way, that it totally destroys [a child's] peace of mind." In other words, Freud's observations led her to conclude that children are not instinctively afraid of war but that they are extremely afraid of (and damaged by) being separated from their families. War orphans needed protection, Freud felt, "not because horrors and atrocities are so strange to them, but because we want them at this decisive stage of their development to overcome and estrange themselves from the primitive and atrocious wishes of their own infantile nature."

After the war ended, the war nursery was replaced by the Hampstead Child Therapy Course and Clinic. Under Anna Freud's leadership, the clinic was devoted, explained a London *Times* writer, "to training, treatment, teaching and research in the field of child development." Freud's work and writings continued to reflect her interest in education and child development. Later, she became interested in children's legal rights, and she applied concepts of analytic child psychology to such legal issues as child custody, foster care, and adoption. In the 1960s Freud worked during various periods at Yale University's law school and child-study center, where she investigated the law as it relates to and affects children. Her discoveries in this area led her to write, with Yale professors Joseph Goldstein and Albert Solnit, *Beyond the Best Interests of the Child* in 1973 and *Before the Best Interests of the Child* in 1979. In these volumes Freud and her co-authors argue against removing children from their homes in all but the most extreme circumstances. According to a London *Times* writer, the authors' work has had "a remarkable impact on all workers . . . whose difficult task it is to administer the law in both Britain and the United States."

In a review of *Before the Best Interests of the Child* for the *Washington Post Book World* David Chambers summarized the book's central point: "The authors believe that children suffer irremediable trauma from disruptions in ties with their parents, even parents of whom most of us disapprove. . . . Their primary message is: Stay out, leave the child where she or he is, hands off. The consequences of intervention are likely to be more damaging to the child than the parental conduct complained of." Chambers was critical of the authors' extreme position regarding legal intervention in abusive situations: "By using examples only of shockingly inappropriate removals, . . . the authors may delude some readers into accepting their position, but judges and social workers will have no difficulty remembering much harder cases when a child seemed clearly harmed or severely endangered but had no broken bones to show for it." Nonetheless, Chambers concluded, many children are too hastily removed from their homes, and the authors' message regarding legal intervention in cases of suspected child abuse "is important and needs to be heard everywhere."

In addition to her own work, Anna Freud devoted considerable attention to defending and explaining her father's teachings. She also helped edit a number of his writings, including *The Origins of Psychoanalysis: Letters to Wilhelm Fliess,* which was first published in English in 1954. During the early 1980s that work became the focus of controversy when a researcher found that significant portions of Freud's letters to his friend Dr. Wilhelm Fliess had been omitted by Anna Freud and her co-editors when they published *The Origins of Psychoanalysis.* The omissions contained references to Sigmund Freud's seduction theory—an early theory that he later abandoned. Jeffrey M. Masson, the researcher who discovered the omissions, was convinced that Freud's renunciation of the seduction theory had been a mistake, and that the entire premise of psychoanalytic thought was therefore faulty.

In 1977, eager to examine the original Freud-Fliess correspondence, Masson had approached Anna Freud for permission to do so. At first, Masson told Janet Malcolm in an interview for the *New Yorker,* Freud was reluctant, but finally she agreed to his request. Three years later Masson was elected by the board of the Sigmund Freud archives to become its director. That position gave him additional access to Freud's unpublished work, and he continued his efforts to uncover an explanation for Freud's abandonment of the seduction theory. This theory, which Freud had discussed in letters to Fliess between 1895 and 1897, proposed that mental illness in adults resulted from sexual abuse suffered during childhood. According to *New York Times* writer Ralph Blumenthal, Freud later decided that his patients' accounts of abuse were wishes, rather than memories of actual events, and this idea led him to develop his theory of the Oedipus complex, which "has dominated psychoanalysis, with far-reaching implications ever since."

Masson's research convinced him that Freud's patients had in fact been sexually abused, and that Freud had been wrong to doubt them. After examining the original letters and discovering that most references to the seduction theory had been omitted from the published collection, Masson asked Anna Freud to explain the omissions. He reported her reply in his book *The Assault on Truth: Freud's Suppression of the Seduction Theory,* which was excerpted in the *Atlantic.* "Miss Freud indicated that since her father had eventually abandoned the seduction theory, it would only prove confusing to readers to be exposed to his early hesitations and doubts." "I, on the other hand," Masson wrote, "felt that these passages not only were of great historical importance but might well represent the truth. Nobody, it seemed to me, had the right to decide for others, by altering the record, what was truth and what was error." Anna Freud further told Masson that "keeping up the seduction theory would mean to abandon the Oedipus complex, and with it the whole importance of phantasy life, conscious or unconscious phantasy. In fact," she told him, "I think there would have been no psychoanalysis afterwards."

Masson's findings generated a great deal of controversy and led to his dismissal as director of the Freud archives. "I regret this publicity," Anna Freud said when asked to comment on Masson's research. Other responses to Masson's claims that Freud had mistakenly abandoned the seduction theory were varied. In a *New York Times* article, Daniel Goleman assessed the controversy and its implications: "The dispute, as Dr. Masson depicts it, is over how an analyst treats the traumatic events of a patient's life. . . . Freud's abandonment of the seduction theory, in this light, has been interpreted to mean that the analyst ignores those realities, that the most traumatic events of real life carry no weight, compared to one's fantasies." But according to Goleman, most practicing psychoanalysts disagree with Masson. In practice, asserted Goleman, the majority of analysts do not adhere to strict Freudian theory. Instead, they "take into account both the real events of a patient's life and the emotional meaning the patient gives to them." Frank R. Hartman, a Manhattan psychiatrist, is another who disagreed with Masson's claims. "Freud realized he made a mistake in attributing all neurosis to repressed memories of actual abuse," Hartman told the *New York Times.* "He discovered a much broader theory which explained much more."

Anna Freud and her co-editors were perhaps misguided in their decision to delete references to the seduction theory from *The Origins of Psychoanalysis,* Goleman nonetheless concluded. "If the motive of the handful who participated in deleting information from Freud's published papers was in fact to protect a particular psychoanalytic ideology, it can be seen as a cover-up." However, Goleman also noted, "the whole Byzantine edifice of psychoanalytic theory simply does not rise or fall on the issue of the seduction theory. It is not so much a cornerstone of psychoanalysis as a pathway that led to its discovery, a pioneering track that modern travelers are not required to follow."

Some observers feel that Anna Freud was needlessly zealous in her efforts to preserve the integrity of orthodox psychoanalytic theory. "It could be argued that Anna Freud . . . respect[ed] the letter of her father's work, but not its spirit," commented David Ingleby in the *Times Literary Supplement.* "For Sigmund Freud, in keeping with his scientific ideals, made wholesale changes in his theory when confronted with awkward data." But psychoanalysis "took second place to nothing in Anna Freud's life," Ingleby wrote, and her contributions to the profession were considerable. "As well as developing new ideas on the adaptive functioning of the ego, . . . she acquired a legendary reputation as a child analyst, and (through the Hampstead Clinic, and her widespread following in America) . . . placed that profession firmly on the map."

BIOGRAPHICAL/CRITICAL SOURCES:

BOOKS

Peters, Uwe Henrik, *Anna Freud: A Life for Children,* Weidenfeld & Nicolson, 1985.
Robinson, Donald, *Miracle Finders,* McKay, 1976.

PERIODICALS

Atlantic, February, 1984.
Los Angeles Times, October 23, 1986.
New Yorker, December 5, 1983, December 12, 1983.
New York Times, August 18, 1981, August 25, 1981, January 24, 1984.
New York Times Book Review, January 23, 1972.
Time, April 26, 1968.
Times (London), April 18, 1985.
Times Literary Supplement, June 25, 1970, April 14, 1972, January 5, 1973, March 9, 1973, July 18, 1975, April 9, 1982.
Washington Post Book World, March 9, 1980.

OBITUARIES:

PERIODICALS

Newsweek, October 18, 1982.
New York Times, October 10, 1982.
Time, October 25, 1982.
Times (London), October 11, 1982.
Washington Post, October 10, 1982.

*   *   *

FREUD, Sigmund 1856-1939

PERSONAL: Name originally Sigismund Solomon Freud; born May 6, 1856, in Freiberg, Moravia (now Pribor, Czechoslovakia); died of cancer, September 23, 1939, in London, England; cremated; son of Jacob (a merchant) and Amalia Freud; married Martha Bernays, 1886; children: Martin, Anna, four others. *Education:* University of Vienna, M.D., 1881; studied with neurologist J. M. Charcot in Paris, 1885-86.

CAREER: Worked at the Physiological Institute of Vienna, 1876-1882; Vienna Central Hospital, Vienna, assistant physician, 1882-85; private psychiatric practice in Vienna, 1886-1938; University of Vienna, Vienna, 1886-1938, began as lecturer in neuropathology, became professor of neurology. Co-founder of the Vienna Psycho-Analytic Society and the International Psychoanalytical Association; visiting lecturer at universities in the United States and Europe, including Clark University and the University of London.

AWARDS, HONORS: Honorary member of the American Psychiatric Association, the American Psychoanalytic Association, the New York Neurological Society, the French Psychoanalytic Society, and the Royal Medico-Psychological Association; honorary doctoral degree from Clark University; Goethe Prize, 1930; fellow of the Royal Society of Medicine (London).

WRITINGS:

Zur Auffassung der Aphasien: Eine kritische Studie, Deuticke, 1891, translation with introduction by E. Stengel published as *On Aphasia: A Critical Study,* International Universities Press, 1953.
(With Josef Breuer) *Studien uber Hysterie,* Deuticke, 1895, translation by A. A. Brill published as *Selected Papers on Hysteria and Other Psychoneuroses,* Journal of Nervous and Mental Disease Publishing Co., 1909, enlarged edition translated by James Strachey published as *Studies on Hysteria,* Basic Books, 1957.
Die infantile Cerebrallaehmung, Hoelder, 1897, translation by Lester A. Russin published as *Infantile Cerebral Paralysis,* University of Miami Press, 1968.
Die Traumdeutung, Deuticke, 1900, translation by Brill published as *The Interpretation of Dreams,* Macmillan, 1913, reprinted, Random House, 1978, translation by James Strachey published under the same title, Basic Books, 1955.
Zur Psychopathologie des Alltagslebens (Ueber Vergessen, Versprechen, Vergreifen, Aberglaube und Irrtum), Karger, 1904, translation by Brill published as *Psychopathology of Everyday Life,* Macmillan, 1914, translation by Alan Tyson published as *The Psychopathology of Everyday Life,* Norton, 1965.
Drei Abhandlungen zur Sexualtheorie, Deuticke, 1905, translation by Brill published as *Three Contributions to the Sexual Theory,* Journal of Nervous and Mental Disease Publishing Co., 1910, 2nd enlarged edition published as *Three Contributions to the Theory of Sex,* 1916, translation by J. Strachey published as *Three Essays on the Theory of Sexuality,* Imago Publishing Co., 1949, Basic Books, 1962.
Der Witz und seine Beziehung zum Unbewussten, Deuticke, 1905, translation by Brill published as *Wit and Its Relation to the Unconscious,* Moffat, 1916, translation by James Strachey published as *Jokes and Their Relation to the Unconscious,* Norton, 1960.
Ueber Psychoanalyse: Fuenf Vorlesungen gehalten zur zwanzigjaehrigen Gruendungsfeier der Clark University in Worcester, Massachussetts, September, 1909, Deuticke, 1910, translation published as *The Origin and Development of Psychoanalysis,* Clark University Press, 1910, reprinted, Regnery Gateway, 1987, translation by J. Strachey published as *Five Lectures on Psycho-Analysis,* Norton, 1977.
Eine Kindheitserinnerung des Leonardo da Vinci, Deuticke, 1910, translation by Brill published as *Leonardo da Vinci: A Psychosexual Study of Infantile Reminiscence,* Moffat, 1916, reprinted, Vintage, 1961, translation by Tyson published as *Leonardo da Vinci and A Memory of His Childhood,* Norton, 1966.
Ueber den Traum, Bergmann, 1911, translation by M. D. Eder published as *On Dreams,* Rebman, 1914, translation by James Strachey published under the same title, Norton, 1952, reprinted, 1980.

Totem und Tabu: Ueber einige Ueberinstimmungen im Seelenleben der Wilden und der Neurotiker, Heller, 1913, translation by Brill published as *Totem and Taboo: Resemblances Between the Psychic Lives of Savages and Neurotics*, Moffat, 1917, reprinted, Vintage, 1961, translation by J. Strachey published as *Totem and Taboo: Some Points of Agreement Between the Mental Lives of Savages and Neurotics*, Routledge & Paul, 1950, Norton, 1952.

"Zeitgemaesses ueber Krieg und Tod," originally published in German periodical *Imago*, 1915, translation by Brill and Alfred B. Kuttner published as *Reflections on War and Death*, Moffat, 1918.

Vorlesungen zur Einfuehrung in die Psychoanalyse, three volumes, Heller, 1916, translation by Joan Riviere published as *A General Introduction to Psychoanalysis*, Boni & Liveright, 1920.

The History of the Psychoanalytic Movement, translated by Brill, Journal of Nervous and Mental Disease Publishing Co., 1917.

Dream Psychology: Psychoanalysis for Beginners, translated by Eder, McCann, 1920.

Jenseits des Lustprinzips, Internationaler Psychoanalytischer Verlag, 1920, translation by C. J. M. Hubback published as *Beyond the Pleasure Principle*, International Psychoanalytic Press, 1922, translation by J. Strachey published under the same title, Liveright, 1961.

Massenpsychologie und Ich-Analyse, Internationaler Psychoanalytischer Verlag, 1921, translation by J. Strachey published as *Group Psychology and the Analysis of the Ego*, International Psychoanalytic Press, 1922, Norton, 1975.

Das Ich und das Es, Internationaler Psychoanalytischer Verlag, 1923, translation by Riviere published as *The Ego and the Id*, Hogarth Press, 1927, Norton, 1962.

Selbstdarstellungen, Meiner, 1925, translation by J. Strachey published as *An Autobiographical Study*, Hogarth Press, 1935, Norton, 1952.

Hemmung, Symptom und Angst, Internationaler Psychoanalytischer Verlag, 1926, translation supervised by L. Pierce Clark published as *Inhibition, Symptom and Anxiety*, Psychoanalytic Institute, 1927, translation by Alix Strachey published as *Inhibitions, Symptoms and Anxiety*, Hogarth Press, 1936, revised edition, Norton, 1959.

Die Frage der Laienanalyse: Underredung mit einem Unparteiischen, Internationaler Psychoanalytischer Verlag, 1926, translation by A. Paul Maerker-Branden published as *The Problem of Lay-Analysis*, Brentano, 1927, translation by J. Strachey published as *The Question of Lay-Analysis: An Introduction to Psycho-Analysis*, Imago Publishing Co., 1947, reprinted, Norton, 1969.

Zie Zukunft einer Illusion, Internationaler Psychoanalytischer Verlag, 1927, translation by W. D. Robson-Scott published as *The Future of an Illusion*, Liveright, 1928, translation by J. Strachey published under the same title, Norton, 1975.

Das Unbehagen in der Kultur, Internationaler Psychoanalytischer Verlag, 1930, translation by Riviere published as *Civilization and Its Discontents*, J. Cape and H. Smith, 1930, translation by J. Strachey published under the same title, Norton, 1961.

Neue Folge der Vorlesungen zur Einfuehrung in die Psychoanalyse, Internationaler Psychoanalytischer Verlag, 1933, translation by W. J. H. Sprott published as *New Introductory Lectures on Psycho-Analysis*, Norton, 1933, translation by J. Strachey published under the same title, Hogarth, 1974.

(With Albert Einstein) *Why War?*, International Institute of Intellectual Cooperation, 1933.

The Problem of Anxiety, translated by Henry Alden Bunker, Norton, 1936.

Der Mann Moses und die monotheistiche Religion: Drei Abhandlungen, Allert de Lange, 1939, translation by Katherine Jones published as *Moses and Monotheism*, Knopf, 1939.

An Outline of Psycho-Analysis, translated by J. Strachey, Norton, 1949.

The Origins of Psycho-Analysis: Letters to Wilhelm Fliess, Drafts and Notes, 1889-1902, translated by Erich Mosbacher and James Strachey, Basic Books, 1954, reprinted, 1977.

(With D. E. Oppenheim) *Dreams in Folklore*, translated by A. M. O. Richards, International Universities Press, 1958.

On Creativity and the Unconscious: Papers on the Psychology of Art, Literature, Love, Religion, selected by Benjamin Nelson, Harper, 1958.

Briefe 1873-1939, edited by E. L. Freud, Fischer, 1960, translation by Tania and James Stern published as *The Letters of Sigmund Freud*, Basic Books, 1960.

The Cocaine Papers, Dunquin Press, 1963, Stonehill, 1975.

Sigmund Freud/Oskar Pfister: Briefe 1909 bis 1939, edited by E. L. Freud and H. Meng, Fischer, 1963, translation by Erich Mosbacher published as *Psychoanalysis and Faith: The Letters of Sigmund Freud and Oskar Pfister*, Basic Books, 1963.

Character and Culture, Collier Books, 1963.

Freud: A Dictionary of Psychoanalysis, edited by Nandor Fodor and Frank Gaynor, Fawcett, 1963.

Sigmund Freud/Karl Abraham: Briefe 1907 bis 1926, edited by H. C. Abraham and E. L. Freud, Fischer, 1965, translation by Bernard Marsh and Hilda C. Abraham published as *A Psychoanalytic Dialogue: The Letters of Sigmund Freud and Karl Abraham, 1907-1926*, Basic Books, 1965.

General Psychological Theory: Papers on Metapsychology, Collier Books, 1966.

Sigmund Freud/Lou Andreas-Salome, Briefwechsel (letters), edited by E. Pfeiffer, Fischer, 1966, translation by William and Elaine Robson-Scott published as *Sigmund Freud and Lou Andrea-Salome*, Harcourt, 1972.

(With William C. Bullitt) *Thomas Woodrow Wilson, Twenty-Eighth President of the United States: A Psychological Study*, Houghton, 1967.

The Complete Introductory Lectures on Psychoanalysis, translated by J. Strachey, Norton, 1967.

Briefwechsel von Sigmund Freud und Arnold Zweig, 1927-1939, edited by E. L. Freud, Fischer, 1968, translation published as *The Letters of Sigmund Freud and Arnold Zweig, 1927-1939*, Harcourt, 1970.

Briefwechsel, edited by William McGuire and Wolfgang Sauerlaender, Fischer, 1974, translation by Ralph Manheim and R. F. C. Hull published as *The Freud/Jung Letters: The Correspondence Between Sigmund Freud and C. G. Jung*, Princeton University Press, 1974.

The Complete Letters of Sigmund Freud to Wilhelm Fliess, 1887-1904, edited by Jeffrey Moussaieff Masson, Harvard University Press, 1985.

Works also published in multi-titled volumes.

COLLECTIONS

Sammlung kleiner Schriften zur Neurosenlehre, five volumes, Volumes 1-3, Deuticke, Volume 4, Heller, Volume 5, Internationaler Psychoanalytischer Verlag, 1906-22.

Gesammelte Schriften, twelve volumes, Internationaler Psychoanalytischer Verlag, 1924-34.

Collected Papers, five volumes, translation supervised by Riviere, International Psychoanalytic Press, 1924-50, Basic Books, 1959.

The Basic Writings of Sigmund Freud, edited by Brill, Random House, 1938, reprinted, 1965.

Gesammelte Werke, seventeen volumes, Imago Publishing Co., 1940-52.

The Standard Edition of the Complete Psychological Works of Sigmund Freud, twenty-four volumes, edited by J. Strachey, Macmillan, 1953-74, *Abstracts* published by National Institute of Mental Health, 1971, *A Concordance to the Standard Edition,* edited by Samuel A. Cuttman, et. al. published by G. K. Hall, 1980.

Civilization, War and Death: Selections From Three Works by Sigmund Freud, edited by John Rickman, Hogarth Press, 1968.

The Essentials of Psychoanalysis, Hogarth Press, 1986.

OTHER

Contributor to psychology journals; editor of psychoanalytic journals, including the *International Journal of Psychoanalysis;* translator into the German of works by J. M. Charcot, H. M. Bernheim, and Marie Bonaparte.

SIDELIGHTS: Sigmund Freud, the Viennese father of psychoanalysis, began his career as a medical neurologist studying the nervous system. He became an internationally-recognized expert on the causes of children's paralysis and collaborated with the noted neurologist J. M. Charcot and the physician Josef Breuer on research to determine the origin and nature of hysteria. Breuer broke new ground by recognizing this nervous disorder as a psychological rather than a physical disturbance, and he and Freud had some success treating patients with hypnosis. Freud's work with hysterics led him to the strikingly original insight that would form the core of psychoanalysis: the idea that neurotic behavior is motivated by unconscious desires that can be revealed through the discursive method of free association.

Early on, Freud hypothesized that the sexual drive (or "libido") lay behind many of these unconscious desires, a view that was deeply shocking to nineteenth-century European society. The radical theorist found himself isolated from the main currents in academic psychology, and he labored alone in the 1890s to refine his theories by analyzing himself and a succession of patients. The psychoanalytic method Freud pioneered sought to reveal the unconscious conflicts and frustrations, often stemming from childhood, that he believed to be responsible for much irrational behavior. By talking spontaneously about his or her feelings under the analyst's guidance, the psychoanalytic patient undertook the slow and painful process of discovering and resolving these unconscious conflicts.

Freud published the results of his work in a series of groundbreaking books, beginning with *Die Traumdeutung* (*The Interpretation of Dreams*) in 1900. In this book, which remains one of his most widely read works, the psychiatrist postulated that dreams often express unconscious desires in symbolic form. Freud theorized that the mechanism of repression, whereby the mind keeps unconscious material from surfacing into consciousness, relaxed during sleep: dream interpretation thus offered an important way of making contact with the deep recesses of the psyche. Freud explored other possible paths to the unconscious in *Zur Psychopathologie des Alltagslebens* and *Der Witz und seine Beziehung zum Unbewussten* (respectively translated as *The Psychopathology of Everyday Life* and *Wit and Its Relation to the Unconscious*). These innovative works suggested that such seemingly innocuous behavior as slips of the tongue, superstitious

quirks, and joke telling could yield psychoanalytic clues to unconscious desires. Freud concluded that psychoanalysis could render useful insights about normal as well as neurotic behavior.

Drei Abhandlungen zur Sexualtheorie, published in 1905 and translated five years later as *Three Contributions to the Sexual Theory,* secured Freud's international reputation and notoriety. The Viennese psychiatrist outlined here the childhood stages of sexual development whose successful passage he thought vital to adult happiness and psychic equilibrium. Dismissing the Victorian image of the sexually innocent child, Freud saw childhood as consisting of stages charged with sexual feelings, focused successively on the mouth, the anus, and the genitals. These bodily organ stages are associated with a developing psychosexual orientation from love of the self to love of the image of the self in another person and, finally, sexual attraction to another person recognized as such. Freud postulated that a development watershed is generally reached between the ages of three and five, when the child feels a strong attraction to the parent of opposite sex and intense rivalry toward the same-sex parent (the so-called Oedipal and Electra stages). Freud theorized that unresolved conflicts in negotiating these developmental stages were major contributors to adult neurosis.

This bold and original sexual theory provoked controversy that continues even today. Freud's insistence on the libido as the dominant human drive led to breaks with some of his illustrious followers, notably Alfred Adler and Carl Jung, who respectively emphasized a "will to power" and a mythic/spiritual questing as important sources of unconscious energy. But the Freud-led international psychoanalytic movement gained considerable influence in professional circles in the period before World War I, and Freudian theory had been popularized in Europe and the United States by the 1920s. Freud's *Vorlesungen zur Einguehrung in die Psychoanalyse* (*General Introduction to Psychoanalysis*), published in 1916 and translated into English four years later, introduced his basic ideas about dreams, errors, sexual development, and neurosis to a general readership.

While continuing to give prime importance to sexual energy and individual childhood development, Freud refined and extended psychoanalytic theory significantly during the early 1920s. Responding in part to the carnage of World War I, he wrote of a powerful human aggressive drive and death instinct in *Jenseits des Lustprinzips* (*Beyond the Pleasure Principle*). The deepest instinct of life, he theorized, is to return to an original state of relative equilibrium or stable diffusion in the broader world—that is, death. In *Das Ich und das Es,* translated as *The Ego and the Id,* Freud introduced a conceptual framework for the basic structure of the psyche. According to this theory, the individual experiences a basic conflict between the instinctual, gratification-driven *id* and the inhibitory controls derived from parents and society and internalized in the *superego.* The task of the third psychic structure, the ego, is to reconcile—as much as possible—these conflicting demands according to the opportunities and constraints presented by the outside world. "A neurosis," Freud wrote, "is the result of a conflict between the ego and the id; the person is at war with himself. A psychosis is the outcome of similar disturbance between the ego and the outside world."

In his other writings Freud devoted attention to cultural and historical influences in psychic development. In *Totem und Tabu* (*Totem and Taboo*), published in 1913, the psychologist analyzed, as indicated by the book's subtitle, the "resemblances between the psychic lives of savages and neurotics," as shown especially in their approaches to totemic or proscribed objects. "The book is extraordinarily provocative," wrote a *New Republic* reviewer in 1918. "There is a thrilling sense of having had contact with a mind at work on the root-problems of human behavior." *Das Unbehagen in der Kultur,* translated as *Civilization and Its Discontents* and one of Freud's best-known works, discusses the basic, irreconcilable conflict between the claims of society and the individual. The very essence of civilization is frustration and denial, Freud argues, and all the products of art, science, and culture in general owe their existence to rechannelled (or "sublimated") sexual energy. Yet Freud did not deny the value of civilization or the fact that culture and its products could become independently desirable. "If Mr. Freud's is not a thoroughly trustworthy mind, it is none the less, one need hardly add, an immensely interesting one, and surely one of the most seminal of our era," wrote Henry Hazlitt in a 1930 *Nation* review. " 'Civilization and Its Discontents,' in spite of its few vagaries, must be set down an impressive and absorbing contribution to the great problem of happiness under our civilization."

While Freudian concepts and language now suffuse Western culture, psychoanalytic theory remains highly controversial fifty years after the psychologist's death. Freud continues to be criticized for exaggerating unconscious sexual motivations, and many of his theories about female sexuality are now widely dismissed. Freud's ideas have also come under fire for what critics see as their narrow positivism and antispiritualism; cited in particular are his characterizations of art as essentially neurotic and religion as "the collective neurosis." More fundamentally, the very concept of an unconscious yet communicative mind has been challenged and psychoanalysis itself belittled as an unfalsifiable and empirically vacuous pseudoscience.

But Freud himself by no means viewed psychoanalysis as a closed, immutable or complete doctrine, and he made only limited claims for its therapeutic value. He also had no patience with those who wished to use his ideas to justify superficial pleasure seeking or to evade personal responsibility for their lives. The whole point of psychoanalysis, in its founder's view, is to *extend* the domain of rational control, and hence, of responsibility, into formerly unconscious parts of the psyche, not to blame early life experiences for adult problems. Whether or not Freud's theories hold up empirically—and there is still much argument on both sides—his genius in introducing an entirely new paradigm for thinking about human behavior is universally acknowledged.

BIOGRAPHICAL/CRITICAL SOURCES:

BOOKS

Abramson, Jeffrey B., *Liberation and Its Limits: The Moral and Political Thought of Freud,* Free Press, 1984.

Berliner, Arthur K., *Psychoanalysis and Society: The Social Thought of Sigmund Freud,* University Press of America, 1983.

Bernheimer, Charles and Claire Kahane, editors, *In Dora's Case: Freud, Hysteria, Feminism,* Columbia University Press, 1985.

Bloom, Harold, editor, *Sigmund Freud,* Chelsea House, 1985.

Bocock, Robert, *Freud and Modern Society,* Nelson, 1976.

Bocock, *Sigmund Freud,* Travistock, 1983.

Chasseguet-Smirgel, Janine and Bela Grunberger, *Freud or Reich? Psychoanalysis and Illusion,* Yale University Press, 1986.

Clark, Ronald W., *Freud: The Man and the Cause,* Random House, 1980.

Cohen, Ira H., *Ideology and Consciousness: Reich, Freud, and Marx,* New York University Press, 1982.

Dilham, Ilham, *Freud and Human Nature,* Blackwell, 1983.

Dilman, *Freud and the Mind,* Blackwell, 1984.

Draenos, S., *Freud's Odyssey,* Yale University Press, 1982.

Erdelyi, Matthew Hugh, *Freud's Cognitive Psychology,* W. H. Freeman, 1985.

Fast, Irene, *Event Theory: A Piaget-Freud Interpretation,* L. Erlbaum, 1985.

Feffer, Melvin, *The Structure of Freudian Thought: The Problem of Immutability and Discontinuity in Development Theory,* International Universities Press, 1982.

Fischer, Seymour and Roger P. Greenberg, *The Scientific Credibility of Freud's Theories and Therapy,* Columbia University Press, 1985.

Freud, Martin, *Sigmund Freud: Man and Father,* Vanguard, 1958.

Freud, Sigmund, *The Ego and the Id,* translated by Joan Riviere, Norton, 1962.

Freud, Sigmund, *Totem and Taboo: Resemblances Between the Psychic Drives of Savages and Neurotics,* translated by James Strachey, Norton, 1952.

Fromm, Erich, *The Greatness and Limitations of Freud's Thought,* Harper, 1980.

Gabriel, Yiannis, *Freud and Society,* Routledge, 1983.

Gay, Peter, *A Godless Jew: Freud, Atheism, and the Making of Psychoanalysis,* Yale University Press, 1987.

Gay, *Freud: A Life for Our Time,* Norton, 1988.

Grinstein, Alexander, *Freud's Rules of Dream Interpretation,* International Universities Press, 1983.

Grunbaum, Adolf, *The Foundations of Psychoanalysis: A Philosophical Critique,* University of California Press, 1984.

Harris, Jay and Jean Harris, *The One-Eyed Doctor, Sigmund Freud: Psychological Origins of Freud's Works,* J. Aronson, 1984.

Hogenson, George B., *Jung's Struggle with Freud,* University of Notre Dame Press, 1983.

Holt, Robert, *Freud Reappraised,* Guilford Press, 1989.

Isbister, J. N., *Freud: An Introduction to His Life and Work,* Polity Press, 1985.

Jones, Ernest, *The Life and Work of Sigmund Freud,* three volumes, Basic Books, 1953-57.

Kline, Paul, *Fact and Fantasy in Freudian Theory,* Methuen, 1981.

Kline, *Psychology and Freudian Theory: An Introduction,* Methuen, 1984.

Kofman, Sarah, *The Enigma of Woman: Woman in Freud's Writings,* Cornell University Press, 1985.

Lewis, Helen Block, *Freud and Modern Psychology,* Plenum, 1983.

Mahoney, Patrick, *Freud as a Writer,* International Universities Press, 1982.

Mahoney, *Freud and the Rat Man,* Yale University Press, 1986.

Malcolm, Janet, *In the Freud Archives,* Knopf, 1984.

Mann, Thomas, *Freud, Goethe, Wagner,* Knopf, 1937.

Masson, Jeffrey Moussaieff, *The Assault on Truth: Freud's Suppression of the Seduction Theory,* Farrar, 1984.

McCaffrey, Phillip, *Freud and Dora: The Artful Dream,* Rutgers University Press, 1984.

McGrath, William J., *Freud's Discovery of Psychoanalysis,* Cornell University Press, 1986.

Meynell, Hugo, *Freud, Marx, and Morals,* Barnes and Noble, 1981.

Ricoeur, Paul, *Freud and Philosophy,* Yale University Press, 1970.

Rieff, Philip, *Freud: The Mind of the Moralist,* Viking, 1959.

Roazen, Paul, *Freud: Political and Social Thought,* Knopf, 1968.

Robert, Marthe, *The Psychoanalytic Revolution: Sigmund Freud's Life and Achievement,* Harcourt, 1967.

Steele, Robert S., *Freud and Jung: Conflicts of Interpretation,* Routledge, 1982.

Stepansky, Paul E., editor, *Freud: Appraisals and Reappraisals: Contributions to Freud Studies,* Analytic Press, 1986.

Stevens, Richard, *Freud and Psychoanalysis: An Exposition and Appraisal,* St. Martin's, 1983.

Sulloway, *Freud, Biologist of the Mind,* Basic Books, 1970.

Trossman, Harry, *Freud and the Imaginative World,* Analytic Press, 1985.

Wallace, Edwin R., *Freud and Antrhopology: A History and Reappraisal,* International Universities Press, 1983.

Wollheim, Richard, editor, *Freud: A Collection of Critical Essays,* Anchor, 1974.

Wollheim and James Hopkins, editors, *Philosophical Essays on Freud,* Cambridge University Press, 1982.

PERIODICALS

Atlantic, January, 1962.
Nation, September 17, 1930.
New Republic, July 20, 1918.
New York Review of Books, August 18, 1988.
New York Times Book Review, March 12, 1967, January 29, 1989.
New York Times Magazine, May 6, 1956, October 4, 1970.
Times Literary Supplement, May 10, 1974.

—*Sketch by Curtis Skinner*

*   *   *

FRIDAY, Nancy   1937-

PERSONAL: Born August 27, 1937, in Pittsburgh, Pa.; daughter of Walter (a financier) and Jane (Colbert) Friday; married W. H. Manville (a writer), October 20, 1967 (marriage ended); married Norman Pearlstine (an editor), July, 1988. *Education:* Attended Wellesley College.

ADDRESSES: Home—1108 Southard St., Key West, Fla. 33040. *Agent*—Betty Anne Clarke, International Creative Management, 20 West 51st St., New York, N.Y. 10019.

CAREER: San Juan Island Times, San Juan, Puerto Rico, reporter, 1960-61; editor, *Islands in the Sun* (magazine), 1961-63; free-lance writer, 1963—.

WRITINGS:

NONFICTION

My Secret Garden: Women's Sexual Fantasies, Trident, 1973.
Forbidden Flowers: More Women's Sexual Fantasies, Pocket Books, 1975.
My Mother/My Self: The Daughter's Search for Identity, Delacorte, 1977.
Men in Love: Men's Sexual Fantasies; The Triumph of Love over Rage, Delacorte, 1980.
Jealousy, Perigord, 1985.

SIDELIGHTS: Nancy Friday entered the ranks of "pop-psychology" in the early 1970s with her books *My Secret Garden: Women's Sexual Fantasies* and *Forbidden Flowers: More Women's Sexual Fantasies.* Though non-scientific, both books broke ground as forums for women who might not otherwise suspect that their fantasies could be shared by others. But even before these works were published, Friday had been researching questions on the theme of mother-daughter relationships in contemporary times. In 1977, after interviewing three hundred mothers and daughters nationwide, Friday published perhaps her best-known book to date, *My Mother/My Self: The Daughter's Search for Identity.*

A quick bestseller, *My Mother/My Self* generated controversy because of the frank and often disturbing conclusions the author offered. "In effect, Friday is saying that our mothers molded us to fit the preliberation ideal of woman, and thus burdened us with the task of freeing ourselves," writes Amy Gross in a *Village Voice* review. "She is also saying that until we do free ourselves, we will define happiness in terms of the symbiotic relationship we had with mother, no matter how unhappy that was." Gross faults *My Mother/My Self* for the author's "demands that we accept her every point as the truth about our lives," adding that in this book Friday's "focus is on the psychologically pathological. Her focus is on rage." But to *New York Times Book Review* critic Doris Grumbach, *My Mother/My Self* is "rich in anecdote, memories, testimonials, confessions, opinions by experts. . . . [The author] tells us that we inherit from our mothers much of what we are: our physical selves, our capacities, our whole baggage of repressions, insecurities and guilts," continues Grumbach. "Friday instructs us to look at ourselves not so much as the victims of a discriminatory patriarchy, but of an inevitable and unavoidable and destructive maternalism."

Friday followed *My Mother/My Self* with *Men in Love: Men's Sexual Fantasies; The Triumph of Love over Rage.* Similar in format to her first two books (the author solicited responses by including a mailing address within the two volumes) *Men in Love* includes two hundred male fantasies culled from three thousand letters. As the book was being released, Friday predicted it would be more controversial than her previous works because "people found it easy to talk about [female fantasies]; they're easily dismissed as trivial. This time you're dealing with *men,* the bedrock of society, you're talking about the deepest vulnerabilities of the so-called powerful sex," as Friday told John F. Baker in a *Publishers Weekly* interview. In the same article, the author revealed that *Men in Love* deals with "very powerful, primitive feelings, which arouse deep anxiety. The way I see it, the fantasies and feelings don't need an intellectual response; they need a gut-level deeply felt reaction, and that's how I treat them."

A number of critics fault Friday's analytics in *Men in Love. Newsweek's* Peter S. Prescott, for one, reports that the volume features a "stupefying quantity of testimony to various agitated states of mind interleaved with brief essays in which the author repeats what we have just read and ventures her interpretations. . . . Her thesis, that men's love of women is filled with rage, is pretty enough, but entirely unsupported by any of the evidence she has assembled." But Prescott does confess his "affection for this woman. Her charm, surely has much to do with her lack of credentials, with her distrust of statistical method, with her conviction that she has become in our society a liberating force, and with her refusal to disbelieve whatever her excited informers tell her to be true. I particularly like her just-folks prose style," the critic adds.

Jealousy, Friday's 1985 publication, postulates that jealousy and envy, two emotions that may seem synonymous, are in fact vastly different. The author makes an important distinction in this respect, says Susan Wood of *Washington Post Book World.* Jealousy "arises from a fear of losing something we have," while envy "is a desire to have something someone else has," as Wood relates. "Envy is by far the most destructive emotion and it is envy that is most often at work when we spoil what we love."

Again, critical reaction proved mixed. *Los Angeles Times* reviewer Carolyn See, taking the negative viewpoint, calls *Jealousy* "long, too long, way too long" at 524 pages, and adds that the author's "own diligent work habits may have finally betrayed her. She may have worked so long on 'Jealousy' that her . . . finger has slipped off the pulse of the nation: While she was working the temper of the times may have changed." Noting a passage in the book's introduction, where Friday describes a lustful encounter with a man who introduces her to *huevos rancheros,* See remarks that "no woman in the 1980s—when the rest of the nation is contemplating monogamy, children, 'the new chastity' and the sinister specter of AIDS—can hope to establish authority and credibility with tales of picking up other women's underwear and eating Mexican breakfasts." Wood, while sharing See's opinion that the book's length "might seem daunting," nonetheless adopts a more positive viewpoint overall. In *Jealousy,* she says, "nearly every page is readable, intelligent and full of insight and information. Most of all, *Jealousy* is big in importance. Relatively little has been written on the subject, certainly for the general reader, and Friday is convincing in her argument of jealousy's central role in our lives and the ways in which our lack of understanding, even our denial of the 'green-eyed monster' often cripples our most intimate relationships."

BIOGRAPHICAL/CRITICAL SOURCES:

BOOKS

Friday, Nancy, *My Mother/My Self: The Daughter's Search for Identity,* Delacorte, 1977.
Friday, Nancy, *Jealousy,* Perigord, 1985.

PERIODICALS

Chicago Tribune Book World, May 18, 1980.
Esquire, March, 1980.
Los Angeles Times, November 26, 1985.
Ms., May, 1980.
Nation, May 31, 1980.
Newsweek, March 17, 1980.
New York Review of Books, May 13, 1976.
New York Times, December 30, 1977.
New York Times Book Review, October 7, 1973, February 12, 1978, February 22, 1981, October 6, 1985.
People, December 19, 1977.
Publishers Weekly, February 28, 1980.
Times Literary Supplement, October 24, 1975.
Village Voice, November 28, 1977.
Washington Post Book World, August 19, 1973, March 23, 1980, September 29, 1985.

*   *   *

FRIEDAN, Betty (Naomi) 1921-

PERSONAL: Born February 4, 1921, in Peoria, Ill.; daughter of Harry (a jeweler) and Miriam (Horowitz) Goldstein; married Carl Friedan (a theatrical producer), June, 1947 (divorced May, 1969); children: Daniel, Jonathan, Emily. *Education:* Smith College, A.B. (summa cum laude), 1942; further study at University of California, Berkeley, University of Iowa, and Esalen Institute. *Politics:* Democrat.

ADDRESSES: Home—31 West 93rd St., New York, N.Y. 10023. *Office*—One Lincoln Plaza, New York, N.Y. 10023.

CAREER: Feminist organizer, writer, and lecturer at more than fifty universities, institutes, and professional associations worldwide, including Harvard Law School, University of Chicago, Vassar College, Smithsonian Institution, New York Bar Association, U.S. Embassy in Bogota, Colombia, and in Sweden, the Netherlands, Brazil, Israel, and Italy, beginning in the 1960s;

writer. Organizer and director, First Women's Bank & Trust Co., New York City, 1974—.

Teacher of creative nonfiction writing, New York University, and New School for Social Research, 1965-1970; taught course on women and urban problems, 1972-73. Visiting professor, Yale University, 1974, and Queens College of the City University of New York, 1975. Organizer of Women's Strike for Equality, 1970, International Feminist Congress, 1973, and Economic Think Tank for Women, 1974. Consultant to President's Commission on the Status of Women, 1964-65, Rockefeller Foundation project on education of women, 1965, University of California at Los Angeles project on continuing education for women, 1965, Philadelphia Psychiatric Center, 1972, and Harvard University, Kennedy Institute of Political Science, 1972.

MEMBER: National Organization for Women (NOW; founding president, 1966-70; member of board of directors of legal defense and education fund), National Women's Political Caucus (founder; member of national policy council, 1971-73), National Association to Repeal Abortion Laws (vice-president, 1972-74), National Conference of Public Service Employment (member of board of directors), Girl Scouts of the U.S.A. (member of national board), Women's Forum, American Sociological Association, Association for Humanistic Psychology, Gerontological Society of America, PEN, American Federation of Television and Radio Artists (AFTRA), American Society of Journalists and Authors, Author's Guild, Authors League of America, Society of Magazine Writers, Phi Beta Kappa, Coffee House.

AWARDS, HONORS: New World Foundation-New York State Education Department grant, 1958-62; Wilhelmina Drucker prize for contribution to emancipation of men and women, 1971; Humanist of the Year award, 1975; American Public Health Association citation, 1975; L.H.D., Smith College, 1975; Mort Weisinger Award for outstanding magazine article, American Society of Journalists and Authors, 1979; "Author of the Year," American Society of Journalists and Authors; L.H.D., State University of New York at Stony Brook, 1985; L.H.D., Cooper Union, 1987.

WRITINGS:

The Feminine Mystique, Norton, 1963, new edition, 1974, twentieth-anniversary edition, 1983.
(Contributor) Mary Lou Thompson, editor, *Voices of the New Feminism,* Beacon Press, 1970.
It Changed My Life: Writings on the Women's Movement, Random House, 1976, published with a new introduction by the author, Norton, 1985.
The Second Stage, Summit Books, 1981, revised edition, 1986.

Contributor to anthologies, including *Anatomy of Reading,* edited by L. L. Hackett and R. Williamson, McGraw, 1966, *Gentlemen, Scholars, and Scoundrels: Best of "Harper's" 1850 to the Present,* and *A College Treasury.* Contributor of articles to *Saturday Review, New York Times Magazine, Harper's, Redbook, Mademoiselle, Ladies' Home Journal, Social Policy, Good Housekeeping, New York, Newsday, Working Woman,* and other periodicals. Contributing editor and columnist, *McCall's,* 1971-74; member of editorial board, *Present Tense.*

The Schlesinger Library of Radcliffe College maintains a collection of Friedan's personal papers.

WORK IN PROGRESS: A book about growing older, entitled *The Fountain of Age.*

SIDELIGHTS: In the early 1960s, Betty Friedan was a wife and mother who had lost her job as a newspaper reporter after requesting her second maternity leave. She continued to write, though, contributing articles to women's magazines. It was in the pages of these magazines that Friedan first perceived a pattern. "Her editors would cut references to her subjects' careers," notes Marilyn French in an *Esquire* article. "They claimed a woman painting a crib was interesting to their readers, but a woman painting a picture was not. . . . The reality of women's lives—physical, intellectual, emotional—was censored; what appeared was a fantasy, a picture-book image of happy female domesticity." French continues: "Friedan began to analyze the fantasy; she interviewed housewives about the reality of their lives; she thought about the reasons for the promotion of such a false notion. She gave the image a name: the Feminine Mystique."

Her resulting book, *The Feminine Mystique,* was an immediate and controversial success when it was published in 1963. The main tenet of the work is that the boredom and fatigue experienced by many American women resulted from their lot as housebound wives without any outside interests. The postwar boom of suburban homes and labor-saving appliances, argues the author, produced a generation of women who "changed the sheets on the beds twice a week instead of once, took the rug-hooking class in adult education, and pitied their poor frustrated mothers, who had dreamed of having a career. Their only dream was to be perfect wives and mothers; their highest ambition to have five children and a perfect house, their only fight to get and keep their husbands." But the eventual dissatisfaction with this life style made these same women embarrassed and confused. Friedan also documents the great number of wives who visited psychiatrists and ended up "taking tranquilizers like cough drops."

Friedan's solution for what she termed "the problem that has no name" involves education and new opportunities for women outside the home. As she declares in her book, "Drastic steps must now be taken to re-educate the women who were deluded or cheated by the feminine mystique." Moreover, "it is time to stop giving lip service to the idea that there are no battles left to be fought for women in America, that women's rights have already been won. It is ridiculous to tell girls to be quiet when they enter a new field, or an old one, so the men will not notice they are there. In almost every professional field, in business and in the arts and sciences, women are still treated as second-class citizens. . . . A girl should not expect special privileges because of her sex, but neither should she 'adjust' to prejudice and discrimination."

While the struggle for women's equality in America predates even the 1920s suffrage movement, *The Feminine Mystique* was seen as a new unifying force. Thousands of copies sold in hardcover and more than a million in paperback, and its author gained both fame and status as a leading figure in the emerging women's movement. The years following *The Feminine Mystique* were busy ones for Friedan. In 1966 she was a founder of the National Organization for Women and served as its president until 1970. As *New Republic* writer Jane Howard describes, Friedan "has picketed the White House, been subpoenaed, helped to 'liberate' the Oak Room of the Plaza Hotel for women at lunchtime, talked herself hoarse from 1000 lecterns and before innumerable television cameras, and overcome her fear of flying." However, "not all her adventures have been upbeat." As the most visible representative of what was then called "Women's Lib," Friedan was often the target of heated emotions and even personal disdain. "A lot of people treated me like a leper," she tells Howard.

Twenty years after *The Feminine Mystique* was published, Friedan wrote in a 1983 *New York Times Magazine* piece that she

is "still awed by the revolution that book helped spark." Those two decades saw many changes in the movement that Friedan helped initiate. The emergence of activists like Gloria Steinem, the splintering of the women's movement into special-interest groups, the defeat of the Equal Rights Amendment in Congress, and the continued debates about the rights to legal abortions all affected Friedan personally and professionally. She aptly summed up the impact of her experiences in the title of her 1976 book, *It Changed My Life.* By 1981 Friedan had formulated a continuum for the women's movement that she describes in her book *The Second Stage.* Essentially, the new thesis calls for women to accept both their men and their families as allies in their quest for equality. She in fact feels the family is the new synthesis in the movement. "The second stage cannot be seen in terms of women alone," Friedan states in the work. "The second stage involves coming to new terms with the family—new terms with love and with work. The second stage may not even be a women's movement. Men may be at the cutting edge of the second stage."

Part of what influenced Friedan to write *The Second Stage* was the emergence of the Superwoman myth—the image of the woman who effortlessly juggles her career, marriage, and children. The author even finds a term to describe this phenomenon: The Feminist Mystique. She warns that the Superwoman, as far removed from reality as the perfect housewives depicted in the magazines of the 1960s, could have lasting negative effects on the women's movement. But the biggest controversy about the book was in reaction to the author's implied message that women have succeeded in gaining equality to the degree that men can now play a significant part in the women's movement. This caused a backlash from more militant feminists, as well as charges that Friedan had lost touch with the basic goals of the movement that she helped establish.

One of the most vocal detractors is writer Ellen Willis, who has this to say about *The Second Stage* in a *Nation* article: "It is absurd . . . for Friedan to call the family the 'new frontier' of feminism. The family is and always has been a central concern of feminism. Friedan is really saying that feminists should embrace the current trend toward mindless sentimentality about the family and abandon our abrasive habit of analyzing and criticizing it." Noting that the author sees no need "to discuss how the conventional family oppresses women," Willis goes on to state that in her own view, Americans must first be willing to accept alternative forms of family life (including the freedom to "separate sex from procreation and both from marriage, to be single, childless or lesbian") without subjecting anyone to social or legal pressures. "And it is exactly this set of demands," says Willis, "that Friedan devotes much of her book to condemning as love-denying, individualistic, hedonist, offensive to right-thinking Americans and injurious to respectable feminist goals."

To Judith Barnard, writing in *Chicago Tribune Book World,* the essential weakness in *The Second Stage* "is Friedan's failure to treat the women's movement in the sociological context of other movements. Seeing it as unique, she does not consider the wide, sometimes violent pendulum swings that characterize revolutions, small and large, and so sees only despair and confusion now that the early exhilaration is fading, and the momentum faltering, in the reactionary climate fostered by government and the holdouts who will always be with us." But in the opinion of Erica Jong, author of feminist novel *Fear of Flying,* Friedan "criticizes the women's movement with the desperate concern of a loving mother." Reviewing *The Second Stage* for *Saturday Review,* Jong continues: "[The author] wants to bring us to our senses. Many women are still so insecure that they hear any analysis as criticism, constructive criticism as destructive criticism, a call to self-analysis as a call to retreat."

Los Angeles Times critic Nancy Shiffrin and *Washington Post Book World* critic Webster Schott cite flaws in *The Second Stage,* but both ultimately recommend the work. Schott in particular points out stylistic faults—the author "tells us too often that she is at the power center of the women's movement" and "her material is repetitious, disorganized, and written in a hurry"—but concludes that "one only notes the flaws to dismiss them. *The Second Stage* is intelligent, compassionate, and pertinent. It's an education. And it provides a course of action, especially for men." And Jong sums up that Friedan's "understanding of the doubleness of things, her refusal to be conned by slogans, her insistence on psychological truth rather than political polemicizing, her insistence on seeing the feminist movement in historical perspective, her refusal, in all instances, to throw out the baby with the bathwater, make the reading of this book a supremely optimistic experience. For those of us seeking a new direction for feminism, it is here."

The activist who once wrote, "I am not that far from everywoman," has approached standard retirement age with unflagging commitment to equality. Friedan, states French, has throughout the years "remained true to her principles, personal and political. She has been and remains a bridge between conservative and radical elements in feminism, and an ardent advocate of harmony and humane values. Her affirmation of the family in *The Second Stage* is a passionate plea for general awareness of the inclusive nature of feminism: its vision of human wholeness; its repudiation of laws and customs that deny men expression of their emotions, sensitivity, and nurturing qualities and deny women expression of assertive intellect, action, and a voice in society. Friedan will stand in history as an initiator of the 'second wave' of feminism and as one who has never wavered in fidelity to its larger vision."

BIOGRAPHICAL/CRITICAL SOURCES:

BOOKS

Contemporary Issues Criticism, Volume 2, Gale, 1984.
Friedan, Betty, *The Feminine Mystique,* Norton, 1963, new edition, 1974, twentieth-anniversary edition, 1983.
Friedan, Betty, *It Changed My Life: Writings on the Women's Movement,* Random House, 1976.
Friedan, Betty, *The Second Stage,* Summit Books, 1981.
Mitchell, Juliet, *Psychoanalysis and Feminism,* Random House, 1974.

PERIODICALS

Chicago Tribune, June 13, 1985, December 14, 1986, February 7, 1988.
Chicago Tribune Book World, November 8, 1981.
Esquire, December, 1983.
Los Angeles Times, December 27, 1981.
Nation, November 14, 1981, November 28, 1981.
National Review, February 5, 1982.
New Republic, April 27, 1974, January 20, 1982, July 1, 1983.
New York Times, August 3, 1976, April 25, 1983, June 2, 1986.
New York Times Book Review, July 4, 1976, November 22, 1981.
New York Times Magazine, July 5, 1981, February 27, 1983, November 3, 1985.
Saturday Review, July 24, 1976, October, 1981.
Times Literary Supplement, May 31, 1963, July 30, 1982.
Village Voice, June 28, 1976.
Washington Post Book World, November 1, 1981, October 19, 1983.

Yale Review, spring, 1963.

* * *

FRIEDMAN, Milton 1912-

PERSONAL: Born July 31, 1912, in New York, N.Y.; son of Jeno Saul and Sarah Ethel (Landau) Friedman; married Rose Director, June 25, 1938; children: Janet, David. *Education:* Rutgers University, A.B., 1932; University of Chicago, A.M., 1933; Columbia University, Ph.D., 1946. *Avocational interests:* Tennis, carpentry.

ADDRESSES: Office—Hoover Institution, Stanford, CA 94305-6010.

CAREER: University of Chicago, Social Science Research Committee, Chicago, Ill., research assistant, 1934-35; National Resources Committee, Washington, D.C., associate economist, 1935-37; National Bureau of Economic Research, New York City, member of research staff, 1937-45, 1948-81; U.S. Treasury Department, Division of Tax Research, Washington, D.C., principal economist, 1941-43; Columbia University, Division of War Research, New York City, associate director of statistical research group, 1943-45; University of Minnesota, Minneapolis, associate professor of economics and business administration, 1945-46; University of Chicago, Chicago, associate professor, 1946-48, professor, 1948-62, Paul Snowden Russell Distinguished Service Professor of Economics, 1962-82, Paul Snowden Russell Distinguished Service Professor Emeritus, 1982; Hoover Institution, Stanford, Calif., senior research fellow, 1977.

Columbia University, part-time lecturer, 1937-40, and Wesley Clair Mitchell Research Professor of Economics, 1964-65. Visiting Fulbright lecturer, Cambridge University, 1953-54; visiting professor, University of California, Los Angeles, 1967, and University of Hawaii, 1972; visiting scholar, Federal Reserve Bank of San Francisco, 1977. Member of President's Commission on White House Fellows, 1971-73, and Federal Reserve System advisory committee on monetary statistics, 1974. Host of ten-part television series "Free to Choose," Public Broadcasting Service, 1980, and discussion leader of three-part series "Tyranny of the Status Quo," Public Broadcasting Service, 1984. Chief economic advisor to Senator Barry Goldwater, 1964. Consultant to Economic Cooperation Administration, Paris, 1950, and International Cooperation Administration, India, 1955.

MEMBER: National Academy of Sciences, American Statistical Association (fellow), American Economic Association (member of executive committee, 1955-57; president, 1967), Econometric Society (fellow), Institute of Mathematical Statistics (fellow), American Philosophical Society, Mont Pelerin Society (American secretary, 1957-62; member of council, 1962-65; vice-president, 1967-70, 1972-; president, 1970-72), American Enterprise Institute for Public Policy Research (member of council of academic advisors, 1956-78), Royal Economic Society, Western Economic Association (president, 1984-85), Philadelphia Society (member of board of trustees, 1965-67, 1970-72, 1976-), Quadrangle Club (Chicago).

AWARDS, HONORS: John Bates Clark Medal, American Economic Association, 1951; Center for Advanced Study in the Behavioral Sciences fellow, 1957-58; Ford faculty research fellow, 1962-63; LL.D. from St. Paul's University, Tokyo, 1963, Kalamazoo College, 1968, Rutgers University, 1968, Lehigh University, 1969, Loyola University, 1971, University of New Hampshire, 1975, Harvard University, 1979, Brigham Young University, 1980, Dartmouth College, 1980, and Gonzaga University,

1981; L.H.D. from Rockford College, 1969, Roosevelt University, 1975, and Hebrew Union College, Los Angeles, 1981; D.Sc. from University of Rochester, 1971; named Chicagoan of the Year, Chicago Press Club, 1972; named Educator of the Year, Chicago United Jewish Fund, 1973; Nobel Prize for Economic Science, 1976; Scopus Award from American Friends of the Hebrew University, 1977; Ph.D. from Hebrew University of Jerusalem, 1977; D.C.S. from Francisco Marroquin University, 1978; Freedoms Foundation, Private Enterprise Exemplar Medal, 1978, Valley Forge Honor Certificate, 1978, for speech "The Future of Capitalism," and George Washington Honor Medal, 1978, for television series "Open Mind," WPIX, New York City; gold medal from National Institute of Social Sciences, 1978; Statesman of the Year Award, Sales and Marketing Executives International, 1981; Ohio State Award, New Perspectives Award, and Tuck Media Award, all 1981, all for television series "Free to Choose"; Grand Cordon Sacred Treasure, Japan, 1986; National Medal of Science, 1988; Presidential Medal of Freedom, 1988.

WRITINGS:

(With Carl Shoup and Ruth P. Mack) *Taxing to Prevent Inflation,* Columbia University Press, 1943.

(With Simon Kuznets) *Income from Independent Professional Practice,* National Bureau of Economic Research, 1945.

(With H. A. Freeman, F. Mosteller, and W. Allen Wallis) *Sampling Inspection,* McGraw, 1948.

Essays in Positive Economics, University of Chicago Press, 1953.

(Editor and contributor) *Studies in the Quantity Theory of Money,* University of Chicago Press, 1956, reprinted, 1973.

A Theory of the Consumption Function, Princeton University Press, 1957.

A Program for Monetary Stability, Fordham University Press, 1960, reprinted, Fordham, 1983.

Price Theory: A Provisional Text, Aldine, 1962, revised edition, 1976.

(With wife, Rose D. Friedman) *Capitalism and Freedom,* University of Chicago Press, 1962, reprinted with new preface, 1981.

Inflation: Causes and Consequences, Asia Publishing House (Bombay), 1963.

(With Anna I. Schwartz) *A Monetary History of the United States, 1867-1960* (also see below), Princeton University Press, 1963.

The Great Contraction, 1929-1933: Chapter Seven of "Monetary History of the United States, 1867-1960", National Bureau of Economic Research, 1965.

(With Robert V. Roosta) *The Balance of Payments: Free Versus Fixed Exchange Rates,* American Enterprise Institute for Public Policy Research, 1967.

Dollars and Deficits: Inflation, Monetary Policy, and the Balance of Payments, Prentice-Hall, 1968.

The Optimum Quantity of Money and Other Essays, Aldine, 1969.

(With Walter W. Heller) *Monetary Versus Fiscal Policy,* Norton, 1969.

(With Schwartz) *Monetary Statistics of the United States: Estimates, Sources, Methods,* Columbia University Press, 1970.

The Counter-Revolution in Monetary Theory, Institute of Economic Affairs, 1970, Transatlantic, 1972.

(With Wilbur I. Cohen) *Social Security: Universal or Selective?,* American Enterprise Institute for Public Policy Research, 1972.

An Economist's Protest: Columns on Political Economics (collection of magazine columns), Thomas Horton, 1972, 2nd edi-

tion, 1975, 2nd edition also published as *There's No Such Thing as a Free Lunch,* Open Court, 1975, 3rd edition published as *Bright Promises, Dismal Performance: An Economist's Protest,* edited by William R. Allen, Harcourt, 1983.

Money and Economic Development, Praeger, 1973.

Milton Friedman's Monetary Framework: A Debate with His Critics, edited by Robert I. Gordon, University of Chicago Press, 1974.

Essays on Inflation and Indexation, American Enterprise Institute for Public Policy Research, 1974.

Indexing and Inflation, American Enterprise Institute for Public Policy Research, 1974.

Monetary Correction, Transatlantic Arts, 1975.

Unemployment Versus Inflation, Institute of Economic Affairs, 1975.

The Nobel Prize in Economics, Hoover Institute Press, 1976.

From Galbraith to Economic Freedom, Institute of Economic Affairs, 1977.

(Contributor) Frederick E. Webster, editor, *The Business System: A Bicentennial View,* University Press of New England, 1977.

Tax Limitation, Inflation, and the Role of Government, Fisher Institute, 1979.

(With R. D. Friedman) *Free to Choose: A Personal Statement* (Book-of-the-Month Club alternate selection), Harcourt, 1980.

The Invisible Hand in Economics and Politics, Institute of Southeast Asian Studies [Singapore], 1981.

(With Schwartz) *Monetary Trends in the United States and the United Kingdom: Their Relation to Income, Prices, and Interest Rates, 1867-1975,* University of Chicago Press, 1982.

(With R. D. Friedman) *Tyranny of the Status Quo,* Harcourt, 1984.

Politics and Tyranny: Lessons in Pursuit of Freedom, Pacific Institute for Public Policy Research, 1985.

Also author of *Theoretical Framework for Monetary Analysis, Inflation and Unemployment: The New Dimension of Politics,* and other monographs, published speeches, and booklets. Columnist, *Newsweek,* 1966-84. Contributor of articles and reviews to economic and statistics journals. Member of board of directors, Aldine Publishing Co., 1961-76. Member of board of editors, *American Economic Review,* 1951-53, and *Econometrica,* 1957-69. Member of advisory board, *Journal of Money, Credit, and Banking,* 1968.

SIDELIGHTS: "Economic freedom," Milton Friedman declares in *Free to Choose: A Personal Statement,* "is an essential requisite for political freedom. By enabling people to cooperate with one another without coercion or central direction, it reduces the area over which political power is exercised. In addition, by dispersing power, the free market provides an offset to whatever concentration of political power may arise. The combination of economic and political power in the same hands is a sure recipe for tyranny." Friedman's defense of freedom is the foundation of his economic thought. It has led him in his many books, his years of teaching at the University of Chicago, and in two widely-seen educational television series, to promote the ideas of a free market economic system.

As the leader of the Chicago School of economics, a school of economic thought that calls for an end to government intervention in all aspects of the economy, Friedman has seen his position gain the ascendency in recent years. "Events in Eastern Europe, the experience of prolonged inflation, disillusion with the welfare state in particular, resentment at the spread of bureaucratic intrusion and alarm at the unchecked growth of government expenditures along with a concommitant growth in the popularity of tax evasion—all have undoubtedly contributed to the change in political climate," E. I. Mishan explains in the *Times Literary Supplement.* Friedman was awarded the Nobel Prize for Economic Science in 1976. And with the election of President Ronald Reagan in the United States and Prime Minister Margaret Thatcher in England, both of whom are followers of Friedman, some of Friedman's economic proposals have become government policy.

Friedman's belief in the free market system is argued in his book *Capitalism and Freedom,* co-written with his wife, Rose D. Friedman. The book's major theme, the authors state, "is the role of competitive capitalism—the organization of the bulk of economic activity through private enterprise operating in a free market as a system of economic freedom and a necessary condition for political freedom." The book also delineates the proper role of government in a free market system. Two broad principles define this ideal government, the Friedmans write: "First, the scope of government must be limited. Its major function must be to protect our freedom both from the enemies outside and from our fellow-citizens. . . . The second broad principle is that government power must be dispersed. If government is to exercise power, better in the county than in the state, better in the state than in Washington."

Because Friedman holds these beliefs, he criticizes much of the social legislation enacted by the United States Government since the New Deal of the 1930s. Friedman fears that those who promote current social legislation are all too ready "to rely on the state for the furtherance of welfare and equality," Abba P. Lerner writes in the *American Economic Review.* This reliance on the state results in an encroachment on individual liberty, as it gives power over individual decisions to the government.

Friedman believes that many of the social problems targeted by government legislation can be better dealt with by the private sector. "He is not suggesting that all the reforms of the last half-century be repudiated, with nothing to take their place; in each case he offers a substitute that he believes will fulfill the objectives of the discarded program yet will maximize individual freedom and minimize coercion by government," Frank R. Bruel explains in the *Social Service Review. Capitalism and Freedom,* Lerner writes, presents "an impressive number of ways in which both freedom and welfare could be increased by a fuller utilization of the price mechanism" of the free market.

Another of Friedman's primary beliefs is that fluctuations in the quantity of money in circulation is of great importance in determining a nation's economic health. Sharp declines produce recession and depression; sharp increases, inflation. To prevent both depression and inflation, he proposes increasing the nation's money supply at a fixed rate each year in order to ensure a steady rate of growth.

In *A Monetary History* of the United States, 1867-1960, cowritten with Anna J. Schwartz, Friedman traces the history of the nation's money supply. In doing so, he also writes extensively about the Federal Reserve System, the government agency regulating the nation's money supply. Organized in 1914 in response to alleged banking abuses, the Federal Reserve has caused, Friedman believes, even more serious abuses. The Great Depression of the 1930s would not have been so catastrophic, Friedman argues, had not the Federal Reserve stepped in and worsened the situation. Friedman's *A Monetary History* of the United States is considered to be "the definitive history and is as useful to his critics as to his cohorts," according to Eliot Janeway of the *Los Angeles Times Book Review.*

In *Free to Choose* and *Tyranny of the Status Quo,* both written with his wife, Friedman presents his economic views for a popular audience. Both books were companions to nationally broadcast television programs and are meant not for the academic audience of Friedman's previous books but for the general reader. Mishan describes *Free to Choose* as "a popular version of the more fastidious but no less cogently argued statement of his views elaborated in Friedman's *Capitalism and Freedom.*" As such, the book is meant to "persuade readers to embrace a certain set of principles," Donald J. Yankovic explains in the *Journal of Economic Literature.*

Sidney Weintraub of the *New York Times Book Review* describes *Free to Choose* as "clear, cogent, sure and humorless," and believes that it is "sweeping and surgical in cutting up economic absurdities perpetrated by government agencies since the New Deal." Although he is "skeptical of its message," Weintraub nonetheless concludes that *Free to Choose* is "noteworthy for its clarity, logic, candor and unequivocal stand on political implications." Yankovic sees the Friedmans' strong defense of the free market system as a prime aspect of the book's importance. "The Friedmans offer," Yankovic writes, "a sound prescription for improving the economic well-being of the bulk of the population by widening the range of individual choices. . . . [*Free to Choose*] reminds us that there are many protections for us, in our various economic roles, in the market itself. It also reminds us that when we turn to government for protection, good intentions can lead to perverse results."

Many of the same arguments found in *Free to Choose* are restated in *Tyranny of the Status Quo,* but the focus of the book is on the economic policies of President Reagan's first term in office. Though Reagan came to the presidency with the idea "that Big Government is the sworn enemy of economic progress and individual freedom . . . the bureaucrats survived the first years of his regime unscarred," writes Ron Grossman in the *Chicago Tribune Book World.* The Friedmans try to determine why Reagan, who was elected in part because he sought to limit the size of government, was able to reform relatively little of it. They find that "a new administration has six to nine months to achieve major changes." Any changes attempted beyond this initial period will probably fail, although Reagan was able to institute a sweeping tax reform in his second term. "In the end," Susan Lee states in the *New York Times Book Review,* "the Friedmans blame Mr. Reagan for not being bold enough during his honeymoon period." To insure a limited federal government, since even a president is limited in what he can accomplish in this area, the Friedmans propose several constitutional amendments, including one requiring a balanced budget.

"Whatever your political persuasion," Marjorie Lewellyn Marks writes of the book in the *Los Angeles Times,* "many Friedman arguments, backed by statistical and historical documentation, are quite convincing." But Wayne Godley of the *Times Literary Supplement* disagrees. *Tyranny of the Status Quo,* Godley states, "is full of simple, plausible and dogmatic statements. . . . I disagree totally with the Friedmans' economics and passionately with their political beliefs." Grossman, too, has some reservations about the book. He sees it as calling for institutional change yet failing to present a workable strategy for this change. But he does believe that "Rose and Milton Friedman offer a compelling description of what ails American society."

Evaluations of Friedman's career point to his many contributions to economic science. James Tobin of the *Economist* explains that "Friedman was a pioneer in developing and applying the fruitful idea of 'human capital'. In 1957, Friedman showed how the distinction between permanent and transient income resolved puzzles in consumption and saving statistics for whole economies and for samples of households. His monumental monetary history . . . is an indispensable treatise packed with theoretic insights and policy analysis as well as historical and statistical narrative." Writing in the *New Statesman,* Wilfred Beckerman maintains: "If Nobel prizes are awarded according to the intellectual power of the recipients and the extent to which they have stimulated research and analysis in their fields . . . Milton Friedman certainly deserves one. If they are awarded according to the extent to which the recipients have correctly analysed some aspects of the phenomena they have studied, he may still deserve one, but it is not yet possible to be sure about this."

But Friedman's most tremendous contribution to economics has been his leadership of the Chicago School to dominance in the field. Mishan explains that "Friedman master-minded a counterrevolution in macro-economics which eventually succeeded in rolling back the once-triumphant Keynesian revolution and, through the lucidity of his writings and teaching, created countless disciples to spread the gospel." H. Erich Heinemann, writing in the *New York Times,* believes that "one of the most profound intellectual changes in the last decade has been the emergence of the monetarist school [the Chicago School] of economics, led by Professor Milton Friedman." According to Arthur Kemp in the introduction to Friedman's *Contemporary Issues Criticism* entry, few economists "have had as great or greater impact on professional economic thought in the twentieth century" as Milton Friedman.

MEDIA ADAPTATIONS: Free to Choose: A Personal Statement was written in conjunction with the television series "Free to Choose," Public Broadcasting Service, 1980; *Tyranny of the Status Quo* was written in conjunction with the television series "Tyranny of the Status Quo," Public Broadcasting Service, 1984. The texts of the books and series are different.

BIOGRAPHICAL/CRITICAL SOURCES:

BOOKS

Contemporary Issues Criticism, Volume 1, Gale, 1982.
Friedman, Milton and Rose D. Friedman, *Capitalism and Freedom,* University of Chicago Press, 1962.
Friedman, Milton and Rose D. Friedman, *Free to Choose: A Personal Statement,* Harcourt, 1980.
Friedman, Milton and Rose D. Friedman, *Tyranny of the Status Quo,* Harcourt, 1984.

PERIODICALS

American Economic Review, June, 1963, September, 1965.
American Political Science Review, March, 1977.
Annals of the American Academy of Political and Social Science, November, 1963.
Business History Review, fall, 1971.
Business Week, July 19, 1969, November 1, 1976.
Canadian Journal of Political Science, March, 1968.
Chicago Tribune Book World, March 11, 1984.
Christian Century, November 25, 1970.
Christian Science Monitor, February 11, 1980.
Commentary, July, 1969.
Commonweal, February 23, 1973.
Economist, July 1, 1972, October 9, 1976, October 23, 1976.
Esquire, September, 1970.
Fortune, June 1, 1967.
Journal of American History, June, 1964.
Journal of Economic History, March, 1975, June, 1981.
Journal of Political Economy, December, 1963.
Listener, September 26, 1974.
Los Angeles Times, May 6, 1984, September 14, 1988.
Los Angeles Times Book Review, May 29, 1983.
Money, September, 1976.
Nation, November 20, 1976, January 22, 1977.
National Review, September 10, 1971, November 9, 1973, September 16, 1977.
New Republic, November 6, 1976, March 22, 1980.
New Statesman, October 22, 1976.
Newsweek, January 31, 1972, October 25, 1976.
New York Review of Books, April 17, 1980.
New York Times, July 12, 1970, January 14, 1980, July 14, 1981.
New York Times Book Review, February 24, 1980, February 26, 1984.
New York Times Magazine, January 25, 1970.
Saturday Evening Post, May, 1977.
Science, November 5, 1976.
Scientific American, December, 1976.
Social Service Review, March, 1963.
Time, January 10, 1969, December 19, 1969, February 1, 1971.
Times Literary Supplement, April 16, 1970, September 5, 1980, September 14, 1984.
U.S. News & World Report, April 4, 1966, March 7, 1977.
Wall Street Journal, May 23, 1968, January 10, 1969.
Washington Post, November 24, 1963, February 1, 1980.

*   *   *

FRIEL, Brian 1929-

PERSONAL: Birth-given name, Bernard Patrick Friel; born January 9, 1929, in Omagh, Tyrone, Northern Ireland; son of Patrick (a teacher) and Christina (MacLoone) Friel; married Anne Morrison, December 27, 1955; children: Paddy (daughter), Mary, Judy, Sally, David. *Education:* Attended St. Columb's College, 1941-46; St. Patrick's College, Maynooth, Ireland, B.A., 1948; St. Joseph's Teachers Training College (now St. Joseph's College of Education), graduate study, 1949-50. *Avocational interests:* Reading, trout fishing, slow tennis.

ADDRESSES: Home—Drumaweir House, Greencastle, Donegal, Ireland. *Agent*—International Creative Management, 40 West 57th St., New York, NY 10019; Curtis Brown, 162-168 Regent St., London W1R 5TB, England.

CAREER: Teacher at primary and post-primary schools in and around Derry City, Northern Ireland, 1950-60; writer, 1960—. Tyrone Guthrie Theater, observer, 1963; co-founder of Field Day Theatre Company, 1980. Member of Irish Senate.

MEMBER: Irish Academy of Letters, Aosdana.

AWARDS, HONORS: Macauley fellowship from Irish Arts Council, 1963; Christopher Ewart-Biggs Memorial Prize, British Theatre Association Award, and *Plays and Players* Award for best new play, all 1981, for *Translations; Evening Standard* award for best play of the season, 1988, for *Aristocrats.* D.Litt., Rosary College (Chicago), 1974, National University of Ireland, 1983, New University of Ulster, 1986.

WRITINGS:

PLAYS

The Francophile, produced in Belfast, 1960; produced as *The Doubtful Paradise,* Belfast, 1960.
The Enemy Within (three-act; produced in Dublin, 1962), Proscenium Press, 1975.
The Blind Mice, produced in Dublin, 1963.

Philadelphia, Here I Come! (first produced in Dublin at Gaiety Theatre, September 28, 1964; produced on Broadway at Helen Hayes Theatre, February 16, 1966), Faber, 1965, Farrar, Straus, 1966.

The Loves of Cass McGuire (first produced on Broadway at Helen Hayes Theatre, October 6, 1966), Farrar, Straus, 1967.

Lovers (two one-acts, *Winners* and *Losers;* first produced in Dublin at Gate Theatre, summer, 1967; produced on Broadway at Vivian Beaumont Theatre, June 25, 1968), Farrar, Straus, 1968.

Crystal and Fox [and] *The Mundy Scheme* (*Crystal and Fox* first produced in Dublin, 1968; produced in Los Angeles at Mark Taper Forum, February, 1969; produced in New York, March, 1972; *The Mundy Scheme* first produced in Dublin at Olympia Theatre, June 11, 1969; produced on Broadway at Royale Theatre, December 11, 1969), Farrar, Straus, 1970.

The Gentle Island (two-act; first produced in Dublin at Olympia Theatre, 1971), Davis-Poynter, 1973.

The Freedom of the City (two-act; first produced in Dublin at Abbey Theatre, 1972; produced in Chicago at Goodman Theatre, 1974; produced on Broadway, 1974), S. French, 1974.

Volunteers (first produced in Dublin at Abbey Theatre, 1975), Faber, 1979.

Living Quarters (first produced in Dublin at Abbey Theatre, 1977), Faber, 1978.

The Faith Healer (produced in New York City, 1979), Faber, 1980.

Aristocrats (three-act; produced in Dublin, 1979), Gallery Press, 1980.

Translations (produced in Derry, 1980), Faber, 1981.

American Welcome (produced in New York City, 1980), published in *The Best Short Plays 1981,* Chilton, 1981.

(Translator) Anton Chekhov's *"Three Sisters"* (produced in Derry, 1981), Gallery Books, 1981.

The Communication Cord (produced in Derry, 1982), Faber, 1983.

Selected Plays of Brian Friel, Faber, 1984, Catholic University Press, 1986.

(Adapter) *Fathers and Sons* (based on a novel by Ivan Turgenev), first produced in London, 1987; produced in New Haven, CT, 1988.

Making History, produced in London, 1988.

OTHER

A Saucer of Larks (stories), Doubleday, 1962.

The Gold in the Sea (stories), Doubleday, 1966.

Selected Stories, Gallery Books, 1979.

The Diviner: Brian Friel's Best Short Stories, Devin, 1983.

(Editor) Charles McGlinchey, *The Last of the Name,* Blackstaff Press, 1986.

Author of screen adaptation of his play *Philadelphia, Here I Come!,* c. 1970; also has written for British and Irish radio and television. Contributor of stories to periodicals, including *New Yorker.*

MEDIA ADAPTATIONS: The Loves of Cass McGuire was produced on television in Dublin.

SIDELIGHTS: Brian Friel is noted for his deft use of language and his interest in Irish life and history; among his best-known plays are *Philadelphia, Here I Come!,* from 1964, and the more recent *Translations,* first produced in 1980. The story of a hopeful but heretofore luckless Irishman who immigrates to the

United States, *Philadelphia* was Friel's first major success, remarkable for its adept use of a dual role: the lead actor plays both the private and public sides of the character as individual entities. The play was a long-running success in New York City and was eventually filmed as well. *Translations* was a widely welcomed, "vibrant, deeply moving work of art in which everything seems to have come together for its author," according to *Chicago Tribune* critic Richard Christiansen. Set in 1833, when British authorities mapped and renamed Ireland's old Gaelic towns, the play shows the beginning of the end of traditions and cultural identity and the roots of the modern divided Ireland. Christiansen deemed it "glorious," writing that in this work Friel "found the theme, the period of history, the language and the passion to create a work that resonates with poetic metaphor, taking a specific incident and turning it into a profound and moving drama of universal meaning."

BIOGRAPHICAL/CRITICAL SOURCES:

BOOKS

Contemporary Literary Criticism, Gale, Volume 5, 1976, Volume 42, 1987.

Dantanus, Ulf, *Brian Friel: The Growth of an Irish Dramatist,* Faber, 1987.

Dictionary of Literary Biography, Volume 13: *British Dramatists since World War II,* Gale, 1982.

Maxwell, D. E. S., *Brian Friel,* Bucknell University Press, 1973.

PERIODICALS

Chicago Tribune, September 24, 1982.

Los Angeles Times, February 3, 1984, September 19, 1989.

New York Times, April 7, 1979, December 11, 1979, April 15, 1981, February 24, 1983, November 12, 1983, April 26, 1989, April 30, 1989.

Times (London), May 9, 1983, July 11, 1987, June 4, 1988, December 7, 1988.

Times Literary Supplement, October 15, 1982, June 3, 1983.

* * *

FRISCH, Max (Rudolf) 1911-

PERSONAL: Born May 15, 1911, in Zurich-Hottingen, Switzerland; son of Franz Bruno (an architect) and Lina (Wildermuth) Frisch; married Gertrud Anna Constance von Meyenburg, July 30, 1942 (divorced, 1959); married Marianne Oellers, December, 1968 (divorced); children: (first marriage) Ursula, Hans Peter, Charlotte. *Education:* Attended University of Zurich, 1931-33; Federal Institute of Technology, Zurich, diploma in architecture, 1940.

ADDRESSES: Home—CH-6611 Berzona Tessin, Switzerland.

CAREER: Free-lance journalist for various Swiss and German newspapers, including *Neue Zuercher Zeitung* and *Frankfurter Zeitung,* beginning 1933; architect in Zurich, Switzerland, 1945-55; full-time writer, 1955—. *Military service:* Swiss Army, 1939-45, served as cannoneer and later as border guard on the Austrian and Italian frontiers.

MEMBER: Deutsche Akademie fuer Sprache und Dichtung, Akademie der Kuenste, PEN, American Academy and Institute of Arts and Letters (honorary member), American Academy of Arts and Sciences (honorary member), Comunita degli Scrittori.

AWARDS, HONORS: Conrad Ferdinand Meyer Prize, 1938; Rockefeller Foundation grant for drama, 1951; Georg Buechner Prize, German Academy of Language and Poetry, 1958; Literature Prize of the City of Zurich, 1958; Literature Prize of Northrhine-Westphalia, 1963; Prize of the City of Jerusalem, 1965; Grand Prize, Swiss Schiller Foundation, 1974; Peace Prize, German Book Trade, 1976; Commandeur de l'Ordre des Arts et des Lettres, 1985; Common Wealth Award, Modern Language Association of America, 1986; International Neustadt Prize for Literature, University of Oklahoma, 1987. Has received honorary doctorates from the City University of New York, 1982, Bard College, Philipps University, Marburg, West Germany, and Technische Universitaet, Berlin.

WRITINGS:

NOVELS

Juerg Reinhart: Eine sommerliche Schicksalsfahrt, Deutsche Verlags-Anstalt, 1934, revised edition published as *J'adore ce qui me brule; oder, Die Schwierigen: Roman,* Atlantis (Zurich), 1943, 2nd revised edition published as *Die Schwierigen; oder, J'adore ce qui me brule,* Atlantis, 1957.

Antwort aus der Stille: Eine Erzaehlung aus den Bergen (title means "Answer Out of the Silence: A Tale from the Mountains"), Deutsche Verlags-Anstalt, 1937.

Bin; oder, Die Reise nach Peking, (title means "Am; or, the Trip to Peking"), Atlantis, 1945.

Stiller: Roman, Suhrkamp (Frankfurt on the Main), 1954, translation by Michael Bullock published as *I'm Not Stiller,* Abelard, 1958.

Homo Faber: Ein Bericht, Suhrkamp, 1957, translation by Bullock published as *Homo Faber: A Report,* Abelard, 1959.

Meine Name sei Gantenbein, Suhrkamp, 1964, translation by Bullock published as *A Wilderness of Mirrors,* Methuen, 1965, Random House, 1966.

Montauk: Eine Erzaehlung, Suhrkamp, 1975, translation by Geoffrey Skelton published as *Montauk,* Harcourt, 1976.

Der Mensch erscheint im Holozaen: Eine Erzaehlung, Suhrkamp, 1979, translation by Skelton published as *Man in the Holocene: A Story,* Harcourt, 1980.

Blaubart: Eine Erzaehlung, Suhrkamp, 1982, translation by Skelton published as *Bluebeard,* Harcourt, 1984.

PLAYS

Nun singen sie wieder: Versuch eines Requiems (two-act; title means "Now They Sing Again: An Attempt at a Requiem"; first produced in Zurich at the Schauspielhaus, March 29, 1945), Schwabe (Switzerland), 1946, translation by David Lommen published as "Now They Sing Again" in *Contemporary German Theatre,* edited by Michael Roloff, Avon, 1972.

Santa Cruz: Eine Romanz (five-act; first produced at the Schauspielhaus, March 7, 1946), Suhrkamp, 1946.

Die chinesische Mauer: Eine Farce (also see below; first produced at the Schauspielhaus, October 10, 1946), Schwabe, 1947, 2nd revised edition, 1972, translation by James L. Rosenberg published as *The Chinese Wall,* Hill & Wang, 1961.

Als der Kriege zu Ende war: Schauspiel (also see below; title means "When the War Was Over"; first produced at the Schauspielhaus, January 8, 1948), Schwabe, 1949, edited by Stuart Friebert, Dodd, 1967.

Graf Oederland: Ein Spiel in Zehn Bildern (also see below; title means "Count Oederland: A Play in Ten Scenes"; first produced at the Schauspielhaus, February 10, 1951; produced in Washington, D.C., at Arena Stage as "A Public Prosecutor Is Sick of It All," 1973), Suhrkamp, 1951, revised edition published as *Graf Oederland: Eine Moritat in zwoelf Bildern,* Suhrkamp, 1963, edited by George Salamon, Harcourt, 1966.

Don Juan; oder, die Liebe zur Geometrie: Eine Komoedie in fuenf Akten (also see below; title means "Don Juan; or, The Love of Geometry: A Comedy in Five Acts"; first produced at the Schauspielhaus, May 5, 1953), Suhrkamp, 1953.

Rip van Winkle: Hoerspiel (radio play; first produced in Germany, 1953), Reclam (Stuttgart), 1969.

Herr Biedermann und die Brandstifter: Hoerspiel (also see below; radio play; first produced in Germany, 1953; first stage adaptation produced as *Biedermann und die Brandstifter: Eine Lehrstueck ohne Lehre, mit einem Nachspiel* at the Schauspielhaus, March 29, 1958; produced in London as *The Fire Raisers,* 1961; produced at the Maidman Playhouse as *The Firebugs,* February, 1963), Suhrkamp, 1958, translation by Bullock published as *The Fire Raisers: A Morality without Moral, with an Afterpiece,* Methuen, 1962, translation by Mordecai Gorelick published as *The Firebugs: A Learning Play without a Lesson,* Hill & Wang, 1963.

Die grosse Wut des Philipp Hotz (also see below; one-act; first produced at the Schauspielhaus, March 29, 1958; produced at the Barbizon-Plaza Theatre as "The Great Fury of Philipp Hotz," November, 1969), translation published as "Philipp Hotz's Fury" in *Esquire,* October, 1962.

Andorra: Stueck in zwoelf Bildern (also see below; one-act radio play; first broadcast in West Germany, 1959; stage adaptation first produced at the Schauspielhaus, November 2, 1961; produced on Broadway at the Biltmore Theatre, February 9, 1963), Suhrkamp, 1962, translation by Bullock published as *Andorra: A Play in Twelve Scenes,* Hill & Wang, 1964.

Three Plays (contains "The Fire Raisers," "Count Oederland," and "Andorra"), translation by Bullock, Methuen, 1962.

Zurich-Transit: Skizze eines Films (television play; first produced on German television, January, 1966), Suhrkamp, 1966.

Biografie: Ein Spiel (also see below; two-act; first produced at the Schauspielhaus, February 1, 1968), Suhrkamp, 1967, revised edition, 1968, translation by Bullock published as *Biography: A Game,* Hill & Wang, 1969.

Three Plays (contains "Don Juan; or, the Love of Geometry," "The Great Rage of Philipp Hotz," and "When the War Was Over"), translation by J. L. Rosenberg, Hill & Wang, 1967.

Four Plays: The Great Wall of China, Don Juan; or, the Love of Geometry, Philipp Hotz's Fury, Biography: a Game, translation by Bullock, Methuen (London), 1969.

Triptychon: Drei szenische Bilder, Suhrkamp, 1978, translation by Skelton published as *Triptych: Three Scenic Panels,* Harcourt, 1981.

Also author of plays "Stahl" (title means "Steel"), 1927, and "Judith," 1948, and "Herr Quixote," a radio play, 1955.

OTHER

Geschrieben im Grenzdienst 1939, [Germany], 1940.

Blaetter aus dem Brotsack (diary; title means "Pages from the Knapsack"), Atlantis (Zurich), 1940, reprinted, 1969.

Marion und die Marionetten: Ein Fragment, Gryff-Presse (Basel, Switzerland), 1946.

Das Tagebuch mit Marion (title means "Diary with Marion"), Atlantis, 1947, revised and expanded version published as *Tagebuch, 1946-1949,* Droemer Knaur (Munich), 1950, translation by Skelton published as *Sketchbook, 1946-49,* Harcourt, 1977.

(Author of annotations) Robert S. Gessner, *Sieben Lithographien,* Huerlimann (Zurich), 1952.

(With Lucius Burckhardt and Markus Kutter) *Achtung, die Schweiz: Ein Gespraech ueber unsere Lage und ein Vorschlag zur Tat,* Handschin (Basel), 1956.

(Author of foreword) Markus Kutter and Lucius Burckhardt, *Wir selber bauen unsere Stadt: Ein Hinweis auf die Moeglichkeiten staatlicher Baupolitik,* Handschin (Basel), 1956.

(With Burckhardt and Kutter) *Die Neue Stadt: Beitraege zur Diskussion,* Handschin, 1956.

(Author of afterword) Bertold Brecht, *Drei Gedichten,* [Zurich], 1959.

(Contributor) Albin Zollinger, *Gesammelte Werke,* Volume 1, Atlantis (Zurich), 1961.

Ausgewaehlte Prosa, edited by Stanley Corngold, Suhrkamp, 1961, Harcourt, 1968.

Stuecke, two volumes, Suhrkamp, 1962.

(Author of texts with Kurt Hirschfeld and Oskar Waelterlin) Teo Otto, *Skizzen eines Buehnenbildners: 33 Zeichnungen,* Tschudy (St. Gallen, Switzerland), 1964.

(Contributor) Alexander J. Seiler, *Siamo italiani/Die Italiener: Gespraeche mit italienischen Arbeitern in der Schweiz,* EVZ Verlag (Zurich), 1965.

(Author of preface) Gody Suter, *Die grossen Staedte: Was sie zerstoert und was sie retten kann,* Luebbe (Bergisch Gladbach, West Germany), 1966.

Oeffentlichkeit als Partner (essays), Suhrkamp, 1967.

Erinnerungen an Brecht, Friedenauer (West Berlin), 1968.

Dramaturgisches: Ein Briefwechsel mit Walter Hoellerer, Literarisches Colloquium (West Berlin), 1969.

(Author of postscript) Andrei Sakharov, *Wie ich mir die Zukunft vorstelle: Gedanken ueber Fortschritt, friedliche Koexistenz und geistige Freiheit,* Diogenes (Zurich), 1969.

(With Rudolf Immig) *Der Mensch zwischen Selbstentfremdung und Selbstverwirklichung,* Calwer (Stuttgart), 1970.

Glueck: Eine Erzaehlung, Brunnenturm-Presse, 1971.

Wilhelm Tell fuer die Schule, Suhrkamp, 1971.

Tagebuch, 1966-71, Suhrkamp, 1972, translation by Skelton published as *Sketchbook, 1966-71,* Harcourt, 1974.

Dienstbuchlein, Suhrkamp, 1974.

Stich-Worte, Suhrkamp, 1975.

(With Hartmut von Hentig) *Zwei Reden zum Friedenspreis des Deutschen Buchhandels 1976,* Suhrkamp, 1976.

Gesammelte Werke in zeitlicher Folge, six volumes, Suhrkamp, 1976.

Frisch: Kritik, Thesen, Analysen, Francke (Bern, Switzerland), 1977.

Erzaehlende Prosa, 1939-1979, Volk und Welt (West Berlin), 1981.

Stuecke, two volumes, Volk und Welt, 1981.

Forderungen des Tages, Suhrkamp, 1983.

Contributor to periodicals in West Germany and Switzerland, including *Neue Schweizer Rundschau, Der Spiegel,* and *Atlantis;* contributor to newspapers, including *Neue Zuercher Zeitung* and *Sueddeutsche Zeitung.*

SIDELIGHTS: Along with fellow Swiss dramatist Friedrich Duerrenmatt, Max Frisch "has been a major force in German drama for the generation since 1945," declares Arrigo Subiotto in *The German Theatre: A Symposium.* Best known for such works as *I'm Not Stiller* and *The Firebugs,* Frisch is esteemed as both a novelist and playwright. Winning numerous literary awards, including the Georg Buechner Prize and Neustadt International Prize, he has been a perennial candidate for the Nobel Prize for several years. His writing, characterized by its surrealistic style, "is a sort of poetry," remarks Joseph McLellan in the *Washington Post Book World,* "but a poetry of the mind rather than the senses—sparse and austere, with every detail chosen for its resonances." Several critics have commented on not only the remarkable consistency of this style, which *Dictionary of Literary Biography* contributor Wulf Koepke avers to be "discernable since the early 1940s," but also on Frisch's inventiveness in expressing "a single theme: the near impossibility of living truthfully," concludes Sven Birkerts in his *New Republic* article.

As a student of German literature at the University of Zurich, Frisch admired such writers as Albin Zollinger and Gottfried Keller. His father's death, however, made it necessary for him to leave school to support himself and his mother. Becoming a free-lance journalist for various German and Swiss newspapers, he traveled widely in Europe throughout the 1930s. During this time, Frisch also wrote fiction; but, as Koepke notes, he "grew increasingly disenchanted with his writing, and in 1937 he burned all his manuscripts." Opting for a more utilitarian career, he temporarily abandoned his writing goals to attend architecture classes at the Federal Institute of Technology in Zurich, where he received his diploma in 1940. However, he was not able to refrain totally from writing, and, while serving as a border guard in the Swiss army, he wrote *Juerg Reinhart: Eine sommerliche Schicksalsfahrt, Antwort aus der Stille: Eine Erzaehlung aus den Bergen, Blaetter aus dem Brotsack,* and *Bin; oder, die Reise nach Peking.*

These lesser-known works, considering they were written during the time of Hitler's Third Reich, "astound the reader by their absolutely apolitical character," observe Mona and Gerhard Knapp in *World Literature Today.* Frisch was by no means unconcerned with the war's effects, however. Characterized by *New York Times Book Review* contributor Richard Gilman as "politically liberal, a pacifist," the author "was very much aware of his own unique position regarding the war; as a Swiss, apparently unaffected by the conflict surrounding his own country, Frisch could only attempt to present the lessons of the war from a bipartisan point of view," observes Manfred Jurgensen in *Perspectives on Max Frisch.* This is precisely what the dramatist attempts to do in his first plays written after the war.

Invited in 1945 by the director of the Zurich Schauspielhaus, Kurt Hirschfield, to write plays for his theater, the author's *Nun singen sie wieder: Versuch eines Requiems* ("Now They Sing Again: An Attempt at a Requiem") explores prejudice by placing characters from both the Axis and Ally countries into the world of the afterlife, where they become equals. In his next play about the war, *Als der Krieg zu Ende war* ("When the War Was Over"), Frisch writes of a German woman who falls in love with a Russian soldier, demonstrating, as Carol Petersen says in his book, *Max Frisch,* "that by true human feelings all kinds of prejudices can and must be overcome."

However, "Frisch has no real hope that [such social] evils can be remedied," remarks Koepke, and his plays and novels are therefore largely pessimistic. For example, in *The Theater of Protest and Paradox: Developments in the Avant-Garde Drama,* George Wellwarth asserts that "Frisch's two best plays, [*The Chinese Wall*] and [*The Firebugs: A Learning Play without a Lesson*], are consciously foredoomed pleas for a better world. The irony implicit in them no longer sounds like the scornful laughter of the gods we hear in Duerrenmatt; it sounds like the self-reproaching wailing of the damned." Underlying this pessimism is, as Jurgensen remarks, Frisch's frustration with "man's incorrigible selfishness and his inability or unwillingness to learn, to change, to think dynamically." According to Petersen, the lesson of *The Chinese Wall* is therefore that "freedom is only in the realm of the spirit; for, in the real world, the possessors of power end up by doing the same things over and over again."

Approaching this theme from another angle in what *World Literature Today* contributor Adolf Muschg calls Frisch's "most successful play internationally," *The Firebugs* creates a character who, instead of trying to prevent disaster, actually fosters it. In this play, a weak-willed hair lotion manufacturer named Gottlieb Biedermann is unable to admit to himself the true intentions of two arsonists, and knowingly allows them to enter and destroy his home. Several interpretations of the political implications of this play have been proposed, as Subiotto explains: "[*The Firebugs*] can be seen as a metaphor of Hitler's legitimate 'seizure of power' or of the way in which the nations of the world are playing with nuclear bombs as deterrents. . . . It also offers a 'model' of liberal societies allowing freedom of action, in the name of liberty, to extremist elements in their midst (whether of right or left) whose avowed aim is to destroy those societies." According to Koepke, the author endorses the interpretation that *The Firebugs* is about "the weakness of capitalist society." What is also significant about *The Firebugs* is how it further develops Frisch's "theme of the true identity behind an artificial mask, the destruction of false conventions, and the feeling of the self from deeply ingrained prejudices," writes Alex Natan in his introduction to *German Men of Letters: Twelve Literary Essays.*

One of the main obstacles to living truthfully, in Frisch's view, is the inability of people to accept their true identities. The theme of concealed or lost identity, then, has become the central theme of much of the author's work. Martin Esslin reveals in his *Reflections: Essays on Modern Theatre,* that this human shortcoming is for the author "the ultimate sin, the extinction of [people's] true existence, the origin of all the troubles of our time." And the main obstacle to this discovery of the true self are the images we create for ourselves and others to hide reality. In his diary, *Sketchbook, 1946-49,* Frisch summarizes his beliefs this way: "It is written: thou shalt make no graven images of God. But we can also understand the commandment thus: 'god' as that part of every human being which is intangible and ever-changing. To make graven images of each other is a sin which is committed against us and which we almost continually commit against others—except, that is, when we love." Because of his interest in this theme, the central character in many of Frisch's novels and plays, explicates *New York Times Book Review* critic George Stade, is often "either someone who tries to escape from himself, . . . or who writhes in the nets of definition others cast over him, . . . or who finds out, too late, that he is not what he took himself to be."

One example of such a play is *Andorra: A Play in Twelve Scenes,* which, along with *The Firebugs,* the Knapps say "catapulted [Frisch] to international theatrical prominence." *Andorra* revolves around the theme of anti-semitism to illustrate the imposition of images. The story concerns the deception of a schoolteacher, living in fictional Andorra, who hides the identity of his illegitimate son Andri by telling his neighbors that Andri is a Jewish boy whom he has saved from the oppressive "Blacks." With the increasing strength of the Blacks, the Andorrans begin to impose more and more stereotypes on Andri until he eventually accepts himself as Jewish. Even when he learns the truth about who he really is, however, Andri is unable to shed this false identity; and, when the Blacks invade Andorra, he chooses to die under their persecution.

The struggle for self-truth in a world which prefers the stereotypes and simplicity of the image to an authentic existence is also evident in *Don Juan; or, the Love of Geometry.* Here, in what

Petersen calls "an uncommonly clever, wittily pointed play, which offers a broad view of the relativity of all human sentiment," Frisch twists the legend of Don Juan by describing Juan as a lover of geometry who is forced into the role of philanderer by the demands and expectations of society. He actually prefers the logic and precision of geometry to the capricious ways of the women who surround him. Compared to the traditional version of Don Juan, critics like Petersen believe that "the twentieth-century man, inclined to rationalism, can more readily recognize himself in Frisch's Don Juan."

The three novels that deal with the theme of identity on its most introspective, individual level are *I'm Not Stiller, Homo Faber: A Report,* and *A Wilderness of Mirrors.* Along with a number of other critics, Charles Hoffman, a contributor to *The Contemporary Novel in German: A Symposium,* feels that with these books, Frisch "has created three of the most important novels of [the mid-nineteenth century]. Taken together, these books are perhaps the most meaningful [in] recent German writing." The years in which they were written, from 1954 to 1964, were also "of singular importance in establishing Frisch's international reputation," add the Knapps.

Like *Don Juan, Homo Faber* appeals to the modern man, but on a much more serious note. Submerging himself in a love of technology over actual human emotions, Frisch's protagonist, engineer Walter Faber, unwittingly enters into a relationship with a woman whom he later discovers to be his illegitimate daughter. Because he cannot face the emotions that result from this discovery, Faber "is punished for his 'blindness' by her loss" when she dies of a snake bite, explain the Knapps. In this description of a man who becomes alienated from his own identity through his reverence for modern technology, "Frisch has captured that essential anguish of modern man which we find in the best of Camus," asserts Richard Plant in *Spectator.* But *Homo Faber* is also one of Frisch's more optimistic works because, notes Koepke, in the "last period of his life, characterized by a growing awareness of human existence, [Faber] not only comes into contact with his own past failures and their long-term consequences but also begins to see the truth of nontechnological realities."

I'm Not Stiller, which Michael Butler in his *The Novels of Max Frisch* says "established [for Frisch] a claim to major status in the history of the novel in post-war Germany and Switzerland," is his most critically acclaimed novel concerning the theme of escape from the self. Told mostly through the point-of-view of the sculptor Anatol Stiller, *I'm Not Stiller* is the story of a man who assumes the identity of an American named White in an effort to flee his feelings of failure as an artist, husband, and lover. Confronted with his true identity by the Swiss government, which has accused him of having worked with the Communists, Stiller is forced to face his true identity, and the resulting personal struggle that Frisch chronicles in Stiller's journal, "consumes not only all his own moral and artistic energy," say the Knapps, "but also that of his frail wife Julika, who soon dies." The last section of *I'm Not Stiller* is told by Stiller's prosecutor, who moralizes: "As long as a person does not accept himself, he will always have the fear of being misunderstood and misconstrued by his environment." Although some critics like Plant feel that the novel's "provocative idea [has] been spoiled . . . by excessive detail and overdecoration," a number of others think that *I'm Not Stiller* is one of Frisch's best works. Butler opines, for example, that in *I'm Not Stiller* "Frisch suddenly produced a narrative work of unsuspected depth and fascination."

In what Hoffman calls a "brilliant demonstration" of writing, *A Wilderness of Mirrors* also deals with the manipulation of identities in order to deal with emotional relationships. The most experimental of the three loosely related novels about identity, *A Wilderness of Mirrors* explores a multitude of plots while characters are cast and recast in a variety of roles. The extremely complex storyline of this book, however, has caused some critics, like *Observer* reviewer D. J. Enright, to remark that "for all the insights and vividness, the ponderous machinery [of the plot] is out of proportion to the final product." Others, like Butler, however, applaud the novel as "an intensely private exploration of personal dislocation and inadequacy."

Although Frisch's more recent works, *Montauk, Triptych: Three Scenic Panels,* and *Man in the Holocene,* address some of the usual Frisch themes, they "mark a turning point in his writing," claims Barbara Saunders in *Forum for Modern Language Studies. Triptychon* and *Man in the Holocene,* says Saunders, "substantiate Frisch's own assertion that he is 'finished' with the autobiographical form he used in such books as *I'm Not Stiller* and *Homo Faber.*" Saunders continues: "*Montauk* indicates the climax of a progression towards positive self-appraisal and has enabled Frisch to develop beyond the preoccupations of ambivalent personal identity." Frisch has given himself the opportunity to write about his own thoughts and experiences in this thinly veiled autobiographical book concerning an ageing writer's weekend with his American girlfriend. Ironically, though, some critics like *Book Forum* contributor Steven Kellman believe that in this book "it is to flee [his own identity] that the Swiss novelist finds himself in Montauk." The author writes in *Montauk* how this is due to a fear that his image as a writer has begun to obscure the real Max Frisch as if he were one of his own characters. In one chapter of the book, for example, he declares: "I have been serving up stories to some sort of public, and in these stories I have, I know, laid myself bare—to the point of non-recognition."

After *Montauk* the author's books betray his awareness of his advancing years. Koepke explains: "While in *Montauk* numerous quotes from Frisch's earlier works indicate self-acceptance, the past has become threatening in the last works. Old age and death are dominant themes, but even more prevalent may be regret of the past—one's own and that of the human race." For example, Jurgensen states that in *Triptychon* "Frisch shows . . . how all acts, thoughts, and misunderstandings are repeated in death; death becomes the stage for re-enacting our lives. The finality does not lie in death but in our unthinking life, in our inability to do anything other than repeat ourselves." "*Triptychon*'s real subject is a social death," Jurgensen concludes, "in fact: the death of society."

Jurgensen also notes that this pessimistic theme is similar to that in *The Firebugs;* and his next book, *Man in the Holocene,* also resembles *The Firebugs* in its "unsettling notion that some rational, well-meaning force is actually *willing* catastrophe," according to *Nation* reviewer Arthur Sainer. In what McLellan asserts to be "a small book but a major achievement," *Man in the Holocene* relates the last few days in the life of a ageing man named Geiser who becomes trapped in his alpine valley home by a landslide. Battling against his own encroaching senility and a dwindling food supply, Geiser ironically passes up the chance to escape his isolation, eventually suffering from a stroke before he finally dies. *Man in the Holocene,* like *Triptychon,* reiterates Frisch's suspicion of the transience of the human race. McLellan phrases it this way: In *Man in the Holocene* "the old man's life itself is being eroded, as are all men's lives—as is, perhaps, the life of the entire species."

Frisch returns to his more familiar theme of identity in *Bluebeard.* But, avers Sven Birkerts in a *New Republic* review, the author "is not so much returning to earlier themes as he is bringing the preoccupations of a lifetime under a more calculated and intense pressure." As in *I'm Not Stiller,* the story's events are related by the protagonist, Dr. Schaad, through his memories about his trial. This time, the main character is accused of being a wife murderer, like the infamous Bluebeard; and this role is forced upon him to the point where he eventually assimilates it. Marga I. Weigel notes the similarity between Dr. Schaad's identity crisis and that of another Frisch character. Writing in *World Literature Today,* Weigel observes: "[Dr. Schaad] works himself more and more into the role of the murderer. He is now convinced he is the person others consider him to be—an attitude identical to the reaction of Andri in *Andorra.*"

Similarities such as this in Frisch's work have been noted by other critics, but the resemblances of *Bluebeard* to other Frisch works do not detract from their value, according to Butler. In an article in the *Times Literary Supplement,* Butler comments: "Although Max Frisch can no longer avoid producing texts which are resonant of earlier achievements, this latest work demonstrates once again his skill in creating new and fascinating ways of exploring old truths." Birkerts also comments: "The structural and stylistic shifts [in the author's work] mark his maturing, the varying of his concerns, his need for increasingly direct statement. The man grows, but his is the same man." *Bluebeard,* like Frisch's other works, reminds the reader that "there is no simple prescription for truthful living," asserts Birkerts. Frisch, instead, desires to force people to think about what he is writing. As he declares in his *Sketchbook, 1946-49,* "I should consider that I had done my duty if I had put a question in such a way that from then on the members of the audience could not bear to live without the answer. But it must be their answer, their own, which they can provide only in the framework of their own lives."

MEDIA ADAPTATIONS: Homo Faber: A Report has been adapted for the screen by Paramount.

BIOGRAPHICAL/CRITICAL SOURCES:

BOOKS

Butler, Michael, *The Novels of Max Frisch,* Oswald Wolff, 1976.

Contemporary Literary Criticism, Gale, Volume 3, 1975, Volume 9, 1978, Volume 14, 1980, Volume 18, 1981, Volume 32, 1985, Volume 44, 1987.

Daemmrich, Horst S., and Diether H. Haenicke, *The Challenge of German Literature,* Wayne State University Press, 1971.

Dictionary of Literary Biography, Volume 69: *Contemporary German Fiction Writers,* Gale, 1988.

Esslin, Martin, *Reflections: Essays on Modern Theatre,* Doubleday, 1969.

Frisch, Max, *Sketchbook, 1946-49,* Harcourt, 1977.

Garten, Hugh Frederic, *Modern German Drama,* Methuen, 1959.

Hayman, Ronald, *The German Theatre: A Symposium,* Barnes & Noble, 1975.

Heitner, Robert R., editor, *The Contemporary Novel in German: A Symposium,* University of Texas Press, 1967.

Lumley, Frederick, *New Trends in 20th Century Drama,* Oxford University Press, 1967.

Natan, Alex, editor, *German Men of Letters: Twelve Literary Essays,* Volume 3, Oswald Wolff, 1968.

Petersen, Carol, *Max Frisch,* translated by Charlotte La Rue, Ungar, 1972.

Probst, Gerhard F., and Jay F. Bodine, editors, *Perspectives on Max Frisch,* University Press of Kentucky, 1982.

Weber, Brom, editor, *Sense and Sensibility in Twentieth-Century Writing,* Southern Illinois University Press, 1970.

Weisstein, Ulrich, *Max Frisch,* Twayne, 1967.

Wellwarth, George, *The Theater of Protest and Paradox: Developments in the Avant-Garde Drama,* New York University Press, 1964.

PERIODICALS

Biography News, June, 1974.

Books Abroad, winter, 1968.

Chicago Sun-Times, May 5, 1974.

Chicago Tribune Book World, September 28, 1980.

Christian Science Monitor, February 12, 1968.

Forum for Modern Language Studies, July, 1982.

German Life and Letters, October, 1974.

Los Angeles Times Book Review, August 10, 1980.

Modern Drama, December, 1975.

Nation, July 3, 1976, September 20, 1980.

New Republic, July 11, 1983.

New Statesman, August 6, 1982.

New Yorker, May 24, 1976, July 11, 1977.

New York Review of Books, September 24, 1981.

New York Times, July 2, 1968, November 27, 1969, May 17, 1970, May 22, 1980.

New York Times Book Review, February 20, 1966, April 28, 1974, May 16, 1976, May 27, 1976, April 3, 1977, March 19, 1978, May 11, 1980, June 22, 1980, July 10, 1983, September 29, 1983.

Observer, July 25, 1982, March 13, 1983.

Saturday Review, April 12, 1958, May 7, 1960, February 26, 1966.

Spectator, April 11, 1958, May 7, 1960.

Times (London), February 24, 1983.

Times Literary Supplement, November 11, 1965, January 25, 1968, September 29, 1972, September 12, 1980, June 4, 1982, July 30, 1982.

Tulane Drama Review, March, 1962.

Village Voice, July 11, 1968.

Washington Post Book World, July 18, 1976, July 27, 1980, July 17, 1983.

World Literature Today, spring, 1977, spring, 1979, spring, 1983, autumn, 1984, autumn, 1986.

—*Sketch by Kevin S. Hile*

*   *   *

FROMM, Erich   1900-1980

PERSONAL: Born March 23, 1900, in Frankfurt, Germany; died of a heart attack March 18, 1980, in Muralto, Switzerland; came to United States in 1934; naturalized citizen, 1940; son of Naphtali (a wine merchant) and Rosa (Krause) Fromm; married Frieda Reichmann, June 16, 1926 (divorced); married Henny Gurland, July 24, 1944 (died, 1952); married Annis Freeman, December 18, 1953. *Education:* University of Heidelberg, Ph.D., 1922; attended University of Munich, 1923-24, Institute of the German Psychoanalytic Society, 1928-31, Psychoanalytic Institute (Berlin), and University of Frankfurt.

ADDRESSES: Home—180 Riverside Dr., New York, N.Y. 10024; and Locarno, Switzerland.

CAREER: Psychoanalyst, philosopher, and writer, 1925-80. Psychoanalytic Institute and University of Frankfurt, Frankfurt, Germany, lecturer in social psychology at Institute for Social Research, 1929-32; Columbia University, International Institute for Social Research, New York City, lecturer, 1934-39, guest lecturer, 1940-41; Bennington College, Bennington, Vt., member of faculty, 1941-50; William Alanson White Institute for Psychiatry, Psychoanalysis and Psychology, New York City, cofounder, member of faculty, 1946-50, chairman of faculty, 1947-50; National Autonomous University of Mexico, Medical School, Frontera, professor of psychoanalysis, 1951-80, head of department, 1955-80; Mexican Institute for Psychoanalysis, Mexico City, Mexico, director, 1955-65; Michigan State University, East Lansing, professor, 1957-61, founder of Institute of Psychology; New York University, New York City, adjutant professor of psychology, 1962-80. Lecturer, American Institute for Psychoanalysis, 1941-42, and New School for Social Research, 1946-56; Terry Lecturer, Yale University, 1949-50. Diplomate in clinical psychology, American Psychological Association.

MEMBER: Mexican National Academy of Medicine (honorary member), New York Academy of Science (fellow), Washington Psychoanalytic Society.

AWARDS, HONORS: Fellow at Washington School of Psychiatry, 1940, and at William Alanson White Institute for Psychiatry, Psychoanalysis and Psychology, 1945.

WRITINGS:

Die Entwicklung des Christusdogmas (title means "The Development of the Dogma of Christ"), Internationaler Psychoanalytischer Verlag (Vienna), 1931.

Escape from Freedom, Farrar & Rinehart, 1941, Avon, 1971 (published in England as *The Fear of Freedom,* Kegan Paul, Trench, Trubner & Co., 1942).

Man for Himself: An Inquiry into the Psychology of Ethics, Rinehart, 1947, reprinted, Fawcett, 1978.

Psychoanalysis and Religion, Yale University Press, 1950.

The Forgotten Language: An Introduction to the Understanding of Dreams, Fairy Tales, and Myths, Rinehart, 1951.

The Sane Society, Rinehart, 1955, reprinted, Fawcett, 1977.

The Art of Loving: An Enquiry into the Nature of Love, Harper, 1956, reprinted, 1974.

Sigmund Freud's Mission: An Analysis of His Personality and Influence, Harper, 1959.

(Editor with Daisetz T. Suzuki and Richard De Martino) *Zen Buddhism and Psychoanalysis,* Harper, 1960.

Let Man Prevail: A Socialist Manifesto and Program (booklet), Lambert Schneider (Heidelberg), 1961.

(Editor with Hans Herzfeld) *Der Friede: Idee und Verwirklichung* (title means "Peace: Theory and Reality"), Lambert Schneider, 1961.

(Editor) *Marx's Concept of Man,* Ungar, 1961.

Is World Peace Still Possible?: An Enquiry into the Facts and Fictions of Foreign Policy, [New York], c. 1962.

Beyond the Chains of Illusion: My Encounter with Marx and Freud, Simon & Schuster, 1962, reprinted, 1985.

War within Man: A Psychological Enquiry into the Roots of Destructiveness, American Friends Service Committee, 1963.

The Dogma of Christ and Other Essays on Religion, Psychology, and Culture, Holt, 1963.

May Man Prevail?: An Enquiry into the Facts and Fictions of Foreign Policy, Doubleday, 1964.

The Heart of Man: Its Genius for Good and Evil, Harper, 1964, reprinted, 1980.

(Editor) *Socialist Humanism: An International Symposium,* Doubleday, 1965.

You Shall Be as Gods: A Radical Interpretation of the Old Testament and Its Tradition, Holt, 1966.

(Editor with Raymond Xirau) *The Nature of Man,* Macmillan, 1968.

The Revolution of Hope: Toward a Humanized Technology, Harper, 1968.

(With Michael Maccoby) *Social Character in a Mexican Village: A Socio-Psychoanalytic Study,* Prentice-Hall, 1970.

The Crisis of Psychoanalysis (essays), J. Cape, 1970, Fawcett, 1971.

The Anatomy of Human Destructiveness, Holt, 1973.

(With Hans Juergen Schultz) *Im Namen des Lebens: Ein Portraet im Gespraech mit Hans Juergen Schultz* (booklet; title means "In the Name of Life: A Portrait in Conversation with Hans Juergen Schultz"), Deutsche Verlags-Anstalt, 1974.

To Have or To Be?, Harper, 1976.

Greatness and Limitations of Freud's Thought, Harper, 1980.

Gesamtsausgabe (title means "Complete Works"), Deutsche Verlags-Anstalt, 1980-81.

On Disobedience and Other Essays, Seabury, 1981.

The Working Class in Weimar Germany: A Psychological and Sociological Study, edited by Wolfgang Bonss, translated by Barbara Weinberger, Harvard University Press, 1984.

For the Love of Life, translated by Robert and Rita Kimber, Free Press, 1985.

CONTRIBUTOR

Ruth N. Anshen, *Moral Principle of Action: Man's Ethical Imperative,* Harper, 1952.

James R. Newman, editor, *What Is Science?,* Simon & Schuster, 1955.

Clark E. Moustakas, editor, *The Self: Explorations in Personal Growth,* Harper, 1956.

Anshen, editor, *Language: An Enquiry into Its Meaning and Function,* Harper, 1957.

William Phillips, editor, *Art and Psychoanalysis,* Criterion, 1957.

Abraham H. Maslow, editor, *New Knowledge in Human Values,* Harper, 1959.

Anshen, editor, *Family: Its Function and Destiny,* revised edition, Harper, 1959.

Michael Harrington and Paul Jacobs, editors, *Labor in a Free Society,* University of California Press, 1959.

Huston Smith, editor, *Search for America,* Prentice-Hall, 1959.

Richard A. Condon and Burton O. Kurth, editors, *Writing from Experience,* Harper, 1960.

Hiram Collins Haydn and Betsy Saunders, editors, *The American Scholar Reader,* Atheneum, 1960.

Donald G. Brennan, editor, *Arms Control, Disarmament, and National Security,* Braziller, 1961.

Irving Louis Horowitz, editor, *The New Sociology: Essays in Social Science and Social Theory in Honor of C. Wright Mills,* Oxford University Press, 1964.

Steven E. Deutsch and John Howard, editors, *Where It's At: Radical Perspective in Sociology,* Harper, 1969.

Summerhill: For and Against, Hart Publishing, 1970.

Contributor of articles to professional journals.

WORK IN PROGRESS: A sequel to *To Have or To Be?;* a book on "godless religion," a study of religious experience in which the concept of god is "unnecessary and undesirable"; a book on self-analysis.

SIDELIGHTS: Critics, disciples, and objective analysts alike have been hard pressed to define Erich Fromm's role in the world of letters. As John Dollard pointed out in the *New York Herald Tribune,* Fromm was "at once sociologist, philosopher, historian, psychoanalyst, economist, and anthropologist—and, one is tempted to add, lover of human life, poet, and prophet." Fromm himself indicated the vast scope of his concerns in the foreword to his most famous book, *Escape from Freedom,* when he wrote that "this book is part of a broad study concerning the character structure of modern man and the problems of the interaction between psychological and sociological factors which I have been working on for several years."

Throughout his career Fromm strove toward an understanding of human existence based upon the breaking down of barriers— between individuals as well as between schools of thought. In a *Los Angeles Times* obituary article of the famous psychologist, a reviewer summarizes: "Fromm's lifelong concern was how people could come to terms with their isolation, insignificance and doubts about life's meaning." As his theories developed over the decades into what would later be collectively labeled "social humanism," he incorporated knowledge and information culled from such diverse fields as Marxist socialism and Freudian psychology. The psychologist used these schools of thought as building blocks for developing original theories which, like his idiosyncratic life, often ran against popular beliefs.

A descendent of a Jewish family whose members had often become rabbis, Fromm ceased practicing Judaism when he was twenty-six. In a quote from the *New York Times,* he once told a reporter, "I gave up my religious convictions and practices because I just didn't want to participate in any division of the human race, whether religious or political." As a pacifist, Fromm protested against the use of military force during World War I, helped organize the National Committee for a Sane Nuclear Policy (SANE) in 1957, and strove to encourage understanding between the Soviet Union and the United States. As a psychologist, he diverged from the Freudian school, in which the unconscious was the main factor in understanding human actions, by pointing out the importance of the influence of social and economic factors.

Fromm's numerous and varied interests are revealed in the over twenty publications which he completed during his lifetime. For instance, *May Man Prevail?: An Enquiry into the Facts and Fictions of Foreign Policy* is an analysis of the cold war between the United States and the Soviet Union, while *The Forgotten Language: An Introduction to the Understanding of Dreams, Fairy Tales, and Myths* is an early examination of the role of fantasy and myth in the interplay between social control and individual imaginative freedom. In 1956, he published *The Art of Loving: An Enquiry into the Nature of Love,* in which he maintained that "love is the only sane and satisfactory answer to the problem of human existence" and examined the many varieties and forms of the emotion. *The Art of Loving* enjoyed enormous popularity during the 1960s, and many sociologists believe it has had a significant influence on the lifestyles of Americans. Within these pages, the psychologist asserted that "love is not primarily a relationship to a specific person; it is an attitude, an orientation of character, which determines the relatedness of a person to the world as a whole, not toward one 'object' of love." Fromm believed that love could only be called a mature emotion when it "preserves one's integrity."

Most of Fromm's work has been an application of psychoanalysis, sociology, philosophy, and religion to the peculiar problems of man in modern industrialized society. In *Escape from Free-*

dom he postulated that "modern man, freed from the bonds of pre-individualistic society, which simultaneously gave him security and limited him, has not gained freedom in the positive sense of the realization of his individual self; that is, the expression of his intellectual, emotional and sensuous potentialities. Freedom, though it has brought him independence and rationality, has made him isolated and, thereby, anxious and powerless." This problem, the individual's tenuous relationship to institutions and society, became the core of such later works as *Man for Himself: An Enquiry into the Psychology of Ethics* and *The Sane Society.*

Fromm's penultimate book, *To Have or To Be?,* presents "the viewpoint and challenge of 'radical humanistic psychoanalysis,' " explains Paul Roazen in *Nation.* The volume has been seen as the culmination of Fromm's work at that time and maintains, according to a publisher's note, "that two modes of existence are struggling for the spirit of humankind; the *having* mode, which concentrates on material possession, acquisitiveness, power, and aggression and is the basis of such universal evils as greed, envy, and violence; and the *being* mode, which is based in love, in the pleasure of sharing, and in meaningful and productive rather than wasteful activity. Dr. Fromm sees the *having* mode bringing the world to the brink of psychological and ecological disaster, and he outlines a program for socio-economic change [to] turn the world away from its catastrophic course."

Although some of Fromm's work has been collected and published since his death, the last book to be completed during his lifetime is *Greatness and Limitations of Freud's Thought.* This work echoes the sentiment of his 1962 publication, *Beyond the Chains of Illusion: My Encounter with Marx and Freud,* in which he wrote that Marx was superior to Freud because he believed in the possibility that mankind could be perfected. As the author says in a *Spectator* article by Hans Keller, "If Freud could have imagined a classless and free society he would have dispensed with the ego and id as universal categories of the human mind." Because of this lack of confidence in Freud's theories as well as his methods, Fromm developed a new approach to psychoanalysis. Dr. Earl G. Witenberg, director of the William Alanson White Institute for Psychiatry, Psychoanalysis and Psychology that Fromm co-founded in 1946, relates in a *New York Times* article by Dava Sobel that Fromm was interested in "working face to face with [his patient] and dynamically engaging him with insights about his condition and working actively toward the goal of getting those things clarified."

This method of psychoanalysis which Fromm devised was never described by him in print, however. His theories in this area are instead preserved only in the memories of his colleagues. Nevertheless, the psychoanalyst and philosopher will be remembered as one "who sought to apply the lessons of psychology to the social and political problems of the 20th century," according to J. Y. Smith of the *Washington Post.* "His theory of human nature cut a middle path between the instinctivists, who held that innate qualities were fixed at birth, and the behaviorists, who taught that all responses are the result of learning," says Sobel. Erich Fromm, concludes Dr. Witenberg in Sobel's article, "was a great man, both by his presence and his firm ideas."

BIOGRAPHICAL/CRITICAL SOURCES:

BOOKS

Butz, Otto, editor, *To Make a Difference,* Harper, 1967.
Evans, Richard I., *Dialogue with Erich Fromm,* Harper, 1966.
Fromm, Erich, *Escape from Freedom,* Farrar & Rinehart, 1941.
Fromm, Erich, *The Art of Loving: An Enquiry into the Nature of Love,* Harper, 1956.
Fromm, Erich, *Greatness and Limitations of Freud's Thought,* Harper, 1980.
Glen, J. S., *Erich Fromm: A Protestant Critique,* Westminster, 1966.
Gotesky, Rubin, *Personality: The Need for Liberty and Rights,* Libra, 1967.
Hammond, G. B., *Man in Estrangement,* Vanderbilt University Press, 1965.
Hausdorff, Don, *Erich Fromm,* Twayne, 1972.
Landis, Bernard, and Edward S. Tauber, editors, *In the Name of Life: Essays in Honor of Erich Fromm,* Holt, 1971.
Montague, Ashley, editor, *Culture and the Evolution of Man,* Oxford University Press, 1962.
Schaar, J. H., *Escape from Authority: The Perspectives of Erich Fromm,* Basic Books, 1961.

PERIODICALS

Book World, November 10, 1968.
Choice, October, 1984.
Commonweal, March 14, 1969, March 15, 1974, May 19, 1976.
Kirkus Review, November 15, 1985.
Nation, September 1, 1969.
New Republic, December 7, 1968.
New York Herald Tribune, September 4, 1955.
Publishers Weekly, September 13, 1976.
Saturday Review, April 11, 1959, December 14, 1968.
Spectator, January 10, 1981.
Times Literary Supplement, December 7, 1969, April 28, 1972, December 27, 1974.

OTHER

"Focus on Erich Fromm; the Eminent Psychologist talks with Heywood Hale Broun" (cassette recording), Center for Cassette Studies, c. 1976.
"Childhood" (cassette recording), Pacifica Tape Library.

OBITUARIES:

PERIODICALS

AB Bookman's Weekly, April 14, 1980.
Chicago Tribune, March 19, 1980.
Los Angeles Times, March 19, 1980.
Newsweek, March 31, 1980.
New York Times, March 19, 1980.
Publishers Weekly, April 4, 1980.
Time, March 31, 1980.
Times (London), March 19, 1980.
Washington Post, March 19, 1980.

*   *   *

FROST, Robert (Lee) 1874-1963

PERSONAL: Born March 26, 1874, in San Francisco, Calif.; died January 29, 1963, in Boston, Mass.; son of William Prescott (a newspaper reporter and editor) and Isabel (a teacher; maiden name, Moodie) Frost; married Elinor Miriam White, December 19, 1895 (died, 1938); children: Elliott (deceased), Lesley (daughter), Carol (son; deceased), Irma, Marjorie (deceased), Elinor Bettina (deceased). *Education:* Attended Dartmouth College, 1892, and Harvard University 1897-99.

CAREER: Poet. Held various jobs between college studies, including bobbin boy in a Massachusetts mill, cobbler, editor of a country newspaper, schoolteacher, and farmer. Lived in England, 1912-15. Tufts College, Medford, Mass., Phi Beta Kappa poet, 1915 and 1940; Amherst College, Amherst, Mass., professor of English and poet-in-residence, 1916-20, 1923-25, and 1926-28; Harvard University, Cambridge, Mass., Phi Beta Kappa poet, 1916 and 1941; Middlebury College, Middlebury, Vt., co-founder of the Bread-Loaf School and Conference of English, 1920, annual lecturer, beginning 1920; University of Michigan, Ann Arbor, professor and poet-in-residence, 1921-23, fellow in letters, 1925-26; Columbia University, New York City, Phi Beta Kappa poet, 1932; Yale University, New Haven, Conn., associate fellow, beginning 1933; Harvard University, Charles Eliot Norton Professor of Poetry, 1936, board overseer, 1938-39, Ralph Waldo Emerson Fellow, 1939-41, honorary fellow, 1942-43; associate of Adams House; fellow in American civilization, 1941-42; Dartmouth College, Hanover, N.H., George Ticknor Fellow in Humanities, 1943-49, visiting lecturer.

MEMBER: International PEN, National Institute of Arts and Letters, American Academy of Arts and Letters, American Philosophical Society.

AWARDS, HONORS: Levinson Prize, *Poetry* magazine, 1922; Pulitzer Prize for poetry, 1924, for *New Hampshire,* 1931, for *Collected Poems,* 1937, for *A Further Range,* and, 1943, for *A Witness Tree;* Golden Rose Trophy, New England Poetry Club, 1928; Russell Loines Prize for poetry, National Institute of Arts and Letters, 1931; Mark Twain medal, 1937; Gold Medal of the National Institute of Arts and Letters, 1939; Gold Medal of the Poetry Society of America, 1941 and 1958; Gold Medal, Limited Editions Club, 1949; unanimous resolution in his honor and gold medal from the U.S. Senate, March 24, 1950; American Academy of Poets Award, 1953; Medal of Honor, New York University, 1956; Huntington Hartford Foundation Award, 1958; Emerson-Thoreau Medal, American Academy of Arts and Sciences, 1958; participated in President John F. Kennedy's inauguration ceremonies, 1961, by reading his poems "Dedication" and "The Gift Outright"; Congressional Gold Medal, 1962; Edward MacDowell Medal, 1962; Bollingen Prize in Poetry, 1963; inducted into American Poet's Corner at Cathedral of St. John the Divine, 1986. Chosen poet laureate of Vermont by the State League of Women's Clubs; more than forty honorary degrees from colleges and universities, including Oxford and Cambridge Universities, Amherst College, and the University of Michigan.

WRITINGS:

POETRY

Twilight, [Lawrence, Mass.], 1894, reprinted, University of Virginia, 1966.
A Boy's Will, D. Nutt, 1913, Holt, 1915.
North of Boston, D. Nutt, 1914, Holt, 1915, reprinted, Dodd, 1977.
Mountain Interval, Holt, 1916.
New Hampshire, Holt, 1923, reprinted, New Dresden Press, 1955.
Selected Poems, Holt, 1923.
Several Short Poems, Holt, 1924.
West-Running Brook, Holt, 1928.
Selected Poems, Holt, 1928.
The Lovely Shall Be Choosers, Random House, 1929.
The Lone Striker, Knopf, 1933.
Two Tramps in Mud-Time, Holt, 1934.
The Gold Hesperidee, Bibliophile Press, 1935.
Three Poems, Baker Library Press, 1935.
A Further Range, Holt, 1936.
From Snow to Snow, Holt, 1936.
A Witness Tree, Holt, 1942.

A Masque of Reason (verse drama), Holt, 1942.
Steeple Bush, Holt, 1947.
A Masque of Mercy (verse drama), Holt, 1947.
Greece, Black Rose Press, 1948.
Hard Not to Be King, House of Books, 1951.
Aforesaid, Holt, 1954.
The Gift Outright, Holt, 1961.
"Dedication" and "The Gift Outright" (poems read at the presidential inaugural, 1961; published with the inaugural address of J. F. Kennedy), Spiral Press, 1961.
In the Clearing, Holt, 1962.
Stopping by Woods on a Snowy Evening, Dutton, 1978.
Early Poems, Crown, 1981.
A Swinger of Birches: Poems of Robert Frost for Young People (with audio cassette), Stemmer House, 1982.
Spring Pools, Lime Rock Press, 1983.
Birches, illustrated by Ed Young, Holt, 1988.

Also author of *And All We Call American,* 1958.

POEMS ISSUED AS CHRISTMAS GREETINGS

Christmas Trees, Spiral Press, 1929.
Neither Out Far Nor In Deep, Holt, 1935.
Everybody's Sanity, [Los Angeles], 1936.
To a Young Wretch, Spiral Press, 1937.
Triple Plate, Spiral Press, 1939.
Our Hold on the Planet, Holt, 1940.
An Unstamped Letter in Our Rural Letter Box, Spiral Press, 1944.
On Making Certain Anything Has Happened, Spiral Press, 1945.
One Step Backward Taken, Spiral Press, 1947.
Closed for Good, Spiral Press, 1948.
On a Tree Fallen Across the Road to Hear Us Talk, Spiral Press, 1949.
Doom to Bloom, Holt, 1950.
A Cabin in the Clearing, Spiral Press, 1951.
Does No One but Me at All Ever Feel This Way in the Least, Spiral Press, 1952.
One More Brevity, Holt, 1953.
From a Milkweed Pod, Holt, 1954.
Some Science Fiction, Spiral Press, 1955.
Kitty Hawk, 1894, Holt, 1956.
My Objection to Being Stepped On, Holt, 1957.
Away, Spiral Press, 1958.
A-Wishing Well, Spiral Press, 1959.
Accidentally on Purpose, Holt, 1960.
The Woodpile, Spiral Press, 1961.
The Prophets Really Prophesy as Mystics, the Commentators Merely by Statistics, Spiral Press, 1962.
The Constant Symbol, [New York], 1962.

COLLECTIONS

Collected Poems of Robert Frost, Holt, 1930, new edition, 1939, reprinted, Buccaneer Books, 1983.
Selected Poems, Holt, 1934, reprinted, 1963.
Come In, and Other Poems, edited by Louis Untermeyer, Holt, 1943, reprinted, F. Watts, 1967, enlarged edition published as *The Road Not Taken: An Introduction to Robert Frost,* reprinted as *The Pocket Book of Robert Frost's Poems,* Pocket Books, 1956.
The Poems of Robert Frost, Modern Library, 1946.
You Come Too: Favorite Poems for Young Readers, Holt, 1959, reprinted, 1967.
A Remembrance Collection of New Poems by Robert Frost, Holt, 1959.
Poems, Washington Square Press, 1961.

Longer Poems: The Death of the Hired Man, Holt, 1966.
Selected Prose, edited by Hyde Cox and Edward Connery Lathem, Holt, 1966, reprinted, Collier Books, 1968.
Complete Poems of Robert Frost, Holt, 1968.
The Poetry of Robert Frost, edited by Lathem, Holt, 1969.
Robert Frost: Poetry and Prose, edited by Lawrence Thompson and Lathem, Holt, 1972.
Selected Poems, edited by Ian Hamilton, Penguin, 1973.

LETTERS

The Letters of Robert Frost to Louis Untermeyer, Holt, 1963.
Selected Letters, edited by Thompson, Holt, 1964.

OTHER

A Way Out: A One-Act Play, Harbor Press, 1929.
The Cow's in the Corn: A One-Act Irish Play in Rhyme, Slide Mountain Press, 1929.
(Contributor) John Holmes, editor, *Writing Poetry,* Writer, Inc., 1960.
(Contributor) Milton R. Konvitz and Stephen E. Whicher, editors, *Emerson,* Prentice-Hall, 1962.
Robert Frost on "Extravagance" (the text of Frost's last college lecture, Dartmouth College, November 27, 1962), [Hanover, N.H.], 1963.
Robert Frost: A Living Voice (contains speeches by Frost), edited by Reginald Cook, University of Massachusetts Press, 1974.
(With Caroline Ford) *The Less Travelled Road,* Bern Porter, 1982.
Stories for Lesley, edited by Roger D. Sell, University Press of Virginia, 1984.

Frost's papers are collected at the libraries of the University of Virginia, Amherst College, and Dartmouth College, and the Huntington Library in San Marino, California.

SIDELIGHTS: Robert Frost holds a unique and almost isolated position in American letters. "Though his career fully spans the modern period and though it is impossible to speak of him as anything other than a modern poet," writes James M. Cox, "it is difficult to place him in the main tradition of modern poetry." In a sense, Frost stands at the crossroads of nineteenth-century American poetry and modernism, for in his verse may be found the culmination of many nineteenth-century tendencies and traditions as well as parallels to the works of his twentieth-century contemporaries. Taking his symbols from the public domain, Frost developed, as many critics note, an original, modern idiom and a sense of directness and economy that reflect the imagism of Ezra Pound and Amy Lowell. On the other hand, as Leonard Unger and William Van O'Connor point out in *Poems for Study,* "Frost's poetry, unlike that of such contemporaries as Eliot, Stevens, and the later Yeats, shows no marked departure from the poetic practices of the nineteenth century." Although he avoids traditional verse forms and only uses rhyme erratically, Frost is not an innovator and his technique is never experimental.

Frost's theory of poetic composition ties him to both centuries. Like the nineteenth-century Romantics, he maintained that a poem is "never a put-up job. . . . It begins as a lump in the throat, a sense of wrong, a homesickness, a loneliness. It is never a thought to begin with. It is at its best when it is a tantalizing vagueness." Yet, "working out his own version of the 'impersonal' view of art," as Hyatt H. Waggoner observed, Frost also upheld T. S. Eliot's idea that the man who suffers and the artist who creates are totally separate. In a 1932 letter to Sydney Cox, Frost explained his conception of poetry: "The objective idea is all I ever cared about. Most of my ideas occur in verse. . . . To be too subjective with what an artist has managed to make objec-

tive is to come on him presumptuously and render ungraceful what he in pain of his life had faith he had made graceful."

To accomplish such objectivity and grace, Frost took up nineteenth-century tools and made them new. Lawrence Thompson has explained that, according to Frost, "the self-imposed restrictions of meter in form and of coherence in content" work to a poet's advantage; they liberate him from the experimentalist's burden—the perpetual search for new forms and alternative structures. Thus Frost, as he himself put it in "The Constant Symbol," wrote his verse regular; he never completely abandoned conventional metrical forms for free verse, as so many of his contemporaries were doing. At the same time, his adherence to meter, line length, and rhyme scheme was not an arbitrary choice. He maintained that "the freshness of a poem belongs absolutely to its not having been thought out and then set to verse as the verse in turn might be set to music." He believed, rather, that the poem's particular mood dictated or determined the poet's "first commitment to metre and length of line."

Critics frequently point out that Frost complicated his problem and enriched his style by setting traditional meters against the natural rhythms of speech. Drawing his language primarily from the vernacular, he avoided artificial poetic diction by employing the accent of a soft-spoken New Englander. In *The Function of Criticism,* Yvor Winters faulted Frost for his "endeavor to make his style approximate as closely as possible the style of conversation." But what Frost achieved in his poetry was much more complex than a mere imitation of the New England farmer idiom. He wanted to restore to literature the "sentence sounds that underlie the words," the "vocal gesture" that enhances meaning. That is, he felt the poet's ear must be sensitive to the voice in order to capture with the written word the significance of sound in the spoken word. "The Death of the Hired Man," for instance, consists almost entirely of dialogue between Mary and Warren, her farmer-husband, but critics have observed that in this poem Frost takes the prosaic patterns of their speech and makes them lyrical. To Ezra Pound "The Death of the Hired Man" represented Frost at his best—when he "dared to write . . . in the natural speech of New England; in natural spoken speech, which is very different from the 'natural' speech of the newspapers, and of many professors."

Frost's use of New England dialect is only one aspect of his often discussed regionalism. Within New England, his particular focus was on New Hampshire, which he called "one of the two best states in the Union," the other being Vermont. In an essay entitled "Robert Frost and New England: A Revaluation," W. G. O'Donnell noted how from the start, in *A Boy's Will,* "Frost had already decided to give his writing a local habitation and a New England name, to root his art in the soil that he had worked with his own hands." Reviewing *North of Boston* in the *New Republic,* Amy Lowell wrote, "Not only is his work New England in subject, it is so in technique. . . . Mr. Frost has reproduced both people and scenery with a vividness which is extraordinary." Many other critics have lauded Frost's ability to realistically evoke the New England landscape; they point out that one can visualize an orchard in "After Apple-Picking" or imagine spring in a farmyard in "Two Tramps in Mud Time." In this "ability to portray the local truth in nature," O'Donnell claims, Frost has no peer. The same ability prompted Pound to declare, "I know more of farm life than I did before I had read his poems. That means I know more of 'Life.' "

Frost's regionalism, critics remark, is in his realism, not in politics; he creates no picture of regional unity or sense of community. In *The Continuity of American Poetry,* Roy Harvey Pearce describes Frost's protagonists as individuals who are constantly forced to confront their individualism as such and to reject the modern world in order to retain their identity. Frost's use of nature is not only similar but closely tied to this regionalism. He stays as clear of religion and mysticism as he does of politics. What he finds in nature is sensuous pleasure; he is also sensitive to the earth's fertility and to man's relationship to the soil. To critic M. L. Rosenthal, Frost's pastoral quality, his "lyrical and realistic repossession of the rural and 'natural,' " is the staple of his reputation.

Yet, just as Frost is aware of the distances between one man and another, so he is also always aware of the distinction, the ultimate separateness, of nature and man. Marion Montgomery has explained, "His attitude toward nature is one of armed and amicable truce and mutual respect interspersed with crossings of the boundaries" between individual man and natural forces. Below the surface of Frost's poems are dreadful implications, what Rosenthal calls his "shocked sense of the helpless cruelty of things." This natural cruelty is at work in "Design" and in "Once by the Pacific." The ominous tone of these two poems prompted Rosenthal's further comment: "At his most powerful Frost is as staggered by 'the horror' as Eliot and approaches the hysterical edge of sensibility in a comparable way. . . . His is still the modern mind in search of its own meaning."

The austere and tragic view of life that emerges in so many of Frost's poems is modulated by his metaphysical use of detail. As Frost portrays him, man might be alone in an ultimately indifferent universe, but he may nevertheless look to the natural world for metaphors of his own condition. Thus, in his search for meaning in the modern world, Frost focuses on those moments when the seen and the unseen, the tangible and the spiritual intersect. John T. Napier calls this Frost's ability "to find the ordinary a matrix for the extraordinary." In this respect, he is often compared with Emily Dickinson and Ralph Waldo Emerson, in whose poetry, too, a simple fact, object, person, or event will be transfigured and take on greater mystery or significance. The poem "Birches" is an example: it contains the image of slender trees bent to the ground-temporarily by a boy's swinging on them or permanently by an ice-storm. But as the poem unfolds, it becomes clear that the speaker is concerned not only with child's play and natural phenomena, but also with the point at which physical and spiritual reality merge.

Such symbolic import of mundane facts informs many of Frost's poems, and in "Education by Poetry" he explained: "Poetry begins in trivial metaphors, pretty metaphors, 'grace' metaphors, and goes on to the profoundest thinking that we have. Poetry provides the one permissible way of saying one thing and meaning another. . . . Unless you are at home in the metaphor, unless you have had your proper poetical education in the metaphor, you are not safe anywhere."

Frost's own poetical education began in San Francisco where he was born in 1874, but he found his place of safety in New England when his family moved to Lawrence, Massachusetts, in 1884 following his father's death. The move was actually a return, for Frost's ancestors were originally New Englanders. The region must have been particularly conducive to the writing of poetry because within the next five years Frost had made up his mind to be a poet. In fact, he graduated from Lawrence High School, in 1892, as class poet (he also shared the honor of covaledictorian with his wife-to-be Elinor White); and two years later, the *New York Independent* accepted his poem entitled "My Butterfly," launching his status as a professional poet with a check for $15.00.

To celebrate his first publication, Frost had a book of six poems privately printed; two copies of *Twilight* were made—one for himself and one for his fiancee. Over the next eight years, however, he succeeded in having only thirteen more poems published. During this time, Frost sporadically attended Dartmouth and Harvard and earned a living teaching school and, later, working a farm in Derby, New Hampshire. But in 1912, discouraged by American magazines' constant rejection of his work, he took his family to England, where he could "write and be poor without further scandal in the family." In England, Frost found the professional esteem denied him in his native country. Continuing to write about New England, he had two books published, *A Boy's Will* and *North of Boston,* which established his reputation so that his return to the United States in 1915 was as a celebrated literary figure. Holt put out an American edition of *North of Boston,* and periodicals that had once scorned his work now sought it.

Since 1915 Frost's position in American letters has been firmly rooted; in the years before his death he came to be considered the unofficial poet laureate of the United States. On his seventy-fifth birthday, the U.S. Senate passed a resolution in his honor which said, "His poems have helped to guide American thought and humor and wisdom, setting forth to our minds a reliable representation of ourselves and of all men." In 1955, the State of Vermont named a mountain after him in Ripton, the town of his legal residence; and at the presidential inauguration of John F. Kennedy in 1961, Frost was given the unprecedented honor of being asked to read a poem, "The Gift Outright," which he wrote for the occasion.

Though Frost allied himself with no literary school or movement, the imagists helped at the start to promote his American reputation. *Poetry: A Magazine of Verse* published his work before others began to clamor for it. It also published a review by Ezra Pound of the British edition of *A Boy's Will,* which Pound said "has the tang of the New Hampshire woods, and it has just this utter sincerity. It is not post-Miltonic or post-Swinburnian or post Kiplonian. This man has the good sense to speak naturally and to paint the thing, the thing as he sees it." Amy Lowell reviewed *North of Boston* in the *New Republic,* and she, too, sang Frost's praises: "He writes in classic metres in a way to set the teeth of all the poets of the older schools on edge; and he writes in classic metres, and uses inversions and cliches whenever he pleases, those devices so abhorred by the newest generation. He goes his own way, regardless of anyone else's rules, and the result is a book of unusual power and sincerity." In these first two volumes, Frost introduced not only his affection for New England themes and his unique blend of traditional meters and colloquialism, but also his use of dramatic monologues and dialogues. "Mending Wall," the leading poem in *North of Boston,* describes the friendly argument between the speaker and his neighbor as they walk along their common wall replacing fallen stones; their differing attitudes toward "boundaries" offer symbolic significance typical of the poems in these early collections.

Mountain Interval marked Frost's turn to another kind of poem, a brief meditation sparked by an object, person or event. Like the monologues and dialogues, these short pieces have a dramatic quality. "Birches," discussed above, is an example, as is "The Road Not Taken," in which a fork in a woodland path transcends the specific. The distinction of this volume, the *Boston Transcript* said, "is that Mr. Frost takes the lyricism of 'A Boy's Will' and plays a deeper music and gives a more intricate variety of experience."

Several new qualities emerged in Frost's work with the appearance of *New Hampshire,* particularly a new self-consciousness and willingness to speak of himself and his art. The volume, for which Frost won his first Pulitzer Prize, "pretends to be nothing but a long poem with notes and grace notes," as Louis Untermeyer described it. The title poem, approximately fourteen pages long, is a "rambling tribute" to Frost's favorite state and "is starred and dotted with scientific numerals in the manner of the most profound treatise." Thus, a footnote at the end of a line of poetry will refer the reader to another poem seemingly inserted to merely reinforce the text of "New Hampshire." Some of these poems are in the form of epigrams, which appear for the first time in Frost's work. "Fire and Ice," for example, one of the better known epigrams, speculates on the means by which the world will end. Frost's most famous and, according to J. McBride Dabbs, most perfect lyric, "Stopping by Woods on a Snowy Evening," is also included in this collection; conveying "the insistent whisper of death at the heart of life," the poem portrays a speaker who stops his sleigh in the midst of a snowy woods only to be called from the inviting gloom by the recollection of practical duties. Frost himself said of this poem that it is the kind he'd like to print on one page followed with "forty pages of footnotes."

West-Running Brook, Frost's fifth book of poems, is divided into six sections, one of which is taken up entirely by the title poem. This poem refers to a brook which perversely flows west instead of east to the Atlantic like all other brooks. A comparison is set up between the brook and the poem's speaker who trusts himself to go by "contraries"; further rebellious elements exemplified by the brook give expression to an eccentric individualism, Frost's stoic theme of resistance and self-realization. Reviewing the collection in the *New York Herald Tribune,* Babette Deutsch wrote: "The courage that is bred by a dark sense of Fate, the tenderness that broods over mankind in all its blindness and absurdity, the vision that comes to rest as fully on kitchen smoke and lapsing snow as on mountains and stars—these are his, and in his seemingly casual poetry, he quietly makes them ours."

A Further Range, which earned Frost another Pulitzer Prize and was a Book-of-the-Month Club selection, contains two groups of poems subtitled "Taken Doubly" and "Taken Singly." In the first, and more interesting, of these groups, the poems are somewhat didactic, though there are humorous and satiric pieces as well. Included here is "Two Tramps in Mud Time," which opens with the story of two itinerant lumbermen who offer to cut the speaker's wood for pay; the poem then develops into a sermon on the relationship between work and play, vocation and avocation, preaching the necessity to unite them. Of the entire volume, William Rose Benet wrote, "It is better worth reading than nine-tenths of the books that will come your way this year. In a time when all kinds of insanity are assailing the nations it is good to listen to this quiet humor, even about a hen, a hornet, or Square Matthew. . . . And if anybody should ask me why I still believe in my land, I have only to put this book in his hand and answer, 'Well-here is a man of my country.'"

Most critics acknowledge that Frost's poetry in the forties and fifties grew more and more abstract, cryptic, and even sententious, so it is generally on the basis of his earlier work that he is judged. His political conservatism and religious faith, hitherto informed by skepticism and local color, became more and more the guiding principles of his work. He had been, as Randall Jarrell points out, "a very odd and very radical radical when young" yet became "sometimes callously and unimaginatively conservative" in his old age. He had become a public figure, and in the

years before his death, much of his poetry was written from this stance.

Reviewing A Witness Tree in *Books,* Wilbert Snow noted a few poems "which have a right to stand with the best things he has written": "Come In," "The Silken Tent," and "Carpe Diem" especially. Yet Snow went on: "Some of the poems here are little more than rhymed fancies; others lack the bullet-like unity of structure to be found in 'North of Boston.'" On the other hand, Stephen Vincent Benet felt that Frost had "never written any better poems than some of those in this book." Similarly, critics were let down by *In the Clearing.* One wrote, "Although this reviewer considers Robert Frost to be the foremost contemporary U.S. poet, he regretfully must state that most of the poems in this new volume are disappointing. . . . [They] often are closer to jingles than to the memorable poetry we associate with his name." Another maintained that "the bulk of the book consists of poems of 'philosophic talk.' Whether you like them or not depends mostly on whether you share the 'philosophy.'"

Indeed, many readers do share Frost's philosophy, and still others who do not nevertheless continue to find delight and significance in his large body of poetry. In October, 1963, President John F. Kennedy delivered a speech at the dedication of the Robert Frost Library in Amherst, Massachusetts. "In honoring Robert Frost," the President said, "we therefore can pay honor to the deepest source of our national strength. That strength takes many forms and the most obvious forms are not always the most significant. . . . Our national strength matters; but the spirit which informs and controls our strength matters just as much. This was the special significance of Robert Frost." The poet would probably have been pleased by such recognition, for he had said once, in an interview with Harvey Breit: "One thing I care about, and wish young people could care about, is taking poetry as the first form of understanding. If poetry isn't understanding all, the whole world, then it isn't worth anything."

BIOGRAPHICAL/CRITICAL SOURCES:

BOOKS

Anderson, Margaret, *Robert Frost and John Bartlett: The Record of a Friendship,* Holt, 1963.
Barry, Elaine, compiler, *Robert Frost on Writing,* Rutgers University Press, 1973.
Barry, Elaine, *Robert Frost,* Ungar, 1973.
Breit, Harvey, *The Writer Observed,* World Publishing, 1956.
Concise Dictionary of American Literary Biography: The Twenties, 1917-1929, Gale, 1989.
Contemporary Literary Criticism, Gale, Volume 1, 1973, Volume 3, 1975, Volume 4, 1975, Volume 9, 1978, Volume 10, 1979, Volume 13, 1980, Volume 15, 1980, Volume 26, 1983, Volume 34, 1985, Volume 44, 1987.
Cook, Reginald L., *The Dimensions of Robert Frost,* Rinehart, 1958.
Cook, Reginald L., *Robert Frost: A Living Voice,* University of Massachusetts Press, 1974.
Cox, James M., *Robert Frost: A Collection of Critical Essays,* Prentice-Hall, 1962.
Cox, Sidney, *Swinger of Birches: A Portrait of Robert Frost,* New York University Press, 1957.
Dictionary of Literary Biography, Volume 54: *American Poets, 1880-1945, Third Series,* Gale, 1987.
Dodd, Loring Holmes, *Celebrities at Our Hearthside,* Dresser, 1959.
Doyle, John R., Jr., *Poetry of Robert Frost: An Analysis,* Hallier, 1965.

Evans, William R., editor, *Robert Frost and Sidney Cox: Forty Years of Friendship,* University Press of New England, 1981.

Francis, Robert, recorder, *A Time to Talk: Conversations and Indiscretions,* University of Massachusetts Press, 1972.

Frost, Lesley, *New Hampshire's Child: Derry Journals of Lesley Frost,* State University of New York Press, 1969.

Gerber, Philip L., *Robert Frost,* Twayne, 1966.

Gould, Jean, *Robert Frost: The Aim Was Song,* Dodd, 1964.

Grade, Arnold, editor, *Family Letters of Robert and Elinor Frost,* State University of New York Press, 1972.

Greiner, Donald J., *Checklist of Robert Frost,* Charles E. Merrill, 1969.

Greiner, Donald J. and Charles Sanders, *Robert Frost: The Poet and His Critics,* American Library Association, 1974.

Hall, Donald, *Remembering Poets,* Hater, 1977.

Isaacs, Emily Elizabeth, *Introduction to Robert Frost,* A. Swallow, 1962, reprinted, Haskell House, 1972.

Jarrell, Randall, *Poetry and the Age,* Vintage, 1955.

Jennings, Elizabeth, *Frost,* Barnes & Noble, 1966.

Lathem, Edward C. and Lawrance Thompson, editors, *Robert Frost: Farm Poultryman; The Story of Robert Frost's Career As a Breeder and Fancier of Hens,* Dartmouth Publishers, 1963.

Lathem, Edward C., editor, *Interviews with Robert Frost,* Rinehart, 1966.

Lathem, Edward C., editor, *A Concordance to the Poetry of Robert Frost,* Holt Information Systems, 1971.

Lentricchia, Frank, *Robert Frost: Modern Poetics and the Landscapes of Self,* Duke University Press, 1975.

Lowell, Amy, *Tendencies in Modern American Poetry,* Macmillan, 1917.

Mertins, Marshall Louis and Esther Mertins, *Intervals of Robert Frost: A Critical Bibliography,* University of California Press, 1947, reprinted, Russell, 1975.

Mertins, Marshall Louis, *Robert Frost: Life and Talks— Walking,* University of Oklahoma Press, 1965.

Munson, Gorham B., *Robert Frost: A Study in Sensibility and Good Sense,* G. H. Doran, 1927, reprinted, Haskell House, 1969.

Newdick, Robert Spangler, *Newdick's Season of Frost: An Interrupted Biography of Robert Frost,* edited by William A. Sutton, State University of New York Press, 1976.

Orton, Vrest, *Vermont Afternoons with Robert Frost,* Tuttle, 1971.

Pearce, Roy Harvey, *The Continuity of American Poetry,* Princeton, 1961.

Poirier, Richard, *Robert Frost,* Oxford University Press, 1977.

Pound, Ezra, *The Literary Essays of Ezra Pound,* New Directions, 1954.

Pritchard, William H., *Frost: A Literary Life Reconsidered,* Oxford University Press, 1984.

Reeve, Franklin D., *Robert Frost in Russia,* Little, Brown, 1964.

Rosenthal, M. L., *The Modern Poets,* Oxford University Press, 1965.

Shepley, Elizabeth, *Robert Frost: The Trial by Existence,* Holt, 1960.

Sohn, David A. and Richard Tyre, *Frost: The Poet and His Poetry,* Holt, 1967.

Spiller, Robert E. and others, *Literary History of the United States,* 4th revised edition, Macmillan, 1974.

Squires, Radcliffe, *Major Themes of Robert Frost,* University of Michigan Press, 1969.

Tharpe, Jac, editor, *Frost: Centennial Essays II,* University Press of Mississippi, 1976.

Thompson, Lawrence, *Fire and Ice: The Art and Thought of Robert Frost,* Holt, 1942, reprinted, Russell, 1975.

Thompson, Lawrence, *Robert Frost,* University of Minnesota Press, 1959.

Thompson, Lawrence, editor, *Selected Letters of Robert Frost,* Holt, 1964.

Thompson, Lawrence, *Robert Frost: The Early Years, 1874-1915,* Holt, 1966.

Thompson, Lawrence, *Robert Frost: The Years of Triumph, 1915-1938,* Holt, 1970.

Thompson, Lawrence and R. H. Winnick, *Robert Frost: The Later Years, 1938-1963,* Holt, 1976.

Unger, Leonard and William Van O'Connor, *Poems for Study,* Holt, 1953.

Untermeyer, Louis, *Makers of the Modern World,* Simon & Schuster, 1955.

Untermeyer, Louis, *Lives of the Poets,* Simon & Schuster, 1959.

Untermeyer, Louis, *Robert Frost: A Backward Look,* U.S. Government Printing Office, 1964.

Van Egmond, Peter, *The Critical Reception of Robert Frost,* G. K. Hall, 1974.

Waggoner, Hyatt H., *American Poetry from the Puritans to the Present,* Houghton, 1968.

Wagner, Linda Welshimer, editor, *Robert Frost: The Critical Reception,* B. Franklin, 1977.

West, Herbert Faulkner, *Mind on the Wing,* Coward, 1947.

Winters, Yvor, *The Function of Criticism,* A. Swallow, 1957.

PERIODICALS

America, December 24, 1977.
American Literature, January, 1948.
Atlantic, February, 1964, November, 1966.
Bookman, January, 1924.
Books, May 10, 1942.
Boston Transcript, December 2, 1916.
Commonweal, May 4, 1962, April 1, 1977.
New Republic, February 20, 1915.
New York Herald Tribune, November 18, 1928.
New York Times, October 19, 1986.
New York Times Book Review, July 17, 1988.
New York Times Magazine, June 11, 1972, August 18, 1974.
Poetry, May, 1913.
Saturday Review of Literature, May 30, 1936, April 25, 1942.
South Atlantic Quarterly, summer, 1958.
Times Literary Supplement, December 14, 1967.
Virginia Quarterly Review, summer, 1957.
Wisconsin Library Bulletin, July, 1962.
Yale Review, spring, 1934, summer, 1948.

OBITUARIES:

PERIODICALS

Current Biography, March, 1963.
Illustrated London News, February 9, 1963.
Newsweek, February 11, 1963.
New York Times, January 30, 1963.
Publishers Weekly, February 11, 1963.

*   *   *

FRY, Christopher 1907-

PERSONAL: Name originally Christopher Fry Harris; born December 18, 1907, in Bristol, England; son of Charles John (a builder and later a church reader) and Emma Marguerite Fry (Hammond) Harris; married Phyllis Marjorie Hart, December

3, 1936; children: one son. *Education:* Attended Bedford Modern School, Bedford, England, 1918-26. *Religion:* Church of England.

ADDRESSES: Home—The Toft, East Dean, near Chichester, West Sussex PO18 0JA, England. *Agent*—ACTAC Ltd., 16 Cadogan Ln., London S.W.1., England.

CAREER: Bedford Froebel Kindergarten, teacher, 1926-27; Citizen House, Bath, England, actor and office worker, 1927; Hazelwood Preparatory School, Limpsfield, Surrey, England, schoolmaster, 1928-31; secretary to H. Rodney Bennett, 1931-32; Tunbridge Wells Repertory Players, founding director, 1932-35, 1940, 1944-46; Dr. Barnardo's Homes, lecturer and editor of schools magazine, 1934-39; Oxford Playhouse, director, 1940; Arts Theatre Club, London, England, director, 1945, staff dramatist, 1947. Visiting director, Oxford Playhouse, 1945-46, Arts Theatre Club, 1947. Composer. *Military service:* Pioneer Corps, 1940-44.

MEMBER: Dramatists Guild, Garrick Club.

AWARDS, HONORS: Shaw Prize Fund award, 1948, for *The Lady's Not for Burning;* William Foyle Poetry Prize, 1951, for *Venus Observed;* New York Drama Critics Circle Award, 1951, for *The Lady's Not for Burning,* 1952, for *Venus Observed,* and 1956, for *Tiger at the Gates;* Queen's Gold Medal for Poetry, 1962; Heinemann Award, Royal Society of Literature, 1962, for *Curtmantle;* D.A., 1966, and Honorary Fellow, 1988, Manchester Polytechnic, 1966; Writers Guild Best British Television Dramatization award nomination, 1971, for "The Tenant of Wildfell Hall"; Doctor of Letters, Lambeth and Oxford University, 1988; Royal Society of Literature Fellow.

WRITINGS:

PLAYS

(With Monte Crick and F. Eyton) "She Shall Have Music," first produced in London, England, 1934.

"Open Door," first produced in London, England, 1936.

The Boy with a Cart: Cuthman, Saint of Sussex (also see below; first produced in Coleman's Hatch, Sussex, England, 1938; produced on the West End at Lyric Theatre, January 16, 1950), Oxford University Press, 1939, 2nd edition, Muller, 1956.

(Author of libretto) "Robert of Sicily: Opera for Children," first produced in 1938.

"The Tower" (pageant), first produced at Tewkesbury Festival, Tewkesbury, England, July 18, 1939.

Thursday's Child: A Pageant (first produced in London, 1939), Girl's Friendly Press (London), 1939.

(Author of libretto) "Seven at a Stroke: A Play for Children," first produced in 1939.

A Phoenix Too Frequent (comedy; also see below; first produced in London at Mercury Theatre, April 25, 1946; produced on Broadway with "Freight," 1950), Hollis & Carter, 1946, Oxford University Press, 1949.

The Firstborn (also see below; tragedy; broadcast on radio, 1947; first produced at Gateway Theatre, Edinburgh, Scotland, September 6, 1948), Cambridge University Press, 1946, 3rd edition, Oxford University Press, 1958.

The Lady's Not for Burning (also see below; comedy; first produced in London at Arts Theatre, March 10, 1948; produced on the West End, May 11, 1949, produced on Broadway at Royale Theatre, November 8, 1950), Oxford University Press, 1949, revised edition, 1973.

Thor, with Angels (also see below; first produced at Chapter House, Canterbury, England, June, 1948; produced on the West End at Lyric Theatre, September 27, 1951), H. J. Goulden, 1948, Oxford University Press, 1949.

Venus Observed (also see below; first produced in London at St. James Theatre, January 18, 1950; produced on Broadway at Century Theatre, February 13, 1952), Oxford University Press, 1950.

A Sleep of Prisoners (also see below; first produced in Oxford, England, at University Church, April 23, 1951; produced in London at St. Thomas's Church, May 15, 1951), Oxford University Press, 1951, 2nd edition, 1965.

The Dark Is Light Enough: A Winter Comedy (also see below; first produced on the West End at Aldwych Theatre, April, 30, 1954; produced on Broadway at ANTA Theatre, February 23, 1955) Oxford University Press, 1954.

Curtmantle: A Play (also see below; first produced in Dutch in Tilburg, Netherlands, at Stadsschouwburg, March 1, 1961, produced on the West End at Aldwych Theatre, October 6, 1962), Oxford University Press, 1961.

A Yard of Sun: A Summer Comedy (first produced at Nottingham Playhouse, Nottingham, England, July 11, 1970; produced on the West End at Old Vic Theatre, August 10, 1970), Oxford University Press, 1970.

One Thing More, or Caedmon Construed (first produced at Chelmsford Cathedral, England, 1986; broadcast on radio, 1986), Oxford University Press, 1985, Dramatists Play Service, 1987.

Also author of "Youth of the Peregrines," produced at Tunbridge Wells with premiere production of George Bernard Shaw's "Village Wooing." Author of radio plays for "Children's Hour" series, 1939-40, and of "Rhineland Journey," 1948.

SCREENPLAYS AND TELEPLAYS

"The Canary," British Broadcasting Corp. (BBC-TV), 1950.

"The Queen Is Crowned" (documentary), Universal, 1953.

(With Denis Cannan) "The Beggar's Opera," British Lion, 1953.

"Ben Hur," Metro-Goldwyn-Mayer, 1959.

"Barabbas," Columbia, 1961.

(With Jonathan Griffin, Ivo Perilli, and Vittorio Bonicelli) "The Bible: In the Beginning," Twentieth Century-Fox, 1966.

"The Tenant of Wildfell Hall," BBC-TV, 1968.

"The Brontes of Haworth" (also see below; four teleplays), BBC-TV, 1973.

"The Best of Enemies," BBC-TV, 1976.

"Sister Dora," BBC-TV, 1977.

"Star Over Bethlehem," BBC-TV, 1981.

TRANSLATOR

(And adaptor from *L'Invitation au Chateau* by Jean Anouilh), *Ring Round the Moon: A Charade with Music* (first produced on the West End at Globe Theatre, January 26, 1950), Oxford University Press, 1950.

(And adaptor) Jean Giraudoux, *Tiger at the Gates* (also see below; first produced on the West End at Apollo Theatre, October 3, 1955), Methuen, 1955, 2nd edition, 1961, Oxford University Press, 1956, produced as *The Trojan War Will Not Take Place* (London, 1983), Methuen, 1983.

(And adaptor) Anouilh, *The Lark* (first produced on the West End at Lyric Theatre, May 11, 1955; produced on Broadway at Longacre Theatre, November 17, 1955), Methuen, 1955, Oxford University Press, 1956.

(And adaptor from *Pour Lucrece* by Giraudoux), *Duel of Angels* (also see below; first produced on the West End at Apollo Theatre, April 22, 1958; produced on Broadway at Helen Hayes Theatre, April 19, 1960), Methuen, 1958, Oxford University Press, 1959.

(And adaptor) Giraudoux, *Judith* (also see below; first produced
   on the West End at Her Majesty's Theatre, June 20, 1962),
   Methuen, 1962.
Sidonie Gabrielle Colette, *The Boy and the Magic,* Dobson, 1964,
   Putnam, 1965.
(And adaptor) Henrik Ibsen, *Peer Gynt* (first produced at Chich-
   ester Festival Theatre, Chichester, England, May 13, 1970),
   Oxford University Press, 1970, revised edition, 1989.
(And adaptor) Edmond Rostand, *Cyrano de Bergerac* (first pro-
   duced at Chichester Festival Theatre, May 14, 1975), Ox-
   ford University Press, 1975.

OMNIBUS VOLUMES

*Three Plays: The Firstborn; Thor, with Angels; A Sleep of Prison-
   ers,* Oxford University Press, 1960.
(Translator) Giraudoux, *Plays* (contains *Judith, Tiger at the
   Gates,* and *Duel of Angels*), Methuen, 1963.
Plays (contains *Thor, with Angels* and *The Lady's Not for Burn-
   ing*), Oxford University Press, 1969.
Plays (contains *The Boy with a Cart: Cuthman, Saint of Sussex,
   The Firstborn,* and *Venus Observed*), Oxford University
   Press, 1970.
Plays (contains *A Sleep of Prisoners, The Dark Is Light Enough,*
   and *Curtmantle*), Oxford University Press, 1971.
Selected Plays (contains *The Boy with a Cart: Cuthman, Saint of
   Sussex, A Phoenix Too Frequent, The Lady's Not for Burn-
   ing, A Sleep of Prisoners, Curtmantle*), Oxford University
   Press, 1985.
(Translator with Timberlake Wertebaker) *Jean Anouilh: Five
   Plays,* Heinemann, 1986.

OTHER

(Contributor) Kaye Webb, editor, *An Experience of Critics and
   the Approach to Dramatic Criticism,* Perpetua, 1952, Oxford
   University Press, 1953.
(Author of libretto) "Crown of the Year" (cantata), first pro-
   duced in 1958.
(Contributor) Robert W. Corrigan, editor, *The Modern Theatre,*
   Macmillan, 1964.
The Boat That Mooed (juvenile fiction), Macmillan, 1965.
(Contributor) H. F. Rubinstein, editor, *The Drama Bedside
   Book,* Atheneum, 1966.
(With Jonathan Griffin) *The Bible: Original Screenplay,* Pocket
   Books, 1966.
The Brontes of Haworth, published in two volumes, Davis-
   Poynter, 1975.
Can You Find Me: A Family History, Oxford University Press,
   1978.
(Adaptor) *Paradise Lost* (first produced in Chicago, 1978),
   Schott, 1978.
Death Is a Kind of Love (lecture; drawings by Charles E. Wads-
   worth), Tidal Press, 1979.
Charlie Hammond's Sketch Book, Oxford University Press,
   1980.
Genius, Talent and Failure (lecture), King's College, 1987.

Also contributor to anthology, *Representative Modern Plays:
Ibsen to Tennessee Williams,* edited by Robert Warnock, Scott,
Foresman, 1964. Contributor to *Theatre Arts* and *Plays and
Players.*

SIDELIGHTS: British playwright, screenwriter, translator, and
critic Christopher Fry is best known for his elegant verse plays,
which emerged in the 1940s and 1950s as a sharp contrast to the
naturalism and realism popular since the late nineteenth century.
When Fry's blank-verse comedy "The Lady's Not for Burning"

first appeared on stage in London during the 1950s, it became
an immediate sensation. According to Harold Hobson in *Drama:*
"It is difficult to exaggerate the sense of freshness and excitement
that swept through the theatrical world when *The Lady's Not for
Burning,* with the extraordinary brilliance of the fancies, the conceits, and the imagination of its dialogue, the originality of its
verse-form, and the joyous mediaeval paradox of its story seemed
to shatter the by then somnolent reign of naturalism on the British stage." Derek Stanford recalls in *Christopher Fry:* "Without
the creaking machinery of any cranked-up manifesto, the plays
of Fry appeared on the stage, receiving a progressive succession
of applause. For the first time for several centuries, we were
made to realise that here was a poet addressing the audience
from the boards with that immediacy of effect which had seemed
to have deserted the muse as far as its dramatic office was concerned. . . . Like a man who is conscious of no impediment, and
does not anticipate embarrassing rebuffs, Fry spoke out with a
power natural to him. He was heard—with surprise, with pleasure, and relief."

Fry's style attracted as many detractors as devotees; some complained that his rapidly moving, glittering language masked non-
existent plots and shallow characterizations. In a *Times Literary
Supplement* review of *The Lady's Not for Burning,* a critic finds
the play "without the comparatively pedestrian power of developing character and situation," and adds: "It is surprising how
rich a play may be in fine speeches and yet be a bad play because
the speeches alter nothing." But Stanford determines that "so
readily magniloquent and rich, in fact, is Fry that in an age of
verbal paucity his own Elizabethan munificence of diction appears to our 'austerity' reviewers as suspect. None of these critics, it is true, has been able to deny the impact of his language,
but have rather tended to minimise its import by treating it as
the playwright's sole talent."

"The Lady's Not for Burning," directed by and starring John
Gielgud, was the first installment of a series of four comedies,
each corresponding to a different season. The series continued
with "Venus Observed" (autumn), "The Dark Is Light Enough"
(winter), and concluded, twenty-two years after its commence-
ment, with "A Yard of Sun" (summer). While the other plays,
especially "Venus Observed," received critical acclaim, none
surpassed "The Lady's Not for Burning" in popularity. "The
Lady's Not for Burning" is set in a somewhat fantastic medieval
world, and primarily concerns two characters: Thomas, an embittered ex-soldier who wishes to die, and Jennet, a wealthy
young orphan who loves life, but has been sentenced to burn on
a trumped-up witchcraft charge so that the town may inherit her
property. The play intertwines irony and comedy, with a dense
mayor, his practical wife, and their two quarrelling sons all playing clownish roles. In *Dictionary of Literary Biography,* Audrey
Williamson describes the play as "a lyric of spring: it has an
April shimmer, like the dust of pollination shot by sunlight."
Williamson continues: "There is a kind of golden haze about it
that is penetrated by the occasional bawdiness of the humor: for
Fry has combined the robustness of the Elizabethans with
touches of the cheerful blasphemy that mingled with piety in the
medieval morality play. But the sense of the abundance, mystery,
and poetry of life is unimpaired."

"Venus Observed" involves an emotionally remote and aging
duke who intends to choose a wife from his many ex-lovers. But
in the process he becomes infatuated with the young woman his
son also loves. The role of the elderly stargazer was played by
Laurence Olivier in London and Rex Harrison in New York;
Theatre Arts contributor L. N. Roditte writes of the character:
"The Duke is a hero of considerable magnitude; his story,

though mild and witty, has an element of tragedy. . . . [Fry] has created an extraordinary part that other great actors will want to play." Although "Venus Observed" was well received by the public and critics, Fry's style again received criticism. According to *Saturday Review* contributor John Mason Brown: "Mr. Fry is blessed with one of the most delightful talents now contributing to the theatre. He has a wit, nimble and original; an agile and unpredictable mind, as playful as it is probing; and a love of language which can only be described as a lust." But Brown continues that Fry "is an anachronism, if you will; a fellow who has wandered from one Elizabethan age into another," and concludes: "Mr. Fry concentrates on all the sensuous splendors of the flesh, ignoring the skeleton of sustained ideas or dramatic structure." Harold Clurman in the *New Republic*, however, strongly objects to this view: "Let no one say that Fry's work consists of playful, euphonious words and no more. The meaning is clear to anyone who will pay attention. . . . And the meaning . . . is historically or (socially) revealing. Fry's plays are poems of resignation in which tragic substance is flattened into lovely ornament."

The Dark is Light Enough delves into the past, this time using the background of revolutions on the Hungarian border in 1848. The heroine, Countess Rosmarin, is an elderly lady who attempts to rescue her ex-son-in-law, an army deserter, from execution. While the play ends in death, "the viewer senses a summer radiance on which winter has set its feathered touch, light and cold as the snowflakes descending outside the window," explains Williamson. In *Ariel*, Stanley Wiersma also sees the conclusion as a positive one: "The Countess . . . finds warmth enough in the winter of our discontent, goodness enough in a wicked world, life enough in death." *Chicago Sunday Tribune* contributor F. E. Faverty sees a conflict between the plot and dialogue, however. "In spite of the heavy themes, the dialogue is light and sparkling," he writes. "There is a quotable epigram on every page. Nonetheless, one's final impression is that there is too much talk and too little action." But Williamson admires the interplay: "Fry adapts his verse to his theme, conveying wisdom and a new verbal austerity," she continues. "It makes for a play of dramatic tension and fascination."

Fry's abhorrence of violence is an important part of *The Dark Is Light Enough*. Wiersma identifies the play's themes as "violence as self-assertion, violence as loyalty to the state, violence as loyalty to God, and, finally, violence to be endured but not to be inflicted," and explains that the playwright sees such violence as "an infection with its own irrational necessities. The violence in the situation and within the people is moving toward a duel; who fights it or against whom is beside the point." Fry's answer to violence is love: love that endures pain but refuses to inflict it. Emil Roy, in his monograph on Fry, finds this treatment unique: "Unlike most of his contemporaries, Fry has not given man's meanness, animality, and evil a central position in his work. If men are selfish, egoistic, and blind to love, it belongs to his more enlightened, self-controlled, and discerning characters to bring their understanding and tolerance to bear upon the pain and anguish that results."

A Yard of Sun ends the quartet; it deals with the return of two absent members of an Italian family: the black sheep and a betrayed friend. A *Times Literary Supplement* reviewer calls the characters and situation "stereotyped" and claims they "receive a thick coating of Fry's Christmas-tree versification which serves to convert cliches into fanciful imagery and camouflage the fact that no issue is being squarely faced." But according to Williamson, the play contains "a concentrated glow of language, pared to a new, more austere structure. The Italianate characterization

is vivid and varied, and the story line taut and gripping." And a *Newsweek* reviewer finds that *A Yard of Sun* "shimmers with poetry and affirms Fry's belief in a basically mystical Christian benevolence."

All of the plays in the quartet are described as comedies, although the "fall" and "winter" episodes are darker than their counterparts. In *Literary Half-Yearly*, J. A. Collins connects the playwright's view of these works with his religious beliefs: "Christopher Fry has defined comedy as 'an escape, not from truth but from despair: a narrow escape into faith.'" Collins finds this view of faith innovative in that it suggests ways of reacting to the universe and does not concern itself with solutions to paradoxes: "The attitude of faith is always love—romantic love, brotherly love, love of God and the universe; but even in love (the acceptance of faith) spirit and flesh refuse to harmonize and the old battle continues."

Overall, Stanford sees Fry as a joyous free-thinker in a narrow world: "In a universe often viewed as mechanic, he has posited the principle of mystery; in an age of necessitarian ethics, he has stood unequivocally for ideas of free-will. In theatre technique, he has gaily ignored the sacrosanct conventions of naturalistic drama; and in terms of speech he has brought back poetry onto the stage with undoctored abandon." Roy states: "Fry has occasionally seemed wordy, sentimental, and lacking in conventional kinds of conflict, but he has more than compensated with vital and compassionate characters, the courage to deal with contemporary human conflicts and issues, and some of the most vital language in the theater today." And Williamson concludes: "In Fry's hands the English theater turned, for an elegantly creative period, away from prosaic reality and explored both the poetry and the mystery of life."

Fry's plays have been translated into French, German, Spanish, Dutch, Norwegian, Finnish, Italian, Swedish, Danish, Greek, Serbo-Croat, Hungarian, Tamil, Portuguese, Flemish, Czech, Polish, and Albanian. A manuscript collection is held by Harvard University Theatre Collection.

BIOGRAPHICAL/CRITICAL SOURCES:

BOOKS

Contemporary Literary Criticism, Gale, Volume 2, 1974, Volume 10, 1979, Volume 14, 1980.
Dictionary of Literary Biography, Volume 13: *British Dramatists since World War II*, Gale, 1982.
Kirkpatrick, D. L., editor, *Contemporary Dramatists*, 4th edition, St. James Press, 1988.
Leeming, Glenda, *Poetic Drama*, Macmillan, 1989.
Roy, Emil, *Christopher Fry*, Southern Illinois University Press, 1968.
Stanford, Derek, *Christopher Fry: An Appreciation*, Peter Nevill, 1951.
Wiersma, Stanley, *More Than the Ear Discovers: God in the Plays of Christopher Fry*, Loyola University Press, 1983.

PERIODICALS

Ariel, October, 1975.
Drama, spring, 1979.
Literary Half-Yearly, July, 1971.
New Republic, August 20, 1951, March 3, 1952, December 2, 1978.
Newsweeek, July 27, 1970.
New York Times Book Review, January 21, 1979.
New York Times Magazine, March 12, 1950.

Plays and Players, December, 1987.
Saturday Review, March 1, 1952, March 21, 1953.
Theatre Arts, L. N. Roditte, September, 1950.
Times Literary Supplement, April 2, 1949, August 21, 1970, October 20, 1978.

—*Sketch by Jani Prescott*

* * *

FRYE, (Herman) Northrop 1912-

PERSONAL: Born July 14, 1912, in Sherbrooke, Quebec, Canada; son of Herman Edward and Catherine Maud (Howard) Frye; married Helen Kemp, August 24, 1937 (deceased). *Education:* University of Toronto, B.A., 1933; Emmanuel College, ordained, 1936; Merton College, Oxford, M.A., 1940. *Religion:* United Church of Canada.

ADDRESSES: Home—127 Clifton Rd., Toronto, Ontario, Canada M4T 2G5. *Office*—Massey College, University of Toronto, Toronto, Ontario, Canada M5S 2E1.

CAREER: University of Toronto, Victoria College, Toronto, Ontario, lecturer in English, 1939-41, assistant professor, 1942-46, associate professor, 1947, professor of English, 1948—, chairman of department, 1952-59, principal, 1959-67, University Professor, 1967—. Chancellor, Victoria University, Toronto, 1978—. Visiting professor at Harvard University, Princeton University, Columbia University, Indiana University, University of Washington, University of British Columbia, Cornell University, University of California, Berkeley, and Oxford University. Andrew D. White Professor-at-Large, Cornell University, 1970-75; Charles Eliot Norton Poetry Professor, Harvard University, 1974-75. Member of board of governors, Ontario Curriculum Institute, 1960-63; chairman of Governor-General's Literary Awards Committee, 1962. Advisory member, Canadian Radio Television and Telecommunications Commission, 1968-77.

MEMBER: Modern Language Association of America (executive council member, 1958-62; president, 1976), English Institute (former chairman), Royal Society of Canada (fellow), American Academy of Arts and Sciences (foreign honorary member), British Academy (corresponding fellow), American Philosophical Society (foreign member), American Academy and Institute of Arts and Letters (honorary member).

AWARDS, HONORS: Guggenheim fellow, 1950-51; Lorne Pierce Medal of the Royal Society of Canada, 1958; Canada Council medal, 1967; Pierre Chauveau Medal of the Royal Society of Canada, 1970; Canada Council Molson Prize, 1971; Companion of the Order of Canada, 1972; honorary fellow, Merton College, Oxford, 1974; Civic Honour, City of Toronto, 1974; Royal Bank Award, 1978. Thirty honorary degrees from colleges and universities in Canada and the United States, including Dartmouth College, Harvard University, Princeton University, and University of Manitoba.

WRITINGS:

Fearful Symmetry: A Study of William Blake, Princeton University Press, 1947.
Anatomy of Criticism: Four Essays, Princeton University Press, 1957.
(With others) *The English and Romantic Poets and Essayists: A Review of Research and Criticism,* Modern Language Association of America, 1957.
Culture and the National Will, Carleton University, for Institute of Canadian Studies, 1957.

(With Kluckhohn and Wigglesworth) *Three Lectures,* University of Toronto, 1958.
By Liberal Things, Clarke, Irwin, 1959.
(Editor) *Shakespeare, The Tempest,* Penguin, 1959.
(Editor) *Design for Learning,* University of Toronto Press, 1962.
(With L. C. Knights and others) *Myth and Symbol: Critical Approaches and Applications,* edited by Bernice Slote, University of Nebraska Press, 1963.
The Developing Imagination (published together with an essay by A. R. MacKinnon), Harvard University Press, 1963.
The Well-Tempered Critic, Indiana University Press, 1963.
T. S. Eliot, Grove, 1963, reprinted, University of Chicago Press, 1982.
Fables of Identity: Studies in Poetic Mythology, Harcourt, 1963.
(Editor) *Romanticism Reconsidered,* Columbia University Press, 1963.
The Educated Imagination, Indiana University Press, 1964.
A Natural Perspective: The Development of Shakespearean Comedy and Romance, Columbia University Press, 1965, recent edition, Peter Smith, 1988.
The Return of Eden: Five Essays on Milton's Epics, University of Toronto Press, 1965.
(Editor) *Blake: A Collection of Critical Essays,* Prentice-Hall, 1966.
Fools of Time: Studies in Shakespearean Tragedy, University of Toronto Press, 1967.
The Modern Century (Whidden Lectures), Oxford University Press, 1967.
A Study of English Romanticism, Random House, 1968, recent edition, University of Chicago Press, 1983.
The Stubborn Structure: Essays on Criticism and Society, Methuen, 1970.
The Bush Garden: Essays on the Canadian Imagination, House of Anansi Press, 1971.
The Critical Path: An Essay on the Social Context of Literary Criticism, Indiana University Press, 1971.
The Secular Scripture: A Study of the Structure of Romance, Harvard University Press, 1976.
Spiritus Mundi: Essays on Literature, Myth and Society, Indiana University Press, 1976.
Northrop Frye on Culture and Literature: A Collection of Review Essays, edited by Robert Denham, Chicago University Press, 1978.
Creation and Recreation, University of Toronto Press, 1980.
The Great Code: The Bible and Literature, Harcourt, 1982.
Divisions on a Ground: Essays on Canadian Culture, House of Anansi Press, 1982.
The Myth of Deliverance: Reflections on Shakespeare's Problem Comedies, University of Toronto Press, 1982.
(Editor with others) *The Harper Handbook to Literature,* Harper, 1985.
Northrop Frye on Shakespeare, Yale University Press, 1986.
On Education, University of Michigan Press, 1988.

Has written educational radio and television programs for the Canadian Broadcasting Co. Work represented in anthologies. Contributor to professional journals. *Canadian Forum,* literary editor, 1947-49, editor, 1949-52.

SIDELIGHTS: Northrop Frye's most important book, *Anatomy of Criticism: Four Essays,* "forced itself" on him when he was trying to write something else. Frye had just completed a comprehensive study of William Blake and was determined to apply Blake's principles of literary symbolism and Biblical analysis to the poet Edmund Spenser. But "the introduction to Spenser became an introduction to the theory of allegory, and that theory obstinately adhered to a much larger theoretical structure," Frye explains in *Anatomy*'s preface. "The basis of argument became more and more discursive, and less and less historical and Spenserian. I soon found myself entangled in those parts of criticism that have to do with such words as 'myth,' 'symbol,' 'ritual,' and 'archetype'. . . . Eventually, the theoretical and the practical aspects of the task I had begun completely separated." But rather than abandon the project, Frye simply shifted his focus, writing not about Spenser in particular, but about literature in general. When he finished, he had produced four essays of what he calls "pure critical theory." Published together in 1957, these essays comprise *Anatomy of Criticism,* a schematic, nonjudgmental theory of literature and the first, according to David Schiller in *Commentary,* "which enables a student to tell where, in the totality of his literary experiences, an individual experience belongs."

One of Frye's motives for writing *Anatomy of Criticism* was to bring some sense of order to the field of literary criticism, an art he considered not only misunderstood, but also in disarray. He found the lack of communication among critics appalling. Each school had its own specific theory, but there was no general framework to measure it by. "It is all very well for Blake to say that to generalize is to be an idiot," Frye writes in his study, "but when we find ourselves in the cultural situation of savages who have words for ash and willow and no word for tree, we wonder if there is not such a thing as being too deficient in the capacity to generalize." To remedy the problem, Frye set out to develop "a coordinating principle, a central hypothesis which, like the theory of evolution in biology, will see the phenomena it deals with as parts of a whole."

His idea was to approach poetry (and by poetry Frye means all literature) the way Aristotle did—"as a biologist [approaching] a system of organisms, picking out its genera and species, formulating the broad laws of literary experience and, in short, writing as though . . . there is a totally intelligible structure of knowledge attainable about poetry which is not poetry itself, or the experience of it, but poetics." To figure out what these "poetics" were, Frye surveyed the whole phenomena of literary experience, isolating each genre, myth and archetypal literary symbol and then relating it to literature as a whole. Frye organized his finding into categories and came up with the four critical approaches that would eventually form the basis of his essays. They are: historical criticism (theory of modes), ethical criticism (theory of symbols), archetypal criticism (theory of myths), and rhetorical criticism (theory of genres). Although Frye allots each of these approaches a place in his hypothetical structure, his own particular emphasis is on literary archetypes and how they relate to myths.

When Frye speaks of archetypes, he is referring not to the Jungian concept of a racial consciousness, but to certain "typical" images that recur in poetry. In literature, the repetition of such common images of physical nature as the sea or the forest cannot be explained away as "coincidence," Frye argues. Instead, he says, each is an "archetype" or "symbol which connects one poem with another and thereby helps to unify and integrate our literary experience." When we study a masterpiece, Frye explains in his study, the work "draws us to a point at which we seem to see an enormous number of converging patterns of significance. We begin to wonder if we cannot see literature, not only as complicating itself in time, but as spread out in conceptual space from some kind of center that criticism could locate." That center represents the primitive myths from which archetypes spring.

Frye contends that archetypal criticism provides an effective means of deriving the structural principles of literature because it assumes a larger context of literature as a whole. Employing an analogy, Frye compares literature to painting, showing that just as the structural principles of painting are related to plane geometry, so too are the structural principles of literature related to religion and mythology. The Biblical archetypes of the "city" the "garden," and the "sheepfold" are as pervasive in religious writing as gods and demons are in myths, Frye maintains. Thus Frye turns to the symbolism of the Bible and to classical mythology employing both "as a grammar of literary archetypes" to use his words.

Harold Bloom, writing in the *New York Times Book Review,* calls Frye's theory of myths "the richest and most persuasive of [his] investigations. . . . He mapped four seasonal myths: Spring or Comedy, Summer or Romance, Autumn or Tragedy, Winter or Irony and Satire. Working entirely from what he took to be the internal characteristics of thousands of literary texts, Frye produced a coherent account of the ways in which themes, ideas and metaphors tended to repeat themselves in each of his seasonal myths."

Although post-classical literature rarely seems mythic, Frye argues that the myth has simply been "displaced" or covered over with a veneer of realism, making the new work "credible, logically motivated, or morally acceptable" to its audience. In Nathaniel Hawthorne's *The Marble Faun,* for example, there is a girl of singular purity and gentleness who lives in a tower surrounded by doves. Writes Frye: "The doves are very fond of her; another character calls her his 'dove,' and remarks indicating some special affinity with doves are made about her by both author and characters. If we were to say that [she] is a dove-goddess like Venus . . . we should not be reading the story quite accurately in its own mode; we should be translating it into straight myth." But, Frye argues, to recognize that Hawthorne employs an archetypal pattern is not irrelevant, or unfair. In fact, he postulates that a person "can get a whole liberal education simply by picking up one conventional poem and following its archetypes as they stretch out into the rest of literature."

One of the most controversial features of Frye's schema is the role it assigns critics. The historical function of criticism, from the time of Samuel Johnson to T. S. Eliot, has been to provide a means of discriminating good writing from bad. But Frye's interest is in what makes works of literature similar to one another, not what makes them different, and he adamantly rejects the notion of critic as judge. It is not, he maintains, the critic's responsibility to evaluate poetry or to say that one poem is better than another because his judgment, while informed, is really nothing more than a reflection of taste. And, "the history of taste is no more a part of the structure of criticism than the Huxley-Wilberforce debate is part of the structure of biological science," Frye writes. Matters of judgment are best left to book reviewers, not critics, in Frye's point of view.

But W. K. Wimsatt, in an essay in *Northrop Frye in Modern Criticism,* charges Frye with inconsistency: "He can and is willing to distinguish 'ephemeral rubbish,' mediocre works, random and peripheral experience, from the greatest classics, the profound masterpieces in which may be discerned the converging patterns of the primitive formulas. At other moments, however, he says that criticism has nothing whatever to do with either the experience of the judging of literature. The direct experience of literature is central to criticism, yet somehow this center is excluded from it." The effect, Wimsatt concludes, is that the reader remains unsure whether Frye "wishes to discredit all critical valuing whatever, or only the wrong kinds of valuing."

Another important feature of Frye's schema is his view in general and poetry in particular. According to A. Walton Litz, writing in the *Harvard Guide to Contemporary American Writing,* Frye "shares with his modern predecessors a poet-Romantic view of the poem as an autonomous organism, which exists independently from the intentions of its creator." And in his study, Frye employs a metaphor that bears out Litz's supposition. "The poet," Frye says, "who writes creatively rather than deliberately, is not the father of his poem; he is at best a midwife, or, more accurately still, the womb of Mother Nature herself. . . . The fact that revision is possible, that a poet can make changes in a poem not because he likes them better, but because they are better, shows clearly that the poet has to give birth to the poem as it passes through his mind. He is responsible for delivering it in as uninjured a state as possible, and if the poem is alive, it is equally anxious to be rid of him, and screams to be cut loose from all the navel-strings and feeding-tubes of his ego."

If the poet is the "midwife" of the poem, the critic, according to Frye, may be conceived of as the nurse who presents the creation to the world. And in this role as a describer and classifier of literature, the critic assumes a position that is not subservient, but equal to that of the artist, as Litz explains: "If *Anatomy of Criticism* is a major work of enduring importance, as I believe it to be, then it is the first great work of English or American literary criticism not produced by a practicing artist, and signals a decisive turn toward the continental model. The critic is no longer the servant of the artist but a colleague, with his own special knowledge and powers. . . . [Frye] provides a system which tempts the critic to interpose himself between the artist and the audience as an independent creative force." Despite his admiration for *Anatomy,* Litz says that Frye's system "when manipulated by less subtle minds—tend[s] to homogenize literature and give the critic a spurious authority."

Nor is this the only objection that has been raised against Frye's theory. Some critics charge that Frye's preoccupation with myth and convention isolates literature from its social context, while others accuse him of ignoring history and imprisoning literature in a timeless vacuum of archetypal myths. W. K. Wimsatt perhaps best articulates this objection when he says: "The Ur-Myth, the Quest Myth, with all its complications, its cycles, acts, scenes, characters, and special symbols, is not a historical fact. And this is so not only in the obvious sense that the stories are not true, but in another sense, which I think we tend to forget and which mythopoeic writing does much to obscure: that such a coherent, cyclic, and encyclopedic system, such a monomyth, cannot be shown ever to have evolved actually either from ritual, anywhere in the world, or ever anywhere to have been entertained in whole or even in any considerable part. We are talking about the myth of myth. As Frye himself, in his moments of cautionary vision, observes, the 'derivation' of the literary genres from the quest myth is 'logical,' not historical. [But,] if we take Frye at his word and attempt to deduce his system 'logically,' we will reject it, for the structure which he shows us is . . . divided between truism and *ad libitum* fantasy."

As a way of countering these charges, Frye, in his subsequent writings, frequently employs subtitles that insist upon the social reference of his criticism, according to Scott Sanders in *Cambridge Review.* Frye's 1970 publication, *The Stubborn Structure: Essays on Criticism and Society,* is one such example, and *The Critical Path: An Essay on the Social Context of Literary Criticism,* which appeared the following year, is another. Sanders says

that in such publications, however, Frye is "less concerned with the communal sources of literature than he is with the potential role of the humanities, informed by literature, in directing social change."

In addition to addressing issues raised by his adversaries, Frye's later writing also elucidates his original theory, and offers some of the practical criticism that was absent in his masterwork. In *A Natural Perspective: The Development of Shakespearean Comedy and Romance,* for instance, Frye turns to Shakespeare to demonstrate his belief that art does not imitate life directly, but instead art imitates art. Writing in the *Times Literary Supplement,* a reviewer explains: "These essays elaborate the thesis that Shakespearean comedy, like modern painting, represents a deliberate departure from the conventions of realism, a distortion or stylization of the subject which indicates an interest in more purely self-contained artistic values. The comedies and romances, so the argument runs, do not hold up the mirror to nature: their *raison d'etre* must be sought in the comic structure itself, as that of music in the musical structure. Indeed, Shakespeare's thematic images and words, echoing, calling, responding, have the same function as similar repeated patterns in music, and sometimes, as in music, a new theme or second subject will be introduced which our ear accepts without explanation—as when Leontes' jealousy burst out unheralded and unforeseen."

In the years that have passed since Frye published his seminal piece, critics have continued to search for its flaws. One common objection, expressed by Morris Dickstein in *Partisan Review,* is that "Frye always establishes a distance, at once heuristic and self-protective between himself and his subject. He aims at the precision of outline rather than the intimacy or concreteness of detail." Another is the point, raised by W. K. Wimsatt, that the analogies Frye depends on to make his major points are not logically valid. Notwithstanding this criticism, many scholars are attracted by the nonjudgmental quality of Frye's system and his genuinely humanistic approach (which proclaims that an understanding of literature is indeed of great human importance). This group has embraced Frye's theories and introduced his methods into the university classroom. And, as Murray Krieger notes in his introduction to *Northrop Frye in Modern Criticism,* "whatever the attitude toward Northrop Frye's prodigious scheme, one cannot doubt that he has had an influence—indeed an absolute hold—on a generation of developing literary critics greater and more exclusive than that of any one theorist in recent critical history." Summarized Harold Bloom in the *New York Times Book Review:* "Frye is the legitimate heir of a Protestant and Romantic tradition that has dominated much of British and American literature, the tradition of the Inner Light, by which each person reads Scripture for himself or herself without yielding to a premature authority imposed by Church or State or School. This is Frye's true greatness, and all who teach interpretations are indebted to him for precept and for example."

BIOGRAPHICAL/CRITICAL SOURCES:

BOOKS

Ayre, John, *Northrop Frye: A Critical Biography,* General Publishing (Don Mills, Canada), 1988.
Contemporary Literary Criticism, Volume 24, Gale, 1983.
Denham, Robert, *Northrop Frye and Critical Method,* Pennsylvania State University Press, 1978.
Denham, Robert, *Northrop Frye: An Annotated Bibliography of Primary and Secondary Sources,* University of Toronto Press, 1988.

Dictionary of Literary Biography, Gale, Volume 67: *Modern American Critics Since 1955,* 1988, Volume 68: *Canadian Writers, 1920-1959, First Series,* 1988.

Hoffman, Daniel, editor, *Harvard Guide to Contemporary American Writing,* Belknap Press, 1979.

Krieger, Murray, editor, *Northrop Frye in Modern Criticism: Selected Papers From the English Institute,* Columbia University Press, 1966.

PERIODICALS

Book Week, July 19, 1964.
Cambridge Review, May 7, 1971.
Commentary, September, 1968.
Commonweal, September 20, 1957.
Criticism, summer, 1967.
Fiddlehead, summer, 1967.
Globe and Mail (Toronto), October 4, 1986.
New York Review of Books, April 14, 1977.
New York Times Book Review, April 18, 1976, April 11, 1982, November 30, 1986.
Partisan Review, winter, 1969.
South Atlantic Quarterly, spring, 1967.
Times Literary Supplement, August 12, 1965, July 2, 1982, February 17, 1984, April 26, 1985.
Washington Post Book World, May 16, 1982.
Yale Review, autumn, 1957, spring, 1964, spring, 1967, March, 1971.

* * *

FUENTES, Carlos 1928-

PERSONAL: Born November 11, 1928, in Panama City, Panama; Mexican citizen; son of Rafael Fuentes Boettiger (a career diplomat) and Berta Macias Rivas; married Rita Macedo (a movie actress), 1959 (divorced, 1969); married Sylvia Lemus (a television journalist), 1973; children: (first marriage) Cecilia; (second marriage) Carlos Rafael, Natasha. *Education:* National University of Mexico, LL.B., 1948; graduate study, Institute des Hautes Etudes, Geneva, Switzerland. *Politics:* Independent leftist.

ADDRESSES: Home—716 Watchung Rd., Bound Brook, N.J. 08805.

CAREER: Writer. International Labor Organization, Geneva, Switzerland, began as member, became secretary of the Mexican delegation, 1950-52; Ministry of Foreign Affairs, Mexico City, Mexico, assistant chief of press section, 1954; National University of Mexico, Mexico City, secretary and assistant director of cultural dissemination, 1955-56; head of department of cultural relations, 1957-59; Mexico's ambassador to France, 1975-77. Fellow at Woodrow Wilson International Center for Scholars, 1974. Norman Maccoll Lecturer, Cambridge University, 1977; Virginia Gildersleeve Professor, Barnard College, 1977; Henry L. Tinker Lecturer, Columbia University, 1978; lecturer or visiting professor at University of Mexico, University of California at San Diego, University of Oklahoma, University of Concepcion in Chile, University of Paris, University of Pennsylvania, Harvard University, and George Mason University.

MEMBER: American Academy and Institute of Arts and Letters (honorary).

AWARDS, HONORS: Centro Mexicano de Escritores fellowship, 1956-57; Biblioteca Breve Prize from Seix Barral (publishing house; Barcelona), 1967, for *Cambio de piel;* Xavier Villaurrutia Prize (Mexico), 1975; Romulo Gallegos Prize (Venezuela), 1977, for *Terra Nostra;* Alfonso Reyes Prize (Mexico), 1979, for body of work; National Award for Literature (Mexico), 1984, for "Orchids in the Moonlight"; nominated for *Los Angeles Times* Book Award in fiction, 1986, for *The Old Gringo;* Miguel de Cervantes Prize from Spanish Ministry of Culture, 1987; Ruben Dario Order of Cultural Independence (Nicaragua) and literary prize of Italo-Latino Americano Institute, both 1988, for *The Old Gringo;* honorary degrees from numerous colleges and universities, including Columbia College, Chicago State University, Harvard University, and Washington University.

WRITINGS:

NOVELS

La region mas transparente, Fondo de Cultura Economica, 1958, translation by Sam Hileman published as *Where the Air Is Clear,* Ivan Obolensky, 1960, Hileman's translation published as *Where the Air Is Clear: A Novel,* Farrar, Straus, 1982.

Las buenas consciencias, Fondo de Cultura Economica, 1959, translation published as *The Good Conscience,* Ivan Oblensky, 1961, reprinted, Farrar, Straus, 1981.

La muerte de Artemio Cruz, Fondo de Cultura Economica, 1962, reprinted, 1983, translation by Hileman published as *The Death of Artemio Cruz,* Farrar, Straus, 1964.

Aura (also see below), Era, 1962, reprinted, 1982, translation by Lysander Kemp, Farrar, Straus, 1965.

Zona sagrada, Siglo XXI, 1967, translation by Suzanne Jill Levine published as *Holy Place* (also see below), Dutton, 1972.

Cambio de piel, Mortiz, 1967, translation by Hileman published as *A Change of Skin,* Farrar, Straus, 1968.

Cumpleanos, Mortiz, 1969, translation published as "Birthday" in *Holy Place & Birthday: Two Novellas,* Farrar, Straus, in press.

Terra Nostra (also see below), Seix Barral, 1975, translation by Levine, afterword by Milan Kundera, Farrar, Straus, 1976.

La cabeza de hidra, Mortiz, 1978, translation by Margaret Sayers Peden published as *Hydra Head,* Farrar, Straus, 1978.

Una familia lejana, Era, 1980, translation by Peden published as *Distant Relations,* Farrar, Straus, 1982.

El gringo viejo, Fondo de Cultura Economica, 1985, translation by Peden and Fuentes published as *The Old Gringo,* Farrar, Straus, 1985.

Christopher Unborn (translation of *Cristobal Nonato*), Farrar, Straus, 1989.

Holy Place & Birthday: Two Novellas, Farrar, Straus, in press.

SHORT STORIES

Los dias enmascarados (also see below), Los Presentes, 1954, reprinted, Era, 1982.

Cantar de ciegos (also see below), Mortiz, 1964.

Dos cuentos mexicanos (title means "Two Mexican Stories"; two short stories previously published in *Cantar de ciegos*), Instituto de Cultura Hispanica de Sao Paulo, Universidade de Sao Paulo, 1969.

Poemas de amor: Cuentos del alma, Imp. E. Cruces (Madrid), 1971.

Chac Mool y otros cuentos, Salvat, 1973.

Agua quemada (anthology), Fondo de Cultura Economica, 1981, translation by Peden published as *Burnt Water,* Farrar, Straus, 1980.

Constancia and Other Stories for Virgins, Farrar, Straus, 1989.

PLAYS

Todos los gatos son pardos (also see below), Siglo XXI, 1970.

El tuerto es rey (also see below; first produced [in French], 1970), Mortiz, 1970.

Los reinos originarios (contains "Todos los gatos son pardos" and "El tuerto es rey"), Seix Barral, 1971.

Orquideas a la luz de la luna (first produced in English as "Orchids in the Moonlight" at American Repertory Theater in Cambridge, Mass., June 9, 1982), Seix Barral, 1982.

NONFICTION

The Argument of Latin America: Words for North Americans, Radical Education Project, 1963.

(Contributor) *Whither Latin America?* (political articles), Monthly Review Press, 1963.

Paris: La revolucion de mayo, Era, 1968.

La nueva novela hispanoamericana, Mortiz, 1969.

(Contributor) *El mundo de Jose Luis Cuevas,* Tudor (Mexico City), 1969.

Casa con dos puertas (title means "House With Two Doors"), Mortiz, 1970.

Tiempo mexicano (title means "Mexican Time"), Mortiz, 1971.

Cervantes; o, La critica de la lectura, Mortiz, 1976, translation published as *Don Quixote; or, The Critique of Reading,* Institute of Latin American Studies, University of Texas at Austin, 1976.

On Human Rights: A Speech, Somesuch Press (Dallas), 1984.

Latin America: At War With the Past, CBC Enterprises, 1985.

Myself With Others: Selected Essays, Farrar, Straus, 1988.

OTHER

(Editor and author of prologue) Octavio Paz, *Los signos en rotacion, y otros ensayos,* Alianza, 1971.

Cuerpos y ofrendas (anthology; includes selections from *Los dias enmascarados, Cantar de ciegos, Aura,* and *Terra Nostra*), introduction by Octavio Paz, Alianza, 1972.

(Author of introduction to Spanish translation) Milan Kundera, *La vida esta en otra parte,* Seix Barral, 1977.

(Author of introduction) Omar Cabezas, *Fire From the Mountain,* Crown, 1988.

Collaborator on several film scripts, including "Pedro Paramo," 1966, "Tiempo de morir," 1966, and "Los caifanes," 1967. Work represented in numerous anthologies, including *Antologia de cuentos hispanoamericanos,* Nueva Decada (Costa Rica), 1985. Contributor to periodicals in the United States, Mexico, and France, including *New York Times, Washington Post,* and *Los Angeles Times.* Founding editor, *Revista Mexicana de Literatura,* 1954-58; co-editor, *El Espectador,* 1959-61, *Siempre,* 1960, and *Politica,* 1960.

WORK IN PROGRESS: A novel about the assassination of Emiliano Zapata; a five-part television series for the Smithsonian Institution, to be called "The Buried Mirror," commemorating the 500th anniversary of Christopher Columbus's voyage, to be broadcast in the fall of 1991.

SIDELIGHTS: "Carlos Fuentes," states Robert Maurer in *Saturday Review,* is "without doubt one of Mexico's two or three greatest novelists." He is part of a group of Latin American writers whose writings, according to Alistair Reid's *New Yorker* essay, "formed the background of the Boom," a literary phenomenon Reid describes as a period in the 1960s when "a sudden surge of hither-to unheard-of writers from Latin America began to be felt among [U.S.] readers." Fuentes, however, is singled out from among the other writers of the Boom in Jose Donoso's autobiographical account, *The Boom in Spanish American Literature: A Personal History,* in which the Chilean novelist calls Fuentes "the first active and conscious agent of the internationalization of the Spanish American novel." And since the 1960s, Fuentes has continued his international influence in the literary world: his 1985 novel, *The Old Gringo,* for example, was the first written by a Mexican to ever appear on the *New York Times* bestseller list.

Although, as Donoso observes, early worldwide acceptance of Fuentes's novels contributed to the internationalization of Latin American literature, his work is an exploration of the culture and history of one nation, his native Mexico. Critics note the thematic presence of Mexico in nearly all Fuentes's writing. Robert Coover comments in the *New York Times Book Review* that in *The Death of Artemio Cruz,* for instance, Fuentes delineates "in the retrospective details of one man's life the essence of the post-Revolutionary history of all Mexico." Mexico is also present in Fuentes's novel *Terra Nostra,* in which, according to *Washington Post Book World* contributor Larry Rohter, "Fuentes probes more deeply into the origins of Mexico—and what it means to be a Mexican—than ever before." Fuentes's *Old Gringo*—published more than twenty years after *The Death of Artemio Cruz*—returns to the same theme as it explores Mexico's relationship with its northern neighbor, the United States.

Fuentes explains his preoccupation with Mexico, and particularly with Mexican history, in a *Paris Review* interview. "Pablo Neruda used to say," he told Alfred MacAdam and Charles Ruas, "that every Latin American writer goes around dragging a heavy body, the body of his people, of his past, of his national history. We have to assimilate the enormous weight of our past so that we will not forget what gives us life. If you forget your past, you die." Fuentes also notes that the development of the same theme in his novels unifies them so that they may be considered part of the same work. The author observes in the same interview, "In a sense my novels are one book with many chapters: *Where the Air Is Clear* is the biography of Mexico City; *The Death of Artemio Cruz* deals with an individual in that city; [and] *A Change of Skin* is that city, that society, facing the world, coming to grips with the fact that it is part of civilization and that there is a world outside that intrudes into Mexico."

Along with thematic unity, another characteristic of Fuentes's work is his innovative narrative style. In a *New Yorker* review, Anthony West compares the novelist's technique to "a rapid cinematic movement that cuts nervously from one character to another." Evan Connell states in the *New York Times Book Review* that Fuentes's "narrative style—with few exceptions—relies on the interruption and juxtaposition of different kinds of awareness." Reviewers Donald Yates and Karen Hardy also comment on Fuentes's experimental style. In the *Washington Post Book World* Yates calls Fuentes "a tireless experimenter with narrative techniques and points of view," while in *Hispania* Hardy notes that in Fuentes's work "the complexities of a human or national personality are evoked through . . . elaborate narrative devices."

Fuentes's novels *The Death of Artemio Cruz* and *Terra Nostra* are especially good examples of his experimental techniques. The first narrative deals with a corrupt Mexican millionaire who on his deathbed relives his life in a series of flashbacks. In the novel Fuentes uses three separate narrations to tell the story, and for each of these narrations he uses a different narrative person. *New York Review of Books* contributor A. Alvarez explains the three-part narration of the novel: "Cruz's story is told in three persons. 'I' is the old man dying on his bed; 'you' is a slightly vatic, 'experimental' projection of his potentialities into an unspecified future . . . ; 'he' is the real hero, the man whose history emerges bit by bit from incidents shuffled around from his seventy-one years."

In John S. Brushwood's *Mexico in Its Novel: A Nation's Search for Identity,* the critic praises Fuentes's technique, commenting: "The changing narrative viewpoint is extremely effective, providing a clarity that could not have been accomplished any other way. I doubt that there is anywhere in fiction a character whose wholeness is more apparent than in the case of Artemio Cruz."

Coover observes that in *Terra Nostra* Fuentes once again uses a variety of narrators to tell his story. Commenting favorably on Fuentes's use of the "you" narrative voice in the novel, Coover writes: "Fuentes's second person [narration] is not one overheard on a stage: the book itself, rather than the author or a character, becomes the speaker, the reader or listener a character, or several characters in succession." Spanish novelist Juan Goytisolo similarly states in *Review:* "One of the most striking and most successful devices [in *Terra Nostra*] is the abrupt shift in narrative point of view (at times without the unwary reader's even noticing), passing from first-person narration to second, . . . and simultaneously rendering objective and subjective reality in one and the same passage with patent scorn for the rules of discourse that ordinarily govern expository prose." In the *Paris Review* Fuentes comments on his use of the second person narrative, calling it "the voice poets have always used and that novelists also have a right to use."

Fuentes's use of the second person narrative and other experimental techniques makes his novels extremely complex. The author's remarks in a *New York Times Book Review* interview with Frank MacShane concerning the structure of *Terra Nostra* describe the intricacy of the work: "My chief stylistic device in 'Terra Nostra' is to follow every statement by a counter statement and every image by its opposite." This deliberate duplicity by the author, along with the extensive scope of the novel, causes some reviewers to criticize *Terra Nostra* for being unaccessible to the average reader. Maurer, for instance, calls the novel "a huge, sprawling, exuberant, mysterious, almost unimaginably dense work of 800 pages, covering events on three continents from the creation of man in Genesis to the dawn of the twenty-first century," and adds that "*Terra Nostra* presents a common reader with enormous problems simply of understanding what is going on." *Newsweek*'s Peter S. Prescott notes: "To talk about [*Terra Nostra*] at all we must return constantly to five words: excess, surreal, baroque, masterpiece, [and] unreadable."

Other critics, however, have written more positive reviews, seeing *Terra Nostra* and other Fuentes works as necessarily complex. *Village Voice* contributor Jonah Raskin finds Fuentes is at his best when the novelist can "plunge readers into the hidden recesses of his characters' minds and at the same time allow language to pile up around their heads in thick drifts, until they feel lost in a blizzard of words that enables them to see, to feel, in a revolutionary way." Fuentes also defends the difficulty of his works in a *Washington Post* interview with Charles Truehart. Recalling the conversation with the Mexican author, Truehart quotes Fuentes as saying: "I believe in books that do not go to a ready-made public. . . . I'm looking for readers I would like to *make*. . . . To *win* them, . . . to *create* readers rather than to give something that readers are expecting. That would bore me to death."

While Fuentes's innovative use of theme and structure has gained the author an international reputation as a novelist, he believes that only since *Terra Nostra* has he perfected his craft. "I feel I'm beginning to write the novels I've always wanted to write and didn't know how to write before," he explains to Philip Bennett in a *Boston Globe Magazine* interview. "There were the novels of youth based on energy, and conceptions derived from energy. Now I have the conceptions I had as a young man, but I can develop them and give them their full value."

MEDIA ADAPTATIONS: Two short stories from *Cantar de ciegos* were made into films in the mid-1960s; *The Old Gringo* was adapted into a film of the same title by Fonda Films, 1989.

AVOCATIONAL INTERESTS: Reading, travel, swimming, visiting art galleries, listening to classical and rock music, motion pictures, the theater.

BIOGRAPHICAL/CRITICAL SOURCES:

BOOKS

Authors in the News, Volume 2, Gale, 1976.
Brushwood, John S., *Mexico in Its Novel: A Nation's Search for Identity,* University of Texas Press, 1966.
Contemporary Literary Criticism, Gale, Volume 3, 1975, Volume 8, 1978, Volume 10, 1979, Volume 13, 1980, Volume 22, 1982, Volume 41, 1987.
Donoso, Jose, *The Boom in Spanish American Literature: A Personal History,* Columbia University Press, 1977.
Plimpton, George, editor, *Writers at Work: The Paris Review Interviews, Sixth Series,* Penguin Books, 1984.

PERIODICALS

Boston Globe Magazine, September 9, 1984.
Hispania, May, 1978.
Los Angeles Times Book Review, October 27, 1985.
Newsweek, November 1, 1976.
New Yorker, March 4, 1961, January 26, 1981, February 24, 1986.
New York Review of Books, June 11, 1964.
New York Times Book Review, November 7, 1976, October 19, 1980, October 27, 1985, August 20, 1989.
Paris Review, winter, 1981.
Review, winter, 1976.
Saturday Review, October 30, 1976.
Village Voice, January 28, 1981, April 1, 1986.
Washington Post, May 5, 1988.
Washington Post Book World, October 26, 1976, January 14, 1979, August 20, 1989.

—*Sketch by Marian Gonsior*

* * *

FUGARD, (Harold) Athol 1932-

PERSONAL: Born June 11, 1932, in Middelburg, Cape Province, South Africa; son of Harold David (an owner of a general store) and Elizabeth Magdalena (a cafe manager) Fugard; married Sheila Meiring (a novelist, poet, and former actress), 1956; children: Lisa. *Education:* Attended Port Elizabeth Technical College, and University of Cape Town, 1950-53.

ADDRESSES: Home—P.O. Box 5090, Port Elizabeth, South Africa. *Agent*—William Morris Agency, 1350 Avenue of the Americas, New York, N.Y. 10019.

CAREER: Actor, director, and playwright. Crew member of a tramp steamer bound from Port Sudan, Sudan, to the Far East, 1953-55; Fordsburg Native Commissioner's Court, Johannesburg, South Africa, clerk, 1958; worked as actor and director in various theatre productions in New York City, London, and South Africa. Actor in television film "The Blood Knot" for British Broadcasting Corp. (BBC-TV), 1968.

AWARDS, HONORS: Obie Award for distinguished foreign play, *Village Voice,* 1971, for "Boesman and Lena"; *Plays &*

Players award for best new play, 1973, for "Sizwe Banzi Is Dead"; New York Critics Circle award for best play, 1982, for "A Lesson from Aloes"; Drama Desk award and Critics Circle award for best play, 1983, and *Evening Standard* award, London, 1984, for " 'Master Harold' . . . And the Boys"; Commonwealth Award, 1984, for contribution to the American theatre; honorary degrees from Yale University, Georgetown University, Natal University, Rhodes University, and Cape Town University.

WRITINGS:

Tsotsi (novel), Collings, 1980, Random House, 1981.
Notebooks, 1960-1977, edited by Mary Benson, Faber, 1983, Knopf, 1984.

PLAYS

"No-Good Friday" (also see below), first produced in Cape Town, South Africa, 1956.
"Nongogo" (also see below), first produced in Cape Town, 1957.
The Blood Knot (first produced in Johannesburg, South Africa, and London, 1961; produced Off-Broadway, 1964; also see below), Simondium, 1963, Odyssey, 1964.
Hello and Goodbye (first produced in Johannesburg, 1965; produced Off-Broadway at Sheridan Square Playhouse, September 18, 1969; also see below), A. A. Balkema, 1966, Samuel French, 1971.
"The Occupation," published in *Ten One-Act Plays,* Heinemann, 1968.
Boesman and Lena (first produced in Grahamstown, South Africa, 1969; produced Off-Broadway at Circle in the Square, June 22, 1970; produced on the West End at Royal Court Theatre Upstairs, July 19, 1971; also see below), Buren, 1969, revised and rewritten edition, Samuel French, 1971 (published with "The Blood Knot," "People Are Living There" [also see below], and "Hello and Goodbye" as *Boesman and Lena, and Other Plays,* Oxford University Press, 1978).
People Are Living There (first produced in Cape Town at Hofmeyr Theatre, June 14, 1969; produced on Broadway at Forum Theatre, Lincoln Center, November 18, 1971), Oxford University Press, 1970, Samuel French, 1976.
(With Don MacLennan) *The Coat* [and] *Third Degree* (the former by Fugard, the latter by MacLennan), A. A. Balkema, 1971.
Statements (contains three one-act plays: [with John Kani and Winston Ntshona] "Sizwe Banzi Is Dead," first produced in Cape Town, 1972, produced in New York City, 1974; [with Kani and Ntshona] "The Island," first produced in South Africa, 1972, produced on the West End at Royal Court Theatre, December, 1973, produced in New York at Edison Theatre, November, 1974; and "Statements After an Arrest under the Immorality Act," first produced in Cape Town, 1972, produced in London, 1974), Oxford University Press, 1974.
"Dimetos," first produced in Edinburgh, 1975, produced in London and New York City, 1976 (published with "No-Good Friday" and "Nongogo" as *Dimetos and Two Early Plays,* Oxford University Press, 1977).
(With Ross Devenish) *The Guest: An Episode in the Life of Eugene Marais,* Donker (Johannesburg), 1977.
A Lesson from Aloes (first produced in Johannesburg, December, 1978, produced in New York, 1980), Oxford University Press, 1981.
"The Drummer," produced in Louisville, 1980.

"Master Harold" . . . And the Boys (first produced in New Haven, Connecticut, March, 1982, produced on Broadway at Lyceum Theatre, May 5, 1982), Oxford University Press, 1983 (published with "The Blood Knot," "Hello and Goodbye," and "Boesman and Lena" as *Selected Plays,* Oxford University Press, 1987).
The Road to Mecca (first produced in New Haven, 1984, produced in London at Lyttelton Theatre, March 1, 1985, produced in New York at Promenade Theatre, April, 1988), Faber, 1985.
"A Place with the Pigs," produced in New Haven, 1987.

OTHER

Author of teleplays "Mille Miglia" and "The Guest at Steenkampskraal." Produced screenplays include "Boesman and Lena" (based on his play), 1972, "The Guest," 1976, "Meetings with Remarkable Men," 1979, "Marigolds in August," 1980, "Gandhi," 1982, and "The Killing Fields," 1984. Plays reprinted in various anthologies.

SIDELIGHTS: "If ever there was a born dramatist," writes Edith Oliver in a *New Yorker* article, "it is the South African Athol Fugard." Besides being the best-known dramatic voice from his native country, Fugard often acts in and directs his own stage works, and is a leading anti-apartheid proponent wherever he travels. Though many critics and playgoers rank Fugard among the political "agitprop" playwrights, he insists that his plays are more humanistic than abstract, and that they merely reflect life in segregated South Africa as it now exists.

In "Boesman and Lena," for instance, the title characters are "coloreds" who have more relative freedom than the South African blacks, but less than the whites; consequently, they cannot relate to either group, and live with constant despair. In this play, as in others, Fugard's tendency to write extended dialogues for two or three characters has caused some critics to label him inaccessible. *New York* magazine's description of "Boesman and Lena" typifies the mixed feelings toward Fugard's works: "Even though short, the play seems slow and long-winded at first. . . . But slowly the language muddles through, the underlying humanity of these dehumanized beings creeps up on us. Against our will, we are drawn into compassionate kinship with them. . . . In the end, it is our sense of solidarity that makes a harsh experience rewarding."

Fugard often earns praise for humanizing the issue of apartheid. One archetypical Fugard work, "The Blood Knot," is "agitprop of the best kind," according to John Corry in a *New York Times* review, adding the play seems "never overt, and always more concerned with people than with politics—but it is a good deal more than that. It is an exploration of the human condition, fairly bursting with soul." The plot centers on two half-brothers, one a dark-skinned black, the other light enough to "pass" for white, and their various political and familial conflicts. (Fugard, who is white, has played the light-skinned brother in a New Haven production. He appeared opposite his longtime collaborator, the actor Zakes Mokae.) In a *New York Times* interview by Samuel G. Freedman, Fugard remembers the 1961 opening of "The Blood Knot," then considered a most controversial work because it mixed a black actor with a white one. What was supposed to be a modest production in a makeshift theatre escalated into a *cause celebre* among South African playgoers. "Words were not sufficient," says Fugard of that time. "I remember people would sit and look at us. They'd either say thank you or they'd cry. It was something so hard to describe. You knew something was happening; you knew something had happened. That's why the Government couldn't stop us."

But the Government has stepped in several times throughout Fugard's career, banning his plays from official South African productions on the grounds that they were subversive. This was also the case with the writer's perhaps best-known play, " 'Master Harold' . . . And the Boys," which opened in New York in 1982. In that year the *New York Times* reported that "South African censors have decreed that it is a criminal offense to import or distribute copies of [this play]." This decree, the article pointed out, did not necessarily apply to performing the play, and a year later "Master Harold" did have its Johannesburg premiere. " 'Master Harold' . . . And the Boys" is acknowledged as Fugard's most autobiographical play to date, focusing as it does on a white South African teenager in 1950, the year Fugard himself would have been eighteen, and set in a tearoom, the likes of which Fugard's mother ran back then in Port Elizabeth. Harold ("Hally") is presented as "an intelligent, witty prep-school student who questions the injustices of his society and already dreams about being an artist," as Frank Rich describes in a *New York Times* review. The other two characters in the play—the "boys"—are middle-aged black employees of the family's restaurant. Sadly for Hally, his relationship with his parents is strained, and in his desperation he turns to the servants, Willie and Sam, for guidance.

The two servants, aware of Hally's personal problems, try to counsel him, but are hampered by the youth's confused hostility toward them, which manifests itself in racial taunts (it is Hally who insists "the boys" call him "Master Harold"). This play "is South Africa to its marrow," according to *Washington Post* reviewer David Richards. "And yet, midway through a drama that never once inflates its humble particulars or indulges in lofty pronouncements, you will realize that Fugard is writing about all of us. His play is about the gulfs that suddenly yawn at our feet and the scapegoats we make to exorcise our pain. It is about the punishment we inflict on others, when we are really inflicting it upon ourselves."

The playwright spoke to *Los Angeles Times* reporter Kevin Kelly about using his own past as the basis for a script. "I am Hallie. . . . Rather, I was Hallie when I was 18, 19, 20," says Fugard. He calls creating "Master Harold" "the most painful writing experience of my life," especially in its attempt "to come to terms with my father and mother. I felt like Eugene O'Neill when he was dealing with his ghosts in 'Long Day's Journey into Night.' The awful fear of revealing myself! And the fear that I was on an ego trip; that the play would turn out to be just too personal." As Kelly points out, Fugard needn't have worried: "Some critics, this writer included, consider 'Master Harold' among the handful of great plays of our time." "Fugard's strength is simplicity," observes *Los Angeles Times* critic Sylvie Drake. "He approaches difficult matters head-on, but with pervasive sensitivity of more than a little depth. Paradoxically, he can also border—and does in 'Master Harold'—on melodrama. Powerful histrionics are very much part of this play. What saves it is Fugard's instinctive sense of when to pull back, when to let silence speak, when to let action make its singular, staggering statement"

Speaking to Kelly, Fugard expresses a hope for the future of both his country and himself. "The government did start . . . to relax itself in terms of theater. Now theaters are open to everyone regardless of color. You can even mix a cast without infringing the law. But that doesn't dictate that the society is changing radically. It's window dressing, really." "When I wrote 'A Lesson from Aloes,' which deals with the absolute necessity of friendship between blacks and whites," he continues, "I found myself trying to discover whether I was an optimist or a pessimist about

the country I love so much. I don't know. In 'Master Harold,' Hally says, 'I oscillate between hope and despair.' That remains as true for me as it did when I was 18."

BIOGRAPHICAL/CRITICAL SOURCES:

BOOKS

Contemporary Literary Criticism, Gale, Volume 5, 1976, Volume 9, 1978, Volume 14, 1980, Volume 25, 1983, Volume 40, 1986.
Fugard, Athol, *Notebooks 1960-1977,* Faber, 1983, Knopf, 1984.

PERIODICALS

Los Angeles Times, March 13, 1982, July 17, 1983, July 29, 1983.
New Republic, July 25, 1970, December 21, 1974.
Newsweek, May 28, 1984.
New York, June 6, 1970, December 2, 1974, February 20, 1978, May 17, 1982, January 6, 1986.
New Yorker, December 11, 1978.
New York Review of Books, February 19, 1981.
New York Times, September 19, 1969, May 17, 1970, June 4, 1970, July 6, 1970, December 17, 1974, February 2, 1977, April 1, 1980, April 5, 1980, November 16, 1980, February 1, 1981, June 6, 1981, March 21, 1982, May 5, 1982, November 12, 1982, December 5, 1982, May 15, 1984, December 11, 1985, April 3, 1987, May 28, 1987, April 10, 1988, April 13, 1988, April 24, 1988.
Times Literary Supplement, May 2, 1980, March 1, 1985.
Village Voice, February 20, 1978.
Washington Post, April 13, 1985, September 29, 1987.

*   *   *

FULLER, Buckminster
See FULLER, R(ichard) Buckminster (Jr.)

*   *   *

FULLER, Charles (H., Jr.) 1939-

PERSONAL: Born March 5, 1939, in Philadelphia, Pa.; son of Charles H. (a printer) and Lillian (Anderson) Fuller; married; two sons. *Education:* Attended Villanova University, 1956-58; La Salle College, B.A., 1967.

ADDRESSES: Home—15 Langford St., Philadelphia, Pa. 19136. *Agent*—Esther Sherman, William Morris Agency, 1350 Avenue of the Americas, New York, N.Y. 10019.

CAREER: Playwright. Co-founder and co-director of Afro-American Arts Theatre, Philadelphia, Pa., 1967-71; writer and director of "The Black Experience," WIP-Radio, Philadelphia, 1970-71; professor of African-American studies at La Salle College, 1970, and at Temple University; lecturer.

MEMBER: Dramatists Guild, P.E.N., Writers Guild East.

AWARDS, HONORS: Creative Artist Public Service Award, 1974; Rockefeller Foundation fellow, 1975; National Endowment for the Arts fellow, 1976; Guggenheim fellow, 1977-78; Obie Award from the *Village Voice,* 1981, for "Zooman and the Sign"; Audelco Award for best writing, 1981, for "Zooman and the Sign"; Pulitzer Prize in drama, New York Drama Critics award for best American play, Audelco Award for best play, Theatre Club Award for best play, and Outer Circle Critics award for best Off-Broadway play, all 1982, all for "A Soldier's Play"; D.F.A. from La Salle College, 1982, and Villanova University, 1983; Hazelitt Award from Pennsylvania State Council on the Arts, 1984; D.F.A. from Chestnut Hill College, 1984.

WRITINGS:

PLAYS

"The Village: A Party" (two-act), first produced in Princeton, N.J., at McCarter Theatre, October, 1968, produced as "The Perfect Party," Off-Broadway at Tambellini's Gate Theatre, March 20, 1969.

"Brother Marcus" (four-act), first produced in 1968; produced as "The Rise" in Philadelphia, Pa., at Afro-American Arts Theatre, c. 1968; produced in New York City at Harlem School of the Arts, 1974.

"The Lay Out Letter" (one-act), first produced in 1968; produced as "The Layout" in Philadelphia, Pa., at Freedom Theatre, spring, 1975.

"The Sunflower Majorette" (one-act), first produced in Philadelphia, Pa., at Afro-American Arts Theatre, 1969.

"Emma" (one-act), produced in Philadelphia, Pa., at Afro-American Arts Theatre, 1970.

"An Untitled Play" (one-act), produced in Philadelphia, Pa., at Afro-American Arts Theatre, 1970.

"First Love" (one-act), first produced in Philadelphia, Pa., at Afro-American Arts Theatre, 1971; produced in New York City at Billie Holiday Theatre, June 1974.

"In My Many Names and Days" (six one-acts), first produced in New York City at Henry Street Settlement, September, 1972.

"The Candidate" (three-act), first produced in New York City at Henry Street Settlement, April, 1974.

"In the Deepest Part of Sleep" (two-act), first produced in New York City at St. Marks Playhouse, June 4, 1974.

"The Brownsville Raid" (three-act), first produced in New York City at the Negro Ensemble Company, December 5, 1976.

"Sparrow in Flight" (two-act), first produced in New York City at the AMAS Repertory Theatre, November 2, 1978.

Zooman and the Sign (two-act; first produced in New York City at the Negro Ensemble Company, November, 1979), Samuel French, 1981.

A Soldier's Play (two-act; first produced in New York City at the Negro Ensemble Company, November 20, 1981), Samuel French, 1982.

Also author of plays "Ain't Nobody Sarah, But Me," 1969, "Cain," 1969, "Indian Giver," 1969, and "J. J.'s Game," 1969. Plays represented in anthologies, including *New Plays From the Black Theatre*, Bullins, 1969.

"WE" SERIES; PLAYS

"Sally," first produced in Atlanta, Ga., August, 1988; produced in New York City at the Negro Ensemble Company, November, 1988.

"Prince," produced in New York City at the Negro Ensemble Company, November, 1988.

"Jonquil," produced in New York City at Theater Four, January, 1990.

"Burner's Frolic," produced in New York City at Theater Four, February, 1990.

SCREENPLAYS

"A Soldier's Story" (adapted from the stageplay "A Soldier's Play"), Columbia Pictures, 1984.

TELEPLAYS

"Roots, Resistance, and Renaissance" (twelve-week series), WHYY-TV (Philadelphia), 1967.

"The Sky is Gray" ("American Short Story Series"), New York, 1980.

OTHER

Contributor of short stories to anthologies and periodicals, including *Black Dialogue* and *Liberator*. Also contributor of nonfiction to periodicals, including *Liberator, Negro Digest,* and *Philly Talk*.

WORK IN PROGRESS: A fifth, concluding play in "We" series.

SIDELIGHTS: Charles Fuller is, according to Walter Kerr in the *New York Times,* "one of the contemporary American theater's most forceful and original voices." In his plays Fuller explores human relationships, particularly between blacks and whites, in what many critics find realistic, unbiased, and poignant terms. "He's not tendentious; the work isn't agitprop or anything near it," Kerr continued. "Mr. Fuller isn't really interested in special pleading, but in simply and directly—and cuttingly—observing what really does go on in this world of ours after you've brushed the stereotypes away."

Fuller first gained notice as a playwright with Princeton's McCarter Theatre production of "The Village: A Party." The "village" is a community comprised of racially-mixed couples. Life is peaceful in the protective society until its black leader falls in love with a black woman. Fearing their image will suffer from their leader's action, the other couples murder the defector and insist that his white widow marry a black man, thus perpetuating their tradition. Fuller examines integration through his play and intimates that integration often magnifies racial tension.

"Mr. Fuller has written a not-too-fanciful fantasy about racial integration that somberly concludes that it will not at present solve anybody's racial problems," wrote Dan Sullivan in a *New York Times* review of "The Village." "The play's originality and urgency are unquestionable and so is the talent of the playwright." A later production of "The Village," presented as "The Perfect Party," moved critic Lawrence Van Gelder, also writing in the *New York Times,* to applaud Fuller's "smooth, natural dialogue and deft characterization."

Another of Fuller's plays, "The Brownsville Raid," was based on a true incident that occurred in 1906 when an entire U.S. Army regiment was dishonorably discharged because none of the 167 black soldiers comprising the unit would confess to inciting a riot in Brownsville, Texas. Witnesses of the attack gave conflicting accounts of what happened, and no evidence was supplied to indict the men, but nevertheless they were released from service. Sixty-six years later the Army cleared the men's records, calling their discharge "a gross injustice." "Though it is Fuller's intention to condemn this incident for the disgrace it was," noted Martin Gottfried in the *New York Post,* "his play is no mere tract. His white characters are not caricatures, his black soldiers are not made to be aware ahead of their times." Gottfried found the play "engrossing, unusual, and strong," while *Village Voice* critic Julius Novick thought the story "a bit dull," but nevertheless deemed "The Brownsville Raid" "scrupulous dramatically as well as ideologically," and "clear" and "methodical."

With his play "Zooman and the Sign," Fuller won an Obie and proved to critic Gerald Weales, writing in the *Georgia Review,* that he is "an obviously talented playwright, ambitious in his attempt to deal with difficult and complex themes." "Zooman" is set in a decaying neighborhood in Philadelphia where a young girl was shot to death while playing jacks on her front porch. The child is dead when the play opens, but the grief of her family, the ambivalence of her neighbors, and the cocky, self-justifying attitude of her teen-aged murderer are demonstrated as the play progresses. "The play never quite succeeds in the ambitious terms in which it is conceived," Weales opined, "but its aspirations and its incidental strengths make it far more fascinating than many a neater, smaller play." In the *Los Angeles Times,* critic Don Shirley deemed "Zooman" "a rarity. Its story is simply but not simplistically told, and it examines vital urban issues with urgency but without hysteria."

In 1982 Fuller became the second black playwright to win the Pulitzer Prize for drama. His prizewinner, "A Soldier's Play," is set at an army base in Louisiana during World War II. The drama opens with the murder of black Technical Sergeant Vernon Waters, a tough and wrathful man who may have been killed by any one of several people or groups. For instance, Waters refused to play Uncle Tom to his white military superiors or to the white Southern community and the Ku Klux Klan surrounding the base, thus an angry Caucasian individual or group may have been responsible. But Waters was also viewed with disdain by some members of his own race; he often degraded his recruits, calling them "shiftless, lazy niggers" and other derogatory names, and chastised them for making their race look like "fools" to whites; therefore the murderer might be one of his black subordinates. Following Waters's murder, the army sends an officer to investigate, an act that is more intended to appease the other black military men than to bring about justice.

To the surprise of the white officers at Fort Neal, the investigating official who arrives is Captain Richard Davenport, the first black officer they have ever seen. As Davenport questions possible suspects, Waters's psychotic self-hatred and the damaging effects of racism on his life are revealed, as well as new episodes of racism as a result of Davenport's presence. "Here as before," wrote Frank Rich in the *New York Times,* "the playwright has a compassion for blacks who might be driven to murder their brothers because he sees them as victims of a world they haven't made." "Yet he doesn't let anyone off the hook," Rich continued. "Mr. Fuller demands that his black characters find the courage to break out of their suicidal, fratricidal cycle just as he demands that whites end the injustices that have locked his black characters into the nightmare." In another *New York Times* piece on the drama, Rich wrote: " 'A Soldier's Play' seems to me a rock-solid piece of architecture, briskly and economically peopled by dimensional blacks, whites and psychological misfits caught between. The work is tough, taut and fully realized." Walter Kerr suggested in the *New York Times:* "You should make Mr. Fuller's acquaintance. Now."

Fuller eventually adapted "A Soldier's Play" as the film "A Soldier's Story," which enjoyed substantial acclaim following its 1984 release. Among his other works of note are the plays comprising the "We" series, which presents the history of American blacks in the second half of the nineteenth century. With the "We" plays, wrote Mel Gussow in the *New York Times,* Fuller "is scrutinizing the economic entrapment of people forced to weight their pragmatic needs against their desire for complete emancipation and integration."

BIOGRAPHICAL/CRITICAL SOURCES:

BOOKS

Contemporary Literary Criticism, Volume 25, Gale, 1983.
Dictionary of Literary Biography, Volume 38: *Afro-American Writers After 1955: Dramatists and Prose Writers,* Gale, 1985.

PERIODICALS

Georgia Review, fall, 1981.
Los Angeles Times, August 15, 1982, July 23, 1983, November 6, 1983.

Nation, January 23, 1982.
New Leader, July 12-26, 1982.
Newsweek, December 21, 1981.
New Yorker, December 20, 1976.
New York Post, December 6, 1976.
New York Times, November 13, 1968, March 21, 1969, June 5, 1974, November 8, 1978, November 17, 1981, November 27, 1981, December 6, 1981, December 27, 1981, January 10, 1982, January 11, 1982, March 24, 1982, April 13, 1982, July 31, 1988, January 15, 1990, February 26, 1990.
Time, January 18, 1982.
Village Voice, December 20, 1976.
Washington Post, October 26, 1983, October 28, 1983, November 8, 1983, August 2, 1988.

*   *   *

FULLER, R(ichard) Buckminster (Jr.)   1895-1983 (Buckminster Fuller)

PERSONAL: Born July 12, 1895, in Milton, Mass.; died of a heart attack, July 1, 1983, in Los Angeles, Calif.; son of Richard Buckminster (a merchant) and Caroline Wolcott (Andrews) Fuller; married Anne Hewlett, July 12, 1917 (died July, 1983); children: Alexandra Willets (deceased), Allegra (Mrs. Robert Snyder). *Education:* Attended Harvard University, 1913-15, and U.S. Naval Academy, 1917.

ADDRESSES: Home—200 Locust, Philadelphia, Pa. 19106. *Office*—P.O. Box 696, Edwardsville, Ill. 62025.

CAREER: Writer and lecturer. Richards, Atkinson & Kaserick, Boston, Mass., apprentice machine fitter, 1914; Armour & Co., New York, N.Y., apprentice, 1915-17, assistant export manager, 1919-21; national account sales manager, Kelly Springfield Truck Co., 1922; president, Stockade Building System, 1922-27; 4-D Co., Chicago, Ill., founder, 1927, president, 1927-32; assistant director of research, Pierce Foundation-American Radiator-Standard Sanitary Manufacturing Co., 1930; Dymaxion Corp., Bridgeport, Conn., founder, 1932, director and chief engineer, 1932-36, vice-president and chief engineer, 1941-42; assistant to director of research and development, Phelps Dodge Corp., 1936-38; technical consultant, *Fortune* magazine, 1938-40; chief of mechanical engineering section, Board of Economic Warfare, 1942-44; special assistant to director, Foreign Economic Administration, 1944; chairman of board and administrative engineer, Dymaxion Dwelling Machines, 1944-46; Fuller Research Foundation, Wichita, Kan., chairman of board of trustees, 1946-54; president, Geodesics, Inc., 1954-56; Synergetics, Inc., Raleigh, N.C., president, 1954-59; Southern Illinois University, Carbondale, 1956-83, began as research professor, became professor emeritus; Plydomes, Inc., Des Moines, Iowa, president, beginning 1957; Tetrahelix Corp., Hamilton, Ohio, chairman of board, beginning 1959. Chairman of board, Buckminster Fuller Institute, beginning 1959; trustee, Research and Design Institute, 1966; director, Temcor Corporation, 1967; University of Detroit, Detroit, Mich., R. Buckminster Fuller Professor of Architecture, beginning 1970; Trowbridge Lecturer, Yale University, 1955; Hill Foundation Lecturer, St. Olaf's College, 1957; Lorado Taft Lecturer, University of Illinois, 1960; Charles Eliot Norton Professor of Poetry, Harvard University, 1961-62; Ullman Lecturer, Brandeis University, 1962; San Jose State College, visiting professor of engineering, 1966, and world fellow in residence, University City Science Center, beginning 1972; visiting professor, Iowa State University, 1966; visiting professor or lecturer at many universities around the world. U.S. representative to American-Russian Protocol Exchange, U.S.S.R., 1959.

Consultant to Time, Inc., 1938-40, Ford Foundation and Calcutta (India) Planning Organization, beginning 1961, the governor of North Carolina, beginning 1962, Space Science Laboratory of General Electric, 1963, U.S. Steel Space Team, 1964, John Deere and Co., 1964, American Association of University Women, 1965, NASA and ASTRA, beginning 1965, and U.S. Institute of Behavioral Research, beginning 1965. Director of Oceanographic Study, New York, N.Y.; member of board of trustees, New York Cancer Research Institute, beginning 1964, and International Corporation, beginning 1964; member of board of trustees of overseers in art, Brandeis University, beginning 1965; architect/trustee for "Denationalized World Man Territory," Cyprus, beginning 1966; president of board of directors, Harmony Hill Music Foundation, beginning 1966; member of council, Internal Advisory Council of the National Pollution Control Foundation, 1966. *Military service:* U.S. Navy, 1917-19; became lieutenant.

MEMBER: World Academy of Art and Science (fellow), World Society for Ekistics (vice-president; international president, 1975-77), International Society for Stereology, Royal Society of Arts (Benjamin Franklin life fellow), Royal Institute of British Architects, Society of Venezuelan Architects, Mexican College and Institute of Architects, Institute for Advanced Philosophic Research, Mensa (international president, 1975-83), Institute of General Semantics (fellow and honorary trustee), Institute of Human Ecology, American Association for the Advancement of Science (life fellow), American Institute of Architects (honorary life member), National Academy of Sciences (member of Building Research Institute), National Institute of Arts and Letters (life member), American Society of Professional Geographers, American Association of University Professors, American Academy of Arts and Letters (academician, 1980), American Society for Metals, Society of Architectural Historians, Harvard Engineering Society, Lincoln Academy of Illinois, Architectural League of New York, Phi Beta Kappa, Sigma Xi, Alpha Rho Chi, Tau Sigma Delta, Century Club (New York), New York Yacht Club, Northeast Harbor Fleet, Camden Yacht Club, Somerset Club (Boston), Authors Club (London).

AWARDS, HONORS: Award of merit from New York chapter of American Institute of Architects, 1952; award of merit from U.S. Marine Corps, 1954; Gran Premio, Trienniale de Milano, 1954 and 1957; Centennial Award, Michigan State University, 1955; gold medal scarab, National Architectural Society, 1958; gold medal, Philadelphia chapter of American Institute of Architects, 1960; Frank P. Brown Medal, Franklin Institute, 1960; Allied Professions gold medal, American Institute of Architects, 1963; Plomade de Oro Award, Society of Mexican Architects, 1963; Brandeis University Special Notable Creative Achievement Award of the Year, 1964; Delta Phi Delta Gold Key Laureate, 1964; Industrial Designers Society of America Award of Excellence, 1966; Graham Foundation fellow, 1966-67; Lincoln Academy of Illinois, fellow and Order of Lincoln Medal, 1967; gold medal, National Institute of Arts and Letters, 1968; named Humanist of the Year, American Association of Humanists, 1969; Dean's Award, State University of New York, 1980; named to Housing Hall of Fame, 1981; Presidential Medal of Freedom, 1983. Recipient of about forty honorary degrees from numerous colleges and universities, including University of North Carolina, 1954, University of Michigan, 1955, Washington University, 1957, Southern Illinois University, 1959, Rollins College, 1960, University of Colorado, 1964, University of New Mexico, 1964, Clemson University, 1964, Monmouth College,

1965, Long Island University, 1966, Clarkson College, 1967. "Buckminster Fuller Recognition Day" declared by University of Colorado, 1963, state of Massachusetts, 1977, cities of Boston and Cambridge, 1977, state of Minnesota, 1978, state of Illinois, 1980, city of Buffalo, 1980, city of Austin, 1981.

WRITINGS:

4D Time-Lock, privately printed, 1927, reprinted, N.M. Lama Foundation, 1972.

Nine Chains to the Moon, Lippincott, 1938, reprinted, Doubleday, 1971.

(With others) *New Worlds in Engineering,* Chrysler Co., 1940.

Industrialization of Brazil, Board of Economic Warfare, 1943.

Survey of the Industrialization of Housing, U.S. Foreign Economics Administration, 1944.

(With Robert W. Marks; under name Buckminster Fuller) *The Dymaxion World of Buckminster Fuller,* Reinhold, 1960.

Geoscope 1960, edited by James Robert Hillier, Princeton University, 1960.

New Approaches to Structure, [Washington, D.C.], 1961.

Untitled Epic Poem of the History of Industrialization, J. Williams, 1962.

No More Second Hand God, and Other Writings, Southern Illinois University Press, 1963.

Ideas and Integrities: A Spontaneous Autobiographical Disclosure, edited by Robert W. Marks, Prentice-Hall, 1963.

Education Automation: Freeing the Scholar to Return to His Studies, Southern Illinois University Press, 1963.

Charles Eliot Norton 1961-1962 Lectures at Harvard University, Harvard University Press, 1963.

Governor's Conference with Buckminster Fuller, Governor's Office (Raleigh), 1963.

(With John McHale) *World Design Science Decade, 1965-1975: Inventory of World Resources, Human Trends, and Needs—Phase 1 of 5 Two-Year Increments of World Retooling Design Decade Proposed to the International Union of Architects,* Southern Illinois University, 1963.

(With McHale) *World Resources Inventory, Human Trends and Needs,* Southern Illinois University, 1963.

World Design Science Decade, 1965-1975: The Design Initiative (includes phase 1, [1964], document 2, also brief outlines of phases 2, 3, 4, and 5), Southern Illinois University, 1964.

Comprehensive Thinking, edited by McHale, Southern Illinois University, 1965.

What I Am Trying to Do, Cape Goliard, 1968.

(Author of foreword) Isamu Noguchi, *A Sculptor's World,* Harper, 1968.

(Contributor) Richard Kostelanetz, editor, *Beyond Left and Right: Radical Thought for Our Times,* Morrow, 1968.

Operating Manual for Spaceship Earth, Southern Illinois University Press, 1969.

(With others) *The Arts and Man,* Prentice-Hall, 1969.

Utopia or Oblivion: The Prospects for Humanity, Bantam, 1969.

Reprints and Selected Articles, Bern Porter, 1969.

Planetary Planning, Jawaharlal Nehru Memorial Fund, 1969.

Fifty Years of the Design Science Revolution and the World Game: A Collection of Articles and Papers on Design, Southern Illinois University, 1969.

(With others) *Approaching the Benign Environment: The Franklin Lectures in the Sciences and Humanities,* University of Alabama Press, 1970.

I Seem to Be a Verb, Bantam, 1970.

(Author of introduction) Samuel Rosenberg, *The Come As You Are Masquerade Party,* Prentice-Hall, 1970.

The Buckminster Fuller Reader, edited by James Miller, J. Cape, 1970.

The World Game: Integrative Resource Utilization Planning Tool, Southern Illinois University, 1971.

Old Man River: An Environmental Domed City, Parsimonious Press, 1972.

(Editor with Henry Dreyfuss) *Symbol Sourcebook: An Authoritative Guide to International Graphic Symbols,* McGraw, 1972.

Intuition, Doubleday, 1972, second revised edition, Impact, 1983.

Buckminster Fuller to Children of Earth, Doubleday, 1972.

Earth, Inc., Doubleday-Anchor, 1973.

Synergetics: Explorations in the Geometry of Thinking, Macmillan, 1975.

And It Came to Pass—Not to Stay, Macmillan, 1976.

(With Edgar J. Applewhite) *Synergetics Two: Explorations in the Geometry of Thinking,* Macmillan, 1979.

R. Buckminster Fuller on Education, edited by Robert D. Kahn and Peter H. Wagschal, University of Massachusetts Press, 1979.

(With Kiyoshi Kuromiya) *Critical Path,* St. Martin's, 1981.

Tetrascroll, St. Martin's, 1982.

Grunch of Giants, St. Martin's, 1983.

Also produced recordings "Designing Environments," Big Sur Recordings, 1976, "Anticipating Tomorrow's Schools," [Philadelphia], 1975, and "R. Buckminster Fuller Thinks Aloud," Credo 2. Contributor to journals. Editor, *Convoy* (magazine), 1918-19; publisher, *Shelter* (magazine), 1931-32; editor and author, "Notes on the Future" column, *Saturday Review,* beginning 1964.

SIDELIGHTS: In 1927, when he was thirty-two years old, Richard Buckminster ("Bucky") Fuller, Jr., stood at the shores of Lake Michigan and contemplated whether to take his life. Despondent over the death of his four-year-old daughter, in disgrace with his family because he was the first Fuller in five generations to have been expelled (twice) from Harvard University, the young man had also just lost his job and was a debt-ridden alcohol abuser. As he would later recall, Fuller paused for a while at the lake's edge on "a jump-or-think basis." The answer came to him, as a *New York Times* article reported, when Fuller realized that "you do not have the right to eliminate yourself. You do not belong to you. You belong to the universe." With that, Fuller turned from the shore and embarked on what would become an illustrious career as one of America's most innovative engineers and inventors, as well as a noted philosopher, poet, educator, and environmentalist.

Best known for his invention of the geodesic dome, the self-described "citizen of the twenty-first century" was a major proponent of using science to improve life on what he coined Spaceship Earth. Acclaim, even acceptance, did not come easily at first; early in his career Fuller was regarded by some as a crackpot because of such utopian inventions as the Dymaxion House, a fully self-sufficient prefabricated dwelling, and the Dymaxion Bathroom, the whole of which could be produced en masse, like an auto body. Perhaps the most controversial of these early innovations was the Dymaxion Car. Built in the 1930s, the car was a fuel efficient egg-shaped three-wheeler (efficiency estimated at 40 miles per gallon) that could reach speeds of up to 120 miles per hour. The promising prototype succumbed to poor publicity after a 1935 accident in which, as the *New York Times* stated, "one of the cars collided with a sedan in Chicago and both vehicles overturned. By the time reporters arrived, the other car had been towed away. The driver of the Dymaxion car was killed,

and under such headlines as 'Three Wheeled Car Kills Driver,' newspaper accounts did not mention that another car had been involved."

Despite such setbacks, Fuller's enthusiasm for Dymaxion products (the word is an amalgam of "dynamic, maximum" [efficiency], and "ion" [of power]) and other futuristic concepts continued unabated. And while the tide of public approval began to turn his way with the production of the Dymaxion Ariocean World Map—the first flat chart that displayed the entire surface of the earth without distortion—Fuller's reputation as an engineer of vision was cemented with the 1947 unveiling of the geodesic dome.

Defining geodesic as "the most economical momentary relationship among a plurality of points and events," the self-taught architect had designed that rare thing—a "structure [that] occurs in nature and can be built by man," according to the *New York Times.* The dome is "as self-sufficient as a butterfly's wing and as strong as an egg shell," the *Times* continued. "It depends on no heavy vaults or flying buttresses to support it. Its strength is derived instead from a complex of alternating squares and triangles which produce a phenomenal strength-to-weight ratio when pressure is applied to any point on the structure. It crops up all over in nature—in viruses, in the cornea of the eye. Fuller patented it in 1953—almost like getting a patent on gravity." Within a short time of its introduction, the geodesic dome was being used as everything from a cover for an automobile plant to a hangar for a Marine Corps helicopter station. "Radomes" housed radar equipment along miles of the Distant Early Warning Lines in the Arctic. Russian premier Nikita Khrushchev was impressed by the structure and invited its inventor to lecture to Soviet engineers.

Indeed, lecturing and generally promoting the wonders of the new technological age were as important to Fuller as were any of his other projects. America's countercultural youth of the 1960s were especially attracted to the scientist-philosopher, who championed the environment with his energy efficient designs. In a 1970 *Saturday Review* article, Harold Taylor explained further Fuller's popularity with the young: "[They] are prepared to accept the fact that the very conception of wealth as accumulation of capital is in the present circumstances obsolete, and that wealth is to be measured not by the amounts of money in banks but [, as Fuller insisted,] by the amounts of energy, physical and mental, that are available to solve the problem of making the world work for its inhabitants." The philosopher himself stated this idea more flatly in a 1976 *New York Times Magazine* profile: "There is no energy shortage. There is no energy crisis. There is a crisis of ignorance."

As an author, Fuller often described a technological utopia waiting for those willing to shed the old ideas about science and society. A passage from his study *Synergetics: Explanations in the Geometry of Thinking,* for instance, predicts a future "moving intuitively toward an utterly classless, raceless, omnicooperative, omniworld humanity." Naturally, some critics took exception to this kind of speculation; Robert Wood and O. B. Hardison, Jr., found *Synergetics* an engrossing if somewhat difficult read. Wood, writing in *Saturday Review,* was "exasperated" by the book's "approach to evidence and validation. [The author] interweaves strangely disparate elements: fact and value, commentary on life and the universe, quantity and quality, evidence and inference. And he does this majestically, carelessly, in a manner calculated to infuriate the conscientious scholar in whatever field he happens to be writing about." However, the critic suggested that the sheer weight of Fuller's arguments (the book runs almost 900 pages) and the enthusiasm with which he expressed them made the work valuable. The author, concluded Wood, infused his book with "a genuinely American idiom, of liberalism and expansion and progress. So *Synergetics* is best *read*, not studied. But this reading should be done in 'takes,' with time in between for contemplation. Fuller's work is best understood as a special celebration of the American experience and as such, it deserves our heartfelt appreciation."

New York Times Book Review critic Hardison called *Synergetics* "a kind of *summa theologica* of Fuller's mathematics, philosophy and design theories." Citing the numerous graphs, charts, and equations the author included in the work, Hardison remarked that as a reader "you grope for analogies. The Notebooks of Leonardo. The Opera of Paracelsus. Pascal's *Pensees.* Or Alexander Pope's remark about Creation: 'A mighty maze, but not without a plan.' [The book] is alternately brilliant and obscure, opaque and shot through with moments of poetry. What becomes clear with patience is that the virtues and the liabilities are one. *Synergetics* could not have been written in any other way because its language and mathematics are vehicles for a vision. They embody the vision and if they were different the vision itself would be different—perhaps impossible to express, but certainly impossible to express convincingly."

One of the last major books published before his death, Fuller's *Critical Path,* was called by its author "by far the most important thing" he had ever done, according to Guy Murchie in the *Chicago Tribune Book World.* Essentially a long-range plan for the revitalization of Spaceship Earth, Critical Path employs some of the author's most startling scientific views, as well as an admonishment for its readers to stop being wary of technology and to start appreciating the potential gifts that science offers. For instance, Fuller wrote that the "most effective educational system for human beings is to be derived from the home video cassette system and supporting books, the pages of which are also to be called forth on world-satellite-interlinked video 'library' screens as published in any language." "Some will consider *Critical Path* too far up in the clouds for practical use because they are biased against technology," stated Murchie, "but if they could only let themselves consider his message with a fully open mind, I think they just might discover something profoundly spiritual there."

Shortly after Fuller's death, Norman Cousins had this to say about the futurist in *Saturday Review:* "The great poets have attempted to describe the human mind and spirit, but I doubt that any of them have done so more provocatively than Bucky. The reason perhaps is that Bucky was not only inspired and nourished by the weightless and all-embracing entity called the human mind, but he had a way of opening our minds to the phenomena within them. In this way, he introduced us to ourselves."

BIOGRAPHICAL/CRITICAL SOURCES:

BOOKS

Close, G. W., *R. Buckminster Fuller,* Council of Planning Libraries, 1977.
Fuller, Buckminster, and Robert W. Marks, *The Dymaxion World of Buckminster Fuller,* Reinhold, 1960.
Hatch, Alden, *Buckminster Fuller: At Home in the Universe,* Crown, 1974.
Kenner, Hugh, *Bucky: A Guided Tour of Buckminster Fuller,* Morrow, 1973.
Lord, Athena V., *Pilot for Spaceship Earth: R. Buckminster Fuller, Architect, Inventor and Poet* (for juveniles), Macmillan, 1978.

McHale, John, R., *Buckminster Fuller,* Braziller, 1962.
Rosen, Sidney, *Wizard of the Dome: R. Buckminster Fuller, Designer for the Future,* Little, Brown, 1969.
Snyder, R., editor, *R. Buckminster Fuller,* St. Martin's, 1980.

PERIODICALS

Architectural Forum, October, 1963.
Business Week, May 10, 1958.
Chicago Tribune Book World, March 22, 1981.
Horizon, summer, 1968.
Los Angeles Times Book Review, April 26, 1981, September 19, 1982.
Life, February 26, 1971.
Nation, June 15, 1970.
National Review, July 22, 1983.
Newsweek, July 13, 1959, August 5, 1963.
New Yorker, October 10, 1959.
New York Times, August 28, 1978.
New York Times Book Review, July 28, 1963, May 5, 1968, April 20, 1969, June 29, 1975, April 19, 1981, July 17, 1983.
New York Times Magazine, August 23, 1959, April 23, 1967, July 6, 1975.
People, July 21, 1980.
Saturday Review, May 2, 1970, May 31, 1975, September-October, 1983.
Science Digest, October, 1964.
Time, October 20, 1958, January 10, 1964, March 10, 1967, March 1, 1968, May 11, 1970.
Times (London), April 14, 1983.
Times Literary Supplement, September 6, 1963, August 6, 1964, September 11, 1969, October 28, 1983.
Washington Post, June 10, 1970.

OBITUARIES:

PERIODICALS

Newsweek, July 11, 1983.
New York Times, July 3, 1983.
Time, July 11, 1983.
Times (London), July 4, 1983.
Washington Post, July 3, 1983.

* * *

FUSSELL, Paul 1924-

PERSONAL: Surname rhymes with "Russell"; born March 22, 1924, in Pasadena, Calif.; son of Paul (an attorney) and Wilhma (Sill) Fussell; married Betty Ellen Harper (a journalist), June 17, 1949 (divorced 1987); married Harriette Behringer, April 11, 1987; children: Rosalind, Sam. *Education:* Pomona College, B.A., 1947; Harvard University, M.A., 1949, Ph.D., 1952.

ADDRESSES: Home—2020 Walnut St., Apt. 4-H, Philadelphia, Pa. 19103. *Office*—Department of English, University of Pennsylvania, Philadelphia, Pa. 19104-6273.

CAREER: Connecticut College, New London, instructor in English, 1951-54; Rutgers University, New Brunswick, N.J., assistant professor, 1955-59, associate professor, 1959-64, professor of English, 1964-76, John DeWitt Professor of English Literature, 1976-83; University of Pennsylvania, Philadelphia, Donald T. Regan Professor of English Literature, 1983—. Fulbright lecturer, University of Heidelberg, 1957-58. Regional chairman, Woodrow Wilson National Fellowship Foundation, 1962-64. Consulting editor, Random House, Inc., 1964-65. *Military ser-*

vice: U.S. Army, Infantry, 1943-47; became first lieutenant; received Bronze Star and two Purple Hearts.

MEMBER: Modern Language Association of America, Academy of Literary Studies, English Institute (secretary, 1964-70), Royal Society of Literature (fellow).

AWARDS, HONORS: James D. Phelan Award, 1965, for nonfiction; Lindback Foundation Award, 1971; National Endowment for the Humanities senior fellowship, 1973-74; National Book Critics Circle Award and National Book Award, both 1976, both for *The Great War and Modern Memory;* Ralph Waldo Emerson Award, Phi Beta Kappa, 1976; Guggenheim fellow, 1977-78; American Academy and Institute of Arts and Letters award, 1980, for excellence in literature; *Abroad: British Literary Traveling between the Wars* was nominated for a National Book Critics Circle Award, 1980; Litt.D., Pomona College, 1981; M.A., University of Pennsylvania, 1983; Rockefeller fellow, 1983-84.

WRITINGS:

Theory of Prosody in Eighteenth-Century England, Connecticut College, 1954.
(Co-author) *The Presence of Walt Whitman,* Columbia University Press, 1962.
The Rhetorical World of Augustan Humanism: Ethics and Imagery from Swift to Burke, Oxford University Press, 1965.
Poetic Meter and Poetic Form, Random House, 1965, revised edition, 1979.
Samuel Johnson and the Life of Writing, Harcourt, 1971, reprinted, 1986.
The Great War and Modern Memory, Oxford University Press, 1975.
(Editor) *The Ordeal of Alfred M. Hale,* Leo Cooper, 1975.
Abroad: British Literary Traveling between the Wars, Oxford University Press, 1980.
The Boy Scout Handbook and Other Observations, Oxford University Press, 1982.
(Editor) *Siegfried Sassoon's Long Journey: Selections from the Sherston Memoirs,* Oxford University Press, 1983.
Class: A Guide through the American Status System, Summit Books, 1983, published as *Class,* Ballantine, 1984 (published in England as *Caste Marks: Style and Status in the USA,* Heinemann, 1984).
(Editor) *The Norton Book of Travel,* Norton, 1987.
Thank God for the Atom Bomb and Other Essays, Summit Books, 1988.
Wartime: Understanding and Behavior in the Second World War, Oxford University Press, 1989.

Also editor of *The Norton Book of Modern War.* Contributor of reviews and essays to *Saturday Review, Encounter, Virginia Quarterly Review, Partisan Review,* and other publications. Contributing editor to *Harper's,* 1979-83, and *New Republic,* 1979-85.

SIDELIGHTS: It was not until Paul Fussell "got tired of writing" what he was "supposed to write," as he told Robert Dahlin of *Publishers Weekly,* that he became a successful author. For twenty years, Fussell wrote critical works on poetic theory and eighteenth-century English literature, none of which sold more than 8,000 copies. But with *The Great War and Modern Memory,* a study of the cultural impact of the First World War, came the realization that he could reach a general audience. *The Great War and Modern Memory* has sold over 50,000 copies and won Fussell a National Book Award and the National Book Critics Circle Award. "It was the perfect moment in a writer's life," he

tells Dahlin, "the right subject, the right time. It was an accidental masterpiece." Since his successful break with academic writing, Fussell has continued to write nonfiction for a general audience.

As Fussell explains in the preface, *The Great War and Modern Memory* is about "the British experience of the Western Front from 1914 to 1918 and some of the literary means by which it has been remembered, conventionalized and mythologized." Fussell argues that the modernist sensibility—what Robert Hughes of *Time* defines as "the sense of absurdity, disjuncture and polarization, the loathing of duly constituted authorities, the despair and the irony"—derives from the horrors of the First World War.

By comparing the art and literature to that about the First World War, Fussell traces the differences between prewar and postwar culture. The war is likened by Hughes to "a fault line [that] had opened in history, and all that had been taken as normal vanished into its rumbling cleft." Writing in the *New York Times Book Review,* Frankas Kermode states that "the national imagination, even the texture of our culture, have been permanently qualified by those years, and by men's understanding of what happened in them."

The dominant change brought about by the war, Fussell states, is the irony common to modernist culture. This irony was inspired by the overwhelming destruction of the First World War—a conflict few people initially thought would last more than a few weeks. Casualties soon reached levels never seen in previous wars—at Vimy Ridge, 160,000 men were lost; 60,000 died at the Somme; and more than 350,000 died at Passchendaele. War in the trenches was bloody, filthy, cold and seemingly endless. Traditional romantic forms of art and literature—depicting war as glamorous and heroic—proved inadequate to express the realities of mass suffering. The flamboyant patriotic appeals of government propaganda were countered with understated and ironic language from the soldiers in the trenches. The war forever changed the common speech, the arts, literature, and journalism of western society. "With invention and wit, Fussell [explores] the most significant themes, myths, and literary resources that are created or called upon by the situation of warfare—more precisely, trench warfare," William H. Pritchard writes in the *Saturday Review.*

The winner of the National Book Award and the National Book Critics Circle Award, *The Great War and Modern Memory* also received praise from the critics. Hughes calls the book "a scrupulously argued and profoundly affecting account of what the Great War changed," while the *New Yorker* critic finds it "a learned and well-balanced book that is also bright and sensitive." Although having doubts about some of Fussell's conclusions, Kermode thinks that "one's sense of the whole book is that on the major issues it is right, skillful and compassionate. . . . This book is an important contribution to our understanding of how we came to make [the First World War] part of our minds."

In *Abroad: British Literary Traveling between the Wars,* Fussell examines the literary record left by the postwar generation of travelers, drawing a clear distinction between the traditional traveler of that time and the modern tourist. Richard Rodriguez of the *Los Angeles Times Book Review* finds that Fussell is "concerned with British travelers and travel writing in the years between the wars. The '20's and '30's were, argues Fussell, the great years of modern travel. After wartime gray, cold, deprivation and confinement, 'imaginative and sensitive' Englishmen sought release in travel to the glittering regions of the sun: the Mediterranean, the Middle East, Africa, and Latin America."

Writing in the *Washington Post Book World,* Peter Stansky observes that the "heyday of travel began in the aftermath of the First World War, about which [Fussell] wrote with so much originality and force in *The Great War and Modern Memory.* The present book, which might serve as a coda to its distinguished predecessor, looks back again and again to the first war to explain the peculiarities and excitements of the postwar reaction, not least among them the phenomena of travel and travel writing." Dahlin believes that in both books Fussell "peels away layers of history and experience to uncover English literary observations underlying them."

Fussell maintains that the period between the world wars was the last great age of travel, now replaced by mere tourism. When travelers wrote books about their experiences, they created what Fussell believes is a distinct literary form. Stansky notes that "it is hard to imagine the case for travel writing, a genre worthy of a place alongside poetry and the novel, being made more impressively." Fussell devotes chapters to the travel writing of D. H. Lawrence, Graham Greene, Evelyn Waugh, and other British literary figures. He also resurrects Robert Byron's *The Road to Oxiana* as a masterpiece of the genre. Jonathan Raban of the *New York Times Book Review* calls *Abroad: British Literary Traveling between the Wars* "an exemplary piece of criticism. It is immensely readable. It bristles with ideas. It disinters a real lost masterpiece from the library stacks. It admits a whole area of writing—at last!—to its proper place in literary history."

When asked why travel writing does not enjoy more critical attention, Fussell told Walter W. Ross in an interview in *CA New Revision Series,* Volume 21, "I think it is because of our superstition about fiction: in general, we assume fiction is good artistically and nonfiction is bad. But that is based upon the naive assumption that nonfiction *is* nonfiction. Actually, everything is fiction that's uttered in a shape which is not a natural shape, by which I mean sentences and paragraphs. Travel writing is really a form of fiction validated by appeals to actual experience. It involves fictional techniques, and it's those which make it pleasurable to read. I think we make a sort of overevaluation of what we take to be fictional experience. . . . I guess it's our continued superstition about the 'artistic' that we get from the nineteenth century that prevents people from seeing that the travel book is artistic." But Michael Ratcliffe of the London *Times* considers Fussell's proposal incorrect. He believes that everything Fussell says on behalf of travel writing and as a separate genre "argues its diversity and binds it more tightly to other forms and to the central intellectual crisis of the age."

Fussell's contention that travel has been replaced by tourism—and that travel books are therefore no longer written—is rebuked by Raban, who points out that "two of the best books ever written in the genre, Mark Twain's *Innocents Abroad* and Evelyn Waugh's own *Labels,* happen to be about tourists on a package holiday." Raban makes clear that the essential condition on travel writing remains with us: "the experience of living among strangers, away from home." Stansky, too, disagrees that travel is dead. "The spirit of travel," he writes, "will prove inextinguishable: the space ship is waiting, the hotel is on Mars."

In *The Boy Scout Handbook and Other Observations* Fussell returns to some of the concerns with war found in *The Great War and Modern Memory.* A collection of reviews and essays on a variety of literary topics, the book is "actually the elaborate, multifaceted working out of traumas suffered during World War II, when Fussell was plunged from boyhood into manhood by his experiences as a line officer in Europe," as Joseph McLellan maintains in the *Washington Post.* Peter Ackroyd of the London

Times believes that "some of the most powerful writing in the book comes from [Fussell's] account of his own experiences as an infantryman in France during the Second World War."

Fussell argues that his own war experiences altered his later life. The war, Ackroyd explains, "left him with a profound irony, a certain detachment, and a scepticism about human motives which runs through this book as its unacknowledged theme." D. Keith Mano agrees with this assessment in a *People* article, noting that "when you read Fussell, you can hear a disgruntled giant talking underneath his elegant and explosive prose style." Mano quotes Fussell as explaining: "I'm proud of that. I've created a character out of myself." Ronald B. Shwartz of the *American Spectator* describes Fussell's character as "a kind of thinking man's John Wayne, wielding prose with a certain fetching swagger and acid humor, and blaming it all on nothing less than his stint as a combat platoon leader in WWII."

This brash personal approach leads Fussell to explore literary byways often overlooked by more conventional academic writers. The title of his book, for example, is taken from one piece in which he reviews the latest edition of *The Boy Scout's Handbook.* Fussell defends the book because the motive behind it "is goodness, and the happiness which is associated with virtue," Judith Chettle notes in the *Christian Science Monitor.* Fussell ends by calling the book "among the very few remaining repositories of something like classical ethics." In other pieces he questions the value of Graham Greene's prose, discusses censorship in South Africa, and draws a comparison between newspaper personal ads and the irate letters authors write to protest bad reviews. "He is a bull in the china shop of American letters," Shwartz maintains.

With the publication of *Class: A Guide through the American Status System,* Fussell turned his attention to a topic touched upon briefly in *The Boy Scout Handbook and Other Observations:* the nature of class distinctions in the United States. He finds these distinctions to be primarily in matters of taste. Fussell claims that our choice of clothes, houses, cars, books, and other items, as well as our language, reveal our class origins. "Of the many guides to social travel that have appeared recently, Mr. Fussell's is surely the most comprehensive, as well as one of the wittiest," Alison Lurie writes in the *New York Times Book Review.*

In his examination of class differences Fussell explains why owning a Mercedes-Benz automobile is hopelessly upper middle class; why red geraniums are gauche; and how a threadbare Oriental rug on your floor can move you into a higher class. Fussell finds American class distinctions so pervasive that he includes a do-it-yourself living room rating test for determining which social class you occupy. Points are awarded for items of furniture, number of books displayed, artwork on the walls, and for other contents. "Most of the author's judgments," Cleveland Amory comments in the *Chicago Tribune Book World,* "are extremely accurate and most of his examples unfailingly interesting."

Although Fussell divides American society into nine classes, "his primary interest is in the upper middle, the middle and the various levels of what he chooses to call the proletarians, or 'proles,' " Jonathan Yardley explains in the *Washington Post Book World.* "Toward the upper middle he displays the ambiguity to be expected of one who is almost certainly a member of it; toward the 'proles' he affects a good-natured egalitarianism that soon enough slides into patronizing. But there is no equivocation or uncertainty in Fussell's attitude toward the middle classes: it is one of unrestrained loathing, utterly unameliorated by sympathy or empathy." Fussell's aim, R. Z. Sheppard writes in *Time*, "is to offend, mainly the middle class, and to decry the decline of culture and taste. He succeeds, with considerable wit and a fine malice."

For those who wish to live outside the class system, Fussell offers an "X" group who are unhindered by class limitations and are able to enjoy true liberty. These X's avoid the pretensions of the upper classes and the insecurities of the proles while commenting ironically on the rest of society. "X's always dress down a peg. . . . They drink cheap but 'excellent' wine; they seldom eat out, . . . ; they favor ironic lawn furniture, if any. In short, they are academics, manfully keeping up with last year's unconventions," as Wilfrid Sheed writes in the *Atlantic.* " 'X people' are just wonderful," Yardley states, "and all the rules for living the X life can be found in [the book]; there seem to be at least as many of them as there are for living middle-class life, and they are every bit as rigid." Similarly, Mary R. Lefkowitz of the *Times Literary Supplement* wonders if the X's, "so long as they feel constrained to comment on the rest of us by their eccentric behavior, can ever truly manage to be free." "Fussell may inspire some of his readers to become X-people," Lurie observes. "Most people, however, will simply enjoy the book as a shrewd and entertaining commentary on American mores today."

Speaking to Elizabeth Mehren of the *Los Angeles Times*, Fussell explained that writing *Class: A Guide through the American Status System* allowed him "to be irresponsible, which I love being," and offered him a chance to write about "the most interesting subject there is, because it's about everybody." Fussell's enthusiasm is shared by the Toronto *Globe & Mail* reviewer, who calls the book an "engaging attempt to chart the American status system. . . . Read and chuckle. And wince. There's no stop to the fun."

Returning to a more disturbing subject, Fussell has gained more critical attention with *Wartime: Understanding and Behavior in the Second World War.* Though spoken of as a "good" war because it put an end to Hitler's holocaust, the war, like any war, was abominable, Fussell maintains. This controversial opinion, supported by numerous examples of needless slaughter, has been hailed by some readers as a long-overdue account of the actual horrors of the war as they experienced it. Others have denounced the book, claiming that Fussell's criticisms stem from sympathy with Nazi Germany. "The reaction to this book . . . shows how precious the second [world] war was to the self-esteem of Americans," Fussell told Richard Bernstein of the *New York Times.* Not claiming, as some have said, that the war should not have been fought, Fussell explained, "the war was both necessary and awful. The war was necessary and just and it caused a mess of intellectual and moral ruin." The ground warfare, he claims, demoralized soldiers who then had a hard time reconciling the brutality of combat experience with their reception as heroes when they came home. *Washington Post Book World* editor Nina King explains, "the war as it was known by the men in the infantry combat units [was] a war of bodies hideously dismembered or blown into a thousand pieces, of grinding, humiliating fear that caused many men to lose control of their bowels and some to go mad. . . . But if the myth of the 'good war' persists 50 years later, it is because many of the survivors who knew the reality accept the myth, either because it is easier to live with, or because

the idealistic, 'highminded' side of the war was also part of their understanding."

Thank God for the Atom Bomb and Other Essays declares that the use of nuclear weapons such as the bomb that destroyed Hiroshima is preferable to the carnage Fussell witnessed in Europe and the Pacific. Critics of the decision to use the bomb can easily forget that the minimization of casualties was a factor in reaching that decision, Fussell points out. He addresses this issue—and other war-related topics—to answer the facile comments of critics whose opinions are not informed by experience. Fussell told John Blades of the *Chicago Tribune* that future books will look at other topics. "I finished what I like to think is my last book on the subject [of war], 'The Norton Book of Modern War,' an anthology of war writings from the First War through Vietnam, with my commentary and interpretation. I found it so depressing, really, that I'd like to write a cheerful book, about the circus or the theater or something a little elevating. I'm tired of writing about mass murder and its meaning. After a while, you're persuaded that it doesn't have any meaning."

BIOGRAPHICAL/CRITICAL SOURCES:

BOOKS

Contemporary Authors, New Revision Series, Volume 21, Gale, 1987.
Fussell, Paul, *The Great War and Modern Memory,* Oxford University Press, 1975.

PERIODICALS

American Spectator, July, 1983, April, 1984.
Atlantic, October, 1983.
Chicago Tribune, October 1, 1980, November 23, 1989.
Chicago Tribune Book World, November 13, 1983.
Christian Science Monitor, September 10, 1982.
Globe and Mail (Toronto), June 24, 1985, September 23, 1989.
Los Angeles Times, November 23, 1980, December 26, 1983, June 23, 1988, December 25, 1989.
Los Angeles Times Book Review, November 6, 1983.
New Yorker, October 20, 1975.
New York Review of Books, October 16, 1975.
New York Times, September 1, 1980, November 2, 1980, December 16, 1980, October 8, 1982, November 18, 1983, August 17, 1989, October 11, 1989.
New York Times Book Review, August 31, 1975, August 31, 1980, August 29, 1982, November 13, 1983, August 7, 1988, September 3, 1989.
People, February 7, 1983.
Publishers Weekly, October 3, 1980, June 23, 1989.
Saturday Review, February 21, 1976.
Time, October 20, 1975, October 31, 1983.
Times (London), March 19, 1981, January 27, 1983.
Times Literary Supplement, March 20, 1981, February 11, 1983, July 6, 1984, September 22, 1989.
Tribune Books (Chicago), July 27, 1988, August 13, 1989.
Voice Literary Supplement, November, 1983.
Washington Post, September 6, 1982, September 28, 1982, July 4, 1988.
Washington Post Book World, September 21, 1980, June 27, 1982, November 6, 1983, August 13, 1989.

G

G. B. S.
See SHAW, George Bernard

*　　*　　*

GADDIS, William 1922-

PERSONAL: Born in 1922, in New York, N.Y.; children: one son, one daughter. *Education:* Attended Harvard University, 1941-45.

ADDRESSES: Agent—Candida Donadio and Associates, 231 West 22nd St., New York, N.Y. 10011.

CAREER: New Yorker, New York, N.Y., fact checker, 1946-47; lived in Latin America, Europe and North Africa, 1947-52; freelance writer of filmscripts, speeches and corporate communications, 1956-70; novelist. Has also worked for magazines and taught at universities. Distinguished visiting professor at Bard College, 1977.

MEMBER: American Academy and Institute of Arts and Letters.

AWARDS, HONORS: National Institute of Arts and Letters grant, 1963; National Endowment for the Arts grants, 1967 and 1974; Rockefeller grant and National Book Award, 1976, for *J R;* Guggenheim Fellowship, 1981; MacArthur Foundation Fellowship, 1982; nomination for PEN/Faulkner Award, 1985, for *Carpenter's Gothic.*

WRITINGS:

NOVELS

The Recognitions, Harcourt, 1955, corrected edition, Penguin Books, 1985.
J R, Knopf, 1975, corrected edition, Penguin Books, 1985.
Carpenter's Gothic, Viking, 1985.

OTHER

Contributor to periodicals, including *Atlantic, New Yorker, New York Times,* and *Harper's.*

WORK IN PROGRESS: A novel about litigation.

SIDELIGHTS: William Gaddis is one of the most highly regarded yet least read novelists in America. Although many readers remain unfamiliar with his work, certain critics have made extravagant claims for it. Richard Toney, in the *San Francisco Review of Books,* describes Gaddis's first book, *The Recognitions,* as "a novel of stunning power, 956 pages of linguistic pyrotechnics and multi-lingual erudition unmatched by any American writer in this century—perhaps in any century." L. J. Davis, in his *National Observer* review, writes that Gaddis's second novel, *J R,* "is the equal of—if not superior to—its predecessor"; but the work remains, as Frederick Karl asserts in his *Conjunctions* essay, "perhaps the great unread novel of the postwar era." Since the publication in 1985 of his third novel, *Carpenter's Gothic* (and with it reissues of the first two), Gaddis has attained some of the recognition so long denied him, yet his position in contemporary American fiction remains unsettled. Most critics group him with such postmodern fabulators as Thomas Pynchon, John Barth, and Robert Coover; others place him in the modernist tradition of James Joyce and Thomas Mann. Gaddis himself sees his work as related in spirit to the great Russian novels of the nineteenth century. One fact is certain: Gaddis's achievement can no longer be ignored.

Gaddis has drawn heavily on his own background for the settings of his novels. Born in Manhattan in 1922, he was raised in Massapequa, Long Island, in the house that was the model for the Bast home in *J R.* Like the Basts, Gaddis's maternal relatives were Quakers, though he himself was raised in a Calvinist tradition, as is Wyatt Gwyon in *The Recognitions.* Like Otto in the same novel and Jack Gibbs in *J R,* Gaddis grew up without a father. Haunting all three novels, in fact, is the spirit of a dead or absent father who leaves a ruinous state of affairs for his children, a situation that can be extrapolated to include Gaddis's vision of a world abandoned by God and plunged into disorder. The youngster's fifth through thirteenth years were spent at a boarding school in Berlin, Connecticut, which not only furnished the fictional Jack Gibbs with the bleak memories recalled in *J R* but also provided the unnamed New England setting for the first chapter of *The Recognitions.* Returning to Long Island to attend Farmingdale High School, Gaddis contracted the illness that debilitates Wyatt in the first novel and that kept Gaddis out of World War II. Instead he attended Harvard and edited the *Harvard Lampoon* until circumstances required him to leave in 1945 without a degree.

Back in New York, Gaddis worked as a fact checker at the *New Yorker,* a job that he later recalled as "terribly good training, a kind of post-graduate school for a writer, checking everything, whether they were stories or profiles or articles. . . . A lot of the complications of high finance and so forth in *J R*—I tried very hard to get them all right. And it was very much that two years at the *New Yorker*," he told Miriam Berkley in a *Publishers Weekly* interview. At this time he also mingled in the Greenwich Village milieu recreated in the middle section of *The Recognitions*. Here he became acquainted with future Beat writers William Burroughs, Allen Ginsberg, Alan Ansen, and Jack Kerouac. (In fact, Kerouac converted Gaddis into a character named Harold Sand in his 1958 novel *The Subterraneans*.) In 1947 Gaddis set off on five years of wandering through Mexico, Central America, Spain, France, and North Africa until in 1952 he returned to America to complete his first novel.

Published in 1955, *The Recognitions* is an account of personal integration amid collective disintegration, of an individual finding himself in a society losing itself. That individual is Wyatt Gwyon, a failed seminarian who turns to forging Old Masters in an earnest but misguided attempt to return to an era when art was authentic and sanctioned by God. Wyatt is set in stark contrast to the other artist figures in the novel: Otto, the playwright; Esme, the poet; Max, the painter; Sinisterra, the counterfeiter—all of whom plagiarize, falsify, or discredit the artistic process. (Only Stanley, the organist, approaches Wyatt's standards, but he perishes for lack of the one thing that saves Wyatt: love.) These figures, along with the rest of the novel's large cast of characters, are representative of a society losing itself in a shoddy world so encrusted with counterfeit that "recognitions" of authenticity are nearly impossible.

The action in *The Recognitions* runs on two narrative planes that occasionally intersect. On one plane is Wyatt, whom Karl calls "an avenging Messiah . . . because he perceives himself as bringing a purifying and cleansing quality, a 'recognition,' to a society that has doomed itself with corruptive sophistication." But Wyatt is hobbled in his pursuit of a "vision of order" (as it is later called in *Carpenter's Gothic*) by a psychologically crippling boyhood that has instilled in him a grim mixture of guilt, secrecy, and alienation. The compromised worlds of religion and art are exposed in the first two chapters, and Wyatt's brief fling with conventionality (complete with wife and nine-to-five job) fails by chapter three, leaving him open to the temptations of the novel's Mephistopheles, Recktall Brown, a corrupt art dealer. Selling his soul to the devil (and losing his name in the process, for in primitive myth the loss of one's name accompanied the loss of one's soul), Wyatt retreats offstage for the entrance of his parodic counterpart, Otto Pivner, whose comic misadventures in Central America and Greenwich Village constitute the second narrative plane of the novel.

Here the "corruptive sophistication" spoken of by Karl comes to the forefront as endless discussions of art and religion are carried on through endless parties and bar conversations by those whom Gaddis lampoons as "the educated classes, an ill-dressed, underfed, overdrunken group of squatters with minds so highly developed that they were excused from good manners, tastes so refined in one direction that they were excused for having none in any other, emotions so cultivated that the only aberration was normality, all afloat here on sodden pools of depravity calculated only to manifest the pricelessness of what they were throwing away, the three sexes in two colors, a group of people all mentally and physically the wrong size." Otto and other characters such as Stanley and Max represent distorted, incomplete versions of Wyatt, and though Wyatt is rarely present during their goings-on, he hovers above them like a Rilkean angel, emblematic of what Gaddis calls in the novel "the self who could do more." As Wyatt realizes, "None of them moves, but it reflects

him, none of them . . . reacts, but to react with him, none of them hates but to hate with him, to hate him, and loving . . . none of them loves, but, loving. . . ." Here he trails off, for the absence of love—in his world and in the world at large—merges as the major cause for the godless, counterfeit condition surrounding modern man. With this realization, Wyatt abandons forgery, travels to Spain (where his mother is entombed), and finds the love necessary to baptize his new life. Spurning love, the rest of the novel's characters are last seen rushing headlong into death, madness, or disintegration.

This oversimplified scenario belies the multi-layered complexity of *The Recognitions*, a complexity necessary to dramatize the novel's thematic concern with imitation versus reality. As Tony Tanner points out in the *New York Times Book Review*, "If at times we feel lost, displaced, disoriented as we move through the complicated edifice of the book, we are only experiencing analogically a lostness that is felt in varying ways by all the characters in the book." Often eschewing traditional narrative exposition, Gaddis abandons the reader at the various scenes of action, forcing him instead to overhear the confused gropings, deliberate lies, and mistaken notions of the characters, to sort them out as best he can. In other words, the reader must participate in the novel and make the same "recognitions" demanded of its characters by the title. An immense network of allusions, references, motifs, and gestures are introduced and repeated in countless funhouse mirror permutations, demanding (as do all of Gaddis's novels) much greater attention from the reader than usual. The novel is also very erudite, but this characteristic has too often been overemphasized: the sense, if not the literal meaning, of Gaddis's hundreds of references, allusions, and foreign language phrases is usually clear enough from the context.

An aspect of the novel that has been underemphasized, however, is its humor. Although Gaddis works in what Karl describes as "the more doomed part of the American tradition, associated with [Herman] Melville's Ahab, [Nathaniel] Hawthorne's fated figures, [Edgar Allan] Poe's nightmarish characters and scenes," *The Recognitions* is animated by a comic brio that adds the kind of desperate hilarity to his grim theme that one finds in Alexander Pope's *Dunciad* or in Nikolai Gogol's *Dead Souls*. Gaddis's themes are often Kafkaesque, but one must read him as the Czechs read Franz Kafka: as a comic realist, rather than as a Joycean artificer of scholarly labyrinths.

The Recognitions had as little immediate impact as *Moby-Dick* did a century earlier. Unfortunately, 1955 was "one of American criticism's weakest hours," as Maurice Dolbier noted in a *New York Herald Tribune* article seven years later, and most reviewers were put off by this gargantuan novel by an unknown writer. A few readers recognized its greatness immediately, but only in later years did a historical perspective allow critics to gauge its importance. In his 1975 *Saturday Review* assessment of Gaddis's second novel, John Aldridge, an early champion, writes from such a perspective: "As is usually the case with abrasively original work, there had to be a certain passage of time before an audience could begin to be educated to accept *The Recognitions*. The problem was not simply that the novel was too long and intricate or its vision of experience too outrageous, but that even the sophisticated reading public of the mid-Fifties was not yet accustomed to the kind of fiction it represented. . . . The most authoritative mode in the serious fiction of the Fifties was primarily realistic, and the novel of fabulation and Black Humor—of which *The Recognitions* was later to be identified as a distinguished pioneering example—had not yet come into vogue. In fact, the writers who became the leaders of the Black Humor movement had either not been heard from in 1955 or remained undiscovered. Their work over the past 20 years has created a context in which it is possible to recognize Gaddis's novel as having helped inaugurate a whole new movement in American fiction. Rereading it with the knowledge of all that this movement has taught us about modern experience and the opening of new possibilities for the novel, one can see that *The Recognitions* occupies a strikingly unique and primary place in contemporary literature."

Aldridge's evaluation has been echoed by others. In 1976 *New York Times Book Review* contributor George Stade described Gaddis as "a presiding genius . . . of post-war American fiction," and each year more readers share professor Frank McConnell's conclusion that *The Recognitions* is "the indispensable novel of the last thirty years in America, and that contemporary fiction makes no real sense without the presence of this strange, perverse, confusing, and ultimately sane book."

Little was heard of Gaddis in the decade and a half after 1955. Denied the life of a "successful" novelist, he began a long line of jobs in industry, working first in publicity for a pharmaceutical firm, then writing films for the army, and later writing speeches for corporate executives (as does Thomas Eigen in *J R*, who has also published an important but neglected novel). With the appearance in a 1970 *Dutton Review* of what would later become the opening pages of his second novel, Gaddis broke his fifteen-year silence. Two more fragments from *J R* appeared, in *Antaeus* and *Harper's*, before the novel was published in the fall of 1975 to much stronger reviews than *The Recognitions* had received. *J R* won the National Book Award for the best fiction of the year and has since earned the praise of such writers as Saul Bellow, Mary McCarthy, William H. Gass, Stanley Elkin, Joseph McElroy, and Don DeLillo.

Although this intricate, 726-page novel resists easy summary, it is essentially a satire of corporate America, a "country" so obsessed with money that failure is all but inevitable for anyone who doesn't sell his soul to Mammon. (The theme of failure in American life and literature is the subject of one of Gaddis's few essays, "The Race for Second Place," which doubles as an excellent companion piece to his fiction.) At the center of the novel is eleven-year-old J. R. Vansant, a slovenly but clever boy who transforms a small "portfolio" of mail order acquisitions and penny stocks into an unwieldy paper empire in an improbably short time. The most radical feature of the novel is its narrative mode: except for an occasional transitional passage, the novel is composed entirely of dialogue. Novels totally in dialogue had been done before—for example, by Ronald Firbank (whom Gaddis has read) and Ivy Compton-Burnett (whom he hasn't)—but never to the extreme lengths Gaddis takes this technique. For the dialogue is not the literary dialogue of most novels, tidied up and helpfully larded with "he said"'s and explanatory asides by the author on what the characters actually mean by what they say. Instead, *J R* reads like a tape-recorded transcription of real voices: ungrammatical, often truncated, with constant interruptions by other characters (and by telephones, radios, and televisions), with rarely an identifying or interpretive remark by the author.

Such a mode makes unusual demands upon the reader; it demands that he read actively with involvement and concentration, rather than passively, awaiting entertainment. Jack Gibbs, a major character, pinpoints this problem during a drunken conversation with Edward Bast, a young composer: " . . . problem most God damned readers rather be at the movies. Pay attention here bring something to it take something away problem most God damned writing's written for readers perfectly happy who

they are rather be at the movies, come in empty-handed go out the same God damned way I told him Bast. Ask them to bring one God damned bit of effort want everything done for them they get up and go to the movies." The phrase "pay attention here" is directed to the reader as much as to Bast. In his interview with *Publishers Weekly*, Gaddis reiterated the point: "For me it is very much a proposition between the reader and the page. That's what books are about. And he must bring something to it or he won't take anything away. . . . Television is hot, it provides everything. In the so-called situation comedies, you go with a completely blank mind, which is preoccupied for a half hour, and then you turn it off. You have brought nothing to it and you take nothing home. Much bad fiction is like this. Everything is provided for you, and you forget it a week later." What the attentive reader takes home from *J R* is a ringing in the ears from what Sarah E. Lauzen, in her *Postmodern Fiction* essay, calls "the constant cacophony of America selling America." The first word of the novel is "money," a word that reappears throughout the novel as its debasing touch besmirches everything from education to science, from politics to marriage, from the arts to warfare.

Just as everyone in the counterfeit cultural world of *The Recognitions* moves in relation to Wyatt, everyone in the phony paper world of *J R* moves in relation to the young title figure, who embodies what Gaddis calls, in the *Publishers Weekly* interview, "simple naked cheerful greed, no meanness, no nastiness, and not a great deal of intelligence, as I say. Just doing what you're supposed to do." Where Huck Finn spurns the corrupt civilization handed down to him, J. R. gleefully accepts it, wanting only to know how fast he can get his share. By following the letter of the law at the expense of its spirit, he is able to build his "family of companies" with the assistance of adults as amoral as he is.

The only adults who attempt to infuse a moral sense into J. R. are his teacher, Amy Joubert, and his reluctant business associate, Edward Bast, a struggling musician. But Amy is too preoccupied with her own problems to be of much help, and Bast causes more problems than he solves. Although one of the major conflicts in the novel is between such outwardly directed people as J. R. and such inwardly directed people as the book's artists, all of the latter figures—Bast, Eigen, Gibbs, Gall, Schramm, and Schepperman—have largely themselves to blame for their artistic failures rather than the crass business world to which they belong. Despite their failures, however, most are seen at work on new art projects at the novel's end, for as Johan Thielemans notes in an essay appearing in *In Recognition of William Gaddis*, "artistic perfection represents the only possible escape from entropic processes."

The term "entropy" is introduced in the novel almost as early as "money," and this concept—the tendency for any system to move from a state of order to one of disorder—operates throughout the novel. "Things fall apart; the centre cannot hold" was William Butler Yeats's poetic formulation of this principle in "The Second Coming," and nearly everyone in Gaddis's novel is caught up in a desperate attempt to hold things together in the face of encroaching disorder and dissolution. But the attempts are largely futile: families break up, artists burn out and/or commit suicide, businesses close or are swallowed up by conglomerates, children are abandoned, coitus is interrupted, and communication breaks down. Entropy is closely related to information theory, and the reader would do well to take Gibbs's advice and "read Wiener on communication, more complicated the message more God damned chance for errors, take a few years of marriage such a God damned complex of messages going both ways can't get a God damned thing across, God damned much entropy going on. . . ." The reference is to Norbert Wiener's *The Human Use of Human Beings,* in which it is argued, "As entropy increases, the universe, and all closed systems in the universe, tend naturally to deteriorate and lose their distinctiveness, to move from the least to the most probable state, from a state of organization and differentiation in which distinctions and forms exist, to a state of chaos and sameness." *J R* itself imitates this state of chaos and sameness: everyone's life in the novel is chaotic, and the exclusive use of dialogue creates what Thomas LeClair, in his *Modern Fiction Studies* essay, calls "a massive consistency in which characters with different backgrounds, moneymen and artists alike, come to have the same rushed habits of speech, the inability to complete a message or act."

Yet, Wiener goes on to say: "But while the universe as a whole, if indeed there is a whole universe, tends to run down, there are local enclaves whose direction seems opposed to that of the universe at large and in which there is a limited and temporary tendency for organization to increase. Life finds its home in some of these enclaves." One of these enclaves is art, and Gaddis's highly organized novel assures the reader that negentropic acts are still possible. As Aldridge writes at the end of his review of *J R:* "It is undoubtedly inevitable that the novel promises at almost every point to fall victim to the imitative fallacy, that it is frequently as turgid, monotonous, and confusing as the situation it describes. Yet Gaddis has a strength of mind and talent capable of surmounting this very large difficulty. He has managed to reflect chaos in a fiction that is not itself artistically chaotic because it is imbued with the conserving and correcting power of his imagination. His awareness of what is human and sensible is always present behind his depiction of how far we have fallen from humanity and sense."

Unless the reader abandons himself to the roller-coaster narrative rush and the giddiness resulting from its outrageous scenario, *J R* will appear more difficult than it actually is. Like its predecessor, *J R* is primarily a comic novel; as Alicia Metcalf Miller writes in her review for the Cleveland *Plain Dealer* (a review Gaddis has quoted with approval), "If Gaddis is a moralist, he is also a master of satire and humor. *J R* is a devastatingly funny book. Reading it, I laughed loudly and unashamedly in public places, and at home, more than once, I saw my small children gather in consternation as tears of laughter ran down my face." Such is the reader response for which *J R* aims.

Gaddis's underground reputation surfaced somewhat after the publication of *J R* in 1975. The National Book Award for fiction was followed by a steady stream of academic essays and dissertations, culminating in 1982 with the first book on Gaddis's work, a special issue of the *Review of Contemporary Fiction,* and a MacArthur Foundation Fellowship (the so-called "genius" award). Two years later, the second book on his work appeared, Gaddis was elected to the American Academy and Institute of Arts and Letters, and he finished his third novel.

For this novel—originally titled "That Time of Year: A Romance" but published in the summer of 1985 as *Carpenter's Gothic*—Gaddis turned away from the "mega-novel" and set out to write a shorter, different sort of book. As he explained in a *Washington Post* interview with Lloyd Grove: "I wanted it to move very fast. Everything that happens on one page is preparing for the next page and the next chapter and the end of the book. When I started I thought, 'I want 240 pages'—that was what set I out for. It preserved the unity: one place, one very small amount of time, very small group of characters, and then, in effect, there's a nicer word than 'cliche,' what is it? Staples. That is, the staples of the marriage, which is on the rocks, the

obligatory adultery, the locked room, the mysterious stranger, the older man and the younger woman, to try to take these and make them work."

Sharing John Barth's practice of reviving old-fashioned novelistic conventions in new, metafictional forms, Gaddis restores to worn-out literary cliches some of the drama and intensity they had before they were spoiled by overuse. Like *The Recognitions,* his third novel is concerned with the ambiguous nature of reality—"There's a very fine line between the truth and what really happens" is an oft-repeated line in *Carpenter's Gothic*—and it also attacks the perversions done in the name of religion. From *J R* it takes its narrative technique—an almost total dependence on dialogue to convey the narrative—and its contempt for the perversions done in the name of capitalism. Gaddis has McCandless, one of two failed novelists in *Carpenter's Gothic,* dismiss his own work as "just an afterthought . . . just a footnote, a postscript," and in one sense Gaddis's third novel is itself just a footnote, a postscript to the two encyclopedic works that preceded it. But seen in its own light, the novel is a tour de force that presents its author's most characteristic themes and techniques with economy and flair.

Carpenter's Gothic is rooted in a specific time and place: the action takes place over a month's time (internal references date it October-November 1983) in a "carpenter gothic" style Victorian house in a small Hudson River Valley town. (Gaddis owned just such a house on Ritie Street in Piermont, New York.) Almost continuously on stage is Elizabeth Booth—Bibbs to her brother Billy, Liz to her husband Paul, and Mrs. Booth to McCandless, the house's owner. These men subject Liz to the bullying, self-serving dialogue that makes up the bulk of the novel and that brings the outside world onto Gaddis's one-set stage. (The novel is so overtly dramatic that theatrical metaphors are irresistible.) With newspapers and telephone calls filling the roles of messengers, a complicated plot quickly unfolds concerning Christian fundamentalism, political chicanery, African mineral rights, and a half-dozen family disputes. Long-suffering Liz endures it all, helpless to prevent her men from rushing headlong into (and even creating) the Armageddon that looms on the final pages of the novel.

"Whatever your grasshoppers know that's one thing," McCandless says to Liz at one point, "you won't hear it from the females, they're practically silent, it's the males that. . . ." Here Liz uncharacteristically interrupts, for in *Carpenter's Gothic,* as in all Gaddis's novels, the males do most of the talking and create most of the problems. Like Esme in *The Recognitions* and Amy in *J R,* Liz is the still point in a frantic male world, "the only thing that holds things together," as her brother Billy admits. Though endearingly flawed, she is perhaps the most sympathetic figure in all three of Gaddis's novels. For that reason, her sudden death at the end of the novel is much more heartrending than Esme's in *The Recognitions* (or Rhoda's in *J R*) and gives *Carpenter's Gothic* its bleaker, more despairing tone.

Liz's husband Paul, a Vietnam veteran once attacked by his own men, is in one sense a grown-up J. R. Vansant—an identification Gaddis encourages when someone dismisses Paul for "know[ing] as much about finance as some snot nosed sixth grader." Like J. R., Paul simply does what people do to "make it" in America, never examining for an instant the ethics or morality of his questionable dealings. But the man who brings the greatest disorder into Liz's life is McCandless, the mysterious owner of the house, whom she transforms into a wearily romantic figure out of Charlotte Bronte's *Jane Eyre* (a movie version of which serves as a backdrop to Liz and Paul's joyless lovemaking). At the end of chapter four, McCandless takes down a copy of V. S. Naipaul's *The Mimic Men* and reads his own fate: "*A man, I suppose, fights only when he hopes, when he has a vision of order, when he feels strongly there is some connexion between the earth on which he walks and himself. But there was my vision of a disorder which it was beyond any one man to put right.*" No longer feeling any connection between his world and himself, outraged at the stupidity that has severed that connection, McCandless can only envision a bleak future of the sort with which Pope closed his *Dunciad*. "Lo! thy dread empire, CHAOS! is restored; / Light dies before thy uncreating word; / Thy hand, great Anarch! lets the curtain fall; / And Universal Darkness buries All."

This vision of deep disorder belongs to Gaddis as well, for *Carpenter's Gothic,* as Peter Prescott declares in his *Newsweek* review, "is surely Gaddis's most pessimistic, his most savage novel." No one in the novel demonstrates any possibility of sidestepping, much less overcoming, the world's crushing stupidity. An escape hatch through which characters such as Wyatt and Bast can save themselves is present in the first two novels, but no such option is available in *Carpenter's Gothic*. As Robert Kelly writes in his review for *Conjunctions,* Gaddis does not seem to have "an optimistic bone in his body—at least not in his writing hand." This pessimism springing from what T. S. Eliot in "Little Gidding" called "the conscious impotence of rage / At human folly"—bothers many readers; but Kelly goes on to make a crucial point: "We are foolish if we expect the skilful anatomist who excoriates vicious folly to provide a cure for it too—and doubly foolish if we credit any panacea he does trick himself into prescribing."

Even art, the panacea prescribed in the first two novels, is suspect in the third book. On one level, *Carpenter's Gothic* is a meditation on fiction, specifically on the dubious motives for writers' fiction-making impulses. For Liz—as perhaps for the younger Gaddis—fiction offers "some hope of order restored, even that of a past life in tatters, revised, amended, fabricated in fact from its very outset to reorder its unlikelihoods, what it all might have been." But McCandless insists on the suspect, compromised nature of art in his commentary on the carpenter gothic style of his house, a passage which doubles as a description of the novel itself: "All they had were the simple dependable old materials, the wood and their hammers and saws and their own clumsy ingenuity bringing those grandiose visions the masters had left behind down to a human scale with their own little inventions, . . . a patchwork of conceits, borrowings, deceptions, the inside's a hodgepodge of good intentions like one last ridiculous effort at something worth doing even on this small a scale." Consequently, any reader who flees the disorder of life for the order of art will find cold comfort in *Carpenter's Gothic*. Ambiguities tease the most attentive of readers: Was McCandless actually in a mental hospital, and should he thus be considered mad? Is a Jew? To whom does the house's furniture, assumed throughout to be Irene McCandless's, really belong, and why does she need to ask directions to the house? There are as few tidy answers in this book as there are in life itself; "disinformation" has supplanted communication in both spheres.

Although *Carpenter's Gothic* was better received than the earlier two novels, nearly every critic berated Gaddis for his bleak outlook. Few if any pointed to the tradition of vitriolic satire to which Gaddis clearly belongs, a tradition that goes back through Nathaniel West and Mark Twain to the great eighteenth-century satirists, back through Ben Jonson and the Shakespeare of *Troilus and Cressida, Timon of Athens,* and even *King Lear,* and finally back to such classical satirists as Juvenal and Persius. All of these writers would respond as McCandless does to Liz's query: "Do you think that's why people write it? fiction I mean?" "From outrage," he responds. But Liz goes on to voice another aspect of Gaddis's aesthetic: "I think people write because things didn't come out the way they're supposed to be." "Or because we didn't," McCandless adds.

Throughout Gaddis's novels there is a sense of bitter disappointment at America for not fulfilling its potential, for not coming out the way it was supposed to. In this regard Gaddis resembles his beloved Russian novelists of the nineteenth century; in the *New York Times Book Review* William H. Gass reports a talk of Gaddis's in Lithuania where he insisted "the comic and satiric side of his work was attempting to save his version of his country as the earlier Russian writers had endeavored to redeem theirs." In the third novel, however, America seems to have reached the yellow dead-end sign planted at the bottom of the book's first page. "It's too late to try to . . .," Liz murmurs late in the novel, only to be interrupted by Paul's more final "Too late." *Carpenter's Gothic,* like F. Scott Fitzgerald's *The Great Gatsby,* seems to be saying that it is too late to reverse the tide, to restore the promise of the American dream, too late for anything more than "one last ridiculous effort at something worth doing." The smirking neighborhood kids who haunt the novel hint at a bleaker future. Even the surging energies of such novels as Gaddis's seem no guarantee against the inevitable entropic fall of America.

Informing all three of Gaddis's novels is what Wallace Stevens in "The Idea of Order at Key West" called the "blessed rage for order." Like Pope before him Gaddis uses satire to lash those institutions and social tendencies responsible for the increasing disorder in modern life. For this reason, it is clearly ridiculous to accuse Gaddis—as some critics have—of contributing to the very moral chaos he deplores. Like the classical satirists exemplified in Maynard Mack's well-known essay "The Muse of Satire," Gaddis "invites us to join . . . [what Louis I. Bredvold called] 'the invisible church of good men' everywhere, 'few though they may be—for whom things matter.' And he never lets us forget that we are at war; there is an enemy."

BIOGRAPHICAL/CRITICAL SOURCES:

BOOKS

Aldridge, John W., *In Search of Heresy,* McGraw, 1956.
Contemporary Literary Criticism, Gale, Volume 1, 1973, Volume 3, 1975, Volume 6, 1976, Volume 8, 1978, Volume 10, 1979, Volume 19, 1981, Volume 43, 1987.
Dictionary of Literary Biography, Volume 2: *American Novelists since World War II,* Gale, 1978.
Gaddis, William, *The Recognitions,* Harcourt, 1955, corrected edition, Penguin Books, 1985.
Gaddis, William, *J R,* Knopf, 1975, corrected edition, Penguin Books, 1985.
Gaddis, William, *Carpenter's Gothic,* Viking, 1985.
Gardner, John, *On Moral Fiction,* Basic Books, 1978.
Kuehl, John and Steven Moore, editors, *In Recognition of William Gaddis,* Syracuse University Press, 1984.
Madden, David, *Rediscoveries,* Crown, 1971.
Magill, Frank N., editor, *Survey of Contemporary Literature,* supplement, Salem Press, 1972.
Magill, Frank N., editor, *Literary Annual,* Salem Press, 1976.
McCaffery, Larry, editor, *Postmodern Fiction,* Greenwood Press, 1986.
Moore, Steven, *A Reader's Guide to William Gaddis's "The Recognitions,"* University of Nebraska Press, 1982.
Tanner, Tony, *City of Words,* Harper, 1971.

Wiener, Norbert, *The Human Use of Human Beings,* Houghton, 1954.

PERIODICALS

Atlantic, April, 1985.
Berkeley Gazette, March 16, 1962.
Chicago Tribune Book World, July 14, 1985.
Commentary, December, 1985.
Commonweal, April 15, 1955.
Conjunctions, Number 7, 1985, Number 8, 1985.
Contemporary Literature, winter, 1975.
Critique, winter, 1962-63, Volume XIX, number 3, 1978, Volume XXII, number 1, 1980.
Genre, Number 13, 1980.
Hollins Critic, April, 1977.
International Fiction Review, Volume X, number 2, 1983.
Los Angeles Times Book Review, July 14, 1985.
Modern Fiction Studies, Number 27, 1981-82.
Nation, April 30, 1955.
National Observer, October 11, 1975.
newspaper, Numbers 12-14, 1962.
Newsweek, March 14, 1955, November 10, 1975, July 15, 1985.
New Yorker, April 9, 1955.
New York Herald Tribune, April 14, 1962.
New York Herald Tribune Book Review, March 13, 1955.
New York Times, July 3, 1985.
New York Times Book Review, March 13,1955, July 14, 1974, November 9, 1975, June 20, 1976, June 6, 1982, July 7, 1985, February 2, 1986.
New York Times Magazine, November 15, 1987.
Observer Weekend Review, September 9, 1962.
Plain Dealer (Cleveland), October, 1975.
Publishers Weekly, July 12, 1985.
Pynchon Notes, Number 11, 1983.
Queen's Quarterly, summer, 1962.
Review of Contemporary Fiction, Volume II, number 2, 1982.
San Francisco Review of Books, February, 1976.
Saturday Review, March 12, 1955, October 4, 1975.
Scotsman, April 10, 1965.
Studies in American Humor, Number 1, 1982.
Time, March 14, 1955, July 22, 1985.
Times Literary Supplement, February 28, 1986.
TREMA, Number 2, 1977.
United States Quarterly Book Review, June, 1955.
Village Voice, November 1, 1962.
Virginia Quarterly Review, summer, 1976.
Washington Post, August 23, 1985.
Washington Post Book World, July 7, 1985.
Western Review, winter, 1956.
Wisconsin Studies in Contemporary Literature, summer, 1965.
Yale Review, September, 1951.

*   *   *

GAINES, Ernest J(ames) 1933-

PERSONAL: Born January 15, 1933, in Oscar, La. (some sources cite River Lake Plantation, near New Roads, Pointe Coupee Parish, La.); son of Manuel (a laborer) and Adrienne J. (Colar) Gaines. *Education:* Attended Vallejo Junior College; San Francisco State College (now University), B.A., 1957; graduate study at Stanford University, 1958-59.

ADDRESSES: Office—Department of English, University of Southwestern Louisiana, East University Ave., Lafayette, La.

70504. *Agent*—JCA Literary Agency, Inc., 242 West 27th St., New York, N.Y. 10001.

CAREER: "Writing, five hours a day, five days a week." Denison University, Granville, Ohio, writer in residence, 1971; Stanford University, Stanford, Calif., writer in residence, 1981; University of Southwestern Louisiana, Lafayette, professor of English and writer in residence, 1983—. Whittier College, visiting professor, 1983, and writer in residence, 1986. *Military service:* U.S. Army, 1953-55.

AWARDS, HONORS: Wallace Stegner Fellow, Stanford University, 1957; Joseph Henry Jackson Award from San Francisco Foundation, 1959, for "Comeback" (short story); award from National Endowment for the Arts, 1967; Rockefeller grant, 1970; Guggenheim fellowship, 1971; award from Black Academy of Arts and Letters, 1972; fiction gold medal from Commonwealth Club of California, 1972, for *The Autobiography of Miss Jane Pittman,* and 1984, for *A Gathering of Old Men;* award from Louisiana Library Association, 1972; honorary doctorate of letters from Denison University, 1980, Brown University, 1985, Bard College, 1985, and Louisiana State University, 1987; award for excellence of achievement in literature from San Francisco Arts Commission, 1983; D.H.L. from Whittier College, 1986; literary award from American Academy and Institute of Arts and Letters, 1987.

WRITINGS:

FICTION

Catherine Carmier (novel), Atheneum, 1964.
Of Love and Dust (novel), Dial, 1967.
Bloodline (short stories; also see below), Dial, 1968.
A Long Day in November (story originally published in *Bloodline*), Dial, 1971.
The Autobiography of Miss Jane Pittman (novel), Dial, 1971.
In My Father's House (novel), Knopf, 1978.
A Gathering of Old Men (novel), Knopf, 1983.

Contributor of stories to anthologies and periodicals.

SIDELIGHTS: The fiction of Ernest J. Gaines, including his 1971 novel *The Autobiography of Miss Jane Pittman,* is deeply rooted in the black culture and storytelling traditions of rural Louisiana where the author was born and raised. His stories have been noted for their convincing characters and powerful themes presented within authentic—often folk-like—narratives that tap into the complex world of Southern rural life. Gaines depicts the strength and dignity of his black characters in the face of numerous struggles: the dehumanizing and destructive effects of racism; the breakdown in personal relationships as a result of social pressures; and the choice between secured traditions and the sometimes radical measures necessary to bring about social change. Although the issues presented in Gaines's fiction are serious and often disturbing, "this is not hot-and-breathless, burn-baby-burn writing," Melvin Maddocks points out in *Time;* rather, it is the work of "a patient artist, a patient man." Expounding on Gaines's rural heritage, Maddocks continues: "[Gaines] sets down a story as if he were planting, spreading the roots deep, wide and firm. His stories grow organically, at their own rhythm. When they ripen at last, they do so inevitably, arriving at a climax with the absolute rightness of a folk tale." Larry McMurtry in the *New York Times Book Review* adds that as "a swimmer cannot influence the flow of a river, . . . the characters of Ernest Gaines . . . are propelled by a prose that is serene, considered and unexcited." Jerry H. Bryant in the *Iowa Review* writes that Gaines's fiction "contains the austere dignity and simplicity of ancient epic, a concern with man's most powerful emotions and the actions that arise from those emotions, and an artistic intuition that carefully keeps such passions and behavior under fictive control. Gaines may be one of our most naturally gifted story-tellers."

Gaines's boyhood experiences growing up on a Louisiana plantation provide many of the impressions upon which his stories are based. Particularly important, he told Paul Desruisseaux in the *New York Times Book Review,* were "working in the fields, going fishing in the swamps with the older people, and, especially, listening to the people who came to my aunt's house, the aunt who raised me." Although Gaines moved to California at the age of fifteen and subsequently went to college there, his fiction has been based in an imaginary Louisiana plantation region named Bayonne, which a number of critics have compared to William Faulkner's Yoknapatawpha County. Gaines has acknowledged looking to Faulkner, in addition to Ernest Hemingway, for language, and to French writers such as Gustave Flaubert and Guy de Maupassant for style. A perhaps greater influence, however, has been the writings of nineteenth-century Russian authors. In a profile by Beverly Beyette for the *Los Angeles Times,* Gaines explains that reading the works of authors such as Nikolai Gogol, Ivan Turgenev, and Anton Chekhov helped unlock the significance of his rural past. "I found something that I had not truly found in American writers," he told Beyette. "They [the Russian writers] dealt with peasantry differently. . . . I did not particularly find what I was looking for in the Southern writers. When they came to describing my own people, they did not do it the way that I knew my people to be. The Russians were not talking about my people, but about a peasantry for which they seemed to show such feeling. Reading them, I could find a way to write about my own people." That Gaines knew a different South from the one he read about in books also provided an incentive to write. "If the book you want doesn't exist, you try to make it exist," he told Joseph McLellan in the *Washington Post.* Gaines later told Beyette: "That's the book that influenced me most. . . . I tried to put it there on that shelf, and I'm still trying to do that."

Gaines's first novel, *Catherine Carmier,* is "an apprentice work more interesting for what it anticipates than for its accomplishments," notes William E. Grant in the *Dictionary of Literary Biography.* The novel chronicles the story of a young black man, Jackson Bradley, who returns to Bayonne after completing his education in California. Jackson falls in love with Catherine, the daughter of a Creole sharecropper who refuses to let members of his family associate with anyone darker than themselves, believing Creoles racially and socially superior. The novel portrays numerous clashes of loyalty: Catherine torn between her love for Jackson and love for her father; Jackson caught between a bond to the community he grew up in and the experience and knowledge he has gained in the outside world. "Both Catherine and Jackson are immobilized by the pressures of [the] rural community," writes Keith E. Byermann in the *Dictionary of Literary Biography,* which produces "twin themes of isolation and paralysis [that] give the novel an existential quality. Characters must face an unfriendly world without guidance and must make crucial choices about their lives." The characters in *Catherine Carmier*—as in much of Gaines's fiction—are faced with struggles that test the conviction of personal beliefs. Winifred L. Stoelting in *CLA Journal* explains that Gaines is concerned more "with how they [his characters] handle their decisions than with the rightness of their decisions—more often than not predetermined by social changes over which the single individual has little control."

Gaines sets *Catherine Carmier* in the time of the Civil Rights movement, yet avoids making it a primary force in the novel. Grant comments on this aspect: "In divorcing his tale from contemporary events, Gaines declares his independence from the political and social purposes of much contemporary black writing. Instead, he elects to concentrate upon those fundamental human passions and conflicts which transcend the merely social level of human existence." Grant finds Gaines "admirable" for doing this, yet also believes Jackson's credibility marred because he remains aloof from contemporary events. For Grant, the novel "seems to float outside time and place rather than being solidly anchored in the real world of the modern South." Byerman concurs, stating that the novel "is not entirely successful in presenting its major characters and their motivations." Nonetheless, he points out that in *Catherine Carmier,* "Gaines does begin to create a sense of the black community and its perceptions of the world around it. Shared ways of speaking, thinking, and relating to the dominant white society are shown through a number of minor characters."

Gaines's next novel, *Of Love and Dust,* is also a story of forbidden romance, and, as in *Catherine Carmier,* a "new world of expanding human relationships erodes the old world of love for the land and the acceptance of social and economic stratification," writes Stoelting. *Of Love and Dust* is the story of Marcus Payne, a young black man bonded out of prison by a white landowner and placed under the supervision of a Cajun overseer, Sidney Bonbon. Possessed of a rebellious and hostile nature, Marcus is a threat to Bonbon, who in turn does all that he can to break the young man's spirit. In an effort to strike back, Marcus pays special attention to the overseer's wife; the two fall in love and plot to run away. The novel ends with a violent confrontation between the two men, in which Marcus is killed. After the killing, Bonbon claims that to spare Marcus would have meant his own death at the hands of other Cajuns. Grant notes a similarity between *Of Love and Dust* and *Catherine Carmier* in that the characters are "caught up in a decadent social and economic system that determines their every action and limits their possibilities." Similarly, the two novels are marked by a "social determinism [which] shapes the lives of all the characters, making them pawns in a mechanistic world order rather than free agents."

Of Love and Dust demonstrates Gaines's development as a novelist, offering a clearer view of the themes and characters that dominate his later work. Stoelting writes that "in a more contemporary setting, the novel . . . continues Gaines's search for human dignity, and when that is lacking, acknowledges the salvation of pride," adding that "the characters themselves grow into a deeper awareness than those of [his] first novel. More sharply drawn . . . [they] are more decisive in their actions." Byerman writes that the novel "more clearly condemns the economic, social, and racial system of the South for the problems faced by its characters." Likewise, the first-person narrator in the novel—a co-worker of Marcus—"both speaks in the idiom of the place and time and instinctively asserts the values of the black community."

Gaines turns to a first-person narrator again in his next novel, *The Autobiography of Miss Jane Pittman,* which many consider to be his masterwork. Miss Jane Pittman—well over one hundred years old—relates a personal history that spans the time from the Civil War and slavery up through the Civil Rights movement of the 1960s. "To travel with Miss Pittman from adolescence to old age is to embark upon a historic journey, one staked out in the format of the novel," writes Addison Gayle, Jr., in *The Way of the New World: The Black Novel in America.* "Never mind that Miss Jane Pittman is fictitious, and that her 'autobiography,' offered up in the form of taped reminiscences, is artifice," adds Josh Greenfield in *Life,* "the effect is stunning." Gaines's gift for drawing convincing characters reaches a peak in *The Autobiography of Miss Jane Pittman.* "His is not . . . an 'art' narrative, but an authentic narrative by an authentic ex-slave, authentic even though both are Gaines's inventions," Bryant comments. "So successful is he in *becoming* Miss Jane Pittman, that when we talk about her story, we do not think of Gaines as her creator, but as her recording editor."

The character of Jane Pittman could be called an embodiment of the black experience in America. "Though Jane is the dominant personality of the narrative—observer and commentator upon history, as well as participant—in her odyssey is symbolized the odyssey of a race of people; through her eyes is revealed the grandeur of a people's journey through history," writes Gayle. "The central metaphor of the novel concerns this journey: Jane and her people, as they come together in the historic march toward dignity and freedom in Sampson, symbolize a people's march through history, breaking old patterns, though sometimes slowly, as they do." The important historical backdrop to Jane's narrative—slavery, Reconstruction, the Civil Rights movement, segregation—does not compromise, however, the detailed account of an individual. "Jane captures the experiences of those millions of illiterate blacks who never had a chance to tell their own stories," Byerman explains. "By focusing on the particular yet typical events of a small part of Louisiana, those lives are given a concreteness and specificity not possible in more general histories."

In his fourth novel, *In My Father's House,* Gaines focuses on a theme which appears in varying degrees throughout his fiction: the alienation between fathers and sons. As the author told Desruisseaux: "In my books there always seems to be fathers and sons searching for each other. That's a theme I've worked with since I started writing. Even when the father was not in the story, I've dealt with his absence and its effects on his children. And that is the theme of this book." *In My Father's House* tells of a prominent civil rights leader and reverend (Phillip Martin) who, at the peak of his career, is confronted with a troubled young man named Robert X. Although Robert's identity is initially a mystery, eventually he is revealed to be one of three offspring from a love affair the reverend had in an earlier, wilder life. Martin hasn't seen or attempted to locate his family for more than twenty years. Robert arrives to confront and kill the father whose neglect he sees as responsible for the family's disintegration: his sister has been raped, his brother imprisoned for the murder of her attacker, and his mother reduced to poverty, living alone. Although the son's intent to kill his father is never carried out, the reverend is forced "to undergo a long and painful odyssey through his own past and the labyrinthine streets of Baton Rouge to learn what really happened to his first family," writes William Burke in the *Dictionary of Literary Biography Yearbook.* McMurtry notes that as the book traces the lost family, "we have revealed to us an individual, a marriage, a community and a region, but with such an unobtrusive marshaling of detail that we never lose sight of the book's central thematic concern: the profoundly destructive consequences of the breakdown of parentage, of a father's abandonment of his children and the terrible and irrevocable consequences of such an abandonment."

Burke writes that *In My Father's House* presents the particular problem of manhood for the black male, which he notes as a recurring theme in Gaines's fiction: "Phillip Martin's failure to keep his first family whole, to honor his and [his companion's] love by marriage, and the dissipation of the first half of his adult life—these unfortunate events are clearly a consequence of Mar-

tin's fear of accepting the responsibilities of black manhood." Burke highlights the accumulated effects of racism on black males, and cites Gaines's comments to Desruisseaux: "You must understand that the blacks who were brought here as slaves were prevented from becoming the men that they could be. . . . A *man* can speak up, he can do things to protect himself, his home and his family, but the slaves could never do that. If the white said the slave was wrong, he was wrong. . . . So eventually the blacks started stepping over the line, [saying] 'Damn what *you* think I'm supposed to be—I will be what I ought to be. And if I must die to do it, I'll die'. . . . Quite a few of my characters step over that line."

A Gathering of Old Men, Gaines's most recent novel, presents a cast of aging Southern black men who, after a life of subordination and intimidation, make a defiant stand against injustice. Seventeen of them, together with the 30-year-old white heiress of a deteriorating Louisiana plantation, plead guilty to murdering a hostile member (Beau Boutan) of a violent Cajun clan. While a confounded sheriff and vengeful family wait to lynch the black they've decided is guilty, the group members—toting recently fired shotguns—surround the dead man and "confess" their motives. "Each man tells of the accumulated frustrations of his life—raped daughters, jailed sons, public insults, economic exploitation—that serve as sufficient motive for murder," writes Byerman. "Though Beau Boutan is seldom the immediate cause of their anger, he clearly represents the entire white world that has deprived them of their dignity and manhood. The confessions serve as ritual purgings of all the hostility and self-hatred built up over the years." Fifteen or so characters—white, black, and Cajun—advance the story through individual narrations, creating "thereby a range of social values as well as different perspectives on the action," notes Byerman. Reynolds Price writes in the *New York Times Book Review* that the black narrators "are nicely distinguished from one another in rhythm and idiom, in the nature of what they see and report, especially in their specific laments for past passivity in the face of suffering." The accumulated effect, observes Elaine Kendall in the *Los Angeles Times Book Review,* is that the "individual stories coalesce into a single powerful tale of subjugation, exploitation and humiliation at the hands of landowners." Price comments that although "some of them, especially at the beginning, are a little long-winded and repetitive, in the manner of country preachers[,] . . . a patient reader will sense the power of their stories through their dead-level voices, which speak not from the heart of a present fear but from lifetimes of humiliation and social impotence. They are choosing now to take a stand, on ground where they've yielded for centuries—ground that is valuable chiefly through their incessant labor."

Another theme of *A Gathering of Old Men,* according to Ben Forkner in *America,* is "the simple, natural dispossession of old age, of the traditional and well-loved values of the past, the old trades and the old manners, forced to give way to modern times." Sam Cornish writes in the *Christian Science Monitor* that the novel's "characters—both black and white—understand that, before the close of the novel, the new South must confront the old, and all will be irrevocably changed. Gaines portrays a society that will be altered by the deaths of its 'old men,' and so presents an allegory about the passing of the old and birth of the new."

Alice Walker writes in the *New York Times Book Review* that Gaines "claims and revels in the rich heritage of Southern Black people and their customs; the community he feels with them is unmistakable and goes deeper even than pride. . . . Gaines is mellow with historical reflection, supple with wit, relaxed and expansive because he does not equate his people with failure." Gaines has been criticized by some, however, who feel his writing does not focus directly on problems facing blacks. Gaines responds to Desruisseaux that he feels "too many blacks have been writing to tell whites all about 'the problems,' instead of writing something that all people, including their own, could find interesting, could enjoy." Gaines has also remarked that more can be achieved than strictly writing novels of protest. In an interview for *San Francisco,* the author states: "So many of our writers have not read any farther back than [Richard Wright's] *Native Son.* So many of our novels deal only with the great city ghettos; that's all we write about, as if there's nothing else." Gaines continues: "We've only been living in these ghettos for 75 years or so, but the other 300 years—I think this is worth writing about."

MEDIA ADAPTATIONS: "The Autobiography of Miss Jane Pittman," adapted from Gaines's novel, aired on the Columbia Broadcasting System (CBS-TV), January 31, 1974, starring Cicely Tyson in the title role; the special won nine Emmy Awards. "The Sky Is Gray," a short story originally published in *Bloodline,* was adapted for public television in 1980. "A Gathering of Old Men," adapted from Gaines's novel, aired on CBS-TV, May 10, 1987, starring Lou Gossett, Jr., and Richard Widmark.

BIOGRAPHICAL/CRITICAL SOURCES:

BOOKS

Authors in the News, Volume 1, Gale, 1976.
Bruck, Peter, editor, *The Black American Short Story in the Twentieth Century: A Collection of Critical Essays,* B. R. Gruner (Amsterdam), 1977.
Concise Dictionary of American Literary Biography: Broadening Views, 1968-1988, Gale, 1989.
Contemporary Literary Criticism, Gale, Volume 3, 1975, Volume 11, 1979, Volume 18, 1981.
Dictionary of Literary Biography, Gale, Volume 2: *American Novelists since World War II,* 1978, Volume 33: *Afro-American Fiction Writers after 1955,* 1984.
Dictionary of Literary Biography Yearbook: 1980, Gale, 1981.
Gayle, Addison, Jr., *The Way of the New World: The Black Novel in America,* Doubleday, 1975.
Hicks, Jack, *In the Singer's Temple: Prose Fictions of Barthelme, Gaines, Brautigan, Piercy, Kesey, and Kosinski,* University of North Carolina Press, 1981.
O'Brien, John, editor, *Interview with Black Writers,* Liveright, 1973.

PERIODICALS

America, June 2, 1984.
Black American Literature Forum, Volume XI, 1977.
Chicago Tribune Book World, October 30, 1983.
Christian Science Monitor, December 2, 1983.
CLA Journal, March, 1971, December, 1975.
Iowa Review, winter, 1972.
Life, April 30, 1971.
Los Angeles Times, March 2, 1983.
Los Angeles Times Book Review, January 1, 1984.
Nation, February 5, 1968, April 5, 1971, January 14, 1984.
Negro Digest, November, 1967, January, 1968, January, 1969.
New Orleans Review, Volume I, 1969, Volume III, 1972.
New Republic, December 26, 1983.
New Statesman, September 2, 1973, February 10, 1984.
Newsweek, June 16, 1969, May 3, 1971.
New Yorker, October 24, 1983.
New York Times, July 20, 1978.

New York Times Book Review, November 19, 1967, May 23, 1971, June 11, 1978, October 30, 1983.
Observer, February 5, 1984.
San Francisco, July, 1974.
Southern Review, Volume X, 1974.
Studies in Short Fiction, summer, 1975.
Time, May 10, 1971, December 27, 1971.
Times Literary Supplement, February 10, 1966, March 16, 1973, April 6, 1984.
Village Voice Literary Supplement, October, 1983.
Washington Post, January 13, 1976.
Washington Post Book World, June 18, 1978, September 21, 1983.

* * *

GALBRAITH, John Kenneth 1908-

PERSONAL: Born October 15, 1908, in Iona Station, Ontario, Canada; son of William Archibald (a politician and farmer) and Catherine (Kendall) Galbraith; married Catherine Atwater, September 17, 1937; children: John Alan, Peter, James, Douglas (deceased). *Education:* University of Toronto, B.S. (agriculture), 1931; University of California, Berkeley, M.S., 1933, Ph.D., 1934; attended Cambridge University, 1937-38. *Politics:* Democrat.

ADDRESSES: Home—30 Francis Ave., Cambridge, Mass. 02138; Newfane, Vt. (summer); Gstaad, Switzerland (winter). *Office*—American Academy and Institute of Arts and Letters, 633 West 155th St., New York, N.Y. 10032-7599.

CAREER: Harvard University, Cambridge, Mass., instructor and tutor, 1934-39; Princeton University, Princeton, N.J., assistant professor of economics, 1939-42; U.S. Office of Price Administration, Washington, D.C., administrator in charge of price division, 1941-42, department administrator, 1942-43; member of board of editors, *Fortune,* 1943-48; Harvard University, lecturer, 1948-49, Paul M. Warburg Professor of Economics, 1949-75, named professor emeritus; U.S. Ambassador to India, 1961-63. Reith Lecturer, 1966; visiting fellow, Trinity College, Cambridge, 1969-70. Director of U.S. Strategic Bombing Survey, 1945, and Office of Economic Security Policy, U.S. Department of State, 1946. Presidential advisor to John F. Kennedy and Lyndon B. Johnson.

MEMBER: American Academy and Institute of Arts and Letters (president, 1984—), American Academy of Arts and Sciences (fellow), American Economic Association (president, 1972), Americans for Democratic Action (chairman, 1967-69), American Farm Economists Association, Twentieth Century Fund (trustee), Century Club (New York), Harvard Club (New York), Federal City (Washington, D.C.), Saturday (Boston).

AWARDS, HONORS: Research fellow, University of California, 1931-34; fellow, Social Science Research Council, 1937-38; Medal of Freedom, 1946; LL.D., Bard College, 1958, Miami University (Ohio), 1959, University of Toronto, 1961, Brandeis University, 1963, University of Massachusetts, 1963, University of Guelph, 1965, University of Saskatchewan, 1965, Rhode Island College, 1966, Boston College, 1967, Hobart and William Smith Colleges, 1967, University of Paris, 1975, in addition to others; Sarah Josepha Hale Award, Friends of the Richards Free Library, 1967; recipient of President's Certificate of Merit.

WRITINGS:

California County Expenditures, University of California Press, 1934.

Branch Banking and Its Bearing upon Agricultural Credit, [Lancaster, Pa.], 1934.

(With Henry Sturgis Dennison) *Modern Competition and Business Policy,* Oxford University Press, 1938.

(Editor with Carl J. Friedrich) *Public Policy, 1953-1955,* Littauer Center, 1940.

(Contributor) *Can Europe Unite?,* Foreign Policy Association (New York City), 1950.

America and Western Europe, Public Affairs Committee (New York City), 1950.

A Theory of Price Control, Harvard University Press, 1952, reprinted with new introduction by Galbraith, 1980.

American Capitalism: The Concept of Countervailing Power, Houghton, 1952, revised edition, 1956, reprinted with new introduction by Galbraith, M. E. Sharpe, 1980.

Economics and the Art of Controversy, Rutgers University Press, 1955.

The Great Crash, 1929, Houghton, 1955, reprinted with new introduction by Galbraith, 1988.

(With Richard H. Holton and in collaboration with others) *Marketing Efficiency in Puerto Rico,* Harvard University Press, 1955.

Economic Planning in India, Indian Statistical Institute, 1956.

(With Luther G. Griffith) *Perspectives on Conservation: Essays on America's Natural Resources,* edited by Henry Jarret, Johns Hopkins Press, 1958.

Journey to Poland and Yugoslavia, Harvard University Press, 1958.

The Affluent Society, Houghton, 1958, 4th edition, 1984.

The Liberal Hour, Houghton, 1960.

(Contributor) Yigael Yadin, *The Past Speaks to the Present,* Granada TV Network Limited, 1962.

Economic Development in Perspective, Harvard University Press, 1962, revised edition published as *Economic Development,* 1964.

The Economics of Banking Operations, McGill University Press, 1963.

(Under pseudonym Mark Epernay) *The McLandress Dimension* (satire), Houghton, 1963, revised edition, New American Library, 1968.

The Scotch (memoir), Houghton, 1964, 2nd edition, 1985 (published in England as *Made to Last,* Hamish Hamilton, 1964, and as *The Non-potable Scotch: A Memoir on the Clansman in Canada,* Penguin, 1964).

(With others) *Economic Strategy and the Third Plan,* Taplinger, 1964.

The Underdeveloped Country (text of five radio broadcasts aired fall, 1965), Canadian Broadcasting Corp., 1965.

Economic Discipline, Houghton, 1967.

The New Industrial State, Houghton, 1967, 4th edition, 1985.

How to Get Out of Vietnam: A Workable Solution to the Worst Problem of Our Time, New American Library, 1967.

Subdesarrollo y conducta social, Ediciones Tercer Mundo (Bogota, Colombia), 1967.

The Triumph: A Novel of Modern Diplomacy (Book-of-the-Month Club selection), Houghton, 1968, reprinted with new introduction, Arbor House, 1984.

(With Mohinder Singh Randhawa) *Indian Painting: The Scene, Themes and Legends,* Houghton, 1968.

How to Control the Military, Doubleday, 1969.

Ambassador's Journal: A Personal Account of the Kennedy Years, Houghton, 1969.

(With others) *National Priorities,* Public Affairs Press, 1969.

Who Needs the Democrats, and What It Takes to Be Needed, Doubleday, 1970.

(Author of introduction) David Levine, *No Known Survivors: David Levine's Political Prank,* Gambit, 1970.

(With others) *La crise des societes industrielles,* [Paris], 1971.

A Contemporary Guide to Economics, Peace, and Laughter (essays), edited by Andrea D. Williams, Houghton, 1971.

Economics and the Public Purpose, Houghton, 1973.

A China Passage, Houghton, 1973, reprinted, Paragon House, 1989.

(Author of introduction) Frank Moraes and Edward Howe, editors, *India,* McGraw-Hill, 1974.

John Kenneth Galbraith Introduces India, edited by Moraes and Howe, Deutsch, 1974.

Of Men and Foreign Policy (sound recording), Center for the Study of Democratic Institutions (Santa Barbara, Calif.), 1974.

Money: Whence It Came, Where It Went, Houghton, 1975.

(With G. G. Johnson, Jr.) *The Economic Effects of the Federal Public Works Expenditures, 1933-1938,* Da Capo, 1975.

The Age of Uncertainty (based on television series produced by British Broadcasting Corp., 1977; Book-of-the-Month Club selection), G. K. Hall, 1977.

The Galbraith Reader: From the Works of John Kenneth Galbraith, selected and with commentary by the editors of Gambit, Gambit, 1977.

(With Nicole Salinger) *Almost Everyone's Guide to Economics,* Houghton, 1978.

Annals of an Abiding Liberal, edited by Williams, Houghton, 1979.

The Nature of Mass Poverty, Harvard University Press, 1979.

A Life in Our Times: Memoirs, Houghton, 1981.

Galbraith na UnB: Conferencias e comentarios de um simposio internacional realizado de 25 a 28 de agosto de 1980, Editora Universidade de Brasilia (Brasilia, Brazil), 1981.

The Anatomy of Power, Houghton, 1983.

The Voice of the Poor: Essays in Economic and Political Persuasion, Harvard University Press, 1983.

Essays from the Poor to the Rich, Bharatiya Vidya Bhavan, 1983.

(With Paul W. McCracken) *Reaganomics: Meaning, Means, and Ends,* Free Press, 1983.

A View from the Stands: Of People, Politics, Military Power, and the Arts, edited by Williams, Houghton, 1986.

Economics in Perspective: A Critical History, Houghton, 1987.

(With Stanislav Menshikov) *Capitalism, Communism and Coexistence: From the Bitter Past to a Better Present,* Houghton, 1988.

Strategy of Export-Led Growth, LBJ School of Public Affairs, 1988.

Balancing Acts: Technology, Finance, and the American Future, Basic Books, 1989.

A Tenured Professor (novel), Houghton, 1990.

Author of numerous drafts of speeches for political leaders, including Franklin D. Roosevelt, Adlai Stevenson, Lyndon B. Johnson, Robert Kennedy, and Edward Kennedy. Editor of "Harvard Economic Studies" series, Harvard University Press. Contributor to scholarly journals. Reviewer, under pseudonym Herschel McLandress, of the pseudonymous *Report from Iron Mountain.*

Galbraith's works have been translated into numerous foreign languages.

SIDELIGHTS: John Kenneth Galbraith is considered among the twentieth century's most influential economists and foremost writers on economics. In addition to authoring over forty books, including such classic economic texts as *The Affluent Society, The New Industrial State,* and *Economics and the Public Purpose,* the versatile Canadian-born Galbraith has also served as advisor to several U.S. presidents, as the U.S. ambassador to India, and is a world-travelled professor and lecturer on economics. Galbraith has introduced several key phrases into the vernacular of economists and layman, terms such as "affluent society," "conventional wisdom," and "countervailing power." Paul A. Samuelson, a Nobel Prize-winning economist and former advisor to President John F. Kennedy, once called John Kenneth Galbraith the "non-economist's economist." R. Z. Sheppard in *Time* summarizes Galbraith's perpsective in this way: "He confronts the world and its problems as a supremely rational man—and something of an entertainer. . . . Behind this elegant raillery, Galbraith maintains a cool, doctor-patient relationship with the world. The combination of wit and seriousness makes him a distinguished popularizer and advocate who can waltz through wars, revolutions, famines, depressions and global follies without ever losing the crease of his Savile Row prose."

The Affluent Society, Galbraith's major assessment of the U.S. economic situation, has become a key economic reference source. First published in 1958, it has appeared on the reading lists of colleges and universities throughout the United States, and has been published in a dozen foreign languages, including Gujarte, Hindu, and Tamil. In *The Affluent Society,* Galbraith raises the question of priorities and how wealth is to be divided; he poses the same question again in *The New Industrial State.* "Galbraith is an antenna and a synthesizer," says Samuelson. "He senses what is in the air and puts it together and packages it." Galbraith's opinions have been the topics of much debate among economists, yet, according to Galbraith, economists are "trapped by assumptions and preconceptions which belong to an economic order that has passed into history," writes Harry Magdoff. Galbraith believes that "economics, as it is conventionally taught, is in part a system of belief designed less to reveal truth than to reassure its communicants about established social arrangements."

Galbraith is also an outspoken critic of governmental policy, and a continual "purveyor of predictions," according to *Time.* He credits John Maynard Keynes with influencing his own conversion to economics and Henry Luce for teaching him to write. Paul Booth remarks that "the bulk of Galbraith's proposals are for intellectuals," because Galbraith "calls for using the power he believes they have to solve the problems he outlines." And it is the work of intellectuals—their strategies for change—that give body and substance to Galbraith's theories. His book, *The Great Crash, 1929,* is one of his first major statements on the importance of change in our economic system, although he had carefully defined his principles of economics in *A Theory of Price Control* and again in *American Capitalism: The Concept of Countervailing Power.*

Before *American Capitalism,* Galbraith had written *A Theory of Price Control,* which, although he claims "maybe fifty people read it had it had absolutely zero influence," was to him "the best book I ever wrote in many ways." He decided at that time to "engage a larger audience . . . [because then,] other economists would have to react to me. My work would not be ignored." In many ways, *The Great Crash, 1929* explains Galbraith's feelings about the need for our present society to be open to criticism and, thus, to want to change for what may be a better way of life. Galbraith admits that "many things in the stock market today grow from the factors that were at work in 1929. . . . We have a new generation of innocents . . . who believe there is something about computers that's certain to make them rich." D. F. Dowd in *Nation* recommends *1929* to "those who have grown complacent about the present."

Galbraith, who describes himself as a writer, has assigned himself the task of explaining to the public the most vital issues: the poor and big business. (Galbraith claims his height, 6 feet 8 inches, has much to do with the responsibilities he has assumed. He observed *The Scotch:* "The superior confidence which people repose in the tall man is well merited. Being tall, he is more visible than other men and being more visible, he is much more closely watched. In consequence, his behavior is far better than that of smaller man. He's lived with the comforting belief that everyone around him is abnormally short.") Victor Navasky in the *New York Times Book Review* recounts Galbraith's method of presenting these issues: "Galbraith told me that his system is four drafts, and then on the fifth, he put in 'that note of spontaneity everybody likes. It is very important to develop your basic system of defense. Many people have a good case but affirm it by overstating it. My device is to put my case in the most moderate form and then draw the attention of the reader to my extreme moderation.' " One of Galbraith's trademarks is his entertaining and witting manner of writing; however, as Walter Russell Mead notes in the *Los Angeles Times Book Review:* "Galbraith's irreverent wit and lucid style lead many to underestimate his importance in the history of economic thought. Like Adam Smith, clearly the economist for whom Galbraith feels the greatest admiration and personal affinity, Galbraith has spent a career attacking the entrenched errors of conventional wisdom."

Undoubtedly, Galbraith's dry wit is one of the reasons for the success of *The Affluent Society.* Gerald Carson in the *Chicago Sunday Tribune* thinks Galbraith has never been in better form "as discussant and epigrammatist. . . . [He demonstrates that] we are fighting our modern economic battles with antique weapons: muskets in the missile age. Galbraith can hit a vested interest at any range and shoot folly as it flies, in business thinking, in Washington circles, even in the professorate." The question Galbraith asks, according to Robert Lekachman in the *New Republic,* is "haven't things got twisted when we produce in order to provide jobs, instead of get jobs in order to produce?" E. L. Dale in the *New York Times* points out that Galbraith finds the urgency of production "a myth." A treatise on the difficulty of avoiding depressions and inflation in our present society, *The Affluent Society* raises, in particular, three issues. Robert L. Heibroner in the *New York Herald Tribune Book Review* (who claims he has referred to *The Affluent Society* more than to any other book in the past 10 years) explains: "One of these is the moral problem of how an Affluent Society may be prevented from becoming merely a Rich one. A second is the efficacy of Mr. Galbraith's reforms to offset the inertia and the vested interests of a powerful social structure. A third is what form of social cohesion can replace our troublesome but useful absorption in Production." Booth writes that, according to Galbraith, "private wants could [have been] satisfied by the pluralistic economy but 'public squalor' was the outcome, for no force represented the general interest of the society in the pluralistic give-and-take of the economy," writes Booth.

"The test of writing about political economy is its ability to explain individual phenomena with a more fundamental analysis," and, according to Booth, Galbraith's *The New Industrial State* "meets that test." S. S. Smith in *Library Journal* finds that "Galbraith is a political economist like Adam Smith, Marx and Keynes. He is also, like Veblen, a social satirist, but possessed of a deadpan Scots Canadian irony and humor." This description seems to accurately characterize Galbraith as author of *The New Industrial State.* Scores of reviewers have concerned themselves with the corporate and government issues Galbraith presents therein. Probably the economic publishing event of the year in

1967, *The New Industrial State* was the stuff of a thousand debates. Galbraith believes, contrary to established liberal doctrine, that "it is no longer possible to accept the view that individual free choice is the guiding force in the economic system." He demonstrates that modern business "uses its political influence to persuade the Government to maintain full employment and total demand for all output of all firms. Moreover, by advertising, it attempts to persuade the consumer to buy what it has to sell," writes Alan Day. Galbraith "addresses himself to the social class which has been gaining in power—'the educational and scientific estate responsible for producing the educated talent and new technological knowledge on which the industrial system increasingly depends'—urging them to understand their society and to use their power to correct its deficiencies," the *Spectator* reviewer writes. *Spectator* points out that, in contrast to Marx, "Galbraith has a unique personal knowledge of the mainsprings of power in modern society and he writes extremely readably."

As a consequence of the economic, social, and political issues he raises, "Galbraith finds the quality of American life defective," writes Saul Maloff. "In an industrial system with its 'peculiar association with weapons of unimaginable ferocity and destructiveness,' he asks, 'if at all, is human personality to be saved?'" Galbraith has no easy answers, "but it [is] his vision, of the good in a humane society, that 'esthetic goals will have pride of place' and the 'subordinate' industrial system will become an 'essentially technical arrangement for providing convenient goods and services in adequate volume.' He calls upon those who agree with his analysis to reject the system's 'monopoly of social purpose.' Therein 'the chance for salvation lies.'"

BIOGRAPHICAL/CRITICAL SOURCES:

BOOKS

Contemporary Issues Criticism, Volume 1, Gale, 1982.
Galbraith, John Kenneth, *A Life in Our Times: Memoirs,* Houghton, 1981.
Hancock, M. D., and G. Sjoberg, editors, *Politics in the Post-Welfare State,* Columbia University Press, 1972.
Reisman, D. A., *Galbraith and Market Capitalism,* New York University Press, 1980.
Reisman, D. A., *Tawney, Galbraith, and Adam Smith,* St. Martin's, 1982.

PERIODICALS

Atlantic Monthly, January, 1987.
Chicago Tribune, June 1, 1958.
Christian Science Monitor, May 29, 1958, June 17, 1967.
Library Journal, September 1, 1960.
Look, March 27, 1970.
Los Angeles Times Book Review, March 4, 1990.
Motive, March, 1968.
Nation, July 30, 1955.
New Republic, June 9, 1958, July 8, 1967.
Newsweek, June 26, 1967, July 3, 1967.
New Yorker, January 6, 1968.
New York Herald Tribune Book Review, June 1, 1958.
New York Times, June 1, 1958, February 24, 1990.
New York Times Book Review, June 25, 1967, February 11, 1990.
Observer Review, June 3, 1967.
Playboy (interview), June, 1968.
Saturday Review, August 13, 1960.
Spectator, November 10, 1967.
Time, February 16, 1968.
Tribune Books (Chicago), February 18, 1990.
Washington Post Book World, February 11, 1990.

GALLANT, Mavis 1922-

PERSONAL: Born Mavis de Trafford Young, August 11, 1922, in Montreal, Quebec, Canada. *Education:* Attended secondary schools in the United States and Canada.

ADDRESSES: Home—14 rue Jean Ferrandi, Paris, France. *Agent*—Georges Borchardt, 136 East 57th St., New York, N.Y. 10022.

CAREER: The Standard, Montreal, Quebec, feature writer and critic, 1944-50; free-lance writer, 1950—. Writer in residence at University of Toronto, 1983-84.

MEMBER: PEN, Authors Guild, Authors League of America.

AWARDS, HONORS: Named Officer of the Order of Canada, 1981; Governor General's Award, 1981, for *Home Truths: Selected Canadian Stories;* honorary doctorates from University of St. Anne, Nova Scotia, and York University, Ontario, both 1984; Canada-Australia Literary Prize, 1985.

WRITINGS:

FICTION

The Other Paris (short stories), Houghton, 1956, reprinted, G. K. Hall, 1986.
Green Water, Green Sky (novel), Houghton, 1959, reprinted, Macmillan, 1982.
My Heart Is Broken: Eight Stories and a Short Novel, Random House, 1964, reprinted, General Publishing Company (Toronto), 1982 (published in England as *An Unmarried Man's Summer,* Heinemann, 1965).
A Fairly Good Time (novel), Random House, 1970, reprinted, G. K. Hall, 1986.
The Pegnitz Junction: A Novella and Five Short Stories, Random House, 1973.
The End of the World and Other Stories, McClelland & Stewart, 1974.
From the Fifteenth District: A Novella and Eight Short Stories, Random House, 1979.
Home Truths: Selected Canadian Stories, Macmillan, 1981.
Overhead in a Balloon: Stories of Paris, Macmillan, 1985.
In Transit: Twenty Stories, Random House, 1989.

OTHER

(Author of introduction) Gabrielle Russier, *The Affair of Gabrielle Russier,* Knopf, 1971.
(Author of introduction) J. Hibbert, *The War Brides,* PMA (Toronto), 1978.
What Is To Be Done? (play; first produced in Toronto at Tarragon Theatre, November 11, 1982), Quadrant, 1983.
Paris Notebooks: Essays and Reviews, Macmillan, 1986.

Contributor of essays, short stories, and reviews to numerous periodicals, including *New Yorker, New York Times Book Review, New Republic,* and *New York Review of Books.*

WORK IN PROGRESS: A novel.

SIDELIGHTS: Canadian-born Mavis Gallant is widely considered one of the finest crafters of short stories in the English language. Her works, most of which appear initially in the *New Yorker* magazine, are praised for sensitive evocation of setting and penetrating delineation of character. In the words of *Maclean's* magazine contributor Mark Abley, Gallant "is virtually unrivalled at the art of short fiction," an exacting artist whose pieces reveal "an ability to press a lifetime into a few resonant pages as well as a desire to show the dark side of comedy and the humor that lurks behind despair." *Time* magazine correspondent Timothy Foote calls Gallant "one of the prose masters of the age," and adds that no modern writer "casts a colder eye on life, on death and all the angst and eccentricity in between." Since 1950 Gallant has lived primarily in Paris, but she has also spent extended periods of time in the United States, Canada, and other parts of Europe. Not surprisingly, her stories and novellas show a wide range of place and period; many feature refugees and expatriates forced into self-discernment by rootlessness. As Anne Tyler notes in the *New York Times Book Review,* each Gallant fiction "is densely-woven, . . . rich in people and plots—a miniature world, more satisfying than many full-scale novels. . . . There is a sense of limitlessness: each story is like a peephole opening out into a very wide landscape."

Dictionary of Literary Biography essayist Ronald B. Hatch observes that the subject of children, "alone, frightened, or unloved," recurs often in Gallant's work. This, he notes, reflects Gallant's own difficult youth. The author underwent a solitary and transient childhood, attending seventeen different schools in the United States and Canada. Her father died while she was in grade school, and her mother, soon remarried, moved to the United States, leaving the child with strangers. Speaking to how her formative years influenced her writing, Gallant told the *New York Times:* "I think it's true that in many, many of the things I write, someone has vanished. And it's often the father. And there is often a sense that nothing is very safe, and you're often walking on a very thin crust." One advantage of Gallant's farflung education has endured, however. As a primary schooler in her native Montreal, she learned French, and she remained bilingual into adulthood.

Gallant matured into a resourceful young woman determined to be a writer. At the age of twenty-one she became a reporter with the Montreal *Standard,* a position that honed her writing talents while it widened her variety of experiences. Journalism, she told the *New York Times,* "turned out to be so valuable, because I saw the interiors of houses I wouldn't have seen otherwise. And a great many of the things, particularly in . . . [fiction] about Montreal, that I was able to describe later, it was because I had seen them, I had gone into them as a journalist. If I got on with the people, I had no hesitation about seeing them again. . . . I went right back and took them to lunch. I could see some of those rooms, and see the wallpaper, and what they ate, and what they wore, and how they spoke, . . . and the way they treated their children. I drew it all in like blotting paper." From these encounters Gallant began to write stories. In 1950 she decided to leave Montreal and begin a new life as a serious fiction writer in Paris. At the same time she began to send stories to the *New Yorker* for publication. Her second submission, a piece called "Madeline's Birthday," was accepted, beginning a four-decade relationship with the prestigious periodical. Gallant used the six hundred dollar check for her story to finance her move abroad. Paris has been her permanent home ever since.

Expatriation provided Gallant with new challenges and insights that have formed central themes in her fiction. In *The Other Paris* and subsequent story collections, her characters are "the refugee, the rootless, the emotionally disinherited," to quote a *Times Literary Supplement* reviewer, who adds: "It is a world of displacement where journeys are allegorical and love is inadequate." Gallant portrays postwar people locked into archaic cultural presuppositions; often dispossessed of their homes by haphazard circumstances, they are bewildered and insecure, seeking refuge in etiquette and other shallow symbols of tradition. *Time* correspondent Patricia Blake maintains that Gallant's "natural subject is the varieties of spiritual exile. . . . All [her characters] are bearers of a metaphorical 'true passport' that transcends na-

tionality and signifies internal freedom. For some this serves as a safe-conduct to independence. For others it is a guarantee of loneliness and despair." Gallant also presents the corollary theme of the past's inexorable grip on its survivors. In her stories, *New York Review of Books* essayist V. S. Pritchett contends, "we are among the victims of the wars in Europe which have left behind pockets of feckless exiles. . . . History has got its teeth into them and has regurgitated them and left them bizarre and perplexed." Whether immersed in the past or on the run from it, vainly trying to "turn over a new leaf," Gallant's characters "convey with remarkable success a sense of the amorphousness, the mess of life," to quote *Books and Bookmen* contributor James Brockway. Spiritually and physically marginal, they yearn paradoxically for safety, order, and freedom. "Hearts are not broken in Mavis Gallant's stories . . .," concludes Eve Auchincloss in the *New York Review of Books.* "Roots are cut, and her subject is the nature of the life that is led when the roots are not fed."

Most critics applaud Gallant's ability to inhabit the minds of her characters without resort to condescension or sentimentality. Abley claims that the author "can write with curiosity and perceptiveness about the kind of people who would never read a word of her work—a rarer achievement than it might sound. She is famous for not forgiving and not forgetting; her unkindness is usually focused on women and men who have grown complacent, never reflecting on their experience, no longer caring about their world. With such people she is merciless, yet with others, especially children bruised by neglect, she is patient and even kind. In the end, perhaps, understanding can be a means of forgiveness. One hopes so, because Mavis Gallant understands us terribly well." In the *Chicago Tribune Book World* Civia Tamarkin suggests that Gallant's works "impose a haunting vision of man trapped in an existential world. Each of the stories is a sensitive, though admirably understated, treatment of isolation, loneliness, and despair. Together they build an accumulating sense of the frustrating indifference of the cosmos to human hopes."

Gallant is best known for her short stories and novellas, but she has also written two novels, *Green Water, Green Sky* and *A Fairly Good Time.* Hatch contends that these works continue the author's "exploration of the interaction between an individual's thoughts and his external world." In *Green Water, Green Sky,* according to Constance Pendergast in the *Saturday Review,* Gallant "writes of the disaster that results from a relationship founded on the mutual need and antagonism of a woman and her daughter, where love turns inward and festers, bringing about inevitably the disintegration of both characters." Lighter in tone, *A Fairly Good Time* follows the blundering adventures of a Canadian, Shirley Perrigny, who lives in France. Hatch notes that the novel "may well be the funniest of all her works. . . . As a satire on the self-satisfied habits of the French, *A Fairly Good Time* proves enormously high-spirited. Yet the novel offers more than satire. As the reader becomes intimately acquainted with Shirley, her attempts to defeat the rigidity of French logic by living in the moment come to seem zany but commendable."

Home Truths: Selected Canadian Stories, first published in 1981, has proven to be one of Gallant's most popular collections. In Abley's view, the volume "bears repeated witness to the efforts made by this solitary, distant writer to come to terms with her own past and her own country." The stories focus on footloose Canadians who are alienated from their families or cultures; the characters try "to puzzle out the ground rules of their situations, which are often senseless, joyless and contradictory," to quote *Nation* reviewer Barbara Fisher Williamson. *New York Times Book Review* contributor Maureen Howard observes that in

Home Truths, Canada "is not a setting, a backdrop; it is an adversary, a constraint, a comfort, the home that is almost understandable, if not understanding. It is at once deadly real and haunting, phantasmagoric." Phyllis Grosskurth elaborates in *Saturday Night:* "Clearly [Gallant] is still fighting a battle with the Canada she left many years ago. Whether or not that country has long since vanished is irrelevant, for it has continued to furnish the world of her imagination. . . . She knows that whatever she writes will be in the language that shaped her sensibility, though the Canada of her youth imposed restraints from which she could free herself only by geographic separation. Wherever she is, she writes out of her roots. . . . Her Montreal is a state of mind, an emotion recalled, an apprenticeship for life." *Home Truths* won the 1981 Governor General's Award, Canada's highest literary honor. *Books in Canada* correspondent Wayne Grady concludes that it is not a vision of Gallant's native country that emerges in the book, but rather "a vision of the world, of life: it is in that nameless country of the mind inhabited by all real writers, regardless of nativity, that Mavis Gallant lives. We are here privileged intruders."

The *New Yorker* has been the initial forum for almost all of Gallant's short fiction—and much of her nonfiction, too—since 1950. Critics, among them *Los Angeles Times* reviewer Elaine Kendall, feel that Gallant's work meets the periodical's high literary standards; in Kendall's words, Gallant's stories "seem the epitome of the magazine's traditional style." Readers of the *New Yorker* expect to find challenging stories, and according to Hatch, Gallant offers such challenges. "The reader finds that he cannot comprehend the fictional world as something given, but must engage with the text to bring its meanings into being," Hatch writes. "As in life, so in a Gallant story, no handy editor exists ready to point the moral." Foote expresses a similar opinion. "Gallant rarely leaves helpful signs and messages that readers tend to expect of 'literature': This way to the Meaning or This story is about the Folly of Love . . .," the critic concludes. "In the end the stories are simply there—haunting, enigmatic, printed with images as sharp and durable as the edge of a new coin, relentlessly specific."

The critical reception for Gallant's work has been very positive, indeed. *Washington Post Book World* reviewer Elizabeth Spencer suggests that there is "no writer in English anywhere able to set Mavis Gallant in second place. Her style alone places her in the first rank. Gallant's firmly drafted prose neglects nothing, leaves no dangling ends for the reader to tack up. . . . She is hospitable to the metaphysics of experience as well as to the homeliest social detail." Grosskurth writes: "Gallant's particular power as a writer is the sureness with which she catches the ephemeral; it is a wry vision, a blend of the sad and the tragi-comic. She is a born writer who happens to have been born in Canada, and her gift has been able to develop as it has only because she could look back in anger, love, and nostalgia." *New York Times Book Review* contributor Phyllis Rose praises Gallant for her "wicked humor that misses nothing, combined with sophistication so great it amounts to forgiveness." The critic concludes: "To take up residence in the mind of Mavis Gallant, as one does in reading her stories, is a privilege and delight."

BIOGRAPHICAL/CRITICAL SOURCES:

BOOKS

Contemporary Literary Criticism, Gale, Volume 7, 1977, Volume 18, 1981, Volume 38, 1986.
Dictionary of Literary Biography, Volume 53: *Canadian Writers since 1960, First Series,* Gale, 1986.

Lecker, Robert and Jack David, editors, *The Annotated Bibliography of Canada's Major Authors,* Volume 5, ECW (Ontario), 1984.
Merler, Grazia, *Mavis Gallant: Narrative Patterns and Devices,* Tecumseh, 1978.
Moss, John, editor, *Present Tense,* NC Press (Toronto), 1985.

PERIODICALS

Atlantis, autumn, 1978.
Books and Bookmen, July, 1974.
Books in Canada, October, 1979, October, 1981, April, 1984, October, 1985.
Canadian Fiction Magazine, Number 28, 1978, Number 43, 1982.
Canadian Forum, February, 1982, November, 1985.
Canadian Literature, spring, 1973, spring, 1985.
Chicago Tribune Book World, November 11, 1979.
Christian Science Monitor, June 4, 1970.
Globe and Mail (Toronto), October 11, 1986, October 15, 1988.
Los Angeles Times, April 15, 1985.
Los Angeles Times Book Review, November 4, 1979, May 24, 1987.
Maclean's, September 5, 1964, November 9, 1981, November 22, 1982.
Nation, June 15, 1985.
New Republic, August 25, 1979, May 13, 1985.
New York Review of Books, June 25, 1964, January 24, 1980.
New York Times, June 5, 1970, October 2, 1979, April 20, 1985, July 9, 1985, March 4, 1987.
New York Times Book Review, February 26, 1956, September 16, 1979, May 5, 1985, March 15, 1987.
Quill and Quire, October, 1981, June, 1984.
Rubicon, winter, 1984-85.
Saturday Night, September, 1973, November, 1981.
Saturday Review, October 17, 1959, August 25, 1979, October 13, 1979.
Spectator, August 29, 1987, February 20, 1988.
Time, November 26, 1979, May 27, 1985.
Times (London), February 28, 1980.
Times Literary Supplement, March 14, 1980, February 28, 1986, January 22-28, 1988, September 25-October 1, 1987.
Virginia Quarterly Review, spring, 1980.
Washington Post Book World, April 14, 1985, March 29, 1987.

*   *   *

GALLEGOS (FREIRE), Romulo   1884-1969

PERSONAL: Born August 2, 1884, in Caracas, Venezuela; died April 4, 1969, in Caracas, Venezuela; son of Romulo Gallegos Osie and Rita Freire Guruceaga; married Teotiste Arocha Egui, April, 1912; children: Alexis, Sonia. *Education:* Attended Colegio Sucre; received B.Ph. from Central University; studied law. *Politics:* Democratic Action.

CAREER: Writer. Worked variously as accountant and railway stationmaster; co-founder and staff member of magazine *La Alborada,* beginning in 1909; Colegio Federal, Barcelona, Venezuela, faculty member, 1911; assistant principal of high school in Caracas, Venezuela, c. 1912-18; subdirector of Normal School for Men, 1918; director of Liceo Andres Bello and professor of philosophy, beginning in 1922; Venezuelan Government, appointed senator by Juan Vicente Gomez, c. 1930, resigned, 1931; salesman for National Cash Register Co. in Spain; Municipal Council, Caracas, member, beginning in 1936, also served briefly as minister of education; elected deputy to Congress from Federal District, 1937; elected president of Venezuela, February, 1948; deposed by army, November, 1948; exiled to Cuba; returned to Venezuela in 1958. Member of National Council of Public Instruction, 1914-21.

AWARDS, HONORS: Prize from Asociacion del Mejor Libro del Mes (Book-of-the-Month Club), Madrid, Spain, 1929, for *Dona Barbara;* LL.D. from Columbia University, 1948; Gold Medal of the Liberator from Bolivarian Society, 1948.

WRITINGS:

"El milagro del ano" (play), first produced c. 1914.
El ultimo Solar (novel), originally published in 1920, published as *Reinaldo Solar,* Araluce (Barcelona, Venezuela), 1930.
La trepadora (novel), Tipografia Mercantil (Caracas, Venezuela), 1925.
Dona Barbara (novel), Araluce, 1929, reprinted, Ayacucho (Caracas), 1982, translation by Robert Malloy, J. Cape and H. Smith, 1931.
Cantaclaro (novel), Araluce, 1934, reprinted, Espasa-Calpe (Madrid), 1982.
Canaima (novel), Araluce, 1935, reprinted, Espasa-Calpe, 1982, translation with notes by Jaime Tello, North American Association of Venezuela (Caracas), 1984.
Pobre negro (novel), Elite (Caracas), 1937.
Programa politico y discursos del candidato popular, Romulo Gallegos, Elite, 1941, reprinted, Comision Centenario del Natalicio de Romulo Gallegos, 1985.
El forastero (novel), Elite, 1942, published as *La primera version de El forastero: Novela inedita,* Equinoccio (Caracas), 1980.
Sobre la misma tierra (novel), Elite, 1943, reprinted, Espasa-Calpe, 1981.
La rebelion, y otros cuentos (stories), del Maestro (Caracas), 1946, reprinted, Espasa-Calpe, 1981.
Obras completas (complete works), Lex (Havana, Cuba), 1949.
La brizna de paja en el viento (novel), Selecta (Havana), 1952.
Una posicion en la vida, Humanismo (Mexico), 1954.
La doncella (drama) y El ultimo patriota (cuentos) (play and stories), Montobar (Mexico), 1957.
Obras selectas (selected works), EDIME (Madrid), 1959.
Sus mejores cuentos (stories), Organizacion Continental de los Festivales del Libro, c. 1959.
Antologia de Romulo Gallegos, edited with introduction by Pedro Diaz Seijas, B. Costa-Amic (Mexico), 1966.
Cuentos venezolanos (stories), Espasa-Calpe Argentina (Buenos Aires), 1966.
Tierra bajo los pies, Alianza, 1971.
Cuentos (stories), Arte y Literatura (Havana), 1973.
Vida y literatura, Embajada de Venezuela, 1977.
Cuentos completos (complete stories), Monte Avila (Caracas), 1981.
Apreciacion de Andres Eloy Blanco: Con apendice de textos del poeta, Gobierno del Estado Miranda (Los Teques, Venezuela), 1985.
Romulo Gallegos, la "segura inmortalidad," Centauro (Caracas), 1985.
Pensamiento y accion politica de Romulo Gallegos, introduction by Marco Tulio Bruni Celli, [Caracas], c. 1985.
Romulo Gallegos, multivision, Ediciones de la Presidencia de la Republica, Comision Ejecutiva Nacional para la Celebracion del Centenario del Natalicio de Romulo Gallegos, 1986.

Also author of story collection *Los aventureros,* 1913.

SIDELIGHTS: Numbered among Venezuela's finest novelists, Romulo Gallegos became known both for his prosaic depictions of the Venezuelan prairies and for his mixed reception in political circles. Gallegos's debut novel, *El ultimo Solar,* features thieves and ruthless politicians in a land said to reflect early twentieth-century Venezuela under the rule of dictator Juan Vicente Gomez. Gomez took no action against Gallegos for this novel or the following one, *La trepadora,* but Gallegos's third, *Dona Barbara,* attracted a great deal of attention.

In *Dona Barbara* Gallegos depicts the Venezuelan prairie ranches, modeling them in part after one of Gomez's; published in 1929, the book describes the rise of the character Barbara from river boat life to head of an empire of estates. *Dona Barbara* was widely praised and is regarded as a classic in Latin American literature. As a result of its success, Gomez named Gallegos a senator, reportedly in an attempt to curb his writing. Gallegos, however, never attended a Senate session; instead he resigned his post and went to live in the United States in 1931. Two other novels, *Cantaclaro* and *Canaima,* were written during this voluntary exile.

Gallegos returned to Venezuela in 1936 after Gomez's death and became increasingly active in politics, at the same time continuing to write. The novel *Pobre negro,* published in 1937, won acclaim for its fine writing and moving portrayal of slavery and the plight of mulattos. Gallegos's political involvement peaked in the 1940s with his election as president of a new government. Taking office in 1948, he was Venezuela's first freely elected leader, but he held the post less than a year before a military junta overthrew his administration. Another period of exile ensued, lasting until the 1958 overthrow of Marcos Perez Jimenez, who had led the junta. By the time of his death a decade later, Gallegos had achieved international recognition as one of his country's foremost men of letters.

OBITUARIES:

BOOKS

Current Biography, H. W. Wilson, 1969.

PERIODICALS

New York Times, April 8, 1969.
Times (London), April 6, 1969.

* * *

GANDALAC, Lennard
See BERNE, Eric (Lennard)

* * *

GANDHI, M. K.
See GANDHI, Mohandas Karamchand

* * *

GANDHI, Mahatma
See GANDHI, Mohandas Karamchand

* * *

GANDHI, Mohandas Karamchand 1869-1948
(M. K. Gandhi, Mahatma Gandhi)

PERSONAL: Born October 2, 1869, in Probandar, Kathiawar, India; assassinated, January 30, 1948, in New Delhi, India; son of Karamchand (a provincial political official) and Putlibai Gandhi; married wife Kasturbai, 1883 (died, 1944); children: four sons; one daughter (adopted). *Education:* Attended University of Bombay; attended Samaldas College, Bhavnagar, India, 1887-88; received law degree from Inner Temple, London, 1891.

CAREER: Called to the bar, London, England, 1891; private law practice in Bombay and Rajkot, India, 1891-93; moved to Natal, South Africa, and worked for an Indian business firm, 1893-94; private law practice in Durban and Johannesburg, South Africa, 1894-1914; founded the Natal Indian Congress, 1894, to advance the political and civil rights of Indians in South Africa and served as the organization's secretary; organized the Indian Ambulance Corps to assist British forces during the Boer War, 1899-1902; launched *satyagraha* non-cooperation campaign for Indian rights, 1906, and led movement until 1914; returned to India and engaged in social work and community organizing in the Indian countryside, c. 1915-18; became president of the Indian National Congress and founded Satyagraha League, 1919; led *satyagraha* non-cooperation campaign for home rule against the British colonial government, 1919-22; imprisoned for seditious conspiracy, 1922-24; led new *satyagraha* campaigns and was repeatedly imprisoned in the 1930s; imprisoned for demanding Indian independence and opposing the British war effort, 1942-44; helped negotiate Indian independence, 1945-47; engaged in social work, 1947; fatally shot in 1948 by a Hindu extremist opposed to Gandhi's policies toward Muslims.

AWARDS, HONORS: Boer War Medal, c. 1902, and Kaisar-i-Hind Medal, 1906, from the British government in South Africa (Gandhi returned both in 1928).

WRITINGS:

WORKS ON POLITICS, SOCIETY, RELIGION, AND MORALITY

Hind Swaraj or Indian Home Rule, [South Africa], 1909, Navajivan, 1939.

Speeches and Writings, Natesan, 1918.

Swaraj and Non-Cooperation, Chakravartty, 1920.

Swaraj in One Year, Ganesh, 1921.

Mahatma Gandhi on Spinning, compiled by Manoranjan Bhattacharya, Bhattacharya, 1921.

Freedom's Battle: Being a Comprehensive Collection of Writings and Speeches on the Present Situation, Ganesh, 1922.

The Wheel of Fortune, Ganesh, 1922.

Non-Cooperation: Recent Speeches and Writings, Ganesh, 1922.

India on Trial, Ahimsa Ashram, 1922.

Mahatma Gandhi's Jail Experiences, Tagore, 1922.

The Tug of War, Book Club (Calcutta), 1922.

Young India (collection of articles published in journal *Young India*), Ganesan, Volume I: *1919-1922,* 1923, Volume II: *1924-1926,* 1927, Volume III: *1927-1928,* 1935.

Mahatma Gandhi: His Life, Writings, and Speeches, Ganesh, 1923.

A Guide to Health, Ganesan, 1923.

Sermon on the Sea, Universal Publishing Co., 1924.

Hindu-Muslim Tension: Its Cause and Cure, Young India Office, 1924.

Is India Different? The Class Struggle in India, Communist Party (London), 1927.

Satyagraha in South Africa, Navajivan, 1928, Academic Reprints, 1954.

Ethical Religion, Ganesan, 1930.

How to Compete With Foreign Cloth, Calcutta Book Co., 1931.

India's Case for Swaraj: Being Selected Speeches, Writings, Interviews, etc., of Mahatma Gandhi in England and India, September 1931-January 1932, Yeshanand, 1932.

My Soul's Agony: Being Statements Issued From Yeravda Prison about the Removal of Untouchability, Servants of Untouchables Society (Bombay), 1932.

The Bleeding Wound! Being a Most Up-to-Date Collection of Gandhiji's Writings and Statements on Untouchability, Shyam Lal, 1932.

Views on Untouchability: Being Extracts From Speeches and Writings, edited by Mukut Beharilal, privately printed (Kashi), 1932.

Self-Restraint Versus Self Indulgence, two volumes, Navajivan, 1933-39.

To the Students, edited by Anand T. Hingorani, Hingorani, 1935, new version edited by Bharatan Kumarappa, Navajivan, 1952.

Cent Percent Swadeshi or the Economics of Village Industries, Navajivan, 1938.

Swadeshi: True or False, Chandrashankar Shukla, 1940.

Birth Control Versus Self Control, edited by Dewan Ram Parkash, Dewan, 1941.

Christian Missions: Their Place in India, Navajivan, 1941, revised edition, 1957.

Economics of Khadi, Navajivan, 1941.

The Indian States' Problems, Navajivan, 1941.

To the Women, edited by Hingorani, Hingorani, 1941.

Non-Violence in Peace and War, two volumes, Navajivan, 1942-49, Garland Publishing, 1972.

To the Hindus and Muslims, edited by Hingorani, Hingorani, 1942.

To the Princes and Their People, edited by Hingorani, Hingorani, 1942.

Women and Social Injustice, Navajivan, 1942.

Our Language Problem, Hingorani, 1942.

Conquest of Self: Being Gleanings From His Writings and Speeches, compiled by R. K. Prabhu and U. R. Rao, Thacker, 1943.

Gandhi Against Fascism, edited by Jag Parvesh Chander, Free India Publications, 1943.

Ethics of Fasting, edited by Chander, Indian Printing Works, 1944.

The Mind of Mahatma Gandhi, compiled by Prabhu and U. R. Rao, Oxford University Press, 1945.

Swaraj Through Charkha, compiled by Kanu Gandhi, All India Spinners' Association, 1945.

Teachings of Mahatma Gandhi, edited by Chander, Indian Printing Works, 1945.

Daridra-Narayana, edited by Hingorani, Hingorani, 1946.

Communal Unity, Navajivan, 1947.

Gita the Mother, edited by Chander, 4th edition, Indian Printing Works, 1947.

India of My Dreams, compiled by Prabhu, Hind Kitabs, 1947.

Ramanama: The Infallible Remedy, edited by Hingorani, Hingorani, 1947.

To the Protagonists of Pakistan, edited by Hingorani, Hingorani, 1947.

Delhi Diary: Prayer Speeches From 10-9-1947 to 30-1-1948, Navajivan, 1948.

Precious Pearls, compiled by R. S. Kaushala, Glifton, 1948.

Selection From Gandhi, compiled by N. K. Bose, Navajivan, 1948.

Why the Constructive Programme, All India Congress Committee, 1948.

Diet and Diet Reform, Navajivan, 1949.

Food Shortage and Agriculture, Navajivan, 1949.

For Pacifists, Navajivan, 1949.

The Mahatma and the Missionary: Selected Writings, edited by Clifford Manshardt, Regnery, 1949.

Conversations of Gandhiji, edited by Chandrashankar Shukla, Vora, 1949.

The Gandhi Sutras: The Basic Teachings of Mahatma Gandhi, edited by D. S. Sarma, Devin-Adair, 1949.

Mohanmala: A Gandhian Rosary: Being a Thought for Each Day of the Year Gleaned From the Writings and Speeches of Mahatma Gandhi, compiled by Prabhu, Hind Kitabs, 1949.

Hindu Dharma, edited by Kumarappa, Navajivan, 1950.

The Good Life, edited by Chander, third enlarged edition, Indian Printing Works, 1950.

Health, Wealth and Happiness, Bharatiya Karmayogi Samaj, 1950.

Thus Spake Mahatma, Vichar Sahitya, 1950.

A Day Book of Thoughts From Mahatma Gandhi, edited by K. T. Narasimha Char, Macmillan, 1951.

Selected Writings of Mahatma Gandhi, edited by Ronald Duncan, Beacon, 1951.

Ruskin's Unto This Last: A Paraphrase, Navajivan, 1951.

Basic Education, Navajivan, 1951.

The Ideology of the Charkha: A Collection of Some of Gandhiji's Speeches and Writings About Khadi, edited by Shrikrishnadas Jaju, All India Spinners' Association, 1951.

Satyagraha: Non-Violent Resistance, edited by Kumarappa, Navajivan, 1951, Schocken, 1961.

Towards Non-Violent Socialism, edited by Kumarappa, Navajivan, 1951.

The Wit and Wisdom of Gandhi, edited by Homer A. Jack, Beacon, 1951.

Rebuilding Our Villages, edited by Kumarappa, Navajivan, 1953.

How to Serve the Cow, edited by Kumarappa, Navajivan, 1954.

Medium of Instruction, edited by Kumarappa, Navajivan, 1954.

Sarvodaya: The Welfare of All, edited by Kumarappa, Navajivan, 1954.

Untouchability, edited by Kumarappa, Navajivan, 1954.

Ashram Observances in Action, Navajivan, 1955.

Gokhale: My Political Guru, Navajivan, 1955.

Khadi: Why and How, edited by Kumarappa, Navajivan, 1955.

My Religion, edited by Kumarappa, Navajivan, 1955.

On Removal of Untouchability, Director of Publicity (Bombay), 1956.

Truth of God: Gleanings From the Writings of Mahatma Gandhi Bearing on God, God-Realization and the Godly Way, compiled by Prabhu, Navajivan, 1956.

Thoughts on National Language, Navajivan, 1956.

The Gandhi Reader: A Source Book of His Life and Writings, edited by Jack, Indiana University Press, 1956.

Towards Lasting Peace, edited by Hingorani, Bharatiya Vidya, 1956.

Economic and Industrial Life and Relations, three volumes, edited by V. B. Kher, Navajivan, 1957.

Food for the Soul, edited by Hingorani, Bharatiya Vidya, 1957.

The Science of Satyagraha, edited by Hingorani, Bharatiya Vidya, 1957.

The Socialism of My Conception, edited by Hingorani, Bharatiya Vidya, 1957.

All Men Are Brothers: Life and Thoughts of Mahatma Gandhi as Told in His Own Words, Columbia University Press, 1958.

A Gandhi Anthology, compiled by Valji Govindji Desai, Navajivan, 1958.

Homage to the Departed, edited by V. B. Kher, Navajivan, 1958.

Women, Navajivan, 1958.

Jawaharlal Nehru: The Jewel of India, edited by Hingorani, Pearl, 1960.

My Non-Violence, edited by Sailesh Kumar Bandyopadhaya, Navajivan, 1960.

Writings and Speeches of Gandhi Relating to Bihar, 1917-1947, edited by K. K. Datta, Government of Bihar, 1960.

The Art of Living, edited by Hingorani, Pearl, 1961.

My Philosophy of Life, edited by Hingorani, Pearl, 1961.

Search of the Supreme, three volumes, edited by V. B. Kher, Navajivan, 1961-62.

Economic Thought, edited by J. S. Mathur and A. S. Mathur, Chaitanya Publishing House, 1962.

Bapu and Children, edited by Prabhu and Shewak Bhojraj, Navajivan, 1962.

All Religions Are True, edited by Hingorani, Pearl, 1962.

Birth Control, edited by Hingorani, Bharatiya Vidya, 1962.

The Law and the Lawyers, edited by S. B. Kher, Navajivan, 1962.

The Problem of Education, Navajivan, 1962.

The Teachings of the Gita, edited by Hingorani, Bharatiya Vidya, 1962.

True Education, Navajivan, 1962.

Varnashramadharma, compiled by Prabhu, Navajivan, 1962.

The Essential Gandhi: An Anthology, edited by Louis Fischer, Random House, 1962, reprinted, Vintage, 1983.

The Message of Jesus Christ, edited by Hingorani, Bharatiya Vidya, 1963.

The Supreme Power, edited by Hingorani, Bharatiya Vidya, 1963.

The Way to Communal Harmony, edited by U. R. Rao, Navajivan, 1963.

Caste Must Go and the Sin of Untouchability, compiled by Prabhu, Navajivan, 1964.

The Law of Continence: Brahmacharya, edited by Hingorani, Bharatiya Vidya, 1964.

The Role of Women, edited by Hingorani, Bharatiya Vidya, 1964.

Stone Walls Do Not a Prison Make, compiled and edited by V. B. Kher, Navajivan, 1964.

Through Self-Control, edited by Hingorani, Bharatiya Vidya, 1964.

Gandhiji Expects: What the Father of the Nation Expected of People's Representatives, compiled by H. M. Vyas, Navajivan, 1965.

Gita My Mother, edited by Hingorani, Bharatiya Vidya, 1965.

Glorious Thoughts of Gandhi, edited by N. B. Sen, New Book Society (New Delhi), 1965.

The Hindu-Muslim Unity, edited by Hingorani, Bharatiya Vidya, 1965.

My Picture of Free India, edited by Hingorani, Bharatiya Vidya, 1965.

The Health Guide, edited by Hingorani, Bharatiya Vidya, 1965.

My Varnashrama Dharma, edited by Hingorani, Bharatiya Vidya, 1965.

Our Language Problem, edited by Hingorani, Bharatiya Vidya, 1965.

Industrialize—and Perish!, compiled by Prabhu, Navajivan, 1966.

The Nature Cure, edited by Hingorani, Bharatiya Vidya, 1966.

Man Versus Machine, edited by Hingorani, Bharatiya Vidya, 1966.

To Be Perplexed, edited by Hingorani, Bharatiya Vidya, 1966.

The Village Reconstruction, edited by Hingorani, Bharatiya Vidya, 1966.

The Gospel of Swadeshi, edited by Hingorani, Bharatiya Vidya, 1967.

The Wisdom of Gandhi, Philosophical Library, 1967.

The Selected Works of Mahatma Gandhi, edited by Shriman Narayan, Navajivan, 1968.

The Message of Mahatma Gandhi, compiled and edited by U. S. Mohan Rao, Publications Division of the Government of India, 1968.

Pen-Portraits and Tributes by Gandhiji: Sketches of Eminent Men and Women by Mahatma Gandhi, compiled and edited by U. S. Mohan Rao, National Book Trust (New Delhi), 1969.

Essential Writings, selected and edited by V. V. Remana Murti, Gandhi Peace Foundation (New Delhi), 1970.

Modern Versus Ancient Civilization, edited by Hingorani, Bharatiya Vidya, 1970.

My Views on Education, edited by Hingorani, Bharatiya Vidya, 1970.

Political and National Life and Affairs, three volumes, compiled and edited by V. B. Kher, Navajivan, 1967-68.

Service Before Self, edited by Hingorani, Bharatiya Vidya, 1971.

Epigrams From Gandhiji, compiled by S. R. Tikekar, Publications Division of the Government of India, 1971.

Pathway to God, compiled by M. S. Deshpande, Navajivan, 1971.

Why Fear or Mourn Death?, edited by Hingorani, Bharatiya Vidya, 1971.

Gandhi and Haryana: A Collection of His Speeches and Writings Pertaining to Haryana, edited by J. Chandra, Usha, 1977.

The Words of Gandhi, selected by Richard Attenborough, Newmarket, 1982.

The Quintessence of Gandhi in His Own Words, compiled by Madhu Muskan, 1984.

The Moral and Political Writings of Mahatma Gandhi, edited by Raghavan Iyer, Oxford University Press, 1986.

Gandhi in India: In His Own Words, University Press of New England, 1987.

Works published under name variation M. K. Gandhi and under title Mahatma Gandhi. Also author of numerous pamphlets on political, social, religious, and moral issues.

CORRESPONDENCE AND OTHER

The Story of My Experiments With Truth, translated by Mahadev Desai, Navajivan, 1927-29, 2nd edition published as *An Autobiography, or the Story of My Experiments With Truth,* 1940, abridged edition, Hind Kitabs, 1950.

My Early Life (1869-1914) (autobiography), arranged and edited by Mahadev Desai, Oxford University Press, 1932.

Songs From Prison (translation of Hindu lyrics made in prison by Gandhi), edited by John S. Hoyland, George Allen, 1934.

Gandhi-Jinnah Talks: Text of Correspondence and Other Relevant Matter, July-October 1944, Hindustan Times, 1944.

Correspondence Between Gandhiji and P. C. Joshi, People's Publishing House, 1945.

Gandhi's Correspondence With the Government, 1942-1944, Navajivan, 1945.

Famous Letters of Mahatma Gandhi, compiled and edited by R. L. Khipple, Indian Printing Works, 1947.

Selected Letters, two volumes, translated by Valji Govindji Desai, Navajivan, 1949-62.

Bapu's Letters to Mira, 1924-1948, Navajivan, 1949, published by Harper as *Gandhi's Letters to a Disciple,* 1950.

(Letters) to a Gandhian Capitalist: Correspondence Between Gandhi and Jamnalal Bajaj and Members of His Family, edited by Kaka Kalelkar, Jamnalal Seva Trust, 1951, second revised and enlarged edition, Sevak Prakashan, 1979.

(Letters) to Ashram Sisters (6-12-1926 to 30-12-1929), edited by Kaka Kalelkar, Navajivan, 1952.

My Dear Child: Letters to Esther Faering, edited by Alice M. Barnes, Navajivan, 1956.

Gandhi-Rajabhoj Correspondence, 1932-1946, edited by M. P. Mangudkar and G. B. Nirantar, Bharat Sevak Sangh, 1956.

Letters to Rajkumari Amrit Kaur, Navajivan, 1961.

Letters to Manibahen Patel, translated and edited by Valji Govindji Desai and Sudarshan V. Desai, Navajivan, 1963.

Works published under name variation M. K. Gandhi and under title Mahatma Gandhi. Contributor of articles to newspapers and magazines, including *Young India.* Founder of and contributor to journal *Indian Opinion,* 1904.

COLLECTED WORKS

Collected Works, ninety volumes (expected), Publications Division of the Government of India, 1958—.

SIDELIGHTS: The Indian independence leader Mohandas Karamchand Gandhi, called the Mahatma ("Great Soul") by many of his countrymen, changed the world far beyond his successful struggle to end British imperial rule in India. Gandhi's philosophy of nonviolent resistance to illegitimate authority and his mass civil disobedience campaigns introduced a new form of popular political struggle that has since been adopted around the globe, notably by the civil rights movement in the United States. The Indian leader's religious and social convictions, centered on the ideals of tolerance, community, equality, simplicity, and self-sacrifice and elaborated in his voluminous writings, have also entered the currency of modern thought. Above all, Gandhi's personal example of self-abnegation, his courage and perseverance, and his tolerance and humanity remain a source of inspiration to millions worldwide.

The son of a provincial official from the *Vaisya* Hindu caste, Gandhi studied law in England and struggled to overcome a painful shyness that threatened to abort his career. His political initiation occurred in Natal, South Africa, where he went to work for an Indian company and found himself victimized by the country's policies of racial discrimination. Gandhi refused to endure this treatment passively and formed the Natal Indian Congress in 1894 to further the large Indian minority's political and civil rights and press reform on the British colonial government. Supported by his now-thriving legal practice in Johannesburg, Gandhi founded the journal *Indian Opinion* in 1904 to rouse support for Indian rights, and he also began exploring spiritually-based paths to social change. Gandhi's innovative melding of political, social, and religious thinking led him to the key concept of *satyagraha,* or nonviolent but often extra-legal resistance to illegitimate authority. He launched a mass civil disobedience campaign in Johannesburg in 1906 to protest the Transvaal government's plan to register and better police the Indian population and continued to promote *satyagraha* until he left the country to return to India eight years later. Gandhi's efforts to improve the lot of South African Indians produced few concrete gains but helped bolster Indian confidence and self-esteem and also encouraged the country's oppressed black majority in its struggle for political and civil rights. The Indian leader described his South African campaign in *Satyagraha in South Africa,* published in 1928.

Gandhi's political work in South Africa had been well-publicized in India, and he returned a recognized leader to his native country. He joined the Indian National Congress, a moderate reformist organization composed largely of the Western-educated Indian elite that sought greater local self-government under British rule. As in South Africa, however, Gandhi found his political *metier* in direct, mass organizing rather than party building and political deal making. He spent two years traveling to remote Indian villages, where he inspired the rural poor with his moral and spiritual teachings as well as by his political vision of a self-reliant, emancipated nation.

Gandhi's developing spiritual politics overturned the traditional political opposition of means and ends and advanced the proposition that individual morality, social justice, and political self-determination are mutually interdependent and must all advance or fall together. He came to regard *satya* (truth) and *ahimsa* (nonviolence) as absolute moral values that transcend any particular creed or philosophy but that can only become real through active individual engagement in social life. Gandhi saw modern industrial society and power politics as often inimical to these values, and he counterposed an Indian vision of decentralized, egalitarian village communities engaged in agriculture and traditional handicrafts. He launched his famous *khadi* (homespun) movement as a symbol of self-reliance and native industry that would also help emancipate India from its dependence on imported cloth. Gandhi's emphasis on spirituality and rejection of Western-styled industrialism struck many progressive Indian independence leaders as reactionary, but he won a wide following among the Indian masses. Humble yet charismatic, a self-deprecating but inspiring leader, Gandhi took up residence in voluntary poverty and celibacy in a remote *ashram* (spiritual commune) near Ahmadabad and was soon known throughout India as the Mahatma, or "great soul."

In 1919, Gandhi became president of the Indian National Congress and formed the Satyagraha League to launch a mass civil disobedience campaign against repressive colonial laws. The non-cooperation movement's broader goal was the achievement of *Swaraj*, or home rule, to be won through such tactics as boycotting British goods and institutions and courting mass arrests and jailings. The generally peaceful movement provoked a savage British response, most notoriously when British troops massacred four hundred Indians attending a nonviolent demonstration in Armitsar, Punjab state. Along with thousands of others, Gandhi himself was arrested in 1922 and sentenced to six years in prison for seditious conspiracy.

Released because of illness after two years, Gandhi confronted a weakened and divided Congress movement in the mid-1920s. Rising religious tensions prompted Muslims to leave the predominantly Hindu organization and form their own Moslem League, while radicals demanded a commitment to complete political independence and a thoroughgoing social reform program. Gandhi and other *satyagraha* leaders were accused of eviscerating the movement and martyring the Congress rank-and-file in their anxiety to avoid violence.

Gandhi suspended much of his activist work in the mid-1920s in response to these criticisms, although he remained very much in the public eye through his widely-circulated writings. Two collections of articles on non-cooperation and the nationalist movement that originally appeared in the journal *Young India* were published during this period, and his *Story of My Experiments With Truth,* written during his years in prison, appeared in 1927. This last work "is extraordinary for candor and quality of self-criticism," remarked *Los Angeles Times Book Review* critic Malcolm Boyd. Writing in the *Yale Review,* Merle Curti commented, "The book is without literary distinction, but it is, nevertheless, great . . . because of the supreme sincerity and humility with which Gandhi reveals his limitations and strength in his never-ending struggle to approach Absolute Truth or God."

Gandhi's political semiretirement was short-lived, however, and he returned to active leadership of the Congress as British intran-

sigence helped the nationalist movement recover strength and unity in the late 1920s. Gandhi joined more radical Congress leaders in raising a new demand for full political independence instead of British dominion status and then launched his famous *satyagraha* campaign against the colonial salt tax in March, 1930. The movement received worldwide press attention when Gandhi led thousands of followers on a dramatic march across India to the seaport of Dandi, where he was arrested for illegally making salt out of sea water. Successive non-cooperation campaigns punctuated by arrest, imprisonment, protest fasts, and inconclusive negotiations with the British authorities defined Gandhi's political activity in the 1930s and early 1940s and brought him and the Congress movement much international attention and respect. Gandhi's nonviolent tactics and moral rectitude sowed self doubt among the British colonists themselves and undermined their willingness to crush the independence movement by force.

The end of the World War II raised the issue of decolonization to the forefront of the international political agenda, and the new British Labour government bowed to political reality by beginning serious negotiations with Indian independence leaders to end British rule in India. The talks culminated in a 1947 tripartite agreement between the British, the Indian National Congress, and the Moslem League to partition the Indian subcontinent into the states of India and Pakistan, with respective Hindu and Muslim majority populations. Gandhi was dismayed by partition and counseled against acceptance of the agreement, but he could not moderate the deep religious hatreds dividing his countrymen. With independence at hand, he turned from politics to the immense task of promoting his program of social justice, which he believed would be achieved through the voluntary actions of morally enlightened individuals. When rising communal violence threatened to make the newly free subcontinent ungovernable, Gandhi spoke out passionately for religious tolerance and began a "fast unto death" to protest the bloodshed. A Hindu fanatic enraged by this plea for brotherhood assassinated the Indian leader in the midst of his fast on January 30, 1948.

Scores of books attributed to Gandhi have appeared since the Mahatma's death, and his collected writings are expected to fill ninety volumes when they are published in their entirety by the Indian government. Some of these books are compilations of overlapping articles on topical political issues, but much of Gandhi's writing is devoted to political, social, and spiritual themes of enduring interest. His better known works include *The Mind of Mahatma Gandhi,* a selection of basic writings from 1909 to 1948, and *All Men Are Brothers: Life and Thoughts of Mahatma Gandhi, as Told in His Own Words,* which was published under the auspices of the United Nations Educational, Scientific, and Cultural Organization (UNESCO). "To read this book is an education in itself," *Saturday Review* critic Ranjee Shahani observed of the latter work. "Gandhi stands out in our murky era as a lighthouse of uncommon commonsense."

BIOGRAPHICAL/CRITICAL SOURCES:

BOOKS

Bakshi, S. R., *Gandhi and the Status of Women,* Criterion, 1987.
Birla, Ghanshyam Dass, *Bapu, a Unique Association,* Bharatiya Vidya Bharan, 1977.
Bose, Nirmal Kumar, *My Days with Gandhi,* Nishana, 1953.
Brown, Judith M., *Gandhi and Civil Disobedience: The Mahatma in Indian Politics, 1928-1934,* Cambridge University Press, 1977.
Chatterjee, Margaret, *Gandhi's Religious Thought,* Macmillan, 1983.

Deshpande, M. S., *Light of India: The Message of the Mahatma,* Wilco, 1958.

Erikson, Erik H., *Gandhi's Truth: On the Origins of Militant Nonviolence,* Norton, 1969.

Gandhi, M. K., *The Story of My Experiments With the Truth,* translated by Mahadev Desai, Navajivan, 1927-29.

Gandhi, M. K., *My Early Life (1869-1914),* arranged and edited by Mahadev Desai, Oxford University Press, 1932.

Gandhi, Prabhudas, *My Childhood with Gandhiji,* Navajivan, 1957.

Gauba, K. L., *The Assassination of Mahatma Gandhi,* Jaico Publishing House, 1969.

Gaur, V., *Mahatma Gandhi: A Study of His Message of Non-Violence,* Sterling, 1977.

Goyal, O. P., *Gandhi: An Interpretation,* Kitab Mahal, 1964.

Green, Martin, *Tolstoy and Gandhi, Men of Peace: A Biography,* Basic Books, 1983.

Jesudasan, Ignatius, *A Gandhian Theology of Liberation,* Orbis, 1984.

Juergensmeyer, Mark, *Fighting with Gandhi,* Harper, 1984.

Mathur, J. S., editor, *Gandhian Thought and Contemporary Society,* Bharatiya Vidya, 1974.

Mehta, Ved, *Mahatma Gandhi and His Apostles,* Viking, 1976.

Moon, Penderel, *Gandhi and Modern India,* Norton, 1969.

Mukherjee, Dhurjati, *The Towering Spirit: Gandhian Revelance Assessed,* Chetana Publications, 1978.

Muzumdar, Haridas T., *Mahatma Gandhi: Peaceful Revolutionary,* Scribner, 1952.

Nanda, B. R., *Gandhi and His Critics,* Oxford University Press, 1985.

Owen, Hugh, *Gandhi,* University of Queensland Press, 1984.

Payne, Robert, *The Life and Death of Mahatma Gandhi,* Dutton, 1969.

Prabhu, R. K., *This Was Bapu: One Hundred and Fifty Anecdotes Relating to Mahatma Gandhi,* Navajivan, 1954.

Prasad, K. M., *Sarvodaya of Gandhi,* Raj Hans Publications, 1984.

Puri, Reshmi-Sudha, *Gandhi on War and Peace,* Praeger, 1987.

Richards, Glyn, *The Philosophy of Gandhi: A Study of His Basic Ideas,* Barnes & Noble, 1982.

Sharma, Bishan Sarup, *Gandhi As a Political Thinker,* Indian Press, 1956.

Sharp, Gene, *Gandhi As a Political Strategist/Essays on Ethics and Politics,* Porter Sargent, 1979.

Sheean, Vincent, *Mahatma Gandhi: A Great Life in Brief,* Publications Department, Government of India, 1954.

Shirer, William L., *Gandhi: A Memoir,* Simon & Schuster, 1979.

Slade, Madeleine, *The Spirit's Pilgrimage,* Coward-McCann, 1960.

Tendulkar, D. G., *Mahatma,* eight volumes, Pradesh, 1951-54.

PERIODICALS

Los Angeles Times Book Review, January 16, 1983.

Nation, January 23, 1924.

New York Herald Tribune Weekly Book Review, November 7, 1948.

New York Times Magazine, May 25, 1969.

Saturday Review, September 26, 1959.

Times Literary Supplement, July 26, 1934; March 31, 1972.

Yale Review, spring, 1949.

—*Sketch by Curtis Skinner*

GARCIA LORCA, Federico   1898-1936

PERSONAL: Commonly known by mother's surname, Lorca; born June 5, 1898, in Fuentevaqueros, Granada, Spain; executed August 19, 1936, in Viznar, Granada, Spain; son of Federico Garcia Rodriguez (a landowner) and Vicenta Lorca (a teacher). *Education:* Attended University of Granada, 1914-19; received law degree from University of Madrid, 1923; attended Columbia University, 1929.

CAREER: Writer. Artistic director, serving as director and producer of plays, for University Theater (state-sponsored traveling theater group, known as *La Barraca* ["The Hut"]), 1932-35. Director of additional plays, including *Blood Wedding,* 1933. Lecturer; illustrator, with work represented in exhibitions; musician, serving as arranger and pianist for recordings of Spanish folk songs, 1931. Helped to organize Festival of *Cante Jondo* (Granada, Spain), 1922.

WRITINGS:

POETRY

Libro de poemas (title means "Book of Poems"), Maroto (Madrid), 1921 (also see below).

Canciones (1921-1924), [Malaga, Spain], 1927, translation by Phillip Cummings published as *Songs,* Duquesne University Press, 1976 (also see below).

Primer romancero gitano (1924-1927), Revista de Occidente (Madrid), 1928, 2nd edition (and most later editions) published as *Romancero gitano,* 1929, translation by Langston Hughes published as *Gypsy Ballads,* Beloit College, 1951, translation by Rolfe Humphries published as *The Gypsy Ballads, With Three Historical Ballads,* Indiana University Press, 1953, translation by Michael Hartnett published as *Gipsy Ballads,* Goldsmith Press (Dublin), 1973, translation and commentary by Carl W. Cobb published as *Lorca's "Romancero gitano": A Ballad Translation and Critical Study,* University Press of Mississippi, 1983 (also see below).

Poema del cante jondo, Ulises (Madrid), 1931, translation by Carlos Bauer published as *Poem of the Deep Song/ Poema del cante jondo* (bilingual edition), City Lights Books, 1987 (also see below).

Llanto por Ignacio Sanchez Mejias (title means "Lament for Ignacio Sanchez Mejias"; commonly known as "Lament for the Death of a Bullfighter"), Arbol, 1935 (also see below).

Seis poemas gallegos (title means "Six Galician Poems"; written in Galician with assistance from others), Nos (Santiago de Compostela), 1935 (also see below).

Primeras canciones (title means "First Songs"), Heroe (Madrid), 1936 (also see below).

Lament for the Death of a Bullfighter, and Other Poems (bilingual edition), translation by A. L. Loyd, Oxford University Press, 1937, reprinted, AMS Press, 1978.

Divan del Tamarit (title means "Divan of the Tamarit"), published in *Obras Completas,* Losada, 1938 (also see below).

Poems, translation by Stephen Spender and J. L. Gili, Oxford University Press, 1939.

Poeta en Nueva York, Seneca (Mexico), 1940, translations published as *Poet in New York,* (bilingual edition) by Ben Belitt, introduction by Angel del Rio, Grove Press, 1955, reprinted, 1983, by Stephen Fredman, Fog Horn Press, 1975, by Greg Simon and Steven F. White, Farrar, Straus, 1988 (also see below).

The Poet In New York, and Other Poems (includes "Gypsy Ballads"), translation by Rolfe Humphries, introduction by J. Bergamin, Norton, 1940.

Selected Poems of Federico Garcia Lorca, translation by Stephen Spender and J. L. Gili, Hogarth Press (London), 1943, Transatlantic Arts (New York), 1947.

Poemas postumos, Canciones musicales, Divan del Tamarit, Mexicanas (Mexico), 1945.

The Selected Poems of Federico Garcia Lorca (bilingual edition), edited by Francisco Garcia Lorca and Donald M. Allen, introduction by Francisco Garcia Lorca, New Directions, 1955.

Lorca, translation and introduction by J. L. Gili, Penguin, 1960-65.

(With Juan Ramon Jimenez) *Lorca and Jimenez: Selected Poems,* translation by Robert Bly, Sixties Press, 1967.

Divan and Other Writings (includes "Divan of the Tamarit"), translation by Edwin Honig, Bonewhistle Press, 1974.

Lorca/Blackburn: Poems, translation by Paul Blackburn, Momo's Press, 1979.

The Cricket Sings: Poems and Songs for Children (bilingual edition), translation by Will Kirkland, New Directions, 1980.

Suites (reconstruction of a collection planned by Lorca), edited by Andre Belamich, Ariel (Barcelona), 1983.

Ineditos de Federico Garcia Lorca: Sonetos del amor oscuro, 1935-1936, (title means "Unpublished Works of Federico Garcia Lorca: Sonnets of the Dark Love, 1935-1936") compiled by Marta Teresa Casteros, Instituto de Estudios de Literatura Latinoamericana (Buenos Aires), c. 1984.

Poems represented in numerous collections and anthologies.

PLAYS

El malefico de la mariposa (two-act; title means "The Butterfly's Evil Spell"; first produced in Madrid at Teatro Esclava, March 22, 1920), published in *Obras completas,* Aguilar, 1954 (also see below).

Mariana Pineda: Romance popular en tres estampas (three-act; first produced in Madrid, Spain, at Teatro Fontalba, October, 1927; first published as *Romance de la muerte de Torrijos* in *El Dia Grafico,* June 25, 1927), Rivadeneyra (Madrid), 1928, translation by James Graham-Lujan published as *Mariana Pineda: A Popular Ballad in Three Prints* in *Tulane Drama Review,* winter, 1962, translation by Robert G. Havard published as *Mariana Pineda: A Popular Ballad in Three Engravings,* Aris & Phillips, 1987 (also see below).

La zapatera prodigiosa: Farsa violenta (two-act; title means "The Shoemaker's Prodigious Wife"; first produced in Madrid at Teatro Espanol, 1930), published in *Obras completas* (also see below).

El publico (one scene apparently missing), excerpts published in *Los Cuatro Vientos,* 1933; enlarged version published in *El publico: Amor, teatro, y caballos en la obra de Federico Garcia Lorca,* edited by R. Martinez Nadal, Dolphin (Oxford), 1970, revised edition published as *El publico: Amor y muerte en la obra de Federico Garcia Lorca,* J. Mortiz (Mexico), 1974, translation published as *Lorca's "The Public": A Study of an Unfinished Play and of Love and Death in Lorca's Work,* Schocken, 1974; Lorca's manuscript published by Dolphin, 1976; revised version published in *El publico y comedia sin titulo: Dos obras postumas,* 1978 (also see below).

Bodas de sangre: Tragedia (three-act; first produced in Madrid at Teatro Beatriz on March 8, 1933), Arbol, 1935, translation by Jose A. Weissberger produced as *Bitter Oleander* in New York City, 1935, translation by Gilbert Neiman published as *Blood Wedding,* New Directions, 1939 (also see below).

Amor de Don Perlimplin con Belisa en su jardin (title means "The Love of Don Perlimplin with Belisa, in His Garden"; first produced in Madrid on April 5, 1933), published in *Obras completas* (also see below).

Yerma: Poema tragico (three-act; first produced in Madrid on December 29, 1934), Anaconda (Buenos Aires), 1937, translation by Ian Macpherson and Jaqueline Minett published as *Yerma: A Tragic Poem* (bilingual edition), general introduction by John Lyon, Aris & Phillips, 1987 (also see below).

Retabillo de Don Cristobal (puppet play; title means "Don Cristobal's Puppet Show"; first produced in Buenos Aires, Argentina, at Teatro Avenida, March, 1934; revised version produced in Madrid at Feria del Libro, May 12, 1935), Subcomisariado de Propaganda del Comisariado General de Guerra (Valencia), 1938 (also see below).

Dona Rosita la soltera; o, El lenguaje de las flores: Poema granadino del novecientos, (three-act; title means "Dona Rosita the Spinster; or, The Language of Flowers: Poem of Granada in the Nineteenth Century"; first produced in Barcelona, Spain, at the Principal Palace, December, 1935), published in *Obras completas* (also see below).

Los titeres de Cachiporra: Tragecomedia de Don Cristobal y la sena Rosita: Farsa (puppet play; title means "The Billy-Club Puppets: Tragicomedy of Don Cristobal and Mam'selle Rosita: Farce"; first produced in Madrid at Zarzuela Theater, December, 1937), published in *Obras completas* (also see below).

Asi que pasen cinco anos (three-act; title means "As Soon as Five Years Pass"), published in *Obras Completas,* Losada, 1938 (also see below).

From Lorca's Theater: Five Plays (contains *The Shoemaker's Prodigious Wife, The Love of Don Perlimplin with Belisa, in His Garden, Dona Rosita the Spinster, Yerma,* and *When Five Years Pass*), translation by Richard L. O'Connell and James Graham-Lujan, introduction by Stark Young, Scribner, 1941.

La casa de Bernarda Alba: Drama de mujeres en los pueblos de Espana (three-act; title means "The House of Bernarda Alba: Drama of Women in the Villages of Spain"; first produced in Buenos Aires at Teatro Avenida, March 8, 1945), Losada, 1944 (also see below).

Three Tragedies (contains *Blood Wedding, Yerma,* and *The House of Bernarda Alba*), translation by Richard L. O'Connell and James Graham-Lujan, introduction by Francisco Garcia Lorca, New Directions, 1947, Greenwood Press, 1977.

Comedies (contains *The Butterfly's Evil Spell, The Shoemaker's Prodigious Wife, The Love of Don Perlimplin with Belisa, in His Garden, Dona Rosita the Spinster*), translation by Richard L. O'Connell and James Graham-Lujan, introduction by Francisco Garcia Lorca, New Directions, 1954, enlarged edition published as *Five Plays: Comedies and Tragicomedies* (includes *The Billy-Club Puppets*), 1963, Penguin, 1987.

Three Tragedies (contains *Blood Wedding, Yerma,* and *The House of Bernarda Alba*), translation by Sue Bradbury, Folio Society (London), 1977.

Comedia sin titulo (one act of an incomplete play; also known as "El sueno de la vida" ["The Dream of Life"]; first produced in Madrid in July, 1989), published in *El publico y comedia sin titulo: Dos obras postumas,* 1978 (also see below).

El publico [and] *Comedia sin titulo: Dos obras postumas,* edited by R. Martinez Nadal and M. Laffranque, Seix Barral, 1978, translation by Carlos Bauer published as *The Public*

[and] *Play Without a Title: Two Posthumous Plays,* New Directions, 1983.

The Rural Trilogy: Blood Wedding [and] *Yerma* [and] *The House of Bernarda Alba,* translation by Michael Dewell and Carmen Zapata, introduction by Douglas Day, Bantam, 1987.

Three Plays (contains *Blood Wedding, Dona Rosita the Spinster,* and *Yerma*), translation by Gwynne Edwards and Peter Luke, introduction by Edwards, Methuen, 1987.

Once Five Years Pass, and Other Dramatic Works, translation by William B. Logan and Angel G. Orrios, Station Hill Press, 1989.

Two Plays of Misalliance: The Love of Don Perlimplin [and] *The Prodigious Cobbler's Wife,* Aris & Phillips, 1989.

Also author of short dramatic sketches, including "La doncella, el marinero, y el estudiante" (title means "The Maiden, the Sailor, and the Student") and "El paseo de Buster Keaton" (title means "Buster Keaton's Stroll"), both 1928, and "Quimera" (title means "Chimera"). Adapter of numerous plays, including *La dama boba* and *Fuenteovejuna,* both by Lope de Vega. Plays represented in collections and anthologies.

OMNIBUS VOLUMES

Obras completas, (title means "Complete Works"), edited by Guillermo de Torre, Losada (Buenos Aires), 1938-46.

Obras completas, edited with commentary by Arturo de Hoyo, introductions by Jorge Guillen and Vicente Aleixandre, Aguilar, 1954, recent edition, 1986.

Obras (title means "Works"), edited with commentary by Mario Hernandez, several volumes, Alianza, 1981—, 2nd edition, revised, 1983—.

OTHER

Impresiones y paisajes (travelogue), P. V. Traveset (Granada), 1918, translation by Lawrence H. Klibbe published as *Impressions and Landscapes,* University Press of America, 1987.

Federico Garcia Lorca: Cartas a sus amigos (letters), edited by Sebastian Gasch, Cobalto (Barcelona), 1950.

Garcia Lorca: Cartas, postales, poemas, y dibujos (includes letters and poems), edited by Antonio Gallego Morell, Monedo y Credito (Madrid), 1968.

Deep Song, and Other Prose, translation by Christopher Maurer, New Directions, 1980.

From the Havana Lectures, 1928: "Theory and Play of the Duende" and "Imagination, Inspiration, Evasion" (lectures; bilingual edition), translation by Stella Rodriguez, preface by Randolph Severson, introduction by Rafael Lopez Pedraza, Kanathos (Dallas, Tex.), 1981.

Selected Letters, edited with translation by David Gershator, New Directions, 1983.

How a City Sings from November to November (lecture; bilingual edition), translation by Christopher Maurer, Cadmus Editions, 1984.

Also author of the filmscript "Trip to the Moon." Illustrator of several books, including *El fin del viaje* by Pablo Neruda; drawings represented in collections, including *Federico Garcia Lorca: Dibujos,* Ministerio de Cultura (Granada), 1986, and Helen Oppenheimer, *Lorca—The Drawings: Their Relation to the Poet's Life and Work,* F. Watts, 1987. Co-editor of *gallo* (Granada literary magazine; title means "rooster"), 1928.

SIDELIGHTS: Federico Garcia Lorca was "a child of genius beyond question," declared Jorge Guillen in *Language and Poetry.* A Spanish poet and dramatist, Lorca was at the height of his fame in 1936 when he was executed by fascist rebels at the age of thirty-eight; in the years thereafter, Guillen suggested, the writer's prominence in European culture matched that of his countryman Pablo Picasso. Lorca's work has been treasured by a broad spectrum of the reading public throughout the world. His complete works have been reprinted in Spain almost every year since the 1950s, and observers believe he is more widely recognized in the English-speaking world than any Spanish writer except Miguel de Cervantes, author of *Don Quixote.* Lorca was familiar with the artistic innovators of his time, and his work shares with theirs a sense of sophistication, awareness of human psychology, and overall pessimism. But while his contemporaries often preferred to appeal to the intellect, Lorca gained wide popularity by addressing basic human emotions. He possessed an engaging personality and a dynamic speaking style, and he imbued his writing with a wide range of human feeling, including awe, lust, nostalgia, and despair. "Those who knew him," wrote his brother Francisco in a foreword to *Three Tragedies,* "will not forget his gift . . . of enlivening things by his presence, of making them more intense."

The public image of Lorca has varied greatly since he became famous in the 1920s. Known primarily for works about peasants and gypsies, he was quickly labeled a simple poet of rural life—an image he felt oversimplified his art. His death enraged democratic and socialist intellectuals, who called him a political martyr; but while Lorca sympathized with leftist causes, he avoided direct involvement in politics. In the years since Lorca died, his literary biographers have grown more sophisticated, revealing his complexity both as a person and as an artist. To biographer Carl Cobb, for instance, Lorca's "life and his work" display a "basic duality." Despite friends and fame Lorca struggled with depression, concerned that his homosexuality, which he hid from the public, condemned him to live as a social outcast. While deeply attached to Spain and its rural life, he came to reject his country's social conservatism, which disdained his sexuality. Arguably, Lorca's popularity grew from his conscious effort to transform his personal concerns into comments on life in general, allowing him to reach a wide audience.

During his youth Lorca experienced both Spain's traditional rural life and its entry into the modern world. Born in 1898, he grew up in a village in Andalusia—the southernmost region of Spain, then largely untouched by the modern world. Such areas were generally dominated by the traditional powers of Spanish society, including political conservatism, the Catholic church, and affluent landowners. Lorca's father, a landowning liberal, confounded his wealthy peers by marrying a village schoolteacher and by paying his workers generously. Though Lorca was a privileged child he knew his home village well, attending school with its children, observing its poverty, and absorbing the vivid speech and folktales of its peasants. "I have a huge storehouse of childhood recollections in which I can hear the people speaking," Lorca observed, according to biographer Ian Gibson. "This is poetic memory, and I trust it implicitly." The sense of lost innocence that recurs in Lorca's writings, Gibson averred, focuses on his early rural years, probably the happiest of his life.

But once Lorca moved with his parents to the Andalusian city of Granada in 1909, many forces propelled him into the modern world. Spain was undergoing a lengthy crisis of confidence, spurred by the country's defeat by the United States in the War of 1898. Some Spaniards wished to strengthen traditional values and revive past glory, but others hoped their country would moderate its conservatism, foster intellectual inquiry, and learn from more modernized countries. With his parents' encouragement Lorca encountered Spain's progressives through his schooling, first at an innovative, nonreligious secondary school, and then at the University of Granada, where he became a protege of such intellectual reformers as Fernando de los Rios and Martin Dominguez Berrueta. By his late teens Lorca was already known as a multi-talented artist—his first book, the travelogue *Impresiones y paisajes* (*Impressions and Landscapes*), appeared before he was twenty—but he was also a poor student. Skilled as a pianist and singer, he would probably have become a musician if his parents had not compelled him to stay in school and study law. "I am a great Romantic," he wrote to a friend at the time, according to Gibson. "In a century of Zeppelins and idiotic deaths, I weep at my piano dreaming of the Handelian mist."

In 1919 Lorca's parents let him transfer to the University of Madrid, where he ignored classes in favor of socializing and cultural life. The move helped Lorca's development as a writer, however, for some of the major trends of modern European culture were just beginning to reach Spain through Madrid's intellectual community. As Western writers began to experiment with language, Madrid became a center of ultraism, which sought to change the nature of poetry by abandoning sentiment and moral rhetoric in favor of "pure poetry"—new and startling images and metaphors. Surrealism, aided by Sigmund Freud's studies of psychology, tried to dispense with social convention and express the hidden desires and fears of the subconscious mind. New ideas surrounded Lorca even in his dormitory—an idealistic private foundation, the Residencia de Estudiantes, which tried to recreate in Spain the lively intellectual atmosphere found in the residence halls of England's elite universities. At the Residencia Lorca met such talented students as Luis Bunuel and Salvador Dali, who soon became prominent in the surrealist movement. The friendship between Lorca and Dali became particularly close, and at times painful to both. Dali, somewhat withdrawn in his youth, resisted becoming Lorca's lover but was clearly drawn to Lorca's ebullient personality. Lorca, who came to view Dali with feelings of unrequited love, was impressed by his friend's audacity as a social critic and as a painter. "You are a Christian tempest," Dali told Lorca, according to Gibson, "and you need my paganism."

Lorca's early poems, Carl Cobb suggested, show his "search . . . for a permanent manner of expression"; the results are promising but sometimes awkward. Lorca quickly showed a gift for imagery and dramatic imagination, adeptly describing, for instance, the experience of a bird being shot down by a hunter. But he had to struggle to shed the vague, overemotional style of romanticism—a difficult task because he often seemed to be making veiled comments about his unhappiness as a homosexual. For example, Lorca's poem about the doomed love of a cockroach for a butterfly became an artistic disaster when it was presented in 1920 as the play "El malefico de la mariposa" ("The Butterfly's Evil Spell"). Lorca's Madrid audience derided the play, and even when he became a successful dramatist he avoided discussing the experience. A more successful poem, which Gibson called "one of Lorca's most moving," is "Encuentro" ("Meeting"), in which the poet speaks with the loving wife he might have known as a heterosexual. (At his death Lorca left behind many unpublished works—generally dominated by frustration or sadness—on homosexual themes, apparently presuming that the general public would not accept the subject matter.) Lorca tried many poetic forms, particularly in *Canciones* (*Songs*), which contains poems written between 1921 and 1924. He wrote several extended odes, including the "Ode to Salvador Dali," which was widely praised as a defense of modern art although it can also be read as a love poem. The form and rhythm of music inspired a group of poems titled *Suites,* which were not published as a unified collection until 1983.

Eventually Lorca achieved great success as a poet by describing the traditional world of his childhood with a blend of very old and very contemporary writing techniques. The impetus came from his friendship with Manuel de Falla, a renowned composer who moved to Granada to savor the exotic music of Andalusia's gypsies and peasants. The two men rediscovered the gypsies' *cante jondo* or "deep song," a simple but deeply felt form of folk music that laments the struggles of everyday life. For Lorca, the ancient *cante jondo* became a model for innovative poetry: it expressed human feeling in broad terms while avoiding the rhetorical excess of romanticism. While helping Falla to organize a 1922 *cante jondo* festival that drew folk singers from throughout Spain, Lorca wrote a poetry collection titled *Poema del cante jondo* (*Poem of the Deep Song*). In these verses, Gibson observed, Lorca tried to convey the emotional atmosphere of the folk songs while avoiding the awkward pretense that he was an uneducated gypsy. Thereafter Lorca discovered that he could increase the dramatic impact of his folk-inspired poetry by using the narrative form of old Spanish ballads to tell poetic stories about gypsies and other characters; the poems could retain a twentieth-century outlook by using innovative language and a sophisticated understanding of the human mind. The resulting work, *Romancero gitano* (*Gypsy Ballads*), appeared in 1928 and soon made Lorca famous throughout the Hispanic world.

Gypsy Ballads shows Lorca at the height of his skill as a poet, in full control of language, imagery, and emotional suggestion. The characters inhabit a world of intense, sometimes mysterious, emotional experience. In the opening ballad a gypsy boy taunts the moon, which appears before him as a sexually attractive woman; suddenly the moon returns to the sky and takes the child with her, while other gypsies wail. Observers have tried to explain the ballad as everything from a comment on Lorca's sense of being sexually "different" to a metaphor for death. Some of the ballads appear to celebrate sexual vitality. In an unusually delicate poem, Lorca describes a gypsy nun who is fleetingly aroused by the sound of men on horseback outside her convent; in another a gypsy man describes his nighttime tryst with a woman by a riverbank. Much of the book conveys menace and violence: a girl runs through the night, her fear of being attacked embodied by the wind, which clutches at her dress; a gypsy is murdered by others who envy his good looks; in the final ballad, derived from the Bible, a prince rapes his sister. In his lecture "On the Gypsy Ballads," reprinted in *Deep Song and Other Prose*, Lorca suggests that the ballads are not really about gypsies but about pain—"the struggle of the loving intelligence with the incomprehensible mystery that surrounds it." "Lorca is not deliberately inflicting pain on the reader in order to shock or annoy him," wrote Roy Campbell in *Lorca*, but the poet "feels so poignantly that he has to share this feeling with others." Observers suggest that the collection describes the force of human life itself—a source of both energy and destructiveness.

The intensity of *Gypsy Ballads* is heightened by Lorca's mastery of the language of poetry. "Over the years," observed Cobb in his translation of the work, "it has become possible to speak of the 'Lorquian' metaphor or image, which [the poet] brought to fruition" in this volume. When Lorca says a gypsy woman bathes "with water of skylarks," Cobb explained, the poet has created a stunning new image out of two different words that describe something "soothing." Sometimes Lorca's metaphors boldly draw upon two different senses: he refers to a "horizon of barking dogs," for instance, when dogs are barking in the distance at night and the horizon is invisible. Such metaphors seem to surpass those of typical avant-garde poets, who often combined words arbitrarily, without concern for actual human experience.

Lorca said his poetic language was inspired by Spanish peasants, for whom a seemingly poetic phrase such as "oxen of the waters" was an ordinary term for the strong, slow current of a river. Campbell stressed that Lorca was unusually sensitive to "the *sound* of words," both their musical beauty and their ability to reinforce the meaning of a poem. Such skills, practiced by Spain's folksingers, made Lorca "musician" among poets, Campbell averred; interestingly, Lorca greatly enjoyed reading his work aloud before audiences and also presented Spanish folk songs at the piano. Reviewers often lament that Lorca's ear for language is impossible to reproduce in translation.

Lorca's newfound popularity did not prevent him from entering an unusually deep depression by 1929. Its causes, left vague by early biographers, seem to have been the breakup of Lorca's intense relationship with a manipulative lover and the end of his friendship with Dali. At Bunuel's urging Dali had moved to Paris, where the two men created a bizarre surrealist film titled "Un Chien andalou" ("An Andalusian Dog"). Lorca was convinced that the film, which supposedly had no meaning at all, was actually a sly effort to ridicule him. The poet, who knew no English and had never left Spain, opted for a radical change of scene by enrolling to study English at New York City's Columbia University. In New York Lorca's lively and personable manner charmed the Spanish-speaking intellectual community, but some have surmised that inwardly he was close to suicide. Forsaking his classes Lorca roamed the city, cut off from its citizens by the language barrier. He found most New Yorkers cold and inhuman, preferring instead the emotional warmth he felt among the city's black minority, whom he saw as fellow outcasts. Meanwhile he struggled to come to terms with his unhappiness and his sexuality.

The first product of Lorca's turmoil was the poetry collection *Poeta en Nueva York* (*Poet in New York*). In the book, Cobb observed, New York's social problems mirror Lorca's personal despair. The work opens as the poet reaches town, already deeply unhappy; he surveys both New York's troubles and his own; finally, after verging on hopelessness, he regathers his strength and tries to resolve the problems he has described. *Poet in New York* is far more grim and difficult than *Gypsy Ballads,* as Lorca apparently tries to heighten the reader's sense of alienation. The liveliness of the earlier volume gives way to pessimism; the verse is unrhymed; and, instead of using vivid metaphors about the natural world, Lorca imitates the surrealists by using symbols that are strange and difficult to understand. In poems about American society Lorca shows a horror of urban crowds, which he compares to animals, but he also shows sympathy for the poor. Unlike many white writers of his time, he is notably eloquent in describing the oppression of black Americans, particularly in his image of an uncrowned "King of Harlem"—a strong-willed black man humiliated by his menial job. Near the end of the collection he predicts a general uprising in favor of economic equality and challenges Christianity to ease the pain of the modern world. In more personal poems Lorca contrasts the innocent world of his childhood with his later unhappiness, alludes to his disappointments in love, and rails at the decadence he sees among urban homosexuals. He seems to portray a positive role model in his "Ode to Walt Whitman," dedicated to a nineteenth-century American poet—also a homosexual—who attempted to celebrate common people and the realities of everyday life. Lorca's final poem is a song about his departure from New York for Cuba, which he found much more hospitable than the United States. Commentators disagreed greatly about the merits of *Poet in New York,* which was not published in its entirety until after Lorca's death. Many reviewers, disappointed by the book's ob-

scure language and grim tone, dismissed it as a failed experiment or an aberration. By contrast, Cobb declared that "with the impetus given by modern critical studies and translations, *Poet in New York* has become the other book which sustains Lorca's reputation as a poet."

Before Lorca returned to Spain in 1930, he had largely completed what many observers would call his first mature play, *El publico* (*The Public*). Written in a disconcerting, surrealist style comparable to *Poet in New York,* the play confronts such controversial themes as the need for truth in the theater and for truth about homosexuality, in addition to showing the destruction of human love by selfishness and death. After his disastrous experience with "The Butterfly's Evil Spell," Lorca had spent the 1920s gradually mastering the techniques of drama, beginning with the light, formulaic Spanish genres of farce and puppet plays. From puppet theater, observers have suggested, Lorca learned to draw characters rapidly and decisively; in farces for human actors, he developed the skills required to sustain a full-length play. For instance, the farce *La zapatera prodigiosa* (*The Shoemaker's Prodigious Wife*), begun in the mid-1920s, shows Lorca's growing ease with extended dialogue and complex action. In *Amor de Don Perlimplin con Belisa en su jardin* (*The Love of Don Perlimplin with Belisa, in His Garden*), begun shortly thereafter, Lorca toys with the conventions of farce, as the play's object of ridicule—an old man with a lively young wife—unexpectedly becomes a figure of pity. By 1927 Lorca gained modest commercial success with his second professional production, *Mariana Pineda.* The heroine of this historical melodrama meets death rather than forsake her lover, a rebel on behalf of democracy. By the time the play was staged, however, Lorca said he had outgrown its "romantic" style.

Accordingly, in *The Public* Lorca proposed a new theater that would confront its audience with uncomfortable truths. As the play opens, a nameless Director of popular plays receives three visitors, who challenge him to present the "theater beneath the sand"—drama that goes beneath life's pleasing surface. The three men and the Director rapidly change costumes, apparently revealing themselves as unhappy homosexuals, locked in relationships of betrayal and mistrust. The Director then shows his audience a play about "the truth of the tombs," dramatizing Lorca's pessimistic belief that the finality of death overwhelms the power of love. Apparently the Director reshapes William Shakespeare's "Romeo and Juliet," in which young lovers die rather than live apart from each other. In *The Public* Juliet appears on stage after her love-inspired suicide, realizing that her death is meaningless and that she will now remain alone for eternity. The Director's audience riots when faced with such ideas, but some theater students, perhaps representing the future of drama, are intrigued. Back in Spain Lorca read *The Public* to friends, who were deeply shocked and advised him that the play was too controversial and surrealistic for an audience to accept. Lorca apparently agreed: he did not release the work and, according to biographer Reed Anderson, dismissed it in interviews as "a poem to be booed at." Nonetheless, Lorca observed, it reflected his "true intention."

Lorca remained determined to write plays rather than poetry, but he reached what some have called an unspoken compromise with his audience, presenting innovative theater that would not provoke general outrage. He became artistic director of the University Theater, a state-supported group of traveling players known by its Spanish nickname, *La barraca* ("The Hut"). The troupe, which presented plays from the "Golden Age" of Spanish drama in the seventeenth century, was welcomed by small villages throughout Spain that had never seen a stage performance. Lorca, who gained invaluable experience in theater by directing and producing the programs, decided that an untapped audience for challenging drama existed among Spain's common people. In a manner reminiscent of the *Gypsy Ballads,* he wrote a series of plays set among the common people of Spain, discussing such serious themes as human passion, unrequited love, social repression, the passing of time, and the power of death. Rather than shock by discussing homosexuality as in *The Public,* he focused on the frustrations of Spain's women. As the plays emerged, Lorca spoke of bringing "poetry" to the theater. But his characters often speak prose, and observers suggest he was speaking somewhat metaphorically. Like other playwrights of his time, Lorca seems to have felt that nineteenth-century dramatists' emphasis on realism—accurate settings, everyday events—distracted writers from deeper, emotional truths about human experience. To make theater more imaginative and involving, Lorca used a variety of effects: vivid language, visually striking stage settings, and heightened emotions ranging from confrontation to tension and repression. By adding such "poetry" to scenes of everyday Spanish life, he could show audiences the underlying sorrows and desires of their own lives.

In accord with such aims, Lorca's four best-known plays from the 1930s—*Dona Rosita la soltera* (*Dona Rosita the Spinster*), *Bodas de sangre* (*Blood Wedding*), *Yerma,* and *La casa de Bernarda Alba* (*The House of Bernarda Alba*)—show notable similarities. All are set in Spain during Lorca's lifetime; all spotlight ordinary women struggling with the impositions of Spanish society. *Dona Rosita* is set in the Granada middle class that Lorca knew as a teenager. In three acts set from 1885 to 1911, Lorca first revels in nostalgia for turn-of-the-century Spain, then shows Rosita's growing despair as she waits helplessly for a man to marry her. By the play's end, as Rosita faces old age as an unwanted, unmarried woman, her passivity seems as outdated as the characters' costumes. The three remaining plays, called the "Rural Trilogy," are set in isolated villages of Lorca's Spain. *Yerma*'s title character is a woman whose name means "barren land." She dutifully allows relatives to arrange her marriage, then gradually realizes, to her dismay, that her husband does not want children. Torn between her desire for a baby and her belief in the sanctity of marriage, Yerma resorts to prayer and sorcery in a futile effort to become a mother. Finally she strangles her husband in a burst of uncontrollable frustration. In *The House of Bernarda Alba,* the repressive forces of society are personified by the play's title character, a conservative matriarch who tries to confine her unmarried daughters to the family homestead for eight years of mourning after the death of her husband. The daughters grow increasingly frustrated and hostile until the youngest and most rebellious commits suicide rather than be separated from her illicit lover. *Blood Wedding* is probably Lorca's most successful play with both critics and the public. A man and woman who are passionately attracted to each other enter loveless marriages out of duty to their relatives, but at the woman's wedding feast the lovers elope. In one of the most evocative and unconventional scenes of all Lorca's plays, two characters representing the Moon and Death follow the lovers to a dark and menacing forest, declaring that the couple will meet a disastrous fate. The woman's vengeful husband appears and the two men kill each other. The play ends back at the village where the woman, who has lost both her husband and her lover, joins other villagers in grieving but is isolated from them by mutual hatred. In each of the four plays, an individual's desires are overborne by the demands of society, with disastrous results.

After *Blood Wedding* premiered in 1933, Lorca's fame as a dramatist quickly matched his fame as a poet, both in his home-

land and in the rest of the Hispanic world. A short lecture tour of Argentina and Uruguay stretched into six months, as Lorca was greeted as a celebrity and his plays were performed for enthusiastic crowds. He was warmly received by such major Latin American writers as Chile's Pablo Neruda and Mexico's Alfonso Reyes. Neruda, who later won the Nobel Prize for his poetry, called Lorca's visit "the greatest triumph ever achieved by a writer of our race." Notably, while Lorca's most popular plays have achieved great commercial success with Spanish-speaking audiences, they have been respected, but not adulated, by the English-speaking public. Some observers suggested that the strength of the plays is limited to their language, which is lost in translation. But others, including Spaniard Angel del Rio and American Reed Anderson, have surveyed Lorca's stagecraft with admiration. In the opening scenes of *Blood Wedding,* for instance, Lorca skillfully contrasts the festive mood of the villagers with the fierce passions of the unwilling bride; in *Yerma* he confronts his heroine with a shepherd whose love for children subtly embodies her dreams of an ideal husband. In an article that appeared in *Lorca: A Collection of Critical Essays,* del Rio wondered if the plays were too steeped in Hispanic culture for other audiences to easily appreciate.

Lorca's triumphs as a playwright were marred by growing troubles in Spain, which became divided between hostile factions on the political left and right. Though Lorca steadily resisted efforts to recruit him for the Communist party, his social conscience led him to strongly criticize Spanish conservatives, some of whom may have yearned for revenge. Meanwhile Lorca seemed plagued by a sense of foreboding and imminent death. He was shocked when an old friend, retired bullfighter Ignacio Sanchez Mejias, was killed by a bull while attempting to revive his career in the ring. Lorca's elegy—*Llanto por Ignacio Sanchez Mejias* (*Lament for the Death of a Bullfighter*)—has often been called his best poem, endowing the matador with heroic stature as he confronts his fate. Later, friends recalled Lorca's melodramatic remark that the bullfighter's death was a rehearsal for his own. In 1936 civil war broke out in Spain as conservative army officers under General Francisco Franco revolted against the liberal government. Lorca, who was living in Madrid, made the worst possible decision by electing to wait out the impending conflict at his parents' home in Granada, a city filled with rebel sympathizers. Granada quickly fell to rebel forces, who executed many liberal politicians and intellectuals. One was Lorca, who was arrested, shot outside town, and buried in an unmarked grave.

Franco's regime, which controlled all of Spain by 1939, never accepted responsibility for Lorca's death. But Lorca remained a forbidden subject in Spain for many years: "We knew there had been a great poet called Garcia Lorca," recalled film director Carlos Saura in the *New York Times,* "but we couldn't read him, we couldn't study him." By the 1950s Lorca's work was again available in Spain, but it was still difficult to research either his life or his death. Those who knew him avoided discussing his sexuality or releasing his more controversial work; residents of Granada who knew about his execution were afraid to speak. Gradually there emerged a new willingness to understand Lorca on his own terms, and after Franco died in 1975, Lorca could be openly admired in his homeland as one of the century's greatest poets—a status he had never lost elsewhere. His legacy endures as a unique genius whose personal unhappiness enabled him to see deeply into the human heart. "When I met him for the first time, he astonished me," Guillen recalled, according to Anderson. "I've never recovered from that astonishment."

MEDIA ADAPTATIONS: Several of Lorca's plays have been adapted for opera and ballet, including *Blood Wedding, Yerma,* and *The Love of Don Perlimplin with Belisa, in His Garden. Blood Wedding* was adapted by Antonio Gades for a ballet, which was in turn adapted by Carlos Saura for a film of the same title, 1981.

BIOGRAPHICAL/CRITICAL SOURCES:

BOOKS

Adams, Mildred, *Garcia Lorca: Playwright and Poet,* Braziller, 1977.

Allen, Rupert C., *The Symbolic World of Garcia Lorca,* University of New Mexico Press, 1972.

Anderson, Reed, *Federico Garcia Lorca,* Grove, 1984.

Berea, Arturo, *Lorca: The Poet and His People,* translation by Ilsa Berea, Harcourt, 1949.

Bowra, C. M., *The Creative Experiment,* Macmillan, 1949.

Byrd, Suzanne Wade, *Garcia Lorca, La Barraca, and the Spanish National Theater,* Abra, 1975.

Campbell, Roy, *Lorca: An Appreciation of His Poetry,* Yale University Press, 1952.

Cobb, Carl W., *Federico Garcia Lorca,* Twayne, 1967.

Cobb, Carl W., *Contemporary Spanish Poetry (1898-1963),* Twayne, 1976.

Colecchia, Francesca, editor, *Garcia Lorca: A Selectively Annotated Bibliography of Criticism,* Garland Publishing, 1979.

Colecchia, Francesca, editor, *Garcia Lorca: An Annotated Primary Bibliography,* Garland Publishing, 1982.

Duran, Manuel, editor, *Lorca: A Collection of Critical Essays,* Prentice-Hall, 1962.

Edwards, Gwynne, *Lorca: The Theatre Beneath the Sand,* Boyars, 1980.

Garcia Lorca, Federico, *Three Tragedies,* translation by Richard L. O'Connell and James Graham-Lujan, introduction by Francisco Garcia Lorca, New Directions, 1947.

Garcia Lorca, Federico, *Five Plays: Comedies and Tragicomedies,* translation by Richard L. O'Connell and James Graham-Lujan, introduction by Francisco Garcia Lorca, New Directions, 1963.

Garcia Lorca, Federico, *Deep Song, and Other Prose,* translation by Christopher Maurer, New Directions, 1980.

Garcia Lorca, Federico, *Lorca's "Romancero gitano": A Ballad Translation and Critical Study,* translation and commentary by Carl W. Cobb, University Press of Mississippi, 1983.

Garcia Lorca, Federico, *Poet in New York,* translation by Greg Simon and Steven F. White, edited with an introduction by Christopher Maurer, Farrar, Straus, 1988.

Garcia Lorca, Francisco, *In the Green Morning: Memories of Federico,* translation by Christopher Maurer, New Directions, 1986.

Gibson, Ian, *The Assassination of Federico Garcia Lorca,* W. H. Allen, 1979.

Gibson, Ian, *Federico Garcia Lorca: A Life,* Pantheon, 1989.

Guillen, Jorge, *Language and Poetry: Some Poets of Spain,* Harvard University Press, 1961.

Honig, Edwin, *Garcia Lorca,* New Directions, 1944.

Laurenti, Joseph L. and Joseph Siracusa, *Federico Garcia Lorca y su mundo: Ensayo de una bibliografia general/ The World of Federico Garcia Lorca: A General Bibliographic Survey,* Scarecrow Press, 1974.

Lima, Robert, *The Theatre of Garcia Lorca,* Las Americas, 1963.

Londre, Felicia Hardison, *Federico Garcia Lorca,* Ungar, 1984.

Morris, C. B., *A Generation of Spanish Poets, 1920-1936,* Cambridge University Press, 1969.

Pollin, Alice M. and Philip H. Smith, editors, *A Concordance to the Plays and Poems of Federico Garcia Lorca,* Cornell University Press, 1975.

Stanton, Edward F., *The Tragic Myth: Lorca and Cante Jondo,* University Press of Kentucky, 1978.

Trend, J. B., *Lorca and the Spanish Poetic Tradition,* Russell & Russell, 1971.

Twentieth-Century Literary Criticism, Gale, Volume 1, 1978, Volume 7, 1982.

Young, Howard T., *The Victorious Expression: A Study of Four Contemporary Spanish Poets,* University of Wisconsin Press, 1966.

PERIODICALS

Commonweal, November 3, 1939, April 20, 1945, August 12, 1955, September 2, 1955, October 21, 1955.

Kenyon Review, summer, 1955.

Nation, September 18, 1937, November 1, 1941, December 27, 1947.

New Republic, February 27, 1935, November 10, 1937, October 11, 1939, September 2, 1940, October 13, 1941.

New York Times, October 19, 1980, July 5, 1989.

New York Times Book Review, September 3, 1939, June 14, 1953, October 9, 1955, November 20, 1988, October 8, 1989.

Parnassus, spring, 1981.

Poetry, December, 1937, September, 1940.

Saturday Review, October 2, 1937, August 26, 1939, January 13, 1940, November 26, 1960.

Time, December 22, 1947, April 17, 1964.

Times Literary Supplement, October 16, 1937, May 27, 1939, September 2, 1965, September 2, 1977, November 21, 1980, August 2, 1984.

—*Sketch by Thomas Kozikowski*

*   *   *

GARCIA MARQUEZ, Gabriel (Jose) 1928-

PERSONAL: Surname pronounced "Gar-*see*-a *Mar*-kez"; born March 6, 1928, in Aracataca, Colombia; son of Gabriel Eligio Garcia (a telegraph operator) and Luisa Santiaga Marquez Iguaran; married Mercedes Barcha, March 21, 1958; children: Rodrigo, Gonzalo. *Education:* Attended Universidad Nacional de Colombia, 1947-48, and Universidad de Cartagena, 1948-49.

ADDRESSES: Home—P.O. Box 20736, Mexico City D.F., Mexico. *Office*—Apartado Postal 20736 Deleyacion Alvaro Bregon 01000, Mexico. *Agent*—Agencia Literaria Carmen Balcells, Diagonal 580, Barcelona 21, Spain.

CAREER: Worked as a journalist, 1947-65, including job with *El heraldo,* Baranquilla, Colombia; film critic and news reporter, *El espectador,* Bogota, Colombia, Geneva, Switzerland, Rome, Italy, and Paris, France, Prensa Latina news agency, Bogota, 1959, and as department head in New York City, 1961; writer, 1965—. Founder, Cuban Press Agency, Bogota; Fundacion Habeas, founder, 1979, president, 1979—. Mediator between Colombian government and leftist guerrillas in early 1980s.

MEMBER: American Academy of Arts and Letters (honorary fellow), Foundation for the New Latin American Film (Havana; president, 1985—).

AWARDS, HONORS: Colombian Association of Writers and Artists Award, 1954, for story "Un dia despues del sabado"; Premio Literario Esso (Colombia), 1961, for *La mala hora;* Chianciano Award (Italy), 1969, Prix de Meilleur Livre Etranger (France), 1969, and Romulo Gallegos prize (Venezuela), 1971, all for *Cien anos de soledad;* LL.D., Columbia University, 1971; *Books Abroad*/Neustadt International Prize for Literature,

1972; Common Wealth Award for Literature, Bank of Delaware, 1980; Nobel Prize for Literature, 1982; *Los Angeles Times* Book Prize nomination for fiction, 1983, for *Chronicle of a Death Foretold; Los Angeles Times* Book Prize for fiction, 1988, for *Love in the Time of Cholera.*

WRITINGS:

FICTION

La hojarasca (novella; title means "Leaf Storm"; also see below), Ediciones Sipa (Bogota), 1955, reprinted, Bruguera (Barcelona), 1983.

El coronel no tiene quien le escriba (novella; title means "No One Writes to the Colonel"; also see below), Aguirre Editor (Medellin, Colombia), 1961, reprinted, Bruguera, 1983.

La mala hora (novel; also see below), Talleres de Graficas "Luis Perez" (Madrid), 1961, reprinted, Bruguera, 1982, English translation by Gregory Rabassa published as *In Evil Hour,* Harper, 1979.

Los funerales de la Mama Grande (short stories; title means "Big Mama's Funeral"; also see below), Editorial Universidad Veracruzana (Mexico), 1962, reprinted, Bruguera, 1983.

Cien anos de soledad (novel), Editorial Sudamericana (Buenos Aires), 1967, reprinted, Catedra, 1984, English translation by Rabassa published as *One Hundred Years of Solitude,* Harper, 1970.

Isabel viendo llover en Macondo (novella; title means "Isabel Watching It Rain in Macondo"; also see below), Editorial Estuario (Buenos Aires), 1967.

No One Writes to the Colonel and Other Stories (includes "No One Writes to the Colonel," and stories from *Big Mama's Funeral*), translated by J. S. Bernstein, Harper, 1968.

La increible y triste historia de la candida Erendira y su abuela desalmada (novella; title means "Innocent Erendira and Her Heartless Grandmother"; also see below), Barral Editores, 1972.

El negro que hizo esperar a los angeles (short stories), Ediciones Alfil (Montevideo), 1972.

Ojos de perro azul: Nueve cuentos desconocidos (short stories; also see below), Equisditorial (Argentina), 1972.

Leaf Storm and Other Stories (includes "Leaf Storm," and "Isabel Watching It Rain in Macondo"), translated by Rabassa, Harper, 1972.

La increible y triste historia de la candida Erendira y su abuela desalmada (short stories; includes *El coronel no tiene quien le escriba*), Libreria de Colegio (Buenos Aires), 1975.

El otono del patriarca (novel), Plaza & Janes Editores (Barcelona), 1975, translation by Rabassa published as *The Autumn of the Patriarch,* Harper, 1976.

Todos los cuentos de Gabriel Garcia Marquez: 1947-1972 (title means "All the Stories of Gabriel Garcia Marquez: 1947-1972"), Plaza & Janes Editores, 1975.

Innocent Erendira and Other Stories (includes "Innocent Erendira and Her Heartless Grandmother" and stories from *Ojos de perro azul*), translated by Rabassa, Harper, 1978.

Dos novelas de Macondo (contains *La hojarasca* and *La mala hora*), Casa de las Americas (Havana), 1980.

Cronica de una muerte anunciada (novel), La Oveja Negra (Bogota), 1981, translation by Rabassa published as *Chronicle of a Death Foretold,* J. Cape, 1982, Knopf, 1983.

Viva Sandino (play), Editorial Nueva Nicaragua, 1982, 2nd edition published as *El asalto: El operativo con que el FSLN se lanzo al mundo,* 1983.

El rastro de tu sangre en la nieve: El verano feliz de la senora Forbes, W. Dampier Editores (Bogota), 1982.

El secuestro: Guion cinematografico (unfilmed screenplay), Oveja Negra, 1982.

"Erendira" (filmscript; adapted from his novella *La increible y triste historia de la candida Erendira y su abuela desalmada*), Les Films du Triangle, 1983.

Collected Stories, translated by Rabassa and Bernstein, Harper, 1984.

El amor en los tiempos del colera, Oveja Negra, 1985, English translation by Edith Grossman published as *Love in the Time of Cholera,* Knopf, 1988.

El cataclismo de Damocles, Editorial Universitaria Centroamericana (Costa Rica), 1986.

"A Time to Die" (filmscript), ICA Cinema, 1988.

"Diatribe of Love against a Seated Man" (play), first produced at Cervantes Theater, Buenos Aires, 1988.

El general en su laberinto, Mondadori Espana, 1989, English translation published as *The General in His Labyrinth,* Knopf, 1990.

NONFICTION

(With Mario Vargas Llosa) *La novela en America Latina: Dialogo,* Carlos Milla Batres (Lima), 1968, published as *Dialogo sobre la novela Latinoamericana,* Peru Andino (Lima), 1988.

El relato de un naufrago (journalistic pieces), Tusquets Editor (Barcelona), 1970, English translation by Randolph Hogan published as *The Story of a Shipwrecked Sailor,* Knopf, 1986.

Cuando era feliz e indocumentado (journalistic pieces; title means "When I Was Happy and Undocumented"), Ediciones El Ojo de Camello (Caracas), 1973.

Cronicas y reportajes (journalistic pieces), La Oveja Negra, 1978.

Periodismo militante (journalistic pieces), Son de Maquina Editores (Bogota), 1978.

De viaje por los paises socialistas: 90 dias en las "Cortina de hierro" (journalistic pieces), Ediciones Macondo (Colombia), 1978.

(Contributor) *Los sandanistas,* Oveja Negra, 1979.

(Contributor) Soledad Mendoza, editor, *Asi es Caracas,* Editorial Ateneo de Caracas, 1980.

Obra periodistica (journalistic pieces), edited by Jacques Gilard, Bruguera, Volume 1: *Textos constenos,* 1981, Volumes 2-3: *Entre cachacos,* 1982, Volume 4: *De Europa y America (1955-1960),* 1983.

(With P. Mendoza) *El olor de la guayaba: Conversaciones con Plinio Apuleyo Mendoza* (interviews), La Oveja Negra, 1982, English translation by Ann Wright published as *The Fragrance of Guava,* edited by T. Nairn, Verso, 1983.

(With Guillermo Nolasco-Juarez) *Persecucion y muerte de minorias: Dos perspectivas,* Juarez Editor (Buenos Aires), 1984.

(Contributor) *La Democracia y la paz en America Latina,* Editorial El Buho (Bogota), 1986.

1928-1986, presencia de Jovito Villalba en la historia de la democracia venezolana, Ediciones Centauro, 1986.

La aventura de Miguel Littin, clandestino en Chile: Un reportaje, Editorial Sudamericana, 1986, English translation by Asa Zatz published as *Clandestine in Chile: The Adventures of Miguel Littin,* Holt, 1987.

OTHER

Also co-author and producer of six screenplays made for Spanish television, "Fable of the Beautiful Pigeon Fancier," "I'm the One You're Looking For," "Miracle in Rome," "The Summer of Miss Forbes," "Letters from the Park," and "A Happy Sunday," together titled "Amores Dificiles" (title means "Dangerous Loves"); two screenplays, "Letters from the Park" and "Miracle in Rome" were scheduled to appear on Public Television's "Great Performance" series, 1989 and 1990. Author of weekly syndicated column.

WORK IN PROGRESS: Co-writing new works with Guerra, Duque, and director Sergio Toledo; adapting a Colombian novel, "La Maria," for television.

SIDELIGHTS: "I knew [*One Hundred Years of Solitude*] would please my friends more than my other [books] had," said Gabriel Garcia Marquez in a *Paris Review* interview with Peter H. Stone. "But when my Spanish publisher told me he was going to print eight thousand copies, I was stunned because my other books had never sold more than seven hundred. I asked him why not start slowly, but he said he was convinced that it was a good book and that all eight thousand copies would be sold between May and December. Actually they were sold within one week in Buenos Aires."

Winner of the 1982 Nobel Prize for Literature, Garcia Marquez "is one of the small number of contemporary writers from Latin America who have given to its literature a maturity and dignity it never had before," asserts John Sturrock in the *New York Times Book Review. One Hundred Years of Solitude* is perhaps Garcia Marquez's best-known contribution to the awakening of interest in Latin American literature, for the book's appearance in Spanish in 1967 prompted unqualified approval from readers and critics. It has sold more than ten million copies, has been translated into over thirty languages and, according to an *Antioch Review* critic, the popularity and acclaim for the novel "mean that Latin American literature will change from being the exotic interest of a few to essential reading and that Latin America itself will be looked on less as a crazy subculture and more as a fruitful, alternative way of life." So great was the novel's initial popularity, writes Mario Vargas Llosa in *Garcia Marquez: Historia de un deicido,* that not only was the first Spanish printing of the book sold out within one week, but for months afterwards Latin American readers alone would exhaust each successive printing. Translations of the novel similarly elicited enthusiastic responses from critics and readers around the world.

In this outpouring of critical opinion, which *Books Abroad* contributor Klaus Muller-Bergh refers to as "an earthquake, a maelstrom," various reviewers have termed *One Hundred Years of Solitude* a masterpiece of modern fiction. For example, Chilean poet Pablo Neruda, himself a Nobel laureate, is quoted in *Time* as calling the book "the greatest revelation in the Spanish language since the *Don Quixote* of Cervantes." Similarly enthusiastic is William Kennedy, who writes in the *National Observer* that "*One Hundred Years of Solitude* is the first piece of literature since the Book of Genesis that should be required reading for the entire human race." And Regina Janes, in her study *Gabriel Garcia Marquez: Revolutions in Wonderland,* describes the book as "a 'total novel' that [treats] Latin America socially, historically, politically, mythically, and epically," adding that *One Hundred Years of Solitude* is also "at once accessible and intricate, lifelike and self-consciously, self-referentially fictive."

The novel is set in the imaginary community of Macondo, a village on the Colombian coast, and follows the lives of several generations of the Buendia family. Chief among these characters are Colonel Aureliano Buendia, perpetrator of thirty-two rebellions and father of seventeen illegitimate sons, and Ursula Buendia, the clan's matriarch and witness to its eventual decline. Besides following the complicated relationships of the Buendia family, *One Hundred Years of Solitude* also reflects the political, social, and economic troubles of South America. Many critics believe that the novel, with its complex family relationships and extraordinary events, is a microcosm of Latin America itself. But as *Playboy* contributor Claudia Dreifus states in her interview with the author, Garcia Marquez has facetiously described the plot as "just the story of the Buendia family, of whom it is prophesied that they shall have a son with a pig's tail; and in doing everything to avoid this, the Buendias *do* end up with a son with a pig's tail."

The mixture of historical and fictitious elements that appear in *One Hundred Years of Solitude* places the novel within that type of Latin American fiction that critics term magical or marvelous realism. Janes attributes the birth of this style of writing to Alejo Carpentier, a Cuban novelist and short story writer, and concludes that Garcia Marquez's fiction follows ideas originally formulated by the Cuban author. The critic notes that Carpentier "discovered the duplicities of history and elaborated the critical concept of 'lo maravilloso americano' the 'marvelous real,' arguing that geographically, historically, and essentially, Latin America was a space marvelous and fantastic . . . and to render that reality was to render marvels." Garcia Marquez presents a similar view of Latin America in his *Paris Review* interview with Stone: "It always amuses me that the biggest praise for my work comes for ·the imagination while the truth is that there's not a single line in all my work that does not have a basis in reality." The author further explained in his *Playboy* interview with Dreifus: "Clearly, the Latin American environment is marvelous. Particularly the Caribbean. . . . The coastal people were descendants of pirates and smugglers, with a mixture of black slaves. To grow up in such an environment is to have fantastic resources for poetry. Also, in the Caribbean, we are capable of believing anything, because we have the influences of all those different cultures, mixed in with Catholicism and our own local beliefs. I think that gives us an open-mindedness to look beyond apparent reality."

The first line of *One Hundred Years of Solitude* introduces the reader into this world of imagination. According to James Park Sloan in the *Chicago Tribune Book World:* "Few first lines in literature . . . have comparable force: 'Many years later, as he faced the firing squad, Colonel Aureliano Buendia was to remember that distant afternoon when his father took him to discover ice.' It contains so much of what [makes] the work magical, including a steadily toneless background in which everyday events become marvelous and marvelous events are assimilated without comment into everyday life. Equally important, it establishes a time scheme," continues the critic, which "simultaneously [looks] backward at a present seen as memory in light of that future." Gordon Brotherson also notes the magical quality of *One Hundred Years of Solitude* and the book's relationship with Carpentier's fiction. In *The Emergence of the Latin American Novel,* Brotherson refers to the "skillful vagueness" of the opening sentence and writes, "Phrases like 'many years later' and 'that distant afternoon' lead back through the prehistoric stones to a timeless world where (in an allusion to Carpentier and his magic realism) we are told many things still needed to be named."

Muller-Bergh believes that Garcia Marquez's particular gift for inserting the magical into the real is responsible for his popularity as a writer. The critic comments that "Latin American and Spanish readers . . . as well as European critics who have heaped unprecedented praise on the author" have found that this "penchant for plausible absurdities [is] one of Garcia Marquez's most enduring qualities." Alan Weinblatt explains the novelist's technique in the *New Republic,* noting that for Garcia Marquez "the key to writing *One Hundred Years of Solitude* was the idea of saying incredible things with a completely unperturbed face." The author credits this ability to his maternal grandmother: "She was a fabulous storyteller who told wild tales of the supernatural with a most solemn expression on her face," he told Dreifus. "As I was growing up, I often wondered whether or not her stories were truthful. Usually, I tended to believe her because of her serious, deadpan facial expression. Now, as a writer, I do the same thing; I say extraordinary things in a serious tone. It's possible to get away with *anything* as long as you make it believable. That is something my grandmother taught me." The straightforward manner in which the author tells of Aureliano Buendia and his father going out "to discover ice" is repeated throughout the novel and throughout Garcia Marquez's fiction. For example, in *One Hundred Years of Solitude* Remedios the Beauty ascends into heaven while outside shaking out some sheets, yellow flowers fall all night when a family patriarch dies, and when a young man dies, his blood runs through the streets of the town and into his parents' house where, avoiding the rugs, it stops at the feet of his mother. In other works, Garcia Marquez tells of a woman "so tender she could pass through walls just by sighing" and of a general who sires five thousand children.

But along with the fantastic episodes in Garcia Marquez's fiction appear the historical facts or places that inspired them. An episode involving a massacre of striking banana workers is based on a historical incident; in reality, Garcia Marquez told Dreifus, "there were very few deaths . . . [so] I made the death toll 3000 because I was using certain proportions in my book." But while *One Hundred Years of Solitude* is the fictional account of the Buendia family, the novel is also, as John Leonard states in the *New York Times,* "a recapitulation of our evolutionary and intellectual experience. Macondo is Latin America in microcosm." Robert G. Mead, Jr. similarly observes in *Saturday Review* that "Macondo may be regarded as a microcosm of the development of much of the Latin American continent." Adds the critic: "Although [*One Hundred Years of Solitude*] is first and always a story, the novel also has value as a social and historical document." Garcia Marquez responds to these interpretations in his interview with Dreifus, commenting that his work "is not a history of Latin America, it is a *metaphor* for Latin America."

The "social and historical" elements of *One Hundred Years of Solitude* reflect the journalistic influences at work in Garcia Marquez's fiction. Although known as a novelist, the author began as a reporter and still considers himself one. As he remarked to Stone, "I've always been convinced that my true profession is that of a journalist." Janes believes that the evolution of Garcia Marquez's individual style is based on his experience as a correspondent; in addition, this same experience leads Janes and other critics to compare the Colombian with Ernest Hemingway. "[The] stylistic transformation between *Leaf Storm* and *No One Writes to the Colonel* was not exclusively an act of will," Janes claims. "Garcia Marquez had had six years of experience as a journalist between the two books, experience providing practice in the lessons of Hemingway, trained in the same school." And George R. McMurray, in his book *Gabriel Garcia Marquez,* maintains that Hemingway's themes and techniques have "left their mark" on the work of the Colombian.

Garcia Marquez has also been compared to another American Nobel-winner, William Faulkner, who also elaborated on facts to create his fiction. Faulkner based his fictional territory Yoknapatawpha County on memories of the region in northern Mississippi where he spent most of his life; Garcia Marquez based Macondo, the town appearing throughout his fiction, on Aracataca, the coastal city of his birth. A *Time* reviewer calls

Macondo "a kind of tropical Yoknapatawpha County" while *Review* contributor Mary E. Davis points out further resemblances between the two authors. Davis notes: "Garcia Marquez concentrates on the specific personality of place in the manner of the Mississippean, and he develops even the most reprehensible of his characters as idiosyncratic enigmas." Concludes the critic: "Garcia Marquez is as fascinated by the capacity of things, events, and characters for sudden metamorphosis as was Faulkner."

Nevertheless, *Newsweek* writer Peter S. Prescott maintains that it was only after Garcia Marquez shook off the influence of Faulkner that he was able to write *One Hundred Years of Solitude;* in this novel the author's "imagination matured: no longer content to write dark and fatalistic stories about a Latin Yoknapatawpha County, he broke loose into exuberance, wit and laughter." Thor Vilhjalmsson similarly observes in *Books Abroad* that while "Garcia Marquez does not fail to deal with the dark forces, or give the impression that the life of human beings, one by one, should be ultimately tragic, . . . he also shows every moment pregnant with images and color and scent which ask to be arranged into patterns of meaning and significance while the moment lasts." While the Colombian has frequently referred to Faulkner as "my master," Luis Harss and Barbara Dohmann add in their *Into the Mainstream: Conversations with Latin-American Writers* that in his later stories, "the Faulknerian glare has been neutralized. It is not replaced by any other. From now on Garcia Marquez is his own master."

In *The Autumn of the Patriarch* Garcia Marquez uses a more openly political tone in relating the story of a dictator who has reigned for so long that no one can remember any other ruler. Elaborating on the kind of solitude experienced by Colonel Aureliano Buendia in *One Hundred Years,* Garcia Marquez explores the isolation of a political tyrant. "In this fabulous, dreamlike account of the reign of a nameless dictator of a fantastic Caribbean realm, solitude is linked with the possession of absolute power," describes Ronald De Feo in the *National Review.* Rather than relating a straightforward account of the general's life, however, *The Autumn of the Patriarch* skips from one episode to another, using dense and detailed descriptions. *Times Literary Supplement* contributor John Sturrock finds this approach appropriate to the author's subject; calling the work "the desperate, richly sustained hallucination of a man rightly bitter about the present state of so much of Latin America," Sturrock notes that "Garcia Marquez's novel is sophisticated and its language is luxuriant to a degree. Style and subject are at odds because Garcia Marquez is committed to showing that our first freedom—and one which all too many Latin American countries have lost—is of the full resources of our language." *Time* writer R. Z. Sheppard similarly comments on Garcia Marquez's elaborate style, observing that "the theme is artfully insinuated, an atmosphere instantly evoked like a puff of stage smoke, and all conveyed in language that generates a charge of expectancy." The critic concludes: "Garcia Marquez writes with what could be called a stream-of-consciousness technique, but the result is much more like a whirlpool."

Some critics, however, find both the theme and technique of *The Autumn of the Patriarch* lacking. J. D. O'Hara, for example, writes in the *Washington Post Book World* that for all his "magical" realism Garcia Marquez "can only remind us of real-life parallels; he cannot exaggerate them. For the same reason," adds the critic, "although he can turn into grisly cartoons the squalor and paranoia of actual dictatorships, he can scarcely parody them; reality has anticipated him again." *Newsweek*'s Walter Clemons similarly finds the novel somewhat disappointing:

"After the narrative vivacity and intricate characterization of the earlier book [*The Autumn of the Patriarch*] seems both oversumptuous and underpopulated. It is—deadliest of compliments—an extended piece of magnificent writing," concludes Clemons. But other critics believe that the author's skillful style enhances the novel; referring to the novel's disjointed narrative style, Wendy McElroy comments in *World Research INK* that "this is the first time I have seen it handled properly. Gabriel Garcia Marquez ignores many conventions of the English language which are meant to provide structure and coherence. But he is so skillful that his novel is not difficult to understand. It is bizarre; it is disorienting," continues the critic. "But it is not difficult. Moreover, it is appropriate to the chaos and decay of the general's mind and of his world." Similarly, De Feo maintains that "no summary or description of this book can really do it justice, for it is not only the author's surrealistic flights of imagination that make it such an exceptional work, but also his brilliant use of language, his gift for phrasing and description." Concludes the critic: "Throughout this unique, remarkable novel, the tall tale is transformed into a true work of art."

"With its run-on, seemingly free-associative sentences, its constant flow of images and color, Gabriel Garcia Marquez's last novel, *The Autumn of the Patriarch,* was such a dazzling technical achievement that it left the pleasurably exhausted reader wondering what the author would do next," comments De Feo in the *Nation*. This next work, *Chronicle of a Death Foretold* "is, in miniature, a virtuoso performance," states Jonathan Yardley of the *Washington Post Book World*. In contrast with the author's "two masterworks, *One Hundred Years of Solitude* and *The Autumn of the Patriarch,*" continues the critic, "it is slight; . . . its action is tightly concentrated on a single event. But in this small space Garcia Marquez works small miracles; *Chronicle of a Death Foretold* is ingeniously, impeccably constructed, and it provides a sobering, devastating perspective on the system of male 'honor.'" In the novella, describes Douglas Hill in the Toronto *Globe and Mail*, Garcia Marquez "has cut out an apparently uncomplicated, larger-than-life jigsaw puzzle of passion and crime, then demonstrated, with laconic diligence and a sort of concerned amusement, how extraordinarily difficult the task of assembling the pieces can be." The story is based on a historical incident in which a young woman is returned after her wedding night for not being a virgin; her brothers then set out to avenge the stain on the family honor by murdering the man she names as her "perpetrator." The death is "foretold" in that the brothers announce their intentions to the entire town; but circumstances conspire to keep all but Santiago Nasar, the condemned man, from this knowledge, and he is brutally murdered.

"In telling this story, which is as much about the townspeople and their reactions as it is about the key players, Garcia Marquez might simply have remained omniscient," observes De Feo. But instead "he places himself in the action, assuming the role of a former citizen who returns home to reconstruct the events of the tragic day—a day he himself lived through." This narrative maneuvering, claims the critic, "adds another layer to the book, for the narrator, who is visible one moment, invisible the next, could very well ask himself the same question he is intent on asking others, and his own role, his own failure to act in the affair contributes to the book's odd, haunting ambiguity." This recreation after the fact has an additional effect, as Gregory Rabassa notes in *World Literature Today:* "From the beginning we know that Santiago Nasar will be and has been killed, depending on the time of the narrative thread that we happen to be following, but Garcia Marquez does manage, in spite of the repeated foretelling of the event by the murderers and others, to maintain the sus-

pense at a high level by never describing the actual murder until the very end." The critic explains: "Until then we have been following the chronicler as he puts the bits and pieces together ex post facto, but he has constructed things in such a way that we are still hoping for a reprieve even though we know better." "As more and more is revealed about the murder, less and less is known," writes Leonard Michaels in the *New York Times Book Review*. "Yet the style of the novel is always natural and unselfconscious, as if innocent of any paradoxical implication."

In approaching the story from this recreative standpoint, Garcia Marquez is once again making use of journalistic techniques. As *Chicago Tribune Book World* editor John Blades maintains, "Garcia Marquez tells this grisly little fable in what often appears to be a straight-faced parody of conventional journalism, with its dependence on 'he-she-they told me' narrative techniques, its reliance on the distorted, contradictory and dreamlike memories of 'eyewitnesses.'" Blades adds, however, that "at the same time, this is precision-tooled fiction; the author subtly but skillfully manipulates his chronology for dramatic impact." The *New York Times*'s Christopher Lehmann-Haupt similarly notes a departure from the author's previous style: "I cannot be absolutely certain whether in 'Chronicle' Gabriel Garcia Marquez has come closer to conventional storytelling than in his previous work, or whether I have simply grown accustomed to his imagination." The critic determines that "whatever the case, I found 'Chronicle of a Death Foretold' by far the author's most absorbing work to date. I read it through in a flash, and it made the back of my neck prickle." "It is interesting," remarks *Times Literary Supplement* contributor Bill Buford, that Garcia Marquez has chosen to handle "a fictional episode with the methods of a journalist. In doing so he has written an unusual and original work: a simple narrative so charged with irony that it has the authority of political fable." Concludes the critic: "If it is not an example of the socialist realism [Garcia] Marquez may claim it to be elsewhere, *Chronicle of a Death Foretold* is in any case a mesmerizing work that clearly establishes [Garcia] Marquez as one of the most accomplished, and the most 'magical' of political novelists writing today."

Despite this journalistic approach to the story, *Chronicle of a Death Foretold* does contain some of the "magical" elements that characterize Garcia Marquez's fiction. As Robert M. Adams observes in the *New York Review of Books*, there is a "combination of detailed factual particularity, usually on irrelevant points, with vagueness, confusion, or indifference on matters of more importance." The result, suggests Adams, is that "the investigation of an ancient murder takes on the quality of a hallucinatory exploration, a deep groping search into the gathering darkness for a truth that continually slithers away." But others find that this combination of journalistic detail and lack of explanation detracts from the novel; D. Keith Mano, for example, comments in the *National Review* that because the narrator "has been sequestered as a juror might be . . . , he cannot comment or probe: and this rather kiln-dries the novel." The critic elaborates by noting that the primary characters "are left without development or chiaroscuro. They seem cryptic and surface-hard: film characters really. . . . Beyond a Warren Report-meticulous detective reconstruction, it is hard to care much for these people. Emotion, you see, might skew our clarity." But Edith Grossman asserts in *Review* that this reconstruction is meant to be enigmatic: "Garcia Marquez holds onto the journalistic details, the minutiae of the factual, that constitute the great novelistic inheritance of Western realism, and at the same time throws doubt on their reliability through his narrative technique and by means of the subtle introduction of mythic elements." Concludes the critic:

"Once again Garcia Marquez is an ironic chronicler who dazzles the reader with uncommon blendings of fantasy, fable and fact."

Another blending of fable and fact, based in part on Garcia Marquez's recollections of his parents's marriage, *Love in the Time of Cholera* "is an amazing celebration of the many kinds of love between men and women," characterizes Elaine Feinstein in the London *Times.* "In part it is a brilliantly witty account of the tussles in a long marriage, whose details are curiously moving; elsewhere it is a fantastic tale of love finding erotic fulfilment in ageing bodies." The novel begins with the death of Dr. Juvenal Urbino, whose attempt to rescue a parrot from a tree leaves his wife of fifty years, Fermina Daza, a widow. Soon after Urbino's death, however, Florentino Ariza appears on Fermina Daza's doorstep; the rest of the novel recounts Florentino's determination to resume the passionate courtship of a woman who had given him up over half a century ago. In relating both the story of Fermina Daza's marriage and her later courtship, *Love in the Time of Cholera* "is a novel about commitment and fidelity under circumstances which seem to render such virtues absurd," recounts *Times Literary Supplement* contributor S. M. J. Minta. "[It is] about a refusal to grow old gracefully and respectably, about the triumph sentiment can still win over reason, and above all, perhaps, about Latin America, about keeping faith with where, for better or worse, you started out from."

Although the basic plot of *Love in the Time of Cholera* is fairly simple, some critics accuse Garcia Marquez of over-embellishing his story. Calling the plot a "boy-meets-girl" story, Chicago *Tribune Books* contributor Michael Dorris remarks that "it takes a while to realize this core [plot], for every aspect of the book is attenuated, exaggerated, overstated." The critic also notes that "while a Harlequin Romance might balk at stretching this plot for more than a year or two of fictional time, Garcia Marquez nurses it over five decades," adding that the "prose [is] laden with hyperbolic excess." In addition, some observers claim that instead of revealing the romantic side of love, *Love in the Time of Cholera* "seems to deal more with libido and self-deceit than with desire and mortality," as Angela Carter terms it in the *Washington Post Book World.* Dorris expresses a similar opinion, writing that while the novel's "first 50 pages are brilliant, provocative, . . . they are overture to a discordant symphony" which portrays an "anachronistic" world of machismo and misogyny. In contrast, Toronto *Globe and Mail* contributor Ronald Wright believes that the novel works as a satire of this same kind of "hypocrisy, provincialism and irresponsibility of the main characters' social milieu." Concludes the critic: "Love in the Time of Cholera is a complex and subtle book; its greatest achievement is not to tell a love story, but to meditate on the equivocal nature of romanticism and romantic love."

Other reviewers agree that although it contains elements of his other work, *Love in the Time of Cholera* is a development in a different direction for Garcia Marquez. Author Thomas Pynchon, writing in the *New York Times Book Review,* comments that "it would be presumptuous to speak of moving 'beyond' 'One Hundred Years of Solitude' but clearly Garcia Marquez has moved somewhere else, not least into deeper awareness of the ways in which, as Florentino comes to learn, 'nobody teaches life anything.' " Countering criticisms that the work is overemotional, Minta claims that "the triumph of the novel is that it uncovers the massive, submerged strength of the popular, the cliched and the sentimental." While it "does not possess the fierce, visionary poetry of 'One Hundred Years of Solitude' or the feverish phantasmagoria of 'The Autumn of the Patriarch,'" as *New York Times* critic Michiko Kakutani describes it, *Love in the Time of Cholera* "has revealed how the extraordinary is contained in the ordinary, how a couple of forgotten, even commonplace lives can encompass the heights and depths of grand and eternal passion. The result," concludes the critic, "is a rich commodious novel, a novel whose narrative power is matched only by its generosity of vision." "The Garcimarquesian voice we have come to recognize from the other fiction has matured, found and developed new resources," asserts Pynchon, "[and] been brought to a level where it can at once be classical and familiar, opalescent and pure, able to praise and curse, laugh and cry, fabulate and sing and when called upon, take off and soar." Concludes the critic: "There is nothing I have read quite like [the] astonishing final chapter, symphonic, sure in its dynamics and tempo. . . . At the very best [this remembrance] results in works that can even return our worn souls to us, among which most certainly belongs 'Love in the Time of Cholera,' this shining and heartbreaking novel."

Although he has earned literary fame through his fiction, Garcia Marquez has also gained notoriety as a reporter; as he commented to Stone, "I always very much enjoy the chance of doing a great piece of journalism." The Colombian elaborated in his interview with Dreifus: "I'm fascinated by the relationship between literature and *journalism.* I began my career as a journalist in Colombia, and a reporter is something I've never stopped being. When I'm not working on fiction, I'm running around the world, practicing my craft as a reporter." His work as a journalist, however, has produced some controversy, for in it Garcia Marquez not only sees a chance to develop his "craft," but also an opportunity to become involved in political issues. His self-imposed exile from Colombia was prompted by a series of articles he wrote in 1955 about the sole survivor of a Colombian shipwreck, for the young journalist related that the government ship had capsized due to an overloading of contraband. Garcia Marquez has more recently written *Clandestine in Chile: The Adventures of Miguel Littin,* a work about an exile's return to the repressive Chile of General Augusto Pinochet; the political revelations of the book led to the burning of almost 15,000 copies by the Chilean government. In addition, Garcia Marquez has maintained personal relationships with such political figures as Cuban President Fidel Castro, French President Francois Mitterand, and the late Panamanian leader General Omar Torrijos.

Because of this history of political involvement, Garcia Marquez has often been accused of allowing his politics to overshadow his work; he has also encountered problems entering the United States. When asked by the *New York Times Book Review*'s Marlise Simons why he is so insistent on becoming involved in political issues, the author replied that "If I were not a Latin American, maybe I wouldn't [become involved]. But underdevelopment is total, integral, it affects every part of our lives. The problems of our societies are mainly political." The Colombian further explained that "the commitment of a writer is with the reality of all of society, not just with a small part of it. If not, he is as bad as the politicians who disregard a large part of our reality. That is why authors, painters, writers in Latin America get politically involved."

Despite the controversy that his politics and work stir, Garcia Marquez's *One Hundred Years of Solitude* is enough to ensure the author "a place in the ranks of twentieth century masters," claims Curt Suplee of the *Washington Post.* The Nobel-winner's reputation, however, is grounded in more than this one masterpiece; as the Swedish Academy's Nobel citation states, "Each new work of his is received by critics and readers as an event of world importance, is translated into many languages and published as quickly as possible in large editions." "At a time of dire predictions about the future of the novel," observes McMurray,

Garcia Marquez's "prodigious imagination, remarkable compositional precision, and wide popularity provide evidence that the genre is still thriving." And as *Chicago Tribune Book World* contributor Harry Mark Petrakis describes him, Garcia Marquez "is a magician of vision and language who does astonishing things with time and reality. He blends legend and history in ways that make the legends seem truer than truth. His scenes and characters are humorous, tragic, mysterious and beset by ironies and fantasies. In his fictional world, anything is possible and everything is believable." Concludes the critic: "Mystical and magical, fully aware of the transiency of life, his stories fashion realms inhabited by ghosts and restless souls who return to those left behind through fantasies and dreams. The stories explore, with a deceptive simplicity, the miracles and mysteries of life."

MEDIA ADAPTATIONS: "Erendira" was produced by Les Films du Triangle in 1984; "Chronicle of a Death Foretold" was filmed by Francesco Rossi in 1987; the play "El Coronel No Tiene Quien Le Escriba" was adapted from Garcia Marquez's novel of the same title by Carlos Gimenez, and was first produced Off-Broadway at the Public/Newman Theater; a play, "Blood and Champagne," has been based on Garcia Marquez's *One Hundred Years of Solitude.*

BIOGRAPHICAL/CRITICAL SOURCES:

BOOKS

Authors & Artists for Young Adults, Volume 3, Gale, 1990.
Bestsellers 1989, Number 1, Gale, 1989.
Brotherson, Gordon, *The Emergence of the Latin American Novel,* Cambridge University Press, 1979.
Contemporary Literary Criticism, Gale, Volume 2, 1974, Volume 3, 1975, Volume 8, 1978, Volume 10, 1979, Volume 15, 1980, Volume 27, 1984, Volume 47, 1988, Volume 55, 1989.
Dictionary of Literary Biography Yearbook: 1982, Gale, 1983.
Fernandez-Braso, Miguel, *Gabriel Garcia Marquez,* Editorial Azur (Madrid), 1969.
Gabriel Garcia Marquez, nuestro premio Nobel, La Secretaria de Informacion y Prensa de la Presidencia de la Nacion (Bogota), 1983.
Gallagher, David Patrick, *Modern Latin American Literature,* Oxford University Press, 1973.
Guibert, Rita, *Seven Voices,* Knopf, 1973.
Harss, Luis and Barbara Dohmann, *Into the Mainstream: Conversations with Latin-American Writers,* Harper, 1967.
Janes, Regina, *Gabriel Garcia Marquez: Revolutions in Wonderland,* University of Missouri Press, 1981.
Mantilla, Alfonso Renteria, compiler, *Garcia Marquez habla de Garcia Marquez,* Renteria (Colombia), 1979.
McGuirk, Bernard and Richard Cardwell, editors, *Gabriel Garcia Marquez: New Readings,* Cambridge University Press, 1988.
McMurray, George R., *Gabriel Garcia Marquez,* Ungar, 1977.
Porrata, Francisco E. and Fausto Avedano, *Explicacion de Cien anos de soledad [de] Garcia Marquez,* Editorial Texto (Costa Rica), 1976.
Pritchett, V. S., *The Myth Makers,* Random House, 1979.
Rodman, Selden, *Tongues of Fallen Angels,* New Direction, 1974.
Vargas Llosa, Mario, *Garcia Marquez: Historia de un deicido,* Barral Editores, 1971.

PERIODICALS

Books Abroad, winter, 1973, summer, 1973, spring, 1976.
Book World, February 22, 1970, February 20, 1972.
Chicago Tribune, March 6, 1983.
Chicago Tribune Book World, November 11, 1979, November 7, 1982, April 3, 1983, November 18, 1984, April 27, 1986.
Christian Science Monitor, April 16, 1970.
Commonweal, March 6, 1970.
Detroit News, October 27, 1982, December 16, 1984.
El Pais, January 22, 1981.
Globe and Mail (Toronto), April 7, 1984, September 19, 1987, May 21, 1988.
Hispania, September, 1976.
London Magazine, April/May, 1973, November, 1979.
Los Angeles Times, October 22, 1982, January 25, 1987, August 24, 1988.
Los Angeles Times Book Review, April 10, 1983, November 13, 1983, December 16, 1984, April 27, 1986, June 7, 1987, April 17, 1988.
Nation, December 2, 1968, May 15, 1972, May 14, 1983.
National Observer, April 20, 1970.
National Review, May 27, 1977, June 10, 1983.
New Republic, April 9, 1977, October 27, 1979, May 2, 1983.
New Statesman, June 26, 1970, May 18, 1979, February 15, 1980, September 3, 1982.
Newsweek, March 2, 1970, November 8, 1976, July 3, 1978, December 3, 1979, November 1, 1982.
New York Review of Books, March 26, 1970, January 24, 1980, April 14, 1983.
New York Times, July 11, 1978, November 6, 1979, October 22, 1982, March 25, 1983, December 7, 1985, April 26, 1986, June 4, 1986, April 6, 1988.
New York Times Book Review, September 29, 1968, March 8, 1970, February 20, 1972, October 31, 1976, July 16, 1978, September 16, 1978, November 11, 1979, November 16, 1980, December 5, 1982, March 27, 1983, April 7, 1985, April 27, 1986, August 9, 1987, April 10, 1988.
Paris Review, winter, 1981.
Playboy, February, 1983.
Publishers Weekly, May 13, 1974, December 16, 1983.
Review, Number 24, 1979, September/December, 1981.
Saturday Review, December 21, 1968, March 7, 1970.
Southwest Review, summer, 1973.
Time, March 16, 1970, November 1, 1976, July 10, 1978, November 1, 1982, March 7, 1983, December 31, 1984, April 14, 1986.
Times (London), November 13, 1986, June 30, 1988.
Times Literary Supplement, April 15, 1977, February 1, 1980, September 10, 1982, July 1, 1988.
Tribune Books (Chicago), June 28, 1987, April 17, 1988.
Washington Post, October 22, 1982.
Washington Post Book World, February 22, 1970, November 14, 1976, November 25, 1979, November 7, 1982, March 27, 1983, November 18, 1984, July 19, 1987, April 24, 1988.
World Literature Today, winter, 1982.
World Press Review, April, 1982.
World Research INK, September, 1977.

—*Sketch by Marian Gonsior and Diane Telgen*

*   *   *

GARDAM, Jane   1928-

PERSONAL: Born July 11, 1928, in Coatham, Yorkshire, England; daughter of William (a schoolmaster) and Kathleen (Helm) Pearson; married David Gardam (a Queen's counsel), April 20, 1952; children: Timothy, Mary, Thomas. *Education:* Bedford College, London, B.A. (with honors), 1949, graduate study, 1949-52. *Politics:* "Ecology." *Religion:* Anglo-Catholic.

ADDRESSES: Home—Haven House, Sandwich, Kent, England.

CAREER: Weldons Ladies Journal, London, England, subeditor, 1952-53; *Time and Tide,* London, assistant literary editor, 1953-55; writer. Organizer of hospital libraries for Red Cross, 1950.

AWARDS, HONORS: David Higham Prize for fiction and W. Holtby Award, both 1977, both for *Black Faces, White Faces;* runner-up citation, Booker Prize, 1978, for *God on the Rocks;* Whitbread Award, 1983, for *The Hollow Land;* Katherine Mansfield Award, 1984, for *The Pangs of Love.*

WRITINGS:

JUVENILE FICTION

A Few Fair Days (short stories), Macmillan, 1971.
A Long Way from Verona (novel), Macmillan, 1971, reprinted, Hamish Hamilton, 1986.
The Summer after the Funeral (novel), Macmillan, 1973.
Bilgewater (novel), Hamish Hamilton, 1976.
God on the Rocks (novel), Morrow, 1979.
Bridget and William, illustrated by Janet Rawlings, Julia MacRae, 1981.
The Hollow Land, illustrated by Rawlings, Julia MacRae, 1981.
Horse, illustrated by Rawlings, Julia MacRae, 1982.
Kit, illustrated by William Geldart, Julia MacRae, 1984.
Kit in Boots, Julia MacRae, 1986.
Swan, Julia MacRae, 1986.
Through the Doll's House Door (novel), Julia MacRae, 1987.

ADULT FICTION

Black Faces, White Faces (short stories), Hamish Hamilton, 1975, published as *The Pineapple Bay Hotel,* Morrow, 1976.
The Sidmouth Letters (short stories), Morrow, 1980.
The Pangs of Love (short stories; also see below), Hamish Hamilton, 1983.
Crusoe's Daughter (novel), Atheneum, 1986.
Showing the Flag (short stories), Penguin, 1989.

OTHER

Also author of scripts for television films, including "The Easter Lilies," based on the author's book *The Pangs of Love.* Contributor of short stories to magazines.

SIDELIGHTS: Hailed in Great Britain as a writer of talent and originality, Jane Gardam has enjoyed success with children's fiction as well as with short stories and novels expressly for adults. In fact, in an essay for the *Dictionary of Literary Biography* critic Patricia Craig expresses the opinion that categorizing Gardam's fiction strictly as "juvenile" or "adult" does the writer's work a disservice. The appeal of Gardam's fiction, writes Craig, "should not be restricted by any factor of age in the reader. . . . All of Gardam's work is marked by certain admirable characteristics: economy of style, exuberance and humor, a special relish for the startling and the unexpected."

Proof of Gardam's ability to touch readers of various ages can be found in the awards she has won: the David Higham Prize for *Black Faces, White Faces,* short stories for adults, and the prestigious Whitbread Award for *The Hollow Land,* a work ostensibly for juveniles. Jane Miller outlines Gardam's strengths in a *Times Literary Supplement* review: "[She] has a spectacular gift for detail, of the local and period kind, and for details which make characters so subtly unpredictable that they ring true, and her humor is tough as well as delicate."

Young teens on the brink of adult discovery are often the central characters in Gardam's juvenile fiction. Craig feels that Gardam's works "recreate directly the sensations and impressions of childhood." Craig also notes a slightly autobiographical cast in a number of the juvenile novels: "Although to an extent transformed in the course of writing, certain elements of Gardam's early life seem to have made a fairly consistent pattern in her books: the girl with a much younger brother; the schoolmaster or clergyman father; the Yorkshire or Cumbria locations. Each book, however, has a distinctive feeling, a mood and atmosphere all its own. Gardam repeats her motifs but not her effects. . . . [She] makes high comedy of the fidgets and fancies of adolescence, with her heroine constantly on the brink of some contretemps or social disaster; but the narrative is charged as well with a kind of muted fairy-tale glamour."

Gardam received critical acclaim for her first three children's books, but she was still virtually unknown as an author when she published her first work for adults, *Black Faces, White Faces.* The short story collection, which appeared in the United States as *The Pineapple Bay Hotel,* won Britain's David Higham for best first novel, even though it was Gardam's fourth book and not a novel at all. Craig explains that the stories in Gardam's story collections are interrelated within each volume, but "what is important is not the classification [as novel or collection] but the degree of acuity brought to bear on a theme." Indeed, publication of *Black Faces, White Faces* expanded Gardam's critical audience considerably and accorded her highly favorable reviews that have continued with subsequent story collections and novels.

Victoria Glendinning describes Gardam in the *Times Literary Supplement,* with emphasis on her adult themes: "She is a very English writer, in that her observation is at its sharpest on matters of class and status, and her most poisonous darts reserved for the upper middle classes, or rather for the female residue who no longer have servants to exploit and are ending their days in seedy stinginess." "Her manifold traps are hidden away under glass and satin," notes Raymond Sokolov in the *Washington Post Book World.* "The voice you hear is an odd combination of girl and grande dame, a voice that trills out the most sinister truths as if they were part of the court circular." In a London *Times* review of *The Pangs of Love,* Elaine Feinstein suggests that Gardam "is a spare and elegant master of her art, which is neither genteel nor gentle, and she spares the well-bred less than the vulgar, and the predictably English abroad least of all."

Throughout Gardam's fiction, juvenile and adult alike, the author explores eccentric behavior in central characters as well as supporting ones. In Craig's words, "she is interested in the discrepancy between the face one presents to the world and one's actual feelings, and the comedy which results from lack of face." A *Times Literary Supplement* reviewer also notes that Gardam's characters, "young and old, are observed with unwavering directness, their emotional hang-ups and outlets quietly understated so that the adolescent reader can take or leave the undertones." According to Craig, however, "the fanciful and highly colored in Gardam's work are always disciplined by a northern toughness and plainness of expression. . . . One of [her] greatest strengths as a writer is the ability to confine her observations to the most telling; every detail is there for a purpose."

Perhaps the most incisive comment on Gardam's talent comes from a *Times Literary Supplement* review of *A Long Way from Verona:* "Jane Gardam is a writer of such humorous intensity—glorious dialogue, hilarious set-pieces—that when one reads her for the first time one laughs aloud and when rereading her, the acid test for funny books, one's admiration increases a hundred-fold." In the years since Gardam began publishing fiction, Craig concludes, she "has shown herself to be a novelist of rare inventiveness and power."

BIOGRAPHICAL/CRITICAL SOURCES:

BOOKS

Blishen, Edward, editor, *The Thorny Paradise: Writers on Writing for Children,* Kestrel, 1975.
Children's Literature Review, Volume 12, Gale, 1987.
Contemporary Literary Criticism, Volume 43, Gale, 1987.
Dictionary of Literary Biography, Volume 14: *British Novelists since 1960,* Gale, 1983.

PERIODICALS

Horn Book, October, 1978, December, 1978.
Los Angeles Times Book Review, December 21, 1980.
New Statesman, November 12, 1971, October 13, 1978, April 11, 1980.
New York Times, December 19, 1980.
New York Times Book Review, May 7, 1972, February 17, 1974, August 11, 1974, May 2, 1976, April 27, 1986.
Observer, February 13, 1983.
Spectator, November 13, 1971, December 22, 1973, November 29, 1975, December 11, 1976, November 25, 1978, May 3, 1980, February 19, 1983.
Times (London), February 10, 1983, February 9, 1985.
Times Educational Supplement, November 20, 1981.
Times Literary Supplement, November 22, 1971, December 3, 1971, November 23, 1973, September 19, 1975, December 10, 1976, October 13, 1978, April 18, 1980, March 27, 1981, September 18, 1981, February 10, 1984, May 31, 1985, July 10, 1987, July 7, 1989.
Washington Post, April 21, 1986.
Washington Post Book World, May 2, 1976, January 8, 1978.

*   *   *

GARDNER, Erle Stanley   1889-1970
(A. A. Fair, Carleton Kendrake, Charles J. Kenny)

PERSONAL: Born July 27, 1889, in Malden, Mass.; died March 11, 1970, in Temecula, Calif.; son of Charles Walter (a mining engineer) and Grace Adelma (Waugh) Gardner; married Natalie Talbert, April 9, 1912 (separated, 1935; died, February, 1968); married Agnes Jean Bethell, August 7, 1968; children: (first marriage) Natalie Grace (Mrs. Toby Naso).

CAREER: Writer. Admitted to California Bar, 1911; attorney, Oxnard, Calif., 1911-16; Consolidated Sales Co., president, 1918-21; Sheridan, Orr, Drapeau, and Gardner, Ventura, Calif., attorney, 1921-33; founder and member, Court of Last Resort, 1948-60; founder, Paisano Productions, 1957; consultant and editor, "Perry Mason" television show, 1957-66.

MEMBER: American Bar Association, American Judicature Society, American Academy of Forensic Sciences, Law Science Academy of America, American Society of Criminology, American Polygraph Association (honorary life member), Academy of Scientific Interrogation, California Bar Association, New Hampshire Medico Society, Kansas Peace Officers Association, Harvard Association of Political Science, Elks, Adventurers (Chicago and New York).

AWARDS, HONORS: Mystery Writers of America, Edgar Allan Poe Award, 1953, for *The Court of Last Resort,* Grand

Master Award, 1961; honorary alumnus, Kansas City University; Doctor of Law, McGeorge College of Law, 1956, and New Mexico University.

WRITINGS:

"PERRY MASON" SERIES; PUBLISHED BY MORROW, EXCEPT AS INDICATED

The Case of the Velvet Claws, 1933, reprinted, Aeonian Press, 1976.
The Case of the Sulky Girl, 1933, reprinted, Aeonian Press, 1976.
The Case of the Lucky Legs, 1934, reprinted, Aeonian Press, 1976.
The Case of the Howling Dog, 1934, reprinted, Aeonian Press, 1976.
The Case of the Curious Bride, 1934, reprinted, Aeonian Press, 1976.
The Case of the Counterfeit Eye, 1935, reprinted, Aeonian Press, 1976.
The Case of the Caretaker's Cat, 1935, reprinted, Aeonian Press, 1976.
The Case of the Sleepwalker's Niece, 1936, reprinted, Aeonian Press, 1976.
The Case of the Stuttering Bishop, 1936, reprinted, Aeonian Press, 1976.
The Case of the Dangerous Dowager, 1937, reprinted, Aeonian Press, 1976.
The Case of the Lame Canary, 1937.
The Case of the Substitute Face, 1938, reprinted, Pocket Books, 1960.
The Case of the Shoplifter's Shoe, 1938.
The Case of the Perjured Parrot, 1939, reprinted, Ballantine, 1982.
The Case of the Rolling Bones, 1939.
The Case of the Baited Hook, 1940, reprinted, Pocket Books, 1961.
The Case of the Silent Partner, 1940, reprinted, Pocket Books, 1962.
The Case of the Haunted Husband, 1941, reprinted, Ballantine, 1981.
The Case of the Empty Tin, 1941, reprinted, Pocket Books, 1958.
The Case of the Drowning Duck, 1942.
The Case of the Careless Kitten, 1942.
The Case of the Buried Clock, 1943.
The Case of the Drowsy Mosquito, 1943.
The Case of the Crooked Candle, 1944, reprinted, Garland Publishing, 1976.
The Case of the Black-Eyed Blonde, 1944, reprinted, Pocket Books, 1968.
The Case of the Golddigger's Purse, 1945.
The Case of the Half-Wakened Wife, 1945.
The Case of the Borrowed Brunette, 1946.
The Case of the Fan Dancer's Horse, 1947.
The Case of the Lazy Lover, 1947.
The Case of the Lonely Heiress, 1948, reprinted, Pocket Books, 1965.
The Case of the Vagabond Virgin, 1948, reprinted, Ballantine, 1982.
The Case of the Dubious Bridegroom, 1949.
The Case of the Cautious Coquette, 1949.
The Case of the Negligent Nymph, 1950, reprinted, Ballantine, 1982.
The Case of the One-Eyed Witness, 1950.
The Case of the Fiery Fingers, 1951, reprinted, Ballantine, 1981.
The Case of the Angry Mourners, 1951.
The Case of the Moth-Eaten Mink, 1952.

The Case of the Grinning Gorilla, 1952, reprinted, Ballantine, 1982.
The Case of the Hesitant Hostess, 1953.
The Case of the Green-Eyed Sister, 1953.
The Case of the Fugitive Nurse, 1954.
The Case of the Runaway Corpse, 1954.
The Case of the Restless Redhead, 1954, reprinted, Ballantine, 1982.
The Case of the Glamorous Ghost (also see below), 1955.
The Case of the Sun Bather's Diary, 1955, reprinted, Ballantine, 1982.
The Case of the Nervous Accomplice, 1955.
The Case of the Terrified Typist (also see below), 1956.
The Case of the Demure Defendant, 1956, reprinted, Pocket Books, 1970.
The Case of the Gilded Lily, 1956, reprinted, Robert Bentley, 1981.
The Case of the Lucky Loser (also see below), 1957.
The Case of the Screaming Woman (also see below), 1957.
The Case of the Daring Decoy, 1957.
The Case of the Long-Legged Models (also see below), 1958.
The Case of the Foot-Loose Doll (also see below), 1958.
The Case of the Calendar Girl, 1958.
The Case of the Deadly Toy, 1959, reprinted, Robert Bentley, 1981.
The Case of the Mythical Monkeys, 1959, reprinted, Robert Bentley, 1981.
The Case of the Singing Skirt, 1959, reprinted, Robert Bentley, 1981.
The Case of the Waylaid Wolf (also see below), 1960.
The Case of the Duplicate Daughter, 1960.
The Case of the Shapely Shadow, 1960, reprinted, Ballantine, 1991.
The Case of the Spurious Spinster, 1961, reprinted, G. K. Hall, 1982.
The Case of the Bigamous Spouse, 1961.
The Case of the Reluctant Model, 1962.
The Case of the Blonde Bonanza, 1962.
The Case of the Ice-Cold Hands, 1962, reprinted, G. K. Hall, 1980.
Mischievous Doll, 1963, reprinted, G. K. Hall, 1981.
The Case of the Stepdaughter's Secret, 1963.
The Case of the Amorous Aunt, 1963.
The Case of the Daring Divorcee, 1964.
The Case of the Phantom Fortune, 1964.
The Case of the Horrified Heirs, 1964.
The Case of the Troubled Trustee, 1965.
The Case of the Beautiful Beggar, 1965.
The Case of the Worried Waitress, 1966.
The Case of the Queenly Contestant, 1967.
The Case of the Careless Cupid, 1968.
The Case of the Fabulous Fake, 1969.
The Case of the Fenced-in Woman, 1972.
The Case of the Postponed Murder, 1973.

"DOUG SELBY" SERIES; PUBLISHED BY MORROW

The D.A. Calls It Murder, 1937.
The D.A. Holds a Candle, 1938.
The D.A. Draws a Circle, 1939.
The D.A. Goes to Trial, 1940.
The D.A. Cooks a Goose, 1942.
The D.A. Calls a Turn, 1944.
The D.A. Breaks a Seal, 1946.
The D.A. Takes a Chance, 1948.
The D.A. Breaks an Egg, 1949.

SHORT STORIES

The Case of the Murderer's Bride, and Other Stories, edited by Ellery Queen, Davis Publications, 1969.
The Case of the Crimson Kiss, Morrow, 1971.
The Case of the Crying Swallow, and Other Stories, Morrow, 1971.
The Case of the Irate Witness, Morrow, 1972.
The Amazing Adventures of Lester Leith, Dial, 1981.

Contributor to *The Art of the Mystery Story,* edited by Howard Haycroft, Simon & Schuster, 1946; *The President's Mystery Plot,* Prentice-Hall, 1967; and *The Fear Merchant,* New English Library, 1974.

NONFICTION; PUBLISHED BY MORROW

The Land of Shorter Shadows, 1948.
The Court of Last Resort, 1952.
Neighborhood Frontiers, 1954.
The Case of the Boy Who Wrote "The Case of the Missing Clue" with Perry Mason, 1959.
Hunting the Desert Whale, 1960.
Hovering over Baja, 1961.
The Hidden Heart of Baja, 1962.
The Desert Is Yours, 1963.
The World of Water: Exploring the Sacramento Delta, 1964.
Hunting Lost Mines by Helicopter, 1965.
Off the Beaten Track in Baja, 1967.
Gypsy Days on the Delta, 1967.
Mexico's Magic Square, 1968.
Drifting Down the Delta, 1969.
Host with the Big Hat, 1970.
Cops on Campus and Crime in the Streets, 1970.
Whispering Sands: Stories of Gold Fever and the Western Desert, edited by Charles G. Waugh and Martin H. Greenberg, 1981.

UNDER PSEUDONYM A. A. FAIR; PUBLISHED BY MORROW, EXCEPT AS INDICATED

The Bigger They Come, 1939, reprinted, Pocket Books, 1971 (published in England as *Lam to the Slaughter,* Hamish Hamilton, 1939).
Turn on the Heat, 1940.
Gold Comes in Bricks, 1940, reprinted, Dell, 1971.
Spill the Jackpot, 1941, reprinted, Dell, 1971.
Double or Quits, 1941, reprinted, Dell, 1972.
Owls Don't Blink, 1942.
Bats Fly at Dusk, 1942, reprinted, Dell, 1972.
Cats Prowl at Night, 1943.
Give 'em the Ax, 1944, reprinted, Dell, 1974 (published in England as *An Axe to Grind,* Heinemann, 1951).
Crows Can't Count, 1946.
Fools Die on Friday, 1947, reprinted, Dell, 1971.
Bedrooms Have Windows, 1949, reprinted, Dell, 1972.
Top of the Heap, 1952.
Some Women Won't Wait, 1953, reprinted, Dell, 1972.
Beware the Curves, 1956, reprinted, Pocket Books, 1971.
You Can Die Laughing, 1957, reprinted, Pocket Books, 1975.
Some Slips Don't Show, 1957.
The Count of Nine, 1958.
Pass the Gravy, 1959.
Kept Women Can't Wait, 1960.
Bachelors Get Lonely, 1961.
Shills Can't Cash Chips, 1961 (published in England as *Stop at the Red Light,* Heinemann, 1962).
Try Anything Once, 1962.

Fish or Cut Bait, 1963.
Up for Grabs, 1964.
Cut Thin to Win, 1965.
Widows Wear Weeds, 1966.
Traps Need Fresh Bait, 1967.
All Grass Isn't Green, 1970.

OTHER

(Under pseudonym Carleton Kendrake) *The Clue of the Forgotten Murder,* Morrow, 1935.
(Under pseudonym Charles J. Kenny) *This Is Murder,* Morrow, 1935.
Murder Up My Sleeve, Morrow, 1938.
The Case of the Turning Tide, Morrow, 1941.
The Case of the Smoking Chimney, Morrow, 1943.
The Case of the Backward Mule, Morrow, 1946.
Two Clues (novellas), Morrow, 1947.
The Case of the Musical Cow, Morrow, 1950.
Seven Complete Novels (omnibus volume; contains *The Case of the Glamorous Ghost, The Case of the Terrified Typist, The Case of the Lucky Loser, The Case of the Screaming Woman, The Case of the Long-Legged Models, The Case of the Foot-Loose Doll,* and *The Case of the Waylaid Wolf*), Crown, 1979.

Also author of radio scripts. Contributor to various magazines.

SIDELIGHTS: Mystery writer Erle Stanley Gardner "often insisted," Albin Krebs stated in the *New York Times,* "that he was 'not really a writer at all,' and to be sure, there were many critics who enthusiastically agreed with him. But millions of readers . . . looked upon Mr. Gardner . . . as a master storyteller." Gardner enjoyed being called a "fiction factory" or "the Henry Ford of detective novelists," references to the assembly-line nature of his prolific literary output. With more than two-hundred million copies of his books sold, and sales at one time peaking at twenty-six thousand copies a day, Gardner ranked as the best-selling American author of all time. "In terms of total readership," Hank Burchard of the *Washington Post* reported, "he ranks right up there with Homer, Matthew, Mark, Luke, and John."

The hard-hitting defense lawyer Perry Mason was easily Gardner's most popular character, appearing in some eighty of his novels. Mason, Otto Penzler stated in *The Private Lives of Private Eyes, Spies, Crimefighters, and Other Good Guys,* "is the most famous lawyer in fiction." "Perry Mason," Isaac Anderson of the *New York Times* believed, "is not only a shrewd lawyer and a brilliant detective, he is a master of stagecraft, who knows how to stage dramatic climaxes in the courtroom when they will do the most good for his client." The Mason books are based on Gardner's years as a lawyer in rural California, with each novel being a composite of several actual cases. Many of the techniques employed by Mason were first used by Gardner himself who was, Burchard stated, "noted for his deft use of little-known statutes, penetrating cross-examination and colorful courtroom demeanor." On one occasion Gardner defended a group of Chinese accused of illegal gambling by filling the courtroom with Chinese and daring the prosecuting attorney to match the indictments with the accused men. The charges were dropped. On another occasion Gardner's client was accused of causing a woman's nervous breakdown with his loose talk about her. A small earthquake shook the California courthouse during the proceedings and Gardner quickly used the unexpected event to his advantage, pointing out to the jury that the plaintiff had been the only person in the courthouse to stay calm during the quake. His client was acquitted. Gardner's clients were usually poor, members

of minority groups, or those whom Gardner considered unjustly accused. *Time* quoted him as saying that he defended "vagrants, peeping Toms and chicken thieves as if they were statesmen." In 1948, Gardner founded the Court of Last Resort, an organization of lawyers who took on seemingly hopeless cases from across the country. In the twelve years of its existence, the Court of Last Resort was responsible for saving a number of defendants from prison terms.

In the 1920s, Gardner began to write fiction at night while working by day as a lawyer. His hectic schedule at the time included a full day of court appearances, several hours of researching points of law at the library, and then writing a self-imposed quota of four thousand words of fiction when he returned home in the evening. His determination soon paid off. In 1921, the pulp magazine *Breezy Stories* published "Nellie's Naughty Nightie," Gardner's first published work. He was soon selling his stories to a wide variety of pulp magazines at such a steady rate that he cut back his legal practice to two days a week to devote more time to writing. At its peak, Gardner's output reached some one million words of published fiction per year, with his stories appearing in the pulp magazines at a rate of better than one per week.

In these early days Gardner experimented with a variety of story genres, including westerns, confession stories, and mysteries. Out of these writing experiments came the publication in 1933 of *The Case of the Velvet Claws,* the first Perry Mason novel. With the publication of this book Gardner's writing career took a new turn. Thayer Hobson, the president of Gardner's publishing house, suggested that Gardner concentrate his efforts on his new character, turning Perry Mason into a series character. Gardner took the advice. Although he would later write mysteries featuring other characters and some nonfiction books, the bulk of Gardner's later writing concerned Perry Mason. "It is a matter of loyalty to the characters one has created," *Newsweek* quoted Gardner as explaining, "and loyalty to one's associates."

The Perry Mason books, Burchard explained, "are formula books." In each one Mason defended a client charged with murder. The client is always entangled in a set of suspicious circumstances which makes him look guilty. When it seems as if all is lost and his client will be convicted, Mason risks everything—his life, disbarment, and/or a jail sentence—on a desperate last bid, confident that he can win acquittal. In a surprise ending, Mason's desperate bid pays off and he saves his client in a climactic courtroom scene, producing evidence at the last moment which not only clears the defendant but reveals the real murderer as well. "Defying all odds," Penzler observed, "Mason never loses a case." This despite Mason's own admission in *The Case of the Counterfeit Eye:* "I don't ask a client if he's guilty or innocent. Either way he's entitled to a day in court." Cyril Ray of *Spectator* described the Mason books as coming "off a conveyor-belt, of course, but with all the neatness and finish of the machine-made article."

The typical Perry Mason book, Burchard believed, "isn't great, but it isn't bad, either. The prose is mostly workmanlike, with a clinker here and there, the plot turns are less outrageous than many that can be found on any bookstand. . . . Gardner always [puts] in interesting and often informative factual detail . . . and the legal details are always scrupulously accurate." This attention to detail was noted by several critics, including James Sandoe of the *New York Herald Tribune Book Review.* Sandoe wrote that Gardner's "real assurance lies in the tricks of plotting and the accurate language of trial law." O. L. Bailey of the *Saturday Review of the Arts* stated that Gardner "never pretended to be anything but a commercial writer. His stock in trade was the great care he took to make sure that all the details of his complex plots were right." Gardner went so far as to purchase a new gun for each murder mystery he wrote. During a court trial, he said, the murder weapon's serial number must be entered into the court record. "If I give a phony one [in a Perry Mason book]," Gardner told *Newsweek*, "people write in and say there isn't any such serial number. If I give a real serial number, I face a lawsuit. So every time I commit a murder, I have to buy the gun." At the time of his death, Gardner was reported to have had a large gun collection.

The Perry Mason formula was popular. By the mid-1960s, Gardner books were selling some twenty-six thousand copies a day. Krebs reported that Gardner once complained about his phenomenal success: "I have become chained to my fiction factory because my audience can't get enough of my stories, no matter how fast I write them." And Gardner wrote them fast. To help him prepare his usual production of four or five new books a year, he hired a staff of six secretaries to type manuscripts from his recorded dictation. Because he worked on several books at the same time, and because his prolific production was backlogged by his publisher, Gardner was reported to have never been sure which was his most recently published book.

In the 1940s, a Perry Mason radio show was broadcast five days a week in soap opera fashion. This show was superceded in 1957 by "Perry Mason," a television series starring Raymond Burr. Gardner served as consultant and editor to the series, which used many of his original Perry Mason novels as sources for its episodes. The show was a tremendous success, running nine seasons in prime time and becoming the most popular lawyer series in television history. Because Gardner was the majority owner of Paisano Productions, the packagers of "Perry Mason" for the Columbia Broadcasting System, he was said to have earned some fifteen million dollars from the show. "Perry Mason" is still broadcast in reruns in nearly every major American city and broadcast overseas in sixteen different languages.

The continuing popularity of Gardner's work was evidenced in 1973 when the country of Nicaragua issued a series of postage stamps honoring the great detectives of literature. One of the twelve postage stamps featured Gardner's character Perry Mason. The University of Texas at Austin, which owns a collection of Gardner's manuscripts, letters, and papers, announced in 1970 that it would build a replica of Gardner's study, where most of his many books were written.

"I write to make money," Krebs quoted Gardner as once saying, "and I write to give the reader sheer fun." Burchard quoted Gardner explaining his popularity this way: "Ordinary readers see in me somebody they can identify with. I'm for the underdog. Justice is done in my books. The average man is always in a state of supreme suspense because his life is all complications with no conclusions. In my books, he sees people in trouble get out of trouble."

MEDIA ADAPTATIONS: Warner Brothers filmed *The Case of the Howling Dog* in 1934, *The Case of the Curious Bride* in 1935, *The Case of the Lucky Legs* in 1935, *The Case of the Velvet Claws* in 1936, *The Case of the Black Cat* in 1936, and *The Case of the Stuttering Bishop* in 1937. Columbia Broadcasting System ran a Perry Mason radio series, 1943-55, the television series "Perry Mason," 1957-66, and "The New Adventures of Perry Mason," 1973-74.

BIOGRAPHICAL/CRITICAL SOURCES:

BOOKS

Frugate, Francis L. and Roberta B. Frugate, *Secrets of the World's Best-Selling Writer: The Storytelling Techniques of Erle Stanley Gardner*, Morrow, 1980.
Gardner, Erle Stanley, *The Case of the Counterfeit Eye*, Morrow, 1935.
Gardner, *Host with the Big Hat*, Morrow, 1969.
Hughes, Dorothy B., *Erle Stanley Gardner: The Case of the Real Perry Mason*, Morrow, 1978.
Johnson, Alva, *The Case of Erle Stanley Gardner*, Morrow, 1947.
Mott, Frank Luther, *Golden Multitudes*, Macmillan, 1947.
Mundell, E. H., *Erie Stanley Gardner: A Checklist*, Kent State University Press, 1969.
Penzler, Otto, *The Private Lives of Private Eyes, Spies, Crimefighters, and Other Good Guys*, Grosset, 1977.

PERIODICALS

Atlantic, January, 1967.
Books and Bookmen, March, 1971.
Christian Science Monitor, January 17, 1973.
Coronet, February, 1956.
Newsweek, October 25, 1943, October 7, 1957, January 18, 1960.
New Yorker, November 11, 1950.
New York Herald Tribune Book Review, November 16, 1952, May 25, 1958.
New York Times, June 24, 1934, November 18, 1934, January 6, 1957, May 11, 1958.
New York Times Book Review, September 13, 1959, February 4, 1973.
New York Times Magazine, March 21, 1965.
Publishers Weekly, January 27, 1958, August 11, 1958.
Reader's Digest, August, 1963.
Saturday Evening Post, May 30, 1942, September 1, 1956, January 30, 1960.
Saturday Review of Literature, July 16, 1938.
Saturday Review of the Arts, February, 1973.
Spectator, March 28, 1970.
Time, May 9, 1949.
Variety, April 1, 1970.

OBITUARIES:

PERIODICALS

American Bookman, March 23, 1970.
L'Express, March 16-22, 1970.
National Observer, March 23, 1970.
Newsweek, March 23, 1970.
New York Times, March 12, 1970.
Publishers Weekly, March 23, 1970.
Time, March 23, 1970.
Variety, March 18, 1970.
Washington Post, March 12, 1970.

*   *   *

GARDNER, John (Edmund) 1926-

PERSONAL: Born November 20, 1926, in Seaton Delaval, England; son of Cyril John (a priest of Church of England) and Lena (Henderson) Gardner; married Margaret Mercer, September 15, 1952; children: Alexis Mary Walmsley, Simon Richard John. *Education:* St. John's College, Cambridge, B.A., 1950, M.A., 1951; attended St. Stephen's House, Oxford, 1951-52.

ADDRESSES: Home—Charlottesville, Va. *Office*—Whitington Books Inc., 1156 Avenue of the Americas, Suite 750, New York, N.Y. 10036. *Agent*—Desmond Elliott, 15/17 King Street St. James's, London SW1Y 6QU, England.

CAREER: Writer. Ordained priest of Church of England, 1953, legally released from obligations of the priesthood, 1958; magician with American Red Cross, Entertainments Department, 1943-44; curate in Evesham, England, 1952-58; *Herald,* Stratford-upon-Avon, England, theatre critic and arts editor, 1959-64. Lecturer in the United States and Soviet Union. *Military service:* Royal Navy, Fleet Air Arm, 1944-46. Royal Marines, Commandos, 1946; served in Hong Kong and Malta; became chaplain.

MEMBER: Author's Guild, Crime Writers Association, Mystery Writers of America.

WRITINGS:

NOVELS; EXCEPT AS INDICATED

Spin the Bottle (autobiography), Muller, 1963.
The Liquidator, Viking, 1964.
Understrike, Viking, 1965.
Amber Nine, Viking, 1966.
Madrigal, Viking, 1968.
Hideaway (stories), Corgi, 1968.
Founder Member, Muller, 1969.
A Complete State of Death, J. Cape, 1969, Viking, 1970.
Traitor's Exit, Muller, 1970.
Air Apparent, Putnam, 1970 (published in England as *The Airline Pirates,* Hodder & Stoughton, 1970).
The Censor, New English Library, 1970.
Every Night's a Festival, Morrow, 1971 (published in England as *Every Night's a Bullfight,* M. Joseph, 1971).
The Assassination File (stories), Corgi, 1972.
The Corner Men, Doubleday, 1974.
The Return of Moriarty, Putnam, 1974 (published in England as *Moriarty,* Pan Books, 1976).
The Revenge of Moriarty, Putnam, 1975.
A Killer for a Song, Hodder & Stoughton, 1975.
To Run a Little Faster, M. Joseph, 1976.
The Werewolf Trace, Doubleday, 1977.
The Dancing Dodo, Doubleday, 1978.
The Nostradamus Traitor (first novel in "Kruger Trilogy"), Doubleday 1979.
The Garden of Weapons (second novel in "Kruger Trilogy"), Hodder & Stoughton, 1980, McGraw, 1981.
The Last Trump, McGraw, 1980 (published in England as *Golgotha,* W. H. Allen, 1980).
The Quiet Dogs (third novel in "Kruger Trilogy"), Hodder & Stoughton, 1982, Berkley Publishing, 1989.
Flamingo, Hodder & Stoughton, 1983.
The Secret Generations, Putnam, 1985.
The Secret Houses, Putnam, 1988.
The Secret Families, Putnam, 1989.

JAMES BOND NOVELS

License Renewed, R. Marek, 1981 (also see below).
For Special Services, Coward, McCann & Geoghegan, 1982 (also see below).
Icebreaker, Putnam, 1983 (also see below).
Role of Honor, Putnam, 1984.
Nobody Lives For Ever, Putnam, 1986.
No Deals, Mr. Bond, Putnam, 1987.
Scorpius, Putnam, 1988.
License Revoked, Berkley Publishing, 1989.

Win, Lose or Die, Putnam, 1989.

OTHER

Ian Fleming's James Bond: Three Complete Novels (contains *Licence Renewed, For Special Services,* and *Icebreaker*), Crown, 1987.

Works have been translated into more than fourteen languages.

WORK IN PROGRESS: A long novel titled *Maestra;* another James Bond novel; research on the history of Russia for a work to be published in 1991.

SIDELIGHTS: John Gardner's suspense novels have enjoyed steady success since the early 1960s, but in 1981 this established author received international attention when his novel *License Renewed* became a major best-seller. The reason for its immediate popularity: *License Renewed* was a new James Bond adventure, the first to appear in sixteen years. Bond, a fictional agent for England's Secret Service, was created by the late Ian Fleming in 1951 and quickly gained a loyal following. Fans are familiar with the most trivial details concerning Bond, or Agent 007 as he is also known; therefore, any flaws in a re-creation of Fleming's hero were certain to be noticed. The public's eager reception of *License Renewed* attests to Gardner's skill in performing his difficult task.

Gardner's interest in writing began early in life; he was an avid reader from the age of three. He once told *CA:* "At the age of nine I announced that I would be a writer, and my father presented me with a notebook. On the title page I wrote, 'The Complete Works of John Gardner.' The book remained empty for a long while, but I knew that I should really be an actor or a writer." Before realizing that ambition, Gardner followed his father into the Anglican priesthood. He had been in the ministry for five years when he realized that he had taken "the wrong turning." He explained to Fred Hauptfuhrer in *People* magazine: "It came to me the way some others have a conversion . . . only mine was in reverse. I was preaching one Sunday and realized I didn't believe a word I was saying." He left the priesthood in 1958. At that time, with the aid of hypnosis and aversion therapy, he was also able to overcome a heavy drinking habit. Gardner's first professional writing was done for the Stratford-upon-Avon *Herald,* where he acted as theatre critic and arts editor for six years. The experience was valuable, but, he told *CA,* "I realized I would not be happy forever acting as a critic of other people's work." Accordingly, in 1963, he published his first book, *Spin the Bottle,* an account of his struggle with alcohol. The next year, he published *The Liquidator,* a book that established him in the suspense genre in which he was to become so successful.

Spy novels, including Ian Fleming's Bond series, were at the height of their popularity in the early 1960s. According to Anthony Boucher of the *New York Times Book Review,* Gardner had written "a deliberate (and skillful) parody of James Bond" in *The Liquidator.* That novel's protagonist was the cowardly, inept Boysie Oakes, who was faint-hearted enough to have to hire others to do his killing. Yet Boucher maintains that the book is more than a comedy, writing, "Mr. Gardner succeeds in having it both ways; he has written a clever parody which is also a genuinely satisfactory thriller." Some years later Gardner created another spy quite unlike Bond. *The Nostradamus Traitor, The Garden of Weapons,* and *The Quiet Dogs* all featured Big Herbie Kruger, a German-born British intelligence agent who sees himself as a failure in both his life and work. The Kruger trilogy found an enthusiastic audience and drew praise from reviewers for Gardner's fine workmanship. T. J. Binyon describes *The Garden of Weapons* in the *Times Literary Supplement* as "a solid, finely detailed and intricately constructed piece of work," and Henry McDonald, writing in the *Washington Post Book World,* calls the same book "a skillfully crafted novel which sustains a high level of suspense from start to finish."

When the owners of the copyright to the James Bond character, Gildrose Publications, decided to hire an author to continue the Bond series some fourteen years after Fleming's last novel was published, Gardner's background made him a natural candidate for the job. His facility in imitating the style of other writers is noted by Derrick Murdoch in the Toronto *Globe and Mail:* "John Gardner is technically a highly competent thriller novelist who never seems to be quite at ease unless he is writing in the same vein as another writer. . . . It's what makes him so well-qualified to continue the James Bond Saga." Gildrose's board of directors agreed, finally selecting Gardner from a list of twelve authors. Peter Janson-Smith, one of Gildrose's directors and formerly Ian Fleming's agent, told *People* magazine, "We wanted someone with a respect for Fleming, not someone who'd start saying where Ian had gone wrong and threaten to walk out if we altered a word."

Gardner understood the difficulties inherent in the project. He explained to Hauptfuhrer, "[Bond is] a household name. Fans know how he cuts his fingernails, so the writer is a target for nitpickers. Mr. Fleming is a very difficult act to follow." Nevertheless, the author accepted the challenges of the assignment and began to write. He told Edwin McDowell in the *New York Times Book Review,* "I supplied [Gildrose] with four possible narrative outlines, and they picked one of them and asked me to do certain things. What they wanted was for me to think in terms of Bond having been on ice for a while, but being quite up to date about what's been going on in the world during the past two decades." He elaborated in *People,* "Then there's the matter of character. He's got to be the same man, but much more aware of women's position in society."

The result of these considerations was a Bond who drank less, drove a fuel-efficient Saab, and smoked low-tar cigarettes. Not unexpectedly, some critics reacted indignantly to this updating of the spy character. Michael Malone's *New York Times Book Review* article states, "Bond was so suited to his times, so right in [the 1950s,] that age of astronauts and Thunderbirds, perhaps he should have decided you only live once. . . . For Bond to be worrying about gas mileage is like shipping the Scarlet Pimpernel to Plymouth Colony." And, although praising Gardner's skill, T. J. Binyon and Stanley Ellin, writing respectively in the *Times Literary Supplement* and *New York Times Book Review,* both express the opinion that because Bond originated as Fleming's alter ego, no other author could satisfactorily re-create him. Gardner's third Bond book, *Icebreaker,* is, according to Binyon, "full of good action; his torture scenes are splendidly painful; his villain is adequately megalomaniac, though perhaps not sufficiently *outre;* his girls are pretty, sexy, and available, and the courting routines as embarrassingly obvious as anything in the original. . . . But in the end Gardner's Bond doesn't really measure up to Fleming's. There isn't that maniacal snobbery about trivial and useless detail which the original so endearingly manifests. And, furthermore, Gardner simply hasn't grasped Bond's most important trait: he only takes assignments where his creator would like to take a holiday. And who on earth would want to holiday in the 'desolate Arctic wastes of Lapland'? Certainly not the luxurious Bond." Ellin writes that Gardner is somewhat overqualified for the job of following Fleming: "Ian Fleming was a dreadful writer, a creator of books for grown-up boys, a practitioner of tin-eared prose. As evidenced by his writing, he was also by nature a ferocious and humorless snob, a political primitive,

a chauvinist in every possible area." Gardner, continues Ellin, is "a writer of style and wit and a sharp-eyed, acidulous and yet appreciative view of humanity and its foibles. Fleming's shoes are simply too tight and misshapen for Mr. Gardner to wear comfortably."

But Mel Watkins of the *New York Times Book Review* feels that Gardner's Bond is certainly equal to Fleming's original, and is perhaps superior, thanks to his more believable personality. "Although Mr. Gardner's Bond is less raffishly macho and arrogant than previously depicted, the spirit of the 007 series remains intact, and few Fleming admirers are likely to object. There is, in fact, something appealing about a James Bond who can react to women with some sympathy and confusion at a crucial moment." Bond fans, perhaps the sternest critics of all, made the final judgment: they bought and read the books eagerly. *License Renewed* sold over 130,000 copies in hardcover alone, inspiring such confidence in its publishers that the sequel, *For Special Services,* enjoyed a first printing of 95,000 copies.

Gardner went on to produce more successful James Bond novels that include *Nobody Lives For Ever, No Deals, Mr. Bond, Scorpius,* and *Win, Lose or Die.* In addition, the author has earned acclaim for other books of mystery and intrigue published in the late 1980s, such as *The Secret Generations, The Secret Houses,* and *The Secret Families.*

Gardner described his writing technique to *CA:* "I work rather like an actor, taking on a theme or role so that it, eventually, envelops me. After that, I need to work with a good editor, who I use as an actor uses a director. . . . Work is life and life is work, though I have no pretensions about being 'literary'—I greatly mistrust any so-called 'Literary Establishment.' I am a story-teller, a professional wordsmith—it is a job, like that of a carpenter or any other craftsman. Sometimes the piece works, sometimes not."

MEDIA ADAPTATIONS: "The Liquidator" was released as a feature film by Metro-Goldwyn-Mayer in 1965. *A Complete State of Death* was released as "The Stone Killer" by Columbia in 1973.

AVOCATIONAL INTERESTS: Reading, music.

BIOGRAPHICAL/CRITICAL SOURCES:

BOOKS

Contemporary Literary Criticism, Volume 30, Gale, 1984.

PERIODICALS

Globe and Mail (Toronto), December 24, 1983, October 27, 1984, July 30, 1988, July 22, 1989.
New York Times, April 9, 1983.
New York Times Book Review, October 18, 1964, August 1, 1965, June 7, 1981, June 14, 1981, May 30, 1982, April 24, 1983, December 1, 1985.
People, June 21, 1982.
Punch, May 20, 1981, July 27, 1983.
Time, July 6, 1981, July 5, 1982.
Times Literary Supplement, December 26, 1980, June 5, 1981, September 17, 1982, July 22, 1983.
Washington Post Book World, April 5, 1981, January 5, 1986.

*   *   *

GARDNER, John (Champlin), Jr.   1933-1982

PERSONAL: Born July 21, 1933, in Batavia, N.Y.; died in a motorcycle accident, September 14, 1982, in Susquehanna, Pa.; son of John Champlin (a dairy farmer) and Priscilla (a high school literature teacher; maiden name, Jones) Gardner; married Joan Louise Patterson, June 6, 1953 (divorced, 1976); married Liz Rosenberg, 1980 (divorced); children: Joel, Lucy. *Education:* De Pauw University, student, 1951-53; Washington University, St. Louis, A.B., 1955; State University of Iowa, M.A., 1956, Ph.D., 1958.

ADDRESSES: Office—c/o Boskydell Artists Ltd., 72 Monument Ave., Bennington, Vt. 05201.

CAREER: Oberlin College, Oberlin, Ohio, instructor, 1958-59; Chico State College (now California State University), Chico, Calif., instructor, 1959-62; San Francisco State College (now San Francisco State University), San Francisco, Calif., assistant professor of English, 1962-65; Southern Illinois University, Carbondale, professor of English, 1965-74; Bennington College, Vt., instructor, 1974-76; Williams College, Williamstown, Mass., and Skidmore College, Saratoga Springs, N.Y., instructor, 1976-77; George Mason University, Fairfax, Va., instructor, 1977-78; founder and director of writing program, University of New York at Binghamton, 1978-82; author, 1976-82. Distinguished visiting professor, University of Detroit, 1970-71; visiting professor, Northwestern University, Evanston, Ill., 1973.

MEMBER: Modern Language Association of America, American Association of University Professors.

AWARDS, HONORS: Woodrow Wilson fellowship, 1955-56; Danforth fellowship, 1972-73; Guggenheim fellowship, 1973-74; National Education Association award, 1972; *Grendel* named one of 1971's best fiction books by *Time* and *Newsweek; October Light* named one of the ten best books of 1976 by *Time* and *New York Times;* National Book Critics Circle award for fiction, 1976, for *October Light;* Armstrong Prize, 1980, for *The Temptation Game.*

WRITINGS:

NOVELS

The Resurrection, New American Library, 1966, reprinted, Random House, 1987.
The Wreckage of Agathon, Harper, 1970.
Grendel, Knopf, 1971, reprinted, Random House, 1989.
The Sunlight Dialogues, Knopf, 1972.
Jason and Medeia (novel in verse), Knopf, 1973, reprinted, Random House, 1986.
Nickel Mountain: A Pastoral Novel, Knopf, 1973, reprinted, Random House, 1989.
October Light, Knopf, 1976, reprinted, Random House, 1989.
Freddy's Book, Knopf, 1980.
Mickelsson's Ghost, Knopf, 1982.

JUVENILES

Dragon, Dragon and Other Timeless Tales, Knopf, 1975.
Gudgekin the Thistle Girl and Other Tales (Junior Literary Guild selection), Knopf, 1976.
In the Suicide Mountains, Knopf, 1977.
A Child's Bestiary (light verse), Knopf, 1977.
King of the Hummingbirds, and Other Tales, Knopf, 1977.
Vlemk, the Box Painter, Lord John Press, 1979.

CRITICISM

(Editor with Lennis Dunlap) *The Forms of Fiction,* Random House, 1961.
(Editor and author of introduction) *The Complete Works of the Gawain-Poet in a Modern English Version with a Critical Introduction,* University of Chicago Press, 1965.

(Editor with Nicholas Joost) *Papers on the Art and Age of Geoffrey Chaucer,* Southern Illinois University Press, 1967.
(Editor and author of notes) *The Gawain-Poet: Notes on Pearl and Sir Gawain and the Green Knight, with Brief Commentary on Purity and Patience,* Cliffs Notes, 1967.
Morte D'Arthur Notes, Cliffs Notes, 1967.
Sir Gawain and the Green Knight Notes, Cliffs Notes, 1967.
(Editor and author of notes) *The Alliterative Morte Arthure, The Owl and the Nightingale and Five Other Middle English Poems* (modern English version), Southern Illinois University Press, 1971.
The Construction of the Wakefield Cycle, Southern Illinois University Press, 1974.
The Construction of Christian Poetry in Old English, Southern Illinois University Press, 1975.
The Life and Times of Chaucer, Knopf, 1977.
The Poetry of Chaucer, Southern Illinois University Press, 1978.
On Moral Fiction, Basic Books, 1978.
On Becoming a Novelist, Harper, 1983.
The Art of Fiction: Notes on Craft for Young Writers, Knopf, 1984.

OTHER

The King's Indian and Other Fireside Tales (novellas), Knopf, 1974, reprinted, McKay, 1989 (published in England as *The King's Servant,* J. Cape, 1975).
(Contributor) Matthew Bruccoli and C. E. Frazer Clark, Jr., editors, *Pages,* Volume 1, Gale, 1976.
William Wilson (libretto; also see below), New London Press, 1978.
Poems, Lord John Press, 1978.
Three Libretti (includes *William Wilson, Frankenstein,* and *Rumpelstiltskin*), New London Press, 1979.
MSS: A Retrospective, New London Press, 1980.
The Art of Living and Other Stories, Knopf, 1981.
(Editor with Shannon Ravenel) *The Best American Short Stories of 1982,* Houghton, 1982.
(Translator with Nobuko Tsukui) Kikuo Itaya, *Tengu Child,* Southern Illinois University Press, 1983.
(Translator with John R. Maier) *Gilgamesh: A Translation,* Knopf, 1984.
Stillness and Shadows, edited by Nicholas Delbanco, Knopf, 1986.

Also author of *The Temptation Game* (radio play), 1980. Contributor of short stories to *Southern Review, Quarterly Review of Literature,* and *Perspective;* of poetry to *Kenyon Review, Hudson Review,* and other literary quarterlies; and of articles to *Esquire, Saturday Evening Post,* and other magazines. Founder and editor, *MSS* (a literary magazine).

SIDELIGHTS: John Champlin Gardner—not to be confused with the John Edmund Gardner who writes satiric mystery novels or John L. Gardner who was once the head of the Department of Health, Education and Welfare—was a philosophical novelist, a medievalist well versed in the classics, an educator, and an opinionated critic. Described by *Village Voice* contributor Elizabeth Stone as "Evel Knievel at the typewriter," Gardner stood for conservation of values from the past yet maintained a lifelong love-hate relationship with "the rules." Though he championed the moral function of literature, his long hair, leather jacket, and motorcycle classed him with nonconformists. The typical conflict in his work pits individual freedom against institutions that dominate by means of cultural "myths." In novels and stories, Paul Gray of *Time* summarizes, "Gardner sets conflicting metaphysics whirling, then records the patterns thrown out by their lines of force. One situation consistently recurs, . . . an inherited past must defend itself against a plotless future.''

Gardner's novels provoked a wide range of critical responses, and, unlike many "academic" fictions, were appreciated by a large audience. Three of his novels were bestsellers. "Very few writers, of any age, are alchemist enough to capture the respect of the intellectual community *and* the imagination of others who lately prefer [Jacqueline] Susann and [Judith] Krantz. Based on critical acclaim, and sales volume, it would seem that this man accomplished both," Craig Riley wrote in *Best Sellers*. Carol A. MacCurdy reported in *Dictionary of Literary Biography Yearbook, 1982*, "Many critics consider *Grendel* (1971) a modern classic, *The Sunlight Dialogues* an epic of the 1970s, and *October Light* [which won the National Book Critics Circle Award for fiction in 1976] a dazzling piece of Americana."

Gardner spent his apprenticeship in literature as a medievalist, devoting himself to the writings of Chaucer and Dante, stories about King Arthur and Sir Gawain, and other classics. His studies were largely well received. Walter Clemons of *Newsweek* called *The Life and Times of Chaucer* "a very appealing investigative biography." Adding to the reader's interest, he said, was the fact that "Gardner's scholarship is solid and thorough, but he wears his mortarboard in a rakish tilt." Of *The Poetry of Chaucer* Clemons declared, "the energy, enthusiasm and complexity of Gardner's argument stirs one to read Chaucer afresh."

Gardner's notes on *Morte D'Arthur, Sir Gawain and the Green Knight,* and the Gawain poet have helped younger readers to appreciate these classics. His books for children also draw from his knowledge of medieval literature. They are fairy tales retold with original twists, "hip" tales in which familiar characters speak in today's cliches, or where unlikely contemporary characters are revived by the magic of the past. For example, in *Dragon, Dragon and Other Tales,* losers win and heroes lose. "Kings prove powerless, young girls mighty. The miller wins the princess, but she proves to be a witch. Tables are turned this way and that, with consequences that are hilarious and wonderful," Jonathan Yardley related in the *New York Times Book Review*. Like most of Gardner's fairy tales, *In the Suicide Mountains*—the story of three outcasts who find happiness after hearing some old folktales—is for adults as well.

Gardner always worked on several book projects at a time and did not publish his novels in the order that they were finished. Gardner's first published novel, *The Resurrection,* traces a philosophy professor's thoughts after he learns his life will be shortened by leukemia. David Cowart observed in *Dictionary of Literary Biography,* "The book asks the question Gardner would ask in every succeeding novel: how can existential man—under sentence of death—live in such a way as to foster life-affirming values, regardless of how ultimately provisional they may prove?" *The Resurrection* introduces features that recur in later books: an embedded second narrative, usually a "borrowed" text; a facility with fictional techniques; and an emotional impact Cowart describes as "harrowing."

Gardner's second published novel, *The Wreckage of Agathon,* proved his skill as an antiquarian, as a writer who could bring forward materials from ancient history and weave them into "a novel transcending history and effectively embracing all of it, a philosophical drama that accurately describes the wreckage of the 20th century as well as of Agathon, and a highly original work of imagination," wrote Christopher Lehmann-Haupt of the *New York Times*. Built of mostly dialogue, it exposed Gardner's "manic glee in disputation," or "delight in forensic and rhe-

torical flashiness for its own sake," Cowart observed. Its themes include the relation between individuals and the social orders they encounter. *The Wreckage of Agathon* "delineates the mental motion of the individual as sacred, whether he's a seer or not . . . and it exuberantly calls into question society's categorical insistances—the things brought into being at our own expense to protect us against ourselves, other people, and, putatively, other societies," Paul West wrote in the *New York Times Book Review.*

The Sunlight Dialogues also grapples with this theme. In a *Washington Post Book World* review, Geoffrey Wolff called *The Sunlight Dialogues* "an extended meditation on the trench warfare between freedom and order." The Sunlight Man—a policeman-turned-outlaw embittered by the loss of his family—and Police Chief Fred Clumly, obsessed with law and order, duel to the death in this novel. Emerging in the conflict between them is Gardner's examination of how these two forces impinge on art. Wolff commented, "While all men wish for both—freedom and order—the conflict between them is dramatized by every decision that an artist makes. The artist will do what he will. . . . No: the artist does what he must, recognizes the limits, agrees to our rules so that we can play too. No; . . . it's *his* cosmos. And so it goes."

Grendel retells the *Beowulf* tale from the monster's point of view. This new tack on the sea of the familiar hero myth allowed Gardner to fathom new insights into the conflict between order and chaos. In the *New York Times,* Richard Locke explained how the uncivil behavior of "civilized" man contributed to Grendel's murderous career: "Though twice he attempts to shed his monsterhood, become human, join these other verbal creatures, . . . he's misunderstood on both occasions, and the rat-like humans attack him in fear. So, racked with resentment, pride and vengeful nihilism, outraged by mankind's perversity (for the noble values of the poet's songs are betrayed in a trice by the beery warlords), Grendel commences his cynical war." Though confirmed in cynicism, the monster remains haunted by the words of The Shaper, the poet who revives inspiration and hope in the hearts of his listeners. In this way, Gardner demonstrated the power of art and its role in Western culture.

Gardner employed symbolism on many levels in *Grendel.* By breaking the novel into twelve sections corresponding to the signs of the zodiac, Gardner constructed a "cosmic" novel, since twelve is a symbol of the cosmos. By setting his story into this construction, the progression of the twelve signs became at the same time the twelve years of Grendel's conflict with civilization. "In numerology a number multiplied by itself represents an intensification of the original symbolism," Cowart pointed out; and this structure intensifies the ending, in which "Grendel learns that he too—death itself, symbolically—is mortal." The monster's last words—"Poor Grendel's had an accident. . . . *so may you all*"—hint at the complexity of moral questions, since it implies both the momentary monstrosity of the executioner Beowulf and the monster's relief at his release from a life of despair and violence. Other critics also recognize that by placing the monster's reign on a cyclical form, Gardner meant to affirm the regenerative power of life that puts death—and all that is monstrous—into perspective. Thus, "In this short novel," Cowart wrote, "Gardner burnishes the classic at the same time that he creates a new masterpiece."

Nickel Mountain: A Pastoral Novel explored again the complex relationship between order and chaos, particularly as they relate to human responsibility for events in a world that seems to give random accident free play. Narrator Henry Soames, proprietor of an all-night diner, has a ringside seat to the "horror of the random," to cite Cowart, in the lives of his patrons. Slow-moving and dominated by routine, the pastoral life around the diner is interrupted by a series of fatal accidents, including auto wrecks and house fires. Touching Henry more closely is the man who fell to his death on the stairs while recoiling from Henry's shout. Debates ensue about limits to the assignment of blame. Some of Gardner's characters feel that the assignment of guilt, though painful, is preferable to seeing themselves as victims of mere chance. As *London Magazine* contributor Herbert Lomas put it, recognitions of personal failure or weakness are "what lead you to love, brotherhood and God. It's through weakness and failure that you find warmth, . . . see your need for mercy and forgiveness, and thus everyone's, and feel the beginnings of sacramental consciousness." "Here, as in his other fiction," wrote Michael Wood in the *New York Review of Books,* "Gardner shows a marvelous gift for making *stories* ask balanced, intricate questions, for getting his complex questions into tight stories."

Henry's bout with guilt in *Nickel Mountain* stemmed from a personal tragedy Gardner suffered early in his life. The eleven-year-old Gardner was at the wheel of a tractor that ran over and killed his seven-year-old brother David. Though it was an accident, he believed he could have prevented it. Daily flashbacks to the accident troubled him until he had written the story "Redemption" in 1979, a story based on his memory of the accident. Because writing the story demanded concentration on the scene in order to take narrative control of it, his terror was diffused. But the question of human responsibility versus chance continued to surface in many of Gardner's novels and stories, suggesting that this question had become, for him, a habit of mind.

What was an internal conflict in *Nickel Mountain* became open debate in Gardner's next bestseller. *October Light* pits American conservativism against liberalism embodied in a seventy-year-old Vermont farmer and his eighty-year-old feminist sister. In a characteristic rage about declining morals, James shoots Sally's television set and locks her into an upstairs room. They shout their arguments through the closed door. Sally finds a store of apples in the attic and parts of a "trashy" book about marijuana smugglers, *The Smugglers of Lost Soul's Rock,* and refuses to come out, even after her niece unlocks the door. She sees correspondences between the book's plot and her conflict with James. More vulnerable to his intimidating anger is James's son Richard, who commits suicide. Gardner exposed the regrettable stubbornness of both sides of their conflict and at the same time implied the paucity of absurdist literature in the "trashy" parody of postmodern literature Sally reads.

By the novel's end, James revises his opinions to accommodate a wider range of sensibility. "In *October Light,* then," reasoned Cowart, "we have a rustic world where the same horrors obtain as in the black-comic, nihilistic, 'smart-mouth satirical' novels typified by *Smugglers,* but Gardner convinces us that James Page can, at the age of seventy-two, come to self-knowledge—and that the thawing of this man's frozen heart holds much promise for all people who, bound in spiritual winter, have ever despaired of the spring."

"Using one obsession to attack another, [Gardner's] novels move with a pacing and complexity that are remarkable in current fiction," Josephine Hendin remarked in the *New Republic.* However, the novelist does not take sides. "Gardner's irresolution takes the form of an irony so pervasive it seems to stem from that well of American bitterness that made Herman Melville and Mark Twain, creators of distinctive American heroes, finally black about America's possibilities. Gardner presses his ambivalences into *October Light,* forcing his chauvinism and his nihilism against each other like monuments to two American civilizations. He achieves a disturbing, utterly original novel that gets as close as any book can to that acid cartoon, Grant Wood's 'American Gothic.' " Other critics suggested that Gardner was motivated to promote the exercise of moral sense more than to side with any particular philosophical stance.

Freddy's Book is a frame tale, a long story set into the "frame" of another narrative. A professor introduces a guest to his "monster" son, an eight-foot-tall recluse who has written a book. The shy giant's tome is the retelling of Sweden's liberation from Danish rule in the sixteenth century, glossed with the Devil's role as instigator of conflict on both sides who is eventually murdered by the knight Lars-Goren Bergkvist. "The final scene, in which the Devil is scaled like a mountain, is a marvelously virtuosic piece of narrative, with juxtapositions and counterpoints smacking as much of the screenwriter's art as the novelist's. Gardner is a masterful storyteller, even when, as in 'Freddy's Book,' he is curiously lacking in tone," John Romano wrote in the *New York Times Book Review.*

Lars-Goren, though flatly drawn in comparison to other Gardner characters, does his share of philosophical introspection. He ponders over his sudden fear of the Devil, and over the question, if evil can be destroyed, should it? The argument that evil is a foil against which good defines and proves itself is not a simple resolution, Lehmann-Haupt points out in *Books of the Times,* since Gardner let the Devil make this suggestion. Lars-Goren understands that since the Devil "is inherent in us or in our situation," evil may not be easily destroyed, Romano explained. However, added Romano, "Lars-Goren . . . acts *in spite of* what he knows, because, one gathers, the gesture itself is worth something, is perhaps worth everything."

In a *Chicago Tribune Book World* review, William Logan charged Gardner with plagiarism for using passages from a history of Sweden by Michael Roberts nearly verbatim in sections of *Freddy's Book.* Gardner rebutted that his attribution at the beginning of the book ("Numerous passages here are drawn, slightly altered, from other sources") should have been sufficient. His letter to the *Chicago Tribune* explained, "I used hundreds of sources. . . . To have acknowledged my hundreds of quotations and allusions would have been lunacy." He went on to explain that allusiveness is a trait of all medievalist literature: "The first step in literary composition, according to medieval rhetorical theory, is *inventio,* which is sometimes defined as 'the collection of old materials to be used in a new way.' Collage technique, the technique I practice, has nothing to do with plagiarism." Rather, he claimed, it was his homage paid to the vast store of literature that came before—his way of acknowledging the "dependency" of contemporary novelists on the accomplishments of earlier writers.

While writing *Mickelsson's Ghost,* Gardner deliberately tried to make the novel radically different from his prior works. The result, by comparison, said Curt Suplee of the *Washington Post,* "is a highbrow potboiler. . . . And it takes a wide-bodied and fast-moving narrative to carry all Gardner's themes, aiming them at the totalitarian threats in modern culture (metaphorically embedded in the Mormons and tax men) and a grand theological synthesis." Gardner explained to Suplee, "The two sort of big ghosts in the thing are Nietzsche and Luther: Luther's saying none of your works mean anything; and Nietzsche's saying works are everything. And if you get those two things together, you have courtly love. The lover does the most that he can possibly do, and then the grace of the lady saves him."

The title character, a philosophy professor, is troubled with a proliferation of "ghosts." The farm on which he has taken refuge from the world is haunted by apparitions of its previous owners, including the founder of Mormonism, Joseph Smith, and the still-living Hell's Angel who sold him the farm. Harassed by the Internal Revenue Service and the Sons of Dan (a fictional group of fanatic assassins), Mickelsson is haunted by his own crimes. After a teen he sleeps with gets pregnant, he robs an elderly man, hoping to pay the girl not to have an abortion. During the robbery, the man dies of a heart attack. Should Mickelsson, or should he not, think of himself as the murderer of the elderly miser? This and other questions of ethics—including how to assess the worth of individual human lives, Jack Miles noted in the *Los Angeles Times Book Review*—are the center of "this huge and ambitious book," Woiwode suggested, "and its grappling hook at your heart . . . is its questioning of our premises of what is real, or what 'reality' is; and in its brave examination of this, and of borderline states of supposed health, it becomes the kind of book that can alter one's way of looking at life."

Henry is also haunted by "hundreds of literary and philosophical and socio-historical echoes, most of them knit seamlessly into the story's unfurling," Woiwode related in the *Chicago Tribune Book World*. The ruling principle of the novel is excess as suggested in the title, *mickel* being the medieval word for "much." *New York Review of Books* contributor Robert Towers called it "an immense, baggy novel, loosely packed with four or five plots, several competing genres, a small army of characters, and enough thematic material to fuel a dozen all-night bull-sessions." Some readers found the excesses tedious while others found them delightful.

In addition to these novels, Gardner wrote a number of thought-provoking works on the purpose and craft of fiction. His criticism was hailed, as were his novels, as "disturbing." *On Moral Fiction,* written in part before his novels were published, contained many blunt statements that negatively assessed the works of other major novelists. Some of his statements contradicted others, such that his position was at times overstated, understated, or unclear. Some took these judgments as insults; and some critics, picking up the gauntlet, evaluated Gardner's subsequent works from a fighting stance. Yet others forgave the book's faults because they agreed with Gardner about the essentially humane quality of great literature.

Convinced that fiction exerts an important influence on our daily lives, Gardner claimed that novelists "should think always, of what harm they might inadvertently do, and not do it. If there is good to be said, the writer should remember to say it. If there is bad to be said, he should say it in a way that reflects the truth that, though we see the evil, we choose to continue among the living." For Gardner, "true" and "moral" art was art that "clarifies life, establishes models of human action, casts nets toward the future, carefully judges our right and wrong directions, celebrates and mourns. . . . It does not sneer or giggle in the face of death, it invents prayers and weapons. It designs visions worth trying to make fact." His comment that "real art creates myths a society can live instead of die by" has been cited often. He said in an interview with Joe David Bellamy in *The New Fiction* that fiction was furthermore a weapon against evil, which is overcome, as William Blake said, "by acts of imagination." His preface explaining his selections for *The Best American Short Stories of 1982* would later assert that the best fiction communicates its author's sincere and "serious personal concern" for others. Literary ambition alone is not enough to produce great literature, he claimed. "Eight million people died while we were thinking about how to become 'great writers,'" he told writers at a Bread Loaf conference, according to the *Washington Post*'s Chuck Cascio. Gardner declared, "You cannot be a great writer unless you feel greatly."

Having stated his standard so boldly, Gardner was judged by it himself. For instance, Romano maintained that while *Freddy's Book* was philosophical fiction, it wasn't moral, since it appeared to encourage the kind of exuberant destruction of evil that was "moved by vagrant, unexamined feelings" and is therefore prone to "slip over into immorality at any turn." Furthermore, Romano claimed, Gardner was "a better modernist than he [knew]." The complex structures and labyrinthine plots belonging to postmodernist literature such as that of John Barth and Jorge Luis Borges also flourish in Gardner's books. *National Review* critic Don Crinklaw observed that Gardner's work shares with that of Barth and William Gass a dependence on earlier literature, characters identified by their philosophical positions, and independence from the literary tastes of critics and casual readers. On a deeper level, Romano observed that the novelist's moral aesthetic fought with his love for "the fabulous, the enchanted," which was his "by training and inclination" as a medievalist. About this elemental contradiction, Romano stated, "It is fascinating and a little droll to see him struggling against his own gifts."

On Becoming a Novelist expressed Gardner's many thoughts about his vocation and outlined what it takes to be a professional novelist. Most important, he claimed, are "drive"—an unyielding persistence to write and publish; and faith—confidence in one's own abilities, belief in one's eventual success. The book restated his moral aesthetic. *Los Angeles Times Book Review* contributor Richard Rodriguez was struck by Gardner's passionate rejection of fictions that substitute "inconclusiveness," "pointlessly subtle games," or obsessive "puzzle-making" for essential storytelling. *The Art of Fiction: Notes on Craft for Young Writers* "originated as the so-called 'Black Book,' an underground text passed from hand to hand in university creative-writing departments," Stuart Schoffman noted in the *Los Angeles Times Book Review,* citing Gardner's comment from its preface that "it is the most helpful book of its kind." John L'Heureux remarked in the *New York Times Book Review* that "Gardner was famous for his generosity to young writers, and 'The Art of Fiction' is his posthumous gift to them."

Gardner's gift to literature, Charles Johnson noted in *Dictionary of Literary Biography Yearbook, 1982,* was "the literary strategy that fused theory and technique in his tales and novels. . . . Classical forms as vehicles infused with dignity, an affirmative worldview, and a timeless sense of value. . . . [He] offered us the achievements of the past—artistic and metaphysical—as models for the future."

MEDIA ADAPTATIONS: An animated film version of *Grendel* called *Grendel, Grendel, Grendel* was produced by Victorian Film Corporation in Australia in 1981.

BIOGRAPHICAL/CRITICAL SOURCES:

BOOKS

Bellamy, Joe David, editor, *The New Fiction: Interviews with Innovative American Writers,* University of Illinois Press, 1974.

Contemporary Literary Criticism, Gale, Volume 2, 1974, Volume 3, 1975, Volume 5, 1976, Volume 7, 1977, Volume 8, 1978, Volume 10, 1979, Volume 18, 1981, Volume 28, 1984, Volume 34, 1985.

Cowart, David, *Arches and Light: The Fiction of John Gardner,* Southern Illinois University Press, 1983.

Dictionary of Literary Biography, Volume 2: *American Novelists since World War II,* 1978.
Dictionary of Literary Biography Yearbook, 1982, Gale, 1983.
Gardner, John, *Grendel,* Knopf, 1971.
Gardner, *On Moral Fiction,* Basic Books, 1978.
Gardner, *Freddy's Book,* Knopf, 1980.
Gardner, *On Becoming a Novelist,* Harper, 1983.
Gardner, *The Art of Fiction: Notes on Craft for Young Writers,* Knopf, 1984.
Plimpton, George, editor, *Writers at Work: The Paris Review Interviews,* Viking, 1981.

PERIODICALS

Atlantic, January, 1984.
Books of the Times, May, 1980.
Chicago Tribune, March 16, 1980, April 13, 1980.
Chicago Tribune Book World, May 24, 1981, April 13, 1980, June 13, 1982, April 1, 1984.
Esquire, January, 1971, June, 1982.
Best Sellers, April, 1984.
Los Angeles Times Book Review, May 30, 1982, December 5, 1982, June 12, 1983, May 30, 1982, February 12, 1984.
National Review, November 23, 1973.
New Republic, February 5, 1977.
Newsweek, December 24, 1973, April 11, 1977.
New York Review of Books, March 21, 1974, June 24, 1982.
New York Times, September 4, 1970, November 14, 1976, December 26, 1976, January 2, 1977.
New York Times Book Review, November 16, 1975, March 23, 1980, May 17, 1981, May 31, 1981, June 20, 1982, February 26, 1984, July 20, 1986.
Time, January 1, 1973, December 30, 1974, December 20, 1976.
Times Literary Supplement, October 23, 1981, October 22, 1982, July 29, 1983.
Village Voice, December 27, 1976.
Washington Post, July 25, 1982, March 1, 1983.
Washington Post Book World, December 24, 1972, March 23, 1980, May 3, 1981, May 14, 1982.

OBITUARIES:

PERIODICALS

Chicago Tribune, September 16, 1982.
Publishers Weekly, October 1, 1982.
Newsweek, September 27, 1982.
New York Times, September 15, 1982.
School Library Journal, November, 1982.
Time, September 27, 1982.
Times (London), September 18, 1982.

*　　*　　*

GARDONS, S. S.
See SNODGRASS, William D(e Witt)

*　　*　　*

GARNER, Alan 1934-

PERSONAL: Born October 17, 1934, in Cheshire, England; son of Colin and Marjorie Garner; married first wife, Ann Cook, in 1956; married Griselda Greaves, 1972; children: (first marriage) one son, two daughters; (second marriage) one son, one daughter. *Education:* Attended Magdalen College, Oxford.

ADDRESSES: Home—"Toad Hall," Blackden-cum Goostrey, Cheshire CW4 8BY, England.

CAREER: Writer. *Military service:* British Army; became second lieutenant.

AWARDS, HONORS: Carnegie Medal, 1967, and Guardian Award, 1968, both for *The Owl Service;* Lewis Carroll Shelf Award, 1970, for *The Weirdstone of Brisingamen;* first prize, Chicago International Film Festival, for *Images.*

WRITINGS:

The Weirdstone of Brisingamen: A Tale of Alderley, Collins, 1960, published as *The Weirdstone: A Tale of Alderley,* F. Watts, 1961, revised edition, Walck, 1969.
The Moon of Gomrath, Walck, 1963.
Elidor, Walck, 1965.
Holly from the Bongs, Collins, 1966.
The Owl Service, Walck, 1967.
The Old Man of Mow, illustrated by Roger Hill, Doubleday, 1967.
(Editor) *A Cavalcade of Goblins,* illustrated by Krystyna Turska, Walck, 1969 (published in England as *The Hamish Hamilton Book of Goblins,* Hamish Hamilton, 1969).
Red Shift, Macmillan, 1973.
The Breadhorse, Collins, 1975.
The Guizer, Greenwillow Books, 1976.
The Stone Book, Collins, 1976, Collins & World, 1978.
Tom Fobble's Day, Collins, 1977, Collins & World, 1979.
Granny Reardun, Collins, 1977, Collins & World, 1979.
The Aimer Gate, Collins, 1978, Collins & World, 1979.
The Golden Brothers, Collins, 1979.
The Girl of the Golden Gate, Collins, 1979.
The Golden Heads of the Well, Collins, 1979.
The Princess and the Golden Mane, Collins, 1979.
Alan Garner's Fairytales of Gold, Philomel Books, 1980.
The Lad of the Gad, Collins, 1980, Philomel Books, 1981.
Alan Garner's Book of British Fairytales, Collins, 1984.
A Bag of Moonshine (folk stories), Delacorte, 1986.
The Stone Book Quartet, Dell, 1988.

Also author of dance drama, *The Green Mist,* 1970; also author of libretti for *The Bellybag* (music by Richard Morris), 1971, and *Potter Thompson* (music by Gordon Crosse), 1971; also author of plays, *Lamaload,* 1978, *Lurga Lom,* 1980, *To Kill a King,* 1980, *Sally Water,* 1982, and *The Keeper,* 1983; also author of documentary films, *Places and Things,* 1978, and *Images,* 1981; also author, with John Mackenzie, of film adaptation of *Red Shift,* 1978.

SIDELIGHTS: Though Alan Garner was once considered a "children's" author, the increasing complexity of his stories has led many reviewers to reevaluate their original assessment of his work. For most, the turning point in his status was the publication of *The Owl Service,* an eerie tale of supernatural forces that interweaves ancient symbolism from Welsh folklore with a modern plot and original details. A story "remarkable not only for its sustained and evocative atmosphere, but for its implications," *The Owl Service* is "a drama of young people confronted with the challenge of a moral choice; at the same time it reveals, like diminishing reflections in a mirror, the eternal recurrence of the dilemma with each generation," according to the *Children's Book World.* A critic from the *Christian Science Monitor* describes it as "a daring juxtaposition of legend from the *Mabinogion,* and the complex relationship of two lads and a girl [in which] old loves and hates are . . . reenacted. Mr. Garner sets his tale in a Welsh valley and touches with pity and terror the minds of the reader who will let himself feel its atmosphere. This is not a book 'for children'; its subtle truth is for anyone who will reach for it." A writer for the *Times Literary Supplement* echoes this sentiment, noting that with *The Owl Service* "Alan Garner has moved away from the world of children's books and has emerged as a writer unconfined by reference to age-groups; a writer whose imaginative vein is rich enough to reward his readers on several different levels."

In an essay excerpted in the *Times Literary Supplement,* Garner himself alludes to the many levels of meaning in his work. Speaking of his readers, he says: "The age of the individual does not necessarily relate to the maturity. Therefore, in order to connect, the book must be written for all levels of experience. This means that any given piece of text must work at simple plot level, so that the reader feels compelled to turn the page, if only to find out what happens next; and it must also work for me, and for every stage between. . . . I try to write onions."

One book so complex that some critics find it almost impenetrable is *Red Shift,* a novel comprised of three different stories with separate sets of characters who are linked only by a Stone Age axe-head, which functions as a talisman, and a rural setting in Cheshire. Composed almost wholly of dialogue, *Red Shift* jump-cuts from the days of the Roman conquest to the seventeenth century to the present time. Writing in *Horn Book,* Aidan Chambers compares the book to "a decorated prism which turns to show—incident by incident—first one face, then another. In the last section, the prism spins so fast that the three faces merge into one color, one time, one place, one set of people, one meaning." Michael Benton believes that "*Red Shift* expresses the significance of place and the insignificance of time. . . . Certainly in style and structure the book is uncompromising: the familiar literary surface of the conventional novel is stripped away and one is constantly picking up hints, catching at clues, making associations and allowing the chiselled quality of the writing to suggest new mental landscapes."

Despite the fact that Garner's novels are difficult, especially for young American readers unfamiliar with the local British dialects he employs so freely, Garner "takes his craft very seriously, gives far more time to each book than the majority of present-day writers and has probably given more thought to the theory and practice of writing for children than anyone else," writes Frank Eyre in *British Children's Books in the Twentieth Century.*

BIOGRAPHICAL/CRITICAL SOURCES:

BOOKS

British Children's Books in the Twentieth Century, Dutton, 1971.
Contemporary Literary Criticism, Volume 17, Gale, 1981.

PERIODICALS

Chicago Tribune Book World, November 10, 1985.
Children's Book World, November 3, 1968.
Children's Literature in Education, March, 1974.
Christian Science Monitor, November 2, 1967.
Globe and Mail (Toronto), April 4, 1987.
Horn Book, October, 1973.
New York Times Book Review, October 28, 1973, July 22, 1979.
Times Literary Supplement, November 30, 1967, September 28, 1973, March 25, 1977, December 2, 1977, September 29, 1978, November 30, 1984.
Village Voice, December 25, 1978.
Washington Post Book World, July 8, 1979, November 10, 1985.

* * *

GARRISON, Frederick
See SINCLAIR, Upton (Beall)

GASCOYNE, David (Emery) 1916-

PERSONAL: Born October 10, 1916, in Harrow, England; son of Leslie Noel (a bank official) and Winfred Isabel (Emery) Gascoyne; married Judy Tyler Lewis, May 17, 1975; children: two stepsons, two stepdaughters. *Education:* Attended Salisbury Cathedral Choir School ("this had a lasting influence on my life") and Regent Street Polytechnic.

ADDRESSES: Home—48 Oxford St., Northwood, Cowes, Isle of Wight PO31 8PT, England. *Agent*—Alan Clodd, 22 Huntington Rd., London N29 DV, England.

CAREER: Poet and writer. Has given poetry reading tours in the United States, 1951-52, and 1981, and in Ireland, 1984. Representative on international committee, *Nuova Revista Europa,* Milan; president, Third European Festival of Poetry, Belgium, 1981. Attended poetry festivals in Rome, Paris, Amsterdam, Florence, Belgrade, and other cities, 1978-88.

MEMBER: Royal Society of Literature (fellow), World Organization for Poets (member of cultural committee), Committee of Belgian Biennales Internationales de Poesi (honorary member).

AWARDS, HONORS: Rockefeller-Atlantic Award, 1949; the British Council and the Centre Georges Pompidou presented a "Homage to David Gascoyne" in 1981; Biella European Poetry Prize, 1982, for *La Mano de Poeta.*

WRITINGS:

POEMS

Roman Balcony, and Other Poems, Lincoln Williams, 1932.
Man's Life Is This Meat, Parton Press, 1936.
Hoelderlin's Madness, Dent, 1938.
Poems, 1937-1942, Editions Poetry, 1943.
A Vagrant, and Other Poems, Lehmann, 1950.
Night Thoughts (verse play; first broadcast on radio by the British Broadcasting Corp., December 7, 1955), Grove, 1956.
Collected Poems, edited and with an introduction by Robin Skelton, Oxford University Press, 1965, enlarged edition published as *Collected Poems, 1988,* 1988.
The Sun at Midnight: Aphorisms, with Two Poems, Enitharmon Press, 1970.
Three Poems, Enitharmon Press, 1976.
Early Poems, Greville Press, 1980.
La Mano de Poeta, Edizioni S. Marco dei Giustiniani, 1982.
Tankens Doft, Ellerstroms, 1988.

TRANSLATOR

Salvador Dali, *Conquest of the Irrational,* J. Levy, 1935.
(With Humphrey Jennings) Benjamin Peret, *A Bunch of Carrots: Twenty Poems,* Roger Roughton, 1936, revised edition published as *Remove Your Hat,* 1936.
(With others) Paul Eluard, *Thorns of Thunder,* Europa/Nott, 1936.
Andre Breton, *What Is Surrealism?,* Faber, 1936.
Collected Verse Translations, edited by Skelton and Alan Clodd, Oxford University Press, 1970.
(With others) Paul Auster, editor, *The Random House Book of 20th Century French Poetry,* Random House, 1982.
Breton and Philippe Soupault, *The Magnetic Fields,* Atlas Press, 1985.

CONTRIBUTOR TO ANTHOLOGIES

Poets of Tomorrow, Hogarth Press, 1942.
Penguin Modern Poets, No. 17, Penguin, 1970.

A Garland of Poems for Leonard Clark on His 75th Birthday, Lomond Press/Enitharmon Press, 1980.
Free Spirits I, City Lights, 1982.

Also contributor to anthologies published in France, Germany, Italy, Yugoslavia, Argentina, and Hong Kong.

OTHER

Opening Day (novel), Cobden-Sanderson, 1933.
A Short Survey of Surrealism, Cobden-Sanderson, 1935, City Lights, 1982.
(Editor and author of introduction) Kenneth Patchen, *Outlaw of the Lowest Planet,* Grey Walls Press, 1946.
"The Hole in the Fourth Wall; or, Talk, Talk, Talk" (play), first produced in London at the Watergate Theatre, 1950.
Thomas Carlyle, Longmans, Green, 1952.
Paris Journal, 1937-1939, preface by Lawrence Durrell, Enitharmon Press, 1978.
Journal, 1936-1937, Enitharmon Press, 1980.
Rencontres avec Benjamin Fondane, Editions Arcane, 1984.

Contributor to periodicals, including *New English Weekly, Partisan Review, Cahiers du Sud, Times Literary Supplement, Literary Review, Two Rivers, Ambit, Poetry Review, PN Review, Temenos, Malahat Review, Botteghe Oscure,* and other publications in England, France, Belgium and Italy.

SIDELIGHTS: The poetry of David Gascoyne has undergone several major changes during his long career. At first an imagist, then a dedicated surrealist, Gascoyne's early poems were visionary, fantastic works filled with hallucinatory images and symbolic language. By the 1940s, he was writing mystical poems in which Christian imagery played a large part and the ecstatic pain of the religious seeker was paramount. Since publishing a few more poems in the late 1940s, Gascoyne has published little new work. Since the 1950s, his writing has been curtailed due to a mental breakdown and continuing bouts of severe depression. But Gascoyne's place in modern British poetry is secure; writing in *Twentieth Century,* Elizabeth Jennings describes Gascoyne as the "only living English poet in the true tradition of visionary or mystical poetry." In an article for the *Dictionary of Literary Biography,* Philip Gardner calls Gascoyne's *Poems, 1937-1942* "among the most distinguished and powerful collections of the last fifty years."

According to Gardner, in an article for the *Times Literary Supplement,* Gascoyne "was the literary prodigy of the 1930s." *Roman Balcony, and Other Poems,* Gascoyne's first book of poetry, appeared when the author was sixteen, and was followed by a novel, a nonfiction study entitled *A Short Survey of Surrealism,* several volumes of work translated from the French, and, before Gascoyne was twenty, a second volume of poems. This initial burst of activity was never to be repeated.

Roman Balcony, and Other Poems was published in 1936 while Gascoyne was still attending school. He had received a small legacy and used the money to finance the book's publication. Strongly influenced by the imagist poets and the fin-de-siecle writings of the 1890s, these early poems are "highly impressionistic, introspective, and word-conscious," Gardner explains in the *Dictionary of Literary Biography.* Robin Skelton, in his introduction to Gascoyne's *Collected Poems,* calls *Roman Balcony* "an astonishing performance for an adolescent. . . . Already in this book there is that interest in hallucinatory obsessive symbolism which gave so many of [Gascoyne's] poems of the later thirties their individual and disturbing quality."

Gascoyne's early interest in symbolism and the hallucinatory led him to study the surrealist writers of the 1930s, a school little known in England at that time. He was one of the first British poets to take note of the surrealists, and is generally credited with introducing their work to the English-speaking world. In 1935 and 1936, Gascoyne translated collections by the surrealists Salvador Dali, Benjamin Peret, and Andre Breton. His nonfiction introduction to the group's beliefs, *A Short Survey of Surrealism,* is described by Stephen Spender in the *Times Literary Supplement* as "a delightful book conveying, almost for the first time in English, the fascination of this movement."

This interest in surrealism is evident in the second collection of Gascoyne's poems, *Man's Life Is This Meat,* a book which contains works dedicated to such surrealists as Max Ernst, Rene Magritte, and Salvador Dali. The poems utilize the juxtapositions, intense imagery, and dream logic found in many surrealist works. Skelton says of the poems in this collection that "Gascoyne employed surrealist techniques to good effect. . . . Some poems look like products of a free-association game, [but] a second glance shows them to be full of profound implications."

With *Poems, 1937-1942,* published during the Second World War, Gascoyne first won widespread critical acclaim. "It was with the publication of *Poems, 1937-1942* . . . that Gascoyne's stature became fully apparent," Skelton believes. The book, Derek Stanford maintains in *Poetry Review,* represents "the high-water-mark of Gascoyne's career." Containing poems which are more mystical than those he wrote during his brief association with the surrealists, the book is the first expression, according to Jennings, of Gascoyne's mature poetic voice. "I do not think, . . . that he really found his own voice or his own individual means of expression until he started writing the poems which appeared in the volume entitled *Poems, 1937-42,*" Jennings writes.

In these mystical poems Gascoyne writes as an agonized Christian seeker desperate for a transcendent realm beyond the mortal world. "The theme which emerges most clearly," Skelton states, ". . . is that of man's despair at his mortality, and his confusion; but often it seems that some illumination of the darkness is imminent." Speaking of the poem series entitled "Miserere" which forms part of the book, Kathleen Raine of the *Sewanee Review* explains that these works "are in praise of the 'Eternal Christ'; the poet speaks from those depths into which the divine Presence has descended in order to redeem our fallen world, in a voice of sustained eloquence, as if at last the angel spoke." Commenting on this same group of poems, Spender explains that Gascoyne was inspired to write these works by the outbreak of the Second World War. Gascoyne, Spender states, "employs the Christian theme of the Miserere to express and transform the agony of war. . . . The poems which Gascoyne wrote early in the war have the immediacy of terrifying events which, acting upon the poet's sensibility like a hand upon an instrument, produce music and images that become part of the larger religious history of mankind."

Gascoyne's ability to combine his visionary poetry with an awareness of the real world around him is remarked upon by Skelton, who states that in *Poems, 1937-1942,* Gascoyne "achieved a religious poetry which combines powerful symbolism with contemporary relevance." Writing in *The Freedom of Poetry: Studies in Contemporary Verse,* Stanford believes that "the poetry of Gascoyne creates a world that is no escape from or substitute for the world we already know. All the problems reality makes us face, we face again in this poetry; and meeting them here for a second time we find them no longer modified by the small distractions of daily life, or the comic relief which existence offers. In this verse we are made to experience the total impact of wickedness—evil itself assumes an image. So, without mercy or mitigation, we are forced to look on this picture of our guilt and inhabit a sphere that seems to be sealed against the possible entry of hope."

Gascoyne's affiliation with the surrealists of the 1930s left its mark on these later poems, although the works are not strictly in the surrealist style. As Michael Schmidt writes in *A Reader's Guide to Fifty Modern British Poets,* "Gascoyne, in his mature work, adapted elements of surrealist technique to an English tradition." Raine comments that "from the surrealists Mr. Gascoyne learned to find, everywhere mirrored in objective reality, subjective states." Writing in *The Ironic Harvest: English Poetry in the Twentieth Century,* Geoffrey Thurley finds that Gascoyne's "capacity for feeling in the presence of rare affinities . . . springs from the same sensibility as created the Surrealist poems, tutored by the Surrealist discipline." Schmidt sees two major influences from the surrealists: "In [Gascoyne's] later poems the surreal elements serve to intensify a mental drama which is powerful for being rooted in the real. . . . The tension is between what he can say and what a language, wrenched and disrupted, can only hope to imply. . . . The main lesson he learned from surrealism was rhythmical. Throughout his work, his sense of line and rhythm units is subtle. In the surreal poems, it is rhythm alone that renders the distorted imagery effective, that fuses disparate elements into an apparent whole."

Beginning with *Poems, 1937-1942,* Gascoyne began to write in a distinctive narrative voice. As a writer for the *Times Literary Supplement* observes, "what makes Gascoyne's poetry so remarkable is its oracular quality." Raine believes that Hoelderlin's work inspired Gascoyne. She cites the metaphysical poems in the *Poems, 1937-1942* volume as bearing "the evident mark of Hoelderlin's influence; whose imaginative flights David Gascoyne from this time dared, finding in his own wings an eagle-strength upon which he outsoared, in sublimity, all his contemporaries."

A Vagrant, and Other Poems appeared in 1950 and contains works written between 1943 and 1950. "Though it contains nothing finer than [the poems found in *Poems, 1937-1942*], the high level of pure poetry, the perfect command of language, never falters," Raine states. "The tone," Skelton notes, "is generally more quiet. The same beliefs are expressed, but with greater delicacy, and often with humor." Gardner, too, sees a quieter mood in *A Vagrant, and Other Poems.* Many of the poems in this collection, he states in the *Dictionary of Literary Biography,* "transmit a quiet inner beauty one would call mellow, if that word did not carry overtones of a temperament too easily satisfied. Perhaps one may suggest their spiritual quality by saying that they convey a new acceptance of human limitations, a reconciliation."

Several critics believe that *Night Thoughts,* Gascoyne's lone attempt at a dramatic verse play, is among his finest works. Skelton, for example, calls it "his single greatest achievement." The play, written for and first broadcast on radio, is meant to "break through to those other islands of humanity, to reach the drifting rafts of those who, being alone, are also ready to make contact," as Thurley explains. This attempted union with members of the listening audience has a mystical connotation. Stanford believes that the most successful section of *Night Thoughts* is called "Encounter with Silence." This section of the play "is one of the most subtle expositions of man as a spiritually communicative animal to be found in contemporary literature," Stanford writes. "The

voice we hear speaking is that of the Solitary, who slowly realises that silence is the music not of the Void but of the Spirit."

During the 1960s and 1970s, Gascoyne published little new work. His *Collected Poems* appeared in 1965 to general critical appreciation, and two volumes of his journals appeared in the late 1970s and early 1980s. But problems in his personal life prevented Gascoyne from writing new work. Bouts of severe depression and paranoia, along with a brief drug addiction, hindered his efforts. He suffered, too, Gardner notes in the *Dictionary of Literary Biography,* "three serious breakdowns in the course of his life." During one such episode in 1973, Gascoyne met Judy Tyler Lewis, a part-time hospital worker, who he married in 1975. Gascoyne has said that since that time, his life has vastly improved.

Gascoyne's *Paris Journal, 1937-1939* and *Journal, 1936-37* were written just after his initial burst of creative activity. They record his move to Paris in the mid-1930s, his break with the surrealists and brief affiliation with communism, and provide a fascinating insight into his thoughts and observations of the time. As Spender notes about *Paris Journal,* "On several levels, Gascoyne's journal is a classic example of this genre." "Taken together," Gardner writes in the *Times Literary Supplement,* "the two journals offer admirers of Gascoyne's work an engrossing record of his self-realization and artistic growth."

Especially noted by critics was Gascoyne's success at rendering the tone and flavor of the time, as well as his revealing expression of his own moods and thoughts. "Few at 20, which was Gascoyne's age when he began [*Paris Journal, 1937-1939*], could have known themselves so fully or have had the literary maturity for such a self-portrait . . .," Ronald Blythe comments in the *Listener.* "The *Journal* certainly charms, but with something more than talent—perhaps by its ability to describe, with neither conceit nor tedium, all the initial *longueur* of a writer's existence." Spender finds in *Paris Journal* "some beautiful passages of prose poetry evoking Paris street scenes and the French countryside—and also some very somber ones. The young Gascoyne is a marvelously truthful and exact recorder of impressions made on him at concerts and art exhibitions." Alan Ross, writing in *London Magazine,* sees the appearance of Gascoyne's journals as a hopeful sign that the poet may soon begin writing new work. "What is encouraging about the journals," he states, "is that they suggest a shrewd and amusing observer of contemporary foibles, to the extent that one could envisage a late period in the poetry that might be more anecdotal and idiomatic as well as lighter in mood. Gascoyne's literary career, after so long and distressing an interruption, deserves a happy ending. There are few writers from whom one would more welcome poems out of the blue."

In a letter to *CA,* Gascoyne comments on the possibility of his writing new poetry: "After about 15 years of complete non-production, and hospitalizations following three severe mental breakdowns, I have at the age of 72 recovered sufficient self-confidence to make me feel I may be entering a new, closing period of creativity."

BIOGRAPHICAL/CRITICAL SOURCES:

BOOKS

Bedford, Colin, *David Gascoyne: A Bibliography of His Works (1929-1985),* Heritage Books, 1986.
Contemporary Literary Criticism, Volume 45, Gale, 1987.
Dictionary of Literary Biography, Volume 20: *British Poets, 1914-1945,* Gale, 1983.
Gascoyne, David, *Collected Poems,* Oxford University Press, 1965.

Gascoyne, David, *Paris Journal, 1937-1939,* Enitharmon Press, 1978.

Gascoyne, David, *Journal, 1936-37,* Enitharmon Press, 1980.

Raine, Kathleen, *Defending Ancient Springs,* Oxford University Press, 1967.

Remy, Michel, *David Gascoyne, ou l'urgence de l'inexprimé,* Presses Universitaires de Nancy, 1984.

Scarfe, Francis, *Auden and After: The Liberation of Poetry, 1930-1941,* Routledge, 1942.

Schmidt, Michael, *A Reader's Guide to Fifty Modern British Poets,* Heinemann Educational, 1979.

Stanford, Derek, *The Freedom of Poetry: Studies in Contemporary Verse,* Falcon Press, 1947.

Stanford, Derek, *Inside the Forties: Literary Memoirs, 1937-1957,* Sidgwick & Jackson, 1977.

Thurley, Geoffrey, *The Ironic Harvest: English Poetry in the Twentieth Century,* Edward Arnold, 1974.

PERIODICALS

Book Forum, fall, 1978.
Listener, September 7, 1978.
London Magazine, July, 1957, November, 1965, June, 1981.
New Statesman, September 22, 1978.
Observer, December, 1950.
Poetry, September, 1966.
Poetry Review, Volume 56, 1965.
Sewanee Review, spring, 1967.
Temenos, Number 7.
Times Literary Supplement, August 12, 1965, October 1, 1971, October 27, 1978, February 6, 1981, August 26, 1988.
Twentieth Century, June, 1959.

*   *   *

GASS, William H(oward) 1924-

PERSONAL: Born July 30, 1924, in Fargo, N.D.; son of William Bernard and Claire (Sorensen) Gass; married Mary Patricia O'Kelly, June 17, 1952; married Mary Alice Henderson, September 13, 1969; children: (first marriage) Richard G., Robert W., Susan H.; (second marriage) Elizabeth, Catherine. *Education:* Kenyon College, A.B., 1947; Cornell University, Ph.D., 1954.

ADDRESSES: Home—6304 Westminster Pl., St. Louis, Mo. 63130. *Office*—Department of Philosophy, Washington University, St. Louis, Mo. 63130. *Agent*—Lynn Nesbit, International Creative Management, 40 West 57th St., New York, N.Y. 10019.

CAREER: College of Wooster, Wooster, Ohio, instructor in philosophy, 1950-54; Purdue University, Lafayette, Ind., assistant professor, 1954-60, associate professor, 1960-66, professor of philosophy, 1966-69; Washington University, St. Louis, Mo., professor of philosophy, 1969-79, David May Distinguished University Professor in the Humanities, 1979—. Visiting lecturer in English and philosophy, University of Illinois, 1958-59. Member of Rockefeller Commission on the Humanities, 1978-80; member of literature panel, National Endowment for the Arts, 1979-82. *Military service:* U.S. Navy, 1943-46; served in China and Japan; became ensign.

MEMBER: PEN, American Philosophical Association, American Academy and Institute of Arts and Letters, National Academy of Arts and Sciences.

AWARDS, HONORS: Longview Foundation Award in fiction, 1959, for "The Triumph of Israbestis Tott"; Rockefeller Foundation grant for fiction, 1965-66; Standard Oil Teaching Award, Purdue University, 1967; Sigma Delta Chi Best Teacher Award, Purdue University, 1967 and 1968; *Chicago Tribune* award for Big-Ten teachers, 1967; Guggenheim fellowship, 1969-70; Alumni Teaching Award, Washington University, 1974; National Institute for Arts and Letters prize for literature, 1975; National Medal of Merit for fiction, 1979; National Book Critics Circle award for criticism, 1986, for *The Habitations of the Word.* Honorary degrees include D.Litt., Kenyon College, 1974; D.Litt., George Washington University, 1982; D.Litt., Purdue University, 1985.

WRITINGS:

FICTION

Omensetter's Luck (novel), New American Library, 1966.
In the Heart of the Heart of the Country (short stories), Harper, 1968, revised edition, David R. Godine, 1981.
Willie Masters' Lonesome Wife (novella; first published in *Tri-Quarterly* magazine, 1968), Knopf, 1971 .

NONFICTION

Fiction and the Figures of Life, Knopf, 1970.
(Author of introduction) *The Geographical History of America,* Random House, 1973.
On Being Blue, David R. Godine, 1975.
The World within the Word, Knopf, 1978.
The Habitations of the Word: Essays, Simon & Schuster, 1984.

OTHER

Contributor to numerous periodicals, including *New York Review of Books, New York Times Book Review, New Republic, Nation, TriQuarterly, Salmagundi,* and to philosophical journals. William Gass's manuscripts have been collected in the Washington University Library.

WORK IN PROGRESS: The Tunnel (novel); *The Master of Secret Revenges and Other Stories; The Surface of No City* (photographs); essays on architecture.

SIDELIGHTS: "Both as an essayist and as a writer of fiction, William Gass has earned the reputation of being one of the most accomplished stylists of his generation," writes Arthur M. Saltzman in *Contemporary Literature.* Gass, who is the David May Distinguished Professor in the Humanities at Washington University, is a principal advocate of the primacy of language in literature and of the self-referential integrity of literary texts. *Times Literary Supplement* reviewer Robert Boyers contends that Gass's fictions—represented by novels, novellas, and short stories—"give heart to the structuralist enterprise," while his essays "may be said to promote the attack on realist aesthetics." Viewed as a whole, Boyers concludes, Gass's work constitutes "the most vigorous anti-realist literary 'programme' we have had in our time." A philosopher by training, Gass "maintains an art-for-art's-sake 'ethic' of infinite aesthetic value, in a structure of the sublime grotesque, as his principle of creativity," to quote *Criticism* contributor Reed B. Merrill. Merrill adds: "His interest lies in the pleasures of the imagination, in model making, and in aesthetic projections composed in the face of an all-pervasive determinism." Whatever his views, Gass remains one of the most respected creative literary minds in modern American letters. In the *New York Times Book Review,* Robert Kiely notes that the author "has written some of the freshest and most finely disciplined fictional prose to have appeared in America since World War II. . . . The unlikely combination of criticism, philosophy and metaphorical inventiveness has resulted in a kind of poetry."

As a collegian Gass studied philosophy, specializing in the philosophy of language. This training manifests itself in his later work principally in a sense of the musical and intellectual nature of words, sentences, and paragraphs. *Los Angeles Times Book Review* correspondent Jonathan Kirsch observes that Gass "does not merely celebrate language; quite the contrary, he is gifted with the nagging intellectual curiosity that prompts a precocious child to take apart a pocket watch to see what makes it tick." In the *Saturday Review,* Brom Weber comments on the fusion of fiction and philosophy in Gass's view. "Gass holds that philosophy and fiction are alike in that both are fictional constructions, systems based on concepts expressed linguistically, worlds created by minds whose choice of language specifies the entities and conditions comprising those worlds," Weber explains. "The reality of these fictional worlds does not depend upon correspondence with or reflection of other worlds, such as the sociophysical one customarily regarded as the 'real' world. Consequently, such concepts as cause and effect—designed to explain the 'real' world—are not necessarily relevant to a fictional world if its creator's language does not encompass causality." Kiely puts it more succinctly when he suggests Gass holds that "philosophy and fiction are both 'divine games,' that they do not so much interpret reality as contribute to it."

To call Gass's opinion on fiction a "theory" is perhaps to overstep the bounds of his intentions. He told the *Southwest Review* that especially in his own fiction, he is "not interested in trying to write according to some doctrine." He continued: "When I'm writing fiction, it's very intuitive, so that what happens, or what I do, or how it gets organized, is pretty much a process of discovery, not a process of using some doctrine that you can somehow fit everything into." Gass merely feels that fictions should constitute their own worlds of words and not necessarily attempt to represent some external reality. Weber notes that the author "is dissatisfied with 'character,' 'plot,' 'realism,' and similar conceptual terms that relate fiction to more than itself, and dislikes explication and paraphrase as analytic methods that superimpose 'meaning' upon fiction." Boyers elaborates: "We all know what Gass is writing against, including the tiresome use of novels for purposes of unitary moral uplift and penetrating 'world-view.' What he detests is the goody sweepstakes, in which works of art are judged not by their formal complexity or nuances of verbal texture but by their ability to satisfy easy moral imperatives." The critic declares that, as essayist and fiction writer, Gass "has had some hand in discrediting the kind of righteous moralism that so corrupts ordinary apprehension of the literary arts."

"The esthetic aim of any fiction is the creation of a verbal world, or a significant part of such world, alive through every order of its Being," Gass writes in *Fiction and the Figures of Life.* "The artist's task is therefore twofold. He must show or exhibit his world, and to do this he must actually make something, not merely describe something that might be made." Obviously, Gass is calling for a literature that makes demands of both its creator and its readers; reaching beyond reportage, it is its own reality unfolding on the page. In *Critique: Studies in Modern Fiction,* Richard J. Schneider claims that Gass "suggests that any philosophic separation of spirit from body, reason from emotion, experience from innocence, and words from deeds is destructive of life. He reminds us (and we need reminding) that fiction, like poetry, should not merely mean but, above all, be." *New York Times Book Review* contributor Frederic Morton addresses the ways in which Gass's fictions reflect this concept. Gass, notes Morton, "chooses the small gray lulls in life: rural twilights, small-town still-lifes, shadowed backyards. From them he draws dolor and music and a resonance touching us all. Gass is, in fact,

a virtuoso with homely textures. They are the perfect foils for the nightmare leaps of his language. You are about to relax in those hick locales, even to feel comfortably bored, when the ambush of metaphors starts together with the shock of jagged elisions. . . . It's a tension that keeps the reader revealingly off-balance. . . . In brief, Gass engenders brand-new abrupt vulnerabilities. We read about the becalmed Midwest, about farmers mired in their dailiness, and realize too late that we've been exposed to a deadly poetry."

Omensetter's Luck, Gass's first novel, was "immediately recognized as a stunning achievement," according to Larry McCaffery in the *Dictionary of Literary Biography.* Published in 1966 after numerous rejections, the book established the unique verbal qualities that would come to be associated with all of Gass's work. The novel resists summarization; set in an Ohio river town, it explores the relationship between Brackett Omensetter, a happily unselfconscious "prelapsarian Adam," to quote McCaffery, and two conscious and thoughtful men, Henry Pimber and Jethro Furber. A *Newsweek* correspondent calls the book "a masterpiece of definition, a complex and intricate creation of level within level, where the theme of Omensetter's luck becomes an intense debate on the nature of life, love, good and evil, and finally, of death. . . . [It] is a story of life and death in the little countries of men's hearts." Richard Gilman offers a different interpretation in *The Confusion of Realms.* The novel, writes Gilman, "*is* Gass's prose, his style, which is not committed to something beyond itself, not an instrument of an idea. In language of amazing range and resiliency, full of the most exact wit, learning and contemporary emblems, yet also full of lyric urgency and sensuous body, making the most extraordinary juxtapositions, inventing, coining, relaxing at the right moments and charging again when they are over, never settling for the rounded achievement or the finished product, he fashions his tale of the mind, which is the tale of his writing a novel."

Given the difficulty Gass endured trying to find a publisher for *Omensetter's Luck,* he must have been immensely gratified by the critical reception the work received once it found its way into print. Gilman has called it "the most important work of fiction by an American in this literary generation . . . marvelously original, a whole Olympic broad jump beyond what almost any other American has been writing, the first full replenishment of language we have had for a very long time, the first convincing fusion of speculative thought and hard, accurate sensuality that we have had, it is tempting to say, since [Herman] Melville." *Nation* reviewer Shaun O'Connell describes *Omensetter's Luck* as "a difficult, dazzling first novel, important in its stylistic achievement and haunting in its dramatic evocation of the most essential human questions." Not every assessment has been entirely favorable, however. In his *Bright Book of Life: American Novelists & Storytellers from Hemingway to Mailer,* Alfred Kazin writes: "Everything was there in *Omensetter's Luck* to persuade the knowing reader of fiction that here was a great step forward: the verve, the bursting sense of possibility, the gravely significant atmosphere of contradiction, complexity of issue at every step. But it was all in the head, another hypothesis to dazzle the laity with. Gass had a way of dazzling himself under the storm of his style." Conversely, *Harper's* reviewer Earl Shorris praises Gass's stylistic achievement. *Omensetter's Luck,* Shorris declares, is, "page after page, one of the most exciting, energetic, and beautiful novels we can ever hope to read. It is a rich fever, a parade of secrets, a novel as American as [Mark Twain's] *Huckleberry Finn* and as torturously comic as [James Joyce's] *Ulysses.*"

Gass followed *Omensetter's Luck* with *In the Heart of the Heart of the Country,* a short story collection "whose highly original form exactly suits its metafictional impulses," to quote McCaffery. McCaffery describes the book as a development of the related themes of isolation and the difficulties of love through the use of experimental literary forms. The characters "control their lives only to the extent that they can organize their thoughts and descriptions into meaningful patterns. Not surprisingly, then, we come to know them mainly as linguistic rather than psychological selves, with their actions usually less significant to our understanding of them than the way they project their inner selves through language." Again critics have praised the volume as a significant contribution to American letters. *Hudson Review* correspondent Robert Martin Adams notes that Gass's techniques, "which are various and imaginative, are always in the service of vision and feeling. Mr. Gass's stories are strict and beautiful pieces of writing without waste or falsity or indulgence." In the *New Republic,* Richard Howard writes: "This is a volume of fictions which tell the truth, and speak even beyond the truth they tell; it is in that outspokenness, the risk of leaving something standing in his mind, that the authority of William Gass persists." *Nation* contributor Philip Stevick concludes that *In the Heart of the Heart of the Country* "finally amounts to an eccentric and ingratiating book, like no other before it, full of grace and wit, displaying a mind in love with language, the human body, and the look of the world."

No Gass work reveals "a mind in love with language" more clearly than *Willie Masters' Lonesome Wife,* the author's 1971 novella. Merrill feels that the piece "stands, along with his fascinating, impressionistic literary criticism, as perhaps [Gass's] best work to date. . . . Structurally, it is clear from the beginning that the subject of this book is the act of creation, and that [the narrator] Babs is William Gass's 'experimental structure' composed of language and imagination. The book *is* literally Babs. The book is a woman from beginning to end. The covers are the extrinsic flesh, the pages are the intrinsic contents of Bab's consciousness—her interior world. It would be difficult to find a better example of the use of structural principles than in Gass's stylistic combination of form and content in his book." In a *Critique* essay, McCaffery calls the novella "a remarkably pure example of metafiction" and adds: "As we watch 'imagination imagining itself imagine,' . . . we are witnessing a work self-consciously create itself out of the materials at hand—words. As the best metafiction does, *Willie Masters' Lonesome Wife* forces us to examine the nature of fiction-making from new perspectives. If Babs (and Gass) have succeeded, our attention has been focused on the act of reading words in a way we probably have not experienced before. The steady concern with the *stuff* of fiction, words, makes Gass's work unique among metafictions which have appeared thus far." *New York Review of Books* contributor Michael Wood observes that the work reveals "a real urgency, a powerful vision of the loneliness inherent in writing . . . and of writing as a useful and articulate image for loneliness of other kinds."

Whatever the subject at hand, Gass's essays are invariably artistic creations in and of themselves. *Village Voice* reviewer Sam Tanenhaus notes that each piece "is a performance or foray: [Gass] announces a topic, then descants with impressive erudition and unbuttoned ardor for the surprising phrase. The results often dazzle, and they're unfailingly original, in the root sense of the word—they work back toward some point of origin, generally a point where literature departs from the external world to invent a world of its own." Gass may serve as a spokesman for technical experimentation in fiction and for the value of innovative form, but his nonfiction also "asks us to yield ourselves in loving attentiveness to the being of language, poetic word, and

concept, as it unfolds and speaks through us," according to Jeffrey Maitland in *Modern Fiction Studies.* V. S. Pritchett offers a similar view in the *New Yorker.* Writes Pritchett, "Gass is a true essayist, who certainly prefers traveling to arriving, who treats wisdom as a game in which no one wins. . . . His personality, his wit and affectations are part of the game." Kiely, on the other hand, finds a common core in Gass's meditations. The critic contends that in a variety of ways "—by means of startling metaphor and philosophical cajolery—he does the same thing in each essay: he calls our attention to art." The "art" to which attention is called is one that resists ease and proves imagination—beginning and ending with itself. "Gass is not 'ordering experience,' sending us on to higher morality;" explains Shorris, "he is not documenting anything. The work is there, and the work is beautiful. The experience of it is a significant and exciting ordeal from which we cannot emerge unchanged."

The cumulative impression left by Gass's essays is, to quote Kiely, "that of a man thinking." Gass calls his whole imagination into play and then develops his obsessions stylistically with complicated flights of prose. *New Republic* essayist Robert Alter calls Gass "clearly a writer willing to take chances" with a "freewheeling inventiveness." Alter suggests, however, that the "casting aside of inhibitions also means that unconscious materials are constantly popping through the surface of the writing, often in ways that subvert its effectiveness." *New York Times Book Review* correspondent Denis Donoghue also admits a certain discomfort with some of Gass's assertions. Still, Donoghue claims, "his sentences, true or false, are pleasures. Reading them, I find myself caring about their truth or error to begin with, but ending up not caring as much as I suppose I ought, and taking them like delicacies of the palate." Boyers remarks: "Gass's books are wonderful books because they raise all of the important aesthetic issues in the starkest and most inventive way. The writing is informed by a moral passion and a love of beautiful things that are never compromised by the author's compulsive addiction to aestheticizing formulations." Wood puts it another way: "The writer speaks tenderly to his paper, and, by caring for his words, constructs a world for his readers."

As Candyce Dostert notes in the *Wilson Library Bulletin,* to read William Gass "is to accompany an extraordinary mind on a quest for perfection, an invigorating voyage for the strong of heart." Gass is acclaimed equally for his ground-breaking fiction and for the essays that defend the fiction's aesthetics. In the *Dictionary of Literary Biography,* McCaffery states: "Certainly no other writer in America has been able to combine his critical intelligence with a background as a student of both the literary and philosophical aspects of language and to make this synthesis vital." Edmund White arrives at a similar conclusion in the *Washington Post Book World.* Gass's "discursive prose always reminds us that he is an imaginative writer of the highest order," White contends. "Indeed, among contemporary American writers of fiction, he is matched as a stylist only by a very select group." Another *Washington Post Book World* contributor, Paul West, observes that Gass's world "*is* words, *his* way of being. . . . Gass sings the flux, under this or that commercial pretext, and in the end renders what he calls 'the interplay of genres . . . skids of tone and decorum' into cantatas of appreciative excess. A rare gift that yields startling art."

Gass has given numerous interviews on his art to scholarly periodicals. In one for the *Chicago Review,* he said of his fiction: "What you want to do is create a work that can be read non-referentially. There is nothing esoteric or mysterious about this. It simply means that you want the work to be self-contained. A reader can do with a work what he or she wants. You can't force interpretations and you can't prevent them." He added: "I'm interested in how the mind works—though not always well—by sliding off into sneakily connected pathways, parking the car at another level of discourse, arriving by parachute."

BIOGRAPHICAL/CRITICAL SOURCES:

BOOKS

Bellamy, Joe David, editor, *The New Fiction: Interviews with Innovative American Writers,* University of Illinois Press, 1974.
Contemporary Fiction in America and England, 1950-1970, Gale, 1976.
Contemporary Literary Criticism, Gale, Volume 1, 1973, Volume 2, 1974, Volume 8, 1978, Volume 11, 1979, Volume 15, 1980, Volume 39, 1986.
Dictionary of Literary Biography, Volume 2: *American Novelists since World War II,* Gale, 1978.
Gass, William H., *Fiction and the Figures of Life,* Knopf, 1970.
Gilman, Richard, *The Confusion of Realms,* Random House, 1969.
Kazin, Alfred, *Bright Book of Life: American Novelists & Storytellers from Hemingway to Mailer,* Little, Brown, 1973.
McCaffery, Lawrence, *Metafictional Muse,* Pittsburgh University Press, 1982.
Vidal, Gore, *Matters of Fact and of Fiction: Essays 1973-1976,* Random House, 1977.

PERIODICALS

Book World, November 21, 1971.
Bulletin of Bibliography, July-September, 1974.
Chicago Daily News, February 1, 1969.
Chicago Review, autumn, 1978.
Contemporary Literature, summer, 1984.
Criticism, fall, 1976.
Critique: Studies in Modern Fiction, December, 1972, summer, 1976.
Delaware Literary Review, Volume 1, 1972.
Falcon, winter, 1972.
Harper's, May, 1972, October, 1978.
Harvard Advocate, winter, 1973.
Hudson Review, spring, 1968.
Iowa Review, winter, 1976.
Los Angeles Times Book Review, March 24, 1985, January 26, 1986.
Modern Fiction Studies, autumn, 1973, winter, 1977-78, winter, 1983.
Nation, May 9, 1966, April 29, 1968, March 22, 1971, January 29, 1977.
New Republic, May 7, 1966, May 18, 1968, March 20, 1971, October 9, 1976, May 20, 1978, March 11, 1985.
Newsweek, April 18, 1966, February 15, 1971, March 25, 1985.
New Yorker, January 10, 1977.
New York Review of Books, June 23, 1966, April 11, 1968, December 14, 1972, July 15, 1974, April 17, 1975, May 1, 1975, May 15, 1975, August 5, 1976, October 14, 1976.
New York Times, October 4, 1976, February 14, 1985.
New York Times Book Review, April 17, 1966, April 21, 1968, February 21, 1971, November 14, 1971, November 7, 1976, July 9, 1978, June 3, 1979, March 10, 1985.
Pacific Coast Philology, Volume 9, 1974.
Partisan Review, summer, 1966.
Salmagundi, fall, 1973.
Saturday Review, March 2, 1968, September 21, 1968, May 29, 1971.
Shenandoah, winter, 1976.

Southern Review, spring, 1967.
Southwest Review, spring, 1979, autumn, 1985.
Time, November 15, 1976.
Times Literary Supplement, May 18, 1967, August 14, 1969, April 22, 1977, November 3, 1978.
Twentieth Century Literature, May, 1976.
Village Voice, June 4, 1985.
Washington Post Book World, July 9, 1978, March 3, 1985.
Western Humanities Review, winter, 1978.
Wilson Library Bulletin, May, 1985.
World Literature Today, spring, 1979, winter, 1987.

—*Sketch by Anne Janette Johnson*

*   *   *

GASSET, Jose Ortega y
    See ORTEGA y GASSET, Jose

*   *   *

GAWSWORTH, John
    See BATES, H(erbert) E(rnest)

*   *   *

GEISEL, Theodor Seuss 1904-
    (Theo. LeSieg, Dr. Seuss; Rosetta Stone, a joint pseudonym)

PERSONAL: Surname is pronounced *Guy-*zel; born March 2, 1904, in Springfield, Mass.; son of Theodor Robert (superintendent of Springfield public park system) and Henrietta (Seuss) Geisel; married Helen Palmer (an author and vice-president of Beginner Books), November 29, 1927 (died, October 23, 1967); married Audrey Stone Diamond, August 6, 1968. *Education:* Dartmouth College, A.B., 1925; graduate study at Lincoln College, Oxford, 1925-26, and Sorbonne, University of Paris.

ADDRESSES: Home—La Jolla, Calif. *Office*—Random House, Inc., 201 East 50th St., New York, N.Y. 10022. *Agent*—International Creative Management, 40 West 57th St., New York, N.Y. 10019.

CAREER: Author and illustrator. Free-lance cartoonist, beginning 1927; advertising artist, Standard Oil Company of New Jersey, 1928-41; *PM* (magazine), New York, N.Y., editorial cartoonist, 1940-42; publicist, War Production Board of U.S. Treasury Department, 1940-42; Beginner Books, Random House, Inc., New York, N.Y., founder and president, 1957—. Correspondent in Japan, *Life* (magazine), 1954. Trustee, La Jolla (Calif.) Town Council, beginning 1956. One-man art exhibitions at San Diego Arts Museum, 1950, Dartmouth College, 1975, Toledo Museum of Art, 1975, La Jolla Museum of Contemporary Art, 1976, and Baltimore Museum of Art, 1987. *Military service:* U.S. Army Signal Corps, Information and Education Division, 1942-46; became lieutenant colonel; received Legion of Merit.

MEMBER: Authors League of America, American Society of Composers, Authors and Publishers (ASCAP), Sigma Phi Epsilon.

AWARDS, HONORS: Academy Award, 1946, for "Hitler Lives," 1947, for "Design for Death," and 1951, for "Gerald McBoing-Boing"; Randolph Caldecott Honor Award, Association for Library Services for Children, American Library Association, 1948, for *McElligot's Pool,* 1950, for *Bartholomew and the Oobleck,* and 1951, for *If I Ran the Zoo;* Young Reader's Choice

Award, Pacific Northwest Library Association, 1950, for *McElligot's Pool;* L.H.D., Dartmouth College, 1956, American International College, 1968, and Lake Forest College, 1977; Lewis Carroll Shelf Award, 1958, for *Horton Hatches the Egg,* and 1961, for *And to Think That I Saw It on Mulberry Street;* Boys' Club Junior Book Award, Boys' Club of America, 1966, for *I Had Trouble in Getting to Solla Sollew.*

Peabody Award, 1971, for animated cartoons "How the Grinch Stole Christmas" and "Horton Hears a Who"; Critics' Award from International Animated Cartoon Festival and Silver Medal from International Film and Television Festival of New York, both 1972, both for "The Lorax"; Los Angeles County Library Association Award, 1974; Southern California Council on Literature for Children and Young People Award, 1974, for special contribution to children's literature; named "Outstanding California Author," California Association of Teachers of English, 1976; Emmy Award, 1977, for "Halloween Is Grinch Night"; Roger Revelle Award, University of California, San Diego, 1978; winner of Children's Choice Election, 1978; grand marshall of Detroit's Thanksgiving Day Parade, 1979.

D.Litt., Whittier College, 1980; Laura Ingalls Wilder Award, Association for Library Services for Children, American Library Association, 1980; "Dr. Seuss Week" proclaimed by State Governors, March 2-7, 1981; Regina Medal, Catholic Library Association, 1982; National Association of Elementary School Principals special award, 1982, for distinguished service to children; Pulitzer Prize, 1984, for his "special contribution over nearly half a century to the education and enjoyment of America's children and their parents"; PEN Los Angeles Center Award for children's literature, 1985, for *The Butter Battle Book;* D.H.L., University of Hartford, 1986.

WRITINGS:

UNDER PSEUDONYM DR. SEUSS; SELF-ILLUSTRATED

And to Think That I Saw It on Mulberry Street, Vanguard, 1937.
The 500 Hats of Bartholomew Cubbins, Vanguard, 1938.
The Seven Lady Godivas, Random House, 1939, reprinted, 1987.
The King's Stilts, Random House, 1939.
Horton Hatches the Egg, Random House, 1940.
McElligot's Pool, Random House, 1947.
Thidwick, the Big-Hearted Moose, Random House, 1948.
Bartholomew and the Oobleck, Random House, 1949.
If I Ran the Zoo, Random House, 1950.
Scrambled Eggs Super! (also see below), Random House, 1953.
The Sneetches and Other Stories, Random House, 1953.
Horton Hears a Who! (also see below), Random House, 1954.
On Beyond Zebra, Random House, 1955.
If I Ran the Circus, Random House, 1956.
Signs of Civilization! (booklet), La Jolla Town Council, 1956.
The Cat in the Hat (also see below), Random House, 1957, French/English edition published as *La Chat au chapeau,* Random House, 1967, Spanish/English edition published as *El Gato ensombrerado,* Random House, 1967.
How the Grinch Stole Christmas (also see below), Random House, 1957.
The Cat in the Hat Comes Back!, Beginner Books, 1958.
Yertle the Turtle and Other Stories, Random House, 1958.
Happy Birthday to You!, Random House, 1959.
One Fish, Two Fish, Red Fish, Blue Fish, Random House, 1960.
Green Eggs and Ham, Beginner Books, 1960.
Dr. Seuss' Sleep Book, Random House, 1962.
Hop on Pop, Beginner Books, 1963.
Dr. Seuss' ABC, Beginner Books, 1963.

(With Philip D. Eastman) *The Cat in the Hat Dictionary, by the Cat Himself,* Beginner Books, 1964.
Fox in Socks, Beginner Books, 1965.
I Had Trouble in Getting to Solla Sollew, Random House, 1965.
Dr. Seuss' Lost World Revisited: A Forward-Looking Backward Glance (nonfiction), Award Books, 1967.
The Cat in the Hat Songbook, Random House, 1967.
The Foot Book, Random House, 1968.
I Can Lick 30 Tigers Today! and Other Stories, Random House, 1969.
Mr. Brown Can Moo! Can You?, Random House, 1970.
I Can Draw It Myself, Random House, 1970.
The Lorax, Random House, 1971.
Marvin K. Mooney, Will You Please Go Now?, Random House, 1972.
Did I Ever Tell You How Lucky You Are?, Random House, 1973.
The Shape of Me and Other Stuff, Random House, 1973.
There's a Wocket in My Pocket!, Random House, 1974.
Oh, the Thinks You Can Think!, Random House, 1975.
The Cat's Quizzer, Random House, 1976.
I Can Read with My Eyes Shut, Random House, 1978.
Oh Say Can You Say?, Beginner Books, 1979.
The Dr. Seuss Storybook (includes *Scrambled Eggs Super!*), Collins, 1979.
Hunches in Bunches, Random House, 1982.
The Butter Battle Book (also see below), Random House, 1984.
You're Only Old Once, Random House, 1986.
The Tough Coughs as He Ploughs the Dough: Early Writings and Cartoons by Dr. Seuss, edited by Richard Marschall, Morrow, 1986.
Oh, the Places You'll Go!, Random House, 1990.

UNDER PSEUDONYM THEO. LeSIEG

Ten Apples up on Top!, illustrated by McKie, Beginner Books, 1961.
I Wish That I Had Duck Feet, illustrated by B. Tokey, Beginner Books, 1965.
Come Over to My House, illustrated by Richard Erdoes, Beginner Books, 1966.
The Eye Book, illustrated by McKie, Random House, 1968.
(Self-illustrated) *I Can Write—By Me, Myself,* Random House, 1971.
In a People House, illustrated by McKie, Random House, 1972.
The Many Mice of Mr. Brice, illustrated by McKie, Random House, 1973.
Wacky Wednesday, illustrated by George Booth, Beginner Books, 1974.
Would You Rather Be a Bullfrog?, illustrated by McKie, Random House, 1975.
Hooper Humperdink . . .? Not Him!, Random House, 1976.
Please Try to Remember the First of Octember!, illustrated by Arthur Cummings, Beginner Books, 1977.
Maybe You Should Fly a Jet! Maybe You Should Be a Vet, illustrated by Michael J. Smullin, Beginner Books, 1980.
The Tooth Book, Random House, 1981.

SCREENPLAYS

"Your Job in Germany" (documentary short subject), U.S. Army, 1946, released under title "Hitler Lives," Warner Bros., 1946.
(With wife, Helen Palmer Geisel) "Design for Death" (documentary feature), RKO Pictures, 1947.
"Gerald McBoing-Boing" (animated cartoon), United Productions of America (UPA)/Columbia, 1951.
(With Allen Scott) "The 5,000 Fingers of Dr. T" (musical), Columbia, 1953.

Also author of screenplays for "Private Snafu" film series, for Warner Bros.

TELEVISION SCRIPTS

"How the Grinch Stole Christmas," Columbia Broadcasting System, Inc. (CBS-TV), first aired December 18, 1966.
"Horton Hears a Who," CBS-TV, first aired March 19, 1970.
"The Cat in the Hat," CBS-TV, first aired March 10, 1971.
"Dr. Seuss on the Loose," CBS-TV, first aired October 15, 1973.
"Hoober-Bloob Highway," CBS-TV, first aired February 19, 1975.
"Halloween Is Grinch Night," American Broadcasting Companies, Inc. (ABC-TV), first aired October 28, 1977.
"Pontoffel Pock, Where Are You?," ABC-TV, first aired March 2, 1980.
"The Grinch Grinches the Cat in the Hat," ABC-TV, first aired May 20, 1982.
"The Butter Battle Book," Turner Network Television (TNT-TV), first aired November 13, 1989.

OTHER

(Illustrator) *Boners,* Viking, 1931.
(Illustrator) *More Boners,* Viking, 1931.
(Under pseudonym, Dr. Seuss) *My Book about Me, by Me, Myself: I Wrote It! I Drew It,* illustrated by Roy McKie, 1969.
(Under pseudonym, Dr. Seuss) *Great Day for Up!,* illustrated by Quentin Blake, Random House, 1974.
(With Michael Frith, under joint pseudonym Rosetta Stone) *Because a Little Bug Went Ka-Choo!,* illustrated by Frith, Beginner Books, 1975.
Dr. Seuss from Then to Now (museum catalog), Random House, 1987.
(Under pseudonym, Dr. Seuss) *I Am Not Going to Get Up Today!,* illustrated by James Stevenson, Random House, 1987.

Contributor of cartoons and prose to magazines, including *Judge, College Humor, Liberty, Vanity Fair,* and *Life.* Editor, *Jack-o'-Lantern* (Dartmouth College humor magazine), until 1925. The manuscript of *The 500 Hats of Bartholomew Cubbins* is in the collection of Dartmouth College in Hanover, New Hampshire. Other manuscripts are in the Special Collections Department of the University of California Library in Los Angeles.

WORK IN PROGRESS: A musical based on *The Seven Lady Godivas.*

SIDELIGHTS: Theodor Seuss Geisel, better known under his pseudonym "Dr. Seuss," is "probably the best-loved and certainly the best-selling children's book writer of all time," writes Robert Wilson of the *New York Times Book Review.* Seuss has entertained several generations of young readers with his zany nonsense books. Speaking to Herbert Kupferberg of *Parade,* Seuss claims: "Old men on crutches tell me, 'I've been brought up on your books.'" His "rhythmic verse rivals Lewis Carroll's," states Stefan Kanfer of *Time,* "and his freestyle drawing recalls the loony sketches of Edward Lear." Because of his work in publishing books for young readers and for the many innovative children's classics he has himself written, Seuss "has had a tremendous impact," Miles Corwin of the *Los Angeles Times* declares, "on children's reading habits and the way reading is taught and approached in the school system."

Seuss had originally intended to become a professor of English, but soon "became frustrated when he was shunted into a particularly insignificant field of research," reports Myra Kibler in the *Dictionary of Literary Biography.* After leaving graduate school

in 1926, Seuss worked for a number of years as a free-lance magazine cartoonist, selling cartoons and humorous prose pieces to the major humor magazines of the 1920s and 1930s. Many of these works are collected in *The Tough Coughs as He Ploughs the Dough.* One of Seuss' cartoons—about "Flit," a spray-can pesticide—attracted the attention of the Standard Oil Company, manufacturers of the product. In 1928 they hired Seuss to draw their magazine advertising art and, for the next fifteen years, Seuss created grotesque, enormous insects to illustrate the famous slogan "Quick, Henry! The Flit!" He also created monsters for the motor oil division of Standard Oil, including the Moto-Raspus, the Moto-Munchus, and the Karbo-Nockus, that, says Kibler, are ancestral to his later fantastic creatures.

It was quite by chance that Seuss began writing by children. Returning from Europe by boat in 1936, Seuss amused himself during the long voyage by putting together a nonsense poem to the rhythm of the ship's engine. Later he drew pictures to illustrate the rhyme and in 1937 published the result as *And to Think That I Saw It on Mulberry Street,* his first children's book. Set in Seuss' home town of Springfield, Massachusetts, *Mulberry Street* is the story of a boy whose imagination transforms a simple horse-drawn wagon into a marvelous and exotic parade of strange creatures and vehicles. Many critics regard it as Seuss' best work.

Mulberry Street, along with *The 500 Hats of Bartholomew Cubbins, Horton Hatches the Egg* and *McElligot's Pool,* introduces many of the elements for which Seuss has become famous. *Mulberry Street* features rollicking anapestic tetrameter verse that compliments Seuss's boisterous illustrations. Jonathan Cott, writing in *Pipers at the Gates of Dawn: The Wisdom of Children's Literature,* declares that "the unflagging momentum, feeling of breathlessness, and swiftness of pace, all together [act] as the motor for Dr. Seuss's pullulating image machine." Whimsical fantasy characterizes *The 500 Hats of Bartholomew Cubbins,* while *Horton Hatches the Egg* introduces an element of morality and *McElligot's Pool* marks the first appearance of the fantasy animal characters for which Seuss has become famous.

The outbreak of World War II forced Seuss to give up writing for children temporarily and to devote his talents to the war effort. Working with the Information and Education Division of the U.S. Army, he made documentary films for American soldiers. One of these Army films—"Hitler Lives"—won an Academy Award, a feat Seuss repeated with his documentary about the Japanese war effort "Design for Death," and the UPA cartoon "Gerald McBoing-Boing," about a little boy who can only speak in sound effects. "The 5,000 Fingers of Dr. T," which Seuss wrote with Allen Scott, achieved cult status during the 1960s among music students on college campuses. Later, Seuss adapted several of his books into animated television specials, the most famous of which—"How the Grinch Stole Christmas"—has become a holiday favorite.

The success of his early books confirmed Seuss as an important new children's writer. However, it was *The Cat in the Hat* that really established his reputation and revolutionized the world of children's book publishing. By using a limited number of different words, all simple enough for very young children to read, and through its wildly iconoclastic plot—when two children are alone at home on a rainy day, the Cat in the Hat arrives to entertain them, wrecking their house in the process—*The Cat* provided an attractive alternative to the simplistic "Dick and Jane" primers then in use in American schools, and critics applauded its appearance. For instance, Helen Adams Masten of *Saturday Review* marveled at the way Seuss, using "only 223 different words, . . . has created a story in rhyme which presents an impelling incentive to read.'' The enthusiastic reception of *The Cat in the Hat* led Seuss to found Beginner Books, a publishing company specializing in easy-to-read books for children. In 1960, Random House acquired the company and made Seuss president of the Beginner Books division.

In the years since 1960 Seuss and Beginner Books have created many modern classics for children, from *Green Eggs and Ham,* about the need to try new experiences, and *Fox in Socks,* a series of increasingly boisterous tongue-twisters, to *The Lorax,* about environmental preservation, and *The Butter Battle Book,* a fable based on the nuclear arms race. In 1986, at the age of 82, however, Seuss produced *You're Only Old Once,* a book for the ''obsolete children'' of the world. The story follows an elderly gentleman's examination at ''The Golden Age Clinic on Century Square,'' where he's gone for ''Spleen Readjustment and Muffler Repair.'' The gentleman, who is never named, is subjected to a number of seemingly pointless tests by merciless physicians and grim nurses, ranging from a diet machine that rejects any appealing foods to an enormous eye chart that asks, ''Have you any idea how much these tests are costing you?'' Finally, however, he is dismissed, the doctors telling him that ''You're in pretty good shape/For the shape that you're in!''

In its cheerful conclusion *You're Only Old Once* is typically Seuss; ''The other ending is unacceptable,'' Seuss confides to *New York Times Book Review* contributor David W. Dunlap. In other ways, however, the book is very different. Seuss tells Dunlap that *You're Only Old Once* is much more autobiographical than any of his other stories. Robin Marantz Henig, writing in the *Washington Post Book World,* says *You're Only Old Once* ''is lighthearted, silly, but with an undertone of complaint. Being old is sometimes tough, isn't it . . . Seuss seems to be saying.'' *Los Angeles Times Book Review* contributor Jack Smith declares that in it Seuss ''reveals himself as human and old, and full of aches and pains and alarming symptoms, and frightened of the world of geriatric medicine, with its endless tests, overzealous doctors, intimidating nurses, Rube Goldberg machines and demoralizing paperwork.'' Nonetheless, Henig concludes, ''We should all be lucky enough to get old the way this man, and Dr. Seuss himself, has gotten old.''

MEDIA ADAPTATIONS: Dr. Seuss' animated cartoon character Gerald McBoing-Boing appeared in several other UPA pictures, including ''Gerald McBoing-Boing's Symphony,'' 1953, ''How Now McBoing-Boing,'' 1954, and ''Gerald McBoing-Boing on the Planet Moo,'' 1956. In December of 1956, Gerald McBoing-Boing appeared in his own animated variety show, ''The Gerald McBoing-Boing Show,'' which aired on CBS-TV on Sunday evenings. The program ran through October of 1958.

BIOGRAPHICAL/CRITICAL SOURCES:

BOOKS

Children's Literature Review, Gale, Volume 1, 1976, Volume 9, 1985.
Cott, Jonathan, *Pipers at the Gates of Dawn: The Wisdom of Children's Literature,* Random House, 1983.
Dictionary of Literary Biography, Volume 61: *American Writers for Children since 1960: Poets, Illustrators, and Nonfiction Authors,* Gale, 1987.
Lanes, Selma G., *Down the Rabbit Hole: Adventures and Misadventures in the Realm of Children's Literature,* Atheneum, 1972.

PERIODICALS

Chicago Tribune, May 12, 1957, April 15, 1982, April 17, 1984, June 29, 1986, January 14, 1987.
Los Angeles Times, November 27, 1983, October 7, 1989.
Los Angeles Times Book Review, March 9, 1986.
New York Times, May 21, 1986, December 26, 1987.
New York Times Book Review, November 11, 1952, May 11, 1958, March 20, 1960, November 11, 1962, November 16, 1975, April 29, 1979, February 26, 1984, March 23, 1986.
Parade, February 26, 1984.
Publishers Weekly, February 10, 1984.
Saturday Review, May 11, 1957, November 16, 1957.
Time, May 7, 1979.
Washington Post, December 30, 1987.
Washington Post Book World, March 9, 1986.

—*Sketch by Kenneth R. Shepherd*

* * *

GENET, Jean   1910-1986

PERSONAL: Born December 19, 1910, in Paris, France; died of throat cancer, April 15, 1986 in Paris, France; never knew his parents; was abandoned by his mother, Gabrielle Genet, to the *Assistance publique,* and was raised by a family of peasants.

CAREER: Novelist, dramatist, and poet. Joined the French Foreign Legion under a false name and subsequently deserted; was a beggar, thief, and homosexual prostitute; was thrown out of five countries and spent time in thirteen jails before the age of thirty-five.

AWARDS, HONORS: Village Voice Off-Broadway (Obie) awards, 1960, for ''The Balcony,'' and 1961, for ''The Blacks.''

WRITINGS:

Notre-Dame-des-Fleurs (novel), dated from Fresnes prison, 1942, limited edition, L'Arbalete, 1943, revised edition, Gallimard (Paris), 1951, French & European Publications (New York), 1966, translation by Bernard Frechtman published as *Our Lady of the Flowers,* Morihien (Paris), 1949, published with introduction by Jean-Paul Sartre, Grove, 1963.
Miracle de la rose (prose poem), dated from La Sante and Tourelles prisons, 1943, L'Arbalete, 1946, 2nd edition, 1956, translation by Frechtman published as *Miracle of the Rose,* Blond, 1965, Grove, 1966, recent edition, 1988.
Chants secrets (poems), privately printed (Lyons), 1944.
Querelle de Brest, privately printed, 1947, translation by Gregory Streatham published as *Querelle of Brest,* Blond, 1966, translation by Anselm Hollo published as *Querelle,* Grove, 1974.
Pompes funebres, privately printed, c. 1947, revised edition, 1948, translation by Frechtman published as *Funeral Rites,* Grove, 1969, recent edition, 1987.
Poemes, L'Arbalete, 1948, 2nd edition, 1962.
Journal du voleur, Gallimard, 1949, French & European Publications, 1966, translation by Frechtman published as *The Thief's Journal,* foreword by Sartre, Olympia Press, 1954, Grove, 1964, recent edition, 1987.
Haute Surveillance (play; first produced at Theatre des Mathurins, February, 1949), Gallimard, 1949, French & European Publications, 1965, translation by Frechtman published as *Deathwatch: A Play* (also see below; produced as ''Deathwatch,'' Off-Broadway at Theatre East, October 9, 1958), Faber, 1961.
L'Enfant criminel et 'Adame Miroir, Morihien, 1949.

Les Beaux Gars, [Paris], 1951.

Les Bonnes (play; first produced in Paris, April 17, 1947), Pauvert, 1954, French & European Publications, 1963, translation by Frechtman published as *The Maids* (also see below; produced in New York at Tempo Playhouse, May 6, 1955), introduction by Sartre, Grove, 1954, augmented French edition published as *Les Bonnes et comment jouer Les Bonnes,* M. Barbezat, 1963.

The Maids [and] *Deathwatch,* introduction by Sartre, Grove, 1954, revised edition, 1962, recent edition, 1988.

Le Balcon (play; produced in Paris at Theatre du Gymnase, May 18, 1960), illustrated with lithographs by Alberto Giacometti, L'Arbalete, 1956, French & European Publications, 1962, translation by Frechtman published as *The Balcony* (produced in London at London Arts Theatre Club, April 22, 1957; produced on Broadway at Circle in the Square, March 3, 1960), Faber, 1957, Grove, 1958, revised edition, Grove, 1960, reprint of French edition edited by David Walker, published under original title, Century Texts, 1982.

Les Negres: Clownerie (play; first produced at Theatre de Lutece, October 28, 1959), M. Barbezat, 1958, 3rd edition, published with photographs, M. Barbezat, 1963, translation by Frechtman published as *The Blacks: A Clown Show* (produced as "The Blacks" Off-Broadway at St. Mark's Playhouse, May 4, 1961), Grove, 1960, recent edition, 1988.

Les Paravents (play; produced in Stockholm, Sweden, at Alleteatem Theatre, 1964), M. Barbezat, 1961, French & European Publications, 1976, translation by Frechtman published as *The Screens* (produced in Brooklyn, N.Y., at Brooklyn Academy of Music, November, 1971), Grove, 1962, recent edition, 1987.

Lettres a Roger Blin, Gallimard, 1966, translation by Richard Seaver published as *Letters to Roger Blin: Reflections on the Theater,* Grove, 1969 (same translation published in England as *Reflections on the Theatre, and Other Writings,* Faber, 1972).

May Day Speech (delivered in 1970 at Yale University), with description by Allen Ginsberg, City Lights, 1970.

The Complete Poems of Jean Genet, Man-Root, 1980.

Treasures of the Night: Collected Poems of Jean Genet, translated by Steven Finch, Gay Sunshine, 1981.

Un Captif amoreux, Gallimard, 1986, translation by Barbara Bray published as *Prisoner of Love,* Harper & Collins, 1989.

What Remains of a Rembrandt Torn into Four Equal Parts and Flushed Down the Toilet, Hanuman Books, 1988.

Lettres a Olga et Marc Barbezat, L'Arbalete, 1988.

OMNIBUS VOLUMES

Oeuvres completes, Volume I (contains "Saint Genet: Comedien et martyr," by Jean-Paul Sartre), Volume II (contains "Notre-Dame-des-Fleurs," "Le Condamne a mort," "Miracle de la rose," and "Un Chant d'amour"), Volume III (contains "Pompes funebres," "Le Pecheur du suquet," and "Querelle de Brest"), Volume IV (contains "Les Bonnes," "Le Balcon," and "Haute Surveillance"), Volume V (contains "Le Funambule," "Le Secret de Rembrandt," "L'Atelier d'Alberto Giacometti," "Les Negres," "Les Paravents," and "L'Enfant criminel"), Gallimard, 1951-79, Volumes I-IV (with Volume IV containing additional works, "L'Etrange Mot d'. . .," "Ce qui est reste d'un Rembrant dechire en petits carres," "Comment jouer Les Bonnes," and "Comment jouer Le Balcon"), French & European Publications, 1951-53.

L'Atelier d'Alberto Giacometti; Les Bonnes, suivi d'une lettre; L'Enfant criminel [and] *Le Funambule,* L'Arbalete, 1958.

OTHER

Work is represented in anthologies, including *Seven Plays of the Modern Theatre,* edited by Harold Clurman, Grove, 1962. Creator of film "A Song of Love," based on Genet's poem "Un Chant d'amour." Author of scenario "Mademoiselle," Woodfall Films, 1966. Contributor to *Esquire.*

SIDELIGHTS: Jean Genet's works rarely inspire indifference. For some readers, he was a creative genius; for others, he was a mere pornographer. Indeed, his works, his attitudes, his theories, and the criticism written about him seem founded on irreconcilable oppositions.

Although the facts of Genet's life are mixed with fiction, it is certain that he was born in 1910 in Paris. His father was unknown, and his mother, Gabrielle Genet, abandoned him at birth. As a ward of the *Assistance publique,* he spent his early childhood in an orphanage. As a young boy he was assigned to a peasant family in the Morvan region of France. The foster parents, who were paid by the state to raise him, accused him of theft, and some time between the age of ten and fifteen he was sent to the Mettray Reformatory, a penal colony for adolescents. After escaping from Mettray and joining and deserting the Foreign Legion, Genet spent the next twenty years wandering throughout Europe where he made his living as a thief and male prostitute.

According to the legend, he began writing his first novels in jail and quickly rose to literary prominence. Having been sentenced to life in prison for a crime he did not commit, he received a presidential pardon from Vincent Auriol in 1948, primarily because of a petition circulated by an elite group of Parisian writers and intellectuals. After 1948 Genet devoted himself to literature, the theatre, the arts, and various social causes, particularly those espoused by the Black Panthers.

Francois Mauriac, a fervent opponent of Genet's work, rebuked him in a 1949 article "The Case of Jean Genet" ("Le Cas Jean Genet") for what Mauriac considered "worse than vice and crime, namely the *literary* utilization of vice and crime, their methodical exploitation." Mauriac, in conceding Genet's talent but deploring its use, ironically helped confirm Genet's stature as a writer. At the opposite end of the critical pole were the Parisian intellectuals, led by Jean-Paul Sartre and Jean Cocteau, who quickly became ardent defenders of Genet and his work. Sartre's 1952 portrayal of the writer as existential hero in *Saint Genet: Actor and Martyr* (*Saint Genet, comedien et martyr*) elevated him to the status of cult hero and his work to a legitimate object of scholarly research.

Unfortunately, Sartre's seminal work fostered almost as many legends about Genet as Genet himself had created; Sartre accommodated Genet's life, theories, and early works to his own existential philosophy. To give but one example, Sartre maintained that Genet loathed "history and historicity," an idea that is easily refuted given the historical content of so much of his creative work. Sartre's use of Genet for his own purposes, however, in no way detracted from the value of *Saint Genet* as a source for valid interpretation of the writer. For, be it the thesis (Genet as existential saint), or the antithesis (Genet as Mauriacian Lucifer), modern criticism clearly agrees that Genet and his works are best represented by the concept, first identified by Sartre, of the "eternal couple of the criminal and the saint."

Recent analyses of Genet's works have become less occupied with their morality than with their complexities of style, thematic structures, aesthetic theories, and transformations of the life into the legend. In addition, scholarship has revised many of the early opinions of his works. It is now clear, for example, that

Genet purposely created myths about his life and art. The once widely accepted story of the uneducated convict creating works of genius in a jail cell was undoubtedly created to enhance his opportunities for financial and literary success. It is now certain that Genet had read Proust and that he was aware of his literary ancestors, such as de Sade, Rimbaud, Lautreamont, Celine, Jouhandeau, Pirandello, and the surrealists.

One useful aspect of the Genet myth is the idea that his development as a writer was from poetry to novels to plays. According to the legend, his initial creative effort was a poem written in prison, and, in fact, his first published work was his poem "The Condemned Man" ("Le Condamne a mort"), of 1942. The period from 1942 to 1948 was dominated by four major novels and one fictionalized autobiography. He also wrote two plays, of which one, "The Maids" ("Les Bonnes"), was produced by Louis Jouvet in 1947. Although Genet made two films between 1949 and 1956 ("Imagenetions" and "Song of Love"), he commented in a 1965 *Playboy* interview that "Sartre's book created a void which made for a kind of psychological deterioration . . . [and I] remained in that awful state for six years." His most successful theatrical period was from 1956 to 1962. During that time, he wrote and presented three plays—all successful major productions. Various ballets, mimes, films, aesthetic criticism, and sociopolitical statements were interspersed throughout his years of productivity, from about 1937 to 1979. Weakened by ill health, Genet published little after 1979.

From his first poem "The Condemned Man," to his last work, the play "The Screens" ("Les Paravents"), Genet dealt with constant subjects: homosexuality, criminality (murder, theft, corruption), saintliness, reality and illusion, history, politics, racism, revolution, aesthetics, solitude. Many people have been shocked not only by his themes but also by his attitude toward himself, his life, and his material—and most of all by his stated intention to corrupt. He openly professed his homosexuality, his admiration for crime and criminals, his joy in theft, and his contempt for the society that rejected him. His vitriolic and scatological attacks on accepted social values made him the target of innumerable moralists.

Genet, whose work is often defended on the basis of its poetic style and inspiration, has been very little studied as a poet. In Richard C. Webb's *Jean Genet: An Annotated Bibliography, 1943-1980*, the section devoted to studies of the poetry consists of one page: two entries and ten cross-references. By comparison, entries for the plays require 295 pages. Clearly, the poetry has been seen as the least important part of Genet's work. Scholars point out that his poetic style and structure follow nineteenth-century models and that there are obvious borrowings from Valery, Verlaine, Hugo, and Baudelaire. Camille Naish in *A Genetic Approach to Structures in the Work of Jean Genet* established that the poems could be specifically linked in theme and structure with his subsequent works. However, Naish also quoted Genet as disparaging his own poems, "finding them 'too much influenced by Cocteau and neo-classicism.'"

Genet's early success as a novelist may certainly be attributed to various factors—to the support of Cocteau and Sartre, to the scandal arising from his subject matter, and to the notoriety of the thief as novelist. The critics long continued to accept the simplistic legend of the unlettered convict genius despite the classical references and other literary allusions, the sophisticated structures, and the sheer volume of work purportedly created between 1942 and 1948. The legend persisted until 1970 when Richard N. Coe published, in *The Theatre of Jean Genet: A Casebook*, an essay by Lily Pringsheim in which she reported that the

Genet she had known in Germany in 1937 was of "a truly astonishing intelligence. . . . I could scarcely believe the extent of his knowledge of literature." She also revealed that Genet begged her "to store away a number of manuscripts and that he shared [with her friend Leuschner] an uncontrollable thirst for knowledge, for Leuschner, like Genet, carried books about with him everywhere he went: Shakespeare, language textbooks, scientific treatises."

A simple count of the major works supposedly created by Genet between 1942 and 1948, when he was in and out of prison, should have led some critics to question the legend. The staggering production of this period allegedly included four novels, an autobiography, two plays, three poems, and a ballet. Pringsheim's testimony supports the idea that a major portion of the work was done at an earlier date and in libraries with reference sources. In his very first novel, *Our Lady of the Flowers* (*Notre-Dame-des-Fleurs*), supposedly written in Fresnes prison, Genet accurately quoted from *The Constitutional and Administrative History of France* by the nineteenth-century historian Jean-Baptiste-Honore-Raymond Capefigue. Furthermore, in a letter to the author of this essay, Genet confirmed that he had read *The Memoires on the Private Life of Marie Antoinette* by Madame Genet-Campan. The fact that Genet had read these rather unusual works, had quoted accurately from one of them (supposedly while in prison), and had used the other as a source for material in his play "The Maids," leads one to several conclusions: major portions of *Our Lady* were written outside prison, Genet was extremely well read and undoubtedly an habitue of libraries, and he probably received the basics of a traditional French education while incarcerated as a boy at the Mettray reformatory.

Of the five novels, counting the fictionalized autobiography *The Thief's Journal* (*Journal du voleur*), critics consider *Our Lady of the Flowers* and *Miracle of the Rose* (*Miracle de la rose*) to be the best. Genet's first novel was brought to Cocteau's attention by three young men who had become acquainted with Genet who was then selling books (some stolen) from a bookstall along the Seine. Cocteau recognized the literary merit of *Our Lady*, which is a tour de force. This novel is unique for several reasons: its basic philosophy, its sophisticated literary technique, and its composite central character Genet-Divine-Culafroy. Some critics think that Genet, the uneducated convict, should be considered a precursor of the "new novel"—that literary movement which came into being as a protest against the traditional novel. Genet's works, like those of the well-known "new novelists" Alain Robbe-Grillet and Michel Butor, may be considered untraditional in their disregard of conventional psychology, their lack of careful transitions, their confused chronologies, and their disdain for coherent plot structures.

To understand *Our Lady*, or any of Genet's works, one must turn to Sartre's *Saint Genet* for an explanation of the "sophistry of the Nay." Sartre explained Genet's view of the world by relating it to the concept of the saint. According to Sartre saintliness results from refusing something—honors, power, or money, for example—and the seekers after saintliness soon "convince themselves and others that they have refused everything": "With these men appeared the sophistry of the Nay . . . [and] in a destructive society which places the blossoming of being at the moment of its annihilation, the Saint, making use of divine meditation, claims that a Nay carried to the extreme is necessarily transformed into a Yea. Extreme poverty is wealth, refusal is acceptance, the absence of God is the dazzling manifestation of his presence, to live is to die, to die is to live, etc. One step further and we are back at the sophisms of Genet: sin is the yawning chasm of God. In going to the limit of nothingness, one finds being, to love is to betray, etc." From this concept, Sartre postulated the concept of the "eternal couple of the criminal and the saint": hence, the legitimacy of the pursuit of saintliness by the homosexual thief Genet-Divine-Culafroy, the hero/heroine of *Our Lady*. The plot of this "epic of masturbation," as Sartre first labeled it, is difficult to follow because Genet wanders from past to present without transition in an episodic celebration of perversity. Louis Culafroy, a twenty-year-old peasant, arrives in Paris from the provinces. He assumes the name Divine and makes his living as a thief and male prostitute. Through the story of Our Lady's conviction for the murder of a helpless old pederast, it is the development of the Genet-Divine-Culafroy character which focuses the novel and provides its true literary merit.

Genet's seeking to canonize this homosexual thief and his use of metaphors combining the sacred and the obscene caused the moralists to rally to the defense of the traditional and the acceptable. Francis L. Kunkle in his *Passion and the Passion: Sex and Religion in Modern Literature* is representative of those critics who reject Genet's work; Kunkle finds *Our Lady* to be "a kind of endless linguistic onanism which often collapses into obscene blasphemy." Most critics, however, consider *Our Lady* innovative in its treatment of time and its concept of gesture-as-act, sophisticated in its self-conscious aesthetic, and poetic in its use of incantatory language. In *Jean Genet: A Critical Appraisal,* Philip Thody defends the worth of the book: "There are a number of reasons for considering *Our Lady of the Flowers* as Genet's best novel, and the work in which his vision of reality is given its most effective expression. It has a unity which stems from its concentration upon a single character, and Genet's projection of his own problems on to Divine creates a detachment and irony that are not repeated in any other of his works."

In his next two "novels," Genet followed the successful formula used in *Our Lady. Miracle of the Rose* relates the story of Harcamone, "graduate" of the Mettray reformatory, who, betrayed by a fellow convict, murders a prison guard in order to die "gloriously" rather than serve a life sentence. The novel concludes with the mystical experience that Genet, the work's narrator, supposedly underwent the night prior to Harcamone's execution. Although this novel provides certain insights into Genet's life, the reader must be cautious about regarding the work as strictly autobiographical. The writer stipulated that his life must "be a legend, in other words, legible, and the reading of it must give birth to a certain new emotion that I call poetry." *Miracle,* which is easier to follow than *Our Lady,* may be marred by the excessive self-consciousness of its technique. Yet, as in *Our Lady,* Genet set forth in *Miracle* his inversion of good and evil, his longing for deification through degradation, and his homoeroticism.

In *The Thief's Journal* Genet revealed much about his incredible odyssey through the criminal underworld and the sordid prisons of Europe in the 1930s and 1940s. Even if only partially factual, the book remains a fascinating social document. But whether Genet's works are primarily social documents or private mythologies is a question that frequently occupies critics. For example, Lucian Goldmann, in *La Creation culturelle dans la societe moderne* (*Cultural Creation in Modern Society*), labels Genet the "greatest advocate of social revolt in contemporary French literature." Yet, in *Narcissus Absconditus, the Problematic Art of Autobiography in Contemporary France,* Germaine Bree stresses the mythological aspect of his work saying that *Journal* "gyrates upon itself, proclaiming its symbol-laden ceremonies to be fiction."

Funeral Rites (*Pompes funebres*) and *Querelle of Brest* (*Querelle de Brest*) are Genet's least successful works. *Funeral* is Genet's lament for a lover killed during the liberation of Paris, and *Querelle* relates the depressing story of a sailor who is a murderer, thief, and opium smuggler. Both works concentrate on homosexuality, and *Querelle* is the only Genet novel that is not fictionalized autobiography. The critical judgments about his novels reflect the antitheses so often associated with the author and his works: the novels are considered poetic eroticism or pornographic trash, lyrical incantations or demented exhibitionism, sociological documents or masturbatory fantasies. They have been described—and this is only a partial catalogue of labels employed—as existentialist, solipsistic, ambiguous, mythological, homosexual, popular, Freudian, semimystical, humorous, basically romantic, adolescent, obscene, blasphemous, ahistorical, archetypal.

After the publication of *The Thief's Journal* Genet turned to the theatre for the presentation of his radical views of the world. Perhaps because of his obsession with religion, the theatre proved a better vehicle for his ideas and techniques than did the novel, since the theatrical experience is, by definition and tradition, a form of ceremony, a rite. However, Genet had some problems in adjusting to the new medium, in seeing his fantasies corrupted by realistic treatment; during Peter Zadek's 1957 London production of "The Balcony" ("Le Balcon"), for example, he was barred from the theatre for disrupting the production. Yet he soon learned to stage his fantasies within the context of theatrical reality. More importantly, he met and accepted Roger Blin as his future director and interpreter. Under Blin's guidance, his theatrical genius blossomed in the productions of "The Blacks" and "The Screens."

Critical reactions to the plays are as divergent as they are to the novels. In *Theatre and Anti-Theatre: New Movements since Beckett,* Ronald Hayman labels Genet's plays "anti-theatrical." Lucien Goldmann focuses on the socio-political aspects of the plays, which he considers examples of revolutionary, social realism. Between those two extremes exists a wide range of terms often applied to Genet's drama, including ritualistic, absurd, metaphysical, neurotic, nonrealistic, and cruel.

Genet's works for the theatre may be divided into two periods— 1947 to 1949 and 1956 to 1962. It is generally accepted that although "The Maids" was the first play produced, "Deathwatch" ("Haute Surveillance") was written earlier. The several revisions that Genet made of "Deathwatch" suggest that he was little satisfied with the original version of the play so often compared to Sartre's "No Exit." This first play by the "convict-genius" is tightly constructed, almost classical in conception and presentation. The unities of time, place, and action are strictly observed. However, the concept of decorum is violated by the on-stage murder of Maurice by Lefranc, and the language and premise of the author are definitely not classical. Once again, the spectators and the critic are confronted with the concept of the "criminal and the saint."

Genet established a criminal-religious hierarchy—that is, the more serious the crime the more "saintly" the criminal. Within this hierarchy Genet developed those subjects consistently found throughout his work: betrayal, murder, homosexuality, theft, and solitude. Although there is some dispute over who the "hero" really is, it seems obvious that Lefranc, not Green Eyes, is the preferred Genetian hero because he chooses his murder and opts for prison, whereas Green Eyes repudiates his murder. Furthermore, Lefranc admits that he is provoked to murder Maurice by an imaginary spray of lilacs, symbol of fate and death. Lefranc seeks to become the "Lilac Murderer" in imitation of other thugs who have acquired exotic nicknames appropriate to their crimes—the Avenger, the Panther, the Tornado, for example. "Deathwatch" thus serves as an excellent example of Genet's creative process. As the author of this essay has commented in the *French Review,* "he began with a basic symbol, that is, it is unlucky to take lilacs into a house for they will cause a death, and then expanded this symbol to include the basic themes of the play—murder, betrayal, fate, sex, and the criminal-religious hierarchy. By bedecking his criminals with lilacs, Genet has created a gigantic and a new flower-symbol."

"The Maids," based on an actual murder committed by the Papin sisters, is a one-act play that serves as a brilliant example of Genet's ability to create complex structures for what Sartre called his "whirligig of reality and illusion." Genet wanted very much to have the female roles performed by young men. He also wanted a sign posted to inform the audience of the deception. This would have added two more levels of illusion to the already complicated role-playing wherein one of the maids assumes the guise of their mistress and her sister plays the role of the sister playing the mistress. As the author of this essay discusses in *Kentucky Romance Quarterly,* a remarkably complicated work results: "The complexity of Genet's genius is such that he can create a play such as *The Maids* based on 'historical materials' which is at the same time an illustration of the philosophical concept of the eternal couple of the criminal and the saint, a 'Fable' based on the history of Marie Antoinette and the French Revolution, and an example of a black mass."

"The Balcony," unlike the first two plays in which there is a certain classical simplicity of form, is a long and complex series of scenes that take place primarily in Madame Irma's "House of Illusions," a brothel where various rooms are reserved for the ritualized performance of erotic fantasies based on such equations as sex/power, sex/religion, and sex/revolution. In the preface to the definitive edition of the play, Genet stressed that his play was not a satire but the "glorification of the Image and the Reflection." Richard N. Coe, in *The Vision of Jean Genet,* considers "The Balcony" an example of Genet's essential conception of drama: "The highest, most compelling form of experience—the experience which Genet describes as sacred and which forms the basis of all his mysticism—occurs when the human consciousness becomes simultaneously aware of the two co-existent dimensions of existence: the real and the transcendental. This, as Genet sees it, is the underlying miracle of the Christian Eucharist; and it is also the principle of all true theatre." Given Genet's obsession with religion and saintliness, it becomes more understandable why he objected so strenuously to Zadek's realistic London production of "The Balcony." For, as Martin Esslin points out in *The Theatre of the Absurd,* Genet desired that "his fantasies of sex and power . . . be staged with the solemnity and the outward splendor of the liturgy in one of the world's great cathedrals."

In a real sense, the first and last scenes of this complex play are summations of Genet's theories and theatrical techniques. The first tableau opens with a character wearing bishop's vestments in a whore house (attack on conventional morality). The bishop is a fake who turns out to be a gas-meter reader (whirligig of illusion and reality). Like the other Western power figures (the judge, the general, the chief of police, and the revolutionary), the bishop's existence is predicated on its opposite. The cleric can exist only if sin exists, for his function, which is to forgive sinners, depends on the antithesis of holiness (antithetical power relationship of the sinner and the saint). Within this same antithetical concept, the bishop later seeks to betray the chief of police

(betrayal as necessary adjunct to saintliness). Concomitantly, the bishop is "holy" because he plays the role of a clergyman in a whorehouse, but he is less "holy" than the prostitutes because they are not playing the roles of but are truly prostitutes. Thus in Genet's upside-down world they are saints (sophistry of the Nay).

After a series of tableaux illustrating various Genetian subjects—betrayal, murder, the nature of royalty, illusion and reality, sex and power, the futility of revolution, function versus appearance—Madame Irma, the sole character who is not a victim of the need to live an "illusion," turns to the audience and advises them to "go home, where everything—you may be quite sure—will be falser than here. . . ." By breaking the theatrical conventions in addressing the audience directly, by blurring the distinction between the illusion of the theatre and the "reality" outside the theatre, the conclusion thereby reflects Genet's desire that the play be the "glorification of the Image and the Reflection." Genet the thief has once again "robbed" the bourgeois audience. An experienced crook, he diverts their attention with shock tactics while he tries to strip them of their values. The irony is that he not only tries to undermine their moral certainties but that he is enriched by their willingness to pay to be insulted and deceived. There is, in his mind, very little difference between picking a victim's pocket and doing what he does in the theatre. As the play ends, the sounds of a new revolution are heard, by which Genet intended that smug, self-righteous men be reminded that thieves, murderers, and revolutionaries will constantly strive to wreck their complacency.

Genet's last two major artistic creations, "The Blacks" ("Les Negres") and "The Screens," may well have provided him with his most satisfying moments in his war on society. Both plays, in which racism or colonialism are presented within the context of Genetian ritual and ceremony, are vitriolic attacks on bourgeois values. "The Blacks," written in 1957 and performed in 1959, is a play within a play. The audience, which must always include a white person or an effigy of one, is entertained with a ritual re-enactment of the murder of a white woman by a black man. The murderer is convicted by a white court—blacks wearing white masks. However, the trial of the murderer is a diversion from the real crime—a black traitor's execution—that is supposedly taking place off-stage. Presenting blacks acting out their hatred of whites and of white society, the play had its greatest success and most profound impact at the time of the race riots in America in the late 1960s. Although Bettina Knapp declares in *Jean Genet* that nothing real occurs on stage, that "the whole ritual on stage, then, is a big joke, a game, a 'clownerie' (the subtitle of the play)," it is more often believed that Genet's play was one of the first theatrical productions in which black actors confronted a primarily white audience with an expression of their suppressed hatreds and prejudices. It was certainly instrumental in the creation of a true black theatre movement.

Criticism of "The Blacks" attests that, even in the black community, there was, as usual, a wide divergence of opinion. E. Bullins, the editor of *Black Theatre,* attacked the play and its author: "Jean Genet is a white, self-confessed homosexual with dead, white Western ideas—faggoty ideas about Black Art, Revolution, and people. His empty masochistic activities and platitudes on behalf of the Black Panthers should not con Black people. . . . Beware of whites who plead the Black cause." However, most critics, black or white, saw the play as an expression of black liberation, of black psychology, and of the bitterness in race relations. Very few critics accepted what director Roger Blin insisted was Genet's intention: to present a play that was an exercise in aesthetics, not in politics or psychology.

Genet's last work, "The Screens," must also have provided him with endless hours of amused satisfaction at critical reactions. The play, an obvious attack on French colonialism and a virulent condemnation of the war in Algeria, naturally provoked hostile reactions from the right-wing element in France. Published in 1961, the play was not performed in its entirety until 1964 in Stockholm. Due to its explosive content, "The Screens" was banned in France until 1966, when it was presented for a total of forty performances at the behest of Andre Malraux, Minister of Culture. It must have delighted Genet's sense of irony to see his play produced at the Odeon, the theatre of France, for the play is an attack on the nation. Even more ironic was the need for police protection because of the violence directed at the actors and the author by "honest patriots." The outcast, the rejected orphan, the despised homosexual and thief, had had the last word.

It is a difficult if not impossible task to summarize "The Screens," Genet's most complex play. Some ninety-six characters create "artistic" patterns on screens during the performance of a very complicated plot while dressed, for the most part, in fantastic costumes. The plot concerns Said, the poorest man in Algeria, who can afford to marry only the ugliest woman. An ascetic figure, Said wishes to become as abject as possible through self-degradation; Leila, Said's intended, supports his intentions and seeks to become even uglier in order to help him achieve his goal. Having stolen, not from the French but from his Arab neighbors, Said is cast out by his own kind and ultimately arrested. The "hero" of this play is not only poor and ugly, a thief and an outcast, he is loathsome—or worse—dull. Of all of Genet's plays and of all of his heroes, "The Screens" and Said are the most calculatedly vile. Genet's images of filth and excrement abound, and both the French and the Arabs are portrayed as vermin. As Richard N. Coe writes in *The Vision of Jean Genet:* "One might almost suspect that Genet, in a last desperate attempt to reconcile his artist's aestheticism with politics, is trying to use the conventional concept of Beauty—which he himself now identifies unhesitatingly with the enemy society—as an argument in favour of the outcast. But, in spite of the ingenious twists of logic involved . . . in the long run the argument defeats itself. For if beauty is sufficient to invalidate the claim of Monsieur Blankensee to so many kilometers of Algerian countryside, unfortunately it invalidates the claims of the Arabs simultaneously. What remains is not Arab-owned economy, but simply a Void, a *zero.*" If the play espouses anything at all, it is anarchy, nihilism, and filth.

Indeed, it is quite possible that interest in the play will focus more on the scandal it caused and on the politics it examined than on the play itself. Although Genet and Blin insisted that the play was nonpartisan, that it was a poetic and not a political statement, the hostilities began soon after the opening performance. The stage became a target for stink bombs and rotten eggs; numerous fights broke out between actors and spectators and between partisan spectators. In particular, a scene where French soldiers break wind in the face of a dead French officer caused howls of protest, mostly from cadets of Saint Cyr and from members of various veterans' organizations.

Although a definitive judgment of Genet and his works is difficult to make, a quantitative statement about the critical attention to him is revealing. Webb's *Jean Genet: An Annotated Bibliography, 1943-1980,* lists some 1,790 books, articles, theses, and other scholarly works; and this number does not count the many critical reviews of specific productions that Webb includes—for example, the seventy-two write-ups of the 1959 Paris production of "The Blacks." Genet and his works are clearly the subject of much critical interest. Both author and works were catapulted to international fame primarily because of the scandal created by his "pornography" and because of Genet's association with Sartre. Yet, rather than debating the "pornographic" aspect of the works, most modern critics argue about their meanings. Any effort to categorize Genet's work may appear arrogant, but it seems appropriate to identify three subjects or characteristics—nihilism, complexity, and antithesis—pertaining to his entire canon.

Perhaps the most easily defined characteristic is negativism. Although the obvious nihilism may be a pose, it is one which serves several purposes. Ultimately one suspects that Genet used the sordid facts of his life as a means to escape it and that he recognized very early on that success is often founded on a loud, provocative, scandalous attack on bourgeois society. Some critics theorize that he created his own scandal based on nihilism and eroticism in order to become rich and famous and to gain a measure of revenge upon society. But whatever the source or motive, Genet's works reflect his unwavering pursuit of his ideals of nothingness and absolute solitude.

The word "complexity" is constantly present in critics' discussions of Genet's works. Whether the complexity was intentional or the result of literary, educational, or philosophic insufficiency depends on what education Genet received while at the Mettray reformatory and on when exactly he began writing. If we accept Pringsheim's statements, Genet was not only experimenting with verse and prose in 1937, he had already written several manuscripts and was in possession of and reading Shakespeare, language textbooks, and other material—all of this many years before he supposedly wrote *Our Lady of the Flowers* in Fresnes prison and long before he had met either Cocteau or Sartre. His first published novel does clearly reveal sophisticated techniques and classical allusions indicating that the legend of the uneducated convict genius was greatly exaggerated by Sartre, Cocteau, and Genet himself. He may have been primarily self-taught, and it is certain that he spent long hours reading and doing research in libraries. But the story that he was miraculously endowed in prison with literary talent and a vast store of classical and literary knowledge is clearly apocryphal.

Finally, antithesis was the foundation of Genet's literary theories and techniques as well as the basis for his view of the world. Whether they treat the eternal couple of the criminal and the saint or the "sophistry of the Nay," his works are best understood through the figure of the mirror, long a symbol of thesis and antithesis, wherein everything is at once itself and its own opposite. Genet, like the dancer in his ballet "Adame Mirror," creates a series of gestures in front of a mirror that reflects a reversed image of reality. Certainly he used the mirror image throughout his works—Stilitano lost in the house of mirrors at the amusement park in *The Thief's Journal,* the vital role of mirrors in "The Balcony." Perhaps even more pertinent is the symbol of opposing mirrors, mirrors which reflect reality reversed time and time again; indeed, Genet used just such a technique in "The Balcony" when the gas-meter reader plays the role of the bishop in the whore house, the fake bishop is then forced by the chief of police to play the role of the real bishop who has been killed during the revolution, and then after seeking to betray the chief of police in order to assume power in the real world, the would-be bishop rejects function in favor of "sublime appearance." The entire sequence may be interpreted as a series of reversed reflections of reality caught in opposing mirrors.

Genet was undoubtedly a part of that literary tradition in France called "le poete maudit" (the accursed or outcast poet) and represented by Villon, the Marquis de Sade, Baudelaire, Rimbaud, Verlaine, and even Gide and Proust. Generally rejected by society, these writers sought justification, vengeance, or something comparable by rejecting or attacking that society. If there is redemption for these authors, it takes place because of a commitment to art. One can not say that Genet and his works are less acceptable than were Baudelaire and his works in the mid-nineteenth century. Baudelaire was even convicted of pornography for *The Flowers of Evil,* now considered a masterpiece and a source for much twentieth-century poetry. Genet should he read and studied for those same reasons we now read and study those other writers in rebellion—as a way to understand ourselves and our times. Genet—the orphan, the professed homosexual, the convicted criminal—forces his readers to face certain facts of human nature and history. His language and his beliefs may be offensive to some, but his work reflects the reality of the world of criminals and prison life. Genet must not, however, he considered a mere writer of social documents, for his genius lay in his ability to create works of great complexity in a style that interests the reader and challenges the critic. Finally, there is no doubt that his subject matter and his innovative techniques and structures made him one of the most significant and controversial French authors of the twentieth century.

MEDIA ADAPTATIONS: Le Balcon was filmed and released as "The Balcony" by Continental in 1963; *Querelle de Brest* was filmed as "Querelle of Brest" and *Haute surveillance* was filmed as "Deathwatch"; a filmed stage performance of "The Maids" was released in 1975. Selections from Genet's works have been recorded on Caedmon Records, including a reading by Genet, in French, from *Journal du voleur.*

BIOGRAPHICAL/CRITICAL SOURCES:

BOOKS

Abel, Lionel, *Metatheatre: A New View of Dramatic Form,* Hill & Wang, 1963.

Bree, Germaine, *Narcissus Absconditus, the Problematic Art of Autobiography in Contemporary France,* Clarendon Press, 1978.

Brophy, Brigid, *Don't Never Forget: Collected Views and Reviews,* Holt, 1966.

Brustein, Robert, *Seasons of Discontent: Dramatic Opinions, 1959-1965,* Simon & Schuster, 1965.

Burgess, Anthony, *The Novel Now: A Guide to Contemporary Fiction,* Norton, 1967.

Coe, Richard N., *The Vision of Jean Genet,* Grove, 1968.

Coe, Richard N., editor, *The Theatre of Jean Genet: A Casebook,* Grove, 1970.

Contemporary Literary Criticism, Gale, Volume I, 1973, Volume II, 1974, Volume V, 1976, Volume X, 1979, Volume XIV, 1980, Volume ILIV, 1987, Volume ILVI, 1988.

Dictionary of Literary Biography, Volume 72: *French Novelists, 1930-1960,* Gale, 1988.

Driver, Tom F., *Jean Genet,* Columbia University Press, 1966.

Esslin, Martin, *The Theatre of the Absurd,* Anchor Books, 1961.

Glicksberg, Charles I., *Modern Literary Perspectives,* Southern Methodist University Press, 1970.

Goldmann, Lucien, *La Creation culturelle dans la societe moderne,* Denoel, 1971.

Grossvogel, D. I., *Four Playwrights and a Postscript,* Cornell University Press, 1962.

Hassan, Ihab, *The Dismemberment of Orpheus,* Oxford University Press, 1971.

Hayman, Ronald, *Theatre and Anti-theatre: New Movements since Beckett,* Oxford University Press, 1979.

Knapp, Bettina, *Jean Genet,* Twayne, 1968.

Kostelanetz, Richard, editor, *On Contemporary Literature,* Avon, 1964.

Kunkle, Francis, *Passion and the Passion: Sex and Religion in Modern Literature,* Westminister, 1975.

Littlejohn, David, *Interruptions,* Grossman, 1970.

Mandel, Siegfried, editor, *Contemporary European Novelists,* Southern Illinois University Press, 1968.

McMahon, J. H., *The Imagination of Jean Genet,* Yale University Press, 1964.

Nadeau, Maurice, *The French Novels since the War,* Methuen, 1967.

Naish, Camille, *A Genetic Approach to Structures in the Work of Jean Genet,* Harvard University Press, 1978.

Pronko, Leonard Cabell, *Avant Garde: The Experimental Theatre in France,* University of California Press, 1962.

Pronko, Leonard Cabell, *Theater East and West: Perspectives toward a Total Theater,* University of California Press, 1967.

Sartre, Jean-Paul, *Saint Genet, comedien et martyr,* Gallimard, 1952, translation by Bernard Frechtman published as *Saint Genet: Actor and Martyr,* Braziller, 1963.

Thody, Philip, *Jean Genet: A Critical Appraisal,* Stein & Day, 1968.

Webb, Richard C., *Jean Genet: An Annotated Bibliography, 1943-1980,* Scarecrow, 1982.

Weightman, John, *The Concept of the Avant-Gard: Explorations in Modernism,* Alcove, 1973.

Wellwarth, George, *Theatre of Protest and Paradox: Developments in the Avant-Garde Drama,* New York University Press, 1964.

PERIODICALS

American Cinematographer, May, 1963.

Atlantic, January, 1965.

Black Theatre, Number 5, 1971.

Book Week, October 6, 1963.

Contemporary Literature, autumn, 1975.

Dance, December, 1969.

Dance News, September, 1957.

Drama, summer, 1972.

Drama Review, fall, 1969.

Drama Survey, spring-summer, 1967.

French Review, December, 1971, October, 1974, December, 1974, April, 1980, December, 1981, May, 1984.

Globe and Mail (Toronto), April 19, 1986, July 29, 1989.

Harper, January, 1965, September, 1974.

Holiday, June, 1965.

Horizon, November 29, 1964.

Kentucky Romance Quarterly, Number 3, 1985.

Kenyon Review, March, 1967.

Le Figaro Litteraire, March 26, 1949, October 15, 1951.

Modern Drama, September, 1967, September 1969, March, 1974, September, 1976.

Nation, March 20, 1954, November 2, 1963, January 14, 1964, December 27, 1971.

New Leader, October 28, 1974.

New Republic, November 23, 1963.

New Statesman, January 10, 1964.

Newsweek, December 20, 1971, May 9, 1983.

New Yorker, January 16, 1965, October 21, 1974.

New York Times, January 19, 1986, October 26, 1986.

New York Times Book Review, September 29, 1963, February 19, 1967, June 15, 1969, September 8, 1974.

Partisan Review, April, 1949.

Playboy, April, 1965.

Plays and Players, May, 1974.
Saturday Review, June 18, 1960, November 14, 1964, July 12, 1969, November 15, 1969.
Southern Review, March, 1975, March, 1978.
Times (London), July 17, 1987.
Times Literary Supplement, October 31, 1958, April 8, 1965, June 12, 1987, April 21, 1989.
TriQuarterly 30, spring, 1974.
Village Voice, March 18, 1965.
Washington Post Book World, November 3, 1974.
Wisconsin Studies in Contemporary Literature, summer, 1969.

OBITUARIES:

PERIODICALS

Chicago Tribune, April 16, 1986.
New York Times, April 16, 1986.
Time, April 28, 1986.
Washington Post, April 16, 1986.

*   *   *

GEORGES, Georges Martin
See SIMENON, Georges (Jacques Christian)

*   *   *

GEROME
See THIBAULT, Jacques Anatole Francois

*   *   *

GIBB, Lee
See WATERHOUSE, Keith (Spencer)

*   *   *

GIDE, Andre (Paul Guillaume)   1869-1951

PERSONAL: Born November 22 (one source says November 21), 1869, in Paris, France; died of pneumonia, February 19, 1951, in Paris, France; buried in Cuverville-en-Caux, Normandy, France; son of Paul (a professor) and Juliette (Rondeaux) Gide; married cousin, Madeleine Rondeaux, in 1895; children: (with Elisabeth van Rysselberghe) Catherine. *Education:* Educated privately and in public schools in Paris, France.

CAREER: Novelist, playwright, essayist, diarist, and translator. Co-founder of *La Nouvelle Revue francaise* in 1909 and of *L'Arche,* a literary magazine in North Africa; literary critic for *La Revue blanche.* Mayor of La Roque, a commune in Normandy, France, 1896; juror in Rouen, France, 1912; special envoy of the Colonial Ministry in Africa, 1925-26. Worked with the Red Cross and, later, in a convalescent home for soldiers, and became director of the Foyer Franco-Belge during World War I. Traveled extensively in Europe and Africa.

MEMBER: Royal Society of London (elected honorary fellow, 1924), American Academy of Arts and Letters (elected honorary corresponding member, 1950).

AWARDS, HONORS: Goethe Medal, 1932; honorary doctorate in letters from University of Oxford, 1947; Nobel Prize in literature from Nobel Foundation, 1947; Goethe Plaque from the city of Frankfort on the Main, 1949.

WRITINGS:

NOVELS AND NOVELLAS

Le Voyage d'Urien, Librairie de l'Art Independant, 1893, second edition, 1894, translation with introduction and notes by Wade Baskin published as *Urien's Voyage,* Philosophical Library, 1964.
Paludes (satire; also see below), Librairie de l'Art Independant, 1895, Gallimard, 1973.
Le Promethee mal enchaine (satire; also see below), Mercure, 1899, new edition, Gallimard, 1925, translation by Lilian Rothermere published as *Prometheus Illbound,* Chatto & Windus, 1919.
L'Immoraliste, Mercure, 1902, translation by Dorothy Bussy published as *The Immoralist,* Knopf, 1930, translation by Richard Howard published as *The Immoralist,* Knopf, 1970.
La Porte etroite, Mercure, 1909, revised edition, 1959, translation by Dorothy Bussy published as *Strait Is the Gate,* Knopf, 1924.
Isabelle (also see below), Gallimard, 1911, translation by Dorothy Bussy published as *Isabelle,* Knopf, 1968.
Les Caves du Vatican: Sotie (satire; also see below), Gallimard, 1914, Macmillan, 1956, translation by Dorothy Bussy published as *The Vatican Swindle,* Knopf, 1925, published as *Lafcadio's Adventures,* Knopf, 1928 (published in England as *The Vatican Cellars,* Cassell, 1952).
La Symphonie pastorale (also see below), Editions de la Nouvelle Revue Francaise, 1919, translation by Dorothy Bussy published as *The Pastoral Symphony,* Knopf, 1968.
Les Faux-Monnayeurs, Gallimard, 1926, translation by Dorothy Bussy published as *The Counterfeiters* (also see below), Knopf, 1927 (published in England as *The Coiners,* Cassell, 1950).
L'Ecole des femmes (also see below), Gallimard, 1929, translation by Dorothy Bussy published as *The School for Wives,* Knopf, 1929.
Robert: Supplement a "L'Ecole des femmes" (also see below), Gallimard, 1929.
Genevieve; ou, La Confidence inachevee (also see below), Gallimard, 1936.
L'Ecole des femmes [suivi de] *Robert* [et de] *Genevieve,* Gallimard, 1944, translation by Dorothy Bussy published as *The School for Wives, Robert,* [and] *Genevieve; or, The Unfinished Confidence,* Knopf, 1950.
Thesee (also see below), Pantheon, 1946, translation by John Russell published as *Theseus,* New Directions Publishing, 1949.
Marshlands [and] *Prometheus Misbound: Two Satires,* translation by George D. Painter, New Directions Publishing, 1953, McGraw, 1965.
Two Symphonies: Isabelle [and] *The Pastoral Symphony,* translation by Dorothy Bussy, Knopf, 1931 (published in England as *La Symphonie pastorale* [and] *Isabelle,* Penguin Books, 1963).

LYRICAL WORKS IN VERSE AND PROSE

Les Cahiers d'Andre Walter (title means "The Notebooks of Andre Walter"; also see below), Librairie de l'Art Independant, 1891, translation of first half with introduction by Wade Baskin published as *The White Notebook,* Philosophical Library, 1964, translation with introduction and notes by Baskin published as *The Notebooks of Andre Walter,* Philosophical Library, 1968.

Le Traite du Narcisse: Theorie du symbole (title means "Treatise of the Narcissus: Theory of the Symbol"; also see below), Librairie de l'Art Independant, 1891.

Les Poesies d'Andre Walter (title means "The Poems of Andre Walter"; also see below), Librairie de l'Art Independent, 1892.

La Tentative Amoureuse; ou, Le Traite du vain desir (title means "The Attempt at Love; or, The Treatise of Vain Desire"; also see below), Librairie de l'Art Independant, 1893.

Les Nourritures terrestres, Mercure, 1897.

Les Nouvelles Nourritures, Gallimard, 1935.

The Fruits of the Earth, translated by Dorothy Bussy, Knopf, 1949 (published in England as *Fruits of the Earth,* Secker & Warburg, 1962, published as *Fruits of the Earth* [and] *Later Fruits of the Earth,* Penguin Books/Secker & Warburg, 1970).

Les Nourritures terrestres [et] *Les Nouvelles Nourritures,* Club des Libraires de France, 1956.

PLAYS

"Philoctete" (also see below), first performed privately, April 3, 1919.

Le Roi Candaule (first produced in Paris, France, at Nouveau Theatre, May 9, 1901; also see below), Editions de la Revue Blanche, 1901.

Saul: Drame en cinq actes (first produced in Paris, France, at Theatre du Vieux-Colombier, June 16, 1922; also see below), Mercure, 1903, enlarged edition, 1904.

Le Retour de l'enfant prodigue (first produced in Monte Carlo, Monaco, at Theatre de Monte-Carlo, December 4, 1928; text first published in *Vers et Prose,* 1907; also see below), Bibliotheque de l'Occident, 1909, translation by Aldyth Thain published as *The Return of the Prodigal Son,* Utah State University Press, 1960.

Bethsabe (first published in *L'Ermitage,* 1903; also see below), Bibliotheque de l'Occident, 1912.

Oedipe: Drame en trois actes (first produced in Antwerp, Belgium, at Cercle Artistique, December 10, 1931; also see below), Gallimard, 1931.

Persephone (first produced in Paris, France, at l'Opera, April, 1934; also see below), Gallimard, 1934, translation by Samuel Putnam published as *Persephone,* Gotham Book Mart, 1949.

"Le Treizieme Arbre" (title means "The Thirteenth Tree"; one-act farce), first produced in Marseilles, France, at Rideau Gris, May 8, 1935.

Le Retour (title means "The Return"), Ides et Calendes, 1946.

(With Jean-Louis Barrault) *Le Proces: Piece tiree du roman de Kafka* (dramatization of Franz Kafka's novel *Der Prozess;* first produced October 10, 1947), Gallimard, 1947, translation and adaptation by Jacqueline and Frank Sundstrom published as *The Trial,* Secker & Warburg, 1950, translation by Leon Katz and Joseph Katz published as *The Trial: A Dramatization Based on Franz Kafka's Novel,* Schocken, 1964.

Robert; ou, L'Interet general (title means "Robert; or, The General Interest"; five-act play; first produced in Tunis, Tunisia, at Theatre Municipal, April 30, 1946), Ides et Calendes, 1949.

Les Caves du Vatican: Farce en trois actes et dix-neuf tableaux (first produced in Montreux, Switzerland, at Societe des Belles-Lettres, December 9, 1933; revised script produced in Paris, France, at the Comedie-Francaise, December 13, 1950), Ides et Calendes, 1948, Gallimard, 1950.

Persephone: Melodrame en trois tableaux d'Andre Gide (opera libretto), music by Igor Fedorovich Stravinski, Boosey & Hawkes, 1950.

COLLECTED WORKS

Philoctete; Le Traite du Narcisse; La Tentative amoureuse; El Hadj (includes "El Hadj; ou, Le Traite du faux prophete" [title means "El Hadj; or, The Treatise of the False Prophet"]), Mercure, 1899.

Morceaux choisis (title means "Selections"; collection of previously published and unpublished works), Editions de la Nouvelle Revue Francaise, 1921.

Pages choisise (collection of previously published and unpublished works), Georges Cres, 1921.

Divers: Caracteres; Un Esprit non prevenu; Dictees; Lettres, Gallimard, 1931.

Oeuvres completes, fifteen volumes, edited by Louis Martin Chauffier, Gallimard and Editions de la Nouvelle Revue Francaise, 1932-39.

Le Retour de l'enfant prodigue, precede de cinq autres traites: Le Traite du Narcisse, La Tentative amoureuse, El Hadj, Philoctete, Bethsabe, Gallimard, 1932, reprinted, 1967, translation by Dorothy Bussy published as *The Return of the Prodigal, Preceded by Five Other Treatises; With "Saul," a Drama in Five Acts* (contains "Narcissus," "The Lover's Attempt," "El Hadj," "Philoctetes," "Bathsheba," "The Return of the Prodigal," "Saul"), Secker & Warburg, 1953.

Theatre (contains *Saul, Le Roi Candaule, Oedipe, Persephone, Le Treizieme Arbre*), Gallimard, 1942.

Theatre complet, eight volumes, Ides et Calendes, 1947-49.

Recits, roman, soties (collection of prose and poetry), Gallimard, 1948.

My Theater: Five Plays and an Essay (contains "Saul," "Bathsheba," "Philoctetes," "King Candaules," "Persephone," "The Evolution of the Theater"), translation by Jackson Mathews, Knopf, 1952.

Poesie; Journal; Souvenirs (collection of lyrical and autobiographical works), Gallimard, 1952.

Ne jugez pas; Souvenirs de la cour d'assises; L'Affaire Redureau; La Sequestree de Poitiers, Gallimard, 1957.

Romans, recits, et soties: Ouevres lyriques (collection of works, including *Le Voyage d'Urien, Paludes, La Porte etroite, La Symphonie pastorale, Les Faux-Monnayeurs, Le Journal des Faux-Monnayeurs, Le Traite du Narcisse, El Hadj*), edited with notes and bibliography by Yvonne Davet and Jean-Jacques Thierry, La Pleiade/Gallimard, 1958.

Oeuvres (collection of journals and lyrical works), Gallimard, 1960.

OTHER

Si le grain ne meurt (autobiography; first part printed privately, Imprimerie Ste. Catherine, 1920, second part printed privately, 1921), Gallimard, 1926, translation by Dorothy Bussy published as *If It Die: An Autobiography,* Random House, 1935 (published in England as *If It Die,* Secker & Warburg 1950).

The Journals of Andre Gide, four volumes, selected, edited, and translated by Justin O'Brien, Knopf, 1947-51 (published in England as *Journals,* Secker & Warburg, 1948-55, and as *Journals, 1889-1949,* Penguin Books, 1967), published as *The Journals of Andre Gide, 1889-1949,* Vintage Trade, 1956, abridged edition published as *The Journals of Andre Gide,* Volume 1: *1889-1924,* Volume 2: *1924-1949,* Northwestern University Press, 1987.

Also author of volumes of essays, criticism, travel writings, and correspondence. Translator of numerous works into French.

SIDELIGHTS: As a master of prose narrative, occasional dramatist and translator, literary critic (particularly of Fyodor Dostoevsky), letter writer, essayist, and diarist, Andre Gide provided twentieth-century French literature with one of its most intriguing examples of the man of letters. Gide continued the tradition of reflection on culture—its books and its institutions—established by the sixteenth-century essayist Michel de Montaigne, who had introduced the record of the self as a subject for serious literature in France. Inasmuch as it reflects the complex personality behind it, Gide's work enlarges this permission to take the self as subject. Inasmuch as that personality is ironic, however, the record of the self is deliberately subverted. While Gide lent the authorial pronoun "I" to any number of heroes and heroines in his narratives, he simultaneously cast aspersions on their credibility; while he recorded in his voluminous *Journal* the activities and thought of an eighty-year lifetime, he refused to recognize his authentic portrait in anything he had written if it were considered separately from the self-examinations in the rest of his works. "Hardly a day goes by that I don't put everything back into question," he wrote in his *Journal* in 1922. Each volume was intended to challenge itself, what had preceded it, and what could conceivably follow it. This characteristic, according to Daniel Moutote in his *Cahiers Andre Gide* essay, is what makes Gide's work "essentially modern": the "perpetual renewal of the values by which one lives."

Gide's earliest works participate in what is generally known as the symbolist aesthetic. A literary and philosophical movement determined to break the hold of realism and rationalism on French poetry through the use of suggestion and allusive, emotionally charged language, symbolism was an important training element for the writers of Gide's generation who, as young men in their twenties, were just beginning to establish their careers during the last decade of the nineteenth century in France. The high seriousness of the movement, its goal of revolutionizing French literature, and its circle of intellectuals who gathered weekly in the living room of the master poet Stephane Mallarme to discuss the future of poetry appealed to the young Gide, who, like many of his companions at that time, thought of himself primarily as a poet and intellectual. Of rigorous Protestant stock, Gide approached his writing as a highly moral interrogation of the conventions of morality, as a labor in service of ideas created by the intellect first and the imagination second: "Imagination (with me)," he wrote in his *Journal* in the 1890s, "rarely precedes the idea; it's the latter, and not at all the former, that excites me. . . . For me, the idea of a work often precedes its *imagination* by several years."

By "imagination," Gide meant the actual elaboration of a work with plot, characters, and other elements that would bring the "idea" to life. For most of Gide's writing, the "idea" required a long maturation before its "imagination." Though he was accustomed by inclination and exercise to the written expression of ideas, Gide did not necessarily think of himself as one who wrote easily. His *Journal* through the years records the occasional bouts of nervous agitation that preceded the creation of new works; the procrastination, false starts, and abandoned projects; his complaints of scratchy pens, crooked tables, forgotten notebooks, inconsiderate visitors, and reluctant sentences that often made the work of writing difficult; and above all his frustration at wishing to say everything at once and having, necessarily, to say only part at a time. In an article reprinted in *Gide: A Collection of Critical Essays,* Alain Girard pointed out that the published *Journal* is not the complete private diary of its author,

who admittedly tore out or withheld parts of it. Nevertheless, the *Journal* faithfully records the importance Gide gave to sincerity and truthfulness to the self as moral values mediating between culturally defined notions of good and evil. It is also clear to what extent sincerity and obligation to the self required the author's discipline and effort of will: "Certainly I could have been more easily a naturalist, doctor or pianist . . . than a writer," Gide wrote in his *Journal* in 1910, "but I can bring more diverse qualities to this career; the others would have been more exclusive; but it's to this one that I must bring the most willpower."

Gide's pseudonymic *Cahiers d'Andre Walter,* a confessional work presented as a journal published posthumously, marked in 1891 Gide's entry into literary Paris. *Les Poesies d'Andre Walter* was published in 1892. In 1910, Gide remarked in his *Journal* that his present undertaking, *Corydon,* was his first work in twenty years to restore to him the "feeling of indispensability" that had dictated *Andre Walter.* Again in his 1924 *Journal* Gide recalled his earliest prose experiment: "I began to write before knowing French very well—and especially: before knowing how to use it well. But I was bursting. . . . At that time, I thought I could bend the language to my purposes." From the beginning, however, the French classical tradition of the word in obedience to the idea dominated Gide's concept of style; the tone and language of each work had to be perfectly suited to the subject being dealt with. He defined the beauty of a work in terms of the harmony of its composition and the exactitude and rigorousness of its style, writing, for example, in undated *Journal* notes this defense of the lack of imagery in *Andre Walter:* "Beginning with my *Notebooks of Andre Walter* I practiced a style that aimed toward a more secret and more essential beauty. . . . I wanted this language 'poorer' still, more strict, more refined, judging that the only purpose of ornamentation is to hide one's faults and that only thoughts insufficiently beautiful in themselves should fear perfect nudity [of style]."

Gide characterized much of his later narrative fiction not as "novels" but as "recits," or "accounts," stories spoken or written by first-person narrators about themselves and directed at specific audiences of listeners or readers. Gide's skill as narrator is evident in his ability to suggest multiple perspectives on the events recounted while remaining technically within the limits implied by the first-person point of view. One of these means of suggestion is the *mise en abyme,* a process of mirroring one story within another for which the play-within-a-play in William Shakespeare's *Hamlet* serves as the classic example. Gide understood the *mise en abyme* as a dramatization of the subject of the work within the experiences of the characters themselves; one of his favorite uses of this device eventually was to represent within the work a character/novelist writing or planning to write a novel on the exact subject as the novel (by Gide) in which the character appears. Still in his symbolist phase, however, and reflecting on *Andre Walter* in his *Journal* for 1893, Gide considered the *mise en abyme* the most effective way to convey the essence of the "typical psychological novel"—that is, the influence of the story upon the storyteller, or, in terms closer to Gide's own willfully philosophical ones, the reaction of what is imagined upon the imagining subject.

Gide's first major narrative work, *L'Immoraliste,* is flanked, on one side, by a short novel and a group of plays, and on the other, by a period of depression and difficulty during which Gide reworked much of his old material and wrote and rewrote *La Porte etroite,* which, in 1909, brought him his first real success. In 1899, the short novel *Le Promethee mal enchaine* introduced what would be Gide's major theme of the "gratuitous act"; the play *Philoctete* was published in the same year, followed by a second play, *Le Roi Candaule,* in 1901 and a third, *Saul,* in 1903. Although they met with little critical success and are not considered major works, Gide's plays from this period are, according to Germaine Bree in *Andre Gide: L'Insaissisable protee,* so original as to bear little resemblance to classical, naturalist, or symbolist theater. Rather, with their "ambiguity unresolved by the denouement" and Gide's evocation of a "special world in which language and gesture approach an encoded language," Bree declared, they "opened the way" for French theater as Sartre and Camus would develop it after World War II. During this period between *L'Immoraliste* and *La Porte etroite,* there also appeared, to little critical fanfare, *Pretextes,* a collection of articles and short pieces; the evocative *Amyntas,* that Gide in his 1910 *Journal* called his "most perfect" work to date; and *Le Retour de l'enfant prodigue,* a parable that Gide completed, contrary to his usual practice, within just three weeks during the winter of 1907, partly because, he explained in his *Journal* at the time, "I was tired of not writing any more and all the other subjects I have within me presented too many difficulties to be dealt with right away." His most important contribution to literature during this interim, however, turned out to be not a written work but the literary journal and publishing house he co-founded in 1909. With its goal of publishing the best of contemporary writing (of course, including Gide's), the history of the *Nouvelle Revue francaise* became, in the words of Gide's biographer Pierre de Boisdeffre in his *Cahiers Andre Gide* essay, "the history of all of French literature from the 1910's to the 1950's."

In 1931, when his *Journal* and even his correspondence were being widely published, Gide reflected in the *Journal* that "the absence of echo"—or critical attention—for his earliest works had been the true guarantee of their value; writing for future readers, he said, he had written for timelessness. Pierre de Boisdeffre estimated in his *Vie d'Andre Gide, 1869-1951* that *L'Immoraliste* had had "only a handful" of reviewers, and Gide himself pessimistically predicted in his 1902 *Journal* that an edition of only three hundred copies would be sufficient to meet demand; however, Claude Martin has documented in *La Maturite d'Andre Gide* the fairly extensive critical "echo" the book received in 1902 and 1903, pointing out that Gide was upset not that his book wasn't being read, but that it wasn't being read well. Among the flurry of articles about *L'Immoraliste,* Martin cites an essay by Marcel Drouin (Gide's brother-in-law writing under the pseudonym "Michel Arnauld") in *La Revue blanche* of November, 1902, an essay that constituted the authorized response to what Gide perceived as his readers' errors. Drouin wrote that the book would give rise to fewer misconceptions if "more people knew how to read, within the lines and between the lines, then reread, then reflect on their reading" of this book in which "the antithesis is next to the thesis, the objection with the argument, . . . united in the same soul and the single life [of the protagonist]." Among the false perceptions attending the book was one that attributed its derivation, suggested by its title, from Friedrich Nietzsche's "immoralism." Gide himself later insisted in his *Journal* for 1922 that his recit had not been so much "influenced" as "confirmed" by Nietzsche, whom he had discovered only after beginning to write the book; on the other hand, the *Journal* for 1905 records his satisfaction that at least one perceptive reader had praised him for having, with his protagonist Michel, peered through "the cracks in culture."

Gide's sensitivity to the critical reaction aroused by his works is well documented. Charles Du Bos described in *Le Dialogue avec Andre Gide* the author's "fear of and passion for compromising himself "; according to an entry in Gide's 1922 *Journal,* Madeleine Gide wrote to her husband in January of that year: "What

very much disturbs me is the nasty campaign begun against you . . . if you were invulnerable, I wouldn't worry. But you are vulnerable, and you know it, and I know it." It was precisely by his refusal to choose a definitive ethical position within his works that Gide rendered himself most vulnerable to critical attack by partisan thinkers and keepers of public morality. He, in fact, repeatedly provoked such attacks, as demonstrated by this comment about *La Porte etroite,* which Thierry quotes in his "Notice" to the Pleiade edition: "It's to the gratuitousness of the work of art that the Protestant remains refractory; he wants the work to have meaning, instruction, usefulness." By his term "gratuitousness," Gide suggested the function of his works as art, proposing with his heroes and heroines—"against whom [I] cannot side any more than [I] set them up as exemplary"—not solutions, but enigmas and stimuli to his readers' reflection. The Catholic critic Henri Massis, a principal adversary whose articles always appeared, Gide complained in his *Journal* for 1921, the very day the writer's books went on sale, refused in his *Jugements* to accept an argument from aesthetic grounds in defense of moral nonpartisanship; for Massis, Gide's "classicism" and the "gratuitousness of [his] art" were simply code words for hypocrisy, moral turpitude, and evasion of responsibility.

Gide responded to attacks of this nature by affirming, first, that his intention had never been to "influence," and, second, that anyone who attributed this intention to him wasn't reading him properly. In Massis's case, misreading involved misquoting— "Curious, this inability of Massis to quote a text exactly or without falsifying its meaning," he observed ruefully in his 1931 *Journal*; more seriously, as Gide protested in a 1921 entry, the critic interpreted the novelist's fictional characters as spokesmen for their creator. The basis of Gide's objection was thus the extreme literality with which his opponents tended to read his work, mistaking art as doctrine and directly envisaging an army of Gide disciples who would interpret his works as strict blueprints for anarchy. With the exception of *The Fruits of the Earth,* Gide eventually insisted, all of his works had to be read "ironically" or "critically," and even in this book, he wrote in his *Journal* for 1926, "there is, for whoever consents to read well and without prejudice, the critique of the book within the book itself, as it should be." In a 1950 letter to Pierre Lafille, a letter quoted by Lafille in his *Cahiers Andre Gide* essay, Gide wrote, "You have admirably noted that in each of my books there coexist and are juxtaposed, at one and the same time, the depiction of a psychological state and the critique of that very state." Jean Hytier, in *Andre Gide,* explained this irony as a play of sympathy and antipathy, identification and distance, skillfully balanced in the recits: "By sympathy, [Gide] makes these first persons singular speak with an accent of truth unequaled in French fiction; . . . by antipathy, he maintains all his reserve, marks the distances which separate him from his creatures. . . . Readers let themselves be carried away, and react naively to the story they are being told, . . . but [Gide] also intends the reader to withdraw his identification, either by the story's end, or . . . as it is being told." The characters themselves are the first victims of Gide's irony, for as Germaine Bree observed in a 1951 *Yale French Studies* essay, they "are rather like players who, in a football game, persist in playing basketball, with the conviction that that is the game being played."

Moutote contended that Gide's difficulties with his critics represented the "drama of an avant-garde thinker" who had to wait for the public to catch up with him. In moments of equanimity, Gide would show himself resigned to the wait and confident of its results; writing in his *Journal* in 1921, he declared: "I would have stopped writing long ago if I were not convinced that those to come will discover in my writings what those today refuse to see, and what I know, however, I have put in them. . . . I will let my books patiently choose their readers; the small number of today will be the opinion-makers of tomorrow." "Being out of step with his time," he summarized in the 1937 *Journal,* "is what gives an artist his reason for being. . . . He opposes, he initiates." Even during the campaigns against him, Gide appreciated that bad press was better than no press at all, remarking wryly in a 1924 *Journal* entry that the "diabolical uproar" of Massis and his clan "made me more famous in three months than my books . . . in thirty years." In fairness to Massis, however, it must be recognized that this critic was right about Gide's refusal to be pinned down by any single one of his books: "If anyone thinks that in my latest work he has finally grasped what I am like," Gide wrote in his 1909 *Journal,* "let him think again: it's always from my last-born that I am the most different."

A happier critical fate attended the memoirs, published in 1926 as *Si le grain ne meurt,* and recounting Gide's life up to his engagement to Madeleine in 1895. A number of Gide's friends, who were in a position to judge the completed work against his expressed desire for clarity and sincerity, expressed either their disappointment at his excessive discretion or their opinion that too great a concern for clarity had vastly oversimplified Gide's portrait of himself. For Du Bos in the *Dialogue, Si le grain ne meurt* was long on preparation and short on revelation, finally only "caricatural" of a "Gide larger, fuller, more moving, I was going to say than his entire work, in any case than this rasping and grating sketch." More perceptively, however, Gide's friend Jacques Raverat acknowledged—as Gide approvingly noted in his *Journal* for 1920—that the only way to have a full portrait of the author was to read all of Gide's works at the same time, since "all the states that, for artistic reasons, you depict as successive can be simultaneous with you." Gide's biographers, particularly Jean Delay, have drawn attention to the numerous inaccuracies and omissions in Gide's recollections of his past in this work; tantalizingly related to both autobiography and fiction (Gide's own and fiction as a genre), however, *Si le grain ne meurt* has been regarded as a masterpiece of the genre called "literary autobiography" by C. D. E. Tolton in his *Andre Gide and the Art of Autobiography.*

As if in reaction to his increasing notoriety, Gide's *Journal* for the years preceding World War I records his sense that, approaching his fortieth birthday, he had not yet said the most important of what he wanted to say. "If I died today," he wrote in May of 1910, "my entire opus would disappear in favor of *Strait Is the Gate,* that's the only [work] that would be given any consideration." Two years later he again lamented in the *Journal,* "If I were to disappear now, no one could suspect, from what I've written, the better things I have yet to say. By what boldness, by what presumption of a long life, have I still kept the most important for the end?"

In 1919 Gide began his early sketches for *The Counterfeiters,* explaining to van Rysselberghe that what he had in mind was "a work, a novel that would make people say: 'Ah yes! we understand why he claimed not to have written any before this.' " *The Counterfeiters* was intended to leave behind the "monographs" of the recits in favor of multiplicity and counterpoint: "I conceive of the novel in the same manner as Dostoevsky, [as] a struggle between points of view," he told van Rysselberghe in a 1919 interview. Still working on the book in 1923, he wrote at that time in his *Journal,* "What I want a novel to be? an intersection—a rendez-vous of problems." From its inception, the notion of "journal" was integral to this work. To help keep track of his uncharacteristicly broad range of material ("there's

enough here to feed half a dozen novels," he observed in the 1921 *Journal*), Gide kept a special journal detailing his plans for and progress on the novel; the resulting *Journal des Faux-Monnayeurs* is Gide's record of, in Thierry's description, "the architecture of the novel [that shows] not a plot as it develops but a novel as it is being written." In addition, a fictional journal kept within the novel by the character Edouard (in preparation for his novel, also entitled *The Counterfeiters*) is the means by which Gide intended to decenter his narrative focus and make of *The Counterfeiters* "the critique of the novel . . . in general," as he explained to van Rysselberghe: "There isn't one center to my novel, there are two, as in an ellipse: the events on the one hand and their reaction in 'Edouard.' Ordinarily, when one writes a novel, one either starts with the characters and makes up events to develop them, or starts with the events and creates characters as needed to explain them. But 'Edouard,' who holds the psychological strings of a series of beings who confide in him, rather than writing a novel, dreams of making them act in reality, and he doesn't succeed in substantiating the characters by the events. These characters give him events, that he can't do anything with! and that becomes part of the subject."

While *The Counterfeiters* was in press, Gide went on an extended tour of the Congo, the first of many voyages he would undertake and write about during the final third of his life. "All the long trips I haven't taken are like remorse within me," van Rysselberghe overheard him say before this departure, "traveling seems to me almost a duty, a kind of piety; I think the Good Lord must not be very happy with the way we honor Him, He must think, 'What! I gave them all that and look how little they make of it!' " Gide's *Voyage au Congo* and *Retour du Tchad* have been presented in support of a social conscience that had first surfaced in his *Souvenirs de la cour d'assises* before largely disappearing from the intervening works; Gide's descriptions in the *Voyage* of the economic exploitation of French equatorial Africa led to a public debate on colonialism upon his return to Paris. Similarly, his observations on his trip to Moscow as an honored guest at Maxim Gorki's funeral, the *Retour de l'U.R.S.S.,* and its supplement, *Retouches a mon "Retour de l'U.R.S.S.,"* sharply critiqued the Soviet system and announced Gide's estrangement from the Communist movement, which he had supported financially and ideologically during the early 1930s.

Although *Les Nouvelles Nourritures* is a work that Gide had been anticipating writing since the 1920s, Pierre de Boisdeffre has characterized it in *Metamorphoses de la litterature* as Gide's "Marxist Gospel"; a volume of letters, articles, and speeches from 1930 to 1938 grouped under the title *Litterature engagee* records Gide's flirtation with Communism, including the eminently forgettable play *Robert; ou, L'Interet general,* of which the Moscow debut was hastily canceled after the apostasy of the *Retour de l'U.R.S.S.* Like Catholicism, Marxism ultimately proved too doctrinaire for Gide; despite their differing principles—the first, he judged, preaching charity and ignoring justice, the second announcing justice at the expense of love—their doctrinal similarity is brought out in this objection to Marx's writing in his *Journal* for summer, 1937: "It's the Latin Mass. Where one doesn't understand, one bows down."

Finally, a trio of recits from this period was also intended to respond to social issues. *L'Ecole des femmes, Robert,* and *Genevieve* present the complex portrait of a courtship and marriage judged from the respective viewpoints of the fiancee become wife and mother, the husband, and ultimately the daughter. Through these three figures Gide intended, according to a *Journal* entry for 1930, "to meet head-on the whole question of feminism." Yet even Albert J. Guerard who, in his *Andre Gide,* had judged *The*

Immoralist "one of the greatest realistic novels of the century" and parts of *The Counterfeiters* and *Lafcadio's Adventures* "among the triumphs of modern anti-realism," had to admit that "surely few important novelists have written books as superficial and as dull as *L'Ecole des femmes, Robert,* and *Genevieve.*" It would appear that Gide agreed with Guerard. Arthur E. Babcock calls attention in his *Portraits of Artists: Reflexivity in Gidean Fiction, 1902-1946* to a 1947 letter in which Gide explained to Guerard, "My *School for Wives,* or at least the third part (*Genevieve*), is of all my books (and by far) the most painfully written. . . . At the time I was poisoned by the social question. Let's let it drop."

Gide's final works returned to what had always been for him a fertile source, equal to Christianity in imaginative possibility and moral instruction: Greek mythology. His version of *Oedipe,* which added, he said in his 1932 *Journal,* "jokes, trivialities and incongruities" to Sophocles' classic text, seemed to him a dramatization of the tragic "struggle between individualism and submission to religious authority"; his intention, he wrote in a *Journal* entry for 1933, was to evoke not terror and pity—the aims of the original Greek tragedy—but reflection. Evaluating his *Oedipe* in his 1931 *Journal,* he envisioned as a separate work a "decisive meeting" between the mythological king Theseus, whose life he had long wanted to write, and Oedipus, "each measuring himself against the other and illuminating, each under cover of the other, their two lives"; the meeting takes place near the end of Gide's final recit, his "testament" *Thesee,* which Claude Martin called, in *Andre Gide par lui-meme,* "at the evening of his life, . . . an intelligent extract of his wisdom."

Gide's contributions to contemporary literature were publicly recognized during the last years of his life: an honorary fellow of the Royal Society of London since 1924, he was awarded both an honorary doctorate from the University of Oxford and the Nobel Prize in literature in 1947. His intimate writings continued to his death: *Et nunc manet in te (Madeleine),* published in 1951, is a poignant memorial to his wife, who had died in 1938; it completes the image Gide wished to leave of himself by including those previously unpublished pages of his *Journal* in which he discussed his relationship with "Emmanuele"/Madeleine. *Ainsi soit-il; ou, Les Jeux sont faits* ends six days before Gide's death in 1951. Jean Delay considered this last work, along with *Andre Walter,* "aesthetically the least successful" and "psychologically the most interesting, [*Andre Walter*] because the twenty-year-old poet does not yet know how to create art, [*Ainsi soit-il*] because the octogenarian, sensing death approach, disdains to create it and allows his pen to run free." Gide's final work concluded with a characteristic refusal to conclude—writing or, as it turned out, living: "No! I can't affirm that with the end of this notebook, all will be closed; that it will be over. Maybe I will want to add something more. . . . At the last minute, add something more." *Ainsi soit-il* was published posthumously in 1952.

MEDIA ADAPTATIONS: La Symphonie pastorale was adapted into a motion picture script of the same title by Pierre Bost and Jean Aurenche and published by Nouvelle Edition, with a preface by J. Delannoy, in 1948; the book was adapted into a play in three acts and published by F. De Wolfe & Robert Stone in 1954. *L'Immoraliste* was adapted into a play titled *Andre Gide's "The Immoralist"* by Ruth and Augustus Goetz and published by Dramatists Play Service in 1962.

BIOGRAPHICAL/CRITICAL SOURCES:

BOOKS

Arland, Marcel, and Jean Mouton, editors, *Entretiens sur Andre Gide,* Mouton, 1967.
Babcock, Arthur E., *Portraits of Artists: Reflexivity in Gidean Fiction, 1902-1946,* French Literature Publications, 1982.
Boisdeffre, Pierre de, *Metamorphoses de la litterature,* Alsatia, 1950, excerpted in *Les Critiques de notre temps et Gide,* edited by Michel Raimond, Garnier, 1971.
Boisdeffre, Pierre de, *Vie d'Andre Gide, 1869-1951: Essai de biographie critique,* Hachette, 1970.
Bree, Germaine, *Andre Gide: L'Insaisissable protee,* Belles Lettres, 1953, English revision and translation published as *Andre Gide,* Rutgers University Press, 1963, excerpted in *Les Critiques de notre temps et Gide,* edited by Michel Raimond, Garnier, 1971.
Cahiers Andre Gide, Gallimard, 1969—.
Cordle, Thomas, *Andre Gide,* Twayne, 1969.
Davet, Yvonne, editor, *Litterature engagee,* by Andre Gide, Gallimard, 1950.
Davet, Yvonne and Jean-Jacques Thierry, editors and authors of notes, *Romans, recits, et soties: Oeuvres lyriques,* texts by Andre Gide, La Pleiade/Gallimard, 1958.
Delay, Jean, *La Jeunesse d'Andre Gide,* two volumes, Gallimard, 1956, translation by June Guicharnaud published as *The Youth of Andre Gide,* University of Chicago Press, 1963.
Dictionary of Literary Biography, Volume 65: *French Novelists, 1900-1930,* Gale, 1988.
Du Bos, Charles, *Approximations,* Fayard, 1965, excerpted in *Les Critiques de notre temps et Gide,* edited by Michel Raimond, Garnier, 1971.
Du Bos, Charles, *Le Dialogue avec Andre Gide,* Correa, 1947, excerpted in *Les Critiques de notre temps et Gide,* edited by Michel Raimond, Garnier, 1971.
Fay, Bernard, *Les Precieux,* Perrin, 1966.
Fowlie, Wallace, *Andre Gide: His Life and Art,* Macmillan, 1965.
Gide, Andre, *Journal, 1889-1939,* La Pleiade/Gallimard, 1948.
Gide, Andre, *Journal, 1939-1949: Souvenirs,* La Pleiade/Gallimard, 1954.
Gide, Andre, *The Journals of Andre Gide,* four volumes, selected, edited, translated, introduced, and annotated by Justin O'Brien, Knopf, 1947-51.
Guerard, Albert J., *Andre Gide,* Harvard University Press, 1969.
Hytier, Jean, *Andre Gide,* Charlot, 1945, translation by R. Howard excerpted in *Gide: A Collection of Critical Essays,* edited by David Littlejohn, Prentice-Hall, 1970.
Ireland, G. W., *Gide: A Study of His Creative Writings,* Oxford University Press, 1970.
Littlejohn, David, *The Andre Gide Reader,* Knopf, 1971.
Littlejohn, David, editor and author of introduction, *Gide: A Collection of Critical Essays,* Prentice-Hall, 1970.
Magny, Claude-Edmonde, *Histoire du roman francais depuis 1918,* Seuil, 1950, excerpted in *Les Critiques de notre temps et Gide,* edited by Michel Raimond, Garnier, 1971.
Martin, Claude, *Andre Gide par lui-meme,* Seuil, 1964, excerpted in *Les Critiques de notre temps et Gide,* edited by Michel Raimond, Garnier, 1971.
Martin, Claude, *La Maturite d'Andre Gide: De "Paludes" a "L'Immoraliste,"* Klincksieck, 1977.
Martin du Gard, Roger, *Recollections of Andre Gide,* translation by John Russell, Viking, 1953.
Massis, Henri, *Jugements,* Plon, 1924.
Mauriac, Claude, *Conversations With Andre Gide,* translation by Michael Lebeck, Braziller, 1965.

Mauriac, Francois, *Memoires Interieurs,* translation by G. Hopkins, Eyre & Spottiswoode, 1960, excerpted in *Gide: A Collection of Critical Essays,* edited by David Littlejohn, Prentice-Hall, 1970.

O'Brien, Justin, *Index detaille des quinze volumes de l'Edition Gallimard des "Oeuvres completes" d'Andre Gide,* Pretexte, 1954.

O'Brien, Justin, *Portrait of Andre Gide,* Knopf, 1953.

Painter, George D., *Andre Gide: A Critical Biography,* Atheneum, 1968.

Raimond, Michel, editor, *Les Critiques de notre temps et Gide,* Garnier, 1971.

Riviere, Jacques, *Etudes,* Gallimard, 1944, excerpted in *Les Critiques de notre temps et Gide,* edited by Michel Raimond, Garnier, 1971.

Rysselberghe, Maria van, *Les Cahiers de la petite dame: Notes pour l'histoire authentique d'Andre Gide,* Gallimard, 1973.

Tolton, C. D. E., *Andre Gide and the Art of Autobiography: A Study of "Si le grain ne meurt,"* Macmillan (Toronto), 1975.

Twentieth-Century Literary Criticism, Gale, Volume 5, 1981, Volume 12, 1984.

PERIODICALS

Contemporary Review, September, 1909.
New York Times, December 27, 1983, November 3, 1987.
New York Times Book Review, October 2, 1983.
Perspectives on Contemporary Literature, number 8, 1982.
Revue blanche, July 15, 1902, November 15, 1902.
Revue de Paris, August 15, 1927.
Times Literary Supplement, June 26, 1981, March 7, 1986.
Yale French Studies, number 7, 1951.

* * *

GILBERT, Sandra M(ortola) 1936-

PERSONAL: Born December 27, 1936, in New York, NY; daughter of Alexis Joseph (a civil engineer) and Angela (Carvso) Mortola; married Elliot Lewis Gilbert (a professor of English), December 1, 1957; children: Roger, Katherine, Susanna. *Education:* Cornell University, B.A., 1957; New York University, M.A., 1961; Columbia University, Ph.D., 1968.

ADDRESSES: Office—Department of English, University of California, Davis, CA 95616.

CAREER: Queens College of the City University of New York, Flushing, lecturer in English, 1963-64, 1965-66; Sacramento State College (now California State University, Sacramento), lecturer in English, 1967-68; California State College (now California State University), Hayward, assistant professor of English, 1968-71; St. Mary's College, Moraga, CA, lecturer in English, 1972; Indiana University at Bloomington, associate professor of English, 1973-75; University of California, Davis, 1975-85, began as associate professor, became professor of English; Princeton University, Princeton, NJ, professor of English, 1985-89; University of California, Davis, professor of English, 1989—.

MEMBER: Modern Language Association of America.

AWARDS, HONORS: National Endowment for the Humanities fellowship, 1980-81; Rockefeller Foundation fellowship, 1982; Guggenheim fellowship, 1983.

WRITINGS:

Shakespeare's *"Twelfth Night,"* Thor Publishing, 1964.
Two Novels by E. M. Forster, Thor Publishing, 1965.
D. H. Lawrence's *"Sons and Lovers,"* Thor Publishing, 1965.

The Poetry of W. B. Yeats, Thor Publishing, 1965.
Two Novels by Virginia Woolf, Thor Publishing, 1966.
Acts of Attention: The Poems of D. H. Lawrence, Cornell University Press, 1973.
In the Fourth World: Poems, University of Alabama Press, 1978.
(With Susan Gubar) *The Madwoman in the Attic: The Woman Writer and the Nineteenth-Century Literary Imagination,* Yale University Press, 1979.
(Editor with Gubar) *Shakespeare's Sisters: Feminist Essays on Women Poets,* Indiana University Press, 1979.
The Summer Kitchen: Poems, Heyeck, 1983.
Emily's Bread: Poems, Norton, 1984.
(Editor with Gubar) *The Norton Anthology of Literature by Women: The Tradition in English,* Norton, 1985.
Blood Pressure: Poems, Norton, 1988.
(With Gubar) *No Man's Land: The Place of the Woman Writer in the Twentieth Century,* Yale University Press, Volume 1: *The War of the Words,* 1988, Volume 2: *Sexchanges,* 1989.

Also editor of Kate Chopin's *The Awakening and Other Stories,* Peter Smith. Contributor to anthologies, including *Best Little Magazine Fiction,* 1971, *Bicentennial Poetry Anthology,* 1976, *Contemporary Women Poets,* 1978, and *The Poetry Anthology,* 1978. Contributor of fiction and poetry to *Mademoiselle, Poetry, Epoch, Nation, New Yorker,* and other magazines.

WORK IN PROGRESS: The Tidal Wave: Poems; Mother Rights: Studies in Maternity and Creativity; (with Gubar) *No Man's Land: The Place of the Woman Writer in the Twentieth Century,* Volume 3: *Letters from the Front.*

SIDELIGHTS: In *The Madwoman in the Attic: The Woman Writer and the Nineteenth-Century Literary Imagination,* "Sandra Gilbert and Susan Gubar offer a bold new interpretation of the great 19th-century woman novelists, and in doing so they present the first pervasive case for the existence of a distinctly female imagination," writes Le Anne Schreiber in the *New York Times Book Review.* As Carolyn See notes in the *Los Angeles Times Book Review,* the authors examine how attitudes toward women and woman writers held by men and women alike shaped the literature of Jane Austen, Charlotte and Emily Bronte, Emily Dickinson, George Eliot, and Mary Shelley. According to See, Gilbert and Gubar reveal how these woman novelists used the "essentially destructive myth [that a woman writer was an aberration, 'the Devil Herself ']—and their own fears about it to create their own myths, their own world views."

Rosemary Ashton describes *The Madwoman in the Attic* in the *Times Literary Supplement* as a "purposefully written book essentially without a thesis," whose "authors exhaust the reader with . . . formidable but unconvincing rhetoric." She adds, "It is hard not to suspect that they found just what they were looking for, and equally hard to give acceptance to their 'findings.' " Yet, in a *Washington Post Book World* review, Carolyn G. Heilbrun writes, "At last, feminist criticism, no longer capable of being called a fad, is clearly and coherently mapped out." Heilbrun concludes, "*The Madwoman in the Attic,* by revealing the past, will profoundly alter the present, making it possible, at last, for woman writers to create their own texts."

More recently, Gilbert and Gubar have been working on a three volume book of feminist criticism entitled *No Man's Land: The Place of the Woman Writer in the Twentieth Century.* In a *Globe and Mail* review of the first volume, *The War of the Words,* Janice Kulyk Keefer calls the study a "thoroughly provocative (and provocatively thorough) revisioning of the genesis of modernism." Noting that *No Man's Land* was written to be a sequel to *The Madwoman in the Attic, New York Times Book Review* contributor Walter Kendrick remarks that if this latest work "achieves its complementary goal, it will set the direction of feminist criticism for the next generation of students and scholars."

Gilbert, who is also the author of a number of poetry collections, told *CA:* "I see myself as a poet, a critic, and a feminist, hoping that each 'self' enriches the others. As a poet, however, I'm superstitious about becoming too self-conscious; as a critic, I want to stay close to the sources of poetry; and as a feminist, I try to keep my priorities clear without sermonizing. Those *caveats* mean that a statement like this one necessarily has to be short—at least for now."

BIOGRAPHICAL/CRITICAL SOURCES:

PERIODICALS

Globe and Mail (Toronto), February 13, 1988.
Los Angeles Times Book Review, March 2, 1980, May 12, 1985.
Newsweek, July 15, 1985.
New York Times Book Review, December 9, 1979, April 28, 1985, February 19, 1989, March 12, 1989.
Times Literary Supplement, August 8, 1980, April 18, 1986, June 3, 1988.
Washington Post Book World, November 25, 1979, June 2, 1985, January 17, 1988.

*   *   *

GILCHRIST, Ellen 1935-

PERSONAL: Born February 20, 1935, in Vicksburg, Miss.; daughter of William Garth (an engineer) and Aurora (Alford) Gilchrist; children: Marshall, Garth, Pierre. *Education:* Millsaps College, B .A., 1967; attended University of Arkansas, 1976.

ADDRESSES: Home and office—Fayetteville, Ark. *Agent*—Don Congdon Associates, 177 East 70th St., New York, N.Y. 10021.

CAREER: Poet and fiction writer. Journalist. *Vieux Carre Courier,* contributing editor, 1976-79. Weekly commentator on National Public Radio's daily "Morning Edition" show, 1984 and 1985.

MEMBER: Authors Guild.

AWARDS, HONORS: Poetry award from the Mississippi Arts Festival, 1968; craft in poetry award from *New York Quarterly,* 1978; National Endowment for the Arts grant in fiction, 1979; Pushcart prizes from Pushcart Press, 1979-80, for the story "Rich," and 1983, for the story "Summer, An Elegy"; fiction award from the *Prairie Schooner,* 1981; *In the Land of Dreamy Dreams* was named an honor book of the Louisiana Library Association, 1981; fiction awards from the Mississippi Academy of Arts and Science, 1982 and 1985; Saxifrage Award, 1983; American Book Award for fiction from the Association of American Publishers, 1984, for *Victory Over Japan;* J. William Fulbright Award for literature, 1985; national scriptwriting award from the National Educational Television network, for the play "A Season of Dreams."

WRITINGS:

The Land Surveyor's Daughter (poems), Lost Roads (Fayetteville, Ark.), 1979.
In the Land of Dreamy Dreams (short stories), University of Arkansas Press, 1981, reissued, Little, Brown, 1985.
The Annunciation (novel; Book-of-the-Month Club alternate selection), Little, Brown, 1983.
Victory Over Japan (short stories), Little, Brown, 1984.
Drunk With Love (short stories), Little, Brown, 1986.

Falling Through Space: The Journals of Ellen Gilchrist, Little, Brown, 1987.
The Anna Papers (novel), Little, Brown, 1988.
Light Can Be Both Wave and Particle (short stories), Little, Brown, 1989.

Also author of the play "A Season of Dreams" (based on short stories by Eudora Welty), produced by the Mississippi Educational Network. Work represented in anthologies, including *The Pushcart Prize: Best of the Small Presses,* Pushcart, 1979-80, 1983. Contributor of poems, short stories, and articles to magazines and journals, including *Atlantic Monthly, California Quarterly, Cincinnati Poetry Review, Cosmopolitan, Iowa Review, Ironwood, Kayak, Mademoiselle, New Laurel Review, New Orleans Review, New York Quarterly, Poetry Northwest, Pontchartrain Review, Prairie Schooner,* and *Southern Living.*

WORK IN PROGRESS: A novel; short stories; a play; a screenplay.

SIDELIGHTS: With the fall 1981 publication of her first short story collection, *In the Land of Dreamy Dreams,* Ellen Gilchrist gained the attention of the reading public, literary critics, and publishers. During the first few months after the book's publication, about ten thousand copies sold in the Southwest alone, a phenomenon particularly impressive since the book was published by a small university press, was launched with no advertising or promotional campaigns, and was reviewed by major publications only after its public appeal proved itself through sales. The book's acclaim continued to spread by word of mouth, finally reaching an editor at a major trade publishing house—Little, Brown—who offered Gilchrist a cash advance on a novel and second short story collection. In the meantime, critics began to review *In the Land of Dreamy Dreams* in major periodicals, and their assessment concurred with that of the public. As Susan Wood remarked in her *Washington Post Book World* review of *In the Land of Dreamy Dreams:* "Henceforth, Gilchrist may serve as prime evidence for the optimists among us who continue to believe that few truly gifted writers remain unknown forever. And Gilchrist is the real thing all right. In fact, it's difficult to review a first book as good as this without resorting to every known superlative cliche—there are, after all, just so many ways to say 'auspicious debut.' "

In the Land of Dreamy Dreams is a collection of fourteen short stories, most of which are set in New Orleans, and many of which focus on the lives and concerns of adolescents. According to Wood: "They are 'traditional' stories, of real people to whom things really happen—set, variously, over the last four decades among the rich of New Orleans, the surviving aristocracy of the Mississippi Delta, and southerners transplanted—a step or so down in status, it would seem—to southern Indiana. The book's jacket says that the 'prime ingredients' [of Gilchrist's stories] are 'envy, greed, lust, terror, and self-deceit,' and although these are certainly present, there is also humor and self-knowledge and love. It is more accurate to say that *In the Land of Dreamy Dreams* is about the stratagems, both admirable and not so, by which we survive our lives." Jim Crace, in his *Times Literary Supplement* review of *In the Land of Dreamy Dreams,* indicated that the reader's first impression of the book is not necessarily the most valid assessment, noting that Gilchrist's text "is obsessively sign posted with street names and Louisiana landmarks. . . . But *In the Land of Dreamy Dreams* cannot be dismissed as little more than an anecdotal street plan. . . . The self-conscious parading of exact Southern locations is a protective screen beyond which an entirely different territory is explored and mapped. Gilchrist's 'Land of Dreamy Dreams' is Adolescence." Wood likewise noted that many of "the stories in *In the Land of Dreamy Dreams* are peopled with children and adolescents" and commented that "it is unusual to find a writer who understands them as well as Gilchrist does."

The young people depicted by Gilchrist are struggling to come to terms with the way their dreams and aspirations meet with reality and its limitations. Among these characters are an eight-year-old girl who delights in pretending to be an adult in a bar while commiserating with a newly widowed wartime bride; a girl who dreams up a variety of disasters that could befall her brothers, who have excluded her from their Olympic-training plans; a young woman who convinces her father to help her obtain an abortion; another girl who discovers her father's extramarital love affair; and an unruly teenager who disrupts the order of her adoptive father's world, challenges his self-esteem, and so aggravates him that he finally shoots her and then commits suicide. The "chief subject" of the stories featuring these and other characters, according to Jonathan Yardley of the *Washington Post Book World*, "is domestic life among the bored, purposeless, self-indulgent and self-absorbed rich." But domestic is not to be confused with tame. As Yardley observed, the "brutal realities that Gilchrist thrusts into these lives are chilling, and so too is the merciless candor with which she discloses the emptiness behind their glitter." And John Mellors similarly remarked in the *Listener*: "*In the Land of Dreamy Dreams* has many shocks. The author writes in a low, matter-of-fact tone of voice and then changes key in her dramatic, often-bloody endings."

Critics praised Gilchrist's perception, characterization, and style. Yardley remarked of the collection, "Certainly it is easy to see why reviewers and readers have responded so strongly to Gilchrist; she tells home truths in these stories, and she tells them with style." Crace concluded that her "stories are perceptive, her manner is both stylish and idiomatic—a rare and potent combination." Miranda Seymour, reviewing *In the Land of Dreamy Dreams* for the London *Times*, concluded that "Gilchrist's stories are elegant little tragedies, memorable and cruel" and compared her writing to that of fellow southerners Carson McCullers and Tennessee Williams in that all three writers share "the curious gift for presenting characters as objects for pity and affection." And Wood observed: "Even the least attractive characters become known to us, and therefore human, because Gilchrist's voice is so sure, her tone so right, her details so apt."

In 1983 Gilchrist's first novel, *The Annunciation*, was published. It tells the story of Amanda McCamey, beginning with her childhood on a Mississippi Delta plantation, where she falls in love with and, at the age of fourteen, has a child by her cousin Guy. She later marries a wealthy New Orleans man, for whom she represents a Faulknerian character incarnated, and leads a life of high society and heavy drinking for a number of years. She eventually turns away from this lifestyle and returns to school, where she discovers a gift for languages that has lain dormant during the forty-some years of her life. After demonstrating this skill in small literary publications, Amanda is offered the chance to translate the rediscovered poetry of an eighteenth-century Frenchwoman. She divorces her husband and moves to a university town in Arkansas to pursue her translating. Here, in addition to her work, Amanda finds love and friendship among a commune of hippie-type poets and philosophers in the Ozarks. She also becomes pregnant by her twenty-five-year-old lover, who eventually leaves her.

The Annunciation received mixed reviews from critics. Jonathan Yardley, in his *Washington Post Book World* critique of the book, asserted that for "130 pages . . . *The Annunciation* is a complex, interesting, occasionally startling novel; but as soon as Gilchrist moves Amanda away from the conflicts and discontents of New Orleans, the book falls to pieces." Describing the dialogue of Amanda and her fellow philosopher-poets as "sentimental nonsense of the sort that passed for profundity on the college campuses in the '60s and '70s," Yardley explained that once Amanda moves to the Ozarks *The Annunciation* "loses its toughness and irony. Amid the potters and the professors and the philosopher-poets of the Ozarks, Amanda McCamey turns into mush." Frances Taliaferro, on the other hand, reviewing *The Annunciation* in Harper's, deemed Gilchrist's novel " 'women's fiction' par excellence" and described the book as "a cheerful hodgepodge of the social and psychological fashions of the past three decades." Moreover, Taliaferro explained, "Amanda is in some ways a receptacle for current romantic cliches, but she is also a vivid character of dash and humor. . . . Even a skeptical reader pays her the compliment of wondering what she will do next in this surprisingly likable novel." Taliaferro also concluded that, despite some tragedy, the "presiding spirit of this novel is self-realization, and Amanda [in the end] has at last made her way to autonomy."

Gilchrist's next book, the short story collection *Victory Over Japan,* won the 1984 American Book Award for fiction. In their reviews of the collection, critics hailed Gilchrist's return to the genre, style, and even some of the characters of *In the Land of Dreamy Dreams.* Jonathan Yardley remarked, in his *Washington Post* review of *Victory Over Japan:* "Not merely is this humdinger of a book as good as 'In the Land of Dreamy Dreams,' it is even better." Beverly Lowry, reviewing *Victory Over Japan* in the *New York Times Book Review,* commented: "Those who loved 'In the Land of Dreamy Dreams' will not be disappointed. Many of the same characters reappear. . . . Often new characters show up with old names. . . . These crossovers are neither distracting nor accidental. . . . Ellen Gilchrist is only changing costumes, and she can 'do wonderful tricks with her voice.' "

With regard to her "voice," critics noted the writing style used in *Victory Over Japan* to emulate the speech patterns of the New Orleans area. David Sexton remarked in his *Times Literary Supplement* review of *Victory Over Japan,* "Ellen Gilchrist's stories are made from the talk of the Mississippi Delta," and "the drawly 'whyyyyyy not' world of the modern South which she creates is a great pleasure to visit." Gene Lyons, writing in *Newsweek,* deemed Gilchrist a "natural teller of tales" and related her speaking style to her writing, noting: "The minute Ellen Gilchrist begins to talk, a listener knows just where she got the singular vernacular voice that draws readers directly into *Victory Over Japan.*" And Lowry concluded: "The stories are wonderful to tell aloud."

Lowry further noted of Gilchrist's writing in *Victory Over Japan:* "Without much authorial manicuring or explanation, she allows her characters to emerge whole, in full possession of their considerable stores of eccentricities and passion." These characters, most of them women, include Nora Jane, who robs a New Orleans bar to finance a trip to San Francisco to visit her lover and ends up entertaining a carload of children on the Golden Gate Bridge during an earthquake; Crystal, whom Lowry described as a "once rich, very bright and hard drinking" girl with a "dark and crackling sense of humor" and whose escapades are recounted by her black maids; and Rhoda, who appears three times in the collection, first as an eight-year-old more impressed by her classmate's fourteen rabies shots than by the bombing of Hiroshima, then as a frustrated fourteen-year-old Lucky Strikes smoker whose "desire for beauty and romance drove her all day long and pursued her if she slept," and finally as a thirty-four-year-old, sexually adventuresome divorcee who was "poorer than she was accustomed to being."

Commenting on Gilchrist's characters, Lowry noted that the central character is usually a woman and is typically "out on some limb . . . commenting on the view, trying to think of a way down." Yardley, after describing some of what he termed "the many spoiled, willful yet captivating women" in *Victory Over Japan,* remarked: "All of these women, and their men as well, are out for a good time, though what they're more likely to get is a surprise." With regard to Gilchrist's book as a whole, Yardley concluded: "Because many of the stories are connected in ways both obvious and subtle, you feel as though you are reading a novel; at the end you have that satisfied, contented feeling only a good novel can give. . . . 'Victory Over Japan' is an absolute knockout." Lowry concurred, "If we're lucky, there will be yet another [collection], with yet more overlapping tales."

Gilchrist's subsequent volumes—including the short story collections *Drunk With Love* and *Light Can Be Both Wave and Particle,* the novel *The Anna Papers,* and the nonfiction volume *Falling Through Space*—have earned her further recognition as one of America's leading writers. As Betsy Kline reported in her *Chicago Tribune* review of *Drunk With Love,* "There are few pleasures . . . that can match the satisfaction of a collection of short stories by Ellen Gilchrist."

Gilchrist told *CA:* "I write to learn and to amuse myself and out of joy and because of mystery and in praise of everything that moves, breathes, gives, partakes, is. I like the feel of words in my mouth and the sound of them in my ears and the creation of them with my hands. If that sounds like a lot of talk, it is. What are we doing here anyway, all made out of stars and talking about everything and telling everything? The more one writes the clearer it all becomes and the simpler and more divine. A friend once wrote to me and ended the letter by saying: 'Dance in the fullness of time.' I write that in the books I sign. It may be all anyone needs to read."

AVOCATIONAL INTERESTS: "Love affairs (mine or anyone else's), all sports, children, inventions, music, rivers, forts and tents, trees."

BIOGRAPHICAL/CRITICAL SOURCES:

PERIODICALS

Chicago Tribune, October 14, 1986.
Contemporary Literary Criticism, Gale, Volume 34, 1985, Volume 48, 1988.
Harper's, June, 1985.
Listener, January 6, 1983.
Ms., June, 1985.
New Statesman, March 16, 1984.
Newsweek, January 14, 1985, February 18, 1985.
New Yorker, November 19, 1984.
New York Times Book Review, September 23, 1984.
Times (London), November 25, 1982.
Times Literary Supplement, October 15, 1982, April 6, 1984, May 24, 1985.
Washington Post, September 12, 1984.
Washington Post Book World, January 24, 1982, March 21, 1982, May 29, 1983, December 31, 1987.

*   *   *

GILL, Brendan 1914-

PERSONAL: Born October 4, 1914, in Hartford, Conn.; son of Michael Henry Richard and Elizabeth (Duffy) Gill; married

Anne Barnard, June 20, 1936; children: Brenda, Michael, Holly, Madelaine, Rosemary, Kate, Charles. *Education:* Yale University, B.A., 1936.

ADDRESSES: Office—New Yorker, 25 West 43rd St., New York, N.Y. 10036.

CAREER: New Yorker, New York, N.Y., regular contributor, 1936—, film critic, 1960-67, drama critic, 1968—.

MEMBER: Irish Georgian Society (board member), Institute for Art and Urban Resources (president), Victorian Society (vice-president), New York Landmark Conservancy (board chairman), Municipal Art Society (board chairman), Film Society of Lincoln Center (vice-president).

AWARDS, HONORS: National Institute and American Academy of Arts and Letters grant, 1951; National Book Award, 1951, for *The Trouble of One House.*

WRITINGS:

Death in April and Other Poems, Hawthorne House, 1935.
The Trouble of One House (novel), Doubleday, 1950.
The Day the Money Stopped (novel), Doubleday, 1957.
"La Belle," (play), first produced in Philadelphia, 1962.
(With Robert Kimball) *Cole: A Book of Cole Porter Lyrics and Memorabilia,* Holt, 1972.
Tallulah, Holt, 1972.
(Author of introduction) *The Portable Dorothy Parker,* Viking, 1973.
The Malcontents, Harcourt, 1973.
(Editor) *Happy Times,* photography by Jerome Zerbe, Harcourt, 1973.
Ways of Loving: Two Novellas and Eighteen Short Stories, Harcourt, 1974.
(Editor) Philip Barry, *States of Grace: Eight Plays,* Harcourt, 1975.
Here at the New Yorker, Random House, 1975.
Lindbergh Alone, Harcourt, 1977.
Summer Places, photography by Dudley Witney, Stewart & McClelland, 1977.
(Author of introduction) *St. Patrick's Cathedral: A Centennial History,* Quick Fox, 1979.
(Author of foreword) Gene Schermerhorn, *Letters to Phil: Memories of a New York Boyhood,* New York Bound, 1982.
A Fair Land to Build In: The Architecture of the Empire State, Press League of New York State, 1984.
Many Masks: A Life of Frank Lloyd Wright, Putnam, 1987.

Also author, with Derry Moore, of *The Dream Come True,* and of *Wooings,* both 1980. Contributor of short stories to *Saturday Review, New Yorker, Collier's,* and *Virginia Quarterly Review.*

WORK IN PROGRESS: A biography of Stanford White, for Viking; a collection of essays, *Thirties People,* for Harcourt.

SIDELIGHTS: Disdaining the tortured artist myth, Brendan Gill writes fondly of his career at the *New Yorker:* "I started out at the place where I wanted most to be and with much pleasure and very little labor have remained here since." Unlike his colleagues, whom he describes as "lonely, molelike creatures, who work in their own portable if not peasant darkness and who seldom utter a sound above a groan," Gill is amused by his talent. "I am always so ready to take a favorable view of my powers," writes Gill, "that even when I am caught out and made a fool of, I manage to twist this circumstance about until it becomes a proof of how exceptional I am."

Gill, a diversified writer who has produced novels, short stories, essays, film and drama reviews, told *CA:* "Fiction is my chief interest, followed by architectural history, followed by literary and dramatic criticism. If these fields were to be closed to me, I would write copy for a bird-seed catalogue. In any event, I would write."

Author of the popular bestseller, *Here at the New Yorker,* which the *New York Times Book Review* called "delightful" and *Time* termed an "account laced with some acid," Gill is sentimental of the past spent there: "Looking back, I shake my head, not without wonder, at that arrogant, confident beginner." But he is not cynical of the future. "Today I feel emerging on the threshold of old age the latest of the many persons I have been, and even this person may prove, with luck and discipline, only the latest me and not the last."

MEDIA ADAPTATIONS: Gill's *The Day the Money Stopped* was produced as a play by Maxwell Anderson.

BIOGRAPHICAL/CRITICAL SOURCES:

BOOKS

Gill, Brendan, *Here at the New Yorker,* Random House, 1975.

PERIODICALS

Globe and Mail (Toronto), February 6, 1988.
Los Angeles Times, November 29, 1987, December 13, 1987.
Los Angeles Times Book Review, September 20, 1987, November 22, 1987, November 29, 1987.
New York Times, December 9, 1987.
New York Times Book Review, February 16, 1975, December 13, 1987.
Time, February 24, 1975.
Times Literary Supplement, March 24-30, 1989.
Tribune Books (Chicago), November 8, 1987.
Washington Post Book World, November 22, 1987.

* * *

GILL, Patrick
    See CREASEY, John

* * *

GILRAY, J. D.
    See MENCKEN, H(enry) L(ouis)

* * *

GINSBERG, Allen 1926-

PERSONAL: Born June 3, 1926, in Newark, N.J.; son of Louis (a poet and teacher) and Naomi (Levy) Ginsberg. *Education:* Columbia University, A.B., 1948. *Politics:* "Space Age Anarchist." *Religion:* "Buddhist-Jewish."

ADDRESSES: Home—P.O. Box 582, Stuyvesant Station, New York, N.Y.

CAREER: Poet. Spot welder, Brooklyn Naval Yard, Brooklyn, N.Y., 1945; dishwasher, Bickford's Cafeteria, New York City, 1945; worked on various cargo ships, 1945-56; literary agent, reporter for New Jersey union newspaper, and copy boy for *New York World Telegram,* 1946; night porter, May Co., Denver, Colo., 1946; book reviewer, *Newsweek,* New York City, 1950; market research consultant in New York City and San Francisco, Calif., 1951-53; instructor, University of British Columbia,

Vancouver, 1963; founder and treasurer, Committee on Poetry Foundation, 1966—; organizer, Gathering of the Tribes for a Human Be-In, San Francisco, 1967; co-founder, co-director, and teacher, Jack Kerouac School of Disembodied Poetics, Naropa Institute, Boulder, Colo., 1974—. Has given numerous poetry readings at universities, coffee houses, and art galleries in the United States, England, Russia, India, Peru, Chile, Poland, and Czechoslovakia; has addressed numerous conferences, including Group Advancement Psychiatry Conference, 1961, Dialectics of Liberation Conference, 1967, LSD Decade Conference, 1977, and World Conference on Humanity, 1979; has appeared in numerous films, including "Pull My Daisy," 1960, "Guns of the Trees," 1962, "Couch," 1964, "Wholly Communion," 1965, "Allen for Allen," 1965, "U.S.A. Poetry: Allen Ginsberg and Lawrence Ferlinghetti" (TV film), 1966, "Joan of Arc," 1966, "Galaxie," 1966, "Herostratus," 1967, "The Mind Alchemists," 1967, "Chappaqua," 1967, "Don't Look Back," 1967, (narrator) "Kaddish" (TV film), 1977, and "Renaldo and Clara," 1978.

MEMBER: National Institute of Arts and Letters, P.E.N., New York Eternal Committee for Conservation of Freedom in the Arts.

AWARDS, HONORS: Received Woodbury Poetry Prize; Guggenheim fellow, 1963-64; National Endowment for the Arts grant, 1966; National Institute of Arts and Letters award, 1969; National Book Award for Poetry, 1974, for *The Fall of America;* National Arts Club Medal of Honor for Literature, 1979; National Endowment for the Arts fellowship, 1986.

WRITINGS:

POETRY

Howl and Other Poems, introduction by William Carlos Williams, City Lights, 1956, revised edition, Grabhorn-Hoyem, 1971.
Siesta in Xbalba and Return to the States, privately printed, 1956.
Kaddish and Other Poems, 1958-1960, City Lights, 1961.
Empty Mirror: Early Poems, Corinth Books, 1961, new edition, 1970.
Reality Sandwiches: 1953-1960, City Lights, 1963.
The Change, Writer's Forum, 1963.
Kral Majales (title means "King of May"), Oyez, 1965.
Wichita Vortex Sutra, Housmans, 1966, Coyote Books, 1967.
TV Baby Poems, Cape Golliard Press, 1967, Grossman, 1968.
Airplane Dreams: Compositions From Journals, House of Anansi (Toronto), 1968, City Lights, 1969.
(With Alexandra Lawrence) *Ankor Wat,* Fulcrum Press, 1968.
Scrap Leaves, Tasty Scribbles, Poet's Press, 1968.
Wales—A Visitation, July 29, 1967, Cape Golliard Press, 1968.
The Heart Is a Clock, Gallery Upstairs Press, 1968.
Message II, Gallery Upstairs Press, 1968.
Planet News, City Lights, 1968.
For the Soul of the Planet Is Wakening . . . , Desert Review Press, 1970.
The Moments Return: A Poem, Grabhorn-Hoyem, 1970.
Ginsberg's Improvised Poetics, edited by Mark Robison, Anonym Books, 1971.
New Year Blues, Phoenix Book Shop, 1972.
Open Head, Sun Books (Melbourne), 1972.
Bixby Canyon Ocean Path Word Breeze, Gotham Book Mart, 1972.
Iron Horse, Coach House Press, 1972, City Lights, 1974.
The Fall of America: Poems of These States, 1965-1971, City Lights, 1973.
The Gates of Wrath: Rhymed Poems, 1948-1952, Grey Fox, 1973.

Sad Dust Glories: Poems during Work Summer in Woods, 1974, Workingman's Press, 1975.

First Blues: Rags, Ballads, and Harmonium Songs, 1971-1974, Full Court Press, 1975.

Mind Breaths: Poems, 1972-1977, City Lights, 1978.

Poems All Over the Place: Mostly Seventies, Cherry Valley, 1978.

Mostly Sitting Haiku, From Here Press, 1978, revised and expanded edition, 1979.

Careless Love: Two Rhymes, Red Ozier Press, 1978.

(With Peter Orlovsky) *Straight Hearts' Delight: Love Poems and Selected Letters,* Gay Sunshine Press, 1980.

Plutonium Ode: Poems, 1977-1980, City Lights, 1982.

Collected Poems, 1947-1980, Harper, 1984.

White Shroud, Harper, 1986.

OTHER

(Author of introduction) Gregory Corso, *Gasoline* (poems), City Lights, 1958.

(With William Burroughs) *The Yage Letters* (correspondence), City Lights, 1963.

(Contributor) David Solomon, editor, *The Marijuana Papers* (essays), Bobbs-Merrill, 1966.

Prose Contribution to Cuban Revolution, Artists Workshop Press, 1966.

(Translator with others) Nicanor Parra, *Poems and Antipoems,* New Directions, 1967.

(Contributor) Charles Hollander, editor, *Background Papers on Student Drug Abuse,* U.S. National Student Association, 1967.

(Author of introduction) John A. Wood, *Orbs: A Portfolio of Nine Poems,* Apollyon Press, 1968.

(Contributor) Bob Booker and George Foster, editors, *Pardon Me, Sir, but Is My Eye Hurting Your Elbow?* (plays), Geis, 1968.

(Author of introduction) Louis Ginsberg, *Morning in Spring* (poems), Morrow, 1970.

(Compiler) *Documents on Police Bureaucracy's Conspiracy against Human Rights of Opiate Addicts and Constitutional Rights of Medical Profession Causing Mass Breakdown of Urban Law and Order,* privately printed, 1970.

(Contributor of commentary) Jean Genet, *May Day Speech,* City Lights, 1970.

Indian Journals: March 1962-May 1963; Notebooks, Diary, Blank Pages, Writings, City Lights, 1970.

Notes after an Evening with William Carlos Williams, Portents Press, 1970.

(Author of introduction) William Burroughs, Jr., *Speed* (novel), Sphere Books, 1971.

(Author of foreword) Ann Charters, *Kerouac* (biography), Straight Arrow Books, 1973.

(Contributor of interview) Donald M. Allen, editor, *Robert Creeley, Contexts of Poetry: Interviews 1961-1971,* Four Seasons Foundation, 1973.

The Fall of America Wins a Prize (text of speech), Gotham Book Mart, 1974.

Gay Sunshine Interview: Allen Ginsberg with Allen Young, Grey Fox, 1974.

The Visions of the Great Rememberer (correspondence), Mulch Press, 1974.

Allen Verbatim: Lectures on Poetry, Politics, and Consciousness, edited by Gordon Ball, McGraw, 1975.

Chicago Trial Testimony, City Lights, 1975.

To Eberhart from Ginsberg (correspondence), Penmaen Press, 1976.

Journals: Early Fifties, Early Sixties, edited by Ball, Grove, 1977.

(With others) *Madeira and Toasts for Basil Bunting's 75th Birthday,* edited by Jonathan Williams, Jargon Society, 1977.

(With Neal Cassady and author of afterword) *As Ever: Collected Correspondence of Allen Ginsberg and Neal Cassady,* Creative Arts, 1977.

(Author of introduction) Anne Waldman and Marilyn Webb, editors, *Talking Poetics from Naropa Institute: Annals of the Jack Kerouac School of Disembodied Poetics,* Volume I, Shambhala, 1978.

Composed on the Tongue (interviews), edited by Donald Allen, Grey Fox Press, 1980.

(With others) *Nuke Chronicles,* Contact Two, 1980.

Performer on numerous recordings, including "San Francisco Poets," Evergreen Records, 1958; and "Howl and Other Poems," Fantasy, 1959. Work appears in numerous anthologies, including *The Beat Generation and the Angry Young Men,* edited by Gene Feldman and Max Gartenberg, Citadel Press, 1958 (published in England as *Protest,* Panther Books, 1960); and *The New Oxford Book of American Verse,* edited by Richard Ellmann, Oxford University Press, 1976. Contributor of poetry and articles to periodicals, including *Evergreen Review, Journal for the Protection of All Beings, Playboy, New Age, Atlantic, Partisan Review,* and *Times Literary Supplement.* Correspondent, *Evergreen Review,* 1965; former contributing editor, *Black Mountain Review;* former advisory guru, *Marijuana Review.*

SIDELIGHTS: Although an influential figure in contemporary poetry, Allen Ginsberg is also known for his political activities and his interest in the visionary.

Ginsberg first came to public attention in 1956 with the publication of *Howl and Other Poems.* "Howl," a long-line poem in the tradition of Walt Whitman, is an outcry of rage and despair against a destructive, abusive society. The poem's raw, honest language and its "Hebraic-Melvillian bardic breath," as Ginsberg calls it, stunned many traditional critics. James Dickey, for instance, refers to "Howl" as "a whipped-up state of excitement" and concludes that "it takes more than this to make poetry. It just does." Critic Walter Sutton dubs "Howl" "a tirade revealing an animus directed outward against those who do not share the poet's social and sexual orientation." Other critics responded more positively. Richard Eberhart, for example, calls "Howl" "a powerful work, cutting through to dynamic meaning. . . . It is a howl against everything in our mechanistic civilization which kills the spirit. . . . Its positive force and energy come from a redemptive quality of love." Paul Carroll judges it "one of the milestones of the generation." Appraising the impact of "Howl," Paul Zweig notes that it "almost singlehandedly dislocated the traditionalist poetry of the 1950's." Reed Whittemore, although noting that "Howl" is one of "a small number of earth-moving angry poems of this century, poems that poets (and people) who come after have been unable to ignore," nonetheless believes it to be "a sort of natural disaster" for American poetry. "Rightly or wrongly," he writes, " 'Howl' knocked hell out of earlier images of what best minds say and do."

In addition to stunning many critics, *Howl* also stunned the San Francisco Police Department. Because of the graphic sexual language of the poem, they declared the book obscene and arrested the publisher, poet Lawrence Ferlinghetti. The ensuing trial attracted national attention as such prominent literary figures as Mark Schorer, Kenneth Rexroth, and Walter Van Tilberg Clark spoke in defense of *Howl.* Schorer testified that "Ginsberg uses the rhythms of ordinary speech and also the diction of ordinary speech. I would say the poem uses necessarily the language of vulgarity." Clark called *Howl* "the work of a thoroughly honest poet, who is also a highly competent technician." The testimony eventually persuaded Judge Clayton W. Horn to rule that *Howl* was not obscene.

Howl became the manifesto of the Beat literary movement. The Beats, popularly known as Beatniks, included poets and novelists who wrote in the language of the street about previously forbidden and unliterary topics. Ginsberg and such poets as Gregory Corso, Michael McClure, and Gary Snyder were prominent figures in this movement.

In 1961, Ginsberg published *Kaddish and Other Poems*. "Kaddish," a poem similar in style and form to "Howl," is based on the traditional Hebrew prayer for the dead and tells the life story of Ginsberg's mother, Naomi. It is considered to be one of Ginsberg's better poems. Thomas F. Merrill dubs it "Ginsberg at his purest and perhaps at his best." Helen Vendler considers "Kaddish" Ginsberg's "great elegy for his mother." Louis Simpson simply refers to it as "a masterpiece."

Ginsberg's early poems were greatly influenced by fellow Paterson, New Jersey, resident William Carlos Williams. Ginsberg recalls being taught at school that Williams "was some kind of awkward crude provincial from New Jersey," but upon talking to Williams about his poetry, Ginsberg "suddenly realized [that Williams] was hearing with raw ears. The sound, pure sound and rhythm—as it was spoken around him, and he was trying to adapt his poetry rhythms out of the actual talk-rhythms he heard rather than metronome or sing-song archaic literary rhythms." Ginsberg acted immediately on his sudden understanding. "I went over my prose writings," he told an interviewer, "and I took out little four-or-five line fragments that were absolutely accurate to somebody's speak-talk-thinking and rearranged them in lines, according to the breath, according to how you'd break it up if you were actually to talk it out, and then I sent 'em over to Williams. He sent me back a note, almost immediately, and he said 'These are it! Do you have any more of these?' "

Another major influence was Ginsberg's friend Jack Kerouac, who wrote novels in a "spontaneous" style that Ginsberg admired and adapted in his own work. Kerouac had written some of his books by putting a roll of white paper into a typewriter and typing continuously in a "stream of consciousness." Ginsberg began writing poems not, as he states, "by working on it in little pieces and fragments from different times, but remembering an idea in my head and writing it down on the spot and completing it there."

Both Williams and Kerouac emphasized a writer's emotions and natural mode of expression over traditional literary structures. Ginsberg has cited as historical precedents for this idea the works of poet Walt Whitman, novelist Herman Melville, and writers Henry David Thoreau and Ralph Waldo Emerson.

A major theme in Ginsberg's poetry has been politics. Kenneth Rexroth calls this aspect of Ginsberg' work "an almost perfect fulfillment of the long, Whitman, Populist, social revolutionary tradition in American poetry." In a number of poems, Ginsberg refers to the union struggles of the 1930's, popular radical figures, the McCarthy red hunts, and other leftist touchstones. In "Wichita Vortex Sutra," Ginsberg attempts to end the Vietnam War through a kind of magical, poetic evocation. In "Plutonium Ode," he attempts a similar feat—this time ending the dangers of nuclear power through the magic of a poet's breath. Other poems, such as "Howl," although not expressly political in nature, are nonetheless considered by many critics to contain strong social criticism.

Ginsberg's political activities have been called strongly libertarian in nature, echoing his poetic preference for individual expression over traditional structure, In the mid-sixties, he became closely associated with the hippie and antiwar movements. He created and advocated "flower power," a strategy in which antiwar demonstrators would promote positive values like peace and love to dramatize their opposition to the death and destruction caused by the Vietnam War. The use of flowers, bells, smiles, and mantras (sacred chants) became common among demonstrators for some time. In 1967, Ginsberg was an organizer of the "Gathering of the Tribes for a Human Be-In," an event modeled after the Hindu mela, a religious festival. It was the first of the hippie festivals and served as an inspiration for hundreds of others. In 1969, when some antiwar activists staged an "exorcism of the Pentagon," Ginsberg composed the mantra they chanted. He testified for the defense in the Chicago 7 Conspiracy Trial in which antiwar activists were charged with "conspiracy to cross state lines to promote a riot."

Sometimes, Ginsberg's politics ran afoul of the authorities. He was arrested at an antiwar demonstration in New York City in 1967 and teargassed at the Democratic National Convention in Chicago in 1968. In 1972, he was jailed for demonstrating against President Richard Nixon at the Republican National Convention in Miami. In 1978, he and longtime companion Peter Orlovsky were arrested for sitting on train tracks in order to stop a trainload of radioactive waste coming from the Rocky Flats Nuclear Weapons Plant in Colorado.

Ginsberg's political activities have caused him problems in other countries as well. In 1965, he visited Cuba as a correspondent for *Evergreen Review*. After he complained about the treatment of gays at the University of Havana, the government asked Ginsberg to leave the country. In the same year, Ginsberg traveled to Czechoslovakia where he was elected "King of May" by thousands of Czech citizens. The next day, the Czech government requested that he leave, ostensibly because he was "sloppy and degenerate." Ginsberg attributes his expulsion to the Czech secret police who were embarrassed by the acclaim given to "a bearded American fairy dope poet."

Another continuing concern reflected in Ginsberg's poetry has been his interest in the spiritual and visionary. His interest in these matters stems back to a series of visions he had while reading William Blake's poetry. Ginsberg recalls hearing "a very deep earthen grave voice in the room, which I immediately assumed, I didn't think twice, was Blake's voice . . . the peculiar quality of the voice was something unforgettable because it was like God had a human voice, with all the infinite tenderness and anciency and mortal gravity of a living Creator speaking to his son."

These visions prompted an interest in mysticism that led Ginsberg, for a time, to experiment with various drugs. He has said that some of his best poetry was written under the influence of drugs: the second part of "Howl" with peyote, "Kaddish" with amphetamines, and "Wales—A Visitation" with LSD. After a trip to India in 1962, however, during which he was introduced to meditation and yoga, Ginsberg changed his mind about drugs. He has since maintained that meditation and yoga are far superior to drugs in raising one's consciousness, although he still believes that psychedelics could prove helpful in writing poetry. Psychedelics, he has said, are "a variant of yoga and [the] exploration of consciousness."

Ginsberg's study of Eastern religions was spurred on by his discovery of mantras, rhythmic chants used for spiritual effects. Their use of rhythm, breath, and elemental sounds seemed to him a kind of poetry. In a number of poems, he has incorporated mantras into the body of the text, transforming the work into a kind of poetic prayer. During poetry readings, he often begins by chanting a mantra in order to set the proper mood.

Ginsberg's interest in Eastern religions eventually led him to the Venerable Chogyam Trungpa, Rinpoche, a Buddhist abbot from Tibet who has had a strong influence on Ginsberg's writing. The early seventies found Ginsberg taking classes at Trungpa's Naropa Institute in Colorado as well as teaching poetry classes there. In 1972, Ginsberg took the Refuge and Boddhisattva vows, formally committing himself to the Buddhist faith.

A primary aspect of Trungpa's teaching is a form of meditation called shamatha in which one concentrates on one's own breathing. This meditation, Ginsberg says, "leads first to a calming of the mind, to a quieting of the mechanical production of fantasy and thought-forms; it leads to sharpened awareness of them and to taking an inventory of them." Ginsberg's book *Mind Breaths,* dedicated to Trungpa, contains several poems written with the help of shamatha meditation.

In 1974, Ginsberg and poet Anne Waldman co-founded the Jack Kerouac School of Disembodied Poetics as a branch of Trungpa's Naropa Institute. "The ultimate idea is to found a permanent arts college," Ginsberg says of the school, "sort of like they have in Tibetan tradition where you have teachers and students living together in a permanent building which would go on for hundreds of years. Sort of a center where you'd have a poet old enough to really be a teacher or guru poet." Ginsberg has attracted such prominent writers as Diane di Prima, Ron Padgett, and William Burroughs to speak and teach at the school. "Trungpa wants the presence of poets at Naropa," Ginsberg has said, "to inspire the Buddhists towards becoming articulate, and he also sees the advantage of having the large scale Buddhist background to inspire the poets to silence; to the appreciation of silent space in meditation and breath."

Relating his poetry to his interest in the spiritual, Ginsberg once said: "Writing poetry is a form of discovering who I am, and getting beyond who I am to free awakeness of consciousness, to a self that isn't who I am. It's a form of discovering my own nature, and my own identity, or my own ego, or outlining my own ego, and also seeing what part of me is beyond that."

Ginsberg has lived a kind of literary "rags to riches"—from his early days as the feared, criticized, and "dirty" poet to his present position within what Richard Kostelanetz calls "the pantheon of American literature." He has been one of the most influential poets of his generation and, in the words of James F. Mersmann, "a great figure in the history of poetry." Paul Carroll has even speculated that Ginsberg "may become the first American poet to win the Nobel Prize."

How would Ginsberg like to be remembered? "As someone in the tradition of the oldtime American transcendentalist individualism," he has said, "from that old gnostic tradition . . . Thoreau, Emerson, Whitman . . . just carrying it on into the 20th century."

Ginsberg told *CA* that among human faults he is most tolerant of anger; in his friends he most appreciates tranquillity and sexual tenderness; his ideal occupation would be "articulating feelings in company"; his favorite authors are William Burroughs, Hubert Selby, Jack Kerouac, and Jean Genet; he would like to die peacefully.

MEDIA ADAPTATIONS: "Kaddish" was adapted as a film, with Ginsberg as narrator, and broadcast by National Educational Television in 1977.

BIOGRAPHICAL/CRITICAL SOURCES:

BOOKS

Carroll, Paul, *The Poem in Its Skin,* Follett, 1968.

Charters, Ann, *Scenes Along the Road,* Gotham Book Mart, 1971.

Charter, Ann, *Kerouac,* Straight Arrow Books, 1973.

Charters, Samuel, *Some Poems/Poets: Studies in American Underground Poetry Since 1945,* Oyez, 1971.

Concise Dictionary of Literary Biography: 1941-1968, Gale, 1987.

Contemporary Literary Criticism, Gale, Volume 1, 1973, Volume 2, 1974, Volume 3, 1975, Volume 4, 1975, Volume 6, 1976, Volume 13, 1980, Volume 36, 1986.

Cook, Bruce, *The Beat Generation,* Scribner, 1971.

Dictionary of Literary Biography, Gale, Volume 5: *American Poets since World War II,* 1980, Volume 16: *The Beats: Literary Bohemians in Postwar America,* 1983.

Erlich, J. W., editor, *Howl of the Censor,* Nourse Publishing, 1961.

Faas, Ekbert, editor, *Towards a New American Poetics: Essays and Interviews,* Black Sparrow Press, 1978.

Fielder, Leslie A., *Waiting for the End,* Stein & Day, 1964.

Gay Sunshine Interview: Allen Ginsberg with Allen Young, Grey Fox Press, 1974.

Gross, Theodore L., editor, *Representative Men,* Free Press, 1970.

Kramer, Jane, *Allen Ginsberg in America,* Random House, 1969.

Kraus, Michelle P., *Allen Ginsberg: An Annotated Bibliography, 1969-1977,* Scarecrow, 1980.

Lipton, Lawrence, *The Holy Barbarians,* Messner, 1959.

McNally, Dennis, *Desolate Angel: Jack Kerouac, the Beats, and America,* Random House, 1979.

Merrill, Thomas F., *Allen Ginsberg,* Twayne, 1969.

Mersmann, James F., *Out of the Vietnam Vortex: A Study of Poets and Poetry against the War,* University Press of Kansas, 1974.

Mottram, Eric, *Allen Ginsberg in the Sixties,* Unicorn Bookshop, 1972.

Parkinson, Thomas F., *A Casebook on the Beats,* Crowell, 1961.

Portuges, Paul, *The Visionary Poetics of Allen Ginsberg,* Ross-Erikson, 1978.

Rather, Lois, *Bohemians to Hippies: Waves of Rebellion,* Rather Press, 1977.

Rexroth, Kenneth, *American Poetry in the Twentieth Century,* Herder, 1971.

Rosenthal, Mocha L., *The Modern Poets: A Critical Introduction,* Oxford University Press, 1960.

Rosenthal, Mocha L., *The New Poets: American and British Poetry since World War II,* Oxford University Press, 1967.

Roszak, Theodore, *The Making of a Counter Culture,* Doubleday, 1969.

Shaw, Robert B., editor, *American Poetry since 1960: Some Critical Perspectives,* Dufour, 1974.

Simpson, Louis, *A Revolution in Taste,* Macmillan, 1978.

Stepanchev, Stephen, *American Poetry since 1945,* Harper, 1965.

Sutton, Walter, *American Free Verse: The Modern Revolution in Poetry,* New Directions, 1973.

Tyrell, John, *Naked Angels,* McGraw, 1976.

Widmer, Kingsley, *The Fifties: Fiction, Poetry, Drama,* Everett/Edwards, 1970.

PERIODICALS

American Poetry Review, September, 1977.
Best Sellers, December 15, 1974.
Black Mountain Review, autumn, 1957.
Book World, May 25, 1969.
Carolina Quarterly, spring-summer, 1975.
Chicago Review, summer, 1975.
Denver Post, July 20, 1975.
East West Journal, February, 1978.
Encounter, February, 1970.
Esquire, April, 1973.
Evergreen Review, July-August, 1961.
Globe and Mail (Toronto), February 23, 1985.
Harper's, October, 1966.
Hudson Review, autumn, 1973.
Journal of Popular Culture, winter, 1969.
Library Journal, June 15, 1958.
Life, May 27, 1966.
Los Angeles Times, April 18, 1985.
Nation, February 25, 1957, November 11, 1961, November 12, 1977.
National Review, September 12, 1959.
National Screw, June, 1977.
National Observer, December 9, 1968.
New Age, April, 1976.
New York Times, February 6, 1972.
New York Times Book Review, September 2, 1956, May 11, 1969, August 31, 1969, April 15, 1973, March 2, 1975, October 23, 1977, March 19, 1978.
New York Times Magazine, July 11, 1965.
New Republic, July 25, 1970, October 12, 1974, October 22, 1977.
New Times, February 20, 1978.
New Yorker, August 17, 1968, August 24, 1968, May 28, 1979.
Parnassus: Poetry in Review, spring-summer, 1974.
Partisan Review, Number 2, 1959, Number 3, 1967, Number 3, 1971, Number 2, 1974.
People, July 3, 1978.
Philadelphia Bulletin, May 19, 1974.
Playboy, April, 1969.
Plays and Players, April, 1972.
Poetry, September, 1957, July, 1969, September, 1969.
Salmagundi, spring-summer, 1973.
San Francisco Oracle, February, 1967.
Saturday Review, October 5, 1957.
Small Press Review, July-August, 1977.
Thoth, winter, 1967.
Time, February 9, 1959, November 18, 1974, March 5, 1979.
Times Literary Supplement, July 7, 1978.
Unmuzzled Ox, Volume III, Number 2, 1975.
Village Voice, April 18, 1974.
Washington Post, March 17, 1985.

*   *   *

GINZBURG, Natalia 1916-
(Alessandra Tournimparte)

PERSONAL: Born July 14, 1916, in Palermo, Italy; daughter of Carlo (a novelist and professor of biology) and Lidia (Tanzi) Levi; married Leone Ginzburg (an editor and political activist), 1938 (died, 1944); married Gabriele Baldini, 1950.

ADDRESSES: Home—Piazza Camp Marzio 3, Rome, Italy.

CAREER: Novelist, short story writer, dramatist, and essayist. Worked for Einaudi (publisher), Turin, Italy. Member of Italian parliament.

AWARDS, HONORS: Strega Prize, 1964, for *Lessico famigliare;* Marzotto Prize for European Drama, 1968, for *The Advertisement.*

WRITINGS:

(Under pseudonym Alessandra Tournimparte) *La strada che va in citta* (two short novels), Einaudi (Turin, Italy), 1942, reprinted under own name, 1975, translation by Frances Frenaye published under own name as *The Road to the City* (contains "The Road to the City" and "The Dry Heart"), Doubleday, 1949.
E stato cosi, Einaudi, 1947, reprinted, 1974.
Valentino (novella; also see below), Einaudi, 1951.
Tutti i nostri ieri (novel), Einaudi, 1952, translation by Angus Davidson published as *A Light for Fools,* Dutton, 1956, translation published as *Dead Yesterdays,* Secker & Warburg, 1956.
(With Giansiro Ferrata) *Romanzi del 900,* Ediziono Radio Italiana (Turin), 1957.
Sagittario (novella; also see below), Einaudi, 1957, translation published as *Sagittarius,* 1975.
Le voci della sera, Einaudi, 1961, new edition edited by Sergio Pacilici, Random House, 1971, translation by D. M. Low published as *Voices in the Evening,* Dutton, 1963.
Le piccole virtu (essays), Einaudi, 1962, translation by Dick Davis published as *The Little Virtues,* Seaver Books, 1986.
Lessico famigliare (novel), Einaudi, 1963, translation by Low published as *Family Sayings,* Dutton, 1967.
Cinque romanzi brevi (short novels and short stories), Einaudi, 1964.
Ti ho sposato per allegria (plays), Einaudi, 1966.
The Advertisement (play; translation by Henry Reed first produced in London at Old Vic Theatre, September 24, 1968), Faber, 1969.
Teresa (play), [Paris], 1970.
Mai devi domandarmi (essays), Garzanti (Milan) 1970, translation by Isabel Quigly published as *Never Must You Ask Me,* M. Joseph, 1973.
Caro Michele (novel), Mondadori (Milan), 1973, translation by Sheila Cudahy published as *No Way,* Harcourt, 1974, published as *Dear Michael,* Owen, 1975.
Paese di mare e altre commedie, Garzanti, 1973.
Vita immaginaria (essays), Mondadori, 1974.
Famiglia (contains novellas "Borghesia" and "Famiglia"), 1977, translation by Beryl Stockman published as *Family,* Holt, 1988.
La citte e la casa, 1984, translation by Davis published as *The City and the House,* Seaver Books, 1987.
All Our Yesterdays, translation by Davidson, Carcanet, 1985.
The Manzoni Family, translation by Marie Evans, Seaver Books, 1987.
Valentino and Sagittarius, translation by Avril Bardoni, Holt, 1988.

Also author of *Fragola e panna,* 1966, *La segretaria,* 1967, and "I Married You for the Fun of It," 1972.

SIDELIGHTS: Natalia Ginzburg is one of the best-known postwar Italian writers. Her cool, controlled, simple style of writing has impressed critics, while her intimate explorations of domestic life are praised for their authenticity and concern for traditional values. Annapaola Concogni of the *New York Times Book Review* explains that Ginzburg possesses an "ear tuned in to the subtlest frequencies of domestic life, its accents, its gestures, its ups and downs and constant contradictions." Isabel Quigly compares Ginzburg to Chekhov, finding that, when reading Ginzburg's fiction, "Inevitably, Chekhov comes to mind: not only because the long summer days, the endless agreeable but unrewarding chat, the whole provincial-intellectual set-up, recall him, but because the Italian charm, and volatility, and loquacity, and unselfconscious egocentricity, and inability to move out of grooves, and so on, that Miss Ginzburg so brilliantly captures, are all Chekhovian qualities."

"Natalia Ginzburg is at her best when dealing with detail," Marc Slonim writes of *A Light for Fools,* "and her descriptions of children and adolescents have a definite poetic flavor. Most of the incidents and characters are seen through the eyes of an adolescent, and the book has much of the naivete and charm of a child's vision. This 'point of view' in the Jamesian sense gives a unity of diction to the whole narrative." Similarly, Quigly comments, "She has an extraordinary gift for what you might call cumulative characterization-a method that dispenses almost entirely with description and builds up solid and memorable people by the gradual mounting up of small actions, oblique glances, other people's opinions."

Other reviewers are critical of Ginzburg's method of characterization. Thomas G. Bergin writes that the characters in *Voices in the Evening* "are, for the most part, like excellent line drawings, quite real but somehow not 'filled in.' Their bone structure is magnificent, but there is no flesh." And although Otis K. Burger finds the same novel to be "crisp, brittle, entertaining, and informative," he also remarks that "the very coolness of the style tends to defeat the subtle theme of the death of a family (and a love) through sheer lack of gumption. The brevity of the book and its semicomic treatment of a muted tragedy come to seem, not a strength but part of the general, fatal weariness. The 'voices in the evening' tend to cancel each other out—succeeding only too well in presenting people who, pallid to begin with, end as mere phantoms."

Although *Family Sayings* is on the surface a simple family tale, what is beneath and between the lines reveals the weight and worth of the novel. Raymond Rosenthal writes that "what started as a simple family chronicle takes on the timeless, magnificent aspect of an ancient tale, a Homeric saga. It is magical, exhilarating. In the last pages, after all is accomplished and the deaths, the bereavements, the terrible losses of war and social struggle have been counted up, so to speak, the mere fact that Natalia's mother is still telling the same old stories, and that her father—the counter-muse, the rationalistic ogre—is still there to provide the antiphonic accompaniment of grumbles and complaints, becomes mythical in the truest sense. The surface of this book is also its depths."

Gavin Ewart also praises *Family Sayings.* The book exhibits, Ewart notes, "a simple, distilled style, a reliance on the virtues of repetition, an awareness of the ridiculousness of human beings; a great love (reading between the lines) for both her father and her mother; the shadow of Proust. All these are in it. Dealing with more 'tragic' material, it has the control and the only slightly edited reality that one finds in *My Life and Hard Times* (remember Thurber?). Though this is verbal comedy and not farce, it still seems, like that masterpiece, to imply that life can be terrible, but also terribly funny."

No Way concerns Michael, a young revolutionary living in a basement apartment. Ginzburg develops the relationships between Michael and his friends through letters (most of which are written to Michael, few of which he answers). "While Michael is expending what turn out to be his last days," Martin Levin comments, "his father dies, his girlfriend Mara runs through a half dozen patrons, and his mother is jilted by her lover Philip. All of these relationships are assembled by epistolary connections that have the intricacy and the fragility of an ant city. The wit is mordant and comes directly out of paradox." Lynne Sharon Schwartz notes, "The contours of [Ginzburg's] sentences linger in the ear like phrases from great music, familiar, basic truths. Her characters, sad, thwarted, often drab types, are memorable in the manner of people one knew very long ago."

"What makes this book so wonderful," L. E. Sissman declares, "magical even—is that we are never bored by the imprisoned pacings and abortive flights of its people. They all become real and individual and fascinating through the technical gifts of the author. . . . *No Way* is a novel of the curdling of aspirations and the enfeebling of powers among those who heretofore held sway. Its quality lies in its reportorial accuracy, in its fine, warm, rueful equanimity, in its balance in the face of toppling worlds. It is a most remarkable book."

Writing in the *Los Angeles Times Book Review,* Peter Brunette calls Ginzburg "the undisputed doyenne of contemporary Italian letters. Both a successful playwright and essayist, she has also become, through a steady outpouring of quietly memorable fiction over the last four decades, a world-class novelist."

BIOGRAPHICAL/CRITICAL SOURCES:

BOOKS

Contemporary Literary Criticism, Gale, Volume 5, 1976, Volume 11, 1979, Volume 54, 1989.

PERIODICALS

London Magazine, May, 1967.
Los Angeles Times Book Review, December 27, 1987.
New Leader, March 13, 1967.
New Republic, September 14, 1974.
New Yorker, October 21, 1974.
New York Review of Books, January 23, 1975.
New York Times, January 5, 1957, October 6, 1963.
New York Times Book Review, September 1, 1974, June 26, 1988.
Saturday Review, September 21, 1963.
Spectator, August 24, 1956.
Times Literary Supplement, February 5, 1971, April 13, 1973, June 15, 1973, February 21, 1975, March 28, 1975, June 2, 1978.

*   *   *

GIONO, Jean 1895-1970

PERSONAL: Born March 30, 1895, in Manosque, Basses-Alpes (now Alpes-de-Haute Provence), France; died October 9(?), 1970, in Manosque, Alpes-de-Haute Provence, France; son of Jean-Antoine (a cobbler) and Pauline (Pourcin) Giono; married Elise Maurin, June 20, 1920; children: Aline, Sylvie (Mrs. Gerard Durbet). *Education:* Attended College de Manosque, 1911.

ADDRESSES: Home—Manosque, Alpes-de-Haute Provence, France.

CAREER: Banque au Comptoir National d'Escompte de Paris, Manosque, France, clerk, 1911-14, 1918-29; novelist, poet, and playwright. Member of jury, l'Acadamie Goncourt, 1954-70; president of jury, Festival de Cannes, 1961. Director of own film "Cresus," 1960. *Military service:* French Army, 1914-18.

MEMBER: Rotary Club de Manosque.

AWARDS, HONORS: Prix litteraire de Monaco, 1953; Chevalier de la Legion d'Honneur; Chevalier d'Orange et Nassau; Commandeur de l'Ordre Culturel de Monaco.

WRITINGS:

Accompagnes de la flute (poems; also see below), Editions Saint-Paul, 1924, French & European Publications, 1959.

Colline (novel; also see below), B. Grasset, 1929, French & European Publications, 1960, translation and introduction by Jacques Le Clercq published as *Hill of Destiny*, Brentano's, 1929, French-language edition, published with a preface by Raoul Audibert and a response by Giono published under original title, Amis du Club du Livre du Mois, 1958, text edition by Brian Nelson, Basil Backwell, 1987.

Un de Baumugnes (novel; also see below), B. Grasset, 1929, French & European Publications, 1961, translation by Le Clercq, with a preface by Andre Maurois, published as *Lovers Are Never Losers*, Coward, 1931.

Manosque-des-plateaux, Emile-Paul, 1930, reprinted, 1954, published as *Manosque-des-Plateaux, suivi de Poeme de l'olive*, Gallimard, 1986.

Presentation de Pan (also see below), B. Grasset, 1930.

Regain (novel; also see below), B. Grasset, 1930, translation by Henri Fluchere and Geoffrey Myers published as *Harvest*, Viking, 1939, revised French-language edition, edited with notes by Dominique Baudouin, published under original title, B. Grasset, 1967.

Naissance de l'Odyssee, B. Grasset, 1930, reprinted, 1965, new edition, with two works by Pablo Picasso, Club des Librairies de France (Paris), 1960.

Le Grand troupeau (novel; also see below), Gallimard, reprinted, 1972, translation by Norman Glass published in England as *To the Slaughterhouse*, P. Owen, 1969.

Jean le bleu (novel; also see below), B. Grasset, 1932, translation by Katherine Allen Clarke published as *Blue Boy*, Viking, 1946, reprinted, North Point Press, 1982.

Solitude de la pitie (stories), Gallimard, 1932, reprinted, with a preface by Jean Vagne, Editions Rencontre, 1962, new edition, Gallimard, 1970, French & European Publications, 1973.

Le Serpent d'etoiles (also see below), B. Grasset, 1933, French & European Publications, 1962.

Le Chant du monde (novel; also see below), Gallimard, 1934, Macmillan, 1935, reprinted, French & European Publications, 1976, translation by Fluchere and Myers published as *The Song of the World*, Viking, 1937, reprinted, North Point Press, 1982.

Que ma joie demeure (novel; also see below), B. Grasset, 1935, French & European Publications, 1959, translation by Katherine Allen Clarke published as *Joy of Man's Desiring*, Viking, 1940, reprinted, North Point Press, 1982.

Les Vraies Richesses (also see below), B. Grasset, 1936, reprinted, 1960. *Refus d'obeissance* (essay; includes four chapters from *Le Grand troupeau*), Gallimard, 1937.

Batailles dans la montagne (novel; also see below), Gallimard, 1937.

Lettre aux paysans sur la pauvrete et le paix, B. Grasset, 1938.

Le Poids du ciel, Gallimard, 1938, French & European Publications, 1971. *Vivre libre*, two volumes, [Paris], volume 1, 1938, volume 2, 1939.

Precisions, B. Grasset, 1939.

Triomphe de la vie (also see below), B. Grasset, 1942.

(Translator with Lucien Jacques) Herman Melville, *Moby Dick*, Gallimard, 1942.

L'Eau vive (stories), Gallimard, 1943, French & European Publications, 1973, Volume 1: *Rondeur desjours*, Volume 2: *L'Oiseau bague*.

Pour saluer Melville, Gallimard, 1943.

Le Voyage en caleche: Divertissement romantique en 3 actes (play), Editions du Rocher (Monaco), 1946.

Un Roi sans divertissement (fiction; also see below), Gallimard, 1947, French & European Publications, 1972.

Noe (fiction), Table Ronde, 1947, French & European Publications, 1973. *Fragments d'un paradis*, Coulet, 1948.

Mort d'un personnage (also see below), B. Grasset, 1949.

Les Ames fortes (novel), Gallimard, 1949, French and European Publications, 1972.

Village, Prochaska, 1950.

Les Grands chemins (novel; also see below), Gallimard, 1951, French & European Publications, 1973.

Le Hussard sur le toit (novel; also see below), Gallimard, 1951, French & European Publications, 1972, translation by Jonathan Griffin published in England as *The Husser on the Roof*, Museum Press, 1953, published as *The Horseman on the Roof*, Knopf, 1954, reprinted, North Point Press, 1982.

Le Moulin de Pologne (also see below), Gallimard, 1952, French & European Publications, 1972, translation by Peter de Mendelssohn published as *The Malediction*, Criterion, 1955, French language edition, with an afterword by Giono, published under original title, Gallimard, 1958.

La Chasse au bonheur, Berto (Marseilles), 1953.

Voyage en Italie, Gallimard, 1953.

(With Georges Monmarche) *Provence* (travel guide), Hachette, 1954.

Notes sur l'affaire Dominici: Suivi d'un essai sur caractere des personnages, Gallimard, 1955, translation by de Mendelssohn published in England as *The Dominici Affair*, Museum Press (London), 1956.

Jean Giono, ce solitaire (includes previously unpublished work by Giono), edited by Romee de Villeneuve, Presses Universelles, (Avignon), 1955.

L'Ecossais, ou La Fin des heros, Aux depens du Rotary-Club, 1955.

Giono par lui-meme (autobiography), Editions du Seuil, 1956.

Lundi, Dutilleul, 1956.

Le Bonheur fou (novel; also see below), Gallimard, 1957, reprinted, 1976, translation by Phyllis Johnson published as *The Straw Man*, Knopf, 1959. (With others) *Rome*, French & European Publications, 1958.

Angelo (novel; also see below), Gallimard, 1958, translation by Alma E. Murch published in England under same title, P. Owen, 1960.

(With Alain Allioux) *Hortense; ou. L'Eau vive*, Editions France Empire, 1958, reprinted, Livre de Poche, 1974.

Oppede le vieux, Roco & Auphan, 1959.

Sur les oliviers morts, P. Fanlac, 1959.

(Editor and author of notes) Virgil, *Les Pages immortelles de Virgile*, Buchet-Chastel, 1960.

Camargue (travel book guide), Editions Claire-fontaine, 1960.

Menagerie enigmatique de Giono, Aux Depens d'un Amateur, 1961.

Cresus: Livre de conduite du metteur en scene (screenplay), Rico & Auphan, 1961.

(Editor and author of introduction) Yves Brayer, *Carnet du Maroc*, La Bibliotheque des Arts (Paris), 1963.

Le Desastre de Pa vie, 24 fevrier 1525, introduction by Gerard Walter, Gallimard, 1963, translation by Murch, introduction by Walter, published as *The Battle of Pavia, 24th February 1525*, P. Owen, 1965, Hillary, 1966.

Animalites, B. Klein, 1965.

Le Deserteur (also see below), Editions de Fontainemore, 1966.

Deux Cavaliers de l'orage (novel), Gallimard, 1965, translation by Alan Brown published in England as *Two Riders of the Storm,* P. Owen, 1967.

Il Disertore Jacques Joseph Fourny (includes an English translation as a separate folder), Franco Maria Ricci, 1966, Wittenborn, 1967.

Provence perdue, Edition du Rotary Club Manosque, 1967.

Preface a "l'Iliade" (an introduction to Homer's *Iliad*), Ecole Estienne, 1967.

The Man Who Planted Hope and Grew Happiness, translation, introduction by Gaylord Nelson, Friends of Nature, 1967, published as *The Man Who Planted Trees,* Chelsea Green Publications, 1987.

Le Genie du Sud, edited by Claude Annick Jacquet, John Didier, 1967.

Ennemonde et autre caracteres (novel), Gallimard, 1968, translation by David Le Vay published in England as *Ennemonde,* P. Owen, 1970.

Une Histoire d'amour (also see below), French & European Publications, 1969.

(Adaptor) *Les Chute des Anges, Un Deluge, Le Coeur cerf fragments traduit du bulgare,* Editions de Manosque, 1969.

L'Iris de suse, Gallimard, 1970, French & European Publications, 1974.

La Mission (also see below), Editions de Manosque, 1971.

Faust au village (originally published in *Les Oeuvres libres,* Volume 282, number 56, 1951), French & European Publications, 1977.

Ecrits pacifistes, French & European Publications, 1978.

Les Terrasses de l'Ile d'Elbe, Gallimard, 1978.

Angelique (novel), Gallimard, 1980.

Dragoon, suivi de Olympe, Gallimard, 1982.

Les Trois Arbres de Palzem, Gallimard, 1984.

Correspondance Jean Giono-Lucien Jacques (letters), 2 volumes, edited by Pierre Citron, Gallimard, 1981-83.

Correspondance Andre Gide-Jean Giono (letters), edited by Roland Bourneuf and Jacques Cotnam, Centre d'Etudes Gidiennes, 1983.

AUTHOR OF PREFACE OR INTRODUCTION

Marie Borrely, *Le Dernier Feu,* Gallimard, 1931.

Anton Coolen, *Le Bon Assassin,* B. Grasset, 1936.

Leon Isnardy, *Geographie du department des Basse-Alpes,* Mollet, 1939.

J. Poucel, *A la decouverte des orchidees de France,* Stock, Delamain & Boutelleau, 1942.

Anton Hansen Tammsaare, *Le Terre-du-voleur* (novel), translated by Elisabeth Desmarest and edited by Pierre Tremois, [Paris], 1944.

Samivel, *L'Opera des pics,* Arthaud, 1944.

L'Iliad d'Homere, Bordas, 1950.

Maurice Chauvet, *La Route du vin,* Editions des Arceaux, 1950.

Charles Agniel, *Les Compagnons de la Bonne Auberge,* Table Ronde, 1950.

Niccolo Machiavelli, *Oeurvres completes,* Gallimard, 1952.

Albert Detaille, *La Provence merveilleuse,* Detaille, 1953.

Felix Leclerc, *Moi, mes souliers,* Amoit-Dumont, 1955.

Maurice Pezet, *Les Alpilles,* Horizons de France, 1955.

Bernard Buffet, Hazan, 1956.

Romee de Villeneuve, *Dix Ans d'erreurs,* Universelles, 1956.

Maurice Chevaly, *Fleurs artificielles,* Presses Universelles, 1956.

Rome que j'aime, Sun, 1958.

Regina Wallet, *Le Sang de la vigne,* Editions du Scorpion, 1958.

Georges Navel, *Chacun son royaume* (short story), Gallimard, 1960.

Peintres de La realite du XXe siecle, Hades (Paris), 1960.

Tableau de la litterature francaise, volume 1, Gallimard, 1962.

Blaise de Monluc, *Commentaires, 1521-1576,* edited with critical material and notes by Paul Courteault, Gallimard, 1964.

Tristan, Livre de Poche, 1964.

Juan Ramon Jimenez, *Platero et moi,* Rombaldi, 1964.

Merveilles des palais italiens, Hachette, 1968, translation published as *Great Houses of Italy,* Weidenfeld & Nicolson, 1969.

COLLECTIONS AND OMNIBUS VOLUMES

Le Lanceur de graines [and] *Le Bout de la route* [and] *Le Femme du boulanger* (plays; the latter an adaptation of Giono's *Jean le bleu* by Marcel Pagnol), Nouvelle Revue Francaise, 1943, reprinted, Pastorelly, 1974.

Theatre de Jean Giono (contains "Le Lanceur de graines," "Le Bout de la route," "Le Femme du boulanger," and "Esquisse d'une mort d'Helene"), Gallimard, 1943.

Triomphe de la vie [and] *Les Vraies richesses,* B. Grasset, 1943.

Chroniques (includes "Un Roi sans divertissement" and "Noe"), Gallimard, 1947.

Romans (contains "Colline," "Un de Baumugnes," "Regain," "Le Grand troupeau," "Le Chant du monde," "Que majoie demeure," and "Batailles dans la montagne"), Gallimard, 1956.

Domitien, suivi de Joseph a Dothan (plays; the latter an adaptation of the work by Joost van den Vondel), Gallimard, 1959.

Accompagnes de la flute [and] *Lettres a Lucien Jacques,* [Manosque], 1959.

Regain [and] *Presentation de Pan,* Le Club du Meilleur Livre, 1960.

Chroniques romanesques (contains "La Nuit du decembre 1826," "Une Histoire d'amour," "Un Roi sans divertissement," "Noe," "Le Moulin de Pologne," and "Les Grande chemins"), Gallimard, 1962.

Giono Selections, edited by Maxwell A. Smith, Heath, 1965.

Le Bal [and] *L'Ecossais; ou, La Fin des heros* [and] *Angelo* [and] *Le Hussard sur le toit,* Gallimard, 1965.

Cycle du Hussard (contains "Le Bonheur fou" and "Mort d'un personnage"), Gallimard, 1965.

Oeuvres, Rombaldi (Paris), 1965, Volume 1: *Hommage a Jean Giono, by Marcel Achard, [and] Regain [and] Le Serpent d'etoiles;* Volume 2: *Que majoie demeure;* Volume 3: *Jean le bleu [and] Mort d'un personnage;* Volume 4: *Un de Baumugnes [and] Le Vraies richesses;* Volume 5: *Colline [and] Triomphe de Ia vie.*

Oeuvres romanesques completes, six volumes, edited by Robert Ricatte and Pierre Citron, Gallimard, 1971-83, reprinted, 1984.

Le Recits de la demi-brigade (contains "Noe," "Une Histoire d'amour," "Le Bal," "La Mission," "La Belle hotesse," and "L'Ecossais; ou, La Fin des heroes"), Gallimard, 1972.

Le Deserteur et autres recits (contains "Le Deserteur," "La Pierre," "Arcadie . . . Arcadie," and "Le Grand Theatre"), Gallimard, 1973.

Oeuvres cinematographiques, edited by Jacques Meny, Gallimard, 1980.

Coeurs, Passions, caracteres, Gallimard, 1982.

OTHER

Also author of *Images de Provence* (travel guide); Heures Claires, *Recherche de la Purete,* French & European Publications; (with George Pillement) *The Rome I Love,* Tudor; and of preface to *Carnets de moleskin,* by Jacques, 1939. Author of plays "Le Bout de la route" (also see below), 1941, and "Le Lanceurs de Graines" (also see below).

SIDELIGHTS: In *French Novelists of Today,* Henri Peyre wrote: "At the very moment when her political and economic leaders seemed powerless to avert an impending catastrophe, France produced a number of writers whose robust audacity and faith were scarcely equaled elsewhere in Europe. Jean Giono [was] probably the most original among these men." Giono's lifelong home was Manosque, a small provincial town in southern France. It is this pastoral environment that forms the background for much of his work. To a great extent, Giono was also influenced by the ancient Greek tragedies, and he sought to adapt the complex themes of those classics to his provincial setting. He is also known as "a luxury writer," Walter Redfern wrote in *Dictionary of Literary Biography.* "One of [Giono's] texts, 'Le Grand Theatre,' appeared in possibly the most exclusive book ever, encrusted with gems by Salvador Dali, weighing 460 pounds, and valued over a million dollars," reported Redfern. Malcolm Scott of *French Studies* explained, "The fusion of Giono's love of classical literature and his adoration of the Provencal countryside are the two dynamic impulses behind his work."

Throughout his work, Giono displayed a deep love of and respect for nature. He thought of nature as being in a state of constant motion and change, and he endeavored to convey his joy in nature and his belief that it and man are inseparable. Peyre stated that "the chief actors in Giono's stories are the great elemental forces: The wind, the torrents of spring unleashed over field and marsh, the parched earth in summer, the Dionysian dance of reeling odors, which intoxicate his men and his women, and above all, the stars that guide their works and their humble meditations." And Maxwell A. Smith remarked in his study of Giono that, in his earlier novels, "Giono is especially effective in his sense of the movement of natural forces, such as the wind rolling clouds into fantastic and monstrous images, or the melting of mountain glaciers and snowfields in the spring."

Some critics, however, believed that Giono over-emphasized his view of an animated universe. "[Giono's] absorption with natural forces sometimes [tends] to diminish his human figures until they [are] scarcely distinguishable from plant or animal creation," Smith contended. Germaine Bree and Margaret Guiton, authors of *An Age of Fiction: The French Novel from Gide to Camus,* agreed: "Giono's universe is animated to the point of agitation. Everything in his novels is in motion, and everyone is engaged in some precise action. . . . No stream of water, no small seed, no large glacier, fails to vibrate with human feeling. . . . So persistent is this trait that the grandeur of Giono's natural world often gives way to a sort of crowded fussiness."

Despite such criticism, many reviewers praised Giono's early novels for their sense of wonder and delight in the unity of man and nature. According to Peyre, "[Giono] rejected much of our urban and analytical civilization; but he held out hope for despairing moderns. He aimed at rebuilding a new unity in man and endeavored to instil in him the sweet, or bitter, 'lore that nature brings.' " Norma L. Goodrich expressed a similar view in *Giono: Master of Fictional Modes.* She found that one of the author's "chief themes [is] the happiness of man released from society into the wide world as a free adventurer." Goodrich further commented that Giono's novels "afford shelter and comfort by reminding the modern reader, with whom the world is much too much, that beyond his routine and narrow horizons lies a vast, adventuresome universe of freedom and pure delight."

In *The Private World of Jean Giono,* Redfern suggested that by rejecting modern civilization and offering an alternative, primitive view of man and nature in harmony, Giono cut himself off from the modern reader. "Convinced that this century's civilization has been commercialized and atomized, he has tried to construct in opposition a fictional world, self-contained and internally coherent. Yet this is to foster hermiticism. He cannot share this with readers who do live in their times, at least not the whole of it." On the other hand, Smith believed that although Giono set his novels "in the comparatively wild and primitive" countryside of France, his themes "are universal and timeless—the struggle of man for survival against the great forces of nature; the elemental and eternal instincts of love and friendship, ambition and revenge."

During the late 1930s, Giono's work underwent a change in theme and outlook. Some critics suggested that this was the result of the onslaught of the war. A confirmed pacifist upon his return from the first World War, Giono was imprisoned for refusing to serve during World War II. (Giono was also accused of collaborating with the Nazis, a charge which led to his ostracism from French literary circles for several years.) Peyre noted that while the "early novels of Giono [reflect] the radiant search for joy," his later works display his "[obsession] with the memories of the war." Peyre added that in *Batailles dans la montagne* "the dramatic and even the plain human quality of Giono's earlier works seem gone." Scott found that *Que ma joie demeure* is "the last novel to present [Giono's] romantic . . . vision of the peasant's world," and that its successor, *Batailles dans la montagne,* "stresses instead the hardships of a peasant community struggling against a hostile nature." Moreover, Giono was "soon . . . to abandon his *cycle paysan* and embark on his chroniques and historical novels," according to Scott. "He was largely to abandon also the rich imagery of his prewar books."

Maurice Nadeau, author of *The French Novel since the War,* once argued that although Giono shifted the focus of his novels from the grandeur of village life to the grandeur of history, he was still guilty of avoiding the reality of the times. "This escape into the past saves Giono from having to take sides in the controversies of our time and allows him even more than before to turn away from a world that has disappointed him and which he totally rejects."

Regardless of his approach to dealing with the realities of his time, Giono is considered one of the most important French novelists of the century. "Giono [was] first of all a great poet in prose," according to Smith. "It is now generally recognized that he . . . brought . . . a new freshness, warmth, and color to the French language." In writing of Giono's earlier novels, Peyre asserted: "They [ignore] academic subtleties and the fashion of the day. Their heroes [are] not poisoned by complexities. . . . In them the tone of a psychological dissector [has] given way to that of a poetical master of suggestive language and an epic storyteller." And, finally, in discussing the profusion of Giono's work, Smith commented: "What will remain will in all likelihood be only a handful of his novels—but enough to assure him a permanent and distinguished rank among the great novelists of France."

MEDIA ADAPTATIONS: The films "Angele," 1934, "Regain," 1937, and "La Femme du boulanger," 1938, all directed by Marcel Pagnol, were based on Giono's novels. Film adaptations have also been made of *L'Eau vive, Les Grands chemins,* and *Un Roi sans divertissement.*

BIOGRAPHICAL/CRITICAL SOURCES:

BOOKS

Bourneuf, Roland, editor, *Les Critiques de notre temps et Giono,* Garnier, 1977.
Bree, Germaine, and Margaret Guiton, *An Age of Fiction: The French Novel from Gide to Camus,* Rutgers "University Press, 1957.
Carriere, Jean, *Jean Giono,* La Manufacture, 1985.
Clayton, Alan, *Pour une poetique de la parole chez Giono,* Minard, 1978.
Clayton, editor, *Jean Giono, imaginaire et ecriture,* Edisud, 1985.
Contemporary Literary Criticism, Gale, Volume 4, 1975, Volume 11, 1979.
de Villeneuve, Romee, *Jean Giono, ce solitaire* (includes previously unpublished work by Giono), Presses Universelles, (Avignon), 1955.
Dictionary of Literary Biography, Volume 72: *French Novelists, 1930-1960,* Gale, 1988.
Godard, Henri, editor, *Album Giono,* Gallimard, 1980.
Goodrich, Norma L., *Giono: Master of Fictional Modes,* Princeton University Press, 1973.
Meny, Jacques, *Jean Giono et le cinema,* Simoen, 1978.
Michefelder, Christian, *Jean Giono et les religioni de la terre,* Gallimard, 1938.
Nadeau, Maurice, *The French Novel since the War,* translated by A. M. Sheridan-Smith, Methuen, 1967, Grove, 1969.
Peyre, Henri, *The Contemporary French Novel,* Oxford University Press, 1955. Peyre, *French Novelists of Today,* Oxford University Press, 1967.
Pugnet, Jaques, *Jean Giono,* Editions Universitaires, 1955.
Redfern, W. D., *The Private World of Jean Giono,* Duke University Press, 1967.
Robert, Pierre R., *Jean Giono et les techniques du roman,* University of California, 1961.
Smith, Maxwell A., *Jean Giono,* Twayne, 1966.
Ullmann, Stephen, *Style in the French Novel,* Cambridge University Press, 1957.

PERIODICALS

French Studies, July, 1972.
Los Angeles Times Book Review, June 6, 1982, April 5, 1987.
New York Times Book Review, May 30, 1982, July 4, 1982.
Times Literary Supplement, April 17, 1981, May 25, 1984.
Washington Post Book World, July 5, 1981, May 2, 1982.

*   *   *

GIOVANNI, Nikki 1943-

PERSONAL: Birth-given name, Yolande Cornelia Giovanni, Jr.; born June 7, 1943, in Knoxville, Tenn.; daughter of Jones (a probation officer) and Yolande Cornelia (a social worker; maiden name, Watson) Giovanni; children: Thomas Watson. *Education:* Fisk University, B.A. (with honors), 1967; also attended University of Pennsylvania, Social Work School; and Columbia University, School of the Arts.

CAREER: Poet, writer, lecturer; Queens College of the City University of New York, Flushing, N.Y., assistant professor of black studies, 1968; Rutgers University, Livingston College, New Brunswick, N.J., associate professor of English, 1968-72. Visiting professor of English at Ohio State University, 1984; professor of creative writing at Mount St. Joseph on the Ohio, 1985. Founder of publishing firm, Niktom Ltd., 1970. Has given numerous poetry readings and lectures at universities in the United

States and Europe, including the University of Warsaw, Poland; has made television appearances on numerous talk shows; participated in "Soul at the Center," Lincoln Center for the Performing Arts, 1972. Co-chair of Literary Arts Festival for State of Tennessee Homecoming, 1986.

MEMBER: National Council of Negro Women, Society of Magazine Writers, National Black Heroines for PUSH, Winnie Mandela Children's Fund Committee, Delta Sigma Theta.

AWARDS, HONORS: Grants from Ford Foundation, 1967, National Endowment for the Arts, 1968, and Harlem Cultural Council, 1969; named one of ten most admired black women by the *Amsterdam News,* 1969; *Mademoiselle* award for outstanding achievement, 1971; Omega Psi Phi Fraternity award for outstanding contribution to arts and letters, 1971; Meritorious Plaque for Service, Cook County Jail, 1971; Prince Matchabelli Sun Shower Award, 1971; life membership and scroll, National Council of Negro Women, 1972; National Association of Radio and Television Announcers award for best spoken word album, 1972, for *Truth Is on Its Way;* Woman of the Year Youth Leadership Award, *Ladies Home Journal,* 1972; Doctorate of Humanities, Wilberforce University, 1972; National Book Award nomination, 1973, for *Gemini;* American Library Association commendation for one of the best books for young adults, 1973, for *My House;* Doctorate of Literature from University of Maryland, Princess Anne Campus, 1974, Ripon University, 1974, Smith College, 1975, and Mount St. Joseph on the Ohio, 1983; Cincinnati Chapter YWCA Woman of the Year, 1983; elected to Ohio Women's Hall of Fame, 1985; named Outstanding Woman of Tennessee, 1985. Keys to numerous cities, including Lincoln Heights, Ohio, Dallas, Tex., and Gary, Ind., all 1972; New York, N.Y., 1975; Buffalo, N.Y., and Cincinnati, Ohio, both 1979; Savannah, Ga., and Clarksdale, Miss., both 1981; Miami, Fla., 1982; New Orleans, La., Monroe, La., Fort Lauderdale, Fla., and Los Angeles, Calif., all 1984.

WRITINGS:

POETRY

Black Feeling, Black Talk (also see below), Broadside Press, 1968, 3rd edition, 1970.
Black Judgement (also see below), Broadside Press, 1968.
Black Feeling, Black Talk/Black Judgement (contains *Black Feeling, Black Talk* and *Black Judgement*), Morrow, 1970.
Re: Creation, Broadside Press, 1970.
Poem of Angela Yvonne Davis, Afro Arts, 1970.
Spin a Soft Black Song: Poems for Children, illustrations by Charles Bible, Hill & Wang, 1971, reprinted with illustrations by George Martin, Lawrence Hill, 1985, revised edition, Farrar, Straus, 1987.
My House, foreword by Ida Lewis, Morrow, 1972.
Ego Tripping and Other Poems for Young People, illustrations by George Ford, Lawrence Hill, 1973.
The Women and the Men, Morrow, 1975.
Cotton Candy on a Rainy Day, introduction by Paula Giddings, Morrow, 1978.
Vacation Time: Poems for Children, illustrations by Marisabina Russo, Morrow, 1980.
Those Who Ride the Night Winds, Morrow, 1983.
Sacred Cows . . . and Other Edibles, Morrow, 1988.

NONFICTION

Gemini: An Extended Autobiographical Statement on My First Twenty-five Years of Being a Black Poet, Bobbs-Merrill, 1971, reprinted, Penguin Books, 1980.

(With James Baldwin) *A Dialogue: James Baldwin and Nikki Giovanni,* Lippincott, 1973.

(With Margaret Walker) *A Poetic Equation: Conversations Between Nikki Giovanni and Margaret Walker,* Howard University Press, 1974.

SOUND RECORDINGS

Truth Is on Its Way, Right-On Records, 1971.
Like A Ripple on a Pond, Niktom, 1973.
The Way I Feel, Atlantic Records, 1974.
Legacies: The Poetry of Nikki Giovanni, Folkways Records, 1976.
The Reason I Like Chocolate, Folkways Records, 1976.
Cotton Candy on a Rainy Day, Folkways Records, 1978.

OTHER

(Editor) *Night Comes Softly: An Anthology of Black Female Voices,* Medic Press, 1970.

Contributor to numerous anthologies. Author of columns "One Woman's Voice," for Anderson-Moberg Syndicate of the *New York Times,* and "The Root of the Matter," in *Encore American and Worldwide News.* Contributor to magazines, including *Black Creation, Black World, Ebony, Essence, Freedom Ways, Journal of Black Poetry, Negro Digest,* and *Umbra.* Editorial consultant, *Encore American and Worldwide News.*

A selection of Giovanni's public papers are at Mugar Memorial Library of Boston University, Boston, Massachusetts.

SIDELIGHTS: Since establishing herself as one of the preeminent figures in the 1960s black literary renaissance, Nikki Giovanni has achieved international prominence as a poet, essayist, and lecturer. Her speaking tours of the United States and Europe have earned her the nickname "Princess of Black Poetry," as she often attracts sizeable and enthusiastic crowds to her readings. Best known for her books of poems on the themes of self-discovery and black consciousness, Giovanni has also received critical acclaim for her several volumes of children's verse as well as for her albums of poetry read to music, including the best-selling *Truth Is on Its Way.*

In the course of twenty years, Giovanni's work has evolved from the "open, aggressive, and explosive revolutionary tendencies that characterized her early verses" to "expressions of universal sensitivity, artistic beauty, tenderness, warmth, and depth," according to Mozella G. Mitchell in the *Dictionary of Literary Biography.* A central theme remains constant in Giovanni's poetry, however. Mitchell notes that Giovanni has a deep concern "about her own identity as a person . . . and what her purpose in life should be." This introspection often blends quite naturally with social and political activism, as Giovanni herself explains in *Ebony* magazine: "I write out of my own experiences—which also happen to be the experiences of my people. But if I had to choose between my people's experiences and mine, I'd choose mine because that's what I know best. That way I don't have to trap the people into some kind of dreams that I have about what they should be into. An artist's job is to show what he sees."

Giovanni was born Yolande Cornelia Giovanni, Jr., in Knoxville, Tennessee, the younger of two daughters in a close-knit family. She was particularly devoted to her sister Gary and to her maternal grandmother, Louvenia Terrell Watson, who was, Mitchell states, "assertive, militant, and terribly intolerant of white people." Mitchell feels that Louvenia Watson was instrumental in teaching Giovanni responsibility to her own race. When Giovanni was still young, her family moved to Cincinnati, Ohio, the city she still considers home, but she remained very close to her grandmother and spent several of her teen years in Knoxville. In her poetry, essays, and speeches, Giovanni celebrates the warmth of her formative years in Cincinnati and Knoxville. She told *Ebony:* "I had a really groovy childhood and I'm really pleased with my family. . . . Essentially everything was groovy." Mitchell characterizes Giovanni's poetry about her youth as "a return to the source, to the beginning, to the mother's womb, so to speak, from which a glorious rebirth is to be expected."

Giovanni entered Fisk University in 1960 at the age of seventeen. Mitchell describes the poet's ideology at that stage in her life: "Coming from a middle-class family residing in a suburb of Cincinnati, Ohio, she was then a Goldwater supporter who had read much of, among other books, Ayn Rand, cheap novels, and fairy tales. Yet, she was in a state of growth." The independent-minded Giovanni came into conflict with Fisk's dean of women and was released from the school because her "attitudes did not fit those of a Fisk woman." After a hiatus of several years, Giovanni returned to Fisk and became a serious student as well as a budding black rights activist. One of her first achievements on campus was her organization of a successful demonstration to restore the Fisk chapter of the Student Nonviolent Coordinating Committee that had lost its charter.

The 1960s saw a great expansion of the American civil rights movement, as blacks and other minority groups began to call more stridently for recognition, equality, and respect. Soon after her graduation with honors from Fisk University, and following the death of her beloved grandmother, Giovanni began to find a place in the ranks of the black literary movement that sought to raise black consciousness through poetry and prose. In a passage from *Gemini: An Extended Autobiographical Statement on My First Twenty-five Years of Being a Black Poet,* Giovanni credits a roommate named Bertha with bringing about her conversion to revolutionary ideals: "Before I met [Bertha] I was Ayn Rand-Barry Goldwater all the way. Bertha kept asking, how could Black people be conservative? What have they got to conserve? And after awhile (realizing that I had absolutely nothing, period) I came around." Though this passage suggests levity, Giovanni embraced the Black Power movement with great seriousness. According to Mitchell, "Her encounters in the Southern environment and her close observations of the progressive developments in the nation of the civil rights demonstrations, especially in the South, along with the great popularity of Malcolm X and the Nation of Islam around the country, among other things, captured the imagination and enthusiasm of this sensitive young woman."

Giovanni's first three books of poetry, *Black Feeling, Black Talk; Black Judgement;* and *Re: Creation,* were published between 1968 and 1970. The poems in these volumes cover many aspects of Giovanni's life at the time: her commitment to the revolution and anger over society's reaction to the revolutionary leaders, her lovers and the romantic feelings she experiences for them, and her family and emotionally secure childhood. Mitchell describes the poems in these books as "a kind of ritualistic exorcism of former nonblack ways of thinking and an immersion in blackness. Not only are they directed at other black people whom she wanted to awaken to the beauty of blackness, but also at herself as a means of saturating her own consciousness." This poetic "immersion in blackness" becomes evident, Mitchell feels, in the "daring questions, interspersed with ironic allusions to violent actions blacks have committed for the nation against their own color across the world." Giovanni's vision, however, "goes beyond . . . violent change to a vision of rebuilding." According to Alex Batman in the *Dictionary of Literary Biography,* Giovanni is "not so much urging violence for itself [in this poetry] as she is demanding black assertiveness, although one finds it hard to acknowledge that she may be willing to accept violence, even if she is not enthusiastic about it."

Critical reaction to Giovanni's early volumes centers upon her more revolutionary poems. In *Dynamite Voices I: Black Poets of the 1960s,* Don L. Lee observes that "Nikki writes about the familiar: what she knows, sees, experiences. It is clear why she conveys such urgency in expressing the need for Black awareness, unity, solidarity. . . . What is perhaps more important is that when the Black poet chooses to serve as political seer, he must display a keen sophistication. Sometimes Nikki oversimplifies and therefore sounds rather naive politically." Mitchell has a related criticism: "In this early stage of her commitment of her talent to the service of the black revolution, her creativity is bound by a great deal of narrowness and partiality from which her later work is freed." Batman is also one of several critics who find in Giovanni's early books an indebtedness to an oral rather than a literary tradition. "The poems . . . reflect elements of black culture, particularly the lyrics of rhythm-and-blues music," writes Batman. "Indeed, the rhythms of her verse correspond so directly to the syncopations of black music that her poems begin to show a potential for becoming songs without accompaniment." Lee comments: "Nikki is at her best in the short, personal poem. . . . Her effectiveness is in the area of the 'fast rap.' She says the right thing at the right time. Orally this is cool, but it doesn't come across as printed poetry." Batman concludes similarly that in reaching to create "a blues without music," Giovanni "repeats the worst mistake of the songwriter—the use of language that has little appeal of its own in order to meet the demands of the rhythm."

Despite the difficulties Batman and Lee note in the poet's early work, they both praise her as an artist of great potential. Lee writes: "She is definitely growing as a poet," and Batman claims that a careful reading of her verse "shows that the talent is indeed there." Critical reservations notwithstanding, Giovanni's earliest works were enormously successful, given the relatively low public demand for modern poetry. In an article for *Mademoiselle* magazine, Sheila Weller notes that *Black Judgement* sold six thousand copies in three months, making that volume five to six times more sellable than the average. Mitchell suggests that Giovanni's poems of the period brought her prominence "as one of the three leading figures of the new black poetry between 1968 and 1971," and speaking engagements began to fill much of her time.

In 1969 Giovanni took a teaching position at Rutgers University. During the summer of that year, her son Thomas was born. Describing in Ebony magazine her choice to have a baby out of wedlock, she said: "Tommy is what is fashionably known as 'an illegitimate baby' and there's no reason for my going on any other trip. I had a baby at 25 because I wanted to have a baby and I could afford to have a baby. I did not get married because I didn't want to get married and I could afford not to get married." She also told *Harper's Bazaar* that Tommy's birth caused her to reevaluate her priorities. "To protect Tommy there is no question I would give my life," she said. "I just cannot imagine living without him. But I can live without the revolution."

Giovanni's work through the mid-1970s reflects this change in focus. In addition to her collection of autobiographical essays, *Gemini,* she published two books of poetry for children and two books of adult poetry, *My House* and *The Women and the Men.* Mitchell writes of this period in Giovanni's career: "We see evidence of a more developed individualism and greater introspec-

tion, and a sharpening of her creative and moral powers, as well as of her social and political focus and understanding." Reflecting on *The Women and the Men,* published in 1975, Batman notes: "The revolution is fading from the new poems, and in its place is a growing sense of frustration and a greater concern with the nature of poetry itself. Throughout these poems is a feeling of energy reaching out toward an object that remains perpetually beyond the grasp."

The themes of family love, loneliness, frustration, and introspection explored in Giovanni's earlier works find further expression in *My House* and *The Women and the Men.* In the foreword to *My House,* Ida Lewis describes the key to understanding the poet's conviction: "The central core [of Giovanni's work] is always associated with her family: the family that produced her and the family she is producing. She has reached a simple philosophy more or less to the effect that a good family spirit is what produces healthy communities, which is what should produce a strong (Black) nation." Mitchell discusses *The Women and the Men* with emphasis upon Giovanni's heightened sense of self: "In this collection of poems, . . . she has permitted to flower fully portions of herself and her perception which have been evident only in subdued form or in incompletely worked-through fragments. Ideas concerning women and men, universal human relatedness, and the art of poetry are seen here as being in the process of fuller realization in the psyche of the author." Noting the aspects of personal discovery in *My House,* critic John W. Connor suggests in the *English Journal* that Giovanni "sees her world as an extension of herself . . . sees problems in the world as an extension of her problems, and . . . sees herself existing amidst tensions, heartache, and marvelous expressions of love. . . . When a reader enters *My House,* he is invited to savor the poet's ideas about a meaningful existence in today's world." "*My House* is not just poems," writes Kalumu Ya Salaam in *Black World.* "*My House* is how it is, what it is to be a young, single, intelligent Black woman with a son and no man. Is what it is to be a woman who has failed and is now sentimental about some things, bitter about some things, and generally always frustrated, always feeling frustrated on one of various levels or another."

Concurrent with her poetry for adults, Giovanni has published three volumes of poetry for children, *Spin a Soft Black Song, Ego-Tripping and Other Poems for Young People,* and *Vacation Time.* According to Mitchell, the children's poems have "essentially the same impulse" as Giovanni's adult poetry; namely, "the creation of racial pride and the communication of individual love. These are the goals of all of Giovanni's poetry, here directed toward a younger and more impressionable audience." In a *New York Times Book Review* article on *Spin a Soft Black Song,* Nancy Klein writes: "Nikki Giovanni's poems for children, like her adult works, exhibit a combination of casual energy and sudden wit. No cheek-pinching auntie, she explores the contours of childhood with honest affection, sidestepping both nostalgia and condescension." A *Booklist* reviewer, commenting on *Ego-Tripping,* claims: "When [Giovanni] grabs hold . . . it's a rare kid, certainly a rare black kid, who could resist being picked right up." Critics of *Vacation Time* suggest that some of the rhyme is forced or guilty of "an occasional contrivance to achieve scansion," in the words of Zena Sutherland for the *Bulletin of the Center for Children's Books,* but praise is still forthcoming for the theme of Giovanni's verses. "In her singing lines, Giovanni shows she hadn't forgotten childhood adventures in . . . exploring the world with a small person's sense of discovery," writes a *Publishers Weekly* reviewer. Mitchell, too, claims: "One may be dazzled by the smooth way [Giovanni] drops all political and personal concerns [in *Vacation Time*] and completely enters the world of the child and brings to it all the fanciful beauty, wonder, and lollipopping."

As early as 1971, Giovanni began to experiment with another medium for presenting her poetry—sound recording. Recalling how her first album, *Truth Is on Its Way,* came to be made, Giovanni told *Ebony:* "Friends had been bugging me about doing a tape but I am not too fond of the spoken word or of my voice, so I hesitated. Finally I decided to try it with gospel music, since I really dig the music." Giovanni also told *Ebony* that she chose gospel music as background for her poetry because she wanted to make something her grandmother would listen to. *Truth Is on Its Way* was the best selling spoken-word album of 1971, contributing greatly to Giovanni's fame nationwide. "I have really been gratified with the response [to the album] of older people, who usually feel that black poets hate them and everything they stood for," Giovanni told *Ebony.* The popularity of *Truth Is on Its Way* encouraged Giovanni to make subsequent recordings of her poetry as well as audio- and videotapes of discussions about poetry and black issues with other prominent poets.

In 1978 Giovanni published *Cotton Candy on a Rainy Day,* which Mitchell describes as "perhaps her most sobering book of verse. . . . It contains thoughtful and insightful lyrics on the emotions, fears, insecurities, realities, and responsibilities of living." Mitchell detects a sense of loneliness, boredom, and futility in the work, caused in part by the incompleteness of the black liberation movement. Batman, too, senses a feeling of despair in the poems: "What distinguishes *Cotton Candy on a Rainy Day* is its poignancy. One feels throughout that here is a child of the 1960s mourning the passing of a decade of conflict, of violence, but most of all, of hope." In her introduction to the volume, Paula Giddings suggests that the emotional complacency of the 1970s is responsible for Giovanni's apparent sense of despondency: "Inevitably, the shining innocence that comes from feeling the ideal is possible is also gone, and one must learn to live with less. . . . The loneliness carries no blame, no bitterness, just the realization of a void. . . . Taken in the context of Nikki's work [*Cotton Candy on a Rainy Day*] completes the circle: of dealing with society, others, and finally oneself."

Those Who Ride the Night Winds, Giovanni's 1983 publication, represents a stylistic departure from her previous works. "In this book Giovanni has adopted a new and innovative form; and the poetry reflects her heightened self-knowledge and imagination," writes Mitchell. The subject matter of *Those Who Ride the Night Winds* tends once more to drift toward a subdued but persistent political activism, as Giovanni dedicates various pieces to Phillis Wheatley, Martin Luther King, Jr., Rosa Parks, and the children of Atlanta, Georgia, who were at the time of the writing living in fear of a serial murderer. Mitchell suggests that the paragraphs punctuated with ellipses characteristic of the volume make the poems "appear to be hot off the mind of the author. . . . In most cases the poems are meditation pieces that begin with some special quality in the life of the subject, and with thoughtful, clever, eloquent and delightful words amplify and reconstruct salient features of her or his character."

In addition to citing Giovanni's thoughtfulness and creativity throughout the body of her published material, Mitchell praises the poet's capacity for growth as "a singular quality exhibited in her works as a whole. A steady progression toward excellence in craftsmanship is one of the key elements in her development." As Paula Giddings notes in the introduction to *Cotton Candy on a Rainy Day,* "Nikki Giovanni is a witness. Her intelligent eye has caught the experience of a generation and dutifully recorded

it. She has seen enough heroes, broken spirits, ironies, heartless minds and mindless hearts to fill several lifetimes." Later in the essay, Giddings concludes: "I have never known anyone who cares so much and so intensely about the things she sees around her as Nikki. That speaks to her humanity and to her writing. Through the passion and the cynicism of the last two decades she has cared too much to have either a heartless mind or, just as importantly, a mindless heart."

MEDIA ADAPTATIONS: A television film entitled "Spirit to Spirit: The Poetry of Nikki Giovanni," featuring the poet reading from her published works, was produced by the Public Broadcasting Corporation, the Corporation for Public Broadcasting, and the Ohio Council on the Arts. It first aired in 1986 on public television stations.

BIOGRAPHICAL/CRITICAL SOURCES:

BOOKS

Authors in the News, Volume 1, Gale, 1976.
Children's Literature Review, Volume 6, Gale, 1984.
Contemporary Literary Criticism, Gale, Volume 2, 1974, Volume 4, 1975, Volume 9, 1981.
A Dialogue: James Baldwin and Nikki Giovanni, Lippincott, 1972.
Dictionary of Literary Biography, Gale, Volume 5: *American Poets Since World War II,* 1980, Volume 41: *Afro-American Poets Since 1955,* 1985.
Evans, Mari, editor, *Black Women Writers, 1950-1980: A Critical Evaluation,* Doubleday, 1984.
Gibson, Donald B., editor, *Modern Black Poets: A Collection of Critical Essays,* Prentice-Hall, 1973.
Giovanni, Nikki, *Black Judgement,* Broadside Press, 1968.
Giovanni, Nikki, *Gemini: An Extended Autobiographical Statement on My First Twenty-five Years of Being a Black Poet,* Bobbs-Merrill, 1971.
Giovanni, Nikki, *My House,* foreword by Ida Lewis, Morrow, 1972.
Giovanni, Nikki, *Cotton Candy on a Rainy Day,* introduction by Paula Giddings, Morrow, 1978.
Henderson, Stephen, *Understanding the New Black Poetry: Black Speech and Black Music as Poetic References,* Morrow, 1973.
Lee, Don L., *Dynamite Voices I: Black Poets of the 1960s,* Broadside Press, 1971.
Noble, Jeanne, *Beautiful, Also, Are the Souls of My Black Sisters: A History of the Black Woman in America,* Prentice-Hall, 1978.
Tate, Claudia, *Black Women Writers at Work,* Crossroad Publishing, 1983.

PERIODICALS

Best Sellers, September 1, 1973, January, 1976.
Black World, December, 1970, January, 1971, February, 1971, April, 1971, August, 1971, August, 1972, July, 1974.
Bulletin of the Center for Children's Books, October, 1980.
Choice, May, 1972, March, 1973, September, 1974, January, 1976.
Christian Science Monitor, June 4, 1970, June 19, 1974.
CLA Journal, September, 1971.
Ebony, February, 1972, August, 1972.
Encore, spring, 1972.
English Journal, April, 1973, January, 1974.
Essence, August, 1981.
Harper's Bazaar, July, 1972.
Ingenue, February, 1973.

Jet, May 25, 1972.
Los Angeles Times, December 4, 1985.
Los Angeles Times Book Review, April 17, 1983.
Mademoiselle, May, 1973, December, 1973, September, 1975.
Milwaukee Journal, November 20, 1974.
New York Times, April 25, 1969, July 26, 1972.
New York Times Book Review, November 7, 1971, November 28, 1971, February 13, 1972, May 5, 1974.
Partisan Review, spring, 1972.
Publishers Weekly, November 13, 1972, May 23, 1980.
Saturday Review, January 15, 1972.
Time, April 6, 1970, January 17, 1972.
Washington Post, January 30, 1987.
Washington Post Book World, May 19, 1974, March 8, 1981, February 14, 1988.

OTHER

The Poet Today (sound recording), The Christophers, 1979.

*   *   *

GLASSCOCK, Amnesia
See STEINBECK, John (Ernst)

*   *   *

GODOY ALCAYAGA, Lucila   1889-1957
(Gabriela Mistral)

PERSONAL: Born April 7, 1889, in Vicuna, Chile; died in 1957 in Hempstead, N.Y.; daughter of Jeronimo Godoy Villanueva (a schoolteacher and minstrel) and Petronila Alcayaga; children: Yin Yin (adopted; deceased). *Education:* Attended Pedagogical College, Santiago, Chile.

CAREER: Poet and author. Primary and secondary school teacher and administrator in Chile, including position as principal of Liceo de Senoritas, Santiago, 1910-22; adviser to Mexican minister of education Jose Vasconcelos, 1922; visiting professor at Barnard and Middlebury colleges and the University of Puerto Rico. League of Nations, Chilean delegate to Institute of Intellectual Cooperation, member of Committee of Arts and Letters; consul in Italy, Spain, Portugal, Brazil, and the United States.

AWARDS, HONORS: Juegos Florales laurel crown and gold medal from the city of Santiago, Chile, 1914, for *Sonetos de la muerte;* Nobel Prize for literature from the Swedish Academy, 1945; honorary degree from the University of Chile.

WRITINGS:

UNDER PSEUDONYM GABRIELA MISTRAL

Desolacion (poetry and prose; title means "Desolation"; also see below), preliminary notes by Instituto de las Espanas, Instituto de las Espanas en los Estados Unidos (New York), 1922, 2nd edition augmented by Mistral, additional prologue by Pedro Prado, Nascimento, 1923, 3rd edition, prologues by Prado and Hernan Diaz Arrieta (under pseudonym Alone), 1926, new edition with prologue by Roque Esteban Scarpa, Bello, 1979 (variations in content among these and other editions).
(Editor and contributor) *Lecturas para mujeres* (essays; also see below), introduction by Mistral, Secretaria de Educacion (Mexico), 1923, 4th edition, edited with an apology by Palma Guillen de Nicolau, Porrua (Mexico), 1967.
Ternura: Canciones de ninos (title means "Tenderness"; also see below), Saturnino Calleja (Madrid), 1924, enlarged edition, Espasa Calpe, 1945, 8th edition, 1965.

Nubes blancas (poesias), y la oracion de la maestra (poetry and prose; includes selections from *Desolacion* and *Ternura* and complete text of "Oracion de la maestra"), B. Bauza (Barcelona), 1925.
Poesias, Cervantes (Barcelona), c. 1936.
Tala (poetry; title means "Felling"; also see below), Sur (Buenos Aires), 1938, abridged edition, Losada, 1946, reprinted with introduction by Alfonso Calderon, Bello, 1979.
Antologia: Seleccion de la autora (includes selections from *Desolacion, Tala,* and *Ternura*), selected by Mistral, prologue by Ismael Edwards Matte, ZigZag, 1941, 3rd edition published as *Antologia,* prologue by Alone, 1953.
Pequena antologia (selected poetry and prose), Escuela Nacional de Artes Graficas, 1950.
Poemas de las madres, epilogue by Antonio R. Romero, illustrations by Andre Racz, Pacifico, 1950.
Lagar (poetry; title means "Wine Press"), Pacifico, 1954.
Obras selectas, Pacifico, 1954.
Los mejores versos, prologue by Simon Latino, Nuestra America (Buenos Aires), 1957.
Canto a San Francisco, El Eco Franciscano, 1957.
Epistolario, introduction by Raul Silva Castro, Anales de la Universidad de Chile, 1957.
Mexico maravilloso (essays and poetry originally published in *Lecturas para mujeres* and periodical *El Maestro*), selected with an introduction by Andres Henestrosa, Stylo (Mexico), 1957.
Produccion de Gabriela Mistral de 1912 a 1918 (poetry, prose, and letters, most previously unpublished), edited by Silva Castro, Anales de la Universidad de Chile, 1957.
Recados: Contando a Chile, selected with prologue by Alfonso M. Escudero, Pacifico, 1957.
Selected Poems of Gabriela Mistral, translated by Langston Hughes, Indiana University Press, 1957.
Croquis mexicanos: Gabriela Mistral en Mexico (contains prose selections from *Lecturas para mujeres,* poetry, and a pedagogical lecture titled "Imagen y palabra en la educacion"), B. Costa-Amic (Mexico), c. 1957, reprinted, Nascimento, 1978.
Poesias completas, edited by Margaret Bates, prologues by Julio Saavedra Molina and Dulce Maria Loynaz, Aguilar (Madrid), 1958, 3rd edition, introduction by Esther de Caceres, 1966.
Poema de Chile, revisions by Doris Dana, Pomaire, 1967.
Antologia de Gabriela Mistral, selected with prologue by Emma Godoy, B. Costa-Amic, 1967.
Poesias, edited with a prologue by Eliseo Diego, Casa de las Americas, 1967.
Homenaje a Gabriela Mistral, Orfeo, 1967.
Selected Poems of Gabriela Mistral, translated by Dana, Johns Hopkins Press, 1971.
Todas ibamos a ser reinas, Quimantu, 1971.
Antologia general de Gabriela Mistral (poems, essays, and letters; portions originally published in periodical *Orfeo,* 1969), Comite de Homenaje a Gabriela Mistral, 1973.
Antologia poetica de Gabriela Mistral, selected with a prologue by Calderon, Universitaria, 1974.
Cartas de amor de Gabriela Mistral, Bello, 1978.
Prosa religiosa de Gabriela Mistral, notes and introduction by Luis Vargas Saavedra, Bello, 1978.
Gabriela presente, selected by Ines Moreno, Literatura Americana Reunida, 1987.

Also author of *Sonetos de la muerte,* 1914, and "An Appeal to World Conscience: The Genocide Convention," 1956. Author of fables, including *Grillos y ranas,* translation by Dana published as *Crickets and Frogs,* Atheneum, 1972, and *Elefante y su secreto,* adaptation and translation by Dana published as *The Elephant and His Secret,* Atheneum, 1974. Poetry for children published as *El nino en la poesia de Gabriela Mistral,* 1978. Correspondence between Mistral and Matilde Ladron de Guevara published as *Gabriela Mistral, "rebelde magnifica,"* 1957.

Contributor to periodicals, including *Bulletin, Commonweal, Living Age,* and *Poetry.*

SIDELIGHTS: Nobel laureate Gabriela Mistral—whose actual name was Lucila Godoy Alcayaga—was a prominent Latin American poet, educator, and diplomat. A Chilean native of Spanish, Basque, and Indian descent, she was raised in a northern rural farming community. Following the example of her father, Mistral initially pursued a career in education, beginning as a primary school teacher at the age of fifteen. Over the next decade, she went on to become a secondary school professor, inspector general, and ultimately a school director. A leading authority on rural education, Mistral served as an adviser to Mexican minister of education Jose Vasconcelos in the early 1920s. Her background in teaching and value as an educational consultant led to her active service in the Chilean government. Mistral is probably best known, however, for her brand of rich but unpretentious lyrical poetry.

The tragic suicide of her fiance in the early 1900s prompted Mistral to compose her first lines of melancholy verse. Within several years she completed a small body of poetry that she would later publish under the Mistral pseudonym (which is said to be either a tribute to poets Gabriele D'Annunzio and Frederic Mistral or a combined reference to the archangel Gabriel and the brutal northerly wind, or "mistral," of southern France). Having entered her *Sonetos de la muerte* ("Sonnets on Death") in a Santiago writing contest in 1914, she earned first prize and instant fame, developing in ensuing years a reputation as one of Latin America's most gifted poets.

Critics have noted the joint influences of biblical verse and the works of Hindu poet Rabindranath Tagore and Nicaraguan poet Ruben Dario on the literary development of Mistral. She frequently expressed through her verse an urgent concern for outcasts, underprivileged or otherwise impoverished people, and ancestors—the poet donated profits from her third book to Basque children orphaned in the Spanish Civil War. Her simple, unadorned writings evoke a sense of mystery and isolation, centering on themes of love, death, childhood, maternity, and religion. Mistral had turned to religion for solace in her despair over the loss of her intended husband. Her first volume of poetry, *Desolacion* ("Desolation"), is imbued with the spirit of an individual's struggle to reconcile personal fulfillment with the will of God. In expressing her grief and anguish throughout the collection with characteristic passion and honesty, Mistral "talks to Christ as freely as to a child," commented Mildred Adams in *Nation.*

Several critics on Mistral, including Adams, have suggested that both her lover's death and her failure to bear his child inspired in the poet a fervent dedication to children. *Ternura* ("Tenderness"), her 1924 volume of children's poetry, is a celebration of the joys of birth and motherhood. While *Desolacion* reflects the pain of a lost love and an obsession with death, *Ternura* is generally considered a work of renewed hope and understanding. Infused with a decidedly Christian temper, the poems in the latter collection are among the most sentimental written by Mistral, and they evoke the poet's overriding desire to attain harmony and peace in her life.

Correlating Mistral's treatment of the love theme with her frequent depiction of mother and child, Sidonia Carmen Rosenbaum theorized in *Modern Women Poets of Spanish America:* "Her conception of love is . . . profoundly religious and pure. Its purpose is not to appease desire, to satisfy carnal appetites, but soberly to give thought to the richest, the most precious, the most sacred heritage of woman: maternity." *Saturday Review* contributor Edwin Honig expressed a similar view, noting that for Mistral, "Childbearing . . . approximates a mystic condition: it is like finding union with God. . . . The experience of gestating another life inside oneself is the supreme act of creation."

Though consistently stark, simple, and direct, Mistral's later verse is marked by a growing maturity and sense of redemption and deliverance. The 1938 collection *Tala* ("Felling"), according to Rosenbaum, possesses "a serenity that reveals an emotion more contained (whose key note is hope) and . . . an expression less tortured" than the early works and therefore continues Mistral's path toward renewal. The poet achieved a greater objectivity in both this work and her final volume of poetry, *Lagar* ("Wine Press"), which was published in 1954. Through pure and succinct language, *Lagar* conveys Mistral's acceptance of death and marks her growing freedom from bitterness. Several critics have implied that this collection—the culmination of her literary career—is both a refinement of her simple and skillful writing style and a testament to her strengthened faith and ultimate understanding of God. As Fernando Alegria explained in *Las fronteras del realismo: Literatura chilena del siglo XX,* "Here we have the secret dynamism [of the poet's verse]; it contains a salvation."

In *Gabriela Mistral: The Poet and Her Work,* Margot Arce de Vazquez concluded: "[Mistral's] poetry possesses the merit of consummate originality, of a voice of its own, authentic and consciously realized. The affirmation within this poetry of the intimate 'I,' removed from everything foreign to it, makes it profoundly human, and it is this human quality that gives it its universal value."

BIOGRAPHICAL/CRITICAL SOURCES:

BOOKS

Alegria, Fernando, *Las fronteras del realismo: Literatura chilena del siglo XX,* ZigZag, 1962.
de Vazquez, Margot Arce, *Gabriela Mistral: The Poet and Her Work,* translated by Helene Masslo Anderson, New York University Press, 1964.
Foster, David William and Virginia Ramos Foster, editors, *Modern Latin American Literature,* Volume 2, Ungar, 1975.
Mistral, Gabriela, *Selected Poems of Gabriela Mistral,* translated by Doris Dana, Johns Hopkins Press, 1971.
Rosenbaum, Sidonia Carmen, *Modern Women Poets of Spanish America: The Precursors, Delmira Agustini, Gabriela Mistral, Alfonsina Storni, Juana de Ibarbourou,* Hispanic Institute in the United States, 1945.
Szmulewicz, Efraim, *Gabriela Mistral: Biografia emotiva,* Sol de Septiembre, 1967.
Taylor, Martin C., *Gabriela Mistral's Religious Sensibility,* University of California Press, 1968.
Twentieth-Century Literary Criticism, Volume 2, Gale, 1979.
Vargas Saavedra, Luis, editor, *El otro suicida de Gabriela Mistral,* Universidad Catolica de Chile, 1985.

PERIODICALS

Cuadernos Americanos, September-October, 1962.
Living Age, November 29, 1924.

Nation, December 29, 1945.
Poet Lore, winter, 1940.
Saturday Review, March 22, 1958, July 17, 1971.

—*Sketch by Barbara Carlisle Bigelow*

*   *   *

GODWIN, Gail (Kathleen) 1937-

PERSONAL: Born June 18, 1937, in Birmingham, Ala.; daughter of Mose Winston and Kathleen (a teacher and writer; maiden name, Krahenbuhl) Godwin; married Douglas Kennedy (a photographer), 1960 (divorced); married Ian Marshall (a psychotherapist), 1965 (divorced, 1966). *Education:* Attended Peace Junior College, 1955-57; University of North Carolina, B.A., 1959; University of Iowa, M.A., 1968, Ph.D., 1971.

ADDRESSES: Home—R.D. Box 248, Woodstock, N.Y. 12498. *Agent*—John Hawkins, Paul R. Reynolds, Inc., 71 West 23rd St., New York, N.Y. 10010.

CAREER: Miami Herald, Miami, Fla., reporter, 1959-60; U.S. Embassy, London, England, travel consultant in U.S. Travel Service, 1962-65; University of Iowa, Iowa City, instructor in English literature, 1967-71, instructor in Writer's Workshop, 1972-73; University of Illinois, Center for Advanced Studies, Urbana-Champaign, fellow, 1971-72; writer. Special lecturer in Brazil for United States Information Service, State Department Cultural Program, spring, 1976; lecturer in English and creative writing at colleges and universities, including Vassar College, spring, 1977, and Columbia University, beginning in fall, 1978.

MEMBER: P.E.N. Authors Guild, National Book Critics Circle, A.S.C.A.P., Modern Language Association of America.

AWARDS, HONORS: National Endowment for the Arts grant in creative writing, 1974-75; nominated for a National Book Award, 1974, for *The Odd Woman;* Guggenheim fellowship in creative writing, 1975-76; National Endowment for the Arts grant for librettists, 1977-78; nominated for American Book awards, 1980, for *Violet Clay,* and 1982, for *A Mother and Two Daughters;* Award in Literature, American Institute and Academy of Arts and Letters, 1981.

WRITINGS:

NOVELS

The Perfectionists, Harper, 1970.
Glass People, Knopf, 1972.
The Odd Woman, Knopf, 1974.
Violet Clay (Book-of-the-Month Club alternate selection), Knopf 1978.
A Mother and Two Daughters (Book-of-the-Month Club alternate selection), Viking, 1982.
The Finishing School (Book-of-the-Month Club alternate selection), Viking, 1985.
A Southern Family, Morrow, 1987.

OTHER

Dream Children (short stories), Knopf, 1976.
(Contributor) Janet Sternburg, editor, *The Writer on Her Work* (essays), Norton, 1980.
(Contributor) *Real Life* (short stories), Doubleday, 1981.
Mr. Bedford and the Muses (a novella and short stories), Viking, 1983.
(Editor with Shannon Ravenel) *The Best American Short Stories, 1985,* Houghton, 1985.

Librettist of musical works by Robert Starer, "The Last Lover," first produced in Katonah, New York, 1975, "Journals of a Songmaker," first produced in Pittsburgh with Pittsburgh Symphony Orchestra, 1976, "Apollonia," first produced in Minneapolis, 1979, "Anna Margarita's Will," recorded by C.R.I., 1980, and "Remembering Felix," 1987.

Contributor of essays and short stories to periodicals, including *Atlantic, Antaeus, Ms., Harper's, Writer, McCall's, Cosmopolitan, North American Review, Paris Review,* and *Esquire.* Reviewer for *North American Review, New York Times Book Review, Chicago Tribune Book World,* and *New Republic.* Member of editorial board of *Writer.*

SIDELIGHTS: "More than any other contemporary writer, Gail Godwin reminds me of 19th century pleasures, civilized, passionate about ideas, ironic about passions," Carol Sternhell states in a *Village Voice* review of *The Finishing School.* "Her characters—sensible, intelligent women all—have houses, histories, ghosts; they comfortably inhabit worlds both real and literary, equally at home in North Carolina, Greenwich Village and the England of *Middlemarch.*" Godwin's protagonists are modern women, though, often creative and frequently Southern. And like many other writers of her era, she tends to focus "sharply on the relationships of men and women who find their roles no longer clearly delineated by tradition and their freedom yet strange and not entirely comfortable," Carl Solana Weeks says in *Dictionary of Literary Biography.*

The characters in her first published novels, *The Perfectionists* and *Glass People,* deal with the conflicting pulls of marriage and individuality, while *The Odd Woman, Violet Clay, Mr. Bedford and the Muses,* and *The Finishing School* concern the relationship of the world of art and literature to women's lives. *Mother and Two Daughters* is a comedy of manners which portrays women who "are able to achieve a kind of balance, to find ways of fully becoming themselves that don't necessitate a rejection of everything in their heritage," Susan Wood relates in *Washington Post Book World.*

Mother and Two Daughters is a "panoramic story," Godwin's "biggest and most popular book so far," Sternhell indicates, and some of its appeal may be due to its optimism. For example, although the plots of both *The Finishing School* and *A Mother and Two Daughters* are "set in motion by the death of a father and the adjustments demanded of the women he protected," Paul Gray notes in *Time,* he argues that Godwin has made things easier on the survivors in *A Mother and Two Daughters.* "In this spacious, harmonious book—an expansive and imaginative celebration of American life—Gail Godwin retrieves her heroines from impasses," Josephine Hendin says in the *New York Times Book Review.* "Through characters who are recognizable contemporaries, she takes us back to an Emersonian faith in the human capacity for good, for betterment."

The book is also "the richest, and most universal" of Godwin's works, "with a wholeness about its encompassing view of a large Southern family," according to Louise Sweeney in *Christian Science Monitor,* and is widely regarded as an unusually artful bestseller, appealing not only to the general public but also to Godwin's longtime followers. Godwin told John F. Baker in *Publishers Weekly* that she thinks of the novel as "a broadening of my canvas," while *Washington Post Book World* reviewer Jonathan Yardley finds the novel "a work of complete maturity and artistic control, one that I'm fully confident will find a permanent and substantial place in our national literature," as well as "a populous, exuberant expansive novel in the victorian tradition." Godwin "turns out—this was not really evident in her four previous books—to be a stunningly gifted novelist of manners," Yardley comments.

Set against a current events background of the Iranian revolution, Three Mile Island, and Skylab, *A Mother and Two Daughters* opens in the changing town of Mountain City, North Carolina (a fictional city), with the death of Leonard Strickland of a heart attack as he is driving home with his wife from a party. The book records "the reactions and relationships of his wife Nell and daughters Cate and Lydia, both in their late thirties, as the bereavement forces each of them to evaluate the achievement and purpose of their own lives," Jennifer Uglow writes in *Times Literary Supplement.* "As each woman exerts her claims on the others, as each confronts the envy and anger the others can inspire," Hendin relates, "Gail Godwin orchestrates their entanglements with great skill." And "for the first time," according to Baker, "Godwin enters several very different minds and personalities, those of her three protagonists."

Lydia, the more conventional, younger daughter, well-organized and efficient, was married young to a loving, financially successful husband. She has just walked out on their marriage, taking one of her sons, to return to college. "We see her begin a love relationship," Marge Piercy comments in *Chicago Tribune,* "cement a new friendship with her black sociology professor Renee," and, in Uglow's words, transform "both her domestic virtues and her ladylike inheritance into media chic by starring in a television cookery show." Cate, the unconventional, politically radical daughter, is twice-divorced, and the small college at which she teaches is failing. An abrasive, perpetually dissatisfied and intolerant woman approaching the age of forty, she's never published and faces the prospect of having to start over again. She must now decide whether to solve all her problems by marrying a wealthy man who loves her.

The "life of an affluent white woman with her book club, volunteer work and parties is seen with wry affection, through the eyes of Nell," reports Piercy. "It most surprised me that I could get into the head of an elderly woman," Godwin told Baker, "but in fact it was easy. Her state of calm acceptance, her ability to sense the stillness at the center of things, is what most aspire to." Nell, Lisa Schwarzbaum comments in *Detroit News,* "raised to be a gracious gentlewoman—albeit sharper, more direct, less genteel, more 'North-thinking' than the other good ladies of Mountain City, N.C.—faces her future without the philosophical, steadying man on whom she had relied so thoroughly for support and definition." Here, according to Anne Tyler in *New Republic,* Godwin provides the reader with a "meticulous" documentation of small-town life with its "rituals of Christmas party and book club meeting."

Not content to focus only on the three main characters, though, Godwin portrays "one great enormous pot of people," declares Caroline Moorhead in *Spectator,* a whole "series of characters in all their intertwined relationships with each other, each other's lovers, children, parents, acquaintances." According to Uglow, the cast includes "a Southern grande dame with a pregnant teenage protege; a pesticide baron with two sons, one retarded, the other gay; a hillbilly relative whose nose was bitten off in a brawl; [and] a one-legged Vietnam veteran whose wife runs a local nursery school." Christopher Lehmann-Haupt in the *New York Times* says that these characters are amazingly vivid, citing "the sense one gets that their lives are actually unfolding in the same world as yours." As Godwin told Baker, the rich man's retarded son "loves to look at the boats passing in the river below their castle," leading her editor to suggest, " 'Wouldn't he buy him a really great telescope?' And of course

he would, so I wrote it in." Tyler indicates that "there's an observant, amused, but kindly eye at work here, and not a single cheap shot is taken at these people who might so easily have been caricatures in someone else's hands."

The story is "a comedy in the classic sense," John B. Breslin writes in *America,* "moving from dispersion to reunion." In Godwin's epilogue, set in 1984, the "intense, often contentious characters assemble for a sort of utopian jamboree on a mountaintop in North Carolina," *New York Times Book Review* critic Judith Gies writes, "and the author is able to make us believe, with them, in the possibility of harmony." *Village Voice* critic Mary Logue argues that "the happy endings [Godwin] provides deny these characters the freedom of their own fate," while *Time* reviewer Paul Gray maintains that the ending is "preposterous, and why not? Despite its abundance of realistic details, *A Mother and Two Daughters* is at heart an old story in brand-new clothes. This time around, Rochester does not get Jane Eyre; she tells him to keep his distance while she manages the estate. Godwin's version of this turnabout is entertaining and stereoscopic. Her novel can be read as a straightforward account of three plucky women imposing their wills on a receptive world; it can also be seen as a gentle comedy of the unfettered consciousness. Viewed both ways at once, it is engrossing and deep."

Mr. Bedford and the Muses is "an interim work in which [Godwin] pauses to look backward and forward" after *A Mother and Two Daughters,* reports Daphne Athas in *Chicago Tribune Book World.* The book consists of a novella and five short stories, and "all the stories are about the relationship of artists to their material," comments Lehmann-Haupt. Several of these artists are young women, says *New Republic* writer Kathleen Kearns, "hungry for experiences and unceasingly observant, ambitiously eager to turn life into art. But experiencing always seems to get in the way of their writing, or else writing in the way of truly experiencing." And, according to Kathleen Leverich in *Christian Science Monitor,* "Godwin so values a tidy symmetry that she sometimes sacrifices too much of life's randomness to it. Therefore, some of Godwin's stories, almost too neatly shaped, are ingenious diversions rather than affecting epiphanies."

In an author's note, Godwin "reflects upon the sources—the 'Muses'—from which all of these tales arose," explains a *Washington Post Book World* critic: "Both in this note and in the stories themselves, Godwin invites the reader into her mind, into the mysterious process through which fiction is created." Here, Athas comments, Godwin allows the reader to "view these stories as more than themselves, as testimony to her remarkable continuing career, and as evidence of the distinction between literature and life." And Godwin reflects in this note on the need for muses, observes Lehmann-Haupt, "particularly when writer's block attacks in any of its unpleasant guises; on one muse in particular, a turtle named Mr. Bedford, who helped the author to finish the long story, really a novella, that is named after its boxy, slow-moving inspiration."

The novella "Mr. Bedford" is based on Godwin's experiences at a boardinghouse in London where she lived during the 1960s while she worked at a job at the U.S. Travel Service at the American Embassy. In the opinion of *Los Angeles Times* writer Valerie Miner, the book "is irresistible reading if you have ever known the adventures and traumas of being a young American living abroad. Gail Godwin has just the right distance from her expatriation to conjure youthful passions and to distill them in the irony of experience."

"The American diarist in this novella revisits her younger self, an eager student of the world," Joanna Motion reports in *Times*

Literary Supplement. Carrie Ames, the main character of title novella, is "a young woman from North Carolina with what she calls a 'glamorous lifeboat' job . . . in London that she says would 'keep me financially afloat till the winds of love and accomplishment bestirred themselves and set me on my course,'" Gene Lyons reports in *Newsweek.* Carrie is secretly divorced, and as Lyons relates, her "ambition is to write the American 'Madame Bovary' about how and why." Her life soon becomes entangled with those of an expatriate American couple, manipulative parent figures who run the boardinghouse in which she lives.

With *The Finishing School* Godwin expands the first person voice she used in "Mr. Bedford" into "a narrative of humanly impressive energies, as happy-sad in its texture as life itself may be said to be," William H. Pritchard writes in *New Republic.* Shifting from one age perspective to another, Justin Stokes, a successful forty-year-old actress, tells the story of the summer she turns fourteen and her life is changed forever when she undergoes what Gray calls "a brief but harrowing rite of passage toward maturity." After her father and grandparents die in quick succession, the young Justin, her mother, and her brother leave Fredericksburg, Virginia, to live with her aunt in an upstate New York town populated with people who work for the local division of International Business Machines. There she makes friends with the local bohemian, Ursula DeVane, a forty-four-year-old failed actress who lives with her brother Julian, a talented musician of little consequence, in an old rundown home the two inherited from their parents.

Ursula DeVane takes Justin on as her protegee, and they begin to meet in an old stone hut in the woods where Ursula often retreats, the "Finishing School" in which Ursula "enthralls Justin with tales of her past and encourages her artistic aspirations," as Wood puts it. The novel "charts the exhilaration, the enchantment, the transformation, then the inevitable disillusionment and loss inherent in such a friendship and such self-discovery," according to Frances Taliaferro in *New York Times Book Review.* And, as Sternhell relates, it is essentially "the tale of a daughter with two mothers." Where *A Mother and Two Daughters* "was symphonic—many movements, many instruments—*The Finishing School* plays a gentle, chilling theme with variations. . . . Its form is clearly that of a realistic novel," Sternhell writes. But *The Finishing School* "often reads like a fable, a contemporary myth; daughters love mothers, and—variations on a theme—daughters betray mothers, repeatedly inevitably."

The Finishing School may be "old fashioned," according to Lehmann-Haupt, "in its preoccupation with such Aristotelian verities as plot, reversal, discovery, and the tragic flaw. But Miss Godwin's power to isolate and elevate subtle feelings makes her traditional story seem almost innovative." Although it doesn't quite meet the definition of true tragedy, the book is "a finely nuanced, compassionate psychological novel, subtler and more concentrated" than *A Mother and Two Daughters,* Taliaferro maintains. And Lehmann-Haupt points out that Godwin's characters serve to lend the novel a variety "as well as to distinguish the two worlds that Justin Stokes inhabits—the two dimensional world of the I.B.M. lookalikes and the rich, mysterious kingdom where 'art's redemptive power' is supposed to prevail." The characterization of Justin "is one of the most trustworthy portraits of an adolescent in current literature," says Taliaferro, and the book itself, she concludes, is "a wise contribution to the literature of growing up."

Literature has figured in Godwin's life from an early age. She grew up in Asheville, North Carolina, in the shadow of another writer, Thomas Wolfe. During the war her mother was a reporter, and Godwin recalls in an essay in *The Writer on Her Work* that "whenever Mrs. Wolfe called up the paper to announce, 'I have just remembered something else about Tom,'" her mother "was sent off immediately to the dead novelist's home on Spruce Street." Godwin's parents were divorced, and while Godwin was growing up, her mother taught writing and wrote love stories on the weekend to support her daughter while Godwin's grandmother ran the house. And although her mother never sold any of her novels, Godwin writes in the essay, "already, at five, I had allied myself with the typewriter rather than the stove. The person at the stove usually had the thankless task of fueling. Whereas, if you were faithful to your vision at the typewriter, by lunchtime you could make two more characters happy—even if you weren't so happy yourself. What is more, if you retyped your story neatly in the afternoon and sent it off in a manila envelope to New York, you'd get a check back for $100 within two or three weeks (300 words to the page, 16-17 pages, 2¢ a word: in 1942, $100 went a long way)."

Not that her grandmother was dispensable. Godwin indicates in *The Writer on Her Work* that "in our manless little family, she also played the mother and could be counted on to cook, sew on buttons, polish the piano, and give encouragement to creative endeavors. She was my mother's first reader, while the stories were still in their morning draft; 'It moves a little slowly here,' she'd say, or 'I didn't understand why the girl did this.' And the tempo would be stepped up, the heroine's ambiguous action sharpened in the afternoon draft; for if my grandmother didn't follow tempo and motive, how would all those other women who would buy the magazines?"

Godwin didn't meet her father until he showed up many years later at her high school graduation when, she recalls in the essay, he introduced himself, and she flung herself, "weeping," into his arms. He invited her to come and live with him, which she did, briefly, before he shot and killed himself like the lovable ne'er-do-well Uncle Ambrose in *Violet Clay*—a character inspired, at least in part, by Godwin's father, according to Weeks in *Dictionary of Literary Biography.*

After graduating from the University of North Carolina, Godwin was hired as a reporter for the *Miami Herald* and was reluctantly fired a year later by a bureau chief who felt he had failed to make a good reporter out of her. She married her first husband, newspaper photographer Douglas Kennedy, around that time. After her divorce, she completed her first novel, *Gull Key,* the story of "a young wife left alone all day on a Florida island while her husband slogs away at his job on the mainland," according to Godwin in *The Writer on Her Work.* (She worked on the book during her slow hours at the U.S. Travel Service in London.) Having submitted that work to several English publishers without good results, she relates that she even sent a copy to a fly-by-night agency that advertised in a magazine, "WANTED: UNPUBLISHED NOVELS IN WHICH WOMEN'S PROBLEMS AND LOVE INTERESTS ARE PREDOMINANT. ATTRACTIVE TERMS." She was never able to track down the agency or anyone associated with it.

Godwin was not totally satisfied with her work at the time and found focussing on characters and themes outside of herself to be helpful. She got the idea for one of her most highly-regarded short stories, "An Intermediate Stop" (now included in her collection *Dream Children*), in a writing class at the London City Literary Institute after the teacher instructed the students to write a 450-word story beginning with the sentence: "'*Run away,*' *he muttered to himself, sitting up and biting his nails.*"

Godwin writes in *The Writer on Her Work* that "when that must be your first sentence, it sort of excludes a story about a woman in her late twenties, adrift among the options of wifehood, career, vocation, a story that I had begun too many times already—both in fiction and reality—and could not resolve. My teacher wisely understood Gide's maxim for himself as writer: 'The best means of learning to know oneself is seeking to understand others.' "

Godwin describes "An Intermediate Stop" as a story "about an English vicar who has seen God, who writes a small book about his experience, and becomes famous. He gets caught up in the international lecture-tour circuit. My story shows him winding up his exhausting American tour at a small Episcopal college for women in the South. He is at his lowest point, having parroted back his own written words until he has lost touch with their meaning. He fears that, given the present pace and pressure of his public life, he will never again approach that private, meditative state of mind that brought God into focus in the first place." *New York Times* writer Anatole Broyard indicates that, here, "another kind of epiphany—in the form of a Texas debutante—restores his faith. The brilliance with which this girl is evoked reminds us that love and religion both partake of the numinous." A draft of that story also got the author accepted into the University of Iowa Writer's Workshop, and some of Godwin's early work about women like herself did begin to take shape successfully.

Her first published novel, *The Perfectionists,* which Godwin says is somewhat reflective of her second marriage, is described by Robert Scholes in *Saturday Review* as "an excellent piece of work, shrewdly observed and carefully crafted. . . . *The Perfectionists* is, in fact, too good, too clever, and too finished a product to be patronized as a 'first novel.' " Joyce Carol Oates in *New York Times Book Review* calls it "a most intelligent and engrossing novel" about "the paranoid tragedy of our contemporary worship of self-consciousness, of constant analysis." The book relates the story of the disintegrating "perfect" marriage of a psychiatrist and his wife, Dane, while they are on vacation in Majorca with the man's son. The vision the man has offered his wife of "a continuously developing relationship, lived from the head, the heart and the gut, has already soured," comments a *Times Literary Supplement* reviewer. Scholes writes that "the eerie tension that marks this complex relationship is the great achievement of the novel. It is an extraordinary accomplishment, which is bound to attract and hold many readers."

In Godwin's *Glass People,* Francesca Bolt, pampered and adored wife in a flawless but sterile marital environment, leaves her husband in a brief bid for freedom. This book, too, is praised as "a formally executed, precise, and altogether professional short novel" by Joyce Carol Oates in *Book World.* Weeks indicates, however, that in *Glass People,* Godwin is exploring "a theme introduced in *The Perfectionists,* that of a resolution of woman's dilemma through complete self-abnegation; but the author, already suspicious of this alternative in her first novel, presents it here as neither fully convincing nor ironic." As the *New York Times Book Review* critic asks: "Are we really to root for blank-minded Francesca to break free, when her author has promised us throughout that she's totally incapable of doing so?" Genevieve Stuttaford, though, in *Saturday Review,* argues that "the characters in *Glass People* are meticulously drawn and effectively realized, the facets of their personalities subtly, yet precisely, laid bare. The author is cooly neutral, and she makes no judgements. This is the way it is, Godwin is saying, and you must decide who the villains are."

"Marking a major advance in Godwin's development as a novelist," Weeks reports, "her third book, *The Odd Woman,* is twice as long as either of her previous novels, not from extension of plot but from a wealth of incidents told in flashback and in fantasy and a more thorough realization of present action." The book's major theme, Anne Z. Mickelson suggests in *Reaching Out: Sensitivity and Order in Recent American Fiction by Women,* is "how to achieve freedom while in union with another person, and impose one's own order on life so as to find self-fulfillment." Literature is explored in the novel as one means of giving shape to life, and thus, the book is generally regarded as cerebral and allusive, and in *Times Literary Supplement* critic Victoria Glendinning's words, it is "too closely or specifically tied to its culture" to be considered universal. Lore Dickstein, however, in *New York Times Book Review,* indicates that the novel is "a pleasure to read. Godwin's prose is elegant, full of nuance and feeling, and sparkling with ironic humor."

The odd woman of the book, "odd" in this case meaning not paired with another person, is Jane Clifford, a thirty-two-year-old teacher of Romantic and Victorian literature at a midwestern college. Thomas R. Edwards in *New York Review of Books* characterizes her as "untenured and unsure of reappointment, insomniac . . ., unmarried but in the midst of an affair with Gabriel Weeks, an art historian who teaches elsewhere and whom she sees only infrequently, at MLA meetings, for example." For Jane, Mickelson writes, "through whose consciousness the story unfolds, order and control, and organization are vital words." Jane reads and rereads George Gissing's *The Odd Woman,* a nineteenth-century book she is teaching in her classes about "a poor, uneducated, unmarried woman"; researches George Eliot's life, "which seems to Jane a model of order"; and observes "the lives of grandmother, mother, half-sister, colleagues, and friends," attempting "to formulate a comprehensive statement from all this and use it to impose order on her own life," Mickelson says.

Thus, for Jane, Susan E. Lorsch points out in *Critique,* "the worlds of fiction and the 'real' world are one." Jane "interweaves her life with books," remarks Lorsch, "she experiences her life through literature, through the books she has so entirely assimilated." And not only does Jane experience "literary worlds as real," Lorsch continues, "she treats the actual world as if it were an aesthetic creation. The anecdotes of her family history become the formative stories of Jane's present as well as her past, serving as simply so much more fiction for her to analyze and interpret."

Jane's mother, Kitty, "whom she adores, wrote in her youth romantic fiction of the most unreal kind," Glendinning comments. But according to Lorsch, Kitty "distinguishes between what we find in books which is subject to economic necessities and what we find in life. . . . Kitty understands that the worlds of literature and everyday life are discontinuous, separate, and that she cannot carry expectations from the one to the other." Lorsch indicates that "the entire book moves toward the climax and the completion of Jane's perception that the worlds of life and art are far from identical." But "despite her convincing quarrel with the literary imagination," Lorsch says, Godwin ends *The Odd Woman* with what *Dictionary of Literary Biography* critic Weeks describes as an affirmation of "Godwin's belief in the power of art to give shape to existence."

Violet Clay, Weeks comments, confirms Godwin's "mastery of the full, free narrative technique of *The Odd Woman*—the integration of fantasy and flashback into the narrative line—while also recalling the clean, classic structure of her two earlier novels." Furthermore, continues Weeks, "In *Violet Clay* Godwin raises a question that is central to understanding her work as a whole: what is the relationship between the artist and her art? The answer implied in Violet Clay's achievement as painter reflects directly Godwin's ideals as a writer."

The main character of the novel, Violet Clay, leaves the South for New York at age twenty-four to become a great artist, but "nine years later," John Leonard explains in *New York Times*, "all that she paints are covers on Gothic romances for a paperback publishing house." The novel opens as Violet, divorced and temporarily manless, "is putting the finishing touches to her nth cover for Harrow House Gothics, which shows, like all the others, a terrified girl in a velvet cloak and unsuitable shoes running away from the dark, beetle-browed mansion whose dark, beetle-browed owner she will marry in the last chapter," *Times Literary Supplement* writer Loma Sage says.

Violet finally loses her job at Harrow House because the new art director wants to use photographs of terrorized women on the jackets of the romances rather than the idealized paintings Violet creates. When Violet finds out her only living relative, Uncle Ambrose, a failed writer, has shot himself, she journeys to the Plommet Falls, New York, cabin in which her uncle died to claim his body and bury him. And, in *Washington Post Book World* critic Susan Shreve's words, "she decides to stay on and face the demons with her paint and brush." She makes friends in Plommet Falls with a woman she will later paint, a totally self-sufficient carpenter who is a victim of incest and rape.

The book reflects "the old-fashioned assumption that character develops and is good for something besides the daily recital to one's analyst," points out a *Harper's* critic. According to Leonard, however, *Violet Clay* is "too intelligent for its own good. It is overgrown with ideas. You can't see the feelings for the ideas." Katha Pollitt in *New York Times Book Review* comments that *Violet Clay* "has the pep-talk quality of so many recent novels in which the heroine strides off the last page, her own woman at last. Read as a cautionary tale, it's pretty scarifying: If you have artistic ambitions, it will probably make you start getting up earlier." As Sternhell argues, though, Godwin's novels "are not about book-ness, not about the idea of literature, but about human beings who take ideas seriously. Clever abstracts are not her medium: her 'vital artistic subject,' like Violet Clay's is, will always be the 'living human figure.' "

With her seventh novel, 1987's *A Southern Family*, Godwin returns to the setting of Mountain City first found in *A Mother and Two Daughters*. Another book of manners in the Victorian tradition, the work revolves around the death of a member of the Quick family. Twenty-eight-year-old Theo, divorced and father of a young son, is found dead after he apparently killed his girlfriend and committed suicide. Subsequently focussing on reactions from family members who include novelist Clare, her quirky mother Lily, and Clare's alcoholic half-brother Rafe, *A Southern Family*, according to Susan Heeger in the *Los Angeles Times Book Review*, "takes off from Theo's death on a discursive exploration of family history and relationships as the Quicks struggle to measure their blame and—belatedly—to know the brother and son they failed in life."

Several reviewers consider *A Southern Family* to be Godwin's most accomplished work. "Suffice it to say that *A Southern Family* is an ambitious book that entirely fulfills its ambitions," declares Yardley in his review for the *Washington Post Book World*. "Not merely is it psychologically astute," the critic continues, "it is dense with closely observed social and physical detail that in every instance is exactly right." Likewise, Beverly

Lowry in the *New York Times Book Review* proclaims that Godwin's book "is the best she's written." Deeming *A Southern Family* "a rich, complex book," Lowry concludes that Godwin's works "all give evidence of a supple intelligence working on the page. In this one she's in full bloom and at her mindful best."

BIOGRAPHICAL/CRITICAL SOURCES:

BOOKS

Contemporary Literary Criticism, Gale, Volume V, 1976, Volume VIII, 1978, Volume XXXI, 1985.
Dictionary of Literary Biography, Volume VI: *American Novelists since World War II,* Gale, 1981.
Godwin, Gale, *Violet Clay,* Knopf, 1978.
Godwin, Gale, *Mr. Bedford and the Muses,* Viking, 1983.
Godwin, Gale, *The Finishing School,* Viking, 1985.
Mickelson, Anne Z., *Reaching Out: Sensitivity and Order in Recent American Fiction by Women,* Scarecrow, 1979.
Sternburg, Janet, editor, *The Writer on Her Work,* Norton, 1980.

PERIODICALS

America, December 21, 1974, April 17, 1982.
Atlantic, May, 1976, October, 1979.
Book World, October 1, 1972.
Boston Globe, February 21, 1982.
Chicago Tribune Book World, January 10, 1982, October 16, 1983, January 27, 1984.
Christian Science Monitor, November 20, 1974, April 1, 1976, June 23, 1978, July 21, 1983, September 2, 1983.
Commonweal, June 1, 1984.
Critique, winter, 1978.
Critique: Studies in Modern Fiction, Number 3, 1980.
Detroit Free Press, March 10, 1985.
Detroit News, April 11, 1982, October 16, 1983, February 10, 1985.
Harper's, July, 1978.
Listener, June 9, 1977.
Los Angeles Times, November 13, 1981.
Los Angeles Times Book Review, September 11, 1983, February 24, 1985, February 9, 1986, October 4, 1987.
Miami Herald, February 29, 1976.
Ms., January, 1982.
National Review, September 15, 1978.
New Republic, January 25, 1975, July 8, 1978, February 17, 1982, December 19, 1983, February 25, 1985.
New Statesman, August 15, 1975.
Newsweek, February 23, 1976, January 11, 1982, September 12, 1983, February 25, 1985.
New Yorker, November 18, 1974, January 18, 1982.
New York Review of Books, February 20, 1975, April 1, 1976, July 20, 1978.
New York Times, September 21, 1972, September 30, 1974, February 16, 1976, May 18, 1978, December 22, 1981, September 6, 1983, October 4, 1983, January 24, 1985, September 21, 1987.
New York Times Book Review, June 7, 1970, October 15, 1972, October 20, 1974, February 22, 1976, May 21, 1978, January 10, 1982, September 18, 1983, January 27, 1985, October 11, 1987.
Observer, February 5, 1984.
Pacific Sun, September 23-29, 1983.
Progressive, October, 1978.
Publishers Weekly, January 15, 1982.
Saturday Review, August 8, 1970, October 28, 1972, February 21, 1976, June 10, 1978, January, 1982.

Spectator, January 15, 1977, September 2, 1978, February 6, 1982.
Sunday Star-Telegram (Ft. Worth), February 14, 1982.
Time, January 25, 1982, February 11, 1985, October 5, 1987.
Times (London), February 18, 1982, March 28, 1985.
Times Literary Supplement, July 23, 1971, July 4, 1975, September 15, 1978, March 5, 1982, February 17, 1984.
Village Voice, March 30, 1982, February 26, 1985.
Washington Post, February 7, 1983.
Washington Post Book World, May 21, 1978, December 13, 1981, September 11, 1983, February 3, 1985, September 13, 1987.
The Writer, September, 1975, December, 1976.

*   *   *

GOLDING, William (Gerald) 1911-

PERSONAL: Born September 19, 1911, in St. Columb, Cornwall, England; son of Alex A. (a schoolmaster) and Mildred A. Golding; married Ann Brookfield, 1939; children: David, Judith. *Education:* Brasenose College, Oxford, B.A., 1935, M.A., 1960.

ADDRESSES: Home—Cornwall, England.

CAREER: Writer. Was a settlement house worker after graduating from Oxford University; taught English and philosophy at Bishop Wordsworth's School, Salisbury, Wiltshire, England, 1939-40, 1945-61; wrote, produced, and acted for London equivalent of "very, very far-off-Broadway theatre," 1934-40, 1945-54. Writer in residence, Hollins College, 1961-62; honorary fellow, Brasenose College, Oxford University, 1966. *Military service:* Royal Navy, 1940-45; became rocket ship commander.

MEMBER: Royal Society of Literature (fellow), Savile Club.

AWARDS, HONORS: Commander, Order of the British Empire, 1965; D.Litt., University of Sussex, 1970, University of Kent, 1974, University of Warwick, 1981, Oxford University, 1983, and University of Sorbonne, 1983; James Tait Black Memorial Prize, 1980, for *Darkness Visible;* Booker McConnell Prize, 1981, for *Rites of Passage;* Nobel Prize for Literature, 1983, for body of work; LL.D., University of Bristol, 1984; knighted, 1988.

WRITINGS:

FICTION

Lord of the Flies, Faber, 1954, published with an introduction by E. M. Forster, Coward, 1955, casebook edition with notes and criticism, edited by James R. Baker and Arthur P. Ziegler, Jr., Putnam, 1964.
The Inheritors, Faber, 1955, Harcourt, 1962.
Pincher Martin, Faber, 1955, new edition, 1972, published as *The Two Deaths of Christopher Martin,* Harcourt, 1957.
Free Fall, Harcourt, 1960.
The Spire, Harcourt, 1964.
The Pyramid (novellas), Harcourt, 1967.
The Scorpion God: Three Short Novels (includes "Clonk Clonk," "Envoy Extraordinary" [also see below], and "The Scorpion God"), Harcourt, 1971.
Darkness Visible, Farrar, Straus, 1979.
Rites of Passage (first novel in trilogy), Farrar, Straus, 1980.
The Paper Men, Farrar, Straus, 1984.
Close Quarters (second novel in trilogy), Farrar, Straus, 1987.
Fire Down Below (third novel in trilogy), Farrar, Straus, 1989.

OTHER

Poems, Macmillan, 1934.
(Contributor) *Sometimes, Never* (anthology), Ballantine, 1956.
The Brass Butterfly: A Play in Three Acts (based on "Envoy Extraordinary"; first produced in Oxford, England at New Theatre, 1958; produced in London, England at Strand Theatre, April, 1958; produced in New York at Lincoln Square Theatre, 1965), Faber, 1958.
"Break My Heart" (play), BBC Radio, 1962.
The Hot Gates, and Other Occasional Pieces (nonfiction), Harcourt, 1965.
A Moving Target (essays and lectures), Farrar, Straus, 1982.
An Egyptian Journal (travel), Faber, 1985.

Contributor to periodicals.

SIDELIGHTS: William Golding has been described as pessimistic, mythical, spiritual—an allegorist who uses his novels as a canvas to paint portraits of man's constant struggle between his civilized self and his hidden, darker nature. With the appearance of *Lord of the Flies,* Golding's first published novel, the author began his career as both a campus cult favorite and one of the late twentieth-century's most distinctive—and debated—literary talents. Golding's appeal is summarized by the Nobel Prize committee, who issued this statement when awarding the author their literature prize in 1983: "[His] books are very entertaining and exciting. They can be read with pleasure and profit without the need to make much effort with learning or acumen. But they have also aroused an unusually great interest in professional literary critics [who find] deep strata of ambiguity and complication in Golding's work, . . . in which odd people are tempted to reach beyond their limits, thereby being bared to the very marrow."

Golding was born in England's west country in 1911. His father, Alex, was a follower in the family tradition of schoolmasters; his mother, Mildred, was a suffragette. The family home in Marlborough is characterized by Stephen Medcalf in *William Golding* as "darkness and terror made objective in the flint-walled cellars of their fourteenth-century house . . . and in the graveyard by which it stood." By the time Golding was seven years old, Medcalf continues, "he had begun to connect the darkness . . . with the ancient Egyptians. From them he learnt, or on them he projected, mystery and symbolism, a habit of mingling life and death, and an attitude of mind sceptical of the scientific method that descends from the Greeks."

When he was twelve, Golding "tried his hand at writing a novel," reports Bernard Oldsey in his *Dictionary of Literary Biography* article. "It was to be in twelve volumes and, unlike the kinds of works he had been reading [adventure stories of the Edgar Rice Burroughs and Jules Verne ilk], was to incorporate a history of the trade-union movement. He never forgot the opening sentence of this magnificent opus: 'I was born in the Duchy of Cornwall on the eleventh of October, 1792, of rich but honest parents.' That sentence set a standard he could not maintain, he playfully admitted, and nothing much came of the cycle."

Despite this setback the young man remained an enthusiastic writer and, on entering Brasenose College of Oxford University, abandoned his plans to study science, preferring to read English literature. At twenty-two, a year before taking his B.A. in English, Golding saw his first literary work published—a poetry collection simply titled *Poems.* In hindsight, the author called the pieces "poor, thin things," according to Medcalf. But, in fact, Medcalf remarks, "They are not bad. They deal with emotions—as they come out in the poems, rather easy emotions—of loss and grief, reflected in nature and the seasons."

After graduating from Oxford, Golding perpetuated family tradition by becoming a schoolmaster in Salisbury, Wiltshire. His teaching career was interrupted in 1940, however, when World War II found "Schoolie," as he was called, serving five years in the Royal Navy. Lieutenant Golding saw active duty in the North Atlantic, commanding a rocket launching craft. "What did I do?," he responds in Oldsey's article about his wartime experiences. "I survived." Present at the sinking of the *Bismarck,* and participating in the D-Day invasion, Golding later told Joseph Wershba of the *New York Post:* "World War Two was the turning point for me. I began to see what people were capable of doing."

On returning to his post at Bishop Wordsworth's School in 1945, Golding, who had enhanced his knowledge of Greek history and mythology by reading while at sea, attempted to further his writing career. He produced three novel manuscripts that remained unpublished. "All that [the author] has divulged about these [works] is that they were attempts to please publishers and that eventually they convinced him that he should write something to please himself," notes Oldsey. That ambition was realized in 1954, when Golding created *Lord of the Flies.*

The novel which established Golding's reputation, *Lord of the Flies* was rejected by twenty-one publishers before Faber & Faber accepted the forty-three-year-old schoolmaster's book. While the story has been compared to such previous works as *Robinson Crusoe* and *High Wind in Jamaica,* Golding's novel is actually the author's "answer" to nineteenth-century writer R. M. Ballantyne's children's classic *The Coral Island: A Tale of the Pacific Ocean.* These two books share the same basic plot line and even some of the same character names (two of the lead characters are named Ralph and Jack in both books). The similarity, however, ends there. Ballantyne's story, about a trio of boys stranded on an otherwise uninhabited island, shows how, by pluck and resourcefulness, the young castaways survive with their morals strengthened and their wits sharpened. *Lord of the Flies,* on the other hand, is "an allegory on human society today, the novel's primary implication being that what we have come to call civilization is, at best, not more than skin-deep," as James Stern explains in a *New York Times Book Review* article.

Initially, the tale of a group of schoolboys stranded on an island during their escape from atomic war received mixed reviews and sold only modestly in its hardcover edition. But when the paperback edition was published in 1959, thus making the book more accessible to students, the novel began to sell briskly. Teachers, aware of the student interest and impressed by the strong theme and stark symbolism of the work, assigned *Lord of the Flies* to their literature classes. And as the novel's reputation grew, critics reacted by drawing scholarly theses out of what was previously dismissed as just another adventure story.

Golding provides in *Time* a simple exegis of his book. "The theme," he says, "is an attempt to trace the defects of society back to the defects of human nature." Indeed, the book begins with a company of highly-bred young men ("We've got to have rules and obey them. After all, we're not savages. We're English, and the English are best at everything," one of them states) and in just a few weeks strips them of nearly every aspect of "civilization," revealing what Golding describes as man's "true" nature underneath. In *Lord of the Flies,* religion becomes pagan ritual—the boys worship an unknowable, pervading power that they call The Beast; even a group of choirboys becomes a chanting warrior troupe. Democratic society crumbles under barbarism. "Like

any orthodox moralist Golding insists that Man is a fallen creature, but he refuses to hypostatize Evil or to locate it in a dimension of its own. On the contrary Beelzebub, Lord of the Flies, is Roger and Jack and you and I, ready to declare himself as soon as we permit him to," John Peter points out in *Kenyon Review.* "One sees what Golding is doing," says Walter Allen in his book *The Modern Novel.* "He is showing us stripped man, man naked of all the sanctions of custom and civilization, man as he is alone and in his essence, or at any rate, as he can be conceived to be in such a condition."

In his study *The Tragic Past,* David Anderson, like many critics, sees Biblical implications in Golding's novel. "*Lord of the Flies,*" writes Anderson, "is a complex version of the story of Cain—the man whose smoke-signal failed and who murdered his brother. Above all, it is a refutation of optimistic theologies which believed that God had created a world in which man's moral development had advanced *pari passu* with his biological evolution and would continue so to advance until the all-justifying End was reached. What we have in [the book] is not moral achievement but moral regression. And there is no all-justifying End: the rescue-party which takes the boys off their island comes from a world in which regression has occurred on a gigantic scale—the scale of atomic war. The human plight is presented in terms which are unqualified and unrelieved. Cain is not merely our remote ancestor: he is contemporary man, and his murderous impulses are equipped with unlimited destructive power."

The work has also been called Golding's response to the popular artistic notion of the 1950s, that youth was a basically innocent collective, victims of adult society (as in J. D. Salinger's *Catcher in the Rye,* a novel that rivals *Lord of the Flies* in student popularity). In 1960, C. B. Cox deemed *Lord of the Flies* as "probably the most important novel to be published . . . in the 1950s." Cox, writing in *Critical Quarterly,* continued: "[To] succeed, a good story needs more than sudden deaths, a terrifying chase and an unexpected conclusion. *Lord of the Flies* includes all these ingredients, but their exceptional force derives from Golding's faith that every detail of human life has a religious significance. This is one reason why he is unique among new writers in the '50s. . . . Golding's intense conviction [is] that every particular of human life has a profound importance. His children are not juvenile delinquents, but human beings realising for themselves the beauty and horror of life."

Not every critic responded with admiration to *Lord of the Flies,* however. One of Golding's more vocal detractors is Kenneth Rexroth, who had this to say in *Atlantic:* "Golding's novels are rigged. All thesis novels are rigged. In the great ones the drama escapes from the cage of the rigging or is acted out on it as on a skeleton stage set. Golding's thesis requires more rigging than most and it must by definition be escape-proof and collapsing." Rexroth elaborates: "[The novel] functions in a minimal ecology, but even so, and indefinite as it is, it is wrong. It's the wrong rock for such an island and the wrong vegetation. The boys never come alive as real boys. They are simply the projected annoyances of a disgruntled English schoolmaster."

Jean E. Kennard voiced a different view in her study *Number and Nightmare: Forms of Fantasy in Contemporary Fiction:* "Golding's ability to create characters which function both realistically and allegorically is illustrated particularly well in *Lord of the Flies.* It is necessary for Golding to establish the boys as 'real' children early in the novel—something he achieves through such small touches as Piggy's attitude to his asthma and the boys' joy in discovering Piggy's nickname—because his major thesis is, after all, about human psychology and the whole force of the fable would be lost if the characters were not first credible to us as human beings."

The wide variety of critical reaction to Golding's first novel is assessed by Bernard Oldsey. In his article, Oldsey cites such writers as E. L. Epstein and Claire Rosenfield, who "analyzed the work as a fictionalized version of primitive psychology and anthropology. Frederick Karl," Oldsey goes on, "oversimplifying the political allegory, declared that 'When the boys on the island struggle for supremacy, they re-enact a ritual of the adult world, as much as the Fellows in [C. P.] Snow's *The Masters* work out the ritual power in the larger world.' The temptation to force the novel into an allegorical box was strong, since the story is evocative and the characters seem to beg for placement within handy categories of meaning. But Golding is a simply complicated writer; and . . . none of the boxes fits precisely. [Critics Ian Gregor and Mark Kinkead-Weekes] wisely concluded that 'Golding's fiction has been too complex and many sided to be reducible to a thesis and a conclusion. *Lord of the Flies* is imagined with a flexibility and depth which seem evidence of finer art than the polish and clarity of its surface.' "

Golding took his theme of tracing the defects of society back to the defects of human nature a step further with his second novel, *The Inheritors.* This tale is set at the beginning of human existence itself, during the prehistoric age. A tribe of Neanderthals, as seen through the characters of Lok and Fa, live a peaceful primitive life. Their happy world, however, is doomed: evolution brings in its wake the new race, *Homo sapiens,* who demonstrate their acquired skills with weapons by killing the Neanderthals. The book, which Golding has called his favorite, is also a favorite with several critics. And, inevitably, comparisons were made between *The Inheritors* and *Lord of the Flies.*

To Peter Green, in *A Review of English Literature,* for example, "it is clear that there is a close thematic connection between [the two novels]: Mr. Golding has simply set up a different working model to illustrate the eternal human verities from a new angle. Again it is humanity, and humanity alone, that generates evil; and when the new men triumph, Lok, the Neanderthaler, weeps as Ralph wept for the corruption and end of innocence [in *Lord of the Flies*]." Oldsey sees the comparison in religious terms: "[The *Homo sapiens*] represent the Descent of Man, not simply in the Darwinian sense, but in the Biblical sense of the Fall. Peculiarly enough, the boys [in *Lord of the Flies*] slide backward, through their own bedevilment, toward perdition; and Lok's Neanderthal tribe hunches forward, given a push by their *Homo sapiens* antagonists, toward the same perdition. In Golding's view, there is precious little room for evolutionary slippage: progression in *The Inheritors* and retrogression in *Lord of the Flies* have the same results. The Descent of Man and Man's Fall (that is to say, rationalism versus religion, the scientific view versus spiritual vision) constitute the crux of Golding's constant thematic structuring. This is true for all of his literary endeavors, but nowhere is it more apparent than in *The Inheritors.*"

Just as *Lord of the Flies* is Golding's rewriting, in his own terms, of *The Coral Island,* the author "said that he wrote *The Inheritors* to refute [H. G. Wells's controversial sociological study] *Outline of History,* and one can see that between the two writers there is a certain filial relation, though strained, as such relations often are," comments a *Times Literary Supplement* critic. "They share the same fascination with past and future, the extraordinary capacity to move imaginatively to remote points in time, the fabulizing impulse, the need to moralize. There are even similarities in style. And surely now, when Wells's reputation as a great writer is beginning to take form, it will be understood as high praise of Golding if one says that he is our Wells, as good in his own individual way as Wells was in his." Taken together, the author's first two novels are, according to Lawrence R. Ries, "studies in human nature, exposing the kinds of violence that man uses against his fellow man. It is understandable why these first novels have been said to comprise [Golding's] 'primitive period,' " as Ries states in his book *Wolf Masks: Violence in Contemporary Fiction.*

Golding's "primitive period" ended with the publication of his third novel, *Pincher Martin* (published in America as *The Two Deaths of Christopher Martin,* out of the publishers' concern for American readers who would not know that "pincher" is British slang for "petty thief "). Stylistically similar to Ambrose Bierce's famous short story "An Occurrence at Owl Creek Bridge," *Pincher Martin* is about a naval officer who, after his ship is torpedoed in the Atlantic, drifts aimlessly before latching on to a barren rock. Here he clings for days, eating sea anemones and trying his best to retain consciousness. Delirium overtakes Pincher Martin, though, and through his rambling thoughts he relives his past. The discovery of the sailor's corpse at the end of the story in part constitutes what has been called a "gimmick" ending, and gives the book a metaphysical turn—the reader learns that Pincher Martin has been dead from the beginning of the narrative.

The author's use of flashbacks throughout the narrative of *Pincher Martin* is discussed by Avril Henry in *Southern Review:* "On the merely narrative level [the device] is the natural result of Martin's isolation and illness, and is the process by which he is gradually brought to his ghastly self-knowledge." In fact, says Henry, the flashbacks "function in several ways. First the flashbacks relate to each other and to the varied forms in which they themselves are repeated throughout the book; second, they relate also to the details of Martin's 'survival' on [the rock]. . . . Third, they relate to the six-day structure of the whole experience: the structure which is superficially a temporal check for us and Martin in the otherwise timeless and distorted events on the rock and in the mind, and at a deeper level is a horrible parody of the six days of Creation. What we watch is an unmaking process, in which man attempts to create himself his own God, and the process accelerates daily."

And, while acknowledging the influences present in the themes of *Pincher Martin*—from Homer's *Odysseus* to *Robinson Crusoe* again—Medcalf further suggests that the novel is Golding's most autobiographical work to date. The author, says Medcalf, "gave Martin more of the external conditions of his own life than to any other of his characters, from [his education at] Oxford . . . through a period of acting and theatre life to a commission in the wartime Navy." Golding, too, has added another dimension from his own past, notes Medcalf: "His childhood fear of the darkness of the cellar and the coffin ends crushed in the walls from the graveyard outside [his childhood home]. The darkness universalizes him. It becomes increasingly but always properly laden with symbolism: the darkness of the thing that cannot examine itself, the observing ego: the darkness of the unconscious, the darkness of sleep, of death and, beyond death, heaven."

Each of Golding's first three novels, according to James Gindin in his *Postwar British Fiction: New Accents and Attitudes,* "demonstrates the use of unusual and striking literary devices. Each is governed by a massive metaphorical structure—a man clinging for survival to a rock in the Atlantic ocean or an excursion into the mind of man's evolutionary antecedent—designed to assert something permanent and significant about human nature. The metaphors are intensive, far-reaching; they permeate all the details and events of the novels. Yet at the end of each novel the metaphors, unique and striking as they are, turn into 'gimmicks' [Golding's own term for the device], into clever tricks that shift the focus or the emphasis of the novel as a whole." In Gindin's further criticism of Golding's "gimmicks," the critic states that such endings fail "to define or to articulate fully just how [the author's] metaphors are to be qualified, directed, shaped in contemporary and meaningful terms."

Gimmick endings notwithstanding, V. S. Pritchett sums up Golding's early books as romantic "in the austere sense of the term. They take the leap from the probable to the possible." Pritchett elaborates in a *New Statesman* review: "All romance breaks with the realistic novelist's certainties and exposes the characters to transcendent and testing dangers. But Golding does more than break; he bashes, by the power of his overwhelming sense of the detail of the physical world. He is the most original of our contemporaries."

To follow *Pincher Martin,* the author "said that he next wanted to show the patternlessness of life before we impose our patterns on it," according to Green. However, the resulting book, *Free Fall,* Green continues, "avoids the amoebic paradox suggested by his own prophecy, and falls into a more normal pattern of development: normal, that is, for Golding." Not unlike *Pincher Martin, Free Fall* depicts through flashbacks the life of its protagonist, artist Sammy Mountjoy. Imprisoned in a darkened cell in a Nazi prisoner-of-war camp, Mountjoy, who has been told that his execution is imminent, has only time to reflect on his past.

Despite the similarity in circumstance to *Pincher Martin,* Oldsey finds one important difference between that novel and *Free Fall.* In *Free Fall,* a scene showing Sammy Mountjoy's tortured reaction on (symbolically) reliving his own downfall indicates a move toward atonement. "It is at this point in Golding's tangled tale that the reader begins to understand the difference between Sammy Mountjoy and Pincher Martin," Oldsey says. "Sammy escapes the machinations of the camp psychiatrist, Dr. Halde, by making use of man's last resource, prayer. It is all concentrated in his cry of 'Help me! Help me!'—a cry which Pincher Martin refuses to utter. In this moment of desperate prayer, Sammy spiritually bursts open the door of his own selfishness."

Medcalf sees the story as Dantesque in nature (Mountjoy's romantic interest is even named Beatrice) and remarks: "Dante, like Sammy, came to himself in the middle of his life, in a dark wood [the cell, in Sammy's case], unable to remember how he came there. . . . His only way out is to see the whole world, and himself in its light. Hell, purgatory and heaven are revealed to him directly, himself and this world of sense in glimpses from the standpoint of divine justice and eternity." In *Free Fall* the author's intent "is to show this world directly, in other hints and guesses. He is involved therefore in shewing directly the moment of fall at which Dante only hints. He has a hero without reference points, who lives in the vertigo of free fall, therefore, reproachful of an age in which those who have a morality or a system softly refuse to insist on them: a hero for whom no system he has will do, but who is looking for his own unity in the world—and that, the real world, is 'like nothing, because it is everything.' Golding, however, has the advantage of being able to bring Dante's world in by allusion: and he does so with a Paradise hill on which Beatrice is met."

Several critics have taken special notice of Golding's use of names in *Free Fall*—and his selection of the novel's title itself. Peter M. Axthelm, in his book *The Modern Confessional Novel,* finds that "almost every proper name . . . implies something about the character it identifies." The name Sammy Mountjoy, with its hedonistic ring, for example, contrasts sharply with that of his childhood guardian, Father Watts-Watt. The most crucial name in the book, though, states Axthelm, is that of the woman whom Sammy loves and abuses, Beatrice Ifor. Sammy reads her surname as "I-for," an extension of his own sexual passion. But her name can also be read as "If-or," indicating a spiritual choice—"in other words, she is the potential bridge between Sammy's two worlds," as Axthelm notes. Unable to reconcile the two sides of her character, Sammy "ignores the spiritual side of the girl and grasps only the 'I-for,' the self-centered, exploitative lust. He upsets the balance and destroys the bridge," says the critic.

"Many critics have commented that the title [*Free Fall*] has both a theological and a scientific significance," declares Kennard, "but Golding himself has, as usual, expressed it best: 'Everybody has translated this in terms of theology; well, okay, you can do it that way, which is why it's not a bad title, but it is in fact a scientific term. It is where your gravity has *gone;* it is a man in a space ship who has no gravity; things don't fall or lift, they float about; he is completely divorced from the other idea of a thing up *there* and centered on *there* in which he lives.' Sammy Mountjoy, narrator of *Free Fall,* has more insight and perhaps more conscience than Pincher Martin, but basically his is Pincher's problem. He is islanded, trapped in himself, 'completely divorced from the other idea of a thing up there.' " "Sammy is the character through whom Mr. Golding, one suspects, is beginning to be reconciled to the loss of his primal Eden," offers Green.

In Golding's fifth novel, *The Spire,* "the interest is all in the opacity of the man and in a further exploration of man's all-sacrificing will," writes Medcalf. Fourteenth-century clergyman Dean Jocelin "is obsessed with the belief that it is his divine mission to raise a 400-foot tower and spire above his church," as Oldsey describes. "His colleagues protest vainly that the project is too expensive and the edifice unsuited for such a shaft. His master builder (obviously named Roger Mason) calculates that the foundation and pillars of the church are inadequate to support the added weight, and fruitlessly suggests compromises to limit the shaft to a lesser height. The townspeople—amoral, skeptical, and often literally pagan—are derisive about 'Jocelin's Folly.' " Dean Jocelin, nonetheless, strives on. The churchman, in fact, "neglects all his spiritual duties to be up in the tower overseeing the workmen himself, all the while choosing not to see within and without himself what might interrupt the spire's dizzying climb," Oldsey continues. The weight of the tower causes the church's foundations to shudder; the townspeople increasingly come to see Jocelin as a man dangerously driven.

Finally, despite setbacks caused by both the workers (they "drink, fornicate, murder, and brawl away their leisure hours," according to Oldsey) and by the elements of nature (storms ravage the tower in its building stage), the spire nears completion. Dean Jocelin himself drives the final nail into the top of the edifice—and as he does, succumbs to a disease and falls from the tower to his death. "Whether he has been urged by Satan, God, or his own pride (much like that of Pincher Martin) is a moot question," stresses Oldsey, who also notes that "again Golding returns to the most obsessive subject in his fiction—The Fall."

The Spire "is a book about vision and its cost," observes *New York Review of Books* critic Frank Kermode. "It has to do with the motives of art and prayer, the phallus turned spire; with the deceit, as painful to man as to God, involved in structures which are human but have to be divine, such as churches and spires.

But because the whole work is a dance of figurative language such an account of it can only be misleading." Characteristic of all Golding's work, *The Spire* can be read on two levels, that of an engrossing story and of a biting analysis of human nature. As Nigel Dennis finds in the *New York Times Book Review,* Golding "has always written on these two levels. But 'The Spire' will be of particular interest to his admirers because it can also be read as an exact description of his own artistic method. This consists basically of trying to rise to the heights while keeping himself glued to the ground. Mr. Golding's aspirations climb by clinging to solid objects and working up them like a vine. This is particularly pronounced in [*The Spire*], where every piece of building stone, every stage of scaffolding, every joint and ledge, are used by the author to draw himself up into the blue."

With this book Golding completed his first decade in the literary eye. The author's prolific output—five novels in ten years—and the high quality of his work established him as one of the late twentieth-century's most distinguished writers. This view of Golding was cemented in 1965, when the author was named a Commander of the British Empire.

Thus, by 1965, Golding was evidently on his way to continuing acclaim and popular acceptance—but "then matters changed abruptly," as Oldsey relates. The writer's output dropped dramatically: for the next fifteen years he produced no novels and only a handful of novellas, short stories, and occasional pieces. Of this period—what Boyd refers to as the "hiatus in the Golding oeuvre"—*The Pyramid,* a collection of three related novellas (and considered a novel proper by some critics), is generally regarded as one of the writer's weaker efforts. The episodic story of a man's existence in the suspiciously-named English town of Stilbourne, *The Pyramid* proved a shock to "even Golding's most faithful adherents [who] wondered if the book was indeed a novel or if it contributed anything to the author's reputation. To some it seemed merely three weak stories jammed together to produce a salable book," says Oldsey. *The Pyramid,* however, does have its admirers, among them John Wakeman of the *New York Times Book Review,* who feels the work is Golding's "first sociological novel. It is certainly more humane, exploratory, and life-size than its predecessors, less Old Testament, more New Testament." And to a *Times Literary Supplement* critic the book "will astonish by what it is not. It is not a fable, it does not contain evident allegory, it is not set in a simplified or remote world. It belongs to another, more commonplace tradition of English fiction; it is a low-keyed, realistic novel of growing up in a small town—the sort of book H. G. Wells might have written if he had been more attentive to his style."

The Scorpion God, another collection of novellas, was somewhat better received. One *Times Literary Supplement* reviewer, while calling the work "not major Golding," nevertheless finds the book "a pure example of Golding's gift. . . . The title story is from Golding's Egyptological side and is set in ancient Egypt. . . . By treating the unfamiliar with familiarity, explaining nothing, he teases the reader into the strange world of the story. It is as brilliant a *tour de force* as *The Inheritors,* if on a smaller scale."

Golding's reintroduction to the literary world was acknowledged in 1979 with the publication of *Darkness Visible.* Despite some fifteen years absence from the novel, the author "returns unchanged," Samuel Hynes observes in a *Washington Post Book World* article. "[He is] still a moralist, still a maker of parables. To be a moralist you must believe in good and evil, and Golding does; indeed, you might say that the nature of good and evil is his only theme. To be a parable-maker you must believe that

moral meaning can be expressed in the very fabric of the story itself, and perhaps that some meanings can only be expressed in this way; and this, too, has always been Golding's way."

The title *Darkness Visible* derives from Milton's description of Hell in *Paradise Lost,* and from the first scenes of the book Golding confronts the reader with images of fire, mutilation, and pain—which he presents in Biblical terms. For instance, notes *Commonweal* reviewer Bernard McCabe, the novel's opening describes a small child, "horribly burned, horribly disfigured, [who walks] out of the flames at the height of the London blitz. . . . The shattered building he emerges from . . . is called 'a burning bush,' the firemen stare into 'two pillars of lighted smoke,' the child walks with a 'ritual gait,' and he appears to have been 'born from the sheer agony of a burning city.' " The rescued youth, dubbed Matty, the left side of whose face has been left permanently mutilated, grows up to be a religious visionary.

"If Matty is a force for light, he is opposed by a pair of beautiful twins, Toni and Sophy Stanhope," continues Susan Fromberg Schaeffer in her *Chicago Tribune Book World* review. "These girls, once symbols of innocence in their town, discover the seductive attractions of darkness. Once, say the spirits who visit Matty, the girls were called before them, but they refused to come. Instead, obsessed by the darkness loose in the world, they abandon morality, choosing instead a demonic hedonism that allows them to justify anything, even mass murder." "Inevitably, the two girls will . . . [embark on a] spectacular crime, and just as inevitably, Matty, driven by his spirit guides, must oppose them," sums up *Time*'s Peter S. Prescott. "The confrontation, as you may imagine, ends happily for no one."

Darkness Visible received mixed reviews overall, with much of the negative reaction focusing on the author's "embarrassing fictional stereotypes . . . and his heavy-handedly ironic attempt to create a visionary-moron in [Matty]," as Joyce Carol Oates relates in *New Republic.* And McCabe finds that although the novel "has its undeniable fascinations . . . [nevertheless] what I end up with is an impression of a very earnest writer, blessed with remarkable skills and up to all sorts of ingenuities, struggling with a dark vision of man, trying to express it through a complex art, making another attempt at another *tour de force,* and getting nowhere."

On the other hand, Hynes, who concedes that *Darkness Visible* is a "difficult novel," adds that "unlike many other contemporary novels, it is difficult because its meaning is difficult: it is not a complicated word game, or a labyrinth with a vacuum at the center. Golding, the religious man, has once more set himself the task of finding the signs and revelations, the parable, that will express his sense of the human situation. Difficult, yes—isn't morality difficult?—but worth the effort."

While *Darkness Visible* "could not by itself restore Golding to prominence," as Robert Towers points out in the *New York Review of Books,* the wave of renewed interest the book generated in its author paved the way for Golding's following novel, *Rites of Passage.* A tale of high-seas adventure, *Rites of Passage,* according to Towers, is "a first-rate historical novel that is also a novel of ideas—a taut, beautifully controlled short book with none of the windiness or costumed pageantry so often associated with fictional attempts to reanimate the past."

Some of the ideas explored in this book trace back to *Lord of the Flies* "and to the view [the author] held then of man as a fallen being capable of a 'vileness beyond words,' " as *New Statesman* writer Blake Morrison sees it. Set in the early nineteenth-century, *Rites of Passage* tells of a voyage from England to Australia as recounted through the shipboard diary of young aristocrat Edmund Talbot. "He sets down a vivid record of the ship and its characters," explains Morrison. They include "the irascible Captain Anderson . . . , the 'wind-machine Mr Brockleband,' the whorish 'painted Magdalene' called Zenobia, and the meek and ridiculous 'parson,' Mr Colley, who is satirised as mercilessly as the clerics in [Henry] Fielding's *Joseph Andrews*." This latter character is the one through which much of the dramatic action in *Rites of Passage* takes place. For Colley, this "country curate . . . this hedge priest," as Golding's Talbot describes him, "is the perfect victim—self-deluding, unworldly, sentimentally devout, priggish, and terrified. Above all he is ignorant of the powerful homosexual streak in his nature that impels him toward the crew and especially toward one stalwart sailor, Billy Rogers," says Towers. Driven by his passion yet torn by doubt, ridiculed and shunned by the other passengers on the ship, Colley literally dies of shame during the voyage.

"It should be clear . . . that the ship is a microcosm of sorts, encapsulating an entire society or nation," Towers notes. "It may even have occurred to some that the concealed name of this obsolete old ship of the line, with its female figurehead obscenely nicknamed by the crew, might well be *Britannia*. At this hint of allegorizing I can imagine a shudder passing through certain prospective readers. But they need not fear. Though there is indeed a schoolmasterish streak in Golding, inclining him toward the didactic, tempting him to embellish his work with literary references . . . , he has in *Rites of Passage* constructed a narrative vessel sturdy enough to support his ideas. And because his ideas—about the role of class, about the nature of authority and its abuses, about cruelty (both casual and deliberate) and its consequences—because these themes and others are adequately dramatized, adequately incorporated, they become agents within the novel, actively and interestingly, at work within the fictional setting."

The author faced his harshest criticism to date with the publication of his 1984 novel *The Paper Men*. A farce-drama about an aging, successful novelist's conflicts with his pushy, overbearing biographer, *The Paper Men* "tells us that biography is the trade of the con man, a fatuous accomplishment, and the height of impertinence in both meanings of the word," according to London *Times* critic Michael Ratcliff. Unfortunately for Golding, most critics find *The Paper Men* to be sorely lacking in the qualities that distinguish the author's best work. Typical of their commentary is this observation from Michiko Kakutani of the *New York Times*: "Judging from the tired, petulant tone of [the novel], Mr. Golding would seem to have more in common with his creation than mere appearance—a 'scraggy yellow-white beard, yellow-white thatch and broken-toothed grin.' He, too, seems to have allowed his pessimistic vision of man to curdle his view of the world and to sour his enjoyment of craft."

Some reviewers call *The Paper Men* a work unworthy of a Nobel Prize winner (Golding had received the award just months prior to the book's publication); reacting to the outpouring of negative criticism, Blake Morrison says in the *Times Literary Supplement* that "all that can be said with confidence is that Golding's previous novels, even those that were coolly received on publication, have stood up well to subsequent re-readings, and that *The Paper Men* is certain to get a more patient treatment from future explicators than it has had from its reviewers. As for the author, he will have to console himself with [his lead character's] rather specious piece of reasoning on the poor reception of [his own novel]: 'You have to write the bad books if you're going to write the good ones.' "

Departing briefly from fiction, Golding has produced two books of "occasional pieces," works containing essays, reviews, and lectures. *The Hot Gates, and Other Occasional Pieces* was published in 1965; *A Moving Target* appeared in 1982, one year prior to the author's receipt of the Nobel Prize. Literary observations pervade *A Moving Target*. Golding speaks not only of the works of such authors as Samuel Richardson, Alexander Pope, and Jane Austen, he offers "advice" to aspiring writers and, "with pristine clarity, he answers critics, academics and 'dangerous' postgraduate students who have subjected his 'Lord of the Flies' to 'Freudian analysis, neo-Freudian analysis, Jungian analysis, Roman Catholic approval, . . . Protestant apprisal, nonconformist surmise, and Scientific Humanist misinterpretation," as *Los Angeles Times Book Review* contributor John Rechy observes.

But the most moving passage in the book, according to Gabriel Josipovici, writing in the *Times Literary Supplement*, is a pair of mood pieces that find Golding reliving his youthful infatuation with Egyptology, and a travel essay that finds the boy, a lifetime later, finally exploring Egypt in person. The critic opined: "This volume is fascinating . . . because it gives us a glimpse of two Goldings. The pieces about place, about Homer, about fairytales, convey the power of his imagination, his extraordinary ability to enter into and convey to us the strangeness and incomprehensibility of the world we live in. The lectures, on the other hand, give us a glimpse of the writer turning into a monument, not graciously but uneasily."

While he has faced extensive criticism and categorization in his writing career, the author is able to provide a brief, simple description of himself in Jack I. Biles's *Talk: Conversations with William Golding*: "I'm against the picture of the artist as the starry-eyed visionary not really in control or knowing what he does. I think I'd almost prefer the word 'craftsman.' He's like one of the old-fashioned shipbuilders, who conceived the boat in their mind and then, after that, touched every single piece that went into the boat. They were in complete control; they knew it inch by inch, and I think the novelist is very much like that."

MEDIA ADAPTATIONS: Pincher Martin was produced as a radio play for the British Broadcasting Corp. in 1958; *Lord of the Flies* was filmed by Continental in 1963, and by Castle Rock Entertainment in 1990.

AVOCATIONAL INTERESTS: Sailing, archaeology, and playing the piano, violin, viola, cello, and oboe.

BIOGRAPHICAL/CRITICAL SOURCES:

BOOKS

Allen, Walter, *The Modern Novel*, Dutton, 1964.
Anderson, David, *The Tragic Past*, John Knox Press, 1969.
Axthelm, Peter M., *The Modern Confessional Novel*, Yale University Press, 1967.
Babb, Howard S., *The Novels of William Golding*, Ohio State University Press, 1970.
Baker, James R., *William Golding: A Critical Study*, St. Martin's, 1965.
Biles, Jack I., *Talk: Conversations with William Golding*, Harcourt, 1971.
Biles, Jack I. and Robert O. Evans, editors, *William Golding: Some Critical Considerations*, University Press of Kentucky, 1979.
Burgess, Anthony, *The Novel Now: A Guide to Contemporary Fiction*, Norton, 1967.

Contemporary Literary Criticism, Gale, Volume 1, 1973, Volume 2, 1974, Volume 3, 1975, Volume 8, 1978, Volume 10, 1979, Volume 18, 1981, Volume 27, 1984.

Dick, Bernard F., *William Golding,* Twayne, 1967.

Dictionary of Literary Biography, Volume 15: *British Novelists, 1930-1959,* Gale, 1983.

Dictionary of Literary Biography Yearbook: 1983, Gale, 1984.

Gindin, James, *Postwar British Fiction: New Accents and Attitudes,* University of California Press, 1962.

Gindin, James, *Harvest of a Quiet Eve: The Novel of Compassion,* Indiana University Press, 1971.

Golding, William, *Lord of the Flies,* Faber, 1954, published with an introduction by E. M. Forster, Coward, 1955, reprinted, 1978.

Golding, William, *The Spire,* Harcourt, 1964.

Golding, William, *The Hot Gates, and Other Occasional Pieces,* Harcourt, 1965.

Golding, William, *Darkness Visible,* Farrar, Straus, 1979.

Golding, William, *Rites of Passage,* Farrar, Straus, 1980.

Golding, William, *A Moving Target,* Farrar, Straus, 1982.

Green, Peter, *A Review of English Literature,* Longmans, Green, 1960.

Hynes, Samuel, *William Golding,* Columbia University Press, 1964.

Johnson, Arnold, *Of Earth and Darkness: The Novels of William Golding,* University of Missouri Press, 1980.

Kennard, Jean E., *Number and Nightmare: Forms of Fantasy in Contemporary Fiction,* Archon Books, 1975.

Kinkead-Weekes, Mark and Ian Gregor, *William Golding: A Critical Study,* Faber, 1967.

Medcalf, Stephen, *William Golding,* Longman, 1975.

Oldsey, Bernard S. and Stanley Weintraub, *The Art of William Golding,* Harcourt, 1965.

Ries, Lawrence R., *Wolf Masks: Violence in Contemporary Fiction,* Kennikat Press, 1975.

Tiger, Virginia, *William Golding: The Dark Fields of Discovery,* Calder & Boyars, 1974.

PERIODICALS

Atlantic, May, 1965, April, 1984.

Chicago Tribune, October 7, 1983.

Chicago Tribune Book World, December 30, 1979, October 26, 1980, April 8, 1984.

Commentary, January, 1968.

Commonweal, October 25, 1968, September 26, 1980.

Critical Quarterly, summer, 1960, autumn, 1962, spring, 1967.

Critique: Studies in Modern Fiction, Volume 14, number 2, 1972.

Detroit News, December 16, 1979, January 4, 1981, April 29, 1984.

Kenyon Review, autumn, 1957.

Life, November 17, 1967.

Listener, October 4, 1979, October 23, 1980, January 5, 1984.

London Magazine, February-March, 1981.

London Review of Books, June 17, 1982.

Los Angeles Times Book Review, November 9, 1980, June 20, 1982, June 3, 1984.

New Republic, December 8, 1979, September 13, 1982.

New Statesman, August 2, 1958, April 10, 1964, November 5, 1965, October 12, 1979, October 17, 1980, June 11, 1982.

Newsweek, November 5, 1979, October 27, 1980, April 30, 1984.

New Yorker, September 21, 1957.

New York Post, December 17, 1963.

New York Review of Books, April 30, 1964, December 7, 1967, February 24, 1972, December 6, 1979, December 18, 1980.

New York Times, September 1, 1957, November 9, 1979, October 15, 1980, October 7, 1983, March 26, 1984, June 22, 1987.

New York Times Book Review, October 23, 1955, April 19, 1964, November 18, 1979, November 2, 1980, July 11, 1982.

Saturday Review, March 19, 1960.

South Atlantic Quarterly, autumn, 1970.

Southern Review, March, 1976.

Spectator, October 13, 1979.

Time, September 9, 1957, October 13, 1967, October 17, 1983, April 9, 1984, June 8, 1987.

Times (London), February 9, 1984, June 11, 1987.

Times Literary Supplement, October 21, 1955, October 23, 1959, June 1, 1967, November 5, 1971, November 23, 1979, October 17, 1980, July 23, 1982, March 2, 1984.

Twentieth Century Literature, summer, 1982.

Village Voice, November 5, 1979.

Washington Post, July 12, 1982, October 7, 1983, January 12, 1986.

Washington Post Book World, November 4, 1979, November 2, 1980, April 15, 1984.

Yale Review, spring, 1960.

* * *

GOLDSMITH, Peter
See PRIESTLEY, J(ohn) B(oynton)

* * *

GOODALL, Jane   1934-
(Jane van Lawick-Goodall)

PERSONAL: Born April 3, 1934, in London, England; daughter of Mortimer Herbert (a businessman and motor car racer) and Myfanwe (an author under name Vanne Goodall; maiden name Joseph) Goodall; married Hugo van Lawick (a nature photographer), March 28, 1964 (divorced); married Derek Bryceson (a member of Parliament and director of Tanzania National Parks), 1973 (deceased); children: (first marriage) Hugo Eric Louis. *Education:* Attended Uplands School, England; Cambridge University, Ph.D., 1965. *Religion:* Church of England.

ADDRESSES: Home and office—Gombe Stream Research Centre, P.O. Box 185, Kigoma, Tanzania, East Africa.

CAREER: Gombe Stream Research Centre, Tanzania, East Africa, ethologist, 1960—; writer, 1965—. Assistant secretary to Dr. Louis S. B. Leakey, 1960; assistant curator of National Museum of Natural History, Nairobi, Kenya, 1960. Visiting professor of psychiatry and human biology, Stanford University, 1970-75; honorary visiting professor of zoology, University of Dar Es Salaam, Tanzania, 1972—.

MEMBER: American Academy of Arts and Sciences (honorary foreign member, 1972—).

AWARDS, HONORS: Wilkie Brothers Foundation grant, 1960; two Franklin Burr prizes from National Geographic Society; gold medal for conservation from San Diego Zoological Society; conservation award from New York Zoological Society; J. Paul Getty Wildlife Conservation Prize, 1984; R. R. Hawkins Award from Association of American Publishers, 1987, for *The Chimpanzees of Gombe: Patterns of Behavior.*

WRITINGS:

UNDER NAME JANE van LAWICK-GOODALL

(Contributor) Irven De Vore, editor, *Primate Behavior,* Holt, 1965.

My Friends the Wild Chimpanzees, with photographs by Hugo van Lawick, National Geographic Society, 1967.

(Contributor) Desmond Morris, editor, *Primate Ethology,* Aldine, 1967.

The Behavior of Free-Living Chimpanzees in the Gombe Stream Reserve (monograph), Tindall & Cassell, 1968.

(With Hugo van Lawick) *Innocent Killers,* Collins, 1970, Houghton, 1971.

In the Shadow of Man, with photographs by Hugo van Lawick, Houghton, 1971, revised edition published under name Jane Goodall, 1988.

(With Hugo van Lawick) *Grub: The Bush Baby* (story of authors' son), Houghton, 1972.

UNDER NAME JANE GOODALL

The Chimpanzees of Gombe: Patterns of Behavior, Harvard University Press, 1986.

My Life with the Chimpanzees, Simon & Schuster, 1988.

The Chimpanzee Family Book, Picture Book Studio, 1989.

Through a Window, Houghton, 1990.

EDITOR; "JANE GOODALL'S ANIMAL WORLD" SERIES

Jane Goodall's Animal World: Chimpanzees, Macmillan, 1989.

Jane Goodall's Animal World: Lions, Macmillan, 1989.

Jane Goodall's Animal World: Hippos, Macmillan, 1989.

Jane Goodall's Animal World: Pandas, Macmillan, 1989.

OTHER

Contributor to *National Geographic, Nature, Annals of the New York Academy of Science,* and other journals.

WORK IN PROGRESS: Continued research and teaching on chimpanzee behavior.

SIDELIGHTS: Naturalist Jane Goodall has spent more than three decades in the jungles of Tanzania studying the behavior of wild chimpanzees. An animal lover since birth, the gentle Goodall has devoted herself to a quest for deeper understanding of the rich social, biological, and cultural interaction among the species most closely related to man. *New York Times* contributor John Noble Wilford calls Goodall "something of a celebrity: the young Englishwoman who plunges into Africa, spends the days and years in communion with chimpanzees, . . . dispatches occasional learned reports and keeps right on studying the animals she finds so fascinating." Wilford concludes that by virtue of her tenacious and inspiring work, Goodall has become "an authority of the first rank in the study of animal behavior."

Many youngsters dream of becoming wildlife biologists in the wilds of Africa. Goodall was one such child—she spent hours observing the animals in or near her London home and delighted in a toy chimpanzee someone had given her. Soon after graduating from high school, Goodall took an extended trip to Kenya in East Africa. There she became acquainted with Louis S. B. Leakey, a noted naturalist and paleontologist. Leakey was so impressed with Goodall's devotion to wildlife that he gave her a job so she could stay in Africa. Goodall served as an assistant secretary, accompanied the Leakeys on fossil-hunting trips to the remote Olduvai Gorge region, and helped to improve the National Museum of Natural History in Nairobi. In 1960, Leakey proposed a project that proved irresistible to Goodall: a six-month field study of the wild chimpanzees on a reserve in Tanzania.

Goodall had no formal training in ethology (the study of animal behavior) when she began her duties in the Gombe Stream Chimpanzee Reserve. What she did have was a fierce curiosity about her subject and a high tolerance for primitive living conditions in rugged, inhospitable terrain. Fighting malaria and the constant intrusion of cobras, centipedes, and thieving baboons, Goodall attempted to follow the activities of an elusive band of chimps that lived in the Gombe area. For months she observed the animals through binoculars, slowly moving closer as they became accustomed to her presence. After six months she realized that her task, if done properly, would take years and years. The Leakey family helped to find further funding for the project, and Goodall patiently and painstakingly began to compile a wealth of original observations of wild chimpanzee behavior.

Goodall's many fascinating discoveries are documented in the books she has written, most notably *In the Shadow of Man* and *The Chimpanzees of Gombe: Patterns of Behavior.* Goodall has also been featured in several *National Geographic* television specials. As John H. Crook notes in the *New York Times Book Review,* Goodall's "careful documentation puts the necessary flesh on much that has been merely speculation and corrects earlier accounts of chimpanzee behavior." Among other things, Goodall has observed wild chimps making and using simple tools, stalking and killing small animals for food, battling rival troops of chimps for terrain, and cooperating in such group activities as hunting and defending territory. Most critics agree that the value of Goodall's research lies in the longevity of the project—her unbroken observation of individual animals for a decade or more has led to a number of important discoveries about chimpanzee child rearing, aggression, and personality development. "Jane Goodall's popular books on chimpanzees have the family lines of Tolstoy and the addictive intrigue of a soap opera—the 'Dynasty' of chimps," writes *Washington Post* correspondent Carla Hall.

Goodall did not seek to become a celebrity. Her earliest work—and much of her subsequent writing—is scholarly, aimed at the university-trained specialist. She does realize, however, that lay readers, especially children, are fascinated by primates. According to Denise R. Majkut in *Best Sellers,* throughout Goodall's work the author "comes across as a great lover of nature—loving the beauty of the wild jungles of Africa, the continuing struggle for survival there of the chimps, and man's typical behavior." Indeed, Goodall has taken numerous leaves from her field studies in recent years in order to become a spokesperson for conservation of chimpanzee habitat as well as for humane treatment of captive primates. Goodall especially likes to impart these ideas to children. "I feel it's something I want to spend more time telling children: that animals are like us," she told *Publishers Weekly.* "They feel pain like we do. We want to make people understand that every chimp is an individual, with the same kinds of intellectual abilities."

Goodall is only the eighth person in the history of Cambridge University to have received a Ph.D. without first earning a baccalaureate. The honor was based on a thesis she produced after her first five years in the Gombe Stream Reserve. Bettyann Kevles claims in the *Los Angeles Times Book Review* that Goodall has done more than any other scientist to enlighten humankind about the rich life of chimpanzees. Kevles writes: "Thanks to the painstaking efforts of Goodall and her colleagues, we admire the chimpanzees of Gombe because we understand the complexity of their lives." Now an international traveller who lectures and writes in addition to her field work, Goodall hopes her work will help win new respect for members of the animal kingdom. "I want to make [people] aware that animals have their own needs, emotions, and feelings—they matter," she told *Publishers Weekly.* ". . . I want to give kids a passion, an understanding and awareness of the wonder of animals."

MEDIA ADAPTATIONS: Several television specials have featured Goodall and her work, including "Miss Goodall and the Wild Chimpanzees," Columbia Broadcasting System, 1965.

AVOCATIONAL INTERESTS: Riding, photography, reading, classical music.

BIOGRAPHICAL/CRITICAL SOURCES:

BOOKS

Coerr, Eleanor B., *Jane Goodall,* Putnam, 1976.
Fox, Mary Virginia, *Jane Goodall: Living Chimp Style,* Dillon, 1981.
Goodall, Jane van Lawick, *In the Shadow of Man,* Houghton, 1971, revised edition, 1988.
Goodall, Jane and Hugo van Lawick, *Grub: The Bush Baby,* Houghton, 1972.
Goodall, Jane, *My Life with the Chimpanzees,* Simon & Schuster, 1988.
Green, Timothy, *The Restless Spirit: Profiles in Adventure,* Walker & Co., 1970 (published in England as *The Adventurers,* M. Joseph, 1970).

PERIODICALS

Best Sellers, November 15, 1971.
Booklist, January 1, 1972.
Chicago Tribune, August 24, 1986, February 15, 1987.
Chicago Tribune Book World, October 17, 1971.
Choice, January, 1972.
Christian Science Monitor, October 14, 1971.
Economist, October 30, 1971.
Kirkus Reviews, August 15, 1971.
Ladies' Home Journal, October, 1971, February, 1975.
Library Journal, December 1, 1971, March 1, 1972.
Listener, November 25, 1971.
Los Angeles Times Book Review, December 28, 1986.
McCall's, August, 1970.
Nation, January 17, 1972.
Natural History, December, 1967.
New Statesman, December 4, 1970, December 3, 1971.
Newsweek, June 2, 1975.
New York Times, November 26, 1971, August 19, 1986.
New York Times Book Review, August 24, 1986.
New York Times Magazine, February 18, 1973.
Publishers Weekly, November 22, 1970, August 9, 1971, October 2, 1972, January 29, 1988.
Saturday Review of Science, February, 1973.
Time, November 30, 1970, November 8, 1971.
Times Literary Supplement, November 20, 1970, November 19, 1971, May 1, 1987.
Tribune Books (Chicago), November 9, 1986, June 5, 1988.
U.S. News and World Report, November 5, 1984.
Voice Literary Supplement, September, 1986.
Washington Post, September 18, 1984, January 24, 1987.
Washington Post Book World, March 13, 1988.

*   *   *

GOODMAN, Paul 1911-1972

PERSONAL: Born September 9, 1911, in New York, N.Y.; son of Barnett (a businessman) and Augusta Goodman; died August 3, 1972, in North Stratford, N.H.; married (common-law) to second wife, Sally; children: (first marriage) Susan; (second marriage) Mathew R., Daisy J. *Education:* City College of New York (now City College of the City University of New York), B.A., 1931; attended lectures at Columbia and Harvard, though he was never officially registered at either institution; University of Chicago, Ph.D., 1940 (received, 1954).

ADDRESSES: Home—New York, N.Y.; and North Stratford, N.H.

CAREER: Worked as an outside reader for Metro-Goldwyn-Mayer, 1931; University of Chicago, instructor, 1939-40; Manumit School of Progressive Education, Pawling, N.Y., instructor in Latin, physics, history, and mathematics; later an instructor at Black Mountain College, Black Mountain, N.C.; has taught at New York University and Sarah Lawrence College; was Knapp Professor, University of Wisconsin, 1964; taught at Experimental College of San Francisco State College, 1966, and University of Hawaii, 1971-72. Lecturer on college campuses. Conducted seminars on "Education and the Great Society" at Institute for Policy Studies, Washington, D.C. Practiced as lay psychotherapist with the New York Institute for Gestalt Therapy.

AWARDS, HONORS: American Council of Learned Societies fellowship, 1940; Harriet Monroe Memorial Prize from *Poetry* magazine, 1949; award from the National Institute of Arts and Letters, 1953.

WRITINGS:

POETRY

Stop-light, Vinco Publishing, 1941.
(Contributor) *Five Young American Poets,* New Directions, 1945.
The Well of Bethlehem, privately printed, c. 1950.
Red Jacket, privately printed, c. 1956.
The Lordly Hudson: Collected Poems, Macmillan, 1962.
Day, and Other Poems, privately printed, c. 1960.
Hawkweed, Random House, 1967.
North Percy, Black Sparrow, 1968.
Homespun of Oatmeal Gray, Random House, 1970.
Collected Poems, Random House, 1974.

FICTION

The Grand Piano, or, The Almanac of Alienation (novel), Colt, 1942.
The Facts of Life (stories), Vanguard, 1945.
State of Nature (novel), Vanguard, 1946.
The Break-Up of Our Camp and Other Stories, New Directions, 1949.
The Dead of Spring (novel), privately printed, 1950.
Parents' Day (novel), 5x8 Press, 1951, recent edition, Black Sparrow, 1985.
The Empire City (collected novels), Bobbs-Merrill, 1959.
Our Visit to Niagara (stories), Horizon Press, 1960.
Making Do (novel), Macmillan, 1963.
Adam and His Works (stories), Random House, 1968.
The Collected Stories and Sketches of Paul Goodman, edited by Taylor Stoehr, Black Sparrow, Volume 1: *The Break-Up of Our Camp: Stories, 1932-1935,* 1978, Volume 2: *A Ceremonial: Stories, 1936-1940,* 1978, Volume 3: *The Facts of Life: Stories, 1940-1949,* 1979, Volume 4: *The Galley to Mytilene: Stories, 1949-1960,* 1980.
Don Juan: or, The Continuum of the Libido, edited by Taylor Stoehr, Black Sparrow, 1979.

NONFICTION

(With Meyer Leben and Edward Roditi) *Pieces of Three,* 5x8 Press, 1942.
Art and Social Nature (essays), Arts and Science Press, 1946.

Kafka's Prayer (criticism), Vanguard, 1947.

(With brother, Percival Goodman) *Communitas: Means of Livelihood and Ways of Life,* University of Chicago Press, 1947, 2nd edition, Vintage, 1960.

(With Frederick S. Perls and Ralph Hefferline) *Gestalt Therapy,* Messner, 1951.

The Structure of Literature (criticism), University of Chicago Press, 1954.

Censorship and Pornography on the Stage and Are Writers Shirking Their Political Duty? [New York], c. 1959.

Growing Up Absurd: Problems of Youth in the Organized System, Random House, 1960.

The Community of Scholars, Random House, 1962.

Utopian Essays and Practical Proposals, Random House, 1962.

Drawing the Line, Random House, 1962.

The Society I Live in Is Mine, Horizon Press, 1963.

Compulsory Mis-Education, Horizon Press, 1964.

People or Personnel: Decentralizing and the Mixed System, Random House, 1965.

Five Years: Thoughts During a Useless Time (partial autobiography), Brussell & Brussell, 1967.

Like a Conquered Province: The Moral Ambiguity of America (Massey Lectures, Canadian Broadcasting Corp.), Random House, 1967.

The Open Look, Funk, 1969.

The Individual and Culture, Dorsey, 1969.

New Reformation: Notes of a Neolithic Conservative, Random House, 1970.

Speaking and Language: Defense of Poetry (criticism), Random House, 1971.

Little Prayers and Finite Experience, Harper, 1972.

Drawing the Line: The Political Essays of Paul Goodman, edited by Taylor Stoehr, Free Life Editions (New York), 1977.

Nature Heals: The Psychological Essays of Paul Goodman, edited by Taylor Stoehr, Free Life Editions, 1977.

Creator Spirit Come! The Literary Essays of Paul Goodman, edited by Taylor Stoehr, Free Life Editions, 1977.

The Black Flag of Anarchism, Kropotkin's Lighthouse (London, England), 1978.

PLAYS

Childish Jokes: Crying Backstage (first produced in New York by Living Theatre, August, 1951), 5x8 Press, 1958.

"The Cave at Machpelah", first produced in New York at Living Theatre Playhouse, June, 1959.

Three Plays: The Young Disciple (first produced in New York by Living Theatre, October, 1955), *Faustina* (first produced in New York at Cherry Lane Theatre, May, 1952), *Jonah* (first produced in New York at American Place Theater, February, 1966), Random House, 1965.

Tragedy and Comedy: Four Cubist Plays, Black Sparrow, 1970.

OTHER

(Contributor) M. R. Stein, A. J. Vidick, and D. M. White, editors, *Identity and Anxiety,* Free Press, 1960.

(Contributor) Herbert Gold, editor, *First Person Singular: Essays for the Sixties,* Dial, 1963.

(Editor) *Seeds of Liberation,* Braziller, 1965.

(Compiler) *Essays in American Colonial History,* Holt, 1967.

Contributor to *Dissent, Commentary, Harper's, Commonweal, Poetry, Playboy, Salmagundi, Esquire, Symposium, Mademoiselle, Nation, New York Review of Books,* and other publications. Edited *Complex* magazine; former film editor, *Partisan Review;* served as television critic, *New Republic.* An editor of *Liberation,* 1960-72.

SIDELIGHTS: During the wave of radicalism which swept college campuses in the 1960s, students who believed they could trust no one over thirty made an exception for Paul Goodman. Journalists have noted that Goodman was the only writer consistently quoted by the Free Speech Movement in Berkeley. According to George Steiner, "Goodman's is about the only American voice that young English pacifists and nuclear disarmers find convincing." Students see him "as the prophet and exemplar of a free life in a bureaucratic society," wrote Richard Kostelanetz. He in turn saw the students as "the major exploited class," whose education is for the most part a waste of time. "To Goodman, drop-outs, delinquents, and college beatniks are all victims of the same process," said Peter Schrag, "and have all refused to accept the terms of organized society and the empty rat race (his phrase) which it imposes."

Society's terms are precisely what Goodman always refused to accept. He was what Michael Harrington calls "a devotee of that genuinely American cult of experience in which the natural man refuses to obey, or rather, seeks to destroy conventional society." He admired the individual and despised organizational personnel and any "enterprises extrinsically motivated and interlocked with other centralized systems." (Goodman said that his liberalism often took him close to the position held by the radical Right.) All of the instances of dissatisfaction that Goodman enumerated were directly concerned with his belief that, as Steiner explains, "the health of society [is] indivisible from the mental state and psychopathology of the individual," an individual who is always a social animal. To arrive at his philosophical position, Goodman "linked doctrines of anarchism, non-violence, and decentralization derived from Kropotkin, Gandhi, and Jefferson, to the heritage of Freud and, more specifically, of Wilhelm Reich." Kostelanetz noted that "essentially, Goodman believes that man is creative, loving, and communal; but often the institutions and roles of behavior that he creates serve to alienate him from his natural self. Moreover, once society's organizations become more important than the individuals who comprise them, then man must suppress his humanity to suit the inhuman system." Kostelanetz added that, throughout Goodman's lectures, books, and public statements, "what particularly impresses the young (and perhaps disturbs the old) is Goodman's personal integrity. He has always lived by his ideals, defying whatever bureaucratic systems he touched, practicing conspicuously the non-conformist sexual behavior he preached (resulting in his being fired from his first three teaching positions), forbidding editors to bowdlerize what he had written, attaining such a mastery over poverty that he could never succumb to money, and having a sense of purpose that made him resistant to flattery or vanity."

Steiner felt that he continued to "sustain dialogue amid the chaotic loudness of mass society. . . . Between the closing walls of technological determinism and political cliche, he is trying to hack out elbow room for the imagination. The novels, the poems, the polemics, the tough-minded reveries of the utopian, spring from an axiom of hope: from the assertion that the imperatives of our social and political condition are only apparent, that they do not enshrine the only possibility." Goodman once said "It is false that I write about many subjects. I have only one, the human beings I know in their man-made scene." He was a self-described "community anarchist" whose concern was the improvement of society through the efforts of individuals and voluntary groups. He said optimistically: "If ten thousand people in all walks of life will stand up on their two feet and talk out and insist, we shall get back our country."

Writing was Goodman's principal vocation, though it was not a profitable one until the publication of *Growing Up Absurd.*

Steiner believes that "roughly, Goodman's career falls into three periods: a stage of intellectually brilliant but not unconventional radicalism in the 1930s, culminating in his novel, *The Empire City* (1942); a fairly long eclipse, during which his work was known to a small circle of passionate admirers; . . . and the breakthrough, after *Growing Up Absurd* in 1960, and the re-issue of *Communitas.*" *Growing Up Absurd,* an argument in defense of America's youth, "defines the chaos of society that they sense but cannot clarify," writes Kostelanetz. Goodman continued to write about the young, especially in relation to education. "Fundamentally," he said, "there is no right education except growing up into a worthwhile world. Indeed, our excessive concern with problems of education at present simply means that the grown-ups do not have such a world." He favors small colleges where students would be guided by "intrinsic motivation," and has proposed voluntary attendance on all levels of education. The components of our present system, he believed, "are a uniform world-view, the absence of any viable alternative, confusion about the relevance of one's own experience and feelings, and a chronic anxiety, so that one clings to the one world-view as the only security. This is brainwashing." Dropping-out, as he saw it, is a sound alternative. In *Compulsory Mis-Education,* Goodman, a Ph.D., states that "long schooling is not only inept, it is psychologically, politically and professionally damaging." He further believes that we should be experimenting with "different kinds of schools, no school at all, the real city as school, farm schools, practical apprenticeships, guided travel, work camps, little theaters and local newspapers, community service."

On the basis of his proposals for an improved educational system, Goodman's critics labeled him a romantic, a dreamer, an anti-intellectual. Schrag notes that "his chief villains—men like James B. Conant—are people who see education as training ground for the demands that this culture makes." While reviewing *The Community of Scholars,* wherein Goodman advocated a return to the ideal of the medieval university, D. M. Grunschlag was disconcerted because Goodman apparently showed a greater concern for "student happiness, administrative fluency, and 'growing up' than [for] education." On the other hand, Goodman has become "a sort of roving prophet," says Schrag, "for the independent students who are establishing free universities and similar para-academic organizations."

Yet even those who admire his ideas find some of his solutions unworkable. Nat Hentoff writes: "Goodman's solutions to the various problems he confronts are often debatable and are sometimes impossible of achievement without a prior social revolution that he does not know how to instigate. His highest and most stimulating function, therefore, is as a nay-sayer. What makes him so readable is that all his years in exacerbated opposition have not made him chronically self-righteous or humorless. . . . However one may disagree with Goodman's theories, it is invigorating to attend his indignant, sardonic, and often devastatingly accurate assaults on specific examples of obtuseness in the culture." Some of his discourses have also been attacked as either poorly written or lacking in sound judgment. In response to one attack on his alleged imprecision and wooliness, he wrote: "I suppose I ought to say something about the [charge] that I don't do my homework, since other profound scholars . . . have accused me of the same. (Indeed, I seem to some people to be a village idiot.) Now Aristotle points out that it is the sign of an ignorant man to be more precise than the subject warrants. In books like *Growing Up, Gestalt Therapy,* and *Communitas* I am trying to say something about the whole man in an indefinitely complicated organism/environment field. My experience in reading in this interesting subject is that those au-

thors say the best things who keep their visions central and concrete, . . . who draw on what they know intimately, and are not afraid to risk being passionately involved. Their strong errors, as St. Thomas says, are better than weak truths."

Goodman's books teem with suggestions for man's improvement. He proposed, instead of a reliance on drugs, a return to revitalizing leisure activity; the non-interference of the state in one's sexual life ("to license sex is absurd"); withdrawal from Vietnam; banning private automobiles in Manhattan; building dormitories in housing projects to allow children to safely get away from home; and removing national boundaries by encouraging economic regionalism and international functions. Certain critics, such as Edmund Fuller, believe that Goodman is "a sage in some areas and a screwball in others." Goodman simply held to his position that "to make positive decisions for one's community, rather than being regimented by others' decisions, is one of the noble acts of man."

"First, I'm a humanist," said Goodman. "Anything I write on society is pragmatic—it aims to accomplish something. . . . Apart from that I'm also an artist. That's a different internal spring. You don't create an artwork from the same motivation. I write songs, for instance, but that's the same as writing a poem. Also, it's impossible to be a dramatist without being a musician or a choreographer. I'm a man of letters."

His fiction, poetry, and literary criticism are as provocative and inventive as his social essays. Robert Phelps called *Empire City,* which includes Goodman's favorite book, *The Dead of Spring,* "a book originating in good will, mature candor, and an urgently fermenting, more than secular morality. . . . The spirit inside, and the text itself, which seems not so much written as whistled, laughed, teased, prayed, come as close to imparting a man's gratuitous love for his own kind as mere language ever can." Denise Levertov wrote of his poems: "Rhythmically, most of the story poems tend to go flat, and inventive though Paul Goodman is he cannot put me, for me, into the long-since-dead ballade. But the sonnets are among the few readable sonnets of the century. . . . [Some of the other poems are] marvels of true, peculiar, irreducible poetry." Laurence Lieberman wrote of Goodman's poetry: "It is his lover's quarrel with the country that I'm grateful to find he's keeping alive in the poems, and that is what gives his poetry a kind of superabundant life that is rare today." Goodman once said: "I must write, freely, the kind of poems and stories that belong to a person who dutifully takes on these other responsibilities of citizenship. Yet the task is too much for me." Steiner sees "both the moral choice and the statement of defeat [as] Jewish. But as one looks at the prodigious amount of work done, there is no sense of failure; only the exhilarating sight of a man fighting windmills which have, in fact, turned out to be Philistine giants. Mr. Goodman is a *mensch.* The species is getting rare."

BIOGRAPHICAL/CRITICAL SOURCES:

BOOKS

Contemporary Issues Criticism, Gale, Volume 1, 1982.
Contemporary Literary Criticism, Gale, Volume 1, 1973, Volume 2, 1974, Volume 4, 1975, Volume 7, 1977.
Nicely, Tom, *Adam and His Work: A Bibliography of Sources by and About Paul Goodman (1911-1972),* Scarecrow Press, 1979.
Parisi, Peter, editor, *Artist of the Actual: Essays on Paul Goodman,* Scarecrow Press, 1986.
Widmer, Kingsley, *Paul Goodman,* Twayne, 1980.

PERIODICALS

Atlantic, August, 1965.
Commentary, June, 1960, August, 1963.
Nation, April 13, 1963.
New York Herald Tribune Book Review, June 28, 1959, November 18, 1962.
New York Herald Tribune Lively Arts, January 15, 1961.
New York Times Book Review, September 27, 1964.
New York Times Magazine, April 3, 1966.
Reporter, July 18, 1963, January 26, 1967.
Saturday Review, February 17, 1962, February 18, 1967.
Times Literary Supplement, October 22, 1954.
Washington Post Book World, January 4, 1981.

OBITUARIES:

PERIODICALS

Newsweek, August 14, 1972.
New York Times, August 4, 1972.
Publishers Weekly, August 14, 1972.
Time, August 14, 1972.

*   *   *

GORBACHEV, Mikhail (Sergeyevich) 1931-

PERSONAL: Born March 2, 1931, in Privolnoye, Stavropol, U.S.S.R.; son of Sergei (a combine driver) and Maria (Panteleyevna) Gorbachev; married Raisa Maksimovna Titorenko (a former professor of Marxist-Leninist theory at Moscow State University), 1954; children: Irina (daughter). *Education:* Moscow State University, law degree, 1955; Stavropol Agricultural Institute, degree in agriculture, 1967.

ADDRESSES: Home—Moscow, U.S.S.R. *Office*—Central Communist Party of the Soviet Union, Staraya Place 4, Moscow, U.S.S.R.

CAREER: Soviet politician and statesman. Agricultural worker in Stavropol Krai, U.S.S.R., 1946-50; Communist Party of the Soviet Union, Stravropol City Committee, Stavropol, member of Komsomol (Young Communist League), beginning 1956, first secretary, 1956-58, 1966-68, second secretary, 1968-70, Stravropol Krai Committee, Komsomol, second secretary and first secretary, 1958-62, first secretary, 1970-78, deputy to U.S.S.R. Supreme Soviet, beginning 1970, Central Committee, Moscow, member, 1971—, secretary for agriculture, beginning 1978, candidate member of Politburo, 1979, full member of Politburo, 1980, chairman of foreign affairs committee, beginning 1984, general secretary, 1985—. Presidium of the Supreme Soviet of U.S.S.R., member, 1985—, chairman, 1988—.

AWARDS, HONORS: Has received many awards and decorations, including three Order of Lenin citations, Order of the October Revolution, Order of the Red Banner of Labor, 1949, and named *Time* magazine's Man of the Decade for the 1980s, January, 1990.

WRITINGS:

(And author of introduction) *A Time for Peace* (collection of Gorbachev's speeches), Richardson & Steirman, 1985.
Perestroika: New Thinking for Our Country and the World, Harper, 1987.

SIDELIGHTS: "To do something better, you must work an extra bit harder," writes Soviet Union leader Mikhail Gorbachev in his book *Perestroika: New Thinking for Our Country and the World.* "I like this phrase: working an *extra bit harder.* For me,

it is not just a slogan, but a habitual state of mind." It is precisely this type of dedication to his ideals and goals, that has lead Gorbachev from a position as a harvester operator in southern Russia to general secretary of the Soviet Central Committee making Gorbachev one of the most powerful and influential leaders in the world today.

Gorbachev was virtually unknown to much of the world until he was chosen successor to Konstantin U. Chernenko as general secretary of the Soviet Union. Since his appointment on March 11, 1985, he has become internationally recognized as a fearless, aggressive, intelligent, and personable politician striving to revitalize the Soviet Union by introducing the concepts of *glasnost,* or openness, and *perestroika,* or restructuring, within the U.S.S.R. While his major concern is the stagnation of the Soviet economy and the implementation of key economic reforms, Gorbachev has also been working diligently on plans to better Soviet life by improving its technology and science, and promoting its arts and literature. Gorbachev's book, *Perestroika: New Thinking for Our Country and the World* outlines the reforms he believes are necessary for the Soviet Union to undertake to further develop and strengthen its political, social, and economic system.

Essential to bringing about the economic successes hoped for and discussed in *Perestroika,* the complete revision of the old five-year economic plan designed during the Brezhnev years was necessary. The new plan, conceived by Gorbachev and his economic advisers, calls for decreased bureaucratic control and involvement in state enterprises and the total elimination of corruption and incompetence in all levels of the Communist party and the government. At the same time, increased emphasis on improving the quality of Soviet products, updating plant equipment and machinery, encouraging the importance of research and development, accenting both short- and long-term innovative planning are vitally important and essential. As Gorbachev summarizes in a speech he delivered to the Soviet Central Committee in December of 1984: "We cannot remain a major power in world affairs unless we put our domestic house in order."

In *Perestroika,* Gorbachev also expresses his desire for better cooperation and involvement in the world community. In the spirit of *glasnost,* the Soviet Union is working toward improving communication, increasing understanding, and suggesting the possibility of joint projects and ventures to be undertaken with other nations. Gorbachev is especially interested in possible trade agreements and discussing defense and military options between the Soviets and the other major countries in the world such as the United States and England.

In the *Washington Post,* a spokesperson for *Perestroika*'s American publisher, Harper & Row, provides this quote from Gorbachev to describe his purpose in writing this book: "This book is not a scientific treatise, nor a base of propaganda. . . . This book is about our plans and how we are going to implement them." Gorbachev was also quoted as saying: "We want people of every country to enjoy prosperity, welfare and happiness. The road to this lies through proceeding to a nuclear-free, nonviolent world. We have embarked on this road and call on other countries and nations to follow suit."

In a review of *Perestroika,* Toronto's *Globe & Mail* reviewer Charles Taylor remarks: "In the first half of his book, Gorbachev explains and defends his doctrine of *perestroika*: the restructuring of the Soviet Union's economic and political system, which he launched three years ago. With some frankness, he describes how the bureaucratic mentality had led to lethargy and stagnation, and how dramatic changes had become essential." Taylor continues to comment: "[Gorbachev's commitment to *detente*] dominates the second half of his book, and is the main object of the exercise. Nuclear war is unthinkable, since it would mean the end of civilization. For this reason, neither the United States nor the Soviet Union can seek to dominate the world. Instead, they must actively pursue arms control and avoid confrontations."

"*Perestroika,* or restructuring, as vividly and conversationally described in this remarkable manifesto," writes Robert Scheer in the *Los Angeles Times Book Review,* "is based on a profound criticism of the 'stagnation' of Soviet society and an insistence on radically reordering its essential economic mechanisms. But *perestroika* requires for its success a breeze of *glasnost* blowing through the country's stultified intellectually and political life." Scheer continues to remark: "If *perestroika*—for now a top-down movement with all of the limitations thus implied—succeeds in cutting through the morass of bureaucratic inefficiency and stupidity to ignite grass-roots support, it will represent a second Soviet 'revolution.' Or so Gorbachev claims, writing as a new Lenin in this modern rendition (or revision) of the Soviet Founding Father's 'What Is to Be Done?' "

Writing about *Perestroika* in the *New York Times Book Review,* Robert Legvold notes that "no Soviet leader has ever before written anything like it: a long, impassioned, self-justifying letter to the American people. . . . None ever addressed us directly, laying out the disasters and challenges preoccupying him at home, trying to convey his understanding of international realities, and inviting a joint effort to think through what truly matters in the contest between our two societies." Legvold goes on to write that "Gorbachev is up to something enormously important within his own land, and, if we will hear him out, we may begin to understand what drives him, and what is in it for us. Mr. Gorbachev believes deeply in the Soviet system, but he also knows that the system is in profound trouble, and he accepts the need for thoroughgoing change. His book shows us both sides of the man."

Although promoting controversial reforms, laboring to end corruption on all levels, and working to improve Soviet relations with the other super powers in the world, Gorbachev is not seeking to fundamentally change the Soviet Union's political system. He is seeking to revitalize and strengthen, and build a more effective party organization and government. Gorbachev comments in *Perestroika:* "We carry out all our transformations in accordance with socialist options, and we are looking for answers to questions brought up by life within the framework of socialism. . . . We are measuring all our successes and mistakes by socialist yardsticks." Gorbachev is still a staunch believer and loyal member in the Soviet system that he became involved in while attending law school at Moscow State University.

Gorbachev was so committed to the Communist Party that after graduation he began working professionally for the Komsomol (Young Communist League) after earning his law degree. Gorbachev was routinely given more responsibility and awarded with a number of key promotions that brought him to the attention of influential party members and made him part of the Kremlin's inner circle. Arkady N. Shevchenko, a high ranking Soviet official who has since defected, described Gorbachev in his book, *Breaking with Moscow,* as "intelligent, well educated, and well mannered." Shevchenko also stated that Gorbachev had "earned a reputation as an energetic regional Party leader and manager. . . . He was also known as a reasonable man, with less arrogance than most professional Party [workers]."

In 1982, Yuri Andropov was selected general secretary after long-time Soviet leader Leonid Brezhenev died. Although thought by some party officials as a possible candidate for the

position, Gorbachev instead became Yuri Andropov's chief lieutenant. As chief lieutenant, Gorbachev was responsible for carrying out many of the reforms that the general secretary felt was necessary to strengthen the government and the Communist Party. When Andropov died fifteen months after taking office, the Politburo, unsure whether to continue Andropov's campaign for reform, chose conservative seventy-two-year-old Konstantin U. Chernenko to succeed Andropov.

Under Chernenko's command, Gorbachev became chairman of the foreign affairs committee of the Supreme Soviet often filling in for the ailing general secretary at public leadership functions. On March 11, 1985, the day after Chernenko died, Gorbachev was chosen to succeed Chernenko as general secretary of the Soviet Union. As head of the largest country on the globe—one that extends across eleven time zones—and with a population of over 273 million people, Gorbachev is in a key position to effect world affairs.

Gorbachev has proved to be a quite different leader than his predecessors. Considered by many to be an eloquent and effective speaker and an intelligent and thoughtful politician, Gorbachev has somewhat softened many people's views concerning the Soviet Union and communism. Before Gorbachev, the world was accustomed to seeing very little of Soviet leaders and when they did appear in public they were elderly, frequently in poor health, a bit rough, aggressive, and uncompromising. Gorbachev has changed this image by his promotion of *glasnost*. Repeatedly referred to as "a master at public relations," Gorbachev began appearing regularly on Soviet television, officially visiting numerous countries and meeting with their leaders, attending conferences on global issues, and even stopping to chat with the citizens on the street in both the Soviet Union and abroad.

In a lengthy *Time* article, George J. Church sums up his thoughts on Gorbachev: "He could be the most dangerous adversary the U.S. and its allies have faced in decades—or the most constructive. Molded by famine and war, promised a measure of hope after Stalin's demise and then abruptly disillusioned, Gorbachev is not the sort of man who would willingly drag his country back into the dark days of repression, economic hardship and international obloquy. If there is a lesson in the 56-year education of Mikhail Sergeyevich Gorbachev, it is that a new, unfamiliar kind of leader has risen in the Soviet Union, and that the old rules of dealing with that long-suffering land are suddenly outdated. For the West, the education is just beginning."

While *perestroika* seems to be somewhat improving the image of the Soviet Union in the West, the process of reform is going rather slowly in the Soviet Union. Many of the changes approved by the Politburo as long ago as 1983 have not yet been uniformly put into effect. The average Soviet citizen—whether in the cities or in the agricultural regions—is not yet experiencing any benefits from Gorbachev's ideas. Daily life is still very difficult for the majority of Soviet citizens—there are long lines and very little choice of food, very limited and poor housing conditions available, extremely high costs for most consumer goods, and low compensation of salaries for work done.

This growing frustration was evident at the 1990 annual May Day event. Traditionally, an orchestrated show of worker solidarity, the celebration held in Red Square in Moscow turned out to be a historical happening. In the spirit of *glasnost,* the parade and related festivities were opened for the first time in history to include any organization that wished to participate. Over tens of thousands of people marched in the parade, representing a variety of groups, including Hare Krishnas, social democrats, and anti-Stalinists. As many of these marchers passed the spot where the top leaders of the Soviet Union sat, they booed, jeered, and carried banners that condemned Gorbachev and other leaders, their policies, and the communist party.

In an interview conducted by senior executives and editors of the *Washington Post* and *Newsweek,* Gorbachev explains what he feels is the current feeling among Soviets concerning *perestroika:* "When such huge undertakings as *perestroika* take place, when we need to develop not only the strategy but also the tactics of moving forward, that requires not only active dialogue in the leadership but in the whole society. And that is what has been happening. The whole country is now an enormous debating society. . . . We, together with our society, are seeking answers to all questions. And this is accompanied by discussions, and sometimes by heated debate, and that is normal. Our problem has been that for many years there was no such debate in the society, in the party, not in the Central Committee, not in the government itself or the Politburo. This absence of debate led to many losses, mistakes and omissions."

Recently, the politics of the world seem to be changing very quickly. East and West Germany are no longer divided by the Berlin War, the people of several Soviet bloc countries, including Lithuania and Romania, are strongly expressing their desire for independence from Soviet rule. The outcome from these events, coupled with future political changes and the internal upheaval in the Soviet Union, indicate exciting and uncertain times ahead for Gorbachev.

"With remarkable imagination and daring [Gorbachev] has embarked on a course, perhaps now irreversible, that is reshaping the world," declares Lance Morrow in *Time.* "He is trying to transform a government that was not just bad or inept but inherently destructive, its stupidity regularly descending into evil. He has been breaking up an old bloc to make way for a new Europe, altering the relationship of the Soviet empire with the rest of the world and changing the nature of the empire itself. He has made possible the end of the cold war and diminished the danger that a hot war will ever break out between the superpowers."

BIOGRAPHICAL/CRITICAL SOURCES:

BOOKS

Gorbachev, Mikhail, *Perestroika: New Thinking for Our Country and the World,* Harper, 1987.
Shevchenko, Arkady N., *Breaking with Moscow,* Knopf, 1985.
Sullivan, George, *Mikhail Gorbachev,* Messner, 1988.

PERIODICALS

Detroit Free Press, May 2, 1990.
Globe & Mail (Toronto), January 9, 1988.
Los Angeles Times, September 26, 1987.
Los Angeles Times Book Review, November 15, 1987.
Newsweek, May 6, 1985, December 4, 1989, December 11, 1989.
New York Times Magazine, March 3, 1985.
New York Times Book Review, December 13, 1987.
Time, January 4, 1988, January 1, 1990.
Washington Post, September 26, 1987, May 22, 1988.

*   *   *

GORDIMER, Nadine   1923-

PERSONAL: Born November 20, 1923, in Springs, South Africa; daughter of Isidore (a jeweler) and Nan (Myers) Gordimer; married Gerald Gavronsky, March 6, 1949 (divorced, 1952); married Reinhold H. Cassirer (owner and director of art gallery), January 29, 1954; children: (first marriage) Oriane Tara-masco; (second marriage) Hugo. *Education:* Attended private schools and the University of the Witwatersrand.

ADDRESSES: Home—7 Frere Rd., Parktown West, Johannesburg 2193, South Africa. *Agent*—Russell & Volkening, Inc., 50 West 29th St., New York, N.Y. 10001.

CAREER: Writer. Ford Foundation visiting professor, under auspices of Institute of Contemporary Arts, Washington, D.C., 1961; lecturer, Hopwood Awards, University of Michigan, Ann Arbor, 1970; writer in residence, American Academy in Rome, 1984; has also lectured and taught writing at Harvard, Princeton, Northwestern, Columbia, and Tulane universities.

MEMBER: International PEN (vice-president), Congress of South African Writers, Royal Society of Literature, American Academy of Arts and Sciences (honorary member), American Academy of Literature and Arts (honorary member).

AWARDS, HONORS: W. H. Smith & Son Literary Award, 1961, for short story collection *Friday's Footprint, and Other Stories;* Thomas Pringle Award, 1969; James Tait Black Memorial Prize, 1973, for *A Guest of Honour;* Booker Prize for Fiction, National Book League, 1974, for *The Conservationist;* Grand Aigle d'Or, 1975; CNA Award, 1975; Neil Gunn fellowship, Scottish Arts Council, 1981; Common Wealth Award for Distinguished Service in Literature, 1981; Modern Language Association of America award, 1982; Premio Malaparte, 1985; Nelly Sachs Prize, 1985; Bennett Award, *Hudson Review,* 1986; Officier de l'Ordre des Arts et des Lettres (France), 1986. D.Litt., University of Leuven, 1980, Smith College, City College of the City University of New York, and Mount Holyoke College, all 1985, and honorary degrees from Harvard University and Yale University, both 1987, and New School for Social Research, 1988.

WRITINGS:

NOVELS

The Lying Days, Simon & Schuster, 1953, published with new introduction by Paul Bailey, Virago, 1983.
A World of Strangers, Simon & Schuster, 1958, reprinted, Penguin, 1984.
Occasion for Loving, Viking, 1963, published with new introduction by Bailey, Virago, 1983.
The Late Bourgeois World, Viking, 1966, reprinted, Penguin, 1982.
A Guest of Honour, Viking, 1970, reprinted, Penguin, 1988.
The Conservationist, Cape, 1974, Viking, 1975.
Burger's Daughter, Viking, 1979.
July's People, Viking, 1981.
A Sport of Nature (Book-of-the-Month Club dual selection), Knopf, 1987.
My Son's Story, Farrar, Straus, 1990.

SHORT STORIES

Face to Face (also see below), Silver Leaf Books (Johannesburg), 1949.
The Soft Voice of the Serpent, and Other Stories (contains many stories previously published in *Face to Face*), Simon & Schuster, 1952.
Six Feet of the Country (also see below), Simon & Schuster, 1956.
Friday's Footprint, and Other Stories, Viking, 1960.
Not for Publication, and Other Stories, Viking, 1965.
Livingstone's Companions, Viking, 1971.
Selected Stories (contains stories from previously published collections), Cape, 1975, Viking, 1976 (published in England as *No Place Like: Selected Stories,* Penguin, 1978).
Some Monday for Sure, Heinemann Educational, 1976.

A Soldier's Embrace, Viking, 1980.

Town and Country Lovers, Sylvester and Orphanos (Los Angeles), 1980.

Six Feet of the Country (contains stories from previously published collections selected for television series of same title), Penguin, 1982.

Something Out There, Viking, 1984.

CONTRIBUTOR OF SHORT STORIES TO ANTHOLOGIES

Stories from the New Yorker, 1950-1960, Simon & Schuster, 1960.

David Wright, editor, *South African Stories,* Faber, 1960.

Gerda Charles, *Modern Jewish Stories,* Prentice-Hall, 1963.

C. L. Cline, editor, *The Rinehart Book of Short Stories,* alternate edition, Holt, 1964.

Penguin Modern Stories 4, Penguin, 1970.

James Wright, editor, *Winter's Tales 22,* St. Martin's, 1977.

Robert Kalechofsky and Roberta Kalechofsky, editors, *Echad 2: South African Jewish Voices,* Micah Publications, 1982.

Marie R. Reno, editor, *An International Treasury of Mystery and Suspense,* Doubleday, 1983.

Short Story International 46: Tales by the World's Great Contemporary Writers, International Cultural Exchange, 1984.

Chinua Achebe and C. L. Innes, editors, *African Short Stories,* Heinemann, 1985.

Nancy Sullivan, editor, *The Treasury of English Short Stories,* Doubleday, 1985.

Stephen Gray, editor, *The Penguin Book of Southern African Stories,* Penguin, 1985.

Clifton Fadiman, editor, *The World of the Short Story: A Twentieth Century Collection,* Houghton, 1986.

Daniel Halpern, editor, *The Art of the Tale: An International Anthology of Short Stories,* Viking, 1986.

Alberto Manguel, editor, *Dark Arrows: Great Stories of Revenge,* Potter, 1987.

Also contributor of previously published short stories to numerous other anthologies.

OTHER

(Editor with Lionel Abrahams) *South African Writing Today,* Penguin, 1967.

African Literature: The Lectures Given on This Theme at the University of Cape Town's Public Summer School, February, 1972, Board of Extra Mural Studies, University of Cape Town, 1972.

The Black Interpreters: Notes on African Writing, Spro-Cas/Ravan (Johannesburg), 1973.

On the Mines, photographs by David Goldblatt, C. Struik (Cape Town), 1973.

(Author of appreciation) *Kurt Jobst: Goldsmith and Silversmith; Art Metal Worker,* G. Bakker (Johannesburg), 1979.

(With others) *What Happened to Burger's Daughter; or, How South African Censorship Works,* Taurus (Johannesburg), 1980.

Lifetimes Under Apartheid, photographs by Goldblatt, Knopf, 1986.

The Essential Gesture: Writing, Politics and Places, edited and introduced by Stephen Clingman, Knopf, 1988.

Also author of television plays and documentaries, including "A Terrible Chemistry," 1981, "Choosing for Justice: Allan Boesak," with Hugo Cassirer, 1985, "Country Lovers," "A Chip of Glass Ruby," "Praise," and "Oral History," all part of "The Gordimer Stories" series adapted from stories of the same title, 1985. Contributor to periodicals, including *Atlantic, Encounter,* *Granta, Harper's, Holiday, Kenyon Review, Mother Jones, New Yorker, Paris Review,* and *Playboy.*

SIDELIGHTS: "Nadine Gordimer has become, in the whole solid body of her work, the literary voice and conscience of her society," declares Maxwell Geismar in *Saturday Review.* In numerous novels, short stories, and essays, she has written of her South African homeland and the apartheid under which its blacks, coloreds, and whites subsist; and from her prolific pen has flowed a cultural collage upon which readers worldwide have gazed sentiently for decades. "This writer, several times rumored to be under consideration for the Nobel Prize in Literature, has made palpable the pernicious, pervasive character of that country's race laws, which not only deny basic rights to most people but poison many relationships," maintains Miriam Berkley in *Publishers Weekly.* Her insight, integrity, and compassion inspire unreserved and unabated critical admiration; and, internationally honored for having written what some critics consider social history, she is acclaimed as well for the elegance and meticulousness with which she records it. "She has mapped out the social, political and emotional geography of that troubled land with extraordinary passion and precision," says Michiko Kakutani of the *New York Times,* observing in a later essay that "taken chronologically, her work not only reflects her own evolving political consciousness and maturation as an artist—an early lyricism has given way to an increased preoccupation with ideas and social issues—but it also charts changes in South Africa's social climate." As Merle Rubin remarks in the *Los Angeles Times Book Review,* "Gordimer is a voice worth listening to."

Born in South Africa to Jewish emigrants from London, Gordimer experienced a typical European middle-class colonial childhood, the solitude of which was relieved by extensive and eclectic reading at her local library—an activity she delighted in "like a pig in clover," she recalls in a *Los Angeles Times* interview with Berkley. She settled into political awareness slowly, explaining to Carol Sternhell in *Ms.:* "I think when you're born white in South Africa, you're peeling like an onion. You're sloughing off all the conditioning that you've had since you were a child." Having begun to write as a child, she published her first short story at the age of fifteen and gained an American audience from fiction appearing in such periodicals as the *New Yorker* and *Harper's.* "Her extraordinary gifts," writes Rubin, "were evident from the start: a precise ear for spoken language that lent great authenticity to her dialogue; a sensitivity to the rhythms and texture of the written word that gave her prose the power of poetry; a keen eye that made her a tireless observer; an even keener sense of social satire based upon her ability to see through appearances to the heart of the matter, and a strong feeling of moral purpose, composed in equal parts of her indignation at the sheer injustice of South Africa's entrenched racial oppression and of her commitment to speak the truth as she saw it."

Much of Gordimer's fiction focuses upon white middle-class lives and frequently depicts what Geismar describes as "a terrified white consciousness in the midst of a mysterious and ominous sea of black humanity"; but the "enduring subject" of her writing has been "the consequences of apartheid on the daily lives of men and women, the distortions it produces in relationships among both blacks and whites," says Kakutani. Margo Jefferson finds the pieces in *Selected Stories* "marked by the courage of moral vision and the beauty of artistic complexity," adding in *Newsweek* that "Gordimer examines, with passionate precision, the intricacies both of individual lives and of the wide-ranging political and historical forces that contain them." Culling from several of her previously published collections of the early fifties through the middle seventies, *Selected Stories* opens with "Is There Nowhere Else We Can Meet?," a glimpse of a white woman's fears of sexual attack during a mugging by a black male, and closes with "Africa Emergent," a candid exploration of reluctance to assist a politically imprisoned black artist. Noting in the introduction that the collection's "chronological order turns out to be an historical one," Gordimer continues that "the change in social attitudes unconsciously reflected in the stories represents both that of the people in my society—that is to say, history—and my apprehension of it; in the writing, I am acting upon my society, and in the manner of my apprehension, all the time history is acting upon me."

"Gordimer splendidly observes the remnants of persons beneath the repulsive stereotypes, an imaginative effort paralleled by her view of Africa itself, its extraordinary beauty showing through the obscene mess that has been dumped on it," writes Frank Kermode in the *New York Review of Books* about *Selected Stories*. Anatole Broyard concurs in a *New York Times* review of *A Soldier's Embrace:* "Nobody else writes about contemporary Africa as well as Nadine Gordimer does. . . . She, almost alone, achieves what Saul Bellow called 'the esthetic consumption of the environment.' Her Africa does not disappear into metaphors: in her books, metaphors disappear into Africa, like the early explorers and missionaries." Despite avowed attempts to avoid "adulation" in his critical study of her shorter work, *Nadine Gordimer,* Robert F. Haugh nonetheless recognizes that "her gifts are so diverse, her range so astonishingly broad, her gallery of places and people so various, that one cannot speak of her world in a phrase, as one would say [William] Faulkner's South, or [Thomas] Hardy's Wessex." Haugh maintains that "to read her stories is to know Africa."

From the first, reviewers hailed Gordimer's promise as a writer—a promise quickly realized, for each successive novel or collection of stories elicits critical accolades and further enhances her literary stature. In a *New York Times* review of *The Lying Days,* about a young white woman raised in a mining suburb of Johannesburg, James Stern deems her first novel "as void of conceit and banality, as original and as beautifully written as a novel by Virginia Woolf." Particularly esteemed, though, as a master of short fiction, Gordimer is called "one of the most gifted practitioners of the short story anywhere in English" by Edward Weeks in an *Atlantic* review of the award-winning *Friday's Footprint, and Other Stories.* As Robert E. Kuehn proclaims in a *Chicago Tribune Book World* review of her collection *Something Out There,* "Her best stories . . . deserve a place on the same shelf as the masterpieces of the genre. And even her less than perfect pieces command attention and admiration for their characteristic chastity of language, emotion and gesture."

Critics praise Gordimer's prose for its sustained poetic elegance and clarity, but they occasionally detect in her early work what Irving Howe refers to as "literary self-consciousness" in a *New Republic* review of Gordimer's second novel, *A World of Strangers,* in which a young Oxford-educated publishing employee on assignment in Johannesburg confronts the disparity in lives of privilege and deprivation decided solely by skin pigmentation. Although Edmund Fuller contends in a *Chicago Sunday Tribune* review that "Gordimer is an artist of marked skill and control, with perceptive insights into character and moral dilemmas," Howe observes that "she spins her sentences immaculately; she never drops into anger or vital passion; the satiny flow of similes and metaphors, modestly calling attention to themselves, survives every pressure of her subject." As Whitney Balliett describes it in the *New Yorker,* "One is always conscious of a pleased deliberation, as if her prose were continually hugging itself."

However, in a *Washington Post Book World* review of *A Soldier's Embrace,* Lynne Sharon Schwartz describes Gordimer's technique as "this elliptical poet's way with metaphor as a shortcut to meaning, together with a compression of language that can render the core of a life or a situation in a few sentences," sentences which, according to Vivian Gornick in the *Village Voice,* "accumulate slowly into a concentrate of thoughtful feeling that is reserved and quiet." *Newsweek*'s Peter S. Prescott suggests that despite Gordimer's "occasionally eccentric" syntax, her "stories are so thickly textured and of such high specific gravity as to demand, and repay, a second reading." Calling her prose "meticulous yet earthily sensual, a blend of metaphor and minute detail," Eric Redman of the *Washington Post Book World* thinks that "while her writing is oblique, it is never obscure." In Gornick's opinion, "Gordimer's work—like that of a good doctor trying to find out where it hurts—applies steady pressure to external circumstance until the live places beneath the surface stir with surprised feeling."

Critics also point to what they perceive to be a certain detachment or stoicism in Gordimer's early work; but her fourth novel, *The Late Bourgeois World,* which transpires during a weekend in which a divorced woman must explain to her child the suicide of his father who betrayed the cause of African nationalism to which he was once committed, prompts a *Newsweek* reviewer to acknowledge, "In this slim, nervous novel about tensions in racially torn South Africa, Miss Gordimer—usually so cool and distant—bristles openly with angry frustration." A *Times Literary Supplement* contributor thinks that despite its atmosphere of horror, the novel is not an overtly political one: "Only incidentally, and after one has put down the book, does one reflect on the situation out of which so fine, compassionate, and exquisitely written a work has emerged." Stuart Evans suggests in the London *Times* that "Gordimer's achievement is the way in which the importance of personal feelings are represented in the context of real and present political and social malaise; and more broadly in the light of moral and ethical questions which complacency and comfort, exemplary nannies of another age, ensure are heard but not noticed." Noting that Gordimer includes in her work "the heroic and the base, the public and the private, politics and love and the clashes endemic to both," Schwartz proposes that "for Gordimer, the public and private zones are not neatly separable; perhaps this integrity is one source of her artistic strength."

The essence of Gordimer's value as an artist rests in "her ability to meet the demands of her political conscience without becoming a propagandist and the challenges of her literary commitment without becoming a disengaged esthete," as J. B. Breslin determines in an *America* review of *A Soldier's Embrace.* "She is never trivial, she never rejoices, she never groans," states Kuehn. "She is above all a truthful writer. Her abiding subject is the politics of everyday life." And she is particularly praised for the way in which she politicizes her fiction. Veronica Geng suggests in *Ms.* that the manner in which "Gordimer's fiction connects to her political views and activities" illustrates "what the literary critic Leslie Fiedler has called 'the relationship between the truth of art, the truth of conscience, and the truth of facts.' " Although her work is political, it is neither didactic nor propagandistic. "I was writing before politics impinged itself upon my consciousness," Gordimer remarks in a *Paris Review* interview, adding: "But the real influence of politics on my writing is the influence of politics on people. Their lives, and I believe their very personalities, are changed by the extreme political circumstances one lives under in South Africa. I am dealing with people; here are people who are shaped and changed by politics. In that way my material is profoundly influenced by politics.''

Newsweek's Walter Clemons notes that "she says she tries to make the political implications of her works grow out of the lives of particular characters"; and she is especially commended for those characters that epitomize specific aspects of South African society itself. In *The Conservationist,* for instance, Gordimer explores the rapacity of white rule through the characterization of Mehring, a wealthy South African industrialist whose interests are clearly material and whose privilege as a white in a country of suppressed blacks denies him little. Calling the novel "an evocation of the whole South African nightmare," Paul Theroux declares in the *New Statesman* that "it is not often that lyrical intelligence and political purpose are combined in so effective a way."

In *The Burger's Daughter,* Gordimer examines white ambivalence about apartheid through the characterization of Rosa, whose irresolution about the anti-apartheid cause of her imprisoned Afrikaner father surfaces when he dies and she leaves the country to establish a new life. The novel provides "multiple views of a complex, uncertain person and of the complex cause that formed her," comments Anne Tyler in the *Saturday Review.* Calling it her "most political and most moving novel, going to the heart of the racial conflict in South Africa," Anthony Sampson points out in the *New York Times Book Review:* "Its politics come out of its characters, as part of the wholeness of lives that cannot evade them." And in a *Christian Science Monitor* review of this novel, David Winder indicates that "what ennobles Gordimer's riveting poetic prose is her intellectual and political honesty—the scrupulous unsentimentality with which she affixes blame or despair, irrespective of color, status, or political orientation."

Referring to Gordimer as "the most influential home-grown critic of her country's repressive racial policies," Paul Gray continues in a *Time* review of *Something Out There:* "But that reputation tends to blur some of the finer distinctions of her art. She is not really a polemicist. The portraits of her native land shade softly into irony and indirection; an overriding injustice must be deduced from small, vividly realized details." Deeming this to be particularly true about *The Burger's Daughter,* Tyler thinks that Gordimer "has a special reverence for the particular, for that one small, glittering facet that will cast light on the whole." Observing, also, that in *The Burger's Daughter* "the political moments are always illuminated by the intense observation of people and places," Sampson feels that this universalizes Gordimer's writing: "People, landscapes and politics are blended in this evocative style, and through the eyes of the young, bewildered daughter the wide arc of South African politics comes into sudden focus." In the *Hudson Review,* Joseph Epstein compares reading this novel to "looking at a mosaic very close up, tile by tile; and it is only toward the end that one gets a feel for the whole—that one stands back and says, My, this is really quite impressive."

"Microscopic observation, language so sharp it stings" is how Edmund Morris, in the *New York Times Book Review,* expresses the way in which Gordimer's "writing lingers in the mind." However, some critics believe that her writing merely iterates the dilemma without offering alternatives to it. For example, although Melvyn Hill finds Gordimer "truly passionate in her loyalty to experience and dedication to craft," he suggests in a *Voice Literary Supplement* discussion of *Something Out There* that her "premises are not truly revolutionary. She shows the structure of apartheid but cannot offer a vision of the future." Alice

Digilio, though, conversely contends in the *Washington Post Book World* that "Gordimer's role as an artist is not to offer answers or scenarios for the future. She goes on telling her stories, finding new ways to present them and recording through the imagination the personal sides of political and historical journeys." Yet Gordimer's fiction, especially her most recent work, does envision and convey a South African future.

In *A Guest of Honour,* for example, Gordimer sketches a newly independent African country and a former colonial administrator whose invitation to return is complicated by the opposing factions of two of his former proteges; the conflicts are no longer between black and white, but among blacks themselves. In an *Encounter* review, Derwent May especially admires Gordimer's description of Africa—"a wonderfully rich description, drawing on a fine feeling both for nature and history, and an exceptional knowledge of individual African character." And in the *New York Times Book Review,* Theroux suggests that "Gordimer's vision of Africa is the most complete one we have, and in time to come, when we want to know everything there is to know about a newly independent black African country, it is to this white South African woman and 'Guest of Honor' that we will turn."

"It is a commonplace to say of serious writers that they have only one tale to tell, and they write it again and again," comments Cynthia Propper Seton in the *Washington Post Book World.* "But the mind of Nadine Gordimer has a reach so wide, that each of her books, indeed each of her stories, seems to be new ground, freshly observed." In *July's People,* Gordimer peers into South Africa's future to discover a toppled government, besieged cities, and a liberal white family rescued from the wreckage of their suburban Johannesburg home by their black house servant, July, who takes them to his own village home. In this novel, Gordimer "shows us convincingly, rather than tells us, that black rule *must* come to South Africa, and even with the best will in the world on both sides, when it does come it won't be easy," remarks Bruce Cook in the *Detroit News.* As Bette Howland assesses it in the *Chicago Tribune Book World:* "When Nadine Gordimer imagines and creates a situation, you are going to experience it—like it or not. Her gift is not particularly ingratiating, but it is commanding. 'July's People' does something that novels used to do, before newspapers, radio, TV, and movies took over; and it proves that the novel still does it better. It shows us how things are; the privilege of experience." And Seton numbers the novel "among those seemingly slighter novels that become a benchmark in one's understanding, not only of South African realities, but of all good people in Western society, and how we buckle."

In Gordimer's most recent novel, *A Sport of Nature,* she offers "a panoramic view not only of what has already taken place in South Africa but of what the future, inevitably or at least imaginatively, will become," writes *Time*'s Paul Gray, adding that once again, Gordimer "has fused her native land's agonies and contradictions into intense portraits of ordinary lives." The novel, which is about a white woman who is raised in South Africa and inherits the revolutionary cause of her assassinated black husband, "imagines, in its triumphal ending, a black African state in the place of South Africa, with Hillela and her second husband, a revolutionary general and reinstated president, standing for the wished-for integration within it," summarizes Patricia Craig in the *Times Literary Supplement.* And although Stuart Evans of the London *Times* feels that *A Sport of Nature* is flawed by Gordimer's projection of a "South African future which few of us can really believe in," Gray considers her novel to be "both richly detailed and visionary, a brilliant reflection of a world that exists and an affirmation of faith in one that could be born."

Rubin suggests that "as Gordimer's reputation has steadily and deservedly risen, there have been signs of falling off in her most recent work." Considering *A Sport of Nature* "as weak in purely literary terms as it is lacking in positive political wisdom," the critic also ponders whether these weaknesses could possibly be "reflections of her deepening pessimism about the future of her country and a growing disillusionment, not only with liberalism, which she dismissed decades ago, but with all kinds of human endeavor from rationalism to radicalism." Although similarly referring to Gordimer as a writer "who has been developing an apparently justifiable contempt for her own kind," Marq de Villiers adds in the Toronto *Globe and Mail* that she "has not given up on them altogether." Despite "the pessimism and the contempt, this is not a book with hopelessness as its tone," says de Villiers. As Maureen Howard observes in the *New York Times Book Review,* "Never a polemic, the novel is the mature achievement of the once isolated provincial child, the once politically uninvolved writer of accomplished New Yorker stories."

Finding her work "exhilarating," Mark Abley writes in the Toronto *Globe and Mail* about *Something Out There:* "One of Gordimer's extraordinary qualities as a writer is her knack of seeming authoritative about nearly all classes and social groups—young and old; rural and urban; female and male; Afrikaans, English and black. She works with her formidable intelligence and all her senses at full pitch." This is especially evidenced by her depiction of Mehring in *The Conservationist,* for in Jonathan Raban's estimation in *Encounter,* Gordimer "writes about being a man with more curiosity, passion and intelligence than any man could bring to the subject." In a *Times Literary Supplement* review of *A Soldier's Embrace,* Frank Tuohy suggests that "on one level her writing can be seen as the most sensitive record we have of the various shifts in attitude—breaths, rather than winds, of change—as they have occurred in South Africa throughout the past forty or so years," but adds that "we see her world most clearly and movingly as it affects women, especially good-hearted young girls."

According to a *People* contributor, Gordimer "suggests that only people like Hillela, shrewd and perceptive and infinitely adaptable, can survive the insanity." Regarding her fascination with people like the character of Hillela, Gordimer tells Sternhell: "There *are* people who live instinctively, who act first and think afterward. And they are great survivors. And I think that cerebral people like myself have often been inclined to look down on them. And then you find that really you've been quite wrong." Yet "Gordimer is not a feminist," Sternhell points out: "The Women's Movement, she says, 'doesn't seem irrelevant to me in other places in the world, but it does seem at the present time to be kind of a luxury in South Africa. Every black woman has more in common with a black man than she has with her white sisters.' " Commenting on her belief that writers are "androgynous beings," Gordimer tells Sternhell that "the real thing that makes a writer a writer is the ability to intuit other people's states of mind. . . . I think there is a special quality a writer has that is not defined by sex."

According to Brigitte Weeks in the *Washington Post Book World,* "Gordimer insists that her readers face South African life as she does: with affection and horror." And noting Gordimer's perception of apartheid as "a personal as well as a political tragedy," Weeks feels that "her characters define her moral position with devastating clarity: humanity and apartheid cannot coexist. Inevitably, one must destroy the other." Noting that Gordimer's

books are no longer banned by the South African government, Dan Bellm indicates in *Mother Jones,* "A deeper dilemma thus comes to light: a white writer is committed to black liberation, but is in no more than a marginal position to help bring it about and is declared harmless by apartheid itself. Now what?" Gordimer tells Beth Austin in a *Chicago Tribune* interview that her greatest hope is that blacks gain political power and "come into their own in South Africa, come into their own heritage." She cares little whether whites will survive as a group in that country, indicating: "But if you're a white born in South Africa, I believe that there is a place for you—if you prove it, by your actions, by the way you live—primarily by the fight you put up against oppressive government. If you do this, you then prove that it is possible to opt out of class and color. . . . You can be part of the new South Africa."

In her introduction to *Selected Stories,* Gordimer considers the "tension between standing apart and being fully involved" as that which at once creates and serves as a writer's point of departure. However, as she indicates to Austin, "I feel that as a citizen, as a human being, I also have other responsibilities. I can't say that these are all discharged by my work." Indicating in a *U.S. News & World Report* conversation with Alvin P. Sanoff that she admires those individuals with "that extra passion and courage" who have sacrificed their own careers and have "put every energy into the struggle," Gordimer points out: "Everybody treads a kind of line of how far they will go and measures that against what use they can be. Yet, I think that anybody who is still lucky enough to be able to go out of the country, who still has a passport, couldn't come out and refuse to be interviewed about these things."

Kakutani states that Gordimer, who has helped establish the South African Anti-Censorship Action Group, and has granted numerous interviews, proposes that the essential question is how much influence do writers have at all: "My observation is that writers are not taken seriously in America—they're regarded as entertainers. And in Eastern Europe and the Soviet Union, they're taken so seriously that sometimes they can't be published at all. In South Africa, as writers, I doubt whether we have any influence on the Government at all. But I do think South African fiction writers, if we've been of any use at all, have helped rouse and raise the consciousness of the outside world to the longterm effects of life in our country. To put it very simplistically, a newspaper account, however good, tells you what happened. But it's the playwright, the novelist, the poet, the short-story writer who gives you some idea of why."

"I began to write, I think, out of the real source of all art, and that is out of a sense of wonderment about life, and a sense of trying to make sense out of the mystery of life," Gordimer tells Austin. "That hasn't changed in all the years that I've been writing. That is the starting point of everything that I write." Gordimer explains that in writing, one attempts to "build the pattern of his own perception out of chaos," continuing in the introduction of *Selected Stories,* "To make sense of life: that story, in which everything, novels, stories, the false starts, the half-completed, the abandoned, has its meaningful place, will be complete with the last sentence written before one dies or imagination atrophies."

MEDIA ADAPTATIONS: "City Lovers," based on Gordimer's short story of the same title, was filmed by TeleCulture Inc./ TelePool in South Africa in 1982.

BIOGRAPHICAL/CRITICAL SOURCES:

BOOKS

Clingman, Stephen R., *The Novels of Nadine Gordimer: History From the Inside,* Allen & Unwin, 1988.
Contemporary Literary Criticism, Gale, Volume 3, 1975, Volume 5, 1976, Volume 7, 1977, Volume 10, 1979, Volume 18, 1981, Volume 33, 1985, Volume 51, 1989.
Gordimer, Nadine, *Selected Stories,* Viking, 1976.
Haugh, Robert F., *Nadine Gordimer,* Twayne Publishers, 1974.
Heywood, Christopher, *Nadine Gordimer,* Profile, 1983.
Nell, Racilia Jilian, *Nadine Gordimer, Novelist and Short Story Writer: A Bibliography of Her Works,* University of the Witwatersrand, 1964.
Tucker, Martin, *Africa in Modern Literature: A Survey of Contemporary Writing,* Ungar, 1967.
Wade, Michael, *Nadine Gordimer,* Evans, 1978.

PERIODICALS

America, April 17, 1976, October 11, 1980.
Atlantic, January, 1960.
Bestsellers, December 15, 1970, November 15, 1971, March 15, 1975.
Booklist, October 1, 1958, January 10, 1960.
Chicago Sunday Tribune, September 21, 1958.
Chicago Tribune, May 18, 1980, December 7, 1986, November 12, 1987.
Chicago Tribune Book World, September 9, 1979, June 7, 1981, July 29, 1984.
Christian Science Monitor, January 10, 1963, November 4, 1971, May 19, 1975, September 10, 1979.
Commonweal, October 23, 1953, July 9, 1965, November 4, 1966.
Detroit News, September 2, 1979, June 7, 1981, May 31, 1989.
Encounter, August, 1971, February, 1975.
Globe and Mail (Toronto), July 28, 1984, June 6, 1987.
Harper's, February, 1963, April, 1976.
Hudson Review, spring, 1980.
Library Journal, September 1, 1958.
London Magazine, April/May, 1975.
Los Angeles Times, July 31, 1984, December 7, 1986.
Los Angeles Times Book Review, August 10, 1980, April 19, 1987, April 3, 1988, April 2, 1989.
Modern Fiction Studies, summer, 1987.
Mother Jones, December, 1988.
Ms., July, 1975, September, 1987.
Nation, June 18, 1971, August 18, 1976, May 2, 1987.
New Republic, July 7, 1952, November 10, 1958, May 8, 1965, September 10, 1966, September 13, 1975.
New Statesman, May 24, 1958, May 14, 1971, November 8, 1974, November 28, 1975.
New Statesman and Nation, August 18, 1956.
Newsweek, May 10, 1965, July 4, 1966, March 10, 1975, April 19, 1976, September 22, 1980, June 22, 1981, July 9, 1984, May 4, 1987.
New Yorker, June 7, 1952, November 21, 1953, November 29, 1958, May 12, 1975.
New York Herald Tribune Book Review, May 25, 1952, October 4, 1953, October 21, 1956, September 21, 1958, January 10, 1960, April 7, 1963.
New York Review of Books, June 26, 1975, July 15, 1976.
New York Times, June 15, 1952, October 4, 1953, October 7, 1956, September 21, 1958, May 23, 1965, October 30, 1970, September 19, 1979, August 20, 1980, May 27, 1981, July 9, 1984, January 14, 1986, April 22, 1987, December 28, 1987.
New York Times Book Review, January 10, 1960, September 11, 1966, October 31, 1971, April 13, 1975, April 18, 1976, August 19, 1979, August 24, 1980, June 7, 1981, July 29, 1984, May 3, 1987.
Paris Review, summer, 1983.
People, May 4, 1987.
Publishers Weekly, March 6, 1987, April 10, 1987, September 30, 1988.
San Francisco Chronicle, May 26, 1952, November 9, 1953, January 24, 1960.
Saturday Review, May 24, 1952, October 3, 1953, September 13, 1958, January 16, 1960, May 8, 1965, August 20, 1966, December 4, 1971, March 8, 1975, September 29, 1979.
Sewanee Review, spring, 1977.
Spectator, February 12, 1960.
Time, October 15, 1956, September 22, 1958, January 11, 1960, November 16, 1970, July 7, 1975, June 8, 1981, July 23, 1984, April 6, 1987.
Times (London), December 16, 1982, March 22, 1984, April 2, 1987.
Times Literary Supplement, October 30, 1953, July 13, 1956, June 27, 1958, February 12, 1960, March 1, 1963, July 22, 1965, July 7, 1966, May 14, 1971, May 26, 1972, January 9, 1976, July 9, 1976, April 25, 1980, September 4, 1981, March 30, 1984, April 17, 1987, September 23-29, 1988.
Tribune Books (Chicago), April 26, 1987.
U.S. News & World Report, May 25, 1987.
Village Voice, September 17, 1980.
Voice Literary Supplement, September, 1984.
Washington Post, December 4, 1979.
Washington Post Book World, November 28, 1971, April 6, 1975, August 26, 1979, September 7, 1980, May 31, 1981, July 15, 1984, May 3, 1987, November 20, 1988.
World Literature Today, autumn, 1984.
Yale Review, winter, 1988.

*   *   *

GORDON, Caroline 1895-1981

PERSONAL: Born October 6, 1895, in Trenton, Ky.; died April 11, 1981, in San Cristobal de las Casas, Chiapas, Mexico, following surgery; daughter of James (director of a school for boys) and Nancy Minor (Meriwether) Morris; married Allen Tate (a poet and critic), November 2, 1924 (divorced, 1954); children: Nancy Meriwether (Mrs. Percy H. Wood, Jr.). *Education:* Bethany College, A.B., 1916. *Religion:* Roman Catholic.

CAREER: High school teacher, 1917-20; *Chattanooga News,* Chattanooga, Tenn., reporter, 1920-24; University of North Carolina, Woman's College, Greensboro, professor of English, 1938-39; Columbia University, School of General Studies, New York, N.Y., lecturer in creative writing, beginning 1946; University of Dallas, Dallas, Tex., director of master's creative writing program. Visiting professor of English at University of Washington, Seattle, 1953, University of Kansas, 1956, and Purdue University; writer-in-residence at University of California, Davis, 1962-63; lecturer in creative writing at New School for Social Research, University of Utah, and University of Virginia.

MEMBER: Alpha Xi Delta.

AWARDS, HONORS: Guggenheim fellowship for creative writing, 1932; second prize, O. Henry Memorial Awards, 1934; Litt.D., Bethany College, 1946; National Institute Grant in Literature, 1950; D.Litt., St. Mary's College, Notre Dame, Ind., 1964; grants from National Arts Council, 1966, National Endowment for the Arts, 1967.

WRITINGS:

The Forest of the South (stories), Scribner, 1945.
(Editor with Allen Tate) *The House of Fiction: An Anthology of the Short Story, with Commentary,* Scribner, 1950, 2nd edition, 1960.
How to Read a Novel, Viking, 1957.
(Contributor) Thomas E. Connolly, editor, *Joyce's Portrait: Criticism and Critiques,* Appleton, 1962.
Old Red and Other Stories, Scribner, 1963.
A Good Soldier: A Key to the Novels of Ford Madox Ford, University of California Library (Davis), 1963.
The Collected Stories of Caroline Gordon, Farrar, Straus, 1981.
Southern Mandarins: Letters of Caroline Gordon to Sally Wood, 1924-1937, Louisiana State University Press, 1984.

NOVELS

Penhally, Scribner, 1931.
Aleck Maury, Sportsman, Scribner, 1934, reprinted, Southern Illinois University Press, 1980 (published in England as *The Pastimes of Aleck Maury: The Life of a True Sportsman,* Dickson, 1935).
The Garden of Adonis, Scribner, 1937, reprinted, Cooper Square, 1972.
None Shall Look Back, Scribner, 1937 (published in England as *None Shall Look Back: A Story of the American Civil War,* Constable, 1937).
Green Centuries, Scribner, 1941.
The Women on the Porch, Scribner, 1944.
The Strange Children, Scribner, 1951, reprinted, Cooper Square, 1972.
The Malefactors, Harcourt, 1956.
The Glory of Hera, Doubleday, 1972.

Contributor to periodicals, including *Harper's, Sewanee Review,* and *Kenyon Review.*

SIDELIGHTS: In his introduction to *The Collected Stories of Caroline Gordon,* Robert Penn Warren grouped Caroline Gordon with such other Southern women writers as Eudora Welty, Flannery O'Connor and Katherine Anne Porter—writers "who have been enriching our literature uniquely in this century." A member of the Southern Renaissance of the 1920s and 1930s, Gordon wrote of the traditional values of the American South. Her novel *Aleck Maury, Sportsman* was called by Ashley Brown, in the *Dictionary of Literary Biography Yearbook, 1981,* "an American classic." A *Nation* reviewer described the same book as "one of the most distinguished and beautiful novels to come out of the South." Writing in the *Dictionary of Literary Biography,* W. J. Stuckey claimed that at their best, Gordon's novels "are written with a lucidity that makes them timeless as well as moving accounts of human conduct."

An opponent of the more experimental fiction advocated by such writers as Gertrude Stein, whom she had met during the 1930s in Paris, Gordon asserted the primacy of personal experience as a source for fiction. Her stories and novels are often based on her own life. *Penhally* tells of the decline of a Southern aristocratic family and is inspired in part by Gordon's own family. *Aleck Maury* is based on Gordon's father, an avid sportsman and a teacher of classical literature, while *The Strange Children* and *The Malefactors* draw from Gordon's circle of friends in Paris during the 1930s. As Cynthia H. Rogers commented in the *Dic-*

tionary of Literary Biography, Gordon believed that "the only proper subject for fiction is the realistic portrayal of experience."

Gordon also believed in rendering personal experience in an objective style. Stuckey credited her with being "a master of the impersonal manner." This objectivity led critics like Andrew Lytle to ascribe a certain "coldness" to her writing: "Her tension at times seems too severe, as if her image as mask penetrates the passion and, instead of objectifying, freezes it. It causes her characters at times to appear immobile or cold." E. H. Walton believed that "Gordon fails to interest one crucially in any of her characters. She portrays them perfunctorily and without real warmth."

Critics like D. B. Collins, however, exemplify a more favorable critical judgment of Gordon's writing. Her work, Collins wrote, "is shapely, it has vitality, it illuminates a major aspect of American life, it is written in a style so perfectly suited to its matter that it goes straight to that heaven of all lovers of style: although . . . one feels a constant quiet reassurance running so deep that it rarely emerges into conscious appreciation; it is overlooked, and only seen in retrospect for the remarkable literary feat that it really is." Writing in the *Dictionary of Literary Biography Yearbook, 1981,* Howard Baker called Gordon "a stylist of the highest order."

BIOGRAPHICAL/CRITICAL SOURCES:

BOOKS

Contemporary Literary Criticism, Gale, Volume 6, 1976, Volume 13, 1980, Volume 29, 1984.
Dictionary of Literary Biography, Gale, Volume 4: *American Writers in Paris, 1920-1939,* 1980, Volume 9: *American Novelists, 1910-1945,* 1981.
Dictionary of Literary Biography Yearbook, 1981, Gale, 1982.
McDowell, Frederick P. W., *Caroline Gordon,* University of Minnesota Press, 1966.
O'Connor, William Van, *The Grotesque: An American Genre and Other Essays,* Southern Illinois University Press, 1962.
Rubin, Louis D. and Robert D. Jacobs, editors, *South: Modern Southern Literature in Its Cultural Setting,* Doubleday, 1961.
Stuckey, William J., *Caroline Gordon,* Twayne, 1972.
Tate, Allen, *Memoirs and Opinions, 1926-1974,* Swallow Press, 1975.
Walker, William Edward and Robert L. Walker, editors, *Reality and Myth: Essays in American Literature,* Vanderbilt University Press, 1964.

PERIODICALS

Books, September 27, 1931, November 4, 1934, February 21, 1937, November 2, 1941.
Book Week, May 21, 1944, October 20, 1963.
Christian Science Monitor, March 8, 1937.
Commonweal, October 26, 1945.
Critique, winter, 1956.
Library Journal, September 15, 1957.
Nation, October 7, 1931, January 9, 1935, March 20, 1937.
National Review, December 31, 1963.
New Republic, November 4, 1931, January 2, 1935, March 31, 1937, January 5, 1942, April 20, 1956.
New Yorker, November 1, 1941, June 3, 1944, September 22, 1945, March 17, 1956.
New York Times, September 20, 1931, December 2, 1934, February 21, 1937, November 2, 1941, May 21, 1944, October 7, 1945, July 30, 1950, March 4, 1956, October 27, 1957.
New York Times Book Review, October 20, 1963.

Saturday Review, November 21, 1931, February 20, 1937, May 27, 1944, October 27, 1945, June 17, 1950, November 16, 1957.
Southern Review, summer, 1937, spring, 1971.
Times Literary Supplement, August 7, 1937.
Wilson Library Bulletin, September, 1937.

OBITUARIES:

PERIODICALS

AB Bookman, May 4, 1981.
Newsweek, April 27, 1981.
New York Times, April 14, 1981.
Publishers Weekly, May 1, 1981.
Time, April 27, 1981.

*   *   *

GORDON, Mary (Catherine) 1949-

PERSONAL: Born December 8, 1949, in Long Island, N.Y.; daughter of David (a writer and publisher) and Anna (a legal secretary; maiden name, Gagliano) Gordon; married James Brian (an anthropologist), 1974 (marriage ended); married Arthur Cash (a professor of English), 1979; children: Anna Gordon Cash. *Education:* Barnard College, B.A., 1971; Syracuse University, M.A., 1973. *Religion:* Catholic.

ADDRESSES: Home—Poughkeepsie, N.Y. *Agent*—Peter Matson, 32 West 40th St., New York, N.Y. 10023.

CAREER: Dutchess Community College, Poughkeepsie, N.Y., teacher of English, 1974-78; Amherst College, Amherst, Mass., teacher of English, 1979. Novelist and author of short stories.

AWARDS, HONORS: Janet Heidinger Kafka Prize from University of Rochester, 1979, for *Final Payments,* and 1981, for *The Company of Women.*

WRITINGS:

Final Payments (novel), Random House, 1978.
The Company of Women (novel), Random House, 1981.
Men and Angels (novel), Random House, 1985.
Temporary Shelter (stories), Random House, 1987.
The Other Side (novel), Viking, 1989.

Contributor of short stories to periodicals, including *Atlantic Monthly, Harper's, Ladies' Home Journal, Mademoiselle, Redbook,* and *Virginia Quarterly Review.*

SIDELIGHTS: Mary Gordon made a name for herself with her first novel, *Final Payments,* and has continued to impress critics and readers with three subsequent novels and one collection of short stories. By showing an adept use of language and a willingness to probe unfashionable themes, she has already been acclaimed "one of the most gifted writers of her generation."

Final Payments is the story of Isabel Moore, a woman of thirty who is about to leave home for the first time. For eleven years she has nursed her domineering and devoutly Catholic father through a series of strokes, and upon his death she sets out to live a life of her own. Isabel finds a social service job, develops friendships, and involves herself with married men, but eventually feels remorse for her "self-indulgence." To atone for her presumptuousness, she steps back into the caretaker's role, devoting herself to a woman she despises, Margaret Casey, her father's former housekeeper. Finally, Isabel is saved from self-torment by an alcoholic priest.

Critics found Gordon's treatment of the theme of sacrifice both surprising and compelling. "All of a sudden," said Nan Robert-

son, "this first novel has surged up out of the 'me generation' of self-absorbed, navel-contemplating, dropout American children, and has knocked the critics for a loop." Certain paradoxes, however, surround Isabel's life of devotion. To Wilfred Sheed, the book was "about such matters as the *arrogance* of loving the unlovable, and the resourcefulness of the latter in breaking their saviors." Doris Grumbach saw Isabel "caught in a web of Christian virtues: the need for sacrifice, the desirability of celibacy." Altogether, said Sheed, *Final Payments* "gives a picture of certain Catholic lives . . . more ambiguous than anything either a loyalist or a heretic would have had a mind to produce a few years ago."

One unambiguous aspect of the novel, critics seem to agree, is Gordon's strength as a writer. "From the opening rites of burial," remarked Martha Duffy, "the reader relaxes, secure in the hands of a confident writer." *Sewanee Review* critic Bruce Allen praised "Gordon's spectacular verbal skill [which] allows her heroine to express complex emotional and intellectual attitudes with great precision." And Pearl K. Bell contended that "it is no small thing, at twenty-nine, to write with Mary Gordon's phenomenal assurance and metaphoric authority."

Comparisons have already been made between Gordon and other masters of fiction. Critics Sheed and John Leonard both cited similarities between Gordon and Jane Austen. "It is no accident that her model is Austen, the patron writer of the cloistered," noted Sheed. Leonard, meanwhile, added that Gordon is "as good on friendship as Jane Austen." *Washington Post* reviewer Edmund White paid further tribute to Gordon when he said, "It is the most intelligent and convincing first novel I have read in years, one that combines the high moral seriousness of Doris Lessing and the stylistic elegance of Flannery O'Connor."

Along with the abundance of praise for *Final Payments* has come some criticism. Isabel's "sojourn in the big world is a lot less interesting than her bondage," said Maureen Howard, and her ensuing "lightning conversion" to caring for the despised Margaret Casey has been called unconvincing. Others have objected to the book's "forced" cleverness and its "too schematic" plot. James F. Rawley and Robert F. Moss, too, had doubts about the story line, but still labeled the book "a sturdy hybrid: a relatively trashy plot, marked by contrivance and sensationalism, but handled with the tools of high art, specifically a technical sophistication and an allusive, savagely ironic tone."

In her second novel, *The Company of Women,* Gordon tells the story of Felicitas Taylor and the circle of Catholic women around her: Felicitas's widowed mother, two spinsters, and two women who have lost their husbands to alcohol and an asylum. At the center of their lives is a "fiercely conservative" priest, Father Cyprian, who has abandoned parish work because "he detests the permissiveness of the contemporary church." Similar in many ways to *Final Payments, The Company of Women* has reinforced Gordon's reputation as a penetrating writer of Catholic life. "If there was any doubt that Mary Gordon was her generation's preeminent novelist of Roman Catholic mores and manners when she published her remarkable first novel," contended Francine du Plessix Gray of the *New York Times Book Review,* "it is dispelled by her new book."

As the novel opens, the worldly hope for the circle of women is Felicitas, an exceptionally bright girl of fourteen. Her mother "could see Felicitas only among elders, the child in the temple, amazing the scribes with learning," writes Gordon. The story moves on in part two to cover Felicitas's life after she leaves a Catholic college to attend Columbia University. There, according to du Plessix Gray, Felicitas "rebels against the idols of her childhood . . . [and] shacks up with a trendy, philandering Columbia professor and lets her classical studies fall by the wayside." She becomes pregnant, returns to the company of women, and, as *Time*'s R. Z. Sheppard pointed out, "pursues a career in ordinariness with a grudging acceptance." Seven years later, seeking a father for her child, Felicitas marries a hardware store owner. The women, meanwhile, see in Felicitas's daughter their hope for the future.

A question raised by du Plessix Gray is typical of the response to *The Company of Women:* "Is Miss Gordon's craft as a novelist keeping up with the grand and virginal boldness of her vision?" Du Plessix Gray cited Gordon's "problems creating fully fleshed, noncelibate male characters"; she complained about "frequent lapses into solemnity and self-righteousness"; she argued that Gordon's prose "in this novel is as prodigiously uneven as are her characterizations." But, du Plessix Gray continued, "If I've been harsh with 'The Company of Women' it is because of my enormous admiration for Miss Gordon's earlier book, for the purity, ambition and grandeur of vision offered in both her books."

Christopher Lehmann-Haupt, too, had reservations about some of Gordon's prose, but the *New York Times* critic felt that the clearness of Gordon's insight made her second novel a significant achievement. "The problem is simply that the new novel is technically more ambitious than the earlier one," thought Lehmann-Haupt. "For in telling her story from at least seven different points of view, Miss Gordon is trying to achieve a narrative far more complex and modulated than she did in 'Final Payments.'" Lehmann-Haupt concluded by saying, "'The Company of Women,' for all its intelligence and moral insight, remains a disappointment. Next to the incandescence of 'Final Payments,' it merely glows."

Gordon's work after *The Company of Women* has continued to elicit widespread praise from critics. In novels such as *Men and Angels* and *The Other Side,* Gordon has maintained her focus on several themes—religion, relations among women, and familial conflict—while widening the scope of her plots. In *Men and Angels,* for instance, a woman experiences freedom in her blossoming career, only to find that her family is threatened as a result of her choices, while in *The Other Side,* members of a large, Irish-Catholic family struggle with their Irish past and their American present. In a collection of short stories titled *Temporary Shelter,* Gordon probes the dangers that surround discontented characters torn by abuse, vengeance, and cruelty. Reviewers of these three volumes lauded Gordon's careful, revealing prose and her ability to draw complex characters. *New York Times* critic Michiko Kakutani called *Men and Angels* "fierce" and "shining" and added that the book "is essentially a beautifully written and highly ambitious novel . . . that marks a new turn in Miss Gordon's brilliant career." Christopher Lehmann-Haupt, also writing in the *New York Times,* commented on the drama, tension, and sadness that Gordon evokes in *Temporary Shelter,* a collection that he termed "versatile and eloquent." "In Ms. Gordon's able hands," noted Lehmann-Haupt, "[artistic form] is not in the least temporary."

AVOCATIONAL INTERESTS: Theology, musical comedy.

BIOGRAPHICAL/CRITICAL SOURCES:

BOOKS

Contemporary Literary Criticism, Gale, Volume 13, 1980, Volume 22, 1982.
Dictionary of Literary Biography, Volume 6: *American Novelists Since World War II, Second Series,* Gale, 1980.

Dictionary of Literary Biography Yearbook: 1981, Gale, 1982.

PERIODICALS

Chicago Tribune, April 14, 1985.
Chicago Tribune Book World, February 22, 1981.
Commentary, September, 1978.
Commonweal, October 27, 1978.
Detroit News, March 15, 1981.
Feature, March, 1979.
Globe and Mail (Toronto), November 16, 1985, June 21, 1986, August 22, 1987.
Los Angeles Times, December 17, 1989.
Los Angeles Times Book Review, February 22, 1981, April 14, 1985, July 12, 1987, October 22, 1989.
Newsweek, April 10, 1978, February 16, 1981, April 1, 1985.
New York Review of Books, June 1, 1978.
New York Times, April 4, 1978, May 31, 1978, February 13, 1981, March 20, 1985, April 9, 1987, October 10, 1989.
New York Times Book Review, April 16, 1978, February 15, 1981, March 31, 1985, April 19, 1987, October 15, 1989.
Publishers Weekly, February 6, 1981.
Saturday Review, March 4, 1978.
Sewanee Review, fall, 1978.
Spectator, January 13, 1979.
Time, April 24, 1978, February 16, 1981, April 1, 1985.
Times (London), October 31, 1985, January 25, 1990.
Times Literary Supplement, September 1, 1978, October 25, 1985, July 17, 1987, January 26, 1990.
Tribune Books (Chicago), March 29, 1987, October 15, 1989.
Washington Post Book World, April 9, 1978, February 22, 1981, March 31, 1985, April 26, 1987, October 8, 1989.

*   *   *

GORDONE, Charles 1925-

PERSONAL: Born October 12, 1925, in Cleveland, Ohio; son of William and Camille (Morgan) Gordon; married Jeanne Warner (a stage and film producer), 1959; children: Stephen, Judy, Leah Carla, David. *Education:* Los Angeles State College of Applied Arts and Sciences (now California State University, Los Angeles), B.A., 1952; also attended University of California, Los Angeles.

ADDRESSES: Home—17 West 100th St., New York, N.Y. 10025. *Office*—c/o Springer-Warner Productions, 365 West End Ave., New York, N.Y. 10024. *Agent*—Rosenstone/Wender, 3 East 48th St., New York, N.Y. 10017.

CAREER: Playwright, actor, and director. As actor, has appeared in plays, including "Of Mice and Men," 1953, "The Blacks," 1961-65, and "The Trials of Brother Jero," 1967. Director of about twenty-five plays, including "Rebels and Bugs," 1958, "Peer Gynt," 1959, "Tobacco Road," 1960, "Detective Story," 1960, "No Place to Be Somebody," 1967, "Cures," 1978, and "Under the Boardwalk," 1979. Co-founder of Committee for the Employment of Negro Performers, 1962, and chairman; member of Commission on Civil Disorders, 1967; instructor at Cell Block Theatre, Yardville and Bordontown Detention Centers, New Jersey, 1977-78; judge, Missouri Arts Council Playwriting Competition, 1978; instructor at New School for Social Research, 1978-79; member of Ensemble Studio Theatre and Actors Studio. *Military service:* U.S. Air Force.

AWARDS, HONORS: Obie Award for best actor, 1953, for performance in "Of Mice and Men"; Pulitzer Prize for drama, Los Angeles Critics Circle Award, and Drama Desk Award, all

1970, all for "No Place to Be Somebody"; grant from the National Institute of Arts and Letters, 1971.

WRITINGS:

PLAYS

(With Sidney Easton) "Little More Light Around the Place," first produced in New York City at Sheridan Square Playhouse, 1964.

No Place to Be Somebody: A Black-Black Comedy (first produced in New York City at Sheridan Square Playhouse, November, 1967; produced Off-Broadway at New York Shakespeare Festival Public Theatre, May, 1969; produced on Broadway at American National Theatre and Academy (ANTA) Theatre, December 30, 1969; produced in Los Angeles at the Matrix, July, 1987), introduction by Joseph Papp, Bobbs-Merrill, 1969.

"Willy Bignigga" [and] "Chumpanzee," first produced together in New York City at Henry Street Settlement New Federal Theatre, July, 1970.

"Gordone Is a Muthah" (collection of monologues; first produced in New York City at Carnegie Recital Hall, May, 1970), published in *The Best Short Plays of 1973*, edited by Stanley Richards, Chilton, 1973.

"Baba-Chops," first produced in New York City at Wilshire Ebel Theatre, 1975.

"The Last Chord," first produced in New York City at Billie Holliday Theatre, 1977.

"A Qualification for Anabiosis," first produced in New York City, 1978; revised as "Anabiosis," produced in St. Louis, 1979.

Also author of an unproduced musical, "The Block," and of screenplays "No Place to Be Somebody" (adapted from the play), "The W.A.S.P.," (adapted from the novel by Julius Horwitz), "From These Ashes," "Under the Boardwalk," and "Liliom."

SIDELIGHTS: Charles Gordone's "No Place to Be Somebody," a production of Joseph Papp's Public Theatre, opened on Broadway to rave reviews. Walter Kerr, reviewing the play in the *New York Times,* hailed Gordone as "the most astonishing new American playwright since Edward Albee," while other critics compared him to Eugene O'Neill. Like O'Neill, they posited, Gordone finds his truths in bars, where pretending is too troublesome. Set in a tawdry bar in Greenwich Village, "No Place" belongs in the category of American saloon dramas and follows in the tradition of such plays as "The Iceman Cometh" and "The Time of Your Life." But, as a *Time* critic pointed out, " 'Johnny's Bar' is no oasis for gentle day-dreamers. It is a foxhole of the color war—full of venomous nightmares, thwarted aspirations and trigger-quick tempers."

The owner of the bar, Johnny Williams, is also a pimp who takes on the syndicate in an effort to obtain control of the local rackets. His ambition is to organize his own black mafia, and he uses the affections of a white female student to further his aims. Although he has "learned early to hate white society and not to trust anybody," Johnny supports an out-of-work actor and retains an incompetent white employee. Other characters include a bartender who has "drug-induced daydreams of having once been a jazz musician," Johnny's two whores, a disillusioned ex-dancer and short-order cook, and Gabe Gabriel, an unemployed, light-skinned black actor who is too white for black roles. Gabe is Gordone's spokesman, introducing the acts of the play, and reciting monologues that "use humor and candor to express the absurdity and tragedy of racism." He is also an observer rather than a participant. At the end of the play, however, he shoots Johnny, at the request of Machine Dog, a black militant who exists only in Gabe's mind.

Although many critics noted that the play had some flaws, all praised Gordone's ability for characterization and dialogue. Some indicated that the play's only problem came from Gordone's ambition of trying to say too much in one work. As Edith Oliver noted in the *New Yorker:* "There are several plots . . . and subplots running through the script, but what is more important is the sense of life and intimacy of people in a place, and of the diversity of their moods—the sudden, sometime inexplicable, spurts of anger and wildness and fooling—and their understanding of one another." Kerr highlighted Gordone's "excellent habit" of pressing "his confrontations until they become reversals, until the roles are changed."

"Written with a mixture of white heat and intellectual clarity," wrote *Newsweek* contributor Jack Kroll, "It is necessarily and brilliantly grounded in realism but takes off from there with high courage and imagination; it is funny and sad and stoical, revolutionary and conciliatory." In a review for the *New Yorker,* Brendon Gill concurred: "Mr. Gordone is as fearless as he is ambitious, and such is the speed and energy with which he causes his characters to assault each other—every encounter is, in fact, a collision—that we have neither the time nor the will to catch our breath and disbelieve. The language is exceptionally rough and exceptionally eloquent; it is a proof of Mr. Gordone's immense talent that the excrementitious gutterances of his large cast of whores, gangsters, jailbirds, and beat-up drifters stamp themselves on the memory as beautiful."

Criticism from black reviewers was not, however, totally favorable. Along with Clayton Riley and Peter Bailey, some black critics found evidence of self-hate—"a hint of contempt for black people"—in Gordone's play. But most critics were quick to stress Gordone's concern with all people—black and white alike—who feel despair but continue to hope.

BIOGRAPHICAL/CRITICAL SOURCES:

BOOKS

Contemporary Literary Criticism, Gale, Volume 1, 1973, Volume 4, 1975.
Dictionary of Literary Biography, Volume 7: *Twentieth-Century American Dramatists,* Gale, 1981.

PERIODICALS

Black World, December, 1972.
Christian Science Monitor, September 21, 1970.
Critic's Choice, September, 1969.
Journal of Negro Education, spring, 1971.
Los Angeles Times, July 17, 1987, July 24, 1987.
Negro Digest, April, 1970.
Newsweek, June 2, 1969.
New York, June 9, 1969.
New Yorker, May 17, 1969, January 10, 1970.
New York Times, May 18, 1969, December 31, 1969, May 17, 1970.
Saturday Review, May 31, 1969.
Time, May 16, 1969.
Variety, May 28, 1969, January 14, 1970, June 10, 1970, August 26, 1970, September 15, 1971.
Village Voice, May 8, 1969, May 22, 1969.

GORYAN, Sirak
See SAROYAN, William

* * *

GOTTESMAN, S. D.
See POHL, Frederik

* * *

GOULD, Lois
(Lois Benjamin)

PERSONAL: Daughter of E. J. Regensburg (a cigar company executive) and Jo Copeland (a fashion designer); married Philip Benjamin (a reporter and novelist), 1959 (deceased); married Robert E. Gould (a psychiatrist and psychoanalyst), September 14, 1967; children: (first marriage) Anthony, Roger. *Education:* Wellesley College, B.A.

ADDRESSES: Home—144 East End Ave., New York, N.Y. 10028. *Agent*—Brandt and Brandt Literary Agency, 1501 Broadway, New York, N.Y. 10036.

CAREER: Journalist and writer. *New York Times,* New York, N.Y., columnist, 1977. Former reporter, *Long Island Star Journal;* former executive editor and columnist, *Ladies Home Journal;* columnist and senior editor, *McCall's;* founder and editor, *Insider's Newsletter* (*Look* Magazine). Lecturer and teacher at Wesleyan University, Northwestern University, and New York University. Board member, Wesleyan Writers Conference.

WRITINGS:

(Under name Lois Benjamin; with Waldo L. Fielding) *Sensible Childbirth: The Case Against Natural Childbirth* (nonfiction), Viking, 1962.
(Under name Lois Benjamin) *So You Want to Be a Working Mother!* (nonfiction), McGraw, 1966.
Such Good Friends (novel), Random House, 1970, reissued, Farrar, Straus, 1988.
Necessary Objects (novel), Random House, 1972.
Final Analysis (novel), Random House, 1974.
A Sea-Change (novel), Simon & Schuster, 1976.
Not Responsible for Personal Articles (essays), Random House, 1978.
X: A Fabulous Child's Story (fiction), illustrated by Jacqueline Chwast, Daughters Publishing, 1978.
La Presidenta (novel), The Linden Press/Simon & Schuster, 1981.
Subject to Change (novel), Farrar, Straus, 1988.

Author of column "Hers" for the *New York Times;* contributor of articles to *New York, Newsday, Ms., New York Times* magazine, and the North American Newspaper Alliance.

SIDELIGHTS: Despite Lois Gould's reputation for giving a "sharply etched presentation of a female viewpoint" in her writing, as *Publishers Weekly* contributor John F. Baker calls it, Gould told *CA:* "My fiction works represent neither a popularization of feminism nor a politicization of literature, nor are they intended to achieve either of these dubious purposes. I have been reviewed by feminist critics who say my work is anti-feminist and by anti-feminist critics who say the reverse." She is interested in gender roles in society and how these roles are formed, but not to the exclusion of exploring other ideas about which to write. In addition to her works about gender roles and society with which she is often associated, she has written everything from nonfiction to adult fairy tales.

Her book *X: A Fabulous Child's Story* is an example of the author's handling of the gender role issue in allegorical form. The plot involves a government experiment in which a child named X is raised to be androgynous, and relates how the frustration of not being able to identify X's sex reveals people's gender prejudices. Although the illustrations by Jacqueline Chwast suggest the book is for children, a *New York Times Book Review* critic says "the message of Lois Gould's narrative is very grown-up." Some adult readers, remarks Susan Jacoby in the *Washington Post,* "are disturbed by the serious questions about gender identity that are woven throughout 'X.' The book has already been criticized on grounds that it evokes fantasies of 'genital mutilation,' that it is authoritarian because the scientists are government scientists, and that it is too upper-middle-class" because so many toys are bought for X. *Village Voice* contributor Eliot Fremont-Smith realizes, however, that "the book is intended to be sunny and cheerful. . . . It's less against sexist toys and gender roles than for all toys and roles; kids' psyches shouldn't be stupidly restricted by these things."

On a more serious note, Gould's *A Sea-Change* is also an allegorical story, but one meant exclusively for adults. Like her earlier books *Such Good Friends* and *Final Analysis, A Sea-Change* deals with a relationship between two adults, but uses more direct imagery in describing the sexual identity changes that the female character, Jessie Waterman, goes through. In this novel, explains *Chicago Tribune Book World* critic Doris Grumbach, the woman undergoes "a curious and fascinating [female to male] metamorphosis effected not only from within, but also from the external, masculine cultural pressures upon her." Grumbach concludes that *A Sea-Change* is "an entirely meaningful study, in contemporary terms, of the problem of being a woman." However, to critics like Anne Tyler, who discusses the book in the *New York Times Book Review,* the novel's maze of symbols makes it difficult to understand. Tyler also objects to what she feels is Gould's generalization that "men are brutal, and women love it." In *Harper's,* reviewer Ella Leffland says that the book's central idea is that of "the concept of exploitee-turning-exploiter"; beyond this point she feels that "clarity ends." But the idea, Leffland adds, "is a good one, psychologically valid."

Gould does not limit herself to fictional works about gender roles in society, though. She has written nonfiction books about subjects such as childbirth and the working woman, as well as fiction dealing with politics and other social issues. *La Presidenta,* for example, is "an evocative study of sex and politics based loosely on the Perons of Argentina," summarizes Baker in his *Publishers Weekly* interview with Gould. The novel is also interested in the role of the media in society. Rosa, whose life in the book reflects that of Eva Peron, begins her career as an actress and radio personality before becoming a political figure, her elevation in status being aided by "key political developments touched off by hints in newspaper gossip columns," says Baker. "Gould sees the media's role in America today as similar." She tells Baker: "It's hardly just a Latin thing. We now have a movie star as a President."

Although *Washington Post Book World* contributor Anita Desai feels that the author's language "wears cinematic make-up too heavy for daylight and employs smooth, silken strings of cliches," *Chicago Tribune Book Review* contributor Diane M. Ross believes the strength of *La Presidenta* lies in its ability to raise itself above the "merely . . . historical novel, or worse, a thinly disguised celebrity life." Ross maintains that Gould "holds the uncertain facts of history and the trivial rumors of celebrity at arm's length, uncovering for study the skeleton of fear and aspiration beneath the artificial flesh of legend."

In 1988, seven years after *La Presidenta,* Gould published *Subject to Change,* an adult fairy tale which marked an even greater departure from the author's early novels. MacDonald Harris describes it in the *New York Times Book Review* as a "fantasy, but hard-minded, ironic and concise." It is a tale about a "30-year old child-king . . . [and a] frigid young queen," says *Washington Post Book World* reviewer Octavia E. Butler. They live in an imaginary Renaissance kingdom in need of an heir and finances. The cast of characters includes a female dwarf and a scheming sorcerer who involve themselves in the royal couple's problems.

The style of the book, notes Richard Eder in the *Los Angeles Times Book Review,* is "dreamlike," so that "what happens precisely is not precisely clear." Eder continues: "The book is a carousel; importance lies not in what or where each figure is itself, but in its ornamental revolutions. . . . The book stops but the carousel doesn't. The last line tells us that 'the ending is subject to change.' " Butler finds that not only the ending, but also the tense and narrative voices are "subject to change," and remarks that this is a distracting feature of the novel. She also believes that the characters "are never permitted quite enough humanity to be liked or cared about in any way for more than a few minutes at a time." The most significant feature of the novel, says Butler, is the book's tone, which is "cool, clever, and distant." Harris categorizes the author's work as "an erudite book." Furthermore, he writes, the story is meant "to exercise not our liberal sentiments, but our power of laughter." It is, he concludes, "curiously wise."

Subject to Change demonstrates Gould's willingness to try new things. "Gould is a writer who determinedly resists pigeonholing and in each new book strikes out in fresh directions," remarks a *Publishers Weekly* reviewer. Over the years, the author has concerned herself less with the issue of gender roles in society in order to explore other issues; and sometimes she abandons issues altogether in favor of pure storytelling. "After each book I've always felt that this was not what I was trying to do," Gould tells Baker in her interview. "I think that each time I've had a change of viewpoint, and I like to think I've always moved on."

BIOGRAPHICAL/CRITICAL SOURCES:

BOOKS

Contemporary Literary Criticism, Gale, Volume 4, 1975, Volume 10, 1979.

PERIODICALS

Chicago Tribune Book Review, September 19, 1976, May 31, 1981.
Harper's, October, 1976.
Los Angeles Times Book Review, July 17, 1988.
New York Times Book Review, September 19, 1976, June 29, 1980, May 31, 1981, July 10, 1988.
Publishers Weekly, April 17, 1981, May 27, 1988.
Village Voice, July 10, 1978.
Washington Post, July 29, 1978.
Washington Post Book World, May 24, 1981, July 17, 1988.

*   *   *

GOULD, Stephen Jay 1941-

PERSONAL: Born September 10, 1941, in New York, N.Y.; son of Leonard (a court reporter) and Eleanor (an artist; maiden name, Rosenberg) Gould; married Deborah Lee (an artist and writer), October 3, 1965; children: Jesse, Ethan. *Education:* Antioch College, A.B., 1963; Columbia University, Ph.D., 1967.

ADDRESSES: Office—Museum of Comparative Zoology, Harvard University, Cambridge, Mass. 02138.

CAREER: Antioch College, Yellow Springs, Ohio, instructor in geology, 1966; Harvard University, Cambridge, Mass., assistant professor, 1967-71, associate professor, 1971-73, professor of geology and curator of invertebrate paleontology at Museum of Comparative Zoology, 1973—, Alexander Agassiz Professor of Zoology, 1982—. Harvard University, assistant curator, 1967-71, associate curator of invertebrate paleontology, 1971-73.

MEMBER: American Association for the Advancement of Science, American Academy of Arts and Sciences, American Society of Naturalists (president, 1979-80), Paleontological Society (president, 1985-86), Society for the Study of Evolution (vice president, 1975, president, 1990), Society of Systematic Zoology, Society of Vertebrate Paleontology, History of Science Society, European Union of Geosciences (honorary foreign fellow), Linnaean Society of London (foreign member), Sigma Xi.

AWARDS, HONORS: National Science Foundation, Woodrow Wilson, and Columbia University fellows, 1963-67; principal investigator for various grants, National Science Foundation, 1969—; Schuchert Award, Paleontological Society, 1975; National Magazine Award in essays and criticism, 1980, for "This View of Life"; "Notable Book" citation, American Library Association, 1980, and American Book Award in science, 1981, both for *The Panda's Thumb;* "Scientist of the Year" citation, *Discover,* 1981; National Book Critics Circle Award in general nonfiction, 1981, American Book Award nomination in science, 1982, and outstanding book award, American Educational Research Association, all for *The Mismeasure of Man;* MacArthur Foundation Prize fellowship, 1981-86; medal of excellence, Columbia University, 1982; F. V. Haydn Medal, Philadelphia Academy of Natural Sciences, 1982; Joseph Priestley Award and Medal, Dickinson College, 1983; Neil Miner Award, National Association of Geology Teachers, 1983; silver medal, Zoological Society of London, 1984; Bradford Washburn Award and gold medal, Museum of Science (Boston), 1984; distinguished service award, American Humanists Association, 1984; Tanner Lectures, Cambridge University, 1984, and Stanford University, 1989; meritorious service award, American Association of Systematics Collections, 1984; Founders Council Award of Merit, Field Museum of Natural History, 1984; John and Samuel Bard Award, Bard College, 1984; Phi Beta Kappa Book Award in science, 1984, for *Hen's Teeth and Horse's Toes;* Sarah Josepha Hale Medal, 1986; creative arts award (citation in nonfiction), Brandeis University, 1986; Terry Lectures, Yale University, 1986; distinguished service award, American Geological Institute, 1986; Glenn T. Seaborg Award, International Platform Association, 1986; In Praise of Reason Award, Committee for the Scientific Investigation of Claims of the Paranormal, 1986; H. D. Vursell Award, American Academy and Institute of Arts and Letters, 1987; National Book Critics Circle Award nomination in general nonfiction, 1987, for *Time's Arrow, Time's Cycle;* Anthropology in Media Award, American Anthropological Association, 1987; History of Geology Award, Geological Society of America, 1988; T. N. George Medal, University of Glasgow, 1989. Recipient of over twenty honorary degrees from colleges and universities.

WRITINGS:

An Evolutionary Microcosm: Pleistocene and Recent History of the Land Snail P. (Poecilozonites) in Bermuda, [Cambridge, Mass.], 1969.
Ontogeny and Phylogeny, Belknap Press, 1977.

Ever Since Darwin: Reflections in Natural History (essays), Norton, 1977.

The Panda's Thumb: More Reflections in Natural History (essays), Norton, 1980.

(With Salvador Edward Juria and Sam Singer) *A View of Life,* Benjamin-Cummings, 1981.

The Mismeasure of Man, Norton, 1981.

Hen's Teeth and Horse's Toes: Further Reflections in Natural History (essays), Norton, 1983.

The Flamingo's Smile: Reflections in Natural History (essays), Norton, 1985.

(With Rosamund Wolff Purcell) *Illuminations: A Bestiary,* Norton, 1986.

Time's Arrow, Time's Cycle: Myth and Metaphor in the Discovery of Geological Time, Harvard University Press, 1987.

An Urchin in the Storm: Essays About Books and Ideas, Norton, 1987.

Wonderful Life: The Burgess Shale and the Nature of History, Norton, 1989.

Author of monthly column, "This View of Life," in *Natural History.*

OTHER

(Contributor with Niles Eldredge) T. J. M. Schopf, editor, *Models in Paleobiology,* Freeman, Cooper, 1972.

(Contributor) Ernst Mayr, editor, *The Evolutionary Synthesis: Perspectives on the Unification of Biology,* Harvard University Press, 1980.

(General editor) *The History of Paleontology* (contains thirty-four different works), twenty volumes, Ayer, 1980.

(Editor with Eldredge) Mayr, *Systematics and the Origin of Species,* Columbia University Press, 1982.

(Editor with Eldredge) Theodosius Dobzhansky, *Genetics and the Origin of Species,* Columbia University Press, 1982.

(Contributor) Charles L. Hamrum, editor, *Darwin's Legacy: Nobel Conference XVIII, Gustavus Adolphus College, St. Peter, Minnesota,* Harper, 1983.

(Author of foreword) Gary Larson, *The Far Side Gallery 3,* Andrews & McMeel, 1988.

Contributor to proceedings of International Congress of Systematic and Evolutionary Biology Symposium, 1973; contributor to *Bulletin of the Museum of Comparative Zoology,* Harvard University. Contributor of more than one hundred articles to scientific journals. Associate editor, *Evolution,* 1970-72; member of editorial board, *Systematic Zoology,* 1970-72, *Paleobiology,* 1974-76, and *American Naturalist,* 1977-80; member of board of editors, *Science,* 1986— . Member of advisory board, Children's Television Workshop, 1978-81, and "Nova," 1980— .

SIDELIGHTS: Harvard University professor and evolutionary biologist Stephen Jay Gould is renowned for his ability to translate difficult scientific theories into understandable terms. In his books and essays on natural history, Gould, a paleontologist and geologist by training, popularizes his subjects without trivializing them, "simultaneously entertaining and teaching," writes James Gorman in the *New York Times Book Review.* With his essay collections *Ever Since Darwin, The Panda's Thumb, Hen's Teeth and Horse's Toes,* and *The Flamingo's Smile,* in addition to book-length studies on specific topics, such as *The Mismeasure of Man* and *Time's Arrow, Time's Cycle,* Gould has won critical acclaim for bridging a gap between the front lines of science and the literary world. "As witty as he is learned, Gould has a born essayist's ability to evoke the general out of fascinating particulars and to discuss important scientific questions for an audience of educated laymen without confusion or condescen-

sion," Gene Lyons comments in *Newsweek.* "He is a thinker and writer as central to our times as any whose name comes to mind." Lee Dembart offers similar praise in the *Los Angeles Times:* "Stephen Jay Gould is one of our foremost expositors of science, a man of extraordinary intellect and knowledge and an uncanny ability to blend the two. He sees familiar things in fresh ways, and his original thoughts are textured with meaning and powerfully honed. . . . The publication of a new book by Gould is a cause for celebration."

Gould's essay collections feature pieces written for his popular monthly column, "This View of Life," which appears in the magazine *Natural History.* His column "communicates the excitement of Gould's field of evolutionary biology in superbly witty and literate fashion to anyone willing to grapple with slippery and subtle ideas," David Graber comments in the *Los Angeles Times Book Review.* As both his column and books demonstrate, a frequent technique of Gould's is to illuminate scientific principles by way of interesting, often peculiar, examples within nature. "When he writes about such biological oddities as the inverted jellyfish Cassiopea, the praying mantis's mating habits, the giant panda's extra 'thumb' or the flamingo's inverted jaw, he does so with a double purpose—to entertain us with fascinating details while teaching us a few general concepts," remarks David Quammen in the *New York Times Book Review.* "Every oddity he describes stands on its own as a discrete fact of nature, an individual mystery, as well as yielding an example of some broader principle."

Gould's focus on the unexpected within nature reflects a view that permeates his work: that natural history is significantly altered by events out-of-the-ordinary and is largely revealed by examining its "imperfections." "Catastrophes contain continuities," explains Michael Neve in the *Times Literary Supplement.* "In fact Gould has made it his business to see the oddities and small-scale disasters of the natural record as the actual historical evidence for taking evolution seriously, as a real event." Through imperfections, "we can . . . see how things have altered by looking at the way organic life is, as it were, cobbled together out of bits and pieces some of which work, but often only just." The panda's "thumb," highlighted in Gould's 1981 American Book Award-winning essay collection *The Panda's Thumb: More Reflections in Natural History,* particularly demonstrates this. Not really a thumb at all, the offshoot on the panda's paw is actually an enlarged wristbone that enables the panda to strip leaves from bamboo shoots. "If one were to design a panda from scratch, one would not adapt a wrist bone to do the job of a thumb," observes *Times Literary Supplement* reviewer D. M. Knight. An imperfection, the appendage "may have been fashioned by a simple genetic change, perhaps a single mutation affecting the timing and rate of growth."

That nature does not always display the expected is also behind "punctuated equilibrium," the noted evolutionary theory formulated by Gould with paleontologist Niles Eldredge. Punctuated equilibrium, familiarly known as "punk eke," holds that evolution does not occur in the steady incremental stages assumed by adherents of "gradualism"—but in rapidly sweeping leaps of change initiated in small segments of a population. Gould and Eldredge's theory proposes that "new species usually arise, not by the slow and steady transformation of entire ancestral populations, but by the splitting off of small isolates from an unaltered parental stock," continues Knight. Adds Richard Rhodes in the *Chicago Tribune Book World:* "They don't run from one to the next like melting cheese. They're more revolutionary than that: changing at the edges and the changed forms lying in wait to overwhelm the main body when it fails." Punctuated equilibrium also highlights a discrepancy that for years has daunted the traditionalists of Darwinian studies. According to Knight, "Gradualism should lead to the finding of transitional forms in the fossil record, but there are extremely few. . . . [Punctuated equilibrium] raises the problem of what is the use of a half-developed organ; and it seems as though some more jerky mechanism must be invoked, the evolution of a species being a matter of rapid changes in small populations followed by long periods of stability." Commenting on the theory in a 1988 *CA* interview, Gould said it has gained increasing acceptance amongst colleagues: "It was new in 1972, and now it's a part of any paleontological discussion of the nature of pattern in life's history. I don't think anyone would deny that it happens often. The remaining issue is its relative frequency."

The sway that gradualism has held over the field of evolution is something Gould attributes to human expectations of harmony and progress. "Our standard view of the history of life is more based on our hopes and expectations than the realities of nature," he told Michelle Green in *People*. "We try so hard to see nature as a progressive process leading in a predictable and determined way towards us—the pinnacle of creation . . . but a closer examination . . . shows nothing of the sort. History is quirky, full of random events." In a *New York Times Magazine* profile of Gould, James Gleick reports: "For Homo sapiens, Gould and some of his colleagues believe, biological evolution is already over." He quotes Gould: "We're not just evolving slowly, . . . for all practical purposes we're not evolving. There's no reason to think we're going to get bigger brains or smaller toes or whatever—we are what we are."

Gould's writings emphasize science as a discipline "culturally embedded." "Science is not a heartless pursuit of objective information," he is quoted in the *New York Times Book Review*, "it is a creative human activity." Raymond A. Sokolov, in the same publication, remarks that Gould's "method is at bottom, a kind of textual criticism of the language of earlier biologists, a historical analysis of their 'metaphors,' their concepts of the world." Gould frequently examines science as the output of individuals working within the confines of specific time periods and cultures. In a *New Yorker* review of *The Flamingo's Smile: Reflections in Natural History*, John Updike writes of "Gould's evangelical sense of science as an advancing light [which] gives him a vivid sympathy with thinkers in the dark." Updike continues: "Gould chastens us ungrateful beneficiaries of science with his affectionate and tactile sense of its strenuous progress, its worming forward through fragmentary revelations and obsolete debates, from relative darkness into relative light. Even those who were wrong win his gratitude." Sue M. Halpern notes in *Nation*: "Gould is both a scientist and a humanist, not merely a scientist whose literary abilities enable him to build a narrow-bridge between the two cultures in order to export the intellectual commodities of science to the other side. [His writing] portrays universal strivings, it expresses creativity and it reveals Gould to be a student of human nature as well as one of human affairs."

Gould also demonstrates instances where science, by factually "verifying" certain cultural prejudices, has been misused. *The Flamingo's Smile* contains several accounts of individuals victimized as a result of cultural prejudices used as scientific knowledge, such as the "Hottentot Venus," a black southern African woman whose anatomy was put on public display in nineteenth-century Europe, and Carrie Buck, an American woman who was legally sterilized in the 1920s because of a family history of mentally "unfit" individuals. And in *The Mismeasure of Man*, his 1981 National Book Critics Circle Award-winning study, Gould focuses on the development of IQ testing and debunks the work of scientists purporting to measure human intelligence objectively. "This book," writes Gould, "is about the abstraction of intelligence as a single entity, its location within the brain, its quantification as one number for each individual, and the use of these numbers to rank people in a single series of worthiness, invariably to find that oppressed or disadvantaged groups—races, classes or sexes—are innately inferior and deserve their status." Halpern points out a theme that runs throughout Gould's work: "Implicit in Gould's writing is a binding premise: while the findings of science are themselves value-free, the uses to which they are put are not."

In a *London Review of Books* essay on *Hen's Teeth and Horse's Toes: Further Reflections in Natural History*, John Hedley Brooke summarizes some of the major themes, all pointing "towards a critique of neo-Darwinian gradualism," that appear in Gould's writings. He cites: "The 'fact' of evolution is 'proved' from those imperfections in living organisms which betray a history of descent. The self-styled 'scientific creationists' have no leg to stand on and are simply playing politics. Natural selection must not be construed as a perfecting principle in any strong sense of perfection. Neo-Darwinists who look to adaptive utility as the key to every explanation are as myopic as the natural theologians of the early 19th century who saw in the utility of every organ the stamp of its divine origin. . . . Another recurrent theme is the extent to which the course of evolution has been constrained by the simple fact that organisms inherit a body structure and style of embryonic development which impose limits on the scope of transformation." This last principle is enhanced by Gould's field work with the Bahamian land snail genus *Cerion*, a group that displays a wide variety of shapes, in addition to a permanent growth record in its shell. "More orthodox evolutionists would assume that the many changes of form represent adaptations," notes Gleick. "Gould denies it and finds explanations in the laws of growth. Snails grow the way they do because there are only so many ways a snail *can* grow."

Some reviewers have commented that Gould's writings display a repetition of key principles and themes—in reviewing *Hen's Teeth and Horse's Toes*, Hedley remarks that "the big implications may begin to sound familiar"—however, Gould earns consistent praise for the diversity of his interests and subject matter through which he illustrates evolutionary principles. "Gould entices us to follow him on a multifaceted Darwinian hunt for answers to age-old questions about ourselves and the rest of the living world," writes John C. McLoughlin in the *Washington Post Book World*. "Like evolution itself, Gould explores possibilities—any that come to hand—and his range of interest is stupendous. . . . Throughout, he displays with force and elegance the power of evolutionary theory to link the phenomena of the living world as no other theory seems able." Steven Rose writes in the *New York Times Book Review*: "Exploring the richness of living forms, Mr. Gould, and we, are constantly struck by the absurd ingenuity by which fundamentally inappropriate parts are pressed into new roles like toes that become hooves, or smell receptors that become the outer layer of the brain. Natural selection is not some grandiose planned event but a continual tinkering. . . . Mr. Gould's great strength is to recognize that, by demystifying nature in this way, he increases our wonder and our respect for the richness of life."

BIOGRAPHICAL/CRITICAL SOURCES:

BOOKS

Gould, Stephen Jay, *The Mismeasure of Man*, Norton, 1981.

PERIODICALS

America, May 24, 1986.
Antioch Review, spring, 1978.
Chicago Tribune, December 2, 1981, January 20, 1988.
Chicago Tribune Book World, November 30, 1980, June 26, 1983.
Christian Science Monitor, July 15, 1987.
Detroit News, May 22, 1983.
Economist, May 16, 1987.
Listener, June 11, 1987.
London Review of Books, December 1, 1983.
Los Angeles Times, June 2, 1987.
Los Angeles Times Book Review, July 17, 1983, November 29, 1987.
Nation, June 18, 1983, November 16, 1985.
Natural History, January, 1988.
Nature, November 19, 1987.
New Republic, December 3, 1977, November 11, 1981.
Newsweek, November 9, 1981, August 1, 1983.
New Yorker, December 30, 1985.
New York Review of Books, June 1, 1978, February 19, 1981, October 22, 1981, May 28, 1987.
New York Times, October 17, 1987.
New York Times Book Review, November 20, 1977, September 14, 1980, November 1, 1981, May 8, 1983, September 22, 1985, December 7, 1986, September 11, 1987, November 15, 1987.
New York Times Magazine, November 20, 1983.
People, June 2, 1986.
Rolling Stone, January 15, 1987.
Science, May, 1983.
Time, May 30, 1983, September 30, 1985.
Times Literary Supplement, May 22, 1981, February 10, 1984, October 25, 1985, June 6, 1986, September 11-17, 1987.
Voice Literary Supplement, June, 1987.
Washington Post Book World, November 8, 1981, May 8, 1983, September 29, 1985, April 26, 1987.

OTHER

"Stephen Jay Gould: This View of Life" (segment of television series, "Nova"), first aired on Public Broadcasting System (PBS-TV), December 18, 1984.

* * *

GOULDNER, Alvin W(ard) 1920-1980

PERSONAL: Born July 29, 1920, in New York, N.Y.; died of a heart attack, December 15, 1980, in Madrid, Spain; son of Louis and Estelle (Fetbrandt) Gouldner; married second wife, Janet Lee Walker, February 5, 1966; children: Richard, Alan, Andrew, Alessandra. *Education:* City College (now City College of the City University of New York), B.B.A., 1941; Columbia University, M.A., 1945, Ph.D., 1953.

ADDRESSES: Home—7260 Creveling Dr., St. Louis, Mo. 63130. *Office*—Department of Sociology, Washington University, St. Louis, Mo. 63130.

CAREER: American Jewish Committee, New York, N.Y., resident sociologist, 1945-47; State University of New York College for Teachers (now State University of New York College at Buffalo), assistant professor of sociology, 1947-51; Standard Oil Co. of New Jersey, New York, N.Y., consulting sociologist, 1951-52; Antioch College, Yellow Springs, Ohio, associate professor of sociology, 1952-54; University of Illinois at Urbana-Champaign,

associate professor, 1954-57, professor of sociology, 1957-59; Washington University, St. Louis, Mo., research professor of sociology, 1959-67, Max Weber Research Professor of Social Theory, 1967-80, chairman of department of sociology and anthropology, 1959-64. Visiting lecturer, Harvard University, 1956; visiting professor at Free University, Berlin, 1965, School of Economics, Stockholm, 1965, 1977, Hebrew University, Jerusalem, 1966, Warsaw University, 1966, University of Amsterdam, 1972-76, University of Lund, 1972, University of Puerto Rico, 1972, Goldsmith's College, London, 1977, University of Copenhagen, 1977, and University of Zagreb, 1977. Chief principal investigator, Pruitt-Igoe Project, National Institute of Mental Health, 1963-67. Consulting editor, Penguin Books (London), 1969-74.

MEMBER: American Sociological Association (member of council), Society for the Study of Social Problems (president, 1960-61, 1962), Society for the Psychological Study of Social Issues, Sociological Research Association.

AWARDS, HONORS: Social Science Research Council award 1952, research award, 1959; Fellow of the Center for Advanced Study in the Behavioral Sciences, Stanford University, 1961-62.

WRITINGS:

(Editor) *Studies in Leadership: Leadership and Democratic Action,* Harper, 1950.
Patterns of Industrial Bureaucracy, Free Press of Glencoe, 1954.
Wildcat Strike, Antioch, 1954.
(Editor) Emile Durkheim, *Socialism and Saint-Simon,* Antioch, 1958.
(With Richard Peterson) *Notes on Technology and the Moral Order,* Bobbs-Merrill, 1962.
(With H. P. Gouldner) *Modern Sociology: An Introduction to the Study of Human Interaction,* Harcourt, 1963.
Enter Plato: Classical Greece and the Origins of Social Theory, Basic Books, 1965, part 1 published as *The Hellenic World: A Sociological Analysis,* Harper, 1969.
(Editor with S. M. Miller) *Applied Sociology: Opportunities and Problems,* Free Press, 1965.
A Preliminary Report on Housing and Community Experiences of Pruitt-Igoe Residents, Social Science Institute, Washington University, 1966.
The Coming Crisis of Western Sociology, Basic Books, 1970.
For Sociology: Renewal and Critique in Sociology Today, Basic Books, 1973.
The Dialectic of Ideology and Technology: The Origins, Grammar, and Future of Ideology, Seabury, 1976.
The Future of Intellectuals and the Rise of the New Class: A Frame of Reference, Theses, Conjectures, Arguments, and an Historical Perspective on the International Class Contest of the Modern Era, Seabury, 1979.
The Two Marxisms: Contradictions and Anomalies in the Development of Theory, Seabury, 1980.
Against Fragmentation: The Origins of Marxism and the Sociology of Intellectuals, edited by Janet Gouldner and Cornelis Disco, Oxford University Press, 1984.

Editor, Bobbs-Merrill reprint series in sociology, 1960-80. Founder and editor-in-chief, *Trans-Action,* 1963-66; editor-in-chief, *New Critics Press,* St. Louis, 1969-80; co-founder and editor, *Theory and Society,* Amsterdam, 1973-80. Also associate editor of *Social Problems, Sociological Abstracts,* and *Journal of the History of the Behavioral Sciences.*

SIDELIGHTS: Turning the analytical eye of the sociologist on sociology itself, closely observing the behavior of the sociologist and the social theorist, Alvin W. Gouldner became an outspoken opponent of the convention that the sociologist could or should be an objective observer, removed from the object of study. In his book *The Coming Crisis of Western Sociology,* Gouldner advocated what he called "Reflexive Sociology." "A Reflexive Sociology means that we sociologists must . . . acquire the ingrained habit of viewing our own beliefs as we now view those held by others," he wrote.

"Many practitioners [of sociology] stress that it is a social *science* and regard its scientific side as its most distinguishing and important feature," Gouldner observed in *The Coming Crisis of Western Sociology.* "They wish to become, and to be thought of as, scientists; they wish to make their work more rigorous, more mathematical, more formal, and more powerfully instrumented. To them it is the scientific method of study itself, not the object studied or the way the object is conceived, that is the emotionally central if not the logically defining characteristic of sociology." For these sociologists, writes Bennett M. Berger in the *New York Times Book Review,* "the purpose of [social] theory is to explain the known facts of society and culture." In this view, sociology, like other natural sciences, is "value-neutral," adds Berger.

Gouldner argued in *The Coming Crisis of Western Sociology,* however, that objectivity emerged and has continued not out of a need for neutrality but as "the ideology of those who are alienated and politically homeless." Similarly, notes Berger, "Gouldner sees most of modern sociology as an effort by theorists to create social worlds they could accommodate themselves to, because they could not change the world they in fact confronted." Gouldner hoped that a "Reflexive Sociology" would convince sociologists that they use social theories to advance their own interests. He commented, "The ultimate goal of a Reflexive Sociology is the deepening of the sociologist's own awareness, of who and what he is, in a specific society at any given time, and of how both his social role and his personal praxis affect his work as a sociologist."

Unlike the scientist/sociologist, Gouldner believed that "the major significance of [social] theory is ideological," Berger indicates, "because every explanation of given social facts sustains or undermines specific political interests and the definitions of the socially 'real' in which those interests are rooted." In Gouldner's view, the sociologist should be engaged and take an active role in confronting contemporary social issues. He saw "the task of the sociologist as the establishment of a new community with its own radical critical conceptualizations, which emancipate through the understanding they give *beyond that available in everyday life,*" writes a *Times Literary Supplement* reviewer.

Even so, as Gouldner wrote, "It will be impossible either to emancipate men from the old society or to build a humane new one, without beginning here and now the construction of a total counter-culture, including new social theories; and it is impossible to do this without a critique of the social theories dominant today." Gouldner offered his critique in *The Coming Crisis of Western Sociology;* he examined Soviet Marxism and American functionalism, especially in the ideas of Talcott Parsons. "It is the most learned, the most closely reasoned, and the most eloquently written sociological history of sociological ideas to have appeared in the 20 years that I have been reading sociology," maintains Berger.

In two later books, *The Future of Intellectuals and the Rise of the New Class* and *Against Fragmentation: The Origins of Marxism and the Sociology of Intellectuals,* Gouldner examined how Marxism has been employed not by the proletariat but rather by a "New Class" to acquire and consolidate its authority. According to Gouldner, notes Norman Birnbaum in the *New York Times Book Review,* "Marx made a significant mistake when he thought that the bourgeoisie would be replaced by the proletariat. He failed to see that culture, a more important form of capital than money, would become the driving force of history." Those who control culture, the intellectuals (including sociologists) and the technical intelligentsia, form this "New Class." Gouldner suggested in *The Future of Intellectuals and the Rise of the New Class,* "The New Class believes that the world should be governed by those possessing superior competence, wisdom and science—that is, themselves. The Platonic Complex, the dream of the philosopher king with which Western philosophy begins, is the deepest wish-fulfilling fantasy of the New Class."

The posthumously published *Against Fragmentation* represents "a sociological analysis of the way [Marxism] has been used by some intellectuals and how it may be used by intellectuals in the future," Andrzej Walicki comments in the *New York Review of Books.* According to Gouldner, Karl Marx was the first to see scientific Marxism as "an ideology that intellectuals could and did use against their artisan competitors." Marxism, Gouldner indicated, "served to justify intellectuals' presence in a workers' movement in which they were all too obviously aliens." Gouldner added that Marxist socialism has provided "a strategy for optimizing the life chances of the new cultural bourgeoisie— intellectuals—by removing the moneyed class and old institutions that limit its upward mobility, and . . . a political strategy through which the New Class can attract allies to accomplish this."

"Although Gouldner's thesis is not new," Walicki points out, "his elaboration of it is certainly more thorough and impressive than that of his various predecessors." He adds, "It may lead some Marxist or radical intellectuals in the West to become more aware of the implications of their own views."

BIOGRAPHICAL/CRITICAL SOURCES:

BOOKS

Gouldner, Alvin W., *The Coming Crisis of Western Sociology,* Basic Books, 1970.
Gouldner, Alvin W., *The Future of Intellectuals and the Rise of the New Class: A Frame of Reference, Theses, Conjectures, Arguments, and an Historical Perspective on the International Class Contest of the Modern Era,* Seabury, 1979.
Gouldner, Alvin W., *Against Fragmentation: The Origins of Marxism and the Sociology of Intellectuals,* edited by Janet Gouldner and Cornelis Disco, Oxford University Press, 1984.

PERIODICALS

New York Review of Books, March 11, 1971, April 25, 1985.
New York Times, April 16, 1979.
New York Times Book Review, October 25, 1970, April 15, 1979.
Times Literary Supplement, January 11, 1974, July 25, 1980, September 6, 1985.

OBITUARIES:

PERIODICALS

New York Times, January 11, 1981.

*   *   *

GOYTISOLO, Juan 1931-

PERSONAL: Born January 5, 1931, in Barcelona, Spain; immigrated to France, 1957. *Education:* Attended University of Barcelona and University of Madrid, 1948-52.

CAREER: Writer. Worked as reporter in Cuba, 1965; associated with Gallimard Publishing Co., France. Visiting professor at universities in the United States.

AWARDS, HONORS: Received numerous awards for *Juegos de manos;* Premio Europalia, 1985.

WRITINGS:

NOVELS

Juegos de manos, Destino, 1954, recent edition, 1975, translation by John Rust published as *The Young Assassins,* Knopf, 1959.

Duelo en el paraiso, Planeta, 1955, Destino, 1981, translation by Christine Brooke-Rose published as *Children of Chaos,* Macgibbon & Kee, 1958.

El circo (title means "The Circus"), Destino, 1957, recent edition, 1982.

Fiestas, Emece, 1958, Destino, 1981, translation by Herbert Weinstock published as *Fiestas,* Knopf, 1960.

La resaca (title means "The Undertow"), Club del Libro Espanol, 1958, J. Mortiz, 1977.

La isla, Seix Barral, 1961, reprinted, 1982, translation by Jose Yglesias published as *Island of Women,* Knopf, 1962 (published in England as *Sands of Torremolinos,* J. Cape, 1962).

Senas de identidad, J. Mortiz, 1966, translation by Gregory Rabassa published as *Marks of Identity,* Grove, 1969.

Reivindicacion del Conde don Julian, J. Mortiz, 1970, Catedra, 1985, translation by Helen R. Lane published as *Count Julian,* Viking, 1974.

Juan sin tierra, Seix Barral, 1975, translation by Lane published as *Juan the Landless,* Viking, 1977.

Makbara, Seix Barral, 1980, translation by Lane published as *Makbara,* Seaver Books, 1981.

Paisajes despues de la batalla, Montesinos, 1982, translation by Lane published as *Landscapes After the Battle,* Seaver Books, 1987.

SHORT STORIES

Para vivir aqui (title means "To Live Here"), Sur, 1960, Bruguera, 1983.

Fin de fiesta: Tentativas de interpretacion de una historia amorosa, Seix Barral, 1962, translation by Yglesias published as *The Party's Over: Four Attempts to Define a Love Story,* Weidenfeld & Nicolson, 1966, Grove, 1967.

TRAVEL NARRATIVES

Campos de Nijar, Seix Barral, 1960, Grant & Cutler, 1984, translation by Luigi Luccarelli published as *The Countryside of Nijar* in *The Countryside of Nijar* [and] *La chanca,* Alembic Press, 1987.

La chanca, Libreria Espanola, 1962, Seix Barral, 1983, translation by Luccarelli published in *The Countryside of Nijar* [and] *La chanca,* Alembic Press, 1987.

Pueblo en marcha: Instantaneas de un viaje a Cuba (title means "People on the March: Snapshots of a Trip to Cuba"), Libreria Espanola, 1963.

Cronicas sarracinas (title means "Saracen Chronicles"), Iberica, 1982.

OTHER

Problemas de la novela (literary criticism; title means "Problems of the Novel"), Seix Barral, 1959.

Las mismas palabras, Seix Barral, 1963.

Plume d'hier: Espagne d'aujourd'hui, compiled by Mariano Jose de Larra, Editeurs Francais Reunis, 1965.

El furgon de cola (critical essays; title means "The Caboose"), Ruedo Iberico, 1967, Seix Barral, 1982.

Spanien und die Spanien, M. Bucher, 1969.

(Author of prologue) Jose Maria Blanco White, *Obra inglesa,* Formentor, 1972.

Obras completas (title means "Complete Works"), Aguilar, 1977.

Libertad, libertad, libertad (essays and speeches), Anagrama, 1978.

(Author of introduction) Mohamed Chukri, *El pan desnudo* (title means "For Bread Alone"), translation from Arabic by Abdellah Djibilou, Montesinos, 1982.

Coto vedado (autobiography), Seix Barral, 1985, translation by Peter Bush published as *Forbidden Territory: The Memoirs of Juan Goytisolo,* North Point Press, 1989.

En los reinos de taifa (autobiography), Seix Barral, 1986.

(Author of commentary) Omar Khayyam, *Estances,* translation into Catalan by Ramon Vives Pastor, del Mall, 1985.

Contracorrientes, Montesinos, 1985.

Space in Motion (essays), translation by Lane, Lumen Books, 1987.

Work represented in collections and anthologies, including *Juan Goytisolo,* Ministerio de Cultura, Direccion General de Promocion del Libro y la Cinematografia, 1982. Contributor to periodicals.

SIDELIGHTS: "Juan Goytisolo is the best living Spanish novelist," wrote John Butt in the *Times Literary Supplement.* The author, as Butt observed, became renowned as a "pitiless satirist" of Spanish society during the dictatorship of Francisco Franco, who imposed his version of conservative religious values on the country from the late 1930s until his death in 1975. Goytisolo, whose youth coincided with the rise of Franco, had a variety of compelling reasons to feel alienated from his own country. He was a small child when his mother was killed in a bombing raid, a casualty of the civil war that Franco instigated to seize power from a democratically elected government. The author then grew up as a bisexual in a country dominated, in Butt's words, by "frantic machismo." Eventually, said Goytisolo in his memoir *Coto vedado* (*Forbidden Territory*), he became "that strange species of writer claimed by none and alien and hostile to groups and categories." In the late 1950s, when his writing career began to flourish, he left Spain for Paris and remained in self-imposed exile until after Franco died.

The literary world was greatly impressed when Goytisolo's first novel, *Juegos de manos* (*The Young Assassins*), was published in 1954. David Dempsey found that it "begins where the novels of a writer like Jack Kerouac leave off." Goytisolo was identified as a member of the Spanish "restless generation" but his first novel seemed as much akin to Fedor Dostoevski as it did to Kerouac. The plot is similar to Dostoevski's *The Possessed:* a group of students plot the murder of a politician but end up murdering the fellow student chosen to kill the politician. Dempsey wrote, "Apparently, he is concerned with showing us how self-destructive and yet how inevitable this hedonism becomes in a society dominated by the smug and self-righteous."

Duelo en el paraiso (*Children of Chaos*) was seen as a violent extension of *The Young Assassins.* Like Anthony Burgess's *A Clockwork Orange* and William Golding's *Lord of the Flies, Children of Chaos* focuses on the terror wrought by adolescents. The children have taken over a small town after the end of the Spanish Civil War causes a breakdown of order.

Fiestas begins a trilogy referred to as "The Ephemeral Morrow" (after a famous poem by Antonio Machado). Considered the best volume of the trilogy, it follows four characters as they try to escape life in Spain by chasing their dreams. Each character meets with disappointment in the novel's end. Ramon Sender called *Fiestas* "a brilliant projection of the contrast between Spanish official and real life," and concluded that Goytisolo "is without doubt the best of the young Spanish writers."

El circo, the second book in "The Ephemeral Morrow," was too blatantly ironic to succeed as a follow-up to *Fiestas.* It is the story of a painter who manages a fraud before being punished for a murder he didn't commit. The third book, *La resaca,* was also a disappointment. The novel's style was considered too realistic to function as a fitting conclusion to "The Ephemeral Morrow."

After writing two politically oriented travelogues, *Campos de Nijar (The Countryside of Nijar)* and *La chanca,* Goytisolo returned to fiction and the overt realism he'd begun in *La resaca.* Unfortunately, critics implied that both *La isla (Island of Women)* and *Fin de Fiesta (The Party's Over)* suffered because they ultimately resembled their subject matter. *The Party's Over* contains four stories about the problems of marriage. Although Alexander Coleman found that the "stories are more meditative than the full-length novels," he also observed, "But it is, in the end, a small world, limited by the overwhelming ennui of everything and everyone in it." Similarly, Honor Tracy noted, "Every gesture of theirs reveals the essence of the world, they're absolutely necessary, says another: we intellectuals operate in a vacuum. . . . Everything ends in their all being fed up."

Goytisolo abandoned his realist style after *The Party's Over.* In *Senas de identidad (Marks of Identity),* wrote Barbara Probst Solomon, "Goytisolo begins to do a variety of things. Obvious political statement, he feels, is not enough for a novel; he starts to break with form—using a variety of first, second and third persons, he is looking and listening to the breaks in language and . . . he begins to break with form—in the attempt to describe what he is really seeing and feeling, his work becomes less abstract." Robert J. Clements called *Marks of Identity* "probably his most personal novel," but also felt that the "most inevitable theme is of course the police state of Spain." Fusing experimentation with a firm political stance, Goytisolo reminded some critics of James Joyce while others saw him elaborating his realist style to further embellish his own sense of politics.

Reivindicacion del Conde don Julian (Count Julian), Goytisolo's next novel, is widely considered to be his masterpiece. In it, he uses techniques borrowed from Joyce, Celine, Jean Genet, filmmaker Luis Bunuel, and Pablo Picasso. Solomon remarked that, while some of these techniques proved less than effective in many of the French novels of the 1960s, "in the hands of this Spanish novelist, raging against Spain, the results are explosive." *Count Julian* is named for a legendary Spanish nobleman who betrayed his country to Arab invaders in the Middle Ages. In the shocking fantasies of the novel's narrator, a modern Spaniard living as an outcast in Africa, Julian returns to punish Spain for its cruelty and hypocrisy. Over the course of the narration, the Spanish language itself gradually transforms into Arabic. Writing in the *New York Times Book Review,* Carlos Fuentes called *Count Julian* "an adventure of language, a critical battle against the language appropriated by power in Spain. It is also a search for a new/old language that would offer an alternative for the future."

With the publication of *Juan sin tierra (Juan the Landless),* critics began to see Goytisolo's last three novels as a second trilogy. However, reviews were generally less favorable than those for either *Marks of Identity* or *Count Julian.* Anatole Broyard, calling attention to Goytisolo's obsession with sadistic sex and defecation, remarked, "Don Quixote no longer tilts at windmills, but

toilets." A writer for *Atlantic* suggested that the uninformed reader begin elsewhere with Goytisolo.

Even after the oppressive Franco regime was dismantled in the late 1970s, Goytisolo continued to write novels that expressed deep alienation by displaying an unconventional, disorienting view of human society. *Makbara,* for example, is named for the cemeteries of North Africa where lovers meet for late-night trysts. "What a poignant central image it is," wrote Paul West in *Washington Post Book World,* "not only as an emblem of life in death . . . but also as a vantage point from which to review the human antic in general, which includes all those who go about their daily chores with their minds below their belts." "The people [Goytisolo] feels at home with," West declared, "are the drop-outs and the ne'er do wells, the outcasts and the misfits." In *Paisajes despues de la batalla (Landscapes After the Battle),* the author moved his vision of alienation to Paris, where he had long remained in exile. This short novel, made up of seventy-eight nonsequential chapters, displays the chaotic mix of people—from French nationalists to Arab immigrants—who uneasily coexist in the city. "The Paris metro map which the protagonist contemplates . . . for all its innumerable permutations of routes," wrote Abigail Lee in the *Times Literary Supplement,* "provides an apt image for the text itself." *Landscapes* "looked like another repudiation, this time of Paris," Butt wrote. "One wondered what Goytisolo would destroy next."

Accordingly, Butt was surprised to find that the author's memoir of his youth, published in 1985, had a markedly warmer tone than the novels that had preceded it. "Far from being a new repudiation," Butt observed, *Forbidden Territory* "is really an essay in acceptance and understanding. . . . Gone, almost, are the tortuous language, the lurid fantasies, the dreams of violation and abuse. Instead, we are given a moving, confessional account of a difficult childhood and adolescence." Goytisolo's recollections, the reviewer concluded, constitute "a moving and sympathetic story of how one courageous victim of the Franco regime fought his way out of a cultural and intellectual wasteland, educated himself, and went on to inflict a brilliant revenge on the social system which so isolated and insulted him."

BIOGRAPHICAL/CRITICAL SOURCES:

BOOKS

Contemporary Literary Criticism, Gale, Volume 5, 1976, Volume 10, 1979, Volume 23, 1983.
Goytisolo, Juan, *Forbidden Territory,* translation by Peter Bush, North Point Press, 1989.
Schwartz, Kessel, *Juan Goytisolo,* Twayne, 1970.
Schwartz, Ronald, *Spain's New Wave Novelists 1950-1974: Studies in Spanish Realism,* Scarecrow Press, 1976.

PERIODICALS

Atlantic, August, 1977.
Best Sellers, June 15, 1974.
Los Angeles Times Book Review, January 22, 1989.
Nation, March 1, 1975.
New Republic, January 31, 1967.
New York Times Book Review, January 22, 1967, May 5, 1974, September 18, 1977, June 14, 1987, July 3, 1988, February 12, 1989.
Saturday Review, February 14, 1959, June 11, 1960, June 28, 1969.
Texas Quarterly, spring, 1975.
Times Literary Supplement, May 31, 1985, September 9, 1988, May 19, 1989, November 17, 1989.
Washington Post Book World, January 17, 1982, June 14, 1987.

GRAHAM, James
See PATTERSON, Harry

*   *   *

GRAHAM, Tom
See LEWIS, (Harry) Sinclair

*   *   *

GRASS, Guenter (Wilhelm) 1927-

PERSONAL: Born October 16, 1927, in the Free City of Danzig (now Gdansk, Poland). *Education:* Attended Kunstakademie, Duesseldorf, Germany (now West Germany); attended Berlin Academy of Fine Arts, 1953-55. *Politics:* Social Democrat. *Religion:* Roman Catholic.

ADDRESSES: Home—Hamburg, West Germany. *Office/studio*—Niedstrasse 13, Berlin-Grunewald 41, Germany.

CAREER: Novelist, poet, playwright, graphic artist, and sculptor. Former farm laborer in the Rhineland; worked in potash mine near Hildesheim, Germany (now West Germany); black marketeer; apprentice stonecutter during the late 1940s, chiseling tombstones for firms in Duesseldorf, Germany; worked as a drummer and washboard accompanist with a jazz band. Speechwriter for Willy Brandt during his candidacy for the election of Bundeskanzler in West Germany. Visited the United States in 1964 and 1965, giving lectures and readings at Harvard University, Yale University, Smith College, Kenyon College, and at Goethe House and Poetry Center of YM and YWCA, New York, N.Y.; writer in residence at Columbia University, 1966. Has exhibited his drawings, lithographs, and sculptures. *Military service:* Drafted into the German Army during World War II; aide with the Luftwaffe; prisoner of war in Marienbad, Czechoslovakia, 1945-46.

MEMBER: American Academy of Arts and Sciences, Berliner Akademie der Kuenste (president, 1983-86), Deutscher PEN, Zentrum der Bundesrepublik, Verband Deutscher Schriftsteller, Gruppe 47.

AWARDS, HONORS: Lyrikpreis, Sueddeutscher Rundfunk, 1955; prize from Gruppe 47, 1958; Bremen Literary Award, 1959; literary prize from the Association of German Critics, 1960; *Die Blechtrommel (The Tin Drum)* was selected by a French jury as the best foreign-language book of 1962; a plaster bust of Grass was placed in the Regensburger Ruhmestempel Walhalla, 1963; Georg Buechner Prize, 1965; Thedor Heuss Preis, 1969; Berliner Fontane Preis, 1969; *Local Anaesthetic* was selected as one of 1970's ten best books by *Time,* 1970; Carl von Ossiersky Medal, 1977; Premio Internazionale Mondello, Palermo, 1977; International Literatur Award, 1978; *The Flounder* was selected as one of 1978's best books of fiction by *Time,* 1979; Antonio Feltrinelli Award, 1982; awarded distinguished service medal from the Federal Republic of Germany (but Grass declined to accept award), 1980; honorary doctorates from Harvard University and Kenyon College.

WRITINGS:

Die Vorzuege der Windhuehner (poems, prose, and drawings; title means "The Advantages of Windfowl"; also see below), Luchterhand, 1956, 3rd edition, 1967.

(Author of text) *O Susanna: Ein Jazzbilderbuch: Blues, Balladen, Spirituals, Jazz,* Kiepenheuer & Witsch, 1959.

Die Blechtrommel (novel; also see below), Luchterhand, 1959, reprinted, 1984, translation by Ralph Manheim published as *The Tin Drum,* Vintage Books, 1962, reprinted, 1980.

Gleisdreieck (poems and drawings; title means "Rail Triangle"), Luchterhand, 1960.

Katz und Maus (novella; also see below), Luchterhand, 1961, reprinted, 1981, translation by Manheim published as *Cat and Mouse,* Harcourt, 1963.

Hundejahre (novel; also see below), Luchterhand, 1963, translation by Manheim published as *Dog Years,* Harcourt, 1965.

Rede ueber das Selbstverstaendliche (speech), Luchterhand, 1965.

(Illustrator) Ingeborg Buchmann, *Ein Ortfuer Zufaelle,* Wagenbach, 1965.

Dich singe ich, Demokratie, Luchterhand, 1965.

Fuenf Wahlreden (speeches; contains "Was ist des Deutschen Vaterland?," "Loblied auf Willy," "Es steht zur Wahl," "Ich klage an," and "Des Kaisers neue Kleider"), Nuewied (Berlin), 1965.

Selected Poems (in German and English; includes poems from *Die Vorzuege der Windhuehner* and *Gleisdreieck;* also see below), translations by Michael Hamburger and Christopher Middleton, Harcourt, 1966, published as *Poems of Guenter Grass,* Penguin, 1969.

Ausgefragt (poems and drawings; title means "Questioned") Luchterhand, 1967.

Der Fall Axel C. Springer am Beispiel Arnold Zweig: Eine Rede, ihr Anlass, und die Folgen, Voltaire Verlag, 1967.

New Poems (includes poems from *Ausgefragt;* also see below), translation by Hamburger, Harcourt, 1968.

Ueber das Selbstverstaendliche: Reden, Aufsaetze, offene Briefe, Kommentare (title means "On the Self-Evident"; also see below), Luchterhand, 1968, revised and supplemented edition published as *Ueber das Selbstverstaendliche: Politische Schriften,* Deutscher Taschenbuch-Verlag 1969.

Briefe ueber die Grenze: Versuch eines Ost-West-Dialogs by Guenter Grass and Pavel Kohout (letters), C. Wegner, 1968.

Ueber meinen Lehrer Doeblin und andere Vortraege (title means "About My Teacher Doeblin and Other Lectures"), Literarisches Collequium Berlin, 1968.

Guenter Grass: Ausgewaehlte Texte, Abbildungen, Faksimiles, Bio-Bibliographie, edited by Theodor Wieser, Luchterhand, 1968, also published as *Portraet und Poesie,* 1968.

Kunst oder Pornographie?, J. F. Lehmann, 1969.

Speak Out: Speeches, Open Letters, Commentaries (includes selections from *Ueber das Selbsrverstaertdliche: Reden, Aufsaetze, offene Briefe Kommentare*), translated by Manheim, Harcourt, 1969.

oertlich betaeubt (novel), Luchterhand, 1969, translation by Manheim published as *Local Anaesthetic,* Harcourt, 1970.

Die Schweinekopfsuelze, Merlin Verlag, 1969.

Originalgraphik (poem with illustrations), limited edition, Argelander, 1970.

Gesammelte Gedichte (collected poems; also see below), Luchterhand, 1971.

Dokumente zur politischen Wirkung, edited hy Heinz Ludwig Arnold and Franz Josef Goertz, Richard Boorherg, 1971.

Aus dem Tagebuch einer Schnecke, Luchterhand, 1972, translation by Manheim published as *From the Diary of a Snail,* Harcourt, 1973.

Mariazuehren Hommageamarie Inmarypraise, Bruckmann, 1973, bilingual edition with translation by Middleton published as *Inmarypraise,* Harcourt, 1974.

Liebe geprueft (poems), [Bremen], 1974.

Der Buerger und seine Stimme (title means "The Citizen and His Voice"), Luchterhand, 1974.

Guenter Grass Materialienbuch, edited by Rolf Geissler, Luchterhand, 1976.

Der Butt, Luchterhand, 1977, translation by Manheim published as *The Flounder,* Harcourt, 1978.

Denkzettel (title means "Note for Thought"), Luchterhand, 1978.

In the Egg and Other Poems (contains poems from *Selected Poems* and *New Poems*), translated by Hamburger and Middleton, Secker & Warburg, 1978.

Das Treffen in Telgte, Luchterhand, 1978, translation by Manheim published as *The Meeting at Telgte,* Harcourt, 1981.

Werkverzeichnis der Radierungen (catalogue), A. Dreher, 1979.

(With Volker Schloendorff) *Die Blechtrommel als Film,* Zweitausendeins, 1979.

(Contributor) *Danzig 1939: Treasures of a Destroyed Community,* Wayne State University Press, 1980.

Aufsaetze zur Literatur, 1957-1979 (title means "Essays on Literature, 1957-1979"), Luchterhand, 1980.

Danziger Trilogie (title means "Danzig Trilogy"; contains *Die Blechtrommel, Katz und Maus,* and *Hundejahre*), Luchterhand, 1980.

Kopfgeburten; oder Die Deutschen sterben aus, Luchterhand, 1980, translation by Manheim published as *Headbirths; or, The Germans Are Dying Out,* Secker & Warburg, 1982.

Zeichnen and Schreiben: Das bildnerische Werk des Schriftstellers Guenter Grass, Luchterhand, 1982, translation published as *Graphics and Writing,* Harcourt, 1983.

Kinderlied (poems and etchings; originally published in *Gesammelte Gedichte*), Lord John, 1982.

Zeichnunger und Texte, 1954-1977, Luchterhand, 1982, translation by Hamburger and Walter Arndt published as *Drawings and Words, 1954-1977,* Harcourt, 1983.

Ach, Butt!: Dein Maechen geht bose aus, Luchterhand, 1983.

Radierungen und Texte, 1972-1982, Luchterhand, 1984, translation by Hamburger and others published as *Etchings and Words, 1972-1982,* Harcourt, 1985.

Widerstand lernen: Politische Gegenreden, 1980-1983 (title means "Learning Resistance: Political Countertalk"), Luchterhand, 1984.

On Writing and Politics: 1967-1983 (essays), translated by Manheim, Harcourt, 1985.

Geschenkt Freiheit, Akademie der Kueunste, 1985.

Die Raettin, Luchterhand, 1986, translation by Manheim published as *The Rat,* Harcourt, 1987.

Werkausgabe, ten volumes, edited by Volker Neuhaus, Luchterhand, 1987.

Zunge Zeigen, Luchterhand, 1988, translation by John E. Woods published as *Show Your Tongue,* Harcourt, 1989.

Two States, One Nation?: Against the Unenlightened Clamoring for German Reunification, Harcourt, 1990.

PLAYS

Die boesen Koeche: Ein Drama in fuenf Akten (first produced in West Berlin in 1961; translation by A. Leslie Willson produced as "The Wicked Cooks" on Broadway at Orpheum Theatre, January 23, 1967), Luchterhand, 1982.

Hochwasser: Ein Stueck in zwei Akten (two acts; also see below), Suhrkamp, 1963, 4th edition, 1968.

Onkel, Onkel (four acts; title means "Mister, Mister"; also see below), Wagenbach 1965, reprinted, Luchterhand, 1983.

Die Plebejer proben den Aufstand: Ein deutsches Trauerspiel (also see below; first produced in West Berlin at Schiller Theatre, January 15, 1966), Luchterhand, 1966, reprinted, 1985, translation by Manheim published as *The Plebeians Rehearse the Uprising: A German Tragedy* (produced in Cambridge, Mass., at the Harvard Dramatic Club, 1967), Harcourt, 1966.

"The World of Guenter Grass," adapted by Dennis Rosa, produced Off-Broadway at Pocket Theatre, April 26, 1966.

Hochwasser [and] *Noch zehn Minuten bis Buffalo* (title of second play means "Only Ten Minutes to Buffalo"; also see below), edited by Wilson, Appleton, 1967.

Four Plays (includes "The Flood" [produced in New York at Project III Ensemble Theater, June, 1986], "Onkel, Onkel," [cited in some sources as "Mister, Mister"], "Only Ten Minutes to Buffalo," and "The Wicked Cooks"), Harcourt, 1967.

"Davor" (also see below), first produced in West Berlin at Schiller Theatre, February 16, 1969, translation by Wilson and Manheim produced as "Uptight" in Washington, D.C., at Kreeger Theatre, March 22, 1972, published as *Davor: Ein Stuck in dreizehn Szenen,* Harcourt, 1973 translation published as *Max: A Play,* Harcourt, 1972.

Theaterspiele (includes "Hochwasser," "Onkel, Onkel," "Die Plebejer proben den Aufstand," and "Davor"; first produced in West Berlin at the German Opera, 1970), Luchterhand, 1970.

Other plays include "Beritten hin und zurueck" (title means "Rocking Back and Forth"), "Goldmaeulchen," 1964, and "Zweiunddreizig Zaehne."

OTHER

Also collaborator with Jean-Claude Carriere, Volker Schlondorff and Franz Seitz on screenplay for film adaptation of *Katz und Maus,* released by Modern Art Film, 1967. Author of material for catalogues to accompany his art work. Work represented in anthologies, including *Deutsche Literatur seit 1945 in Einzeldorstellunger,* edited by Dietrich Weber, Kroener, 1968. A recording of selected readings by the author, "oertlich betaeubt," has been produced by Deutsche Grammophon Gesellschaft, 1971. Editor with Heinrich Boell and Carola Stern, *L-80.*

WORK IN PROGRESS: Two States—One Nation?, a book arguing against the reunification of Germany.

SIDELIGHTS: Guenter Grass, together with such other authors as Heinrich Boell, Uwe Johnson, and Martin Walser, represents a generation of post-World War II German writers, all of whom joined an informal workshop named Group 47. When, in 1955, Grass first attended a meeting of this group, at the invitation of its founder Hans Werner Richter, he had no other literary credentials than a third prize from a radio network poetry contest. But his verse was well received by the members of Group 47, and the following year Grass published his first volume, a slim book of drawings and poetry entitled *Die Vorzuege der Windhuehner* ("The Advantages of Windfowl"). While this collection of apparently surrealistic poems and fine-lined drawings of oversized insects was hardly noticed at the time (an English translation of certain of its poems was first published in *Selected Poems* in 1965), it contains the seed of much of his future work. To this day, Grass's specific kind of creative imagination can be identified as the graphic and plastic arts combined with lyric inspiration. As Kurt Lothar Tank writes in *Guenter Grass:* "One thinks of Paul Klee when one takes . . . lines in this volume of poetry and, instead of actually reading them, visualizes them. One feels with tender fervor the gaiety, light as a dream with which the poet nourishes the windfowl of his own invention that lend wings to his creative act."

In 1958 Grass won the coveted prize of Group 47 for a reading from his manuscript *Die Blechtrommel (The Tin Drum),* published the following year. This book transformed the author into a controversial international celebrity. Grass commented on the inspiration for and evolution of the book, which he wrote while living with his wife in a basement apartment in Paris, in a 1973 radio lecture, "Retrospective on 'The Tin Drum' or The Author as Questionable Witness" (reprinted in *Guenter Grass Materialienbuch*). He said that while he was travelling in France in 1952 and constantly occupied with drawing and writing, he conceived a poem whose protagonist was a "Saint on a Column" and who, from this "elevated perspective," would describe life in the village. But, later, tiny Oskar Matzerath, the tin-drummer, became the exact reverse of a pillar-dweller. By staying closer to the earth than normal, the protagonist of *The Tin Drum* acquired a unique point of view. Presumably it took not merely an adventurer in imagination but also a student of sculpture and drawing (as Grass had been since 1948 at the academies of Duesseldorf and Berlin) to discover this unusual perspective.

The viewpoint of a precocious three-year-old allowed Grass an honest insider's approach to the problem that all the writers of Group 47 were struggling with: the task of coming to grips with the overwhelming experience of World War II, with what had led up to it, and with what had followed in its wake as "economic miracle." In January of 1963, shortly before *The Tin Drum* was published in the United States, a writer for *Time* pronounced Grass's work the "most spectacular example" of recent German literature "trying to probe beneath the surface prosperity to the uneasy past." The reviewer called Grass, whose *Tin Drum* was winning prizes and stirring anger all over Europe, "probably the most inventive talent to be heard from anywhere since the war" and described his central character, Oskar, as "the gaudiest gimmick in his literary bag of tricks. . . . For Oskar is that wildly distorted mirror which, held up to a wildly deformed reality, gives back a recognizable likeness." Two decades later, while reviewing Grass's latest volume, John Irving wrote in *Saturday Review:* "In the more than 20 years since its publication, *Die Blechtrommel*—as it is called in German—has not been surpassed; it is the greatest novel by a living author."

Like Grass, the fictional Oskar was born in Danzig (now Gdansk, Poland) to middle-class parents who owned a grocery store. Unlike Grass, however, Oskar stops growing at the age of three as a self-willed act of protest against the adult world surrounding him. He continues to give expression to this protest on the tin drum he receives for his third birthday. His shrill, three-year-old voice shatters at will his teacher's spectacles, a doctor's lab ware, grandfather clocks, and windowpanes. By the time the war ends, Oskar has lost his mother and both his real and his presumed fathers, for whose unheroic deaths he bears some responsibility. He now feels compelled to submit to the agonizing process of growing up, but in spite of his own fatherhood and his transferral to a challenging postwar existence in the west, he remains a cripple, a hunchback, a presumed murderer, a mental patient, and an unerring artist on the tin drum.

In Germany, reaction to Grass's bestselling novel ranged from critical endorsement to moral outrage. Characteristic of the honors and scandals surrounding the book was the literature prize of Bremen, voted by the jury but withheld by the city senate on moral grounds. Similar charges against Grass's writings took the form of law suits in 1962, were repeated with political overtones on the occasion of the Buechner Prize award in 1965, and continued as confrontations with the Springer Press and others.

The formidable task of coming to grips with his country's past, however, is not something Grass could accomplish in one novel no matter how incisive. By 1963 when *The Tin Drum* appeared in the United States, he had published a second volume of poetry and drawings, *Gleisdreieck* ("Rail Triangle"); a novella, *Katz und Maus* (translated as *Cat and Mouse*); and another novel of epic dimensions, *Hundejahre* (translated as *Dog Years*). The drawings and poems of *Gleisdreieck* (which are translated in *Selected Poems* and in *In the Egg and Other Poems*) make up a volume of more imposing format than Grass's first poetry collection and clearly show his development from a playful style obsessed with detail to a bolder, more encompassing form of expression.

In the novella *Cat and Mouse,* set as is *The Tin Drum* in the region around the city of Danzig, the central focus and, with it, a sense of guilt are diverted from the first person narrator, Pilenz, to Mahlke, his high school friend. Mahlke's protruding adam's apple causes his relentless pursuit of the Iron Cross—never referred to by name—with which he intends to cover up his "mouse." But in the end the narrator, who has set up the cat-and-mouse game, can no longer fathom the depth of his friend's fatal complex nor his own role in it.

The years from the prewar to the postwar era are presented in *Dog Years* through the perspective of three different narrators, a team directed by Amsel, alias Brauxel, who makes scarecrows in man's image. The seemingly solid childhood friendship of Amsel and Matem evolves into the love-hate relationship between Jew and non-Jew under the impact of Nazi ideology. When the former friends from the region of the Vistula finally meet again in the west, the ominous Fuehrer dog, who followed Matem on his odyssey, is left behind in Brauxel's subterranean world of scarecrows. While *Dog Years,* like *The Tin Drum,* again accounts for the past through the eyes of an artist, the artist is no longer a demonic tin-drummer in the guise of a child but the ingenious maker of a world of objects reflecting the break between the creations of nature and those of men. Referring to Amsel's "keen sense of reality in all its innumerable forms," John Reddick writes in *The Danzig Trilogy of Guenter Grass:* "Any serious reader of Grass's work will need little prompting to recognize that Grass is in fact describing his own, as well as his persona's art."

In 1961, well into his *Tin Drum* fame, Grass revealed at a meeting of theatre experts in Hamburg that, departing from his early poetry he had written four long plays and two one-act plays during "the relatively short time, from 1954 to 1957." Not all of the plays to which he referred had heen staged or published at that time; some, like *Onkel, Onkel* (*Mister, Mister*), appeared later in revised editions. Grass's earliest plays, *Beritten hin und zurueck* (*Rocking Back and Forth*) and *Noch zehn Minuten bis Buffalo* (*Only Ten Minutes to Buffalo*), have clearly programmatic character. They stage diverse attitudes about approaches to drama or poetry. As presentations of Grass's "poetics" they belong in the same category as his important early essays, "Die Ballerina" ("The Ballet Dancer") of 1956 and "Der Inhalt als Widerstand" ("Content as Resistance") of 1957.

Grass's two early one-act plays share the paradoxical feature of stationary travel. In *Rocking Back and Forth,* a clown insistent on riding his rocking horse defies all attempts on the part of a critic, a playwright, an actor, and a film-cutter to get some kind of action going on the stage. Hence, with the clown clinging to his toy horse, the play revolves around going nowhere. In *Only Ten Minutes to Buffalo,* the stage centerpiece is an "old locomotive and tender, overgrown with moss." Engineer and fireman, Krudewil and Pempelfort, of course, never arrive in Buffalo. A painter on the scene perceives their restless activity as "Jacob wrestling with the angel . . . timely and timeless"; but in the down-to-earth vision of a cowherd "all they can do is chase cows." Eventually though, the cowherd also fancies a trip to Buffalo and simply drives the rusty old locomotive off the stage.

Die boesen Koeche (*The Wicked Cooks*), written in 1956 in Paris and initially performed in 1961 in Berlin, is Grass's first play to have been staged in the United States (New York, 1967). In 1961 Martin Esslin had included discussion of Grass's early dramatic works in *The Theatre of the Absurd*. But in 1966 Peter Spycher argued in a *Germanisch-Romanische Monatsschrift* article that, at least in the case of *The Wicked Cooks,* the criteria of absurdist theatre do not apply. In the play a team of five restaurant cooks find their reputations threatened by the popular "Gray Soup" cooked on occasion by a guest referred to as "the Count." The play revolves around the intrigues of the cooks to obtain the Count's soup recipe. They even try to trade him a nurse, the girl-friend of one of them, in return for the secret. Unfortunately for the cooks, the Count and the nurse fall in love, and when the cooks invade their idyllic existence, the Count shoots both the woman and himself. Spycher justifiably sees the play as an "allegorical parable" or "anti-tale," for the Count assures the cooks that "it is not a recipe, it's an experience, a living knowledge, continuous change—."

Grass's initial limited success as a playwright took on the dimensions of a scandal with the 1966 production in Berlin of *Die Plebejer proben den Aufstand: Ein deutsches Trauerspiel* (*The Plebeians Rehearse the Uprising*), subtitled *A German Tragedy*. Andrzej Wirth in his essay for *A Guenter Grass Symposium* explains why this "semi-documentary" drama, based on the 1953 workers' revolt in Berlin, provoked a negative reaction in that city: "In Berlin's Schiller Theater Grass's *Plebeians* tested Bertolt Brecht's credibility *vis a vis* the Uprising. The outcome of this test was a negative one. The Boss [of the play] was a Versager [failure], a Hamletic victim of his own theorems which confused his insights of reality. . . . And the Berlin audience interpreted the play as a challenge to Brecht's image, as a case of Gunter Grass versus Bertolt Brecht." However, as Wirth continues, "the American premiere of *The Plebeians Rehearse the Uprising* (1967) in the Harvard Dramatic Club presented an interesting alternative." Due to the English translation and certain changes in the staging, "the play succeeded in exposing a more universal theme—the dilemma of the artist: the aesthetic man versus the man of action, ideal versus reality." Although "the play was thus more impoverished than embellished," it could arrive at such an interpretation.

The reception of Grass's 1966 play was partially a result of his decision to participate actively in politics by campaigning for the Social Democrats. That Grass took up residence in Berlin in 1960, a year after the sudden fame of *The Tin Drum,* can be seen as a political statement. His relation to Berlin is documented in three major poems of the 1960 volume *Gleisdreieck* (the name of a railroad station between East and West Berlin). In 1961 he began to assist Willy Brandt, then mayor of Berlin, with speech writing. When the Berlin wall went up during that year, Grass wrote an open letter to Anna Seghers, president of the German Democratic Republic writers' association, asking for a public statement. Regarding his decision to get involved with politics, Grass, as he records in *Aus dem Tagebuch einer Schnecke* (translated as *From the Diary of a Snail*), explained to his children: "When I was thirty-two I became famous. Since then, Fame has been with us as a roomer. . . . It's only because he's so lazy, and so useless when he besieges my writing desk, that I've taken him with me into politics and put him to work as a receptionist: he is good at that. Everybody takes him seriously, even my opponents and enemies."

Grass's third volume of poetry and drawings, *Ausgefragt* ("Questioned," selections translated in *New Poems*), reflects the political controversies of the 1960s. One cycle of poems in this volume is entitled "Indignation, Annoyance, Rage" and is inspired by the protest songs of the early sixties. Intoning the "powerlessness" of the guitar protesters, Grass points to the futility of their ritualistic peace marches. But the student protests gained momentum after 1966 and became a force to be reckoned with. Thus Grass's hope of engaging the protesters in constructive election activity was crushed by the demands of the new, increasingly radical Left. Within the literary developments of the 1960s, Grass's *New Poems,* which ranged in subject matter from the private to the public sphere, and from aesthetics to politics, have been described by H. Vormweg—in the introduction to Grass's *Gesammelte Gedichte* ("Collected Poems")—as reality training. The perception of individual and social reality has been exceptional in German literature, and as Vormweg points out, Grass, in his poems, ignores the most obvious change in the literature of the late 1950s and 1960s. The new objective of literature, as reflected for example in "concrete poetry," has been to expose language itself as an unreliable medium, inadequate for identifying things and situations as they are. Grass, however, evinces a fundamental trust in language and its ability to communicate reality. In his *New Poems* he attempts to make perfectly visible the inescapable contradictions and conflicts of everyday life, including his own.

Grass's political essays of this period are collected in the volume *Ueber das Selbstverstaendliche* (translated as *On the Self-Evident*). The title comes from his acceptance speech for the prestigious Buechner Prize in 1965; in that year the Social Democrats had lost the elections, and Grass was dubbed a bad loser by critics of his speech. Another collection of his speeches, open letters, and commentaries from the 1960s is translated in the volume, *Speak Out!,* which also contains Grass's 1966 address— "On Writers as Court Jesters and on Non-Existent Courts"—at the meeting of Group 47 in Princeton. While Grass's references to some of his writing colleagues and himself were rigorously criticized in Germany, the last statement of his Princeton speech became renowned: "A poem knows no compromise, but men live by compromise. The individual who can stand up under this contradiction and act is a fool and will change the world." Three more volumes of political essays and commentaries—*Der Buerger und seine Stimme* ("The Citizen and His Voice"), *Denkzettel* ("Note for Thought") and *Widerstand lernen: Politische Gegenreden* ("Learning Resistance: Political Countertalk")—show that Grass remained politically outspoken through the 1970s and 1980s.

In 1969, six years after *Dog Years,* Grass published another novel, *oertlich betaeubt* (translated as *Local Anaesthetic*). For the first time he left the Danzig origins of his earlier prose works, concentrating instead on his new home town, the Berlin of the 1960s, and on the student protests against the Vietnam War. Starusch, a high school teacher, while undergoing extensive dental treatment, is confronted with the plan of his favorite student Scherbaum to set fire to his dog on Kurfuerstendamm. By this act the seventeen-year-old hopes to awaken the populace to the realities of the war. Yet in the end the dog is not burned, and the student is about to undergo a dental treatment similar to his teacher's.

The reception of this novel in Germany was predictably negative. War protest reduced to the level of a dachshund was conceived as belittlement of the real problems at hand. In the United States, however, *Local Anaesthetic* earned Grass some enthusiastic reviews and a *Time* cover story. The caption read, "Novelist between the Generations: A Man Who Can Speak to the Young." Perhaps the only problem with this hopeful statement was that "the young" didn't listen, nor did they read the book;

they preferred Hesse's "Siddharta." However, the *Time* essay provided a lucid interpretation of *Local Anaesthetic* while other reviewers of the book found it difficult to make the switch from the generous epic panorama of the "Danzig Trilogy" to the contemporary outrages of the 1960s.

However, a play preceding the book, "Davor," was performed successfully as "Uptight" in Washington, D.C., in 1972. (The English translation was published as *Max: A Play.*) The play, based on the dialectics of the middle part of *Local Anaesthetic,* portrays the conflicts among the three major characters and two of their female partners: the middle-aged, liberal but sceptical, teacher and his dentist who believe in talk to prevent action and the student who wants to act to the point of sacrificing his dog. The teacher's female colleague and the student's Maoist girlfriend provide, as Henry Hewes declares in his *Saturday Review* essay, "the more emotionally radical attitudes of the World War II and present generations."

In some monographs on Grass's works, *Local Anaesthetic* and *From the Diary of a Snail* are grouped together as "Contemporary Political Novels" (as in *Guenter Grass: The Writer in a Pluralist Society*) or presented as examples of "The Political Activist as Writer" (as in Irene Leonard's *Guenter Grass*). These labels oversimplify the form and content of both works. Addressing itself directly to his children, *From the Diary of a Snail* contains his most openly autobiographical statements to date. It is also a diary recording his experience during Willy Brandt's election campaign of 1969 for the Social Democrats. Most important, however, this book marks a change of emphasis from politics to the more private occupation with the visual arts. Grass writes in the *Diary:* "It's true: I am not a believer; but when I draw, I become devout. . . . But I draw less and less. It doesn't get quiet enough any more. I look out to see what the clamor is; actually it's me that's clamoring and somewhere else." In the context of this self-portrait in the *Diary,* we also find revealing remarks about Grass's inspiration and technique as graphic artist: "I draw what's left over. . . . A rich, that is, broken line, one that splits, stutters in places, here passes over in silence, there thickly proclaims. Many lines. Also bordered spots. But sometimes niggardly in disbursing outlines."

The image of the snail indicates Grass's withdrawal into an increasingly meditative phase. Although he adopted the snail as his political emblem ("the snail is progress"), his entire field of vision is affected by it. The snail replaces one of the eyeballs in two self-portraits, etchings in copper produced in 1972. Moreover, the English version of the *Diary* contains a reproduction of Duerer's engraving "Melancolia I." The "Variations on Albrecht Duerer's Engraving" are summarized in a speech celebrating the Duerer anniversary of 1971 and appended to the *Diary.* The personifications of both "Melancholy" and her twin sister, "Utopia," are supplemented by a narrative on "Doubt," whose story provides an excursion into the past—a report to the children about the fate of the Jewish community of Danzig during the war. With the exception of this narrative thread, the *Diary* dispenses almost entirely with plot; yet the importance of this book in defining Grass's concerns and motivations has gradually become clear to critics of his work.

Around 1974 Grass again began work on a major novel. At first he referred to it as a "Cookbook." Already in *The Diary of a Snail* he had toyed with plans of writing "a narrative cookbook: about ninety-nine dishes, about guests, about man as an animal who can cook." At a later stage, the working title for the new novel was modified: "The (female) cook in me." At a still later stage the book was said to be a variation on the Grimms' tale of

"The Fisherman and His Wife." When after numerous public readings, including one in New York, the work was published in August 1977, it was entitled *Der Butt* (translated as *The Flounder*) and comprised 699 pages of prose laced with forty-six poems.

The Flounder is structured around the nine months of a pregnancy and "nine or eleven" female cooks, each representing a major phase in prehistory and history from the neolithic to the present. The talking flounder functions as an archetypal male element, the tempter, who gradually destroys the mythic golden age of the matriarch. He is duly sentenced and punished by a group of feminists but will resume his destructive influence as future advisor and assistant to womankind instead of mankind. Clearly, the novel is purporting to correct some misconceptions about the roles of women in history and in the present. But the strength of this epic account lies not in its feminist argument but rather, as is usual with Grass, in its historical panorama. The setting for the mythical and historical events, all told by an ever-present first person narrator, is once again the Baltic shore around the mouth of the Vistula. The representation of major cultural phases and personages, through individual female characters who provide life and nourishment, accounts for much of the fascination the work exerts. In the context of historical settings and figures, many of the images Grass had etched in copper—the fishheads, the mushrooms, and the portraits of women—became dynamic agents of the narrative.

In Germany, the popular reception of the new book exceeded all expectations. For eight months *Der Butt* remained at the top of the bestseller lists. According to H. Vormweg, in the 1978 edition of *Text & Kritik,* Grass proved himself not only as a great writer but also as a writer of and for the people. Ralph Manheim provided a masterful English translation in the record time of one year. But the reception of the English *The Flounder* was much less enthusiastic than that of the German version. In an attempt to explain the "critical resistance to this insistently ambitious work" by "the old pervasions of genre," Richard Howard observes in his *New Leader* review: "It is difficult to be comfortable with a novel that has no mortal characters, no plot, and no modesty." A majority of reviewers, including *New Yorker* contributor John Updike, feel that the richness of the "stew" demands too much digestion. They object to its length, its preoccupation with food and cooking, with sex and scatology. For some readers, Grass's cooks do not come across as real characters. Nigel Dennis in the *New York Review of Books* labels *The Flounder* "a very bad novel." Morris Dickstein, on the other hand, concludes in the *New York Times:* "Mr. Grass's cooks save him for they give body to his politics. . . . The cooks bring together Grass the novelist and Grass the socialist." With regard to the issue of feminism, *The Flounder* is labeled by Howard both "an antifeminist tract" and "a feminist tract." In a more thorough study of *The Flounder* within the context of Grass's overall work, Michael Hollington speculates "that critical reaction to the book in English-speaking countries was short-sighted" and "that as the novel is digested its distinction will gradually be recognized." *Time* magazine listed *The Flounder* under "Best Fiction of 1978" and under "Editor's Choice" through May 1979.

In 1978, the year following the completion of *The Flounder,* Grass exercised a long-standing option. Since 1959 he had received numerous offers to film *The Tin Drum.* However as he declared in a June 1978 interview—reprinted in *"Die Blechtrommel": Tagebuch einer Verfilmung*—Franz Seitz received the right to film *The Tin Drum* only after he presented Grass with a written plan followed by a prize-winning screenplay. But it was his acquaintance with the director, Volker Schloendorff, that really won Grass over for work on the movie. Schloendorff found the ideal actor for Oskar Matzerath in the twelve-year-old David Brennent, and Grass heartily approved this choice. He worked closely with Schloendorff on dialogue, accompanied the team during the filming in Gdansk, and produced two portrait etchings of young David as the tin drummer. The movie won a Cannes film festival prize and also an American Oscar as best foreign film for 1979-1980. Richard Schickel wrote in *Time:* "From the interplay of literary conceit and hard-edged, artfully compressed observations of a very real world, [Schloendorff] has created a film that has the dislocating immediacy of a nightmare that anyone anywhere might conjure up."

In 1979 Grass published *Das Treffen in Telgte* (translated as *The Meeting at Telgte*). This relatively short narrative is dedicated to Hans Werner Richter, founder of Group 47, in honor of his seventieth birthday. *The Meeting at Telgte,* like *The Flounder,* employs historical material, but because of its compact action, provides more suspenseful reading. Set in 1647, the novel portrays some twenty historical German writers who undertake a fictitious journey to Westphalia because they wish to contribute their share to the peace negotiations toward the end of the devastating Thirty Years War. Clearly, the situation parallels that of the writers of Group 47 after World War II. But the story is not a *roman a clef,* although several of the seventeenth-century writers in Grass's "meeting" have twentieth-century counterparts in Group 47. For example, the mischievous Gelnhausen, who becomes the author of the *Simplicissimus* epic, reflects certain traits of Grass himself, and Simon Dach functions as a seventeenth-century image of Richter. The iconography on the dust jacket, a human hand with a quill rising above a sea of rubble, may represent as wishful a dream for the modern age as it was for the seventeenth century. But its execution in *The Meeting at Telgte* produces a masterpiece, as *German Quarterly* contributor Richard Schade has shown, by means of the thistle and writer's hand imagery.

In the summer and fall of 1979 the Grasses and the Schloendorffs undertook a tour of East Asia sponsored by the Goethe Institute, and in November and December of that year, Grass wrote *Kopfgeburten; oder Die Deutschen sterben aus (Headbirths; or, The Germans are Dying Out)*. *Headbirths* is an account of the Asia trip projected into the following year, i.e. the election year 1980 and the first year of "Orwell's decade." Grass's fictional travellers, Harm and Doerte, are happily married teachers who were born after World War II and met as students in the 1960s. They travel to Asia under a group plan to educate themselves, but all the while they are torn by two major concerns: the forthcoming elections in West Germany and the decision whether or not to have a child. The resolution of both concerns remains uncertain. As they return from their trip their cat has had five kittens, but the elections are still imminent and Doerte has resumed taking birth control pills.

To characterize *Headbirths* as an "election manifesto," even "an election manifesto a la Grass," as Noel Thomas has done in *The Narrative Works of Guenter Grass,* does not do justice to this volume, nor does the label, attached to it by F. J. Raddatz in *Die Zeit,* as "Maerchen" (a fairy tale) about Harm and Doerte. The author/narrator occasionally refers to his writing as a tentative new film script for Volker Schloendorff but realizes that it cannot qualify as such. Raddatz's description of the book as "narrative essay" perhaps could be modified to the more accurate term "essayistic narrative." Writing in *Saturday Review* John Irving recommends *Headbirths* as the best "general introduction to Grass's genius." This opinion is especially valid if Grass's genius is perceived in its ironic mode—at times gross and outright satir-

ical, at times subtly melancholic. There is irony even in the two aspects of the title. While Grass refers to his fictional protagonists as his particular "headbirths," he also makes fun of their "child yes, child no" dilemma. While he toys with the statistical possibility that the Germans are dying out, he pokes fun at it as a campaign issue of the Christian Democrats under F. Strauss. While he sympathizes with certain of Harm and Doerte's political activities, he characterizes through them some typical generational phenomena. He doesn't even shy away from loading the couple's travel luggage with a German liver sausage that remains "symbolically undelivered," as Irving points out, concluding that "Within this deceptively plain narrative, Grass uncovers insoluble, irreducible complexity; he writes at his baroque best."

MEDIA ADAPTATIONS: Die Blechtrommel (The Tin Drum) was filmed and released by New World Pictures, April, 1980 and won several awards, including the Golden Palm Award from the Cannes Film Festival and an Oscar for the best foreign picture from the Academy of Motion Picture Arts and Sciences, both 1980.

BIOGRAPHICAL/CRITICAL SOURCES:

BOOKS

Arnold, Heniz Ludwig, *Gespraeche mit Schriftstellern,* C. H. Beck, 1975.

Bauer Pickar, Gertrud, editor, *Adventures of a Flounder: Critical Essays on Guenter Grass' "Der Butt,"* Wilhelm Fink Verlag, 1982.

Burgess, Anthony, *The Novel Now: A Guide to Contemporary Fiction,* Norton, 1967.

Casanova, Nicole, *Guenter Grass: Atelier des Metamorphoses,* Pierre Belfond, 1979.

Contemporary Literary Criticism, Gale, Volume 1, 1973, Volume 2, 1974, Volume 4, 1975, Volume 6, 1976, Volume 11, 1979, Volume 15, 1980, Volume 22, 1982, Volume 32, 1985, Volume 49, 1988.

Cunliffe, W. Gordon, *Guenter Grass,* Twayne, 1969.

Daemmrich, Horst S., and Diether H. Haenicke, editors, *The Challenge of German Literature,* Wayne State University Press, 1971.

Der deutsche Roman der Gegenwart, 3rd edition, Kohlhammer, 1971.

Dictionary of Literary Biography, Volume 75: *Contemporary German Fiction Writers,* second series, Gale, 1988.

Diller, Edward, *A Mythic Journey: Guenter Grass's "Tin Drum,"* University Press of Kentucky, 1974.

Enright, D. J., *Conspirators and Poets: Reviews and Essays,* Dufour, 1966.

Enright, D. J., *Man Is an Onion: Reviews and Essays,* Open Court, 1972.

Esslin, Martin, *Reflections: Essays on Modern Theatre,* Doubleday, 1960.

Esslin, Martin, *The Theatre of the Absurd,* Doubleday, 1961.

Grass, Guenter, *Aus dem Tagebuch einer Schnecke,* Luchterhand, 1972, translation by Manheim published as *From the Diary of a Snail,* Harcourt, 1973.

Grass, Guenter, *Dokumente zur politischen Wirkung,* edited by Heinz Ludwig Arnold and Franz Josef Goertz, Richard Boorberg, 1971.

Grass, Guenter, *Four Plays,* Harcourt, 1967.

Grass, Guenter, *Gesammelte Gedichte* (collected poems), Luchterhand, 1971.

Grass, Guenter, *Guenter Grass Materialienbuch,* edited by Rolf Geissler, Luchterhand, 1976.

Grass, Guenter, *Kinderlied* (poems and etchings; originally published in *Gesammelte Gedichte*), Lord John Press, 1982.

Grass, Guenter, *Werkverzeichnis der Radierungen* (catalogue), A. Dreher, 1979.

Grass, Guenter, and Volker Schloendorff, *Die Blechtrommel als Film*, Zweitausendeins, 1979.

Guenter Grass Radierungen, 1972-1974, A. Dreher, 1974.

Hamburger, Michael, *Art As Second Nature: Occasional Pieces, 1950-1974*, Carcanet New Press, 1975.

Heitner, Robert R., editor, *The Contemporary Novel in German: A Symposium*, University of Texas Press, 1967.

Hollington, Michael, *Guenter Grass: The Writer in a Pluralistic Society*, Marion Boyars, 1980.

Jurgensen, Manfred, editor, *Grass: Kritik-Thesen-Analysen*, Francke, 1973.

Jurgensen, Manfred, *Ueber Guenter Grass: Untersuchungen zur sprachbildlichen Rollenfunktian*, Francke, 1974.

Leonard, Irene, *Guenter Grass*, Oliver & Boyd, 1974.

Loschuetz, Gert, editor, *Von Buch zu Buch—Guenter Grass in der Kritik: Eine Dokumentation*, Luchterhand, 1968.

Mason, Ann L., *The Skeptical Muse: A Study Of Guenter Grass' Conception of the Artist*, Herbert Lang, 1974.

Mayer, Hans, *Steppenwolf and Everyman*, translated by Jack D. Zipes, Crowell, 1971.

Mews, Siegfried, editor, *Guenter Grass's "The Flounder" in Critical Perspective*, AMS Press, 1983.

Miles, Keith, *Guenter Grass*, Barnes & Noble, 1975.

Neuhaus, Volker, *Guenter Grass*, Metzler, 1979.

Nonnenmann, Klaus, editor, *Schriftsteller der Gegenwart*, Walter, 1963.

O'Neill, Patrick, *Guenter Grass: A Bibliography, 1955-1975*, University of Toronto Press, 1976.

Panichas, George, editor, *The Politics of Twentieth Century Novelists*, Hawthorn, 1971.

Reddick, John, *The Danzig Trilogy of Guenter Grass*, Harcourt, 1974.

Schloendorff, Volker, *"Die Blechtrommel": Tagebuch einer Verfilmung*, Luchterhand, 1979.

Steiner, George, *Language and Silence*, Atheneum, 1967.

Tank, Kurt Lothar, *Guenter Grass*, 5th edition, Colloquium, 1965, translation by John Conway published as *Guenter Grass*, Ungar, 1969.

Thomas, Noel, *The Narrative Works of Guenter Grass*, John Benjamins, 1982.

Wieser, Theodor, *Guenter Grass: Portrait und Poesie*, Luchterhand, 1968.

Willson, A. Leslie, editor, *A Guenter Grass Symposium*, University of Texas Press, 1971.

PERIODICALS

Akzente, Number 3, 1956, Number 4, 1957, Number 5, 1958.
Atlantic, June, 1981.
Books Abroad, spring, 1972.
Chicago Review, winter, 1978.
Chicago Tribune, October 29, 1978, June 27, 1980.
Chicago Tribune Book World, May 10, 1981, March 21, 1982.
Commonweal, May 8, 1970.
Contemporary Literature, summer, 1973, winter, 1976.
Critique: Studies in Modern Fiction, Number 3, 1978.
Cross Currents, winter, 1977.
Detroit News, May 9, 1982.
Diacritics, Number 3, 1973.
Die Zeit, May 23, 1980, October 8, 1982, December 10, 1982.
Dimension, summer, 1970.
Encounter, April, 1964, November, 1970.

Germanisch-Romanische Monatsschrift, Number 47, 1966.
German Quarterly, Number 54, 1981, Number 55, 1982.
Harper's, December, 1978.
Journal of European Studies, September, 1979.
Literary Review, summer, 1974.
London Magazine, October, 1978.
London Review of Books, February 5-18, 1981, May 6-19, 1982.
Los Angeles Times, May 22, 1981, April 18, 1982, May 20, 1983, July 21, 1985.
Michigan Quarterly Review, winter, 1975.
Modern Fiction Studies, spring, 1971.
Nation, December 23, 1978, April 24, 1982.
Natur, Number 11, 1984.
New German Critique, Number 5, 1975.
New Leader, October 29, 1973, December 4, 1978.
New Republic, June 20, 1970, April 14, 1982.
New Review, May, 1974,
New Statesman, June 7, 1974, June 26, 1981.
New Yorker, April 25, 1970, October 15, 1973, November 27, 1978, June 14, 1982.
New York Review of Books, November 23, 1978, June 11, 1981.
New York Times, April 15, 1977, November 9, 1978, November 25, 1978, May 31, 1979, January 26, 1980, April 30, 1981, March 6, 1983, June 2, 1986.
New York Times Book Review, August 14, 1966, March 29, 1970, September 30, 1973, November 12, 1978, November 23, 1978, May 17, 1981, March 14, 1982, May 16, 1982, February 27, 1983, March 27, 1983, February 19, 1984, June 23, 1985.
San Francisco Review of Books, July/August, 1981.
Saturday Review, May 20, 1972, November 11, 1978, May, 1981, March, 1982. *Scala*, Number 6, 1981, Number 1, 1982.
Spectator, May 18, 1974.
Time, January 4, 1963, April 13, 1978, April 28, 1980, May 18, 1981, January 27, 1986.
Times (London), June 22, 1981, April 22, 1982, September 19, 1985.
Times Literary Supplement, October 13, 1978, September 26, 1980, June 26, 1981, April 23, 1982.
University of Toronto Quarterly, fall, 1977.
Village Voice, October 25, 1973.
Virginia Quarterly Review, spring, 1975.
Washington Post, March 2, 1972, April 10, 1982.
Washington Post Book World, September 23, 1973, November 5, 1978, August 9, 1981, August 11, 1985.
Wisconsin Studies, Number 7, 1966.
World, October 24, 1972.
World Literature Today, spring, 1981, autumn, 1981.

*   *   *

GRAU, Shirley Ann 1929-

PERSONAL: Born July 8, 1929, in New Orleans, La.; daughter of Adolph Eugene and Katherine (Onions) Grau; married James Kern Feibleman (a professor at Tulane University), August 4, 1955; children: Ian James, Nora Miranda, William Leopold, Katherine Sara. *Education:* Tulane University, B.A. (with honors in English), 1950. *Politics:* Democrat. *Religion:* Unitarian Universalist.

ADDRESSES: Office—1314 First National Bank of Commerce Bldg., New Orleans, La. 70112. *Agent*—Brandt & Brandt, 1501 Broadway, New York, N.Y. 10036.

CAREER: Novelist and short story writer. Board member, St. Martin's Episcopal School, New Orleans, La.

MEMBER: Authors Guild, Authors League of America, Phi Beta Kappa.

AWARDS, HONORS: Pulitzer Prize, 1965, for *The Keepers of the House.*

WRITINGS:

SHORT STORY COLLECTIONS

The Black Prince and Other Stories, Knopf, 1955, reprinted in *Three by Three: Masterworks of the Southern Gothic,* introduction by Lewis P. Simpson, Peachtree Publications, 1985.
The Wind Shifting West, Knopf, 1973.
Nine Women, Knopf, 1985.

NOVELS

The Hard Blue Sky, Knopf, 1958.
The House on Coliseum Street, Knopf, 1961, reprinted, Avon, 1986.
The Keepers of the House, Knopf, 1964.
The Condor Passes, Knopf, 1971.
Evidence of Love, Random House, 1977.

OTHER

(Author of foreword) George Washington Cable, *Old Creole Days,* New American Library, 1961.
(Author of introduction) Marjorie Kinnan Rawlings, *Cross Creek,* Time, 1966.

Contributor of stories and articles to journals and magazines, including *Atlantic, New Yorker, Redbook, Mademoiselle,* and *Reporter.*

WORK IN PROGRESS: More fiction (novels and short stories).

SIDELIGHTS: Novelist and short story writer Shirley Ann Grau has been described as a fictional anthropologist for her authentic portraits of the people and atmosphere of the South. When she made her literary debut in 1955, Grau was hailed as one of the year's most promising new writers. Her first book, *The Black Prince and Other Stories,* received praise that "was little short of adulation," according to Paul Schlueter in his study *Shirley Ann Grau.* Fulfilling that early promise, Grau won the Pulitzer Prize for fiction nine years later with her novel *The Keepers of the House.* Reflecting on this period in Grau's career, *Time* critic R. Z. Sheppard observes: "[Grau] has avoided the dangers of early acclaim that might have thrust her into the footsteps of such belles of Southern *lettres* as Flannery O'Conner and Eudora Welty. Instead, Grau has usually played to her strength—a cautious application of talent to the Southern traditions and people she knows best."

Although her novels and stories are often Southern in setting and theme, Grau resists being labeled a Southern or regional writer. Critics who have studied Grau's work in detail maintain that she is, indeed, more than a regional writer. Mary Rohrberger comments in *Women Writers of the Contemporary South:* "Southern female writer [Grau] is, by accident of birth and genes. Southern regionalist writer, she is not. Nor are her skills confined to revealing and commenting on 'the genuinely native particulars of a scene' in time, as Frederick J. Hoffman would have it. Rather, like that of other important writers, her work transcends particulars, excellent as she is at rendering them." Schlueter notes: "If any label were to be placed on Grau as an artist, it would be as one with a strong sense of 'place,' an emphasis in her work . . . on the locale in which her work is set and the identification the reader has with that locale." He adds that while some of Grau's work "is regional writing, . . . this does not imply a pejorative

diminishing of the talent necessary to render the locale so vividly that it becomes a universal experience."

Grau's ability to evocatively describe nature has been noted by other critics as well. Ann Pearson, for instance, observes in *Critique* that "nature is her vision, the focal point of her best fiction." Grau depicts nature as an impersonal though dominant force in her characters' lives. Pearson adds: "Unlike [other Southern writers] who romanticize and personify nature to suit their purpose, Grau's treatment of natural surroundings has a chilly impersonality—in spite of the steamy earth that is her region, the bayous of Louisiana and the Gulf Coast of Alabama. Her innumerable swamps, marshes, and forests are described objectively, never filtered through an imagination given to moonlight and magnolia."

In no other work does nature play a more important role than in Grau's novel *The Hard Blue Sky.* According to Pearson the title itself "indicates the dominance of the elements over the lives of the poor fishermen of the Isle aux Chiens," the primitive island at the mouth of the Mississippi where the story is set. In this isolated world live an inbred populace of French and Spanish descent who endure the hazards of nature and their own volatile passions. Instead of a central plot, Grau uses interwoven episodes and flashbacks to dramatize a series of crises in the lives of individual islanders, while the community as a whole awaits the first hurricane of summer. In one episode Henry Livaudais vanishes into a swamp with a girl from a neighboring island. The incident sets off violent warfare between the two rival island groups, but it also leads Henry's mother to reaffirm her love for her husband by accepting his bastard son as her own. Another narrative strand focuses on the confusion and sexual anxieties of young Annie Landry, emphasizing "the psychological experiences that are typical of the adolescent in contemporary fiction," Louise Y. Gossett remarks in her book *Violence in Recent Southern Fiction.*

The Hard Blue Sky has been favorably compared to *The Black Prince and Other Stories.* "Even more than in her first book," observes Jean W. Ross in the *Dictionary of Literary Biography,* "Grau captures in *The Hard Blue Sky* a general authenticity of folkways, largely through a skilled rendition of speech patterns and customs." She adds: "The fine control and careful natural description seen in Grau's earlier book are the real virtues of this one, a more ambitious undertaking; these strengths are not obscured by the novel's lack of dramatic force." A *Kirkus Reviews* contributor writes: "This island world, alien and apart and tempered by the whims of the sea and sky, has a somnolent fascination, the vitality and the violence of the lives it shapes are retained and reflected with a very realistic but unquestionable lyricism." Elizabeth Bartelme concludes in *Commonweal:* "You come off this island knowing the people intimately, the pattern and rhythm of their speech, the things that have shaped their lives, their fortitude, humor, simplicity. They are fortunate to have a chronicler like Shirley Ann Grau. She is an extraordinarily fine writer."

Grau's "most ambitious—and in some respects most successful—novel to date," according to Schlueter, is *The Keepers of the House.* Published in 1964 and subsequently awarded the Pulitzer Prize for fiction, *The Keepers of the House* is set in a mythical town in the southern Delta country and chronicles three generations of the Howland family. "Again nature, in this case the land which comprises most of the Howland fortune, is of great importance, but with a difference," Ross observes. "It is now bound up with the history in which the story is rooted, and it provides purpose and conflict for the central characters."

Years after the death of his first wife, plantation owner William Howland takes a black woman, Margaret, into his home as his mistress and housekeeper. Will and Margaret have three children of their own, and they also give shelter to his granddaughter, Abigail, after her mother's death. Their offspring are eventually sent North to school; meanwhile, Abigail marries a segregationist politician who builds his career on the Howland name and the exploitation of racial prejudice. Their marriage collapses when, just before the gubernatorial primary, one of Will and Margaret's children returns to provide proof that Will and Margaret were actually husband and wife.

"With rich and bitter irony Miss Grau shows us how Will Howland's domestic arrangement is tolerated by the white community only because he is assumed to be exploiting a helpless girl," writes Frederick C. Crews in the *New York Times Book Review*. "When it is discovered, after his death, that he regarded her as his true wife and in fact secretly married her, the delicate fabric of caste hypocrisy in the town rips apart." Abigail's husband deserts her and their children, angry whites attack the Howland plantation, and Abigail moves to defend her inheritance and take revenge on the town.

Schlueter observes that upon publication of *The Keepers of the House*, Grau was "immediately, though in respects misleadingly, compared by various critics to the likes of Faulkner." He adds: "But Grau is not a Faulkner, and though such parallels exist, her work can stand by itself simply as a beautifully realized and executed work in which her lyrical power as a writer has almost perfect control and development." Expressing a similar opinion, Crews writes: "Her lucidity, her narrative directness, her reliance on the bare details of her plot instead of on ponderous philosophizing—all are non-Faulknerian traits, and in her hands they are agreeable virtues." Other reviews of the book have been equally laudatory. Granville Hicks, for example, writes in *Saturday Review:* "It is a novel of considerable dramatic force. Miss Grau makes her point—the absurdities as well as the cruelties to which prejudice leads—sharply enough, but this is a story not a tract. . . . All the virtues of Miss Grau's earlier books are here, together with a new power."

Although most of Grau's novels have been favorably received, Schlueter believes that "her lasting status as a writer may be more as a writer of the shorter form than of the novel." Mary Rohrberger comments in *Women Writers of the Contemporary South:* "As a short story writer, Grau's talent is immense though not revealed by a simple surface reading; for what is beneath the surfaces and interacting with them is what is characteristic of the short story genre, and Grau has mastered the genre."

Her first collection, *The Black Prince and Other Stories,* was published when Grau was twenty-four years old and has been described by a *Time* critic as "the most impressive U.S. short story debut between hard covers since J. D. Salinger's *Nine Stories.*" *The Black Prince and Other Stories* describes a primitive world and the conditions of survival for its white and black inhabitants. Set along the bayous of the Mississippi, the stories record "frustration and violence and death," but also "serenity and achievement and life," according to *Saturday Review* critic William Peden. Louise Y. Gossett comments in *Violence in Recent Southern Fiction* that while Grau usually limits herself to observable facts, she occasionally introduces the supernatural, as in her title story. In "The Black Prince," violence erupts around a black Lucifer-figure who mints coins from wax, seduces women with his wealth and power, and is finally dispatched with a magic silver bullet. In other stories, observes Gossett, "she sketches the primal roots of all human experience" and details the rudimentary

conflict between man and nature, "depicting a direct relationship which has become increasingly rare in a mechanized world."

Reflecting on *The Black Prince and Other Stories,* Ross writes, "Already apparent in this first book were qualities which would characterize Grau's work: the lean prose which has been compared by several critics to that of Hemingway; the precise, impersonal descriptions of nature; the meticulous craftsmanship; the use of various points of view." John Nerber, likening Grau's literary debut to that of Eudora Welty, says in the *New York Times:* "Without being in the least like Miss Welty . . ., Miss Grau has the same unmistakable authority, the instinctive feeling for form and language (obviously strengthened by a lot of hard work) and that pervasive relish for the wonderful particularities of human nature that are part of the equipment of the born writer."

In her third collection, *Nine Women,* Grau "moves beyond the more insistent regionalism of her previous work to delineate the lives of nine very different women living in widely disparate worlds—tony, blue-blooded summer resorts, in-grown Roman Catholic communities, poor black neighborhoods and isolated bayou towns . . .," notes *New York Times* critic Michiko Kakutani. "Where the sense of 'Southernness' remains in these stories is in their preoccupation with the past, with the passing of time and its incalculable losses. Nearly every heroine is now poised on the brink of change, and each is somehow engaged in the sad, sweet business of remembering her life."

In the highly acclaimed "Letting Go," for example, a woman named Mary Margaret breaks away from her cold, demanding parents and comfortable but monotonous marriage "and begins to shape a life that can truly be her own," writes Jonathan Yardley in the *Washington Post Book World.* Several of the other stories are concerned with aging and death. "Even when death is not involved," writes *Los Angeles Times* critic Richard Eder, "the climactic moment is usually a relinquishing of some kind." Edward J. Curtin, Jr., comments in *America* that "almost without exception, the characters in these stories suffer the living deaths of frozen hearts; affectless and fatalistic, they seek false refuge in the physical houses they call home."

The characters' fatalism and hopelessness makes *Nine Women* "a curious but disappointing book," according to Curtin. He explains: "[Grau] is attuned to issues of great import, but her vision of life is redolent of a weary resignation that borders on the nihilistic. . . . Nearly all the characters in this book share in that helpless passivity and childishness, in that love of easeful death. Resignation, hopelessness and weariness mark them. It is as though Grau cannot imagine people fierce enough to fight for authentic existence. Rather than live in possibility, they dwell inertly in houses of hopelessness."

Other reviewers, however, maintain that Grau's characters are indeed spirited, but that their spiritedness is no match for fate. Writes Yardley: "In all of these stories there is an awareness that fate is capricious. . . . Even as these women seek to master their lives, they know they cannot. . . . There is in their lives 'a thing that crouched waiting in the shadows,' a fate they have no choice but to accept, however shocking and painful it may prove to be." *Ms.* contributor Diane Cole notes that "Grau dramatizes the lives of women . . . who share only their common heritage in the South and their determined spirit. . . . They are gritty, outwardly cool, yet passionately methodical in pursuing their goals." She concludes, "At its best, *Nine Women* should send new readers to discover Shirley Ann Grau's world of strong women of the South."

BIOGRAPHICAL/CRITICAL SOURCES:

BOOKS

Contemporary Literary Criticism, Gale, Volume IV, 1975, Volume IX, 1978.
Dictionary of Literary Biography, Volume II: *American Novelists since World War II,* Gale, 1978.
Gossett, Louise Y., *Violence in Recent Southern Fiction,* Duke University Press, 1965.
Grau, Shirley Ann, *Nine Women,* Knopf, 1985.
Prenshaw, Peggy Whitman, editor, *Women Writers of the Contemporary South,* University Press of Mississippi, 1984.
Schlueter, Paul, *Shirley Ann Grau,* Twayne, 1981.

PERIODICALS

America, April 26, 1986.
Atlantic, October, 1971.
Catholic World, March, 1955.
Chicago Tribune Book Week, March 22, 1964.
Chicago Tribune Book World, February 9, 1986.
Commonweal, July 11, 1958.
Contempora, Volume II, number 2, 1972.
Critique, Volume VI, number 1, 1963, Volume XVII, number 2, 1975.
Hudson Review, autumn, 1977.
Kirkus Reviews, April 15, 1958, April 15, 1961.
Listener, January 19, 1978.
Los Angeles Times, January 22, 1986.
New Republic, April 18, 1964, September 18, 1971, November 24, 1973.
New Statesman, September 30, 1977.
Newsweek, December 26, 1955.
New Yorker, March 21, 1977.
New York Herald Tribune Book Review, January 16, 1955, June 22, 1958.
New York Review of Books, December 2, 1971.
New York Times, January 16, 1955, September 9, 1971, November 1, 1973, January 4, 1986.
New York Times Book Review, July 10, 1955, March 22, 1964, September 19, 1971, December 23, 1973, October 16, 1977, February 9, 1986.
Observer, October 2, 1977.
Publishers Weekly, January 10, 1986.
Saturday Review, January 29, 1955, March 21, 1964, September 18, 1971, February 19, 1977.
Sewanee Review, October/December, 1962, fall, 1974.
Southern Review, winter, 1974.
Time, January 24, 1955, June 23, 1958, April 10, 1964, September 6, 1971, February 7, 1977.
Times Literary Supplement, November 15, 1974, December 9, 1977.
Village Voice, April 15, 1986.
Washington Post Book World, October 10, 1971, November 27, 1973, January 12, 1986.

*   *   *

GRAVES, Robert (von Ranke) 1895-1985
(John Doyle, a pseudonym; Barbara Rich, a joint pseudonym)

PERSONAL: Born July 24, 1895, in London, England; died after a long illness, December 7, 1985, in Deya, Majorca, Spain; buried in village cemetery in Deya, Majorca, Spain; son of Alfred Perceval (an Irish poet and ballad writer) and Amalia (von Ranke) Graves; married Nancy Nicholson, 1918 (divorced, 1929); married Beryl Pritchard, 1950; children: (first marriage) Jenny, David, Catherine, Samuel; (second marriage) William, Lucia, Juan, Tomas. *Education:* Attended Charterhouse School; Oxford University, B.Litt., 1926. *Religion:* None.

ADDRESSES: Home—Majorca, Spain. *Agent*—A. P. Watt Ltd., 20 John St., London WC1N 2DL, England.

CAREER: Egyptian University, Cairo, Egypt, professor of English literature, 1926; co-founder of Seizin Press, 1928; Clarke Lecturer, Trinity College, Cambridge University, 1954-55; lecturer in United States, 1958; Oxford University, Oxford, England, professor of poetry, 1961-65; lecturer in United States, 1966-67. Arthur Dehon Little Memorial Lecturer at Massachusetts Institute of Technology, 1963. *Military service:* Royal Welch Fusiliers, 1914-18; served in France; became captain.

MEMBER: American Academy of Arts and Sciences (honorary member).

AWARDS, HONORS: Bronze Medal for poetry at Olympic Games in Paris, 1924; James Tait Black Memorial Prize, 1935, for *I, Claudius* and *Claudius, the God and His Wife Messalina;* Hawthornden Prize, 1935, for *I, Claudius;* Femina-Vie Heureuse Prize and the Stock Prize, 1939, for *Count Belisarius;* Russell Loines Memorial Fund Award, 1958; Gold Medal of Poetry Society of America, 1959; Foyle Poetry Prize, 1960; M.A., Oxford University, 1961; Arts Council award, 1962; Italia Prize for radio play, 1965; Gold Medal for poetry at Cultural Olympics in Mexico City, 1968; Queen's Gold Medal for Poetry, 1969; honorary fellow of St. John's College, 1971.

WRITINGS:

POETRY

Over the Brazier, Poetry Bookshop, 1916.
Goliath and David, Chiswick Press, 1916.
Fairies and Fusiliers, Heinemann, 1917, Knopf, 1918.
Country Sentiment, Knopf, 1920.
The Pier-Glass, Knopf, 1921.
The Feather Bed, L. and V. Woolf, 1923.
Whipperginny, Knopf, 1923.
Mock Beggar Hall, Hogarth Press, 1924.
Welchman's Hose, The Fleuron, 1925.
Robert Graves, Benn, 1925.
(Under pseudonym John Doyle) *The Marmosite's Miscellany,* Hogarth Press, 1925.
Poems, 1914-1926, Heinemann, 1927, Doubleday, Doran & Co., 1929.
Poems, 1929, Seizin Press, 1929.
Ten Poems More, Hours Press (Paris), 1930.
Poems, 1926-1930, Heinemann, 1931.
To Whom Else?, Seizin Press, 1931.
Poems, 1930-1933, Barker, 1933.
Collected Poems, Random House, 1938.
No More Ghosts, Faber, 1940.
(With Alan Hodge and Norman Cameron) *Work in Hand,* Hogarth, 1942.
Poems, 1938-1945, Creative Age Press, 1946.
Collected Poems, 1914-1947, Cassell, 1948.
Poems and Satires, Cassell, 1951.
Poems, 1953, Cassell, 1953.
Collected Poems, 1955, Doubleday, 1955.
Robert Graves: Poems Selected by Himself, Penguin Books, 1957.
The Poems of Robert Graves Chosen by Himself, Doubleday, 1958.

Collected Poems, 1959, Cassell, 1959, Doubleday, 1961, 3rd edition, Cassell, 1962.
The Penny Fiddle: Poems for Children, Cassell, 1960, Doubleday, 1961.
More Poems, 1961, Cassell, 1961.
Selected Poetry and Prose, edited, introduced, and annotated by James Reeves, Hutchinson, 1961.
Poems, Collected by Himself, Doubleday, 1961.
The More Deserving Cases: Eighteen Old Poems for Reconsideration, Marlborough College Press, 1962.
New Poems, Cassell, 1962, Doubleday, 1963.
Ann at Highwood Hall: Poems for Children, Cassell, 1964.
Man Does, Woman Is, Doubleday, 1964.
Love Respelt, Cassell, 1965, Doubleday, 1966.
Collected Poems, 1965, Cassell, 1965.
Collected Poems, 1966, Doubleday, 1966.
Seventeen Poems Missing From Love Respelt, Stellar Press, 1966.
Colophon to "Love Respelt," Bertram Rota, 1967.
(With D. H. Lawrence) *Poems,* edited by Leonard Clark, Longman, 1967.
Poems, 1965-1968, Cassell, 1968.
Beyond Giving, Bertram Rota, 1969.
Love Respelt Again, Doubleday, 1969.
Poems About Love, Cassell, 1969.
Poems, 1968-1970, Cassell, 1970, Doubleday, 1971.
Advice From a Mother, Poem-of-the-Month Club, 1970.
Green-Sailed Vessel, Bertram Rota, 1971.
Poems, 1970-1972, Cassell, 1972.
Timeless Meeting, Bertram Rota, 1973.
At the Gate, Bertram Rota, 1974.
Collected Poems, Cassell, 1975.
New Collected Poems, Doubleday, 1977.

FICTION

My Head! My Head! Being the History of Elisha and the Shunamite Woman; With the History of Moses as Elisha Related It, and Her Questions Put to Him, Secker, 1925.
The Shout, Mathews and Marrot, 1929.
(With Laura Riding, under joint pseudonym Barbara Rich) *No Decency Left,* J. Cape, 1932.
The Real David Copperfield, Barker, 1933.
I, Claudius, Smith & Haas, 1934, reprinted, Vintage, 1989.
Claudius, the God and His Wife Messalina, Barker, 1934, Smith & Haas, 1935, reprinted, Vintage, 1989.
"Antigua, Penny, Puce," Seizin Press and Constable, 1936, published as *The Antigua Stamp,* Random House, 1937.
Count Belisarius, Random House, 1938, reprinted, Farrar, Straus, 1982.
Sergeant Lamb of the Ninth, Methuen, 1940, published as *Sergeant Lamb's America,* Random House, 1940, reprinted, Academy Chicago, 1986.
Proceed, Sergeant Lamb, Random House, 1941.
The Story of Marie Powell, Wife to Mr. Milton, Cassell, 1943, published as *Wife to Mr. Milton: The Story of Marie Powell,* Creative Age Press, 1944.
The Golden Fleece, Cassell, 1944, published as *Hercules, My Shipmate,* Creative Age Press, 1945.
King Jesus, Creative Age Press, 1946, 6th edition, Cassell, 1962.
The Islands of Unwisdom, Doubleday, 1949 (published in England as *The Isles of Unwisdom,* Cassell, 1950).
Watch the North Wind Rise, Creative Age Press, 1949 (published in England as *Seven Days in New Crete,* Cassell, 1949).
Homer's Daughter, Doubleday, 1955, reprinted, Academy Chicago, 1987.
Catacrok! Mostly Stories, Mostly Funny, Cassell, 1956.

They Hanged My Saintly Billy: The Life and Death of Dr. William Palmer, Doubleday, 1957.
Collected Short Stories, Doubleday, 1964, published as *The Shout and Other Stories,* Penguin Books, 1978.

NONFICTION

On English Poetry; Being an Irregular Approach to the Psychology of This Art, From Evidence Mainly Subjective, Knopf, 1922.
The Meaning of Dreams, Palmer, 1924.
Poetic Unreason and Other Studies, Palmer, 1925.
Contemporary Techniques of Poetry: A Political Analogy, Hogarth Press, 1925.
Another Future of Poetry, Hogarth Press, 1926.
Impenetrability; or, The Proper Habit of English, L. and V. Woolf, 1926.
Lawrence and the Arabs, J. Cape, 1927, published as *Lawrence and the Arabian Adventure,* Doubleday, Doran & Co., 1928.
Lars Porsena; or, The Future of Swearing and Improper Language, Dutton, 1927, revised edition published as *The Future of Swearing and Improper Language,* K. Paul, Trench, Trubner & Co., 1936.
Mrs. Fisher; or, The Future of Humour, K. Paul, Trench, Trubner & Co., 1928.
(With Riding) *A Pamphlet Against Anthologies,* J. Cape, 1928.
Goodbye to All That: An Autobiography, J. Cape, 1929, J. Cape & H. Smith, 1930, revised edition, Doubleday, 1957.
T. E. Lawrence to His Biographer, Doubleday, 1938, published with Liddell Hart's work as *T. E. Lawrence to His Biographers,* Doubleday, 1963, 2nd edition, Cassell, 1963.
(With Alan Hodge) *The Long Week-End: A Social History of Great Britain, 1918-1939,* Faber, 1940, Macmillan, 1941.
(With Hodge) *The Reader Over Your Shoulder: A Handbook for Writers of English Prose,* Macmillan, 1943.
The White Goddess: A Historical Grammar of Poetic Myth, Creative Age Press, 1948, amended and enlarged edition, Vintage Books, 1958, reprinted, Peter Smith, 1983.
The Common Asphodel: Collected Essays on Poetry, 1922-1949, H. Hamilton, 1949.
(With Joshua Podro) *The Nazarene Gospel Restored,* Cassell, 1953, Doubleday, 1954.
(With Podro) *Nazarene Gospel,* Cassell, 1955.
Adam's Rib, and Other Anomalous Elements in the Hebrew Creation Myth: A New View, Trianon Press, 1955, Yoseloff, 1958.
The Greek Myths, two volumes, Penguin Books, 1955, reprinted, Moyer Bell, 1988.
The Crowning Privilege: The Clark Lectures, 1954-1955 (includes sixteen new poems), Cassell, 1955, Doubleday, 1956.
(With Podro) *Jesus in Rome: A Historical Conjecture,* Cassell, 1957.
5 Pens in Hand, Doubleday, 1958.
Steps: Stories, Talks, Essays, Poems, Studies in History, Cassell, 1958.
Food for Centaurs: Stories, Talks, Critical Studies, Poems, Doubleday, 1960.
Greek Gods and Heroes, Doubleday, 1960 (published in England as *Myths of Ancient Greece,* Cassell, 1961).
Oxford Addresses on Poetry, Doubleday, 1962.
The Siege and Fall of Troy, Cassell, 1962, Doubleday, 1963.
Nine Hundred Iron Chariots, Massachusetts Institute of Technology, 1963.
(With Raphael Patal) *Hebrew Myths: The Book of Genesis,* Doubleday, 1964, reprinted, Doubleday, 1989.
Mammon (lecture; also see below), London School of Economics, 1964.

Mammon and the Black Goddess (one section previously published as *Mammon*), Doubleday, 1965.
Majorca Observed, Doubleday, 1965.
Spiritual Quixote, Oxford University Press, 1967.
Poetic Craft and Principle (collection of Oxford lectures), Cassell, 1967.
(Author of introduction) *Greece, Gods, and Art,* Viking, 1968.
The Crane Bag, Cassell, 1969.
Difficult Questions, Easy Answers, Cassell, 1972, Doubleday, 1973.
Selected Letters of Robert Graves, edited by Paul O'Prey, Hutchinson, Volume I: *In Broken Images: 1914-1946,* 1982, Volume II: *Between Moon and Moon: 1946-1972,* 1984.

FOR CHILDREN

The Big Green Book, illustrated by Maurice Sendak, Crowell, 1962.
Two Wise Children, Harlin Quist, 1966.
The Poor Boy Who Followed His Star, Cassell, 1968, Doubleday, 1969.
The Ancient Castle, P. Owen, 1980.

EDITOR

The English Ballad: A Short Critical Survey, Benn, 1927.
(Compiler) *The Less Familiar Nursery Rhymes,* Benn, 1927.
(And author of foreword) Algernon Charles Swinburne, *An Old Saying,* J. S. Mayfield, 1947.
English and Scottish Ballads, Macmillan, 1957.
(And author of foreword) *The Comedies of Terence,* Doubleday, 1962, published as *Comedies,* Aldine, 1962.

Condensed Merrill P. Paine's edition of *David Copperfield,* by Charles Dickens, Harcourt, 1934. Edited, with Laura Riding, a semi-annual called *Epilogue: A Critical Summary,* 1935-37.

TRANSLATOR

(With Laura Riding) Georg Schwarz, *Almost Forgotten Germany,* Random House, 1937.
Lucius Apuleius, *The Transformations of Lucius, Otherwise Known as "The Golden Ass,"* Farrar, Straus, 1951.
Manuel de Jesus Galvan, *The Cross and the Sword,* Indiana University Press, 1954.
Pedro Antonio de Alarcon, *The Infant With the Globe,* Faber, 1955.
Marcus Annaeus Lucanus, *Pharsalia: Dramatic Episodes of the Civil Wars,* Penguin Books, 1956.
George Sand, *Winter in Majorca,* Cassell, 1956, reprinted, Academy Chicago, 1989.
Suetonius, *The Twelve Caesars,* Cassell, 1957.
The Anger of Achilles: Homer's "Iliad" (produced at Lincoln Center, New York, 1967), Doubleday, 1959.
Hesiodu Stamperia del Santuccio, *Fable of the Hawk and the Nightingale,* 1959.
(With Omar Ali-Shah) *The Rubaiyyat of Omar Khayaam* (based on the 12th-century manuscript), Cassell, 1967, published as *The Original Rubaiyyat of Omar Khayaam,* Doubleday, 1968.
Solomon's "Song of Songs," Cassell, 1968, Doubleday, 1969.

OTHER

John Kemp's Wager: A Ballad Opera, S. French, 1925.
But It Still Goes On: An Accumulation (includes the play "But It Still Goes On"), J. Cape, 1930, J. Cape & H. Smith, 1931.
Occupation: Writer (includes the play "Horses"), Creative Age Press, 1950.

Nausicaa (opera libretto adapted from his novel *Homer's Daughter;* music by Peggy Glanville-Hicks), produced in Athens, Greece, 1961.

SIDELIGHTS: Robert Graves often stirred controversy in his endeavors as a poet, novelist, critic, mythographer, translator, and editor. Stephen Spender of the *New York Times Book Review* characterized Graves as a free thinker: "All of his life Graves has been indifferent to fashion, and the great and deserved reputation he has is based on his individuality as a poet who is both intensely idiosyncratic and unlike any other contemporary poet and at the same time classical." A rebel socially, as well as artistically, Graves left his wife and four children in 1929 to live in Majorca with Laura Riding, a Russian Jewish poet. Douglas Day commented on the importance of this move in his *Swifter Than Reason: The Poetry and Criticism of Robert Graves:* "The influence of Laura Riding is quite possibly the most important single element in his poetic career: she persuaded him to curb his digressiveness and his rambling philosophizing and to concentrate instead on terse, ironic poems written on personal themes. She also imparted to him some of her own dry, cerebral quality, which has remained in much of his poetry. There can be little doubt that some of his best work was done during the years of his literary partnership with Laura Riding."

It has been suggested that one of Graves's debts to Riding was his long-standing fascination with the Muse of poetry. Anne Fremantle noted in *Nation* that T. S. Matthews gives Riding credit for Graves's "mystical and reverent attitude to the mother goddess," that muse to whom he refers by a variety of names, including Calliope and the White Goddess. In his *Third Book of Criticism,* Randall Jarrell notes that Muse symbolism permeates Graves's writing: "All that is finally important to Graves is condensed in the one figure of the Mother-Mistress-Muse, she who creates, nourishes, seduces, destroys; she who saves us—or, as good as saving, destroys us—as long as we love her, write poems to her, submit to her without question, use all our professional, Regimental, masculine qualities in her service. Death is swallowed up in victory, said St. Paul; for Graves Life, Death, everything that exists is swallowed up in the White Goddess."

Critics often described the White Goddess in paradoxical terms. Patrick Callahan, writing in the *Prairie Schooner,* called her a blend of the "cruelty and kindness of woman." He contended: "Cerridwen, the White Goddess, is the apotheosis of woman at her most primitive. Graves finds the women he has loved an embodiment of her. If Cerridwen is to be adored, she is also to be feared, for her passing can rival the passing of very life, and the pendulum of ecstasy and anguish which marks human love reaches its full sweep in her." Martin Seymour-Smith also noted the complex personality of the Muse, describing her in his *Robert Graves* as "the Mother who bears man, the Lover who awakens him to manhood, the Old Hag who puts pennies on his dead eyes. She is a threefold process of Birth, Copulation, and Death." Brian Jones, however, found the Goddess one-dimensional. He wrote in *London Magazine:* "It is interesting that it is often impossible to tell whether the feminine pronoun [in *Poems, 1965-1968*] refers to woman or Goddess or both; not that this is necessarily an adverse criticism, but in Graves both the woman and the Goddess [are] sentimental, belittled, simplified male creation[s]. The dignity and 'otherness' of the woman is missing."

Graves explored and reconstructed the White Goddess myth in his book *The White Goddess: A Historical Grammar of Poetic Myth.* J. M. Cohen noted in his *Robert Graves:* "The mythology of The White Goddess, though its elements are drawn from a vast field of ancient story and legends, is in its assemblage

Graves's own creation, and conforms to the requirements of his own poetic mind." One of Graves's prerequisites is spontaneity. Muse poetry, wrote Graves in his *Oxford Addresses on Poetry,* "is composed at the back of the mind; an unaccountable product of a trance in which the emotions of love, fear, anger, or grief are profoundly engaged, though at the same time powerfully disciplined." Graves gave an example of such inspiration, explaining that while writing *The Golden Fleece* he experienced powerful feelings of "a sudden enlightenment." According to Cohen, this insight was into a subject Graves knew "almost nothing" about. Cohen wrote that "a night and day of furious cogitation was followed by three weeks of intense work, during which the whole 70,000 words of the original were written." Monroe K. Spears deplored this method of composition in the *Sewanee Review:* "Graves's theory of poetry—if it can be dignified by the name of theory—is essentially a perfectly conventional late Romantic notion of poetry as emotional and magical; it is remarkable only in its crude simplicity and vulnerability." Still, Randall Jarrell asserted that "Graves's richest, most moving, and most consistently beautiful poems—poems that almost deserve the literal *magical*—are his mythic/archaic pieces, all those the reader thinks of as 'White Goddess' poems."

"Unsolicited enlightenment" also figured in Graves's historical method. Peter Quennell wrote in his *Casanova in London:* "The focal point of all of [Graves's] scholarly researches is the bizarre theory of Analeptic Thought, based on his belief that forgotten events may be recovered by the exercise of intuition, which affords sudden glimpses of truth 'that would not have been arrived at by inductive reasoning.' In practice . . . this sometimes means that the historian first decides what he would *like* to believe, then looks around for facts to suit his thesis." Quennell suggested a hazard of that method: "Although [Graves's] facts themselves are usually sound, they do not always support the elaborate conclusions that Graves proceeds to draw from them; two plus two regularly make five and six; and genuine erudition and prophetic imagination conspire to produce some very odd results." Spears also questioned Graves's judgment, claiming that "he has no reverence for the past and he is not interested in learning from it; instead, he re-shapes it in his own image . . . he displays much ingenuity and learning in his interpretations of events and characters, but also a certain coarseness of perception and a tendency to oversimplify."

The story of Graves's translation of *The Rubaiyyat of Omar Khayaam* served to exemplify the stir he was capable of making when he brought his own theories about history to his writing. First, critics and scholars questioned the veracity of his text. Graves had worked from an annotated version of the poem given him by Ali-Shah, a Persian poet; although Ali-Shah alleged that the manuscript had been in his family for 800 years, L. P. Elwell-Sutton, an Orientalist at Edinburgh University, decried it as a "clumsy forgery." Next came the inevitable comparisons with Edward FitzGerald's standard translation, published in 1859. FitzGerald's depiction of romanticized Victorian bliss is epitomized by the much-quoted lines, "A Book of Verse underneath the Bough / A Jug of Wine, a Loaf of Bread, and Thou." Graves's translation, on the other hand, reads: "Should our day's portion be one mancel loaf, / a haunch of mutton and a gourd of wine." A *Time* critic defended FitzGerald's translation by quoting FitzGerald himself: " 'A translation must live with a transfusion of one's own worse life if he can't retain the original's better. Better a live sparrow than a stuffed eagle.' " The critic added that "Graves's more dignified *Rubaiyyat* may be an eagle to FitzGerald's sparrow. But FitzGerald's work is still in living flight, while Graves's already sits there on the shelf—stuffed."

Philip Toynbee concurred in the *Observer Review:* "This is another case in which Graves's 'improvement' looks a poorish thing beside the original." And Martin Dodsworth commented in *Listener:* "Graves does not convince here. He has produced a prosy New English Bible sort of Khayaam, whose cloudy mysticism raises more questions than it answers."

Despite his detractors, Graves maintained his characteristically independent stance (he once told his students that "the poet's chief loyalty is to the Goddess Calliope, not to his publisher or to the booksellers on his publisher's mailing list") in defending his translation against the more commercially directed attempt he felt FitzGerald made. In Graves's opinion, the poet was writing about the ecstasy of Sufi mysticism, not—as he says FitzGerald implies—more earthly pleasures. In an extensive apologia for his translation, Graves wrote in *Observations:* "Any attempt at improving or altering Khayaam's poetic intentions would have seemed shocking to me when I was working on the *Rubaiyyat.* . . . My twin principles were: 'Stick as strictly to the script as you can' and 'Respect the tradition of English verse as first confirmed by the better Tudor poets: which is to be as explicit as possible on every occasion and never play down to ignorance.' "

Some critics felt that such statements revealed an admirable strength of character. John Wain, for one, felt that Graves demonstrated an unswerving dedication to his ideals in his writing. He commented in the *New York Times Magazine:* "Robert Graves's long, eventful and productive life has certainly been marked by plenty of fighting spirit, whatever name you give to it—combativeness, magnificent independence or just plain cussedness. He has faith in his own vision and his own way of doing things—legitimately, since they are arrived at by effort and sacrifice, by solitude and devotion—and when he has arrived at them, he cares nothing for majority opinion. He has never been in the least daunted by the discovery that everybody else was out of step. Whatever is the issue—the choice of a life style, a knotty point in theological controversy, a big literary reputation that should be made smaller, or a smaller one that should be made bigger—Graves has reached his own conclusions and never worried if no one agreed with him." Considering Graves's output, Wain concluded: "He is not an easy writer. He does not make concessions. He has achieved a large readership and a great fame because of the richness of what he has to offer—its human depth, its range, its compelling imaginative power—rather than by fancy packaging or deep-freeze convenience."

BIOGRAPHICAL/CRITICAL SOURCES:

BOOKS

Cohen, J. M., *Robert Graves,* Oliver & Boyd, 1960.
Contemporary Literary Criticism, Gale, Volume 1, 1973, Volume 2, 1974, Volume 6, 1976, Volume 11, 1979, Volume 39, 1986, Volume 44, 1987, Volume 45, 1987.
Day, Douglas, *Swifter Than Reason: The Poetry and Criticism of Robert Graves,* University of North Carolina Press, 1963.
Dictionary of Literary Biography, Volume 20, *British Poets, 1914-1945,* Gale, 1983.
Dictionary of Literary Biography Yearbook: 1985, Gale, 1986.
Enright, D. J., *Conspirators and Poets,* Dufour, 1966.
Graves, Robert, *Goodbye to All That: An Autobiography,* J. Cape, 1929.
Graves, Robert, *Oxford Addresses on Poetry,* Doubleday, 1962.
Higginson, F. H., *A Bibliography of the Works of Robert Graves,* Shoe String, 1966.
Hoffman, D. G., *Barbarous Knowledge,* Oxford University Press, 1967.

Jarrell, Randall, *The Third Book of Criticism,* Farrar, Straus, 1969.

Nemerov, Howard, *Poetry and Fiction,* Rutgers University Press, 1963.

Quennell, Peter, *Casanova in London,* Stein & Day, 1971.

Seymour-Smith, Martin, *Robert Graves,* Longman Group, revised edition, 1965.

Swinnerton, Frank, *The Georgian Literary Scene,* Dent, 1951.

PERIODICALS

Atlantic, January, 1966.
Commentary, February, 1967.
Harper's, August, 1967.
Horizon, January, 1962.
Hudson Review, spring, 1967.
Life, June 24, 1963, October 15, 1965.
Listener, May 4, 1967, November 9, 1967, December 24, 1970.
Literary Times, April, 1965.
London Magazine, February, 1969.
Los Angeles Times Book Review, December 28, 1980, January 23, 1983.
Nation, March 18, 1978.
National Observer, March 17, 1969.
New Leader, October 27, 1969.
New Statesman, December 3, 1965.
Newsweek, May 20, 1968, July 28, 1969.
New York Times, December 1, 1966, October 26, 1967, September 20, 1979, December 25, 1981.
New York Times Book Review, July 20, 1969, October 12, 1969, March 11, 1973, April 29, 1979, May 30, 1982, October 17, 1982.
New York Times Magazine, October 30, 1966.
Observations, July, 1968.
Playboy, December, 1970.
Poetry, January, 1969.
Prairie Schooner, summer, 1970.
Publishers Weekly, August 11, 1975.
Sewanee Review, fall, 1965.
Shenandoah, spring, 1966.
Time, November 3, 1967, May 31, 1968.
Times (London), May 27, 1982, July 26, 1985.
Times Literary Supplement, October 7, 1965, December 7, 1967, June 26, 1969, November 21, 1980, September 27, 1985.
Variety, July 26, 1972.
Washington Post Book World, November 29, 1981.
Yale Review, autumn, 1968.

OBITUARIES:

BOOKS

Current Biography, H. W. Wilson, 1986.

PERIODICALS

Chicago Tribune, December 9, 1985.
Daily Variety, December 10, 1985.
Los Angeles Times, December 8, 1985.
National Review, December 31, 1985.
Newsweek, December 16, 1985.
New York Times, December 8, 1985.
Publishers Weekly, December 20, 1985.
School Library Journal, February, 1986.
Time, December 16, 1985.
Times (London), December 9, 1985.
Washington Post, December 8, 1985, December 9, 1985.

GRAY, Alasdair (James) 1934-

PERSONAL: Born December 28, 1934, in Glasgow, Scotland; son of Alex (a machine operator) and Amy (a homemaker; maiden name, Fleming) Gray; children: Andrew. *Education:* Glasgow Art School, received diploma, 1957. *Politics:* "Devolutionary Scottish C.N.D. [Campaign for Nuclear Disarmament] Socialist." *Religion:* None.

ADDRESSES: Home—39 Kersland St., Glasgow G12 8BP, Scotland.

CAREER: Part-time art teacher in area of Glasgow, Scotland, 1958-62; theatrical scene painter in Glasgow, 1962-63; free-lance playwright and painter in Glasgow, 1963-75; People's Palace (local history museum), Glasgow, artist-recorder, 1976-77; University of Glasgow, Glasgow, writer in residence, 1977-79; free-lance painter and maker of books in Glasgow, 1979—.

MEMBER: Scottish Society of Playwrights, Glasgow Print Workshop, various organizations supporting coal miners and nuclear disarmament.

AWARDS, HONORS: Three grants from Scottish Arts Council, between 1968 and 1981; award from Saltire Society, 1982, for *Lanark: A Life in Four Books;* award from Cheltenham Literary Festival, 1983, for *Unlikely Stories, Mostly;* award from Scottish branch of P.E.N., 1986.

WRITINGS:

Lanark: A Life in Four Books (novel), author-illustrated, Harper, 1981, revised, Braziller, 1985.
Unlikely Stories, Mostly (short stories), author-illustrated, Canongate, 1983, revised, Penguin, 1984.
1982 Janine (novel), Viking, 1984, revised, Penguin, 1985.
The Fall of Kelvin Walker: A Fable of the Sixties (novel; adapted from his television play of the same title; also see below), Canongate, 1985, Braziller, 1986.
(With James Kelman and Agnes Owens) *Lean Tales* (short story anthology), author-illustrated, J. Cape, 1985.
Saltire Self-Portrait 4, Saltire Society Publications, 1988.
Old Negatives (poems), author-illustrated, J. Cape, 1989.
The Anthology of Prefaces, Canongate, 1989.
McGrotty and Ludmilla; or, The Harbinger Report: A Romance of the Eighties, White Leaf, 1989.

Contributor to periodicals, including *Chapman* and *The Edinburgh Review.*

PLAYS FOR THE STAGE

"Dialogue" (one-act), first produced in Edinburgh at Gateway Theatre, 1971.
"The Fall of Kelvin Walker" (two-act; adapted from his television play of the same title; also see below), first produced in Stirling at McRoberts Centre, University of Stirling, 1972.
"The Loss of the Golden Silence" (one-act), first produced in Edinburgh at Pool Theatre, 1973.
"Homeward Bound" (one-act), first produced in Edinburgh at Pool Theatre, 1973.
(With Tom Leonard and Liz Lochhead) "Tickly Mince" (two-act), first produced in Glasgow at Tron Theatre, 1982.
(With Liz Lochhead, Tom Leonard and James Kelman) "The Pie of Damocles" (two-act), first produced in Glasgow at Tron Theatre, 1983.

RADIO PLAYS

"Quiet People," British Broadcasting Corporation (BBC), 1968.

"The Night Off," BBC, 1969.
"Thomas Muir of Huntershill," BBC, 1970.
"The Loss of the Golden Silence," BBC, 1974.
"McGrotty and Ludmilla," BBC, 1976.
"The Vital Witness," BBC, 1979.
"Near the Driver," translation into German by Berndt Rullkotter broadcast by Westdeutsche Rundfunk, 1983, original text broadcast by BBC, 1988.

TELEVISION PLAYS

"The Fall of Kelvin Walker," BBC, 1968.
"Dialogue," BBC, 1972.
"Triangles," Granada, 1972.
"The Man Who Knew About Electricity," BBC, 1973.
"Honesty," BBC, 1974.
"Today and Yesterday" (series of three 20-minute educational documentaries), BBC, 1975.
"Beloved," Granada, 1976.
"The Gadfly," Granada, 1977.
"The Story of a Recluse," BBC, 1987.

SIDELIGHTS: After more than twenty years as a painter and a scriptwriter for radio and television, Alasdair Gray rose to literary prominence with the publication of several of his books in the 1980s. His works have been noted for their mixture of realistic social commentary and vivid fantasy, augmented by the author's own evocative illustrations. Jonathan Baumbach wrote in the *New York Times Book Review* that Gray's work "has a verbal energy, an intensity of vision, that has been mostly missing from the English novel since D. H. Lawrence." And David Lodge of *New Republic* said that Gray "is that rather rare bird among contemporary British writers—a genuine experimentalist, transgressing the rules of formal English prose . . . boldly and imaginatively."

In his writing Gray often draws upon his Scottish background, and he is regarded as a major force in the literature of his homeland. Author Anthony Burgess, for instance, said in the *Observer* that he considered Gray the best Scottish novelist since Walter Scott became popular in the early nineteenth century. Unlike Scott, who made his country a setting for historical romance, Gray focuses on contemporary Scotland, where the industrial economy deteriorates and many citizens fear that their social and economic destiny has been surrendered to England. Critics praised Gray, however, for putting such themes as decline and powerlessness into a larger context that any reader can appreciate. "Using Glasgow as his undeniable starting point," Douglas Gifford wrote in *Studies in Scottish Literature*, "Gray . . . transforms local and hitherto restricting images, which limited [other] novelists of real ability, . . . into symbols of universal prophetic relevance."

Gray's first novel, *Lanark,* is a long and complex work that some reviewers considered partly autobiographical. It opens in Unthank, an ugly, declining city explained in reviews as a comment on Glasgow and other Western industrial centers. As in George Orwell's *Nineteen Eighty-four,* citizens of Unthank are ruled by a domineering and intrusive bureaucracy. Lanark is a lonely young man unable to remember his past. Along with many of his fellow-citizens, he is plagued with "dragonhide," an insidious, scaly skin infection seen as symbolic of his emotional isolation. Cured of his affliction by doctors at a scientific institute below the surface of the earth, Lanark realizes to his disgust that the staff is as arrogant and manipulative as the ruling elite on the surface. Before escaping from this underworld, Lanark has a vision in which he sees the life story of a young man who mysteriously resembles him—Duncan Thaw, an aspiring artist who lives in twentieth-century Glasgow.

Thaw's story, which comprises nearly half the book, is virtually a novel within a novel. It echoes the story of Lanark while displaying a markedly different literary technique. As William Boyd explained in the *Times Literary Supplement,* "the narration of Thaw's life turns out to be a brilliant and moving evocation of a talented and imaginative child growing up in working-class Glasgow. The style is limpid and classically elegant, the detail solidly documentary and in marked contrast to the fantastical and surrealistic accoutrements of the first 100 pages." Like Gray, Thaw attends art school in Glasgow, and as with Lanark, Thaw's loneliness and isolation are expressed outwardly in a skin disease, eczema. With increasing desperation Thaw seeks fulfillment in love and art, and his disappointment culminates in a violent outburst in which he kills—or at least thinks he kills—a young woman who had abandoned him. Bewildered and hopeless, he commits suicide. Boyd considered Thaw's story "a minor classic of the literature of adolescence," and Gifford likened it to James Joyce's novel *A Portrait of the Artist as a Young Man.* The last part of Gray's book focuses once more on Lanark, depicting his futile struggle to improve the world around him.

Critics have generally lauded *Lanark,* although some expressed concern that it was hampered by its size and intricacy. Boyd, for instance, felt that the parallel narratives of Thaw and Lanark "do not happily cohere." *Washington Post Book World*'s Michael Dirda said that *Lanark* was "too baggy and bloated," but he stressed that "there are such good things in it that one hardly knows where it could be cut." Many critics echoed Boyd's overall assessment that "*Lanark* is a work of loving and vivid imagination, yielding copious riches." Moreover, Burgess featured *Lanark* in his book *Ninety-nine Novels: The Best in English Since 1939,* declaring, "It was time Scotland produced a shattering work of fiction in the modern idiom. This is it."

Although *Lanark* rapidly achieved critical recognition in Britain, Gray's second novel, *1982 Janine,* was the first to be widely known in the United States. The novel records the thoughts of Jock McLeish, a disappointed, middle-aged Scottish businessman, during a long night of heavy drinking. In his mind Jock plays and replays fantasies in which he sexually tortures helpless women, and he gives names and identities to his victims, including the Janine of the title. Burgess spoke for several reviewers when he wrote in the *Observer* that such material was offensive and unneeded. But admirers of the novel, such as Richard Eder of the *Los Angeles Times,* felt that Jock's sexual fantasies were a valid metaphor for the character's own sense of helplessness. Jock, who rose to a managerial post from a working-class background, now hates himself because he is financially dependent on the ruling classes he once hoped to change.

As Eder observed, Jock's powerlessness is in its turn a metaphor for the subjugation of Scotland. Jock expounds on the sorry state of his homeland in the course of his drunken railings. Scotland's economy, he charges, has been starved in order to strengthen the country's political master, England; what is more, if war with the Soviet Union breaks out, Jock expects the English to use Scotland as a nuclear battlefield. As the novel ends, Jock resolves to quit his job and change his life for the better. Eder commended Gray for conveying a portrait of helplessness and the search for self-realization "in a flamboyantly comic narrator whose verbal blue streak is given depth by a winning impulse to self-discovery, and some alarming insight."

Gray's short story collection, *Unlikely Stories, Mostly,* is "if anything more idiosyncratic" than *1982 Janine,* according to Jonathan Baumbach of the *New York Times Book Review*. Many reviewers praised the imaginativeness of the stories while acknowledging that the collection, which includes work dating back to Gray's teenage years, is uneven in quality. As Gary Marmorstein observed in the *Los Angeles Times Book Review*, some of the stories are "slight but fun," including "The Star," in which a boy catches a star and swallows it, and "The Spread of Ian Nicol," in which a man slowly splits in two like a microbe reproducing itself. By contrast, "Five Letters From an Eastern Empire" is one of several more complex tales that received special praise. Set in the capital of a powerful empire, the story focuses on a talented poet. Gradually readers learn the source of the poet's artistic inspiration: the emperor murdered the poet's parents by razing the city in which they lived, then ordered him to write about the destruction. "The tone of the story remains under perfect control as it darkens and deepens," Adam Mars-Jones noted in the *Times Literary Supplement*, "until an apparently reckless comedy has become a cruel parable about power and meaning."

Gray's third novel, *The Fall of Kelvin Walker*, was inspired by personal experience. Still struggling to establish his career several years after his graduation from art school, Gray was tapped as the subject of a documentary by a successful friend at the British Broadcasting Corporation (BBC). Gray, who had been living on welfare, suddenly found himself treated to airline flights and limousine rides at the BBC's expense. In *Kelvin Walker* the title character, a young Scotsman with a burning desire for power, has a similar chance to use the communications media to fulfill his wildest fantasies. Though Walker arrives in London with few assets but self-confidence and a fast-talking manner, his persistence and good luck soon win him a national following as an interviewer on a television show. But in his pride and ambition Walker forgets that he exercises such influence only at the whims of his corporate bosses, and when he displeases them his fall from grace is as abrupt as his rise.

Kelvin Walker, which Gray adapted from his 1968 teleplay of the same title, is shorter and less surrealistic than his previous novels. The *Observer*'s Hermione Lee, though she stressed that Gray "is always worth attending to," felt that this novel "doesn't allow him the big scope he thrives on." By contrast, Larry McCaffery of *New York Times Book Review* praised *Kelvin Walker* for its "economy of means and exquisite control of detail." Gray "is now fully in command of his virtuoso abilities as a stylist and storyteller," McCaffery said, asserting that Gray's first four books—"each of which impresses in very different ways—indicate that he is emerging as the most vibrant and original new voice in English fiction."

Gray told *CA:* "I write to extend an excitement by giving it to others. I get ideas by conversing with others or by reading them. I have been influenced by most of the usual books, frequently in translation; by some very fine films; and by several kinds of popular and commercial rubbish."

BIOGRAPHICAL/CRITICAL SOURCES:

BOOKS

Burgess, Anthony, *Ninety-nine Novels: The Best in English Since 1939—A Personal Choice*, Allison & Busby, 1984.
Contemporary Literary Criticism, Volume 41, Gale, 1987.

PERIODICALS

Christian Science Monitor, October 5, 1984.
Los Angeles Times, November 21, 1984.
Los Angeles Times Book Review, December 9, 1984.
New Republic, November 12, 1984.

New York Times Book Review, October 28, 1984, May 5, 1985, December 21, 1986.
Observer (London), April 15, 1984, March 31, 1985.
Spectator, February 28, 1981.
Stage, November 30, 1972.
Studies in Scottish Literature, Volume 18, 1983.
Times (London), April 1, 1986.
Times Literary Supplement, February 27, 1981, March 18, 1983, April 13, 1984, March 29, 1985, May 10, 1985.
Voice Literary Supplement, December, 1984.
Washington Post Book World, December 16, 1984, August 31, 1986.

*   *   *

GRAY, Francine du Plessix 1930-

PERSONAL: Born September 25, 1930, in Warsaw, Poland (some sources say France); came to United States in 1941; naturalized citizen, 1952; daughter of Bertrand Jochaud (a diplomat and pilot for the Resistance) and Tatiana (Iacovleff) du Plessix; married Cleve Gray (a painter), April 23, 1957; children: Thaddeus Ives, Luke Alexander. *Education:* Attended Bryn Mawr College, 1948-50, and Black Mountain College, summers, 1951-52; Barnard College, B.A., 1952. *Politics:* Democrat. *Religion:* Roman Catholic.

ADDRESSES: Home—Greystones, Cornwall Bridge, CT 06754. *Agent*—Georges Borchardt, Inc., 136 East 57th St., New York, NY 10022.

CAREER: United Press International, New York City, reporter at night desk, 1952-54; *Realities* (magazine), Paris, France, editorial assistant for French edition, 1954-55; free-lance writer, 1955—; *Art in America*, New York City, book editor, 1964-66; *New Yorker*, New York City, staff writer, 1968—. Distinguished visiting professor at City College of the City University of New York, spring, 1975; visiting lecturer at Saybrook College, Yale University, 1981; adjunct professor, School of Fine Arts, Columbia University, 1983—. Judge of 1974 National Book Award in philosophy and religion. Attended Soviet-American Writers' Workshop in Batumin, U.S.S.R., 1979.

MEMBER: International PEN, Authors Guild, Authors League of America, National Book Critics Circle.

AWARDS, HONORS: Putnam Creative Writing Award from Barnard College, 1952; National Catholic Book Award from Catholic Press Association, 1971, for *Divine Disobedience: Profiles in Catholic Radicalism;* Front Page Award from Newswomen's Club of New York, 1972, for *Hawaii: The Sugar-Coated Fortress;* LL.D. from City University of New York, 1981, Oberlin College, 1985, University of Santa Clara, 1985.

WRITINGS:

Divine Disobedience: Profiles in Catholic Radicalism, Knopf, 1970.
Hawaii: The Sugar-Coated Fortress, Random House, 1972.
Lovers and Tyrants (novel), Simon & Schuster, 1976.
World Without End (novel), Simon & Schuster, 1981.
October Blood (novel), Simon & Schuster, 1985.
Adam and Eve and the City: Selected Nonfiction, Simon & Schuster, 1987.
Soviet Women: Walking the Tightrope, Doubleday, 1990.

Contributor of articles, stories, and reviews to periodicals, including *Vogue, New Yorker, Saturday Review, New York Review of Books, New York Times Book Review,* and *New Republic.*

WORK IN PROGRESS: A novel.

SIDELIGHTS: In 1976 *New Yorker* columnist Francine du Plessix Gray published *Lovers and Tyrants,* a book Caryl Rivers describes in *Ms.* as being "as rich in its texture as the lace tablecloths women of my grandmother's generation used to crochet." The novel, a startling and often touching autobiographical *bildungsroman,* gained the attention of many critics. "Every woman's first novel about her own break-through into adulthood is significant—liberation of any kind is significant—but Francine du Plessix Gray has created, in hers, something memorable," comments Kathleen Cushman in the *National Observer.* "To the cathartic throes of autobiography she has added a good dose each of humor, irony, and skill; *Lovers and Tyrants* transcends its limited possibilities as a book about *Woman Oppressed* and crosses into the realm of art."

The eight parts of this novel of "ascent and liberation," as Joan Peters calls it in the *Nation,* describe various periods in the life of Stephanie, the heroine. It begins with her childhood in Paris as the daughter of a Russian mother and an aristocratic French father who wanted her to be a boy. She is raised by a hypochondriac governess and her childhood, she writes in the opening lines of the book, was "muted, opaque, and drab, the color of gruel and of woolen gaiters, its noises muted and monotonous as a sleeper's pulse. . . . My temperature was taken twice a day, my head was perpetually wrapped in some woolen muffler or gauze veiling. I was scrubbed, spruced, buffed, combed, polished, year round, like a first communicant." After her father's death in the Resistance, Stephanie and her mother move to New York where Stephanie attends a fancy boarding school. Later, a young adult, she returns to France to visit her relatives and has an affair with a French prince who describes himself as "style incarnate." Nearing thirty, she marries an architect, bears two sons, and continues her career as a journalist. She feels confined and dissatisfied in her marriage and leaves to tour the Southwest, writing about bizarre religious cults and taking up with a twenty-five-year-old homosexual who longs to be both a bisexual and a photographer and who continuously begs Stephanie to feed him. The theme of the novel, as Stephanie points out, is the tyranny of love: "Every woman's life is a series of exorcisms from the spells of different oppressors: nurses, lovers, husbands, gurus, parents, children, myths of the good life. The most tyrannical despots can be the ones who love us the most."

That theme, Gray acknowledges, came from experiences in her own life. In an essay for the *New York Times Book Review,* Gray writes that her late start in writing fiction was partially due to fear of disapproval from her father—even though he had died when she was eleven. *Lovers and Tyrants* grew out of her frustration as a young wife and mother. "I was married and had two children," Gray stated in the *New York Times Book Review* "The Making of an Author" column, "and since I live deep in the country and in relative solitude, encompassed by domestic duties, the journal [that I kept] became increasingly voluminous, angry, introspective. The nomad, denied flight and forced to turn inward, was beginning to explode. One day when I was 33, after I'd cooked and smiled for a bevy of weekend guests whom I never wished to see again, I felt an immense void, a great powerlessness, the deepest loneliness I'd ever known. I wept for some hours, took out a notebook, started rewriting one of the three stories that had won me my Barnard prize. It was the one about my governess. . . . It was to become, 12 years and two books of nonfiction later, the first chapter for *Lovers and Tyrants.* The process of finishing that book was as complex and lengthy as it was painful."

"There is something very French—Cartesian—in the orderly, rigid pattern that Francine's novel imposes on the random rich-

ness of Stephanie's life," remarks Audrey Foote in *Washington Post Book World.* "It is convenient, too; Gray herself has compared it to stringing beads. Once the themes are established, Stephanie-Francine is absolved of all problems of plot construction, free to proceed methodically yet meaningfully through the heroine's life, devoting every stage, every chapter to the unmasking of another 'jailer.' *Lovers and Tyrants* is an apt and total title; the book is a litany of oppressors, a rosary of named identities." It is that process of naming her oppressors that is central to Stephanie's story, for, to her, that is the way to liberation. "We must name the identities of each jailer before we can crawl on toward the next stage of freedom," Stephanie writes in her journal. "To herself, and to me," says Peters, "Stephanie is simply a person trying to acknowledge and accommodate the forces that have acted on her and which remain a part of her."

The process of naming her oppressors and liberating herself from them (and from the strangling memories of past 'jailers') forms the crux of *Lovers and Tyrants.* But it is not only a personal liberation that Stephanie seeks. She views her situation as part of the historical oppression of women. When she leaves her husband and takes to the road, she says that she rebels "for all women, because we are killing each other in our doll's houses." Her ultimate desire, she tells the reader, is "to be free, to be a boy, to be God." Comments Rivers in *Ms.:* "[Stephanie] sees dropping out as the prelude to rebirth. She will be Kerouac, Dean; she will infringe on male territory. . . . *Lovers and Tyrants* may be a classic in a new genre of literature—the woman as wanderer, seeker of truth. . . . To take this journey with her is to confront not only the questions of love and freedom, but those of death and immortality and existence as well." Sara Sanborn considers the novel to be a feminist fable. "The theme of this novel," Sanborn writes in *Saturday Review,* "[is] the perpetual seduction of women by those who will offer tenderness and authority, the feminine materials of feminine transcendence."

The first three-fourths of the novel—the first-person sections describing her childhood, her return to France, and her marriage—is widely praised for its wit, fine writing, and evocative detail. "The author has no trouble persuading the reader that there was once a small girl in Paris named Stephanie," says *Time*'s Timothy Foote, as he notes the similarities between Stephanie's life and that of her creator's (the French and Russian parentage, the immigration to New York, the private schools, the fling in Paris, the career as a journalist, an artistic husband two sons, even, notes Foote, the same high cheekbones and large eyes). "Stephanie's remembrance of things past flashes with literary style and wit. Remarkable siblings, and sexual suitors are summoned up, often in hilarious detail, though they are mostly kept frozen at the edge of caricature by Stephanie's satiric perceptions." These early sections of the novel, writes Julian Moynahan in the *New York Times Book Review,* "are crammed with unforgettably drawn characters, rich emotion and complex social portraiture. In counterpoint they bring out contrasted aspects of French life that are both immemorial and contemporary, and that perhaps only a cultural 'amphibian' like Mrs. du Plessix Gray would clearly see." Joan Peters in *Nation* deems "the depiction of Stephanie's relationship with Paul . . . as complex a portrait of love and marriage as I have seen in recent novels."

While critical opinion of the beginning sections of *Lovers and Tyrants* is overwhelmingly favorable, reviews of the last chapters tend to be negative. Michael Wood, for example, in his *New York Review of Books* article calls the final chapters of *Lovers and Tyrants* "truly lamentable," citing sloppy writing and a final section that "has expanded too far into fantasy" as his reasons for such harsh criticism. "There is a great deal that goes on in the eighth, last, longest, and presumably climactic chapter of *Lovers and Tyrants*," Christopher Lehmann-Haupt comments in the *New York Times.* "There is abundant activity. . . . There is sex. . . . But nowhere in that concluding chapter is it possible to find anything to rouse the reader from his intensifying somnolence. Nowhere is there an interesting unanswered question about the plot or the heroine's development. Nowhere is there activity or thought that one hasn't long since been able to predict. Nowhere is there articulation of Stephanie's problem that we haven't heard uttered before. ('God, I hate puritanism, wasp puritanism, all kinds. Do you realize it's puritanism got us into Vietnam?') Nowhere is there surprise. And that is why *Lovers and Tyrants,* for all the wit and thrust of its prose, is finally so exasperating. The drone of its intelligence ultimately bores."

Village Voice book editor Eliot Fremont-Smith also finds *Lovers and Tyrants* intelligent but at the same time lacking because of that intelligence. "I think something more basic is wrong," he remarks, referring to the abrupt change in the book's tone in the last sections, "and it has to do with intelligence and class. And tone. And tonyness. *Lovers and Tyrants* is nothing if not wonderfully intelligent. For much of the novel, the intelligence is presumed and shared; the reader is in really interesting company, and feels there by right of respectful invitation, and is so honored. But toward the end, the intelligence—not so much of Stephanie or her witty companion, but of the *book*—turns into something else, a sort of shrill IQ-mongering. Intellectual references from the very best places are tossed around like Frisbees; it becomes a contest, and a rather exclusionary one, with the reader on the sidelines. This subverts, first, credibility. (Such *constant* smartness, such unflagging articulation of sensibility, such memories! Don't they ever say Stekel when they mean Ferenczi? Don't they ever get tired?) It subverts, second, a sense of caring. A defensive reaction but that's what happens when one feels snubbed, or made the fool. In the end, *Lovers and Tyrants* seems more crass than Class; there is an unpleasant aftertaste of having been unexpectedly and for no deserving reason, insulted. This is inelegant."

Credibility is also seen as a problem by other reviewers of *Lover and Tyrants.* A major criticism of the novel is that, in the end, the story is not believable. "There is so much in this book to admire that I wish I could believe Stephanie's story. I don't," says Sara Sanborn in *Saturday Review.* "Stephanie seems twice-born, her sensibility as narrator formed more by other writers, from Henry James to Kate Millet, than by the events recounted, which also have their haunting familiarity. I don't believe for one minute that Stephanie really has two children: in twenty years the chief effect they have on her is to supply her with wise-child sayings. Finally, I don't believe in Stephanie's unvarying superiority. Even in her bad moments, she is more thoughtful, sensitive, and self-perceptive, more humorous, open, and finally free than anyone she encounters. The other characters seem to have their existence only to further her self-exploration." *Newsweek* reviewer Peter S. Prescott also agrees: "For three-quarters of its route, *Lovers and Tyrants* is a remarkably convincing, even exhilarating performance. [However,] toward the end, in a long section in the third person, I sensed the author striking poses, lecturing us a bit to emphasize points already amply developed, introducing two characters—a radical Jesuit and a homosexual youth—who are not as engaging as I suspect the author means them to be."

Time's Timothy Foote questions Stephanie's credibility as a character and narrator because, he says, "Stephanie's cries rise to heaven like those of De Sade's Justine, a girl one recollects, with far more justification for complaint." At the point Stepha-

nie leaves her husband (who, Foote mentions, is a "fine husband, a kind man, a devoted father") and goes on the road, "Mrs. Gray abruptly switches from the first-person 'I' narrative form that has preserved whatever degree of credibility the story maintains. Stephanie in the third-person, Stephanie as 'she,' makes fairly ludicrous fiction. . . . This is an age that has learned any grievance must be accepted as both genuine and significant if the public weeping and wailing are long and loud enough. It would therefore be wise to take seriously Mrs. Gray's passionate meditation on the tyranny of love. Not as a novel, though." In the end, Michael Wood in *New York Review of Books* finds that "this hitherto solid and patient novel has expanded too far into fantasy, and has lost even the truth of seriously entertained wishes."

Concomitant to the lack of credibility that Stephanie suffers is what is perceived by some critics as her inability to reconcile her feminist beliefs with her actions. Writing in the *Nation,* Joan Peters observes that "one of the problems with *Lovers and Tyrants* is that not all the contradictions are accounted for or, it seems, planned for. Among the most perplexing of these is the tension between Stephanie's feminist analysis of her life and her persistent identification with men. On the one hand, she is quite strong in her analysis of how confining it is to be a woman, how discrimination operates, how few models women have, etc. . . . On the other hand, the actual record of Stephanie's life is a Freudian's delight and a feminist's nightmare. Again and again Stephanie realizes that she wants to be a boy." Peters then points out contradictions that belie Stephanie's words: "[her] need to be with men, her desire to be a boy, the absence of female friends, the Henry Milleresque sexual descriptions, her assumption that it is because Mishka couldn't love men that she was so cruel." Moynahan calls Stephanie "the unsatisfactory representation or symbol of modern woman in the throes of an unprecedented process of liberation." Earlier in his article, Moynahan had questioned the value of Stephanie's liberation, noting that despite her access to almost every pleasure desired and freedom from most worries, Stephanie slips "into madness out of a conviction that her freedom is obstructed."

Audrey Foote in *Washington Post Book World* says, "Gray writes with such passion, grace and wit, and her themes are so fashionable, that the reader is swept along in sympathetic credulity until he begins to scrutinize these tyrants." Stephanie's tyrants—governess, family, husband, lovers, friends—Foote points out, are hardly that, loving and indulging Stephanie in any way they can. Continues Foote: "Surely none of these 'lovers' in the wide sense she intends, can seriously be classified as 'tyrants.'. . . *En fin,* there is only one clue that her obsession with tyranny is not pure paranoia: the sex scenes. . . . They are significant in showing that Stephanie, so heroic if quixotic in defiance of imagined oppression, is, alas, a sexual masochist. 'He ordered,' 'she asked permission,' 'he commanded'—she *chooses* these dominating lovers, and her compliance, her collaboration explains her conviction: 'Our enslavers segregate us into zoos, with our full consent.' Speak for yourself, Stephanie! Thus finally the provocative title and grand design of this novel turn out to be based on little more than a retrogressive sexual taste, a dreary and dubious cliche. . . . She is in search of freedom—to do what? What does she want? What do women want? Francine never quite tells us about Stephanie (does *she* know?)"

Despite reservations about *Lovers and Tyrants,* most critics have, in the end, judged it favorably. Peters concludes that in spite of the book's limitations, "what *Lovers and Tyrants* does do, and does beautifully, is exploit the limited strength of the autobiographical genre. Gray presents a fascinating, intelligent woman whose personal contradictions concerning tradition, freedom, sex, culture, and religion shed light on the larger society in a way that is sometimes inadvertant, more often artistically controlled." Michael Wood concedes that *Lovers and Tyrants* "is an absorbing and intelligent book, if a little too icy to be really likable." Finally, the *Village Voice*'s Fremont-Smith observes: "*Lovers and Tyrants* has all sorts of problems and gets tiresomely narcissistic and irritating; still, it is one of the very truly interesting and stimulating—one wants to argue with it and about it—books I've read all year. . . . If Gray's book burns a bit, and it does, that should suggest fire as well as ice at its core."

World Without End, Gray's second novel, is also noted for its sensitivity and intelligence. The story of three lifelong friends who reunite in middle age to tour Russia and, hopefully, to "learn how to live the last third of our lives," *World Without End* is "an ambitious novel about love and friendship, faith and doubt, liberty and license," comments Judith Gies in *Saturday Review.* D. M. Thomas, writing in the *Washington Post Book World,* considers *World Without End* to be "clearly the work of a richly talented writer. . . . The book is struggling with an important subject: the conflict within each of us between the psychological hungers symbolized by America and Russia—individualism and brotherhood, anarchy and order. It is no small achievement to have explored interestingly one of the most crucial dilemmas of our age."

Doris Grumbach in *Commonweal* calls *World Without End* "a prime entry in the novel of intelligence. It is just that: the lives [Gray] tells about ring with authenticity for their times and their place." It is the novel's "intelligence"—its lengthy discourses on a variety of subjects and the articulate growing self-awareness of its characters—that holds the attention of many of its reviewers. The *New York Times*'s John Leonard notes the "lyric excess" of the characters's musings, but believes that Gray "has chosen to satirize the art, the religion and the politics of the last 35 years" through characters Sophie, Claire, and Edmund. "[Gray] has also chosen to forgive the creatures of her satire," says Leonard. "They are more disappointed in themselves than readers will be in them as characters."

For other critics, the intellectual discussions in *World Without End* are a hindrance to an appreciation of the novel. "Anyone not conversant with the intellectual and esthetic upheavals in American art and politics over the last 30 years ought not attempt to read this novel," suggests Henrietta Epstein in the *Detroit News,* "for these concerns, along with those of friendship and love, are at the heart of Francine du Plessix Gray's work. "*Newsweek* reviewer Annalyn Swan concurs with Leonard that "some of this is obviously satire" and says that "when Gray is not trying to be wry, or brilliant, she can be wonderful." Swan concludes that Gray, "like many social critics who cross the line into fiction, . . . has not yet mastered the difference between show and tell, between writing fiction that lives and using fiction as a forum for ideas. What she aspires to here is a highbrow critique of art and society in the last twenty years. What she has written is a novel that strives too hard to impress. The prose is full of bad breathiness, the characters suffer from terminal solipsism, and the social criticism is often as cliched as the attitudes it attacks."

Esquire columnist James Wolcott also comments on Gray's satiric designs: "Tripping through *World Without End,* I kept telling myself that the book might be a spoofy lark—a Harlequin romance for art majors—but I have a lurking suspicion that Gray is serious. After all, the novel's theme—the pull and persistence of friendship—is butressed by quotations from Catullus and from Roland Barthes, and floating through the text are the

sort of flowery phrases only a tremulously sincere epicurean would use." *Commentary*'s Pearl K. Bell is also highly critical of Gray's second novel. "Francine Gray's sententious dialogue about love and death and self-fulfillment does not blind us to the poverty of thought in what seems to have been conceived as a novel of ideas," the critic contends. "*World Without End* is not a novel of ideas, it is an adolescent daydream, an orgy of pseudo-intellectual posturing, a midnight bull session in a college dorm."

Grumbach finds that a distance is placed between the reader and the characters because of the intense intellectualism of the novel. She asserts that "despite the impressive and always accurate documentation of place (Edmund's visit to the Hermitage and the art he looks at there consumes five dense pages) and the character, social movements, parental backgrounds, lovers, husbands, visits with each other, letters and postcards [the three friends] exchange for all those years, do we ever feel close to these people? Curiously, not really. They are so detailed and cerebral, their talk is so elevated and informed, we know so many facts about their milieus that, somehow, passion is smothered." But, other critics disagree. Reynolds Price in the *New York Times Book Review,* for instance, finds that in *World Without End,* Gray "displays the one indispensable gift in a novelist—she generates slowly and authoritatively a mixed set of entirely credible human beings who shunt back and forth through credible time and are altered by the trip. Ample, generous and mature, the book is stocked with the goods a novel best provides."

Leonard also finds the book—and the characters in it—touching. "The reader chooses sides," he writes. "In this novel about Renaissance art and Puritanism, about Anglican convents and academic departments of art about friendship and that televised soap opera General Hospital—about lust and literature and missing fathers and saints full of greed and pride and envy—in this popcorn-popper of ideas, in which Edmund is the tourist of art, Claire the tourist of suffering and Sophie the tourist of everything, we are blessed with real people in the middle of an important argument about art and religion and sexuality. We are persuaded. . . . I chose Sophie to root for. It's been a long time in novels since I was a fan. Mrs. Gray tells us that 'Orpheus dismembered will continue to sing, his head floating down our rivers.' A real friend will either scoop up the head or hit it with a stick. Mrs. Gray scoops and sings."

Gray's second father was artist Alexander Liberman, art director of *Vogue* magazine. Her mother once worked at Saks Fifth Avenue, New York City, in the fashion industry. Drawing from this heritage, *October Blood* satirizes "the peculiar world of high fashion" and "sets out to tell a serious, even painful, story about three generations of remarkable women," Judith Viorst remarks in the *New York Times Book World Review.* Though *October Blood* received mixed reviews, Joanne Kaufman of *Book World* notes that "Gray is successful at showing that the concerns of the fashion world are as lightweight as a Chanel chemise."

Gray's next bestselling nonfiction book looks at another facet of her heritage, the Soviet ancestry of her mother and the other emigres who raised her in Paris. *Soviet Women: Walking the Tightrope* records Gray's observations of contemporary Soviet life and women's concerns she gathered on a visit to her mother's homeland. "The distinguished American journalist and novelist Francine du Plessix Gray has now brought us a rich and contradictory selection of Soviet women's opinions," Mary F. Zirin comments in the *Los Angeles Times Book Review.* Reading it, says Zirin, "is like turning a kaleidoscope—a new pattern emerges with every chapter. . . . Gray uses her novelistic skills to record talks with some women in which psychological pressure and suppressed rage can be sensed under a facade of stoic cheer." The government encourages women to hold jobs and to raise large families; abortion is the most well-known method of birth control, Gray reports. Each woman expects to have between seven and fourteen abortions before menopause; there are between five and eight abortions for every live birth, and one out of five babies is born with a defect. Women form deep commitments to each other but tend to see men as crude liabilities.

Carroll Bogert of *Newsweek* relates that *Soviet Women* offers some surprises: "Gray turns a predictable tale of oppression upside down. . . . Traditions have ensured a peculiar female dominance in a society where tremendous male chauvinism persists. . . . Ninety-two percent of Soviet women work, and they do nearly all domestic chores. One woman admits many women have 'a need to control that verges on the tyrannical, the sadistic.'" Furthermore, though the reforms of *glasnost* are viewed by outsiders as a move toward greater personal liberty for Soviet citizens, "the Bolshevik ideal of sexual equality is being trampled in the retreat from socialism," Bogert points out. Bogert concludes, "For Westerners who think Gorbachev's reforms will make Them more like Us, this fine writer has a valuable lesson to teach."

AVOCATIONAL INTERESTS: Tennis, gardening, cooking Provencal food.

BIOGRAPHICAL/CRITICAL SOURCES:

BOOKS

Contemporary Authors Autobiography Series, Volume 2, Gale, 1985.
Contemporary Literary Criticism, Volume 22, Gale, 1982.
Gray, Francine du Plessix, *Lovers and Tyrants,* Simon & Schuster, 1976.
Gray, *World Without End,* Simon & Schuster, 1981.

PERIODICALS

Book World, October 13, 1985.
Books and Bookmen, March, 1971.
Chicago Tribune Book World, May 31, 1981, August 15, 1982, March 25, 1990.
Commentary, August, 1981.
Commonweal, May 22, 1981.
Detroit News, December 16, 1981.
Esquire, June, 1981.
Harpers, November, 1976.
Listener, February 25, 1971, June 2, 1977.
Los Angeles Times Book Review, March 25, 1990.
Ms., November, 1976, July, 1981.
Nation, February 1, 1971, November 20, 1976.
National Observer, December 18, 1976.
National Review, November 12, 1976.
New Republic, June 27, 1970.
Newsweek, October 11, 1976, June 22, 1981, March 26, 1990.
New York Review of Books, November 11, 1976.
New York Times, October 8, 1976, September 15, 1979, May 19, 1981, August 20, 1981.
New York Times Book Review, May 31, 1970, October 17, 1976, May 24, 1981, September 12, 1982, October 6, 1985, March 11, 1990.
Progressive, November, 1981.
Saturday Review, June 13, 1970, October 30, 1976, May, 1981.
Time, November 1, 1976.
Times Literary Supplement, May 20, 1977.
Village Voice, November 22, 1976.
Wall Street Journal, October 25, 1976, June 1, 1981.

Washington Post Book World, August 29, 1976, October 24, 1976, May 24, 1981, March 11, 1990.

* * *

GRAY, Simon (James Holliday) 1936-
(Hamish Reade)

PERSONAL: Born October 21, 1936, in Hayling Island, Hampshire, England; son of James Davidson (a pathologist) and Barbara Cecelia Mary (Holliday) Gray; married Beryl Mary Kevern (a picture researcher), August 20, 1964; children: Benjamin, Lucy. *Education:* Dalhousie University, B.A. (honors in English), 1958; Trinity College, Cambridge, B.A. (honors in English), 1962. *Politics:* None. *Religion:* None.

ADDRESSES: Home—London, England. *Agent*—Judy Daish, 83 Eastbourne Mews, London W2 6LQ, England.

CAREER: Author and playwright. Teacher of English in France, 1960-61, and Spain, 1962-63; lecturer, University of British Columbia, 1963-64; supervisor in English, Trinity College, Cambridge University, 1964-66; lecturer in drama and literature, Queen Mary College, University of London, 1966-86.

MEMBER: Dramatists Guild, Societe des Auteurs (France).

AWARDS, HONORS: Writers Guild Award for best play, 1967, for "Death of a Teddy Bear"; *Evening Standard* Award for best play, 1972, for "Butley"; *Evening Standard* Award, *Plays and Players* Award, and New York Drama Critics Circle Award, all for best play, all 1976, for "Otherwise Engaged"; Cheltenham Prize for Literature, 1981, for "Quartermaine's Terms."

WRITINGS:

Colmain (novel), Faber, 1962.
Simple People (novel), Faber, 1964.
Little Portia (novel), Faber, 1966.
(Editor with Keith Walker) *Selected English Prose,* Faber, 1967.
(Under pseudonym Hamish Reade) *A Comeback for Stark,* Putnam, 1968.
An Unnatural Pursuit and Other Pieces (journal), Faber, 1985, St. Martin's, 1986.
How's That for Telling 'Em, Fat Lady? (journal), Faber, 1988.

TELEVISION PLAYS

"The Caramel Crisis," British Broadcasting Corp. (BBC-TV), 1966.
"Death of a Teddy Bear" (also produced as "Molly"; also see below), BBC-TV, 1967.
"A Way with the Ladies," BBC-TV, 1967.
Sleeping Dog (first broadcast on BBC-TV, 1967), Faber, 1968.
"Spoiled" (also see below), BBC-TV, 1968.
"Pig in a Poke" (also see below), BBC-TV, 1969.
"The Dirt on Lucy Lane," BBC-TV, 1969.
"Style of the Countess," BBC-TV, 1970.
"The Princess," BBC-TV, 1970.
"Man in a Side-Car" (also see below), BBC-TV, 1971.
"Plaintiffs and Defendants" (also see below), BBC-TV, 1975.
"Two Sundays" (also see below), BBC-TV, 1975.
"After Pilkington," BBC-TV, 1987.

PLAYS

Wise Child (first produced on the West End at Wyndham's Theatre, October 10, 1967; produced on Broadway at Helen Hayes Theatre, January 27, 1972), Faber, 1968, Samuel French, 1974.
Dutch Uncle (first produced in Brighton, England, at Theatre Royal, March 3, 1969; produced on the West End at Na-

tional Theatre, 1969, and at Aldwych Theatre, March 26, 1969), Faber, 1969.

Spoiled (first produced in Glasgow, Scotland, at Close Theatre Club, 1970; produced on the West End at Haymarket Theatre, February 24, 1971; produced on Broadway at Morosco Theatre, October 31, 1972), Methuen, 1971.

The Idiot (adapted from the novel by Fyodor Dostoevsky; first produced on the West End at National Theatre, July 15, 1970), Methuen, 1971.

Butley (first produced in Oxford, England, at Oxford Playhouse, July 7, 1971; produced on the West End at Criterion Theatre, July 14, 1971; produced on Broadway at Morosco Theatre, 1972; also see below), Methuen, 1971, Viking, 1972.

"Otherwise Engaged," first produced on the West End at Queen's Theatre, July 30, 1975; published as *Otherwise Engaged, and Other Plays* (also contains *Two Sundays* and *Plaintiffs and Defendants*), Methuen, 1975.

Dog Days (produced in Oxford at Oxford Playhouse, October 26, 1976; produced Off-Broadway at Hudson Guild Theatre [directed by Gray], 1985), Eyre Methuen, 1976.

"The Rear Column," produced on the West End at Globe Theatre, February 23, 1978; produced in New York at Manhattan Theatre Club, November, 1978; published as *The Rear Column, and Other Plays* (also contains *Molly* [also see below] and *Man in a Side-Car*), Eyre Methuen, 1978, Heinemann, 1985.

Molly (produced in Watford, England, at Palace Theatre, November 23, 1977; produced Off-Broadway at Hudson Guild Theatre, January, 1978), Samuel French, 1979.

Stage Struck (produced on the West End at Vaudeville Theatre, November 21, 1979), Eyre Methuen, 1979, Seaver, 1981.

Close of Play (produced on the West End at Lyttleton Theatre, May 24, 1979; produced in New York at Manhattan Theatre Club, 1981), Methuen, 1980, published as *Close of Play* [and] *Pig in a Poke*, Heinemann, 1984.

Quartermaine's Terms (produced on the West End at Queen's Theatre, July 28, 1981; produced in New Haven, Conn., at Long Wharf Theatre, 1982; produced in New York at Playhouse 91, February, 1983), Eyre Methuen, 1981, Heinemann, 1983.

The Common Pursuit: Scenes from the Literary Life (first produced in London at Lyric Hammersmith Theatre, July, 1984; produced in New Haven at Long Wharf Theatre, February, 1985), Methuen, 1984, Heinemann, 1985.

Plays, Methuen, 1986.

Melon (produced on the West End at Royal Haymarket Theatre, 1987), Methuen, 1987.

OTHER

"Butley" (screenplay; adapted from his play), American Film Theatre, 1974.

Also author of play adaptation of *Tartuffe,* produced at Kennedy Center, Washington, D.C., 1982, and of screen adaptation of *A Month in the Country.*

SIDELIGHTS: No one has ever accused Simon Gray of writing plays that are too mainstream. In fact, the Briton's first stage work, "Wise Child," was originally written for television but was "considered too bizarre for home viewing," according to Anthony Stephenson in a *Dictionary of Literary Biography* article on the writer. Gray was a product of Cambridge University during the early 1960s, a place and an era that produced a notable group of creative talent, including novelists Frederick Raphael and Margaret Drabble, satirist Peter Cook, comedian-turned-interviewer David Frost, and actor Derek Jacobi. "Many of these people were already beginning to make their mark in the world at large while still pursuing their studies," observes Stephenson. "Gray was no exception." Though he lived abroad for several years, teaching the English language to natives of France and Spain, Gray returned to his homeland in 1965 to lecture in drama and literature at Queen Mary College, London University, and worked there for twenty years.

Journeyman television writing prepared Gray for his first West End opening. "When Gray began writing ['Wise Child'], he conceived the central character as a woman, but gradually the character evolved into a man dressed as a woman," Stephenson relates. "The character, Mrs. Artminster, . . . is in fact a male criminal wearing women's clothing to evade the police, who want him for a brutal mail robbery. He is staying with his young accomplice, Jerry, who poses as Mrs. Artminster's son, at a shabby provincial hotel run by a homosexual. The curious interdependence of the pair reaches its climax when, after murdering the homosexual landlord, Jerry dresses in the maid's clothes and Mrs. Artminster reverts to his male attire."

Several successful if not so memorable Gray plays followed "Wise Child" until 1971, when "Butley" opened at London's Criterion Theatre. Considered one of the playwright's best works, its title character, says Stephenson, is a "viper-tongued teacher of English at London University," inviting comparisons with the author himself. The play takes place in one day, when Butley's raw wit and skepticism cause problems for virtually everyone in his life, including his wife, his students, his office-mate and another faculty member. As Stephenson notes: "His technique is to put them in the wrong by demonstrating through satire the woolliness of their thinking and the insincerity of their motives. In striking out at everyone around him, [Butley] reveals the emptiness and hollowness of his own life."

To *New York Times* critic Clive Barnes, in "Butley" Gray has "written about this half-baked academic with astonishing compassion. Butley goes around 'spreading futility.' He slouches like a lost soul, and yet uses his wit like a sledgehammer to ward off the world and reality. And despite his glorious and desperate faults, he remains oddly likable and strangely sympathetic. Even his pompousness and mad egoism have been made in some way attractive." In a *Midwest Quarterly* review of the play, Sophia B. Blaydes sees the anti-protagonist in a different light. "[The work] has as much laughter as any comedy could evoke," she writes, "but it is a laughter generated by literary allusions, by wit, and by skilled word play that were used as weapons of defense and attack. Butley's skill is verbal, and for a while his wit captures our sympathies and our admiration, yet he manages to create a distance so that ultimately he is isolated from us, too." Blaydes also notes that "in a perverse manner, Butley demonstrates those qualities we believe essential to the English professor: sensitivity, kindness, perceptiveness, eloquence, but he uses them on this day to annihilate, destroy, or dismiss those around him and to reject and sever his professional ties." "Butley" enjoyed a healthy run both on the West End and on Broadway. It is the only original Gray play yet to have been produced as a film.

A subsequent stage work, "Otherwise Engaged," has met with equal critical and popular success. "Essentially the idea [behind the play] is to present a character preoccupied with a single, simple activity and have the activity delayed by a series of increasingly dramatic interruptions," as Stephenson describes. "Otherwise Engaged" thus presents Hench, a publisher, at home attempting to merely listen to a recording of Richard Wagner's opera *Parsifal.* But, as Stephenson continues, poor Hench is "interrupted by his brother, who is anxious about his prospects of becoming a deputy headmaster; by Jeff, a literary critic, who, like Butley, launches a series of verbal attacks on a variety of targets; by Jeff's mistress, who tries to seduce him; by Wood, a failure, who at one time had attended a private boarding school, reveals Hench's homosexual activities as a schoolboy and accuses Hench of seducing his fiancee; by his wife, who tells him she is pregnant by either Hench or her lover, Ned; by his tenant Dave, who denounces him as a complacent fake liberal and moves squatters [illegal tenants] into Hench's house; and by a telephoned suicide message from Wood, which Hench switches off in mid-sentence."

In "Butley" and "Otherwise Engaged," John Bush Jones sees a shift away from the kind of farce Gray originally presented in plays like "Wise Child." "Gone is the complex plotting and overt stage action of the early pieces in favor of in-depth examinations of character through a drama whose movement comes largely through its dialogue," writes Jones in *West Virginia University Philological Papers.* "It is this dominance of language, especially the incessant exercise of wit by the protagonists [Butley and Hench], that has led to the popular labeling of these plays as comedies of manners. Perhaps to some extent this is accurately descriptive; the witty banter and the occasional exposure of the posturing types that inhabit twentieth-century academia and literary circles do partially admit these plays to that genre. And yet, their underlying structure does not."

Jones goes on to explain that both "Butley" and "Otherwise Engaged" more approach the tragic in tone than the comic. "To begin with, in [both works] Gray has economically compressed the action into one climactic day in the life of the protagonist. The alleged unities of time and place are rigorously adhered to as the unity of action: all events . . . work toward the ultimate overwhelming of the hero. Very little 'happens' in either play, at least in the sense of stage action or permutations of plot. In both, most everything 'has happened' already, largely because of the behavior of the protagonists, and what occurs on stage is the unveiling to the audience of his destructive behavior and the gradual revelation to him himself of the finally disastrous consequences of that mode of conduct." Jones sees everything necessary for tragic implications "is present in the fate of Ben Butley and Simon Hench. Both are permitted to come to that condition not allowed by protagonists of Gray's farces—the moment of recognition that they themselves are the causes of their present state."

As with his other notable plays, Gray drew upon his own early experience as an English-language teacher abroad to create the atmosphere for "Quartermaine's Terms." The title character of "Quartermaine's Terms"—a single, middle-aged teacher of English to foreigners at a British university—"has a tendency to doze off in mid-conversation, to drift away early from his own classes, to miss the punch line of any joke," as Frank Rich puts it in a *New York Times* review. "But he's one of those benign fellows who can be carried on indefinitely by arcane British institutions. Though professionally incompetent, Quartermaine is unfailingly polite, loyal and undemanding." This play takes place over three years, while Quartermaine and his fellow teachers, a singularly disillusioned lot with names like Meadle, Sackling and Windscape, face various crises of career and life. But as the story progresses, it is Quartermaine who gets the sack, fired abruptly for lackluster performance even after he has devoted his entire career to this one school. "Grim as that may sound," says *Washington Post* critic David Richards, "Gray's play manages to be acutely funny. The humor comes not from the particular misfortunes, but from the way one character invariably manages to elbow another's problems aside in favor of his own." Interviewed

by Nan Robertson for the *New York Times,* Gray professed a strong affection for his once and future backup career: "It's extremely depressing not to be making progress with writing a play, and I do really deeply love reading poems and plays and the discipline of doing it for and with students. It's stimulating."

John Russell Taylor, in a *Plays & Players* article, has mixed feelings about the play. Though "Quartermaine's Terms" "is very respectable and not actually boring, Gray seems to be holding his characters at a distance, filling out the picturesque details of their mostly horrible out-of-school lives with great ingenuity but never actually persuading us to believe, much less to care." But to *New York* magazine's John Simon, the work "keeps us suspended between laughter and melancholy, [and also melds] primal (almost primitive) emotions with fastidious speculations about the compromises, contradictions, numbing paradoxes of existence, and allows each spectator to enjoy the show according to his intellectual means." Simon concludes that if "Gray's understatedly heartbreaking ending does not get you where you live, either you or I don't know what theater—and art—is."

Gray again visits his alma mater, Cambridge, with "The Common Pursuit," a where-are-they-now comedy centering on the reunion of a handful of 1960s collegiate *artistes* turned 1980s sellouts. The circle of friends includes the editor and staff of a Cambridge literary magazine ("The Common Pursuit"), and what happens when the campus intelligentsia become hack writers, television critics, and professional money-mongerers. "We witness the moral, emotional and spiritual ravages inflicted by the [twenty years] on the editor, his associates and the journal itself," notes Benedict Nightingale in a *New York Times* piece. In another *New York Times* article, Mel Gussow remarks that toward the end of the play, Stuart, the editor who serves as main character, "stands looking at unpublished, perhaps unpublishable poems by a friend, recently deceased, who may have been the best of their misfortunate lot. Stuart's silence touchingly communicates his own despair." The author, Gussow also observes, "has sometimes been criticized for writing undramatic plays about inconsequential people, a charge that could of course also be raised against [famed Russian playwright Anton] Chekhov. One of several differences is that Chekhov's characters often become violent about vaunting their unhappiness; Mr. Gray's characters are more resigned to accept their fate. But in the Chekhovian sense, he writes plays of indirect action; the characters are the action."

In the Robertson interview, Gray tells of his passion for "found" dialogue. "I can't resist listening," he says, citing the time on a London subway when he overheard a woman describing a date to her girlfriend: "And then he put his hand up my skirt—you know the one—the blue dirndl skirt." In such inspiration does Gray begin his plays. He always opens "with a bit of dialogue: a character in a room who says something, and I hope someone else will say something," as Gray explains. Robertson adds that a typical Gray play can go through 35 or 40 revisions: "It is 'grinding' agony until then," but as the author puts it, "the last draft is always effortless, which is how I know it's finished."

BIOGRAPHICAL/CRITICAL SOURCES:

BOOKS

Authors in the News, Volume 1, Gale, 1976.
Contemporary Authors Autobiography Series, Volume 3, Gale, 1980.
Contemporary Literary Criticism, Gale, Volume 9, 1978, Volume 14, 1980, Volume 36, 1986.

Dictionary of Literary Biography, Volume 13: *British Dramatists since World War II,* Gale, 1982.

Kerensky, Oleg, *The New British Drama: Fourteen Playwrights since Osborne and Pinter,* Hamish Hamilton, 1977.

Taylor, John Russell, *The Second Wave: British Drama for the Seventies,* Hill & Wang, 1971.

PERIODICALS

American Theatre, June, 1986.
Drama, winter, 1981.
Los Angeles Times, February 10, 1986.
Midwest Quarterly, summer, 1977.
Newsweek, February 11, 1985.
New York, January 24, 1983.
New York Times, November 1, 1972, February 4, 1977, February 9, 1977, February 25, 1981, January 7, 1983, February 25, 1983, February 28, 1983, March 6, 1983, February 2, 1985, February 22, 1986, September 30, 1986, October 19, 1986, October 20, 1986, November 2, 1982, May 10, 1987.
Plays and Players, October, 1981.
Time, November 3, 1986.
Times Literary Supplement, September 6, 1985, December 11, 1987, April 22, 1988.
Washington Post, April 23, 1982, March 29, 1983.
West Virginia University Philological Papers, Volume 25, 1979.

*   *   *

GREELEY, Andrew M(oran)   1928-

PERSONAL: Born February 5, 1928, in Oak Park, Ill.; son of Andrew T. (a corporation executive) and Grace (McNichols) Greeley. *Education:* St. Mary of the Lake Seminary, A.B., 1950, S.T.B., 1952, S.T.L., 1954; University of Chicago, A.M., 1961, Ph.D., 1962. *Politics:* Democrat.

ADDRESSES: Home—1012 East 47th St., Chicago, Ill. 60653. *Office*—National Opinion Research Center, University of Chicago, 6030 South Ellis Ave., Chicago, Ill. 60637; and Department of Sociology, University of Arizona, Tucson, Ariz. 85721.

CAREER: Ordained Roman Catholic priest, 1954. Church of Christ the King, Chicago, Ill., assistant pastor, 1954-64; University of Chicago, National Opinion Research Center, Chicago, senior study director, 1961-68, program director for higher education, 1968-70, director of Center for the Study of American Pluralism, 1971—; University of Arizona, Tucson, professor of sociology, 1978—. Lecturer in sociology of religion, University of Chicago, 1962-72; professor of sociology of education, University of Illinois at Chicago. Member of planning committee, National Conference on Higher Education, 1969. Has made a number of appearances on radio and television programs. Consultant to Hazen Foundation Commission; member of board of advisers on student unrest, National Institute of Mental Health.

MEMBER: American Sociological Association, American Catholic Sociological Society (former president), Society for the Scientific Study of Religion, Religious Research Association.

AWARDS, HONORS: Thomas Alva Edison Award, 1962, for "Catholic Hour" radio broadcasts; Catholic Press Association award for best book for young people, 1965; LL.D., St. Joseph's College (Rensselaer, Ind.), 1967; Litt.D., St. Mary's College (Winona, Minn.), 1967.

WRITINGS:

The Church and the Suburbs, Sheed, 1959.

Strangers in the House, Catholic Youth in America, Sheed, 1961, revised edition, Doubleday, 1967.

(Editor with Michael E. Schlitz) *Catholics in the Archdiocese of Chicago,* Chicago Archdiocesan Conservation Council, 1962.

Religion and Career, Sheed, 1963.
Letters to a Young Man, Sheed, 1964.
Letters to Nancy, Sheed, 1964.
(With Peter H. Rossi) *The Education of Catholic Americans,* Aldine, 1966.
The Hesitant Pilgrim: American Catholicism After the Council, Sheed, 1966.
The Catholic Experience: An Interpretation of the History of American Catholicism, Doubleday, 1967.
Changing Catholic College, Aldine, 1967.
And Young Men Shall See Visions, Doubleday, 1968.
Crucible of Change: The Social Dynamics of Pastoral Practice, Sheed, 1968.
Uncertain Trumpet: The Priest in Modern America, Sheed, 1968.
Youth Asks, "Does God Talk?," Nelson, 1968, published as *Youth Asks, "Does God Still Speak?,"* 1970.
(With Martin E. Marty) *What Do We Believe?,* Meredith, 1968.
From Backwater to Mainstream: A Profile of Catholic Higher Education, McGraw, 1969.
A Future to Hope In: Socio-Religious Speculations, Doubleday, 1969.
Life for a Wanderer: A New Look at Christian Spirituality, Doubleday, 1969.
Religion in the Year 2000, Sheed, 1969.
Why Can't They Be Like Us?: Facts and Fallacies about Ethnic Differences and Group Conflicts in America (also see below), Institute of Human Relations Press, 1969.
A Fresh Look at Vocations, Clarentian, 1969.
The Friendship Game, Doubleday, 1970.
New Horizons for the Priesthood, Sheed, 1970.
The Life of the Spirit (also the Mind, the Heart, the Libido), National Catholic Reporter, 1970.
(With William E. Brown) *Can Catholic Schools Survive?,* Sheed, 1970.
(With Joe L. Spaeth) *Recent Alumni and Higher Education,* McGraw, 1970.
Why Can't They Be Like Us?: American's White Ethnic Groups (includes portions of *Why Can't They Be Like Us?: Facts and Fallacies about Ethnic Differences and Group Conflicts in America*), Dutton, 1971.
Come Blow Your Mind With Me, Doubleday, 1971.
The Jesus Myth, Doubleday, 1971.
The Touch of the Spirit, Herder & Herder, 1971.
What a Modern Catholic Believes About God, Thomas More Press, 1971.
The Denominational Society: A Sociological Approach to Religion in America, Scott, Foresman, 1972.
Priests in the United States: Reflections on a Survey, Doubleday, 1972.
The Sinai Myth, Doubleday, 1972.
That Most Distressful Nation: The Taming of the American Irish, Quadrangle, 1972.
The Unsecular Man: The Persistence of Religion, Schocken, 1972.
What a Modern Catholic Believes About the Church, Thomas More Press, 1972.
The Catholic Priest in the United States: Sociological Investigations, United States Catholic Conference, 1972.
The New Agenda, Doubleday, 1973.
Sexual Intimacy, Thomas More Press, 1973.

(Editor with Gregory Baum) *The Persistence of Religion,* Seabury, 1973.

Building Coalitions: American Politics in the 1970s, New Viewpoints, 1974.

The Devil, You Say! Man and His Personal Devils and Angels, Doubleday, 1974.

Ecstasy: A Way of Knowing, Prentice-Hall, 1974.

Ethnicity in the United States: A Preliminary Reconnaissance, Wiley, 1974.

(With Baum) *The Church as Institution,* Herder & Herder, 1974.

MEDIA: Ethnic Media in the United States, Project IMPRESS (Hanover, N.H.), 1974.

Love and Play, Thomas More Press, 1975.

May the Wind Be at Your Back: The Prayer of St. Patrick, Seabury, 1975.

The Sociology of the Paranormal: A Reconnaissance, Sage Publications, 1975.

(With William C. McCready and Kathleen McCourt) *Catholic Schools in a Declining Church,* Sheed, 1976.

The Communal Catholic: A Personal Manifesto, Seabury, 1976.

Death and Beyond, Thomas More Press, 1976.

Ethnicity, Denomination, and Inequality, Sage Publications, 1976.

The Great Mysteries: An Essential Catechism, Seabury, 1976.

Nora Maeve and Sebi, illustrations by Diane Dawson, Paulist/Newman, 1976.

(With McCready) *The Ultimate Values of the American Population,* Sage Publications, 1976.

The American Catholic: A Social Portrait, Basic Books, 1977.

The Mary Myth: On the Femininity of God, Seabury, 1977.

Neighborhood, Seabury, 1977.

No Bigger Than Necessary: An Alternative to Socialism, Capitalism, and Anarchism, New American Library, 1977.

An Ugly Little Secret: Anti-Catholicism in North America, Sheed Andrews, 1977.

Everything You Wanted to Know About the Catholic Church but Were Too Pious to Ask, Thomas More Press, 1978.

(Editor with Baum) *Communication in the Church Concilium,* Seabury, 1978.

(With J. N. Kotre) *The Best of Times, the Worst of Times,* Nelson Hall, 1978.

Crisis in the Church: A Study of Religion in America, Thomas More Press, 1979.

The Making of the Popes 1978: The Politics of Intrigue in the Vatican, Sheed Andrews, 1979.

Women I've Met, Sheed Andrews, 1979.

The Magic Cup: An Irish Legend, McGraw, 1979.

(Editor) *The Family in Crisis or in Transition: A Sociological and Theological Perspective,* Seabury, 1979.

Death in April (novel), McGraw, 1980.

The Irish Americans: The Rise to Money and Power, Times Books, 1980.

(With McCready) *Ethnic Drinking Subcultures,* Praeger, 1980.

The Cardinal Sins (novel), Warner Books, 1981.

Thy Brother's Wife (novel), Warner Books, 1982.

Catholic High Schools and Minority Students, Transaction Publications, 1982.

The Bottom Line Catechism for Contemporary Catholics, Thomas More Press, 1982.

Religion: A Secular Theory, Free Press, 1982.

How to Save the Catholic Church, Penguin, 1984.

Ascent Into Hell (novel), Warner Books, 1984.

American Catholics Since the Council: An Unauthorized Report, Thomas More Press, 1985.

Happy Are the Meek, Warner Books, 1985.

Virgin and Martyr (novel), Warner Books, 1985.

Confessions of a Parish Priest: An Autobiography, Simon & Schuster, 1986.

Angels of September (novel), G. K. Hall, 1986.

God Game (novel), Warner Books, 1986.

Patience of a Saint, Warner Books, 1986.

Catholic Contributions, Sociology and Policy, Thomas More Press, 1987.

The Final Planet, Warner Books, 1987.

Happy Are Those Who Thirst for Justice, Mysterious Press, 1987.

Lord of the Dance (novel), Warner Books, 1987.

When Life Hurts: Healing Themes From the Gospels, Thomas More Press, 1988.

Angel Fire (novel), Random House, 1988.

Love Song, Warner Books, 1988.

Rite of Spring, Warner Books, 1988.

Religious Indicators, 1940-1985, Harvard University Press, 1989.

Andrew Greeley's Chicago, Contemporary Books, 1989.

God in Popular Culture, Thomas More Press, 1989.

Myths of Religion, Warner Books, 1989.

Religious Change in America, Harvard University Press, 1989.

St. Valentine's Night (novel), Warner Books, 1989.

The Search for Maggie Ward (novel), Warner Books, 1991.

Also author of *Teenage World: Its Crises and Anxieties,* Divine Word Publications, and of a number of shorter works. Author of a syndicated column, appearing in approximately eighty newspapers. Contributor to Catholic magazines and to sociology and education journals.

SIDELIGHTS: Andrew Greeley is, according to a *Time* writer, "a Roman Catholic priest, a sociologist, a theologian, a weekly columnist, the author of [numerous] books, and a celibate sex expert. He is an informational machine gun who can fire off an article on Jesus to the *New York Times Magazine,* on ethnic groups to the *Antioch Review,* and on war to *Dissent.*" *Time* reports that Greeley's friend, psychologist-priest Eugene Kennedy, calls him "obsessive, compulsive, a workaholic. . . . He's a natural resource. He should be protected under an ecological act." While dividing his time between the National Opinion Research Center at the University of Chicago, where he has been involved in sociological research since 1961, and the University of Arizona, where he holds a professorship, Greeley has also published scores of books and hundreds of popular and scholarly articles, making him one of the nation's leading authorities on the sociology of religion.

The adjective "controversial" arises often in articles on Greeley and in reviews of his many books. (Kennedy calls him "the Howard Cosell of the Catholic church.") Much of the controversy surrounding Greeley stems from the difficulty critics have experienced in trying to label him. As another *Time* reporter explains: "On practically any topic, Greeley manages to strike some readers as outrageously unfair and others as eminently fair, as left wing and right wing, as wise and wrong-headed." Greeley advocates a great many changes within the Catholic church, including the ordination of women, liberalized policies on birth control and divorce, and a more democratic process for selecting popes, cardinals, and bishops; as a result, he is often at odds with church leaders. On the other hand, he feels that priests are most effective in serving the people when they remain celibate and that the church has taken the correct stand on abortion; he is, therefore, open to criticism from his more liberal colleagues. He maintains, *Time* continues, that "the present leadership of the church is morally, intellectually, and religiously bankrupt" and has referred to the hierarchy as "mitred pinheads." At the same time, he feels no affinity for the more radical element within the church and has said of activist Jesuit Daniel Berrigan, "As a political strategist, he's a great poet."

Greeley's writings have covered myriad topics, many of which deal with the role of religion in modern life. His subjects have included ethnicity, religious education, church politics, secular politics, the family, death and dying, vocations, history, and the future. His opinions in most of these areas have proven controversial to some extent, but when he tackles the subject of sex—particularly as it relates to religion today—he stirs up more than the usual amount of critical commentary. A good example is his book *Sexual Intimacy,* which the *Time* writer calls "a priest's enthusiastic endorsement of inventive marital sex play," and which J. W. Gartland of *Library Journal* recommends to Catholics who "seek a 'sexier' sexual relationship with their spouse and need supportive religious sanctions." In a much-quoted chapter entitled "How to Be Sexy," Greeley portrays a wife greeting her husband "wearing only panties and a martini pitcher—or maybe only the martini pitcher." According to *Time,* "One right-wing Catholic columnist declared that even discussing the book would be an occasion of sin." But, Greeley explained to Pamela Porvaznik in an interview for the *Detroit News Sunday Magazine,* "a vigorous sexual life is one of the biggest problems confronting married couples. How can people grow in intimacy? How can they consistently reassure themselves and each other of their own worth? These are real issues, and it's time the Church put them into perspective."

In a review of *Sexual Intimacy* for *America,* T. F. Driver writes: "Whatever scholarship may lie behind the book's judgments has been carefully (or do I mean carelessly) hidden. Though the book contains precious little theological reflection, it is based, I think, on an erroneous theological assumption namely, that the God we have known all along as Yahweh is the same who presides over the modern sexual revolution. It sounds to me like the old game of baptizing everything in sight." However, Charles Dollen of *Best Sellers* calls it "by far one of the best books on marriage and sexuality that has been published in many, many years. . . . [Greeley's] style is witty, charming and far above average. But it is the content that sets this book apart. He has some vital insights into what sex and sexuality are all about." *Commentary*'s John Garvey finds *Sexual Intimacy* to be "a mixed thing. At its worst it offers incredibly bad taste ('it is no exaggeration . . . to say that the wife clad in panties and martini pitcher is imitating Yahweh's behavior'). . . . But Greeley is often very good. [His] comparisons of erotic and divine love are often to the point, especially the relationship between divine and human vulnerability."

One of Greeley's best-known works is *The Making of the Popes, 1978: The Politics of Intrigue in the Vatican.* In this book he details the series of startling events that took place in Rome beginning in the summer of 1978: the death of Pope Paul VI in July; the subsequent election of John Paul I, who died after only thirty-three days in office; and the election of John Paul II, the first non-Italian pope since 1522. The book is particularly noteworthy for its inclusion of little-known "inside information" on the process of electing a new pope, much of it supplied by an informant that Greeley calls "Deep Purple." The title of the book and the use of stylistic devices such as a diary format are intentionally reminiscent of Theodore H. White's *Making of the President* books, reinforcing Greeley's thesis that papal elections have all of the mystery, the jockeying for power, and the behind-the-scenes intrigue of an American presidential election. Several reviewers, including R. A. Schroth of the *New York Times Book Review,* note that Greeley's choice of the name "Deep Purple" for his unnamed source suggests that "he clearly identifies with

Woodward and Bernstein." Thus, although the author sees himself as a journalist covering what is, essentially, a political event, he still leaves himself the option of injecting personal comments (as White is known to do) on the various candidates, the election process, and the diverse political powers that subtly influence the voting. "The White model works pretty well," writes Robert Blair Kaiser of the *New York Times,* "freeing the author to present an account of [the] doings in Rome, which, for all its ambiguous partisanship, tells us more about the election of two popes (and the future of the church) than less knowing reporters ever could."

Greeley's partisanship leads him to offer the opinion that the church didn't need another leader like Paul VI, "a grim, stern, pessimistic, solemn-faced pope who did not appeal to the world as a man who is really possessed by the 'good news' he claims to be teaching." He would prefer, Kaiser says, "a hopeful holy man who smiles," a man "whose faith makes him happy and whose hope makes him joyful." Greeley was satisfied with the choice of John Paul I and just as happy with his successor, John Paul II, but his approval of the cardinals' choices has not altered his view of papal elections. He told Linda Witt of *People:* "The cardinals are a closed group of men who have spent their whole lives strictly in ecclesiastical activities. Their average age is over sixty, and they are extremely cautious and conservative. In many cases they are totally out of touch with the world. There were between thirty and thirty-five cardinals—about one-third of those voting—who had no notion of what was going on, and who drifted from candidate to candidate depending on who seemed likely to win." Asked what kind of election process he would prefer, Greeley replied: "In the early church, the Pope and all the bishops were elected by the people of their diocese. The cardinals would go into St. Peter's and pick a man and bring him out. If the faithful applauded, he was the Pope. If they booed, the cardinals went back inside and tried again. I'm not suggesting we revert to that, but I would like to see a gradual sharing of power with the rest of the church." J. J. Hughes of *America,* while expressing a few misgivings about Greeley's reportage, concludes that "the book is a remarkable achievement. We are fools, and guilty fools, if we dismiss it as unworthy of serious consideration."

Greeley achieved widespread popularity in the early 1980s with several novels, three of which became best-sellers: *The Cardinal Sins,* depicting a corrupt bisexual archbishop, *Thy Brother's Wife,* the story of a priest who falls in love with his sister-in-law, and *Ascent Into Hell,* about a young priest struggling to remain true to his vows. Although Greeley maintains that each of his novels contains a spiritual message, the books sparked controversy with their pointed criticisms of the Catholic church and their sex scenes. In 1984, the priest published *Lord of the Dance,* another best-seller, this time centering on Irish Catholics in Chicago. Among his numerous other works of the 1980s, Greeley also wrote an autobiography—*Confessions of a Parish Priest*—in 1986.

BIOGRAPHICAL/CRITICAL SOURCES:

BOOKS

Contemporary Literary Criticism, Volume 28, Gale, 1984.

PERIODICALS

America, December 8, 1973, May 15, 1976, April 9, 1977, May 26, 1979.
Best Sellers, November 15, 1973.
Chicago Tribune, March 3, 1985, August 22, 1989.

Chicago Tribune Book World, May 24, 1981, May 2, 1982, June 26, 1983, November 25, 1984, August 31, 1986.

Commonweal, December 14, 1973, June 18, 1976, August 31, 1979.

Detroit News, September 7, 1980, May 20, 1984, February 23, 1986.

Detroit News Sunday Magazine, February 2, 1975.

Globe and Mail (Toronto), March 2, 1985, August 20, 1988.

Library Journal, November 15, 1973.

Los Angeles Times Book Review, March 28, 1982, December 9, 1984, March 16, 1986, September 14, 1986, April 30, 1989.

National Review, April 15, 1977.

New York Review of Books, March 4, 1976.

New York Times, March 13, 1972, March 6, 1977, September 21, 1979, March 22, 1981, October 31, 1985.

New York Times Book Review, June 24, 1979, July 26, 1981, April 11, 1982, January 6, 1985, March 10, 1985, March 30, 1986, February 8, 1987, July 31, 1988, August 14, 1988, January 22, 1989, September 17, 1989.

New York Times Magazine, May 6, 1984.

People, July 9, 1979.

Time, January 7, 1974, July 16, 1978, August 10, 1981.

Times Literary Supplement, August 31, 1984.

Washington Post, June 11, 1981, January 24, 1984, April 6, 1984, July 21, 1986, August 19, 1986, June 13, 1987, November 16, 1987.

Washington Post Book World, March 24, 1985, January 27, 1986.

*   *   *

GREEN, Brian
See CARD, Orson Scott

*   *   *

GREEN, Julien (Hartridge) 1900-
(Theophile Delaporte, David Irland)

PERSONAL: Born September 6, 1900, in Paris, France; christened Julian, but has used the French spelling, Julien, since the late 1920s; son of U.S. citizens, Edward Moon (a business agent) and Mary Adelaide (Hartridge) Green; children: Eric Jourdan (adopted). *Education:* Attended Lycee Janson-de-Sailly, Paris; attended University of Virginia, 1919-22; studied drawing at La Grande Chaumiere, Paris, 1922-23. *Religion:* Roman Catholic.

ADDRESSES: c/o Le Seuil, 27 rue Jacob, Paris 6e France.

CAREER: Writer, 1924—. Stayed several times in the United States, including a visit to Virginia, 1933-34; went to America in 1940 after France fell to Germany; lectured on French writers at Princeton University, Goucher College, Mills College, and a Jesuit college, 1940-1942; returned to Paris, 1945. *Wartime service:* World War I—Volunteered for the American Field Service, 1917; served on the French front at Verdun; later worked for six months with the Norton-Harjes Service (now the Red Cross) in Italy until May, 1918; joined the French Army as an American, training at the artillery school, Fontainebleau; served in the region of Metz, and, after the armistice, went with his regiment to the Saar on occupation duty; demobilized, 1919. World War II—Joined U.S. Army, 1942; later held post in the U.S. Office of War Information; made radio broadcasts to France, 1943.

MEMBER: Academie de Baviere, L'Academie Royale de Belgique, Academie Francaise, Academy of Arts and Letters, Academie of Mainz, Conseil litteraire de Monaco, Phi Beta Kappa.

AWARDS, HONORS: Prix Paul Flat, Academie Francaise, and Femina-Bookman Prize, both 1928, both for *Adrienne Mesurat;* Harper Prize, 1929-30, for *Leviathan;* Harper 125th Anniversary Award, 1942, for *Memory of Happy Days;* Officier de la Legion d'Honneur; Grand Prix Litteraire de Monaco, 1951, for the whole of his work; Grand Prix National des Lettres, 1966; Prix Ibico Reggino, 1968; Grand Prix, Academie Francaise, 1970; James Biddle Eustace Franco-American Award, 1972; Grand Prix Litterature de Pologne, 1985; Prix des Universites Alemaniques; Grand Prix Arts, Sciences et Lettres de Paris.

WRITINGS:

FICTION

Mont-Cinere (novel), Plon, 1926, translation of complete version by Marshall A. Best published as *Avarice House,* Harper, 1927, complete French edition, Plon, 1928, new English edition published as *Monte-Cinere,* edited by C. T. Stewart, Harper, 1937.

Adrienne Mesurat (novel), Plon, 1927, translation by Henry Longan Stuart published as *The Closed Garden,* Harper, 1928, new French edition (containing some manuscript pages), Club des Libraires de France, 1957, revised edition, Holmes & Meier, 1989.

Le Voyageur sur la terre (story; illustrated with a portrait of the author by Jean Cocteau), Gallimard, 1927, translation by Courtney Bruerton published as *The Pilgrim on the Earth,* Harper, 1929.

Christine (story), F. Paillart, 1927.

La Traversee inutile (story), Plon, 1927, published as "Leviathan" in *Christine, suivi de Leviathan,* Editions des Cahiers Libres, 1928.

Les Clefs de la mort (story; title means "The Keys of Death"), J. Schiffrin (Paris), 1928.

Leviathan (novel; not the same work as the story, "Leviathan"), Plon, 1929, revised edition with a preface by J. C. Brisville, Editions Recontre (Lausanne), 1962, translation by Vyvyan Holland published as *The Dark Journey,* Harper, 1929.

Le Voyageur sur la terre (collection; contains "Leviathan," "Christine," "The Keys of Death," and "The Pilgrim on the Earth"), Plon, 1930, translation by Bruerton published as *Christine, and Other Stories,* Harper, 1930.

L'Autre Sommeil (novel), Gallimard, 1931.

Epaves (novel), Plon, 1932, translation by Holland published as *The Strange River,* Harper, 1932.

Le Visionnaire (novel), Plon, 1934, translation by Holland published as *The Dreamer,* Harper, 1934.

Minuit (novel), Plon, 1936, translation by Holland published as *Midnight,* Harper, 1936.

Varouna (novel), Plon, 1940, translation by James Whitall published as *Then Shall the Dust Return,* Harper, 1941.

Si j'etais vous (novel), Plon, 1947, revised edition, 1970, translation by J. H. F. McEwen published as *If I Were You,* Harper, 1949.

Moira (novel), Plon, 1950, translation by Denise Folliot published under same title, Macmillan, 1951.

Le Malfaiteur (novel), Plon, 1955, general edition, 1956, augmented edition, 1974, translation by sister, Anne Green, published as *The Transgressor,* Pantheon 1957.

Chaque homme dans sa nuit (novel), Plon, 1960, translation by A. Green published as *Each in His Darkness,* Pantheon, 1961.

L'Autre (novel), Plon, 1971, translation by Bernard Wall published as *The Other One,* Harcourt, 1973.

La Nuit des fantomes (children's book; title means "Halloween"), Plon, 1976.

Le Mauvais Lieu (novel), Plon, 1977.

L'apprenti psychiatre (story; first published in English as *The Apprentice Psychiatrist* in *Quarterly Review,* 1920), translation by son, Eric Jourdan, Le Livre de Poche, 1977.
Histoires de vertige (stories), Le Seuil, 1984.
Les Pays lointains (novel), Le Seuil, 1987.

Also author of *Les Etioles du Sud,* 1989.

AUTOBIOGRAPHY

Journal, Volume 1: *Les Annees faciles, 1928-34,* Plon, 1938, revised edition published as *Les Annees faciles, 1926-34,* 1970; Volume 2: *Derniers beaux jours, 1935-39,* Plon, 1939; Volume 3: *Devant la porte sombre, 1940-43,* Plon, 1946; Volume 4: *L'Oeil de l'ouragan, 1943-46,* Plon, 1949; Volume 5: *Le Revenant, 1946-50,* Plon, 1951; Volume 6: *Le Miroir interieur, 1950-54,* Plon, 1955; Volume 7: *Le Bel aujourd'hui, 1955-58,* Plon, 1958; Volume 8: *Vers l'invisible, 1959-66,* Plon, 1967; Volume 9: *Ce qui reste de jour, 1966-72,* Plon, 1972; Volume 10: *La bouteille a la Mer, 1972-76,* Plon, 1976; Volume 11: *La terre est si belle, 1976-78,* Le Seuil, 1982; Volume 12: *La lumiere du monde, 1978-81,* Le Seuil, 1982, Volume 13: *L'arc-en-ciel, 1981-88,* 1988.
Personal Record, 1928-39 (contains *Journal,* Volumes 1 and 2), translation by Jocelyn Godefroi, Harper, 1939.
Memories of Happy Days (memoir), Harper, 1942.
(Contributor) *Les Oeuvres nouvelles* (includes "Quand nous habitions tous ensemble," reminiscences), Editions de la Maison Francaise (New York), 1943.
Journal: 1928-1958 (omnibus edition; contains Volumes 1-7), Plon, 1961, translation by A. Green published in abridged edition as *Diary, 1928-57,* edited by Kurt Wolff, Harcourt, 1964, new omnibus edition published as *Journal, 1928-66* (contains Volumes 1-8), two volumes, Plon, 1969.
Jeunes Annees (autobiography), Volume 1: *Partir avant le jour,* Grasset, 1963, translation by A. Green published as *To Leave before Dawn,* Harcourt, 1967; Volume 2: *Mille chemins ouverts,* Grasset, 1964; Volume 3: *Terre Lointaine,* Grasset, 1966; *Jeunesse,* Plon, 1974; published in two volumes, Le Seuil, 1984.
Memories of Evil Days, edited by Jean-Pierre J. Piriou, University Press of Virginia, 1976.
Dans la gueule de Tempo (journals), illustrated with 500 photographs, Plon, 1978.
Ce qu'il faut d'amour a l'homme, Plon, 1978.

PLAYS

Sud (three-act; produced in Paris, 1953), Plon, 1953, translation produced as "South," London, 1955, published in *Plays of the Year,* Volume 12, Elek, 1955, operatic version, with music by Kenton Coe, produced at Opera de Paris, 1973.
L'Ennemi (three-act; produced in Paris, 1954), Plon, 1954.
L'Ombre (three-act; produced at Theatre Antoine, 1956), Plon, 1956.
Demain n'exite pas; L'Automate (three- and four-act), Le Seuil, 1985.

NONFICTION

(Under pseudonym Theophile Delaporte) *Pamphlet contre les Catholiques de France* (essay), Editions de la Revue des Pamphletaires (Paris), 1924, new edition, preface by Jacques Maritain, Plon, 1963.
Suite anglaise (essays), Cahiers de Paris, 1927.
Un Puritain homme de lettres: Nathaniel Hawthorne, Editions des Cahiers Libres, 1928.
Liberte (essay), Plon, 1974.
Paris (essay), Editions du Champ Vallon, 1983.

Frere Francois, Le Seuil, 1983, translation by Peter Heinegg published as *God's Fool: The Life and Times of Francis of Assisi,* Harper, 1985.
Le Langage et son double/The Language and Its Shadow (essays; bilingual edition with translations by the author), Editions de la Difference, 1985.

OTHER

(Translator with A. Green) Charles Peguy, *Basic Verities: Prose and Poetry,* Pantheon, 1943.
(Translator with Anne Green) Peguy, *Men and Saints,* Pantheon, 1944.
(Translator) Peguy, *God Speaks: Religious Poetry,* Pantheon, 1945.
(Translator) Peguy, *The Mystery of the Charity of Joan of Arc,* Pantheon, 1949.
Oeuvres Completes (collected works), ten volumes, Plon, 1954-65.
Bibliotheque de la Pleiade (collected works), five volumes, Gallimard, 1971-75.
Pamphlet contre les catholiques de France, suivi de Ce qu'il faut d'amour a l'homme; L'Appel du desert; La Folie de Dieu, Gallimard, 1982.
(With Jacques Maritain) *Un grande amitie: Correspondance, 1926-1972,* edited by Piriou, Plon, 1979, complete edition, Gallimard, 1982, English translation by Bernard Doering published as *The Story of Two Souls: The Correspondence of Jacques Maritain and Julien Green,* edited by Henry Bars and Jourdan, Fordham University Press, 1988..

Also author of filmscripts *Leviathan,* 1962, and, with Jourdan, *La Dame de pique,* 1965; author, with Jourdan, of television and radio scripts *Je est un autre,* 1954, and *La Mort de Ivan llytch,* 1955. Contributor to *Revue Hebdomadaire, Revue Europeenne, Nouvelle Revue Francaise, Revue Universelle, La Parisienne, Revue des Deux Mondes, University of Virginia Magazine, American Scholar,* and other periodicals.

WORK IN PROGRESS: A sequel to *Les Pays lointains;* Volume 6 of *Bibliotheque de la Pliade;* a play; a book on poets, with Eric Jourdan.

MEDIA ADAPTATIONS: Extracts from Green's work, including a reading by Green himself, have been recorded in the series "Auteurs du 20e Siecle," Philips.

SIDELIGHTS: In 1930 Courtney Bruerton wrote: "As Julien Green is the first American novelist to choose French as his medium of expression, so he is the first American to be ranked by competent critics as a great French writer." L. Clark Keating comments on the "irresistible appeal" which Green's work has held for critics, "many of whom have tried to find American sources and models for his characters and situations." Among his works which have American settings is *Avarice House;* this story, notes Keating, "is laid in a Virginia farmhouse, modeled on an uncle's manor house near Warrenton [where] Green spent several weeks during his first American sojourn." Discussing the similarities between Green and novelist Nathaniel Hawthorne, the critic suggests that "Green's sombre and fantastic imagination, and his preoccupation with violence and death, are often reminiscent of the nineteenth-century New Englander." He concludes that Hawthorne, "if not a model, has been an inspiration."

Andre Maurois, on the other hand, does not recognize a predominant English or American influence on Green's work: "For my part," writes Maurois, "I see very well wherein Green resembles the Brontes, but I see also wherein he resembles Balzac." According to I. W. Brock, Green is "unmistakably French" and "may be called American only because of his parentage. His ideas, language and philosophy are primarily French." Recognized for this, in 1971 Green became the first foreign member of the Academie Francaise.

The unusual nature of Green's background, however, tends to elude classification. Marilyn Gaddis points out: "By temperament and training Green was perhaps as much as ten years behind most boys of his generation. To begin with, he was the most confirmed French-speaking member of a household that was a miniature bilingual community. . . . Teased about his Confederate sympathies and Protestantism by his French schoolmates, Green withdrew into his own creative fantasy world." Samuel Stokes writes that Green's parents "brought to Europe all sorts of furniture which caused considerable consternation among their French friends, but," he continues, "its appearance created an atmosphere." James Lord similarly affirms: "The emotional stress of this formative duality had a decisive effect upon the young author" which is "starkly reflected" in his works. For instance, Peter Hall, the London producer of *South,* has said that it is a play about "extremes: North versus South, white man against coloured man, the old world of Europe in contrast with the new world of America, the difficulty that the sexually normal have in understanding the sexually abnormal."

For Brock, the main strength of Green's work lies in its "psychological naturalism." Robert Kanters, emphasizing a different aspect, feels that the use of dreams in Green's work "is a natural way less between reality and the fantastic than between two different levels of reality."

L. Clark Keating says of Green as a man, that he is "solitary and takes pains to avoid a crowd. Although a traveler he has few of the earmarks of the tourist. Even in his diary he does not choose to write of the issues of the day." Defending this position, Marilyn Gaddis states: "It would be incorrect—and basically unfair—to call either his solitude or his lack of social commitment an escape. On the contrary he has faced and transcended the alienation which most of his readers bury or ignore." After a period of doubt and religious crisis, Green became "reconverted" to the Roman Catholic faith in 1939, and James Lord writes: "His personal, intellectual and moral adherence to the tenets of Roman Catholicism appears to be complete."

Although he is bilingual in English and French, Green found that when he tried to write in English, it was like "wearing clothes that were not made for me." His only imaginative story in English is "The Apprentice Psychiatrist," published in 1920. He has mastered a number of other languages; Robert de Saint-Jean reports: "During a voyage in Italy, I had the surprise of hearing Julien Green express himself easily in Italian: I knew he was reading Dante in the original text, but thought that he understood the language without being able to speak it, and especially to make himself understood. In Germany, the same experience." The critic also reports that Green has studied Greek and Latin assiduously. In 1935, he took lessons in Hebrew from a rabbi in Paris "after much time spent in floundering among contradictory versions of the Bible."

BIOGRAPHICAL/CRITICAL SOURCES:

BOOKS

Burne, Glenn S., *Julian Green,* Twayne, 1972.
Contemporary Literary Criticism, Gale, Volume 3, 1975, Volume 11, 1979.
Cooke, M. G., *Hallucination and Death as Motifs of Escape in the Novels of Julien Green,* Catholic University of America Press, 1960.
Dunaway, John M., *The Metamorphoses of the Self: The Mystic, the Sensualist, and the Artist in the Works of Julien Green,* University Press of Kentucky, 1978.
Dictionary of Literary Biography, Gale, Volume 4: *American Writers in Paris, 1920-1939,* 1980, Volume 72: *French Novelists, 1930-1960,* 1988.
Gaddis, Marilyn, *The Critical Reaction to Julien Green (1926-56),* unpublished thesis, University of Missouri, 1958.
Green, Anne, *With Much Love,* Harper, 1948.
Green, Julien, *Journal* Volumes 1-10, Plon, 1938-76, Volumes 11-12, Le Seuil, 1982, translation of Volumes 1-7 by Anne Green published in an abridged edition as *Diary, 1928-57,* edited by Kurt Wolff, Harcourt, 1964.
Green, Julien, *Memories of Happy Days,* Harper, 1942, reprinted, Greenwood Press, 1969.
Green, Julien, *Jeunes Annees* (autobiography), Volume 1: *Partir avant le jour,* Grasset, 1963, translation by A. Green published as *To Leave before Dawn,* Harcourt, 1967; Volumes 2-3, Grasset, 1964-66, Volume 4, Plon, 1974.
Saint Jean, Robert de, *Julien Green,* Editions du Seuil, 1967.
Stokes, Samuel, *Julian Green and the Thorn of Puritanism,* King's Crown Press, Columbia University, 1955.

PERIODICALS

Biblio, December, 1949.
Bookman, August, 1932.
Emory University Quarterly, March, December, 1945.
French Review, March, 1950, May, 1955.
L'Express, February 15-21, 1971.
Livres de France, February, 1967.
London Magazine, January, 1967.
New Yorker, September 1, 1951.
New York Times Book Review, May 11, 1941, October 1, 1967.
PMLA, June, 1939.
Saturday Review of Literature, November, 1939.
Sewanee Review, April, 1932.

*   *   *

GREENE, Graham 1904-

PERSONAL: Born October 2, 1904, in Berkhamsted, Hertfordshire, England; son of Charles Henry (headmaster of Berkhamsted School) and Marion Raymond Greene; married Vivien Dayrell Browning, 1927; children: one son, one daughter. *Education:* Attended Berkhamsted School; Balliol College, Oxford, B.A., 1925. *Religion:* Catholic convert, 1926.

CAREER: Writer. *Times,* London, England, sub-editor, 1926-30; film critic for *Night and Day* during the 1930s; *Spectator,* London, England, film critic, 1935-39, literary editor, 1940-41; with Foreign Office in Africa, 1941-44; Eyre & Spottiswoode Ltd. (publishers), London, England, director, 1944-48; Indo-China correspondent for *New Republic,* 1954; Bodley Head (publishers), London, England, director, 1958-68. Member of Panamanian delegation to Washington for signing of Canal Treaty, 1977.

AWARDS, HONORS: Hawthornden Prize, 1940, for *The Labyrinthine Ways* (published in England as *The Power and the Glory*); James Tait Black Memorial Prize, 1949, for *The Heart of the Matter;* Catholic Literary Award, 1952, for *The End of the Affair;* Boys' Clubs of America Junior Book Award, 1955, for

The Little Horse Bus; Pietzak Award (Poland), 1960; D.Litt., Cambridge University, 1962; Balliol College, Oxford, honorary fellow, 1963; Companion of Honour, 1966; D.Litt., University of Edinburgh, 1967; Shakespeare Prize, 1968; Legion d'Honneur, chevalier, 1969; John Dos Passos Prize, 1980; medal of the city of Madrid, 1980; Jerusalem Prize, 1981; Grand Cross of the Order of Vasco Nunez de Balboa (Panama), 1983; named commander of the Order of Arts and Letters (France), 1984; named to British Order of Merit, 1986; named to the Order of Ruben Dario (Nicaragua), 1987; Royal Society of Literature Prize.

WRITINGS:

FICTION, EXCEPT AS INDICATED

Babbling April (poems), Basil Blackwell, 1925.

The Man Within, Doubleday, 1929.

The Name of Action, Heinemann, 1930, Doubleday, 1931.

Rumour at Nightfall, Heinemann, 1931, Doubleday, 1932.

Orient Express, Doubleday, 1932 (published in England as *Stamboul Train,* Heinemann, 1932).

It's a Battlefield, Doubleday, 1934, reprinted with new introduction by author, Heinemann, 1970.

The Basement Room, and Other Stories, Cresset, 1935, title story revised as "The Fallen Idol" and published with *The Third Man* (also see below), Heinemann, 1950.

England Made Me, Doubleday, 1935, published as *The Shipwrecked,* Viking, 1953, reprinted under original title with new introduction by author, Heinemann, 1970.

The Bear Fell Free, Grayson & Grayson, 1935.

Journey Without Maps (travelogue; also see below), Doubleday, 1936, 2nd edition, Viking, 1961.

This Gun for Hire, Doubleday, 1936 (also see below; published in England as *A Gun for Sale,* Heinemann, 1936).

Brighton Rock, Viking, 1938, reprinted with new introduction by author, Heinemann, 1970, reprinted, 1981.

The Confidential Agent (also see below), Viking, 1939, reprinted with new introduction by author, Heinemann, 1971.

Another Mexico, Viking, 1939, reprinted, 1982 (published in England as *The Lawless Roads,* Longmans, Green, 1939; also see below).

The Labyrinthine Ways, Viking, 1940 (published in England as *The Power and the Glory,* Heinemann, 1940), reprinted under British title, Viking, 1946, reprinted under British title with new introduction by author, Heinemann, 1971, reprinted, Viking, 1982.

British Dramatists (nonfiction), Collins, 1942, reprinted, Folcroft, 1979.

The Ministry of Fear (also see below), Viking, 1943.

Nineteen Stories, Heinemann, 1947, Viking, 1949, later published with some substitutions and additions as *Twenty-one Stories,* Heinemann, 1955, Viking, 1962.

The Heart of the Matter, Viking, 1948, reprinted with new introduction by author, Heinemann, 1971.

The Third Man (also see below), Viking, 1950, reprinted, 1983.

The Lost Childhood, and Other Essays, Eyre & Spottiswoode, 1951, Viking, 1952.

The End of the Affair, Viking, 1951.

The Living Room (two-act play; produced in London, 1953), Heinemann, 1953, Viking, 1957.

The Quiet American, Heinemann, 1955, reprinted, Viking, 1982.

Loser Takes All, Heinemann, 1955, Viking, 1957.

The Potting Shed (three-act play; produced in New York, 1957, and in London, 1958), Viking, 1957.

Our Man in Havana (also see below), Viking, 1958, reprinted with new introduction by author, Heinemann, 1970.

The Complaisant Lover (play; produced in London, 1959), Heinemann, 1959, Viking, 1961.

A Burnt-Out Case, Viking, 1961.

In Search of a Character: Two African Journals, Bodley Head, 1961, Viking, 1962.

Introductions to Three Novels, Norstedt (Stockholm), 1962.

The Destructors, and Other Stories, Eihosha Ltd. (Japan), 1962.

A Sense of Reality, Viking, 1963.

Carving a Statue (two-act play; produced in London, 1964, and in New York, 1968), Bodley Head, 1964.

The Comedians, Viking, 1966.

(With Dorothy Craigie) *Victorian Detective Fiction: A Catalogue of the Collection,* Bodley Head, 1966.

May We Borrow Your Husband?, and Other Comedies of the Sexual Life, Viking, 1967.

(With Carol Reed) *The Third Man: A Film* (annotated filmscript), Simon & Schuster, 1968.

Collected Essays, Viking, 1969.

Travels With My Aunt, Viking, 1969.

(Author of introduction) Al Burt and Bernard Diederich, *Papa Doc,* McGraw, 1969.

A Sort of Life (autobiography), Simon & Schuster, 1971.

Graham Greene on Film: Collected Film Criticism, 1935-1940, Simon & Schuster, 1972 (published in England as *The Pleasure Dome,* Secker & Warburg, 1972).

The Portable Graham Greene (includes *The Heart of the Matter,* with a new chapter; *The Third Man;* and sections from eight other novels, six short stories, nine critical essays, and ten public statements), Viking, 1972.

The Honorary Consul, Simon & Schuster, 1973.

Collected Stories, Viking, 1973.

Lord Rochester's Monkey, Being the Life of John Wilmot, Second Earl of Rochester, Viking, 1974.

The Return of A. J. Raffles (three-act comedy based on characters from E. W. Hornung's *Amateur Cracksman;* produced in London, 1975), Simon & Schuster, 1976.

The Human Factor, Simon & Schuster, 1978.

Dr. Fischer of Geneva; or, The Bomb Party, Simon & Schuster, 1980.

Ways of Escape, Simon & Schuster, 1981.

Monsignor Quixote, Simon & Schuster, 1982.

J'accuse: The Dark Side of Nice, Bodley Head, 1982.

Yes and No [and] *For Whom the Bell Chimes* (comedies; produced together in Leicester, England, at Haymarket Studio, March, 1980), Bodley Head, 1983.

Getting to Know the General: The Story of an Involvement, Simon & Schuster, 1984.

The Tenth Man, Bodley Head, 1985.

(Author of preface) *Night and Day* (selections from London periodical), edited by Christopher Hawtree, Chatto & Windus, 1985.

Granta 17, Penguin, 1986.

Collected Short Stories, Penguin, 1988.

The Captain and the Enemy, Viking, 1988.

Yours, etc.: Letters to the Press, 1945-1989, edited by Hawtree, Reinhardt, 1989.

OMNIBUS VOLUMES

3: This Gun for Hire; The Confidential Agent; The Ministry of Fear, Viking, 1952, reprinted as *Three by Graham Greene: This Gun for Hire; The Confidential Agent; The Ministry of Fear,* 1958.

Three Plays, Mercury Books, 1961.

The Travel Books: Journey Without Maps [and] *The Lawless Roads,* Heinemann, 1963.

Triple Pursuit: A Graham Greene Omnibus (includes *This Gun for Hire, The Third Man,* and *Our Man in Havana*), Viking, 1971.

Works also published in additional multititle volumes.

JUVENILE

This Little Fire Engine, Parrish, 1950, published as *The Little Red Fire Engine,* Lothrop, Lee & Shepard, 1952.
The Little Horse Bus, Parrish, 1952, Lothrop, Lee & Shepard, 1954.
The Little Steamroller, Lothrop, Lee & Shepard, 1955.
The Little Train, Parrish, 1957, Lothrop, Lee & Shepard, 1958.

EDITOR

The Old School (essays), J. Cape, 1934.
H. H. Munro, *The Best of Saki,* 2nd edition, Lane, 1952.
(With brother, Hugh Greene) *The Spy's Bedside Book,* British Book Service, 1957.
(Author of introduction) Marjorie Bowen, *The Viper of Milan,* Bodley Head, 1960.
The Bodly Head Ford Madox Ford, Volumes 1 and 2, Bodley Head, 1962.
(And author of epilogue) *An Impossible Woman: The Memories of Dottoressa, Moor of Capri,* Viking, 1976.
(With brother, Hugh Greene) *Victorian Villanies,* Viking, 1984.

CONTRIBUTOR

24 Short Stories, Cresset, 1939.
Alfred Hitchcock's Fireside Book of Suspense, Simon & Schuster, 1947.
Why Do I Write?, Percival Marshall, 1948.

Contributor to *Esquire, Commonweal, Spectator, Playboy, Saturday Evening Post, New Statesman, Atlantic, London Mercury, New Republic, America, Life,* and other publications.

MEDIA ADAPTATIONS: Screenplays based on his books and stories: "Orient Express," 1934; "This Gun for Hire," 1942; "The Ministry of Fear," 1944; "The Confidential Agent," 1945; "Brighton Rock," screenplay by Greene and Terrence Rattigan, 1947; "The Smugglers," 1948; "The Fallen Idol" (based on Greene's 1935 short story "The Basement Room"), screenplay by Greene, 1949; "The Third Man," screenplay by Greene, 1950; "The Heart of the Matter," 1954; "The End of the Affair," 1955; "Loser Takes All," 1957; "The Quiet American," 1958; "Across the Bridge," 1958; "Our Man in Havana," screenplay by Greene, 1960; "The Power and the Glory," 1962; "The Comedians," screenplay by Greene, 1967; "The Living Room," 1969; "The Shipwrecked," 1970; "May We Borrow Your Husband?," 1970; "The End of the Affair," 1971; "Travels with My Aunt," 1973; "England Made Me," 1973; "A Burned-Out Case," 1973; "The Human Factor," screenplay by Tom Stoppard, directed by Otto Preminger, 1980; "Beyond the Limit," 1983; "Strike It Rich" (based on Greene's 1955 novella *Loser Takes All*), 1990.

SIDELIGHTS: Graham Greene is among the most widely read of all major English novelists of the twentieth century. Yet Greene's popular success—which David Lodge in *Graham Greene* holds partly responsible for a "certain academic hostility" towards Greene—came neither quickly nor easily. Of Greene's initial five novels, the first two were never published; and two others, *The Name of Action* and *Rumour at Nightfall* sold very poorly and have never been reprinted. In his first autobiographical volume, *A Sort of Life,* Greene laments that, in his earliest novels, he did not know "how to convey physical excitement": the ability to write a "simple scene of action . . . was

quite beyond my power to render exciting." Even as late as 1944, Greene confessed in his introduction to *The Tenth Man,* he had "no confidence" in sustaining his literary career.

Greene's string of literary failures drove him to write *Stamboul Train,* a thriller that Greene hoped would appeal to film producers. The novel, filmed two years later as *Orient Express,* is recognized by critics as Greene's coming-of-age work. Writing in a taut, realistic manner, Greene set *Stamboul Train* in contemporary Europe; gathered a train load of plausibly motivated characters; and sent them on their journey. Retaining such stock melodramatic devices as cloak-and-dagger intrigue, flight and pursuit, hair-breadth escapes, and a breakneck narrative space, Greene shifted the focus away from the conventional hero—the hunter—and onto the villain and/or ostensible villain. What emerged was less a formula than a set of literary hardware that Greene would be able to use throughout the rest of his career, not just to produce further entertainments, but to help give outward excitement to his more morally centered, more philosophic novels.

Stamboul Train is the first of several thrillers Greene refers to as "entertainments"—so named to distinguish them from more serious novels. In his next two entertainments, *A Gun for Sale* (published in the United States as *This Gun for Hire*) and *The Confidential Agent,* Greene incorporated elements of detective and spy fiction, respectively. He also injected significant doses of melodrama, detection, and espionage into his more serious novels *Brighton Rock, The Power and the Glory* (published in the United States as *The Labyrinthine Ways), The Heart of the Matter, The End of the Affair, The Quiet American, A Burnt-Out Case, The Comedians, The Honorary Consul,* and *The Human Factor.* Indeed, so greatly did Greene's entertainments influence his other novels that, after 1958, he dropped the entertainment label.

Intrigue and contemporary politics are key elements of Greene's entertainments. In at least two of his thrillers Greene eulogizes the tranquility of European life before the First World War. "It was all so peaceful," Dr. Hasselbacher muses about Germany in *Our Man in Havana,* "in those days. . . . Until the war came." And Arthur Rowe, dreaming in *The Ministry of Fear,* notes that his mother, who "had died before the first great war, . . . could [not] have imagined" the blitz on London of the second. He tells his mother that the sweet Georgian twilight—"Tea on the lawn, evensong, croquet, the old ladies calling, the gentle unmalicious gossip, the gardener trundling the wheelbarrow full of leaves and grass"—"isn't real life any more." He continues: "I'm hiding underground, and up above the Germans are methodically smashing London to bits all round me. . . . It sounds like a thriller, doesn't it, but the thrillers are like life . . . spies, and murders, and violence . . . that's real life."

Suffering, seediness, and sin are also recurring motifs that typify the tone of Greene's work. When, in one of the very early novels Greene later disowned, a character moans, "I suffer, therefore I am," he defines both the plight and the habit of mind of many protagonists who would follow him. In *A Burnt-Out Case* Dr. Colin sees suffering as a humanizing force: "Sometimes I think that the search for suffering and the remembrance of suffering are the only means we have to put ourselves in touch with the whole human condition." And he adds—what none of Greene's other characters would dispute—"suffering is not so hard to find."

Greene's characters inhabit a world in which lasting love, according to the narrator of the story "May We Borrow Your Husband?" means the acceptance of "every disappointment, every failure, every betrayal." By Greene's twenty-second novel, *Doctor Fischer of Geneva; or, The Bomb Party,* suffering has become a sufficient cause for having a soul. When the narrator of *Doctor Fischer* tells his wife, "If souls exist you certainly have one," and she asks, "Why?" he replies, "You've suffered." This statement may well sound masochistic—"Pain is part of joy," the whiskey priest asserts in *The Power and the Glory*, "pain is a part of pleasure"; but as Greene says in the essay "Hans Anderson," it is really the "Catholic ideal of the acceptance of pain for a spiritual benefit." This ideal is behind the saintly Sarah's striking statement in *The End of the Affair:* "How good You [God] are. You might have killed us with happiness, but You let us be with You in pain."

According to Kenneth Allott and Miriam Farris in their 1951 study *The Art of Graham Greene*, "seediness . . . seems to Greene the most honest representation of the nature of things." One typical recurring character, for example, appeared as early as the opening chapters of *The Man Within.* From the "shambling," bored priest in that novel who sniffles his way through the burial service for Elizabeth's guardian; to the wheezing old priest smelling of eucalyptus at the end of *Brighton Rock;* to the whiskey priest in *The Power and the Glory;* to the broken-down Father Callifer in *The Potting Shed* with his "stubbly worn face," "bloodshot eyes," and "dirty wisp of a Roman collar," Greene has annointed a small cathedral of seedy priests. Francis Wyndham summarizes an objection whose validity each reader must judge for himself: "Some find [Greene's] continual emphasis on squalor and seediness . . . overdone."

Also typical of Greene's characters is their predilection for sin. Greene "seems to have been born with a belief in Original Sin," John Atkins suggests in *Graham Greene,* and certainly his characters have been tainted by it. Raven in *A Gun for Sale* is but one of many Greene protagonists who "had been marked from birth." Another is the whiskey priest's illegitimate daughter in *The Power and the Glory:* "The world was in her heart already, like the small spot of decay in the fruit." Likewise, D. the "confidential agent": "Give me time," he thinks, "and I shall infect anything." Atkins "can almost hear [Greene's] teeth gnashing at those who omitted to sleep with someone else's wife or husband . . . it is difficult to read Greene's fiction without sensing a contempt for sinlessness." Atkins concludes: Greene's "concern with sin has become so intense he finds a life without sin to be devoid of meaning." But George Orwell's witty complaint about Greene in *The Collected Essays, Journalism and Letters of George Orwell* is the best known. Labeling his subject the leader of the "cult of the sanctified sinner," Orwell declares that Greene shows a Catholic's "snobbishness" about sin: "there is something *distingue* in being damned; Hell is a sort of high-class nightclub, entry to which is reserved for Catholics only."

Though Greene's Catholicism has generated the most intense critical debate, only five or six of his more than twenty novels actually focus on the religion: *Brighton Rock, The Power and the Glory, The Heart of the Matter* (the so-called "Catholic trilogy" analyzed by R. W. B. Lewis in *The Picaresque Saint* and by Marie-Beatrice Mesnet in *Graham Greene and the Heart of the Matter),* *The End of the Affair, Monsignor Qnor Quixote,* and, perhaps, *A Burnt-Out Case.* In exploring Catholicism in his fiction, Greene eschews propaganda. He notes in *Ways of Escape,* his second volume of autobiography, *Ways of Escape,* notes that he is "not a Catholic writer but a writer who happens to be a Catholic." That is, Catholicism does not provide a dogma he wishes to promulgate in his novels but instead supplies a framework within which he can measure the human situation. "I'm not a religious man," Greene told *Catholic World* interviewer

Gene D. Phillips, "though it interests me. Religion is important, as atomic science is."

Despite the attention paid his Catholicism, Greene told Phillips that religion has occupied only "one period" of his writing career: "My period of Catholic novels was preceded and followed by political novels." Greene's first successful novels were written in the 1930s, a decade G. S. Fraser in *The Modern Writer and His World* has said "forced the writer's attention back on the intractable public world around him." In *Ways of Escape* Greene defines the mid-1930s as "clouded by the Depression in England . . . and by the rise of Hitler. It was impossible in those days not to be committed, and it is hard to recall details of ones' private life as the enormous battlefield was prepared around us." Greene's earlier political novels are set in Europe, usually in England (Smith calls *It's a Battlefield,* published in 1934, and *England Made Me,* published in 1935, "condition-of-England" novels); but the later political novels move from one third-world trouble spot to another, even as they explore the themes found throughout Greene's work: commitment, betrayal, corruption, sin, suffering, and the nature of human sexuality, often against a backdrop of Catholicism.

In both religion and politics Greene is against the dogmatic and the doctrinaire, against those who sacrifice the corrupt but living human spirit for a grand but bloodless thesis. For example, in *Monsignor Quixote,* however much the good-natured priest and the equally good-natured communist politician quibble, both reject the intellectual rigidities of those who commitment to their respective causes is ideologically absolute. Politics and religion, then, are closely related. *Monsignor Quixote* is at once political and religious in nature; and, while nobody denies that *The Power and the Glory* is one of Greene's Catholic works, it can also be studied as a political novel.

Not only a novelist, Greene has written in more than a dozen other genres: novella, short story, play, radio play, screenplay, essay, memoir, biography, autobiography, travel book, poetry, polemic, children's literature. This remarkable output, Smith says, testifies "to a creative energy that has sought to explore the forms open to the literary imagination, and to the fact that Greene is a writer in the deepest, as well as the widest, sense of the term." Although Greene has made his mark primarily in the novel, at least his stories, plays, and nonfiction prose, as well as his work in the film, deserve consideration.

About the short story genre Greene writes in *Ways of Escape:* "I remain in this field a novelist who happens to have written short stories." Unfailingly modest in appraising his own literary efforts, Greene says in a note to his collection *Nineteen Stories,* "I am only too conscious of the defects of these stories. . . . The short story is an exacting form which I have not properly practised." His stories, he says, are "merely . . . the by-products of a novelist's career." However true this evaluation might be for *Nineteen Stories,* and however correct Lodge might be in calling the short story a "form in which [Greene] has never excelled," some of Greene's stories do merit reading. Even John Atkins, who in *Graham Greene* concurs with Lodge that the "short story is not one of Greene's successful forms," concedes that the four new works in *Twenty-One Stories* "show an improvement" over those in the earlier volume. And in *Ways of Escape* Greene registers contentment with "The Destructors," "A Chance for Mr. Lever," "Under the Garden," and "Cheap in August": "I have never written anything better than" these works, he declares.

Less distinguished than his fiction, Greene's dramas have provided him with, if nothing else, diversion. He has often recorded, almost bragged about, his life-long attempt to escape depression and boredom, starting with Russian roulette as a teenager and culminating in a career as a restless, wandering novelist who, when his mainstay produces boredom, tries to escape by shifting genres. Writing plays, he declares in *Ways of Escape,* "offered me novelty, an escape from the everyday": "I needed a rest from novels."

As with the stories, critics have not expressed general enthusiasm for Greene's plays. *The Complaisant Lover,* however, has attracted applause. Stratford calls it an "outstanding and original achievement," and to Atkins it is as "vital as many of the Restoration comedies." But Smith is acute in pointing to a "curious lack in the plays, that of memorable characters"—certainly not a problem in Greene's novels. On the whole most critics would agree with Lodge's assessment: "it does not seem likely that Greene will add a significant chapter to the history of British drama."

Greene's nonfiction prose, although not widely analyzed, has been more appreciated. Metaphorical and speculative, the travel books are distinctly literary; Greene's narratives record spiritual no less than physical journeys. Greene's first travel book, *Journey Without Maps,* is representative of his work in the genre. Believing Africa to be "not a particular place, but a shape, . . .that of the human heart," Greene imagines his actual trip as, simultaneously, a descent, with Freud as guide, into the collective soul of humanity in quest of "those ancestral threads which still exist in our unconscious minds." Greene finds in Africa "associations with a personal and racial childhood"; and when in the end he returns to civilization, the conclusion he draws about his experience affirms the "lost childhood" theme about which he has so frequently written: "This journey, if had done nothing else, had reinforced a sense of disappointment with what man had made out of the primitive, what he had made out of childhood."

Commentators frequently turn to Greene's critical essays as an aid to understanding his fiction; "Fresh and stimulating," as Wyndham says, the essays throw "much light on [Greene's] own work as a novelist." But the essays are worth reading in their own right. Atkins contends that "When Greene's criticism is gathered together we realize how very good it is," that Greene "has unerring good judgment in all literary matters. He can always be relied upon to see through falsity and to detect the ring of truth in others." And Atkins offers a startling evaluation: Greene's "criticism is much more free of fault than his fiction."

Many critics believe that, among serious novelists, Greene has had the closest contact with the film. From 1935 to 1940 for the *Spectator* and in 1937 for *Night and Day* he wrote film reviews. In addition, more than twenty of his own novels and stories have been filmed, some with his own screenplays. Furthermore, Greene has written original screenplays, including the 1949 classic *The Third Man.* It is, then, understandable that to the *Paris Review* interviewers he should call himself a "film man."

At least since 1945, when James Agee in *The Nation* noticed that "Greene achieves in print what more naturally belongs in films, and in a sense does not write novels at all, but verbal movies," critics have been discussing the cinema's impact on Greene's fiction. To Evelyn Waugh, in a review printed in both *The Tablet* and *Commonweal, The Heart of the Matter* seems to have been created "out of an infinite length of film" from which "sequences had been cut": "The writer has become director and producer. Indeed, the affinity to the film is everywhere apparent . . . the cinema . . . has taught a new habit of narrative." Fraser picks up this point: "Greene is present in his novels as a producer is present in a film. . . . He cuts, like a film director, from episode to episode."

Greene's cinematic prose method is evident in his first successful novel, *Stamboul Train.* In creating this work with an eye on the film camera, Greene interspersed passages of extended narrative with brief cuts from one character or group of characters to another. This device both sustains the novel's full-throttle pace by generating a sense of motion—appropriate to a story whose center is a speeding express train—and, with great economy, evokes the stew of humanity thrown together at a railway station or on a train. The union of film and fiction is even pondered in *Stamboul Train* by the character Q. C. Savory, who seems to describe Greene's own ambition to incorporate aspects of the film into his fiction: "One thing the films had taught the eye, Savory thought, the beauty of the landscape in motion, how a church tower moved behind and above the trees, how it dipped and soared with the uneven human stride, the loveliness of a chimney rising towards a cloud and sinking behind the further cowls. That sense of movement must be conveyed in prose."

Though acclaimed for his work in various genres, it is as a novelist that he is most respected. Some critics even recognize him as the leading English novelist of his generation. In Lodge's words, among British novelists who are Greene's contemporaries, "it is difficult to find his equal." Smith's evaluation that Greene's is "one of the more remarkable careers in twentieth-century fiction" is understated, especially alongside the judgment of the anonymous *Times Literary Supplement* reviewer of the Collected Edition that Greene is the "principal English novelist now writing in [the 'great'] tradition" of Henry James, Joseph Conrad, and Ford Madox Ford. But it is, perhaps, Wyndham who comes closest to explaining Greene's sustained popularity when he states, simply, that "everything [Greene] writes is readable."

BIOGRAPHICAL/CRITICAL SOURCES:

BOOKS

Allen, Walter, *The Modern Novel,* Dutton, 1965.

Allott, Kenneth, and Miriam Farris Allott, *The Art of Graham Greene,* Hamish Hamilton, 1951, Russell & Russell, 1965.

Atkins, John, *Graham Greene,* Roy, 1958.

Bestsellers 89, Issue 4, Gale, 1989.

Contemporary Literary Criticism, Gale, Volume 1, 1973, Volume 3, 1975, Volume 6, 1976, Volume 9, 1978, Volume 14, 1980, Volume 18, 1981, Volume 27, 1984, Volume 37, 1986.

DeVitis, L. A., *Graham Greene,* Twayne, 1964.

Dictionary of Literary Biography, Gale, Volume 13: *British Dramatists Since World War II,* 1982, Volume 15: *British Novelists, 1930-1959,* 1983, Volume 77: *British Mystery Writers, 1920-1939,* 1989.

Dictionary of Literary Biography Yearbook: 1985, Gale, 1986.

Evans, R. O., editor, *Graham Greene: Some Critical Considerations,* University of Kentucky Press, 1963.

Hynes, Samuel, editor, *Graham Greene: A Collection of Critical Essays,* Prentice-Hall, 1973.

Kermode, Frank, *Puzzles and Epiphanies,* Chilmark, 1962.

Kunkel, Francis L., *The Labyrinthine Ways of Graham Greene,* Sheed, 1959.

Living Writers, Sylvan Press, 1947.

Lodge, David, *Graham Greene,* Columbia University Press, 1966.

Mauriac, Francois, *Great Men,* Rockliff, 1952.

Mesnet, Maire-Beatrice, *Graham Greene and the Heart of the Matter,* Cresset, 1954.

Mueller, Walter R., *The Prophetic Voice in Modern Fiction,* Association Press, 1959.

Newby, P. H., *The Novel: 1945-1950,* Longmans, Green, 1951.

O'Faolain, Dean, *The Vanishing Hero,* Atlantic Monthly Press, 1956.

Prescott, Orville, *In My Opinion,* Bobbs-Merrill, 1952.

Reed, Henry, *The Novel Since 1939,* Longmans, Green, 1947.

Rostenne, Paul, *Graham Greene: Temoin des temps tragiques,* Julliard, 1949.

Sherry, Norman, *The Life of Graham Greene, Volume 1: 1904-1939,* Viking, 1989.

Stratford, Philip, *Faith and Fiction,* University of Notre Dame Press, 1964.

Wyndham, Francis, *Graham Greene,* Longmans, Green, 1955.

Zabel, Morton Dauwen, *Craft and Character in Modern Fiction,* Viking, 1957.

PERIODICALS

America, January 25, 1941.

Globe and Mail (Toronto), September 29, 1984.

Life, February 4, 1966.

Los Angeles Times, September 25, 1980, January 2, 1981, March 20, 1985.

Los Angeles Times Book Review, October 23, 1988.

New York Review of Books, March 3, 1966.

New York Times, February 27, 1978, May 19, 1980, January 18, 1981, September 24, 1982, October 25, 1984, March 4, 1985, June 6, 1985, October 17, 1988.

New York Times Book Review, January 23, 1966.

Time, September 20, 1982.

Times (London), September 6, 1984, September 7, 1984, March 14, 1985, February 5, 1990.

Times Literary Supplement, January 27, 1966, March 28, 1980, March 15, 1985.

Washington Post, April 3, 1980, September 20, 1988.

Washington Post Book World, May 18, 1980, October 16, 1988.

* * *

GREER, Germaine 1939-
(Rose Blight)

PERSONAL: Born January 29, 1939, near Melbourne, Australia; daughter of Eric Reginal (a newspaper advertising manager) and Margaret May Mary (Lanfrancan) Greer; married Paul de Feu (a journalist), 1968 (divorced, 1973). *Education:* University of Melbourne, B.A., 1959; University of Sydney, M.A., 1961; Newnham College, Cambridge, Ph.D., 1967. *Politics:* Anarchist. *Religion:* Atheist.

ADDRESSES: Home—Tuscany, Italy. *Agent*—Curtis Brown Ltd., 162-68 Regent St., London W1R 5TA, England.

CAREER: Taught at a girls' school in Australia; University of Warwick, Coventry, England, lecturer in English, 1967-73; founder and director of Tulsa Centre for the Study of Women's Literature, 1979-82; writer. Has been an actress on a television comedy show in Manchester, England.

WRITINGS:

The Female Eunuch, MacGibbon & Kee, 1970, McGraw, 1971.

The Obstacle Race: The Fortunes of Women Painters and Their Work, Farrar, Straus, 1979.

Sex and Destiny: The Politics of Human Fertility, Harper, 1984.

Shakespeare (literary criticism), Oxford University Press, 1986.

The Madwoman's Underclothes: Essays and Occasional Writings, Picador, 1986, Atlantic Monthly Press, 1987.

(Editor with Jeslyn Medoff, Melinda Sansone, and Susan Hastings) *Kissing the Rod: An Anthology of Seventeenth-Century Women's Verse,* Farrar, Straus, 1989.

Daddy, We Hardly Knew You, Viking Penguin, 1989.

Contributor to *River Journeys,* Hippocrene Books, c. 1985. Contributor to periodicals, including *Esquire, Listener, Oz, Spectator,* and, under pseudonym Rose Blight, *Private Eye.* Columnist, *London Sunday Times,* 1971-73. Co-founder of *Suck.*

SIDELIGHTS: Germaine Greer's writings, which include *The Female Eunuch, The Obstacle Race: The Fortunes of Women Painters and Their Work, Sex and Destiny: The Politics of Human Fertility,* a literary study titled *Shakespeare,* and the essay collection *The Madwoman's Underclothes,* have earned her both praise and disparagement from mainstream, academic, and feminist critics. The praise has typically been offered for her scholarly insight—which is perhaps most notable in *Shakespeare* and her study of great but unrecognized women artists, *The Obstacle Race*—and the criticism for her refusal to routinely espouse whatever literary or feminist ideas are most popular at a given time. In 1989 she published a more personal book than her previous volumes, *Daddy, We Hardly Knew You,* which records the investigations into her father's life and personality that she began after her father's death in 1983.

Greer had become a media success upon the American publication of *The Female Eunuch* in 1971. Such celebrity was consistent with her roles as a television performer and as a self-avowed London "groupie" (her enthusiasm for jazz and popular music had brought her into contact with musicians and other members of Britain's underground culture); but critics seized upon her slick and frankly sexual image as counterproductive to the feminist cause she espoused. While her book climbed the best-seller charts in both the United States and England and *Vogue* magazine hailed her as "a super heroine," many members of the women's liberation movement questioned her authority. While *Newsweek* described her as "a dazzling combination of erudition, eccentricity and eroticism," some feminist writers wondered whether an indisputably attractive Shakespearean scholar could speak with understanding about the plight of women in general.

Nevertheless, *The Female Eunuch* sold. It was made a Book-of-the-Month Club alternate and a Book Find Club selection and was ultimately translated into twelve languages. During a United States promotional tour in the spring of 1971, Greer furthered her message on television and radio talk shows, in *Life* magazine, and in a well-publicized debate with Norman Mailer, a novelist and self-confirmed "male chauvinist."

Greer's basic argument, as explained in the book's introduction, is that women's "sexuality is both denied and misrepresented by being identified as passivity." She explains that women, urged from childhood to live up to an "Eternal Feminine" stereotype, are valued for characteristics associated with the castrate—"timidity, plumpness, languor, delicacy and preciosity"—hence the book's title. From the viewpoint of this primary assumption, Greer examines not only the problems of women's sexuality, but their psychological development, their relationships with men, their social position, and their cultural history. What most struck early critics of the book was that she considered "the castration of our true female personality . . . not the fault of men, but our own, and history's." Thus *Newsweek* considered Greer's work "women's liberation's most realistic and least anti-male manifesto"; and Christopher Lehmann-Haupt called it "a book that combines the best of masculinity *and* femininity."

BIOGRAPHICAL/CRITICAL SOURCES:

PERIODICALS

Detroit News, May 9, 1971.

Globe and Mail (Toronto), February 25, 1984, October 17, 1987, April 29, 1989, August 5, 1989.
Life, May 7, 1971.
Listener, October 22, 1970.
Los Angeles Times, March 7, 1984, November 26, 1987.
Los Angeles Times Book Review, September 6, 1987.
Newsweek, March 22, 1971.
New York Times, April 20, 1971, November 1, 1979, March 5, 1984, April 23, 1984.
New York Times Book Review, October 11, 1987, January 28, 1990.
Observer (London), October 11, 1970.
Publishers Weekly, May 25, 1984.
Time, April 16, 1984.
Times (London), March 20, 1986, October 23, 1986, March 20, 1989, March 25, 1989.
Times Literary Supplement, June 17, 1988, March 17, 1989.
Washington Post, November 22, 1979, January 24, 1990.

*   *   *

GREER, Richard
See SILVERBERG, Robert

*   *   *

GREGOR, Lee
See POHL, Frederik

*   *   *

GRENVILLE, Pelham
See WODEHOUSE, P(elham) G(renville)

*   *   *

GREY, Zane   1872-1939

PERSONAL: Name originally Pearl Zane Gray; born January 31, 1872, in Zanesville, Ohio; died October 23, 1939, in Altadena, Calif.; son of Lewis M. (a travelling preacher and dentist) and Josephine (Zane) Gray; married Lina Elise Roth, November 21, 1905; children: Romer, Elizabeth, Loren. *Education:* University of Pennsylvania, Philadelphia, D.D.S., 1896.

CAREER: Writer. Practiced dentistry in New York City, 1896-1904; traveled in the West, 1907-18.

WRITINGS:

WESTERN WRITINGS

Betty Zane, Charles Francis Press, 1903, abridged edition, Saalfield, 1940.
The Spirit of the Border: A Romance of the Early Settlers in the Ohio Valley, A. L. Burt, 1906, abridged edition, Saalfield, 1940.
The Last of the Plainsmen, Outing, 1908.
The Last Trail: A Story of Early Days in the Ohio Valley, A. L. Burt, 1909, abridged edition, Saalfield, 1940.
The Heritage of the Desert: A Novel, Harper, 1910.
Riders of the Purple Sage: A Novel, Harper, 1912.
Desert Gold: A Romance of the Border, Harper, 1913, abridged edition published as *Prairie Gold,* Sphere Books, 1967.
The Light of Western Stars: A Romance, Harper, 1914.
The Rustlers of Pecos County, Munsey, 1914.
The Lone Star Ranger: A Romance of the Border, Harper, 1915.
The Rainbow Trail: A Romance, Harper, 1915.

The Border Legion, Harper, 1916.
Wildfire, Harper, 1917.
The U.P. Trail: A Novel, Harper, 1918, published in England as *The Roaring U.P. Trail,* Hodder & Stoughton, 1918.
The Desert of Wheat: A Novel, Harper, 1919.
The Man of the Forest: A Novel, Harper, 1920.
The Mysterious Rider: A Novel, Harper, 1921.
To the Last Man: A Novel, Harper, 1922.
Wanderer of the Wasteland, Harper, 1923.
The Call of the Canyon, Harper, 1924.
Roping Lions in the Grand Canyon, Harper, 1924.
The Thundering Herd, Harper, 1925.
The Vanishing American, Harper, 1925, published in England as *The Vanishing Indian,* Hodder & Stoughton, 1926.
Under the Tonto Rim, Harper, 1926.
Forlorn River: A Romance, Harper, 1927.
Nevada: A Romance of the West, Harper, 1928.
Wild Horse Mesa, Harper, 1928.
Fighting Caravans, Harper, 1929.
The Shepherd of Guadaloupe, Harper, 1930.
Sunset Pass, Harper, 1931.
Arizona Ames, Harper, 1932.
Robber's Roost, Harper, 1932.
The Drift Fence, Harper, 1933.
The Hash Knife Outfit, Harper, 1933.
The Code of the West, Harper, 1934.
Thunder Mountain, Harper, 1935.
The Trail Driver, Harper, 1936.
The Lost Wagon Train, Harper, 1936.
West of the Pecos, Harper, 1937.
Majesty's Rancho, Harper, 1938.
Raiders of Spanish Peaks, Harper, 1938.
Knights of the Range, Harper, 1939.
Western Union, Harper, 1939.
30,000 on the Hoof, Harper, 1940.
Twin Sombreros, Harper, 1941.
Stairs of Sand, Harper, 1943.
Shadow on the Trail, Harper, 1946.
Valley of Wild Horses, Harper, 1947.
Rogue River Feud (originally serialized under title "Rustlers of Silver River"), Harper, 1948.
The Deer Stalker, Harper, 1949.
The Maverick Queen, Harper, 1950.
The Dude Ranger, Harper, 1951.
Captives of the Desert, Harper, 1952.
Wyoming, Harper, 1953.
Lost Pueblo, Harper, 1954.
Black Mesa, Harper, 1955.
Stranger from the Tonto, Harper, 1956.
The Fugitive Trail, Harper, 1957.
The Arizona Clan, Harper, 1958.
Horse Heaven Hill, Harper, 1959.
Boulder Dam, Harper, 1963.
Zane Grey's Greatest Western Stories, edited by Loren Grey, Belmont, 1975.
Zane Grey's Greatest Indian Stories, edited by Loren Grey, Belmont, 1975.
Zane Grey's Greatest Animal Stories, edited by Loren Grey, Belmont, 1975.
The Big Land, edited by Loren Grey, Belmont, 1976.
Yaqui and Other Great Indian Stories, edited by Loren Grey, Belmont, 1976.
The Buffalo Hunter, edited by Loren Grey, Belmont, 1977.
The Westerner, edited by Loren Grey, Belmont, 1977.
Savage Kingdom, Henry, 1979.

JUVENILES

The Short-Stop, McClurg, 1909.
The Young Forester, Harper, 1910.
The Young Pitcher, Harper, 1911.
The Young Lion Hunter, Harper, 1911.
Ken Ward in the Jungle: Thrilling Adventures in Tropical Wilds, Harper, 1912.
The Red-Headed Outfield and Other Baseball Stories, Grosset & Dunlap, 1920.
Tappan's Burro and Other Stories, Harper, 1923.
Don: The Story of a Lion Dog, Harper, 1928.
The Wolf Tracker, Harper, 1930.
Zane Grey's Book of Camps and Trails, Harper, 1931.
The Ranger and Other Stories, Harper, 1960.
Blue Feather and Other Stories, Harper, 1961.
The Adventures of Finspot, D-J Books, 1974.

Also author of seven volumes of "King of the Royal Mounted" series of "Big-Little" books for Whitman, 1936-46.

OTHER

Nassau, Cuba, Yucatan, Mexico: A Personal Note of Appreciation of These Nearby Foreign Lands, New York and Cuba Mail, 1909.
Tales of Fishes, Harper, 1919.
Tales of Lonely Trails, Harper, 1922.
The Day of the Beast, Harper, 1922.
Tales of Southern Rivers, Harper, 1924.
Tales of Fishing Virgin Seas, Harper, 1925.
Tales of an Angler's Eldorado—New Zealand, Harper, 1926.
Tales of Swordfish and Tuna, Harper, 1927.
(With others) *Zane Grey: The Man and His Work*, Harper, 1928.
Tales of Fresh-Water Fishing, Harper, 1928.
Tales of Tahitian Waters, Harper, 1931.
An American Angler in Australia, Harper, 1937.
The Zane Grey Omnibus, edited by Ruth G. Gentles, Harper, 1943.
Wilderness Trek: A Novel of Australia, Harper, 1944.
Adventures in Fishing, edited and with notes by Ed Zern, Harper, 1952.
Zane Grey, Outdoorsman: Zane Grey's Best Hunting and Fishing Tales, Prentice-Hall, 1972.
Shark! Zane Grey's Tales of Man-Eating Sharks, edited by Loren Grey, Belmont, 1976.
The Reef Girl: A Novel of Tahiti, edited by Loren Grey, Harper, 1977.
Zane Grey's Tales from the Fisherman's Log, Hodder & Stoughton, 1979.

Also coauthor of screenplays "The Vanishing Pioneer," 1928, and "Rangle River," 1936.

SIDELIGHTS: "Perhaps more than any other modern American novelist," declares Ann Ronald in the *Dictionary of Literary Biography*, "Zane Grey caught the imaginations of several generations of readers." In books such as *The Heritage of the Desert* and *Riders of the Purple Sage*, Grey helped popularize the American West as a subject for fiction. Although writers such as James Fenimore Cooper (with *The Deerstalker* and *The Last of the Mohicans*) and Owen Wister (with *The Virginian*) also used the American frontier as the setting for their stories, Grey's vivid descriptions of Western landscapes and popular, formulaic plots established the "Western" genre. "From 1910 until 1925," Ronald continues, "his books appeared regularly on best-seller lists, and even today, in both hardcover and paperback, his fiction remains popular."

In his Western novels, Grey broke free from the nineteenth-century dime novel approach to adventure stories. He made three important innovations: he created the figure of the mysterious outlaw or gunfighter enlisted to fight for good; he wrote Western stories—particularly *The Light of Western Stars*—from a woman's point of view, and examined the love between an Indian chief and a white girl in *The Vanishing American;* and he established the Western environment as a test of character. Critics now believe that Grey should be read as a romantic rather than a realistic writer—that, although he gained his knowledge of the West through firsthand experience, making many trips there, and performed extensive research on historical background, especially in *The U.P. Trail* (his history of the transcontinental railroad), he was in fact more interested in portraying types rather than characters pitted against forces of evil or forces of nature, to triumph or perish.

Riders of the Purple Sage, the novel that brought Grey his greatest popular acclaim, demonstrates some of these elements. In Lassiter, the taciturn gunslinger, and Jane Withersteen, the proud Mormon heiress, the book "matched a superhuman hero with a virginal heroine and placed them against a backdrop of ruggedness and violence in a struggle against unmitigated evil," states Danney Goble in the *Journal of Arizona History*. Another pattern Grey frequently used, Ronald states, was "an adaptation of the 'easterner goes West to learn about life' embellished with his own richly pictorial imagination." Yet, although other authors had used these formulas before, says Ronald in her *Zane Grey*, Grey's work is different because it is "an outgrowth of the author's personal experiences, a reiteration of his own journey to the frontier." "Within a few years the plots and characters would become standard," Goble concludes. "But Grey's combination of brutal violence and saccharine romance—a heady mixture all but unknown to his predecessors in the writing of frontier fiction—established his claim to a gold mine which he exploited time and again."

Grey's vivid depiction of the Western landscape was one of the strongest elements of his writing, critics agree. "He portrays it as an acid test of those elemental traits of character which he admires," writes T. K. Whipple in *Study Out the Land: Essays*. "It kills off the weaklings, and among the strong it makes the bad worse and the good better. Nature to him is somewhat as God is to a Calvinist—ruthlessly favoring the elect and damning the damned." "Grey may have fallen short of what Emerson had in mind in 'The American Scholar' in calling for a literature on indigenous American themes," declares Gary Topping in *Western American Literature*, "but for millions of readers he did provide an introduction, at least, to the literary potential of many common aspects of Western life."

"My long labors have been devoted to making stories resemble the times they depict," Grey wrote in the foreword to his novel *To the Last Man*. "I have loved the West for its vastness, its contrasts, its beauty and color and life, for its wildness and violence, and for the fact that I have seen how it developed great men and women who died unknown and unsung." "Romance," he continued, "is only another name for idealism; and I contend that life without ideals is not worth living. . . . Walter Scott wrote romance; so did Victor Hugo; and likewise Kipling, Hawthorne, Stevenson. It was Stevenson, particularly, who wielded a bludgeon against the realists. People live for the dream in their hearts." "We are all dreamers," he concluded, "if not in the heavy-lidded wasting of time, then in the meaning of life that makes us work on."

BIOGRAPHICAL/CRITICAL SOURCES:

BOOKS

Dictionary of Literary Biography, Volume 9: *American Novelists, 1910-1945,* Gale, 1981.
Garland, Hamlin, *Hamlin Garland's Diaries,* edited by Donald Pizer, Huntington Library, 1968.
Grey, Zane, *To the Last Man: A Novel,* Harper, 1922.
Gruber, Frank, *Zane Grey: A Biography,* World Publishing, 1970.
Jackson, Carlton, *Zane Grey,* Twayne, 1973.
Karr, Jean, *Zane Grey: Man of the West,* Greenberg, 1949.
Mott, Frank Luther, *Golden Multitudes: The Story of Best Sellers in the United States,* Macmillan, 1947.
Nye, Russel B., *The Unembarrassed Muse: The Popular Arts in America,* Dial, 1970.
Powell, Lawrence Clark, *Southwest Classics: The Creative Literature of the Arid Lands—Essays on the Books and Their Writers,* Ward Ritchie Press, 1974.
Ronald, Ann, *Zane Grey,* Boise State University, 1975.
Scott, Kenneth W., *Zane Grey, Born to the West: A Reference Guide,* G. K. Hall, 1979.
Twentieth-Century Literary Criticism, Volume 6, Gale, 1982.
Twentieth-Century Western Writers, Gale, 1982.
Whipple, T. K., *Study Out the Land: Essays,* University of California Press, 1943.

PERIODICALS

American Review of Reviews, June, 1912.
Journal of Arizona History, spring, 1973.
New York Times, September 12, 1908, October 8, 1910, February 18, 1912.
Saturday Review of Literature, November 11, 1939.

*　　*　　*

GRIEVE, C(hristopher) M(urray) 1892-1978
(Hugh MacDiarmid; other pseudonyms: Isobel Guthrie, A. K. Laidlaw, James MacLaren, Pteleon)

PERSONAL: Born August 11, 1892, in Langholm, Dumfriesshire, Scotland; died of cancer, September 9, 1978, in Edinburgh, Scotland; son of James (a postman) and Elizabeth (Graham) Grieve; married Margaret Skinner, June, 1918 (divorced, January, 1932); married Valda Trevlyn, September 12, 1934; children: (first marriage) Christine, Walter; (second marriage) James Michael Trevlyn. *Education:* Attended Langholm Academy, Broughton Junior Student Centre (Edinburgh) and University of Edinburgh. *Politics:* Communist (formally, from 1934 to 1938 when he was expelled; rejoined Party, 1957).

ADDRESSES: Home—The Cottage, Brownsbank, Candymill, Biggar, Lanarkshire, Scotland.

CAREER: Joined Independent Labour Party at 16; became a journalist, 1912, working for a number of papers in Scotland and near the Welsh-English border; worked as a chief reporter and general factotum for *Montrose Review,* Montrose, Scotland, 1920-29; worked on *Vox,* London, England, 1929; lived in Liverpool, England, 1930, working as a public relations officer with the Organization for Advancing the Interests of Merseyside; returned to London to work for Unicorn Press; moved to Whalsay, Shetland Islands, 1933, and stayed until 1941; worked as manual laborer on a war job, Clydeside, 1941-43; worked on ships engaged in estuarial duties, British Merchant Service, 1943-45; moved to Glasgow, Scotland, 1945, then to Strathhaven, moved

to Biggar, 1951. Labour member of town council of Montrose, 1923-28; justice of the peace, Angus, with life appointment, 1923-78; one of the founders of the National Party of Scotland, 1928; was a defeated candidate in the 1964 General Election, opposing Sir Alec Douglas-Home. Regular lecturer for Scottish University extramural departments, Workers' Educational Association, and Rationalist Press Association. Vice-president, British Peace Committee; founder-member, Committee of 100; director of theater workshop for Pioneer Theatres Ltd. *Military service:* Royal Army Medical Corps, 1915-20; served in Salonika, Italy, and France.

MEMBER: PEN (one of the founders of the Scottish Centre, 1927), World Burns Federation (life member), Saltire Society (life member).

AWARDS, HONORS: Civil List pension for services to literature, 1951; LL.D., University of Edinburgh, 1957.

WRITINGS:

Annals of the Five Senses (poetry and prose), C. M. Grieve, 1923, Faber, 1930.
Contemporary Scottish Studies (prose), L. Parsons (London), 1926, enlarged edition, Scottish Educational Journal, 1976.
Albyn; or, Scotland and the Future (prose), Dutton, 1927.
The Present Position of Scottish Music (prose), C. M. Grieve, (Montrose), 1927.

POETRY; UNDER PSEUDONYM HUGH MacDIARMID

Sangschaw, Blackwood (Edinburgh), 1925, 2nd edition, 1937.
Penny Wheep, Blackwood, 1926, 2nd edition, 1937.
A Drunk Man Looks at the Thistle, Blackwood, 1926, new edition, edited by John C. Weston, University of Massachusetts Press, 1971.
The Lucky Bag, Porpoise Press (Edinburgh), 1927.
To Circumjack Cencrastus; or, The Curly Snake, Blackwood, 1930.
First Hymn to Lenin and Other Poems, introduction by AE (George William Russell), Unicorn Press, 1931.
Second Hymn to Lenin, Valda Trevlyn (Thakeham), 1932, published in *Second Hymn to Lenin and Other Poems,* Nott, 1935.
Scots Unbound and Other Poems (also see below), E. Mackay (Stirling), 1932.
Tarras, [Edinburgh], 1932.
Stony Limits and Other Poems (also see below), Gollancz, 1934.
Selected Poems, Macmillan (London), 1934, enlarged edition published as *Speaking for Scotland: Selected Poems of Hugh MacDiarmid,* Contemporary Poetry (Baltimore), 1946.
Direadh, [Dunfermline], 1938, limited edition published as *Direadh I, II, and III,* K. Duvan and C. H. Hamilton, 1974.
Cornish Heroic Song for Valda Trevlyn, Caledonian Press (Glasgow), 1943.
Selected Poems of Hugh MacDiarmid, edited by R. Crombie Saunders, Maclellan (Glasgow), 1945.
Poems of the East-West Synthesis, Caledonian Press, 1946.
A Kist of Whistles: New Poems by Hugh MacDiarmid, Maclellan, 1947.
Selected Poems, edited by Oliver Brown, Maclellan, 1954.
In Memoriam James Joyce: From a Vision of World Language (also see below), Maclellan, 1955.
Stony Limits and Scots Unbound and Other Poems (composite volume), Castle Wynd (Edinburgh), 1956.
The Battle Continues, Castle Wynd, 1957.
Three Hymns to Lenin, Castle Wynd, 1957.
The Kind of Poetry I Want, K. D. Duval (Edinburgh), 1961.

Collected Poems of Hugh MacDiarmid, Macmillan (New York), 1962, revised edition, prepared by John C. Weston, 1967.

Bracken Hills in Autumn, C. H. Hamilton (Edinburgh), 1962.

Poetry like the Hawthorn (from *In Memoriam James Joyce*), [Hemel Hempstead, Hertfordshire], 1962.

Poems to Paintings by William Johnstone, 1933, K. D. Duval, 1963.

An Apprentice Angel, New Poetry Press, 1963.

The Ministry of Water, D. Glen (Glasgow), 1964.

Six Vituperative Verses, Satire Press, 1964.

The Terrible Crystal [and] *A Vision of Scotland,* D. Glen (Ayrshire), 1964.

The Fire of the Spirit, D. Glen (Glasgow), 1965.

Whuchulls, Akros (Preston, Lancashire), 1966.

(With Norman MacCaig) *Poems by Hugh MacDiarmid and Norman MacCaig,* University of Massachusetts, 1967.

Early Lyrics by Hugh MacDiarmid, edited by J. K. Annand, Akros, 1968, 2nd edition, 1969.

A Lap of Honour, MacGibbon & Kee, 1967, Swallow Press, 1969.

On a Raised Beach, Harris Press, 1967.

A Clyack-Sheaf, MacGibbon & Kee, 1969.

More Collected Poems, Swallow Press, 1970.

Selected Poems, edited by David Craig and John Manson, Penguin, 1970.

The Hugh MacDiarmid Anthology: Poems in Scots and English, edited by Michael Grieve and Alexander Scott, Routledge & Kegan Paul, 1972.

Poems, edited by Alistair Keith Campsie, Famedram, 1972.

Song of the Seraphion, Covent Garden Press, 1973.

Selected Lyrics, edited by Kulgin D. Duval and Colin H. Hamilton, Officina Bodoni (Verona), 1977.

The Socialist Poems of Hugh MacDiarmid, edited by T. S. Law and Thurso Berwick, Routledge & Kegan Paul, 1978.

Complete Poems, 2 volumes, edited by Michael Grieve and W. R. Aitken, Brian & O'Keeffe, 1978.

PROSE; UNDER PSEUDONYM HUGH MacDIARMID

The Present Condition of Scottish Arts and Affairs, PEN Club, 1927.

The Scottish National Association of April Fools, The University Press, Aberdeen, 1928.

Fidelity in Small Things, 1929.

Five Bits of Miller, privately printed (London), 1934.

At the Sign of the Thistle: A Collection of Essays, Nott, 1934.

Scotland in 1980, privately printed (Montrose), 1935.

Charles Doughty and the Need for Heroic Poetry, [St. Andrews], 1936.

Scottish Eccentrics, Routledge & Kegan Paul, 1936.

Scotland and the Question of a Popular Front against Fascism and War, Hugh MacDiarmid Book Club, 1938.

The Islands of Scotland: Hebrides, Orkneys, and Shetlands, Scribner, 1939.

Lucky Poet: A Self-Study in Literature and Political Ideas, Being the Autobiography of Hugh MacDiarmid, Methuen, 1943, enlarged edition, J. Cape, 1972.

Cunninghame Graham: A Centenary Study, Caledonian Press, 1952.

Francis George Scott: An Essay on the Occasion of His Seventy-Fifth Birthday, 25th January 1955, M. Macdonald (Edinburgh), 1955.

Burns Today and Tomorrow, Castle Wynd, 1959.

David Hume, Scotland's Greatest Son, Paperback Booksellers (Edinburgh), 1962.

The Man of (Almost) Independent Mind (on David Hume), Gordon (Edinburgh), 1962.

The Ugly Birds without Wings, Allan Donaldson (Edinburgh), 1962.

Sydney Goodsir Smith, C. H. Hamilton, 1963.

Tribute to Harry Miller, [Edinburgh], 1963.

The Company I've Kept, Hutchinson, 1966, University of California Press, 1967.

(With Owen Dudley Edwards, Gwynfor Evans, and Joan Rhys) *Celtic Nationalism,* Routledge & Kegan Paul, 1968.

The Uncanny Scot: A Selection of Prose, edited by Kenneth Buthlay, MacGibbon & Kee, 1968.

Selected Essays, edited by Duncan Glen, J. Cape, 1969, University of California Press, 1970.

John Knox, Ramsey Head, 1976.

Aesthetics in Scotland, edited by Alan Bold, B & N Imports, 1985.

EDITOR; UNDER PSEUDONYM HUGH MacDIARMID

Northern Numbers, three series, T. N. Foulis (Edinburgh), 1920 and 1921, third series privately printed (Montrose), 1922.

Robert Burns, 1759-1796, Benn, 1926.

Living Scottish Poets, Benn, 1931.

(And author of introduction) *The Golden Treasury of Scottish Poetry,* Macmillan (London), 1940.

Douglas Young, *Auntran Blads: An Outwale o Verses,* Maclellan, 1943.

(And author of introduction) William Soutar, *Collected Poems,* A. Dakers (London), 1948.

(With Maurice Lindsay) *Poetry Scotland,* number 4, Serif, 1949.

(And author of introduction) William Dunbar, *Selected Poems,* Maclellan, 1955.

(Author of foreword) *Sculpture & Drawings by Benno Schotz,* [Edinburgh], 1961.

Robert Burns, *Love Songs,* Vista Books (London), 1962.

Editor of *Scottish Chapbook* (monthly), 1922-23. Former editor of *Scottish Nation* and *Northern Review.*

OTHER; UNDER PSEUDONYM HUGH MacDIARMID

(Contributor of research) *The Rural Problem,* Constable, for Fabian Research Department, 1913.

(Translator from the Spanish) Ramon Maria de Tenreiro, *The Handmaid of the Lord,* Secker & Warburg, 1930.

(Contributor) *New Tales of Horror,* Hutchinson, 1934.

(With Lewis Grassic Gibbon) *Scottish Scene; or, The Intelligent Man's Guide to Albyn* (poetry and prose), Jarrolds, 1934.

(Translator from the Gaelic) Alexander MacDonald, *The Berlinn of Claranald,* Abbey Bookshop (St. Andrews), 1935.

(Contributor) John Rowland, editor, *Path and Pavement,* [London], 1937.

(Translator from the Swedish and editor, with Elspeth Harley Schubert) Harry Martinson, *Aniara: A Review of Man in Time and Space* (epic poem), Knopf, 1963.

(Translator from the German) Bertolt Brecht, *The Threepenny Opera,* Eyre Methuen, 1973.

Metaphysics and Poetry, Lothlorien, 1975.

Short plays include "Some Day," 1923, "The Purple Patch," 1924, "Jenny Spells," 1924, "The Candidate," 1924, "The Morning Post," 1924. Writer of scripts for radio and television. Contributor to *New Age, Glasgow Herald,* and other publications.

SIDELIGHTS: C. M. Grieve, best known under his pseudonym Hugh MacDiarmid, is credited with effecting a Scottish literary revolution which restored an indigenous Scots literature, and has been acknowledged as the greatest poet that his country has produced since Robert Burns. As a writer, political theorist, revolutionary, prophet, and multifarious personality, he was a man to be reckoned with, even by those who did not agree that he was one of Great Britain's greatest poets. Ian Hamilton wrote that MacDiarmid made enemies largely because "he makes his own rules, contemns categories, cracks open water-tight compartments, bestraddles disciplines, scorns social, cultural, and academic cliques and claques, and affirms . . . that it is not failure but low aim that is criminal."

MacDiarmid's opinions, Hamilton continued, "display in bewildering profusion the contradictions inherent in the Scottish character; but his poetry holds them all in the tension of Gregory Smith's 'Caledonian antisyzygy'. . . . He stands wherever extremes meet and clash, to absorb the turmoil. 'And damn consistency!' He has dedicated himself to the enlargement of human consciousness, and that is no neat and tidy business." Hamilton further stated that "Goethe is the only writer with whom Hugh MacDiarmid can be compared in intellectual audacity and imaginative voracity. It is impossible for a Scotsman . . . to see MacDiarmid simply as a poet. He is, also, more judiciously appreciated abroad than at home—except in England, where he is accorded the indifferent indulgence due to outstanding eccentrics. Politer and more considered noises have been made lately, but only, I suspect, to mark his graduation to Grand Old Man status. MacDiarmid, however, is no Grand Old Man. He is still as Douglas Young saw him: 'at bay on his native heath, sprouting fresh tines at every angle and bellowing to quell the pack'—an indomitable, irreconcilable, unpredictable, paradoxical, and unpuffable genius."

MacDiarmid's poetry is like he was—lyrical, argumentative, polemical, and contradictory. Unable to believe, as W. H. Auden does, that poetry makes nothing happen, MacDiarmid in 1926 stated that "the function of art is the extension of human consciousness." When he published *Direadh* he noted: "I turn from the poetry of beauty to the poetry of wisdom—of 'wisdom,' that is to say, the poetry of moral and intellectual problems, and the emotions they generate." Kenneth Buthlay, writing in *Hugh MacDiarmid (C. M. Grieve),* calls this later poetry, such as that contained in *In Memoriam James Joyce,* the "poetry of information." The early MacDiarmid, according to Iain Crichton Smith in *Hugh MacDiarmid: A Critical Survey,* began like Blake, with lyrics which contain "a fusion of the intellect and feeling which is highly unusual and at times hallucinatory. [Then both went on] to write long poems based rather insecurely on systems which are fairly private (even MacDiarmid's communism doesn't seem to be all that orthodox)." The change in MacDiarmid's poetry occurred about 1930. MacDiarmid explained: "I, like Heine after the success of his lyrics found . . . I could no longer go on with that sort of thing but required to break up the unity of the lyric and introduce new material of various kinds on different levels of significance. It took Heine years of agonized effort to find the new form he needed, and his later work, in which he did find it, never won a measure of esteem like that secured by his early work. So in my case."

Much of the strength of MacDiarmid's reputation still rests on his early lyrics. Crichton Smith notes that the lyrical fusion of the masculine and feminine sensibility was later replaced by an attitude that was entirely masculine, dour, and willful, and, he believes, weaker as a result. An early volume, *A Drunk Man Looks at the Thistle,* was hailed by Oliver St. John Gogarty as "the most virile and vivid poetry written in English or any dialect thereof for many a long day." *A Drunk Man* is still considered to be one of the finest contemporary poems. According to Buthlay, the poem, "without quite bursting at the seams, is able

to hold all or almost all of MacDiarmid—which is to say that it is crammed full of fine lyrics, satire, flyting, parody, burlesque, occasional verse, Rabelaisian jokes, metaphysical conceits, translations and adaptations, sustained meditations and speculations on philosophical and religious problems, elemental symbols, and allusions recondite and otherwise. . . . The ultimate subject of the work is the creative process itself. . . . When not deeply imaginative, . . . he has astonishing resources of metaphysical wit and satirical, fantastic, or grotesque humour at his command. Wit in the sense that Donne had wit, a mental and emotional and verbal agility in juggling with the mutations of possibility, permeates the whole poem."

Buthlay has also pointed out that MacDiarmid was, in a special sense, an eclectic poet. "One cannot derive his style from particular sources because the sources are so many and so fantastically varied. This has obvious dangers, and [MacDiarmid] speaks of his fear of having 'paralysed his creative faculties by overreading.' What saved him from this in the end was the intense activity of a 'tiny specialist cell in his brain' which constantly experimented with an 'obscure ray . . . emanating from his subtle realisation that beyond the individual mind of each man was a collective mind'—that is, the 'collective unconscious' of Jung."

In his later poems MacDiarmid turned from imaginative to intellectual verse. He no longer said, as he had in 1923, that he was "quite certain that the imagination had some way of dealing with the truth which the reason had not, and that commandments delivered when the body is still and the reason silent are the most binding that the souls of men can ever know." Many critics were disappointed with MacDiarmid's intellectualism. Crichton Smith bemoaned the fact that MacDiarmid should think that "a poetry of ideas must necessarily be a more 'serious' poetry. These long poems may be intellectually exciting but they are not serious. They do not confront us with serious things. They do not, I think, react on us as whole human beings. . . . Now it is true that the movement of MacDiarmid's verse recognizes the difficulty of arriving at the truth. . . . There are times however, when MacDiarmid gives the idea that he himself knows the truth and that his ideas are essentially right."

"The weakness of MacDiarmid's use of facts," writes Buthlay, "is that he is oftener content to catalogue them with Whitman than to follow Thoreau's hint of the need to transmute them imaginatively into 'the substance of the human mind.' " Ian Gordon lamented the change to "a style that is inconsequent always, incoherent very often, and is all too seldom poetry." His admirers, according to Hamilton, "claim that MacDiarmid has triumphantly fashioned a loose, discursive, open-ended kind of meditative vehicle which is hospitable to ideas, facts and arguments, that he has marvellously broken free of fiddling post-symbolist constraints. The unconvinced, [however,] complain that he has merely granted himself a licence to be boringly opinionated, that he has ditched rhythm, metaphor and formal discipline in order to make room for muddled, self-admiring chat."

Then there are those who admit, as Louis Simpson does, that "in spite of everything, he is a superb poet." Even though, as Buthlay says, MacDiarmid wrote too much and discriminated too little, "he is a major poet, and there is no book he has written that does not, however partially or intermittently, testify to that fact." Late in life he turned to what the *Times Literary Supplement* called "infinitely expansible poetry on an epic scale." In Hamilton's opinion, the range of poetry to be found in *Collected Poems* "is breathtaking; and the faults, flaws, and fissures serve not to diminish but (as always with genius) to enhance its superhuman scale."

MacDiarmid's abiding interest was language, particularly its aural qualities. He originally wrote in English even though he disliked what he felt to be the English domination of Scottish literature and hoped that his countrymen would look to Europe for literary inspiration. He later decided that his own country's language should be revived, and became the leading figure in the Scottish Renaissance of the twenties, encouraging others to write in the eclectic Scots that he himself had chosen as a means of expression. During the early thirties he moved from this synthetic Scots, or "Lallans," to what Buthlay calls "synthetic English," a combination of English scientific terminology and "recondite elements of the English vocabulary." This experiment was short-lived, for by 1935, when *Second Hymn to Lenin and Other Poems* appeared, he no longer employed "synthetic English," and only the title poem was written (three years previously) in Scots. From about 1935 until shortly before his death he wrote almost entirely in English, although he did compose several longer poems in Scots, principally because he felt that, to quote T. S. Eliot, "many things can be expressed in Scots which cannot be expressed in English at all."

MacDiarmid turned to Scots not merely because he was a Scottish nationalist. To write in Scots was an act of faith, what MacDiarmid called "an experience akin to religious conversion." Moreover, he used Scots, as David Daiches explains, not as an alternative to English; he used it "for effects which are unobtainable in English." This un-Englishness in his writings led to comparisons with James Joyce. Edwin Muir in 1923 noted that "except Mr. Joyce, nobody at present is writing more resourceful English prose." Muir called *Sangschaw* "the product of a realistic, or more exactly a materialistic, imagination, which seizing upon everyday reality shows not the strange beauty which that sometimes takes on, but rather the beauty which it possesses normally and in use." MacDiarmid said about the aesthetic values of Scots: "One of the most distinctive characteristics of the Vernacular, part of its very essence, is its insistent recognition of the body, the senses. . . . This explains the unique blend of the lyrical and the ludicrous in primitive Scots sentiment. . . . The essence of the genius of our race is, in our opinion, the reconciliation it effects between the base and the beautiful, recognising that they are complementary and indispensable to each other." Buthlay notes, however, that by 1934, some former admirers were no longer enthusiastic about Vernacular poetry, and were, in fact, "expressing grave doubts about the possibilities of Scots as a literary medium." In 1936 Muir wrote: "[MacDiarmid] has written some remarkable poetry; but he has left Scottish verse very much where it was before."

The English never understood why a man capable of writing in English would choose to employ another language. (Buthlay reports that not one important English critic had anything favorable to say about *A Drunk Man Looks at the Thistle* until it appeared in *Collected Poems* 36 years later.) Yet it is undeniable that MacDiarmid made Scots a reputable medium for poetry. M. L. Rosenthal still believes that MacDiarmid's best work was executed in Scots. Other critics say that he surpasses Burns. "Certainly he has a range of reference that has not been in Scottish poetry since Dunbar," writes Simpson. "He has written fine lyrics and discursive poems, in English as well as Scots."

Alan Denson notes that MacDiarmid was no mere theorist. "Like all true artists his concern and his language have been directed to the betterment of economic and educational conditions." He is not a humanitarian, however, and refuses to be called a humanist. He has been called everything from a Scottish nationalist and a Marxist internationalist to a Nietzschean communist. (The *Times Literary Supplement* once conjectured that "the years on Whalsay were perhaps a Zarathustran self-conquering.") His communism was, in any event, highly individualistic, "a stage on the way to Anarchism." He wrote in his autobiography: "I am . . . interested only in a very subordinate way in the politics of Socialism as a political theory; my real concern with Socialism is as an artist's organised approach to the interdependencies of life." Buthlay notes that MacDiarmid was "especially preoccupied with the source of 'inspiration' and the mysterious factors that go to produce 'genius,' because he believed the hope of mankind to lie in the possibility of evolving a race of men to whom what is now called 'genius' would be the norm. The tremendous significance of Lenin's revolution (*and* Douglas's economics) was that it promised to clear 'bread-and-butter problems' out of the way and establish much more favourable conditions for this all-important evolutionary process." As might be expected, these opinions were not universally well received. As Simpson says, MacDiarmid "was driven out of the market place; for years he lived in actual poverty on an island off the coast of Scotland. . . . In the thirties when the university Marxists—W. H. Auden, Spender and their friends—became fashionable, MacDiarmid remained obscure. He came from the working class; he meant what he said; he was embarrassing."

"You cannot read MacDiarmid 'just for the poetry'," writes Simpson; "he doesn't want to be read that way; he flings his opinions in your teeth." The *Times Literary Supplement* reviewer adds: "From his very beginnings Mr. MacDiarmid has never been interested in mere literature or even, whatever his gifts for it, in mere poetry; writing for him has been an aspect, an instrument, of political and cultural struggle, and his poems have increasingly tended towards the condition of the manifesto or the prophecy. Mere art he now sees as a temptation." In his instructional essays, for example, "he demonstrates the intrinsic interest in ideas and principles which has been the hidden descant to all his writings," writes Denson. "Warm in sentiment, genial in manner, every stratum in [his] essays is deeper, richer, and stronger than queasy appetites could stomach."

His principal pseudonym, Hugh MacDiarmid (he used others early in his career in order to review his own works), "is more of a *nom de guerre* than a *nom de plume*," writes Buthlay. "Hugh MacDiarmid is the scourge of the Philistines, the ruthless intellectual tough looking for a rumble." A *Times Literary Supplement* writer noted that, roughly, "C. M. Grieve was the professional journalist, the editor, the critic and publicist, the man who expressed hopes but also realistic doubts; Hugh MacDiarmid was the bard, the prophet, the enemy of compromise. The two identities, and the possibility of disagreement and discussion between them, saved their owner also from getting tied too sharply down to one narrow position."

"My story," MacDiarmid once said, ". . . is the story of an absolutist whose absolutes came to grief in his private life." In his last years he led "a quiet, rustic, ascetic life," according to Buthlay. In Scotland he became a legendary figure. Denson writes: "The spirit is everything, the letter a mere translation of the man. Is there elsewhere an emblem more apt to describe Hugh MacDiarmid's quality, as a man, than his own words? Perhaps only Mozart's music could depict such a poet."

BIOGRAPHICAL/CRITICAL SOURCES:

BOOKS

Aitken, William R., and others, *Hugh MacDiarmid: A Festschrift,* Dufour, 1963.
Buthlay, Kenneth, *Hugh MacDiarmid (C. M. Grieve),* Oliver & Boyd, 1964, revised edition, Scottish Academic Press, 1982.

Contemporary Literary Criticism, Gale, Volume 2, 1974, Volume 4, 1975, Volume 11, 1979, Volume 19, 1981.
Dictionary of Literary Biography, Volume 20: *British Poets, 1914-1945,* Gale, 1983.
Glen, Duncan, *Hugh MacDiarmid (Christopher Murray Grieve) and the Scottish Renaissance,* Chambers (Edinburgh), 1964.
Glen, Duncan, editor, *Hugh MacDiarmid: A Critical Survey,* Scottish Academic Press, 1972.
Poems Addressed to Hugh MacDiarmid (festschrift), edited by Duncan Glen, Akros, 1967.
Scott, P. C., and A. C. Davis, editors, *The Age of MacDiarmid: Essays on Hugh MacDiarmid and His Influence on Contemporary Scotland,* Mainstream, 1980.

PERIODICALS

Agenda (special MacDiarmid double number), autumn-winter, 1967-68.
Books Abroad, summer, 1967.
Harper's, August, 1967.
Irish Statesman, January 8, 1927.
Listener, August 10, 1967.
Nation, June 5, 1967.
New York Times Book Review, June 25, 1967.
Observer, August 13, 1967.
Poetry, July, 1948.
Punch, July 19, 1967.
Scottish Field, August, 1962.
Times Literary Supplement, December 31, 1964, August 24, 1967.

*   *   *

GRIGSON, Geoffrey (Edward Harvey) 1905-1985

PERSONAL: Born March 2, 1905, in Pelynt, Cornwall, England; died November 28, 1985; son of William Shuckforth (a canon) and Mary (Boldero) Grigson; married Frances Galt, 1929 (died, 1937); married Burta Kunert, 1938 (marriage dissolved); married Jane McIntire (a writer); children: (first marriage) one daughter; (second marriage) one son, one daughter; (third marriage) one son. *Education:* St. Edmund Hall, Oxford, graduated. *Politics:* Labour. *Religion:* None.

ADDRESSES: Home—Broad Town Farm, Broad Town, Swinton, Wiltshire, England. *Agent*—David Higham Associates, 5-8 Lower John St., London W1R 4HA, England.

CAREER: Poet and professional writer. After college became member of London staff of *Yorkshire Post;* in 1929 began working on *Morning Post,* London, became literary editor; founded and edited *New Verse,* 1933-39, an avant-garde poetry magazine which published early poems of Auden, MacNeice, Dylan Thomas, and others; had worked in publishing formerly in Talks Department of British Broadcasting Corp. and member of BBC Literary Advisory Committee.

AWARDS, HONORS: Duff Cooper Memorial Prize, 1971; Oscar Blumenthal Prize, 1971.

WRITINGS:

POETRY

Several Observations: Thirty-Five Poems, Cresset Press (London), 1939.
Under the Cliff and Other Poems, Routledge, 1943.
The Isles of Scilly and Other Poems, Routledge, 1946.
Legenda Suecana, privately printed, 1953.
The Collected Poems of Geoffrey Grigson: 1924-1962, Phoenix House (London), 1963.

A Skull in Salop and Other Poems, Dufour, 1967.
Ingestion of Ice-Cream and Other Poems, Macmillan, 1969.
Discoveries of Bones and Stones, and Other Poems, Macmillan, 1971.
Sad Grave of an Imperial Mongoose, Macmillan, 1973.
Angles and Circles and Other Poems, Gollancz, 1974.
The Fiesta and Other Poems, Secker & Warburg, 1978.
History of Him, Secker & Warburg, 1980.
Collected Poems, 1963-1980, Allison & Busby, 1982.
The Cornish Dancer and Other Poems, Secker & Warburg, 1983.
Montaigne's Tower and Other Poems, Secker & Warburg, 1984.
Persephone's Flowers and Other Poems, Secker & Warburg, 1986.

NONFICTION

Henry Moore, Penguin, 1943.
Wild Flowers in Britain, Hastings House, 1944.
Samuel Palmer: The Visionary Years, Kegan Paul, 1947.
English Romantic Art (catalogue prepared for an Arts Council of Great Britain Exhibition), [London], 1947.
An English Farmhouse and Its Neighbourhood, Parrish, 1948.
The Scilly Isles, with drawings and watercolors by Fred Uhlman, Elek, 1948, revised edition, Duckworth, 1977.
The Harp of Aeolus, and Other Essays on Art, Literature, and Nature, Routledge, 1948.
Places of the Mind (essays, some originally appeared in periodicals), Routledge & Kegan Paul, 1949.
Flowers of the Meadow, with illustrations by Robin Tanner, Penguin, 1950.
The Crest on the Silver: An Autobiography, Cresset, 1950.
Wessex, Collins, 1951.
A Master of Our Time: A Study of Wyndham Lewis, Methuen, 1951, reprinted, Gordon Press, 1989.
Essays from the Air (radio talks), Routledge & Kegan Paul, 1951.
West Country, Collins, 1951.
Gardenage; or, The Plants of Ninhursaga, Routledge & Kegan Paul, 1952.
(With Jean Cassou) *The Female Form in Painting,* Harcourt, 1953.
Freedom of the Parish, Phoenix House, 1954, reprinted, The Cornish Library, 1982.
Gerard Manley Hopkins, Longmans, for the British Council, 1955, revised edition, 1968.
The Englishman's Flora, Phoenix House, 1955, revised edition, 1975.
English Drawing from Samuel Cooper to Gwen John, Thames & Hudson, 1955.
The Shell Guide to Flowers of the Countryside (also see below), Phoenix House, 1955.
Jean Baptiste Camille Corot (Book-of-the-Month Club selection), Metropolitan Museum, 1956.
England, photographs by Edwin Smith, Thames & Hudson, 1957, Studio Publications, 1958.
(Author of commentary) Stevan Celebonovic, *Old Stone Age,* Philosophical Library, 1957.
(Author of commentary) Celebonovic, *The Living Rocks,* preface by Andre Maurois, translation by Joyce Emerson and Stanley Pococks, Philosophical Library, 1957.
Fossils, Insects, and Reptiles (also see below), Phoenix House, 1957.
The Painted Caves, Phoenix House, 1957.
Art Treasures of the British Museum, preface by Sir Thomas Kendrick, Abrams, 1957.
The Wiltshire Book, Thames & Hudson, 1957.
(Author of commentary) Henry Moore, *Heads, Figures and Ideas,* New York Graphic Society, 1958.

Looking and Finding and Reading and Investigating and Much Else (juvenile), drawings by Christopher Chamberlin, Phoenix House, 1958, reprinted, J. Baker, 1970.

Shell Guide to Trees and Shrubs (also see below), Phoenix House, 1958.

English Villages in Colour, Batsford, 1958.

A Herbal of All Sorts, Macmillan, 1959.

Shell Guide to Wild Life (also see below), Phoenix House, 1959.

English Excursions, Macmillan, 1959.

Samuel Palmer's Valley of Vision, Phoenix House, 1960.

Christopher Smart, Longmans, for the British Council, 1961.

The Shell Country Book, Phoenix House, 1962, Dent, 1973.

Poets in Their Pride, Phoenix House, 1962, Basic Books, 1964.

(With others) *The Shell Nature Book* (contains *The Shell Guide to Flowers of the Countryside, Fossils, Insects, and Reptiles, Shell Guide to Trees and Shrubs,* and *Shell Guide to Wild Life*), Basic Books, 1964.

The Shell Book of Roads, illustrated by David Gentleman, Ebury Press, 1964.

(With wife, Jane Grigson) *Shapes and Stories: A Book about Pictures* (juvenile), J. Baker, 1964, Vanguard, 1965.

The Shell Country Alphabet, M. Joseph, in association with George Rainbird, 1966.

(With J. Grigson) *Shapes and Adventures,* Marshbank, 1967, published as *More Shapes and Stories: A Book about Pictures,* Vanguard, 1967.

Ben Nicholson: Twelve New Works (brochure for exhibition), Marlborough Fine Art Ltd. and Marlborough New London Gallery, 1967.

Poems and Poets, Dufour, 1969.

Shapes and People: A Book about Pictures (juvenile), Vanguard, 1969.

Notes from an Odd Country, Macmillan, 1970.

Shapes and Creatures: A Book about Pictures (juvenile), Black, 1973.

The Contrary View: Glimpses of Fudge and Gold, Rowman & Littlefield, 1974.

A Dictionary of English Plant Names (and Some Products of Plants), Allen Lane, 1974.

Britain Observed: The Landscape through Artists' Eyes, Phaidon, 1975.

The Englishman's Flora, Hart-Davis MacGibbon, 1975.

The Goddess of Love: The Birth, Triumph, Death, and Return of Aphrodite, Constable, 1976, Stein & Day, 1977.

Twists of the Way, Mandeville, 1981.

Blessings, Kicks and Curses, Allison & Busby, 1982.

The Private Art: A Poetry Notebook, Allison & Busby, 1982.

Recollections: Mainly of Artists and Writers (memoir), Chatto & Windus, 1984.

(With J. Grigson) *Shapes, Animals and Special Creatures,* Vanguard, in press.

EDITOR

(With Denys Kilham Roberts, Gerald Gould, and John Lehmann) *The Year's Poetry,* John Lane, 1934.

(And author of introduction) *The Arts Today,* John Lane, 1935, reprinted, Kennikat, 1970.

(With Roberts) *The Year's Poetry, 1937-38,* John Lane, 1938.

New Verse: An Anthology (originally appeared in the first six years of the periodical *New Verse*), Faber, 1939.

(And author of introduction) *The Journals of George Sturt,* Cresset, 1941.

The Romantics: An Anthology, Routledge, 1942, Granger, 1978.

Visionary Poems and Passages; or, The Poet's Eye, with original lithographs by John Craxton, F. Muller (London), 1944.

The Mint: A Miscellany of Literature, two volumes, Routledge, 1946-48.

Before the Romantics: An Anthology of the Enlightenment, Routledge, 1946, reprinted, Salamander, 1984.

Poetry of the Present: An Anthology of the Thirties and After, Phoenix House, 1949.

Poems of John Clare's Madness, Routledge & Kegan Paul, 1949, Harvard University Press, 1951.

(And author of introduction) William Barnes, *Selected Poems,* Harvard University Press, 1950 (published in England as *Selected Poems of William Barnes,* Routledge & Kegan Paul, 1950).

(And author of introduction) *Selected Poems of John Dryden,* Grey Walls Press (London), 1950.

(And author of introduction) George Crabbe, *Poems,* Grey Walls Press, 1950.

(And author of introduction) John Clare, *Selected Poems,* Routledge & Kegan Paul, 1950.

The Victorians: An Anthology, Routledge & Kegan Paul, 1950.

(And author of commentary) Robert John Thomton, *Temple of Flora,* Collins, 1951.

About Britain, thirteen volumes, Collins, 1951.

(And author of introduction) Samuel Taylor Coleridge, *Poems,* Grey Walls Press, 1951.

(With Charles Harvard Gibbs-Smith) *People, Places, and Things,* four volumes, Grosvenor Press, 1954, published as *People, Places, and Things,* Hawthorn, Volume I: *People,* 1954, 2nd edition, 1957, Volume II: *Places,* 1954, 2nd edition, 1957, Volume III: *Things,* 1954, 2nd edition, 1957, Volume IV: *Ideas,* 1954, 2nd edition, 1957.

The Three Kings: A Christmas Book of Carols, Poems, and Pieces, G. Fraser (Bedford), 1958.

The Cherry Tree: A Collection of Poems (juvenile), Vanguard, 1959.

Country Poems, Hutton, 1959.

The Concise Encyclopedia of Modern World Literature, Hawthorn, 1963, revised 2nd edition, 1970.

O Rare Mankind!: A Short Collection of Great Prose, Phoenix House, 1963.

Watter Savage Landor, *Poems,* Centaur Press, 1964, Southern Illinois University Press, 1965.

The English Year from Diaries and Letters, Oxford University Press, 1967, reprinted, 1984.

A Choice of William Morris's Verse, Faber, 1969.

A Choice of Thomas Hardy's Poems, Macmillan (London), 1969.

A Choice of Robert Southey's Verse, Faber, 1970.

Pennethorne Hughes, *Thirty-Eight Poems,* Baker, 1970.

(And author of introduction) *Faber Book of Popular Verse,* Faber, 1971, published as *Gambit Book of Popular Verse,* Gambit, 1971.

Rainbows, Fleas, and Flowers: A Nature Anthology Chosen by Geoffrey Grigson (juvenile), Baker, 1971, Vanguard, 1974.

Unrespectable Verse, Allen Lane, 1971.

The Faber Book of Love Poems: Love Expected, Love Begun, The Plagues of Loving, Love Continued, Absences, Doubts, Division, Love Renounced, and Love in Death, Faber, 1973, reprinted, 1983.

Poet to Poet: Charles Cotton, Penguin, 1975.

The Penguin Book of Ballads, Penguin, 1975.

The Faber Book of Epigrams and Epitaphs, Faber, 1977.

The Faber Book of Nonsense Verse, Faber, 1979.

The Oxford Book of Satirical Verse: Chosen by Geoffrey Grigson, Oxford University Press, 1980.

The Faber Book of Poems and Places, Faber, 1980.

The Faber Book of Reflective Verse, Faber, 1984.

AUTHOR OF INTRODUCTION

Francis Bacon, *Essays,* Oxford University Press, 1937.

Horse and Rider: Eight Centuries of Equestrian Paintings, Thames & Hudson, 1950.

R. B. Beckett, *John Constable and the Fishers,* Routledge Kegan Paul, 1952.

English Country: A Series of Illustrations, Batsford, 1952.

William Allingham's Diary, Centaur, 1967.

Faber Book of Poems and Places, Faber, 1980.

Thomas Tusset, *Five Hundred Points of Good Husbandry,* Oxford University Press, 1983.

Henry James, *A Little Tour in France,* Oxford University Press, 1984.

OTHER

Contributor to *New Statesman, Listener, Encounter, Times Literary Supplement, Guardian, Observer, Sunday Times, New York Review of Books,* and other periodicals.

SIDELIGHTS: The poet Geoffrey Grigson remained in Britain's literary forefront for half a century, though his poetry often received less recognition than his critical essays and numerous anthologies of others' works. As a critic Grigson established a considerable reputation in the 1930s, when he simultaneously edited his prestigious periodical *New Verse* and served as the literary editor of the conservative newspaper *Morning Post.* In both of these publications, and subsequently in the pages of the *Times Literary Supplement, New Statesman,* the *New York Review of Books* and other journals, Grigson reviewed with "a ferocity and personal animus foreign to the general, indulgent tone of modern criticism," according to a London *Times* reporter. In a *Times Literary Supplement* article, Samuel Hynes wrote of Grigson: "Every review is . . . a headlong charge with beaver down and lance at the ready, against the slackness, the wrong-headedness, the vulgarity, the un-Grigsonness of the rest of the world." In his later years, however, Grigson increased his output of published poetry, and Hynes noted: "If posterity, that shadowy reader, returns to Grigson, it will probably not be for his prose. The poetry has a better chance. . . . For Grigson belongs to the class of habitual poets, the kind who write poetry all the time, as other people write journals or diaries or letters, as a means of self-definition and self-sustenance, a way of arresting the daily losses that time exacts."

Grigson was born in Pelynt, Cornwall in 1905, when his father, a canon, was fifty-nine years old. Perceiving a distance between himself and his natural parents, the young Grigson adopted a surrogate mother named Bessie from amongst the Pelynt villagers, and she nurtured within him a delight for the Cornish landscape and for gardening. *Dictionary of Literary Biography* contributor Douglas Loney suggested that Grigson's love for the vicarage garden of his childhood became "the deepest foundation stone of his eclectic, observing, curious poetry. . . . The young Grigson had discovered that the nature which he so loved could be ordered by a careful and patient art and so could achieve a significance reaching beyond its own borders." At every opportunity throughout the years of schooling he called "long purgatory," Grigson escaped to favorite rural areas to observe wildlife and indulge in amateur archaeology. He then brought with him to Oxford University, Loney wrote, "an intense appreciation of the poetry of Herbert, Coleridge, and Hopkins, for the vigor of their poetic language and their stylistic discipline, for their romantic questing, for their insistence . . . on the immediate and the particular, on nature, and on nature's reflection of something rather more elusive, something of the spirit."

After graduating from Oxford, Grigson briefly held a position with the *Yorkshire Post,* writing short articles and book reviews. In 1929 he moved to the *Morning Post,* where he eventually became literary editor. Using the proceeds from the sales of review copies sent to the *Morning Post,* he founded *New Verse* in 1933. The avant-garde periodical, published for six years and never boasting a circulation greater than one thousand, achieved a prestige that far outstripped its modest dimensions. According to Loney, *New Verse* "made in its brief life an important contribution to letters, more perhaps in providing a forum for the works of some of England's finest young poets between the wars than for Grigson's attacks upon critics and authors who dared to disagree with him." Hynes conversely claimed: "In his early *New Verse* days, Grigson marred his achievement as an editor by abusing writers whose only offense was not to please him; *New Verse* was an extraordinarily good journal, and the editing of it was a heroic act, but what one remembers most clearly about it now is likely to be not the high quality of its verse, but the violence of its attacks." In retrospect, Grigson castigated himself for the venomous reviews he penned for *New Verse.* Loney has quoted the author as saying, "I had not grown up enough . . . to realize that the neck of a beheaded fool grows three more foolish heads. The fun and slaughter now make me, if I recall them, rather sick."

Even after he discontinued *New Verse* in 1939 and began to publish his own poetry in books, Grigson maintained his reputation as an assessor of literary works. Other critics welcomed his forthright approach. In the *Spectator,* Peter Levi wrote: "Grigson fulfills perfectly the most important function of a critic even if he muffs some of the others. That is, he extends the reader's range and understanding, he shows one new things, he points to what is alive." P. J. Kavanagh stated in the *Spectator:* "Geoffrey Grigson has been a figure of such general cultural utility, . . . for so long . . . that it is odd to realize that anyone who praises him acquires a large number of unseen enemies. . . . This is because, in his detestation of the false, the merely fashionable, he has never been able to resist putting the boot in or, if that metaphor is too inelegant, planting a poisoned dart in the tenderest place, and then twisting." In 1974 a *Times Literary Supplement* reviewer claimed: "It would he hard to point to any critic who has so successfully combined an educated traditional taste with an acute awareness of what is going on around him. He has never succumbed either to the ineptitudes of academic criticism or to the standards of the flea-market by which most contemporary verse is judged."

Though a London *Times* writer suggests that the bitter tone of Grigson's criticism "may have sprung partly from the comparative non-recognition of his poetry," Grigson's verse was widely, and generally favorably, reviewed. Hynes described the work as springing from a tradition of "quotidian poetry . . . the poetry of the small, the homely, the contingent, the low-voiced, the ordinary. . . . It is a private record, a self alone in the world: there is rarely another person present, not many poems are direct address, almost none are third person narratives. The observations are exact but reticent, visual but not descriptive, and though they are full of natural details, they are painterly rather than nature poems." A *Times Literary Supplement* reviewer likewise noted Grigson's "interest in small, compact, isolated objects" in poems where "the density is pared down by his finely-wrought verse to a set of clean, separate perceptions, half-lights and ambiguities dispelled by a fastening on silhouetted shapes." "Quirky Mr. Grigson certainly is," wrote another *Times Literary Supplement* critic, who explained: "he enjoys oddments and oddities, and he seems to feel and think in short, sharp bursts, so that his poems are moments of delight and of irritation, little scraps and brief petulances. His touch is surer with objects and creatures than it is with people, even in the love poems." Loney concluded of Grigson's verse: "Although he may find it impossible to affirm any lasting reality beyond that which his senses reveal, he continues to celebrate the fleeting graces which he observes in the objects and events surrounding him." Roger Garfitt offered a similar assessment in *London Magazine:* "Grigson is particularly good at catching moments of subjective illumination and relating them to precise backgrounds, so that they form a kind of critique and history of present times. . . . The result is a poetry, of positive humanism, a redoubt of humane sensibility."

Unimpressed by the British academic community, Grigson never sought to align himself with a university. He worked instead at preparing anthologies, writing nature books, editing art books and museum catalogues, and even publishing an occasional book for children. The author of a *Times Literary Supplement* profile wrote of Grigson's eclectic oeuvre: "Under the often considerable pressures of earning a living he has never given way to the temptations of middlebrow literary good fellowship." Hynes noted that although "it is the criticism that has made his reputation," the best of Grigson's work "has been written in celebration of pictures, of places, of artists, of moments of vision, of the star that the black seeds make in a halved pear." More than one critic commented on a "Grigson paradox," as Valentine Cunningham termed it in the *Times Literary Supplement.* Cunningham cited the "mix of literary naturalist and nature-watching poet-critic," while another *Times Literary Supplement* contributor, after listing the natural history topics common to Grigson's essays, commented: "It seems strange that this Geoffrey Grigson should live in the same skin with the writer of sharp reviews and often sharper letters to periodicals." Hynes expressed the hope that readers in the future would award more attention to the positive side of Grigson's work. "It is a sad irony," Hynes concluded, "that because he has been so quick to attack and condemn others, he should not be recognized in his essential role, as one of the true celebrators of what is."

BIOGRAPHICAL/CRITICAL SOURCES:

BOOKS

Contemporary Literary Criticism, Gale, Volume 7, 1977, Volume 39, 1986.
Dictionary of Literary Biography, Volume 27: *Poets of Great Britain and Ireland, 1945-1960,* Gale, 1984.
Grigson, Geoffrey, *The Crest on the Silver: An Autobiography,* Cresset, 1950.
Grigson, *Recollections: Mainly of Artists and Writers,* Chatto & Windus, 1984.
Scarfe, Francis, *Auden and After,* Routledge, 1942.
Thwaite, Anthony, *Poetry Today, 1960-1973,* British Council, 1973.

PERIODICALS

Books Abroad, winter, 1967.
Book Week, December 19, 1965.
Book World, March 17, 1968.
Christian Science Monitor, November 30, 1967.
Economist, February 8, 1969.
Encounter, May, 1975.
Harper's, July, 1963.
Listener, November 16, 1967.
London Magazine, June, 1967, February/March, 1975.
New Review, February, 1975.

New Statesman, July 21, 1967, February 2, 1969, May 15, 1970, March 14, 1975.
New York Times Book Review, January 7, 1968.
Observer, June 18, 1967.
Poetry, April, 1970.
Review, September 3, 1970.
Saturday Review, November 13, 1965.
Spectator, June 14, 1968, August 2, 1975, December 18, 1976, December 1, 1982, September 22, 1984.
Times (London), October 23, 1980, November 4, 1982, December 16, 1982, October 27, 1983, January 24, 1985.
Times Literary Supplement, December 7, 1962, December 12, 1963, August 10, 1967, October 10, 1967, November 30, 1967, December 21, 1967, March 13, 1969, July 31, 1969, December 4, 1969, September 4, 1970, November 30, 1970, February 4, 1972, June 1, 1973, April 19, 1974, July 25, 1975, November 10, 1978, September 12, 1980, January 16, 1981, May 28, 1982, October 22, 1982, February 11, 1983, December 14, 1984.

OBITUARIES:

PERIODICALS

Observer, December 1, 1985.
Times (London), November 30, 1985.
Times Literary Supplement, January 17, 1986.

[Sketch verified by wife, Jane Grigson]

* * *

GRIMBLE, Reverend Charles James
See ELIOT, T(homas) S(tearns)

* * *

GRIMES, Martha

PERSONAL: Born in Pittsburgh, Pa.; daughter of D. W. (a city attorney) and June (a hotel owner; maiden name, Dunnington) Grimes; divorced; children: Kent Van Holland. *Education:* University of Maryland, B.A., M.A.

ADDRESSES: Home—Silver Spring, Md. *Office*—Department of English, Montgomery College, Takoma and Fenton St., Takoma Park, Md. 20012.

CAREER: Instructor in English at University of Iowa, Iowa City; assistant professor of English at Frostburg State College, Frostburg, Md.; Montgomery College, Takoma Park, Md., professor of English, 1970—.

MEMBER: Authors Guild.

AWARDS, HONORS: Nero Wolfe Award for best mystery of the year from the Wolf Pack, 1983, for *The Anodyne Necklace.*

WRITINGS:

MYSTERY NOVELS

The Man With a Load of Mischief, Little, Brown, 1981.
The Old Fox Deceiv'd, Little, Brown, 1982.
The Anodyne Necklace, Little, Brown, 1983.
The Dirty Duck (also see below), Little, Brown, 1984.
The Jerusalem Inn (also see below), Little, Brown, 1984.
Help the Poor Struggler (also see below), Little, Brown, 1985.
The Deer Leap: A Richard Jury Mystery, Little, Brown, 1985.
I Am the Only Running Footman, Little, Brown, 1986.
Martha Grimes: The Dirty Duck, Help the Poor Struggler, Jerusalem Inn, Dell, 1986.

The Five Bells and Bladebone, Little, Brown, 1987.
The Old Silent, Little, Brown, 1989.
The Old Contemptibles, Little, Brown, 1991.

OTHER

Send Bygraves (a mystery in poems), Putnam, 1989.

SIDELIGHTS: Martha Grimes's mystery novels have prompted critics to commend the wit and elegance of her writing and to compare her work to that of such masters of the classic British detective story as Dorothy Sayers, Margery Allingham, Ngaio Marsh, and Agatha Christie. Unlike her celebrated predecessors, however, Grimes is an American rather than a native Briton and relies on frequent trips to England and knowledge gleaned from reading and research to supply her with materials from which to create her stories' settings and her characters' backgrounds and dialects.

Grimes's idea for her first novel was sparked by a British pub name, and she has continued in each subsequent novel to use a British pub as both the title and part of the setting. Grimes told *Washington Post* reporter Sarah Booth Conroy in 1983: "I remember vividly when I decided to write my first mystery. I had written a narrative poem and another novel, neither published. But in 1977, I was sitting in a Hot Shoppe in Bethesda [Maryland], looking at a book about English pub names, and I came across 'The Man With a Load of Mischief.' Suddenly I knew that's what I wanted to do: write books set in English pubs. . . . Now, unless I have the pub name first, I can't write the book." In addition to bearing the name of a pub, all of Grimes's novels feature as their main characters Richard Jury, a handsome, dedicated, sensitive, and urbane Scotland Yard detective; Jury's aristocratic, agreeable, yet dilettantish assistant, Melrose Plant, whom critics consider a literary descendant of Dorothy Sayers's Lord Peter Wimsey; and Plant's obnoxious, snobby, interfering, American-born Aunt Agatha.

Grimes's first detective novel concerns five murders in the English village of Long Piddleton. One of the murder victims is drowned in a keg of ale at the village pub called The Man With a Load of Mischief. In the course of his investigation into the Long Piddleton murders, Inspector Jury and the reader make the acquaintance of a number of eccentric villagers who are suspects in the case. According to Jean M. White, in her *Washington Post Book World* review of *The Man With a Load of Mischief,* the denouement of Grimes's "tangled plot" is "untidy." But White, who commented that Grimes "has learned her sleight-of-hand from Christie and delights in the rich characterization of Marsh," concluded that this untidiness was "a minor complaint for readers who value wit, atmosphere, and charm in their mysteries."

In Grimes's second novel, *The Old Fox Deceiv'd,* Jury solves a series of mysterious deaths and disappearances connected with the Crael family household. Set in a Yorkshire fishing village, the story opens with the discovery of a corpse wearing a costume from a Shakespearean play in an alley near the pub that gives this book its name. A *New Yorker* critic judged *The Old Fox Deceiv'd* "a pleasure from that classic start to its equally classic finish." White remarked that Grimes had improved upon the plot of her first novel and concluded: "This time Grimes has put it all together with a tidy plot with a clever twist, an assortment of fetching characters," and "sly wit and atmosphere." Charles Champlin, in his *Los Angeles Times Book Review* critique of *The Old Fox Deceiv'd,* deemed Grimes "a new and charming American disciple" of the classic detective novel genre whose writing "con-

firms that the spirit of Mmes. Christie, Allingham and Sayers . . . lives on."

In 1983 Grimes won the Nero Wolfe Award for best mystery of the year and garnered much critical acclaim for her third mystery, *The Anodyne Necklace.* The book's setting is divided between London's East End and the British village of Littleborne. Its plot centers on murders in both locations and their connection to a jewelry theft. Jury performs much of his detective work while watching gamesters play Wizards and Warlocks in the Littleborne pub called The Anodyne Necklace. *New York Times Book Review* critic Newgate Callendar noted that the plot of this book "is carefully structured, including the surprise ending." He considered Grimes to be "a superior writer who brings a strong touch of poetry to her imagery." White, reviewing *The Anodyne Necklace* in the *Washington Post Book World,* called attention to the eccentric villagers of Littleborne and the "marvelously alive characters" with which Grimes peoples London's East End, noting that Grimes's "rowdies are masters of communication in street jargon." White further remarked that Grimes possesses a "sharply observant eye for social comedy while offering sly detection" and deemed *The Anodyne Necklace* "a literate, witty, stylishly crafted mystery of detection in the finest British tradition." Callendar, however, qualified Grimes's part in this tradition, refuting the idea that Grimes is a "combination of Agatha Christie and Dorothy L. Sayers" and asserting that *The Anodyne Necklace* "is stamped with the author's own exquisite sensibility."

Callendar considered Grimes's next book, *The Dirty Duck,* to be "even better than 'The Anodyne Necklace.'" Commenting that "it is hard to overpraise this book," the critic described it as a "beautifully written" and "well-worked-out murder mystery with something of a surprise ending." White also praised Grimes's writing in *The Dirty Duck,* noting that the author "is in good form with her literate style and witty eye" and that she "could hardly miss" with the "assortment of colorful characters" portrayed in *The Dirty Duck.* Many of these characters, aside from the usual trio of Jury, Plant, and Plant's Aunt Agatha, are rich Americans touring Britain who are themselves the targets of a razor-brandishing murderer. One of the tourists, a computer buff, is determined to prove that Shakespeare was involved in the 1593 slaying of his literary rival Christopher Marlowe. Coincidentally, the murders, which take place in London and Stratford-on-Avon, home of Britain's Royal Shakespeare Theatre, are linked by quotations from Elizabethan poetry that the murderer leaves next to the victims' bodies. In the end, the controversy surrounding Marlowe's death, in conjunction with the killer's poetic clues, provides the key to the identity of the tourists' slayer.

The Jerusalem Inn, Grimes's fifth mystery, features a classic British mystery situation—the house party—and begins with aborted romance. While Jury spends the Christmas season with unpleasant relatives in the English countryside, he shares a poignant moment with a woman he meets in a graveyard. Before their acquaintance can develop, however, she is found murdered. Jury joins the investigation into the woman's death, but shortly thereafter another killing occurs in a nearby hall, where Jury's assistant, Plant, his Aunt Agatha, and their friend Vivian are staying as part of a holiday house party composed of eccentric, artsy aristocrats. Jury solves the two murder cases, which turn out to be connected, and does so in part through clues to the victims' past that he finds in the local Jerusalem Inn.

Help the Poor Struggler is a tale of revenge and child murder near Dorset, England. In this book Grimes introduces Brian Macalvie, a cynical, experienced chief constable with whom Jury must work to find the party responsible for a series of child killings. Macalvie, meeting Jury at a bleak, shabby pub called Help the Poor Struggler, aids Jury by linking the recent murders to one that occurred twenty years earlier and resulted in an erroneous murder conviction. According to a *Time* critic, the book is written with "a deadly earnest tone and a climactic burst of violence befitting its story of long-calculated revenge." Robert Barnard, reviewing *Help the Poor Struggler* in the *Washington Post Book World,* also noticed a shift towards solemnity in Grimes's tone and viewed it with favor, commenting: "The best thing about [Grimes's] early books is a Sayers-like boisterous humor, and it is odd to find that growing seriousness suits Grimes as it never did Sayers. Where Sayers became dull, Grimes takes on a new tautness and purpose." Barnard, an Englishman, also remarked that in *Help the Poor Struggler* Grimes fine-tuned her portrayals of English society, which, according to Barnard, had in earlier books been a "slight but disconcerting bit off-key, out of focus." Concluded Barnard: "There are still mistakes, often in dialogue . . ., but the feel is now right, the narrative confident and convincing. . . . One hopes that Martha Grimes' readership will grow so large that she can take a sabbatical year or two in Britain . . . and add that top layer of total confidence to her picture of British life."

Grimes told *CA:* "I like to tell stories—traditional English stories with a Scotland Yard superintendent. The only unusual thing about this is that I am an American."

BIOGRAPHICAL/CRITICAL SOURCES:

PERIODICALS

Armchair Detective, summer, 1985, spring, 1988.
Atlantic Monthly, February, 1985.
Chicago Tribune Book World, September 25, 1983.
Globe and Mail (Toronto), January 5, 1985, December 21, 1985.
Los Angeles Times, December 13, 1989.
Los Angeles Times Book Review, September 12, 1982, January 19, 1986.
New Yorker, September 20, 1982, August 22, 1983, June 18, 1984.
New York Times Book Review, September 25, 1983, May 13, 1984, March 17, 1985, September 29, 1985, January 26, 1986, September 13, 1987.
Time, July 15, 1985, February 24, 1986.
Washington Post, October 3, 1983.
Washington Post Book World, November 15, 1981, November 21, 1982, July 17, 1983, May 20, 1984, December 16, 1984, May 19, 1985.

*   *   *

GRIZZARD, Lewis (M., Jr.) 1946-

PERSONAL: Surname is pronounced "Griz-*zard*"; born October 20, 1946, in Columbus, Ga.; son of Lewis McDonald (a soldier, coach, and teacher) and Christine (a schoolteacher; maiden name, Word) Grizzard; married, July 17, 1966 (divorced, 1969); married Fay Rentz (divorced, 1976); married Kathy Taulman, February 10, 1979 (divorced, 1982). *Education:* University of Georgia, A.B.J., 1967.

ADDRESSES: Office—Atlanta *Journal* and Atlanta *Constitution,* 72 Marietta St., Atlanta, Ga. 30303; and Grizzard Enterprises, 2000 Riveredge Pkwy. N.W., Atlanta, Ga. 30328.

CAREER: Journal, Atlanta, Ga., 1968-70s, began as sportswriter, became executive sports editor; worked as free-lance writer, staff member of Atlanta *Constitution,* and sports editor

of Chicago *Sun-Times,* all in 1970s; columnist for Atlanta *Constitution* and Atlanta *Journal,* 1979—. Commentator for WSB-TV, 1980; owner of Grizzard Enterprises, Atlanta, 1980—. Actor in television programs, including "Designing Women," 1988.

WRITINGS:

Kathy Sue Loudermilk, I Love You (collected columns), Peachtree Publishers, 1979.
Won't You Come Home, Billy Bob Bailey? (collected columns), Peachtree Publishers, 1980.
Don't Sit under the Grits Tree with Anyone Else but Me (collected columns), Peachtree Publishers, 1981.
(With Loran Smith) *Glory! Glory! Georgia's 1980 Championship Season: The Inside Story,* Peachtree Publishers, 1981.
They Tore out My Heart and Stomped That Sucker Flat, Peachtree Publishers, 1982.
If Love Were Oil, I'd Be about a Quart Low: Lewis Grizzard on Women, Peachtree Publishers, 1983.
Elvis Is Dead and I Don't Feel So Good Myself, Peachtree Publishers, 1984.
Shoot Low, Boys—They're Ridin' Shetland Ponies: In Search of True Grit, Peachtree Publishers, 1985.
My Daddy Was a Pistol and I'm a Son of a Gun (biography), Villard Books, 1986.
When My Love Returns from the Ladies Room, Will I Be Too Old to Care? (collected columns), Villard Books, 1987.
Don't Bend over in the Garden, Granny, You Know Them Taters Got Eyes, Villard Books, 1988.
Lewis Grizzard on Fear of Flying: Avoid Pouting Pilots and Mechanics Named Bubba, Longstreet Press, 1989.
Lewis Grizzard's Advice to the Newly Wed . . . and the Newly Divorced: I Can't Remember the Names of My Ex-Wives: I Just Call Them Plaintiff, Longstreet Press, 1989.
Chili Dawgs Always Bark at Night, Villard Books, 1989.
If I Ever Get Back to Georgia, I'm Gonna Nail My Feet to the Ground, Villard Books, 1990.

Several of Grizzard's works, read by the author, have been recorded on audio cassette for Random House Sound Editions. Contributor to periodicals, including *TV Guide.*

SIDELIGHTS: Lewis Grizzard, who described himself in the *Washington Post* as "a quintessential southern male," is a columnist for the Atlanta *Constitution* and its sister newspaper, the Atlanta *Journal.* Though he had only limited experience as a writer when he began his column in the late 1970s, his popularity soon burgeoned, first in the South and then throughout the United States. By the late 1980s his commentaries were syndicated in hundreds of newspapers, he had speaking engagements nationwide, and his books appeared regularly on bestseller lists. Grizzard's writing, a mixture of humor, satire, and sentiment, focuses on the problems of day-to-day living and often draws on the author's life for material. In the *Post,* publishing executive Chuck Perry called Grizzard "a Faulkner for just plain folks," referring to the prize-winning novelist of Southern life. As Perry explained, Grizzard "strikes a chord common people feel every day."

Early in his career Grizzard was primarily an editor, but success in management left him personally unfulfilled. Executive sports editor of the Atlanta *Journal* when only twenty-three, he soon moved to Chicago as sports editor of the *Sun-Times.* At the age of thirty he was about to become managing editor, but he realized that he disliked the weather and the folkways of Chicago and that two divorces had left him feeling homesick for the South. He spoke to Jim Minter, the man who first hired him at the *Journal,* beseeching his former boss for a writing job. Minter offered a cut in pay and a sports column; Grizzard accepted and returned to Atlanta. He soon found sportswriting too formulaic, however, so he transformed the column by offering his personal opinions on life in general. "There's just not enough personal journalism any more," he lamented in the *Detroit News,* "where you can actually get a feel for the individual doing the writing."

Grizzard writes with a Southern accent, as his notorious book titles suggest. (His volume about sex is called *Don't Bend over in the Garden, Granny, You Know Them Taters Got Eyes.*) The author's public image, observed Art Harris of the *Post,* "is Confused '50s Man adrift in a post-60s world." In *Elvis Is Dead and I Don't Feel So Good Myself,* Grizzard uses the demise of Southern rock idol Elvis Presley as a symbol of his unhappiness with contemporary America. Presley seemed thrillingly rebellious to Grizzard and other teenagers in the more conservative America of the early 1960s, but by the time the singer died in 1977, overweight and in decline, America had changed greatly. "Here is one Baby Boomer who liked it better when it was simpler," Grizzard writes of himself in the book. "The everlasting dilemma facing me is that although I live in a new world, I was reared to live in the old one." He labels himself an "in-betweener."

Accordingly, Grizzard picks and chooses among the aspects of American society he will accept and those he will reject. "There's nothing I won't write about," he said in the *Detroit News.* "I don't have any sacred cows." He accepts the desire of many women to have a career, but says he still wants his wife to cook dinner sometimes—and not just in a microwave. Moreover, "I don't understand the gay movement," he writes in *Elvis Is Dead.* "I don't care if you make love to Nash Ramblers, as long as you're discreet about it." His opinions have outraged many readers, including feminists, gays, and ethnic minorities. When Grizzard wrote a column in defense of a man jailed for patting a woman's bottom, dozens of co-workers at the *Constitution* signed a petition against him. Nor is Grizzard a reliable friend to political conservatives, for he has questioned foes of abortion, television evangelists, and the National Rifle Association—he thinks animals should have guns. The author's ambiguous appeal is perhaps exemplified by his relationship to Andrew Young, who was elected Atlanta's second black mayor in 1981. Grizzard, who twitted the mayor regularly in his column, averred that he would do the same with anyone in Young's position of power. In turn Mayor Young, according to the *Chicago Tribune*'s Jim Spencer, "consider[ed] many of Grizzard's broadsides against him . . . to be racist." But in the *Post,* Young called his nemesis a "downright funny" man who "makes an art of poor-white-trash culture."

Grizzard's up-and-down relationships with women have become part of his legend. He has been married and divorced three times, most recently to Kathy Taulman, an ex-debutante who married him before he became famous. As he acknowledges, his third wife brought some style and sophistication to his down-home manner, improving his appearance and taking him to nightclubs in New York and Paris. Then he had open-heart surgery, they were divorced, and Grizzard wrote about his emotional and medical heart trouble in the book *They Tore out My Heart and Stomped That Sucker Flat.* His next volume, *If Love Were Oil, I'd Be about a Quart Low,* is specifically about women, and he discussed his marriages on national television. Taulman, suggesting she was the butt of too many Grizzard jokes, decided to write her own book. Her *How to Tame a Wild Bore and Other Facts of Life with Lewis,* which she published under the name Kathy Grizzard Schmook, was displayed beside her ex-husband's work in bookstores and was bought by interested

Grizzard fans. In his column Grizzard said her book "was at least based on the truth." Of her next book, an autobiography, Grizzard wrote, "I howled as I read [it], I cried and I missed her."

For in addition to the satirical edge that riles his detractors, Grizzard has an unabashedly sentimental side. He has been praised repeatedly for his ability to mix humor and tears, most notably in a memoir about his father, *My Daddy Was a Pistol and I'm a Son of a Gun.* Despite the book's boisterous title, it was apparently written with much pain. Grizzard's father and namesake was a career soldier who served in World War II, earning a Bronze Star, and again in Korea, where he escaped from behind enemy lines with the aid of a Communist Chinese defector. But the stress of war, Grizzard believes, destroyed his father's ability to cope with life. Not long after the Korean War, the elder Lewis became an alcoholic, divorced, and received a less-than-honorable discharge from the army. Grizzard saw little of his father for the remainder of his childhood, but later on, as the older man suffered the ravages of alcoholism, Grizzard provided what help he could. Grizzard's father died an untimely death in 1970, at the age of fifty-six.

In *My Daddy Was a Pistol* Grizzard circles between past and present, nostalgia and regret, often prompted by finding a memento or meeting one of his father's old acquaintances. The book makes clear that Grizzard loved his father deeply, despite the older man's flaws as a parent. "I cannot drink and talk about my father," Grizzard writes, "or I will cry"; but at the same time, he calls his father a hilarious observer of human foibles, whose sense of humor informs Grizzard's own writing. The *Tribune*'s Spencer called *My Daddy Was a Pistol* "a heartfelt and hardfelt look at unconditional love."

"It's beyond my wildest dreams what's happened to me," said Grizzard in the *News,* alluding to his widespread popularity. No longer an obscure sportswriter in a bachelor apartment, the author owns an ample home with a pickup truck and a Mercedes in the driveway. He has established a management company, Grizzard Enterprises, to coordinate his finances and public appearances. Throughout the 1980s his typical production was four columns every week and a book every year. While the *Tribune*'s Jack Hurst enjoyed Grizzard's 1987 offering—*When My Love Returns from the Ladies' Room, Will I Be Too Old to Care?*—he suggested that Grizzard should publish such collections of columns a little less often, selecting only the funniest. "A 'Best of Grizzard' no doubt would be hilarious from cover to cover," Hurst declared. " 'Half of Last Year's Grizzard,' however, is more of an impressive testament to the man's indefatigability." As Grizzard told the *News,* being productive isn't his most difficult task—"doing all this and trying to live your life is what's tough."

BIOGRAPHICAL/CRITICAL SOURCES:

BOOKS

Grizzard, Lewis, *They Tore out My Heart and Stomped That Sucker Flat,* Peachtree Publishers, 1982.

Grizzard, Lewis, *If Love Were Oil, I'd Be about a Quart Low: Lewis Grizzard on Women,* Peachtree Publishers, 1983.

Grizzard, Lewis, *Elvis Is Dead and I Don't Feel So Good Myself,* Peachtree Publishers, 1984.

Grizzard, Lewis, *My Daddy Was a Pistol and I'm a Son of a Gun,* Villard Books, 1986.

Schmook, Kathy Grizzard, *How to Tame a Wild Bore and Other Facts of Life with Lewis: The Semi-True Confessions of the Third Mrs. Grizzard,* Peachtree Publishers, 1986.

PERIODICALS

Chicago Tribune, October 16, 1986, November 10, 1987.
Detroit News, February 20, 1983, September 12, 1984.
New York Times, February 9, 1986, October 19, 1986, April 8, 1990.
Publishers Weekly, October 3, 1986.
Southern Living, August, 1985.
Washington Post, January 13, 1985, January 5, 1988.

*   *   *

GROSSMAN, Vasily (Semenovich) 1905-1964

PERSONAL: Some sources transliterate given name as Vasilii or Vassili and middle name as Semyonovich; born in 1905 in Berdichev, Ukraine, Russia (now U.S.S.R.); died of cancer, September 14, 1964, in Moscow, U.S.S.R.; son of Ekaterina Grossman. *Education:* Graduate of Moscow University (now Moscow M. V. Lomonosov State University).

CAREER: Industrial safety engineer and chemical engineer until 1934; professional writer, 1934-64; *Krasnaya zvezda* (military newspaper), Moscow, U.S.S.R., World War II correspondent, 1941-45.

MEMBER: Soviet Writers' Union (member of presidium, 1954-64).

AWARDS, HONORS: Received Banner of Labor decoration for his writings, 1955.

WRITINGS:

Rasskazy, Sovetskii Pisatel, 1937.
Stepan Kol'chugin (fiction), illustrations by V. Konovalova, Detizdat, 1937.
Yunost Kol'chugina, Detskaya Literatura, 1939, translation by Rosemary Edmonds published as *Kol'chugin's Youth,* Hutchinson International Authors, 1946.
Narod bessmerten (novel), Pravda, 1942, translation by Elizabeth Donnelly published as *The People Immortal,* Foreign Languages Publishing House, 1943, translation by Leo Lerman published as *No Beautiful Nights,* Messner, 1944.
Stalingrad: Sentyabr' 1942-yanvar' 1943 (title means "Stalingrad: September 1942-January 1943"), Sovetskii Pisatel, 1943.
With the Red Army in Poland and Byelorussia (First Byelorussian Front, June-July, 1944), translation from the Russian by Helen Altschuler, Hutchinson, 1945.
Gody voiny, Khudozhestvennaya Literatura, 1946, translation by Donnelly and Rose Prokofiev published as *The Years of War (1941-1945),* Foreign Languages Publishing House, 1946.
Povesti i rasskazy, Sovetskii Pisatel, 1950.
Za pravoe delo (novel), Voennoe, 1955.
Povesti, rasskazy, ocherki, introduction by F. Levin, Voennoe, 1958.
Staryi uchitel' (short stories), Sovetskii Pisatel, 1962.
Osenniaia buria (short stories), Sovetskii Pisatel, 1965.
Dobro vam! (short stories), Sovetskii Pisatel, 1967.
Vse techet (novel), Possev, 1970, translation by Thomas P. Whitney published as *Forever Flowing,* Harper, 1972.
(Editor with Ilya Ehrenburg) *Chernaia kniga: O zlodeiskom povsemestnom ubiistve evreev nemetsko-fashistskimi zakhvachikami vo vremenno-okkupirovannykh raionakh Sovetskogo Soiuza i v lageriakh unichtozheniia Pol'shi vo vremia voiny 1941-1945 gg.,* compiled by Margarita Aliger, Tarbut, 1980, translation by John Glad and James S. Levine published as *The Black Book: The Ruthless Murder of Jews by German-Fascist Invaders Throughout the Temporarily-Occupied Regions of the Soviet Union and in the Death Camps of Poland During the War of 1941-1945,* Holocaust Publications, 1981.
Zhizn' i sud'ba (novel), [Lausanne, Switzerland], 1980, translation by Robert Chandler published as *Life and Fate,* Harper, 1985.
Na evreiskie temy: Izbrannoe v dvukh tomakh, Aliia, 1985.

Also author of the novel *Glyukauf,* 1934, and the play "Esli verit' pifagoreitsam," 1946.

Contributor of sketches and short stories to periodicals, including *Krasnaya zvezda, Literaturnaya gazeta,* and *Novy mir.*

SIDELIGHTS: An esteemed member of the Soviet literary establishment for most of his career, author Vasily Grossman underwent a personal and artistic transformation toward the end of his life that caused his later writings to be censored by Soviet officials and, eventually, praised by Western readers. Before his change Grossman distinguished himself in the Soviet Union with his short stories, journalistic sketches, and epic novels that reflected the ideals of the Communist party and won the favor of Maxim Gorky, the father of the officially sanctioned form of Soviet literature, socialist realism. As a World War II correspondent Grossman was, "along with Ilya Ehrenburg, the most famous and best-loved journalist of the war years," according to literary historian Simon Markish in *Commentary.* In spite of this adulation, Grossman, a Russian-born Jew, became increasingly critical of his country when Joseph Stalin, the general secretary of the Communist party Central Committee, began to openly encourage anti-Semitism in the late 1940s. Because he identified more with his Russian than his Jewish heritage, Grossman did not fully appreciate Soviet discrimination against Jews until his Stalingrad war novel *Za pravoe delo* was attacked by party officials for its Jewish content. Facing probable deportation or execution in the early 1950s as a result of the book, Grossman was spared from both by the death of Stalin in 1953. Grossman subsequently abandoned his belief in the benevolence of the state and its rulers and spent his final years writing works critical of the country he once praised—works that remained unpublished when he died of cancer in 1964.

Western readers first learned of Grossman's work through the 1970 publication in West Germany of *Vse techet,* a novel published in 1972 in the United States as *Forever Flowing.* The book, which Grossman began writing in 1955 and revised during the last three and a half years of his life, tells the story of Ivan Grigoryevich's return to Moscow after spending thirty years in a Siberian labor camp. Ivan finds that in spite of their relative material prosperity, his friends are prisoners of the fear that they will be brutalized by Stalin's forces. As *New York Times* contributor Thomas Lask observed, Grossman painted a picture of the Soviet state under Stalin as "a rapacious, relentless, soul-crushing adversary—an enemy of the people." Grossman tied the emergence of the "soul-crushing" Soviet government to revolutionary Communist leader Nikolai Lenin—several critics felt this was the book's major achievement—and to the country's history of serfdom, which according to Grossman conditioned the Soviet people to enslavement. "Grossman is remarkable among Soviet writers for seeing [Stalinism] not as some kind of error in development or interruption of progress but as the essential culmination of the whole course of Russian history," a *Times Literary Supplement* reviewer noted, adding that Grossman "sees Stalin as the true successor of Lenin, and Lenin as the destroyer of the liberty which had become possible for the first time in 1917."

In 1985 Grossman's epic novel *Zhizn' i sud'ba,* a work hailed by many reviewers as his best, was published in English as *Life and Fate.* Depicting the lives of family members in Europe during World War II, *Life and Fate* focuses on the struggle for freedom amidst the similarly repressive regimes of Stalin and Hitler. Grossman submitted the book for official publication in 1960, but its open criticism of the Soviet Union's anti-Semitism caused the Communist party Central Committee to confiscate all copies of the novel along with Grossman's notes, outlines, and type-writer ribbon in 1961. A microfilm copy of the book was smuggled out of the country, however, and a Russian language edition was published in Switzerland in 1980. While the novel did much to familiarize the West with Grossman and the effects of Stalin-ism, not all the book's reviews were favorable. "Too many in the West have come to equate criticism of the Soviet regime with 'good' literature," W. Bruce Lincoln pointed out in *Chicago Tri-bune Book World,* adding that "too few of the novel's subplots rise above the level of the wartime newspaper reporting at which Grossman excelled." Saying that Grossman had written a work of "artistic witness" rather than a "work of art," Richard Eder complained in the *Los Angeles Times Book Review* that the "woodenness of many of Grossman's characters, and the flights of rhetoric, and sometimes sentimentality, that he engages in, are serious flaws."

On the other hand, some critics felt *Life and Fate* was good enough to merit comparison with Leo Tolstoy's *War and Peace.* John Bayley contended in his *London Review of Books* article that Grossman captured some of the inner spirit of Tolstoy, not-ing further that the "genius of both novelists appears in the com-pelling and spontaneous way they juxtapose the human and the non-human in scenes of swift unspoken analysis." Even several reviewers who thought the comparison between the two Russian authors was unjustified nonetheless agreed that Grossman's ex-periences from World War II and Stalinist Russia, reflected in *Life and Fate,* made the author an important historical witness. Ronald Hingley, for instance, wrote in the *New York Times Book Review* that translator Robert Chandler's "long labors have made available a work that substantially justifies his own de-scription of it as 'the most complete portrait of Stalinist Russia we have or are ever likely to have.' " In addition, *Washington Post Book World* contributor Fernanda Eberstadt reflected on the book's powerful theme: "Its great subject is human freedom, as exercised in those minute acts of 'senseless kindness' by which ordinary men and women wage war against the forces of enslave-ment, forces which are embodied in our own time by commu-nism, fascism, and their common scourge, anti-Semitism. Gross-man's excoriation of these evils is the more effective and the more ennobling for being clothed in a gently majestic humanism which renders this work not only an evocation of an era, but a novel for all time."

BIOGRAPHICAL/CRITICAL SOURCES:

BOOKS

Contemporary Literary Criticism, Volume 41, Gale, 1987.
Lipkin, Semen, *Stalingrad Vasiliia Grossmana,* Ardis, 1986.

PERIODICALS

Chicago Tribune Book World, March 23, 1986.
Commentary, April, 1986.
Encounter, December, 1986.
Globe and Mail (Toronto), March 29, 1986.
Harper's, March, 1986.
London Review of Books, September 19, 1985.
Los Angeles Times Book Review, March 30, 1986.
New York Times, April 1, 1972, May 12, 1982.
New York Times Book Review, March 26, 1972, March 14, 1982, March 9, 1986.
Times (London), December 19, 1985, November 27, 1986.
Times Literary Supplement, February 23, 1973, November 22, 1985.
Washington Post, April 12, 1972, December 11, 1987.
Washington Post Book World, April 6, 1986.

OBITUARIES:

PERIODICALS

New York Times, September 18, 1964.

*　　　*　　　*

GUARE, John 1938-

PERSONAL: Born February 5, 1938, in New York, N.Y.; son of Edward and Helen Claire (Grady) Guare; married Adele Chatfield-Taylor (an artist), May 20, 1981. *Education:* George-town University, A.B., 1961; Yale University, M.F.A., 1963.

ADDRESSES: Home—New York, N.Y. *Agent*—R. Andrew Boose, One Dag Hammarskjold Plaza, New York, N.Y. 10017.

CAREER: Playwright. Playwright-in-residence at New York Shakespeare festival, 1977; Yale University, New Haven, Conn., adjunct professor of playwriting, 1978-81. Member of board of directors, Municipal Arts Society of New York City. *Military service:* U.S. Air Force Reserve, 1963.

MEMBER: American Institute of Arts and Letters, Authors League of America, Dramatists Guild (member of board of di-rectors), Eugene O'Neill Playwrights' Conference (founding member).

AWARDS, HONORS: Obie Award, 1968, for "Muzeeka"; Obie Award as New York Drama Critics Most Promising Playwright, 1968-69, for "Cop-Out"; New York Drama Critics Circle Award for Best American Play, 1971, for "The House of Blue Leaves"; Outer Critics Circle Prize for playwriting, 1971; New York Drama Critics Circle Award for Best Musical of 1971-72, for "Two Gentlemen of Verona"; Antoinette Perry (Tony) Awards for Best Musical and for Best Libretto, 1972, for "Two Gentlemen of Verona"; Rockefeller grant in playwriting; Joseph Jefferson award for playwriting, 1977, for "Landscape of the Body"; Award of Merit for drama, American Academy of Arts and Letters, 1981; New York Film Critics Award, Los Angeles Film Critics Award, National Society of Film Critics Award, Venice Film Festival Grand Prize, and Academy Award nomi-nation for best original screenplay, all 1981, all for "Atlantic City"; New York Institute of the Humanities fellowship, 1982.

WRITINGS:

(Author of preface) *From Ibsen: Workshop,* Da Capo Press, 1978.

PLAYS

"Universe," first produced in New York, 1949.
"Did You Write My Name in the Snow?," first produced in New Haven, Conn., 1962.
"To Wally Pantoni, We Leave a Credenza," first produced in New York, 1964.
The Loveliest Afternoon of the Year [and] *Something I'll Tell You Tuesday* (both first produced Off-Off-Broadway at Cafe Cino, 1966), Dramatists Play Service, 1968.
Muzeeka and Other Plays: Cop-Out, Home Fires (includes "Muzeeka," first produced in Waterford, Conn., 1967, pro-

duced in New York, 1968, and "Cop-Out" and "Home Fires," both first produced in Waterford, 1968, produced in New York, 1969), Grove, 1969.

(Contributor) John Lahr, editor, *Showcase I: Plays from the Eugene O'Neill Foundation,* Grove, 1969.

"A Play by Brecht" (a musical based on Bertolt Brecht's "The Exception and the Rule"; music by Leonard Bernstein, lyrics by Stephen Sondheim), first produced on Broadway at Broadhurst Theatre, February 18, 1969.

(Contributor) *Off-Broadway Plays,* Volume I, Penguin (London), 1970.

Kissing Sweet [and] *A Day for Surprises: Two Short Plays* ("Kissing Sweet," first produced on television, 1969; "A Day for Surprises," first produced in London, 1971), Dramatists Play Service, 1970.

(With Milos Forman) *Taking Off* (screenplay; produced by Universal, 1971), New American Library, 1971.

"Un Pape a New York," first produced in Paris at Gaiete-Montparnasse, 1972.

The House of Blue Leaves (first produced Off-Broadway at Truck and Warehouse Theatre, February 10, 1971, produced on Broadway at Plymouth Theatre, October, 1986), Viking, 1972.

(With Mel Shapiro and Galt MacDermot) *Two Gentlemen of Verona* (based on Shakespeare's play; produced in New York at Delacorte Theatre, July 22, 1971; produced on Broadway at St. James Theatre, December 1, 1971), Holt, 1973.

Marco Polo Sings a Solo (first produced in Nantucket, Mass., at Cyrus Pierce Theatre, August 6, 1973, produced Off-Broadway at New York Shakespeare Festival Public Theatre, January 12, 1977), Dramatists Play Service, 1977.

(With Harold Stone) "Optimism; or, The Adventures of Candide" (based on Voltaire's novel *Candide*), produced in Waterford at Eugene O'Neill Foundation Theatre, September, 1973.

Rich and Famous (first produced Off-Broadway at Estelle Newman Public Theatre, February 19, 1976), Dramatists Play Service, 1977.

Landscape of the Body (first produced in Lake Forest, Ill., at Academy Festival Theatre, 1977, produced Off-Broadway at Shakespeare Festival Public Theatre, October 12, 1977), Dramatists Play Service, 1978.

Bosoms and Neglect (first produced Off-Broadway at Longacre Theatre, May 3, 1979, revised version produced in New Haven at Yale Repertory Theatre, October, 1979, and Off-Broadway at New York Theatre Workshop, April 8, 1986), Dramatists Play Service, 1979.

"In Fireworks Lie Secret Codes," first produced Off-Broadway at Mitzi E. Newhouse Theatre, March 5, 1981.

"Atlantic City" (screenplay), produced by Paramount Pictures, 1981.

"Lydie Breeze" (first play of a projected historical tetralogy), first produced in New York at American Place Theatre, February, 1982.

Gardenia (second play of a projected historical tetralogy; first produced in New York at Manhattan Theatre Club, April 28, 1982), Dramatists Play Service, 1982.

Three Exposures (collected plays, including "The House of Blue Leaves," "Bosoms and Neglect," and "Landscape of the Body"), Harcourt, 1982.

"Hey, Stay a While," produced in Chicago, Ill., at Goodman Theatre, 1984.

"Women and Water" (third play of a projected historical tetralogy), first produced in Washington, D.C., at Arena Stage, November 29, 1985.

(With Wendy Wasserstein, David Mamet, Maria Irene Fornes, Michael Weller, Samm-Art Williams, and Spalding Gray) "Orchards" (seven one-act plays based on stories by Anton Chekhov), first produced in New York at Lucille Lortel Theatre, April 22, 1986.

"Moon over Miami," first produced in New Haven at Yale Repertory Theatre, February, 1989.

"Six Degrees of Separation," first produced in London by the Royal Shakespeare Company, 1989, produced in New York at Lincoln Center Theatre, 1990.

SIDELIGHTS: John Guare has been called "the great romantic poet of contemporary American theatre" by Richard Christiansen in the *Chicago Tribune,* as well as "the world's oldest living promising young playwright," a line from one of Guare's own plays, which he now regrets having mentioned to a literal-minded interviewer. "Whatever you say about John Guare's preeminence among major American dramatists, he is by far the funniest," states *Los Angeles Times* writer Lawrence Christon. "There is an antic, unpredictable, indirect quality to his people, who are so self-absorbed that they're almost dreamlike, and fairly impervious to the ruin they generate around them."

Guare is that rare playwright who has never needed to make a living doing anything but his chosen work. He wrote his first play at age 11—and showed as much aptitude for promotion as he did for playwriting. Guare and a friend called *Life* magazine and said, "There are two boys putting on a play in a garage," and *Life* magazine hung up on them, recounts a *New York Times* article. So they called *Newsday,* a newspaper in Long Island, New York, and tried again: "There are two boys putting on a play in a garage and giving all the money to orphans." The newspaper promptly dispatched a photographer whose pictures of the youngsters' production ran in July of 1949.

Since then, Guare has solidly established himself as an award-winning playwright, although his works often open to mixed reviews, and sometimes are better received in revivals than in their original productions. His darkly humorous vision of modern America is reflected in such works as "The House of Blue Leaves" and "Bosoms and Neglect," both of which contain scenes of illness, slow death, and even murder. To *Dictionary of Literary Biography* writer Suzanne Dieckman, the "exploration of the desperate need for success is a major thematic preoccupation in [Guare's] work. Tracing the sources of this need through a tangled web of parent-child relationships, the media, literature, commercialized Catholicism, psychiatry, global politics, and a host of other contemporary fantasies, Guare creates a cartoon-like dramatic world that at its best is both agonizing and outrageously funny."

"The House of Blue Leaves" illustrates Dieckman's point. The play's protagonist is Artie, a zookeeper who yearns to sell his Tinpan Alley types of songs but instead must cope with an insane wife, a demanding girlfriend, and a son whose idea of rebellion is to kill the pope. Eventually, after one rejection too many, Artie kills his wife and retreats into a fantasy world. "This nightmarish farce appears to derive in part from Guare's relationship with his own parents; the play is autobiographical not only in inspiration but also in some of its details," Dieckman contends. "[The son's] story of his childhood humiliation . . . for instance, Guare claims to be 'an exact word-for-word' report of [his] own experience." However dark the comedy, the playwright "is not simply a prankster," notes Harold Clurman in a *Nation* review. "What motivates him is scorn for the fraudulence of our way of life. In *The House of Blue Leaves,* he has been aroused by the obsession with big shots, 'personalities,' stars, the 'in' tribe. That is a way of saying that we no longer see people as human beings; we worship 'names.' The imbecile, the villainous, the irredeemably mediocre possess glamour . . . if they have been sufficiently publicized."

"Bosoms and Neglect" is another in Guare's stable of black comedies, in this case dealing with a blind, cancer-ridden octogenarian whose last days are spent in verbal duels with her son, a middle-aged man called Scooper. While *New York Times* critic Mel Gussow diagnoses the play as having "theatrical schizophrenia" in its disjointed two acts, the reviewer also finds that "Bosoms and Neglect" "is more interesting than many other current plays." "Beneath its quirky surface, [the work] tells us that unrequited love between children and parents is potentially more catastrophic than it is between lovers," Christon says in another *Los Angeles Times* article. "But it also shows us how no moral or message or insight is enough to maintain the godawful slipperiness of our emotional equilibrium. With Guare the line between insanity and reason flickers like a hairline cut on an old film. That's what makes his comedy so special."

In 1982 Guare left the realm of modern times to begin a historical tetralogy. The first three plays of the tetralogy encompass a period in America from post-Civil War times to the turn of the century, and they examine the lives of a young woman, Lydie Breeze, and the three men who share her world. "Lydie Breeze," "Gardenia," and "Women and Water" are all set on Nantucket island, where the main characters attempt to form a utopian commune that disintegrates with jealousy and murder. "The imagery that runs through this frantic family history—disease, insanity, mutilation, death, decay, poisoned sex—is not new in [the author's] work, even though the period idiom is," Frank Rich points out in the *New York Times*. Rich has mixed reactions to Guare's efforts in "Lydie Breeze," calling the play "a literate ambitious experiment" that nonetheless has "luminous and savage theatrical bits [floating] within a murky, incorporeal whole."

To a *New Yorker* critic, "Lydie Breeze" has "an elaborate plot and contains a great deal of whizzing, cometlike dialogue, but it also has within it a great stillness, an immense silence, which amounts to a statement of reverence. (The stillness makes the play, full of action though it is, something like a painting. After it is over, it lives on in one's imagination as if it were a single object—or, rather, a still space with objects in it, a tableau.)" *Newsweek*'s Jack Kroll feels that Guare "has seized on the turn of the century as the pivotal moral moment in American history. He's taken the Ibsen-like themes of tainted blood and skeleton-stuffed closets and turned them into a Yankee Doodle Deadly saga of broken promises. Because he's John Guare, he has also had a lot of fun doing this. The glory of Guare is his unabashed (or perhaps abashed) romanticism, his bifocal vision of the tragic and the absurd, his natural instinct for the theatrical. It may be that the true contemporary form of tragedy is one that triggers a laugh as its proper response—a new kind of laugh, a slapstick sob at the Strangelovian nature of our fate."

The events in "Gardenia" take place twenty years before those dramatized in "Lydie Breeze," while "Women and Water" is set in an even earlier era, with Guare "trying to parallel the complex family saga with the Civil War itself," according to Gussow in his *New York Times* review. Gussow notes that "while it is intriguing to follow the continuing family chronicle . . . one cannot say that the journey has been overly enlightening, or that it has taken profitable advantage of [the author's] considerable talent as a playwright." Nevertheless, "even as the play makes its rocky crossing, there are moments that remind us of Mr. Guare's perceptive eye for physical detail . . . and for momentous emo-

tional disturbances. . . . After three plays, Lydie remains dramatically elusive, as [Guare] continues to aspire to be a playwright as architect." While Christiansen's praise for "Women and Water" is likewise measured, the *Chicago Tribune* critic finds it "thrilling indeed to see an artist of Guare's stature paint on such a broad canvas, to reach for the surge and sweep of man's history in a production that calls for all-out theatrical effects."

"Guare forces a critical review of all those aspects of society which drive people to live in fantasy instead of being honest with themselves and with each other," Dieckman concludes. "If his plays sometimes seem bogged down with the weight of too many words, too many ideas, they are themselves an accurate reflection of contemporary life—bombarded from all directions with information, dreams, and conflicting demands."

BIOGRAPHICAL/CRITICAL SOURCES:

BOOKS

Contemporary Literary Criticism, Gale, Volume VIII, 1978, Volume XIV, 1980, Volume XXIX, 1984.
Dasgupta, Guatam, *American Playwrights: A Critical Survey,* Volume I, Drama Book Specialists, 1981.
Dictionary of Literary Biography, Volume VII: *Twentieth-Century American Dramatists,* Gale, 1981.

PERIODICALS

Chicago Tribune, December 20, 1985.
Los Angeles Times, June 22, 1982, October 9, 1984, October 22, 1984, February 7, 1986.
Nation, March 1, 1971.
Newsweek, February 14, 1977, May 14, 1979, February 1, 1982.
New Yorker, February 14, 1977, October 24, 1977, March 15, 1982.
New York Times, March 7, 1971, May 4, 1979, October 14, 1979, December 7, 1979, May 29, 1981, February 21, 1982, February 25, 1982, April 29, 1982, May 2, 1982, May 9, 1984, December 8, 1985, March 16, 1986, March 20, 1986, April 6, 1986, April 9, 1986, April 13, 1986, April 23, 1986, April 9, 1988, February 24, 1989, May 18, 1989.
Saturday Review, November 20, 1973.
Village Voice, April 24, 1974, February 14, 1977, May 14, 1979.
Washington Post, May 31, 1984, January 17, 1986.

* * *

GUBAR, Susan (David) 1944-

PERSONAL: Born in 1944.

ADDRESSES: Office—Department of English, Indiana University, Bloomington, Ind. 47401.

CAREER: Associate professor of English at Indiana University, Bloomington.

AWARDS, HONORS: Joint nomination, with Sandra M. Gilbert, for outstanding book of criticism, National Book Critics Circle, 1979, for *The Madwoman in the Attic: The Woman Writer and the Nineteenth-Century Literary Imagination.*

WRITINGS:

(Editor and author of introduction with Sandra M. Gilbert) *Shakespeare's Sisters: Feminist Essays on Women Poets,* Indiana University Press, 1979.
(With Gilbert) *The Madwoman in the Attic: A Study of Women and the Nineteenth-Century Literary Imagination,* Yale University Press, 1979.

(Editor with Gilbert) *The Norton Anthology of Literature by Women: The Tradition in English,* Norton, 1985.

(With Gilbert) *No Man's Land: The Place of the Woman Writer in the Twentieth Century,* Yale University Press, Volume 1: *The War of the Words,* 1988, Volume 2: *Sexchanges,* 1989.

(Editor with Joan Hoff-Wilson) *For Adult Users Only: The Dilemma of Violent Pornography,* Indiana University Press, 1989.

SIDELIGHTS: In *The Madwoman in the Attic,* authors Susan Gubar and Sandra Gilbert argue that nineteenth-century women writers were forced to write within the confines of a male-dominated literary tradition. Artistic creativity, notes *Washington Post Book World*'s Carolyn G. Heilbrun, was viewed by men such as Gerard Manly Hopkins as "a male gift, a male quality," whereas it was believed that women suffered from literary sterility. Viewed as trespassers in the domain of male literary tradition, women who took up the pen risked being condemned as unfeminine. At the same time, female authors who attempted to defy or move away from the established male tradition were ridiculed as "lady novelists" or "female poetasters." Consequently, say the authors, women became fearful that they were incapable of true artistic expression and were angry because they were trapped within the patriarchal structure.

Repressing their rage and fear, women writers of the nineteenth century began to subvert the male tradition in which they were forced to write, clandestinely developing a literary style that was distinctly their own. A "socially acceptable" veneer, the authors maintain, concealed the deeper meanings in the works of great female writers, including Charlotte and Emily Bronte, Jane Austen, Mary Shelley, George Eliot, and Emily Dickinson. "Thus," writes Patricia Meyer Spacks in *Yale Review,* "the woman writer manages simultaneously to conform to and subvert patriarchal standards." What is more, says Heilbrun, the write often "revised male genres to record her own story in disguise." Her disguise was frequently that of an alter ego, or "madwoman," who acted upon the destructive impulses that the author could not permit herself or her heroine to manifest openly.

The scheming, strong-willed matrons in Jane Austen's books represent a defiant aspect of the author that contrasts sharply with her ostensibly submissive side. While Austen appears to advise young women to yield to male authority, in the words of *New York Times Book Review* critic LeAnne Schreiber, although "Austen may seem to be writing variations on 'The Taming of the Shrew' in her novels, . . . through her series of mad matriarchs she conveys the hidden message that the shrew is never really tamed." Like Austen, George Eliot appears to counsel acquiescence on the part of her young heroines. Gubar and Gilbert assert that Eliot was a "madwoman in the attic" who, by manipulating her plots, exacted vengeance on the male tyrants. And Dickinson, they suggest, more directly assumed the role of "madwoman" by feigning insanity so that she would be free to write her unorthodox poetry. "Even the most apparently conservative and decorous women writers," contend Gubar and Gilbert, "obsessively create fiercely independent characters who seek to destroy all the patriarchal structures which both their authors and their authors' submissive heroines seem to accept as inevitable."

New Leader's Phoebe Pettingell finds the authors's "close textual readings . . . insightful and valuable." Schreiber elaborates that in developing a "complex and compelling understanding of the subterfuges that have made the work of women such as Emily Bronte and Mary Shelley seem puzzling and odd," Gubar and Gilbert present "the first persuasive case for the existence of a distinctly female imagination." Heilbrun concurs, hailing *The Madwoman in the Attic* as "a pivotal book, one of those after which we will never think the same again."

BIOGRAPHICAL/CRITICAL SOURCES:

BOOKS

Gilbert, Sandra, and Susan Gubar, *The Madwoman in the Attic: A Study of Women and the Nineteenth-Century Literary Imagination,* Yale University Press, 1979.

PERIODICALS

Ms., January, 1986.
New Leader, February 25, 1980.
New York Times Book Review, December 9, 1979.
Washington Post Book World, November 25, 1979.
Yale Review, winter, 1980.

*   *   *

GUEST, Judith (Ann) 1936-

PERSONAL: Born March 29, 1936, in Detroit, Mich.; daughter of Harry Reginald (a business person) and Marion Aline (Nesbit) Guest; married husband, Larry (a data processing executive), August 22, 1958; children: Larry, John, Richard. *Education:* University of Michigan, B.A., 1958.

ADDRESSES: Home—4600 West 44th St., Edina, Minn. 55424.

CAREER: Writer. Employed as a teacher in public schools in Birmingham, Mich., 1959-60 and 1969, Royal Oak, Mich., 1964 and 1969-70, and Troy, Mich., 1974-75.

MEMBER: P.E.N. American Center, Authors Guild, Detroit Women Writers.

AWARDS, HONORS: Janet Heidinger Kafka Prize from University of Rochester, 1977, for *Ordinary People.*

WRITINGS:

NOVELS

Ordinary People (Book-of-the-Month Club selection), Viking, 1976.
Second Heaven (Book-of-the-Month Club selection), Viking, 1982.
(With Rebecca Hill) *Killing Time in St. Cloud,* Delacorte, 1988.
"Rachel River" (screenplay based on stories by Carol Bly), Taurus Entertainment, 1989.

Also author of a screenplay adaptation of *Second Heaven.* Contributor to periodicals, including *The Writer, Palatine Press,* and *Arlington Heights Herald.*

WORK IN PROGRESS: Another novel, tentatively entitled *Errands;* two original screenplays.

SIDELIGHTS: Judith Guest is a popular novelist who achieved startling success with *Ordinary People,* her first book. Contrary to custom, Guest sent the manuscript to Viking Press without a preceding letter of inquiry and without the usual plot synopsis and outline that many publishing houses require. The manuscript was read by an editorial assistant who liked it well enough to send Guest a note of encouragement and pass the story along to her superiors for a second reading. Months passed. Then, in the summer of 1975, when Guest was in the midst of moving from Michigan to Minnesota, came the word she'd been waiting for: Viking would be "honored" to publish *Ordinary People,* the first unsolicited manuscript they had accepted in twenty-six years. Guest's book went on to become not only a best-selling novel—selected by four book clubs, serialized in *Redbook*, and sold to Ballantine for paperback rights for $635,000—but also an award-winning film that captured the 1980 Oscar for best movie of the year. Since that time, Guest has published another novel, *Second Heaven*, which also deals with family relationships and problems of communication.

The story of a teenage boy's journey from the brink of suicide back to mental health, *Ordinary People* shows the way that unexpected tragedy can destroy even the most secure of families. Seventeen-year-old Conrad Jarrett, son of a well-to-do tax lawyer, appears to have everything: looks, brains, manners, and a good relationship with his family. But when he survives a boating accident that kills his older brother, Conrad sinks into a severe depression, losing touch with his parents, teachers, friends, and just about everyone else in the outside world. His attempt to kill himself by slashing his wrists awakens his father to the depth of his problems, but it also cuts Conrad off from his mother—a compulsive perfectionist who believes that his bloody suicide attempt was intended as a punishment for her. With the help of his father and an understanding analyst, Conrad slowly regains his equilibrium. "Above all," writes *New York Review of Books* contributor Michael Wood, "he comes to accept his mother's apparent failure to forgive him for slashing his wrists, and his own failure to forgive her for not loving him more. It is true that she has now left his father, because he seemed to be cracking up under the strain of his concern for his son, but Conrad has learned 'that it is love, imperfect and unordered, that keeps them apart, even as it holds them somehow together.' "

"The form, the style of the novel dictate an ending more smooth than convincing," according to Melvin Maddocks in *Time*. "As a novelist who warns against the passion for safety and order that is no passion at all, Guest illustrates as well as describes the problem. She is neat and ordered, even at explaining that life is not neat and ordered." While *Newsweek*'s Walter Clemons agrees that *Ordinary People* "solves a little too patly some of the problems it raises," he also allows that "the feelings in the book are true and unforced. Guest has the valuable gift of making us like her characters; she has the rarer ability to move a toughened reviewer to tears." *Village Voice* contributor Irma Pascal Heldman also has high praise for the novel, writing that "Guest conveys with sensitivity a most private sense of life's personal experiences while respecting the reader's imagination and nurturing an aura of mystery. Without telling all, she illuminates the lives of 'ordinary people' with chilling insight."

Guest's insights into her male protagonist is particularly keen, according to several reviewers, including Lore Dickstein, who writes in the *New York Times Book Review:* "Guest portrays Conrad not only as if she has lived with him on a daily basis—which I sense may be true—but as if she has gotten into his head. The dialogue Conrad has with himself, his psychiatrist, his friends, his family, all rings true with adolescent anxiety. This is the small, hard kernel of brilliance in the novel." But while acknowledging that Guest's male characters are well defined, several reviewers believe that Beth, the mother, is not fully developed. "The mother's point of view, even though she is foremost in the men's lives, is barely articulated," writes Dorothea D. Braginsky in *Psychology Today*. "We come to know her only in dialogue with her husband and son, and through their portrayals of her. For some reason Guest has given her no voice, no platform for expression. We never discover what conflicts, fears and aspirations exist behind her cool, controlled facade."

Guest herself has expressed similar reservations about the character, telling a *Detroit News* contributor that Beth is "pretty enig-

matic in the novel. The reader might have been puzzled by her." But Guest also believes that Mary Tyler Moore's portrayal of Beth Jarrett in the film adaptation of the novel did much to clarify the character. "[Mary Tyler Moore] just knocks me out," Guest told John Blades in a *Chicago Tribune* interview. "She's a terrific actress, a very complex person, and she brought a complexity to the character that I wish I'd gotten into the book. I fought with that character for a long time, trying to get her to reveal herself, and I finally said this is the best I can do. When I saw Mary in the movie, I felt like she'd done it for me."

Guest was also pleased with the movie's ending, which was more inconclusive than the book's. "The more things get left open-ended the better," Guest told Blades. "If you tie everything into a neat little bow, people walk out of the theater and never give it another thought. If there's ambiguity, people think about it and talk about it." She believes director Robert Redford's sensitive presentation "leaves the viewer to his own conclusions," which is how it should be.

In 1982, Guest published *Second Heaven*, a novel that shares many of its predecessor's concerns. "Again, a damaged adolescent boy stands at the center of the story; again, the extent of his wounds will not be immediately apparent," notes Peter S. Prescott in *Newsweek*. "Again, two adults with problems of their own attempt to save the boy from cooperating in his own destruction." In an interview with former *Detroit Free Press* book editor Barbara Holliday, Guest reflects on her fascination with what she calls this "crucial" period known as adolescence: "It's a period of time . . . where people are very vulnerable and often don't have much experience to draw on as far as human relationships go. At the same time they are making some pretty heavy decisions, not necessarily physical but psychological decisions about how they're going to relate to people and how they're going to shape their lives. It seems to me that if you don't have sane sensible people around you to help, there's great potential for making irrevocable mistakes."

The way that signals can be misinterpreted, leading to a breakdown in communication between people who may care deeply for one another, is a theme of both her novels and a topic she handles well, according to novelist Anne Tyler. "[Guest] has a remarkable ability to show the unspoken in human relationships—the emotions either hidden or expressed so haltingly that they might as well be hidden, the heroic self-control that others may perceive as icy indifference," Tyler writes in the *Detroit News*.

In *Second Heaven* it is Gale Murray, abused son of a religiously fanatic father and an ineffectual mother, who hides his feelings behind a facade of apathy. After a brutal beating from his dad, Gale runs away from home, seeking shelter with Catherine (Cat) Holzmann, a recently divorced parent with problems of her own. When Gale's father tries to have his son institutionalized, Cat enlists the aid of Mike Atwood, a disenchanted lawyer, who is falling in love with Cat. He takes on the case largely as a favor to her. According to Norma Rosen in the *New York Times Book Review*, "Cat and Michael must transcend their personal griefs and limits in order to reach out for this rescue. In saving another's life they are on the way to saving their own."

Because of the story's clear delineation of good versus evil and its melodramatic courtroom conclusion, *Second Heaven* strikes some critics as contrived. "Everything in the book is so neat and polished; so precisely timed and calibrated," suggests *New York Times* reviewer Christopher Lehmann-Haupt, "the way the newly divorced people dovetail, conveniently providing a surrogate mother and a fatherly counselor for battered Gale Murray. . . . The reader continually gets the feeling that Mrs. Guest is working with plumb line and level and trowel to build her airtight perpendicular walls of plot development." Or, as Rosen puts it: "On the one hand there are the clear evils of control, rules, order. They are associated with inability to love, fanaticism, brutality. Clutter and lack of organization are good. . . . Yet in the context of the author's antineatness and anticontrol themes, the technique of the novel itself appears at times to he almost a subversion: the quick-march pace, the click-shot scenes, the sensible serviceable inner monologues unvaried in their rhythms."

While acknowledging the book's imperfections, Jonathan Yardley maintains in the *Washington Post* that "the virtues of 'Second Heaven' are manifold, and far more consequential than its few flaws. . . . Neither contrivance nor familiarity can disguise the skill and, most particularly, the sensitivity with which Guest tells her story. She is an extraordinarily perceptive observer of the minutiae of domestic life, and she writes about them with humor and affection." Concludes *Chicago Tribune Book World* contributor Harry Mark Petrakis: "By compassionately exploring the dilemmas in the lives of Michael, Catherine, and Gale, Judith Guest casts light on the problems we often endure in our own lives. That's what the art of storytelling and the craft of good writing are all about."

MEDIA ADAPTATIONS: Ordinary People was filmed by Paramount in 1980.

BIOGRAPHICAL/CRITICAL SOURCES:

BOOKS

Contemporary Literary Criticism, Gale, Volume 8, 1978, Volume 30, 1984.

PERIODICALS

Chicago Tribune, November 4, 1980.
Chicago Tribune Book World, October 3, 1982.
Detroit Free Press, October 7, 1982.
Detroit News, September 26, 1982, October 20, 1982.
Los Angeles Times, February 28, 1988, February 24, 1989.
Los Angeles Times Book Review, October 30, 1988.
Ms., December, 1982.
Newsweek, July 12, 1976, October 4, 1982.
New Yorker, July 19, 1976, November 22, 1982.
New York Review of Books, June 10, 1976.
New York Times, July 16, 1976, October 22, 1982, February 17, 1989.
New York Times Book Review, July 18, 1976, October 3, 1982.
Psychology Today, August, 1976.
Publishers Weekly, April 19, 1976.
Saturday Review, May 15, 1976.
Time, July 19, 1976, October 25, 1982.
Tribune Books, November 20, 1988.
Village Voice, July 19, 1976.
Washington Post, September 22, 1982, December 16, 1988.

*   *   *

GUIRALDES, Ricardo (Guillermo) 1886-1927

PERSONAL: Born in Buenos Aires, Argentina, February 13, 1886; died of Hodgkin's disease in Paris, France, October 8, 1927; son of Manuel Guiraldes (ranchowner); married Adelina del Carril, 1913. *Education:* Attended college courses in architecture and law.

CAREER: Writer. Co-founder of Editorial Proa (publishing house), Buenos Aires, Argentina.

AWARDS, HONORS: Gran Premio Nacional de la Literatura (Argentina) for *Don Segundo Sombra.*

WRITINGS:

El cencerro de cristal (title means "The Crystal Cowbell"; prose and poetry), 1915, reprinted, Losada (Buenos Aires), 1952.
Cuentos de muerte y de sangre (title means "Stories of Death and Blood"; short stories; also see below), 1915, reprinted, Losada, 1958.
Raucho: Momentos de una juventud contemporanea (title means "Raucho: Moments in a the Life of a Contemporary Youth"; novel), 1917, Centro Editor de America Latina (Buenos Aires), 1968.
Rosaura (novel; also see below), 1922, reprinted with prologue by Victoria Ocampo, Sudamericana (Buenos Aires), 1960.
Xaimaca (title means "Jamaica"; novel written as prose poem), 1923, reprinted, Losada, 1967.
Don Segundo Sombra (novel), Proa (Buenos Aires), 1926, reprinted with preliminary note by wife, Adelina del Carril, Losada, 1940, reprinted, G. Kraft (Buenos Aires), 1960, translation by Harriet de Onis of original Spanish edition published as *Don Segundo Sombra: Shadows on the Pampas,* introduction by Waldo Frank, Farrar & Rinehart, 1935, abridged Spanish edition edited by Ethel W. Plimpton and Maria T. Fernandez published under original title, Holt, 1945.
Poemas misticos (title means "Mystical Poems"), 1928, reprinted, Ricardo Guiraldes, 1969.
Poemas solitarios (title means "Solitary Poems"), edited by del Carril, Colon, 1928, reprinted, Ricardo Guiraldes, 1970.
Seis relatos con un poema de Alfonso Reyes y una fotografia (title means "Six Stories with a Poem by Alfonso Reyes and a Photograph"), Proa, 1929, reprinted, Perrot (Buenos Aires), 1957.
El sendero: Notas sobre mi evolucion espiritualista en vista de un futuro (title means "The Path: Notes on My Spriritual Evolution in Light of the Future"), Maestricht (The Netherlands), 1932, reprinted, Ricardo Guiraldes, 1977.
Cuentos de muerte y de sangre, seguidos de Aventuras grotescas y una trilogia cristiana (title means "Stories of Death and Blood followed by Grotesque Adventures and a Christian Trilogy"), Espasa-Calpe (Madrid), 1933, reprinted, Losada, 1978.
Rosaura (novela corta) y siete cuentos (title means "Rosaura (Short Novel) and Seven Stories"), Losada, 1952.
Obras completas (title means "Complete Works"), Emece, 1962.
Croquis, dibujos y poema de Ricardo Guiraldes: Obra inedita (title means "Sketches, Drawings and Poem by Ricardo Guiraldes: Unedited Works"), edited by del Carril, Ricardo Guiraldes (Buenos Aires), 1967.
El libro bravo, Ricardo Guiraldes, 1970.

Also author of *Pampa,* 1954. Contributor of short stories in English translation to numerous anthologies, including *Tales from the Argentine,* 1930, *The Golden Land,* edited by de Onis, 1948, and *Short Stories of Latin America,* edited by A. Torres-Rioseco, 1963. Founding editor, with Jorge Luis Borges and Pablo Rojas Paz, of *Proa* (Buenos Aires literary review), 1924-25.

SIDELIGHTS: "He was a wealthy man, son of a ranchowner, and knew how to combine his enthusiasm for contemporary French and German literature with an authentic if slightly exalted love for his native country." This was how Argentine poet, short story writer, and novelist Ricardo Guiraldes was described by Emir Rodriguez Monegal in his biography of another Argentine author entitled *Jorge Luis Borges: A Literary Biography.*

Borges was both Guiraldes's friend and his collaborator on the Buenos Aires literary review *Proa* but their friendship and collaboration came to an early end with Guiraldes's premature death at age forty-one. Shortly before he died, Guiraldes published what many consider his crowning achievement, *Don Segundo Sombra,* a novel that, according to Rodriguez Monegal's assessment, "was to make [Guiraldes] the most famous Argentine novelist of the first half of the century."

Guiraldes, like Borges and many of Argentina's most important authors of the early years of the twentieth century, felt a strong attraction for the new forms of literature being introduced in Europe at the time, but refused to abandon Argentine themes. Guiraldes was keenly aware of European ways and literature, having been taken on his first trip abroad when he was only two and having spoken fluent French and German along with his native Spanish since early childhood. In his early twenties, he took a two-year trip around the world, pausing to live in Europe for a while (Guiraldes is credited with introducing the Argentine tango to Parisian society). In between trips to Europe, Guiraldes spent most of his time on the family ranch, La Portena, located in the province of Buenos Aires.

Both European and Argentine influences were to be important throughout Guiraldes's short literary career. In 1915, his first two books were published: *El cencerro de cristal* (title means "The Glass Cowbell") and *Cuentos de muerte y sangre* (title means "Tales of Death and Blood"). Each of the two works seemed to represent one side in the dual nature of Guiraldes's background: the former, a book of poetry, showed a strong European influence, especially that of French symbolist poet Jules Laforgue; the latter was a collection of short stories of Argentine farm life. The same dichotomy can be seen unified in *Don Segundo Sombra:* although it is essentially a story of Argentine life (a fact that Guiraldes emphasized by using the rustic dialect of the gauchos to tell the story), it is written employing the techniques, including metaphors and synesthesia, Guiraldes learned from his avid reading of European literature.

In his *Spanish-American Literature: A History* Enrique Anderson-Imbert commented on how Guiraldes's choice of images converted the novel from being an expression of Argentine nationalism into an important work of Latin American fiction: "Even the most realistic details are doubly artistic: because they are chosen for their starkness and because of their evocative effect. Guiraldes combined the language spoken from birth by the Creoles with the language of the Creolist educated in European impressionism, expressionism, and ultraism. In spite of his realist dialogs, his folklore, his rural comparisons, his pampa dialect of cowhands and cattlemen, *Don Segundo Sombra* is an artistic novel." Ethel W. Plimpton and Maria T. Fernandez explained in the introductory notes to their edition of *Don Segundo Sombra* some of the evocative power of the Argentine's prose, calling the book "one of the finest examples of how rudimentary and primitive literary material can be transformed in the hands of a conscious artist. In it the two planes of crude yet beautiful reality and of poetic fancy intersect in a way that inevitably recalls *Don Quijote.*"

Along with comparisons to Cervantes's seventeenth-century masterpiece, *Don Segundo Sombra* has also been likened to a classic of U.S. literature, Mark Twain's *The Adventures of Huckleberry Finn.* In Waldo Frank's introduction to the English translation of Guiraldes's novel, the critic notes that both Guiraldes's and Twain's books concern the adventures of a young boy accompanied only by an older man from whom he learns a great deal. Frank also sees both books as dealing with the passing away of an era. *Don Segundo Sombra* is the tale of Fabio Caceres, a boy who runs away from the Buenos Aires home of his aunts to live with a gaucho named Don Segundo Sombra. Fabio recounts episodes in their five years together. The adventures cease when the boy discovers he is the illegitimate son of a wealthy landowner who has died and left him his estate. At this point, no longer needed, Don Segundo Sombra says good-bye to his friend.

The gaucho life Guiraldes described in the book was much like that of the American cowboy of the Old West. Gauchos were horsemen, many of mixed Spanish and Indian blood, who lived on the pampas, the fertile grassy plains that make up the middle-section of Argentina, and made their living off the cattle they raised. Through Caceres's commentary on gaucho life, Guiraldes is able to include a myriad of colorful details—including cockfights, dances, fairs, and knife duels—in his novel. As the *Don Segundo Sombra* was being published, the gauchos' picturesque form of life was starting to change, brought on by the laying of railroad tracks and the fencing of pasture land. Written in highly lyrical prose, the book became an evocation of the disappearing gaucho lifestyle. The reasons for the novel's popularity, according to Anderson-Imbert "were factors other than literary merits . . ., such as the nationalist feelings of the reader, the surprise of finding, in gaucho clothes, a metaphoric language fashionable in postwar literature, and a conception of the novel, also fashionable in those years, according to which the poetic tone was more important than the action and the characterization."

MEDIA ADAPTATIONS: Don Segundo Sombra was adapted by Augusto Roa Bastos for a film of the same title, 1968.

BIOGRAPHICAL/CRITICAL SOURCES:

BOOKS

Anderson-Imbert, Enrique, *Spanish-American Literature: A History,* Volume 2: *1910-1963,* 2nd edition revised and updated by Elaine Malley, Wayne State University Press, 1969.

Guiraldes, Ricardo, *Don Segundo Sombra: Shadows on the Pampas,* translation by Harriet de Onis, Farrar & Rinehart, 1935.

Plimpton, Ethel W. and Maria T. Fernandez, editors, Ricardo Guiraldes, *Don Segundo Sombra,* Holt, 1945.

Rodriguez Monegal, Emir, *Jorge Luis Borges: A Literary Biography,* Dutton, 1978.

—*Sketch by Marian Gonsior*

*　　*　　*

GUNN, Thom(son William) 1929-

PERSONAL: Born August 29, 1929, in Gravesend, England; son of Herbert Smith (a journalist) and Ann Charlotte (Thomson; a journalist) Gunn; unmarried. *Education:* Trinity College, Cambridge, B.A., 1953, M.A., 1958; attended Stanford University, 1954-55, 1956-58. *Religion:* Atheist.

ADDRESSES: Home—1216 Cole St., San Francisco, CA 94117.

CAREER: Lived in Paris, 1950, and Rome, 1953-54; resident of California since 1954, except for one year in San Antonio, Tex.; visited Berlin, 1960. University of California, Berkeley, 1958-66, began as lecturer, became associate professor of English, visiting lecturer, 1973—. Freelance writer, 1966—. *Military service:* British Army, National Service, 1948-50.

AWARDS, HONORS: Levinson Prize, 1955; Somerset Maugham Award, 1959; American Institute of Arts and Letters grant, 1964; National Institute and American Academy Awards in Literature, 1964; Rockefeller award, 1966; Guggenheim fellowship, 1971; W. H. Smith Award 1980; PEN/Los Angeles Prize for poetry, 1983, for *Passages of Joy;* Robert Kirsch Award, 1988, for body of work focused on the American West.

WRITINGS:

(Editor) *Poetry from Cambridge,* Fortune Press, 1953.
Thom Gunn (poetry), Fantasy Press, 1953.
Fighting Terms: A Selection, Fantasy Press, 1954, revised edition, Faber, 1962, original edition reprinted, Bancroft Press, 1983.
The Sense of Movement, Faber, 1957, University of Chicago Press, 1959.
My Sad Captains, and Other Poems (also see below), University of Chicago Press, 1961.
(With Ted Hughes) *Selected Poems,* Faber, 1962.
(Editor with Ted Hughes) *Five American Poets,* Faber, 1963.
A Geography, Stone Wall Press, 1966.
(With Ander Gunn) *Positives* (photographs by Ander Gunn; verse captions by Thom Gunn), Faber, 1966, University of Chicago Press, 1967.
Touch, Faber, 1967, University of Chicago Press, 1968.
The Garden of the Gods, Pym-Randall Press, 1968.
(Editor and author of introduction) Fulke Greville Brooke, *Selected Poems of Fulke Greville,* University of Chicago Press, 1968.
Poems, 1950-1966: A Selection, Faber, 1969.
The Explorers, R. Gilbertson, 1969.
The Fair in the Woods, Sycamore Press, 1969.
Sunlight, Albondocani Press, 1969.
Moly (also see below), Faber, 1971.
Moly [and] *My Sad Captains,* Farrar, Straus, 1973.
To the Air, David R. Godine, 1974.
(Editor) *Ben Jonson: Poems,* Penguin, 1974.
Jack Straw's Castle and Other Poems, Farrar, Straus, 1976.
Selected Poems 1950-1975, Farrar, Straus, 1979.
Talbot Road, Helikon Press, 1981.
The Passages of Joy, Farrar, Straus, 1982.
The Occasions of Poetry: Essays in Criticism and Autobiography, edited by Clive Wilmer, Farrar, Straus, 1982, expanded edition, North Point Press, 1985.
Lament, Doe Press, 1985.
Sidewalks, Albondocani Press, 1985.
The Hurtless Trees, Jordan Davies, 1986.
Night Sweats, R. Barth, 1987.
Undesirables, Pig Iron Press, 1988.

Also author of *Games of Chance,* 1982. Contributor of memoir to *My Cambridge,* 1977. Work represented in many anthologies, including: *Springtime,* edited by G. S. Fraser and I. Fletcher, Peter Owen, 1953, and *Mark in Time,* edited by R. Johnson and N. Harvey, Glide Publications, 1971. Poetry reviewer, *Yale Review,* 1958-64, and *London Magazine.* Contributor to *Encounter, New Statesman, Poetry, Times Literary Supplement,* and other publications.

SIDELIGHTS: An English poet long resident in California, Thom Gunn combines a respect for traditional poetic forms with an interest in popular topics, such as the Hell's Angels, LSD, and homosexuality. While Gunn wrote most of his early verses in iambic pentameter—a phase when his ambition was "to be the John Dunne of the twentieth century"—his more recent poems assume a variety of forms, including syllabic stanzas and free verse. The course of his development is recorded in *Selected Poems 1950-1975,* in which "the language begins as English and

progresses toward American," according to *Nation* reviewer Donald Hall.

Gunn told *CA* that students of his work should read Paul Giles's article "Landscapes of Repetition" in *Critical Quarterly.* He explained, "I find it valuable because he reads me as I would want to be read, i.e. taking my later books for themselves rather than in light of the earlier books." Of his personal life, he wrote in 1983, "I am a completely anonymous person—my life contains no events, and I lack any visible personality. My books are so commonplace that I was once mistaken for an antique hat-stand (and I was wearing no hat). I lack motivation, circumstances, viewpoints on vital subjects, and illuminating personal data." As this comment reveals, Gunn is known for his reticence—and irony.

In fact, Gunn's personal life—that of the radical nonconformist—is far more interesting than he claims. Born in England to a journalist with socialist sympathies, Gunn's early life was peripatetic; after his parents' divorce when he was nine, he traveled with his father to various assignments. Back in England, the family kept moving, evading German bombs. His early poetry, focused on the upheavals of war and the freedom of life on the road, was considered violent against the tradition of gentility maintained in the 1940s. The young Gunn felt more at home in California, where he studied poetry with Yvor Winters and lived with his homosexual lover. *Village Voice* contributor Mark Caldwell claims that Gunn's experiences have been notably less tame than his poems might suggest. "If he belongs to a nation it is San Francisco; or perhaps homosexuality is his country—but I do not find him pledging allegiance to anything except his own alert, unforgiving, skeptical independence," Hall observes in a *Los Angeles Times Book Review* piece about Gunn. Gunn's characteristic understatement about his life resurfaces in *The Occasions of Poetry: Essays in Criticism and Autobiography,* Ian Hamilton reports in the *Times Literary Supplement:* "The book's effort is to present the author as reflective and benign. We see him as fond and skilful explicator of Hardy and Fulke Greville, and as awed apprentice to Robert Duncan and William Carlos Williams."

Gunn's masterful fusion of "modern" and "traditional" elements has brought him critical acclaim. Writing in the *New York Times Book Review,* M. L. Rosenthal praises *Selected Poems 1950-1975,* noting that "Gunn has developed his craft so that by now even his freest compositions have a disciplined music." And, echoing this sentiment, *New York Review of Books* critic Stephen Spender suggests that the contradiction between the "conventional form" of Gunn's poems and their "often Californian 'with it' subject matter" is what distinguishes his work. Frank representations of violence, deviance, and the life of the counterculture based in San Francisco connect with "yesterday and tomorrow" in Gunn's art, remarks Charles Champlin of the *Los Angeles Times.* "It is," Spender elaborates, "as though A. E. Housman were dealing with the subject matter of *Howl,* or Tennyson were on the side of the Lotus Eaters."

In a *Poetry* article, Robert B. Shaw speculates that Gunn's fluctuation between metrical poems and free verse reflects an internal struggle: "On the one hand, the poet feels the attraction of a life ruled by traditional, even elitist values, and by purely individual preferences a private life in the classic sense, the pursuit of happiness. On the other hand, he feels a visionary impulse to shed his isolated individuality and merge with a larger whole." Commenting on the same tension in Gunn's work, Jay Parini notes in the *Massachusetts Review* that rule and energy (the two forces Winters once advised Gunn to keep in view), "potentially counterdestructive principles, exist everywhere in [Gunn's] work, not sapping the poems of their strength but creating a tensed climate of balanced opposition. Any poet worth thinking twice about possesses *at least* an energetic mind; but it is the harnessing of this energy which makes for excellence. In Gunn's work an apparently unlimited energy of vision finds, variously, the natural baoundaries which make expression—and clarity—possible."

Selected Poems 1950-1975 features examples of both metrical and free verse styles, prompting Rosenthal to conclude that it is "fortunate that American readers now have a single volume of Thom Gunn's selected poems. With their undemonstrative virtuosity, their slightly corrupt openness, their atmosphere of unfathomable secrets and their intimacy, so like that of a reticent friend who has something crucial to confess, these poems strike a chord at once insinuatingly familiar and infinitely alien."

Neither British nor American, Gunn resolutely evades easy classification, Hall observes in the *Los Angeles Times Book Review.* "The point is not legalities of citizenship (Gunn remains a resident alien, fitting a poet both domestic and estranged) but that he may not be labeled by nationality or anything else. His identity is his resistance to the limitations of identity. He belongs to uncertainty, exploration, movement and ongoingness. . . . Here is the man without conventional supports who refuses title and easychair, political party and national identity. For Gunn," who told *CA* "I join nothing," "affiliation seems a lie; change alone endures."

AVOCATIONAL INTERESTS: Reading, films, drinking.

BIOGRAPHICAL/CRITICAL SOURCES:

BOOKS

Bixby, George and Jack W. C. Hagstrom, *Thom Gunn: A Bibliography, 1940-78,* Rota (London), 1979.
Bold, Alan, *Thom Gunn and Ted Hughes,* Oliver & Boyd (Edinburgh), 1976.
Contemporary Literary Criticism, Gale, Volume 3, 1975, Volume 6, 1976, Volume 18, 1981, Volume 32, 1985.
Dictionary of Literary Biography, Volume 27: *Poets of Great Britain and Ireland, 1945-1960,* Gale, 1984.

Haffenden, John, editor, *Viewpoints: Poets in Conversation,* Faber, 1981.
King, P. R., *Nine Contemporary Poets: A Critical Introduction,* Methuen, 1979.

PERIODICALS

Book World, September 16, 1973.
British Book News, April, 1987.
Critical Quarterly, summer, 1987.
Encounter, January, 1983.
Guardian, September 1, 1961.
Listener, August 12, 1982.
London Review of Books, July 15, 1982.
Los Angeles Times, November 7, 1988.
Los Angeles Times Book Review, November 6, 1988.
Massachusetts Review, spring, 1982.
Nation, November 10, 1979.
New Statesman, October 6, 1961, August 13, 1982.
New York Review of Books, September 20, 1973.
New York Times Book Review, June 16, 1974, January 20, 1980.
Observer, July 10, 1988.
Poetry, August, 1958, May, 1974, September, 1975.
Saturday Review, June 1, 1961.
Sewanee Review, January, 1985.
Spectator, September 1, 1961.
Stand, spring, 1989.
Times Literary Supplement, September 29, 1961, January 1, 1967, October 5, 1967, April 24, 1969, April 16, 1971, August 30, 1974, July 23, 1982.
Village Voice, October 26, 1982.
World Literature Today, summer, 1986.

*   *   *

GUT, Gom
   See SIMENON, Georges (Jacques Christian)

*   *   *

GUTHRIE, Isobel
   See GRIEVE, C(hristopher) M(urray)

H

H. D.
See DOOLITTLE, Hilda

* * *

HAIG, Fenil
See FORD, Ford Madox

* * *

HAILEY, Arthur 1920-

PERSONAL: Born April 5, 1920, in Luton, England; immigrated to Canada, 1947, naturalized citizen (retaining British citizenship), 1952; son of George Wellington (a factory worker) and Elsie Mary (Wright) Hailey; married Joan Fishwick, 1944 (divorced, 1950); married Sheila Dunlop, July 28, 1951; children: (first marriage) Roger, John, Mark; (second marriage) Jane, Steven, Diane. *Education:* Attended elementary school in England. *Avocational interests:* Travel, reading, music, boat handling, fishing.

ADDRESSES: Home—Lyford Cay, P.O. Box N-7776, Nassau, Bahamas. *Office*—Seaway Authors Ltd., First Canadian Place-6000, P.O. 130, Toronto, Ontario, Canada M5X 1A4.

CAREER: Office boy in London, England, 1934-39; clerk in London, 1939; Maclean-Hunter Publishing Co., Toronto, Ontario, assistant editor of *Bus and Truck Transport,* 1947-49, editor, 1949-53; Trailmobile Canada Ltd., Toronto, sales promotion manager, 1953-56; full-time writer, 1956—. *Military service:* Royal Air Force, fighter pilot, 1939-47; served in Europe, the Middle East, and the Far East; became flight lieutenant.

MEMBER: Writers Guild of America, Authors League of America, Association of Canadian Television and Radio Artists (honorary life member), Lyford Cay Club (Bahamas).

AWARDS, HONORS: Gold medal of Canadian Council of Authors and Artists, 1956; Best Canadian Playwright Award, 1957 and 1958; Emmy Award, c. 1957, for "No Deadly Medicine"; Doubleday Canadian Prize Novel Award, 1962, for *In High Places;* gold medal of Commonwealth Club of California, 1968, for *Airport.*

WRITINGS:

NOVELS

(With John Castle) *Flight into Danger* (based on "Zero Hour!," film version of Hailey's television play "Flight into Danger" [also see below]), Souvenir Press (London), 1958, published as *Runway Zero Eight,* Doubleday, 1959.
The Final Diagnosis (based on his television play "No Deadly Medicine" [also see below]), Doubleday, 1959.
In High Places, Doubleday, 1962.
Hotel, Doubleday, 1965.
Airport, Doubleday, 1968.
Wheels, Doubleday, 1971.
The Moneychangers, Doubleday, 1975.
Overload, Doubleday, 1979.
Strong Medicine, Doubleday, 1984.
The Evening News, Doubleday, 1990.

OTHER

(With Hall Bartlett and John Champion) "Zero Hour!" (screenplay based on his television play "Flight into Danger"), Paramount, 1957.
Close-up on Writing for Television (collection of television plays), Doubleday, 1960.

Author of over twenty television plays, including "Flight into Danger," 1956, "No Deadly Medicine," 1957, and "Course for Collision," 1962, performed on numerous programs, including "Westinghouse Studio One," "Playhouse 90," and "Kraft Theatre."

All of Hailey's novels have appeared in foreign editions, and most have been published in as many as thirty-one languages.

MEDIA ADAPTATIONS: Films based on Hailey's novels include "The Young Doctors," based on *The Final Diagnosis,* United Artists, 1961, "Hotel," Warner Brothers, 1967, "Airport," Universal, 1969, "Wheels," Universal, 1977, "The Moneychangers," Paramount, 1977, and "Overload." In addition, the films "Airport 1975," "Airport 1977," and "Concorde—Airport 1979," although not based on Hailey's work, were produced as sequels to the original "Airport." *Strong Medicine* was produced as a mini-series.

SIDELIGHTS: Arthur Hailey's career as a professional writer began in 1955 when, on a business flight across Canada, he began to fantasize about what might happen if both the pilot and copilot suddenly became incapacitated—leaving him, a rather rusty World War II fighter pilot, the only person able to land the plane. It took Hailey just six evenings and two weekends to turn the daydream into his first television play, "Flight into Danger." Being unfamiliar with the conventions of television writing, he wrote the play in standard theatrical form without camera directions; and not knowing anyone in the TV industry, he simply mailed it to "Script Department, Canadian Broadcasting Corp." The play reached Nathan Cohen, script editor of CBC's "General Motors Theatre," who ironically noticed it amidst countless other unsolicited scripts precisely because of the peculiar style in which it was written. The initial broadcast on April 7, 1956, drew rave reviews and extraordinary viewer response; it was subsequently presented on networks in the United States and Great Britain where it was equally well received. Since then, Hailey's success as a writer for television and especially as a novelist has been phenomenal. He has had six consecutive best sellers, and several major motion pictures have been based on his books.

Strangely it is Hailey's success that has caused the most discourse among critics. In an attempt to explain the author's ability to turn out consistent best-sellers, some reviewers accuse him of writing "formula" or "programmed" novels, and others say that he sets out to write books that will make good films. Joseph McLellan outlines the supposed Hailey formula: "Start with something large and complicated, a business or institution that touches the lives of large numbers of people and is not fully understood by the public. Ideally, the subject should have a touch of glamour and some element of risk in its routine activities. The writer takes the reader inside this subject, letting him see it from various points of view and tossing in an occasional little sermon on public responsibilities. Numerous characters are formed out of available material (cardboard will do nicely) and they are set in motion by a series of crises, small, medium, and large, which illustrate the nature and particularly the weaknesses of the activity that is the real subject (in a sense the real hero) of the book." And yet, if there is a formula that Hailey follows, it seems to have little effect on his readers who flock to the bookstores at the mere hint of a press release from his publisher. As Peter Andrews puts it: "Hailey's novels are such genuine publishing events that to criticize them is like putting the slug on the Rockettes. It's not going to change anything. No sooner is his contract inked than mighty lumberjacks start to make their axes ring. Paperback houses and book clubs fairly whimper to give him money while the work is still in progress, and Ross Hunter calls up the old actors' home to begin casting his next blockbuster. At the publication party itself the last deviled egg is still to be consumed when his book busts through on the best-seller list."

Most criticism Hailey takes philosophically; he admits that he prefers good reviews to bad, but concedes that the critics have made a few good points. He does, however, take offense at the charge that he writes programmed fiction. In an interview with Ned Smith, Hailey says: "The word formula is used frequently in reviews and commentaries. And I react to it. Maybe oversensitively. But I feel that if the books I write are formulas, then why doesn't someone else take the same formula, if it's that evident? Well, it isn't a formula. As I see it, what I write is a cut, a profile of a section of the life and times in which we live. And just as some writers use a profile of an individual—one person—so I take a profile that involves the technology, the dilemmas, the shortcomings, the science of our time, and write about that." He is also quick to respond to those who accuse him of writing with the best-seller list in mind. He told Smith: "People say 'Hailey sets out to write, (a) a best seller, (b) something that

book clubs will want, (c) to sell to the movies.' But I really don't think of these things. I pick a subject that interests me, one that I think will interest readers. I try to find something with a fairly basic common denominator, but there has to be some chemistry in me that arouses interest and enthusiasm, because if I haven't that myself, I can't translate it to the reader over the three years that I'm working on a book. But I don't try to outguess the best-seller lists or book clubs or movies. Because you can't outguess them all, and if I tried it, I'd fall flat on my face."

No doubt the formula accusations stem from certain characteristics that are evident in all of Hailey's writing: the meticulous attention to detail, the multiple plots and subplots, and his penchant for choosing as subjects monolithic structures (a hotel, an airport, the automobile industry) about which most people know little, but with which they are unquestionably fascinated. Hailey's ability to research a subject with unusual vigor and tenacity has resulted in a group of books that truly take the reader into the hearts of these otherwise unapproachable institutions. Patricia MacManus, in a review of *Hotel*, says that the book "undoubtedly covers every department in the curriculum of Cornell's School of Hotel Administration." And she feels that there are "enough intersecting story-lines to keep even the most plot-addicted readers scurrying to stay abreast of the multi-layered goings-on at the St. Gregory, the fictitious New Orleans hostelry of *Hotel*." Robert Cromie writes that Hailey covers his subject in *Airport* with such great detail that the book is likely "to upset airline executives, managers of non-mythical airports, and perhaps the Federal agencies." Some of the sensitive areas include "the dangers inherent in too-short runways, the curtailing of power during the vital early stages of takeoff as a sop to nearby homeowners, the possibility that the easy availability of insurance at every major field may encourage bomb-for-profit schemes, the frantic efficiency which *usually* prevails in the radar room as traffic is supervised, and even the airlines' pregnancy plan for unwed stewardesses."

If there can be said to be a formula or pattern to Hailey's work, it is the now-famous system he has developed in order to garner the vast quantity of detail and technical information with which he packs his books. He spends about a year researching his subject, six months reviewing notes and planning, and eighteen months writing. While researching *Hotel*, he read twenty-seven books about hotels and twelve on New Orleans. At the same time he collected numerous clippings from hotel trade publications as well as those sent to him by his agent and friends. He studied five large hotels in depth (including a six-week stay as a paying guest at an old hotel in New Orleans), and twenty-eight smaller ones. During his research for *Airport*, Hailey spent hours in the airports of New York, Los Angeles, Chicago, Washington, D.C., Tampa, Toronto, Montreal, London, Paris, and Brussels, interviewing airport and airline employees and absorbing the atmosphere. Hailey's interviews with people inside an industry are noted for their relaxed nature; he carries no tape recorder and takes no notes. Instead he waits until after the session to record his impressions into a dictation machine for later transcription by his secretary. One especially noteworthy conversation yielded eight pages of single-spaced notes; he is, as he says, a bit precise. His writing technique is equally exacting. He is known to write six hundred words, more or less, per day, a rather small amount in comparison to many authors. Hailey's six hundred words, however, are ready for publication; he does his rewriting as he goes along, sometimes revising a paragraph as many as twenty times. Reports of his researching and writing methods have appeared in print so often that Hailey has begun to tire of having them presented as a set of unbreakable rules. He insists that he does not feel bound by this or any other system. Yet he is undeniably a careful planner and it is with this type of structured method that he works most effectively.

One facet of Hailey's craft that induces some agreement among the critics is his ability to weave an interesting tale. Frank Cameron, in an explanation of the author's rise to success, writes: "For one thing, no one has yet devised a satisfactory substitute for innate talent and Hailey is a born story teller. In this sense he is reminiscent of Somerset Maugham although without Maugham's urbanity of style. Hailey is Hailey. He has his own crisp style which has the twin virtues of economy and sustained suspense. A Hailey novel or a Hailey television play is meant to entertain. There is no emphasis on the introspective agonizing of any character. An obscure reference or bit of *avant-garde* rhetoric does not exist in his works. Moralizing he leaves to other writers unless he can weave it into his own story in ways that do not interrupt the plot and pace." Hailey told Patricia Farrell: "It is very obvious that people like reading facts as a background to fiction and this I try to do. It just seems that I happen to have the ability to do it, but I don't strive to be a proselytizer, a crusader, an educator, a consumer advocate; I'm none of those things. I'm a story teller and anything else is incidental."

BIOGRAPHICAL/CRITICAL SOURCES:

BOOKS

Bestsellers 90, Issue 3, Gale, 1990.
Contemporary Literary Criticism, Volume 5, Gale, 1976.
Dictionary of Literary Biography, Volume 88: *Canadian Writers, 1920-1959, Second Series,* Gale, 1989.
Dictionary of Literary Biography Yearbook, 1982, Gale, 1983.
Hailey, Sheila, *I Married a Bestseller,* Doubleday, 1978.

PERIODICALS

America, May 8, 1965, November 20, 1971.
American Way, July, 1975.
Best Sellers, February 15, 1965, April 1, 1968, October 15, 1971, April, 1975.
Booklist, March 1, 1965, April 15, 1968, November 15, 1971, April 15, 1975.
Books and Bookmen, May, 1965, September, 1975.
Book Week, January 24, 1965.
Book World, January 24, 1965, April 14, 1968.
Chicago Sunday Tribune, December 13, 1959.
Flying, May, 1968.
Kirkus Reviews, January 15, 1959, November 1, 1978.
Library Journal, March 1, 1962, March 1, 1968.
Miami Herald, June 1, 1975.
National Observer, April 1, 1968, November 6, 1971, May 3, 1975.
National Review, June 20, 1975.
New Republic, October 23, 1971.
New Statesman, July 4, 1975.
New Yorker, October 3, 1959, January 27, 1962.
New York Herald Tribune, October 18, 1959.
New York Times, April 5, 1959, April 20, 1968, July 28, 1975, December 18, 1978.
New York Times Book Review, September 20, 1959, February 21, 1965, April 7, 1968, September 19, 1971, May 18, 1975, February 11, 1979.
Observer, May 2, 1965.
Publishers Weekly, October 30, 1975.
San Francisco Chronicle, April 19, 1959, December 13, 1959, February 4, 1962.
Saturday Evening Post, November, 1975.
Time, March 26, 1965, March 22, 1968, October 11, 1971, April 14, 1975.
Wall Street Journal, September 21, 1971, March 20, 1975.
Washington Post, July 25, 1969, March 23, 1975.
Washington Post Book World, March 23, 1975, January 15, 1979.
Writer's Digest, August, 1972.
Writer's Yearbook, Number 39, 1967.

*   *   *

HALEY, Alex(ander Murray Palmer) 1921-

PERSONAL: Born August 11, 1921, in Ithaca, N.Y.; son of Simon Alexander (a professor) and Bertha George (a teacher; maiden name, Palmer) Haley; married Nannie Branch, 1941 (divorced, 1964); married Juliette Collins, 1964 (divorced); children: (first marriage) Lydia Ann, William Alexander; (second marriage) Cynthia Gertrude. *Education:* Attended Alcorn Agricultural & Mechanical College (now Alcorn State University); attended Elizabeth City Teachers College, 1937-39.

ADDRESSES: Office—Kinte Corporation, P.O. Box 3338, Beverly Hills, Calif. 90212.

CAREER: U.S. Coast Guard, 1939-59, retiring as chief journalist; free-lance writer, 1959—. Founder and president of Kinte Corporation, Los Angeles, Calif., 1972—. Script consultant for television miniseries "Roots," "Roots: The Next Generation," and "Palmerstown, U.S.A."; has lectured extensively and appeared frequently on radio and television; adviser to African American Heritage Association, Detroit, Mich.

MEMBER: Authors Guild, Society of Magazine Writers.

AWARDS, HONORS: Litt.D. from Simpson College, 1971, Howard University, 1974, Williams College, 1975, and Capitol University, 1975; honorary doctorate from Seaton Hill University, 1974; special citation from National Book Award committee, 1977, for *Roots;* special citation from Pulitzer Prize committee, 1977, for *Roots;* Spingarn Medal from NAACP, 1977; nominated to Black Filmmakers Hall of Fame, 1981, for producing "Palmerstown, U.S.A.," 1981.

WRITINGS:

(With Malcolm X) *The Autobiography of Malcolm X,* Grove, 1965.
Roots: The Saga of an American Family, Doubleday, 1976.
A Different Kind of Christmas, Doubleday, 1988.

Initiated "Playboy Interviews" feature for *Playboy,* 1962. Contributor to periodicals, including *Reader's Digest, New York Times Magazine, Harper's,* and *Atlantic.*

WORK IN PROGRESS: My Search for Roots, an account of how *Roots* was researched and written; a study of Henning, Tenn., where Haley was raised.

SIDELIGHTS: Haley's book *Roots* is seldom mentioned without the word "phenomenon" tacked on. Combined with the impact of the televised miniseries, *Roots* has become a "literary-television phenomenon" and a "sociological event," according to *Time.* By April, 1977, almost two million people had seen all or part of the first eight-episode sequence.

Although critics generally lauded Haley for his accomplishment, they seemed unsure whether to treat *Roots* as a novel or as a historical account. While it is based on factual events, the dialogue, thoughts, and emotions of the characters are fictionalized. Haley himself described the book as "faction," a mixture of fact and fiction. Most critics concurred and evaluated *Roots* as a blend of history and entertainment. And despite the fictional characterizations, Willie Lee Rose suggested in the *New York Review of Books* that Kunte Kinte's parents Omoro and Binte "could possibly become the African proto-parents of millions of Americans who are going to admire their dignity and grace." *Newsweek* found that Haley's decision to fictionalize was the right approach: "Instead of writing a scholarly monograph of little social impact, Haley has written a blockbuster in the best sense—a book that is bold in concept and ardent in execution, one that will reach millions of people and alter the way we see ourselves."

Some concern was voiced, especially at the time of the first television series, that racial tension in America would be aggravated by *Roots*. But while *Time* reported several incidents of racial violence following the telecast, it commented that "most observers thought that in the long term, *Roots* would improve race relations, particularly because of the televised version's profound impact on whites. . . . A broad consensus seemed to be emerging that *Roots* would spur black identity, and hence black pride, and eventually pay important dividends." Some black leaders viewed *Roots* "as the most important civil rights event since the 1965 march on Selma," according to *Time*. Vernon Jordan, executive director of the National Urban League, called it "the single most spectacular educational experience in race relations in America."

Haley has heard only positive comments from both blacks and whites. He told William Marmon in a *Time* interview: "The blacks who are buying books are not buying them to go out and fight someone, but because they want to know who they are. *Roots* is all of our stories. It's the same for me or any black. It's just a matter of filling in the blanks—which person, living in which village, going on what ship across the same ocean, slavery, emancipation, the struggle for freedom. . . . The white response is more complicated. But when you start talking about family, about lineage and ancestry, you are talking about every person on earth. We all have it; it's a great equalizer. . . . I think the book has touched a strong, subliminal cord."

But there was also concern, according to *Time*, that "breast-beating about the past may turn into a kind of escapism, distracting attention from the present. Only if *Roots* turns the anger at yesterday's slavery into anger at today's ghetto will it really matter." And James Baldwin wrote in the *New York Times Book Review:* "*Roots* is a study of continuities, of consequences, of how a people perpetuate themselves, how each generation helps to doom, or helps to liberate, the coming one—the action of love, or the effect of the absence of love, in time. It suggests, with great power, how each of us, however unconsciously, can't but be the vehicle of the history which has produced us. Well, we can perish in this vehicle, children, or we can move on up the road."

For months after the publication of *Roots* in October, 1976, Haley signed at least five hundred books daily, spoke to an average of six thousand people a day, and traveled round trip coast-to-coast at least once a week, according to *People*. Stardom took its toll on Haley. *New Times* reported that on a trip to his ancestral village in Africa, Haley complained: "You'll find that people who celebrate you will kill you. They forget you are blood and flesh and bone. I have had days and weeks and months of schedules where everything from my breakfast to my last waking moment was planned for me. . . . Someone has you by the arm and is moving you from room to room. Then people *grab* at you. You're actually pummeled—hit with books—and you ask yourself, My God, what *is* this?"

Although Haley now wishes that he were famous "one day a month," stardom was not always a problem. Upon retiring from the Coast Guard in 1959, he decided to become a free-lance writer and headed for Greenwich Village, rented a basement apartment, and "prepared to starve," as he told John F. Baker in a *Publishers Weekly* interview. Unwilling to take a job because he wanted to devote his full energies to writing, he came close to starving. "One day," he related to Baker, "I was down to 18 cents and a couple of cans of sardines, and that was *it*." The next day a check came for an article he had written and he struggled on. Today the 18 cents and sardine cans are framed and hang in the library of his home as symbols of his "determination to be independent."

MEDIA ADAPTATIONS: Roots was adapted as two television miniseries by American Broadcasting Companies (ABC), as "Roots," 1977, and "Roots: The Next Generation," 1979.

BIOGRAPHICAL/CRITICAL SOURCES:

BOOKS

Contemporary Literary Criticism, Gale, Volume 8, 1978, Volume 12, 1980.
Dictionary of Literary Biography, Volume 38: *Afro-American Writers After 1955: Dramatists and Prose Writers,* Gale, 1985.

PERIODICALS

Ebony, April, 1977.
Forbes, February 15, 1977.
Ms., February, 1977.
National Review, March 4, 1977.
New Republic, March 12, 1977.
Newsweek, September 27, 1976, February 14, 1977.
New Yorker, February 14, 1977.
New York Review of Books, November 11, 1976.
New York Times, October 14, 1976.
New York Times Book Review, September 26, 1976, January 2, 1977, February 27, 1977.
People, March 28, 1977.
Publishers Weekly, September 6, 1976.
Saturday Review, September 18, 1976.
Time, October 18, 1976, February 14, 1977.

*   *   *

HALL, Cameron
See del REY, Lester

*   *   *

HALL, Willis 1929-

PERSONAL: Born April 6, 1929, in Leeds, England; son of Walter (a fitter) and Gladys (Gomersal) Hall; married Valerie Shute, 1973; children: Peter, Macer, Daniel, James. *Education:* Educated in Leeds, England.

ADDRESSES: Home—64 Clarence Rd., St. Albans, Hertfordshire, England. *Agent*—London Management, 235-241 Regent St., London W1A 2JT, England.

CAREER: Writer. *Military service:* British Regular Army, 1947-52; served as radio playwright for Chinese Schools Department of Radio Malaya.

MEMBER: Garrick Club, Savage Club, Lansdowne Club.

AWARDS, HONORS: Drama award for play of the year from *Evening Standard,* 1959, for "The Long and the Short and the Tall."

WRITINGS:

(With I. O. Evans) *They Found the World* (juvenile), Warne, 1959.

A Glimpse of the Sea: Three Short Plays (contains "A Glimpse of the Sea," one-act, first produced in London, England, 1959; "The Last Day in Dreamland," one-act, first produced in London, 1959; and "Return to the Sea," television play, first broadcast in 1959), M. Evans, 1960.

The Royal Astrologers: Adventures of Father Mole-Cricket; or, The Malayan Legends (juvenile), Heinemann, 1960, Coward, 1962.

(With Michael Parkinson) *The A to Z of Soccer,* Pelham, 1970.

(With Bob Monkhouse) *The A to Z of Television,* Pelham, 1971.

My Sporting Life, Luscombe, 1975.

Incredible Kidnapping (juvenile), Heinemann, 1975.

The Last Vampire (juvenile), Bodley Head, 1982.

The Irish Adventures of Worzel Gummidge (juvenile), Severn House, 1984.

Dragon Days, illustrated by Alison Claire Darke, Bodley Head, 1985.

Also author of *The Summer of the Dinosaur,* 1977; *The Inflatable Shop,* 1984; *The Return of the Antelope,* 1985; *Spooky Rhymes,* 1987; *The Antelope Company at Large,* 1987; *Dr. Jekyll and Mr. Hollins,* 1988; and *Henry Hollins and the Dinosaur,* 1989.

PUBLISHED PLAYS

Final at Furnell (radio play; first broadcast in 1954), M. Evans, 1956.

The Long and the Short and the Tall (first produced in Edinburgh, Scotland, 1958; produced in London, England, 1959; produced in New York, N.Y., 1962; also see below), Heinemann, 1959, Theatre Arts, 1961.

(With Lewis Jones) *Poet and Pheasant* (radio play; first broadcast in 1955), Deane, 1959.

The Play of the Royal Astrologers (first produced in Birmingham, England, 1958; produced in London, 1968), Heinemann, 1960.

The Day's Beginning: An Easter Play, Heinemann, 1963.

The Gentle Knight (radio play; first broadcast in 1964), Blackie, 1966.

The Railwayman's New Clothes (television play; first broadcast in 1971), S. French, 1974.

Kidnapped at Christmas (first produced in London, 1975), Heinemann, 1975.

Walk On, Walk On (first produced in Liverpool, England, 1975), S. French, 1976.

A Right Christmas Caper (first produced in 1977), S. French, 1978.

Treasure Island (musical; based on novel by Robert Louis Stevenson; first produced in 1985), S. French, 1986.

Wind in the Willows (musical; based on story by Kenneth Grahame; first produced in 1985), S. French, 1986.

PUBLISHED PLAYS; WITH PETER WATERHOUSE

Billy Liar (adaptation of novel by Waterhouse; first produced in London, 1960; produced in New York, 1963; also see below), Norton, 1960.

Celebration: The Wedding and the Funeral (first produced in Nottingham, England, 1961; produced in London, 1961), M. Joseph, 1961.

England, Our England (musical; first produced in London, 1962), M. Evans, 1964.

The Sponge Room [and] *Squat Betty* (the former: one-act, first produced in Nottingham, 1962, produced in New York, 1964; the latter: one-act, first produced in London, 1962, produced in New York, 1964), M. Evans, 1963.

All Things Bright and Beautiful (first produced in Bristol, England, 1962; produced in London, 1962), M. Joseph, 1963.

Come Laughing Home (first produced as "They Called the Bastard Stephen" in Bristol, 1964; produced as "Come Laughing Home" in Wimbledon, England, 1965), M. Evans, 1965.

Say Who You Are (first produced in London, 1965), M. Evans, 1967, also published as *Help Stamp Out Marriage* (first produced in New York, 1966), S. French, 1966.

(Also translators) *Saturday, Sunday, Monday* (adaptation of a play by Eduardo de Filippo; first produced in London, 1973; produced in New York), Heinemann, 1974.

Who's Who (first produced in Coventry, England, 1971; produced in London, 1973), S. French, 1974.

Children's Day (first produced in Edinburgh, 1969; produced in London, 1969), S. French, 1975.

Worzel Gummidge (musical; adaptation of television series based on characters created by Barbara Euphan Todd; first produced in 1981; also see below), S. French, 1984.

UNPUBLISHED PLAYS

"Chin-Chin" (adaptation of play, "Tchin-Tchin," by Francois Billetdoux), first produced in London, 1960.

(With Robin Maugham) "Azouk" (adaptation of play by Alexandre Rivemale), first produced in Newcastle-Upon-Tyne, England, 1962.

(Co-author) "Yer What?" (revue), first produced in Nottingham, 1962.

"The Love Game" (adaptation of play by Marcel Archard), first produced in London, 1964.

(With Waterhouse) "Joey, Joey" (musical), first produced in London, 1966.

(With Waterhouse) "Whoops-a-Daisy," first produced in Nottingham, 1968.

(With Waterhouse) "The Card" (musical; adaptation of novel by Arnold Bennett), first produced in Bristol, 1973, produced in London, 1973.

"Christmas Crackers," first produced in London, 1976.

"Stag-Night," first produced in London, 1976.

"Filumena" (adaptation of work by de Filippo), first produced in 1977.

"The Water Babies" (musical; based on work by Charles Kingsley), first produced in 1987.

(With Waterhouse) "Budgie" (musical), first produced in 1989.

Author of screenplays, including: "The Long and the Short and the Tall," 1961; (with Waterhouse) "Whistle Down the Wind," 1961; (with Waterhouse) "A Kind of Loving," 1961; "The Valiant," 1962; (with Waterhouse) "Billy Liar" (adapted from novel by Waterhouse), 1963; "West Eleven," 1963; (with Waterhouse) "Man in the Middle," 1964; (with Waterhouse) "Pretty Polly," 1968; and "Lock Up Your Daughters," 1969.

Author of television plays, including: "Air Mail From Cyprus," 1958; "On the Night of the Murder," 1962; "By Endeavour Alone," 1963; (with Waterhouse) "Happy Moorings," 1963; "How Many Angels," 1964; "The Ticket," 1969; "They Don't All Open Men's Boutiques," 1972; "The Villa Maroc," 1972; "Song at Twilight," 1973; "Friendly Encounter," 1974; "The Piano-Smashers of the Golden Sun," 1974; "Illegal Approach," 1974; "Midgley," 1975; "Match-Fit," 1976; and "The Road to 1984."

Author of radio plays, including: "The Nightingale," 1954; "Furore at Furnell," 1955; "Frenzy at Furnell," 1955; "Friendly at Furnell," 1955; "Fluster at Furnell," 1955; "One Man Absent," 1955; "A Run for the Money," 1956; "Afternoon for Antigone," 1956; "The Long Years," 1956; "Any Dark Morning," 1956; "Feodor's Bride," 1956; "One Man Returns," 1956; "A Ride on the Donkeys," 1957; "The Calverdon Road Job," 1957; "Harvest the Sea," 1957; "Monday at Seven," 1957; "Annual Outing," 1958; "The Larford Lad," 1958; and (with Leslie Halward) "The Case of Walter Grimshaw," 1958.

Editor of books, including: (With Waterhouse) *Writers' Theatre,* Heinemann, 1967; (with Parkinson) *Football Report: An Anthology of Soccer,* Pelham, 1973; *Football Classified: An Anthology of Soccer,* Luscombe, 1975; and *Football Final,* Pelham, 1975.

Work represented in anthologies, including: Michael Barry, editor, *The Television Playwright: Ten Plays for BBC Television,* Hill & Wang, 1960; Stanley Richards, editor, *Modern Short Plays From Broadway and London,* Random House, 1969; John Foster, editor, *Drama Study Units,* Heinemann, 1975; and Alan Durband, editor, *Prompt Three,* Hutchinson, 1976.

Writer for television shows, including: "Inside George Webley," 1968; "Queenie's Castle," 1970; "Budgie," 1971-72; "The Upper Crusts," 1973; "Three's Company," 1973; "Billy Liar," 1973-74; "The Fuzz," 1977; "Worzel Gummidge," 1979; "The Danedyke Mystery," 1979; "Stan's Last Game," 1983; "The Bright Side," 1985; and "The Return of the Antelope," 1986.

* * *

HALLIDAY, Michael
   See CREASEY, John

* * *

HAMILTON, Clive
   See LEWIS, C(live) S(taples)

* * *

HAMILTON, Ernest
   See MERRIL, Judith

* * *

HAMILTON, Franklin
   See SILVERBERG, Robert

* * *

HAMILTON, Mollie
   See KAYE, M(ary) M(argaret)

* * *

HAMILTON, Virginia   1936-

PERSONAL: Born March 12, 1936, in Yellow Springs, Ohio; daughter of Kenneth James (a musician) and Etta Belle (Perry) Hamilton; married Arnold Adoff (an anthologist and author), March 19, 1960; children: Leigh Hamilton (daughter), Jaime Levi (son). *Education:* Studied at Antioch College, 1952-55, Ohio State University, 1957-58, and at New School for Social Research.

ADDRESSES: Home—Yellow Springs, Ohio. *Agent*—Dorothy Markinko, McIntosh & Otis, Inc., 475 Fifth Ave., New York, N.Y. 10017.

CAREER: "Every source of occupation imaginable, from singer to bookkeeper."

AWARDS, HONORS: Zeely appeared on the American Library Association's list of notable children's books of 1967 and received the Nancy Block Memorial Award of Downtown Community School Awards Committee, New York; Edgar Allan Poe Award for best juvenile mystery, 1969, for *The House of Dies Drear;* Ohioana Literary Award, 1969; John Newbery Honor Book Award, 1971, for *The Planet of Junior Brown;* Lewis Carroll Shelf Award, *Boston Globe-Horn Book* Award, 1974, John Newbery Medal and National Book Award, both 1975, all for *M. C. Higgins, the Great;* John Newbery Honor Book Award, Coretta Scott King Award, *Boston Globe-Horn Book* Award, and American Book Award nomination, all 1983, all for *Sweet Whispers, Brother Rush; Horn Book* Fanfare Award in fiction, 1985, for *A Little Love;* Coretta Scott King Award, *New York Times* Best Illustrated Children's Book Award, and *Horn Book* Honor List selection, all 1986, all for *The People Could Fly: American Black Folktales.*

WRITINGS:

(Editor) *The Writings of W. E. B. Du Bois,* Crowell, 1975.
The People Could Fly: American Black Folktales, Knopf, 1985, published with cassette, 1987.
In the Beginning: Creation Stories from around the World, Harcourt, 1988.

JUVENILE BIOGRAPHIES

W. E. B. Du Bois: A Biography, Crowell, 1972.
Paul Robeson: The Life and Times of a Free Black Man, Harper, 1974.
Anthony Burns: The Defeat and Triumph of a Fugitive Slave, Knopf, 1988.

JUVENILE NOVELS

Zeely, Macmillan, 1967, reprinted, 1986.
The House of Dies Drear, Macmillan, 1968, reprinted, 1985.
The Time-Ago Tales of Jahdu, Macmillan, 1969.
The Planet of Junior Brown, Macmillan, 1971, reprinted, 1986.
Time-Ago Lost: More Tales of Jahdu, illustrated by Ray Prather, Macmillan, 1973.
M. C. Higgins, the Great, Macmillan, 1974, published with teacher's guide by Lou Stanek, Dell, 1986.
Arilla Sun Down, Greenwillow, 1976.
Jahdu, pictures by Jerry Pinkney, Greenwillow, 1980.
Hugo Black: The Alabama Years, University of Alabama Press, 1982.
Sweet Whispers, Brother Rush, Philomel, 1982.
The Magical Adventures of Pretty Pearl, Harper, 1983.
Willie Bea and the Time the Martians Landed, Greenwillow, 1983.
A Little Love, Philomel, 1984.
Junius over Far, Harper, 1985.
The Mystery of Drear House, Greenwillow, 1987.
A White Romance, Philomel, 1987.

"JUSTICE" TRILOGY

Justice and Her Brothers, Greenwillow, 1978.
Dustland, Greenwillow, 1980.
The Gathering, Greenwillow, 1981.

ADAPTATIONS: The House of Dies Drear was adapted for the Public Broadcasting Service series "Wonderworks" in 1984.

SIDELIGHTS: Virginia Hamilton is one of the most prolific and influential authors of books about black children. In an essay published in *Children's Literature Review,* Rudine Sims names Hamilton, along with four other respected black authors, as one of today's foremost image-makers for black Americans. Hamilton is also recognized as a gifted and demanding storyteller. Ethel L. Heins, for example, writes in *Horn Book:* "Few writers of fiction for young people are as daring, inventive, and challenging to read—or to review—as Virginia Hamilton. Frankly making demands on her readers, she nevertheless expresses herself in a style essentially simple and concise."

Throughout her writing career, Hamilton has struggled "to find a certain form and content to express black literature as American literature and perpetuate a pedigree of American black literature for the young," she told Wendy Smith in the *Chicago Tribune Book World.* Her struggle has resulted in the creation of stories woven of elements of history, myth, and folklore. Although these elements are a reflection of her black heritage, Hamilton believes that they are also an essential part of American culture and should, therefore, be important to all Americans. In a *Horn Book* essay, Hamilton explains her subject matter this way: "What I am compelled to write can best be described as some essence of the dreams, lies, myths, and disasters befallen a clan of my blood relatives whose troubled footfall is first discernible on this North American continent some one hundred fifty years ago. . . . I claim the right (and an accompanying responsibility) by dint of genealogy to 'plumb the line' of soul and ancestry."

Hamilton's vision has been deeply influenced by her background. "Time, place, the hometown become almost mythical for me," she told the Children's Literature Association Conference, as reported by Marilyn Apseloff in *Children's Literature in Education.* Hamilton grew up in southern Ohio, where her family has lived for generations. As a result, "I see that locale through my eyes, my mother's eyes, and my grandmother's eyes," she commented to Apseloff. Hamilton absorbed the history and folklore of her people from reading books and magazines and listening to the stories told by her kin. She continues to celebrate this heritage in her own writing in an effort to counteract the "feeling that anything having to do with black history or culture is somehow humiliating, as if it were all part of slavery, and we don't want to deal with it," she told Smith.

In *Sweet Whispers, Brother Rush,* Hamilton uses the supernatural to illustrate how important an awareness of the past is in understanding the present. The book centers on Tree (short for Teresa), a teenager isolated from friends and school activities because she is responsible for caring for her brother Dab, who is stricken with a painful, debilitating illness. Tree and Dab have never known their father or any extended family; their mother Viola is a live-in nurse who comes home only occasionally to buy groceries and leave the children money. So when the ghost of Viola's brother appears, Tree, who has known "quiet for years, the way other children knew noise and lots of laughter," welcomes both his company and the opportunity to learn about her family's unfortunate past.

Interracial Books for Children Bulletin contributor Geraldine Wilson compares *Sweet Whispers, Brother Rush* to "a thoughtfully designed African American quilt." She elaborates: "It is finely stitched, tightly constructed and rooted in cultural authenticity. Hamilton uses humor that is sometimes finely wrought into a sharp pathos. She clips the fabric of tragedy, turning it into an arresting applique that makes her handling and revelation of human error, of human inability to cope, of tragedy, memorable."

Sweet Whispers, Brother Rush is written in dialect, and although several reviewers state that they had difficulty understanding the language, *New York Times Book Review* contributor Katherine Paterson believes it is one of Hamilton's more accessible books. She writes: "To the more timid reader, young or old, who may feel inadequate to Miss Hamilton's always demanding fiction, I say: Just read the first page, just the first paragraph, of 'Sweet Whispers, Brother Rush.' Then stop if you can."

One of Hamilton's most notable books is *M. C. Higgins, the Great,* recipient of several awards, including the National Book Award and the John Newbery Medal. The story portrays the Higginses, a close-knit family who reside on Sarah's Mountain in southern Ohio. The mountain has special significance to the Higginses, for it has belonged to their family since M. C.'s great-grandmother Sarah, an escaped slave, settled there. The conflict in the story arises when a hugh spoil heap, created by strip mining, threatens to engulf their home. M. C. is torn between his love for his home and his concern for his family's safety, and he searches diligently for a solution that will allow him to preserve both.

M. C. Higgins, the Great was highly praised by critics, including poet Nikki Giovanni, who writes in the *New York Times Book Review:* "Once again Virginia Hamilton creates a world and invites us in. 'M. C. Higgins, the Great' is not an adorable book, not a lived-happily-ever-after kind of story. It is warm, humane and hopeful and does what every book should do—creates characters with whom we can identify and for whom we care." Carol Vassallo expresses a similar opinion in *Children's Literature: Annual of the Modern Language Association Seminar on Children's Literature and the Children's Literature Association:* "The beauty of the writing, the poetic imagery, the characters, each unique yet completely believable, and the original themes all make the reading of this book an unforgettable experience, and mark Virginia Hamilton as one of the most important of today's writers for children."

Although black folklore and myth play important roles in all of Hamilton's books, *The People Could Fly: American Black Folktales* is devoted entirely to restoring this literary heritage. The book is comprised of animal fables, supernatural tales, and slave narratives—stories that "belong to all of us," Hamilton remarked to Wendy Smith in the *Chicago Tribune Book World.* The subtitle itself, Hamilton told Smith, is "a political statement." Her editor wanted to call the stories black American folktales; Hamilton, however, maintains that they are "American first and black second."

To give *The People Could Fly* a universal appeal, Hamilton tells the stories in simple dialect, and she uses "multiple voices to give American children, black and white, a sense of the richness and complexity of black culture," writes Smith. *The People Could Fly* was welcomed by critics because, as Ishmael Reed observes in the *New York Times Book Review,* it "makes these tales available to another generation of readers." Kristiana Gregory comments in the *Los Angeles Times Book Review:* "Told in easy-to-understand dialect, the stories echo the voices of fugitives and slaves, some of whom were the authors' ancestors. We are reminded of the deep sorrow and fears of an oppressed people, but also that the human spirit, however enslaved, still feels love and hope. It is this spirit Hamilton celebrates."

Since she began her writing career, Hamilton has had her books published consistently, but Rudine Sims believes that on the whole, publication of literature about black children is declining. In a guest essay for *Children's Literature Review* entitled "Children's Books about Blacks: A Mid-Eighties Status Report," Sims writes: "The heyday of publishing children's books about blacks is past. Since the mid-seventies, the number of available children's books dealing with black life has declined steadily." The conservatism of the eighties, maintains Sims in the *Christian Science Monitor,* has slowed publication of these books "to a trickle, and the list of black authors remains small."

Hamilton alludes to Sims's statement in the *Chicago Tribune Book World* interview with Smith, but she emphasizes what is, from her point of view, a more critical issue: distribution. Although Hamilton's books are written about black children, her books are more easily distributed, and thus sold, in white communities. Her solution, she told Smith, is to travel. "So I go out all over the country all the time; that's what you have to do. They may say black books are dead, but we keep proving they aren't by winning awards and doing whatever else we have to. That's what I'm committed to."

BIOGRAPHICAL/CRITICAL SOURCES:

BOOKS

Authors in the News, Volume 1, Gale, 1976.
Butler, Francelia, editor, *Children's Literature: Annual of the Modern Language Association Seminar on Children's Literature and the Children's Literature Association,* Volume 4, Temple University Press, 1975.
Children's Literature Review, Gale, Volume 1, 1976, Volume 8, 1985, Volume 11, 1986.
Contemporary Literary Criticism, Volume 26, Gale, 1983.
Dictionary of Literary Biography, Gale, Volume 33: *Afro-American Fiction Writers after 1955,* 1984, Volume 52: *American Writers for Children since 1960: Fiction,* 1986.
Hamilton, Virginia, *Sweet Whispers, Brother Rush,* Philomel, 1982.

PERIODICALS

Best Sellers, January, 1983.
Chicago Tribune Book World, November 10, 1985.
Children's Literature in Education, winter, 1983.
Christian Science Monitor, May 12, 1980, August 3, 1984.
Cincinnati Enquirer, January 5, 1975.
Horn Book, February, 1970, February, 1972, June, 1973, April, 1975, August, 1975, October, 1982, June, 1983.
Interracial Books for Children Bulletin, Numbers 1 and 2, 1983, Number 5, 1984.
Kirkus Reviews, July 1, 1974, April 1, 1983, October 1, 1985.
Library Journal, September 15, 1971.
Listener, November 6, 1975.
Los Angeles Times Book Review, March 23, 1986.
New York Times Book Review, October 13, 1968, September 22, 1974, December 22, 1974, December 17, 1978, May 4, 1980, September 27, 1981, November 14, 1982, September 4, 1983, November 10, 1985, November 8, 1987.
School Library Journal, April, 1983.
Times (London), November 20, 1986.
Times Literary Supplement, May 23, 1975, September 19, 1980, November 20, 1981, February 28, 1986, October 30-November 5, 1987, November 20-26, 1987.
Village Voice, December 14, 1975.
Washington Post Book World, November 10, 1974, November 11, 1979, September 14, 1980, November 7, 1982, November 10, 1985.

HAMMETT, (Samuel) Dashiell 1894-1961

PERSONAL: Born May 27, 1894, in St. Mary's County, Md.; died of lung cancer January 10, 1961; son of Richard Thomas (a farmer and politician) and Annie (Bond) Hammett; married Josephine Dolan, July 6, 1921 (separated, 1927; divorced, 1937); children: Mary Jane, Josephine. *Education:* Attended Baltimore Polytechnic Institute. *Politics:* Marxist.

ADDRESSES: Home—Katonah, N.Y.; and New York, N.Y.

CAREER: Writer. Worked as freight clerk, stevedore, timekeeper, yardman, and railroad worker; private detective with Pinkerton National Detective Agency, c. 1914-18 and 1919-21; Albert S. Samuels Jewelers, San Francisco, Calif., advertising copywriter, 1922-27; worked sporadically as screenwriter for various motion picture studios from 1930 until after World War II. Active in various left-wing organizations, beginning 1937; member of Civil Rights Congress, New York state president, 1946, national vice-chairman, 1948, New York state chairman, 1951; convicted and imprisoned for contempt of Congress, 1951. Jefferson School of Social Sciences, faculty member, 1946-47 and 1949-56, member of board of trustees, 1948. *Military service:* U.S. Army Ambulance Corps, 1918-19, became sergeant; U.S. Army Signal Corps, 1942-45, became sergeant.

WRITINGS:

Red Harvest (novel; serialized in *Black Mask,* 1927), Knopf, 1929, reprinted, J. Curley, 1983.
The Dain Curse (novel; based on Hammett's short story "The Scorched Face"), Knopf, 1929, reprinted, J. Curley, 1983.
The Maltese Falcon (novel), Knopf, 1930, reprinted, North Point Press, 1984.
The Glass Key (novel), Knopf, 1931, reprinted, Vintage Books, 1972.
(Editor) *Creeps by Night* (stories), John Day, 1931 (published in England as *Modern Tales of Horror,* Gollancz, 1932; selections published in England as *The Red Brain and Other Thrillers,* Belmont, 1961, and as *Breakdown and Other Thrillers,* New English Library, 1968).
The Thin Man (novel), Knopf, 1934, reprinted, Vintage Books, 1972.
Secret Agent X-9 (comic strip), McKay, 1934, reprinted, International Polygonics, 1983.
Dashiell Hammett Omnibus: "Red Harvest," "The Dain Curse," "The Maltese Falcon," Knopf, 1935.
The Complete Dashiell Hammett (contains *The Thin Man, The Glass Key, The Maltese Falcon,* and *Red Harvest*), Knopf, 1942.
$106,000 Blood Money (stories), Spivak, 1943, published as *Blood Money,* Dell, 1944, and as *The Big Knockover,* Jonathan Press, 1948.
"Watch on the Rhine" (screenplay; adapted from the play by Lillian Hellman), Warner Bros., 1943.
The Battle of the Aleutians (history), U.S. Army, 1944.
The Adventures of Sam Spade (stories), Spivak, 1944, published as *They Can Only Hang You Once,* Spivak, 1949.
The Continental Op (stories), Spivak, 1945, Franklin Library, 1984.
A Man Called Spade (stories), Dell, 1945.
The Return of the Continental Op (stories), Spivak, 1945.
Hammett Homicides (stories), Spivak, 1946.
Dead Yellow Women (stories), Spivak, 1947.
Nightmare Town (stories), Spivak, 1948.
Creeping Siamese (stories), Spivak, 1950.
Woman in the Dark (stories), Spivak, 1951, reprinted, Random House, 1989.

A Man Named Thin (stories), Ferman, 1962.
Novels (contains *Red Harvest, The Dain Curse, The Maltese Falcon, The Glass Key,* and *The Thin Man*), Knopf, 1965.
The Big Knockover (stories), edited by Lillian Hellman, Random House, 1966 (published in England as *The Dashiell Hammett Story Omnibus,* Cassell, 1966).
The Continental Op: More Stories From "The Big Knockover," Dell, 1967.
The Continental Op (stories; different from two collections above with same title), edited by Steven Marcus, Random House, 1974.

Works represented in numerous anthologies of detective fiction.

Contributor of stories and articles to more than thirty magazines, including *Black Mask, Smart Set, Brief Stories, True Detective Stories, Argosy All-Story Monthly, Saturday Review of Literature, Bookman, American Magazine, Collier's, Liberty, Redbook,* and *Ellery Queen's Mystery Magazine.*

SIDELIGHTS: Dashiell Hammett is widely considered the father of hard-boiled detective fiction. Along with those of Caroll John Daley, Hammett's stories in *Black Mask* magazine helped to bring about a major movement in detective fiction away from the genteel detectives solving crimes perpetrated by masterminds, to rough, believable private eyes dealing with common crooks. In the words of Raymond Chandler, "Hammett took murder out of the Venetian vase and dropped it into the alley! . . . Hammett gave murder back to the kind of people that commit it for reasons, not just to provide a corpse; and with the means at hand, not with hand-wrought duelling pistols, curare, and tropical fish."

Hammett's importance as a writer lies in his influence as an innovator, his impact as a stylist, and his skill in characterization. In 1948, Raymond Chandler wrote in a letter to fellow crime fiction writer Cleve F. Adams: "I did not invent the hard boiled murder story and I have never made any secret of my opinion that Hammett deserves most or all of the credit." Along with Chandler, Hammett is the most imitated writer of the genre. Erle Stanley Gardner declared: "I think of all the early pulp writers who contributed to the new format of the detective story, the word 'genius' was more nearly applicable to Hammett than to any of the rest. Unfortunately however, because Hammett's manner was so widely imitated it became the habit for the reviewers to refer to 'the Hammett School' as embracing the type of story as well as the style."

Hammett was important as more than simply a genre writer. As Howard Haycraft observed, Hammett's novels "are also character studies of close to top rank in their own right, and are penetrating if often shocking as novels of manners as well. They established new standards for realism in the genre. Yet they are as sharply stylized and deliberately artificial as Restoration Comedy, and have been called an inverted form of romanticism."

In one sense Hammett's detectives are romantics. They dare to believe in and hold firmly to a strict code of behavior which is in opposition to that of the world in which they move. Realistic and resourceful enough to be able to operate effectively among thieves, murderers, kidnappers, and blackmailers, Hammett's Continental Op, Sam Spade, Ned Beaumont, and Nick Charles are incorruptible in their belief that criminals ought to pay for their acts. When the unnamed Continental Op is tempted with money and sex to let a Russian princess guilty of murder and theft go free, he explains: "You think I'm a man and you're a woman. That's wrong. I'm a manhunter and you're something that's been running in front of me. There's nothing human about

it. You might just as well expect a hound to play tiddly-winks with the fox he's caught." That sentiment presages the famous farewell of Sam Spade to Brigid O'Shaughnessy, the murderess he loves but turns over to the police: "I'm going to send you over. The chances are you'll get off with life. That means you'll be out again in twenty years. You're an angel. I'll wait for . . . . If they hang you I'll always remember you." Ellery Queen noticed the seeming paradox of Hammett's romanticism early on: "The skin of realism hides the inner body of romance. All you see at first glance is that tough outer skin. But inside—deep in the core of his plots and counterplots—Hammett is one of the purest and most uninhibited romantics of all."

But Hammett was most of all a realist, and he was successful because, unlike his predecessors, he knew the world about which he wrote. When he was an operative for the Pinkerton National Detective Agency, Hammett "rated at the very top." As a detective, Hammett searched for accused securities thief Nick Arnstein; he worked for the defense during Fatty Arbuckle's celebrated trial for rape and murder; and he once found $125,000 in stolen gold stuffed down the smoke stack of a ship about to embark for Australia. In 1921, tuberculosis contracted during World War I forced Hammett to give up detective work for a more sedate occupation. He apparently was determined to be a poet and sought to support himself by writing detective stories. In 1922, he began writing about the characters and the life he had been forced to abandon. Hammett remarked in 1929: "The 'op' I use . . . is the typical sort of private detective that exists in our country today. I've worked with half a dozen men who might be he with a few changes."

Black Mask magazine, begun by H. L. Mencken and George Jean Nathan, was the most important forum for writers of the hard-boiled school, and Hammett quickly became the most popular of the *Black Mask* writers with the magazine's readership. Between 1923 and 1927, thirty-two of his stories were published there. *Black Mask* editors took their work and their writers seriously; they demanded quality material and freely suggested new avenues for their writers' work. In 1926, Captain Joseph T. Shaw became editor of Black Mask and encouraged Hammett to write longer fiction. As a result, in November, 1927, the first installment of the four-part *Red Harvest,* Hammett's first novel, was published in *Black Mask.*

The opening lines of *Red Harvest* illustrate well the major elements of Hammett's style: "I first heard Personville called Poisonville by a red-haired mucker named Hickey Dewey in the Big Ship in Butte. He also called a shirt a shoit. I didn't think anything of what he had done to the city's name. Later I heard men who could manage their r's to give it the same pronunciation." Careful attention to vernacular speech, use of criminal argot, and a knowledgeable, objective point of view characterize Hammett's fiction.

In *Red Harvest* the unnamed Continental Op tells the story of one of his cases. Typically, he goes into Personville, a totally lawless community, and by manipulating one group of criminals against another causes them to kill off each other. William F. Nolan pointed out that by the end of the novel "more than thirty deaths are toted up, a total which includes twelve of the nineteen main characters." During the course of the novel, the op breaks some laws, tells some lies, betrays some confidences, but he does so in a criminal environment where, he is realist enough to know, an honest man wouldn't stand a chance.

Red Harvest was a critical success. Herbert Asbury in *Bookman* declared: "It is doubtful if even Ernest Hemingway has ever written more effective dialogue than may be found within the pages of this extraordinary tale of gunmen, gin and gangsters. The author displays a style of amazing clarity and compactness, devoid of literary frills and furbelows, and his characters, who race through the story with the rapidity and destructiveness of machine guns, speak the crisp hard-boiled language of the underworld." W. R. Brooks in *Outlook* echoed those remarks: "It is written by a man who plainly knows his underworld and can make it come alive for his readers."

Those comments are typical, and they forecast the success Hammett would achieve upon the publication in 1930 of his third novel, *The Maltese Falcon. The Dain Curse,* published in 1929, was not up to Hammett's standards. Though it received a share of reviewers' compliments, most contemporary readers might agree with William Nolan's description: "Lacking the cohesive element of a single locale, this story jumps from seacoast to city to country, while the reader is forced to cope with over thirty characters." Based on Hammett's short story "The Scorched Face," *The Dain Curse* is the story of a family curse caused by incest which links the op's client's daughter with her blackly religious captor. The story is of drugs and, most of all, murder in a gothic setting. Elizabeth Sanderson reported that Hammett himself considered *The Dain Curse* "a silly story."

If *The Dain Curse* was Hammett's least successful novel, *The Maltese Falcon* ranked with his very best. The novel brought Hammett instant fame and prosperity. Sam Spade, the novel's protagonist, has served as a standard of hard-boiled characterization. Tough, calloused, competent, and operating according to his own code of justice, Sam Spade is the epitome of the lone detective working without reward to make things right. When Spade was accused of murder by an incompetent district attorney, the private eye explained his position: "As far as I can see my best chance of clearing myself of the trouble you're trying to make for me is by bringing in the murderers-all tied up. And my only chance of ever catching them is by keeping away from you and the police, because neither of you show any signs of knowing what in hell it's all about." Spade perhaps best illustrates the emotional callousness characteristic of Hammett's detectives. Somerset Maugham complained that Spade was hardly recognizable from the crooks he chased. That observation is critical to an understanding of Spade and his work. As Spade tells Brigid O'Shaughnessy: "Don't be too sure I'm as crooked as I'm supposed to be. That kind of reputation might be good business . . . making it easier to deal with the enemy." Good men can't deal with bad ones because being good, they obey a different set of rules. Spade deals with the enemy on his own terms.

In 1930, W. R. Brooks wrote in *Outlook* that *The Maltese Falcon* "is not only probably the best detective story we have ever read, it is an exceedingly well written novel." That opinion has worn well for more than half a century. *The Maltese Falcon* is widely considered a standard by which American mysteries are judged.

Hammett is said to have liked *The Glass Key* best among his novels. As Oliver Pilat has suggested, Ned Beaumont, the protagonist of *The Glass Key,* is "closer to the character of the author than some of Hammett's brassier detectives." Beaumont is tubercular, a gambler, a man with an intense sense of loyalty to his friend, yet a man who lives by a private code. Like Sam Spade, he is not impervious to human relationships, but he will not allow his personal feelings to blind him to the truth. When a U.S. senator, father of the woman Beaumont respects, if not loves, is proven to have murdered his son, he asks Beaumont for "the return of my revolver and five minutes—a minute—alone in this room" so that he may take the honorable Way out. Beaumont's

reply has the force of unrefined justice about it: "You'll take what's coming to you."

As Hammett's plots became less complex, his characters more realistic, his writing more mature, the heroes of his fiction continued to see that people got what they deserved. *The Glass Key* is a novel about justice, friendship, and priorities. Ned Beaumont's friend, Paul Madvig, is a political boss who very nearly lets his attraction to Senator Ralph B. Henry's daughter, Janet, ruin him. Beaumont serves his friend well by saving him, against Madvig's will, from a murder charge by exposing Senator Henry as his son's murderer and by saving Madvig from Janet Henry, who "hates him like poison." Madvig is unwilling to face the truth and Beaumont is too good a friend to allow him not to. Beaumont serves to make people accept reality—whether it be to take what's coming to them or to give up what they have no claim to.

M. I. Cole writing in *Spectator* called *The Glass Key* "the work of a man who knows exactly what he means to do, and who knows, also, why the current tradition of English detective fiction cannot be translated into American. . . . His people are violent, grafty, and full of sex appeal and responsiveness thereto: he is a clever writer."

After *The Glass Key,* it was three years before Hammett's next and last novel, *The Thin Man,* was written. Five years earlier he had literally been a starving writer. In 1931, his income was estimated at over $50,000; it would soon double. He rode in a chauffeur-driven Rolls Royce (he was said to have refused to drive after he dumped an ambulance load of wounded soldiers during World War I) and tipped his barber with twenty-dollar bills. He had become a celebrity—and he had met perhaps the most influential woman in his life who was to be his companion until his death, Lillian Hellman.

While *The Maltese Falcon* was shocking to the readers of its day because it featured a homosexual villain, one line in *The Thin Man* which referred to a man's sexual arousal while wrestling with a young girl created such a furor that the publisher felt obliged to run an ad in the *New York Times Book Review* defending the book's popularity: "Twenty thousand people don't buy a book within three weeks to read a five-word question." The sex in Hammett's work is very mild by today's standards; what is more interesting about *The Thin Man* is the change of tone and the change in the character of the detective. Nick Charles hates his work. A former detective, he has married a rich woman and wants to enjoy liquor and leisure. In many ways Hammett was, in 1934, much like Nick Charles. He was wealthy, an alcoholic, and his interest in his work was waning. Curiously *The Thin Man,* a light mystery with a self-indulgent hero, was Hammett's bestselling and most lucrative book. The movie starring William Powell and Myrna Loy was so successful that five sequels were made. Hammett no longer had to write to survive.

Hammett wrote *The Thin Man* at a hotel run by writer Nathanael West. Lillian Hellman recalled the process: "I had known Dash when he was writing short stories, but I had never been around for a long piece of work. Life changed: the drinking stopped; the parties were over. The locking-in time had come and nothing was allowed to disturb it until the book was finished. I had never seen anyone work that way: the care for every word, the pride in the neatness of the typed page itself, the refusal for ten days or two weeks to go out even for a walk for fear something would be lost." Later, in a letter to Hellman, who served as the model for Nora Charles, Hammett wrote: "Maybe there are better writers in the world, but nobody ever invented a more insufferably smug pair of characters. They can't take that away from me, even for $40,000." The $40,000 referred to the money he made from one of the *Thin Man* sequels.

After 1934, movies played an important part in Hammett's life. F. Scott Fitzgerald called Hammett one of the good writers "ruined" by Hollywood. Raymond Chandler concurred: "He was one of the many guys who couldn't take Hollywood without trying to push God out of the high seat."

Whatever the reason, Hammett stopped writing after *The Thin Man.* All of the books that appeared under his name after 1934 are collections of stories written earlier. The extent of his literary activities appears to have been as a screenwriter—including the only screenplay for which he was credited, the adaptation of Lillian Hellman's *Watch on the Rhine*—a script doctor for stage plays, consultant for radio scripts, and occasional book reviewer. He did attempt a novel, but returned the advance he had accepted from Random House when it became clear that the novel would never be completed (the unfinished novel, *Tulip,* appears in *The Big Knockover*). William Nolan suggested that one clue to Hammett's silence lies in the words of Pop, *Tulip*'s Hammett-like narrator: "If you are tired you ought to rest, I think, and not try to fool yourself and your customers with colored bubbles."

Though Hammett's writing career effectively ended in 1934, he remained a nationally prominent man until his death. About 1937, Hammett apparently joined the Communist party and he figured in Communist party affairs for the next twenty years. At the height of the paranoia which accompanied McCarthyism, the FBI reported that Hammett was a sponsor, member, or supporter of over forty organizations sympathetic to communism; in 1948 he served as national vice-chairman of the Civil Rights Congress (CRC), declared by the U.S. Attorney General to be a subversive organization. Lillian Hellman faced squarely the subject of Hammett's politics: "I don't know if Hammett was a Communist Party member: most certainly he was a Marxist. But he was a very critical Marxist, often contemptuous of the Soviet Union in the same hick sense that many Americans are contemptuous of foreigners. He was often witty and bitingly sharp about the American Communist Party, but he was, in the end, loyal to them." On February 23, 1955, testifying before the joint legislative committee Investigation of Charitable and Philanthropic Agencies and Organizations at the Supreme Court-New York City, Hammett stated: "Communism to me is not a dirty word. When you are working for the advance of mankind it never occurs to you whether a guy is a Communist."

In 1951, Hammett was called to testify before the New York State Supreme Court as a trustee of the Bail Bond Committee of CRC in the wake of the violation of bail by eleven members of the Communist Party for whom the CRC had posted bond, four of whom could not be located. When Hammett refused to testify—even to identify his signature—he was sentenced to six months in federal prison for contempt of court. He served his term between July and December of 1951.

In April of 1953, Hammett was called to testify before the Senate Permanent Subcommittee on Investigations of the Committee on Government Operations, chaired by Joseph McCarthy. His testimony before that committee is often quoted. Asked by McCarthy if he would "purchase the works of some seventy-five Communist authors and distribute their works throughout the world," Hammett replied, "If I were fighting communism, I don't think I would do it by giving people any books at all."

Royalties from Hammett's work supported him well into the 1950s. Before he was jailed, Hammett still earned $1000 per week from royalties. But after his release, the Internal Revenue Service took an increasing interest in his affairs, resulting in February, 1957, in a $140,796 default judgment for tax deficiencies. Tubercular and physically exhausted, Hammett was unable to pay the judgment and his income was attached for the rest of his life. In 1957, he listed his income as less than $30. In November, 1960, he was found to have lung cancer. He died on January 10, 1961. At his funeral Lillian Hellman said of Dashiell Hammett: "He never lied, he never faked, he never stooped. He seemed to me a great man."

MEDIA ADAPTATIONS: The Maltese Falcon, The Thin Man, Woman in the Dark, and *The Glass Key* were adapted for films in the 1930s and 1940s.

BIOGRAPHICAL/CRITICAL SOURCES:

BOOKS

Authors in the News, Volume 1, Gale, 1976.
Contemporary Literary Criticism, Gale, Volume 3, 1975, Volume 5, 1976, Volume 10, 1979, Volume 19, 1981, Volume 47, 1988.
Concise Dictionary of American Literary Biography: The Twenties, 1917-1929, Gale, 1989.
Dictionary of Literary Biography Documentary Series, Volume 6, Gale, 1989.
Gardiner, Dorothy, and Katherine Sorley Walker, editors, *Raymond Chandler Speaking,* Houghton, 1962.
Gores, Joe, *Hammett,* Putnam, 1975.
Hammett, Dashiell, *The Maltese Falcon,* Knopf, 1930.
Hammett, Dashiell, *The Glass Key,* Knopf, 1931.
Hammett, Dashiell, *The Continental Op,* Spivak, 1945.
Hammett, Dashiell, *They Can Only Hang You Once,* Spivak, 1949.
Haycraft, Howard, *Murder for Pleasure,* Appleton-Century, 1941.
Haycraft, Howard, editor, *The Art of the Mystery Story,* Simon & Schuster, 1946.
Hellman, Lillian, *An Unfinished Woman,* Little, Brown, 1969.
Hellman, Lillian, *Pentimento,* Little, Brown, 1973.
Hellman, Lillian, *Scoundrel Time,* Little, Brown, 1976.
Mundell, E. H., *A List of the Original Appearances of Dashiell Hammett's Magazine Work,* Kent State University Press, 1968.
Nolan, William F., *Dashiell Hammett: A Casebook,* McNally & Loftin, 1969.

PERIODICALS

Atlantic Monthly, December, 1944.
Baltimore News-American, August 19, 1973.
Bookman, March, 1929.
City of San Francisco, November 4, 1975.
Esquire, September, 1934.
Miami Herald, March 17, 1974.
New York Times, January 11, 1961, August 25, 1988.
Outlook, February 13, 1929, February 26, 1930.
Spectator, February 14, 1931.
Washington Post Book World, October 2, 1988.

*   *   *

HAMPTON, Christopher (James) 1946-

PERSONAL: Born January 26, 1916, in Fayal, Azores; son of Bernard Patrick (with Cable & Wireless Ltd.) and Dorothy (Herrington) Hampton; married Laura de Holesch (a social worker), 1971; children: two. *Education:* New College, Oxford, M.A., 1968.

ADDRESSES: Home—2 Kensington Park Gardens, London W11, England. *Agent*—Margaret Ramsay Ltd., 14-A Goodwin's Ct., St. Martin's Ln., London WC2, England.

CAREER: Playwright and screenwriter. Resident Dramatist, Royal Court Theatre, London, England, 1968-70.

MEMBER: Royal Society of Literature (fellow), Dramatists' Club.

AWARDS, HONORS: Evening Standard Drama award for best comedy, 1970, *Plays and Players* London Theatre Critics' award for best play, 1970, Antoinette Perry (Tony) award nominations for best play and best author, 1971, and *Variety*'s Thirty-third Annual Poll of Broadway Drama Critics most promising playwright award, 1971, all for "The Philanthropist"; *Plays and Players* London Theatre Critics' award for best play, 1973, and Los Angeles Drama Critics' award for Distinguished Playwriting, 1974, both for "Savages"; *Screen International* award for best screenplay, 1980, for "Tales From the Vienna Woods"; *Plays and Players* London Theatre Critics' award for best play, 1985, Tony award nomination for best play, 1987, and New York Drama Critics Circle award for best new foreign play, 1987, all for "Les Liaisons Dangereuses"; Academy Award (Oscar) for best screenplay adapted from another medium, and Writers Guild of America award, both 1988, for "Dangerous Liaisons."

WRITINGS:

PLAYS

When Did You Last See My Mother? (first produced in Oxford, England, February, 1966; produced on the West End at Comedy Theatre, July 4, 1966; produced Off-Broadway at Sheridan Square Playhouse, January, 1967; produced in revised version at Royal Court Theatre, August 11, 1970), Grove, 1967.

"Marya," translation by Michael Glenny and Harold Shukman (adapted from the work by Isaac Babel; first produced in England at Royal Court Theatre, October, 1967; produced on BBC-TV, 1981), published in *Plays of the Year: Volume 35*, Elek Books, 1969.

Total Eclipse (three-act; first produced in England at Royal Court Theatre, September, 1968; produced in revised version at Lyric Theatre, Hammersmith, England, April, 1981; produced on BBC2-TV, April 10, 1973), Faber, 1969, Samuel French, 1972, revised version, Faber, 1981.

The Philanthropist: A Bourgeois Comedy (two-act; first produced in England at Royal Court Theatre, August 3, 1970; produced on Broadway at Ethel Barrymore Theatre, March 15, 1971; produced at Manhattan Theater Club, 1983; produced on BBC2-TV, 1975), Faber, 1970, Samuel French, 1971.

"Uncle Vanya," translation by Nina Froud (adapted from the work by Anton Chekhov; first produced in England at Royal Court Theatre, February 24, 1970; radio production, London, October 12, 1970), published in *Plays of the Year: Volume 39*, Elek Books, 1971.

Hedda Gabler (adapted from the work by Henrik Ibsen; first produced in Stratford, Ontario, 1970; produced on Broadway at Playhouse Theatre, February 17, 1971), Samuel French, 1972.

A Doll's House (adapted from the work by Ibsen; first produced on Broadway at Playhouse Theatre, February, 1971; produced on the West End at Criterion Theatre, February 20, 1973), Samuel French, 1972.

Savages (two-act; first produced in England at Royal Court Theatre, April 12, 1973; produced on the West End at Comedy Theatre, June 20, 1973; revised version produced in Los Angeles at Mark Taper Forum, August, 1974; produced on BBC2-TV, 1975), Fraser, 1973, revised edition, Samuel French, 1976.

Don Juan (adapted from the work by Moliere; first produced in Bristol, England, 1972; produced on BBC Radio, 1972), Faber, 1974.

Treats (two-act; first produced in England at Royal Court Theatre, February 3, 1976; produced on the West End at Mayfair Theatre, March 6, 1976; produced in New York City at Hudson Guild Theater, October, 1977; produced on Yorkshire Television, 1977), Faber, 1976.

(Translator) Oedoen von Horvath, "Tales From the Vienna Woods," first produced in England at National Theatre, 1977.

(Translator) von Horvath, *Don Juan Carlos Comes Back From the War* (first produced in England at National Theatre, April 18, 1978; produced in New York City at Manhattan Theater Club, 1979), Faber, 1978.

(Translator) Ibsen, *The Wild Duck* (first produced in England at National Theatre, December 13, 1979), Faber, 1979, Samuel French, 1983.

"After Mercer," first produced in England at National Theatre, 1980.

(Translator) Ibsen, *Ghosts* (first produced, 1978), Samuel French, 1983.

The Portage to San Cristobal of A. H. (two-act; adapted from the novel by George Steiner; first produced in England at Mermaid Theatre, February 17, 1982; produced in the United States in 1983), Faber, 1983.

Tales From Hollywood (two-act; first produced in Los Angeles at Mark Taper Forum, March 25, 1982), Faber, 1983.

(Translator) Moliere, "Tartuffe," first produced in England, July 28, 1983.

Les Liaisons Dangereuses (adapted from the novel by Choderlos de Laclos; first produced in England, September, 1985; produced in New York City at Music Box Theater, 1987), Faber, 1985.

SCREENPLAYS

"A Doll's House" (adapted from the work by Henrik Ibsen), released by Paramount Pictures, 1973.

"Beyond the Limit" (adapted from a novel by Graham Greene), released by Paramount Pictures, 1983.

"The Good Father" (adapted from the novel by Peter Prince), released by Skouras Pictures, 1987.

"Gauguin: Wolf at the Door," released by International Film Marketing, 1987.

"Dangerous Liaisons" (adapted from the novel by Choderlos de Laclos), released by Warner Bros., 1988.

Also author of "Tales From the Vienna Woods," 1979.

OTHER

"Able's Will," produced on BBC-TV, 1977.

"The History Man" (television serial; adapted from the novel by Malcolm Bradbury), produced on BBC2-TV, 1981.

(Translator) Patrice Chereau and Ariane Mnouchkine, "The Prague Trial," produced on BBC Radio, October, 1983.

"Hotel du Lac" (adapted from the work by Anita Brookner), produced on BBC-TV, 1986.

SIDELIGHTS: Clive Barnes comments: " 'The Philanthropist' is a good, funny, literate and literary play. Mr. Hampton is dazzlingly clever. He writes dialogue that has the bright artificiality of Wilde and yet, also like Wilde, with just sufficient humanity in it to remain bearable. His play—despite strange random outgrowths in its structure and very definite lapses of tension—has a construction that is both brilliant and apt. This is high comedy, even if some of the lines could find their bedfellows in low farce." Continuing on "The Philanthropist," Harold Clurman writes that "Hampton . . . succeeds in making a humane comedy out of the sorry fellow. Other English playwrights—Pinter, David Storey, Osborne—write tense, grotesque, startling or oppressive images close to nightmares about such men. Hampton cleverly toys a bit, skims the surface with bright undergraduate effrontery and nonchalance, but at bottom he is still an honest observer, a common sense realist. The combination of arch teasing and sympathy add up to a most agreeably intelligent play. The future will tell which of Hampton's traits will prevail: the cleverness or the sensibility."

Writing on "Savages," R. B. Marriott says: "It is good to see a play that is blazing with passion directed in a humanitarian cause, which uncompromisingly attacks political and social corruption, and tries to present a vision of a world which could be happy, decent and good; and then to have this accomplished with quiet simplicity and moving words. So it is with Christopher Hampton's 'Savages'."

Hampton's 1985 play, "Les Liaisons Dangereuses," was similarly well received. Adapted from a 1792 novel by French writer Choderlos de Laclos, "Les Liaisons Dangereuses"—a chronicle of cruel and destructive power struggles among the French aristocracy—was a success in both London and New York City and was nominated for a Tony award for best play. *New York Times* critic Mel Gussow called the play "brilliant" and noted that "Hampton transcends his previous work with 'Les Liaisons Dangereuses.' His indictment of the last days of the ancien regime becomes an extraordinary dance of decadence." Hampton's screenplay for the film version, "Dangerous Liaisons," earned him an Academy Award for best screenplay in 1988.

On writing, Christopher Hampton began by telling W. Stephen Gilbert that the best thing about being a writer is: " 'actually being able to do it and to do nothing else. . . . But there's a longer list of bad things about being a writer. Mainly, it's difficult. I get very few ideas that I really want to use. I used to get many more than I do now but I've got better at recognising them when they're no good. I just find it a real battle, a temperamental battle. There are plenty of writers who plunge ahead and produce a lot of work and I feel that they're the people who are the real instinctive writers whereas with me it's a fight to get the thing on paper. I love finishing. I feel wonderful for weeks afterwards. But I'm rather lazy, I think, You only work for yourself, which is the advantage and disadvantage of writing, and if you can't force yourself to work, you get very depressed and into a vicious circle. . . . I become very easily discouraged. I don't know what would have happened if the plays hadn't been done. . . . It depended on a fantastic amount of good fortune. Now it's a different matter. If you're good you go on, if you're not good you don't go on.' "

BIOGRAPHICAL/CRITICAL SOURCES:

BOOKS

Contemporary Literary Criticism, Volume 4, Gale, 1975.
Clurman, Harold, *The Divine Pastime: Theatre Essays,* Macmillan, 1974.
Dictionary of Literary Biography, Volume 13: *British Dramatists Since World War II,* Gale, 1982.

PERIODICALS

Bookseller, January 30, 1971.
Chicago Tribune, March 4, 1987, April 27, 1987, January 13, 1989.
Globe and Mail (Toronto), June 20, 1987.
Los Angeles Times, September 29, 1983, October 18, 1984, February 13, 1987, May 10, 1987, July 31, 1987, August 7, 1988, December 21, 1988.
Nation, April 5, 1971.
Newsweek, March 29, 1971, March 2, 1987.
New York Times, March 21, 1971, March 1, 1977, October 7, 1977, January 7, 1983, October 14, 1983, October 30, 1983, February 11, 1987, April 26, 1987, May 1, 1987, May 10, 1987, May 17, 1987, July 21, 1987, July 31, 1987, July 31, 1988, December 21, 1988, January 22, 1989, July 31, 1989.
Observer Review, August 9, 1970, January 10, 1971.
Plays & Players, October, 1970, January, 1971, May, 1973.
Punch, September 18, 1968.
Show Business, October 31, 1970.
Stage, April 19, 1973.
Statesman, September 20, 1968.
Times (London), April 14, 1982, September 3, 1983, January 6, 1984, July 12, 1985, October 3, 1986, April 3, 1988, March 9, 1989.
Transatlantic Review, Number 31.
Variety, March 10, 1971, March 17, 1971, April 21, 1971, July 14, 1971, September 20, 1972.
Washington Post, October 20, 1978, March 7, 1987, March 13, 1987, September 19, 1987, January 13, 1989.

*   *   *

HAMSUN, Knut
See PEDERSEN, Knut

*   *   *

HAMSUND, Knut Pedersen
See PEDERSEN, Knut

*   *   *

HANDKE, Peter 1942-

PERSONAL: Born December 6, 1942, in Griffen, Carinthia, Austria; married Libgart Schwarz, 1966 (separated, 1972); children: one daughter. *Education:* Attended a Jesuit seminary, and University of Graz, 1961-65.

ADDRESSES: Home—53 rue Cecille-Dinant, F-92140 Clamart, France. *Office*—c/o Suhrkamp Verlag, Postfach 4229, 6000 Frankfurt am Main, Federal Republic of Germany.

CAREER: Dramatist, novelist, poet, essayist, and screenwriter, 1966—.

AWARDS, HONORS: Gerhart Hauptmann Prize, 1967; Schiller Prize, 1972; Buechner Prize, 1973; Kafka Prize, 1979 (refused).

WRITINGS:

FICTION

Die Hornissen (novel; title means "The Hornets"), Suhrkamp, 1966.
Der Hausierer (novel; title means "The Peddler"), Suhrkamp, 1967. *Begruessung des Aufsichtsrats* (experimental prose pieces; title means, "Welcoming the Board of Directors"),

Residenz Verlag, 1967, also published in *Peter Handke* (see below).

Die Angst des Tormanns beim Elfmeter (novel), Suhrkamp, 1970, translation by Michael Roloff published as *The Goalie's Anxiety at the Penalty Kick,* Farrar, Straus, 1972 (also see below).

Der kurze Brief zum langen Abschied (novel), Suhrkamp, 1972, translation by Ralph Manheim published as *Short Letter, Long Farewell,* Farrar, Straus, 1974.

Die Stunde der wahren Empfindung (novel), Suhrkamp, 1975, translation by Manheim published as *A Moment of True Feeling,* Farrar, Straus, 1977.

Die linkshaendige Frau: Erzaehlung (novel), Suhrkamp, 1976, translation published as *The Left-Handed Woman,* Farrar, Straus, 1978 (also see below).

Langsame Heimkehr (title means "The Long Way Round"), Suhrkamp, 1979, translation by Manheim published in *Slow Homecoming* (also see below), Farrar, Straus, 1983.

Die Lehre der Sainte-Victoire (title means "The Lesson of Mont Saint-Victoire), Suhrkamp, 1980, translation by Manheim published in *Slow Homecoming* (also see below), Farrar, Straus, 1983.

Kindergeschichte (title means "Children's Stories"), Suhrkamp, 1981, translation by Manheim published in *Slow Homecoming* (also see below), Farrar, Straus, 1983.

Slow Homecoming, translated by Manheim, Farrar, Straus, 1983.

Across (novella), translated by Manheim, Farrar, Straus, 1986.

Repetition (novel), translated by Manheim, Farrar, Straus, 1988.

The Afternoon of a Writer (novel), translated by Manheim, Farrar, Straus, 1989.

PLAYS

"Publikumsbeschimpfung" (first produced in Frankfurt at Theater am Turm, June 8, 1966), published in *Publikumsbeschimpfung und Andere Sprechstuecke* (see below), translation by Roloff published as "Offending the Audience" in *Kaspar and Other Plays* (see below).

"Selbstbezichtigung" (first produced in Oberhausen at Staedtische Buehnen, October 22, 1966), published in *Publikumsbeschimpfung und Andere Sprechstuecke* (see below), translation by Roloff published as "Self-Accusation" in *Kaspar and Other Plays* (see below).

"Weissagung" (first produced in Oberhausen at Staedtische Buehnen, October 22, 1966), published in *Publikumsbeschimpfung und Andere Sprechstuecke* (see below), translation by Roloff published as "Prophecy" in *The Ride Across Lake Constance and Other Plays* (see below).

"Hilferufe" (first produced in Stockholm, September 12, 1967), published in *Deutsches Theater der Gegenwart 2,* 1967, translation by Roloff published as "Calling for Help" in *Drama Review,* fall, 1970, and in *The Ride Across Lake Constance and Other Plays* (see below).

Kaspar (produced simultaneously in Frankfurt at Theater am Turm and in Oberhausen at Staedtische Buehnen, May 11, 1968), Suhrkamp, 1968, translation by Roloff under same title (produced in New York at the Brooklyn Academy of Music, February, 1973) published in *Kaspar and Other Plays* (see below), also published separately, Methuen, 1972.

"Das Mundel will Vormund sein" (first produced in Frankfurt at Theater am Turm, January 31, 1969), published in *Theatre Heute,* February, 1969, and in *Peter Handke* (see below), translation by Roloff published as "My Foot My Tutor" in *Drama Review,* fall, 1970, and in *The Ride Across Lake Constance and Other Plays* (see below).

Quodlibet (first produced in Basle at Basler Theater, January 24, 1970), published in *Theater Heute,* March, 1970, also privately printed, 1970, translation by Roloff published under same title in *The Ride Across Lake Constance and Other Plays* (see below).

Wind und Meer: 4 Hoerspiele (title means "Wind and Sea: Four Radio Plays"), Suhrkamp, 1970.

Der Ritt ueber den Bodensee (first produced in Berlin at Schaubuehne am Halleschen Ufer, January 23, 1971), Suhrkamp, 1971, translation by Roloff as *The Ride Across Lake Constance* (produced in New York at the Forum, Lincoln Center, January, 1972) published in *The Contemporary German Drama,* edited by Roloff, Equinox Books, 1972, published separately, Methuen, 1973 (also see below).

Die Unvernuenftigen sterben aus (first produced in Zurich, April, 1974), Suhrkamp, 1973, translation by Roloff and Karl Weber published as *They Are Dying Out,* Methuen, 1975 (also see below).

"A Sorrow Beyond Dreams," produced in New York City at Marymount Manhattan Playhouse, June, 1977.

Ueber die Doerfer: Dramatisches (dramatic poem; first produced in Salzburg, 1982), Suhrkamp, 1981.

(With Wim Wenders) "Wings of Desire" (screenplay), Orion, 1988.

GERMAN COLLECTIONS

Publikumsbeschimpfung und Andere Sprechstuecke (includes "Publikumsbeschimpfung," "Selbstbezichtigung," and "Weissagung), Suhrkamp, 1966.

Peter Handke: Prosa, Gedichte, Theaterstuecke, Hoerspiel, Aufsaetze (includes "Begruessung des Aufsichtsrats," "Publikumsbeschimpfung," and "Das Mundel will Vormund sein"), Suhrkamp, 1969.

Stuecke (title means "Plays"), Suhrkamp, 1972.

Stuecke 2, Suhrkamp, 1973.

ENGLISH COLLECTIONS

Kaspar and Other Plays (includes "Kaspar," "Offending the Audience," and "Self-Accusation"), translated by Roloff, Farrar, Straus, 1969.

Offending the Audience (includes "Offending the Audience" and "Self-Accusation"), translated by Roloff, Methuen, 1971.

The Ride Across Lake Constance and Other Plays (includes "Prophecy," "Calling for Help," "My Foot My Tutor," "Quodlibet," and "They Are Dying Out"), translated by Roloff and Karl Weber, Farrar, Straus, 1976.

OTHER

Die Innenwelt der Aussenwelt der Innenwelt (poems), Suhrkamp, 1969, abridged translation by Roloff published as *The Innerworld of the Outerworld of the Innerworld,* Seabury, 1974.

(Compiler) *Der gewoehnliche Schrecken* (title means "The Ordinary Terror"), Residenz Verlag, 1969.

Deutsche Gedichte (title means "German Poems"), Euphorion-Verlag, 1969.

Chronik der laufenden Ereignisse (film scenario; title means "Chronicle of Current Events"), Suhrkamp, 1971.

Ich bin ein Bewohner des Elfenbeinturms (essays; title means "I Live in an Ivory Tower"), Suhrkamp, 1972.

Wunschloses Ungluock (biography), Residenz Verlag, 1972, translation by Manheim published as *A Sorrow Beyond Dreams,* Farrar, Straus, 1975.

Als das Wuenschen noch geholfen hat (poems), Suhrkamp, 1974, translation by Roloff published as *Nonsense and Happiness,* Urizen Books, 1976.

Falsche Bewegung (film scenario; title means "False Move"), Suhrkamp, 1975.

Three by Peter Handke (contains *A Sorrow Beyond Dreams, Short Letter Long Farewell, The Goalie's Anxiety at the Penalty Kick*), Avon, 1977.

(And director) "The Left-Handed Woman" (screenplay; adaptation of Handke's novel), 1978.

The Weight of the World (diary), translated by Manheim, Farrar, Straus, 1984.

WORK IN PROGRESS: A journal; also a novel—"a personal odyssey"—set in the Rocky Mountains and in Austria.

SIDELIGHTS: Nicholas Hern is one of a number of critics who have suggested that Peter Handke's legal training may have been an important influence on his prose style, pointing out that "most of his plays and novels consist of a series of affirmative propositions each contained within one sentence. . . . The effect . . . is not unlike the series of clauses in a contract or will or statute-book, shorn of linking conjunctions. It is as if a state of affairs or a particular situation were being defined and constantly redefined until the final total definition permits of no mite of ambiguity." Handke's prose has reminded other readers of the propositions making up Ludwig Wittgenstein's *Tractatus Logico-Philosophicus,* and the inquiries into language of Wittgenstein and the French structuralists touch on themes that are central to Handke's work. Discussing his more strictly literary masters, Handke said in 1977 that American novelist William Faulkner remains the most important of all writers to him.

Handke's remarkable style was first displayed in the experimental prose pieces he wrote and published in magazines while still at the university, and in *Die Hornissen,* which reminded reviewers of the French "new novel." This first novel appeared in the spring of 1966 and was generally well received, but it was not this alone that made him overnight a figure to be reckoned with on the German literary scene. In April, 1966, Handke went to the United States to participate in the twenty-eighth convention of Group 47, the famous association of German writers, which that year met in Princeton, New Jersey. On the last day of the conference Handke, then aged twenty-four, made the first move in a deliberate campaign of what came to be called "Handke-Publicity." In his book on Group 47 Siegfried Mandel wrote: "Shaking his Beatle-mane, Handke . . . railed against what he had been listening to: impotent narrative; empty stretches of descriptive (instead of analytical) writing pleasing to the ears of the older critics; monotonous verbal litanies, regional and nature idyllicism, which lacked spirit and creativeness. The audience warmed up to the invective with cheers, and later even those whose work had been called idiotic, tasteless, and childish came over to congratulate the Group 47 debutant and to patch things up in brotherly fashion. . . . As he stood among a circle of interviewers—a thin, energetic figure with thick, dark sunglasses—it became clear that he had arrived as a spokesman for the young and hitherto silent clique and reestablished confidence in the rejuvenating capacity of the group."

This assessment was fully confirmed a few months later, when Handke's first play was the major hit in a week of experimental new drama in Frankfurt. *Offending the Audience,* in which all the comfortable assumptions of bourgeois theatre are called in question and the audience is systematically mocked and insulted, was and has remained highly popular in German theatres. To a lesser extent, the same is true of Handke's other early "sprechst-

uecke"—plays which all in various ways investigate the role of language in defining the individual's social identity.

The power of language is the theme also of *Kaspar,* Handke's first full-length play. It is a matter of record that in 1828 in Nuremberg a sixteen-year-old boy was discovered who had apparently been confined all his life in a closet, and who was physically full-grown but mentally a baby. This was Kaspar Hauser, whose story has intrigued a number of writers, and who in Handke's play is indoctrinated with conventional moral precepts in the process of being taught to speak. As Nicholas Hern put it, "the play is an abstract demonstration of the way an individual's individuality is stripped from him by society, specifically by limiting the expressive power of the language it teaches him." Robert Brustein rejected the play's thesis, but found it all the same "sometimes penetrating, sometimes brilliant, always permeated by a fierce, if rather cold, intensity." In Germany *Kaspar* was voted play of the year, and it is regarded as one of the most important postwar German plays.

A number of other plays have followed, for radio, television, and the stage. The most discussed of these was Handke's second full-length play, *The Ride Across Lake Constance,* which, most critics thought, also dealt with the problems of communication, though in a baroque and bewildering fashion that fascinated even some reviewers, like Clive Barnes, who could make no sense of it at all. Hern wrote that in this play "Handke has moved from a Wittgensteinian distrust of language to a Foucaultian distrust of what our society calls reason. His play is by no means surrealist in externals only: it parallels the surrealists' cardinal desire—the liberation of men's minds from the constraints of reason. Thus Handke continues to demonstrate that the consistently *anti*-theatrical stance which he has maintained throughout his dramatic writing can none the less lend concrete theatrical expression to abstract, philosophical ideas, thereby generating a new and valid form of theatre."

Meanwhile, Handke had been establishing a second reputation as one of the most important of the young German novelists. His first success in this form was *The Goalie's Anxiety at the Penalty Kick,* which reflects the same preoccupations as his plays. As Russell Davies wrote, when Handke's alienated hero Bloch commits an apparently pointless murder, "it is the problem of language itself which upsets his mind and stomach. . . . One comes to realise that Handke is demonstrating how similar to the toils of madness are the inner wranglings of the writer as he fights to order his world." Frank Conroy called the book "an ambitious tour de force in which Handke deals with the interrelationships of man, external reality and time."

The partly autobiographical novel *Short Letter, Long Farewell,* about a young Austrian writer's haphazard journey across the United States to a dangerous meeting with his estranged wife, had a mixed but generally favorable reception. And there was little but praise for *A Sorrow Beyond Dreams,* Handke's profoundly sensitive account of his mother's life, which ended in suicide. Michael Wood wrote of it that "Handke's objective tone is a defense against the potential flood of his feelings, of course, but it is also a act of piety, an expression of respect: this woman's bleak life is not to be made into 'literature'. . . . Handke's mother is important not because she is an especially vivid case but because she is not, because she is one of many." Dramatized as a monologue by Daniel Freudenberger, it was staged by the Phoenix Theatre at the Marymount Manhattan Theatre early in 1977, and greatly praised.

Some reviewers were disappointed by *A Moment of True Feeling,* another fictional study in alienation, but Stanley Kauffmann was deeply impressed. He suggested that Handke was moving toward "the novel as poem" and concluded that "this new book proves further that, in power and vision and range, he is the most important new writer on the international scene since Beckett."

Handke has written: "I myself would support Marxism every time as the only possibility of solution but not its pronouncement in play, in the theatre." His refusal to use his plays and novels as vehicles for political propaganda has been much criticized by the New Left in Germany, but Handke maintains that literature and political commitment are incompatible. "It would be repugnant to me to twist my criticism of a social order into a story or to aestheticize it into a poem," he says in one of his essays. "I find that the most atrocious mendacity: to manipulate one's commitment into a poem or to make literature out of it, instead of just saying it loud."

BIOGRAPHICAL/CRITICAL SOURCES:

BOOKS

Boa, Elizabeth and J. H. Reid, *Critical Strategies: German Fiction in the Twentieth Century,* McGill-Queens University Press, 1972.
Contemporary Literary Criticism, Gale, Volume 5, 1976, Volume 8, 1978, Volume 10, 1979, Volume 15, 1980, Volume 38, 1986.
Falkenstein, Henning, *Peter Handke,* Colloquium Verlag, 1974.
Gilman, Richard, *The Making of Modern Drama,* Farrar, Straus, 1974.
Heintz, Guenter, *Peter Handke,* Klett, 1971.
Hern, Nicholas, *Peter Handke: Theatre and Anti-Theatre,* Wolff, 1971.
Mandel, Siegfried, *Group 47,* Southern Illinois University Press, 1973.
Rischbieter, Henning, *Peter Handke,* Friedrich, 1972.
Scharang, Michael, editor, *Uber Peter Handko,* Suhrkamp, 1973.
Schultz, Uwe, *Peter Handke,* Friedrich, 1973.
Ungar, Frederick, editor, *Handbook of Austrian Literature,* F. Ungar, 1973.

PERIODICALS

Chicago Tribune, December 1, 1989, December 15, 1989.
Drama Review, fall, 1970.
London Times, May 15, 1972, November 13, 1973, December 9, 1973.
Los Angeles Times, May 22, 1985, June 25, 1986, May 20, 1988.
Los Angeles Times Book Review, July 16, 1989.
New Republic, February 28, 1970, September 28, 1974.
Newsweek, July 3, 1978.
New York Review of Books, May 1, 1975, June 23, 1977.
New York Times, January 30, 1977, March 22, 1971, June 17, 1978, January 25, 1980, April 2, 1980, July 12, 1984, June 25, 1986, April 29, 1988, August 28, 1989.
New York Times Book Review, May 21, 1972, September 15, 1974, April 27, 1975, July 31, 1977, June 18, 1978, July 22, 1984, August 4, 1985, July 17, 1986, August 7, 1988.
Performance, September-October 1972.
Publishers Weekly, September 12, 1977.
Text und Kritik, Number 24, 1969 (Handke issue).
Times (London), April 3, 1980, July 25, 1985, August 4, 1988, July 8, 1989.
Times Literary Supplement, April 21, 1972, December 1, 1972, April 18, 1980, July 17, 1981, November 15, 1985, October 3, 1986.
Tribune Books (Chicago), July 3, 1988.
Universitas, February 25, 1970.

Washington Post Book World, July 28, 1985.

*   *   *

HANLEY, James   1901-1985
(Patric Shone)

PERSONAL: Born September 3, 1901, in Dublin, Ireland; died November 11, 1985, in London, England.

CAREER: Novelist, short story writer, and playwright. Went to sea in 1915, jumped ship in Canada, 1917; after World War I worked a variety of jobs, including free-lance journalist, railway porter, and racecourse cashier; full-time author in Wales, 1930-85. *Military service:* Canadian Expeditionary Force, during the First World War.

WRITINGS:

NOVELS

Drift, Eric Partridge, 1930, complete and limited edition, Boriswood, 1931.
Boy, Boriswood, 1931, Knopf, 1932.
Ebb and Flood, John Lane, 1932.
Captain Bottell, limited edition, Boriswood, 1933, Panther Books, 1965.
Resurrexit Dominus, limited edition, privately printed, 1934.
The Furys (first book of "The Furys" chronicle), Macmillan, 1935.
Stoker Bush, Chatto & Windus, 1935, Macmillan, 1936.
The Secret Journey (second book of "The Furys" chronicle), Macmillan, 1936.
Hollow Sea, John Lane, 1938, reprinted, Panther Books, 1965.
Our Time Is Gone (third book in "The Furys" chronicle), John Lane, 1940, revised edition, Phoenix House, 1949, published as a trilogy with first two books of "The Furys" chronicle, Dent, 1949.
The Ocean, Morrow, 1941, reprinted, Mayflower Books, 1965.
No Directions, Faber, 1943.
Sailor's Song, Nicholson & Watson, 1943.
What Farrar Saw, Nicholson & Watson, 1946.
Emily, Nicholson & Watson, 1948.
Winter Song (fourth book of "The Furys" chronicle), Dent, 1950.
(Under pseudonym Patric Shone) *The House in the Valley,* J. Cape, 1951.
The Closed Harbour, Macdonald & Co., 1952, published as *The Closed Harbor,* Horizon Press, 1953.
The Welsh Sonata: Variations on a Theme, Derek Verschoyle, 1954.
Levine, Horizon Press, 1956.
An End and a Beginning, Horizon Press, 1958.
Say Nothing (adapted from his own play), Horizon Press, 1962.
Another World, Horizon Press, 1972.
A Woman in the Sky, Horizon Press, 1973.
A Dream Journey, Horizon Press, 1976.
Against the Stream, Horizon Press, 1982.

STORY COLLECTIONS

A Passion before Death, privately printed, 1930.
The Last Voyage: A Tale, limited edition, William Jackson, 1931.
Men in Darkness: Five Stories, preface by John Cowper Powys, John Lane, 1931, Knopf, 1932, reprinted, Books for Libraries Press, 1970.
Stoker Haslett: A Tale, Joiner & Steele, 1932.
Aria and Finale and Other Stories, Boriswood, 1932.
Quartermaster Clausen, Arlan, 1934.

The German Prisoner, introduction by Richard Aldington, privately printed, c. 1935.
At Bay, Grayson, 1935.
Half an Eye: Sea Stories, John Lane, 1937.
People Are Curious: Short Stories, John Lane, 1938.
At Bay: Tales, Faber, 1944.
Crilly and Other Stories, Nicholson & Watson, 1945.
Selected Stories, Fridberg (Dublin), 1947.
A Walk in the Wilderness, Dent, 1950.
Collected Stories, Macdonald & Co., 1953.
Don Quixote Drowned, Macdonald & Co., 1953.
The Darkness, Covent Garden Press, 1973.

PLAYS

"Say Nothing," first broadcast, 1961, first produced in Stratford at Theatre Royal, August 14, 1962, produced in New York, 1965.
The Inner Journey: A Play in Three Acts (also see below; first produced in Hamburg, 1967; produced in New York at Forum Theatre, March 20, 1969), Horizon Press, 1965.
"Forever and Forever," first produced in Hamburg, 1966.
Plays One (includes "The Inner Journey" and "A Stone Flower"), Kaye & Ward, 1968.
"It Wasn't Me," first produced in London, 1968.
"Leave Us Alone," first produced in London, 1972.

Also author of television scripts, including "The Inner World of Miss Vaughan," 1964, "Another Port, Another Town," 1964, "Mr. Ponge," 1965, "Day Out for Lucy," 1965, "A Walk in the Sea," 1966, "That Woman," 1967, and "Nothing Will Be the Same Again," 1968. Also author of radio scripts, including "S. S. Elizabethan," 1941, "Freedom's Ferry," 1941, "Open Boat," 1941, "Return to Danger," 1942, "A Winter Journey," 1958, "I Talk to Myself," 1958, "A Letter in the Desert," 1958, "Gobbet," 1959, "The Queens of Ireland," 1960, "Miss Williams," 1960, "Say Nothing," 1961, "A Pillar of Fire," 1962, "A Walk in the World," 1962, "A Dream," 1963, "One Way Out," 1967, "The Silence," 1968, "Sailor's Song," 1970, and "One Way Only," 1970.

OTHER

Broken Water: An Autobiographical Excursion, Chatto & Windus, 1937.
Grey Children: A Study in Humbug and Misery (sociological study of unemployment among coal miners in South Wales), Methuen, 1937.
Between the Tides, Methuen, 1939.
Towards Horizons (on life at sea), Mellifont Press, 1949.
(Editor and compiler with Nina Froud) Fedor Ivanovich Shaliapin, *Chaliapin: An Autobiography as Told to Maxim Gorky,* Stein & Day, 1967.
J. C. Powys: A Man in the Corner, limited edition, K. A. Ward, 1969.
The Face of Winter (poem), limited edition illustrated by wife, Liam Hanley, K. A. Ward, 1969.
Herman Melville: A Man in the Customs House, limited edition, Dud Norman Press, 1971.

Plays anthologized in *Plays of the Year,* Volume 27, edited by J. C. Trewin, Elek, 1963, and *Plays and Players,* volumes 10 and 11, edited by Peter Roberts, Hansom Books, 1963. Also author with others of special issue on John Cowper Powys of *Dock Leaves* (literary journal), spring, 1956.

SIDELIGHTS: Praised by such writers as Herbert Read, John Cowper Powys, and C. P. Snow, James Hanley published novels, plays, and short stories for nearly five decades. Yet, for most of his life Hanley was little known by the general public. The diversity of his work made it difficult for readers and critics to place him; his books ranged from superior sea stories to a five-volume portrait of a Liverpool working class family. Hanley's subject matter and prose style also limited his audience. His stories were unyielding in their portrayal of difficult lives; Ruth Mathewson of *New Leader* described Hanley as being "concerned with exploring self-imprisonment and spiritual deprivation." His prose was spare and demanding; Thomas R. Edwards of the *New York Review of Books* called *A Dream Journey* "a hard book to learn to read, being resolutely unamusing, severely undecorated, unresponsive to expectations of 'story.' It is to be liked, if at all, only on its own intransigent terms."

Praise for Hanley's books came not from the reading public but from critics and fellow novelists. Irving Howe, writing in the *New York Times Book Review,* called Hanley "that rarity of rarities: a genuine original. No one has ever quite used the English language with such bruising abrasiveness, nor quite worked out the same vision of human existence." Bruce Allen of the *Chicago Tribune Book World* claimed that Hanley "has produced more good novels than most of the 20th-Century writers who are far more celebrated. . . . I predict that Hanley will be acclaimed as one of the greatest living novelists, and perhaps placed in serious contention for the Nobel Prize he so richly deserves."

AVOCATIONAL INTERESTS: Fishing, music.

BIOGRAPHICAL/CRITICAL SOURCES:

BOOKS

Contemporary Literary Criticism, Gale, Volume 3, 1975, Volume 5, 1976, Volume 8, 1978, Volume 13, 1980.

PERIODICALS

Chicago Tribune Book World, March 18, 1979.
New Leader, January 3, 1977.
New York Times Book Review, December 19, 1976.
Publishers Weekly, December 27, 1976.
Time, February 18, 1974.

OBITUARIES:

PERIODICALS

Chicago Tribune, November 15, 1985, November 17, 1985.
Daily Variety, November 15, 1985.
Detroit Free Press, November 13, 1985.
New York Times, November 13, 1985.
Times (London), November 12, 1985.

*　　　*　　　*

HANNAH, Barry 1942-

PERSONAL: Born April 23, 1942, in Meridian, Miss.; son of William (an insurance agent) and Elizabeth (King) Hannah; divorced; children: Barry, Jr., Ted, Lee. *Education:* Mississippi College, B.A., 1964; University of Alabama, M.A., 1966, M.F.A., 1967.

ADDRESSES: Home—Route 2, Box 197, Oxford, Miss. 38655.

CAREER: Writer. Clemson University, Clemson, S.C., teacher of literature and fiction, 1967-73; Middlebury College, Middlebury, Vt., writer in residence, 1974-75; University of Alabama, Tuscaloosa, teacher of literature and fiction, 1975-80; worked as writer with filmmaker Robert Altman in Hollywood, Calif., 1980; University of Iowa, Iowa City, writer in residence, 1981; University of Mississippi, University, writer in residence, 1982;

University of Montana, Missoula, writer in residence, 1982-83; University of Mississippi, writer in residence, 1984 and 1985.

AWARDS, HONORS: Award in fiction from Bellaman Foundation, 1970; Atherton fellowship from Bread Loaf Writers Conference, 1971; nomination for National Book Award, 1972, for *Geronimo Rex;* Arnold Gingrich Award for short fiction from *Esquire,* 1978, for *Airships;* special award in fiction from American Academy of Arts and Letters, 1978.

WRITINGS:

Geronimo Rex (novel), Knopf, 1972.
Nightwatchmen (novel), Viking, 1973.
Airships (short stories), Knopf, 1978.
Ray (novel), Knopf, 1981.
Two Stories (short stories), Nouveau Press, 1982.
Black Butterfly (short stories), Palaemon Press, 1982.
The Tennis Handsome (novel), Knopf, 1983.
Power and Light (novella), Palaemon Press, 1983.
Captain Maximus (short stories), Knopf, 1985.
Hey Jack! (novel), Seymour Lawrence, 1987.
(Co-editor) *Boomerang,* Houghton, 1989.

Contributor to periodicals, including *Esquire.*

SIDELIGHTS: Barry Hannah is among the most prominent writers to emerge from the American South since World War II. His novels and short stories reveal a preoccupation with violence and sex that marks him as a disturbing and often demanding author. His first novel, *Geronimo Rex,* details the struggles and adventures of Harry Monroe, a romantic youth with literary aspirations in Louisiana. Amidst the turbulent racial struggle of the early 1960s, Monroe abandons his plans to write and begins a period of disappointment and depravity with a succession of local whores. At his spiritual nadir, he desperately adopts the legendary Indian warrior Geronimo as his inspiration. "What I especially liked about Geronimo," Monroe declares, "was that he had cheated, lied, stolen, usurped, killed, burned, raped. . . . I thought I would like to get into that line of work." At college, Monroe befriends Bobby Dove Fleece, a pallid youth cowed by domineering parents. The two students eventually oppose an avid racist, Whitfield Peter, in a wild shootout culminating in the bigot's defeat. Monroe then marries and enrolls in graduate school.

Geronimo Rex was received with great enthusiasm by most critics and was nominated for a National Book Award. Jim Harrison, writing in the *New York Times Book Review,* called it "almost a totally successful book" and declared, "The writing is intricate enough to make it hard to believe that it's really a first novel." Although John Skow, in the *Washington Post,* protested that the book's momentum was disrupted by the subplots, he agreed that the language was "raucously good" and anticipated Hannah's next work.

Hannah returned to Harry Monroe in the following novel, *Nightwatchmen.* While studying for his doctorate, Monroe meets Thorpe Trove, a rich but strange figure whose estate functions as a meeting place for several of Monroe's fellow students. Thorpe is obsessed with the Knocker, a mysterious killer plaguing the academic community of Southern Mississippi University. *Nightwatchmen* focuses on Thorpe's efforts to expose the Knocker, for which purpose he recruits an equally eccentric detective, the elderly Howard Hunter.

Nightwatchmen abounds in scenes or speeches of mutilation and death. In taped accounts, provided by acquaintances of the Knocker's victims, gruesome acts are related in a manner that both reinforces the notion of society as violent and underscores its callous acceptance of mayhem. In addition, hurricane Camille wreaks havoc on the area, accounting for more grisly deaths and chaos. Despite these sensational aspects, *Nightwatchmen* failed to entice critics and was ultimately ignored.

In 1978 Hannah produced his first collection of short stories, *Airships.* Equally comprised of new work and stories previously featured in *Esquire,* the volume served to confirm Hannah's standing as one of the South's most unique writers. Several stories in *Airships* were culled from Hannah's abandoned novel on the adventures of Confederate General Jeb Stuart. Centering on the recollections of maimed survivors of Stuart's campaigns, these stories range in subject from the brutality of war to the obsessive love for Stuart harbored by a homosexual Confederate. Other tales show a similar preoccupation with violence and deviant behavior in events ranging from tennis tournaments to the apocalypse. In the particularly unsettling "Eating Wife and Friends," Hannah portrays an impending world in which the 1930s are referred to as the "Mild Depression." It is a nightmare of ghoulish depravity, however humorously represented, in which trespassers of private property are shot and eaten, and in which impoverished wanderers are compelled to eat grass and even poison ivy to survive. Writing in the *New York Times Book Review,* Michael Wood hailed the collection's longer works for their "careful, sympathetic wit [in depicting] the string of unlikely shocks and half-hearted enthusiasms that often make up a life." *Time*'s Paul Gray agreed, noting that most of the tales "are artfully rounded-off vignettes humping with humor and menace."

Hannah's third novel, *Ray,* recounts the experiences of an apparently immortal, and slightly unhinged, protagonist who served in both the Civil War and the Vietnam War, and who also worked in Alabama as a doctor. Like the preceding novels and *Airships, Ray* emphasizes violence and death as its title character recalls a gruesome event in Vietnam, contemplates suicide, and reflects on a defeat suffered in Virginia during the Civil War. *Newsweek*'s Walter Clemons described *Ray* as "a griper, but also an accepter," adding that "he wakes up every morning voracious for more sex, more fights, more disappointments." Clemons characterized the novel as a work "of brilliant particulars, dizzying juxtapositions and no reassuring narrative transitions." Benjamin DeMott was exuberant in praising *Ray* as "the funniest, weirdest, soul-happiest work of fiction by a genuinely young American writer that I've read in a long while."

In *The Tennis Handsome,* Hannah further pursued his interest in graphic, and often absurd, violence. Ostensibly concerned with the exploits of an incredibly attractive tennis player, French Edward, and his twisted mentor, Baby Levaster, *The Tennis Handsome* abounds in scenes of perverse mayhem—including a woman raped by a walrus—and absurd humor. A reviewer in *New Republic* complained that the overwhelmingly violent nature of the novel—which also features gouged eyes, death by incineration, suicide, a stroke victim, broken bones, and death from a crossbow—resulted in "a lurid gumbo of inconsequence." The reviewer added, "There is no plot, no unfolding logic of development, no growth of character." Ivan Gold, writing in the *New York Times Book Review,* was less critical of the novel. He conceded that *The Tennis Handsome* "may not be [Hannah's] 'best' book already assembled," but added that "it's as good a place to start as any." Gold was impressed with the bizarre tone of the novel, and, noting that it was partially derived from works first featured in *Airships,* declared that "the stories are worth repeating." But Christopher Lehmann-Haupt, writing in the *New York Times,* was exhausted by the book's frantic pace. He declared that "the manic language palls eventually, and there is little in the way of credible characterization to bring us relief." Lehmann-Haupt added: "Finally, the only living thing in 'The Tennis Handsome' is the author's fierce determination to stun us with his zaniness. This works for a while, but it's simply not enough to sustain us for the length of a novel."

Hannah's 1985 story collection, *Captain Maximus,* represented to some reviewers a powerful step forward from the failings of *The Tennis Handsome.* Observed Peter Ross in the *Detroit News,* Hannah "serves up an unimpeachably original imagination, a mature sense of self-mockery and an abundance of technical and pyrotechnic skill." While reprising some of the violence of earlier books and once again showcasing Hannah's "vital" prose, the book also features "more narrative movement" than *Ray* and *The Tennis Handsome,* lauded Lehmann-Haupt in the *New York Times.* Praising the stories' brilliant wit and surges of energy, Ross placed Hannah among such noted literary figures as Raymond Carver and Frederick Barthelme, "at the forefront of America's latest crop of experimental writers."

BIOGRAPHICAL/CRITICAL SOURCES:

BOOKS

Contemporary Literary Criticism, Gale, Volume 23, 1983, Volume 38, 1986.
Dictionary of Literary Biography, Volume 6: *American Novelists since World War II, Second Series,* Gale, 1980.

PERIODICALS

Chicago Tribune Book World, November 23, 1980, July 3, 1983.
Detroit News, August 4, 1985.
Los Angeles Times Book Review, September 6, 1987, September 13, 1987.
Nation, November 29, 1980.
New Republic, December 13, 1980, April 18, 1983.
Newsweek, May 8, 1978, December 15, 1980.
New York Review of Books, April 23, 1978.
New York Times, April 15, 1978, April 18, 1983, April 29, 1985, November 18, 1987.
New York Times Book Review, May 14, 1972, April 23, 1978, May 21, 1978, November 16, 1980, December 21, 1981, May 1, 1983, June 9, 1985, November 1, 1987.
New Yorker, September 9, 1972.
Saturday Review, June 10, 1978, November, 1980.
Time, May 15, 1978, January 12, 1981, July 22, 1985.
Washington Post, April 19, 1972, August 26, 1987.
Washington Post Book World, June 23, 1985, March 16, 1986, August 17, 1986.

*   *   *

HANNON, Ezra
See HUNTER, Evan

*   *   *

HANSBERRY, Lorraine (Vivian)   1930-1965

PERSONAL: Born May 19, 1930, in Chicago, Ill.; died of cancer, January 12, 1965, in New York, N.Y.; buried in Beth-El Cemetery, Croton-on-Hudson, N.Y.; daughter of Carl Augustus (a realtor and banker) and Nannie (Perry) Hansberry; married Robert B. Nemiroff (a music publisher and songwriter), June 20, 1953 (divorced March, 1964). *Education:* Attended University of Wisconsin, Art Institute of Chicago, Roosevelt College, New

School for Social Research, and studied in Guadalajara, Mexico, 1948-50.

ADDRESSES: Home—New York, N.Y. *Agent*—c/o Vivian Productions, 137 West 52nd St., New York, N.Y. 10019.

CAREER: Playwright. Worked variously as clerk in a department store, tag girl in a fur shop, aide to a theatrical producer, and as waitress, hostess, and cashier in a restaurant in Greenwich Village run by the family of Robert Nemiroff; associate editor, *Freedom* (monthly magazine), 1952-53.

MEMBER: Dramatists Guild, Ira Aldrich Society, Institute for Advanced Study in the Theatre Arts.

AWARDS, HONORS: New York Drama Critics Circle Award for Best American play, 1959, for "A Raisin in the Sun"; named "most promising playwright" of the season, *Variety,* 1959; Cannes Film Festival special award and Screen Writers Guild nomination, both 1961, both for screenplay "A Raisin in the Sun."

WRITINGS:

PLAYS

A Raisin in the Sun: A Drama in Three Acts (produced on Broadway, 1959; also see below), Random House, 1959.
The Sign in Sidney Brustein's Window: A Drama in Three Acts (first produced on Broadway, 1964), Random House, 1965.
Les Blancs (two-act; first produced on Broadway, 1970), Hart Stenographic Bureau, 1966, published as *Lorraine Hansberry's "Les Blancs": A Drama in Two Acts,* adapted by Robert Nemiroff, Samuel French, 1972.
"A Raisin in the Sun," "The Sign in Sidney Brustein's Window," [and] *"The 101 Final Performances of 'Sidney Brustein': Portrait of a Play and Its Author,"* by Robert Nemiroff, New American Library, 1966.
To Be Young, Gifted and Black: A Portrait of Lorraine Hansberry in Her Own Words (play; also see below; produced Off-Broadway, 1969), adapted by Nemiroff, Samuel French, 1971.
Les Blancs: The Collected Last Plays of Lorraine Hansberry (includes "The Drinking Gourd" and "What Use Are Flowers?"), edited by Nemiroff, Random House, 1972, published as *Lorraine Hansberry: The Collected Last Plays,* New American Library, 1983.
A Raisin in the Sun (expanded twenty-fifth anniversary edition) [and] *The Sign in Sidney Brustein's Window,* New American Library, 1987.

OTHER

"A Raisin in the Sun" (screenplay), Columbia, 1960.
(Author of text) *The Movement: Documentary of a Struggle for Equality* (collection of photographs), Simon & Schuster, 1964 (published in England as *A Matter of Colour: Documentary of the Struggle for Racial Equality in the U.S.A.,* Penguin, 1965).
(Self-illustrated) *To Be Young, Gifted and Black: Lorraine Hansberry in Her Own Words,* edited by Nemiroff, introduction by James Baldwin, Prentice-Hall, 1969.
A Raisin in the Sun (recording), three cassettes, Caedmon, 1972.
Lorraine Hansberry Speaks Out: Art and the Black Revolution (recording), Caedmon, 1972.

Contributor to anthologies, including *American Playwrights on Drama,* 1965, and *Three Negro Plays,* Penguin, 1969, and to *Black Titan: W. E. B. DuBois.* Contributor to periodicals, including *Negro Digest, Freedomways, Village Voice,* and *Theatre Arts.*

SIDELIGHTS: Lorraine Hansberry was born into a middle-class black family on Chicago's south side in 1930. She recalled that her childhood was basically a happy one; "the insulation of life within the Southside ghetto, of what must have easily been half a million people, protected me from some of the harsher and more bestial aspects of white-supremacist culture," the playwright stated in *Portraits in Color.* At the age of seven or eight, Hansberry and her upwardly-mobile family deliberately attempted to move into a restricted white neighborhood. Her father fought the civil-rights case all the way to the U.S. Supreme Court, eventually winning his claim to a home within the restricted area. "The Hansberrys' determination to continue to live in this home in spite of intimidation and threats from their angry, rock-throwing white neighbors is a study in courage and strength," Porter Kirkwood assessed in *Freedomways.* "Lorraine's character and personality were forged in this atmosphere of resistance to injustice." "Both of my parents were strong-minded, civic-minded, exceptionally race-minded people who made enormous sacrifices in behalf of the struggle for civil rights throughout their lifetimes," Hansberry remembered.

While in high school, Hansberry first became interested in the theatre. "Mine was the same old story—" she recollected, "sort of hanging around little acting groups, and developing the feeling that the theatre embraces everything I liked all at one time." When Lorraine attended the University of Wisconsin she became further acquainted with great theatre, including the works of August Strindberg, Henrik Ibsen, and Sean O'Casey. She was particularly taken with the Irish dramatist's ability to express in his plays the complex and transcendent nature of man, to achieve "the emotional transformation of people on stage."

After studying painting in Chicago and abroad, Hansberry eschewed her artistic plans and moved to New York City in 1950 to begin her career as a writer. Politically active in New York, Hansberry wrote for Paul Robeson's *Freedom* magazine and participated in various liberal crusades. During one protest concerning practices of discrimination at New York University, Lorraine met Robert Nemiroff, himself a writer and pursuer of liberal politics. Although Nemiroff was white, a romance developed between the two, and in 1953 they married.

Nemiroff encouraged Hansberry in her writing efforts, going so far as to salvage her discarded pages from the wastebasket. One night in 1957, while the couple was entertaining a group of friends, they read a scene from Hansberry's play in progress, "A Raisin in the Sun." The impact left by the reading prompted Hansberry, Nemiroff, and friends to push for the completion, financing, and production of the drama within the next several months.

Enjoying solid success at tryout performances on the road, "A Raisin in the Sun" made its New York debut at the Ethel Barrymore Theatre, becoming the first play written by a black woman to be produced on Broadway; it was the first to be directed by a black director in more than fifty years. When "A Raisin in the Sun" won the New York Drama Critics Circle Award, Hansberry became the youngest writer and the first black artist ever to receive the honor, competing that year with such theatre luminaries as Tennessee Williams, Eugene O'Neill, and Archibald MacLeish. In June, 1959, Hansberry was named the "most promising playwright" of the season by *Variety*'s poll of New York drama critics.

"A Raisin in the Sun" tells the story of a black family attempting to escape the poverty of the Chicago projects by buying a house in the suburbs with the money left from the insurance policy of their dead father. Conflict erupts when the son, Walter Lee,

fights to use the money instead to buy his own business—a life's ambition. Yet when a white representative from the neighborhood that the family plans to integrate attempts to thwart their move, the young man submerges his materialistic aspirations—for a time, at least—and rallies to support the family's dream. Still Hansberry wonders, as expressed in the lines of poet Langston Hughes from which she takes her title, what will become of Walter Lee's frustrated desires: "What happens to a dream deferred? / Does it dry up like a raisin in the sun? / Or fester like a sore—and then run?"

Because the play explored a universal theme—the search for freedom and a better life—the majority of its audience loved it. According to Gerald Weales in *Commentary,* it reflected neither the traditional Negro show, folksy and exotic, or the reactionary protest play, with black characters spouting about the injustices of white oppression. Rather, "A Raisin in the Sun" was a play about a family that just happened to be black. "The thing I tried to show," Hansberry told Ted Poston in the *New York Post,* "was the many gradations in even one Negro family, the clash of the old and the new."

New York Times critic Brooks Atkinson admired "A Raisin in the Sun" because it explored serious problems without becoming academic or ponderous. "[Hansberry] has told the inner as well as outer truth about a Negro family in Chicago," the critic observed. "The play has vigor as well as veracity and is likely to destroy the complacency of anyone who sees it." Weales labeled "Raisin" "a good play" whose "basic strength lies in the character and the problem of Walter Lee, which transcends his being a Negro. If the play were only the Negro-white conflict that crops up when the family's proposed move is about to take place, it would be editorial, momentarily effective, and nothing more. Walter Lee's difficulty, however, is that he has accepted the American myth of success at its face value, that he is trapped, as Willy Loman was trapped, by a false dream. In planting so indigenous an American image at the center of her play, Miss Hansberry has come as close as possible to what she intended—a play about Negroes which is not simply a Negro play." The reviewer also found the play "genuinely funny and touching," with the dialogue between family members believable.

"A Raisin in the Sun" ran for 530 performances. Shortly thereafter a film version of the drama was released; Hansberry won a special award at the Cannes Film Festival and was nominated for an award from the Screen Writers Guild for her screenplay. She then began working on a second play about a Jewish intellectual who vacillates between social commitment and paralyzing disillusionment. Entitled "The Sign in Sidney Brustein's Window," the play ran on Broadway for 101 performances despite mixed reviews and poor sales. "Its tenure on Broadway parallels the playwright's own failing health," Kirkwood noted. The play closed on January 12, 1965, the day Hansberry died of cancer at the age of thirty-five.

Although Hansberry and her husband divorced in 1964, Nemiroff remained dedicated to the playwright and her work. Appointed her literary executor, he collected his ex-wife's writings and words after her death and presented them in the autobiographical *To Be Young, Gifted and Black.* He also edited and published her three unfinished plays, which were subsequently produced: "Les Blancs," a psychological and social drama of a European-educated African who returns home to join the fight against Colonialism; "The Drinking Gourd," a drama on slavery and emancipation expressed through the story of a black woman; and "What Use Are Flowers?," a fable about an aging hermit who, in a ravaged world, tries to impart to children his remembrances of the past civilization he had once renounced. "It's true that there's a great deal of pain for me in this," Nemiroff told Arlynn Nellhaus of the *Denver Post* about his custodianship, "but there's also a great deal of satisfaction. There is first-class writing and the joy of seeing [Lorraine's] ideas become a contemporary force again . . . [is] rewarding. . . . She was proud of black culture, the black experience and struggle. . . . But she was also in love with all cultures, and she related to the struggles of other people. . . . She was tremendously affected by the struggle of ordinary people—the heroism of ordinary people and the ability of people to laugh and transcend."

To Be Young, Gifted and Black was made into a play that ran Off-Broadway in 1969, keeping the memory of Hansberry and critical examination of her small body of work alive. Martin Goffried, in *Women's Wear Daily*, hypothesized that "Miss Hansberry's tragically brief playwriting career charted the postwar steps in the racial movement, from working within the system ('A Raisin in the Sun') to a burgeoning distrust of white liberals ('The Sign in Sidney Brustein's Window') to the association with Africa in 'Les Blancs' that would evolve, after her death, from the ashes of passive resistance into the energy and danger of militant activism." Writing in *Beautiful, Also, Are the Souls of My Black Sisters,* Jeanne L. Noble examined the author in a similar sociological light, wondering where, in today's political continuum, Hansberry would stand in comparison with the new breed of black writers. Yet she concluded: "Certainly for [Hansberry's] works to leave a continuing legacy—though she died at age 35, just before the fiercest testing period of the black revolution—is itself monumental. And we will always ponder these among her last words: 'I think when I get my health back I shall go into the South to find out what kind of revolutionary I am.' "

But most critics did not perceive of Hansberry as a particularly political or "black" writer, but rather as one who dealt more with human universals. Gerald Weales speculated in *Commonweal* that "it is impossible to guess how she might have grown as a writer, but her two [finished] plays indicate that she had wit and intelligence, a strong sense of social and political possibility and a respect for the contradictions in all men; that she could create a milieu (the family in *Raisin,* the Greenwich Village circle in *Sign*) with both bite and affection; that she was a playwright—like Odets, like Miller—with easily definable flaws but an inescapable talent that one cannot help admiring." And *Life* magazine's Cyclops concluded that Hansberry's gentle and intelligent sensibilities could best be read in these lines from "The Sign in Sidney Brustein's Window," when Sidney describes himself: "A fool who believes that death is a waste and love is sweet and that the earth turns and men change every day and that rivers run and that people wanna be better than they are and that flowers smell good and that I hurt terribly today, and that hurt is desperation and desperation is energy and energy can *move* things."

MEDIA ADAPTATIONS: A musical version of "The Sign in Sidney Brustein's Window" was produced on Broadway in 1972; a musical version of "A Raisin in the Sun," entitled "Raisin," was produced on Broadway in 1973.

AVOCATIONAL INTERESTS: Ping-pong, skiing, walking in the woods, reading biographies, conversation.

BIOGRAPHICAL/CRITICAL SOURCES:

BOOKS

Authors in the News, Volume 2, Gale, 1976.

Bigsby, C. W. E., and others, *Confrontation and Commitment: A Study of Contemporary American Drama,* MacGibbon & Kee, 1967.
Bigsby, C. W. E., editor, *The Black American Writer,* Volume 2, Penguin, 1969.
Cherry, Gwendolyn, and others, *Portraits in Color,* Pageant Press, 1962.
Concise Dictionary of American Literary Biography: The New Consciousness, 1941-1968, Gale, 1987.
Contemporary Authors Bibliography Series, Volume 3: *American Dramatists,* Gale, 1989.
Contemporary Literary Criticism, Volume 17, Gale, 1981.
Dictionary of Literary Biography, Gale, Volume 7: *Twentieth-Century American Dramatists,* 1981, Volume 38: *Afro-American Writers after 1955: Dramatists and Prose Writers,* 1985.
Noble, Jeanne L., *Beautiful, Also, Are the Souls of My Black Sisters: A History of the Black Women in America,* Prentice-Hall, 1978.
Scheader, Catherine, *They Found a Way: Lorraine Hansberry,* Children's Press, 1978.

PERIODICALS

Commentary, June, 1959.
Commonweal, September 5, 1969, January 22, 1971.
Denver Post, March 14, 1976.
Esquire, November, 1969.
Freedomways, winter, 1963, summer, 1965, fourth quarter, 1978.
Life, January 14, 1972.
New Yorker, May 9, 1959.
New York Post, March 22, 1959.
New York Times, March 8, 1959, March 12, 1959, April 9, 1959, November 9, 1983, August 15, 1986.
Washington Post, November 16, 1986, December 2, 1986.
Women's Wear Daily, November 16, 1970.

OBITUARIES:

PERIODICALS

Antiquarian Bookman, January 25, 1965.
Books Abroad, spring, 1966.
Newsweek, January 25, 1965.
New York Times, January 13, 1965.
Publishers Weekly, February 8, 1965.
Time, January 22, 1965.

*   *   *

HARDWICK, Elizabeth 1916-

PERSONAL: Born July 27, 1916, in Lexington, Ky.; daughter of Eugene Allen and Mary (Ramsey) Hardwick; married Robert Lowell (a poet), July 28, 1949 (divorced, 1972); children: Harriet. *Education:* University of Kentucky, A.B., 1938, M.A., 1939; Columbia University, additional study.

ADDRESSES: Home—15 West 67th St., New York, N.Y. 10023.

CAREER: Writer; adjunct associate professor of English, Barnard College, New York, N.Y.

MEMBER: American Academy and Institute of Arts and Letters.

AWARDS, HONORS: Guggenheim fellowship in fiction, 1948; George Jean Nathan Award for dramatic criticism (first woman recipient), 1967; National Academy and Institute of Arts and

Letters award in literature, 1974; National Book Critics Circle Award nomination, 1980, for *Sleepless Nights.*

WRITINGS:

The Ghostly Lover (novel), Harcourt, 1945.
The Simple Truth (novel), Harcourt, 1955.
(Editor) *The Selected Letters of William James,* Farrar, Straus, 1960.
A View of My Own: Essays on Literature and Society, Farrar, Straus, 1962.
Seduction and Betrayal: Women and Literature (essays), Random House, 1974.
(Editor) *Rediscovered Fiction by American Women: A Personal Selection* (series; 18 volumes), Ayer, 1977.
Sleepless Nights (novel), Random House, 1979.
Bartleby in Manhattan (essays), Random House, 1984.
(Editor) *The Best American Essays 1986,* Ticknor & Fields, 1986.

OTHER

Contributor to periodicals, including *Partisan Review, New Yorker,* and *Harper's.* Founder and advisory editor, *New York Review of Books.*

SIDELIGHTS: An accomplished essayist and novelist, Elizabeth Hardwick is perhaps best known "primarily for brilliant literary and social criticism, which has graced the pages of many of the country's leading liberal journals, most notably the *Partisan Review* and the *New York Review of Books,*" according to Joseph J. Branin, in a *Dictionary of Literary Biography* article on Hardwick. Hardwick was born and raised in Kentucky, but found her way to New York City during her young adult years; she's lived in New York ever since.

Her first novel, *The Ghostly Lover,* mirrors this aspect of the author's life: the protagonist, Marian, grew up in the South and moved to Manhattan. As the story goes on, Marian returns to her hometown to care for her ailing grandmother, but so misses New York that she moves there for good following her grandmother's death. "Throughout the novel, Marian is presented as a profoundly lonely young person," notes Branin. "[She] longs for connection and intimacy with another person but finds it impossible to break through the separateness of the characters in the novel. She is especially disappointed with her mother, whom she adores from a distance."

As Branin reports, *The Ghostly Lover* garnered mixed critical reaction. But soon after its publication, Hardwick was contacted by Philip Rahv, an editor of the avant-garde *Partisan Review,* to become a contributor. "She accepted the offer eagerly and thus began her long and successful career as a social and literary critic," Branin writes. As Hardwick's reputation as a writer grew, so did her fame outside the editorial offices. She married the poet Robert Lowell in 1949, a union that lasted until 1972, when Lowell divorced Hardwick to marry Caroline Blackwood, an Irish writer. "In 1977, the last year of his life, Lowell returned to Hardwick," relates Branin. "They summered together in Castine, Maine, before Lowell died of heart failure in New York." The piece continues with Hardwick telling a *New York Times* reporter at that time that her former husband was "the most extraordinary person I have ever known, like no one else—unplaceable, unaccountable."

Hardwick's published works include a second novel, *The Simple Truth,* a story of speculation and accusation surrounding a sensational murder trial. That novel, like the author's first, was greeted with mixed reviews. Hardwick continued publishing, first a selection of William James' letters, then an collection called *A View of My Own: Essays on Literature and Society.* A 1974 collection, *Seduction and Betrayal: Women and Literature,* caught the attention of several critics, including Rosemary Dinnage, who remarks in a *Times Literary Supplement* article that the book "is so original, so sly and strange, but the pleasure in embedded in the style, in the way [the author] flicks the English language around like a whip." Hardwick's concern in *Seduction and Betrayal,* Dinnage goes on to say, "is to present her own angry and witty view of the sexes, and for this she has more scope with the fictional beings and the companions of writers than with the great creative women, for these less easily align themselves with the victims." Hardwick "is no hand-wringer," says *Books and Bookmen* critic Jean Stubbs. "She is a literary surgeon, admirably equipped to expose the nerves." And in the opinion of Joan Didion, writing in *New York Times Book Review,* "Perhaps no one has written more acutely and poignantly about the ways in which women compensate for their relative physiological inferiority, about the poetic and practical implications of walking around the world deficient in hemoglobin, deficient in respiratory capacity, deficient in muscular strength and deficient in stability of the vascular and autonomic nervous systems."

By the time Hardwick's collection *Bartleby in Manhattan* came out, in 1984, she was almost universally acclaimed as a major essayist, prompting *New York Times* reviewer Christopher Lehmann-Haupt to remark, "One is interested in anything that Elizabeth Hardwick writes. That is a given." For this volume of social and literary musings, however, Lehmann-Haupt does have some reservations: "The subjects . . . give one a moment or two of pause. The atmosphere in the South during the civil rights movement of the 1960's? The significance of Martin Luther King, Jr. and of Lee Harvey Oswald and his family? . . . It isn't so much that we've lost interest in these topics as that they've become as familiar to us by now as our fingers and our toes." Another reviewer finds more to recommend in *Bartleby in Manhattan.* "As these essays of the past 20 years show, Hardwick's [concerns] have two qualities that make her one of our finest critics: a heart that wants to be moved and a critical intelligence that refuses to indulge it," finds *Los Angeles Times Book Review* writer Richard Eder. "Much that she deals with produces more disquiet in her than reward; she looks for values in the fiery writing of the '60s and the distanced writing of the '70s and finds them poor or limited. Our reward is the record of her search." "Whatever her subject," says novelist Anne Tyler, acting as critic for *New Republic,* Hardwick "has a gift for coming up with descriptions so thoughtfully selected, so exactly right, that they strike the reader as inevitable." As Tyler also notes, "Mere aptitude of language, of course, is not sufficient. What makes *Bartleby in Manhattan* memorable is the sense of the author's firm character. 'Pull yourself together,' she says briskly to a racist who tells her he feels sick at the sight of an integrated crowd."

The author's third novel, *Sleepless Nights,* "is a difficult work to classify," comments Branin. One possible definition may be "autobiographical": the fiction centers on a writer named Elizabeth, who grew up in Kentucky and moved to Manhattan. In the course of the story the narrator "remembers certain people and places from her past. . . . [Her] compassion for her old acquaintances and her careful observations as she brings these memories to life give the work its power and unity," Branin states.

Elizabeth Hardwick "is the voice of toughminded gentility," says Joan Joffe Hall in a *New Republic* review from 1974. "She inspires confidence because she seems just like the reader, a shade smarter perhaps, able to turn the commonplace into reve-

lation, talking in someone's living room with an earnest casual-
ness beyond personality. It's the quality most of us aspire to."

BIOGRAPHICAL/CRITICAL SOURCES:

BOOKS

Contemporary Literary Criticism, Volume 13, Gale, 1980.
Dictionary of Literary Biography, Volume 6: *American Novelists
    since World War II,* Gale, 1980.

PERIODICALS

Books and Bookmen, January, 1976.
Chicago Tribune, November 25, 1986.
Los Angeles Times Book Review, May 29, 1983.
New Republic, May 25, 1974, June 20, 1983.
Newsweek, June 17, 1974, May 30, 1983.
New York Review of Books, January 27, 1974, April 29, 1979.
New York Times, April 2, 1982, May 24, 1983.
New York Times Book Review, May 5, 1974, June 12, 1983.
Times Literary Supplement, November 29, 1974.
Village Voice, May 7, 1979.
Washington Post Book World, May 12, 1974, May 29, 1983.

*   *   *

HARDY, Thomas   1840-1928

PERSONAL: Born June 2, 1840, in Higher Bockhampton, Dorset, England; died after a short illness, January 11, 1928, in Dorchester, Dorset, England; cremated and ashes buried in Poets'
Corner, Westminster Abbey, London, England; heart buried in
Stinsford, Dorset, England; son of Thomas (a stonemason) and
Jemima (Hand) Hardy; married Emma Lavinia Gifford, September 17, 1874 (died, 1912); married Florence Emily Dugdale
(a teacher and children's author), February 10, 1914. *Education:*
Educated privately in Dorchester, Dorset, England.

ADDRESSES: Home—Max Gate, Dorchester, Dorset, England.

CAREER: Writer. Worked as an architect in Dorchester and
London, beginning as an apprentice.

AWARDS, HONORS: Medal of the Royal Institute of British
Architects, 1863, for "On the Application of Colored Bricks and
Terra Cotta in Modern Architecture"; LL.D., University of Aberdeen, 1905; Order of Merit, 1910, from the British Government; Litt.D., Cambridge University, 1913; D.Litt., Oxford University, 1920; LL.D., University of St. Andrews, 1922; D.Litt.,
University of Bristol, 1925.

WRITINGS:

NOVELS

Desperate Remedies (anonymously; three volumes), Tinsley
    Brothers, 1871, revised one volume edition, Henry Holt &
    Company, 1874, recent edition, St. Martin's, 1977.
Under the Greenwood Tree (anonymously; two volumes), Tinsley
    Brothers, 1872, one volume edition, Holt & Williams, 1873,
    recent edition, Oxford University Press, 1986.
A Pair of Blue Eyes (first published serially in *Tinsley's Maga-
    zine,* September, 1872-July, 1873), three volumes, Tinsley
    Brothers, 1873, one volume edition, Holt & Williams, 1873,
    revised edition, Macmillan, 1919, recent edition, Penguin
    Books, 1986.
Far from the Madding Crowd (first published serially in *Cornhill
    Magazine,* January, 1874-December, 1874), two volumes,
    Smith, Elder & Company, 1874, one volume edition, Henry

Holt & Company, 1874, revised edition, Smith, Elder, &
    Company, 1875, recent edition, Norton, 1986.
The Hand of Ethelberta (first published serially in *Cornhill Mag-
    azine,* July, 1875-May, 1876), two volumes, Smith, Elder &
    Company, 1876, one volume edition, Henry Holt & Com-
    pany, 1876, revised edition, Osgood, McIlvaine & Com-
    pany, 1896, recent edition, St. Martin's, 1978.
The Return of the Native (first published serially in *Belgravia,*
    January, 1878-December, 1878), three volumes, Smith,
    Elder & Company, 1878, one volume edition, Henry Holt
    & Company, 1878, revised edition, Osgood McIlvaine &
    Company, 1895, recent edition, Garland Publishing, 1986.
The Trumpet-Major (first published serially in *Good Words,* Jan-
    uary, 1880-December, 1880), three volumes, Smith, Elder
    & Company, 1880, one volume edition, Henry Holt & Com-
    pany, 1880, recent edition, Penguin Books, 1985.
A Laodicean (first published serially in *Harper's New Monthly
    Magazine,* December, 1880-December, 1881), Harper &
    Brothers, 1881, three volume edition, Sampson Low, Mar-
    ston, Searle & Rivington, 1881, recent edition, St. Martin's,
    1978.
Two on a Tower (first published serially in *Atlantic Monthly,*
    May, 1882-December, 1882), three volumes, Sampson Low,
    Marston, Searle & Rivington, 1882, one volume edition,
    Henry Holt & Company, 1882, revised edition, Sampson
    Low, Marston, Searle & Rivington, 1883, recent edition,
    Macmillan, 1976.
The Romantic Adventures of a Milkmaid (also see below; first
    published serially in *Graphic,* summer, 1883), Harper &
    Brothers, 1883.
The Mayor of Casterbridge (first published serially in *Graphic,*
    January 2, 1886-May 15, 1886), two volumes, Smith, Elder
    & Company, 1886, revised one volume edition, Henry Holt
    & Company, 1886, recent edition, Chelsea House, 1987.
The Woodlanders (first published serially in *Macmillan's Maga-
    zine,* May, 1886-April, 1887), three volumes, Macmillan,
    1887, one volume edition, Harper & Brothers, 1887, recent
    edition, Oxford University Press, 1985.
Tess of the d'Urbervilles: A Pure Woman Faithfully Presented
    (first published serially in *Graphic,* July 4, 1891-December
    26, 1891), three volumes, Osgood, McIlvaine Company,
    1891, one volume edition, Harper & Brothers, 1892, revised
    editions, Osgood, McIlvaine & Company, 1892, 1895, re-
    cent edition, Buccaneer Books, 1987.
Jude the Obscure (first published serially in *Harper's New
    Monthly Magazine,* December, 1894-November, 1895),
    Harper & Brothers, 1896, revised edition, Macmillan, 1902,
    recent edition, Chelsea House, 1987.
The Well-Beloved (first published serially in *Illustrated London
    News,* October 1, 1892-December 17, 1892), Harper &
    Brothers, 1897, recent edition, St. Martin's, 1978.
An Indiscretion in the Life of an Heiress (first published in *New
    Quarterly Magazine,* July, 1878), privately printed, 1934.

Also author of unpublished novel *The Poor Man and the Lady.*

SHORT STORY COLLECTIONS

Wessex Tales, two volumes, Macmillan, 1888, one volume edi-
    tion, Harper & Brothers, 1888, revised edition, Osgood,
    McIlvaine & Company, 1896, 2nd revised edition, Macmil-
    lan, 1912, recent edition, Franklin Library, 1982.
A Group of Noble Dames, Harper & Brothers, 1891, recent edi-
    tion, St. Martin's, 1957.
Life's Little Ironies, Harper & Brothers, 1894, revised edition,
    Macmillan, 1912, recent edition, Academy Chicago Pub-
    lishers, 1985.

A Changed Man, The Waiting Supper, and Other Tales, Harper & Brothers, 1913, recent edition, Academy Chicago Publishers, 1986.

Old Mrs. Chundle and Other Stories, With The Tragedy of the Famous Queen of Cornwall, St. Martin's, 1977.

POETRY

(And illustrator) *Wessex Poems and Other Verses,* Harper & Brothers, 1898.

Poems of the Past and the Present, Harper & Brothers, 1901.

Time's Laughingstocks and Other Verses, Macmillan, 1909.

Satires of Circumstance, Macmillan, 1914.

Moments of Vision and Miscellaneous Verses, Macmillan, 1917.

Late Lyrics and Earlier With Many Other Verses, Macmillan, 1922.

Human Shows, Far Phantasies, Songs, and Trifles, Macmillan, 1925.

Winter Words in Various Moods and Metres, Macmillan, 1928.

POETRY—OMNIBUS EDITIONS

Selected Poems, Macmillan, 1916.

Collected Poems, Macmillan, 1919, enlarged edition, 1930, Macmillan, 1931.

Chosen Poems, Macmillan, 1929.

The Complete Poems, Macmillan, 1976, Macmillan, 1978.

The Variorum Edition of the Complete Poems of Thomas Hardy, Macmillan, 1979.

The Complete Poetical Works of Thomas Hardy, Oxford University Press, 1982-85.

PLAYS

The Mistress of the Farm (adapted from *Far from the Madding Crowd;* first produced as "Far from the Madding Crowd" in Liverpool at the Prince of Wales Theatre, February 27, 1882, produced in the West End at the Globe Theatre, April 29, 1882), privately printed, c. 1879.

The Three Wayfarers (one act; first produced in London at Terry's Theatre, June 3, 1893), Harper & Brothers, 1893, revised edition, Fountain Press, 1930, recent edition, Scholars' Facsimiles and Reprints, 1979.

"Tess of the d'Urbervilles" (five acts; adapted from the novel of the same name), first produced in New York at the Fifth Avenue Theatre, March 2, 1897; later published in *Tess in the Theatre,* edited by Marguerite Roberts, University of Toronto Press, 1950.

The Dynasts (nineteen acts; selected revised scenes first produced in London at Kingsway Theatre, November 25, 1914), Macmillan, Volume 1, 1904, Volume 2, 1905, Volume 3, 1908, one volume edition, 1910, recent edition, 1978.

(Adapter) *The Play of "Saint George,"* privately printed, 1921.

The Famous Tragedy of the Queen of Cornwall (one-act; first produced in Dorchester, England, November, 1923), Macmillan, 1923, revised edition, 1924, recent edition, Folcroft, 1980.

OTHER

(With wife, Florence Emily Hardy) *The Early Life of Thomas Hardy, 1840-1891* (autobiography), Macmillan, 1928.

(With F. Hardy) *The Later Years of Thomas Hardy, 1892-1928* (autobiography), Macmillan, 1930.

Thomas Hardy's Personal Writings: Prefaces, Literary Opinions, Reminiscences, University of Kansas, 1966.

The Literary Notes of Thomas Hardy, Acta Universitatis Gothoburgensis, 1974.

The Personal Notebooks of Thomas Hardy, Macmillan, 1978, Columbia University Press, 1979.

The Collected Letters of Thomas Hardy, edited by Richard L. Purdy and Michael Millgate, Oxford University Press, Volume 1, 1978, Volume 2, 1980, Volume 3, 1982, Volume 4, 1984, Volume 5, 1985, Volume 6, 1987, Volume 7, 1988.

Also author of nonfiction prose works such as "Candour in English Fiction," 1890.

COLLECTED WORKS

The Penguin Thomas Hardy, Penguin Books, 1983.

The Works of Thomas Hardy in Prose: With Prefaces and Notes, eighteen volumes, AMS Press, 1984.

Works of Thomas Hardy, Smith Publications, 1989.

MEDIA ADAPTATIONS: Tess of the d'Urbervilles was adapted for film and released under the title "Tess," starring Nastassia Kinski, by Columbia Pictures, 1980.

SIDELIGHTS: Thomas Hardy was both a great poet and a great novelist. Although, as Laurence Lerner and John Holstrom point out in *Thomas Hardy and His Readers,* Hardy "was a classic of the English novel long before he died," he was not celebrated as a poet of the very first rank until after his death. Helmut E. Gerber's brief synopsis, in the first volume of *Thomas Hardy: An Annotated Bibliography of Writings about Him,* gives some indication of the evolution of Hardy's reputation: "In the first period, 1871-1896, Hardy established himself with critics and general readers as an important novelist, but recurring storms of controversy made his life difficult at times. During the second, 1897-1928, Hardy the poet and dramatist lost some of this 'celebrity,' but by the time of his death in 1928 he had gained a measure of national respect tendered to few English authors of the last one hundred years. The third period, 1929-1939, was a time of falling reputation for Hardy. In the fourth, 1940-1969, beginning with a centenary celebration curtailed by the incipient World War, the rediscovery of much that had been undervalued and the reassessment of Hardy the man and artist proceeded without pause."

This brief summary, however, only partially suggests the controversy that has enveloped judgments of Hardy's works, both his poetry and prose. If there is at present a "Hardy industry" producing dozens of books and hundreds of articles, it arose, in part, as Jean Brooks suggests in *Thomas Hardy: The Poetic Structure,* because Hardy's "place in literature has always been controversial, [and] constant reassessment is essential to keep the balance between modern and historical perspective." Lerner and Holstrom's collection of reviews written about Hardy's works during the author's lifetime demonstrates the kinds of responses his novels engendered initially. But characteristics of Hardy's works that may have disturbed his contemporaries prompting an anonymous reviewer of Hardy's novel *Jude the Obscure* (1895) to entitle his article "Jude the Obscene"—may not trouble modern readers. As Albert J. Guerard indicates in *Thomas Hardy:* "We are in fact attracted by much that made the post-Victorian realist uneasy." Even today, however, Hardy's works evoke an especially powerful subjective response in critics. Brooks believes that the "strong disagreements about what is 'good' or 'bad' in Hardy's work prove only the relativity of judgement and the vitality of the author." As Donald Davie suggests in *Thomas Hardy and British Poetry,* "Each reader finds in the poems what he brings to them; what he finds there is his own pattern of preoccupations and preferences. If this is true of every poet to some degree, of Hardy it is exceptionally true."

The variety of opinions about Hardy's works has been expressed by several of the most famous modern writers; Lerner and Holstrom record that Henry James, writing about *Tess of the d'Urbervilles* (1891) to Robert Louis Stevenson, asserted: *Tess* "is vile. The pretense of 'sexuality' is only equalled by the absence of it, and the abomination of the language by the author's reputation for style." In *After Strange Gods* T. S. Eliot commented: "[Hardy] seems to me to have written as nearly for the sake of 'self-expression' as a man well can; and the self which he had to express does not strike me as a particularly wholesome or edifying matter of communication." By contrast D. H. Lawrence, in his perceptive "Study of Thomas Hardy" included in *Phoenix: The Posthumous Papers of D. H. Lawrence,* claimed that the writer's "feeling, his instinct, his sensuous understanding is . . . very great and deep, deeper than that, perhaps, of any other English novelist." Moreover, Virginia Woolf, in *The Second Common Reader,* declared: "Thus it is no mere transcript of life at a certain time and place that Hardy has given us. It is a vision of the world and of man's lot as they revealed themselves to a powerful imagination, a profound and poetic genius, a gentle and humane soul." Quite clearly, then, the quality of Hardy's writing has been variously assessed; but as Irving Howe notes in *Thomas Hardy,* any "critic can, and often does, see all that is wrong with Hardy's poetry but whatever it was that makes for his strange greatness is hard to describe."

The variation in responses to Hardy's work is due in part to the writer's extraordinarily prolific output. In the twenty-six years between 1871 and 1897, he wrote fourteen novels, three volumes of short stories, and several poems that would be published later. Not even illness curtailed his productivity: *A Laodicean* (1881) was dictated to his wife when Hardy was bedridden with what Michael Millgate in *Thomas Hardy: A Biography* speculates was kidney stones complicated by typhoid fever. From 1898 until his death in 1928 Hardy published eight volumes of poetry; about one thousand poems were published in his lifetime. Moreover, between 1903 and 1908 Hardy published *The Dynasts*—a huge poetic drama in 3 parts, 19 acts, and 130 scenes. In a canon of this size, some works will not measure up to the highest standard. Indeed, only five or six of the novels and some frequently anthologized poems are familiar to most American readers.

Although criticism of Hardy's works varies considerably, certain subjects recur in commentary discussing both the novels and the poems. First, there is the question of Hardy's style. Eliot's opinion of the writer's techniques has been discussed since it was first published in 1934's *After Strange Gods:* "[Hardy] was indifferent even to the prescripts of good writing: he wrote sometimes overpoweringly well, but always very carelessly; at times his style touches sublimity without ever having passed through the stage of being good." Hardy insisted that he purposely created the strange effects that critics have labeled as lapses. His technique, Hardy explained in his autobiography, engendered in critics "the inevitable ascription to ignorance of what was really choice after full knowledge. That the author [Hardy] loved the art of concealing art was undiscerned." Brooks notes: "Time has revealed Hardy's antirealistic devices to be imaginative truths about cosmic Absurdity rather than the author's incompetence."

Second, Hardy's subjects have drawn much critical attention. Many of his early critics disapproved of certain topics or motifs that run throughout Hardy's novels, poems, and stories. Guerard identifies some of these: "The inventiveness and improbability, the symbolic use of reappearance and coincidence, the wanderings of a macabre imagination, the suggestions of supernatural agency; the frank acknowledgement that love is basically sexual and marriage usually unhappy; the demons of plot, irony

and myth." The contemporary reader, on the other hand, may not be disturbed by these particular issues but may find others more difficult to accept.

In Hardy's time, as now, readers complained of what they perceived in the author's tone and stance as pessimism, a word he especially disliked to have applied to his works. This complaint charges that the novels are too gloomy and that most end unhappily. Although modern readers would phrase their responses differently, an anonymous 1892 reviewer of *Tess of the d'Urbervilles* expressed feelings that are echoed today: "Nor do we believe that any person reads novels to reform himself—he reads them for pleasure. . . . In this view the story of Tess appeals to human sympathy very strongly and directly; it harrows our hearts, it arouses our anger, it fills us with indignation, and it leaves us depressed and sorrowful. . . . No way out of shame and sin has been shown us, and we already knew the way to death. . . . A sense of this superb workmanship is the only pure pleasure the book affords; every other effect is as black as night, as cheerless as a tomb, as hopeless as the scaffold."

Hardy's long career spanned the Victorian and the modern eras. He described himself in "In Ten Ebris II" as a poet "who holds that if way to the Better there be, it exacts a full look at the Worst" and during his nearly eighty-eight years he lived through too many upheavals—among them the Boer War and World War I—to have become optimistic with age. Nor did he seem by nature to be cheerful. J. Hillis Miller, who in *Thomas Hardy: Distance and Desire* sees the writer as a "spectator," suggests, "The tone of voice natural to a spectator who sees things from such a position imparts its slightly acerb flavor throughout his work as a compound of irony, cold detachment, using reminiscent bitterness, an odd kind of sympathy which might be called 'pity at a distance,' and, mixed with these, a curious joy, a grim satisfaction that things have, as was foreseen, come out for the worst in this worst of all possible worlds." Miller believes that Hardy's stance had its roots in his early childhood, reflecting what many contemporary critics have come to recognize: in spite of Hardy's frequent denials, his works are strongly autobiographical and reveal events and feelings of his youth and early manhood.

Born in 1840 in the English village of Higher Bockhampton in the county of Dorset, Hardy died in 1928 at Max Gate, a house he built for himself and his first wife, Emma Lavinia Gifford, in Dorchester, a few miles from his birthplace. As a youth, Hardy traversed the distance on foot between Bockhampton and Dorchester, where he attended school; as an adult he frequently traveled from Dorchester to Bockhampton to visit his family, especially his mother, Jemima Hand Hardy, whom Robert Gittings in *Young Thomas Hardy* calls the real guiding star of his early life. Until he was in his seventies, Hardy usually stayed from April to July of each year in London, where he attended the theater, concerts, operas, his clubs, and the many gatherings of his literary associates and aristocratic friends. But Dorset was his home; his family, the people of his childhood, his memories, the land itself with heath and river—all these made him a rooted man.

Living in Dorset, one of the poorest and most backward of the counties, Hardy was exposed to patterns of rural life little changed in hundreds of years, which he described in his essay "The Dorsetshire Labourer" (1883) and explored through the rustic characters in many of his novels. A local dialect similar to German was spoken in the vicinity at least by the older inhabitants. Stonehenge was only the most famous of the many remains of the past with which the English south abounded. There Hardy could explore and contemplate Druid and Roman, ancient and medieval ruins.

For Hardy, the Napoleonic Wars constituted the great event of the historical past; Dorset tradition, which he imbibed, told of the fear of Bonaparte's invasion of England. Hardy's novel *The Trumpet Major* (1880) and his epical, poetical drama *The Dynasts* reflect a lifetime of involvement with this historical material. The author interviewed elderly soldiers who had fought in the Napoleonic campaigns so that, as Richard H. Taylor notes in his introduction to *The Personal Notebooks of Thomas Hardy,* "impressions of the Napoleonic era were passed down to Hardy by word of mouth"; Hardy also visited the field of the battle of Waterloo, where Napoleon's forces were defeated.

But if Hardy were alive to the past, he was also sensitive to the future, at least as a writer; scores of younger authors, including William Butler Yeats, Siegfried Sassoon, and Virginia Woolf, visited him, and he discussed poetry with Ezra Pound. Furthermore, Hardy spoke eloquently against some of the horrors of his present, notably the Boer War and World War I, in such works as "Drummer Hodge" and "In Time of 'The Breaking of Nations,'" to name only the best known of his many war poems.

Strongly identifying himself and his work with Dorset, Hardy saw himself as a successor to the Dorset dialect poet William Barnes, who had been a friend and mentor. Moreover, Hardy called his novels the Wessex Novels, after one of the kingdoms of Anglo-Saxon Britain. He provided a map of the area, with the names of the villages and towns he coined to represent actual places—for example, Hardy's fictional Casterbridge is Dorchester, Budmouth is Weymouth, and Melchester is Salisbury—and he helped his friend Hermann Lea to locate scenes from the novels for Lea's book *Thomas Hardy's Wessex,* published in 1925. Interest in Hardy country has remained high, and the literary pilgrims to Dorset have contributed to what Gerber, in the introduction to the first volume of his bibliography, calls the "'Hardy of Wessex' cult."

In spite of what turned out to be a highly productive career as both novelist and poet, Hardy had not decided initially to become a writer. After his schooling he was apprenticed, at the age of sixteen, to the Dorchester architect John Hicks. In Hardy's choice of architecture, he seemed to have continued in the line of work pursued by his father and grandfather; both men were stonemasons and builders. Like his father, too, Hardy played the violin and accompanied the senior Thomas Hardy at country dances.

During the years of his apprenticeship Hardy was not only studying architecture and playing the violin but satisfying his curiosity in other ways. At sixteen he took pains to witness the hanging of a young woman. His description of her rain-drenched body dangling from the rope had, according to Gittings, "distinctly sexual overtones." The incident satisfied voyeuristic tendencies and echoed in his writing. Guerard suggests that Hardy's presentation of almost pathologically unaggressive male characters reveals "unconscious autobiography" and equates the "unaggressive spectator" with the "neurotic voyeur." Hardy recreated the spectacle of the execution in his conclusion for *Tess of the d'Urbervilles* in which Tess is hanged; and the event remained vivid in Hardy's memory: Gittings notes in *Thomas Hardy's Later Years* that when the writer was in his eighties, "his mind and his tongue reverted to some of the less seemly obsessional topics of his youth. One was the hanging and public execution of women."

Hardy's other interests during the time of his apprenticeship seem to have been decidedly intellectual in nature. He awakened early in the morning to read Latin or Greek before his walk to John Hicks's office, a pattern of study his fictional character Jude was also to follow in *Jude the Obscure.* Hardy was aided in his studies by his friend Horatio Mosley, known as Horace Moule, eight years his senior. As H. C. Webster notes in *On a Darkling Plain,* Hardy's friendship with Moule "was primarily responsible for his early contact with the thought of his time." As a result he read the *Origin of Species* by Charles Darwin, whose funeral Hardy was to attend, and Herbert Spencer's *First Principles,* John Stuart Mill's *On Liberty,* and Ernest Renan's and John Colenso's biblical criticism. Moule, however, was a deeply troubled man; his suicide in 1873 was a "cataclysmic event" in Hardy's life, according to Gittings in *Young Thomas Hardy:* following Moule's death Hardy was unable to portray in his novels "a man who was not, in some way, maimed by fate."

After his apprenticeship to Hicks ended in 1862, Hardy was employed by Arthur Blomfield, a distinguished London architect, and spent the next five years in London continuing his extensive reading and his architectural work but also availing himself of the opportunities that London afforded to a young man of literary, musical, and artistic talents. But London could also satisfy Hardy's taste for the bizarre and macabre. One day when he was overseeing the removal of coffins from the graveyard of Old St. Pancras Churchyard prior to church restoration, Hardy observed an open coffin with one skeletal body and two skeletal heads, a sight which made a vivid impression on him and subsequently on his writing. Richard C. Carpenter, in a 1960 *Modern Fiction Studies* essay, traces the grotesque in Hardy's novels-"the kind of situation, scene, or image which yokes man and his environment together in strange relationships." The "gurgoyle" that spouts torrents of water and washes away the flowers planted on a freshly dug grave in *Far from the Madding Crowd* (1874) or the clergyman who is late to perform a wedding ceremony and is found wandering in a graveyard because he thought he was to officiate at a funeral in *Two on a Tower* (1882) are only two of many examples of Hardy's use of the grotesque, what can be called his nightmare vision.

Much is known about the places Hardy visited and what he observed during these London years and the years immediately afterward when he returned to Dorset because of ill health and continued his architectural work there. Much is also known about his intellectual growth, about the books he read. In *Thomas Hardy: A Study of His Writings and Their Background,* William R. Rutland cites the Bible, the Romantic poets—especially Percy Bysshe Shelley, John Keats, and William Wordsworth—and the Dorset poet William Barnes as early influences on Hardy. Adding to the writers whom he read under Moule's tutelage during the years of his apprenticeship, Hardy turned to the classics, reading Homer, Sophocles, Euripides, and Aeschylus, whose recurring theme "call no man happy while he lives" Rutland believes to have had a strong influence on the development of Hardy's "twilight view" of life. Hardy also studied Virgil, Horace, and Catullus among the Latin writers.

Many critics point to an influence of German philosopher Arthur Schopenhauer on Hardy, although Hardy himself dismissed such speculation; both critics and the author are partially correct. Hardy was forty-three in 1883 when Schopenhauer's *The World as Will and Idea* was first translated and published in English, and the English writer had already published nine novels. Naturally, his views, his stance, his cast of mind were by then well developed. On the other hand, Schopenhauer's and other German philosophic works were almost certainly absorbed and incorporated in Hardy's view. Indeed, Rutland shows how Hardy grappled with the German philosophers and demonstrates their influence on the evolution of *The Dynasts.* Nonetheless, as Miller notes in *Thomas Hardy: Distance and Desire:* "[It] is impossible to demonstrate, however, that any one of these sources is uniquely important in determining Hardy's view of life. He read many of the writers who formulated the late Victorian outlook, and his notions were undoubtedly also acquired in part from newspapers, periodicals and other such reading." No matter how "philosophic" his novels seem, Hardy was not a philosopher, as he clearly revealed in his preface to *Jude the Obscure:* "Like former productions of this pen, *Jude the Obscure* is simply an endeavour to give shape and coherence to a series of seemings, or personal impressions, the question of their consistency or their discordance, of their permanence of their transitoriness, being regarded as not of the first moment." John Holloway notes in *The Victorian Sage: Studies in Argument* that Hardy's novels and works in general are impressionistic; they are not philosophic documents, not arguments.

In spite of the destruction of many of Hardy's notebooks, critics can trace his intellectual growth and development. About his private life, however, the writer was extremely reticent, indeed, secretive. Gittings says in *Young Thomas Hardy* that Hardy was "determined to set up a barrier against biography." The two-volume official biography—*The Early Life of Thomas Hardy,* published in 1928, and *The Later Years of Thomas Hardy,* published in 1930—listed Hardy's second wife, Florence, whom he married in 1914 after the death of his first wife, Emma, as the author of the two volumes, commonly labeled "The Life." However, in 1954 Richard L. Purdy, in *Thomas Hardy: A Bibliographic Study,* revealed that the majority of "The Life" had actually been composed by Hardy himself. Although Florence added the last four chapters and some other material after Hardy's death, "The Life" is, with some qualifications, an autobiography written in the third person.

Autobiographical and biographical material is of great significance to an understanding of Hardy's work because it has become increasingly clear that, in spite of the writer's denials, his novels are very strongly autobiographical. His poems, on the other hand, have always been more intimately and directly connected with their author; the subjects alone make this link inevitable. The great poems of 1912 to 1913 were written after the death of Emma on November 27, 1912. Some of these works are dated as early as December, 1912, a month after her death, and others were composed in March of the following year, after Hardy had visited St. Juliot, Cornwall, where he first met Emma. Some poems bear initials identifying the person or persons referred to; certain travel poems clearly mark places Hardy visited; several poems are dedicated to writers Hardy knew, such as George Meredith, Algernon Charles Swinburne, and Leslie Stephen; and among his greatest works are occasional poems—for example, "The Convergence of the Twain" on the sinking of the Titanic in 1912—and his war poetry.

Moving beyond obvious connections between the author's life and his verse, scholarship of the 1960s and 1970s has ever more explicitly revealed the autobiographical basis for much of the poetry. Davie notes that "whatever the rights or wrongs of using biographical information to assist explication of other poets, in the case of an author so secretive as Hardy it has already proved itself indispensable." The writer's extraordinary ability to retain a moment, an impression, a seemingly trivial event in his memory for forty years and then to bring it forth in verse is attested to by J. O. Bailey in *The Poetry of Thomas Hardy.* Bailey writes that Hardy seemed "to think of the past as present and of the

dead in their graves as somehow alive." As Kenneth Marsden declares in *The Poems of Thomas Hardy,* the writer's "chief resource [was] memory and his chief modes, meditation and reminiscence."

Hardy's extraordinary memory of events of the past should not obscure the fact that, as Gittings notes in *Young Thomas Hardy,* "if one were to believe 'The Life,' Hardy had no contact at all with young women from the time he was sixteen to the age of twenty-nine, when he met his first wife." Lack of first-hand information about his relationships with women has encouraged speculation and conjecture. In *Providence and Mr. Hardy,* Lois Deacon and Terry Coleman contend that Hardy was in love with his cousin Tryphena and had a child with her. Gittings—as well as other biographers—agrees that Tryphena was very important to Hardy, but does not support the theory about the child; he does believe that Hardy loved not only Tryphena, but two of her sisters as well, and that this situation was reflected in his novel *The Well-Beloved* (1897), in which the hero is in love with a woman, her daughter, and her granddaughter at intervals of twenty years.

In spite of Hardy's apparent attraction to other women throughout the years, Emma Lavinia Gifford, Hardy's first wife, was the most significant of his attachments, both for his life and for his art. Hardy met Emma in 1870 when he was sent to St. Juliot, Cornwall, to plan and oversee a church restoration. It was to the early days of their courtship that the poet so frequently turned in the memorial verses which Carl J. Weber in *Hardy of Wessex* declares may "outlive anything else that Hardy has done." Emma strongly supported Hardy's decision to give up architecture and turn to writing, for at the time they first met, he had a number of poems to his credit and was working on his first novel.

Hardy's career as a novelist technically began in the 1860s. His first novel, *The Poor Man and the Lady,* was completed in 1867 but was never published, although George Meredith, who read it for the publishing house of Chapman & Hall, recognized the writer's talents. Sections of it, however, were cannibalized for use in *Desperate Remedies,* published anonymously in 1871 after Hardy helped defray the costs by giving the publisher Tinsley seventy-five pounds. This book is a love story and mystery thriller. Howe says that the novel reveals a "repeated upsurge of barely controlled psychic materials." Hardy, in years to come, learned to control and to refine his material, but even in this apprentice work certain characteristics of his best novels are found. H. C. Duffin, in *Thomas Hardy: A Study of the Wessex Novels, the Poems and "The Dynasts,"* notes the erotic situation around which almost all Hardy's novels are built, a situation also reflected in most of his short stories and many of his poems. As Pierre d'Exideuil suggests in *The Human Pair in the Works of Thomas Hardy,* the writer "sees in love at once the creative and motor force, [and] accords it first place among human preoccupations." Lawrence, in his study of Hardy, describes this theme as the characters' "struggle into love."

In *Desperate Remedies* the heroine Cytherea Graye has two suitors—Edward Springrove, whom she loves, and Aeneas Manston, to whom she is strongly attracted. This situation, a heroine with two, or perhaps three, lovers occurs frequently in Hardy's works. One of the writer's earliest admirers, Havelock Ellis, noted in an 1883 *Westminster Review* article this "persistent repetition of the same situations."

Although *Desperate Remedies* seemed barely under the author's control, Hardy's next novel, *Under the Greenwood Tree* (1872), is a model of form. Taking its title, as Geoffrey Grigson explains in his introduction to the 1974 Macmillan edition of the novel, "from the broadside ballad of 'Under the Greenwood Tree,' in which countrymen and country girls . . . have rural fun under the greenwood tree," the narrative is composed of four parts representing the seasonal divisions of the year. In Douglas Brown's view expressed in his *Thomas Hardy,* the value of the agricultural life is here elaborated by the novelist for the first time. Although "the old, stable order is passing," Brown notes, the "loss, the dismay, is not yet tragic, and the deliberate framing of the tale to suggest hope balances the insistence upon dying traditions." The love story, in which the heroine, Fancy Day, is attracted to two men, is only in part a private affair, for the novel conveys a constant sense of community. As Perry Meisel suggests in *Thomas Hardy: The Return of the Repressed,* the love story is symbolic of broader social forces. The theme of betrayal, which came to dominate Hardy's work, is sounded here, but *Under the Greenwood Tree* is his sunniest novel.

His next novel, *A Pair of Blue Eyes,* published in 1873, is of special interest because it presents a slightly fictionalized account of Hardy's first meeting with Emma. But the best of his early novels, and the one that has received the greatest critical attention and acclaim, is *Far from the Madding Crowd.* However, as astute a reviewer as Henry James, whose *Nation* article is reprinted in Lerner and Holstrom's collection, was not favorably disposed: "Everything human in the book strikes us as factitious and insubstantial; the only things we believe in are the sheep and the dogs."

The publishing history of *Far from the Madding Crowd* is significant. During the nineteenth century novels tended to be serialized in magazines before being published in volume form. Magazine editors were highly concerned that nothing in the serial version of the novel be offensive to their primarily female readers or to an editor's idea of what material was appropriate for women. Hardy, as well as William Makepeace Thackeray, Charles Dickens, and other writers, submitted to this procedure. In the case of *Far from the Madding Crowd,* Hardy was asked for a novel by Leslie Stephen, editor of *Cornhill,* a prestigious magazine whose first editor was Thackeray. Stephen's invitation to Hardy was, according to Millgate, an "extraordinary moment for a hitherto unknown writer." Moreover, Stephen—editor of the *Dictionary of National Biography* and the father of Virginia Woolf—eventually became Hardy's close friend and admired associate. Stephen's influence on the writer was greater than that of any other contemporary, according to Millgate, and one of Hardy's loveliest poems is the sonnet he wrote on Stephen's death, "The Schreckhorn."

The problems of censorship implicit in serialization for a family magazine did not disappear simply because Hardy and Stephen were friends, although the difficulties were eased. Stephen suggested changes which the novelist made, knowing that when the book was published in volume form he would be able to restore the original version if he chose. In *Thomas Hardy from Serial to Novel,* Mary Ellen Chase traces some of the changes appearing in the serial publication, alterations which, on occasion, completely undermined the novel in question.

Although Hardy gave vent to his frustration with censorship in his essay "Candour in English Fiction" (1890), the problem was one that continued to plague him: "What this practically amounts to is that the patrons of literature, . . . acting under the censorship of prudery, rigorously exclude from the pages they regulate subjects that have been made, by general approval of the best judges, the bases of the finest imaginative compositions since literature rose to the dignity of an art." Sensible and intelligent readers and critics certainly understood the seriousness with which Hardy wrote, yet some prepared to burn Hardy's books on the grounds that they pandered to lascivious tastes, degraded the institution of marriage, or were antireligious. As virtually all Hardy biographers note, he was extremely sensitive to criticism and very vulnerable to attacks, even by readers who appeared to be deranged.

Far from the Madding Crowd is called by Dale Kramer in *Thomas Hardy: The Forms of Tragedy* "the non-tragic predecessor." The novel ends happily when the steadfast hero, Gabriel Oak, marries Bathsheba Everdene, the woman he has loved and served for many years, although the darker side of life is never at far remove. Once again the heroine is given a choice of men—Oak, Farmer Boldwood, and Sergeant Troy—who are very different from one another. Kramer declares that this situation is based on the idea of dichotomy: "The assumption of the aesthetic in the novel is that any and all reactions to situations will be between two extremes, or on one of two extremes." Brown also responds to this division, but sees it in terms of Bathsheba's major choice between Troy, who is an outsider, and Oak, who knows such enduring things as the land, his sheep, the weather, the cycle of the seasons: "value inheres in the persistence itself. Oak embodies that persistence." Hardy's skill in describing the countryside, the farms, and the setting of the novel is emphasized by Joseph W. Beach in *The Technique of Thomas Hardy:* "we know by evidence of all our senses that we are dealing here with 'substantial things.' "

Bathsheba is the most memorable of the heroines of Hardy's early novels, and he lavished care on his portrayal of her. However, in her flightiness, her inability to run her farm without Gabriel Oak's help, her general dependence on men, and her attraction to Sergeant Troy—who is handsome, dashing, and skilled with his sword, but a womanizer—some critics have seen a depreciation of women. J. I. M. Stewart writes in *Thomas Hardy: A Critical Biography,* "If Hardy does shake a slightly obsessed fist in *Far from the Madding Crowd* it is neither at Crass Causality nor at the decay of the times but at Woman"; Hardy is afflicted, Stewart suggests, by "sexual pessimism and [an] inclination to misogyny."

Hardy's women have fascinated critics of the novels. Samuel C. Chew suggests in *Thomas Hardy: Poet and Novelist* that "Hardy's women are all of one type, differing only in degree." Although many other critics hold similar views, few state them so absolutely. Guerard, for example, sees Hardy's women as "charming, impulsive, and dangerously contradictory"; they fall into several categories ranging from those who are fickle to those who are pure. Howe notes that Hardy liked women and that he was "thoroughly traditional in celebrating the maternal, the protective, the fecund, the tender, the lifegiving." Lascelles Abercrombie declares in *Thomas Hardy: A Critical Study* that for the writer the "first requirement of feminine nature seems to be, on the whole, the *maintenance* of personal integrity (this desire typifying itself in purity, chastity, virginity)." With the exception of Arabella Donn in *Jude the Obscure* and a few less important characters, most of Hardy's women are young and sexually inexperienced, of marriageable age, and eager to attach themselves to some man. Since most either have no parents or highly unreliable ones, the heroines are looking, as Ruth Milberg-Kaye writes in *Thomas Hardy—Myths of Sexuality,* for "substitutes for the fathers they miss, and most discover that the ideal Hardy hero is a perfect paternal substitute, although not an adequate lover."

Hardy's men, on the other hand, fall into two general categories: the dependable, enduring, somewhat stolid, and sexually unaggressive men, such as Gabriel Oak, who tend to idealize women; and the rakish, devilish, sexually aggressive users of women, such as Sergeant Troy, to whom the heroines are inevitably attracted. Howe suggests that although Hardy valued the virtues associated with passivity, his creativity was stirred by assertiveness. Guerard feels that Hardy liked pathologically unaggressive men: "Those who do seem normally aggressive, or of normal sexuality, are either grotesquely unreal" or are rakes or stage villains. Lawrence suggests that this division of character represents a split between the spirit and the flesh and that Hardy believed "that which is physical, of the body, is weak, despicable, bad"; at the same time, according to Lawrence, Hardy maintains an "unconscious adherence to the flesh."

The composition of Hardy's *Far from the Madding Crowd,* Millgate contends, can be seen in retrospect as "marking the end of the earliest, happiest, and in certain respects most generously creative period in his career." Webster notes that from 1878 on Hardy "became increasingly melancholic." With the exception of *The Trumpet Major,* the novels that followed are darker, more ironic, bitter, tragic. During the years between 1874, which saw the publication of *Far from the Madding Crowd,* and 1886, when *The Mayor of Casterbridge* appeared, Hardy wrote one of his best-known works, *The Return of the Native* (1878), and a number of lesser-known novels that are useful in tracing Hardy's development as a writer but of somewhat limited interest to a general readership.

Unlike the other novels written during this second period, *The Return of the Native* breaks new ground. In it Hardy described the various forces—personal and elemental—that seem to be beyond the characters' control. He wrote of the destructive relationship between a mother, Mrs. Yeobright, who, according to Millgate, resembles Jemima Hardy, and her son, Clym Yeobright; this sort of attachment Hardy never explored in writing again in any detail. He portrayed sexual involvements—Clym and Eustacia Vye, Damon Wildeve and Eustacia Vye—that are resolved only when the lovers, Wildeve and Eustacia, drown. He showed the power of the land itself, Egdon Heath, which, according to Brown, "nourishes the very vitality and stability it would threaten to destroy." A growing sense that man is driven by impulses that are not under rational control asserts itself more strongly here than in Hardy's previous novels; Beach describes this theme as the "tragedy of irreconcilable ideals": "What happens is subordinate to what is felt." Webster believes that *The Return of the Native* represents a "sudden break from the effort to balance social and cosmic evils." These dichotomies are still present in *The Return of the Native,* but, as Ian Gregor notes in *The Great Web: The Form of Hardy's Major Fiction,* they are now somewhat different: "The characters tend to perceive they are acting in two plots, one of their own devising, one of vast impersonal forces, but in this novel they see no relationship between the two."

Even the ending of the novel is problematic. For one thing, the marriage of Diggory Venn to Clym's cousin Thomasin—Wildeve's widow—was not a conclusion Hardy wanted; he claimed that it was contrived to satisfy readers' desire for a happy ending. Of more importance, however, is the ambiguity of Hardy's view of his protagonist Clym Yeobright at the end of *The Return of the Native.* Has Clym achieved a modest success or is he a minor failure? Has he gained wisdom or is he deluded? Are such terms meaningful in these circumstances? These are questions with which critics have grappled.

Although in *The Return of the Native* Hardy explores what Millgate suggests is a "road he had not taken," in the novel he returns

to his childhood, to the memories of his mother, and to Egdon Heath, the expanse of heathland between Dorchester and Warham. In *The Mayor of Casterbridge* (1886), on the other hand, Hardy treats the Dorchester of the 1820s, thirty years and more before his youth and years of apprenticeship there. While writing this novel Hardy returned both to the actual Dorchester that was to be his home until his death, and to Casterbridge, the fictional Dorchester of his imagination; the novelist prepared by reading the *Dorset County Chronicle* for 1826, the era portrayed in *The Mayor of Casterbridge.* He noted in the novel's preface three historical events which came together for him in the composition of the novel: "They were the sale of a wife by her husband, the uncertain harvests which immediately preceded the repeal of the Corn Laws, and the visit of a Royal personage to the aforesaid part of England."

But in *The Mayor of Casterbridge* Hardy also developed themes already in evidence in *The Return of the Native.* Starting from the German Romantic poet Novalis's dictum "Character is fate," Hardy traced in the person of Michael Henchard the rise to and fall from power of a man who, from the very beginning of the novel, carries the seeds of destruction within himself. His tragic plight, according to Brooks, is threefold: "cosmic (representative of man's predicament in an uncaring universe), social (showing the plight of a rural community when old methods are swept away by new) and personal."

Of central interest to critics of *The Mayor of Casterbridge* is the character of Henchard, a man capable in a moment of drunken abandon of selling his wife and young daughter, Elizabeth-Jane, to the highest bidder; in repentance for his inhumanity, Henchard vows to give up alcohol for twenty-one years, and with the strength gained from guilt and sobriety, he goes on to become mayor in the town of Casterbridge, only to be supplanted by a Scotsman named Donald Farfrae. Judgments of Henchard range from that of Beach, who believes that Henchard's vanity is everyman's vanity and that to condemn him is to condemn ourselves, to that of Miller, who speculates that Henchard's soul casts a shadow between himself and all others he meets.

The unique position of *The Mayor of Casterbridge* in Hardy's canon is suggested by the writer's preface to the novel: "The story is more particularly a study of one man's deeds and character than, perhaps, any other of those included in my Exhibition of Wessex life." Gregor believes the *Mayor* to be a "rare novel" in the history of English fiction because "it must be one of the very few major novels . . . where sexual relationships are not, in one way or another, the dominant element."

Critics view the novel as reflecting change. For Kramer, one feature of *The Mayor of Casterbridge* is "the presentation of an individual struggle as but one occurrence of timeless rhythm, the cycle of change within the organization of society." Farfrae, who supplants Henchard, can, Kramer suggests, "be toppled by a man" just as he upset Henchard. Brown, on the other hand, sees the conflict between the two men as the "struggle between the native countryman and the alien invader." Gregor believes that the conflict is both public and private and "finds dramatic expression in the idea of generation," which connotes both history as well as development. Gregor finds change, the movement from youth to adulthood and maturity, emphasized in the novel's final sentence: "And in being forced to class herself [Elizabeth-Jane] among the fortunate she did not cease to wonder at the persistence of the unforeseen, when the one to whom such unbroken tranquillity had been accorded in the adult stage was she whose youth had seemed to teach that happiness was but the occasional episode in a general drama of pain." Although both

Roy Morrell, in *Thomas Hardy: The Will and the Way,* and Gregor stress the importance of reading this sentence in its entirety, its final part—"happiness was but the occasional episode in a general drama of pain"—has been frequently used as a clear and simple thematic expression of Hardy's view of the human condition.

Webster declares that the novels written after *The Mayor of Casterbridge* come "closer to striking a mean between what is comprehensible (natural law) and what is incomprehensible ('Chance')" because they are more balanced between optimism and pessimism than the earlier works. Certainly *The Woodlanders,* published in 1887, does fit Webster's characterization. In his 1960 *Modern Fiction Studies* essay, Robert Y. Drake, Jr., describes *The Woodlanders* as a "traditional pastoral" and states that the novel ends on a happy note. Little in the novel is determined by forces outside the characters; what happens to them is, for the most part, not a matter of chance, but of choice.

In *The Woodlanders* the heroine, Grace Melbury, marries Edred Fitzpiers, a doctor who is above her in station, rather than the man who has loved her for years, Giles Winterbourne. Fitzpiers falls in love with Grace when he sees her face in a mirror. He explains that love is innate; all it needs is a face—an image—on which to be projected. Fitzpiers says: "I am in love with something in my own head, and no thing-in-itself outside it at all." Many of Hardy's characters, especially the men, fall in love in this way, reflecting a tendency toward idealization that Miller has studied in Hardy's novels. *The Woodlanders* suggests, however, that "loving kindness, unlike love," is based upon understanding people's "true shape": "The woman herself [Grace Melbury] was a conjectural creature who had little to do with the outlines presented; . . . a shape in the gloom, whose true quality could only be approximated by putting together a movement now and a glance then, in that patient attention which nothing but watchful loving-kindness ever troubles itself to give."

This conflict between the self-involvement of love and the generosity of loving-kindness is most fully worked out in Hardy's next novel, *Tess of the d'Urbervilles* (1891), which bears the subtitle *A Pure Woman Faithfully Presented.* Tess Durbeyfield, the novel's title character, has left her lover, Alec d'Urberville, and borne him a child who dies; some years later, she is deserted by her husband, Angel Clare, when she tells him about her former lover. Throughout the novel, each of her lovers sees Tess as a projection of himself and makes no attempt to see her as she is.

Hardy's attempts to allow the reader to see Tess as she is and as no one in the novel is able to see her—may account for the diversity of critical views about the character. P. N. Furbank, in spite of his enthusiasm for the novel, suggests in his introduction to the 1974 Macmillan edition that "Tess is so many things that we may forget what she is not—I mean, a rounded character in the nineteenth-century novelist's sense. She is so vivid to us, we know so exactly what she looks like and what her voice sounds like, that we credit her with more coherence as a character than she possesses." Milberg-Kaye contends that there is "something of a made-up quality about her. . . . She is incomplete, made up of bits and pieces, because Hardy wanted to do more with her and have her stand for more than his representation of her warrants." Another way of looking at this problem is suggested by Bernard J. Paris who, in an essay collected in The Victorian Experience, observes that Hardy seems "particularly blind to the contribution which their [the characters'] neuroses make to their unhappy lives." And a number of critics have identified masochistic impulses in Tess.

Tess is drawn to two men who are very different from one another. Alex d'Urberville is, as Guerard notes, a stage villain, and Angel Clare, as his name implies, is spiritual to a fault; according to Lawrence, Hardy himself was "something of an Angel Clare." Angel, however, unlike Alec, is able to mature and develop. In *Ethical Perspectives in the Novels of Thomas Hardy,* Virginia R. Hyman declares that during Angel's reunion with Tess his perception of her "utter reliance upon him arouses his own feelings, which are, at last, adequate to the situation: 'Tenderness was absolutely dominant in him at last.'" He is now able to protect Tess, although what she has done—her murder of Alec—is far worse than what he had deserted her for in the past—her affair with Alec. Although Angel supports her, the law finds her guilty, and Tess is hanged. In the last paragraph of the novel, Hardy writes: "'Justice' was done, and the President of the Immortals, in Aeschylean phrase, had ended his sport with Tess." Hardy's involvement with Tess (he called her "my" Tess, and Paris says that her creator was in love with her), the intensity with which she is portrayed, and the sympathy Hardy evokes for her plight create the novel's special quality. Stewart declares that "*Tess of the d'Urbervilles* is not merely an emotional novel; it is one of the greatest distillations of emotion into art that English literature can show."

Tess of the d'Urbervilles initially aroused much strong opposition, but the truly vitriolic responses were reserved for *Jude the Obscure.* Titles of review articles, as reprinted in Lerner and Holstrom's collection, included not only "Jude the Obscene" but also "Hardy the Degenerate." However, writers Havelock Ellis and H. G. Wells were strong supporters, recognizing the novel's great powers. Hardy responded briefly to his severe critics in the 1912 preface to *Jude the Obscure* and ironically noted an unexpected consequence of the attacks: "the experience completely curing me of further interest in novel-writing."

Much critical discussion of the novel centers on the three major characters—Jude Fawley, Sue Bridehead, and Arabella Donn. Stewart contends that in this "innovatory novel" there is much literary stereotype—an honorable man, Jude, falls for an earthy, sexual woman, Arabella; disgusted by her, he turns to her opposite, a spiritual type, Sue. In his afterword to the New American Library edition of the novel, A. Alvarez suggests that the women are projections of Jude's inner needs. Jude and Sue, on the other hand, were seen by Hardy as counterparts, images of one another.

As Frank R. Giordano, Jr., notes in his 1972 *Studies in the Novel* essay, *Jude the Obscure* is a *Bildungsroman,* a novel of development. It is the only novel of Hardy's that traces, albeit briefly, a child's development from youth to adulthood. The reader follows Jude's study of the classics, his desire to go to Christminster (Oxford), his attraction to Arabella, his yearning for Sue, and, after Sue's departure, his self-destructive urges and early death. Lawrence writes that Jude becomes "exhausted in vitality, bewildered, aimless, lost, pathetically nonproductive." And Stewart says that perhaps "no work of the English imagination since *Samson Agonistes* at once suggests so much power and so much fatigue." When he finished *Jude the Obscure* in 1895, Hardy seems to have come to the end of what he had to say in the novel and to have explored all the problems he felt were within the scope of his fiction. Liberated from the novel, he turned to poetry, devoting considerable effort to *The Dynasts.*

According to John Wain's introduction to the 1965 St. Martin's Press edition of the dramatic poem, in composing *The Dynasts* Hardy took "one of those sudden jumps which characterize the man of genius. . . . He wrote his huge work in accordance with conventions of an art that had not yet been invented: the art of cinema." *The Dynasts,* following this view, is "neither a poem, nor a play, nor a story. It is a shooting-script." Walter F. Wright suggests in *The Shaping of "The Dynasts"* that the work "epitomizes his [Hardy's] world view after he had secured from the philosophers the metaphorical structure for expressing what he had long felt to be true."

In *The Dynasts* Hardy confronted the problem of reconciling determinism and man's capacity for making moral choices, as Wright points out. What, in short, is Hardy's philosophy? Bailey describes three stages in the writer's philosophic development: the first, influenced by Darwin, expressed the view that "natural law rules the world"; the second, influenced by Schopenhauer, "tended to personify natural law as the Universal Will or an Unconscious Mind capable of being waked to consciousness through human agency"; and the third, Hardy's "evolutionary meliorism," presented the hope that human action could make life better.

But how is the Universal Will or the Immanent Will, which is unconscious, to become conscious? As Rutland notes, there is conflict between the "limited and fallible, but conscious and directed, will of the individual towards ordered well being; and the unlimited and all-powerful but unconscious and senseless, urge of an 'Immanent Will' to continuing but purposeless existence." Hardy's answer to this problem is to be found in the concluding verses of *The Dynasts,* which Bailey calls a "paean of hope": "But—a stirring thrills the air / Like to sounds of joyance there / That the rages / Of the ages / Shall be cancelled, and deliverance offered from the darts that were, / Consciousness the Will informing, till It fashion all things fair!" A work of such size and scope as *The Dynasts,* which was published in three parts over five years, engendered varied, and sometimes bewildered, responses. But by 1908, with the publication of the third part, most reviewers were enthusiastic.

In his remaining years, Hardy turned almost exclusively to poetry. Samuel Hynes, in *The Pattern of Hardy's Poetry,* points to two productive poetic periods: the 1860s, and 1910 to 1920. In the latter period, Hardy most fully developed his poetic talents. He published eight volumes of poetry, beginning in 1898 with *Wessex Poems,* containing lyrics dating from the 1860s, and ending with *Winter Words,* published in 1928 and including poems written during the last year of his life.

When Hardy died in 1928, his ashes were deposited in the Poets' Corner of Westminster Abbey and his heart, having been removed before cremation, was interred in the graveyard at Stinsford Church where his parents, grandparents, and his first wife were buried. Although his family were understandably distressed by these somewhat bizarre arrangements, this double burial—a reflection of the duality of the public and the private man—seems quite fitting for Thomas Hardy.

BIOGRAPHICAL/CRITICAL SOURCES:

BOOKS

Abercrombie, Lascelles, *Thomas Hardy: A Critical Study,* Martin Secker, 1912.

Bailey, J. O., *The Poetry of Thomas Hardy: A Handbook and Commentary,* University of North Carolina Press, 1970.

Beach, Joseph W., *The Technique of Thomas Hardy,* Chicago University Press, 1922.

Blunden, Edmund, *Thomas Hardy,* Macmillan, 1942.

Brennecke, Ernest, *Thomas Hardy's Universe: A Study of a Poet's Mind,* Small, Maynard & Company, 1924.

Brooks, Jean, *Thomas Hardy: The Poetic Structure,* Cornell University Press, 1971.

Brown, Douglas, *Thomas Hardy,* Longmans, Green, 1962.

Carpenter, R. C., *Thomas Hardy,* Twayne, 1964.

Casagrande, Peter, *Unity in Hardy's Novels: "Repetitive Symmetries,"* Regents Press of Kansas, 1982.

Cecil, Lord David, *Hardy, the Novelist: An Essay in Criticism,* Constable, 1943.

Chase, Mary Ellen, *Thomas Hardy from Serial to Novel,* University of Minnesota Press, 1927.

Chew, Samuel C., *Thomas Hardy: Poet and Novelist,* Allen & Unwin, 1921.

Cox, R. G., editor, *Thomas Hardy: The Critical Heritage,* Barnes & Noble, 1970.

Davie, Donald, *Thomas Hardy and British Poetry,* Oxford University Press, 1972.

Deacon, Lois and Terry Coleman, *Providence and Mr. Hardy,* Hutchinson, 1966.

d'Exideuil, Pierre, *The Human Pair in the Works of Thomas Hardy,* Toulmin, 1930.

Dictionary of Literary Biography, Gale, Volume 18: *Victorian Novelists,* 1983, Volume 19: *British Poets, 1840-1914,* 1983.

Duffin, H. C., *Thomas Hardy: A Study of the Wessex Novels, the Poems, and "The Dynasts,"* Manchester University Press, 1937.

Eliot, T. S., *After Strange Gods: A Primer of Modern Heresy,* Harcourt & Brace, 1934.

Firor, Ruth A., *Folkways in Thomas Hardy,* University of Pennsylvania Press, 1931.

Gerber, Helmut E. and Eugene W. Davis, editors, *Thomas Hardy: An Annotated Bibliography of Writings about Him,* North Illinois University Press, Volume 1, 1973, Volume 2, 1983.

Gittings, Robert, *Young Thomas Hardy,* Heinemann, 1975.

Gittings, Robert, *Thomas Hardy's Later Years,* Heinemann, 1978.

Gregor, Ian, *The Great Web: The Form of Hardy's Major Fiction,* Rowman & Littlefield, 1974.

Guerard, Albert J., *Thomas Hardy: The Novels and Stories,* Harvard University Press, 1949.

Hardy, Evelyn, *Thomas Hardy: A Critical Biography,* St. Martin's, 1954.

Hardy, Thomas, *The Personal Notebooks of Thomas Hardy,* introduction by Richard H. Taylor, Columbia University Press, 1979.

Hardy, Thomas and Florence Emily Hardy, *The Early Life of Thomas Hardy, 1840-1891,* Macmillan, 1928.

Hardy, Thomas and Florence Emily Hardy, *The Later Years of Thomas Hardy, 1892-1928,* Macmillan, 1930.

Holloway, John, *The Victorian Sage: Studies in Argument,* St. Martin's, 1953.

Hornback, Bert G., *The Metaphor of Chance: Vision and Technique,* Ohio University Press, 1971.

Howe, Irving, *Thomas Hardy,* Macmillan, 1967.

Hyman, Virginia R., *Ethical Perspective in the Novels of Thomas Hardy,* Kennikat Press, 1975.

Hynes, Samuel, *The Pattern of Hardy's Poetry,* University of North Carolina Press, 1961.

Johnson, Lionel, *The Art of Thomas Hardy,* Dodd, Mead, 1894.

Kay-Robinson, Denys, *The Landscape of Thomas Hardy,* Salem House, 1984.

Kramer, Dale, *Thomas Hardy: The Forms of Tragedy,* Wayne State University Press, 1975.

Lawrence, D. H., *Phoenix: The Posthumous Papers of D. H. Lawrence,* Viking Press, 1936.

Lea, Hermann, *Thomas Hardy's Wessex,* Macmillan, 1925.

Lerner, Laurence and John Holstrom, editors, *Thomas Hardy and His Readers: A Selection of Contemporary Reviews,* Barnes & Noble, 1968.

Levine, Richard A., editor, *The Victorian Experience,* Ohio University Press, 1976.

Marsden, Kenneth, *The Poems of Thomas Hardy: A Critical Introduction,* Oxford University Press, 1969.

Meisel, Perry, *Thomas Hardy: The Return of the Repressed,* Yale University Press, 1972.

Milberg-Kaye, Ruth, *Thomas Hardy—Myths of Sexuality,* John Jay Press, 1983.

Miller, J. Hillis, *Thomas Hardy: Distance and Desire,* Harvard University Press, 1970.

Millgate, Michael, *Thomas Hardy: A Biography,* Random House, 1982.

Morrell, Roy, *Thomas Hardy: The Will and the Way,* University of Malaya Press, 1965.

Orel, Harold, *Thomas Hardy's Epic Drama: A Study of "The Dynasts,"* University of Kansas Press, 1963.

Pinion, F. B., *A Hardy Companion: A Guide to the Works of Thomas Hardy and Their Background,* Macmillan, 1968.

Purdy, Richard L., *Thomas Hardy: A Bibliographic Study,* Oxford University Press, 1954.

Rutland, William R., *Thomas Hardy: A Study of His Writings and Their Background,* Basil Blackwell, 1938.

Stewart, J. I. M., *Thomas Hardy: A Critical Biography,* Dodd, Mead, 1971.

Twentieth-Century Literary Criticism, Volume 4, Gale, 1981.

Weber, Carl J., *Hardy in America: A Study of Thomas Hardy and His American Readers,* Colby College Press, 1946.

Weber, Carl J., *Hardy of Wessex: His Life and Literary Career,* revised edition, Columbia University Press, 1965.

Webster, H. C., *On a Darkling Plain: The Art and Thought of Thomas Hardy,* University of Chicago Press, 1947.

Woolf, Virginia, *The Second Common Reader,* Harcourt & Brace, 1932.

Wright, Walter F., *The Shaping of "The Dynasts": A Study in Thomas Hardy,* University of Nebraska Press, 1967.

PERIODICALS

Hopkins Review, Volume 5, number 4, 1952.
Kenyon Review, Volume 13, 1951.
Modern Fiction Studies, Volume 6, 1960.
New York Review of Books, November 14, 1974.
Nineteenth Century Fiction, Volume 9, 1954, Volume 24, 1969.
Publications of the Modern Language Association, Volume 61, 1946.
Southern Review, Volume 6, 1940.
Studies in Philology, Volume 60, 1963.
Studies in the Novel, Volume 4, 1972.
Westminster Review, April, 1883.

* * *

HARE, David 1947-

PERSONAL: Born June 5, 1947, in Bexhill, Sussex, England; son of Clifford Theodore Rippon (a sailor) and Agnes Cockburn (Gilmour) Hare; married Margaret Matheson, 1970 (divorced, 1980); children: Joe, Lewis, Darcy. *Education:* Attended Lancing College, Sussex, England; Jesus College, Cambridge, M.A. (honors), 1968.

ADDRESSES: Home—33 Ladbroke Rd., London W11, England. *Agent*—Margaret Ramsey Ltd., 14a Goodwin's Court, London WC2N 4LL, England.

CAREER: Playwright, director, and filmmaker. A. B. Pathe, London, England, film editor, 1968; Portable Theatre (traveling company), founder and director, 1968-71; Royal Court Theatre, literary manager, 1969-70, resident dramatist, 1970-71; Nottingham Playhouse, resident dramatist, 1973; Joint Stock Theatre (traveling company), director, 1974-80; Greenpoint Films, founder, 1982; National Theatre, associate director, 1984-88.

MEMBER: Royal Society of Literature (fellow).

AWARDS, HONORS: Evening Standard awards, for most promising playwright, 1970, for *Slag,* and 1985, for *Pravda;* John Llewellyn Rhys Memorial Award, 1975, for *Knuckle;* British Academy of Film and Television Arts award for best television play of the year, 1979, for *Licking Hitler;* New York Drama Critics Circle award for best foreign play and Antoinette Perry ("Tony") award nomination for best play, both 1983, for *Plenty; Plays and Players* award for best new play and City Limits award, both 1985, for *Pravda;* Golden Bear award from Berlin Film Festival, 1985, for *Wetherby.*

WRITINGS:

PUBLISHED PLAYS

How Brophy Made Good (one-act; first produced in Brighton, England, at Brighton Combination Theatre, 1969), published in *Gambit,* 1970.

Slag (two-act; first produced in London at Hampstead Theatre Club, April 6, 1970; produced on Broadway at Public Theatre, March, 1971), Faber, 1971.

(With others) *Lay By* (one-act; first produced in Edinburgh, Scotland, at Traverse Theatre, 1971; produced in London, England, at Open Space Theatre, 1971), Calder & Boyars, 1972.

The Great Exhibition (two-act; first produced in London at Hampstead Theatre Club, February 28, 1972), Faber, 1972.

(With Howard Brenton) *Brassneck* (three-act; first produced in Nottingham, England, at Nottingham Playhouse, 1973), Eyre Methuen, 1974.

Knuckle (two-act; first produced in the West End at Comedy Theatre, 1974; produced Off-Broadway at Phoenix Theatre, 1975), Faber, 1974, revised, 1978.

Fanshen (two-act; adapted from work by William Hinton; first produced in London at ICA Theatre, 1975), Faber, 1976.

Teeth 'n' Smiles (two-act; first produced in London at Royal Court Theatre, 1975), Faber, 1976.

Plenty (two-act; first produced in London at National Theatre, 1978), French, 1978.

(With others) *Deeds* (produced in Nottingham, 1978), published in *Plays and Players,* 1978.

A Map of the World (produced at Adelaide Festival, 1982), Faber, 1982, revised, 1983.

(With Howard Brenton) *Pravda* (produced in London at National Theatre, 1985), Methuen, 1985.

"The Bay at Nice," and "Wrecked Eggs" (produced in London at National Theatre, 1986), Faber, 1986.

The Asian Plays: "Fanshen," "Saigon," "A Map of the World," Faber, 1986.

The History Plays: "Plenty," "Knuckle," "Licking Hitler," Faber, 1986.

The Secret Rapture (produced in London, 1988; produced off-Broadway, 1989; produced on Broadway, 1989), Grove, 1989.

UNPUBLISHED PLAYS

(With Tony Bicat, and director) *Inside Out* (one-act; adapted from diaries of Franz Kafka), first produced in London at Arts Laboratory, 1968.

What Happened to Blake? (one-act), first produced in London at Royal Court Theatre, September 29, 1970.

The Rules of the Game (three-act; adapted from a play by Luigi Pirandello), first produced in London at National Theatre, June 15, 1971.

Deathsheads (one-act), first produced in Edinburgh at Traverse Theatre, 1971.

(With others) *England's Ireland* (two-act), first produced in Amsterdam, Netherlands, at Mickery Theatre, 1972; produced in London at Roundhouse Theatre, 1972.

The Madman Theory of Deterrence (sketch), produced in London, 1983.

(Author of libretto, and director) *The Knife* (opera), produced Off-Broadway at Public Theatre, 1987.

TELEVISION PLAYS

Man above Men, British Broadcasting Corp. (BBC), 1973.

(And director) *Licking Hitler* (broadcast by BBC, January 10, 1978), Faber, 1978.

(And director) *Dreams of Leaving,* BBC, January 17, 1980.

Saigon: Year of the Cat (broadcast by Thames Television, 1983), Faber, 1983.

OTHER

(And director) *Wetherby* (screenplay; released by Metro-Goldwyn-Mayer/United Artists Classics, 1985), Faber, 1985.

Plenty (screenplay based on his play of the same title), Twentieth Century-Fox, 1985.

(And director) *Strapless* (screenplay), Granada, 1989.

Also author of screenplay *Paris by Night,* 1988; author of *Racing Demon,* 1989.

WORK IN PROGRESS: A Gift of Honey, a three-act stage play.

SIDELIGHTS: Michael Billington of the *New York Times* ranked David Hare among those contemporary British playwrights who "believe in the power of the stage as a medium of social and political analysis." Like such writers as Trevor Griffiths, David Edgar, Howard Barker, and Howard Brenton, Hare is "instinctively left wing," and he works his plays around a core of political ideas. In an interview with *Theatre Quarterly,* Hare explained: "Journalism, however intelligent, will always fail you. It is glib by nature. Words can *only* be worked in real situations. That is why the theatre is the best court society has."

Nevertheless, Hare is not a propagandist, due in large part to his sense of disillusion with the possibility of social change. He once told a reporter for *Theatre Quarterly:* "I was very pissed off with life while I was at University, and very disillusioned about the activities of the left. It's really only as a writer that I've begun to think myself straight, work out for myself the answer to political questions . . . which are never answered by polemic or journalism or propaganda." In his play *Plenty,* for example, he "showed how the ringingly defiant optimism of post-World War II Britain had turned to dust and ashes," noted Billington.

By his own admission, Hare has never been a technically innovative writer: "It's always the content of the work that determines everything," he maintains. Billington suggested that, like his contemporaries, Hare has been "more influenced by the techniques of film and television than . . . by traditional Ibsenite

methods." To some extent, his work is characterized by a multiplicity of scenes and a sense of swift cutting. *Plenty,* for instance, switches at one point from an enormous room in the Foreign Office to a bed-sitting room in Blackpool.

Hare's first full-length play, *Slag,* is a successful comedy set in a private girls' school which is gradually falling apart as its three teachers battle over sex and power. While their students steadily dwindle away, the three women become bound to each other by their view of society. And, according to Mary Holland, "a society of women may come up with some better solutions to the problems of people living together than one dominated by male egoism and traditions." The central concern, as Marilyn Stasio observed, is "crumbling traditions and powerless authority"; but the comic perspective on feminist issues—women trying to go it alone not only politically but sexually—led several critics to dismiss Hare as a "male chauvinist." Hare himself, however, maintained both that the play was written in praise of women and "that it's really a play about institutions, not about women at all."

Hare's other plays similarly zero in on individuals as manifestations of larger social truths. Of the source for *The Great Exhibition* he has explained: "The only political experience I had had was believing passionately in the Labour Government of 1964, and watching that government sell everything down the river." Hence, the play was about a disillusioned Labour member of Parliament who sees his life as merely a performance. A reviewer for *Stage* called the play "a wry, funny, sad cartoon on the emotional bewilderment and moral vacuity of sections of the liberal, pacific, intellectual middle-class."

In Hare's own words, *Teeth 'n' Smiles* is about " 'the new man'; whether we have any chance of changing ourselves." It deals with the class war in the context of a collapsing rock and roll music group. To Richard Eder, the core of the play was a sense of class guilt, an angry judgment on the intelligentsia that forced its characters to stand too rigidly for its author's arguments. Yet such an effect might seem to be Hare's purpose as a playwright: "To write a play at all," he has insisted, "you have to work extremely hard on what you believe about the subject—and the writing process is finding out the truth or otherwise of what you believe by testing it on the stage."

BIOGRAPHICAL/CRITICAL SOURCES:

BOOKS

Contemporary Literary Criticism, Volume 29, Gale, 1984.

Dictionary of Literary Biography, Volume 13: *British Dramatists since World War II,* Gale, 1982.

PERIODICALS

Chicago Tribune, September 25, 1985, September 27, 1985, August 13, 1988, November 13, 1988, January 15, 1989, April 7, 1989.

Cue, March 6, 1971.

Film Comment, October, 1985.

Hudson Review, summer, 1971.

Los Angeles Times, September 6, 1985, September 18, 1985, September 28, 1985, December 19, 1989.

Ms., October, 1985.

Nation, March 8, 1971.

New Republic, March 13, 1971.

New Statesman, June 4, 1971.

Newsweek, August 5, 1985, September 23, 1985.

New York, March 22, 1971.

New Yorker, March 6, 1971.

New York Times, November 4, 1977, March 18, 1979, August 14, 1979, March 10, 1981, October 17, 1982, October 22, 1982, January 13, 1983, January 31, 1983, February 3, 1983, March 13, 1983, June 20, 1985, July 19, 1985, September 19, 1985, October 2, 1985, October 11, 1985, October 13, 1985, March 8, 1987, March 11, 1987, March 15, 1987, July 31, 1988, September 23, 1989, October 22, 1989, October 27, 1989.

New York Times Magazine, September 29, 1985.

Plays and Players, May, 1970, July, 1971, April, 1978.

Stage, June 24, 1971, March 2, 1972.

Theatre Quarterly, September-November, 1975.

Time, June 10, 1985, October 28, 1985.

Times (London), January 31, 1983, March 2, 1985, March 8, 1985, May 4, 1985, November 22, 1985, September 11, 1986, October 6, 1988.

Times Literary Supplement, February 11, 1983.

Washington Post, April 5, 1983, August 26, 1985, September 20, 1985, November 27, 1988.

*   *   *

HARGRAVE, Leonie
See DISCH, Thomas M(ichael)

*   *   *

HARRIS, (Theodore) Wilson 1921-
(Kona Waruk)

PERSONAL: Born March 24, 1921, in New Amsterdam, British Guiana (now Guyana); immigrated to England, 1959; son of Theodore Wilson (an insurer and underwriter) and Millicent Josephine (Glasford) Harris; married Cecily Carew, 1945; married second wife, Margaret Nimmo Burns (a writer), April 2, 1959. *Education:* Queen's College, Georgetown, British Guiana, 1934-39; studied land surveying and geomorphology under government auspices, 1939-42.

ADDRESSES: Home—London, England. *Office*—c/o Faber & Faber, 3 Queen Sq., London WC1N 3AU, England.

CAREER: British Guiana Government, government surveyor, 1942-54, senior surveyor, 1955-58; full-time writer in London, England, 1958—. Visiting lecturer, State University of New York at Buffalo, 1970, Yale University, 1970; guest lecturer, Mysore University (India), 1978; regents' lecturer, University of California, 1983; writer in residence, University of West Indies, 1970, University of Toronto, 1970, Newcastle University, Australia, 1979, University of Queensland, Australia, 1986; visiting professor, University of Texas at Austin, 1972, 1981-82, 1983, University of Aarhus, Denmark, 1973, and in Cuba. Delegate, UNESCO Symposium on Caribbean Literature in Cuba, 1968, and National Identity Conference in Brisbane, Australia, 1968.

AWARDS, HONORS: English Arts Council grants, 1968 and 1970; Commonwealth fellow at University of Leeds, 1971; Guggenheim fellow, 1972-73; Henfield writing fellow at University of East Anglia, 1974; Southern Arts fellow, Salisbury, 1976; D.Lit., University of West Indies, 1984; Guyana Prize for Fiction, 1985-87; D.Litt., University of Kent at Canterbury, 1988.

WRITINGS:

FICTION

Palace of the Peacock (Book I of the "Guiana Quartet"), Faber, 1960.

The Far Journey of Oudin (Book II of the "Guiana Quartet"), Faber, 1961.

The Whole Armour (Book III of the "Guiana Quartet"), Faber, 1962.

The Secret Ladder (Book IV of the "Guiana Quartet"), Faber, 1963.

The Whole Armour [and] *The Secret Ladder,* Faber, 1963.

Heartland, Faber, 1964.

The Eye of the Scarecrow, Faber, 1965.

The Waiting Room, Faber, 1967.

Tamatumari, Faber, 1968.

Ascent to Omai, Faber, 1970.

The Sleepers of Roraima (short stories), Faber, 1970.

The Age of the Rainmakers (short stories), Faber, 1971.

Black Marsden: A Tabula Rasa Comedy, Faber, 1972.

Companions of the Day and Night, Faber, 1975.

Da Silva da Silva's Cultivated Wilderness [and] *Genesis of the Clowns* (also see below), Faber, 1977.

Genesis of the Clowns, Faber, 1978.

The Tree of the Sun, Faber, 1978.

The Angel at the Gate, Faber, 1982.

Carnival, Faber, 1985.

The Guyana Quartet (boxed set), Faber, 1985.

OTHER

(Under pseudonym Kona Waruk) *Fetish* (poetry), privately printed (Georgetown, Guyana), 1951.

The Well and the Land (poetry), British Guiana, 1952.

Eternity to Season (poetry), privately printed (Georgetown), 1954, 2nd edition, New Beacon Books, 1978.

Tradition and the West Indian Novel (lecture), New Beacon, 1965.

Tradition, the Writer and Society: Critical Essays, New Beacon, 1967.

History, Fable and Myth in the Caribbean and Guianas (booklet), National History and Arts Council (Georgetown), 1970.

Fossil and Psyche (criticism), African and American Studies and Research Center, University of Texas, 1974.

Explorations: A Series of Talks and Articles, 1966-1981, edited with introduction by Hena Maes-Jelinek, Dangaroo Press, 1981.

The Womb of Space: The Cross-Cultural Imagination, Greenwood Press, 1983.

The Infinite Rehearsal, Faber, 1987.

Contributor to anthologies, including *Caribbean Rhythms,* 1974, and *Critics on Caribbean Literature,* 1978; contributor to periodicals, including *Literary Half-Yearly, Kyk-over-al,* and *New Letters.*

SIDELIGHTS: Novelist Wilson Harris blends philosophy, poetic imagery, symbolism and myth to create new visions of reality. His fiction shows the reader a world where the borders between physical and spiritual reality, life and death have become indistinguishable. In *World Literature Today,* Richard Sander states that Harris has "realized a new, original form of the novel that in almost all respects constitutes a radical departure from the conventional novel." Reed Way Dasenbrock, also writing in *World Literature Today,* claims that Harris "has always operated at a very high level of abstraction, higher than any of his fellow West Indian novelists, higher perhaps than any other contemporary novelist in English. . . . And whether one regards Harris's evolution as a rich and exciting development or a one-way trip down an abstractionist cul-de-sac, there is no denying his unique vision or dedication to that vision." The constant use of abstraction has brought Harris both praise and criticism; while some find his work rewarding and challenging, others think his unorthodox methods alienate the reader.

Harris is perhaps best known to the general public for *The Guyana Quartet*. Important to all four works of the quartet is the landscape of the Guyanese interior, which Harris came to know well during his years as a government surveyor. "Two major elements seem to have shaped Harris's approach to art and his philosophy of existence: the impressive contrasts of the Guyanese landscapes, . . . and the successive waves of conquest which gave Guyana its heterogeneous population polarised for centuries into oppressors and their victims," writes Hena Maes-Jelinek in *West Indian Literature*. "The two, landscape and history, merge in his work into single metaphors symbolising man's inner space saturated with the effects of historical—that is, temporal—experiences."

Harris's works are frequently difficult for critics to summarize because they move so far from the accepted definition of a novel. Harris uses dream, hallucination, psychic experiences, and various historical times without clearcut divisions, and critics often find it necessary to invent a genre for Harris's works in order to discuss them. Michael Thorpe in *World Literature Today* calls the author's more recent books "psychical 'expeditions.'" A *Times Literary Supplement* contributor terms *Palace of the Peacock*, the first volume of the "Guyana Quartet," "a 150-page definition of mystical experience given in the guise of a novel." And an *Encounter* contributor describes Harris's work as "a metaphysical shorthand on the surface of a narrative whose point cannot readily be grasped by any but those thoroughly versed in his previous work and able at once to recognise the recurrent complex metaphors."

Reviewers frequently mention that to fully grasp Harris's work it is necessary to be familiar with his metaphors, since the elaborately written passages and complex symbolism can make the writing nearly impenetrable for readers used to more traditional fiction. A *Times Literary Supplement* contributor warns, "no reader should attempt Mr. Harris's novels unless he is willing to work at them." Reviewing *Palace of the Peacock*, another *Times Literary Supplement* contributor says it is "a difficult book to read, yet it is the very concreteness of Mr. Harris's imagery that makes its denseness so hard to penetrate." Thorpe agrees, writing, "The uninitiated reader may become discouraged, wrestling with opaque ideas attached to tantalizing shadows of what he seeks in fiction: engagement with deeply apprehended lives and moving action." But according to J. P. Durix, also a *Times Literary Supplement* contributor, the reader who stays with Harris is rewarded by his "dense style and meticulous construction, his attention to visual and rhythmic effects, [which] are matched by an inventiveness which few contemporary novelists can equal."

Harris also writes literary criticism; in *The Womb of Space*, he expands upon many of the ideas contained in his novels. But in his general theory as well as in his fictional works, Harris's points can be hard to understand. Steven G. Kellman writes in *Modern Fiction Studies*, "I take it that Wilson Harris' theme is the ability of consciousness to transcend a particular culture. But his articulation of that theme is so turgid, so beset by mixed and obscure metaphors and by syntactical convolutions that much of the book simply remains unintelligible even to a sympathetic reader." Harris's goal in the work is to establish parallels between writers of various cultural backgrounds. He observes in *The Womb of Space* that "literature is still constrained by regional and other conventional but suffocating categories." His vision is of a new world community, based on cultural heterogeneity, not homogeneity, which, "as a cultural model, exercised by a ruling ethnic group, tends to become an organ of conquest and division because of imposed unity that actually subsists on the suppression of others." Sander believes that *The Womb of Space* is "an attack on the traditional critical establishment." A *Choice* contributor agrees, claiming, "*The Womb of Space* issues a direct challenge to the intellectual provincialism that often characterises literary study in the US."

But critics who applaud Harris's work believe he has contributed greatly to the understanding of art and consciousness. John Hearne writes in *The Islands in Between*, "No other British Caribbean novelist has made quite such an explicit and conscious effort as Harris to reduce the material reckonings of everyday life to the significance of myth." And speaking of the breadth of Harris's work, Louis James states in the *Times Literary Supplement*, "The novels of Wilson Harris . . . form one ongoing whole. Each work is individual; yet the whole sequence can be seen as a continuous, ever-widening exploration of civilization and creative art."

BIOGRAPHICAL/CRITICAL SOURCES:

BOOKS

Baugh, Edward, editor, *Critics on Caribbean Literature: Readings in Literary Criticism,* St. Martin's, 1978.
Contemporary Literary Criticism, Volume 25, Gale, 1983.
Drake, Sandra E., *Wilson Harris and the Modern Tradition: A New Architecture of the World,* Greenwood Press, 1986.
Gilkes, Michael, *The West Indian Novel,* Twayne, 1981.
Gilkes, Michael, *Wilson Harris and the Caribbean Novel,* Longman, 1975.
Harris, Wilson, *The Tree of the Sun,* Faber, 1978.
Harris, Wilson, *The Womb of Space: The Cross-Cultural Imagination,* Greenwood Press, 1983.
James, Louis, editor, *The Islands in Between,* Oxford University Press, 1968.
Maes-Jelinek, Hena, *The Naked Design,* Dangaroo Press, 1976.
Maes-Jelinek, Hena, *Wilson Harris,* Twayne, 1982.
Munro, Ian and Reinhard Sander, editors, *Kas-Kas: Interviews with Three Caribbean Writers in Texas,* African and Afro-American Research Institute, The University of Texas at Austin, 1972.

PERIODICALS

Choice, March, 1984.
Encounter, May, 1987.
Modern Fiction Studies, summer, 1984.
Observer, July 7, 1985.
Quill and Quire, October, 1985.
Spectator, March 25, 1978.
Times Literary Supplement, December 9, 1965, July 4, 1968, May 21, 1970, October 10, 1975, May 25, 1977, May 19, 1978, October 15, 1982, July 12, 1985, September 25-October 1, 1987.
World Literature Today, winter, 1984, summer, 1985, spring, 1986.

*   *   *

HARRISON, Tony 1937-

PERSONAL: Born April 30, 1937, in Leeds, Yorkshire, England; son of Harry Ashton (a baker) and Florence (Homer) Harrison; married Rosemarie Crossfield Dietzsch (an artist), January 16, 1960; children: Jane, Max. *Education:* University of Leeds, B.A., 1958. *Religion:* None.

ADDRESSES: Home—9 Grove, Gosforth, Newcastle-upon-Tyne NE3 1NE, England. *Agent*—Kenneth Ewing, Fraser & Dunlop, 91 Regent St., London W1R 3RU, England.

CAREER: Poet, playwright, and translator. Lecturer at Ahmadu Bello University (Nigeria), 1962-66, and Charles University (Prague), 1966-67. Northern Arts fellow in poetry at Universities of Newcastle and Durham, 1967-68, and 1976-77; UNESCO traveling fellow in poetry, 1969; Gregynog Arts Fellow at University of Wales, 1973-74; resident dramatist at National Theatre, London, 1977-79.

MEMBER: Writers' Action Group.

AWARDS, HONORS: Cholmondeley Award for Poetry from Society of Authors, 1969; Geoffrey Faber Memorial Prize, 1972, for *The Loiners.*

WRITINGS:

POETRY

Earth works, Northern House, 1964.
Newcastle Is Peru, Eagle Press, 1969.
The Loiners, London Magazine Editions, 1970.
From 'The School of Eloquence' and Other Poems, Rex Collings, 1978.
Continuous: Fifty Sonnets From 'The School of Eloquence', Rex Collings, 1981.
A Kumquat for John Keats, Bloodaxe Books, 1981.
U.S. Marshall, Bloodaxe Books, 1981.
Selected Poems, Viking, 1984.

Poems have been included in *Corgi Modern Poets in Focus,* Volume 4, Corgi, 1971, and *Rex Collings Christmas Book,* Rex Collings, 1976.

OTHER

(Adapter with James Simmons) *Aikin Mata* (play; based on Aristophanes's *Lysistrata;* first produced in Zaria, Nigeria, 1965), Oxford University Press, 1966.
(Translator and adapter) *The Misanthrope* (play; based on Moliere's *Le Misanthrope;* first produced in London at National Theatre, February 22, 1973), Rex Collings, 1973.
(Translator and adapter) *Phaedra Britannica* (play; based on Racine's *Phedre;* first produced in London at Old Vic Theatre, September 9, 1975; produced in New York City at CSC Repertory Theater, December 1988), Rex Collings, 1975.
(Translator) *The Poems of Palladas,* Anvil Press, 1975.
The Passion (play; first produced in London at Cottesloe Theatre, April 21, 1977), Rex Collings, 1977.
Bow Down (play; first produced at Cottesloe Theatre, July 5, 1977), Rex Collings, 1977.
(Translator) *The Bartered Bride* (libretto for opera; based on the work by Bedrich Smetana; first produced in New York City, October, 1978), E. C. Schirmer, 1978.
(With Philip Sharpe) *Looking Up,* Migrant Press, 1979.
(Translator and Adapter) *The Oresteia* (play; based on the work by Aeschylus; first produced in London at Olivier Theatre, November 28, 1981), Rex Collings, 1981.
The Mysteries, Faber, 1985.
Dramatic Verse, 1973-1985, Bloodaxe Books, 1985.

Author of the lyrics for the film "Bluebird," 1976. Contributor to British magazines and newspapers.

SIDELIGHTS: Tony Harrison has enjoyed significant success as a poet, playwright, and translator. C. E. Lamb notes in *Dictionary of Literary Biography* that "[Harrison] has through his work as a poet and translator developed a technical skill of extraordinary brilliance, wit, and vigor, which has recently allowed him to support in his poetry themes of immense personal and historical pain. As a translator, he has enormous range; he has had

equal success with Racine, Moliere, and Aeschylus, always rendering the plays completely new while retaining the essential qualities of the originals."

Harrison has traveled all over the world, including Cuba, the Soviet Union and much of Africa.

BIOGRAPHICAL/CRITICAL SOURCES:

BOOKS

Contemporary Literary Criticism, Volume 43, Gale, 1987.
Dictionary of Literary Biography, Volume 40: *Poets of Great Britain and Ireland Since 1960,* Gale, 1985.

PERIODICALS

Honest Ulsterman, September-October, 1970.
Listener, October 8, 1970.
New York Times, December 17, 1988.
New York Times Book Review, November 29, 1987.
Spectator, December 9, 1978.
Times (London), December 22, 1984, January 18, 1985.
Times Literary Supplement, January 15, 1982, January 4, 1985, June 6, 1986.
Washington Post Book World, January 31, 1988.

* * *

HARSON, Sley
   See ELLISON, Harlan

* * *

HART, Ellis
   See ELLISON, Harlan

* * *

HARTLEY, L(eslie) P(oles)   1895-1972

PERSONAL: Born December 30, 1895, in Whittesley, Cambridgeshire, England; died December 13, 1972; son of Harry Bark (a justice of the peace) and Mary Elizabeth (Thompson) Hartley. *Education:* Balliol College, Oxford, B.A., 1922.

ADDRESSES: Home—Avondale, Bathford, Somerset SW7, England.

CAREER: Literary critic, novelist, and short story writer, 1923-72. Tutor in preparatory school in Northdown, England, during the early 1920s; Clark Lecturer, Trinity College, Cambridge, 1964. *Military service:* Served in World War II, 1916-18.

MEMBER: Athenaeum Club and Beefsteak Club (both London), Bath and County Club (Bath).

AWARDS, HONORS: James Tait Black Memorial Prize, 1947, for *Eustace and Hilda;* Catholic Book of the Year Award, 1951, for *My Fellow Devils;* W. H. Heinemann Foundation Award and *Daily Mail's* Book of the Year Award, both 1953, both for *The Go-Between;* Commander of Order of the British Empire, 1956; Companion of Literature Award from Royal Society of Literature, 1972.

WRITINGS:

Night Fears, and Other Stories (short stories), Putnam, 1924.
Simonetta Perkins (novel), Putnam, 1925.
The Killing Bottle, Putnam, 1932.
The Shrimp and the Anemone (first novel in trilogy; also see below), Putnam (London), 1944, published in America as

West Window, Doubleday, 1945, new edition with commentary and notes by Patricia D'Arcy, Bodley Head, 1967.

The Sixth Heaven (second novel in trilogy; also see below), Putnam (London), 1946, Doubleday, 1947, reprinted, Faber, 1964.

Eustace and Hilda (third novel in trilogy; also see below), Putnam (London), 1947.

The Travelling Grave, and Other Stories (short stories), Arkham House, 1948.

The Boat (novel), Putnam (London), 1949, Doubleday, 1950.

My Fellow Devils (novel), James Barrie, 1951, British Book Centre, 1959.

The Go-Between (novel), Hamish Hamilton, 1953, Knopf, 1954, revised edition with introduction by Hartley, Heinemann, 1963, reprinted, Scarbrough House, 1980.

The White Wand, and Other Stories (short stories), Hamish Hamilton, 1954.

A Perfect Woman (novel), Hamish Hamilton, 1955, Knopf, 1956.

The Hireling (novel), Hamish Hamilton, 1957, Rinehart, 1958.

Eustace and Hilda: A Trilogy (includes *The Shrimp and the Anenione, The Sixth Heaven, Hilda's Letter,* and *Eustace and Hilda*), introduction by David Cecil, Putnam, 1958, Dufour, 1961.

Facial Justice (science fiction novel), Hamish Hamilton, 1960, Doubleday, 1961.

Two for the River, Hamish Hamilton, 1961.

The Brickfield (novel; also see below), Hamish Hamilton, 1964.

The Betrayal (novel; also see below), Hamish Hamilton, 1966.

The Novelist's Responsibility: Lectures and Essays, Hamish Hamilton, 1967, Hillary House, 1968.

The Collected Short Stories of L. P. ley, introduction by David Cecil, Hamish Hamilton, 1968, published as *The Complete Short Stories of L. P. Hartley,* 1973, Beaufort Books, 1986.

Poor Clare (novel), Hamish Hamilton, 1968.

(Author of foreword) Cynthia Asquith, *Diaries 1915-1918,* Hutchinson, 1968, Knopf, 1969.

The Love-Adept: A Variation on a Theme (novel), Hamish Hamilton, 1969.

My Sister's Keeper, Hamish Hamilton, 1970.

The Harness Room (novel), Hamish Hamilton, 1971.

Mrs. Carteret Receives, and Other Stories (short stories), Hamish Hamilton, 1971.

The Collections, Hamish Hamilton, 1972.

The Will and the Way (novel), Hamish Hamilton, 1973.

The Brickfield [and] *The Betrayal,* Hamish Hamilton, 1973.

(Contributor of screenplay) Harold Pinter, editor, *Five Screenplays,* Grove, 1989.

Fiction reviewer for *Spectator, Observer, Week-End Review, Sketch,* and *Time and Tide.*

SIDELIGHTS: L. P. Hartley has been recognized as one of the major English authors of this century. A prolific writer, Hartley is author of novels, short stories, and literary criticism that have been praised for their intelligence, realism, and sensitivity.

"L. P. Hartley has a high reputation in England and deservedly so," stated Frederick R. Karl in *A Reader's Guide to the Contemporary English Novel.* "What he starts out to do he accomplishes admirably; his novels are models of intelligent writing, good sense, sharp feeling for proportion, and clean design. His world of upper middle-class gentility unfolds without fuss or affection. Hartley is that rare novelist who knows what he whats to do and goes about it with a minimum of waste."

Walter Allen described Hartley in his book, *The Modern Novel: In Britain and the United States,* in this manner: "Hartley is one of a number of contemporary novelists who strike one as being very much at the centre of the English tradition of the novel. They are concerned with the behaviour of men and women in society, with the making of choices; and they are also scholarly novelists in the way that some painters and musicians are called scholarly. They approach the writing of fiction with a full knowledge of what has been done in the art before. They are conscious of the great exemplars. They are not the less original for this, but it means that generally they know precisely what it is they are doing, and what they are doing may very well be ambitious indeed."

Richard Jones once wrote that L. P. Hartley was "one of the last gentleman-writers with a sensibility schooled at a time when a limited number of people could spend a good deal of time being complex about very little."

MEDIA ADAPTATIONS: The Go-Between was produced as a motion picture starring Julie Christie and Alan Bates, by Columbia Pictures in 1971.

AVOCATIONAL INTERESTS: Rowing, swimming, walking.

BIOGRAPHICAL/CRITICAL SOURCES:

BOOKS

Allen, Walter, *The Modern Novel: In Britain and the United States,* Dutton, 1964.

Bien, Peter Adolph, *L. P. Hartley,* Pennsylvania State University Press, 1962.

Bloomfield, Paul, *L. P. Hartley,* Longman, 1962, revised edition, 1970.

Contemporary Literary Criticism, Gale, Volume 2, 1974, Volume 22, 1982.

Dictionary of Literary Biography, Volume 15: *British Novelists, 1930-1959,* Gale, 1983.

Karl, Frederick R., *A Readers Guide to the Contemporary English Novel,* Farrar, Straus, 1962.

PERIODICALS

Books and Bookmen, July 1969.
Listener, November, 7, 1968.
London Magazine, February, 1969.
New York Times, July 25, 1954.
Observer, October 27, 1968.
Spectator, November 3, 1944.
Yale Review, autumn, 1954.

OBITUARIES:

PERIODICALS

AB Bookman, March 19, 1973.
Time, December 25, 1973.
Variety, January 17, 1973.

*   *   *

HASEK, Jaroslav (Matej Frantisek) 1883-1923 (Benjamin Franklin, Vojtech Kapristian z Hellenhofferu, M. Ruffian)

PERSONAL: Born April 24 (some sources say April 30), 1883, in Prague, Bohemia (now Czechoslovakia); died January 3, 1923, in Lipnice, Czechoslovakia; son of Josef (a schoolmaster and bank employee) and Katerina Hasek; married Jarmila Mayerova, May, 1910 (separated, 1912); children: Richard. *Ed-*

ucation: Graduated from Czechoslavonic Commercial Academy, 1902. *Politics:* Communist.

ADDRESSES: Home—Lipnice, Czechoslovakia.

CAREER: Writer, 1901-23. Worked at pharmacies; clerk at Insurance Bank of Slavie, 1902-03; editor of journal *Svet zvirat,* 1909-10; co-owner of dog-selling business; cabaret performer, 1912-15 and 1921-23. *Military service:* Austrian Army, received Silver Medal; Russian prisoner of war, 1915-16; Free Czechoslovak Legion, 1916-18; Red Army, 1918-20.

MEMBER: Party of Moderate Progress Within the Limits of the Law (founder).

WRITINGS:

Ze stare drogerie (short stories; title means "From the Old Pharmacy"), first published c. 1901, translation by Cecil Parrott published in *The Red Commissar,* Dial Press, 1981 (also see below).

(With Ladislav Hajek) *Majove vykriky* (poems; title means "Cries of May"), [Prague], 1903.

Kdyz clovek spadne v Tatrach, [Prague], 1912.

Dobry vojak Svejk, a jine podivne historky (short stories; title means "The Good Soldier Svejk, and Other Strange Stories"), [Prague], 1912, translation by Parrott published in *The Red Commissar,* Dial Press, 1981 (also see below).

Utrpeni pana Tenkrata (title means "The Tribulations of Mr. That-Time"), [Prague], 1912, Odeon (Prague), 1973.

Pruvodci cizincu, a jine satiry (short stories), [Prague], 1913, A. Synek (Prague), 1925, translation by I. T. Havlu published as *The Tourist Guide: Twenty-six Stories* (includes "Affable Persuasion," "Among Bibliophilists," "The Austrian Customs Authorities," "Bogumirov, the Serbian Pope, and Mufti Isrim's Goat," "The End of Saint Jura," "An Experiment in Giving a Teetotal Party," "Mr. Florentin Versus Chocholka," "My Friend Hanuska," "The Sad Fate of the Railway Station Mission," "Something Spicy About Legal Arbiters," and "The Struggle for Souls"), Artia, 1961.

Muj obchod se psy, a jine humoresky (short stories; title means "My Trade With Dogs"), [Prague], 1915, A. Synek, 1924.

Dobry vojak Svejk v zajeti (novel; title means "The Good Soldier Svejk in Captivity"), [Russia], 1917.

Osudy dobreho vojaka Svejka za svetove valky (novel), four volumes (last volume completed by Karel Vanek), [Prague], 1920-23, abridged translation by Paul Selver published as *The Good Soldier: Schweik,* illustrated by Josef Lada, Doubleday, 1930, reprinted, with foreword by Leslie A. Fiedler, New American Library, 1963, new and unabridged translation—excluding Vanek's additions—by Parrott published as *The Good Soldier Svejk and His Fortunes in the World War,* Heinemann, 1973, Crowell, 1974.

Tri muzi se zralokem, a jine poucne historky (title means "Three Men and a Shark, and Other Instructive Stories"), [Prague], 1920.

Pepicek Novy, a jine povidky (title means "Pepicek Novy, and Other Stories"), [Prague], 1921, Statni Nakladatelstvi Krasne Literatury, Hubny a Umeni (Prague), 1963.

Velitelem mesta Bugulmy (short stories; title means "The City Commander of Bugulma"), [Prague], c. 1921, Ceskoslovensky Spisovatel, 1966, Sixty-Eight Publishers (Toronto), 1976, translation by Parrott published in *The Red Commissar,* Dial Press, 1981 (also see below).

Mirova Konference (title means "The Peace Conference"), [Prague], 1922.

Skola humoru, Svoboda, 1949.

Mala zoologicka zahrada: Povidky o zviratkach znamych i nove objevenych (short stories), Prace, 1950.

Afera s kreckem, a jine povidky (short stories), Mlada Fronta, 1954, reprinted, 1973.

Utrapy vychovatele, Albatros (Prague), 1969.

Praha ve dne v noci, Ceskoslovensky Spisovatel, 1973.

Vetrny mlynar a jego dcera: Kabaretni sceny a hry Bohemske druziny Jaroslava Haska, edited by Radko Pytlik, illustrated by Zdenek Mezl, Ceskoslovensky Spisovatel, 1976.

Lidsky profil Jaroslava Haska: Korespondence a dokumenty (correspondence), commentary and notes by Pytlik, Ceskoslovensky Spisovatel, 1979.

Also author of *Historky z razicke basty* (title means "Stories From the Water Bailiff's Watch-Tower at Razice"), translation by Parrott published in *The Red Commissar,* Dial Press, 1981 (also see below). Author of incomplete volumes of *Osudy dobreho vojaka Svejka za svetove valky.*

Works represented in anthologies, including *War or Peace,* edited by Alfred Brandt and Frederick H. Law, Harper, 1938. Contributor, under eighty pseudonyms, including Benjamin Franklin, Vojtech Kapristian z Hellenhofferu, and M. Ruffian, of short stories to periodicals, including *Karikatury.* Assistant editor of *Ceske slovo,* 1911; staff member of *Cechoslovan,* 1916-18; editor of *Nash put* and *Red Europe,* both 1919.

COLLECTED WORKS

Spisy (title means "Works"), sixteen volumes, [Prague], 1924-29, reprinted, Statni Nakladatelstvi Krasne Literatury, Hubny a Umeni, 1955-68.

Panoptikum mest'aku, byrokratu a jinych zkamenelin, compiled by Zdena Ancik, ROH (Prague), 1950.

Skolni citanky a jine satiry, introduction and notes by Radko Pytlik, Prace, 1956.

Abeceda humoru, compiled by Ancik, Milan Jankovic, and Pytlik, two volumes, Ceskoslovensky Spisovatel, 1960.

Dekameron humoru a satiry, compiled by Ancik, Ceskoslovensky Spisovatel, 1968.

Vybor z dila Jaroslava Haska (title means "Selections"), four volumes, Ceskoslovensky Spisovatel, 1976-82.

The Red Commissar, Including Further Adventures of the Good Soldier Svejk and Other Stories (includes "The Criminals' Strike," "Hasek's Effort to Improve the Finances of the Monarchy," "How I Met the Author of My Obituary," "The Judicial Reform of Mr. Zakon," "Justice and the Lesser Bodily Needs," "The Procession of the Cross," "The City Commander of Bugulma," "From the Old Pharmacy," "The Good Soldier Svejk and Other Strange Stories," and "Stories From the Water Bailiff's Watch-Tower at Razice"), translation by Cecil Parrott, original illustrations by Josef Lada, Dial Press, 1981.

Little Stories by a Great Master, translation by Doris Koziskova, Orbis Press Agency (Prague), 1984.

SIDELIGHTS: Jaroslav Hasek is an internationally famous Czech author. Though he is credited with more than twelve hundred stories—as well as poems, dramatic fragments, and political writings—his reputation rests almost entirely on his four-volume, incomplete novel *Osudy dobreho vojaka Svejka za svetove valky* (*The Good Soldier Svejk and His Fortunes in the World War*), which is prized for its cynical and satirical treatment of all forms of ideology. The work has earned Hasek comparisons with a range of satirists, including Jonathan Swift and Francois Rabelais, and with contemporary masters such as Karl Kraus and Franz Kafka, and it has been hailed by contemporary critics such as Leslie Fiedler, who called it the twentieth-century's first war novel.

Hasek was born in 1883 in Prague, capital of disadvantaged Bohemia within the Austrian Habsburg empire. Bohemian culture was dominated by the Germanic minority. Consequently, the majority Czechs called for the formation of their own state. Various political crises ensued, but no real progress was made toward Czech autonomy. Thus many Czechs, including young Hasek, felt contempt for Prague's Germanic citizens.

In his youth Hasek suffered from feelings of inferiority due to family circumstances. His father, a failed schoolmaster who became a bank worker, died from alcoholism, and Hasek's mother desperately struggled to maintain the family's tenuous position of social respectability. She was, however, unable to control young Hasek, who participated in street demonstrations and failed to hold steady employment.

A pharmacist employer eventually took an interest in Hasek and recommended his enrollment in Prague's Czechoslavonic Commercial Academy, a leading secondary school counting Czech intellectuals among its faculty. Although Hasek proved a less-than-model student, he managed to pass his final examination with distinction. He also wrote and published stories, and with his younger brother he toured Hungary, Moravia, and Slovakia. These tours provided Hasek with more material for many of his early works.

When Hasek left the academy, he was already contributing fiction to leading periodicals. Nevertheless, his mother persuaded him to take a bank position, which he promptly lost by leaving without permission. During this period he continued writing, collaborating with his friend Ladislav Hajek on a 1903 poetry collection, *Majove vykriky* ("Cries of May"), and producing several stories, but he failed to earn sufficient income to support himself or help his family. In 1904 he even jeopardized his own livelihood by joining an anarchist movement. This affiliation made it difficult for him to place his stories in newspapers, most of which were tied to the traditional political parties.

By this time, Hasek had developed a reputation as a hard-drinking vagabond who rebelled against both Prague's Austrian establishment and traditional Czech political movements. Some critics have suggested that this image was, at least to some extent, merely a mask, for Hasek was a highly intelligent and sensitive artist who desired a settled bourgeois existence. This desire was reflected in his relationship with Jarmila Mayerova, whom he met in 1906. Mayerova admired Hasek's writing and shared some of his subversive political views. But her father, who had risen from poverty to the middle class, feared that his daughter would lose hard-won social status upon marriage to Hasek. A stormy, on-and-off courtship ensued for several years, stabilizing only when Hasek's friend Hajek found him steady employment as editor of *Svet zvirat,* a journal devoted to animals. This change in status apparently satisfied Mayerova's father, and in May, 1910, the couple finally married.

Despite the newlyweds' mutual affection, Hasek soon felt cramped by circumstances at home and at work. Initially, he submitted to his wife's attempts to control his grooming and dress, and he also worked diligently, even increasing his journal's circulation. Within a few months, however, Hasek lapsed into his former behavior, frequenting pubs and showing little enthusiasm for work. At *Svet zvirat,* he began writing apparently serious articles about such zoological fantasies as werewolves and prehistoric fleas. The publisher discovered Hasek's fabrications and fired him, whereupon Hasek founded a dog-selling business

called the Cynological Institute. Unfortunately, he may have indulged in suspicious practices, for the business soon failed amid lawsuits.

Around February, 1911, an incident occurred that remains a mystery to Hasek's biographers. Nearly two hours past midnight, the heavily intoxicated Hasek was found leaning over the side of the Charles Bridge in Prague, apparently preparing to jump. Although he was forcibly restrained and temporarily confined to an asylum, Hasek treated the whole affair as a hoax, later using the incident as material for the hilarious fourth chapter of *The Good Soldier Svejk and His Fortunes in the World War.* But some critics have speculated that he was actually in a state of despair bordering on mental illness. During Hasek's confinement, his wife moved back with her parents, and although the couple made sporadic attempts to reconcile, the marriage was over.

1911 was also the year in which Hasek founded the Party of Moderate Progress Within the Bounds of Law and declared himself a candidate for an ultimately unimportant seat in the Austrian Parliament. Hasek and some friends had established the new party to both parody traditional factions and lure customers to a pub. At party meetings held there, Hasek strengthened his reputation as the clown of the counterculture by delivering outrageous speeches. Notable was the "Lecture on the Rehabilitation of Animals," which derided animal-related name-calling as cruel and insulting to the animals involved.

Hasek tried to capitalize on his speech-making prowess by becoming a cabaret entertainer, but he was only successful when performing before his circle of friends. During this period—from 1912 to 1915—Hasek continued writing and publishing prolifically, but his income was scarcely sufficient to support his eating and drinking. Separated from his wife, he exploited his friends to sustain his lifestyle.

It was supposedly while wallowing in alcoholic excess that Hasek conceived the character Svejk. One evening Hasek scrawled a note with the heading "The Idiot in the Company," under which was the sentence: "He had himself examined to prove that he was capable of serving as a regular soldier." (Before World War I, Czechs were routinely resorting to every conceivable means to *avoid* serving in the Austrian Army.) Hasek soon produced several tales featuring this idiot, named Josef Svejk. He initially published the stories in the magazine *Karikatury,* then collected them in the 1912 volume *Dobry vojak Svejk, a jine podivne historky* (included in the English-language work *The Red Commissar*).

Hasek's life as a cabaret performer and writer was interrupted in January, 1915, when he received his draft notice. As a university graduate, Hasek could have become an officer, but he forfeited this status—through misconduct—and joined the Austrian Army's Ninety-first Regiment in Ceske Budejovice, thus beginning what many critics consider the most remarkable period of his career. While in the Austrian military Hasek became involved in various scrapes, some of which he later attributed to Svejk, and he also saw action at the front—at Sokal in Galicia in July, 1915—and received a Silver Medal and a promotion.

In September, 1915, Hasek was captured by the Russians. Evidence indicates that he deliberately allowed himself to be caught, perhaps allying himself with other Czechs who actually opposed the Austrians. Eventually, the Russian czar permitted the formation of the Free Czechoslovak Legion, which consisted largely of anti-Austrian Czechs recruited from the prison camps. Legion recruiters arrived in Totskoye, where Hasek was interned after barely surviving a cholera epidemic. He joined immediately and traveled to Kiev to assist with recruitment, a task that he undertook wholeheartedly and with considerable success.

In February, 1917, the Russian revolution occurred: The czar was overthrown and the communists assumed control. These events were followed by the Bolshevik revolution and a civil war pitting the revolutionary Red Army against the pro-czarist White Army. Hasek, who had supported the Czar, defied the Czech government-in-exile and joined the Red Army, which eventually assigned the production of propaganda to him. Throughout the next three years—1918 to 1920—Hasek proved a responsible and effective official, and he even abstained from alcohol. But in 1920, with the Red Army victorious and the Czechoslovak Republic established, he agreed to return to Prague.

When Hasek came home in December, 1920, he found himself in an unenviable position. For deserting the Czech Legion, he was deemed a traitor; for joining the Red Army, he was called a dangerous subversive; and for establishing relations with a Russian woman, Alexandra Lvova, he was decried as a bigamist. The hostile reception he received seriously affected his spirits. He soon returned to drink and his former Prague lifestyle. In the last two years of his life, he made another unsuccessful attempt as a cabaret performer, but he also published many stories and completed the first three volumes of the final version of *The Good Soldier Svejk.* These volumes, published separately, achieved considerable popular success and earned Hasek sufficient money to purchase a small house in Lipnice. But he was already seriously ill, and he died on January 3, 1923, with his finest literary work unfinished.

Although incomplete, *The Good Soldier Svejk* is undoubtedly Hasek's greatest literary achievement—without which his name would constitute only a footnote in the history of Czech literature. The novel opens with a report of the assassination of the Archduke Franz Ferdinand, the event that precipitated the war, and with Svejk's arrest for subversion by the police spy Bretschneider. Svejk is shuffled from police headquarters to jail, to a medical board, to an insane asylum, to the police station again, then back home. Several months later he is drafted even though he suffers from rheumatism. Once in the service, Svejk is consigned to the garrison jail under suspicion of malingering. He is released to the spectacularly corrupt chaplain Otto Katz, who ultimately forfeits Svejk's services in a card game to Lieutenant Lukas. Eventually, both Svejk and Lukas are ordered to serve with the Ninety-first Regiment in Ceske Budejovice. Svejk becomes separated from Lukas, however, and commences a futile, adventure-filled trek through Hungary and Galicia. While traveling he is captured by Austrian soldiers and accused of being a Russian spy. Later, after further escapades, Svejk is declared a certified imbecile by an army medical board. He leaves the service and begins supporting himself by selling ugly mongrels with forged pedigrees.

While *The Good Soldier Svejk* has been hailed as a masterwork, its protagonist has been the subject of a critical debate: Is he *really* the idiot he seems, or is his idiocy a mask deliberately assumed to thwart the Austrian military bureaucracy? Ample evidence exists for either point of view. Hasek's original inspiration, under the heading "The Idiot in the Company," seems to point to genuine idiocy; but in the epilogue to Part I, where Hasek comments on public reaction to portions of the novel already published, he seems to point the other way: "I do not know whether I shall succeed in achieving my purpose with this book. The fact that I have already heard one man swear at another and

say 'You're about as big an idiot as Svejk' does not prove that I have."

But the assertion that Svejk's idiocy is a deliberately assumed mask points to a crucial issue concerning the character, the author, and the very nature of writing under an oppressive regime. Though Hasek wrote the final version of *The Good Soldier Svejk* in the relatively free atmosphere of the Czechoslovak Republic, his literary style and even his personality, as Gustav Janouch has suggested in *Jaroslav Hasek,* was formed by living under a repressive system—one that imposed censorship—and by the resulting need to mask one's true sentiments. At the same time, through a curious paradox, Hasek the satirist is concerned always with unmasking, with revealing the reality hidden behind the pretense or the rhetoric of the State.

With *The Good Soldier Svejk* Hasek was not concerned, though, with delving deeply into the minds of his characters, who are all lovingly sketched *types.* The crucial factor is the situation created by the juxtaposition of these types and their collective involvement in the insanity of the world war. Thus it is probably irrelevant to ask whether Svejk's stupidity is real or assumed: his idiotic, literal-minded obedience to orders from his superiors is a device used by Hasek to reveal the absurdity of the Austrian empire, its military bureaucracy, and ultimately the futility of war in general. This inimitable technique of subverting a military machine through excessive zeal, whether genuine or pretended, has inspired the term "Svejkism," familiar to most Central Europeans, even those who have not read the novel.

The originality of *The Good Soldier Svejk* is unquestionable, as is its status as a uniquely Czech work responding to particular historical circumstances. But *Svejk* is hardly just historical fiction. It is clearly satirical, and it has been compared to the satires of British writer Jonathan Swift. Similarly, in his boisterous and often obscene humor Hasek has been compared to French satirist Francois Rabelais. And Robert Pynsent, in editor Holger Klein's book *The First World War in Fiction: A Collection of Literary Essays,* compared Hasek's attack on the Austrian war effort to that of the Viennese satirist Karl Kraus, while J. P. Stern, in *Forum for Modern Language Studies,* likened *Svejk* to American writer Joseph Heller's antiwar novel *Catch-22.*

The Good Soldier Svejk also belongs to another subgenre, possibly fiction's oldest: the picaresque novel, which relates the adventures of a wanderer. *Svejk*'s episodic plot, its depiction of a central character from the underclass, and, above all, its perspective mark it as a classic twentieth-century example of this genre. The picaresque perspective exposes pretense, and in *Svejk* codes of honor receive particular scorn, as do any notions that causes are worth human lives. But this perspective is limited to the current state of society—Svejk himself is only interested in self-preservation, and the narration never points to any ideological or revolutionary solution to the problems depicted.

In his other fiction, including work in the English-language collections *The Tourist Guide* and *The Red Commissar,* Hasek was equally provocative. The characters and settings in these accounts offer a panorama of life in central and eastern Europe, from Bavaria to Russia, and are mostly based on legends and Hasek's own experiences. Characterized by irreverence, they range from gentle irony to vicious satire. Hasek was most pointed when dealing with religious institutions, particularly the Roman Catholic church, as in "The Struggle for Souls" and "The End of Saint Jura." As an anti-Austrian and pan-Slavist, Hasek was considerably more gentle in depicting the Russian Orthodox church in stories such as "Bogumirov, the Serbian Pope, and Mufti Isrim's Goat" and "The Procession of the

Cross." His sympathies for the poor and dispossessed, instead of for the ruling classes, are exemplified in "My Friend Hanuska" and the cycle "Stories From the Water Bailiff's Watch-Tower at Razice." He favored lawbreakers over a judicial system he found contemptible and ridiculous—as in "Affable Persuasion," "Something Spicy about Legal Arbiters," "The Criminals' Strike," and "The Judicial Reform of Mr. Zakon"—and he championed the individual against any bureaucracy in such pieces as "The Austrian Customs Authorities" and "Hasek's Effort to Improve the Finances of the Monarchy." In addition, he showed hostility toward artistic and moral pretensions of all kinds in "Among Bibliophilists," "The Sad Fate of the Railway Station Mission," and "An Experiment in Giving a Teetotal Party," while his much-noted penchant for bathroom humor is evident in tales such as "Mr. Florentin Versus Chocholka" and "Justice and the Lesser Bodily Needs."

Despite the impressive nature of his satirical perspective, particularly in *The Good Soldier Svejk,* Hasek did not initially find favor with most Czech critics. Apart from the expected condemnations prompted by Hasek's personal reputation, objections were raised concerning *The Good Soldier Svejk*'s vulgar expressions, allegedly obscene subject matter, invariably blasphemous treatment of religion, the crudeness of prose, and—above all—the unflattering light that the novel's protagonist cast on the Czech national character. Those who took pride in the heroic exploits of the Czech Legion and justified World War I because it led to Czech independence did not wish to see Czechs presented as antimilitarist malingerers and saboteurs, least of all by a Legion deserter.

Only the enthusiastic reception of *The Good Soldier Svejk* abroad—most notably in Germany, where Grete Reiner's 1926 translation and subsequent theatrical versions created a genuine craze—compelled many Czech critics to reexamine Hasek's novel. This revaluation, completed under the Communist regime, eventually led to Hasek's reputation as a literary master. Perhaps Hasek would appreciate this final irony—that the work of an antiestablishment author, one generally reviled and rejected by his own society, has won international recognition and the official approval of his country's governing elite.

MEDIA ADAPTATIONS: Grete Reiner's 1926 German translation of *The Adventures of The Good Soldier Schwejk* was adapted for the stage by Erwin Piscator and produced in Berlin at the Theater Am Nollendorfplatz in 1928. Bertolt Brecht also adapted the novel for the drama *Schweyk in the Second World War.*

BIOGRAPHICAL/CRITICAL SOURCES:

BOOKS

Frynta, Emanuel, *Hasek: The Creator of Schweik,* translated by Jean Layton and George Theiner, Artia, 1965.
Hasek, Jaroslav, *The Tourist Guide: Twenty-six Stories,* translated by I. T. Havlu, Artia, 1961.
Hasek, Jaroslav, *The Good Soldier: Schweik,* translated by Paul Selver, introduction by Leslie A. Fiedler, New American Library, 1963.
Hasek, Jaroslav, *The Good Soldier Svejk and His Fortunes in the World War,* translated by Cecil Parrott, Heinemann, 1973.
Hasek, Jaroslav, *The Red Commissar, Including Further Adventures of the Good Soldier Svejk and Other Stories,* translated by Parrott, Dial Press, 1981.
Janouch, Gustav, *Jaroslav Hasek: Der Vater des Braven Soldaten Schwejk,* Francke, 1966.
Klein, Holger, *The First World War in Fiction: A Collection of Critical Essays,* Barnes & Noble, 1977.
Kopeczi, Bela and Peter Juhasz, editors, *Litterature et Realite,* Akademiai Kiado, 1963.
Parrott, Cecil, *The Bad Bohemian: The Life of Jaroslav Hasek, Creator of The Good Soldier Svejk,* Bodley Head, 1978.
Parrott, Cecil, *Jaroslav Hasek: A Study of "Svejk" and the Short Stories,* Cambridge University Press, 1982.
Pytlik, Radko, editor, *Jaroslav Hasek in Briefen, Bildern und Erinnerungen,* translated by Gustav Just, Aufbau, 1983.
Twentieth-Century Literary Criticism, Volume 4, Gale, 1981.

PERIODICALS

Archiv fur das Studium der neueren Sprachen und Literaturen, Volume 215, number 1, 1978.
Canadian Slavonic Papers, Volume 22, number 1, 1980.
Comparative Literature, summer, 1968.
Forum for Modern Language Studies, Volume 2, number 1, 1966.
Germano-Slavica, spring, 1984.
New Republic, May 21, 1930, July 20, 1974.
Newsweek, March 11, 1974.
New York Times, February 16, 1930.
Osteuropa, Volume 12, numbers 4-5, 1962.
Saturday Review of Literature, February 15, 1930.
Scando-Slavica, Number 10, 1964.
Slavic and East-European Studies, autumn-winter, 1962.
Studia Slavica, November 9, 1963.
Times Literary Supplement, May 29, 1930, September 7, 1962, September 21, 1973, December 2, 1977, February 24, 1978.
World Literature Today, winter, 1978.
Zeitschrift fur Slawistik, Volume 25, number 3, 1980.

*   *   *

HATTERAS, Amelia
See MENCKEN, H(enry) L(ouis)

*   *   *

HATTERAS, Owen
See MENCKEN, H(enry) L(ouis)

*   *   *

HAVEL, Vaclav 1936-

PERSONAL: Born October 5, 1936, in Prague, Czechoslovakia; son of Vaclav M. (a property owner) and Bozena (Vavreckova) Havel; married Olga Splichalova. *Education:* Attended technical college, 1955-57, and Academy of Art, Prague, 1962-67.

ADDRESSES: Home—Udejvickeho rybnicku 4, 1600 Prague 6, Czechoslovakia.

CAREER: Playwright and political leader. ABC Theatre, Prague, Czechoslovakia, stagehand, 1959-60; Theatre on the Balustrade, Prague, stagehand, 1960-61, assistant to artistic director, 1961-63, literary manager, 1963-68, resident playwright, 1968; elected president of Czechoslovakia by parliament, 1989.

MEMBER: PEN, Union of Writers (Czechoslovakia).

AWARDS, HONORS: Austrian State Prize for European Literature, 1969; *Village Voice* Off-Broadway award, 1970, for "The Increased Difficulty of Concentration"; Obie Award for playwriting, 1984, for "A Private View"; prize from German Booksellers Association, 1989.

WRITINGS:

PLAYS IN ENGLISH TRANSLATION

Zahradni slavnost (first produced in Prague, Czechoslovakia, at Theatre on the Balustrade, 1963), [Czechoslovakia], 1964, translation by Vera Blackwell published as *The Garden Party* (also see below), J. Cape, 1969.

Vyrozumeni (first produced in Prague at Theatre on the Balustrade, 1965; produced Off-Broadway at Anspacher Theatre, April 23, 1968), Dilia, 1965, translation by Blackwell published as *The Memorandum*, J. Cape, 1967.

Ztizena noznost soustredeni (first produced in Prague at Theatre on the Balustrade, April, 1968; produced in New York City at Lincoln Center, December 4, 1969), Dilia, 1968, translation by Blackwell published as *The Increased Difficulty of Concentration,* J. Cape, 1972.

"Audience" and "Vernisaz," translations by Blackwell published in *Sorry: Two Plays* (also see below), Methuen, 1978.

"A Private View," translation by Blackwell produced in New York at Public Theater, 1983.

Largo Desolato (produced in Bristol at Theatre Royal, translation by Marie Winn produced in New York at Public Theater, 1986), translation by Tom Stoppard, Faber, 1987.

Temptation (first produced in Vienna, 1985, produced in England by the Royal Shakespeare Company at the Other Place, translation by Marie Winn produced in New York at the Public Theater, 1989), translation by George Thiener, Faber, 1988.

Also author of plays, "The Mountain Hotel," "The Conspirators," "The Guardian Angel," and the one-act, "Protest."

IN CZECH

(With Ivan Vyskocil) "Autostop" (play; title means "Hitchhike"), first produced in Prague in 1961.

Protokoly (title means "Protocols"; contains "Zahradni slavnost," "Vyrozumeni," two essays, and selected poems), Mlanda Fronta, 1966.

Hry 1970-1976 (contains "Spiklenci," "Zebracka Opera," "Horsky Hotel," "Audience," and "Vernisaz"), Sixty-Eight Publishing House (Toronto), 1977.

OTHER

(With others) *The Power of the Powerless: Citizens Against the State in Central Eastern Europe,* edited by John Keane, M. E. Sharpe (Armonk, N.Y.,) 1985.

Vaclav Havel, or Living in Truth (essay collection), edited by Jan Vladislav, Faber, 1987.

Letters to Olga (nonfiction), translated by Paul Wilson, Knopf, 1988.

Long Distance Interrogation (interviews conducted by Karel Hvizdala), translated by Paul Wilson, Knopf, 1990.

Work represented in anthologies, including *Three Eastern European Plays,* Penguin, 1970, and *Vanek Plays: Four Authors, One Character,* translated by M. Pomichalek and A. Mozga, University of British Columbia. Contributor to *New York Review of Books.*

SIDELIGHTS: Vaclav Havel, whom Horace Judson described in *Time* as "one of the most fearless Czech playwrights," is also considered one of the most important playwrights of eastern and central Europe. Writing in *Tulane Drama Review,* Henry Popkin ranked Havel as "the leading Czech dramatist since Karel Capek." Since 1968, however, following the Russian invasion of Czechoslovakia, Havel's works have been banned from the Czech stage. Despite harassment and arrest, Havel remained ac-

tive in the political reform movement that began in the spring of 1968. He also continued to write plays, even though he was under police surveillance.

Denied a higher education because his father had been a wealthy landowner before the Communist takeover in Czechoslovakia, Havel began to support himself by working in a chemical factory. He was able to complete his secondary education, however, by attending night classes and was permitted to attend a technical college, during which time he wrote and published his first essays on poetry and drama. In 1963, while attending the Academy of Arts in Prague, he published a monograph on the writer and painter Joseph Capek.

After his military service, Havel began his successful association with the Theatre on the Balustrade, an avant-garde acting ensemble. Under the leadership of Jan Grossman, who served as producer from 1962 to 1968, the Balustrade became the leading dramatic ensemble in Prague. Grossman, a renowned drama critic and translator, was considered a nonconformist and was officially barred from public theatrical work. But his productions were highly successful with the public despite the criticism and condemnation by both the Czech Communist party and the Soviet cultural attache in Prague. Some of Havel's own difficulties with the authorities were described by Popkin in "Theatre in Eastern Europe": "Vaclav Havel, the leading Czech dramatist, was expected at the New York meeting of PEN in 1966, but he did not get there. It was charged that his passport had been withdrawn; official sources replied that no Czech citizen is normally in possession of his passport and that Havel was free to travel abroad. And yet, later in the year, Havel did not turn up at an Austrian conference at which he was expected." Havel was permitted to visit the United States in 1968, but his passport was again confiscated in the summer of 1969. On August 26, 1969, as reported by the *New York Times,* Havel made a radio appeal "from an underground station in Liberec, a town in northern Bohemia, monitored by Radio Free Europe in Munich, begging Western intellectuals to raise their voices in condemnation of the Russian occupation of his country."

After the Soviet invasion of Czechoslovakia, Havel and Grossman were forbidden to work in the Czech theatre. Havel received many invitations to continue his work in the West, but he chose to remain in Czechoslovakia, where he continued his fight for freedom. In 1969, for example, he visited the steel mills in Ostrava and spoke to the unions about workers and intellectuals cooperating to defend the freedoms gained in 1968. As *Time* reported, "The meeting was banned by the police and locked out by management, but was held anyway out of doors." Havel remarked at the time: "They haven't arrested me—not yet. As long as I am invited to these meetings, I will go."

Havel was later arrested many times, however, and was continually harassed. When his adaptation of "The Beggar's Opera" was produced by amateurs in 1975, even members of the audience became victims of police reprisals. In 1977 he became one of the three principal spokesmen for the Charter 77 manifesto, which charged the Czech Government with human and civil rights violations and called for compliance with the provisions of the Helsinki agreement. After joining with the artists, writers, intellectuals, and working people of the Charter 77 movement, Havel was arrested and imprisoned several times. In March, 1979, the *New York Review of Books* reported that he "has recently been kept under tight surveillance by the political police."

Critics have noted the universality of Havel's plays. E. J. Czerwinski observed in *Books Abroad* that "Havel rarely refers to his country in his works." Havel explains this quality in terms of the political climate in which he wrote his early plays: "They might not have been directly political, but they confronted everyday realities and were a manifestation of freedom where there was no freedom." Because his plays deal with the dehumanization of man within the increasing mechanization of society, he has been labeled an absurdist and, in fact, credited with bringing the absurdist method to Czechoslovakia. But, as the critic for *Plays and Players* noted, out of "the need to deal with current issues through allegory," Havel uses absurdist technique not, like Western absurdists, to explore mental states, but "to disguise public social issues."

Jan Grossman considered Havel's drama not absurd but "appellative." In the introduction to a 1965 collection of Havel's work, Grossman wrote: "I do not know whether Havel's theatre belongs to the 'absurd'. . . . His plays are inventive, artificial; but this quality has nothing to do with romantic fantasies or . . . unbridled insanity. . . . Havel's artificial structuring of the world is made up of real, even commonplace and banal, components, joined most reasonably into a whole."

Thus grounded in reality, Havel's plays remain decidedly allegorical, and, as noted in both *Plays and Players* and *Time,* for the Czech audience the allusions are immediately recognizable. The protagonist of a Havel play is political bureaucracy itself, or a mechanism of bureaucracy which controls not only the characters, but also the plot and action of the play. For Havel, Grossman maintained, the mechanization of man is not just a theme, "but the central subject, from which his technique derived and on which it is focused."

According to Popkin, Havel's first play, "The Garden Party," "touches upon the discomforts endured by political bureaucracy as it makes its transition from Stalinism to an awkward and severely limited liberalism." It concerns the career of Hugo Pludek who, continually mouthing platitudes and political slogans, rises rapidly to control of the Office of Liquidation and the Office of Inauguration. The central problem involves the attempt to dissolve the Office of Liquidation, which, however, can only dissolve itself—an impossible accomplishment since, once the process was begun, the Office would no longer exist to finish the job. Grossman described "The Garden Party" as dominated by cliche: "Man does not use cliche, cliche uses man. Cliche is the hero, it causes, advances, and complicates the plot, determining human action, and deviating further and further from our given reality, creates its own."

"The Memorandum" also concerned the political power of language, the distortion of language by bureaucracy. A writer for the *Times Literary Supplement* commented: "In *The Garden Party* Havel showed us words dominating human beings: the phrase is the real hero of the piece, creating the situations and complicating them, directing human destinies instead of being their tool. In *Vyrozumeni*—to use the original Czech title of *The Memorandum*—man finds himself enmeshed not merely in a succession of phrases but in a whole language." The play revolves around an artificial and incomprehensible language aimed at making all office communication precise and unemotional; the fall and rise of the office manager, as a result of his inability to use the new language, constitutes the play's main action.

Clive Barnes, in the *New York Times,* called "The Memorandum" a "witty, funny and timely" political satire, while Robert Hatch, in the *Nation,* considered it a "bureaucratic burlesque." The critic for *Prompt,* however, wrote: "I would prefer to describe *The Memorandum* as a comedy of hypothesis. The world Havel creates in the play, is a hypothetical one, and therefore possible. Yet, our awareness of the comic, is an awareness of deviations from a concrete normality, either of physical behavior, or vested in certain general ideas: truth, honesty, charity. Thus, in the play there is established a tension between the opposing poles of hypothesis and actuality, possibility and accepted normality, into which the audience is thrust."

After Havel was silenced by the Czech authorities, "The Increased Difficulty of Concentration" was produced in New York City by the Lincoln Center Repertory Theatre. Jules Irving, director of the theatre, described the play as "an abrasive satire which couples bureaucratic farce, involving an effeminate computer called Puzuk, with an unorthodox structure where events are played back like a film rewinding." The play depicts the attempts of an intellectual to establish a viable way of living within his mechanized and meaningless environment. It consists of a day in the life of Dr. Edouard Huml, a social scientist, for whom romantic excesses have become a last refuge.

Marilyn Stasio, in *Cue,* called the work a "potent satiric drama" that, "for all its ominous undertones, [is] an inescapably funny play." Mell Gussow, of the *New York Times,* found the play "gentler" than "The Memorandum," and *Variety* considered it "a better play than Havel's earlier work, . . . with application beyond the border of eastern Europe." In his review for the *Nation,* Harold Clurman noted the play's importance for the Czech audience: "The speech that seems almost embarrassingly out of place with us, a speech in which the central character declares his conviction that the truth of life cannot be measured by computers or bureaucratic dictates but only by the motivations of the human heart, is what Havel meant his play to say. That is what gave it social force in his country. . . . Thus the play, a farce of no great subtlety, becomes something vital to the Czech citizen forever under the vigilant and evil eye—of who can say just what."

In the 1970's Havel managed to get some of his work out of Czechoslovakia, and a few pieces broadcast in Great Britain and published in Canada. The *Times Literary Supplement* praised Havel as a playwright of great promise: "In his preoccupation with the logical and the illogical Havel is a second Lewis Carroll, except that many people in Prague who saw his plays came out laughing 'with a chill up their spine.' His theatre could be the theatre of the absurd but it is not: his central theme is mechanization and what it makes a man, but mechanization is a gimmick rather than an inescapable factor in progress (as Capek might have seen it). It is clear that Havel's master in ideas was Kafka and in expression Ionesco. His is something of a genius whose promise is even greater than his performance."

Havel's political protests continued. He spent four months in prison in 1978, and the following year he was found guilty of subversion and imprisoned for agitating that the government respect human rights, as expressed in the Helsinki Agreement. Four years later, in 1982, he was transferred from prison to a civilian hospital and released because of illness. Soon afterwards, Havel again succeeded in sending writing out of Czechoslovakia and three of his plays, "Private View," 1983, "Temptation," 1985, and "Largo Desolato," 1986, were produced. Additionally, Havel published in England a collection of essays, *Vaclav Havel, or Living in Truth* and *Letters to Olga,* a book of reminiscences based on letters he wrote to his wife from prison.

Later in the decade, during the political upheaval in Czechoslovakia and other European communist countries in 1989, Havel emerged as the leader of the opposition to his country's government, and was elected president by the parliament in December of that year. Havel, who in recent years has maintained that he wanted to be a playwright, rather than a political figure, is quoted by Henry Kamm in the *New York Times* concerning his political office: "I have repeatedly said my occupation is writer. . . . I have no political ambitions. I don't feel myself to be a professional politician. But I have always placed the public interest above my own. . . . And if, God help us, the situation develops in such a way that the only service that I could render my country would be to do this, then of course I would do it."

BIOGRAPHICAL/CRITICAL SOURCES:

BOOKS

Contemporary Literary Criticism, Volume 25, Gale, 1983.

PERIODICALS

Books Abroad, spring, 1971.
Chicago Tribune, December 30, 1989, February 22, 1990.
Cue, December 13, 1969.
Globe and Mail (Toronto), April 30, 1988, October 28, 1989, December 30, 1989, January 6, 1990.
Los Angeles Times, February 22, 1989, February 15, 1989, December 4, 1989, December 17, 1989, January 13, 1990, February 23, 1990.
Los Angeles Times Book Review, April 3, 1988.
Nation, May 27, 1968, December 22, 1969.
New Yorker, May 18, 1968.
New York Review of Books, August 4, 1977, March 22, 1979.
New York Times, May 6, 1968, October 22, 1969, December 5, 1969, December 14, 1969, November 20, 1983, November 21, 1983, March 23, 1986, March 26, 1986, March 31, 1988, February 5, 1989, April 9, 1989, December 8, 1989, December 17, 1989, December 18, 1989, December 23, 1989, December 30, 1989, January 13, 1990.
New York Times Book Review, May 8, 1988.
New York Times Magazine, October 25, 1989.
Observer Review, December 17, 1967.
Plays and Players, August, 1971.
Prompt, number 12, 1968.
Time, June 14, 1968, July 25, 1969.
Times (London), October 15, 1986, February 12, 1987, May 2, 1987, April 27, 1988, February 29, 1989, March 4, 1989, February 17, 1990.
Times Literary Supplement, March 7, 1968, March 10, 1972.
Tulane Drama Review, spring, 1967.
Variety, December 17, 1969.
Washington Post, August 26, 1988 , February 22, 1989, May 15, 1989, October 27, 1989, January 7, 1990, January 9, 1990, March 4, 1990.

*   *   *

HAWKES, John (Clendennin Burne, Jr.) 1925-

PERSONAL: Born August 17, 1925, in Stamford, Conn.; son of John Clendennin Burne and Helen (Ziefle) Hawkes; married Sophie Goode Tazewell, September 5, 1947; children: John Clendennin Burne III, Sophie Tazewell, Calvert Tazewell, Richard Urquhart. *Education:* Harvard University, A.B., 1949.

ADDRESSES: Home—18 Everett Ave., Providence, R.I. 02906. *Agent*—Lynn Nesbit, International Creative Management, 40 West 57th St., New York, N.Y. 10019.

CAREER: Harvard University Press, Cambridge, Mass., assistant to production manager, 1949-55; Harvard University, Cambridge, visiting lecturer, 1955-56, instructor in English, 1956-58; Brown University, Providence, R.I., assistant professor, 1958-62, associate professor, 1962-67, professor of English, be-

ginning in 1967, T. B. Stowell University Professor, beginning in 1973. Visiting assistant professor of humanities, Massachusetts Institute of Technology, 1959; leader of novel workshop, Utah Writers' Conference, Salt Lake City, summer, 1962; special guest, Aspen Institute for Humanistic Studies, summer, 1962; staff member, Bread Loaf Writers' Conference, summer, 1963; writer in residence, University of Virginia, April, 1965; visiting professor of creative writing, Stanford University, 1966-67; visiting distinguished professor of creative writing, City College of the City University of New York, 1971-72. Member of Panel on Educational Innovation, Washington, D.C., 1966-67. *Wartime service:* American Field Service, 1944-45.

MEMBER: American Academy of Arts and Sciences, American Academy and Institute of Arts and Letters.

AWARDS, HONORS: M.A. from Brown University, 1962; Guggenheim fellowship, 1962-63; American Academy and Institute of Arts and Letters grant, 1962; Ford Foundation fellowship in theater, 1964-65; Rockefeller Foundation grant, 1966; Prix du Meilleur Livre Etranger, 1973; Prix Medicis Etranger for best foreign novel translated into French, 1986, for *Adventures in the Alaskan Skin Trade.*

WRITINGS:

Fiasco Hall (poems), Harvard University Printing Office, 1949.
(Editor with Albert J. Guerard and others) *The Personal Voice: A Contemporary Prose Reader,* Lippincott, 1964.
Innocent Party: Four Short Plays (contains "The Questions," first produced in Stanford, California, at Stanford Repertory Theatre, January 13, 1966; produced by NBC-TV, 1967; produced Off-Broadway at Players Workshop, January 14, 1972; "The Wax Museum," first produced in Boston, Massachusetts, at Theatre Company of Boston, April 28, 1966; produced Off-Broadway at Brooklyn Academy of Music, April 4, 1969; "The Undertaker," first produced at Theatre Company of Boston, March 28, 1967; "The Innocent Party," first produced at Theatre Company of Boston, February, 1968; produced Off-Broadway at Brooklyn Academy of Music, April 4, 1969), New Directions, 1967.
(Editor with others) *The American Literary Anthology I: The First Annual Collection of the Best from the Literary Magazines,* Farrar, Straus, 1968.
Lunar Landscapes: Stories and Short Novels, 1949-1963 (includes *The Owl, The Goose on the Grave,* and *Charivari;* also see below), New Directions, 1969.
Humors of Blood & Skin: A John Hawkes Reader (autobiographical notes), introduction by William H. Gass, New Directions, 1984.

NOVELS

The Cannibal, New Directions, 1949.
The Beetle Leg, New Directions, 1951, reprinted, 1967.
The Goose on the Grave: Two Short Novels (contains *The Goose on the Grave* and *The Owl;* also see below), New Directions, 1954.
The Lime Twig, New Directions, 1961.
Second Skin, New Directions, 1964.
The Blood Oranges, New Directions, 1971.
Death, Sleep, and the Traveler, New Directions, 1974.
Travesty, New Directions, 1976.
The Owl, New Directions, 1977.
The Passion Artist, Harper, 1979.
Virginie: Her Two Lives, Harper, 1982.
Adventures in the Alaskan Skin Trade, Simon & Schuster, 1985.
Innocence in Extremis (novella), Burning Deck, 1985.

Whistlejacket, Random House, 1988.

Also author of novella *Charivari.*

OTHER

Contributor to volumes, including *New Directions in Prose and Poetry II; The World of Black Humor: An Introductory Anthology of Selections and Criticism,* edited by Douglas M. Davis, 1967; *Write and Rewrite: A Story of the Creative Process,* edited by John Kuehl, 1967; *Flannery O'Connor,* edited by Robert E. Reiter; *The American Novel since World War II;* and *Writers as Teachers, Teachers as Writers.* Contributor of short stories, poems, articles, and reviews to periodicals, including *Audience, Voices: A Journal of Poetry, Sewanee Review, Massachusetts Review,* and *Tri-Quarterly.*

SIDELIGHTS: John Hawkes is most often characterized as an avant-garde writer. Hawkes's own declarations about his work and methods in an interview for *Wisconsin Studies in Contemporary Literature* support this assessment: "I began to write fiction on the assumption that the true enemies of the novel were plot, character, setting, and theme, and having once abandoned these familiar ways of thinking about fiction, totality of vision or structure was really all that remained. And structure—verbal and psychological coherence—is still my largest concern as a writer."

Hawkes's rejection of traditional novelistic methods results in books which critics call nightmarish and dreamlike. S. K. Oberbeck remarks: "Flannery O'Connor has said that one 'suffers [*The Lime Twig*] like a dream.' This is true of each of Hawkes's novels. His narratives move with the pace and color of a dream. Something in the dream reassures us; something either draws us on or repels us. Attraction or repulsion: these two violent reactions become suddenly mixed in the narrative as Hawkes writes it." Similarly, W. M. Frohock believes that "Hawkes's specialty is weaving little bits of authentic reality into a fabric of deep-textured nightmare." David Littlejohn adds that "the writer, since Kafka, who most purely offers a 'distortion of real experience in the manner of dreams'—our basic definition of anti-realism—is the . . . American John Hawkes."

Each of Hawkes's works has been attacked by critics who object to his unconventional methods. Alexander Klein, writing in the *New Republic,* contends that in *The Cannibal* "John Hawkes presents a 'surrealistic novel' which manages for long stretches to make dullness and surrealism appear practically synonymous. Actually the book is a series of related images (some fresh and sharp) and fragmentary sketches (a few vividly effective), gimcracked together with a semblance of plot and allegory." In like manner, a *New Yorker* reviewer finds that *The Lime Twig* "is struck through with bright flashes of emotion and imagery, but they do not compensate for the general murkiness of his prose, and they are not well enough balanced with the proportion and perspective that it very badly needs."

Yet many critics find both method and purpose in the seeming madness of Hawkes's novels. Charles Matthews argues that the "essence of Hawkes' technique is to destroy the conventional linkages and unifying forces of narrative. . . . For Hawkes, the destruction of the unity of perception is a particularization of that greater sense of destruction, deracination, decomposition, and dissolution which modern man feels when confronted with all those former sources of meaning: church, state, science, art, in short, all human institutions, ideals, and ideologies. The reader of Hawkes faces the abyss indeed, but it is the abyss which he must face every day." Robert Scholes feels that "Hawkes means to use conscious thought and art to illuminate the unconscious, to show us things about ourselves which may be locked in our own unconscious minds, avoiding the scrutiny of our consciousness."

In an interview with Scholes, Hawkes's remarks about the nightmares evinced in his writing echo the contentions of Matthews and Scholes: "We can't deny the essential crippling that is everywhere in life. I don't advocate crippling; I'm an opponent of torture. I deplore the nightmare; I deplore terror. I happen to believe that it is only by traveling those dark tunnels, perhaps not literally but psychically, that one can learn in any sense what it means to be compassionate." "My fiction," Hawkes concludes in the interview, "is generally an evocation of the nightmare or terroristic universe in which sexuality is destroyed by law, by dictum, by human perversity, by contraption, and it is this destruction of human sexuality which I have attempted to portray and confront in order to be true to human fear and to human ruthlessness, but also in part to evoke its opposite, the moment of freedom from constriction, constraint, death."

In addition to discussing the psychological elements in his novels, Hawkes has also commented on his concern with structure. "My novels are not highly plotted," he observes in *Wisconsin Studies,* "but they're elaborately structured." Donald J. Greiner points out that "structure often holds the key to Hawkes' difficult fiction. . . . Structure in his work is based upon cross-references, parallels, and contrasts, rather than upon the development of plot and character. It is this technique that enriches the nightmarish overtones of the novels and gives them their poetic quality." Scholes also notes the novels' meticulously wrought structures; *The Lime Twig,* for example, "which seems so foggy and dreamlike, is actually as neatly put together as the electrical circuitry of the human nervous system." Scholes stresses in particular the careful interweaving of recurring images and verbal patterns. In a discussion of *The Beetle Leg,* Lucy Frost also emphasizes Hawkes's use of images: "Images become crucial. . . . In the image the power of the novel resides." Not all critics, however, praise the elaborate structures of Hawkes's writing. Randall Green, for example, calls *The Lime Twig* "an academic exercise."

Reviewers also point to a pictorial quality in Hawkes's work. David Dillon feels that Hawkes is "at his best when he is closest to the spirit of the grotesque painters—Bosch to Brueghel. . . . The juxtaposed incongruities and monstrosities and enigmatic figures in the paintings have the same effect that Hawkes has, in his earlier writing, where he delights and thoroughly disconcerts his reader all at the same time." Earl Ganz makes a similar comment: "If you wish to understand John Hawkes, a painter friend once told me, think of Brueghel. . . . As with Brueghel, there is a beauty in this terrible world, a beauty the painter expresses in color and that Hawkes is able to do through description, his ability to describe painfully vivid scenes and, at certain moments, even to share that ability with his characters." Hawkes describes, in a *Massachusetts Review* interview, the centrality of visual images to his creative method: "I write out of a series of pictures that literally and actually do come to mind, but I've never seen them before. It is perfectly true that I don't know what they mean, but I feel and know that they have meaning. *The Cannibal* is probably the clearest example of this kind of absolute coherence of vision of anything I have written, when all the photographs do add together or come out of the same black pit."

Another element of Hawkes's work is its humor. As Greiner shows, many reviewers are disconcerted by Hawkes's "black humor" and the bleakness of his comedy, but other critics see the humor as a central, important part of the novels. Greiner, for instance, finds that Hawkes "daringly mixes a horror with humor, the grotesque with the heroic, creating a complex tone which some readers find hard to handle." Greiner contends that Hawkes rejects traditional comedy, which usually aims to mock aberrant behavior and assert a "benevolent social norm." Hawkes's characters, "while they perform ridiculous acts and reveal absurd personal defects in the manner of traditional comedy, rarely discover their faults in time so as to be safely reestablished with society." In fact, Hawkes dismisses orthodox social norms. Fiction, he says, "should be an act of rebellion against all the constraints of the conventional pedestrian mentality around us. Surely it should destroy conventional morality." While Hawkes spurns conventional morality, his "contemporary humor," Greiner argues, "maintains faith in the invulnerability of basic values: love, communication, sympathy. Given a world of fragmentation, self-destruction, and absurdity, Hawkes tries to meet the terrors with a saving attitude of laughter so as to defend and celebrate these permanent values." In the *Massachusetts Review* interview, Hawkes insists on his comic intentions: "I have always thought that my fictions, no matter how diabolical, were comic. I wanted to be very comic—but they have not been treated as comedy. They have been called 'black, obscene visions of the horror of life' and sometimes rejected as such, sometimes highly praised as such."

In addition to considering particular elements in his fiction, Hawkes has examined the relationship between fiction and life: "I think that we read for joy, for pleasure, for excitement, for challenge. It would seem pretty obvious, however, that fiction is its own province. Fiction is a made thing—a manmade thing. It has its own beauties, its own structures, its own delights. Its only good is to please us and to relate to our essential growth. I don't see how we could live without it. It may be that the art of living is no more than to exercise the act of imagination in a more irrevocable way. It may be that to read a fiction is only to explore life's possibilities in a special way. I think that fiction and living are entirely separate and that the one could not exist without the other." Furthermore, when asked by Scholes to comment on W. H. Auden's belief that the world would be no different if Shakespeare and Dante had never lived, Hawkes replies: "I don't agree with the idea. It seems obvious that the great acts of the imagination are intimately related to the great acts of life—that history and the inner psychic history must dance their creepy minuet together if we are to save ourselves from total oblivion. I think it's senseless to attempt to talk as Auden talked. The great acts of the imagination create inner climates in which psychic events occur, which in themselves are important, and also affect the outer literal events in time and space through what has occurred in the act of reading."

BIOGRAPHICAL/CRITICAL SOURCES:

BOOKS

Bellamy, Joe David, editor, *The New Fiction: Interviews with Innovative American Writers,* University of Illinois Press, 1974.

Busch, Frederick, *Hawkes: A Guide to His Works,* Syracuse University Press, 1973.

Contemporary Literary Criticism, Gale, Volume 1, 1973, Volume 2, 1974, Volume 3, 1975, Volume 4, 1975, Volume 7, 1977, Volume 9, 1978, Volume 14, 1980, Volume 15, 1980, Volume 27, 1984, Volume 49, 1988.

Dictionary of Literary Biography, Gale, Volume 2: *American Novelists since World War II,* 1978, Volume 7: *Twentieth-Century American Dramatists,* 1981.

Dictionary of Literary Biography Yearbook: 1980, Gale, 1981.

Greiner, Donald J., *Comic Terror: The Novels of John Hawkes,* Memphis State University Press, 1973.

Hawkes, John, *Humors of Blood & Skin: A John Hawkes Reader,* introduction by William H. Gass, New Directions, 1984.

Hryciw, Carol A., *John Hawkes: An Annotated Bibliography,* Scarecrow, 1977.

Kuehl, John, *John Hawkes and the Craft of Conflict,* Rutgers University Press, 1975.

Littlejohn, David, *Interruptions,* Grossman, 1970.

Malin, Irving, *New American Gothic,* Southern Illinois University Press, 1962.

Moore, Harry T., editor, *Contemporary American Novelists,* Southern Illinois University Press, 1964.

Santore, Anthony C., and Michael Pocalyko, editors, *A John Hawkes Symposium: Design and Debris,* New Directions, 1977.

Scholes, Robert, *The Fabulators,* Oxford University Press, 1967.

PERIODICALS

American Scholar, summer, 1965.

Audience, spring, 1960.

Book Week, September 26, 1965.

Chicago Tribune Book World, September 16, 1979.

Commonweal, July 2, 1954.

Contemporary Literature, Volume 11, number 3, 1970.

Critique: Studies in Modern Fiction, Volume 6, number 2, 1963, Volume 14, number 3, 1973.

Daedalus, spring, 1963.

Encounter, June, 1966.

Harvard Advocate, March, 1950.

Life, September 19, 1969.

Listener, July 18, 1968, May 5, 1970.

Los Angeles Times Book Review, May 9, 1982.

Massachusetts Review, summer, 1966.

Mediterranean Review, winter, 1972.

Minnesota Review, winter, 1962.

Nation, September 2, 1961, November 16, 1985.

National Observer, June 19, 1971.

New Leader, December 12, 1960, October 30, 1961.

New Republic, March 27, 1950, November 10, 1979, November 18, 1985.

New Statesman, March 11, 1966, November 10, 1967, May 1, 1970.

Newsweek, April 3, 1967.

New Yorker, April 29, 1961.

New York Review of Books, July 13, 1967, June 10, 1982.

New York Times, September 15, 1971.

New York Times Book Review, May 14, 1961, May 29, 1966, September 19, 1971, April 21, 1974, March 28, 1976, September 16, 1979, June 27, 1982, November 25, 1984, September 29, 1985, November 25, 1985.

Saturday Review, August 9, 1969, October 23, 1971.

Southwest Review, winter, 1965, autumn, 1971, summer, 1974.

Time, February 6, 1950, September 24, 1979.

Times Literary Supplement, February 17, 1966, October 15, 1971, February 14, 1975, February 28, 1986.

Village Voice, April 10, 1969, May 23, 1974, September 3, 1979, May 18, 1982, September 17, 1985.

Washington Post, October 1, 1969.

Washington Post Book World, October 14, 1979, September 29, 1985, July 24, 1988.

Wisconsin Studies in Contemporary Literature, summer, 1965.

HAYASECA y EIZAGUIRRE, Jorge
See ECHEGARAY (y EIZAGUIRRE), Jose (Maria Waldo)

*   *   *

HAYDEN, Robert E(arl) 1913-1980

PERSONAL: Name originally Asa Bundy Sheffey; name legally changed by foster parents; born August 4, 1913, in Detroit, Mich.; died February 25, 1980, in Ann Arbor, Mich.; son of Asa and Gladys Ruth (Finn) Sheffey; foster son of William and Sue Ellen (Westerfield) Hayden; married Erma I. Morris, June 15, 1940; children: Maia. *Education:* Detroit City College (now Wayne State University), B.A., 1936; University of Michigan, M.A., 1944. *Religion:* Baha'i.

CAREER: Federal Writers' Project, Detroit, Mich., researcher, 1936-40; University of Michigan, Ann Arbor, teaching fellow, 1944-46; Fisk University, Nashville, Tenn., 1946-69, began as assistant professor, became professor of English; University of Michigan, professor of English, 1969-80. Bingham Professor, University of Louisville, 1969; visiting poet, University of Washington, 1969, University of Connecticut, 1971, and Denison University, 1972. Member, Michigan Arts Council, 1975-76; Consultant in Poetry, Library of Congress, 1976-78.

MEMBER: American Academy and Institute of Arts and Letters, Academy of American Poets, PEN, American Poetry Society, Authors Guild, Authors League of America, Phi Kappa Phi.

AWARDS, HONORS: Jules and Avery Hopwood Poetry Award, University of Michigan, 1938 and 1942; Julius Rosenwald fellow, 1947; Ford Foundation fellow in Mexico, 1954-55; World Festival of Negro Arts grand prize, 1966, for *A Ballad of Remembrance;* Russell Loines Award, National Institute of Arts and Letters, 1970; National Book Award nomination, 1971, for *Words in the Mourning Time;* Litt.D., Brown University, 1976, Grand Valley State College, 1976, Fisk University, 1976, Wayne State University, 1977, and Benedict College, 1977; Academy of American Poets fellow, 1977; Michigan Arts Foundation Award, 1977; National Book Award nomination, 1979, for *American Journal.*

WRITINGS:

POEMS

Heart-Shape in the Dust, Falcon Press (Detroit), 1940.
(With Myron O'Higgins) *The Lion and the Archer,* Hemphill Press (Nashville), 1948.
Figure of Time: Poems, Hemphill Press, 1955.
A Ballad of Remembrance, Paul Breman (London), 1962.
Selected Poems, October House, 1966.
Words in the Mourning Time, October House, 1970.
The Night-Blooming Cereus, Paul Breman, 1972.
Angle of Ascent: New and Selected Poems, Liveright, 1975.
American Journal, limited edition, Effendi Press, 1978, enlarged edition, Liveright, 1982.
Robert Hayden: Collected Poems, edited by Frederick Glaysher, Liveright, 1985.

OTHER

(Editor and author of introduction) *Kaleidoscope: Poems by American Negro Poets* (juvenile), Harcourt, 1967.
(With others) "Today's Poets" (recording), Folkways, 1967.
(Author of preface) Alain LeRoy Locke, editor, *The New Negro,* Atheneum, 1968.

(Editor with David J. Burrows and Frederick R. Lapides) *Afro-American Literature: An Introduction,* Harcourt, 1971.
(Editor with James Edwin Miller and Robert O'Neal) *The United States in Literature,* Scott, Foresman, 1973, abridged edition published as *The American Literary Tradition, 1607-1899,* 1973.
(Contributor) *The Legend of John Brown,* Detroit Institute of Arts, 1978.
Collected Prose, edited by Glaysher, University of Michigan Press, 1984.

Contributor to periodicals, including *Atlantic, Negro Digest,* and *Midwest Journal.* Drama and music critic, *Michigan Chronicle,* late 1930s.

SIDELIGHTS: Robert E. Hayden was the first black poet to be chosen as Consultant in Poetry to the Library of Congress, a position described by Thomas W. Ennis of the *New York Times* as "the American equivalent of the British poet laureate designation." Hayden's formal, elegant poems about the black historical experience earned him a number of other major awards as well. "Robert Hayden is now generally accepted," Frederick Glaysher stated in Hayden's *Collected Prose,* "as the most outstanding craftsman of Afro-American poetry."

The historical basis for much of Hayden's poetry stemmed from his extensive study of American and black history. Beginning in the 1930s, when he researched black history for the Federal Writers' Project in his native Detroit, Hayden studied the story of his people from their roots in Africa to their present condition in the United States. "History," Charles T. Davis wrote in *Modern Black Poets: A Collection of Critical Essays,* "has haunted Robert Hayden from the beginning of his career as a poet." As he once explained to Glenford E. Mitchell of *World Order,* Hayden saw history "as a long, tortuous, and often bloody process of becoming, of psychic evolution."

Other early influences on Hayden's development as a poet were W. H. Auden, under whom Hayden studied at the University of Michigan, and Stephen Vincent Benet, particularly Benet's poem "John Brown's Body." That poem describes the black reaction to General Sherman's march through Georgia during the Civil War and inspired Hayden to also write of that period of history, creating a series of poems on black slavery and the Civil War that won him a Hopwood Award in 1942.

After graduating from college in 1944, Hayden embarked on an academic career. He spent some twenty-three years at Fisk University, where he rose to become a professor of English, and ended his career with an eleven-year stint at the University of Michigan. Hayden told Mitchell that he considered himself to be "a poet who teaches in order to earn a living so that he can write a poem or two now and then."

Although history plays a large role in Hayden's poetry, many of his works are also inspired by the poet's adherence to the Baha'i faith, an Eastern religion which believes in a coming world civilization. Hayden served for many years as the poetry editor of the group's *World Order* magazine. The universal outlook of the Baha'is also moved Hayden to reject any narrow racial classification for his work. James Mann of the *Dictionary of Literary Biography* claimed that Hayden "stands out among poets of his race for his staunch avowal that the work of black writers must be judged wholly in the context of the literary tradition in English, rather than within the confines of the ethnocentrism that is common in contemporary literature written by blacks." As Lewis Turco explained in the *Michigan Quarterly Review,* "Hayden has always wished to be judged as a poet among poets, not one to whom special rules of criticism ought to be applied in order to make his work acceptable in more than a sociological sense."

This stance earned Hayden harsh criticism from other blacks during the polarized 1960s. He was accused of abandoning his racial heritage to conform to the standards of a white, European literary establishment. "In the 1960s," William Meredith wrote in his foreword to *Collected Prose*, "Hayden declared himself, at considerable cost in popularity, an American poet rather than a black poet, when for a time there was posited an unreconcilable difference between the two roles. . . . He would not relinquish the title of American writer for any narrower identity."

Ironically, much of Hayden's best poetry is concerned with black history and the black experience. "The gift of Robert Hayden's poetry," Vilma Raskin Potter remarked in *MELUS*, "is his coherent vision of the black experience in this country as a continuing journey both communal and private." Hayden wrote of such black historical figures as Nat Turner, Frederick Douglass, Malcolm X, Harriet Tubman, and Cinquez. He also wrote of the Underground Railroad, the Civil War, and the American slave trade. Edward Hirsch, writing in the *Nation*, called Hayden "an American poet, deeply engaged by the topography of American myth in his efforts to illuminate the American black experience."

Though Hayden wrote in formal poetic forms, his range of voices and techniques gave his work a rich variety. "Hayden," Robert G. O'Meally wrote in the *Washington Post Book World*, "is a poet of many voices, using varieties of ironic black folk speech, and a spare, ebullient poetic diction, to grip and chill his readers. He draws characters of stark vividness as he transmutes cardinal points and commonplaces of history into dramatic action and symbol." "His work," Turco wrote, "is unfettered in many ways, not the least of which is in the range of techniques available to him. It gives his imagination wings, allows him to travel throughout human nature." Speaking of Hayden's use of formal verse forms, Mann explained that Hayden's poems were "formal in a nontraditional, original way, strict but not straight-jacketed" and found that they also possessed "a hard-edged precision of line that molds what the imagination wants to release in visually fine-chiseled fragmental stanzas that fit flush together with the rightness of a picture puzzle."

It wasn't until 1966, with the publication of *Selected Poems*, that Hayden first enjoyed widespread attention from the nation's literary critics. As the *Choice* critic remarked at the time, *Selected Poems* showed Hayden to be "the surest poetic talent of any Negro poet in America; more importantly, it demonstrated a major talent and poetic coming-of-age without regard to race or creed." With each succeeding volume of poems his reputation was further enhanced until, in 1976 and his appointment as Consultant in Poetry to the Library of Congress, Hayden was generally recognized as one of the country's leading black poets.

Critics often point to Hayden's unique ability to combine the historical and the personal when speaking of his own life and the lives of his people. Writing in *Obsidian: Black Literature in Review*, Gary Zebrun argued that "the voice of the speaker in Hayden's best work twists and squirms its way out of anguish in order to tell, or sing, stories of American history—in particular the courageous and plaintive record of Afro-American history—and to chart the thoughts and feelings of the poet's own private space. . . . Hayden is ceaselessly trying to achieve . . . transcendence, which must not be an escape from the horror of history or from the loneliness of individual mortality, but an ascent that somehow transforms the horror and creates a blessed permanence."

BIOGRAPHICAL/CRITICAL SOURCES:

BOOKS

Concise Dictionary of Literary Biography, Volume 1: *The New Consciousness, 1941-1968,* Gale, 1987.
Contemporary Authors Bibliographical Series, Volume 2, Gale, 1986.
Contemporary Literary Criticism, Gale, Volume 5, 1976, Volume 9, 1978, Volume 14, 1980, Volume 37, 1986.
Conversations with Writers, Volume 1, Gale, 1977.
Dictionary of Literary Biography, Gale, Volume 5: *American Poets since World War II,* 1980, Volume 76: *Afro-American Writers, 1940-1955,* 1988.
Fetrow, Fred M., *Robert Hayden,* Twayne, 1984.
Gibson, Donald B., editor, *Modern Black Poets: A Collection of Critical Essays,* Prentice-Hall, 1973.
Hatcher, John, *From the Auroral Darkness: The Life and Poetry of Robert Hayden,* George Ronald, 1984.
Hayden, Robert E., *Collected Prose,* edited by Frederick Glaysher, University of Michigan Press, 1984.
O'Brien, John, *Interviews with Black Writers,* Liveright, 1973.

PERIODICALS

Choice, May, 1967, December, 1984.
MELUS, spring, 1980, spring, 1982.
Michigan Quarterly Review, spring, 1977, winter, 1982, fall, 1983.
Nation, December 21, 1985.
New York Times Book Review, January 17, 1971, February 22, 1976, October 21, 1979.
Obsidian: Black Literature in Review, spring, 1981.
Virginia Quarterly Review, autumn, 1982.
Washington Post Book World, June 25, 1978.
World Order, spring, 1971, summer, 1975, winter, 1976, fall, 1981.

OBITUARIES:

PERIODICALS

AB Bookman's Weekly, April 21, 1980.
Black Scholar, March/April, 1980.
Chicago Tribune, February 27, 1980.
Encore, April, 1980.
Los Angeles Times, March 3, 1980.
New York Times, February 27, 1980.
Time, March 10, 1980.
Washington Post, February 27, 1980.

* * *

HAYEK, F(riedrich) A(ugust von) 1899-

PERSONAL: Born May 8, 1899, in Vienna, Austria; immigrated to Great Britain, 1931; naturalized British citizen, 1938; son of August (a physician and botany professor) and Felizitas (von Juraschek) von Hayek; married Helene von Fritsch, 1926 (marriage ended); married Helene Bitterlich, 1950; children: (first marriage) Christine M. F., Laurence J. H. *Education:* University of Vienna, Dr. Jur., 1921, Dr. Sc.Pol., 1923; graduate study at New York University, 1923-24.

ADDRESSES: Home—Urachstrasse 27, D-7800, Freiburg in Breisgau, Federal Republic of Germany. *Office*—University of Freiburg, D-7800, Kozzegiengebaude II, Federal Republic of Germany.

CAREER: Employed with the Austrian Civil Service, 1921-26; Austrian Institute for Economic Research, Vienna, Austria, director, 1927-31; University of Vienna, Vienna, lecturer in economics and statistics, 1929-31; University of London, London, England, Tooke Professor of Economic Sciences and Statistics, 1931-50; University of Chicago, Chicago, Ill., professor of social and moral sciences, 1950-62; University of Freiburg, Freiburg, Federal Republic of Germany, professor of economics, 1962-69, professor emeritus, 1969—. Visiting professor at University of Salzburg, Salzburg, Austria, 1970-77.

MEMBER: British Academy (fellow), Austrian Academy of Science (honorary fellow), Academia Sinaica (honorary fellow), Reform Club (London).

AWARDS, HONORS: Nobel Prize for economic science, 1974; Austrian Distinction for Science and Art, 1975; Medal of Merit from Baden-Wuerttemberg, 1981; Ring of Honor from City of Vienna, 1983; Gold Medal from City of Paris, 1984. Honorary degrees: D.Sc., University of London, 1941; Dr. Jur., University of Rikkyo, Tokyo, 1964; Dr.Jur., University of Salzburg, 1974; Dr.Lit.Hum., University of Dallas, 1975; Dr.Soc.Sci., Marroquin University, Guatemala, 1977; also received degrees from Santa Maria University, Valparaiso, 1977, University of Buenos Aires, 1977, and University of Giessen, 1982.

WRITINGS:

Geldtheorie und Konjunkturtheorie, Hoelder-Pichler-Tempsky, 1929, translation by N. Kaldor and H. M. Cromme published as *Monetary Theory and the Trade Cycle,* Harcourt, 1933, reprinted, Augustus Kelley, 1966.
Prices and Production, G. Routledge & Sons, 1931, 2nd edition, 1935, reprinted, Augustus Kelley, 1967.
Monetary Nationalism and International Stability, Longmans, Green, 1938, reprinted, Cato Institute, 1989.
Freedom and the Economic System, University of Chicago Press, 1939.
Profits, Interest, and Investment, and Other Essays on the Theory of Industrial Fluctuations, G. Routledge & Sons, 1939.
The Pure Theory of Capital, Macmillan, 1941, reprinted, University of Chicago Press, 1975.
The Road to Serfdom, University of Chicago Press, 1944.
Individualism and Economic Order, University of Chicago Press, 1948, reprinted, Routledge & Kegan Paul, 1977.
The Sensory Order: An Inquiry into the Foundation of Theoretical Psychology, University of Chicago Press, 1952, reprinted, 1976.
The Counter-Revolution of Science: Studies on the Abuse of Reason, Free Press (England), 1952, reprinted, Liberty Fund, 1980.
The Political Ideal of the Rule of Law, [Cairo], 1955.
The Constitution of Liberty, University of Chicago Press, 1960.
Dr. Bernard Mandeville, Oxford University Press, c. 1966.
Studies of Philosophy, Politics, and Economics, University of Chicago Press, 1967.
Confusion of Language in Political Thought, Transatlantic, 1968.
Freiburger Studien (title means "Freiburg Studies": includes ten essays translated from the original English), Mohr, 1969.
Roads to Freedom, Routledge & Kegan Paul, 1969.
Toward Liberty, California Institute for Humane Studies, 1971.
A Tiger by the Tail: The Keynesian Legacy of Inflation, Transatlantic, 1972.
Verdict on Rent Control, London Institute of Economic Affairs, 1972.
Economic Freedom and Representative Government, Transatlantic, 1973.
Law, Legislation, and Liberty: A New Statement of the Liberal Principles of Justice and Political Economy, University of

Chicago Press, Volume 1: *Rules and Order,* 1973, Volume 2: *The Mirage of Social Justice,* 1977, Volume 3: *The Political Order of a Free People,* 1979.
Full Employment at Any Price?, Transatlantic, 1975.
Rent Control, Fraser Institute, 1975.
Denationalization of Money: An Analysis of the Theory and Practice of Concurrent Currencies, London Institute of Economic Affairs, 1976, 2nd edition, Transatlantic, 1977.
A Choice in Currency: A Way to Stop Inflation, Transatlantic, 1977.
New Studies: In Philosophy, Politics, Economics, and the History of Ideas, University of Chicago Press, 1978.
Three Sources of Human Values, London School of Economics, 1978.
Unemployment and Monetary Policy: Government as Generator of the "Business Cycle," Cato Institute, 1979.
1980s Unemployment and the Unions, Transatlantic, 1980.
Money, Capital, and Fluctuations: Early Essays, University of Chicago Press, 1984.
The Essence of Hayek, edited by Chiaki Nishiyama and Kurt Leube, Hoover Institution, 1984.
The Collected Works of F. A. Hayek, Volume 1: *The Fatal Conceit: The Errors of Socialism,* edited by W. W. Bartley III, University of Chicago Press, 1988.

Also author of *The Reactionary Character of the Socialist Conception,* Hoover Institution.

EDITOR

Beitraege zur Geldtheorie, J. Springer, 1933.
Collectivist Economic Planning: Critical Studies on the Possibilities of Socialism, G. Routledge & Sons, 1935, reprinted, Augustus Kelley, 1967.
John Stuart Mill, *John Stuart Mill and Harriet Taylor: Their Correspondence,* University of Chicago Press, 1951, reprinted, Richard West, 1979.
Capitalism and the Historians, University of Chicago Press, 1954.
Henry Thornton, *An Enquiry into the Nature and Effects of the Paper Credit of Great Britain,* Augustus Kelley, 1962.
Rules, Perception, and Intelligibility, British Academy, 1976.

OTHER

Contributor of articles to *Economic Journal, Economica,* and other publications in the United States and Europe.

SIDELIGHTS: A Nobel Prize-winning economist, F. A. Hayek advocates the classic liberal economic principles of the nineteenth century. These principles include an unhindered free enterprise system, a free market, and political democracy. These beliefs have led him to suggest that the form of government most conducive to freedom is one with impartial laws which guarantee social order and the unregulated expression of human life. Hayek is a major figure in contemporary economic thought and is generally credited with inspiring England's shift away from a government-controlled economy. But because his ideas ran counter to the prevailing collectivist views of other economists for several decades, Hayek's "fame and his influence have been achieved very much against the flow of fashionable opinion," Michael Ivens writes in the *Spectator.* Hayek has written on such diverse subjects as monetary theory, inflation, socialism, political freedom, unemployment, and scientific methodology, but he is most highly regarded for his books examining the relationship between economic systems and personal freedom.

Hayek first made his reputation in the 1930s as a monetary theorist. In *Monetary Theory and the Trade Cycle* (originally published as *Geldtheorie und Konjunkturtheorie*) and *Monetary Nationalism and International Stability,* Hayek presented his views on the subject. In *Monetary Theory and the Trade Cycle* he argues that business cycles are not caused by fluctuations in currency value but by the volume of currency in circulation. The reviewer for the *Times Literary Supplement* finds the book of "unquestioned importance" and praises "the great erudition, the logical austerity and the unusual power of sustained abstract reasoning which [Hayek] has at his command." In *Monetary Nationalism and International Stability,* Hayek calls for an international monetary standard. He argues that national currencies, with their varying exchange rates, inhibit free trade between nations. An international currency would lower trade barriers and thereby decrease international tensions. Honor Croome of *Spectator* believes that Hayek "treats his difficult subject both conscientiously and stimulatingly" and judges the book to be "intellectually satisfying."

In the 1930s, too, Hayek first turned his attention to the issue of government economic planning, a subject that would increasingly occupy a central position in his later work. His initial effort in this area was the 1935 anthology *Collectivist Economic Planning: Critical Studies on the Possibilities of Socialism.* This book brought together a number of articles debunking the efficiency of government economic planning. The *Economist* reviewer believes that "the case is a very strong one," while the critic for the *Times Literary Supplement* calls *Collectivist Economic Planning* "a book of outstanding interest."

Hayek's study of economic planning culminated in 1944 with the publication of perhaps his most famous book, *The Road to Serfdom.* Here he argues against state planning of the economy not because it is inefficient, as he had shown in *Collectivist Economic Planning,* but because it concentrates too much power in the hands of the state. Hayek holds that all state-controlled economies—including socialism, communism, fascism, and the welfare state—inevitably lead to totalitarian dictatorship because they require a strong, central government with enormous powers. Such a government, Hayek believes, is antithetical to personal freedom.

The book met with an enthusiastic response, even from many who found it essentially incorrect in its analysis. Henry Hazlitt of the *New York Times* calls *The Road to Serfdom* "one of the most important books of our generation" and "an arresting call to all well-intentioned planners and socialists, to all those who are sincere democrats and liberals at heart, to stop, look and listen." Hans Kohn of the *Saturday Review of Literature* describes the book as "cogent in its reasoning, gracious in its presentation, forceful in its plea." But T. V. Smith in *Ethics* calls the book "hysterical" because "it is agitated at heart and in turn agitates others." Eric Roll, writing in *American Economic Review,* finds that "Hayek presents his thesis with considerable skill" but that his "strong political prejudices show through the veneer of reasonableness coupled with high-mindedness with which he tries to impress the reader." But even John Maynard Keynes, an economist whose views are far removed from Hayek's own, admits, according to Ivens, that he was "in agreement with virtually the whole of [the book]; and not only in agreement but in deeply moved agreement." Writing forty years after the initial publication of *The Road to Serfdom,* Edwin J. Feulner, Jr., of *American Spectator* describes the book in glowing terms. "I have never read a more profound work, nor a more eloquent warning against the dangers of government intervention," Feulner maintains. *The Road to Serfdom* has been surprisingly successful for a book of economic theory. It was a best-seller in both the United States and England, was adapted for radio, condensed in *Read-*

ers' Digest, serialized by the King Features Syndicate, reprinted in pamphlet form by the Book-of-the-Month Club, and translated into a dozen languages.

In subsequent volumes Hayek continues to examine the relationship between freedom and economics, maintaining that only a free enterprise system is compatible with personal liberty. His *Individualism and Economic Order* covers a number of topics, ranging from socialist planning to the meaning of economic competition. Sidney Ratner of the *American Political Science Review* admits that "though many will disagree with some or all of his views, few will deny that he writes with vigor, considerable freshness and originality, and wide learning." George Soule of *Nation* believes that because Hayek is "among the most thoughtful and consistent supporters of a market economy, as against planning either by the state or by private monopoly, those who disagree with him cannot afford to ignore him."

In 1954 Hayek edited *Capitalism and the Historians,* a collection of essays on the effects the industrial revolution had on the British working class. These essays disprove the widely held idea that industrialization had harmed the working class. In fact, industrialization substantially improved the lives of the workers. Filled with contemporary eyewitness accounts and case histories, the book details the improvement in living standards for those who became factory workers. It shows that most of these workers had been poor farm laborers living in barns or ditches. They were often hungry; their health was poor. The conditions in the urban slums, where they moved after becoming factory workers, although unpleasant by today's standards, were a vast improvement over their previous lives. Leo Teplow of *Management Review* thinks the book is "a hundred years late, [but it] is still very badly needed and deserves a wide audience." Writing in the *Christian Science Monitor,* H. C. Kenney declares that "it is refreshing to have established experts provide a thoughtful, scholarly debunking of the long popular myth." Leo Rosten of the *Saturday Review/World* suggests reading this book, "and you will revise the stereotypes about socialism and capitalism that we all learned." He finds, too, that *Capitalism and the Historians* "makes hash out of our traditional picture of the evils, the horrors, and the 'inhumane' impact of the factory system."

Hayek extended the ideas first expressed in *The Road to Serfdom* in *The Constitution of Liberty.* This study of the nature of freedom and how it can be preserved under law examines the relationship between systems of government and citizens' personal freedom. Hayek outlines what he sees as the necessary prerequisites for a free society, primary among these being a free market. Milton Friedman, writing in the *New York Times Book Review,* believes the book "provides a comprehensive restatement of the fundamental values underlying a liberal view and applies those values to the concrete problems of our times." Commenting in the *Chicago Sunday Tribune,* George Morgenstern calls *The Constitution of Liberty* "the book of the year in the field of ideas. . . . Hayek's far ranging work, encyclopedic in scope and disclosing a staggering learning, is written with coolness and clarity." Not all reviewers agreed with Hayek's formula for a free society. But as Sidney Hook observes in the *New York Times Book Review,* "even those who accept little of his argument will find . . . Hayek's comprehensive analysis of the nature of freedom an interesting and provocative work."

The three-volume work *Law, Legislation, and Liberty: A New Statement of the Liberal Principles of Justice and Political Economy* is, M. Stanton Evans writes in the *National Review,* "the crowning achievement of [Hayek's] career." In it, Hayek elaborates upon his economic and political beliefs concerning a free society. As in previous works, he expresses his distrust of socialist economic systems, believing that they inevitably lead to dictatorial government. In the first volume of the massive work, entitled *Rules and Order,* Hayek stresses the necessity for government to serve as a legal framework to preserve the essentially spontaneous nature of human life. Evan Simpson of *Library Journal* finds that in *Rules and Order,* "the eminent economist and philosopher [Hayek] champions the free, spontaneous social order against attempts to direct society in desired paths."

In the second volume of the work, *The Mirage of Social Justice,* Hayek dismisses all arguments that justify government intervention into the economic or social life of its citizens. Such intervention is often sanctioned by the idea of social justice—the belief that the distribution of wealth in a society must meet some ethical or moral standard. Hayek emphasizes that the effects of a free market system—the distribution of wealth—cannot be found to be just or unjust because those effects are not the predetermined intentions of any individual. Evans describes *The Mirage of Social Justice* as "a work of sustained intellection that is truly awesome." The *Economist* critic agrees, stating that "it is impossible to give more than the slightest flavour of a work of this importance. The main task of the reviewer is not to assess it, but simply to underline how important it is as a contribution to the existing debate on social and political philosophy, and in particular on the meaning of and foundation of freedom and, dare one say it, justice."

The Political Order of a Free People completes *Law, Legislation, and Liberty.* Having examined in the first two volumes the tendency of government to intervene in the lives of its citizens and thereby inhibit personal freedom, Hayek in this book details the type of government needed to insure freedom. One chapter, entitled "A Model Constitution," proposes a return to the original form of the American government—a bicameral congress and a separation of political powers, something Hayek believes we have lost. These measures would return control of the legislative process, now in the hands of the politicians, back to the people again. The foundation for such a government, Hayek maintains, is "the recovery of the free market as the basis of politics and policy," as G. L. McDowell writes in the *Virginia Quarterly Review.* "Hayek," writes L. M. Lachmann in the *Journal of Economic Literature,* "is a bitterly disappointed, life-long democrat to whom the discrepancy between the ideals of his youth . . . and the daily practice of contemporary democratic governments . . . is not merely a spectacle painful to behold, but a symptom of a serious disease of modern society." McDowell finds Hayek "more polemical than philosophical" in this book, but judges *The Political Order of a Free People* "an important contribution to the dialectic of social thought."

For several decades Hayek has been a leading proponent of economic and political freedom, a role that earned him a Nobel Prize in economic science in 1974. His influence, particularly in England, has been substantial. British prime ministers Winston Churchill and Margaret Thatcher have both cited Hayek as the primary inspiration for their economic policies. His ideas have also inspired the Chicago school of economics, of which Milton Friedman is a prominent member, as well as many contemporary advocates of libertarianism. Hook describes Hayek as "one who is passionately opposed to the coercion of human beings by the arbitrary will of others, who puts liberty above welfare and is sanguine that greater welfare will thereby ensue." Simpson calls Hayek "an eloquent defender of classical liberalism in a period more receptive to an egalitarian understanding of liberal values." In his book *Hayek on Liberty,* John Gray praises Hayek as a philosopher who "gives us a defence of individual freedom without

equal in modern thought," while Friedman finds Hayek to be "the leading philosopher of a liberal society (in the 19th-century sense of a society devoted to promoting freedom)." Ivens concludes that Hayek is "a model political and economic philosopher for the late 20th century."

BIOGRAPHICAL/CRITICAL SOURCES:

BOOKS

Butler, Eamonn, *Hayek: A Study of His Life and Work,* Temple Smith, 1983.
Butler, Eamonn, *Hayek: His Contribution to the Political and Economic Thought of Our Time,* Temple Smith, 1984.
Essays on Hayek, Routledge & Kegan Paul, 1977.
Gray, John, *Hayek on Liberty,* Basil Blackwell, 1984.
Hayek's Social and Economic Philosophy, Macmillan, 1979.

PERIODICALS

American Economic Review, March, 1945.
American Political Science Review, February, 1949, September, 1968.
American Spectator, December, 1984.
Annals of the American Academy of Political and Social Science, May, 1945, January, 1949, November, 1952, May, 1954.
Atlantic, December, 1944.
Chicago Sunday Tribune, February 14, 1960.
Christian Science Monitor, March 10, 1954.
Commonweal, September 29, 1944.
Economist, April 20, 1935, October 6, 1973, February 5, 1977.
Ethics, April, 1945.
Journal of Economic Literature, September, 1980.
Journal of Political Economy, April, 1932, February, 1942.
Library Journal, February 1, 1974, June 1, 1977.
Management Review, August, 1954.
Manchester Guardian, October 24, 1952.
Nation, September 25, 1948.
National Review, December 22, 1978, December 7, 1979.
New Statesman, November 24, 1967, January 14, 1977.
New Yorker, September 25, 1948.
New York Times, September 24, 1944, September 5, 1948.
New York Times Book Review, February 21, 1960, September 12, 1965, June 8, 1980.
Political Science Quarterly, September, 1945.
Saturday Review, April 2, 1960.
Saturday Review of Literature, October 21, 1944.
Saturday Review/World, May 18, 1974.
Spectator, December 17, 1937, March 31, 1944, July 1, 1960, May 5, 1979, August 18, 1984.
Times Literary Supplement, May 4, 1933, June 20, 1935, February 5, 1938, April 1, 1944, December 12, 1952, July 22, 1960, July 25, 1968, August 9, 1985.
Virginia Quarterly Review, winter, 1980.
Weekly Book Review, October 29, 1944.

*   *   *

HAZZARD, Shirley 1931-

PERSONAL: Born January 30, 1931, in Sydney, Australia; daughter of Reginald (a government official) and Catherine (Stein) Hazzard; married Francis Steegmuller (a novelist and biographer), December 22, 1963. *Education:* Educated at Queenwood College, Sydney, Australia.

ADDRESSES: Home—200 East 66th St., New York, N.Y. 10021. *Agent*—McIntosh & Otis, Inc., 475 Fifth Ave., New York, N.Y. 10017

CAREER: Writer. Worked for British Intelligence in Hong Kong, 1947-48, and for British High Commissioner's Office, Wellington, New Zealand, 1940-50; United Nations, New York, N.Y., general service category, Technical Assistance to Under-developed Countries, 1952-62, serving in Italy, 1957.

MEMBER: American Academy and Institute of Arts and Letters.

AWARDS, HONORS: U.S. National Institute of Arts and Letters award in literature, 1966; National Book Award nomination, 1971; National Book Critics Circle Award, American Book Award nomination, and P.E.N./ Faulkner Award nomination, all 1981, for *The Transit of Venus*.

WRITINGS:

Cliffs of Fall, and Other Stories, Knopf, 1963.
The Evening of the Holiday (novel), Knopf, 1966.
People in Glass Houses: Portraits from Organization Life (nonfiction), Knopf, 1967.
The Bay of Noon (novel), Atlantic-Little, Brown, 1970.
Defeat of an Ideal: A Study of the Self-Destruction of the United Nations (nonfiction), Atlantic-Little, Brown, 1973.
The Transit of Venus (novel), Viking, 1980.
Countenance of Truth: The United Nations and the Waldheim Case (nonfiction), Viking, 1990.

Contributor to periodicals, including *New Yorker*.

WORK IN PROGRESS: A novel.

SIDELIGHTS: Even before the publication of her best-selling novel *The Transit of Venus*, Shirley Hazzard's work met with unusual critical approval. For example, Robie Macauley writes in the *New York Times Book Review* that Hazzard's *The Bay of Noon* is "one of those rare novels that tries to address itself to the reader's intelligence rather than his nightmares. Its assumptions are fine and modest: That the reader will enjoy a sense of place if that place is drawn for him so perfectly that it seems to breathe, that the reader will understand a story based on the interactions of personality rather than mere violence, that the reader will take pleasure in a style that is consciously elegant and literary." Laurence La Fore, also of the *New York Times Book Review*, asserts that "Shirley Hazzard's writing is like some electronic mechanism, enormously intricate in design and function, charged with great power, but so refined by skill that it may be contained in a small case and exhibit a smooth and shapely surface." And a *Time* reviewer describes Hazzard's earlier prose as "so understated that it forces the reader to become uncommonly attentive. But mostly it is because she chooses her words with such delicacy and precision that even ordinary situations acquire poetic shadings."

But it was with the release of *The Transit of Venus* that Hazzard gained a wider and more diverse readership. Writing in the *Chicago Tribune*, Lynne Sharon Schwartz remarks: "If the literary establishment were given to pageantry, [*The Transit of Venus*] ought to be welcomed with a flourish of trumpets. Last year John Gardner clamored for moral fiction: Here is a book that ventures confidently amid the abiding themes of truth, beauty, goodness, and love, and is informed, moreover, by stringent intelligence and lacerating irony. Hazzard spares no one, not even her reader."

New York Times Book Review critic Michiko Kakutani explains that "during the last decade and a half, Shirley Hazzard has achieved much critical acclaim for her fiction—fiction distinguished by its sculptured prose and its civilized portrayals of love and loss. Yet with her self-consciously literary style, the author

. . . neither sought nor expected to cultivate a wider public. Considerably longer and more complex than her previous work, *The Transit of Venus* suddenly appeared on the Best Seller List."

Los Angeles Times critic Doris Grumbach writes that she was very moved by *The Transit of Venus*. She feels that it "is an impressive, mature novel, full and satisfying, by a novelist whose earlier work—two novels and two collections of stories . . . did not prepare us for this book. Without fear of exaggeration I can say it is the richest fictional experience I have had in a long time, so sumptuous a repast that it may not be to every reader's taste."

Although characterization plays a vital role in all of her writings, Hazzard exhibits particular skill in this area in *The Transit of Venus*. Webster Schott points out in the *Washington Post*: "Her purpose is to reveal [the characters] in the act of living and to make their pleasure, anguish and confusion rise out of their personalities as they respond to change. . . . All of *The Transit of Venus* is human movement, and seen from near the highest level art achieves."

New York Times Book Review critic Gail Godwin points out that "Hazzard has even managed to forge a sort of 'godlike grammar' to contain her ambitious design. This is reflected in her precise, frequently elliptical style and in a certain *distanced* outlook, the 'godlike' overview that spots the movements of people, then picks out and connects the salient details over fastmoving, curved sweep of time."

However, John Leonard suggests that Hazzard's skill not only lies in her characterizations but in her literary style in general. "Miss Hazzard writes as well as Stendhal," Leonard remarks in the *New York Times*. "No matter the object—a feeling, a face, a room, the weather—it is stripped of its layers of paint, its clots of words, down to the original wood; oil is applied; grain appears, and a glow. Every epigram and apostrophe is earned. A powerful intelligence is playing with a knife. It is an intelligence that refuses to be deflected by ironies; irony isn't good enough."

The feature that several critics have identified as the underlying factor of Hazzard's skillful characterization and literary style is her sensitivity. One such critic, Webster Schott, writes in the *Washington Post*: "Her perceptions of gesture, voice, attitude bespeak an omniscient understanding of human personality. The story she tells is, for the most part, so usual as to sound irrelevant. What she brings to it is virtually everything that story alone cannot tell about human lives." Agreeing with this premise, Lynne Sharon Schwartz remarks in the *Chicago Tribune* that "*The Transit of Venus* evidences the wisdom of one not only well traveled but well acquainted with truth and falsehood in their numberless guises. Interwoven with the story of Caro's and Grace's lives and loves are a devastating representation of British class structure, with barriers and loopholes clearly marked; an acerbic, satirical view of a governmental bureaucracy that scoops the marrow out of men and leaves them empty bone; a glimpse at underground activists struggling for fundamental political decencies in Latin America, as well as a survey of various modes of contemporary marriage."

Hazzard relayed her own opinion as to the reason for the success of *The Transit of Venus*. She tells Michiko Kakutani in an interview published in the *New York Times Book Review* that "I think there is a tendency now to write jottings about one's own psyche and then call it a novel. My book, though, is really a *story*—and that might have contributed to its success."

BIOGRAPHICAL/CRITICAL SOURCES:

BOOKS

Contemporary Literary Criticism, Volume XVIII, Gale, 1981.
Dictionary of Literary Biography Yearbook: 1982, Gale, 1983.
Geering, R. G., *Recent Fiction,* Oxford University Press (Melbourne), 1973.

PERIODICALS

Australian Literary Studies, October, 1979.
Chicago Tribune, March 9, 1980.
Globe and Mail (Toronto), September 24, 1988.
Listener, October 19, 1967.
Los Angeles Times, March 9, 1980.
Meanjin, summer, 1970.
National Review, February 27, 1968.
New Statesman, October 20, 1967.
New Yorker, April 13, 1970.
New York Times, February 26, 1980.
New York Times Book Review, January 9, 1966, November 12, 1967, April 5, 1970, March 16, 1980, May 11, 1980, April 29, 1990.
Saturday Review, January 8, 1966.
Time, January 14, 1966, November 24, 1967.
Times Literary Supplement, July 7, 1966, October 19, 1967, May 7, 1970.
Village Voice, March 3, 1980.
Washington Post, March 9, 1980.
Washington Post Book World, April 8, 1990.

*   *   *

HEAD, Bessie 1937-1986

PERSONAL: Original name Bessie Amelia Emery; born July 6, 1937, in Pietermaritzburg, South Africa; died of hepatitis, April 17, 1986, in Botswana; married Harold Head (a journalist), September 1, 1961 (divorced); children: Howard. *Education:* Educated in South Africa as a primary school teacher. *Politics:* None ("dislike politics"). *Religion:* None ("dislike formal religion").

ADDRESSES: Home—P.O. Box 15, Serowe, Botswana, Africa. *Agent*—John Johnson, Clerkenwell House, 45/47 Clerkenwell Green, London EC1R 0HT, England.

CAREER: Teacher in primary schools in South Africa and Botswana for four years; journalist at Drum Publications in Johannesburg for two years; writer. Represented Botswana at international writers conference at University of Iowa, 1977-78, and in Denmark, 1980.

AWARDS, HONORS: The Collector of Treasures and Other Botswana Village Tales was nominated for the Jock Campbell Award for literature by new or unregarded talent from Africa or the Caribbean, *New Statesman,* 1978.

WRITINGS:

When Rain Clouds Gather (novel), Simon & Schuster, 1969.
Maru (novel), McCall, 1971.
A Question of Power (novel), Davis Poynter, 1973, Pantheon, 1974.
The Collector of Treasures and Other Botswana Village Tales (short stories), Heinemann, 1977.
Serowe: Village of the Rain Wind (historical chronicle), Heinemann, 1981.
A Bewitched Crossroad: An African Saga (historical chronicle), Donker (Craighall), 1984, Paragon House, 1986.

Contributor to periodicals, including the London *Times, Presence Africane, New African,* and *Transition.*

SIDELIGHTS: "Unlike many exiled South African writers," said a London *Times* contributor, "[Bessie Head] was able to root her life and her work anew in a country close to her tormented motherland." Born of racially mixed parentage in South Africa, Head lived and died in her adopted Botswana, the subject of much of her writing; in 1979, after fifteen years as part of a refugee community located at Bamangwato Development Farm, she was granted Botswanan citizenship. In *World Literature Written in English,* Betty McGinnis Fradkin described Head's meager existence after a particularly lean year: "There is no electricity yet. At night Bessie types by the light of six candles. Fruit trees and vegetables surround the house. Bessie makes guava jam to sell, and will sell vegetables when the garden is enlarged." Despite her impoverished circumstances, Head acknowledged to Fradkin that the regularity of her life in the refugee community brought her the peace of mind she sought: "In South Africa, all my life I lived in shattered little bits. All those shattered bits began to grow together here. . . . I have a peace against which all the turmoil is worked out!"

"Her novels strike a special chord for the South African diaspora, though this does not imply that it is the only level at which they work or produce an impact as novels," observed Arthur Ravenscroft in *Aspects of South African Literature.* "They are strange, ambiguous, deeply personal books which initially do not seem to be 'political' in any ordinary sense of the word." Head's racially mixed heritage profoundly influenced both her work and her life, for an element of exile as well as an abiding concern with discrimination, whatever its guise, permeate her writing. Noting in *Black Scholar* that Head has "probably received more acclaim than any other black African woman novelist writing in English," Nancy Topping Bazin added that Head's works "reveal a great deal about the lives of African women and about the development of feminist perspectives." According to Bazin, Head's analysis of Africa's "patriarchal system and attitudes" enabled her to make connections between the discrimination she experienced personally from racism and sexism, and the root of oppression generally in the insecurity that compels one to feel superior to another.

Head is "especially moving on the position of women, emerging painfully from the chrysalis of tribalist attitudes into a new evaluation of their relationship to men and their position in society," stated Mary Borg in a *New Statesman* review of Head's first novel, *When Rain Clouds Gather.* Considered "intelligent and moving" by one *Times Literary Supplement* contributor, it is described by another as combining "a vivid account of village life in Botswana with the relationship between an Englishman and an embittered black South African who try to change the traditional farming methods of the community." The black male flees South African apartheid only to experience discrimination from other blacks as a refugee in Botswana. For this novel, Head drew upon her own experience as part of a refugee community, which she indicated in *World Literature Written in English* had been "initially, extremely brutal and harsh." Head explained that she had not experienced oppression by the Botswanan government itself in any way, but because South African blacks had been "stripped bare of every human right," she was unaccustomed to witnessing "human ambition and greed . . . in a black form." Calling *When Rain Clouds Gather* "a tale of innocence and experience," Ravenscroft acknowledged that "there are moments of melodrama and excessive romanticism, but the real life of the novel is of creativity, resilience, reconstruction, fulfilment." Most of the major characters "are in one sense or another handicapped exiles, learning how to mend their lives," said Ravenscroft, adding that "it is the vision behind their effortful embracing of exile that gives Bessie Head's first novel an unusual maturity."

Ravenscroft found that in addition to the collective, cooperative enterprise that the village itself represents in *When Rain Clouds Gather,* it speaks to an essential concern of Head's writing by offering a solution for personal fulfillment: "Against a political background of self-indulgent, self-owning traditional chiefs and self-seeking, new politicians more interested in power than people, the village of Golema Mmidi is offered as a difficult alternative: not so much a rural utopia for which the Africa of the future could aim, as a means of personal and economic independence and interdependence, where the qualities that count are benign austerity, reverence for the lives of ordinary people (whether university-educated experts or illiterate villagers), and, above all, the ability to break out of the prison of selfhood without destroying individual privacy and integrity."

Head's second novel, *Maru,* is also set in a Botswanan village. According to Ravenscroft, though, in this book, "workaday affairs form the framework for the real novel, which is a drama about inner conflict and peace of mind and soul." *Maru* is about the problems that accompany the arrival of the well-educated new teacher with whom two young chiefs fall in love. It is "about interior experience, about thinking, feeling, sensing, about control over rebellious lusts of the spirit," said Ravenscroft, who questioned whether or not "the two chief male characters . . . who are close, intimate friends until they become bitter antagonists, are indeed two separate fictional characters, or . . . symbolic extensions of contending character-traits within the same man?" Although the new teacher has been raised and educated by a missionary's wife, she belongs to the "lowliest and most despised group in Botswana, the bushmen," explained the London *Times* contributor. "Problems of caste and identity among black Africans are explored with sensitivity," remarked Martin Levin in the *New York Times Book Review.* Ravenscroft suggested that while the novel is a more personal one than Head's first, it is also a more political one, and he was "much impressed and moved by the power . . . in the vitality of the enterprise, which projects the personal and the political implications in such vivid, authentic parallels that one feels they are being closely held together."

Head's critically well-received third novel, *A Question of Power,* relates the story of a young woman who experiences a mental breakdown. In a *Listener* review, Elaine Feinstein observed that "the girl moves through a world dominated by strange figures of supernatural good and evil, in which she suffers torment and enchantment in turn: at last she reaches the point where she can reject the clamorous visions which beset her and assert that there is 'only one God and his name is Man.'" According to Bazin, Head acknowledged in an interview with Lee Nichols in her *Conversations with African Writers: Interviews with Twenty-six African Authors* that *A Question of Power* is largely autobiographical. "Like Elizabeth, the protagonist in *A Question of Power,* Bessie Head was born in a South African mental hospital," explained Bazin. "Her mother, a wealthy, upperclass, white woman, was to spend the rest of her life there, because in an apartheid society, she had allowed herself to be made pregnant by a black stableman. Until age thirteen, Bessie Head, like Elizabeth, was raised by foster parents and then put in a mission orphanage." Paddy Kitchen pointed out in the *New Statesman,* though, that the novel merely "contains parallels and winnowings from life, not journalist records," adding that "the incredible part is the clarity of the terror that has been rescued from such private, muddled nightmares." Similarly, Ravenscroft discerned no "confusion of identity" between the character and her creator: "Head makes one realize often how close is the similarity between the most fevered creations of a deranged mind and the insanities of deranged societies."

Lauded for the skill with which she recreated the hellish world of madness, Head was also credited by critics such as Jean Marquard in *London Magazine* with having written "the first metaphysical novel on the subject of nation and a national identity to come out of Southern Africa." In his *The Novel in the Third World,* Charles R. Larson credits the importance of *A Question of Power* not just to the introspection of its author but to her exploration of subjects hitherto "foreign to African fiction as a subdivision of the novel in the Third World: madness, sexuality, guilt." Noting that the protagonist's "Coloured classification, her orphan status at the mission, and her short-lived marriage" represent the origin of most of her guilt, Larson attributed these factors directly to "the South African policy of apartheid which treats people as something other than human beings." Further, Larson felt that Head intended the reader to consider all the "variations of power as the evils that thwart each individual's desire to be part of the human race, part of the brotherhood of man."

A Question of Power, wrote Roberta Rubenstein in the *New Republic,* "succeeds as an intense, even mythic, dramatization of the mind's struggle for autonomy and as a symbolic protest against the political realities of South Africa." And in *Books Abroad,* Robert L. Berner considered it "a remarkable attempt to escape from the limitations of mere 'protest' literature in which Black South African writers so often find themselves." Berner recognized that Head could have "written an attack on the indignities of apartheid which have driven her into exile in Botswana," but instead chose to write a novel about the "response to injustice first in madness and finally in a heroic struggle out of that madness into wholeness and wisdom." Ravenscroft perceived in *A Question of Power* "an intimate relationship between an individual character's private odyssey of the soul and public convulsions that range across the world and from one civilization to another," and deemed the novel "a work of striking virtuosity—an artistically shaped descent into the linked bells of madness and oppression, and a resolution that provides the hope of both internal and external reconciliation."

Critics have analyzed Head's first three novels, *When Rain Clouds Gather, Maru,* and *A Question of Power,* collectively in terms of their thematic concerns and progression. Suggesting that the three novels "deal in different ways with exile and oppression," Marquard noted that "the protagonists are outsiders, new arrivals who try to forge a life for themselves in a poor, under-populated third world country, where traditional and modern attitudes to soil and society are in conflict." Unlike other African writers who are also concerned with such familiar themes, said Marquard, Head "does not idealize the African past and . . . she resists facile polarities, emphasizing personal rather than political motives for tensions between victim and oppressor." Ravenscroft recognized "a steady progression from the first novel to the third into ever murkier depths of alienation from the currents of South African, and African, matters of politics and power." Similarly, Marquard detected an inward movement "from a social to a metaphysical treatment of human insecurities and in the last novel the problem of adaptation to a new world, or new schemes of values, is located in the mind of a single character." Ravenscroft posited that "it is precisely this journeying into the various characters' most secret interior recesses of mind and (we must not fight shy of the word) of soul, that gives the three novels a quite remarkable cohesion and makes them a sort of trilogy."

Considering *When Rain Clouds Gather, Maru,* and *A Question of Power* to be "progressive in their philosophical conclusion about the nature and source of racism," Cecil A. Abrahams suggested in *World Literature Written in English* that "ultimately, Head examines . . . sources of evil and, conversely, of potential goodness. The most obvious source is the sphere of political power and authority; it is clear that if the political institutions which decree and regulate the lives of the society are reformed or abolished a better or new society can be established." According to Ravenscroft, the elements of imprisonment and control provide thematic unity among the novels. Pointing to the "loneliness and despair of exile" in each of them, Ravenscroft found the resilience of their characters "even more remarkable," and concluded that "what the three novels do say very clearly is that whoever exercises political power, however laudable his aims, will trample upon the faces and limbs of ordinary people, and will lust in that trampling. That horrible obscenity mankind must recognize in its collective interior soul." And Head, said Ravenscroft, "refuses to look for the deceiving gleam that draws one to expect the dawn of liberation in the South, but accepts what the meagre, even parched, present offers."

Head's collection of short stories, *The Collector of Treasures and Other Botswana Village Tales,* which was considered for the *New Statesman*'s Jock Campbell Award, explores several aspects of African life, especially the position of women. Linking Head to the "village storyteller of the oral tradition," Michael Thorpe noted in *World Literature Today* that her stories are "rooted, folkloristic tales woven from the fabric of village life and intended to entertain and enlighten, not to engage the modern close critic." In the *Listener,* John Mellors related Head's statement that "she has 'romanticised and fictionalized' data provided by old men of the tribe whose memories are unreliable." In its yoking of present to past, the collection also reveals the inevitable friction between old ways and new. The world of Head's work "is not a simply modernizing world but one that seeks, come what may, to keep women in traditionally imprisoning holes and corners," said Valerie Cunningham in the *New Statesman*. "It's a world where whites not only force all blacks into an exile apart from humanity but where women are pushed further still into sexist exile." In *The Collector of Treasures and Other Botswana Village Tales,* added Cunningham, "Head puts a woman's as well as a black case in tales that both reach back into tribal legend and cut deep into modern Africa."

Head's last two books, *Serowe: Village of the Rain Wind* and *A Bewitched Crossroad: An African Saga,* are categorized as historical chronicles and combine historical accounts with the folklore of the region. The collected interviews in *Serowe* focus on a time frame that spans the eras of Khama the Great (1875-1923) and Tshekedi Khama (1926-1959) through the Swaneng Project beginning in 1963 under Patrick Van Rensburg, "a South African exile who, like Head herself, has devoted his life in a present-day Botswana to make some restitution for white rapacity," wrote Thorpe. Larson, who considers "reading any book by Bessie Head . . . always a pleasure," added that *Serowe* "falls in a special category." Calling it a "quasi-sociological account," Larson described it as "part history, part anthology and folklore." "Its citizens give their testimonies, both personal and practical, in an unselfconscious way," said Paddy Kitchen in the *Listener,* "and Bessie Head—in true African style—orders the information so that, above all, it tells a story." *Serowe* is "a vivid portrait of a remarkable place . . . one wishes there were many more studies of its kind," remarked a *British Book News* contributor. Kitchen

believed it to be "a story which readers will find themselves using as a text from which to meditate on many aspects of society." And discussing her last book, *A Bewitched Crossroad,* which examines on a broader scope the African tribal wars in the early nineteenth century, Thorpe found that "in her moral history humane ideals displace ancestor-worship, and peace-loving strength displaces naked force."

Questioned by Fradkin about the manner in which she worked, Head explained: "Every story or book starts with something just for myself. Then from that small me it becomes a panorama—the big view that has something for everyone." Head "stresses in her novels the ideals of humility, love, truthfulness, freedom, and, of course, equality," wrote Bazin. At the time of her death, she had achieved an international reputation and had begun to write her autobiography. Head obviously endured much difficulty during her life; despite her rejection of and by South Africa as well as the hardships of her exiled existence, however, she emerged from the racist and sexist discrimination that she both witnessed and experienced, to the affirmation she told Fradkin represented the only two themes present in her writing—"that love is really good . . . and . . . that it is important to be an ordinary person." She added, "More than anything I want to be noble." According to Kitchen, "a great deal has been written about black writers, but Bessie Head is surely one of the pioneers of brown literature—a literature that includes everybody."

BIOGRAPHICAL/CRITICAL SOURCES:

BOOKS

Contemporary Literary Criticism, Volume 25, Gale, 1983.
Heywood, Christopher, editor, *Aspects of South African Literature,* Heinemann, 1976.
Larson, Charles R., *The Novel in the Third World,* Inscape Publishers, 1976.
Nichols, Lee, editor, *Conversations with African Writers: Interviews with Twenty-six African Authors,* Voice of America (Washington, D.C.), 1981.
Zell, Hans M., and others, *A New Reader's Guide to African Literature,* Holmes & Meier, 2nd edition, 1983.

PERIODICALS

Best Sellers, March 15, 1969.
Black Scholar, March/April, 1986.
Books Abroad, winter, 1975.
British Book News, November, 1981.
Listener, February 4, 1971, November 22, 1973, April 20, 1978, July 2, 1981.
London Magazine, December/January, 1978-79.
New Republic, April 27, 1974.
New Statesman, May 16, 1969, November 2, 1973, June 2, 1978.
New York Times Book Review, September 26, 1971.
Times Literary Supplement, May 2, 1969, February 5, 1971.
World Literature Today, winter, 1982, summer, 1983, winter, 1983, winter, 1986.
World Literature Written in English, Volume 17, number 1, 1978, Volume 17, number 2, 1978, Volume 18, number 1, 1979.

OBITUARIES:

PERIODICALS

Journal of Commonwealth Literature, Volume 21, number 1, 1986.
Ms., January, 1987.
Times (London), May 1, 1986.

HEANEY, Seamus (Justin) 1939-

PERSONAL: Name is pronounced "*Shay*-moos *Hee*-knee"; born April 13, 1939, in County Derry, Northern Ireland; son of Patrick (a farmer) and Margaret Heaney; married Marie Devlin, 1965; children: Michael, Christopher, Catherine. *Education:* Attended St. Columb's College, Derry; Queen's University of Belfast, B.A. (first class honors), 1961, St. Joseph's College of Education, teacher's certificate, 1962.

ADDRESSES: Office—Department of English and American Literature and Language, Harvard University, Warren House, 11 Prescott St., Cambridge, MA 02138.

CAREER: Poet, 1960—. Worked as secondary school teacher in Belfast, 1962-63; St. Joseph's College of Education, Belfast, Northern Ireland, lecturer, 1963-66; Queen's University of Belfast, lecturer in English, 1966-72; free-lance writer, 1972-75; Carysfort College, Dublin, Ireland, lecturer, 1976-82; Harvard University, Cambridge, MA, visiting lecturer, 1979, visiting professor, 1982-86, Boylston Professor of Rhetoric and Oratory, 1986—. Visiting lecturer, University of California, Berkeley, 1970-71. Has given numerous lectures and poetry readings at universities in England, Ireland, and the United States.

MEMBER: Irish Academy of Letters.

AWARDS, HONORS: Eric Gregory Award, 1966, Cholomondeley Award, 1967, Somerset Maugham Award, 1968, and Geoffrey Faber Memorial Prize, 1968, all for *Death of a Naturalist;* Poetry Book Society Choice citation, 1969, for *Door into the Dark;* writer in residence award from American Irish Foundation and Denis Devlin Award, both 1973, for *Wintering Out;* E. M. Forster Award from American Academy and Institute of Arts and Letters, 1975; W. H. Smith Award, Duff Cooper Memorial Prize, and Poetry Book Society Choice citation, all 1976, for *North;* Bennett Award from *Hudson Review,* 1982; D.H.L. from Fordham University and Queen's University of Belfast, both 1982; *Los Angeles Times* Book Prize nomination, 1984, and PEN Translation Prize for Poetry, 1985, both for *Sweeney Astray: A Version from the Irish;* Whitbread Award, 1987, for *The Haw Lantern.*

WRITINGS:

POETRY COLLECTIONS

Death of a Naturalist, Oxford University Press, 1966.
Door into the Dark, Oxford University Press, 1969.
Wintering Out, Faber, 1972, Oxford University Press, 1973.
North, Faber, 1975, Oxford University Press, 1976.
Field Work, Farrar, Straus, 1979.
Poems: 1965-1975, Farrar, Straus, 1980 (published in England as *Selected Poems 1965-1975,* Faber, 1980).
(Adapter and translator) *Sweeney Astray: A Version from the Irish,* Farrar, Straus, 1984.
Station Island, Farrar, Straus, 1984.
The Haw Lantern, Farrar, Straus, 1987.

POETRY CHAPBOOKS

Eleven Poems, Festival Publications (Belfast), 1965.
(With David Hammond and Michael Longley) *Room to Rhyme,* Arts Council of Northern Ireland, 1968.
A Lough Neagh Sequence, edited by Harry Chambers and Eric J. Morten, Phoenix Pamphlets Poets Press (Manchester), 1969.
Boy Driving His Father to Confession, Sceptre Press (Surrey), 1970.
Night Drive: Poems, Richard Gilbertson (Devon), 1970.

Land, Poem-of-the-Month Club, 1971.
Servant Boy, Red Hanrahan Press (Detroit), 1971.
Stations, Ulsterman Publications (Belfast), 1975.
Bog Poems, Rainbow Press (London), 1975.
(With Derek Mahon) *In Their Element,* Arts Council of Northern Ireland, 1977.
After Summer, Deerfield Press, 1978.
Hedge School: Sonnets from Glanmore, C. Seluzichi (Oregon), 1979.
Sweeney Praises the Trees, [New York], 1981.

PROSE

The Fire i' the Flint: Reflections on the Poetry of Gerard Manley Hopkins, Oxford University Press, 1975.
Robert Lowell: A Memorial Address and Elegy, Faber, 1978.
Preoccupations: Selected Prose 1968-1978, Farrar, Straus, 1980.
The Government of the Tongue: Selected Prose, 1978-1987, Farrar, Straus, 1988.

EDITOR

(With Alan Brownjohn) *New Poems: 1970-71,* Hutchinson, 1971.
Soundings: An Annual Anthology of New Irish Poetry, Blackstaff Press (Belfast), 1972.
Soundings II, Blackstaff Press, 1974.
(With Ted Hughes) *The Rattle Bag* (poetry), Faber, 1982.
The Essential Wordsworth, Ecco Press, 1988.

OTHER

(With John Montague) *The Northern Muse* (sound recording), Claddagh Records, 1969.
(Contributor) *The Writers: A Sense of Ireland,* O'Brien Press (Dublin), 1979.

Contributor of poetry and essays to periodicals, including *New Statesman, Listener, Guardian, Times Literary Supplement,* and *London Review of Books.*

SIDELIGHTS: Seamus Heaney is widely recognized as one of Ireland's finest living poets. A native of Northern Ireland who divides his time between a home in Dublin and a teaching position at Harvard University, Heaney has attracted a readership on two continents and has won prestigious literary awards in England, Ireland, and the United States. As Blake Morrison notes in his work *Seamus Heaney,* the author is "that rare thing, a poet rated highly by critics and academics yet popular with 'the common reader.' " Part of Heaney's popularity stems from his subject matter—modern Northern Ireland, its farms and cities beset with civil strife, its natural culture and language overrun by English rule. *Washington Post Book World* contributor Marjorie Perloff suggests that Heaney is so successful "because of his political position: the Catholic farm boy from County Derry transformed into the sensitive witness to and historian of the Irish troubles, as those troubles have shaped and altered individual lives." Likewise, *New York Review of Books* essayist Richard Murphy describes Heaney as "the poet who has shown the finest art in presenting a coherent vision of Ireland, past and present."

To call Heaney a poet of the Irish countryside is to oversimplify his sensibility, however. According to Robert Pinsky in the *New Republic,* the author also incorporates "a *literary* element into his work without embarrassment, apology, or ostentation." Indeed, Heaney takes delight in the sounds and histories of words, using language to create "the music of what happens," to quote from one of his poems. "The poet's triumph is to bring the ingredients of history and biography under the control of his music," writes Irvin Ehrenpreis in the *New York Review of Books.*

"Heaney's expressive rhythms support his pleasure in re-echoing syllables and modulating vowels through a series of lines to evoke continuities and resolutions." Nor is Heaney's subject matter merely provincial and pastoral, insulated from broader human perspectives. Morrison notes: "One does not have to look very deeply into Heaney's work . . . to see that it is rather less comforting and comfortable than has been supposed. Far from being 'whole,' it is tense, torn, divided against itself; far from being straightforward, it is layered with often obscure allusions; far from being archaic, it registers the tremors and turmoils of its age, forcing traditional forms to accept the challenge of harsh, intractable material. . . . A proper response to Heaney's work requires reference to complex matters of ancestry, nationality, religion, history, and politics." This is not to say that Heaney's work is difficult or inaccessible, though. Pinsky concludes that the poems "give several kinds of pleasure: first of all, [Heaney] is a talented writer, with a sense of language and rhythm as clean, sweet, and solid as new-worked hardwood. Beyond that, . . . his talent [has] the limberness and pluck needed to take up some of the burden of history—the tangled, pained history of Ireland. Heaney's success in dealing with the murderous racial enmities of past and present, avoiding all the sins of oratory, and keeping his personal sense of balance, seems to me one of the most exhilarating poetic accomplishments in many years."

Inevitably, Heaney has been compared with the great Irish poet William Butler Yeats; in fact, several critics have called Heaney "the greatest Irish poet since Yeats." Such praise-by-comparison makes the poet uncomfortable, and it serves to obscure the uniqueness of his work. *New York Review of Books* contributor Richard Ellmann once wrote: "After the heavily accented melodies of Yeats, and that poet's elegiac celebrations of imaginative glories, Seamus Heaney addresses his readers in a quite different key. He does not overwhelm his subjects; rather he allows them a certain freedom from him, and his sharp conjunctions with them leave their authority and his undiminished." Elizabeth Jennings makes a similar observation in the *Spectator*. To Jennings, Heaney is "an extremely Irish poet most especially in language, but he is not a poet in the Yeatsian mould.... He is serious, of course, but it is the gravity which grows in his roots, not one which is obtrusive in the finished artefact." In the *Listener*, Conor Cruise O'Brien analyzes the source from which the comparison might have stemmed. "Heaney's writing is modest, often conversational, apparently easy, low-pitched, companionably ironic, ominous, alert, accurate and surprising," notes O'Brien. "An Irish reader is not automatically reminded of Yeats by this cluster of characteristics, yet an English reader may perhaps see resemblances that are there but overlooked by the Irish— resemblances coming, perhaps, from certain common rhythms and hesitations of Irish speech and non-speech." *Newsweek* correspondent Jack Kroll finds similarities in Heaney's subject matter: "Like Yeats, Heaney combines all the conflicting poles of the Irish experience into a rich, embattled language: paganism and Christianity, repression and expansion, desire and chastity, country and city, ignorance and enlightenment, hope and despair."

Kroll is not the only critic who notes "the conflicting poles of Irish experience" in Heaney's work. London *Times* contributor Bel Mooney also delineates the inner divisions that define and intensify the poet's writing. "Again and again," contends Mooney, "we observe him poised on a pivot, a one-man dialectic in whom opposites are—uncomfortably—unified. Ulster v Eire; English learning v Irish culture; education v roots; the language of debate v silence and acceptance; liberalism v Catholicism; comfort v guilt; love v loneliness and restlessness; belonging v

exile. . . . It is all there. He knows it well." Ehrenpreis elaborates: "Speech is never simple in Heaney's conception. He grew up as an Irish Catholic boy in a land governed by Protestants whose tradition is British. He grew up on a farm in his country's northern, industrial region. As a person, therefore, he springs from the old divisions of his nation. At the same time, the theme that dominates Heaney's work is self-definition, the most natural subject of the modern lyric; and language, from which it starts, shares the old polarities. For Heaney, it is the Irish speech of his family and district, overlaid by British and urban culture which he had acquired as a student." In a *Harper's* essay, Terrence Des Pres suggests that Heaney has had "to accommodate, but also shove against, the expansive beauty of the conqueror's tongue in order to recover the rooted speech of his own society and place." *Critical Quarterly* correspondent John Wilson Foster describes how Heaney remains "suspended between the English and (Anglo-) Irish traditions and cultures. Correlatives of ambivalence proliferate in his verse: the archetypal sound in his work (and to be savoured in the reading) is the guttural spirant, half-consonant, half-vowel; the archetypal locale is the bog, half-water, half-land; the archetypal animal is the eel which can fancifully be regarded (in its overland forays) as half-mammal, half-fish."

Heaney is well aware of the dual perspective afforded him by his upbringing and subsequent experiences. He once described himself in the *New York Times Book Review* as one of a group of Catholics in Northern Ireland who "emerged from a hidden, a buried life and entered the realm of education." This process began for Heaney at age eleven; that year he left the family farm to study on scholarship at a boarding school in Belfast. Access to the world of English, Irish, and American letters—first at St. Columb's College and then at Queen's University of Belfast— was "a crucial experience," according to the poet. He was especially moved by artists who created poetry out of their local and native backgrounds—authors such as Ted Hughes, Patrick Kavanagh, and Robert Frost. Heaney said: "From them I learned that my local County Derry [childhood] experience, which I had considered archaic and irrelevant to 'the modern world' was to be trusted. They taught me that trust and helped me to articulate it." Searching his cultural roots, but also letting his English literary education enrich his expression, Heaney began to craft "a poetry concerned with nature, the shocks and discoveries of childhood experience on a farm, the mythos of the locale—in short, a regional poetry," to quote Robert Buttel in his book *Seamus Heaney*. This sort of poetry, Buttel continues, was, in the early 1960s, "essentially a counter-poetry, decidedly not fashionable at the time. To write such poetry called for a measure of confidence if not outright defiance."

According to Morrison, a "general spirit of reverence towards the past helped Heaney resolve some of his awkwardness about being a writer: he could serve his own community by preserving in literature its customs and crafts, yet simultaneously gain access to a larger community of letters." Indeed, Heaney's earliest poetry collections—*Death of a Naturalist* and *Door into the Dark*—evoke "a hard, mainly rural life with rare exactness," in the words of *Parnassus: Poetry in Review* contributor Michael Wood. Using descriptions of rural laborers and their tasks and contemplations of natural phenomena—filtered sometimes through childhood and sometimes through adulthood—Heaney seeks the self by way of the perceived experience, celebrating the life force through earthly things. Buttel writes: "Augmenting the physical authenticity and the clean, decisive art of the best of the early poems, mainly the ones concerned with the impact of the recollected initiatory experiences of childhood and youth, is the human voice that speaks in them. At its most distinctive it is un-pretentious, open, modest, and yet poised, aware." Kroll notes that in these first poems, Heaney "makes you see, hear, smell, taste this life, which in his words is not provincial, but parochial; provincialism hints at the minor or the mediocre, but all parishes, rural or urban, are equal as communities of the human spirit. So Heaney's poems dig away, filled with a grunting vowel music that evokes the blunt ecstasy of physical work."

In *Northern Voices: Poets from Ulster,* Terence Brown expresses the view that it is a mistake "to think of Heaney as merely a descriptive poet, endowed with unusual powers of observation. From the first his involvement with landscape and locale, with the physical world, has been both more personal and more remarkable in its implications than any mere act of observation and record could be." Heaney's early poems are not burdened with romantic notions about nature; rather they present nature "as a random power that sometimes rewards but more often frustrates human [efforts]," to quote Arthur E. McGuinness in *Eire-Ireland. New York Times Book Review* correspondent Nicholas Christopher likewise finds "no folksy, down-home or miniaturist tendencies in [Heaney's] presentation of natural subjects. His voice is complex and his eye keen, but as with any inspired poet, he is after transformations, not reproductions. Nature is neither antagonist nor sounding board but a component of the human imagination." This latter description outlines the direction Heaney's poetry has taken since he "began to open, both to the Irish, and to his own abyss," in the words of *Times Literary Supplement* reviewer Harold Bloom. In the poems collected in *Wintering Out* and *North,* according to Des Pres, "rural integrity remains intact, but images of violent intent intrude all the same. Which is to say that the structure of Heaney's poetry reflects the shape of life as he knows it to be, a fusion of history and the land, politics colliding with life's daily round. This could hardly be otherwise for a poet growing up in Northern Ireland, where religious and political tensions always threatened to break, as they have since 1969, into madness and bloodshed."

"Seamus Heaney comes from the north of Ireland, and his career has almost exactly coincided with the present span of the 'troubles,' " claims Seamus Deane in the *Sewanee Review.* The "troubles" to which Deane refers are, of course, the violent political struggles between Northern Ireland's Protestants and their British allies and the militant Irish Republican Army. Heaney was living in Belfast when the fighting erupted in 1969; as a Catholic partisan, notes Morrison, "he felt the need to write poetry that would be not necessarily propagandist but certainly urgent in tone." In *Critical Quarterly,* Damian Grant suggests that Heaney "is no protest poet, but nor can he remain indifferent to the bombs, snipers, and internment camps that maim the body of his land." The poet has sought, therefore, to weave the current Irish troubles into a broader historical frame embracing the general human situation. Deane writes that in *Wintering Out* and *North,* "the ancient past and the contemporary present, myth and politics, are in fact analogues for one another. . . . Mr. Heaney is very much in the Irish tradition in that he has learned, more successfully than most, to conceive of his personal experience in terms of his country's history. . . . Accent, etymologies, old ritual murders and invasions, contemporary assassinations and security systems—these and other related elements swarm now more and more thickly, the lethal infusoria in this pellucid verse." *New York Review of Books* correspondent Richard Murphy suggests that the poetry "is seriously attempting to purge our land of a terrible blood-guilt, and inwardly acknowledging our enslavement to a sacrificial myth. I think it may go a long

way toward freeing us from the myth by portraying it in its true archaic shape and color, not disguising its brutality."

Heaney has found a powerful metaphor for current violence in the archaeological discoveries made in peat bogs in Ireland and northern Europe. The chemical nature of the water in the bogs preserves organic material buried in them—including human beings. In 1969 Heaney read *The Bog People,* by P. V. Glob, an archaeologist who had unearthed the preserved remains of several ritually slaughtered Iron Age Europeans. Des Pres quotes Heaney on the impact this work had on his poetry: "The unforgettable photographs of these victims blended in my mind with photographs of atrocities, past and present, in the long rites of Irish political and religious struggles." Heaney's well-known "bog poems," according to Murphy, trace "modern terrorism back to its roots in the early Iron Age, and mysterious awe back to the 'bonehouse' of language itself. . . . He looks closely . . . at our funeral rites and our worship of the past. . . . The central image of this work, a symbol which unifies time, person, and place, is bogland: it contains, preserves, and yields up terror as well as awe." "What makes Heaney different is the archetypal dimension of his poetic involvement with Irish culture," writes Gregory A. Schirmer in *Eire-Ireland.* "Nowhere is this more evident—and nowhere is Heaney's art more transcendent—than in the poems that Heaney has written about the peat bogs of Ireland and Jutland and the treasures and horrors that they have preserved. Heaney has developed the image of the bog into a powerful symbol of the continuity of human experience that at once enables him to write about the particularities of his own parish, past and present, and to transcend, at the same time, those particularities."

Some critics have detected another dimension to the bog imagery in Heaney's poems. According to Helen Vendler in the *New Yorker,* these works "represent Heaney's coming to grips with an intractable element deep both in personal life (insofar as the bog and its contents represent the unconscious) and in history. They lift him free from a superficial piety that would put either sectarian or national names to the Ulster killings, and they enable a hymn to the 'ruminant ground.'. . . He remarks dissolution and change by tasting things as they grow sour, feeling them sink in himself, losing part of himself bubbling in the acrid changes of fermentation." *Stand* contributor Terry Eagleton likewise feels that the bog landscape "furnishes the imagery for a self-exploration, as the movement of sinking into the bog becomes symbolic of a meditative psychological return to the roots of personal identity; and it does all this while preserving and deepening the kind of discourse which has always been Heaney's chief poetic strength—the discourse of material Nature itself." Brown writes: "The imagination has its dark bog-like depths, its sediments and strata from which images and metaphors emerge unbidden into the light of consciousness. . . . Such a sense of self as bound up with, and almost indistinguishable from, the dense complex of Irish natural and historical experience, obviously allows Heaney to explore Ulster's contemporary social and political crisis through attending to his own memories and obsessions." McGuinness suggests that digging into the "bog" of his imagination as well as into the sediments of the real bog "has convinced Heaney that, even in these desperate times, one might hope to connect with life-enhancing elemental powers and, through the discipline of language, to give these connections shape."

Morrison suggests that the role of political spokesman has never particularly suited Heaney. The author "has written poems directly about the Troubles as well as elegies for friends and acquaintances who have died in them; he has tried to discover a historical framework in which to interpret the current unrest; and he has taken on the mantle of public spokesman, someone looked to for comment and guidance," notes Morrison. "Yet he has also shown signs of deeply resenting this role, defending the right of poets to be private and apolitical, and questioning the extent to which poetry, however 'committed,' can influence the course of history." In the *New Boston Review,* Shaun O'Connell contends that even Heaney's most overtly political poems contain depths that subtly alter their meanings. "Those who see Seamus Heaney as a symbol of hope in a troubled land are not, of course, wrong to do so," O'Connell states, "though they may be missing much of the undercutting complexities of his poetry, the backwash of ironies which make him as bleak as he is bright." Deane makes a similar assessment, claiming that under sustained reading "the poems express no politics and indeed they flee conceptual formulations with an almost indecent success. Instead they interrogate the quality of the relationship between the poet and his mixed political and literary traditions. . . . Relationship is unavoidable, but commitment, relationship gone sour, is a limiting risk." *Partisan Review* contributor Deborah Tall feels that, in Heaney's poetry, "the burden is not so much to act politically as to speak for his unspoken-for peasant countrymen."

In 1972 Heaney left Belfast for the opportunity to live in a cottage outside Dublin, where he could write full time. The move had political overtones even though Heaney made it for financial reasons; Morrison observes that the subsequent poetry in *Field Work* "is deeply conscious of that move into the countryside." Morrison adds: "It was not surprising that the move should have been seen by some as a betrayal of the Northern Catholic community and should have aroused in Heaney feelings of unease and even guilt. One important consequence was the new seriousness he brought to his thinking about the writer and his responsibilities." At his retreat in Glanmore, Heaney reasserted his determination to produce fresh aesthetic objects, to pursue his personal feelings as member of—and not spokesman for—church, state, and tribe. Denis Donoghue suggests in the *New York Times Book Review* that in *Field Work* "Heaney is writing more powerfully than ever, more fully in possession of his feeling, more at home in his style. He has given up, at least for the moment, the short line of his earlier poems, which often went along with a brittle, self-protective relation to his experience. The new long line is more thoughtful, it brings a meditative music to bear on fundamental themes of person and place, the mutuality of ourselves and the world."

A further liberating experience occurred at Glanmore when Heaney began to undertake the translation and adaptation of the Irish lyric poem *Buile Suibhne.* The work concerns an ancient king who, cursed by the church, is transformed into a mad birdman and forced to wander in the harsh and inhospitable countryside. Heaney's translation of the epic was published as *Sweeney Astray: A Version from the Irish;* in the *Dictionary of Literary Biography* Buttel contends that the poem "reveals a heartfelt affinity with the dispossessed king who responds with such acute sensitivity, poetic accuracy, and imaginative force to his landscape." *New York Times Book Review* contributor Brendan Kennelly also deems the poem "a balanced statement about a tragically unbalanced mind. One feels that this balance, urbanely sustained, is the product of a long, imaginative bond between Mr. Heaney and Sweeney." Indeed, this bond is extended into Heaney's 1984 volume *Station Island,* where a series of poems entitled "Sweeney Redivivus" take up Sweeney's voice once more. Buttel sees these poems as part of a larger theme in *Station Island;* namely, "a personal drama of guilt, lost innocence, and lost moral and religious certainty played against the redemptions

of love, faith in the integrity of craft and of dedicated individuals, and ties with the universal forces operating in nature and history."

Language—and the action of writing—have always been central preoccupations for Heaney, but especially so in his more recent works. Morrison contends that the author's poetry has been shaped "by the modes of post-war Anglo-American poetry" as well as by the romantic tradition. Moreover, continues Morrison, "Heaney's preoccupation with language and with questions of authorial control makes him part of a still larger modern intellectual movement which has emphasized that language is not a transparent medium by means of which a writer says what he intends to, but rather something self-generating, infinitely productive, exceeding us as individuals." As A. Alvarez puts it in the *New York Review of Books,* Heaney "is not rural and sturdy and domestic, with his feet planted firmly in the Irish mud, but is instead an ornamentalist, a word collector, a connoisseur of fine language for its own sake." *Washington Post Book World* contributor John B. Breslin writes: "Like every poet, Heaney is a professional deceiver, saying one thing and meaning another, in a timeless effort at rescuing our language from the half-attention we normally accord it. Words matter because they are his matter, and ours, the inescapable medium of exchange between two otherwise isolated sets of experience." This fascination with words is evident in *The Haw Lantern,* published in 1987; *Times Literary Supplement* reviewer Neil Corcoran feels that the poems in that work "have a very contemporary sense of how writing is elegy to experience." W. S. DiPiero explains Heaney's intent in the *American Scholar:* "Whatever the occasion—childhood, farm life, politics and culture in Northern Ireland, other poets past and present—Heaney strikes time and again at the taproot of language, examining its genetic structures, trying to discover how it has served, in all its changes, as a culture bearer, a world to contain imaginations, at once a rhetorical weapon and nutriment of spirit. He writes of these matters with rare discrimination and resourcefulness, and a winning impatience with received wisdom."

Critical reaction to Heaney's work has been almost universally positive. "Only the most gifted poets can start from their peculiar origin in a language, a landscape, a nation, and from these enclosures rise to impersonal authority," writes Ehrenpreis. "Seamus Heaney has this kind of power. . . . One may enter his poetry by a number of paths, but each joins up with others. Nationality becomes landscape; landscape becomes language; language becomes genius." Des Pres concludes that Heaney's audience should "read him for his excellence, and then for the way he meets the challenge of politics and manages to honor beauty's plea. Then read him again for a perspective on our own predicament. For to judge from most recent American poetry, we stick to flowers and sidestep the rage, ignoring *what we know* or turning it to metaphor merely. . . . What we need is what he gives—a poetry that allows the spirit to face and engage, and thereby transcend, or at least stand up to, the murderous pressures of our time. This need is not a question of praxis or ideology, but of imagination regaining authority and of spirit bearing witness to its own misfortune and struggle." In *Seamus Heaney,* Buttel remarks: "Heaney continues to write his own poetry, carrying on his essential contribution to the flourishing state of Irish poetry today. For all its native authenticity, however, his is not an insular poetry. Seamus Heaney's best poems define their landscape and human experience with such visceral clarity, immediacy, and integrity of feeling that they transcend their regional source and make a significant contribution to contemporary poetry written in English."

In an interview published in *Viewpoints: Poets in Conversation with John Haffenden,* Heaney offered some insight into his craftsmanship. "One thing I try to avoid ever saying at readings is '*my* poem,' " he said, "—because that sounds like a presumption. The poem *came, it came.* I didn't go and fetch it. To some extent you wait for it, you coax it in the door when it gets there. I prefer to think of myself as the host to the thing rather than a big-game hunter." Elsewhere in the same interview he commented: "You write books of poems because that is a fulfillment, a making; it's a making sense of your life and it gives achievement, but it also gives you a sense of growth."

BIOGRAPHICAL/CRITICAL SOURCES:

BOOKS

Abse, Dannie, editor, *Best of the Poetry Year 6,* Robson, 1979.

Begley, Monie, *Rambles in Ireland,* Devin-Adair, 1977.

Broadbridge, Edward, editor, *Seamus Heaney,* Danmarks Radio (Copenhagen), 1977.

Brown, Terence, *Northern Voices: Poets from Ulster,* Rowman & Littlefield, 1975.

Buttel, Robert, *Seamus Heaney,* Bucknell University Press, 1975.

Contemporary Literary Criticism, Gale, Volume 5, 1976, Volume 7, 1977, Volume 14, 1980, Volume 25, 1983, Volume 37, 1986.

Curtis, Tony, editor, *The Art of Seamus Heaney,* Poetry Wales Press, 1982.

Dictionary of Literary Biography, Volume 40: *Poets of Great Britain and Ireland since 1960,* Gale, 1985.

Harmon, Maurice, editor, *Image and Illusion: Anglo-Irish Literature and Its Contexts,* Wolfhound Press (Dublin), 1979.

Longley, Michael, editor, *Causeway: The Arts in Ulster,* Arts Council of Northern Ireland, 1971.

Morrison, Blake, *Seamus Heaney,* Methuen, 1982.

Viewpoints: Poets in Conversation with John Haffenden, Faber, 1981.

Weathers, William, editor, *The Nature of Identity: Essays Presented to Donald E. Haydon by the Graduate Faculty of Modern Letters,* University of Tulsa Press, 1981.

PERIODICALS

American Scholar, autumn, 1981.

Chicago Tribune Book World, April 19, 1981, September 9, 1984.

Crane Bag, Volume 1, number 1, 1977, Volume 3, number 2, 1979.

Critical Inquiry, spring, 1982.

Critical Quarterly, spring, 1974, spring, 1976.

Eire-Ireland, summer, 1978, winter, 1980.

Encounter, November, 1975.

Fortnight, December, 1980.

Globe and Mail (Toronto), September 3, 1988.

Harper's, March, 1981.

Hollins Critic, October, 1970.

Honest Ulsterman, winter, 1975.

Irish Times, December 28, 1973, December 6, 1975.

Listener, December 7, 1972, November 8, 1973, September 25, 1975, December 20-27, 1984.

London Review of Books, November 1-14, 1984.

Los Angeles Times, May 16, 1984, January 5, 1989.

Los Angeles Times Book Review, March 2, 1980, October 21, 1984, June 2, 1985, October 27, 1987.

Midwest Quarterly, summer, 1974.

Nation, November 10, 1979.

New Boston Review, August-September, 1980.

New Republic, March 27, 1976, December 22, 1979, April 30, 1984, February 18, 1985.

New Review, August, 1975.

New Statesman, July 11, 1975.

Newsweek, February 2, 1981, April 15, 1985.

New Yorker, September 28, 1981, September 23, 1985.

New York Review of Books, September 20, 1973, September 30, 1976, March 6, 1980, October 8, 1981, March 14, 1985.

New York Times, April 22, 1979, January 11, 1985.

New York Times Book Review, March 26, 1967, April 18, 1976, December 2, 1979, December 21, 1980, May 27, 1984, March 10, 1985, March 5, 1989.

New York Times Magazine, March 13, 1983.

Observer, June 22, 1969, November 4, 1979, November 11, 1979.

Parnassus: Poetry in Review, spring-summer, 1974, fall-winter, 1977, fall-winter, 1979.

Partisan Review, Number 3, 1986.

Philadelphia Inquirer, January 24, 1988.

Phoenix, July, 1973.

Ploughshares, Volume 5, number 3, 1979.

Quest, January-February, 1978.

Saturday Review, July-August, 1985.

Sewanee Review, winter, 1976.

Shenandoah, summer, 1974.

Southern Review, January, 1980.

Spectator, September 6, 1975, December 1, 1979, November 24, 1984, June 27, 1987.

Stand, Volume 17, number 1, 1975-76, Volume 22, number 3, 1981.

Time, March 19, 1984, February 25, 1985.

Times (London), October 11, 1984, January 24, 1985, October 22, 1987, June 3, 1989.

Times Literary Supplement, June 9, 1966, July 17, 1969, December 15, 1972, August 1, 1975, February 8, 1980, October 31, 1980, November 26, 1982, October 19, 1984, June 26, 1987, July 1-7, 1988.

Tribune Books (Chicago), November 8, 1987.

Twentieth Century Studies, November, 1970.

Washington Post Book World, January 6, 1980, January 25, 1981, May 20, 1984, January 27, 1985.

World Literature Today, summer, 1977, autumn, 1981, summer, 1983.

*   *   *

HEARNE, John (Edgar Caulwell) 1926- (John Morris, a joint pseudonym)

PERSONAL: Born February 4, 1926, in Montreal, Quebec, Canada; son of Maurice Vincent and Doris (May) Hearne; married Joyce Veitch, September 3, 1947 (divorced); married Leeta Mary Hopkinson (a teacher), April 12, 1955; children: two. *Education:* Attended Jamaica College; Edinburgh University, M.A., 1950; University of London, teaching diploma, 1950. *Religion:* Christian.

ADDRESSES: Home—P.O. Box 335, Kingston 8, Jamaica. *Office*—Creative Arts Centre, University of the West Indies, Kingston 7, Jamaica. *Agent*—Claire Smith, Harold Ober Associates, Inc., 40 East 49th St., New York, N.Y. 10017.

CAREER: Teacher at schools in London, England, and in Jamaica, 1950-59; information officer, Government of Jamaica, 1962; University of the West Indies, Kingston, Jamaica, resident tutor in extramural studies, 1962-67, head of Creative Arts Centre, 1968—. Visiting Gregory Fellow in Commonwealth Literature at University of Leeds, England, 1967; Colgate University, New York, visiting O'Connor Professor in Literature, 1969-70, and visiting professor in literature, 1973. *Military service:* Royal Air Force, air gunner, 1943-46.

MEMBER: International PEN.

AWARDS, HONORS: John Llewelyn Rhys Memorial Prize, 1956, for *Voices under the Window;* Silver Musgrave Medal from Institute of Jamaica, 1964.

WRITINGS:

NOVELS

Voices under the Window, Faber, 1955.
Stranger at the Gate, Faber, 1956.
The Faces of Love, Faber, 1957, published as *The Eye of the Storm,* Little, Brown, 1958.
The Autumn Equinox, Faber, 1959, Vanguard Press, 1961.
Land of the Living, Faber, 1961, Harper, 1962.
(With Morris Cargill, under joint pseudonym John Morris) *Fever Grass,* Putnam, 1969.
(With Cargill, under joint pseudonym John Morris) *The Candywine Development,* Collins, 1970, Lyle Stuart, 1971.
The Sure Salvation, Faber, 1981, St. Martin's, 1982.

OTHER

(With Rex Nettleford) *Our Heritage,* University of the West Indies, 1963.
(Editor and author of introduction) *Carifesta Forum: An Anthology of Twenty Caribbean Voices,* Carifesta 76 (Kingston, Jamaica), 1976.
(Editor and author of introduction) *The Search for Solutions: Selections from the Speeches and Writings of Michael Manley,* Maple House Publishing Co., 1976.
(With Lawrence Coote and Lynden Facey) *Testing Democracy through Elections: A Tale of Five Elections,* edited by Marie Gregory, Bustamante Institute of Public and International Affairs (Kingston), 1985.

Also author of teleplays, including "Soldiers in the Snow," with James Mitchell, 1960, and "A World Inside," 1962; author of stage play "The Golden Savage," 1965. Contributor to anthologies, including *West Indian Stories* (includes "The Wind in This Corner" and "At the Stelling"), 1960, and *Stories from the Caribbean* (includes "A Village Tragedy" and "The Lost Country"), 1965, published as *Island Voices: Stories From the West Indies,* 1970, both edited by Andrew Salkey. Contributor of short stories and articles to periodicals, including *Atlantic Monthly, New Statesman,* and the *Trinidad Guardian.*

SIDELIGHTS: A West Indian writer who sometimes collaborates with Morris Cargill as the pseudonymous John Morris, John Hearne is known for his vivid depictions of life among the West Indies and their people. In particular, several of his writings focus on Jamaica—the native land of his parents—and address complex social and moral issues affecting both individual relationships and, to a lesser extent, the cultural and political aspects of the island. Much of Hearne's fiction—including the novels *Stranger at the Gate, The Faces of Love, The Autumn Equinox,* and *Land of the Living*—also takes place on Cayuna, a mythical counterpart of Jamaica. More generally, his work relates a broad, first-hand account of the Caribbean experience and features elements of racial and social inequities as well as recurrent themes of betrayal and disenchantment. Especially noteworthy are Hearne's acclaimed narrative skill and descriptive style, which distinguish his fiction as characteristically evocative and lifelike.

Hearne's 1981 novel, *The Sure Salvation,* takes place in the southern Atlantic Ocean aboard a sailing ship of the same name. Set in the year 1860, the story chronicles the illegal buying and selling of negroes more than fifty years after England first enacted laws prohibiting the practice commonly known as the slave trade. Through a "series of deft flashbacks," observed Times Literary Supplement critic T. O. Treadwell, Hearne recounts individual circumstances that led to his characters' unlawful fraternity on board the *Sure Salvation.* Risking constant danger and the death penalty if they are caught, the captain and crew hope to amend their ill-fated lives with monies paid for the vessel's charge of five hundred Africans. While the "beastliness isn't played down," Treadwell noted, we come "to understand, and even sympathize with" these men and their despicable dealings due to Hearne's successful literary craftsmanship and execution. Treadwell further announced that the "author's gift for irony . . . that the slavers are no freer than" their shackled cargo, provides this "absorbing" tale with its utmost pleasures, and he concluded that *The Sure Salvation* proves the "power of the sea story . . . as potent as ever."

Hearne commented that his writing is influenced by his growing up in an island society large enough to be interesting but small enough for "characters" to be known intimately. He added: "I have been much concerned with politics (as a commentator) as Jamaica has tried to fashion itself into a newly independent society since the early 1960s."

BIOGRAPHICAL/CRITICAL SOURCES:

BOOKS

James, Louis, editor, *The Islands In Between: Essays on West Indian Literature,* Oxford University Press, 1968.
Ramchand, Kenneth, *The West Indian Novel and Its Background,* Barnes & Noble, 1970.

PERIODICALS

Times Literary Supplement, June 19, 1981.

* * *

HEATH, Roy A(ubrey) K(elvin) 1926-

PERSONAL: Born August 13, 1926, in Georgetown, British Guiana (now Guyana); son of Melrose A. (a teacher) and Jessie R. (a teacher) Heath; married Aemilia Oberli; children: three. *Education:* University of London, B.A., 1956.

ADDRESSES: Agent—Bill Hamilton, A. M. Heath & Co. Ltd., 40-42 William IV St., London WC2N 4DD, England.

CAREER: Worked in civil service in Guyana, 1942-50; held various clerical jobs in London, England, 1951-58; teacher of French and German in London, 1959—. Called to the Bar, Lincoln's Inn, 1963.

AWARDS, HONORS: Drama Award from Theatre Guild of Guyana, 1971, for *Inez Combray;* fiction prize from London *Guardian,* 1978, for *The Murderer.*

WRITINGS:

Inez Combray (play), produced in Georgetown, Guyana, 1972.
A Man Come Home (novel), Longman, 1974.
The Murderer (novel), Allison & Busby, 1978.
From the Heat of the Day (novel), Allison & Busby, 1979.
One Generation (novel), Allison & Busby, 1980.
Genetha (novel), Allison & Busby, 1981.
Kwaku; or, The Man Who Could Not Keep His Mouth Shut (novel), Allison & Busby, 1982.

Orealla (novel), Allison & Busby, 1984.
Art and History (lectures), Ministry of Education (Georgetown, Guyana), 1984.
The Shadow Bride (novel), Collins, 1988.

Also author of short stories.

WORK IN PROGRESS: A novel.

SIDELIGHTS: Roy A. K. Heath told *CA:* "My work is intended to be a dramatic chronicle of twentieth-century Guyana."

BIOGRAPHICAL/CRITICAL SOURCES:

PERIODICALS

New York Times Book Review, January 15, 1984.
Times Literary Supplement, November 12, 1982, July 27, 1984.

*   *   *

HEBERT, Anne 1916-

PERSONAL: Born August 1, 1916, in Sainte-Catherine-de-Fossambault, Quebec, Canada; daughter of Maurice-Lang (a literary critic) and Marguerite Marie (Tache) Hebert. *Education:* Privately educated.

ADDRESSES: Home—Paris, France. *Agent*—c/o Musson Book Co., 30 Lesmill Rd., Don Mills, Ontario, Canada M3B 2T6.

CAREER: Poet and novelist. Worked for Radio Canada, 1950-53, and for National Film Board, 1953-60.

MEMBER: Royal Society of Canada.

AWARDS, HONORS: Grants from the Canadian government, 1954, Canadian Council of Arts, 1961, Guggenheim Foundation, 1963, and the province of Quebec, 1965; Prix de la Province de Quebec, France Canada prize, and Duvernay prize, all 1958, all for *Les Chambres de bois;* Governor General award, 1975; grand prix de Monaco, 1975; award from the French Academy, 1975; Prix David of the province of Quebec, 1978; Prix Femina, 1982, for *Les Fous de Bassan.*

WRITINGS:

POETRY

Les Songes en equilibre (title means "Dreams in Equilibrium"), Les Editions de l'Arbre, 1942.
Le Tombeau des rois, Institut Litteraire du Quebec, 1953, translation by Peter Miller published as *The Tomb of the Kings,* Contact Press (Toronto), 1967, augmented French edition published as *Poemes,* Editions du Seuil, 1960, translation by Alan Brown published as *Poems,* Musson, 1975.
Selected Poems, Boa Editions, 1987.

Contributor of poems to literary journals.

NOVELS

Les Chambres de bois, Editions du Seuil, 1958, translation by Kathy Mezei published as *The Silent Rooms,* Musson, 1974.
Le Torrent: Nouvelles, Editions du Seuil, 1963, new edition published as *Le Torrent, suivi de Deux nouvelles inedites,* Editions HMH (Montreal), 1963, translation by Gwendolyn Moore published as *The Torrent: Novellas and Short Stories,* Harvest House (Montreal), 1973.
Kamouraska, Editions du Seuil, 1970, translation by Norman Shapiro published under same title, Crown, 1973.
Les Enfants du sabbat, Editions du Seuil, 1975, translation by Carol Dunlop-Hebert published as *Children of the Black Sabbath,* Musson, 1977.

Heloise, Editions du Seuil, 1980, translation by Sheila Fischman published under the same title, Stoddart (Toronto), 1982.
Le Fous de Bassan, Editions du Seuil, 1982, translation by Fischman published as *In the Shadow of the Wind,* Stoddart, 1982.

OTHER

"Les Invites au proces, Le Theatre du grand prix" (radio play), Radio-Canada, 1952.
(With others) "Trois de Quebec" (radio play), Radio-Canada, 1953.
"Les Indes parmi nous" (screenplay), National Film Board, 1954.
"La Canne a peche" (screenplay), National Film Board, 1959.
"Saint-Denys Garneau" (screenplay), National Film Board, 1960.
Saint-Denys Garneau and Anne Hebert (selected works), Klanak Press (Vancouver, British Columbia), 1962.
Le Temps sauvage, La Merciere assassinee, Les Invites au proces: Theatre (plays; "Le Temps sauvage" first produced in Quebec, Canada, at the Theatre du Nouveau Monde at the Palais Montcalm, October 8, 1966), Editions HMH, 1967.

SIDELIGHTS: Anne Hebert was born into an intellectually stimulating environment. Her father, Maurice-Lang Hebert, was a distinguished literary critic, and among his friends were some of the finest minds in Quebec. Due to a childhood illness Hebert was educated privately and spent most of her time at the family's country home in Sainte-Catherine-de-Fossambault.

She began writing poetry in her adolescence with the advice and guidance of her father and her cousin, the poet Hector de Saint-Denys Garneau. Unlike Saint-Denys Garneau, Hebert emerged from the spiritual struggle described in her first two books of poetry; her cousin remained in self-isolation until his death. *Les Songes en equilibre,* Hebert's first book of poetry, chronicled the experiences of a young woman who traveled from the easiness of childhood fun to the renunciation of pleasure and the acceptance of a lonely life of spiritual and poetic duty. Hebert received a strict Roman Catholic training as a child, and believed the poet to be a spiritual force in man's salvation.

In her second book of poetry, Hebert revealed that the austere life she had chosen for herself was stifling her work. It is in this volume of her poetry that Hebert emerged from a dark and deep spiritual struggle. Samuel Moon observed: "[*The Tomb of the Kings*] is a book closely unified by its constant introspection, by its atmosphere of profound melancholy, by its recurrent themes of a dead childhood, a living death cut off from love and beauty, suicide, the theme of introspection itself. Such a book would seem to be of more interest clinically than poetically, but the miracle occurs and these materials are transmuted by the remarkable force of Mlle. Hebert's imagery, the simplicity and directness of her diction, and the restrained lyric sound of her *vers libre.*"

Although known primarily as a poet, Hebert has also written for the stage and television, and is the author of three published novels. Characteristic of Hebert's novels in the theme of the inhibiting burden of the past, which binds any freedom for future actions. Many critics have noted that this theme is a French-Canadian phenomenon.

Kamouraska is Hebert's second novel and it has drawn praise from both Canadian and American critics. A *Choice* reviewer noted: "[This novel] conveys the same sense of mounting and almost unendurable excitement that one felt on first reading a Bronte novel—except that *Kamouraska* is modern in style and explicitness. The events are a stream-of-consciousness re-creation of a murder of passion that actually occurred in 1840. Hebert's poetic vision draws the thoughtful reader to be one with each of the frenzied characters." A *Canadian Forum* critic compared Hebert's "highly complex style and imagery" with that of Proust, Kafka, and Joyce, and stated that "the greatness of this work resides in the happy mixture of particularity and universality, unity and complexity, vitality and artistic originality, and, above all, in the way the author makes simplistic moral judgment of the characters impossible."

Mel Watkins of the *New York Times* called Hebert a "stylist of the first rank" in his review of *Children of the Black Sabbath,* a novel that deals with a young novice who is possessed by the devil. Watkins observed that Hebert "both complements and heightens this eerie, aphotic atmosphere with the verity and density of her minor characters and with the restrained elegance of her prose. The result is an impressionistic tale that moves smoothly. . . . The vitality of the prose, of itself, makes it one of the best of its kind."

BIOGRAPHICAL/CRITICAL SOURCES:

BOOKS

Contemporary Literary Criticism, Gale, Volume 4, 1975, Volume 29, 1984.
Dictionary of Literary Biography, Volume 68: *Canadian Writers, 1920-1959, First Series,* Gale, 1988.

PERIODICALS

Canadian Forum, November/December, 1973.
Choice, September, 1973.
New York Times, September 7, 1977.
New York Times Book Review, July 22, 1984.
Poetry, June, 1968.

*   *   *

HEIDEGGER, Martin   1889-1976

PERSONAL: Born September 26, 1889, in Messkirch, Germany (now West Germany); died May 26, 1976, in Messkirch, West Germany; son of Friedrich (a sexton) and Johanna (Kempf) Heidegger; married Elfride Petri, 1917; children: Joerg, Hermann, Erika. *Education:* Received doctorate from University of Freiburg.

ADDRESSES: Home—Roetebuckweg 47, Freiburg im Breisgau, West Germany.

CAREER: Philosopher. University of Freiburg, Freiburg, Germany, *Privatdozent,* 1915, seminar leader, 1916-20, assistant to Edmund Husserl, 1920-23; University of Marburg, Marburg, Germany, professor ordinarius, 1923-28; University of Freiburg, professor ordinarius, 1928-33, rector, 1933-34, lecturer, 1945-50, professor emeritus, 1951-57; lecturer.

MEMBER: Academy of Fine Arts of Berlin, Academy of Sciences of Heidelberg, Bavarian Academy of Fine Arts.

AWARDS, HONORS: Named honorary citizen of Messkirch, 1959; Hebel prize of Baden-Wuerttemberg, 1960.

WRITINGS:

IN ENGLISH

Sein und Zeit: Erste Haelfte, Halle, 1927, translation by John Macquarrie and Edward Robinson published as *Being and Time,* Harper, 1962.

Was Ist Metaphysiks?, F. Cohen, 1929, translation by R. F. C. Hull and A. Crick published as "What Is Metaphysics" in *Existence and Being* (also see below), Regnery, 1949.

Vom Wesen des Grundes, published in *Festschrift fuer Edmund Husserl,* M. Niemeyer, 1929, bilingual edition with translation by Terrence Malick published as *The Essence of Reasons,* Northwestern University Press, 1969.

Kant und das Problem der Metaphysik, F. Cohen, 1929, translation by James S. Churchill published as *Kant and the Problem of Metaphysics,* Indiana University Press, 1962.

Vom Wesen der Wahrheit, V. Klostermann, 1943, translation published as "On the Essence of Truth" in *Existence and Being* (also see below), Regnery, 1949.

Erlaeuterungen zu Hoelderlins Dichtung, V. Klostermann, 1944, translation by D. Scott published as "Hoelderlin and the Essence of Poetry" in *Existence and Being* (also see below), Regnery, 1949.

Platons Lehre von der Wahrheit: Mit einem Brief uber den "Humanismus," A. Francke, 1947, translations published as "Plato's Doctrine of Truth" and "Letter on Humanism" in *Philosophy in the Twentieth Century,* Volume 2, edited by William Barrett and Henry D. Aiden, Random House, 1962.

Existence and Being (contains "Remembrance of the Poet," "Hoelderlin and the Essence of Poetry," "On the Essence of Truth," and "What Is Metaphysics"), edited by Edward Brock, Regnery, 1949.

Holzwege (title means "Woodpaths"), V. Klostermann, 1950, translation published as "The Origin of the Work of Art" in *Poetry, Thought, Language* (also see below), Harper, 1971.

Einfuehrung in die Metaphysik, M. Niemeyer, 1953, translation by Ralph Manheim published as *An Introduction to Metaphysics,* Yale University Press, 1959.

Was heisst Denken?, M. Niemeyer, 1954, translation by J. Glenn Gray and Fred D. Wieck published as *What Is Called Thinking?,* Harper, 1968.

Zur Seinsfrage, [Frankfurt], 1956, translation by William Kluback and Jean T. Wilde published as *The Question of Being,* Twayne, 1958.

Was ist das—die Philosophie?, G. Neske, 1956, translation by Kluback and Wilde published as *What Is Philosophy?,* Twayne, 1958.

Identitaet und Differenz, G. Neske, 1957, translation by Kurt F. Leidecker published as *Essays in Metaphysics: Identity and Difference,* Philosophical Library, 1960.

Gelassenheit, G. Neske, 1959, translation by John M. Anderson and E. Hans Freund published as *Discourse on Thinking,* Harper, 1966.

Unterwegs zur Sprache, G. Neske, 1959, translation by Peter D. Hertz published as *On the Way to Language,* Harper, 1971.

Nietzsche, two volumes, G. Neske, 1961, translation published in four volumes, Harper, Volume 1: *Nietzsche: The Will to Power as Art,* translated by David Farrell Krell, 1979, Volume 2: *Nietzsche: The Eternal Recurrence of the Same,* translated by Krell, 1984, Volume 3: *Nietzsche: Will to Power as Knowledge [and] As Metaphysics,* edited by Krell, translated by Joan Stambaugh and Frank Capuzzi, in press, Volume 4: *Nietzsche: Nihilism,* translated by Capuzzi, 1982.

Die Frage nach dem Ding: Zu Kants Lehre von den transzendentaler Grundsaetzen, M. Niemeyer, 1962, translation by W. B. Barton, Jr., and Vera Deutsch published as *What Is a Thing?,* Regnery, 1967.

Die Technik und die Kehre, G. Neske, 1962, translation by William Lovitt published as *The Question Concerning Technology and Other Essays,* Harper, 1976.

(Editor) Edmund Husserl, *Phenomenology of Internal Time Consciousness,* translated by Churchill, Midland Books, 1964.

German Existentialism, translated by Dagobert D. Runes, Wisdom Library, 1965.

Zur Sache des Denkens, M. Niemeyer, 1969, translation by Stambaugh published as *On Time and Being,* Harper, 1972, selections translated and published in *The End of Philosophy* (also see below), Harper, 1973.

(With Eugen Fink) *Heraklit: Seminar Wintersemester 1966/67,* V. Klostermann, 1970, translation by Charles H. Seibert published as *Heraclitus Seminar, 1966-1967,* University of Alabama Press, 1979.

Hegel's Concept of Experience, Harper, 1970.

Schellings Abhandlung, M. Niemeyer, 1971, translation by Stambaugh published as *Schelling's Treatise on the Essence of Human Freedom,* Ohio University Press, 1985.

Poetry, Language, Thought, translated by Albert Hofstadter, Harper, 1971.

The End of Philosophy (contains excerpts from *Zur Sache des Denkens, Nietzsche,* and *Vortraege und Aufsatze*), translated by Stambaugh, Harper, 1973.

Early Greek Thinking, translated by Krell and Capuzzi, Harper, 1975.

Die Grundprobleme der Phaenomenologie, V. Klostermann, 1975, translation with introduction by Hofstadter published as *The Basic Problems of Phenomenology,* University of Indiana Press, 1982.

Martin Heidegger: Basic Writings From "Being and Time" (1927) to "The Task of Thinking" (1964), edited and translated by Krell, Harper, 1976.

The Piety of Thinking: Essays by Martin Heidegger, Indiana University Press, 1976.

Metaphysische Anfangsgruende der Logik im Ausgang von Leibniz, V. Klostermann, 1978, translation by Michael Heim published as *The Metaphysical Foundations of Logic,* Indiana University Press, 1984.

Prolegomena zur Geschichte des Zeitbegriffs, V. Klostermann, 1979, translation by Theodore Kisiel published as *The History of the Concept of Time,* Indiana University Press, 1985.

Hegels Phaenomenologie des Geistes, V. Klostermann, 1980, translation by Parvis Emad and Kenneth Maly published as *Hegel's Phenomenology of Spirit,* Indiana University Press, 1988.

OTHER

Die Lehre vom Urteil im Psychologismus: Ein kritisch-positiver Beitrag zur Logik, Barth, 1914.

Die Kategorien und Bedeutungslebre des Duns Scotus, Mohr, 1916.

Der Feldweg, V. Klostermann, 1953.

Aus der Erfahrung des Denkens, G. Neske, 1954.

Vortraege und Aufsatze (title means "Lectures and Essays"), three volumes, G. Neske, 1954.

Der Satz vom Grund (title means "The Law of Explanation"), G. Neske, 1957.

Hebel—Der Hausfreund, G. Neske, 1957.

Der Ursprung des Kunstwerkes, P. Reclam, 1960.

Kants These ueber das Sein, V. Klostermann, 1962.

Vermittlung und Kehre, K. Alber, 1965.

Wegmarken (title means "Trail Marks"), V. Klostermann, 1967.

Martin Heidegger, V. Klostermann, 1969.

Phaenomenologie und Theologie, V. Klostermann, 1971.

Fruehe Schriften, V. Klostermann, 1972.

Gesamtausgabe (collection), Klostermann, 1975.

Logik: Die Frage nach der Wahrheit, V. Klostermann, 1976.

Hoederlins Hymne "Germanien" und "Der Rhein," V. Klostermann, 1980.

Aristotles, Metaphysik, V. Klostermann, 1981.

Aus der Erfahrung des Denkens, G. Neske, 1981.

Grundbegriffe, V. Klostermann, 1981.

Hoelderlins Hymne, V. Klostermann, 1982.

Grundbegriffe der Metaphysik, V. Klostermann, 1983.

Denkenfahrungen, 1910-1976, V. Klostermann, 1983.

Grundfragen der Philosophie, V. Klostermann, 1984.

Hoelderlins Hymne "Der Ister," V. Klostermann, 1984.

Also author of *Die Selbstbehauptung der Deutschen Universitaet* (title means "Self-Determination of the German University"), 1933.

SIDELIGHTS: Martin Heidegger is regarded by many scholars as one of the most innovative and inquisitive thinkers concerned with the posing of philosophical questions. Living at a time when the nihilism coined by Turgenev had blossomed into a movement, Heidegger chose to question the definition of "existence," rather than apply the term to refute other concepts. His major asset lay, according to Edward B. Fiske, in his ability to "rethink the entire history of Western philosophy and to restore confidence in man's ability to ask the big questions."

Heidegger felt that it was man's primary duty to define the word "being." "Do we have an answer today to the question, what do we really mean by the word 'being'?" he asked in *Being and Time.* "By no means, and it behooves us to pose anew the question."

Heidegger was driven to "pose anew the question" by his belief that man—in the classical Greek period—had hastily applied the assumption that truth was whatever was intellectually perceived as correct. He interpreted the classical Greek scholars' definition as a distortion of reality. For Heidegger, it was not enough to say simply that something existed. He devoted most of his lifetime to addressing this difficult problem of metaphysics.

Although the bulk of Heidegger's writings deal obsessively with the term "being," he defined it for himself in his first major work, *Being and Time.* After an interminable amount of philosophical diatribes (Heidegger was known as an excessive and wordy writer), he resolved in *Being and Time* that "being," for man, was an endless quest to define that very term. Put simply, Heidegger had, through complex and highly evolved concepts, reduced the incomprehensible act of being to a finite state. If the act of being is to ceaselessly attempt to define the term, then being must be finite, for all those that exist die. Heidegger termed this cycle of life-quest-death *Dasein* or "being there." Heidegger separated man from all else by claiming only those who experienced *Dasein* could exist. Cleverly, Heidegger had used the principle of the opposite to define: in order to exist, one must cease to exist.

Heidegger proposed his complex philosophy at a time when existentialism was also taking a hold among European scholars. By concerning himself with the definition of being as it applies to man, Heidegger was incorrectly associated with other existentialists, notably Jean Paul Sartre, whose own work was heavily influenced by Heidegger's. Heidegger argued that, unlike the existentialists, he was not concerned with man but with being. His own conclusions had forced him to accept man as an integral part of his concept, but his major concern was with existence and the finiteness of being.

Heidegger had made a sufficient name for himself by 1930 and was periodically offered positions outside the one he held with the University of Freiburg. However, after taking a new position at Freiburg, Heidegger spoke about the obligations of the German race to history. Soon after, he embraced a neo-Nietzschean stance and frequented Nazi rallies. After declaring that Adolf Hitler "alone is the German reality," Heidegger even denied one of his former teachers, a Jew, access to the university. "Heidegger behaved disgracefully," wrote Sidney Hook, "towards his teacher and other Jewish colleagues."

Many scholars and critics were stung by Heidegger's bizarre political stance, though it noticeably cooled towards the late 1930s. He became disillusioned by Hitler and resigned from his position at Freiburg. Still, the association with Nazism had been established and it haunted him for many years. After the war, a tribunal ruled that Heidegger was merely a sympathizer and, though his colleagues protested, he returned to teach at Freiburg.

While he never abandoned his pursuit of being, Heidegger's later years were devoted more to hermeneutics, defined by Fiske as an approach to linguistics that "focuses on language as revelational and conceives of words as events." He saw language as essential to being and wrote that "only where there is language is there world."

Working essentially from the poetry of Hoelderlin, Heidegger determined that "to write poetry is to make a discovery." As Alvin Rosenfeld observed, "The poem enacts a reality which has no existence prior to language but rises contemporaneously with it. What is manifest in the poem is the real: poetry is 'the transmutation of the world into word.' " Heidegger saw language as a proof of existence. "Language is the house of Being," he wrote, "the whole sphere of presence is present in saying."

The relation between language and being was a preoccupation with Heidegger in his last years. Aside from giving occasional lectures at Freiburg, he rarely wandered from his home in the Black Forest. But his works, long slighted because of his past association with Nazism, regained the attention that had been deprived them by vindictive scholars. "Even when we say that we greet him with gratitude and reverence, we do not know exactly what that means," acknowledged Karl Rahner. "But certainly he has taught us this: that in any and every unutterable mystery we can and should seek what holds sway over us, even when we can hardly express it in words."

BIOGRAPHICAL/CRITICAL SOURCES:

BOOKS

Contemporary Literary Criticism, Volume 24, Gale, 1983.
Decleve, Henri, *Heidegger und Kant,* Kluwer, 1970.
Fay, Thomas Aquinas, *Heidegger: The Critique of Logic,* Kluwer, 1977.
Frings, Manfred S., *Heidegger and the Quest for Truth,* Time Books, 1968.
Heidegger, Martin, *Being and Time,* Harper, 1962.
Marx, Werner, *Heidegger and the Tradition,* Northwestern University Press, 1971.
Murray, Michael, *Heidegger and Modern Philosophy,* Yale University Press, 1978.
Perotti, James L., *Heidegger on the Divine: The Thinker, the Poet, and God,* Ohio University Press, 1974.
Sallis, John, editor, *Heidegger and the Path of Thinking,* Duquesne University Press, 1970.
Sheehan, Thomas, editor, *Heidegger: The Man and the Thinker,* Precedent Publishing, 1978.
Sherover, Charles M., *Heidegger, Kant, and Time,* Indiana University Press, 1971.
Vail, L. M., *Heidegger and Ontological Difference,* Pennsylvania State University Press, 1972.
White, David A., *Heidegger and the Language of Poetry,* University of Nebraska Press, 1978.

PERIODICALS

American Poetry Review, January/February, 1974.
New York Review of Books, December 4, 1980.
Times Literary Supplement, February 15, 1980.

OBITUARIES:

PERIODICALS

Current Biography, July, 1976.
Detroit Free Press, May 27, 1976.
Newsweek, June 7, 1976.
New York Times, May 27, 1976.
Time, June 7, 1976.
Washington Post, May 27, 1976.

* * *

HEINLEIN, Robert A(nson) 1907-1988
(Anson MacDonald, Lyle Monroe, John Riverside, Caleb Saunders, Simon York)

PERSONAL: Surname rhymes with "fine line"; born July 7, 1907, in Butler, Mo.; died in 1988 in Carmel, Calif.; son of Rex Ivar (an accountant) and Bam (Lyle) Heinlein; married Leslyn McDonald (divorced); married Virginia Gerstenfeld, October 21, 1948. *Education:* Attended University of Missouri, 1925; U.S. Naval Academy, graduate, 1929; University of California, Los Angeles, graduate study, 1934.

ADDRESSES: Home—Bonny Doon Rd., Santa Cruz, Calif. 95060.

CAREER: Writer, 1939-88. Commissioned ensign, U.S. Navy, 1929, became lieutenant, retired because of physical disability, 1934; aviation engineer at Naval Air Experimental Station, Philadelphia, Pa., 1942-45. Owner of Shively & Sophie Lodes silver mine, 1934-35; candidate for California State Assembly, 1938; James V. Forrestal Lecturer, U.S. Naval Academy, 1973; guest commentator during Apollo lunar landing, Columbia Broadcasting System, 1969.

MEMBER: American Institute of Astronautics and Aeronautics, Authors' League of America, Navy League, Air Force Association, Air Power Council, Association of the Army of the United States, United States Naval Academy Alumni Association, American Association for the Advancement of Science.

AWARDS, HONORS: Guest of Honor, World Science Fiction Convention, 1941, 1961, and 1976; Hugo Award, World Science Fiction Convention, 1956, for *Double Star,* 1960, for *Starship Troopers,* 1962, for *Stranger in a Strange Land,* and 1967, for *The Moon Is a Harsh Mistress;* Boys' Clubs of America Book Award, 1959; Sequoyah Children's Book Award of Oklahoma, Oklahoma Library Association, 1961, for *Have Space Suit, Will Travel;* named best all-time author, Locus magazine readers' poll, 1973 and 1975; Nebula Grand Master Award, Science Fiction Writers of America, 1975; National Rare Blood Club Humanitarian Award, 1974; Council of Community Blood Centers Award, 1977; American Association of Blood Banks Award,

1977; Inkpot Award, 1977; L.H.D., Eastern Michigan University, 1977; the Rhysling Award of the Science Fiction Poetry Association is named for a character in a Heinlein story; Tomorrow Starts Here Award, Delta Vee Society.

WRITINGS:

SCIENCE FICTION NOVELS

Rocket Ship Galileo (also see below), Scribner, 1947, reprinted, Ballantine, 1977.
Beyond This Horizon, Fantasy Press, 1948, reprinted, Gregg, 1981.
Space Cadet, Scribner, 1948, reprinted, Ballantine, 1978.
Red Planet, Scribner, 1949, reprinted, Ballantine, 1977.
Sixth Column, Gnome Press, 1949, published as *The Day After Tomorrow,* New American Library, 1951.
Farmer in the Sky, Scribner, 1950, reprinted, Ballantine, 1975.
Waldo [and] *Magic, Inc.* (also see below), Doubleday, 1950, reprinted, Gregg, 1979, published as *Waldo: Genius in Orbit,* Avon, 1958.
Between Planets, Scribner, 1951, reprinted, Ballantine, 1978.
Universe, Dell, 1951, published as *Orphans of the Sky,* Gollancz, 1963, Putnam, 1964, reprinted, Berkley Publishing, 1983.
The Puppet Masters (also see below), Doubleday, 1951.
Rolling Stones, Scribner, 1952, reprinted, Ballantine, 1977 (published in England as *Space Family Stone,* Gollancz, 1969).
Revolt in 2100, Shasta, 1953.
Starman Jones, Scribner, 1953, reprinted, Ballantine, 1975.
Star Beast, Scribner, 1954, reprinted, Ballantine, 1977.
Tunnel in the Sky, Scribner, 1955, reprinted, Ballantine, 1977.
Double Star, Doubleday, 1956, reprinted, Gregg, 1978.
Time for the Stars, Scribner, 1956, reprinted, Ballantine, 1978.
Citizen of the Galaxy, Scribner, 1957 reprinted, Ballantine, 1978.
The Door into Summer, Doubleday, 1957, reprinted, Gregg, 1979.
Have Space Suit, Will Travel, Scribner, 1958, reprinted, 1977.
Methuselah's Children, Gnome Press, 1958.
Starship Troopers, Putnam, 1959, reprinted, Berkley Publishing, 1984.
Stranger in a Strange Land, Putnam, 1961, unabridged edition published as *Stranger in a Strange Land: The Uncut Version,* Putnam, 1991.
Glory Road, Putnam, 1963, reprinted, Gregg, 1979.
Podkayne of Mars: Her Life and Times, Putnam, 1963.
Farnham's Freehold, Putnam, 1964.
Three by Heinlein (contains *The Puppet Masters, Waldo,* and *Magic, Inc.*), Doubleday, 1965 (published in England as *A Heinlein Triad,* Gollancz, 1966).
A Robert Heinlein Omnibus, Sidgwick & Jackson, 1966.
The Moon Is a Harsh Mistress, Putnam, 1966.
I Will Fear No Evil, Putnam, 1971.
Time Enough for Love: The Lives of Lazarus Long, Putnam, 1973.
The Notebooks of Lazarus Long, Putnam, 1978.
The Number of the Beast, Fawcett, 1980.
Friday, Holt, 1982.
Job: A Comedy of Justice, Ballantine, 1984.
The Cat Who Walks Through Walls: A Comedy of Manners, Putnam, 1985.

STORY COLLECTIONS

The Man Who Sold the Moon, Shasta, 1950, reprinted, New American Library, 1973.
The Green Hills of Earth, Shasta, 1951, reprinted, Amereon, 1976.

Assignment in Eternity, Fantasy Press, 1953 reprinted, New American Library, 1970.
The Menace from Earth, Gnome Press, 1959, reprinted, Amereon, 1976.
The Unpleasant Profession of Jonathan Hoag, Gnome Press, 1959, reprinted, Berkley Publishing, 1976, published as *6 x H,* Pyramid Publications, 1962.
The Worlds of Robert A. Heinlein, Ace Books, 1966.
The Past through Tomorrow: Future History Stories, Putnam, 1967.
The Best of Robert Heinlein, 1939-1959, edited by Angus Wells, two volumes, Sidgwick & Jackson, 1973.
Destination Moon, Gregg, 1979.
Expanded Universe: The New Worlds of Robert A. Heinlein, Ace Books, 1980.

OTHER

(Contributor) Lloyd Arthur Eshbach, editor, *Of Worlds Beyond: The Science of Science Fiction,* Fantasy Press, 1947, reprinted, Dobson, 1967.
(Editor) *Tomorrow, the Stars,* Doubleday, 1952, reprinted, Berkley Publishing, 1984.
(With others) *Famous Science Fiction Stories,* Random House, 1957.
(With others) *The Science Fiction Novel: Imagination and Social Criticism,* Advent, 1959.
(Author of preface) Daniel O. Graham, *High Frontier: A Strategy for National Survival,* Pinnacle Books, 1983.

Also author of engineering report, *Test Procedures for Plastic Materials Intended for Structural and Semi-Structural Aircraft Uses,* 1944. Contributor to anthologies and to the *Encyclopaedia Britannica.* Contributor of over 150 short stories and articles, some under pseudonyms, to *Saturday Evening Post, Analog, Galaxy, Astounding Science Fiction,* and other publications.

SCREENPLAYS

"Destination Moon" (based on *Rocket Ship Galileo*), Eagle Lion, 1950.
"Project Moonbase," Lippert Productions, 1953.

Also author of scripts for television and radio programs.

SIDELIGHTS: "The one author who has raised science fiction from the gutter of pulp space opera . . . to the altitude of original and breathtaking concepts," Alfred Bester maintains in *Publishers Weekly,* "is Robert A. Heinlein." Heinlein's influence in his field has been so great that Alexei Panshin states in his *Heinlein in Dimension: A Critical Analysis* that "the last twenty-five years of science fiction may even be taken in large part as an exploration by many writers of the possibilities inherent in Heinlein's techniques."

Heinlein's influence began with his fiction of the 1940s and, as Panshin points out, derives from his "insistence in talking clearly, knowledgeably, and dramatically about the real world [which] destroyed forever the sweet, pure, wonderful innocence that science fiction once had. . . . In a sense, Heinlein may be said to have offered science fiction a road to adulthood." Speaking of this early work, Daniel Dickinson writes in *Modern Fiction Studies* that Heinlein possessed "a vast knowledge of science, military affairs, and politics" which enabled him to write "stories that shimmered gemlike amid the vast mass of middling, amateurish tales that choked the pulp SF journals. Heinlein's influence was enormous; dozens of young writers strove to imitate his style, and editors refashioned their publications to reflect the new sense of sophistication Heinlein and a few others were bringing to the field." Heinlein's impact on younger science fiction writers can be seen in a poll taken by *Astounding Science Fiction* magazine in 1953: eighteen top science fiction writers of the time cited Heinlein as the major influence on their work.

Despite his great importance in science fiction, Heinlein's explanations of his work belied his own stature. He explained in several interviews that he only began to write when his career as a naval officer was cut short by tuberculosis. After his forced retirement from the Navy, Heinlein tried his hand at several unsuccessful ventures, including a silver mine in Colorado. In 1939, to supplement his modest retirement pay, he wrote and submitted a short story to *Astounding Science Fiction* magazine. They sent him a check for seventy dollars, and Heinlein began his career. He told *CA:* "I started writing for a reason many writers have had: I was in poor health and unable to work steadily. I continued because it turned out to be a gratifying way of supporting myself and my dependents." "Look," Heinlein told Curt Suplee of the *Washington Post,* "I write stories for money. What I wanted to be was an admiral."

"Heinlein's following was ardent and instant with the appearance of his first short story in *Astounding Science Fiction* magazine more than 40 years ago," Theodore Sturgeon explains in the *Los Angeles Times Book Review.* In his early stories, Heinlein concentrated on a particular kind of science fiction—logically extrapolating current science into the near-future. His speculations were so accurate that his work of this time predicts a host of developments years before they came to be, including the atom bomb, nuclear power plants, the waterbed, moving sidewalks, and an electronic space defense shield. As Suplee explains it, Heinlein "pioneered the extrapolative story format, in which present trends are projected into a plausible future," and he "couched his scientific problems in human terms."

After working as an engineer during World War II, Heinlein returned to writing in the late 1940s. It was during this time that he moved from the genre magazines in which he had made his reputation to the slick magazines, particularly the *Saturday Evening Post.* As Joseph Patrouch writes in the *Dictionary of Literary Biography,* "Heinlein was the first major science-fiction writer to break out of category and reach the larger general-fiction market, and therefore he was the first to start breaking down the walls that had isolated science fiction for so long."

Heinlein also began to publish novels for young people in the late 1940s. Dickinson calls this work "a series of well-crafted novels that continue to attract readers both young and old." Sturgeon believes that Heinlein's "series of 'juveniles' had a great deal to do with raising that category from childish to what is now called YA—'Young adult.' " Several reviewers deem Heinlein's ostensibly "juvenile" books to be better than much of what is marketed as adult science fiction. H. H. Holmes, for example, writes in the *New York Herald Tribune Book Review* that "the nominally 'teenage' science-fiction novels of Robert A. Heinlein stand so far apart from even their best competitors as to deserve a separate classification. These are no easy, adventurous, first-steps-to-space boys' books, but mature and complex novels, far above the level of most adult science fiction both in characterization and in scientific thought." "A Heinlein book," Villiers Gerson observes in the *New York Times Book Review,* "is still better than 99 per cent of the science-fiction adventures produced every year." Heinlein's novels of this time have been reprinted and marketed to adult readers since their initial appearances.

In the 1950s, Heinlein entered the field of television and motion pictures. His novel *Space Cadet* was adapted as the television program "Tom Corbett: Space Cadet." He wrote the screenplay

and served as technical adviser for the film "Destination Moon," described by Peter R. Weston as "the first serious *and* commercially successful space flight film" which "helped to pave the way" for the Apollo space program of the 1960s.

Heinlein's belief in man's eventual exploration of outer space, and his proselytizing on behalf of space travel, was a primary concern in his postwar fiction. Donald A. Wollheim notes in his *The Universe Makers: Science Fiction Today* that Heinlein "believes in the future of mankind and in the endless frontier of the galactic civilization that is to be." Writing in *Extrapolation,* Diane Parkin-Speer comments that "Heinlein assumes that technology will continue to develop, [that] the cosmos is infinite, [and that] with increased scientific knowledge man may roam the universe."

By writing for young people about space travel, Heinlein hoped to prepare them for the future. Patrouch quotes Heinlein as explaining: "Youths who build hot-rods are not dismayed by spaceships; in their adult years they will build such ships. In the meantime they will read stories of interplanetary travel." Patrouch maintains that Heinlein was essentially correct about the effect he had on his young readers: "Heinlein's stories convinced a whole generation that man will really be able to do things he can only imagine now—and that generation grew up and sent Apollo to the moon."

In the late 1950s Heinlein turned away from his juvenile fiction and published the first of what became a string of controversial novels. This novel, *Starship Troopers,* is the first of Heinlein's books to speculate not on future scientific changes, but on future societal changes. It postulates a world run by military veterans; the novel's protagonist is an army infantryman. Military law takes precedent over civil law in this world, and military discipline is the norm. As Heinlein explained to Suplee, the society depicted in the novel is "a democracy in which the poll tax is putting in a term of voluntary service—which could be as a garbage collector." *Starship Troopers* has been attacked by some critics for its supposed fascistic and militaristic tendencies and earned Heinlein a reputation as a right-winger. But Dennis E. Showalter counters critical attacks on *Starship Troopers* in an article for *Extrapolation.* Although he agrees that the pervasive military presence in the hypothetical society would "chill the heart of the civil libertarian," Showalter maintains that the novel is "neither militaristic nor fascist in the scholarly sense of these concepts." Despite the controversy, *Starship Troopers* is still one of Heinlein's most popular novels. It won a Hugo Award and has remained in print for more than two decades.

Heinlein followed *Starship Troopers* with another controversial novel that met with strong opposition, this one quite different in its speculations about the future. *Stranger in a Strange Land* tells the story of Valentine Michael Smith, a Martian with psi powers who establishes a religious movement on Earth. Members of his Church of All Worlds practice group sex and live in small communes. *Stranger in a Strange Land* is perhaps Heinlein's best known work. It has sold over three million copies, won a Hugo Award, created an intense cult following, and even inspired a real-life Church of All Worlds, founded by some devoted readers of the book.

Stranger in a Strange Land was, David N. Samuelson writes in *Critical Encounters: Writers and Themes in Science Fiction,* "in some ways emblematic of the Sixties. . . . It fit the iconoclastic mood of the time, attacking human folly under several guises, especially in the person or persons of the Establishment: government, the military, organized religion. By many of its readers, too, it was taken to advocate a religion of love and of incalculable power, which could revolutionize human affairs and bring about an apocalyptic change, presumably for the better." Robert Scholes and Eric S. Rabkin, writing in their *Science Fiction: History, Science, Vision,* believe that "the values of the sixties could hardly have found a more congenial expression."

Heinlein explained his intentions in writing *Stranger in a Strange Land* as being, R. A. Jelliffe quotes him in the *Chicago Tribune,* "to examine every major axiom of the western culture, to question each axiom, throw doubt on it—and, if possible, to make the anti-thesis of each axiom appear a possible and perhaps desirable thing—rather than unthinkable." This ambitious attack caused a major upheaval in science fiction. *Stranger in a Strange Land,* Patrouch explains, "broke out of category and forced a reevaluation of what science fiction could be and do. As he had done immediately before World War II, Heinlein helped to reshape the genre and make it more significant and valuable than it had been."

In subsequent novels Heinlein continued to speculate on social changes of the future, dealing with such controversial subjects as group marriage and incest. In *The Moon Is a Harsh Mistress,* lunar colonists practice a variety of marriage forms because of the shortage of women on the moon. Variations on group marriage are necessary. In *I Will Fear No Evil,* an elderly, dying businessman has his brain transplanted into the body of a young woman. He then impregnates himself with his own sperm, previously stored in a sperm bank. *Time Enough for Love: The Lives of Lazarus Long* explores varieties of future incest through the immortal character Lazarus Long. Long rescues a young girl from a fire, raises her as his daughter, then marries her and has children. He also creates two female clones of himself with whom he has sex. In another episode, Lazarus travels back in time two thousand years and has intercourse with his own mother. In these novels of the 1960s and 1970s, Parkin-Speer writes, "a defense of unconventional sexual love is [Heinlein's] central theme. . . . The ideal sexual love relationship, first presented in *Stranger in a Strange Land,* is heterosexual, nonmonogamous, and patriarchal, with an emphasis on procreation. The protagonists of the novels and their various sexual partners express unorthodox sexual views and have no inhibitions or guilt."

Although several of these more controversial novels have won major awards, some critics have expressed misgivings about Heinlein's work from this period. "Instead of concerning himself with facts," Panshin says of several of these books, Heinlein "has treated his opinions as though they were facts. More than that, he has so concentrated on presenting his opinions with every narrative device he knows that he has neglected story construction, characterization, and plot." Parkin-Speer believes that "as Heinlein the preacher has come to the forefront the quality of his fiction has declined." Norman Spinrad allows in a *Washington Post Book World* review that some critics "have used these latter-day works as springboards for a rather extreme revisionism which seeks to discredit [Heinlein's] entire oeuvre." But Elizabeth Anne Hull insists in *Extrapolation* that in his controversial novels Heinlein does not force his opinions on his reader. Hull believes that he "raises issues for the serious adult mind to consider and trusts the reader to draw his or her own conclusions."

Beginning with his novel *Friday,* published in 1982, Heinlein tempered his social speculations by presenting them in the context of a science fiction adventure. The novel tells the story of Friday, a female "artificial person"—a genetically designed human—working for a government spy agency of the next century. In her interplanetary travels as a courier of secret docu-

ments, Friday enjoys sexual exploits with both men and women. But as an artificial person, she is insecure about herself and uneasy about the role she must play to pass in human society. When assassinations and terrorism rock the Earth, Friday must fight her way back home across several foreign countries. This journey becomes a symbolic quest for her own identity.

Many critics welcomed the change in Heinlein's writing. Dickinson calls it a "paean to tolerance that Heinlein sings through the Friday persona. . . . With this book, Heinlein once again pulled the rug out from under those who had him pegged." Sturgeon finds *Friday* a "remarkable and most welcome book" that is "as joyous to read as it is provocative."

Job: A Comedy of Justice and *The Cat Who Walks Through Walls: A Comedy of Manners* continued to combine serious subject matter with rollicking interplanetary adventure. *Job* is a science fiction cover of the biblical story of a man who is tested by God. In this novel, Alex Hergensheimer shifts between alternate worlds without warning. These jarring disruptions force him to continually reassess himself and adapt his behavior to new and sometimes dangerous conditions. Gerald Jonas of the *New York Times Book Review,* while finding *Job* not as fine as earlier, "classic Heinlein," still describes the book as "an exhilarating romp through the author's mental universe (or rather universes), with special emphasis on cultural relativism, dogmatic religion (treated with surprising sympathy) and the philosophical conundrum of solipsism. . . . Heinlein has chosen to confront head on the question posed by the original story: why do bad things happen to good people?" Although Sue Martin of the *Los Angeles Times Book Review* calls *Job* "another dreadful wallow in the muddy fringe of a once-great, if not the greatest, SF imagination," Kelvin Johnston of the *Observer* claims that Heinlein is a "veteran raconteur who couldn't bore you if he tried."

The Cat Who Walks Through Walls also ranges through vast stretches of time and space. When Colonel Colin Campbell is wrongly accused of murder, he and his wife escape in a spaceship, hide out on the moon, and eventually join the Time Corps, a group of time-travelers who revise human history by intervening at crucial moments. David Bradley of the *New York Times Book Review* finds that *The Cat Who Walks Through Walls* contains "dialogue as witty as Oscar Wilde's, action as rollicking as Edgar Rice Burrough's and satire as spicy as Jonathan Swift's, and it gives a troubling glimpse of the future that may be ours." James and Eugene Sloan, writing of the novel in the *Chicago Tribune Book World,* claim that "no writer is better or clearer with science and technology. When Heinlein describes the physics of an airless landing (you speed up to slow down), it's like an old cowboy telling you how to break broncos."

Evaluations of Heinlein's career often point out the polarized critical reaction to his work. Though Heinlein "set the tone for much of modern science fiction," as Jonas reports, and Sturgeon believes "his influence on science fiction has been immense," there are critics who characterize him as right wing or even fascistic and, based on their reaction to his politics, denigrate the value of Heinlein's work. Heinlein's belief in self-reliance, liberty, individualism, and patriotism make him appear, Joseph D. Olander and Martin Harry Greenberg admit in their *Robert A. Heinlein,* "to adopt positions favored by the American political right."

Bud Foote of the *Detroit News* defines Heinlein's political thought, which he sees as having stayed consistent after the 1950s, in this way: "The greatest thing to which a human can aspire is living free. Enslaving one's fellow-human physically, mentally or spiritually is the unforgivable sin; allowing oneself so to be enslaved is nearly as bad. Honorable people meet their obligations; there's no such thing as a free lunch. All systems are suspect; all forms of government are terrible, with rule by the majority low on the list." Suplee sees much of Heinlein's fiction as concerned with "how freedom of will and libertarian self-reliance can coexist with devotion to authority and love of country." Olander and Greenberg find "some of the perennial concerns of philosophy, such as the best form of government, whether and to what extent political utopias are possible, and the dimensions of power, liberty, equality, justice, and order" to be confronted in Heinlein's best work.

Central to Heinlein's vision is the strong and independent hero found in much of his fiction. The Heinlein hero, Olander and Greenberg maintain, "is always tough, just, relatively fearless when it counts, and endowed with extraordinary skills and physical prowess." Johnston describes the typical Heinlein protagonist as a "lone male genius on the Last Frontier who prevails against any organized authority that dares to restrict his potential." Writing in his study *The Classic Years of Robert A. Heinlein,* George Edgar Slusser argues that Heinlein's protagonists are "elite" men born with inherently superior traits. "Heinlein elite are not known by physical signs, nor do they bear the traditional hero's stamp," Slusser writes. "[They possess] a common mental disposition: they believe in individual freedom, and are willing to band together to fight entangling bureaucracy and mass strictures."

Although Heinlein remained a controversial writer until his death in 1988, he was undoubtedly one of the most popular and influential writers in the field of science fiction. His books have sold over forty million copies and have been translated into twenty-nine languages, and virtually everything he has published is still in print. Heinlein's influence in the field continues to be enormous. Olander and Greenberg describe him as "an outstanding figure in modern American science fiction." Jonas maintains that he "has probably influenced the development of science fiction more than any other writer." And, because of his importance in shaping the modern science fiction genre, Bradley believes that Heinlein "is gradually being recognized as one of the most influential writers in American literature."

MEDIA ADAPTATIONS: The television series "Tom Corbett: Space Cadet" was based on Heinlein's novel *Space Cadet;* television, radio, and film rights to many of Heinlein's works have been sold.

AVOCATIONAL INTERESTS: Stone masonry and sculpture, cats, ballistics, fiscal theory.

BIOGRAPHICAL/CRITICAL SOURCES:

BOOKS

Aldiss, Brian W., *Billion Year Spree: The True History of Science Fiction,* Doubleday, 1973.
Atheling, William, Jr., *The Issue at Hand,* Advent, 1964.
Atheling, William, Jr., *More Issues at Hand,* Advent, 1970.
Clareson, Thomas D., editor, *Voices for the Future: Essays on Major Science Fiction Writers,* Volume 1, Bowling Green University, 1976.
Contemporary Literary Criticism, Gale, Volume 1, 1973, Volume 3, 1975, Volume 8, 1978, Volume 14, 1980, Volume 26, 1983, Volume 55, 1989.
Dictionary of Literary Biography, Volume 8: *Twentieth Century American Science Fiction Writers,* Gale, 1981.
Franklin, H. Bruce, *Robert A. Heinlein: America as Science Fiction,* Oxford University Press, 1980.

Gunn, James, *The Road to Science Fiction: From Heinlein to the Present,* New American Library, 1979.
Knight, Damon, *In Search of Wonder: Critical Essays on Science Fiction,* Advent, 1956.
Maskowitz, Sam, *Seekers of Tomorrow: Masters of Modern Science Fiction,* World Publishing, 1966.
Nicholls, Peter, *Robert A. Heinlein,* Scribner, 1982.
Olander, Joseph D. and Martin Harry Greenberg, editors, *Robert A. Heinlein,* Taplinger, 1978.
Panshin, Alexei, *Heinlein in Dimension: A Critical Analysis,* Advent, 1968.
Riley, Dick, editor, *Critical Encounters: Writers and Themes in Science Fiction,* Ungar, 1978.
Rose, Lois and Stephen Rose, *The Shattered Ring: Science Fiction and the Quest for Meaning,* John Knox, 1970.
Scholes, Robert and Eric S. Rabkin, *Science Fiction: History, Science, Vision,* Oxford University Press, 1977.
Slusser, George Edgar, *Robert A. Heinlein: Stranger in His Own Land,* Borgo, 1976.
Slusser, George Edgar, *The Classic Years of Robert A. Heinlein,* Borgo, 1977.
Wollheim, Donald A., *The Universe Makers: Science Fiction Today,* Harper, 1971.

PERIODICALS

American Mercury, October, 1960.
Analog, May, 1954, September, 1964.
Author and Journalist, January, 1963.
CEA Critic, March, 1968.
Chicago Tribune, August 6, 1961.
Chicago Tribune Book World, August 17, 1980, January 7, 1984.
Christian Science Monitor, November 7, 1957.
Detroit News, July 25, 1982.
Extrapolation, December, 1970, May, 1975, spring, 1979, fall, 1979, fall, 1982.
Galaxy, February, 1952, December, 1966.
Journal of Popular Culture, spring, 1972.
Los Angeles Times, December 19, 1985.
Los Angeles Times Book Review, June 20, 1982, October 21, 1984.
Magazine of Fantasy and Science Fiction, June, 1956, November, 1961, March, 1971, October, 1980.
Modern Fiction Studies, spring, 1986.
National Observer, November 16, 1970.
National Review, March 26, 1963, November 16, 1970, December 12, 1980.
New Statesman, July 30, 1965.
New Worlds, June, 1962.
New Yorker, July, 1974.
New York Herald Tribune Book Review, November 28, 1954, November 13, 1955, November 18, 1956, May 12, 1962.
New York Times, March 3, 1957, August 22, 1973.
New York Times Book Review, October 23, 1949, November 14, 1954, December 29, 1957, December 14, 1958, January 31, 1960, March 23, 1975, August 24, 1980, September 14, 1980, July 4, 1982, November 1984, December 22, 1985.
Observer, December 23, 1984.
Publishers Weekly, July 2, 1973.
Punch, August 25, 1965, November 22, 1967.
San Francisco Chronicle, November 8, 1959.
Saturday Review, November, 1958.
Science Fiction Review, November, 1970.
SF Commentary, May, 1976.
Spectator, June 3, 1966, July 3, 1977.
Speculation, August, 1969.

Times Literary Supplement, October 6, 1969, December 1, 1970, April 2, 1971, June 14, 1974.
Washington Post, September 5, 1984.
Washington Post Book World, May 11, 1975, June 27, 1982.

* * *

HELD, Peter
See VANCE, John Holbrook

* * *

HELFORTH, John
See DOOLITTLE, Hilda

* * *

HELLENHOFFERU, Vojtech Kapristian z
See HASEK, Jaroslav (Matej Frantisek)

* * *

HELLER, Joseph 1923-

PERSONAL: Born May 1, 1923, in Brooklyn, N.Y.; son of Isaac (a truck driver) and Lena Heller; married Shirley Held, September 3, 1945 (divorced); children: Erica Jill, Theodore Michael. *Education:* Attended University of Southern California; New York University, B.A., 1948; Columbia University, M.A., 1949; graduate study, Oxford University, 1949-50.

ADDRESSES: Home—East Hampton, Long Island, New York. *Agent*—Candida Donadio & Associates, 111 West 57th St., New York, N.Y. 10019.

CAREER: Novelist. Pennsylvania State University, University Park, instructor in English, 1950-52; *Time* magazine, New York City, advertising writer, 1952-56; *Look* magazine, New York City, advertising writer, 1956-58; *McCall's* magazine, New York City, promotion manager, 1958-61; former teacher of fiction and dramatic writing at Yale University and University of Pennsylvania; City College of the City University of New York, New York City, Distinguished Professor of English, until 1975; full-time writer, 1975—. Has worked in the theater, movies, and television. *Military service:* U.S. Army Air Forces, World War II; served as B-25 wing bombardier; flew sixty missions; became first lieutenant.

MEMBER: Phi Beta Kappa.

AWARDS, HONORS: Fulbright scholar, 1949-50; National Institute of Arts and Letters grant in literature, 1963; Prix Interallie (France) and Prix Medicis Etranger (France), both 1985, both for *God Knows.*

WRITINGS:

(Contributor) *Nelson Algren's Own Book of Lonesome Monsters,* Lancer, 1960.
Catch-22 (novel; also see below; chapter one originally published in *New World Writing,* 1955), Simon & Schuster, 1961, critical edition, edited by Robert M. Scotto, Dell, 1973.
Something Happened (novel; excerpt originally published in *Esquire,* September, 1966), Knopf, 1974.
Good as Gold (novel; Literary Guild selection), Simon & Schuster, 1979.
God Knows (novel), Knopf, 1984.
(With Speed Vogal) *No Laughing Matter* (autobiography), Putnam, 1986.

Picture This, Putnam, 1988.

Contributor of short stories to periodicals, including *Atlantic Monthly, Esquire,* and *Cosmopolitan;* contributor of reviews to periodicals, including *New Republic.*

PLAYS

We Bombed in New Haven (two-act; first produced in New Haven, Conn., at the Yale School of Drama Repertory Theater, December 4, 1967, produced on Broadway at the Ambassador Theater, October 16, 1968), Knopf, 1968.
Catch-22: A Dramatization (one-act play based on novel of same title; first produced in East Hampton, N.Y., at the John Drew Theater, July 23, 1971), Samuel French, 1971.
Clevinger's Trial (based on chapter eight of novel *Catch-22;* produced in London, 1974), Samuel French, 1973.

SCREENPLAYS

(With David R. Schwartz) "Sex and the Single Girl" (based on book of same title by Helen Gurley Brown), Warner Brothers, 1964.
(Uncredited) "Casino Royale" (based on novel of same title by Ian Fleming), Columbia Pictures, 1967.
(With Tom Waldman and Frank Waldman) "Dirty Dingus Magee" (based on novel *The Ballad of Dingus Magee* by David Markson), Metro-Goldwyn-Mayer, 1970.
(Contributor) "Of Men and Women" (television drama), American Broadcasting Companies, 1972.

Also author, under pseudonym, of other television screenplays during the 1960s.

WORK IN PROGRESS: A sequel to *Catch-22,* for Putnam.

SIDELIGHTS: "There was only one catch . . . and that was Catch-22," Doc Daneeka informs Yossarian. As Yossarian, the lead bombardier of Joseph Heller's phenomenal first novel, soon learns, this one catch is enough to keep him at war indefinitely. After pleading with Doc Daneeka that he is too crazy to fly any more missions, Yossarian is introduced to Catch-22, a rule which stipulates that anyone rational enough to want to be grounded could not possibly be insane and therefore must return to his perilous duties. The novel *Catch-22* is built around the multifarious attempts of Captain John Yossarian to survive the Second World War, to escape the omnipresent logic of a regulation which somehow stays one step ahead of him.

At the time of its publication in 1961, Heller's antiwar novel met with modest sales and lukewarm reviews. But by mid-decade, the book began to sell in the American underground, becoming a favored text of the counter-culture. "[*Catch-22*] came when we still cherished nice notions about WW II," Eliot Fremont-Smith recalls in the *Village Voice.* "Demolishing these, it released an irreverence that had, until then, dared not speak its name." With more than ten million copies now in print, *Catch-22* is generally regarded as one of the most important novels of our time. It "is probably the finest novel published since World War II," Richard Locke declares in the *New York Times Book Review.* "*Catch-22* is the great representative document of our era, linking high and low culture." The title itself has become part of the language, and its "hero" Yossarian, according to Jack Schnedler of the *Newark Star-Ledger,* "has become the fictional talisman to an entire generation."

In the *New York Times Book Review,* Heller cites three reasons for the success of *Catch-22:* "First, it's a great book. I've come to accept the verdict of the majority. Second, a whole new generation of readers is being introduced to it. . . . Third, and most important: Vietnam. Because this is the war I had in mind; a war fought without military provocation, a war in which the real enemy is no longer the other side but someone allegedly on your side. The ridiculous war I felt lurking in the future when I wrote the book." "There seems no denying that though Heller's macabre farce was written about a rarefied part of the raging war of the forties during the silent fifties," Josh Greenfeld wrote in a 1968 *New York Times Book Review* article, "it has all but become the chapbook of the sixties." As Joseph Epstein summarizes in *Book World, Catch-22* "was a well-aimed bomb."

In his *Bright Book of Life,* Alfred Kazin finds that "the theme of *Catch-22* . . . is the total craziness of war . . . and the struggle to survive of one man, Yossarian, who knows the difference between his sanity and the insanity of the system." After his commanding officer repeatedly raises the number of bombing missions required for discharge, Yossarian decides to "live forever or die in the attempt." "Yossarian's logic becomes so pure that everyone thinks him mad," Robert Brustein writes in the *New Republic,* "for it is the logic of sheer survival, dedicated to keeping him alive in a world noisily clamoring for his annihilation." Brustein continues: "According to this logic, Yossarian is surrounded on all sides by hostile forces. . . . [He] feels a blind, electric rage against the Germans whenever they hurl flak at his easily penetrated plane; but he feels an equally profound hatred for those of his own countrymen who exercise an arbitrary power over his life."

"The urgent emotion in Heller's book is . . . every individual's sense of being directly in the line of fire," Kazin believes. In the *Dictionary of Literary Biography,* Inge Kutt views Pianosa, the fictional island in the Mediterranean Sea which is the setting of the novel, as a microcosm of "the postwar world which not only includes the Korean and Vietnam wars but also the modern mass society." "Heller's horrifying vision of service life in World War II is merely an illustration of the human condition itself," Jean E. Kennard asserts in *Mosaic.* "The world has no meaning but is simply there [and] man is a creature who seeks meaning," Kennard elaborates. "Reason and language, man's tools for discovering the meaning of his existence and describing his world, are useless."

Language, as presented in *Catch-22,* is more than useless; it is dangerous, a weapon employed by the authorities to enslave individuals in a world of institutionalized absurdity, a world where pilots lose their lives because their commanding officer wants to see prettier bombing patterns or his name in the *Saturday Evening Post.* Language, in the form of Catch-22, is the mechanism which transforms military doublethink into concrete reality, into commands which profoundly affect human life and death. Catch-22, as the novel states, is the rule "which specified that a concern for one's safety in the face of dangers that were real and immediate was the process of a rational mind. Orr was crazy and could be grounded. All he had to do was ask; and as soon as he did, he would no longer be crazy and would have to fly more missions." As Jerry H. Bryant notes in his book *The Open Decision:* "Only the insane voluntarily continue to fly. This is an almost perfect catch because the law is in the definition of insanity. . . . The system is closed." In the *Arizona Quarterly,* Marcus K. Billson III examines Catch-22: "There is no way out of the tautological absurdity of [this] regulation. . . . The will of authority predominates by the force of language. Man is caught in an unrelenting cycle of oppression and brutality disguised in the convolutions of Catch-22." "Catch-22," Billson continued, "is law deriving its power from a universal faith in language as presence. The world of the novel projects the horrific, yet all too real, power of language to divest itself from any necessity of reference,

to function as an independent, totally autonomous medium with its own perfect system and logic. That such a language pretends to mirror anything but itself is a commonplace delusion which Heller satirizes masterfully throughout the novel. Yet, civilization is informed by this very presence, and Heller shows how man is tragically and comically tricked and manipulated by such an absurdity."

The acquiescence of men to language in *Catch-22,* Carol Pearson observes, is rooted in their failure to find any "transcendental comfort to explain suffering and to make life meaningful. . . . People react to meaninglessness by renouncing their humanity, becoming cogs in the machine. With no logical explanation to make suffering and death meaningful and acceptable, people renounce their power to think and retreat to a simple-minded respect for law and accepted 'truth.' " Writing in the *CEA Critic,* Pearson cites one of the book's many illustrations of this moral retreat: "The M.P.'s exemplify the overly law-abiding person who obeys law with no regard for humanity. They arrest Yossarian who is AWOL, but ignore the murdered girl on the street. By acting with pure rationality, like computers programmed only to enforce army regulations, they have become mechanical men." This incident, this "moment of epiphany," Raymond M. Olderman writes in *Beyond the Waste Land,* symbolizes "much of the entire novel's warning—that in place of the humane, . . . we find the thunder of the marching boot, the destruction of the human, arrested by the growth of the military-economic institution."

In the novel, the character Milo Minderbinder is the personification of this military-economic system. An enterprising mess officer, Minderbinder creates a one-man international syndicate whose slogan, "What's good for M&M Enterprises is good for the country," is used to justify a series of war-profiteering schemes. Minderbinder forms a private army of mercenaries (available to the highest bidder), corners the market on food and makes enormous profits selling it back to army mess halls, and convinces the U.S. government that it must buy up his overstock of chocolate-coated cotton balls in the interest of national security. Milo's empire soon stretches across Europe and North Africa. "His deals have made him mayor of every town in Sicily, Vice-Shah of Oran, Caliph of Baghdad, Imam of Damascus, and the Sheik of Araby," Brustein notes. Minderbinder's ambitions culminate in one final economic boom. As Olderman observes: "His wealth, influence, and sphere of action become enormous, until he and his profit-seeking are omnipotent and omnipresent. For business purposes he takes gas pellets from life jackets and morphine from first aid kits, leaving the drowning and the wounded without aid, but with the comforting message that 'what's good for M & M Enterprises is good for the country.' The ultimate inversion comes when Milo bombs and strafes his own camp for the Germans, who pay their bills more promptly than some, and kills many Americans at an enormous profit. In the face of criticism, he reveals the overwhelming virtue of his profit." In the *Canadian Review of American Studies,* Mike Franks concludes that "for Milo, contract, and the entire economic structure and ethical system it embodies and represents, is more sacred than human life."

"The military-economic institution rules, and the result is profit for some, but meaningless, inhuman parades for everyone else," Olderman writes. Confronted with this "totally irrelevant and bureaucratic power that either tosses man to his death or stamps out his spirit," Yossarian must make a moral decision. Olderman surveys Yossarian's alternatives: "He can be food for the cannon; he can make a deal with the system; or he can depart, deserting not the war with its implications of preserving political freedom, but abandoning a waste land, a dehumanized inverted, military-economic machine."

Yossarian, whose only wish is to stay alive, will not stand still for the "cannon." Kennard recounts Yossarian's second alternative: "[He] is given the chance to save his own life if he lies about Colonels Cathcart and Korn to their superior officers. He will, in accepting the offer, probably act as an incentive to his fellow officers to fly more missions in which many of them may be killed. He is given a chance . . . to join forces with the pestilences. After accepting the offer he is stabbed by Nately's whore and realizes that by joining those who are willing to kill, he has given them the right to kill him." Nately's whore, who shadows Yossarian after his fellow pilot Lt. Nately is killed in action, "pops out of every bush and around every corner to attack him because of Nately's death," Olderman writes. "However guiltless Yossarian may be of that one death, he is not guiltless—he has suffered as a victim, but has also been a victimizer. So Nately's whore will follow him forever, a kind of universal principle reminding him that he will always be unjustly beset and will probably always deserve it." In the book, Yossarian sympathizes with his determined pursuer: "Someone had to do something. Every victim was a culprit, every culprit a victim, and somebody had to stand up and do something and break the lousy chain of inherited habit that was imperiling them all."

As Bryant notes, "The only way that the circular justification of Catch-22 can be dealt with is by breaking out of the circle." Yossarian's friend Orr had broken free by sailing off into the Mediterranean in a rowboat, bound for neutral Sweden. Guided by Orr's example and by the wisdom imparted by the death of a young gunner named Snowden, Yossarian reneges on his agreement with the colonels and decides to desert. "In the course of the narrative," Olderman says, "occasional references are made to Snowden, . . . whose insides are shot out as his plane flies over Italy and who dies in Yossarian's arms. The experience profoundly affects Yossarian. As the narrative advances, the reader is given longer and longer glimpses of the incident. But not until Yossarian decides to try another way of getting out of combat than to agree with Korn and Cathcart do we get Snowden's full story. As the boy whimpers, 'I'm cold,' Yossarian, horrified, sees his entrails slither to the floor. There is a message in those entrails that teaches Yossarian, finally, what he must do. The message reads: 'Man was matter, that was Snowden's secret. Drop him out of a window and he'll fall. Set fire to him and he'll burn. Bury him like other kinds of garbage and he'll rot. The spirit gone, man is garbage.' " Yossarian refuses to discard his spirit; he heads for Sweden, the only place left in the world, he believes, which is free of mob rule. The impossibility of reaching Scandinavia via rowboat does not deter him. What is important is the act, the attempt, not the destination, Ronald Wallace observes in *The Last Laugh.* As Frank concludes, "The Sweden he aims for is located, perhaps, not so much in the real world as in the geography of the moral imagination." And Yossarian "is still at large," Heller surmises in an interview in the *Newark Star-Ledger.* "He hasn't been caught."

In the *Partisan Review,* Morris Dickstein comments: "The insanity of the system . . . breeds a defensive counter-insanity. . . . [Yossarian is] a protagonist caught up in the madness, who eventually steps outside it in a slightly mad way." Heller remarks in *Pages* that much of the humor in his novel arises out of his characters' attempts to escape, manipulate, and circumvent the logic of Catch-22. Before deserting, Yossarian tries to outwit Catch-22 in order to survive; he employs "caution, cowardice, defiance, subterfuge, stratagem, and subversion, through feigning illness, goofing off, and poisoning the company's food with laundry soap," Brustein writes. "He refuses to fly, goes naked, walks backward," adds Olderman.

"Heller's comedy is his artistic response to his vision of transcendent evil, as if the escape route of laughter were the only recourse from a malignant world," Brustein states. "[He] is concerned with that thin boundary of the surreal, the borderline between hilarity and horror. . . . Heller often manages to heighten the macabre obscenity of war much more effectively through its gruesome comic aspects than if he had written realistic descriptions. And thus, the most delicate pressure is enough to send us over the line from farce to phantasmagoria."

"I never thought of *Catch-22* as a comic novel," Heller says in the *New York Times.* "[But] . . . I wanted the reader to be amused, and . . . I wanted him to be ashamed that he was amused. My literary bent . . . is more toward the morbid and the tragic. Great carnage is taking place and my idea was to use humor to make ridiculous the things that are irrational and very terrible." Dickstein cites the profiteering of Minderbinder as one example of the tragic underpinning of Heller's comedy: "[Milo's] amoral machinations, so hilarious at first, become increasingly sombre, ugly and deadly—like so much else in the book—that we readers become implicated in our own earlier laughter." "Below its hilarity, so wild that it hurts, *Catch-22* is the strongest repudiation of our civilization, in fiction, to come out of World War II," Nelson Algren states in *Nation.* As Brustein concludes, Heller is "at war with much larger forces than the army. . . . [He] has been nourishing his grudges for so long that they have expanded to include the post-war American world. Through the agency of grotesque comedy, Heller has found a way to confront the humbug, hypocrisy, cruelty, and sheer stupidity of our mass society. . . . Through some miracle of prestidigitation, Pianosa has become a satirical microcosm of the macrocosmic idiocies of our time."

Heller's subsequent novels have continued this "war," extending the field of battle to governmental and corporate life. *Good as Gold,* Fremont-Smith notes in the *Village Voice,* is "touted . . . as doing for the White House what *Catch-22* did for the military," while the absurdity and alienation of the American business community is the focus of *Something Happened,* the story of Bob Slocum, a middle-level manager who describes himself as "one of those many people . . . who are without ambition already and have no hope."

"He is restless," Kurt Vonnegut, Jr., writes of Slocum in the *New York Times Book Review.* "He mourns the missed opportunities of his youth. He is itchy for raises and promotions, even though he despises his company and the jobs he does. He commits unsatisfying adulteries now and then at sales conferences in resort areas, during long lunch hours, or while pretending to work late at the office. He is exhausted," Vonnegut concludes. "He dreads old age." In the *New Republic,* William Kennedy analyzes Heller's restless protagonist: "Bob Slocum is no true friend of anybody's. He is a woefully lost figure with a profound emptiness, a sad, absurd, vicious, grasping, climbing, womanizing, cowardly, sadistic, groveling, loving, yearning, anxious, fearful victim of the indecipherable, indescribable malady of being born human." John W. Aldridge describes Slocum as "a man raging in a vacuum." In the *Saturday Review/World,* Aldridge examines Slocum's plight: "His mental state is shaped by chronic feelings of loss divorced from an understanding of what precisely has been lost. . . . The elements that are most real in Slocum's life are precisely those that might be considered conducive to peace of mind: material affluence and comfort, abundant leisure time, professional success, satisfactory marital relations, and considerable extracurricular sex with a number of attractive women. Yet these are the primary sources of his suffering because he is forever searching them for meaning and can find none." Aldridge continues: "He is haunted by the sense that at some time in the past something happened to him, something that he cannot remember but that changed him from a person who had aspirations for the future, who believed in himself and his work, who trusted others and was able to love, into the person he has since unaccountably become, a man who aspires to nothing, believes in nothing and no one, least of all himself, who no longer knows if he loves or is loved."

Slocum's loss of meaning is symbolized by his search for Virginia, for the lost dreams of his youth. "As Yossarian kept flashing back to that primal, piteous scene in the B-25 where his mortally wounded comrade, Snowden, whimpered in his arms, so Slocum keeps thinking back, with impacted self-pity and regret, to the sweetly hot, teasing, slightly older girl in the insurance office where he worked after graduating from high school, whom he could never bring himself to 'go all the way' with," Edward Grossman writes in *Commentary*. "He blew it," D. Keith Mano remarks in the *National Review,* "and this piddling missed opportunity comes to stand for loss in general. He makes you accompany him again and again, and again and again to the back staircase for a quiet feel that never matures." As Mano notes, "Slocum becomes semi-obsessed: telephones the insurance company to ascertain if his . . . girlfriend is still employed there, if *he* is still employed there. And he isn't." Instead, Slocum finds that this haunting figure of a girl, like his own spirit, has committed suicide.

"What he wants now is to want something the way he once wanted Virginia," Kennedy declares. "Why can't some things other than stone remain always as they used to be, he wonders. Sad. What happened is that something happened. . . . [Slocum] spends the whole book trying to recreate what was and what is, speculating endlessly on what caused the ruin of such glorious innocence, such exciting desire. He has no more desire, only a stale, processed lust."

Clearly, something happened to create such unhappiness. "Something happened indeed," Benjamin DeMott finds, "namely the death of the heart." In the novel, Slocum says he wants "to continue receiving my raise in salary each year, and a good cash bonus at Christmastime . . . to be allowed to take my place on the rostrum at the next company convention . . . and make my three minute report to the company of the work we have been doing in my department." In the *Atlantic Monthly,* DeMott attributes Slocum's pain to the fact that "caring at levels deeper than these is beyond him." Melvin Maddocks points out that "it is not what has happened, but what has not happened to Slocum that constitutes his main problem." In a *Time* review, Maddocks describes Slocum as "a weightless figure with no pull of gravity morally or emotionally" who can love only his nine-year-old son, and then only for "brief, affecting moments."

Slocum's life revolves around his office and home; in both of these worlds he folds, under the weight of external pressures and inner fears, into a helpless state of alienation. "Money and power and the corporation [are] for Bob Slocum what war and death and the Air Force had been for Yossarian," John Leonard notes in the *New York Times.* Just as Yossarian feared his own commanders and compatriots, so does Slocum, in the more secure confines of the business organization, live in fear of his associates. "He's afraid of closed doors and of accident reports. He's afraid of five people in his office," Jerome Klinkowitz observes. "At home Slocum fears and distrusts his family, although he

loves them in his way," Aldridge says. "Slocum's wife is attractive and intelligent but bored and without a sense of meaning in her life. She has begun to drink in the afternoon and to flirt at parties." The Slocums, as Kennedy details, are the parents of "an insecure and nasty 16-year-old daughter whose shins [Slocum] wants to kick, an idiot son he is sick of and would like to unload, another son, aged nine, who is the principal joy of his life and whom he ruins by allowing the company's values (get to the top, don't give your money away, compete, compete) smother the boy's wondrously selfless and noncompetitive good nature." "One cannot but recognize that many of the pressures on Slocum are generated by the nuclear family itself and by the establishments in which the family is trained," Elaine Glover writes in *Stand*. With the exception of Derek, the mentally retarded son, none of Slocum's family have names, Fremont-Smith points out. "All of them are unhappy in various ways, and Slocum knows it is largely his fault." "Slocum does his deadly best to persuade us, with his tap-tap-tapping of facts, that he is compelled to be as unhappy as he is, not because of . . . flaws in his own character, but because of the facts," Vonnegut states.

However much the "facts" may conspire against Slocum, the real pressure is exerted from within. As Heller comments in the *Newark Star-Ledger:* "All the threats to Bob Slocum are internal. His enemy is his own fear, his own anxiety." According to an *America* review, "Heller has replaced the buzzing, booming world of an army at war with the claustrophobic universe of Bob Slocum's psyche, where all the complications, contradictions and absurdities are generated from within. . . . Like Yossarian, Slocum always feels trapped—by his wife, by his children, but mostly by himself." Slocum, who giggles inwardly at the thought of rape and glances over his shoulder for sodomists, confesses, "Things are going on inside me I cannot control and do not admire." "Within and without, his world is an unregenerate swamp of rack and ruin," Pearl K. Bell asserts in the *New Leader.* "Pathologically disassociated from himself, Slocum is a chameleon, taking on the gestures and vocabularies of whichever colleague he is with; even his handwriting is a forgery, borrowed from a boyhood friend." This disassociation is more than a middle-age malaise; it is symptomatic of a deeper affliction, a crippling of the spirit that leaves Slocum barely enough strength to lament, "I wish I knew what to wish."

As the novel draws to a close, Slocum finally and tragically expresses his love for his favorite son. As the boy lies bleeding after being struck by a car, someone yells, "Something happened!" Slocum rushes towards the child, horrified: "He is dying. A terror, a pallid, pathetic shock more dreadful than any I have been able to imagine, has leaped into his face. I can't stand it. He can't stand it. He hugs me. He looks beggingly at me for help. His screams are piercing. I can't bear to see him suffering such agony and fright. I have to do something. I hug his face deeper into the crook of my shoulder. I hug him tightly with both my arms. I squeeze. 'Death,' says the doctor, 'was due to asphyxiation. The boy was smothered. He had superficial lacerations of the scalp and face, a bruised face, a deep cut on his arm. That was all.' "

According to *Playboy, Something Happened* "unleashed a fusillade of violently mixed reviews. . . . Nearly three quarters of the critics viewed Heller's looping, memory-tape narrative as a dazzling, if depressing, literary tour de force." Fremont-Smith, for instance, calls *Something Happened* a "very fine, wrenchingly depressing" novel. "It gnaws at one, slowly and almost nuzzlingly at first, mercilessly toward the end. It hurts. It gives the willies." In his *New York Times Book Review* article, Vonnegut finds that the book is "splendidly put together and hypnotic to read. It is as clear and hard-edged as a cut diamond." Maddocks, however, labels Heller's second novel "a terrific let-down," while Grossman believes it is "a lump compared with *Catch-22.*" L. E. Sissman of the *New Yorker,* who calls *Something Happened* "a painful mistake," cites a frequent criticism of the novel: "[Heller] indulges in overkill. When we have seen Bob Slocum suffer a failure of nerve (or a failure of common humanity) in a dozen different situations, we do not need to see him fail a dozen times more." Mano asserts that "you can start *Something Happened* on page 359, read through to the end, and still pass a multiple choice test in plot, character, style. . . . [It] is overlong, a bit of an imposition."

Slocum's repetitive monologue has been criticized by certain reviewers, but, as George J. Searles points out in *Critique,* "Slocum, a businessman rather than a man of letters, is by necessity a limited narrator. Although articulate and aware of the fundamentals of language . . ., he is not a *writer.* His mode of speech—and the book has the feel of being spoken, rather than written—is flat, ordinary, and unexciting, and is an accurate reflection of his personality." Caroline Blackwood is uncomfortable with the narrative voice of the story for a different reason. In the *Times Literary Supplement,* she asks: "Is it possible [that such a man as Slocum] would be capable of viewing himself, his values, his work, and his relationship with his family, with the brutal and humorous introspection of Mr. Heller's central character? . . . Slocum asks for an enormous suspension of disbelief. Quite often he appears schizophrenic; the superior wit, insights, and sensibilities of his creator are superimposed so erratically and unsuitably on this commonplace and tiresome man." Schroth, however, finds Slocum a convincing narrator. He writes in *Commonweal:* "Who can read the paranoid utterances of Robert Slocum . . . and not recognize to some degree his own share in the competitive madness and chronic anxiety of American life? . . . [*Something Happened*] is a book which sums up the spiritual emptiness of the 1970s so excruciatingly that it may be another decade before many critics adequately appreciate it and most Americans can read it with sufficient detachment." Finally, Aldridge believes Heller "has discovered and possessed new territories of the imagination, and he has produced a major work of fiction, one that is as distinctive of its kind as *Catch-22* but more ambitious and profound, an abrasively brilliant commentary on American life that must surely be recognized as the most important novel to appear in this country in at least a decade."

Heller's third novel "indicts a class of clerks," Leonard writes in the *New York Times. Good as Gold* is a fictional expose of the absurd workings of the machinery of government, of a politics reduced to public relations, of a President who spends most of his first year in office penning *My Year in the White House,* of an administrative aide who mouths such wisdom as "Just tell the truth . . . even if you have to lie" and "This President doesn't want yes-men. What we want are independent men of integrity who will agree with all our decisions after we make them." Into this world stumbles Bruce Gold, a professor of English who is called to public service after writing a favorable review of the Presidential book. Gold is rewarded for his kind words with a "spokesman" position but yearns for higher duty; specifically, he wants to be Secretary of State, more specifically, he wants to be the first *real* Jewish Secretary of State (Gold is convinced that Henry Kissinger, who prayed with Richard Nixon and "made war gladly," cannot possibly be Jewish). For his part, Gold chips in by coining such expressions as "You're boggling my mind" and "I don't know," phrases that enter the lexicon of the press conference and earn Gold the admiration of his superiors. As *Time*'s R. Z. Sheppard observes: "[Gold] is no stranger to dou-

ble-think. A literary hustler whose interest in government is a sham, he does not even vote, a fact 'he could not publicly disclose without bringing blemish to the image he had constructed for himself as a radical moderate.' " Gold was schooled in absurdity during his tenure at a New York City university, where he devised a curriculum such that "it was now possible . . . for a student to graduate with an English major after spending all four years of academic study watching foreign movies in a darkened classroom." With this experience as a huckster of the academy, Gold, it would appear, is ready for Washington.

In the beginning, Gold flourishes in his new environment, where, according to Sheppard, "catch-22 is now Potomac newspeak." He meets the Important People, elbows his way onto a Presidential Commission, and prepares to exchange his homey Jewish wife for the promiscuous daughter of a wealthy bigot in order to ease his advance to the upper echelons of the Administration. Along the way he is more than willing to endure the anti-Semitic prattle of his potential father-in-law and others, learning, as Leonard says, "to lick the boots that specialize in stepping on you."

Like *Something Happened, Good as Gold* is "another painful portrait of a bright but almost empty man watching his soul melt in his hands," writes Schroth. "The book is essentially about Jews, especially those like Gold, who wants to escape his identity while exploiting it, particularly by making a lot of money on a big book about Jews," Leonard Michaels comments in the *New York Times Book Review.* (Gold, despite his ignorance of his heritage, has received a substantial advance from a publisher for a book on "The Jewish Experience in America.") "It is one of the main themes of *Good as Gold* that Jews violate themselves in their relations with such unreal creatures of their own minds, especially when Jews yearn for tall blondes and jobs in Washington where successful Jews are slaves," Michaels continues. "Gold yearns to escape what he is so that he can become what he isn't, which is precisely what he hates. He nearly succeeds, nearly becomes a Washington non-Jewish Jew, a rich, powerful slave with a tall blonde wife." Gold, unlike other characters in the story, is very much aware of his moral degeneration; a passage from the book reads: "How much lower would he crawl to rise to the top? he asked himself with wretched self-reproval. Much, much lower, he answered in improving spirit, and felt purged of hypocrisy by the time he was ready for dinner." "Unlike Heller's earlier hero, Yossarian, Gold pants to embrace the insanity of our time," Peter S. Prescott observes in *Newsweek.* "His need for money and the chance to escape his suffocating family prick his ambition."

"He is totally out of sync with his family," Alex Taylor says in the *Detroit Free Press.* In the *Los Angeles Times Book Review,* Darryl Ponicsan explains: "He's got two sons away at college and he's not crazy about them. . . . He won't let them come home for a weekend. He's afraid of his daughter, who lives at home. He's bored with his wife, Belle. He has an older brother, Sid, who sets him up at every opportunity. . . . He has four older sisters and their mates harping about, an aged father who admits to having liked him briefly when he was a baby and a stepmother who suffers—if that's the word, and it isn't—insanity, ceaselessly knitting wool and talking just like a Joseph Heller character." Jack Beatty finds that "the scenes of the Golds at dinner belong to the heights of comedy. . . . These family dinners are torture for Gold. Yet underneath [all the eating] and the practiced taunts, the feverish intimacy of the Gold family, there are some abiding values at work which Heller wants us to recognize and, I think, celebrate." In the *New Republic,* Beatty sees Gold's brother Sid as an example of such values:

"Sid, a prosperous businessman, is no hero; he's just a good man. He hated his father, yet bailed the old man out of his last business, and still pays the bills for his Florida retirement. He resented his smarter kid brother but paid his way through Columbia nonetheless. Sid has done his duty." "The scenes with the family might at first seem disconnected from the Washington scenes," Ronald Hayman points out, "but the pivotal joke is that someone who can fly so high as Gold should be treated with such savage contempt by his family, should be so inept at defending himself, and so incapable of staying away."

In his *New York Times* article, Leonard elaborates on Gold's dilemma: "What is being proposed is that being brought up lower middle-class Jewish in this country means being humiliated by your own family; that you assimilate, by groveling, a vacuum and a lie; that you have masturbatory dreams of acquiring the power to exact revenge on the father who disdains you; that to acquire such power you will be willing to mortgage every morsel of your capacity for critical discrimination; that you lick the boots that specialize in stepping on you, and hate yourself in the morning." Leonard adds: "Those critics who, over the years, have suggested that [Heller] be more Jewish in his fiction are going to be sorry they asked."

Indeed, Heller's treatment of "The Jewish Experience in America" has aroused criticism, including accusations that *Good as Gold* is anti-Semitic. According to Sheppard, the book "is a savage, intemperately funny satire on the assimilation of the Jewish tradition of liberalism into the American main chance. It is a delicate subject, off-limits to non-Jews fearful of being thought anti-Semitic and unsettling to successful Jewish intellectuals whose views may have drifted to the right in middle age. Heller, who is neither a Gentile or a card-carrying intellectual, goes directly for the exposed nerve." Lyons observes that "it was not so long ago . . . when a book dealing in such cultural stereotypes as Heller employs throughout would have been closely scrutinized by a self-appointed committee of rabbis and Jewish intellectuals to determine whether, on the balance, the portraits presented were 'good for the Jews' or 'bad for the Jews'. . . . Such stereotypes are nothing but peasant superstition and ought to be dismissed as such." In *Books and Bookmen,* Hayman points out that the Gentiles in Heller's satirical novel are "even more obnoxious" than the Jewish characters. "Both, fortunately, are extremely entertaining." But Fremont-Smith asserts in the *Village Voice* that *Good as Gold* is not "without offensiveness. It does bore. It is also anti-Semitic. If Heller believes (and I'm willing to think he thinks he does) that everything is rotten to the core, this goes double for the Jews. . . . The Jews in *Good as Gold* are uniformly portrayed as snivelling, deceitful, self-aggrandizing, and ambitious beyond their worth: *Much, much lower, he answered in improving spirit.*"

In the novel, Heller depicts Henry Kissinger as the epitome of the "non-Jewish Jew" and examines, as Schroth notes, "the germ of Kissingerism within each of us." "Gold's real tension comes from the fact that his own morality dangles barely a ledge above his enemy's. He knows the corrupting tendency within himself, in every intellectual and journalist to become corrupted by the mere smell of power, to become a Kissinger . . . and, worst of all," Schroth adds, "to forsake his heritage, to forget or deny he is a Jew." In the *New York Review of Books,* Thomas R. Edwards finds that Gold's political aspirations have "one distinct drawback. Gold hates everything connected with Henry Kissinger, sees him as a loathsomely pushy cartoon-Jew and a closet Nazi. . . . Whatever the merits of this view of Kissinger's character, Gold's assault on his good name . . . is exhilaratingly energetic and winning. Its single-mindedness serves the purposes

not only of comedy and moral outrage but also gives the novel its structure." Similarly, Jack Beatty of the *New Republic* comments: "The risk Gold runs in trying to become the first real Jewish Secretary of State is that he will be forced to act like Henry Kissinger, and that would mean his moral destruction. . . . *Good as Gold* is a cultural event. A major novelist takes on our greatest celebrity with all the wit and language at his command, and . . . a central historical figure [has] been .. intimately castigated by the Word. Score one for literature." Gene Lyons in *Nation,* however, believes that the attack on Kissinger is only "occasionally funny, [and] often slides over into what seems like simple malice, and pretty much for its own sake. . . . Satirizing the man by presenting clippings from Anthony Lewis is not very funny or effective. They were much better the first time around." In the end, Gold is finally offered his alter ego's former cabinet position but, as Beatty observes, "is recalled to New York and to himself " by the death of his brother Sid. Like Yossarian, Gold decides to "desert" his absurd world; he refuses the coveted post, choosing instead to preside over the funeral of his brother, the grief of his family, and, finally, the restoration of his own integrity. "He is a man with a profound moral sense," William McPherson asserts in *Book World.* "Once in a while he is reminded of it, and reminds us."

The critical reaction to *Good as Gold* has been divided. Edwards remarks that "*Good as Gold,* if hardly a perfect novel, is continuously alive, very funny, and finally coherent. . . . Like Heller's other novels, [it] is a book that takes large risks: it is sometimes rambling, occasionally self-indulgent, not always sure of the difference between humor and silliness. But this time the risks pay off. . . . Heller is among the novelists of the last two decades who matter." The *Hudson Review* describes it as a "big, ugly book," and Aram Bakshian, Jr., of the *National Review* calls it "an embarrassing flop. . . . The best [Heller] has to offer us in his latest novel is fool's gold." Hayman finds the novel is flawed but says that "nothing is unforgivable when a book makes you laugh out loud so often," and McPherson concludes: "When I didn't hate it, I loved it. Joseph Heller, of all people, would understand that." Finally, Mel Brooks in *Book World* rates *Good as Gold* as "somewhere between *The Brothers Karamazov* and those dirty little books we used to read . . . It's closer to *Karamazov.*"

Five years after publishing *Good as Gold* Heller produced *God Knows,* a satiric novel whose tone has been likened to that of a stand-up comedy routine. The narrator of *God Knows* is the Old Testament's David—the killer of Goliath, poet and singer for Biblical royalty, king of Israel, and father of the wise ruler Solomon (who is portrayed in the book as an idiot). Despite some critics' objections that the book lacks a unifying point, reviewers have overwhelmingly proclaimed it, as does Stuart Evans in the London *Times,* "a very funny, very serious, very *good* novel." *Picture This,* published in 1988, is a reflection on such figures in Western history as Dutch painter Rembrandt, Greek philosophers Socrates and Plato, and twentieth-century U.S. presidents. Similar in tone to *God Knows, Picture This* revels in anachronisms, mentioning the "freedom fighters" of the war between Athens and Sparta, for example, and of "police actions" in the fifth century B.C. A few of the author's main themes, according to Richard Rayner of the London *Times,* are that "power and intellect are incompatible, that politicians wage disastrous wars for no good reason, . . . and that humanity learns nothing from its mistakes." Rayner adds, though, that "Heller does all this in *Picture This* and gets away with it most of the time, for the simple reason that he is funny. . . . He refuses to take institutions seriously; or rather, . . . he takes them *so* seriously they become hilarious."

While working on *God Knows* during the early 1980s, Heller was stricken with a nerve disease, Guillain-Barre syndrome, that left him paralyzed for several months. Though the author became too weak to move and almost too weak to breathe on his own, he eventually regained his strength and recovered from the often fatal disorder. After completing *God Knows,* Heller began writing his first nonfiction book, *No Laughing Matter,* with Speed Vogel, a friend who helped him considerably during his illness. *No Laughing Matter* tells the story of Heller's convalescence and his friendship with Vogel in sections that are written alternately by the two men. Noting that Vogel's observations "provide comic relief to Mr. Heller's medical self-absorption," *New York Times* writer Christopher Lehmann-Haupt praises the book as both serious and comic. "It was indeed no laughing matter," Lehmann-Haupt observes. "And yet we do laugh, reading this account of his ordeal. We laugh because as well as being an astute observer of his suffering . . . Heller can be blackly funny about it." The reviewer adds that "most of all, we laugh at the way Mr. Heller and his friends relate to each other. . . . [Their] interaction is not only richly amusing, it is positively cheering."

MEDIA ADAPTATIONS: Catch-22 was produced as a motion picture by Paramount in 1970. The film was directed by Mike Nichols, adapted by Buck Henry, and starred Alan Arkin as Yossarian.

BIOGRAPHICAL/CRITICAL SOURCES:

BOOKS

A Dangerous Crossing, Southern Illinois University Press, 1973.

Aichinger, Peter, *The American Soldier in Fiction, 1880-1963,* Iowa State University Press, 1975.

American Novels of the Second World War, Mouton, 1969.

Authors in the News, Volume 1, Gale, 1976.

Bergonzi, Bernard, *The Situation of the Novel,* University of Pittsburgh Press, 1970.

Bier, Jesse, *The Rise and Fall of American Humor,* Holt, 1968.

Bruccoli, Matthew J. and C. E. Frazer Clark, Jr., editors, *Pages: The World of Books, Writers, and Writing,* Gale, 1976.

Bryant, Jerry H., *The Open Decision: The Contemporary American Novel and Its Intellectual Background,* Free Press, 1970.

Burgess, Anthony, *The Novel Now: A Guide to Contemporary Fiction,* Norton, 1967.

Colmer, John, editor, *Approaches to the Novel,* Rigby (Adelaide), 1967.

Contemporary Literary Criticism, Gale, Volume 1, 1973, Volume 3, 1975, Volume 5, 1976, Volume 8, 1978, Volume 11, 1979, Volume 36, 1986.

Dictionary of Literary Biography, Gale, Volume 2: *American Novelists since World War II,* 1978, *Yearbook: 1980,* 1981, Volume 28: *Twentieth-Century American Jewish Fiction Writers,* 1984.

Friedman, Bruce Jay, editor, *Black Humor,* Bantam, 1965.

Harris, Charles B., *Contemporary American Novelists of the Absurd,* College and University Press, 1971.

Harrison, Gilbert A., editor, *The Critic as Artist: Essays on Books, 1920-1970,* Liveright, 1972.

Hauck, Richard Boyd, *A Cheerful Nihilism: Confidence and the Absurd in American Humorous Fiction,* Indiana University Press, 1971.

Heller, Joseph, *Catch-22,* Simon & Schuster, 1961.

Heller, Joseph, *Something Happened,* Knopf, 1974.

Heller, Joseph, *Good as Gold,* Simon & Schuster, 1979.

Kazin, Alfred, *The Bright Book of Life: American Novelists and Storytellers from Hemingway to Mailer,* Little, Brown, 1973.

Kiley, Frederick and Walter McDonald, editors, *A Catch-22 Casebook,* Crowell, 1973.

Kostelanetz, Richard, editor, *On Contemporary Literature,* Avon, 1964.

Literary Horizons: A Quarter Century of American Fiction, New York University Press, 1970.

Littlejohn, David, *Interruptions,* Grossman, 1970.

Miller, James E., Jr., *Quests Surd and Absurd: Essays in American Literature,* University of Chicago Press, 1967.

Miller, Wayne Charles, *An Armed America, Its Face in Fiction: A History of the American Military Novel,* New York University Press, 1970.

Moore, Harry T., editor, *Contemporary American Novelists,* Southern Illinois University Press, 1964.

Moore, Harry T., editor, *American Dreams, American Nightmares,* Southern Illinois University Press, 1970.

Nagel, James, editor, *Critical Essays on Catch-22,* Dickenson, 1974.

Nelson, Gerald B., *Ten Versions of America,* Knopf, 1972.

New American Arts, Horizon Publishing, 1965.

Number and Nightmare: Forms of Fantasy in Contemporary Fiction, Archon, 1975.

Olderman, Raymond M., *Beyond the Waste Land: The American Novel in the Nineteen-Sixties,* Yale University Press, 1972.

Podhoretz, Norman, *Doings and Undoings: The Fifties and After in American Writing,* Farrar, Straus, 1964.

Richter, D. H., *Fable's End: Completeness and Closure in Rhetorical Fiction,* University of Chicago Press, 1974.

Scott, Nathan A., editor, *Adversity and Grace: Studies in Recent American Literature,* University of Chicago Press, 1968.

Scotto, Robert M., editor, *A Critical Edition of Catch-22,* Delta, 1973.

Tanner, Tony, *City of Words,* Harper, 1971.

Wallace, Ronald, *The Last Laugh,* University of Missouri Press, 1979.

Whitbread, Thomas B., editor, *Seven Contemporary Authors,* University of Texas Press, 1966.

PERIODICALS

America, October 26, 1974, May 19, 1979.

Arizona Quarterly, winter, 1980.

Atlantic Monthly, January, 1962, October, 1974, March, 1979.

Book Digest, May, 1976.

Books, October, 1967.

Books and Bookmen, June, 1979.

Book Week, February 6, 1966.

Book World, October 6, 1974, March 11, 1979, December 9, 1979.

Canadian Review of American Studies, spring, 1976.

CEA Critic, November, 1974.

Chicago Tribune Book World, March 18, 1979.

Christian Science Monitor, October 9, 1974, March 28, 1979, April 9, 1979.

Commentary, November, 1974, June, 1979.

Commonweal, December 5, 1974, May 11, 1979.

Critique, Volume 5, number 2, 1962, Volume 7, number 2, 1964-65, Volume 9, number 2, 1967, Volume 22, number 2, 1970, Volume 17, number 1, 1975, Volume 18, number 3, 1977.

Detroit Free Press, March 18, 1979.

Harper's, March, 1979.

Hudson Review, winter, 1979-80.

Life, January 1, 1968.

Listener, October 24, 1974, May 10, 1979.

Los Angeles Times Book Review, March 25, 1979.

Mademoiselle, August, 1963.

Midwest Quarterly, winter, 1974.

Mosaic, fall, 1968, spring, 1971.

Motive, February, 1968.

Nation, November 4, 1961, October 19, 1974, June 16, 1979.

National Review, November 22, 1974, July 20, 1979.

Newark Star-Ledger, October 6, 1974.

New Leader, October 28, 1974, March 26, 1979.

New Republic, November 13, 1961, October 19, 1974, March 10, 1979.

New Statesman, October 25, 1974.

Newsweek, October 14, 1974, December 30, 1974, March 12, 1979.

New York, September 30, 1974.

New Yorker, December 9, 1961, November 25, 1974, April 16, 1979.

New York Review of Books, October 17, 1974, April 5, 1979.

New York Times, October 23, 1961, December 3, 1967, December 7, 1967, June 19, 1970, October 1, 1974, March 5, 1979, September 19, 1984, February 13, 1986, September 1, 1988.

New York Times Book Review, October 22, 1961, September 9, 1962, March 3, 1968, October 6, 1974, February 2, 1975, May 15, 1977, March 11, 1979.

New York Times Sunday Magazine, March 4, 1979, January 12, 1986.

Paris Review, winter, 1974.

Partisan Review, Volume 43, number 2, 1976.

Playboy, June, 1975.

Publishers Weekly, November 1, 1985.

Richmond Times-Dispatch, December 8, 1974.

Rolling Stone, April 16, 1981.

Saturday Review, October 14, 1961, August 31, 1968, February 6, 1971.

Saturday Review/World, October 19, 1974.

Spectator, June 15, 1962, October 26, 1974, May 5, 1979.

Stand, Volume 16, number 3, 1975.

Studies in the Novel, spring, 1971, spring, 1972.

Time, October 27, 1961, February 1, 1963, June 15, 1970, October 14, 1974, March 12, 1979.

Times (London), November 29, 1984, October 19, 1988, October 20, 1988.

Times Literary Supplement, October 25, 1974.

Twentieth Century Literature, January, 1967, October, 1973.

U.S. News and World Report, April 9, 1979.

Village Voice, March 5, 1979.

Vogue, January 1, 1963.

Washington Post, October 8, 1984, August 31, 1988.

Yale Review, summer, 1975.

*   *   *

HELLMAN, Lillian (Florence) 1906-1984

PERSONAL: Born June 20, 1906, in New Orleans, La.; died of cardiac arrest June 30, 1984, in Martha's Vineyard, Mass.; daughter of Max Bernard (a businessman) and Julia (Newhouse) Hellman; married Arthur Kober (a writer), December 30, 1925 (divorced, 1932). *Education:* Attended New York University, 1922-24, and Columbia University, 1924.

ADDRESSES: Home—630 Park Avenue, New York, N.Y. 10021; and Vineyard Haven, Mass. 02568. *Agent*—Harold Matson, 22 East 40th St., New York, N.Y. 10016.

CAREER: Playwright and author. Horace Liveright, Inc. (publisher), New York City, manuscript reader, 1924-25; theatrical

playreader in New York City, 1927-30; Metro-Goldwyn-Mayer, Hollywood, Calif., scenario reader, 1930-31; returned to New York City, 1932, working as part-time playreader for producer Harold Shulman. Taught or conducted seminars in literature and writing at Yale University, 1966, and at Massachusetts Institute of Technology and Harvard University. Director of plays in New York City, including "Another Part of the Forest," 1946, and "Montserrat," 1949. Narrator, Marc Blitzstein Memorial Concert, New York City, 1964.

MEMBER: American Academy of Arts and Letters, American Academy of Arts and Sciences (fellow), Dramatists Guild (member of council), American Federation of Television and Radio Artists.

AWARDS, HONORS: New York Drama Critics Circle Award, 1941, for "Watch on the Rhine," and 1960, for "Toys in the Attic"; Academy Award nominations for screenplays "The Little Foxes," 1941, and "The North Star," 1943; M.A. from Tufts University, 1950; Brandeis University Creative Arts Medal in Theater, 1960-61; LL.D. from Wheaton College, 1961, Douglass College of Rutgers University, Smith College, and New York University, all 1974, Franklin and Marshall College, 1975, and Columbia University, 1976; Gold Medal for drama from National Institute of Arts and Letters, 1964; National Book Award in Arts and Letters, 1969, for *An Unfinished Woman,* and nomination, 1974, for *Pentimento: A Book of Portraits;* elected to Theatre Hall of Fame, 1973; MacDowell Medal, 1976.

WRITINGS:

(Editor and author of introduction) Anton Chekhov, *Selected Letters,* Farrar, Straus, 1955, reprinted, 1984.

(Editor and author of introduction) Dashiell Hammett, *The Big Knockover* (selected stories and short novels), Random House, 1966 (published in England as *The Dashiell Hammett Story Omnibus,* Cassell, 1966).

An Unfinished Woman (memoirs; also see below), Little, Brown, 1969, reprinted, Macmillan (London), 1987.

Pentimento: A Book of Portraits (memoirs; also see below), Little, Brown, 1973.

Scoundrel Time (memoirs; also see below), introduction by Garry Wills, Little, Brown, 1976.

Three (contains *An Unfinished Woman, Pentimento: A Book of Portraits, Scoundrel Time,* and new commentaries by author), Little, Brown, 1979.

Maybe (memoirs), Little, Brown, 1980.

(With Peter S. Feibleman) *Eating Together: Recollections and Recipes,* Little, Brown, 1984.

PLAYS

The Children's Hour (first produced in New York City at Maxine Elliott's Theatre, November 20, 1934; also see below), Knopf, 1934, acting edition, Dramatists Play Service, 1953, reprinted, 1988.

Days to Come (first produced in New York City at Vanderbilt Theatre, December 15, 1936; also see below), Knopf, 1936.

The Little Foxes (three-act; first produced in New York City at National Theatre, February 15, 1939; also see below), Random House, 1939, acting edition, Dramatists Play Service, 1942, reprinted, 1986.

Watch on the Rhine (three-act; first produced on Broadway at Martin Beck Theatre, April 1, 1941; also see below), Random House, 1941, limited edition with foreword by Dorothy Parker, privately printed, 1942, acting edition, Dramatists Play Service, 1944, reprinted, 1986.

Four Plays (contains *The Children's Hour, Days to Come, The Little Foxes,* and *Watch on the Rhine*), Random House, 1942.

The Searching Wind (two-act; first produced in New York City at Fulton Theatre, April 12, 1944; also see below), Viking, 1944.

Another Part of the Forest (three-act; first produced at Fulton Theatre, November 20, 1946; also see below), Viking, 1947.

Montserrat (two-act; adapted from Emmanuel Robles's play; first produced at Fulton Theatre, October 29, 1949; also see below), Dramatists Play Service, 1950.

The Autumn Garden (three-act; first produced in New York City at Coronet Theatre, March 7, 1951; also see below), Little, Brown, 1951, revised acting edition, Dramatists Play Service, 1952.

The Lark (adapted from Jean Anouilh's play *L'Alouette;* first produced on Broadway at Longacre Theatre, November 17, 1955; also see below), Random House, 1956, acting edition, Dramatists Play Service, 1957.

(Author of book) Leonard Bernstein, *Candide: A Comic Opera Based on Voltaire's Satire* (first produced on Broadway at Martin Beck Theatre, December 1, 1956; also see below), Random House, 1957.

Toys in the Attic (three-act; first produced Off-Broadway at Hudson Theatre, February 25, 1960; also see below), Random House, 1960, acting edition, Samuel French, 1960.

Six Plays (contains *Another Part of the Forest, The Autumn Garden, The Children's Hour, Days to Come, The Little Foxes,* and *Watch on the Rhine*), Modern Library, 1960, limited edition with illustrations by Mark Bellerose, Franklin Library, 1978.

My Mother, My Father and Me (adapted from Burt Blechman's novel *How Much?;* first produced on Broadway at Plymouth Theatre, April 6, 1963; also see below), Random House, 1963.

Collected Plays (contains *The Children's Hour, Days to Come, The Little Foxes, Watch on the Rhine, The Searching Wind, Another Part of the Forest, Montserrat, The Autumn Garden, The Lark, Candide, Toys in the Attic,* and *My Mother, My Father and Me*), Little, Brown, 1972.

The Little Foxes [and] *Another Part of the Forest,* Viking, 1973.

Also author of unpublished and unproduced play, "Dear Queen."

SCREENPLAYS

(With Mordaunt Shairp) "Dark Angel," United Artists, 1935.

"These Three" (based on "The Children's Hour"), United Artists, 1936.

"Dead End," United Artists, 1937.

"The Little Foxes" (based on her play), RKO, 1941.

The North Star, a Motion Picture about Some Russian People (released by RKO, 1943; later released for television broadcast as "Armored Attack"), introduction by Louis Kronenberger, Viking, 1943.

"The Searching Wind," Paramount, 1946.

"The Chase," Columbia, 1966.

CONTRIBUTOR OF PLAYS TO ANTHOLOGIES

Four Contemporary American Plays, Random House, 1961.
Six Modern American Plays, Random House, 1966.
A Treasury of the Theatre: Modern Drama from Oscar Wilde to Eugene Ionesco, Simon & Schuster, 1967.

OTHER

Pentimento: Memory as Distilled by Time (sound recording), Center for Cassette Studies, c. 1973.

Lillian Hellman: The Great Playwright Candidly Reflects on a Long Rich Life (sound recording), Center for Cassette Studies, c. 1977.

Conversations with Lillian Hellman, edited by Jackson R. Bryer, University Press of Mississippi, 1986.

Contributor of sketches to "Broadway Revue," produced in New York City, 1968; contributor of articles to *Collier's, New York Times, Travel and Leisure,* and other publications. Hellman's manuscripts are collected at the University of Texas at Austin.

SIDELIGHTS: She has been called one of the most influential female playwrights of the twentieth century; the voice of social consciousness in American letters; the theatre's intellectual standard-bearer—and yet Lillian Hellman always prided herself on avoiding easy labels. At the time of her death in 1984, the author/playwright could claim more long-running Broadway dramas—five—than could other renowned American writers like Tennessee Williams, Edward Albee, and Thornton Wilder. Ironically, though, Hellman was perhaps best remembered by a later generation of Americans for posing in a mink coat in an advertisement titled "What Becomes a Legend Most?"

Born in turn-of-the-century New Orleans to a struggling shoe merchant and his upper-middle-class wife, Hellman had the advantages of a solid education and a well-traveled childhood. Her ties to her mother had Hellman pondering well into adulthood. "So far apart were the temperaments of mother and daughter—for Hellman was always a spirited, independent child—that only after her mother had been dead for five years did [Hellman] realize how much she had loved her," according to Carol MacNicholas in a *Dictionary of Literary Biography* article on the playwright.

By the early 1920s Hellman had left college to work as a manuscript reader for a New York City publishing firm—her first professional foray into the world of writing that she would later dominate. For the ambitious Hellman, the benefits of working in publishing ran beyond five o'clock. "After working hours, [the publishers'] parties gave Hellman her firsthand acquaintance with the adventurous, often reckless life of the literary world of the 1920s," said MacNicholas. "The bohemian life appealed to the young woman who was just advancing into her own twenties; she enjoyed the glamour of the writer's world and nurtured the impulse to find excitement in whatever she did."

For Hellman, that impulse led her into an early marriage to press agent Arthur Kober, and career jumps into playreading and book reviewing. Following her husband to Paris, Hellman made side trips to 1929 Germany, where the embryonic Nazi movement gave the woman her first exposure to anti-Semitism, a theme that would later emerge in her plays "Watch on the Rhine" and "The Searching Wind." By 1930 the Kobers had moved to Hollywood, where Hellman read scripts for Metro-Goldwyn-Mayer. It was there, too, that she met the mystery novelist/screenwriter Dashiell Hammett.

Sensing that her marriage to Kober was failing, Hellman turned to Hammett, best known for the stylish suspense novel *The Thin Man* (some critics believe that Hammett based his suave detectives Nick and Nora Charles on himself and Hellman), and he became her lover and mentor. Hammett encouraged Hellman's first produced play, "The Children's Hour," in 1933 (an earlier play, "Dear Queen," was neither published nor produced). "A play about the way scandalmongering can ruin people's lives,

['The Children's Hour'] focuses on two young women, Karen Wright and Martha Dobie, who have set up a private boarding school," explained MacNicholas. "Their prospects for a happy and secure future are shattered when one of their pupils, Mary Tilford, a spoiled and vicious problem child, tells her grandmother, . . . a pillar of local society, about an abnormal sexual relationship between Karen and Martha." "The Children's Hour" caused a sensation in its time, not merely for its controversial subject matter (for a movie remake in 1936, a "safe" heterosexual triangle was substituted for the play's original theme), but also for its writer's obvious talent. "So far as sheer power and originality are concerned, [Hellman's] play is not merely the best of the year but the best of many years past," wrote J. W. Krutch in a 1935 *Nation* review.

With that success behind her, Hellman ushered in an era, from the late 1930s through the late 1940s, of classic dramas that helped shape a golden age of American theatre. Chief among them is "The Little Foxes," perhaps the playwright's best known work. An excoriating look at the rivalries and disloyalty among a turn-of-the-century Southern family, the play explores how the wealthy Hubbard clan of New Orleans schemes to keep itself rich and powerful, at the expense of both outsiders and each other. In this tale, "William Marshall, a visiting Chicago businessman, has displayed a willingness to establish a local cotton mill to be controlled by the Hubbards if they can raise enough money to buy fifty-one percent of the new company," as MacNicholas explained. "An intense power struggle ensues, dividing the family into two camps: the powerful and cruel Hubbard siblings (Regina and her two brothers, Ben and Oscar), and those brought into the family by marriage (Horace, Regina's husband; Alexandra, their fair-minded daughter; and Birdie, Oscar's wife)." By the second act, added MacNicholas, every Hubbard is out for him- or herself.

"The Little Foxes," both in its stage and film incarnations, was a great popular and critical success. Some critics took its theme of greed as a parable for the rise of the industrial South; others saw the play as Hellman's look back at the turmoil within her own family. In 1946, seven years after "The Little Foxes" had premiered, Hellman produced what today is known as a "prequel": "Another Part of the Forest," which takes a look at the Hubbard clan twenty years earlier than when audiences had first met them. "Twenty years does not transport them to the age of innocence; their evil natures are already well cultivated," noted Richard Moody in his book *Lillian Hellman: Playwright.*

The mixed reviews of "Another Part of the Forest" focused on critics' speculation that Hellman had packed too much melodrama into the play. Moody found that the follow-up work did "not match the earlier play in concentrated power. [Hellman] has followed too many paths. If fewer crises had been packed into the two days [in which the story takes place], if the voices had been less strident, . . . [then the characters] might have become more fully realized, and our hearts might have become more committed." For all its structural faults, though, Moody called "Another Part of the Forest" "a strong and exciting play."

In between "The Little Foxes" and "Another Part of the Forest," Hellman premiered the political drama "Watch on the Rhine." This 1941 production focused on a Washington family and the war refugees they harbor. Among the boarders are a Rumanian count and his American wife, and an anti-Nazi German. Fear and prejudice follow the characters, resulting in tragedy. Except "for those who suffered through the Hitler years," remarked Moody, "the fierce impact of the play in 1941 cannot be fully sensed. If it appears melodramatic now, it appeared melo-

dramatic then, but with a difference: the world was boiling with melodrama. Cruelty and villainy were not figments of the playwright's imagination, and it was almost impossible for a writer to tell us anything we didn't already know or to dramatize atrocities more effectively than events had already dramatized them." Hellman "knew that her fiction must do more than demonstrate the strange and awful truth that screamed from the front pages of every daily paper," he added. A critic of the day, Rosamond Gilder of *Theatre Arts,* called "Watch on the Rhine" "more faulty in structure" than "The Children's Hour" and "The Little Foxes," and also noted that Hellman, "whose hallmark has been an almost brutal cynicism, who has excelled in delineating mean, ruthless and predatory types, [here indulges] in a tenderness, an emotionalism that borders on the sentimental."

The 1950s saw Hellman writing three play adaptations—"Montserrat," "The Lark," and "Candide," the latter a musical—plus an original work, "The Autumn Garden." It wasn't until 1960, however, that the playwright had her next important original drama produced. "Toys in the Attic" examines the psychological effects of sudden wealth an a poor family. One of Hellman's best plays, according to Moody, "Toys in the Attic" "achieves the magnitude and human revelation that have always been the mark of serious drama." The plot revolves around two sisters, Carrie and Anna Berniers, who have devoted their lives to their ne'er-do-well younger brother, Julian. They find that he has married a wealthy but neurotic woman, and when Julian returns home to visit, he brings his bride and virtual fistfuls of cash, which he distributes indiscriminately. "The sudden reversal of fortune is too shocking to accept, and Carrie is convinced that her brother has gone crazy," noted MacNicholas.

With "Toys in the Attic," Hellman "picked up the sword of judgment many playwrights of the period [had] laid aside and [wielded] it with renewed vigor," said John Gassner in his book *Dramatic Soundings: Evaluations and Retractions Culled from 30 Years of Dramatic Criticism.* Gassner also found that it is "the special merit of Lillian Hellman's work that dreadful things are done by the onstage characters out of affectionate possessiveness, rather than out of ingrained villainy. Although the author's corresponding view of life is ironic and is trenchantly expressed, there is no gloating over human misery, no horror-mongering, no traffic with sensationalism in *Toys in the Attic.*"

"Toys in the Attic" was Hellman's last major play (she produced one more drama, "My Mother, My Father and Me," an adaptation of Burt Blechman's novel *How Much?,* but it ran only briefly in 1963). From 1969 on, Hellman became well regarded for a quartet of books recounting events in her life. From the beginning of her public life, the writer's politics had been intertwined with her career. As MacNicholas pointed out, "The origins of [Hellman's] liberalism are traced to her childhood: on the one hand, she witnessed her mother's family increase their fortunes at the expense of Negroes; on the other, she admired the dignity and tough-mindedness of her black nurse Sophronia. Dashiell Hammett, of course, was a radical who shared and influenced much of her life in the 1930s and 1940s."

With Hellman's first book of memoirs, *An Unfinished Woman,* the author took an unconventional approach to traditional autobiography, as Moody described it. "Only in the first third of the book does she allow chronology to govern her narrative. After that she swings freely among her remembrances of places, times, and people—all intimately observed, all colored with some special personal involvement."

The word "pentimento" describes a phenomenon in art wherein a painting fades to the point that one can see the rough sketches and previous drafts through the surface of the finished work. The word also serves as the title of Hellman's second book of memoirs, a look at the friends and relations that fueled Hellman's adult years. This book garnered much critical notice, most notably for its sophisticated writing style. "It is now apparent that *An Unfinished Woman* was the beginning—a try-out, if you will, and more hesitant than arrogant—of a new career for Lillian Hellman," declared *New York* critic Eliot Fremont-Smith. "*Pentimento: A Book of Portraits* . . . , is its realization." Fremont-Smith also called the work one of "extraordinary richness and candor and self-perception, and triumph considering the courage such a book requires, a courage that lies, [the author] shows by example, far deeper than one is usually inclined to accept."

Muriel Haynes, in a *Ms.* review, called *Pentimento* "a triumphant vindication of the stories the author threw away in her twenties because they were 'no good.' These complex, controlled narratives profit from the dramatist's instinct for climax and immediate, sharp characterization; but they have an emotional purity her plays have generally lacked." Less impressed was *London Magazine* reviewer Julian Symons, who said that the memoir "is not, as American reviewers have unwisely said, a marvel and a masterpiece and a book full of perceptions about human character. It is, rather, a collection of sketches of a fairly familiar kind, which blend real people known to history and Lillian Hellman . . . with people known only by their Christian names in the book, who may be real or partly fictionalized." By far the best known section of the book is "Julia," the story of Hellman's friendship during the 1930s with a rich young American woman working in the European underground against the Nazis. The story was adapted into the popular film "Julia" in 1977.

In *Pentimento,* as in her other books, Hellman was occasionally criticized by the press for presenting her facts unreliably, "bending" the truth to support her views. Paul Johnson, a writer for the British journal *Spectator,* cited an article casting doubt whether "Julia" actually existed. "What [Boston University's Samuel McCracken] demonstrates, by dint of checking Thirties railway timetables, steamship passenger lists, and many other obscure sources, is that most of the facts Hellman provides about 'Julia's' movement and actions, and indeed her own, are not true." Johnson further suggested that what Hellman had been presenting all along is a left-wing apologia for World War II and the McCarthy era that followed.

Hellman, though no Stalinist, had in fact rebelled against the Cold War communism investigations during the postwar era—in one of her most memorable lines, she informed the House Un-American Activities Committee that she had no intention of cutting her conscience to fit that year's fashion. *Scoundrel Time* is based on the story of "the 67 minutes that [the author] spent before the [HUAC] in Washington in 1952, of what preceded the hearings, and what its consequences were," according to *Listener* critic David Hunt. Even though Hellman was "scrupulously specific in what she [said] in *Scoundrel Time,* carefully limiting her text to what she herself experienced, thought, said, and did, this memoir nevertheless applies directly to the essential experience of her time—in other words, to history," noted Bruce Cook in a *Saturday Review* article. "There are a couple of good reasons for this. First, and probably most important, is that this is a work of *literary* quality. As with . . . *An Unfinished Woman* and *Pentimento, Scoundrel Time* is a triumph of tone. No writer I know can match the eloquence of her ah-what-the-hell as she looks back over the whole sorry spectacle and tells with restraint and precision just what she sees." *Scoundrel Time,* in Maureen Howard's view, "is not a confessional book. Hellman has seldom told more than her work required. [HUAC figureheads] are sketched

in, and she gives us the details of her own bewildering sadness during those hard times. . . . Her stories are guarded and spare by design," as Howard wrote in *New York Times Book Review. Ms.* critic Vivian Gornick shared this view, calling *Scoundrel Time* "a valuable piece of work. The kind of work that stands alone, untouched, in the midst of foolish criticism and foolish praise alike."

Among the Hellman memoirs, her last work, *Maybe: A Story,* represents the most obvious tie between fact and fiction. *New Republic* critic Maggie Scarf, who couldn't decide if the book were a novelized autobiography or an autobiographical novella, called "monumental despair" the "true subject of *Maybe.* For Lillian Hellman has gone swimming in the waters of time and memory and found herself adrift in a vast sea of unreliability—the shore of solid information . . . seems to recede each time she believes she has the true details in sight." The narrative covers the life of Sarah Cameron, "a woman whom Hellman knew very slightly but over a long period of time," according to Scarf. "Sarah may or may not have taken Lillian Hellman's first lover away from her; this malicious young man, Alex . . . , had devastated [the author] on their fourth and final session in bed by recommending that she take a bath," offered Robert Towers in a *New York Times Book Review* piece. "But absorbing as this autobiographical material is, it does not compensate, in my opinion, for the emptiness at the heart of the book. Miss Hellman fails to bring Sarah Cameron into existence as even a remotely comprehensible woman. The evidence is so scattered, so inconsistent, so blurred by time and alcohol, that we are left with a wraith to insubstantial to evoke even a sense of mystery, much less to support a valid point about the ultimate unknowability of figures in our past."

To Gornick, this time in a *Village Voice* review, Hellman's digressions into her past seem unworthy of the author's talent. "The association between Hellman and Sarah herself has no substance whatever; it's all fragments and fancy speculations and peripheral incidents and mysterious allusions that seem only to provide the writer with an excuse to call up once again Hammett and the drinking years, the aunts in New Orleans, making movies for Sam Goldwyn. The effort to surround Sarah with metaphoric meaning is strained and painfully obvious." Walter Clemons, in a *Newsweek* review, saw the inconsistencies in *Maybe* in another way: "Her nonstory, for that is what her tale of Sarah turns out to be, is a tricky, nervy meditation on the fallibility of memory, the failure of attention, the casual aplomb of practiced liars, the shivery unpredictability of malice." Clemons also praised Hellman's sharp voice, given her advanced years and alcoholic history.

Even as she moved into her seventies, Hellman remained a vibrant force in the public eye. She fueled this reputation in 1980 when she sued her contemporary, Mary McCarthy (author of *The Group*), after McCarthy told Dick Cavett on his talk show that she found Hellman an overrated and dishonest writer. Hellman sought damages in excess of $1.7 million for "mental pain and anguish"; the suit, however, "died when she did," as Frank Rich put it in *New York Times Book Review.*

Maybe was Hellman's last major published work; a cookbook, co-written with longtime friend Peter Feibleman, came out shortly after her June, 1984, death. The news of Hellman's passing brought out a string of testimonials from notable writers, including these words by *Newsweek*'s David Ansen: "In her 60s, looking back on her life in her memoirs, Hellman found her indelible voice. The gallery of portraits in *Pentimento*—especially 'Julia'—are unforgettable: whether they prove to be as much fiction as fact, as some have accused, cannot diminish their power and glamour. She may have called herself 'unfinished,' but a more appropriate title would have been 'An Unmellowed Woman'. . . . The Hellman anger arose from her clear-eyed view of social injustice and strong moral convictions, and she remained true to her passion throughout her rich and tumultuous life. Not for her the modernist halftones of alienation and equivocation. The fire within her lit up the cultural landscape; its heat will be deeply missed."

MEDIA ADAPTATIONS: Marc Blitzstein adapted "The Little Foxes" as an opera, "Regina," in 1949. "Another Part of the Forest" was filmed by Universal in 1948, and "Toys in the Attic" was adapted for film by United Artists, 1963. Television adaptations include "Montserrat," 1971, and "The Lark." A section of Hellman's memoir *Pentimento* was adapted into the film "Julia" and released in 1977. In 1986, William Luce wrote a one-woman play, "Lillian," based on Hellman's life; the production ran briefly in New York City.

BIOGRAPHICAL/CRITICAL SOURCES:

BOOKS

Adler, Jacob H., *Lillian Hellman,* Vaughn, 1969.
Authors in the News, Gale, Volume 1, 1976, Volume 2, 1976.
Contemporary Literary Criticism, Gale, Volume 2, 1974, Volume 4, 1975, Volume 8, 1978, Volume 14, 1980, Volume 18, 1981, Volume 33, 1985, Volume 44, 1987, Volume 52, 1989.
Dictionary of Literary Biography, Gale, Volume 7: *Twentieth-Century American Dramatists,* 1981.
Dictionary of Literary Biography Yearbook: 1984, Gale, 1985.
Falk, Doris V., *Lillian Hellman,* Ungar, 1978.
Gassner, John, *Dramatic Soundings: Evaluations and Retractions Culled from 30 Years of Dramatic Criticism,* Crown, 1968.
Lederer, Katherine, *Lillian Hellman,* Twayne, 1979.
Moody, Richard, *Lillian Hellman: Playwright,* Bobbs-Merrill, 1972.
Wright, William, *Lillian Hellman: The Image, the Woman,* Simon & Schuster, 1986.

PERIODICALS

Chicago Tribune, March 30, 1980.
Listener, November 18, 1986.
London Magazine, August/September, 1974.
Ms., January, 1974, August, 1976.
Nation, May 22, 1935.
New Republic, August 2, 1980, August 13, 1984.
Newsweek, June 2, 1980.
New York, September 17, 1973.
New York Review of Books, June 10, 1976.
New York Times, November 13, 1980, August 26, 1984.
New York Times Book Review, September 23, 1973, April 25, 1976, June 1, 1980.
Saturday Review, April 17, 1976.
Spectator, July 14, 1984.
Theatre Arts, June, 1941.
Time, May 19, 1980.
Village Voice, May 19, 1980.
Washington Post, May 19, 1980.

OBITUARIES:

PERIODICALS

Chicago Tribune, July 1, 1984.
Los Angeles Times, July 1, 1984.
Newsweek, July 9, 1984.

New York Times, July 1, 1984.
Washington Post, July 1, 1984.

*   *   *

HELPRIN, Mark 1947-

PERSONAL: Born June 28, 1947, in New York, N.Y.; son of Morris (a motion picture executive) and Eleanor (Lynn) Helprin; married Lisa Kennedy (a tax attorney), June 28, 1980; children: two daughters. *Education:* Harvard College, A.B., 1969, A.M., 1972; postgraduate study at Magdelan College, University of Oxford, 1976-77. *Religion:* Jewish. *Politics:* Republican.

CAREER: Writer. Former instructor at Harvard University. *Military service:* Israeli Infantry and Air Corps, border guard, 1972-73; also served in British Merchant Navy.

AWARDS, HONORS: American Academy, Rome, Italy, fellow; PEN/Faulkner Award, National Jewish Book Award, and nomination for American Book Award, all 1982, all for *Ellis Island and Other Stories;* American Academy and Institute of Arts and Letters award, 1982; Prix de Rome, 1982; Guggenheim fellow, 1984.

WRITINGS:

A Dove of the East and Other Stories, Knopf, 1975.
Refiner's Fire: The Life and Adventures of Marshall Pearl, a Foundling (novel), Knopf, 1977.
Ellis Island and Other Stories, Seymour Lawrence/Delacorte, 1981.
Winter's Tale (novel), Harcourt, 1983.
(Editor with Shannon Ravenel) *The Best American Short Stories,* Houghton, 1988.
(Adaptor) *Swan Lake* (juvenile), with illustrations by Chris Van Allsburg, Houghton, 1989.

Work anthologized in *The O. Henry Prize Stories.* Contributor to *New Yorker, Esquire,* and the *New York Times Magazine.*

SIDELIGHTS: "In whatever form [Mark] Helprin writes, he demonstrates a literary talent that deserves appreciation, a talent to make language evoke a sense of the beauty and wonder of majestic nature," according to William J. Scheick in the *Dictionary of Literary Biography Yearbook: 1985.* Best known for his short stories, Helprin has published two collections of his work in that form, *A Dove of the East and Other Stories* and *Ellis Island and Other Stories.* Both collections have earned him high critical praise, and the latter won several prestigious literary awards.

Commenting on *A Dove of the East,* Dorothy Rabinowitz contends that the stories are "immensely readable" and that some are "quite superb." She writes: "Mr. Helprin's old-fashioned regard shines through all his characters' speeches, and his endorsement gives them eloquent tongues. Now and again the stories lapse into archness, and at times, too, their willed drama bears down too heavily. But these are small flaws in works so estimably full of talent and—the word must out—of character." Dan Wakefield was even more appreciative of Helprin's work. "The quality that pervades these stories," he writes, "is love—love of men and women, love of landscapes and physical beauty, love of interior courage as well as the more easily obtainable outward strength. The author never treats his subjects with sentimentality but always with gentleness of a kind that is all too rare in our fiction and our lives."

Helprin's *Ellis Island and Other Stories* won the PEN/Faulkner Award, a National Jewish Book Award, and a nomination for the American Book Award, as well as critical acclaim. Scheick reports that "reviewers were struck by the power of imagination in these stories as well as by their rich texture and their delicate and economic style." Anatole Broyard of the *New York Times,* in his review of the book, compares Helprin with "Marc Chagall, Isaac Bashevis Singer, Franz Kafka: there is something of each of these in 'Ellis Island and Other Stories.' There is even a bit of Louis Ferdinand Celine. Yet these are only peripheries. Mr. Helprin is ferociously original." Seymour Krim of the *Washington Post Book World* notes that Helprin has "a fresh voice and vision" while his stories are a "combination of the realistic and fantastic intertwining of experience, guided by compassion and a prose style as clear and shining as a northern star."

AVOCATIONAL INTERESTS: Mountain climbing.

BIOGRAPHICAL/CRITICAL SOURCES:

BOOKS

Contemporary Literary Criticism, Gale, Volume 7, 1977, Volume 10, 1979, Volume 22, 1982, Volume 32, 1985.
Dictionary of Literary Biography Yearbook: 1985, Gale, 1986.

PERIODICALS

Atlantic, October, 1975, September, 1983.
Commentary, June, 1981.
Harper's, November, 1977.
Los Angeles Times, November 8, 1984.
New Statesman, February 13, 1976.
Newsweek, September 19, 1983.
New Yorker, October 17, 1977.
New York Review of Books, February 23, 1978.
New York Times, January 30, 1981, March 5, 1981, September 2, 1983.
New York Times Book Review, November 2, 1975, January 1, 1978, March 25, 1981, September 4, 1983.
Openers, fall, 1984.
Publishers Weekly, February 13, 1981.
Saturday Review, September 20, 1975.
Spectator, April 24, 1976.
Washington Post Book World, September 23, 1983.

* * *

HEMINGWAY, Ernest (Miller)   1899-1961

PERSONAL: Born July 21, 1899, in Oak Park, Ill.; committed suicide, July 2, 1961, in Ketchum, Idaho; son of Clarence Edmunds (a physician) and Grace (a music teacher; maiden name, Hall) Hemingway: married Hadley Richardson, September 3, 1921 (divorced March 10, 1927); married Pauline Pfeiffer (a writer), May 10, 1927 (divorced November 4, 1940); married Martha Gellhorn (a writer), November 21, 1940 (divorced December 21, 1945); married Mary Welsh (a writer), March 14, 1946; children: (first marriage) John Hadley Nicanor; (second marriage) Patrick, Gregory. *Education:* Educated in Oak Park, Ill.

ADDRESSES: Home—Ketchum, Idaho; and Finca Vigia, Cuba.

CAREER: Writer, 1917-61. *Kansas City Star,* Kansas City, Mo., cub reporter, 1917-18; ambulance driver for Red Cross Ambulance Corps in Italy, 1918-19; *Co-operative Commonwealth,* Chicago, Ill., writer, 1920-21; *Toronto Star,* Toronto, Ontario, covered Greco-Turkish War, 1920, European correspondent, 1921-24; covered Spanish Civil War for North American Newspaper Alliance, 1937-38; war correspondent in China, 1941; war correspondent in Europe, 1944-45.

AWARDS, HONORS: Pulitzer Prize, 1953, for *The Old Man and the Sea;* Nobel Prize for Literature, 1954; Award of Merit from American Academy of Arts & Letters, 1954.

WRITINGS:

NOVELS

The Torrents of Spring: A Romantic Novel in Honor of the Passing of a Great Race (parody), Scribner, 1926, published with a new introduction by David Garnett, J. Cape, 1964, reprinted, Scribner, 1972.
The Sun Also Rises, Scribner, 1926, published with a new introduction by Henry Seidel Canby, Modern Library, 1930, reprinted, Scribner, 1969 (published in England as *Fiesta,* J. Cape, 1959).
A Farewell to Arms, Scribner, 1929, published with new introductions by Ford Madox Ford, Modern Library, 1932, Robert Penn Warren, Scribner, 1949, John C. Schweitzer, Scribner, 1967.
To Have and Have Not, Scribner, 1937, J. Cape, 1970.
For Whom the Bell Tolls, Scribner, 1940, published with a new introduction by Sinclair Lewis, Princeton University Press, 1942, reprinted, Scribner, 1960.
Across the River and Into the Trees, Scribner, 1950, reprinted, Penguin with J. Cape, 1966.
The Old Man and the Sea, Scribner 1952.
Islands in the Stream, Scribner, 1970.
The Garden of Eden, Scribner, 1986.

SHORT STORIES, EXCEPT AS INDICATED

Three Stories & Ten Poems, Contact (Paris), 1923.
In Our Time, Boni & Liveright, 1925, published with additional material and new introduction by Edmund Wilson, Scribner, 1930, reprinted, Bruccoli, 1977 (also see below).
Men Without Women, Scribner, 1927.
Winner Take Nothing, Scribner, 1933.
Fifth Column and the First Forty-nine Stories (stories and a play), Scribner, 1938, stories published separately as *First Forty-nine Stories,* J. Cape, 1962, play published separately as *The Fifth Column: A Play in Three Acts,* Scribner, 1940, J. Cape, 1968 (also see below).
The Short Stories of Ernest Hemingway, Scribner, 1938.
The Snows of Kilimanjaro and Other Stories, Scribner, 1961.
The Short Happy Life of Francis Macomber and Other Stories, Penguin, 1963.
Hemingway's African Stories: The Stories, Their Sources, Their Critics, compiled by John M. Howell, Scribner, 1969.
The Nick Adams Stories, preface by Philip Young, Scribner, 1972.
(Contributor) Peter Griffin, *Along With Youth* (biography that includes five previously unpublished short stories: "Crossroads," "The Mercenaries," "The Ash-Heel's Tendon," "The Current," and "Portrait of the Idealist in Love"), Oxford University Press, 1985.
The Complete Short Stories of Ernest Hemingway: The Finca Vigia Edition, Scribner, 1987.

OTHER

in our time (miniature sketches), Three Mountain Press (Paris), 1924 (also see above).
Today Is Friday (pamphlet), As Stable Publications (Englewood, N.J.), 1926.
Death in the Afternoon (nonfiction), Scribner, 1932.
God Rest You Merry Gentlemen, House of Books, 1933.
Green Hills of Africa (nonfiction), Scribner, 1935, reprinted, Penguin with J. Cape, 1966.

The Spanish Earth (commentary and film narration), introduction by Jasper Wood, J. B. Savage (Cleveland, Ohio), 1938.

The Spanish War (monograph), Fact, 1938.

(Editor and author of introduction) *Men at War: The Best War Stories of All Time* (based on a plan by William Kozlenko), Crown, 1942.

Voyage to Victory, Crowell-Collier, 1944.

The Secret Agent's Badge of Courage, Belmont Books, 1954.

Two Christmas Tales, Hart Press, 1959.

A Moveable Feast (reminiscences), Scribner, 1964.

Collected Poems, Haskell, 1970.

The Collected Poems of Ernest Hemingway, Gordon Press, 1972.

Ernest Hemingway: Eighty-Eight Poems, Harcourt, 1979.

Ernest Hemingway, Selected Letters, 1917-1961, Scribner, 1981.

Complete Poems, edited by Nicholas Gerogiannis, University of Nebraska Press, 1983.

Hemingway on Writing, Scribner, 1984.

The Dangerous Summer (nonfiction), introduction by James A. Michener, Scribner, 1985.

Conversations With Ernest Hemingway, University Press of Mississippi, 1986.

OMNIBUS VOLUMES

The Portable Hemingway (contains *The Sun Also Rises, A Farewell to Arms, To Have and Have Not, For Whom the Bell Tolls,* and short stories), edited by Malcolm Cowley, Viking, 1944.

The Essential Hemingway (contains one novel, novel extracts, and twenty-three short stories), J. Cape, 1947, reprinted, 1964.

The Hemingway Reader, edited with foreword by Charles Poore, Scribner, 1953.

Three Novels: The Sun Also Rises, A Farewell to Arms, and The Old Man and the Sea, each with separate introductions by Malcolm Cowley, Robert Penn Warren, and Carlos Baker, respectively, Scribner, 1962.

The Wild Years (collection of journalism), edited by Gene Z. Hanrahan, Dell, 1962.

By-line, Ernest Hemingway: Selected Articles and Dispatches of Four Decades, edited by William White, Scribner, 1967.

Fifth Column and Four Stories of the Spanish Civil War, Scribner, 1969 (also see above).

Ernest Hemingway, Cub Reporter: Kansas City Star Stories, edited by Matthew J. Bruccoli, University of Pittsburgh Press, 1970.

Ernest Hemingway's Apprenticeship: Oak Park, 1916-1917, edited by Bruccoli, Bruccoli Clark NCR Microcard Editions, 1971.

The Enduring Hemingway: An Anthology of a Lifetime in Literature, edited by Charles Scribner, Jr., Scribner, 1974.

Dateline—Toronto: Hemingway's Complete Toronto Star Dispatches, edited by White, Scribner, 1985.

SIDELIGHTS: "The writer's job is to tell the truth," Ernest Hemingway once said. When he was having difficulty writing he reminded himself of this, as he explained in his memoirs, *A Moveable Feast.* "I would stand and look out over the roofs of Paris and think, 'Do not worry. You have always written before and you will write now. All you have to do is write one true sentence. Write the truest sentence that you know.' So finally I would write one true sentence, and then go on from there. It was easy then because there was always one true sentence that I knew or had seen or had heard someone say."

Hemingway's personal and artistic quests for truth were directly related. As Earl Rovit noted: "More often than not, Heming-

way's fictions seem rooted in his journeys into himself much more clearly and obsessively than is usually the case with major fiction writers. . . . His writing was his way of approaching his identity—of discovering himself in the projected metaphors of his experience. He believed that if he could see himself clear and whole, his vision might be useful to others who also lived in this world."

The public's acquaintance with the personal life of Hemingway was perhaps greater than with any other modern novelist. He was well known as a sportsman and *bon vivant* and his escapades were covered in such popular magazines as *Life* and *Esquire.* Hemingway became a legendary figure, wrote John W. Aldridge, "a kind of twentieth-century Lord Byron; and like Byron, he had learned to play himself, his own best hero, with superb conviction. He was Hemingway of the rugged outdoor grin and the hairy chest posing beside a marlin he had just landed or a lion he had just shot; he was Tarzan Hemingway, crouching in the African bush with elephant gun at ready, Bwana Hemingway commanding his native bearers in terse Swahili; he was War Correspondent Hemingway writing a play in the Hotel Florida in Madrid while thirty Fascist shells crashed through the roof; later on he was Task Force Hemingway swathed in ammunition belts and defending his post singlehanded against fierce German attacks." Anthony Burgess declared: "Reconciling literature and action, he fulfilled for all writers, the sickroom dream of leaving the desk for the arena, and then returning to the desk. He wrote good and lived good, and both activities were the same. The pen handled with the accuracy of the rifle; sweat and dignity; bags of *cojones.*"

Hemingway's search for truth and accuracy of expression is reflected in his terse, economical prose style, which is widely acknowledged to be his greatest contribution to literature. What Frederick J. Hoffman called Hemingway's "esthetic of simplicity" involves a "basic struggle for absolute accuracy in making words correspond to experience." For Hemingway, William Barrett commented, "style was a moral act, a desperate struggle for moral probity amid the confusions of the world and the slippery complexities of one's own nature. To set things down simple and right is to hold a standard of rightness against a deceiving world."

In a discussion of Hemingway's style, Sheldon Norman Grebstein listed these characteristics: "first, short and simple sentence constructions, with heavy use of parallelism, which convey the effect of control, terseness, and blunt honesty; second, purged diction which above all eschews the use of bookish, latinate, or abstract words and thus achieves the effect of being heard or spoken or transcribed from reality rather than appearing as a construct of the imagination (in brief, verisimilitude); and third, skillful use of repetition and a kind of verbal counterpoint, which operate either by pairing or juxtaposing opposites, or else by running the same word or phrase through a series of shifting meanings and inflections."

One of Hemingway's greatest virtues as a writer was his self-discipline. He described how he accomplished this in *A Moveable Feast.* "If I started to write elaborately, or like someone introducing or presenting something, I found that I could cut that scrollwork or ornament out and throw it away and start with the first true simple declarative sentence I had written. . . . I decided that I would write one story about each thing that I knew about. I was trying to do this all the time I was writing, and it was good and severe discipline." His early training in journalism as a reporter for the *Kansas City Star* and the *Toronto Star* is often mentioned as a factor in the development of his lean style.

Later, as a foreign correspondent he learned the even more rigorously economic language of "cablese," in which each word must convey the meaning of several others. While Hemingway acknowledged his debt to journalism in *Death in the Afternoon* by commenting that "in writing for a newspaper you told what happened and with one trick and another, you communicated the emotion to any account of something that has happened on that day," he admitted that the hardest part of fiction writing, "the real thing," was contriving "the sequence of motion and fact which made the emotion and which would be valid in a year or ten years or, with luck and if you stated it purely enough, always."

Although Hemingway has named numerous writers as his literary influences, his contemporaries mentioned most often in this regard are Ring Lardner, Sherwood Anderson, Ezra Pound, and Gertrude Stein. Malcolm Cowley assessed the importance of Stein and Pound (who were both friends of Hemingway) to his literary development, while stressing that the educational relationship was mutual. "One thing he took partly from her [Stein] was a colloquial—in appearance—American style, full of repeated words, prepositional phrases, and present participles, the style in which he wrote his early published stories. One thing he took from Pound—in return for trying vainly to teach him to box—was the doctrine of the accurate image, which he applied in the 'chapters' printed between the stories that went into *In Our Time;* but Hemingway also learned from him to bluepencil most of his adjectives." Hemingway has commented that he learned how to write as much from painters as from other writers. Cezanne was one of his favorite painters and Wright Morris has compared Hemingway's stylistic method to that of Cezanne. "A Cezanne-like simplicity of scene is built up with the touches of a master, and the great effects are achieved with a sublime economy. At these moments style and substance are of one piece, each growing from the other, and one cannot imagine that life could exist except as described. We think only of what is there, and not, as in the less successful moments, of all of the elements of experience that are not."

While most critics have found Hemingway's prose exemplary (Jackson J. Benson claimed that he had "perhaps the best ear that has ever been brought to the creation of English prose"), Leslie A. Fiedler complained that Hemingway learned to write "through the eye rather than the ear. If his language is colloquial, it is *written* colloquial, for he was constitutionally incapable of hearing English as it was spoken around him. To a critic who once asked him why his characters all spoke alike, Hemingway answered, 'Because I never listen to anybody.'"

Hemingway's earlier novels and short stories were largely praised for their unique style. Paul Goodman, for example, was pleased with the "sweetness" of the writing in *A Farewell to Arms.* "When it [sweetness] appears, the short sentences coalesce and flow, and sing—sometimes melancholy, sometimes pastoral, sometimes personally embarrassed in an adult, not adolescent, way. In the dialogues, he pays loving attention to the spoken word. And the writing is meticulous; he is sweetly devoted to writing well. Most everything else is resigned, but here he makes an effort, and the effort produces lovely moments."

But in his later works, particularly *Across the River and Into the Trees* and the posthumously published *Islands in the Stream,* the Hemingway style degenerated into near self-parody. "In the best of early Hemingway it always seemed that if exactly the right words in exactly the right order were not chosen, something monstrous would occur, an unimaginably delicate internal warning system would be thrown out of adjustment, and some princi-

ple of personal and artistic integrity would be fatally compromised," John Aldridge wrote. "But by the time he came to write *The Old Man [and the Sea]* there seems to have been nothing at stake except the professional obligation to sound as much like Hemingway as possible. The man had disappeared behind the mannerism, the artist behind the artifice, and all that was left was a coldly flawless facade of words." Foster Hirsch found that Hemingway's "mawkish self-consciousness is especially evident in *Islands in the Stream.*" *Across the River and Into the Trees,* according to Philip Rahv, "reads like a parody by the author of his own manner—a parody so biting that it virtually destroys the mixed social and literary legend of Hemingway." And Carlos Baker wrote: "In the lesser works of his final years . . . nostalgia drove him to the point of exploiting his personal idiosyncrasies, as if he hoped to persuade readers to accept these in lieu of that powerful union of objective discernment and subjective response which he had once been able to achieve."

But Hemingway was never his own worst imitator. He was perhaps the most influential writer of his generation and scores of writers, particularly the hard-boiled writers of the thirties, attempted to adapt his tough, understated prose to their own works, usually without success. As Clinton S. Burhans, Jr., noted: "The famous and extraordinarily eloquent concreteness of Hemingway's style is inimitable precisely because it is not primarily stylistic: the how of Hemingway's style is the what of his characteristic vision."

It is this organicism, the skillful blend of style and substance, that made Hemingway's works so successful, despite the fact that many critics have complained that he lacked vision. Hemingway avoided intellectualism because he thought it shallow and pretentious. His unique vision demanded the expression of emotion through the description of action rather than of passive thought. In *Death in the Afternoon,* Hemingway explained, "I was trying to write then and I found the greatest difficulty, aside from knowing truly what you really felt, rather than what you were supposed to feel, was to put down what really happened in action; what the actual things were which produced the emotion you experienced."

Even morality, for Hemingway, was a consequence of action and emotion. He stated his moral code in *Death in the Afternoon:* "What is moral is what you feel good after and what is immoral is what you feel bad after." Lady Brett Ashley, in *The Sun Also Rises,* voices this pragmatic morality after she has decided to leave a young bullfighter, believing the break to be in his best interests. She says: "You know it makes one feel rather good deciding not to be a bitch. . . . It's sort of what we have instead of God."

Hemingway's perception of the world as devoid of traditional values and truths and instead marked by disillusionment and moribund idealism, is a characteristically twentieth-century vision. World War I was a watershed for Hemingway and his generation. As an ambulance driver in the Italian infantry, Hemingway had been severely wounded. The war experience affected him profoundly, as he told Malcolm Cowley. "In the first war I was hurt very badly; in the body, mind, and spirit, and also morally." The heroes of his novels were similarly wounded. According to Max Westbrook they "awake to a world gone to hell. World War I has destroyed belief in the goodness of national governments. The depression has isolated man from his natural brotherhood. Institutions, concepts, and insidious groups of friends and ways of life are, when accurately seen, a tyranny, a sentimental or propagandistic rationalization."

Both of Hemingway's first two major novels, *The Sun Also Rises* and *A Farewell to Arms,* were "primarily descriptions of a society that had lost the possibility of belief. They were dominated by an atmosphere of Gothic ruin, boredom, sterility and decay," John Aldridge wrote. "Yet if they had been nothing more than descriptions, they would inevitably have been as empty of meaning as the thing they were describing." While Alan Lebowitz contended that because the theme of despair "is always an end in itself, the fiction merely its transcription, . . . it is a dead end," Aldridge believed that Hemingway managed to save the novels by salvaging the characters' values and transcribing them "into a kind of moral network that linked them together in a unified pattern of meaning."

In the search for meaning Hemingway's characters necessarily confront violence. Omnipresent violence is a fact of existence, according to Hemingway. Even in works such as *The Sun Also Rises* in which violence plays a minimal role, it is always present subliminally—"woven into the structure of life itself," William Barrett remarked. In other works violence is more obtrusive: the wars in *A Farewell to Arms* and *For Whom the Bell Tolls,* the hostility of nature which is particularly evident in the short stories, and the violent sports such as bullfighting and big game hunting that are portrayed in numerous works.

"Hemingway is the dramatist of the extreme situation. His overriding theme is honour, personal honour: by what shall a man live, by what shall a man die, in a world the essential condition of whose being is violence?" Walter Allen wrote. "These problems are posed rather than answered in his first book *In Our Time,* a collection of short stories in which almost all of Hemingway's later work is contained by implication."

The code by which Hemingway's heroes must live (Philip Young has termed them "code heroes") is contingent on the qualities of courage, self-control, and "grace under pressure." Irving Howe has described the typical Hemingway hero as a man "who is wounded but bears his wounds in silence, who is defeated but finds a remnant of dignity in an honest confrontation of defeat." Furthermore, the hero's great desire must be to "salvage from the collapse of social life a version of stoicism that can make suffering bearable; the hope that in direct physical sensation, the cold water of the creek in which one fishes or the purity of the wine made by Spanish peasants, there can be found an experience that can resist corruption."

Hemingway has been accused of exploiting and sensationalizing violence. However, Leo Gurko remarked that "the motive behind Hemingway's heroic figures is not glory, or fortune, or the righting of injustice, or the thirst for experience. They are inspired neither by vanity nor ambition nor a desire to better the world. They have no thoughts of reaching a state of higher grace or virtue. Instead, their behavior is a reaction to the moral emptiness of the universe, an emptiness that they feel compelled to fill by their own special efforts."

If life is an endurance contest and the hero's response to it is prescribed and codified, the violence itself is stylized. As William Barrett asserted: "It is always played, even in nature, perhaps above all in nature, according to some form. The violence erupts within the patterns of war or the patterns of the bullring." Clinton S. Burhans, Jr., is convinced that Hemingway's "fascination with bullfighting stems from his view of it as an art form, a ritual tragedy in which man confronts the creatural realities of violence, pain, suffering, and death by imposing on them an esthetic form which gives them order, significance, and beauty."

It is not necessary (or even possible) to understand the complex universe—it is enough for Hemingway's heroes to find solace in beauty and order. Santiago in *The Old Man and the Sea* cannot understand why he must kill the great fish he has come to love, Burhans noted. Hemingway described Santiago's confusion: "I do not understand these things, he thought. But it is good we do not try to kill the sun or the moon or the stars. It is enough to live on the sea and kill our brothers."

Despite Hemingway's pessimism, Ihab Hassan declared that it is "perverse to see only the emptiness of Hemingway's world. In its lucid spaces, a vision of archetypal unity reigns. Opposite forces obey a common destiny; enemies discover their deeper identity; the hunter and the hunted merge. The matador plunges his sword, and for an instant in eternity, man and beast are the same. This is the moment of truth, and it serves Hemingway as symbol of the unity which underlies both love and death. His fatalism, his tolerance of bloodshed, his stoical reserve before the malice of creation, betray a sacramental attitude that transcends any personal fate."

Death is not the ultimate fear: the Hemingway hero knows how to confront death. What he truly fears is *nada* (the Spanish word for nothing)-existence in a state of nonbeing. Hemingway's characters are alone. He is not concerned with human relationships as much as with portraying man's individual struggle against an alien, chaotic universe. His characters exist in the "island condition," Stephen L. Tanner has noted. He compared them to the islands of an archipelago "consistently isolated [and] alone in the stream of society."

Several critics have noted that Hemingway's novels suffer because of his overriding concern with the individual. *For Whom the Bell Tolls,* a novel about the Spanish Civil War, has engendered controversy on this matter. While it is ostensibly a political novel about a cause that Hemingway believed in fervently, critics such as Alvah C. Bessie were disappointed that Hemingway was still concerned exclusively with the personal. "The cause of Spain does not, in any *essential* way, figure as a motivating power, a driving, emotional, passional force in this story." Bessie wrote. "In the widest sense, that cause is actually irrelevant to the narrative. For the author is less concerned with the fate of the Spanish people, whom I am certain he loves, than he is with the fate of his hero and heroine, who are himself. . . . For all his groping the author of the *Bell* has yet to integrate his individual sensitivity to life with the sensitivity of every living human being (read the Spanish people); he has yet to expand his personality as a novelist to embrace the truths of other people, everywhere; he has yet to dive deep into the lives of others, and there to find his own." But Mark Schorer contended that in *For Whom the Bell Tolls* Hemingway's motive is to portray "a tremendous sense of man's dignity and worth, an urgent awareness of the necessity of man's freedom, a nearly poetic realization of man's *collective* virtues. Indeed, the individual vanishes in the political whole, but vanishes precisely to defend his dignity, his freedom, his virtue. In spite of the ominous premium which the title seems to place on individuality, the real theme of the book is the relative unimportance of individuality and the superb importance of the political whole."

Hemingway's depiction of relationships between men and women is generally considered to be his weakest area as a writer. Leslie A. Fiedler has noted that he is only really comfortable dealing with men without women. His women characters often seem to be abstractions rather than portraits of real women. Often reviewers have divided them into two types: the bitches such as Brett and Margot Macomber who emasculate the men in their lives, and the wish-projections, the sweet, submissive women such as Catherine and Maria (in *For Whom the Bell Tolls*). All of the characterizations lack subtlety and shading. The love affair between Catherine and Frederic in *A Farewell to Arms* is only an "abstraction of lyric emotion," Edmund Wilson commented. Fiedler complained that "in his earlier fiction, Hemingway's descriptions of the sexual encounter are intentionally brutal, in his later ones, unintentionally comic; for in no case, can he quite succeed in making his females human. . . . If in *For Whom the Bell Tolls* Hemingway has written the most absurd love scene in the history of the American novel, this is not because he lost momentarily his skill and authority; it is a give-away—a moment which illuminates the whole erotic content of his fiction."

In 1921, when Hemingway and his family moved to the Left Bank of Paris (then the literature, art, and music capital of the world), he became associated with other American expatriates, including F. Scott Fitzgerald, Archibald MacLeish, E. E. Cummings, and John Dos Passos. These expatriates and the whole generation which came of age in the period between the two world wars came to be known as the "lost generation." For Hemingway the term had more universal meaning. In *A Moveable Feast* he wrote that being lost is part of the human condition—that all generations are lost generations.

Hemingway also believed in the cyclicality of the world. As inscriptions to his novel *The Sun Also Rises*, he used two quotations: first, Gertrude Stein's comment, "You are all a lost generation"; then a verse from Ecclesiastes which begins, "One generation passeth away, and another generation cometh; but the earth abideth forever. . . ." The paradox of regeneration evolving from death is central to Hemingway's vision. The belief in immortality is comforting, of course, and Hemingway evidently found comfort in permanence and endurance. According to Steven R. Phillips, Hemingway discovered permanence in "the sense of immortality that he gains from the otherwise impermanent art of the bullfight, in the fact that the 'earth abideth forever,' in the eternal flow of the gulf stream and in the permanence of his own works of art." Hemingway's greatest depiction of endurance is in *The Old Man and the Sea* in which "he succeeds in a manner which almost defeats critical description," Phillips claimed. "The old man becomes the sea and like the sea he endures. He is dying as the year is dying. He is fishing in September, the fall of the year, the time that corresponds in the natural cycle to the phase of sunset and sudden death. . . . Yet the death of the old man will not bring an end to the cycle; as part of the sea he will continue to exist."

Hemingway was inordinately proud of his own powers of rejuvenation, and in a letter to his friend Archibald MacLeish, he explained that his maxim was: "*Dans la vie, il faut (d'abord) durer.*" ("In life, one must [first of all] endure.") He had survived physical disasters (including two near-fatal plane crashes in Africa in 1954) and disasters of critical reception to his work (*Across the River and Into the Trees* was almost universally panned). But due to his great recuperative powers he was able to rebound from these hardships. He made a literary comeback with the publication of *The Old Man and the Sea*, which is considered to be among his finest works. In 1954 he was awarded the Nobel Prize for Literature. But the last few years of his life were marked by great physical and emotional suffering. He was no longer able to write—to do the thing he loved the most. Finally Hemingway could endure no longer and, in 1961, he took his own life.

In the 1980s Scribner published two additional posthumous works—*The Dangerous Summer* and *The Garden of Eden*. Written in 1959 while Hemingway was in Spain on commission for *Life* magazine, *The Dangerous Summer* describes the intense and bloody competition between two prominent bullfighters. *The Garden of Eden*, a novel about newlyweds who experience marital conflict while traveling through Spain on their honeymoon, was begun by Hemingway in the 1940s and finished fifteen years later. While interest in these works was high, critics judged neither book to rival the thematic and stylistic achievements of his earlier works, which have made Hemingway a major figure in modern American literature.

MEDIA ADAPTATIONS: Several of Hemingway's works have been adapted for motion pictures, including *For Whom the Bell Tolls; To Have and Have Not; The Sun Also Rises,* screenplay by Peter Viertel, Twentieth Century-Fox, 1956; *A Farewell to Arms,* screenplay by Ben Hecht, The Selznick Co., 1957; and *The Old Man and the Sea,* screenplay by Peter Viertel, Warner Bros., 1957.

BIOGRAPHICAL/CRITICAL SOURCES:

BOOKS

Aldridge, John W., *Time to Murder and Create: The Contemporary Novel in Crisis,* McKay, 1966.

Allen, Walter, *The Modern Novel,* Dutton, 1964.

Astro, Richard and Jackson J. Benson, editors, *Hemingway in Our Time,* Oregon State University Press, 1974.

Baker, Carlos, *Hemingway: The Writer as Artist,* Princeton University Press, 1956.

Baker, *Ernest Hemingway: A Life Story,* Scribner, 1969.

Baker, editor, *Ernest Hemingway: Critiques of Four Major Novels,* Scribner, 1962.

Baldwin, Kenneth H. and David K. Kirby, editors, *Individual and Community: Variations on a Theme in American Fiction,* Duke University Press, 1975.

Barrett, William, *Time of Need: Forms of Imagination in the Twentieth Century,* Harper, 1972.

Benson, Jackson J., editor, *The Short Stories of Ernest Hemingway: Critical Essays,* Duke University Press, 1975.

Bruccoli, Matthew J. and C. E. Frazer Clark, Jr., editors, *Fitzgerald-Hemingway Annual,* Bruccoli Clark Books, 1969-76, Gale, 1977.

Burgess, Anthony, *Urgent Copy: Literary Studies,* Norton, 1968.

Burgess, *The Novel Now: A Guide to Contemporary Fiction,* Norton, 1967.

Burgess, Anthony, *Ernest Hemingway and His World,* Scribner, 1978.

Castillo-Puche, Jose L., *Hemingway in Spain,* Doubleday, 1974.

Concise Dictionary of American Literary Biography: The Twenties, 1917-1929, Gale, 1989.

Contemporary Literary Criticism, Gale, Volume 1, 1973, Volume 3, 1975, Volume 6, 1976, Volume 8, 1978, Volume 13, 1980, Volume 19, 1981, Volume 30, 1984, Volume 34, 1985, Volume 39, 1986, Volume 41, 1987, Volume 44, 1987, Volume 50, 1988.

Cowley, Malcolm, *A Second Flowering: Works and Days of the Lost Generation,* Viking, 1973.

Dictionary of Literary Biography, Gale, Volume 4: *American Writers in Paris, 1920-1939,* 1978, Volume 9: *American Novelists, 1910-1945,* 1981.

Donaldson, Scott, *By Force of Will: The Life in Art and Art in the Life of Ernest Hemingway,* Viking, 1977.

Fiedler, Leslie A., *Love and Death in the American Novel,* Criterion, 1960.

Fiedler, *Waiting for the End,* Stein & Day, 1964.

Frohock, W. M., *The Novel of Violence in America,* Southern Methodist University Press, 1957.

Geisman, Maxwell, *American Moderns: From Rebellion to Conformity,* Hill & Wang, 1958.

Grebstein, Sheldon N., *Hemingway's Craft,* Southern Illinois University Press, 1973.

Griffin, Peter, *Along With Youth,* Oxford University Press, 1985.

Gurko, Leo, *Ernest Hemingway and the Pursuit of Heroism,* Crowell, 1968.

Hardy, Richard E. and John G. Cull, *Hemingway: A Psychological Portrait,* Banner Books, 1977.

Hassan, Ihab, *The Dismemberment of Orpheus: Toward a Postmodern Literature,* Oxford University Press, 1971.

Hemingway, Ernest, *A Moveable Feast,* Scribner, 1964.

Hemingway, *Death in the Afternoon,* Scribner, 1932.

Hemingway, Gregory H., *Papa: A Personal Memoir,* Houghton, 1976.

Hemingway, Leicester, *My Brother, Ernest Hemingway,* Fawcett, 1972.

Hemingway, Mary Welsh, *How It Was,* Knopf, 1976.

Hoffman, Frederick J., *The Modern Novel in America,* Regnery, revised edition, 1963.

Hotchner, A. E., *Papa Hemingway: A Personal Memoir,* Bantam, 1966.

Howe, Irving, *A World More Attractive: A View of Modern Literature and Politics,* Horizon Press, 1963.

Kazin, Alfred, *Bright Book of Life: American Novelists and Storytellers from Hemingway to Mailer,* Little, Brown, 1973.

Madden, David, editor, *Tough Guy Writers of the Thirties,* Southern Illinois University Press, 1968.

Morris, Wright, *The Territory Ahead: Critical Interpretations in American Literature,* Harcourt, 1958.

Nahal, Chaman, *The Narrative Pattern in Ernest Hemingway's Fiction,* Fairleigh Dickinson, 1971.

Priestley, J. B., *Literature and Western Man,* Harper, 1960.

Rahv, Philip, *The Myth and the Powerhouse,* Farrar, Straus, 1965.

Reynolds, Michael S., *Hemingway's First War: The Making of "A Farewell to Arms,"* Princeton University Press, 1976.

Rovit, Earl R., *Ernest Hemingway,* Twayne, 1963.

Seward, William, *My Friend Ernest Hemingway,* A. S. Barnes, 1969.

Stephens, Robert O., *Hemingway's Nonfiction: The Public Voice,* University of North Carolina Press, 1968.

Unfried, Sarah P., *Man's Place in the Natural Order: A Study of Ernest Hemingway's Major Works,* Gordon Press, 1976.

Updike, John, *Picked-Up Pieces,* Knopf, 1975.

Wagner, Linda W., editor, *Ernest Hemingway: Five Decades of Criticism,* Michigan State University Press, 1974.

Waldhorn, Arthur, *Ernest Hemingway,* McGraw, 1973.

Westbrook, Max, editor, *The Modern American Novel: Essays in Criticism,* Random House, 1966.

Wylder, Delbert E., *Hemingway's Heroes,* University of New Mexico Press, 1969.

Young, Philip, *Ernest Hemingway,* University of Minnesota Press, revised edition, 1965.

Young, *Ernest Hemingway: A Reconsideration,* Pennsylvania State University Press, 2nd edition, 1966.

PERIODICALS

American Scholar, summer, 1974.
Arizona Quarterly, spring, 1973.
Chicago Tribune, July 17, 1986.
Chicago Tribune Book World, October 13, 1985, May 4, 1986, August 24, 1986.
Detroit News, June 9, 1985.
Georgia Review, summer, 1977.
Globe and Mail (Toronto), November 30, 1985, May 31, 1986.
Kenyon Review, winter, 1941.
Los Angeles Times, May 22, 1986, January 25, 1987.
Los Angeles Times Book Review, June 23, 1985.
Mediterranean Review, spring, 1971.
Midwest Quarterly, spring, 1976.
Modern Fiction Studies, summer, 1975.
New Masses, November 5, 1940.
Newsweek, May 19, 1986.
New Yorker, May 13, 1950.
New York Review of Books, December 30, 1971.
New York Times, June 1, 1985, May 21, 1986, July 24, 1989, August 17, 1989.
New York Times Book Review, June 9, 1985, May 18, 1986.
New York Times Magazine, August 18, 1985.
Observer, February 8, 1987.
Publishers Weekly, January 11, 1985.
Southwest Review, winter, 1976.
Time, May 26, 1986.
Times (London), July 18, 1985, August 1, 1986, February 12, 1989.
Washington Post, July 29, 1987.
Washington Post Book World, June 30, 1985, November 3, 1985, June 1, 1986.
Yale Review, spring, 1969.

*   *   *

HENDERSON, F. C.
See MENCKEN, H(enry) L(ouis)

*   *   *

HENDERSON, Sylvia
See ASHTON-WARNER, Sylvia (Constance)

*   *   *

HENLEY, Beth
See HENLEY, Elizabeth Becker

*   *   *

HENLEY, Elizabeth Becker 1952-
(Beth Henley)

PERSONAL: Born May 8, 1952, in Jackson, Miss.; daughter of Charles Boyce (an attorney) and Elizabeth Josephine (an actress; maiden name, Becker) Henley. *Education:* Southern Methodist University, B.F.A., 1974; attended University of Illinois, 1975-76.

ADDRESSES: Home—Los Angeles, Calif. *Agent*—Gilbert Parker, William Morris Agency, 1350 Avenue of the Americas, New York, N.Y. 10019.

CAREER: Actress and playwright. Theatre Three, Dallas, Tex., actress, 1972-73; Southern Methodist University, Directors Colloquium, Dallas, member of acting ensemble, 1973; Dallas Minority Repertory Theatre, Dallas, teacher of creative dramatics, 1974-75; University of Illinois, Urbana, teacher of beginning acting, Lessac voice technique, 1975-76. Actress, Great American People Show, summer, 1976.

AWARDS, HONORS: Co-winner of Great American Playwriting Contest, Actor's Theatre of Louisville, 1978, nominee for Susan Smith Blackburn Award, 1979, New York Drama Critics Circle Award for best new American play, 1981, Guggenheim Award from *Newsday,* 1981, Pulitzer Prize for drama, 1981, and Antoinette Perry (Tony) Award nomination for best play, 1981, all for "Crimes of the Heart"; Academy Award nomination for best adapted screenplay, 1986, for movie version of "Crimes of the Heart."

WRITINGS:

ALL UNDER NAME BETH HENLEY

Am I Blue (one-act play; first produced in Dallas, Tex., at Southern Methodist University Margo Jones Theatre, fall, 1973), Dramatists Play Service, 1982.

Crimes of the Heart (three-act play; first produced in Louisville, Ky., at Actors Theatre, February 18, 1979; produced on Broadway at John Golden Theatre, November 4, 1981; also see below), Dramatists Play Service, 1981.

"Morgan's Daughters" (script for television pilot), Paramount, 1979.

The Miss Firecracker Contest (two-act play; first produced in Los Angeles, Calif., at Victory Theatre, spring, 1980; produced Off-Broadway at Manhattan Theatre Club, June, 1980; also see below), Dramatists Play Service, 1985.

The Wake of Jamey Foster (two-act play; first produced in Hartford, Conn., at Hartford Stage Theatre, January 1, 1982; produced on Broadway at Eugene O'Neill Theatre, October 14, 1982), Dramatists Play Service, 1985.

"The Debutante Ball" (play), first produced in Costa Mesa, Calif., at South Coast Repertory, April, 1985.

(With Budge Threlkeld) "Survival Guides" (television script), Public Broadcasting System, 1985.

"Crimes of the Heart" (screenplay; based on author's play of the same title), De Laurentiis Entertainment Group, 1986.

"Nobody's Fool" (screenplay), Island Pictures, 1986.

(With David Byrne and Stephen Tobolowsky) "True Stories" (screenplay), Warner Bros., 1986.

The Lucky Spot (play; first produced in Williamstown, Mass., at Williamstown Theatre Festival, summer, 1986; produced on Broadway at City Center Theatre, April, 1987), Dramatists Play Service, 1987.

"Miss Firecracker" (screenplay), Corsair Pictures, 1988.

SIDELIGHTS: Elizabeth Becker Henley—Beth Henley to theatregoers—is a member of the new breed of American playwrights dedicated to preserving regional voices on the stage. In Henley's case, her Mississippi upbringing provides the background for a host of Southern-accented plays, one of which, the black comedy "Crimes of the Heart," went on to win its author a Pulitzer Prize when she was 29. Like many playwrights before her, Henley originally set her sights on being an actress. She ventured into writing, though, after deciding there weren't many good contemporary roles for Southern women. A product of Southern Methodist University, Henley got her first play produced there, a one-act work called "Am I Blue." In 1976, the playwright moved to Los Angeles to live with actor/director Stephen Tobolowsky (with whom she would later collaborate on the screenplay "True Stories"). Three years later Henley submitted a three-act play to the Great American Play Contest sponsored by Actors Theatre of Louisville, Kentucky. Henley's play— "Crimes of the Heart"—won the contest and there began the first of its many successful stagings.

Set in Hazlehurst, Mississippi, "five years after Hurricane Camille," the story centers on three eccentric sisters who converge in the home of the youngest, Babe, after she has shot her well-to-do husband because, as Babe puts it, "I didn't like his looks." The other sisters include Meg, a would-be singer who has struck out in Hollywood; and Lenny, single and desperate at age 30. These sisters, according to Edith Oliver in a *New Yorker* review, "walking wounded, who are in tears at one moment and giggling and hugging at the next, . . . are very much of the South, of Mississippi, and [novelist] Eudora Welty has prepared us for them." John Simon reviewed the production for *New York* magazine and finds "the play is an essence, *the* essence of provincial living." Simon further calls "Crimes of the Heart" a "loving and teasing look back at deep-southern, small-town life, at the effect of constricted living and confined thinking on three different yet not wholly unalike sisters amid Chekhovian boredom in honeysuckle country, and, above all, at the sorely tried but resilient affection and loyalty of these sisters for one another."

Some critics took exception to Henley's use of ironic black-humor in "Crimes of the Heart." Michael Feingold, writing in *Village Voice,* for instance, thinks the playwright's attitude toward her three main characters, with its "pity and mockery aimed at them in laser-gun bursts," has "no organic connection and no deep roots. The play gives the impression of gossiping about its characters rather than presenting them, and [Henley's] voice, though both individual and skillful, is the voice of a small-town southern spinster yattering away on the phone, oozing pretended sympathy and real malice for her unfortunate subjects, and never at any point coming close to the truth of their lives." And to *New Leader* reviewer Leo Sauvage, "I find nothing enthralling in spending an evening with three badly adjusted, if not mentally retarded sisters, who are given free rein to exhibit their individual eccentricities." Sauvage concludes that he would label Henley's humor as "sick, not black."

But others see great value in Henley's work. "Crimes of the Heart" may be "overlong, occasionally cliched and annoyingly frivolous at moments," notes *Daily News* critic Don Nelson, "but Henley keeps intriguing us with a delightfully wacky humor plus a series of little mysteries played out by characters we can never dismiss as superficial on a set that absorbs us into their lives." "The physical modesty of her play belies the bounty of plot, peculiarity, and comedy within it," concludes *Saturday Review* writer Scot Haller of Henley's effort. "Like Flannery O'Connor [another Southern novelist], Henley creates ridiculous characters but doesn't ridicule them. Like Lanford Wilson [a contemporary playwright], she examines ordinary people with extraordinary compassion. Treating the eccentricities of her characters with empathy, [Henley] manages to render strange turns of events not only believable but affecting."

"Crimes of the Heart" was eventually adapted into movie form, as was another Henley play, "The Miss Firecracker Contest." In the latter story, a ne'er-do-well young woman, Carnelle Scott, seeks to uplift her station in her small Mississippi town. She figures the best way to gain respect would be to win the "Miss Firecracker" beauty contest, a rather cheesy local affair. To that end, Carnelle enlists other outcasts in her town to aid in her quest. As the play opens, Carnelle is seen on a bare stage dressed in a leotard and draped in an American flag, tap-dancing and baton-twirling her way through the "Star-Spangled Banner." "Though [the playwright's] territory looks superficially like the contemporary American South," writes *Time*'s Richard Schickel, "it is really a country of the mind: one of Tennessee Williams' provinces that has surrendered to a Chekhovian raiding party, perhaps. Her strength is a wild anecdotal inventiveness, but her people, lost in the ramshackle dreams and tumble-down ambitions with which she invests them, often seem to be metaphors waywardly adrift. They are blown this way and that by the gales of laughter they provoke, and they frequently fail to find a solid connection with clear and generally relevant meaning." Unfortunately for Henley, "The Miss Firecracker Contest" did not last long on the boards.

"It is not often that a girl from Jackson, Mississippi, can accomplish so much in what might be called a 'big city' world of film and theatre," declares Lucia Tarbox in a *Dictionary of Literary Biography Yearbook: 1986* article on the playwright. "However, Beth Henley has managed to succeed by bringing her southern small-town past with her. [Though she's known both financial success and failure], she does not allow the negative to overcome that which is positive." Quoting Henley, Tarbox concludes with the observation, "Something I'm sure has to do with the South's defeat in the Civil War, which is that you should never take yourself too seriously. You may be beaten and defeated, but your spirit cannot be conquered. The South has the gall to still be able to say we have our pride, but as a human characteristic it is admirable."

BIOGRAPHICAL/CRITICAL SOURCES

BOOKS

Contemporary Literary Criticism, Gale, Volume 23, 1983.
Dictionary of Literary Biography Yearbook: 1986, Gale, 1987.

PERIODICALS

Daily News (New York), November 5, 1981.
Los Angeles Times, April 16, 1983.
New Leader, November 30, 1981.
Newsweek, December 22, 1986.
New York, November 16, 1981.
New Yorker, January 12, 1981.
New York Times, June 8, 1979, December 22, 1980, February 15, 1981, April 14, 1981, June 10, 1981, June 11, 1981, October 25, 1981, November 5, 1981, December 28, 1981, April 14, 1982, May 28, 1984, November 2, 1986.
New York Times Magazine, May 1, 1983.
Saturday Review, November, 1981, January, 1982.
Time, June 11, 1984, December 22, 1986.
Village Voice, November 18, 1981.
Washington Post, December 12, 1986.

* * *

HENRI, Adrian (Maurice) 1932-

PERSONAL: Surname is pronounced as the English "Henry"; born April 10, 1932, in Birkenhead, Cheshire, England; son of Arthur Maurice (a civil servant) and Emma (Johnson) Henri; married Joyce Wilson (a model), November 29, 1959 (divorced). *Education:* University of Durham, B.A. (honors), 1955. *Politics:* "Non-doctrinaire anarchist." *Religion:* None.

ADDRESSES: Home—21 Mount St., Liverpool L1 9HD, England. *Agent*—Deborah Rogers Ltd., 20 Powis Mews, W11 England.

CAREER: Writer, artist, and singer. Worked as fairground worker, teacher, and scenic artist, 1955-61; Manchester College of Art and Design, Manchester, England, part-time lecturer, 1961-64; Liverpool College of Art, Liverpool, England, lecturer in department of foundation studies, 1964-67; full-time per-

former with the Liverpool Scene (a poetry/pop music group), 1967-70; toured the U.S. as solo performer, 1973 and 1976, and Canada, 1980; writer-in-residence at Tattenhall Schools' Centre, Cheshire, England, 1980-82, and Liverpool University, 1989. Has exhibited paintings at Institute of Contemporary Arts, 1968, Art Net, 1975, Wolverhampton, 1976, and Demarco Gallery, 1977. Visiting lecturer, Bradford College.

MEMBER: Liverpool Academy of Arts (president, 1972-81).

AWARDS, HONORS: Prize for painting from Arts Council of Northern Ireland, 1964; John Moores Liverpool prize for painting, 1972.

WRITINGS:

(With Michael Kustow) "I Wonder: A Guillaume Apollinaire Show," first produced in London, 1968.
(With Nell Dunn) *I Want* (novel; also see below), J. Cape, 1972.
Total Art: Environments, Happenings, and Performances, Praeger, 1974 (published in England as *Environments and Happenings,* Thames & Hudson, 1974).
(With Carol Ann Duffy) *Beauty and the Beast,* Glasshouse Press, 1977.
(With Roger Wade Walker) *Eric the Punk Cat* (juvenile), Hodder & Stoughton, 1982.
(With Dunn) "I Want" (based on novel of the same title), produced in Liverpool, 1983.
(With Walker) *Eric and Frankie in Las Vegas* (juvenile), Hodder & Stoughton, 1987.

Also author of *The Postman's Palace* (juvenile), 1990.

POETRY

(With Roger McGough and Brian Patten) *The Mersey Sound: Penguin Modern Poets 10,* Penguin, 1967, new edition, 1983.
Tonight at Noon, Rapp & Whiting, 1968, McKay, 1969.
City, Rapp & Whiting, 1969.
Talking after Christmas Blues, with music by Wallace Southam, Turret Books, 1969.
Poems for Wales and Six Landscapes for Susan, Arc Publications, 1970.
Autobiography, J. Cape, 1971.
America, Turret Books, 1972.
The Best of Henri: Selected Poems, 1960-70, J. Cape, 1975.
One Year, Arc Publications, 1976.
City Hedges: Poems, 1970-76, J. Cape, 1977.
Words without a Story, Glasshouse Press, 1979.
From the Loveless Motel: Poems, 1976-79, J. Cape, 1980.
Penny Arcade: Poems, 1978-82, J. Cape, 1983.
Collected Poems: Nineteen Sixty-seven to Nineteen Eighty-five, Allison & Busby, 1986.
The Phantom Lollipop Lady, and Other Poems (juvenile), Methuen, 1986.

Also author of *Rhinestone Rhino* (juvenile), 1989, and *Wish You Were Here,* 1990.

Also performer on recordings. Work appears in anthologies, including *Liverpool Scene,* edited by Edward Lucie Smith, Rapp & Carroll, 1967; and *The Oxford Book of Twentieth-Century English Verse,* Oxford University Press, 1973. Also author of television script "Yesterday's Girl," 1973.

SIDELIGHTS: Adrian Henri told *CA:* "I was trained as a painter and still paint and exhibit. I think my fine art background has had a considerable effect on my writing. Painters tend to be more aware of international movements and how they relate to them than are writers. In my case, the movements of the Fifties and Sixties—Abstract Expressionism and Pop Art—had a decisive influence on my approach to writing. So too has modern jazz, rock and roll, country music, the blues, and the language of advertising, particularly for television.

"I began to write in a manner now recognizable as my own through being involved in weekly poetry readings in the early Sixties in Liverpool. For me, poetry is, very much, a heightened form of my own speech. Many of my poems have been set to music. Working with sympathetic musicians has increased my awareness of the rhythms in my work.

"Paradoxically, perhaps, although I believe there is no substitute for hearing the poet's voice out loud, I believe *mis-en-page* and the opportunity to study words and images at leisure—that the printed page affords—to be equally important.

"Writing plays or songs or, indeed, exhibiting paintings seems to be all part of the same activity: the business of conveying images as clearly as possible."

AVOCATIONAL INTERESTS: Soccer, travel, old movies, genre fiction.

BIOGRAPHICAL/CRITICAL SOURCES:

BOOKS

Conversations, Flat Earth Press, 1975.
Nuttall, Jeff, *Bomb Culture,* McGibbon & Kee, 1969.
Raban, Jonathan, *The Society of the Poem,* Harrup, 1971.
Willett, John, *Art in a City,* Metheun, 1967.

PERIODICALS

Encounter, February, 1970, November, 1972, April, 1978.
Listener, February 24, 1972.
Observer, January 19, 1969, February 13, 1972.
Punch, November 13, 1968.
Times (London), November 15, 1986.
Times Literary Supplement, July 13, 1967, January 13, 1978, July 18, 1980, April 13, 1984.

* * *

HENRY, Marion
See del REY, Lester

* * *

HENRY, O.
See PORTER, William Sydney

* * *

HENRY, Oliver
See PORTER, William Sydney

* * *

HERBERT, Frank (Patrick) 1920-1986

PERSONAL: Born October 8, 1920, in Tacoma, Wash.; died of cancer, February 11, 1986, in Madison, Wis.; son of Frank and Eileen Marie (McCarthy) Herbert; married Flora Parkinson, March, 1941 (divorced, 1945); married Beverly Ann Stuart, June 23, 1946; children: Penny (Mrs. D. R. Merritt), Brian Patrick, Bruce Calvin. *Education:* Attended University of Washington, 1946-47.

ADDRESSES: Home—Port Townsend, Wash. *Agent*—Lurton Blassingame, 60 East 42nd St., New York, N.Y. 10017; and Ned Brown, P.O. Box 5020, Beverly Hills, Calif. 90210.

CAREER: Novelist. Lecturer in general and interdisciplinary studies, University of Washington, Seattle, 1970-72; consultant in social and ecological studies, Lincoln Foundation, and to countries of Vietnam and Pakistan, 1971; director and photographer of television show, "The Tillers," 1973.

MEMBER: World without War Council (member of national council, 1970-73; member of Seattle council, beginning 1972).

AWARDS, HONORS: Nebula Award, Science Fiction Writers of America, 1965, and Hugo Award, World Science Fiction Convention, 1966, both for *Dune;* Doctor of Humanities, Seattle University, 1980.

WRITINGS:

SCIENCE FICTION NOVELS

The Dragon in the Sea, Doubleday, 1956, reprinted, Gregg, 1980, published as *21st Century Sub,* Avon, 1956, published as *Under Pressure,* Ballantine, 1974.
Dune (also see below), Chilton, 1965.
The Green Brain, Berkley Publishing, 1966.
Destination: Void (also see below), Berkley Publishing, 1966, revised edition, 1978.
The Eyes of Heisenberg, Berkley Publishing, 1966.
The Heaven Makers, Avon, 1968.
The Santaroga Barrier, Berkley Publishing, 1968.
Dune Messiah (also see below), Berkley Publishing, 1970.
Whipping Star (also see below), Berkley Publishing, 1970.
The God Makers (also see below), Berkley Publishing, 1971.
Hellstrom's Hive, Doubleday, 1973.
Children of Dune (also see below), Berkley Publishing, 1976.
The Dosadi Experiment (also see below), Berkley Publishing, 1977.
The Illustrated Dune, Berkley Publishing, 1978.
(With Bill Ransom) *The Jesus Incident* (also see below), Berkley Publishing, 1979.
The Great Dune Trilogy (contains *Dune, Dune Messiah,* and *Children of Dune*), Gollancz, 1979.
Direct Descent, Ace Books, 1980.
Priests of Psi (also see below), Gollancz, 1980.
God, Emperor of Dune (Literary Guild selection), Berkley Publishing, 1981.
The White Plague, Putnam, 1982.
(With Bill Ransom) *The Lazarus Effect,* Putnam, 1983.
Heretics of Dune, Putnam, 1984.
Chapterhouse: Dune, Putnam, 1985.
Worlds beyond Dune: The Best of Frank Herbert (contains *The Jesus Incident, Whipping Star, Destination: Void, The God Makers,* and *The Dosadi Experiment*), Berkley Publishing, 1987.
(With Brian Herbert) *Man of Two Worlds,* Ace Books, 1987.

OTHER

(With others) *Five Fates* (short stories), Doubleday, 1970.
(Editor) *New World or No World* (interviews), Ace Books, 1970.
The Worlds of Frank Herbert (short stories), Ace Books, 1970.
Soul Catcher, Berkley Publishing, 1972.
The Book of Frank Herbert (short stories), DAW Books, 1972.
Threshold: The Blue Angels Experience (nonfiction), Ballantine, 1973.
The Best of Frank Herbert (short stories), Sphere Books, 1974.
(Editor with others) *Tomorrow, and Tomorrow, and Tomorrow . . . .,* Holt, 1974.
"Sandworms of Dune" (recording), Caedmon, 1978.
"The Truths of Dune" (recording), Caedmon, 1979.
"The Battles of Dune" (recording), Caedmon, 1979.

The Priests of Psi and Other Stories (short stories), Gollancz, 1980.
(With Max Barnard) *Without Me You're Nothing: The Essential Guide to Home Computers* (nonfiction), Simon & Schuster, 1981.
(Editor) *Nebula Awards Fifteen* (anthology), Harper, 1981.
The Maker of Dune, edited by Timothy O'Reilly, Berkeley Publishing, 1987.

Contributor of fiction to *Esquire, Galaxy, Amazing Stories, Analog,* and other magazines.

SIDELIGHTS: Frank Herbert's science fiction novel *Dune* has been highly praised for its detailed rendering of an imaginary world—the desert planet of Arrakis. A winner of both the Hugo and Nebula Awards, *Dune* is one of the best-known and most influential science fiction novels. Joseph McClellan of the *Washington Post Book World* describes *Dune* as "a portrayal of an alien society . . . more complete and deeply detailed than any author in the [science fiction] field had ever managed or attempted before." John Leonard of the *New York Times* writes that "J. R. R. Tolkien and C. S. Lewis, with their readymade Christian moralizing to fall back on, are not in Mr. Herbert's inventive league. For *Dune,* [Herbert] dreamed up several complete religions, an alien ecology and technology, entire histories and cultures and black arts." D. Douglas Fratz of the *Washington Post Book World* calls Herbert "a master world builder [who, in *Dune*], used a strong narrative—a struggle for political control of Arrakis—almost solely as framework for presenting the marvelous details of his creation."

Dune concerns the prophecy of a coming messiah and the eventual fulfillment of that prophecy. "[*Dune*] began," Timothy O'Reilly quotes Herbert in his book *Frank Herbert* as saying, "with a concept: to be a long novel about the messianic convulsions which periodically inflict themselves on human societies." *Dune Messiah, Children of Dune,* and *God Emperor of Dune,* further novels in the *Dune* series, explore the ramifications of the fulfilled prophecy and, in particular, what happens to a society that abdicates its decision-making powers to follow the dictates of a hero. In *Dream Makers,* Herbert states: "The bottom line in the *Dune* [series] is: beware of heroes. [It is] much better to rely on your own judgement, and your own mistakes." O'Reilly comments that "many of the features of the superhero mystique that [Herbert] unveils in *Dune* haunt our own culture. By increasing our awareness of a problem, science fiction can be a powerful tool for change. When it reaches the subconscious levels [as *Dune* does], it goes beyond being even a cautionary fable and becomes, in Herbert's own words, a 'training manual for consciousness.' "

Dune also reflects Herbert's concern with environmental preservation. The Fremen, a tribe of the planet Arrakis, must be vigilant in all of their actions so as not to upset the delicate balance of the planet's ecology. They are, as Gerald Jonas of the *New York Times* states, "a people forced by circumstances into total ecological awareness." In their efforts to save what little their barren planet provides them and to improve its fragile ecology, the Fremen graphically demonstrate the interdependence between man and his environment. "In the hands of skilled writers like Herbert," Willis E. McNelly states in *America,* "science fiction becomes a tool or a device to say something meaningful about our contemporary world. . . . We need to understand what we are doing to our own environment, Herbert seems to be saying [in his *Dune* series], because some of the things we've done . . . may already be beyond redemption with disastrous consequences for the earth and for human life."

John Ower of *Extrapolation* admires the way Herbert presents these matters of serious concern while providing his readers with an entertaining story. Ower praises "the complexity, the depth, and the symbolic virtuosity of [*Dune*]," while noting that Herbert's "art is rooted in the naive elements of good storytelling. . . . *Dune* is an adventure. . . . However, it coheres perfectly in its solidity of specification, never abandoning the concreteness and verisimilitude which are primal sources of pleasure." Ower finds that through *Dune*'s "appeal to our curiosity and wonder, Herbert leads us beyond a childlike fascination with his fictional surface to the intellectual and visionary depths behind it." He concludes that the novel is "a subtle, complex, and carefully crafted work of art. It thus constitutes an eloquent comment on the increasing maturity of science fiction as a form."

In contrast to this view, Robert Scholes writes in *Structural Fabulation* that "*Dune* is a romance of adventure, and it is not my intention . . . to suggest that this romance hides great speculative profundities." Scholes goes on to state: "Herbert wisely avoids loading the story with a greater conceptual weight than the romance of adventure can comfortably handle, nor does he often try to philosophize beyond his own intellectual range." He concludes that "tact, consistency, and restraint are what make this adventure story an exceptionally mature and interesting one."

Dune has become a powerful influence in the science fiction field, inspiring other novels that share its ecological concern. "So completely," Jonas writes, "did Mr. Herbert work out the interactions of man and beast and geography and climate that [*Dune*] became the standard for a new subgenre of 'ecological' science fiction." It has also proved its popularity with readers; the *Dune* books have sold over one million copies in hardcover and paperback editions.

Speaking of the *Dune* series as a whole, Jonas writes: "To read the *Dune* [books] is to plunge into someone else's obsession. As in Tolkien's *The Lord of the Rings,* nothing in these books is real, yet everything has a life-or-death importance. . . . I would personally rate the *Dune* [series] an unqualified success." Similarly, Leonard judges the series to be "the finest sustained fantasy I know of in imaginative literature."

For an interview with this author, see *Contemporary Authors New Revision Series,* Volume 5.

MEDIA ADAPTATIONS: "Dune" was filmed in 1984 by David Lynch; released by Dino de Laurentis/Universal, it starred Jose Ferrer as the Emperor of the Known Universe and Kyle MacLachlan as Paul Atreides.

BIOGRAPHICAL/CRITICAL SOURCES:

BOOKS

Aldiss, Brian W., *Billion Year Spree: The True History of Science Fiction,* Doubleday, 1973.
Allen, Louis David, *Herbert's 'Dune' and Other Works,* Cliff's Notes, 1975.
Berger, Harold L., *Science Fiction and the New Dark Age,* Popular Press, 1976.
Contemporary Literary Criticism, Gale, Volume 12, 1980, Volume 23, 1983, Volume 35, 1985, Volume 44, 1987.
Dictionary of Literary Biography, Volume 8: *Twentieth-Century Science Fiction Writers,* Gale, 1981.
McNelly, Willis E., *The Dune Encyclopedia,* Putnam, 1984.
O'Reilly, Timothy, *Frank Herbert,* Ungar, 1981.

Platt, Charles, *Dream Makers: The Uncommon People Who Write Science Fiction,* Berkley Publishing, 1980.

Riley, Dick, editor, *Critical Encounters: Writers and Themes in Science Fiction,* Ungar, 1978.

Scholes, Robert, *Structural Fabulation: An Essay on Fiction of the Future,* University of Notre Dame Press, 1975.

Scholes, Robert and Eric S. Rabkin, *Science Fiction: History, Science, Vision,* Oxford University Press, 1977.

PERIODICALS

Amazing Stories, July, 1956.
America, June 10, 1972, June 26, 1976.
Analog, July, 1956, April, 1966, June, 1970.
Booklist, May 1, 1976.
Chicago Tribune Book World, June 14, 1981.
Extrapolation, December, 1971, May, 1974, December, 1974, May, 1976.
Future Life, Number 14, 1979.
Galaxy, April, 1966, September, 1976, August, 1977.
Magazine of Fantasy and Science Fiction, March, 1966, April, 1969, May, 1971, February, 1977.
National Observer, May 23, 1977.
New Worlds, October, 1966.
New York Times, September 2, 1977, April 27, 1981.
New York Times Book Review, March 11, 1956, September 8, 1974, August 1, 1976, November 27, 1977, May 17, 1981.
Observer, October 3, 1976.
Psychology Today, August, 1974.
School Library Journal, March, 1973.
Science Fiction Review, August, 1970, August, 1979.
Spectator, August 26, 1978.
Time, March 29, 1971.
Times Literary Supplement, January 14, 1977.
Washington Post, December 14, 1984.
Washington Post Book World, May 9, 1976, May 24, 1981.

OBITUARIES:

PERIODICALS

Arlington USA, February 13, 1986.
Chicago Tribune, February 14, 1986.
Detroit Free Press, February 13, 1986.
Los Angeles Times, February 13, 1986.
Newsweek, February 24, 1986.
New York Times, February 13, 1986.
Publishers Weekly, February 28, 1986.
Time, February 24, 1986.
Washington Post, February 13, 1986.

*   *   *

HERBERT, Zbigniew 1924-

PERSONAL: Born October 29, 1924, in Lwow, Poland; son of Boleslaw (an attorney) and Maria (Kaniak) Herbert; married Katarzyna Dzieduszyska, April 30, 1968. *Education:* University of Krakow, M.A. (economics), 1947; Nicholas Copernicus University of Torun, M.A. (law), 1948; University of Warsaw, M.A. (philosophy), 1950.

ADDRESSES: Home—ul. Promenady 21m 4, 00-778 Warsaw, Poland.

CAREER: Poet, dramatist, and essayist. Also worked as a bank clerk, manual laborer, and journalist; did free-lance work for *Tworczosc* (literary review), 1955-76; co-editor of *Poezja* (poetry journal), 1965-68, resigned in protest of anti-Semitic policies.

Professor of modern European literature at California State College (now University), Los Angeles, 1970; professor at University of Gdansk, Gdansk, Poland, 1972. Has given poetry readings at universities and for national organizations throughout the United States, including the World Poetry Conference, State University of New York at Stony Brook, 1968, and Lincoln Center Festival, 1968. *Wartime service:* Member of Polish underground during World War II.

MEMBER: Polish Writers' Association (board member), P.E.N., Akademie der Kuenste, Bayerische Akademie der Schoenen Kuenste (corresponding member).

AWARDS, HONORS: Millenium Prize, Polish Institute of Arts and Sciences (United States), 1964; Nicholas Lenau Prize (Austria), 1965, for his contribution to European literature; Knight's Cross, Order of Polonia Restituta, 1974 (refused to accept); Bruno Schulz Prize, 1988.

WRITINGS:

IN ENGLISH TRANSLATION

Selected Poems, translated from the original Polish by Czeslaw Milosz and Peter Dale Scott, Penguin, 1968.

Selected Poems (includes selections from *Pan Cogito* [also see below]), translated from the original Polish by John Carpenter and Bogdana Carpenter, Oxford University Press, 1977.

Report from the Besieged City, translated from the original Polish by John Carpenter and Bogdana Carpenter, Ecco Press, 1985.

Barbarian in the Garden (essays; also see below), translated from the original Polish by Michael March and Jaroslaw Anders, Carcanet, 1985.

IN POLISH

Struna swiatla (poems; title means "A String of Light"), Czytelnik (Warsaw), 1956.

Hermes, pies i gwiazda (poems; title means "Hermes, a Dog and a Star"), Czytelnik, 1957.

Studium przedmiotu (poems; title means "The Study of an Object,"), Czytlenik, 1961.

Barbarzyna w ogrodzie (essays; title means "Barbarian in the Garden"), Czytelnik, 1962.

Dramaty (plays; title means "Dramas"; includes "The Philosophers' Den" and "The Reconstruction of the Poet"), Panstwowy Instytut Wydawniczy (Warsaw), 1970.

Pan Cogito (poems; title means "Mr. Cogito"), Czytelnik, 1974.

Author of *Napis* (title means "The Inscription"), 1969, *Wiersze zebrane* (title means "Collected Verse"), 1971, and *Wybor wiersze,* 1983; also author of radio plays and dramas, including *Inny pokoj* (title means "The Other Room"), *Jaskinia filozofow* (title means "Cove of Philosophers"), and *Lalek, rekonstrukcja poety,* 1973. Work represented in anthologies, including *The Broken Mirror,* edited by Pawel Mayewski, Random House (Toronto), 1958; *Introduction to Modern Polish Literature: An Anthology of Fiction and Poetry,* edited by Adam Gillon and Kudwik Krzyzanowski, Twayne, 1964; and *Postwar Polish Poetry: An Anthology,* edited by Czeslaw Milosz, Doubleday, 1965.

SIDELIGHTS: Although Zbigniew Herbert's surname is English, he considers himself a Polish writer, "even an unfashionably patriotic one." In an interview with *New Leader,* Herbert discussed his diversified family background: "There is a legend in my family to the effect that one of my paternal forebearers left England during the 16th century at a time of religious controversy. One of my grandmothers was Armenian. I come of a family of military people, mostly, and lawyers."

Herbert began writing poetry when he was seventeen, but did not publish until 1956, "after fifteen years of writing for the drawer." Certainly one factor in the late publication of his work was the political climate in Poland during the forties and fifties: the suppression of all publishing during the Nazi occupation and the severe literary censorship of the repressive Stalinist regime. And as Czeslaw Milosz pointed out: "Before 1956 the price for being published was to renounce one's own taste and he [Herbert] did not wish to pay it." Herbert, however, is not bitter about the fifteen-year wait; on the contrary, he considers it "a period of fasting" which gave him time to work on his attitudes without external pressures.

Described by Stephen Stepanchev as "a witness to his time," Herbert can be considered a political poet. But as Stephen Miller advised: "The word political may be misleading for it brings to mind the bad verse of the thirties, verse damaged by causes. . . . The political poet who deals directly with the events of contemporary history usually plays a losing game. His moral outrage will probably overwhelm his poetry, making it self-righteous, predictable, and shrill. . . . Although Herbert's poetry is preoccupied with the nightmares of recent history . . . it is not public speech. Subdued and casual, his poems shun both hysteria and apocalyptic intensity." According to A. Alvarez, Herbert "is political by virtue of being permanently and warily in opposition. . . . His opposition is not dogmatic: during the Nazi occupations he was not, to my knowledge, a Communist, nor during the Stalinist repression was he ever noticeably even Catholic or nationalist. Herbert's opposition is a party of one; he refuses to relinquish his own truth and his own standards in the face of any dogma."

Perhaps Herbert's "political" attitude can be found in his interpretation of the role of the poet. "In Poland," Herbert once stated, "we think of the poet as prophet; he is not merely a maker of verbal forms or an imitator of reality. The poet expresses the deepest feelings and the widest awareness of people. . . . The language of poetry differs from the language of politics. And, after all, poetry lives longer than any conceivable political crisis. The poet looks over a broad terrain and over vast stretches of time. He makes observations on the problems of his own time, to be sure, but he is a partisan only in the sense that he is a partisan of the truth. He arouses doubts and uncertainties and brings everything into question."

Although Herbert's purpose as a poet and the subjects of his poetry are serious, he mixes humor and satire effectively. "The most distinctive quality of Herbert's imagination," wrote Laurence Lieberman, "is his power to invest impish fantasy, mischievously tender nonsense, with the highest seriousness. His humorous fantasy is the armor of a superlatively healthy mind staving off political oppression. Fantasy is an instrument of survival: it is the chief weapon in a poetry arsenal which serves as a caretaker for the individual identity, a bulwark against the mental slavery of the totalitarian church and state." Miller also saw Herbert's humor as "a way of resisting the dehumanizing and impersonal language of the state. . . . Keeping a sense of humor means keeping a private language and avoiding the total politicization of the self."

Herbert's poetry is also laced with biblical and Greek mythological allusions. Miller contended that "the lens of myth reduces the glare of contemporary experience, placing it in a perspective that enables [Herbert] to view it without losing his sanity and sense of humor." He also pointed out that the use of myth "liberates

[Herbert] from the confines of particular historical events. . . . At the same time the use of myth fleshes out the thin bones of the satire, making it sly and elegant, not obvious and heavy-handed." For example, a poem entitled "Preliminary Investigation of an Angel" offers a comparison between totalitarian regimes and biblical mythology: an "angel" of the state, a member of the hierarchy, is put on trial and judged to be guilty of crimes against the "heavenly" government. The poem is reminiscent of the Stalin purges when no "faithful" member of the party was free from suspicion. In another poem, "Why the Classics," Herbert contrasts Thucydides, the Greek historian who accepted the responsibility for the failure of his mission to capture Amphipolis, with the "generals of most recent wars" who wallow in their self-pity and state that everyone, and therefore no one, is responsible for *their* failures and actions.

Pan Cogito is, according to Ruel K. Wilson, one of Herbert's most pessimistic works. Wilson, who sees Herbert as "Poland's finest postwar poet," noted that his "concern [in *Pan Cogito*] . . . is for humanity rather than for ideologies, which so often betray those who naively embrace them." To Bogdana Carpenter and John Carpenter, Herbert's concern is self-identity: "If Herbert discovers in himself traces of others and feels menaced by biological and historical determinism, he has at the same time an acute awareness of his separation from other human beings. In his earlier books Herbert frequently used the pronoun 'we' with a feeling of great solidarity and compassion for others, while in his recent work he tends to use the first-person singular pronoun. This is surprising—the ability to identify with other people . . . is one of Herbert's most striking traits."

Mr. Cogito, the main character in the book, is a problem to many critics. Unable to determine satisfactorily the relationship between Herbert and Cogito, critics have labeled the character petty and mediocre. His concerns are practical and his life ordinary. Cogito enjoys reading sensationalist newspaper features, fails when he tries transcendental meditation, and "his stream of consciousness brings up detritus like a tin can." But both Wilson and the Carpenters have dismissed such criticisms by noting that Cogito is a very human and universal man. According to Wilson, Cogito is "a modern intellectual who reads the newspapers, recalls his childhood, his family; he also muses on pop-art, America, alienation, magic, an aging poet, the creative process." For the Carpenters Cogito "is a device allowing Herbert to admit this ordinariness we all share, to establish it and, once this is done, to build upon it. Herbert wants to underline ordinariness and imperfection because he wants to deal with practical, not transcendent, morality. The poems of *Pan Cogito* consistently apply ethics not only to action but to the possible, viable action of everyday life, taking human failings into account. The poems are tolerant and humane in their approach, and they are less categorical than the earlier poems, embracing a greater sense of contradictions." Wilson noted that "in the last analysis, Cogito's 'weaknesses'—his incapacity for abstract thought, his rejection of dogmaticism, his very human petty fears and anxieties, his feelings of inadequacy and the concomitant self-irony—become his greatest strengths and virtues." With regard to the role of characters in his work, Herbert once stated: "The speaker of my poems is a generalized figure who speaks not for himself or for me but for humanity. He is representative; he speaks for a generation, if you like; he makes historical and moral judgements."

BIOGRAPHICAL/CRITICAL SOURCES:

BOOKS

Alvarez, A., *Under Pressure,* Penguin, 1965.

Alvarez, *Beyond All This Fiddle: Essays 1955-1967,* Random House, 1969.

Cheuse, Alan, and Richard Koffler, editors, *The Rare Action: Essays in Honor of Francis Fergusson,* Rutgers University Press, 1970.

Contemporary Literary Criticism, Gale, Volume 9, 1978, Volume 43, 1987.

PERIODICALS

Books Abroad, winter, 1972, spring, 1975.
Los Angeles Times, September 11, 1985.
Mosaic, fall, 1969.
New Leader, August 26, 1968.
Poetry, April, 1969.
World Literature Today, spring, 1977, autumn, 1978.

*   *   *

HERR, Michael   1940(?)-

PERSONAL: Born c. 1940.

ADDRESSES: Home—New York, N.Y. *Office*—c/o Alfred A. Knopf, Inc., 201 East 50th St., New York, N.Y. 10022.

CAREER: Writer.

WRITINGS:

Dispatches (nonfiction), Knopf, 1977.
(Author of narration) Francis Coppola and John Milius, "Apocalypse Now" (screenplay), United Artists, 1979.
(With Guy Peellaert) *The Big Room,* Simon & Schuster, 1987.
(With Gustav Hasford and Stanley Kubrick) "Full Metal Jacket" (screenplay), Warner Bros., 1987.
Walter Winchell: A Novel, Knopf, 1990.

Contributor of articles to *Rolling Stone, Esquire,* and *New American Review.*

MEDIA ADAPTATIONS: Dispatches was adapted into a musical by Elizabeth Swados and produced in New York City at the Martinson Hall/Public Theater, April 18, 1979.

SIDELIGHTS: In 1967 Michael Herr arrived in Vietnam to cover the war there for *Esquire.* Ten years later, *Dispatches,* his impressions of that time, was hailed by literary critics as perhaps the finest documentation of what it was like in Vietnam during the late 1960s. *Dispatches* has been called "convulsively brilliant," "nightmarish," and "awesome." C. D. B. Bryan called it "the best book to have been written about the Vietnam War."

Reporting the war was a difficult task. "I went to cover the war," Herr noted, "and the war covered me." Herr discovered that he actually enjoyed being there. As Paul Gray wrote, "Herr came to realize that Viet Nam was the most intense experience life was ever likely to offer him." Reveling in the danger of war, Herr wrote: "There were choices everywhere, but they were never choices that you could hope to make. There was even some small chance for personal style in your recognition of the one thing you feared more than any other. You could die in a sudden blood-burning crunch as your chopper hit the ground like dead weight, you could fly apart so that your pieces would never be gathered, you could take one neat round in the lung and go out hearing only the bubble of the last few breaths, you could die in the last stage of malaria with that faint tapping in your ears, and that could happen to you after months of firefights and rockets and machine guns. . . . You could be shot, mined, grenaded, rocketed, mortared, sniped at, blown up and away so that your leavings had to be dropped into a sagging poncho and carried to

Graves Registration, that's all she wrote. It was almost marvelous."

As a correspondent, Herr was an oddity in Vietnam for he was there by choice. "A GI would walk clear across a firebase for a look at you if he'd never seen a correspondent before," wrote Herr, "because it was like going to see the Geek, and worth the walk." Another passage reflects the disbelief Herr encountered among soldiers: " 'Oh man, you *got* to be kidding me. You guys *asked* to come here?' 'Sure.' 'How long do you have to stay?' he asked. 'As long as we want.' 'Wish *I* could stay as long as *I* want,' the Marine called Love Child said. '*I'd* been home las' March.' 'When did you get here?' I asked. 'Las' March.' "

Although he romanticized many of his own experiences in Vietnam, Herr was still able to see the war as a "story that was as simple as it had always been, men hunting men, a hideous war and all kinds of victims." He wrote of one soldier who escaped death by hiding under the corpses of his fellow soldiers while the enemy went about bayoneting the dead. In another episode, American troops escaping by helicopter were forced to shoot their Vietnamese allies who'd jeopardized the take-off by also trying to jump aboard.

Herr's writing throughout is oddly detached yet subjective. "He preaches no sermons, draws no morals, enters no ideological disputes," declared Gray. "He simply suggests that some stories must be told—not because they will delight and instruct but because they happened." However, John Leonard called *Dispatches* "a certain kind of reporting come of age—that is, achieving literature. It is the reporting of the 1960's at last addressing itself to great human issues, subjective, painfully honest, scaled of abstractions down to the viscera, the violence and the sexuality understood and transcended." He concluded with one word: "Stunning."

Critics also praise Herr's ear for dialogue. Alfred Kazin wrote, "Herr caught better than anyone else the kooky, funny, inventively desperate code in which the men in the field showed that they were well and truly in shit." Another critic, Geoffrey Wolff, reported that Herr "had ears like no one else's ears over there, and he brought an entire language back alive." Typical of the dialogue in *Dispatches* is one GI's comment when he learns that another soldier will only be in Vietnam for four months. "Four Months?" comes the reply. "Baby, four *seconds* in this whorehouse'll get you greased." Another soldier exclaims, "A dead buddy is some tough shit, but bringing your own ass out alive can sure help you to get over it."

Kazin reserved his highest praise for the political aspects of *Dispatches.* Despite his enthusiasm for the language, Kazin claimed that Herr's "big effort is not literary but political. To his generation, Vietnam did come down to so much self-enclosed, almost self-deafened, despair. No one gets above that specific cruel environment." He cites one soldier's rationale for being in Vietnam, "I mean, if we can't shoot these people, what . . . are we doing here?" Explaining why he can't die in Vietnam, another soldier contends, "'Cause it don't exist." Herr contrasts his own position with that of a "young soldier speaking in all bloody innocence, saying, 'All that's just a *load,* man. We're here to kill gooks. Period.' " Herr amends the soldier's comment by insisting that that "wasn't at all true of me. I was there to watch."

Upon returning to America, Herr had to deal with his memories of the war. "Was it possible that they were there and not haunted?," he wondered of his friends from the war. "No, not possible, not a chance. I know I wasn't the only one. Where are they now? (Where am I now?) I stood as close to them as I could without actually being one of them, and then I stood as far back as I could without leaving the planet." While sharing departure with other correspondents, Herr observed: "A few extreme cases felt that the experience there had been a glorious one, while most of us felt that it had been merely wonderful. I think that Viet Nam was what we had instead of happy childhoods."

Gray concluded his review of *Dispatches* by noting, "Herr dared to travel to that irrational place and to come back with the worst imaginable news: war thrives because men still love it." But Bryan defended Herr's position: "To Michael Herr's credit he never ceased to feel deeply for the men with whom he served; he never became callous, always worried for them, agonized over them, on occasion even took up arms to defend them. His greatest service, I'm convinced, is this book."

BIOGRAPHICAL/CRITICAL SOURCES:

BOOKS

Herr, Michael, *Dispatches,* Knopf, 1977.

PERIODICALS

Atlantic, January, 1978.
Book World, November 6, 1977.
Esquire, March 1, 1978.
Los Angeles Times, June 21, 1987, June 26, 1987.
Los Angeles Times Book Review, September 20, 1987.
Newsweek, November 14, 1977, June 29, 1987.
New Times, November 11, 1977.
New York Review of Books, December 8, 1977.
New York Times, October 28, 1977, April 19, 1979, June 26, 1987, May 14, 1990.
New York Times Book Review, November 20, 1977.
Saturday Review, January 7, 1978.
Time, November 7, 1977, June 29, 1987.
Tribune Books (Chicago), May 13, 1990.
Washington Post, June 26, 1987, June 28, 1987.

* * *

HERSEY, John (Richard) 1914-

PERSONAL: Born June 17, 1914, in Tientsin, China; son of Roscoe Monroe (a Y.M.C.A. secretary in China) and Grace (a missionary; maiden name Baird) Hersey; married Frances Ann Cannon, April 27, 1940 (divorced, February, 1958); married Barbara Day Addams Kaufman, June 2, 1958; children: (first marriage) Martin, John, Ann, Baird; (second marriage) Brook (daughter). *Education:* Yale University, B.A., 1936; attended Clare College, Cambridge, 1936-37. *Politics:* Democrat.

ADDRESSES: Home—420 Humphrey St., New Haven, Conn. 06511.

CAREER: Private secretary, driver, and factotum for Sinclair Lewis, summer, 1937; writer, editor, and correspondent, *Time* magazine, 1937-44, correspondent in China and Japan, 1939, covered South Pacific warfare, 1942, correspondent in Mediterranean theater, including Sicilian campaign, 1943, and in Moscow, 1944-45; editor and correspondent for *Life* magazine, 1944-45; writer for *New Yorker* and other magazines, 1945—; made trip to China and Japan for *Life* and *New Yorker,* 1945-46; fellow, Berkeley College, Yale University, 1950-65; master, Pierson College, Yale University, 1965-70, fellow, 1965—; writer-in-residence, American Academy in Rome, 1970-71; lecturer, Yale University, 1971-75, professor, 1975—. Chairman, Connecticut Volunteers for Stevenson, 1952; member of Adlai Stevenson's campaign staff, 1956. Editor and director of writers' co-operative

magazine, '47. Member of Westport (Conn.) School Study Council, 1945-50, of Westport Board of Education, 1950-52, of Yale University Council Committee on the Humanities, 1951-56, of Fairfield (Conn.) Citizens School Study Council, 1952-56, of National Citizens' Commission for the Public Schools, 1954-56; consultant, Fund for the Advancement of Education, 1954-56; chairman, Connecticut Committee for the Gifted, 1954-57; member of Board of Trustees, Putney School, 1953-56; delegate to White House Conference on Education, 1955; trustee, National Citizens' Council for the Public Schools, 1956-58; member, visiting committee, Harvard Graduate School of Education, 1960-65; member, Loeb Theater Center, 1980—; Yale University Council Committee on Yale College, member, 1959-61, chairman, 1964-69; trustee, National Committee for Support of the Public Schools, 1962-68.

MEMBER: National Institute of Arts and Letters, American Academy of Arts and Letters (secretary, 1961-78, chancellor, 1981—), American Academy of Arts and Sciences, Authors League of America (member of council, 1946-70, vice-president, 1949-55, president, 1975-80), Authors Guild (member of council, 1946—), PEN.

AWARDS, HONORS: Pulitzer Prize, 1945, for *A Bell for Adano;* Anisfield-Wolf Award, 1950, for *The Wall;* Daroff Memorial Fiction Award, Jewish Book Council of America, 1950, for *The Wall;* Sidney Hillman Foundation Award, 1951, for *The Wall;* Howland Medal, Yale University, 1952; National Association of Independent Schools Award, 1957, for *A Single Pebble;* Tuition Plan Award, 1961; Sarah Josepha Hale Award, 1963; named honorary fellow of Clare College, Cambridge University, 1967. Honorary degrees: M.A., Yale University, 1947; L.H.D., New School for Social Research, 1950, Syracuse University, 1983; LL.D., Washington and Jefferson College, 1950; D.H.L., Dropsie College, 1950; Litt.D., Wesleyan University, 1954, Bridgeport University, 1959, Clarkson College of Technology, 1972, University of New Haven, 1975, Yale University, 1984, Monmouth College, 1985, William and Mary College, 1987.

WRITINGS:

Men on Bataan, Knopf, 1942.
Into the Valley: A Skirmish of the Marines, Knopf, 1943.
Hiroshima (first published in *New Yorker,* August 31, 1946), Knopf, 1946, school edition, Oxford Book Co., 1948.
Here to Stay: Studies on Human Tenacity, Hamish Hamilton, 1962, Knopf, 1963.
The Algiers Motel Incident, Knopf, 1968.
(With others) *Robert Capa,* Paragraphic, 1969.
Letter to the Alumni, Knopf, 1970.
(Editor) *Ralph Ellison: A Collection of Critical Essays,* Prentice-Hall, 1973.
(Editor) *The Writer's Craft,* Knopf, 1974.
The President, Knopf, 1975.
Aspects of the Presidency: Truman and Ford in Office, Ticknor & Fields, 1980.
Blues, Knopf, 1987.
(Author of commentary) John Armour and Peter Wright, *Manzanar,* Times, 1988.
Life Sketches, Knopf, 1989.

NOVELS

A Bell for Adano, Knopf, 1944, with new foreword by Hersey, Modern Library, 1946.
The Wall, Knopf, 1950.
The Marmot Drive, Knopf, 1953.
A Single Pebble, Knopf, 1956.

The War Lover, Knopf, 1959.
The Child Buyer, Knopf, 1960.
White Lotus, Knopf, 1965.
Too Far to Walk, Knopf, 1966.
Under the Eye of the Storm, Knopf, 1967.
The Conspiracy, Knopf, 1972.
My Petition for More Space, Knopf, 1974.
The Walnut Door, Knopf, 1977.
The Call: An American Missionary in China, Knopf, 1985.

SIDELIGHTS: In his article "The Novel of Contemporary History" for the *Atlantic Monthly* in 1949, John Hersey states: "Fiction is a clarifying agent. It makes truth plausible. Who had even a tenable theory about the Soviet purge trials until he had read Koestler's *Darkness at Noon?* Who understood the impact of Italian Fascism upon peasants, on the one hand, and upon thinking men, on the other, until he had read Silone's *Fontamara* and *Bread and Wine?* What is argued here is only this much: among all the means of communication now available, imaginative literature comes closer than any other to being able to give an impression of the truth."

This use of imaginative literature to present historical truth has been one of Hersey's major concerns. His Pulitzer Prize-winning *A Bell for Adano* is set in an Italian village occupied by American troops during World War II; *The Wall* is set in the Jewish ghetto in Warsaw at the close of that war; and Hersey's nonfictional work *Hiroshima* uses fictional techniques to present its story of Japanese atom bomb survivors. "Hersey [has] dedicated himself to the goal of chronicling the events and issues of his time," Sam B. Girgus notes in the *Dictionary of Literary Biography.*

"Hersey is an impressive figure in contemporary American letters," writes Nancy L. Huse in her study *The Survival Tales of John Hersey.* Huse finds in Hersey's work "a mind rebelling at the age's acceptance of nuclear weapons, the Holocaust, racism, and the annihilation of the individual in a technological society." This attitude "places Hersey as an intellectual contemporary of Bellow, Wright, Mailer and Agee," Huse argues. Similarly, Eva Hoffman, writing in the *New York Times,* notes that "it has been John Hersey's virtue as teacher and public figure . . . that, against all odds and the grain of the times, he has sustained the idea of writing as a moral mission." Jonathan Yardley of the *Washington Post Book World* finds that "Hersey's decency is both transparent and transcendent. He cares about matters that deserve to be cared about, and he writes about them with palpable passion."

MEDIA ADAPTATIONS: A Bell for Adano was adapted as a stage play by Paul Osborn and was first produced at the Cort Theater in New York in December, 1944, and was filmed by Twentieth Century-Fox in 1945; *The Wall* was dramatized by Millard Lampell and was first produced at the Billy Rose Theater in New York in December, 1960, and was filmed for television by Columbia Broadcasting System in 1982; *The War Lover* was filmed by Columbia Pictures in 1962; *The Child Buyer* was adapted as a stage play by Paul Shyre and was first produced at the University of Michigan Professional Theater Program in Ann Arbor in 1964.

AVOCATIONAL INTERESTS: Sailing, gardening, fishing, reading.

BIOGRAPHICAL/CRITICAL SOURCES:

BOOKS

Contemporary Literary Criticism, Gale, Volume 1, 1973, Volume 2, 1974, Volume 7, 1977, Volume 9, 1978, Volume 40, 1986.

Dictionary of Literary Biography, Volume 6: *American Novelists since World War II,* Gale, 1980.
Huse, Nancy Lyman, *John Hersey and James Agee: A Reference Guide,* G. K. Hall, 1978.
Huse, Nancy Lyman, *The Survival Tales of John Hersey,* Whitston, 1983.
Sanders, David, *John Hersey,* Twayne, 1967.

PERIODICALS

Atlantic Monthly, November, 1949, April, 1966.
Book Week, September 26, 1965.
Commonweal, March 5, 1965.
Life, March 18, 1966.
National Observer, February 8, 1965.
Newsweek, January 25, 1965, June 7, 1965.
New York Herald Tribune Book Review, August 29, 1946, March 5, 1950, August 20, 1950, June 3, 1956, September 25, 1960.
New York Times, April 22, 1985.
New York Times Book Review, February 6, 1944, February 26, 1950, June 10, 1956, September 25, 1960, January 19, 1965, February 28, 1966, May 10, 1987.
Publishers Weekly, May 10, 1985.
Saturday Review, November 2, 1946, March 4, 1950, June 2, 1956, January 23, 1965.
Time, June 4, 1956, January 29, 1965, March 25, 1966.
Times Literary Supplement, December 7, 1946.
Washington Post Book World, October 16, 1977.
Yale Review, winter, 1987.

*   *   *

HERVEY, Evelyn
   See KEATING, H(enry) R(eymond) F(itzwalter)

*   *   *

HERZOG, E.
   See MAUROIS, Andre

*   *   *

HESSE, Hermann   1877-1962
(Hermann Lauscher, Emil Sinclair)

PERSONAL: Born July 2, 1877, in Calw, Wuerttemberg, Germany; died August 9, 1962; Swiss citizen, 1924-62; son of Johannes (a religious journalist, publisher, and missionary) and Marie (Gundert) Hesse; married Maria Bernoulli, 1904 (divorced, 1923); married Ruth Wenger, January, 1924 (divorced, 1927); married Ninon Auslaender Dolbin, November, 1931 (died September 22, 1966); children: (first marriage) Bruno, Heiner, Martin. *Education:* Attended preparatory Latin school of Rector Otto Bauer, Goeppingen, Germany, 1890-1891; studied theology at Seminar Maulbronn, 1891-92; attended Gymnasium at Cannstadt, expelled in 1893.

ADDRESSES: Home—Montagnola, near Lugano, Switzerland.

CAREER: Apprenticed to a bookseller in Esslingen, Germany; worked in Calw, Germany for six months as assistant to his father at Calwer Verlagsverein (a publishing association); apprentice in the clock factory of Heinrich Perrot, in Calw, 1894; Heckenhauer book shop in Tuebingen, Germany, apprentice, 1895-98, assistant, 1898-1899; worked with a book dealer in Basel, Switzerland, 1899-1901; author, 1903-62; *Maerz* (periodical), editor, 1907-12; during World War I edited *Sonntagsbote fuer deutsche Kriegsgefangene,* the periodical for prisoners of war; co-editor of *Deutsche Internierten-Zeitung,* 1916-17, and of *Vivos Voco,* 1919-20. *Wartime service:* Served as a volunteer worker through the German consulate in Bern, Switzerland, on behalf of the German prisoners of war, 1914-18.

MEMBER: Prussian Academy of Poets (resigned in 1926 when he lost faith in German politics), Schweizerischer Schriftstellerverein ("Swiss Writers Club"; Zuerich).

AWARDS, HONORS: Wiener Bauernfeldpreis, 1904; Fontanepreis, 1920, for *Demian* (Hesse declined this award as it was intended for new writers); Gottfried-Keller Prize for literature (Zuerich) 1936; Nobel Prize for Literature, 1946; Goethe-Preis (Frankfurt), 1946; honorary doctorate, University of Bern, 1947; Wilhelm Raabe-Preis, 1950; Peace Prize of the German Book Trade, 1955; Knight of the order Pour le Merite (Friedensklasse), 1955.

WRITINGS:

POETRY

Romantische Lieder, E. Pierson, 1899.
(Under pseudonym Hermann Lauscher) *Hinterlassene Schriften und Gedichte,* Reich, 1901, published under name Hermann Hesse as *Hermann Lauscher,* S. Fischer, 1933.
Gedichte, G. Grote, 1902.
Unterwegs, Mueller, 1911, supplement with title *Zeitgedichte,* 1915.
Aus Indien: Aufzeichnungen von einer indischen Reise, S. Fischer, 1913.
Musik des Einsamen, E. Salzer, 1915.
Gedichte des Malers, Verlag Seidwyla, 1920.
Ausgewaehlte Gedichte, S. Fischer, 1921.
Italien, Euphorion-Verlag, 1923.
Verse im Krankenbett, Staempfli, 1927.
Vom "grossen" und vom "kleinen" Dichtertum, O. Harrassowitz, 1928.
Trost der Nacht: Neue Gedichte, S. Fischer, 1929.
Jahreszeiten, Gebrueder Fretz, 1931.
Blumengiessen, 1933.
Besinnung, Erasmusdruck, 1934.
Lehen einer Blume, Erasmusdruck, 1934.
Vom Baum des Lebens, Insel Verlag, 1934.
Schmerzen, Erasmusdruck, 1935.
Jahreslauf, Orell Fuessli, 1936.
Ein Traum Josef Knechts, privately printed by Erasmusdruck, 1936.
Das Haus der Traeume (an incomplete poem), Vereinigung Oltner Buecherfreunde, 1936.
Stunden im Garten: Eine Idylle, Bermann-Fischer, 1936.
Chinesisch, S. Fischer, 1937.
Orgelspiel, Erasmusdruck, 1937.
Der lahme Knabe: Eine Erinnerung aus der Kindheit, Gebrueder Fretz, 1937.
Neue Gedichte, S. Fischer, 1937.
Foehnige Nacht, S. Fischer, 1938.
Der letzte Glasperlenspieler, S. Fischer, 1938.
Zehn Gedichte, privately printed by Staempfli, 1939.
Die Gedichte (collected poems), Fretz & Wasmuth, 1942, 5th enlarged edition, 1956.
Fuenf Gedichte, privately printed by Franz Schmitt, 1942.
Krankennacht, 1942.
Stufen: Noch ein Gedicht Josef Knechts, Bezirksschule fuer das graphische Gewerbe in Thueringen, 1943.
Der Bluetenzweig, Fretz & Wasmuth, 1945.

Friede 1914 [and] *Dem Frieden entgegen 1945: Zwei Friedensgedichte,* K. H. Silomon, 1945.
Spaete Gedichte, privately printed by Tschudy, 1946.
In Sand geschrieben, Neue Zuercher Zeitung, 1947.
Drei Gedichte, Conzett & Huber, 1948.
Jugendgedichte, G. Grote, 1950.
Zwei Gedichte, privately printed by Tschudy, 1951.
Rueckblick (fragment), Conzett & Huber, 1951.
Zwei Idyllen: Stunden im Garten [and] *Der lahme Knabe,* Suhrkamp, 1952.
Gedichte, Suhrkamp, 1953.
Alter Maler in der Werkstatt (for Hans M. Purrmann), 1954.
Klage und Trost, 1954.
Zum Frieden, Tschudy, 1956.
Wanderer im Spaetherbst, [Montagnola], 1956, Staempfli, 1958.
Wenkenhof: Eine romantische Jugenddichtung, National-Zeitung, 1957.
Das Lied von Abels Tod, [Montagnola], 1957.
24 ausgewaehlte Gedichte, edited by Hans R. Hilty, Tschudy, 1958.
Treue Begleiter, Tschudy, 1958.
Gedichte, Tschudy, 1958.
Besinnung [and] *Stufen,* Tschudy, 1959.
Vier spaete Gedichte, privately printed by Tschudy, 1959.
Freund Peter: Bericht an die Freunde, privately printed by Gebrueder Fretz, 1959, published as *Bericht an die Freunde: Letzte Gedichte,* Vereinigung Oltner Buecherfreunde, 1960.
Stufen: Alte und neue Gedichte in Auswahl, Suhrkamp, 1961, 2nd edition, 1966.
Die spaeten Gedichte, Insel Verlag, 1963.
Buchstaben, Kumm, 1965.
Poems, selected and translated by James Wright, Farrar, Straus, 1970.
Stufen: Ausgewaehlte Gedichte, Suhrkamp, 1972.
Poems, Bantam, 1974.

NOVELS

Peter Camenzind, S. Fischer, 1904, translation by Walter J. Strachan, P. Owen, 1961, translation by Michael Roloff, Farrar, Straus, 1969.
Unterm Rad, S. Fischer, 1906, translation by Strachan published as *The Prodigy,* Vision Press, 1957, translation by Roloff published as *Beneath the Wheel,* Farrar, Straus, 1969.
Gertrud, A. Langen, 1910, translation by Hilda Rosner published as *Gertrude,* Vision Press, 1955, revised translation, Farrar, Straus, 1969.
Rosshalde, S. Fischer, 1914, translation by Ralph Manheim, Farrar, Straus, 1970.
(Under pseudonym Emil Sinclair) *Demian: Die Geschichte von Emil Sinclairs Jugend,* S. Fischer, 1919, translation by N. H. Friday published as *Demian,* Boni & Liveright, 1923, new edition with foreword by Thomas Mann published as *Demian: The Story of a Youth,* Holt, 1948, new translation by Roloff and Michael Lebeck, with introduction by Mann, published as *Demian: The Story of Emil Sinclair's Youth,* Harper, 1965, reprinted as *Demian,* Bantam, 1981.
Siddhartha: Eine indische Dichtung, S. Fischer, 1922, translation by Rosner published as *Siddhartha,* New Directions, 1951.
Aufzeichnungen eines Herrn im Sanatorium (fragment), Phaidon-Verlag, 1925, published as *Haus zum Frieden: Aufzeichnungen eines Herrn im Sanatorium,* Johannespresse, 1947.
Der Steppenwolf, S. Fischer, 1927, translation by Basil Creighton published as *Steppenwolf,* Holt, 1929, revised edition, 1963.

Narziss und Goldmund, S. Fischer, 1930, translation by Geoffrey Dunlop published as *Death and the Lover,* Dodd, 1932 (later published in England by P. Owen as *Goldmund,* 1959, and as *Narziss and Goldmund,* 1965), new translation by Ursule Molinaro published as *Narcissus and Goldmund,* Farrar, Straus, 1968.

Die Morgenlandfahrt: Eine Erzaehlung, S. Fischer, 1932, translation by Rosner published as *The Journey to the East,* Vision Press, 1956, Noonday, 1957.

Das Glasperlenspiel: Versuch einer Lebensbeschreibung des Magister Ludi Josef Knecht samt Knechts hinterlassenen Schriften, two volumes, Fretz & Wasmuth, 1943, translation by Mervyn Savill published as *Magister Ludi,* Holt, 1949, 2nd edition, Aldus, 1957, new translation by Richard Winston and Clara Winston published as *The Glass Bead Game (Magister Ludi),* Holt, 1969, and as *Magister Ludi (The Glass Bead Game),* Bantam, 1970.

Berthold (fragment), Fretz & Wasmuth, 1945.

SHORT FICTION

Eine Stunde hinter Mitternacht, E. Diederichs, 1899.

Diesseits (five tales), S. Fischer, 1907, new edition, 1930.

Nachbarn (five tales), S. Fischer, 1908.

Umwege (five tales), S. Fischer, 1912.

Der Hausierer, Stuttgart, 1914.

Anton Schievelbeyns ohn-freiwillige Reise nachher ost-Indien, H. F. S. Bachmair, 1914.

Knulp: Drei Geschichten aus dem Leben Knulps (published in part in 1908), S. Fischer, 1915, new edition, Oxford University Press, 1932, translation by Ralph Manheim published as *Knulp: Three Tales from the Life of Knulp,* Farrar, Straus, 1971.

Am Weg (eight tales), Reuss & Itta, 1915, published as *Am Weg: Erzaehlungen,* W. Classen, 1946, enlarged edition published as *Am Weg: Fruehe Erzaehlungen,* 1970.

Schoen ist die jugend (two tales), S. Fischer, 1916, new edition, Prentice-Hall, 1932, original edition published as *Schoen ist die jugend und der Zyklon: Zwei Erzaehlungen,* Suhrkamp, 1961.

Hans Dierlamms Lehrzeit (a tale), Kuenstierdank-Gesellschaft, 1916.

Alte Geschichten (two tales), Buecherzentrale fuer deutsche Kriegsgefangene, 1918.

Zwei Maerchen (two tales), Buecherei fuer deutsche Kriegsgefangene, 1918.

Maerchen, S. Fischer, 1919, translation by Denver Lindley published as *Strange News from Another Star and Other Tales,* Farrar, Straus, 1972.

Im Presselschen Gartenhaus: Eine Erzaehlung dem alten Tuebingen (a tale), Lehmann, 1920.

Klingsors letzter Sommer (three tales), S. Fischer, 1920, translation by R. Winston and C. Winston published as *Klingsor's Last Summer,* Farrar, Straus, 1970.

Die Offizina Bodoni (miscellany), J. Hegner, 1923.

Psychologia balnearia oder Glossen eines Badener Kurgastes, privately printed in Montagnola, 1924, published as *Kurgast: Aufzeichnungen von einer Badener Kur,* S. Fischer, 1925.

Die Verlobung (tales), Verein fuer Verbreitung guter Schriften, 1924.

Piktors Verwandlungen (a tale), Gesellschaft deutsche Buecherfreunde, 1925.

Die Nuernberger Reise (a tale), S. Fischer, 1927.

Der Zyklon und andere Erzaehlungen (tales), S. Fischer, 1929.

Weg nach Innen: Vier Erzaehlungen (four tales), S. Fischer, 1932.

Hermann Hesse (selections), edited by Alfred Simon, E. Reinhardt, 1932.

Kleine Welt (seven revised tales and poems from *Nachbarn, Umwege* and *Aus Indien*), S. Fischer, 1933.

Fabulierbuch (tales), S. Fischer, 1935.

Tragisch (a tale), H. Reichner, 1936.

In der alten Sonne (a tale), P. Reclam, 1943.

Der Pfirsichbaum und andere Erzaehlungen (tales), Buechergilde Gutenberg, 1945.

Traumfaehrte: Neue Erzaehlungen und Maerchen (early tales, 1910-32), Fritz & Wasmuth, 1945.

Kurgast [and] *Die Nuernberger Reise: Zwei Erzaehlungen* (two tales), Fretz & Wasmuth, 1946.

Heumond [and] *Aus Kinderzeiten: Erzaehlungen,* Gute Schriften, 1947.

Weg nach Innen: Vier Erzaehlungen (four tales; different selection than *Weg nach Innen* above), Suhrkamp, 1947.

Geheimnisse (tales), Conzett & Huber, 1947, published as *Geheimnisse: Letzte Erzaehlungen,* Suhrkamp, 1955.

Kinderseele (three tales), Duckworth, 1948.

Fruehe Prosa, Fretz & Wasmuth, 1948.

Kinderseele und Ladidel (two tales), edited by W. M. Dutton, Harrap, 1948, Heath, 1952.

Zwei Erzaehlungen: Der Novalis [and] *Der Zwerg,* edited by Anna Jacobson and Anita Asher, Appleton, 1948, 2nd edition, 1950.

Der Bettler (a tale), privately printed by Tschudy, 1949.

Glueck (a tale), privately printed by Tschudy, 1949.

Hermann Hesse (collection of early tales), two volumes, edited by Ernst Rheinwald and Otto Hartmann [Tuebingen and Stuttgart], 1949.

Drei Erzaehlungen (three tales), edited by Waldo C. Peebles, American Book Co., 1950.

Weihnacht mit zwei Kindergeschichten, Neue Zuercher Zeitung, 1951.

Bericht aus Normalien (fragment) [Montagnola], 1951.

Die Verlobung und andere Erzaehlungen (tales), Deutsche Buch-Gemeinschaft, 1951.

Spaete Prosa (collected tales, 1944-50), Suhrkamp, 2nd edition, 1967, American text edition edited by Theodore Ziolkowski, Harcourt, 1966.

Glueck (eleven tales), [Vienna], 1952.

Diesseits. Kleine Welt. Fabulierbuch, Suhrkamp, 1954.

Diesseits: Erzaehlungen, with a foreword by the author, Diogenes Verlag, 1954.

Der Wolf und andere Erzaehlungen (tales), edited by Martha Ringier, Schweizer, 1955.

Floetentraum, Arethusa Pers, 1955, 8th edition, 1969.

Zwei jugendliche Erzaehlungen (two tales), Vereinigung Oltner Buecherfreunde, 1956.

Der Zwerg [Bamberg], 1956.

Augustus, Der Dichter [and] *Ein Mensch mit Namen Ziegler,* edited by Thomas E. Colby, Norton, 1957, published as *Drei Erzaehlungen: Augustus, Der Dichter,* [and] *Ein Mensch mit Namen Ziegler,* Methuen, 1960.

Klein und Wagner (a tale), Suhrkamp, 1958, 2nd edition published as *Klein und Wagner: Novelle,* 1973.

Der Lateinschueler, Gute Schriften, 1958.

Tractat vom Steppenwolf, Suhrkamp, 1961.

Drei Erzaehlungen (three tales), Suhrkamp, 1961.

Tessiner Erzaehlungen (tales), with watercolors by the author, Fretz, 1962.

Weg nach Innen: Fuenf Erzaehlungen (five tales), Deutscher Buecherbund, 1965.

Prosa aus dem Nachlass, edited by Ninon Hesse, Suhrkamp, 1965.

Der vierte Lebenslauf Josef Knechts, edited by Ninon Hesse, Suhrkamp, 1966.

Aus Kinderzeiten und andere Erzaehlungen, Verlag der Arche, 1968.

Der Dichter, Arethusa Pers, 1969.

Stories of Five Decades, edited, with introduction, by Theodore Ziolkowski, translation by Ralph Manheim and Denver Linley, Farrar, Straus, 1972.

Weg nach Innen: Hermann Hesse (five tales; different selection than *Weg nach Innen* with five tales above), Suhrkamp, 1973.

Iris: Ausgewaehlte Maerchen (selected tales), Suhrkamp, 1973.

Tales of Student Life, edited, with introduction, by Ziolkowski, translation by Manheim, Farrar, Straus, 1975.

(And illustrator) *Pictor's Metamorphosis and Other Fantasies,* edited and with introduction by Ziolkowski, translated by Rika Lesser, Farrar, Straus, 1982.

NONFICTION

Boccaccio (monograph), Schuster & Loeffler, 1904.

Franz von Assisi (monograph), Schuster & Loeffler, 1904.

Faust und Zarathustra, Bremer Verlag, 1909.

Zum Sieg, [Stuttgart], 1915.

Kriegslektuere, Thomas, 1915.

Lektuere fuer Kriegsgefangene, Staempfli, 1916.

(With sister, Adele Hesse) *Zum Gedaechtnis unseres Vaters* (biography of their father, Johannes Hesse), Polygraphisches Institut, 1916, Wunderlich, 1930.

(Under pseudonym Emil Sinclair) *Eigensinn,* 1918.

(Published anonymously) *Zarathustras Wiederkehr: Ein Wort an die deutsche Jugend,* Staempfli, 1919.

(With Richard Woltereck) *Kindergenesungsheim Milwaukee: Ein Aufruf an die gebuertigen Deutschen im Ausland,* Seemann, 1920.

Wanderung, Aufzeichnungen: Mit farbigen Bildern vom Verfasser, S. Fischer, 1920, translation by James Wright published as *Wandering: Notes and Sketches,* Farrar, Straus, 1972.

Blick ins Chaos (three essays), Verlag Seldwyla, 1920, translation by Stephen Hudson published as *In Sight of Chaos,* Verlag Seldwyla, 1923.

Erinnerung an Lektuere, Braumueller, 1925.

Betrachtungen, S. Fischer, 1928.

Eine Bibliothek der Weltliteratur, Reclam-Verlag, 1929, Ungar, 1945, supplemented edition includes *Magie des Buches,* W. Classen, 1946.

Magie des Buches, Poeschel & Trepte, 1930.

Beim Einzug ins neue Haus, privately printed in Montagnola, 1931.

Gedenkblaetter, S. Fischer, 1937, 3rd edition, Suhrkamp, 1950.

Der Novalis: Aus dem Papieren eines Altmodischen, Vereinigung Oltner Buecherfreunde, 1940.

Kleine Betrachtungen (six essays), Staempfli, 1941.

Das seltene Buch, K. H. Silomon, 1942.

Gedenkblatt fuer Franz Schall, Fretz & Wasmuth, 1943.

Nachruf auf Christoph Schrempf, Fretz & Wasmuth, 1944.

Zwischen Sommer und Herbst, privately printed in Zurich, 1944.

Erinnerung an Klingsors Sommer, Fretz & Wasmuth, 1944.

Zwei Aufsaetze (two essays), privately printed by Gebrueder Fretz, 1945.

Maler und Schriftsteller, Museum Solothum, 1945.

Danksagung und moralisierende Betrachtung, [Montagnola], 1946.

Statt eines Briefes, [Montagnola], 1946.

Dank an Goethe (four essays), W. Classen, 1946.

Der Europaer (five essays), Suhrkamp, 1946.

Feuerwerk (essay), privately printed by Vereinigung Oltner Buecherfreunde, 1946.

Krieg und Frieden: Betrachtungen zu Krieg und Politik seit dem Jahre 1914 (twenty-nine essays), Fretz & Wasmuth, 1946, supplemented edition, [Berlin], 1949, translation by Manheim published as *If the War Goes On: Reflections on War and Politics,* Farrar, Straus, 1971.

Mein Glaube, Conzett & Huber, 1946.

Ansprache in der ersten Stunde des Jahres 1946, Neue Zuercher Zeitung, 1946.

Eine Konzertpause, Neue Zuercher Zeitung, 1947.

Stufen der Menschwerdung (first published in *Neue Rundschau,* number 43, 1932), Vereinigung Oltner Buecherfreunde, 1947.

Antwort auf Bittbriefe, privately printed in Montagnola, 1947.

Die kulturellen Werte des Theaters, 1947.

Berg und See, Buechergilde Gutenberg, 1948.

Ueber Romain Rolland, 1948.

Traumtheater, National-Zeitung, 1948.

Begegnungen mit Vergagenem, [Montagnola], 1949.

Gedenkblatt fuer Martin, Neue Zuercher Zeitung, 1949.

Gedenkblatt fuer Adele, privately printed by Gebrueder Fretz, 1949.

Stunden am Schreibtisch, National-Zeitung, 1949.

Wege zu Hermann Hesse (essay; excerpt from *Gedichten und Prosa*), edited by Walter Haussmann, Metzler, 1949.

Erinnerung an Andre Gide, Tschudy, 1951.

Ueber "Peter Camenzind," Neue Zuercher Zeitung, 1951.

Gedanken ueber Gottfried Keller, National-Zeitung, 1951.

Die Dohle, Neue Zuercher Zeitung, 1951.

Grossvaeterliches, privately printed by Tschudy, 1952.

Herbstliche Erlebnisse: Gedenkblatt fuer Otto Hartmann, Tschudy, 1952.

Lektuere fuer Minuten: Ein paar Gedanken aus meinen Buechern und Briefen, privately printed by Staempfli, 1952.

Nachruf fuer Marulla, Gebrueder Fretz, 1953.

Kaminfegerchen, privately printed by Tschudy, 1953.

Ueber das Alter, Vereinigung Oltner Buecherfreunde, 1954.

Notizblaetter um Ostern, Neue Zuercher Zeitung, 1954.

Abendwolken [and] *Bei den Massageten* (two essays), Tschudy, 1956.

Hilfsmaterial fuer den Literaturunterricht, Volk und Wissen Volksigener, 1956.

Der Trauermarsch: Gedenkblatt fuer einen Jugendfreund, Tschudy, 1957.

Tessin, Verlag der Arche, 1957.

(With Gunter Boehmer) *Festliches Tessin,* [Frankfurt-am-Main], 1957.

In Italien vor fuenfzig Jahren, National-Zeitung, 1958.

Eine Bodensee-Erinnerung, [Basel], 1961.

Aerzte: Ein paar Erinnerungen, Vereinigung Oltner Buecherfreunde, 1963.

Ein Blatt von meinem Baum, Hyperion-Verlag, 1964.

Neue deutsche Buecher: Literaturberichte fuer Bonniers Litteraera Magasin, 1935-36, edited by Bernard Zeller, Schiller Nationalmuseum, 1965.

Politische Betrachtungen, compiled by Siegfried Unseld, Suhrkamp, 1970.

Mein Glaube: Eine Dokumentation, compiled, with afterword, by Siegfried Unseld, Suhrkamp, 1971.

Autobiographical Writings, edited, with introduction, by Ziolkowski, translation by Lindley, Farrar, Straus, 1972.

Eigensinn: Autobiographische Schriften, compiled, with afterword, by Siegfried Unseld, Suhrkamp, 1972.

Schriften zur Literatur, two volumes, Suhrkamp, 1972.

Die Kunst des Mussiggangs: Kurze Prosa aus dem Nachlass, edited, with afterword, by Volker Michels, Suhrkamp, 1973.

My Belief: Essays on Life and Art, edited, with introduction, by Ziolkowski, translated by Lindley and Manheim, Farrar, Straus, 1974.

LETTERS

Der Junge Dichter: Ein Brief an Viele, A. Langen, 1910, published as *An einen jungen Dichter,* Callwey, 1932.

Zwei Briefe (correspondence with Thomas Mann), Tschudy, 1945.

Ein Brief nach Deutschland, National-Zeitung, 1946.

Brief an Adele, Neue Zuercher Zeitung, 1946.

Der Autor an einen Korrektor, Kantonales Amt fuer berufliche Ausbildung, 1947.

Zwei Briefe ueber das Glasperlenspiel, National-Zeitung, 1947.

An einen jungen Kollegen in Japan, privately printed by Gebrueder Fretz, 1947.

Versuch einer Rechtfertigung (correspondence with Max Brod), Conzett & Huber, 1948.

Blaetter vom Tage, privately printed by Gebrueder Fretz, 1948.

Preziositaet (letter to Eduard Korrodi), Neue Zuercher Zeitung, 1948.

Auszuege aus zwei Briefen, Conzett & Huber, 1949.

An einen jungen Kuenstler, privately printed at Montagnola, 1949.

Zwei Briefe: An einen jungen Kuenstler [and] *Das junge Genie,* Tschudy, 1950, published as *Das junge Genie: Brief an einen Achtzehnjaehrigen,* 1950, also published as *Das junge Genie: Antwort an einen Achtzehnjaehrigen,* Neue Zuercher Zeitung, 1950.

An einen "einfachen Mann aus dem arbeitenden Volk," National-Zeitung, 1950.

Ein Brief zu Thomas Manns 75. Geburtstag, S. Fischer, 1950.

Kriegsangst: Antwort auf Briefe aus Deutschland, National-Zeitung, 1950.

An die Herausgeber der "Dichterbuehne", E. Blaschker Verlag, 1950.

Brief an einen schwaebischen Dichter (letter to Otto Heuschele), Vereinigung Oltner Buecherfreunde, 1951.

Glueckwunsch fuer Peter Suhrkamp, 1951.

Briefe (collection), Suhrkamp, 1951, 2nd enlarged edition, 1964.

Eine Handvoll Briefe (collection), Buechergilde Gutenberg, 1951.

Ahornschatten, Neue Zuercher Zeitung, 1952.

Letzter Gruss an Otto Hartmann, 1952.

Allerlei Post: Rundbrief an Freunde, Neue Zuercher Zeitung, 1952.

Geburtstag: Ein Rundbrief, 1952.

Engadiner Erlebnisse: Ein Rundbrief, Conzett & Huber, 1953.

[Correspondence with Romain Rolland], Fretz & Wasmuth, 1954.

Beschwoerungen: Rundbrief im Februar 1954, Tschudy, 1954.

Rundbrief aus Sils-Maria, Neue Zuercher Zeitung, 1954.

Ueber Gewaltpolitik, Krieg und das Boese in der Welt, National-Zeitung, 1955.

Ein paar Leserbrief an Hermann Hesse, privately printed in Montagnola, 1955.

Antworten, privately printed by Tschudy, 1958.

Ein paar indische Miniaturen, National-Zeitung, 1959.

An einen Musiker, Vereinigung Oltner Buecherfreunde, 1960.

Kindheit und Jugend vor Neunzehnhundert: Hermann Hesse in Briefen und Lebenszeugnissen, 1877-95, compiled and edited by Ninon Hesse, Suhrkamp, 1966.

Briefwechsel: Hermann Hesse-Thomas Mann, edited by Anni Carlsson, Suhrkamp, 1968.

Briefwechsel, 1945-59: [Von] Hermann Hesse [und] Peter Suhrkamp, edited by Siegfried Unseld, Suhrkamp, 1969.

Hermann Hesse, Helene Voigt-Diederichs: Zwei Autorenportraets in Briefen, 1897 bis 1900, Diederichs, 1971, also published as *Zwei Autorenportraets in Briefen, 1897 bis 1900: Hermann Hesse [und] Helen Voigt-Diederichs,* 1971.

Briefwechsel aus der Naehe [bei] Hermann Hesse [und] Karl Kerenyi, edited, with commentary, by Magda Kerenyi, Langen-Mueller, 1972.

D'une rive a l'autre: Hermann Hesse et Romain Rolland, Albin Michel, 1972.

COLLECTED WORKS

Gesammelte Dictungen, six volumes, Suhrkamp, 1952.

Gesammelte Schriften, seven volumes, Suhrkamp, 1957.

Gesammelte Werke, twelve volumes, Suhrkamp, 1970, 3rd edition, 1973.

Die Erzaehlungen: Hermann Hesse, compiled by Volker Michels, Suhrkamp, 1973.

Gesammelte Briefe, edited by Volker Michels and Ursula Michels, with Heiner Hesse, Suhrkamp, 1973.

EDITOR

(With Martin Lang and Emil Strauss) *Der Lindenbaum* (German folksongs), S. Fischer, 1910.

August J. Liebeskind, *Morgenlaendische Erzaehlungen,* Insel Verlag, 1913, 2nd edition, 1957.

Josef von Eichendorff, *Gedichte und Novellen,* Deutsche Bibliothek, 1913, new edition, 1945.

Jean Paul, *Titan,* Insel Verlag, 1913.

Ludwig Achim von Amim and Clemens Brentano, compilers, *Des Knaben Wunderhorn* (old German songs), Deutsche Bibliothek, 1913.

Das Meisterbuch, Deutsche Bibliothek, 1913, new edition, 1918.

Christian Wagner, *Gedichte,* Georg Mueller, 1913.

Der Zauberbrunnen (German romantic songs), Kiepenheuer, 1913.

Lieder deutscher Dichter, A. Langen, 1914.

Matthias Claudius, *Der Wandsbecker Bote,* Insel Verlag, 1915.

Gesta Romanorum, Insel Verlag, 1915.

Alemannenbuch, Verlag Seldwyla, 1919, new edition, 1920.

(With Walter Stich) *Ein Schwabenbuch fuer die deutschen Kriegsgefangenen,* Verlag der Buecherzentrale fuer deutsche Kriegsgefangene, 1919.

Xaver Schnyder von Wartensee, *Ein Luzerner Junker vor hundert Jahren* (excerpt from memoirs), Verlag Seldwyla, 1920.

Salomon Gessner, *Dichtungen,* Haessel, 1922.

Geschichten aus dem Mittelalter, K. Hoenn, 1925.

Maerchen und Legenden aus der Gesta Romanorum, Insel Verlag, 1926.

Goethe, *30 Gedichte,* Lesezirkel Hottingen, 1932.

SERIES EDITOR

(With Richard Woltereck) "Buecherei fuer deutsche Kriegsgefangene," twenty titles, Verlag der Buecherzentrale fuer deutsche Kriegsgefangene, 1918-19.

"Merkwuerdige Geschichten," six titles, Verlag Seldwyla, 1922-24.

"Merkwuerdige Geschichten und Menschen," seven titles, S. Fischer, 1925-27.

OTHER

Selma Lagerlof (excerpt from *Hinterlassene Schriften und Gedichte*), A. Langen, 1908.

Kleiner Garten: Erlebnisse und Dichtungen (miscellany), E. P. Tal, 1919.

Heimkehr (first act of a play), 1920.

Elf Aquarelle aus dem Tessin, O. C. Recht, 1921.

(Under pseudonym Emil Sinclair) *Sinclairs Notizbuch: Mit einer mehrfarbigen Tafel nach einem Aquarelle des Verfassers,* Rasher, 1923.

Bilderbuch, S. Fischer, 1926.

Krisis: Ein Stueck Tagebuch, S. Fischer, 1928.

Kurzgefasster Lebenslauf, edited by Erwin Ackerknecht, Herrcke & Lebeling, 1929.

Kastanienbaeume, Kunstgewerbeschule, 1932.

Mahnung: Erzaehlungen und Gedichte, privately printed by Werkstatt der Gothaer gewerbliche Berufsschule (Gotha), 1933.

Hieroglyphen, Erasmusdruck, 1936.

Drei Bilder aus einem alten Tessiner Park, Oprecht, 1938.

Prosa: Auf einen Dichter, Fretz & Wasmuth, 1942.

Bildschmuck im Eisenbahnwafen, Weltwoche-Verlag, 1944.

Rigi-Tagebuch, 1945, Staempfli, 1945.

Indischer Lebenslauf (excerpts from *Das Glasperlenspiel*), Gute Schriften, 1946.

Spaziergang in Wuerzburg, privately printed by Tschudy, 1947.

Fuer Max Wassmer, zum 60. Geburtstag, Der Bund, 1947.

Beschreibung einer Landschaft: Ein Stueck Tagebuch, privately printed by Staempfli, 1947.

Legende vom indischen Koenig, Bemer Handpresse E. Jenzer, 1948.

Der Stimmen und der Heilige (first published as "Ein Stueck Tagebuch" in *Betrachtungen*), privately printed by Johannespresse, 1948.

Fragment aus der Jugendzeit, Neue Zuercher Zeitung, 1948.

Notizen aus diesen Sommertagen, National-Zeitung, 1948.

Musikalische Notizen, Conzett & Huber, 1948.

Gerbersau (collected early writings), two volumes, R. Wunderlich, 1949.

Alle Buecher dieser Welt: Ein Almanach fuer Buecherfreunde, edited by K. H. Silomon, Verlag die Wage, 1949.

Aus vielen Jahren (poetry, stories, pictures, and other items), Staempfli, 1949.

Das Lied des Lebens, Neue Zuercher Zeitung, 1950.

Eine Arbeitsnacht, Neue Zuercher Zeitung, 1950.

Aus dem "Tagebuch eines Entgleisten," National-Zeitung, 1950.

Aus einem Notizbuch, Tschudy, 1951.

Noergeleien, National-Zeitung, 1951.

Eine Sonate, National-Zeitung, 1951.

Das Werk von Hermann Hesse: Ein Brevier (selections of fiction with excerpts from letters), edited by Siegfried Unseld, Suhrkamp, 1952.

Aprilbrief, Neue Zuercher Zeitung, 1952.

Dank fuer die Briefe und Glueckwuensche zum 2 Juli 1952, privately printed in Montagnola, 1952.

Kauf einer Schreibmaschine, National-Zeitung, 1952.

Regen im Herbst (Gruss und Glueckwunsch), privately printed in Montagnola, 1953.

Der Schlossergeselle, National-Zeitung, 1953.

Doktor Knoelges Ende, National-Zeitung, 1954.

Die Nikobaren, National-Zeitung, 1954.

Knopf-Annaehen, National-Zeitung, 1955.

Tagebuchblatt: Ein Maulbronner Seminarist, Tschudy, 1955.

Aquarelle aus dem Tessin, W. Klein, 1955.

Beschwoerungen: Spaete Prosa, neue Folge, Suhrkamp, 1955.

Magie des Buches: Betrachtungen und Gedichte, Hoehere Fachschule fuer das Graphische Gewerbe, 1956.

Gedichte und Prosa, Schroedel, 1956.

Cesco und der Berg, National-Zeitung, 1956.

Weihnachtsgaben und anderes, privately printed in Montagnola, 1956.

Wiederbegegnung mit zwei Jugendgedichten, Westermann, 1956.

Welkes Blatt, Schiller-National-Museum, 1957.

Gute Stunde, Laetare-Verlag, 1957.

Malfreunde, Malsorgen, Neue Zuercher Zeitung, 1957.

Betrachten und Briefe, Suhrkamp, 1957.

Hermann Hesse: Ein Auswahl, edited by Reinhard Buchward, Velhagen & Klasing, 1957.

Knulp, Peter Camenzind, [und] Briefe, edited, with notes by A. Rossen, Kastalia, 1958.

Chinesische Legende, privately printed by Tschudy, 1959.

Sommerbrief aus dem Engadin, privately printed by Tschudy, 1959.

Rueckgriff, privately printed by Tschudy, 1960.

Ein Paar Aufzeichnungen und Briefe, privately printed by Tschudy, 1960.

Aus einem Tagebuch des Jahres 1920, Verlag der Arche, 1960.

Das Wort, Conzett & Huber, 1960.

Schreiben und Schriften, privately printed by Tschudy, 1961.

Zen, privately printed by Tschudy, 1961.

Dichter und Weltburger (selections), edited by Gisela Stein, Holt, 1961.

Der Beichvater (selection from *Das Glasperlenspiel*), Furche-Verlag, 1962.

Prosa und Gedichte, compiled, with interpretation, by Franz Baumer, Koesel-Verlag, 1963.

Erwin, William Matheson, 1965.

Hermann Hesse: Eine Auswahl fuer Auslaender (selections in German for foreigners), compiled, with supplement, by Gerhard Kirchhoff, Hueber, 1966.

Lectuerefuer Minuten: Gedanken aus seinen Buechern und Briefen, compiled by Volker Michels, Suhrkamp, 1971.

Beschreibung einer Landschaft, Neske, 1971.

Glueck, Spaete Prosa, und Betrachtungen: Hermann Hesse, Suhrkamp, 1973.

Hermann Hesse und der ferner Osten, Buechergilde Gutenberg, 1973.

Reflections: Selections from his Books and Letters, compiled by Volker Michels, translated by Ralph Manheim, Farrar, Straus, 1974.

Also editor of numerous books. Work represented in many anthologies.

SIDELIGHTS: When Hermann Hesse was twelve years old, he read Hoelderlin's poem "Die Nacht" and decided that he must become a poet. Eva J. Engel wrote: "Quite clearly such an experience is something like a miracle which can be encountered only once in a lifetime. The individual thus summoned, alone and wondering, doubting his own fitness, is suddenly aware that he is completely set apart from all those around him by a heightened capacity, the capacity of 'individuation.' As part of this painful and yet wonderful process of 'coming into being' he will experience shocks which reveal things that were hidden to him and stood in the way of his inner progress."

As a young poet, Hesse attempted to escape from modern civilization. He was "overcome by an intensity of suffering," noted Miss Engel, and he refused to face the antitheses engendered by civilization. He felt himself incapable of either choosing or rejecting the "essential loneliness of the artist" (Engel). Thus, Hesse sought the serenity of nature, and his earliest work fell within the tradition of German Romanticism. He began by observing, feeling, and recording. The observation of nature brought insight into the beauty and mystery of nature and Hesse progressed to a recognition of self as external to the natural world of his observations. Hesse's early poetry, documenting his first interpretations of this duality of self and world, became the Goethean poetry of confession. He had begun to impose the discipline of ratiocination upon the spontaneity of observation. Miss Engel wrote: "the content of Hesse's work began to show more and more clearly that it was groping towards 'Erkenntnis' [In a footnote Engel added: "For Hesse this word would seem to stand for 'gaining insight into existence and its meaning'"]. This search begins with innumerable attempts to seek and describe the individual self, the real self, the essential self."

Hesse's search for self-definition eventually led to a more cogent definition of his opponent—the external world. Ralph Freedman stated: "This alien reality or 'world' is variously identified with anything seemingly external to the self, including objects of perception, non-intuitive reasoning, social pressures, or mercantilism; in short, it is a very wide concept and includes the very world of perception as well as contemporary reality." Once conscious of the adversary, Hesse began his lifelong pursuit of the ultimate acceptance or resolution of the conflict. His quest, however, was not wholly selfish. Miss Engel commented that Hesse wrote: "I am a poet, I seek and profess. It is my task to serve sincerity and truth. . . . I have a mission: those who also search must help to understand and to endure life." But he was yet unable to comprehend the nature of his goal. He became critical of his Romantic sentiments, of Christianity, and of Western thought, and he began the study of Eastern religions and philosophies in an effort to learn the technique of impersonal analysis through which the wisdom and depth of Chinese poetry is manifested. Ernst Rose said: "The Romantic quatrains were replaced by free verse and a more involved syntax. But Hesse still could not overcome his self. . . . There emerged a new clarity and simplicity, no longer naive, and almost brittle in its observation of distance. These mature poems still let the poetic self shine through, but the objective image now claimed the center of attention. Their quality is that of a wise serenity. . . . In such poems the real world has become ephemeral, a shell and a dress for the infinite. Hesse now seeks to be nothing more than a mirror, in which passing visions and images momentarily appear." Rose commented that Hesse himself said: "I had advanced far enough on the Eastern path of Lao-tse and of the *I Ching,* so I knew exactly how accidental and changeable was this so-called reality."

The influence of his study of Oriental philosophy was reflected in *Siddhartha.* "For Western readers," explained Rose, "*Siddhartha* climaxed centuries of effort to penetrate Eastern thought and religion and to understand that God had revealed himself to mankind in different ways." But as Hesse had become discontented with the formal religions of the West, so he concluded that Oriental dogma did not define the ultimate relationship between self and world in a fully acceptable manner. The "East" which he sought became a metaphor for the transcendental self. He was, nevertheless, assured of the existence of an omnipresent *divinity* (not a *deity* in the sense of a certain being) which, according to Rose, "could never be expressed in concrete anthropomorphic images, but was always accessible to mystic intuition." Hesse's study of the various formalized systems thus became part of a process of individuation; he realized that the goal of his personal quest could only be derived from his own interpretations of self and externality. Miss Engel noted: "Though he would never join Nietzsche in his clamouring for a 'revaluing of all values,' Hesse does accept, with distress, that 'God is dead';

he accepts the consequences that the individual must rethink metaphysical concepts by himself, that is without the support of recognized religions." Ralph Freedman stated: "As it confronts the world, the self seeks to absorb its opponent." And it was the necessity for selectivity in this absorption that forced Hesse to assume various stances in his confrontation with the world. His technique, then, must be the postulation, by an act of will, of creative illusion in which self and world are imposed upon one another. Freedman believes that, if Hesse's goal is to be the projection of the conflict between self and world into an ego that can unify them, he must employ either "mystical revelation" or "the illusion induced by art." Freedman remarked: "For Hesse, these two realms are interdependent—the mystic's vision encompassing more fully any unity achieved by art, the poet's apprehension sustaining in time the harmonies briefly envisioned in the mystic's trance. . . . The moment of reconciliation must be frozen in time. To elicit 'magic' from the materials of crude experience, Hesse must represent unity within the flow of time. The artist must capture the mystic's vision through his medium of words." (Rose told us that "in his most inspired moments, Hesse did not want to be called a poet or an artist, but a magician.") "Throughout Hesse's novels, stories, and fairy tales," Freedman continued, "idyllic moments and scenes occur as essential structural elements through which the hero's quest is accentuated and ultimately defined. . . . Hesse's protagonists, and occasionally the author himself, depict their experiences so as to unify past, present, and future in a single moment of apprehension."

It was through the medium of his fiction, then, that Hesse presented himself in opposition to the world. But his work is not autobiographical in the usual sense. Rather, he used "aesthetic self-portraits achieved through representative heroes" (Freedman). Freedman explained Hesse's employment of this device thus: "The perennial split between the individual and the world beyond him is portrayed, not in dramatic action, but in symbolic or allegorical self-representation. Echoing Novalis' idea of the artist as a supreme mimic dissolving alien existence in himself, Hesse renders his conflicts as symbolic 'self-portraits'. . . . These psychological self-portraits include particularly Hesse's versions of the 'eternal self' regulating the 'I' of poet and hero. Besides functioning as a Freudian superego, or, more pertinently, as a Jungian collective unconscious, this higher aspect of self acts as a *daemon* who guards its activities and comments upon them ironically. . . . Hermann Hesse's lyrical novels reconcile an inner vision with a universe of consecutive events. His success in creating an adequate form in the spirit of Novalis is his most important distinction as a modern writer and transcends many of his difficulties and imperfections. Combining allegorical narrative with psychological and philosophical self-portraits, he achieved a vision of man and ideas with an immediacy usually unobtainable in conventional narrative."

Thus Hesse's fiction uses the terms and processes of the real world to approach an ego operative in the realm of illusion. *Steppenwolf* was an important product of Hesse's thinking at this time. Rose commented: "It was the first German novel to include a descent into the cellars of the subconscious in its search for spiritual integration. With Freud it recognized the *libido,* and with Jung it discovered in the subconscious a reservoir of spiritual archetypes and formative ideas." But Hesse realized that his achievement in *Steppenwolf* was merely another step toward his goal. Miss Engel observed that twenty years later he wrote in *Das Glasperlenspiel:* "To transcend, rather like to awake, too, was a truly magic term for me. It was demanding, encouraging; it consoled and promised. My life, so I decided, was to consist of transcendence. It was to move with measured tread from step to step.

It was to pass through and leave behind one zone after another in the way in which a piece of music deals with theme after theme and different tempi by playing them, completing them, dismissing them, never wearying or falling asleep, on the contrary, fully awake and alert." Rose concluded: "With *Steppenwolf,* Hesse reached the end of his 'confessional' period. The poet realized that an exclusive concern with his own soul would never lead to the desired integration of man and society. Unity could be reached only by his immersion in the full stream of life, and in his last novels he chose to depict life as a whole."

At one time Hesse considered, although not seriously, becoming a musician and abandoning his writing. Music, for Hesse, functioned as the integration of the conflicting elements in self and world, producing either dissonance, which the artist must hopelessly attempt to resolve, or harmony in the achievement of art. Freedman believed that Hesse expressed his desire to be a musician in *Der Kurgast:* "If I were a musician I could write without difficulty a melody in two voices, a melody which consists of two notes and sequences which correspond to each other, which in any event stand to one another in the closest and liveliest reciprocity and mutual relationship. And anyone who could read music, could read my double melody, could see and hear in each tone its counterpoint, the brother, the enemy, the antipode." Freedman further explained that "as a writer, Hesse longs to be a musician, not because he might feel more at home in a non-literary metier, but because music embodies the very concept of harmony within dissonance which is his prevailing theme. The clash of opposites and their reconciliation is not only heard and made visually apparent to the reader of musical notations; it is also dramatized. . . . In its function of presenting simultaneously the harmony and dissonance of opposing motifs, music seems to solve the conflicts in self and world."

In 1931, Hesse began *Das Glasperlenspiel* ("The Bead Game"), a novel on which he worked for eleven years. "As early as 1935," related Rose, "Hesse called [this work] the final goal of his life and poetic activity." The novel postulates the achievement of a transcendental harmony of self and divinity wherein human existence finds its ultimate meaning. Miss Engel said of the novel: "By the Utopian nature of this ideal alliance Hesse refers us to accomplishment, to endeavor in a foreseeable future. He would not have turned to the future if he had considered the present congenial to such ideas. He could not reject the present without looking at it closely. Hence, his search is no longer concerned with the 'self in the past' but with the self in the present-day world. We are first of all concerned with the ego and the intellectual stimulus it received." Rose explained the premise and function of the novel for Hesse: "Since man is forever removed from [divinity], he can attain the ultimate only in symbolic form. This form is embodied in the bead game, a game played with glass beads strung on wires, with each bead representing a special theme or idea. . . . Things are set in proper perspective and are recognized in their transcendental relationship. They become translucent glass beads which anticipate the cosmic unity meant by the deity. The dreams of the subconscious are correlated to the abstractions of the intellect; the revelations of art to the systems of philosophy; romantic and Platonic visions to Chinese and Indian speculations; Nicholas of Cusa to Leibnitz and Hegel. The idea is to pursue the disparate elements of modern culture, and of every culture, to a common divine fountainhead. The bead game is no mere sport for jaded intellectuals. . . . For in Hesse's view, the elements of culture are by no means unimportant. They are not the inconsequential veil of Maya, but retain their weight and individuality. . . . This time Hesse wants to live life in earnest and find an applicable and practical solution

for the problem of human existence." Miss Engel summarized: "It is Hesse's extraordinary achievement, and good fortune, to have been able to jettison belief in dualism and to attempt to see life in terms of integration of phenomenon and idea. From a belief in opposites . . ., he advanced to the acceptance of polarity." "Hesse's view of man," wrote Rose, "can best be described as a poetic image of the total personality adumbrated by anthropological psychology. Here the individual stands in the spheres of nature and society just as much as he is indissolubly linked with history and with the forces of transcendency."

Music also functions as a symbol integral to the progress of the novel. Freedman stated: "It resolves dissonance by organizing experience and directing it toward a total vision rather than toward its consecutive or analytic explication. In this way, music can be seen . . . as the quintessence of imagination. It is 'the infinite within the finite, the element of genius present in all forms of art.' Its language, composed of magic formulae, is apt to frighten away philistines as new, indefinable worlds are opened up. An example of this view of music is Hesse's famous distinction in *Der Steppenwolf* between *rauschende* and *heitere* Musik. The former is chaotic music, likened to that of Wagner. A deceptive vision of unity is achieved by massive sound which blurs boundaries between contradictory elements and themes. Its chaos, apparently triumphant, merely reflects diversity in an indistinguishable mass. The latter is clear, detached music likened to that of Mozart. Its ordered harmonies show the interplay of contrasting motifs with precision; its detachment prevents the blurring of boundaries between self and world and so reflects an independent unity. Music deepens the melody of life and catches it in art."

In whatever manner Hesse presented his philosophical convictions, however, "he never wrote in the abstract terms of rational philosophy. His was the more suggestive language of art." (Rose). Miss Engel wrote: "[His was] a predilection for specific, generally onomatopoeic words, and, above all, for the rhythmic pattern of his prose. The prose is as flexible as the theme, and yet has a recognizable musicality of its own (only the *Glasperlenspiel* must be excepted). The sentence structure is beautifully clear, characterized by a throng of adjectives and a complex differentiation of content and emphasis by paraphrase. Antithetical structure has as much symbolic significance as the tripartite, graduated statement." The result of such writing, observed Rose, is the "achievement of transparency. The clarity of the vision gains depth and becomes mysterious." Rose believed, however, that Hesse's simplicity is often misunderstood. "The clarity of Hesse's language," he asserted, "was meant as a defense against chaos. . . . A transparent world is no accidental array of realistic details to which one has to adapt by compromise. It demands commitment."

Robin White, in the early 1960s, wrote: "Although Hermann Hesse received the Nobel Prize for literature in 1946, his work, with the possible exception of *Steppenwolf* has remained relatively unknown in the United States." Freedman explored this lack of interest among non-German-speaking readers: "The reasons are not too far to seek; they lie in his choice of the lyrical genre. In the English-speaking world, for example, this form appears alien to the novel, vaguely experimental, without the substance of character and plot required even of poetic novelists like Hardy or D. H. Lawrence. Nor does Hesse seem to be a 'symbolic' writer like Faulkner or Joyce."

In the following decade, however, Hesse's work sold well over six million copies in English translation. The *Times Literary Supplement* explained his rise from unknown lyrical experimentalist to literary cult hero: "The Hesse we read today is in fact no longer the bittersweet elegist of Wilhelmine Germany, the anguished intellectual entre deux guerres, the serene hermit of Montagnola apres Nobel. The cult has adjusted the kaleidoscope of Hesse's works in such a way as to bring into focus a Hesse for the 1970s: environmentalist, war opponent, enemy of a computerized technocracy, who seeks heightened awareness and who is prepared to sacrifice anything but his integrity for the sake of his freedom."

Although it is doubtful that he was aware of his illness, Hesse had leukemia. At the age of eighty-five, he died in his sleep from a brain hemorrhage.

MEDIA ADAPTATIONS: Siddhartha was filmed in 1972 by Lotus Films; *Der Steppenwolf* was filmed in 1974 by D/R Films, Inc. A cassette, "Beneath the Wheel," was released by G. K. Hall, 1985, and "Hesse between Music," by Caedmon; sections of Hesse's fiction have also been recorded. Hesse's work has been scored or adapted for numerous musical compositions.

AVOCATIONAL INTERESTS: Watercolor painting, music.

BIOGRAPHICAL/CRITICAL SOURCES:

BOOKS

Baumer, F., *Hermann Hesse,* Ungar, 1969.
Boulby, Mark, *Hermann Hesse: His Mind and Art,* Cornell University Press, 1967.
Contemporary Literary Criticism, Gale, Volume 1, 1973, Volume 2, 1974, Volume 3, 1975, Volume 6, 1976, Volume 11, 1979, Volume 17, 1981, Volume 25, 1983.
Dictionary of Literary Biography, Volume 66: *German Fiction Writers, 1885-1913,* Gale, 1988.
Farquharson, R. H., *An Outline of the Works of Hermann Hesse,* Forum House, 1973.
Field, G. W., *Hermann Hesse,* Twayne, 1970.
Freedman, Ralph, *The Lyrical Novel: Studies in Hermann Hesse, Andre Gide, and Virginia Woolf,* Princeton University Press, 1963.
Michels, Volker, compiler, *Materialien zu Hermann Hesses "Der Steppenwolf,"* Suhrkamp, 1972.
Michels, Volker, compiler, *Materialien zu Hermann Hesses "Das Glasperlenspiel,"* Suhrkamp, 1973.
Michels, Volker, *Hermann Hesse: Leben und Werk im Bild,* Insel-Verlag, 1973.
Mileck, Joseph, *Hermann Hesse and His Critics,* University of North Carolina Press, 1958.
Natan, Alex, editor, *German Men of Letters, Volume II,* Oswald Wolff, 1963.
Pfeifer, Martin, *Hermann Hesse-Bibliographie: Primarschrifttum und Sekundaerschrifttum in Auswahl,* Erich Schmidt, 1973.
Rose, Ernst, *Faith from the Abyss,* New York University Press, 1965.
Seidlin, Oskar, *Essays in German and Comparative Literature,* University of North Carolina Press, 1961.
Serrano, M., *C. G. Jung and Hermann Hesse,* Routledge & Kegan Paul, 1971.
Unseld, Siegfried, *Hermann Hesse: Eine Werkgeschichte,* Suhrkamp, 1973.
Waibler, Helmut, *Hermann Hesse: Eine Biblographie,* Francke-Verlag, 1962.
Zeller, Bernard, *Portrait of Hesse: An Illustrated Biography,* translation by Mark Hollebone, McGraw, 1971.
Ziolkowski, Theodore, *The Novels of Hermann Hesse: A Study in Theme and Structure,* Princeton University Press, 1967.
Ziolkowski, Theodore, editor, *Hesse,* Prentice-Hall, 1973.

PERIODICALS

Chicago Tribune Book World, January 17, 1982.
Comparative Literature, fall, 1970.
Times Literary Supplement, September 10, 1982.

*   *   *

HEYER, Georgette 1902-1974
(Stella Martin)

PERSONAL: Born August 16, 1902, in London, England; died July 4, 1974, in London, England; daughter of George and Sylvia (Watkins) Heyer; married George Ronald Rougier (a barrister), August 18, 1925; children: Richard George. *Education:* Privately educated.

ADDRESSES: Office—c/o Deborah Owen, 78 Narrow St. Limehouse, London NW 8, England.

CAREER: Writer, 1921-74; lived in Africa, 1925-28, and Yugoslavia, 1928-29.

WRITINGS:

The Black Moth, Houghton, 1921.
The Great Roxhythe, Hutchinson, 1922.
Instead of the Thorn, Hutchinson, 1923, Buccaneer Books, 1976.
(Under pseudonym Stella Martin) *The Transformation of Philip Jettan,* [London], 1923, published as *Powder and Patch: The Transformation of Philip Jettan,* Heinemann, 1930.
Simon the Coldheart, Small, Maynard, 1925.
These Old Shades, Heinemann, 1926, Dutton, 1966.
Helen, Longmans, Green, 1928.
The Masqueraders, Heinemann, 1928.
Beauvallet, Heinemann, 1929.
Pastel, Longmans, Green, 1929.
The Barren Corn, Longmans, Green, 1930.
The Conqueror, Heinemann, 1931, Dutton, 1964.
The Convenient Marriage, Heinemann, 1934, Dutton, 1966.
Devil's Cub, Heinemann, 1934, Dutton, 1966.
Regency Buck, Heinemann, 1935, Dutton, 1966.
An Infamous Army (historical novel), Heinemann, 1937, Dutton, 1965.
Royal Escape, Heinemann, 1938, Dutton, 1967.
No Wind of Blame, Hodder & Stoughton, 1939, Dutton, 1970.
The Spanish Bride (historical novel), Heinemann, 1940, Dutton, 1965.
The Corinthian, Heinemann, 1940, Dutton, 1966.
Faro's Daughter, Heinemann, 1941, Dutton, 1967.
Beau Wyndham, Doubleday, 1941.
Friday's Child, Heinemann, 1944, Putnam, 1946.
The Reluctant Widow, Putnam, 1946.
The Foundling, Putnam, 1948.
Arabella, Putnam, 1949.
The Grand Sophy, Putnam, 1950.
The Quiet Gentleman, Heinemann, 1951, Putnam, 1952.
Cotillion, Putnam, 1953.
The Toll-Gate, Putnam, 1954.
Bath Tangle, Putnam, 1955.
Sprig Muslin, Putnam, 1956.
April Lady, Putnam, 1957.
Sylvester; or, The Wicked Uncle, Putnam, 1957.
Venetia, Heinemann, 1958, Putnam, 1959.
The Unknown Ajax, Heinemann, 1959, Putnam, 1960.
A Civil Contract, Heinemann, 1961, Putnam, 1962.

Pistols for Two and Other Stories, Heinemann, 1962, Dutton, 1964.
The Nonesuch, Heinemann, 1962, Putnam, 1963.
False Colours, Bodley Head, 1963, Dutton, 1964.
Frederica, Dutton, 1965.
Black Sheep, Bodley Head, 1966, Dutton, 1967.
Cousin Kate, Bodley Head, 1968, Dutton, 1969.
Charity Girl, Dutton, 1970.
Lady of Quality, Dutton, 1972.
My Lord John, Dutton, 1975.

MYSTERIES

Footsteps in the Dark, Longmans, Green, 1932, Buccaneer Books, 1976.
Why Shoot a Butler?, Longmans, Green, 1933.
The Unfinished Clue, Longmans, Green, 1934, Harmondsworth, 1943.
Merely Murder, Doubleday, 1935 (published as *Death in the Stocks,* Longmans, Green, 1935, Harmondsworth, 1942).
Behold, Here's Poison!, Doubleday, 1936.
The Talisman Ring, Heinemann, 1936, Dutton, 1967.
They Found Him Dead, Hodder & Stoughton, 1937, Dutton, 1973.
A Blunt Instrument, Doubleday, 1938.
Envious Casca, Hodder & Stoughton, 1941, Sun Dial Press, 1942.
Penhallow, Heinemann, 1942, Doubleday, 1943.
Duplicate Death, Heinemann, 1951, Bantam, 1977.
Detection Unlimited, Heinemann, 1953, Dutton, 1969.

OMNIBUS VOLUMES

The Georgette Heyer Omnibus (contains *Faro's Daughter, The Corinthian,* and *The Nonesuch*), Dutton, 1973.
These Old Shades [and] *Sprig Muslin* [and] *Sylvester* [and] *The Corinthian* [and] *The Convenient Marriage,* Heinemann, 1977.

SIDELIGHTS: Author of nearly sixty romance and mystery novels, Georgette Heyer attracted a large and devoted readership in both England and the United States. From her first book, written when she was seventeen, to her last, Heyer entertained her readers for over fifty years with her "waggishly frolicsome, pertly paced" novels.

Most of Heyer's novels are set in the Regency period of early nineteenth-century England and are filled with descriptions of customs, clothes, and manners of that era. Some critics have complained that her books are "overstuffed" because of her tendency to "give her readers too much rather than too little history" and have claimed that a few of her romances, such as *April Lady,* contain inaccurate details. Nevertheless, other reviewers have agreed with I. W. Lawrence that Heyer "knows her history thoroughly and seldom takes liberties with it." In 1964 a *Time* writer declared: "By knowing more about Regency fops, rakes, routs and blades than anyone else alive, Georgette Heyer has turned what otherwise could be dismissed as a long series of sugary historical romances into a body of work that will probably be consulted by future scholars as the most detailed and accurate portrait of Regency life anywhere."

One of Heyer's techniques for setting the historical tone of her period pieces was to liberally sprinkle the dialogue with Regency slang. Some critics found this irritating and suggested that readers skip over it. Others thought this aspect of dialogue delightful, and Lucille Crane noted that "the slang which should puzzle the American reader, does not. In itself it brings alive an era."

Throughout the years, Heyer has often been compared to English novelist Jane Austen because of her wit, her leisurely detailed manner, and her tongue-in-cheek description of early nineteenth-century manners. "Like Jane Austen (to whom she can hold a dim candle) Miss Heyer has a gift for painting one or two magnetic characters who stand out in bright relief among a host of lesser ones, always well and amusingly drawn," noted Nancie Matthews. A few critics, however, pointed out that Heyer's books did not contain enough ironic commentary to qualify as social satire in the tradition of Austen.

Regardless of their historically accurate accounts of the Regency period, Heyer's novels are for many readers best known as lively and entertaining "escape" literature. *Chicago Sunday Tribune* critic Henry Cavendish observed that Heyer's stories stack up "as something of a literary bubble bath wherein readers so inclined may take a delightful and frothy dip."

Although some reviewers have complained of her stock characters and predictable conclusions, Heyer earned a better reputation for quality than did many other romance writers of her time. A *Times Literary Supplement* reviewer declared that Heyer's works are "redeemed from the ruck of such productions by the author's light-hearted wit and her peculiar skill in the delineation of silly women." Richard Match agreed that Heyer's stories are rescued from the category of "trashy novels" by several saving graces, including her "sardonic, elegantly turned eighteenth-century prose." Discussing an early Heyer romance, *Instead of the Thorn,* a *Literary Review* critic declared: "It is so easy to read, it is so recognizably human, the characters are so completely in their role, and the conclusions grow so quietly out of the premises that one has gone straight through the story almost without realizing what skill and insight have gone into its creation."

Heyer's humor and characterization helped make her mysteries as popular as her romances. Critics such as Isaac Anderson maintained that even though "there are not so many shudders in Georgette Heyer's murder mysteries as there are in those of some other writers, . . . there is a lot more fun." And although a few reviewers complained that her plots were hardly mysterious, others noted that they were logical, ingenious, and free from messy details. The *Times Literary Supplement* declared that *Death in the Stocks* "is an excellent example of what can be achieved when the commonplace material of detective fiction is worked up by an experienced novelist."

Stephanie Nettell has attributed Heyer's tremendous popularity to her wit, charm, warmth, and gusto, her good story lines and talented use of language, and most of all her sharp delineation of character. "All the characters are attractive, even the villains. They are all alive," exclaimed Nettell. Heyer is one of those people "who like[s] to write, never mind the actual chore of it, and this gets across to the reader." Her steady stream of best sellers testifies to Crane's observation that "Heyer's efforts are always enjoyable . . . in spite of the defects in technique we are all so fond of criticising. My recommendation is: Read and Enjoy!"

BIOGRAPHICAL/CRITICAL SOURCES:

BOOKS

Dictionary of Literary Biography, Volume 77: *British Mystery Writers, 1920-1939,* Gale, 1988.
Hodge, Jane Aiken, *The Private World of Georgette Heyer,* Bodley Head, 1984.

PERIODICALS

Best Sellers, March 1, 1964, September 15, 1967, December 1, 1967, March 1, 1968, June 15, 1968, October 15, 1970, April 15, 1973, May 15, 1973.

Books and Bookmen, September, 1965, November, 1968.

Book Week, March 15, 1964.

Boston Transcript, May 23, 1925, July 10, 1937, September 25, 1937.

Chicago Daily Tribune, March 6, 1937.

Chicago Sun Book Week, March 2, 1947.

Chicago Sunday Tribune, October 22, 1950, April 12, 1953, September 1, 1957, May 22, 1960.

Christian Science Monitor, April 24, 1958, May 12, 1960, January 4, 1962, November 5, 1964.

Commonweal, June 17, 1949.

Library Journal, July, 1957, March 15, 1958.

Literary Review, June 21, 1924.

Manchester Guardian, June 23, 1936, June 25, 1937.

New Statesman and Nation, June 25, 1938.

New Yorker, October 15, 1938, May 28, 1949, October 7, 1950, September 4, 1954.

New York Herald Tribune Book Review, August 26, 1956, June 5, 1960.

New York Times, April 12, 1924, February 21, 1937, June 13, 1937, August 8, 1937, October 9, 1938, February 17, 1946, March 21, 1948, April 6, 1952, April 12, 1953, August 29, 1954, September 4, 1955.

Saturday Review, March 22, 1952.

Saturday Review of Literature, June 6, 1925.

Spectator, June 17, 1938.

Time, February 21, 1964.

Times (London), August 31, 1984.

Times Literary Supplement, April 18, 1935, June 12, 1937, October 1, 1938, November 8, 1941, January 18, 1957.

Weekly Book Review, February 24, 1946.

OBITUARIES:

PERIODICALS

New York Times, July 6, 1974.

Publishers Weekly, July 29, 1974.

Washington Post, July 6, 1974.

*　*　*　*　*

HEYERDAHL, Thor 1914-

PERSONAL: Born October 6, 1914, in Larvik, Norway; son of Thor (president of brewery and mineral water plant) and Alison (chairman of Larvik Museum; maiden name, Lyng) Heyerdahl; married Liv Coucheron Torp, 1936; married Yvonne Dedekam-Simonsen, 1949; children: (first marriage) Thor, Bjorn; (second marriage) Anette, Marian, Elisabeth. *Education:* Attended University of Oslo, 1933-36.

ADDRESSES: Home—Colla Micheri, 17020 Laigueglia, Italy.

CAREER: Anthropologist and explorer; conducted expeditions to Polynesia, 1937-38, 1947, 1955-56, British Columbia, 1939-40, Galapagos Islands, 1953, Andes area, 1954, Africa and Asia Minor, 1968-70, 1973-77, Atlantic Ocean, 1969, 1970, and Indian Ocean, 1977-78. Has appeared on radio and television in Europe, the United States, and Latin America. Board director, Kon-Tiki Museum, Oslo, Norway, 1948. International trustee, World Wildlife Fund, 1977; international patron, United World Colleges, 1978. *Military service:* Free Norwegian Forces, 1942-45; became lieutenant.

MEMBER: World Association of World Federalists (vice-president), Royal Norwegian Academy of Sciences, New York Academy of Sciences (fellow; honorary member), Geographical Societies of Norway, Sweden, Belgium, Brazil, Peru, and U.S.S.R., Explorers Club (New York), Travellers Club (Oslo), Club des Explorateurs (Paris).

AWARDS, HONORS: Commander, Order of St. Olav (Norway); Officer of Distinguished Merits (Peru); Officer of Merit, First Class (Egypt); Great Officer of Royal Alauites Order (Morocco); Kiril i Metodi, Order of First Class (Bulgaria); Order of the Golden Ark (Holland); Patrons Gold Medal from Royal Geographical Society; Vega Gold Medal from Royal Anthropological and Geographical Society (Sweden); Great Officer of Distinguished Merit (Italy); also medalist of geographical and anthropological societies in France, Scotland, and the United States; Academy Award for documentary film, "Kon-Tiki," 1951; Ph.D. from University of Oslo, 1961; International Pahlavi Environment Prize from United Nations, 1978; Magellan Award from Circumnavigators Club, 1981.

WRITINGS:

Pa Jakt efter Paradiset (title means "On the Hunt for Paradise"), Gyldendal, 1938.

Kon-Tiki Ekspedisjonen, Gyldendal, 1948, translation by F. H. Lyon published as *Kon-Tiki: Across the Pacific by Raft,* Rand McNally, 1950, young people's edition published as *Kon-Tiki for Young People,* Rand McNally, 1960, 2nd edition, G. Allen, 1965, new edition published as *The Kon-Tiki Expedition,* 1968.

American Indians in the Pacific: The Theory behind the Kon-Tiki Expedition, Allen & Unwin, 1952, Rand McNally, 1953.

Great Norwegian Expeditions, Dreyers Forlag, 1956.

(With Arne Skjolsvold) *Archaeological Evidence of Pre-Spanish Visits to the Galapagos Islands,* Society for American Archaeology, 1956, reprinted, Kraus Reprint, 1974.

Aku-Aku: Paaskeoeyas Hemmelighet, Gyldendal, 1957, translation published as *Aku-Aku: The Secret of Easter Island,* Rand McNally, 1958, reprinted, Ballantine, 1974.

(Editor and contributor with Edwin N. Ferdon) *Norwegian Archaeological Expedition to Easter Island, and the East Pacific Reports,* Rand McNally, Volume I: *Archaeology of Easter Island,* 1961, Volume II: *Miscellaneous Subjects,* 1965.

(Co-author) *Vanished Civilizations,* Thames & Hudson, 1963.

Indianer and Altasiaten im Pazifik, Wollzeilen Verlag (Vienna), 1966, translation published as *Sea Routes to Polynesia,* Rand McNally, 1968.

Ra, Gyldendal, 1970, translation published as *The Ra Expeditions,* Doubleday, 1970.

Fatu-Hiva: Back to Nature, Allen & Unwin, 1974, Doubleday, 1975.

The Art of Easter Island, Doubleday, 1975.

Early Man and the Ocean: A Search for the Beginnings of Navigation and Seaborne Civilizations, Doubleday, 1978.

The Tigris Expedition: In Search of Our Beginnings, Allen & Unwin, 1980, Doubleday, 1981.

The Maldive Mystery, Allen & Unwin, 1986.

Easter Island: The Mystery Solved, Random House, 1989.

DOCUMENTARY FILMS

"Kon-Tiki" (based on his *Kon-Tiki Ekspedisjonen*), RK0, 1951.

"Ra" (based on his book of same title), Swedish Broadcasting Corp., 1971.

OTHER

Contributor to scientific journals.

SIDELIGHTS: Thor Heyerdahl's adventure tales have captured the hearts of millions around the world. *Kon-Tiki Ekspedisjonen,* more popularly known in English as *Kon-Tiki,* has been translated into sixty-six languages, while *Aku-Aku, Ra,* and *Fatu-Hiva* have been translated into more than thirty languages with huge sales reported for most of these editions.

Kon-Tiki really started Heyerdahl on his writing career, a career that has been enlightening and challenging to literary critics and scientists alike. In *Kon-Tiki,* Heyerdahl relates how a balsa raft, built as men of the stone age might have built it, successfully completed a trip from Peru to a small island east of Tahiti. According to Emmett Dedmon of the *Chicago Sun-Times, Kon-Tiki* "is as great an adventure as is possible to imagine, . . . as good as *Robinson Crusoe,* plus the fact that *Kon-Tiki* is true."

In *Kon-Tiki* Heyerdahl describes his efforts to prove to scientists that Polynesia may originally have been settled by men from Peru who crossed the 4,000 miles of ocean in rafts made of balsa. Heyerdahl further challenges his peers in *American Indians in the Pacific: The Theory behind the Kon-Tiki Expedition* which, according to a *Times Literary Supplement* contributor, "demonstrated beyond any doubt that the pre-European inhabitants of South America could have reached Polynesia." While Wendell C. Bennett of the *New York Times Book Review* stresses that Heyerdahl had not resolved the question of the Polynesian origins of American Indians, in 1961 the Tenth Pacific Science Congress in Honolulu agreed that South America constituted a main source area of Pacific Island peoples and cultures.

In 1955 Heyerdahl led a Norwegian archaeological expedition to Easter Island, the Polynesian island lying closest to South America. The scientists in the expedition discovered that civilizations dating as far back as A.D. 380 had existed on the island, and also that the island had experienced three distinct waves of migration. A reviewer for the *Springfield Republican* writes of *Aku-Aku: The Secret of Easter Island,* the book that detailed this expedition: "It would require something pretty substantial now to refute these plausible and convincing conclusions, based on the expedition's findings. . . . More static than *Kon-Tiki,* most of the activity being in one locality, *Aku-Aku* . . . is no less engrossing and rewarding, except for an excess of palaver with the natives. Some portions are pure archaeology, furnishing information available nowhere else, others are justifiable conjecture."

For almost twenty years the idea that papyrus rafts could have carried ancient Egyptians or other early travelers across the Atlantic some 4,000 years ago intrigued Heyerdahl. So in 1969, after several years of research and planning, Heyerdahl made his first attempt to recreate this voyage by building a papyrus reed boat named *Ra,* in honor of the Egyptian sun god, selecting an international crew of seven men, and setting sail across the Atlantic. *Ra* sailed 2,700 nautical miles in eight weeks before it began breaking up 600 miles off Barbados. With faith that the voyage could indeed take place as planned, Heyerdahl and his crew again set sail in 1970 with a new papyrus reed boat named *Ra II.* This time Heyerdahl and his crew completed the 3,270 nautical-mile journey in fifty-seven days, traveling from Safi in Morocco to Barbados in the West Indies.

As a result of this adventure, Heyerdahl published *Ra* in 1970. Geoffrey Bibby writes of *Ra* in the *New York Times Book Review:* "Let it be said immediately that Thor Heyerdahl has pulled it off again. He has written a superb adventure-book about a superb adventure. . . . [He] has lost none of his magic of phrase, and the translation renders faithfully the laconic playing-down of real danger and hard work which comes almost naturally to Norwegians. . . . The book is compelling reading as the vessel gradually approaches America and gradually falls more and more to pieces. Nor is the Ra II voyage, which ends the book, anticlimactical. . . . Heyerdahl's experiment shows . . . that we cannot take wooden construction for granted. Representation of Indian Ocean ships of the third millennium B.C. are few and inaccurate but we must now look at them with fresh eyes."

Heyerdahl told *CA* that it was in this same review that Bibby, a leading world authority on the archaeology of the Persian Gulf area, challenged Heyerdahl "to test the seaworthiness of a Sumerian reed ship which was built from a Mesopotamian reed [called berdi] deemed highly water absorbent and unfit for ocean travels by modern scientists." In 1977 Heyerdahl, with the aid of Marsh Arabs from Iraq and Titicaca Indians from South America, built the reed ship *Tigris* and with an international crew of eleven men sailed down the River Tigris, through the Persian Gulf, and by way of Oman and Pakistan across the Indian Ocean to Djibouti at the entrance of the Red Sea. This reed-ship voyage, lasting five months and covering 4,200 miles, showed that as early as 3,000 B.C. there could have been direct contact between the three oldest known civilizations: those of Mesopotamia, the Indus Valley, and Egypt.

Then in 1982 Heyerdahl received an invitation from the government of the Maldive Islands to aid in resolving some gaps in the islands' pre-twelfth-century history. With several archaeologists, Heyerdahl led an excursion to these islands in the Indian Ocean and met with unexpected success. Lee Dembart of the *Los Angeles Times* notes that the carved stonework and temples unearthed by Heyerdahl and his colleagues provided "conclusive evidence that many people had lived there before, including Buddhists before the Muslims and sun worshipers before them, . . . [and that] directly and indirectly the prehistoric Maldives had been involved in global trade." *Washington Post* reviewer James T. Yenckel finds "an engrossing detective story" in *The Maldive Mystery,* which evolved out of Heyerdahl's Maldive excursion, and Dervla Murphy says in the *Times Literary Supplement* that "because so little has been written about the Maldives . . . this book is well worth reading, and the author's excitement on being challenged by the Maldive mystery is unmistakably genuine—and therefore infectious."

Heyerdahl's readership, both inside and outside the scientific community, is strong and devoted. Heyerdahl's lay followers find in his writings captivating accounts of the courage, ability, and trust exhibited while fighting the perils and the mysteries of the open sea. For example, in his review of *Kon-Tiki: Across the Pacific by Raft,* Roland Sawyer writes in the *Christian Science Monitor* that "while this is not the first time that a log has been turned into literature, it has seldom been done so superbly. The book is cast in terms of men-against-the-sea, which gives it a general rather than particular appeal. Specialists in archaeology, ethnology, ichthyology, and other fields will be among its avid readers." Agreeing with Sawyer, a *Times Literary Supplement* critic explains further that "given the imaginative birth of this adventure, its brilliant audacity, its gambler's throw with death, its resource in peril and its success, any book about it would perhaps write itself. Mr. Heyerdahl has made it a superb adventure story which all the world may, and probably will, read. He has woven into many pages a particular enchantment which proves him a writer as well as a dreamer and man of action."

Although Heyerdahl achieved literary and scientific prominence with *Kon-Tiki,* many critics and readers also praise Heyerdahl's other exploration books. For instance, M. C. Scoggin writes in *Horn Book* that *Aku-Aku* is "fast and fascinating. . . . This is a long book and I can't vouch for its archaeology but it is a vigorous adventure story with all the lure of mysteries to be solved." And a *Kirkus Reviews* contributor feels that "with a rare gift of communication, Heyerdahl keeps one reading even when the material seems somewhat repetitive, and one longs for more of the natives of today—and less of their grisly treasures. The individuals come through the story—and their strange traditions and ancestor worship and the incredible continuity of inherited abilities, scarcely sensed themselves, and make a unique contribution to understanding."

As *Atlantic* reporter P. L. Adams explains in his review of *Early Man and the Ocean: A Search for the Beginnings of Navigation and Seaborne Civilizations,* many of Heyerdahl's books were written "on the whole for a professional audience but [they are] by no means too technical for the general reader. . . . He is less romantic and less dogmatic than his more exuberant followers, and much more careful to distinguish possibility from probability and both of these from solid archaeological evidence."

After almost reaching America from Africa with his papyrus ship *Ra* in 1969 and crossing the entire Atlantic from Morocco to Barbados with his second papyrus ship *Ra II* in 1970, Heyerdahl was the first to call world attention to ocean pollution through his messages to the United Nations. At the United Nations First Law of the Sea Conference in Stockholm in 1972, Secretary General U-Thant included Heyerdahl's detailed report as appendix to his own report on the state of the oceans, and Heyerdahl has since testified for national governments and warned the general public in twenty-two nations through personal appearances concerned with environmental protection and the threat to a living ocean.

In 1958, Heyerdahl moved with his family to his present residence in Italy, where he has restored the little medieval village of Colla Micheri on a hilltop on the Ligurian coast. In 1981, Heyerdahl told *CA* that his motto is: "A united mankind in a healthy biosphere."

MEDIA ADAPTATIONS: The Tigris Expedition was made into a documentary film produced by the British Broadcasting Corp. in collaboration with the National Geographic Society in 1979. *Archaeological Evidence of Pre-Spanish Visits to the Galapagos Islands, Aku-Aku: The Secret of Easter Island,* and *The Maldive Mystery* have been filmed.

AVOCATIONAL INTERESTS: Outdoor life, woodcarving, cartooning.

BIOGRAPHICAL/CRITICAL SOURCES:

BOOKS

Bailey, Bernadine, *Famous Modern Explorers,* Dodd, 1963.
Contemporary Literary Criticism, Volume XXVI, Gale, 1983.
Jacoby, Arnold, *Senor Kon-Tiki: Boken om Thor Heyerdahl,* Cappelen (Oslo), 1965, translation published as *Senor Kon-Tiki: The Biography of Thor Heyerdahl,* Rand McNally, 1967.

PERIODICALS

Atlantic, July, 1976, March, 1979.
Booklist, September 1, 1953.
Chicago Sunday Tribune, September 3, 1950, July 26, 1953.
Chicago Sun-Times, September 5, 1950.
Christian Science Monitor, September 7, 1950, August 20, 1975.
Holiday, March, 1977.
Horn Book, February, 1959.
Kirkus Reviews, July 1, 1958.
Life, August 15, 1969.

Los Angeles Times, October 21, 1986, September 17, 1989.
Los Angeles Times Book Review, January 21, 1990.
Manchester Guardian, April 8, 1958.
National Geographic, December, 1978.
New Statesman, April 5, 1958, May 7, 1971.
Newsweek, September 8, 1958.
New York Herald Tribune Book Review, September 10, 1950, October 18, 1950.
New York Times Book Review, August 9, 1953, November 27, 1960, December 8, 1968, August 22, 1971, August 16, 1981.
Observer, August 20, 1970.
Saturday Review, September 27, 1958, October 4, 1958, May 13, 1961, August 2, 1969.
Spectator, March 31, 1950.
Springfield Republican, September 14, 1958.
Time, September 8, 1958, August 30, 1971, November 28, 1977.
Times Literary Supplement, April 7, 1950, June 25, 1971, October 17, 1980, September 12, 1986, January 19, 1990.
Washington Post, August 29, 1986, December 16, 1987.
Washington Post Book World, December 9, 1984.

*   *   *

HIGGINS, George V(incent)   1939-

PERSONAL: Born November 13, 1939, in Brockton, Mass.; son of John Thompson and Doris (Montgomery) Higgins; married Elizabeth Mulkerin, September 4, 1965 (divorced January, 1979); married Loretta Lucas Cubberley, August 23, 1979; children: (first marriage) Susan, John. *Education:* Boston College, B.A., 1961, J.D., 1967; Stanford University, M.A., 1965.

ADDRESSES: Home—15 Brush Hill Lane, Milton, Mass. 02186.

CAREER: Journal and Evening Bulletin, Providence, R.I., reporter, 1962-63; Associated Press, bureau correspondent in Springfield, Mass., 1963-64, newsman in Boston, Mass., 1964; Guterman, Horvitz & Rubin (law firm), Boston, researcher, 1966-67; admitted to the Massachusetts Bar, 1967; Commonwealth of Massachusetts, Office of the Attorney General, Boston, legal assistant in the administrative division and organized crime section, 1967, deputy assistant attorney general, 1967-69, assistant attorney general, 1969-70; U.S. District Court of Massachusetts, Boston, assistant U.S. attorney, 1970-73, special assistant U.S. attorney, 1973-74; George V. Higgins, Inc. (law firm), Boston, president, 1973-78; Griffin & Higgins (law firm), Boston, partner, 1978-82; writer. Instructor in law enforcement programs, Northeastern University, Boston, 1969-71; instructor in trial practice, Boston College Law School, 1973-74, 1978-79. Consultant, National Institute of Law Enforcement and Criminal Justice, Washington, D.C., 1970-71.

MEMBER: Writers Guild of America.

AWARDS, HONORS: The Friends of Eddie Coyle was chosen one of the top twenty postwar American novels by the Book Marketing Council, 1985.

WRITINGS:

NOVELS

The Friends of Eddie Coyle (also see below), Knopf, 1972.
The Digger's Game, Knopf, 1973.
Cogan's Trade (also see below), Knopf, 1974.
A City on a Hill, Knopf, 1975.
The Judgement of a Deke Hunter, Little, Brown, 1976.
Dreamland, Little, Brown, 1977.
A Year or So With Edgar, Harper, 1979.

Kennedy for the Defense, Knopf, 1980.
The Rat on Fire (also see below), Knopf, 1981.
The Patriot Game, Knopf, 1982.
A Choice of Enemies, Knopf, 1984.
Penance for Jerry Kennedy, Knopf, 1985.
The Friends of Eddie Coyle, Cogan's Trade, The Rat on Fire, Robinson, 1985.
Imposters, Holt, 1986.
Outlaws, Holt, 1987.
Wonderful Years, Wonderful Years, Holt, 1988.
Trust, Holt, 1989.

The Friends of Eddie Coyle has been translated into Italian, Spanish, French, Danish, Norwegian, Finnish, German, Flemish, and Turkish; *The Digger's Game* has been translated into Spanish and Norwegian; *Cogan's Trade* has been translated into Norwegian.

OTHER

(Contributor) Martha Foley, editor, *The Best American Short Stories 1973* (anthology), Houghton, 1973.
(Contributor) James Ross, editor, *They Don't Dance Much* (anthology), Southern Illinois University Press, 1975.
The Friends of Richard Nixon (nonfiction), Little, Brown, 1975.
Style Versus Substance: Boston, Kevin White, and the Politics of Illusion, Macmillan, 1984.
Old Earl Died Pulling Traps: A Story, limited edition, Bruccoli Clark, 1984.
The Progress of the Seasons: A Partisan's View of Forty Years of Baseball at Fenway Park, Holt, 1989.

Columnist, *Boston Herald American,* 1977-79; author of magazine criticism column, *Boston Globe,* 1979-85; author of biweekly television column, *Wall Street Journal,* 1984—. Contributor of essays and short fiction to journals and magazines, including *Arizona Quarterly, Cimarron Review, Esquire, Atlantic, Playboy, Gentleman's Quarterly, New Republic,* and *Newsweek.*

SIDELIGHTS: A lawyer who has served as a prosecutor and defense lawyer in both state and federal courts, George V. Higgins has an intimate knowledge of the American criminal justice and political systems. As a novelist, Higgins draws from his experience, creating detailed examinations of crime, justice, and politics. Higgins told Nicholas Shakespeare of the *London Times,* "The disability of much American literature is that it's written by college professors sitting on their big fat rusty-dusties who don't know anything about law, politics, or any subject in which real people make real livings." Higgins has worked with real criminals, real policemen, real lawyers, and real politicians; his fiction has ben praised for its authentic depictions of these people and their lives.

As Hugh M. Ruppersburg points out in the *Dictionary of Literary Biography,* "George V. Higgins' work has two notable features: its analysis of the motives underlying human character and behavior, and its reliance on dialogue for the revelation of plot, character, and theme." Although he focuses on characters who live outside the mainstream of society, Higgins demonstrates that these people are plagued by the same ambitions and frustrations as those in more mundane walks of life. He allows each character to speak for himself and then arranges the conversations like the testimony in a trial to convey the larger story. The author uses dialogue so extensively that "the plot of a Higgins novel—suspense, humor and tragedy—is a blurrily perceived skeleton within the monsoon of dialogue," comments Roderick MacLeish in the *Washington Post Book World.* Higgins's novels are spoken, and therefore "lacking in figurative or heavily imagistic language," writes Ruppersburg. "The result is a concrete style, economical and to the point."

His first three novels—*The Friends of Eddie Coyle, The Digger's Game,* and *Cogan's Trade*—established Higgins as "an impressive chronicler of the life style of the small-time hoodlum for whom crime is the only thing that does pay," notes O. L. Bailey in the *New York Times Book Review.* Some reviewers immediately placed his fiction in the crime genre; yet, unlike the traditional crime novelist, Higgins "forgoes sentimentality, private eyes and innocent victims to write exclusively of criminals who work on each other in a community where sin is less talked of than are mistakes," relates Peter S. Prescott in *Newsweek.* The author's scrutiny of this often unseen yet real segment of society puts his novels in the company of serious mainstream fiction. Similarly, by uncovering the obscure world of the criminal, Higgins allows its comparison to mainstream society. "Money, family pressures, and the desire for a middle-class life-style motivate the behavior of the criminal as well as the average citizen," indicates Ruppersburg. "Kids grow up," J. D. O'Hara adds in *New Republic,* "customs change, new men take over from the dying or incompetent old men, power changes hands, deals succeed or fail." Yet the tone of this subsociety is different. "The criminal world is . . . realistically depicted as a pitiless jungle where self-preservation depends on constant vigilance, and everyone leads a twitching knife-edge existence," Leo Harris observes in *Books and Bookmen.*

Higgins received immediate critical approval for his writing with the publication of *The Friends of Eddie Coyle,* "one of the best of its genre I have read since Hemingway's 'The Killers,' " claims Christopher Lehmann-Haupt of the *New York Times.* It "is fiction of a most convincing order," according to Harvey Gardner in the *New York Times Book Review.* "The story of Eddie and his hood friends, and of the cops and lawyers who belong in their world as much as the crooks do, is told in short, beautifully-made episodes, full of nicely heard talk." Eddie Coyle is a struggling middleman in Boston's underworld economy whose specialty is dealing guns. "There is nothing glamorous or humorous about Eddie Coyle, and nothing remotely adventurous about the life he leads," Joe McGinniss observes in the *New York Times Book Review.* "It is seamy; it is drab."

The Friends of Eddie Coyle introduced what would become the trademark of Higgins's fiction, a "unique virtuosity in exploiting an uncanny ear for the argot of the underworld," explains Bailey. By using the language of the criminal and emphasizing dialogue, Higgins creates a book that is "flat toneless, and positively reeking with authenticity," writes McGinniss. "Its dialogue eats at one's nerve endings," adds Lehmann-Haupt. However, not all reviewers praise Higgins's use of dialogue to relate his story. One complaint is that because all these criminals speak the same slang, they sound alike; character distinctions become blurred. McGinniss admits that "all of Eddie's friends . . . seem not so much individuals as facets of the same personality." The reviewer adds, however, "Rather than a weakness, I suspect that this may well be Higgins's main point." In Harris's opinion, *The Friends of Eddie Coyle* "is expressed in dialogue that is perhaps just a shade too good, too redolent of Hemingway . . . and Runyon." Yet Harris finds that Higgins's style "makes a literary tragedy out of a small time crook and his fate." McGinniss concludes, "With 'The Friends of Eddie Coyle,' [Higgins has] given us the most penetrating glimpse yet into what seems the real world of crime."

The Digger's Game "confirms that Higgins writes about the world of crime with an authenticity that is unmatched," comments Jonathan Yardley in the *Washington Post Book World.* "In [his first two] novels," adds Yardley, "the central character is an obscure man who has done something fairly stupid but quite understandable, and is trying to pay the price without getting killed in the process." The Digger's mistake is gambling away eighteen thousand dollars in Las Vegas, putting him in debt to a loan shark. Higgins follows Digger; the things he does and the people he sees while trying to pay his debt tell his story. "Higgins has done more than write a fast, gripping story about Boston's underworld," James Mills notes in *The New York Times Book Review.* "He has created in the Digger a deeply touching character who . . . would be equally moving if he were out of crime and struggling for survival in a bank or an automobile factory." Mills adds, "A lot of writers have taken a shot at the Vegas madness, but none has described it with more humor, sadness and pathos than Higgins."

The critical debate surrounding Higgins's third novel, *Cogan's Trade,* has centered on the author's continued evolution toward a novel told completely through the dialogue of its characters. Understanding is difficult in the opinion of Bailey because the reader must glean information from the conversations of characters who speak in unfamiliar slang. "The flaw in 'Cogan,' " he writes in the *New York Times Book Review,* "is that there is not enough of our mother tongue to keep confusion at bay." What prose there is offers primarily physical description and very little interpretation or judgment of the criminal behavior of Higgins's characters. But a *Times Literary Supplement* reviewer maintains that "in Higgins, violence is always committed in cold blood; people are just doing their job, and so the prose can afford to remain disinterested."

Higgins employs dialogue for more than its realistic effect, believe some reviewers. "Like [James] Joyce, Higgins uses language in torrents, beautifully crafted, ultimately intending to create a panoramic impression," writes Roderick MacLeish. Adds a contributor to the *Times Literary Supplement,* "For all their surface authenticity, the speeches have more in common with dramatic monologues than with conversations that are merely 'overheard'; brutal and obscene though they unquestionably are, their effect is still one of stylization." "He's drawing the fewest possible lines on his canvas in order to conjure up in the reader's imagination the details of the spaces in between," explains Lehmann-Haupt. "Lines that provoke the imagination so actively are what entertaining art is all about."

In summary writes MacLeish: "As a novel, *Cogan's Trade* is a brilliant exposition of Higgins's Boston underworld as the flipside of all respectable lives of desperation. As a thriller it is that taut story whose drama is heightened by our own understanding of how it has to end." "*Cogan's Trade* . . . firmly establishes [Higgins] as a novelist of wit, intelligence and disquieting originality," concludes a *Times Literary Supplement* reviewer.

In his fourth novel, *A City on a Hill,* Higgins "has abandoned Boston lowlife for the more complex and intellectually treacherous milieu of Washington politics," Pearl K. Bell comments in the *New Leader.* The United States had entered the Watergate era and Higgins tuned his ear for the power struggles and corruption of the political arena. "In politics as in crime, Higgins' interest lies with those who work in the shadows. He is as concerned as ever with hopes that go unrealized, prospects that never materialize, ambitions that prove excessive," Yardley relates in the *New Republic.* Politics has remained a major concern of Higgins's fiction; it has also been the topic of a nonfiction work, an examination of the Watergate incident entitled *The Friends of Richard Nixon.*

A City on a Hill "may be the definitive novel of Washington at the staff level," Christopher Lydon writes in the *New York Times Book Review,* "the world of driven, dependent campaign hotshots who so quickly become power junkies and then political tramps and almost never leave the capital." Yardley finds that although this novel "contains many perceptive observations about the machinations of politics and political people . . . Higgins does not seem secure of his territory." Yardley adds: "*A City on a Hill* simply does not have the authenticity, the sureness, of the earlier novels. When it does have authenticity, Higgins has moved from Washington back to Boston, to the people he knows."

Higgins concentrates on the people and the city he knows best in another novel of the political scene, *A Choice of Enemies.* The story is that of Bernie Morgan, speaker of the state house, his fall from power, and the people responsible. "Certain [is Higgins's] feeling for the corridor and cloakroom dynamics of Massachusetts politics," writes Charles Champlin in the *Los Angeles Times Book Review.* As a novel, *A Choice of Enemies* received a mixed critical response, primarily because of its form; "all information, personal background, emotion (everything but interior decoration and clothing) is expressed through dialogue," explains *National Review* contributor D. Keith Mano.

Some reviewers believe that with this novel Higgins's continuing experiment with form exceeded its limits. "Every monotonous obscenity, every dropped word, every cliche and catch phrase, has an initial ring of taped reality," Champlin concedes. He adds, however, "Like transcripts, it needs careful pruning or the sound overruns the sense and, even more damaging, grows dull." In his article in the *New York Times Book Review,* Peter Andrews is strongly critical of the book: " 'A Choice of Enemies' represents the final collapse of [Higgins's] ongoing experiment in trying to create a kind of gutter prose-poetry as a vehicle for narrative storytelling." Andrews remarks, "The author has told his tale in such an opaque fashion that I could never get a handle on the story."

Higgins responded to his critics in a letter to *CA:* "What I am doing is replacing the omniscient author with the omniscient reader. The requisite suspension of disbelief consists wholly of the reader's agreement that for his money he has gotten not only a batch of search warrants valid everywhere, to listen in on what the characters say, but the remarkable good fortune to attend only those conversations in which they hatch their plots, betray themselves, and doublecross each other. If the reader is acute, the characters will tell him the story, leaving him to judge for himself the morality, ethics, and decency of their actions."

Some reviewers do respond favorably to Higgins's efforts. "In gradually moving toward a story told entirely by dialogue, Higgins has pulled off a remarkable transition," writes D. Keith Mano, "from distinctive realist crime writer to serious, long-reach novelist, still distinctive." "Hemming, hawing, tortuous circumlocutions, and the endless maundering excursuses of quotidian conversation are the devices that Higgins expertly uses to build suspense and tension," explains Nick Tosches in the *Village Voice.* And according to Mano, Higgins has overcome one of the faults that weakened his earlier novels: "Where, in *Cogan's Trade* (1974), each voice sounded like the same marvelous Boston Glib Person, here you have differentiation, variety, and social ecumenism." "Higgins is the master of what he does, and *A Choice of Enemies* contains some of the most brilliant and outrageous passages he has ever brought forth," concludes Tosches.

Jerry Kennedy, the protagonist of two Higgins novels, lives at the intersection of crime, politics, justice, and middle-class

America. Like Higgins, Kennedy is a Boston criminal lawyer. *Kennedy for the Defense* and *Penance for Jerry Kennedy* offer the expected insights into criminal behavior and political infighting, but they also examine the role of the criminal trial lawyer in the American justice system. Kennedy "makes his living providing the Constitutionally guaranteed defense for the victims and/or perpetrators of the rampant socioeconomic chaos prevalent in various levels of society in and around Boston," observes Tom McNevin in *Best Sellers*. Kennedy defends not by proving his clients innocent; his cases seldom go to trial. The offenders he represents are usually guilty, and more often than not he advises them to plead so. Higgins explains in a *Time* article: "There is a good reason why 85% to 90% of all criminal cases brought by a competent prosecutor end up in defense pleas; nobody can win them." What Kennedy does is use the various mechanisms of justice to obtain for his clients lesser charges, reduced sentences, and accelerated probations. "Higgins argues that experts like Kennedy fill a vital function in the criminal justice system as indispensable agents of the plea bargaining in whose absence the courts would surely collapse," comments Robert Lekachman in the *Nation*. "Higgins claims further that justice is more likely to be served by the ministrations of cynical, greedy but invariably astute lawyers than by the more formal processes of trial and sentence."

Beyond their portraits of the criminal trial lawyer and the justice system, the Jerry Kennedy novels have gained attention for their characterization. As John Jay Oshom, Jr., notes in *Washington Post Book World*, "Because the characters ruminate instead of react, there is never much tension in the novel. Yet some of what is lost in the way of tension is gained in the careful depiction of character." Jeremiah Francis Kennedy is a man caught between his desire to lead a relaxed, middle-class life-style and his fascination with his work. Kennedy, his colleagues, and clients make *Kennedy for the Defense* "a variegated yarn of third-rate perpetrators, second-class citizens and first-person encounters," *Time* reviewer Peter Stoler remarks. Although they may not be likable, Stoler adds that this "tangled cast is instantly credible and permanently delightful." Evan Hunter echoes Stoler's view. He writes in the *New York Times Book Review:* "George V. Higgins has created a genre of his own, in which the people are so real that it doesn't matter what they're doing or how they go about doing it; just being in their company is pleasure enough."

In *Penance for Jerry Kennedy*, Higgins presents an older Kennedy plagued by difficulties, "a decent, hard-working lawyer who has not lived up to the expectations of his professors, his clients, his colleagues or his wife, and who knows it," says Elaine Kendall in the *Los Angeles Times*. Kennedy commits a mistake that earns him the disfavor of an influential judge and makes him the object of a television reporter's investigation. Kennedy compounds his troubles by drinking to excess. He is at the depths of his personal and professional life. His values are going out of style. "*Penance for Jerry Kennedy* is a novel about a dying breed—lawyers who think on their feet rather than from behind desktop computer terminals and who fight with reasoned words instead of endless streams of documents," Douglas E. Winter remarks in *Washington Post Book World*. "But Jerry Kennedy is unstoppable," concludes Winter, "the kind of fictional lawyer one meets all too rarely—one whose life and work are made real."

Higgins has been called by some a crime novelist and by others the creator of a new genre. He has at times been compared to major literary figures of the twentieth century. For Hugh M. Ruppersburg, "his skill in characterization and realistic dialogue, his success at portraying individuals in a crisis of identity, his understanding of the influences which form human character, and his development of a unique, effective novelistic form appropriate to his talents establish George V. Higgins as a writer of considerable stature."

Higgins continues to write prolifically, publishing approximately one novel every year. His recent fiction includes *Imposters, Outlaws, Wonderful Years, Wonderful Years,* and *Trust*. In a 1984 *CA* interview, Higgins reflected on his writing career: "All I wanted to do was tell stories. I thought that reading stories was an absorbing, happy way to spend your time and therefore that telling them must be even more fun, even more absorbing; and I was right."

MEDIA ADAPTATIONS: The Friends of Eddie Coyle was filmed by Paramount in 1973.

BIOGRAPHICAL/CRITICAL SOURCES:

BOOKS

Contemporary Literary Criticism, Gale, Volume 4, 1975, Volume 7, 1977, Volume 10, 1979, Volume 18, 1981.
Dictionary of Literary Biography, Volume 2: *American Novelists Since World War II,* Gale, 1978.
Dictionary of Literary Biography Yearbook: 1981, Gale, 1982.

PERIODICALS

Best Sellers, August, 1980.
Books and Bookmen, September, 1972.
Los Angeles Times, February 28, 1985.
Los Angeles Times Book Review, March 4, 1984, August 16, 1987, January 1, 1989.
Nation, April 26, 1980.
National Review, November 7, 1975, May 18, 1984.
New Republic, March 30, 1974, April 12, 1975.
Newsweek, March 25, 1974, April 28, 1975, September 6, 1976, March 3, 1980.
New Yorker, June 24, 1974, March 18, 1985.
New York Times, January 25, 1972, March 23, 1973, April 10, 1974, March 14, 1975, May 12, 1986, September 15, 1987.
New York Times Book Review, February 6, 1972, February 11, 1973, March 25, 1973, March 31, 1974, March 30, 1975, October 26, 1975, March 2, 1980, February 12, 1984, February 24, 1985, January 21, 1990.
Time, April 1, 1974, April 14, 1975, August 23, 1976, March 31, 1980, September 14, 1987.
Times (London), May 16, 1985, March 6, 1986.
Times Literary Supplement, August 16, 1974, November 7, 1980, June 19, 1987, December 29, 1989.
Tribune Books, December 11, 1988, November 26, 1989.
Village Voice, January 31, 1984.
Washington Post Book World, April 1, 1973, March 31, 1974, March 2, 1980, March 17, 1985, June 13, 1986, August 23, 1987, October 2, 1988, April 29, 1989, October 22, 1989.

*   *   *

HIGGINS, Jack
See PATTERSON, Harry

*   *   *

HIGHET, Helen
See MacINNES, Helen (Clark)

HIGHSMITH, (Mary) Patricia 1921-
(Claire Morgan)

PERSONAL: Born January 19, 1921, in Ft. Worth, Tex.; daughter of Jay Bernard Plangman and Mary (Coates) Plangman Highsmith. *Education:* Barnard College, B.A., 1942.

ADDRESSES: Agent—Marianne Ligginstorfer, Diogenes Verlag, Sprechstrasse 8, 8032 Zurich, Switzerland.

CAREER: Writer, 1942—.

MEMBER: Detection Club.

AWARDS, HONORS: Mystery Writers of America Scroll and Grand Prix de Litterature Policiere, both 1957, both for *The Talented Mr. Ripley;* Crime Writers Association of England Silver Dagger Award for best foreign crime novel of the year, 1964, for *The Two Faces of January;* Le Prix Litteraire, 1987.

WRITINGS:

Strangers on a Train, Harper, 1950, Penguin, 1979.
(Under pseudonym Claire Morgan) *The Price of Salt,* Coward, 1952, reprinted with a new afterword by the author, Naiad Press, 1984.
The Blunderer, Coward, 1954, published as *Lament for a Lover,* Popular Library, 1956, reprinted under original title, Hamlyn, 1978.
The Talented Mr. Ripley (also see below), Coward, 1955, reprinted, Penguin, 1981.
Deep Water, Harper, 1957 (published in England as *Deep Water: A Novel of Suspense,* Heinemann, 1957), reprinted, Penguin, 1979.
A Game for the Living, Harper, 1958, reprinted, Hamlyn, 1978.
(With Doris Sanders) *Miranda the Panda Is on the Veranda* (juvenile), Coward, 1958.
This Sweet Sickness, Harper, 1960, reprinted, Penguin, 1982.
The Cry of the Owl, Harper, 1962.
The Two Faces of January, Doubleday, 1964.
The Glass Cell, Doubleday, 1964, reprinted, Penguin, 1980.
The Story-Teller, Doubleday, 1965 (published in England as *A Suspension of Mercy,* Heinemann, 1965, reprinted, Penguin, 1981).
Plotting and Writing Suspense Fiction, Writer, Inc., 1966, enlarged and revised edition, 1981.
Those Who Walk Away, Doubleday, 1967.
The Tremor of Forgery, Doubleday, 1969.
The Snail-Watcher, and Other Stories, Doubleday, 1970 (published in England as *Eleven: Short Stories,* Heinemann, 1970).
Ripley under Ground (also see below), Doubleday, 1970.
A Dog's Ransom, Knopf, 1972.
Little Tales of Misogyny (short stories; in German), Diogenes Verlag, 1974, English language edition, Heinemann, 1977, Mysterious Press, 1986.
Ripley's Game (also see below), Knopf, 1974.
The Animal-Lover's Book of Beastly Murder (short stories), Heinemann, 1975.
Edith's Diary, Simon & Schuster, 1977.
Slowly, Slowly in the Wind (short stories), Heinemann, 1979.
The Black House, David & Charles, 1979 (published in England as *The Black House, and Other Stories,* Heinemann, 1981).
The Boy Who Followed Ripley, Crowell, 1980.
People Who Knock on The Door, Heinemann, 1983, Mysterious Press, 1985.
The Mysterious Mr. Ripley (contains *The Talented Mr. Ripley, Ripley under Ground,* and *Ripley's Game*), Penguin, 1985.

Mermaids on the Golf Course, and Other Stories, Heinemann, 1985.
Found in the Street, Heinemann, 1986, Atlantic Monthly Press, 1987.
Tales of Natural and Unnatural Catastrophes, Heinemann, 1987.

Also author of material for television, including the "Alfred Hitchcock Presents" program.

SIDELIGHTS: The author of numerous short story collections and novels, including the well-known *Strangers on a Train,* American-born Patricia Highsmith has enjoyed much greater critical and commercial success in England, France, and Germany than in her native country. As Jeff Weinstein speculates in the *Village Voice Literary Supplement,* the reason for this is that Highsmith's books have been "misplaced"—relegated to the mystery and suspense shelves instead of being allowed to take their rightful place in the literature section. As far as her ardent admirers here and abroad are concerned, Patricia Highsmith is more than just a superb *crime* novelist. In fact, declares Brigid Brophy in *Don't Never Forget: Collected Views and Reviews,* "there's the injustice. . . . As a novelist *tout court* she's excellent. . . . Highsmith and Simenon are alone in writing books which transcend the limits of the genre while staying strictly inside its rules: they alone have taken the crucial step from playing games to creating art."

The art in Highsmith's work springs from her skillful fusion of plot, characterization, and style, with the crime story serving primarily "as a means of revealing and examining her own deepest interests and obsessions," according to a *Times Literary Supplement* reviewer. Among her most common themes are the nature of guilt and the often symbiotic relationship that develops between two people (almost always men) who are at the same time fascinated and repelled by each other. "Highsmith's works therefore dig down very deeply into the roots of personality," says Julian Symons in the *London Magazine,* exposing the dark side of people regarded by society as normal and good. Or, as Thomas Sutcliffe explains in the *Times Literary Supplement,* Highsmith writes "not about what it feels like to be mad, but what it feels like to remain sane while committing the actions of a madman."

Highsmith's preoccupations with guilt and contrasting personalities surfaced as early as her very first novel. *Strangers on a Train* chronicles the relationship between Guy Haines, a successful young architect, and Charles Bruno, a charming but unstable man slightly younger than Haines. The two men first meet on a train journey when Bruno repeatedly tries to engage his traveling companion in conversation. He eventually persuades Haines to open up and talk about feelings he usually keeps to himself, including the fact that he harbors considerable resentment toward his wife. Bruno, who has long fantasized about killing his much-hated father, then suggests to Haines that they rid themselves of their "problems" once and for all: Bruno will kill Haines's wife for him, and Haines in turn will kill Bruno's father. Since there is no connection between the victims and their killers, Bruno theorizes, the police will be at a loss to solve the murders. With more than a hint of reluctance, Haines rejects the plan, but to no avail; Bruno remains intrigued by it and proceeds to carry out his part.

As Paul Binding observes in a *Books and Bookmen* article, "the relation of abnormal Bruno to normal [Haines] is an exceedingly complex one which is to reverberate throughout Patricia Highsmith's output. On the one hand Bruno is a *doppelgaenger* figure; he embodies in repulsive flesh and blood form what [Haines's] subconscious has long been whispering to him. . . . On the other hand Bruno exists in his own perverse right, and [Haines] can have no control over him. . . . As a result of [Bruno's] existence, and of its coincidence with [Haines's] own, the rational, moral [Haines] becomes entangled in a mesh which threatens to destroy his entire security of identity. . . . [Haines is a man] tormented by guilt—guilt originally inspired by interior elements. Yet [he becomes], in Society's eyes, guilty for exterior reasons." With the exception of the "Ripley" books (*The Talented Mr. Ripley, Ripley under Ground, Ripley's Game,* and *The Boy Who Followed Ripley*), which focus on the activities of the opportunistic and amoral Tom Ripley, a man incapable of feeling guilt, these themes are at the heart of Highsmith's fiction.

According to Symons, Highsmith typically launches her stories with the kind of "trickily ingenious plot devices often used by very inferior writers." He hastens to add, however, that these only serve as starting points for the "profound and subtle studies of character that follow." As Burt Supree observes in the *Village Voice Literary Supplement,* most of Highsmith's characters—none of whom are "heroes" in the conventional sense—are likely to be "obsessive, unquestioning, humdrum men with no self-knowledge, no curiosity, and Byzantine fantasy lives—respectable or criminal middle-class, middle-brow people of incredible shallowness. Nowhere else will you find so many characters you'd want to smack. . . . Like lab animals, [they] come under careful scrutiny, but [Highsmith] doesn't care to analyze them or beg sympathy for them. They go their independent ways with the illusion of freedom. Contact seems only to sharpen their edges, to irk and enrage." Yet as Craig Brown points out in the *Times Literary Supplement,* "it is a rare villain or psychopath [in Highsmith fiction] whom the reader does not find himself willing toward freedom, a rare investigator or victim (sometimes the one becomes the other) whom the reader is unhappy to see dead. Those she terms her 'murderer-heroes' or 'hero-psychopaths' are usually people whose protective shells are not thick enough to deaden the pain as the world hammers at their emotions. . . . Some live, some die, some kill, some crack up."

Sutcliffe echoes this assessment of Highsmith's characters as basically sane people who commit apparently insane acts, usually while under considerable strain. "What she observes so truthfully is not the collapse of reason but its persistence in what it suits us to think of as inappropriate conditions," declares the critic. "Even Ripley, the least scrupulous and likable of her central characters, has motives for his actions, and though they are venal and vicious they are not irrational. Her suburban killers remain calculatingly evasive until the end. . . . They don't hear voices and they don't have fun. Indeed in the act of killing their attitude is one of dispassionate detachment, of a sustained attempt to rationalize the intolerable. . . . In all the books death is contingent and unsought, almost never meticulously planned and very rarely the focus for our moral indignation."

In fact, notes Francis Wyndham, the actual violent act of murder takes a back seat to what has led up to it and, to a lesser extent, what follows. "It is rare for a death to occur . . . until at least a third of the book is past; often it is reserved for the very end," writes Wyndham. "When it takes place, her readers are made aware not only of the horror, but also of the *embarrassment* following an act of destructive violence; it is as if a person one knows quite well were suddenly killed by somebody else one knows quite well. And although Miss Highsmith makes the most scrupulous psychological preparation for her murders, so that their eruption is never unconvincing, yet the effect on her readers is shocking in the same kind of way as the experience of murder would be in life."

In the eyes of most critics, it is Highsmith's skill at depicting a character's slide into derangement or death that distinguishes her "in a field where imitative hacks and dull formula-mongers abound," to quote a *Times Literary Supplement* reviewer. Symons declares: "The quality that takes her books beyond the run of intelligent fiction is not [the] professional ability to order a plot and create a significant environment, but rather the intensity of feeling that she brings to the problems of her central figures. . . . From original ideas that are sometimes farfetched or even trivial she proceeds with an imaginative power that makes the whole thing terrifyingly real." The world she creates for her characters has a "relentless, compulsive, mutedly ominous quality," says Hermione Lee in the *Observer,* one that leaves the reader "in a perpetual state of anxiety and wariness."

Binding views Highsmith's fiction in a similar fashion. "[Her] characters spin or fall into (and sometimes both) proliferating webs of plot: the humdrum world, so meticulously built up by the author, recedes, and the reader enters another, metaphorical one, of menace, suspense, irresolution compounded by experience of the murderous. . . . Her faculty for observation is preternaturally acute, her gift for analysis of reaction or train of thought almost painfully developed. At the same time a mood of nervous anticipation is what one principally associates with each novel, and none of them would be aesthetically satisfactory without a deed of violence."

The prose Highsmith uses to communicate a sense of chilling dread and almost claustrophobic desperation is flat and plain, devoid of jargon, cliches, and padding. Some find it reminiscent of a psychological case history—a detailed and dispassionate account of a life moving out of control. According to Reg Gadney in *London Magazine,* "It is a characteristic skill of Miss Highsmith to convey unease and apprehension with an understated narrative style and painstaking description of domestic practicalities. Her characters often seem to counter-balance their expectation of fear by entrenching themselves in domestic routines. . . . [Their] tenacious efforts . . . to keep hold of everyday reality and logic serve to heighten the menace and chaos." *New Statesman* reviewer Blake Morrison, in fact, believes Highsmith is "at her most macabre when most mundane."

In Brown's opinion, "her style, on the surface so smooth and calm, underneath so powerful and merciless," is precisely what "entices the reader in and then sends him, alongside the 'psychopath-hero,' tumbling against the rocks." Weinstein agrees that "the reader has no choice but to follow the work, nothing could go another way. You are trapped in the very ease of reading. The result is like suffocation, losing breath or will." Supree views Highsmith's appeal as a combination of "repellent fascination and inexorable design"; like Brown and Weinstein, he, too, feels a compulsion to continue reading once caught in her fictional web. Explains the reviewer: "Highsmith's descriptions have a kind of neutral distance, but even so one reads her stories, as Graham Greene says, with a sense of 'personal danger,' or, perhaps, of contamination. I often find myself loath to turn the page, lest I find out more than I want to. Then I do, and I do." All in all, concludes Wyndham, the author's "unemphatic style makes a highly effective medium for the unsettling view of life which she expresses"—a view that H. R. F. Keating points out "will not please every reader [, especially] those of us who want there to be happy endings." But as Keating goes on to note in the *Times Literary Supplement,* "her view has its truth, and truth makes you free."

Symons identifies several qualities in Highsmith's work that make her, in his words, "such an interesting and unusual novelist." He has particular praise for "the power with which her male characters are realized" as well as for her ability to portray "what would seem to most people abnormal states of minds and ways of behaviour." Continues the critic: "The way in which all this is presented can be masterly in its choice of tone and phrase. [Highsmith's] opening sentences make a statement that is symbolically meaningful in relation to the whole book. . . . The setting is also chosen with great care. . . . [She seems to be making the point that] in surroundings that are sufficiently strange, men become uncertain of their personalities and question the reason for their own conduct in society." In short, declares Symons, Highsmith's work is "as serious in its implications and as subtle in its approach as anything being done in the novel today."

Similar plaudits come from J. M. Edelstein in a *New Republic* article. "Low-key is the word for Patricia Highsmith," Edelstein states. "Low-key, subtle, and profound. It is amazing to me that she is not better known, for she is superb and is a master of the suspense novel. . . . [The body of her work] should be among the classics of the genre."

A *Times Literary Supplement* reviewer reflects on the dilemma facing those who attempt to evaluate Patricia Highsmith's work. In essence, explains the reviewer, "it is difficult to find ways of praising [her] that do not at the same time do something to diminish her. With each new book, she is ritually congratulated for outstripping the limitations of her genre, for being as much concerned with people and ideas as with manipulated incident, for attempting a more than superficial exploration of the psychopathology of her unpleasant heroes—for, in short, exhibiting some of the gifts and preoccupations which are elementarily demanded of competent straight novelists." According to this same reviewer, Highsmith can best be described in the following terms: "She is the crime writer who comes closest to giving crime writing a good name."

MEDIA ADAPTATIONS: Strangers on a Train was made into a film by Alfred Hitchcock for Warner Brothers in 1951; it also served as the basis for another Warner Brothers movie in 1969 entitled "Once You Kiss a Stranger." *The Talented Mr. Ripley* was filmed as "Purple Noon" by Times Film Corp., in 1961; *The Blunderer* was first filmed as "Le Meurtrier" in 1963 and then as "Enough Rope" by Artixo Productions in 1966; *This Sweet Sickness* inspired the French film "Tell Her I That Love Her" in 1977; and *Ripley's Game* was filmed as "The American Friend" in 1978. All but a few of the rest of Highsmith's novels have been optioned for film.

AVOCATIONAL INTERESTS: Drawing, painting, woodworking, snail-watching, traveling by train.

BIOGRAPHICAL/CRITICAL SOURCES:

Brody, Brigid, *Don't Never Forget: Collected View and Reviews,* Holt, 1966.
Contemporary Literary Criticism, Gale, Volume 2, 1974, Volume 14, 1975, Volume 42, 1987.
Symons, Julian, *Mortal Consequences: A History—From the Detective Story to the Crime Novel,* Harper, 1972.

PERIODICALS

Books and Bookmen, March, 1971, March, 1983.
Globe and Mail (Toronto), January 21, 1984.
Listener, July 9, 1970, February 17, 1983.
London Magazine, June, 1969, June-July, 1972.
New Republic, May 20, 1967, June 29, 1974.
New Statesman, May 31, 1963, February 26, 1965, October 29, 1965, January 24, 1969, March 30, 1979, October 2, 1981.
Newsweek, July 4, 1977.
New Yorker, May 27, 1974.
New York Herald Tribune Books, February 7, 1960.
New York Review of Books, September 15, 1974.
New York Times Book Review, January 30, 1966, April 1, 1967, April 30, 1967, July 19, 1970, July 7, 1974, April 6, 1986.
Observer, February 12, 1967, January 19, 1969, July 12, 1970, January 9, 1983.
Punch, January 29, 1969, March 10, 1971, June 2, 1982.
Spectator, February 21, 1969, December 5, 1981, February 12, 1983.
Times (London), February 24, 1983, April 3, 1986.
Times Literary Supplement, June 1, 1967, September 24, 1971, April 25, 1980, October 2, 1981, February 4, 1983, September 27, 1985, April 18, 1986.
Village Voice Literary Supplement, August, 1982.
Washington Post, June 28, 1980.
Washington Post Book World, September 15, 1985, October 6, 1985.
Washington Star-News, November 25, 1973.

*   *   *

HILL, Geoffrey (William) 1932-

PERSONAL: Born June 18, 1932, in Bromsgrove, Worcestershire, England. *Education:* Graduated from Keble College, Oxford.

ADDRESSES: Home—England. *Office*—Emmanuel College, Cambridge, England.

CAREER: Poet. University of Leeds, Leeds, Yorkshire, England, 1954-80, became senior lecturer in English; fellow of Emmanuel College and University Lecturer, Cambridge University, Cambridge, England.

MEMBER: Royal Society of Literature (fellow, 1972).

AWARDS, HONORS: E. C. Gregory Award for Poetry, 1961, for *For the Unfallen;* Hawthornden Prize, 1969, and Geoffrey Faber Memorial Prize, 1970, both for *King Log;* Whitbread Award, 1971, Alice Hunt Bartlett Prize from the Poetry Society, 1971, and Heinemann Award from the Royal Society of Literature, 1972, all for *Mercian Hymns;* Duff Cooper Memorial Prize, 1979, for *Tenebrae;* Loines Award from the American Academy and Institute of Arts and Letters, 1983; Ingram Merrill Foundation award in literature, 1985.

WRITINGS:

POETRY

Poems (pamphlet), Oxford University Poetry Society, 1952.
For the Unfallen: Poems 1952-1958 (also see below), Deutsch, 1959, Dufour, 1960.
Preghiere (pamphlet), Northern House, 1964.
(With Edwin Brock and Stevie Smith) *Penguin Modern Poets Eight,* Penguin, 1966.
King Log (also see below), Dufour, 1968.
Mercian Hymns (also see below), Deutsch, 1971.
Somewhere Is Such a Kingdom: Poems 1952-1971 (includes *For the Unfallen, King Log,* and *Mercian Hymns*), Houghton, 1975.
Tenebrae, Deutsch, 1978, Houghton, 1979.
The Mystery of the Charity of Charles Peguy, Agenda Editions, 1983, Oxford University Press (New York), 1984.
Collected Poems, Penguin, 1985, Oxford University Press (New York), 1986.

OTHER

Brand (five-act version of Henrik Ibsen's play of the same name; first produced in London at the National Theatre, April, 1978), Heinemann, 1978, revised edition, University of Minnesota Press, 1981.

The Lords of Limit: Essays on Literature and Ideas, Oxford University Press, 1984.

Also featured on the recording "The Poetry and Voice of Geoffrey Hill," Caedmon, 1979.

SIDELIGHTS: "Geoffrey Hill is a poet with a capacity for paradox," writes Vincent B. Sherry, Jr., in a *Dictionary of Literary Biography* profile. "He combines the two opposing tendencies of British verse in the postwar period, displaying an excellent formal control, like the Movement poets of the 1950s, and an awareness of the violence of language in relation to history, like Ted Hughes and others writing since the 1960s." But what Hill is perhaps best noted for is his dedication to historical poetry, a genre that has seen few practitioners in recent years. In such collections as *Preghiere, King Log,* and *Mercian Hymns,* Hill seeks "to convey extreme emotions by opposing the restraint of established form to the violence of his insight or judgment," notes *New York Review of Books* critic Irvin Ehrenpreis. "He deals with violent public events. Appalled by the moral discontinuities of human behavior, he is also shaken by his own response to them, which mingles revulsion with fascination."

Hill's *For the Unfallen: Poems 1952-1958* was published in 1959 and earned the poet wide recognition: the poems within display "a new, deepened sense of history as well as a continued interest in religion and myth," says Sherry. "Thus the title refers to the unfallen in the recent war as well as to those unfallen from grace. But the consolations of religion do not diminish the anxieties of history." Critical response to *For the Unfallen* was enthusiastic, but not unanimously so. Sherry mentions in his article that Hill's "characteristic syntax—discontinuous, abrasive, jagged—" caused some reviewers to label his work impenetrable. Nevertheless, *For the Unfallen* was hailed as a major work by the young talent and garnered the E. C. Gregory Award for Poetry in 1961.

Further successful collections followed, including *King Log* and *Mercian Hymns,* both acclaimed for their use of Christian symbolism combined with what Craig Raine calls the "high seriousness" of the poet's style. In a *New Statesman* review of *Mercian Hymns,* Raine adds that a reader of Hill's work "can't miss the noble application of scruples to life. The purged cadences, the bitter medicine of his syntax appeals to the puritan in us: even when the poetry is difficult, obscure and painful to read, we know it is doing us good. It makes no concessions to our intellectual and moral self-esteem."

"All of Hill's poems are individual acts of perception and reflection expressed in the image and rhythm of a particular language," finds Thomas Getz in his book *Modern Poetry Studies.* "We can only read *Mercian Hymns* by learning the language from the poems themselves. The poems are most interesting when the reader attends to the quality of individualization and the quality of language, which is itself an almost physical act of archaeology, the creation of an idiom that digs out an imagery of the past and articulates it as contemporary." Getz also relates that "the mark of Hill's integrity is his acceptance of the pain involved in examining the forces of historical process and of religious imagination that break apart the contingency of man and his world."

But history and religion are not Hill's only subjects. *Poetry* reviewer Donald Hall mentions the theme of sexual love as Hill's

strongest of all. "Of course it is intertwined with suffering and suspicion and everything else," says Hall, "but [Hill's] is a poetry of sensuality as well as sensuousness. The natural world in Hill's poems is fecund and thick with the blood of sex, wounds, and sexual wounds, both attractive and repellent. . . . I am aware of no recent poetry which more belongs to the body, both in its texture of mouthy rhythm and in its imagery, yet it is also a poetry repelled by body."

Tenebrae, "meaning 'darkness' in Latin," as Sherry points out, was published in 1978. The collection "refers to the somber ritual on Good Friday evening, when candles are ceremonially extinguished to symbolize the death of Christ," Sherry continues. "There is a kind of liturgical propriety in *Tenebrae,* matched by a literary decorum unseen since *King Log:* a return to closed forms, especially the sonnet, and extensive echoing and paraphrasing of earlier literature." As in the poet's earlier works, remarks Getz, the images in *Tenebrae* are "associated with the crucifixion and acts of martyrdom, as though human sacrifice were a cynosure of the basic feeling of Christian belief. . . . There is not the almost physical interaction of subject and object as in *Mercian Hymns* or some of the earlier social and historical poems. For Hill, faith can only engage the language as that which is longed for but not fully assented to." *Harper's* critic Hayden Carruth simply calls *Tenebrae* "the best book of devotional poetry in the modern high style since [T. S.] Eliot's Ash-Wednesday."

The Mystery of the Charity of Charles Peguy is a long-form poem—"an even hundred quatrains of off-rhymed pentameter verse," as Tom Disch describes it—based on a real incident in French history. "Readers whose memory of the news, and of French poetry, doesn't stretch back to 1914 and earlier will need more than the footnotes and a two-page biographical sketch provided by Hill in order to fathom what the poem is talking about," Disch states in his *Washington Post Book World* review of the work. "Reading it cold the first time though, I came away with a sense that it was gorgeous poetry but that the title was all too apt."

The real Charles Peguy was a poet who "began his literary career as a polemicist for the Dreyfusard Party, underwent an extreme but not unnatural conversion from socialism to the France of 'the old republic,' and died in 1914, a patriotic soldier in the war he had urged his country to fight," according to David Bromwich's *New Republic* article on Hill's book. The critic says that there is an air of "unfamiliarity" to Hill's verse. "It has none of the unction of geniality; does not weaken itself with whimsies, or otherwise truckle for patronage. . . . [Hill] does not want to be loved for his poems, or search out ways of being likable in his poems."

What Bromwich calls this "distinct negative appeal" is a "source of Hill's endurance thus far. And it has encouraged him to try for an uncommon success, and write a long poem about another poet. Like no other poem of the age, *The Mystery of the Charity of Charles Peguy* sustains its meditation with continuous intensity. Its motive may be described as an attempt to hold poetry and history in a single thought. Yet its eloquence is straightforward, chaste, and declarative, checked only by the thought that all eloquence terminates in action."

The Lords of Limit: Essays on Literature and Ideas, a collection of nine essays—some originally lectures—was published in 1984. Bromwich reviewed the book for *New Republic* and reports that "though Hill's reading includes all sorts of literature, metaphysics, moral philosophy, and sermons, as well as poems and novels, he has no patience for intellectual argument, in any common understanding of the term. He makes his paragraphs of a tissue of quotations—sometimes striking, sometimes rather dull—from critics, philosophers, and historians. These he then weaves together with the texts of his subject, and contemporary observers of his subject, pestering some of his authorities and praising others with brief comments and judicial summaries." Bromwich further points out that this style is "well-designed to conceal from the author himself whatever distinction may exist between that which he knows deeply and that which he knows less deeply. It lacks or, perhaps, eschews the available graces of prose. Yet it provides a serious setting for some thoughtful aphorisms, and may be said to exhibit all the strictly privative virtues of Hill's temperament. It is never facile, careless, or merely ingratiating, and it is free of cant."

That Hill has received so much critical notice in his career yet remains all but unknown to the general public is a matter addressed by Sherry, who concludes in the *Dictionary of Literary Biography* that "the degree of difficulty in [Hill's] poetry, it is now commonly agreed, measures the individuality of his attitudes, the uniqueness of his voice. These qualities should sustain a growing body of critical commentary. Hill remains, however, a rather isolated, unassignable genius; his high standards have prescribed but limited his fame: only a select clerisy of devoted 'fellow-labourers' has attempted to penetrate his sometimes imposing surfaces. But to confront the work is to be impressed, moved, and awed even before understanding it. The consensus is that Hill's reputation will accrue like his own poems, at his own pace: he does not write quickly, and throw away; he shapes slowly, and saves."

BIOGRAPHICAL/CRITICAL SOURCES:

BOOKS

Bloom, Harold, editor, *Geoffrey Hill*, Chelsea House, 1986.
Brown, Merle, *Double Lyric: Divisiveness and Communal Creativity in Recent English Poetry*, Columbia University Press, 1980.
Contemporary Literary Criticism, Gale, Volume 5, 1976, Volume 8, 1980, Volume 13, 1981, Volume 45, 1987.
Dictionary of Literary Biography, Volume 40: *Poets of Great Britain and Ireland Since 1960*, Gale, 1985.
Getz, Thomas H., *Modern Poetry Studies*, Media Study, Inc., 1980.
Hart, Henry, *The Poetry of Geoffrey Hill*, Southern Illinois University Press, 1986.
Robinson, Peter, editor, *Geoffrey Hill: Essays on His Work*, Open University Press, 1985.
Waterman, Andrew, *British Poetry Since 1970: A Critical Survey*, edited by Peter Jones and Michael Schmidt, Persea Books, 1980.

PERIODICALS

Atlantic, June, 1979.
Critical Quarterly, spring/summer, 1984.
Encounter, March, 1979.
Essays in Criticism, July, 1979.
Globe and Mail (Toronto), January 17, 1987.
Harper's, January, 1980.
Hudson Review, spring, 1976.
Iowa Review, summer, 1972.
Nation, February 9, 1985.
New Republic, September 16, 1985.
New Statesman, January 5, 1979.
New York Review of Books, January 22, 1976.
New York Times Book Review, January 11, 1976, April 1, 1979.

Parnassus: Poetry in Review, spring/summer, 1973, spring/summer, 1976.
Poetry, July, 1976, May, 1980.
Sewanee Review, summer, 1976.
Southern Review, January, 1979, January, 1981.
Spectator, October 23, 1971, December 7, 1985.
Times Literary Supplement, August 25, 1966, October 31, 1968, August 27, 1971, May 4, 1984.
Washington Post Book World, December 30, 1984.
Yale Review, March, 1976.

*   *   *

HILL, John
   See KOONTZ, Dean R(ay)

*   *   *

HILL, Susan (Elizabeth) 1942-

PERSONAL: Born February 5, 1942, in Scarborough, England; daughter of R. H. and Doris Hill; married Stanley W. Wells (a Shakespearean scholar), April 23, 1975; children: Jessica, Clemency. *Education:* King's College, University of London, B.A. (with honors), 1963. *Religion:* Anglican.

ADDRESSES: Home—Midsummer Cottage, Church Lane, Beckley, Oxford, England. *Agent*—Curtis Brown, Ltd., 1 Crave Hill, London W2 3EW, England; and John Cushman Associates, Inc., 25 West 43rd St., New York, N.Y. 10036.

CAREER: Novelist, playwright, and critic, 1960—. *Coventry Evening Telegraph*, Coventry, England, 1963-68; *Daily Telegraph*, London, England, monthly columnist, 1977—.

MEMBER: King's College (fellow).

AWARDS, HONORS: Somerset Maugham Award, 1971, for *I'm the King of the Castle;* Whitbread Literary Award for fiction, 1972, for *The Bird of Night;* John Llewelyn Rhys Memorial Prize, 1972, for *The Albatross;* fellow of the Royal Society of Literature, 1972.

WRITINGS:

The Albatross (short stories), Hamish Hamilton, 1971, published as *The Albatross and Other Stories*, Saturday Review Press, 1975.
The Custodian (short stories), Covent Garden Press, 1972.
A Bit of Singing and Dancing (short stories), Hamish Hamilton, 1973.
(Contributor) A. D. Maclean, editor, *Winter's Tales 20*, Macmillan (London), 1974, St. Martin's, 1975.
The Elephant Man, Cambridge University Press, 1975.
(Editor and author of introduction) Thomas Hardy, *The Distracted Preacher and Other Tales*, Penguin, 1980.
(Editor with Isabel Quigly) *New Stories 5*, Hutchinson, 1980.
(Translator with Jonathan Tittler) *Juyungo: The First Black Ecuadorian Novel*, Three Continents, 1982.
The Magic Apple Tree: A Country Year, Hamish Hamilton, 1982, Holt, 1983.
(Editor) *People: Essays and Poems*, Chatto & Windus, 1983.
(Editor) *Ghost Stories*, Hamish Hamilton, 1983.
Through the Kitchen Window, illustrated by Angela Barrett, Hamish Hamilton, 1984, Stemmer House, 1986.
One Night at a Time (juvenile), illustrated by Vanessa Julian-Ottie, Hamish Hamilton, 1984.
Go Away, Bad Dreams! (juvenile), illustrated by Julian-Ottie, Random House, 1985.

The Lighting of the Lamps, David & Charles, 1986.
Shakespeare Country, photographs by Rod Talbot, Penguin, 1987.
(Editor with Joelie Hancock) *Literature-Based Reading Programs at Work,* Heinemann Educational, 1988.
Can It Be True? A Christmas Story, illustrated by Barrett, Viking, 1988.
Lanterns Across the Snow, Crown, 1988.
Mother's Magic, illustrated by Alan Marks, David & Charles, 1988.
Through the Garden Gate, David & Charles, 1988.
The Spirit of the Cotswolds, Penguin, 1988.
Family, Viking, 1990.

NOVELS

The Enclosure, Hutchinson, 1961.
Do Me a Favour, Hutchinson, 1963.
Gentleman and Ladies, Hamish Hamilton, 1968, Walker & Co., 1969.
A Change for the Better, Hamish Hamilton, 1969, Penguin, 1980.
I'm the King of the Castle, Viking, 1970.
Strange Meetings, Saturday Review Press, 1972.
The Bird of the Night, Saturday Review Press, 1972.
In the Springtime of the Year, Saturday Review Press, 1974.
The Woman in Black: A Ghost Story, Hamish Hamilton, 1983, Godine, 1986.

RADIO PLAYS

"Miss Lavender is Dead," British Broadcasting Corp. (BBC Radio), 1970.
"Taking Leave," BBC Radio, 1971.
"The End of the Summer" (also see below), BBC Radio, 1971.
"Lizard in the Grass" (also see below), BBC Radio, 1971.
"The Cold Country," BBC Radio, 1972.
"Winter Elegy," BBC Radio, 1973.
"Consider the Lilies" (also see below), BBC Radio, 1973.
"A Window on the World," BBC Radio, 1974.
"Strip Jack Naked" (also see below), BBC Radio, 1974.
"Mr. Proudham and Mr. Sleight," BBC Radio, 1974.
"On the Face of It," BBC Radio, 1975.
The Cold Country and Other Plays for Radio (includes "The Cold Country," "The End of Summer," "Lizard in the Grass," "Consider the Lilies," and "Strip Jack Naked"), BBC Publications, 1975.
On the Face of It (BBC Radio, 1975), published in *Act 1,* edited by David Self and Ray Speakman, Hutchinson, 1979.
"The Summer of the Giant Sunflower," BBC Radio, 1977.
"The Sound that Time Makes," BBC Radio, 1980.
"Here Comes the Bride," BBC Radio, 1980.
Chances, BBC Radio, 1981, stage adaptation first produced in London, 1983.
"Out in the Cold," BBC Radio, 1982.
"Autumn," BBC Radio, 1985.
"Winter," BBC Radio, 1985.

OTHER

Author of "The Badness Within Him," a television play, first broadcasted in 1980, and "The Ramshackle Company," a children's play, first produced in London in 1981. Contributor of two stories to *Penguin New Short Stories.*

MEDIA ADAPTATIONS: Gentleman and Ladies was adapted as a radio play in 1970.

SIDELIGHTS: Susan Hill's novels tend to deal with people who live outside what is considered to be the mainstream lifestyle. She tends to place these characters in isolated spots, characterizing them with her use of language and portraying their situations with a strong emphasis on atmosphere. For example, Jonathan Raban writes in *London Magazine* that Hill's *A Change for the Better* "is artfully composed of the dead and rotting language of Westbourne itself; a destitute society finds its linguistic correlative in a dialect of sad cliches. . . . The language of the narrative strictly follows the airless corridors of the characters' own thoughts, reproduced in every colourless detail—mean, complaining, platitudinous. . . . But the tone of *A Change for the Better* is rooted in its dialogue: Miss Hill has created a stylized, yet brilliantly accurate grammar and vocabulary for her distressed gentlefolk—an entirely authentic idiom to be spoken by the living dead as they inhabit their shabby-genteel wasteland. Their language is rigid, archaic, and metrical, a mixture of drab proverbs, oratorical flourishes borrowed from popular romance, and catch phrases from the more sober varieties of adman's English." Raban finds that Miss Hill has "a fine sense of pace and timing and a delicious eye for incongruous detail."

In keeping with the tradition of the horror story, the author's *The Woman in Black: A Ghost Story,* first published in 1983, "could almost pass for a Victorian ghost novel," remarks E. F. Bleiler in the *Washington Post Book World.* Outside of its setting in the early twentieth century, the novel may seem like "a routine horror story" of the late nineteenth century, suggests Bleiler. However, the reviewer continues, "the sustained mood and the depth of emotion that the author evokes with minimal means" make it atypical. Similarly, *Times Literary Supplement* contributor Patricia Craig feels that "the fullest flavour is extracted from every ingredient that goes into *The Woman in Black.*" Bleiler's only objections to the story are its initially slow plot development and the somewhat "confusing, perhaps even unnecessary" circumstances of the main character's situation. But the story as a whole, Bleiler concludes, "is certainly memorable, one of the strongest stories of supernatural horror that I have read in many years."

Other critics have also noted, while reviewing Hill's books, the author's special ability in creating an atmosphere to help set a novel's mood. In one case, *Books and Bookmen* contributor J. A. Cuddon remarks that the title story of *The Albatross and Other Stories* is "about fear, anxiety and inadequacy in which the atmosphere and environment are evoked with great skill and feeling and the characters are presented and developed with a kind of austere compassion." Cuddon later continues: "The language is spare, the dialogue terse and the tone beautifully adjusted to the severe vision. . . . The narrative, the events, are simple enough, but long after one has read these stories one is left with a curious, hard-edged almost physical sensation; a feeling of chill and desolation. But not depression. Miss Hill's art brings an elation of its own."

In a review of *Strange Meetings* in *Books and Bookmen,* Diane Leclercq writes: "Coming hard on the heels of Susan Hill's very considerable achievements in her most recent work, one expects great things from [this book]. In many respects one gets them: the hard-edged prose, the painstaking detail, some aspects of the portrayal of Hilliard, and many of the minor characters. But the book has inbuilt defects that make it, in the final analysis, a failure. . . . The radical weakness is, perhaps, a failure to realize any of the attitudes that people must have had in the situation at the Western Front."

New Republic reviewer Michele Murray believes that "*The Bird of the Night* lacks all those elements that automatically stamp a new novel as 'profound' or 'important,' and worth noticing.

What it has instead are qualities rarely found in contemporary fiction and apparently not much valued, which is a pity. It is a thoroughly *created* piece of work, a novel wrought of language carefully designed to tell a story drawn, not from the surface of the author's life or fragments of her autobiography, but from the heart of the imagination. . . . The careful shaping of material to make its effect with the utmost economy, adhered to and practiced by such modern masters as Gide, Woolf, Colette, and Pavese, seems to have fallen into abeyance, and it is good to see it once again employed with such great skill."

Murray calls *In the Springtime of the Year* "another triumph by an artist who, in her quiet, steady way, is fast becoming one of the outstanding novelists of our time." She goes on to say that Susan Hill "has already demonstrated her mastery of character-drawing and fictional technique in her earlier novels, but *In the Springtime of the Year*, with its deliberate stripping away of almost all the elements of conventional fiction, represents a remarkable advance in what is turning out to be a considerable *oeuvre* for such a young writer. . . ." Margaret Atwood concludes in a *New York Times Book Review* article that despite "lapses into simplemindedness, *In the Springtime of the Year* justifies itself by the intensity of those things it does well: moments of genuine feeling, moments of vision. It is less a novel than the portrait of an emotion, and as this it is poignant and convincing."

BIOGRAPHICAL/CRITICAL SOURCES:

PERIODICALS

Best Sellers, October 1, 1970.
Books and Bookmen, April, 1971, January, 1972, June, 1974.
Bookseller, October 23, 1971.
Listener, October 8, 1970.
London Magazine, November, 1969.
New Republic, February 16, 1974, May 18, 1974.
New Statesman, January 31, 1969, January 25, 1974.
New York Times Book Review, March 30, 1969, May 27, 1973, May 18, 1974.
Times Literary Supplement, October 14, 1983.
Washington Post, May 19, 1974.
Washington Post Book World, August 24, 1986.

*   *   *

HIMES, Chester (Bomar)   1909-1984

PERSONAL: Born July 29, 1909, in Jefferson City, Mo.; died November 12, 1984, of Parkinson's disease, in Moraira, Spain; son of Joseph Sandy (a teacher) and Estelle (a teacher; maiden name, Bomar) Himes; married Jean Lucinda Johnson, August 13, 1937 (divorced); married wife Lesley. *Education:* Attended Ohio State University, 1926-28.

ADDRESSES: Home—Casa Griot, Pla del Mar 123, Moraira, Alicante, Spain. *Agent*—Rosalyn Targ, 250 West 57th St., New York, NY 10019.

CAREER: Writer. Convicted of armed robbery of $53,000 at the age of nineteen and sentenced to twenty years in Ohio State Penitentiary; while in prison, began to write and contributed prison stories to magazines; released from prison about 1935, after serving six years; worked for Federal Writer's Project, subsequently completing a history of Cleveland (never published); worked briefly as a journalist for the Cleveland *Daily News,* as a writer for the labor movement and the Communist party, and at odd jobs; during World War II, worked in shipyards and for aircraft companies in Los Angeles and San Francisco; left the United States to travel and live abroad in 1953; lived in Paris for many years; suffered a stroke in Mexico, 1965, and was temporarily inactive; made a film in Harlem for French television, 1967; lived in Spain for the last fifteen years of his life.

AWARDS, HONORS: Julius Rosenwald fellowship in creative writing, 1944-45; Yaddo fellowship, 1948; Grand Prix Policier, 1958.

WRITINGS:

NOVELS

If He Hollers, Let Him Go, Doubleday, 1945, new edition, Berkley Publishing, 1964.
Lonely Crusade, Knopf, 1947, reprinted, Thunder's Mouth, 1987.
Cast the First Stone, Coward, 1952, reprinted, New American Library, 1975.
The Third Generation, World Publishing, 1954, reprinted, Chatham Bookseller, 1973.
The Primitive, New American Library, 1955, reprinted, New American Library, 1971.
Pinktoes, Olympia Press (Paris), 1961, Putnam, 1965.
Ne nous enervons pas! (title means "Be Calm"), translation by J. Fillon, Gallimard, 1961.
Mamie Mason; ou, Un Exercise de la bonne volonte, translation by Andre Mathieu, Editions Les Yeux Ouverts, 1963.
Une Affaire de viol, translation by Mathieu, Editions Les Yeux Ouverts, 1963, published in the original English as *A Case Of Rape,* Howard University Press, 1984.

"SERIE NOIR"/"HARLEM DOMESTIC" SERIES; TRANSLATED INTO FRENCH FROM ORIGINAL ENGLISH MANUSCRIPTS

For Love of Imabelle, Fawcett, 1957, translation by Minnie Danzas published as *La Reine des Pommes* (title means "The Five-Cornered Square"), Gallimard, 1958, revised English edition published as *A Rage in Harlem,* Avon, 1965.
Il pleut des coups durs, translation by C. Wourgaft, Gallimard, 1958, published as *The Real Cool Killers,* Avon, 1959.
The Crazy Kill (originally published in French by Gallimard, 1958), Avon, 1959.
Couche dans le pain (title means "A Jealous Man Can't Win"), translation by J. Herisson and H. Robillot, Gallimard, 1959.
Tout pour plaire, translation by Yves Malartic, Gallimard, 1959, published as *The Big Gold Dream,* Avon, 1960.
Dare-dare, translation by Pierre Verrier, Gallimard, 1959, published as *Run Man, Run,* Putnam, 1966.
Imbroglio negro, translation by Fillon, Gallimard, 1960, published as *All Shot Up,* Avon, 1960.
Retour en Afrique, translation by Pierre Sergent, Plon, 1964, published as *Cotton Comes to Harlem,* Putnam, 1965, translation published as *La Casse de l'Oncle Tom,* Plon, 1971.
The Heat's On (originally published in French by Gallimard, 1960), Putnam, 1966, published as *Come Back, Charleston Blue,* Dell, 1967.
Blind Man with a Pistol, Morrow, 1969, published as *Hot Day Hot Night,* Dell, 1970, translation by Robillot published as *L'Aveugle au pistolet,* Gallimard, 1970.

OTHER

The Autobiography of Chester Himes, Doubleday, Volume 1: *The Quality of Hurt,* 1972, Volume 2: *My Life of Absurdity,* 1977.
Black on Black: Baby Sister and Selected Writings (stories), Doubleday, 1973.

Work represented in many anthologies, including *Black Writers of America, Negro Caravan, Right On!, American Negro Short Stories,* and *The Best Short Stories by Negro Writers.* Contributor to periodicals, including *Atlanta Daily World, Coronet, Esquire,* and *Pittsburgh Courier.*

SIDELIGHTS: Chester Himes wrote successfully in many genres, including novels of social protest, autobiographies, and popular crime thrillers. But whatever form his writing took, it was always dedicated to one subject—"racism, the hurt it inflicts, and all the tangled hates," according to Stephen F. Milliken's book *Chester Himes: A Critical Appraisal.* Himes wrote about racial oppression with a bitter, unrelenting anger that earned him comparisons to Richard Wright and James Baldwin. "He writes with the same intense ferocity with which he might knock a man down," declared *Virginia Quarterly Review* writer Raymond Nelson. This sense of rage and the unforgiving strokes with which he painted both black and white characters alienated many readers of both races; as a result, Himes was for years almost unknown in this country, though he was highly respected in Europe even during his lifetime.

Himes was born to socially successful parents, but his early life was troubled due to the constant fighting between his light-skinned mother and his dark-skinned father. The racial tension between the couple was to form one of the recurring themes in Himes's fiction, that of discrimination by light-skinned blacks against those of darker color. He attended Ohio State University for two years before being expelled for leading his fraternity on a romp through Columbus's red light district that ended in a speakeasy brawl. Drifting into a life of petty crime, he was arrested for armed robbery in less than a year and sentenced to twenty years in Ohio State Penitentiary. There, Himes witnessed beatings, killings, riots, and a fire that took the lives of over three hundred convicts. He began to write short stories based on these experiences; they were soon accepted for publication in *Esquire* magazine, where they appeared signed with Himes's name and prison identification number.

Released from prison after serving six years of his sentence, Himes worked variously for the Federal Writers Project, the labor movement, the Communist party and the Cleveland *Daily News* over the next few years. In 1941 he set out for California, lured by the prospect of profitable work in wartime industry. The government shipyards had a reputation for fair hiring and employment practices, but Himes found discriminatory "Jim Crow" policies as prevalent there as anywhere else. He later wrote in his autobiography that the hypocrisy of Los Angeles sickened him more than the outright hostility of the South. He expressed his bitter reaction to his Los Angeles experiences in *If He Hollers, Let Him Go,* his first novel.

In this work, the author used a naturalistic style to describe five days of steadily mounting tension in the life of Bob Jones, a black foreman in a wartime shipyard. Each day Bob awakes with his nerves taut, "struggling to keep from lashing back violently against a hateful environment," as *Dictionary of Literary Biography* essayist Frank Campenni described it. Various characters illustrate different attitudes adopted by blacks to get along in the white world. For example, Bob's light-skinned girlfriend, Alcie, sometimes passes as white; his co-worker, Smitty, adopts an "Uncle Tom"-like demeanor; and UCLA graduate Ben strives for equal achievements in a separate black community. Unable to accept any of these compromises, Bob feels completely at odds with himself and the world.

Taunted with a racial slur from one of his workers, Bob responds in kind. The incident results in a demotion for Bob, while Madge, his antagonist, goes unreprimanded. Madge is a bigoted Texan who pretends to fear Bob while secretly desiring him. Bob finds his hatred and disgust for her tinged with an inexplicable sexual attraction. Tension mounts between the two, culminating in Madge's attempted seduction of Bob; when he rejects her advances, she cries rape and he is nearly lynched. Himes convincingly depicted Bob's defeat as unavoidable, "the product not only of his environment but of the tortured desires and twisted fears of his damaged psyche," wrote Campenni. "The organization of the novel lends its stereotyped situation unexpected power. Each night during the five days encompassed, Jones has violent nightmares in which he is trapped or endangered, so that the actual events are not merely foreshadowed, but given an internalized inevitability. The surrealistic quality of these nightmares underscores vividly . . . the doom which hangs over Jones."

Himes followed *If He Hollers, Let Him Go* with *Lonely Crusade,* a novel similar in plot and theme to his first. *Lonely Crusade* is less powerful than its predecessor, however, due to "Himes's tendency toward melodrama and overstatement," in Campenni's opinion. Next came a trio of novels that were largely autobiographical: *Cast the First Stone, The Third Generation* and *The Primitive. Cast the First Stone* is regarded by many critics to be the classic prison novel. It relates the harrowing events of Himes's term in Ohio State Penitentiary. In *The Third Generation,* the author skillfully reduced "the traumas generated within the black American Community itself by the pressures of racism to the story of a single black family, rent by the conflict between a black-hating mother and a black-accepting father, and the sons caught in between—Himes's own story," explained Milliken.

Himes regarded *The Primitive* as his favorite work. Like *If He Hollers, Let Him Go, The Primitive* used disturbing nightmares to foreshadow the violent and tragic end of the relationship between Jesse Robinson, the writer-protagonist, and Kriss, his white mistress. Based on Himes's real-life love affair with Vandi Haywood, this painful story blended "surrealistic and obsessive patterns quite successfully into what may well be the author's most profound novel," wrote Michel Fabre in *Black World.* Milliken reserved particular praise for Himes's compassionate portrait of Kriss, writing that her characterization represented "the most complete exposition [Himes] gave in his writing of his conviction that the hurts of the white woman are at least comparable to those of the black man, and that she endures a roughly similar, and equally pitiable, minority status."

Today these early novels are ranked among the classics of black American protest literature. At the time of their publication, however, they received scant critical attention and sold very few copies. Unable to support himself by writing, Himes was also barred from all but the most menial jobs because of his prison record. Completely disillusioned with what American society had to offer him, Himes left the country permanently in 1953. For many years he lived in Paris in the company of other black American expatriates, including Himes's literary model, Richard Wright. But while Wright lived as something of a Parisian celebrity, Himes was penniless and unknown when he arrived in France.

In his autobiography, Himes states that he was leading a "desperate" life in "a little crummy hotel" when he was contacted by French publisher Marcel Duhamel in 1956. Duhamel was familiar with Himes's work and wanted the author to produce a novel set in Harlem for his popular series of crime thrillers, "Serie Noir." Himes responded by locking himself in his room with two or three bottles of wine each day and within three weeks handed Duhamel a finished manuscript entitled *For Love of Imabelle.* Translated into French and published as *La Reine des Pommes,* the book was a tremendous success, winning the Grand Prix Policier in 1958. Himes went on to produce a total of ten novels for "Serie Noir"; he called the books his "Harlem Domestic" series.

All ten novels followed the same formula: a violent and inexplicable crime, enacted in private, touches off a wave of equally violent reactions in anarchy-ridden Harlem. Black detectives "Coffin" Ed Jones and "Grave Digger" Johnson try to bring order to the scene, usually by methods as illegal and deadly as those of the criminals. More often than not, they are only partially successful. French readers loved the irony and mordant humor which marked these fast-paced novels. Several of the books were eventually published in English under such titles as *A Rage in Harlem, The Real Cool Killers,* and *The Heat's On.* American critics at first voiced many objections to the graphic excesses of Himes's stories, but the books sold well, and it was through the "Harlem Domestic" series that the author first received some measure of recognition in the United States.

Himes found it quite ironic that he achieved his greatest success with the "Harlem Domestic" series, for he wrote each of the novels within a matter of weeks, motivated strictly by his need for cash. But while the author "may have thought he cut his own forebrain out when he began to write genre novels, . . . these works complement, rather than contradict, the agonized nostalgia of his other novels," asserted a *Voice Literary Supplement* contributor. Today, many critics feel that almost in spite of himself, Himes produced some of his strongest work in his detective fiction. While the "Harlem Domestic" series contained no overt social messages, as Himes's other books had, their grim portrayal of ghetto life was itself a powerful statement on the failure of America's promises for blacks. Campenni commented that Himes's work was strengthened when he eliminated the obvious preaching that occasionally marred his earlier novels, for "by objectifying and externalizing his rage against racism, [he] seems paradoxically to have liberated his imagination and his exuberant sense of life."

An additional strength of the Harlem detective stories is their absurdist humor, believed Edward Margolies, contributor to *Studies in Black Literature.* "It is humor—resigned, bitter, earthy, slapstick, macabre—that protects author, readers and detectives from the gloom of omnipresent evil." Margolies added that Himes's humor was perfectly appropriate to the setting of his novels, for it is "the hard cynical wit of the urban poor who know how to cheat and lie to the white world to survive physically, and cheat and lie to themselves to survive psychologically." A *Times Literary Supplement* reviewer added: "Even in a book like [*Cotton Comes to Harlem*]—with a laugh on nearly every page—it is evident [Himes] is concerned with the Negro's plight in Harlem, aware of every corruption from whores and dope-addiction to mere urine-stained walls, aware of the unkillable hope in the minds of many of these people and of the hopelessness of their situation as it is now. . . . It is his value as a writer, and it makes this book a novel, that he can jest at all of it, make stiletto social comments, and keep his story running."

The "Harlem Domestic" novels have been criticized for perpetrating negative images of blacks, but a *Voice Literary Supplement* writer stressed that Himes's "women dressed in red, his jazzmen, pimps, and scam artists partying on barbecue and weed are saved from being reverse stereotypes because of the bitter density of the rage and humor from which they spring." In all his fiction Himes "drove deeper into the subject [of racism] than

anyone ever had before," affirmed Milliken. "He recorded what happens to a man when his humanity is questioned, the rage that explodes within him, the doubts that follow, and the fears, and the awful temptation to yield, to embrace degradation. . . . [He] has produced . . . the most complete and perfect statement of the nature of native American racism to be found in American literature, and one of the most profound statements about the nature of social oppression, and the rage and fear it generates in individuals, in all of modern literature."

Yale University has a major collection of Himes's literary manuscripts and letters. His works have been published in France, Germany, Denmark, Sweden, Italy, Holland, Portugal, Norway, and Japan.

MEDIA ADAPTATIONS: Cotton Comes to Harlem was produced as a film, starring Godfrey Cambridge and Raymond St. Jacques, by United Artists, 1970; *The Heat's On* was produced as "Come Back, Charleston Blue," starring the same actors, by Warner Brothers, 1972.

BIOGRAPHICAL/CRITICAL SOURCES:

BOOKS

Amistad I, Knopf, 1970.
Contemporary Literary Criticism, Gale, Volume 2, 1974, Volume 4, 1975, Volume 7, 1977, Volume 18, 1981.
Dictionary of Literary Biography, Gale, Volume 2: *American Novelists since World War II,* 1978, Volume 76: *Afro-American Writers, 1940-1955,* 1988.
Himes, Chester, *The Autobiography of Chester Himes,* Doubleday, Volume 1: *The Quality of Hurt,* 1972, Volume 2: *My Life of Absurdity,* 1977.
Hughes, Carl Milton, *The Negro Novelist, 1940-1950,* Citadel, 1970.
Littlejohn, David, *Black on White: A Critical Survey of Writing by American Negroes,* Viking, 1966.
Lundquist, James, *Chester Himes,* Ungar, 1976.
Margolies, Edward, *Native Sons,* Lippincott, 1968.
Milliken, Stephen, *Chester Himes: A Critical Appraisal,* University of Missouri Press, 1976.
Symons, Julian, *Mortal Consequences: A History—From the Detective Story to the Crime Novel,* Harper, 1972.

PERIODICALS

America, April 15, 1972, July 21, 1973.
American Libraries, October, 1972.
Best Sellers, July 15, 1965, December 1, 1966, March 15, 1969.
Black World, July, 1970, March, 1972, July, 1972.
Booklist, July 15, 1972.
Books and Bookmen, September, 1967, August, 1968, October, 1971.
Book Week, March 28, 1965, August 8, 1965.
Book World, February 22, 1970, March 26, 1972.
Chicago Review, Volume 25, number 3, 1973.
College Language Association Journal, number 15, 1972.
Commonweal, December 1, 1972.
Critique: Studies in Modern Fiction, Volume 16, number 1, 1974.
Esquire, May, 1972.
Journal of American Studies, April, 1978.
Journal of Popular Culture, spring, 1976.
L'Express, April 5-11, 1971.
Nation, December 20, 1971.
Negro Digest, July, 1967.
New Statesman, April 11, 1975.
New York Times, March 6, 1972, March 8, 1972.

New York Times Book Review, February 7, 1965, August 15, 1965, November 27, 1966, February 23, 1969, March 12, 1972, April 30, 1972, June 4, 1972, February 13, 1977.
Observer Review, June 18, 1967, June 29, 1969.
Prairie Schooner, winter, 1974-75.
Publishers Weekly, January 17, 1972, January 31, 1972, April 3, 1972, June 23, 1975.
Punch, July 23, 1969.
Saturday Review, March 22, 1969, April 15, 1972.
Spectator, July 12, 1969.
Studies in Black Literature, summer, 1970.
Studies in Short Fiction, summer, 1975.
Times (London), June 28, 1969, August 11, 1985.
Times Literary Supplement, April 25, 1975.
Variety, April 9, 1969, March 15, 1972, July 5, 1972.
Virginia Quarterly Review, spring, 1972, summer, 1972, summer, 1973.

OBITUARIES:

PERIODICALS

Detroit Free Press, November 14, 1984.
Los Angeles Times, November 15, 1984.
Newsweek, November 16, 1984.
New York Times, November 14, 1984.
Publishers Weekly, November 30, 1984.
Times (London), November 14, 1984.
Washington Post, November 16, 1984.

* * *

HINTON, S(usan) E(loise) 1950-

PERSONAL: Born in 1950 in Tulsa, Okla.; married David E. Inhofe (a mail order businessman), September, 1970; children: Nicholas David. *Education:* University of Tulsa, B.S., 1970.

ADDRESSES: Home—Tulsa, Okla. *Office*—c/o Press Relations, Dell Publishing Co., 666 Fifth Ave., 10th Fl., New York, N.Y. 10103.

CAREER: Began writing at the age of sixteen; author of young adult novels. Has consulted on and appeared in film adaptations of her novels, including "Tex" and "The Outsiders."

AWARDS, HONORS: New York Herald Tribune best teen-age books list, 1967, *Chicago Tribune Book World* Spring Book Festival Honor Book, 1967, *Media & Methods* Maxi Award, 1975, and Massachusetts Children's Book Award, 1979, all for *The Outsiders;* American Library Association (ALA) Best Books for Young Adults list, 1971, *Chicago Tribune Book World* Spring Book Festival Honor Book, 1971, and Massachusetts Children's Book Award, 1978, all for *That Was Then, This Is Now;* ALA Best Books for Young Adults list, 1975, *School Library Journal* Best Books of the Year list, 1975, and Land of Enchantment Award, New Mexico Library Association, 1982, all for *Rumble Fish;* ALA Best Books for Young Adults list, 1979, *School Library Journal* Best Books of the Year list, 1979, New York Public Library Books for the Teen-Age, 1980, American Book Award nomination for children's paperback, 1981, Sue Hefly Honor Book, Louisiana Association of School Libraries, 1982, California Young Reader Medal nomination, California Reading Association, 1982, and Sue Hefly Award, 1983, all for *Tex;* Golden Archer Award, 1983; ALA Young Adult Services Division/*School Library Journal* Author Award, 1988, for body of work.

WRITINGS:

The Outsiders (young adult novel), Viking, 1967, reprinted, Dell, 1989.
That Was Then, This Is Now (young adult novel), Viking, 1971, reprinted, Dell, 1989.
Rumble Fish (young adult novel; also see below), Delacorte, 1975.
Tex (young adult novel), Delacorte, 1979.
(With Francis Ford Coppola) "Rumble Fish" (screenplay; adapted from her novel of same title), Universal, 1983.
Taming the Star Runner (young adult novel), Delacorte, 1988.

SIDELIGHTS: As a teenager in Tulsa, Oklahoma, S. E. Hinton enjoyed reading but often found her options limited, as she told *Newsweek*'s Gene Lyons: "A lot of adult literature was older than I was ready for. The kids' books were all Mary Jane-Goes-to-the-Prom junk. I wrote 'The Outsiders' so I'd have something to read." Angered by the random beating of a friend, Hinton was inspired to write a story of an escalating class conflict between "greasers" and "socs" that ends in tragedy. Published in 1967 when Hinton was seventeen, *The Outsiders* "gave birth to the new realism in adolescent literature" and launched its author toward achieving "almost mythical status as the grand dame of young adult novelists," Patty Campbell relates in the *New York Times Book Review.* Hinton's frank depiction of the cruelty and violence that teens can perpetrate upon one another was a new development in books for adolescents, and led some adult critics to condemn the novel's realism. Teenagers, however, responded overwhelmingly to the book and Hinton became an overnight success.

The Outsiders opens with a group of "greasers" preparing for one of their habitual fights with their upper-middle-class rivals, the "socs"; with their parents indifferent or absent, the boys, including narrator Ponyboy Curtis, substitute their gang for family. But when one of Ponyboy's friends kills a soc in self-defense, it sets off a chain of events that eventually tears the group apart. "By almost any standard," writes Thomas Fleming in the *New York Times Book Review,* "Miss Hinton's performance is impressive. . . . She has produced a book alive with the fresh dialogue of her contemporaries, and has wound around it a story that captures, in vivid patches at least, a rather unnerving slice of teen-age America." *Saturday Review* critic Zena Sutherland similarly observes that *The Outsiders* is "written with distinctive style by a teen-ager who is sensitive, honest, and observant." A *Times Literary Supplement* reviewer, however, notes that "the plot creaks and the ending is wholly factitious," and remarks that the language "is both arresting and tiring to read in its repetitiousness." While likewise faulting the author for unlikely plot twists and occasional overwriting, Lillian N. Gerhardt nevertheless comments in *School Library Journal* that Hinton is a writer "seeing and saying more with greater storytelling ability than many an older hand."

"For all its weaknesses, this young writer's first novel *The Outsiders* made a considerable impact and offered an uncomfortable glimpse into the world of teenage violence in America," David L. Rees states in *Children's Book Review.* "We are still in that world, but here," in *That Was Then, This Is Now,* "it is even more strikingly drawn," says Rees. Instead of a conflict between rich and poor teens, *That Was Then, This Is Now* presents two foster brothers, Bryon and Mark, moving apart as one becomes more involved in school and girlfriends while the other moves deeper into a career of crime and drugs. "The phrase 'if only' is perhaps the most bittersweet in the language, and Miss Hinton uses it skillfully to underline her theme: growth can be a dangerous process," Michael Cart summarizes in the *New York Times Book Review. Book World* contributor Polly Goodwin also considers Hinton's novel "a powerful story, which pulls no punches in portraying a way of life its protagonists casually accept as normal," although she feels that Bryon's eventual decision to turn his friend in to the police is not very believable. Cart similarly faults the author for portraying Bryon's decisions as "made not intellectually but emotionally," but states that "otherwise she has written a mature, disciplined novel, which excites a response in the reader. Whatever its faults, her book will be hard to forget." "*That Was Then, This Is Now* is a searing and terrible account of what life can be like [for teens]," a *Times Literary Supplement* writer comments, concluding that the novel is "a starkly realistic book, a punch from the shoulder which leaves the reader considerably shaken."

While Hinton's next novel, *Rumble Fish,* demonstrates her usual aptitude for memorable dialogue and fast-paced narrative, many critics feel that this story of a disillusioned young man who gradually loses everything meaningful to him does not match the quality of her previous work. In *Tex,* however, Hinton "has taken a larger canvas on which to group more varied characters," asserts Margery Fisher of *Growing Point.* The author moves her setting from Tulsa to California to explore the relationship of fourteen-year-old Tex and his older brother Mason, who must take the place of the boys' traveling cowboy father. Resentful of his brother's authority at home and having difficulties at school, Tex's problems multiply when he and Mason are kidnapped by a hitchhiker; Tex later gets into a confrontation with a drug pusher. *New York Times Book Review* contributor Paxton Davis believes that the number of unusual events occurring in the story strains credulity: "There's too much going on here. Even by the standards of today's fiction, S. E. Hinton's vision of contemporary teen-age life is riper than warrants belief. . . . [*Tex* is] busier and more melodramatic than the real life it purports to show." Lance Salway agrees that *Tex* is very theatrical, but comments in *Signal* that "a writer as good as Hinton can carry it off effortlessly; one believes implicitly in the characters and cares what happens to them." "In this new book," Fisher concludes, "Susan Hinton has achieved that illusion of reality which any fiction writer aspires to and which few ever completely achieve."

Hinton spent the ten-year interval between *Tex* and her latest novel, *Taming the Star Runner,* advising on the sets of several film adaptations of her books and starting a family. But after just "one paragraph [of *Taming the Star Runner*] the reader is back in familiar Hinton country," notes Campbell. "Once again," a *Kirkus Reviews* writer observes, "Hinton puts a bright, rebellious teen-ager, stubbornly pushing against society's expectations, into a powerful story lashed together with bands of irony." After nearly killing his stepfather in a fight, young Travis is dispatched to his uncle's farm, where he must adjust to a "country" lifestyle unfamiliar to him. While trying to maintain his tough exterior, Travis is also working on a novel and falling in love with Casey, an older girl who is a riding instructor at the horse ranch. *School Library Journal* contributor Charlene Strickland considers the plot "sparse" and built "around a predominantly bleak theme." Campbell, however, states that *Taming the Star Runner* "is remarkable for its drive and the wry sweetness and authenticity of its voice." Because the novel "is also a more mature and difficult work," the critic continues, "it may not be as wildly popular as the other Hinton books have continued to be with succeeding generations. . . . But S. E. Hinton continues to grow in strength as a young adult novelist."

Although Hinton's work has frequently been characterized as representative of teenage life, some critics believe that her novels are more graphic than factual. Michael Malone, for instance, in a *Nation* essay on the author's work, notes that the language used by Hinton's characters is often "heightened" and poetical; in addition, most of the characters are situated outside their families, thus avoiding the problem of parental authority and conflict. "Far from strikingly realistic in literary form, these novels are romances," the critic explains, "mythologizing the tragic beauty of violent youth." Campbell similarly observes that the typical Hinton novel includes "a tough young Galahad in black T-shirt and leather jacket," but the critic maintains that each variation Hinton creates is distinctive in itself: "The pattern is familiar, but [Hinton's] genius lies in that she has been able to give each of the five protagonists she has drawn from this mythic model a unique voice and a unique story." And as Hinton told Jay Scott of *American Film,* it is the people, not the circumstances, of her novels that concern her most: "I don't know what the latest hot trend is. I hate the 'problem' approach. Problems change. Character remains the same. I write character."

Hinton has not been as prolific as other young adult novelists, but that hasn't prevented her from becoming a consistent favorite with her audience; two of the movies adapted from her books, "Tex" and "The Outsiders," were filmed in response to suggestions from adolescent readers. Even though she is no longer a teenager involved in the world about which she writes, Hinton believes that she is suited to writing adolescent fiction: "I don't think I have a masterpiece in me, but I do know I'm writing well in the area I choose to write in," she commented to *Los Angeles Times* writer Dave Smith. "I understand kids and I really like them. And I have a very good memory. I remember exactly what it was like to be a teen-ager that nobody listened to or paid attention to or wanted around. I mean, it wasn't like that with my own family, but I knew a lot of kids like that and hung around with them. . . . Somehow I always understood them. They were my type." And while other young adult novelists have branched out into mainstream fiction, Hinton has no ambitions to write an "adult" best seller, she related to Stephen Farber in the *New York Times:* "If I can ever find any adults who are as interesting as the kids I like, maybe I'll write about adults some day. The reason I keep writing about teen-agers is that it's a real interesting time of life. It's the time of most rapid change, when ideals are clashing against the walls of compromise." "After all," she told Smith, "I was born and raised in Tulsa, never wanted to live anywhere else and still don't, and never wanted to be anything but a writer."

MEDIA ADAPTATIONS: Tex was adapted by Buena Vista/Walt Disney Productions in 1982; *The Outsiders* inspired the 1983 Warner Brothers adaptation by Francis Ford Coppola, as well as a Fox Television weekly series scheduled to begin in 1990; actor Emilio Estevez adapted and starred in a Paramount production of *That Was Then, This Is Now* in 1985.

BIOGRAPHICAL/CRITICAL SOURCES:

BOOKS

Children's Literature Review, Volume 3, Gale, 1978.
Contemporary Literary Criticism, Volume 30, Gale, 1984.
Daly, Jay, *Presenting S. E. Hinton,* Twayne, 1987.

PERIODICALS

American Film, April, 1983.
Book World, May 9, 1971.
Children's Book Review, December, 1971.
Growing Point, May, 1980.

Kirkus Reviews, August 15, 1988.

Los Angeles Times, July 15, 1982, October 14, 1983.

Nation, March 8, 1986.

Newsweek, October 11, 1982.

New York Times, March 20, 1983, March 23, 1983, October 7, 1983, October 23, 1983.

New York Times Book Review, May 7, 1967, August 8, 1971, December 14, 1975, December 16, 1979, April 2, 1989.

Saturday Review, May 13, 1967, January 27, 1968.

School Library Journal, May, 1967, October, 1988.

Signal, May, 1980.

Times Literary Supplement, October 30, 1970, October 22, 1971, April 2, 1976, March 20, 1980.

Village Voice, April 5, 1983.

Washington Post, October 8, 1982, October 18, 1983.

Washington Post Book World, February 12, 1989.

—*Sketch by Diane Telgen*

*   *   *

HIRAOKA, Kimitake 1925-1970
(Yukio Mishima)

PERSONAL: Born January 14, 1925, in Tokyo, Japan; died by his own hand, November 25, 1970, in Tokyo, Japan; son of Azusa (a public official) and Shizue (Hashi) Hiraoka; married Yoko Sugiyama, June 1, 1958; children: Noriko (daughter), Iichiro (son). *Education:* Tokyo University, degree in jurisprudence, 1947. *Religion:* Zen.

CAREER: Writer, 1948-70. Civil servant with Japanese Finance Ministry, 1948. Founder of Tate No Kai (Shield Society). Lecturer, swordsman, singer, actor, director of plays, director of motion pictures, including "Yukoku," 1965, and "Enjo."

MEMBER: PEN (Japan), Tate No Kai (Shield Society; founder).

AWARDS, HONORS: Shincho Prize from Shinchosha Publishing, 1954, for *The Sound of Waves;* Kishida Prize for Drama from Shinchosha Publishing, 1955; Yomiuri Prize from Yomiuri Newspaper Co., for best novel, 1957, for *The Temple of the Golden Pavilion,* and for best drama, 1961, for "Toka no kiku."

WRITINGS:

UNDER PSEUDONYM YUKIO MISHIMA

Kamen no kokuhaku, [Japan], 1949, translation by Meredith Weatherby published as *Confessions of a Mask,* New Directions, 1958.

Ai no kawaki, [Japan], 1950, translation by Alfred H. Marks published as *Thirst for Love,* introduction by Donald Keene, Knopf, 1969.

Yoru no himawari (four-act play), [Japan], 1953, translation by Shigeho Shinozaki and Virgil A. Warren published as *Twilight Sunflower,* Hokuseido Press (Tokyo), 1958.

Kinjiki (fiction), two volumes, [Japan], 1954, translation by Marks published as *Forbidden Colors,* Secker & Warburg, 1968, Berkley Publishing, 1974.

Shiosai, [Japan], 1954, translation by Weatherby published as *The Sound of Waves,* Knopf, 1956.

Kindai nogaku shu, [Japan], 1956, translation by Keene published as *Five Modern No Plays* (contains "The Damask Drum," "Hanjo," "Kantan," "The Lady Aoi," and "Sotoba komachi"), Knopf, 1957.

Kinkakuji, [Japan], 1956, translation by Morris published as *The Temple of the Golden Pavilion,* Knopf, 1959.

Utage no ato, [Japan], 1960, translation by Keene published as *After the Banquet,* Knopf, 1963.

Gogo no eiko (fiction), [Japan], 1963, translation by John Nathan published as *The Sailor Who Fell from Grace with the Sea,* Knopf, 1965.

Sado koshaku fujin (play), [Japan], 1965, translation by Keene published as *Madame de Sade,* P. Owen, 1968 (first produced in New York City at Playhouse 46, April, 1988).

Death in Midsummer and Other Stories (contains "Death in Midsummer," "Three Million Yen," "Thermos Bottles," "The Priest of Shiga Temple and His Love," "The Seven Bridges," "Patriotism," "Dojoji," "Onnagata," "The Pearl," and "Swaddling Clothes"), translated by Seidensticker, Keene, Morris, and Sargent, New Directions, 1966.

Hagakure nyumon, [Japan], c. 1967, translation by Kathryn N. Sparling published as *The Way of Samurai: Yukio Mishima on Hagakure in Modern Life,* Basic Books, 1977.

Taido, [Japan], 1967, translation and introduction by Weatherby and Paul T. Konya published as *Young Samurai,* Grove, 1967.

Taiyo to tetsu, [Japan], 1968, translation by John Bester published as *Sun and Steel,* Grove, 1970.

Hojo no umi, [Japan], 1969-71, Volume I: *Haru no yuki,* Volume II: *Homba,* Volume III: *Akatsuki no tera,* Volume IV: *Tennin gosui,* translation published as *The Sea of Fertility: A Cycle of Four Novels,* Knopf, Volume I: *Spring Snow,* translated by Michael Gallagher, 1972, Volume II: *Runaway Horses,* translated by Gallagher, 1973, Volume III: *The Temple of Dawn,* translated by E. Dale Saunders and Cecilia S. Seigle, 1973, Volume IV: *The Decay of the Angel,* translated by Seidensticker, 1974.

(Editor with Geoffrey Bownas) *New Writing in Japan,* Penguin, 1972.

Yukio Mishima on 'Hagakure': The Samurai Ethic and Modern Japan, Souvenir Press, 1978.

Acts of Worship (stories), translation by Bester, Kodansha, 1989.

OTHER

Also author of *Hanazakari no mori,* 1944, reprinted, 1968; *Misaki nite no monogatari,* 1947; *Ma gun no tsuka,* 1949; *Toadai,* 1950; *Kaibutsu,* 1950; *Seijo,* 1951; *Kamen no kokuhaku sona ta,* 1951; *Kari to emono,* 1951; *Mishima Yukio tampen shu,* 1951; *Tonorikai,* 1951; *Mishima Yukio shu,* 1952; *Aporo no sakazuki,* 1952; *Mishima Yukio sakuhin shu,* six volumes, 1953-54; *Wakodo yo yomigaere,* 1954; *Koi no miyako,* 1954; *Shosetsuka no kyuka,* 1955; *Megami,* 1955; *Seishun O do ikiru ka,* 1955; *Shiroari no su,* 1956; *Rokumeikan,* 1956; *Kofuku go shuppan,* 1956; *Mishima Yukio senshu,* nineteen volumes, 1957-59; *Gendai shosetsu wa koten tari-uru ka,* 1957; *Rara to kaizoku,* 1957; *Hashizukushi,* 1958; *Fudotoku kyoiku koza,* 1959; *Bunsho tokuhon,* 1959, new edition, 1969; *Natsukonoboken,* 1960; *Ojosan,* 1960; *Nagasugita haru,* 1961; *Toka no kiku,* 1961; *Mishima Yukio gikyoku zenshu,* 1962; *Shisumoru taki,* 1963; *Ai no shisso,* 1963; *Mishima Yukio shu,* 1964; *Nikutai no gakko,* 1964; *Mishima Yukio tampen senshu,* 1964, six volumes, 1971; *Ongaku,* 1965; *Hanteijo daigaku,* 1966; *Mishima Yukio hyoron zenshu,* 1966; *Yakaitfuku,* 1967; *Mishima Yukio chohen zenshu,* 1967; *Koya yori,* 1967; *Inochi urimasu,* 1968; *Kindai nogaku shu,* 1968; (with Mitsuo Nakamura) *Taidan, ningen to bungaku,* 1968; *Waga tomo Hittora,* 1968; *Mishima Yukio reta kyoshitsu,* 1968; *Toron Mishima Yukio vs. Todai Zenkyoto,* 1969; *Raio no Terasu,* 1969; *Sado koshaku fujin,* 1969; *Chinsetsu yumiharizuki,* 1969; *Bunka boei ron,* 1969; *Gikyoku kurotokage,* 1969; *Fudutoku kyoiku kosa,* 1969; *Wakaki samurai no tame ni,* 1969; *Mishima Yukio bungaku ronshu,* 1970; *Mishima Yukio kenkyu,* 1970;

Sakkaron, 1970; *Gensen no kanjo,* 1970; *Mishima Yukio ten,* 1970; *Kodogaku nyumon,* 1970; *Shobu no kororo,* 1970; *Mishima Yukio* (volume of "Nihon bungaku kenkyu shiryo sosho" series), 1971; *Santao Yuchifu tuan p'ien chieh tso hsuan,* 1971; *Mishima Yukio no ningenzo,* 1971; *Mishima Yukio no ski a do miru ka,* 1971; *Ranryo O,* 1971; *Kemono no tawamure,* 1971; *Ao no jidai,* 1971; *Shishi,* 1971; *Mishima Yukio judai sakuhin shu,* 1971; *Mishima Yukio,* 1972; *Shosetsu to wa nani ka,* 1972; *Nihon bungaku shoshi,* 1972; *Mishima Yukio shonen shi,* edited by Kazusuke Ogawa, 1973; *Waga shishunki,* 1973; *Mishima Yukio,* edited by Ken'ichi Adachi, 1973; *Daiichi no sei,* 1973; *Mishima Yukio zenshu,* thirty-six volumes, edited by Shoichi Saeki and Jun Ishikawa, 1973-76; *Mishima Yukio goroku* (title means "Invitation to Mishimalogy"), edited by Ken Akitsu, 1975; and (with Teiji Ito and Takeji Iwamiya) *Sento Gosho,* 1977. Also editor of *Rokusei nakamura utaemon,* 1959; Bungei tokuhon, *Kawabata Yasunari* (short stories), 1962; and Yoshitoshi Taiso, *Chi no bansan,* 1971. Also author of screenplays, including "Yukoku," 1965.

MEDIA ADAPTATIONS: Screen adaptations of Mishima's works include a Japanese production of *Temple of the Golden Pavilion,* entitled "Enjo," and a 1976 English language version of *The Sailor Who Fell from Grace with the Sea,* which featured actors Kris Kristofferson and Sarah Miles. In 1965 Mishima wrote, directed, and played the leading role in a film version of *Yukoku.* His portrayal of the lieutenant's suicide so eerily foreshadowed his own that in 1971 his family had the film destroyed.

SIDELIGHTS: Renowned for his flamboyant personality, eccentric political beliefs, and spectacular ritual suicide, Yukio Mishima is nevertheless best remembered for his contributions to Japanese literature. A prolific writer, Mishima's mastery of novels, essays, and plays earned him a reputation as the literary genius of Japan's postwar generation as well as a place among the world's finest authors.

Mishima's reputation was established in 1949 with his popular first novel, *Confessions of a Mask.* Although not considered an autobiography, the book is an obvious chronicle of Mishima's life from early childhood through his wartime experiences. The novel focused on the narrator's growing awareness that he would have to mask his abnormal sexual preferences from those around him. A *Time* reviewer called it a "fierce portrait of homosexuality—a subject with which Mishima had a lifelong fascination and, some say, involvement." When *Confessions of a Mask* was published, Edwin McClellan asserted, "no Japanese novelist before him had written about a sexual deviant with such elegant abandon. What a book it was, for its time and place. It burst out like a gust of fresh air, seemingly from nowhere, blowing away all the cobwebs left from the war. It was truly a book without nationality; it dazzled, perhaps even touched us all, Americans, Englishmen, and Japanese alike."

In his second book, *Thirst for Love,* Mishima discarded the self-confessional style and told the story of a young widow who moves in with her father-in-law and becomes his mistress. She then develops an obsessive but unreciprocated passion for the household servant boy. Paul Doyle complained that Mishima's "ability to handle character waivers erratically and his plotting is—on at least four or five occasions—obviously artificial and contrived." He added that, "in general, the characters arouse little interest." Other critics commented that Mishima's descriptions of a bourgeois Japanese household were "fascinatingly well done." *Forbidden Colors,* written in 1954, is another novel about homosexuality, but "it is almost totally devoid of the sensitive nuances and affecting honesty of the earlier novel [*Confessions*

of a Mask]," asserted Ivan Morris. Edward Seidensticker found it "a cold, repellent book"; likewise, Dick Wagner and Yoshio Iwamoto thought it was "one of the most stilted and contrived" books Mishima ever wrote. "In it, the mind-body duality is so accentuated, so obviously pushed and dragged to the forefront by whatever devices of plot, scene, and character seem serviceable, that the entire enterprise creaks like some ancient and cumbrous machine." Maurice Capitanchik, however, stated that *Forbidden Colors* "is a work of literature—the enigmatic, frightening and ultimately compassionate product of a complex and dominating intelligence."

Considered one of Mishima's best early books, *The Temple of the Golden Pavilion* won the Yomiuri Prize in 1957. The novel is based on the true story of a young Buddhist acolyte whose ugliness and stutter have made him grow to hate anything beautiful. He becomes obsessed with the idea that the golden temple where he studies is the ideal of beauty, and in envy he burns the temple to the ground. Mishima based his story on information he gathered from the actual court trial, with the protagonist acting as narrator. "But although Mishima has made use of the reported details of the real-life culprit's arrogant and desperate history, culminating in the final willful act of arson," wrote Nancy Wilson Ross in the book's introduction, "he has employed the factual record merely as a scaffolding on which to erect a disturbing and powerful story of a sick young man's obsession with a beauty he cannot attain, and the way in which his private pathology leads him, slowly and fatefully, to self-destruction and a desperate deed of pyromania."

Nearly as popular as his novels were Mishima's modernized versions of traditional Japanese No plays. Developed in the fourteenth century, No plays generally featured four or five actors who tell their story with a recitation and dance accompanied by flute and drums. The plays' stylized gestures and deliberate dialogues became so much a ritual that audiences were able to detect the slightest variation in a performance.

Mishima was the first contemporary author to work successfully in this medium. In adapting some of the plays he painstakingly recreated the details of the story; in others, he followed only the general theme. The plot of *The Damask Drum,* for example, resembles that of the original play. Donald Keene compared the two versions: In the original story an old gardener in a palace falls in love with a princess and is told he will win her favor if he can beat a drum loud enough for her to hear. But the drum is made of damask and can make no sound, so the old man commits suicide. Mishima's version concerns a janitor in a Tokyo law office who falls in love with "the client of a fashionable couturiere in the building across the way," stated Keene. The janitor, too, is told to beat the drum in order to win the girl's affection, but it makes no sound and he commits suicide. In the conclusions, "the No ghost returns to torment the cruel princess with the ceaseless beating of the drum, but in the modern play the lady's inability to love makes her deaf to the beating of the drum, and the janitor's ghost is driven a second time to despair."

The No plays are considered among Mishima's most interesting works. Gwenn Boardman commented that "modern No plays take the poetic spirit of the past, shatter the illusion, and replace the poetry with an ugly vocabulary of destruction and disillusion." Gore Vidal remarked that although Mishima is also proficient as a novelist, "only in his reworking of the No plays does he appear to transcend competence and make (to a foreign eye) literature."

Ten of Mishima's best short stories and plays were translated in *Death in Midsummer and Other Stories.* The longest entry is the title story about a woman whose two small children and sister-in-law drown at a beach. Mishima studies the jealousy, resentment, and guilt of the woman and her husband over their inability to mourn. Howard Hibbett commented that "in this simple but profound and beautifully finished story" Mishima has "vividly . . . succeeded in investing an 'incident' with imaginative life. Psychological analysis in the classic French tradition is enhanced by awareness of the changing seasons, by a sensibility fusing passions, meditations, and landscapes in the great tradition of Japanese literature."

Another notable inclusion in this volume is the short novella "Yukoku." It tells of the ritual suicides of a young army officer and his wife after a coup in which he is involved fails to overthrow reigning politicians. The couple, both "perfect specimens, of physique, of sexual beauty, of loyalty," make passionate love before their suicides. Roy Teele declared that "the juxtaposition of the erotic passages and the brutally described suicide scenes is profoundly moving," and Robert Trumbull considered this "blood-drenched exposition of the old *bushido* spirit" to be a "tour de force in its grim genre."

Mishima's last work, considered by many his magnum opus, was the *Sea of Fertility* tetralogy, the final portions of which he completed and submitted to his publishers on the day of his suicide. In a letter written to an American friend just before his death, Mishima explained: "I wrote everything in it, and I believe I expressed in it everything I felt and thought about through my life. I just finished the novel on the very day of my action in order to realize my Bunbu-Ryodo." (Bunbu-Ryodo is a synthesis of the culture arts and the warrior arts.)

The tetralogy begins with *Spring Snow,* the tragic love story of Kiyoaki and Satoko, both children of Japanese aristocrats. When Satoko is chosen to marry the emperor's grandson, each of Kiyoaki's liaisons with her becomes more dangerous yet all the more passionate. "The book ends in a blaze of romanticism," observed John Spurling, "with Satoko entering a buddhist monastery and Kiyoaki dying of tuberculosis almost at its gates."

Continuing on from Kiyoaki's story in 1912, the rest of the series spans the history of Japan through the 1970's. In each new volume, Kiyoaki is reincarnated as a different person—as a political fanatic, a Thai princess, and then an evil young orphan. The final three volumes are told from the viewpoint of a school friend of Kiyoaki's, "a wonderfully subtle spiritual voyeur named Honda, a rationalist Japanese judge and lawyer," who follows the progress of Kiyoaki's spirit into three new bodies, each bearing a certain pattern of three moles and each dying at the age of twenty. Lance Morrow explained that "Honda, like a principle of embattled moral intelligence, acts as Mishima's civilized guide through the mysteries of love, death, political tragedy and reincarnation."

Although the simple love story of *Spring Snow* made it the most popular book of the tetralogy, the other volumes were also highly regarded. Many readers were drawn to *Runaway Hero* because the suicide of its protagonist, Isao, foreshadowed in almost exact detail the author's own suicide. *The Temple of Dawn* was acclaimed by Capitanchik, who thought it included "some of Mishima's finest descriptive writing, especially concerning Honda's visit to Benares." Morrow also considered this passage "a small masterpiece." The final volume, *The Decay of the Angel,* "raises more questions than it answers," Susan Heath observed, but she also noted that it "brilliantly epitomizes Mishima's pessimistic outlook." Morrow also praised the book, calling it "a wonderfully frigid dance of death in which Mishima, like a Japanese

Prospero, gathers all his artistic belongings together. In its austerity it is among the best of Mishima's novels."

Because Mishima knew this tetralogy was to be his last work, it is often considered a suicide note to the world. Critics disagree, however, on Mishima's intended message. Some reviewers, including Paul Theroux, thought the tetralogy's theme was reincarnation and that Mishima evidently "expects to be back with us in one form or another." Donald Richie agreed, theorizing that Mishima was so concerned with maintaining perfect physical condition and avoiding the decay of aging that he believed in reincarnation as "a promise of eternal youth." Others were convinced that the author did not actually believe in rebirth because, as Heath noted, in the last pages of *Decay of the Angel* "he manages only to cast doubt on the very concept that supposedly lies at the heart of the tetralogy—the idea of reincarnation, a concept in which, as it turns out, he never believed and for which he has not persuasively argued."

Another interpretation, offered by Wagner and Iwamoto, was that Mishima's final work professed the same belief as did his *Temple of the Golden Pavilion:* beauty equals nothingness. "As paradoxical as it may sound, it may be said that he redeemed his life by suicide and his art by installing within it its own negation." Thus in the conclusion of the series we find that by questioning the very concepts he writes about, Mishima, "rather than pulling the rug out from under Honda's feet . . . plucks the wool from his eyes, removing the veil of ignorance and forcing him to experience the void underlying everything."

Spurling asserted that the two major themes of the *Sea of Fertility* tetralogy are the dissolution of the individual and "the dissolution of the old aristocratic culture and the values which it supported," both of which Mishima had vigorously crusaded against during his life. The tetralogy could therefore be considered a written expression of the beliefs for which the author had lived and died.

Mishima's fascination with death and suicide can be traced to his childhood. Born to a family of samurai nobility, he attempted even as a young man to follow the samurai tradition which emphasized expertise in the martial arts, control over mind and body, and a following of the bushido code of self-sacrifice, indifference to pain, and complete loyalty to Japan's emperor. Young Mishima had been convinced that he would die for the emperor during World War II, as did the kamikaze pilots, but because he failed the army physical his death wish remained unfulfilled. After his rejection, he began to build up his frail physique and thereafter maintained his body in the perfect physical condition of the samurai by lifting weights, practicing karate, and engaging in the ancient sword-fighting game of kendo.

When Japan was defeated by the Allies in World War II, the country was forced to adopt a new constitution that stripped the emperor of his power. Under foreign influence Japanese culture began to change in ways that both pleased and horrified Mishima. His home, once described as "almost determinedly un-Japanese," was full of English antiques. Even his writing contained more references to classic French than Japanese literature. But Mishima grew to hate the Westernization that he felt was causing the dissolution of old Japanese ideals. In 1968 he formed a private army of eighty-three university men who were also interested in the martial arts and who believed in the way of the samurai. The goal of the Tate No Kai, or Shield Society, was to return Japan to the samurai tradition, "which he saw as an ethical and esthetic system truer to the spirit of Japan than a modern army," noted Philip Shabecoff. "Although his private army . . . led many Westerners to believe that he sought to revive Japanese militarism, he actually loathed the militarism represented by the Japanese Army of pre-World War II years. He regarded that militarism as a foreign import alien to the Japanese spirit."

One of the ancient samurai rituals that Mishima and his followers believed in was seppuku, a form of suicide reserved for the samurai warrior. In this painful ritual, the subject kneels and slices open his abdomen, releasing the intestines. "Standing behind the subject is a samurai with a sword," a writer for the *New Yorker* explained, "whose function is to behead the subject at the first sign of pain, or even the slightest alteration of the traditional posture."

Seppuku, Richard Halloran pointed out, is "the ultimate protest against that which one cannot accept, the ultimate affirmation of that in which one believes, and the ultimate reconciliation between the two." Many Westerners confuse seppuku with hara-kiri, but there is a difference between the two. Although the two Japanese ideographs that compose the words are the same, their order is reversed and they therefore take on distinct shades of meaning. Hara-kiri literally means "to cut the stomach," whereas seppuku "connotes an inner being or the spirit of a man, roughly with the same sense that Americans intend when they use the inelegant term 'guts.'" So seppuku could be most accurately defined as "the cutting of the spirit."

Apparently Mishima began to plan his suicide several years in advance. Shabecoff reported that during the spring of 1970, "Mishima said that he worked so hard on body building because he intended to die before he was 50 and wanted to have a good-looking corpse." Perhaps to prove his perfect physical condition, Mishima posed in 1969 for a photographic study of various postures of death, including death by drowning, by duel, and by hara-kiri. In addition, a few weeks before his suicide he displayed at a Tokyo department store a series of photographs of himself in the nude. The author was also prepared mentally for the final act. In a letter to Ivan Morris just before his death, Mishima wrote: "After thinking and thinking through four years, I came to wish to sacrifice myself for the old, beautiful tradition of Japan, which is disappearing very quickly day by day."

On November 25, 1970, Mishima and four of his followers from the Shield Society entered the headquarters of Japan's Eastern Ground Self-Defense Forces, took its commander, Lt. General Kanetoshi Mashida, hostage, and demanded that soldiers be assembled on a parade ground below. As twelve hundred men quickly gathered, Mishima went out on a balcony, his kamikaze-style headband fluttering in the breeze, and shouted: "Listen to me! I have waited in vain for four years for you to take arms in an uprising. Are you warriors? If so, why do you strive to guard the constitution that is designed to deny the very reason for the existence of your organization? Why can't you realize that so long as this constitution exists, you cannot be saved? Isn't there anyone among you willing to hurl his body against the constitution that has turned Japan spineless? Let's stand up and fight together and die together for something that is far more important than our life. That is not freedom or democracy, but the most important thing for us all, Japan."

When his words were greeted with angry heckling by the soldiers, Mishima shouted "Tenno Heika Banzai!" ("Long live the Emperor!"), stepped back from the balcony, and proceeded to perform in exact detail the traditional seppuku ceremony. *Time* related the dramatic event: "Mishima stripped to the waist and knelt on the floor. . . . Probing the left side of his abdomen, he put the ceremonial dagger in place, then thrust it deep into his flesh. Standing behind him, Masakatsu Morita, 25, one of his

most devoted followers, raised his sword and with one stroke sent Mishima's severed head rolling to the floor. To complete the ceremony, Morita plunged a dagger into his own stomach, and yet another student lopped off Morita's head. Shedding tears, the three surviving students saluted the two dead men and surrendered to the general's aides." The *New Yorker* pointed out later that Mishima's seventeen-centimeter incision displayed "a degree of mastery over physical reflex, and over pain itself, unparalled in modern records of this ritual."

Ironically, this man so obsessed with death had been greatly admired for his charisma and vitality. Throughout his life he had followed a hectic schedule of writing, acting, singing, directing, exercising, running his private army, and pursuing an active social life. John Nathan described the energetic author: "Mishima has a rare capacity for enjoying himself, and he loves nothing better than a party. He has only to walk into a room full of people and it belongs to him. He is not a large man, but his presence is so palpable it can be stifling. . . . Mishima weighs into a party with gusto, delighting over the food, mixing experimental drinks, neighing hoarsely at all the jokes, including his own. . . . Mishima is clever, amusing, astute, catty."

Although many critics pointed out the paradox of Mishima's captivation with both life and death, East and West, Masao Miyoshi averred that the author "was an amazingly consistent person, who never forgot his wartime catechism—the myth of Japan as a ritually ordered state, the samurai way of life characterized by manly courage and feminine grace, and the vision of imminent death as the catalyst of life." Richie agreed: "Mishima is a man who compares things as they are with things as they have been or could be and who, in the face of public indifference and private doubt, has the strength of character to live by those standards he himself finds suitable. When he also has the strength to die by them the act is astonishing because . . . suddenly the man is all of a piece. . . . Mishima's suicide was the final stone in the arch of his life."

BIOGRAPHICAL/CRITICAL SOURCES:

BOOKS

Contemporary Literary Criticism, Gale, Volume 2, 1974, Volume 4, 1975, Volume 6, 1976, Volume 9, 1978, Volume 27, 1984.
Mishima, Yukio, *Five Modern No Plays,* introduction by Donald Keene, Knopf, 1957.
Mishima, Yukio, *The Temple of the Golden Pavilion,* introduction by Nancy Wilson Ross, Knopf, 1959.
Miyoshi, Masao, *Accomplices of Silence: The Modern Japanese Novel,* University of California Press, 1974.
Nathan, John, *Mishima: A Biography,* Little, Brown, 1974.
Stokes, Henry Scott, *Life and Death of Yukio Mishima,* Farrar, Straus, 1974.

PERIODICALS

Atlantic, April, 1968; September, 1977.
Best Sellers, April 15, 1968; September 1, 1969.
Books Abroad, winter, 1968; spring, 1969.
Books and Bookmen, August, 1970; February, 1971; December, 1974.
Commonweal, March 19, 1971.
Contemporary Literature, winter, 1975.
Critique, Volume X, number 2, 1968; Volume XII, number 1, 1970.
Detroit News, August 20, 1972.
Encounter, May, 1975.
Esquire, May, 1972.
Harper's, September, 1972.

Life, September 2, 1966.
Listener, May 5, 1967; April 25, 1968.
Nation, June 12, 1972.
New Republic, June 24, 1972.
New Statesman, April 7, 1967; November 30, 1973; July 19, 1974.
Newsweek, February 8, 1971.
New Yorker, June 15, 1968.
New York Review of Books, September, 25, 1969; June 17, 1971.
New York Times, March 1, 1967; January 7, 1970; November 26, 1970; November 27, 1970; December 10, 1970; March 24, 1971; July 6, 1972; November 1, 1972; September 15, 1985.
New York Times Book Review, May 1, 1966; June 28, 1968; January 3, 1971; November 12, 1972; June 24, 1973; October 14, 1973; December 2, 1973; May 12, 1974.
Observer Review, September 1, 1968; May 31, 1970; March 14, 1971.
Saturday Review, May 7, 1966; December 12, 1970; June 10, 1972; December 2, 1972.
Saturday Review/World, June 1, 1974.
Spectator, August 30, 1968.
Time, May 24, 1968; October 15, 1973; June 10, 1974.
Times Literary Supplement, April 20, 1967; September 19, 1968; July 2, 1970; March 12, 1971; August 20, 1971; November 10, 1972; November 30, 1973; July 26, 1974.
Variety, July 15, 1970; December 9, 1970; December 30, 1970; April 7, 1971.
Virginia Quarterly Review, autumn, 1968; winter, 1970; autumn, 1973.
Voice Literary Supplement, October, 1982.
Washington Post Book World, June 2, 1968; September 21, 1969; July 2, 1972; July 22, 1973; May 19, 1974.
Yale Review, summer, 1975.

OTHER

Mishima: A Life in Four Chapters (film), 1985.

OBITUARIES:

PERIODICALS

AB Bookman's Weekly, January 4, 1971.
Books Abroad, spring, 1971.
Life, December 11, 1970.
Newsweek, December 7, 1970.
New Yorker, December 12, 1970.
New York Times, November 25, 1970; November 26, 1970.
Time, December 7, 1970.

*   *   *

HIRSCH, E(ric) D(onald), Jr. 1928-

PERSONAL: Born March 22, 1928, in Memphis, Tenn.; son of Eric Donald (a businessman) and Leah (Aschaffenburg) Hirsch; married Mary Pope, 1958; children: John, Frederick, Elizabeth. *Education:* Cornell University, B.A., 1950; Yale University, M.A., 1953, Ph.D., 1957.

ADDRESSES: Home—2006 Pine Top Rd., Charlottesville, Va. 22903. *Office*—Department of English, University of Virginia, Charlottesville, Va. 22901.

CAREER: Yale University, New Haven, Conn., instructor, 1956-60, assistant professor, 1960-63, associate professor of English, 1963-66; University of Virginia, Charlottesville, professor, 1966-72, William R. Kenan Professor of English, 1973—, chairman of department, 1968-71 and 1981-82, director of composi-

tion, 1971—. Member of faculty, School of Criticism and Theory, Northwestern University, summer, 1981; Bateson Lecturer, Oxford University, 1983. Trustee and founder, Cultural Literacy Foundation. *Military service:* U.S. Naval Reserve, 1950-54; active duty, 1950-52.

MEMBER: American Academy of Arts and Sciences (fellow), Modern Language Association of America, Keats-Shelley Association, Byron Society, American Rhododendron Society.

AWARDS, HONORS: Fulbright fellow, 1955; Morse fellow, 1960-61; Guggenheim fellow, 1964-65; *Explicator* (magazine) Prize, 1964, for *Innocence and Experience: An Introduction to Blake;* National Endowment for the Humanities senior fellow, 1971-72 and 1980-81; Wesleyan University Center for the Humanities fellow, 1973 and 1974; Princeton University Council of the Humanities fellow, 1976; Stanford University Center for Advanced Study in the Behavioral Sciences fellow, 1980-81; Australian National University Humanities Research Centre fellow, 1982.

WRITINGS:

Wordsworth and Schelling: A Typological Study of Romanticism, Yale University Press, 1960.
Innocence and Experience: An Introduction to Blake, Yale University Press, 1964.
(Contributor) Harold Bloom and Frederick W. Hilles, editors, *From Sensibility to Romanticism: Essays Presented to Frederick A. Pottle,* Oxford University Press, 1965.
Validity in Interpretation, Yale University Press, 1967.
The Aims of Interpretation, University of Chicago Press, 1976.
The Philosophy of Composition, University of Chicago Press, 1977.
(Contributor) Thomas F. Rugh and Erin R. Silva, editors, *History as a Tool in Critical Interpretation: A Symposium,* Brigham Young University Press, 1978.
(Contributor) Paul Hernadi, editor, *What Is Literature?,* Indiana University Press, 1978.
Cultural Literacy: What Every American Needs to Know, Houghton, 1987.
(With Joseph Kett and James Trefil) *The Dictionary of Cultural Literacy: What Every American Needs to Know* (Literary Guild selection), Houghton, 1988.
(For young people) *The First Dictionary of Cultural Literacy,* Houghton, 1989.

Contributor of essays and articles to *American Educator, Times Literary Supplement, Critical Inquiry, College English,* and *American Scholar.*

SIDELIGHTS: After spending a quarter of a century publishing works that have had a "significant impact on recent American literary criticism and theory," according to Brian G. Caraher of the *Dictionary of Literary Biography,* E. D. Hirsch, Jr., published *Cultural Literacy: What Americans Need to Know,* a book that hit the bestseller lists and raised a storm of controversy. Hirsch argues in the book that many Americans are ignorant of the shared terms and concepts of their society, and that this renders them incapable of participating fully in that society. *Cultural Literacy* brought Hirsch to the attention of a wide reading audience and pushed him into founding the Cultural Literacy Foundation, an organization promoting the teaching of a shared core of knowledge in the nation's schools.

Cultural Literacy begins with a recitation of just how ill-informed contemporary students are. Hirsch quotes studies showing that the majority of high school students do not know when the American Civil War took place; half cannot identify

Winston Churchill or Joseph Stalin; three-fourths do not recognize Walt Whitman or Henry David Thoreau; and many are unaware of when Christopher Columbus discovered America. Their knowledge of science, geography, the arts, and other subjects is also weak. Such a lack of basic information renders much of what these students read meaningless. They are not illiterate, but they are unable to identify people and places discussed in what they read, and are baffled by historic, scientific, and literary terms or allusions. "That so many people should be stumbling around in this kind of fog," writes John Gross in the *New York Times,* "is an obvious cause for concern. It implies a coarsening in the quality of life, and a drying-up of invaluable common traditions. It makes it harder for us to communicate with one another. For the children of the poor and disadvantaged, it represents a formidable barrier to progress." "Most Americans can make out the words," James W. Tuttleton explains in *Commentary.* "The literacy we need, according to Hirsch, is *cultural* literacy."

As a means of identifying some of the information that cultural illiterates lack, Hirsch includes a 63-page list of 5,000 names, terms, and phrases he considers to be essential to cultural literacy. Compiled with the assistance of two academic colleagues, historian Joseph Kett and physicist James Trefil, the list includes such varied items as "absolute zero," "flapper," "Sherlock Holmes," "critical mass," and "empiricism." A complete and thorough knowledge of each item is not needed, Hirsch explains. To understand a text a reader needs schemata, thumbnail explanations of these terms. David Gates in *Newsweek* defines schemata as "simple, superficial ideas suggested by words." Studies show that these are enough to allow a literate person to comprehend newspapers, books, and other media, and more importantly, to participate in his society. According to Tuttleton, Hirsch "points out that the culturally illiterate—and the same goes for those not having a command of standard English—can exercise no effect on discourse concerning social policy." As Hirsch writes in the book, "We will be able to achieve a just and prosperous society only when our schools ensure that everyone commands enough shared background knowledge to be able to communicate effectively with everyone else."

To reach this goal, Hirsch calls for a drastic change in America's educational system. He argues that the idea of reading as an abstract skill divorced from any specific content is a major cause of the present dilemma. According to Hirsch, content is essential to reading and is especially vital for comprehending what is read. Citing recent studies of how we read, Hirsch explains that "every text, even the most elementary, implies information that it takes for granted and doesn't explain. Knowing such information is *the* decisive skill of reading." He calls for schools to supply that necessary background information as it teaches students reading skills. To assist in this effort, Hirsch founded the Cultural Literacy Foundation.

Not all critics have appreciated *Cultural Literacy;* some claim that the book calls for a return to "teaching names, dates and places by rote and providing a context later," as Stefan Kanfer of *Time* puts it. And the list of needed cultural information has prompted "accusations of elitism," Charles Trueheart reports in the *Washington Post.* Robert Pattison of *Nation* argues that "a culture index poses a fundamental political question: How far are the wishes of the people to be consulted in determining the nature of culture itself?" But even harsh critics admit that the book raises some serious questions about the failure of American education.

In *The Dictionary of Cultural Literacy: What Every American Needs to Know,* written with Kett and Trefil, Hirsch provides definitions of the items listed in his earlier book, along with the definitions of many other terms. "The dictionary is more ambitious and really more important," Hirsch tells Trueheart, "because it will suggest to people who are outsiders in the literate culture, 'What do these characters really know that I'm being excluded from?'" The book is arranged into twenty-three sections which cover the major categories of knowledge, providing definitions of hundreds of terms, ideas, events, and names.

Many of Hirsch's ideas about cultural literacy are derived from his years as a literary critic, during which time he has shown "an enduring concern for *types* and for the *typicality* of expressive and interpretive behavior," according to Caraher. As a critic, Hirsch does not isolate a text from its author. Rather, he focuses his attention on the author's worldview, knowledge, and cultural situation. In order to understand an author's work, a critic "must familiarize himself with the typical meanings of the author's mental and experiential world," as Hirsch states in *Validity in Interpretation.* That is, a critic must enter into the author's perceptual framework. Caraher finds that Hirsch's "most singular contribution to modern American criticism and theory . . . might very well be his persistent iteration of the philosophical inevitability and the heuristic power of *typology.*"

BIOGRAPHICAL/CRITICAL SOURCES:

BOOKS

Dictionary of Literary Biography, Volume 67: *Modern American Critics since 1955,* Gale, 1988.
Hirsch, E. D., Jr., *Validity in Interpretation,* Yale University Press, 1967.
Hirsch, E. D., Jr., *Cultural Literacy: What Every American Needs to Know,* Houghton, 1987.
Lentricchia, Frank, *After the New Criticism,* University of Chicago Press, 1980.
Ray, William, *Literary Meaning: From Phenomenology to Deconstruction,* Blackwell, 1984.

PERIODICALS

College English, November, 1977.
Commentary, July, 1987.
Journal of Aesthetics and Art Criticism, fall, 1984.
Journal of Reading, May, 1988.
Nation, May 30, 1987.
Newsweek, April 20, 1987.
New York Times, April 17, 1987, June 14, 1987.
New York Times Book Review, March 15, 1987, December 17, 1989.
Partisan Review, fall, 1967.
Pre/Text, Number 1, spring/fall, 1980.
Time, July 20, 1987.
Virginia Quarterly Review, summer, 1967, winter, 1988.
Washington Post, April 20, 1987.

*   *   *

HITE, Shere 1942-

PERSONAL: First name pronounced "share"; given name Shirley Diana; born November 2, 1942, in St. Joseph, Mo.; daughter of Paul Gregory (a flight controller); legally adopted by Raymond Hite (a truck driver); married Friedrich Hoericke (a concert pianist), 1985. *Education:* University of Florida, B.A. (cum laude), 1964, M.A., 1968; further graduate study at Columbia University, 1968-69.

ADDRESSES: Home—New York, N.Y.; and Laffont, 6 Place St., Sulpice, Paris 75006, France. *Office*—P.O. Box 5282, FDR Station, New York, N.Y. 10022.

CAREER: Model for Wilhelmina Agency, late 1960s; National Organization for Women (NOW), New York City, director of Feminist Sexuality Project, 1972-78; Hite Research International, New York City, director, 1978—. Instructor in female sexuality, New York University, 1977—; lecturer, Harvard University, McGill University, Columbia University, and women's groups, 1977-83. Member of advisory board, American Foundation of Gender and Genital Medicine, Johns Hopkins University.

MEMBER: National Organization for Women (NOW), American Historical Association, American Sociological Association, American Association for the Advancement of Science, Society for the Scientific Study of Sex, Women's Health Network, Academy of Political Science, Women's History Association.

WRITINGS:

(Compiler and editor) *Sexual Honesty: By Women for Women,* Warner Paperback Library, 1974.
The Hite Report: A Nationwide Study of Female Sexuality, Macmillan, 1976.
The Hite Report on Male Sexuality (Book-of-the-Month Club alternate selection), Knopf, 1981, published as *The Hite Report: A Study of Male Sexuality,* Ballantine, 1982.
Women and Love: A Cultural Revolution in Progress, Knopf, 1987.

Consulting editor, *Journal of Sex Education and Therapy* and *Journal of Sexuality and Disability.*

SIDELIGHTS: Shere Hite, who prefers to be called a cultural historian rather than a sex researcher or sexologist, has written three controversial, best-selling books on the topic of human sexuality—*The Hite Report: A Nationwide Study of Female Sexuality, The Hite Report on Male Sexuality,* and *Women and Love: A Cultural Revolution in Progress.* Each book was generated from lengthy questionnaires completed by either female or male respondents from across the nation, and each presents insightful, and even novel, information about this charged topic. With each of these publications, however, critics have called her research methods into question and some have criticized her for what they deem her strong feminist bias. Nevertheless, a thread of appreciation runs through the commentary, for many feel Hite has listened with compassion to the sexual frustrations of contemporary women and men. For instance, Arlie Russell Hochschild maintains in his *New York Times Book Review* assessment of *Women and Love* that "[Hite] sets us next to her in a kind of confessional booth to listen through the curtain. . . . She makes [the women] know they are not alone, she articulates their discontent."

Hite was born Shirley Diana Gregory in 1942 in St. Joseph, Missouri, but her mother and father divorced shortly after the end of World War II. When her mother remarried, Hite was legally adopted by Raymond Hite. This second marriage ended in divorce, as well, and for many years thereafter Hite lived on and off with her grandparents. Hite's earliest desire was to be a classical composer, "but how many women have you heard of becoming composers, right?," she asked *Chicago Tribune* interviewer Cheryl Lavin; accordingly, Hite says her second choice was "trying to figure out how society got where it is and why is it so irrational." Thus, after moving to Florida to stay with some relatives, Hite pursued her B.A. and M.A. degrees in history at the University of Florida. In 1968, she moved to New York City to further her study of history at Columbia University but with-

drew early on and began modeling at the Wilhelmina Agency for the money. Her first link with the feminist movement developed shortly thereafter when she modeled as a secretary in a typewriter advertisement that proclaimed: "The typewriter is so smart she doesn't have to be," notes Martha Smilgis for *Time.* Because the ad incensed her, Hite joined the National Organization for Women (NOW) which was protesting the ad at the time. Then in 1971, according to Smilgis, "Hite read a pamphlet in the NOW office, *The Myth of Female Orgasm,* and decided to create a questionnaire on the issue for a NOW-sponsored 'speak up.'" As she read the women's responses about their sexuality, 'a whole picture of the universe began to fall into place,' says Hite. 'Without feminism I don't know what I would be doing today. It gave me the belief in myself.'" It was this belief in herself and other women that motivated Hite to tap into the subject of contemporary sexual problems.

The first book in Hite's trilogy, *The Hite Report: A Nationwide Study of Female Sexuality,* was an immediate bestseller and was placed in the company of such classic works on sexuality as the Kinsey report and the Masters and Johnson reports. For a period of four years Hite distributed approximately 100,000 lengthy questionnaires to women through such sources as NOW, church newsletters, and *Mademoiselle, Oui,* and *Ms.* magazines. She based the resultant book on the responses of approximately 3,000 women ranging in age from fourteen to seventy-three, with representation from forty-nine states. According to Jean Seligmann for *Newsweek,* whereas the Kinsey and the Masters and Johnson reports were the product of interviews and laboratory research conducted by these authority figures, "the women themselves are presented as the authorities on their own sexuality" in *The Hite Report.* Thus, "reading *The Hite Report,*" notes Karen Durbin for *Mademoiselle,* "is rather like sitting in on a mass-consciousness raising session about female sexuality. Women talk in unusual detail about their sexual experiences and feelings—graphically, factually, rapturously, glumly, and sometimes brutally."

Hite's general conclusion in this first book is that current notions on sexuality must be revised if women are to achieve sexual fulfillment. Hite faults a male-oriented pattern of sexual expression for many of women's sexual difficulties: "There has rarely been any acknowledgement that female sexuality might have a complex nature of its own which would be more than just the logical counterpart of (what we think of as) male sexuality," she writes in the text. Hite also insists that the sexual revolution of the 1960s and 1970s created pressure for women to say "yes" to sex, but that it did not liberate women in any substantial way; that is, women did not find it any easier to say what they really wanted sexually from their partners.

Critical reaction to *The Hite Report,* as well as to the succeeding works in Hite's trilogy, is mixed. *Village Voice* contributor James Wolcott blasts the book, which he sees as a "feminist anthem. . . . *The Hite Report* is a bull session to which [the male writer] has not been invited. Nonetheless, I intend to intrude, for I think *The Hite Report* is a bum book, useful as a masturbation manual perhaps, but dubious as sociology, drear and dry as literature, and hopelessly muddled as polemic." Wolcott begins his criticism by questioning Hite's methodology. He feels the questionnaire Hite employed "bulges with questions so nebulous, so ludicrously open-ended, that it is a wonder the replies didn't run the riverrun length of *Finnegans Wake.*" He also questions the representativeness of Hite's sample after taking into consideration the organizations and magazines involved in distributing the questionnaire. He distrusts Hite's conclusions and proclaims that the "cant is never thicker than when Hite is chanting about the freedom to do your own you-know-what." Likewise, *Washington Post Book World* reviewer Barbara G. Harrison's analysis of the work is generally pessimistic. One of her chief complaints is Hite's overemphasis on the physiological: "I have no prudish objection to reading . . . about the sexual activities and preferences of the 3000 women Hite surveyed. I do, however, think it's daft to act, as Hite does, on the assumption that sex and love are unrelated phenomena. . . . With few exceptions, the questions call for bald physiological fact rather than for psychological nuance . . . which, as good sense ought to tell anybody, is boring." Harrison additionally feels that the many "fancy, flimsy, and unreadable statistical charts and appendices" included in the work as a means of assuring the book's scientific credibility instead "serve only to cast doubt on her methodology." However, Harrison goes on to maintain that doubtful methodology is not the book's main flaw: "What is more detrimental to the integrity of *The Hite Report* is the absence of any synthesizing, reflective intelligence to help us interpret the data . . . which is another way of saying that Hite did not know how to organize her material, or—which is worse—organized it according to her own transparent biases." In the end, though, Harrison recommends the book because she feels the authentic voices of the confused and pained women ought to be heard. "Read it," Harrison writes, "because the answers of many women transcend the limitations imposed on them by the nuts-and-bolts questions Hite asked. Read it because it is frequently provocative and affecting. . . . Read it because, while no one can swear to the honesty of all the answers, even the lies we tell one another are instructive."

Presenting the book from a more positive overall stance are Durbin for *Mademoiselle* and *New York Times Book Review* contributor Erica Jong. Durbin explains that "whatever the limitations of *The Hite Report*, its intentions are more than mechanistic hedonism. If it lobbies for anything, it's for illumination and understanding of a dimension of women's experience that may always remain somewhat mysterious but has so far only been needlessly mystified." In turn, Jong optimistically comments that *The Hite Report* represents the culmination in terms of books that allow women to speak for themselves. According to Jong, women who read *The Hite Report* "will feel enormously reassured about their own sexuality and if enough young men read it, the quality of sex in America is bound to improve."

Hite followed her report on female sexuality with her equally controversial book *The Hite Report on Male Sexuality*. Like the previous work, this book chiefly presents verbatim questionnaire responses, but this time from men—more than 7,000 of them from ages thirteen to ninety-seven. Lynn Langway writes in her *Newsweek* commentary that this is a "larger [1,129 pages], more ambitious and provocative work than its predecessor" and she quotes Hite as saying: " 'I think it will definitely enrage and enlighten. The book was trying to ask how men feel about sexuality. The answer was they like it and they treasure it—but at the same time they dislike it and feel very put upon by it'. . . . Like the women depicted in her first book, many of the 7,239 men who participated in the second study said they felt trapped by sexual stereotypes, craved emotional intimacy—and found themselves unable to talk openly about their sexual angers, anxieties and desires."

Time reviewer John Leo thinks that Hite presents some bizarre theories on male sexuality in the book. For one, he says she "persistently applies a hard-line feminist interpretation. Most sexual problems and sexual differences, she argues, are the result of the 'patriarchal culture,' the age-old male suppression of women. Men like to have intercourse not because of biology, but because they are 'brought up to feel that [this is] a vital part of being a man.' " For another, according to Leo, Hite claims that many men have extramarital affairs because "they come to think of their wives as their mothers, and the incest taboo obviously inhibits sex with mothers." Leo concludes that occasionally "Hite descends from the soapbox long enough to notice what her men are saying. 'The basic feeling that comes through,' she writes, 'is that men feel they are not getting enough love, affection or appreciation.' "

Regarding critical reception to her second book, Hite commented in her interview with Lavin: "On my first book I had mostly women reviewers, and 95 percent of them liked it. On the second I had mostly men reviewers, and 95 percent of them didn't like it. I thought I was saying all these things about masculinity and the patterns of men's lives, and in the press all I'd see is, 'Is she scientific?' and 'Is she just trying to make money?' " According to Roger L. Gould in the *New York Times Book Review,* "For all her efforts, 'The Hite Report on Male Sexuality' is based on a nonrepresentative sample of the American male population. . . . Hite's book . . . informs us only about a specific fraction of our adult male population, and the professional therapist or counselor will find nothing new in it." Nevertheless, Gould goes on to say that "for the nonprofessional, [the book] may be an eye opener in the tradition of the original reports of Alfred Kinsey. . . . [It] pulverizes any remaining myths about 'normal' male sexuality that have not already been reduced to dust by earlier reports." And although Eliot Fremont-Smith claims in his *Village Voice* analysis that Hite overemphasizes what males dislike about sexual intercourse and downplays what they like, he does defend her feminist tone: "Hite's feminism . . . has to be accepted in the natural course of things—it's a contradiction of terms to think of her doing these books and *not* being feminist. It's dumb, too; I would say that a lot of critics of Hite are dumb, thinking she could be neuter or something." In turn, Langway concludes her review by quoting John Money, a Johns Hopkins University psychologist: "Hite has 'uncovered the extraordinary, romantic sentimentality of men who have been brainwashed to feel that they don't *have* these feelings.' " As Langway comments, "Such insights are profoundly important."

In her *Time* contribution, Claudia Wallis estimates that the first two books in Hite's trilogy garnered $2.5 million for the author and that the third, the 900-page "tome" *Women and Love,* is "characteristically grandiose in scope, murky in methodology—and right on target for commercial appeal." The book stirred up a controversy as surely as the previous two had, with some critics blasting Hite for being anti-male and others lauding her for relaying an important message about the disillusionment women experience in their relationships with men. Again, focus was on Hite's research methodology—with complaints centering on the small return rate of 4.5 percent, which many claim cannot provide a fair representation of the U.S. population as a whole, particularly when it is believed that only the most discontented would take the time to answer some 120 essay questions. In general, critics were split on this issue of methodology. For example, in the *Los Angeles Times,* Carol Tavris is especially judgmental of Hite's statistics: "The numbers are, to put it simply, a joke. . . . [Hite] devotes a chapter to defending subjective routes to truth, and then tries to convince the reader that her work is objective and scientifically accurate as well. . . . Well, what is wrong with subjective routes to truth? . . . The answer, I think, lies in the growing popularity of what Robert Asahina, a writer and editor, calls 'social-science fiction'—books that are not really social science but 'naive personal journalism'. . . . The impression that they are based on 'research' adds a veneer of respectability and seriousness, and supposedly elevates them above the authors' personal experiences." Also questioning Hite's statistical validity is *Los Angeles Times* staff writer Elizabeth Mehren who reports that the results of a Washington Post-ABC News public opinion survey are very much at odds with Hite's findings. Whereas Hite's statistics indicate that 98 percent of the women in her study are unhappy with some aspect of their relationship with men, this telephone survey of 1,505 men and women from across the nation found that 93 percent of the women called their relationships with men good or excellent.

Supportive viewpoints do abound, however, as evidenced by Mehren's commentary. She quotes University of Toronto psychiatrist Dr. Frank Sommers as saying that the debate surrounding Hite's book is "part of a defensive reaction where you shoot the messenger." Mehren further quotes Max Siegal, a former president of the American Psychiatric Association: "The big flaw I don't think is methodological. I think it's in society, in a society that is not willing to look at itself and the problems we have in relating to each other." Hite agrees, according to London *Times* reviewer Victoria McKee: "Hite believes that the attacks on her methods have been launched almost entirely by men in order to conjure up a smoke screen to obscure the 'real' issues raised by her book."

The "real" issues of *Women and Love* are summed up by *Ms.* contributor Lisa Duggan when she writes: "[Hite] argues that we are in a difficult phase of a cultural revolution, that women are extending the fight for meaningful equality into the innermost recesses of personal relationships, demanding that life be transformed to incorporate their deeply held values of equality, cooperation, communication, and caring." The chief complaint of the women in Hite's survey seems to be the failure of men to respond to their emotional needs. As Toronto *Globe and Mail* critic Michele Landsberg explains, "The voices of the women . . . are not so much feminist or male-hating as puzzled, depressed, humorous, loving or rueful. But most of them agree: they're tired of doing all the emotional housework." Indeed, Hite reports that 87 percent of her respondents are emotionally closer to their women friends than to their husbands or lovers, and also that 70 percent of women married more than five years reported having extramarital affairs.

In the end, there are those who find Hite's work purposeful and compassionate, and there are those who challenge its very foundation. With respect to *Women and Love*, William Robertson for the *Chicago Tribune* calls it a "monument to dim-wittedness" and also a "bore. There's not an original thought anywhere in sight. . . . In the past, . . . the war between the sexes wasn't so carefully overburdened with mathematical evidence that attempts to convey the impression of truth. . . . She even ignores the evidence of her own research: The hopeless women in her survey don't seem to believe much is changing at all." The complaint that Mariana Valverde voices in her *Globe and Mail* analysis, which Robertson also shares, is that the book's structure obliterates the uniqueness of Hite's individual respondents: "The thousands of pages penned by women, often with great care, are simply put on the floor, cut into bits, and pasted into a mosaic without regard for the integrity of the person whose innermost feelings are . . . being utilized."

Those who are optimistic about *Women and Love* are generally so because Hite let the women themselves tell their stories of pain and disillusionment. "If 'Women and Love' isn't good social science," remarks Hochschild, "it is a valuable, provocative, loosely argued, searching meditation on how culture influences love, illustrated by many hypnotizing, sad, sweet, chilling and lurid stories." Although Hochschild believes that Hite is dealing

with "fishy statistics," "what is wonderfully worthwhile about 'Women and Love' are the moving stories of women and the continuous stream of deep, probing questions Ms. Hite raises about them. . . . She also helps women make sense of their feelings. . . . She articulates their discontent." Landsberg also supports this work. She expresses her viewpoint that many critics "can't have read the book very seriously. Few researchers have ever listened so deeply to the innermost thoughts of their subjects. In fact, the . . . book . . . strikes me as a good deal more thorough and 'scientific' than the idiotic multiple-choice quizzes, the market surveys and opinion polls that reporters usually accept so reverentially. Scientific or not, the book is significant." Scientific or not, liked or not, Hite's trilogy on human sexuality has provided men and women the freedom to voice their opinions on this matter.

AVOCATIONAL INTERESTS: Playing and listening to music, old movies, reading Proust, interior decoration.

BIOGRAPHICAL/CRITICAL SOURCES:

BOOKS

Hite, Shere, *The Hite Report: A Nationwide Study of Female Sexuality*, Macmillan, 1976.
Hite, Shere, *The Hite Report on Male Sexuality*, Knopf, 1981, published as *The Hite Report: A Study of Male Sexuality*, Ballantine, 1982.
Hite, Shere, *Women and Love: A Cultural Revolution in Progress*, Knopf, 1987.

PERIODICALS

Chicago Tribune, November 28, 1982.
Globe and Mail (Toronto), January 2, 1988, January 9, 1988.
Los Angeles Times, October 29, 1987, November 1, 1987, November 16, 1987.
Maclean's, October 19, 1987.
Mademoiselle, January, 1977.
Ms., October, 1981, December, 1987.
Newsweek, October 18, 1976, June 15, 1981, October 19, 1987, November 23, 1987.
New York Times, November 13, 1987, November 15, 1987.
New York Times Book Review, October 3, 1976, July 21, 1981, November 15, 1987.
Psychology Today, December, 1976.
Spectator, March 12, 1988.
Time, October 25, 1976, June 15, 1981, October 12, 1987.
Times (London), November 16, 1987, February 19, 1988, February 25, 1988.
Tribune Books (Chicago), December 2, 1987.
Village Voice, November 1, 1976, June 24, 1981.
Washington Post, November 10, 1987, November 14, 1987.
Washington Post Book World, March 13, 1977, June 21, 1981.

* * *

HOBAN, Russell (Conwell) 1925-

PERSONAL: Born February 4, 1925, in Lansdale, Pa.; son of Abram T. (an advertising manager for the *Jewish Daily Forward*) and Jeanette (Dimmerman) Hoban; married Lillian Aberman (an illustrator), January 31, 1944 (divorced, 1975); married Gundula Ahl (a bookseller), 1975; children: (first marriage) Phoebe, Abrom, Esme, Julia; (second marriage) Jachin Boaz, Wieland, Benjamin. *Education:* Attended Philadelphia Museum School of Industrial Art, 1941-43.

ADDRESSES: Home and office—Fulham, London, England. *Agent*—David Higham Associates Ltd., 5-8 Lower John St., Golden Sq., London WlR 4HA, England.

CAREER: Artist and illustrator for magazine and advertising studios, New York City, 1945-51; Fletcher Smith Film Studio, New York City, story board artist and character designer, 1951; Batten, Barton, Durstine & Osborn, Inc., New York City, television art director, 1952-57; J. Walter Thompson Co., New York City, television art director, 1956; free-lance illustrator for advertising agencies and magazines, including *Time, Life, Fortune, Saturday Evening Post, True,* 1957-65; Doyle, Dane, Bembach, New York City, copywriter, 1965-67. Art instructor at the Famous Artists Schools, Westport, Conn., and School of Visual Arts, New York City. Writer. *Military service:* U.S. Army, Infantry, 1943-45; served in Italian campaign; received Bronze Star.

MEMBER: Authors Guild, Authors League of America, Society of Authors, PEN.

AWARDS, HONORS: The Sorely Trying Day, The Mouse and His Child, How Tom Beat Captain Najork and His Hired Sportsmen, and *Dinner at Alberta's* have all been named notable books by the American Library Association; *Bread and Jam for Frances* was selected as a Library of Congress Children's book, 1964; Boys' Club Junior Book Award, 1968, for *Charlie the Tramp; Emmet Otter's Jug-Band Christmas* was selected as one of *School Library Journal's* Best Books, 1971, and received the Lewis Carroll Shelf Award and the Christopher Award, both 1972; Whitbread Literary Award, 1974, and International Board on Books for Young People Honor List, 1976, both for *How Tom Beat Captain Najork and His Hired Sportsmen; A Near Thing for Captain Najork* was selected as one of the best illustrated children's books of the year by the *New York Times,* 1976; *Riddley Walker* received John W. Campbell Memorial Award for the best science fiction novel of the year from Science Fiction Research Association, 1981, and was nominated as the most distinguished book of fiction by National Book Critics Circle and for the Nebula Award by Science Fiction Writers of America, both 1982; Recognition of Merit, George G. Stone Center for Children's Books, 1982, for his contributions to books for younger children.

WRITINGS:

NOVELS

The Lion of Boaz-Jachin and Jachin-Boaz, Stein & Day, 1973.
Kleinzeit: A Novel, Viking, 1974.
Turtle Diary, J. Cape, 1975, Random House, 1976.
Riddley Walker, J. Cape, 1980, Summit Books, 1981.
Pilgermann, Summit Books, 1983.
The Medusa Frequency, edited by Gary Fisketjohn, Atlantic Monthly, 1987.

JUVENILES

What Does It Do and How Does It Work?: Power Shovel, Dump Truck, and Other Heavy Machines, illustrations by the author, Harper, 1959.
The Atomic Submarine: A Practice Combat Patrol under the Sea, illustrations by the author, Harper, 1960.
Bedtime for Frances, illustrations by Garth Williams, Harper, 1960, reprinted, 1976.
Herman the Loser, illustrations by Lillian Hoban, Harper, 1961.
The Song in My Drum, illustrations by L. Hoban, Harper, 1961.
(With L. Hoban) *London Men and English Men,* Harper, 1962.
(With L. Hoban) *Some Snow Said Hello,* Harper, 1963.
The Sorely Trying Day, illustrations by L. Hoban, Harper, 1964.

A Baby Sister for Frances, illustrations by L. Hoban, Harper, 1964.
Nothing to Do, illustrations by L. Hoban, Harper, 1964.
Bread and Jam for Frances, illustrations by L. Hoban, Harper, 1964, reprinted, 1986.
Tom and the Two Handles, illustrations by L. Hoban, Harper, 1965, reprinted, 1984.
The Story of Hester Mouse Who Became a Writer and Saved Most of Her Sisters and Brothers and Some of Her Aunts and Uncles from the Owl, illustrations by L. Hoban, Norton, 1965.
What Happened When Jack and Daisy Tried to Fool the Tooth Fairies, illustrations by L. Hoban, Scholastic Book Services, 1965.
Henry and the Monstrous Din, illustrations by L. Hoban, Harper, 1966.
The Little Brute Family, illustrations by L. Hoban, Macmillan, 1966.
Goodnight (verse), illustrations by L. Hoban, Norton, 1966.
(With L. Hoban) *Save My Place,* Norton, 1967.
Charlie the Tramp, illustrations by L. Hoban, Four Winds, 1967 (book and record) Scholastic Book Services, 1970.
The Mouse and His Child (novel), illustrations by L. Hoban, Harper, 1967, reprinted, Avon, 1986.
A Birthday for Frances, illustrations by L. Hoban, Harper, 1968.
The Pedaling Man, and Other Poems, illustrations by L. Hoban, Norton, 1968.
The Stone Doll of Sister Brute, illustrations by L. Hoban, Macmillan, 1968. *Harvey's Hideout,* illustrations by L. Hoban, Parents' Magazine Press, 1969.
Best Friends for Frances, illustrations by L. Hoban, Harper, 1969.
Ugly Bird, illustrations by L. Hoban, Macmillan, 1969.
The Mole Family's Christmas, illustrations by L. Hoban, Parents' Magazine Press, 1969, reprinted, Scholastic, Inc., 1986.
A Bargain for Frances, illustrations by L. Hoban, Harper, 1970.
Emmet Otter's Jug-Band Christmas, illustrations by L. Hoban, Parents' Magazine Press, 1971.
Egg Thoughts, and Other Frances Songs, illustrations by L. Hoban, Harper, 1972.
The Sea-Thing Child, illustrations by son, Abrom Hoban, Harper, 1972.
Letitia Rabbit's String Song (Junior Literary Guild selection), illustrations by Mary Chalmers, Coward, 1973.
How Tom Beat Captain Najork and His Hired Sportsmen, illustrations by Quentin Blake, Atheneum, 1974.
Ten What?: A Mystery Counting Book, illustrations by Sylvie Selig, J. Cape, 1974, Scribner, 1975.
Crocodile and Pierrot: A See the Story Book, illustrations by S. Selig, J. Cape, 1975, Scribner, 1977.
Dinner at Alberta's, pictures by James Marshall, Crowell, 1975.
A Near Thing for Captain Najork, illustrations by Q. Blake, J. Cape, 1975, Atheneum, 1976.
Arthur's New Power, illustrations by Byron Barton, Crowell, 1978.
The Twenty-Elephant Restaurant, illustrations by Emily Arnold McCully, Atheneum, 1978, published in England with illustrations by Q. Blake, J. Cape, 1980.
La Corona and the Tin Frog (originally published in *Puffin Annual,* 1974), illustrations by Nicola Bayley, J. Cape, 1978, Merrimack Book Service, 1981.
The Dancing Tigers, illustrations by David Gentlemen, J. Cape, 1979, Merrimack Book Service, 1981.
Flat Cat, illustrations by Clive Scruton, Philomel, 1980.

Ace Dragon Ltd., illustrations by Q. Blake, J. Cape, 1980, Merrimack Book Service, 1981.

They Came from Aargh!, illustrations by Colin McNaughton, Philomel, 1981.

The Serpent Tower, illustrations by David Scott, Methuen/Walker, 1981.

The Great Fruit Gum Robbery, illustrations by C. McNaughton, Methuen, 1981, published as *The Great Gum Drop Robbery,* Philomel, 1982.

The Battle of Zormla, illustrations by C. McNaughton, Philomel, 1982.

The Flight of Bembel Rudzuk, illustrations by C. McNaughton, Philomel, 1982.

Big John Turkle, illustrations by Martin Baynton, Walker Books, 1983, Holt, 1984.

Jim Frog, illustrations by M. Baynton, Walker Books, 1983, Holt, 1984.

Lavinia Bat, illustrations by M. Baynton, Holt, 1984.

Charlie Meadows, illustrations by M. Baynton, Holt, 1984.

The Rain Door, J. Cape, 1986.

The Marzipan Pig, J. Cape, 1986.

Ponders, illustrated by M. Baynton, Walker, 1988.

Monsters, Gollanez, 1989.

OTHER

(Illustrator) W. R. Burnett, *The Roar of the Crowd: Conversations with an Ex-Big-Leaguer,* C. N. Potter, 1964.

(Contributor) Edward Blishen, editor, *The Thorny Paradise: Writers on Writing for Children,* Kestrel, 1975.

Also contributor of articles to *Holiday.* Hoban's papers are included in the Kerlan Collection at the University of Minnesota.

MEDIA ADAPTATIONS: The Mouse and His Child was made into a feature-length animated film by Fario-Lockhart-Sanrio Productions in 1977 and starred the voices of Cloris Leachman, Andy Devine, and Peter Ustinov (who also read an abridged version of the novel for a Caedmon recording in 1977); Glynnis Johns recorded selections from *Bedtime for Frances, A Baby Sister for Frances, Bread and Jam for Frances,* and *A Birthday for Frances* in a sound recording entitled "Frances," as well as selections from *A Bargain for Frances, Best Friends for Frances,* and *Egg Thoughts, and Other Frances Songs* in a sound recording entitled "A Bargain for Frances and Other Stories," both by Caedmon in 1977; *Turtle Diary* was adapted for the screen by United British Artists/Brittanic in 1986, featuring a screenplay by Harold Pinter and starring Glenda Jackson and Ben Kingsley; *Riddley Walker* was staged by the Manchester Royal Exchange Theatre Company, also in 1986.

SIDELIGHTS: "Russell Hoban is a writer whose genius is expressed with equal brilliance in books both for children and for adults," writes Alida Allison in the *Dictionary of Literary Biography.* Peter S. Prescott reports in *Newsweek* that in England, where Hoban's work is particularly successful, he shows signs of becoming a cult writer, and "like other cult writers . . . he writes about ordinary decent people making life-affirming gestures in a world that threatens to dissolve in madness; like them, he writes a prose that is often fresh and funny, occasionally precious." Largely self-educated, Hoban has moved masterfully from artist and illustrator to the author of children's fables and adult allegorical fiction. Praising his "unerring ear for dialogue," his "memorable depiction of scenes," and his "wise and warm stories notable for delightful plots and originality of language," Allison considers Hoban to be "much more than just a clever and observant writer. His works are permeated with an honest, often painful, and always uncompromising urge toward self-

identity." Noting that "this theme of identity becomes more apparent, more complex as Hoban's works have become longer and more penetrating," Allison states, "Indeed, Hoban's writing has leaped and bounded—paralleling upheavals in his own life."

Although Hoban has originated several well-known characters in children's literature, including Charlie the Tramp, Emmet Otter, the Mouse and his Child, and Manny Rat, he is especially recognized for a series of bedtime books about an anthropomorphic badger named Frances. Reviewers generally concur that these stories depict ordinary family life with much humor, wit, and style. Benjamin DeMott suggests in the *Atlantic* that "these books are unique, first, because the adults in their pages are usually humorous, precise of speech, and understandingly conversant with general life, and second, because the author confronts—not unfancifully but without kinky secret garden stuff—problems with which ordinary parents and children have to cope." *Bedtime for Frances,* for instance, concerns nighttime fears and is regarded by many as a classic in children's literature. A contributor to *Junior Bookshelf* thinks that Hoban tells this tale with "beautiful economy," adding that "this is the rarest kind of picture-book text, rhythmic, natural, unalterable." And according to a *Saturday Review* contributor, "The exasperated humor of this book could only derive from actual parental experience, and no doubt parents will enjoy it."

"Hoban has established himself as a writer with a rare understanding of childhood (and parental) psychology, sensitively and humorously portrayed in familiar family situations," writes Allison. Hoban and his first wife, Lillian, also an illustrator and author of books for children, collaborated on many successful works, including several in the Frances series. Allison notes that although their work together was usually well-received, "there were pans as well as paeans." While some books have been faulted for "excessive coziness, for sentimentality, and for stereotyped male-female roles," Allison adds that a more general criticism of their work together is that "it tends toward repetition." However, in their *Children and Books,* May Hill Arbuthnot and Zena Sutherland find that all of Hoban's stories about Frances show "affection for and understanding of children" as well as "contribute to a small child's understanding of himself, his relationships with other people, and the fulfillment of his emotional needs." Further, they say, "These characters are indeed ourselves in fur." Yet as a *Times Literary Supplement* contributor observes, "Excellent as [the Frances books] are, they give no hint that the author had in him such a blockbuster of a book as *The Mouse and His Child.*"

Revered in England as a modern children's classic, *The Mouse and His Child* is described in the *New York Times Book Review* by Barbara Wersba as a story about two wind-up toy mice who are discarded from a toyshop and are then "buffeted from place to place as they seek the lost paradise of their first home—a doll house—and their first 'family,' a toy elephant and seal." Ill-equipped for the baffling, threatening world into which they are tossed, the mouse and his child innocently confront the unknown and its inherent treachery and violence, as well as their own fears. The book explores not only the transience and inconstancy of life but the struggle to persevere also. "Helpless when they are not wound up, unable to stop when they *are,* [the mice] are fated like all mechanical things to breakage, rust and disintegration as humans are to death," writes Margaret Blount in her *Animal Land: The Creatures of Children's Fiction.* "As an adult," says Blount, "it is impossible to read [the book] unmoved." Distressed, however, by the "continuing images of cruelty and decay," Penelope Farmer remarks in *Children's Literature in Education* that *The Mouse and His Child* is "like Beckett for children." But assessing whatever cruelty and decay there is in the novel as the "artful rendering of the facts of life," Allison affirms, "If there is betrayal, there is also self-sacrifice. If there is loss, there is also love. If there is homelessness, there is also destination. The mouse child gets his family in the end; children's literature gets a masterpiece."

"Like the best of books, [*The Mouse and His Child*] is a book from which one can peel layer after layer of meaning," says the *Times Literary Supplement* contributor. Some critics, however, wonder whether it is a children's book at all. Wersba, for instance, feels that "it is the mouse, his child and their search we care about—not metaphysics—and the intellectual trappings of this story are unnecessary." Hoban responds to such assessments in an essay for *Books for Your Children:* "When I wrote [*The Mouse and His Child*] I didn't think it was [a children's book]. I was writing as much book as I was capable of at the time. No concessions were made in style or content. It was my first novel and . . . it was the fullest response I could make to being alive and in the world." Believing the book reveals "an absolute respect for its subject—which means its readers as well," Isabel Quigley adds in the *Spectator,* "I'm still not sure just who is going to read it but that hardly seems to matter. . . . It will last." Hoban feels that within its limitations, the book is suitable for children, though. "Its heroes and heroines found out what they were and it wasn't enough, so they found out how to be more," he says in his essay. "That's not a bad thought to be going with."

Hoban moved to England in 1969 and continues to reside there with his family from a second marriage. Some critics conjecture about the emotional impact that the dissolution of Hoban's first marriage, as well as subsequent estrangements from his children, may have had upon his work, particularly since it was during this period of time that he began to write for an adult audience. Steven Rattner, who interviewed Hoban for the *New York Times,* indicates that because of the extensive publicity that this subject has generated, Hoban declines to discuss it further, stating, "I no longer want to see anything in print about my saying this or that about my first marriage." However, in a *Publishers Weekly* interview, Hoban relates to Barbara A. Bannon that frequent discussions with an analyst about his writing have afforded him an opportunity to become "good friends" with his head. Consequently, Hoban's children's fables have evolved into works that probe beneath the surface of ordinary experience and ponder questions of psychology, philosophy, and theology. Allison thinks that "the presence in Hoban's novels of that impersonal, vast, and random power—call it the mindless flow of birth and death and circumstance—reveals itself in images which seem drawn from depth psychology, from a genius who has traveled through his own muck confronting the fact of his helplessness."

The Lion of Boaz-Jachin and Jachin-Boaz, his first novel for an adult audience, is the "most autobiographical novel I've written," Hoban acknowledges to Bannon. It is described by Allison as the story of a mapmaker who promises his son a master map in which everything that the father has learned and that the son will ever need to know is revealed. However, because of the father's quest for a more meaningful life, he deserts his family and takes the map with him instead. The son follows in anger, and from his own imagination, materializes an extinct lion. "Hoban excels in the clash of the physical and metaphysical," says a *Times Literary Supplement* contributor; and although Noel Perrin feels that "where the book is fabulous, it tends to work," he adds in the *New York Times Book Review* that "the magic simply does not fit into the modern world [Hoban] insists on interpenetrating." Nevertheless, Perrin suggests that the book seems to

"celebrate a release from the kinds of constraints a writer of books for small children—even a distinguished one like . . . Hoban—must work under. Everything he couldn't do in [the Frances books] he does here. If those books were innocent, here he delights in being raunchy. If they were simple, these are complex. . . . The one thing that carries over is a vein of fantasy."

Departing, however, from fantasy as well as autobiography in his *Turtle Diary,* Hoban writes about a man and woman who meet through their pursuit of a common goal to release captive turtles into the sea. The story unfolds simultaneously from the diaries of the two somewhat reclusive individuals; and according to Paul Gray in *Time,* these alternating diary entries "crackle with witty detail, mordant intelligence and self-deprecating irony." Gillian McMahon-Hill considers "*Turtle Diary,* in some ways Hoban's finest writing yet," in that it "provides the best marriage of his concise, poetic and rhythmic expression with his dry, witty observation," and continues in *Children's Literature in Education* that "stylistically the novel is more ambitious and more accomplished than anything previously written."

Suggesting that in *Turtle Diary,* Hoban is "fighting free of the 'lie' at the heart of his past work," Edmund White explains in the *New York Times Book Review:* "No affection is wasted on the turtles. They are chillingly unhuman, mere shells for living instinct. . . . Nor are the people especially endearing. Hoban is at pains to make them unappetizing." Gray thinks that Hoban "argues gently but profoundly that human lives are really composed of details as mysterious in their power as the force that tugs the turtles." Prescott feels that the novel is about the "recovery of life"; but, "unlike the humans," notes Gray, "the creatures know where they must go and venture without questioning." White believes, however, that "not only are [Hoban's] characters dim, but the thematic underpinnings of the book seem flimsy." Yet Perrin maintains that Hoban's early books are "best regarded as part of the learning process by which . . . Hoban prepared himself to write 'Riddley Walker.' And that is a book so shimmering with power, a fantasy so darkly perfect, as to excuse any little errors its author may have made en route."

Nominated as the most distinguished book of fiction by the National Book Critics Circle, and for the Nebula Award by the Science Fiction Writers of America, *Riddley Walker* received the John W. Campbell Memorial Award from the Science Fiction Research Association as the year's best science fiction novel. *Riddley Walker* imagines a world and civilization decades after a nuclear holocaust; the story of what remains is narrated in a fragmented, phonetical English by a twelve-year-old boy struggling to comprehend the past so that its magnificence might be recaptured. "Set in a remote future and composed in an English nobody ever spoke or wrote," writes DeMott in the *New York Times Book Review,* "this short, swiftly paced tale juxtaposes preliterate fable and Beckettian wit, Boschian monstrosities and a hero with Huck Finn's heart and charm, lighting by El Greco and jokes by Punch and Judy. It is a wrenchingly vivid report on the texture of life after Doomsday."

Detecting similarities in *Riddley Walker* to other contemporary works such as Anthony Burgess's *The Clockwork Orange,* John Gardner's *Grendel,* and the complete works of William Golding, DeMott believes that "in vision and execution, this is an exceptionally original work, and Russell Hoban is actually his own best source." *Riddley Walker* "is not 'like' anything," concurs Victoria Glendinning in the *Listener.* As A. Alverez expresses in the *New York Review of Books,* Hoban has "transformed what might have been just another fantasy of the future into a novel of exceptional depth and originality." And according to Joel

Conarroe in the *New York Times Book Review,* "There were critics, including myself, who thought . . . Hoban had produced the year's most distinguished fiction."

Critically lauded and especially popular in England, *Riddley Walker* has been particularly commended for its inventive language, which Alverez thinks "reflects with extraordinary precision both the narrator's understanding and the desolate landscape he moves through." Reviewing the novel in *Time,* Gray finds that the book's narrative generates its own suspense—"the fascination of watching a strange world evolve out of unfamiliar words." Similarly, in the *Washington Post Book World,* Michael Dirda believes that "what is marvelous in all this is the way Hoban makes us experience the uncanny familiarity of this world, while also making it a strange and animistic place, where words almost have a life of their own." "What Hoban has done," suggests Bannon, "is to invent a world and a language to go with it, and in doing both he remains a storyteller, which is the most significant achievement of 'Riddley Walker.'"

Alverez calls *Riddley Walker* an "artistic tour de force in every possible way," but Natalie Maynor and Richard F. Patteson suggest in *Critique* that even more than that, it is "perhaps the most sophisticated work of fiction ever to speculate about man's future on earth and the implications for a potentially destructive technology." Eliot Fremont-Smith maintains in the *Village Voice* that "the reality of the human situation now is so horrendous and bizarre that to get a hold on it requires all our faculties, including the imaginative. We can't do it through plain fact and arms controllers' reasoning alone. . . . Read *Riddley,* too." Although Kelly Cherry refers to the novel in the *Chicago Tribune Book World* as a "philosophical essay in fictional drag," Philip Howard writes in the London *Times* that *Riddley Walker* is a "powerful vision and a true fiction, in that it tells us something about ourselves and the indomitable spirit of man." Similarly, DeMott thinks that Hoban's focus on what has been lost in civilization "summons the reader to dwell anew on that within civilization which is separate from, opposite to, power and its appurtenances, ravages, triumphs." *Riddley Walker,* says DeMott, is "haunting and fiercely imagined and—this matters most—intensely ponderable."

According to a *Harper's* contributor, *Riddley Walker* apparently left Hoban "in a place where there was further action pending and this further action was waiting for the element that would precipitate it into the time and place of its own story." *Pilgermann* was precipitated by a night spent "under the stars" in Galilee, says the *Harper's* contributor, who deems the novel "both *Riddley Walker*'s complement and mirror image." Set in the eleventh century, *Pilgermann* is narrated by a "young European Jew who, made a eunuch by Christian peasants, decides his going to Jerusalem may keep God from leaving the world," writes Thomas LeClair in the *Washington Post Book World.* Pilgermann, from the German for pilgrim, is what the narrator calls himself, but his pilgrimage is one that he does not complete. As Michiko Kakutani explains in the *New York Times,* "Killed during the siege of Antioch in 1098, he is now a disembodied spirit—'a whispering out of the dust'—who speaks with the patchy, retrospective knowledge of history." "Reduced to 'waves and particles,' [the narrator] nonetheless survives as a sentient memory," notes Francis King in a *Spectator* review of the novel. King discusses *Pilgermann*'s "mystical disquisitions, often difficult to follow, on such subjects as predestination or the nature of good and evil, or of symbolical events." Finding the book "dense with mythic allusions and metaphysical speculation," Kakutani observes that "between the rather portentous theorizings, there are clever, philosophical pranks and strangely brilliant passages of description that have the visual impact of paintings glimpsed in a museum."

"Like everything that Russell Hoban writes, 'Pilgermann' is striking and strange," remarks Anthony Thwaite in the London *Observer,* adding that it also suggests a parody of Bunyan—"a series of dark sayings." While Conarroe thinks the novel borrows from several literary genres, including pilgrimage narrative, allegory, and historical fiction, he maintains that "what we have here is not so much a tale of adventure as a meditation on history, loss and grief, a dark treatise on the mysterious nature of things narrated by a 'microscopic chip in that vast circuitry in which are recorded all the variations and permutations thus far.' The novel is a network of small interlocking essays on matters no less significant than mutability and mortality." In his interview with Rattner, Hoban discusses the religious theme of *Pilgermann,* pointing also to the religious aspects of *Riddley Walker,* whose narrator, "confused in a continually wondering way," similarly attempts "to get to the heart of the matter . . . where God is in one form or another." *Pilgermann,* Hoban continues, is comprised of "answers to that question, many of which are contradictory." And although Gray finds the theological aspects of the novel tedious, he considers that "the quality of [Hoban's] ideas is less important than the restless energy of the mind that forms them. He is trying to grasp what cannot be known." "Hoban is a writer who, in his idiosyncratic boldness, never overreaches himself," states King. "One would no more call this book an easy read than one would call an ascent of Mont Blanc an easy walk; but in each case the views are magnificent."

Some critics examine the scholarly and profusely footnoted *Pilgermann* in the shadow of the overwhelmingly successful *Riddley Walker.* Thwaite, for instance, thinks that as powerful as *Pilgermann* is, it lacks the "total rightness of Hoban's best work" and suggests that "some of the effects seem too willed, some of the messages too incoherent, as if he had grabbed too eagerly for a dream that was fading even as he tried to set it down." However, Gray does not believe that it was Hoban's purpose to "pursue a single train of logic or evidence" but rather "to make sense of the universe that contains him. He is not a thinker but an artist." Conarroe, who finds *Riddley Walker* "more consistently riveting" than *Pilgermann,* nevertheless concludes: "To say, though, that . . . Hoban's novel does not measure up to its predecessor is not to suggest that it is an unworthy work of art. 'Riddley Walker,' after all, is miraculous: 'Pilgermann' is merely remarkable."

Hoban is the author of nearly sixty books; although most are for children, for whom he continues to write, adults have found much in his books to appreciate as well. The world that Hoban often explores may be a child's world, but it is a world seen in its complexity. "In my books there aren't characters who are simply bad or simply good," Hoban tells Fred Hauptfuhrer in *People.* "Nothing in life is that simple." Writing for adults has added both breadth and depth to Hoban's work; and as his work has grown in complexity, he has commented upon the process by which an idea evolves into a book. In his interview with Rattner, for example, Hoban recalls: "In all the novels I've written, something I see gets me started. Usually that starting element is a nucleus that gathers other things to itself." And as he explains further to Bannon: "There always seems to be something in my mind waiting to put something together with some primary thought I will encounter. It's like looking out of the window and listening to the radio at the same time. I am committed to what comes to me, however it links up."

In an essay appearing in *The Thorny Paradise: Writers on Writing for Children,* Hoban addresses what appears to be an intrinsic characteristic of his writing for both children and adults: "If in my meandering I have seemed to offer tangled thinking more than worked-out thoughts, it has not been through self-indulgence; I have wanted to join the action of my being with that of my readers in a collective being. Collectively we must possess and be repossessed by the past that we alter with our present, must surrender the vanity of personal identity to something more valuable." More recently, in the Rattner interview, Hoban expresses what he understands to be his function as a writer—"to offer what I hope will be a fruitful confusion"—adding that "all kinds of stupid people are offering sterile clarity. What needs to be recognized is the confusion." Underlying the most powerful of Hoban's works, according to Allison, is the idea that "we must struggle for meaning and identity and place against the random element of loss in the attempt to gain 'self-winding.'" She considers Hoban a "great writer because he makes unsentimental reality into art."

BIOGRAPHICAL/CRITICAL SOURCES:

BOOKS

Arbuthnot, May Hill and Zena Sutherland, *Children and Books,* 4th edition, Scott, Foresman, 1972.

Blishen, Edward, editor, *The Thorny Paradise: Writers on Writing for Children,* Kestrel, 1975.

Blount, Margaret, *Animal Land: The Creatures of Children's Fiction,* Morrow, 1974.

Children's Literature Review, Volume 3, Gale, 1978.

Contemporary Literary Criticism, Gale, Volume 7, 1977, Volume 25, 1983.

Dictionary of Literary Biography, Volume 52: *American Writers for Children since 1960,* Gale, 1986.

PERIODICALS

American Artist, October, 1961.

Antioch Review, summer, 1982.

Atlantic, August, 1976, December, 1983.

Books for Your Children, winter, 1976.

Chicago Tribune Book World, July 12, 1981.

Children's Literature in Education, March, 1972, spring, 1976.

Critique, fall, 1984.

Educational Foundation for Nuclear Science, June, 1982.

Encounter, June, 1981.

Globe and Mail (Toronto), March 29, 1986.

Harper's, April, 1983.

Junior Bookshelf, July, 1963.

Listener, October 30, 1980.

Los Angeles Times, February 14, 1986.

New Statesman, May 25, 1973, April 11, 1975.

Newsweek, March 1, 1976, June 29, 1981, December 7, 1981, May 30, 1983, February 17, 1986.

New Yorker, March 22, 1976, July 20, 1981, August 8, 1983.

New York Review of Books, November 19, 1981.

New York Times, June 26, 1981, November 1, 1981, June 20, 1983, February 14, 1986.

New York Times Book Review, February 4, 1968, March 21, 1976, June 28, 1981, June 6, 1982, May 29, 1983, November 27, 1983.

Observer (London), March 13, 1983.

People, August 10, 1981.

Publishers Weekly, May 15, 1981.

Saturday Review, May 7, 1960, May 1, 1976, December, 1981.

Spectator, May 16, 1969, April 5, 1975, March 12, 1983.

Time, February 16, 1976, June 22, 1981, May 16, 1983.

Times (London), January 7, 1982, March 24, 1983.

Times Literary Supplement, April 3, 1969, March 16, 1973, March 29, 1974, October 31, 1980, March 7, 1986, April 3, 1987, September 4, 1987.

Village Voice, June 15, 1982.

Washington Post, February 28, 1986.

Washington Post Book World, June 7, 1981, June 27, 1982, May 29, 1983, July 12, 1987.

Wilton Bulletin (Wilton, Conn.), September 26, 1962.

*   *   *

HOCHHUTH, Rolf 1931-

PERSONAL: Born April 1, 1931, in Eschwege, Germany (now West Germany); son of Walter (a shoe-factory owner and accountant) and Ilse (Holzapfel) Hochhuth; married Marianne Heinemann, June 29, 1957 (divorced, 1972); children: Martin, Friedrich. *Education:* Studied bookkeeping at a vocational school; attended universities of Marburg, Munich, and Heidelberg, 1952-55. *Religion:* German Evangelical Church.

ADDRESSES: P.O. Box 661, 4002 Basel, Switzerland.

CAREER: Acted as city-hall runner for first postwar mayor (his uncle) of Eschwege, Germany; Verlag C. Bertelsmann (publisher), Guetersloh, Westphalia, Germany, reader and editor, beginning in 1955; Municipal Theatre, Basel, Switzerland, assistant director and playwright, 1963.

MEMBER: P.E.N. of Federal Republic of Germany.

AWARDS, HONORS: Gerhart Hauptmann Prize and Berliner Kunstpreis for *Der Stellvertreter;* Basel Art Prize, 1976.

WRITINGS:

Der Stellvertreter: Schauspiel (play; first produced in West Berlin at Volksbuehne Theatre, February 20, 1963; produced as "The Representative" by Royal Shakespeare Company, 1963; produced as "The Deputy" at Brooks Atkinson Theatre, New York City, February 26, 1964), foreword by Erwin Piscator, Rowohlt Taschenbuch, 1963, translation by Robert David MacDonald published as *The Representative,* Methuen, 1963, translation by Richard Winston and Clara Winston published as *The Deputy,* foreword by Albert Schweitzer, Grove, 1964.

Soldaten: Nekrolog auf Genf (play; first produced in West Berlin at Volksbuehne Theatre, October 9, 1967; translation produced as "Soldiers" at Royal Alexandra Theater, Toronto, Ontario, February 28, 1968; produced in New York at Billy Rose Theatre, May 1, 1968), Rowohlt Taschenbuch, 1967, translation by MacDonald published as *Soldiers: An Obituary for Geneva,* Grove, 1968.

Guerillas: Tragoedie in fuenf Akten (five-act play; first produced in Stuttgart, West Germany, May 15, 1970), Rowohlt Taschenbuch, 1970.

Krieg und Klassenkrieg (essays; title means "War and Class War"), foreword by Fritz J. Raddatz, Rowohlt Taschenbuch, 1971.

Die Hebamme: Komoedie (play; title means "The Midwife"; first produced in May, 1972), Rowohlt Taschenbuch, 1971.

Lysistrate und die NATO (play; title means "Lysistrata and NATO"; first produced February 22, 1974), Rowohlt Taschenbuch, 1973.

Zwischenspiel in Baden-Baden, Rowohlt Taschenbuch, 1974.

Die Berliner Antigone: Prosa und Verse (novella; title means "The Berlin Antigone"), Rowohlt Taschenbuch, 1975.

Tod eines Jaegers (play; title means "Death of a Hunter"), Rowohlt Taschenbuch, 1976.

Eine Liebe in Deutschland (novel), Rowohlt Taschenbuch, 1978.

Juristen: Drei Akte fuer sieben Spieler (play), Rowohlt Taschenbuch, 1979.

Tell '38, Rowohlt Taschenbuch, 1979, translated from the German, Little, Brown, 1984.

A German Love Story (novel), translated by John Brownjohn, Little, Brown, 1980.

"Judith" (play), first produced in Glasgow, Scotland, at Citizens' Theatre, November 9, 1984.

EDITOR

Wilhelm Busch, *Saemtliche Werke, und eine Auswahl der Skizzen und Gemaelde,* Volume I, S. Mohn, 1959, Volume II, C. Bertelsmann, 1960.

Wilhelm Busch, *Lustige Streiche in Versen und Farben,* Ruetten & Loening, 1960.

Wilhelm Busch, *Saemtliche Bildergeschichten mit 3380 Zichnungen und Fachsimilies,* Ruetten & Leoning, 1961.

Liebe in unserer Zeit: Sechzehn Erzaehlungen (short story anthology), two volumes, Bertelsmann Lesering, 1961.

Theodor Storm, *Am grauen Meer,* Mosaik-Verlag, 1962.

Die grossen Meister: Deutsche Erzaehler des 20. Jahrhunderts (short story anthology), two volumes, Bertelsmann Lesering, 1964.

Des Lebens Uberfluss, R. Mohn, c. 1969.

Ruhm und Ehre, Bertelsmann, 1970.

Oscar Tellgmann, *Kaisers Zeiten: Bilder einer Epoche,* Herbig, 1973.

Also editor of Otto Flake's *Die Deutschen,* 1962, and Thomas Mann's *Dichter und Herrscher,* 1963.

OTHER

Author of plays "The Employer," 1965, and "Anatomy of Revolution," 1969.

SIDELIGHTS: Critics almost universally agreed that no previous post-World War II dramatic work shook the conscience of Europe as did Rolf Hochhuth's "Deputy." The impact was equated with that, in their times, of Emile Zola's letter "J'Accuse" and Erich Maria Remarque's novel *All Quiet on the Western Front.* It was propitious in timing, arriving on the scene shortly after Adolf Eichmann's war crimes trial and between sessions of the Second Vatican Council.

The thesis of the play is that Pope Pius XII should have spoken out more strongly and firmly than he did against the mass executions of the Jews during the Nazi period in Germany, especially against *die Endloesung* (the Final Solution). The dramatis personae are not for the most part, at least according to Hochhuth, actual historical people. The main protagonist, Jesuit Father Riccardo Fontana, is considered the most fictional, although the writer was inspired in creating the role by the martyred Father Maximilian Kolbe (Prisoner Number 16670 in Auschwitz) and Bernhard Lichtenberg, prelate of St. Heldwig's Cathedral in Berlin; the work is dedicated to them.

Hochhuth has said that he became interested in the subject on which he has written because, as a member of the young generation in Germany, he shared a great feeling of guilt about the past which he couldn't explain, but about which he felt he must seek to become informed. One of the books that stimulated him to begin work on the play was *The Final Solution,* by Gerald Reitlinger, and, after the death of Pope Pius XII, he spent three years in research preparation, three months in Rome (although secret Vatican archives were open only to the year 1846). He also studied the Nuremburg Trial and Wehrmacht archives. A "Sidelights on History," composed of documentation and stage direc-

tions, was appended to the end of the published version of the play.

Performance of this published version would take six to eight hours; most actual performances last from two to three hours, and adaptations vary in different cities and languages. Hochhuth said in New York that "the most comprehensive version was shown in Vienna, the shortest in Berlin, the most modern in Paris."

Demonstrations accompanied many performances of the play. Especially intense was the one at the Theatre Athenee in Paris, where protesting persons showered pamphlets on the audience, threw stench bombs, and even clambered onto the stage. On the Broadway premiere, about 150 persons demonstrated outside the Brooks Atkinson Theater, including members of the American Nazi party who carried placards reading "Ban the Hate Show"; the doors of the theater were locked during intermission as a protective measure.

Producer and director Herman Shumlin reported that efforts were made to prevent presentation of "The Deputy" in the United States. Billy Rose withdrew his cooperation from the production. An interfaith group, however, headed by Edward Keating, editor of *Ramparts,* then a Roman Catholic paper for laymen, asked the public to regard the play with an open mind; Catholic reaction generally was more restrained than might have been expected, and, in some cases, contrite.

The play itself (its dramaturgy, blank verse and free rhythms), was not considered by critics as exceptional. It was described as old-fashioned, using late nineteenth-century techniques in weak German classical tradition. Hochhuth was, however, credited with recreating the flavor of Nazi jargon. A coincidental relationship between it and Johann von Schiller's *Don Carlos* was noted. It was also compared to Bertolt Brecht's *Heilige Johanne der Schlachthofe.*

Although critics tended to feel that "The Deputy" left a good bit to be desired artistically, most also saw other meaningful aspects to the work. David Boroff wrote in the *National Observer:* "Though it is both flawed and arguable, it has restored seriousness to the Broadway theater. Not since 'Death of a Salesman' or 'The Diary of Anne Frank' have audiences been so profoundly shaken." Walter Kerr, drama critic for the *New York Herald Tribune,* concurred in the opinion that the play is deficient as a play. But he, too, commented: "We are also left with the aftermath of 'The Deputy,' making a clamor in the world which may, hopefully, become the equivalent of a call to prayer. Any virtues the work possesses are extra-theatrical. They may indeed become virtues."

Hochhuth pointed out that the subject of his play has been discussed ever since 1946 by such men as Albert Camus in France and the Catholic thinkers Friedrich Heer and Reinhold Schneider in the German-speaking nations. In regard to his personal feelings about Catholicism he has stated: "My best school friend is a Catholic. In fact, so strict a Catholic that his parents were very much afraid that he would enter the priesthood. He is now in the Federal Department of Justice at Bonn. He is also my son's sponsor." Hochhuth was shocked to see the American Nazis demonstrating at the New York opening and asked: "Why is this permitted in a city that has so many survivors? However, I do understand that democracy permits such things."

The controversy that ensued over the production of his second play, "The Soldiers," was even greater. On April 24, 1967, against the protests of literary manager Kenneth Tynan and artistic director Laurence Olivier, who wanted the play performed,

London's National Theatre decided that the play was unsuitable for production because it allegedly maligned certain notable Englishmen, principally Sir Winston Churchill. In the play, Hochhuth suggests that the death of General Wladyslaw Sikorski, the Polish exile leader during World War II, was not accidental but rather the result of the machinations of the British secret service and was, furthermore, the result of a plot about which Churchill had full knowledge. The Lord Chamberlain, Britain's theatrical censor at the time, suggested that he would allow the play to be publicly performed only if the relatives of the characters in the play gave their consent.

Hochhuth maintained that the play is "against the immorality of air warfare. . . . I cannot blame Churchill. I blame the rules. That is exactly my point in the play. That a great and very human man like Churchill should yet be ready, according to the rules, to blast a city like Hamburg." Hochhuth, in fact, had great admiration for Churchill and kept his portrait in his study in Basel. D. A. N. Jones believed that the play "does not disparage Churchill but concerns itself with the choices men have to make in times of national crisis." Frank Marcus maintained that it "strives for the unvarnished truth and finishes up as a tribute. The method is Schillerian: free verse and constructed in a series of confrontations. Abstract concepts like Honour, Truth, and Fame volley across the net: it's like a Wimbledon of the spirit. The domination of Churchill is made absolute by surrounding him with an entourage of cardboard figures." Marcus added, "With almost Quixotic courage [Hochhuth] has dared to tackle the great moral issues of our time. For this he deserves our unqualified respect, if not our unqualified approval."

When asked whether he specializes in attacking prominent figures Hochhuth replied: "Not at all. When you are writing of great issues and dramas of history, great figures are necessary." Yet primarily because of these attacks his controversial plays received mixed reviews while at the same time succeeding at the box office. He claimed he always has documentary evidence to back his theories and he contended that an author of historical plays has no right to invent incidents or to suppress facts. He said, however, that he does not believe in the "Theater of Documentation" as such. He told Martin Esslin: "I became the champion of 'documentary theater' quite unintentionally. I only noticed what had happened when Piscator wrote a program note in which he used the term 'documentary theater.' I am very unhappy about this catchphrase, for I believe it means very little. Pure documentation can never be more than a bunch of documents. Something must always be *added* to make a play."

MEDIA ADAPTATIONS: Eine Liebe in Deutschland was adapted as the film "A Love in Germany," starring Hanna Schygulla, directed by Andrzei Wajda, Triumph Films, 1984.

BIOGRAPHICAL/CRITICAL SOURCES:

BOOKS

Contemporary Literary Criticism, Gale, Volume 4, 1975, Volume 11, 1979, Volume 18, 1981.
Der Streit un Hochhuths "Stellvertreter," Basilius Presse, 1963.
Summa Inuria; oder, Durfte der Papst schweigen? Hochhuths "Stellvertreter" in der oeffentlichen Kritik, Rowohlt Taschenbuch, 1963.
Ward, M. E., *Rolf Hochhuth,* G. K. Hall, 1977.

PERIODICALS

After Dark, August, 1970.

America, October 12, 1963, November 2, 1963, November 9, 1963, January 4, 1964, January 11, 1964, January 18, 1964, March 7, 1964, March 14, 1964.
Chicago Tribune, January 30, 1985.
Chicago Tribune Book World, June 15, 1980.
Christian Century, September 18, 1963, October 16, 1963.
Christian Science Monitor, May 6, 1968, July 1, 1972.
Commentary, March, 1964.
Commonweal, February 28, 1964, March 20, 1964, May 31, 1968.
Der Spiegel, February 27, 1963.
Detroit Free Press, March 29, 1964, September 24, 1967.
Drama, spring, 1968.
Globe and Mail (Toronto), February 26, 1968.
L'Express, October 3, 1963, December 19, 1963.
Life, March 13, 1964, June 7, 1968.
Listener, October 12, 1967.
London Magazine, January, 1968.
Los Angeles Times, November 15, 1984.
Los Angeles Times Book Review, June 22, 1980.
Nation, March 16, 1964, May 20, 1968, August 25, 1969, August 17, 1970.
National Observer, March 2, 1964, March 4, 1968.
New Leader, March 16, 1964.
New Republic, March 14, 1964.
New Statesman, October 4, 1963.
Newsweek, March 2, 1964, March 11, 1968, January 20, 1969, June 1, 1970.
New York Daily News, February 27, 1964.
New Yorker, December 28, 1963, March 7, 1964, May 11, 1968.
New York Herald Tribune, February 27, 1964.
New York Journal-American, February 27, 1964.
New York Post, February 27, 1964.
New York Review of Books, March 19, 1964.
New York Times, February 27, 1964, February 28, 1964, February 12, 1967, April 26, 1967, September 11, 1967, December 14, 1968, November 9, 1984.
New York Times Book Review, March 1, 1964.
New York Times Magazine, November 19, 1967.
New York World-Telegram, February 27, 1964.
Observer Review, October 15, 1967, May 12, 1968, October 27, 1968, December 15, 1968.
Reporter, January 30, 1964.
Saturday Night, March, 1968.
Saturday Review, March 14, 1964.
Spectator, October 4, 1963, December 20, 1968.
The Saturday Evening Post, February 29, 1964.
Time, November 1, 1963, March 6, 1964, May 10, 1968.
Times (London), April 10, 1980, November 9, 1984, November 12, 1984, May 10, 1985, October 7, 1986.
Times Literary Supplement, May 28, 1970, May 2, 1980.
Transatlantic Review, autumn, 1968.
Variety, August 5, 1970.
Village Voice, March 12, 1964.
Washington Post, January 19, 1969, May 3, 1972.
Zuericher Woche, September 27, 1963.

* * *

HOCHWAELDER, Fritz 1911-1986

PERSONAL: Born May 28, 1911, in Vienna, Austria; died October 20, 1986, in Zurich, Switzerland; son of Leonhard (an upholsterer) and Therese (Koenig) Hochwaelder; married Ursula Buchi, July 26, 1951; married second wife, Susan Schreiner, July 20, 1960; children: (second marriage) Monique. *Education:* Attended elementary school in Vienna, Austria, and later studied in classes.

ADDRESSES: Home—Am Oeschbrig 27, 8053 Zurich, Switzerland.

CAREER: Playwright. Served apprenticeship as an upholsterer in Vienna, Austria, where his first plays were performed in small theaters, 1932, 1936; emigrated to Switzerland in 1938; writer in Zurich, Switzerland, 1945-86.

MEMBER: PEN (Austrian center), Societe des Auteurs (Paris), Schweizer Schriftsteller-Verein, Vereinigung Oesterreichischer Dramatiker.

AWARDS, HONORS: Literary Prize of City of Vienna, 1955; Grillparzer Prize of Austrian Academy of Sciences, 1956; Anton Wildgans Prize of Austrian Industry, 1963; Austrian State Prize for Literature, 1966; Oesterreichisches Ehrenkreuz fuer Kunst und Wissenschaft, 1971; Ehrenring der Stadt Wien, 1972.

WRITINGS:

PLAYS

Jehr, first produced in Vienna at Kammerspiele, March 1, 1933.
Liebe in Florenz (comedy; title means "Love in Florence"), first produced in Vienna at Theater fuer 1949, March 5, 1936.
Das heilige Experiment (five-act; first produced, 1943, subsequently presented in Paris in two acts as "Sur la Terre comme au Ciel," and then in London and New York as "The Strong Are Lonely"; also see below), Volksverlag Elgg (Zurich), 1947, translation of the French play by Eva le Gallienne published as *The Strong Are Lonely,* Samuel French, 1954, German version published in *Oesterreichisches Theater,* Buechergilde Gutenberg, 1964.
Der Unschuldige (title means "The Innocent One"; three-act comedy; first produced at in Vienna at Burgtheater, December 22, 1958; also see below), privately printed in Zurich, 1949, Volksverlag Elgg, 1958.
Virginia, first produced in Hamburg, West Germany, at Grosses Schauspielhaus, December 5, 1951.
Donadieu (three-act; based on the ballad "Die Fuesse im Feuer" by Conrad Ferdinand Meyer; first produced at Burgtheater, October 3, 1953; also see below), Paul Zsolnay (Hamburg), 1953, edition in German with introduction by Richard Thieberger published in England by Harrap, 1967.
Der oeffentliche Anklaeger (three-act; first produced in Stuttgart, West Germany, at Neues Theater, November 10, 1948; also see below), Paul Zsolnay, 1954, acting edition with translation by Kitty Black published as *The Public Prosecutor,* Samuel French, 1958, television adaptation by Theodore Apstein, produced on "U.S. Steel Hour," 1958, edition in German with introduction and notes by J. R. Foster in English published under original title, Methuen, 1962.
Hotel du commerce (comedy; first produced, 1944; also see below), Volksverlag Elgg, 1954.
Der Fluechtling (title means "The Fugitive"; taken from a scenario by George Kaiser; first produced, 1945; also see below), Volksverlag Elgg, 1955.
Die Herberge (title means "The Shelter"; three-act; first produced at Burgtheater, March 30, 1957; also see below), Volksverlag Elgg, 1956.
Meier Helmbrecht (first produced, 1946; also see below), Volksverlag Elgg, 1956.
Esther (five-act comedy; first produced, 1940; also see below), Volksverlag Elgg, 1960.
Der Himbeerpfluecker (three-act comedy; first produced in Zurich at Schauspielhaus, September 24, 1965; translation by

Michael Bullock produced in London as "The Raspberry Picker," June, 1967; also see below), Albert Langen/Georg Mueller, 1965.
Der Befehl (title means "The Command"; first produced for television, British Broadcasting Corp. [BBC-TV], 1967; book contains notes by the author and by Franz Theodor Csokor and Theodor W. Adorno; translation by Robin Hirsch published in *Modern International Drama,* Volume 3, number 2, Pennsylvania State University Press, 1970; also see below), Stiasny (Graz), 1967.
Lazaretti; oder, Der Saebeltiger (three-act; title means "Lazaretti; or, the Saber-toothed Tiger"; produced at Salzburg Festival, 1975; also see below), Verlag Styria, 1975.
Im Wechsel der Zeit: Autobiographische Skizzen und Essays, Verlag Styria, 1980.
Die Prinzessin von Chimay (three-act comedy; also see below), Verlag Styria, 1981.
Der verschwundene Mond (also see below), first produced in 1982.
Die Buergschaft (also see below), first produced in 1984.

Also author of radio play *Der Reigen* based on the play *Weinsberger Ostern 1525* by Arthur Schnitzler; author of unproduced plays *Die verschleierte Frau* (title means "The Veiled Woman"), 1946, and *Schicksalskomoedie* (title means "A Comedy of Fate"), 1960.

OMNIBUS EDITIONS

Dramen I (includes "Das heilige Experiment," "Die Herberge," and "Donnerstag" [a modern miracle play]; "Donnerstag" first produced in Salzburg at Landestheater, July 29, 1959), Albert Langen/Georg Mueller (Munich and Vienna), 1959.
Dramen II (includes "Der oeffentliche Anklaeger," "Der Unschuldige," and "1003" [three-act]; "1003" first produced in Vienna at Theater in der Josefstadt, January 9, 1964), Albert Langen/Georg Mueller, 1964.
Dramen (includes "Das heilige Experiment," "Die Herberge," "Der Himbeerpfluecker"), Albert Langen/Georg Mueller, 1968.
Stuecke (includes "Das heilige Experiment," "Die Herberge," "Der Unschuldige," "Der Himbeerpfluecker"), [Berlin], 1968.
Dramen, Verlag Styria (Graz), Volume 1 (includes "Esther," "Das heilige Experiment," "Hotel du commerce," "Meier Helmbrecht," "Der oeffentliche Anklaeger"), 1975, Volume 2, (includes "Donadieu," "Die Herberge," "Der Unschuldige," "Der Himbeerpfluecker," and "Der Befehl"), 1975, Volume 3, (includes "Die unziemliche Neugier," "Der Fluechtling," "Donnerstag," "1003," "Lazaretti; oder, Der Saebeltiger"), 1979, Volume 4 (includes "Die Prinzessin von Chimay," "Der verschwundene Mond," "Die Buergschaft"), 1985.

ENGLISH TRANSLATIONS

(Contributor) Martin Esslin, translator, *The New Theatre of Europe* (includes "Das heilige Experiment," "Der oeffentliche Anklaeger," "Donadieu," "Die Herberge," and "Der Himbeerpfluecker"), Delta, 1970.
The Public Prosecutor and Other Plays, Ungar, 1979.

SIDELIGHTS: Fritz Hochwaelder presents unusual twists of religious and moral themes in "Das heilige Experiment" and most of his later plays. According to Frederick Lumley, the Viennese-born playwright first attracted attention in 1952 when "Das heilige Experiment" was presented in Paris, where it "caused an immediate stir through the relationship of its theme with that of the worker-priest controversy then topical." Lumley mentions Hochwaelder's constant experiment both in ideas and form; the play "1003," for instance, has only two characters—the author and his imagination, with the author in the process of losing his creation, who seems more alive than himself. The development of Hochwaelder, Lumley says, "makes him not only an important dramatist for the German-speaking theatre, but together with Duerrenmatt and Frisch, also living in Switzerland, and Peter Weiss, another 'exile' living in Sweden, it may be said that the most interesting living dramatists anywhere today are to be found in these [four] representatives of the German language." Three of Hochwaelder's plays have been published in Buenos Aires, and several in Paris.

BIOGRAPHICAL/CRITICAL SOURCES:

BOOKS

Contemporary Literary Criticism, Volume 36, Gale, 1986.
Demetz, Peter, *Post-War German Literature,* Western Publishing, 1970.
Feret, H. M., *"Sur la terre comme au ciel," le vrai drame de Hochwaelder,* Edition du Cerf, 1953.
Litteratur du vingtieme siecle, Volume 4, Casterman, 1960.
Lumley, Frederick, *New Trends in 20th Century Drama,* Oxford University Press, 1967.
McGraw-Hill Encyclopedia of World Drama, 2nd edition, McGraw, 1984.
Wellwarth, George, *The Theater of Protest and Paradox,* New York University Press, 1964.

OBITUARIES:

PERIODICALS

Times (London), October 24, 1986.

*   *   *

HOFFMAN, Abbie   1936-1989
(Free, Barry Freed, George Metesky)

PERSONAL: Original name Abbott Hoffman; born November 30, 1936, in Worcester, Mass.; committed suicide, April 12, 1989, with a barbiturate overdose, in New Hope, Pa.; son of John (founder of Worcester Medical Supply Co.) and Florence (Schanberg) Hoffman; married, 1960 (divorced, 1966), wife's name Sheila; married Anita Kushner, June 10, 1967 (divorced, September, 1980); lived with Johanna Lawrenson for 15 years; children: (first marriage) Andrew, Amy Ilya; (second marriage) america (son). *Education:* Brandeis University, B.A., 1959; University of California, Berkeley, M.A., 1960.

CAREER: Worcester State Hospital, Worcester, Mass., psychologist, 1960-62; pharmaceuticals salesman, 1963-65; founder of Prospect Community House, Worcester; civil rights worker for the Student Non-Violent Coordinating Committee (SNCC) in Mississippi, 1964-66; founder of Liberty House, New York, N.Y., 1966; co-founder of the Youth International Party (Yippies), 1968; founder of Save the River, Thousand Islands, N.Y., 1978; founder of CIA on Trial Project, Northampton, Mass., 1987.

WRITINGS:

F— the System (pamphlet), privately printed, 1968.
(Under pseudonym Free) *Revolution for the Hell of It,* Dial, 1968.
Woodstock Nation: A Talk-Rock Album, Vintage Books, 1969.
Steal This Book, Pirate Editions, 1971.

(With Jerry Rubin and Ed Sanders) *Vote!,* Warner Paperback, 1972.
(With wife, Anita Hoffman) *To america with Love: Letters from the Underground,* Stonehill Publishing, 1976.
Soon to Be a Major Motion Picture, Putnam, 1980.
Square Dancing in the Ice Age: Underground Writings, Putnam, 1982.
(With Jonathan Silvers) *Steal This Urine Test: Fighting the Drug Hysteria in America,* Penguin, 1987.
(With Silvers) *Preserving Disorder: The Faking of the President, 1988,* Penguin, 1989.
The Best of Abbie Hoffman: Selections from "Revolution for the Hell of It," "Woodstock Nation" and "Steal This Book," Four Walls Eight Windows, 1989.

Also author of *Son of Steal This Book.* Contributor of articles, some under pseudonyms, to *East Village Other, Village Voice, Los Angeles Free Press, Eye, Realist, Harper's, Esquire, Parade,* and *Sports Illustrated.* Former travel editor, *Crawdaddy.*

SIDELIGHTS: Described by *Time* as the "Puck of the 1960s underground [and] the frizzy-haired, war-painted Yippie leader who preached revolution against the American establishment," Abbie Hoffman personified the youthful rebellion of the late 1960s with his outlandish guerrilla theatrics, political pranks, and colorful lifestyle. His activities against the Vietnam War combined the revolutionary politics of the New Left with the cultural exuberance of the hippies.

Hoffman first became politically active in the civil rights movement of the early 1960s, working as an organizer for several civil rights organizations and founding Liberty House, a store selling the products of the poor people's co-ops of Mississippi. With the decline of the civil rights movement and the increasing U.S. military presence in Vietnam, Hoffman turned his attention to the fledgling peace movement, organizing opposition to the Vietnam War among the hippies of New York's East Village. Hoffman's brand of political opposition took its cue from Madison Avenue. "Again and again," Morris Dickstein wrote in the *New York Times Book Review,* "[Hoffman] describes himself as a super salesman for radical ideas." This "selling" of radical ideas was done by grabbing as much media attention as possible through wild political pranks, guerilla theater, and media events. As Eva Hoffman wrote in the *Washington Post,* Hoffman "was engaging in an 'image war' in which symbolic desecrations were the weapons and sanctified institutions were the targets." "Even Hoffman's most outrageous performances. . . .," Dickstein pointed out, "had a clear political goal: to remove the aura of legitimacy from what he saw as unjust and oppressive authority."

One of Hoffman's most successful events involved dumping a flurry of dollars into the midst of the New York Stock Exchange during a busy trading day. The resulting mad scramble by stockbrokers for the money garnered worldwide media attention and made a political statement about the American economic system. When appearing as a guest on the "Merv Griffin" television program, Hoffman showed up wearing an American flag shirt, causing the network censors to blank out his half of the television screen. Despite the success of Hoffman's media events in attracting national attention and making statements about what he perceived as societal shortcomings, Hoffman "never for a moment [believed] guerrilla theater . . . could alone stop the war in Vietnam," he wrote in *Soon to Be a Major Motion Picture.* "But it did extend the possibilities of involving the senses and penetrating the symbolic world of fantasy." Hoffman maintained that the modern revolutionary movement must concentrate "on infiltrating and changing the image system." And, of course, "one of the greatest mistakes any revolution can make is to become boring."

In his early books, Hoffman presented the ideas that motivated his unorthodox and dramatic political behavior. Irreverent, humorous, provocative, and sometimes soberingly thoughtful, Hoffman's writings have inspired a very mixed critical reaction. Jack Newfield, writing in the *New York Times Book Review,* found *Revolution for the Hell of It* "a serious manifesto for the growing counter-culture of mind drugs, rock bands, sexual freedom, mixed media, communes, Free Stores, astrology, colorful costumes, and casual nudity. . . . It is a recipe for private amusement and public catastrophe." Describing the same book as a "disjointed but somehow engaging nonbook" and "a slender, acid-infused account of the rise of the nonviolent yippies," a *Time* reviewer went on to find that "the book trips along most gaily on currents of aphorism and imagination. Between its often outrageous put-ons and put-downs lies much that is of significance." Hoffman's books sold over three million copies.

In 1968, Hoffman founded the Youth International Party with fellow revolutionary Jerry Rubin. The party was intended, as a *Saturday Night* writer stated, to "bring together the hippies who were beginning to turn political and the New Left types who were getting bored with picket lines and parades." Known as Yippies (for "Yiddish hippies," as Hoffman once defined the term), supporters of the party had no official membership rolls, no platform, and no leaders. They lived the hippie lifestyle, denounced the Vietnam War and the American political and economic system, and called for a revolution to replace the present system with an anarchistic, communal society. The party first tested its strength at the Democratic Party National Convention in Chicago in 1968, where the Yippies were one of several groups to organize demonstrations against the war. These demonstrations ended in a bloody street battle between protesters and police in what many observers labeled a "police riot." The fighting was so chaotic that television newsmen sent to the scene found themselves being beaten by police. As a result of the violence, eight radicals, including Hoffman, were arrested and charged with conspiracy to incite a riot for their roles in organizing the demonstrations. Though it was not the first time Hoffman had been arrested—he had been arrested some thirty times before for various civil rights and antiwar protest activities—it was the most serious charge he had faced and, with the national media focused on the trial, the one that made his name synonymous with radical activism.

Popularly termed the Chicago Conspiracy Trial, the court proceedings were "as spectacular and outrageous as anything seen in an American courtroom," James Gleick states in *New Times.* Defendant Bobby Seale of the Black Panther Party was bound and gagged in the courtroom after refusing to keep quiet during the proceedings; former Attorney General Ramsey Clark was refused permission to testify before the jury on behalf of the accused; FBI agents were allegedly discovered with eavesdropping equipment outside of a private meeting between the defendants and their lawyers. *Newsweek* reported that "the trial . . . was a landmark in American life and law—and not just for its almost daily pyrotechnics. It had produced the most devastating use of a judge's contempt-of-court power that any lawyer could remember, raised questions about the proper limits on that power and opened up the possibility that the trial system itself might have to be modified in order to cope with defendants and lawyers who refuse to observe its fragile rules of decorum. It had offered the first court test of the controversial 'Rap Brown law' which makes it a crime simply to cross a state line with riotous intent. And it had locked Attorney General John Mitchell's Justice De-

partment into its starkest confrontation with the radical movement, prompting charges from radicals and some liberals that the Administration was embarked on a campaign of political repression against the militant left." All of the defendants, and their lawyers, were found guilty of contempt charges; Hoffman was sentenced to five years in prison. The convictions were appealed and, with the aid of documents obtained under the Freedom of Information Act, eventually dismissed. Defense attorney William Kunstler stated in the *Nation* that the government had tapped their phones, opened their mail, and either bugged or infiltrated their private meetings. The judge and the F.B.I., Kunstler claimed, regularly met in collusion. These actions, together with such things as the jury selection process, which higher courts ruled was "unconstitutional," were grounds for the defendants to be acquitted.

At the conclusion of a drug deal on August 28, 1973—a deal involving Hoffman, $36,000 worth of cocaine, and two undercover police officers—Hoffman again found himself in trouble with the law. Hoffman claimed he had been framed, but he was arrested and charged with possession of cocaine, a charge that carried a minimum sentence of fifteen years in prison. The *New Yorker* noted at the time of the arrest that Hoffman was "in the worst trouble of his life. Although many medical authorities regard cocaine as a non-narcotic drug, relatively innocuous in comparison to heroin, the laws of New York State make no distinction." Despite Hoffman's charges of a frame-up (both buyer and seller of the drug were police officers; Hoffman acted as their middleman), he believed his chances for a fair trial seemed slim, and he jumped bail to avoid standing trial. Hoffman explained his decision to go underground: "We didn't have the money to put on an adequate defense." He further explained: "I was the Devil's naughty son charged with selling the Devil's dandruff."

For the next seven years Hoffman's whereabouts were unknown, although he granted clandestine interviews to several leftist magazines, served as by-mail travel editor for *Crawdaddy* magazine, and published two books and some thirty-five articles. After he resurfaced in 1980—first on television with Barbara Walters to hype his new book, then at the police station—it was learned that Hoffman had lived the previous four years under the alias "Barry Freed," working as an environmental activist in Thousand Islands, New York. As Freed, Hoffman had appeared on local television and radio, been commended by the governor of New York for his conservation work, testified before a U.S. Senate subcommittee on the environment, and been appointed to a federal water resources commission. After serving a year in prison on a reduced charge relating to his drug arrest, Hoffman was released in early 1982 and returned to Thousand Islands where, adopting his old alias of Barry Freed, he continued to work against the transporting of nuclear waste material on the St. Lawrence River. He also became a popular speaker on college campuses.

Hoffman's life underground modified his political views. He dropped the hippie theatrics of his earlier years in favor of a more doctrinaire radicalism. Dickstein believed that "isolation and flight cut Abbie off from his 'image,' like the man in the fable who lost his shadow. This brought out the more serious and thoughtful self that always lurked just behind the clownish facade." During the 1980s, he organized trips to Marxist-run Nicaragua for American journalists and opinion-makers. At the University of Massachusetts, Hoffman worked with Amy Carter, daughter of former president Jimmy Carter, in protesting CIA recruitment on campus. For a time he tried a stand-up comedy act, and he even hosted a weekly talk show for National Public Radio.

Hoffman described himself in *Square Dancing in the Ice Age* as "the most famous relatively poor person in America who hasn't killed a whole bunch of people or assassinated a political candidate." He once explained that he was "just a person who wants to make America a better place for all." At the time of his suicide in 1989, it was revealed that Hoffman had been diagnosed as manic-depressive, prone to wild mood swings, and had apparently been despondent.

BIOGRAPHICAL/CRITICAL SOURCES:

BOOKS

Hoffman, Abbie, *Soon to Be a Major Motion Picture,* Putnam, 1980.
Hoffman, Abbie, *Square Dancing in the Ice Age,* Putnam, 1982.

PERIODICALS

Chicago Tribune, June 9, 1980, February 20, 1985, October 14, 1987, April 28, 1989.
Chicago Tribune Book World, October 26, 1980.
Commonweal, February 7, 1969.
Esquire, April, 1976.
Eve, January, 1969.
Globe and Mail (Toronto), October 4, 1986.
Harper's, May, 1974, September, 1980.
Life, December 31, 1971.
Los Angeles Times, September 5, 1980, May 11, 1988, May 14, 1988, April 14, 1989.
Los Angeles Times Book Review, December 7, 1980, June 20, 1982.
Nation, January 11, 1971, September 29, 1979, May 3, 1980, June 19, 1982.
National Observer, January 13, 1969.
National Review, March 25, 1969, April 7, 1970, June 1, 1971.
New Republic, November 29, 1969.
Newsday, November 6, 1971.
Newsweek, March 2, 1970, July 13, 1970, September 15, 1980.
New Times, May 30, 1975.
New York, September, 1968.
New York Daily News, October 5, 1980.
New Yorker, May 6, 1974.
New York Review of Books, November 6, 1980.
New York Times, January 10, 1969, November 5, 1969, September 1, 1980, February 1, 1987, April 19, 1989.
New York Times Book Review, December 29, 1968, February 22, 1970, July 12, 1970, July 18, 1971, September 21, 1980, August 15, 1982.
People, September 22, 1980.
Playboy, May, 1976.
Progressive, November, 1969.
Saturday Night, July, 1969.
Saturday Review, December 13, 1969.
Time, December 20, 1968, September 15, 1980.
Variety, November 19, 1969.
Village Voice, December 10, 1979.
Wall Street Journal, September 5, 1980.
Washington Monthly, June, 1976.
Washington Post, January 30, 1969, October 5, 1971, September 5, 1980, August 31, 1988, April 14, 1989, July 14, 1989.

OBITUARIES:

PERIODICALS

Chicago Tribune, April 13, 1989.
Los Angeles Times, April 13, 1989.
New York Times, April 14, 1989.
Times (London), April 14, 1989.
Washington Post, April 14, 1989.

*   *   *

HOFFMAN, Alice   1952-

PERSONAL: Born March 16, 1952, in New York, N.Y.; married Tom Martin (a writer); children: Jake, Zack. *Education:* Adelphi University, B.A., 1973; Stanford University, M.A., 1975.

ADDRESSES: Home—Brookline, Mass. *Agent*—Elaine Markson Literary Agency, 44 Greenwich Ave., New York, N.Y. 10011.

CAREER: Writer, 1975—.

AWARDS, HONORS: Mirelles fellow, Stanford University, 1975; Bread Loaf fellowship, summer, 1976; Notable Books of 1979 list, *Library Journal,* for *The Drowning Season.*

WRITINGS:

Property Of (novel), Farrar, Straus, 1977.
The Drowning Season (novel), Dutton, 1979.
Angel Landing (novel), Putnam, 1980.
White Horses (novel), Putnam, 1982.
"Independence Day" (screenplay), Warner Bros., 1983.
Fortune's Daughter (novel), Putnam, 1985.
Illumination Night (novel), Putnam, 1987.
At Risk (novel), Putnam, 1988.

Also author of other screenplays. Contributor of stories to *Ms., Redbook, Fiction, American Review,* and *Playgirl.*

WORK IN PROGRESS: A screenplay adaptation of *At Risk,* for Twentieth Century-Fox.

SIDELIGHTS: Through the course of several novels, Alice Hoffman's work has been characterized by "a shimmering prose style, the fusing of fantasy and realism, [and] the preoccupation with the way the mythic weaves itself into the everyday," Alexandra Johnson summarizes in the *Boston Review.* "Hoffman's narrative domain is the domestic, the daily. Yet her vision—and voice—are lyrical," the critic continues. "She is a writer whose prose style is often praised as painterly, and, indeed, Hoffman's fictional world is like a Vermeer: a beautifully crafted study of the interior life." Hoffman's characters "tend to be rebels and eccentrics," Stella Dong states in a *Publishers Weekly* interview with the author; Hoffman explained that she writes about such people "because they're outsiders and to some extent, we all think of ourselves as outsiders. We're looking for that other person—man, woman, parent or child—who will make us whole." As the author once told *CA:* "I suppose my main concern is the search for identity and continuity, and the struggle inherent in that search."

The protagonist of Hoffman's first novel *Property Of,* for instance, is an unnamed seventeen-year-old girl enamored of McKay, the leader of an urban gang involved in violence and drugs; the story of their year-long relationship is what *Times Literary Supplement* contributor Zachary Leader calls "a sort of punk or pop-gothic *Jane Eyre.*" Despite the "harsh and gritty" quality of the world it portrays, *Property Of* is nevertheless "a remarkably envisioned novel, almost mythic in its cadences, hypnotic," Richard R. Lingeman observes in the *New York Times.* "McKay and the heroine are like tragic lovers in a courtly romance played out in candy stores, clubhouses and mean streets. . . . Hoffman imbues her juvenile delinquents with a romantic intensity that lifts them out of sociology." Edith Milton concurs with this assessment, commenting in the *Yale Review* that "the narrative is engrossing because Hoffman creates characters touched by legend." The critic further elaborates that Hoffman is able to balance "parody and sentiment, cutting her own flights of panting prose with acid self-mockery."

While the writing in *Property Of* "had speed, wit, and a mordant lyricism," Margo Jefferson comments in *Ms.,* "*The Drowning Season* has extravagance and generosity as well." Tracing "a legacy of lovelessness from frozen White Russia to modern New York," as *Newsweek* contributor Jean Strouse describes it, *The Drowning Season* follows Esther the White and Esther the Black, a grandmother and granddaughter who overcome a past of failed communication to slowly establish a relationship. Similar to Hoffman's first novel, *The Drowning Season* functions on two levels, as Susan Wood suggests in the *Washington Post:* " 'The Drowning Season,' just as hypnotic and mythic in its language and rhythms, reverberates with situations and characters that suggest ancient myths and European folk tales and seems on one level to function as a symbolic, allegorical tale in a modern setting. Yet it is very much a novel about believable and imperfect human beings, as concrete and individualized as the family next door." Barry Siegel finds Esther the White in particular "a truly compelling character," writing in the *Los Angeles Times Book Review* that while "she is the source of her family's malaise . . . Hoffman sees in her something much more complex than a villain." The critic concludes that Hoffman "is a superb writer who brings us to understand and to care about all her characters. . . . Hoffman at all times remains in control of her fine narrative."

Hoffman followed *The Drowning Season* with *Angel Landing,* a romance set near a nuclear power plant, and *White Horses,* the story of a young girl's obsession with her older brother. Teresa, the protagonist of *White Horses,* has been brought up hearing the family legend of the *Arias,* dangerous and beautiful young outlaws who carry women off to exciting lives; this legend led Teresa's mother into an unhappy marriage, and Teresa herself into an incestuous love for Silver, who she sees as her ideal *Aria.* "Incest may be the most difficult theme for a novelist to undertake," states *Newsweek* reviewer Peter S. Prescott, "yet Hoffman here makes it tolerable by the mythic mold in which she has cast her story." *New York Times Book Review* contributor Anne Tyler likewise sees a mythic dimension in the novel: " 'White Horses' combines the concrete and the dreamlike. Its characters are people we think we recognize at first; but then on second thought we're not so sure," the critic continues. "There's an almost seamless transition from the real to the unreal, back and forth and back again." Stephanie Vaughn, however, faults the novel's symbolism as "ask[ing] us to see an epic dimension that the story does not quite deliver," as she remarks in her *Washington Post* review. And while Tyler also thinks that the novel is at times "burdened by the very musicality that was so appealing in the beginning," she admits that "these are quibbles, and very minor quibbles at that. The overall impression is one of abundant life, masterfully orchestrated by the author." *White Horses,* Tyler concludes, "is a satisfying novel, at the same time mysterious and believable, and it marks a significant advance for Alice Hoffman."

While *Fortune's Daughter,* in the vein of Hoffman's earlier novels, "has the quality of folk tale—of amazing events calmly recounted," Perri Klass asserts in the *New York Times Book Review* that unlike *White Horses* it has "no . . . explicit myth. Instead, the sense of magic and elemental force arises from the central mystery of childbirth," Klass continues. "This novel's great strength lies in its two heroines, who both find themselves

drawn, without plans, hopes or full understanding, into the inevitably mythological process of pregnancy and childbirth." Rae, pregnant with her first child, has just been deserted by the man for whom she left her home and traveled across a continent; seeking reassurance, she finds Lila, a fortune teller who reads a child's death in Rae's tea leaves. Against Lila's wishes, Rae enlists the older woman's assistance with her pregnancy, evoking Lila's memories of the child she gave up for adoption over twenty years ago. The result, observes Robin Hemley in the *Chicago Tribune Book World,* is "an elegant and evocative novel that conjures up a kind of modern-day female mythology."

Some critics, however, such as *Boston Review* contributor Patricia Meyer Spacks, feel the plot of *Fortune's Daughter* verges on "soap-opera sentimentalities." Nevertheless they acknowledge, as Klass writes, that "the peculiar offbeat humor keeps the narrative from drifting into melodrama." The critic elaborates: "It is in its juxtaposition of the mythic, the apocalyptic, with the resolutely ordinary, in its portrait of eccentric characters living in a very familiar world, that this novel finds its unique voice. It is beautifully and matter-of-factly told, and it leaves the reader with an almost bewildered sense that this primal mythological level does exist in everyday reality, and that there is no event, from the standard miracle of childbirth to the most bizarre magic imaginable, that cannot occur in a setting of familiar, everyday details."

"*Illumination Night,* Hoffman's sixth novel, is in many ways her most subtle," Johnson claims, describing it as "a powerful if often disturbing look at the interior lives, domestic and emotional, of a young family and the teenage girl set on destroying them all." Andre and Vonny are a young couple concerned about their son's lack of growth and the tension in their marriage caused by the unwanted attentions of Jody, a neighboring sixteen-year-old, towards Andre. "This may sound like soap opera," *New York Times* critic Christopher Lehmann-Haupt declares, but Hoffman "has enough power of empathy to make her characters matter to us. Daringly mixing comedy with tragedy, and the quotidian with the fabulous, she has created a narrative that somehow makes myth out of the sticky complexities of contemporary marriage." Hoffman "has a penchant for finding a near-gothic strangeness and enchantment on the edges of everyday experience," Jack Sullivan likewise comments in the *Washington Post Book World.* "Here the mystery starts when the younger characters begin seeing an abnormally huge and beautiful young man—referred to throughout the novel simply as the Giant. This myth-like character becomes as convincingly real as anyone else, especially when Jody begins a secret love affair with him." Throughout the book "is the sure sense that magic and spirituality infuse our lives, and that this magic is as readily available to the poor as to the rich," *Los Angeles Times* critic Carolyn See similarly reports.

"Subtle touches here and there make this intelligent novel shine," Gwyneth Cravens maintains in the *New York Times Book Review.* "Ms. Hoffman knows how to tell a story in clear language and how to avoid subordinating the meanderings of temperament to logic or plot. The characters suddenly, and believably, change their behavior toward one another in the presence of the irrational." Other critics have also remarked on the quality of the author's characterizations; Lehmann-Haupt, for example, observes that "Hoffman writes so simply about human passions that her characters are branded onto one's memory," while London *Times* reviewer Philip Howard states that Hoffman "hits bull's eyes on the incomprehensions between the young and the old, on the magic and pain of ordinary life." As Candice Russell notes in her *Chicago Tribune* review, the author's "omniscient voice . . . explores the underpinnings of her characters, who become increasingly connected and interdependent." Sullivan similarly praises Hoffman's narrative for its "unusually fluid form of subjectivity that becomes a kind of total omniscience . . . without breaking the rhythm of her prose or storyline. From a technical as well as emotional standpoint," the critic concludes, "this is an impressive, stirring performance."

With *At Risk,* the story of a young girl whose AIDS precipitates a family crisis, Hoffman "is mainstreaming a refined literary talent," *Time*'s R. Z. Sheppard recounts. By taking as her subject such a topical social concern, however, Hoffman has drawn criticism from some reviewers for letting the issue of AIDS overcome the story; *Washington Post* writer Jonathan Yardley, for example, contends that the novel "is very much wrought from material offered by the headlines, yet it fails to shape that material into anything approximating life." But Lehmann-Haupt believes that *At Risk* "does succeed in overcoming these obstacles [of topicality]. From its opening sentence, we know we are in a world that is specific and alive." The critic goes on to explain that Hoffman's "simple, brick-solid prose . . . soon establishes that the Farrell family of Morrow, Cape Ann, Mass., is made up not of stick figures, but unique living people." The novel's plot "sounds like by-the-numbers fiction," Jim Shepard remarks in the *New York Times Book Review.* "But what saves it over and over again is Ms. Hoffman's ability to reshape the contours of the experience to achieve something with the pain and freshness of our own childhood memories."

Because the issues in *At Risk* are more self-evident than in the author's other work, some reviewers have suggested that the novel does not contain as much of a "magical" element as do her other books. *Los Angeles Times Book Review* critic Richard Eder, for instance, says that Hoffman "has a style that can be delicately bewitching and capable of a streak of wildness. Sometimes the streak and the delicacy are evident in 'At Risk,' but they have a lot to contend with." "Oddly, this wonderful book isn't markedly different in style or imagination from Hoffman's last novel," Laura Shapiro counters in *Newsweek.* Michele Souda likewise sees in the novel "several perfectly distilled dream sequences, dark and bizarre experiences that remind us how much Hoffman has always trusted her characters' dreams and how well she has invented them." And, as the author explained to London *Times* writer Catherine Bennett, "part of the reason [for the diminished emphasis on magic] is that Aids took the place of that, that was the inexplicable part of it. Aids is like something you'd invent, it's bizarre, it's horrible, it's kind of like a spaceship—this disease just landing. I felt that anything else I was going to add was going to reduce it."

Despite the effect of the AIDS issue, "the novel's true power does not derive from the facts of Amanda's story—as devastating as they are," writes Souda; "it derives from Hoffman's choice of narrative structure and her flawless prose." "What saves [the story] from banality is Hoffman's gift for attaching memorable and often striking images to the [family's] angst," *Village Voice* contributor Ralph Sassone similarly comments, while Shepard adds that "such is Ms. Hoffman's tenderness and perceptiveness that we come to care about her creations despite their imperfections the way we would care about those we love despite theirs." "Alice Hoffman's fine work gets better and better," concludes Souda. "She has often shown us characters driven to desperation by their own feelings and desires, and [in *At Risk*] she shows us, again, how awful that desperation can be. She has taken the nightmare of our time, stripped it of statistics and social rhetoric, and placed it in the raw center of family life."

BIOGRAPHICAL/CRITICAL SOURCES:

BOOKS

Contemporary Literary Criticism, Volume 51, Gale, 1989.

PERIODICALS

Boston Review, September, 1985, October, 1987.
Chicago Tribune, August 31, 1987.
Chicago Tribune Book World, May 5, 1985.
Los Angeles Times, December 5, 1980, May 28, 1982, May 9, 1985, August 24, 1987, June 30, 1988.
Los Angeles Times Book Review, August 19, 1979, July 10, 1988.
Ms., August, 1979, May, 1982, June, 1985.
Newsweek, May 23, 1977, April 12, 1982, August 1, 1988.
New Yorker, May 3, 1982, July 15, 1985.
New York Times, July 14, 1977, July 25, 1987, July 4, 1988.
New York Times Book Review, July 15, 1979, November 9, 1980, March 28, 1982, March 24, 1985, August 9, 1987, July 17, 1988.
Publishers Weekly, April 12, 1985.
Time, July 18, 1988.
Times (London), November 28, 1985, October 1, 1987, October 1, 1988.
Times Literary Supplement, April 21, 1978, March 11, 1988.
Tribune Books (Chicago), June 26, 1988.
Village Voice, July 19, 1988.
Washington Post, August 2, 1979, April 13, 1982, June 29, 1988.
Washington Post Book World, December 21, 1980, August 2, 1987.
Yale Review, winter, 1978.

—*Sketch by Diane Telgen*

*   *   *

HOFSTADTER, Douglas R(ichard) 1945-

PERSONAL: Born February 15, 1945, in New York, N.Y.; son of Robert (a professor) and Nancy (Givan) Hofstadter. *Education:* Stanford University, B.S. (with distinction), 1965; University of Oregon, M.S., 1972, Ph.D., 1975.

ADDRESSES: Home—712 South Henderson St., Bloomington, Ind. 47401. *Office*—Department of Computer Science, Indiana University, Bloomington, Ind. 47405.

CAREER: Indiana University, Bloomington, assistant professor, 1977-80, associate professor of computer science, 1980—.

MEMBER: American Association for Artificial Intelligence, Association for Computing Machinery, Association of Computational Linguistics, Cognitive Science Society.

AWARDS, HONORS: Nomination for National Book Critics Circle Award for nonfiction, 1979, Pulitzer Prize for general nonfiction, and American Book Award, 1980, all for *Goedel, Escher, Bach: An Eternal Golden Braid;* Guggenheim fellowship, 1980-81, for study of computer perception of style in letter forms.

WRITINGS:

Goedel, Escher, Bach: An Eternal Golden Braid (nonfiction), Basic Books, 1979.
(With Daniel C. Dennett) *The Mind's I: Fantasies and Reflections on Self and Soul* (nonfiction), Basic Books, 1981.
Metamagical Themas: Questing for the Essence of Mind and Pattern (magazine columns), Basic Books, 1985.

Author of column "Metamagical Themas" for *Scientific American.*

WORK IN PROGRESS: Research on artificial intelligence.

SIDELIGHTS: Douglas R. Hofstadter told *CA* that he is "split by a combination of scientific and artistic interests." In addition to his work as a computer scientist, Hofstadter plays the piano, writes musical compositions, and studies languages. He speaks "French fluently, also German, Italian, Spanish, and Swedish to a lesser extent." The eclectic range of Hofstadter's interests is reflected in his Pulitzer Prize-winning book, *Goedel, Escher, Bach: An Eternal Golden Braid,* about consciousness and the abstractions underlying its explanation. In the book, Hofstadter uses ideas from many fields of human activity, including art and music, to illustrate metaphorically the subtle mechanisms that allow the human psyche to emerge from mere matter.

"The originality of the book, which is considerable," said *Observer*'s Anthony Burgess, "consists in its attempt to relate various fields of human enterprise in which the basic principle of paradox may be observed." The book is centered on a discussion of Kurt Goedel's Incompleteness Theorem, which reveals that a related, near-paradoxical phenomenon occurs in mathematics by demonstrating that in any sufficiently complex axiomatic system there exist true but unprovable mathematical statements. Hofstadter calls the structures giving rise to such incompleteness "strange loops" and gives examples of them in several areas of human knowledge and endeavor. For example, loops can be seen in the art of Maurits Cornelis Escher, whose drawing "Print Gallery" depicts a man looking at a picture in an art gallery; at the same time, however, the man and the gallery are a part of the picture. A loop can also be found in the music of Johann Sebastian Bach. His "modulating canon" from the "Musical Offering" begins in the key of C and "modulates upward in whole tones to end where it began—in C, only this time an octave higher"; but it can be played on a computer in such a way that "the return to C is made at the original pitch. Thus movement ever farther and farther away from home succeeds only in bringing you home," wrote Burgess.

Hofstadter goes on to argue that these loops and their relationship to one another form patterns that suggest ways to think about how human consciousness and intelligence are organized and how models of them can perhaps someday be artificially created. *Commonweal* reporter James Gips wrote, "The idea is this: If we truly understand some process . . . that requires intelligence, then we can write a computer program that embodies that process."

Hofstadter's ideas are complex, and his book, explained Burgess, "assumes an ability to follow mathematical arguments, hold symbols in the mind, and read complicated music." But, according to the *New York Times Book Review*'s Brian Hayes, Hofstadter's "presentation of [his] ideas is not rigorous." Harry Sumrall of *New Republic* described Hofstadter's technique: "Each chapter is prefaced by a dialogue. These dialogues . . . are witty, playful exchanges that metaphorically describe the subjects treated in the chapters. The chapters then go on to elaborate the dialogues with historical and scientific concepts. These in turn are reinforced by a series of mind games, prints, and musical examples."

Gips hailed *Goedel, Escher, Bach* as "a wondrous book that unites and explains, in a very entertaining way, many of the important ideas of recent intellectual history." The book sold more than one hundred thousand copies during the year following its publication and "has become something of a classic," according to *Psychology Today*'s Howard Gardner.

BIOGRAPHICAL/CRITICAL SOURCES:

BOOKS

Contemporary Issues Criticism, Volume 1, Gale, 1982.

PERIODICALS

Byte, February, 1980.
Chicago Tribune, May 12, 1985.
Ethics, January, 1980.
Globe and Mail (Toronto), May 4, 1985.
Los Angeles Times Book Review, March 21, 1982.
Music Educators Journal, February, 1980.
New Republic, July 21, 1979.
New York Review of Books, December 6, 1979.
New York Times, January 8, 1980, April 15, 1980.
New York Times Book Review, April 29, 1979, November 25, 1979, December 30, 1979, June 6, 1982, November 14, 1982.
New York Times Magazine, August 21, 1983.
Observer, September 23, 1979.
Psychology Today, December, 1979, March, 1980.
Scientific American, July, 1979.
Village Voice, November 19, 1979.
Washington Post Book World, December 20, 1981.
Yale Review, winter, 1980.

*   *   *

HOGARTH, Charles
    See CREASEY, John

*   *   *

HOLBROOK, John
    See VANCE, John Holbrook

*   *   *

HOLLANDER, Paul
    See SILVERBERG, Robert

*   *   *

HOLROYD, Michael (de Courcy Fraser) 1935-

PERSONAL: Born August 27, 1935, in London, England; son of Basil (a businessman) and Ulla (Hall) Holroyd; married Margaret Drabble (a novelist, playwright, and short story writer), September 17, 1982. *Education:* Attended Eton College. *Politics:* Apolitical. *Avocational interests:* Listening to stories, music, watching people dance.

ADDRESSES: Home—London, England. *Agent*—A. P. Watt & Son, 26/28 Bedford Row, London WC1R 4HL, England.

CAREER: Writer. Visiting fellow, Pennsylvania State University, 1979. Member of archives advisory committee, British Broadcasting Systems, 1976-79. *Military service:* British Army, Royal Fusiliers.

MEMBER: Royal Society of Literature (fellow; member of council, 1977—), Royal Historical Society (fellow), P.E.N. (president of British branch, 1985—), Society of Authors (chairman, 1973-74), National Book League (chairman, 1976-78), Arts Council (vice-chairman of literature panel, 1981-82).

AWARDS, HONORS: Saxton Memorial fellowship, 1964; Bollingen fellowship, 1966; Book of the Year award from *Yorkshire Post,* 1968, for *Lytton Strachey;* Winston Churchill fellowship, 1971.

WRITINGS:

Hugh Kingsmill: A Critical Biography, Unicorn Press, 1964, revised edition, Heinemann, 1971.

Lytton Strachey: A Critical Biography (Book-of-the-Month Club and Literary Guild selections), Heinemann, Volume I: *The Unknown Years, 1880-1910*, 1967, Volume II: *The Years of Achievement, 1910-1932*, 1968, both volumes published by Holt, 1968, revised edition published in two volumes as *Lytton Strachey: A Biography*, Penguin, 1971, revised edition, Heinemann, 1973, revised edition published as *Lytton Strachey and the Bloomsbury Group: His Work, Their Influence*, Penguin, 1971.

A Dog's Life (novel), Holt, 1969.

Unreceived Opinions (essays), Heinemann, 1973, Holt, 1974.

Augustus John (biography), Heinemann, Volume I: *The Years of Innocence*, 1974, Volume II: *The Years of Experience*, 1975, published as one volume, Holt, 1975, revised edition published as *Augustus John: A Biography*, Penguin, 1976.

(With Malcolm Easton) *The Art of Augustus John*, Secker & Warburg, 1974, Godine, 1975, published as *Autobiography [of] Augustus John*, J. Cape, 1975.

Bernard Shaw, Random House, Volume 1: *The Search for Love, 1856-1898*, 1988, Volume 2: *The Pursuit of Power, 1898-1918*, 1989.

EDITOR

The Best of Hugh Kingsmill, Gollancz, 1970, Herder & Herder, 1971.

Lytton Strachey by Himself: A Self-Portrait, Holt, 1971.

The Genius of Shaw, Holt, 1979.

(With Paul Levy) *The Shorter Strachey*, Oxford University Press, 1980.

(With Robert Skidelsky) *William Gerhardie, God's Fifth Column: A Biography of the Age, 1890-1940*, Simon & Schuster, 1981.

Essays by Divers Hands, Volume XLII, Longwood, 1982.

Peter Harvest: The Private Diary of David Peterley, Secker & Warburg, 1985.

OTHER

Also author of numerous radio and television scripts. Contributor to periodicals, including *Times* (London), *New York Times Book Review*, *Spectator*, and *London Review of Books*.

WORK IN PROGRESS: The third and final volume in his biography of George Bernard Shaw.

SIDELIGHTS: Michael Holroyd has won international recognition for his biographies of author Lytton Strachey, painter Augustus John, and playwright George Bernard Shaw. "Holroyd," Michele Field explains in *Publishers Weekly*, "approaches biography as a storyteller first and as an historian second." For the rights to his Shaw biography, Holroyd received 625,000 pounds, the highest price ever paid by a British publisher for a biography.

Holroyd's *Lytton Strachey: A Critical Biography* is considered by many reviewers to be a major achievement of the genre. Described by Eliot Fremont-Smith in the *New York Times* as an "enormous, sensitive and . . . definitive biography," *Lytton Strachey* was originally published in England in two volumes. The first volume, entitled *The Unknown Years, 1880-1910*, explores Strachey's youth through his college days at Cambridge University. The second volume, entitled *The Years of Achievement, 1910-1932*, looks at his early failures and disappointments as a writer and historian and chronicles the eventual success and fame he enjoyed until his death in 1932.

A *Times Literary Supplement* reviewer comments: "Together Mr. Holroyd's two volumes form a portrait of an epoch in literature which will not be superseded. Clear-cut, comprehensive, highly coloured and convincing, it will be recognized by contemporary readers and by those who come after as a splendid piece of work. . . . In addition to a portrait of Strachey Mr. Holroyd gives us a far-ranging survey of the most influential minds of the first three decades of this century whose sway is still felt over the background of our lives today." John Rothenstein of the *New York Times Book Review* considers Holroyd's study of Strachey "the best literary biography to appear for many years. It may well prove revolutionary in its effects by quickening the reading public's impatience with biographies that lack detailed treatment of the most intimate aspects of the subjects' lives."

Leonard Woolf, on the other hand, perhaps from his perspective as an actual acquaintance of Strachey, criticizes several elements of the first volume in a *New Statesman* review: "First, there is Mr. Holroyd's style. He is a heavy-handed and heavyminded writer. . . . [Secondly], Mr. Holroyd was ill-advised in his choice of a microscopic scale for Lytton's love affairs. Mr. Holroyd gives them to us at inordinate length and often recapitulates them with a commentary of his own. The book has a third, and still more serious, defect. . . . I think that Mr. Holroyd continually fails to understand people. . . . His misreading of Lytton's character is really fundamental." However, Volume II of the biography prompted Woolf, again writing in the *New Statesman*, to revise his original opinion: "In his second volume [Holroyd] does succeed in bringing Lytton to life, his strange character, his wit and brilliance—and—what was even more difficult—he brings to life the galaxy of strange men and women who for fifteen years circled round Lytton." And Robert Hughes states in *Time:* "With an imposing biography of Lytton Strachey, Holroyd became one of our best guides to the cultural life of England in the early 20th century. No one of his generation has done more to clarify the achievements and emotional imbrications of the Bloomsbury group, or to deflate its more self-enchanted pieties."

Holroyd's *Augustus John* is also recognized by most reviewers to be a major biographical work. This study of the artistic career and personal life of the British painter was also originally published in England in two volumes. According to Hilton Kramer in the *New York Times Book Review*, *Augustus John* is "at once extremely dramatic and extremely poignant, touched throughout by the humor that was an integral part of his hero's extravagant appetite for life, yet in the end a very sad story of wasted vitality and talent. Holroyd handles the rise and fall of this failed hero with consummate skill and an unfailing sympathy." "[Augustus John] was a remarkable character, taken by himself, and his family taken as a whole community is still more interesting," believes a reviewer for the *Economist*. The critic goes on to write that this "story is absorbing. . . . The book deserves nothing but praise." Keith Cushman comments in *Library Journal* that Holroyd did "an impressive job of research and interpretation" in writing *Augustus John*. "Holroyd vividly brings his subject to life and, along with him, the late Victorian and early twentieth century English artistic milieu."

Called by Dan H. Laurence in the Toronto *Globe and Mail* "the most thoughtfully and engagingly written" of Holroyd's biographies, *Bernard Shaw* is a massive three-volume work that took some twelve years to complete. The first major biography of Shaw since the 1950s, Holroyd's work was officially sanctioned by Shaw's estate. It draws upon a host of letters, diaries, and other personal papers to present the career and private life of the noted playwright. According to John Gross of the *New York*

Times, Holroyd "writes with insight, humor and a firm grasp of human—and Shavian—perversity. The book is not without its imperfections, but they don't count for very much in comparison with his achievement as a whole."

Discussing Holroyd's talents as a biographer, Eric Korn remarks in the *New Statesman:* "Holroyd, whose biographical manners are excellent, is like a knowledgeable guest, always ready with an introduction or a whispered biographical footnote, slyly encouraging his host to greater extravagances, relishing the disorder but never overwhelmed by it." A reviewer for the *Economist* comments that "Holroyd's virtues as a biographer are well known: among them are immense thoroughness and excellent marshalling of his data." Finally, Hughes writes in *Time:* "A great deal of the truth about a society lies in the lives of its minor artists. To write about them without falling into postures of condescension, gossip or overpraise is one of the toughest of all biographical feats. It requires a lack of sentiment, a close eye for social nuance and a sense of balance which not many biographers possess. Holroyd has it all."

Speaking of his background, Holroyd once explained: "I was partly brought up by grandparents and compensated for a life of passionate inactivity by filling my head with book-adventures. I have been much influenced by the work of Kingsmill which encouraged me to step from my own life into other peoples', where there appeared to be more going on."

BIOGRAPHICAL/CRITICAL SOURCES:

PERIODICALS

Antioch Review, spring, 1969.
Atlantic, April, 1969.
Book World, July 25, 1971.
Christian Science Monitor, January 30, 1969.
Economist, December 2, 1967, February 24, 1968, August 15, 1970, September 21, 1974, March 29, 1975.
Globe and Mail (Toronto), October 1, 1988, October 21, 1989.
Library Journal, September 15, 1975.
Los Angeles Times, November 4, 1988.
Nation, May 20, 1968.
New Republic, May 18, 1968, December 29, 1973, February 3, 1982.
New Statesman, October 6, 1967, February 23, 1968, March 26, 1971, September 27, 1974, April 18, 1975.
New York Review of Books, March 4, 1976, April 1, 1982.
New York Times, April 29, 1968, August 18, 1975, September 27, 1988, September 15, 1989.
New York Times Book Review, April 28, 1968, June 6, 1968, April 13, 1969, August 10, 1975, December 7, 1975, August 2, 1976, February 17, 1980.
New York Times Magazine, September 11, 1988.
Observer, October 7, 1979.
Publishers Weekly, October 14, 1988.
Saturday Review, April 27, 1968, January 12, 1974.
Spectator, September 21, 1974, March 29, 1975.
Time, May 10, 1968, September 29, 1975.
Times Literary Supplement, November 9, 1967, February 29, 1968, September 11, 1970, March 19, 1971, September 7, 1973, October 18, 1974, March 28, 1975, February 15, 1980, April 3, 1981.
Virginia Quarterly Review, winter, 1977.
Wall Street Journal, May 28, 1968.
Washington Post Book World, August 10, 1975, April 6, 1980.

HOPE, A(lec) D(erwent) 1907-

PERSONAL: Born July 21, 1907, in Cooma, New South Wales, Australia; son of Percival (a clergyman) and Florence Ellen (Scotford) Hope; married Penelope Robinson, May 27, 1937 (some sources say May 21, 1938); children: Emily, Andrew, Geoffrey. *Education:* Sydney University, B.A., 1928; Oxford University, B.A., c. 1930. *Politics:* None.

ADDRESSES: Home—66 Arthur Circle, Forrest, Canberra, Australian Capital Territory 2603, Australia. *Office*—Australian National University, Canberra, G.P.O. Box 4, Canberra 2601, Australia. *Agent*—Curtis Brown Ltd., 27 Union St., Paddington, Sydney, New South Wales 2021, Australia.

CAREER: New South Wales Department of Education, New South Wales, Australia, teacher of English, c. 1933-36; New South Wales Department of Labor and Industry, administrator of vocational tests and guidance counselor for Youth Employment Bureau, two years during the period, 1933-36; Sydney Teachers' College, Sydney, New South Wales, lecturer in English and education, c. 1937-45; University of Melbourne, Melbourne, New South Wales, senior lecturer in English, c. 1945-50; Canberra University College, Canberra, Australian Capital Territory, professor of English, c. 1950-60; Australian National University, Canberra, professor of English, c. 1960-68; library fellow, 1967-72, visiting fellow, beginning in 1973; Sweet Briar College, Sweet Briar, Va., Sue Read Slaughter Professor of Poetry, 1970-71.

MEMBER: Australian Academy of Humanities, Australian Society of Authors (president, 1966), American Academy and Institute of Arts and Letters (honorary member).

AWARDS, HONORS: Grace Levin Prize for Poetry, 1956; Arts Council of Great Britain award for poetry, 1965; Britannica Australian Award for Literature, 1966 (some sources say 1965); Volkswagen Award for Literature, 1966; Myer Award for Australian Literature, 1967; Levinson Prize for Poetry, 1969; Ingram Merrill Award for Literature, 1969; Officer of the Order of the British Empire, 1972; Litt.D., Australian National University, 1972, University of New England, 1973, Monish University, Melbourne, 1976, University of Melbourne, 1976; Companion of the Order of Australia, 1981.

WRITINGS:

The Wandering Islands (poems), Edwards Shaw (Sydney), 1956.
(Compiler) *Australian Poetry, 1960,* Angus & Robertson (Sydney), 1960.
Poems, Hamish Hamilton, 1960, Viking, 1961.
(And author of introduction) *Selected Poems,* Angus & Robertson (Sydney), 1963.
Australian Literature, 1950-1962, Melbourne University Press, 1963.
The Cave and the Spring (essays), Rigby (Adelaide), 1965, University of Chicago Press, 1970, 2nd edition, Sydney University Press, 1974.
Collected Poems, 1930-1965, Viking, 1966.
New Poems: 1965-1969, Angus & Robertson, 1969, Viking, 1970.
Dunciad Minor: An Heroick Poem, Melbourne University Press, 1970.
Midsummer Eve's Dream: Variations on a Theme by William Dunbar (essays), Viking, 1970.
Collected Poems: 1930-1970, Angus & Robertson, 1972.
Selected Poems, Angus & Robertson, 1973.
Native Companions: Essays and Comments on Australian Literature, 1936-1966, Angus & Robertson, 1974.
A Late Picking: Poems, 1965-1974, Angus & Robertson, 1975.

A Book of Answers (poems), Angus & Robertson, 1978.
The Pack of Autolycus (essays), Australian National University Press, 1978.
The New Cratylus: Notes on the Craft of Poetry, Oxford University Press, 1979.
The Drifting Continent, and Other Poems, illustrations by Arthur Boyd, Brindalbella Press (Canberra), c. 1979.
Antechinus: Poems, 1975-1980, Angus & Robertson, 1981.
The Tragical History of Doctor Faustus, Australian National University Press, 1982.
The Age of Reason (poems), Melbourne University Press, 1985.
Selected Poems, edited by Ruth Morse, Carcanet, 1986.
Ladies From the Sea (play), Melbourne University Press, 1987.

SIDELIGHTS: A. D. Hope, Australia's foremost poet, has been called "one of the two or three best poets writing in English." David Kalstone notes that "his poise and sophistication remind one often of Auden," and Samuel French Morse claims that "of the books to own from 1966, Hope's [*Collected Poems, 1930-1965*] is certainly the one."

Jean Garrigue has said that, "in a sense, Hope is literary the way many poets have ceased to be. He is not breaking down form and inviting chaos." Morse explains: "The powerful satiric thrust, the extraordinary sense of self-possession, the sensuality of his imagination, and the all but arrogant clarity of his poems are apparent from the beginning; and these qualities and characteristics are the more surprising in a time when the significant rhetorical gesture has grown increasingly flabby." Garrigue adds: "Syntax is never ambiguous [in Hope's poems]; he favors coherence and logical connections. . . . He rhymes, he works in stanzaic forms. He seems grandly at home in his orderly arrangements. The right word is usually in the right place, but since the poems move in terms of the line, not in terms of the word, the emphasis is on the large unit."

Hope himself, according to Garrigue, has said that "poetry is principally concerned to 'express' its subject and in doing so to create an emotion which is the feeling of the poem and not the feeling of the poet." His success in creating such a poetry might be confirmed by Kalstone, who writes: "It is rare to find—as one does with Hope—poems that depend so successfully on a shared sense of community. His audience is fixed in position, ready to follow the action within the proscenium his poems assume."

Kalstone believes that Hope's skill is "partly one of reinterpretation. The literary scene is one we know, but the characters have been assigned new positions on stage." Kalstone continues: "We are led through a very familiar gallery of mythological, historical and Biblical subjects, and we are asked to see the flash of energy behind the traditional pose. . . . To put it another way, modern settings draw forward Hope the satirist, jaunty but rather uniformly critical of mechanized, overcivilized lives. But he rises to the challenge of the fable. His real gift is for narrative—not so much telling a story, as retelling it with an air of wisdom and experience. The story is a *tableau vivant,* action halted at a moment of high feeling, nuances revealed by the measured order in which we are directed to gestures and landscapes. It is an index of the success of recent American poetry, introspective, often jagged, that declarative sentences, direct syntax, firmly rhymed stanzas should sound now a little strange. These last are precisely Hope's resources, his assured way of drawing us from detail to detail, finishing a picture which stands powerful and separate."

Marius Bewley, on the other hand, adds qualification to his praise of Hope, although he agrees that the poet is "an accomplished and attractive writer." Bewley writes: "Hope is usually, but not always, intelligent in his poetry. One of the hesitations one feels about him is that he often seems to arrive at his intelligent ideas and clever arguments first, and wraps them up in skillful metrics later." And "only very rarely does his language and thought seem organically fused, to share one bloodstream, one flesh, one life." But, Bewley adds, "at his best—and [Hope] is often at his best—his poems achieve a sustained, assured, and musical rhetorical mode of speech."

Both Kalstone and Garrigue believe that Hope's love poems are his best; "they are sensual, sumptuous, dazzling," writes Garrigue. "Without bizarreries or mad touches, they are 'square,' if you will, dedicated to the myth of beauty and joy."

Hope told *CA* that he is interested in philosophy, biology, and history, and that he has no interest in hobbies or sports. He has "some knowledge" of Latin, French, German, Italian, and Spanish. He adds that he has "no very fixed convictions on anything" and adjures us to "see Keats on negative capability."

BIOGRAPHICAL/CRITICAL SOURCES:

BOOKS

A. D. Hope: A Bibliography, Libraries Board of South Australia, 1968.
Contemporary Literary Criticism, Gale, Volume 3, 1975, Volume 51, 1989.

PERIODICALS

Contemporary Literature, winter, 1968.
New Leader, March 27, 1967.
New York Review of Books, May 18, 1967.
Partisan Review, fall, 1967.
Times Literary Supplement, April 7, 1978, February 22, 1980, August 22, 1986.
Village Voice, June 15, 1967.

* * *

HOPE, Brian
See CREASEY, John

* * *

HORATIO
See PROUST, (Valentin-Louis-George-Eugene-)Marcel

* * *

HORGAN, Paul 1903-

PERSONAL: Born August 1, 1903, in Buffalo, N.Y.; son of Edward Daniel and Rose Marie (Rohr) Horgan. *Education:* Attended New Mexico Military Institute, 1920-23. *Religion:* Roman Catholic.

ADDRESSES: Home—77 Pearl St., Middletown, Conn. 06457. *Office*—Wesleyan University, Middletown, Conn. 06457.

CAREER: Novelist, biographer, and writer on national, regional, and church history. Eastman Theatre, Rochester, N.Y., member of production staff, 1923-26; New Mexico Military Institute, Roswell, librarian, 1926-42, assistant to president, 1947-49; Wesleyan University, Middletown, Conn., fellow of Center for Advanced Studies, 1959 and 1961, director of Center, 1962-67, adjunct professor of English, 1967-71, professor emeritus and author-in-residence, 1971—. Visiting lecturer at University of Iowa, 1946, and Yale University, 1969; Saybrook College of Yale University, Hoyt fellow, 1965, associate fellow, 1966—; Aspen Institute for Humanistic Studies, scholar-in-residence, 1968, 1971, and 1973, fellow, 1973—; Pierpont Morgan Library, fellow, 1974—, member of council of fellows, 1975-79 and 1982, life fellow, 1977—.

President of board of directors, Roswell Museum, 1948-55; member of board of directors, Roswell Public Library, 1958-62, and Witter Bynner Foundation, 1972-79; chairman of board of directors, Santa Fe Opera, 1958-71; School of American Research, member of board of managers, 1959—, fellow, 1978; member of advisory board, John Simon Guggenheim Foundation, 1961-67; lay trustee, St. Joseph's College, West Hartford, Conn., 1964-68; Book-of-the-Month Club, member of board of judges, 1969-72, associate, 1972-73; trustee, Associates of Yale University Library, 1976-79; founding trustee, Lincoln County (N.M.) Heritage Trust, 1976—; member of national advisory board, Center for the Book, Library of Congress, 1978—. *Military service:* U.S. Army, chief of Army Information Branch, 1942-46; became lieutenant colonel; received Legion of Merit; recalled for temporary active duty with U.S. Army general staff, 1952.

MEMBER: American Catholic Historical Association (president, 1960), American Academy of Arts and Sciences (fellow), National Institute of Arts and Letters, Connecticut Academy of Arts and Sciences (fellow), Phi Beta Kappa, Athenaeum Club (London), Century Club, Yale Club (New York).

AWARDS, HONORS: Harper Prize Novel Award, 1933, for *The Fault of Angels;* Guggenheim fellow, 1945 and 1959; Pulitzer Prize in history, 1955, for *Great River,* and 1976, for *Lamy of Santa Fe;* Carr P. Collins Award, Texas Institute of Letters, 1955, for *Great River,* and 1976, for *Lamy of Santa Fe;* Bancroft Prize, Columbia University, 1955, for *Great River;* Campion Award for eminent service to Catholic letters, Catholic Book Club, 1957, for *The Centuries of Santa Fe;* created Knight of St. Gregory, 1957; National Catholic Book Award in fiction, Catholic Press Association, 1965, for *Things as They Are,* and 1969, for *Everything to Live For;* Jesse H. Jones Award, Texas Institute of Letters, 1971, for *Whitewater;* Western Writers of America Award and Christopher Book Award, both 1976, for *Lamy of Santa Fe;* Laetare Medal, University of Notre Dame, 1976; Baldwin Medal, Wesleyan University, 1982; Robert Kirsch Award for a body of work on the American West, *Los Angeles Times,* 1987; library at New Mexico Military Institute, Art Center of Roswell Museum, and gallery of Roswell Museum all named for Horgan.

Honorary degrees include Litt.D. from Wesleyan University, 1956, Southern Methodist University, 1957, University of Notre Dame, 1958, Boston College, 1958, New Mexico State University, 1961, College of the Holy Cross, 1962, University of New Mexico, 1963, Fairfield University, 1964, St. Mary's College, 1976, and Yale University, 1977; D.H.L. from Canisius College, 1960, Georgetown University, 1963, Lincoln College, 1968, Loyola College, Baltimore, 1968, D'Youville College, 1968, Pace University, 1968, St. Bonaventure University, 1970, La Salle University, 1971, and Catholic University of America, 1973.

WRITINGS:

A Tree on the Plains: A Music Play for Americans (score by Ernst Bacon; first produced in Spartanburg, S.C., May, 1942; produced in New York, 1943), A. L. Williams, 1942.
Songs after Lincoln (poems), Farrar, Straus, 1965.
The Clerihews of Paul Horgan (biographical poems), Wesleyan University Press, 1985.

NONFICTION

(Self-illustrated) *Men of Arms* (juvenile), McKay, 1931.
From the Royal City of the Holy Faith of St. Francis of Assissi: Being Five Accounts of Life in That Place (sketches originally published in *Yale Review*), Rydal, 1936.
(Author of preface) Robert Hunt, editor, *Selected Poems by Witter Bynner,* Knopf, 1936.
(Editor with Maurice Garland Fulton) *New Mexico's Own Chronicle: Three Races in the Writing of Four Hundred Years,* Upshaw, 1937.
(Author of biographical introduction) *Diary and Letters of Josiah Gregg,* University of Oklahoma Press, Volume I, 1941, Volume II, 1943.
(With the editors of *Look* magazine) *Look at America: The Southwest,* Houghton, 1947.
Great River: The Rio Grande in North American History (Book-of-the-Month Club alternate selection), two volumes, Rinehart, 1954, limited edition with Horgan's watercolor illustrations, 1954, published in a single volume, Holt, 1960.
(Self-illustrated) *The Centuries of Santa Fe,* Dutton, 1956, reprinted, Gannon, 1976.
Rome Eternal, Farrar, Straus, 1959.
Citizen of New Salem (biography; Book-of-the-Month Club selection), Farrar, Straus, 1961 (published in England as *Abraham Lincoln, Citizen of New Salem,* Macmillan, 1961).
Conquistadors in North American History, Farrar, Straus, 1963 (published in England as *Conquistadors in North America,* Macmillan, 1963).
Andrew Wyeth: An Exhibition of Watercolors, Temperas, and Drawings, Art Gallery, University of Arizona, 1963.
Peter Hurd: A Portrait Sketch from Life, University of Texas Press, 1965.
Memories of the Future, Farrar, Straus, 1966.
(Contributor) Bessie A. Stuart, compiler, *And Yet, Entirely Different,* Dearborn Public Schools, 1968.
The Heroic Triad: Essays in the Social Energies of Three Southwestern Cultures, Holt, 1970.
(Editor and author of introduction and commentary) *Maurice Baring Restored: Selections from His Work,* Farrar, Straus, 1970.
Encounters with Stravinsky: A Personal Record, Farrar, Straus, 1972.
Approaches to Writing, Farrar, Straus, 1973, 2nd edition, Wesleyan University Press, 1988.
Ernst Bacon: A Contemporary Tribute, [Orinda, Calif.], 1974.
Lamy of Santa Fe: His Life and Times, Farrar, Straus, 1975.
Josiah Gregg and His Vision of the Early West, Farrar, Straus, 1979.
A Certain Climate: Essays in History, Arts, and Letters, Wesleyan University Press, 1988.
A Writer's Eye: Field Notes and Watercolors, Abrams, 1988.

FICTION

The Fault of Angels, Harper, 1933.
No Quarter Given, Harper, 1935.
Main Line West (also see below), Harper, 1936.
The Return of the Weed (short stories), Harper, 1936 (published in England as *Lingering Walls,* Constable, 1936), reprinted, Northland Press, 1980.
A Lamp on the Plains, Harper, 1937, reprinted, Popular Library, 1964.
Far from Cibola (also see below), Harper, 1938, reprinted, University of New Mexico Press, 1974.
The Habit of Empire, Rydal, 1938.
Figures in a Landscape (short stories), Harper, 1940.

The Common Heart (also see below), Harper, 1942.

The Devil in the Desert (also see below), Longmans, Green, 1952.

One Red Rose for Christmas (also see below), Longmans, Green, 1952.

Humble Powers (contains *The Devil in the Desert, One Red Rose for Christmas,* and "To the Castle"), Macmillan (London), 1954, Image Books, 1956.

(Self-illustrated) *The Saintmaker's Christmas Eve,* Farrar, Straus, 1957, reprinted, Paperback Library, 1971.

A Distant Trumpet, Farrar, Straus, 1960.

Mountain Standard Time (contains *Main Line West, Far from Cibola,* and *The Common Heart*), Farrar, Straus, 1962.

Toby and the Nighttime (juvenile), Ariel Books, 1963.

Things as They Are, Farrar, Straus, 1964.

The Peach Stone: Stories from Four Decades (includes *The Devil in the Desert*), Farrar, Straus, 1967.

Everything to Live For, Farrar, Straus, 1968.

Whitewater (Reader's Digest Condensed Book Club selection; Book-of-the-Month Club and Literary Guild alternate selection), Farrar, Straus, 1970.

The Thin Mountain Air, Farrar, Straus, 1977.

Mexico Bay: A Novel of the Mid-Century (Book-of-the-Month Club alternate selection), Farrar, Straus, 1982.

Of America, East and West: Selections from the Writings of Paul Horgan, Farrar, Straus, 1984.

Under the Sangre de Cristo (sketches originally published in the *Yale Review* and elsewhere), Rydal Press, 1985.

Short stories represented in many anthologies, including *Folk-Say: A Regional Miscellany,* four volumes, edited by B. A. Botkin, University of Oklahoma Press, 1929-32; *O. Henry Memorial Award Prize Stories of 1931,* edited by Blanche Colton Williams, Doubleday, 1931; *Prose, Poetry and Drama for Oral Interpretation,* edited by W. J. Forma, Harper, 1936; *O. Henry Memorial Award Prize Stories of 1936,* edited by Harry Hansen, Doubleday, 1936; *Short Stories from the "New Yorker,"* Simon & Schuster, 1940.

Author of play "Yours, A. Lincoln," first produced in New York, July 9, 1942. Contributor of stories, articles, and essays to periodicals, including *Harper's, Atlantic, Yale Review, North American Review, Direction, America, Good Housekeeping, Ladies' Home Journal, Southwest Review, Theatre Arts, Horizon, Vanity Fair, Saturday Evening Post,* and *Collier's.*

SIDELIGHTS: Though a prolific writer exercising his talents in a wide variety of genres, Paul Horgan is known "primarily [as] a novelist and historian of the West," writes Jonathan Yardley in the *Washington Post Book World.* "His is not the West of Zane Grey and Louis L'Amour," Yardley explains, "but that of Willa Cather: a West of pioneers and settlers, of priests and ranchers, of ordinary people set down in an extraordinary landscape." Horgan's works on the land and people of the West, particularly the Southwest, have received much praise and many awards—including two Pulitzer Prizes in history—because of his knowledge of the region and his solid craftsmanship. "Few men know the Southwest as well as Paul Horgan," says J. F. Bannon in *America,* "[but] fewer still can write of it, its history and its peoples, with [the] same feeling and understanding." Horgan's success also stems from the larger concerns in his works. "Horgan is at once regional and transcontinental," notes Robert Gish in the *Chicago Tribune Book World,* for he is preoccupied with "the great American themes of the East's contact with the West." He has become, according to *Publishers Weekly* editor John F. Baker, "one of the Grand Old Men of American literature."

Much of Horgan's fiction is set in the Southwest, the region in which he has spent over half his life since moving to New Mexico at the age of twelve. The characters are often descendants of the Indians and Spaniards who first tried to control the land as well as Anglo-Americans of a later generation who impose new ways and traditions upon the old. "For both groups Horgan shows infinite understanding and sympathy," states James M. Day in his critical study *Paul Horgan.* "Having lived in New Mexico for so many years himself, he could hardly escape the mingling of the two traditions and the effect they have on the people. Although a historian of stature, it is less his grasp of the facts of the Southwestern past than his absorption of the atmosphere of the place that distinguishes his fiction."

Horgan's greatest mark of success as a Southwestern fiction writer is, according to Day, his ability to capture the spirit of both the Indian-Spanish and the Anglo-American cultures without judging either. Specifically, Day cites Horgan's expression of their radically different approaches to the land itself: "Unlike those descended from Indians and Spaniards, [the Anglo-Americans who are the main characters in Horgan's novels] do not merely accept their place as part of the land, but they must consciously adopt a relationship to it. For them it is almost a matter of will to accept the land, while for the native the relationship simply *is.* For the Indian, his entire life is part of a great whole, encompassing past, present, and future in the eternal face of the land itself, about which there is no necessity to think. . . . Horgan's recognition of the distinction between these two modes of thought marks the depth of his understanding of the people of the Southwest."

A characteristic of Horgan's fiction "remarked upon most frequently," claims Day, "is his descriptive power, particularly when writing of the land itself." Also illustrator for several of his books and many of the jackets, Horgan has been widely praised for his capacity to evoke a scene through words as well as through watercolors. Nevertheless, "the heart of Horgan's books is not the land or what it represents," concludes Day, "but the people who inhabit it. . . . Set against the unchanging background of the plains and mountains of the Southwest, this [approach] is particularly effective."

Horgan's characteristic focus on the people who inhabit the Southwest is also evident in his nonfiction works, particularly in *Great River* and *Lamy of Santa Fe,* both winners of the Pulitzer Prize in history. *Great River* is an account of the Rio Grande and the people who have lived beside it through two thousand years of history. Divided chronologically by the four cultures that dominate the river valley—Indian, Spanish, Mexican, and Anglo-American—the book includes chapters on the elements of belief, custom, group behavior, and social energy that give each culture its unique style. Writing in *Saturday Review,* Walter Prescott Webb claims, "these chapters on social history may in time prove to be the most valuable portions of the work because [Horgan brings] to bear here a keen insight into the lives of those who have lived on and near the river's bank. . . . His acquaintance with the sources, and with individuals along the river and away from it that know them, is amazing."

The expertise Horgan acquired for *Great River* did not come quickly or easily. Traveling the river's full length of 1,800 miles three times and making dozens of shorter trips, he spent ten years researching and writing the two-volume opus. Moreover, Webb says, "Horgan tells us that [*Great River* had] been in the making since he came to Albuquerque at the age of [twelve]. I for one understand what he means. I doubt that anyone can really know an arid land who has not lived long in it, lived there when young to absorb its spirit before he can convey its charm and mystery."

In praising *Great River,* reviewers single out not only Horgan's knowledge of the subject but also his ability to effectively, and often poetically, communicate that knowledge. William deBuys, who in the *New Republic* calls the book "as good a digest of the American frontier experience as one may hope to find," believes that what "sets *Great River* apart [from other histories] and is its finest virtue is Horgan's ability to inspirit human events with the flavor and feeling of the land that spawned them. The stage he sets is broad, permanent. In the background one feels the pulse of the land and its river; they endure." "Paul Horgan is an artist," states J. Frank Dobie in the *New York Times Book Review,* "which means that he is a master of proportions, perspective, and details. [*Great River*] is an unfoldment of life with stretches of narrative as vivid as 'Livy's pictured page' and essays as bold as the divagations of Henry Fielding." Orville Prescott comments in the *New York Times:* "Horgan writes about [each culture and its way of life] with harsh realism and every appearance of objective judgment. But he writes so well, with such skill in capturing the typical emotion of the past, that *Great River* seems almost a romantic book in spite of his best efforts—which is only fitting and proper, for all history, if regarded correctly as the amazing story of men, is romantic."

James M. Day states that *Great River* has been charged with weakness in bibliography and questionable statements of historical interpretation, but he defends Horgan against all these charges: "Horgan suffers the inevitable fate of any man who tries to combine the discipline of history and the imagination of literature. The historians condemn him for sacrificing facts for a personal interpretation of truth, and the critics condemn him for sacrificing literary design to the undisciplined pattern of man's past. Both are right, in a sense, though the criticism is somewhat unjustified because it attacks the writer on grounds of not accomplishing what he has no intention of doing to begin with."

One of Horgan's intentions for *Great River* was to include a sketch he had written on the life of Jean Baptiste Lamy, first bishop of Santa Fe and the inspiration for Willa Cather's novel *Death Comes for the Archbishop.* But Horgan decided to withdraw it from *Great River* and keep it for later expansion. A few years later he began detailed research for a biography of the priest, after gaining access to the archives of the Catholic Church in the Vatican. Containing correspondence dealing with church affairs and missions around the world, the archives "gave him a great deal of hitherto unavailable information about Lamy's early life," notes John F. Baker. Horgan also utilized the archives of American church history at the University of Notre Dame and traveled to Mexico in his quest for information. "Writing this one man's life," Horgan told Baker, "took even more research than writing the whole history and geography of a river spanning thousands of miles." But as with *Great River,* Horgan's efforts were rewarded with a Pulitzer Prize in history and much critical acclaim.

Reviewing *Lamy of Santa Fe* in the *Washington Post Book World,* Jonathan Yardley believes that in Horgan, "Lamy has found his fit biographer, a man devoted as he to the Southwest and as firm in thought and language." "Horgan does better than serve his subject," insists Dennis Halac in *Commonweal.* "This illuminating study," continues Halac, "rises out of its regional interest, not only because of its associations with Cather and Horgan, but as a work of biographical art. The reader is given an excursion into Lamy's life . . . to express a biography with the finest literary standards and, thus, the greatest possible satis-

faction." Colman McCarthy, writing in the *New Republic,* also praises Horgan's technique: "Horgan's scholarship avoids heaviness, and he also stays clear of the candlestick prose that all too often drips the wax of piety whenever the life of a holy man is recounted. Solid and detached biographies of the saintly are uncommon, [and] the excellence of Horgan's work is not accidental."

Lamy of Santa Fe separates much fact about the archbishop from the fiction of Cather's novel, *Death Comes for the Archbishop,* according to Michael Rogin in the *New York Times Book Review.* "Cather invented Lamy's relationship to Indian culture," notes Rogin, "along with the vignettes and Indian friendships to sustain it. . . . Lamy's opposition to the reservation policy is also fiction, not history. So, too, apparently, his criticism of slavery. . . . The historical Lamy promoted the railroad and other instruments of Yankee progress; newcomers blamed him for changing the traditional Southwest. Nostalgia for the architecture and life of old New Mexico, Horgan warns, reads twentieth-century attitudes back into Lamy's time."

Yet, as Halac points out, *Lamy of Santa Fe* contains some improvisations of its own: "the ceremony of Lamy's investiture derived from the ordinals; a sidetrip by young French missionaries to Niagara Falls where they reflect upon Chateaubriand's impressions, which were popular then; Lamy's pious view of Rome contrasted by a contemporary account of Henry James." Halac considers "these inspired innovations" to be the "finest touches in the book," because they "flesh out a story that, in less sensitive hands, could become tedious or spotty. I cannot recall a biography that uses its material so suggestively, not with distortion or as mere embellishment but to knit it into one piece."

"From Mr. Horgan's pages," surmises F. D. Reeve in the *Yale Review,* "emerges a portrait of a wise, patient, tolerant, self-sacrificing, faithful administrator whose design was to improve the physical and moral conditions of all men in the society in which he served. Mr. Horgan's affectionate re-creation of Archbishop Lamy, splendidly documented in rich detail yet portrayed with a master novelist's skill, shows that the West was won in a final sense not by the guns that killed the Indians but by the faith that directed the conquerors' labors." "The life of Lamy," concludes Jonathan Yardley, "with its beguiling mixture of deep spirituality and frontier courage, seems to epitomize the characteristics that Horgan admires, in the desert setting with which he is most comfortable."

MEDIA ADAPTATIONS: Horgan's novel *One Red Rose for Christmas* was adapted into a one-act play, *One Red Rose,* by Sister Mary Olive O'Connell, which was published by Longmans, Green in 1954 and produced on television in 1958. In other television presentations of *One Red Rose* at Christmastime, Helen Hayes appeared twice, and a later dramatic reading was given by Horgan and Ruth Hill on ABC-TV. *A Distant Trumpet* was filmed by Warner Bros. in 1964, and the movie starred Troy Donahue.

BIOGRAPHICAL/CRITICAL SOURCES:

BOOKS

Contemporary Literary Criticism, Gale, Volume IX, 1978, Volume LIII, 1989.
Day, James M., *Paul Horgan,* Steck-Vaughn, 1967.
Dictionary of Literary Biography Yearbook: 1985, Gale, 1986.
Horgan, Paul, *Encounters with Stravinsky: A Personal Record,* Farrar, Straus, 1972.

PERIODICALS

America, October 10, 1970, October 11, 1975.
Atlantic, April, 1961, October, 1970, October, 1975.
Best Sellers, September 1, 1964, August 1, 1970, October 1, 1970.
Books, August 27, 1933, February 3, 1935, March 22, 1936, March 21, 1937, April 21, 1940.
Christian Science Monitor, October 14, 1954, January 24, 1963, October 1, 1970, June 28, 1972.
Commonweal, June 19, 1936, June 24, 1960, October 23, 1970, March 26, 1976.
Critic, winter, 1975.
Life, October 9, 1970.
Los Angeles Times, March 4, 1982.
Los Angeles Times Book Review, May 29, 1988.
Nation, November 2, 1970.
New Republic, March 23, 1938, December 21, 1942, February 7, 1976.
Newsweek, November 29, 1954, September 12, 1977.
New Yorker, December 4, 1954, September 12, 1977.
New York Herald Tribune Book Review, January 30, 1935, October 10, 1954, October 24, 1954, May 5, 1957, April 17, 1960.
New York Review of Books, November 5, 1970.
New York Times, August 27, 1933, February 3, 1935, March 22, 1936, March 14, 1937, March 6, 1938, April 21, 1940, November 22, 1942, March 23, 1952, October 11, 1954, December 18, 1955, October 7, 1956, September 22, 1957, July 10, 1969, September 1, 1970, September 26, 1970, May 8, 1976.
New York Times Book Review, October 10, 1954, May 5, 1957, April 17, 1960, April 23, 1961, August 2, 1964, June 19, 1966, May 14, 1967, August 25, 1968, August 27, 1970, September 27, 1970, July 2, 1972, October 5, 1975, September 11, 1977, January 18, 1981, March 28, 1982.
Publishers Weekly, July 14, 1975.
Reporter, April 25, 1963.
San Francisco Chronicle, September 23, 1957.
Saturday Review, September 16, 1954, October 16, 1954, December 8, 1956, October 5, 1957, April 23, 1960, August 8, 1964, August 12, 1967, August 31, 1968, October 3, 1970, August 9, 1975, September 17, 1977.
Saturday Review of Literature, August 26, 1933, February 9, 1935, March 21, 1936, April 9, 1937, January 2, 1943.
Saturday Review of the Society, July 29, 1972.
Spectator, August 9, 1935.
Time, January 24, 1955, May 2, 1960, October 12, 1970, November 10, 1975.
Times Literary Supplement, July 25, 1935, March 26, 1971, December 22, 1972.
Washington Post, December 1, 1979.
Washington Post Book World, September 8, 1968, January 31, 1971, June 18, 1972, August 17, 1975, October 23, 1977, February 21, 1982.
Yale Review, winter, 1973, winter, 1976.

*   *   *

HORSELY, Ramsbottom
See BERNE, Eric (Lennard)

*   *   *

HOUDINI
See LOVECRAFT, H(oward) P(hillips)

HOUSMAN, A(lfred) E(dward)   1859-1936
(Tristram)

PERSONAL: Born March 26, 1859, in Fockbury, Worcestershire, England; died April 30 (some sources say May 1; one source says October 30), 1936, in Cambridge, England; son of Edward (a solicitor) and Sarah Jane (Williams) Housman. *Education:* St. John's College, Oxford, pass degree, 1882; received M.A. *Politics:* Tory.

CAREER: Her Majesty's Patent Office, London, England, civil servant, 1882-92; University of London, University College, London, professor of Latin, 1892-1911; Cambridge University, Trinity College, Cambridge, England, Kennedy Professor of Latin, 1911-36.

WRITINGS:

POETRY

A Shropshire Lad, Kegan Paul, 1896, J. Lane, 1900, reprinted, with notes and biography by Carl J. Weber, Greenwood Press, 1980.
Last Poems, Holt, 1922.
More Poems, edited by brother, Laurence Housman, Knopf, 1936.
The Collected Poems of A. E. Housman, J. Cape, 1939, Holt, 1940, revised edition published as *Collected Poems,* Penguin Books, 1956, Holt, 1965.
Manuscript Poems: Eight Hundred Lines of Hitherto Uncollected Verse from the Author's Notebooks, edited by Tom Burns Haber, University of Minnesota Press, 1955 (published in England as *The Manuscript Poems of A. E. Housman: Eight Hundred Lines of Hitherto Uncollected Verse from the Author's Notebooks,* Oxford University Press, 1955).
Complete Poems: Centennial Edition, introduction by Basil Davenport, commentary by Tom Burns Haber, Holt, 1959.

EDITOR

(With others) *M. Manilii Astronomica,* five volumes, Grant Richards, 1903-30, published as *Astronomicon,* Georg Olms, 1972.
D. Junii Juvenalis Saturae, Grant Richards, 1905, revised edition, Cambridge University Press, 1931, published as *Saturae,* Greenwood Press, 1969.
M. Annaei Lucani Belli civilis libri decem, Basil Blackwell, 1926, Harvard University Press, 1950.

LECTURES

Introductory Lecture, Delivered Before the Faculties of Arts and Laws and of Science in University College, London, October 3, 1892, Cambridge University Press, 1892, Macmillan, 1937.
The Name and Nature of Poetry, Macmillan, 1933.
The Confines of Criticism: The Cambridge Inaugural, 1911, notes by John Carter, Cambridge University Press, 1969.

LETTERS

Thirty Housman Letters to Witter Bynner, edited by Tom Burns Haber, Knopf, 1957.
A. E. Housman to Joseph Ishill: Five Unpublished Letters, edited by William White, Oriole Press, 1959.
The Letters of A. E. Housman, edited by Henry Maas, Harvard University Press, 1971.
Sir James G. Frazer and A. E. Housman: A Relationship in Letters, Duke University Press, 1974.

Fifteen Letters to Walter Ashburner, introduction and notes by Alan S. Bell, Tragara Press, c. 1976.

COLLECTIONS

A Centennial Memento, commentary by William White, Oriole Press, 1959.

A. E. Housman: Selected Prose, edited by John Carter, Cambridge University Press, 1961.

Poetry and Prose: A Selection, edited by F. C. Horwood, Hutchinson, 1971.

The Classical Papers of A. E. Housman, three volumes, collected and edited by J. Diggle and F. R. D. Goodyear, Cambridge University Press, 1972.

Collected Poems and Selected Prose, edited by Christopher Ricks, Allen Lane, 1988.

OTHER

Co-founder, with A. W. Pollard, of undergraduate periodical *Ye Rounde Table.* Contributor of more than one hundred articles to scholarly journals, including *Classical Review* and *Journal of Philology;* contributor, under pseudonym Tristram, to *Ye Rounde Table.*

SIDELIGHTS: At first glance nothing seems more unlikely than that the poet of the enormously popular *A Shropshire Lad* should be the classical scholar A. E. Housman. This Cambridge University professor of Latin left no doubt as to his priorities: the emendation of classical texts was both an intellectual search for the truth and his life's work; poetry was an emotional and physiological experience that began with a sensation in the pit of the stomach. The apparent discrepancies in this man who became both a first-rate scholar and a celebrated poet should be a reminder that, whatever else poetry does, it also records the interior life, a life that has its roots well beneath the academic gown or the business suit. Furthermore, in Housman's case, though he did aspire to be a great scholar first, scrutiny of his life and work reveals that he valued poetry more highly than he often admitted and that many of the presumed conflicts between the classical scholar and the romantic poet dissolve in the personality of the man.

Though the modern student is usually more interested in Housman's poetry than his textual criticism, some survey of his scholarship is important for an appreciation of his overall contribution and of the cast of mind that could be so devoted—and so imperious—in the search for truth. From his early work on Propertius at Oxford University through his professorship at University College, London, and culminating in his office as Kennedy Professor of Latin at Cambridge University, Housman was not interested in the interpretation of the works of the classical writers he treated. Instead, he was solely involved in the establishment of reliable texts of their works. This process usually required the peeling away of centuries of error made by previous editors, whom Housman frequently treated with unmitigated scorn. In "The Application of Thought to Textual Criticism," a paper presented to the Classical Association at Cambridge in 1921 and collected in John Carter's 1961 edition of the writer's prose, Housman described textual criticism as both a science and an art, requiring reason and common sense. As a science, however, it was not exact, he declared: "A textual critic engaged upon his business is not at all like Newton investigating the motion of the planets: he is much more like a dog hunting for fleas." Housman railed against the prevailing practice of accepting earlier manuscripts as better manuscripts or of accepting all readings—however inane—within a manuscript simply because of the authority of the whole. In this regard he criticized scholars

for being lazy, and this tone of moral rectitude permeated the entire paper. Many scholars, he said, are stupid, lazy, vain—or all three. His last sentence put a cap on it: "Knowledge is good, method is good, but one thing beyond all others is necessary; and that is to have a head, not a pumpkin, on your shoulders, and brains, not pudding, in your head."

Concerning Housman's own reputation as a classical scholar, D. R. Shackleton Bailey in a 1959 *Listener* article said that he was "beyond serious dispute, among the greatest of all time." Bailey spoke of the scholar's "passionate zeal to see each one of the innumerable problems in his text not as others had presented it or as he might have preferred it to appear but exactly as it was." Housman's greatest single textual work was his five-volume edition of the *Astronomica* of Manilius, a first century A.D. Latin poet. The first volume of this work was published in 1903 and the last in 1930. That Housman chose Manilius, a second-rate poet, over Propertius or any of the other better writers with whom he was familiar reveals his desire to establish for himself an unassailable reputation, for as Andrew S. F. Gow declared in *A. E. Housman,* the scholar realized that the *Astronomica* of Manilius provided him the greatest opportunity "of approaching finality in the solution of the problems presented." In a letter to Housman's biographer Graves, G. P. Goold, a later holder of the Latin chair at University College, summed up the scholar's accomplishments: "The legacy of Housman's scholarship is a thing of permanent value; and that value consists less in obvious results, the establishment of general propositions about Latin and the removal of scribal mistakes, than in the shining example he provides of a wonderful mind at work. . . . He was and may remain the last great textual critic. . . . And if we accord [Richard] Bentley the honour of being England's greatest Latinist, it will be largely because Housman declined to claim the title for himself."

It was at University College that Housman experienced his most sustained period of poetry composition, and the main fruit of this period was the publication of *A Shropshire Lad* in 1896. First offered to Macmillan Company in 1896 under the title "Poems by Terence Hearsay," *A Shropshire Lad* was rejected by that publisher: it was subsequently brought out in the same year by Kegan Paul, with the change in the title suggested by Housman's friend Alfred Pollard. The book was published at the author's own expense, and he insisted that he receive no royalties. There wouldn't have been many anyway, since Kegan Paul printed only five hundred copies, and, as Maude M. Hawkins noted in *A. E. Housman: Man Behind a Mask,* the book "sold so slowly that Laurence Housman at the end of two years bought up the last few copies." Though the volume was better appreciated in the United States than in England—Hawkins called most of the critical reviews "lukewarm or adverse." *A Shropshire Lad* did not sell well until it was published by Grant Richards, a man with whom Housman became lifelong friends. Richards's first edition was five hundred copies in 1897, which sold out; he then printed one thousand copies in 1900 followed by two thousand in 1902. Hawkins summed up the volume's early public reception: "After the slow stream of Housman readers from 1896 to 1903, the momentum of popularity increased rapidly. During this period *A Shropshire Lad* had been reviewed in thirty-three periodicals with both praise and condemnation."

During the twentieth century *A Shropshire Lad* has been more of a popular than a critical success. Looking back to the heyday of the book's success, George Orwell remarked in *Inside the Whale and Other Essays:* "Among people who were adolescent in the years 1910-25, Housman had an influence which was enormous and is now [1957] not at all easy to understand. In 1920, when I was about seventeen, I probably knew the whole of *A Shropshire Lad* by heart." In accounting for this popularity, Orwell spoke of certain elements in the poetry: a snobbism about belonging to the country; the adolescent themes of murder, suicide, unhappy love, and early death; and a "bitter, defiant paganism, a conviction that life is short and the gods are against you, which exactly fitted the prevailing mood of the young."

In all of his poetry, Housman continually returns to certain favorite themes. The predominant theme, discussed by Cleanth Brooks in the Ricks collection of essays, is that of time and the inevitability of death. As Brooks said, "Time is, with Housman, always the enemy." In the first poem of *A Shropshire Lad,* "1887," one of the few to be titled, the conventional patriotism of the Queen's jubilee is shot through with the irony that God can only save the Queen with the help of those who have died for her sake: "The saviours come not home tonight: / Themselves they could not save." Housman frequently deals with the plight of the young soldier, and he is usually able to maintain sympathy both for the youth who is the victim of war and for the patriotic cause of the nation. Robert B. Pearsall suggested in a 1967 *PMLA* essay that Housman dealt frequently with soldiers because "the uniform tended to cure isolation and unpopularity, and soldiers characteristically bask in mutual affection."

It is not only war but nature, too, that brings on thoughts of death in Housman's poetry. In the famous *Shropshire Lad* lyric beginning "Loveliest of trees, the cherry now," the speaker says that since life is all too short, he will go out "To see the cherry hung with snow," an obvious suggestion of death. In a well-known verse from *Last Poems,* a particularly wet and old spring causes the speaker to move from a description of nature—"The chestnut casts his flambeaux, and the flowers stream from the hawthorn on the wind away"—to a sense that his lost spring brings one closer to the grave, which, in turn, occasions a splenetic remark about the deity: "Whatever brute and blackguard made the world." To his credit, Housman often does not merely wallow in such pessimistic feelings but counsels a kind of stoical endurance as the proper response: "Shoulder the sky, my lad, and drink your ale." When the sky cannot be shouldered, a type of Roman suicide may be appropriate, as in "Shot? so quick, so clean an ending?" or in another *Shropshire Lad* poem, which ends with the lines: "But play the man, stand up and end you, / When your sickness is your soul."

Another frequent theme in Housman's poetry, one that is related to the death motif, is the attitude that the universe is cruel and hostile, created by a God who has abandoned it. In the poem "Epitaph on an Army of Mercenaries" in *Last Poems,* mercenaries must take up the slack for an uncaring deity: "What God abandoned, these defended, / And saved the sum of things for pay." In such a world where "malt does more than Milton can / To justify God's ways to man," as the lyricist wrote in *A Shropshire Lad,* poetry can serve the purpose of inuring one to the harshness of reality. R. Kowalczyk, in a 1967 *Cithara* essay, summed up this prevalent theme: "Housman's poetic characters fail to find divine love in the universe. They confront the enormity of space and realize that they are victims of Nature's blind forces. A number of Housman's lyrics scrutinize with cool, detached irony the impersonal universe, the vicious world in which man was placed to endure his fated existence."

Within such a universe, the pastoral theme of the preciousness of youth and youthful beauty is everywhere to be found. In "To an Athlete Dying Young," the youth is praised for leaving a world with his accomplishments intact. Like the young girl Lucy in romantic poet William Wordsworth's lyrics, Housman's

youths sometimes die into nature and become part of the natural surroundings: "By brooks too broad for leaping / The lightfoot boys are laid; / The rose-lipt girls are sleeping / In fields where roses fade." But as Brooks declared, as recorded in Ricks's collection of essays, Housman's nature cannot be the same as Wordsworth's after the century's achievement in science: "Housman's view of nature looks forward to our time rather than back to that of Wordsworth. If nature is lovely and offers man delight, she does not offer him solace or sustain him as Wordsworth was solaced and sustained. For between Wordsworth and Housman there interpose themselves Darwin and Huxley and Tindall—the whole achievement of Victorian science."

Furthermore, society sometimes intrudes into Housman's world of nature, and when it does, the rustic youth frequently comes in conflict with it. As Oliver Robinson noted in *Angry Dust: The Poetry of A. E. Housman,* "Housman is especially sympathetic with the man who is at odds with society, the man who cannot keep 'these foreign laws of God and man.'" In one poem from *A Shropshire Lad,* the speaker pities the condemned man in Shrewsbury jail whom he calls "a better lad, if things went right, / Than most that sleep outside."

The themes of his poetry and his emotional handling of them mark Housman as an extension of the romantic movement that flourished in England in the early part of the nineteenth century and had a resurgence in the aesthetic movement of the 1890s. The critical evaluation of Housman's work in the two decades after his death in 1936 is tinged with the anti-romanticism of the period. The directness and simplicity of much of Housman's poetry were viewed as faults. In *A. E. Housman and W. B. Yeats* Richard Aldington reported a rumor that circulated about Cambridge University to the effect that when influential critic I. A. Richards left Housman's Cambridge inaugural lecture he was heard to say: "This had put us back ten years." And Cyril Connolly, in a 1936 *New Statesman* article reprinted in Ricks's collection, said that Housman's poems "are of a triteness of technique equalled only by the banality of thought." He also talked about the limitations of the poet's themes of man's mortality and rebellion against his lot.

By seeing irony in Housman's poetic technique, however, one can mitigate some of what would otherwise be considered faults: the adolescent nature of some of the thought and the sentimental handling of it. Christopher Ricks, in the essay in his collection on Housman, noted that "everyone seems to take it for granted that Housman's poems unwaveringly endorse the pessimistic beliefs which they assert. To me his poems are remarkable for the ways in which rhythm and style temper or mitigate or criticize what in bald paraphrase the poem would be saying."

Regardless of whether one finds irony in the author's poetic technique, it is true that Housman tried to place some distance between himself and his work. Referring to *A Shropshire Lad* in a letter written in 1933, Housman stated that "very little in the book is biographical" and said that his view of the world was "owing to my observation of the world, not to personal circumstances." As to the county of Shropshire itself, Housman admitted in a letter to Maurice Pollet: "I was born in Worcestershire, not Shropshire, where I have never spent much time."

In his roles as classical scholar and as poet, Housman exhibited an unswerving integrity. While this integrity served him well in his classical endeavors, in his poetry it may have relegated him to a rank below that of the major poets of his age. His poetry, based as it is on emotion, never went beyond what he could verify with his own feelings. As Edmund Wilson said in an essay appearing in the Ricks collection, "His world has no opening horizons; it is a prison that one can only endure. One can only come the same painful cropper over and over again and draw from it the same bitter moral." But few writers have expressed this dark if limited vision with more poignancy and clarity than Housman.

BIOGRAPHICAL/CRITICAL SOURCES:

BOOKS

Aldington, Richard, *A. E. Housman and W. B. Yeats,* Peacock Press, 1955.

Carter, John, editor, *A. E. Housman: Selected Prose,* Cambridge University Press, 1961.

Dictionary of Literary Biography, Volume 19: *British Poets, 1840-1914,* Gale, 1983.

Empson, William, *Some Versions of Pastoral,* New Directions, 1960.

Gow, Andrew S. F., *A. E. Housman,* Macmillan, 1936.

Graves, Richard Perceval, *A. E. Housman: The Scholar-Poet,* Scribner, 1979.

Haber, Tom Burns, editor, *The Making of "A Shropshire Lad": A Manuscript Variorum,* University of Washington Press, 1966.

Haber, Tom Burns, *A. E. Housman,* Twayne, 1967.

Hawkins, Maude M., *A. E. Housman: Man Behind a Mask,* Henry Regnery, 1958.

Housman, A. E., *A Shropshire Lad,* Kegan Paul, 1896.

Housman, A. E., *Last Poems,* Holt, 1922.

Housman, A. E., *More Poems,* edited by Laurence Housman, Knopf, 1936.

Housman, A. E., *Manuscript Poems: Eight Hundred Lines of Hitherto Uncollected Verse from the Author's Notebooks,* edited by Tom Burns Haber, University of Minnesota Press, 1955.

Housman, Laurence, *My Brother, A. E. Housman,* Scribner, 1938.

Leggett, B. J., *Housman's Land of Lost Content: A Critical Study of "A Shropshire Lad,"* University of Tennessee Press, 1970.

Leggett, B. J., *The Poetic Art of A. E. Housman: Theory and Practice,* University of Nebraska Press, 1978.

Marlow, Norman, *A. E. Housman: Scholar and Poet,* Routledge & Kegan Paul, 1958.

Orwell, George, *Inside the Whale and Other Essays,* Penguin Books, 1957.

Page, Norman, *A. E. Housman: A Critical Biography,* Schocken, 1983.

Richards, Grant, *Housman, 1897-1936,* Oxford University Press, 1942.

Ricks, Christopher, editor, *A. E. Housman: A Collection of Critical Essays,* Prentice-Hall, 1968.

Robinson, Oliver, *Angry Dust: The Poetry of A. E. Housman,* Bruce Humphries, 1950.

Scott-Kilvert, Ian, *A. E. Housman,* Longman, 1955.

Sparrow, John, *Controversial Essays,* Chilmark House, 1966.

Symons, Katharine E. and others, *Alfred Edward Housman: Recollections,* Holt, 1937.

Twentieth-Century Literary Criticism, Gale, Volume 1, 1978, Volume 10, 1983.

Wallace-Hadrill, F., editor, *Alfred Edward Housman,* Holt, 1937.

PERIODICALS

Cithara, Volume 6, number 2, 1967.
Listener, Volume 61, 1959.
Modern Language Quarterly, June, 1963; March, 1971.
PMLA, June, 1945; March, 1967.

Victorian Poetry, spring, 1972; summer, 1972; autumn, 1976; winter, 1976; autumn, 1983.

* * *

HOWARD, Maureen 1930-

PERSONAL: Born June 28, 1930, in Bridgeport, Conn.; daughter of William L. (a county detective) and Loretta (Burns) Kearns; married Daniel F. Howard (a professor of English), August 28, 1954 (divorced, 1967); married David J. Gordon (a professor), April 2, 1968 (divorced); married Mark Probst (a stockbroker and novelist), 1981; children: (first marriage) Loretta Howard. *Education:* Smith College, B.A., 1952.

ADDRESSES: Home—New York, N.Y. *Agent*—Gloria Loomis, Watkins, Loomis Agency, 150 East 35th St., Suite 530, New York, N.Y. 10016.

CAREER: Author of novels, literary criticism, and book reviews; editor. Worked in publishing and advertising, 1952-54; University of California, Santa Barbara, lecturer in English and drama, 1968-69; New School for Social Research, New York, N.Y., lecturer in English and creative writing, 1967-68, 1970-71, 1974—. Member of staff in English department, Columbia University. Visiting writer at Amherst College, Boston University, Brooklyn College, Princeton, and Yale.

AWARDS, HONORS: Guggenheim fellowship, 1967-68; fellow of Radcliffe Institute, 1967-68; National Book Critics Circle Award in general nonfiction, 1980, and American Book Award nomination in autobiography/biography, 1981, both for *Facts of Life;* PEN/Faulkner Award for Fiction nominations, 1983, for *Grace Abounding,* and 1987, for *Expensive Habits;* Ingram Merrill Fellowship, National Endowment of the Arts, 1988; D.Litt., Bridgeport University.

WRITINGS:

NOVELS

Not a Word about Nightingales, Atheneum, 1961, reprinted, Penguin, 1980.
Bridgeport Bus, Harcourt, 1966.
Before My Time, Little, Brown, 1975.
Grace Abounding, Little, Brown, 1982.
Expensive Habits, Summit Books, 1986.

OTHER

(Editor) *Seven American Women Writers of the Twentieth Century,* University of Minnesota Press, 1977.
Facts of Life (autobiography), Little, Brown, 1978.
(Author of introduction) Virginia Woolf, *Mrs. Dalloway,* centenial edition, Harcourt, 1981.
(Editor) *Contemporary American Essays,* Viking, 1984, published as *The Penguin Book of Contemporary American Essays,* Penguin, 1985.

Also author of a produced play and of screenplays. Represented in numerous anthologies, including *The Best American Short Stories, 1965,* edited by Martha Foley and David Burnett, Houghton, 1965, and *Statements,* edited by Jonathan Baumbach, Braziller, 1975. Contributor to various periodicals, including *New York Times Book Review, New Republic, New Yorker, Hudson Review, Yale Review,* and *Vogue.*

WORK IN PROGRESS: Another novel.

AVOCATIONAL INTERESTS: Gardening, cooking.

SIDELIGHTS: Maureen Howard's literary talents are considered by many to be expansive. She is recognized as a thoroughly professional, perceptive, and sensitive literary critic and editor, and a much admired lecturer sharing her experience and thoughts on creative writing. Her novels are also praised for their clarity, linguistic precision, and character development. Peter S. Prescott declares in *Newsweek* that Howard is "a grand writer of English prose; she's witty and (a rarer quality in novelists) she's intelligent as well." Often compared to the writings of Henry James and Virginia Woolf, Howard's five novels, in addition to her autobiography, have been described as brilliantly sensitive commentaries on contemporary American society. Howard's books, according to Geoffrey Stokes in the *Voice Literary Supplement,* "are subtly scaffolded, intelligent, unsparing-shading-into-sneering chronicles of domestic and national madness."

Howard's first novel, *Not a Word about Nightingales,* portrays a family's unsuccessful attempt to achieve happiness and personal fulfillment. While on a research trip to Pergugia, Italy, college professor Albert Sedgely discards his respected and secure middleclass life and family, and decides to remain in the small village. After completely changing his priorities and his lifestyle, Sedgely takes a mistress and strives to find inner peace and happiness. Meanwhile, his wife sends their eighteen-year-old daughter, Rosemary, to convince Sedgely to return home. While Rosemary quickly becomes enchanted with the colorful Italian life, Sedgely becomes increasing disenchanted. Back in the United States, Sedgely's wife is beginning to enjoy her new independence. However, Rosemary's attraction to her new lifestyle is short lived. Father and daughter return home and the three family members settle back into their safe and orderly life together. Doris Grumbach explains in the *New York Times Book Review* that Howard's intent in *Not a Word about Nightingales* is to write "about the deadly continuity of the marital condition," a condition from which "there is no permanent exit, only acceptance and repetition of marriage's inexorable routine."

Not a Word about Nightingales perfectly highlights a recurring theme found in most of Howard's works of fiction—that the individual must accept the fact that the events that make up and shape his or her life are predetermined. While no one can change their destiny, each one of us is free to grow, develop, and make choices within the limits our character allows. Remarks David M. Taylor in the *Directory of Literary Biography Yearbook: 1983,* "[Howard's] characters have limited control of their fates, but the exercise of will to effect change is championed rather than discouraged. It appears that the author believes that things will generally turn out badly, but the attempt at change is worthwhile." Howard explains her philosophy in a *Publishers Weekly* interview: "I want my characters to echo the excitement of real lives—lives that appear placid and ordinary on the surface but are really heroic efforts of will."

In *Bridgeport Bus,* Howard's second novel, a major life change comes for thirty-five-year-old, Mary Agnes Keely, an aspiring writer who after an argument with her stifling widowed mother, leaves the home they both share and moves to New York City. Obtaining employment as a copywriter and showing real talent as a fledgling author, Mary Agnes takes in a troubled roommate, begins an affair with an advertising-agency artist, and keeps company with a group of bohemian artists. Towards the end of the book, she finds herself pregnant and totally alone. Mary Agnes accepts her situation, gives birth, and comes to the realization that being alone in this world is not as frightening or as tragic as she once thought.

While Elaine Ruben describes *Bridgeport Bus* in the *New Republic* as "a funny, sad work some readers were fortunate to discover and then eager to pass on to friends," Daniel Stern writes in the *Saturday Review,* "that such a diverse and sensitized imagination should exist in the captive body of an Irish Catholic spinster in fruitless rebellion against the paucity of experience to which she appears to be condemned is merely the cream of the irony." Stern continues: "In arriving at the concluding insight that 'it was no great sin to be, at last, alone,' the reader has been rewarded for his attention in a thousand subtle but tangible ways."

Writing novels populated with solid characters, such as Mary Agnes in *Bridgeport Bus,* and other strong-willed woman as Laura Quinn in *Before My Time,* Maud Dowd in *Grace Abounding,* and Margaret Flood in *Expensive Habits,* in addition to the powerful cast found in her autobiography, *Facts of Life,* Howard is referred to by some critics as a "woman's writer." These reviewers remark that her novels systematically revolve around women who are searching for their identity and their place within society's accepted boundaries. These female characters often work hard to grow and strive towards self-awareness even against seemingly very difficult odds. A reviewer for the *Washington Post Book World* describes Howard's novels as "meticulously observed and beautifully written short studies of women caught in the world of men, lost to themselves, and finding little meaning in what they do."

Other reviewers concede that while she does write about women trying to "find themselves," Howard should not be labeled solely a woman's writer since they feel her writings reflect all of contemporary society and not just women. "Howard is a writer in the feminist tradition only because the dominant sensibility is most often that of a woman," states Grumbach in the *Washington Post Book World.* "But she suffers no myopia when it comes to men: husbands, lover, priest-son are all very real and very central to the whole splendidly arranged and securely conceived structure. Women without men, to turn Hemingway's phrase about, is never her subject but rather women searching for their lost selves in a male world in which most of the men are also adrift." In seeming agreement with the premise that Howard's ability to mold and develop such full and deep personalitites is not limited only to her female characters, a reviewer writes in the *New Yorker,* "Maureen Howard has the knack of capturing the essence of people's lives in a shorter time than it takes most authors to usher their characters into a room."

Howard addresses the issue of being called a "woman's writer" in the *Voice Literary Supplement:* "You write a book at least partly because you feel these matters are so important that you want to bring them to life through your characters' stories, and then it's talked about as 'mothers and daughter' or 'a woman's book.' It's as though they decided they were not going to notice 'all that' because the lady writes pretty paragraphs."

Howard's third novel, *Before My Time,* tells the story of a woman forced to confront her past when her cousin's son stays with her family while awaiting arraignment on a drug charge. Laura Quinn attempts to frame a vision of the past for Jimmy Cogan in an effort to help him realize the error of his ways. As they trade stories of their pasts, each episode becomes a vignette of character development. A *New Yorker* critic observes that the book is "full of moral intelligence, wit, and fresh insights into the way people live," adding, "the sketches . . . are so rich that one can only wish they were twice as long." About the novel's content, Paul Gray writes in *Time,* "Without warning, what might have been just another serving of tea and sympathy has become a documentary on U.S. civilization and its discontents." Gray continues to note: "*Before My Time* conveys a range of details and events that would be impressive in a novel twice as long. Although the design appears casual, the book's power is in its language. Time and again, a part is successfully substituted for a whole."

Most critics seem to agree with Gray that one of Howard's most identifiable and admired talents lies in her ability to successfully shape and structure the language in each of her books. This task is accomplished without distracting attention away from her novel's other elements. "Certainly Miss Howard's stylistic virtuosity cannot be disputed," states Pearl K. Bell in the *New Leader,* "every inch of her prose . . . is trimmed and polished with meticulous skill." However, *Publishers Weekly's* Sybil S. Steinberg observes "that critics have generally praised Howard's impeccable command of language, her exact and tartly humorous prose, somewhat surprises [Howard.]" As Howard explains to Steinberg: "Of course I am fascinated with language, but I don't think that is so unusual. I should think all writers who are serious about what they're doing *would* care a lot about language. I think it's very odd when I pick up a novel and see that language has not been honored or used well, or played with."

In her *New York Times Book Review* article on *Before My Time* Grumbach points to another element that seems constant in Howard's writings. Reviewers have longed praised her talent for delicately manipulating characters and plot, gently guiding the reader to the point where they will be required to interpret and draw their own conclusions concerning the characters and the story. As Grumbach writes of *Before My Time:* "Howard has the gift of being unobtrusively present in her fictions, like the good children who are neither seen nor heard. But her hand is felt, controlling events, keeping them in their assigned comic or poignant rings, preventing excess and promoting restrained yet agonized, circular movement. Reading her, one is made to return to the inevitable, to the conclusions that things do not end satisfactorily so much as they happen; they seem to mean something for the moment and then disappear into memory, which is what fiction is to this extraordinary talented writer." *Newsweek's* Prescott also acknowledges Howard's talent: "Howard organizes each scene with artistry, expertly cutting in and out of her narrative and casting no words as she studs her prose with dour wit."

In her award-winning autobiography, *Facts of Life,* Howard recounts her life as daughter of Irish-Catholic parents, a college professor's wife, and tells of the experiences that have shaped her life. Karen Durbin writes in *Ms.:* "When I first read *Facts of Life,* I was immediately gripped by the sheer quality of the writing. Howard's memories of, among other things, her parents, her youth in Irish-Catholic Bridgeport, her experiences later as a faculty wife, are crouched in a vigorous, rushing prose. She uses words with the focused intensity and precision of a poet. . . . Her wit is everywhere. *Facts of Life* is at once painful and humorous." "Howard is a talented novelist who has never written anything so concentrated and properly disturbing as this memoir," states Alfred Kazin in the *New Republic.* "The style is very, very bright; the other characters are wonderfully alive; the suffering and resentment out of which the book was written stick to it like a burr. . . . A painfully strong, good book." And Walter Clemons writes in *Newsweek* that *Facts of Life* "is brief, witty and utterly original. Its candor and conspicuous reticences are exciting and puzzling. . . . It exemplifies Howard's unsettling combination of elegance and earthiness."

In her fourth novel, *Grace Abounding,* Howard follows the path of Maud Dowd's life beginning with her very colorless and spiritless existence as a forty-three-year-old widow and mother of a teenage daughter, Elizabeth. Maud spends much of her time spying on her neighbors—a pair of spinster sisters—and visiting her

dying mother. Maud's life dramatically changes after her mother dies and, after ending a brief and dreadful relationship with an unworthy man, she moves to New York City to pursue vocal training for the talented Elizabeth. Maud remarries a successful and loving man, earns a Ph.D. in psychology and becomes a children's therapist. Elizabeth, in turn, happily gives up her promising singing career to marry and have children. Life for Maud is not entirely golden however, as she copes with the death of a 3-year-old patient and wrestles with her own morality.

Robert Dawidoff writes in the *Los Angeles Times* that *Grace Abounding* "conveys a shrewd feeling for how life changes, how things affect and happen to people, how some stories have endings and meanings and some do not, staying, rather, unresolved in several memories—and how, where faith had best be, grace had better be." "It does give a sense of lives as they are really lived such as only a small minority of novelists in each generation can or even want to manage," remarks Noel Perrin in the *New York Times Book Review.* "Howard . . . is a writer to read. Here the sensibility. There the intelligence." Diane M. Ross comments in the *Chicago Tribune* that "meant to involve us in the irregular rhythms of particular lives, the structure of [*Grace Abounding*] allows for shifting points of view and for chronological gaps in the narrative," Ross continues: "[*Grace Abounding*] depends upon an accumulation of detail and a pattering of scenes rather than a straightforward plot. . . . Howard crosscuts between characters and locations, and blithely elides large chunks of time. . . . Her details are epiphanies, and they range from the ridiculous to the graceful."

At the beginning of Howard's most recent novel, *Expensive Habits,* seemingly successful and well-known writer, Margaret Flood, lays in a hospital room after learning she has a deteriorating heart disease. The forty-five-year-old returns to her Manhattan apartment and through a sequence of flashback scenes, the reader sees Margaret's life as a continual series of episodes—many involving loyalty and betrayal—that leave her searching for her true identity and self-worth. Margaret hopes this search will bring her the peace and contentment she so desperately desires.

Jonathan Yardley suggests in the *Washington Post Book World* that *Expensive Habits* "is a serious and accomplished piece of work. Here as in her other work Howard writes about the fads and fashions of the day, about a society eager to cash in on any passing joy or sorrow, but she is having none of that herself; she stands apart, observing 'the dumb glory of it all' with an eye that is sharp but kind. [*Expensive Habits*] is certainly a book rich in integrity and elegance, by a writer who matters." "Maureen Howard's fine fifth novel attempts more, and accomplishes more, than all the others, marking her steady progress toward the highest rank of American fiction writers," remarks Nora Johnson in the *Los Angeles Times Book Review.* "The prose in [*Expensive Habits*] is dense, complex, disturbing, authoritative. Its several voices suit her story and vividly demonstrate her literary intelligence. It's dazzling to see how deftly she wields her author's tools." And Gray writes in *Time:* "As she had done in her other novels and in the prizewinning autobiography *Facts of Life* . . . the author smuggles more subjects into a book than its length seems to allow. . . . [Howard] has skills that do not comfortably translate into screaming paperback covers and megabuck reprints. She is one of those rare contemporaries whose work demands, and deserves, rereadings."

Although her talent has long been acknowledged and applauded by reviewers and a loyal following, Howard has not yet achieved the measure of success many feel she deserves. "It is hard to understand how a writer of Maureen Howard's elegance, sharpness, sensibility and tenderness has escaped widespread public notice for so long," a critic states in the *Washington Post Book Review*. Durbin remarks in *Ms.*: "I can only hope that soon one of her books will achieve the kind of popular success that (via the publishing miracle of reissues) would rescue all of her work from the elite near-obscurity it now enjoys. Howard is too important a writer to miss. Talking about Willa Cather, Howard wrote: 'She had the nerve to confront big issues—the transience of youth and beauty, love relinquished for ambition, the bitter triumphs of success—what the past will yield if we are truthful.' She might have been describing herself."

BIOGRAPHICAL/CRITICAL SOURCES:

BOOKS

Contemporary Literary Criticism, Gale, Volume 5, 1976, Volume 14, 1980, Volume 46, 1988.
Dictionary of Literary Biography Yearbook: 1983, Gale, 1984.
Howard, Maureen, *Facts of Life,* Little, Brown, 1978.

PERIODICALS

Chicago Tribune Book World, November 14, 1982.
Critics, February 1, 1979.
Harper's, November, 1978.
Los Angeles Times, December 7, 1982.
Los Angeles Times Book Review, May 18, 1986.
New Leader, January 20, 1975.
New Republic, February 8, 1975, September 9, 1978, October 4, 1982.
Newsweek, January 20, 1975, September 25, 1978, October 11, 1982.
New York Times Book Review, January 19, 1975, September 26, 1982, October 2, 1982, December 2, 1982, May 24, 1986, June 8, 1986.
Partisan Review, Volume 56, number 1, 1987.
Saturday Review, October 28, 1978.
Sewanee Review, winter, 1974-75.
Spectator, November 8, 1986.
Time, January 27, 1975.
Washington Post Book World, October 10, 1982, May 11, 1986.

—*Sketch by Margaret Mazurkiewicz*

*   *   *

HOWARD, Warren F.
See POHL, Frederik

*   *   *

HOWE, Irving 1920-

PERSONAL: Born June 1, 1920, in New York, N.Y.; son of David and Nettie (Goldman) Howe; married Arien Hausknecht; married Ilana Wiener; children: Nina, Nicholas. *Education:* City College of New York (now City College of the City University of New York), B.Sc., 1940; Brooklyn College (now Brooklyn College of the City University of New York), graduate study. *Politics:* Socialist.

ADDRESSES: Office—English Programs, Graduate Center, City University of New York, 33 West 42nd St., New York, N.Y. 10036.

CAREER: Brandeis University, Waltham, Mass., 1953-61, began as associate professor, became professor of English; Stanford University, Stanford, Calif., professor of English, 1961-63;

Hunter College of the City University of New York, New York, N.Y., professor of English, 1963-70, distinguished professor, 1970—. Visiting professor, University of Vermont and University of Washington; Christian Gauss Seminar Chair Professor, Princeton University, 1953. *Military service:* U.S. Army, 1942-45.

MEMBER: Modern Language Association of America.

AWARDS, HONORS: Indiana University, School of Letters, fellow; Longview Foundation prize for literary criticism; *Kenyon Review* fellow, 1953; Bollingen Award, 1959-60; National Institute of Arts and Letters award, 1960; Guggenheim fellow, 1964-65, 1971; Jewish Heritage Award, 1975, for excellence in literature; Brandeis University Creative Arts Award, 1975-76; National Book Award, 1976, for *World of Our Fathers: The Journey of the Eastern European Jews to America and the Life They Found and Made;* Present Tense/Joel H. Cavior Award for lifetime achievement, American Jewish Committee, 1986; MacArthur Foundation fellow, 1987.

WRITINGS:

LITERARY CRITICISM

Sherwood Anderson: A Critical Biography, Sloane, 1951.
William Faulkner: A Critical Study, Random House, 1952.
Politics and the Novel, Horizon Press, 1957.
A World More Attractive: A View of Modern Literature and Politics, Horizon Press, 1963.
Thomas Hardy: A Critical Study, Macmillan, 1967.
Decline of the New, Harcourt, 1970.
The Critical Point: On Literature and Culture, Horizon Press, 1973.
Celebrations and Attacks: Thirty Years of Literary and Cultural Commentary, Horizon Press, 1978.
The American Newness: Culture and Politics in the Age of Emerson, Harvard University Press, 1986.

EDITOR

Leo Baeck, *The Essence of Judaism,* Schocken, 1948.
Modern Literary Criticism: An Anthology, Beacon Press, 1958.
Edith Wharton, *The House of Mirth,* Holt, 1962.
Edith Wharton: A Collection of Critical Essays, Prentice-Hall, 1962.
George Gissing, *New Grub Street,* Houghton, 1962.
George Orwell, *Nineteen Eighty-Four: Text, Sources, Criticism,* Harcourt, 1963.
Leon Trotsky, *Basic Writings,* Random House, 1963.
(And author of introduction) *The Radical Papers,* Doubleday, 1966.
Isaac Bashevis Singer, *Selected Short Stories,* Modern Library, 1966.
Thomas Hardy, *Selected Writings: Stories, Poems, and Essays,* Fawcett, 1966.
The Radical Imagination: An Anthology from Dissent Magazine, New American Library, 1967.
Student Activism, Bobbs-Merrill, 1967.
Literary Modernism, Fawcett, 1967.
The Idea of the Modern in Literature and the Arts, Horizon Press, 1968.
Classics of Modern Fiction: Eight Short Novels, Harcourt, 1968, 3rd edition published as *Classics of Modern Fiction: Ten Short Novels,* 1980.
(With Jeremy Larnier) *Poverty: Views from the Left,* Morrow, 1968.
A Dissenter's Guide to Foreign Policy, Praeger, 1968.

Beyond the New Left: A Confrontation and Critique, McCall, 1970.

Essential Works of Socialism, Holt, 1970 (published in England as *A Handbook of Socialist Thought,* Gollancz, 1972).

The Literature of America: Nineteenth Century, McGraw, 1970.

(With Carl Gershman) *Israel, the Arabs, and the Middle East,* Quadrangle Books, 1972.

(With Michael Harrington) *The Seventies: Problems and Proposals,* Harper, 1972.

The World of the Blue-Collar Worker, Times Books, 1973.

Saul Bellow, *Herzog,* Viking, 1976.

Jewish-American Stories, New American Library, 1977.

Fiction as Experience: An Anthology, Harcourt, 1978.

(With others) *Literature as Experience: An Anthology,* Harcourt, 1979.

(With Ruth Wisse) *The Best of Sholem Aleichem,* Simon & Schuster, 1980.

The Portable Kipling, Viking, 1982, published as *The Portable Rudyard Kipling,* Penguin, 1982.

(With wife, Ilana W. Howe) *Short Shorts: An Anthology of the Shortest Stories,* David Godine, 1982.

"1984" Revisited: Totalitarianism in Our Century, Harper, 1983.

Alternatives: Proposals for America from the Democratic Left, Pantheon, 1984.

(With Khone Shmeruk and Wisse) *The Penguin Book of Modern Yiddish Verse,* Viking, 1989.

EDITOR WITH ELIEZER GREENBERG

A Treasury of Yiddish Stories, Viking, 1954, reprinted, Schocken, 1973, revised edition, 1989.

A Treasury of Yiddish Poetry, Holt, 1969.

Voices from the Yiddish: Essays, Memoirs, Diaries, University of Michigan Press, 1972.

Yiddish Stories Old and New, Holiday House, 1974.

Ashes Out of Hope: Fiction by Soviet-Yiddish Writers, Schocken, 1978.

OTHER

The U.A.W. and Walter Reuther, Random House, 1949.

(With Lewis Coser) *The American Communist Party: A Critical History, 1919-1957,* Beacon Press, 1957, reprinted, Da Capo Press, 1974.

Steady Work: Essays in the Politics of Democratic Radicalism, 1953-1966, Harcourt, 1966.

(Author of introduction) William O'Neill, editor, *Echoes of Revolt: The Masses, 1911-1917,* Quadrangle Books, 1967.

(Author of introduction) Henry James, *The American Scene,* Horizon Press, 1968.

(With Coser) *The New Conservatives: A Critique from the Left,* Quadrangle Books, 1968.

World of Our Fathers: The Journey of the Eastern European Jews to America and the Life They Found and Made, Harcourt, 1976 (published in England as *The Immigrant Jews of New York: 1881 to the Present,* Routledge, 1976).

Leon Trotsky, Viking, 1978.

(With Kenneth Libo) *How We Lived: A Documentary History of Immigrant Jews in America, 1880-1930,* Marek, 1979.

(Author of introduction) *Images of Labor,* Pilgrim Press, 1981.

A Margin of Hope: An Intellectual Autobiography, Harcourt, 1982.

Beyond the Welfare State, Schocken, 1982.

(With Libo) *We Lived There, Too: In Their Own Words and Pictures, Pioneer Jews and the Westward Movement of America,* St. Martin's, 1984.

Socialism and America, Harcourt, 1985 (published in Canada as *Socialism in America,* Harcourt, 1986).

Contributor to *Partisan Review, New Republic, New York Review of Books, Harper's, New York Times Book Review,* and other publications. Editor and co-founder, *Dissent,* 1953—.

SIDELIGHTS: Irving Howe is known in a variety of roles. He is a distinguished literary critic; the editor of *Dissent,* an influential left-wing journal of opinion; a historian whose *World of Our Fathers: The Journey of Eastern European Jews to America and the Life They Found and Made* was a winner of the National Book Award and a bestseller; and as a prominent spokesman for the democratic socialist position in the United States. Julian Symons, writing in the *Times Literary Supplement,* defines Howe as "a man primarily involved throughout much of his adult life with politics who has retained a deep interest in literary creation."

Howe first joined the socialist movement as a teenager in 1934, following the faction led by Russian revolutionary leader Leon Trotsky. He wrote for the leftist newspaper Labor Action and participated in political debates on behalf of the Trotskyists and the Independent Socialist League. As he explains in *A Margin of Hope: An Intellectual Autobiography,* "Only radicalism seemed to offer the prospect of coherence, only radicalism could provide a unified view of the world."

With the advent of the Second World War, Howe's political activity was cut short. He was drafted into the United States army and for three years was stationed at a military base in Alaska. "Enforced isolation and steady reading together brought about a slow intellectual change," Howe writes in *A Margin of Hope.* "I lost the singleness of mind that had inspired the politics of my youth." Howe turned to a less dogmatic socialist position which emphasized the necessity for democracy.

When the war ended Howe began to write for *Partisan Review, Commentary,* and other leftist political journals of the late 1940s. This led him in 1953 to co-found the magazine *Dissent,* a political and literary journal which he still edits. "Despite its circulation of about 5,000," Peter Steinfels writes in the *New York Times Book Review,* "*Dissent* ranks among the handful of political journals read most regularly by American intellectuals. And it is virtually alone in its explicit affirmation of democratic socialism."

Howe has written a number of books about American radicalism, including *The American Communist Party: A Critical History, 1919-1957* and *Socialism and America.* His study of Leon Trotsky has also garnered critical acclaim. Howe's history of the American Communist Party, written with Lewis Coser, was the first complete party history to be published. Although several reviewers cite the authors' obvious prejudice against the party— Robert Claiborne of the *Nation* admits that the "lively account is biased, as any book on the subject must be"—most observers find the work to be of great value. "The major merit of this new book," Michael Harrington states in *Commonweal,* "is that it puts the question of the Communist Party into some kind of a historical and political perspective. As history this is a first-rate introduction to a stormy and important subject." Philip Green, writing in the *New Republic,* calls it "a brilliant book, entertaining, lucid, and composed with real style. Though marred by occasional defects of historical method, it remains the most penetrating analysis of the subject matter that I have seen." Harry Schwartz of the *New York Times* concludes that "there is no other single volume of comparable merit and scope available."

Socialism and America is a related study in which Howe writes the history of socialism in the United States, documenting its evolution from the heyday of Eugene Debs at the turn of the century to its present eclipse on the political scene. It is, writes Nicholas Xenos of the *Nation,* "a history of defeat and decline." Howe cites the distinctive nature of American culture, with its strong belief in individualism, for the failure of socialism in the United States. His vision of socialism's future in America is a modest one: to be a moderating force in a capitalist society, curbing the system's worst excesses. Howe "has culled the voluminous scholarship available and summarized it with superb economy, maintaining a level of commentary that nearly always strikes a judicious balance between criticism of the errors and the shortcomings of the socialists of the past and a large-spirited allowance for the particular historical constraints under which they acted," Dennis Wrong states in the *New Republic.*

In *Leon Trotsky,* Howe examines the life and thought of a major figure in the Russian Revolution. The book is, Howe states in the introduction, a "political essay." As a one-time Trotskyist, Howe brings a unique perspective to his account, which is sympathetic to many of Trotsky's goals but critical of his methods. Trotsky and Vladimir Lenin were the primary leaders of the Russian Revolution of 1917 that brought the Communist Party to power. During the subsequent civil war Trotsky led the Red Army to ultimate victory, displaying great skill as a military tactician. The author of seventeen books of socialist theory and a spellbinding orator, Trotsky was "one of the two founding fathers of Soviet Russia, and one of the greatest political thinkers of the century," W. Warren Wagar maintains in the *Saturday Review.* "Trotsky," Webster Schott explains in the *Washington Post Book World,* "was much of the brains, most of the voice, and all of the arms of the revolution."

After the communists assumed control of Russia, it was Trotsky who "provided the ideological base for Lenin's exclusion of other parties from the ruling center," Schott writes. By excluding from power other socialist parties, Trotsky and Lenin created the political framework for an all-encompassing dictatorship. "Trotsky," Wagar explains, "helped construct the Soviet state as a bureaucratized one-party dictatorship in which all dissent, and ultimately even his own, was crushed." In the struggle for power following Lenin's death, Trotsky lost to Joseph Stalin and was forced into exile. He was assassinated by a Soviet agent in Mexico in 1940.

Because of his struggle against Stalin and his forced exile, Trotsky's role in the Russian Revolution is not mentioned in official Soviet histories of the period. Trotsky's life "has been completely obliterated in Soviet historical works," Alexander Rabinowitch writes in the *Nation.* Howe's account is one of the few scholarly works published to deal seriously with Trotsky's life and thought. "Leon Trotsky is the kind of work one expects from Irving Howe," Schott believes. "It is wise, beautifully written, and emotionally informed. . . . He gives us a man, a time, a condition." The critic for the *New York Review of Books* describes the biography as "a tough-minded and fair introduction both to the life of Trotsky and to issues surrounding 'Trotskyism.' " Jack Beatty of the *New Republic* believes that "what Howe has given us here is an admirably compact account of Trotsky's life as well as something far more urgent: he has subjected the political ideas of Trotsky to a discriminating historical and political criticism . . . from the social-democratic point of view. The result is a work full of the rarest sort of political wisdom."

Howe claims that his long political involvement prepared him to write about his other great interest, modern literature. The so-cialist movement, Howe writes in *A Margin of Hope,* "taught us to grasp the structure of an argument . . . to speak and think, and to value discipline of mind." Symons believes that "it was a training that prepared the young Howe . . . for entry into the literary world as critic and social commentator." In his role as critic, Howe approaches literature as a social phenomenon. He insists, Robert Towers claims in the *New Republic,* "upon the rootedness of literature in history, society, and psychology, upon its connection with ideas and the use that has been made of them." Howe is also, Towers writes, a critic "who refuses to insulate his literary concerns from his social and political commitments."

In the late 1940s Howe began to contribute essays and book reviews to journals, becoming one of the New York Jewish intelligentsia. Howe has since made, James Atlas writes in the *New York Times Book Review,* "the familiar pilgrimage through an American literary vocation, making all the stops: He contributed to *Partisan Review,* became a book reviewer for *Time,* wrote ambitious literary essays, eventually got a teaching job at Brandeis, edited *Dissent,* and is now a professor at the City University of New York." Howe has written studies of Sherwood Anderson, William Faulkner, and Thomas Hardy, several collections of essays, and the study *Politics and the Novel.*

A continuing concern in Howe's literary criticism has been the conflict between modernist literature, with its conservative and even reactionary basis, and his own leftist political beliefs. As John Leonard of the *New York Times* writes, "No American critic has struggled more manfully in the last 30 years to reconcile the taste for high art and the temptation to radical politics. Can't we have Ezra Pound and socialism, too?" "To appreciate Howe's critical faculty to its fullest," C. David Heymann admits in the *Chicago Tribune Book World,* "it is perhaps necessary to identify to some degree with his political sympathies. Throughout the years he has adamantly maintained his strong political views in which he continues to admire the dissident in history . . . and to profess his libertarian socialism without rancor toward those of alternate persuasion."

Howe's usually unerring ability to discern the merits and demerits of a literary work, along with his distinguished writing style, have made him a respected critic. "Those who read, write or think about literature turn to Irving Howe," Schott maintains. "He is what we mean by 'critic' instead of 'reviewer'. . . . Howe writes magnificently and has exquisite sensibilities." Towers believes that Howe "has a trained eye for what is meretricious, flashy or merely crackpot in literary discourse and goes after it with the speed and assurance of a leopard." Heymann calls Howe "a literary stylist of the first order" and "unique among his contemporaries for his amazing intellectual versatility."

In his National Book Award-winning *World of Our Fathers,* Howe traces the history of Eastern European Jewish immigrants to America. In so doing, he recreates the history of his own family and friends. Writing in *National Review,* Jacob Neusner praises *World of Our Fathers.* "In this stunning, elegant, monumental work—a triumph of sustained and brilliant narrative—Irving Howe recaptures the intense and vivid life of the immigrant generation," Neusner writes. "His book is, quite simply, the finest work of historical literature ever written on American Jews."

Howe begins the book by recounting Jewish life in Eastern Europe in the 1880s and the conditions that led them to immigrate to the United States. Between 1880 and the outbreak of the First World War, some two million Jews came to the United States from Eastern Europe, most of them to escape a series of bloody pogroms. "Their story," Peter Shaw writes in the *Saturday Review,* "is recounted masterfully by the distinguished literary critic Irving Howe, who marshals the major elements—history, politics, culture, life-style—in a narrative that serves as both a chronicle and an interpretation." Howe draws upon published memoirs, scholarly studies, personal interviews, and official government records for his story. "Massive as it is," Walter Clemons writes in *Newsweek,* "Howe's epic history is a model of distillation and clarity."

After covering the decades of Jewish immigration to America at the turn of the century, Howe speaks of the assimilation of Jews into American society since that time and the resultant disintegration of traditional Jewish culture that this entailed. Howe, Christopher Lehmann-Haupt explains in the *New York Times,* "is both hopeful about the future and surprisingly forgiving for the watering-down that Jewish culture has undergone in the present. . . . All the same, one can't ignore the scope and energy and richness of anecdotal detail with which Mr. Howe has recalled every aspect of the East European immigrant past. . . . This speaks a love far more powerful than the sympathy he grants the Jewish present. Obviously he mourns the death of this past. So he has built a monument to it." Writing in the *New York Review of Books,* Leon Wieseltier calls *World of Our Fathers* "a masterly social and cultural history, a vivid, elegiac, and scrupulously documented portrait of a complicated culture, from its heroic beginnings to its unheroic end."

In *A Margin of Hope* Howe traces the course of his own career, recalling the ideas and issues with which he has been engaged. It is not a personal account, Symons explains: "This is the life of an American radical, not of a husband or father." The publication of the book gave several reviewers occasion to evaluate Howe's contributions over the years. Vivian Gornick, writing in the *Nation,* believes that *"A Margin of Hope* reveals a man for whom idea is event, position engagement. The life of the mind fills these pages, and within that life this man has struggled to be serious, to cohere, to make sense of things; he has risen from the bed seven mornings out of seven to grapple, in his thoughts, with history. Such a person may not necessarily compel love, but he commands recognition and respect." Symons calls *A Margin of Hope* "the record of an admirable life, the testimony of a decent, honest man." "As he has grown older," Monroe K. Spears writes in the *Washington Post Book World,* "[Howe] has come to appreciate the ideal of the gentleman, of being quiet and unassertive, and modest."

Other evaluations of Howe's career praise his varied accomplishments. Lehmann-Haupt characterizes him as "one of our leading historians and theoreticians of the Left," while Clemons calls him "our most capable man of letters since Edmund Wilson." In the *New York Times Book Review,* Roger Sales states that "Irving Howe has had a long, admirable and increasingly enviable career. An academic who is never musty and a journalist who is never merely quick or content with flash, he seems to have grown over the years, and his prose is sharper, his insights more precise and flexible." Towers sees Howe as one of "a line of honorable, engaged, incisive and pugnacious critics that includes Edmund Wilson and [F. R.] Leavis and reaches back to Dr. Johnson—a line that has done as much to invigorate the literary life as any number of theorists or aestheticians." Irving Howe, R. Z. Sheppard states in *Time,* "is one of those writers for whom the designation 'a gentleman and a scholar' was minted."

BIOGRAPHICAL/CRITICAL SOURCES:

BOOKS

Dictionary of Literary Biography, Volume 67: *Modern American Critics since 1955,* Gale, 1988.
Howe, Irving, *Leon Trotsky,* Viking, 1978.
Howe, Irving, *A Margin of Hope: An Intellectual Autobiography,* Harcourt, 1982.

PERIODICALS

Atlantic, November, 1985.
Chicago Tribune Book World, May 20, 1979, March 6, 1983.
Christian Science Monitor, April 25, 1957, October 27, 1966, July 22, 1967.
Commentary, February, 1969.
Commonweal, August 1, 1958.
Los Angeles Times Book Review, November 3, 1985.
Nation, September 24, 1949, September 20, 1958, September 23, 1978, January 1, 1983, November 16, 1985.
National Review, May 14, 1976, December 10, 1982.
New Republic, January 26, 1959, October 28, 1978, June 2, 1979, November 1, 1982, November 25, 1985.
Newsweek, February 2, 1976, December 20, 1982.
New York Review of Books, July 15, 1976, September 28, 1978.
New York Times, September 28, 1949, April 8, 1951, June 22, 1958, March 18, 1970, February 5, 1976, January 29, 1979, March 27, 1979, October 28, 1982.
New York Times Book Review, April 12, 1970, January 6, 1974, November 26, 1978, January 13, 1980, October 31, 1982.
New York Times Magazine, June 17, 1984.
Partisan Review, winter, 1975, fall, 1976.
Saturday Review, February 21, 1976, September 2, 1978.
Time, January 26, 1976.
Times Literary Supplement, August 4, 1978, March 4, 1983.
Village Voice, January 12, 1967.
Washington Post Book World, September 24, 1978, June 10, 1979, December 26, 1982.
World Literature Today, autumn, 1983.

*   *   *

HOYLE, Fred 1915-

PERSONAL: Born June 24, 1915, in Bingley, Yorkshire, England; son of Ben and Mabel (Pickard) Hoyle; married Barbara Clark, December 28, 1939; children: Geoffrey, Elizabeth Jeanne (Mrs. N. J. Butler). *Education:* Emmanuel College, Cambridge, M.A., 1939.

ADDRESSES: Office—St. John's College, Cambridge University, Cambridge, England.

CAREER: Cambridge University, Cambridge, England, research fellow of St. John's College, 1939-72, honorary fellow, 1973—, university lecturer in mathematics, 1945-58, Plumian Professor of Theoretical Astronomy and Experimental Philosophy, 1958-73, director of Institute of Theoretical Astronomy, 1966-72. California Institute of Technology, visiting professor of astrophysics, 1953 and 1954, visiting associate in physics, 1963—, and Sherman Fairchild Distinguished Scholar, 1974-75. Professor of astronomy, Royal Institution, 1969-72; Andrew D. White Professor-at-Large, Cornell University, 1972-78. Honorary research professor, University of Manchester, 1972—, and University of Cardiff, 1975—; honorary fellow, Emmanuel College, Cambridge, 1983. Member of staff, Mount Wilson and Palomar Observatories in California, 1956-58. Senior exhibitioner of the Royal Commission of the Exhibition of 1851, 1939; member of science research council, 1967-72. *Wartime service:* British Admiralty, wartime research, 1940-45.

MEMBER: Royal Astronomical Society (fellow; president, 1971-73), Royal Society (fellow; vice-president, 1970-71), American Academy of Arts and Sciences (honorary member), American Philosophical Society, National Academy of Sciences (foreign associate).

AWARDS, HONORS: Smith Prize, 1939; D.Sc. from University of Norwich, 1967, University of Leeds, 1969, University of Bradford, 1975, and University of Newcastle, 1976; Gold Medal from Royal Astronomical Society, 1968; Kalinga Prize, 1968; Bruce Medal, Astronomical Society of the Pacific, 1970; knighted, 1972; Royal Medal from Royal Society, 1974; Dorothea Klumpke-Roberts Award, Astronomical Society of the Pacific, 1977.

WRITINGS:

Some Recent Researches in Solar Physics, Cambridge University Press, 1949.
The Nature of the Universe, Harper, 1951, revised edition, 1960.
A Decade of Decision, Heinemann, 1953, published as *Man and Materialism,* Harper, 1956.
Frontiers of Astronomy, Heinemann, 1955, New American Library, 1957.
The Black Cloud (science fiction), Harper, 1957.
Ossian's Ride (science fiction), Harper, 1959.
(With John Elliott) *A for Andromeda,* Harper, 1962.
Astronomy, Doubleday, 1962.
Star Formation, H.M.S.O., 1963.
Contradiction in the Argument of Malthus, University of Hull, 1963.
Of Men and Galaxies, University of Washington Press, 1964.
(With Elliott) *Andromeda Breakthrough* (science fiction), Harper, 1964.
Encounter with the Future, Trident, 1965.
Galaxies, Nuclei, and Quasars, Harper, 1965.
Man in the Universe, Columbia University Press, 1966.
October the First Is Too Late (science fiction), Harper, 1966.
Element 79 (science fiction), New American Library, 1967.
From Stonehenge to Modern Cosmology, W. H. Freeman, 1972.
Copernicus, Harper, 1973.
The Relation of Physics and Cosmology, W. H. Freeman, 1973.
(With J. V. Narlikar) *Action-at-a-Distance in Physics and Cosmology,* W. H. Freeman, 1973.
Astronomy and Cosmology, W. H. Freeman, 1975.
Highlights in Astronomy, W. H. Freeman, 1975, published in England as *Astronomy Today,* Heinemann, 1975.
Ten Faces of the Universe, W. H. Freeman, 1977.
Stonehenge: A High Peak of Prehistoric Culture, W. H. Freeman, 1977.
On Stonehenge, W. H. Freeman, 1977.
Energy or Extinction?, Heinemann, 1977, 2nd edition, 1980.
(With Chandra Wickramasinghe) *Lifecloud,* Harper, 1978.
The Cosmogony of the Solar System, Enslow, 1978.
(With Wickramasinghe) *Diseases from Space,* Harper, 1979.
(With son, Geoffrey Hoyle) *Commonsense in Nuclear Energy,* Heinemann, 1979, W. H. Freeman, 1980.
(With Norlikar) *The Physics-Astronomy Frontier,* W. H. Freeman, 1980.
Steady-State Cosmology Re-Visited, Longwood, 1980.
Space Travellers, University College Cardiff Press, 1981.
The Quasar Controversy Resolved, Longwood, 1981.
Facts and Dogmas in Cosmology and Elsewhere, Cambridge University Press, 1982.
Ice, New English Library, 1982.

Evolution from Space and Other Papers on the Origin of Life, Enslow Publishers, 1982.
The Intelligent Universe: A New View of Creation and Evolution, Holt, 1984.
(With Wickramasinghe) *Evolution from Space: A Theory of Cosmic Creationism,* Simon & Schuster, 1984.
From Grains to Bacteria, Longwood, 1984.
(Editor with Wickramasinghe) *Fundamental Studies and the Future of Science,* University College of Cardiff Press, 1984.
Comet Halley, St. Martin's, 1985.
Living Comets, Longwood, 1985.
(With others) *Viruses from Space,* University College Cardiff Press, 1986.
The Small World of Fred Hoyle (autobiography), Joseph, 1986.
(With Wickramasinghe) *Archaeopteryx, the Primordial Bird: A Case of Fossil Forgery,* Longwood, 1987.

SCIENCE FICTION NOVELS; WITH GEOFFREY HOYLE

Fifth Planet, Harper, 1963.
Rockets in Ursa Major, Harper, 1969.
Seven Steps to the Sun, Harper, 1970.
The Molecule Man: Two Short Novels, Harper, 1971.
The Inferno, Harper, 1973.
Into Deepest Space, Harper, 1974.
The Incandescent Ones, Harper, 1977.
The Westminster Disaster, Harper, 1978.
The Energy Pirate, illustrated by Martin Aitchison, Ladybird, 1982.
The Frozen Planet of Azuron, illustrated by Aitchison, Ladybird, 1982.
The Giants of Universal Park, illustrated by Aitchison, Ladybird, 1982.
The Planet of Death, illustrated by Aitchison, Ladybird, 1982.

BOOKLETS

The Origin of Life, University College Cardiff Press, 1980.
(With Wickramasinghe) *Why Neo-Darwinism Does Not Work,* University College Cardiff Press, 1982.
Evolution from Space, University College Cardiff Press, 1982.
The Anglo-Austrian Telescope, University College Cardiff Press, 1982.

OTHER

Author of libretto, "The Alchemy of Love." Contributor of numerous articles to scientific and professional journals.

SIDELIGHTS: Internationally renowned astronomer and professor Fred Hoyle has "published a string of books challenging first one and then another of the basic tenets of modern cosmology," writes John Durant in the *Times Literary Supplement.* In his 1951 book *The Nature of the Universe,* for example, Hoyle rejects the long-standing big bang theory of the origin of the universe in favor of the steady state theory developed by him and his colleagues at Cambridge University.

Hoyle expounds further upon the steady state and other theories in *The Intelligent Universe,* published in 1977. "Writing with the moral indignation of one who believes himself to be up against a conservative and conspiratorial establishment, and who consequently does not expect a fair hearing, Hoyle dismisses one piece of 'orthodox science' after another, replacing each with ingenious alternatives that pop up from page to page like so many rabbits out of a conjurer's hat," writes Durant. In *The Intelligent Universe,* writes *Science Fiction Review* critic Gene Deweese, Hoyle "presents both old and new evidence for [his steady state theory] and shows how the Big Bang has at least as many shortcomings and problems as the Steady State is supposed to have." Hoyle also presents an argument against Charles Darwin's theory of evolution, claiming that "living organisms are too complex to have been produced by chance," relates Durant. Hoyle suggests, instead, that "we owe our existence to another intelligence which created a structure for life as part of a deliberate plan," writes John R. Kalafut in *Best Sellers,* who adds that "in describing the attributes of an intelligence superior to ourselves, [Hoyle] admits that we may have to use the word forbidden in science, 'God.'" Durant finds Hoyle's argument inadequate, stating that the chapter on Darwinism reads "more like the feeble meanderings of a latter-day fundamentalist than like the work of a major scientist." Kalafut, on the other hand, maintains that "this part of the book is extremely well done and the case against traditional evolution is argued most persuasively."

Hoyle and co-author Chandra Wickramasinghe's 1981 book *Diseases from Space* introduced a similarly controversial theory. The authors hypothesize that viruses and bacteria fall into the atmosphere after being incubated in the interiors of comet heads, and that people become ill by breathing the infected air. They support their theory by stating that the spread of disease is frequently far too rapid to attribute to person-to-person contact. Several reviewers express skepticism that Hoyle and Wickramasinghe's thesis will be accepted by the medical profession. Podgorny, for instance, comments that their "hypothesis, though engaging, is most likely farfetched." Expressing a like opinion in the *Antioch Review,* Robert Bieri writes, "This is a fascinating, humorous, challenging book, but few biologists will buy the thesis."

Reviewers do, however, express their admiration for the author's statistical data. Maddox writes: "Like everything Hoyle writes, this book is a splendid read. It is rich in classical quotations . . ., in data gathered from old shipping records, with the outcome of a questionnaire survey among British schools in 1978 on the incidence of influenza, and with simple explanations of statistical arguments well worth reading for their own sake." Bieri concludes, "Even if one can't follow all of their arguments, the almost offhand historical comments throughout the book are amusing, challenging, enlightening."

Hoyle has also written a number of science fiction novels, many of which were coauthored with his son Geoffrey Hoyle. Several critics suggest that Hoyle's highly technical and scientific background enhances the credibility and appeal of his novels. For example, *Listener* reviewer Robert Garioch comments that *Seven Steps to the Sun* "is a remarkable story, well-told, and too credible for comfort. . . . The science in *Seven Steps to the Sun* is correct, as a middle-aged reviewer may learn by consulting his 15-year-old son. The main interest, however, is in the anthropology. . . . It is not at all far-fetched."

Jeanne Cavallini concurs with Garioch and explains in *Library Journal* that "Fred Hoyle is considered one of the world's foremost astrophysicists . . .; his distinguished scientific background is evident in [*The Molecule Man: Two Short Novels*]. Science fiction buffs who like their science fiction to take place in the present and to have the stamp of scientific accuracy will enjoy these stories."

BIOGRAPHICAL/CRITICAL SOURCES:

BOOKS

The Small World of Fred Hoyle (autobiography), Joseph, 1986.

PERIODICALS

Antioch Review, spring, 1981.

Best Sellers, April, 1984.
Books and Bookmen, December, 1979.
Books of the Times, September, 1980.
British Book News, September, 1986.
Listener, September 13, 1979.
New York Review of Books, October 23, 1980.
New York Times Book Review, April 29, 1984.
Observer, August 10, 1986.
Science Books and Films, March, 1981.
Science Fiction Review, February, 1986.
Spectator, August 23, 1986.
Times Literary Supplement, February 10, 1978, December 9, 1983.

* * *

HUDSON, Jeffery
   See CRICHTON, (John) Michael

* * *

HUEFFER, Ford Madox
   See FORD, Ford Madox

* * *

HUGHES, Colin
   See CREASEY, John

* * *

HUGHES, (James) Langston 1902-1967

PERSONAL: Born February 1, 1902, in Joplin, Mo.; died May 22, 1967, of congestive heart failure in New York, N.Y.; son of James Nathaniel (a businessman, lawyer, and rancher) and Carrie Mercer (a teacher; maiden name, Langston) Hughes. *Education:* Attended Columbia University, 1921-22; Lincoln University, A.B., 1929.

ADDRESSES: Home—20 East 127th St., New York, N.Y. *Agent*—Harold Ober Associates, Inc., 40 East 49th St., New York, N.Y. 10017.

CAREER: Poet, novelist, short story writer, playwright, song lyricist, radio writer, translator, author of juvenile books, and lecturer. In early years worked as assistant cook, launderer, busboy, and at other odd jobs; worked as seaman on voyages to Africa and Europe. Lived at various times in Mexico, France, Italy, Spain, and the Soviet Union. Madrid correspondent for *Baltimore Afro-American,* 1937; visiting professor in creative writing, Atlanta University, 1947; poet in residence, Laboratory School, University of Chicago, 1949.

MEMBER: Authors Guild, Dramatists Guild, American Society of Composers, Authors, and Publishers, P.E.N., National Institute of Arts and Letters, Omega Psi Phi.

AWARDS, HONORS: Opportunity magazine literary contest, first prize in poetry, 1925; Witter Bynner undergraduate poetry prize contests, first prize, 1926; *Palms* magazine Intercollegiate Poetry Award, 1927; Harmon Gold Medal for Literature, 1931; Guggenheim fellowship for creative work, 1935; Rosenwald fellowship, 1941; Litt.D., Lincoln University, 1943; American Academy of Arts and Letters grant, 1947; Anisfeld-Wolfe Award for best book on racial relations, 1954; Spingarn Medal, National Association for the Advancement of Colored People, 1960.

WRITINGS:

POETRY; PUBLISHED BY KNOPF, EXCEPT AS INDICATED

The Weary Blues, 1926.
Fine Clothes to the Jew, 1927.
The Negro Mother and Other Dramatic Recitations, Golden Stair Press, 1931.
Dear Lovely Death, Troutbeck Press, 1931.
The Dream Keeper and Other Poems, 1932.
Scottsboro Limited: Four Poems and a Play, Golden Stair Press, 1932.
A New Song, International Workers Order, 1938.
(With Robert Glenn) *Shakespeare in Harlem,* 1942.
Jim Crow's Last Stand, Negro Publication Society of America, 1943.
Freedom's Plow, Musette Publishers, 1943.
Lament for Dark Peoples and Other Poems, Holland, 1944.
Fields of Wonder, 1947.
One-Way Ticket, 1949.
Montage of a Dream Deferred, Holt, 1951.
Ask Your Mama: 12 Moods for Jazz, 1961.
The Panther and the Lash: Poems of Our Times, 1967.

NOVELS

Not Without Laughter, Knopf, 1930, reprinted, Macmillan, 1986.
Tambourines to Glory, John Day, 1958, reprinted, Hill & Wang, 1970.

SHORT STORIES

The Ways of White Folks, Knopf, 1934, reprinted, Random House, 1971.
Simple Speaks His Mind, Simon & Schuster, 1950.
Laughing to Keep from Crying, Holt, 1952.
Simple Takes a Wife, Simon & Schuster, 1953.
Simple Stakes a Claim, Rinehart, 1957.
Something in Common and Other Stories, Hill & Wang, 1963.
Simple's Uncle Sam, Hill & Wang, 1965.

AUTOBIOGRAPHY

The Big Sea: An Autobiography, Knopf, 1940 reprinted, Thunder's Mouth, 1986.
I Wonder as I Wander: An Autobiographical Journey, Rinehart, 1956, reprinted, Thunder's Mouth, 1986.

NONFICTION

A Negro Looks at Soviet Central Asia, Co-operative Publishing Society of Foreign Workers in the U.S.S.R., 1934.
(With Roy De Carava) *The Sweet Flypaper of Life,* Simon & Schuster, 1955, reprinted, Howard University Press, 1985.
(With Milton Meltzer) *A Pictorial History of the Negro in America,* Crown, 1956, 4th edition published as *A Pictorial History of Blackamericans,* 1973.
Fight for Freedom: The Story of the NAACP, Norton, 1962.
(With Meltzer) *Black Magic: A Pictorial History of the Negro in American Entertainment,* Prentice-Hall, 1967.
Black Misery, Paul S. Erickson, 1969.

JUVENILE

(With Arna Bontemps) *Popo and Fifina: Children of Haiti,* Macmillan, 1932.
The First Book of Negroes, F. Watts, 1952.
The First Book of Rhythms, F. Watts, 1954.
Famous American Negroes, Dodd, 1954.
Famous Negro Music Makers, Dodd, 1955.

The First Book of Jazz, F. Watts, 1955, revised edition, 1976.
The First Book of the West Indies, F. Watts, 1956 (published in England as *The First Book of the Caribbean,* E. Ward, 1965).
Famous Negro Heroes of America, Dodd, 1958.
The First Book of Africa, F. Watts, 1960, revised edition, 1964.

EDITOR

Four Lincoln University Poets, Lincoln University, 1930.
(With Bontemps) *The Poetry of the Negro, 1746-1949,* Doubleday, 1949, revised edition published as *The Poetry of the Negro, 1746-1970,* 1970.
(With Waring Cuney and Bruce M. Wright) *Lincoln University Poets,* Fine Editions, 1954.
(With Bontemps) *The Book of Negro Folklore,* Dodd, 1958, reprinted, 1983.
An African Treasury: Articles, Essays, Stories, Poems by Black Africans, Crown, 1960.
Poems from Black Africa, Indiana University Press, 1963.
New Negro Poets: U.S., foreword by Gwendolyn Brooks, Indiana University Press, 1964.
The Book of Negro Humor, Dodd, 1966.
The Best Short Stories by Negro Writers: An Anthology from 1899 to the Present, Little, Brown, 1967.

TRANSLATOR

(With Mercer Cook) Jacques Roumain, *Masters of Dew,* Reynal & Hitchcock, 1947, second edition, Liberty Book Club, 1957.
(With Frederic Carruthers) Nicolas Guillen, *Cuba Libre,* Ward Ritchie, 1948.
Selected Poems of Gabriela Mistral, Indiana University Press, 1957.

OMNIBUS VOLUMES

Selected Poems, Knopf, 1959, reprinted, Vintage Books, 1974.
The Best of Simple, Hill & Wang, 1961.
Five Plays by Langston Hughes, edited by Webster Smalley, Indiana University Press, 1963.
The Langston Hughes Reader, Braziller, 1968.
Don't You Turn Back (poems), edited by Lee Bennett Hopkins, Knopf, 1969.
Good Morning Revolution: The Uncollected Social Protest Writing of Langston Hughes, edited by Faith Berry, Lawrence Hill, 1973.

OTHER

(With Bontemps) *Arna Bontemps-Langston Hughes Letters: 1925-1967,* edited by Charles H. Nichols, Dodd, 1980.

Author of numerous plays (most have been produced), including "Little Ham," 1935, "Mulatto," 1935, "Emperor of Haiti," 1936, "Troubled Island," 1936, "When the Jack Hollers," 1936, "Front Porch," 1937, "Joy to My Soul," 1937, "Soul Gone Home," 1937, "Little Eva's End," 1938, "Limitations of Life," 1938, "The Em-Fuehrer Jones," 1938, "Don't You Want to Be Free," 1938, "The Organizer," 1939, "The Sun Do Move," 1942, "For This We Fight," 1943, "The Barrier," 1950, "The Glory Round His Head," 1953, "Simply Heavenly," 1957, "Esther," 1957, "The Ballad of the Brown King," 1960, "Black Nativity," 1961, "Gospel Glow," 1962, "Jericho-Jim Crow," 1963, "Tambourines to Glory," 1963, "The Prodigal Son," 1965, "Soul Yesterday and Today," "Angelo Herndon Jones," "Mother and Child," "Trouble with the Angels," and "Outshines the Sun."

Also author of screenplay, "Way Down South," 1942. Author of libretto for operas, "The Barrier," 1950, and "Troubled Island." Lyricist for "Just Around the Corner," and for Kurt Weill's "Street Scene," 1948. Columnist for *Chicago Defender* and *New York Post*. Poetry, short stories, criticism, and plays have been included in numerous anthologies. Contributor to periodicals, including *Nation, African Forum, Black Drama, Players Magazine, Negro Digest, Black World, Freedomways, Harlem Quarterly, Phylon, Challenge, Negro Quarterly,* and *Negro Story.*

SIDELIGHTS: Langston Hughes was first recognized as an important literary figure during the 1920s, a period known as the "Harlem Renaissance" because of the number of emerging black writers. Du Bose Heyward wrote in the *New York Herald Tribune* in 1926: "Langston Hughes, although only twenty-four years old, is already conspicuous in the group of Negro intellectuals who are dignifying Harlem with a genuine art life. . . . It is, however, as an individual poet, not as a member of a new and interesting literary group, or as a spokesman for a race that Langston Hughes must stand or fall. . . . Always intensely subjective, passionate, keenly sensitive to beauty and possessed of an unfaltering musical sense, Langston Hughes has given us a 'first book' that marks the opening of a career well worth watching."

Despite Heyward's statement, much of Hughes's early work was roundly criticized by many black intellectuals for portraying what they thought to be an unattractive view of black life. In his autobiographical *The Big Sea,* Hughes commented: "*Fine Clothes to the Jew* was well received by the literary magazines and the white press, but the Negro critics did not like it at all. The Pittsburgh *Courier* ran a big headline across the top of the page, *LANGSTON HUGHES' BOOK OF POEMS TRASH.* The headline in the New York *Amsterdam News* was *LANGSTON HUGHES—THE SEWER DWELLER.* The Chicago *Whip* characterized me as 'the poet low-rate of Harlem.' Others called the book a disgrace to the race, a return to the dialect tradition, and a parading of all our racial defects before the public. . . . The Negro critics and many of the intellectuals were very sensitive about their race in books. (And still are.) In anything that white people were likely to read, they wanted to put their best foot forward, their politely polished and cultural foot—and only that foot."

An example of the type of criticism of which Hughes was writing is Estace Gay's comments on *Fine Clothes to the Jew.* "It does not matter to me whether every poem in the book is true to life," Gay wrote. "Why should it be paraded before the American public by a Negro author as being typical or representative of the Negro? Bad enough to have white authors holding up our imperfections to public gaze. Our aim ought to be [to] present to the general public, already mis-informed both by well meaning and malicious writers, our higher aims and aspirations, and our better selves."

Commenting on reviewers like Gay, Hughes wrote: "I sympathized deeply with those critics and those intellectuals, and I saw clearly the need for some of the kinds of books they wanted. But I did not see how they could expect every Negro author to write such books. Certainly, I personally knew very few people anywhere who were wholly beautiful and wholly good. Besides I felt that the masses of our people had as much in their lives to put into books as did those more fortunate ones who had been born with some means and the ability to work up to a master's degree at a Northern college. Anyway, I didn't know the upper class Negroes well enough to write much about them. I knew only the people I had grown up with, and they weren't people whose

shoes were always shined, who had been to Harvard, or who had heard of Bach. But they seemed to me good people, too."

Hoyt W. Fuller commented that Hughes "chose to identify with plain black people—not because it required less effort and sophistication, but precisely because he saw more truth and profound significance in doing so. Perhaps in this he was inversely influenced by his father—who, frustrated by being the object of scorn in his native land, rejected his own people. Perhaps the poet's reaction to his father's flight from the American racial reality drove him to embrace it with extra fervor." (Langston Hughes's parents separated shortly after his birth and his father moved to Mexico. The elder Hughes came to feel a deep dislike and revulsion for other American blacks.)

In Hughes's own words, his poetry is about "workers, roustabouts, and singers, and job hunters on Lenox Avenue in New York, or Seventh Street in Washington or South State in Chicago—people up today and down tomorrow, working this week and fired the next, beaten and baffled, but determined not to be wholly beaten, buying furniture on the installment plan, filling the house with roomers to help pay the rent, hoping to get a new suit for Easter—and pawning that suit before the Fourth of July." In fact, the title *Fine Clothes to the Jew,* which was misunderstood and disliked by many people, was derived from the Harlemites Hughes saw pawning their own clothing; most of the pawn shops and other stores in Harlem at that time were owned by Jewish people.

Lindsay Patterson, a novelist who served as Hughes's assistant, believed that Hughes was "critically, the most abused poet in America. . . . Serious white critics ignored him, less serious ones compared his poetry to Cassius Clay doggerel, and most black critics only grudgingly admired him. Some, like James Baldwin, were downright malicious about his poetic achievement. But long after Baldwin and the rest of us are gone, I suspect Hughes' poetry will be blatantly around growing in stature until it is recognized for its genius. Hughes' tragedy was double-edged: he was unashamedly black at a time when blackness was demode, and he didn't go much beyond one of his earliest themes, black *is* beautiful. He had the wit and intelligence to explore the black human condition in a variety of depths, but his tastes and selectivity were not always accurate, and pressures to survive as a black writer in a white society (and it was a miracle that he did for so long) extracted an enormous creative toll. Nevertheless, Hughes, more than any other black poet or writer, recorded faithfully the nuances of black life and its frustrations."

Although Hughes had trouble with both black and white critics, he was the first black American to earn his living solely from his writing and public lectures. Part of the reason he was able to do this was the phenomenal acceptance and love he received from average black people. A reviewer for *Black World* noted in 1970: "Those whose prerogative it is to determine the rank of writers have never rated him highly, but if the weight of public response is any gauge then Langston Hughes stands at the apex of literary relevance among Black people. The poet occupies such a position in the memory of his people precisely because he recognized that 'we possess within ourselves a great reservoir of physical and spiritual strength,' and because he used his artistry to reflect this back to the people. He used his poetry and prose to illustrate that 'there is no lack within the Negro people of beauty, strength and power,' and he chose to do so on their own level, on their own terms."

Hughes brought a varied and colorful background to his writing. Before he was twelve years old he had lived in six different American cities. When his first book was published, he had already been a truck farmer, cook, waiter, college graduate, sailor, and doorman at a nightclub in Paris, and had visited Mexico, West Africa, the Azores, the Canary Islands, Holland, France, and Italy. As David Littlejohn observed in his *Black on White: A Critical Survey of Writing by American Negroes:* "On the whole, Hughes' creative life [was] as full, as varied, and as original as Picasso's, a joyful, honest monument of a career. There [was] no noticeable sham in it, no pretension, no self-deceit; but a great, great deal of delight and smiling irresistible wit. If he seems for the moment upstaged by angrier men, by more complex artists, if 'different views engage' us, necessarily, at this trying stage of the race war, he may well outlive them all, and still be there when it's over. . . . Hughes' [greatness] seems to derive from his anonymous unity with his people. He *seems* to speak for millions, which is a tricky thing to do."

Hughes reached many people through his popular fictional character, Jesse B. Semple (shortened to Simple). Simple is a poor man who lives in Harlem, a kind of comic no-good, a stereotype Hughes turned to advantage. He tells his stories to Boyd, the foil in the stories who is a writer much like Hughes, in return for a drink. His tales of his troubles with work, women, money, and life in general often reveal, through their very simplicity, the problems of being a poor black man in a racist society. "White folks," Simple once commented, "is the cause of a lot of inconvenience in my life."

Donald C. Dickinson wrote in his *Bio-Bibliography of Langston Hughes* that the "charm of Simple lies in his uninhibited pursuit of those two universal goals, understanding and security. As with most other humans, he usually fails to achieve either of these goals and sometimes once achieved they disappoint him. . . . Simple has a tough resilience, however, that won't allow him to brood over a failure very long. . . . Simple is a well-developed character, both believable and lovable. The situations he meets and discusses are so true to life everyone may enter the fun. This does not mean that Simple is in any way dull. He injects the ordinary with his own special insights. . . . Simple is a natural, unsophisticated man who never abandons his hope in tomorrow."

A reviewer for *Black World* commented on the popularity of Simple: "The people responded. Simple lived in a world they knew, suffered their pangs, experienced their joys, reasoned in their way, talked their talk, dreamed their dreams, laughed their laughs, voiced their fears—and all the while underneath, he affirmed the wisdom which anchored at the base of their lives. It was not that ideas and events and places and people beyond the limits of Harlem—all of the Harlems—did not concern him; these things, indeed, were a part of his consciousness; but Simple's rock-solid commonsense enabled him to deal with them with balance and intelligence. . . . Simple knows *who* he is and *what* he is, and he knows that the status of expatriate offers no solution, no balm. The struggle is here, and it can only be won here, and no constructive end is served through fantasies and illusions and false efforts at disguising a basic sense of inadequacy. Simple also knows that the strength, the tenacity, the commitment which are necessary to win the struggle also exist within the Black community."

Hoyt W. Fuller believed that, like Simple, "the key to Langston Hughes . . . was the poet's deceptive and *profound* simplicity. Profound because it was both willed and ineffable, because some intuitive sense even at the beginning of his adulthood taught him that humanity was of the essence and that it existed undiminished in all shapes, sizes, colors and conditions. Violations of that

humanity offended his unshakable conviction that mankind is possessed of the divinity of God."

It was Hughes's belief in humanity and his hope for a world in which people could sanely and with understanding live together that led to his decline in popularity in the racially turbulent latter years of his life. Unlike younger and more militant writers, Hughes never lost his conviction that "*most* people are generally good, in every race and in every country where I have been." Reviewing *The Panther and the Lash: Poems of Our Times* in *Poetry,* Laurence Lieberman recognized that Hughes's "sensibility [had] kept pace with the times," but he criticized his lack of a personal political stance. "Regrettably, in different poems, he is fatally prone to sympathize with starkly antithetical politics of race," Lieberman commented. "A reader can appreciate his catholicity, his tolerance of all the rival—and mutually hostile—views of his outspoken compatriots, from Martin Luther King to Stokely Carmichael, but we are tempted to ask, what are Hughes' politics? And if he has none, why not? The age demands intellectual commitment from its spokesmen. A poetry whose chief claim on our attention is moral, rather than aesthetic, must take sides politically."

Despite some recent criticism, Langston Hughes's position in the American literary scene seems to be secure. David Littlejohn wrote that Hughes is "the one sure Negro classic, more certain of permanence than even Baldwin or Ellison or Wright. . . . His voice is as sure, his manner as original, his position as secure as, say Edwin Arlington Robinson's or Robinson Jeffers'. . . . By molding his verse always on the sounds of Negro talk, the rhythms of Negro music, by retaining his own keen honesty and directness, his poetic sense and ironic intelligence, he maintained through four decades a readable newness distinctly his own."

Hughes's poems have been translated into German, French, Spanish, Russian, Yiddish, and Czech; many of them have been set to music. Donald B. Gibson noted in the introduction to *Modern Black Poets: A Collection of Critical Essays* that Hughes "has perhaps the greatest reputation (worldwide) that any black writer has ever had. Hughes differed from most of his predecessors among black poets, and (until recently) from those who followed him as well, in that he addressed his poetry to the people, specifically to black people. During the twenties when most American poets were turning inward, writing obscure and esoteric poetry to an ever decreasing audience of readers, Hughes was turning outward, using language and themes, attitudes and ideas familiar to anyone who had the ability simply to read. He has been, unlike most nonblack poets other than Walt Whitman, Vachel Lindsay, and Carl Sandburg, a poet of the people. . . . Until the time of his death, he spread his message humorously—though always seriously—to audiences throughout the country, having read his poetry to more people (possibly) than any other American poet."

BIOGRAPHICAL/CRITICAL SOURCES:

BOOKS

Baker, Houston A., Jr., *Black Literature in America,* McGraw, 1971.

Bone, Robert A., *The Negro Novel in America,* Yale University Press, 1965.

Children's Literature Review, Volume 17, Gale, 1989.

Concise Dictionary of Literary Biography: The Age of Maturity, 1929-1941, Gale, 1989.

Contemporary Literary Criticism, Gale, Volume 1, 1973, Volume 5, 1976, Volume 10, 1979, Volume 15, 1980, Volume 35, 1985, Volume 44, 1987.

Davis, Arthur P. and Saunders Redding, editors, *Cavalcade*, Houghton, 1971.

Dekle, Bernard, *Profiles of Modern American Authors*, Charles E. Tuttle, 1969.

Dickinson, Donald C., *A Bio-Bibliography of Langston Hughes, 1902-1967*, Archon Books, 1967.

Dictionary of Literary Biography, Gale, Volume 4: *American Writers in Paris, 1920-1939*, 1980, Volume 7: *Twentieth-Century American Dramatists*, 1981, Volume 48: *American Poets, 1880-1945, Second Series*, 1986, Volume 51: *Afro-American Writers From the Harlem Renaissance to 1940*, 1987.

Emanuel, James, *Langston Hughes*, Twayne, 1967.

Gibson, Donald B., editor, *Five Black Writers*, New York University Press, 1970.

Gibson, Donald B., editor and author of introduction, *Modern Black Poets: A Collection of Critical Essays*, Prentice-Hall, 1973.

Hart, W., editor, *American Writers' Congress*, International, 1935.

Hughes, Langston, *The Big Sea: An Autobiography*, Knopf, 1940.

Hughes, Langston, *I Wonder as I Wander: An Autobiographical Journey*, Rinehart, 1956.

Jackson, Blyden and Louis D. Rubin, Jr., *Black Poetry in America: Two Essays in Historical Interpretation*, Louisiana State University, 1974.

Jahn, Janheinz, *A Bibliography of Neo-African Literature from Africa, America and the Caribbean*, Praeger, 1965.

Littlejohn, David, *Black on White: A Critical Survey of Writing by American Negroes*, Viking, 1966.

Meltzer, Milton, *Langston Hughes: A Biography*, Crowell, 1968.

Myers, Elizabeth P., *Langston Hughes: Poet of His People*, Garrard, 1970.

O'Daniel, Thermon B., editor, *Langston Hughes: Black Genius, a Critical Evaluation*, Morrow, 1971.

Rollins, Charlamae H., *Black Troubador: Langston Hughes*, Rand McNally, 1970.

Something About the Author, Gale, Volume 4, 1973, Volume 33, Gale, 1983.

PERIODICALS

American Mercury, January, 1959.
Black Scholar, June, 1971, July, 1976.
Black World, June, 1970, September, 1972, September, 1973.
Booklist, November 15, 1976.
CLA Journal, June, 1972.
Chicago Tribune Book World, April 13, 1980.
Crisis, August-September, 1960, June, 1967, February, 1969.
Ebony, October, 1946.
English Journal, March, 1977.
Life, February 4, 1966.
Nation, December 4, 1967.
Negro American Literature Forum, winter, 1971.
Negro Digest, September, 1967, November, 1967, April, 1969.
New Leader, April 10, 1967.
New Republic, January 14, 1974.
New Yorker, December 30, 1967.
New York Herald Tribune, August 1, 1926.
New York Herald Tribune Books, November 26, 1961.
New York Times, May 24, 1967, June 1, 1968, June 29, 1969, December 13, 1970.
New York Times Book Review, November 3, 1968.
Philadelphia Tribune, February 5, 1927.
Poetry, August, 1968.

San Francisco Chronicle, April 5, 1959.
Saturday Review, November 22, 1958, September 29, 1962.
Washington Post, November 13, 1978.
Washington Post Book World, February 2, 1969, December 8, 1985.

* * *

HUGHES, Richard (Arthur Warren) 1900-1976

PERSONAL: Born April 19, 1900, in Weybridge, Surrey, England; died April 28, 1976 of leukemia; son of Arthur and Louisa Grace (Warren) Hughes; married Frances Catharine Ruth Bazley, January 8, 1932; children: Robert Elystan-Glodrydd, Penelope Hughes Minney, Lleky Susanna Hughes Papastavrou, Catharine Phyllida Hughes Wells, Owain Gardner Collingwood. *Education:* Oriel College, Oxford, B.A., 1922.

CAREER: Novelist, poet, and playwright. As a young man, lived (more for amusement than of necessity) as a tramp, a beggar, and a pavement artist in Europe and, during two brief visits, in the United States; once conducted an expedition through Central Europe and traveled on his own through Canada, the West Indies, and the Near East, as well as Europe and America; University of London, London, England, Gresham Professor of Rhetoric, three years during the 1920's. Co-founder of the Portmadoc Players, a Welsh theatrical company, 1923; first vice-chairman of Welsh National Theatre, 1924-36; from the middle 1940's until 1955, he was primarily engaged with writing filmscripts for Ealing Studios, Ealing, London, England. Civilian Deputy Principal Priority Officer, British Admiralty, 1940-45. *Military service:* British Army, 1918; became second lieutenant.

MEMBER: Royal Society of Literature (fellow), American Academy of Arts and Letters (honorary member), National Institute of Arts and Letters (honorary member); United University Club, Pratt's Club (both London); Royal Welsh Yacht Club (Caemavon).

AWARDS, HONORS: Femina-Vie Heureuse Prize, for *A High Wind in Jamaica;* decorated by British Admiralty, 1946; Order of the British Empire, 1946, for wartime service; D.Litt. from University of Wales, 1956; Arts Council Award, 1961, for *The Fox in the Attic.*

WRITINGS:

NOVELS

The Innocent Voyage, Harper, 1929, (published in England as *A High Wind in Jamaica*, Chatto & Windus, 1929), published as *A High Wind in Jamaica*, Harper, 1930, reprinted with new introduction, 1972.

In Hazard, 1938 (published in England as *In Hazard: A Sea Story*, Chatto & Windus, 1938).

The Fox in the Attic (first volume in "The Human Predicament" series), Harper, 1961.

The Wooden Shepherdess (second bolume in "The Human Predicament" series), Harper, 1973.

POETRY

Lines Written Upon First Observing an Elephant Devoured by a Roc, Golden Cockerel Press, 1922.

Gipsy Night and Other Poems, W. Ransom, 1922.

Ecstatic Ode on Vision, privately printed, 1923.

Meditative Ode on Vision, privately printed, 1923.

Confessio Juvenis: Collected Poems, Chatto & Windus, 1926.

STORY COLLECTIONS

A Moment of Time, Chatto & Windus, 1926.

Burial, and the Dark Child, privately printed, 1930.

The Wonder Dog: The Collected Children's Stories of Richard Hughes, Greenwillow Books, 1977.

In the Lap of Atlas: Stories of Morocco, Chatto & Windus, 1979.

PLAYS

The Sisters' Tragedy (one-act; also see below; first produced in London, 1922), Basil Blackwell, 1922.

A Rabbit and a Leg (includes "The Sisters' Tragedy," "A Comedy of Good and Evil" [produced in London at Birmingham Repertory Theatre, 1924, revived and produced on Broadway as "Minnie and Mr. Williams," 1948], "The Man Born to Be Hanged," "Danger" [radio play; produced on British Broadcasting Corp., 1924]), Knopf, 1924 (published in England as *The Sisters' Tragedy, and Other Plays,* Chatto & Windus, 1924), reprinted as *Plays,* Harper, 1966.

OTHER

(Editor with Robert Graves and Alan Porter) *Oxford Poetry,* Basil Blackwell, 1921.

(Editor) John Skelton, *Poems,* Heinemann, 1924, reprinted, Heinemann, 1977. *Richard Hughes: An Omnibus,* Harper, 1931.

The Spider's Palace, and Other Stories (juvenile), Harper, 1932, reprinted, Penguin, 1972.

Don't Blame Me, and Other Stories (juvenile), Harper, 1940.

(With John Dick Scott) *The Administration of War Production,* H.M.S.O., 1955.

Liturgical Language Today, Church in Wales Publication, 1962.

Gertrude's Child, Harlin Quist, 1966, W. H. Allen, 1967.

Gertrude and the Mermaid (juvenile), Harlin Quist, 1967.

The Lively Image: Four Myths in Literature, Winthrop Publishing, 1975.

Zion Building, Herald House, 1978.

Also author of numerous radio scripts. Contributor to *Atlantic Monthly, Encounter, Listener, New Statesman,* and *New York Herald Tribune.*

SIDELIGHTS: Many critics feel it is unfortunate that Richard Hughes never finished the third volume in his "The Human Predicament" series. While the first two volumes, *The Fox in the Attic* and *The Wooden Shepherdess,* were heralded by many as possibly Hughes' greatest works, many reviewers feel the third volume would be necessary to complete the tale satisfactorily. Hughes intended the series to be a historical trilogy about events between the two World Wars. Besides his novels, Hughes also wrote plays, children's books, and poetry, and he is credited with having written the first radio play, which was broadcast by the British Broadcasting Corp. in 1924.

Walter Sullivan felt Hughes attempted a difficult task when he began his most ambitious project, "The Human Predicament" historical series. As Sullivan explained in the *Sewanee Review:* "Writing about historical figures and hewing the line of historical fact is not easy. The novelist is bound by the dimensions of what was: His imagination is strictly circumscribed by reality. The case of Nazi Germany is a special problem; good writers . . . have failed in trying to write about it out of an excess of feeling against the material they seek to employ. Hughes succeeds. His dramatization of the Night of the Long Knives is masterful—cleanly written, balanced, totally convincing, and moving in a way that no adjective can describe. . . . The joining of the public and private themes is in the final scene [in *The Wooden Shepherdess*] extrapolated, enlarged, transfigured into a melding of the metaphysical and the mundane. All of our realities are encompassed in a scene that is absolutely successful. We could not

legitimately ask for more." *New Statesman*'s Goronwy Rees believed that Hughes was able to accomplish this difficult task of writing an historical trilogy because he had "as deep a passion for history as he has for literature, and he records it with . . . accuracy and respect for truth."

A critic for the *Economist* wrote that the second volume, *The Wooden Shepherdess,* "reinforces the feeling . . . that an obscure relationship exists between ['The Human Predicament'] and 'La Condition Humaine'. . . . Such is its quality that the reader is forever desperate to go on and desperate to go back to find the beginnings of the characters who here surface like drowning men in the sea of history and go under for the second time in 1934. . . . It is wonderfully done, the central panel of an undoubted masterpiece." A *Times Literary Supplement* reviewer called the first volume in this series, *The Fox in the Attic,* "a magnificent, authoritative, compassionate, ironic, funny and tragic book."

Several critics regretted that Hughes' literary output was so small. Specifically, in relation to the trilogy, many critics felt that too much time elapsed between the two published volumes in this trilogy. The first volume of the series was published in 1961 while the second was published in 1973. Rees explained that "so long a gap in publication presents the reader with its own difficulties, particularly as 'The Human Predicament' is designed. . . . The most a reviewer can do . . . is to report progress, rather than pass any final judgment. For Mr. Hughes is a very conscious and deliberate artist, and if there are certain episodes in the present volume whose significance we do not entirely grasp, we can be confident that it will not be concealed by the time the novel is completed."

However, Rees went on to say that "Hughes triumphantly surmounts the difficulties he has imposed on himself by his method of publication. He is . . . a very slow writer. . . . But slowness has its rewards as well as its penalties, and in Mr. Hughes' case one of them is that the novel's long process of gestation has given birth to certain scenes of almost hallucinatory vividness and power. It is as if the writer had sunk into some profound slumber in which, as in a dream, the imagination was set free to conjure up visions and images unaffected by the passage of time. Such a gift makes Mr. Hughes almost unique among contemporary novelists, but like so many precious gifts, it also has its dangers, of which one is that certain scenes stand out so sharply in our minds that we are not always able—as yet—to see how they are related to what comes before and after."

In 1976, the *New York Times* reprinted an explanation Hughes gave to the periodical in 1962 concerning the modest amount of his published work. He told the interviewer: "I am a very slow writer. Everyone tells me that. But a writer does not choose his subjects or his stories." Concerning the time gap between the volumes in his historical series, Hughes explained that "in an enterprise of this sort, it is always a race between the publisher and the undertaker."

Although Hughes was not an extremely prolific poet and novelist, he did earn a reputation as a novelist of distinction. *The Innocent Voyage,* or *A High Wind in Jamaica,* as it is probably better known, was a tremendous success for Hughes, selling more than three million copies. Writing in the *Times Literary Supplement,* Alastair Forbes called the novel "that seamless non-pareil work of genius in which, after no matter how many rereadings, one wishes no single word altered." T. J. Henighan of *Critique: Studies in Modern Fiction* wrote: "I believe [much] can be said for *A High Wind in Jamaica* as a work of fiction, and that as such, it not only stands up to close analysis, but reveals itself as a novel of profound irony, closer to Conrad than to Lewis Carroll. . . . *A High Wind in Jamaica* is a profoundly moving book, funny, beautiful, and finally terrifying."

Some critics, however, including *New Statesman's* Cyril Connolly, believed that it was Hughes' lack of style in *A High Wind in Jamaica* that distinguished his writing. As Connolly explained: "The art of the writer is shown, not in the style so much as in the avoidance of style, in his skill in never 'writing up' incidents which are preposterous enough in themselves, in always making the right transition from one extraordinary pen-picture to the next." And R. B. Macdougall of the *Saturday Review of Literature* believed "no reader will be untouched by the novel's freshness and far-spreading vitality. No one can set it down without thinking some long, long thoughts."

Hughes once admitted that, in a sense, he relinquished his own style to the fictive "style" of each character. "All characters are different facets of the author," he told the *Christian Science Monitor.* "I use a stream of consciousness to describe [an incident] as it appeared to the last person who spoke, though not in his words." By this method Hughes achieved, according to the *Times Literary Supplement,* a language which is "simple, clear, precise to the point of being faintly scientific—and at the same time astonishingly evocative. His verbal control is in itself a *tour de force.*"

In his later years, Hughes had little enthusiasm for his early work, even though critics still praised *A High Wind in Jamaica.* "*A High Wind in Jamaica* and *In Hazard* are both so remote from me," he once wrote. "Now I am only interested in what I am going to write. I want to bring 'The Human Predicament' down to the end of the war. The next volume is going rather faster—should be ready in a couple of years. There should be three or four volumes more, but I will be about 140 years old when I finish them."

James Gray of the *Saturday Review* recognized Hughes' effort as well as his accomplishment: "Hughes [was] inspired as Tolstoy was by the compulsion to create. Everything that he touches comes to life in a gusty, laughing, tender, tragic interpretation of the weird contradictions that jostle each other so pitifully in the human heart." Belinda Humfrey, in her article for the *Dictionary of Literary Biography,* found that Hughes' "reputation for extraordinary brilliance as a writer rests mainly on [four novels], all vividly daring in choice of plot, highly wrought yet brilliantly readable in style, ambitious in their variety of scene and dramatic action, each challenging basic contemporary moral, religious, social and human assumptions."

MEDIA ADAPTATIONS: The Innocent Voyage was dramatized by Paul Osborn and produced on Broadway in 1943; the novel was also filmed by Twentieth Century-Fox Film Corp. and released as "A High Wind in Jamaica" in 1965.

BIOGRAPHICAL/CRITICAL SOURCES:

BOOKS

Contemporary Literary Criticism, Gale, Volume 1, 1973, Volume 11, 1979.
Dictionary of Literary Biography, Volume 15: *British Novelists, 1930-1959,* Gale, 1983.

PERIODICALS

Book Week, April 23, 1967.
Catholic World, May, 1962.
Christian Science Monitor, August 10, 1938, March 2, 1967.
Commonweal, March 30, 1962.

Critique: Studies in Modern Fiction, Volume IX, number 1, 1967.
Economist, May 5, 1973.
New Statesman, October 5, 1929, April 6, 1973.
Newsweek, May 10, 1976.
New Yorker, October 8, 1938.
New York Times, April 30, 1976.
New York Times Book Review, February 4, 1962.
Publishers Weekly, May 24, 1976.
Saturday Review, February 3, 1962.
Saturday Review of Literature, April 13, 1929.
Sewanee Review, winter, 1974.
Springfield Republican, October 9, 1938.
Times Literary Supplement, September 26, 1929, July 9, 1938, October 6, 1961, November 30, 1979.
Washington Post, April 30, 1976.

*　　*　　*

HUGHES, Ted 1930-

PERSONAL: Full name, Edward James Hughes; born August 17, 1930, in Mytholmroyd, West Yorkshire, England; son of William Henry (a carpenter) and Edith (Farrar) Hughes; married Sylvia Plath (a poet), 1956 (died, 1963); married Carol Orchard, 1970; children: (first marriage) Frieda Rebecca, Nicholas Farrar. *Education:* Pembroke College, Cambridge, B.A., 1954, M.A., 1959.

ADDRESSES: Home—Court Green, North Tawton, Devonshire, England. *Office*—c/o Faber & Faber Ltd., 3 Queen's Square, London WC1N 3AU, England.

CAREER: Writer. Instructor, University of Massachusetts—Amherst, Amherst, 1957-59. *Military service:* Royal Air Force, 1948-50.

AWARDS, HONORS: First prize, Young Men's and Young Women's Hebrew Association Poetry Center contest, 1957, and first prize, Guinness Poetry Awards, 1958, both for *The Hawk in the Rain;* Guggenheim fellowship, 1959-60; Somerset Maugham Award, 1960, Hawthornden Prize, 1961, and Abraham Wonsell Foundation awards, 1964-69, all for *Lupercal;* City of Florence International Poetry Prize, 1969, for *Wodwo;* Premio Internazionale Taormina, 1972; Queen's Medal for Poetry, 1974; *Season Songs* was a Children's Book Showcase Title, 1976; Officer, Order of the British Empire, 1977; voted Britain's best poet in 1979 poll by *New Poetry* magazine; Signal Poetry awards, 1979, for *Moon-Bells and Other Poems,* 1981, for *Under the North Star,* and 1983, for *The Rattle Bag: An Anthology of Poetry;* Royal Society of Literature Heinemann Award, 1980, for *Moortown;* runner-up for 1981 Neustadt International Prize for Literature; honorary doctorate degrees from Exeter College, 1982, Open University, 1983, Bradford College, 1984, and Pembroke College, 1986; named Poet Laureate of England, 1984; Kurt Maschler/Emil Award, National Book League (Great Britain), 1985, for *The Iron Man;* Guardian Award for children's fiction, 1985, for *What Is the Truth?: A Farmyard Fable for the Young.*

WRITINGS:

POETRY

The Hawk in the Rain, Harper, 1957.
Pike, Gehenna Press (Northampton, Mass.), 1959.
Lupercal, Harper, 1960.
(With Thom Gunn) *Selected Poems,* Faber, 1962.
Animal Poems, Gilbertson, 1967.
Gravestones, Exeter College of Art, 1967, published as *Poems,* 1968.

I Said Goodbye to the Earth, Exeter College of Art, 1969.

The Martyrdom of Bishop Farrer, Gilbertson, 1970.

Crow: From the Life and Songs of the Crow, Faber, 1970, Harper, 1971, revised edition, Faber, 1972, Harper, 1981.

Fighting for Jerusalem, Mid-NAG, 1970.

Selected Poems, 1957-1967, Faber, 1972, Harper, 1973.

Cave Birds (limited edition), Scolar Press, 1975, enlarged edition published as *Cave Birds: An Alchemical Drama,* Faber, 1978, Viking, 1979.

The Interrogator: A Titled Vulturess, Scolar Press, 1975.

Guadete, Harper, 1977.

Remains of Elmet: A Pennine Sequence, Rainbow Press, 1979, revised edition, Faber, 1979.

(Contributor) Michael Morpurgo, *All Around the Year,* J. Murray, 1979.

Moortown (also see below), Faber, 1979, Harper, 1980.

Selected Poems: 1957-1981, Faber, 1982, enlarged edition published as *New Selected Poems,* Harper, 1982.

Primer of Birds: Poems, Phaedon Press, 1982.

River, Faber, 1983, Harper, 1984.

Flowers and Insects: Some Birds and a Pair of Spiders, Knopf, 1986.

Tales of the Early World, Faber, 1988.

Wolfwatching, Faber, 1989.

Moortown Diary (originally published in *Moortown*), Faber, 1989.

POETRY; LIMITED EDITIONS

The Burning of the Brothel, Turret Books, 1966.

Recklings, Turret Books, 1966.

Scapegoats and Rabies: A Poem in Five Parts, Poet & Printer, 1967.

Poems: Ted Hughes, Fainlight, and Sillitoe, Rainbow Press, 1967.

A Crow Hymn, Sceptre Press, 1970.

A Few Crows, Rougemont Press (Exeter, Devon), 1970.

Amulet, privately printed, 1970.

Four Crow Poems, privately printed, 1970.

Autumn Song, privately printed, 1971.

Crow Wakes: Poems, Poet & Printer, 1971.

(With Ruth Fainlight and Alan Sillitoe) *Poems,* Rainbow Press, 1971.

In The Little Girl's Angel Gaze, Steam Press, 1972.

Prometheus on His Crag: 21 Poems, Rainbow Press, 1973.

Eclipse, Sceptre Press, 1976.

Sunstruck, Sceptre Press, 1977.

Chiasmadon, C. Seluzicki (Baltimore), 1977.

Orts, Rainbow Press, 1978.

Moortown Elegies, Rainbow Press, 1978.

A Solstice, Sceptre Press, 1978.

Calder Valley Poems, Rainbow Press, 1978.

Adam and the Sacred Nine, Rainbow Press, 1979.

Henry Williamson: A Tribute, Rainbow Press, 1979.

Four Tales Told by an Idiot, Sceptre Press, 1979.

PLAYS

"The Calm," first produced in Boston, Mass., 1961.

"The Wound," (also see below; radio play) produced, 1962, revised version produced on stage in London, 1972.

"Epithalamium," first produced in London, 1963.

"The House of Donkeys," first broadcast in 1965.

"The Price of a Bride" (juvenile), first broadcast in 1966.

(Adapter) *Seneca's Oedipus* (first produced in London at National Theatre, 1968), Faber, 1969, Doubleday, 1972.

The Coming of the Kings and Other Plays (juvenile; contains "Beauty and the Beast" [first broadcast, 1965; produced in London, 1971], "Sean, the Fool" [first broadcast in 1968; first produced in London, 1971], "The Devil and the Cats" [first broadcast, 1968; first produced in London, 1971], "The Coming of the Kings" [first televised, 1967; first produced in London, 1972; also see below], and "The Tiger's Bones" [first broadcast November 26, 1965]), Faber, 1970, enlarged edition (also contains "Orpheus" [first broadcast, 1971; also see below]) published as *The Tiger's Bones and Other Plays for Children,* Viking, 1975.

"Orghast," first produced in Persepolis, Iran, 1971.

Eat Crow, Rainbow Press, 1971.

The Coming of the Kings: A Christmas Play in One Act, Dramatic Publishing, 1972.

The Iron Man (based on his juvenile book; also see below; televised, 1972), Faber, 1973.

Orpheus, Dramatic Publishing, 1973.

Also author of radio plays, "The House of Aries," 1960, "A Houseful of Women," 1961, "Difficulties of a Bridegroom," 1963, "Dogs," 1964, and "The Head of Gold," 1967.

JUVENILE

Meet My Folks! (verse), Puffin, 1961, Bobbs-Merrill, 1973, enlarged edition, Faber, 1987.

The Earth-Owl and Other Moon-People (verse), Faber, 1963, Antheneum, 1964, published as *Moon-Whales and Other Moon Poems,* Viking, 1976, revised edition published as *Moon Whales,* Faber, 1988.

How the Whale Became and Other Stories, Faber, 1963, with new illustrations, Atheneum, 1964.

Nessie, The Mannerless Monster (verse), Chilmark, 1964, published with new illustrations as *Nessie the Monster,* Bobbs-Merrill, 1974.

The Iron Giant: A Story in Five Nights, Harper, 1968 (published in England as *The Iron Man: A Story in Five Nights,* with different illustrations, Faber, 1968), published with new illustrations, 1984.

Five Autumn Songs for Children's Voices, Gilbertson, 1968.

The Demon of Adachigahara (libretto), Oxford University Press, 1969.

Spring, Summer, Autumn, Winter (verse; limited edition), Rainbow Press, 1974, revised and enlarged edition published as *Season Songs,* Viking, 1975.

Earth-Moon (limited edition), with illustrations by the author, Rainbow Press, 1976.

Moon-Bells and Other Poems, Chatto & Windus, 1978.

"The Pig Organ; or, Pork with Perfect Pitch" (opera), first performed by English Opera Company at the Round House in London, January, 1980.

Under the North Star (verse), Faber, 1981.

(Editor with Seamus Heaney) *The Rattle Bag: An Anthology of Poetry,* Faber, 1982.

What Is Truth?: A Farmyard Fable for the Young (verse), Harper, 1984.

Ffangs the Vampire Bat and the Kiss of Truth, Faber, 1986.

EDITOR

(With Patricia Beer and Vernon Scannell) *New Poems 1962,* Hutchinson, 1962.

(With T. Gunn) *Five American Poets,* Faber, 1963.

Here Today, Hutchinson, 1963.

(With Alwyn Hughes) Sylvia Plath, *Ariel,* Faber, 1965, Harper, 1966.

(And author of introduction) Keith Douglas, *Selected Poems,* Chilmark, 1965.

Poetry in the Making: An Anthology of Poems and Programmes from "Listening and Writing," Faber, 1967, abridged edition published as *Poetry Is,* Doubleday, 1970.

(And author of introduction) Emily Dickinson, *A Choice of Emily Dickinson's Verse,* Faber, 1968.

(And translator with Assia Gutmann) Yehuda Amichai, *Selected Poems,* Cape Goliard Press, 1968, expanded edition published as *Poems,* Harper, 1969.

(And author of introduction; also see below) William Shakespeare, *With Fairest Flowers While Summer Lasts: Poems from Shakespeare,* Doubleday, 1971 (published in England as *A Choice of Shakespeare's Verse,* Faber, 1971).

Plath, *Crossing the Waters: Transitional Poems,* Harper, 1971 (published in England with differing contents as *Crossing the Waters,* Faber, 1971).

Plath, *Winter Trees,* Faber, 1971, Harper, 1972.

(And author of introduction) Plath, *Johnny Panic and the Bible of Dreams, and Other Prose Writings,* Faber, 1977, 2nd edition, Harper, 1979.

(With Janos Csokits and translator) Janos Pilinszky, *Selected Poems,* Persea Books, 1977.

(And translator) Amichai, *Amen,* Harper, 1977.

New Poetry 6, Hutchison, 1980.

(And author of introduction) Plath, *The Collected Poems,* Harper, 1981.

(With Seamus Heaney) *Arvon Foundation Poetry Competition: 1980 Anthology,* Kilnhurst, 1982.

Plath, *Sylvia Plath's Selected Poems,* Faber, 1985.

OTHER

(Contributor) *Writers on Themselves,* BBC Publications, 1964.

Wodwo (miscellany; includes play, "The Wound"), Harper, 1967.

Shakespeare's Poem (originally published as introduction to *With Fairest Flowers While Summer Lasts: Poems from Shakespeare*), Lexham Press, 1971.

(Adapter) *The Story of Vasco* (libretto; adaptation of a play by Georges Schehade; first produced in London, 1974), Oxford University Press, 1974.

(Translator) Charles Simic and Mark Strand, editors, *Another Republic,* Ecco Press, 1977.

(Translator with Amichai) Amichai, *Time,* Harper, 1979.

The Threshold (short story; limited edition), Steam Press, 1979.

(Consulting editor and author of foreword) Frances McCullough, editor, *The Journals of Sylvia Plath,* Dial, 1982.

(Translator with Csokits) Pilinszky, *The Desert of Love,* Anvil Press Poetry, 1988.

Contributor to numerous anthologies. Contributor to periodicals, including *New Yorker, New York Review of Books,* and *Spectator.* Founding editor, with Daniel Weissbrot, *Modern Poetry in Translation* (journal), 1964-71.

SIDELIGHTS: Ted Hughes's reputation as a poet of international stature was secured in the late 1950s with the publication of his first poetry collection, *The Hawk in the Rain.* According to *Dictionary of Literary Biography* contributor Robert B. Shaw: "Hughes's poetry signalled a dramatic departure from the prevailing modes of the period. The stereotypical poem of the time was determined not to risk too much: politely domestic in its subject matter, understated and mildly ironic in style. By contrast, Hughes marshalled a language of nearly Shakespearean resonance to explore themes which were mythic and elemental." Since that time, Hughes's poetry has fallen in and out of fashion

with literary critics—he was excluded, for example, from an important anthology of British poetry published in the early 1980s—but he has continued to make his presence known. Many critics point to his poetic works of the last two decades, *Moortown* and *River,* in particular, as marking a returning to his former brilliance. His 1984 appointment as Poet Laureate of England assures his status as an important British poet for years to come.

Usually written contrary to the prevailing style, Hughes's work has always been controversial. "Critics rarely harbor neutral feelings toward Hughes's poetry," observes Carol Bere in *Literary Review.* "He has been dismissed as a connoisseur of the habits of animals, his disgust with humanity barely disguised; labeled a 'voyeur of violence,' attacked for his generous choreographing of gore; and virtually written off as a cult poet. . . . Others consider him to be the best poet writing today—admired for the originality and command of his approach; the scope and complexity of his mythic enterprise; and the apparent ease and freshness with which he can vitalize a landscape, free of any mitigating sentimentality."

To read Hughes's poetry is to enter a world dominated by nature, especially by animals. This holds true for nearly all of his books from *The Hawk in the Rain* and the bird of the title to *Moortown,* an examination of life on a farm. Apparently, Hughes love of animals was one of the catalysts in his decision to become a poet. According to London *Times* contributor Thomas Nye, Hughes once confessed "that he began writing poems in adolescence, when it dawned upon him that his earlier passion for hunting animals in his native Yorkshire ended either in the possession of a dead animal, or at best a trapped one. He wanted to capture not just live animals, but the aliveness of animals in their natural state: their wildness, their quiddity, the fox-ness of the fox and the crow-ness of the crow."

Hughes's apparent obsession with animals and nature in his poetry has brought the wrath of more than one critic down upon him. In *The Modern Poet: Essays from "The Review,"* Colin Falck, for instance, writes that the "real limitation of Hughes's animal poems is precisely that they conjure emotions without bringing us any nearer to understanding them. They borrow their impact from a complex of emotions that they do nothing to define, an in the end tell us nothing about the urban civilised human world that we read the poems in." Other commentators see Hughes concentration on animals as the poet's attempt to clarify his feelings on the human condition. "Stated in the broadest possible terms," notes Shaw, "Hughes's enterprise is to examine the isolated and precarious position of man in nature and man's chances of overcoming his alienation from the world around him. In pursuit of these interests Hughes focuses frequently (and often brilliantly) upon animals."

According to P. R. King, Hughes's emphasis on wild creatures is not so much evidence of his concern for them as it is a clue to the importance the poet reserves for what animals symbolize in his work. Through animal imagery, Hughes exalts the instinctive power of nature that he finds lacking in human society. "He sees in them," King writes in *Nine Contemporary Poets: A Critical Introduction,* "the most clear manifestation of a life-force that is distinctly non-human or, rather, is non-rational in its source of power. Hughes observes in modern man a reluctance to acknowledge the deepest, instinctual sources of energy in his own being, an energy that is related to the elemental power circuit of the universe and to which animals are closer than man." King believes that in Hughes's poetry written since *Crow* the poet "has moved on to express a sense of sterility and nihilism in modern man's response to life, a response which he connects with the dominance of man's rational, objective intellect at the expense of the life of emotions and imagination."

Hughes's best-known and most intriguing creations is an animal named Crow, who began appearing in his work in 1967 and eventually came to be the main character in several volumes of poetry, including *A Crow Hymn, Crow: From the Life and Songs of the Crow,* and *Crow Wakes.* In a *Time* review, Christopher Porterfield observes: "Crow is a sort of cosmic Kilroy. Alternately a witness, a demon and a victim, he is in on everything from the creation to the ultimate nuclear holocaust. At various times he is minced, dismembered, rendered cataleptic, but always he bobs back. In his graceless, ignoble way, he is the lowest common denominator of the universal forces that obsess Hughes. He is a symbol of the essential survivor, of whatever endures, however battered." In *Ted Hughes* Keith Sagar comments that in Crow he finds an "Everyman who will not acknowledge that everything he most hates and fears—the Black Beast—is within himself. Crow's world is unredeemable." *Newsweek's* Jack Kroll calls *Crow* "one of those rare books of poetry that have the public impact of a major novel or a piece of super-journalism," and summarizes the effect of the character, noting: "In Crow, Ted Hughes has created one of the most powerful mythic presences in contemporary poetry."

Although critics applauded the mythic quality of Hughes's Crow sagas, many feel that in later works the poet's use of myth often met with disastrous results. *New Republic* contributor J. D. Mc-Clatchy, for instance, observed, "When 'The Thought-Fox' first fluttered the henhouse of English poetry in 1957, Hughes seemed a force of nature. . . . But from *Crow* on, the lines seemed to come unstitched, the mythic gestures sounded hollow." Reviewers, such as Richard Murphy and Sandra McPherson find Hughes at his best when he adheres to describing the natural world around him. In his *New York Review of Books* essay on the author, Murphy notes approvingly that in the progression of Hughes's career "demons and mythical birds rightly give way to the real creatures of his imagination." In like fashion, in *American Poetry Review* McPherson finds "when Hughes leaves for the country and helps a halfborn calf in delivery and gets his boots muddy, he gives us rich energized poetry. But few are likely to write anything but a satirical poem at the indoor beach. Similarly, when Hughes writes of mythical animals and heavenly landscapes, the writing is most of the time unpalatable, unattractive, even slightly ridiculous."

Both McPherson and *New Statesman* contributor Blake Morrison lament the appearance of the myth-inspired "Prometheus on His Crag" sequence in Hughes's *Moortown.* According to Mc-Pherson, in this series of poems Hughes strains "to get the point across of a violent, ugly territory of the universe, where understatement has been run out of town." In his *Los Angeles Times Book Review* critique of the volume Peter Clothier notes, "The strength of the book is in the first group of raw poems, the 'Moortown' of the title; its weakness is in flights to myth that dominate later sequences." But despite various objections raised to portions of the book, critics universally acclaim the poems signaled out by Clothier. "The weight and power of the book come in the title sequence," observes *Times Literary Supplement* contributor Peter Scupham, while Christopher Ricks similarly states in the *New York Times Book Review,* "The title sequence, 'Moortown' strikes me as one of [Hughes's] truest achievements in a very long time."

"Moortown" is a group of thirty-four poems which record Hughes's experiences working his Devonshire farm, culminating

in a set of six pieces dedicated to the memory of his late father-in-law, Jack Orchard, who helped him run the farm. Filled with images of sheep and births of lambs and calves, the poems reveal Hughes as a tender observer of nature. The gentle, loving quality noted by critics, gives way at times to brutal descriptions of the harsh realities of farm life. In one poem, for instance, Hughes describes a newborn lamb and its mother lying on the ground "face to face like two mortally wounded duelists." While Joseph Parisi notes in the *Chicago Tribune Book World* that these poems show Hughes "at the height of his powers," McPherson explains that their strength comes from Hughes's respect for and intimate knowledge of his subject matter. "Hughes has to write out of love to make the most of his gifts. . . .," she maintains. "His poems which grow from close contact with their subject have the real healing effect and are as healthy a poetry as being written today."

Observing that four volumes of Hughes's poetry and three critical studies of his work had been published in the first few years of the eighties, Murphy began a review of several of Hughes's poetical offerings with the proclamation, "Ted Hughes is surviving." Hughes's survival as a poet seems to rest on what Mc-Clatchy calls his "capacity to change." Critics see his recent works as turning points in his career, marking the author with a new sensibility as more that just an "animal poet" but rather a poet who uses animals to express his insight into the enduring spirituality of nature. "Hughes's reputation rests on his very individual vision of the natural world. . . .," writes *Listener* contributor Dick Davis. "He is popular for this very reason—he brings back to our suburban, centrally-heated and, above all, *safe* lives reports from an authentic frontier of reality and the imagination. His poems speak to us of a world that is constantly true in a way that we know our temporary comforts cannot be."

BIOGRAPHICAL/CRITICAL SOURCES:

BOOKS

Children's Literature Review, Volume 3, Gale, 1978.
Contemporary Literary Criticism, Gale, Volume 2, 1974, Volume 4, 1975, Volume 9, 1978, Volume 14, 1980, Volume 37, 1986.
Dictionary of Literary Biography, Volume 40: *Poets of Great Britain and Ireland since 1960, Part 1,* Gale, 1985.
Faas, Ekbert, *Ted Hughes: The Unaccommodated Universe,* Black Sparrow Press, 1980.
Gifford, Terry and Neil Roberts, *Ted Hughes: A Critical Study,* Faber, 1981.
Hamilton, Ian, editor, *The Modern Poet: Essays from "The Review,"* MacDonald, 1968.
King, P. R., *Nine Contemporary Poets: A Critical Introduction,* Methuen, 1979.
Sagar, Keith, *Ted Hughes,* Longman, 1972.
Sagar, Keith, *The Art of Ted Hughes,* enlarged edition, Cambridge University Press, 1978.
Sagar, Keith, *The Achievement of Ted Hughes,* Manchester University Press, 1983.

PERIODICALS

American Poetry Review, January-February, 1982.
Chicago Tribune Book World, February 22, 1981.
Listener, January 12, 1984.
Literary Review, spring, 1981.
Los Angeles Times Book Review, August 10, 1980.
New Republic, September 3, 1984.
New Statesman, January 4, 1980.
Newsweek, April 12, 1971.

New York Review of Books, June 10, 1982.
New York Times Book Review, July 20, 1980.
Time, April 5, 1971.
Times (London), January 8, 1987.
Times Literary Supplement, January 4, 1980.

*   *   *

HUNT, Kyle
See CREASEY, John

*   *   *

HUNTER, E. Waldo
See STURGEON, Theodore (Hamilton)

*   *   *

HUNTER, Evan 1926-
(Curt Cannon, Hunt Collins, Ezra Hannon, Richard Marsten, Ed McBain)

PERSONAL: Born October 15, 1926, in New York, N.Y.; son of Charles and Marie (Coppola) Lombino; married Anita Melnick, October 17, 1949 (divorced); married Mary Vann Finley, June, 1973; children: (first marriage) Ted, Mark, Richard; (second marriage) Amanda Eve Finley (stepdaughter). *Education:* Hunter College (now Hunter College of the City University of New York), B.A., 1950. *Politics:* Democrat.

ADDRESSES: Agent—William Morris Agency, 1350 Avenue of the Americas, New York, N.Y. 10019.

CAREER: Writer. Taught at two vocational high schools in New York City for a short time, about 1950; held various jobs, including answering the telephone at night for American Automobile Association and selling lobsters for a wholesale lobster firm, both New York City; worked for Scott Meredith Literary Agency, New York City, for about six months. *Military service:* U.S. Navy, 1944-46.

MEMBER: Phi Beta Kappa.

AWARDS, HONORS: Mystery Writers of America Award, 1957, for short story "The Last Spin"; Grand Master Award, Mystery Writers of America, 1986, for lifetime achievement.

WRITINGS:

The Evil Sleep, Falcon, 1952.
The Big Fix, Falcon, 1952, published under pseudonym Richard Marsten as *So Nude, So Dead,* Fawcett, 1956.
Find the Feathered Serpent, Winston, 1952, reprinted, Gregg, 1979.
Don't Crowd Me, Popular Library, 1953, published in England as *The Paradise Party,* New English Library, 1968.
(Under pseudonym Hunt Collins) *Cut Me In,* Abelard, 1954, published as *The Proposition,* Pyramid, 1955.
The Blackboard Jungle, Simon & Schuster, 1954, reprinted, Avon, 1976.
(Contributor) David Coxe Cook, editor, *Best Detective Stories of the Year 1955,* Dutton, 1955.
(Under pseudonyn Hunt Collins) *Tomorrow's World,* Bouregy, 1956, published as *Tomorrow and Tomorrow,* Pyramid Books, 1956, published in England under pseudonym Ed McBain, Sphere, 1979.
Second Ending, Simon & Schuster, 1956, published as *Quartet in H,* Pocket Books, 1957.
The Jungle Kids (short stories), Pocket Books, 1956.

(With Craig Rice, under pseudonym Ed McBain) *April Robin Murders* (crime novel), Random House, 1958.
(Under pseudonym Curt Cannon) *I'm Cannon—For Hire* (crime novel), Fawcett, 1958.
Strangers When We Meet (also see below), Simon & Schuster, 1958.
(Under pseudonym Curt Cannon) *I Like 'Em Tough* (short stories), Fawcett, 1958.
A Matter of Conviction, Simon & Schuster, 1959, reprinted, Avon, 1976, published as *Young Savages.* Pocket Books, 1966.
The Remarkable Harry (juvenile), Abelard, 1960.
The Last Spin and Other Stories, Constable, 1960.
The Wonderful Button (juvenile), Abelard, 1961.
Mothers and Daughters, Simon & Schuster, 1961.
Happy New Year, Herbie, and Other Stories, Simon & Schuster, 1963.
Buddwing, Simon & Schuster, 1964.
(Under pseudonym Ed McBain) *The Sentries* (crime novel), Simon & Schuster, 1965.
The Paper Dragon, Delacorte, 1966.
A Horse's Head, Delacorte, 1967.
(Editor under pseudonym Ed McBain) *Crime Squad,* New English Library, 1968.
(Editor under pseudonym Ed McBain) *Homicide Department,* New English Library, 1968.
Last Summer, Doubleday, 1968.
(Editor under pseudonym Ed McBain) *Downpour,* New English Library, 1969.
(Editor under pseudonym Ed McBain) *Ticket to Death,* New English Library, 1969.
Sons, Doubleday, 1969.
Nobody Knew They Were There, Doubleday, 1971.
The Beheading and Other Stories, Constable, 1971.
Every Little Crook and Nanny, Doubleday, 1972.
The Easter Man (a Play), and Six Stories (also see below), Doubleday, 1972.
Seven, Constable, 1972.
Come Winter, Doubleday, 1973.
Streets of Gold, Harper, 1974.
(Under pseudonym Ed McBain) *Where There's Smoke* (crime novel), Random House, 1975.
(Under pseudonym Ezra Hannon) *Doors* (crime novel), Stein & Day, 1975.
The Chisholms: A Novel of the Journey West (also see below), Harper, 1976.
(Under pseudonym Ed McBain) *Guns* (crime novel), Random House, 1976.
Me and Mr. Stenner (juvenile), Lippincott, 1977.
Walk Proud (also see below), Bantam, 1979.
Love, Dad, Crown, 1981.
(Under pseudonym Ed McBain) *The McBain Brief* (short stories), Hamish Hamilton, 1982, Arbor House, 1983.
Far From the Sea, Atheneum, 1983.
Lizzie, Arbor House, 1984.
(Under pseudonym Ed McBain) *Another Part of the City,* Mysterious Press, 1987.
(Under pseudonym Ed McBain) *Downtown,* Morrow, 1989.
(Under pseudonym Ed McBain) *Gangs,* Avon, 1989.

UNDER PSEUDONYM ED McBAIN; "87TH PRECINCT" SERIES

Cop Hater (also see below), Simon & Schuster, 1956.
The Mugger (also see below), Simon & Schuster, 1956.
The Pusher (also see below), Simon & Schuster, 1956.
The Con Man (also see below), Simon & Schuster, 1957.

Killer's Choice, Simon & Schuster, 1957.
Killer's Payoff, Simon & Schuster, 1958.
Lady Killer, Simon & Schuster, 1958.
Killer's Wedge, Simon & Schuster, 1959.
'Til Death, Simon & Schuster, 1959.
King's Ransom, Simon & Schuster, 1959.
Give the Boys a Great Big Hand, Simon & Schuster, 1960.
The Heckler, Simon & Schuster, 1960.
See Them Die, Simon & Schuster, 1960.
Lady, Lady, I Did It!, Simon & Schuster, 1961.
Like Love, Simon & Schuster, 1962.
The Empty Hours (three novellas), Simon & Schuster, 1962.
Ten Plus One, Simon & Schuster, 1963.
Ax, Simon & Schuster, 1964.
He Who Hesitates, Delacorte, 1965.
Doll, Delacorte, 1965.
Eighty Million Eyes, Delacorte, 1966.
The 87th Precinct (includes *Cop Hater, The Mugger, The Pusher,* and *The Con Man*), Boardman, 1966.
Fuzz (also see below), Doubleday, 1968.
Shotgun, Doubleday, 1969.
Jigsaw, Doubleday, 1970.
Hail, Hail, the Gang's All Here, Doubleday, 1971.
Sadie When She Died, Doubleday, 1972.
Let's Hear It for the Deaf Man, Doubleday, 1972.
87th Precinct: An Ed McBain Omnibus, Hamish Hamilton, 1973.
Hail to the Chief, Random House, 1973.
Bread, Random House, 1974.
The Second 87th Precinct Omnibus, Hamish Hamilton, 1975.
Blood Relatives, Random House, 1975.
So Long as You Both Shall Live, Random House, 1976.
Long Time No See, Random House, 1977.
Calypso, Viking, 1979.
Ghosts, Viking, 1980.
Heat, Viking, 1981.
Ice, Arbor House, 1983.
Lightning, Arbor House, 1984.
Eight Black Horses, Avon, 1986.
Poison, Morrow, 1987.
Tricks, Morrow, 1987.
McBain's Ladies: The Women of the 87th Precinct, Mysterious Press, 1988.
Lullaby, Morrow, 1989.
McBain's Ladies, Too, Mysterious Press, 1989.
Vespers, Morrow, 1990.

UNDER PSEUDONYM ED McBAIN; "MATTHEW HOPE" SERIES; CRIME NOVELS

Goldilocks, Arbor House, 1978.
Rumpelstiltskin, Viking, 1981.
Beauty and the Beast, Hamish Hamilton, 1982, Holt, 1983.
Jack and the Beanstalk, Holt, 1984.
Snow White and Rose Red, Holt, 1986.
Puss in Boots, Holt, 1987.
The House That Jack Built, Holt, 1988.

UNDER PSEUDONYM RICHARD MARSTEN

Rocket to Luna (juvenile), Winston, 1953.
Danger: Dinosaurs (juvenile), Winston, 1953.
Runaway Black (crime novel), Fawcett, 1954.
Murder in the Navy (crime novel), Fawcett, 1955, published under pseudonym Ed McBain as *Death of a Nurse,* Pocket Books, 1968.
The Spiked Heel (crime novel), Holt, 1956.
Vanishing Ladies (crime novel), Pocket Books, 1957.

Even the Wicked (crime novel), Permabooks, 1957, published in England under pseudonym Ed McBain, Severn House, 1979.
Big Man (crime novel), Pocket Books, 1959, published in England under pseudonym Ed McBain, Penguin, 1978.
(Contributor) Leo Marguiles, editor, *Dames, Danger, and Death,* Pyramid, 1960.

PLAYS; UNDER NAME EVAN HUNTER

"The Easter Man," produced in Birmingham, England, at Birmingham Repertory Theatre, 1964, produced under title "A Race of Hairy Men!" on Broadway at Henry Miller's Theater, April, 1965.
"The Conjuror," produced in Ann Arbor, Mich., at Lydia Mendelssohn Theatre, November 5, 1969.
"Stalemate," produced in New York, 1975.

SCREENPLAYS AND TELEVISION SCRIPTS; UNDER NAME EVAN HUNTER

"Strangers When We Meet" (based on author's novel of same title), Columbia Pictures Industries, Inc., 1960.
"The Birds" (based on short story by Daphne du Maurier), Universal Pictures, 1963.
"Fuzz" (based on author's novel of same title), United Artists Corp., 1972.
"Walk Proud" (based on author's novel of same title), Universal, 1979.
"The Chisholms" (Columbia Broadcasting System television series), Alan Landsburg Productions, 1979-80.

OTHER

Also author of "Appointment at Eleven" for "Alfred Hitchcock Presents," 1955-61. The Mulgar Memorial Library of Boston University holds Hunter's manuscripts.

SIDELIGHTS: With numerous novels, short stories, plays, and film scripts to his credit, Evan Hunter ranks as one of today's most versatile and prolific writers. Known to millions throughout the world under his pseudonym, Ed McBain (originator of the "87th Precinct" detective series), Hunter is also the author (under his own name) of such thought-provoking best-sellers as *The Blackboard Jungle, Strangers When We Meet, Mothers and Daughters,* and *Last Summer.* He prefers to keep these two identities strictly separate, he explains, because "I don't like to confuse critics who are very easily confused anyway. I also do not like to confuse readers. I wouldn't like a woman, for example, who had read *Mothers and Daughters* by Evan Hunter, to pick up *The Heckler* by Evan Hunter and find that it's about mayhem, bloodshed and violence. I think this would be unfair to her and unfair to me as well."

Though it appeared some ten years after Hunter made his first serious attempts to write for publication, *The Blackboard Jungle* caused the twenty-eight-year-old author to be labeled an "overnight" success. A semi-autobiographical work, *The Blackboard Jungle* tells the story of an idealistic young man who confronts the often violent realities of trying to teach a group of sullen, illiterate, delinquent teenagers in a big-city vocational high school. Written in what was then politely termed the "vernacular," Hunter's dramatic indictment of both the inadequacies of teacher training colleges and of the New York City school system is "a nightmarish but authentic first novel," according to a *Time* critic. The *New York Herald Tribune Book Review*'s Barbara Klaw points to Hunter's "superb ear for conversation," "competence as a storyteller," and "tolerant and tough-minded sympathy for his subject" as some of the book's best features, while Nathan Rothman of the *Saturday Review* feels that it is free of the "distortions and dishonesty" of many newspaper articles on the same topic. And even though the *Nation's* Stanley Cooperman believes that Hunter "makes only cursory attempts to probe the wellsprings of the action he photographs so well," he concludes that the ex-substitute teacher "succeeds in dramatizing an area heretofore neglected in fiction."

Frequently praised for the consistently high standard of professionalism evident in his writing, Hunter freely admits that the Ed McBain books are formula novels, novels in which he tries to be "entertaining, suspenseful and exciting, [with] no intention of commenting on the society we live in." He told *CA:* "When I was beginning to write, I wrote a great many detective stories for the pulp magazines. I wrote not only police stories, but private eye and man-on-the-run and woman-in-jeopardy, the whole gamut. After *The Blackboard Jungle* was published, Pocket Books did the reprint of it. I had an old mystery novel kicking around that I had not yet sold, and there was a pseudonym on it, but not Ed McBain. We sent it to Pocket Books as a possibility for a paperback original. The editor there at the time, a man named Herbert Alexander, was a very bright guy. He recognized the style and called my agent and said, 'Is this our friend Hunter?' My agent said, 'Yes, it is,' and Alexander said, 'Well, I'd like to talk to him.'

"We had lunch one day," Hunter continues, "and the gist of the conversation was that the mainstay of Pocket Books was Erle Stanley Gardner; he had sold millions of books and they would just republish each title every three or four years with new jackets. They kept selling as if they were new books all the time. But he was getting old and they were looking for a mystery writer who could replace him, so they asked me if I had any ideas about a mystery series. I said I would think about it. I got back to them and I said that it seemed to me—after all the mysteries I'd written—that the only *valid* people to deal with crime were cops, and I would like to make the lead character, rather than a single *person,* a *squad* of cops instead—so it would be a *conglomerate* lead character. They said, 'OK, we'll give you a contract for three books and if it works we'll renew it.' I started writing the series."

Hunter's "87th Precinct" novels are known as "police procedurals" in the mystery trade. "The nice thing about the '87th Precinct' is that I can deal with any subject matter so long as it's criminally related," Hunter told *CA.* "With the Ed McBain novels, I only want to say that cops have a tough, underpaid job, and they deal with murder every day of the week, and that's the way it is, folks. With the Hunters, the theme varies and I'll usually ponder the next book for a long, long time—until it demands to be written."

Most of Hunter's other novels exhibit definite thematic concerns, occasionally inspired by biographical or autobiographical material, but often just "intellectual concepts that come to me and take a while to develop before they're put down on paper." He has written a great deal about young people, especially the relationship between the young and the old (usually parents). "I don't know why I've been attracted to writing about young people," he once remarked to a *Publishers Weekly* interviewer. "I guess from *Blackboard Jungle,* it's been a situation that's always appealed to me, the idea of adults in conflict with the young. I think part of my fascination is with America as an adolescent nation and with our so-called adult responses that are sometimes adolescent."

Often these same novels contain elements of current topical interest as well—the state of the American educational system in *The Blackboard Jungle,* the emptiness of post-World War II

middle-class life in *Mothers and Daughters,* the Vietnam War in *Sons,* and the anti-Establishment "hippie" movement of the late 1960s and early 1970s in *Love, Dad.* The *New York Times Book Review's* Ivan Gold concludes, "Mr. Hunter is a serious and honorable writer trying to entertain us, and also trying to tell us, now and again, some useful things about our lives." As Hunter himself once explained to the *Publishers Weekly* interviewer, "The whole reason I write anything is so that someone somewhere will say, 'Oh, yeah. I feel that way too. I'm not alone.' "

MEDIA ADAPTATIONS: Several of Hunter's novels have been made into movies, including "The Blackboard Jungle," Metro-Goldwyn-Mayer, Inc., 1955; "Cop Hater," United Artists Corp., 1958; "The Muggers" (based on *The Mugger*), United Artists, 1958; "The Pusher," United Artists, 1960; "The Young Savages" (based on *A Matter of Conviction*), United Artists, 1961; "High and Low" (based on *King's Ransom*), Toho International, 1963; "Mr. Buddwing" (based on *Buddwing*), Metro-Goldwyn-Mayer, 1967; "Last Summer," Twentieth Century-Fox Film Corp., 1969; "Sans Mobile apparent" (title means "Without Apparent Motive"; based on *Ten Plus One*), President Films, 1971; "Le Cri du cormoran le soir au-dessus des jonques" (title means "The Cry of the Cormorant at Night Over the Junks"; based on *A Horse's Head*), Gaumont International, 1971; and "Every Little Crook and Nanny," Metro-Goldwyn-Mayer, 1972.

BIOGRAPHICAL/CRITICAL SOURCES:

BOOKS

Contemporary Literary Criticism, Gale, Volume 11, 1979, Volume 31, 1985.
Dictionary of Literary Biography Yearbook: 1982, Gale, 1982.
Roy Newquist, *Conversations,* Rand McNally, 1967.

PERIODICALS

Best Sellers, June 15, 1968, August 15, 1969, March 15, 1971.
Books and Bookmen, January, 1969.
Books, June, 1970.
Catholic World, August, 1958.
Chicago Sunday Tribune, January 22, 1956, June 8, 1958, May 28, 1961.
Choice, June, 1970.
Detroit News, January 16, 1983.
Globe and Mail (Toronto), October 19, 1985, June 21, 1986, February 28, 1987.
Harper's, December, 1967, June, 1968.
Los Angeles Times, May 14, 1981, February 4, 1983.
Nation, December 4, 1954.
New Yorker, January 13, 1975.
New York Herald Tribune Book Review, October 17, 1954, January 15, 1956, July 20, 1958.
New York Herald Tribune Lively Arts, May 21, 1961.
New York Times, January 8, 1956, June 15, 1958, June 12, 1968, April 10, 1981, April 19, 1985, February 20, 1987, July 3, 1987.
New York Times Book Review, May 28, 1961, October 20, 1968, July 16, 1969, September 28, 1969, September 19, 1976, May 6, 1979, May 10, 1981.
New Statesman, January 10, 1969.
Newsweek, March 8, 1971.
Observer (London), April 5, 1970.
People, December 19, 1977.
Publishers Weekly, April 3, 1981.
San Francisco Chronicle, July 9, 1961.
Saturday Review, October 9, 1954, January 7, 1956, April 24, 1971, September 9, 1972.

Springfield Republican, July 9, 1961.

Time, October 11, 1954, June 9, 1958, March 8, 1971.

Times (London), August 20, 1981, September 11, 1982, July 11, 1985.

Times Literary Supplement, November 21, 1958, July 28, 1961, January 25, 1968, May 28, 1970, July 13, 1973.

Virginia Quarterly Review, summer, 1968.

Washington Post Book World, March 29, 1981, January 19, 1983, June 24, 1984.

Writer, April, 1969.

Writer's Digest, April, 1971.

*   *   *

HURSTON, Zora Neale   1903-1960

PERSONAL: Born January 7, 1891, in Eatonville, Fla.; died January 28, 1960, in Fort Pierce, Fla.; daughter of John (a preacher and carpenter) and Lucy (a seamstress; maiden name, Potts) Hurston; married Herbert Sheen, May 19, 1927 (divorced, 1931); married Albert Price III, June 27, 1939 (divorced). *Education:* Attended Howard University, 1923-24; Barnard College, B.A., 1928; graduate study at Columbia University.

ADDRESSES: Home—Fort Pierce, Fla.

CAREER: Writer and folklorist. Collected folklore in the South, 1927-31; Bethune-Cookman College, Daytona, Fla., instructor in drama, 1933-34; collected folklore in Jamaica, Haiti, and Bermuda, 1937-38; collected folklore in Florida for the Works Progress Administration, 1938-39; Paramount Studios, Hollywood, Calif., staff writer, 1941; collected folklore in Honduras, 1946-48; worked as a maid in Florida, 1950; free-lance writer, 1950-56; Patrick Air Force Base, Fla., librarian, 1956-57; writer for *Fort Pierce Chronicle* and part-time teacher at Lincoln Park Academy, both in Fort Pierce, Fla., 1958-59. Librarian at the Library of Congress, Washington, D.C.; professor of drama at North Carolina College for Negroes (now North Carolina Central University), Durham; assistant to writer Fannie Hurst.

MEMBER: American Folklore Society, American Anthropological Society, American Ethnological Society, Zeta Phi Beta.

AWARDS, HONORS: Guggenheim fellowship, 1936 and 1938; Litt.D. from Morgan College, 1939; Annisfield Award, 1943, for *Dust Tracks on a Road.*

WRITINGS:

(With Clinton Fletcher and Time Moore) "Fast and Furious" (musical play), published in *Best Plays of 1931-32,* edited by Burns Mantle and Garrison Sherwood, 1931.

Jonah's Gourd Vine (novel), with an introduction by Fanny Hurst, Lippincott, 1934, reprinted with a new introduction by Larry Neal, 1971.

Mules and Men (folklore), with an introduction by Franz Boas, Lippincott, 1935, reprinted, Indiana University Press, 1978.

Their Eyes Were Watching God (novel), Lippincott, 1937, reprinted, University of Illinois Press, 1978.

Tell My Horse (nonfiction), Lippincott, 1938, reprinted, Turtle Island Foundation, 1981, published as *Voodoo Gods: An Inquiry into Native Myths and Magic in Jamaica and Haiti,* Dent, 1939.

Moses, Man of the Mountain (novel), Lippincott, 1939, reprinted, University of Illinois Press, 1984.

Dust Tracks on a Road (autobiography), Lippincott, 1942, reprinted with an introduction by Neal, 1971, reprinted, edited by Robert Hemenway, University of Illinois Press, 1984.

(With Dorothy Waring) *Stephen Kelen-d'Oxylion Presents Polk County: A Comedy of Negro Life on a Sawmill Camp with Authentic Negro Music* (three acts), [New York], c. 1944.

Seraph on the Suwanee (novel), Scribner, 1948, reprinted, AMS Press, 1974.

I Love Myself When I Am Laughing . . . And Then Again When I Am Looking Mean And Impressive, edited by Alice Walker, Feminist Press, 1979.

The Sanctified Church, Turtle Island Foundation, 1983.

Spunk: The Selected Stories of Zora Neale Hurston, Turtle Island Foundation, 1985.

The Gilded Six-Bits, Redpath Press, 1986.

Also author of play with Langston Hughes, "Mule Bone: A Comedy of Negro Life in Three Acts," 1931; author of "The First One" (one-act play), published in *Ebony and Topaz,* edited by Johnson, and of "Great Day" (play). Work represented in anthologies, including *Black Writers in America,* edited by Barksdale and Kinnamon; *Story in America,* edited by E. W. Burnett and Martha Foley, Vanguard, 1934; *American Negro Short Stories,* edited by Clarke; *The Best Short Stories by Negro Writers,* edited by Hughes; *From the Roots,* edited by James; *Anthology of American Negro Literature,* edited by Watkins. Contributor of stories and articles to periodicals, including *American Mercury, Negro Digest, Journal of American Folklore, Saturday Evening Post,* and *Journal of Negro History.*

SIDELIGHTS: Although Hurston was closely associated with the Harlem Renaissance and has influenced such writers as Ralph Ellison, Toni Morrison, Gayl Jones, and Toni Cade Bambara, interest in her has only recently been revived after decades of neglect. Hurston's four novels and two books of folklore are important sources of black myth and legend. Through her writings, Robert Hemenway wrote in *The Harlem Renaissance Remembered,* Hurston "helped to remind the Renaissance—especially its more bourgeois members—of the richness in the racial heritage; she also added new dimensions to the interest in exotic primitivism that was one of the most ambiguous products of the age."

Hurston was born and raised in the first incorporated all-black town in America, and was advised by her mother to "jump at de sun." At the age of thirteen she was taken out of school to care for her brother's children. At sixteen, she joined a traveling theatrical troupe and worked as a maid for a white woman who arranged for her to attend high school in Baltimore. Hurston later studied anthropology at Barnard College and Columbia University with the anthropologist Franz Boas, which profoundly influenced her work. After graduation she returned to her hometown for anthropological study. The data she collected would be used both in her collections of folklore and her fictional works.

"I was glad when somebody told me: 'You may go and collect Negro folklore,' " Hurston related in the introduction to *Mules and Men.* "In a way it would not be a new experience for me. When I pitched headforemost into the world I landed in the crib of Negroism. From the earliest rocking of my cradle, I had known about the capers Br'er Rabbit is apt to cut and what the Squinch Owl says from the housetop. But it was fitting me like a tight chemise. I couldn't see it for wearing it. It was only when I was off in college, away from my native surroundings, that I could see myself like somebody else and stand off and look at my garment. Then I had to have the spyglass of anthropology to look through at that."

Hurston was an ambiguous and complex figure. She embodied seemingly antipodal traits, and Hemenway described her in his

Zora Neale Hurston: A Literary Biography as being "flamboyant yet vulnerable, self-centered yet kind, a Republican conservative and an early black nationalist." Hurston was never bitter and never felt disadvantaged because she was black. Henry Louis Gates, Jr., explained in the *New York Times Book Review:* "Part of Miss Hurston's received heritage—and perhaps the traditional notion that links the novel of manners in the Harlem Renaissance, the social realism of the 30s, and the cultural nationalism of the Black Arts movement—was the idea that racism had reduced black people to mere ciphers, to beings who react only to an omnipresent racial oppression, whose culture is 'deprived' where different, and whose psyches are in the main 'pathological'. . . . Miss Hurston thought this idea degrading, its propagation a trap. It was against this that she railed, at times brilliantly and systematically, at times vapidly and eclectically."

Older black writers criticized Hurston for the frequent crudeness and bawdiness of the tales she told. The younger generation criticized her propensity to gloss over the injustices her people were dealt. According to Judith Wilson, Hurston's greatest contribution was "to all black Americans' psychic health. The consistent note in her fieldwork and the bulk of her fiction is one of celebration of a black cultural heritage whose complexity and originality refutes all efforts to enforce either a myth of inferiority or a lie of assimilation." Wilson continued, "Zora Neale Hurston had figured out something that no other black author of her time seems to have known or appreciated so well—that our homespun vernacular and street-corner cosmology is as valuable as the grammar and philosophy of white, Western culture."

Hurston herself wrote in 1928: "I am not tragically colored. There is no great sorrow dammed up in my soul, nor lurking behind my eyes. I do not mind at all. I do not belong to the sobbing school of Negrohood who hold that nature somehow has given them a lowdown dirty deal and whose feelings are all hurt about it. . . . No, I do not weep at the world—I am too busy sharpening my oyster knife."

Their Eyes Were Watching God is generally acknowledged to be Hurston's finest work of fiction. Still, it was controversial. Richard Wright found the book to be "counter-revolutionary" in a *New Masses* article. June Jordan praised the novel for its positiveness. She declared in a *Black World* review: "Unquestionably, *Their Eyes Were Watching God* is the prototypical Black novel of affirmation; it is the most successful, convincing, and exemplary novel of Blacklove that we have. Period. But the book gives us more: the story unrolls a fabulous, written-film of Blacklife freed from the constraints of oppression; here we may learn Black possibilities of ourselves if we could ever escape the hateful and alien context that has so deeply disturbed and mutilated our rightly effloresence—*as people*. Consequently, this novel centers itself on Blacklove—even as *Native Son* rivets itself upon white hatred."

"She was full of sidesplitting anecdotes, humorous tales, and tragicomic stories," Langston Hughes wrote of Hurston, "remembered out of her life in the South as a daughter of a traveling minister of God. She could make you laugh one minute and cry the next. . . .

"But Miss Hurston was clever, too—a student who didn't let college give her a broad 'a' and who had great scorn for all pretensions, academic or otherwise. That is why she was such a fine folklore collector, able to go among the people and never act as if she had been to school at all. Almost nobody else could stop the average Harlemite on Lenox Avenue and measure his head with a strange-looking, anthropological device and not get

bawled out for the attempt, except Zora, who used to stop anyone whose head looked interesting, and measure it."

BIOGRAPHICAL/CRITICAL SOURCES:

BOOKS

Bone, Robert, *Down Home: A History of Afro-American Short Fiction from Its Beginnings to the End of the Harlem Renaissance,* Putnam, 1975.
Contemporary Literary Criticism, Gale, Volume 7, 1977, Volume 30, 1984.
Davis, Arthur P., *From the Dark Tower,* Howard University Press, 1974.
Dictionary of Literary Biography, Volume 51: *Afro-American Writers From the Harlem Renaissance to 1940,* Gale, 1987.
Hemenway, Robert E., *Zora Neale Hurston: A Literary Biography,* University of Illinois Press, 1977.
Hughes, Langston, *The Big Sea,* Knopf, 1940.
Hughes, Langston and Arna Bontemps, editors, *The Harlem Renaissance Remembered,* Dodd, 1972.
Hurston, Zora Neale, *Dust Tracks on a Road* (autobiography), Lippincott, 1942.
Turner, Darwin T., *In a Minor Chord: Three Afro-American Writers and Their Search for Identity,* Southern Illinois University Press, 1971.

PERIODICALS

Black World, August, 1972, August, 1974.
Ms., March, 1975, June, 1978.
Negro American Literature Forum, spring, 1972.
Negro Digest, February, 1962.
New Masses, October 5, 1937.
New Republic, February 11, 1978.
New York Times Book Review, February 19, 1978, April 21, 1985.
Village Voice, August 17, 1972.
Washington Post Book World, July 23, 1978.

OBITUARIES:

PERIODICALS

Britannica Book of the Year, 1961.
Current Biography, Wilson, 1960.
Newsweek, February 15, 1960.
New York Times, February 5, 1960.
Publishers Weekly, February 15, 1960.
Time, February 15, 1960.
Wilson Library Bulletin, April, 1960.

* * *

HUXLEY, Aldous (Leonard) 1894-1963

PERSONAL: Born July 26, 1894, in Godalming, Surrey, England; died November 22, 1963, in California; son of Leonard and Julia (Arnold) Huxley; married Maria Nys, 1919 (died, 1955); married Laura Archera, 1956; children: Matthew. *Education:* Balliol College, Oxford, B.A., 1916.

CAREER: Employed in government office during World War I; Eton College, Eton, England, schoolmaster, 1917-19; staff member of *Athenaeum* and *Westminster Gazette,* 1919-24; writer.

MEMBER: Athenaeum Club.

AWARDS, HONORS: Award of Merit and Gold Medal, American Academy of Arts and Letters, 1959; D.Litt., University of California, 1959.

WRITINGS:

NOVELS

Crome Yellow, Chatto & Windus, 1921, Doran, 1922, reprinted, Chatto & Windus, 1963, Harper, 1965.

(Translator) R. de Gourmont, *A Virgin Heart,* N. L. Brown, 1921.

Antic Hay (also see below), Doran, 1923.

Those Barren Leaves, Doran, 1925, reprinted, Avon, 1964.

Point Counter Point, Doubleday, 1928, reprinted, Harper, 1969.

Brave New World (also see below), Doubleday, 1932, reprinted, Bantam, 1960.

Eyeless in Gaza, Harper, 1936, reprinted, Bantam, 1968.

After Many a Summer Dies the Swan, Harper, 1939, reprinted, 1965.

Time Must Have a Stop, Harper, 1944.

Ape and Essence, Harper, 1948.

The Genius and the Goddess, Harper, 1955.

Antic Hay and The Gioconda Smile (also see below), Harper, 1957.

Brave New World [and] *Brave New World Revisited* (also see below), Harper, 1960.

Island, Harper, 1962.

SHORT STORIES

Limbo: Six Stories and a Play, Doran, 1920.

Mortal Coils: Five Stories (also see below), Doran, 1922, reprinted, Chatto & Windus, 1968.

Little Mexican and Other Stories, Chatto & Windus, 1924, reprinted, 1959.

Young Archimedes and Other Stories, Doran, 1924.

Two or Three Graces: Four Stories, Doran, 1925, reprinted, Chatto & Windus, 1963.

Brief Candles, Doubleday, 1930, reprinted, Chatto & Windus, 1970.

The Gioconda Smile, Chatto & Windus, 1938.

Collected Short Stories, Harper, 1957.

The Crows of Pearblossom, Random House, 1968.

POETRY

The Burning Wheel, B. H. Blackwell, 1916.

The Defeat of Youth and Other Poems, Longmans, Green, 1918.

Leda and Other Poems, Doran, 1920.

Selected Poems, Appleton, 1925.

Arabia Infelix and Other Poems, Fountain Press, 1929.

Apennine, Slide Mountain Press, 1930.

The Cicadas and Other Poems, Doubleday, 1931.

The Collected Poetry of Aldous Huxley, edited by Donald Watt, Harper, 1971.

PLAYS

Francis Sheridan's The Discovery, Adapted for the Modern Stage, Chatto & Windus, 1924, Doran, 1925.

The World of Light: A Comedy in Three Acts, Doubleday, 1931.

The Gioconda Smile (adapted from Huxley's short story), Harper, 1948 (also published as *Mortal Coils,* Harper, 1948).

NONFICTION

Along the Road: Notes and Essays of a Tourist, Doran, 1925, reprinted, Books for Libraries Press, 1971.

Jesting Pilate: An Intellectual Holiday, Doran, 1926, reprinted, Greenwood, 1974 (published in England as *Jesting Pilate: The Diary of a Journey,* Chatto & Windus, 1957).

Essays New and Old, Chatto & Windus, 1926, Doran, 1927, reprinted, Ayer, 1968.

Proper Studies: The Proper Study of Mankind Is Man, Chatto & Windus, 1927, Doubleday, 1928, reprinted, Chatto & Windus, 1957.

Do What You Will (essays), Doubleday, 1929, reprinted, Chatto & Windus, 1970.

Holy Face and Other Essays, Fleuron, 1929.

Vulgarity in Literature: Digressions From a Theme, Chatto & Windus, 1930, Haskell House, 1966.

Music at Night and Other Essays, Chatto & Windus, 1930, Doubleday, 1931, reprinted, Books for Libraries Press, 1970.

On the Margin: Notes and Essays, Doran, 1932, reprinted, Chatto & Windus, 1971.

Beyond the Mexique Bay: A Traveller's Journal, Harper, 1934, reprinted, Greenwood, 1975.

1936 . . . Peace?, Friends Peace Committee (London), 1936.

The Olive Tree and Other Essays, Chatto & Windus, 1936, Harper, 1937, reprinted, Books for Libraries Press, 1971.

What Are You Going to Do About It? The Case for Constructive Peace, Chatto & Windus, 1936.

An Encyclopedia of Pacifism, Harper, 1937, reprinted, Garland, 1972.

Ends and Means: An Inquiry in the Nature of Ideals and Into the Methods Employed for Their Realization, Harper, 1937, reprinted, Greenwood, 1969.

The Most Agreeable Vice, [Los Angeles], 1938.

Words and Their Meanings, Ward Ritchie Press, 1940.

Grey Eminence: A Study in Religion and Politics, Harper, 1941, reprinted, 1975.

The Art of Seeing, Harper, 1942, reprinted, Chatto & Windus, 1964.

The Perennial Philosophy, Harper, 1945, reprinted, Books for Libraries Press, 1972.

Science, Liberty and Peace, Harper, 1946.

(With Sir John Russell) *Food and People,* [London], 1949.

Prisons, With the "Carceri" Etchings by G. B. Piranesi, Grey Falcon Press, 1949.

Themes and Variations, Harper, 1950.

(With Stuart Gilbert) *Joyce, the Artificer: Two Studies of Joyce's Method,* Chiswick, 1952.

The Devils of Loudun, Harper, 1952.

(With J. A. Kings) *A Day in Windsor,* Britannicus Liber, 1953.

The French of Paris, Harper, 1954.

The Doors of Perception, Harper, 1954, reprinted, 1970.

Heaven and Hell, Harper, 1956, reprinted, 1971.

Tomorrow and Tomorrow and Tomorrow and Other Essays, Harper, 1956 (published in England as *Adonis and the Alphabet and Other Essays,* Chatto & Windus, 1956).

A Writer's Prospect—III: Censorship and Spoken Literature, [London], 1956.

Brave New World Revisited, Harper, 1958.

Collected Essays, Harper, 1959.

On Art and Artists: Literature, Painting, Architecture, Music, Harper, 1960.

Selected Essays, Chatto & Windus, 1961.

The Politics of Ecology: The Question of Survival, Center for the Study of Democratic Institutions (Santa Barbara), 1963.

Literature and Science (also see below), Harper, 1963.

New Fashioned Christmas, Hart Press, 1968.

America and the Future, Pemberton Press, 1970.

The Basic Philosophy of Aldous Huxley, American Institute of Psychology, 1984.

COLLECTIONS

Texts and Pretexts: An Anthology With Commentaries, Chatto & Windus, 1932, Harper, 1933, reprinted, Norton, 1962.
Rotunda: A Selection From the Works of Aldous Huxley, Chatto & Windus, 1932.
Retrospect: An Omnibus of His Fiction and Non-Fiction Over Three Decades, Harper, 1947, reprinted, Peter Smith, 1971.
The Letters of Aldous Huxley, Chatto & Windus, 1969, Harper, 1970.
Great Short Works of Aldous Huxley, Harper, 1969.
Collected Works, Chatto & Windus, 1970.
Science, Liberty and Peace (includes *Literature and Science*), Chatto & Windus, 1970.
The Wisdom of the Ages, two volumes, Found Class Reprints, 1989.

OTHER

Jonah, Gotham, 1977.

Author of screenplay "Woman's Vengeance," based on his own novel *The Gioconda Smile,* 1947, and, with others, of screenplays "Pride and Prejudice," 1940, "Jane Eyre," 1944, and "Madame Curie."

Contributor to numerous periodicals, including *Life, Playboy, Encounter,* and *Daedalus.*

SIDELIGHTS: When Aldous Huxley was sixteen he was stricken with a disease of the eyes, which left him temporarily blind and permanently disrupted his plan to enter the medical profession. Yet his scientific training remained a major force in all his future endeavors. He became a renowned and prolific man of letters, writing essays, fiction, and poetry, as well as criticism of painting, music, and literature, all of it touched by his scientific and analytic processes of thought and sense of detail.

Huxley's work is often seen as falling into two periods: his early work, much of it social satire, is arch and occasionally condescending; his later work, essentially mystical, is prophetic but in places self-righteous. The first period includes novels like *Crome Yellow* (1921) and *Antic Hay* (1923), witty and sardonic dissections of British society, particularly the artists and aristocrats. It also includes the well-known *Brave New World* (1932), which Andre Maurois once called "an exercise in pessimistic prognostication, a terrifying Utopia." The later period is marked by the publication in 1936 of the novel *Eyeless in Gaza,* which concerns the transformation of Anthony Beavis from cynic to mystic. A similar theme is explored in the novel *Time Must Have a Stop* (1944) as well as Huxley's later essays (especially *The Perennial Philosophy,* 1945) and his last novel, *Island* (1962).

Yet, at the chronological center of his career, Huxley balanced these two thrusts and produced the novel *Point Counter Point* (1928), which many critics regard as his most accomplished work of fiction. In it he confronted all of contemporary man's ideals—religion and false mysticism, science, art, sex, politics—and the disillusionment that their inadequacy invokes. In *Point Counter Point* Huxley achieved for the first time what he called the "musicalization of fiction." He shifted and juxtaposed moods, scenes, and characters, and he modulated themes, creating through these variations a verbal counterpoint. As the character Philip Quarles puts it: "He shows several people falling in love, or dying, or praying in different ways—dissimilars solving the same problem." In this fashion, each of the characters (who are all representative of an idea or type) is enhanced and more clearly illuminated than he would be through a conventional presentation of events. Moreover, this breaking down of the story, relating the plot gradually and in pieces, parallels Huxley's theme: people who live for ideas and absolutes will be fragmented, unfulfilled human beings. He suggests that the world must be seen as a whole and accepted as it is, just as the novel, while being studied part by part from within, must be grasped in its entirety if any of the characters are to have significance.

As well as representing ideals, the characters in *Point Counter Point* are based on real people, for the book is a *roman a clef.* The most attractive of them is Mark Rampion, the whole man, who strongly resembles D. H. Lawrence, Huxley's lifelong friend. In turn, Rampion's friend Philip Quarles is suggestive of Huxley himself—a novelist concerned with point of view and a man whose problem is "to transform a detached intellectual scepticism into a way of harmonious all-round living."

In his search for such transformation Aldous Huxley went through many stages of mystical belief. His biographers and critics often cite his experiments with such hallucinogenic drugs as mescaline and lysergic acid (which he labeled "psychodelic") as means of discovering new capacities of the human psyche. But his brother Julian best explained his mystic inclinations in the 1965 *Aldous Huxley: A Memorial Volume.* Julian Huxley said that Aldous was equally fascinated by the hard facts of scientific discovery as by the facts of mystical experience. But, he added, the more science discovers and "the more comprehension it gives us of the mechanisms of existence, the more clearly does the mystery of existence itself stand out." That is, the more human beings may comprehend operative details, the more mysterious will seem the process itself. Hence, Aldous Huxley's mysticism was founded upon scientific training and his search for spiritual truth based on the urge, as Julian put it, "to achieve self-transcendence while yet remaining a committed social being."

Several of Huxley's novels have been adapted for the stage and for film. A collection of his original manuscripts is housed at the University of California.

AVOCATIONAL INTERESTS: Painting, walking, playing piano, "riding in fast cars."

BIOGRAPHICAL/CRITICAL SOURCES:

BOOKS

Atkins, John, *Aldous Huxley,* Orion Press, 1968.
Bedford, Sybille, *Aldous Huxley: A Biography,* Knopf, 1974.
Birnbaum, Milton, *Aldous Huxley's Quest for Values,* University of Tennessee Press, 1971.
Bowering, Peter, *Aldous Huxley: A Study of the Major Novels,* Athlone (London), 1968.
Brander, Laurence, *Aldous Huxley: A Critical Study,* Bucknell University Press, 1970.
Brook, Jocelyn, *Aldous Huxley,* Longmans, Green, 1954.
Clark, Ronald W., *The Huxleys,* McGraw, 1968.
Contemporary Literary Criticism, Gale, Volume 1, 1973, Volume 3, 1975, Volume 4, 1975, Volume 5, 1976, Volume 8, 1978, Volume 11, 1979, Volume 18, 1981, Volume 35, 1985.
Dictionary of Literary Biography, Volume 36: *British Novelists, 1890-1929: Modernists,* Gale, 1985.
Firchow, Peter, *Aldous Huxley: A Satirist and Novelist,* University of Minnesota Press, 1972.
Greenblatt, Stephen J., *Three Modern Satirists: Waugh, Orwell, and Huxley,* Yale University Press, 1965.
Holmes, Charles M., *Aldous Huxley and the Way to Reality,* Indiana University Press, 1970.
Huxley, Julian, *Aldous Huxley: A Memorial Volume,* Harper, 1965.

Huxley, Laura Archera, *This Timeless Moment: A Personal View of Aldous Huxley,* Farrar, Straus, 1968.

Meckier, Jerome, *Aldous Huxley: Satire and Structure,* Barnes & Noble, 1969.

Thody, Peter, *Huxley: A Biographical Introduction,* Scribner, 1973.

Woodcock, George, *Dawn and the Darkest Hour: A Study of Aldous Huxley,* Viking, 1972.

PERIODICALS

Atlantic, January, 1975.
Books and Bookmen, March, 1971.
Choice, November, 1970.
Commonweal, March 28, 1975.
Economist, December 20, 1969.
Esquire, April, 1975.
Nation, June 8, 1970.
National Review, January 31, 1975.
New Leader, November, 1968.
New Republic, May 16, 1970, November 16, 1974.
New Statesman, November 28, 1969.
Newsweek, May 4, 1970, December 9, 1974.
New Yorker, July 18, 1970, February 17, 1975.
Review America, February 22, 1975.
Saturday Review, May 2, 1970.
Saturday Review/World, November 16, 1974.
Time, December 2, 1974.
Times Literary Supplement, December 18, 1969, February 17, 1984.
Washington Post Book World, May 31, 1970, June 16, 1985.

*   *   *

HUXLEY, Julian (Sorell)   1887-1975
(Balbus)

PERSONAL: Born June 22, 1887, in London, England; died February 14, 1975, in London, England; son of Leonard (an essayist and master of Charterhouse) and Julia (Arnold) Huxley; married Marie Juliette Baillot, 1919; children: Anthony Julian, Francis John Heathorn. *Education:* Eton College, King's Scholar; Balliol College, Oxford, Brakenbury Scholar, degree in natural science (with first class honors), 1909; Naples Zoological Station Scholar, 1909-10. *Religion:* Humanist.

ADDRESSES: Agent—A. D. Peters, 10 Buckingham St., London W.C.2, England.

CAREER: Balliol College, Oxford University, Oxford, England, lecturer in zoology, 1910-12; Rice Institute, Houston, Tex., research associate, 1912-13, assistant professor, 1913-16; New College, Oxford University, fellow and senior demonstrator in zoology, 1919-25; King's College, University of London, London, England, professor of zoology, 1925-27, honorary lecturer, 1927-35; Royal Institution, London, Fullerian Professor of Physiology, 1926-29; general supervisor of biological films, G. B. Instructional Ltd., 1933-36, and Zoological Film Productions Ltd., 1937; director general, UNESCO, 1946-48. Galton Lecturer, 1937, 1962; Romanes Lecturer, Oxford University, 1943; William Alanson White Lecturer, Washington, D.C., 1951; first Alfred P. Sloan Lecturer, Sloan-Kettering Institute for Cancer Research, 1955; Beatty Lecturer, McGill University, 1956; visiting professor, University of Chicago, 1959. Participated in Oxford University's expedition to Spitsbergen, Norway, 1921; participated in Jordan Expedition, 1963. Visited East Africa to advise on native education, 1929; member of General Committee for Lord Hailey's African Survey, 1933-38; member of Commission on Higher Education in West Africa, 1944; member, Committee on National Parks, 1946; visited East Africa, 1960, and Ethiopia, 1963, to report to UNESCO on wildlife conservation; vice-president of UNESCO Commission for Scientific and Cultural History of Mankind. *Military service:* British Army, General Headquarters in Italy, staff lieutenant, World War I.

MEMBER: Institute of Animal Behaviour (former president), Eugenics Society (former president), Association for the Study of Systematics (former chairman), Academie des Sciences (Paris; corresponding member), Hungarian Academy of Science (foreign member), Zoological Society of London (secretary, 1935-42), Saville Club, Atheneum Club.

AWARDS, HONORS: Academy Award ("Oscar"), Academy of Motion Picture Arts and Sciences, 1934, for "The Private Life of the Gannets"; Anisfield Award, 1935, for *We Europeans;* fellow of the Royal Society, 1938; honorary member of faculty of biology and medicine, University of Santiago de Chile, 1947; honorary member of Society of Biology, University of Montevideo, 1947; Kalinga Prize, UNESCO, 1953, for distinguished popular science writing; Darwin medal, Royal Society, 1957; Darwin-Wallace commemorative medal, Linnean Society, 1958; knighted, 1958; Albert Lasker Award, Albert and Mary Lasker Foundation, 1959, for efforts in publicizing world population crisis; WWF Gold Medal, WWF International, 1970. Recipient of honorary degrees from University of Caracas, 1947, University of San Carlos de Guatemala, 1947, University of Athens, 1949, Columbia University, 1954, and University of Birmingham, 1959.

WRITINGS:

Holyrood (poems), Blackwell, 1908.
The Individual in the Animal Kingdom, Putnam, 1912.
Essays of a Biologist, Knopf, 1923, 3rd edition, 1926, reprinted, Books for Libraries, 1970.
The Outlook in Biology (pamphlet), Rice Institute (Houston), 1924.
(Editor) *Text-Books of Animal Biology,* Sidgwick & Jackson, 1926.
Essays in Popular Science, Chatto & Windus, 1926, Knopf, 1927.
The Stream of Life, Watts & Co., 1926, Harper, 1927.
(With J. B. S. Haldane) *Animal Biology,* Oxford University Press, 1927.
Religion without Revelation, Harper, 1927, revised edition, 1957, reprinted, Greenwood Press, 1979.
Towards the Open, Chatto & Windus, 1927.
Biology and Society, British Social Hygiene Council, 1928.
(With H. G. Wells and G. P. Wells) *The Science of Life,* Amalgamated Press, 1929, revised edition, 1938.
What Darwin Really Said, Routledge, 1929.
Bird-Watching and Bird Behavior, Chatto & Windus, 1930, 2nd edition, Dobson, 1950.
Science, Religion, and Human Nature (Conway Memorial Lecture), Watts & Co., 1930.
Ants, J. Cape and H. Smith, 1930, reprinted, Arden Library, 1978.
Africa View, Harper, 1931, reprinted, Greenwood Press, 1968.
What Dare I Think?, Harper, 1931.
(With others) *Science and Religion,* W. A. Hammond, 1931.
Problems of Relative Growth, Dial, 1932, 2nd edition, Dover, 1972.
A Scientist among the Soviets, Harper, 1932.
A Captive Shrew and Other Poems of a Biologist, Blackwell, 1932, Harper, 1933.

(With H. G. Wells) *Evolution, Fact and Theory,* Doubleday, 1932, reprinted, Arden Library, 1979.

(With Andrade) *Introduction to Science,* Blackwell, 1932, published as *Simple Science,* 1934, Harper, 1935.

If I Were a Dictator, Harper, 1934.

(With Gavin R. De Beer) *The Elements of Experimental Embryology,* Cambridge University Press, 1934, Hafner, 1963.

(With H. G. Wells and G. P. Wells) *Living Body,* Cassell, 1934.

Scientific Research and Social Needs, Watts & Co., 1934, published as *Science and Social Needs,* Harper, 1935, reprinted, Kraus Reprint, 1969.

(With R. M. Lockley) "The Private Life of the Gannets," (film script), produced in 1934.

(With Andrade) *More Simple Science,* Blackwell, 1935, Harper, 1936.

Problems in Experimental Embryology (Robert Boyle Lecture), Oxford University Press, 1935.

(Editor) T. H. Huxley, *Diary of the Voyage of the H.M.S. Rattlesnake,* Chatto & Windus, 1935, reprinted, Kraus Reprint, 1972.

(With A. C. Haddon) *We Europeans: A Survey of 'Racial' Problems,* J. Cape, 1935, Harper, 1936, reprinted, Arden Library, 1979.

At the Zoo, Allen & Unwin, 1936.

(Author of introduction) Adolf Portmann, *The Beauty of Butterflies,* Batsford, 1936, Oxford University Press (New York), 1945.

(With H. G. Wells and G. P. Wells) *Biology of the Human Race,* Cassell, 1937.

(With H. G. Wells) *How Animals Behave,* Cassell, 1937.

(With H. G. Wells and G. P. Wells) *Man's Mind and Behavior,* Cassell, 1937.

Beginnings of Life, Tuck, 1938.

Animal Language, Country Life Ltd., 1938, new edition, Grosset, 1964.

(Contributor) Sandor Forbat, *Love and Marriage,* Liveright, 1938.

'Race' in Europe, Farrar & Rinehart, 1939.

(Editor) *The Living Thoughts of Darwin,* Longmans, Green, 1939, reprinted, Fawcett, 1959.

(Editor) *The New Systematics,* Clarendon Press, 1940, reprinted, Scholarly Press, 1976.

Argument of Blood: The Advancement of Science, Macmillan, 1941.

(Under pseudonym Balbus) *Arm Now against Famine and Pestilence,* Universal Distributors, 1941.

Democracy Marches, Harper, 1941, reprinted, Books for Libraries, 1970.

Man Stands Alone (also see below), Harper, 1941, reprinted, Books for Libraries, 1970 (published in England as *The Uniqueness of Man,* Chatto & Windus, 1941).

(Under pseudonym Balbus) *Reconstruction and Peace: Needs and Opportunities,* K. Paul, Trench, Trubner & Co., 1941, New Republic, 1942.

(Contributor) H. Thomas, editor, *The Brains Trust Book,* Hutchinson, 1942.

(Contributor) A. Low, editor, *Science Looks Ahead,* Oxford University Press, 1942.

Evolution: The Modern Synthesis, Allen & Unwin, 1942, Harper, 1943, 3rd edition, Hafner, 1974.

Evolutionary Ethics (Romanes Lecture), Oxford University Press, 1943.

TVA: Adventures in Planning, Architectural Press, 1943.

(With Phyllis Deane) *The Future of the Colonies,* Pilot Press, 1944.

(With others) *Humanism,* Watts & Co., 1944.

On Living in a Revolution, Harper, 1944, reprinted, Books for Libraries, 1971.

(With others) *Reshaping Man's Heritage,* Allen & Unwin, 1944.

Julian Huxley on T. H. Huxley: A New Judgment, Watts & Co., 1945.

(With others) *Science at Your Service,* Allen & Unwin, 1945.

Religion as an Objective Problem, Watts & Co., 1946.

UNESCO: Its Purpose and Philosophy, Preparatory Commission of UNESCO, 1946, Public Affairs Press, 1947, reprinted, 1979.

Man in the Modern World, Chatto & Windus, 1947, New American Library, 1948.

(With T. H. Huxley) *Touchstone for Ethics, 1893-1943,* Harper, 1947, reprinted, Books for Libraries, 1971 (published in England as *Evolution and Ethics, 1893-1943,* Pilot Press, 1947, reprinted, Kraus Reprint, 1969).

The Vindication of Darwinism, Pilot Press, 1947.

(With Jaime Torres Bodet) *This Is Our Power,* UNESCO Publications, 1948.

Heredity, East and West: Lysenko and World Science, H. Schuman, 1949, reprinted, Kraus Reprint, 1969 (published in England as *Soviet Genetics and World Science,* Chatto & Windus, 1949).

Natural History in Ireland, Smithsonian Institution, 1951.

Evolution in Action, Harper, 1953.

New Bottles for New Wine: Ideology and Scientific Knowledge, [Singapore], 1953, published as *New Bottles for New Wine: Essays,* Harper, 1957, published as *Knowledge, Morality, and Destiny: Essays,* New American Library, 1960.

Evolution as a Process, Allen & Unwin, 1954, 2nd edition, 1958, Collier, 1963.

From an Antique Land: Ancient and Modern in the Middle East, Crown, 1954, 2nd edition, Parrish, 1961, Harper, 1966.

Kingdom of the Beasts, Vanguard, 1956.

Biological Aspects of Cancer, Harcourt, 1958.

(With others) *A Book That Shook the World,* University of Pittsburgh Press, 1958.

The Story of Evolution: The Wonderful World of Life, Rathbone Books, 1958, published as *The Wonderful World of Life: The Story of Evolution,* Doubleday, 1958, 2nd edition published as *The Wonderful World of Evolution,* Macdonald, 1969.

(With others) *The Destiny of Man,* Hodder & Stoughton, 1959.

(Contributor) Corliss Lamont, editor, *A Humanist Symposium on Metaphysics,* American Humanist Association, 1960.

Man's New Vision of Himself, edited by Peter Hey, University of Natal, 1960.

On Population: Three Essays, (contains work by Huxley, Thomas Malthus, and Frederick Osborn), New American Library, 1960.

(Editor with others) *Nature: Earth, Plants, Animals,* Macdonald & Co., 1960, published as *The Doubleday Pictorial Library of Nature: Earth, Plants, Animals,* Doubleday, 1961.

The Conservation of Wild Life and Natural Habitats in Central and East Africa, UNESCO, 1961.

(Editor and contributor) *The Humanist Frame,* Allen & Unwin, 1961, Harper, 1962.

Education and the Humanist Revolution, Fawley Foundation, University of Southampton, 1962.

The Human Crisis, University of Washington Press, 1963.

(Author of introduction and postscript) Marie Juliette Huxley, *Wild Lives of Africa,* Collins, 1963.

Essays of a Humanist, Harper, 1964.

Man in the Modern World: An Eminent Scientist Looks at Life Today (contains selected essays from *Man Stands Alone*), New American Library, 1964.

(Author of foreword) Henry Eliot Howard, *Territory in Bird Life,* Collins, 1964.

(Editor) *Aldous Huxley, 1894-1963: A Memorial Volume,* Harper, 1965.

(With Henry Bernard Davis Kettlewell) *Charles Darwin and His World,* Viking, 1965.

(Editor with others) *Growth of Ideas: Knowledge, Thought, Imagination,* Macdonald & Co., 1965, published as *The Doubleday Pictorial Library of Growth of Ideas: Knowledge, Thought, Imagination,* Doubleday, 1966.

The Future of Man: Evolutionary Aspects, Ethical Culture Publications, 1966.

(Compiler) *A Discussion on Ritualization of Behaviour in Animals and Man,* Royal Society of London, 1966.

(Author of foreword) George Brown Barbour, *Unterwegs mit Teilhard de Chardin: Auf den Spuren des Lebens in drei Kontinenten,* Walter-Verlag, 1967.

The Courtship Habits of the Great Crested Grebe, J. Cape, 1968.

Memories, Volume 1, Allen & Unwin, 1970, Harper, 1971, Volume 2, Harper, 1973.

(Consultant editor and author of foreword) *The Atlas of World Wildlife,* Rand McNally, 1973 (published in England as *The Mitchell Beazley Atlas of World Wildlife,* Mitchell Beazley, 1973).

Contributor to *Animals* magazine. Biological editor of *Encyclopaedia Britannica,* 14th edition; advisory editor, *Animal and Zoo Magazine,* 1935-42; member of editorial board, *New Naturalist,* beginning 1944.

SIDELIGHTS: Through lectures, radio broadcasts, magazine articles, and books, Julian Huxley made scientific information accessible to the general public, thus earning the distinction of being Britain's "public scientist No. 1." Grandson of scientist Thomas Henry Huxley, one of the earliest and strongest proponents of Darwin's theory of evolution, Julian Huxley grew up in an environment of intellectual integrity and inherited a concern for moral responsibility. Later in life, he was also greatly influenced by his younger brother Aldous Huxley, who wrote *Brave New World* and a number of other widely-read books.

Julian Huxley developed and promoted an integrated system of ideas which he called evolutionary humanism. He believed that evolution was at work everywhere and that man was presently in the human or psychosocial stage. According to Huxley, man possessed the capacity to be "the sole agent of further evolutionary advance on this planet." Advocating the use of reason and knowledge to develop evolutionary humanism as a religion,

Huxley offered modern man a set of behavioral, ethical, and religious principles that placed its final faith in human possibilities rather than in mysticism or supernatural beings.

As a humanist and an atheist who thought the concept of God was "not only unnecessary but intellectually dubious," Huxley often inspired controversy, especially when he expressed his views on religion and eugenics (the science of improving hereditary qualities). A most heated debate arose in 1962 after he gave a lecture proposing selective breeding of human beings along genetic lines. Many people were outraged by his idea of improving the human race through artificial insemination by preferred donors; others agreed with Huxley's belief that this would help man reach his highest potential.

Huxley once told *CA* that among the major challenges to man's progress are the threat of nuclear war, the threat of overpopulation, the rise of communist and fascist ideologies, and the widening gap between the rich and the poor nations. On the subject of overpopulation he wrote: "The implications of evolutionary humanism are clear. If the full development of human individuals and the fulfillment of human possibilities are the overriding aims of our evolution, then any overpopulation which brings malnutrition and misery, or which erodes the world's material resources or its resource of beauty or intellectual satisfaction are evil."

AVOCATIONAL INTERESTS: Travel and bird watching.

BIOGRAPHICAL/CRITICAL SOURCES:

BOOKS

Clark, R. W., *Sir Julian Huxley,* Phoenix House, 1960.
Clark, R. W., *The Huxleys,* McGraw, 1968.

PERIODICALS

Atlantic, June, 1971.
Books and Bookmen, June, 1968, August, 1970.
New York Times, October 12, 1969.
New York Times Book Review, May 24, 1964, April 3, 1966.
Saturday Review, April 24, 1971.
Scientific American, October, 1964.
Times Literary Supplement, November 4, 1965, June 28, 1970.

OBITUARIES:

PERIODICALS

Detroit News, February 16, 1975.
Newsweek, February 24, 1975.
New York Times, February 16, 1975.
Time, February 24, 1975.
Washington Post, February 16, 1975.

I

IBANEZ, Vicente Blasco
    See BLASCO IBANEZ , Vicente

* * *

ILLICH, Ivan 1926-

PERSONAL: Born September 4, 1926, in Vienna, Austria; came to United States in 1951; U.S. citizen; son of Ivan Peter (a landowner and civil engineer) and Ellen (Regenstreif-Ortlieb) Illich. *Education:* Attended University of Florence, University of Rome, and University of Munich; Gregorian University, licentiate in theology, 1951; University of Salzburg, Ph.D., 1951.

ADDRESSES: Home and office—Apdo 479, 62000 Cuernavaca, Mexico.

CAREER: Ordained Roman Catholic priest, 1951; became monsignor, 1956. Incarnation Church, New York, N.Y., assistant pastor, 1951-56; Catholic University of Puerto Rico, Ponce, vice rector, 1956-60; Centro Intercultural de Documentacion, Cuernavaca, Mexico, co-founder and director, 1961-76; guest professor, University of Kassel, 1979-82, University of California at Berkeley, 1982, and University of Marburg, 1983-84; Pennsylvania State University, University Park, Pa., professor of humanities and sciences, 1986-87. Member, Berlin Institute for Advanced Studies, 1981-82. Visiting lecturer at various institutions, including Fordham University, Massachusetts Institute of Technology, and University of Puerto Rico. Former vice president, Superior Council of Education, Government of Puerto Rico.

WRITINGS:

Metamorfosi del clero, La Locusta (Vicenza, Italy), 1968.
(Editor with others) *Spiritual Care of Puerto Rican Migrants,* Centro Intercultural de Documentacion, 1970.
Celebration of Awareness: A Call for Institutional Revolution, introduction by Erich Fromm, Doubleday, 1970, reprinted, Heyday, 1988.
De-Schooling Society, Harper, 1971.
(Contributor) Lionel Rubinoff, editor, *Tradition and Revolution,* St. Martin's, 1972.
(Compiler and contributor) *Centro Intercultural de Documentacion Antologia,* eight volumes, Centro Intercultural de Documentacion, c. 1973.
(Contributor) Peter Bruckman, editor, *Education without Schools,* Souvenir Press, 1973.

Retooling Society 111, Centro Intercultural de Documentacion, 1973.
En America Latina para que sirve le escuela?, Ediciones Busqueda (Buenos Aires), 1973.
(With others) *After De-Schooling, What?,* Harper, 1973.
Tools for Conviviality, Harper, 1973, reprinted, Heyday, 1988.
Energy and Equity, J. Calder, 1973, Harper, 1974.
Medical Nemesis: The Expropriation of Health, Calder & Boyars, 1975, revised edition published as *Limits to Medicine: Medical Nemesis, the Expropriation of Health,* 1976.
(With Etienne Verne) *Imprisoned in the Global Classroom,* Writers & Readers, 1976.
The Right to Useful Unemployment and Its Professional Enemies, Marion Boyars, 1978.
Toward a History of Needs, Pantheon, 1978.
(With others) *Disabling Professions,* Marion Boyars, 1978.
Shadow Work, Marion Boyars, 1981.
Gender, Pantheon, 1982.
H2O and the Waters of Forgetfulness, Heyday, 1987.
(With Barry Sanders) *ABC: The Alphabetization of the Popular Mind,* North Point Press, 1988.

Also author of *Church, Change and Development,* Seabury. Contributor to *Esprit, Temps Modernes, Kursbuch, New York Review of Books, New York Times,* and *Le Monde.*

SIDELIGHTS: "Ivan Illich has an uncanny ability to uncover, and then attack, the most sacred cows of Western civilization. He advocates abolishing compulsory education, because he thinks school systems encourage ignorance, not knowledge. He wants medical services drastically reduced, because he believes doctors are responsible more for sickness than for health. He thinks people would save time if transportation were limited to the speed of a bicycle," John Dorschner writes in the *Miami Herald.* In all his writings, Illich attacks modern bureaucracies for promoting self-serving policies that deprive ordinary people of the right to do things for themselves. Writing in the *New York Times Book Review,* Peter L. Berger characterizes the work of this cultural revolutionary as "simultaneously irritating and inspiring. . . . It is impossible to agree completely with Mr. Illich. It is also impossible to ignore him."

A Catholic priest, Illich first became known in the 1960s when he criticized the Catholic church's policies in Latin America. As early as 1956, in his post as vice-chancellor at the Catholic University of Puerto Rico, he associated with what he called "pro-humanist, pro-independence people" and recommended that money not be channelled into the universities until there were sufficient funds for the grammar schools. After being briefly recalled to the United States, Illich was assigned another foreign position—this time in Cuernavaca, a small town fifty miles from Mexico City, where he helped establish the Intercultural Center for Documentation.

A language school and training station, the Intercultural Center for Documentation was intended to teach priests and laymen who wanted to become Latin American volunteers. But Illich wanted neither the Peace Corps nor the Church to interfere in Latin America because he believed such assistance reduced the natives' independence and ultimately made them feel inferior. Consequently, Illich told Dorschner, his real purpose was "to corrupt [volunteers] while they were still with us and ship them home under their own motivation." When called to Rome in 1968 to explain his position on this and other controversial issues such as birth control, Illich refused to answer questions, instead requesting lay status and finally relinquishing his role as a priest in 1969. However, he remained the school's director until its closing in 1976.

With the publication of *De-Schooling Society* in 1971, Illich was back in the public eye, protesting against mandatory public education and the institutionalization of learning in schools. "Most learning happens casually," he writes in this book, "and even most intentional learning is not the result of programmed instruction." Convinced that a child becomes interested in what he is exposed to at home, Illich argues that money poured into programs for the disadvantaged is money wasted. The lack of stimulus in one's home environment cannot be made up for at school. Furthermore, he argues, the concept of knowledge as something "being taught by a teacher" is misleading. "The need for learning . . . then becomes identified as a need for the services of a teacher instead of access to the opportunity to learn," Joseph P. Fitzpatrick explains in his *America* review. More recently, as the co-author of *ABC: The Alphabetization of the Popular Mind*, Illich has also complained about how writing can be used for social manipulation. Written with Pitzer College English professor Barry Sanders, this book especially warns historians about the dangers of perpetuating historical falsehoods by basing their research on previously published works instead of on primary sources.

While few critics agree with Illich's assessment, several express admiration for the compelling tone of his book. "It is not difficult to pick holes in some of Mr. Illich's propositions, because in leaping from peak to peak he sometimes stumbles," says Anatole Broyard in the *New York Times*. "Schools aren't as bad as he maintains; most learning isn't acquired casually, as he says; the 'street education' that he advocates entered schools a long time ago; schools are not entirely self-perpetuating, because even the scholarship students are clamoring for change. . . . But this is like criticizing the grammar of someone who has just delivered a speech that gave us goosepimples. Flaws and all, *De-Schooling Society* ought to be read by everyone."

In his subsequent publications, Illich zeroes in on other flaws of modern society. *Tools for Conviviality*, for example, rails against "manipulative technologies" such as the automobile, which dominate man while purporting to serve him. And *Medical Nemesis: The Expropriation of Health* criticizes the medical establishment—but not doctors personally—as a major threat to health. "I am deeply saddened by the willingness of people to be taken in by the idea that what medical schools produce, in any way, contributes to health," he told Dorschner. Though people

are spending more money on medical care, they are receiving fewer benefits, just as is the case with education and transportation, Illich maintains.

Illich has occasionally been faulted for his selective use of evidence and for presenting a one-sided picture of events. In his review of *Shadow Work*, Berger observes: "Its weaknesses are those of his earlier books. Modernity, with the exception of some technological innovations, appears here in a consistently negative light. It expropriates, alienates, brings into servitude. Mr. Illich seems incapable of perceiving the liberating and humanizing effects of modernity." In his *Los Angeles Times* review, Kenneth Funsten voices another common objection: "Illich lacks an alternative plan of action realizable in today's world. Like so many thinkers from the '50s and '60s his cry implies as its only solution a return somewhere more primitive. But this is no solution at all."

When asked, at a press conference, why he does not offer more detailed alternatives in his writing, Illich replied that he did not want to be "engaged in any party whose ideology I would have to bolster. I want to provide a method which allows people to distinguish the feasible from the infeasible utopia." According to Dorschner, this means "he will tell us what utopia is not; others can suggest what it should be."

BIOGRAPHICAL/CRITICAL SOURCES:

BOOKS

Authors in the News, Volume 2, Gale, 1976.
du Plessix Gray, Francine, *Divine Disobedience: Profiles in Catholic Radicalism*, Knopf, 1970.
Illich, Ivan, *De-Schooling Society*, Harper, 1971.

PERIODICALS

America, December 16, 1978.
Los Angeles Times, May 28, 1981.
Los Angeles Times Book Review, February 21, 1988.
Miami Herald, October 12, 1975.
New York Times, June 4, 1971, March 27, 1978, December 30, 1982.
New York Times Book Review, April 9, 1978, March 8, 1981, January 30, 1983.

*　　*　　*

INCOGNITEAU, Jean-Louis
See KEROUAC, Jean-Louis Lebrid de

*　　*　　*

INFANTE, G(uillermo) Cabrera
See CABRERA INFANTE, G(uillermo)

*　　*　　*

INGE, William Motter 1913-1973

PERSONAL: Surname rhymes with "hinge"; born May 3, 1913, in Independence, Mo.; died June 10, 1973, in Los Angeles, Calif.; son of Luther Clayton (a merchant) and Maude Sarah (Gibson) Inge. *Education:* University of Kansas, A.B., 1935; George Peabody College for Teachers, A.M., 1938.

CAREER: Playwright, whose almost lifelong interest in the stage was sidetracked at various times for periods of more lucrative teaching and journalism. Started as a child monologuist, acted in high school and college plays, in a tent show, and in summer stock; lacking money to further his acting career on Broadway, turned to teaching as high school instructor in Columbus, Kan., 1937-38, instructor at Stephens College, Columbia, Mo., 1938-43, working last three years under Maude Adams in drama department; left to become drama, music, and movie critic for *St. Louis Star-Times,* St. Louis, Mo., 1943-46; returned to teaching at Washington University, St. Louis, Mo., 1946-49. Taught at University of North Carolina, 1969, and at University of California, Irvine, 1970.

AWARDS, HONORS: George Jean Nathan Award and Theatre Time Award, 1950, for *Come Back, Little Sheba;* Pulitzer Prize in Drama, Outer Circle Award, New York Drama Critics Circle Award, and Donaldson Award, 1953, for *Picnic;* Academy Award ("Oscar") from Academy of Motion Picture Arts and Sciences, 1961, for *Splendor in the Grass.*

WRITINGS:

PLAYS

Come Back, Little Sheba (first produced by Theatre Guild in Westport, Conn., September 12, 1949; produced on Broadway at Booth Theatre, February 15, 1950; also see below), Random House, 1950, acting edition published as *Come Back, Little Sheba: a Drama in Two Acts,* S. French, 1951.

Picnic (based on Inge's short play "Front Porch"; one version titled "Summer Brave" produced at Hyde Park, N.Y., August, 1952 [also see below], subsequently revised and retitled version produced on Broadway at Music Box Theatre, February 19, 1953; also see below), Random House, 1953, acting edition, Dramatists Play Service, 1955.

Bus Stop (reworking and expansion of his one-act "People in the Wind"; first produced on Broadway at Music Box Theatre, March 2, 1955; also see below), Random House, 1955, acting edition published as *Bus Stop: A Three-act Romance,* Dramatists Play Service, 1956 (also collaborated on musical adaptation, originally titled "Beau," then changed to "Cherry," canceled prior to Broadway).

The Dark at the Top of the Stairs (typescript; originally a short play titled "Farther Off From Heaven," first produced by Margo Jones's Little Theatre Group in Dallas, Tex., 1947, expanded retitled version first produced on Broadway at Music Box Theatre, December 5, 1957; also see below), A. Meyerson (New York), 1957, published with an introduction by Tennessee Williams, Random House, 1958, acting edition, Dramatists Play Service, 1960.

Four Plays by William Inge: Come Back, Little Sheba, Picnic, Bus Stop, The Dark at the Top of the Stairs, Random House, 1958.

(Contributor) Bennett Cerf and Van H. Cartmell, editors, *24 Favorite One-Act Plays,* Doubleday, 1958.

The Mall (also see below), [Chicago], 1959.

A Loss of Roses (first produced on Broadway at Eugene O'Neill Theatre, November 28, 1959), Random House, 1960, acting edition, Dramatists Play Service, 1963.

Summer Brave and Eleven Short Plays (contains "Summer Brave," "To Bobolink for Her Spirit," "People in the Wind," "A Social Event," "The Boy in the Basement," "The Tiny Closet," "Memory of Summer," "Bus Riley's Back in Town" [also see below], "The Rainy Afternoon," "The Mall," "An Incident at the Standish Arms," and "The Strains of Triumph"), Random House, 1962.

Natural Affection (produced on Broadway at Booth Theatre, January 31, 1963), Random House, 1963.

Where's Daddy? (first produced as "Family Things" in Westport, Conn., 1965, revised version, retitled, produced on Broadway, February 28, 1966), Random House, 1966, acting edition published as *Where's Daddy?: A Two-act Comedy,* Dramatists Play Service, 1966.

Two Short Plays: The Call [and] *A Murder,* Dramatists Play Service, 1968.

"The Last Pad" (originally titled "Don't Go Gentle"), produced Off-Broadway at 13th Street Theatre, December, 1970.

Also author of "Overnight."

SCREENPLAYS

Splendor in the Grass (produced by Warner Brothers, 1961), Bantam, 1961.

"All Fall Down" (based on novel by James Leo Herlihy), produced by Metro-Goldwyn-Mayer, 1962.

"Bus Riley's Back in Town" (from his own short play; he had his name removed from the credits prior to release and the name Walter Gage appears instead), produced by Universal, 1964.

OTHER

"Out on the Outskirts of Town" (television play), produced on "Bob Hope Chrysler Theatre," November 6, 1964.

Good Luck, Miss Wyckoff, Atlantic-Little, Brown, 1970.

My Son Is a Splendid Driver, Atlantic-Little, Brown, 1971.

Also author of two unfinished filmscripts, "Off the Main Road" and "Almost a Love Song." Contributor to *Esquire.* Inge's papers are collected at the Humanities Research Center, University of Texas, at the Independence Community College in Independence, Kansas, and at the University of Kansas.

SIDELIGHTS: William Inge has been called the playwright of the Midwest, since he was the first, and really only person to write exclusively about the people who have lived their ordinary lives away from the mainstream of America. He is perhaps best known for his psychological portraits of these people, whose lives are so important to him. Inge grew up in small-town Kansas, and did not reach New York for the first time until he was twenty-seven. But, he says, he did not consider himself a Kansan until he was away from home. He told Digby Diehl: "I'm one of those people who grew up in Kansas feeling very superior to it. I felt out of place in that forlorn mid-western agricultural state. I had nothing in common with it at all. It was boring as hell and I wanted out. It wasn't until I got to New York that I became Kansan. Everyone there kept reminding me that they were Jewish or Irish, or whatever, so I kept reminding them that I was midwestern. I discovered I had something a bit unique, but it was the nature of New York that forced me to claim my past."

His strong sense of his rural past infuses all his work. Inge originally wanted to be an actor, and Jean Gould says that "he had the kind of countenance that could have made a 'matinee idol': his deep-set eyes, classic nose and full, curving lips combines in round contour to form, according to Tennessee Williams' description, 'the very handsome and outwardly serene face of William Inge.' He was tall and well-proportioned, and moved with the easy gait of an actor." Fortunately he did discover his true role in the theater.

Inge's place was established in the theater with the production of *Come Back, Little Sheba,* which was well-received, although it did not actually have as long a run on Broadway as might be thought. Inge told Digby Diehl: "It was successful, but moderately so. It was a hit as a movie but the play only got about half the New York critics. Happily, Brooks Atkinson liked it. . . .

On the road we had great success. The audiences were much more responsive and alive." R. Baird Shuman stated in *William Inge* that *Come Back, Little Sheba* "is generally considered Inge's best play. In it Inge's primary concern is to present human motivations and behavior; however, the play, based on one of Inge's early short stories, has greater structural unity and a stronger story line than any of his other plays with the possible exception of his scenario, *Splendor in the Grass.*"

Picnic, Inge's second play introduced in New York, solidified his standing in the city's theater. Shuman wrote: "If Inge's first play had established his reputation in the theater, *Picnic* assured the skeptics that *Come Back, Little Sheba* had not been just a unique stroke of good fortune. The widespread recognition which *Picnic* received caused Inge to be favorably compared to [Tennessee] Williams and [Arthur] Miller." *Picnic* was based on a short play which Inge had called "Front Porch," which he developed and expanded for Broadway. Another version of the play, "Summer Brave," was considered by Inge to be the final version, although it was produced before *Picnic* went to Broadway. Jean Gould wrote in *Modern Playwrights on Drama* of *Picnic*: "It has been called by [John] Gassner a 'pathetic pastoral,' but it also possesses the richness, the earthiness of an al fresco bacchanale, in terms of American folkways in the Middle West."

Inge expanded his one-act "People in the Wind" into *Bus Stop,* which he considers a romantic comedy. Miss Gould said that *Bus Stop* "has serious overtones and moments of sadness, and in its way is a commentary on the haphazard lives of those who try to live by their talents, beauty, or wits, without a penny in the world, homeless and rootless." Shuman said that Inge changed the focus from loneliness, in the short play, to the different aspects of love in the longer work. Inge told Digby Diehl that the play is "the closest thing to fantasy that I ever wrote. It's pretty close to being a fairy tale. The town in Kansas was kind of an archetype." Shuman pointed out that in *Bus Stop* the emotions "are, in the final analysis, stark and undramatized. Herein is the greatest strength of Inge's extreme realism. His clinical objectivity increased steadily from *Come Back, Little Sheba* to *The Dark at the Top of the Stairs,* and it was increasingly reinforced by his unadorned use of language and by the classic starkness of his settings."

In *The Dark at the Top of the Stairs* Inge added to the theses that Shuman believed are evident in his work, "that love is to be discovered through sex and that problems are more often to be solved in bed than in the parlor. Inge is aware most fully of what Brooks Atkinson called 'the illusiveness of experience.' His characters often seek to overcome this illusiveness and to escape from their loneliness through sex." The end of the play finds Rubin urging Cora to come upstairs, where they will reconcile their differences in bed. Inge told an interviewer that although *The Dark at the Top of the Stairs* is not an autobiographical play, "I did kind of base a piece of fiction around the members of my family. But they are only a vague resemblance to my family." "Farther off from Heaven," which was expanded to *The Dark at the Top of the Stairs,* was the first play Inge wrote. He had the opportunity to interview Tennessee Williams in 1945, and as a result of that interview confided his interest in writing to Williams. Inge showed him the play, and Williams made it possible for Margo Jones to produce the play in Dallas in 1947. Although they saw each other infrequently, Inge and Williams remained friends.

The plays which followed *The Dark at the Top of the Stairs—A Loss of Roses, Natural Affection,* and *Where's Daddy?*—did not have the success that the earlier plays had. Difficulties with script changes and a substitution of the leading actress turned *A*

Loss of Roses into a virtual disaster when it opened. Inge had been practically the only backer for the production and the financial and personal losses were great. Neither *Natural Affection* nor *Where's Daddy?* proved very successful, although both were thought to have many good sections. In both *Natural Affection* and *A Loss of Roses* Inge was concerned with the mother-son relationship, as he was in *The Dark at the Top of the Stairs,* and had difficulty in focusing on one aspect of the relationships rather than going off in many directions. Many believe that as Inge moved further away from the more familiar territory of the earlier plays he moved away from some of the elements which were the best in his work. Most agree that he is best at writing about ordinary Midwestern townspeople. His naturalistic style, his psychological perceptions all contributed to the success of his plays. His understanding of children and young people, seen especially in the characters in *The Dark at the Top of the Stairs* and *Splendor in the Grass* has been praised by many.

Splendor in the Grass, for which Inge won an Academy Award, proved very successful, especially in the presentation of the adolescent characters. Shuman stated that "Inge's understanding and recording of adolescent behavior is nothing short of amazing. The small touches which were almost entirely lacking in *A Loss of Roses* are present with vigor in *Splendor in the Grass.*" Shuman also pointed out that the dialogue was much more spare than in either *A Loss of Roses* and *Natural Affection,* and thought that this might have something to do with the success or failure of his plays.

Inge produced two novels in his career, both about small people in the Midwest, both strong on character, and more in line with the material of his earlier plays. *Good Luck, Miss Wyckoff,* Haskel Frankel thought, does not contain anything that Inge has not already covered in his plays; he expressed the opinion that the latter form suited Inge better. Frankel said that *Miss Wyckoff* is "either a new girl in town, or an old hat. Or, for those of us who remember four very happy evenings in the theater, a sentimental journey." Eugene J. Linehan wrote: "The language is strong; the sexuality often gross; but the sense of reality is profound." D. Keith Mano wrote in a discussion of *My Son Is a Splendid Driver*: "William Inge writes in the form of a memoir, which, by his own admission, approximates autobiography. . . . This is a sad, clinical tale, written with dignity and imagination and restraint, yet I doubt if many readers would care to have Mr. Inge's depressing, bitter memories of another era imposed on them with such remitting emphasis."

Inge once told Digby Diehl, "I read somewhere, in Robert Graves, I think, about a tribe which created gods in order to destroy them. I think that the instant a person becomes famous in America a machine is set in motion to destroy him. If you look at the personal lives of people in theater in this country most of them are despairingly unhappy people. Some of our most talented actors are miserable. We have no future or security to offer them. We still think of our artists in the *La Boheme* portrait. America can't believe in the artist as a working man. He becomes famous, but he's not respected. I think it's time now that we get respected and quit being famous."

MEDIA ADAPTATIONS: "Come Back, Little Sheba," adapted by Ketti Frings, was produced by Paramount, 1952; "Picnic" was produced by Warner Brothers, 1955; "Bus Stop," adapted by William Axelrod, was produced by Twentieth Century Fox, 1960; "The Dark at the Top of the Stairs" was produced by Warner Brothers, 1960; "A Loss of Roses" was produced as "The Stripper" by Twentieth Century Fox, 1963. Film rights for *Where's Daddy?* and *Good Luck, Miss Wyckoff* have been sold.

"Picnic" was adapted as a musical titled "Hot September," first produced in Boston at Shubert Theatre, September 4, 1965; "Come Back, Little Sheba" has been adapted as a musical titled "The Word Is Love." A television series based on "Bus Stop" was broadcast during the 1961-62 season.

BIOGRAPHICAL/CRITICAL SOURCES:

BOOKS

American Playwrights, Dodd, 1966.
Brustein, Robert, *Seasons of Discontent,* Simon & Schuster, 1967.
Concise Dictionary of American Literary Biography: The New Consciousness, 1941-1968, Gale, 1987.
Contemporary Literary Criticism, Gale, Volume 1, 1973, Volume 8, 1978, Volume 19, 1981.
Dictionary of Literary Biography, Volume 7: *Twentieth-Century American Playwrights,* Gale, 1981.
Gassner, John, *Theatre at the Crossroads,* Holt, 1960.
Gould, Jean, *Modern Playwrights on Drama,* Hill & Wang, 1965.
Lewis, Allan, *American Plays and Playwrights of the Contemporary Theatre,* Crown, 1965.
Lurnley, Frederick, *New Trends in 20th Century Drama,* Oxford University Press, 1967.
Oppenheimer, George, *Passionate Playgoer,* Viking, 1958.
Shuman, R. Baird, *William Inge,* Twayne, 1965.
Wager, Walter, editor, *The Playwrights Speak,* Delacorte, 1967.

PERIODICALS

American Annals, 1954.
American Book Collector, October, 1965.
Best Sellers, June 1, 1970, June 15, 1971.
Book World, June 14, 1970.
Choice, July, 1967.
Life, January 6, 1958.
Los Angeles Times, March 5, 1982.
Nation, December 2, 1957.
National Review, June 29, 1971.
Newsweek, May 14, 1962.
New York Times, November 30, 1979, July 13, 1984, July 29, 1984.
New York Times Book Review, June 14, 1970.
Show Business, December 12, 1970.
Theater Arts, May, 1950.
Time, December 16, 1957.
Transatlantic Review, autumn, 1967.
Vogue, May 1, 1954.

*   *   *

INNES, Michael
See STEWART, J(ohn) I(nnes) M(ackintosh)

*   *   *

IONESCO, Eugene   1912-

PERSONAL: Born November 26 (some sources list November 13), 1912, in Slatina, Romania; now a French citizen; son of Eugene (a lawyer) and Marie-Therese (Icard) Ionesco; married Rodika Burileano, July 12, 1936; children: Marie-France. *Education:* Attended University of Bucharest; University of Paris, Sorbonne, licencie es lettres, agrege des lettres.

ADDRESSES: Home—96 bd Montparnasse, 75014 Paris, France. *Office*—c/o Editions Gallimard, 5 rue Sebastien Bottin, 75007 Paris, France.

CAREER: Playwright, essayist, and author of fiction. Professor of French in Romania, 1936-39; worked for publisher in France. Has directed and acted in his own plays; also acted in a 1951 adaptation of Fedor Dostoevski's *The Possessed.*

MEMBER: Academie Francaise.

AWARDS, HONORS: Prix de la Critique, Tours Festival, 1959, for film *Monsieur Tete;* Chevalier des Arts et Lettres, 1961; Grand Prix Italia, 1963, for ballet version of *La Lecon;* Grand Prix du Theatre de la Societe des Auteurs, 1966, for total body of work; Le Prix National du Theatre, 1969; Prix Litteraire de Monaco, 1969; Chevalier de la Legion d'Honneur, 1970; Austrian Prize for European Literature, 1971; Jerusalem Prize, 1973, for total body of work, with *Rhinoceros* cited as "one of the great demonstrations against totalitarianism"; officer of the French Foreign Legion of Honor, 1984; T. S. Eliot Award for Creative Writing, Ingersoll Foundation Prizes in Literature and Humanities, 1985.

WRITINGS:

PLAYS

La Cantatrice chauve (one-act; first produced in Paris, France, at Theatre des Noctambules, May 11, 1950), Gallimard, 1962, enlarged edition, 1964, translation (produced Off-Broadway as *The Bald Soprano* at Sullivan Street Playhouse, June 3, 1958) by Donald Watson published as *The Bald Prima Donna: A Pseudo-play,* Samuel French, 1961, published as *The Bald Soprano: Anti-play,* Grove, 1965 (published in England as *The Bald Prima Donna: Anti-Play,* Calder, 1966).
La Lecon (one-act; first produced in Paris at Theatre de Poche-Montparnasse, February 20, 1951), translation (produced Off-Broadway as *The Lesson* at Phoenix Theatre, January 9, 1958) by Watson published as *The Lesson,* Samuel French, 1958.
Les Chaises (first produced in Paris at Theatre Nouveau-Lancry, April 22, 1952), Gallimard, 1962, translation (produced Off-Broadway at Phoenix Theatre, January 9, 1958) by Watson published as *The Chairs,* Samuel French, 1958.
Victimes du devoir (one-act), first produced in Paris at Theatre du Quartier Latin, February, 1953, produced Off-Broadway as *Victims of Duty* at Theatre de Lys, January 19, 1960, produced in Zurich, Switzerland, at Theatre am Neumacht, November, 1968, with Ionesco as director.
Le Salon de l'automobile, first produced in Paris at Theatre de la Huchette, September 1, 1953.
Le Maitre, first produced at Theatre de la Huchette, September 1, 1953, produced in London, England, at Theatre Upstairs, August 31, 1970.
La Jeune fille a marier, first produced at Theatre de la Huchette, September 1, 1953, produced Off-Broadway at Barbizon-Plaza Theatre, May, 1970.
La Niece-Epouse (title means "The Niece-Wife"), first produced at Theatre de la Huchette, September 1, 1953, produced in London, March, 1971.
Amedee, ou Comment s'en debarasser (three-act), first produced in Paris at Theatre de Babylone, April 14, 1954, produced in New York City as *Amadee, or How to Disentangle Yourself* at Tempo Playhouse, October 31, 1955.
Jacques, ou la soumission (one-act), first produced at Theatre de la Huchette, October, 1955, produced in New York City as *Jack* at Sullivan Street Playhouse, June 3, 1958.
Le Tableau, first produced at Theatre de la Huchette, October, 1955, first produced in English by British Broadcasting

Corp. (BBC) as *The Picture,* March 11, 1957, produced Off-Off-Broadway at Cafe Deja-vu, September, 1969.

Le Nouveau Locataire (one-act), first produced in Helsinki, Finland, 1955, produced in Paris at Theatre d'Aujourd'hui, 1957, produced in New York City as *The New Tenant* at Royale Playhouse, March 9, 1960.

L'Impromptu de l'Alma, ou Le Cameleon du berger, first produced in Paris at Studio des Champs-Elysees, February, 1956, produced as *Improvisation, or The Shepherd's Chameleon,* at Theatre de Lys, November 29, 1960.

Tuer sans gages (three-act; first produced in Paris at Theatre Recamier, February 27, 1959; produced in New York City as *The Killer* at Seven Arts Theatre, March 22, 1960), University London Press, 1972.

Scene a quatre, first produced in Italy for the Spoleto Festival, 1959, produced at Theatre Upstairs, August 31, 1970.

Le Rhinoceros (three-act; first produced in Dusseldorf, West Germany, 1959; produced in Paris at Theatre l'Odean, January 25, 1960), Gallimard, 1959, translation (first produced by BBC, August 20, 1959; produced in London at Royal Court Theatre, April 28, 1960; produced on Broadway at Longacre Theatre, January 9, 1961) by Derek Prouse published as *Rhinoceros: A Play in Three Acts,* Samuel French, 1960.

Apprendre a marcher, first performed in Paris at Theatre de l'Etoile, April, 1960.

Delire a deux (one-act; first produced at Studio des Champs-Elyssees, 1962), Gallimard, 1966.

Le Roi se meurt (one-act; first produced in Paris, December 15, 1962), Gallimard, 1963, translation (produced at Royal Court Theatre, September 12, 1963) by Watson published as *Exit the King,* Grove, 1963.

Le Pieton de l'air (ballet-pantomime), first produced at Theatre L'Odean, February 8, 1963, produced on Broadway at New York City Center Theatre, February, 1964.

Lecons de francais pout Americains, produced at Theatre de Poche Montparnasse, February, 1965, with Ionesco cast in the role of the teacher.

La Soif et la faim (three-act; first produced in Paris at Comedie-Francaise, February 28, 1966), [Paris], 1966, translation (produced in Stockbridge, MA, at Berkshire Theatre Festival, July, 1969) published as *Hunger and Thirst: A Play in Three Acts,* Samuel French, 1971.

Les Salutations [and] *La Lacune* [and] *L'Oeuf dur, pour preparer un oeuf dur* [and] *Ches [sic] le docteur* [and] *Le Coca tier en flammes* [and] *D'Isidione* [and] *Histoire des bandits* [and] *Il y eut d'abord* [and] *Lecons de francais pour Americains,* all produced at Theatre Upstairs, August 31, 1970.

Jeux de massacre (one-set; first produced in Dusseldorf, 1970; produced at Theatre Montparnasse, October 17, 1970; produced in Washington, DC, as *Wipe-out Games,* at Kreeger Theater, April, 1971), Gallimard, 1970, translation by Helen Gary Bishop published as *Killing Game,* Random House, 1974.

Macbett (version of Shakespeare's *Macbeth*), Gallimard, 1972, translation by Charles Marowitz published as *Macbett: A Play,* Grove, 1973.

Ce formidable bordel! (produced November 14, 1973), Gallimard, 1973, translation by Bishop published as *A Hell of a Mess,* Grove, 1975.

L'homme aux valises (produced December, 1975, at Theatre de l'Atelier) [and] *Ce formidable bordel!,* Gallimard, 1975.

Voyages chez les morts: themes et variations, Gallimard, 1981, translation (produced in London, 1987) published as *Journeys among the Dead,* Riverrun Press, 1985.

Also author of *Les Grandes Chaleurs, Le Connaissez-vous?,* and *Le Rhume Onirique,* all first produced in 1953; of *L'Avenir est dans les oeufs,* first produced in 1957; of *Impromptu pour la Duchesse de Windsor,* privately performed for the Duke and Duchess of Windsor, May, 1957; and of *Melees et demelees.*

OMNIBUS VOLUMES AND COLLECTIONS

Theatre (includes "La Cantatrice chauve," "La Lecon," "Jacques, ou la sournission," and "Le Salon de l'automobile"), Arcanes, 1953.

Theatre (collected plays), seven volumes, Gallimard, 1954-1981.

Three Plays (contains "La Cantatrice chauve," "La Lecon," and "Les Chaises"), edited by H. F. Brookes and C. E. Fraenkel, Heinemann, 1965.

La Cantatrice chauve: anti-piece [and] *La Lecon: drame comique,* Gallimard, 1970, Holt, 1975.

Les Chaises: farce tragique [and] *L'Impromptu de l'Alma, ou, Le cameleon du berger,* Gallimard, 1973.

OMNIBUS VOLUMES AND COLLECTIONS IN TRANSLATION

Plays, translated by Watson, Calder, Volume 1, 1958, Volume 2, 1961, Volume 3, 1962, Volume 4, 1963, Volume 5, 1963, Volume 6, 1965, Volume 7, 1968.

Four Plays: The Bald Soprano [and] *The Lesson* [and] *Jack, or the Submission* [and] *The Chairs,* translated by Donald M. Allen, Grove, 1958.

Amedee [and] *The New Tenant* [and] *Victims of Duty,* translated by Allen, Grove, 1958.

The Killer, and Other Plays (includes "The Killer," "Improvisation, or the Shepherd's Chameleon," and "Maid to Marry"), translated by Watson, Grove, 1960.

Rhinoceros and Other Plays (includes "Rhinoceros," "The Leader" and "The Future Is in Eggs, or It Takes All Sorts to Make a World"), translated by Prouse, Grove, 1960.

The Chairs [and] *The Killer* [and] *Maid to Marry,* translated by Watson, Calder, 1963.

A Stroll in the Air [and] *Frenzy for Two or More,* translated by Watson, Calder, 1965, Grove, 1968.

Hunger and Thirst [and] *The Picture* [and] *Anger* [and] *Salutations,* translated by Watson, Calder and Boyars, 1968, published as *Hunger and Thirst, and Other Plays,* Grove, 1969.

Rhinoceros [and] *La Vase,* Gallimard, 1970.

Here Comes a Chopper [and] *The Oversight* [and] *The Foot of the Wall,* translated by Watson, Calder and Boyars, 1971.

Macbett [and] *The Mire* [and] *Learning to Walk,* translated by Watson, Calder and Boyars, 1973.

OTHER

(Translator with G. Gabrin) Pavel Dan, *Le Vieil Urcan,* Editions Jean Vigneau, 1945.

Ionesco: Les Rhinoceros au theatre (includes a short story and journal selections), R. Julliard, 1960.

La Photo du Colonel (narratives, many of them the basis for plays; includes "Oriflamme," "La Photo du Colonel," "Le Pieton de l'air," "Une Victime du devoir," "Rhinoceros," "La Vase," and "Printemps 1939"), Gallimard, 1962, new edition, 1970, translation by Jean Stewart (except "A Stroll in the Air," translated by John Russell) published as *The Colonel's Photograph,* Faber, 1967, Grove, 1969.

Notes et contre-notes (essays, addresses, lectures), Gallimard, 1962, new edition, 1970, translation by Watson published as *Notes and Counter-Notes: Writings on the Theatre,* Grove, 1964.

(Author of notes) Joan Miro, *Quelques fleurs pour des amis,* Societe Internationale d'Art, 1964.

Journal en miettes (autobiography), Mercure de France, 1967, translation by Stewart published as *Fragments of a Journal,* Grove, 1968.

Present passe, passe present (autobiography), Mercure de France, 1968, translation by Helen R. Lane published as *Present Past, Past Present: A Personal Memoir,* Grove, 1971.

(Also illustrator) *Decouvertes* (essay), Skira (Geneva), 1969.

(With Michel Benamou) *Mise en train: Premiere Annee de francais* (textbook), Macmillan, 1969.

(Author of text) Jan Lenica, *Monsieur Tete* (animated film), Bruckmann (Munich), 1970.

(Author of text) Gerard Schneider, *Catalogo* (art exhibit), [Torino], 1970.

(With Jean Delay) *Discours de reception d'Eugene Ionesco a l'Academie francaise et reponse de Jean Delay,* Gallimard, 1971.

(Contributor) Richard N. Coe, *Ionesco: A Study of His Plays* (contains "The Niece-Wife"), Methuen, 1971.

(Also illustrator) *Victimes du devoir and Une Victime du devoir* (play and short story), edited by Vera Lee, Houghton, 1972.

Le Solitaire (novel), Mercure de France, 1973, translation by Richard Seaver published as *The Hermit,* Viking, 1974.

Antidotes (essays), Gallimard, 1977.

Un homme en question, Gallimard, 1979.

Pour la culture, contre la politique, Erker, 1979.

Hugoliade, Gallimard, 1982.

Le blanc et le noir (essay), Gallimard, 1985.

Also author of *Contes pour enfants* (stories for children), four volumes, translated into English and published by Harlan Quist. Co-author of the filmscript for *Seven Capital Sins,* produced by Embassy in 1962. Adaptor, with Flemming Flindt, of three of his plays as ballets, including *La Lecon,* performed on European television in 1963, *Le Jeune Homme a marier* (based on *Jacques, ou la sournission*), produced in 1965, and *The Triumph of Death* (based on *Jeux de Massacre*), produced in 1971.

Work represented in numerous anthologies and critical studies, including *Absurd Drama,* edited by Martin Esslin, and *New Directions,* edited by Alan Durrand. Contributor to *Les Lettres nouvelles, Les Lettres francaises, Encore, Evergreen Review, Mademoiselle, L'Express, Tulane Drama Review, Theatre Arts, Commentary, London Magazine,* and other publications.

MEDIA ADAPTATIONS: The Great Man, an opera based on *Le Maitre,* was performed in New York in 1963. *L'homme aux valises* was adapted by Israel Horovitz for his play *Man with Bags.* Several of Ionesco's plays, including *Exit the King, The Lesson,* and *The Picture,* have been shown on American television. The film rights to *Rhinoceros* were sold to Woodfall Films in 1971.

SIDELIGHTS: Eugene Ionesco's early failure to appeal to his audiences has been replaced by such resounding success that now he is, along with Brecht, one of the two most widely-performed contemporary playwrights in the world. Unquestionably an original talent, he has discarded plot in order to "rediscover the rhythms of drama in their purest state and to reproduce them in the form of pure scenic movement." Committed to a belief in an absurd universe where everything is contradiction, where "only myth is true," where communication is probably impossible, he must conclude, "what else can one do but laugh at it?"

And laugh he does. Itichard Coe has written: "To a greater or less degree, all Ionesco's drama is a satire upon the bourgeoisie, its speech, its manners, and its morals." "Humor," writes Ionesco, "is my outlet, my release and my salvation." Yet his humor holds no optimism but rather what Coe has called a "pro-found and ineradicable pessimism" inculcated by a world where the senselessness of death is the ultimate absurdity.

Critic Susan Sontag, who considers Ionesco "a minor writer even at his best," does grant him these triumphs: "What Ionesco did—no mean feat—was to appropriate for the theater one of the great technical discoveries of modern poetry: that all language can be considered from the outside, as by a stranger. . . . His next discovery, also long familiar in modern poetry, was that he could treat language as a palpable thing. (Thus, the teacher kills the student in *The Lesson* with the word 'knife.')"

Ionesco's favorite dramatic device is the platitude. By its use he demonstrates the absurdity of language and the futility of communication. "But in my view," he writes in *Cahiers des Quatres Saisons,* "the unusual can spring only from the dullest and most ordinary routine and from our everyday prose, when pursued beyond their limits; . . . nothing surprises me more than banality; the 'surreal' is there, within our reach, in our daily conversation." A master at creating illusion, Ionesco begins with an unrealistic situation, develops it to its limits, engaging himself in "an adventure, a hunt, the discovery of a universe that reveals itself to me, at the presence of which I am the first to be astounded."

Criticized by Kenneth Tynan and Orson Welles for his allegedly apolitical position, Ionesco continues to affirm that the source of his plays is "a mood and not an ideology, an impulse not a program." Coe, however, asserts Ionesco's commitment to the cause of man, though his concern is with ultimates and absolutes, not with ephemeral political situations. Even Utopia cannot eliminate absurdity, death, and loneliness. Moreover, true revolutions are not political, Ionesco maintains. "Science and art have done far more to change thinking than politics have. The real revolution is taking place in the scientists' laboratories and in the artists' studios. Penicillin and the fight against dipsomania are worth more than politics and a change of government."

Though Ionesco continues to believe that "the work of art is untranslatable," his work has appeared in 27 languages.

BIOGRAPHICAL/CRITICAL SOURCES:

BOOKS

Bonnefoy, Claude, *Conversations with Eugene Ionesco,* translated by Jan Dawson, Faber, 1970, Holt, 1971.

Coe, Richard N., *Ionesco,* Grove, 1961, revised and enlarged edition, Methuen, 1971.

Coll, Toby, editor, *Playwrights on Playwriting,* Hill & Wang, 1961.

Contemporary Literary Criticism, Gale, Volume 1, 1973, Volume 4, 1975, Volume 6, 1976, Volume 9, 1978, Volume 11, 1979, Volume 15, 1980, Volume 41, 1987.

Duckworth, C., *Angels of Darkness,* Barnes & Noble, 1972.

Esslin, Martin, *The Theatre of the Absurd,* Doubleday, 1968.

Grossvogel, David I., *Four Playwrights and a Postscript: Brecht, Ionesco, Beckett, Genet,* Cornell University Press, 1962.

Grossvogel, David I., *The Blasphemers,* Cornell University Press, 1965.

Hayman, R., *Eugene Ionesco,* Heinemann, 1972.

Jacobson, J., and W. R. Mueller, *Ionesco and Genet,* Hill & Wang, 1968.

Kitchin, Laurence, *Mid-Century Drama,* Faber, 1960.

Moore, Harry T., *French Literature since World War II,* Southern Illinois University Press, 1966.

Pronko, Leonard C., *Avant-Garde: The Experimental Theatre in France,* University of California Press, 1962.

Pronko, *Eugene Ionesco,* Columbia University Press, 1965.

Southern, Terry, Richard Seaver, and Alexander Trocchi, editors, *Writers in Revolt,* Fell, 1963.
Wager, Walter, editor, *The Playwrights Speak,* Delacorte, 1967.
Wellworth, George, *Theatre of Protest and Paradox,* New York University Press, 1964.
Wulbern, J. H., *Brecht and Ionesco: Commitment in Context,* University of Illinois Press, 1971.

PERIODICALS

Chicago Tribune, March 26, 1980.
Chicago Tribune Book World, December 8, 1985.
Los Angeles Times, February 16, 1988; February 17, 1988.
New York Times, March 12, 1980; June 12, 1987; June 15, 1988.
Times (London), June 22, 1983; January 17, 1987.
Times Literary Supplement, January 22, 1982; February 6, 1987; April 15-21, 1988.

*   *   *

IRLAND, David
See GREEN, Julien (Hartridge)

*   *   *

IRVING, John (Winslow) 1942-

PERSONAL: Born March 2, 1942, in Exeter, N.H.; son of Colin F. N. (a teacher) and Frances (Winslow) Irving; married Shyla Leary, August 20, 1964 (divorced, 1981); married Janet Turnbull, June 6, 1987; children: (first marriage) Colin, Brendan. *Education:* University of New Hampshire, B.A. (cum laude), 1965; University of Iowa, M.F.A., 1967; additional study at University of Pittsburgh, 1961-62, and University of Vienna, 1963-64.

ADDRESSES: c/o William Morrow, 105 Madison Ave., New York, N.Y. 10016.

CAREER: Novelist. Mount Holyoke College, South Hadley, Mass., assistant professor of English, 1967-72, 1975-78; University of Iowa, Iowa City, writer in residence, 1972-75. Teacher and reader at Bread Loaf Writers Conference.

AWARDS, HONORS: Rockefeller Foundation grant, 1971-72; National Endowment for the Arts fellowship, 1974-75; Guggenheim fellow, 1976-77; *The World According to Garp* was nominated for a National Book Award in 1979, and won an American Book Award in 1980; named one of ten "Good Guys" honored for contributions furthering advancement of women, National Women's Political Caucus, 1988, for *Cider House Rules.*

WRITINGS:

Setting Free the Bears (also see below), Random House, 1969.
The Water-Method Man (also see below), Random House, 1972.
The 158-Pound Marriage (also see below), Random House, 1974.
The World According to Garp, Dutton, 1978.
Three by Irving (contains *Setting Free the Bears, The Water-Method Man,* and *The 158-Pound Marriage*), Random House, 1980.
The Hotel New Hampshire (Book-of-the-Month Club main selection), Dutton, 1981.
The Cider House Rules, Morrow, 1985.
A Prayer for Owen Meany (Book-of-the-Month Club main selection), Morrow, 1989.

Also contributor of short stories to *Esquire, Playboy,* and other magazines.

MEDIA ADAPTATIONS: The World According to Garp was released by Warner Bros./Pan Arts in 1982, and starred Robin Williams, Glenn Close, and Mary Beth Hurt, and featured cameo performances by Irving and his sons; *The Hotel New Hampshire* was released by Orion Pictures in 1984, and starred Rob Lowe, Jodie Foster, and Beau Bridges.

SIDELIGHTS: Novelist John Irving is a gifted storyteller with a remarkably fertile imagination and a penchant for meshing the comic and the tragic. *Saturday Review* critic Scot Haller describes Irving's work this way: "Fashioning wildly inventive, delightfully intricate narratives out of his sense of humor, sense of dread and sense of duty, Irving blends the madcap, the macabre, and the mundane into sprawling, spiraling comedies of life." Irving is perhaps best known for his critically-acclaimed bestseller, *The World According to Garp,* which has sold more than three million copies in hardback and paperback together since its 1978 publication. *Garp* achieved a cult status complete with T-shirts proclaiming "I Believe in Garp," and received serious critical attention which ultimately propelled the author "into the front rank of America's young novelists," according to *Time* critic R. Z. Sheppard.

Though a contemporary novelist, Irving's concerns are traditional ones, a characteristic that, critics note, distinguishes his work from that of other contemporary fiction. *Dictionary of Literary Biography* contributor Hugh M. Ruppersburg, for example, writes, "The concerns of Irving's novels are inherently contemporary. Yet often they bear little similarity to other recent fiction, for their author is more interested in affirming certain conventional values—art and the family, for instance—than in condemning the status quo or heralding the arrival of a new age. . . . What is needed, [Irving] seems to suggest, is a fusion of the compassion and common sense of the old with the egalitarian openmindedness of the new." Irving himself likens his fictional values and narrative technique to those of 19th-century writers. "I occasionally feel like a dinosaur in my own time because my fictional values are terribly old-fashioned," Irving states in the *Los Angeles Times.* "They go right back to the deliberately sentimental intentions of the 19th-Century novelist: Create a character in whom the reader will make a substantial emotional investment and then visit upon that character an unbearable amount of pain." Like those nineteenth-century novelists, Irving also believes that he is responsible for entertaining the reader. "I think, to some degree, entertainment is the responsibility of literature," Irving told Haller. "I really am looking upon the novel as an art form that was at its best when it was offered as a popular form. By which I probably mean the 19th century."

Irving's nineteenth-century values are reflected in *The World According to Garp,* a work he describes in the *Washington Post Book World* as "an artfully disguised soap opera." Irving adds: "The difference is that I write well, that I construct a book with the art of construction in mind, that I use words intentionally and carefully. I mean to make you laugh, to make you cry; those are soap-opera intentions, all the way." A lengthy family saga, *Garp* focuses on nurse Jenny Fields, her illegitimate son, novelist T. S. Garp, and Garp's wife and two sons. Described as a "disquieting" work by *New Republic* contributor Terrence Des Pres, *Garp* explicitly explores the violent side of contemporary life. Episodes involving rape, assassination, mutilation, and suicide abound, but these horrific scenes are always infused with comedy. As Irving notes in the *Los Angeles Times,* "No matter how gray the subject matter or orientation of any novel I write, it's still going to be a comic novel."

"A true romantic hero," according to *Village Voice* critic Eliot Fremont-Smith, Garp is obsessed with the perilousness of life, and wants nothing more than to keep the world safe for his family and friends. Ironically, Garp is the one who ultimately inflicts irreversible harm on his children, illustrating Irving's point that "the most protective and unconditionally loving parents can inflict the most appalling wounds on their children," writes Pearl K. Bell in *Commentary*. While Garp is obsessed with protecting his family and friends, his mother's obsession involves promoting her status as a "sexual suspect"—a woman who refuses to share either her life or her body with a man. Through her bestselling autobiography, *A Sexual Suspect,* Jenny becomes a feminist leader. Her home evolves into a haven for a group of radical feminists, The Ellen James Society, whose members have cut out their tongues as a show of support for a young girl who was raped and similarly mutilated by her attackers. Both Garp and Jenny eventually are assassinated—she by an outraged antifeminist convinced that Jenny's influence ruined his marriage, he by an Ellen Jamesian convinced that Garp is an exploiter of women because of a novel he wrote about rape. Discussing these characters in a *Publishers Weekly* interview with Barbara A. Bannon, Irving remarks, "It mattered very fiercely to me that [Garp and Jenny] were people who would test your love of them by being the extremists they were. I always knew that as mother and son they would make the world angry at them."

Critics note that *Garp* demonstrates a remarkable sensitivity to women, because it deals sympathetically with issues such as rape, feminism, and sexual roles. *Nation* contributor Michael Malone writes, "With anger, chagrin and laughter, Irving anatomizes the inadequacies and injustices of traditional sex roles. . . . The force behind a memorable gallery of women characters—foremost among them, Garp's famous feminist mother and his English professor wife—is not empathy but deep frustrated sympathy." A similar opinion is expressed by *Ms.* contributor Lindsy Van Gelder, who expresses admiration for Irving's ability to explore "feminist issues from rape to sexual identity to Movement stardom . . . minus any Hey-I'm-a-man-but-I-really understand self-conscious fanfare." Irving explains in the *Los Angeles Times,* however, that his "interest in women as a novelist is really very simple. . . . I see every evidence that women are more often victims than men. As a novelist I'm more interested in victims than in winners." In fact, Irving flatly disagrees with critics who describe *Garp* in sociological or political terms. He states in the *Contemporary Literature* interview with Larry McCaffery: "Obviously now when people write about *Garp* and say that it's 'about' feminism and assassination and the violence of the sixties, they're ignoring the fact that I lived half of the sixties in another country. I don't know anything about the violence of the sixties; it's meaningless to me. I'm not a sociological writer, nor should I be considered a social realist in any way."

Nor does Irving concur with critics who, noting several significant similarities between Garp and Irving, describe *Garp* as a semi-autobiographical work. Bell, for example, writes: "[Irving] indulges in elaborate games of allusion to his own life and career, as though taunting the reader to guess what has been made up, what taken whole from life. A little of this can be useful and funny, but Irving tends to let it go on too long, and the peekaboo can become much too coy." In a *New York Times Book Review* interview with Thomas Williams, however, Irving maintains: "I make up all the important things. I've had a very uninteresting life. I had a happy childhood. I'm grateful for how ordinary my life is because I'm not ever tempted to think that something that happened to me is important simply because it happened to me. I have no personal axes to grind; I'm free, therefore, to imagine the best possible ax to grind—and I really mean that: that's a sig-

nificant freedom from the tyranny and self-importance of autobiography in fiction."

The World According to Garp was heralded as Irving's finest and most original work; Des Pres observes that "nothing in contemporary fiction matches it." The critic continues: "Irving tells the story of Garp's family with great tenderness and wisdom. By tracing the relationship between wife and husband, and then again between parents and children (and how these two sets intersect to cause catastrophe), Irving is able to handle a large range of human hope and fear and final insufficiency. He is excellent in his portrait of Garp's sons, Duncan and Walt, whose view of their father is often hilarious, whose dialogue is true without fail, and whose vulnerability in a world of numberless hurtful things causes Garp a brooding, prophetic dread."

Several reviewers compliment in particular the narrative flow of *Garp*. "Reading *Garp* was like listening to Homer's account of the Trojan War told in a singsong monotone," writes Doris Grumbach in *Saturday Review*. "I relished every page, every line, of the imaginative feast. To paraphrase Alexander Pope, it has all the force of many fine words." *New York Times Book Review* critic Richard Locke comments: "What is most impressive about the book . . . is its narrative momentum: Irving has a natural narrative gift, and even when the plot is not as cosmic as it tries to be, one can't help wondering what will happen to these people next and reading on." *Times Literary Supplement* contributor Thomas M. Disch similarly notes, "*The World According to Garp* is a novel about the novel, and the novelist, as seducer. . . . What raises the book above its own conundrums is . . . the personality of its author. It is a seductive personality, not in any opprobrious sense, but in the way that John Ridd, the narrator of *Lorna Doone,* is seductive—by the sweetness of his disposition and the lilt of his voice, which, as it rises from the turning pages, commands not just attention but affection." *New York Times Book Review* contributor Julian Moynahan comments that while Irving's "new novel contains some febrile fabulations (the wrong sort of exaggeration) in its handling of the feminist theme, . . . his instincts are so basically sound, his talent for storytelling so bright and strong, that he gets down to the truth of his time in the end."

Other reviewers praise the originality and credibility of Irving's characterizations. "What does matter about *The World According to Garp* is the captivating originality of the characters, the closely drawn entirety of the life that Irving bestows upon them, and the infectious love he feels for these emanations of his head," writes Bell. Concurs Locke, "The characters . . . compel our sympathy. We feel with them—strongly—in the midst of their family lives and lusts and disasters." *New York Times* reviewer Christopher Lehmann-Haupt adds, "The way he filters [the book's violent events] through his hero's unique imagination, we not only laugh at the world according to Garp, but we also accept it and love it."

However, "not everyone who read *Garp* responded to the novel's fun and games," remarks R. Z. Sheppard in *Time*. "Many readers were offended by Irving's mating of the truly tragic and grotesquely comic." Irving responds in the *Saturday Review,* "People who think *Garp* is wildly eccentric and very bizarre are misled about the real world. . . . I can't imagine where they've been living or what they read for news. Five out of seven days I find things in the *New York Times* that seem to me far less explainable than the rather human behavior in *Garp.*" He similarly remarks in a *New York Times Book Review* interview with Thomas Williams, "In just the same way that I don't see comedy and tragedy as contradictions . . . I don't see that unhappy endings undermine rich and energetic lives."

The majority of reviewers embrace Irving's fictional world—violence and all. "If the events seem at times to be too brutal and terrible, if too many violences seem to have been heaped upon already suffering and bloodied persons, that is the way it is," writes Grumbach. "Garp writes and lives as he finds the world. And because John Irving is so subtle and persuasive a writer, we believe in his fictional world." Locke comments, "The horrible violence that plagues this family elicits in the reader something of the large sympathy for the doomed that novelists in the great tradition can summon up." A *Newsweek* reviewer observes, "Irving here deals out Grand Guignol shocks leading to a hushed, heart-stopping revelation of irreparable grief. This is brilliant work." Bell concludes: "Remarkably, none of the slaughter and mayhem that erupt with such bloody frequency in *The World According to Garp* seems sensationalistic or even melodramatic. Irving has taken a capacious and demanding view of his task as a storyteller, and carried it out with sober compassion, adventurous ingenuity, and great intelligence." Ruppersburg determines that "whether [Irving's] future novels climb to the best-seller lists or not, his peculiar synthesis of dark humor, social upheaval, and the tragic tenor of modern life with realistic and likable characters may well exert a profound influence on the fiction of the 1980s. What Irving will ultimately achieve for himself remains to be seen; but his fiction so far—especially his fourth novel—has heralded the arrival of an indisputably significant figure on the American literary scene."

Tucked into the pages of *The World According to Garp* is one of Garp's works, "The Pension Grillparzer," which Locke describes as "a short narrative, given in full, . . . [that] glows at the heart of 'The World According to Garp' like some rich gem or flower." This brief but compelling tale formed the outline for Irving's next work, *The Hotel New Hampshire.* Irving explains in *New York* magazine: "I realized while writing 'Pension' that I wanted to write about hotels—not realistically, as I was doing at the time, but metaphorically. I also wanted to keep the voice of 'Pension,' a straightforward first-person narrative told from a child's point of view that a child could understand. It would be a novel about childhood, about growing up and how the impressions children have of themselves and those closest to them change as they grow older. It is the most fairytale-like novel I have done in that it relies the least on one's understanding of the real world."

Despite its fairytale-like qualities, *The Hotel New Hampshire* explores adult issues like incest, terrorism, suicide, freakish deaths, and gang rape, all infused with Irving's trademark macabre humor. A family saga like *Garp, The Hotel New Hampshire* spans nearly four generations of the troubled Berry family. Headed by Win, a charming but irresponsible dreamer who is ultimately a failure at innkeeping, and Mary, who dies in the early stages of the novel, the Berry family includes five children: Franny, Frank, Egg, Lilly, and John, the narrator. While Egg perishes along with his mother, the remaining children are left to struggle through childhood and adolescence. Irving describes the family this way in *New York:* "[The Hotel New Hampshire] takes a large number of people and says in every family we have a dreamer, a hero, a late bloomer, one who makes it very big, one who doesn't make it at all, one who never grows up, one who is the shit detector, the guide to practicality, and often you don't know who these people will be, watching them in their earlier years."

The Berrys, along with an array of subsidiary characters—human and animal—eventually inhabit three hotels: one in New Hampshire, one in Vienna, and one in Maine. According to Irving, the hotels are symbols for the passage from infancy to maturity. "The first hotel is the only real hotel in the story," states Irving in *New York.* "It is childhood. The one in Vienna is a dark, foreign place, that phase called adolescence, when you begin leaving the house and finding out how frightening the world is. . . . The last one is no hotel at all. . . . It is a place to get well again, which is a process that has been going on throughout the novel."

Since it followed such a phenomenally successful work, *The Hotel New Hampshire* naturally invited comparisons to its predecessor. "There is no question in my mind it's better than *The World According to Garp,*" Irving maintains in *New York.* "It certainly is every bit as big a book, and it means much more. It's a more ambitious novel symbolically but with a different point of view, deliberately narrower than *Garp.*" Irving nevertheless anticipated that critics would reject the novel. As he states in the *Chicago Tribune Book World:* "There will be people gunning for me—they'll call the book lazy, or worse—sentimental. But getting bad press is better than no press. It's better to be hated than to be ignored—even children know that."

In fact, critics' opinions largely fulfilled Irving's dismal prediction. *Chicago Tribune Book World* contributor Judith Rossner, for example, notes, "I found an emptiness at the core of 'The Hotel New Hampshire' that might relate to the author's having used up his old angers and familiar symbols without having found new reasons for his rage and different bodies to make us see it." *Saturday Review* critic Scot Haller writes: "*The Hotel New Hampshire* could not be mistaken for the work of any other writer, but unfortunately, it cannot be mistaken for Irving's best novel, either. It lacks the urgency of *Setting Free the Bears,* the bittersweet wit of *The 158-Pound Marriage,* the sly set-ups of *Garp.* The haphazardness that afflicts these characters' lives has seeped into the storytelling, too." *Time* critic R. Z. Sheppard offers this view: "[Unlike Garp's story,] John Berry's story is not resolved in violent, dramatic action, but in a quiet balancing of sorrow and hope. It is a difficult act, and it is not faultless. The dazzling characterizations and sense of American place in the first part of the novel tend to get scuffed in transit to Europe. There are tics and indulgences. But the book is redeemed by the healing properties of its conclusion. Like a burlesque *Tempest, Hotel New Hampshire* puts the ordinary world behind, evokes a richly allusive fantasy and returns to reality refreshed and strengthened."

Critics also note that *The Hotel New Hampshire* reflects the influence of numerous other writers, notably J. D. Salinger, Vladimir Nabokov, and Kurt Vonnegut. Discussing this issue at length in *Esquire,* James Wolcott writes, "Imagine Salinger's Glass family with fouler mouths and lower brows and you have some notion of how precociously darling and fragile these Berrys are." The critic adds that "Nabokov holds a particularly potent sway over *The Hotel New Hampshire,*" but concludes, "Perhaps the presiding influence, however, is that of Kurt Vonnegut. Irving is a passionate admirer of Vonnegut's . . . and he seems to share Vonnegut's flip sense of doom and irony." Although he concedes that *The Hotel New Hampshire* "can be devilishly readable," Wolcott believes that Irving is ultimately unsuccessful in his attempt to imitate such "modernist" writers. "Whatever its lapses, *The World According to Garp* was an original affront; *The Hotel New Hampshire* is ultratrendy and nakedly—almost desperately—derivative," Wolcott remarks. "By trying to storm the ranks of the modernist giants, Irving only betrays how far he lags behind their lyricism and expressive brilliance. He kneels like a camp follower in the shadows of their greatness, combing the grass for strands of gold."

According to *Newsweek* critic Peter S. Prescott: "The bad news about 'The Hotel New Hampshire'. . . is that the new novel suffers from a terminal case of the cutes. . . . Irving is determined to charm us; he applies charm to his pages as relentlessly as a mason applies cement to an arch he suspects may collapse." Prescott concludes: "Novels don't need messages, but 'The Hotel New Hampshire' is so incessantly didactic, so portentous, that I found myself quite ready to grapple with ideas and furious that Irving offered me only marshmallow whip. 'LIFE IS SERIOUS BUT ART IS FUN!' he writes at the end, and I guess that's what he intends his story to mean, but here he offers little to demonstrate either argument." On the other hand, *New Republic* contributor Jack Beatty compliments Irving's narrative technique. "John Irving is a talented but facile writer. His prose never encounters those resistances—emotional, moral, epistemological— that energise memorable statement. It never strains at meaning; it just sweeps you along, its easy momentum lulling your critical faculty and rocking you back to a childlike state of wonder." Beatty concludes: "We all want to check in to the Hotel New Hampshire. It is 'the sympathy space' where we can be fully known and yet fully loved, and where a powerful imagination holds us fast and won't let us die."

Originally intended to be a saga of orphanage life in early twentieth-century Maine, Irving's sixth novel *The Cider House Rules* became, instead, a statement on abortion. The issue of abortion arose during Irving's research for the novel, when he "discovered that abortion was an integral part of the life of an orphanage hospital at that time," as he remarks in the *Los Angeles Times*. He concedes in that same article, "This is in part a didactic novel, and in part a polemic. I'm not ashamed of that. . . . But I remain uncomfortable at the marriage between politics and fiction. I still maintain that the politics of abortion came to this book organically, came to it cleanly."

Evoking the works of Victorian novelists such as Charles Dickens and Charlotte Bronte, Irving's *The Cider House Rules* is set in an orphanage in dreary St. Cloud, Maine, where the gentle, ether-addicted Dr. Larch and his saintly nurses preside lovingly over their orphans. Larch also provides illegal but safe abortions, and although he is painfully aware of the bleak existence that many of the orphans endure, he doesn't encourage expectant mothers to abort. As he puts it, "I help them have what they want. An orphan or an abortion." One unadopted orphan in particular, Homer Wells, becomes Larch's spiritual son and protege. Larch schools Homer in birth and abortion procedures and hopes that Homer will one day succeed him at the orphanage. When Homer comes to believe that the fetus has a soul, however, he refuses to assist with abortions. A conflict ensues, and Homer seeks refuge at Ocean View apple orchard, located on the coast of Maine.

The book's title refers to the list of rules posted in Ocean View's cider house regarding migrant workers' behavior. Several critics acknowledge the significance of rules, both overt and covert, in the lives of the characters. Toronto *Globe and Mail* contributor Joy Fielding, for example, comments, "*The Cider House Rules* is all about rules; the rules we make and break; the rules we ignore; the rules we post for all to see; the invisible rules we create for ourselves to help us get through life; the absurdity of some of these rules and the hypocrisy of others, specifically our rules regarding abortion." Similarly, *Los Angeles Times* critic Elaine Kendall writes, "Much is made of the literal Cider House Rules,

a typed sheet posted in the migrant workers dormitory, clearly and politely spelling out the behavior expected by the owners of the orchard. Sensible and fair as these rules are, they're made to be broken, interpreted individually or ignored entirely, heavily symbolic of the social and moral codes Irving is exploring." *New York Times* reviewer Christopher Lehmann-Haupt similarly notes that Dr. Larch follows his own rules, and that "the point— which is driven home with the sledgehammer effect that John Irving usually uses—is that there are always multiple sets of rules for a given society. Heroism lies in discovering the right ones, whether they are posted on the wall or carved with scalpels, and committing yourself to follow them no matter what."

Despite the multiplicity of rules and moral codes explored by Irving, critics tend to focus on abortion as the crucial issue of *The Cider House Rules*. They express different opinions, however, concerning Irving's position on the abortion issue. *Time* critic Paul Gray comments that *The Cider House Rules* "is essentially about abortions and women's right to have them," and Susan Brownmiller describes the work in the *Chicago Tribune* as "a heartfelt, sometimes moving tract in support of abortion rights." Kendall, on the other hand, maintains, "Though Dr. Larch's philosophy justifying his divided practice is exquisitely and closely reasoned, the abortion episodes are graphic and gruesome, as if Irving were simultaneously courting both pro-choice and right-to-life factions." *New York Times Book Review* contributor Benjamin DeMott offers this view: "The knowledge and sympathy directing Mr. Irving's exploration of the [abortion] issue are exceptional. Pertinent history, the specifics of surgical procedure, the irrecusable sorrow of guilt and humiliation, the needs and rights of children—their weight is palpable in these pages."

With a few exceptions, *The Cider House Rules* was favorably reviewed; several critics, including DeMott, believe it is Irving's most worthwhile novel. "By turns witty, tenderhearted, fervent and scarifying, 'The Cider House Rules' is, for me, John Irving's first truly valuable book," writes DeMott. "The storytelling is straightforward—not the case with his huge commercial success, 'The World According to Garp'. . . . The theme is in firm focus—not the case with 'The Hotel New Hampshire'. . . . The novelist's often-deplored weakness for the cute and trendy, although still evident, is here less troubling." Christopher Lehmann-Haupt concurs in the *New York Times*: "[Irving's] novels have tended to sprawl both in tone and focus, but in 'The Cider House Rules' he has positively streamlined his form. . . . The familiar elements of the macabre, the violent and the cute all seem more controlled and pointed, more dedicated to the end of advancing Mr. Irving's story toward a definite and coherent resolution. . . . 'The Cider House Rules' has greater force and integrity than either of its two immediate predecessors. It's funny and absorbing and it makes clever use of the plot's seeming predictability."

Spectator reviewer David Profumo, however, comments that while "there are moments of outstanding writing in the book," the novel "proves to be something of a phantom pregnancy in itself, promising to deliver so much more than it does." *Washington Post Book World* critic Jonathan Yardley similarly observes that Irving has "assembled his customary cast of mildly eccentric characters and trotted them through the customary paces, but at the end there is not feeling that they—and therefore you, the reader—have been anywhere or done anything interesting. It's not so much that the trip is unpleasant as that it's pointless." Fielding concurs, "The novel, despite many wonderful moments, is never quite as good as it promises to be. Ultimately it fails to engage our emotions, surprising in light of its volatile subject matter. Often Irving is lecturing, telling readers what to feel, instead of allowing them to draw their own conclusions, to feel things for themselves." Gray, on the other hand, attributes the novel's weaknesses to the cynicism of our times. He writes: "Although Irving admires and emulates the expansive methods of Victorian fiction, he is, after all, a product of this century and all its horrors. He cannot, like Dickens, honestly trick out a story with coincidences that will allow good people to triumph; the best Irving can offer is a tale that concludes with a few survivors who are not entirely maimed or deranged by what they have been through."

Remarking in a *Time* interview that he is "moved and impressed by people with a great deal of religious faith," Irving explains to Michael Anderson in the *New York Times Book Review,* "Jesus has always struck me as a perfect victim and a perfect hero." What impresses him most is that Christ is aware of his own destiny: "That is truly a heroic burden to carry," he tells Phyllis Robinson in the *Book-of-the-Month Club News.* Similarly, in *A Prayer for Owen Meany,* a novel that examines the good and evil—especially the capacity of each to be mistaken for the other, Irving's memorable Christ-like hero knows his destiny, including the date and circumstances of his death. Small in size but large in spirit, Owen Meany has a distinctive but ineffable voice caused by a fixed larynx; and throughout the novel, Irving renders Owen's speech in upper case—suggested to him by the red letters in which Jesus's utterances appear in the New Testament. Believing that nothing in his life is accidental or purposeless, Owen professes himself an instrument of God. Although the foul ball hit off Owen's bat kills the mother of his best friend, Johnny Wheelwright, it ultimately reveals to Johnny the identity of his father. The story of their adolescence and friendship is recalled and narrated by Johnny, who eventually comes to a belief in God because of Owen and his sacrifice. "No one has ever done Christ in the way John Irving does Him in *A Prayer for Owen Meany,*" writes Stephen King in the *Washington Post Book World.* "This is big time, friends and neighbors."

In a *Time* review, Sheppard points out that "anyone familiar with Irving's mastery of narrative technique, his dark humor and moral resolve also knows his fiction is cute like a fox." Sheppard suggests that despite its theological underpinnings, the novel "scarcely disguise[s] his indignation about the ways of the world," and actually represents "a fable of political predestination." Although finding the book flawed in terms of its structure and development, Robert Olen Butler suggests in Chicago *Tribune Books* that it nevertheless contains "some of the elements that made 'The World According to Garp' so attractive to the critics and the bestseller audience alike: flamboyant, even bizarre, characters; unlikely and arresting plot twists; a consciousness of contemporary culture; and the assertion that a larger mechanism is at work in the universe." In the estimation of Brigitte Weeks in the *Book-of-the-Month Club News,* "John Irving is a reader's writer, and *A Prayer for Owen Meany* is a reader's novel, a large, intriguing grab bag of characters and ideas that moves the spirit and fascinates the mind. . . . There is no one quite like him."

Sheppard offers this assessment of Irving's work: "Irving's philosophy is basic stuff: one must live willfully, purposefully and watchfully. Accidents, bad luck, undertoads and open windows lurk everywhere—and the dog really bites. It is only a matter of time. Nobody gets out alive, yet few want to leave early. Irving's popularity is not hard to understand. His world is really the world according to nearly everyone."

BIOGRAPHICAL/CRITICAL SOURCES:

BOOKS

Bestsellers 89, Issue 3, 1989.
Contemporary Literary Criticism, Gale, Volume 13, 1980, Volume 23, 1983, Volume 38, 1986.
Dictionary of Literary Biography, Volume 6: *American Novelists since World War II,* Second Series, Gale, 1980.
Dictionary of Literary Biography Yearbook: 1982, Gale, 1983.

PERIODICALS

Book-of-the-Month Club News, April, 1989.
Chicago Tribune, May 12, 1985.
Chicago Tribune Book World, May 11, 1980, September 13, 1981.
Christian Century, October 7, 1981.
Commentary, September, 1978, June, 1982.
Contemporary Literature, winter, 1982.
Detroit News, August 30, 1981, March 12, 1989.
Esquire, September, 1981.
Globe and Mail (Toronto), March 10, 1984, July 6, 1985.
Los Angeles Times, September 16, 1982, March 20, 1983, June 4, 1985, July 10, 1985.
Los Angeles Times Book Review, March 26, 1989.
Maclean's, June 11, 1979.
Ms., July, 1979.
Nation, June 10, 1978.
New Republic, April 29, 1978, September 23, 1981.
Newsweek, April 17, 1978, September 21, 1981.
New York, August 17, 1981.
New Yorker, May 8, 1978, October 12, 1981, July 8, 1985.
New York Times, April 13, 1978, August 31, 1981, May 20, 1985, March 8, 1989.
New York Times Book Review, April 23, 1978, May 21, 1978, May 26, 1985, March 12, 1989.
People, December 25, 1978.
Prairie Schooner, fall, 1978.
Publishers Weekly, April 24, 1978.
Rolling Stone, December 13, 1979.
Saturday Review, May 13, 1978, September, 1981.
Spectator, June 22, 1985.
Time, April 24, 1978, August 31, 1981, June 3, 1985, April 3, 1989.
Times (London), June 20, 1985.
Times Literary Supplement, October 20, 1978, June 21, 1985.
Tribune Books (Chicago), March 19, 1989.
Village Voice, May 22, 1978.
Wall Street Journal, March 21, 1989.
Washington Post, August 25, 1981.
Washington Post Book World, April 30, 1978, May 19, 1985, March 5, 1989.

*   *   *

IRWIN, P. K.
See PAGE, P(atricia) K(athleen)

*   *   *

ISAACS, Susan   1943-

PERSONAL: Born in 1943 in Brooklyn, N.Y.; married Elkan Abramowitz (a trial lawyer); children: Andrew, Elizabeth. *Education:* Attended Queens College (now Queens College of the City University of New York).

ADDRESSES: Agent—Owen Laster, William Morris Agency, 1350 Avenue of the Americas, New York, N.Y. 10019.

CAREER: Novelist and screenwriter. *Seventeen* magazine, New York City, 1966-70, began as assistant editor, became senior editor; political speech writer for Democratic candidates in Brooklyn and Queens, New York, and for the president of the borough of Queens, New York City.

WRITINGS:

Compromising Positions (mystery novel; Book-of-the-Month Club selection; also see below), Times Books, 1978.
Close Relations (novel; Literary Guild selection), Lippincott & Crowell, 1980.
Almost Paradise (novel; Literary Guild selection), Harper, 1984.
People Like You and Me, Harper, 1987.
Shining Through (novel; Literary Guild selection), Harper, 1988.

SCREENPLAYS

"Compromising Positions" (based on her novel of the same title), Paramount, 1985.
"Hello Again," Buena Vista, 1987.

SIDELIGHTS: Before Susan Isaacs wrote her first novel, her portfolio consisted mainly of writing she had done as an editor for *Seventeen* magazine and as a political speechwriter. So when *Compromising Positions* went beyond best-seller and Book-of-the-Month Club selection status to bring in higher-than-hoped-for amounts for paperback, foreign, and movie rights, Isaacs was stunned. She told *Publishers Weekly* interviewer Sybil S. Steinberg: "All I had hoped to do was just get a mystery published. Suddenly, everybody loved me. It was overwhelming."

The heroine of *Compromising Positions* is Judith Singer, a bored housewife who seeks an outlet for her underemployed intelligence by playing detective when her periodontist is found murdered in his office. Judith's list of suspects grows as she discovers that several of her neighbors—the attractive, upwardly mobile wives of successful men—had not only been seduced, but also photographed by the dentist while arranged in pornographic poses. Judith is romanced by an officer and confronted by her dull but dutiful husband before the mystery unravels.

Compromising Positions—"the seeming result of an Erica Jong-Joan Rivers collaboration on a Nancy Drew mystery," according to *Chicago Tribune* contributor Clarence Petersen—has received generally favorable reviews. "The dialogue is ribald and wise-cracking, the action fast and furious every step of the way," says a *Publishers Weekly* critic who also deems the book a "very funny first novel." Minor criticisms temper the praise from other reviewers. "It is a good idea, and the book starts out well. But it bogs down about halfway through," a *Newsweek* writer believes. What "begins as a splendid parody of suburban potboilers . . . ends by becoming one itself," Jack Sullivan echoes in the *New York Times Book Review,* but he allows that "Miss Isaacs' overall aim is so precise, her one-liners so wonderfully funny, that we can hardly complain."

Isaacs' first spoof was followed by *Close Relations,* "a hilarious satire of ethnic stereotyping," in Steinberg's words. Marcia Green, an independent divorcee and speechwriter for an Italian gubernatorial candidate, decides between Jerry Morrisey, an attractive Irish Catholic bachelor—also her boss—and a perfectly eligible Jewish lawyer, the friend of her cousin Barbara. Isaacs "succeeds in nailing the hothouse vulgarity and oppressive pressure tactics of a certain kind of Jewish family," Susan Cheever notes in the *Washington Post Book World.* The novel's backdrop is the campaign, set in motion when New York's WASP governor chokes to death on a knish given to him by an admirer at a rally in Queens.

Marcia's numerous sexual encounters are graphically depicted throughout the book. She has "the kind of sexual appetites which have traditionally been a male prerogative—at least in literature," Cheever explains. In *Publishers Weekly,* Barbara A. Bannon describes *Close Relations* as "a risible romp throughout—the snappy dialogue yielding up laughs on every page, the love story tender and satisfying, the plot pulsing with adrenalin."

Introducing the author's third novel, a *People* magazine contributor states, "Isaacs' *Almost Paradise* . . . has moral scruples and sentimentality—but also a unique blend of glittery settings and psychologically astute drama." As in her other novels, Isaacs brings together characters from a variety of social classes while providing genealogical background for her main characters, Nicholas Cobleigh and Jane Heissenhuber. Young Nick thwarts his wealthy family's expectations by becoming an actor instead of a lawyer and by marrying lower class Jane, who, like Cinderella, was raised by a persecuting stepmother and an inept but abusive father. Jane forfeits her career; Nick becomes a superstar; Jane develops agoraphobia. A passionately experimental therapist cures Jane's phobia and frigidity, and she becomes a talk-show hostess; meanwhile, Nick succumbs to an affair with an insistent co-star, then leaves Jane for a fragile university student. Even so, love survives. The celebrities are just about to reconcile when Jane, having independently overcome her fear of flying to surprise Nick on location, is hit by a car.

Almost Paradise has been an enormous popular success, reaching bestseller status even before its official publication date, but, critically, the book has not fared so well. "The characters not only speak in cliches—. . . most of them are cliches," *New York Times* contributor Michiko Kakutani believes. In the *Los Angeles Times Book Review,* Kenneth Atchity calls the book "a Dick and Jane Reader . . . enhanced with erotica, troublesome relatives, and grown-up recipes" with "a shockingly happenstance, tragic finish." However, responses have not been all negative. *Washington Post Book World* reviewer Jonathan Yardley concludes that *Almost Paradise* is "considerably more skillfully done than the run-of-the-mill potboiler, and Isaacs does know how to keep a story rolling along." Aside from the book's artistic problems, says Anna Shapiro in the *New York Times Book Review,* Isaacs "keeps the plot boiling, and mostly one is reading too absorbedly to notice."

Isaacs' own comments about her writing are frequently self-effacing. She told *People* magazine, "My son was reading *Charlotte's Web* and asked, 'Do you write as good as E. B. White?' When I said 'No,' he walked out." Even the most severe criticisms of her popular novels are modified by applause for her sassy humor and accurate rendering of contemporary dialogue. Writing about *Almost Paradise* in *Best Sellers,* Joan Oppenheim says: "Susan Isaacs' very direct style and sensitive writing come to the rescue. What she is saying often becomes less significant than how it is being said."

BIOGRAPHICAL/CRITICAL SOURCES:

BOOKS

Bestsellers 89, Issue 1, Gale, 1989.
Contemporary Literary Criticism, Volume 32, Gale, 1985.

PERIODICALS

Best Sellers, August, 1978, March, 1984.
Chicago Tribune, September 1, 1985, September 4, 1985, April 30, 1989.
Chicago Tribune Book World, March 25, 1984.
Detroit News, November 9, 1980, March 18, 1984.

Los Angeles Times, September 1, 1980, August 30, 1985, November 6, 1987.

Los Angeles Times Book Review, March 4, 1984.

Newsweek, May 1, 1978, November 16, 1987.

New York, October 6, 1980.

New Yorker, May 15, 1978.

New York Times, February 1, 1984, August 30, 1985, July 12, 1987, November 6, 1987.

New York Times Book Review, April 30, 1978, February 12, 1984, September 11, 1988.

People, April 24, 1978, April 30, 1984, August 29, 1988.

Publishers Weekly, January 9, 1978, January 23, 1978, July 25, 1980, September 12, 1980, January 4, 1985.

Savvy, August, 1988.

Times Literary Supplement, November 3, 1978.

Tribune Books, August 14, 1988.

Washington Post, August 31, 1980, September 3, 1985, November 9, 1987.

Washington Post Book World, August 31, 1980, February 12, 1984, August 7, 1988.

*　　*　　*

ISHERWOOD, Christopher (William Bradshaw) 1904-1986

PERSONAL: Born August 26, 1904, in High Lane, Cheshire, England; died of cancer, January 4, 1986, in Santa Barbara, Calif.; came to United States, 1939, naturalized citizen, 1946; son of Francis Edward (a military officer) and Kathleen (Machell-Smith) Isherwood. *Education:* Attended Repton School, 1919-22, Corpus Christi College, Cambridge, 1924-25; King's College, University of London, medical student, 1928-29. *Politics:* Democrat. *Religion:* Vedantist.

CAREER: Writer, 1926-86. Worked as a secretary to French violinist Andre Mangeot and his Music Society String Quartet, London, England, 1926-27; private tutor in London, 1926-27; went to Berlin, Germany, in 1929 to visit W. H. Auden, and stayed, on and off, for four years; taught English in Berlin, 1930-33; traveled throughout Europe, 1933-37; did film script work for Gaumont-British; went to China with Auden, 1938; dialogue writer for Metro-Goldwyn-Mayer, Hollywood, Calif., 1940; worked with American Friends Service Committee, Haverford, Pa., in a hostel for Central European refugees, 1941-42; resident student of Vedanta Society of Southern California, Hollywood, and co-editor with Swami Prabhavananda of Society's magazine, *Vedanta and the West,* 1943-45; traveled in South America, 1947-48; guest professor at Los Angeles State College (now California State University, Los Angeles) and at University of California, Santa Barbara, 1959-62; Regents Professor at University of California Los Angeles, 1965, and University of California, Riverside, 1966.

MEMBER: National Institute of Arts and Letters, American Civil Liberties Union, Wider Quaker Fellowship, Screenwriters Guild.

AWARDS, HONORS: Brandeis University creative arts award, 1974-75; PEN Body of Work Award, 1983; Common Wealth Award for distinguished service in literature, 1984.

WRITINGS:

NOVELS

All the Conspirators, J. Cape, 1928, new edition, 1957, New Directions, 1958.

The Memorial: Portrait of a Family, Hogarth, 1932, New Directions, 1946.

The Last of Mr. Norris, Morrow, 1935 (published in England as *Mr. Norris Changes Trains,* Hogarth, 1935).

Sally Bowles, Hogarth, 1937.

Goodbye to Berlin, Random House, 1939.

Prater Violet, Random House, 1945, reprinted, Farrar, Strauss, 1989.

The Berlin Stories (contains *The Last of Mr. Norris* and *Goodbye to Berlin*), J. Laughlin, 1946, New Directions, 1963.

The World in the Evening, Random House, 1954.

Down There on a Visit, Simon & Schuster, 1962.

A Single Man, Simon & Schuster, 1964.

A Meeting by the River (also see below), Simon & Schuster, 1967.

PLAYS

(With W. H. Auden) *The Dog beneath the Skin, or Where is Francis?* (three-act), Random House, 1935.

(With Auden) *The Ascent of F6,* Random House, 1937, 2nd edition, Faber, 1957.

(With Auden) *A Melodrama in Three Acts: On the Frontier,* Faber, 1938, published as *On the Frontier: A Melodrama in Three Acts,* Random House, 1939.

"The Adventures of the Black Girl in Her Search for God" (based on a George Bernard Shaw novella), first produced in Los Angeles at Mark Taper Forum, March, 1969.

"The Legend of Silent Night" (television special; adapted from a story by Paul Gallico), broadcast by American Broadcasting Companies (ABC), 1969.

(With Don Bachardy) "A Meeting by the River" (based on Isherwood's novel), first produced in Los Angeles at Mark Taper Forum, 1972, first produced on Broadway at the Palace Theater, March, 1979.

(With Auden) *Plays and Other Dramatic Writings, 1928-1938,* Faber, 1989.

SCREENPLAYS

(Author of scenario and dialogue with Margaret Kennedy) "Little Friend," Gaumont-British, 1934.

(Contributor) "A Woman's Face," Metro-Goldwyn-Mayer (MGM), 1941.

(With Robert Thoeren) "Rage in Heaven" (based on novel by James Hilton), MGM, 1941.

(Contributor) "Forever and a Day," RKO, 1943.

(With Ladislas Fodor) "The Great Sinner," Loew's, 1949.

"Diane," MGM, 1955.

(With Terry Southern) "The Loved One" (based on the novel by Evelyn Waugh), Filmways, 1965.

(With Don Magner and Tony Richardson) "The Sailor from Gibraltar" (based on the novel by Marguerite Duras), Woodfall, 1967.

(With Bachardy) *Frankenstein: The True Story* (based on the novel by Mary Shelley), produced, 1972, Avon, 1973.

Also author of screenplay "Diane" and of dialogue for other films. Also author, with Lesser Samuels, of original story for "Adventure in Baltimore," RKO, 1949.

TRANSLATOR

Bertolt Brecht, *Penny for the Poor,* Hale, 1937.

(With Swami Prabhavananda) *Bhagavad-Gita,* Rodd, 1944, published as *The Song of God: Bhagavad-Gita,* Harper, 1951, 3rd edition, Vedanta Press, 1951.

(And editor with Prabhavananda) Sankara, *Crest-Jewel of Discrimination,* Vedanta Press, 1947.

Charles Baudelaire, *Intimate Journals,* Rodd, 1947.

(And editor with Prabhavananda) *How to Know God* (Patanjali's *Yoga Aphorisms*), Harper, 1953.

(Translator of verse sections) Brecht, *Threepenny Novel,* Grove, 1956.

OTHER

Lions and Shadows: An Education in the Twenties (autobiography), Hogarth, 1938, New Directions, 1947.

(With Auden) *Journey to War,* Random House, 1939.

(Editor) *Vedanta for the Western World,* Marcel Rodd, 1945, published as *Vedanta and the West,* Harper, 1951.

The Condor and the Cows: A South American Travel Diary, Random House, 1949.

(Editor) *Vedanta for Modern Man,* Harper, 1951.

(Editor) *Great English Short Stories,* Dell, 1957.

An Approach to Vedanta, Vedanta Press, 1963.

Ramakrishna and His Disciples (biography), Simon & Schuster, 1965.

Exhumations: Stories, Articles, Verses, Simon & Schuster, 1966.

Essentials of Vedanta, Vedanta Press, 1969.

Kathleen and Frank (autobiography), Simon & Schuster, 1971.

Christopher and His Kind (autobiography), Farrar, Straus, 1976.

My Guru and His Disciple, Farrar, Straus, 1980.

People One Ought to Know, Doubleday, 1982.

October, limited edition, Twelvetrees Press, 1983.

The Wishing Tree: Christopher Isherwood on Mystical Religion, edited by Robert Adjemian, Vedanta Press, 1987.

Contributor to periodicals, including *Harper's Bazaar* and *Vogue.*

SIDELIGHTS: "Christopher Isherwood," W. J. Tuner observed, "may not be a great writer . . . but at least he is a real writer and not a pretentious bore." Through what David Daiches called "quietly savage dead-pan observation," Isherwood unfolded his social comedies. As a student of the deformities of society, he was, according to Frank Kermode, "farcical about desperate matters" and concentrated on those aspects that are amusing, "almost as if what mattered was their intrinsic comic value." Isherwood's unique view of the comic in art, a theory of "High Camp," is explained by a character in *The World in the Evening:* "True High Camp always has an underlying seriousness. You can't camp about something you don't take seriously. You're not making fun of it; you're making fun out of it. You're expressing what's basically serious to you in terms of fun and artifice and elegance. Baroque art is largely camp about religion. The Ballet is camp about love. . . . It's terribly hard to define. You have to meditate on it and feel it intuitively, like Lao-Tze's *Tao.*"

"I believe in being a serious comic writer," Isherwood once said. "To me, everything is described in those terms. Not in the terms of the unredeemably tragic view of life, but at the same time, not in terms of screwballism. Nor in terms of saying, 'Oh, it's all lovely in the garden.' I think the full horror of life must be depicted, but in the end there should be a comedy which is beyond both comedy and tragedy. The thing Gerald Heard calls 'metacomedy'. . . . All I aspire to is to have something of this touch of 'metacomedy.' To give some description of life as it is lived now, and of what it has been like for me, personally, to have been alive."

Isherwood was probably most successful in his Berlin books, *The Last of Mr. Norris* and *Goodbye to Berlin* (collected as *The Berlin Stories*), in which he fictionalized his visits to the pre-Nazi Berlin of the 1930s. In *The Last of Mr. Norris,* Isherwood's narrator is William Bradshaw; in *Goodbye to Berlin,* the narrator is named Christopher Isherwood. This matter-of-fact blend of fact and fiction reflected the naive, honest style Isherwood was seeking in these stories. In both books he used the phrase "I am a camera" to indicate what he felt his role as narrator should be: a simple recording device. The decadence of Weimar Germany was therefore portrayed in these stories in startling and full detail. Graham Greene, in an article for the *Dictionary of Literary Biography Yearbook: 1986,* described *The Last of Mr. Norris* as "a permanent landmark in the literature of our time." Writing in the *Dictionary of Literary Biography,* Claude J. Summers called *Goodbye to Berlin* an "extraordinary achievement" and "a book of haunting loneliness . . . a masterful study of an inhibited young man." Julian Symons concluded in the *Sunday Times* that the Berlin stories "remain, and they capture a time, a place, and the people of a disintegrating society in a moving and masterly way. They are a unique achievement."

In later works, Isherwood turned more openly to writing about his own life. Isherwood, noted James Atlas in the *New York Times,* "devoted himself to chronicling his life more or less as it happens." In such novels as *A Single Man,* a study of a day in the life of a middle-aged homosexual, he appeared thinly disguised as the narrator. In such nonfiction works as *Kathleen and Frank,* a remembrance of his parents, and *Christopher and His Kind,* an autobiography in which he first admitted his homosexuality, Isherwood wrote about his own life in a novelistic fashion, detailing his childhood, his many years as a Hollywood screenwriter, and such matters as his love relationship with poet W. H. Auden and his embrace of the Eastern philosophy of Vedanta. Isherwood explained in a 1980 interview, quoted by a *New York Times* writer, "All of my autobiographical books are sort of novels." Michael de-la-Noy, writing in *Books and Bookmen,* called Isherwood "the quintessential autobiographical novelist."

MEDIA ADAPTATIONS: The Berlin Stories was adapted by John Van Druten as a play entitled "I Am a Camera," produced in 1951, and published by Random House in 1952. "I Am a Camera" and *The Berlin Stories* were adapted by Joe Masteroff, John Kander, and Fred Ebb as the Broadway musical "Cabaret," first produced in November, 1966. The screenplay for the movie version of "Cabaret," written by Jay Presson Allen, was based on Isherwood's *The Berlin Stories* and released by Allied Artists in 1972.

AVOCATIONAL INTERESTS: "I was a born film fan."

BIOGRAPHICAL/CRITICAL SOURCES:

BOOKS

Contemporary Literary Criticism, Gale, Volume 1, 1973, Volume 9, 1978, Volume 11, 1979, Volume 14, 1980, Volume 44, 1987.

Dictionary of Literary Biography, Volume 15: *British Novelists, 1930-1959,* Gale, 1983.

Heilbrun, Carolyn G., *Christopher Isherwood,* Columbia University Press, 1970.

Isherwood, Christopher, *Christopher and His Kind,* Farrar, Straus, 1976.

Kermode, Frank, *Puzzles and Epiphanies,* Chilmark, 1962.

King, Francis, *Christopher Isherwood,* Longman, 1976.

Newquist, Roy, *Conversations,* Rand McNally, 1967.

Phelps, Gilbert, editor, *Living Writers,* Transatlantic, 1947.

Wilde, Alan, *Christopher Isherwood,* Twayne, 1971.

PERIODICALS

Books and Bookmen, March, 1986.
New York Review of Books, August 20, 1964.

New York Times, August 2, 1979, August 27, 1980.
New York Times Book Review, August 30, 1964, March 25, 1973.
Paris Review, spring, 1974.
Times Literary Supplement, September 10, 1964.
Twentieth Century Literature, October, 1976.

OBITUARIES:

BOOKS

Contemporary Literary Criticism, Gale, Volume 44, 1987.
Dictionary of Literary Biography Yearbook: 1986, Gale, 1987.

PERIODICALS

AB Bookman's Weekly, January 6, 1986.
Chicago Tribune, January 7, 1986.
Daily Variety, January 6, 1986.
Los Angeles Times, January 6, 1986.
Newsweek, January 20, 1986.
New York Times, January 6, 1986.
Observer, January 12, 1986.
Publishers Weekly, January 17, 1986.
Sunday Times, January 12, 1986.
Time, January 20, 1986.
Washington Post, January 6, 1986.

*   *   *

ISHIGURO, Kazuo   1954-

PERSONAL: Born November 8, 1954, in Nagasaki, Japan; resident of Great Britain since 1960; son of Shizuo (a scientist) and Shizuko (a homemaker; maiden name, Michida) Ishiguro; married Lorna Anne MacDougall (a social worker), May 9, 1986. *Education:* University of Kent, B.A. (with honors), 1978; University of East Anglia, M.A., 1980.

ADDRESSES: Home—9 Grange Close, Guildford, Surrey, England. *Agent*—Deborah Rogers Ltd., 49 Blenheim Crescent, London W11 2EF, England.

CAREER: Grouse beater for Queen Mother at Balmoral Castle, Aberdeen, Scotland, 1973; Renfrew Social Works Department, Renfrew, Scotland, community worker, 1976; West London Cyrenians Ltd., London, England, residential social worker, 1979-80, resettlement worker, 1981-83; writer of plays for television, 1984—. Affiliated with British Film Institute.

AWARDS, HONORS: Winifred Holtby Award from Royal Society of Literature, 1983, for *A Pale View of Hills; A Pale View of Hills* included among "notable books of 1982" by the American Library Association; writer's bursary, 1984, from the Arts Council of Great Britain; Chicago Film Festival Best Short Film award, 1985, for "A Profile of Arthur J. Mason"; Whitbread Literary Award for book of the year from Booksellers Association of Great Britain, and Booker Prize nomination, both 1986, both for *An Artist of the Floating World;* Booker Prize, 1989, for *The Remains of the Day.*

WRITINGS:

(Contributor) *Introduction Seven: Stories by New Writers,* Faber, 1981.
A Pale View of Hills (novel), Putnam, 1982.
An Artist of the Floating World (novel), Putnam, 1986.
The Remains of the Day (novel), Knopf, 1989.

Also author of television film scripts, including "A Profile of Arthur J. Mason," broadcast in 1984, and "The Gourmet," broadcast in 1986. Contributor to literary journals, including *London Review of Books, Firebird, Bananas,* and *Harpers and Queen.*

WORK IN PROGRESS: A novel and a screenplay.

SIDELIGHTS: Kazuo Ishiguro's highly acclaimed first novel, *A Pale View of Hills,* is narrated by Etsuko, a middle-aged Japanese woman living in England. The suicide of her daughter, Keiko, awakens somber memories of the summer in the 1950s in war-ravaged Nagasaki when the child was born. Etsuko's thoughts and dreams turn particularly to Sachiko, a war widow there whose unfortunate relationship with an American lover traumatizes that woman's already troubled daughter, Mariko; Etsuko, too, eventually embraces the West, leaving her Japanese husband to marry an English journalist. "Etsuko's memories, though they focus on her neighbor's sorrows and follies, clearly refer to herself as well," wrote Edith Milton in the *New York Times Book Review.* "The lives of the two women run parallel, and Etsuko, like Sachiko, has raised a deeply disturbed daughter; like her, she has turned away from the strangling role of traditional Japanese housewife toward the West, where she has discovered freedom of a sort, but also an odd lack of depth, commitment and continuity." Surrounded that summer by a new order that shattered ancient ways, the two women chose the Western path of self-interest, compromising—to varying degrees—their delicate daughters. "In Etsuko's present life as much as in her past, she is encircled by a chain of death which has its beginning in the war," suggested *New Statesman* reviewer James Campbell.

Reviewing *A Pale View of Hills* for the *Spectator,* Francis King found the novel "typically Japanese in its compression, its reticence and in its exclusion of all details not absolutely essential to its theme"; other critics cited Ishiguro's subtle, elliptical style as well. While some reviewers agreed with *Times Literary Supplement* writer Paul Bailey—who stated "that at certain points I could have done with something as crude as a fact"—most felt that Ishiguro's delicate layering of themes and images grants the narrative great evocative power. "[It] is a beautiful and dense novel, gliding from level to level of consciousness," remarked Jonathan Spence, writing in a *New Society* critique. "Ishiguro develops [his themes] with remarkable insight and skill," concurred Rosemary Roberts in the *Los Angeles Times Book Review.* "They are described in controlled prose that more often hints than explains or tells. The effect evokes mystery and an aura of menace." And King deemed the novel "a memorable and moving work, its elements of past and present, of Japan and England held together by a shimmering, all but invisible net of images linked to each other by filaments at once tenuous and immensely strong."

Similar applause for Ishiguro's achievement in *A Pale View of Hills* came from *Encounter* reviewer Penelope Lively. The critic described her impressions: "[The novel's] strength is a remarkable quality of style in which dialogue and narration are unemphasized and yet oddly powerful. It is the kind of writing in which one searches in frustration for the source of its effects: sparse, precise and plain, the language has a stealth that leaves you with images that are suggested rather than stated. Trying to pin this down, I turned back through the pages looking for the description of a certain room: it was not there, was a product of my own imagination. And this is a subtle power for a writer to have—the ability to prompt a creative response in the reader, to arouse reactions which must be quite individual, so that the book takes as many forms as it has readers."

While Ishiguro's novel depicts the incineration of a culture and the disjointed lives of the displaced, it is not without optimism. "Ishiguro suggests that the honor of the past was itself more than a little tarnished," related Milton. And critics saw in the war survivors' tenacious struggle to resurrect some sort of life, however alien, great hope and human courage. "Sachiko and Etsuko become minor figures in a greater pattern of betrayal, infanticide and survival played out against the background of Nagasaki, itself the absolute emblem of our genius for destruction," Milton continued. "In this book, where what is stated is often less important than what is left unsaid, those blanked-out days around the bomb's explosion become the paradigm of modern life. They are the ultimate qualities which the novel celebrates: the brilliance of our negative invention, and our infinite talent for living beyond annihilation as if we had forgotten it." Reiterated Roberts: "There is nobility in determination to press on with life even against daunting odds. Ishiguro has brilliantly captured this phoenixlike spirit; high praise to him."

In his second novel, *An Artist of the Floating World,* Ishiguro again explores Japan in transition. Set in a provincial Japanese town during 1949 and 1950, the story revolves around Masuji Ono, a painter who worked as an official artist and propagandist for the imperialist regime that propelled Japan into World War II. Knowing that his former ideals were errant does little to help Ono adjust to the bewildering Westernization that is going on all around him; nor does it quell his longings for the past, with its fervent patriotism, professional triumphs, and deep comradeship. "Ishiguro's insights, like his deceptively simple prose, are finely balanced," wrote Anne Chisholm in the *Times Literary Supplement.* "He shows how the old Japanese virtues of veneration for the *Sensei* (the teacher), or loyalty to the group, could be distorted and exploited; he allows deep reservations to surface about the wholesale Americanization of Japan in the aftermath of humiliation and defeat. Without asking us to condone Ono's or Japan's terrible mistakes, he suggests with sympathy some reasons why the mistakes were made."

Admiring how "Ishiguro unravels the old man's thoughts and feelings with exceptional delicacy," Chisholm determined that the story "is not only pleasurable to read but instructive, without being in the least didactic." "The old man's longings for his past become a universal lament for lost worlds," added the critic, who judged *An Artist of the Floating World* a "fine new novel."

Ishiguro's third novel, *The Remains of the Day,* was an American best-seller and won Britain's Booker Prize, generally considered to be that country's top literary award. While stylistically similar to his two previous novels, *The Remains of the Day* differs from them by focusing on British rather than Japanese characters. The main character is a butler named Stevens who undergoes a gradual but revealing self-examination process after his master, Lord Darlington, dies. Stevens had long considered himself a paradigmatic butler because of his sense of dignity and absolute loyalty to Darlington. As he ruminates on the fact that Darlington was a Nazi sympathizer who harmed many people,

however, Stevens questions the worth of his acquired dignity and realizes—too late—that he missed the opportunity to live his own life.

The Remains of the Day was widely praised. Nina King, for example, applauded Ishiguro's sparse but deft writing style in her *Washington Post* review: "Ishiguro is a subtle writer, who manages to make what Stevens does *not* say almost as revealing as his words. He is also brilliant at description, capturing a scene in a few quick strokes without ever stepping out of Stevens's ponderous character." *Times Literary Supplement* contributor Galen Strawson agreed, saying *The Remains of the Day* "is a strikingly original book, and beautifully made. Reading it, one has an unusual sense of being controlled by the author. Each element is unobtrusively anticipated, then released in its proper place." Lawrence Graver, moreover, averred in the *New York Times Book Review* that the novel "is a dream of a book: a beguiling comedy of manners that evolves almost magically into a profound and heart-rending study of personality, class and culture."

Ishiguro told *CA:* "I am interested in England and Japan; in memory and self-deception; in people who believe their lives a failure."

AVOCATIONAL INTERESTS: Playing guitar and piano.

BIOGRAPHICAL/CRITICAL SOURCES:

BOOKS

Bestsellers 90, Issue 2, Gale, 1990.
Contemporary Literary Criticism, Volume 56, Gale, 1989.

PERIODICALS

Encounter, June-July, 1982.
Los Angeles Times, June 20, 1986.
Los Angeles Times Book Review, August 8, 1982.
New Leader, November 13, 1989.
New Society, May 13, 1982.
New Statesman, February 19, 1982.
Newsweek, October 30, 1989.
New York, October 16, 1989.
New Yorker, April 19, 1982.
New York Times, September 22, 1989, October 28, 1989.
New York Times Book Review, May 9, 1982, June 8, 1986, October 8, 1989.
Spectator, February 27, 1982.
Time, October 30, 1989.
Times (London), February 18, 1982, February 28, 1983, May 25, 1989.
Times Literary Supplement, February 19, 1982, February 14, 1986, May 19, 1989.
Tribune Books, October 1, 1989.
Washington Post, October 2, 1989, October 27, 1989.

J

JACOBSON, Dan 1929-

PERSONAL: Born March 7, 1929, in Johannesburg, South Africa; son of Hyman Michael and Liebe (Melamed) Jacobson; married Margaret Pye (a teacher), February, 1954; children: Simon Orde, Matthew Lindsay, Jessica Liebe. *Education:* University of the Witwatersrand, B.A., 1949.

ADDRESSES: c/o A. M. Heath and Co., 79 St. Martins Ln., London WC2N 4AA, England.

CAREER: South African Jewish Board of Deputies, Johannesburg, public relations assistant, 1951-52; Mills & Feeds Ltd., Kimberley, South Africa, correspondence secretary, 1952-54; writer, 1954—. Visiting professor, Syracuse University, 1965-66; University College, University of London, lecturer, 1974-79, reader in English, 1979—. Fellow of Humanities Research Centre, Australian National University, 1981. Vice-chairman of Literature Panel, Arts Council of Great Britain, 1974-76.

MEMBER: Royal Society of Literature (fellow).

AWARDS, HONORS: Fellowship in creative writing, Stanford University, 1956-57; John Llewelyn Rhys award for fiction, National Book League, 1959; W. Somerset Maugham award, Society of Authors, 1964; visiting fellow, State University of New York at Buffalo, summer, 1971; Wingate-Jewish Chronicle Award, 1977; J. R. Ackerly Award, English PEN Centre, 1985; fellowship from Society of Authors, 1986.

WRITINGS:

The Trap, Harcourt, 1955.
A Dance in the Sun, Harcourt, 1956.
The Price of Diamonds, Knopf, 1958.
The Zulu and the Zeide, Atlantic-Little, Brown, 1959.
The Evidence of Love, Atlantic-Little, Brown, 1960.
No Further West, Macmillan, 1961.
Time of Arrival (essays), Macmillan, 1963.
Beggar My Neighbor (short stories), Weidenfeld & Nicolson, 1964.
The Beginners, Macmillan, 1966.
Through the Wilderness and Other Stories, Macmillan, 1968.
The Rape of Tamar, Macmillan, 1970.
Inklings (short stories), Weidenfeld & Nicolson, 1973.
The Wonder-Worker, Weidenfeld & Nicolson, 1973, Atlantic-Little, Brown, 1974.
The Confessions of Josef Baisz, Harper, 1979.

The Story of Stories: The Chosen People and Its God (nonfiction), Harper, 1982.
Time and Time Again: Autobiographies, Atlantic Monthly Press, 1985.
Her Story, Deutsch, 1987.
Adult Pleasures: Essays on Writers and Readers, David & Charles, 1989.

Contributor to magazines.

MEDIA ADAPTATIONS: An adaptation of *The Zulu and the Zeide* was produced on Broadway in 1965; *A Dance in the Sun* was produced as a play entitled "Day of the Lion" in Cleveland in 1968. *The Rape of Tamar* was adapted into a play called "Yonadab," and was produced in London, England, in 1985.

SIDELIGHTS: Race relations, class consciousness, and other themes of morality characterize the writings of Dan Jacobson. A white, Jewish native of apartheid-torn South Africa, Jacobson uses many of his novels to relate the ongoing struggles from different points of view. *The Trap,* Jacobson's first novel, draws on the author's boyhood experiences at the two farms his father owned "and his firsthand familiarity with relations between the white ruling class and black serving class," as Anne Fisher relates in a *Dictionary of Literary Biography article.* "The themes of the novel are corruption, violence, and betrayal," particularly those kinds peculiar to South Africa, Fisher adds.

In telling the story of how white Van Schoor, a ranch owner, is forced to question the trust he has put in Willem, a black servant, after Willem is blamed for a crime he did not commit, Jacobson creates an effective allegory, according to Fisher: "The ranch can be seen as all of South Africa, the [conflict] between Van Schoor and his servant epitomizes the country's racial problems. The worst part about the situation, as described by the novel, is that everyone involved is hurt by what is happening. The 'trap' encompasses all the characters."

Another notable Jacobson work, *The Evidence of Love,* involves an interracial love affair, a controversial topic—especially so in 1960, when the novel was published. *The Evidence of Love* presents a character, Kenneth Makeer, who is officially classified by the South African government as "colored," but whose skin is light enough for him to pass as white. Kenneth courts a white woman who marries him even after his true racial identity is revealed. The result is a prison term for the couple. While "violence makes a strange ending for a love story, even if the setting is South Africa," acknowledges *New Statesman* critic A. Alvarez, the author nonetheless "has the ability to create sensitive, intelligent people and make them act sensitively and intelligently despite the background of guilt and shock. . . . [*The Evidence of Love,* therefore,] is neither propaganda nor sensationalism. It is, instead, a considerable artistic achievement, all the more impressive because it was written calmly out of the same tensions as created the South African explosion."

"Jacobson's most autobiographical novel" to date is the way Fisher describes *The Beginners.* In this book the author follows a Jewish South African family, with "the main theme of the book [being] the idea of human consciousness, which sets humankind above other forms of life," says Fisher. "Jacobson shows, by tracing the individual lives of the [family members], that the most important ideal to follow in life is one's own human individuality."

The Beginners focuses on Joel Glickman, a young man questioning the values of his life. Like the author, the character lives for a while in England and also in Israel, where he works on a *kibbutz* (communal farm). "Like Joel, [Jacobson] decided not to give his life to Zionism; like Joel, his father owned a butter factory. Joel's University of Witwatersrand is Jacobson's also," notes Fisher. In a *Southern Review* piece, critic David Galloway reports that "there is, unhappily, no . . . formal cohesion in *The Beginners,* though Jacobson's efforts to achieve dramatic unity are clearly apparent." Galloway cites as a key flaw the main character, who is "too weak . . . to carry the entire production," with the other characters never achieving "the vividness they deserve, and feeling is repeatedly drowned by chronology and history." But whatever flaws, the critic points out, Jacobson also offers "an abundance of insight, compassion, architecture, chronology, and faultless prose."

Departing from South African themes, Jacobson produced *The Rape of Tamar* in 1970, a modern retelling of the Old Testament story of an incestuous rape of the virginal Tamar by her half-brother Amnon, the brother of Absalom, King David's most well-remembered offspring. Actually, the novel's main character is none of the above-mentioned, but the narrator, Yonadab, "Amnon's friend and counselor, who is characterized in the Biblical account as a 'very wise man'—or, if one prefers another translation, a 'very subtle man,'—" as Robert Alter remarks. Continuing in a *New York Times Book Review* article, Alter finds that "as Jacobson brilliantly develops him, Yonadab is a man of caustic, skeptical intelligence, directing the cutting edge of his irony equally against the protagonists, his modern audience and himself. The pomp and ceremony of the historical novel . . . are an utter bore to him, and he repeatedly reminds us that any relationship between narrator and readers is a tacitly contractual one, depending upon literary conventions with which he for one will simply not be bothered."

To a *Times Literary Supplement* writer, the mix of biblical parable and modern prose "is a delicate balance to sustain but only rarely does [the author] allow himself to slip into the obvious pitfall and overplay the up-to-date deglamorizing. . . . And it is from the interplay between old dignities and fresh debunkeries that the book's funniest and most compassionate effects derive." The critic concludes by calling *The Rape of Tamar* "a tightrope triumph: you are never sure it's going to keep its balance until it's over—and then you can't imagine how he managed it."

"The links between *Tamar* and [Jacobson's 1973 novel] *The Wonder-Worker* are stronger than they at first appear to be," writes *Time*'s R. Z. Sheppard, reviewing the latter. "Sexual obsession, the disintegration of a family, the linkage between love and hate are evident in both. But where the biblical background of *Tamar* lent grief and madness some heroic grandeur, Jacobson's new book is furnished with the banalities and trivia of contemporary life." The unlikely protagonist of *The Wonder-Worker,* Timothy Fogel, is an ambiguity—a schizophrenic personality who may or may not be merely the figment of another's imagination. Whatever the case, Jacobson examines Timothy's life and his creeping obsession with an unsuspecting woman. The character's other obsession constitutes the title of the novel: Timothy believes he can work wonders, changing himself into "the bricks of a garden wall, into iron, into stone, into wood, into many of the inanimacies around him," according to L. E. Sissman in a *New Yorker* review. "The two obsessions are interconnected: rejected by Susie, [the woman of his dreams, Timothy] . . . escapes into the timelessness and painlessness of brick, and soon becomes an adept at escaping into the nature of things, even in the presence of others."

Many critics reacted strongly to *The Wonder-Worker*'s many-layered appeal. One reviewer, Raymond A. Sokolov, in the *New York Times Book Review,* warns that the novel is not for the casual reader. "It is complex, not easily summarized, cannot be imagined as a movie, will certainly not appeal to people looking for a good read, those unencumbered with respect for subtle wavings of perception in fictional form—to say this is to consign this fine novel to quick if honorable obscurity." The book's "dazzling duality" of plot inspires Bruce Allen's praise, and the *Nation* critic echoes Sokolov's sentiments that "readers . . . expect sequence and logic. The narrator, snug in his cell, denies their relevance. Is the man who reasons thus (if he's not Dan Jacobson) a madman, who chooses art? Or an artist, who becomes mad? The sly [author] may be telling us that there isn't all that much difference between them."

"If the characters often seem somewhat attenuated, it is because they are really secondary to Jacobson's purpose," as *Commentary* reviewer Johanna Kaplan sees it. "The substance of [*The Wonder-Worker*] is the working out of the creative process itself, and in order to achieve his end, Jacobson has relied on language. The voice is spare, hard, brilliant, and though it is often exquisitely lyrical, it is never lush. It is always precise, and precisely dizzying: [the author] is leading us, forcing us into that peculiar, unsafe region of the mind where out of memories, dreams, simple fragments of observation and inexplicable distortion, something new, something other than ordinarily recalled or observed reality, is born as a separate entity. . . . It is true that both art and psychosis transform experience, but as this book succeeds in demonstrating, only one endures."

Following *The Confessions of Joseph Baisz,* a novel of foreign intrigue and betrayal, Jacobson published a nonfictional work, *The Story of Stories: The Chosen People and Its God.* Described as the author's "courageous but problematic attempt to report his own highly individual understanding of the Bible" by *New York Times Book Review* writer Harold Bloom, the book examines "a Jewish nonbeliever's analysis of how the Old Testament story was first put together," according to *Partisan Review* critic Morton W. Bloomfield. "He argues that it was created by ancient Jews to justify or explain the ancient Israelites' conquest of Canaan and then, in fuller form, the punishments which overtook the Jews in biblical days." While "difficulties with Jacobson's theory abound," says Bloomfield, maintaining that certain biblical events were just too elaborate in scope to justify their existence merely as fodder for Old Testament stories, the critic also feels that "the most fascinating part of the book and theory is not [the author's] covenant theory—which echoes others—but rather [his] own doubt about the truth of his story. . . . One gets the feeling that behind much of this intriguing and well-written little book is the impact of the twentieth-century history of the Jews on our author. He may also be thinking of his native South Africa."

Jacobson's most personal book to date, *Time and Time Again: Autobiographies,* is a collection of thirteen essays taking the author from his boyhood sites in South Africa to London, where Jacobson has lived for many years. Among the strongest pieces in the book, states Randolph Stow, is "The Boer Lover," a "memory of a Jewish farmer related to Jacobson's mother." This enigmatic character "lingers in the mind because of [his] strange end. He committed suicide with his domestic life in ruins, not for that reason, however, but because he was convinced that the presence of Cubans in Angola portended the destruction of Afrikanerdom [Afrikaners are the Dutch-descended white "ruling class" of modern South Africa]." Continues Stow in his *Times Literary Supplement* review: "There is a tendency for Jacobson to round off anecdotes with a little moralizing on subjects like time and fate and death. It is a sign of his decency, everywhere apparent, but risks sounding automatic."

Similarly, *New York Times Book Review* critic James Kaufmann finds that the author's "punctiliousness influences his prose." However, he adds, "to cast [Jacobson] as a prig would be improper. Certainly he is a moral writer, but he avoids the pulpit. Think of him as an artisan, circumspect and exacting, who is cautious most of all because he wants things to be *just right.* His emotional reserve is further explained by his subjects, for his 'autobiographies' invariably focus on victims and death."

"In the later chapters [of *Time and Time Again*] Jacobson says very little about his wife and children but is painfully total about his uncle and his father, both now very old, the first in London and the latter still in far Kimberley, [South Africa]," sums up Ronald Blythe in a *Listener* review. "Through these cantankerous ancients he reaches back to the Nazi massacres in Lithuania and, almost more unbearably for himself, to the majestic Hebrew culture and [civilization] which contained his family before Fascism, South African racism and 20th-century Western secularism tore it to fragments. The last chapter is that modern moment of truth, the operating theatre. Here is a good writer at full power."

BIOGRAPHICAL/CRITICAL SOURCES:

BOOKS

Contemporary Literary Criticism, Gale, Volume 4, 1975, Volume 14, 1980.
Dictionary of Literary Biography, Volume 14: *British Novelists since 1960,* Gale, 1983.
Jacobson, Dan, *Time and Time Again: Autobiographies,* Atlantic Monthly Press, 1985.
Roberts, Sheila, *Dan Jacobson,* Twayne, 1984.
Yudelman, Myra, *Dan Jacobson: A Bibliography,* University of Witwatersrand, 1967.

PERIODICALS

Chicago Tribune Book World, January 21, 1979.
Commentary, June, 1974.
Commonweal, January 28, 1983.
Encounter, February, 1974, January, 1978.
Listener, September 12, 1985, August 27, 1987.
London Review of Books, October 1, 1987.
Nation, June 21, 1975.
New Republic, November 14, 1970, January 20, 1979.
New Statesman, June 4, 1960.

Newsweek, October 14, 1968, August 17, 1970, April 1, 1974.
New Yorker, June 24, 1974, March 12, 1979.
New York Review of Books, April 28, 1966, July 18, 1974, April 5, 1979, September 29, 1983.
New York Times Book Review, November 24, 1968, February 21, 1979, April 21, 1974, January 28, 1979, October 17, 1982, September 15, 1985.
Partisan Review, fall, 1983.
Saturday Review, December 14, 1968, May 18, 1974, February 3, 1979.
Southern Review, summer, 1968.
Spectator, May 19, 1973, November 5, 1977.
Time, March 25, 1974.
Times Literary Supplement, September 25, 1970, November 5, 1982, September 15, 1985, August 21, 1987, May 27-June 2, 1988.

*   *   *

JAFFE, Rona 1932-

PERSONAL: Born June 12, 1932, in New York, NY; daughter of Samuel (an elementary school teacher and principal) and Diana (a teacher; maiden name, Ginsberg) Jaffe. *Education:* Radcliffe College, B.A., 1951.

ADDRESSES: Home—201 East 62nd St., New York, NY 10021. *Office*—c/o Ephraim London Buttenweiser, 875 Third Ave., New York, NY 10022. *Agent*—Morton Janklow Associates, 598 Madison Ave., New York, NY 10022.

CAREER: File clerk and secretary, New York City, 1952; Fawcett Publications, New York City, associate editor, 1952-56; writer, 1956—.

WRITINGS:

NOVELS

The Best of Everything, Simon & Schuster, 1958.
Away from Home, Simon & Schuster, 1960, published as *Carnival in Rio* in Europe, South America, and Scandinavia.
The Cherry in the Martini, Simon & Schuster, 1966.
The Fame Game, Random House, 1969.
The Other Woman, Morrow, 1972.
Family Secrets, Simon & Schuster, 1974.
The Last Chance, Simon & Schuster, 1976.
Class Reunion: A Novel, Delacorte, 1979.
Mazes and Monsters: A Novel, Delacorte, 1981.
After the Reunion: A Novel, Delacorte, 1985.
An American Love Story, Delacorte, 1990.

OTHER

The Last of the Wizards (juvenile), Simon & Schuster, 1961.
Mr. Right Is Dead (novella and five short stories), Simon & Schuster, 1965.

Contributor of stories, essays, and articles to various magazines.

SIDELIGHTS: "In Rona Jaffe," notes Elaine Dundy in the *Times Literary Supplement,* "we have a good storyteller who is a good storywriter as well." Jaffe has written several bestsellers, including her first novel, *The Best of Everything.* The book, described by Judy Klemesrud in the *Chicago Tribune* as a "novel about New York career girls trying to sleep and claw their way out of the steno pool," brought the author both fame and fortune while still in her twenties.

In several ways *The Best of Everything* is like many of Jaffe's later novels. The book deals with life in New York City, focuses on conflicts in male/female relationships, and follows the stories of several main characters—three characteristics often found in her work. In one of Jaffe's most ambitious novels, *Family Secrets,* for example, some thirty-two characters appear over the course of the story.

Reviewers commenting on Jaffe's later books almost always compare the work being reviewed to Jaffe's first novel, thereby continuing interest in it. Written in the late fifties, the book has a distinctly pre-women's liberation movement slant which places it firmly in that decade. Although the women in *The Best of Everything* have jobs, they are not career women; men and the possibility of marrying one of them are far more important to these women than their work. At one point in the story one of the women characters thinks to herself: "It's hell to be a woman . . . ; to want so much love, to feel like only half a person, to need so much. What was it Plato had said? A man and a woman are each only half a person until they unite. Why hadn't he made that clearer to the men?"

Some critics, such as Judith Christ, objected to Jaffe's depiction of women in *The Best of Everything,* but the author asserts that the work gives an accurate picture of life in the fifties. According to Jaffe, the characters have much in common with people she knew or interviewed while doing research for the book. Jaffe explained to Klemesrud: In the fifties "girls were brought up to fulfill the image of what boys wanted. They feigned great interest in things they hated because they were only supposed to talk about the boys' interest. . . . They always tried to look their best. . . . It was all part of the fifties ratrace toward the altar."

The fifties also play an important role in Jaffe's *Class Reunion,* a novel that has been described as an updated version of Mary McCarthy's story about coming of age in the 1930s, *The Group.* Alluding to McCarthy's title, a *Time* reviewer observes, "Change Vassar to Radcliffe, the '30s to the '50s, take away the wry tone, and you have Rona Jaffe's readable reworking, *Class Reunion.*" In her *Washington Post* review of the book, Lynn Darling notes that in the novel Jaffe "follows the trials and tribulations of eight members of the Class of '57 . . . as they try to crawl out from under the mind-numbing conformity of the '50s." Darling sees Jaffe's novels as a sort of exorcism of unpleasant memories. "Her observations," Darling comments, "are edged in irony, but like any veteran of a vicious war, past skirmishes are with her still, and she is still in the trenches."

In *Class Reunion* and other novels written since *The Best of Everything,* Jaffe deals with married as well as single women and how they cope with more significant dilemmas than how to catch a man. Divorce, cocaine addiction, teenage suicide, and other contemporary problems are dealt with in detail. But, while Jaffe's recent novels are praised for their readability as well as her skill in capturing the essence of life in New York City, reviews are often mixed.

In the *New York Times Book Review* Katha Pollitt, for example, calls *Class Reunion* "a wry and very readable tale," while in Eve Zibert's *Washington Post* review of the same book, the critic finds the novel "like a soap opera, . . . absorbing and embarrassing at the same time." And, while Nora Johnson in her essay on *The Last Chance* in the *New York Times Book Review* comments, "You have to keep reading Jaffe, she's competent and dependable, and she piles on the delicious details," in Nora Peck's review of *After the Reunion* appearing in the same journal, the critic notes, "Though the soul-searching in this novel may be on the level of [the television programs] 'Dynasty' or 'Dallas,' it proves equally entertaining."

While Leslie Garis does not propose a completely positive view of Jaffe's work, her *Ms.* review of *Family Secrets* does offer a brief summary of the qualities in Jaffe's writing that critics and readers alike find most appealing: "Breezy, immediate, conversational, elliptical—Rona Jaffe writes like [French novelist] Francoise Sagan's American cousin. She's more clean-cut, and less arrogant than Sagan, but their detachment, their simple statements that reduce complex emotional development to one measurable moment, their readiness to describe a childhood in a paragraph, are similar in spirit, if not in content. And when their subjects match their style, both writers carry it off brilliantly."

MEDIA ADAPTATIONS: The Best of Everything was made into a 1959 movie produced by Jerry Wald; *Mazes and Monsters* was made into a 1982 CBS-TV movie.

BIOGRAPHICAL/CRITICAL SOURCES:

BOOKS

Bestsellers 90, Issue 3, Gale, 1990.

PERIODICALS

Book World, November 9, 1969.
Chicago Tribune, May 27, 1968.
Detroit News and Free Press, May 13, 1990.
Listener, January 25, 1968.
Los Angeles Times Book Review, November 10, 1985; July 27, 1986; April 15, 1990.
Ms., November, 1974.
New Leader, November 7, 1966.
New Yorker, August 30, 1976.
New York Times, October 2, 1969.
New York Times Book Review, May 2, 1965; October 2, 1966; September 28, 1969; October 29, 1972; October 27, 1974; September 5, 1976; July 31, 1977; July 8, 1979; July 22, 1979; November 8, 1981; September 22, 1985.
Observer, March 8, 1970; June 8, 1975; October 17, 1976.
People, October 19, 1981.
Saturday Review, September 6, 1958; May 8, 1965.
Spectator, February 6, 1982.
Time, May 21, 1965; October 7, 1966; July 2, 1979.
Times Literary Supplement, February 1, 1968; August 8, 1975.
Virginia Quarterly Review, winter, 1977.
Wall Street Journal, November 29, 1985.
Washington Post, June 23, 1979.
Washington Post Book World, June 24, 1973; September 13, 1981; August 25, 1985; July 13, 1986.

*			*			*

JAKES, John (William) 1932-
(Alan Payne, Jay Scotland)

PERSONAL: Born March 31, 1932, in Chicago, Ill.; son of John Adrian (a Railway Express general manager) and Bertha (Retz) Jakes; married Rachel Ann Payne (a teacher), June 15, 1951; children: Andrea, Ellen, John Michael, Victoria. *Education:* DePauw University, A.B., 1953; Ohio State University, M.A., 1954. *Politics:* Independent. *Religion:* Protestant.

ADDRESSES: Home—P.O. Box 3248, Harbour Town Station, Hilton Head Island, S.C. 29928. *Agent*—Rembar & Curtis, 19 West 44th St., New York, N.Y. 10036.

CAREER: Abbott Laboratories, North Chicago, Ill., 1954-60, began as copywriter, became product promotion manager; Rumrill Co. (advertising agency), Rochester, N.Y., copywriter,

1960-61; free-lance writer, 1961-65; Kircher, Helton & Collett, Inc. (advertising agency), Dayton, Ohio, senior copywriter, 1965-68; Oppenheim, Herminghausen, Clarke, Inc. (advertising agency), Dayton, 1968-70, began as copy chief, became vice-president; Dancer-Fitzgerald-Sample, Inc. (advertising agency), Dayton, creative director, 1970-71; freelance writer, 1971—.

MEMBER: Authors Guild, Authors League of America, Dramatists Guild, Science Fiction Writers of America.

AWARDS, HONORS: LL.D., Wright State University, 1976; Litt.D., DePauw University, 1977; Porgie Award for best books in a series, 1977; Ohioana Book Award for fiction, 1978, for "American Bicentennial" series; Friends of the Rochester Library Literary Award, 1983.

WRITINGS:

The Texans Ride North: The Story of the Cattle Trails (juvenile), John C. Winston, 1952.
Wear a Fast Gun, Arcadia House, 1956.
A Night for Treason, Bouregy & Curl, 1956, reprinted, Pinnacle, 1982.
(Under pseudonym Alan Payne) *Murder, He Says,* Ace Books, 1958.
The Devil Has Four Faces, Bouregy, 1958, reprinted, Pinnacle, 1981.
The Imposter, Bouregy, 1959, reprinted, Pinnacle, 1981.
Johnny Havoc, Belmont Books, 1960.
Johnny Havoc Meets Zelda, Belmont Books, 1962.
Johnny Havoc and the Doll Who Had "It," Belmont Books, 1963.
G.I. Girls, Monarch, 1963.
Tiros: Weather Eye in Space, Messner, 1966.
When the Star Kings Die, Ace Books, 1967.
Great War Correspondents, Putnam, 1967.
Famous Firsts in Sports, Putnam, 1967.
Making It Big, Belmont Books, 1968.
Great Women Reporters, Putnam, 1969.
Tonight We Steal the Stars (bound with *The Wagered World* by Laurence M. Janifer and S. J. Treibich), Ace Books, 1969.
The Hybrid, Paperback Library, 1969.
The Last Magicians, Signet, 1969.
Secrets of Stardeep, Westminster, 1969, bound with *Time Gate* (also see below), New American Library, 1982.
The Planet Wizard, Ace Books, 1969.
The Asylum World, Paperback Library, 1969.
Mohawk: The Life of Joseph Brant, Crowell, 1969.
Black in Time, Paperback Library, 1970.
Six Gun Planet, Paperback Library, 1970.
Mask of Chaos (bound with *The Star Virus* by Barrington T. Bayler), Ace Books, 1970.
Monte Cristo 99, Modern Library, 1970.
Master of the Dark Gate, Lancer Books, 1970.
Conquest of the Planet of the Apes (novelization of film of the same title), Award Books, 1972.
Time Gate, Westminster, 1972.
Witch of the Dark Gate, Lancer Books, 1972.
Mention My Name in Atlantis: Being, at Last, the True Account of the Calamitous Destruction of the Great Island Kingdom, Together with a Narrative of Its Wondrous Intercourses with a Superior Race of Other-Worldlings, as Transcribed from the Mss. of a Survivor, Hopter the Vintner, for the Enlightenment of a Dubious Posterity, DAW Books, 1972.
On Wheels, Paperback Library, 1973.
The Best of John Jakes, edited by Martin H. Greenberg and Joseph D. Olander, DAW Books, 1977.

The Bastard Photostory, Jove, 1980.
North and South (first volume in "North and South" trilogy), Harcourt, 1982.
Love and War (second volume in "North and South" trilogy), Harcourt, 1984.
Susanna of the Alamo: A True Story, Harcourt, 1986.
Heaven and Hell (third volume in "North and South" trilogy), Dell, 1988.
California Gold, Random House, 1989.

"BRAK THE BARBARIAN" SERIES; "SWORDS AND SORCERY"

Brak the Barbarian, Avon, 1968.
Brak the Barbarian versus the Sorceress, Paperback Library, 1969.
Brak versus the Mark of the Demons, Paperback Library, 1969.
Brak: When the Idols Walked, Tower, 1978.
Fortunes of Brak, Dell, 1980.

"AMERICAN BICENTENNIAL" SERIES, PYRAMID; PUBLISHED AS "KENT FAMILY CHRONICLES" SERIES, JOVE

The Bastard (also see below), Pyramid, 1974, Jove, 1978 (published in England in two volumes, Volume 1: *Fortune's Whirlwind,* Volume 2: *To an Unknown Shore,* Corgi, 1975).
The Rebels (also see below), Pyramid, 1975, Jove, 1979.
The Seekers (also see below), Pyramid, 1975, Jove, 1979.
The Furies (also see below), Pyramid, 1976, Jove, 1978.
The Titans, Pyramid, 1976, Jove, 1976.
The Patriots (contains *The Bastard* and *The Rebels*), Landfall Press, 1976.
The Pioneers (contains *The Seekers* and *The Furies*), Landfall Press, 1976.
The Warriors, Pyramid, 1977, Jove, 1977.
The Lawless, Jove, 1978.
The Americans, Jove, 1980.

PLAYS

(Author of lyrics) *Dracula, Baby* (musical comedy), Dramatic Publishing, 1970.
(Author of book and lyrics) *Wind in the Willows* (musical comedy), Performance Publishing, 1972.
A Spell of Evil (three-act melodrama), Performance Publishing, 1972.
Violence (two one-acts), Performance Publishing, 1972.
Stranger with Roses (one-act), Dramatic Publishing, 1972.
(Author of book and lyrics) *Gaslight Girl* (musical) Dramatic Publishing, 1973.
(Author of book and lyrics) *Pardon Me, Is This Planet Taken?* (musical), Dramatic Publishing, 1973.
(Author of book and lyrics) *Doctor, Doctor!* (musical), McAfee Music Corp., 1973.
(Author of book and lyrics) *Shepherd Song* (musical), McAfee Music Corp., 1974.

UNDER PSEUDONYM JAY SCOTLAND

The Seventh Man, Mystery House, 1958, reprinted under name John Jakes, Pinnacle, 1981.
I, Barbarian, Avon, 1959, reprinted under name John Jakes, Pinnacle, 1979.
Strike the Black Flag, Ace Books, 1961.
Sir Scoundrel, Ace Books, 1962.
Veils of Salome, Avon, 1962, reprinted under name John Jakes as *King's Crusader,* Pinnacle, 1976.
Arena, Ace Books, 1963.
Traitors' Legion, Ace Books, 1963, reprinted under name John Jakes as *The Man from Cannae,* Pinnacle, 1977.

Also author, under pseudonym Alan Payne, of *This Will Slay You,* 1958. Contributor of short stories to magazines.

ADAPTATIONS: Three of the "Kent Family Chronicles" books, *The Bastard, The Rebels* and *The Seekers,* were adapted for television by Operation Prime Time and Universal Studios; *North and South* has been produced on television.

SIDELIGHTS: John Jakes is well known as the author of the successful "American Bicentennial" series, later published as the "Kent Family Chronicles," eight paperback novels spanning many generations of an American family. These books, which have sold in excess of thirty-six million copies, have made Jakes one of the most popular historical writers in America, and he has become a recognized influence on a recent literary phenomenon known as the family-saga paperbacks.

Prior to writing the "Kent Family Chronicles," Jakes had published almost forty novels in a variety of genres—science fiction, mystery, juvenile adventure—as well as nonfiction books, short stories, plays, and even lyrics to stage musicals. He was a prolific but unrecognized author when he was contracted by veteran book packager Lyle Kenyon Engle and Pyramid Books to produce that company's "American Bicentennial" series. Jakes's first novel for the series, *The Bastard,* soon became a bestseller. This book and its successors (*The Rebels, The Seekers, The Furies, The Titans, The Warriors, The Lawless,* and *The Americans*) are distinguished by the author's extensive historical detail.

The main attraction of the series, however, lies in its vivid plots and memorable characters. As Curt Suplee explains in the *Washington Post,* "The saga takes the picturesque and prolific Kent family through seven generations and the first 100 years of American history, propelled by a psychic storm of lust, ambition and circumstance."

Following the "Kent Family Chronicles," Jakes produced the hardcover novel *North and South.* Set in the antebellum era, the book covers the West Point education of two friends who eventually find themselves on opposite sides during the Civil War. True to his established writing style, Jakes infuses the story with detailed historical background, prompting Grover Sales, in the *Los Angeles Times Book Review,* to call the author "a good amateur historian—amateur in the best sense." But Sales criticizes the book's "Simon Legree villains, Prince Valiant heroes and Scarlett O'Hara bitches churning their endless way through resolutely telegraphed plots." In a *Chicago Tribune Book World* review, Anstiss Drake remarks: "There is no poetry, no subtlety in Jakes's writing, so his novel is weakest in the romantic passages. But he is solid and memorable in his descriptions of [the main characters'] friendship, and in the ordinary details of life. Jakes is at his best describing the personal crisis that every thinking man and woman faced when the choice was not black and white, and ideas conflicted with common sense, convictions were torn away from loyalties, and complacency gave way to doubt."

Reviewing *North and South* in the *Washington Post,* Jonathan Yardley writes: "It's true that Jakes lacks imagination at characterization, that his prose is rarely better (or worse) than competent, that he knows (and pulls) all the old melodramatic tricks. All of that is true, yet it remains that his novels are reliably entertaining in a solid, predictable, comfortably old-fashioned way." Yardley sums up, "Jakes has assembled an intelligent, unpretentious entertainment many readers will find undemandingly enjoyable." And Mel Watkins, in the *New York Times Book Review,* citing Jakes's "straightforward and workmanlike" narrative style, asserts, "If one is looking for an entertaining,

popularized and generally authentic dramatization of American history, [*North and South*] will meet his expectations."

As *North and South* climbed to the top of the hardcover bestseller lists, John Jakes described his position as a chronicler of American history to Curt Suplee: "I feel a real responsibility to my readers. I began to realize about two or three books into the Kent series that I was the only source of history that some of these people had ever had! Maybe they'll never read a [book by historian] Barbara Tuchman, but down at the K Mart, they'll pick up one of mine." Jakes told *CA* that he has received a significant amount of mail indicating that readers "seem to have gained a new appreciation for American history particularly how interesting and dramatic it truly is when removed from the embalming fluid of conventional teaching and textbooks. Time and again this has been expressed in letters, and in person, and with unashamed sentimentality I can say that no author could ask for a greater reward, or greater proof that the writer's only purpose—to reach and move a reader—was achieved."

BIOGRAPHICAL/CRITICAL SOURCES:

BOOKS

Dictionary of Literary Biography Yearbook: 1983, Gale, 1984.
Hawkins, R., *The Kent Family Chronicles Encyclopedia,* Bantam, 1979.

PERIODICALS

Chicago Tribune Book World, February 21, 1982.
Detroit News, February 23, 1982.
Los Angeles Times, September 18, 1989.
Los Angeles Times Book Review, March 21, 1982, December 2, 1984, September 27, 1987, August 20, 1989.
New York Times, May 2, 1986.
New York Times Book Review, March 7, 1982.
People, November 12, 1984.
Publishers Weekly, April 5, 1976, November 30, 1984.
Washington Post, February 3, 1982, February 28, 1982, November 3, 1984.
Washington Post Book World, April 3, 1977, October 18, 1987, September 17, 1989.

*   *   *

JAMES, C(yril) L(ionel) R(obert)   1901-1989
(J. R. Johnson)

PERSONAL: Born January 4, 1901, in Chaguanas, Trinidad and Tobago; died of a chest infection, May 31, 1989, in London, England; son of a schoolteacher; divorced from first wife; married Selma Weinstein, 1955; children (first marriage): one. *Education:* Graduated from Queen's Royal College secondary school (Port of Spain), 1918.

ADDRESSES: Home—Brixton, London, England. *Agent*—c/o Allison & Busby, 6-A Noel St., London W1V 3RB, England.

CAREER: Member of the Maple cricket team, Port of Spain, Trinidad and Tobago; *Trinidad* (literary magazine), Port of Spain, editor, 1929-30; Queen's Royal College, Port of Spain, teacher, until 1932; *Manchester Guardian,* London, England, correspondent, 1932-38; *Fight* (later *Workers' Fight;* Marxist publication), London, editor, until 1938; trade union organizer and political activist in the United States, 1938-53; West Indian Federal Labor Party, Port of Spain, secretary, 1958-60; *The Nation,* Port of Spain, editor, 1958-60. Lecturer at colleges and universities, including Federal City College, Washington, D.C.;

commentator for the British Broadcasting Company (BBC); cricket columnist for *Race Today.*

WRITINGS:

The Life of Captain Cipriani: An Account of British Government in the West Indies, Nelson, Lancashire, Coulton, 1932, abridged edition published as *The Case for West-Indian Self-Government,* Hogarth, 1933, University Place Book Shop, 1967.

(With L. R. Constantine) *Cricket and I,* Allan, 1933.

Minty Alley (novel), Secker & Warburg, 1936, New Beacon, 1971.

Toussaint L'Ouverture (play; first produced in London, 1936; revised version titled *The Black Jacobins* and produced in Ibadan, Nigeria, 1967), published in *A Time and a Season: Eight Caribbean Plays,* edited by Errol Hill, University of the West Indies (Port of Spain), 1976.

World Revolution, 1917-1936: The Rise and Fall of the Communist International, Pioneer, 1937, Hyperion Press, 1973.

A History of Negro Revolt, Fact, 1938, Haskell House, 1967, revised and expanded edition published as *A History of Pan-African Revolt,* Drum and Spear Press, 1969.

The Black Jacobins: Toussaint L'Ouverture and the San Domingo Revolution, Dial, 1938, Random House, 1963.

(Translator from the French) Boris Souvarine, *Stalin: A Critical Survey of Socialism,* Longman, 1939.

State Capitalism and World Revolution (published anonymously), privately printed, 1950, Facing Reality, 1969.

Mariners, Renegades, and Castaways: The Story of Herman Melville and the World We Live In, privately printed, 1953, Bewick Editions, 1978.

Modern Politics (lectures), PNM (Port of Spain), 1960.

Beyond a Boundary, Hutchinson, 1963, Pantheon, 1984.

The Hegelian Dialectic and Modern Politics, Facing Reality, 1970, revised edition published as *Notes on Dialectics: Hegel, Marx, Lenin,* Lawrence Hill, 1980.

Nkrumah and the Ghana Revolution, Lawrence Hill, 1977, revised edition, Allison & Busby, 1982.

The Future in the Present: Selected Writings of C. L. R. James, Lawrence Hill, 1977.

(With Tony Bogues and Kim Gordon) *Black Nationalism and Socialism,* Socialists Unlimited, 1979.

(With George Breitman, Edgar Keemer, and others) *Fighting Racism in World War II,* Monad, 1980.

Spheres of Existence: Selected Writings, Lawrence Hill, 1981.

Eightieth Birthday Lectures, Race Today, 1983.

At the Rendezvous of Victory: Selected Writings, Lawrence Hill, 1985.

Cricket, Allison & Busby, 1986.

Contributor of short stories to the collections *The Best Short Stories of 1928,* Cape, 1928, and *Island Voices,* Liveright, 1970; author, sometimes under pseudonym J. R. Johnson, of numerous political pamphlets; contributor of articles to newspapers and magazines.

WORK IN PROGRESS: An autobiography.

SIDELIGHTS: C. L. R. James was a leading political and literary figure of Trinidad and Tobago whose interests and values were profoundly shaped by his experience growing up in the British West Indian colony at the beginning of the century. The son of a schoolteacher father, James was raised in the capital of Port of Spain in a highly respectable—indeed, rather puritanical—middle-class black family suffused in British manners and culture. The James family home faced the back of a cricket field, and young Cyril developed a lifelong passion for the baseball-like

sport watching matches from his living room window. The boy also grew up with an intense love for English literature—at age ten he had memorized long passages of William Makepeace Thackeray's *Vanity Fair*—and both his reading and his cricket playing often distracted him from his studies at the elite Queen's Royal College in Port of Spain. Dashing his parents' hopes that he would pursue a political career with the colonial administration, James chose instead to play professional cricket and teach at the Queen's Royal College in the 1920s. At the same time, he set about chronicling the lives of his nation's lower class in a series of naturalistic short stories that shocked his peers and foreshadowed his future Marxism. James's firsthand study of the Port of Spain slums also furnished background for his only novel, *Minty Alley,* an affecting but unsentimental look at the complex personal relationships and humble aspirations of the denizens of a rundown boarding house.

In 1932, chafing under the placid routines of a life in a colonial backwater, James accepted an invitation to go to London to help the great black cricketer Learie Constantine of Trinidad and Tobago write his autobiography. With Constantine's help, James secured a job as a cricket correspondent with the *Manchester Guardian* and published his first nonfiction book, *The Life of Captain Cipriani: An Account of British Government in the West Indies* (later abridged and published as *The Case for West-Indian Self-Government*). This influential treatise—one of the first to urge full self-determination for West Indians—introduced James to leading figures in the two political movements that were to profoundly shape his thinking in the years to come: Pan Africanism and Marxism.

James first developed his Pan Africanist ideas in leftist activist George Padmore's London-based African Bureau, where he joined future African independence leaders Jomo Kenyatta and Kwame Nkrumah as a political propogandist in the mid-1930s. James emphasized the importance of West Indians' coming to terms with their African heritage in order to help forge a sense of national identity in their racially and culturally polyglot society. He also came to regard the struggle to liberate and politically unify colonial Africa as a way of inspiring and mobilizing oppressed people of color around the world to seize control of their destinies. James later examined Pan Africanist theory and practice in two historical works, *A History of Negro Revolt* (later revised and published as *History of Pan-African Revolt*), which surveys nearly two centuries of the black liberation struggle against European colonialism, and *Nkrumah and the Ghana Revolution,* an analysis of the first successful independence movement in modern Africa.

While participating in the vanguard of the African liberation movement, James also became a committed Marxist during his sojourn in London in the 1930s. He took the Trotskyist position in the great dispute over Stalinism that split the world communist movement during those years and wrote a history from that perspective in 1937 titled *World Revolution, 1917-1936: The Rise and Fall of the Communist International.* James's Marxism also informed his 1938 historical study *The Black Jacobins: Toussaint L'Ouverture and the San Domingo Revolution.* In this book, generally regarded as his masterwork, James analyzes the socioeconomic roots and leading personalities of the Haitian revolution of 1791 to 1804, the first and only slave revolt to achieve political independence in world history.

At the center of the revolution and the book stands Toussaint L'Ouverture. The self-taught black slave turned charismatic political leader and redoubtable military commander organized and led a disciplined army of former slaves, who defeated crack

French and British expeditionary forces mustered to crush the insurgency. Of particular interest in *The Black Jacobins,* critics noted, is the author's success in relating the Haitian events to the course of the French Revolution, whose ideals inspired Toussaint even as he fought first Maximilien Robespierre and then Napoleon Bonaparte to free France's most important Caribbean sugar colony, then known as Saint Domingue. The democratic ideals of the Haitian revolution, which culminated in full political independence a year after Toussaint's death in 1803, touched off a wave of slave revolts throughout the Caribbean and helped inspire anti-slavery forces in the southern United States. *New York Herald Tribune Books* reviewer Clara Gruening Stillman judged *The Black Jacobins* as gripping as the events it recounted: "Brilliantly conceived and executed, throwing upon the historical screen a mass of dramatic figures, lurid scenes, fantastic happenings, the absorbing narrative never departs from its rigid faithfulness to method and documentation."

Shortly after publishing *The Black Jacobins* James moved to the United States, where he joined the Trotskyist Socialist Workers Party (SWP) and became a full-time political activist, organizing auto workers in Detroit, Michigan, and tenant farmers in the South. He broke with the SWP in the late 1940s over the question of the nature of the Soviet Union, which he dubbed "state capitalist," and co-founded a new Detroit-based Trotskyist political organization with Leon Trotsky's former secretary Raya Dunayevskaya. James's political activities eventually provoked the wrath of the McCarthy-era U.S. government, which denied him American citizenship and deported him to Great Britain in 1953. While awaiting his expulsion on Ellis Island, the everresourceful James managed to write a short study of Herman Melville titled *Mariners, Renegades, and Castaways* that drew a parallel between Ahab's pursuit of the great white whale in Melville's classic, *Moby Dick,* and left-wing intellectuals' infatuation with Soviet political leader Joseph Stalin.

After five years in London, James returned to Trinidad and Tobago in 1958 to join the movement for political independence there. In Port of Spain he edited *The Nation* magazine and served as secretary of the West Indian Federal Labor Party, whose leader, Dr. Eric Williams, became the island nation's first premier in 1960. Like the United States authorities, however, Williams found James's outspoken Marxism politically threatening and soon compelled James, who had once been Williams's schoolmaster, to go back to England. James left Trinidad and Tobago aggrieved that the emerging Caribbean nations had failed to achieve a lasting formula for political federation, which he believed necessary to further their social and economic development.

Back in London, James returned to political writing and lecturing, particularly on the Pan Africanist movement, West Indian politics, and the black question in the United States. He also rekindled his passion for cricket after leading a successful campaign to have Frank Worrell of Trinidad and Tobago named the first black captain of the West Indian international cricket team. Worrell's spectacular playing at the Australian championship competition in 1961 galvanized a sense of national pride and identity among the emerging West Indian nations and partly inspired James to write *Beyond a Boundary,* his much-praised 1963 survey of cricket's social and cultural significance in Great Britain and the Caribbean. The book's title refers both to the game's objective of driving a ball beyond a marked boundary and James's thesis that this gentlemen's sport can help overcome certain false cultural, racial, and political boundaries within society. On a purely aesthetic level, James argues, cricket has "the perfect flow of motion" that defines the essence of all great art; he holds that a good cricket match is the visual and dramatic equivalent of so-called "high art" and that the sport should be recognized as a genuinely democratic art form. Cricket's high standards of fairness and sportsmanship, on the other hand, illustrate "all the decencies required for a culture" and even played a historic role by showing West Indian blacks that they could excel in a forum where the rules were equal for everyone. The integrated Caribbean cricket teams, James believes, helped forge a new black self-confidence that carried the West Indian colonies to independence. The author renders these observations in a lively, anecdotal style that includes both biographical sketches of great cricketers and personal reminiscences from his own lifelong love affair with the sport. "*Beyond a Boundary* is one of the finest and most finished books to come out of the West Indies," remarked novelist V. S. Naipaul in *Encounter.* "There is no more eloquent brief for the cultural and artistic importance of sport," added *Newsweek*'s Jim Miller.

Before his death in 1989, James published two well-received collections of essays and articles that display his broad literary, cultural, and political interests. *The Future in the Present* contains the author's short story "Triumph," about women tenants in a Port of Spain slum, along with essays ranging from critical interpretations of Pablo Picasso's painting "Guernica" and Melville's *Moby Dick* to a political analysis of workers' councils in Hungary and a personal account of organizing a sharecroppers' strike in Missouri in 1942. "The writings are profound, sometimes; cranky, occasionally; stimulating, always," remarked *Village Voice* critic Paul Berman, and *Times Literary Supplement* reviewer Thomas Hodgkin found the book "a mine of richness and variety." *Rendezvous of Victory,* whose title James took from a verse by the great West Indian poet Aime Cesaire, includes an essay on the Solidarity union movement in Poland and critical discussions of the work of black American novelists Toni Morrison and Alice Walker. The more than eighty-year-old James "show[ed] no diminution of his intellectual energies," wrote Alastair Niven in his review of the collection for *British Books News.* "Throughout this book James's elegant but unmannered style, witty and relaxed when lecturing, reflective and analytical when writing for publication, always conveys a sense of his own robust, humane, and giving personality. Was there ever a less polemical or more persuasive radical?"

BIOGRAPHICAL/CRITICAL SOURCES:

BOOKS

Contemporary Literary Criticism, Volume 33, Gale, 1983.
James, C. L. R., *The Future in the Present: Selected Writings of C. L. R. James,* Lawrence Hill, 1977.
James, C. L. R., *Beyond a Boundary,* Pantheon, 1984.
Mackenzie, Alan and Paul Gilroy, *Visions of History,* Pantheon, 1983.

PERIODICALS

American Scholar, summer, 1985.
British Book News, May, 1984.
CLA Journal, December, 1977.
Encounter, September, 1963.
Nation, May 4, 1985.
Newsweek, March 26, 1984.
New Yorker, June 25, 1984.
New York Herald Tribune Books, November 27, 1938.
New York Times Book Review, March 25, 1984.
Radical America, May, 1970.
Times Literary Supplement, December 2, 1977, January 20, 1978, September 25, 1987.

Village Voice, February 11, 1981, July 10, 1984.
Washington Post Book World, April 22, 1984.

OBITUARIES:

PERIODICALS

Los Angeles Times, June 3, 1989.
New York Times, June 2, 1989.
Times (London), June 2, 1989.
Washington Post, June 3, 1989.

* * *

JAMES, Clive (Vivian Leopold) 1939-

PERSONAL: Born October 7, 1939, in Kogarah, New South Wales, Australia; son of Albert Arthur (a mechanic) and Minora May (a seamstress; maiden name, Darke) James. *Education:* Sydney University, B.A., 1960; Pembroke College, Cambridge, M.A., 1967.

ADDRESSES: Office—Observer, 8 St. Andrew's Hill, London EC4V 5JA, England. *Agent—*A. D. Peters & Co., 10 Buckingham St., London WC2N 6BU, England.

CAREER: Morning Herald, Sydney, Australia, assistant editor, 1961; *Observer,* London, England, television critic, 1972-82, feature writer, 1972—; television performer and writer. Worked as a streetcar conductor, librarian, factory hand, statistician, copy editor, and copy writer. President of Footlights (dramatic society) at Cambridge University.

Appeared in numerous television series, including "Cinema," "Up Sunday," "So It Goes," "A Question of Sex," "Saturday Night People," "Clive James on Television," "The Late Clive James," and "Saturday Night Clive," and on television specials and documentaries, including "Shakespeare in Perspective: Hamlet" (1980), "The Clive James Paris Fashion Show" (1981), "Clive James and the Calendar Girls" (1981), "The Return of the Flash of Lightning" (1982), "Clive James Live in Las Vegas" (1982), "Clive James Meets Roman Polanski" (1984), "The Clive James Great American Beauty Pageant" (1984), "Clive James in Dallas" (1985), "Clive James on Safari" (1986), and "Clive James in Japan" (1987). *Military service:* Australian National Service, 1958-60.

WRITINGS:

CRITICISM

The Metropolitan Critic (essays), Faber, 1974 (also see below).
Visions Before Midnight: Television Criticism From the Observer, 1972-1976, J. Cape, 1977 (also see below).
At the Pillars of Hercules (essays), Faber, 1979 (also see below).
First Reactions: Critical Essays, 1968-1979 (contains essays previously published in *The Metropolitan Critic, Visions Before Midnight,* and *At the Pillars of Hercules*), Knopf, 1980.
The Crystal Bucket: Television Criticism From the Observer, 1976-1979, J. Cape, 1981.
From the Land of Shadows (essays), J. Cape, 1982.
Glued to the Box: Television Criticism From the Observer, 1979-1982, J. Cape, 1983.
Snakecharmers in Texas (essays), J. Cape, 1988.

POETRY

Peregrine Prykke's Pilgrimage Through the London Literary World, New Review, 1974, revised version published as *The Improved Version of Peregrine Prykke's Pilgrimage Through the London Literary World: A Tragic Poem in Rhyming Couplets,* illustrations by Russell Davies, J. Cape, 1976.
The Fate of Felicity Fark in the Land of the Media: A Moral Poem in Rhyming Couplets, illustrations by Marc, J. Cape, 1975.
Britannia Bright's Bewilderment in the Wilderness of Westminster: A Political Poem in Rhyming Couplets, illustrations by Marc, J. Cape, 1976.
Fan-Mail: Seven Verse Letters, Faber, 1977.
Charles Charming's Challenges on the Pathway to the Throne: A Royal Poem in Rhyming Couplets, illustrations by Marc, New York Review of Books, 1981.
Poem of the Year, J. Cape, 1983.
Other Passports: Poems, 1958-1985, J. Cape, 1986.

LYRICS FOR RECORD ALBUMS

Beware of the Beautiful Stranger, Philips Fontana, 1970, reissued, RCA, 1973.
Driving Through Mythical America, Philips Fontana, 1971, RCA, 1973.
A King at Nightfall, RCA, 1973.
The Road of Silk, RCA, 1974.
Secret Drinker, RCA, 1974.
Live Libel, RCA, 1975.
The Master of the Revels, RCA, 1976.

OTHER

(With Pete Atkin) *A First Folio* (songbook), Warner Bros., 1974.
Unreliable Memoirs (autobiography), J. Cape, 1980, Knopf, 1981.
Brilliant Creatures: A First Novel, J. Cape, 1983.
Flying Visits: Postcards From the Observer, 1976-1983 (travel essays), J. Cape, 1984, Norton, 1986.
Falling Towards England (Unreliable Memoirs Continued) (autobiography), J. Cape, 1985, published as *Falling Towards England: Unreliable Memoirs II,* Norton, 1986.
The Remake: A Novel, J. Cape, 1987.

Contributor to periodicals, including *Commentary, Encounter, Listener, London Review of Books, Nation, New Review, New Statesman, New Yorker, New York Review of Books, Ritz, Times Literary Supplement,* and *Vogue.* Literary editor of *honi soit,* 1960.

SIDELIGHTS: Clive James, judged "one of the brightest figures in contemporary English intellectual journalism" by Joseph Epstein in the *New York Times Book Review,* is the author of writings that include two novels, three books of literary criticism, five volumes of mock-epic verse, two autobiographies, and three collections of television criticism gathered from his weekly columns for the London *Observer.* James's style of television reviewing, Laurie Taylor of the London *Times* assessed, is well known for its "acerbic self-consciousness, the feeling for the ridiculous, for the simultaneous reality and unreality of images," and it garnered him more than one million daily readers. He gave up criticizing television programs in 1982 to step before the camera, starring in various television talk shows and specials such as "Saturday Night People," "The Late Clive James," "The Return of the Flash of Lightning," and "Clive James Meets Roman Polanski." James continues to write book reviews and feature articles on the British cultural scene and national politics for the *Observer.*

Born in 1939 in Kogarah, a suburb of Sydney, Australia, James recounts his childhood and adolescence in *Unreliable Memoirs,* the first installment of his series of autobiographies. The author tells of how his father, Albert, volunteered to fight the Japanese at the outbreak of World War II and urged his wife, Minora, to avoid possible bombings by taking their son farther inland to the frontier town of Jannali. Albert survived both combat and the duress of being a Japanese prisoner of war, but he was killed in a plane crash when being transported home in August, 1945. James relates in his memoir that his mother's deep mourning affected him greatly, and he claimed that neither of them ever recovered from the loss. They moved back to Kogarah, where Minora supplemented her small war widow's pension by sewing baby clothes.

Unreliable Memoirs reports that in school James was known as the class clown; he writes that he compensated for his small size by being entertaining. "I cultivated the knack of exaggeration. Lying outrageously, I inflated rumour and hearsay into saga and legend," Walter Clemons in *Newsweek* quoted James from his autobiography. *New York Review of Books* critic James Wolcott cited an example of one of the boy's tall tales from the book: "Climaxing a story of my close personal acquaintance with [German Field Marshall Erwin] Rommel, I produced a pair of old sand-goggles." Yet James encountered the same growing pains of a normal youth: "At a dance," *Times Literary Supplement* contributor Randolph Stow commented, "young James was not so much a wallflower as 'a wall-shadow; a wall-stain.'"

James attended Sydney University on a scholarship for war orphans but was unprepared for the complexities of academic life. "What kind of car, I wondered, was a Ford Madox Ford? What sort of conflict was an Evelyn War?," James asked himself during the first semester, according to Clemons. At the university he read profusely and contributed articles to the school literary journal, *honi soit*, becoming its editor in his senior year. James then began reviewing books for the Sydney *Morning Herald* and after graduation worked there as an assistant editor. Bored with the routine of daily writing in Sydney, he bought a one-way ticket to England. *Unreliable Memoirs* concludes with James aboard a steamer bound for London.

Spectator's David Leitch thought *Unreliable Memoirs* "a hilarious and unexpectedly sentimental journey along roads lined with hibiscus and (mainly untouchable) girls named Nola, Gail and Valma." James's often raucous and crass adolescent humor prompted Clemons to write that James was "hearty and noisy," while Stow thought him "a good bloke . . . often witty, and never less than amiable." Jeffrey Scheuer in *New Republic* noted that "comic sense, bound up with a pathos that is never mawkish, makes this a moving and funny book." Epstein agreed, adding, " 'Unreliable Memoirs' one hopes will be the first of several volumes of autobiography."

James satisfied his fans with the second installment of his autobiography, *Falling Towards England (Unreliable Memoirs Continued),* published in 1985. Commencing in London in 1962, *Falling Towards England* follows James through a variety of odd jobs and a steady progression of women and alcohol while he attempts to write great works of literature at night. The memoir concludes with his being accepted to Pembroke College of Oxford University in 1964. Richard Caseby observed that the mood of *Falling Towards England* is more somber than *Unreliable Memoirs,* owing to more mature subject matter. The critic asserted, "the slight shift in tone, though, is no killjoy. James's wickedly funny jokes and jibes make you laugh out loud and feel warm to the man." Whitney Balliett, commenting in the *New Yorker,* found James's second autobiography "a funny, light-footed, affecting book, a kind of laughing, streamlined 'Down and Out in Paris and London.'"

Reviewing *Falling Towards England* in the *Chicago Tribune,* Dale McFeatters judged the book a "rowdy, literate and raunchy autobiography," and Balliett claimed that this is so because "the hyperbolic electricity that endlessly activates James sometimes overpowers him, and he grows bawdy and a little sweaty. Consider, for example, his hilarious description in 'Falling Towards England' of the effects of the British hamburger on the digestive system. These wild passages are all the more remarkable in that his smooth, unadorned prose never lets on that it has said anything uncouth."

While at Pembroke James submitted critical essays and book reviews to the *Times Literary Supplement, Nation,* and *Listener.* He collected many of these articles in his 1974 work, *The Metropolitan Critic,* which features reviews of writings by such authors as D. H. Lawrence, George Bernard Shaw, Edmund Wilson, and Kate Millett. Critics were impressed by James's objective studies and his nonacademic tone, prompting one *Times Literary Supplement* contributor to note that "beyond the plain-man pose, there is a very straightforward, old-fashioned critical effort." *The Metropolitan Critic* earned James a reputation for discussing literature in its social context, both nineteenth-century and contemporary, and comparing the style to works representative of recent literary trends.

In his second critical effort, *At the Pillars of Hercules,* James collected more of his previously published essays, including his thoughts on Lillian Hellman, Norman Mailer, Raymond Chandler, W. H. Auden, and Aleksandr Solzhenitsyn. *From the Land of Shadows,* his third volume of literary criticism, published in 1982, reflects James's deep interest in Russian politics and literature. James began studying the Russian language in 1975, motivated by an eagerness to read writings by early nineteenth-century Russian author Aleksandr Pushkin in their original language. In *From the Land of Shadows* James looks at a recent translation of one of Pushkin's works, and he critiques writings by Soviet dissidents Solzhenitsyn and Andrei Sakharov and by other Western authors, including Erica Jong, John le Carre, and Philip Larkin. Reviewing the book for the *Times Literary Supplement,* T. J. Binyon asserted that "James has a solid and individual critical personality, which is forceful enough to impose a degree of unity on some very disparate pieces." He also noted that James's "outstanding talent is as a cicerone, guiding the ignorant traveller with patience, knowledge and wit round some favourite literary edifice and communicating his own admiration of it to the goggling and fascinated visitor."

James later turned his critical attention to the television media. *Nation*'s Richard Gilman quoted a London *Times* contributor, who summed up James's popularity as a television critic: "Mr. James makes the programmes so much more enjoyable than they can ever have been to watch." James collected many of his *Observer* columns in the books *Visions Before Midnight, The Crystal Bucket,* and *Glued to the Box.* The volumes feature articles on prominent entertainers such as Bob Hope, David Frost, and Jane Fonda; series like "Dallas" and "Kung Fu" and made-for-television movies; coverage of sporting events, including the 1976 Olympic Games in Moscow and the annual Wimbledon tennis matches; and political figures such as former U.S. President Richard Nixon and his secretary of state, Henry Kissinger. Christopher Warman of the London *Times* commented that the *Glued to the Box* television columns are "sharply observed and highly intelligent, but best of all they are funny," while Byron Rogers in the *Spectator* claimed that James "had a good ear, delighted in the medium, and wrote a great deal of sense."

James's criticism was introduced to an American audience via *First Reactions: Critical Essays, 1968-1979.* The work comprises essays from the British volumes *The Metropolitan Critic, Visions*

Before Midnight, and *At the Pillars of Hercules,* focusing mainly on American literary works and television shows. Robert W. Smith in the *Washington Post Book World* deemed the book "a brilliant work of serious and popular criticism which will delight Americans who don't already know James." As well as previously collected essays on Mailer and Solzhenitsyn, *First Reactions* contains fifteen television columns—including one on Princess Anne's wedding and another on yoga—that John Fuldas in *Saturday Review* found to be "madly funny and deft." Edwards observed that James's criticism of television programming is "never dull, routine or unintelligent," and he decided that James is "probably the best, and certainly the funniest, writer on television I've encountered, one who's fairly sure that there's nothing really *good* to be found on the tube but able to discern degrees of badness and find some bad things interesting, like 'Star Trek,' 'Mission Impossible' and Margaret Thatcher."

As a poet James further satirizes the television medium, as well as print journalism, national politics, and the British royalty, in his mock-epic verse, originally published serially in the *Observer.* In 1974, for example, he took on the publishing industry with *Peregrine Prykke's Pilgrimage Through the London Literary World,* which prompted Auberon Waugh in *Books and Bookmen* to praise James for his "robust, knockabout talent" and his "wit and original perception, not to mention an amiable eccentricity of judgment." Peter Porter in the *London Review of Books* found the poem "ebullient, inventive and accurate," adding that "the literary world brings out all [James's] satirical skill."

The Fate of Felicity Fark in the Land of the Media is a poetic exploration of the print and broadcast journalism community, while *Britannia Bright's Bewilderment in the Wilderness of Westminster* is a commentary on national politics. In his 1981 verse offering, *Charles Charming's Challenges on the Pathway to the Throne,* James delivers a guide to the wedding of Prince Charles to Lady Diana Seethrough-Spiffing, introducing such guests as Prime Minister Margo Hatbox, historian A. J. P. Tailspin, and romance writer Barbara Heartburn. Although some reviewers contended that he was not critical enough of the royal family, Waugh claimed that "at his least serious, [James] is one of the funniest and most formidable writers around."

In 1983 James produced his first novel, *Brilliant Creatures,* another work satirizing the book publishing business. Its protagonist, Lancelot Windhover, is an innocent publisher who is corrupted by members of the literati in London and Los Angeles. Four years later James wrote *The Remake,* the story of an Australian television celebrity, Joel Court, who manages the affairs of Chance Jenolan, a writer for films. In the interval between those novels James compiled *Flying Visits: Postcards From the Observer, 1976-1983,* a collection of travel notes originally published in the *Observer.* In *Flying Visits* James offers his impressions of air trips to various parts of the world, including the Soviet Union, Japan, the United States, and Germany. Balliett deemed him "a first-rate travel writer," while Richard Eder of the *Los Angeles Times* claimed, "What is to be prized in James is not the evocation of a place, but the odd insight or imprecation." Reviewing the book in the *Christian Science Monitor,* Merle Rubin opined that James "exhibits that quality so rarely seen in an increasingly cynical world and in an all-too-cynical profession: gusto."

BIOGRAPHICAL/CRITICAL SOURCES:

BOOKS

James, Clive, *Unreliable Memoirs,* J. Cape, 1980.

James, Clive, *Falling Towards England (Unreliable Memoirs Continued),* J. Cape, 1985.

PERIODICALS

Books and Bookmen, August, 1976.
Chicago Tribune, January 19, 1987.
Christian Science Monitor, September 30, 1986.
London Review of Books, January 22, 1987.
Los Angeles Times, June 4, 1986.
Nation, May 2, 1981.
New Republic, March 21, 1981.
Newsweek, February 23, 1981.
New Yorker, December 29, 1986.
New York Review of Books, April 2, 1981.
New York Times, February 14, 1981.
New York Times Book Review, November 9, 1980, February 15, 1981.
Observer (London), November 30, 1986.
Saturday Review, September, 1980.
Spectator, October 23, 1976, June 11, 1977, May 3, 1980, June 6, 1981, July 23, 1983, January 5, 1985, September 14, 1985.
Time, November 17, 1986.
Times (London), April 30, 1980, January 14, 1984, August 12, 1985.
Times Literary Supplement, May 31, 1974, July 15, 1977, April 25, 1980, May 8, 1981, June 12, 1981, May 7, 1982, December 21, 1984, September 13, 1985, June 26, 1987, November 5, 1987.
Washington Post Book World, April 12, 1981, September 21, 1986.

*   *   *

JAMES, Henry   1843-1916

PERSONAL: Born April 15, 1843 in New York, N.Y.; died February 28, 1916 of edema following a series of strokes in London, England; ashes buried in Cambridge, Mass.; son of Henry (a minister) and Mary Robertson (Walsh) James; emigrated to England, naturalized 1915. *Education:* Attended schools in France and Switzerland; Harvard Law School, 1862-63.

CAREER: Literary critic and novelist. Writer for *Nation* and *Atlantic,* 1866-69; art critic for *Atlantic,* 1871-72; writer for *New York Tribune* while living in Paris, 1875-76; volunteer worker among the displaced and wounded during World War I.

AWARDS, HONORS: L.H.D., Harvard University, 1911, Oxford University, 1912; Order of Merit, 1915; commemorated with a James Memorial Stone, Poet's Corner, Westminster Abbey, London.

WRITINGS:

Watch and Ward, serialized in *Atlantic* magazine, 1871, Houghton, Osgood (Boston), 1878, reprinted, edited by Leon Edel, Grove Press, 1960.
Roderick Hudson, Osgood, 1875, revised edition in three volumes, Macmillan (London), 1879, revised edition reprinted in one volume, Houghton, 1882, reprint edited by Edel, Harper, 1960.
The American (also see below), Osgood, 1877, Scribner, 1907, Dell, 1960.
The Europeans (also see below), two volumes, Macmillan (London), 1878, one volume, Houghton, Osgood, 1879.
An International Episode (also see below), Harper, 1879.
Confidence, Houghton, Osgood, 1880, critical edition, Grosset & Dunlap, 1962.

Washington Square, Harper, 1880, published with *The Pension Beaurepas* [and] *A Bundle of Letters,* Macmillan, 1881, published with *The Europeans,* Modern Library, 1950.

The Portrait of a Lady, three volumes, Macmillan (London), 1881, one volume, Houghton, 1882, text edition adapted by Robert J. Dixon, Regents, 1954, original edition reprinted with introduction by Charles R. Anderson, Collier, 1962.

Novels and Tales of Henry James, fourteen volumes, Macmillan, 1883.

The Bostonians: A Novel, three volumes, Macmillan (London and New York), 1886, reprinted, Dial, 1945.

The Princess Casamassima: A Novel (also see below), Macmillan (New York), 1886, reprinted, Harper, 1959.

The Reverberator (also see below), Macmillan (New York), 1888, reprinted, Grove Press, 1957.

The Tragic Muse (also see below), two volumes, Houghton, 1890, reprinted, Peter Smith, 1960.

The Other House, Macmillan, 1896.

The Spoils of Poynton (first printed as "The Old Things" in *Atlantic,* 1896), Houghton, 1897, reprinted, Penguin, 1963.

What Maisie Knew, Stone, 1897, reprinted, Anchor Books, 1954, published with *In the Cage* [and] *The Pupil,* Macmillan, 1922.

The Awkward Age, Harper, 1899, reprinted, Doubleday, 1958.

The Sacred Fount, Scribners, 1901, reprinted with introduction by Edel, Grove Press, 1959.

The Wings of the Dove, Scribners, 1902, reprinted, Dell, 1958.

The Ambassadors, Harper, 1903, reprint edited by Rosenbaum, Norton, 1964.

The Golden Bowl, two volumes, Scribners, 1904, reprinted, Grove Press, c. 1959.

The Novels and Tales of Henry James, twenty-six volumes, Scribners, 1907-18, reprinted as *The New York Edition of Henry James,* twenty-five volumes, 1962-65, reprinted with additional volumes as *The Novels and Stories of Henry James: New and Complete Edition,* edited by Lubbock, thirty-five volumes, Macmillan, 1921-23.

The Outcry, Scribners, 1911.

The Ivory Tower (unfinished), edited by Percy Lubbock, Scribners, 1917.

The Sense of the Past (unfinished, with author's notes), edited by Lubbock, Scribners, 1917.

The Spoils of Poynton; A London Life; The Chaperon, Macmillan (London), 1922.

The Great Short Novels, edited by P. Rahv, Dial, 1944.

The American Novels and Stories of Henry James, edited by F. O. Matthieson, Knopf, 1947.

Four Selected Novels: The Americans, The Europeans, Daisy Miller, An International Episode, Grosset, 1958.

The Short Novels, Dodd, 1961.

Henry James: Novels, 1886-1990, includes *The Princess Casamassima, The Reverberator,* and *The Tragic Muse,* Library of America, 1989.

STORIES

A Passionate Pilgrim, and Other Tales (includes "A Passionate Pilgrim," "The Last of the Valerii," "Eugene Pickering," "The Madonna of the Future," "The Romance of Certain Old Clothes," and "Madame de Mauves"), Osgood, 1875.

Daisy Miller: A Study (also see below), Harper, 1878, illustrated edition, 1901, reprinted, 1916.

The Madonna of the Future and Other Tales, two volumes (includes "Longstaff's Marriage," "Madame de Mauves," "Eugene Pickering," "The Diary of a Man of Fifty," and "Benvolio"), Macmillan (London), 1879, published as *The*

Madonna of the Future and Other Early Stories, Signet, 1962.

A Bundle of Letters (also see below), Loring (Boston), 1880.

The Diary of a Man of Fifty and A Bundle of Letters (also see below), Harper, 1880.

The Siege of London, Madame de Mauves, Macmillan (London), 1883.

The Siege of London, The Pension Beaurepas, and The Point of View, Osgood, 1883.

Daisy Miller: A Study, Four Meetings, Longstaff's Marriage, Benvolio, Macmillan (London), 1883, published as *Daisy Miller: A Study and Other Stories,* Harper, 1883.

The Siege of London; The Point of View; A Passionate Pilgrim, B. Tauchnitz, 1884.

Tales of Three Cities (includes "Lady Barberina," "A New England Winter," and "Impressions of a Cousin"), Osgood, 1884.

Stories Revived, three volumes (includes "The Author of 'Beltraffio,'" "Pandora," "The Path of Duty," "A Light Man," "A Day of Days," "Georgina's Reasons," "A Passionate Pilgrim," "A Landscape Painter," "Rose-Agathe," "Poor Richard," "The Last of the Valerii," "Master Eustace," "The Romance of Certain Old Clothes," and "A Most Extraordinary Case"), Macmillan, 1885.

Henry James: Author of 'Beltraffio,' Pandora, Georgina's Reasons, The Path of Duty, Four Meetings, Osgood, 1885.

The Aspern Papers, Louisa Pallant, The Modern Warning, two volumes, Macmillan, 1888.

A London Life, The Patagonia, The Liar, Mrs. Temperly, two volumes, Macmillan, 1889, reprinted, Grove Press, 1957.

The Lesson of the Master, The Marriages, The Pupil, Brooksmith, The Solution, Sir Edmund Orme, Macmillan, 1892, published as *The Lesson of the Master and Other Stories,* J. Lehmann, 1948.

The Real Thing and Other Tales (includes "Sir Dominick Ferrand," "Nona Vincent," "The Chaperon," and "Greville Fane"), Macmillan, 1893.

The Private Life, The Wheel of Time, Lord Beaupre, The Visits, Collaboration, Owen Wingrave, Harper, 1893.

The Wheel of Time, Collaboration, Owen Wingrave, Harper, 1893.

Terminations, Volume 1: *The Death of the Lion, The Coxon Fund, The Middle Years,* Volume 2: *The Altar of the Dead,* Harper, 1895.

Embarrassments: The Figure in the Carpet, Glasses, The Next Time, The Way It Came, Macmillan, 1896.

John Delavoy, Macmillan, 1897.

In the Cage (also see below), Herbert S. Stone and Co. (Chicago), 1898.

The Two Magics: The Turn of the Screw, Covering End, Macmillan, 1898.

The Soft Side (includes "The Great Good Place," "Europe," "Paste," "The Real Thing," "The Great Condition," "The Tree of Knowledge," "The Abasement of the Northmores," "The Given Case," "John Delavoy," "The Third Person," "Maud-Evelyn," and "Miss Gunton of Poughkeepsie"), Macmillan, 1900.

The Better Sort (includes "Broken Wings," "The Beldonald Holbein," "The Two Faces," "The Tone of Time," "The Special Type," "Mrs. Medwin," "Flickerbridge," "The Story in It," "The Beast in the Jungle," "The Birthplace," and "The Papers"), Scribners, 1903.

Julia Bride, Harper, 1909.

The Finer Grain (includes "The Velvet Glove," "Mora Montavera," "A Round of Visits," "Crapy Cornelia," and "The Bench of Desolation"), Scribners, 1910.

Gabrielle De Bergerac, edited by A. Mordell, Boni & Liveright, 1918.

Travelling Companions (includes "The Sweetheart of M. Briseux," "Professor Fargo," "At Isella," "Guest's Confession," "Adina," and "De Grey: A Romance"), edited by Mordell, Boni & Liveright, 1919.

A Landscape Painter, Scott and Setzer, 1919.

Master Eustace (also see below), T. Setzer, 1920.

Lady Barberina and Other Tales (also see below), Macmillan (London), 1922.

The Diary of a Man of Fifty, A New England Winter, The Path of Duty, and Other Tales, Macmillan (London), 1923.

The Last of the Valerii; Master Eustace; The Romance of Certain Old Clothes, and Other Tales, Macmillan (London), 1923.

Lord Beaupre; The Visits; The Wheel of Time, and Other Tales, Macmillan (London), 1923.

Maud-Evelyn; The Special Type; The Papers, and Other Tales (includes "The Velvet Glove," "Mora Montavera," "Crapy Cornelia," "A Round of Visits," and "The Bench of Desolation"), Macmillan (London), 1923.

Representative Selections, edited by L. N. Richardson, American Book Co., 1941, reprinted, University of Illinois Press, 1966.

Stories of Writers and Artists, edited by Matthieson, New Directions, 1944.

The Short Stories, edited by C. Fadiman, Modern Library, 1945.

Fourteen Stories, selected by D. Garnett, Hart-Davis, 1946.

The Ghostly Tales of Henry James (includes "The Romance of Certain Old Clothes," "De Grey: A Romance," "The Last of the Valerii," "The Ghostly Rental," "Sir Edmond Orme," "Nona Vincent," "The Private Life," "Sir Dominick Ferrand," "Owen Wingrave," "The Altar of the Dead," "The Friends of the Friends," "The Turn of the Screw," "The Real Thing," "The Great Good Place," "Maud-Evelyn," "The Third Person," "The Beast in the Jungle," and "The Jolly Corner"), edited by Edel, Grosset, 1948, reprinted, 1963.

Ten Short Stories, edited by M. Swan, J. Lehmann, 1948.

Selected Short Stories, edited by Quentin Anderson, Holt, 1950, revised edition, 1957.

The Aspern Papers [and] *The Europeans,* New Directions, 1950.

Eight Uncollected Tales (includes "The Story of a Year," "My Friend Bingham," "The Story of a Masterpiece," "A Problem," "Osborne's Revenge," "Gabrielle de Bergerac," "Crawford's Consistency," and "The Ghostly Rental"), Rutgers University Press, 1950.

The Portable Henry James, edited by M. Zabel, Viking, 1951.

Selected Fiction, edited by Edel, Dutton, 1953.

"A Tragedy of Error": James's First Story (first printed anonymously in *Continental Monthly,* February, 1864), with a prefatory note by Edel, [Brunswick, Me.], 1956.

Selected Stories, edited by G. Hopkins, Oxford University Press, 1957.

In the Cage and Other Tales, edited by Zabel, Doubleday, 1958.

The Turn of the Screw, The Aspern Papers, and Seven Other Stories, edited by M. Swan, Collins, 1959.

The Aspern Papers [and] *The Spoils of Poynton,* Dell, 1959.

Fifteen Short Stories, edited by Zabel, Bantam, 1961.

Henry James: Seven Stories and Studies, edited by E. Stone, Appleton-Century-Crofts, 1961.

Lady Barberina, and Other Tales: Benvolio, Glasses, and Three Essays, Vanguard, 1961.

The Marriages and Other Stories, edited by Eleanor M. Tilton, New American Library, 1961.

The Complete Tales of Henry James, twelve volumes, edited by Edel, Lippincott, 1962-65.

The Henry James Reader, edited by Edel, Scribner, 1965.

The Tales of Henry James, edited by Maqbool Aziz, Oxford University Press, 1973—.

PLAYS

Daisy Miller: A Comedy in Three Acts (adapted from the novel), Osgood, 1883.

The American: A Comedy in Four Acts (adapted from the novel; produced 1891), Heinemann, 1891.

Theatricals, Two Comedies: Tenants, Disengaged (produced 1909), Harper, 1894.

Theatricals, Second Series: The Album, The Reprobate (produced 1919), Harper, 1895.

The Complete Plays of Henry James, includes "The High Bid" (produced 1908), "The Saloon" (produced 1911), and "The Outcry" (produced 1917), edited by L. Edel, Lippincott, 1949.

The Innocents (based on *The Turn of the Screw*), Baker, 1951.

Guy Domville (produced 1895), Lippincott, 1960.

CRITICISM

French Poets and Novelists, Macmillan, 1878, reprinted, Grosset, 1964.

Hawthorne, Macmillan (London), 1879, Harper, 1880, reprinted, Collier, 1967.

The Art of Fiction (also see below), Cupples, Upham, 1885.

Partial Portraits, Macmillan, 1888.

Picture and Text, Harper, 1893.

Essays in London and Elsewhere, Harper, 1893.

The Question of Our Speech [and] *The Lesson of Balzac* (two lectures), Houghton, 1905.

Views and Reviews, Ball (Boston), 1908.

Notes on Novelists with Some Other Notes, Scribners, 1914.

Pictures and Other Passages from Henry James, selected by Ruth Head, Frederick A Stokes Co., 1916.

Within the Rim and Other Essays, 1914-15, Collins, 1918.

Notes and Reviews (early essays, 1864-1866), Dunster House, 1921.

The Art of the Novel: Critical Prefaces, edited by R. P. Blackmur, Scribners, 1934.

The Art of Fiction and Other Essays, edited by M. Roberts, Oxford University Press, 1948.

The Scenic Art: Notes on Acting and the Drama, 1872-1901, edited by A. Wade, Rutgers University Press, 1948.

Daumier, A Caricaturist, Rodale Press, 1954.

The Painter's Eye: Notes and Essays on the Pictorial Arts, edited by J. L. Sweeney, Harvard University Press, 1956, reprinted, University of Wisconsin Press, 1990.

The Future of the Novel: Essays on the Art of Fiction, edited by Edel, Vintage, 1956.

The American Essays, edited by Edel, Vintage, 1956.

The House of Fiction: Essays on the Novel by Henry James, edited by Edel, Hart-Davis, 1957.

Literary Reviews and Essays on American, English, and French Literature, edited by A. Mordell, Twayne, 1957.

French Writers and American Women: Essays, edited by P. Buitenhuis, Compass, 1960.

Selected Literary Criticism, edited by M. Shapira, Horizon Press, 1963.

Henry James, Literary Criticism, edited by Edel and Mark Wilson, Volume 1: *Essays on Literature, American Writers, En-*

glish Writers, Volume 2: *French Writers, Other European Writers, The Prefaces to the New York Edition,* Library of America, 1984.
The Art of Criticism, edited by W. Veeder and S. M. Griffin, University of Chicago, 1986.

TRAVEL

Transatlantic Sketches, Osgood, 1875, abridged edition published as *Foreign Parts,* B. Tauchnitz, 1883.
Portraits of Places, Macmillan (London), 1883, Osgood, 1884, published with an essay on James as a traveller, Lear, 1948.
A Little Tour in France (first published as "En Provence" in *Atlantic,* 1883-84), Osgood, 1885, revised edition with illustrations by Joseph Pennell, Houghton, 1900, reprinted with introduction by Michael Swan, Farrar, Straus, 1950.
English Hours, Houghton, 1905, 2nd edition, Orion Press, 1960.
The American Scene, Harper, 1906, published with essays from *Portraits of Places,* edited by W. H. Auden, Scribners, 1946, original edition reprinted, Granville, 1987.
Italian Hours, Houghton, 1909, reprinted, Grove Press, 1959.
The Art of Travel: Scenes and Journeys in America, England, France, and Italy from the Travel Writings of Henry James, edited by Zabel, [New York], 1958.

AUTOBIOGRAPHY

A Small Boy and Others (also see below), Scribners, 1913.
Notes of a Son and Brother (also see below), Scribners, 1914.
The Middle Years (also see below), Scribners, 1917.
Henry James: Autobiography, (includes *A Small Boy and Others, Notes of a Son and Brother,* and *The Middle Years*), Criterion Books, 1956.

LETTERS

Letters to an Editor, privately printed, 1916.
The Letters of Henry James, two volumes, selected and edited by Lubbock, Scribner, 1920.
"A Most Unholy Trade," Being Letters on the Drama by Henry James, Scarab Press, 1923.
Henry James: Letters to A. C. Benson and Auguste Monod, edited by E. F. Benson, Scribner, 1930.
Theatre and Friendship: Some Henry James Letters, ed. E. Robins, Putnam, 1932.
Henry James and Robert Louis Stevenson: A Record of Friendship and Criticism, edited by Janet Adam Smith, Hart-Davis, 1948.
The Selected Letters of Henry James, edited by Edel, Farrar, Straus, 1955.
(Contributor) *Tales of the Criminous* (with fourteen letters from Henry James), Cassell, 1956.
Parisian Sketches: Letters to the New York Tribune, 1875-1876, edited by Edel and Ilse Dusoir Lind, New York University Press, 1957.
Henry James and H. G. Wells: A Record of Their Friendship, Their Debate on the Art of Fiction, and Their Quarrel, edited by Edel and G. N. Ray, University of Illinois Press, 1958.
Switzerland in the Life and Work of Henry James (includes letters to Mrs. Clara Benedict), Berne, 1966.
Henry James: Letters, edited by Edel, four volumes, Harvard University Press, 1974-84.

OTHER

William Wetmore Story and His Friends (biography), two volumes, Houghton, 1903.
The Henry James Year Book, compiled by Evelyn Garnaut Smalley, R. G. Badgers (Boston), 1911.

The Notebooks of Henry James, edited by Matthiessen and K. B. Murdock, Oxford University Press, 1947, reprinted, 1961.
The Complete Notebooks of Henry James, edited by Edel and Lyall H. Powers, Oxford University Press, 1987.

Works represented in hundreds of anthologies. Most of James's novels were serialized in magazines such as *Atlantic* and *North American Review* before being published in book form. Contributor of short stories to *The Yellow Book, Atlantic, New Review, Harper's, Century,* and other magazines. Contributor of more than 300 reviews and essays to the *New York Tribune, Atlantic, Galaxy, Independent, English Illustrated Magazine, Nation, North American Review,* and other periodicals.

SIDELIGHTS: Henry James was an American literary critic and master of fiction. Educated in Europe and in his later years a resident of England, he came to prefer Europe to the United States first in letters and later in politics. His characteristic themes—including cross-cultural relationships, the psychological make-up and affairs of wealthy characters, and women's roles in society—reflect his cosmopolitan outlook. A prolific writer in several genre, James saw himself primarily as a critic. In an essay collected in *Henry James, Literary Criticism,* he maintained that the life of the literary critic "is heroic, for it is immensely vicarious. He has to understand for others." James also felt that writing criticism was intellectually superior to creative writing, though he regarded fiction writing as an intellectual exercise as well. During his lifetime, the author of novels, short stories, plays, and travel books was unpopular because his style demanded that readers pay close attention in order to perceive subtle effects. Though his values engaged him in conflict with other critics, he made contributions to literature that influenced the forms and direction of contemporary fiction.

The grandson of Irish millionaire William James, Henry James, Jr. was born in New York City near Greenwich Village. His father was an anti-Calvinist minister and a permissive parent who raised his children to think of themselves as citizens of the world. In 1844, Henry James, Sr. moved his family to London to be near Thomas Carlyle, J. J. Garth Wilkinson, and other distinguished thinkers. In 1845 they moved back to New York, but Europe had made an indelible impression on the infant James, who retained vivid memories of Paris and London. Continued travel abroad during his formative years stimulated James's imagination; proximity to the authors and artists who visited his parents encouraged his literary interests. In his youth he was an indifferent student but a voracious reader who became proficient in French and French literature.

The James family returned to the States after a financial loss brought on by panic preceding the outbreak of the Civil War. Henry Jr. and his brother William set aside their art classes for more practical studies. While William studied science, Henry enrolled in the Law School at Harvard in order to have access to the library and the lectures of esteemed authors such as James Russell Lowell. Henry expanded his literary contacts, becoming friends with Charles Eliot Norton and his sister Grace, and Oliver Wendell Holmes. He could attend college while others his age were serving in the civil war because of a severe injury sustained while putting out a fire in the Newport stables. He referred to the injury as "horrid," and "obscure"; neglect of the wound led to permanent injury. Some conjectured that the injury was castration, while others suggested he suffered a slipped disk. Like his father who had lost a leg after being burned in a stable fire, Henry Jr. became a keen observer of life and human character, dividing his time between travel and seclusion for the purpose of writing.

In 1864 James made his debut in print with a short story in the *Continental Monthly* and a review in *North American Review*. The next year saw the appearance of his first signed story in the *Atlantic* and a new friendship with the magazine's editor, James T. Fields. He also befriended the editor's assistant, William Dean Howells. James later credited Howells with helping him to develop the critical eye and the creative confidence he needed to become established as a writer and critic.

A traveler with cosmopolitan tastes, James made numerous trips to France and Italy in search of new subjects. The beauty and antiquity of Rome especially inspired him; his travel diaries *Italian Hours* and *A Little Tour in France* are much admired. *The American Scene*, written after James had spent several decades in Europe, is regarded among the best travel books ever written. A tour of the States along the Atlantic Coast, it expressed the author's dismay at the rampant materialism and contrasting poverty in the slums in New York City. It is valued "for its timeless warning to all Americans: treasure old local color, avoid ravaging the land, resist placing commerce above all else, respect your best art, look about, look out," Robert L. Gale wrote in *Concise Dictionary of American Literary Biography, 1865-1917*.

Fascinated with culture and informed by his travels, James wrote a number of novels that show different cultures and social classes in conflict. *The American* and *Daisy Miller* both show young Americans whose romantic endeavors end poorly because their naive behavior in foreign cultures clashes with society's expectations. In *Daisy Miller*, the title character's social adventures are misconstrued both by the American society abroad and by her American suitor, who suspects her of misconduct with an Italian. In *The American*, wealthy Christopher Newman courts a French woman whose family ultimately rejects him. The French woman's family behaves so villainously that their own son helps Newman discover a secret to use against them. However, Newman cannot bring himself to use blackmail. Gale commented that "The main focus of the romantic novel is the contrast of American innocence and Old World Experience." *The American* became the first of several of James's novels that have become known as "international novels."

Also fascinated by the intricacies of psychology, James used fiction to dissect his characters' complex and sometimes aberrant personalities. A number of his early works show the beginnings of a motif called "the sacred fount," in which intimate relationships are shown to contain one resourceful person who is exploited by the other. His first published novel *Roderick Hudson*, for example, showed an artist taking advantage of his patron in order to live an undisciplined life in Europe. The various ways in which financial concerns complicate relationships was another theme fully developed in James's fiction. Later works such as *The Tragic Muse* and *The Real Thing* increasingly examined the relationship of the artist to his art. All the fictional works share in common the author's "sharp probing of psychological reality," Gale observed. Foremost among the stories having a plot based strictly on psychological development is the much-anthologized "The Turn of the Screw," a ghost story related by an unreliable narrator.

James was one of the first male authors to examine women's roles in Western societies. The novel *The Bostonians*, for example, took women's issues as its subject. Disdained by readers when it was first published, the book has more recently gained important critical attention. Gale summarized, "Most readers now praise it for its evocation of old Boston, for its murky depiction of the eternal battle of the sexes, and especially for its prescience with respect to aspects of women's liberation—for example, the misery of male parental dominance, the victimizing of women by women, marriage as cop-out, and the need for radicalism among reformers." Other books by James that treat women's issues include *Washington Square, The Portrait of a Lady*, and *The Princess Casamassima*, which also looked at the political topic of international anarchy.

The novels *The Princess Casamassima, The Reverberator*, and *The Tragic Muse* are "remarkable for the audacity of their subject matter and for the moral delicacy with which it is explored," Hilton Kramer commented in *Insight*. Also "triumphs of style," they are "triumphant in their depiction of the social forces that were shaping not only the destiny of James's characters but, as he very keenly understood, the moral sensibility of the modern world. . . . To everything that Henry James wrote about the life of his time, he brought an acute and disabused awareness of the moral implications of the decisions that shape our fate. . . . Whether he brought his novelistic powers to the subject of revolutionary politics, the new journalism or the life of art, James was always an unfailing connoisseur of this contest between delicacy and brutality," Kramer added.

Prolific but not popular, James chose topics and wrote in a style that limited the size of his audience. Depending upon the accumulation of subtle effects that unraveled slowly, his stories and novels appealed most to readers who enjoyed intellectual challenges and were not put off by his themes. Serialized in popular magazines, his novels did not sell well in book form. Albert Mordell comments in the introduction to *Literary Reviews and Essays by Henry James*: "Certainly one of the reasons for James's unpopularity is that he was an intellectual and particularly interested in developing an idea. He never started on a story unless he had an idea to promulgate. Yet he was not a propagandist. He shows in all his critical writings that he is looking for the ideas at the base of an author's writings. He 'leavens' all writings with thought, even if this was to prove unprofitable, as he once wrote to his brother William."

While his distinctive and elliptical style pleased some critics, it brought him into notable conflict with others. H. G. Wells, for example, said in *Boon* (reprinted in *Henry James and H. G. Wells: A Record of Their Friendship, Their Debate on the Art of Fiction, and Their Quarrel*) that the novelist's "paragraphs sweat and struggle. . . . And all for tales of nothingness. . . . It is leviathan retrieving pebbles. It is a magnificent but painful hippopotamus resolved at any cost . . . upon picking up a pea which had got into a corner of its den." Letters that James wrote in response to Wells's attack registered the author's shock at the critic's public display of "bad manners." Ezra Pound was similarly appalled at the critical response to James's work. He wrote in a 1918 essay collected in *Literary Essays of Ezra Pound*, "I am tired of hearing pettiness talked about Henry James's style. . . . What I have not heard is any word of the major James, the hater of tyranny; book after early book against . . . all the sordid petty personal crushing oppression, the domination of modern life, not worked out in the diagrams of Greek tragedy. . . . The outbursts in *The Tragic Muse*, the whole of 'The Turn of the Screw,' human liberty, personal liberty, the rights of the individual against all sorts of intangible bondage! The . . . continual passion of it in this man who, fools said, didn't 'feel.' I have never yet found a man of emotion against whom idiots didn't raise this cry." Gertrude Stein also maintained in *Four in America* that James's work was a deeply felt response to what was happening in the lives of the people he observed.

James was no stranger to negative reviews; throughout his career, he was the object of divergent opinions, some of them provoked by his own forthrightness in judging the works and weaknesses of others. Though most of his conflicts with critics centered on the proper manner and role of fiction, others berated him for his values. Lack of enthusiasm for his causes (desire for reforms in education and women's rights, for instance) may also account for the poor reception given to his later novels and plays. When James became a British citizen in 1915 to show solidarity with British and French soldiers, he was perceived as disloyal to his American heritage and denounced by his former countrymen. But James had seen the casualties of the war in Europe first-hand, and had soundly rebuked America for remaining neutral while thousands were being maimed and killed. As in the conflict with Wells, it is fair to say that it may have gone better for James had he not been as critical toward others. By the time of his death in 1916, James "had become, for all practical purposes, an unread author," Kramer summed up in *Insight.* Interest in fiction by James did not revive until decades later when the outbreak of World War II compelled readers to seek his insights on international relations. T. S. Eliot, Ezra Pound, Rebecca West, R. P. Blackmur and other distinguished American writers led a campaign that restored James to literary prominence. Since then, critical studies and articles about his life and works have continued to proliferate.

James's criticism defended the same principles that he practiced when writing fiction. Said Mordell, "James wrote in his well-known essay 'The Art of Fiction' that the deepest quality for a work of art will always be the quality of the mind of the producer, that his novel will partake of the substance of beauty and truth in proportion as the intelligence is fine, and that no good novel will ever proceed from a superficial mind." His critical vision focused on the relations between the artist and his art, between art and life, between art and ideals, and between art and morals. He most applauded literature that was tightly composed, that showed the author achieving difficult effects through mastery of technique, and that required the reader's close attention.

"What James would not tolerate was the vulgar, the egotistical and the bogus; and when he suspected that a writer was not making the most of his gifts, he could be sharply dismissive. . . . For the most part, though," Michiko Kakutani noted in the *New York Times,* "James was less interested in passing judgment on a given text than in using it to shed light on an author's overall achievement. . . . He felt that critics had a responsibility to interpret a writer's inner life and public personality. As a result, his essays are filled with wonderful cameos—character sketches almost as vivid as those found in his novels." Hailed by many critics as a thinker who probed most deeply into the philosophy of art, James was also "by far the best American critic of the nineteenth century who . . . is brimful of ideas and critical concepts and has a well-defined theory and a point of view which allow him to characterize sensitively and evaluate persuasively a wide range of writers: largely, of course, the French, English, and American novelists of his own time," Rene Wellek summarized in *American Literature.*

The novelist's comments on his own fiction form a substantial body of important criticism, Richard P. Blackmur maintained in the introduction to *The Art of the Novel.* "There has never been a body of work so eminently suited to criticism as the fiction of Henry James, and there has certainly never been an author who saw the need and had the ability to criticize specifically and at length his own work. . . . James felt that his Prefaces [to the volumes of the New York edition] represented or demonstrated an artist's consciousness and the character of his work in some detail, made an essay in general criticism which had an interest and a being aside from any connection with his own work, and

that finally, they added up to a fairly exhaustive reference book on the technical aspects of the art of fiction."

As a novelist, James contributed developments in technique and content that were expanded by later important novelists. A major contribution to fiction writing was his "scenic progression" technique, in which the writer would follow one character's perceptions through a sequence of settings. A precursor of stream-of-consciousness technique explored by novelists such as James Joyce, this method of narrative composition was a direct result of James's foray into playwriting during the 1890s, and it is best exemplified in the novel *The Ambassadors.* James also contributed his insistence on form and craft. Commenting on his accomplishments in literature, Gale noted, "James disliked shapeless novels, bulky with social or personal protest and holding up a mirror to chaotic reality; he preferred those with balanced parts and a tidied appearance that please through subjective probing and unusual artistic tension and balance." Furthermore, his subject matter anticipated the concerns of literature in the late twentieth century. The philosophical question of how perception limits awareness, the quest for individual freedom against social pressures to conform, and the examination of women's roles seen in his works are themes that belonged to the social movements of later generations. In addition, noted Gale, James "tentatively explored eroticism (especially in the young), imaginative quests through time, nihilism, and absurdist disorientations." Because of these "forward-looking" traits, concluded Gale, the works of Henry James continue to attract interested readers.

MEDIA ADAPTATIONS: Washington Square was adapted for the stage by Ruth and Augustus Goetz and produced as *The Heiress* in 1948; William Archibald's play version of *The Turn of the Screw* was produced as *The Innocents* in 1950; *The Wings of the Dove* was adapted for the stage by Guy Bolton and produced as *Child of Fortune* in 1956; *The Bostonians* was adapted for theater and produced in Los Angeles, Calif. in 1984; Andrew Holmes and the Empty Space Theatre Company staged a play based on *The Aspern Papers* at the Old Red Lion Theatre in England in 1987.

BIOGRAPHICAL/CRITICAL SOURCES:

BOOKS

Anesko, Michael, *"Friction with the Market": Henry James and the Profession of Authorship,* Oxford University Press, 1986.
Armstrong, Paul B., *The Challenge of Bewilderment: Understanding and Representation in James, Conrad and Ford,* Cornell University Press, 1987.
Bradbury, Nicola, *An Annotated Critical Bibliography of Henry James,* St. Martin's Press, 1987.
Concise Dictionary of American Literary Biography, 1865-1917, Gale, 1988.
Conrad, Joseph, *Notes on Life and Letters,* J. M. Dent, 1905.
Dictionary of Literary Biography, Gale, Volume 12: *American Realists and Naturalists,* 1982, Volume 71: *American Literary Critics and Scholars, 1880-1917,* 1988, Volume 74: *American Short-Story Writers before 1880,* 1988.
Dupee, F. W., *Henry James,* Morrow, 1974.
Edel, Leon, *Henry James: A Life,* Harper, 1985.
Gard, Roger, *Henry James: The Critical Heritage,* Routledge & Kegan Paul, 1968, reprinted, 1986.
Great Writers of the English Language: Novelists and Prose Writers, St. Martin's Press, 1979.
Greene, Graham, *Collected Essays,* Viking, 1969.
James, Henry, *The Art of the Novel: Critical Prefaces,* edited by R. P. Blackmur, 1934.

James, *Henry James and H. G. Wells: A Record of Their Friendship, Their Debate on the Art of Fiction, and Their Quarrel,* edited by Edel and G. N. Ray, Hart-Davis, 1958.

James, *Literary Reviews and Essays,* edited by Albert Mordell, Vista House, 1957.

James, *Henry James, Literary Criticism,* two volumes, edited by Edel and Mark Wilson, Library of America, 1984.

Krook, Dorothea, *The Ordeal of Consciousness in Henry James,* Cambridge University Press, 1962.

Pound, Ezra, *Literary Essays of Ezra Pound,* edited by T. S. Eliot, New Directions, 1918.

Stein, Gertrude, *Four in America,* Yale University Press, 1947.

Tanner, Tony, *Henry James,* Volume 1: *1843-1881,* Volume 2: *1882-1898,* Longman, 1979.

Twentieth Century Literary Criticism, Gale, Volume 2, 1979, Volume 11, 1983, Volume 24, 1987.

PERIODICALS

American Literature, November, 1958.
American Scholar, spring, 1972.
Atlantic, June, 1968.
Discussion, August, 1972.
Insight, June 12, 1989.
Los Angeles Times, December 6, 1984.
Nation, April 23, 1960.
New Yorker, November 7, 1959, March 13, 1971.
New York Times, April 9, 1984, January 26, 1985.
South Atlantic Quarterly, winter, 1975.
Time, November 30, 1962.
Times (London), April 23, 1987.
Yale Review, spring, 1974.

*   *   *

JAMES, P. D.
See WHITE, Phyllis Dorothy James

*   *   *

JAMES, Philip
See del REY, Lester and MOORCOCK, Michael (John)

*   *   *

JARRELL, Randall 1914-1965

PERSONAL: Surname accented on second syllable; born May 6, 1914, in Nashville, Tenn.; died October 14, 1965; buried in New Garden Friends Cemetery, Greensboro, N.C.; son of Owen and Anna (Campbell) Jarrell; married Mackie Langham, 1940; married Mary Eloise von Schrader, November 8, 1952. *Education:* Vanderbilt University, A.B., 1935, A.M., 1938.

ADDRESSES: Home—5706 South Lake Dr., Greensboro, N.C.

CAREER: Kenyon College, Gambier, Ohio, instructor, 1937-39; University of Texas Main University (now University of Texas at Austin), instructor in English, 1939-42; Sarah Lawrence College, Bronxville, N.Y., instructor in English, 1946-47; Princeton University, Princeton, N.J., visiting fellow in creative writing, 1951-52; Woman's College of the University of North Carolina (now University of North Carolina at Greensboro), associate professor, 1947-51, 1953-54, professor of English, 1958-65. Taught at the Salzburg Seminar in American Civilization, Salzburg, Austria, 1948; visiting professor, Princeton University,

1951-52, and University of Illinois, 1953; George Elliston Lecturer, University of Cincinnati, 1958-65; Phi Beta Kappa visiting scholar, 1964-65. Consultant in poetry to the Library of Congress, 1956-58. *Military service:* U.S. Army Air Forces, 1942-46; became celestial navigation tower operator.

MEMBER: Academy of American Poets (chancellor), National Institute of Arts and Letters, Phi Beta Kappa.

AWARDS, HONORS: Guggenheim fellowship in poetry, 1946; Levinson prize, 1948; Oscar Blumenthal prize, 1951; National Institute of Arts and Letters grant, 1951; National Book Award, 1961, for *The Woman at the Washington Zoo: Poems and Translations;* O. Max Gardner award, 1962; D.H.L., Bard College, 1962; Ingram-Merrill Literary award, 1965; fellow, Indiana University School of Letters.

WRITINGS:

(Contributor) *Five Young American Poets,* New Directions, 1940.

Blood for a Stranger (poems), Harcourt, 1942.

Little Friend, Little Friend (poems), Dial, 1945.

Losses (poems), Harcourt, 1948.

(Translator) Ferdinand Gregorovius, *The Ghetto and the Jews of Rome,* Schocken, 1948.

The Seven League Crutches (poems), Harcourt, 1951.

Poetry and the Age (criticism), Knopf, 1953, reprinted, Noonday, 1972.

Pictures from an Institution: A Comedy (novel), Knopf, 1954.

Selected Poems, Knopf, 1955.

(Editor) *The Anchor Book of Stories,* Doubleday-Anchor, 1958.

Uncollected Poems, [Cincinnati], 1958.

The Woman at the Washington Zoo: Poems and Translations (also see below), Atheneum, 1960.

(Editor) *The Best Short Stories of Rudyard Kipling,* Doubleday, 1961.

A Sad Heart at the Supermarket: Essays and Fables, Atheneum, 1962.

(Translator) Ludwig Bechstein, *The Rabbit Catcher and Other Fairy Tales of Ludwig Bechstein,* Macmillan, 1962.

(Translator and author of introduction) Jakob and Wilhelm Grimm, *The Golden Bird and Other Fairy Tales of the Brothers Grimm,* Macmillan, 1962.

(Editor) Rudyard Kipling, *The English in England,* Doubleday, 1963.

(Editor) R. Kipling, *In the Vernacular: The English in India,* Doubleday, 1963.

(Editor) *Six Russian Short Novels,* Doubleday, 1963.

The Gingerbread Rabbit (juvenile), illustrations by Garth Williams, Macmillan, 1963.

Selected Poems Including the Woman at the Washington Zoo, Macmillan, 1964.

The Bat-Poet (juvenile), illustrations by Maurice Sendak, Macmillan, 1964.

(Translator) Anton Chekhov, "The Three Sisters," produced at Morosco Theatre, 1964.

The Lost World: New Poems, Macmillan, 1965, published with an appreciation by Robert Lowell, Collier Books, 1966.

The Animal Family, illustrations by Sendak, Pantheon, 1965.

Randall Jarrell, 1914-1965, edited by Lowell, Pete Taylor, and Robert Penn Warren, Farrar, Straus, 1968.

Complete Poems, Farrar, Straus, 1968, reprinted, 1980.

The Death of the Ball Turret Gunner, illustrations by Robert Andrew Parker, David Lewis, 1969.

The Third Book of Criticism, Farrar, Straus, 1969.

The Achievement of Jarrell: A Comprehensive Selection of His Poems, edited by Frederick J. Hoffman, Scott, Foresman, 1970.

Jerome: The Biography of a Poem, illustrations by Albrecht Duerer, Grossman, 1971.

(Translator) Jakob and Wilhelm Grimm, *Snow-White and the Seven Dwarfs: A Tale from the Brothers Grimm,* Farrar, Straus, 1972.

(Translator) Jakob and Wilhelm Grimm, *The Juniper Tree and Other Tales from Grimm,* edited by Lore Segal and Sendak, Farrar, Straus, 1973.

Fly by Night (juvenile), illustrations by Sendak, Farrar, Straus, 1976.

(Translator) *Goethe's Faust, Part I,* Farrar, Straus, 1976.

A Bat Is Born, illustrations by John Schoenherr, Doubleday, 1978.

Kipling, Auden & Co.: Essays and Reviews 1935-1964, Farrar, Straus, 1979.

(Translator) Jakob Grimm, *The Fisherman and His Wife,* Farrar, Straus, 1980.

Jarrell's Letters: An Autobiographical and Literary Selection, edited by wife, Mary Jarrell, and Stuart Wright, Houghton, 1985.

Former acting literary editor of *Nation;* poetry critic, *Partisan Review,* 1949-51, and *Yale Review,* 1955-57; member of editorial board, *American Scholar,* 1957-65. Contributor to *New Republic, New York Times Book Review,* and other publications.

SIDELIGHTS: Best known as a literary critic but also respected as a poet, Randall Jarrell was noted for his acerbic, witty, and erudite criticism. In a volume of essays about Jarrell titled *Randall Jarrell, 1914-1965,* nearly all of the writers praised his critical faculties. They also noted, commented Stephen Spender in the *New York Review of Books,* "a cruel streak in Jarrell when he attacked poets he didn't like." Elizabeth Bishop, a poet and contributor to the volume, wrote that "Jarrell's reviews did go beyond the limit; they were unbelievably cruel, that's true. . . . He hated bad poetry with such vehemence and so vigorously that it didn't occur to him that in the course of taking apart—where he'd take a book of poems and squeeze, like that, twist—that in the course of doing that, there was a human being also being squeezed."

Jarrell could be harsh, critics agreed, but his vehemence was a barometer of his love for literature. Robert Lowell wrote in the *New York Times Book Review* that Jarrell was "almost brutally serious about literature." Lowell conceded that he was famed for his "murderous intuitive phrases," but defended Jarrell by asserting that he took "as much joy in rescuing the reputation of a sleeping good writer as in chloroforming a mediocre one." Helen Vendler also felt that Jarrell's commitment to promoting good writers was the source of his vitriolic reviews. She wrote in the *New York Times Book Review* that "nobody loved poets more or better than Randall Jarrell—and irony, indifference or superciliousness in the presence of the remarkable seemed to him capital sins." Michael Dirda of the *Washington Post Book World* agreed that Jarrell had the best interests of literature in mind when he used invective. According to Dirda, Jarrell defended his willingness to "bury" (Jarrell's word) a work that did not meet his standards by saying that "taste has to be maintained (or elevated if it's at too low a level to make maintenance bearable) and there is no other way of doing it." John K. Roth noted similarly in the *Los Angeles Times* that Jarrell believed "artistic worth is not a relative, let alone a financial matter. There are such traits as trained and scrupulous taste, [and] reasoned critical judgement."

Christopher Lehmann-Haupt attributed a gradual change in Jarrell's approach to his concern for writers. He wrote in the *New York Times:* "Randall Jarrell was in his early years a harsh and witty disparager. . . . Even [later in his career] when he has praise for a poet, he often begins by knocking a work down, and then floors the reader by pronouncing the poet worth reading. Yet somewhere along the way the zingers and twisteroos die out. . . . [Perhaps] part of the reason Jarrell eases up on his fellow poets is simply because he is worried about their extinction." And although he softened his blows, Jarrell maintained his traditionally-based standards. Suzanne Ferguson wrote in her *Poetry of Randall Jarrell* that his criticism, with standards based on "broad, deep reading in *all* kinds of writing," would "ask always, both explicitly and implicitly, whether the poem tells truth about the world; whether it helps the reader see a little farther, a little more clearly the dark and light of his situation."

Jarrell tried to guide the reader not just by the content but also the style of his writing. A straightforward approach was as important to Jarrell in his own writing as in that of the writers he reviewed, noted D. J. Enright in *Listener:* "Just as common feeling informs his best poetry, so what underlies Randall Jarrell's criticism is common sense—that quality derided by frothy phonies who have failed to notice how uncommon it is—strengthened and clarified by exactly remembered reading, considerable knowledge of what is essential to know, and his own experience in the art of writing." Jarrell's insistence on clarity and accessibility in writing alienated him from some academicians; his denouncement of the New Criticism set him even further afield. According to Hilton Kramer in *New Leader,* the advent of the New Criticism "induced a profound despair over the very nature of the critical vocation, and his response to that despair was to adopt a tone and a method markedly different from the despised weightiness and solemnity he saw overtaking the whole literary enterprise. This change in his critical outlook had the unfortunate effect of depriving Jarrell of a certain seriousness." Michael Dirda interpreted Jarrell's stance in a more positive way: "In a time when criticism was already turning professional and academic, Jarrell spoke as a reader, one who tried to convey his enthusiasm or his disappointment in a book as sharply as he could manage."

Jarrell's passion for clarity extended from his criticism to his poetry. Julian Moynahan asserted in the *New York Times Book Review* that "Jarrell was a master of the modern plain style, the style which in poets like Frost, Hardy and Philip Larkin (Jarrell's favorite younger English poet) is used to connect the vicissitudes of ordinary experience with modes of primary feeling which move deep down within, and between, all of us." A *Time* reviewer suggested that in forming his style, Jarrell "rejected what Poet [Karl] Shapiro calls 'Eliot's High Church voice' in favor of 'plain American, which dogs and cats can read.' He demanded plain speech and uttered it." Other critics have commented on the "colloquial, intimate mode of speech" that James Atlas of the *American Poetry Review* identified with Jarrell; for Karl Shapiro, writing in *Book World,* it seemed that "what Jarrell did was to locate the tone of voice of his time and of his class (the voice of the poet-professor-critic who refuses to surrender his intelligence and his education to the undergraduate mentality)."

While Jarrell retained his colloquial voice with no "discernable 'development'" over the years, he did branch out thematically, according to Hugh B. Staples, who asserted in *Contemporary Literature* that his "diversity is reflected in the considerable canon of his work." Ferguson identified Jarrell's themes as "relatively few and closely related as they evolve through his thirty-year writing career: in the poems of the thirties, the 'great Necessity' of the natural world and the evils of power politics; in the poems of the early forties, the dehumanizing forces of war and ways to escape or recover from these through dreams, mythologizing, or Christian faith; in the poems of the fifties, and continuing into the sixties, loneliness and fear of aging and death, again opposed by the imagination in dreams and works of art; and in some of the last poems, the defeat of Necessity and time through imaginative recovery of one's own past."

One of Jarrell's favorite themes was war. Hayden Carruth wrote in *Nation* that out of "a considerable bulk of poetry . . . the war poems make a distinct, superior unit." According to Carruth, World War II (in which Jarrell, too old to serve as a combat pilot, served as a pilot instructor) left a dark psychological imprint on his poetry. Carruth noted the stylistic progression: "His early poems are sometimes mannered or imitative, and often artificially opaque; but from the first, he wrote with ease, and suffered none of the verbal embarrassment customary among young poets. When the war came he already possessed a developed poetic vocabulary and a mastery of forms. Under the shock of war his mannerisms fell away. He began to write with stark, compressed lucidity."

Vendler also believed that the war inspired Jarrell to find a new focus for his writing. She wrote in the *New York Times Book Review* that "his first steady poems date from his experience in the Air Force, when the pity that was his tutelary emotion, the pity that was to link him so irrevocably to Rilke, found a universal scope." Although "ordinarily he resisted any obvious political rhetoric," according to M. L. Rosenthal in his *Randall Jarrell,* the subject of war elicited a fervent emotional response from Jarrell, and his impassioned treatment won him an appreciative audience. Robert Weisberg echoed many critics when he wrote in the *New York Times Book Review* that Jarrell's poems "entered the spirit of the American soldier with . . . subtle empathy," noting that "perhaps his most famous piece of writing is a stark five-line lyric ['The Death of the Ball Turret Gunner'], the ultimate poem of war."

Vernon Scannell asserted that the war poem "Mail Call" was another example of a work in which Jarrell identified the military's "inescapable reduction of man to either animal or instrument by the calculated process of military training and by the uniformed civilian's enforced acceptance of the murderer's role, the cruel larceny of all sense of personal identity." To make his point on this subject about which he felt so strongly, Jarrell used powerful language. Jonathan Galassi noted in *Poetry Nation* that "the grisly irony reminds one of Auden, an inevitable influence on Jarrell's work of this period, but there is a horrible closeness to the event which Auden would not have ventured. Jarrell's best war poems . . . are . . . rich in dramatic tension, and grounded, as his best work always is, in vivid detail. His ubiquitous generalizations earn their significance from gorgeously terrible descriptions of carnage and fear."

Despite the impact of his images, some critics suggested that Jarrell lost force by making specific incidents serve a general rhetoric, in the kind of "ubiquitous generalizations" cited above. A *Times Literary Supplement* reviewer noted that in his war poetry Jarrell "seldom dealt with the carefully shaped, irreplaceable persons the world had lost. Instead, he wrote about the possible life the men had missed. This vanished futurity could hardly be concrete or particular, and the soldier therefore was too often a case rather than a person." J. C. Levenson agreed in the *Virginia Quarterly Review* that "The Death of the Ball Turret Gunner" "establishes the matter-of-factness of flak and fight more suc-

cessfully than it establishes its big generalization about airmen—and boys—as creatures of the State." Vendler defended Jarrell, writing in the *New York Times Book Review* that "it has been charged that Jarrell's poetry of the war shows no friends, only, in James Dickey's words, 'killable puppets'—but, Jarrell's soldiers are of course not his friends because they are his babies, his lambs to the slaughter—he broods over them." Scannell concluded that "there are moments in [Jarrell's] war poetry when the force of his passion results in confusion and overstatement but far more frequently it is directed and controlled through a technical assurance that has produced some of the most relentless indictments of the evil of war since [Siegfried] Sassoon and [Wilfred] Owen."

Even when he was not writing on war themes, Jarrell often viewed his characters with pity. Jerome Mazzaro noted the insecurity of his characters, writing in *Salmagundi* that "Jarrell's personae are always involved with efforts to escape engulfment, implosion, and petrification, by demanding that they somehow be miraculously changed by life and art into people whose ontologies are psychically secure." The passivity Mazzaro alludes to was frequently cited by other critics, often in reference to Jarrell's portrayals of women. Some critics felt that Jarrell held a particular compassion for women because he viewed them as being trapped by society; the poem "The Woman at the Washington Zoo" represents one often-cited example of this view. Jonathan Galassi wrote in *Poetry Nation* that "Jarrell's women, though conscious there is something wrong in their lives, are unable to define precisely or to respond creatively to their predicaments; they are merely witnesses to their victimization." Some critics objected to Jarrell's tone when he wrote about women. Rosenthal asserted that "there is at times a false current of sentimental condescension toward his subjects, especially when they are female." But more often than not, critics valued Jarrell's perspective, appreciating it for its uncommon compassion.

Jarrell's acute sense of involvement with other people permeated both his poetry and his criticism, according to Levenson. "Though his heart might go out to people as they are and things as they are, he had an ingrained drive to make them better. He could not help telling them to change a word, change a line, change their lives, but the demands he made came out of concern and not out of overbearing authority. No one doubted that. 'To Randall's friends,' writes Peter Taylor [in *Randall Jarrell, 1914-1965*], 'there was always the feeling that he was their teacher. To Randall's students, there was always the feeling that he was their friend.' "

BIOGRAPHICAL/CRITICAL SOURCES:

BOOKS

Children's Literature Review, Volume 6, Gale, 1984.

Concise Dictionary of American Literary Biography: The New Consciousness, 1941-1968, Gale, 1987.

Contemporary Authors Bibliography Series, Volume 2: *American Poets,* Gale, 1986.

Contemporary Literary Criticism, Gale, Volume 1, 1973, Volume 2, 1974, Volume 6, 1976, Volume 9, 1978, Volume 13, 1980, Volume 49, 1988.

Dictionary of Literary Biography, Gale, Volume 48: *American Poets, 1880-1945,* 1986, Volume 52: *American Writers for Children since 1960: Fiction,* 1986.

Ferguson, Suzanne, *The Poetry of Randall Jarrell,* Louisiana State University Press, 1971.

Hungerford, Edward, editor, *Poets in Progress,* Northwestern University Press, 1962, new edition, 1967.

Lowell, Robert, Peter Taylor, and Robert Penn Warren, editors, *Randall Jarrell: 1914-1965,* Farrar, Straus, 1967.

Nemerov, Howard, *Poetry and Fiction,* Rutgers University Press, 1963.

Quinn, Sister Bernetta, *Randall Jarrell,* Twayne, 1981.

Rosenthal, M. L., *Randall Jarrell,* University of Minnesota Press, 1972.

Scannell, Vernon, *Not Without Glory: Poets of the Second World War,* Woburn Press Ltd., 1976.

Shapiro, Karl, *Randall Jarrell,* Gertrude Clark Whittall Poetry and Literature Fund, Library of Congress, 1967.

Stepanchev, Stephen, *American Poetry since 1945,* Harper, 1965.

PERIODICALS

American Poetry Review, January/February, 1975.
Books Abroad, winter, 1971.
Book World, January 26, 1969.
Carleton Miscellany, winter, 1967.
Commentary, February, 1966.
Commonweal, April 18, 1969.
Harper's, April, 1967.
Listener, January 23, 1975.
Los Angeles Times, August 4, 1980.
Nation, July 7, 1969.
New Leader, December 8, 1969.
New York Review of Books, November 25, 1965, November 23, 1967.
New York Times, October 16, 1965, March 2, 1966, July 30, 1980.
New York Times Book Review, October 7, 1961, September 3, 1967, February 2, 1969, September 17, 1972.
Partisan Review, winter, 1967.
Poetry Nation, number 4, 1975.
Reporter, September 8, 1966.
Salmagundi, fall, 1971.
Time, September 15, 1967.
Times Literary Supplement, June 19, 1981.
Virginia Quarterly Review, spring, 1968.
Washington Post Book World, July 20, 1980.

*   *   *

JARVIS, E. K.
See ELLISON, Harlan and SILVERBERG, Robert

*   *   *

JEAKE, Samuel, Jr.
See AIKEN, Conrad (Potter)

*   *   *

JEAN-LOUIS
See KEROUAC, Jean-Louis Lebrid de

*   *   *

JEFFERS, (John) Robinson 1887-1962

PERSONAL: Born January 10, 1887, in Pittsburgh, Pa.; died January 20, 1962, in Carmel, Calif.; son of William Hamilton (a Presbyterian minister and professor) and Annie Robinson (Tuttle) Jeffers; married Una Call Kuster, August 2, 1913 (died, 1950); children: Donnan Call, Garth Sherwood (twins). *Education:* Attended University of Western Pennsylvania (now Uni-

versity of Pittsburgh), 1902-03; Occidental College, A.B., 1905; graduate study at University of Zurich, 1906-07; University of Southern California, Los Angeles, M.A., c. 1910; graduate study at University of Washington, 1910-11.

CAREER: Poet and playwright.

MEMBER: National Institute of Arts and Letters, American Academy of Arts and Letters, Authors League of America, Phi Beta Kappa, Sigma Chi, Nu Sigma Nu.

AWARDS, HONORS: D.Litt. from Occidental College, 1937; fellowship from Book-of-the-Month Club, 1937; L.H.D. from University of Southern California, 1939; Levinson Prize, 1940; Eunice Tietjens Memorial Prize, 1951; Union League Civic and Arts Foundation Prize, 1952; Pulitzer Prize, 1954, for *Hungerfield and Other Poems;* fellowship from Academy of American Poets, 1958; Shelley Memorial Award, 1961.

WRITINGS:

POETRY

Flagons and Apples, Grafton Publishing, 1912, reprinted, Cayucos Books, 1970.
Californians, Macmillan, 1916, reprinted, Cayucos Books, 1971.
Tamar and Other Poems, P. G. Boyle, 1924.
Roan Stallion, Tamar and Other Poems, Boni & Liveright, 1925.
The Women at Point Sur, Boni & Liveright, 1927, reprinted, Liveright, 1977.
Poems, The Book Club of California, 1928.
Cawdor and Other Poems, Liveright, 1928, reprinted with play *Medea,* New Directions, 1970.
Dear Judas and Other Poems, Liveright, 1929, reprinted, 1977.
Descent to the Dead: Poems Written in Ireland and Great Britain, Random House, 1931.
Thurso's Landing and Other Poems, Liveright, 1932.
Give Your Heart to the Hawks, and Other Poems, Random House, 1933.
Solstice and Other Poems, Random House, 1935.
Such Counsels You Gave to Me and Other Poems, Random House, 1937.
The Selected Poetry of Robinson Jeffers, Random House, 1938.
Be Angry at the Sun, Random House, 1941.
The Double Axe and Other Poems, Random House, 1948, reprinted, Liveright, 1977.
Hungerfield and Other Poems, Random House, 1954.
The Loving Shepherdess, Random House, 1956.
The Beginning and the End and Other Poems, Random House, 1963.
Selected Poems, Vintage Books, 1965.
The Alpine Christ and Other Poems, Cayucos Books, 1974.
Brides of the South Wind: Poems 1917-1922, Cayucos Books, 1974.
What Odd Expedients and Other Poems, edited by Robert I. Scott, Shoe String Press, 1981.
Rock and Hawk: A Selection of Shorter Poems by Robinson Jeffers, edited by Robert Hass, Random House, 1987.
The Collected Poetry of Robinson Jeffers, edited by Tim Hunt, Stanford University Press, Volume I: *1920-1928,* 1988, Volume II: *1928-1938,* 1989.

PLAYS

Medea (based on Euripides's play of the same name; first produced on Broadway in 1948), Random House, 1946, reprinted with *Cawdor,* New Directions, 1970.

"The Tower Beyond Tragedy" (based on Aeschylus's "Oresteia" and Jeffers's poem of the same name), first produced in 1950.
"The Cretan Woman" (based on Euripides' *Hippolytus*), first produced in 1954.

OTHER

Poetry, Gongorism, and a Thousand Years, Ritchie, 1949, reprinted, Folcroft, 1974.
Themes in My Poems, Book Club of California, 1956.
Ann N. Ridgeway, editor, *The Selected Letters of Robinson Jeffers, 1897-1962,* Johns Hopkins Press, 1968.
The Last Conservative, Quintessence, 1978.
Songs and Heroes, introduction by Robert J. Brophy, Arundel Press, 1988.

SIDELIGHTS: Although Robinson Jeffers did graduate work in both forestry and medicine, his real ambition was to be a poet. A legacy from an uncle enabled him to devote himself to his chosen vocation. After he received his inheritance, Jeffers moved with his wife to Carmel, California, where he built with his own hands a granite house and an observation tower. As he worked in his isolated stone tower, Jeffers could view the ocean and the mountains. This vista was to pervade nearly all the poetry that he produced. "Mr. Jeffers is . . . much admired by Californians for the beauty of his California landscape-painting," James G. Southworth pointed out. "What Wordsworth has done for the Lake District, Frost for New England, Shelley for the Italian sky, he, they feel, has done for California, particularly for the Monterey coastal mountain region."

Nature not only serves as a backdrop for Jeffers's verse; animals and natural objects are frequently compared to man, with man shown to be the inferior. "There is not one memorable person," Jeffers wrote in "Contrast," "there is not one mind to stand with the trees, one life with the mountains." Jeffers preferred nature to man because he felt that the human race was too introverted, that it failed to recognize the significance of other creatures and things in the universe. He termed his philosophy "inhumanism," which he explained was "a shifting of emphasis from man to not man; the rejection of human solipsism and recognition of the transhuman magnificence. . . . It offers a reasonable detachment as a rule of conduct, instead of love, hate, and envy." Humanity had been spurned by an uncaring God, Jeffers believed, so each individual should rid himself of emotion and embrace an indifferent, nonhuman god.

To develop his philosophy of inhumanism, Jeffers drew on the ideas of others. Radcliffe Squires argued that Schopenhauer's philosophy had the biggest impact on Jeffers's thinking. He stated that "the essential concern in Schopenhauer, the relation of matter and idea, is an essential concern in Jeffers" and held that both men came to the same conclusion: "that there exists a superior reality behind appearance, a reality that is discoverable, though not easily so." Arthur B. Coffin refuted this thesis, maintaining that Nietzsche and Lucretius were Jeffers's primary influences: "Robinson Jeffers used the various concepts of Nietzsche's philosophy to clear away outworn intellectual traditions and religious preconceptions in order to develop his own doctrine of Inhumanism. That Nietzscheanism was a useful—though sometimes limited—tool for Jeffers is now obvious. That his Lucretian-derived Inhumanism and its insistence upon transhuman magnificence flourished from inception is equally clear." Ample evidence has been provided to show that the works of such cyclical historicists as Giambattista Vico, Oswald Spengler, and Flinders Petrie also had an effect on Jeffers's work.

Jeffers's pessimistic outlook was reinforced by his reading of Greek tragedy. As a child, Jeffers had been tutored by his father, a theologian and scholar, who familiarized him with ancient Greek and Biblical tales. Many of these tales are used in Jeffers's poetry. "Solstice," for example, is a retelling of the Medea legend set on the California coast, and "Tamar" is based on an Old Testament story. Many commentators feel that Jeffers misunderstood the nature of Greek tragedy. Kenneth Rexroth complained that Jeffers's "reworking of the plots of Greek tragedy make[s] me shudder at their vulgarity, the coarsening of sensibility, the cheapening of the language and the tawdriness of the paltry insight into the great ancient meanings." Frederic I. Carpenter observed that there are contradictions between Jeffers's inhumanism and his use of tragedy: "The ideal Inhumanist . . . symbolically exorcises the human emotions of pity and terror, and this preserves him from reinvolvement in the tragic drama of history. But this exorcism seems to deny the efficacy and value of tragedy itself. For tragedy seeks not to destroy the emotions of pity and terror but to transmute and sublimate them."

In contrast, Robert Boyers felt that Jeffers did indeed achieve a tragic vision: "What is unmistakable . . . is the poet's steadfast refusal to counsel violence among men and his ability to achieve a perspective wherein the violence men would and did commit could be made tolerable, in a way even absorbed into the universe as an element of necessity. It is nothing less than a tragic vision; and if Jeffers in his poetry could not sufficiently examine and evoke the large potentialities of man within his limitations, as could a Shakespeare and a Yeats, he did at least project a vision worthy of our attention and capable of giving pleasure."

Certain motifs and symbols recur in Jeffers's poetry and serve to underline his belief in inhumanism. The incest motif prevalent in many of his poems emphasizes the danger of man's introversion. Hyatt H. Waggoner explained: "To love one's own kind is in effect to love within the human family, hence incestuous. Incest leads to perversions, mass murder, and finally to nameless and all-pervasive horrors like those in a nightmare that are at once real and indefinable." To avoid the dangers of incest, Jeffers felt that humans should develop the qualities symbolized by the hawk and the rock. For him the hawk and the rock represented "bright power, dark peace;/ Fierce consciousness joined with final/ Disinterestedness."

Jeffers was not noted for his technical ingenuity, but he did develop a style that meshed with his philosophy. Boyers held that there were no paradoxes in Jeffers's "mature vision, so finely wrought, no telling nuances to qualify the poet's commitment; but everything is precisely placed, distributed its proper weight, and there are elements of style so subtly woven into the poem's basic structure that they largely escape observation." Louis Untermeyer praised Jeffers for his "gift of biting language and the ability to communicate the phantasmagoria of terror," while Selden Rodman noted that Jeffers wrote his poetry "with a one-dimensional straightforwardness that is almost Homeric. And the similes he uses, if not Homeric, are as primitively American as the flintlock and the Maypole."

Jeffers's favorite genre was the narrative poem, and exegesis has tended to center on his long, philosophic-dramatic poems. Some critics think that more attention should be paid to his shorter poems. Boyers acknowledged that none of Jeffers's long narratives succeed but felt that the shorter poems reveal Jeffers at his best, and thus deserve reexamination. The conflict that existed between Jeffers's commitment to inhumanism and his commitment to narrative realism interested John R. Alexander. "The doctrine of Inhumanism clearly advocates a rejection of all that can be considered human, while narrative realism by definition prescribes detailed attention to it," Alexander wrote.

Many readers have found Jeffers's philosophy, and consequently his poetry, repugnant. Rexroth echoed the opinions of others when he wrote of Jeffers: "His philosophy I find a mass of contradictions—high-flown statements indulged in for their melodrama alone, and often essentially meaningless. The constantly repeated gospel that it is better to be a rock than a man is simply an unscrupulous use of language." Untermeyer, however, cautioned readers that when approaching Jeffers's verse they must "separate the idea and its expression, remembering that the poem transcends the experience and the personality that prompted it. Between Jeffers the philosopher and Jeffers the poet there is a significant dichotomy. The philosophy is negative, repetitive, dismal. The poetry, even when bitterest, is positive as any creative expression must be."

Even those who are most bitterly opposed to Jeffers's ideology grant that he holds a unique place in modern American literature. James Dickey observed that Jeffers "fills a position in this country that would simply have been an empty gap without him: that of the poet as prophet, as large-scale philosopher, as doctrine-giver." Jeffers derived his belief that the poet should be a seer from Shelley, who held that poets are "the unacknowledged legislators of the world." Although one may dislike Jeffers's jeremiads, many of the terrors that he envisioned came true. "The vision of violence which he [Jeffers] first described in the 1920's has become the obsession of the 1960's," Carpenter declared. "His realization of the absolute absurdity of the historic idealism which would make the world safe for democracy by inventing the bomb which would destroy the world, was prophetic in every sense. His repeated warnings that violence is intrinsic in history, and that this unpleasant fact must be faced, rather than repressed, was prophetic."

Jeffers's last book, aptly entitled *The Beginning and the End*, deals with many of the themes that had concerned him throughout his lifetime. The poems in this volume use such contemporary issues as the population explosion and the Cold War to support Jeffers's long-established opinions. When *The Beginning and the End* was published in 1963, a year after Jeffers's death, some critics felt that it would bolster his sagging reputation. "On its own merits and altogether apart from any pious atonement for the undeserved neglect he has suffered in his late years, this most modest of all his works should do much to make clear how remarkable his accomplishment was," Samuel French Morse stated. Joseph Bennet suggested that on the basis of *The Beginning and the End* "Jeffers' reputation might be in for a renaissance." Recently there has been a renewal of interest in Jeffers's work, but he still has both his ardent admirers and vehement detractors. The debate as to the nature and value of his achievement will probably continue for many years to come.

Some of Jeffers's work has been translated into Italian, German, Danish, and several Slavic languages.

AVOCATIONAL INTERESTS: Stone masonry, swimming, walking.

BIOGRAPHICAL/CRITICAL SOURCES:

BOOKS

Bennett, Melba Berry, *Robinson Jeffers and the Sea*, Gelber, Lilienthal, 1936, Norwood, 1976.
Bennett, Melba Berry, *The Stone Mason of Tor House: The Life and Work of Robinson Jeffers*, Ward Ritchie, 1966.

Brophy, Robert J., *Robinson Jeffers: Myth, Ritual and Symbol in His Narrative Poems*, Press of Case Western Reserve, 1973.
Carpenter, Frederic I., *Robinson Jeffers*, Twayne, 1962.
Carpenter, Frederic I., *The Twenties*, Everett/Edwards, 1966.
Coffin, Arthur B., *Robinson Jeffers: Poet of Inhumanism*, University of Wisconsin Press, 1971.
Concise Dictionary of Literary Biography: The Twenties, 1917-1929, Gale, 1989.
Contemporary Literary Criticism, Gale, Volume 2, 1974, Volume 3, 1975, Volume 11, 1979, Volume 15, 1981, Volume 54, 1989.
Dickey, James, *Babel to Byzantium*, Farrar, Straus, 1968.
Dictionary of Literary Biography, Volume 45: *American Poets, 1880-1945, First Series*, Gale, 1986.
Everson, William, *Robinson Jeffers: Fragments of an Older Fury*, Oyez, 1968.
Gilbert, Rudolph, *Shine, Perishing Republic: Robinson Jeffers and the Tragic Sense in Modern Poetry*, Haskell, 1936.
Gilbert, Rudolph, *Four Living Poets*, Unicorn Press, 1944.
Glicksberg, Charles I., *Modern Literary Perspectivism*, Southern Methodist University Press, 1970.
Jartell, Randall, *The Third Book of Criticism*, Farrar, Straus, 1969.
Kreymborg, Alfred, *Our Singing Strength*, Coward, 1929.
Littlejohn, David, *Interruptions*, Grossman, 1970.
Mazzaro, Jerome, editor, *Modern American Poetry: Essays in Criticism*, McKay, 1970.
Powell, Lawrence Clark, *Robinson Jeffers: The Man and His Work*, Primavera Press, 1934, revised edition, Haskell, 1940.
Ransom, John Crowe, editor, *Kenyan Critics*, World Publishing, 1951.
Rexroth, Kenneth, *Assays*, New Directions 1961.
Rosenthal, M. L., *The Modern Poets*, Oxford University Press, 1960.
Southworth, James G., *Some Modern American Poets*, Basil Blackwell, 1950.
Squires, Radcliffe, *The Loyalties of Robinson Jeffers*, University of Michigan Press, 1956.
Sterling, George, *Robinson Jeffers: The Man and the Artist*, Boni & Liveright, 1926.
Untermeyer, Louis, *Modern American Poetry*, Harcourt, 1950.
Van Wyck, William, *Robinson Jeffers*, Ward Ritchie, 1938.
Vardamis, Alex A., *Critical Reputation of Robinson Jeffers: A Bibliographical Study*, Shoe String Press, 1972.
Waggoner, Hyatt H., *American Poets From the Puritans to the Present*, Houghton, 1968.

PERIODICALS

Harvard Review, winter, 1963-64.
Poetry, July, 1954.
Saturday Review, January 16, 1954.
Sewanee Review, summer, 1969, winter, 1972.
Virginia Quarterly Review, summer, 1963.

*   *   *

JEFFERSON, Janet
See MENCKEN, H(enry) L(ouis)

*   *   *

JENNINGS, Elizabeth (Joan) 1926-

PERSONAL: Born July 18, 1926, in Boston, Lincolnshire, England; daughter of Henry Cecil Jennings (a physician). *Educa-*

tion: St. Anne's College, Oxford, M.A. (with honors). *Religion:* Roman Catholic.

ADDRESSES: Home—11 Winchester Rd., Oxford OX2 6NA, England. *Agent*—David Higham Associates Ltd., 5-8 Lower John St., Golden Square, London W1R 4HA, England.

CAREER: Oxford City Library, Oxford, England, assistant, 1950-58; Chatto & Windus (publishing firm), London, England, reader, 1958-60; poet and free-lance writer, 1961—. Guildersleeve Lecturer, Barnard College, Columbia University, 1974.

MEMBER: Society of Authors.

AWARDS, HONORS: Arts Council award, 1953, for *Poems;* Somerset Maugham Award, 1956, for *A Way of Looking;* Arts Council bursary, 1965 and 1968; Richard Hillary Memorial Prize, 1966, for *The Mind Has Mountains;* Arts Council grant, 1972; W. H. Smith award, 1987, for *Collected Poems.*

WRITINGS:

Poems, Fantasy Press, 1953.
A Way of Looking: Poems, Deutsch, 1955, Rinehart, 1956.
(Editor with Dannie Abse and Stephen Spender) *New Poems 1956: A P.E.N. Anthology,* M. Joseph, 1956.
A Child and the Seashell, Feathered Serpent Press, 1957.
(Editor) *The Batsford Book of Children's Verse,* Batsford, 1958.
A Sense of the World: Poems, Deutsch, 1958, Rinehart, 1959.
Let's Have Some Poetry!, Museum Press, 1960.
Song for a Birth or a Death and Other Poems, Deutsch, 1961, Dufour (Pennsylvania), 1962.
(Editor) *An Anthology of Modern Verse, 1940-60,* Methuen, 1961.
Every Changing Shape, Deutsch, 1961.
Poetry Today, Longmans, Green, 1961.
(Translator) *The Sonnets of Michaelangelo,* Folio Society, 1961, revised edition, Allison & Busby, 1969, Doubleday, 1970, reprinted, Carcanet Press, 1989.
(With Lawrence Durrell and R. S. Thomas) *Penguin Modern Poets I,* Penguin, 1962.
Recoveries: Poems, Dufour, 1964.
Frost, Oliver & Boyd, 1964, Barnes & Noble, 1965.
Christian Poetry, Hawthorn, 1965 (published in England as *Christianity and Poetry,* Burns & Oates, 1965).
The Mind Has Mountains, St. Martin's, 1966.
The Secret Brother and Other Poems for Children, St. Martin's, 1966.
Collected Poems, 1967, Dufour, 1967.
The Animals' Arrival, Dufour, 1969.
Lucidities, Macmillan, 1970.
(Editor) *A Choice of Christina Rossetti's Verse,* Faber, 1970.
Hurt, Poem-of-the-Month Club, 1970.
(With others) *Folio,* Sceptre Press, 1971.
Relationships, Macmillan, 1972.
Growing Points: New Poems, (poems), Carcanet Press, 1975.
Seven Men of Vision: An Appreciation (literary criticism), Harper, 1977.
Consequently I Rejoice (poems), Carcanet Press, 1977.
After the Ark (children's poems), Oxford University Press, 1978.
Winter Wind (poems), Janus Press, 1979.
A Dream of Spring (poems), Celandine, 1980.
Selected Poems, Carcanet Press, 1980.
Moments of Grace (poems), Carcanet Press, 1980.
Italian Light and Other Poems, Snake River Press, 1981.
(Editor) *The Batsford Book of Religious Verse,* Batsford, 1981.
Celebrations and Elegies (poems), Carcanet Press, 1982.
(Editor) *In Praise of Our Lady,* Batsford, 1982.

Extending the Territory (poems), Carcanet Press, 1985.
In Shakespeare's Company, Celandine, 1985.
(With others) *Poets in Hand: A Puffin Quintet,* Penguin, 1985.
Collected Poems, 1953-86, Carcanet Press, 1986.
Tributes (poems), Carcanet, 1989.

Contributor of poems and articles to numerous periodicals, including *Agenda, London Magazine, Poetry Review, New Yorker, Scotsman, Vogue,* and *Encounter.*

SIDELIGHTS: Poet Elizabeth Jennings established her literary reputation during the 1950s as part of The Movement, a group of "angry young men" including such writers as Kingsley Amis, Thom Gunn, and Philip Larkin, who used literature as a means of social protest. Jennings "brought the 'sensitive' dimension to the no-nonsense Movement," Alan Brownjohn writes in the *New Statesman.* "Her work was . . . memorable in its quiet, unstrained way." Since then, Brownjohn notes, Jennings has "impressively increased the scope and richness, and the technical variety and command, of her writing."

Jennings has increasingly turned to religious themes in her verse; her "best and natural state is contemplation, and the poems tend to be about the debits and credits of the contemplative attitude," P. N. Furbank points out in a *Listener* review of *Recoveries.* In a review of *Moments of Grace* for *Listener,* Dick Davis finds that Jennings's title refers to the "intimations of a peace glimpsed beyond the fret and frustration of daily existence." "The poet herself," Davis adds, "seems suspended" between the natural and spiritual worlds. Andrew Motion of *New Statesman* finds that "although [Jennings] has always produced excellently-crafted poems, she has also tended to reduce their lyric force by including ruminatively philosophical material," while a *Books and Bookmen* reviewer of *Selected Poems* praises Jennings's attempt to "balance the mental and emotional demands of the priest and poet." And in *Spectator,* Emma Fisher asserts that Jennings is "looking earnestly" for moments of grace, "carefully examining pieces of life as if waiting for them to break open in revelations."

Jennings's manuscripts are in the collections of the Oxford City Library and the University of Washington, Seattle, and Georgetown University Library, Washington, D.C.

AVOCATIONAL INTERESTS: Travel, art, the theater, conversation.

BIOGRAPHICAL/CRITICAL SOURCES:

BOOKS

Contemporary Authors Autobiography Series, Volume 5, Gale, 1987.
Contemporary Literary Criticism, Gale, Volume 5, 1976, Volume 14, 1980.
Dictionary of Literary Biography, Volume 27: *Poets of Great Britain and Ireland, 1945-1960,* Gale, 1984.
Schmidt, Michael, and Grevel Lindop, editors, *British Poetry since 1960,* Carcanet Press, 1972.

PERIODICALS

Books and Bookmen, December, 1972, February, 1980.
Listener, July 23, 1964, January 31, 1980.
New Statesman, October 13, 1967, May 30, 1975, November 2, 1979.
Poetry, March, 1977.
Spectator, December 1, 1979.
Times (London), January 16, 1986, February 11, 1989.

Times Literary Supplement, December 30, 1977, February 1, 1980, July 16, 1982, May 30, 1986, November 28, 1986, May 5, 1989.

* * *

JHABVALA, Ruth Prawer 1927-

PERSONAL: Born May 7, 1927, in Cologne, Germany (now West Germany); came to England, 1939; naturalized British citizen, 1948; naturalized U.S. citizen, 1986; daughter of Marcus (owner of a clothing business) and Eleonora (Cohn) Prawer; married Cyrus S. H. Jhabvala (an architect), 1951; children: Renana, Ava, Firoza. *Education:* Queen Mary College, London, M.A., 1951.

ADDRESSES: Home and office—400 East 52nd St., New York, N.Y. 10022. *Agent*—Harriet Wasserman, 137 East 36th St., New York, N.Y. 10016.

CAREER: Full-time writer, 1951—.

AWARDS, HONORS: Booker Award for Fiction, National Book League, 1975, for *Heat and Dust;* Guggenheim fellow, 1976; Neil Gunn International fellow, 1979; MacArthur Foundation fellow, 1986-89; Writers Guild of America Award for best adapted screenplay, 1986, and Academy Award (Oscar) for best screenplay adapted from another medium, 1987, both for "A Room with a View"; D.Litt., London University.

WRITINGS:

FICTION

To Whom She Will, Allen & Unwin, 1955, reprinted, Penguin, 1985, published as *Amrita,* Norton, 1956, reprinted, Fireside Paperbacks, 1989.
The Nature of Passion, Allen & Unwin, 1956, Norton, 1957, reprinted, Penguin, 1986.
Esmond in India, Allen & Unwin, 1957, Norton, 1958, reprinted, Penguin, 1980.
The Householder (also see below), Norton, 1960, reprinted, 1985.
Get Ready for Battle, J. Murray, 1962, Norton, 1963, reprinted, Fireside Paperbacks, 1989.
Like Birds, Like Fishes and Other Stories, J. Murray, 1963, Norton, 1964, reprinted, Granada, 1984.
A Backward Place, Norton, 1965, reprinted, Penguin, 1980.
A Stronger Climate: Nine Stories, J. Murray, 1968, Norton, 1969, reprinted, Granada, 1983.
An Experience of India (stories), J. Murray, 1971, Norton, 1972.
A New Dominion, J. Murray, 1972, published as *Travelers,* Harper, 1973.
Heat and Dust (also see below), J. Murray, 1975, Harper, 1976.
How I Became a Holy Mother and Other Stories, J. Murray, 1975, Harper, 1976.
In Search of Love and Beauty, Morrow, 1983.
Out of India: Selected Stories, Morrow, 1986.
Three Continents, Morrow, 1987.

SCREENPLAYS

"The Householder" (based on her novel), Royal, 1963.
(With James Ivory) *Shakespeare Wallah* (produced by Merchant-Ivory Productions, 1966), Grove, 1973.
(With Ivory) "The Guru," Twentieth Century-Fox, 1968.
"Bombay Talkie," Merchant-Ivory Productions, 1970.
Autobiography of a Princess, Harper, 1975.
"Roseland," Merchant-Ivory Productions, 1977.
"Hullabaloo over Georgie and Bonnie's Pictures," Contemporary, 1978.

(With Ivory) "The Europeans" (based on the novel by Henry James), Levitt-Pickman, 1979.
"Jane Austen in Manhattan," Contemporary, 1980.
(With Ivory) "Quartet" (based on the novel by Jean Rhys), Lyric International/New World, 1981.
"Heat and Dust" (based on her novel), Merchant-Ivory Productions, 1983.
"The Bostonians" (based on the novel by James), Merchant-Ivory Productions, 1984.
"The Courtesans of Bombay," Channel 4, England/New Yorker Films, 1985.
"A Room with a View" (based on the novel by E. M. Forster), Merchant-Ivory Productions, 1986.
(With John Schlesinger) "Madame Sousatzka" (based on the novel by Bernice Rubens), Universal, 1988.

WORK IN PROGRESS: A screenplay adaptation of Evan S. Connell's *Mr. Bridge and Mrs. Bridge;* a novel.

SIDELIGHTS: Although Ruth Prawer Jhabvala has long been celebrated in Europe and India for her quality fiction and screenplays, it was not until she captured an Academy Award for her adaptation of "A Room with a View" that she began winning widespread attention in the United States for her work. As a German-born, British citizen living in India for over twenty years, and as a New Yorker for over a decade, Jhabvala brings a unique perspective to her novels and stories of East-West conflict. "With a cool, ironic eye and a feeling for social nuance," asserts Bernard Weinraub in a *New York Times Magazine* article, Jhabvala "[has] developed a series of themes—families battered by change in present-day India, the timeless European fascination with the subcontinent—that were probably both incomprehensible and inconsequential to readers who were not intrigued with India in the first place. And yet," continues the critic, "as Mrs. Jhabvala's work darkened and turned more melancholy, as her detachment grew chilling in her later work, critics began to notice that the writer's India had become as universal as Faulkner's Yoknapatawpha and Chekhov's czarist Russia." "Like Jane Austen," notes *Saturday Review* contributor Katha Pollitt, Jhabvala "treats satirically and intimately a world in which conventions are precisely defined and widely accepted, even by those who are most harmed by them."

Indeed, since the appearance of her first work in 1955, *Amrita* (published in England as *To Whom She Will*), Jhabvala has frequently been compared to the great English writer, due to her cutting portrayals of the foibles of the Indian middle-class. In *Amrita,* comments Nancy Wilson Ross in the *New York Herald Tribune Book Review,* Jhabvala "has written a fresh and witty novel about modern India. It is not necessary to know anything about the customs and habits of . . . New Delhi—the setting of Mrs. Jhabvala's lively comedy of manners—to enjoy her ironic social commentary." And in a *Times Literary Supplement* review of *A Backward Place,* one critic maintains that while Jhabvala "has not the sustained brilliance that Jane Austen often rises to . . . all the same her many excellent qualities are nearly all Austenish ones, and they make her a most interesting and satisfactory writer." "At least three British reviewers have compared her to Jane Austen," observes J. F. Muehl in his *Saturday Review* account of Jhabvala's debut novel, "and the comparison is not only just; it is inevitable."

Jhabvala's later fiction, while still set in India, has focused more on the differences and resultant conflicts between Eastern and Western cultures, and has led to comparison with the work of yet another great English novelist. Jhabvala's Booker Prize-winner *Heat and Dust,* for example, which *Washington Post*

Book World contributor calls "crafted with a technical skill as assured as it is unobtrusive," is, "because of its setting and its theme of Anglo-Indian relationships, reminiscent of E. M. Forster's great novel, *A Passage to India.*" The story of a young British woman who is journeying through India in imitation of her grandfather's first wife Olivia, *Heat and Dust* contains "social comedy . . . as funny and as sympathetic as it is in Mrs. Jhabvala's earlier novels, even though she has departed from her more usual theme of middle-class Indian life," states Brigid Allen in the *Times Literary Supplement.* The account presents the parallel experiences of the two women by moving between the journal of the elder and the story of the younger; Pearl K. Bell says in the *New York Times Book Review* that "Jhabvala moves nimbly between the two generations and the divergent points of time and sentiment." The critic elaborates: "Writing with austere emphatic economy, [Jhabvala] does not belabor the parallels between the two levels of narrative—at least not until the end. Like Forster, she renders the barriers of incomprehension and futility that persist between English and Indians with witty precision."

While *New York Review of Books* contributor Frank Kermode agrees that Jhabvala's "two narratives are quite subtly plaited, with magical chiming between the two," he believes that the author writes "impassively, almost incuriously," about her characters' failures. But Julian Barnes finds this distancing appropriate and deliberate, noting in the *New Statesman* that Jhabvala "offers no comment except through the subsequent experiences of the narrator, which gradually flow into a distorted, parallel version of Olivia's life." Barnes adds that "the two halves make up a stylish and gentle exploration of the theme of Anglo-Indian interpenetration, confirming Aziz's prophetic remarks in *A Passage to India* about the relationship between the two nations." Calling *Heat and Dust* "distinguished by a rapier wit and subtlety," Dorothy Rabinowitz likewise concludes in the *Saturday Review* that Jhabvala's novel "is, particularly in its delicate chartings of passion and of the growth of consciousness, a superb story, a gift to those who care for the novel, and to the art of fiction itself."

Although Jhabvala had been securing a name for herself as one of the foremost modern writers about India after the publication of *Heat and Dust,* she was finding it difficult both to remain in and write about her adopted country. Critics began observing an increasing amount of ambivalence toward India in Jhabvala's writing, a change evident in her retrospective collection of stories, *Out of India.* The *New York Times*'s Michiko Kakutani, for example, comments that "bit by bit, . . . the stories in 'Out of India' darken, grow denser and more ambiguous. In choosing narrative strategies that are increasingly ambitious," explains the reviewer, "Mrs. Jhabvala gradually moves beyond the tidy formulations of the comedy of manners, and a strain of melancholy also begins to creep into her writing."

Village Voice contributor Vivian Gornick similarly sees a sense of "oppressiveness" in Jhabvala's writing, and speculates that "Jhabvala is driven to separate herself from India." The critic believes that this need undermines the author's work: "That drive deprives her of empathy and, inevitably, it deprives her characters of full humanness." In contrast, Paul Gray claims in his *Time* review that the stories in *Out of India* "do not demystify India; they pay the place tributes of empathy and grace." "Reading [these stories] is like watching a scene through an exceptionally clear telescope," states Rumer Godden in the *New York Times Book Review.* This distance, however, "does not take away from the stories' sureness of touch," Godden continues. "They

have a beginning, middle and end, but fused so subtly we drift into them—and are immediately at home—and drift out again."

Jhabvala's most recent works, while eschewing the familiar Indian setting, still explore some of her usual themes, such as the search for spiritual fulfillment. *Three Continents,* for example, relates the story of 19-year-old twins Michael and Harriet Wishwell, heirs to a large fortune who are drawn to the promises of a trio of supposed spiritual philosophers. The twins become obsessed with the Rawul, his consort the Rani, and their "adopted son" Crishi, and turn over control of their lives and fortune to the swindlers. "In its geographical scope, its large and far-flung cast and its relentless scrutiny of both sexual and intellectual thralldom," maintains Laura Shapiro in *Newsweek, Three Continents* "is Jhabvala's most ambitious and impressive work." The *Los Angeles Times*'s Elaine Kendall similarly calls the novel "perhaps [Jhabvala's] most ambitious work," remarking that it "not only confronts these issues [from her previous work] directly but in a more contemporary context."

Despite these assessments of Jhabvala's novel as "ambitious," some critics fault the author for her narrative method. "The narrative belongs to Harriet," Nancy Wigston notes in the Toronto *Globe and Mail,* "and therein lies much of the frustration of the book. Harriet may not be a phony," the reviewer explains, "but she is somewhat of an airhead . . . [and] her insights are limited." Kendall likewise observes that "while the youth and naivete of the narrator help our credulity, ultimately we're left with an inescapable skepticism." "This is an intelligent but unsatisfactory novel," Anita Brookner asserts in the *Spectator,* "intelligent because the author is and cannot help but be so, unsatisfactory because the effort of staying inside Harriet's stupid head conveys a certain tedium." Victoria Glendinning, however, believes that Harriet's narration provides an added dimension: "One of the cleverest things about the writing is the way Ruth Prawer Jhabvala shows how on one level Harriet is aware of everything that is happening, while never admitting it to herself," as the critic writes in the London *Times. Three Continents,* she adds, "[is] a book full of urgent messages about the East and West, about the need to belong somewhere, and the sinister pressures of the modern world." "As a meditation on the twin themes of inheritance and family, 'Three Continents' is a significant achievement," comments *New York Times Book Review* contributor Peter Ackroyd, concluding that "as a guidebook to the inner recesses of idealism and desire it is undoubtedly a success."

While Jhabvala has been a consistent force on the literary scene, she is also a member of the longest producer-director-writer partnership in film history. Along with Ismail Merchant and James Ivory, Jhabvala has helped create numerous movies that, while not hits at the box office, have been praised by critics for their consistent literary quality. Although the author was initially reluctant to attempt screenplays, critic Yasmine Gooneratne thinks that the dramatic qualities necessary for films have always been present in Jhabvala's work. Writing in *World Literature Written in English,* Gooneratne states that the author's early novels have "the tight structure of stage plays, and even [contain] casts of characters. The process by which the comparative simplicities of satiric drama yield to the complexity of ironic fiction is hastened, it would appear, through her experience of working repeatedly within the narrow limits of a screenplay." The critic cites the film-like structure of *Heat and Dust* as an example, and adds that "despite the fact that Mrs. Jhabvala's increasing technical skill as a writer of screenplays has helped her to devise ways and means to make the cinema screen yield workable equivalents for her established fictional techniques, it is probable that her artistry as a fiction-writer still outstrips her achievement as a writer for film. So rapid has her development been, however," Gooneratne continues, "that this is unlikely to be the case for very long." This prediction has proved accurate, for recent Merchant-Ivory-Jhabvala productions have been popular as well as critical successes.

For example, about "The Bostonians," the 1984 adaptation of Henry James's novel, Vincent Canby of the *New York Times* remarks that "it's now apparent [that the trio has] enriched and refined their individual talents to the point where they have now made what must be one of their best films as well as one of the best adaptations of a major literary work ever to come onto the screen." The best—until Jhabvala and her collaborators produced the film that would earn the author an Oscar, 1986's "A Room with a View." Director Ivory and screenwriter Jhabvala "have taken E. M. Forster's 1908 novel and preserved its wit, irony and brilliant observation of character," states Lawrence O'Toole in *Maclean's*. "And they never allow its theme—the importance of choosing passion over propriety—to escape their grasp." Calling the trio's film "an exceptionally faithful, ebullient screen equivalent to a literary work that lesser talents would embalm," Canby notes that "maybe more important than anything else [in the film] is the narrative tone." He explains that Ivory and Jhabvala "have somehow found a voice for the film not unlike that of Forster, who tells the story of 'A Room with a View' with as much genuine concern as astonished amusement. That's quite an achievement." Audiences found the film entertaining as well, for "A Room with a View" became the most popular Merchant-Ivory-Jhabvala collaboration ever, setting house records at many theaters.

While she has been compared to several classic writers, Jhabvala has achieved a prominent literary standing with her consistently excellent work, and critics no longer need comparisons to describe its quality. "How does one know when one is in the grip of art, of a literary power?" asks Rabinowitz in the *New York Times Book Review*. "One feels, amongst other things, the force of personality behind the cadence of each line, the sensibility behind the twist of the syllable. One feels the texture of the unspoken, the very accents of a writer's reticence." Jhabvala, maintains the critic, "seems to come naturally by a good deal of that reticence." Godden similarly praises the author for her original voice: "Time has proved [her unique]; she has written [numerous works] . . . and I could wager there is not in any of them one shoddy line or unnecessary word, a standard few writers achieve. Each book," Godden continues, "has her hallmark of balance, subtlety, wry humor and beauty." And Weinraub, in assessing Jhabvala's reputation in the literary community, quotes the late novelist C. P. Snow: "Someone once said that the definition of the highest art is that one should feel that life is this and not otherwise. I do not know of a writer living who gives that feeling with more unqualified certainty than Mrs. Jhabvala."

BIOGRAPHICAL/CRITICAL SOURCES:

BOOKS

Contemporary Literary Criticism, Gale, Volume 4, 1975, Volume 8, 1978, Volume 29, 1984.

Gooneratne, Yasmine, *Silence, Exile, and Cunning: The Fiction of Ruth Prawer Jhabvala*, Orient Longman (New Delhi), 1983.

Pritchett, V. S., *The Tale Bearers: Literary Essays*, Random House, 1980.

Sucher, Laurie, *The Fiction of Ruth Prawer Jhabvala*, St. Martin's, 1988.

PERIODICALS

Globe and Mail (Toronto), July 26, 1986, October 17, 1987.
Los Angeles Times, November 9, 1983, September 4, 1987.
Maclean's, March 31, 1986.
Modern Fiction Studies, winter, 1984.
New Statesman, October 31, 1975, April 15, 1983.
Newsweek, April 19, 1976, March 10, 1986, August 24, 1987.
New York Herald Tribune Book Review, January 15, 1956.
New York Review of Books, July 15, 1976.
New York Times, August 30, 1973, July 19, 1983, September 15, 1983, August 2, 1984, August 5, 1984, March 7, 1986, May 17, 1986, July 5, 1986, August 6, 1987.
New York Times Book Review, January 15, 1956, February 2, 1969, July 8, 1973, April 4, 1976, June 12, 1983, May 25, 1986, August 23, 1987.
New York Times Magazine, September 11, 1983.
People, March 17, 1986, September 28, 1987.
Publishers Weekly, June 6, 1986.
Saturday Review, January 14, 1956, March 1, 1969, April 3, 1976, October 30, 1976.
Spectator, April 23, 1983, October 24, 1987.
Time, May 12, 1986, October 6, 1986.
Times (London), February 4, 1983, April 14, 1983, October 15, 1987.
Times Literary Supplement, May 20, 1965, November 7, 1975, April 15, 1983, April 24, 1987, November 13, 1987.
Twentieth Century Literature, July, 1969.
Village Voice, August 2, 1983, May 8, 1986, September 30, 1986.
Washington Post, October 7, 1983, September 22, 1984, April 5, 1986.
Washington Post Book World, September 12, 1976, September 18, 1983, May 25, 1986.
World Literature Written in English, April, 1978, November, 1979.

* * *

JIMENEZ (MANTECON), Juan Ramon 1881-1958 (Ramon Jimenez, Juan Jimenez Mantecon, Juan Ramon)

PERSONAL: Born December 24, 1881, in Moguer, Huelva, Spain; died May 29, 1958, in San Juan, P.R.; married Zenobia Camprubi Aymar, 1916 (deceased, 1956). *Education:* Studied painting and poetry at Universidad de Sevilla.

CAREER: Poet and educator. Protege of Spanish modernist poet Ruben Dario in Spain and lecturer in Spanish and French poetry, 1900-36; *Residencia de Estudiantes*, Madrid, Spain, resident editor, beginning 1912; lived in self-imposed exile after the outbreak of the Spanish civil war, beginning in 1936; traveled to Puerto Rico, Cuba, and the United States; lecturer in South America, 1948-49; faculty member, University of Puerto Rico, 1951-58.

AWARDS, HONORS: Nobel Prize for literature, 1956.

WRITINGS:

Almas de violeta (title means "Purple Souls"), [Madrid], 1900.
Ninfeas (title means "Water Lilies"), [Madrid], 1900.
Rimas, [Madrid], 1902, reprinted, Taurus, 1981.
Arias tristes, [Madrid], 1903, reprinted, Taurus, 1981.
Jardines lejanos, [Madrid], 1904, reprinted, Taurus, 1982.
Elejias puras (also see below), [Madrid], 1908, edited with prologue by Francisco Garfias, Losada (Buenos Aires), 1964.
Elejias intermedias (also see below), [Madrid], 1908.

Olvidanzas I: Las hojas verdes 1906, [Madrid], 1909, enlarged edition published as *Olvidanzas (1906-1907),* edited by Garfias, Aguilar, 1968.

Elejias lamentables (also see below), [Madrid], 1910.

Baladas de primavera, [Madrid], 1910, enlarged edition published as *Baladas de primavera (1907),* edited by Garfias, Losada, 1964, published with *Las hojas verdes (1906),* Taurus, 1982.

La soledad sonora, [Madrid], 1911, reprinted, Taurus, 1981.

Poemas majicos y dolientes, [Madrid], 1911, enlarged edition edited by Garfias, Losada, 1965.

Pastorales, [Madrid], 1911, enlarged edition edited by Garfias, Losada, 1965, new enlarged edition edited by A. Campoamor and R. Gullon, Taurus, 1982.

Melancolia, [Madrid], 1912, reprinted, Taurus, 1981.

Laberinto, [Madrid], 1913, reprinted, Taurus, 1982.

Platero y yo (also see below), partial edition, [Madrid], 1914, reprinted as *Platero y yo, elegia andaluza,* Losada, 1940, first complete edition, Calleja, 1917, reprinted as *Platero y yo; elegia andaluza, 1907-1916,* with fifty illustrations by Rafael Alvarez Ortega, Aguilar, 1953, published with a new introduction by the author and illustrations by Baltasar Lobo, Librairie des Editions Espagnoles, 1953, translation by William and Mary Roberts published as *Platero and I: An Andalusian Elegy,* with illustrations by Lobo, P.C. Duchenes (New York), 1956, reprinted, Paragon House, 1986.

Estio (also see below), Calleja, 1915, published as *Estio: A punta de espina,* Losada, 1959, reprinted, Taurus, 1982.

Diario de un poeta recien casado (title means "Diary of a Newly Married Poet"; also see below), [Madrid], 1916, enlarged edition edited by Sanchez Barbudo, Labor (Barcelona), 1970, reprinted, Taurus, 1982, published as *Diario de poeta y mar,* A. Aguado (Madrid), 1955, 3rd edition, Losada, 1972.

Sonetos espirituales (also see below), Calleja, 1917, reprinted, Taurus, 1982, published as *Sonetos espirituales (1914-1915),* A. Aguado, 1957, 3rd edition, Losada, 1970.

Obras de Juan Ramon Jimenez, Calleja (Madrid), 1917.

Poesias escojidas (1899-1917) de Juan Ramon Jimenez, Hispanic Society of America (New York), 1917.

Eternidades, verso 1916-1917 (also see below), [Madrid], 1918, reprinted, Losada, 1944, new edition, Taurus, 1982, published as *Obras: Eternidades, verso (1916-1917),* Renacimiento, 1931.

Piedra y cielo (also see below), [Madrid], 1919, published as *Piedra y cielo, 1917-1918,* Losada, 1948, reprinted, Taurus, 1981.

Antolojia poetica, Losada, 1922, reprinted, 1966.

Segunda antolojia poetica, [Madrid-Barcelona], 1922, published as *Segundo antologia poetica 1898-1918,* Espasa-Calpe (Madrid), 1956, reprinted, 1976.

Poesias escojidas, [Mexico], 1923.

Poesia en verso, privately printed (Madrid), 1923, reprinted, Taurus, 1981.

Belleza (also see below), privately printed (Madrid), 1923, reprinted, Taurus, 1981.

Poesias de Juan Ramon Jimenez, compiled by Pedro Henriquez Urena, Mexico Moderno, 1923.

Unidad (eight notebooks; also see below), [Madrid], 1925.

Poesia en prosa y verso (also see below), edited by his children and Z. C. Aymar, Signo, 1932, 2nd edition, 1933, reprinted, Aguilar, 1962.

Sucesion (also see below), [Madrid], 1932.

Presente (also see below), [Madrid], 1933.

Juan Ramon Jimenez: Cancion, Signo, 1936, reprinted as *Cancion,* with introduction by Agustin Caballero, Aguilar, 1961.

(Editor) *La poesia cubana en 1936,* Institucion Hispanocubana de Cultura, 1937.

Ciego ante ciegos (poems), Publicaciones de la Secretaria de Educacion, Direccion de Cultura (Cuba), 1938.

Espanoles de tres mundos, viejo mundo, nuevo mundo, otro mundo: Caricatura lirica, 1914-1940 (poetry), Losada, 1942, reprinted, 1958, edited by Gullon, A. Aguado, 1960.

Voces de mi copla, Editorial Stylo, 1945, reprinted, Molinas de Agua, c. 1980, published with *Romances de Coral Gables,* Taurus, 1981.

La estacion total (poetry; title means "The Total Season"; also see below), [Buenos Aires], 1946.

El zaratan, with etchings by Alberto Beltran, Antigua Libreria Robredo, 1946, commemorative edition published with illustrations by Gregorio Prieto, Direccion General de Archivos y Biblioteca, 1957.

Animal de fondo (poetry; title means "Animal of Depth"; also see below), [Buenos Aires], 1947, published with French translations by Galtier, Editorial Pleamar, 1949.

Romances de Coral Gables (1939-1942), Editorial Stylo (Mexico), 1948, reprinted as *La Florida en Juan Ramon Jimenez,* edited by Ana Rosa Nunez, 1968.

Fifty Spanish Poems, with English translations by J. B. Trend, Dolphin Book Co. (England), 1950, University of California Press, 1951.

Antologia para ninos y adolescentes, selected by Norah Borges and Guillermo de Torre, Losada, 1951.

Tres poemas: De "Dios deseado y deseante" (poems; title means "God Desired and Desiring"; also see below), Santander, 1953.

Los mejores versos de Juan Ramon Jimenez, [Buenos Aires], 1956.

Platero es pequeno, peludo, suave (excerpts from *Platero y yo*), Talleres Grafico Octavio y Felez, 1956.

Libros de poesia: Sonetos spirituales, Estio, Diario de un poeta recien casado, Eternidades, Piedra y cielo, Belleza, Poesia, La estacion total, Animal de fondo, edited with foreword by Caballero, Aguilar, 1957.

Tercera antolojia poetica (1898-1953), Editorial Biblioteca Nueva, 1957, reprinted, 1971.

Antologia poetica (1898-1953) edited by Eugenio Florit, 1957, reprinted, Biblioteca Nueva, 1981, translation by H. R. Hays published as *Selected Writings,* Farrar, Straus and Cudahy, 1957.

Homenaje de la Revista la torre, University of Puerto Rico, 1957.

La estacion total con las canciones de la nueva luz, 1923-1936, Losada, 1958.

Pajinas escojidas, prosa, compiled by Gullon, Editorial Gredos, (Madrid), 1958.

Pajinas escojidas, verso, compiled by Gullon, Editorial Gredos, 1958.

Moguer, illustrations by Jose R. Escassi, Direccion General de Archivos y Bibliotecas, 1958.

El romance, rio de la lengua espanola, Universidad de Puerto Rico, 1959.

Primeros libros de poesia, compiled by Garfias, Aguilar, 1959.

Cuadernos (includes *Sucesion,* "Obra en marcha," *Unidad, Presente* and *Hojas*) edited by Garfias, Taurus, 1960.

Olvidos de Granada, 1924-1928, Universidad de Puerto Rico, 1960, facsimile edition, Gaballo Griego para la Poesia, 1979.

La corriente infinita; critica y evocacion, edited by Garfias, Aguilar, 1961.

Relaciones amistosas y literarias entre Juan Ramon Jimenez y los Martinez Sierra, compiled by Gullon, Ediciones de la Torre, 1961.

Por el cristal amarillo (also see below), compiled by Garfias, Aguilar, 1961.

El trabajo gustoso (lectures), compiled by Garfias, Aguilar, 1961.

Primeras prosas (also see below), compiled by Garfias, Aguilar, 1962.

El modernismo, edited by Gullon and E. F. Mendez, Aguilar, 1962.

Three Hundred Poems, 1903-1953, translations by Eloise Roach, University of Texas Press, 1962, published with poems in original Spanish as *Trecientos poemas,* Plaza & Janes, 1963, published with *Platero y yo,* Editorial Porrua (Mexico), 1968.

Sevilla, edited by Garfias, [Sevilla], 1963.

La colina de los chopos (also see below), Circulo de Lectores, 1963, 2nd edition published as *La colina de los chopos: Madrid posible e imposible,* edited by Garfias, Taurus, 1971.

Poemas revividos del tiempo de Moguer, Ediciones Chapultepec, 1963.

Dios deseado y deseante: Animal de Fondo con numerosos poemas ineditos, with introduction and notes by A. Sanchez Barbudo, Aguilar, 1964, translation by Antonio T. de Nicolas published as *God Desired and Desiring,* Paragon House, 1987.

Libros ineditos de poesia (two volumes), compiled by Garfias, Aguilar, 1964-67.

Retratos liricos, R. Diaz-Casariego, 1965.

Antologia poetica, edited by Vicente Gaos, Anaya (Salamanca), 1965, 10th edition, Catedra, 1984.

Estetica y etica estetica, critica y complemento, edited by Garfias, Aguilar, 1967.

Libros de prosa, (includes *Primeras prosas, Platero y yo, La colina de los chopos,* and *Por el cristal amarillo*), Aguilar, 1969.

Nueva antolojia poetica, Losada, 1969.

Fuego y sentimiento, 1918-1920, Artes Graficas L. Perez, 1969.

Juan Ramon y yo y Rios que se van, selections by wife Zenobia Camprubi Jimenez, Graficas L. Perez, 1971.

Ellos, de mi propia sangre, 1918-1920, [Madrid], 1973.

Death of Death: Poems, translations by Renato J. Gonzalez, P. Lal (Calcutta, India), c. 1973.

Con el carbon del sol; antologia de prosa lirica, edited by Garfias, EMESA, 1973.

Antologia, compiled by A. Gonzalez, Jucar, 1974, 3rd edition, EMESA, 1979.

En el otro costado, compiled by Aurora de Albornoz, Ediciones Jucar, 1974.

El andarin de su orbita: Seleccion de prosa critica, edited by Garfias, EMESA, 1974.

Critica paralela, selections and commentary by Arturo del Villar, Narcea de Ediciones, 1975.

La obra desnuda, edited by del Villar, Aldebaran, 1976, translation by Dennis Maloney published as *The Naked Book! An Illustrated Poem of Juan Ramon Jimenez,* White Pine, 1984, 2nd edition published as *Naked Music: Poems of Juan Ramon Jimenez.*

Leyenda 1896-1958, edited by A. Sanchez Romeralo, CUSPA, 1978.

Don't Run: A Poem of Juan Ramon Jimenez, translations by Maloney, White Pine, 1980.

Edicion del centenario: Juan Ramon Jimenez, twenty volumes, Taurus, 1981-82.

Prosas criticas, compiled by P. Gomez Bedate, Taurus, 1981.

Canta pajaro lejano, Espasa-Calpe, 1981.

Thirty-Five Poemas del Mar, compiled by L. Jimenez Martos, Rialp, 1981.

Antolojia jeneral en prosa (1898-1954), edited by Crespo and Gomez Bedate, Biblioteca Nueva, 1981.

Baladas de amor: Seleccion de baladas para despues y Odas liricas, Aro Artes Graficas, 1981.

Juan Ramon Jimenez en Cuba, compiled by Cintio Vitier, Editorial Arte y Literatura, 1981.

Isla de la simpatia, Ediciones Huracan, 1981.

Poesia: Juan Ramon Jimenez, compiled by Emilio de Armas, Editorial Arte y Literatura, 1982.

Politica poetica, Alianza, 1982.

Poesias ultimas escojidas (1918-1958), edited by Sanchez Romeralo, Espasa-Calpe, 1982.

Elegias (includes *Elejias puras, Elejias intermedias,* and *Elejias lamentables*), edited by Garfias, Taurus, 1982.

Espacio (also see below), edited by Albornoz, Editorial Nacional, 1982.

Flower Scene, translations by J. C. R. Green, Aquila, 1982.

Juan Ramon Jimenez: Antologia poetica, compiled by German Bleiberg, Alianza, 1983.

Alerta (essays), compiled by F. Javier Blasco, Universidad de Salamanca, 1983.

La realidad invisible, Tamesis, 1983, translation by de Nicolas published as *Invisible Reality,* Pergamon, 1986.

Guerra en Espana, 1936-1953 (autobiography), edited by A. Crespo, Seix Barral, 1985.

Juan Ramon Jimenez para ninos, Ediciones de la Torre, 1985.

Stories of Life and Death, translation by de Nicolas, Paragon House, 1986.

Tiempo y espacio, edited by Villar, 1986, translation by de Nicolas published as *Time and Space: A Poetic Autobiography,* Paragon House, 1988.

Hijo de la alegria, El Observatorio, 1986.

Antologia comentada, compiled by Sanchez Barbudo, Ediciones de la Torre, 1986.

Light and Shadows: Selected Poems and Prose, translations by R. Bly and others, edited by Maloney, White Pine, 1987.

LETTERS

The Literary Collaboration and the Personal Correspondence of Ruben Dario and Juan Ramon Jimenez, edited by Donald F. Fogelquist, University of Miami Press, 1956.

Monumento de amor: Cartas de Zenobia Camprubi y Juan Ramon Jimenez, foreword by Gullon, Ediciones de la Torre, 1959.

Cartas de Antonio Machado a Juan Ramon Jimenez, Ediciones de la Torre, 1959.

Cartas; primera seleccion, compiled by Garfias, Aguilar, 1962.

Seleccion de cartas, 1899-1958, Ediciones Picazo, 1973.

Cartas literarias, Bruguera, 1977.

Cartas de Juan Ramon Jimenez al poeta malagueno Jose Sanchez Rodriguez, edited by A. Sanchez Trigueros, Editorial Don Quijote, 1984.

TRANSLATOR

Romain Rolland, *Vida de Beethoven,* [Madrid], 1915.

(With Aymar) John M. Synge, *Jinetes hacia el mar,* [Madrid], 1920.

(With Aymar) Rabindranath Tagore, *El cartero del rey; La luna nueva,* Losada, 1922, 10th edition, 1972.

(With Aymar) Tagore, *Verso y prosa para ninos,* [Puerto Rico], 1936, 3rd edition, Editorial Orion, 1956, reprinted, 1976.

(With Aymar) Tagore, *El naufrajio* (title means "The Wreck"), Editorial Magisterio Espanol, 1974.

OTHER

Also author of *Aristocracia y democracia,* University of Miami, and *Poesia de siempre: Poemas,* Horizonte (Medellin). Works represented in numerous anthologies of Spanish poetry, such as *Antonio Machado, Juan Ramon Jimenez, Federico Garcia Lorca,* edited by Aitana and Rafael Alberti, Ediciones Nauta, 1970. Contributor to newspapers and literary journals in Huelva, Seville, and Madrid, including *Helios, Indice, Espana, El Sol,* and *La Gaceta Literaria.*

SIDELIGHTS: Juan Ramon Jimenez is considered one of the best and most influential of Spanish poets. His early lyric poetry impressed the major modernist poets of his culture who enlisted him in their attempt to revitalize Spanish poetry. Accomplished in the poetic tradition he inherited, Jimenez went on to develop a new poetics that expanded the frontiers of Spanish literature. Critics divide his works into three periods or stages according to changes in his style. Works from the first period showed the influence of his modernist peers; in the second period he developed the personal aesthetic that became a spiritual discipline in the third. "In a nation where art is often associated with a kind of willful roughness, Jimenez will be remembered always for certain exceptionally 'perfect' compositions," Claudio Guillen noted in a *New Republic* review. *Platero y yo,* a collection of prose poems that record a man's conversations with his donkey, was tremendously popular during the author's lifetime and is still being enjoyed by children and adults around the world. His works have been translated into English, French, German, Italian, Swedish, Welsh, Finnish, Portuguese, Romanian, and the language of the East Indian people of Orissa. His achievement was rewarded by the Nobel Prize in 1956.

Jimenez was born in 1881 to a wealthy couple who lived in Moguer near Huelva on the southwestern coast of Spain. He studied at a Jesuit school and though he was often ill, he enjoyed life and took an early interest in literature. He was not yet twenty when his poems first appeared in literary journals in Huelva, Seville, and Madrid. These melodious lyrics are richly embellished with images of the natural beauty of the land near his family home. For Jimenez, the contemplation of natural beauty led to moments of epiphany, moments in which he experienced communion with God. Like the Greek philosopher Plato, Jimenez believed that every physical object is a copy of a pre-existing, conceptual prototype that exists in the world of ideas. As he caught glimpses of this perfect world in nature or art, the poet would experience "a flash of comprehension, a moment of ecstatic oneness with some natural beauty, a wave of emotion disclosing the essence of some thing," Walter T. Pattison wrote in *Hispania.* The beautiful or beloved objects, however, were subject to change or destruction so that the poet was always conscious of loss. His poems were his attempt to extend the life of the natural beauty and the mystical experiences he loved. Though "salvaging something enduring from the wreckage of time" has been a common theme among poets, "the whole of Juan Ramon Jimenez's poetic work may, indeed, be said to be devoted to the problem of this kind of 'salvation,'" Paul R. Olson observed in *Circle of Paradox: Time and Essence in the Poetry of Juan Ramon Jimenez.*

When his father died, the poet's fascination with the eternal as it revealed itself in nature became an obsession. Writing poetry was an essential component of this spiritual quest. In *The Religious Instinct of the Poetry of Juan Ramon Jimenez,* Leo R. Cole explained, "Juan Ramon was in search of a personal God who

would reveal Himself through the poet's creative activity which makes the word part of the living consciousness." Between 1905 and 1912 Jimenez lived alone and worked as a lecturer in Spanish literature and French poetry. During this highly creative period he wrote many of the works he would spend the rest of his life perfecting. Poems he published before 1921 show his mastery of traditional poetic forms. Critics regard his sonnets (published in *Sonetos espirituales*) among the best ever written in Spanish.

During the second stage, Jimenez developed a personal aesthetic he called "la poesia desnuda" (naked poetry). While composing poems, he pruned away excess words formerly included for the sake of filling out patterns of rhyme or meter. Writing in free verse allowed him to zero in on the quintessential elements of his subject matter; the content—the perception he was trying to capture—would find its own best images arranged in their own best order. The resulting short poems, said Guillen, are held together by "the sensibility, the feeling, or the symbol" instead of the usual logic of speech, or the symmetry provided by forms of verse. "These poems seem to me . . . to represent not so much an attempt to create *things* as to seize an almost unseizable experience," Gerald Brenan wrote in *The Literature of the Spanish People From Roman Times to the Present Day.*

In poems from this period, it is clear that the poet's allegiance to his own purpose became so strong that his quest became his principle of composition. Two internal tensions infused the poems with an energy that critics call "mystery." Some tension was created while trying to communicate the eternal in the passing moment; another tension arose from the struggle to express a private inner world in terms of the surrounding reality. In addition, the strong emotions expressed in these shorter poems gave them a tone more urgent than the tone of previous works. Guillen observed, "If one virtue or one method may be considered characteristic of his poetry, it is that of concentration. Concentration on the indispensible effect, surrounded by silences, concentration above all on the single word, on the force and the magic of which language is capable."

Jimenez relished the symbolic capabilities of words in his 1916 work *Diario de un poeta recien casado.* Its poems expressed his meditations during his voyage to the United States for his wedding to Zenobia Camprubi Aymar. Throughout the *Diario,* Jimenez used the sea as the dominant metaphor, to express conflicting desires. He was accustomed to solitude, and the poet's inclination to remain insular fought with his desire to become more open, to share his personal world with his wife, to become vulnerable to intrusions from the outside world. Howard T. Young, writing in *The Victorious Expression: A Study of Four Contemporary Spanish Poets,* called *Diario* "one of the most remarkable books of Spanish poetry."

In *Diario* "a new practice of poetry achieves its maturity," Michael P. Predmore stated in *Contemporary Literature,* ". . . a new kind of ordering and structuring of poems within . . . a symbolic system." This "masterpiece," he explained, "is a highly complex structure of recurring clusters of images and recurring patterns of association. . . . Each recurring image acquires symbolic value and each poem is a symbolic poem" that contributes by means of its position in the sequence to the book's final effect. Because of the prominence of the sea as a symbol in this work, later editions were titled *Diario de un poeta y mar* ("Diary of a Poet and the Sea"). Roses, pine trees, and water images that recur in his poems also took on the significance of personal symbols.

In the poet's third stylistic period, his lifelong spiritual quest was most evident. Changes in his life in the late 1930s contributed a new urgency to his quest. After he broadened his sensibility through marriage, his sense of security was further challenged by the experience of loss. To escape pressures brought about by the Spanish Civil War, in 1936 Jimenez left his homeland, which remained fresh in his memory in the form of his poems. He traveled to Cuba, the United States, and Puerto Rico, where he became a lecturer at the university. While he coped with these challenges, the process of perfecting his poems—of recording his perceptions of the eternal as it revealed itself in nature—became for him a vital spiritual discipline. Guillen reported that Jimenez was a ruthless revisionist, burning manuscripts he felt were inferior and repeatedly going over earlier works to improve them. The process of seeking perfect articulation became a subject in many of these later poems, so that they became a study of poetics. About works from this period, Young commented that "much of his best final poetry is a metaphor of the creative human mind."

The spiritual longing that propelled Jimenez through earlier stages found its fulfillment in his final works. Published in 1946, *La estacion total* includes poems Jimenez worked on between 1923 and 1936. In these poems, the opposite terms of several paradoxes are reconciled into a unified synthesis. For example, instead of perceiving the four seasons as signals of change and loss, Jimenez recognized them as a single unit or circle, a "total season." Carl W. Cobb observed in *Contemporary Spanish Poetry (1898-1963)* that the book's "title is of course meaningful: a *season* is a temporal period of growth and decay, but *total* suggests the poet's attempt to fuse all seasons into one, into a difficult eternity." In these poems, the poet also recognized that his spiritual quest could be satisfied. He came to see loss as a necessary experience, since beauty is not actually perfect until it has transcended its temporal being and become synonymous with its Platonic or spiritual ideal through memory. Though the prospect of death and non-being troubled Jimenez throughout his life, "as poet he struggled through to a position in which death does not negate the soul," related Cobb.

Animal de fondo ("Animal of Depth"), written on a voyage to Buenos Aires and published in 1946, celebrates the resolution of the poet's longing for eternity in a world of endless change. Young noted that its publication marked the poet's "joyful acclamation of mysticism as the final end of poetry." Informed by the teachings of both Christianity and Eastern religions, he affirmed that the traditional gulf between the flesh and the spirit, the temporal and the eternal, did not exist. He expressed this fusion in the word "*cuerpialma*—bodysoul—to describe the intimacy between matter and spirit, or, as he called it, the encounter of reality and its image," stated Young. Cobb explains, "He was to the end an 'Animal of depth,' a soul-and-body forever responsive to the colors, sounds, smells, and tastes of the earth. Yet with his symbols he sought to evoke the inner reality in, above, or beyond the senses. In the intensity of the lived moment he attempted to expand the limits of human consciousness and record it in permanent form in his *Obra*. . . . As a lyric poet this was his 'beautiful vocation,' his final 'ethics through aesthetics.' " Thus having overcome the melancholy that previously attended his sense of loss over the mutable world, in this "spiritual autobiography," Jimenez published a "shout of joy, the exultation that tugs at the reader," added Young. "At the pinnacle of his years, Jimenez saw the labor of a lifetime finally resolved, and wrote his first book in which there is not a trace of despondency nor a touch of shadow."

Jimenez became a figure in the history of the Spanish literature he taught by making a number of important contributions to the art of poetry. Pattison suggested that his "first great contribution to the modern concept of poetry is precisely the idea of the poet as a mystic of nature. . . . In this century most Spanish poets have followed his lead." Jimenez also fostered a new critical and compositional perspective, the understanding that a single poem can best be understood when seen as a component part of a larger body of related symbols. Brenan remarked that because Jimenez found new forms and images to continue the self-examination central to lyric verse, "The whole of contemporary poetry comes out of him." Thus Jimenez is viewed as the essential link between his modernist predecessors and the generations of Spanish poets that came after him.

BIOGRAPHICAL/CRITICAL SOURCES:

BOOKS

Bell, Audrey F. G., *Contemporary Spanish Literature,* Knopf, 1925.
Brenan, Gerald, *The Literature of the Spanish People From Roman Times to the Present Day,* Cambridge University Press, 1951.
Cardwell, Richard, *Juan R. Jimenez: The Modernist Apprenticeship, 1895-1900,* Colloquium Verlag, 1977.
Cobb, Carl W., *Contemporary Spanish Poetry (1898-1963),* Twayne, 1976.
Cole, Leo R., *The Religious Instinct in the Poetry of Juan Ramon Jimenez,* Dolphin Book Co., 1967.
Diego, Gerardo, *Poesia espanola contemporanea (1901-1934),* Taurus, 1974.
Gullon, Ricardo, *Estudios sobre Juan Ramon Jimenez,* Losada, 1960.
Jimenez, Juan Ramon, *Guerra en Espana, 1936-1953* (autobiography), edited by A. Crespo, Seix Barral, 1985.
Olson, Paul R., *Circle of Paradox: Time and Essence in the Poetry of Juan Ramon Jimenez,* Johns Hopkins University Press, 1967.
Twentieth-Century Literary Criticism, Volume 4, Gale, 1981.
Young, Howard T., *The Victorious Expression: A Study of Four Contemporary Spanish Poets,* University of Wisconsin Press, 1964.

PERIODICALS

Books Abroad, autumn, 1961, summer, 1968.
Contemporary Literature, winter, 1972.
Hispania, February, 1950, September, 1971.
Modern Language Notes, June, 1960, November, 1961, January, 1963.
New Republic, December 16, 1957.
PMLA, January, 1970.
Poetry, July, 1953.
Revista Hispanica Moderna: Columbia University Hispanic Studies, Volume 34, number 4, 1970-71.

*   *   *

JIMENEZ, Ramon
    See JIMENEZ (MANTECON), Juan Ramon

*   *   *

JIMENEZ MANTECON, Juan
    See JIMENEZ (MANTECON), Juan Ramon

*   *   *

JOHNSON, Diane (Lain) 1934-

PERSONAL: Born April 28, 1934, in Moline, Ill.; daughter of Dolph and Frances (Elder) Lain; married B. Lamar Johnson, Jr.,

July, 1953 (marriage ended); married John Frederic Murray (a professor of medicine), May 31, 1968 (one source says November 9, 1969); children: (first marriage) Kevin, Darcy, Amanda, Simon. *Education:* Stephens College, A.A., 1953; University of Utah, B.A., 1957; University of California, M.A., 1966, Ph.D., 1968.

ADDRESSES: Home—24 Edith Pl., San Francisco, Calif. 94133. *Office*—Department of English, University of California, Davis, Calif. 95616. *Agent*—Helen Brann, 157 West 57th St., New York, N.Y. 10019.

CAREER: University of California, Davis, 1968-87, began as assistant professor, became professor of English; writer.

MEMBER: International P.E.N., Modern Language Association of America.

AWARDS, HONORS: Woodrow Wilson grant, 1967; National Book Award nomination, 1973, for *Lesser Lives,* and 1979, for *Lying Low;* Guggenheim fellowship, 1977-78; Rosenthal Award, American Academy and Institute of Arts and Letters, 1979; Pulitzer Prize nomination in general nonfiction, 1983, for *Terrorists and Novelists; Los Angeles Times* book prize nomination in biography, 1984, for *Dashiell Hammett: A Life;* Mildred and Harold Strauss Living Award from American Academy and Institute of Arts and Letters, 1988.

WRITINGS:

NOVELS

Fair Game, Harcourt, 1965.
Loving Hands at Home, Harcourt, 1968.
Burning, Harcourt, 1971.
The Shadow Knows (also see below), Knopf, 1974.
Lying Low, Knopf, 1978.
Persian Nights, Knopf, 1987.

BIOGRAPHY

Lesser Lives: The True History of the First Mrs. Meredith, Knopf, 1973 (published in England as *The True History of the First Mrs. Meredith and Other Lesser Lives,* Heinemann, 1973).
Dashiell Hammett: A Life (also see below), Random House, 1983.

SCREENPLAYS

(With Stanley Kubrick) "The Shining" (based on the Stephen King novel of the same title), Warner Bros., 1980.

Also author of unproduced screenplays "Grand Hotel," "The Shadow Knows" (based on her novel of the same title), and "Hammett" (based on her biography *Dashiell Hammett: A Life*).

OTHER

(Author of preface) John Ruskin, *King of the Golden River* [and] Charles Dickens, *A Holiday Romance* [and] Tom Hood, *Petsetilla's Posy,* Garland Publishing, 1976.
(Author of preface) Margaret Gatty, *Parables of Nature,* Garland Publishing, 1976.
(Author of preface) George Sand, *Mauprat,* Da Capo Press, 1977.
Terrorists and Novelists (collected essays), Knopf, 1982.

Also author of preface to *Frankenstein* by Mary Shelley, c. 1979. Contributor of essays and book reviews to periodicals, including the *New York Times, New York Review of Books, San Francisco Chronicle,* and *Washington Post.*

WORK IN PROGRESS: A novel set in Iran.

SIDELIGHTS: In an age when writers tend to be pigeonholed, Diane Johnson remains a difficult author to categorize. Perhaps best known as an essayist and biographer, she got her start as a novelist and continues to write successfully in this vein. She is a teacher and scholar, with an expertise in nineteenth-century literature, yet she also lent a hand in writing "The Shining," a popular horror film. And while her initial focus was on women and their problems in society, she has since written sympathetically of a man who faced similar difficulties in *Dashiell Hammett: A Life.* Even her early works, which have been claimed as the province of feminists, were intended to cast a wider net, as Johnson explained to Susan Groag Bell in *Women Writers of the West Coast:* "The kinds of crises, the particular troubles that I assign to my women characters, these are not necessarily meant to be feminist complaints. . . . In my mind, they may be more metaphysical or general. That sounds awfully pretentious, but I guess what I mean is that I'm not trying to write manifestos about female independence, but human lives."

Like many serious artists, Johnson sees herself as a craftsman whose work should be judged on its merits as literature, not—as is often the case with women writers—on moral or extraliterary grounds. In her highly acclaimed collection of book reviews and essays, *Terrorists and Novelists,* Johnson addresses the particular problems faced by female novelists, chiding those male critics who "have not learned not to read books by women and imagine them all to be feminist polemics." As she told Bell: "The writer wants to be praised for the management of formal and technical aspects of the narrative and wide-ranging perceptions about society and perhaps the quality of her sensibility, not her own character, and, mainly you want your book to be a success on its own terms."

Though all her novels and one of her biographies have California settings, Johnson was born and raised in Moline, Illinois. Her childhood was untroubled: the first child of middle-aged parents, she lived in the same house surrounded by neighboring aunts and uncles until she went away to college at seventeen. She describes herself as a "puny, bookish little child, with thick glasses" and told *Los Angeles Times* reporter Beverly Beyette that she was "the kind of whom you say, 'Let's take her to the library on Saturday.' I was typecast, but I was a type." When she was nineteen, Johnson married her first husband, then a UCLA medical student, and relocated to the West Coast where she has remained.

Despite her long residence in California, Johnson told Bell that "a certain view of life, which I very much obtained from my Illinois childhood, does inform my work. In a couple of my books I have put a middle-western protagonist, always somebody who's displaced like I am, looking at the mess of today. This person remembers an orderly society from which subsequent events have seemed to depart." She maintains that it is the turmoil of modern society, rather than a personal preoccupation with disorder, that leads to the prevalence of violence in her books. "She is not sensational, sentimental, nor simple-minded," suggests *Critique: Studies in Modern Fiction* contributor Marjorie Ryan, who points out that Johnson writes in "the satiric-comic-realistic tradition, in a mode that may not appeal to readers nurtured on the personal, subjective, and doctrinaire."

In her early fiction, *Fair Game, Loving Hands at Home,* and *Burning,* Johnson employs "a comic tone" as well as "a central female character who is uncertain about how to conduct her life," according to Judith S. Baughman in the *Dictionary of Literary Biography Yearbook.* In each of these novels, a woman who has ventured outside the boundaries of convention "has a shocking experience which sends her back inside, but only temporarily until another experience . . . either sends her outside again or changes her whole perspective," Ryan explains.

As is so often the case with a writer's first fruits, these early novels largely escaped the notice of critics—at least initially. By the time *Burning* appeared, there were flickers of interest, though it was Johnson's potential as a novelist rather than the work at hand that attracted praise. Much criticism was leveled at Johnson's choice of subject. A Southern California story of disaster, *Burning* was viewed as a genre novel that had been approached in the same fashion many times before. As R. R. Davies put it, "Group therapy and the drug-induced self-analysis of depressed citizens have been done to death as satirical material." Though *Newsweek*'s Peter Prescott finds her "witty and serious," he points out that she "tries to be both at once and doesn't make it. Her book should have been either much funnier, or much grimmer or, failing that, she should have been much better." *Book World* contributor J. R. Frakes compares the crowded canvas of her apocalyptic tale to "a twelve ring circus" and welcomes its disastrous ending "almost as a relief," but then goes on to praise Johnson's style, noting that she "superintends this asylum with cool disdain and a remarkable neo-classic elegance of phrase, sentence, and chapter. It is comforting to know that someone competent is in charge."

Her competence established, Johnson began to attract more serious attention, and her fourth novel, *The Shadow Knows,* was widely reviewed. Originally set in Los Angeles, the story was relocated to Sacramento because, as Johnson explained to Susan Groag Bell, "I decided after the reception of *Burning* that Los Angeles was too loaded a place in the minds of readers." The novel takes its title from an old radio melodrama (which featured the line, "Who knows what evil lurks in the hearts of men? The Shadow knows.") and focuses on one terror-filled week in the life of a young divorcee and mother of four known simply as N. When someone slashes her tires, leaves a strangled cat on her doorstep, threatens her over the telephone, and beats up her babysitter in the basement laundry room, N. becomes convinced that she is marked for murder. But who is the assailant? Her spiteful former husband? The wife of her married lover? The psychotic black woman who used to care for her children? Her jealous friend Bess, who comes to visit with a hunting knife in her purse? Or, worst of all, is it some nameless stranger, an embodiment of evil she does not even know? N.'s attempt to identify her enemy, and her imaginary dialogue with the Famous Inspector she conjures up to help her, make up the heart of the book.

Writing in the *New Statesman,* A. S. Byatt describes the novel as a "cunning cross between the intensely articulate plaint of the under-extended intelligent woman and a conventional mystery, shading into a psychological horror-story." *Nation* contributor Sandra M. Gilbert calls it "a sort of bitter parody of a genre invented by nineteenth-century men: the detective novel." Though it masquerades as a thriller, most reviewers acknowledge that *The Shadow Knows* is really a woman's story in which N. abandons what she calls her "safe" life to follow one that is "reckless and riddled with mistakes."

"In her attempts to create a fresh, true identity unconfined by the usual social and familial influences, N. must penetrate the evils which lurk in the hearts of men, even in her own heart in order to find her 'way in the dark,' " writes Baughman. "Thus, she has not only to uncover her potential murderer but also to deal with her own considerable problems and confusions. Because the pressures upon her are so great, the possibility arises that N.'s terrors are powerful projections of her own sense of guilt and confusion rather than appropriate responses to the ma-

levolent acts of an outside aggressor." Some reviewers go so far as to suggest that N.'s problems are more imagined than real. "Understandably, N. would like to know who's doing all these bad things to her, if only to be sure that she's not making it all up," writes Thomas R. Edwards in the *New York Review of Books.* "And since we also wonder if she may not be doing that, we share her desire for knowledge."

In her interview with Bell, Johnson makes it clear that such disbelief stems more from readers' biases than from the way the protagonist is portrayed. "There's [a] problem that comes from having as your central character a female person," says Johnson. "The male narrative voice is still accorded more authority. The female narrative voice is always questioned—is she crazy? Are the things she's saying a delusion, or reality? The narrator in *The Shadow Knows* was intended as an exact and trustworthy reporter of what was happening to her. But many reviewers, while in general liking her, also questioned her about her hysteria, her paranoia, her untrustworthiness. Is she mad or sane? So I began to notice that female narrators, if they're of a sexual age, of a reproductive age, of an age to have affairs, aren't considered trustworthy. . . . Nonetheless, I write about women of childbearing age, because I like to fly in the face of these prejudices and hope that I can make them authoritative and trustworthy reporters."

While women still figure prominently in Johnson's next novel, *Lying Low,* the focus has shifted from psychological to political concerns and from one protagonist to several. The book, which covers four days in the lives of four characters who inhabit a boarding house in Orris, California, is a "mosaic-like juxtaposition of small paragraphs, each containing a short description, a bit of action, reflections of one of the principal characters, or a mixture of all three," according to Robert Towers in the *New York Times Book Review.* Praising its artful construction, elegant style, and delicate perceptions, Towers calls it "a nearly flawless performance. Despite the lack of any headlong narrative rush, one's interest in the working out of the story is maintained at a high level by the skillful, unobtrusive distribution of plot fragments." *Newsweek*'s Peter Prescott says it "represents a triumph of sensibility over plot" and observes that, like other feminist novels, it is "most convincing when least dramatic. Condition, not action, is [its] true concern: the problems of women confronting, or trying to ignore, their desperate lot."

Johnson's skill at rendering domestic crises makes *Saturday Review* contributor Katha Pollitt "wish Diane Johnson had kept her canvas small, a comedy or tragicomedy of manners for our decade of extreme political bewilderment. . . . When Johnson aims for a grander drama, though, she is not convincing. The end, [in which a bomb explodes, killing one of the main characters], seems a failure of imagination, an apocalypse produced ex machina so that we all get the point about the violence that smolders beneath the American surface." A *New Yorker* critic pronounces the conclusion "an awkward attempt to endow a cerebral narrative with the action of a thriller." And the *New Republic* likens the ending to "one of those simple-minded 1960s films in which the source of all evil is 'Amerika' " and concludes that it "seems much too jarring in a novel as full of subtleties of observation and atmosphere as this one."

Persian Nights, Johnson's next novel, concerns Americans in Iran during the decline of the ruling Shah's political power. The *New York Times*'s Lehmann-Haupt acknowledged the work's "exotic atmosphere" and added that "the scenes that are on target draw blood."

In addition to novels, Johnson has written two biographies. Her portrait of the first Mrs. George Meredith, *Lesser Lives: The*

True History of the First Mrs. Meredith, grew out of her doctoral dissertation. "In biographies of Meredith, there would always be this little paragraph about how he was first married to Mary Ellen Peacock who ran off and left him and then, of course, died, deserted and forlorn—like the woman in a Victorian story," Johnson told Bell. "I always thought, I bet there is her side of it too. This was when my own marriage was breaking up, and I was particularly interested in the woman's side of things."

Working from evidence she exhumed from letters and diaries, Johnson hypothesizes that the real Mary Ellen was a strong-willed, intelligent, free spirit, whose main sin was being out of step with her times. Raised by her father in the tradition of eighteenth-century individualism, she incited the wrath of her decidedly Victorian second husband, the famous novelist George Meredith, when she abandoned their loveless marriage to lead a life of her own. The portrait that survives of her as a crazed adulterer who lured a much younger man into marriage is more a reflection of Meredith's vindictiveness than an indication of who she was.

Though some critics felt the biography was lacking in evidence, many praised its artful style. "Jump cutting from scene to scene, she shows what she thinks to be true, what she thinks might be true, and what, in all candor, she thinks no one can prove to be either true or false," writes Catharine R. Stimpson in *Ms.* "Like a historian, she recovers pellets of the past. Like a psychologist, she applies theory and common sense to human behavior. Like a novelist, she takes imaginative liberties and worries about the internal coherence of her work of art. . . . *Lesser Lives* has the buoyant vitality of a book in which a writer has taken risks, and won."

Even when her subject is a contemporary figure, about whom concrete facts and anecdotes are readily available, Johnson prefers an artistic to an exhaustive approach. "A biography has a responsibility which is to present the facts and get all of them straight, so that people can get the basic outlines of a person's life," Johnson explained to Miriam Berkley in *Publishers Weekly.* "And then, I think, it has to have a point of view and a shape which has to come out of the biographer as artist. I guess I am arguing for the interpretive biography, you might call it an art biography, as opposed to a compendious . . . presentation of a lot of facts."

Johnson's commitment to biography as art presented especial challenges in her study of mystery writer Dashiell Hammett and the writing of *Dashiell Hammett: A Life.* The first "authorized" Hammett biographer, Johnson had access to all his personal papers and the cooperation of his family and friends. But in exchange for these privileges, Hammett's executrix and long-time companion Lillian Hellman insisted that she be shown the final manuscript and granted the right to decide whether or not the quoted material could stand.

"She set out to be pleasant and wonderful, then, when she stopped being wonderful, I stopped going to see her," Johnson told Beverly Beyette in the *Los Angeles Times.* The problem was one of vision: "She saw him very much as her guru, this wonderfully strong, terrifically honest, fabulously intelligent dream man. I saw him as an intelligent, troubled man, an alcoholic with terrible writer's block. She didn't like to think of his life having been painful, unsuccessful." Johnson eventually obtained Hellman's permission to use Hammett's letters in her own way. "She had to agree, I guess, that it *was* the best way of presenting Hammett," Johnson told Berkley. "He was a difficult man and not entirely sympathetic, but he was certainly at his most sympathetic in his own voice."

Using a novelistic approach, Johnson intersperses excerpts from Hammett's letters with short stretches of narrative that sometimes reflect her viewpoint, sometimes that of his family and friends. *New York Times Book Review* contributor George Stade compares the technique to one Hammett perfected in his own novels, "the method of the camera eye. We see what the characters do, hear what they say, note their gestures and postures, watch them assume positions toward each other, record their suspect attempts to account for themselves and each other." But just as Hammett's readers had to decipher for themselves his protagonists' motives, so, too, must Johnson's readers "decide for themselves what made Hammett tick."

Because so much is left to the reader, some critics suggest that Johnson is withholding judgment; others conclude that she cannot reveal what she does not know. As *New York Times* reviewer Christopher Lehmann-Haupt puts it: "Silence was Hammett's weapon—silence turned against all bullies and lovers, against his readers and himself. At the bottom of that silence was an ocean of anger: that much this biography makes very clear. The mystery that remains that will probably remain forever—is the true source of that anger." Characterizing Hammett as "a fundamentally passive individual who drifted through life with no clear motivations or deep impulses," *Washington Post Book World* Jonathan Yardley speculates, "when you come right down to it, the 'mystery' lies within us rather than him: for expecting more of him, since he wrote good books, than was actually there, and for feeling frustrated when those expectations go unmet."

Ralph B. Sipper, on the other hand, finds Johnson's "tracking of Hammett's inner life the most revealing to date" and speculates in the *Los Angeles Times Book Review* that perhaps her "most delicate accomplishment is the fine line between iffy psychologizing and creative analysis." Describing the interpretative approach to biography as one in which the writer "studies the facts and filters them through her own sensibility," Sipper concludes that "Diane Johnson has done just that with her multifaceted subject and the result is pure light."

BIOGRAPHICAL/CRITICAL SOURCES:

BOOKS

Contemporary Literary Criticism, Gale, Volume 5, 1976, Volume 13, 1983, Volume 48, 1988.
Dictionary of Literary Biography Yearbook: 1980, Gale, 1981.
Johnson, Diane, *Terrorists and Novelists,* Knopf, 1982.
Yalom, Marilyn, editor, *Women Writers of the West Coast: Speaking of Their Lives and Careers,* Capra, 1983.

PERIODICALS

America, March 19, 1983.
Best Sellers, September 1, 1971.
Book World, October 13, 1968, September 5, 1971.
Chicago Tribune Book World, January 9, 1983.
Critique: Studies in Modern Fiction, Volume XVI, number 1, 1974.
Los Angeles Times, October 6, 1982, April 27, 1983.
Los Angeles Times Book Review, October 30, 1983.
Ms., May, 1974, November, 1978.
Nation, June 14, 1975, November 1, 1978, December 17, 1983.
New Republic, November 1, 1972, November 18, 1978.
New Statesman, November 19, 1971, June 6, 1975.
Newsweek, December 23, 1974, May 5, 1975, October 16, 1978, October 17, 1983, March 30, 1987.
New Yorker, March 3, 1975, November 13, 1978, November 14, 1983.

New York Review of Books, November 2, 1972, February 20, 1975, November 23, 1978.

New York Times, November 27, 1974, May 23, 1980, October 16, 1982, October 5, 1983, March 16, 1987.

New York Times Book Review, September 5, 1971, December 31, 1972, December 22, 1974, November 19, 1978, October 31, 1982, October 16, 1983, April 5, 1987.

Publishers Weekly, September 9, 1983.

Saturday Review, October 28, 1978.

Time, November 7, 1983, March 23, 1987.

Times Literary Supplement, June 6, 1975, November 23, 1979, July 3, 1987.

Village Voice, January 8, 1979.

Washington Post Book World, December 22, 1974, November 26, 1978, September 29, 1982, October 9, 1983.

* * *

JOHNSON, J. R.
See JAMES, C(yril) L(ionel) R(obert)

* * *

JOHNSON, James Weldon 1871-1938

PERSONAL: Born June 17, 1871, in Jacksonville, Fla.; died following an automobile accident, June 26, 1938, in Wiscasset, Me.; buried in Brooklyn, N.Y.; son of James (a restaurant headwaiter) and Helen Louise (a musician and schoolteacher; maiden name, Dillette) Johnson; married Grace Nail, February 3, 1910. *Education:* Atlanta University, A.B., 1894, A.M., 1904; graduate study at Columbia University, c.1902-05.

ADDRESSES: Home—Nashville, Tenn.

CAREER: Poet, novelist, songwriter, editor, historian, civil rights leader, diplomat, lawyer, and educator. Stanton Central Grammar School for Negroes, Jacksonville, Fla., teacher, later principal, 1894-1901; *Daily American* (newspaper), Jacksonville, founder and co-editor, 1895-96; admitted to the Bar of the State of Florida, 1898; private law practice, Jacksonville, 1898-1901; songwriter for the musical theater in partnership with brother, J. Rosamond Johnson, and Bob Cole, New York City, 1901-06; United States Consul to Puerto Cabello, Venezuela, 1906-09, and to Corinto, Nicaragua, 1909-13; *New York Age* (newspaper), New York City, editorial writer, 1914-24; National Association for the Advancement of Colored People (NAACP), New York City, field secretary, 1916-20, executive secretary, 1920-30; Fisk University, Nashville, Tenn., professor of creative literature and writing, 1931-38. Elected treasurer of the Colored Republican Club, New York City, and participated in Theodore Roosevelt's presidential campaign, both in 1904; lectured on literature and black culture at numerous colleges and universities during the 1930s, including New York, Northwestern, and Yale universities, Oberlin and Swarthmore colleges, and the universities of North Carolina and Chicago. Served as director of the American Fund for Public Service and as trustee of Atlanta University.

MEMBER: American Society of Composers, Authors, and Publishers (charter member), Academy of Political Science, Ethical Society, Civic Club (New York City).

AWARDS, HONORS: Spingarn Medal from NAACP, 1925, for outstanding achievement by an American Negro; Harmon Gold Award for *God's Trombones;* Julius Rosenwald Fund grant, 1929; W. E. B. Du Bois Prize for Negro Literature, 1933; named first incumbent of Spence Chair of Creative Literature at Fisk University; honorary doctorates from Talladega College and Howard University.

WRITINGS:

The Autobiography of an Ex-Coloured Man (novel), Sherman, French, 1912, Arden Library, 1978.

(Translator) Fernando Periquet, *Goyescas; or, The Rival Lovers* (opera libretto), G. Schirmer, 1915.

Fifty Years and Other Poems, Cornhill, 1917, AMS Press, 1975.

(Editor) *The Book of American Negro Poetry,* Harcourt, 1922, revised edition, Harcourt, 1969.

(Editor) *The Book of American Negro Spirituals,* Viking, 1925.

(Editor) *The Second Book of Negro Spirituals,* Viking, 1926.

(Editor) *The Books of American Negro Spirituals* (contains *The Book of American Negro Spirituals* and *The Second Book of Negro Spirituals*), Viking, 1940, reprinted, 1964.

God's Trombones: Seven Negro Sermons in Verse (poetry), illustrations by Aaron Douglas, Viking, 1927, Penguin, 1976.

Black Manhattan (nonfiction), Knopf, 1930, Arno, 1968.

Along This Way: The Autobiography of James Weldon Johnson, Viking, 1933, Da Capo, 1973.

Negro Americans, What Now? (nonfiction), Viking, 1934, Da Capo, 1973.

Saint Peter Relates an Incident: Selected Poems, Viking, 1935, AMS Press, 1974.

The Great Awakening, Revell, 1938.

Utopian Literature: A Selection, McGraw, 1968.

(Contributor) John H. Franklin, *Three Negro Classics,* Avon, 1976.

Also author of *Selected Poems,* 1936. Contributor of articles and poems to numerous newspapers and magazines, including the *Chicago Defender, Times-Union* (Jacksonville, Fla.), *New York Age, New York Times, Pittsburgh Courier, Savannah Tribune, Century, Crisis, Nation, Independent, Harper's, Bookman, Forum,* and *Scholastic;* poetry represented in many anthologies; songs published by Joseph W. Stern & Co., Edward B. Marks Music Corp., and others; author of numerous pamphlets on current events published by the NAACP, *Nation, Century,* and others.

MEDIA ADAPTATIONS: "God's Trombones" (sound recording with biographical notes by Walter White, and texts of the poems), read by Bryce Bond, music by William Martin, Folkways Records, 1965; "Reading Poetry: The Creation" (motion picture with study guide), read by Raymond St. Jacques and Margaret O'Brien, Oxford Films, 1972; "James Weldon Johnson" (motion picture), includes an adaptation of "The Creation" read by St. Jacques, Oxford Films, 1972.

SIDELIGHTS: James Weldon Johnson distinguished himself equally as a man of letters and as a civil rights leader in the early decades of the twentieth century. A talented poet and novelist, Johnson is credited with bringing a new standard of artistry and realism to black literature in such works as *The Autobiography of an Ex-Coloured Man* and *God's Trombones.* His pioneering studies of black poetry, music, and theater in the 1920s also helped introduce many white Americans to the genuine Afro-American creative spirit, hitherto known mainly through the distortions of the minstrel show and dialect poetry. Meanwhile, as head of the National Association for the Advancement of Colored People (NAACP) during the 1920s, Johnson led determined civil rights campaigns in an effort to remove the legal, political, and social obstacles hindering black achievement. Johnson's multi-faceted career, which also included stints as a diplomat in Latin America and a successful Tin Pan Alley songwriter, testified to his intellectual breadth, self-confidence, and deep-rooted belief that the future held unlimited new opportunities for black Americans.

Johnson was born in Jacksonville, Florida, in 1871, and his upbringing in this relatively tolerant Southern town may help explain his later political moderation. Both his father, a resort hotel headwaiter, and his mother, a schoolteacher, had lived in the North and had never been enslaved, and James and his brother John Rosamond grew up in broadly cultured and economically secure surroundings that were unusual among Southern black families at the time. Johnson's mother stimulated his early interests in reading, drawing, and music, and he attended the segregated Stanton School, where she taught, until the eighth grade. Since high schools were closed to blacks in Jacksonville, Johnson left home to attend both secondary school and college at Atlanta University, where he took his bachelor's degree in 1894. It was during his college years, as Johnson recalled in his autobiography, *Along This Way,* that he first became aware of the depth of the racial problem in the United States. Race questions were vigorously debated on campus, and Johnson's experience teaching black schoolchildren in a poor district of rural Georgia during two summers deeply impressed him with the need to improve the lives of his people. The struggles and aspirations of American blacks form a central theme in the thirty or so poems that Johnson wrote as a student.

Returning to Jacksonville in 1894, Johnson was appointed a teacher and principal of the Stanton School and managed to expand the curriculum to include high school-level classes. He also became an active local spokesman on black social and political issues and in 1895 founded the *Daily American,* the first black-oriented daily newspaper in the United States. During its brief life, the newspaper became a voice against racial injustice and served to encourage black advancement through individual effort—a "self-help" position that echoed the more conservative civil rights leadership of the day. Although the newspaper folded for lack of readership the following year, Johnson's ambitious publishing effort attracted the attention of such prominent black leaders as W. E. B. Du Bois and Booker T. Washington.

Meanwhile Johnson read law with the help of a local white lawyer, and in 1898 he became the first black lawyer admitted to the Florida Bar since Reconstruction. Johnson practiced law in Jacksonville for several years in partnership with a former Atlanta University classmate while continuing to serve as the Stanton School's principal. He also continued to write poetry and discovered his gift for songwriting in collaboration with his brother Rosamond, a talented composer. Among other songs in a spiritual-influenced popular idiom, Johnson penned the lyrics to "Lift Every Voice and Sing," a tribute to black endurance, hope, and religious faith that was later adopted by the NAACP and dubbed "the Negro National Anthem."

In 1901, bored by Jacksonville's provincialism and disturbed by mounting incidents of racism there, the Johnson brothers set out for New York City to seek their fortune writing songs for the musical theater. In partnership with Bob Cole they secured a publishing contract paying a monthly stipend and over the next five years composed some two hundred songs for Broadway and other musical productions, including such hit numbers as "Under the Bamboo Tree," "The Old Flag Never Touched the Ground," and "Didn't He Ramble." The trio, who soon became known as "Those Ebony Offenbachs," avoided writing for racially exploitative minstrel shows but often found themselves obliged to present simplified and stereotyped images of rural black life to suit white audiences. But the Johnsons and Cole also produced works like the six-song suite titled "The Evolution of Ragtime" that helped document and expose important black musical idioms.

During this time James Weldon Johnson also studied creative literature formally for three years at Columbia University and became active in Republican party politics. He served as treasurer of New York's Colored Republican Club in 1904 and helped write two songs for Republican candidate Theodore Roosevelt's successful presidential campaign that year. When the national black civil rights leadership split into conservative and radical factions—headed by Booker T. Washington and W. E. B. Du Bois, respectively—Johnson backed Washington, who in turn played an important role in getting the Roosevelt Administration to appoint Johnson as United States consul in Puerto Cabello, Venezuela, in 1906. With few official duties, Johnson was able to devote much of his time in that sleepy tropical port to writing poetry, including the acclaimed sonnet "Mother Night" that was published in *Century* magazine and later included in Johnson's verse collection *Fifty Years and Other Poems.*

The consul also completed his only novel, *The Autobiography of an Ex-Coloured Man,* during his three years in Venezuela. Published anonymously in 1912, the novel attracted little attention until it was reissued under Johnson's own name more than a decade later. Even then, the book tended to draw more comment as a sociological document than as a work of fiction. (So many readers believed it to be truly autobiographical that Johnson eventually wrote his real life story, *Along This Way,* to avoid confusion.)

The Autobiography of an Ex-Coloured Man bears a superficial resemblance to other "tragic mulatto" narratives of the day that depicted, often in sentimental terms, the travails of mixed-race protagonists unable to fit into either racial culture. In Johnson's novel, the unnamed narrator is light-skinned enough to pass for white but identifies emotionally with his beloved mother's black race. In his youth, he aspires to become a great black American musical composer, but he fearfully renounces that ambition after watching a mob of whites set fire to a black man in the rural South. Though horrified and repulsed by the whites' attack, the narrator feels an even deeper shame and humiliation for himself as a black man and he subsequently allows circumstances to guide him along the easier path of "passing" as a middle-class white businessman. The protagonist finds success in this role but ends up a failure in his own terms, plagued with ambivalence over his true identity, moral values, and emotional loyalties.

Early criticism of *The Autobiography of an Ex-Coloured Man* tended to emphasize Johnson's frank and realistic look at black society and race relations more than his skill as a novelist. Carl Van Vechten, for example, found the novel "an invaluable source-book for the study of Negro psychology," and the *New Republic*'s Edmund Wilson judged the book "an excellent, honest piece of work" as "a human and sociological document" but flawed as a work of literature. In the 1950s and 1960s, however, something of a critical reappraisal of the *Autobiography* occurred that led to a new appreciation of Johnson as a crafter of fiction. In his critical study *The Negro Novel in America,* Robert A. Bone called Johnson "the only true artist among the early Negro novelists," who succeeded in "subordinating racial protest to artistic considerations." Johnson's subtle theme of moral cowardice, Bone noted, set the novel far above "the typical propaganda tract of the day." In a 1971 essay, Robert E. Fleming drew attention to Johnson's deliberate use of an unreliable narrative voice, remarking that *The Autobiography of an Ex-Coloured Man* "is not so much a panoramic novel presenting race relations throughout America as it is a deeply ironic character study of a marginal man." Johnson's psychological depth and concern with aesthetic coherence anticipated the great black literary movement of the

1920s known as the Harlem School, according to these and other critics.

In 1909, before the *Autobiography* had been published, Johnson was promoted to the consular post in Corinto, Nicaragua, a position that proved considerably more demanding than his Venezuelan job and left him little time for writing. His three-year term of service occurred during a period of intense political turmoil in Nicaragua, which culminated in the landing of U.S. troops at Corinto in 1912. In 1913, seeing little future for himself under President Woodrow Wilson's Democratic administration, Johnson resigned from the foreign service and returned to New York to become an editorial writer for the *New York Age,* the city's oldest and most distinguished black newspaper. The articles Johnson produced over the next ten years tended toward the conservative side, combining a strong sense of racial pride with a deep-rooted belief that blacks could individually improve their lot by means of self-education and bard work even before discriminatory barriers had been removed. This stress on individual effort and economic independence put Johnson closer to the position of black educator Booker T. Washington than that of the politically militant writer and scholar W. E. B. Du Bois in the great leadership dispute on how to improve the status of black Americans, but Johnson generally avoided criticizing either man by name and managed to maintain good relations with both leaders.

During this period Johnson continued to indulge his literary love. Having mastered the Spanish language in the diplomatic service, he translated Fernando Periquet's grand opera *Goyescas* into English and the Metropolitan Opera produced his libretto version in 1915. In 1917, Johnson published his first verse collection, *Fifty Years and Other Poems,* a selection from twenty years' work that drew mixed reviews. "Fifty Years," a sonorous poem commemorating the half-century since the Emancipation Proclamation, was generally singled out for praise, but critics differed on the merits of Johnson's dialect verse written after the manner of the great black dialect poet Paul Laurence Dunbar. The dialect style was highly popular at the time, but has since been criticized for pandering to sentimental white stereotypes of rural black life. In addition to his dialect work, Johnson's collection also included such powerful racial protest poems as "Brothers," about a lynching, and delicate lyrical verse on non-racial topics in the traditional style.

In 1916, at the urging of W. E. B. Du Bois, Johnson accepted the newly created post of national field secretary for the NAACP, which had grown to become the country's premier black rights advocacy and defense organization since its founding in 1910. Johnson's duties included investigating racial incidents and organizing new NAACP branches around the country, and he succeeded in significantly raising the organization's visibility and membership through the years following World War I. In 1917, Johnson organized and led a well-publicized silent march through the streets of New York City to protest lynchings, and his on-site investigation of abuses committed by American Marines against black citizens of Haiti during the U.S. occupation of that Caribbean nation in 1920 captured headlines and helped launch a congressional probe into the matter. Johnson's in-depth report, which was published by the *Nation* in a four-part series titled "Self-Determining Haiti," also had an impact on the presidential race that year, helping to shift public sentiment from the interventionist policies associated with the Wilson Democrats toward the more isolationist position of the Republican victor, Warren Harding.

Johnson's successes as field secretary led to his appointment as NAACP executive secretary in 1920, a position he was to hold for the next ten years. This decade marked a critical turning point for the black rights movement as the NAACP and other civil rights organizations sought to defend and expand the social and economic gains blacks had achieved during the war years, when large numbers of blacks migrated to the northern cities and found industrial and manufacturing jobs. These black gains triggered a racist backlash in the early years of the decade that found virulent expression in a sharp rise in lynchings and the rapid growth of the white supremacist Ku Klux Klan terror organization in the North as well as the South. Despite this violent reaction, Johnson was credited with substantially increasing the NAACP's membership strength and political influence during this period, although his strenuous efforts to get a federal anti-lynching bill passed proved unsuccessful.

Johnson's personal politics also underwent change during the postwar years of heightened black expectations. Disappointed with the neglectful minority rights policies of Republican presidents Harding and Calvin Coolidge, Johnson broke with the Republican party in the early 1920s and briefly supported Robert LaFollette's Progressive party. LaFollette also lost the NAACP leader's backing, however, when he refused to include black demands in the Progressives' 1924 campaign platform. Though frustrated in his political objectives, Johnson opposed Marcus Garvey's separatist "Back to Africa" movement and instead urged the new black communities in the northern cities to use their potentially powerful voting strength to force racial concessions from the country's political establishment.

Even with the heavy demands of his NAACP office, the 1920s were a period of great literary productivity for Johnson. He earned critical acclaim in 1922 for editing a seminal collection of black verse, titled *The Book of American Negro Poetry.* Johnson's critical introduction to this volume provided new insights into an often ignored or denigrated genre and is now considered a classic analysis of early black contributions to American literature. Johnson went on to compile and interpret outstanding examples of the black religious song form known as the spiritual in his pioneering *The Book of American Negro Spirituals* and *The Second Book of Negro Spirituals.* These renditions of black voices formed the background for *God's Trombones,* a set of verse versions of rural black folk sermons that many critics regard as Johnson's finest poetic work. Based on the poet's recollections of the fiery preachers he had heard while growing up in Florida and Georgia, Johnson's seven sermon-poems about life and death and good and evil were deemed a triumph in overcoming the thematic and technical limitations of the dialect style while capturing, according to critics, a full resonant timbre. In *The Book of American Negro Poetry,* Johnson had compared the traditional Dunbar-style dialect verse to an organ having only two stops, one of humor and one of pathos, and he sought with *God's Trombones* to create a more flexible and dignified medium for expressing the black religious spirit. Casting out rhyme and the dialect style's buffoonish misspellings and mispronunciations, Johnson's clear and simple verses succeeded in rendering the musical rhythms, word structure, and vocabulary of the unschooled black orator in standard English. Critics also credited the poet with capturing the oratorical tricks and flourishes that a skilled preacher would use to sway his congregation, including hyperbole, repetition, abrupt mood juxtapositions, an expert sense of timing, and the ability to translate biblical imagery into the colorful, concrete terms of everyday life. "The sensitive reader cannot fail to hear the rantings of the fire-and-brimstone preacher; the extremely sensitive reader may even hear the unwritten 'Amens' of the congregation,'' declared Eugenia W. Collier in a 1960 essay for *Phylon.*

Johnson's efforts to preserve and win recognition for black cultural traditions drew praise from such prominent literary figures as H. L. Mencken and Mark Van Doren and contributed to the spirit of racial pride and self-confidence that marked the efflorescence of black music, art, and literature in the 1920s known as the Harlem Renaissance. This period of intense creative innovation forms the central subject of *Black Manhattan,* Johnson's informal survey of black contributions to New York's cultural life beginning as far back as the seventeenth century. The critically well-received volume focuses especially on blacks in the theater but also surveys the development of the ragtime and jazz musical idioms and discusses the earthy writings of Harlem Renaissance poets Langston Hughes, Countee Cullen, and Claude McKay. "*Black Manhattan* is a document of the 1920's—a celebration, with reservations, of both the artistic renaissance of the era and the dream of a black metropolis," noted critic Allan H. Spear in his preface to the 1968 edition of Johnson's book.

In December 1930, fatigued by the demands of his job and wanting more time to write, Johnson resigned from the NAACP and accepted a part-time teaching post in creative literature at Fisk University in Nashville, Tennessee. In 1933, he published his much-admired autobiography *Along This Way,* which discusses his personal career in the context of the larger social, political, and cultural movements of the times. Johnson remained active in the civil rights movement while teaching at Fisk, and in 1934 he published a book-length argument in favor of racial integration titled *Negro Americans, What Now?* The civil rights struggle also figures in the title poem of Johnson's last major verse collection, *Saint Peter Relates an Incident: Selected Poems.* Inspired by an outrageous act of public discrimination by the federal government against the mothers of black soldiers killed in action, Johnson's satirical narrative poem describes a gathering of veterans' groups to witness the Resurrection Day opening of the Tomb of the Unknown Soldier. When this famous war casualty is finally revealed, he turns out to be black, a circumstance that provokes bewilderment and consternation among the assembled patriots. Despite this original conceit, the poem is generally regarded as one of Johnson's lesser efforts, hampered by structural flaws and somewhat bland writing.

Johnson died tragically in June 1938 after a train struck the car he was riding in at an unguarded rail crossing in Wiscasset, Maine. The poet and civil rights leader was widely eulogized and more than two thousand mourners attended his Harlem funeral. Known throughout his career as a generous and invariably courteous man, Johnson once summed up his personal credo as a black American in a pamphlet published by the NAACP: "I will not allow one prejudiced person or one million or one hundred million to blight my life. I will not let prejudice or any of its attendant humiliations and injustices bear me down to spiritual defeat. My inner life is mine, and I shall defend and maintain its integrity against all the powers of hell." Johnson was buried in Brooklyn's Greenwood Cemetery dressed in his favorite lounging robe and holding a copy of *God's Trombones* in his hand.

BIOGRAPHICAL/CRITICAL SOURCES:

BOOKS

Bone, Robert A., *The Negro Novel in America,* Yale University Press, 1958. *Dictionary of Literary Biography,* Volume 51: *Afro-American Writers from the Harlem Renaissance to 1940,* Gale, 1987.

Fleming, Robert E., *James Weldon Johnson and Arna Wendell Bontemps: A Reference Guide,* G. K. Hall, 1978.
Johnson, James Weldon, *Along This Way: The Autobiography of James Weldon Johnson,* Viking, 1933, Da Capo, 1973.
Levy, Eugene, *James Weldon Johnson: Black Leader, Black Voice,* Chicago University Press, 1973.
Twentieth-Century Literary Criticism, Volume 19, Gale, 1986.
Wagner, Jean, *Les Poetes negres des Etats Unis,* Librairie Istra, 1962, translation by Kenneth Douglas published as *Black Poets of the United States: From Paul Laurence Dunbar to Langston Hughes,* University of Illinois Press, 1973.

PERIODICALS

American Literature, March, 1971.
Crisis, June, 1971.
Journal of Popular Culture, spring, 1968.
Nation, July 2, 1938.
New Republic, February 1, 1928, February 21, 1934.
Newsweek, July 4, 1938.
Phylon, December, 1960, winter, 1971.
Time, July 4, 1938.

*   *   *

JOHNSON, Pamela Hansford 1912-1981
(Nap Lombard, a joint pseudonym)

PERSONAL: Born May 29, 1912, in London, England; died of emphysema, June 18, 1981, in London; daughter of Reginald Kenneth (a civil servant) and Amy Clotilda (an actress; maiden name, Howson) Johnson; married Gordon Neil Stewart (an historian and journalist), 1936 (divorced); married Charles Percy Snow (a scientist and author), July 14, 1950 (died July 1, 1980); children: (first marriage) Andrew Morven, Lindsay Jean; (second marriage) Philip Charles Hansford. *Education:* Attended Clapham County Secondary School.

ADDRESSES: Home—85 Eaton Terr., London SW1, England. *Agent*—Curtis Brown Ltd., 575 Madison Ave., New York, N.Y. 10022.

CAREER: Central Hanover Bank & Trust Co., London, England, stenographer, 1930-34; author, 1935-81; literary critic, 1936-81.

MEMBER: PEN, Royal Society of Literature (fellow), Society for European Culture.

AWARDS, HONORS: Sunday Referee Award, 1933, for poetry; fellow, Center for Advanced Studies, Wesleyan University (Middletown, Conn.), and Timothy Dwight College, Yale University, both 1961; Litt.D., Temple University, Philadelphia, 1963, York University, Toronto, 1967, Widener College, Chester, Penn., 1970; Commander, Order of the British Empire, 1975; D.H.L., University of Louisville.

WRITINGS:

NOVELS

This Bed Thy Centre, Harcourt, 1935, reprinted, Macmillan (London), 1963.
Blessed above Women, Harcourt, 1936.
Here Today, Chapman & Hall, 1937.
World's End, Chapman & Hall, 1937, Carrick & Evans, 1938.
The Monument, Carrick & Evans, 1938.
Girdle of Venus, Chapman & Hall, 1939.
Too Dear for My Possessing (first novel in trilogy), Carrick & Evans, 1940, reprinted, Penguin, 1976, Scribner, 1973.
The Family Pattern, Collins, 1942.

Winter Quarters, Collins, 1943, Macmillan (New York), 1944.

The Trojan Brothers, M. Joseph, 1944, Macmillan, 1945.

An Avenue of Stone (second novel in trilogy), M. Joseph, 1947, Macmillan, 1948, reprinted, Scribner, 1973.

A Summer to Decide (third novel in trilogy), M. Joseph, 1948, Scribner, 1975.

The Philistines, M. Joseph, 1949.

Catherine Carter (first novel in trilogy), Knopf, 1952, reprinted, Macmillan (London), 1969, new edition, Penguin, 1971.

An Impossible Marriage (second novel in trilogy), Macmillan (London), 1954, Harcourt, 1955.

The Last Resort (third novel in trilogy), St. Martin's, 1956, published as *The Sea and the Wedding,* Harcourt, 1957.

The Humbler Creation, Macmillan, 1959, Harcourt, 1960.

An Error of Judgement, Harcourt, 1962.

The Survival of the Fittest, Scribner, 1968, reprinted, University of Chicago Press, 1984.

The Honours Board, Scribner, 1970.

The Holiday Friend, Macmillan, 1972, Scribner, 1973.

The Good Listener, Scribner, 1975.

The Good Husband, Scribner, 1978.

The Bonfire, Scribner, 1981.

"DOROTHY MERTON COMEDIES" TRILOGY

The Unspeakable Skipton, Harcourt, 1959, reprinted, Scribner, 1981.

Night and Silence, Who Is Here? An American Comedy, Scribner, 1963.

Cork Street, Next to the Hatter's: A Novel in Bad Taste, Scribner, 1965.

WITH GORDON NEIL STEWART UNDER JOINT PSEUDONYM NAP LOMBARD; MYSTERY NOVELS

Tidy Death, Cassell, 1940.

The Grinning Pig, Simon & Schuster, 1943 (published in England as *Murder's a Swine,* Hutchinson, 1943).

PLAYS

Corinth House: A Play in Three Acts (produced in London at New Lindsay Theatre, May, 1948), Evans Brothers, 1951, reprinted with an essay on the future of prose drama, St. Martin's, 1954.

(With husband, C. P. Snow) *The Supper Dance,* Evans Brothers, 1951.

(With Snow) *Family Party,* Evans Brothers, 1951.

(With Snow) *Spare the Rod,* Evans Brothers, 1951.

(With Snow) *To Murder Mrs. Mortimer,* Evans Brothers, 1951.

(With Snow) *Her Best Foot Forward,* Evans Brothers, 1951.

(With Snow) *The Pigeon with the Silver Foot: A Legend of Venice* (one-act), Evans Brothers, 1951.

(Adapter with Kitty Black) Jean Anouilh, *The Rehearsal* (produced in London, 1961; produced on Broadway at Royale Theatre, September 23, 1963), Methuen, 1961, Coward, 1962.

(Adapter with Snow) Georgi Dzhagarov, *The Public Prosecutor* (produced in London at Hampstead Theatre Club, 1967), translated from the Bulgarian by Marguerite Alexieva, University of Washington, 1969.

CONTRIBUTOR

Reginald Moore and Woodrow Wyatt, editors, *Stories of the Forties,* Nicolson & Watson, 1945.

Winter's Tales 1, Macmillan, 1955.

George D. Painter, editor and translator, *Marcel Proust: Letters to His Mother,* Rider, 1956, Citadel Press, 1958.

Winter's Tales 3, Macmillan, 1957.

Joan Kahn, editor, *Some Things Strange and Sinister,* Harper, 1973.

John Halperin, *C. P. Snow: An Oral Biography; Together with a Conversation with Lady Snow (Pamela Hansford Johnson),* St. Martin's, 1983.

Also contributor to *Essays and Studies* of the English Association, 1960, and 1963, and to *Transactions* of the Royal Society of Literature, 1963. Contributor of short stories, articles, and critical reviews to numerous periodicals, including *Washington Post, Liverpool Post, John O'London's Weekly, Sunday Chronicle, English Review,* and *Spectator.*

OTHER

Symphony for Full Orchestra (poems), Sunday Referee-Parton Press, 1934.

Thomas Wolfe: A Critical Study, Heinemann, 1947, published as *Hungry Gulliver: An English Critical Appraisal of Thomas Wolfe,* Scribner, 1948, published as *The Art of Thomas Wolfe,* 1963.

I. Compton-Burnett, Longmans, Green, 1951, reprinted, 1973.

Proust Recaptured: Six Radio Sketches Based on the Author's Characters (radio plays; based on *Remembrance of Things Past* by Marcel Proust; contains "The Duchess at Sunset," broadcast, 1948; "Swan in Love," broadcast, 1952; "Madame de Charlus," broadcast, 1954; "Albertine Regained," broadcast, 1954; "Saint-Loup," broadcast, 1955; "A Window at Montjaurain," broadcast, 1956), University of Chicago Press, 1958 (published in England as *Six Proust Reconstructions,* Macmillan, 1958).

(Editor with Snow) *Winter's Tales 7: Stories from Modern Russia,* St. Martin's, 1961, published as *Stories from Modern Russia,* 1962.

(Author of introduction) Cecil Woolf and Brocard Sewell, editors, *Corvo, 1860-1960,* St. Albert's Press, 1961, published as *New Quests for Corvo,* Icon, 1965.

(Author of introduction) Anthony Trollope, *Barchester Towers,* Norton, 1962.

Africa, 2nd edition, Oxford University Press, 1966.

On Iniquity: Some Personal Reflections Arising out of the Moors Murder Trial, Scribner, 1967.

Important to Me: Personalia (autobiography), Macmillan, 1974, Scribner, 1975.

WORK IN PROGRESS: Adelaide Bartlett, a novel.

SIDELIGHTS: Pamela Hansford Johnson was "one of England's best-known novelists, whom many American critics regarded as greatly underrated in the United States," according to her obituary in *Publishers Weekly.* Although perhaps better known in America for her marriage to Lord C. P. Snow, the famous scientist, novelist, and social theorist, Johnson was also renowned as a popular author and critic in her own right. She published her first novel, *This Bed Thy Centre,* when she was only twenty-two, and, in a career covering more than forty years, eventually produced twenty-nine others. "Anthony Burgess, the novelist and critic," said her *New York Times* obituary, "once described Miss Johnson's novels as 'witty, satirical and deftly malicious—some of her books characterized by a sort of grave levity, others by a sort of light gravity.' "

In her books Johnson examined ordinary people, in a wide variety of social classes, who are psychologically impaired in some way, unable to cope with everyday life; people who fall in and out of love; and people who are bound by a philosophy of duty or some other moral concept. According to Ishrat Lindblad in her book *Pamela Hansford Johnson,* "her protagonists are usually intelligent young men and women from the 'middle-middle' class, with literary or artistic ability, whose experience has much in common with her own. She also makes frequent use of a dominant mother and a weak or absent father, and the relationships between mother and child, teacher and pupil are among the most poignantly drawn in her fiction. At the same time she displays an interest in the bizarre and abnormal: nymphomaniacs, homosexuals, old men and women painfully in love with the young, crazed passion, and murder all fall within her range."

Johnson favored the psychological novel early in her career, using counterpoint, stream of consciousness, and interior monologues to examine people under stress. She later turned to more traditional English models, rejecting the experimental forms developed and used by James Joyce and others in the early decades of the twentieth century. Reviewers compared her work to that of George Eliot, Anthony Trollope, and Marcel Proust. In the 1940s, said Lindblad, she adopted an objective voice for narration, using it to explore "the perspective that distance and the passing of time lend to an experience, and it is this aspect of her work that most readily comes to mind as evidence of her debt to Marcel Proust." Later, Lindblad continued, she "moved over to the method of the great nineteenth-century novelists with an implied third-person narrator and a traditional chronological sequence of events." In these later works, stated her London *Times* obituary, "she revealed herself as a novelist in the central English tradition of broad realism. They were works which, in their sad, lucid, honest acceptance of life, were in the direct line of descent from George Eliot's fiction and were concerned, as that fiction was, with problems of right doing, of duty."

This Bed Thy Centre, although mild by today's standards, caused a sensation when it was first published because of its forthright examination of sex. It is a character study of Elsie Cotton, a young girl from a lower middle-class family who is growing up in a London suburb and trying to come to terms with her sexual inhibitions. She is attracted to Roly, the son of the town councilor, who returns her affections and eventually marries her. "Instead of the 'happily ever after' ending of the fairy tale, however," stated Lindblad, "the last few pages of the novel record the frightened thoughts of the young bride as she waits for her husband on her wedding night." Isabel Quigly in her study *Pamela Hansford Johnson* regarded *This Bed Thy Center* as showing "nearly all the basic characteristics of [Johnson's] later writing: its realism, its seriousness without solemnity, its use of social colour and atmosphere, its examination of love in many aspects, with very varied lovers and reactions to love, its lifelike dialogue—abrupt, easily embarrassed, totally 'unliterary.'"

Novels that followed *This Bed Thy Center* explore the psychological problems of people living in the 1920s and 1930s. *World's End* and *The Monument,* for instance, tell of young men and women struggling to survive amid the political and financial unrest of the 1930s, while *Blessed above Women* traces the disintegration of an elderly woman into insanity through sexual frustration. In these volumes Johnson successfully examined the problems resulting from "psychic deprivation and suffering, the exploitation of working-class labor, the unemployment of the thirties, the rise of fascism, and the impending war," declared *Dictionary of Literary Biography* contributor Susan Currier. Although these books were not intended to be didactic, stated Marigold Johnson in the *Times Literary Supplement,* Johnson's "sense of the serious moral duty of the novelist, her concern with the consequences of sin, the torture of bad conscience, the retributive agony of guilt, are still observable even in the plethora of surface domestic detail." Currier explained, "Without blurring

the fluid, clear contours of her characters and situations, she bares their irrational and intolerable interiors."

"Possibly the three volumes of the trilogy [*Too Dear for My Possessing, An Avenue of Stone,* and *A Summer to Decide*] are together Pamela Hansford Johnson's most impressive achievement," declared Quigley. "In them, for the first time," the essayist continued, "she used the public and private lives—the outer and inner worlds—of her characters with complete assurance, and manipulated a large number of these characters and worlds, covering a wide social field, without any sense of strain." The narrator of the sequence is Claud Pickering, a young man relating the story of his life and of the lives of those closest to him. However, the dominant character, and the one after whom Johnson named the trilogy, is not Claud but his stepmother Helena Shea, an Irish singer and the former mistress of Claud's father. Other major characters include Charmian, Helena's daughter and Claud's half-sister, Sir Daniel Archer, whom Helena marries after Claud's father dies, and Cecil, Archer's daughter.

Johnson pursued a Proustian theme of love and memory in *Too Dear for My Possessing,* said Quigley. In it, Claud relates the story of his early years from the perspective of a grown man. When the novel opens, Claud's parents have separated. Unable to obtain a divorce, Claud's father has taken Helena and his teenaged son to live in Belgium. When Claud turns thirteen he receives a visit from his mother, accompanied by her friend Archer and Cecil. "Cecil awakens Claud's dormant sexuality but circumstances work against their relationship developing," explained Lindblad. Claud grows up, marries a girl who works in his office, "is successful; but [he is] haunted, always, by a dream, a vision, a reality that life—or he himself or the girl who was the heart of the dream—forces into the background," declared *New York Times Book Review* contributor Jane Spence Southron. Although Claud eventually declares his love to Cecil and discovers that it is returned, Cecil dies before Claud is free to marry her. He then sits down to write the story of his love for Cecil, pondering "man's romantic nature and his tendency to fall in love with an unattainable dream," stated Lindblad.

Claud continues his family's story in *An Avenue of Stone* and *A Summer to Decide.* "More Helena's book than either of the other two," according to Currier, *An Avenue of Stone* tells of the widowed Lady Archer's infatuation with a worthless young man and of her inability to accept her own aging. *A Summer to Decide* traces Claud's progress into a new, successful relationship at the same time as it reveals the failure of Charmian's marriage. In both books, said Currier, "Claud finds himself torn between desires to intervene on Helena's or Charmian's behalf and painful acknowledgement of their rights to their own degrading passions." "Claud's anger and fidelity, frustration and love, and finally his decision to withdraw," she concluded, "—these are precisely what Johnson is best at—psychological process, attached to ordinary life, in motion."

Johnson wrote about women who shared Charmian's problem in three related novels: *Catherine Carter, An Impossible Marriage,* and *The Last Resort.* Each of these books features women whose desires conflict with their concept of marital duty. Although they are quite different in plot and setting—*Catherine Carter* is a story of the Victorian theater, while the other two depict modern domestic life—Johnson examined in them the same situation in three different ways, and with three different results. For example, the heroine and title character in *Catherine Carter* ends her unhappy marriage by divorcing her husband and gains professional acceptance on equal terms with her second husband. Christine Jackson, the protagonist of *An Impossible Mar-*

riage, also chooses divorce to escape her unfaithful and unloving first husband, but she relates her story in the same way Claud did his in *Too Dear for My Possessing,* said Lindblad. *The Last Resort,* on the other hand, features a woman who adopts marriage as a refuge from guilt; it is the story of Celia Baird, "a well-to-do girl who is rejected by her lover after the death of his invalid wife, and marries a homosexual in the desperate need to obtain at least a new name and an unseparate life," according to a *Times Literary Supplement* reviewer.

In the late 1950s and early 1960s, Johnson changed the direction of her work, moving away from mainstream fiction. Books produced during these years include the "Dorothy Merton Comedies"—*The Unspeakable Skipton, Night and Silence, Who Is Here? An American Comedy,* and *Cork Street, Next to the Hatter's: A Novel in Bad Taste*—a series of satirical novels commenting on the literary life of England and America. The first of these, Lindblad stated, "attracted more attention than any of the author's books since *This Bed Thy Centre.* Critics were impressed by her ability to write a successful comic novel so different from her previous work." They were especially impressed with her characterization of a paranoid artist. Daniel Skipton, "a superb comic creation," according to Walter Allen in the *New Statesman,* is an English-born writer living in Belgium who is fully convinced that he is an unappreciated genius. He has written a single, largely ignored, decadent novel, and must earn a living by "scroung[ing] on gullible tourists and pimp[ing]" to supplement his income, Lindblad explained. "He exploits everyone he can," remarked Currier, "including relatives and publishers to whom he owes more gratitude than venom; and he rationalizes his behavior with fantasies of persecution and his own undervalued worth." In the period covered by the novel—the last few weeks of Skipton's life—he joins a group of pseudo-literati English tourists led by Dorothy Merton, a poetic dramatist and self-proclaimed literary expert. Skipton's attempts to embezzle the tourists end in his own ruin. "Insufferable in victory, magnificiently spiteful and enraged in defeat, Skipton on his death bed conquers, but only esthetically, his gross tormentors," declared *Commonweal* contributor Thomas Curley.

Johnson published her last novel, *A Bonfire,* only a few weeks before she died. Its central image is the bonfire fourteen-year-old Emma Sheldrake watches the night she learns about sexual contact; reviewer Marigold Johnson explained, "Emma thinks she'd prefer being a nun." That same night her father dies. Emma marries Stephen Hood several years later and finds release from many of her inhibitions, but that relationship is doomed. Emma's life from then on is dominated by the "half-real fear of the eternal bonfire at the end of the primrose path of sexual self-indulgence," stated *New Statesman* contributor Gillian Wilce. Before she turns twenty-six, she loses Stephen in an automobile accident, has a brief affair with a younger man, remarries, and her second husband commits suicide. Is it any wonder, asked Marigold Johnson, that Emma is convinced "that her sexual gratifications, blessed or unblessed, have irrevocably destined her for 'the everlasting bonfire'?" In her final book, said R. L. Widman in the *Washington Post Book World,* "Johnson writes with depth, compassion and perspicuity about Emma's feelings, sexual desires and thoughts while avoiding graphic descriptions."

Critical opinion suggests that Johnson's abilities were strongest in the creation of realistic characters and the examination of meaningful themes. Throughout Johnson's career as a novelist, stated Lindblad, "she has demonstrated the seriousness of her commitment to her art and explored those aspects of life that touch upon the experience of most readers with a great deal of lucidity and humaneness." Her talent "is not the mild talent called character-drawing," said Quigly; "it is the creation of people who live outside the novels' pages, who enrich our knowledge of others. It is probably the most creative—the most importantly creative—of the novelist's gifts: the ability to fashion people we come to know more vividly and closely and fruitfully than we know most of our friends, people full grown, credible, feeling, responsive, whose unmentioned feelings we can gauge, whose undescribed reactions we can always imagine, who do not fade and diminish when we shut the book."

AVOCATIONAL INTERESTS: Travel, history, and the philosophy of art.

BIOGRAPHICAL/CRITICAL SOURCES:

BOOKS

Allen, Walter, *The Modern Novel,* Dutton, 1964.
Burgess, Anthony, *The Novel Now: A Guide to Contemporary Fiction,* Norton, 1967.
Contemporary Literary Criticism, Gale, Volume 1, 1973, Volume 7, 1977, Volume 27, 1984.
Dictionary of Literary Biography, Volume 15: *British Novelists, 1930-1959,* Gale, 1983.
Halperin, John, *C. P. Snow: An Oral Biography; Together with a Conversation with Lady Snow (Pamela Hansford Johnson),* St. Martin's, 1983.
Johnson, Pamela Hansford, *Important to Me: Personalia,* Macmillan, 1974, Scribner, 1975.
Karl, Frederick R., *A Reader's Guide to the Contemporary English Novel,* Farrar, Straus, 1962.
Lindblad, Ishrat, *Pamela Hansford Johnson,* Twayne, 1982.
Newquist, Roy, *Counterpoint,* Rand McNally, 1984.
Quigly, Isabel, *Pamela Hansford Johnson,* Longmans, Green, 1968.
Snow, Philip, *Stranger and Brother: A Portrait of C. P. Snow,* Macmillan, 1982, Scribner, 1983.

PERIODICALS

Atlantic, November, 1965.
Chicago Tribune, February 1, 1959, September 16, 1962.
Christian Science Monitor, October 22, 1970, August 3, 1979.
Commonweal, October 21, 1938, February 20, 1959, February 11, 1966.
Drama, fall, 1969.
Kirkus Reviews, January 1, 1960.
Listener, May 16, 1968.
Los Angeles Times Book Review, August 19, 1979, September 13, 1981.
Manchester Guardian, January 23, 1959.
Nation, August 19, 1968.
National Review, August 13, 1968, August 3, 1973.
New Leader, November 16, 1971.
New Republic, March 21, 1960, March 25, 1967.
New Statesman, January 10, 1959, October 1, 1965, March 24, 1967, May 17, 1968, August 14, 1970, October 27, 1972, September 20, 1974, April 25, 1975, July 4, 1975, October 27, 1978, May 1, 1981.
New Statesman and Nation, October 9, 1937, August 31, 1940, February 2, 1952.
Newsweek, May 27, 1968.
New Yorker, March 21, 1959, December 11, 1965, May 25, 1968, April 28, 1973, April 21, 1975, June 30, 1975, November 3, 1975, September 14, 1981.
New York Times, February 25, 1967, May 28, 1968.

New York Times Book Review, February 27, 1938, September 11, 1938, July 28, 1940, July 1, 1945, July 20, 1952, February 24, 1957, February 28, 1960, September 16, 1962, November 14, 1965, July 7, 1968, September 20, 1970, December 6, 1970, September 14, 1975, September 28, 1975.

Observer Review, March 12, 1967.

Publishers Weekly, November 30, 1959.

Reporter, May 18, 1967.

Saturday Evening Post, January 14, 1967.

Saturday Review, July 20, 1963, October 9, 1965, April 15, 1967, August 3, 1968, October 24, 1970, February 22, 1975.

Saturday Review of Literature, June 16, 1945.

Spectator, May 30, 1947, June 21, 1975, May 30, 1981.

Time, November 19, 1965, April 7, 1967, January 3, 1969, September 28, 1970.

Times Literary Supplement, May 31, 1947, November 16, 1956, January 9, 1959, July 20, 1962, September 30, 1965, May 16, 1968, August 14, 1970, October 27, 1972, January 3, 1975, May 2, 1975, June 20, 1975, November 3, 1978, May 1, 1981.

Washington Post, July 14, 1979.

Washington Post Book World, January 28, 1973, September 3, 1981.

OBITUARIES:

PERIODICALS

AB Bookman's Weekly, July 13-20, 1981.

Bookseller, July 4, 1981.

Daily Telegraph (London), June 20, 1981, August 5, 1981.

Guardian (London), June 20, 1981.

Newsweek, June 29, 1981.

New York Times, June 20, 1981.

Publishers Weekly, July 3, 1981.

Sunday Times (London), June 21, 1981.

Time, June 29, 1981.

Times (London), June 20, 1981.

Washington Post, June 21, 1981.

[Sketch reviewed by brother-in-law, Philip Snow]

* * *

JOHNSON, Uwe 1934-1984

PERSONAL: First name is pronounced "Oo-veh"; born July 20, 1934, in Kaemmin, Pomerania (now in Poland); died of a heart attack, March, 1984, in Sheerness, England; son of Erich and Erna (Straede) Johnson; married Elizabeth Schmidt, 1962; children: Katharina E. *Education:* Attended University of Rostock, 1952-54; University of Leipzig, diploma in philology, 1956.

ADDRESSES: Home—26 Marine Parade, Sheerness, Kent ME12 2BB, England.

CAREER: Writer. Lecturer at Wayne State University and Harvard University, 1961; Harcourt, Brace & World, New York, N.Y., full-time editor of new German writing, 1966-67.

MEMBER: P.E.N. (Federal Republic of Germany), Akademie d. Kuenste (West Berlin), Deutsche Akademie (Darmstadt), Gruppe 47.

AWARDS, HONORS: Fontane-Preis Westberlin, 1960; Prix International de la Litterature, 1962; Villa Massino grant, 1962; Buechner-Preis, 1971; Raabe-Preis, 1975; Thomas Mann-Preis, 1978.

WRITINGS:

Mutmassungen ueber Jakob (fiction), Suhrkamp, 1959, translation by Ursule Molinaro published as *Speculations About Jakob,* Grove, 1963.

(Translator) Herman Melville, *Israel Potter,* Dieterich, 1960.

Das dritte Buch ueber Achim (fiction), Suhrkamp, 1961, translation by Molinaro published as *The Third Book About Achim,* Harper, 1967.

(Translator) John Knowles, *In diesem Land,* Suhrkamp, 1963.

Karsch und andere Prosa (fiction), Suhrkamp, 1964, translation of part published as *An Absence,* Cape, 1969.

Zwei Ansichten (fiction), Suhrkamp, 1965, translation by Richard Winston and Clara Winston published as *Two Views,* Harcourt, 1966.

(Editor) Bertolt Brecht, *Me-ti: Buch der Wendungen,* Suhrkamp, 1965.

Jahrestage: Aus dem Leben von Gesine Cresspahl (fiction), four volumes, Suhrkamp, 1970-83, translation of Volume I and part of Volume II by Leila Vennewitz published as *Anniversaries: From the Life of Gesine Cresspahl,* Harcourt, 1975, translation of part of Volume II and all of Volumes III and IV by Vennewitz and Walter Arndt published as *Anniversaries II: From the Life of Gesine Cresspahl,* Harcourt, 1987.

Eine Reise nach Klagenfurt, Suhrkamp, 1974.

Berliner Sachen: Aufsaetze, Suhrkamp, 1975.

(Editor with Hans Mayer) *Das Werk von Samuel Beckett: Berliner Colloquium,* Suhrkamp, 1975.

(Editor) Max Frisch, *Stich-Worte,* Suhrkamp, 1975.

Von dem Fischer un syner Fru: Ein Maerchen nach Philipp Otto Runge (fiction), Insel, 1976.

Begleitumstaende: Frankfurter Vorlesungen, Suhrkamp, 1980.

Skizze eines Verunglueckten (fiction), Suhrkamp, 1982.

Ingrid Babendererde: Reifeprufung 1953, Suhrkamp, 1985.

SIDELIGHTS: Webster Schott thought that Uwe Johnson "writes like no one else anywhere. . . . Imagine the [William] Faulkner style with [Ernest] Hemingway-like diction, and studded with Proustian minutiae. That is close but not quite it." John Fletcher noted that, for Johnson, "reality is not grasped by language, but created by it; language not only delimits the world . . . it also structures it. . . . [He] has seized upon this essential truth, and explores it with dazzling virtuosity and invention." Fletcher found Johnson's work "aesthetically the most accomplished to have come out of Germany in recent years." In it are present "the trauma of defeat and subsequent political division of his country, the need to recreate the literary tradition, and the problem of relating to a self-satisfied and philistine society."

The theme of divided Germany is at the center of all Johnson's work, even in *Anniversaries,* which is set in America. As E. R. von Freiburg wrote, "[Johnson's] homeland is not merely divided but kaleidoscopically splintered. In novel after novel, with endless pains, he sweeps the glittering shards of his national identity together and tries to make them function, if not as what they were, then at least as what they are or might be, knowing from the start that even this melancholy compromise must fail."

Another characteristic of Johnson's writing is his controlled detachment. As Joseph McElroy commented: "Even when we are closest to them, Johnson's people are frighteningly private. He has a way of retreating from scenes." A reviewer for the *Times Literary Supplement* put this in another way: "[Johnson's] prose has an incisive, almost sullen reticence in which not a few Germans under forty will recognize their own voices—and silences. . . . He does not parade any sovereign knowledge of what is going on inside his characters' heads."

Richard Howard wrote, "None of [Johnson's] earlier books . . . is much fun to read." But Howard found *Anniversaries* "a book so large in its aspirations, so fresh in its attitudes, so militant in its inventions, and so unmistakable in their realization that I must call it a masterpiece, even though it is not yet the entire work."

Johnson's prose "tends to bypass all the common abstractions which haunt German fiction," wrote another reviewer. "Fictions, for him, are not devised to define some general truth behind the historical situation which he analyzes; they present rather the concrete infinitesimals of all the possibilities of what the truth might be to the characters within that situation. The situation is always Germany divided. The truth is always a scintillation given off, as actions and perceptions collide in the sensibilities of his characters: It is indefinable, in their nerves, like a solution that will not quite crystallize, or some sort of unlocalized ache in the midst of the German present."

BIOGRAPHICAL/CRITICAL SOURCES:

BOOKS

Baumgart, Reinhart, editor, *Ueber Johnson,* Suhrkamp, 1970.
Botheroyd, Paul F., *Ich und Er: First and Third Person Self-Reference and Problems of Identity in Three Contemporary German-Language Novels,* Mouton, 1976.
Boulby, Mark, *Johnson,* Ungar, 1974.
Contemporary Literary Criticism, Gale, Volume 5, 1976, Volume 10, 1979, Volume 15, 1980, Volume 40, 1986.
Dictionary of Literary Biography, Volume 75: *Contemporary German Fiction Writers, Second Series,* Gale, 1988.
Enright, D., *Conspirators and Poets,* Dufour, 1966.

PERIODICALS

Atlantic, May, 1963.
Christian Century, March 1, 1967.
Christian Science Monitor, April 27, 1967.
Commonweal, April 26, 1963, April 14, 1967.
Encounter, January, 1964.
Harper's, August, 1967.
International Fiction Review, July, 1974.
L'Express, October 11, 1962.
Nation, April 6, 1963, February 13, 1967, September 4, 1967.
Neue deutsche Hefte, Number 6, 1959-60.
New Leader, May 22, 1967.
New Republic, May 25, 1963.
New Statesman, September 6, 1963.
New Yorker, May 18, 1963.
New York Herald Tribune Books, April 7, 1963.
New York Times, December 4, 1966.
New York Times Book Review, April 14, 1963, November 20, 1966, November 8, 1987.
Observer Review, July 9, 1967, January 14, 1968.
Saturday Review, April 6, 1963, December 18, 1965.
Time, January 4, 1963, April 12, 1963.
Times Literary Supplement, September 6, 1963, September 30, 1965, October 14, 1983, October 14, 1985.

OBITUARIES:

PERIODICALS

Chicago Times, March 16, 1984.
Publishers Weekly, March 30, 1984.
Time, March 26, 1984.

JONES, David (Michael) 1895-1974

PERSONAL: Born November 1, 1895, in Brockley, Kent, England; died October 28, 1974, in Harrow, London, England; son of James (a printer's overseer) and Alice Ann (Bradshaw) Jones. *Education:* Attended Camberwell School of Art, 1909-14, and 1919, and Westminster Art School, 1919-21. *Religion:* Roman Catholic.

ADDRESSES: Home—c/o Monksdene Hotel, 2 Northwick Park Rd., Harrow, Middlesex, England.

CAREER: Engraver, book illustrator, painter, poet, and water colorist, 1921-74; worked with craftsman Eric Gill at Ditchling Common, Sussex, 1922-24, and at Capel-y-ffin, Wales, 1925-27. Represented at Venice Biennale International Exhibition of the Fine Arts, 1934; exhibitions of work include shows at the Goupil Gallery, 1929, the National Gallery, London, 1940, 1941, 1942, in Paris, 1945, in Brooklyn, N.Y., 1952-53, and one-man shows at St. George's Gallery, 1927, the Tate Gallery, London, 1954-55, the National Book League, London, 1972, and in Edinburgh, Scotland, and Aberystwyth and Swansea, Wales. Works are found in the collections of the Tate Gallery and the Victoria and Albert Museum in London, the Whitworth Gallery, University of Manchester, the Museum of London, the Walker Gallery, the Liverpool Laing Gallery, Newcastle Kelly's Yard, the National Museum of Wales, Cardiff, the Sydney Art Gallery, the Toronto Art Gallery, the Arts Council of Great Britain, London, and the British Council, London. *Military service:* Royal Welch Fusiliers, infantryman, 1915-18; served with 15th Battalion.

MEMBER: Honorable Society of Cymmrodorion, Society for Nautical Research, Royal Society of Painters in Watercolours (honorary member), Royal Society of Literature (fellow).

AWARDS, HONORS: Royal Society Drawing Prize, 1904; Hawthornden Prize, 1938, for *In Parenthesis;* Russell Loines Memorial Award for poetry, National Institute and American Academy of Arts and Letters, 1954, for *The Anathemata;* Commander, Order of the British Empire, 1955; Harriet Monroe Memorial Prize, *Poetry* magazine, 1956, for poem "The Wall"; D.Litt., University of Wales, 1960; Welsh Arts Council Committee prize, 1960, for *Epoch and Artist,* and 1969; Levinson Prize, *Poetry* magazine, 1961, for poem "The Tutelar of Place"; Royal National Eisteddfod of Wales, Visual Arts Section, Gold Medal for Fine Arts, 1964; Midsummer Prize, Corporation of London, 1968; Companion of Honour, 1974.

WRITINGS:

In Parenthesis, Faber, 1937, 2nd edition, with an introduction by T. S. Eliot, Viking, 1961.
The Anathemata: Fragments of an Attempted Writing (poetry), Faber, 1952, 2nd edition, 1955, Chilmark, 1963.
Epoch and Artist: Selected Writings, edited by Harman Grisewood, Chilmark, 1959.
The Fatigue: A.V.C. DCCLXXIV, Tantus labor non sit cassus, Rampant Lions Press, 1965.
The Tribune's Visitation (poetry), Fulcrum Press, 1969.
An Introduction to "The Rime of the Ancient Mariner," Clover Hill Editions, 1972.
The Sleeping Lord and Other Fragments, Faber, 1974.
Use and Sign, Golgonooza Press, 1975.
The Kensington Mass, edited by Rene Hague, Agenda Editions, 1975.
The Dying Gaul and Other Writings, edited and with an introduction by Grisewood, Faber, 1978.
The Roman Quarry and Other Sequences, Agenda Editions, 1981, Sheep Meadow Press, 1982.

ILLUSTRATOR

A Child's Rosary Book, St. Dominic's Press, 1924.

Eleanor Farjeon, *The Town Child's Alphabet,* Poetry Bookshop, 1924.

H. D. C. Pepler, *Libellus Lapidum,* St. Dominic's Press, 1924.

Jonathan Swift, *Gulliver's Travels into Several Remote Nations of the World,* two volumes, Golden Cockerel Press, 1925.

The Book of Jonah, Golden Cockerel Press, 1926.

Francis Coventry, *Pompey the Little,* Golden Cockerel Press, 1926.

Llyfr y pregeth-wr (Welsh translation of Book of Ecclesiastes), Gwasg Gregynog, 1927.

J. Isaacs, editor, *The Chester Play of the Deluge,* Golden Cockerel Press, 1927.

Samuel Taylor Coleridge, *The Rime of the Ancient Mariner,* Douglas Cleverdon, 1929.

Gwen Plunket Green, *The Prophet Child,* Longmans, 1935, Dutton, 1937.

David Jones (paintings), Penguin, 1949.

David Jones Exhibition, National Book League (London), 1972.

David Jones (exhibition catalogue), The Tate Gallery, 1981.

Also illustrator of R. H. J. Stewart, *March, Kind Comrade,* 1931. Contributor of illustrations to magazines and periodicals, including *The Game.*

OTHER

(Contributor) Elizabeth Jennings, editor, *An Anthology of Modern Verse, 1940-1960,* Methuen, 1961.

Excerpts from The Anathemata, In Parenthesis, [and] *The Hunt* (recording; read by the author), Argo, 1967.

David Jones: Letters to Vernon Watkins, edited and with notes by Ruth Pryor, University of Wales Press, 1976.

Letters to William Hayward, edited by Colin Wilcockson, Agenda Editions, 1979.

Introducing David Jones: A Selection of His Writings, edited by John Matthias with an introduction by Stephen Spender, Faber, 1980.

Dai Greatcoat: A Self-Portrait of David Jones in His Letters, edited by Hague, Faber, 1980.

Letters to a Friend, edited by Aneirin Talfan Davies, Triskele, 1980.

Inner Necessities: Letters of David Jones to Desmond Chute, edited by Thomas R. Dilworth, Anson-Cartwright, 1984.

Contributor to publications, including *Anglo-Welsh Review, Poetry, Listener, Agenda, Times* (London), *Times Literary Supplement,* and others.

The manuscripts of *In Parenthesis, The Anathemata* and *The Sleeping Lord,* along with Jones's personal library, are in the National Library of Wales at Aberystwyth. Jones's letters to Rene Hague are in the Fisher Rare Book Library of the University of Toronto, and his letters to Harman Grisewood are held in the collection of the Beinecke Rare Book Library of Yale University. Various prose manuscripts are in the Boston College library.

SIDELIGHTS: While not as well known as other modernist writers such as T. S. Eliot, Ezra Pound, and James Joyce, David Jones "is increasingly regarded as an important, innovative poet, who has extended and refined the techniques of literary modernism," according to *Dictionary of Literary Biography* contributor Vincent B. Sherry, Jr. A graphic artist as well as a poet, Jones is best known for his long narrative poems *In Parenthesis* and *The Anathemata,* and for his engravings and paintings, which have won many awards. "The supreme quality of his art," both literary and graphic, reports Kathleen Raine in the *Sewanee Re-*

view, ". . . has long been apparent to an inner circle of his friends," but, she adds, "he has never at any time been a widely-read, still less a fashionable, writer, nor is he ever likely to become so, for his work is too subtle and learned for popular tastes."

Much of Jones's oeuvre evokes his Welsh heritage and echoes the events of his own life. "At the time of my birth," he once told *CA,* "my father was a printer's overseer and that meant that I was brought up in a home that took the printed page and its illustration for granted. I began drawing when I was aged five and regarded it as a natural activity which I would pursue as I grew older. I was backward at lessons, could not read til I was about seven or eight, and did not take to writing in the sense of writing books until I was thirty-three years old." In January 1915, Jones enlisted in the Royal Welch Fusiliers as an infantryman, and he served on the Western front from December of that year to March of 1918. After the war he embraced Roman Catholicism and joined a small community of Catholic artists headed by craftsman Eric Gill, among whom he began to develop a unique concept of art and the function of the artist. He did not begin to write *In Parenthesis,* a fictionalized account of his activities in the war, until 1928, and almost a decade passed before it was published. Jones's war experiences and his religious conversion permeate his first long poem. Like Jones, John Ball, the protagonist of *In Parenthesis,* served in the British army on the Western Front during World War I. Both Jones and Ball began training late in 1915, and both were wounded in the battle of the Somme in June of 1916. His second long poem, *The Anathemata,* reflects the poet's Catholic faith and understanding of his art. Set during the Consecration of the Mass, it encompasses the entire history of mankind. Other works display Jones's eclectic tastes, depicting scenes from Celtic literature and mythology, Arthurian legend, Greek and Roman antiquity, and scripture.

Complex in organization, rich in vocabulary, *In Parenthesis* demonstrates the intricacies of Jones's work. David Blamires points out in *David Jones: Artist and Writer* that "in length and overall structure . . . [it] may be said to be a novel, but in its use of language it is more akin to poetry." The poem is divided into seven parts, and tells the story of Private John Ball and his company from their embarkation from England in December 1915 to their participation in the Somme battle of July 1916. "But though Ball is usually present as protagonist-spectator," declares Monroe K. Spears in *Contemporary Literature,* "the poem expresses not his thoughts alone but, most of the time, a kind of collective consciousness; and hence many different forms and levels are necessary. . . . All the details of speech and everything else are vivid, precise, and evocative: but literal realism is immediately transcended." "*In Parenthesis* varies in medium from straightforward prose to prose that is highly elliptical, condensed, dislocated, and discontinuous and to verse with a rhythm that is sometimes very strong—allusive, liturgical, or incantory—but that never employs rhyme or any regular pattern," Spears explains. "The result is a profound and shattering disclosure of combat's physical destruction and spiritual outrage," asserts Thomas Dilworth in the *Georgia Review,* "which is sustained by a controlled and variegated tone lacking in the work of the combatant poets who wrote during the war."

Jones draws on his Welsh literary heritage to describe his experiences. Each of the seven parts of the poem is prefaced with a quotation from an ancient Welsh heroic epic, *Y Gododdin,* which commemorates the destruction of a three-hundred-man raiding party by the English at the battle of Catraeth. The poet also takes images from Shakespeare's history plays and Malory's *Morte d'Arthur,* as well as from T. S. Eliot's *The Waste Land,* mingling with them expressions from the early twentieth century and soldiers' slang from the war. Paul Fussell points out in *The Great War and Modern Memory* that at the end of the first section of the poem the newly trained soldiers "set toward France," just as Henry V does in Shakespeare's play. Part IV is titled "King Pellam's Launde," in reference to the desolate country in which King Arthur's knights find the Holy Grail in the *Morte d'Arthur*. Also drawn from Malory is Ball's fellow soldier Dai Greatcoat, who rises after the platoon's meal and delivers a warrior's boast, patterned after those that appear in epic poetry, in which he claims to have participated in every major battle in history and legend from the fall of Lucifer to the present. He declares that his fathers were present at Edward III's victory over the French at Crecy, and asserts that he took part in Arthur's wars and was a member of the Roman legion that crucified Jesus.

Many critics hold that the archetypal figure Dai Greatcoat and indeed all Jones's soldiers represent the human experience in war throughout the ages. *New York Review of Books* contributor D. S. Carne-Ross maintains, "Jones came in retrospect to see the first of our 'great' modern wars (at least up to the battle of the Somme) as the last action of an older world, the last time that the ancient usages still just held, hence it represented what he and his friends called the Break, the point at which man stepped clear of his past and turned his back on all the previous history of the race." "Faced with the disintegration brought about by the First World War, David Jones sought to recover roots, not just for an individual, but for a whole people," declares Atholl C. C. Murray in *Critical Quarterly*. "This he attempted by constantly emphasising the continuity of history, by showing that the present derives from the past and that both are part of the one process. Thus it is that at various times his Londoners and Welshmen may be assimilated to the three hundred who fought at Catraeth, or to the troops under Henry V at Agincourt, or even to the Roman legionaries." Samuel Rees, writing in *David Jones*, states that "the racial or mythic ancestry that Jones provides for them places them in the whole history of recorded time; they share the human psyche of the soldiers at Catraeth, at the Crucifixion, at Malplaquet, at Harfleur, wherever man has organized war against his own kind."

While all commentators recognize *In Parenthesis* as an important literary achievement, they are divided in their assessments of its success in representing the experience of World War I. Some believe, as does Michael Mott of *Poetry* magazine, that "*In Parenthesis* seems an astonishingly successful combining of epic myth and actuality." Yet Jones's verse is decidedly understated compared to that of the heroic bards. "In chronicling the action of which he was a part, [Jones] does not seek to be an epic poet singing hymns of battle in which new heroes reenact the earth-shaking deeds of their ancestors," reports Rees. "Without apology or special pleading, he details from intimate firsthand acquaintance with the present—and from affectionate intimacy with historical man—the minds and actions of those compelled, for whatever reason, whatever 'accidents' of history and geography, to go 'once more into the breach.'" Yet John H. Johnson, writing in *English Poetry of the First World War*, argues that the poem is indeed an epic, and Dilworth agrees; in *The Shape of Meaning in the Poetry of David Jones*, he states that *In Parenthesis* "is the only authentic and successful epic poem in the language since *Paradise Lost*."

In some critics' opinions, *In Parenthesis* presents an ambiguous vision of the war. Carne-Ross remarks, "What is largely missing is the note of protest, the sense of war as an aberration, something that must never be allowed to happen again." Nonetheless, he concludes, the poet's perspective is understandable: "War is

hell, certainly, but Jones never doubted that there is a good deal of hell around and this aspect of the matter did not greatly surprise him." Dilworth acknowledges that the poem is not primarily interested in promoting pacifism but, he declares, "Its ironies are double-edged; they indict war but also stress the essential goodness of the individual combatant." Rees concludes that "*In Parenthesis* is not a poem either to provoke or to end a war . . . except as it adds to the accumulation of testimony to the stupidities and brutality of history that each age much learn from or, more likely, ignore."

Critics also disagree in their interpretations of the poem's attempt to understand the war. Murray, for instance, calls *In Parenthesis* "a book about how man, even in the most appalling circumstances, can still discern beneath the surface of experience an ultimate significance in life." "If one is ready to perceive it," he concludes, "then there is order and beauty to be discovered even in the lice-ridden marshes of Flanders." On the other hand, Fussell disagrees with this interpretation of the war. He believes that *In Parenthesis* suggests, by placing the suffering of modern British soldiers in an epic, heroic context, "that the war, if ghastly, is firmly 'in the tradition.'" It even implies that, once conceived to be in the tradition, the war can be understood. The tradition to which the poem points holds suffering to be close to sacrifice and individual effort to end in heroism; it contains, unfortunately, no precedent for an understanding of war as a shambles and its participants as victims."

"And yet for all these defects," Fussell admits, "*In Parenthesis* remains in many ways a masterpiece impervious to criticism." The poem, he concludes, is "profoundly decent. When on his twenty-first birthday Mr. Jenkins [the commander of Ball's platoon] receives both his promotion to full lieutenant and a nice parcel from Fortnum and Mason's, we are pleased. Details like these pull the poem in quite a different direction from that indicated by its insistent invocation of myth and ritual and romance. Details like these persuade us with all the power of art that the Western Front is not King Pellam's Land, that it will not be restored and made whole, ever, by the expiatory magic of the Grail. It is too human for that."

In Parenthesis was recognized at the time of its publication in 1937 as a work of immense literary importance and continues to be celebrated as such today. In *The Long Conversation: A Memoir of David Jones*, William Blisset reports that, at a party celebrating the poem's winning the Hawthornden Prize, William Butler Yeats "bowed and intoned: 'I salute the author of *In Parenthesis*.'" T. S. Eliot also praised the work, and many critics acclaimed it highly. "Herbert Read, writing for the *London Mercury*," relates Sherry, "found it 'as near a great epic of the war as ever the war generation will reach,' displaying 'the noble ardour of the *Chanson de Roland* and the rich cadences of the *Morte d'Arthur*.'" More recently, *New York Times Book Review* contributor Stephen Spender has called *In Parenthesis* "the most monumental work of poetic genius to come out of World War I." Dilworth echoes his assessment, saying, "By most accounts, *In Parenthesis* . . . is the finest work of literature to emerge from combat experience in the First World War."

Between 1937 and 1952 Jones worked on a variety of poems, but published very little. A nervous disorder developing from his war experiences prevented his holding a steady job, and his income depended mainly on the generosity of his friends. Pressures from his uncertain earnings aggravated his condition, and in 1946 he suffered a mental collapse that required a rest of nearly a year and a half. In the interim Jones worked on his painting and poetry and further developed his theory of art and artistry, expressing his views in letters and essays. It was not until 1952, with the encouragement of T. S. Eliot and other friends, that he published his second long poem, *The Anathemata,* which partly expounds his aesthetic philosophy and partly expresses his personal faith.

Like *In Parenthesis, The Anathemata* is modernistic, allusive, and fragmentive, but it lacks the chronological storyline that characterizes the earlier work. Instead, it consists of eight separate sections, tracing various traditions of British and European culture, and unified by the image of the Mass. "It is the only epic-length work in any language, as far as I know," declares Dilworth in *The Shape of Meaning,* "in which structure successfully replaces narrative as the primary principle of order. And more than merely ordering content, the structure of *The Anathemata* gives it powerful symbolic focus." "*The Anathemata* does not have the confined narrative structure or the clear identification with classical epic of *In Parenthesis,*" asserts Rees. "More ambitious, certainly, than that work, it attempts something approaching the whole cultural history of the British Isles." Nicholas Jacobs declares in *Agenda,* "Whereas in *In Parenthesis* Jones uses a single major theme, the ideal of comradeship in arms from Aneirin through Malory to Shakespeare, in an attempt to give sense and meaning to the terrible waste of the Western Front, in *The Anathemata* he is concerned much more to recall and celebrate a whole tradition which threatens to slip through his fingers." "*In Parenthesis* tested the military and liturgical forms of order and found them lacking, with neither efficacy for salvation nor effectiveness for survival," Rees reminds us. "The Queen of the Woods, the great earth-goddess, the eternal female principle venerated by myth throughout the centuries, alone could restore order—but *post mortem*. In *The Anathemata* Jones renominates and celebrates the liturgy as the redemptive order for the living, as an art form." Rees concludes, "In intention and scope Jones's poem is truly epic and might be said to rival in ambition Milton's attempt to 'justify the ways of God to Men' for an age which urges art to be at the service of the ego, the State, or itself."

"Clearly," Rees asserts, "it is the whole of human history and prehistory as perceived and experienced by Western man that is Jones's province." The "anathemata" of the poem's title refers to the artifacts that an artist produces, including the graphic and plastic arts, poetry, literature, legend—all the things that help define a culture. The work examines the accumulation of these artifacts from earliest times to the present, with special attention paid to that which has had the greatest influence on the poet: the history, both legendary and factual, "of the Island of Britain as a whole, whose various origins, Celtic, Imperial Roman, Western Christian and Saxon, appear there in the form in which the poet himself, by birth, upbringing and conversion a product of the composite tradition, experiences them," Jacobs explains. "To read [the poem]," declares Rees, "is to engage, in a rare, esoteric way, from a most learned and demanding tutor, in a course in Western Civilization, which is something other than learning the sites of famous battles in Greece and being able to recite, in order, the rulers of Rome and the kings and queens of England."

The Anathemata was Jones's attempt to reestablish contact with these roots of British culture, states Seamus Heaney in the *Spectator,* roots that modern Britain had neglected, especially in the years after World War I. Heaney explains: "His effort has been to graft a healing tissue over that wound in English consciousness inflicted by the Reformation and the Industrial Revolution." Jones felt that modern man had lost his understanding of the past by neglecting the history of his culture. Drawing information from the sciences of archaeology and anthropology, he set out to recover the roots of his heritage. The poem, Rees declares, tells the history of the artist from "his emergence from

the reaches of prehistory, from rocks and caves that he decorated, as at Lascaux, adorning burial sites gratuitously, creating objects that are beautiful to an extrautile degree, and continuing, still an artmaker, to the wasted present, 'at the sagging end and chapter's close.' "

Jones uses his traditions in such a way that they become understandable even to those who do not share the poet's background. Kathleen Raine in her book *David Jones and the Actually Loved and Known* states, "The poet does not thrust his facts upon us, but rather uses these to remind us of our own, often untreasured but none the less precious, fragments of the same totality." Instead Jones concentrates on the universal legacies of mankind. "In the larger sense," Rees explains, "man's 'anathemata' defines all that legacy of man that is his, that is he." The critic concludes that the poet's ideal aim "is to discover via surviving art and artifact and written word, and with application of all the modern insights and methods of literary study, anthropology, comparative religion, and linguistics, the essential human heritage that is ours." He says, "David Jones's life work is finally his testimony to this central credo: 'We were then *homo faber, homo sapiens* before Lascaux and we shall be *homo faber, homo sapiens* after the last atomic bomb has fallen.' "

Closely tied to Jones's concept of man-as-artist is his understanding of Christianity. *The Anathemata* demonstrates his belief that art should be a form of worship, and that worship is itself a form of art. Guy Davenport remarks in the *New York Times Book Review,* "For David Jones art was a sacred act and he expected the reading of his work to be as much a rite as he performed in the composing of it." "Art, as Jones's impractical temperament would have it," explains Sherry, "is essentially gratuitous, intransitive; it serves no social purpose; it is, ideally, a free hymn of praise to God, and as such resembles the gift offerings of sacrament."

But if art can be considered a type of sacrament, the sacraments themselves are a form of art—perhaps, in Jones's opinion, the highest form. "At the center of *The Anathemata* is that cross, the 'Axile Tree,' " Rees reports. "Christ being lifted up made an efficacious sign, made 'anathemata' of his own body." Belief in the veracity of the Christian gospel is not necessary for the reader, he continues, because "Western man's whole being, his history, his ancestry, his *'res,'* is wholly bound up in that myth." "The art of the first Eucharist at the Last Supper redefines all preceding art, even as it was an act that with all its reverberations and implications transformed succeeding events and imparted a unique and new order to Western myth, legend, and history," he concludes. "The priest lifting the wafer of bread in the Mass is the supreme artist," Sherry declares. "The Mass thus provides a kind of infinite moment; its sacrament is the timeless archetype of all the artifacts catalogued in the poem." "Like Joyce, [Jones] has made a total anachronism of all history, so that the Crucifixion is both an event in time, upon which all perspectives converge, and an event throughout time," Davenport states. "The purpose of the evolution of the world was to raise the hill Golgotha, grow the wood for the cross, form the iron for the nails and develop the primate species Homo sapiens for God to be born a member of," he asserts. "The paleolithic Willendorf 'Venus' is therefore as valid and eloquent a Madonna as one by Botticelli, and all soldiers belong to the Roman legion that detailed a work group to execute, by slow torture, the Galilean visionary troublemaker."

The Anathemata met with mixed reactions from its reviewers. Some critics felt that the complexity of the poem made it too difficult to understand. Many others, however, agreed with W. H.

Auden, who declared in *Encounter* that *The Anathemata* "is one of the most important poems of our times." According to Blamires, it had been "hailed by one critic as one of the five 'major poetic efforts of our era' in English." Jones particularly enjoyed Raine's assessment of *The Anathemata* which appeared in the *New Statesman,* says Sherry: "Such is the paradox of our time that the more a poet draws on objective tradition, the less on subjective experiences, the more obscure he will seem." Contemporary reviewers continue to appreciate the power of its language. N. K. Sandars, writing in *Agenda,* states, "We have become numbed, anaesthetized to the power and purpose of words and require to be jolted awake, to feel their recessions and transformations. This is exactly what David Jones has done in *The Anathemata* . . . where juxtapositions of English, Welsh and Latin give, not only an incomparable richness of texture and of reference, but also give words the life of icons, 'images not made with hands.'"

In the remaining years of his life, Jones continued to refine his theory of art and the function of the artist, often in letters to friends, but also in his essays collected in *Epoch and Artist.* He also worked on shorter poems and essays, some of which were collected in the books *The Sleeping Lord and Other Fragments, The Dying Gaul and Other Writings,* and *The Roman Quarry and Other Sequences.* Many of them echo the problems that Jones confronted in *The Anathemata:* some reveal the unrest of Roman legionaries on the borders of the decaying Empire, reflecting "the problems of a political order removed from its local origins," says Sherry. Others—many of which are based on figures from Celtic myth and legend—"praise the virtues of local, rooted culture," he continues. Often these poems were published in a consciously unfinished state as works in progress, but even in their fragmentary condition reviewers recognized the power of Jones's work. Heaney concludes his review of *The Sleeping Lord* by calling Jones "an extraordinary writer" who has "returned to the origin and brought something back, something to enrich not only the language but people's consciousness of who they have been and who they consequently are."

Despite his acclaim in poetic circles—Dilworth calls him "the most important native British poet of the twentieth century" in *The Shape of Meaning*—David Jones continues to be unknown to the public at large. This is partly due to the demands the poet's work makes on readers, but also partly the result of his own preference; Rees explains, "There have been few writers of this or any other age so resolutely uninterested in matters of public reputation or recognition." He spent the last years of his life quietly working, trying to salvage the remnants of traditional Western culture from the onslaught of the twentieth century. "Like Thoreau, Melville and Hopkins," Spender concludes, "he was one of literature's saints who speak with an authority that comes more from religion than from the world of letters."

BIOGRAPHICAL/CRITICAL SOURCES:

BOOKS

Bergonzi, Bernard, *Heroes' Twilight: A Study of the Literature of the Great War,* Constable, 1965.

Blamires, D. M., *David Jones: Artist and Writer,* Manchester University Press, 1971.

Blisset, William, *The Long Conversation: A Memoir of David Jones,* Oxford University Press, 1981.

Cleverdon, Douglas, *The Engravings of David Jones,* Clover Hill Editions, 1981.

Contemporary Literary Criticism, Gale, Volume 2, 1974, Volume 4, 1975, Volume 7, 1977, Volume 13, 1980, Volume 42, 1987.

David Jones, Tate Gallery (London), 1981.

Dictionary of Literary Biography, Volume 20: *British Poets, 1914-1945,* Gale, 1983.

Dilworth, Thomas R., *The Liturgical Parenthesis of David Jones,* Golgonooza Press, 1979.

Dilworth, Thomas R., *The Shape of Meaning in the Poetry of David Jones,* University of Toronto Press, 1988.

Deutsch, Babbette, *Poetry in Our Time,* Holt, 1952.

Fussell, Paul, *The Great War and Modern Memory,* Oxford University Press, 1975.

Gray, Nicolete, *The Painted Inscriptions of David Jones,* Fraser, 1981.

Hague, Rene, *David Jones,* University of Wales Press, 1975.

Hague, Rene, *A Commentary on The Anathemata of David Jones,* University of Toronto Press, 1977.

Hooker, Jeremy, *David Jones: An Exploratory Study of the Writings,* Enitharmon, 1975.

Ironside, Robin, *David Jones,* Penguin, 1949.

Johnson, John H., *English Poetry of the First World War,* Princeton University Press, 1964.

Lectures on Modern Novelists, Department of English, Cambridge University, 1963, Books for Libraries Press, 1972.

Mathias, Roland, editor, *David Jones: Eight Essays on His Work as Writer and Artist,* Gomer, 1976.

Matthias, John, editor, *David Jones, Man and Poet,* National Poetry Foundation (Orono, Me.), 1988.

Nemerov, Howard, *Poetry and Fiction,* Rutgers University Press, 1963.

Pacey, Philip, *David Jones and Other Wonder Voyagers,* Poetry Wales Press, 1982.

Raine, Kathleen, *David Jones and the Actually Loved and Known,* Golgonooza Press, 1978.

Rees, Samuel, *David Jones,* Twayne, 1977.

Rosenthal, M. L., and Sally M. Gall, *The Modern Poetic Sequence: The Genius of Modern Poetry,* Oxford University Press, 1983.

Thwaite, Anthony, *Poetry Today 1960-1973,* British Council, 1973.

Selections II, Sheed, 1954.

PERIODICALS

Agenda, spring-summer, 1967 (special David Jones issue), autumn-winter, 1973-74, (special David Jones issue), winter-spring, 1975.

America, December 19, 1981.

Anglo-Welsh Review, 1981, 1984, 1987.

Antigonish Review, summer, 1984.

Apollo, February, 1963.

Atlantic, July, 1962, October, 1963.

Atlantic Monthly, February, 1975.

Blackfriars, April, 1951.

Books and Bookmen, September, 1971.

Chicago Review, Volume 27, number 1, 1975.

Chicago Sunday Tribune, April 8, 1962.

Christian Century, June 6, 1962, October 2, 1963.

Commonweal, October 19, 1962, October 18, 1963, June 19, 1964.

Contemporary Literature, autumn, 1971, spring, 1973.

Critical Quarterly, autumn, 1973, autumn, 1974.

Dublin Review, fourth quarter, 1952.

Encounter, February, 1954, February, 1970.

English, summer, 1982.

English Language Notes, December, 1977.

Georgia Review, summer, 1981.

Iowa Review, summer-fall, 1975.

Listener, May 14, 1959.
Mercury (London), July, 1937.
New Republic, May 21, 1962, October 16, 1971.
New Statesman, November 22, 1952, May 24, 1974, January 5, 1979, June 27, 1980.
New Yorker, August 17, 1963, August 22, 1964, August 22, 1964.
New York Herald Tribune Books, July 8, 1962, June 9, 1963.
New York Review of Books, October 9, 1980.
New York Times Book Review, April 15, 1962, July 21, 1963, February 18, 1979, October 17, 1982.
Partisan Review, winter, 1978.
Poetry, May, 1971, January, 1975.
Poetry Wales, winter, 1972.
San Francisco Chronicle, April 29, 1962.
Saturday Review, April 7, 1962, October 26, 1963.
Sewanee Review, autumn, 1967.
Spectator, May 4, 1974, May 27, 1978, May 31, 1980.
Stand, Volume 16, number 3, 1975.
Studio, April, 1955.
Time, April 6, 1962.
Times Literary Supplement, August 6, 1954, July 22, 1965, July 27, 1967, August 20, 1971, May 10, 1974.
Twentieth Century, July, 1960.
University of Toronto Quarterly, April, 1967, spring, 1973, spring, 1985.
Western Humanities Review, spring, 1981.

OBITUARIES:

PERIODICALS

American Bookman, November 18, 1974.
New York Times, October 30, 1974.
Times (London), October 29, 1974.
Washington Post, October 31, 1974.

*   *   *

JONES, Gayl 1949-

PERSONAL: Born November 23, 1949, in Lexington, Ky.; daughter of Franklin (a cook) and Lucille (Wilson) Jones. *Education:* Connecticut College, B.A., 1971; Brown University, M.A., 1973, D.A., 1975.

ADDRESSES: c/o Lotus Press, P.O. Box 21607, Detroit, Mich. 48221.

CAREER: University of Michigan, Ann Arbor, 1975-83, began as assistant professor, became professor of English; writer.

MEMBER: Authors Guild, Authors League of America.

AWARDS, HONORS: Award for best original production in the New England region, American College Theatre Festival, 1973, for "Chile Woman"; grants from Shubert Foundation, 1973-74, Southern Fellowship Foundation, 1973-75, and Rhode Island Council on the Arts, 1974-75; fellowships from Yaddo, 1974, National Endowment of the Arts, 1976, and Michigan Society of Fellows, 1977-79; award from Howard Foundation, 1975; fiction award from *Mademoiselle,* 1975; Henry Russell Award, University of Michigan, 1981.

WRITINGS:

Chile Woman (play), Shubert Foundation, 1974.
Corregidora (novel), Random House, 1975.
Eva's Man (novel), Random House, 1976.
White Rat (short stories), Random House, 1977.
Song for Anninho (poetry), Lotus Press, 1981.

The Hermit-Woman (poetry), Lotus Press, 1983.
Xarque and Other Poems, Lotus Press, 1985.

Contributor to anthologies, including *Confirmation,* 1983, *Chants of Saints, Keeping the Faith, Midnight Birds,* and *Soulscript.* Contributor to *Massachusetts Review.*

WORK IN PROGRESS: Research on sixteenth- and seventeenth-century Brazil and on settlements of escaped slaves, such as Palmares.

SIDELIGHTS: "Though not one of the best-known of contemporary black writers, Gayl Jones can claim distinction as the teller of the most intense tales," Keith E. Byerman writes in the *Dictionary of Literary Biography.* Jones's novels *Corregidora* and *Eva's Man,* in addition to many of the stories in her collection *White Rat,* offer stark, often brutal accounts of black women whose psyches reflect the ravages of accumulated sexual and racial exploitation. In *Corregidora* Jones reveals the tormented life of a woman whose female forebears—at the hands of one man—endured a cycle of slavery, prostitution, and incest over three generations. *Eva's Man* explores the deranged mind of a woman institutionalized for poisoning and sexually mutilating (by dental castration) a male acquaintance. And in "Asylum," a story from *White Rat,* a young woman is confined to a mental hospital for a series of bizarre behaviors that protest a society she sees bent on personal violation. "The abuse of women and its psychological results fascinate Gayl Jones, who uses these recurring themes to magnify the absurdity and the obscenity of racism and sexism in everyday life," comments Jerry W. Ward, Jr., in *Black Women Writers (1950-1980): A Critical Evaluation.* "Her novels and short fictions invite readers to explore the interior of caged personalities, men and women driven to extremes." Byerman elaborates: "Jones creates worlds radically different from those of 'normal' experience and of storytelling convention. Her tales are gothic in the sense of dealing with madness, sexuality, and violence, but they do not follow in the Edgar Allan Poe tradition of focusing of private obsession and irrationality. Though her narrators are close to if not over the boundaries of sanity, the experiences they record reveal clearly that society acts out its own obsessions often violently."

Corregidora, Jones's first novel, explores the psychological effects of slavery and sexual abuse on a modern black woman. Ursa Corregidora, a blues singer from Kentucky, descends from a line of women who are the progeny, by incest, of a Portuguese slaveholder named Corregidora—the father of both Ursa's mother and grandmother. "All of the women, including the great-granddaughter Ursa, keep the name Corregidora as a reminder of the depredations of the slave system and of the rapacious natures of men," explains Byerman. "The story is passed from generation to generation of women, along with the admonition to 'produce generations' to keep alive the tale of evil." Partly as a result of this history, Ursa becomes involved in abusive relationships with men. The novel itself springs from an incident of violence; after being thrown down a flight of stairs by her first husband and physically injured so that she cannot bear children, Ursa "discharges her obligation to the memory of Corregidora by speaking [the] book," notes John Updike in the *New Yorker.* The novel emerges as Ursa's struggle to reconcile her heritage with her present life. *Corregidora* "persuasively fuses black history, or the mythic consciousness that must do for black history, with the emotional nuances of contemporary black life," Updike continues. "The book's innermost action . . . is Ursa's attempt to transcend a nightmare black consciousness and waken to her own female, maimed humanity."

Corregidora was acclaimed as a novel of unusual power and impact. "No black American novel since Richard Wright's *Native Son* (1940)," writes Ivan Webster in *Time,* "has so skillfully traced psychic wounds to a sexual source." Darryl Pinckney in *New Republic* calls *Corregidora* "a small, fiercely concentrated story, harsh and perfectly told. . . . Original, superbly imagined, nothing about the book was simple or easily digested. Out of the worn themes of miscegenation and diminishment, Gayl Jones *excavated* the disturbingly buried damage of racism." Critics particularly praised Jones's treatment of sexual detail and its illumination of the central character. "One of the book's merits," according to Updike, "is the ease with which it assumes the writer's right to sexual specifics, and its willingness to explore exactly how our sexual and emotional behavior is warped within the matrix of family and race." In the book's final scene, Ursa comes to a reconciliation with her first husband, Mutt, by envisioning an ambivalent sexual relationship between her great-grandmother and the slavemaster Corregidora. *Corregidora* is a novel "filled with sexual and spiritual pain," writes Margo Jefferson in *Newsweek:* "hatred, love and desire wear the same face, and humor is blues-bitter. . . . Jones's language is subtle and sinewy, and her imagination sure."

Jones's second novel, *Eva's Man,* continues her exploration into the psychological effects of brutality, yet presents a character who suffers greater devastation. Eva Medina Canada, incarcerated for the murder and mutilation of a male acquaintance, narrates a personal history which depicts the damaging influences of a society that is sexually aggressive and hostile. Updike describes the exploitative world that has shaped the mentally deranged Eva: "Evil permeates the erotic education of Eva Canada, as it progresses from Popsicle-stick violations to the witnessing of her mother's adultery and a growing awareness of the whores and 'queen bees' in the slum world around her, and on to her own reluctant initiation through encounters in buses and in bars, where a man with no thumb monotonously propositions her. The evil that emanates from men becomes hers." In a narrative that is fragmented and disjointed, Eva gives no concrete motive for the crime committed; furthermore, she neither shows remorse nor any signs of rehabilitation. More experimental than *Corregidora, Eva's Man* displays "a sharpened starkness, a power of ellipsis that leaves ever darker gaps between its flashes of rhythmic, sensuously exact dialogue and visible symbol," according to Updike. John Leonard adds in the *New York Times* that "not a word is wasted" in Eva's narrative. "It seems, in fact, as if Eva doesn't have enough words, as if she were trying to use the words she has to make a poem, a semblance of order, and fails of insufficiency." Leonard concludes: " 'Eva's Man' may be one of the most unpleasant novels of the season. It is also one of the most accomplished."

Eva's Man was praised for its emotional impact, yet some reviewers found the character of Eva extreme or inaccessible. June Jordan in the *New York Times Book Review* calls *Eva's Man* "the blues that lost control. This is the rhythmic, monotone lamentation of one woman, Eva Medina, who is nobody I have ever known." Jordan explains: "Jones delivers her story in a strictly controlled, circular form that is wrapped, around and around, with ambivalence. Unerringly, her writing creates the tension of a problem unresolved." In the end, however, Jordan finds that the fragmented details of Eva's story "do not mesh into illumination." On the other hand, some reviewers regard the gaps in *Eva's Man* as appropriate and integral to its meaning. Pinckney calls the novel "a tale of madness; one exacerbated if not caused by frustration, accumulated grievances" and comments on aspects that contribute to this effect: "Structurally unsettled, more

scattered than *Corregidora, Eva's Man* is extremely remote, more troubling in its hallucinations. . . . The personal exploitation that causes Eva's desperation is hard to appreciate. Her rage seems never to find its proper object, except, possibly, in her last extreme act." Updike likewise holds that the novel accurately portrays Eva's deranged state, yet he points out that Jones's characterization skills are not at their peak: "Jones apparently wishes to show us a female heart frozen into rage by deprivation, but the worry arises, as it did not in 'Corregidora,' that the characters are dehumanized as much by her artistic vision as by their circumstances."

Jordan raises a concern that the inconclusiveness of *Eva's Man* harbors a potentially damaging feature. "There is the very real, upsetting accomplishment of Gayl Jones in this, her second novel: sinister misinformation about women—about women, in general, about black women in particular." Jones comments in *Black Women Writers (1950-1980)* on the predicament faced in portraying negative characters: "To deal with such a character as Eva becomes problematic in the way that 'Trueblood' becomes problematic in [Ralph Ellison's] *Invisible Man.* It raises the questions of possibility. Should a Black writer ignore such characters, refuse to enter 'such territory' because of the 'negative image' and because such characters can be misused politically by others, or should one try to reclaim such complex, contradictory characters as well as try to reclaim the idea of the 'heroic image'?" In an interview with Claudia Tate for *Black Women Writers at Work,* Jones elaborates: " 'Positive race images' are fine as long as they're very complex and interesting personalities. Right now I'm not sure how to reconcile the various things that interest me with 'positive race images.' It's important to be able to work with a range of personalities, as well as with a range within one personality. For instance, how would one reconcile an interest in neurosis or insanity with positive race image?"

Although Jones's subject matter is often charged and intense, a number of critics have praised a particular restraint she manages in her narratives. Regarding *Corregidora,* Updike remarks: "Our retrospective impression of 'Corregidora' is of a big territory—the Afro-American psyche—rather thinly and stabbingly populated by ideas, personae, hints. Yet that such a small book could seem so big speaks well for the generous spirit of the author, unpolemical where there has been much polemic, exploratory where rhetoric and outrage tend to block the path." Similarly, Jones maintains an authorial distance in her fiction which, in turn, makes for believable and gripping characters. Byerman comments: "The authority of [Jones's] depictions of the world is enhanced by [her] refusal to intrude upon or judge her narrators. She remains outside the story, leaving the reader with none of the usual markers of a narrator's reliability. She gives these characters the speech of their religion, which, by locating them in time and space, makes it even more difficult to easily dismiss them; the way they speak has authenticity, which carries over to what they tell. The results are profoundly disturbing tales of repression, manipulation, and suffering."

Reviewers have also noted Jones's ability to innovatively incorporate Afro-American speech patterns into her work. In *Black Women Writers (1950-1980),* Melvin Dixon contends that "Gayl Jones has figured among the best of contemporary Afro-American writers who have used Black speech as a major aesthetic device in their works. Like Alice Walker, Toni Morrison, Sherley Williams, Toni Cade Bambara, and such male writers as Ernest Gaines and Ishmael Reed, Jones uses the rhythm and structure of spoken language to develop authentic characters and to establish new possibilities for dramatic conflict within the text and between readers and the text itself." In her interview with Tate, Jones remarks on the importance of storytelling traditions to her work: "At the time I was writing *Corregidora* and *Eva's Man* I was particularly interested—and continue to be interested—in oral traditions of storytelling—Afro-American and others, in which there is always the consciousness and importance of the hearer, even in the interior monologues where the storyteller becomes her own hearer. That consciousness or self-consciousness actually determines my selection of significant events."

Jones's 1977 collection of short stories, *White Rat*, received mixed reviews. A number of critics noted the presence of Jones's typical thematic concerns, yet also felt that her shorter fiction did not allow enough room for character development. Diane Johnson comments in the *New York Review of Books* that the stories in *White Rat* "were written in some cases earlier than her novels, so they confirm one's sense of her direction and preoccupations: sex is violation, and violence is the principal dynamic of human relationships." Mel Watkins remarks in the *New York Times,* however, on a drawback to Jones's short fictions: "The focus throughout is on desolate, forsaken characters struggling to exact some snippet of gratification from their lives. . . . Although her prose here is as starkly arresting and indelible as in her novels, except for the longer stories such as 'Jeveta' and 'The Women,' these tales are simply doleful vignettes—slices of life so beveled that they seem distorted."

While Jones's writing often emphasizes a tormented side of life—especially regarding male-female relationships—it also raises the possibility for more positive interactions. Jones points out in the Tate interview that "there seems to be a growing understanding—working itself out especially in *Corregidora*—of what is required in order to be genuinely tender. Perhaps brutality enables one to recognize what tenderness is." Some critics have found ambivalence at the core of Jones's fiction. Dixon remarks: "Redemption . . . is most likely to occur when the resolution of conflict is forged in the same vocabulary as the tensions which precipitated it. This dual nature of language makes it appear brutally indifferent, for it contains the source and the resolution of conflicts. . . . What Jones is after is the words and deeds that finally break the sexual bondage men and women impose upon each other."

BIOGRAPHICAL/CRITICAL SOURCES:

BOOKS

Contemporary Literary Criticism, Gale, Volume 6, 1976, Volume 9, 1978.
Dictionary of Literary Biography, Volume 33: *Afro-American Fiction Writers after 1955,* Gale, 1984.
Evans, Mari, editor, *Black Women Writers (1950-1980): A Critical Evaluation,* Anchor Books, 1984.
Tate, Claudia, editor, *Black Women Writers at Work,* Continuum, 1986.

PERIODICALS

Black World, February, 1976.
Esquire, December, 1976.
Kliatt, spring, 1986.
Literary Quarterly, May 15, 1975.
Massachusetts Review, winter, 1977.
National Review, April 14, 1978.
New Republic, June 28, 1975, June 19, 1976.
Newsweek, May 19, 1975, April 12, 1976.
New Yorker, August 18, 1975, August 9, 1976.
New York Review of Books, November 10, 1977.

New York Times, April 30, 1976, December 28, 1977.
New York Times Book Review, May 25, 1975, May 16, 1976.
Time, June 16, 1975.
Washington Post, October 21, 1977.
Yale Review, autumn, 1976.

*   *   *

JONES, James 1921-1977

PERSONAL: Born November 6, 1921, in Robinson, Ill.; died of congestive heart failure, May 9, 1977, in Southampton, N.Y.; son of Ramon (a dentist) and Ada (Blessing) Jones; married Gloria Mosolino, 1957; children: Kaylie Ann, Jamie Anthony. *Education:* Attended University of Hawaii, 1942, and New York University, 1945.

ADDRESSES: Home—Sagaponack, N.Y.

CAREER: Writer. Writer in residence at Florida International University, 1974-77. *Military service:* U.S. Army, 1939-44; became sergeant; received Purple Heart and Bronze Star.

AWARDS, HONORS: National Book Award, 1952, for *From Here to Eternity.*

WRITINGS:

NOVELS

From Here to Eternity, Scribner, 1951, reprinted, Delacorte, 1980.
Some Came Running, Scribner, 1957, reprinted, Dell, 1979.
The Pistol, Scribner, 1959, reprinted, Dell, 1979.
The Thin Red Line, Scribner, 1962.
Go to the Widow-Maker, Delacorte, 1967.
The Merry Month of May, Delacorte, 1971.
A Touch of Danger, Doubleday, 1973.
Whistle, edited by Willie Morris, Delacorte, 1978.

OTHER

(With others) "The Longest Day" (screenplay), 20th Century-Fox, 1962.
The Ice-Cream Headache and Other Stories, Delacorte, 1968.
(With Art Weithas) *Viet Journal,* Delacorte, 1974.
World War II, Grosset, 1975.
To Reach Eternity: The Letters of James Jones, edited by George Hendrick, Random, 1989.

SIDELIGHTS: By most people's standards James Jones's first novel, *From Here to Eternity,* was an enormous success. It won the National Book Award in 1951 and sold more than four million copies. Although Jones's later books reached the best-seller lists, most critics felt that *From Here to Eternity* was his finest. David Sanders wrote that "James Jones was victimized by the success of his novel. . . . He was termed the 'great natural talent' among contemporaries whose talents were presumably more refined. He was compared to [Theodore] Dreiser and Thomas Wolfe. Worse, he was made a celebrity. . . . He was peculiarly vulnerable to adverse criticism as six years passed before the appearance of his second novel."

When asked once about the fact that most readers continued to associate him with *From Here to Eternity,* Jones replied: "I used to say that damn book has become the bane of my life. I've written at least three novels that are better than that, but everything gets compared to it, adversely, usually, because it was such a huge best seller and such a big film. It's being compared by the notoriety it got, rather than as a work of art."

Gene Baro wrote of the book: "James Jones has taken no less than life itself for his theme, and he has written of it in the strongest tradition of realism, seeking truth, sparing nothing. He has transcended the graphic and explicit; he has permitted himself neither ornament nor nicety; he has produced a book entirely adult." And Charles Rolo was impressed with *From Here to Eternity*'s "tremendous vitality and driving power and graphic authenticity."

Critics have argued about the merit of Jones's writing, with a few suggesting that Jones's success was limited to a particular milieu. Milton Viorst felt that Jones "acquired the reputation of being a man's writer, preoccupied with men's urges, men's morality, men's hang-ups. Almost obsessively, Jones explores the nature of virility. His measure of a man seems all but primordial: The ability to withstand pain, the response to danger, the capacity to manage women. . . . Jones's people move in a world of violence, where life tends to be a brutalizing experience. Yet Jones denies that he is an artless admirer of the elemental male, crude and insensitive. He insists that such an interpretation is a profound misreading of what he is trying to convey in his writings. His feelings are mixed and, in fact, tend toward contempt, he says, for the man who is, for instance, merely brave."

Edmond L. Volpe also noticed this recurring theme weaving through Jones's novels. "James Jones's fictional terrain is limited to that peculiar all-male world governed by strictly masculine interests, attitudes, and values," Volpe wrote. "Into this world, no female can step without immediately altering its character. . . . In this atmosphere, men strip themselves of the refinements of sensibility and language that they adopt in their life with women. Not intellect, nor manners, nor moral and aesthetic sensitivity, but technical skill and knowledge, physical strength and endurance, boldness and courage are the coveted virtues of this exclusively male world. . . . Jones's vision of human existence is brutal and unsentimental, and he conveys it with superb artistry. . . . Jones's fictional terrain is limited, but within that limited area he has presented a frightening twentieth-century view of individual man's insignificance in society and in the universe."

Assessing Jones's work, Wilfrid Sheed commented: "With most writers, once you've said the book is bad you've said all there is to say; but with James Jones, you have barely begun at that point. For Jones is the king of the good-bad writers, those writers who seem to be interesting by mistake and in spite of themselves. . . . Yet the body of his work amounts to something, and this very fact thrusts him ahead of his betters and earns him at least some of his money. . . . His vulnerability included a vulnerability to experience, which many of his tight-faced competitors lack, but that by itself would not be enough—we have had our fill of absorbent writers over the years. What Jones adds to it (besides impressive and easy-to-miss gifts for construction and process descriptions) is that rarest of blessings or curses, a private obsession that picks up echoes elsewhere, an obsession of public value."

In answer to some of the negative criticism of his books, Jones remarked: "Naturally these writers object to my writing style. You think I don't know that it's not elegant? But there's a certain method in that. In my view, a well-turned phrase communicates itself as such and not the thought it contains. It becomes an end in itself. I prefer an inelegant sentence with meaning to an elegant one at the price of meaning. . . . I'm the common man's novelist. I'm not writing for Ph.D.'s at Harvard. I'd like to be read and understood by the rank and file of the United States,

by the private in the Army and not just by some professor of English. I'm the last of the proletarian novelists."

An *Esquire* reviewer noted that "Jones is not an observer of humanity but a prober of the soul—principally his own. . . . He writes not of man's current foibles but of his elementary passions and his eternal concerns: Jealousy, integrity, fidelity, honor. On every page of his prose, Jones spreads himself out unselfconsciously in all his wisdom and his foolishness, his cynicism and his romanticism, his dedication to the most conventional values and his insistence on the daring and the risque. Throughout his work, the pain of personal revelation is etched in every line."

The point Jones felt compelled to inject into his novels is that "everybody suffers. . . . That's the lesson I try to hold to in my own writing. Even the worst SOB in the world has suffered. If you can tag on to where and how and why, then you can create empathy for him while you're writing. It's that that makes him a real person rather than a stereotype. If a person is a creep, he's a creep for certain reasons."

As Jones once explained to Harvey Breitin *The Writer Observed*: "I'm no intellectual radical. But I'd always been a rebel. . . . A writer should be everything. He should be able to be everybody."

MEDIA ADAPTATIONS: From Here to Eternity was filmed by Columbia in 1953 and received three Academy Awards, one for best picture and two for the best male and female supporting actors. In 1979, a remake of the original movie "From Here to Eternity" was broadcast on national television. *Some Came Running* was filmed by Metro-Goldwyn-Mayer in 1958, and *The Thin Red Line* was filmed by Allied Artists in 1964.

AVOCATIONAL INTERESTS: Reading, photography, classical ballet, jazz, boxing, skin diving, and collecting Indian carvings, pewter knives, and guns.

BIOGRAPHICAL/CRITICAL SOURCES:

BOOKS

Authors in the News, Gale, Volume 1, 1976, Volume 2, 1976.
Balakian, Nona and Charles Simmons, editors, *The Creative Present,* Doubleday, 1963.
Breit, Harvey, *The Writer Observed,* World Publishing, 1956.
Contemporary Literary Criticism, Gale, Volume 1, 1973, Volume 3, 1975, Volume 10, 1979, Volume 39, 1986.
Dictionary of Literary Biography, Volume 2: *American Novelists since World War II,* Gale, 1978.
Garrett, George, *James Jones,* Harcourt, 1984.
Geismar, Maxwell, *American Moderns,* Hill & Wang, 1958.
Giles, James R., *James Jones,* G. K. Hall, 1981.
Hopkins, John R., *A Checklist—James Jones,* Bruccoli-Clark, 1974.
MacShane, Frank, *Into Eternity: The Life of James Jones, American Writer,* Houghton, 1985.
Moore, Harry T., editor, *Contemporary American Novelists,* Southern Illinois University Press, 1964.
Morris, Willie, *James Jones: A Friendship,* Doubleday, 1978.

PERIODICALS

Atlantic Monthly, March, 1951, June, 1967, June, 1978.
Books, March, 1964.
Commonweal, September 21, 1962.
Detroit News, December 3, 1978.
Esquire, February, 1967.
Globe and Mail (Toronto), August 5, 1989.
Life, August 4, 1967.
Miami Herald, January 5, 1975.

New Yorker, January 18, 1958, November 17, 1962.
New York Herald Tribune Book Review, February 25, 1951, September 9, 1962.
New York Times, January 29, 1965, February 28, 1978, May 29, 1989.
New York Times Book Review, September 8, 1957, January 12, 1962.
Phylon, Number 4, 1953.
Pittsburgh Press, December 14, 1975.
Saturday Review, January 11, 1958, September 15, 1962.
Time, January 13, 1958, September 14, 1962.
Voice Literary Supplement, September, 1984.
Washington Post Book World, September 1, 1985.

OBITUARIES:

PERIODICALS

National Review, May 23, 1977.
Newsweek, May 23, 1977.
New York Times, May 10, 1977, May 16, 1977.
Publishers Weekly, May 23, 1977.
Time, May 23, 1977.

* * *

JONES, John J.
See LOVECRAFT, H(oward) P(hillips)

* * *

JONES, LeRoi
See BARAKA, Amiri

* * *

JONES, Mervyn 1922-

PERSONAL: Born February 27, 1922, in London, England; son of Ernest (a psychoanalyst) and Katharine (Jokl) Jones; married Jeanne Urquhart, April 2, 1948; children: Jacqueline, Marian, Conrad. *Education:* Attended New York University, 1939-41. *Politics:* Socialist. *Religion:* None.

ADDRESSES: Home—10 Waterside Place, Princess Rd., London N.W.1, England. *Agent*—Christine Bernard, 7 Well Rd., London N.W.3, England.

CAREER: Free-lance journalist and novelist, 1947—; *Tribune,* London, England, assistant editor, 1955-60, drama critic, 1958-66; assistant editor of *New Statesman,* 1966-68. *Military service:* British Army, 1942-47; became captain.

AWARDS, HONORS: Traveling scholarship from Society of Authors, 1982.

WRITINGS:

NOVELS, EXCEPT AS NOTED

No Time to Be Young, J. Cape, 1952.
The New Town, J. Cape, 1953.
The Last Barricade, J. Cape, 1953.
Helen Blake, J. Cape, 1955.
On the Last Day, J. Cape, 1958.
A Set of Wives, J. Cape, 1965.
John and Mary, J. Cape, 1966, Atheneum, 1967.
A Survivor, Atheneum, 1968.
Joseph, Atheneum, 1970.
Mr. Armitage Isn't Back Yet, J. Cape, 1971.
Twilight of Our Day, Simon & Schuster, 1973 (published in England as *Holding On,* Quartet, 1973).

The Revolving Door, Quartet, 1973.
Strangers, Quartet, 1974.
Lord Richard's Passion, Knopf, 1974.
The Pursuit of Happiness, Quartet, 1975, Mason/Charter, 1976.
Scenes from Bourgeois Life (short story collection), Quartet, 1976.
Nobody's Fault, Mason/Charter, 1977.
Today the Struggle, Quartet, 1978.
The Beautiful Words, Deutsch, 1979.
A Short Time to Live, Deutsch, 1980, St. Martin's, 1981.
Two Women and Their Man, Deutsch, 1981, St. Martin's, 1982.
Joanna's Luck, Piatkus, 1984.
Coming Home, Piatkus, 1986.

NONFICTION

(With Michael Foot) *Guilty Men, 1957,* Rinehart, 1957.
Potbank (documentary), Secker & Warburg, 1961.
The Antagonists, C. N. Potter, 1962 (published in England as *Big Two: Life in America and Russia,* J. Cape, 1962).
Two Ears of Corn: Oxfam in Action, Hodder & Stoughton, 1965, published as *In Famine's Shadow: A Private War on Hunger,* Beacon Press, 1967.
(Editor) *Kingsley Martin: Portrait and Self-Portrait,* Humanities, 1969.
Life on the Dole, Davis-Poynter, 1972.
(Translator) K. S. Karol, *The Second Chinese Revolution,* Hill & Wang, 1974.
(Editor) *Privacy,* David & Charles, 1974.
The Oil Rush, photographs by Fay Godwin, Quartet, 1976.
Chances: An Autobiography, Verso, 1987.

OTHER

"The Shelter" (play), first produced in London, 1982.

Author of radio plays, including "Anna," 1982, "Taking Over," 1984, "Lisa," and "Generations," 1986. Work represented in *English Story* anthologies numbers 8 and 10, edited by Woodrow Wyatt, Collins, 1948 and 1950. Contributor to periodicals, including *Bananas, Encounter, Sunday Times, Woman,* and London *Observer.*

SIDELIGHTS: One of the most noticeable features of Mervyn Jones's novels, according to critics, is a meticulous writing style combined with a decidedly leftist political or sociological approach to his subject matter. A typical Jones character, rather than being endowed by the author with a distinctly individual personality, usually serves as a representation or embodiment of a general human quality common to the setting in question. As a result of such preoccupations, some commentators criticize Jones for writing novels which seem "lifeless and contrived," as a *Times Literary Supplement* reviewer described *Lord Richard's Passion. Today the Struggle,* a chronicle tracing the lives of several related English families from the 1930s to the 1970s, also garnered criticism for its focus on causes and types rather than on "real" people, but not all critics panned it. Valentine Cunningham, writing in *New Statesman,* called the book "so engrossing that it's hard to put down." Admitting that "it's bound, of course, occasionally to seem a bit too schemed-for, too shrewdly schematising," Cunningham nonetheless deemed such criticism "midget grouses. Many of the people are wonderfully believable in themselves . . .; they are, what's more, placed most convincingly in their time."

Commenting on the author's work in general, a London *Observer* critic stated that "one thing that Mervyn Jones can certainly do is tell a story: his straightforward narrative technique looks simple, reads easily, and keeps you reading. At the same time, he has a good old-fashioned novelist's way with characters. There is no authorial presence, no overt trickery or trickiness. And such things aren't unimportant to the ordinary reader."

Jones told *CA:* "In a forbidding, almost windowless medieval tower by the coast of southern France, Catholic rulers in the eighteenth century imprisoned Protestant women who refused to renounce their faith. The special torment was that each of them could go free, any day, by accepting conversion. One, Marie Durand, stayed in the tower from the age of fifteen to the age of fifty-three, when the persecution ended. Visitors can still read, carved in stone, the word *resister*. I have taken this as the conclusive symbol in my novel *Today the Struggle*. In all my writing, my theme is the defense and possible survival of the integral human personality, assailed by multiform varieties of cruelty and temptation. How difficult it is to live—that is the subject of all serious novels, I suppose, and certainly of mine. I am concerned with both the dignity and the irony of idealism. Even the good are sometimes absurd and sometimes dishonest; but to know this of oneself is part of the difficulty.

"Critics generally define me as a political writer. Perhaps this reflects the general avoidance, especially by British writers, of what's seen as the contamination of politics. Wearing other hats, as a citizen and a journalist, I've made clear my socialist convictions and my concern with the threat of nuclear war. Politics, in the direct sense, does bulk large in my best-known novels. *Joseph* is based on the life of Joseph Stalin and is an attempt to explain the degeneration of revolutionary ideals. *Twilight of the Day* is a record of working-class life in the East End of London. *Today the Struggle* chronicles the experiences of the politically obsessed and the politically involved—Communists, liberals, pro-Nazis—from the time of the Spanish civil war to the recent past. Yet I don't think that the boundaries of the political can be neatly drawn, if the setting of the novel is the *polis*—city or community. *The Beautiful Words* is a simple story of a mentally handicapped boy trying to survive in the bewildering urban jungle. None of the characters could be imagined demonstrating or even voting, and there's no mention of what we normally call politics, but this novel seems to me as political as any of my others.

"I also believe that the problems with which I'm concerned—problems of integrity, loyalty, and self-realization—can be explored within the framework of intimate personal relationships. In this zone, men and women have to resolve the conflict between externally imposed conventions and authentic desires. In the only novel which I have set in an earlier century, *Lord Richard's Passion,* I sought to exploit a Victorian literary cliche, the dilemma of love and ambition, in order to illuminate this dichotomy. (Reviewers, and perhaps other readers, took it too straight—'a tender evocative story, full of compassion and understanding,' one of them said.) In *Nobody's Fault,* which I personally consider to be my best novel, the central situation is that of a woman fatally and inextricably attached to two contrasted men. In *Two Women and Their Man* it is the affection between women who, on conventional assumptions, should be rivals and enemies. I ask myself, are these, too, political novels? It was a surprise to me, on reading an essay collection called *The Socialist Novel in Britain,* to find that a Marxist critic, Kiernan Ryan, singled out *John and Mary* as the Jones novel he found most significant. In this novel, of which the only subject is the mutual interrogation of two young people who have spent the night together, I deliberately omitted all reference to their social or economic background or indeed their work—an omission remedied with predictable clumsiness in the film made from the book. For Ryan, the achievement of this novel was to dramatize 'the power of men and women to surmount the acquired illusions, fears and prejudices barring their way to mutual self-realization.' I should say that—not only in *John and Mary* but in all my writing—this has been my aim."

MEDIA ADAPTATIONS: John and Mary was filmed by 20th Century-Fox Film Corp. in 1969.

BIOGRAPHICAL/CRITICAL SOURCES:

BOOKS

Contemporary Authors Autobiography Series, Volume 5, Gale, 1987.
Contemporary Literary Criticism, Gale, Volume 10, 1979, Volume 52, 1989.
Jones, Mervyn, *Chances: An Autobiography,* Verso, 1987.

PERIODICALS

Books and Bookmen, August, 1979.
Guardian (London), July 9, 1979.
Library Journal, April 15, 1974.
Listener, December 11, 1975, July 12, 1979.
New Statesman, February 17, 1978, July 13, 1979.
New York Times Book Review, October 16, 1977.
Observer (London), July 22, 1979.
Spectator, August 7, 1976, February 18, 1978.
Times (London), February 7, 1985.
Times Literary Supplement, October 25, 1974, November 7, 1975, August 19, 1977, October 3, 1980, December 19, 1986.

* * *

JONG, Erica 1942-

PERSONAL: Born March 26, 1942, in New York City; daughter of Seymour (an importer) and Eda (a painter and designer; maiden name, Mirsky) Mann; married Michael Werthman (divorced); married Allan Jong, 1966 (a child psychiatrist; divorced September 16, 1975); married Jonathan Fast, 1977 (a writer; divorced, 1983); married Kenneth David Burrows (a lawyer), 1989; children: (third marriage) Molly Miranda. *Education:* Barnard College, B.A., 1963; Columbia University, M.A., 1965; post-graduate study at Columbia School of Fine Arts, 1969-70. *Politics:* "Left-leaning feminist." *Religion:* "Devout pagan."

ADDRESSES: Agent—Morton L. Janklow Associates, Inc., 598 Madison Ave., New York, NY 10022.

CAREER: Writer. Member of English faculty, City College of the City University of New York, 1964-65, 1969-70; member of faculty, University of Maryland, Overseas Division, Heidelberg, West Germany, 1966-69; instructor in English, Manhattan Community College, 1969-70; instructor in poetry, YM-YWCA Poetry Center, New York City, 1971—; lecturer. Member, New York State Council on the Arts, 1972-74.

MEMBER: PEN, Authors League of America, Authors Guild, Dramatists Guild of America, Writers Guild of America, Poetry Society of America, Poets and Writers, Phi Beta Kappa.

AWARDS, HONORS: American Academy of Poets Award, 1963; New York State Council on the Arts grant, 1971; Borestone Mountain Award in poetry, 1971; Bess Hokin prize, *Poetry* magazine, 1971; Madeline Sadin Award, *New York Quarterly,* 1972; Alice Faye di Castagnolia Award, Poetry Society of America, 1972; Creative Artists Public Service (CAPS) award, 1973, for *Half-Lives;* National Endowment for the Arts fellowship, 1973-74; Premio International Sigmund Freud, 1979.

WRITINGS:

NOVELS

Fear of Flying: A Novel (Book of the Month Club alternate selection; also see below), Holt, 1973.
How to Save Your Own Life: A Novel, Holt, 1977.
Fanny, Being the True History of the Adventures of Fanny Hackabout-Jones: A Novel, New American Library, 1980.
Parachutes and Kisses, New American Library, 1984.
Serenissima: A Novel of Venice, Houghton, 1987.
Any Woman's Blues, Harper, 1990.

POETRY

Fruits & Vegetables: Poems, Holt, 1971.
Half-Lives, Holt, 1973.
Loveroot, Holt, 1975.
Here Comes and Other Poems, New American Library, 1975.
The Poetry of Erica Jong, 3 volumes, Holt, 1976.
Selected Poetry, Granada, 1977.
The Poetry Suit, Konglomerati Press, 1978.
At the Edge of the Body, Holt, 1979.
Ordinary Miracles: New Poems, New American Library, 1983.

OTHER

Fear of Flying (sound recording; includes selections from poetry and from the novel of the same title; read by the author), Spoken Arts, 1976.
(Contributor) *Four Visions of America,* Capra Press, 1977.
Witches (miscellany), illustrated by Joseph A. Smith, H. A. Abrams, 1981.
Megan's Book of Divorce: A Kid's Book for Adults, illustrated by Freya Tanz, New American Library, 1984.
Serenissima (sound recording of the novel of the same title; read by the author), Brilliance Corp./Houghton Mifflin, 1987.

Also author of introduction to the Book-of-the-Month Club Facsimile first edition of Vladimir Nabokov's *Lolita,* 1988, and author, with Jonathan Fast, of screenplay "Love Al Dente." Contributor of poems and articles to periodicals, including *Esquire, Ladies Home Journal, Ms., Notion, Vogue, Poetry,* and *Redbook;* contributor to *New York Times Book Review, Los Angeles Times, New Republic, New York, Expressen* (Sweden), *Corriere della Sera* (Italy), *News Day, New Yorker,* and many others.

WORK IN PROGRESS: "Currently developing *Fanny* as a Broadway musical."

SIDELIGHTS: "Although Erica Jong is a versatile poet, a novelist and a social critic," states *Interview* magazine contributor Karen Burke, "her fame from the enormous success of *Fear of Flying* has overshadowed these accomplishments." The story of Isadora Wing's escapades in search of sexual realization won Jong "a special place in woman's literary history," in the opinion of *Ms.* reviewer Karen Fitzgerald. "Jong was the first woman to write in such a daring and humorous way about sex," Fitzgerald declares. "She popularized the idea of a woman's ultimate sexual fantasy . . . sex for the sake of sex."

Dictionary of Literary Biography contributor Benjamin Franklin V points out that the success of Jong's novels has "tended to obscure the fact that she is a popular and good poet." Jong was a poet before she became a novelist—her first collection, *Fruits & Vegetables,* appeared two years before the first of her novels and her early work was generally well received by critics. "Welcome Erica Jong," announces *Saturday Review* contributor James Whitehead, reviewing *Fruits & Vegetables,* "and welcome the sensuality she has so carefully worked over in this wonderful book . . . clearly she has worked hard to gain this splendid and various and serious comic vision." "Too frequently commercial success comes to poets of little ability," says Franklin. "Such is not the case with Jong. In deft verse she addresses life's difficulties with ever-increasing maturity. As a poet of substance, she speaks to the human condition."

Jong's poetry, remarks Douglas Dunn in *Encounter,* is written in the confessional mode, the "crazed exposure of the American ego," and resembles the work of Sylvia Plath and Anne Sexton, confessional poets who wrote extensively on existential despair and the relations between men and women, and who both committed suicide. Unlike them, Jong's intent is encouraging. She chooses to affirm life, and, according to Franklin, her work is "generally positive and optimistic about the human condition." John Ditsky, writing for the *Ontario Review,* explains that Jong is "a Sexton determined to survive," and sees the influence of Walt Whitman, another sensualist, in her poems. Above all, says Franklin, "her own work illustrates women's victory and that instead of flaunting their success and subduing men, women and men should work together and bolster each other."

Isadora Zelda White Stollerman Wing, a poet and writer like her creator, is a woman "unblushingly preoccupied with her own libido," according to Elizabeth Peer of *Newsweek. Fear of Flying* tells the story of Isadora's adventures in search of her ideal sexual experience. On her way to a congress of psychoanalysts in Vienna with her Chinese-American Freudian analyst husband Bennett, she meets Adrian Goodlove, an English analyst and self-proclaimed free spirit. He coaxes her to leave her husband and run off with him on an existential holiday across Europe, to gratify sexual appetites without guilt and remorse. In the course of her sensual odyssey, Isadora realizes that Adrian, who epitomized sex-for-the-sake-of-sex to her, is in fact impotent, and that the freedom she sought in the encounter is false; as Carol Johnson writes in the *Dictionary of Literary Biography,* Isadora finds Adrian's "promised 'liberation' to be simply a new style of confinement." After two weeks he deserts her to keep a planned rendezvous with his own family, leaving Isadora to return to her husband unrepentant, if unfulfilled.

While sex plays a major role in *Fear of Flying,* it is only one of the themes Jong explores in the book. Johnson remarks that the story "revolves around themes of feminism and guilt, creativity and sex," and indeed, Jong tells Burke that *Fear of Flying* is "not an endorsement of promiscuity at all. It [is] about a young woman growing up and finding her own independence and finding the right to think her own thoughts, to fantasize." Emily Toth points out in the *Dictionary of Literary Biography* that "*Fear of Flying* is essentially a literary novel, a Bildungsroman with strong parallels to the *Odyssey,* Dante's *Inferno,* and the myths of Daedalus and Icarus." Parts of the book may be regarded as satirical: Johnson states that Jong's most erotic scenes "are parodies of contemporary pornography, her liberated woman [is] openly thwarted and unfulfilled." Other aspects of the novel, according to an *Atlantic* magazine contributor, include a "diatribe against marriage—against the dread dullness of habitual, connubial sex, against the paucity of means of reconciling the desire for freedom and the need for closeness, against childbearing," and a search for personal creativity.

Fear of Flying was a smashing popular success, selling more than two million paperback copies in its first two years. Whether read for its graphic eroticism, for its wry humor, or for its portrayal of women as people with a right to sexual expression, it revolutionized readers' perceptions of female sexuality with its depiction of Isadora's passions. *Detroit Free Press* contributor Donna

Olendorf explains, "By granting Isadora Wing, her irrepressible heroine, the same liberties that men have typically taken for granted, Jong touched a responsive chord with women all over the world." Jong's work declared to a generation of women that they need not be ashamed of their own sensuality. In an interview with Cynthia Wolfson in the *Chicago Tribune Magazine,* Jong declared, "My spirit and the world's spirit happened to be in the same place at the same time, and I was the mouth." As Isa Kapp put it in the *Washington Post Book World,* the women of America "had been endowed with freedoms even the women's liberation movement was afraid to ask for and did not know it wanted: to bathe in steamy fantasies of seduction by strangers, and to turn the tables on men and treat them as sex objects."

Later books continue Isadora's story. In *How to Save Your Own Life* Isadora, now the successful author of the very daring and very explicit novel *Candida Confesses,* strikes out on her own. Her marriage and her life have become stultifying: husband Bennett confesses that he had an affair with another woman early in their marriage. Finally, she leaves Bennett and travels to California to visit the movie producer who wants to film her book. There she meets Josh Ace, an aspiring screenwriter some years younger than herself, and falls in love with him. Convinced that she has found her ideal man, she prepares to settle down. Some seven years later even that relationship has soured, and Isadora, pushing forty and the mother of a three-year-old girl, is deserted by Josh. *Parachutes and Kisses* tells of her attempt to reexamine her identity, to cope with the pressures and problems of being single with children, of approaching middle age, and of supporting a household on a writer's income. In an interview with Gil Pyrah of the London *Times,* Jong describes what she tries to do in this novel: "It is about having it all in the 1980s. Isadora exemplified the 1970s woman and now, in the l980s, we are trying to be single parents, breadwinners and feminine at the same time." In the course of her journey toward self-realization Isadora makes a tour of Russia, partly in search of her roots and partly to honor her recently deceased grandfather. She has a number of sexual adventures on the way, eventually finding contentment of sorts with a young actor named Bean. At the beginning of *Any Woman's Blues,* however, Isadora disappears in a plane over the South Pacific; the book purports to be the manuscript she has left behind.

Many people confuse Isadora with Jong herself; the author and her protagonist come from similar backgrounds and have led similar lives. Both are New York born, were educated at Barnard and Columbia, have Jewish origins, and have published poetry. Jong herself is somewhat ambivalent about the sources she uses for these books; as Peer says: "There are days when Erica Jong flies into a fit at the suggestion that 'Fear of Flying' is autobiographical. 'It's not true,' she protests. 'I resent that question.' There are other days when Jong, with a buoyant giggle, admits, 'I cannibalized real life.' " Jong has also used her readers' confusion in the further adventures of Isadora. Christopher Lehmann-Haupt points out in a *New York Times* article that the main character of Isadora's novel *Candida Confesses,* in *How to Save Your Own Life,* is a promiscuous woman whom her readers insist on confusing with her, "much to her distress, because everyone ought to know the difference between fiction and autobiography." The distinction is very clear in Jong's mind; in a *Publishers Weekly* interview with Barbara A. Bannon, she maintains that "the sophisticated reader who has read Colette, Proust, Henry Miller knows that what I am writing is a mock memoir, allowing for a complete range of interpretations in between fact and fancy." Lehmann-Haupt concludes, finally, that "though 'Fear of Flying' isn't meant to be an autobiography, it certainly has the ring of candid confession."

Fanny, Being the True History of the Adventures of Fanny Hackabout-Jones: A Novel is "a picaresque of intelligence, buoyant invention and wonderful Rabelaisian energy" in the opinion of *New York Times Book Review* contributor Michael Malone. According to Judy Klemesrud in the *New York Times,* it is also "a radical departure from the so-called confessional style of her first two novels." A longtime student of the eighteenth-century English novels of Lawrence Sterne, Henry Fielding, and John Cleland, Jong designed Fanny as "a cross between *Tom Jones* and *Moll Flanders,* with a wink at *Fanny Hill,*" according to Julia M. Klein in the *New Republic.* Like the fiction it resembles, *Fanny* is filled with adventures in the picaresque tradition: "ripped bodices, witchcraft, piracy, torture, murder, suicide, highway robbery, execution at the yardarm, madness, nay cruelty to horses," says *Times Literary Supplement* reviewer Pat Rogers.

But *Fanny* resembles its predecessors in more than plot. Jong adopts archaic language, spelling and diction, as *Washington Post Book World* contributor Judith Martin illustrates: "She also hath this funny Way with Words that can drive the faithful Reader nuts in the extream, but 'tis a pleasant Prose when once the Reader hath accustom'd herself to't." The author, says Anatole Broyard of the *New York Times,* embellishes her work with "didactic reflections in the 18th-century manner, and with the rather emphatic humor that made Henry Fielding and Laurence Sterne popular." However, he adds, the story also exhibits "the bad habits of the 18th-century novel: the inert moralizing, the strenuous diction, the relentless archness, the picaresque construction, which E. M. Forster described as 'and then, and then.' "

In other ways, however, the author's work is more contemporary; notes Toth, "Jong uses the eighteenth-century novel form to satirize both Fanny's century and her own." "At heart," comments *Chicago Tribune Book World* contributor James Goldman, "this novel is a vehicle for Jong's ideas about Woman and Womanhood." Still, Fanny remains a woman of her times; as Alan Friedman in the *New York Times Book Review* says, "It would be naive to insist that an 18th-century heroine who is in confident command of the entire arsenal of 20th-century feminism is a heroine who defies belief." Essentially, he concludes, Fanny is "a contemporary heroine chained to a romantic sage with neoclassical links."

Jong explores a history different from that of eighteenth-century England in *Serenissima: A Novel of Venice,* described by Olendorf as "another carefully blended concoction of eroticism, feminism and poetry." This novel relates the story of Jessica Pruitt, a much-married and much-divorced actress, who has come to Venice ostensibly to judge a film festival, but also to come to terms with her mother's suicide which took place in Venice years before, with her own middle age, and with the lack of direction in her life. She falls ill and, either in the delirium of her fever or through the use of a magic ring given her by a witchlike silent film star, finds herself in the sixteenth century. There she meets William Shakespeare, on tour with his patron and lover, the Earl of Southampton, and becomes the inspiration for the Dark Lady of his sonnets and for Jessica, daughter of Shylock in *The Merchant of Venice.*

Although replete with sexual overtones and local imagery, *Serenissima* expands the genre of the historical novel not through its use of these, but through its doubling of characters and its disregard for a linear sequence of time. Jong told *CA,* "[*Serenissima*] was a book that owed its inspiration to [Virginia

Woolf's] *Orlando* in the sense that I tried to abolish linear time and say that time is a fiction we invent to please ourselves." Jessica is a twentieth-century actress, but, as Jong tells Burke, she is at the same time a woman of the sixteenth century. "This is a novel full of masks, actors, costumes, performances," declares *Times Literary Supplement* contributor Valentine Cunningham. "Persons and personae converge, intersect, get confused at every turn on and off stage, in public and private, in brothels, at balls, in the here and now, back then," Cunningham explains.

Critics praise the novel for its evocation of the atmosphere of Venice; says Olendorf, "[Jong's] evocation of the city is especially beautiful, fairly shimmering with liquid imagery," and Joan Aiken, writing for the *Washington Post Book World*, lauds the author's descriptive prowess: "the Adriatic, the shimmer of Venice—Jong's control of narrative is beautiful, floating, hypnotic." Burke states, "Jong's novel captures for her readers the time-warped, haunted magic of this city of love and death." At the same time, however, other reviewers find her use of sixteenth-century literature overdone and disappointing. For instance, Shakespeare talks in quotes from his as yet unwritten work, "Southampton reels off sonnets, [and] Shylock wails in passages from 'Lear,'" explains Malone. Notes Susan Jacoby in *Tribune Books*, "This would have been a good joke if it were used sparingly, but repetition makes it truly tedious." Malone concludes, "The Renaissance has not served [the author] as well as did the eighteenth century."

While Jong's Jessica resembles the author's other heroines in some ways, her differences are more apparent. Jessica is older than Fanny and Isadora, and many of her problems are rooted in her occupation. As Cunningham explains, Jessica is "approaching middle age in a male-directed celluloid world where the starlets must never droop or wrinkle." Jong told *CA* that she calls her "the girl who starts out to be a Shakespearean actress and somehow winds up in Hollywood, wondering how she got there," unlike Isadora, "the smart Jewish kid on the couch," or Fanny, who is "fearless. . . . She surrenders to her fate, and her fate never disappoints her."

Burke indicates that Erica Jong's books all involve "women who are in an ambiguous position, philosophically confused, emotionally overwrought," and the author uses these women to create "a realistic collage of the woman's situation today." Jong agrees; at the time *Fear of Flying* was published, she tells Burke, there was a void in literature about women: "Nobody was writing honestly about women and the variousness of their experience." What was missing from the American literary scene, she concludes, was "a thinking woman who also had a sexual life," a woman who could be just as much a hero as any man. As Peer observes, Jong's protagonists make it clear "that women and men are less different than literature has led us to believe. With a courage that ranges from deeply serious to devil-may-care, Jong . . . [has] stripped off the pretty masks that women traditionally wear, exposing them as vulgar, lecherous and greedy, frightened and flawed in short, as bewilderingly human. Sort of like men."

MEDIA ADAPTATIONS: Fear of Flying was optioned for film by Columbia Pictures, but never produced.

BIOGRAPHICAL/CRITICAL SOURCES:

BOOKS

Authors in the News, Volume 1, Gale, 1976.
Contemporary Literary Criticism, Gale, Volume 4, 1975, Volume 6, 1976, Volume 8, 1978, Volume 18, 1981.

Dictionary of Literary Biography, Gale, Volume 2: *American Novelists since World War II*, 1978, Volume 5: *American Poets since World War II*, 1980, Volume 28: *Twentieth-Century Jewish-American Fiction Writers*, 1984.
Jong, Erica, *Ordinary Miracles: New Poems*, New American Library, 1983.

PERIODICALS

Atlantic, December, 1973, April, 1977, November, 1981.
Chicago Tribune, April 25, 1990.
Chicago Tribune Book World, June 10, 1979, August 10, 1980, April 5, 1981, October 14, 1984.
Chicago Tribune Magazine, December 12, 1982.
Detroit Free Press, May 17, 1987, January 7, 1990.
Encounter, July, 1974, December, 1974.
Interview, June, 1987.
Los Angeles Times, November 4, 1981, May 16, 1987, May 18, 1987, January 22, 1990.
Los Angeles Times Book Review, August 17, 1980, June 24, 1984, November 11, 1984, December 24, 1989.
Ms., November, 1980, July, 1981, July, 1986, June, 1987.
New Republic, February 2, 1974, September 20, 1980.
Newsweek, November 12, 1973, May 5, 1975, March 28, 1977, November 5, 1984.
New Yorker, December 17, 1973, April 4, 1977, October 13, 1980, November 19, 1984.
New York Times, August 25, 1973, November 6, 1973, September 7, 1974, June 11, 1975, March 11, 1977, August 4, 1980, August 28, 1980, March 8, 1984, October 10, 1984.
New York Times Book Review, August 12, 1973, November 11, 1973, September 7, 1975, March 20, 1977, March 5, 1978, September 2, 1979, August 17, 1980, April 12, 1981, October 31, 1982, July 1, 1984, October 21, 1984, April 19, 1987, June 5, 1988.
Ontario Review, fall/winter, 1975-76.
People, May 25, 1987.
Publishers Weekly, February 14, 1977, January 4, 1985, February 22, 1985.
Saturday Review, December 18, 1971, April 30, 1977, August, 1980, November, 1981, December, 1981.
Time, March 14, 1977, June 22, 1987.
Times (London), November 2, 1984.
Times Literary Supplement, April 27, 1973, July 26, 1974, May 6, 1977, October 24, 1980, September 18-24, 1987.
Tribune Books (Chicago), April 5, 1987, January 7, 1990.
Washington Post Book World, December 19, 1971, July 6, 1975, March 20, 1977, August 17, 1980, October 21, 1984, April 19, 1987, January 23, 1990.

* * *

JORDAN, June 1936-
(June Meyer)

PERSONAL: Born July 9, 1936, in Harlem, N.Y.; daughter of Granville Ivanhoe (a postal clerk) and Mildred Maude (Fisher) Jordan; married Michael Meyer, 1955 (divorced, 1965); children: Christopher David. *Education:* Attended Barnard College, 1953-55 and 1956-57, and University of Chicago, 1955-65. *Politics:* "Politics of survival and change." *Religion:* "Humanitarian."

ADDRESSES: Home—New York, N.Y. *Office*—Department of English, State University of New York, Stony Brook, N.Y. 11794. *Agent*—Joan Daves, 59 East 54th St., New York, N.Y. 10022.

CAREER: Poet, novelist, essayist, and writer of children's books. Assistant to producer for motion picture "The Cool World," New York City, 1963-64; Mobilization for Youth, Inc., New York City, associate research writer in technical housing department, 1965-66; City College of the City University of New York, New York City, instructor in English and literature, 1966-68; Connecticut College, New London, teacher of English and director of Search for Education, Elevation and Knowledge (SEEK Program), 1967-69; Sarah Lawrence College, Bronxville, N.Y., instructor in literature, 1969-74; City College of the City University of New York, assistant professor of English, 1975-76; State University of New York at Stony Brook, professor of English, 1982—.

Visiting poet in residence at MacAlester College, 1980; writer in residence at City College of the City University of New York; playwright in residence, New Dramatists, New York City, 1987—. Visiting lecturer in English and Afro-American studies, Yale University, 1974-75; chancellor's distinguished lecturer, University of California, Berkeley, 1986. Has given poetry readings in schools and colleges around the country and at the Guggenheim Museum. Founder and co-director, Voice of the Children, Inc.; co-founder, Afro-Americans against the Famine, 1973—. Director of Poetry Center, 1986—, and Poets and Writers, Inc. Member of board of directors, Teachers and Writers Collaborative, Inc., 1978—, and Center for Constitutional Rights, 1984—; member of board of governors, New York Foundation for the Arts, 1986—.

MEMBER: American Writers Congress (member of executive board), PEN American Center (member of executive board).

AWARDS, HONORS: Rockefeller grant for creative writing, 1969-70; Prix de Rome in Environmental Design, 1970-71; Nancy Bloch Award, 1971, for *The Voice of the Children; New York Times* selection as one of the year's outstanding young adult novels, 1971, and nomination for National Book Award, 1971, for *His Own Where;* New York Council of the Humanities award, 1977; Creative Artists Public Service Program poetry grant, 1978; Yaddo fellowship, 1979; National Endowment for the Arts fellowship, 1982; achievement award for international reporting from National Association of Black Journalists, 1984; New York Foundation for the Arts fellow in poetry, 1985.

WRITINGS:

Who Look at Me, Crowell, 1969.
(Editor) *Soulscript: Afro-American Poetry,* Doubleday, 1970.
(Editor with Terri Bush) *The Voice of the Children* (a reader), Holt, 1970.
Some Changes (poems), Dutton, 1971.
His Own Where (young adult novel), Crowell, 1971.
Dry Victories (juvenile and young adult), Holt, 1972.
Fannie Lou Hamer (biography), Crowell, 1972.
New Days: Poems of Exile and Return, Emerson Hall, 1973.
New Room: New Life (juvenile), Crowell, 1975.
Things That I Do in the Dark: Selected Poetry, Random House, 1977.
Okay Now, Simon & Schuster, 1977.
Passion: New Poems, 1977-1980, Beacon Press, 1980.
Civil Wars (essays, articles, and lectures), Beacon Press, 1981.
Kimako's Story (juvenile), illustrated by Kay Burford, Houghton, 1981.
Living Room: New Poems, 1980-84, Thunder's Mouth Press, 1985.
On Call: New Political Essays, 1981-1985, South End Press, 1985.
High Tide—Marea Alta, Curbstone, 1987.

Naming Our Destiny: New and Selected Poems, Thunder's Mouth Press, 1989.

PLAYS

"In the Spirit of Sojourner Truth," produced in New York City at the Public Theatre, May, 1979.
"For the Arrow that Flies by Day" (staged reading), produced in New York City at the Shakespeare Festival, April, 1981.

OTHER

Composer of lyrics and libretto, "Bang Bang Ueber Alles," 1985. Contributor of stories and poems, prior to 1969 under name June Meyer, to periodicals, including *Esquire, Nation, Evergreen, Partisan Review, Black World, Black Creation, Essence, Village Voice, New York Times,* and *New York Times Magazine.*

SIDELIGHTS: June Jordan is considered one of the more significant black women writers publishing today. Although better known for her poetry, Jordan writes for a variety of audiences from young children to adults and in a number of genres from essays to plays. However, in all of her writings, Jordan powerfully and skillfully explores the black experience in America. "The reader coming to June Jordan's work for the first time can be overwhelmed by the breadth and diversity of her concern, and by the wide variety of literary forms in which she expresses them," writes Peter B. Erickson in the *Dictionary of Literary Biography.* "But the unifying element in all her activities is her fervent dedication to the survival of black people."

Chad Walsh writes of Jordan in *Washington Post Book World,* "Exploring and expressing black consciousness, [Jordan] speaks to everyman, for in his heart of hearts every man is at times an outsider in whatever society he inhabits." Susan Mernit writes in the *Library Journal* that "Jordan is a poet for many people, speaking in a voice they cannot fail to understand about things they will want to know." In a *Publishers Weekly* interview with Stella Dong, Jordan explains: "I write for as many different people as I can, acknowledging that in any problem situation you have at least two viewpoints to be reached. I'm also interested in telling the truth as I know it, and in telling people, 'Here's something new that I've just found out about.' I want to share discoveries because other people might never know the thing, and also to get feedback. That's critical."

Reviewers have generally praised Jordan for uniquely and effectively uniting in poetic form the personal everyday struggle and the political oppression of blacks. For example, Mernit believes that Jordan "elucidates those moments when personal life and political struggle, two discrete elements, suddenly entwine. . . . [Jordan] produces intelligent, warm poetry that is exciting as literature." Honor Moore comments in *Ms.* that Jordan "writes ragalike pieces of word-music that serve her politics, both personal and public." And Peter B. Erickson remarks: "Given her total commitment to writing about a life beset on all sides, Jordan is forced to address the whole of experience in all its facets and can afford to settle for nothing less. Jordan accepts, rises to, the challenge."

Jordan sees poetry as a valid and useful vehicle to express her personal and political ideas while at the same time masterfully creating art. "Jordan is an accomplished poet, who knows how to express her political views while at the same time practicing her art; hence these poems make for engaging reading by virtue of their rhythm and poignant imagery." And Moore states in *Ms.* that Jordan "never sacrifices poetry for politics. In fact, her craft, the patterning of sound, rhythm, and image, make her art inseparable from political statement, form inseparable from content. [She] uses images contrapuntally to interweave disparate emotions."

Jordan is also noted for the intense passion with which she writes about the struggles against racism. Susan McHenry remarks in *Nation* that "Jordan's characteristic stance is combative. She is exhilarated by a good fight, by taking on her antagonists against the odds. . . . However, Jordan [succeeds] in effectively uniting her impulse to fight with her need and 'I' desire to love." Jascha Kessler comments in *Poetry* that Jordan's literary "expression is developed out of, or through, a fine irony that manages to control her bitterness, even to dominate her rage against the intolerable, so that she can laugh and cry, be melancholic and scornful and so on, presenting always the familiar faces of human personality, integral personality." Kessler adds that Jordan "adapts her poems to the occasions that they are properly, using different voices, and levels of thought and diction that are humanly germane and not disembodied rages or vengeful shadows; thus she can create her world, that is, people it for us, for she has the singer's sense of the dramatic and projects herself into a poem to express its special subject, its individuality. Of course it's always her voice, because she has the skill to use it so variously: but the imagination it needs to run through all her changes is her talent."

Faith and optimism are perhaps the two common threads that weave through all of Jordan's work, whether it be prose or poetry, for juvenile readers or for a more mature audience. For example, in a *Ms.* review of Jordan's *Civil Wars,* Toni Cade Bambara comments that Jordan has written a "chilling but profoundly hopeful vision of living in the USA. Jordan's vibrant spirit manifests itself throughout this collection of articles, letters, journal entries, and essays. What is fundamental to that spirit is caring, commitment, a deep-rooted belief in the sanctity of life. . . . 'We are not powerless,' she reminds us. 'We are indispensable despite all atrocities of state and corporate power to the contrary.' " And as Patricia Jones points out in the *Village Voice:* "Whether speaking on the lives of children, or the victory in Nicaragua, or the development of her poetry, or the consequences of racism in film Jordan brings her faithfulness to bear; faith in her ability to make change. . . . You respect June Jordan's quest and her faith. She is a knowing woman."

BIOGRAPHICAL/CRITICAL SOURCES:

BOOKS

Children's Literature Review, Volume 10, Gale, 1986.
Contemporary Literary Criticism, Gale, Volume 5, 1976, Volume 11, 1979, Volume 23, 1983.
Dictionary of Literary Biography, Volume 38: *Afro-American Writers after 1955: Dramatists and Prose Writers,* Gale, 1985.

PERIODICALS

Black Scholar, January-February, 1981.
Choice, October, 1985.
Christian Science Monitor, November 11, 1971.
Library Journal, December 1, 1980.
Ms., April, 1975, April, 1981.
Nation, April 11, 1981.
Negro Digest, February, 1970.
New York Times, April 25, 1969.
New York Times Book Review, November 7, 1971.
Poetry, February, 1973.
San Francisco Examiner, December 7, 1977.
Saturday Review, April 17, 1971.
Washington Post, October 13, 1977.
Washington Post Book World, July 4, 1971.

JORGENSEN, Ivar
See ELLISON, Harlan

*   *   *

JORGENSON, Ivar
See SILVERBERG, Robert

*   *   *

JOYCE, James (Augustine Aloysius) 1882-1941

PERSONAL: Born February 2, 1882, in Dublin, Ireland; died following surgery for a perforated ulcer, January 13, 1941, in Zurich, Switzerland; son of John Stanislaus (a tax collector) and Mary Jane (a pianist; maiden name, Murray) Joyce; married Nora Barnacle, July 4, 1931; children: Giorgio, Lucia. *Education:* University College, Dublin, B.A., 1902.

CAREER: Novelist, short story writer, poet, and dramatist. Clifton School, Dalkey, Ireland, teacher, 1904; Berlitz School in Pola, Austria-Hungary (now Yugoslavia), and in Trieste, Austria-Hungary (now Italy), language instructor, 1904-06 and 1907; private language instructor in Trieste, 1907-1915, and sporadically in Zurich, Switzerland, 1915-19; Scuola Superiore di Commericio Revoltella, Trieste, language instructor, 1913-15 and 1919-20.

AWARDS, HONORS: Grants from the Royal Literary Fund, 1915, and the Civil List and the Society of Authors, both 1916.

WRITINGS:

NOVELS

A Portrait of the Artist as a Young Man (first published serially in *Egoist,* February 2, 1914-September 1, 1915), B. W. Huebsch, 1916, definitive edition, corrected by Chester G. Anderson, edited by Richard Ellmann, Viking, 1964, reprinted, 1982.
Ulysses (some chapters first published serially in *Little Review,* March, 1918-September/December, 1920, and in *Egoist,* January/February, 1919-December, 1919), Shakespeare and Company (Paris), 1922, Random House, 1934, reprinted, with a foreword by Morris L. Ernst and the decision of the U.S. District Court rendered by Judge John M. Woolsey, Modern Library, 1942; published as *Ulysses: The Corrected Text,* edited by Hans Walter Gabler with Wolfhard Steppe and Claus Melchior, Random House, 1986.
Finnegans Wake (excerpts first published as fragments of "Work in Progress" [also see below]; portions also published in journals and anthologies, 1928-38), Viking, 1939, reprinted, 1967, recent edition, 1982.
Stephen Hero: A Part of the First Draft of "A Portrait of the Artist as a Young Man," edited with an introduction by Theodore Spencer, New Directions, 1944, revised edition with additional material published as *Stephen Hero,* edited by John J. Slocum and Herbert Cahoon, 1963.

SHORT FICTION

Dubliners (short story collection; three stories first published in *Irish Homestead,* 1904; contains "The Sisters," "An Encounter" [also see below], "Araby," "Eveline," "After the Race," "Two Gallants," "The Boarding House" [also see below], "A Little Cloud," "Counterparts," "Clay," "A Painful Case," "Ivy Day in the Committee Room," "A Mother," "Grace," and "The Dead" [also see below]), Grant Richards, 1914, B. W. Huebsch, 1916, reprinted, edited by Robert Scholes and A. Walton Litz, Viking, 1969, recent edition, 1982.

Anna Livia Plurabelle (later published in *Finnegans Wake* [also see above]), preface by Padraic Colum, Crosby Gaige, 1928 (published in England as *Anna Livia Plurabelle: Fragment of "Work in Progress,"* Faber, 1932); published as *Anna Livia Plurabelle: The Making of a Chapter,* edited with an introduction by Fred H. Higginson, University of Minnesota Press, 1960.

Tales Told of Shem and Shaun: Three Fragments From "Work in Progress" (later published in *Finnegans Wake* [also see above]; contains "The Mookse and the Gripes," "The Muddest Thick That Was Ever Heard Dump," and "The Ondt and the Gracehoper"), Black Sun Press (Paris), 1929.

Haveth Childers Everywhere: Fragment of "Work in Progress," Fountain Press, 1930, reprinted, Richard West, 1980.

The Mime of Mick, Nick, and the Maggies: A Fragment From "Work in Progress," Servire Press, 1934.

Storiella as She Is Syung (fragment of "Work in Progress") Corvinus Press, 1937.

The Dead, edited by William T. Moynihan, Allyn & Bacon, 1965.

An Encounter, illustrations by Sandra Higashi, Creative Education, 1982.

Boarding House, illustrations by Sandra Higashi, Creative Education, 1982.

POETRY

Chamber Music, Elkin Mathews, 1907, authorized edition, B. W. Huebsch, 1918, reprinted, edited with an introduction by William York Tindall, Columbia University Press, 1954, recent edition, Hippocrene Books, 1982 (also see below).

Pomes Penyeach, Shakespeare and Company, 1927, Walton Press, 1971, recent edition, Bern Porter, 1986 (also see below).

Collected Poems of James Joyce (contains "Chamber Music," "Pomes Penyeach," and "Ecce Puer"), Black Sun Press (New York), 1936; published as *Collected Poems,* Viking, 1937, reprinted, 1974, recent edition, Penguin Books, 1986.

Also author of "The Holy Office," c. 1904.

CRITICAL WRITINGS

"Ibsen's New Drama," published in *Fortnightly Review,* April, 1900.

(With F. J. C. Skeffington) "The Day of the Rabblement" [and] "A Forgotten Aspect of the University Question" (the former by Joyce, the latter by Skeffington), Gerrard Brothers (Dublin), 1901, Folcroft, 1970.

The Early Joyce: The Book Reviews, 1902-1903, edited with an introduction by Stanislaus Joyce and Ellsworth Mason, Mamalujo Press, 1955, reprinted, Richard West, 1978.

The Critical Writings of James Joyce, edited by Ellsworth Mason and Richard Ellmann, Viking, 1959, reprinted, Cornell University Press, 1989.

CORRESPONDENCE

Letters of James Joyce (includes *The Cat and the Devil* [also see below]), Viking, Volume I, edited by Stuart Gilbert, 1957, reissued with corrections, 1966, Volumes II and III, edited by Richard Ellmann, 1966.

The Cat and the Devil, illustrations by Richard Erdoes, Dodd, 1964, recent edition, with illustrations by Blachon, Schocken, 1981.

Selected Letters of James Joyce, edited by Richard Ellmann, Viking, 1975.

James Joyce's Letters to Sylvia Beach, 1921-1940, edited by Melissa Banta and Oscar A. Silverman, Indiana University Press, 1987.

OTHER

Exiles (three-act play; German language version first produced in Munich, August 7, 1919; English language version first produced in New York at Neighborhood Playhouse, February 19, 1925), B. W. Huebsch, 1918, reprinted, with the author's own notes and an introduction by Padraic Colum, Viking, 1951, revised edition, 1965.

Epiphanies, introduction and notes by O. A. Silverman, Lockwood Memorial Library, 1956, reprinted, Richard West, 1979.

Scribbledehobble: The Ur-workbook for "Finnegans Wake," edited with an introduction by Thomas E. Connolly, Northwestern University Press, 1961.

A First-Draft Version of "Finnegans Wake," edited by David Hayman, University of Texas Press, 1963.

The Workshop of Daedalus: James Joyce and the Raw Materials for "A Portrait of the Artist as a Young Man," collected and edited by Robert Scholes and Richard M. Kain, Northwestern University Press, 1965.

A Shorter "Finnegans Wake," edited by Anthony Burgess, Viking, 1967.

Giacomo Joyce (memoir), introduction and notes by Richard Ellmann, Viking, 1968.

Joyce's "Ulysses" Notesheets in the British Museum, edited by Phillip F. Herring, University Press of Virginia, 1972.

Ulysses: The Manuscript and First Printings Compared [and] *Ulysses: A Facsimile of the Manuscript,* introduction by Harry Levin, annotations and bibliographical preface by Clive Driver, Octagon Books, 1975.

James Joyce in Padua, edited, translated, and with an introduction by Louis Berrone, Random House, 1977.

Joyce's Notes and Early Drafts for "Ulysses": Selections From the Buffalo Collection, edited by Phillip F. Herring, University Press of Virginia, 1977.

The James Joyce Archive (facsimiles of surviving manuscripts), sixty-three volumes, edited by Michael Groden, Hans Walter Gabler, David Hayman, A. Walton Litz, and Danis Rose, Garland Publishing, 1977-79.

MEDIA ADAPTATIONS: Finnegans Wake was filmed by Expanding Cinema, 1965; *A Portrait of the Artist as a Young Man* was filmed by Ulysses/Howard Mahler, 1979; "The Dead" was filmed by Vestron Pictures, 1987.

SIDELIGHTS: Richard Ellmann in the opening passage of his monumental biography, *James Joyce,* aptly summarized the writer's impact on twentieth-century letters: "We are still learning to be James Joyce's contemporaries, to understand our interpreter." Since the publication of *Finnegans Wake,* a critical commonplace has held that no author now writing in English can attempt to create a work of prose fiction without contending with the force of Joyce's reconstitution of the genre; but, as Ellmann's statement implies, such a presumption projects only a small measure of Joyce's intellectual and artistic achievement.

Contemporary readers can hardly take up a work of fiction without falling under the influence of the conventions that Joyce established for experiencing a text. Many feel his influence directly; editors regularly anthologize short stories from his 1914 *Dubliners* collection, and Joyce's first published novel, *A Portrait of the Artist as a Young Man* (1916), has become a popular text in high school and college literature courses. His last two books, *Ulysses* (1922) and *Finnegans Wake* (1939), though not as widely read as *Dubliners* or *A Portrait,* stand as paradigms of aesthetic achievement: often quoted, paraphrased, alluded to, or simply invoked in the name of artistic excellence. Those who do not encounter the influence of Joyce's consciousness through direct exposure to his works most likely absorb it from the writings of one or more of his literary heirs. Elements within the styles of authors as different from one another as Irish novelist and playwright Samuel Beckett, modern American novelist William Faulkner, English fiction writers Malcolm Lowry and John Fowles, and contemporary American novelists Thomas Pynchon and John Irving identify them as some of those most overtly shaped by Joyce's canon. But no author today can begin to compose without confronting in some way the impact on modern literature brought about by Joyce's new methods of composition, and, consequently, no reader today can take up a work of modern fiction without feeling the repercussions of Joyce's influence.

Although critics have argued over the precise elements that give Joyce his prominence, most would agree that the power within his writings comes not so much from the topics that they explore as from their complex formal structures. The fascination he had for the form of his work is very neatly illustrated in an anecdote recorded by Frank Budgen in *James Joyce and the Making of Ulysses.* Budgen tells of meeting Joyce one night on the Bahnhofstrasse in Zurich:

"I've been working hard on [*Ulysses*] all day," said Joyce.

"Does that mean that you have written a great deal?" I said.

"Two sentences," said Joyce.

I looked sideways but Joyce was not smiling. I thought of [French novelist Gustave] Flaubert.

"You've been seeking the *mot juste*?" I said.

"No," said Joyce. "I have the words already. What I am seeking is the perfect order of words in the sentence."

Throughout his canon the style of Joyce's prose commands immediate attention and involvement because it disrupts traditional assumptions about the role and the perceptual abilities of readers while engaging those readers in the attempt to discover alternative methods for experiencing the text. In *Dubliners* Joyce subtly mitigates condemnations of the suffocating atmosphere of society with evocative portrayals of the humanity of its victims. While descriptions in his stories often seem to reflect the detachment characteristic of late nineteenth-century naturalistic fiction, they also introduce descriptive techniques able to draw from readers empathetic responses to the suffering that characters undergo.

A Portrait of the Artist as a Young Man continues to develop methods of rendering alternating points of view and to enhance reader awareness of the limitations in the credibility of the narrative voice within the text. It presents a highly personal depiction of the childhood, the adolescence, and the emergence into maturity of the novel's central character, Stephen Dedalus, who moves from a bright, pious, confused child into a fiercely independent, strong-minded, irreverent young man and fledgling artist. At the same time, Joyce's depiction of his central character retains an ironic detachment that highlights the supercilious points of Stephen's rebellion and compels readers to reconstruct their impressions of his nature as it evolves over each chapter.

In *Ulysses* a deluge of precise and variegated details recreates for readers the tempo of a single Dublin day, but rapidly fluctuating perspectives inhibit full comprehension of the impressions created by Joyce's montage-like construction. Interior monologue makes one intimately aware of the needs, the aspirations, the strengths, and the failings of the major characters—Stephen Dedalus, Leopold Bloom, and Bloom's wife, Molly—but at the same time a protean succession of styles impedes the emergence of a dominant attitude that would serve as a standard for measuring the actions of any individual in the work.

Finally, *Finnegans Wake,* Joyce's last work, displaces all previous stylistic patterns in his canon as it presents a dream vision of Dublin that amalgamates the particular and the universal, the subjective and the objective. Its digressive form overturns the reader's sense of the primacy of a single attitude and instead gives legitimacy to a wide range of impressions and perceptions. Its sardonic yet sensitive presentations of characters, events, issues, and ideas representing the central features of Western culture survey modern society without clearly idealizing or denigrating it. If Joyce shows a reluctance in his writing to interpret, to lecture, or to make pronouncements, he imposes no such restraints upon his readers. Quite the contrary, in each work and with increasing power, Joyce calls upon his audience to impose meaning on the text rather than to embrace an interpretation dictated by the work itself; he thus inverts conventional assumptions of the reader as a docile and pliant individual approaching a piece of literature like a jigsaw puzzler searching for the pattern hidden by the author under its formal layers.

Joyce's education began in 1888 at Clongowes Wood College, a Jesuit school located about twenty miles west of Dublin. The Jesuit influence permeated every aspect of Joyce's early intellectual growth. In 1898 he enrolled at University College, Dublin, and quickly earned a reputation as a brilliant if idiosyncratic student. Joyce graduated in 1902 with a degree in modern languages and left Dublin for Paris with the idea of studying medicine there. His mother's illness brought him back to Ireland in April of 1903, and by this time he had committed himself to becoming an artist. He found, however, the Dublin literati antipathetic to his efforts. Despite Joyce's considerable achievement of publishing at the age of eighteen an essay on Norwegian dramatist Henrik Ibsen in the *Fortnightly Review,* Irish editors seemed to take little interest in his work. Robert Scholes and Richard M. Kain in *The Workshop of Daedalus* record that one such editor, William Magee, refusing an essay Joyce submitted to the journal *Dana,* declared an unwillingness "to publish what was to myself incomprehensible." In 1904, at the invitation of poet and editor George Russell, Joyce did succeed in placing three stories, later to appear in the *Dubliners,* in the *Irish Homestead;* but the parochial intellectual atmosphere of Dublin was becoming too much for him. In June of the same year Joyce had met Nora Barnacle, the woman with whom he would spend the remainder of his life, and he began to form plans for escaping the suffocating intellectual atmosphere of his native city.

Joyce was opposed to the idea of marriage. Writing to Nora Barnacle in an August, 1904, letter collected in *Letters of James Joyce,* he declared: "My mind quite rejects the whole present social order and Christianity—home, the recognized virtues, classes of life, and religious doctrines. How could I like the idea of home? My home was simply a middle-class affair ruined by spendthrift habits which I have inherited." But he was also painfully aware that he could not live openly with Nora in Dublin outside the sanction of the church. Joyce was determined to leave Ireland and seek a more tolerant moral and intellectual climate. (The Joyces were, in fact, married on July 4, 1931, in order to safeguard their children's rights of inheritance.) In October, 1904, on the promise of a position as a language instructor for a Berlitz School, Joyce and Nora left for the continent. After a brief period in Pola, Joyce and Nora settled in Trieste where he gave language lessons and worked on his short stories and a novel. In July of 1905 the Joyces' first child, Giorgio, was born. Although Joyce would return to Ireland briefly in 1909 and again in 1912, for the rest of his life he lived abroad while keeping Dublin before him in his writing.

Dubliners grew out of the core of stories that Joyce began before he left Ireland. Each piece depicts some aspect of middle- and lower middle-class urban life in Dublin. According to Marvin Magalaner's *Time of Apprenticeship,* Joyce explained his choice of setting to his friend, Arthur Power: "For myself, I always write about Dublin, because if I can get to the heart of Dublin I can get to the heart of all the cities of the world. In the particular is contained the universal." The stories in *Dubliners* emphasize the circumscription of the individual consciousness by the social institutions of family, church, and state. The collection divides itself into narratives of childhood ("The Sisters," "An Encounter," "Araby"), adolescence ("Eveline," "After the Race," "Two Gallants," "The Boarding House"), adult life ("A Little Cloud," "Counterparts," "Clay," "A Painful Case"), and public experiences (politics, "Ivy Day in the Committee Room"; the family, "A Mother"; religion, "Grace"), with the final story ("The Dead") acting as a coda.

In many ways the collection is an indictment of the paralysis that Joyce felt gripped his city. As he told his at-first-reluctant publisher Grant Richards in a June, 1906, letter collected in *Letters of James Joyce:* "It is not my fault that the odour of ashpits and old weeds and offal hangs round my stories. I seriously believe that you will retard the course of civilisation in Ireland by preventing the Irish people from having one good look at themselves in my nicely polished looking-glass." At the same time, the stories reflect a sense of the humanity of Dubliners caught in situations that they cannot fully comprehend or overcome. "The Dead," with its ambiguous ending, leaves open the possibility of some sort of salvation for the central character, Gabriel Conroy, projecting most overtly Joyce's sympathy for his fellow citizens, but even in stories with protagonists who are clearly doomed— "Eveline," "Clay," "A Painful Case" are all examples—his depictions retain an empathy for the hopelessness and the apparent inevitability of their condition.

Throughout the collection Joyce's subtle narrative manipulation balances feelings of understanding and detachment. Probing the consciousness of his characters, Joyce forces the reader to share the sense of desolation of these figures, yet he maintains a narrative distance that allows a clear perception of the flaws and the weaknesses in their natures. A passage from "Counterparts" describing a man's reaction to the sudden realization of the sorry state of his finances exemplifies this balance in Joyce's art: "He cursed his want of money and cursed all the rounds he had stood, particularly all the whiskies and Apollinaris which he had stood to Weathers. If there was one thing that he hated it was a sponge." The words, while echoing the feelings of the protagonist of the story, belong to its unnamed narrator. Experiencing the sharp disappointment that the character Farrington feels, the reader also retains enough detachment to see the full irony of the situation Farrington has brought upon himself. This same pattern, combining association and disengagement, repeats itself throughout the book. In each story Joyce delves into his characters' minds while maintaining a sense of distance, bringing to readers a clear rendition of the anxiety and suffering that individuals endure without absolving them of the venality or the complicity that contributed to their condition.

While composing and refining the short stories that would make up *Dubliners,* Joyce was also writing a novel, *Stephen Hero.* It traces the childhood and early adult life of a middle-class Dublin boy, Stephen Daedalus, from precocious intellectualism to the stirrings of an artistic vocation. Joyce's work, a fragment of which survived and was published posthumously in 1944, follows the linear, cause-and-effect pattern of a conventional nineteenth-century novel. Structured around the commonplace frame of self-effacing, third person narrative, it examines the features of Stephen's intellectual and physical maturation with minute attention to detail. Late in 1907, around the same time that he completed the first version of "The Dead," Joyce radically revised his novelistic approach. He decided to abandon his manuscript, at this point over nine hundred pages long and by Joyce's own calculation approximately half completed, and to begin the process again, this time following a much less orthodox method of composition.

In his new novel, *A Portrait of the Artist as a Young Man,* Joyce retained the basic plot and themes of *Stephen Hero.* Even specific scenes like Stephen's discussion of aesthetics with the dean of studies reappeared, though Joyce reconstructed these scenes to suit the emphasis of his new work. At the same time he introduced fundamental changes in the narrative form and structure. Joyce drastically cut the work, dropping the number of chapters from the proposed fifty to five. To accomplish this formidable task of condensation, Joyce eschewed presentation of linked chronological events, depicting instead a series of lyrical episodes illustrating the developing consciousness of the artist. The changes produced an intimate knowledge of the character of Stephen Dedalus (whose surname too goes through a minor condensation with a single vowel replacing its initial diphthong) while preventing the reader's close association with Stephen's attitudes. This process also further distanced the novel from Joyce's own experiences in Dublin, and, although Ireland and Irish life had a profound effect upon Joyce's art, it is a mistake to read *A Portrait* as if it were his autobiography.

To heighten sensitivity to the stages of Stephen's maturation, each episode unfolds in a style that approximates the intellectual level of the protagonist at the time. Every chapter has its unique tone and cadence, but the novel's opening lines provide perhaps the most familiar and accessible example of this technique: "Once upon a time and a very good time it was there was a moocow coming down along the road and this moocow that was coming down along the road met a nicens little boy named baby tuckoo." The story is one that Stephen's father has told him, and the words are those that he, baby tuckoo, could understand, although they are a bit beyond his own ability to form, as the passage of his speech that immediately follows this section demonstrates; for *"O, the wild rose blossoms/On the little green place,"* he sings, *"O, the green wothe botheth."* The narrative thus presents an evolving perspective parallel to but independent from Stephen's own nature. This emphasis on a fluctuating point of view within the narrative stands as the central feature of Joyce's new approach in *A Portrait.* It gives the reader a strong sense of Stephen's maturing consciousness, yet it allows one to maintain a detached and at times ironic perspective on his nature.

This method for establishing the tone of the work also influences the formal design of Joyce's chapters. Each is organized around a series of "epiphanies"—moments of lyrical insight derived from the seemingly banal occurrences of daily life leading towards an event at the close of the chapter which marks a turning point in Stephen's emotional, intellectual, and spiritual growth. To balance these euphoric moments Joyce introduces throughout each chapter a series of "anti-epiphanies"—instances underscoring the misperceptions resulting from certain elevated attitudes. Moreover, he begins chapters two through five with "anti-epiphanies" aimed at directly undercutting the triumphs of the scenes immediately preceding them in the conclusions of chapters one through four.

The path of alternating feelings traced by these epiphanies and anti-epiphanies follows the thematic development of the novel. Chapter one ends with Stephen on the shoulders of his classmates at Clongowes Wood College celebrating his apparent triumph over Father Dolan's unjust punishment, yet the second chapter begins with an account of how the sinking fortunes of his family have forced Stephen to leave the college. The final scene of the second chapter, his encounter with a prostitute, marks the triumph of Stephen's erotic and romantic passion over what he perceives as hypocritical social repression, but the opening of the next chapter shows Stephen's current sense of the tawdriness of these pleasures. The third chapter, with its famous retreat sermon, ends with Stephen's reception of the Eucharist and his temporary, but at the time quite sincere, reconciliation with the forces of conformity. The first scene opening chapter four, however, shows that his religious practices have lost their efficacy; the aesthetic revelation of his vision on the beach of the birdgirl, which closes the chapter, redirects his psychological development by replacing religion with art as the moral center of his life. The shabby circumstances of the Dedalus household at the opening of chapter five seems to belie this sense of liberation, but the novel ends with a final moment of transcendence, Stephen's articulation of his motives behind his decision to leave Ireland: "I go to encounter for the millionth time the reality of experience and to forge in the smithy of my soul the uncreated conscience of my race." The statement summarizes the thematic paradoxes upon which the novel rests, for it marks both Stephen's break with the constraints of the Irish world in which he grew up and his commitment to reform that world through his artistic powers. Stylistic distinction and multiple perspective function in an efficient but muted manner in *A Portrait;* but in mastering their manipulation and in introducing the reader to the demands made by subtle shifts in tone and point of view, Joyce prepared for the more rigorous presentation of the same techniques in *Ulysses.*

In 1914, as Joyce was finishing *Portrait,* he began to receive the public notice that he had been striving to gain for a decade. Grant Richards, who had proposed in 1906 to publish *Dubliners* and who had subsequently abrogated the agreement after a prolonged conflict with Joyce over cuts in particular stories, renewed his offer. (The collection appeared in June of 1914.) American poet and editor Ezra Pound, put in touch with Joyce by Irish poet William Butler Yeats, took an interest in *A Portrait,* and through his influence the *Egoist* began serial publication of the novel in February. Two more years would pass before Joyce found a publisher, B. W. Huebsch, to bring out the novel in book form, but the increased interest in his work reinforced Joyce's determination to continue his writing.

During 1914, as work on *A Portrait* was coming to a close and planning for *Ulysses* had already begun, Joyce abruptly took up a new project, the composition of his play *Exiles* (1918). The drama focuses on the return to Ireland of Richard Rowan, a successful, middle-aged author, after years of self-imposed exile on the continent. *Exiles* highlights the inevitable clash between an individual who values personal freedom above all else and a society whose central concerns are conformity and superficial appearances. Its 1919 premier in Munich was described by Joyce as "A flop!," according to Ellmann's biography, and subsequent performances have met with mixed success at best. Its composi-

tion, however, proved an important stage in Joyce's artistic development, for it enabled him to examine questions of fidelity, loyalty, and control that would stand at the center of the action of *Ulysses.*

Shortly after the completion of the play, Joyce again became an exile himself. With the onset of World War I his British passport made him a hostile alien in Trieste, a city at that time part of the Austro-Hungarian Empire, and he was forced in 1915 to move with his family to neutral Switzerland. From 1915 to 1919 Joyce lived in Zurich, where he completed drafts of the first twelve episodes of *Ulysses.* After the war he returned briefly to Trieste, and in 1920, at the urging of Pound, he went to Paris where he hoped to find accommodations less chaotic than those in postwar Trieste. Joyce intended the move only as a temporary displacement, meant to last no longer than the few months he judged necessary to finish *Ulysses,* but life in Paris proved more congenial than expected. Among the friends whom Joyce made early in his stay was a young American, Sylvia Beach, owner of the book shop Shakespeare and Company, who agreed to bring out *Ulysses* under her own imprint. By the time the book appeared on February 2, 1922, Joyce and his family were firmly established in Paris and would remain in the city for the next twenty years.

Using the *Odyssey* of Homer as a frame, Joyce depicts in *Ulysses* the events of a single day in Dublin—June 16, 1904. Attention settles on three individuals. Stephen Dedalus, a bit older and more disillusioned than he was as the protagonist of *A Portrait,* spends the day seeking recognition from his fellow Dubliners for his artistic talent while drinking up the salary he has just received for teaching duties at Garret Deasy's school in Dalkey. Leopold Bloom, a middle-aged Jewish advertising canvasser for a Dublin newspaper, wanders around the city intent upon driving from his mind feelings of guilt over his father's death, remorse for the loss, eleven years earlier, of his infant son, apprehension over the maturity of his daughter Milly, and despair over his wife's impending infidelity. Molly Bloom, the wife of Leopold and the only one of the three not to spend her day crisscrossing Dublin, passes her time preparing for and conducting her first act of adultery. Joyce overlays this interaction with a masterful depiction of minor characters and a Rabelaisian delight in the seedy details of urban living. (Such details caused the novel to be banned from the United States until December, 1933, when Judge John M. Woolsey delivered the legal verdict that *Ulysses* was not obscene; it was published in America by Random House in early 1934, twelve years after Sylvia Beach's Paris edition appeared.) Despite the banality surrounding the lives of Bloom, Molly, Stephen, and the other Dubliners, Joyce gives each a dignity and fallibility that makes his or her experiences important to the reader.

As in Joyce's earlier works, style endows *Ulysses* with kinetic force. Its evolving form supplies narration with the power to make mundane characters and events interesting while constraining the reader to participate in the creation of the text by attempting to bring meaning (though not certitude) to it. The novel's introductory chapters establish its tone in a fairly conventional, if sometimes baroque, manner; its first lines read, "Stately, plump Buck Mulligan came from the stairhead, bearing a bowl of lather on which a mirror and a razor lay crossed. A yellow dressinggown, ungirdled, was sustained gently behind him by the mild morning air." After progressing through the first third of the work, Joyce begins to vary the form of succeeding episodes, continually shifting narrative perspective and compelling his audience to reconstruct standards for interpretation: for example, the first line of the "Sirens" episode reads, "Bronze by gold heard the hoofirons, steelyringing imperthnthn thnthnthn." Within chapters Joyce confronts readers with the disjointed impressions of the central characters through various forms of interior monologue, as in the following example of Leopold Bloom's ruminations on the household cat: "Cruel. Her nature. Curious mice never squeal. Seem to like it." (This passage, of course, in a rather prosaic way also illustrates how Joyce conditions his readers to impose meaning, since few will read the passage without inserting a comma after Bloom's "Curious.") The interspersion of more straightforward narration produces tension through overlapping depictions of the action, and perhaps most significantly, Joyce alternately presents a range of perspectives throughout the text, giving no voice primacy. As a consequence the reader must establish, without the intervention or guidance of the author, a personal system of values for weighing the significance of events.

Ulysses stands as a vigorous but logical extension of the stylistic innovation begun in Joyce's earlier works. The diffusion of narrative discourse in *Dubliners* and *A Portrait* manifests itself in every facet of *Ulysses*'s textual structure, and the 1922 novel signals the continuing formal experimentation of *Finnegans Wake*. On a broader level, the publication of *Ulysses* also marks the high point of the dominant literary impulse of its time. Critics have come to see the year 1922, with the appearance of *Ulysses*, of T. S. Eliot's *The Waste Land,* and of German poet Rainer Maria Rilke's *Duino Elegies* and *Sonnets to Orpheus,* as the culmination of modernism. Although Joyce avoided association with artistic groups or literary movements, the characteristics distinguishing his novel— antipathy towards the institutions devoted to preserving the status quo, faith in the humanity of individuals, and a deep interest in stylistic experimentation—reflect the concerns animating the works of the major artists of the period.

Almost immediately after the publication of *Ulysses,* Joyce began the project that would occupy him for the remainder of his life, *Finnegans Wake.* As Ellmann recorded in his biography, from the start the nature of this new work puzzled and disturbed many of Joyce's old friends. Early in the process of his writing, he sent a draft of the opening passage to Harriet Shaw Weaver, who had provided financial and moral support since Joyce's Zurich days. She wrote to him, noted Ellmann, that "the poor hapless reader loses a very great deal of your intention; flounders, helplessly, is in imminent danger, in fact, of being as totally lost to view as that illfated vegetation [the shamrock] you mentioned." Ellmann related that Ezra Pound was left equally nonplussed by his encounter with a selection from the manuscript: "I will have another go at it, but up to present I make nothing of it whatever. Nothing so far as I make out, nothing short of divine vision or a new cure for the clapp [sic] can possibly be worth all the circumambient peripherization." Conditions surrounding its composition were as unsettling as the text itself. Financial troubles continued to plague Joyce at sporadic intervals. Problems with his vision that had begun while he was writing *Ulysses* proved steadily debilitating, and his daughter Lucia came increasingly under the influence of the mental disorder that would eventually institutionalize her. Through it all, Joyce proceeded with an unwavering faith in his "Work in Progress" (the name he used to designate *Finnegans Wake,* refusing to divulge its true title until its publication), and the book appeared, after seventeen years of planning, writing, and revising, on May 4, 1939.

As *Ulysses* examines the culture and society of Ireland by recording the events surrounding a single Dublin day, *Finnegans Wake* traces the prominent features of Western culture through its account of the activities of one Dublin night. Putatively the book concerns itself with the family of a Protestant Dublin pub-keeper living near Phoenix Park on the western border of the city: Hum-

phrey Chimpden Earwicker (commonly referred to in the text as HCE), the father; Anna Livia Plurabelle (ALP), his wife; Shem and Shaun, their twin sons; and Issy, their daughter. In fact, from the opening pages Joyce extends the topical limits of the text by using HCE and his family to serve as representative manifestations of a range of psychological, theological, political, and sociological questions. Episodes in the book operate on both the microcosmic and the macrocosmic levels. They present archetypal views of the institutions and of the attitudes that have traditionally shaped the evolution of European society; simultaneously they offer a sensitive rendition of the complex relations that characterize the makeup of the modern family. Earwicker and others in the family assume a variety of transparent roles— historical and mythological—giving a local habitation to Joyce's ideas while at the same time recalling figures and events from history, mythology, and folklore already well known to the reader. By incorporating both the particular and the universal in his depictions of the major themes of the text, Joyce insures that his work will simultaneously appeal to a range of individuals on a variety of levels.

Joyce intended *Finnegans Wake* less as a critique of Western society than as a reflection of its cyclical nature that acted, as the work itself notes, as "one continuous present tense integument [that] slowly unfolded all marryvoising moodmoulded cyclewheeling history." Its sardonic humor and multiplicity of allusions can, however, create the impression that the text aims at censure. By their very nature the central concerns of *Finnegans Wake* lend themselves to clashes between the spectacular and the absurd, and the figurative language that Joyce employs in his descriptions accentuates the reader's sense of the ridiculous elements in the human condition.

As part of Joyce's efforts to encompass in his work as much of Western civilization as possible, the narration makes repeated reference to cataclysmic events, both historical and mythological, that shaped the evolution of our culture—the stock market crash of 1929, the battle of Waterloo, the medieval Irish battle of Clontarf, the resurrection of Jesus, the murder of Abel by Cain. At the same time it defamiliarizes conventional associations with these events through comical distortion: the Duke of Wellington becomes "Sraughter Willingdone"; Napoleon Bonaparte, Wellington's opponent at Waterloo, is now "Lipoleum"; Joyce rechristens Saint Patrick, the patron saint of Ireland, "flop hattrick"; and its last king, Brian Boru, has his name transformed into "Brewinbaroon." The text also explores more personal elements of society—the rise and fall of the father figure; the bitter struggles of sibling rivalry; the impulses, at times conflicting and at times complementary, of sensual love and sexual depravity; and the perceptions of woman as matriarch and concubine—with the same wry tone with which the novel describes public characters and events. If the juxtaposition of these impressions and observations seems haphazard or contradictory, it is because Joyce repeatedly refused to oversimplify the world as he saw it or to take a polemical position regarding the way one should spend one's life.

In *Finnegans Wake* form does not simply follow content; it enhances and, to a large degree, defines it. The syntactical structure of the text adheres to a circular rather than a linear configuration. The final sentence breaks off at its midpoint to be completed by the fragment opening the text. This pattern is repeated on the thematic level by progressively extravagant reintroductions of dominant issues and by the analogies created between individual experience and cultural events. In one instance, for example, Joyce examines the ramifications of the figurative and literal fall of the father by connecting it with the fall of the

Roman Empire, the fall of Adam, and the fall of Humpty-Dumpty, and throughout the entire passage the dissolution of its descriptive language both records and parodies the events it depicts.

In an effort to break the dominance of rigid linguistic codes, Joyce gives words in *Finnegans Wake* a sensuous, organic quality of their own. To emphasize the range of perceptions and feelings conveyed by what passes for straightforward communication, he twists, stretches, supplements, and reshapes ordinary conversations and descriptions to reform them into multilayered statements. Topical puns on the names of psychologists Carl Jung and Sigmund Freud emerge in a sentence expressing concern for preadolescent girls who "were yung and easily freudened." A familiar scriptural passage suffers the variations of etymology and entomology: "In the buginninng is the woid." And in a sentence asking how a man was hurt the words rearrange themselves to extend their range by combining commentary with inquiry: "What then agentlike brought about that tragoady thundersday this municipal sin business?" Through it all Joyce remains aware of the interpretive demands that his methods place on his readers, but even when he offers a bit of comfort he cannot resist the freeplay of language. "You is feeling like you was lost in the bush, boy? You says: It is a puling sample jungle of woods. You most shouts out: Bethicket me for a stump of beech if I have the poultriest notions what the farest he all means."

On first encounter the virtuosity of *Finnegans Wake* can move a reader to perceive it and Joyce as his or her adversaries, sardonically mocking any attempt to bring comprehension to a conglomeration of unfamiliar or newly created words and disconnected imagery. Such a response is understandable and, to some extent, accurate. While Joyce did not write *Finnegans Wake* out of a perverse wish to destroy language or to render meaning superfluous, he did intend to overthrow the notion that a single interpretation of a work of art could enjoy primacy over all others. To achieve this end he attempted to draw the reader into active, creative reconstruction of the text, not the physical artifact but the metaphysical concept: the product of the imagination responding to words on a page. The digressions, the redundancies, the non sequiturs of his book are not meant to impede understanding but rather to enlarge it. Joyce refuses in *Finnegans Wake* to dictate a single, inclusive meaning informed by a faith in the authority of cause-and-effect logic. He aims, instead, as he says in the novel, at "that ideal reader suffering from an ideal insomnia." He wishes to inspire an intense involvement with the work that will reveal the opportunities of interpretation implicit in the ranges of responses that one can make to his polymorphous material. To label this intention as perverse, however, does an injustice to Joyce, for it demands that he conform to the standards set by the tradition of the nineteenth-century English novel. Judged along those lines, *Finnegans Wake* is a hopeless failure, but such methods deny the very imaginative impulse that art is meant to celebrate, for, as the work itself declares, "the unfacts, did we possess them, are too imprecisely few to warrant our certitude." Joyce would rather have readers trust in their instincts and in the text itself, which at one point asserts: "He is cured of faith who is sick of fate."

The advent of World War II quickly followed the publication of *Finnegans Wake*, and Joyce sardonically expressed the opinion that the war was a plot to undermine interest in his book. Late in 1940, after the German Army had occupied Paris, Joyce and his family left France to return again to neutral Switzerland. In Zurich Joyce became ill; Ellmann in his biography noted that the writer suffered a perforated duodenal ulcer. After an apparently successful operation, Joyce lapsed into a coma, and at 2:15 on the morning of January 13, 1941, he died. The final lines of *Finnegans Wake* may provide a fitting epitaph: "We pass through grass behush the bush to. Whish! A gull. Gulls. Far calls. Coming, far! End here. Us then. Finn, again! Take. Bussoftlhee, mememormee! Till thousendsthee. Lps. The keys to. Given! A way a lone a last a love a long the"

BIOGRAPHICAL/CRITICAL SOURCES:

BOOKS

Anderson, Chester G., editor, *Portrait of the Artist as a Young Man: Text and Criticism*, Penguin, 1977.

Budgen, Frank, *James Joyce and the Making of "Ulysses,"* University of Indiana Press, 1960.

Campbell, Joseph and Henry Morton Robinson, *A Skeleton Key to "Finnegans Wake,"* Viking, 1961.

Connolly, Thomas E., editor, *Joyce's Portrait: Criticisms and Critiques*, Appleton-Century-Crofts, 1962.

Dictionary of Literary Biography, Gale, Volume 10: *Modern British Dramatists, 1940-1945*, 1982, Volume 19: *British Poets, 1840-1914*, 1983, Volume 36: *British Novelists, 1890-1929: Modernists*, 1985.

Ellmann, Richard, *James Joyce*, Oxford University Press, 1959, revised edition, 1984.

Ellmann, Richard, *The Consciousness of James Joyce*, Oxford University Press, 1977.

Gilbert, Stuart, *James Joyce's "Ulysses,"* Random House, 1952.

Hayman, David, *"Ulysses": The Mechanics of Meaning*, Prentice-Hall, 1970.

Joyce, James, *Letters of James Joyce*, Viking, Volume I, edited by Stuart Gilbert, 1957, reissued with corrections, 1966, Volumes II and III, edited by Richard Ellmann, 1966.

Joyce, James, *A Portrait of the Artist as a Young Man*, Viking, 1964.

Joyce, James, *Dubliners*, Viking, 1969.

Joyce, James, *Finnegans Wake*, Viking, 1969.

Joyce, James, *Ulysses*, Random House, 1986.

Joyce, Stanislaus, *My Brother's Keeper*, Faber, 1958.

Kenner, Hugh, *Dublin's Joyce*, Chatto & Windus, 1955.

Kenner, Hugh, *Ulysses*, Allen & Unwin, 1980.

Litz, A. Walton, *James Joyce*, Twayne, 1966.

Magalaner, Marvin, *Time of Apprenticeship: The Fiction of Young James Joyce*, Abelard-Schuman, 1959.

Morris, William E. and Clifford A. Nault, Jr., editors, *Portraits of an Artist: A Casebook on James Joyce's "A Portrait of the Artist as a Young Man,"* Odyssey Press, 1962.

Scholes, Robert and Richard M. Kain, *The Workshop of Daedalus*, Northwestern University Press, 1965.

Staley, Thomas F. and Bernard Benstock, editors, *Approaches to Joyce's Portrait*, University of Pittsburgh Press, 1976.

Tindall, William York, *A Reader's Guide to "Finnegans Wake,"* Farrar, Straus, 1959.

Tindall, William York, *A Reader's Guide to James Joyce*, Noonday Press, 1959.

Twentieth-Century Literary Criticism, Gale, Volume 3, 1980, Volume 8, 1982, Volume 16, 1985.

PERIODICALS

Accent, winter, 1952.

Atlantic Monthly, March, 1958.

Chicago Tribune, June 18, 1989.

James Joyce Quarterly, fall, 1968.

Los Angeles Times Book Review, July 20, 1986.

New Republic, February 17, 1982.

New York Times Book Review, December 31, 1944.

Partisan Review, summer, 1939.

Poetry, July, 1930.
Times Literary Supplement, February 10, 1984.

*   *   *

JUDD, Cyril
See MERRIL, Judith and POHL, Frederik

*   *   *

JUNG, C(arl) G(ustav) 1875-1961

PERSONAL: Surname pronounced "Yoong"; born July 26, 1875, in Kesswil, Thurgau, Switzerland; died June 6, 1961, in Kuessnacht, Switzerland; son of Paul (an Evangelical minister and philologist) and Emilie (Preiswerk) Jung; married Emma Rauschenbach (a psychoanalyst), February 26, 1903 (died November 28, 1955); children: Agathe Jung Niehus, Gret Jung Baumann, Franz, Marianne Jung Niehus, Helene Jung Hoerni. *Education:* University of Basel, M.D., 1900; University of Zurich, Ph.D., 1902.

ADDRESSES: Home—Seestrasse 228, Kuessnacht, Switzerland. *Office*—C. G. Jung Institute, Zurich, Switzerland.

CAREER: Burghoelzli Mental Hospital, Zurich, Switzerland, intern, 1900-05, senior staff physician, 1905-09; University of Zurich, Zurich, intern at university psychiatric clinic, 1900-04, lecturer in psychiatry, 1905-13; private practice of psychoanalysis in Kuessnacht, Switzerland, 1909-61; Federal Polytechnical University, Zurich, professor of psychology, 1932-40; University of Basel, Basel, Switzerland, professor of medical psychology, 1944-45. *Military service:* Served with Swiss Army as medical officer in charge of interred British troops during World War I.

WRITINGS:

IN ENGLISH

The Psychology of Dementia Praecox, translation by Frederick Peterson and A. A. Brill, Journal of Nervous and Mental Disease Publishing Co., 1909.
The Theory of Psychoanalysis, Journal of Nervous and Mental Disease Publishing Co., 1915.
Collected Papers on Analytical Psychology, translation by Constance Long, Bailliere, Tindal and Cox (London), 1916, Moffat, Yard (New York), 1917.
Psychology of the Unconscious: A Study of the Transformations and Symbolisms of the Libido, a Contribution to the Evolution of Thought, translation and introduction by Beatrice M. Hinkle, Moffat, Yard, 1916.
(Editor) *Studies in Word-Association: Experiments in the Diagnosis of Psychological Conditions Carried Out at the Psychiatric Clinic of the University of Zurich, Under the Direction of C. G. Jung,* translation by M. D. Elder, W. Heinemann, 1918.
Psychological Types; or, The Psychology of Individuation, translation from original edition, *Psychologische typen* (Rascher [Zurich], 1921), by H. G. Baynes, Harcourt, 1923.
Contributions to Analytical Psychology, translation by H. G. Baynes and Cary F. Baynes, Harcourt, 1928.
Two Essays on Analytical Psychology, translation from original essay, "Das Unbewusste im normalen und kranken Seelenleben," and essay "Die Beziehungen zwischen dem Ich und dem Unbewussten" (based on the original essay "La Stricture de l'inconscient"), by H. G. Baynes and C. F. Baynes, Dodd, 1928.
Modern Man in Search of a Soul, translation of original lectures by William S. Dell and C. F. Baynes, Trench, Trubner, 1933, Harcourt, 1966.

Dream Symbols of the Individuation Process (from a seminar held at Bailey Island, Maine, September 20-26, 1936) privately printed (New York), 1937.
Psychology and Religion: The Terry Lectures, Yale University Press, 1938.
The Integration of the Personality, translation of original lectures delivered at the Eranos meeting at Ascona, Switzerland, by Stanley M. Dell, Farrar & Rinehart, 1939.
Essays on Contemporary Events, translation from the original edition, *Aufsaetze zur Zeitgeschichte* (Zurich, 1946), by Elizabeth Welsh, Barbara Hannah, and Mary Briner, Kegan Paul, 1947.
On the Psychology of the Spirit: Two Lectures Given at Ascona, Switzerland, August, 1945, translation by Hildegard Nagel, Analytical Psychology Club of New York, 1948.
(With C. Kerenyi) *Essays on a Science of Mythology: The Myth of the Divine Child and the Mysteries of Eleusis,* translation of the original manuscript, *Einfuehrung in das Wesen der Mythologie: Das goettliche Kind; Das goettliche Maedchen,* by R. F. C. Hull, Pantheon, 1949.
(Author of foreword) *The I Ching; or, Book of Changes,* Pantheon, 1950.
(Contributor of psychological commentary) Walter Yeeling Evans Wentz, editor, *The Tibetan Book of the Great Liberation,* Oxford University Press, 1954.
The Interpretation of Nature and the Psyche (contains "Synchronicity: An Acausal Connecting Principle"), Pantheon, 1955.
(Contributor of commentary) T'ai i chin hua tsung chih, *The Secret of the Golden Flower: A Chinese Book of Life,* [1929], Wehman Bros., 1955.
Flying Saucers: A Modern Myth of Things Seen in the Sky, translation from original edition, *Ein moderner Mythus: Von Dingen, die am Himmel geschen werden* (Rascher, 1958), by R. F. C. Hull, Harcourt, 1959.
The Undiscovered Self, Little, Brown, 1958.
Memories, Dreams, Reflections, recorded and edited by Aniela Jaffe, translation of the original manuscript, *Erinnerungen, Traeume, Gedanken* (Rascher, 1962), by Richard Winston and Clara Winston, Vintage Books, 1961.
(With Joseph L. Henderson, Jolande Jacobi, Aniela Jaffe, and Marie-Louise von Franz; and editor) *Man and His Symbols,* final editing by von Franz, Doubleday, 1964.
Analytical Psychology: Its Theory and Practice; The Tavistock Lectures, foreword by E. A. Bennett, Pantheon, 1968.
C. G. Jung: Letters, edited by Gerhard Adler and Aniela Jaffe, Volume 1: *1906-1950,* Volume 2: *1951-1961,* Princeton University Press, 1973.
The Freud-Jung Letters: The Correspondence Between Sigmund Freud and C. G. Jung, translation by R. F. C. Hull and Ralph Manheim, Princeton University Press, 1974.
The Visions Seminar: From the Complete Notes of Mary Foote (from a seminar held in Zurich, autumn, 1930), postscript by Henry A. Murray, Spring Publications (Zurich), 1976.
C. G. Jung Speaking: Interviews and Encounters, edited by R. F. C. Hull and William McGuire, Princeton University Press, 1977.
Aspects of the Feminine, Princeton University Press, 1982.
Dream Analysis: C. G. Jung Seminars, edited by W. McGuire, Princeton University Press, 1984.
The Four Basic Psychological Functions of Man and the Establishment of Uniformities in Human Structures and Human Behavior (two volumes), American Institute of Psychology, 1984.

Also author of *Notes on Lectures Given at the Eidgenoessische Technische Hochschule, Zurich,* Volume 1: *October 1933-July 1935,* 1959, Volume 2: *October 1938-March 1940,* 1959, Volume 3: *November 1940-July 1941,* 1960.

COLLECTED AND SELECTED WORKS

The Collected Works of C. G. Jung, edited by Herbert Read, Michael Fordham, Gerhard Adler, and William McGuire, translated by R. F. C. Hull and others, Pantheon, 1953-66, Princeton University Press, 1967—, Volume 1: *Psychiatric Studies,* Volume 2: *Experimental Researches,* Volume 3: *The Psychogenesis of Mental Disease,* Volume 4: *Freud and Psychoanalysis,* Volume 5: *Symbols of Transformation,* Volume 6: *Psychological Types,* Volume 7: *Two Essays on Analytical Psychology,* Volume 8: *The Structure and Dynamics of the Psyche,* Volume 9, Part I: *The Archetypes and the Collective Unconscious,* Volume 9, Part II: *Aion: Researches Into the Phenomenology of the Self,* Volume 10: *Civilization in Transition,* Volume 11: *Psychology and Religion: West and East,* Volume 12: *Psychology and Alchemy,* Volume 13: *Alchemical Studies,* Volume 14: *Mysterium Coniunctionis: An Inquiry Into the Separation and Synthesis of Psychic Opposites in Alchemy,* Volume 15: *The Spirit in Man, Art, and Literature,* Volume 16: *The Practice of Psychotherapy: General Problems of Psychotherapy,* Volume 17: *The Development of Personality,* Volume 18: *The Symbolic Life,* Volume 19: *General Bibliography of C. G. Jung's Writings,* Volume 20: *General Index to the Collected Works.*

Individual essays from *Collected Works* have been extracted, collected with other essays represented in *Collected Works* in various configurations according to theme of subject matter, and published under new titles by Princeton University Press.

Work represented in anthologies, including *Psychological Reflections: An Anthology of the Writings of C. G. Jung,* selected and edited by Jolande Jacobi, Pantheon, 1953, revised edition published as *Psychological Reflections: A New Anthology of His Writings, 1905-1961,* Princeton University Press, 1970; *Psyche and Symbol: A Selection From the Writings of C. G. Jung,* edited by Violet S. de Laszlo, preface by Jung, translation by C. F. Baynes and R. F. C. Hull, Doubleday, 1958; *Basic Writings,* edited by Violet S. de Laszlo, Modern Library, 1959; and *C. G. Jung: Word and Image,* edited by Aniela Jaffe, Princeton University Press, 1979.

SIDELIGHTS: Carl Jung was the most popularly known and influential member of the group that formed the core of the early psychoanalytic movement—students and followers of famed Viennese psychoanalyst Sigmund Freud. "Although Jung is only now beginning to acquire the widespread popular recognition accorded Freud," wrote David Elkind in a *New York Times Magazine* article, "many of his concepts have long since become part of the American idiom." Contributions made by Jung and his fellow pioneers in the exploration of the human psyche extend beyond their applications in medical psychology. As the *New York Times* observed in its obituary of Jung: "Before the coming of [Jung and Freud], the world was little used to rummaging through man's subconscious to find the key to his peace and security. Before Freud and Jung, the Western world was inclined to think of man's conduct in terms of original sin. Dr. Jung was one of those who gave a tremendous impetus to twentieth-century thinking by declaring flatly that this explanation was not good enough."

"My life is a story of the self-realization of the unconscious," Jung declared in the prologue to his psychological autobiogra-

phy *Memories, Dreams, Reflections,* in which he recounts the early experiences that led to his lifelong interest in the phenomenon of existence. Jung's mother was described as emotionally distant, beset by physical and nervous disorders, and recalled by Jung as a semi-invalid. His father, a former scholar of some promise who had become a minister, grew increasingly bitter and disillusioned as his wife's health deteriorated and his personal and religious doubts intensified.

Jung also pondered religious questions as—reared in the solitude and majesty of the Swiss Alps—his sense of personal communion with nature was heightened by contemplation of dreams and fantasies. The resulting experience of a primal, elemental manifestation of deity seemed to Jung to be at variance with his father's somber teachings of the more traditional Christian God.

As Jung matured, he recounted, he was drawn out of the contemplation of his inner world and into the external world of school and social relationships. He began his studies at the University of Basel and prepared to enter medicine, but he still retained a fascination for the mental world, both as it is experienced and as it is manifested. He made a two-year study of a young girl who practiced spiritualistic phenomena, but it was while he was preparing for his state medical examinations that an incident occurred turning him decisively toward psychiatry. In his introduction to *The Portable Jung,* Joseph Campbell related that Jung was reading his psychiatry textbook, Krafft-Ebing's *Lehrbuch der Psychiatrie,* when his heart began to pound and he had to stand and draw a deep breath. His excitement was intense for, as Jung recalled, "it had become clear to me in a flash of illumination that for me the only possible goal was psychiatry." "Here, and here alone," Campbell declared, "was the empirical field common to spiritual and biological facts."

After completing his medical studies, Jung secured an appointment at the Burghoelzli Hospital in Zurich, Switzerland, where, under the supervision of Egen Bleuler, he worked with patients suffering from schizophrenia, a mental disorder characterized by personality disintegration. During this period Jung came to recognize the existence of groups of thoughts, feelings, memories, and perceptions, organized around a central theme, that he termed psychological complexes. This discovery was related to his research into word association, a technique whereby words presented to a patient elicit other word responses that reflect related concepts in the patient's psyche and, in turn, gives clues to his unique psychic make-up. Jung's work in this area strengthened the credibility of word-association tests as a diagnostic tool.

Jung sent a copy of his word-association studies to Sigmund Freud and in 1904 began his first attempts to treat patients with Freud's psychoanalytic technique. Two years later, when Jung wished to consult with Freud on a specific case, Freud invited Jung to visit him in Vienna, and a professional affiliation commenced. Over the course of their association Freud favored Jung over his other followers in the growing psychoanalytic movement. As early as 1909 Freud confided that he wanted to make Jung his eldest son and successor in the movement. A year later, at the Second Congress of the Association of Psycho-Analysis, Freud even insisted, despite organized opposition, that Jung should be appointed Permanent President.

Years later Jung recalled this event, as Campbell documented: " 'My dear Jung,' [Freud] urged on this occasion, as Jung tells, 'promise me never to abandon the sexual theory. That is the most essential thing of all. You see, we must make a dogma of it, an unshakable bulwark. . . .' In some astonishment Jung asked him, 'A bulwark—against what?' To which [Freud] replied, 'Against the black tide of mud . . . of occultism.' " Jung declared that that was the thing that struck at the heart: "I knew that I would never be able to accept such an attitude. What Freud seemed to mean by 'occultism' was virtually everything that philosophy and religion, including the rising contemporary science of parapsychology, had learned about the psyche. To me the sexual theory was just as occult, that is to say, just as unproven a hypothesis, as many other speculative views. As I saw it, a scientific truth was a hypothesis that might be adequate for the moment but was not to be preserved as an article of faith for all time."

In other areas, however, Jung and Freud held similar views. Like Freud, Jung placed great importance on the interpretation of dreams. While working on dream interpretation and other areas of inquiry, Jung began formulating the earliest models of the concepts for which he is best known. As Jung's *London Times* obituary noted, "Jung regarded the symbol, whether found in dreams or elsewhere, as the best possible expression of something not fully understood. But he often noted that the symbols in the dreams of his patients, while highly charged with emotion, had no meaning for the dreamer and Jung himself could elicit little significance by associations." Jung came to realize that many of the same symbols seemed to recur throughout history in religion, the arts, folktales, alchemy, and other forms of human expression.

Jung became convinced that the source of this symbolic material was what he identified as the collective unconscious, a pool of inherited psychic residue accumulated since the beginning of the human race, an echo of the sum of experience accessible to all humans, that manifests itself through archetypes, or patterns of expression. According to Jung's theories, experiences such as the alternation of day and night, the change of the seasons, birth, and death, acquire psychic strength through repetition and become universal images, charged with emotion and serving as readily perceived evidence of the collective unconscious. Jung viewed the collective unconscious as distinct from the personal unconscious, which, according to Jung, serves as a storehouse of experience unique to each individual.

Jung's conception of the personal unconscious comprises various elements, including the shadow, a symbolic representation of a human's animal instincts and darker impulses; the anima, nondominant female traits naturally present in a male's personality; and the animus, a set of male traits similarly natural to female personalities. According to Jung, the spiritual potential of an individual seeks realization in the unity of the whole organism, incorporating the various elements of the personal unconscious and establishing access to the collective unconscious. Jung called the method whereby this state of unity is reached the process of individuation, which requires one to confront the unconscious in order to differentiate between and gradually integrate the various elements of which it is comprised. Since this unconscious material cannot be directly experienced, it manifests itself through such symbols as art, dreams, or external situations upon which the confrontation is projected and played out.

Jung was aware that parallels to the symbols in his own and his patients' dreams were also evident in Oriental cultures as well as European cultures of several hundred years ago. He became convinced that searching for and identifying these parallel symbols would assist in integrating an individual. "A good half of the reasons why things are now what they are is buried in Yesterday," Jung wrote in the preface to Violet S. de Laszlo's *Psyche and Symbol*. "Science in its attempt to establish causal chains has to refer to the past. We teach comparative anatomy, why not comparative psychology?"

It became clear that Jung's theories about individuation and the collective unconscious could be widely applicable to human experience and could embrace areas not previously within the realm of psychological study. "His great achievement is that he has shown psychology a new direction: he has constructed a psychology for human beings who reach out toward the unknown, the intangible, the spiritual," a *Time* article stated. "Even if he is only half right, Jung has suggested to mankind a way of 'adjustment' not merely to his animal instincts and social pressures but to his great paradoxes and his eternal religious needs."

Indeed, Jung's approach went beyond that of Freud's, which was primarily concerned with the treatment of neurosis, to include also psychotics, or the mentally deranged, and "normal" individuals in all aspects of mental life. This wide range of application of Jung's theories is due, in part, to the complexity of his framework, an outgrowth of his reluctance to fall into the reductionist tendencies of science. He chose rather to construct his concepts on the evidence derived from his clinical observations and personal experience, including a long period of intense self-analysis that brought him to the edge of insanity.

This stage of Jung's personal and professional development began when the crumbling relationship between Freud and Jung, complicated by Freud's unwelcome and censorious involvement in one of Jung's private relationships, disintegrated by 1913 into a formal breach with the publication of Jung's *The Psychology of the Unconscious.* Freud openly criticized the role that Jung had ascribed to symbolism in the book and felt personally betrayed by Jung's departure from the views expressed in Freudian psychoanalytic theory. Jung likewise felt betrayed, believing that Freud in his inflexibility had failed to support him in what he felt to be a logical extension of their mutual work.

Campbell recorded Jung's own reactions: "The only thing [Freud] saw in my work . . . was 'resistance to the father'—my wish to destroy the father. When I tried to point out to him my reasoning about the libido, his attitude toward me was one of bitterness and rejection. . . . And then," he continued, "I could not accept Freud's placing authority above truth." Jung assessed that "the explosion of all those psychic contents could find no room, no breathing space, in the constricting atmosphere of Freudian psychology and its narrow outlook."

The schism was painful for Jung. Campbell reported that "when he had renounced Freud's dogma, the whole psychoanalytic community turned against him, launching even a paranoiac campaign of character assassination." Jung, for his part, sought to understand the rift in psychological terms. In the process, he devised a method of classifying variations of personality. He described these classifications in his book *Psychological Types,* identifying introverts and extraverts, terms that reflect a person's general orientation to the world, and detailing four modes of psychological functioning: thinking, feeling, sensation, and intuition. Jung applied these theories to his own life and, labeling Freud an extravert and himself an introvert, reasoned that their rift in large measure resulted from their basically different personality types.

Jung's own recollections of his work *The Psychology of the Unconscious* reveal how far beyond the limits of Freudian psychology he had grown: "Hardly had I finished the manuscript," he states, "when it struck me what it means to live with a myth, and what it means to live without one. Myth, says a Church Father, is 'what is believed always, everywhere, by everybody'; hence the man who thinks he can live without myth, or outside it, is an exception. He is like one uprooted, having no true link either with the past, or with ancestral life which continues within him, or yet with contemporary human society." Jung asserted: "The psyche is not of today; its ancestry goes back millions of years. Individual consciousness is only the flower and the fruit of the season, sprung from the perennial rhizome beneath the earth; and it would find itself in better accord with the truth if it took the existence of the rhizome into its calculations. For the root matter is the mother of all things." The mythical orientation thereafter became characteristic of Jung's psychology.

From 1913 to 1917 Jung embarked upon a psychic self-exploration that some considered a breakdown and that Jung himself called a "confrontation with the unconscious." Elkind described the situation: "On the Zurich lake shore [Jung] began collecting stones and building a miniature village, including a castle, cottages and a church. The building game had the desired effect and released a stream of vivid phantasies. It was a dangerous period, because much of what he encountered was the stuff of psychosis and there was always a danger of being trapped by the imagery and going insane."

But Jung emerged from the ordeal with renewed conviction of his theories on archetypes, the collective unconscious, and the process of individuation. Along with his views on the significance of dream symbolism, these theories formed the basis of his own approach, which he called analytical psychology. From this point on, Jung continued to perfect and expand his theoretical framework through his private clinical practice and through his study of such diverse subjects as alchemy, Zen Buddhism, folktales, extrasensory perception, astrology, and the occult.

As Jung developed these views, much of mainline psychiatry chose to ignore Jung's resulting contributions to the study and understanding of the human mind. Freudians regarded him as a misguided traitor, and subsequent schools of thought dismissed Jung's work as being too mystical, too cognizant of religion, and too populated by demons, fairy tales, and mythical figures to warrant any serious, or, at least, practical consideration. "But when Dr. Jung is accused of having left medicine for mysticism," a 1955 *Time* article recorded, "he replies that psychiatry must take into account all of man's experience, from the most intensely practical to the most tenuously mystical."

After his break with Freud, Jung developed his own following. And, during the last decades of his life, beginning in 1933, scholars from all over the world converged each year in Lake Maggiore, Switzerland, to read and discuss papers on Jungian thought. These were the annual Eranos Lectures, at which many of the principal papers of Jung's later years were presented.

Jung continued to treat patients and worked on his last major writings—*Aion* and a thirty-year study of alchemy, *Mysterium Coniunctionis*—whereupon he stated: "My psychology was at last given its place in reality and established upon its historical foundations. Thus my task was finished, my work done, and now it can stand."

BIOGRAPHICAL/CRITICAL SOURCES:

BOOKS

Campbell, Joseph, editor, *The Portable Jung,* Viking, 1971.
Carotenuto, Aldo, *A Secret Symmetry: Sabina Spielrein Between Jung and Freud,* translated by Arno Pomerans, John Shepley, and Krishna Winston, Pantheon, 1982.
de Laszlo, Violet S., *Psyche and Symbol: A Selection From the Writings of C. G. Jung,* preface by Jung, Anchor Books, 1958.
Hannah, Barbara, *Jung: His Life and Work,* Putnam, 1976.
Jung, C. G., Joseph L. Henderson, Jolande Jacobi, Aniela Jaffe, and Marie-Louise von Franz, *Man and His Symbols,* edited by Jung and von Franz, Doubleday, 1961.
Jung, *Memories, Dreams, Reflections,* Vintage Books, 1961.

PERIODICALS

American Heritage, April-May, 1980.
Discover, September, 1982.
Los Angeles Times, November 21, 1978.
Nation, June 25, 1973, November 15, 1975.
New Republic, May 15, 1976, August 4 and 11, 1979.
Newsweek, April 29, 1974, June 21, 1982.
New Yorker, March 1, 1982.
New York Review of Books, January 16, 1969, April 15, 1976, May 13, 1982, June 30, 1983.
New York Times Book Review, February 25, 1973, June 27, 1976, November 24, 1978, May 16, 1982.
New York Times Magazine, October 4, 1970.
Rolling Stone, November 21, 1985.
Time, February 14, 1955, December 1, 1975.
Times Literary Supplement, September 21, 1973, October 19, 1973, July 20, 1984.
Virginia Quarterly Review, winter, 1984.

OBITUARIES:

PERIODICALS

New York Times, June 7, 1961.
Times (London), June 8, 1961.

K

KAEMPFERT, Wade
See del REY, Lester

*   *   *

KAFKA, Franz 1883-1924

PERSONAL: Born July 3, 1883, in Prague, Bohemia (now Czechoslovakia); died of tuberculosis of the larynx, June 3, 1924, in Kierling, Klosterneuburg, Austria; buried in Jewish cemetery in Prague-Straschnitz, Czechoslovakia; son of Hermann (a merchant and manufacturer) and Julie (Loewy) Kafka; children: one son. *Education:* Ferdinand-Karls University (Prague), earned doctorate in law, 1906; also attended technical institute in Prague.

ADDRESSES: Home—Prague, Czechoslovakia.

CAREER: Writer. Worked for attorney Richard Loewy drafting legal notices, Prague, Bohemia (now Czechoslovakia), 1906; intern in law courts, Prague, 1906-07; staff member of insurance company Assicurazioni Generali, Prague, 1907-08; specialist in accident prevention and work-place safety for Workers' Accident Insurance Institute for the Kingdom of Bohemia, Prague, 1908-22. Worked at Prague Asbestos Works Hermann & Co. (manufacturers), Zizkov, Bohemia (now Czechoslovakia), 1911-17.

WRITINGS:

SHORT FICTION

Der Heizer: Ein Fragment (title means "The Stoker: A Fragment"; also see below), Kurt Wolff Verlag (Leipzig), 1913, limited edition, illustrated by Elisabeth Siefer, Mary S. Rosenberg, 1985.

Betrachtung (title means "Meditations"; includes stories later published in English translation as "Children on a Country Road," "Unmasking a Confidence Trickster," "Excursion into the Mountains," and "The Street Window"; also see below), Rowohlt Verlag, 1913.

Die Verwandlung (also see below), Kurt Wolff Verlag, 1915, new edition edited by Marjorie L. Hoover, Norton, 1960, translation by A. L. Lloyd published as *The Metamorphosis,* Parton, 1937, Vanguard Press, 1946, modern critical edition, Chelsea House, 1988, published as *The Metamorphosis: Including Selections from Kafka's Letters and Diaries, and*

Critical Essays, translation by Stanley Corngold, Bantam, 1972.

Das Urteil: Eine Geschichte (title means "The Judgement: A Story"; also see below), Kurt Wolff Verlag, 1916.

In der Strafkolonie, Kurt Wolff Verlag, 1919, translation by Willa Muir and Edwin Muir and C. Greenberg published as *The Penal Colony: Stories and Short Pieces,* Schocken, 1948.

Ein Landarzt: Kleine Erzaehlungen (also see below), Kurt Wolff Verlag, 1919, translation by Vera Leslie published as *The Country Doctor: A Collection of Fourteen Stories,* Counter-Point, 1945.

Ein Hungerkunstler: Vier Geschichten (includes stories published in English translation as "A Hunger Artist," "A Little Woman," "First Sorrow," and "Josephine the Singer; or, the Mouse Folk"; also see below), Verlag Die Schmiede (Berlin), 1924.

Beim Bau der Chinesischen Mauer, Ungedruckte Erzaehlungen und Prosa aus dem Nachlass (includes "The Great Wall of China," "The Village Schoolmaster [The Giant Mole]," "The Hunter Gracchus," "Investigations of a Dog," and "The Burrow"; also see below), edited by Max Brod and Hans Joachim Schoeps, Gustav Kiepenheuer Verlag, 1931, translation by Willa and Edwin Muir published as *The Great Wall of China and Other Pieces,* Secker & Warburg, 1933, published as *The Great Wall of China: Stories and Reflections,* Schocken, 1970.

Parables in German and English, translation by Willa and Edwin Muir, Schocken, 1947.

Selected Short Stories, translation by Willa and Edwin Muir, Modern Library, 1952.

Description of a Struggle (also see below), Schocken, 1958.

Parables and Paradoxes, in German and English, translation by Willa and Edwin Muir, Schocken, 1958, published as *Parables and Paradoxes: Parabeln und Paradoxe,* 1961.

Erzaehlungen und Skizzen, edited by Klaus Wagenbach, Moderner Buch-Club (Darmstadt), 1959.

Die Erzaehlungen, edited by Wagenbach, S. Fischer Verlag, 1961, edited by Charles W. Hoffman, Norton, 1970.

Metamorphosis and Other Stories, translation by Willa and Edwin Muir, Penguin, 1961.

Er: Prosa, edited by Martin Walser, Suhrkamp (Frankfurt), 1963.

Short Stories, edited by J. M. S. Pasley, Oxford University Press, 1963.

Der Heizer; In der Strafkolonie; Der Bau, edited by J. M. S. Pasley, Cambridge University Press, 1966.

Saemtliche Erzaehlungen, edited by Paul Raabe, S. Fischer Verlag, 1970.

The Complete Stories, translation by Willa and Edwin Muir, Tania Stern and James Stern, and Ernst Kaiser and Eithne Wilkins, postscript by Nahum N. Glatzer, Schocken, 1971, special centennial edition, edited by Glatzer, foreword by John Updike, illustrated by Adele Grodstein, 1983.

Shorter Works, edited with translation by Malcolm Pasley, Secker & Warburg, 1973.

The Bridge, illustrated by Henri Galeron, Schocken, 1983.

The Metamorphosis, The Penal Colony, and Other Stories, translation by Willa and Edwin Muir, Schocken, 1988.

The Sons (contains "The Metamorphosis," "The Judgement," and "The Stoker"), Schocken, 1989.

Stories also published in English translation independently and in additional collections and anthologies.

NOVELS

Der Prozess, edited by Brod, Verlag Die Schmiede, 1925, translation by Willa and Edwin Muir published as *The Trial,* Gollancz, 1935, Knopf, 1937, revised edition with additional chapters in English translation by E. M. Butler, Secker & Warburg, 1956, definitive edition, with illustrations by George Salter, Knopf, 1957, with drawings by Kafka, Schocken, 1968, reprinted, 1988.

Das Schloss, edited by Brod, Kurt Wolff Verlag, 1926, translation by Willa and Edwin Muir published as *The Castle,* Knopf, 1930, new edition with introduction by Thomas Mann, Knopf, 1941, definitive edition with additional material translation by Wilkins and Ernst Kaiser and with introduction by Mann, Secker & Warburg, 1953, Knopf, 1954, revised edition, Schocken, 1974.

Amerika, edited by Brod, Kurt Wolff Verlag, 1927, translation by Willa and Edwin Muir published under same title, with preface by Mann, afterword by Brod, and illustrations by Emlen Etting, Routledge & Kegan Paul, 1938, New Directions, 1946, reprinted with foreword by Updike, Schocken, 1983.

Novels also collected in single-volume editions.

NONFICTION

The Diaries of Franz Kafka, edited by Brod, Volume 1: *1910-1913,* translation by Joseph Kresh from German manuscripts, Schocken, 1948, Volume 2: *1914-1923,* translation by Martin Greenberg with Hannah Arendt from German manuscripts, Schocken, 1949, both volumes reprinted in single volume, 1989.

Brief an den Vater, S. Fischer Verlag (Frankfurt), 1953, bilingual edition with translation by Ernst Kaiser and Wilkins published as *Letter to His Father/Brief an den Vater,* Schocken, 1966.

I Am a Memory Come Alive: Autobiographical Writings, edited by Glatzer from previous translations, Schocken, 1974.

COLLECTED WORKS

Gesammelte Schriften, edited by Brod and Heinz Politzer, Volumes 1-4, Schocken (Berlin), Volumes 5-6, Mercy (Prague), 1935-36, Volume 1: *Erzaehlungen und kleine Prosa,* translation by Kaiser and Wilkins published as *In the Penal Settlement: Tales and Short Prose Works,* Secker & Warburg,

1973, Volume 5: *Beschreibung eines Kampfes: Novellen, Skizzen, Aphorismen aus dem Nachlass,* translation by Willa and Edwin Muir and Tania and James Stern published as *Description of a Struggle and The Great Wall of China,* Secker & Warburg, 1960.

Gesammelte Werke, 11 volumes, edited by Brod, S. Fischer Verlag, 1950-1974, Volume 4: *Briefe an Milena,* edited by Willy Haas, translation by Tania and James Stern published as *Letters to Milena,* Farrar, Straus/Schocken, 1953, Volume 7: *Hochzeitsvorbereitungen auf dem Lande und andere Prosa aus dem Nachlass,* translation by Kaiser and Wilkins published as *Dearest Father: Stories and Other Writings,* Schocken, 1954 (published in England as *Wedding Preparations in the Country, and Other Posthumous Papers,* Secker & Warburg, 1954), Volume 9: *Briefe 1902-1904,* edited by Beverly Colman and others, translation, with additional material, by Richard Winston and Clara Winston published as *Letters to Friends, Family, and Editors,* Schocken, 1977, Volume 10: *Briefe an Felice und andere Korrespondenz aus der Verlobungszeit,* edited by Erich Heller and Juergen Born, translation by James Stern and Elisabeth Duckworth published as *Letters to Felice,* Schocken, 1973, Volume 11: *Briefe an Ottla und die Familie,* edited by Hartmut Binder and Wagenbach, translation by Richard and Clara Winston and edited by Glatzer published as *Letters to Ottla and the Family,* Schocken, 1982.

The Basic Kafka (omnibus volume), edited by Heller, Pocket Books, 1983.

Fiction and nonfiction also published together in other collections.

OTHER

(Contributor) Harry Steinhauer and Helen Jessiman, editors, *Modern German Stories* (contains "The Hunger Artist"), Oxford University Press, 1938.

Contributor to periodicals, including *Arkadia, Bohemia,* and *Hyperion.*

SIDELIGHTS: Franz Kafka, a Jewish Czechoslovakian who wrote in German, ranks among the twentieth century's most acclaimed writers. He is often cited as the author whose works best evoke the bewildering oppressiveness of modern life, and though his writings accommodate a vast range of interpretations, his general perspective is inevitably one of anxiety and alienation. His characters constantly face failure and futility, and they struggle to survive in a world that is largely unfeeling and unfamiliar. This world, rendered with great detachment and detail, is one in which the fantastic is entirely normal, the irrational is rational, and the unreasonable seems reasonable. It is a bizarre, senselessly oppressive world in which characters endure between madness and despair, and between defeat and mere failure. Kafka's protagonists subject themselves to extraordinary torture contraptions, negotiate unfathomable bureaucratic mazes, and execute astounding transformations. It is a world in which a man becomes an insect and an ape becomes a sophisticate. Today, with genocide, madness, and even impending doom seen as everyday possibilities, Kafka's voice sounds vital and prophetic. As Ernst Pawel wrote in *The Nightmare of Reason: A Biography of Franz Kafka,* Kafka articulates "the anguish of being human."

Kafka was born in Prague in 1883, a time when that city was still part of Bohemia within the Austro-Hungarian Empire. Anti-Semitism was rife throughout eastern Europe, and in Prague, as in many European cities, Jews were reduced by economic and social disadvantage to congregating in ghettos. Within Prague's

Jewish ghetto, Kafka's father, Hermann, owned and operated a dry-goods wholesale store. Hermann Kafka was an uneducated but extremely industrious Czech who had married Julie Loewy, an urbane, German-speaking Jew from a slightly higher social class. Although her husband's superior within Prague's Jewish society, Julie Kafka subordinated herself to him helping in the store most days and joining him at card games most evenings.

Hermann Kafka's domineering manner greatly distressed young Kafka, who found his father loud, impatient, unsympathetic, and, consequently, overwhelming and intimidating. Particularly vivid to Kafka was his childhood memory of an incident in which he repeatedly cried from his bed for water, whereupon his father removed him to a balcony and locked him out of the house. Years later, at age thirty six, the event still powerfully haunted Kafka, and in a missive later published as *Letter to His Father* he reproached Hermann Kafka for his crude methods. "For years thereafter," Kafka wrote, "I kept being haunted by fantasies of this giant of a man, my father, the ultimate judge, coming to get me in the middle of the night, and for almost no reason at all dragging me out of bed onto the *pavlatch*—in other words, that as far as he was concerned, I was an absolute Nothing."

With Kafka's parents devoting their time and energy to the dry-goods store, his upbringing was left largely to maids and governesses. He found himself further separated from his parents when he finally began his education, for Prague's schools, known as gymnasiums, operated ten months each year and assigned extensive homework. Student life proved arduous and trying for Kafka, who was a minority as both a German-speaker and a Jew; and the school, which was designed to shape children into functionaries for the empire's ever-flourishing bureaucracy, offered little of insight or interest to him. Kafka coped with this unappealing and even alienating approach to education by daydreaming and, in adolescence, by reading extensively, with a preference for the works of evolutionist Charles Darwin and philosophers Benedict Spinoza and Friedrich Nietzsche.

In adolescence Kafka also dwelled obsessively on his own self-perceived inadequacy, rejecting his intellect as inferior and his body as loathsome. As his self-perception degenerated, his grades suffered accordingly, and only with a great deal of relentless studying, and some cheating, did he survive his school's hellish period of rigorous final examinations and thereby complete his studies.

For a graduation present, Kafka's parents financed his vacation to a town near the North Sea. The vacation was his first venture from Prague and was intended, at least by his father, as his respite before entering the family business. Kafka, however, had already decided to enter Ferdinand-Karls University, a German school where he intended to study philosophy. Upon returning home, Kafka announced his scholastic intentions and met with powerful disapproval from his father. Despite the parent's objections and harangues, Kafka entered the university in 1901, and soon afterwards he decided to pursue a law degree.

At Ferdinand-Karls University, Kafka became acquainted with intellectuals and aspiring artists. Like many German-speaking students, he joined the Hall of Lecture and Discourse for German Studies, an organization widely recognized as Prague's leading institution for German culture. The Hall had been conceived as an anti-Semitic organization, but the steady influx of German-speaking Jews gradually transformed it into a predominantly Judaic body. Through this group Kafka met his closest friends, including Max Brod, a sickly, hunchbacked student who played and composed music and wrote poetry. While delivering

a lecture on philosopher Arthur Schopenhauer, Brod had denounced Nietzsche as a fraud, and when Kafka vehemently protested afterwards, their friendship began.

With Brod Kafka began sampling Prague's cultural offerings, which included theatrical productions and more esoteric events such as theosophic and anthroposophic lectures and spiritualist seances. In addition, Kafka and Brod frequented Prague's cafes, which numbered more than two hundred, and visited the city's brothels, which also numbered in the hundreds. As a result of his carousing and extra-curricular studies, Kafka's grades suffered. The insufferable boredom of the gymnasium had been replaced by the equally lethal monotony of law school, in which information was inevitably conveyed by such dull lecturers that it was rendered appallingly useless to Kafka and his fellow students. Briefly, Kafka abandoned law studies for chemistry, then returned to law before leaving it again for German studies and art history. He then returned once more to law and continued in that field throughout the remainder of his education.

In 1905, one year before finishing his studies, Kafka's hectic and demanding life finally affected his health and compelled him recover at a sanatorium. There he enjoyed one of his rare pleasurable relationships with a woman. Although his lover was considerably older, Kafka apparently toyed with the notion of marriage. Once back in Prague, however, he abandoned the affair and resumed his association with Jewish intellectuals and artists. At night he frequented theaters, bordellos, and cafes, and listened as his friends and acquaintances discussed politics, art, and their own writings. Unlike his peers, though, Kafka showed little interest in politics or political concepts such as socialism, choosing instead to continue reading works by masters such as Goethe, Kleist, Kierkegaard, Flaubert, Dickens, and Dostoyevsky.

Unbeknownst to his friends, Kafka had also begun writing his own novel, one referred to now as "Beschreibung eines Kampfes" ("Description of a Struggle"). This work—eventually abandoned by Kafka and given incomplete to Brod, who later provided the title—is a funny and fantastic account of a nameless narrator's adventures on a winter's evening. Among the notable episodes in the story is "Gespraech mit dem Beter" ("Conversation With the Supplicant"), an unsettling church encounter recalled by a grotesque fat man as four nude servants carry him across a river. Upon reading "Description of a Struggle," Brod immediately recognized that Kafka had already surpassed his peers as a writer, and in a essay for a local journal he placed Kafka in the "sainted company" of German literature's elite. Kafka received Brod's praise with humility and, characteristically, apprehension. He expressed concern that any writings he published henceforth might disappoint readers aware of his allegedly unmerited stature. To Brod, Kafka confessed that he could never "hope to produce an effect to rival that with which your sentence has endowed my name."

Aside from reading and writing, Kafka also devoted considerable time to preparing for his grueling, extensive final examinations. Upon successfully completing his first two tests, Kafka qualified for work in his prospective field, and in the spring of 1906 he began drafting legal notices for a local attorney. In addition, he also assisted his parents at the family store whenever such involvement was required. His jobs, together with his literary pursuits and his ongoing, seemingly endless studies, considerably diminished his other extra-curricular activities, though he managed to continue indulging in one of his rare athletic interests, swimming.

Strained by constant pressure to fulfill familial, professional, and scholastic obligations and expectations, Kafka again succumbed to exhaustion after earning his law doctorate in June, 1906. Shortly thereafter he re-entered the sanatorium, where he briefly revived his affair with the mysterious older woman. But as before, upon returning home he promptly discontinued the relationship and resumed his relatively carefree social life with Brod and other friends.

Back in Prague Kafka also began writing another story, one now known as "Hochzeitsvorbereitungen auf dem Lande" ("Wedding Preparations in the Country"). This tale—left incomplete by Kafka and consequently titled by Brod—recounts a bridegroom's dread as he travels to meet his beloved. Unlike "Description of a Struggle," which only superficially explores alienation, "Wedding Preparations in the Country" offers a disturbing evocation of apprehension in its all-encompassing banality. The protagonist, Raban, even resorts to childlike optimism by imagining that his two-weeks stay in the countryside will actually be the predicament of someone other than himself. Biographer Ronald Hayman, in *Franz Kafka,* asserted that Kafka used this strategy in his own personal life and added that the tale itself served as a vehicle for Kafka's displacement. Hayman wrote: "Raban's belief that everything could be explained is a projection of Kafka's need to explain everything, by means of a story about an *alter ego.*"

Upon returning to Prague Kafka also began one year's unpaid apprenticeship in the city's court system. His position, while apparently a career necessity, afforded him little opportunity to free himself from his father's household and authority. This continued dependence resulted in increased anxiety for Kafka in mid-1907 when his father decided to move the family into a new building, one recently constructed on a razed portion of the ghetto. To Kafka's utter dismay, the new dwelling afforded him only minimal privacy, for his bedroom was situated between the living room and his parents' bedroom, thus serving as a nerve-racking vantage point from which could be heard all noises and conversations occurring within the home. Also distressing to Kafka were his father's seemingly constant interruptions and his parents' ineffective discretion within their own room. Relaxing, much less writing, proved extremely difficult for the already hypersensitive Kafka.

Fortunately for Kafka, his social activities afforded him substantial distraction from his tense home life. After graduating, he devoted more time to recreation, including motorcycling, swimming, sunbathing, and billiards. He also entered into his first sustained love affair, though it is unclear whether this romance inhibited his enthusiasm for prostitutes. He had, by this time, also revealed serious literary aspirations to Brod and others. But with typically curious reasoning, he maintained that his income should derive from an occupation quite dissimilar from his literary pursuits, and he therefore sought an undistracting, undemanding position, preferably one abroad.

The job that Kafka eventually obtained, though, was a tedious post at an Italian insurance company with a Prague office. Offering low pay and long hours, the post was immensely unappealing, and Kafka almost immediately began hoping for a transfer. But such wishes were futile, and Kafka, sensing unending and unendurable boredom and poverty, contemplated suicide. In the throes of anguish, he abandoned writing and became a more frequent patron of bordellos and low-life cafes. In addition, he entered into relations with a Jewish student. But, realizing that he was psychologically incapable of reciprocating a woman's love, he confessed to Brod that, conversely, he could only love women unlikely to share his feelings. Thus his relationships with women were, understandably, impaired by his neurotic perspective.

In 1908 Kafka's fortunes improved when a friend's father, responding to Kafka's pleas for help, secured him a post at the Workmen's Accident Insurance Institute for the Kingdom of Bohemia. Although the firm was steadfastly anti-Semitic—Kafka became only the second Jew of two hundred and fifty employees—he was nonetheless offered a promising job, one with regular hours and with greater pay than was accorded him by the Italian company. Seizing the opportunity, Kafka hastily obtained a medical report certifying him as prone to nervousness and agitation. This certificate assured his departure from the Assicurazioni, and in late July he assumed the post that he would hold until his death sixteen years later.

At the Workmen's Institute Kafka rapidly attained a level of substantial responsibility. Despite only limited seniority, he was selected to formally introduce new administrator Robert Marschner at a company gathering, and in the ensuing years he contributed segments on work-place safety to Marschner's annual report of 1910, and produced press releases. In *The Nightmare of Reason,* Pawel reports that Kafka's work-related writings, including more technical articles on accident prevention, contradict his image as an incompetent and show him, instead, as a serious, forthright employee. Pawel relates that Kafka's articles "combine an astonishing grasp of abstruse detail with a lucidity of presentation seldom encountered in writings of this sort," and he adds that the technical writings "quite incisively refute the caricature of Kafka as a bumbling fool forever sleepwalking in broad daylight and incapable of tying his shoelaces."

Although the change in employment lessened Kafka's anxieties, its increased responsibilities left him little time for writing and carousing. In March, 1908, Kafka had collected eight brief prose pieces under the title "Betrachtung" ("Meditations") and published them in Franz Blei's journal *Hyperion.* But these works brought him little recognition, and some readers even mistook them for those of another writer, Robert Walser. Kafka consequently held little enthusiasm for the distractions of writing, and it was only through Brod's own efforts and encouragement that he agreed to produce a review of one of Blei's books. This enterprize, however, only exposed Kafka's ambivalence to writing, for he produced a twisted, tentative report. He later apologized to Blei, and along with that written apology he enclosed several pages containing his contributions to a company report.

As an alternative to the constant demands of the Workmen's Institute, Kafka renewed his interest in boating and swimming. But these activities offered only minimal respite from the company, and in late summer, 1909—several months after the Jewish student had ended their largely epistolary relationship—Kafka finally took a brief vacation with Brod. Earlier that summer, he had published excerpts from his abandoned novel *Description of a Struggle* in *Hyperion,* but that publication, like his earlier work in *Hyperion,* apparently gained him little attention. The vacation, however, sufficiently inspired him to engage in a writing contest with Brod, and in early autumn his piece, a description of airplanes, appeared in the publication *Bohemia.*

Invigorated by the vacation, Kafka returned to Prague with renewed interest in writing. In January, 1910, he published a book review in *Bohemia;* in March he produced five prose works for the same periodical; and soon afterwards, he also began a diary. Aside from writing, Kafka improved his physical fitness with daily calisthenics, horseback riding and—in summer—swimming and rowing. These activities, however, failed to ease his increasing digestive distress, and he therefore adopted a vegetarian diet. While converting to vegetarianism, Kafka became preoccupied with his bowel regularity, and he maintained both the vegetarian diet and a bowel obsession throughout his life.

1910 was also the year that Kafka began his interest in Yiddish theatre. In May, Brod took him to a performance at a Prague cafe, and Kafka responded enthusiastically. The following autumn—1911—Kafka befriended members of a troupe and even arranged a performance. For Kafka, the Yiddish theatre was appealing for various reasons: its coarse melodramas afforded him insights into his ancestry and allowed him to explore aspects of race and nationality detested and ignored by his father, who considered the ethnic tradition a vulgar reminder of the ghetto. Inspired by the troupe and its performances, Kafka began studying Yiddish literature and Judaism and even attended a musical presentation arranged by Zionists. He also fell in love with actress Mania Tschissik, but his affections were not reciprocated, and when the troupe finally left Prague Kafka turned to Brod for solace.

This period was one of almost constant personal turmoil for Kafka. In October, 1911, his brother-in-law, Karl Hermann, founded Prague's first asbestos factory at the behest of Kafka's father. Kafka offered his assistance, assuming that such involvement would be only occasional and menial. His father, however, perceived the factory as an opportunity for his son to redeem his wasted life through application to a family business. Since Karl Hermann was often traveling to promote business, Kafka soon found himself constantly working at the factory after leaving his insurance post each afternoon. The factory's noise and filth immensely disturbed Kafka's already sensitive disposition, and endless confrontations with his father, who demanded greater commitment from him, further exacerbated his anxiety. Even in his room Kafka was hardly free of unnerving distractions, for his father's apparently constant shouting rang throughout the home, and barely muffled sounds from the parents' bedroom continually undermined the son's sense of privacy and decency.

Perhaps as a result of living in a state of nearly unending anxiety, Kafka soon suffered declining health, including weak breathing, migraine headache, and more stomach distress. In June, 1912, he obtained one week's sick leave from the insurance company, and in July he spent three more weeks in a German sanatorium. His stay at the sanatorium, however, was motivated largely by recreational considerations, for he longed to swim and languish in the summer sun. Evenings at the sanatorium he devoted to writing a novel that he referred to as "Der Verschollene" (which means "the missing one"). But this work, later developed into *Amerika,* came slowly to Kafka, and by autumn, when he had already returned to Prague, he was still at work on the first chapter.

Once back in Prague, Kafka also occupied himself by collecting several prose works for publication as the volume *Betrachtung.* While compiling that work, he realized a sudden burst of creativity, and within three months he produced two of his greatest stories, "Das Urteil" ("The Judgment") and "Die Verwandlung" ("The Metamorphosis"), and completed the first chapter of *Amerika.* "The Judgment" is certainly a key work in Kafka's canon, for it constitutes one of his most incisive renderings of the father-son conflict that so devastated his personal life. In the tale, protagonist Georg Bendemann suffers from total subordination to his totalitarian father, a domineering widower. One afternoon, George nervously considers his wedding engagement while alone with his father. He tells his father of a friend in St. Petersburg. His father doubts the existence of such a friend and criticizes his son for besmirching the memory of his mother by succumbing to his fiance's sexual advances. Upon shaming his son, the father

then reveals that he actually knows of the St. Petersburg friend and has actually kept him abreast of Georg's engagement. Gleefully proclaiming his deception, the father mocks his son's naivete and condemns him to drown himself. The son complies by dropping himself from a bridge, pausing beforehand only to say, "Dear parents, I have always loved you, all the same."

"The Judgment" is hailed as a masterful articulation of a father-son conflict and an extraordinary expression of oppression and anxiety. "The Metamorphosis" is acclaimed for the same qualities, and is prized additionally for its fantastic premise. In perhaps his most memorable and well-known tale, Kafka wrote of Gregor Samsa, a traveling salesman who awakens at home one morning to find that he has become an enormous insect. Like "The Judgment," "The Metamorphosis" is often interpreted as a reflection of Kafka's own anxieties, for like Kafka, protagonist Samsa is repulsed by his physical existence and is overwhelmed with guilt for his very presence. Samsa's father, in turn, is both angered and disgusted by his son's transformation, which he considers a personal effrontery. Eventually, the father arms himself with fruit and bombards the hideous insect, sinking one apple deep into his back. For more than one month Samsa lives on while the apple rots and inflames his back. His parents and sister try to ignore him, and he usually remains in his room, where he had taken to crawling on the ceiling before the apple incident somewhat incapacitated him. One evening, however, his parents and recent lodgers are enjoying music when Samsa suddenly appears and repulses everyone. The family then decides that the gigantic insect that is Gregor Samsa must be destroyed. Sensing his inconvenient presence within the otherwise harmonious household, Samsa retreats to his room and thinks of his family with "tenderness and love." The next morning, a cleaning woman discovers his already dried corpse.

Both "The Judgment" and "The Metamorphosis," like most of Kafka's subsequent writings, have inspired a wide range of interpretations, and both works have been categorized in often contrasting terms. "The Judgment" has been appraised as both realistic and absurd, while "The Metamorphosis," though more consistently considered a fantastic allegory, is nonetheless perceived by some critics as comedy and by others as tragedy. Despite making these diverging assessments, many critics agree that the tales are dream-like masochistic fantasies reflecting Kafka's father-son conflict and his own traumas and insecurities. Ronald Hayman, for instance, notes in his biography *Kafka* that "Kafka draws on his flow of anxieties" in writing "The Metamorphosis" and adds that even the tale's "root idea . . . was a gift from his father—an invitation to think of himself as verminous."

In 1912, aside from writing "The Judgment" and "The Metamorphosis," Kafka also completed "Der Heizer" ("The Stoker"), the first chapter of his novel *Amerika.* Kafka apparently delighted in reading aloud from this novel, which concerns the odd adventures of a naive young man sent to the United States after having seduced a maid. Upon publication in May, 1913, this chapter drew impressive praise from prominent novelist Robert Musil and received comparisons with the work of Heinrich von Kleist, whom Kafka had long admired as an artist. The next month, "The Judgment" appeared in Brod's periodical *Arkadia,* earning Kafka further recognition as a prominent new writer.

But Kafka was not immediately able to enjoy his newfound celebrity, for as early as 1912 the family factory began amassing imposing debts. The factory's problems were hardly Kafka's fault, for he worked regular hours at the insurance company and devoted only afternoons and some weekends to the plant's operations. But as Karl Hermann was constantly away on business, Kafka had been presumed responsible for the factory by his father, who claimed that various employees were swindling funds. Enduring the harangues of his desperate and incompetent parent, Kafka suffered migraine headaches and further stomach pains, and he once again considered suicide. He expressed such thoughts in a letter to Brod, who consequently wrote to Kafka's mother and urged her to intercede on her son's behalf. She responded by secretly hiring Karl Hermann's brother to fulfill Kafka's management duties. The plan ensued without Hermann Kafka's knowledge, and until the outbreak of World War I it enabled Kafka to live his already traumatic life free of the troublesome family business.

Once freed from his duties at the factory, Kafka devoted greater energy to his budding romance with Felice Bauer, an independent woman he met through Brod. Confident and extroverted, Bauer was the opposite of the insecure and inhibited Kafka in temperament, and biographer Pawel notes in *The Nightmare of Reason* that Kafka was attracted to precisely those qualities that he lacked. With Bauer he quickly established a close, and often confused, relationship, soliciting her opinions on his soon-to-be-published short prose works. Their communication was largely epistolary, with Kafka re-introducing himself to her through a missive on which he labored intermittently for ten days. Pawel calls this first letter "a masterpiece . . . of cunning and dissimulation," one designed by Kafka to present an acceptable image of himself as earnest, educated, and fairly sophisticated.

In his first several letters to Bauer, Kafka obsessively pursued her as a correspondent, writing daily and vigorously encouraging her to reciprocate. In *Kafka's Other Trial: The Letters to Felice*, Elias Canetti notes the almost parasitic nature of these initial missives. Kafka, Canetti writes, "was establishing a connection, a channel of communication, between [Bauer's] efficiency and health and his own indecisiveness and weakness." Canetti adds that Kafka derived a great deal of strength from these letters, and that strength, in turn, led to a great increase in his self-assurance as a writer. Shortly after writing his first letter to Bauer, Kafka felt sufficiently invigorated to produce "The Judgment" in one evening-long burst of creativity, and upon completing the tale he was still so euphoric with thoughts of Bauer that he dedicated the story to her.

Initially, Bauer did not share Kafka's obsession for letter writing. Kafka's extraordinary intimacy and sheer volume of correspondence, however, eventually convinced her of his passionate sincerity and prompted her to begin writing on a daily basis too. Increasingly, Kafka used his correspondence with Bauer as a forum for explaining his phobias, fears, and failures. He also began subordinating himself to her, describing himself as unworthy of her affection. Though more worshipful than reasonable, Kafka proposed marriage in the summer of 1913. Bauer accepted, and the couple's largely epistolary relationship—though they lived only six hours apart by train—seemed destined to result in matrimony.

Soon after becoming engaged, though, Kafka questioned the appeal of marriage. He feared the loss of the very solitude that seemed to him so integral to his recent fortunes as a writer, and in his diary he expressed extreme reservations about his suitability as a spouse. His anxieties led to physical distress, including heart pains. Upon soliciting his father's counsel, he was criticized as an unsuitable marriage prospect. Although Kafka had repeatedly tried to persuade Bauer of their folly, his father's words proved disheartening and unsettling.

In the autumn of 1913, seeking a respite from his traumatic personal life, Kafka entered a sanatorium, where he had a brief, inconsequential affair with a young Swiss woman. After returning to Prague he met with Bauer's friend Grete Bloch, who had agreed to help reconcile differences between the engaged couple. Bloch recounted Bauer's own personal difficulties, including dental decay, which Kafka found particularly repellant. Unable to articulate his objections to the impending marriage, Kafka spontaneously departed for Bauer's home in Berlin. But they met there only briefly before Bauer left to fulfill personal obligations, and so Kafka returned home full of doubt and uncertainty about the status of his engagement.

When Bauer failed to write to him after his brief visit to Berlin, Kafka decided that he could not live without her. In his biography *Kafka*, Hayman recounts a letter to Bauer in which Kafka both confessed his recent infidelity and stressed his love as nonetheless strong: "I love you, Felice, with everything in me that's humanly good, everything that makes me worthy of staying among the living." Instead of responding to Kafka, Bauer once again appealed to her friend Bloch, who reacted by disclosing to Kafka the contents of Bauer's letters to her. Soon Kafka and Bloch had developed their own correspondence, and though by mid-1914 he and Bauer had renewed their engagement, shortly thereafter he and Bloch began their own affair.

Bloch, though sexually involved with Kafka, nonetheless continued advocating Bauer as his wife. Kafka, once again confronted with the likelihood of marriage, responded by pursuing Bloch instead of his fiance. Events culminated in a confrontation between Kafka and both Bloch and Bauer in a hotel room, where Bauer berated him for his infidelity and indecisiveness. She ended their engagement and departed with Bloch, who, unbeknownst to Kafka, was pregnant with his child. Seemingly free of romantic ties, Kafka then vacationed with friends at a Danish seaside resort. Around this time, the Archduke Ferdinand, heir to the kingdom of Austro-Hungary, was assassinated. His death sparked World War I.

With Karl Hermann and his brother fighting in the war, Kafka once again entered the family's asbestos factory. He also continued working at the insurance company, where he had earlier been promoted to deputy secretary. Though working these two jobs, Kafka still found time for his writing. By July he had begun another novel, *Der Prozess* (*The Trial*), and in November he wrote "In der Strafkolonie" ("In the Penal Colony"). The latter work, largely viewed as one of Kafka's most disturbing, concerns an interrogating officer who becomes so proud of his mechanistic torture device—which involves long needles writing a proclamation onto victims' flesh—that he voluntarily submits himself to its deathly function. Like most of Kafka's fiction, "In the Penal Colony" has prompted a vast array of interpretations and has consequently been described in terms ranging from realism to absurdity and from comedy to tragedy. Critics analyzing from a psychological perspective see the tale as an expression of Kafka's own susceptibility for self punishment, while Hayman speculates in his biography that the story may have been influenced by accounts of World War I trench fighting.

After completing "In the Penal Colony" in late 1914, Kafka returned to several others stories in various stages of completion. Believing that he could easily lose inspiration, he often worked on his tales long into the night. His concentration, however, was disrupted by his responsibilities at both the insurance company and the family factory. In addition, he experienced continued poor health, including headaches, exhaustion from insomnia, and severe chest pain, though an earlier doctor's examination disclosed no indication of physical abnormality.

As a result of both business obligations and health problems, Kafka completed few works between the winters of 1914, when he produced "In the Penal Colony," and of 1916, when he wrote "Ein Landarzt" ("A Country Doctor"). During that two-year interim he experienced various changes in his personal life. Most significant was his departure from his parents' household: When one of his sisters returned with her children for the duration of her husband's military service, Kafka moved to another sister's apartment, one vacated when she moved in with her in-laws, and he stayed there more than a year before renting an entire flat in March, 1917, around the same time that the factory finally closed. By that time he and Felice Bauer had once again renewed their courtship. Nearly five months later, he again suffered severe stomach pains, and in August, 1917, two months after he and Bauer announced their second official engagement, Kafka experienced his first tubercular hemorrhage.

By the time of his renewed engagement to Bauer, Kafka was once again writing regularly. "A Country Doctor," his first sustained effort since "In the Penal Colony," recounts a doctor's gruesome, surreal experience on a snowy evening. Summoned to a village, the doctor rides through a blizzard until he arrives at a farmhouse in which a young boy is apparently dying. The doctor initially pronounces the boy healthy, though the lad pleads for death. Upon closer examination, the doctor discovers, near the youth's right hip, a gaping hole in which worms wriggle through clotted blood. After noting the source of the boy's distress, the doctor is inexplicably stripped of his clothing and left alone with the youth, who proclaims that his repulsive hole is his "sole endowment" in the world. The doctor reassures the boy that the wound is relatively slight, whereupon the boy falls silent. The doctor then flees and rides home naked, seemingly unable to either retrieve his clothing or return home in time to salvage his medical practice.

Kafka followed "A Country Doctor" with "A Report to an Academy," in which a socially integrated ape recounts his experiences as a wild animal, and "The Great Wall of China," an ultimately uncompleted account of the wall's construction and its suitability as a defense measure. These works signaled the end of Kafka's very brief period of renewed creativity, for by the end of summer his health had declined seriously and his personal life had once again degenerated into despair and confusion. Following his first sign of internal bleeding, Kafka proceeded to the insurance company and only consulted a physician after having worked that day. His ailment was misdiagnosed as bronchial catarrh, and though he bled again that evening, he waited nearly one month before seeing a specialist. By that time he had also experienced fever, particular during evenings, and shortness of breath. His first doctor, however, had assured him that tuberculosis was unlikely.

With his health uncertain, Kafka returned to his parents' residence, and in September, at Brod's behest, he consulted a specialist and learned that both lungs were congested. He appealed to his employers for a leave of absence and received three months leave. Inexplicably, Kafka disregarded sanatoriums and stayed instead with his sister Ottla in the Bohemian countryside. There he met with Bauer, to whom he was once again engaged, and at that meeting he was fairly unresponsive to her presence. He subsequently neglected her correspondence, then wrote to her that death was preferable to their troubling relationship. In December Kafka returned to Prague, and at Christmas he met with Bauer at the home of Brod, who had earlier interceded on

Bauer's behalf. Soon afterwards Kafka and Bauer parted at the train station, whereupon Kafka visited Brod and told him that the engagement was ended. Brod later recalled the occasion as the only one at which he saw Kafka weep.

In explaining to Brod the engagement's demise, Kafka declared that, as a Western Jew, he was unsuited for marriage. But in January, 1919, he entered into a romance with Julie Wohryzek at the Pension Stuedl, where he had begun a four-month convalescence in December. Kafka had entered the Pension Stuedl weak from his tuberculosis and a recent bout of Spanish influenza. His relationship with Wohryzek was initially frivolous, but when the couple rejoined in Prague in March, he found himself once again drawn to marriage. He announced their engagement that summer, much to the disapproval of his father, who implied that Wohryzek was merely a Jewish seductress. Though burdened by poor health and the strain of personal obligations and familial conflict, Kafka pursued the engagement and even found a desirable flat in Prague-Wrschowitz. When the flat proved unattainable, however, Kafka abruptly withdrew from the marriage plans and proposed instead that Wohryzek live with him in Munich, where he hoped to work for publisher Kurt Wolff. Plans for that job failed, though, and both Kafka and Wohryzek remained, separately, in Prague.

During the period of his involvement with Julie Wohryzek, Kafka's relations with his father strained further. In May, 1919, Kafka presented Hermann Kafka with a copy of *In der Strafkolonie* upon its publication by Kurt Wolff. His father paid scant attention to the book, telling Kafka to place it on the bedside table. Kafka was deeply offended by what he perceived as his father's deliberate disregard for the book. Soon afterwards, Kafka's sensitivity was further violated when his father reacted to the engagement announcement by questioning his son's maturity and Wohryzek's integrity. Kafka vented his frustration by writing the missive posthumously published as *Letter to His Father*, in which he tirelessly examined and analyzed the failings of their relationship. In the letter, which Kafka never delivered, he decried his father as grossly inconsiderate and condemned his behavior as dictatorial. But Kafka, inevitably susceptible to self-doubt, also filled the work with recriminations against his own worthiness and dwelled on his own inadequacies and insecurities. Ultimately, Kafka refrained from attributing his shortcomings to his traumatic childhood, and the entire letter is, perhaps, best seen today as an insightful document into Kafka's ambivalence about himself and others. Erich Heller, in his book *Franz Kafka*, notes as much when writing that Kafka "was unable to sustain any particular indictments against anyone except himself—and even not quite against himself."

Though still ill in December, 1919, Kafka returned to the insurance company, and in early 1920 he received a promotion and a salary increase. By April, however, he was once again weak and in need of another leave from work. After failing to secure occupancy at a sanatorium, he stayed briefly at a hotel, then moved to a pension. At this time he began corresponding regularly with Milena Jesenska-Polak, who had earlier written him seeking permission to translate his tales into Czech. Kafka's first letters were cordial and even kindly, with Kafka sympathizing with Jesenska-Polak's own lung disease and warning her not to squander unnecessary energy on translations of his modest works.

After exhausting his sick-leave, Kafka used his vacation time to remain at the pension, from which he soon adopted a more intimate tone in his correspondence with his translator. Undaunted by Jesenska-Polak's marriage, Kafka wrote to her that through their literary relationship he already possessed her and that, though unworthy of her love, he nonetheless demanded it. He felt that Jesenska-Polak understood him more profoundly than had any other woman, and he courted her accordingly. He disclosed as much to Julie Wohryzek, who tearfully withdrew from his life, whereupon Kafka immediately began doubting Jesenska-Polak's sincerity.

Such suspicions were nearly accurate, for Jesenska-Polak refused to leave her husband. She did, however, comply with Kafka's wish that they meet, and in August they shared a weekend. At this time Kafka renewed his interest in writing, producing preliminary drafts for the novel *Das Schloss* (*The Castle*). But his health proved consistently tenuous, and by autumn he was frequently feverish and suffering labored breathing. After a medical examination disclosed further infection in both his lungs, Kafka entered a clinic in the nearby mountains. He intended to leave after three months, but when that time elapsed he was still weak with coughing spasms and breathing difficulties. Deciding to remain through the winter, Kafka grew increasingly lethargic and spent most days reclining and reading. He socialized rarely, as he was easily repulsed by the often advanced state of other patients' physical deterioration, and he wrote not at all, for at the sanatorium—despite his grave state—he was free of the tension and emotional anxiety that was apparently necessary to his creativity. When spring came, Kafka finally began taking walks in the sanatorium's wooded countryside, and by August he recovered sufficiently to leave the institution and return to work in Prague.

Almost immediately upon resuming his insurance work, though, Kafka ran a constant fever. By September, a cold, and consequent cough, had ravaged him still further, and by autumn, doctors once again urged him to enter a sanatorium. But Kafka did not heed his medical counsel, choosing instead to remain in Prague and endure further physical and emotional distress. Now obsessed with his own demise, Kafka was unable to relax or overcome his overwhelming anxiety. In early 1922, despite securing yet another sick leave from the insurance company, he suffered three weeks of only minimal sleep. As that insomnia threatened to undermine his already tenuous mental and emotional equilibrium, he finally left Prague.

In late January, 1922, Kafka arrived at a mountain resort, where he showed surprising enthusiasm and energy for outdoor activities, including mountain climbing. Within a few days, however, he collapsed while outside, and pneumonia seemed inevitable. Though hardly undaunted by his illness, he showed little of the anxiety that normally characterized his reaction to adversity. Instead, he anticipated emancipation from the trials of life, though such emancipation might bring sorrow, at least temporarily, to his loved ones. But he avoided exacerbating his already serious condition, and by February he was back in Prague, though he still had several weeks left of his sick leave.

To distract himself from anxiety and despair, Kafka turned once more to writing, and in February he completed his celebrated tale "Ein Hungerkuenstler" ("A Hunger Artist"), about a man whose celebrity derives from his refusal to eat. This tale, at once both tragic and comedic, and both absurd and disturbingly realistic, culminates in grim humor when the hunger artist explains his motivation. Diminished to a nearly skeletal state, the dying hunger artist reveals that he had refrained from eating simply because he could not obtain palatable food. "If I had found it," he tells an inquisitive fellow, "believe me, I should have made no fuss and stuffed myself like you or anyone else." Like much of Kafka's fiction, "A Hunger Artist" is often perceived by critics as an absurdist perspective on his condition. Kafka's own wast-

ing away from tuberculosis lends credibility to this interpretation of the tale, though other approaches—including allegorical and even literal interpretations—may seem equally valid.

In early 1922 Kafka also wrote both "Forschungen eines Hundes" ("Investigations of a Dog"), an ultimately unfinished tale about a dog's recollections of life in the "canine community," and most of *The Castle,* his account—also unfinished—of a land surveyor's desperate attempt to secure an audience with obscure and distant higher authorities. By this time Kafka, having obtained his employer's permission for temporary retirement, lay bedridden with near-constant fever and exhaustion. Believing that death was near, he wrote to Brod requesting that he destroy any manuscripts left incomplete, including "Investigations of a Dog" and the novels-in-progress *Amerika, The Trial,* and *The Castle.*

By summer, having once again avoided pneumonia, Kafka left Prague to live with his sister Ellie in the German seaside town Mueritz. There he befriended Dora Dymant, a volunteer worker at a nearby camp for Jewish children. Though weak from fever and chronic coughing, Kafka mustered enough energy to enjoy Dymant's company, and by September he was living with her in Berlin-Steglitz. This residence was intended as temporary, for both Kafka and Dymant, who shared his recent interest in Hebrew studies, planned on immigrating to Palestine.

In Berlin-Steglitz, Kafka and Dymant continued their Hebrew readings, and Kafka, despite his frail condition, even attended lectures at the nearby Academy of Hebrew Studies. He also wrote, but only when rare bursts of energy enabled him to produce an entire work in one sitting. Such was the case in November when he produced "Der Bau" ("The Burrow"), his story about an animal and its obsession with its burrow. Initially, the animal is quite confident of its security within its well hidden, expertly organized domain. So proud is the creature—presumably, a mole—that it even conceals itself outside the burrow and marvels at its concealment. But, as one would expect in a Kafka tale, anxiety and suspicion slowly undermine the animal's confidence, and the creature imagines that the burrow is actually part of a much larger one built by a creature that will soon discover the vulnerable intruder. Eventually, the animal discerns whistling from within the burrow and suspects an unwelcome presence. Though Kafka provided an ending for the tale, it was either destroyed or lost, and the story stops with the creature determined to move from the whistle's direction.

Kafka wrote "The Burrow" in November, 1923, after moving with Dymant into two rooms of a home also occupied by a physician. He saw little of his parents, for they disapproved of Dymant and her background of traditional Judaism, and they condemned the couple's living arrangement. Despite these objections, the parents did supply him with occasional funds, which were useful supplements to his own modest pension. But by early 1924, when digestive troubles joined Kafka's continual fever, even the two rooms proved too costly, and in February he and Dymant moved into one inexpensive room. There he continued to study Hebrew on a daily basis, but his health severely diminished his energy for any sustained activity.

In March, when Brod visited him, Kafka suffered from constant fever and bouts of racking coughing. Dying he traveled back to Prague and once again stayed with at his parents' home. There he produced his final tale, "Josefine die Saengerin oder Das Volk der Mauese" ("Josephine the Singer; or, The Mouse Folk"), about a singing mouse and her effect on others in her community. Josephine is prized by other mice for her beautiful singing voice, but when she argues that her talent should exempt her from more menial tasks, she is denied the privilege. She then refrains from singing and withdraws from the community, which, it is expected, will soon forget her.

Soon after completing "Josephine," Kafka experienced extreme swelling in his tubercular larynx. Swallowing became painful and difficult, and eating became impossible. He was moved to a sanatorium, and Dora Dymant was told that Kafka would probably die within three to four months. When a subsequent diagnosis revealed an improved condition, Kafka was so overwhelmed with happiness that he proposed marriage to Dymant. But within two weeks he suffered great pain and pleaded for his physician to administer morphine. Injections were given, and an ice pack was set on Kafka's throat. On June 3, he awoke and threw the ice pack from himself, then lapsed again into unconsciousness and death.

To his credit, Brod ignored Kafka's will and salvaged the incomplete tales and novels. During the next few years he organized and edited these works, occasionally shaping various drafts into coherent texts and even supplying titles and chapter headings. In the mid-1920s Kafka's three incomplete novels were published, and in 1931 a collection of his incomplete tales—including "The Great Wall of China"—was also printed. Additionally, Brod organized editions of Kafka's complete works and edited collections of his diaries and letters. These posthumous volumes, as much as Kafka's previous publications, established Kafka as one of the twentieth century's major literary figures, a master writer whose works, perhaps more than those of any other artist, reflect the alienation and frustration of modern life.

Critically, Kafka's works have prompted a vast and varied array of interpretations. He has been hailed as a realist, an absurdist, a sociologist, and even, by Thomas Mann, as a comedic theologian. Some writers have emphasized the psychological in analyzing his works, others have concentrated on the Judaic aspects; some have traced his fiction as thinly disguised autobiography, and others have noted the same works as full-fledged fantasies. Consistent in these divergent interpretations is the respect accorded Kafka's works as unique and compelling, and the regard for Kafka as a literary master. More than a few critics share the opinion of Vladimir Nabokov, himself a highly regarded writer, who called Kafka, in *Lecturers on Literature,* "the greatest German writer of our time."

MEDIA ADAPTATIONS: The Trial was adapted by writer-director Orson Welles as a film of the same title in 1963; *Amerika* was adapted by writer-directors Jean-Marie Straub and Daniele Huillet for a film released in the United States as "Class Relations" in 1984; works adapted for the stage include "The Metamorphosis" and "The Hunger Artist."

BIOGRAPHICAL/CRITICAL SOURCES:

BOOKS

Anders, Gunther, *Franz Kafka,* translation by A. Steer and A. K. Thorlby, Bowes & Bowes, 1960.

Bauer, Johann, *Kafka and Prague,* Praeger, 1971.

Brod, Max, *Franz Kafka,* translation by G. Humphreys Roberts and Richard Winston, Schocken, 1960.

Buber-Neumann, Margarete, *Mistress to Kafka,* Secker & Warburg, 1966.

Camus, Albert, *The Myth of Sisyphus, and Other Essays,* translation by Justin O'Brien, Knopf, 1955.

Canetti, Elias, *Kafka's Other Trial: The Letters to Felice,* translation by Christopher Middleton, Schocken, 1982.

Carrouges, Michel, *Kafka versus Kafka,* translation by Emmet Parker, University of Alabama Press, 1968.

Dictionary of Literary Biography, Volume 81: *Austrian Fiction Writers, 1875-1913,* Gale, 1989.

Eisner, Pavel, *Franz Kafka and Prague,* Arts, Inc., 1950.

Emrich, Wilhelm, *Franz Kafka,* Ungar, 1968.

Flores, Angel, editor, *The Kafka Problem,* New Directions, 1946.

Flores, Angel, and Homer Swander, editors, *Franz Kafka Today,* University of Wisconsin Press, 1958.

Flores, Angel, editor, *The Kafka Debate: New Perspectives for Our Time,* Gordonian Press, 1977.

Frynta, Emanuel, *Kafka and Prague,* Batchworth Press, 1960.

Goodman, Paul, *Kafka's Prayer,* Vanguard, 1947.

Gray, Ronald, *Kafka: A Collection of Critical Essays,* Prentice-Hall, 1962.

Gray, Ronald, *Franz Kafka,* Cambridge University Press, 1973.

Greenberg, Martin, *The Terror of Art: Kafka and Modern Literature,* Basic Books, 1968.

Hall, Calvin S., and Richard E. Lind, *Dreams, Life, and Literature: A Study of Franz Kafka,* University of North Carolina Press, 1970.

Hayman, Ronald, *Kafka,* Oxford University Press, 1982.

Heller, Erich, *Franz Kafka,* edited by Frank Kermode, Viking, 1974.

Heller, Erich, *The Disinherited Mind,* Harcourt, 1975.

Howe, Irving, *Modern Literary Criticism: An Anthology,* Beacon Press, 1958.

Hughes, Kenneth, *Franz Kafka: An Anthology of Marxist Criticism,* New England University Press, 1981.

Janouch, Gustav, *Conversations with Kafka,* translation by Goronwy Rees, New Directions, 1971.

Kazin, Alfred, *The Inmost Leaf: A Selection of Essays,* Harcourt, 1955.

Kuna, Franz, editor, *On Kafka: Semi-Centenary Perspectives,* Harper, 1976.

Nabokov, Vladimir, *Lectures on Literature,* edited by Fredson Bowers, Harcourt, 1980.

Nagel, Bert, *Franz Kafka,* Schmidt, 1974.

Pascal, Roy, *Kafka's Narrators: A Study of His Stories and Sketches,* Cambridge University Press, 1982.

Pawel, Ernst, *The Nightmare of Reason: A Life of Franz Kafka,* Farrar, Straus, 1984.

Politzer, Heinz, *Franz Kafka: Parable and Paradox,* Cornell University Press, 1966.

Robert, Marthe, *Kafka,* Gallimard, 1968.

Robert, Marthe, *The Old and the New: From Kafka to Don Quixote,* University of California Press, 1977.

Robert, Marthe, *As Lonely as Franz Kafka,* Harcourt, 1982.

Rolleston, James, *Kafka's Negative Theater,* Pennsylvania State University Press, 1974.

Seltzer, Alvin J., *Chaos in the Novel, the Novel in Chaos,* Schocken, 1974.

Sokel, Walter H., *Franz Kafka,* Columbia University Press, 1966.

Spann, Meno, *Franz Kafka,* Twayne, 1976.

Spilka, Mark, *Dickens and Kafka: A Mutual Interpretation,* Indiana University Press, 1963.

Stern, J. P., *The World of Franz Kafka,* Holt, 1980.

Sussman, Henry, *Franz Kafka: Geometrician of Metaphor,* Coda Press, 1979.

Tauber, Herbert, *Franz Kafka: An Interpretation of His Works,* Kennikat, 1968.

Thorlby, Anthony, *Kafka: A Study,* Heinemann, 1972.

Tiefenbrun, Ruth, *Moment of Torment: An Interpretation of Franz Kafka's Short Stories,* Southern Illinois University Press, 1973.

Twentieth-Century Literary Criticism, Gale, Volume 2, 1979, Volume 6, 1982, Volume 13, 1984, Volume 29, 1988.

Urzidil, Johannes, *There Goes Kafka,* Wayne State University, 1968.

West, Rebecca, *The Court and the Castle: Some Treatments of a Recurrent Theme,* Yale University Press, 1957.

Ziolkowski, Theodore, *Dimensions of the Novel: German Texts and European Contexts,* Princeton University Press, 1969.

PERIODICALS

Approach, fall, 1963.
Bookman, November, 1930.
Commonweal, September 4, 1964.
Comparative Literature, fall, 1959.
Criterion, April, 1938.
German Life and Letters, January, 1953.
Jewish Heritage, summer, 1964.
Journal of English and Germanic Philology, January, 1954.
Journal of Modern Literature, September, 1977.
Kenyon Review, winter, 1939.
Literary Review, summer, 1983.
Literature and Psychology, Volume 27, number 4, 1977.
Modern Fiction Studies, summer, 1958.
Modern Language Notes, October, 1970.
Mosaic, spring, 1972.
Nation, December 7, 1946.
New Republic, October 27, 1937.
New Yorker, May 9, 1983.
New York Times, April 12, 1989, April 16, 1989, August 9, 1989.
Quarterly Review of Literature, Volume 2, number 3, 1945, Volume 20, numbers 1-2, 1976.
Reconstructionist, April 3, 1959.
Studies in Short Fiction, summer, 1965, spring, 1973.
Symposium, fall, 1961.
Thought, summer, 1951.
TriQuarterly, spring, 1966.
Washington Post, January 15, 1989.

*   *   *

KAIN, Saul
See SASSOON, Siegfried (Lorraine)

*   *   *

KAMMEN, Michael G(edaliah)   1936-

PERSONAL: Born October 25, 1936, in Rochester, N.Y.; son of Jacob Merson and Blanche (Lazerow) Kammen; married Carol Koyen (a historian), February 26, 1961; children: Daniel Merson, Douglas Anton. *Education:* George Washington University, A.B. (with distinction), 1958; Harvard University, M.A., 1959, Ph.D., 1964.

ADDRESSES: Home—16 Sun Path, Ithaca, NY 14850. *Office*—Department of History, Cornell University, Ithaca, NY 14853.

CAREER: Harvard University, Cambridge, Mass., instructor, 1964-65; Cornell University, Ithaca, N.Y., assistant professor, 1965-67, associate professor, 1967-69, professor of American history, 1969-73, Newton C. Fan Professor of American History and Culture, 1973—, chairman of history department, 1974-76, director of Society of the Humanities, 1977-80. Member, Seminar in Early American History and Culture, Columbia University, 1967-73: fellow of Humanities Center, Johns Hopkins University, 1968-69. Directeur d'Etudes Associe, Ecole des Hautes

Etudes en Sciences Sociale, Paris, France, 1980-81. Host and moderator for "The States of the Union," a series of fifty one-hour radio programs broadcast by National Public Radio, 1975-76. Consultant, Educational Services Inc., Cambridge, 1964-65, 1973—, and Educational Testing Services, princeton, N.J., 1970-71. Member of board of editors, Cornell University Press, 1971-74, New York History, 1973-77.

MEMBER: International Commission for the History of Representative and Parliamentary Institutions, American Academy of Arts and Sciences, American Society of Legal History, American Historical Association, American Antiquarian Society, Society of American Historians, Hakluyt Society Institute of Early American History and Culture, Massachusetts Historical Society, Colonial Society of Massachusetts, Phi Beta Kappa.

AWARDS, HONORS: National Endowment for the Humanities fellowship, 1967, 1972-73; John Anson Kittredge Educational Fund award, 1968-69; American Council of Learned Societies fellowship, 1969; Pulitzer Prize for history, 1973, for *People of Paradox: An Inquiry Concerning the Origins of American Civilization;* George Washington University Alumni Achievement Award, 1974; Center for Advanced Study in the Behavioral Sciences Fellowship, 1976-77; Guggenheim fellow, 1980-81; Francis Parkman Prize and Henry Adams Prize, 1987, for *A Machine That Would Go of Itself: The Constitution in American Culture.*

WRITINGS:

Operational History of the Flying Boat, Open Sea and Seadrome Aspects: Selected Campaigns, World War II, U.S. Navy Department, 1959.

Operational History of the Flying Boat, Open Sea and Seadrome Aspects: Atlantic Theatre, World War II, U.S. Navy Department, 1960.

(Co-editor) *The Glorious Revolution in America: Documents on the Colonial Crisis of 1689,* Institute of Early American History and Culture, 1964, revised edition, 1972.

(Editor) *Politics and Society in Colonial America: Democracy or Deference?,* Holt, 1967, 2nd edition, Krieger, 1978.

A Rope of Sand: The Colonial Agents, British Politics and the American Revolution, Cornell University Press, 1968.

Deputyes and Libertyes: The Origins of Representative Government in Colonial America, Knopf, 1969.

(Contributor) *Essays on Anglo-American Political Relations, 1675-1775,* Rutgers University Press, 1970.

Empire and Interest: The American Colonies and the Politics of Mercantilism, Lippincott, 1970.

(Editor) *The Contrapuntal Civilization: Essays toward a New Understanding of the American Experience,* Crowell, 1971.

(Editor) *The History of the Province of New-York,* two volumes, Harvard University Press, 1972.

People of Paradox: An Inquiry Concerning the Origins of American Civilization, Knopf, 1972.

(Editor) *"What Is the Good of History?" Selected Letters of Clark L. Becker, 1940-1945,* Cornell University Press, 1973.

Colonial New York: A History, Scribner, 1975.

(With J. P. Greene and R. L. Bushman) *Society, Freedom, and Conscience: The Coming of the Revolution in Virginia, Massachusetts, and New York,* Norton, 1976.

(With Kenneth E. Boulding and Seymour Martin Lipset) *From Abundance to Scarcity: Implications for the American Tradition,* Ohio State University Press, 1978.

A Season of Youth: The American Revolution and the Historical Imagination, Knopf, 1978.

(Editor) *The Past before Us: Contemporary Historical Writing in the United States,* Cornell University Press, 1980.

Spheres of Liberty: Changing Perceptions of Liberty in American Culture, University of Wisconsin Press, 1986.
A Machine That Would Go of Itself: The Constitution in American Culture, Knopf, 1986.
(Editor) *The Origins of the American Constitution: A Documentary History,* Viking, 1986.
Selvages and Biases: The Fabric of History in American Culture, Cornell University Press, 1987.
Constitutional Pluralism: Conflicting Interpretations of the Founders' Intentions, American Jewish Community Press, 1987.
Sovereignty and Liberty: Constitutional Discourse in American Culture, University of Wisconsin Press, 1988.

Contributor to *Studies Presented to the International Commission for the History of Representative and Parliamentary Institutions,* 1970, and to numerous periodicals and journals.

SIDELIGHTS: "The most prolific among present-day historians of early America, Michael Kammen has commanded attention and respect with bold generalizations; a wide-ranging and imaginative use of sources; a working familiarity with the theories and concepts of behavioral and humanistic fields of scholarship; a keen eye for anomaly, irony, and paradox; and a sprightly, clear, and concise prose style," writes John K. Nelson in the *South Atlantic Quarterly.* Kammen, a professor at Cornell University, is a Pulitzer Prize-winning historian who has written a series of wide-ranging books investigating American cultural history, particularly during the nineteenth and twentieth centuries.

In his 1973 book, *People of Paradox: An Inquiry Concerning the Origins of American Civilization,* Kammen studies the American character in terms of self-contradictions and unresolved tensions he sees as implicit in the nation's origins. Many critics found favor with the manner in which Kammen approaches the familiar yet elusive problem of defining a nation's character. Claiming "it might seem as easy as falling off a log to produce yet another book about American national character," *New York Times Book Review* contributor Marcus Cunliffe explains the difficulties inherent in such a task and praises *People of Paradox* as "a lively, wide-ranging book" and Kammen's attempt as "a brilliant stab at reforming some ancient yet perennially intriguing problems." A *New Republic* contributor concurs with Cunliffe, deeming *People of Paradox* "an engaging rehash of the national malaise." In comparing Kammen's observations to the work of others, Cunliffe adds, "Kammen has however taken the idea further than anyone else: He has been more systematic, shown more intellectual curiosity, and written with greater gusto." It was for *People of Paradox* that Kammen received the 1973 Pulitzer Prize for history.

Also well-received was *Colonial New York: A History,* Kammen's 1975 study of cultural and political life in old New York from its initial settlement by the Dutch in the early seventeenth century to the signing of the Declaration of Independence. In *Colonial New York* Kammen uses a broad method of investigation to study the importance of ethnic, linguistic, and regional heterogeneity in shaping the colony's early social and political development. Deeming Kammen's illustrations "superb" and praising the author for advancing his themes "without pushing his case too far," Kevin Starr writes in the *New Republic:* "Many regional histories will appear before, during and after the Bicentennial. Let us hope they approach Colonial New York in overall excellence." A *Washington Post Book World* contributor extols *Colonial New York*'s accessibility, calling it "scholarly, but eminently readable." Even higher praise comes from *Times Literary Supplement* critic Jack P. Greene, who maintains, "Certainly

[*Colonial New York* is] the best available one-volume history of the colony and as good a one-volume account as exists for any of Britain's American colonies."

In *A Season of Youth: The American Revolution and the Historical Imagination,* Kammen turns to studying the imaginative impact of the American Revolution on our national culture. He examines Americans' attitudes toward this event from 1776 to the present, drawing from a wealth of sources—histories and biographies, newspaper articles and broadsides, historical novels, orations, theatrical productions, and even film. Critical reaction to *A Season of Youth* was generally positive. In his *South Atlantic Review Quarterly* review of *A Season of Youth,* John K. Nelson lauds Kammen for his "stimulating observations," "sensitive reading of a vast array of sources," and his "vivid illustrative materials." John Leonard, writing in the *New York Times,* praises Kammen's "pleasantly conversational" tone as well as the book's "lively narrative." However, while most critics admired the scope and thoroughness of Kammen's research, some found fault with his methods of analysis. Leonard, for instance, considers much of what the author does in *A Season of Youth* to be a reiteration of observations made by others, notably French writer and politician Alexis de Tocqueville. However, Leonard writes: "I have my qualms about the glossing of popular culture, especially when you know just what you're looking for in advance. Such detritus is particularly susceptible to manipulation and coercion by other social agencies more deserving of study than the pulp they leave behind, e.g. the legal, educational, medical and historical professions; the advertising and newspeak ministries of business and the state." Similar mixed criticism comes from *New Republic* contributor Garry Wills who, while praising Kammen's ability to "give one a new vantage point for studying old events," criticizes the "formulaic" quality of Kammen's approach noting, "The attempt to sketch a large framework forces Kammen to deal with subjects he is weak in-mainly the visual arts." Despite such criticism, however, most critics seem to agree with the appraisal of *Washington Post Book World* critic George Dangerfield when he writes, "Kammen's book is a work of rich and imaginative scholarship, exciting and important for what it explicates and deeply disturbing for what it implies." The critical consensus seems to echo the remark of a *New York Times Book Review* contributor who claims *A Season of Youth* is "a major contribution to the history of our popular culture."

In one of his more recent works, *A Machine That Would Go of Itself: The Constitution in American Culture,* Kammen offers a cultural history of the American Constitution by examining the role this document has played in the national psyche. Chosen by the editors of the *New York Times Book Review* as one of the best books of 1986, *A Machine That Would Go of Itself* met with widespread acclaim. In his *Washington Post Book World* review of *A Machine That Would Go of Itself,* Stanley Katz praises Kammen's "intriguingly detailed revelations" and deems the work "the best Bicentennial book to date." *Chicago Tribune* contributor Jess Bravin commends the scholarship in *A Machine That Would Go of Itself,* finding the book "packed with research and an unending amount of trivia." Bravin goes on to call the work "an important chronicle of how Americans have come to understand and misunderstand [the Constitution]." John Denvir, writing in the *Los Angeles Times Book Review,* sees *A Machine That Would Go of Itself* as "a provocative book [which raises] important issues." He concludes, "I cannot think of anyone who will not learn much both new and important in this book, and I recommend it highly."

BIOGRAPHICAL/CRITICAL SOURCES:

PERIODICALS

Chicago Tribune, October 2, 1986.
Los Angeles Times Book Review, August 28, 1986, October 12, 1986, December 28, 1986.
New Republic, November 4, 1972, February 28, 1976, January 13, 1979
New York Times, December 5, 1978, September 29, 1986.
New York Times Book Review, October 1, 1972, December 17, 1978, August 17, 1980, September 14, 1986, November 15, 1987, January 3, 1988.
South Atlantic Quarterly, autumn, 1979.
Times Literary Supplement, September 2, 1977.
Washington Post Book World, September 10, 1978, July 13, 1980, October 5, 1986.

*   *   *

KARAGEORGE, Michael
See ANDERSON, Poul (William)

*   *   *

KARNOW, Stanley   1925-

PERSONAL: Born February 4, 1925, in New York, N.Y.; son of Harry (a businessman) and Henriette (Koeppel) Karnow; married Claude Sarraute, July 15, 1948 (divorced, 1955); married Annette Kline, April 12, 1959; children: Curtis Edward, Catherine Anne, Michael Franklin. *Education:* Harvard University, A.B., 1947; additional study at the Sorbonne, University of Paris, 1947-48, and Ecole des Sciences Politiques, 1948-49.

ADDRESSES: Home—10850 Springknoll Dr., Potomac, Md. 20854. *Office*—1220 National Press Building, Washington, D.C. 20045. *Agent*—Ronald Goldfarb, 918 16th St. N.W., Washington, D.C. 20006; and Don Cutler, Sterling Lord Agency, 660 Madison Ave., New York, N.Y. 10021.

CAREER: Time, New York City, correspondent in Paris, France, 1950-57; Time-Life, New York City, bureau chief in North Africa, 1958-59, and Hong Kong, 1959-62; Time, Inc., New York City, special correspondent, 1962-63; *Saturday Evening Post,* Philadelphia, Pa., Far East correspondent, 1963-65; *Washington Post,* Washington, D.C., Far East correspondent, 1965-71, diplomatic correspondent, 1971-72; National Broadcasting Corp. (NBC) News, Washington, D.C., special correspondent, 1972-73; *New Republic,* Washington, D.C., associate editor, 1973-75; syndicated columnist, Register & Tribune Syndicate, 1974—, and King Features, 1975-87; correspondent for public television, 1975—; International Writers Service, Washington, D.C., editor in chief, 1975-86; writer. Chief correspondent for PBS-TV series "Vietnam: A Television History," 1983, and "The U.S. in the Philippines: In Our Image," 1989. Correspondent for *London Observer,* 1961-65; columnist for *Le Point,* Paris, 1976-83. Fellow, Institute of Politics, John F. Kennedy School of Government, and East Asian Research Center, Harvard University, both 1970-71. *Military service:* U.S. Army Air Forces, 1943-46.

MEMBER: Council on Foreign Relations, White House Correspondents Association, Authors Guild, Authors League of America, PEN American Center, Foreign Correspondents Club, Signet Society, Harvard Club, Century Association, Shek-O Club (Hong Kong).

AWARDS, HONORS: Citation from Overseas Press Club, 1966, and annual award for best newspaper interpretation of foreign affairs, 1968; Emmy Awards, Polk Award, and Dupont Award, all 1984, all for "Vietnam: A Television History"; Pulitzer Prize in history, 1990, for *In Our Image: America's Empire in the Philippines.*

WRITINGS:

Southeast Asia, Time-Life Books, 1963.
Mao and China: From Revolution to Revolution, Viking, 1972, published as *Mao and China: Inside China's Cultural Revolution,* Penguin Books, 1984.
Vietnam: The War Nobody Won, Foreign Policy Association, 1983.
(With others) "Vietnam: A Television History" (multi-part documentary series; also see below), Public Broadcasting System (PBS-TV), 1983.
Vietnam: A History (companion volume to the television series), Viking, 1983.
(With others, and co-producer) "The U.S. in the Philippines: In Our Image" (multi-part documentary series; also see below), PBS-TV, 1989.
In Our Image: America's Empire in the Philippines (companion volume to the television series), Random House, 1989.

Also author of articles and television scripts.

SIDELIGHTS: Stanley Karnow has a "well-earned reputation as one of the most diligent and disciplined reporters in Asian journalism," notes Allen S. Whiting in his *New Republic* review of *Mao and China: From Revolution to Revolution.* Karnow spent over twenty years in Asia as a reporter, "so it is hardly surprising that [he] has cut through the fog surrounding China with the skill of an acupuncturist and produced the finest, most objective, most comprehensive book on modern China yet to appear," states *Newsweek* contributor Arthur Cooper. *Mao and China* traces the development of China's Cultural Revolution of the mid-1960s, events which led to a major shift in the Communist party makeup and structure; the book focuses in particular on the actions of party leader Mao Tse-tung. Although China has been perceived in the West as a closed society, "amazingly, there was a continuous stream of information flowing out of China during those years of turmoil," including radio broadcasts, speeches, government documents, and eyewitness stories, as Charles Elliott observes in *Time.* "Karnow monitored enough of this material to be able to see it for what it really was—the first approximation of a free press ever in Communist China," Elliott explains. "His idea, brilliantly carried out, was to sort the mess into reliable narrative history."

Whiting concurs with this assessment, and relates that "Karnow mixes a lucid summary of the main events and contending factions with vivid first-hand accounts drawn from personal interviews with refugees and uniquely revealing Red Guard reports of mayhem." Although *Nation* contributor Bert Cochran faults the author for some of his historical interpretations and remarks that "Karnow does not go beyond the essential materials that have been gathered by American and British Sinologists," he admits that the author "has systematically organized these materials into a detailed brief, and has succeeded in fitting the events of 1966-69 into the story of the evolution of Chinese communism." As the critic summarizes, "Karnow's book is an important contribution to this history because it is the first comprehensive account of a unique and little understood insurrection." *Mao and China* is "a sobering reminder of how little the world knew about the clashes and crises which affected every province and most cities of China," concludes Whiting. The continuing mystery of Chinese society makes "especially valuable the sensitivity, patience and sheer effort by which Karnow [has] illuminated the central arena of politics at a critical juncture."

Karnow also uses his extensive Asian experiences as a background for *Vietnam: A History,* a book published in conjunction with the premiere of PBS-TV's documentary "Vietnam: A Television History." In profiling the background of this long-troubled country, Karnow examines its ancient conflicts with the Chinese as well as the era of French colonial rule before describing the clash Westerners term the "Vietnam War." "He supplements his rigorous research with interviewing of hundreds of participants in the war, including a number of present-day Communist leaders," Regina Millette Frawley describes in the *Christian Science Monitor.* "In so doing, Karnow corroborates many closely held perceptions but explodes others—to his credit, even his own." Karnow visited Vietnam in 1981 to interview the country's military leaders, and it is these "personal accounts, eyewitness reports, exclusive interviews—the nuances of history," comments *Detroit News* contributor Robert Pisor, "[which] give life to Karnow's book." In addition, as Bill Stout recounts in the *Los Angeles Times Book Review,* "Karnow goes back into the history of Vietnam—thousands of years, not mere decades as the U.S. and France had measured events there—and he reminds us again that we had virtually no understanding of the country and its people when our leaders decided to go in."

Indeed, many critics praise the large scope and comprehensiveness of *Vietnam: A History.* Even though "Karnow takes on the whole sweep of Vietnamese history," *Chicago Tribune Book World* writer Jack Fuller maintains that "the story does not overlook the personal, biographical forces that played into the tragedy [and] offers fascinating portraits of Vietnamese figures" and "detailed narratives of controversial events and decisions" as well, including some accounts which are "riveting." Karnow's broad approach allows the reader to see that "America's war [was] merely an episode of the still continuing struggle," Richard West asserts in the *Spectator;* and not only are the Vietnamese and their history illuminated, "we feel, after reading Mr. Karnow, that we now know everything that is worth knowing on why decisions were taken about Vietnam by [the American government]."

These assessments notwithstanding, *New York Times Book Review* contributor Douglas Pike remarks that "despite a masterly effort to be comprehensive, Mr. Karnow's account comes out sketchy and abbreviated. Much important history is reduced to a sentence or two, and slightly less important history is ignored entirely." Harry G. Summers, however, believes that *Vietnam: A History* "is a landmark work. Exceptionally well researched and well written, it is the most complete account to date of the Vietnam tragedy." Stout also finds Karnow's work comprehensive, observing that "his is a rich and unusual mixture; he has the master reporter's eye for meaningful detail, an ear for the memorable quote, and he worked hard to give the Indochina epoch a historian's perspective." But what makes Karnow's work "so remarkable," Summers claims, "is its exceptional balance and objectivity."

Leslie H. Gelb concurs, writing in the *New Republic* that Karnow "draws the best [aspects from other histories], plus his own personal experience, and applies to it all a dispassionate and fair-minded attitude. Karnow himself was a critic of the war," the critic elaborates, "but he has the reportorial self-discipline to stand back now and tell the whole story in a manner that raises but does not answer the pivotal questions." Some reviewers are uncomfortable with Karnow's lack of political judgments—including *Nation* contributor Peter Biskind, who faults Karnow

for "little analysis and much waffling"—but others feel this approach is effective. Frawley, for instance, explains that this ambiguity is intentional: "For the most part, [Karnow] is too much the scholar to violate his journalistic integrity. He presents an impressive array of facts and history, . . . but he deliberately stops short of conclusions." As Fuller reports, the author's opening with a description of Vietnam as it is today, impoverished and unable to deal with the legacy of war, "makes it impossible for the reader to choose sides with any conviction and creates a sense of sadness deeper than the mourning of the dead."

Arnold R. Isaacs comments in the *Washington Post Book World* that because of his impartiality, "Karnow makes clear that cruelty and callous strategies existed on all sides—as does the guilt." Gelb, a former supporter of the war, expresses a similar sentiment: "Karnow's book makes us stare these awful truths in the face once again. He does not judge those who gave us Vietnam, caught in a Greek tragedy as we were. He does not pronounce the war as right or wrong. Rather, he lets us see, as we must if we are to learn anything from that nightmare, that it was a tragic mistake." Commending in particular Karnow's "own skilled, personal observation," Frawley calls *Vietnam* "a major achievement, an important contribution, and a meaningful foundation for further research." As Isaacs concludes: "For a single, panoramic view of the [Vietnam] war and its setting, the best book is unquestionably Stanley Karnow's *Vietnam: A History.*"

The journalist has received similar acclaim for another study of an Asian country that has been closely linked to the United States; published in conjunction with a PBS-TV documentary special, *In Our Image: America's Empire in the Philippines* examines the complex history of the former U.S. colony. "While 'In Our Image' covers recorded Philippine history from its discovery by Magellan in 1521 to America's annexation after the Spanish-American War," relates Garry Abrams of the *Los Angeles Times,* "the book is also a detailed account of recent events behind today's headlines," including the ouster of former president Ferdinand Marcos. Karnow uses the same approach as in *Vietnam,* and "in [his] sure hands, the formula is highly successful," Steve Lohr claims in the *New York Times.* "His implicit premise is that the present is ordained by the past. In the Philippines, as in Vietnam, American policy blunders were often explained by Washington's blinkered view or total ignorance of Philippine history and culture." The result of this, as *Time* contributor Howard G. Chua-Eoan observes, is an exploration of "two countries caught in an obsessive parent-child relationship." The critic explains: "It is a tale of how the U.S. tried to re-create itself in the malleable Philippines, . . . [and] also the story of how the U.S., though it succeeded in imbuing the archipelago with aspects of its likeness, failed at imparting its democratic spirit. In *In Our Image,* the sins of the creator are amply reflected in the faults of its creature."

In Our Image contains some of the same virtues as its predecessor, as Lohr recounts: "Karnow's achievement is in combining exhaustive research with the writing skill to fashion more than 450 years of the Philippine experience into a work that is both a page-turning story and authoritative history. It is hard to imagine anyone doing a better job." Although he thinks the author "is often over-detailed and occasionally irrelevant," *Washington Post Book World* contributor James Halsema similarly notes that Karnow "has written the best popular history of America's nine-decade relationship with the Philippines. It is a long book but never dull." "There is no other book even approaching Mr. Karnow's," concludes *New York Times Book Review* contributor Paul Kreisberg, "either in recounting with sensitivity and accuracy the long history of the Philippines or in leaving readers enormously satisfied with the tale. . . . 'In Our Image' is 22-karat gold, and worth the time of anyone interested not just in the Philippines or Asia or how Americans deal with their friends and their dependents, but simply in a terrific read."

BIOGRAPHICAL/CRITICAL SOURCES:

PERIODICALS

Chicago Tribune Book World, October 16, 1983.
Christian Century, November 16, 1983.
Christian Science Monitor, January 3, 1984.
Detroit News, November 13, 1983.
Los Angeles Times, April 24, 1989.
Los Angeles Times Book Review, November 6, 1983.
Nation, December 18, 1972, December 3, 1983.
New Republic, December 9, 1972, November 14, 1983.
Newsweek, November 6, 1972, October 3, 1983, April 10, 1989.
New York Times, March 29, 1989.
New York Times Book Review, October 29, 1972, October 16, 1983, April 2, 1989.
Spectator, April 27, 1985.
Time, November 6, 1972, April 17, 1989.
Tribune Books, April 30, 1989.
Washington Post Book World, October 2, 1983, April 21, 1985, April 2, 1989.

—*Sketch by Diane Telgen*

*   *   *

KASTEL, Warren
See SILVERBERG, Robert

*   *   *

KAVAN, Anna   1901-1968
(Helen Ferguson)

PERSONAL: Original name, Helen Woods; name changed by deed poll; born in 1901 in Cannes, France; died December 5, 1968, in London, England; daughter of C. C. E. and Helen (Bright) Woods; first husband, Donald Ferguson; second husband, Stuart Edmonds; children: (first marriage) one son (deceased). *Education:* Attended church school (Church of England); privately educated.

CAREER: Writer, literary editor, and designer and renovator of houses.

WRITINGS:

NOVELS

(Under name Helen Ferguson) *A Charmed Circle,* J. Cape, 1929.
(Under name Helen Ferguson) *The Dark Sisters,* J. Cape, 1930.
(Under name Helen Ferguson) *Let Me Alone,* J. Cape, 1930, reprinted under name Anna Kavan, P. Owen, 1979.
(Under name Helen Ferguson) *A Stranger Still,* John Lane, 1935.
(Under name Helen Ferguson) *Goose Cross,* John Lane, 1936.
(Under name Helen Ferguson) *Rich Get Rich,* John Lane, 1937.
Change the Name, J. Cape, 1941.
The House of Sleep (science fiction), Doubleday, 1947 (published in England as *Sleep Has His House,* Cassell, 1948, reprinted, Michael Kesend, 1980).
A Scarcity of Love, Angus Downie, 1956, reprinted, McGraw, 1974.
Eagles' Nest, P. Owen, 1957.
Who Are You?, Scorpion Press, 1963, P. Owen, 1975.
Ice (science fiction), P. Owen, 1967, Doubleday, 1970.

SHORT STORIES

Asylum Piece and Other Stories, J. Cape, 1940, Doubleday, 1946, reprinted, Michael Kesend, 1980.
I Am Lazarus, J. Cape, 1945, reprinted, P. Owen, 1978.
A Bright Green Field and Other Stories, P. Owen, 1958.
Julia and the Bazooka and Other Stories, P. Owen, 1970, Knopf, 1975.
My Soul in China: A Novella and Stories, P. Owen, 1975.

Contributor of short stories to periodicals.

OTHER

(With K. T. Bluth) *The Horse's Tale,* Gaberbocchus, 1949.

SIDELIGHTS: Anna Kavan took her name from the fictional heroine of her novel *Let Me Alone.* In the *New Statesman,* Stanley Reynolds comments that this renaming was "rather as if Dickens had changed his name by deed poll to David Copperfield." Reynolds points out that the decision to adopt this particular name "is even more interesting when you consider that Kavan is not the heroine's original surname but the name of the hated and despised husband of the novel."

In the 1920s and 1930s Kavan wrote conventional romantic novels under her first married name, Helen Ferguson. These novels reflect the comfort she felt in her Chilterns home, where she took great satisfaction in breeding bulldogs. Her marriage to her second husband, a moderately rich painter, was also surrounded in comfort. Nothing about her life at this point indicated what was to come: mental breakdowns, drug abuse, compulsions to suicide, and desperate attempts at withdrawal from drug addiction.

As a child Kavan traveled extensively with her wealthy, emotionally cold mother, with whom she maintained a love-hate relationship all her life. This relationship generated a rage which frequently surfaced in her writings. In a short story, "A World of Heroes," she wrote: "What could have been done to make me afraid to grow up out of such a childhood? Later on, I saw things in proportion, I was always afraid of falling back into that ghastly black isolation of an uncomprehending, solitary, oversensitive child."

After her second marriage failed and ended, like the first, in divorce, Kavan entered a Swiss clinic where she received treatment for mental disorders. She recorded her experiences at the clinic and published them as a series of sketches entitled *Asylum Piece,* her first book to bear the name Anna Kavan. In an article in *Books and Bookmen,* Rhys Davies calls *Asylum Piece* "extraordinarily moving and original." He also notes that Kavan's next novel, *Change the Name,* contains traces of the Ferguson style, indicating that "the metamorphosis [of Ferguson to Kavan] was not yet complete."

Davies's friendship with Kavan began when the author was Helen Ferguson. They had lost touch with each other for three or four years, so Davies knew nothing of Kavan's stay in two mental hospitals or of her drug addiction. At their first meeting after these years, he failed to recognize his friend: "This spectral woman, attenuated of body and face, a former abundance of auburn hair shorn and changed to metallic gold, thinned hands restless, was so different that my own need to readjust to her was a strain."

Like Davies, several of Kavan's friends, familiar only with the affable Helen Ferguson, found it difficult to accept this transformed woman. Her drug addiction created a capriciousness that was unpleasant to experience. She wanted isolation yet at the same time expected attention from a select few. In shunning her past identity, Kavan callously rejected many people connected to it. This need for isolation and retreat from a threatening world appears consistently as a theme in much of Kavan's work.

A registered addict for nearly thirty years, Kavan found escape through heroin. She suffered from acute depression and attempted suicide twice. Davies believes that the heroin acted as a preservative of both sanity and physical energy for Kavan. In addition to writing novels and numerous short stories, she purchased and renovated old houses on Campden Hill and did editorial work for a literary magazine. She also designed and presided over the building of the modernistic house in which she spent the last twelve years of her life.

When British authorities imposed new and tighter regulations on drug addicts, Kavan was forced to attend regularly scheduled sessions which she considered to be disciplinary punishment, but she attended them out of fear that the National Health Service workers would hold back her drug supply. This reinforced her idea of the inimical world she often described in her novels. Davies remarks that in spite of this, Kavan always returned to the "valid discipline" of her stories and that "their clarity of style, their spurning of sensationalism, and their own code of logic were another justification of her vision."

Kavan died with a loaded syringe in her hand. Her usual shot of heroin had not obliterated the final moments. Jill Robinson, in an article in the *New York Times Book Review,* comments: "The facts of one's difficult existence do not guarantee literature. Anna Kavan is not interesting because she was a woman, an addict or had silver blond hair. She is interesting because her work comes through with a powerful androgynous individuality and because the stories are luminous and rich with a fresh kind of peril. She knows how to pull us into her world, her dreams and nightmares—how to have all of it become ours."

BIOGRAPHICAL/CRITICAL SOURCES:

BOOKS

Contemporary Literary Criticism, Gale, Volume 5, 1976, Volume 13, 1980.
Kavan, Anna, *Ice,* introduced by Brian W. Aldiss, Doubleday, 1970.
Kavan, Anna, *Julia and the Bazooka,* edited and introduced by Rhys Davies, Knopf, 1975.

PERIODICALS

Books and Bookmen, March, 1971, June, 1978.
Listener, March 12, 1970.
New Statesman, January 11, 1974, March 28, 1975.
New York Times Book Review, May 11, 1975.
Observer Review, January 17, 1971.
Spectator, January 31, 1976.
Times (London), August 14, 1986.
Times Literary Supplement, September 14, 1967, March 12, 1970, February 5, 1971, June 14, 1974.

OBITUARIES:

PERIODICALS

New York Times, December 7, 1968.
Times (London), December 6, 1968.

KAVANAGH, Patrick (Joseph)   1904-1967
(Piers Plowman)

PERSONAL: Born October 21, 1904, in Inniskeen, Monaghan, Ireland; died of pneumonia, November 30, 1967, in Dublin, Ireland; buried at the parish church in Inniskeen, Ireland; son of James (a shoemaker and farmer) and Bridget (Quinn) Kavanagh; married Katharine Barry Maloney, April 19, 1967.

ADDRESSES: Home—Dublin, Ireland.

CAREER: Farmer and shoemaker in Inniskeen, Ireland, until 1939; writer living primarily in Dublin, Ireland, 1939-67. Extramural lecturer at University College, Dublin, beginning in 1955.

AWARDS, HONORS: A. E. Memorial Award, 1940; grant from Arts Council of Great Britain, 1967, for poetry.

WRITINGS:

POETRY

Ploughman and Other Poems, Macmillan (London), 1936.
The Great Hunger: A Poem, Cuala, 1942, Irish University Press, 1971.
A Soul for Sale: Poems, Macmillan (London), 1947.
Recent Poems, Hand Press, 1958.
Come Dance With Kitty Stobling, and Other Poems, Longmans, Green, 1960, Dufour, 1964.
Collected Poems, Devin-Adair, 1964.
The Complete Poems of Patrick Kavanagh, edited by brother, Peter Kavanagh, Hand Press, 1972.
Lough Derg, Goldsmith, 1978, Martin Brian & O'Keefe, 1978.

PROSE

The Green Fool (fictionalized autobiography), M. Joseph, 1938, Harper, 1939, Martin Brian & O'Keefe, 1971.
Tarry Flynn: A Novel, Pilot, 1948, Devin-Adair, 1949, Martin Brian & O'Keefe, 1972.
(Author of afterword) Peter Kavanagh, *Irish Mythology: A Dictionary,* three volumes, Hand Press, 1958-59.
Self Portrait (autobiographical television script), Dolmen, 1964.
(Author of introduction) W. Steuart Trench, *Realities of Irish Life,* MacGibbon & Kee, 1966.
Collected Pruse, MacGibbon & Kee, 1967.
(Author of introduction) *The Autobiography of William Carleton,* MacGibbon & Kee, 1968.
(With Peter Kavanagh) *Lapped Furrows: Correspondence, 1933-1967, Between Patrick and Peter Kavanagh, With Other Documents,* edited by Peter Kavanagh, Hand Press, 1969.
(With Peter Kavanagh and others) *Love's Tortured Headland: A Sequel to Lapped Furrows* (correspondence), edited by Peter Kavanagh, Hand Press, 1974.
By Night Unstarred: An Autobiographical Novel, edited by Peter Kavanagh, Goldsmith, 1977, Hand Press, 1978.
(With Peter Kavanagh and others) *Kavanagh's Weekly: A Journal of Literature and Politics* (anthology), Goldsmith, 1981.

SOUND RECORDINGS

Almost Everything, Claddagh, 1964.

OTHER

November Haggard: Uncollected Prose and Verse of Patrick Kavanagh, edited by Peter Kavanagh, Hand Press, 1971.
A Patrick Kavanagh Anthology, edited by Eugene Robert Platt, Commedia, 1973.

Columnist for *Standard,* 1943 and 1946-49, *Irish Press,* under name Piers Plowman, 1942-44, *Envoy,* 1949-51, *Creation,* 1957,

Irish Farmers' Journal, 1958-63, *National Observer,* 1959-60, and *RTV Guide,* 1964-66. Contributor of numerous poems, articles, and reviews to periodicals, including *Bell, Dublin, Dundalk Democrat, Horizon, Irish Weekly Independent, Irish Times, Irish Writing, Nimbus, Nonplus, Poetry, Studies,* and *X.* Writer, editor, and publisher for *Kavanagh's Weekly: A Journal of Literature and Politics,* 1952.

MEDIA ADAPTATIONS: Tarry Flynn was adapted for the stage by P. J. O'Connor and Pat Layde and performed at the Abbey Theatre, Dublin, Ireland, 1966. "Self-Portrait," narrated by Patrick Kavanagh, was originally broadcast as an episode of the television series of the same name by Radio Telefis Eirann, October 30, 1962.

SIDELIGHTS: Patrick Kavanagh was an Irish poet who also wrote fiction, autobiography, and numerous articles for Irish periodicals. Many critics and Irish literary figures have called him the nation's best poet since William Butler Yeats, and one of his long poems, "The Great Hunger," is widely regarded as a work of major importance. Even Kavanagh's admirers, however, find his writing difficult to characterize. "There is a sense in which Kavanagh may be said to defy criticism," Anthony Cronin wrote in *Heritage Now.* "You can look in vain in his poems for elaborate metaphors, correspondences, symbols and symbolic extensions of meaning . . . neither is there in his poems really anything that turns out to be a coherent life-view in the philosophical sense." As biographer John Nemo observed: "Kavanagh's point of view evolved primarily from his response to life, which was emotional rather than intellectual. . . . In place of the logic that directs the creative vision of poets like T. S. Eliot and W. B. Yeats, Kavanagh's creative faculties rely on inspiration and intuition. Artistically, he reacts rather than acts. Unlike many modern poets, his poems are not assembled piecemeal like contemporary sculptures but are delivered whole from the creative womb." Louise Bogan said in *New Yorker* that the poet had "an astonishing talent" that "kept on renewing itself not so much by a process of orderly growth as by a continual breaching of boundaries."

Kavanagh began his writing career in the last years of the Irish Literary Renaissance, a cultural movement paralleling the rise of nationalism in Ireland that culminated in the country's independence from Great Britain shortly after World War I. The movement freed writers from the burden of conforming to the styles of English literature and allowed them to concentrate on the Irish subjects with which they were familiar. Many participants in the movement also gave it an ideological mission—to secure Irish cultural independence from Great Britain by glorifying those subjects perceived as spiritually uplifting and uniquely Irish, such as the way of life of the nation's impoverished peasants. Because of their isolation, such country people were thought to have retained a more authentic Irish culture. Often, the writers who praised them were prosperous city-dwellers.

Kavanagh grew up in the peasant life that many who took part in the Irish Renaissance had only encountered as a subject for literature. Son of a shoemaker who owned a small farm, Kavanagh was born in a rural area of county Monaghan in the north of Ireland. He left school at about the age of twelve and thereafter largely taught himself about literature. Years later when he talked about his past for the "Self Portrait" series on Irish television, Kavanagh recalled the intellectual deprivation of his youth. "Although the literal idea of the peasant is of a farm labouring person," he said, "in fact a peasant is all that mass of mankind which lives below a certain level of consciousness. They live in the dark cave of the unconscious and they scream when they see the light." Though his native area was poor, he felt that "the real poverty was lack of enlightenment," and he added, "I am afraid this fog of unknowing affected me dreadfully." Over the course of his life Kavanagh often recounted the skepticism, or even ridicule, with which people in his community viewed his interest in poetry. Such early rejection, Nemo stressed, caused Kavanagh to believe that a poet was inevitably alienated from society.

Though he wrote poems regularly for his own enjoyment by the time he was a teenager, Kavanagh seemed likely to become a small farmer. But in his mid-twenties he succeeded in publishing poems in two non-literary periodicals, the *Irish Weekly Independent* and the *Dundalk Democrat.* This was an astonishing accomplishment to his rural neighbors, but critics have seen defects in these early works comparable to those of many other amateur poets, such as an awkward use of language and simplistic appeals to sentiment. Kavanagh, however, soon distinguished himself by surpassing his early limitations.

In 1929 he chanced upon a copy of the *Irish Statesman,* a periodical that regularly published the work of major Irish writers and was edited by George Russell, a leader of the Literary Renaissance. A philosopher devoted to religious mysticism who wrote prose and poetry under the name A.E., Russell made a special effort to develop the talents of promising unknown writers. He rejected Kavanagh's first submissions to the *Statesman* but encouraged the aspiring poet to try again. After Russell published some later submissions in 1929 and 1930, Kavanagh walked fifty miles to Dublin to visit him personally, and as a result Russell became Kavanagh's literary adviser, giving him books by such writers as Victor Hugo, Fyodor Dostoyevsky, Walt Whitman, Ralph Waldo Emerson and Robert Browning. With Russell's help Kavanagh gained access to Dublin's literary society, based largely on his unique status as an authentic peasant and poet.

Shortly after Russell's death in 1935, Kavanagh's first book, *Ploughman and Other Poems,* was published by Macmillan in its series on contemporary poets. In this collection the amateurish quality of Kavanagh's earliest work has yielded to more polished poems, many of which have a dreamy, lyrical quality that often characterizes the poetry of Russell and other writers of the Literary Renaissance. Some critics thought Kavanagh had yet to prove himself a major poet. Two years after *Ploughman* was published, the *Times Literary Supplement* called him "a young Irish poet of promise rather than of achievement," and Derek Verschoyle said in *Spectator* that "like other poets admired by A.E., he writes much better prose than poetry. Mr. Kavanagh's lyrics are for the most part slight and conventional, easily enjoyed but almost as easily forgotten."

Surprisingly, in view of his ambitions as a poet, Kavanagh's first major critical success came with the publication of an autobiographical prose work titled *The Green Fool* (1938). In this book, which he later revealed was as much novel as autobiography, Kavanagh recounts his rural childhood and his struggles as a budding writer, and while doing so he provides a wide-ranging portrait of Irish society. The book gave Kavanagh international recognition, with favorable reviews appearing in prominent publications in England and the United States. Critics have been impressed by Kavanagh's skillful balance between sentiment and humor. Horace Reynolds observed in the *New York Times Book Review* that *The Green Fool* "has both beauty and sharpness in it," and biographer Alan Warner said that Kavanagh's "romanticism is balanced by a shrewd ironic sense of the ridiculous. A passage of sentimental dreaming is quickly followed by the sharp edge of reality." Though reviewers praised the author's fondly detailed portrait of the folkways and speech of the Irish country-side, Kavanagh is also able, Warner noted, to depict the combative or petty side of his peasants' personalities. In other parts of the book, the author provides a witty description of the literary world. Reynolds, for instance, quoted Kavanagh's remarks that Ralph Waldo Emerson was "a sugary humbug" and that Walt Whitman "tried to bully his way to prophecy." The critic concluded, "You can hardly call him gracious or grateful, but he has the great virtue of honesty, and his heresies are refreshing."

Despite the critical success of *The Green Fool,* Kavanagh soon came to reject the work. As Warner remarked, "I think that one reason why he expressed such intense dislike of the book in his later years is that in it he accepts unequivocally, at times even exploits, his position as peasant poet. He speaks of his acute embarrassment in AE's drawing room at his hob-nailed boots and the patches on the knees of his trousers." Responding to this image of a "green fool," Fletcher Pratt informed readers of the *Saturday Review of Literature* that the author "lays no claim to being a literary figure of any kind, even a minor one. He writes his book through the eyes of an Irish peasant who . . . is more interested in potatoes than in prosody." In the coming years, when Kavanagh wished to be respected for his intellect, he found this persona intolerable.

In the late 1930s Kavanagh decided to leave farm life permanently and pursue a literary career in Dublin. The choice was difficult, for, as his brother Peter recalled in the biography *Sacred Keeper,* Kavanagh "loved the fields but detested the society" of his fellow peasants. When Kavanagh moved to Dublin, he hoped that its people would be more hospitable to him as an artist. Instead, as Nemo related, "he realized that the stimulating environment he had imagined was little different from the petty and ignorant world he had left. He soon saw through the literary masks many Dublin writers wore to affect an air of artistic sophistication. To him such men were dandies, journalists, and civil servants playing at art. His disgust was deepened by the fact that he was treated as the literate peasant he had been rather than as the highly talented poet he believed he was in the process of becoming."

Kavanagh's discontent led to a major change in his writing. Uncomfortable in both the urban and rural cultures of Ireland, and painfully aware of the flaws of both, he rejected the role of peasant poet that had helped make him socially acceptable, becoming known instead for his outspoken pronouncements on Irish society. By the time of his "Self Portrait," Kavanagh had come to call the Irish Literary Movement "the Irish thing" under whose "evil aegis" he had written *The Green Fool,* "a stage-Irish lie."

In his biography of Kavanagh, Darcy O'Brien put the author's disillusionment in a larger context. "Kavanagh's work is the product of a very low, dispirited period in Irish life and literature, the sort of psychological slump that most nations emerging from colonial rule experience after the revival of the past fails and people become aware that they have to make do with the rubble left behind by the departed conqueror." After years of often bitter struggle to create and determine the nature of an independent Ireland, "the energies, hopes and ideals of the Revolution had been exhausted. . . . Having seen the nationalist myths dissolve, disheartened by the values of the developing society, the better Irish writers had by 1940 turned caustically critical."

One of Kavanagh's first efforts at social criticism was "The Great Hunger" (1942), a long narrative poem that critics generally consider his finest work. In writing this unsentimental, sometimes bitter look at one peasant's life, Kavanagh not only confronted the unpleasant side of his background but by implica-

tion repudiated those members of the Literary Renaissance who sentimentalized rural Ireland. The poem tells the story of Patrick Maguire, a peasant who, in the cautious way of many Irish peasants after the devastating famines of the mid-nineteenth century, postpones marriage and children while improving his small farm and increasing his meager wealth. Gradually Maguire realizes that his own virtuous self-denial—his industriousness, devotion to an aging mother, and adherence to the moral teachings of the Catholic church—has led him to emotional desolation. Too old and too tied to his land, he will remain unmarried and isolated, a common fate in the Ireland of Kavanagh's day. In this poem, Kavanagh's lyrical evocations of the beauty of the countryside merely heighten the sense of Maguire's sorrow. Critics have praised the skillful mixture of poetic voices and rhythms in the work, ranging from resonant lines reminiscent of an angry prophet to the short, sharp phrases of simple annoyance. When "The Great Hunger" was reprinted in *Collected Poems* in 1964, *New York Times Book Review* contributor Richard Murphy called it "a great work" that conveys "a terrible and moving image of human frustration"; in *Poetry,* Robin Skelton hailed it as "a vision of mythic intensity."

In the decade after he wrote "The Great Hunger," Kavanagh increasingly directed his social criticism against the Dublin writers and intellectuals who had failed to live up to his expectations. Since he supported himself by writing a large amount of prose for periodicals as a free-lancer, columnist, and reviewer of books and films, Kavanagh had many opportunities to judge the state of Irish culture. His enthusiasm for such assessments grew so great that in 1952 he enlisted his brother's aid in publishing a short-lived periodical, *Kavanagh's Weekly,* as a forum for his views. Kavanagh's opinions were often negative, and even the author's admirers acknowledge that he expressed them in a fashion that was blunt, at times harsh. "Because he believed that the level of Irish literary achievement was very low," Nemo wrote, Kavanagh "never ceased stressing his belief that all good criticism was basically destructive. Destruction was necessary because it was the critic's function to save good writing from being submerged in the general flattery of the mediocre." The author's outspokenness brought him enemies in Dublin, and it has also displeased some literary critics. When a selection of his opinion pieces appeared in the humorously-titled *Collected Pruse* (1967), a reviewer for the *Times Literary Supplement* called them "painful to read" and added that "most of the specific judgments are mean." Similarly, when the thirteen issues of *Kavanagh's Weekly* were reprinted as a collection in 1981, *Supplement* contributor John Lucas said that while the work "has about it a brash, school-boyish, nose-thumbing humour . . . it is stuffed out with . . . dreary and opinionated nonsense."

But Warner is among the admirers of the writer who have seen merit in such work while conceding its flaws: "Although Kavanagh's criticism is not sustained or methodical, and it has something of a take-it-or-leave-it air, he sometimes goes to the heart of the matter in one sentence or phrase." Kavanagh, the critic said, can express "a bold, shrewd and vivid judgement that is worth pages from duller and more systematic critics." Noting Kavanagh's hatred of fashionable jargon and his ability to "let a good deal of fresh air into the discussions and debates of [his] time," Warner compared him to an insightful but opinionated literary critic of the eighteenth century, Samuel Johnson.

Kavanagh was less successful, however, when he used poetry to comment on Irish culture. In a series of verse satires, Kavanagh's targets range from individual writers and their work to the whole of his country's literary society. For example, "The Paddiad; or, The Devil as a Patron of Irish Letters" is a long poem modeled on Alexander Pope's satirical epic, "The Dunciad." The work shows a group of popular Irish writers convened in a pub at a meeting presided over by the devil. In the verse play "Adventures in the Bohemian Jungle," Kavanagh depicts himself as a simple, virtuous "Countryman" who journeys through a corrupt and amoral world in a futile search for good art and admirable artists. Critics have generally been disappointed in all these poems, suggesting that the satire is consistently compromised by bitterness. When several of the works appeared in *Collected Poems,* a reviewer for the *Times Literary Supplement* said that they "lack the sting of wit and infallibility of standpoint that true satire demands. [The author] seems to be trying out [Jonathan] Swift's gymnastics without having his physique." Kavanagh's "critical passion," Nemo surmised, "appears to have been too strong for him to maintain control over language when he struck out at ideals and philosophies that offended him."

While Kavanagh played the role of assertive social critic, inwardly he was more and more plagued by self-doubt. In O'Brien's analysis, when the aspiring reformer found himself unsuccessful, a sense of failure and isolation was the natural consequence. "Often, when [Kavanagh] was not writing satire," said the critic, "he would write about failure." He released a poetry collection, *A Soul for Sale* (1947), that takes its title from an image of failure that opens the poem "Pegasus": "My soul was an old horse / Offered for sale in twenty fairs." Nemo pointed out a variety of poems on a similar theme that Kavanagh wrote during this period. For instance, "To Be Dead," later published in *Come Dance With Kitty Stobling* (1960), discusses the death of poetic creativity, and "I Had a Future," later published in *Collected Poems,* shows Kavanagh's feeling that he had not fulfilled the promise he showed as a young author.

Sometimes Kavanagh escaped from the disappointments he found in Dublin by returning in his imagination to the Irish countryside. In the novel *Tarry Flynn* (1948), he examines the same scenes of youth he earlier surveyed in *The Green Fool,* and he has garnered similar praise for an accurate depiction of peasant life. But as Warner suggested, while *The Green Fool* offers an extensive view of Irish society, *Tarry Flynn* focuses more specifically on the dilemma of an aspiring poet who feels isolated from his rural community by his own talent. Reynolds pointed out in *Saturday Review of Literature* that the novel seems more autobiographical than *The Green Fool,* which is supposedly an autobiography. A number of critics have suggested that Kavanagh's confusion of the two genres weakens *Tarry Flynn* as a novel, arguing that the author is so emotionally close to Tarry that he describes both the character's joy and pain with more intensity than readers would find plausible.

Kavanagh's own pain and frustration reached a peak shortly after the failure of his journal in 1952, when he became the target of some biting satire similar to that which he directed at others. With the help of his strong social criticism, Kavanagh had become a well-known and controversial Dublin personality. In the *Leader,* a widely-read Irish weekly, an anonymous article depicted him in terms Warner summarized as "a clown and 'character,' a mixture of inspired idiot and rollicking bar-room prophet, surrounded by admiring young beatniky disciples whom he despised."

Kavanagh sued for libel. But the *Leader* retained as its defense counsel John Costello, a skillful trial lawyer who had also served as prime minister of Ireland. When the dispute came to trial in February of 1954, Costello undermined Kavanagh's case by insistently questioning the writer about his own numerous satires. Kavanagh lost the suit and, seemingly at the lowest point of his

life, entered a hospital the next year to have surgery for lung cancer. Many expected him to die.

Surprisingly, the poet's life began to improve. Before Kavanagh entered the hospital, he and Costello had begun to turn their animosities into friendship, with Kavanagh sending the lawyer part of a poem and Costello, once again prime minister, using his influence to help the poet obtain a lecturing post at University College, Dublin. Kavanagh overcame his cancer, and as he convalesced on the banks of Dublin's Grand Canal he experienced a further change in his personal outlook, one that resulted in some of his most admired poems. "Barely eluding death had a serious and positive effect on [Kavanagh's] poetry," O'Brien wrote. "His sickness deprived him of a lung and much hatred, or let us say that the trauma of his cancer made the targets of his hatred seem as petty as they were and as unworthy of his continuous attention."

Renouncing hatred, Kavanagh committed himself to an acceptance of life as it is and a celebration of its small pleasures. He repudiated his years as a reformer, observing in his "Self Portrait" that "stupid poets and artists think that by taking subjects of public importance it will help their work to survive. . . . The things that really matter are casual, insignificant little things." He also asserted that "in the final simplicity we don't care whether we appear foolish or not. . . . We are satisfied with being ourselves, however small." As an example of the change in his writing, Kavanagh quoted the opening lines of his sonnet "Canal Bank Walk": "Leafy-with-love banks and the green waters of the canal / Pouring redemption for me, that I do / The will of God wallow in the habitual, the banal / Grow with nature again as before I grew." He wrote many other poems expressing such inner tranquility, several of them sonnets, and they were praised in reviews of the collections *Come Dance With Kitty Stobling* (1960) and *Collected Poems.* Discussing the latter book for the *New York Times Book Review,* Richard Murphy called the sonnets "the most positive work [Kavanagh] has done," praising them as "a lyrical celebration of love fulfilled in man by God."

Though Kavanagh's burst of creativity helped renew interest in his poetry, his health failed again after 1960, and he was able to write little in the years remaining before his death in 1967. His last major work was prompted when Radio Telefis Eireann, the Irish broadcasting network, invited him to write and narrate an autobiographical television program for its "Self Portrait" series. The resulting work, which appeared in print soon after its telecast in 1962, is not a detailed record of Kavanagh's life but rather a series of his comments and recollections. Full of strong opinions and sometimes self-contradictory, the script has been assessed by many commentators as an accurate, engaging, and individualistic portrait of the artist. The broadcast "was the high point of Patrick's career," his brother Peter recalled. "First, he had asserted himself as a poet with the authorities and won; second, he had issued his statement to the public both in what he said and in his manner of saying it."

Kavanagh's willingness to make strong personal statements in his writing, even at the risk of being disliked for it, remains a major factor in his appeal. As Nemo observed: "It would not be incorrect to say that one of his more serious handicaps in becoming a successful poet was his personality. At the same time, however, it is his personality that vitalizes his best writing. Had he been able to direct his responses to life and literature in a more orderly and logical fashion he might have produced a more even body of work, but one lacking the intensity and clarity of vision that characterizes his better poems." At the close of his "Self Portrait," Kavanagh seemed to embrace such intensity as a way of life. "Courage," he asserted, "is nearly everything. Our pure impulses are always right."

BIOGRAPHICAL/CRITICAL SOURCES:

BOOKS

Contemporary Literary Criticism, Volume 22, Gale, 1982.
Cronin, Anthony, *Heritage Now: Irish Literature in the English Language,* St. Martin's, 1982.
Dictionary of Literary Biography, Gale, Volume 15: *British Novelists, 1930-1959,* 1983, Volume 20: *British Poets, 1914-1945,* 1983.
Kavanagh, Patrick, *Self Portrait,* Dolmen, 1964.
Kavanagh, Peter, *Sacred Keeper: A Biography of Patrick Kavanagh,* Goldsmith, 1979.
Nemo, John, *Patrick Kavanagh,* Twayne, 1979.
O'Brien, Darcy, *Patrick Kavanagh,* Bucknell University Press, 1975.
Warner, Alan, *Clay Is the Word: Patrick Kavanagh, 1904-1967,* Dolmen, 1973.

PERIODICALS

Commonweal, March 17, 1939.
Irish University Review, spring, 1973.
New Yorker, April 10, 1965, December 9, 1967.
New York Times Book Review, February 26, 1939, August 24, 1947, May 23, 1965.
Poetry, June, 1965.
Saturday Review of Literature, March 25, 1939, September 20, 1947, January 21, 1950.
Spectator, June 3, 1938, July 31, 1964, February 17, 1979.
Times Literary Supplement, October 24, 1936, October 22, 1938, May 17, 1947, August 12, 1960, August 27, 1964, May 4, 1967, June 13, 1980, July 31, 1981.

OBITUARIES:

PERIODICALS

New York Times, December 1, 1967.
Time, December 8, 1967.
Times (London), December 1, 1967.
Washington Post, December 1, 1967.

*   *   *

KAYE, M(ary) M(argaret) 1909-
(Mollie Hamilton, Mollie Kaye)

PERSONAL: Born in 1909, in Simla, India; married Godfrey John Hamilton (an army officer); children: Carolyn. *Education:* Attended schools in England.

ADDRESSES: c/o Allen Lane, Kingsgate House, 536 King's Rd., London SW10, England.

CAREER: Writer; painter.

WRITINGS:

HISTORICAL NOVELS

Shadow of the Moon, Messner, 1956, enlarged edition, St. Martin's, 1979.
Trade Wind, Coward, 1963, revised edition, St. Martin's, 1981.
The Far Pavilions, St. Martin's, 1978.

MYSTERIES

Death Walked in Kashmir, Staples Press, 1953, reprinted as *Death in Kashmir,* St. Martin's, 1984.

Death Walked in Berlin, Staples Press, 1955, reprinted as *Death in Berlin,* St. Martin's, 1985.
Death Walked in Cypress, Staples Press, 1956, reprinted as *Death in Cyprus,* St. Martin's, 1984.
(Under name Mollie Hamilton) *Later Than You Think,* Coward, 1958, reprinted as *Death in Kenya,* St. Martin's, 1983.
House of Shade, Coward, 1959, reprinted as *Death in Zanzibar,* St. Martin's, 1983.
Night on the Island, Longmans, Green, 1960, reprinted as *Death in the Andamans,* St. Martin's, 1984.

Also author of *Six Bars at Seven,* Hutchinson, and *Strange Island,* Thacker.

FOR CHILDREN

(Under name Mollie Kaye) *Potter Pinner Meadow,* illustrations by Margaret Tempest, Collins, 1937.
(Self-illustrated) *The Animals' Vacation,* New York Graphic Society, 1964.
Thistledown, Quartet, 1982.
The Ordinary Princess, Doubleday, 1984.

Also author of *Black Bramble Wood, Willow Witches Brook,* and *Gold Gorse Common,* Collins.

OTHER

The Far Pavilions Picture Book, Bantam, 1979.
(Editor) Emily Bayley, *The Golden Calm: An English Lady's Life in Moghul Delhi,* Viking, 1980.
Moon of Other Days: M. M. Kaye's Kipling, Salem House, 1989.

SIDELIGHTS: Previously a successful author of children's books and mysteries, M. M. Kaye set these genres aside to concentrate on the historical novel *The Far Pavilions.* After fourteen years and a grueling battle against cancer, Kaye finished the book that has been compared to *Gone with the Wind* and other classics of the genre.

The Far Pavilions gives readers a detailed look at life in colonial India. It is a subject on which she is well qualified to write, for she was born in Simla, India, into a British family that had already lived in that country for two generations. Although she was educated in England, Kaye returned to India after her schooling and married a British army officer. While she was thus a part of the ruling class in colonial India, Kaye's writing has been especially praised for its even-handed portrayal of both the native Indians and the English colonists. Brigitte Weeks writes in the *Washington Post Book World* that *The Far Pavilions* is so powerful, its "readers . . . cannot ever feel quite the same about either the Indian subcontinent or the decrepit history of the British Empire."

The Far Pavilions has been compared to Rudyard Kipling's *Kim.* Like Kipling's novel, Kaye's book features a young British boy who is orphaned, then raised as an Indian and a Hindu. Kaye's protagonist, Ash, is sent to live with aristocratic relatives in England when his parentage is finally revealed. Later, he returns to India as a soldier and finds himself torn between his two heritages. While some critics dismiss Kaye's plot as standard romantic-adventure fare, others praise her for skillfully combining Ash's adventures with an accurate historical account of the events between the Indian Mutiny and the Second Afghan War. Furthermore, emphasizes *Spectator* contributor Francis King, Kaye possesses a "gift for narrative"; he finds *The Far Pavilions* "absorbing" in spite of its more than nine hundred pages. A *New Yorker* writer concurs that Kaye is "a topnotch storyteller and historian; . . . she holds the reader in thrall."

But critics most often point to Kaye's comprehensive vision of nineteenth-century India as the key to her novel's success. *Times Literary Supplement* reviewer Theon Wilkinson explains: "[Kaye] writes with the conviction that events must be told in their fullness or not at all, that ever[y] facet of information touching the characters must be embraced; and *The Far Pavilions* is a great oriental pot-pourri from which nothing is left out: Indian lullabys; regimental bawdy songs; regimental history, wars and campaigns; weddings; funerals; poisonous plants—a tribute to much painstaking research, some drawn from original diaries and journals. . . . The length of the book is a challenge but the effort is rewarded." And Rahul Singh writes in *Punch*, "There is none of the romantic sentimentality that saw India as a country of snake charmers and bejewelled princes, with the faithful Gunga Din thrown in. Nor the view of it as one vast, multiplying, putrefying sewer for which there was no possible hope. Ms. Kaye sees India as many Indians do, and for this one must applaud her."

Before publishing *The Far Pavilions*, Kaye had written two other books similar to it. *Shadow of the Moon* dramatizes the events of the Indian Mutiny through the story of an orphaned Anglo-Spanish girl. *Trade Wind* is set in Zanzibar instead of India, but like *Shadow of the Moon* and *The Far Pavilions*, it examines two cultures in conflict while telling the exciting story of a young abolitionist from Massachusetts who is kidnapped by a handsome slave trader when she travels to Zanzibar. Neither book was particularly successful when first published, but when reissued after the publication of *The Far Pavilions*, both *Shadow of the Moon* and *Trade Wind* became best-sellers. Like *The Far Pavilions*, they have been praised for their fine descriptions of their exotic settings. Walter Shapiro, writing in the *Washington Post Book World*, notes that while its storyline might seem conventional, *Trade Wind* "transcends such easy labels as romance or exotic historical novel. It is a sophisticated treat for those traditional readers who favor good writing, subtle character development, clever plotting and a slightly ironic narrative tone."

MEDIA ADAPTATIONS: The Far Pavilions was produced as a mini-series by Home Box Office in 1984.

BIOGRAPHICAL/CRITICAL SOURCES:

BOOKS

Contemporary Literary Criticism, Volume 28, Gale, 1984.

PERIODICALS

Chapter One, May-June, 1979.
Christian Science Monitor, November 13, 1978.
Detroit News, October 7, 1979.
Los Angeles Times, November 2, 1980, October 9, 1984, May 23, 1986.
Maclean's, September 24, 1979.
New Statesman, October 12, 1979.
Newsweek, September 11, 1978.
New Yorker, October 9, 1978, September 24, 1979, July 27, 1981.
New York Herald Tribune Book Review, September 1, 1957, September 20, 1959.
New York Times, October 26, 1958, December 3, 1978, March 25, 1979.
New York Times Book Review, November 18, 1979.
People, November 20, 1978.
Publishers Weekly, June 25, 1979.
Punch, November 14, 1979.
Sewanee Review, summer, 1980.
Spectator, April 12, 1957, September 9, 1978.

Times Literary Supplement, April 19, 1957, August 22, 1958, September 22, 1978, November 21, 1980, March 26, 1982.
Washington Post, September 11, 1979, April 21, 1984.
Washington Post Book World, September 10, 1978, July 12, 1981, November 11, 1984.

* * *

KAYE, Mollie
See KAYE, M(ary) M(argaret)

* * *

KAYMOR, Patrice Maguilene
See SENGHOR, Leopold Sedar

* * *

KAZAKOV, Yuri Pavlovich 1927-

PERSONAL: Given name transliterated in some sources as Iurii, Jurij, or Yuriy; born in 1927 in Moscow, U.S.S.R.; son of a worker. *Education:* Began study of music in 1944; entered Gnesin Music School in 1946; Institute of Literature, Moscow, graduate, 1958.

ADDRESSES: Home—Beskudnikovskii bulvardoi 5, korpue 1, kv 53, Moscow 1-474, U.S.S.R.

CAREER: Taught in music schools; played in opera studio, jazz and symphony orchestras; writer.

MEMBER: Soyuz Pisateley SSSR (Writers' Union U.S.S.R.).

WRITINGS:

Manka (stories), Arkhangelskoe Knigoizdatel'stvo, 1958.
Na Polustanke (stories; title means "At the Whistle-Stop"), Sovietsky Pisatel, 1959.
Po Dorage (stories and a sketch; title means "On the Road"), Sovietsky Pisatel, 1961.
Legkaia Zhizn (stories; title means "Easy Life"), lzdatelstvo "Pravda," 1963.
Goluboe: Zelenoe (stories and sketches; title means "Blue and Green"), Sovietsky Pisatel, 1963.
Going to Town, and Other Stories, compiled and translated by Gabriella Azrael, Houghton, 1964.
Selected Short Stories, Pergamon, 1964.
Zapakh Khleba, Izdatelstvo Sovetskaya Rossyia, 1965, English translation by Manya Harari and Andrew Thomson published as *The Smell of Bread, and Other Stories,* Harvill, 1965.
Dvoe v dekabre, Molodaia Gvardiia, 1966.
Arcturus The Hunting Hound, and Other Stories, translated by Anne Terry White, Doubleday, 1968.

Contributor to *Zhurnal Molodykh, Moskva, Oktyabr, Znamya,* and other Russian magazines, and to anthologies; contributor to European and American magazines, including *Encounter* and *Esquire.* Included in an Italian anthology of the world's best stories.

Books and stories by Kazakov have been translated into Italian, German, Hungarian, Danish, French, and other languages.

SIDELIGHTS: Yuri Kazakov told *CA:* "I entered the Institute of Literature in 1953. I chanced upon the Institute at a propitious time. The political life of the land was changing; and the youth, the students, felt this more acutely than the rest. We read much, and avidly—and thought a great deal. There was no end to the arguments and discussions.

"I graduated from the Institute in 1958. In justifying my diploma (with some ten stories to my credit), I was graded 'E' which means 'Average.' I alone of our class got an 'Average.' The ideological tenor of my stories was deemed wrong, and my worldview in error. Yet, during this same year, I was accepted into the Writers' Union. I was admitted even prior to the publication of my first book, notwithstanding the Union's bylaws, which make membership contingent upon the actual publication of one or more books. This was the first instance in which Union membership was granted an author who had seen print in a magazine only. The poet, Andrei Voznesensky, was similarly accepted.

"I have written little. In general, Russian writers are not as prolific as the Westerners. We find it incredible, for instance, that William Saroyan wrote fifteen-hundred stories, plus tens of tales and novels, within a ten-year period.

"In retrospect, I attribute the success of my early stories to the fact that I was the first, after a long absence from the literary scene, to pay attention to those aspects of life that were ignored by contemporary writers.

"Critics wrongly have looked for my beginnings in Chekhov, Bunin, or Turgenev. I need hardly add that these writers are so unlike one another that it is quite senseless to ascribe influence upon me to any one man."

In her review of *Going to Town* in the *New York Review of Books,* Helen Muchnic commented: "This is the great news about Kazakov: For years it has seemed that no individual in the Soviet Union was entitled to dream, nor that any artist might be expected to care whether any one dreamed or not. But here is a writer who says openly that life may not be entirely fulfilled in 'sports, conferences, vocational training, and exams,' that unwanted dreams come to trouble a boy's peace of mind; and this writer is not only tolerated, but very popular in Russia. The news is so good that it has led to exaggerated praise. In my opinion, Kazakov is neither revolutionary nor is he—not yet, at least—another Chekhov, Turgenev, or Sherwood Anderson. [But] he is certainly gifted."

BIOGRAPHICAL/CRITICAL SOURCES:

PERIODICALS

Atlantic Monthly, March, 1964.
Nation, February 10, 1964.
New York Review of Books, April 2, 1964.
New York Times Book Review, January 12, 1964.
Saturday Review, February 1, 1964.

* * *

KAZANTZAKIS, Nikos 1883(?)-1957

PERSONAL: Surname also transliterated "Kazantzakes" and "Kazantzake"; born February 18, 1883 (one source says December 2, 1885; one says February 2, 1882), in Heraklion (one source says Candia), Crete; died of complications of leukemia, October 26, 1957, in Freiburg, West Germany; buried in Heraklion, Crete; son of Michael (a farmer) and Maria (Christodoulzki) Kazantzakis; married first wife, 1911 (divorced), married Eleni (Helen) Samios, 1945. *Education:* Attended French School of the Holy Cross (Naxos, Crete), 1897-1899, and Gymnasium (Heraklion, Crete), 1899-1902; received law degree from University of Athens, 1906; further study in Paris, Germany, and Italy, 1906-1910.

CAREER: Writer and traveler. Held various posts in the Greek government, c. 1919-46, including director general in the Ministry of Public Welfare, 1919-27, minister of state, 1945, and minister of national education, c. 1945-46; served in Antibes, France, as director of UNESCO's Bureau of Translations of the Classics, 1947-48.

MEMBER: Greek Writers Society (president, beginning in 1950).

AWARDS, HONORS: Received Lenin Peace Prize from the Soviet Union, 1957; nominated several times for Nobel Prize for literature.

WRITINGS:

FICTION

Ophis kai krinos (novella), first published in 1906, translation with introduction and notes by Theodora Vasils published as *Serpent and Lily: A Novella With a Manifesto* (includes essay "The Sickness of the Age"), University of California Press, 1980.
Toda-Raba: Moscou a Crie (novel; originally written in French), first published in 1934, reprinted, Plon, 1962, translation by Amy Mims published as *Toda Raba,* Simon & Schuster, 1964.
Le Jardin des rochers (novel; originally written in French), [Amsterdam], 1936, reprinted, Plon, 1959, translation by Richard Howard published as *The Rock Garden* (includes passages from *The Saviors of God* [also see below]), Simon & Schuster, 1963.
Bios kai politeia tou Alexi Zorba (novel), first published in 1946, reprinted, Diphros, 1957, translation by Carl Wildman published as *Zorba the Greek,* introduction by Ian Scott-Kilvert, J. Lehmann, 1952, Simon & Schuster, 1953.
Ho Kapetan Michales (novel), first published in 1953, reprinted, Diphros, 1957, translation by Jonathan Griffin published as *Freedom or Death,* preface by A. Den Doolaard, Simon & Schuster, 1956, reprinted, 1983 (published in England as *Freedom and Death,* Faber, 1956).
Ho Christos xanastavronetai (novel), first published in 1954, reprinted, Diphros, 1957, translation by Griffin published as *The Greek Passion,* Simon & Schuster, 1954 (published in England as *Christ Recrucified: A Novel,* Cassirer, 1954).
Ho teleftaios peirasmos (novel), first published in 1955, reprinted, Diphros, 1959, translation with afterword by P. A. Bien published as *The Last Temptation of Christ,* Simon & Schuster, 1960 (published in England as *The Last Temptation,* Cassirer, 1961).
Ho phtochoules tou Theou (novel), Diphros, 1956, translation by Bien published as *Saint Francis: A Novel,* Simon & Schuster, 1962 (published in England as *God's Pauper: St. Francis of Assisi,* Cassirer, 1962).
Hoi aderphophades (novel), first published in 1963, translation by Athena Gianakas Dallas published as *The Fratricides,* Simon & Schuster, 1964, reprinted, 1984.
Megas Alexandros (juvenile), first published in 1979, translation by Theodora Vasils published as *Alexander the Great,* Ohio University Press, 1982.
Sta palatia tes Knosou: Historiko mythistorema gia paidia (juvenile), Ekdoseis E. N. Kazantzake, 1981, abridged and edited translation by Themi and Theodora Vasils published as *At the Palaces of Knossos,* Ohio University Press, 1988.

POETRY

Odysseia, first published in 1938, reprinted, Diphros, 1960, translation with synopsis and notes by Kimon Friar published as *The Odyssey: A Modern Sequel,* Simon & Schuster, 1958, reprinted, 1985.

Tertsines, [Athens], 1960.
Symposion, first published in 1971, translation by Theodora and Themi Vasils published as *Symposium,* Crowell, 1973.

Poetry represented in anthologies, including *Synchronoi kretikoi poietes,* Barmpounakes, 1983.

TRAVEL

Te eida set Rousia, two volumes, first published in 1928, 2nd edition published as *Taxideuontas: Rousia,* Diphros, 1956, translation by Michael Antonakes and Thanasis Maskaleris published as *Russia: A Chronicle of Three Journeys in the Aftermath of the Revolution,* Creative Arts Book Co., 1989.
Ho Morias, first published in 1937, translation by F. A. Reed published as *Journey to the Morea,* Simon & Schuster, 1965 (published in England as *Travels in Greece,* Cassirer, 1966).
Ispania, first published in 1937, reprinted, Diphros, 1957, translation by Amy Mims published as *Spain,* Simon & Schuster, 1963, reprinted, Creative Arts Book Co., 1983.
Iaponia-Kina, first published in 1938, reprinted, Diphros, 1956, translation by George C. Pappgeotes published as *Japan, China,* epilogue by Helen Kazantzakis, Simon & Schuster, 1963 (published in England as *Travels in China and Japan,* Cassirer, 1964).
Anglia, first published in 1941, reprinted, Diphros, 1958, translation published as *England: A Travel Journal,* Simon & Schuster, 1965.
Italia, Aigyptos, Sina, Hierousalem, Kypros, ho Morias, [Athens], 1961, translation by Themi and Theodora Vasils published as *Journeying: Travels in Italy, Egypt, Sinai, Jerusalem, and Cyprus,* Little, Brown, 1975.

Travel works published in six-volume collection titled *Taxideuontas.*

PLAYS

Theatro tragodies me Byzantina themata, three volumes, Diphros, 1955-56.
Theatro tragodies me diaphora themata (title means "Theatrical Tragedies With Different Themes"), Diphros, 1956.
Three Plays (contains "Christopher Columbus," "Melissa," and "Kouros"), translated by Athena Gianakas Dallas, Simon & Schuster, 1969.
Christopher Columbus (four-act), Allen Press, 1972.
Two Plays (contains "Sodom and Gomorrah" and "Comedy: A Tragedy in One Act"), translated by Friar and Bien, North Central Pub. Co., 1982.
Buddha, translated by Friar and Athena Dallis-Damis, Avant Books, 1983.

Also author of plays *O Protomastoras,* 1910, *Niceforos Fokas,* 1927, *Christos* and *Odysseas,* both 1928, and *Ioulianos,* 1945.

CORRESPONDENCE

Epistoles pros te Galateia, Diphros, 1958, translation by Philip Ramp and Katerina Anghelaki Rooke published as *The Suffering God: Selected Letters to Galatia and to Papastephanou,* Caratzas Brothers, 1979.

Selected letters also published in *Tetrakosia grammata tou Kazantzakis ston Prebelaki,* three volumes, 1965, and in *Kazantzakes,* 1975.

OTHER

Salvatores Dei (essay), first published in 1927, revised edition published as *Salvatores Dei: Astetiki,* Sympan, c. 1960,

translation with introduction by Friar published as *The Saviors of God: Spiritual Exercises,* Simon & Schuster, 1960.
Historia tes Rosikes logotechnias (history and criticism), two volumes, first published in 1930, reprinted, E. Kazantzake, 1965.
Anaphora ston Gkreko (autobiography), first published in 1961, reprinted, Ekdoseis He. Kazantzake, 1962, translation by Bien published as *Report to Greco,* Simon & Schuster, 1965.

Translator of works by Dante Alighieri, Wolfgang Johann von Goethe, Homer, Friedrich Nietzsche, Machiavelli, Charles Darwin, Charles Dickens, Harriet Beecher Stowe, William James, Johann Peter Eckermann, and Henri Bergson.

MEDIA ADAPTATIONS: The Greek Passion was adapted for film; *Zorba the Greek* was adapted for a Broadway musical with book by Joe Stein, lyrics by Fred Ebb, and first performed in New York City at the Imperial Theater, November 17, 1968; *Zorba the Greek* was also made into a motion picture featuring Anthony Quinn in the title role by Twentieth Century-Fox in 1964; and *The Last Temptation of Christ* was released as a movie starring Willem Dafoe in 1988 by Universal.

SIDELIGHTS: Nikos Kazantzakis is regarded as the most important and controversial writer in twentieth-century Greek literature. The widely translated author of poetry, plays, travel books, and novels, Kazantzakis spent most of his life traveling and studying, seeking to define the purpose of man's existence. In novels such as *Ho teleftaios peirasmos (The Last Temptation of Christ)* and *Bios kai politeia tou Alexi Zorba (Zorba the Greek),* for which he is best known to American readers, Kazantzakis probes the conflicts between man's physical, intellectual, and spiritual natures. "My principal anguish and the source of all my joys and sorrows from my youth onward," he wrote in his prologue to *The Last Temptation of Christ,* "has been the incessant, merciless battle between the spirit and the flesh."

Kazantzakis's writing is often appraised as a single body that reveals the author's philosophical and spiritual values; most critics agree that his writings are in this sense autobiographical. But although Kazantzakis's works seek to reconcile the dualities of human nature—mind and body, affirmation and despair, even life and death—some critics have suggested that the author's ultimate concern lies more in striving to overcome inherent human conflicts than in resolving them. "Every one of Kazantzakis' major works can be read as a portrayal of Man's seeking reintegration," explained C. N. Stavrou in the *Colorado Quarterly.* "Some succeed, some enjoy a partial success, some fail, others are completely indifferent or find integration by a repudiation rather than a reconciliation of the eternal duality. But there is never any question that in Kazantzakis' eyes the *desideratum* was the conciliation, not the subjugation of the opposing selves in the human psyche. . . . In his works more importance attaches to the struggle to arrive than to the fact of arrival itself."

While Kazantzakis's stature as a unique voice in modern literature is uncontested, critical opinion about the literary quality of his individual works is frequently divided. Many hold the view that Kazantzakis subordinated his artistic concerns to the philosophical ideas he wanted to express. But some critics admire what they consider the passionate poetic voice in which the author communicates with his readers, and others appreciate the realistic descriptions, metaphors, and profuse imagery that comprise Kazantzakis's writing style.

Kazantzakis remained relatively unknown as a writer for much of his career, finally achieving popularity during the last decade of his life with the 1946 publication of *Zorba the Greek,* his story of the friendship between a bookish intellectual and an unsophisticated peasant man. Kazantzakis's fame was intensified by the controversy surrounding several of his subsequent works, beginning with his description of modern Christianity as an ineffective, power-hungry institution in the novel *Ho Christos xanastavronetai* (*The Greek Passion*). Further notoriety ensued with the publication of *The Last Temptation of Christ,* Kazantzakis's 1955 portrayal of an uncertain, emotional Christ troubled by the temptation to renounce his calling and live as an ordinary man. The furor raised by Kazantzakis's work, however, brought the author worldwide notice and established his reputation as a significant writer.

Kazantzakis was born in Heraklion, Crete, in the early 1880s. The son of a peasant farmer and feed dealer, Kazantzakis grew up in a rustic community of shepherds, farmers, and fishermen. His Cretan roots—his love for the peasantry and his early exposure to the Cretans' fervent patriotic desire to overthrow their Turkish oppressors—would exert a large influence on his writings. Several of his novels take place in Crete, and one of them, *Ho Kapetan Michales* (*Freedom or Death*), depicts the Cretan fight for independence. Several critics suggest that Kazantzakis's peasant heritage manifests itself in the Demotic Greek—the language of ordinary people—which he used instead of the traditional literary Atticistic Greek. Although Kazantzakis's use of the language met with criticism from the intellectual community, contemporary critics seem to agree that the coarse, more concrete language of the common man enhanced his literary style. Perhaps most importantly, Crete provided Kazantzakis with an outlook from which he could embrace various viewpoints that ultimately provided the foundation for his thematic concerns. Kazantzakis came to characterize himself in his autobiography *Anaphora ston Gkreko* (*Report to Greco*) as the possessor of a "Cretan glance," a way of seeing that encompassed seemingly incompatible philosophies and perspectives. This ability to blend opposing attitudes, Kazantzakis believed, arose from both the geographical and cultural orientation of his Mediterranean homeland, equidistant from what he saw as the more passive spirituality of Eastern religion and the materialism of the West.

After witnessing increasing tension on his native island throughout his childhood, Kazantzakis was sent as a teenager to the Greek island of Naxos when the Cretan people rose in violence against the Turks in 1897. On Naxos, Kazantzakis attended school at a Franciscan monastery, where he learned French and Italian, studied Western philosophy, and became exposed to the mysteries of Christianity as taught by the monks. In 1906, after he received his law degree from the University of Athens, Kazantzakis moved to France and became the pupil of the French philosopher Henri Bergson. He wrote a dissertation on the works of German philosopher Friedrich Nietzsche and then studied for four years in Germany and Italy. It was at this time that Kazantzakis began his writing career, translating the works of Western scientists and thinkers, composing verse dramas, and completing the novella *Ophis kai krinos* (*Serpent and Lily*), the first of his books to be published.

Commentators suggest that Nietzsche and Bergson strongly influenced Kazantzakis's thought. The author was especially interested in the concepts Nietzsche outlined in *The Birth of Tragedy,* wherein Nietzsche postulated that the primary tension in human nature exists between man's physical drives and his intellectual and spiritual impulses; this idea is central to Kazantzakis's themes. The author was also profoundly interested in Bergson's concept of progressive spiritual development as man's attempt to escape the constraints of his physical and social existence and unite with what Bergson termed the *elan vital,* the universal creative force. Both *Serpent and Lily,* about a young man's struggle to balance the physical and spiritual elements of his love for a woman, and *Salvatores Dei: Asketiki* (*The Saviors of God: Spiritual Exercises*), an essay in which the author explains his early philosophical concerns, display these influences, as do many of Kazantzakis's subsequent works.

In 1919 Kazantzakis accepted a position as director general in Greece's Ministry of Public Welfare, marking the beginning of his association with the Greek government. He spent the following years coordinating the rescue and feeding of nearly 150,000 Greeks affected by civil war in the Caucasus region of the southern Soviet Union. During the rest of the decade he continued to study and traveled widely in Europe and Asia. After visiting the devastation in Germany following World War I, Kazantzakis became attracted to the principles of social change furthered by communist leader Vladimir Lenin. He subscribed to Marxist philosophy for the next several years and visited the Soviet Union several times before 1927, when he resigned his position in the Ministry of Public Welfare to concentrate on bringing about greater understanding between the people of different cultures through his travel and writing. Kazantzakis remained a continual traveller for his entire life, accepting numerous invitations from foreign governments to visit and write about their nations. He published books discussing his impressions and thoughts about his journeys through countries such as Japan, China, England, Spain, Italy, the Soviet Union, and Greece.

During the 1930s Kazantzakis worked as a translator and author, concentrating primarily on his epic poem *Odysseia* (*The Odyssey: A Modern Sequel*), which he based on the Greek poet Homer's classic epic of the same title. Kazantzakis wrote several drafts of the Demotic poem before publishing it in 1938. Critics consider the poem an autobiographical work that presents a psychological portrait of Kazantzakis—in the mythic character Odysseus—after the author became disillusioned by what he saw as communism's inability to fulfill man's spiritual needs. According to Andreas K. Poulakidas's *Comparative Literature Studies* article, "It was toward the end of his Russian experience that Kazantzakis realized he was like Odysseus, a man of many philosophies and personalities. Like Odysseus, he had been a homeless, rootless, but robust wanderer. . . . Thus, Odysseus is the best symbol for his philosophy, and *The Odyssey: A Modern Sequel* . . . is able to give us an interpretive account of Kazantzakis' psychic state at the time he had this realization." Considering the poem to be his most important work, Kazantzakis confirmed his identification with Odysseus's journey in *Report to Greco.* "I created [Odysseus] in order to face the abyss calmly," he was quoted by Kimon Friar in *Saturday Review,* "and in creating him I strove to resemble him. I myself was being created. I entrusted all my yearning to this Odysseus."

The Odyssey begins at the point in Homer's epic where Odysseus returns to his native Ithaca, and it narrates the hero's continued adventures around the Mediterranean. Odysseus arrives home and slays his wife's suitors, but he becomes disenchanted with his life and begins a quest for self-understanding and fulfillment that takes him to Sparta, Crete, and Egypt. After unsuccessfully battling an Egyptian pharaoh, he sails inland, dreaming of establishing an ideal community. Odysseus confers directly with God, builds his utopia, and institutes a social order based on spiritual laws, but at the society's dedication, the city is completely destroyed by a massive eruption of the earth, whereupon Odysseus renounces all personal and social ties. He wanders to the southern tip of Africa, where he builds a boat and sails for the South Pole to die alone.

Critics assert that *The Odyssey* functions at an allegorical as well as autobiographical level. As explained by John Ciardi in *Saturday Review,* each episode in the poem is "an allegory of a stage of the soul, and all are threaded together on a series of mythic themes." Odysseus progresses, according to the reviewer, through seven stages of "Bestiality, Battle-Hunger, Lust, Pure Intellect, Despair, Detachment, and finally, Pure Soul." Critics disagree, however, in their interpretations of the poem's ending. Some regard Odysseus's solitary death as Kazantzakis's comment on life's ultimate meaninglessness, while others construe Odysseus's withdrawal as the triumph of man's soul over both his physical existence and the random disasters that endanger it.

Although critics in Greece reportedly reacted negatively to Kazantzakis's use of Demotic language, reception of the work in English translation was generally favorable, with some reviewers admiring the quality of the poetry itself. "The literary achievement of Kazantzakis's *Odyssey* lies in his rich and sonorous language and vivid and original imagery," asserted C. A. Trypanis, for example, in the *Manchester Guardian.* But some critics found the poem outdated and unoriginal. "There is something oddly old-fashioned about this poem. . . . Not a new departure nor a daring experiment, but simply a kind of nostalgia for the days of the grand style and the picaresque epic," noted *Poetry* contributor L. O. Coxe. Still other reviewers were highly enthusiastic in their praise, hailing the epic as a masterpiece. Adonis Decavalles, for instance, in another *Poetry* review, lauded *The Odyssey* as "undoubtedly the greatest long poem of our time, a colossal achievement in art and substance. It is the mature product of Kazantzakes' deep familiarity with the best in world literature and thought, of intense living, traveling, and thinking."

The 1940s saw the publication of perhaps Kazantzakis's best-known novel, *Zorba the Greek.* Kazantzakis wrote the autobiographical work during the early part of the decade as a tribute to his close friend George Zorba, with whom he had undertaken a mining venture in Crete in 1917. The author, as quoted by George T. Karnezis in the *Carnegie Series in English: A Modern Miscellany,* professed a deep admiration for Zorba, whom he felt "possessed 'the broadest soul, the soundest body, and the freest cry I have known in my life.' " The novel's narrator is accepted by critics as Kazantzakis's self-portrait as an artist and philosopher.

A tale of the friendship between two men with sharply contrasting personalities and outlooks, *Zorba the Greek* is arguably Kazantzakis's most concrete illustration of his preoccupation with the split between man's physical and intellectual natures. The book's narrator is an inhibited scholar referred to only as "the boss," who describes himself as having "fallen so low that, if I had to choose between falling in love with a woman and reading a book about love, I should have chosen the book." He decides to participate more fully in life by leaving his studies and reopening his inactive lignite mine in Crete. While awaiting passage to the island from Greece, he meets Zorba, an earthy, uneducated man who seeks experience rather than understanding. Taken with Zorba's vibrant nature and his impulsive offer to accompany him to Crete, the boss hires Zorba as his foreman and personal cook; the remainder of *Zorba the Greek* is a record of how Zorba challenges his employer's outlook. Assuming at first that Zorba is naive, the boss continually misinterprets Zorba's motives. But by the end of the novel, the boss develops a deep reverence for the workman's love for life, which Zorba demonstrates in his ability to dance, work, love, and fight—intensely and wholeheartedly. The boss has come to see him, as quoted by Karnezis, as "a man with warm blood . . . who lets real tears run down his cheeks when he is suffering; and when he is happy

he does not spoil the freshness of his joy by running it through the fine sieve of metaphysics."

Zorba the Greek met with a favorable reception, although a few critics faulted Kazantzakis for sacrificing the novel's literary aspects—such as a strong plot and individualistic characters—to its philosophical ideas. Other reviewers, however, were enthusiastic, commending the symbolism embodied in Kazantzakis's characterizations of both himself and Zorba. Representing both views was *New Republic* contributor Kimon Friar, who commented, "If read on a literal plane alone, Zorba may be said to have no plot worthy of the name, to be deficient in complexity of characterization, [and] to lack motivation. . . . [But] once the point of view is established, the plan is easily grasped in its magnificent boldness and simplicity, the characters and their actions take on symbolic universality."

Some critics, focusing on Zorba as a literary creation, admired Kazantzakis's success in presenting Zorba's joyful and vital character. "Zorba . . . is funny, ferocious, ingenious, unscrupulous, indomitable, bawdy, sacrilegious and frenzied. Above all, he is terrifyingly, disconcertingly alive," Edmund Fuller asserted in the *New York Times.* "It is in the life force of Zorba himself that [the novel's] uniqueness rests." G. D. Painter offered a similar assessment in the *New Statesman and Nation,* proclaiming *Zorba the Greek* "a novel sweet and elate with sunlight, friendship and happiness, with a life full of both sensations and thoughts; . . . and Zorba, one feels, is among the significant and permanent characters in modern fiction."

After completing *Zorba the Greek* Kazantzakis worked in several capacities as a public servant. In 1945 he became the Greek government's minister of state, and he tried for nearly a year to resolve political differences dividing the government before resigning without success. He also served briefly as minister of education during the ensuing civil war before accepting a post in France in 1947 as director of UNESCO's Translation Bureau, which he held until 1948.

The years from 1948 until Kazantzakis's death in 1957 were the most prolific of his career. During this period he published travel essays, plays, and several novels that explored Christian themes, including *Ho Christos xanastavronetai (The Greek Passion), The Last Temptation of Christ, Ho phtochoules tou Theou (St. Francis),* and *Hoi aderphophades (The Fratricides). The Greek Passion,* Kazantzakis's first novel to probe the nature and meaning of Christ's crucifixion, is not one of the author's best-known fictions, but critics consider it among his most powerful and finely crafted. *The Greek Passion* concerns the inhabitants of Lycovrissi, a Greek village under the domination of the Turks in the 1920s. The novel opens with the village elders casting the townspeople in their roles for the following year's enactment of the crucifixion in the annual passion play, and then successfully encouraging the citizens to turn away a group of Greeks seeking refuge from violent Turkish aggression. After the parts have been distributed, however, the actors begin to assume the identities of their characters, and, as a result, crime, hypocrisy, and prostitution in the village begin to decline. Protagonist Manolios, chosen to play the role of Jesus, offers to sacrifice himself as the murderer of the Turkish ruler's son. Further, when the now-starving refugees return, again asking for protection, Manolios accommodates them in Christian fashion by sharing his land and possessions with them. Manolios's deeds infuriate the village priest, who deems him a heretic and incites the residents to demand that the Turkish officials sentence him to death. The villagers, with the aid of the priest, eventually murder Manolios, thereby creating their own twentieth-century version of Christ's martyrdom.

The Greek Passion's negative portrayal of a modern church more concerned with protecting its power than with following Christ's teachings incurred a negative response from the Greek Orthodox Church; Kazantzakis was nearly excommunicated. Reaction to the English translation was mixed, with some critics admiring the passion displayed by the book's characters, message, and presentation, and others panning the novel's violence and complaining that the work's philosophical content diminishes its dramatic effect. Kazantzakis again faced severe criticism from his compatriots with the publication of *Freedom or Death* in 1954. A nonpartisan rendering of Crete's unsuccessful revolt against Turkish rule in 1889, *Freedom or Death* depicts, according to critic and translator P. A. Bien in his afterword to *The Last Temptation of Christ*, "both the good and bad sides of Greek heroism." For his unemotional portrayal, newspapers reportedly labeled Kazantzakis a traitor to Crete and to Greece.

A year later, Kazantzakis followed *Freedom or Death* with his most controversial novel, *The Last Temptation of Christ*. Kazantzakis described his work on the work, as quoted by Theodore Ziolkowski in *Fictional Transfigurations of Jesus,* as "a laborious, sacred, creative endeavor to reincarnate the essence of Christ, setting aside the dross, falsehood and pettiness which all the churchers and all the cassocked representatives of Christianity have heaped upon this figure, thereby distorting it." A surrealistic fictional biography of Christ, whom Kazantzakis considered to be the supreme embodiment of man's battle to overcome his sensual desires in pursuit of a spiritual existence, the novel focuses on what Kazantzakis imagines as the psychological aspects of Jesus's character and how Christ overcomes his human limitations to unite with God. "In order to mount to the Cross, the summit of sacrifice, and to God, the summit of immateriality, Christ passed through all the stages which the man who struggles passes through," Kazantzakis stated in his prologue to the novel. "That is why his suffering is so familiar to us; that is why we share it, and why his final victory seems to us so much our own future victory. . . . If he had not within him this warm human element, he would never be able to touch our hearts with such assurance and tenderness."

The Last Temptation of Christ offers, according to *Atlantic* contributor Phoebe Adams, "the life story of Jesus of Nazareth, . . . the human events from which the worshipful Gospel account was derived and their meaning to the people who experienced them." The novel—which repeatedly departs from *New Testament* accounts—opens with Jesus working as a cross-builder for the ruling Romans in an attempt to repudiate his divinity. The story follows Jesus's struggle to accept God's will, his increasing strength through his realization that he is the Messiah, the gathering of disciples, his preaching and working miracles, his entry into Jerusalem, and ultimately, his crucifixion, during which he experiences his strongest temptation to abandon his commitment to God. Hanging on the cross, Jesus dreams that a guardian angel rescues him and allows him to reject his role as God's representative on earth and live instead as an ordinary carpenter, husband, and father. In his dream he experiences, according to Nancie Matthews in the *New York Times Book Review,* "erotic bliss and a worldly life." Later, however, Judas Iscariot, whom Jesus had ordered to betray him, appears. Angry that Jesus has not carried out the saving of mankind, Judas accuses Jesus of succumbing to Satan, at which point Jesus awakens and affirms his role as Christ.

Angered by *The Last Temptation of Christ*'s presentation of Christ's humanity, the Greek Orthodox Church branded Kazantzakis a heretic and again threatened to excommunicate him. The book was also placed on the Roman Catholic Index of Forbidden Books, most probably because of its depiction of Jesus's desire to marry and beget children. Criticism of the English translation, like that for *Zorba the Greek,* ranged from the disapproving to the highly laudatory. *Christian Century*'s Kyle Haselden expressed disappointment with Christ's characterization, maintaining that Kazantzakis "writes divinely of that which his human. . . . But in depicting that which is divine the novelist is reduced to the human touch." Adams assessed *The Last Temptation*'s Jesus as a literary figure, noting that "this Jesus is not the assured son of God following a preaccepted path, but a man who, in God's service, . . . assumes something of the character of those epic heroes who choose their deaths—Achilles sailing for Troy under the shadow of the prophecy, or Cuchulainn riding on to battle when he knows his magical luck has left him." More impressed was Matthews, who described *The Last Temptation of Christ* as a "mosaic of all the highlights of the Gospel story, vividly colored by . . . extravagant imagery, which is always richly overflowing but at times is distasteful, too." She concluded, "If the book can be read without prejudice, this will be found a powerfully moving story of a great spiritual victory."

Undaunted by *The Last Temptation of Christ*'s fiery reception, Kazantzakis spent his last years traveling and writing. He died from complications of leukemia in 1957 while returning from a visit to China. Because his conflicts with the church resulted in its refusal to conduct a traditional public funeral mass in Greece, the author was buried quietly in Crete. Several more works, including *Ho phtochoules tou Theou* (*St. Francis*), a fictional rendering of the life of St. Francis of Assisi, and *Hoi aderphophades* (*The Fratricides*), an incomplete novel about an elderly priest in civil-war-torn Greece, were published posthumously, along with the autobiographical *Report to Greco* and several works for children.

Discussing Kazantzakis's significance as a writer, Bien noted in his *Nikos Kazantzakis:* "Those who read only sparingly will most likely find Kazantzakis appealing because of the opinions which he promulgated in everything he wrote—more accurately, because of the way he made these ideas incandescent. For some, the ideas themselves will seem less important than the sincerity . . . with which he wrote them. Others, however, will find that he speaks directly to their own needs. . . . If Kazantzakis is still read [fifty years from now], most likely, it will be because of the basically human, and thus abiding, interest we find in him only when we know his *oeuvre* more or less as a whole. It is doubtful whether future generations will suddenly consider him a superb thinker or craftsman; they may, however, consider him a superb man."

BIOGRAPHICAL/CRITICAL SOURCES:

BOOKS

Bien, Peter, *Nikos Kazantzakis,* Columbia Essays on Modern Writers Pamphlet No. 62, Columbia University Press, 1972.
Kazantzakis, Helen, *Nikos Kazantzakis: A Biography Based on His Letters,* translated from the French by Amy Mims, Simon & Schuster, 1968.
Kazantzakis, Nikos, *The Last Temptation of Christ,* translated with afterword by P. A. Bien, Simon & Schuster, 1960.
Kazantzakis, Nikos, *Report to Greco,* translated by P. A. Bien, Simon & Schuster, 1965.

Kazantzakis, Nikos, *Zorba the Greek,* translated by Carl Wild-man, Simon & Schuster, 1953.
Prevalakis, Pandelis, *Nikos Kazantzakis and His Odyssey: A Study of the Poet and the Poem,* translated by Philip Sherrard, Simon & Schuster, 1961.
Twentieth-Century Literary Criticism, Gale, Volume 2, 1974, Volume 5, 1976, Volume 33, 1985.
Ziolkowski, Theodore, *Fictional Transfigurations of Jesus,* Princeton University Press, 1982.

PERIODICALS

Atlantic, February, 1954; September, 1960.
Book Week, January 3, 1965.
Carnegie Series in English: A Modern Miscellany, Volume X, 1970.
Christian Century, October 5, 1960; September 16, 1962.
Colorado Quarterly, spring, 1964.
Comparative Literature Studies, June, 1969.
Journal of Modern Literature: Nikos Kazantzakis Special Number 2, number 2, 1971-72.
Manchester Guardian, March 20, 1959.
Nation, March 31, 1956.
National Review, October 19, 1965.
New Republic, April 27, 1953; January 25, 1954; December 19, 1964.
New Statesman and Nation, September 6, 1952.
New Yorker, February 4, 1956.
New York Herald Tribune Book Review, January 10, 1954.
New York Times, April 19, 1953.
New York Times Book Review, August 7, 1960; June 10, 1962; June 16, 1963; August 15, 1965; May 5, 1985; September 22, 1985.
Poetry, December, 1959.
San Francisco Chronicle, July 8, 1962.
Saturday Review, January 23, 1954; December 13, 1958; August 6, 1960; February 6, 1965; August 14, 1965.
Time, January 11, 1954.
Times Literary Supplement, December 16, 1965; February 25, 1972.
World Literature Today, spring, 1980.

OBITUARIES:

BOOKS

Current Biography, H. W. Wilson, January, 1958.

PERIODICALS

New York Times, October 29, 1957.

—*Sketch by Emily J. McMurray*

*   *   *

KEATING, H(enry) R(eymond) F(itzwalter) 1926- (Evelyn Hervey)

PERSONAL: Born October 31, 1926, in St. Leonards-on-Sea, Sussex, England; son of John Hervey (a schoolmaster) and Muriel Marguerita (Clews) Keating; married Sheila Mary Mitchell (an actress), October 3, 1953; children: Simon, Bryony (daughter), Piers, Hugo. *Education:* Trinity College, Dublin, B.A., 1952.

ADDRESSES: Home—35 Northumberland Pl., London W2 5AS, England. *Agent*—A. D. Peters & Co., 10 Buckingham St., London WC2N 6BU, England.

CAREER: Mystery writer. Subeditor for *Evening Advertiser,* Swindon, Wiltshire, England, 1952-55, *Daily Telegraph,* Lon-don, England, 1955-57, and *London Times,* London, 1957-60. *Military service:* British Army, 1945-48; became acting lance-corporal.

MEMBER: Crime Writers Association (chairman, 1970-71), Society of Authors (chairman, 1982-84), Detection Club (president, 1985).

AWARDS, HONORS: Golden Dagger Award, Crime Writers Association, 1964, for *The Perfect Murder,* and 1980, for *The Murder of the Maharajah;* Edgar Allan Poe Award, Mystery Writers of America, 1965, for *The Perfect Murder,* and 1980, for *Sherlock Holmes: The Man and His World;* Ellery Queen's Mystery Magazine* short story prize, 1970.

WRITINGS:

MYSTERY NOVELS

Death and the Visiting Firemen, Gollancz, 1959.
Zen There Was Murder, Gollancz, 1960, Penguin, 1963.
A Rush on the Ultimate, Gollancz, 1961, reprinted, Doubleday, 1982.
The Dog It Was That Died (also see below), Gollancz, 1962, Penguin, 1968.
Death of a Fat God, Collins, 1963, Dutton, 1966.
The Perfect Murder, Collins, 1964, Dutton, 1965, reprinted, Academy Chicago Publications, 1983.
Is Skin-Deep, Is Fatal, Dutton, 1965.
Inspector Ghote's Good Crusade, Dutton, 1966.
Inspector Ghote Caught in Meshes, Collins, 1967, Dutton, 1968, reprinted, Academy Chicago Publications, 1985.
Inspector Ghote Hunts the Peacock, Dutton, 1968, reprinted, Academy Chicago Publications, 1985.
Inspector Ghote Plays a Joker, Dutton, 1969, reprinted, Academy Chicago Publications, 1984.
Inspector Ghote Breaks an Egg, Collins, 1970, Doubleday, 1971, reprinted, Academy Chicago Publications, 1985.
Inspector Ghote Goes by Train, Collins, 1971, Doubleday, 1972.
Inspector Ghote Trusts the Heart, Collins, 1972, Doubleday, 1973.
Bats Fly Up for Inspector Ghote, Collins, 1974, Doubleday, 1975.
A Remarkable Case of Burglary, Collins, 1975, Doubleday, 1976.
Filmi, Filmi, Inspector Ghote, Collins, 1976, Doubleday, 1977.
Inspector Ghote Draws a Line, Doubleday, 1979.
The Murder of the Maharajah, Doubleday, 1980.
Go West, Inspector Ghote, Doubleday, 1981.
The Sheriff of Bombay, Doubleday, 1984.
Mrs. Craggs: Crimes Cleared Up, Buchan & Enright, 1985.
Under a Monsoon Cloud, Viking, 1986.
The Body in the Billiard Room, Hutchinson, 1987.
Dead on Time: An Inspector Ghote Mystery, Mysterious Press, 1989.

OTHER NOVELS

The Strong Man, Heinemann, 1971.
The Underside, Macmillan, 1974.
A Long Walk to Wimbledon, Macmillan, 1978.
The Lucky Alphonse, Enigma Books, 1982.
(Under pseudonym Evelyn Hervey) *The Governess,* Doubleday, 1983.
(Under Hervey pseudonym) *The Man of Gold,* Doubleday, 1985.
(Under Hervey pseudonym) *Into the Valley of Death,* Doubleday, 1986.

NONFICTION

(With uncle, Maurice Keating) *Understanding Pierre Teilhard de Chardin,* Lutterworth, 1969.

Murder Must Appetize (literary criticism), Lemon Tree Press, 1975, Mysterious Press, 1981.
Sherlock Holmes: The Man and His World, Scribner, 1979.
Great Crimes, Harmony Books, 1982.
Writing Crime Fiction, St. Martin's, 1986.
Crime and Mystery Fiction: The One Hundred Best Books, Caroll & Graf, 1987, 2nd edition, 1988.

Also author of *Inspector Ghote, His Life and Crimes,* 1989.

EDITOR

(And contributor) *Blood on My Mind: A Collection of New Pieces by Members of the Crime Writers Association about Real Crimes, Some Notable and Some Obscure,* Macmillan, 1972.
Agatha Christie: First Lady of Crime, Holt, 1977.
Crime Writers: Reflections on Crime Fiction, BBC Publications, 1978.
(And contributor) *Whodunit?: A Guide to Crime, Suspense, and Spy Fiction,* Van Nostrand, 1982.

PLAYS

"The Dog It Was That Died" (radio play; based on his novel of the same title), British Broadcasting Corp., 1971.
"The Affair at No. 35" (radio play), British Broadcasting Corp., 1972.
"Inspector Ghote and the All-Bad Man" (radio play), British Broadcasting Corp., 1972.
"Inspector Ghote Makes a Journey" (radio play), British Broadcasting Corp., 1973.
"Inspector Ghote and the River Man" (radio play), British Broadcasting Corp., 1974.
(With Zafar Hai) *The Perfect Man* (screenplay adapted from his own novel), Perfect Movie Productions, 1990.

Also author of "The Five Senses of Mrs. Craggs" (radio play), British Broadcasting Corp.

CONTRIBUTOR

Ellery Queen's Mystery Parade, New American Library, 1968.
George Hardinge, editor, *Winter's Crimes 2,* Macmillan (London), 1970.
Ellery Queen's Murdercade, Random House, 1975.
Hardinge, editor, *Winter's Crimes 7,* Macmillan (London), 1975.
Winn, Dilys, editor, *Murder Ink: The Mystery Reader's Companion,* Workman Publishing, 1977.
Harris, Herbert, editor, *John Creasey's Crime Collection,* Gollancz, 1978.
Symons, Julian, editor, *Verdict of Thirteen,* Harper, 1979.

Also contributor to *Dictionary of National Biography, Twentieth-Century Crime and Mystery Writers, Great Detective Stories,* and *Top Crime.* Contributor of short stories to *Ellery Queen's Mystery Magazine* and *Blackwood's.* Crime book reviewer, *Times* (London), 1967-83.

SIDELIGHTS: His popular series of mystery novels featuring Inspector Ganesh Ghote (pronounced "Go-tee") of the Bombay police have brought H. R. F. Keating acclaim in both England and the United States. Ghote is a unique figure in the mystery genre, a "perturbed, lovable, self-doubting, [and] awkwardly heroic" man, as Anthony Boucher describes him in the *New York Times Book Review.* Ghote has proven popular with mystery fans. The reason for his popularity, J. I. M. Stewart speculates in the *Times Literary Supplement,* is that "unlike the majority of fictional detectives, [Ghote] is a man much like ourselves only more so: diffident, misdoubting his own powers, often sadly muddled by the unaccountable happenings assailing him. But at the same time he is endowed with a dim saving obstinacy and occasional flashes of anger." Keating tells Dale Salwak of *Clues: A Journal of Detection* that he and Inspector Ghote share many of the same traits. "I mean, he is me," Keating declares. "All right, he's Indian and he's a slight figure physically, though tough enough, and I'm not. I'm British and we're miles apart in many ways, but inside him is a lot of me." Newgate Callendar of the *New York Times Book Review* calls Ghote "one of the more endearing personalities of contemporary crime fiction." Writing in the *Library Journal,* H. C. Veit maintains that "Ghote can hardly be over-praised; this prim and unsure little Indian policeman is one of the few classical creations."

Keating's nonfiction writing focuses on the mystery genre, too. The award-winning *Sherlock Holmes: The Man and His World* is a detailed analysis of the rapidly changing English society of the 1890s in which the Sherlock Holmes adventures are set. Keating relates Holmes to his society and shows him to be a product of his time. "Keating observes a duality in Holmes' character: his dedication to law and order and reliance on the 'scientific method' in crime detection reflected the rational, moralistic thought of . . . Victorians . . .; while his cocaine indulgence, expressed admiration . . . [for] avant-garde artists . . ., and interest in bizarre cases reflected his affinity with . . . rebellious Edwardians," Cathy Clancy explains in the *School Library Journal.* In *Whodunit?: A Guide to Crime, Suspense, and Spy Fiction,* Keating provides the mystery genre with a wide-ranging reference tome. It is "one of the best," Jon L. Breen states in the *Armchair Detective,* "including some of the most beautifully written and most penetrating . . . essays on mystery fiction."

Keating told Meera Clark of *Clues: A Journal of Detection* that he uses the crime novel to express his philosophical concerns. "For better or worse," Keating explains, "I really think of myself as a novelist, and I'm using the crime form to say what I have to—I like using it, but I am using it."

MEDIA ADAPTATIONS: A film option for *The Murder of the Maharajah* has been sold.

AVOCATIONAL INTERESTS: "Popping round to the post."

BIOGRAPHICAL/CRITICAL SOURCES:

BOOKS

Bargainnier, Earl F., editor, *Twelve Englishmen of Mystery,* Popular Press, 1984.
Contemporary Authors, Autobiography Series, Volume 8, Gale, 1989.
Keating, H. R. F., editor, *Whodunit?: A Guide to Crime, Suspense, and Spy Fiction,* Van Nostrand, 1982.
Symons, Julian, *Bloody Murder,* Harper, 1972, 2nd edition, Viking, 1985.

PERIODICALS

Armchair Detective, winter, 1986.
Best Sellers, January 15, 1968.
Choice, September, 1977, February, 1980.
Clues: A Journal of Detection, fall/winter, 1983, fall/winter, 1984.
Guardian, May 24, 1974.
Library Journal, September 1, 1972, April 1, 1977.
Los Angeles Times, July 18, 1987, September 5, 1987, November 1, 1987.
New York Times, December 11, 1987, March 2, 1990.
New York Times Book Review, September 12, 1965, May 29, 1966, February 4, 1968, July 16, 1972, May 23, 1976, April 10, 1977, October 18, 1981, November 7, 1982.

Publishers Weekly, October 25, 1985.
School Library Journal, January, 1980.
Time, December 22, 1986.
Times (London), January 7, 1971, August 5, 1978, August 24, 1978, November 7, 1985.
Times Literary Supplement, March 17, 1966, June 15, 1967, December 31, 1971, June 5, 1981, October 29, 1982, October 26, 1984, January 17, 1986, November 28, 1986.
Washington Post Book World, January 16, 1983.
World Press Review, October, 1980.

*   *   *

KEILLOR, Garrison
  See KEILLOR, Gary (Edward)

*   *   *

KEILLOR, Gary (Edward) 1942-
  (Garrison Keillor)

PERSONAL: Known professionally as Garrison Keillor; born August 7, 1942, in Anoka, Minn.; son of John Philip (a railway mail clerk and carpenter) and Grace Ruth (a homemaker; maiden name, Denham) Keillor; married Mary C. Guntzel, September 1, 1965 (divorced May, 1976); married Ulla Skaerved (a social worker), December 29, 1985; children: (first marriage) Jason. *Education:* University of Minnesota, B.A., 1966, graduate study, 1966-68.

ADDRESSES: Agent—Ellen Levine, Ellen Levine Literary Agency, 432 Park Ave. S., New York, N.Y. 10016.

CAREER: Writer. KUOM-Radio, Minneapolis, Minn., staff announcer, 1963-68; Minnesota Public Radio, St. Paul, Minn., producer and announcer, 1971-74, host and principal writer for weekly program "A Prairie Home Companion," 1974-87; host for "Garrison Keillor's American Radio Company of the Air," 1989.

AWARDS, HONORS: George Foster Peabody Broadcasting Award, 1980, for "A Prairie Home Companion"; Edward R. Murrow Award from Corporation for Public Broadcasting, 1985, for service to public radio; Association of Logos Bookstores Book Award for fiction, 1986, for *Lake Wobegon Days;* *Los Angeles Times* Book Award nomination, 1986, for *Lake Wobegon Days;* Grammy Award for best non-musical recording, 1987, for "Lake Wobegon Days."

WRITINGS:

UNDER NAME GARRISON KEILLOR

G.K. the DJ, Minnesota Public Radio, 1977.
The Selected Verse of Margaret Haskins Durber, Minnesota Public Radio, 1979.
Happy to Be Here: Stories and Comic Pieces, Atheneum, 1982, expanded edition, Penguin, 1983.
Lake Wobegon Days, Viking, 1985.
Leaving Home: A Collection of Lake Wobegon Stories, Viking, 1987.
We Are Still Married: Stories and Letters, Viking, 1989.

RECORDINGS

"A Prairie Home Companion Anniversary Album," Minnesota Public Radio, 1980.
"The Family Radio," Minnesota Public Radio, 1982.
"News from Lake Wobegon," Minnesota Public Radio, 1982.
"Prairie Home Companion Tourists," Minnesota Public Radio, 1983.

"Ten Years on the Prairie: A Prairie Home Companion 10th Anniversary," Minnesota Public Radio, 1984.
"Gospel Birds and Other Stories of Lake Wobegon," Minnesota Public Radio, 1985.
"A Prairie Home Companion: The Final Performance," Minnesota Public Radio, 1987.
"Lake Wobegon Loyalty Days: A Recital for Mixed Baritone and Orchestra," Minnesota Public Radio, 1989.

Keillor has also recorded his book "Lake Wobegon Days."

OTHER

(Author of foreword) Bob Eliott and Ray Goulding, *The New Improved! Boy and Ray Book,* McGraw-Hill, 1986.
(Author of introduction) Howard Mohr, *How to Talk Minnesotan,* Penguin, 1987.
(Author of foreword) A. J. Liebling, *The Honest Rainmaker: The Life and Times of Colonel John R. Stingo,* North Point Press, 1989.

Contributor of articles and stories to periodicals, including *New Yorker* and *Atlantic Monthly.*

WORK IN PROGRESS: A novel; more stories.

SIDELIGHTS: With the words "It's been a quiet week in Lake Wobegon, my hometown," radio humorist and author Garrison Keillor introduced his monologue on his long-running Minnesota Public Radio program "A Prairie Home Companion." The stories he told over the air, based partly on his memories of growing up in semi-rural Anoka, Minnesota, were among the highlights of the live-broadcast show—an eclectic mixture of comedy and music (including bluegrass, blues, ethnic folk, choral, gospel, opera, and yodeling)—which reached an audience of about four million listeners per week by the time it went off the air in 1987. It reached a great many more people in its last year when the Disney Channel obtained cable television broadcasting rights.

As principle writer and host of the show, Keillor also revealed his humor in the commercials he wrote for the sponsors of his program, including Ralph's Pretty Good Grocery ("If you can't find it at Ralph's, you can probably get along without it"), Bertha's Kitty Boutique ("For persons who care about cats"), the Chatterbox Cafe ("Where the coffeepot is always on, which is why it always tastes that way"), Bob's Bank ("Neither a borrower nor a lender be; so save at the sign of the sock"), the Sidetrack Tap ("Don't sleep at our bar; we don't drink in your bed"), and especially those Powdermilk Biscuits ("Heavens, they're tasty") that "give shy persons the strength to get up and do what needs to be done."

Many critics place Keillor in the tradition of such American humorists as Ring Lardner, James Thurber, and Mark Twain. Like Twain, who gained a reputation traveling on the American lecture circuit in the last years of the nineteenth and first years of the twentieth century, Keillor's audience originally came from his radio program. Roy Blount, Jr., writing in the *New York Times Book Review* about "A Prairie Home Companion," states that it was "*impossible* to describe. Everyone I have met who has heard it has either been dumbfounded by it, or addicted to it, or both." "The same is true of Keillor's prose," Blount continues, referring to a series of pieces written for the *New Yorker,* and collected in *Happy to Be Here.* However, "many of these pieces," writes Peter A. Scholl in the *Dictionary of Literary Biography Yearbook,* ". . . show the witty and urbane Keillor rather than the wistful, wandering storyteller in exile from Lake Wobegon, where 'smart doesn't count for very much.'"

In 1985, the publication of *Lake Wobegon Days* brought Keillor's small town to national prominence. Beginning with the first explorations of the French traders in the eighteenth century, Keillor goes on to describe the town's history up to the present day. But Lake Wobegon is, according to Mary T. Schmich in the *Chicago Tribune*, "a town that lies not on any map but somewhere along the border of his imagination and his memory." Keillor describes it in *Lake Wobegon Days*: "Bleakly typical of the prairie, Lake Wobegon has its origins in the utopian vision of nineteenth-century New England Transcendentalists, but now is populated mainly by Norwegians and Germans. . . . The lake itself, blue-green and sparkling in the brassy summer sun and neighbored by the warm-colored marsh grasses of a wildlife-teeming slough, is the town's main attraction, though the view is spoiled somewhat by a large grain elevator by the railroad track."

Lake Wobegon, in Keillor's stories, becomes a sort of American Everytown, "the ideal American place to come from," writes Scholl. "One of the attributes of home in Keillor's work is evanescence. . . . Dozens of his stories concern flight from Lake Wobegon, and the title of his radio show gains ironic force with the realization that it was adapted from the Prairie Home Lutheran cemetery in Moorhead, Minnesota; we are permanently at home only when we are gone." Yet "the wonderful thing about Keillor's tone in detailing life as it is lived in Lake Wobegon is not derived from his pathos knowing he can never go home again," Scholl continues. "He refuses to emphasize his status as exile in the novel. The wonder flows from his understanding that the complicated person he has become . . . is truly no step up from the guy down in the Sidetrack Tap he might have been had he never left home in the first place."

Keillor left "A Prairie Home Companion" in June of 1987, deciding that he needed more time to devote to his writing, and, suggests Schmich, in order to escape the unwanted fame that dogged his heels in Minnesota. His next book, *Leaving Home*, consisted of edited versions of his monologues from the last months of the show—many of them about people leaving Lake Wobegon. "Every once in a while," declares Richard F. Shepard in the *New York Times*, "the author slips into a poetic mood and you know he is saying goodbye to a world that was, a goodbye he makes clear as he goes along." The book, Shepard concludes, "says what it has to say with a rare, dry humor that is in what we like to believe is the very best American tradition." "His humor," says Scholl, "is sustained by his comic faith, which like Powdermilk Biscuits, helps readers and listeners 'get up and do what needs to be done.'"

Keillor lived briefly in Denmark with his Danish wife Ulla Skaerved, then returned to the United States and set up a residence in New York City. In 1989, he began a new radio program, "Garrison Keillor's American Radio Company of the Air." Although his latest book, *We Are Still Married*, mostly reprints pieces that appeared originally in the *New Yorker*, he has not yet exhausted his stories about the denizens of his quiet hometown. "In some hidden chamber of our hearts," writes David Black in *Rolling Stone*, "most of us, no matter where we live, are citizens of Lake Wobegon"—the place where, as Keillor has told us, "all the women are strong, all the men are good-looking, and all the children are above average."

BIOGRAPHICAL/CRITICAL SOURCES:

BOOKS

Contemporary Literary Criticism, Volume 40, Gale, 1986.
Dictionary of Literary Biography Yearbook: 1987, Gale, 1988.

Keillor, Garrison, *Lake Wobegon Days*, Viking, 1985.

PERIODICALS

Chicago Tribune, March 15, 1987.
Chicago Tribune Book World, January 24, 1982.
Christian Century, July 21-28, 1982, November 13, 1985.
Country Journal, January, 1982.
Detroit Free Press, September 8, 1985.
Detroit News, September 1, 1985.
Esquire, May, 1982.
New York Times, October 31, 1982, August 20, 1985, October 31, 1985, October 21, 1987.
New York Times Book Review, February 28, 1982, August 25, 1985.
Publishers Weekly, September 13, 1985.
Rolling Stone, July 23, 1981.
Saturday Review, May-June, 1983.
Time, November 9, 1981, February 1, 1982, September 2, 1985, November 4, 1985.
Washington Post, August 23, 1989.
Washington Post Book World, January 18, 1982.

—*Sketch by Kenneth R. Shepherd*

* * *

KELL, Joseph
See WILSON, John (Anthony) Burgess

* * *

KELLER, Helen (Adams) 1880-1968

PERSONAL: Born June 27, 1880, in Tuscumbia, Ala.; died June 1, 1968, in Westport, Conn.; buried at St. Joseph's Chapel in Washington Cathedral, Washington, D.C.; daughter of Arthur H. (an editor) and Kate (Adams) Keller. *Education:* Privately tutored by Anne Sullivan Macy, 1887-1936; studied Braille at the Perkins Institution, 1888-90; attended Horace Mann School for the Deaf, 1890-94; attended the Wright-Humason School for the Deaf, 1894-96; attended Cambridge School for Young Ladies, 1896-97; Radcliffe College, B.A. (cum laude), 1904.

ADDRESSES: Home—Westport, Conn.

CAREER: Author, lecturer, social reformer. Served on the Massachusetts state commission for the welfare of the blind, c. 1903; pioneered open discussion of blindness in the new-born in newspapers and magazines such as *Ladies' Home Journal* and *Kansas City Star*, c. 1905; began lecturing in public for the welfare of the handicapped, 1913; reporter for United Press International, 1913; embarked upon her first transcontinental speaking tour with Anne Sullivan Macy, 1914; made the autobiographical motion picture, "Deliverance," 1919; toured vaudeville with the Orpheum Circuit, 1922-24; founded the Helen Keller Endowment Fund for the American Foundation for the Blind, c. 1930; worked with the war-blinded during World War II; served as counselor on national and international relations for the American Foundation for the Blind and the American Foundation for the Overseas Blind; remained active in social reform movement to aid the handicapped of all nations, traveling and lecturing throughout the world.

MEMBER: National Institute of Arts and Letters (trustee of the American Hall of Fame), Phi Beta Kappa.

AWARDS, HONORS: Order of St. Sava (Yugoslavia), 1931; Theodore Roosevelt Distinguished Service Medal, 1936; General

Federation of Women's Clubs, scroll of honor for pioneer work in the relief of the handicapped, 1941; American Association of Workers for the Blind, distinguished service medal, 1951; National Institute of Social Sciences, gold medal, 1952; Medal of Merit (Lebanon), 1952; Legion of Honor (France), 1952; Southern Cross (Brazil), 1953; Presidential Medal of Freedom, 1964; American Academy of Achievement, golden plate award, 1965; and many other civic, national, and international awards. D.H.L., Temple University, 1931; Litt.D. from University of Delhi and Harvard University, both 1955; LL.D. from University of Glasgow, 1932, University of Witwatersrand, Johannesburg, 1951; M.D., Free University of Berlin, 1955.

WRITINGS:

The Story of My Life, edited by John Albert Macy, Doubleday, Page, 1903, revised and enlarged edition, Hodder & Stoughton, 1966.

Optimism: An Essay, Crowell, 1903 (published in England as *My Key of Life, Optimism: An Essay,* Ibister, 1904), also published as *The Practice of Optimism,* Hodder & Stoughton, 1915.

The World I Live In (essays and poems collected from *Century* magazine), Century, 1908.

The Song of the Stone Wall (poetry), Century, 1910.

Out of the Dark: Essays, Letters, and Addresses on Physical and Social Vision, Doubleday, Page, 1913.

My Religion, Doubleday, Page, 1927.

Midstream: My Later Life (autobiography), Doubleday, Doran, 1929.

Helen Keller in Scotland (autobiography), edited by James Ken Love, Methuen, 1933.

Helen Keller's Journal, 1936-1937 (autobiography), Doubleday, Doran, 1938, reprinted with foreword by Augustus Muir, C. Chivers, 1973.

Let Us Have Faith, Doubleday, Doran, 1940.

Teacher, Anne Sullivan Macy: A Tribute by the Foster Child of Her Mind (biography), introduction by Nella Braddy Henney, Doubleday, 1955.

The Open Door, Doubleday, 1957.

Helen Keller, Her Socialist Years: Writings and Speeches, edited by Philip S. Foner, International Publishers, 1967.

Contributor of numerous articles, poems, and essays to various periodicals, including *Ladies' Home Journal, Atlantic Monthly, Youth's Companion, McClure's,* and *Century.*

MEDIA ADAPTATIONS: A play and several films have been based on the story of Keller's life. "The Miracle Worker" by William Gibson was originally written as a play and was later made into a film. The film version starred Anne Bancroft and Patty Duke, who were named best actress and best supporting actress by the Academy of Motion Picture Arts and Sciences in 1962.

SIDELIGHTS: In February, 1882, Helen, the nineteen-month-old daughter of Arthur and Kate Keller, was rendered unconscious by a severe fever. Helen Keller describes the incident in her autobiography, *The Story of My Life:* "They called it acute congestion of the stomach and brain. The doctor thought I could not live. Early one morning, however, the fever left me as suddenly and mysteriously as it had come. There was great rejoicing in the family that morning, but no one, not even the doctor, knew that I should never see or hear again."

Despite her loss of sight and hearing, Keller learned to do many small tasks such as folding the laundry and fetching objects for her mother. In fact, she devised an effective though limited system of signs to make her wishes known. Keller knew she was dif-

ferent from other people; understandably, the girl's frustration was uncontrollable at times. "Sometimes I stood between two persons who were conversing and touched their lips. I could not understand, and was vexed. I moved my lips and gesticulated frantically without result. This made me so angry at times that I kicked and screamed until I was exhausted."

The Kellers were unable to provide Helen with the specialized training required by a child with her handicaps. As the years passed, she became more willful and less responsive to the guidance of her protective parents. "I was strong, active, indifferent to consequences. I knew my own mind well enough and always had my own way, even if I had to fight tooth and nail for it." When Helen was about six years old, her father took her to Washington, D.C., to be examined by Dr. Alexander Graham Bell. Dr. Bell urged him to write to the Perkins Institution for the Blind in Boston requesting that a competent teacher be sent to Tuscumbia to undertake Helen's education.

In answer to this request, twenty-year-old Anne Mansfield Sullivan, a recent graduate of the Perkins Institution, arrived at the Keller home on March 3, 1887. Sullivan was the daughter of poor Irish immigrants. At an early age she and her younger brother were sent to the infamous Tewksbury almshouse in Massachusetts. She was nearly blind as a result of an eye disease, and had entered the Perkins Institution in 1880. Sullivan knew from her own experience that firmness and determination would be required to teach the undisciplined, though intelligent, Helen. Tempering firmness with love, she spent hours each day teaching Helen the manual alphabet, which the child imitated quickly. It took a great deal of time and perseverance, however, for Sullivan to impress upon Keller the significance of the finger symbols. The moving scene of Keller's discovery that everything has a name has been reenacted time and time again in motion pictures, plays, and dramatizations. Her own description of the incident is quite eloquent: "We walked down the path to the well-house, attracted by the fragrance of the honeysuckle with which it was covered. Some one was drawing water and my teacher placed my hand under the spout. As the cool stream gushed over one hand she spelled into the other the word 'water,' first slowly, then rapidly. I stood still, my whole attention fixed upon the motions of her fingers. Suddenly I felt a misty consciousness as of something forgotten—a thrill of returning thought; and somehow the mystery of language was revealed to me. I knew then that 'w-a-t-e-r' meant the wonderful cool something that was flowing over my hand. That living word awakened my soul, gave it light, hope, joy, set it free! There were barriers still, it is true, but barriers that could in time be swept away."

From that time forward, Keller's curiosity was insatiable and Sullivan's patient perseverance unflagging. Little by little, Keller learned to express herself through the manual alphabet and to read Braille. When Keller was ten years old, Mary Swift Lamson, one of Laura Bridgman's teachers, told Keller about Ragnhild Kaata, a deaf and blind Norwegian child who had been taught to speak. Keller immediately resolved to learn to speak. Sullivan took her to Sarah Fuller, principal of the Horace Mann School for the Deaf. Keller made remarkable progress and eventually learned to speak French and German as well as English. While attending the Wright-Humason School for the Deaf and the Cambridge School for Young Ladies, Keller also studied history, mathematics, literature, astronomy, and physics. Her determination to possess as much knowledge as possible took her to Radcliffe College, from which she graduated, cum laude, in 1904.

Keller's triumph over ignorance was followed by her triumph over public indifference to the welfare of the handicapped. She devoted the rest of her life to the promotion of social reforms aimed at bettering the education and treatment of the blind, the deaf, the mute, and, in effect, all handicapped individuals. The recipient of innumerable humanitarian awards and citations, Keller is credited with prompting the organization of many state commissions for the blind. Her efforts were also very influential in putting an end to the practice of committing the deaf and the blind to mental asylums. In addition, she was a pioneer in informing the public in the prevention of blindness of the newborn. Her candid articles in the *Kansas City Star* and *Ladies' Home Journal* were among the very first public discussions of venereal disease and its relationship to newborn blindness. Keller carried her campaign to improve the condition of the handicapped throughout the world, completing several extensive lecture tours in Europe, Asia, North and South America, and Africa. Keller is universally recognized as one of the foremost humanitarians of the century. Through all the triumphs and trials, Keller's constant companion was her teacher, Anne Sullivan. Even the older woman's marriage to John Albert Macy, the literary critic and editor of Keller's autobiography, did not interrupt the friendship. Sullivan assisted Keller all through her school and college days, manually spelling the lectures and reading assignments into Keller's palm. Later, she accompanied Keller on her lecture tours, giving full support to her pupil and their joint cause of aiding the handicapped. The partnership was ended only at Sullivan's death in 1936.

BIOGRAPHICAL/CRITICAL SOURCES:

AUTOBIOGRAPHY

The Story of My Life, edited by John Albert Macy, Doubleday, Page, 1903, revised and enlarged edition, Hodder & Stoughton, 1966.
The World I Live In, Century, 1908.
Out of the Dark, Doubleday, Page, 1913.
My Religion, Doubleday, Page, 1927.
Midstream: My Later Life, Doubleday, Doran, 1929.
Helen Keller in Scotland, edited by James Kerr Love, Methuen, 1933.
Helen Keller's Journal, 1936-1937, Doubleday, Doran, 1938.
The Open Door, Doubleday, 1957.

BIOGRAPHY

Belck, Jack, *The Faith of Helen Keller: The Life of a Great Woman,* Hallmark Editions, 1967.
Bowie, Walter R., *Women of Light,* Harper, 1963.
Brooks, Van Wyck, *Helen Keller: Sketch for a Portrait,* Dutton, 1956.
Harrity, Richard, and Ralph G. Martin, *Three Lives of Helen Keller,* Doubleday, 1962.
Hickok, Lorena A., *Touch of Magic: The Story of Helen Keller's Great Teacher, Anne Sullivan Macy,* Dodd, 1961.
Lash, Joseph P., *Helen and Teacher: The Story of Helen Keller and Anne Sullivan Macy,* Delacorte, 1980.
Ross, Ishbel, *Journey into Light,* Appleton, 1951.

JUVENILE BIOGRAPHY

Bigland, Eileen, *True Book about Helen Keller,* illustrations by Janet Pullan, Muller, 1957, revised and enlarged edition, S. G. Phillips, 1967.
Brown, Marion, and Ruth Crone, *Silent Storm,* illustrations by Fritz Kredel, Abingdon, 1963.
Davidson, Margaret, *Helen Keller,* Hastings House, 1969.

Graff, Stewart, and Polly A. Graff, *Helen Keller: Toward the Light,* illustrations by Paul Frame, Garrard, 1965.
Hickok, Lorena A., *Story of Helen Keller,* illustrations by Jo Polseno, Grosset, 1958.
Peare, Catherine O., *Helen Keller Story,* Crowell, 1959.
Tibble, John W., and Anne Tibble, *Helen Keller,* illustrations by Harper Johnson, Putnam, 1958.
Waite, Helen E., *Valiant Companions: Helen Keller and Anne Sullivan Macy,* Macrae, 1959.
Wilkie, Katharine E., *Helen Keller: Handicapped Girl,* illustrations by Robert Doremus, Bobbs-Merrill, 1969.
Wymer, Norman, *Young Helen Keller,* Roy, 1965.

PERIODICALS

New York Times Magazine, June 26, 1955, June 26, 1960.

OBITUARIES:

BOOKS

Britannica Book of the Year, Cambridge University Press, 1969.

PERIODICALS

Newsweek, June 10, 1968.
New York Times, June 2, 1968.
Publishers Weekly, June 17, 1968.
Time, June 7, 1968.

*   *   *

KENDRAKE, Carleton
See GARDNER, Erle Stanley

*   *   *

KENEALLY, Thomas (Michael) 1935-

PERSONAL: Born October 7, 1935, in Sydney, Australia; married Judith Martin, 1965; children: two. *Education:* Attended St. Patrick's College, New South Wales.

ADDRESSES: Agent—Tessa Sayle Agency, 11 Jubilee Pl., London SW3 3TE, England.

CAREER: Writer. High school teacher in Sydney, Australia, 1960-64; University of New England, New South Wales, Australia, lecturer in drama, 1968-70. *Military service:* Served in Australian Citizens Military Forces.

MEMBER: Royal Society of Literature (fellow), PEN, Australian Society of Authors (chairman).

AWARDS, HONORS: Miles Franklin Award, 1967, 1968; Captain Cook Bi-Centenary Prize, 1970; Heinemann Award for Literature, Royal Society of Literature, 1973, for *The Chant of Jimmie Blacksmith; Confederates* was chosen as a notable book of 1980 by the American Library Association; Booker McConnell Prize for Fiction, 1982, for *Schindler's Ark; Los Angeles Times* book award for fiction, 1983, for *Schindler's List.*

WRITINGS:

NOVELS

The Place at Whitton, Cassell, 1964, Walker & Co., 1965.
The Fear, Cassell, 1965.
Bring Larks and Heroes, Cassell Australia, 1967, Viking, 1968.
Three Cheers for the Paraclete, Angus & Robertson (Sydney), 1968, Viking, 1969.
The Survivor, Angus & Robertson, 1969, Viking, 1970.
The Dutiful Daughter, Viking, 1971.

The Chant of Jimmie Blacksmith, Viking, 1972.
Blood Red, Sister Rose: A Novel of the Maid of New Orleans, Viking, 1974 (published in England as *Blood Red, Sister Rose,* Collins, 1974).
Gossip from the Forest, Collins, 1975, Harcourt, 1976.
Moses the Lawgiver, Harper, 1975.
Season in Purgatory, Collins, 1976, Harcourt, 1977.
A Victim of the Aurora, Collins, 1977, Harcourt, 1978.
Ned Kelly and the City of the Bees (juvenile), J. Cape, 1978, Penguin, 1980.
Passenger, Harcourt, 1979.
Confederates, Collins, 1979, Harper, 1980.
The Cut-Rate Kingdom, Wildcat Press, 1980.
Schindler's List, Simon & Schuster, 1982 (published in England as *Schindler's Ark,* Hodder & Stoughton, 1982).
A Family Madness, Hodder & Stoughton, 1985, Simon & Schuster, 1986.
The Playmaker, Simon & Schuster, 1987.

PLAYS

Halloran's Little Boat (first produced in Sydney, Australia, 1966), Penguin, 1975.
"Childermass," first produced in Sydney, 1968.
"An Awful Rose," first produced in Sydney at Jane Street Theatre, June 1, 1972.
"Gossip from the Forest," first produced in Sydney in 1983.
"Bullie's House," first produced in 1985.

Also author of television play, "Essington," produced in England, 1974.

OTHER

Outback, Hodder & Stoughton, 1983.
To Asmara, Warner Books, 1989.
(With others) *Australia: Beyond the Dreamland,* Facts on File, 1989.

Co-author of screenplay for the film "Silver City," released in 1985.

SIDELIGHTS: Thomas Keneally's novels are characterized by their sensitivity to style, their objectivity, their suspense, and their diverse subject matter. Whether he is writing a murder mystery or a historical novel, this "honest workman"—as Raymond Sokolov calls him in the *New York Times Book Review*—has consistently demonstrated to critics that he deserves consideration as "one of the most talented of current Australian writers," according to George Steiner in the *New Yorker.*

While discussions of Keneally often emphasize his years spent as a seminary student, only one of his novels focuses directly on the subject. In *Three Cheers for the Paraclete* his protagonist is a "doubting priest," Father James Maitland, who "runs afoul of the local taboos" in a Sydney seminary. He pseudonymously writes a book called "The Meanings of God" and then is asked by the local archbishop to attack it; he invites a cousin and his wife to spend a night in the seminary and is sternly reminded that it is "a house for celibates"; he advises a "psychotic seminarian to consult a psychiatrist." Despite these transgressions, Maitland remains committed to his vocation, at one point saying, "The essential is that I remain in the church." "More anchored to the old order than he realizes," he accepts suspension from the church until he is later allowed to assume a minor post.

As in many of his novels, Keneally presents the characters in *Three Cheers for the Paraclete* objectively and compassionately. "The author does not exaggerate his character portrayals," writes Thomas L. Vince in *Best Sellers.* "Neither the Archbishop nor Bishop-Elect Costello are portrayed as vicious or single-minded men. Nor is Fr. Maitland shown to be a paragon of all virtues brutally exploited by an out-dated Church. What is refreshing about this novel is that the priests and bishops are seen in the fullness of their humanity and that neither Maitland nor his friend, Egan, desert the Church." Richard Sullivan shares this view in the *Washington Post Book World:* "Though this admirably sustained novel makes it clear that some structures are too rigid, that the Church is not unflawed in its members, both clerical and lay, and that more windows need opening, at the same time it reveals with fine objectivity that it is human beings who are at fault, each in his own way, Maitland as much as any."

A similar example of Keneally's desire for objectivity is evident in his account of the St. Joan of Arc story, *Blood Red, Sister Rose.* Bruce Cook of the *Washington Post Book World* claims Keneally's "intent, in fact, seems to be to reduce her and her legend to recognizably human dimensions." Placing Keneally's Joan of Arc in a historical perspective, *Time's* Melvin Maddocks saw her standing between the "Joan-too-spiritual" of the original legend and the "Joan-too-earthy" of George Bernard Shaw. She is "less spectacular than the first two but decidedly more convincing and perhaps, at last, more moving."

Though the subjects of Keneally's novels are diverse, ranging from an eighteenth-century British penal colony in Australia to a World War II medical unit in Yugoslavia, war is often used as a backdrop in his work. After *Blood Red, Sister Rose,* wherein, Cook states, Keneally "seemed determined to write a sort of antihistorical novel, one that would expose the pettiness of war's political basis," Keneally wrote two more wartime novels, *Season in Purgatory* and *Gossip from the Forest.* The first book tells the story of a young English surgeon transferred to a Yugoslavian medical unit in World War II. There, Doctor Pelham confronts assorted horrors of war—wounded soldiers, Nazi bombs, "suicidal attacks" ordered by "lunatic brigadiers"—while being transformed "into a mature, compassionate, politically disenchanted paladin" by his lover, Moja. Again Keneally's skill in character portrayal earns praise from reviewers, but it is not the main characters who capture Jane Miller's attention. "Keneally is interesting about almost everything but his hero and heroine," she writes in the *Times Literary Supplement.* "His language falters into cliche whenever he confronts them. Yet they are surrounded by clusters of men and women, some of whom are startlingly understood and visualized." Writing in *Newsweek,* Margo Jefferson also commends Keneally for perceiving "astutely but not harshly that the most wrenching experiences can leave habits of mind and upbringing intact. The horrors survived in *Season in Purgatory* are all the sharper for not leading to catharsis."

Gossip from the Forest, one of Keneally's most highly praised works, combines fiction and historical event—the signing of the armistice ending World War I. As the delegations from France, England, and Germany convene near Compiegne, France, Keneally's "immediate concern," writes Anne Duchine in the *Times Literary Supplement,* "is to convey the isolation of each man in [the] group, the absolute indifference they feel towards each other." *Newsweek's* Peter S. Prescott explains that "the delegates dream, tell stories, write letters, quarrel among themselves. Keneally is a patient, exploratory writer, content to poke at his characters, to let antagonisms develop. His forest is a fateful place, fit to get lost in, and his characters are all lost one way or another—in stupidity, delusion, desperation. His book is about the crushing effects past attitudes have upon present emergencies. It is not a cheerful story." Ultimately, writes Paul Fussell of the *New York Times Book Review, Gossip from the Forest* "is a study of the profoundly civilian and pacific sensibility beleaguered by crude power. Erzberger [the pacifist and liberal member of the Reichstag who led the German delegation] is intelligent, hopeful, studious, unpretentious, absent-minded and easily bored, and Keneally depicts him as a doomed negotiator with no leverage but personal decency, a knack at sympathy and a flair for language. . . . By the end of the novel we are deeply sympathetic with Erzberger's fate and with Keneally's point, that the twentieth century will not tolerate Matthias Erzbergers. They are civilized, and they are sane."

Perhaps Keneally's most ambitious historical novel is *Confederates*, set during the American Civil War and told from a Southern perspective. The book has no central character, but rather focuses on a group of characters who are involved in the preparations for the Second Battle of Antietam, fought in 1862. Keneally "keeps his canvas as vast as possible," writes John Higgins in the *Times Literary Supplement*, "and his concern is as much with the conscripts as with the captains; the volunteers get just as large a show as the likes of Robert E. Lee and Stonewall Jackson."

Several critics find that Keneally's portrayal of the American South is surprisingly realistic. Jeffrey Burke of the *New York Times Book Review*, for example, writes that it "is almost necessary to remind oneself that the author is Australian, so naturally, intrinsically Southern is the narrative voice." Robert Ostermann of the *Detroit News* states that Keneally's account of the Second Battle of Antietam "deserves comparison . . . to Tolstoy's rendering of the Russian defeat and retreat at Borodino and to Hemingway's of the retreat from Caporetto in *Farewell to Arms*. . . . The fact that this massive, absorbing narrative is the work of an Australian—not a Southerner, not even a native American— testifies even further to the stature of his achievement."

With the publication of *Schindler's List*, which was published in England as *Schindler's Ark*, Keneally found himself embroiled in a controversy over whether his book was fiction or nonfiction, an important point since the book was nominated for the Booker McConnell Prize for Fiction, England's most prestigious literary award. Although the story of Oskar Schindler, a German industrialist during World War II who saved the Jews assigned to work in his factory from Nazi gas chambers, is historical truth, Keneally wrote the book as a novel. "The craft of the novelist," Keneally explains in the London *Times*, "is the only craft to which I can lay claim, and . . . the novel's techniques seem suited for a character of such ambiguity and magnitude as Oskar [Schindler]." After deliberation, the judges decided that *Schindler's Ark* was a novel, and awarded it the Booker McConnell Prize for Fiction.

The controversy over the book is understandable. As Richard F. Shepard of the *New York Times* points out, the real life story of Oskar Schindler "is indeed stranger than fiction." The owner of a German armaments factory staffed with forced Jewish laborers from nearby concentration camps, Schindler made a fortune during the war by supplying the German army with war materials. But when the Nazi regime decided to solve the "Jewish question" through mass extermination of Jewish prisoners, Schindler acted to save as many of his workers as possible. He convinced the local S.S. chief to allow him to house his Jewish workers in a compound built on his factory grounds rather than at a concentration camp "so that their labor [could] be more fully exploited," as Schindler explained it. Through the use of bribes and favors, Schindler worked to reunite his workers with their families, provided them with adequate food and medical care, and even managed to get a particularly murderous S.S. officer transferred to the Russian front. When the Russian army threatened to capture the area of southern Poland where Schindler's factory

was located—and the German army made plans to execute the Jewish workers before retreating—Schindler moved his company and his workers to safety in German-held Czechoslovakia. By the end of the war, Schindler had some thirteen hundred Jewish workers under his protection—far more than he needed to operate his factory—and had spent his entire fortune on bribes and favors.

But despite the singular nature of Schindler's wartime activities, few people after the war knew of Schindler or what he had done. Keneally only learned of the story through a chance meeting with Leopold Pfefferberg, one of the Jews Schindler had saved. "With Pfefferberg's constant help," Keneally told the *New York Times*, "I interviewed almost fifty people who survived, thanks to Schindler." From these interviews Keneally pieced together the full story of Schindler's life for the first time.

Critical reaction to *Schindler's List* was generally favorable. Keneally, writes Christopher Lehmann-Haupt of the *New York Times*, "does not attempt to analyze in detail whatever made Oskar Schindler tick," which Lehmann-Haupt finds "a little disconcerting, considering the novelistic technique he employs to tell his story. But this restraint increases the book's narrative integrity. Because the story doesn't try to do what it can't honestly do, we trust all the more what it does do." Jonathan Yardley of the *Washington Post Book World* feels that the book's major flaw is "the author's insistence on employing devices of the 'new' journalism. . . . But *Schindler's List* has about it a strong, persuasive air of authenticity, and as an act of homage it is a most emphatic and powerful document." Phillip Howard of the London *Times* agrees: "The book is a brilliantly detailed piece of historical reporting. It is moving, it is powerful, it is gripping."

BIOGRAPHICAL/CRITICAL SOURCES:

BOOKS

Contemporary Literary Criticism, Gale, Volume 5, 1976, Volume 8, 1978, Volume 10, 1979, Volume 14, 1980, Volume 19, 1981, Volume 27, 1984, Volume 43, 1987.

PERIODICALS

America, November 13 1976, May 28, 1977.
Best Sellers, July 15, 1968, April 1, 1969, July 1, 1971, August 15, 1972, February 1, 1975, August, 1976, July, 1978.
Books and Bookmen, April, 1968, October, 1972, March, 1974, March, 1979.
Chicago Tribune Book World, December 20, 1980, November 14, 1982, March 2, 1986.
Commonweal, October 24, 1969.
Detroit News, September 28, 1980, November 21, 1982.
Globe and Mail (Toronto), February 4, 1984, May 3, 1986.
Guardian Weekly, March 7, 1976, September 12, 1976.
Kirkus Reviews, March 15, 1971, July 1, 1972, February 1, 1976, November 1, 1976.
Los Angeles Times, November 23, 1983, July 17, 1985, April 7, 1986.
Los Angeles Times Book Review, September 27, 1987.
Nation, November 6, 1972.
National Review, April 29, 1977.
New Statesman, September 1, 1972, October 26, 1973, October 11, 1974, September 19, 1975, September 3, 1976, September 9, 1978, January 19, 1979, November 2, 1979.
Newsweek, April 19, 1976, February 7, 1977, June 18, 1979, March 31, 1986.
New Yorker, February 10, 1975, August 23, 1976, May 23, 1977, May 8, 1978.

New York Times, April 4, 1970, September 9, 1972, October 18, 1982, November 22, 1982, May 17, 1985, March 8, 1986, September 22, 1987.

New York Times Book Review, September 27, 1970, September 12, 1971, January 16, 1972, August 27, 1972, December 3, 1972, February 9, 1975, April 11, 1976, February 27, 1977, October 14, 1977, March 26, 1978, July 8, 1979, October 5, 1980, March 16, 1986, September 20, 1987.

Observer, April 25, 1971, September 10, 1971, November 24, 1974, September 21, 1975, December 14, 1975, September 5, 1976, September 4, 1977, January 21, 1979, October 21, 1979.

Punch, February 28, 1968.

Saturday Review, April 12, 1969, July 24, 1971.

Spectator, March 1, 1968, November 25, 1972, September 7, 1974, November 15, 1975, September 4, 1976, September 3, 1977.

Time, August 16, 1968, June 7, 1971, August 28, 1972, February 10, 1975, March 31, 1986.

Times (London), March 7, 1981, October 20, 1982, October 21, 1982, July 19, 1984, June 14, 1985, October 3, 1985, September 3, 1987, September 4, 1987, February 13, 1988.

Times Literary Supplement, May 7, 1970, April 23, 1971, September 15, 1972, October 26, 1973, October 11, 1974, September 19, 1975, September 3, 1976, October 14, 1977, November 2, 1979, November 23, 1979, December 16, 1983, August 24, 1984, October 18, 1985, December 3, 1987.

Tribune Books (Chicago), September 20, 1987.

Washington Post Book World, April 27, 1969, April 19, 1970, August 29, 1971, August 13, 1972, January 26, 1975, February 20, 1977, March 26, 1978, August 31, 1980, October 4, 1981, October 20, 1982, March 30, 1986.

West Coast Review of Books, July, 1978.

World Literature Today, winter, 1977, autumn, 1978, spring, 1980.

* * *

KENNEDY, John Fitzgerald 1917-1963

PERSONAL: Born May 29, 1917, in Brookline, Mass.; assassinated November 22, 1963, in Dallas, Tex.; buried in Arlington National Cemetery, Arlington, Va.; son of Joseph P. and Rose (Fitzgerald) Kennedy; married Jacqueline Lee Bouvier, September 12, 1953; children: Caroline, John F., Jr., Patrick Bouvier (deceased). *Education:* Attended London School of Economics, 1935-36; Harvard University, B.A. (with honors), 1940; Stanford University, graduate study, 1940.

CAREER: Correspondent, *Chicago Herald-American* and International News Service, covering San Francisco United Nations Conference, Potsdam Conference, and British elections of 1945; U.S. House of Representatives, Washington, D.C., congressman from 11th Congressional District of Massachusetts, 1946-52; U.S. Senate, Washington, D.C., senator from Massachusetts, 1952-60; President of the United States, 1960-63. Member of various Senate committees, 1952-60, including Foreign Relations Committee, Labor and Public Welfare Committee, Joint Economic Committees, and Select Committee to Investigate Improper Activities in the Labor-Management Field; chairman, Subcommittee on Labor. Member of board of overseers, Harvard University, 1957. *Military service:* U.S. Navy, PT boat commander, 1941-45; became lieutenant; received Navy and Marine Corps Medal and Purple Heart.

AWARDS, HONORS: Received numerous honorary degrees, including LL.D. from University of Notre Dame, 1950, Tufts Col-

lege, 1954, Boston University, 1955, Harvard University, 1956, Loras College, Rockhurst College, Boston College, and Northeastern University, and D.Sc. from Lowell Technological Institute, 1956; National Conference of Christians and Jews Annual Brotherhood Award; University of Notre Dame Patriotism Award, 1956; Italian Star of Solidarity of the First Order; "Grande Official" of the Italian government; Greek Cross of the Commander of the Royal Order of the Phoenix; Pulitzer Prize, 1956, American Library Association Notable Book Award, Christopher Book Award, 1956, and Secondary Education board Award, all for *Profiles in Courage.*

WRITINGS:

Why England Slept, Funk, 1940.

(Editor and contributor) *As We Remember Joe,* privately printed, 1945.

Profiles in Courage, Harper, 1956, inauguration edition, 1961, abridged edition for young readers, 1961, memorial edition, 1964, memorial edition for young readers, 1964.

A Nation of Immigrants, Anti-Defamation League of B'nai B'rith, 1959, revised and enlarged edition, Harper, 1964.

John W. Gardner, editor, *To Turn the Tide,* foreword by Carl Sandburg, Harper, 1962.

(Contributor) *Creative America,* Ridge Press, 1962.

(Contributor) Robert A. Goldwin, editor, *Why Foreign Aid?,* Rand McNally, 1963.

America, the Beautiful, Country Beautiful Foundation, 1964.

(With others) *Moral Crisis: The Case far Civil Rights,* Gilbert Publishing Co., 1964.

AUTHOR OF PREFACE, FOREWORD, OR INTRODUCTION

The American Heritage Book of Indians, American Heritage Publishing, 1961.

Robert Johns Bulkley, *At Close Quarters: PT Boats in the World War,* U.S. Government Printing Office, 1962.

Adlai E. Stevenson, *Looking Outward: Years of Crisis at the United Nations,* Harper, 1963.

Theodore C. Sorensen, *Decision-making in the White House,* Columbia University Press, 1963.

OTHER

Speeches published in numerous collections, including *The Strategy of Peace,* edited by Allan Nevins, Harper, 1960; *President Kennedy Speaks,* U.S. Information Service, 1961; *John Fitzgerald Kennedy: A Compilation of Statements and Speeches Made during His Service in the United States Senate and House of Representatives,* U.S. Government Printing Office, 1964; *Spoken Arts Treasury of John F. Kennedy Addresses,* edited by Arthur Luce Klein, Spoken Arts, 1972.

Also author of reports, speeches, addresses, and official papers and correspondence published by U.S. Government Printing Office and other publishers.

SIDELIGHTS: "For the brief time they were in power," states Midge Decter in *Commentary,* "John F. Kennedy and that circle of family, employees, political allies, and friends who after his death were to be dubbed the Court-in-Exile did a good deal more than constitute themselves a new administration. In fact, they swamped the national consciousness. Their arrival in the White House in January 1961 very quickly came to be seen as not a changeover but a breakthrough of some kind. Out of power, they succeeded in becoming a Sword of Damocles hanging over Washington. . . . Out of the mess of an assassination that might have been thought to spell the demise of much more than their now fallen leader, the Kennedy clan somehow managed to impose his two surviving brothers as a certain token of the future. . . . In a way, the Kennedy's peculiar hold over the times became all the more potent as it receded into the realm of the potential. Both remembered from the past and portending the future, they could serve as a general, highly flexible standard of invidiousness with the present."

Furthermore, notes Decter, "the first serious attempt to establish the Kennedy's as at once decisively influential and in the literal sense of the word inconsequential . . . was launched immediately after the death of JFK. In 1965 we were presented with two mammoth inside accounts of the Kennedy administration: Arthur Schlesinger, Jr.'s *A Thousand Days* and Theodore C. Sorensen's *Kennedy,* which invited us to believe that the United States under JFK had passed through three decisive years in which everything, and yet strangely enough, almost nothing happened. Both books frankly admitted to partisanship . . . and both, though in very different ways, set a pattern of apology that would prove of lasting value to the Kennedy movement in the years ahead. . . . To boil the proposition down to plain language, we were asked to judge Kennedy as President by his intentions rather than by his achievements."

This "pattern of apology" has only just begun to be challenged by revisionist historians who have discovered, in the words of a *Newsweek* critic, "that there was a good deal less to Camelot than met the eye." The result, it appears, is that "suddenly nothing seems too bad to say about the Kennedy's. Admirers have had their say—it takes a small library to accommodate it—but apparently there is a literary Newtonian law at work: every idolatrous book has an opposite revisionist work."

For the most part, criticism of John F. Kennedy centers around his basic political method—namely, an arrogance combined with a tendency to "manufacture" international crises situations which he could then appear to resolve, creating an illusion of power and competence in the process. As Decter notes: "Besides elegance and gaiety, that which preeminently characterized the New Frontier was a kind of swashbuckling, an arrogant lack of principle. . . . Kennedy and his 'best and brightest people in the country' swooped down on the White House and tackled its problems in the spirit of the belief that these problems continued to persist only because the 'right' people had never before been let loose on them. . . . Any possibility for a greatness of record, as distinguishable from high style and intention, Kennedy avoided. He took no real leadership except in foreign policy, and even there it was largely a matter of making a personal impression and establishing personal relations. . . . What the Kennedy administration wanted, then, what it sought to do, was to impose an image of itself on American society and American history; an image of itself as the rightful, by virtue of intrinsic superiority, American ruling class."

In his book *The Kennedy Promise: The Politics of Expectation,* Henry Fairlie contends that the Kennedy administration was obsessed with not only the politics of expectation but the "politics of confrontation" as well; in other words, the President and his advisers cultivated and enjoyed the prospects of putting rapid and clever counterinsurgency measures into effect whenever possible. Convinced that domestic problems were, for the most part, settled (or at least in the process of working themselves out), Kennedy focused his efforts on his real concern: "the exaltation of the power of the state." He was, in short, determined to restore the United States to "an elevated sense of national purpose," to help it regain its earlier confident lead over the Soviet Union in science, technology, and armaments. To achieve these goals, Fairlie continues, Kennedy used international crises as "a

spectacular display of his power in a situation of maximum peril. . . . It was at one minute to midnight that the Administration believed the hands of the clock always stood, all over the globe; and they were driven by the fear that, if they did not act before the clock struck, they would all be pumpkins. They aspired to greatness not just occasionally, but all the time. . . . All over Washington men would rise early to answer the bidding to crisis and to greatness, and the still slumbering public would awake in the morning to find that they had been summoned to meet danger once more, and once more to be rescued from it. . . . [Kennedy's] legacy was that he had accustomed the American people to an atmosphere of crisis and taught them to seek confrontation, eyeball to eyeball, within it."

Concludes Fairlie: "One cannot study the Administration of John Kennedy, the men and the measures, without deciding that it was a last confident—almost braggart—assertion of the capacity of American positivism to fulfill the prophecy of American puritanism: that the city of man can be built in the image of the City of God on this earth, and that the response of the American people to this assertion was that of men who wished to believe it. When it failed, there was an assassination to blame; when it failed again, there was yet another assassination."

Arthur Schlesinger, Jr. disputes this view of the Kennedy administration. He writes: "It is true, of course, that Kennedy was by temperament an activist. . . . At the same time, [he] was far from incautious. 'Prudent' was a favorite adjective [of his]. . . . Far from believing that personal leadership was irresistible, Kennedy was by nature a conciliator, which meant among other things that he recognized the legitimacy, or at least the existence, of other points of view. . . . [He] simply did not believe there was an American solution to every world problem. On the contrary, he was keenly aware that nationalism was the strongest political emotion of the time, and his essential purpose in foreign affairs was to adjust American policy to what he called the 'revolution of national independence' he saw going on around the world." Yet this same president who was so "keenly aware" of the strong nationalistic forces of his time, according to David Halberstam in his book, *The Best and the Brightest,* once told James Reston that the Soviet Union's arrogance toward the administration meant that "now we have a problem of trying to make our power credible and Vietnam looks like the place."

James Q. Wilson also defends the Kennedy administration against Fairlie's claims of an imperial presidency. He notes: "Almost every Presidential candidate gives way to bombast and fantastical claims about what government can or should accomplish. . . . The 'imperial' rhetoric Kennedy employed was, substantively at least, very much in tune with the prevailing national consensus at the time. . . . When Kennedy spoke, he spoke for a generation that had been in the war, had shared and shaped that purpose, and that was in no mood to see this country once again turn its back on the world or on the possibility of aggression." Nevertheless, Wilson concludes, "Kennedy was not only a poor, but a mischievous political executive, lacking in any experience in the management of large affairs, overly attentive to the verbal skills of 'gifted amateurs' and 'in-and-outers,' wrongly contemptuous of the federal bureaucracy (or at least contemptuous for the wrong reasons), and persistently inclined to attempt to govern by means of personal intervention and the waging of administrative guerrilla warfare on the slopes of a massive, complex, but not incompetent executive establishment. Kennedy not only sent a few thousand 'advisers' to Vietnam without much sense of what they were supposed to do, or how, or to what end; he also . . . sent them all over the globe and indeed into many parts of our own government."

In addition to condemning a political attitude which led to such confrontations as the Cuban Missile Crisis, critics have also questioned Kennedy's domestic record. Summarizes *Newsweek:* "Kennedy's crisis-mongering caused more than 75,000 bomb shelters to sprout up for 60 million Americans and occasioned such over-staged muscle-flexing as the price-rise showdown with U. S. Steel. . . . [His] impatience, [revisionists] say, betrayed him when it came to the long slog of getting legislation through Congress, and the nation's growing problems in housing, education and urban decay were either overlooked or let slide to the second term that never came. And Kennedy, despite his enormous popularity with black voters, gets only indifferent marks from the historians on the racial issue. His civil-rights bill plowed very shallow furrows, and the support he gave Martin Luther King's nonviolent activism was more cosmetic than substantive."

In another *Newsweek* article, Kenneth Auchincloss concludes that "disputes such as these are bootless and unreal. The Kennedy Administration simply didn't have time to be measured by achievements, real or putative. . . . 'He didn't leave much of a record,' Brandeis historian John Roche says. 'But his contribution was that he turned on a whole series of forces in American politics that had been latent. . . . He was responsible for bringing these forces front and center. After the parade come the street sweepers—they were Johnson.'. . . If the New Frontier was a parade, it was one conducted with high style and gusto, and that was hardly a trivial feature in those years. . . . For style is a crucial element in the U.S. Presidency: without the ability to lead, to inspire, to release potential energies and create a sense of hope, a President seems lacking in something vital to the office."

Tom Wicker, author of a 1964 book entitled *Kennedy without Tears,* reflects in a 1977 *Esquire* article that "even in 1964, I did not argue, in any case, that Kennedy was a great man or even a great President—only that we were going to treat him as if he had been. We have, but not, I think, because of some mass American delusion that in a brief, unfinished term he managed to rank himself with Washington, Jefferson, Lincoln, Roosevelt; rather, his murder was a disillusionment. Merely that he was cut down as he was, on a sunlit day, in the bloody mess of his mortality, might have been enough to establish him forever as the symbol of all our incompleted selves, spoiled dreams, blasted hopes. That, I believe, is the key to his meaning for us. Even Americans mindful of the limitations of John Kennedy's thousand days, and of the later revelations of his follies and fallibilities, look back upon him as to their own lost dreams. He is the most fascinating might-have-been in American history, not just for what he was in his time but for what we made of him—not because of what we were but because of what we thought we were, and know now we'll never be."

BIOGRAPHICAL/CRITICAL SOURCES:

BOOKS

Bishop, Jim, *A Day in the Life of President Kennedy,* Random House, 1964.
Bishop, Jim, *The Day Kennedy Was Shot,* 2nd edition, Crowell, 1972.
Buchanan, T. G., *Who Killed Kennedy?,* Putnam, 1964.
Burns, James MacGregor, *John Kennedy: A Political Profile,* Harcourt, 1960.
Dinneen, Joseph Francis, *The Kennedy Family,* Little, Brown, 1959.
Exner, Judith, *My Story,* Grove, 1977.

Fairlie, Henry, *The Kennedy Promise: The Politics of Expectation,* Doubleday, 1973.
Halberstam, David, *The Best and the Brightest,* Random House, 1972.
Lasky, Victor, *J.F.K.: The Man and the Myth,* Arlington House, 1966.
Lowe, Jacques, *Portrait: The Emergence of John F. Kennedy,* McGraw, 1961.
Manchester, William, *Death of a President,* Harper, 1967.
McCarthy, Joseph Weston, *The Remarkable Kennedys,* Dial, 1960.
Noyes, Peter, *Legacy of Doubt,* Pinnacle Books, 1973.
Schlesinger, Arthur M., Jr., *A Thousand Days,* Houghton, 1965.
Schwab, Peter and J. Lee Shneidman, *John F. Kennedy,* Twayne, 1974.
Sorensen, Theodore C., *Kennedy,* Harper, 1965.
Tregaskis, Richard, *John F. Kennedy and PT-109,* Random House, 1962.
White, Theodore, *The Making of the President: 1960,* Atheneum, 1961.
White, Theodore, *In Search of History: A Personal Adventure,* Harper, 1978.
Wicker, Tom, *Kennedy without Tears: The Man Beneath the Myth,* Morrow, 1964.

PERIODICALS

Commentary, January, 1970, June, 1973.
Esquire, June, 1977.
Harper's, December, 1972, January, 1973.
Newsweek, February 1, 1971, February 12, 1973, November 19, 1973, December 6, 1976, September 18, 1978, October 9, 1978.
New York Times Magazine, September 18, 1978, October 9, 1978.
Saturday Review, May 13, 1961.
Time, January 8, 1973, July 3, 1978, September 18, 1978, November 27, 1978.
Washington Post, August 29, 1987.

*   *   *

KENNEDY, William   1928-

PERSONAL: Born January 16, 1928, in Albany, N.Y.; son of William J. (a deputy sheriff) and Mary (a secretary; maiden name, MacDonald) Kennedy; married Ana Daisy (Dana) Sosa (a former actress and dancer), January 31, 1957; children: Dana, Katherine, Brendan. *Education:* Siena College, B.A., 1949.

ADDRESSES: Office—New York State Writers Institute, State University of New York at Albany, 1400 Washington Ave., Albany, N.Y. 12222. *Agent*—Liz Darhansoff, 1220 Park Ave., New York, N.Y. 10028.

CAREER: Post Star, Glen Falls, N.Y., assistant sports editor and columnist, 1949-50; *Times-Union,* Albany, N.Y., reporter, 1952-56; *Puerto Rico World Journal,* San Juan, assistant managing editor and columnist, 1956; Miami *Herald,* Miami, Fla., reporter, 1957; correspondent for Time-Life publications in Puerto Rico, and reporter for Dorvillier (business) newsletter and Knight Newspapers, 1957-59; San Juan *Star,* Puerto Rico, founding managing editor, 1959-61; full-time fiction writer, 1961-63; *Times-Union,* Albany, special writer, 1963-70, and film critic, 1968-70; book editor of *Look* magazine, 1971; State University of New York at Albany, lecturer, 1974-82, professor of English, 1983—.

Writers Institute at Albany, founder, 1983, director, 1984—. Visiting professor of English, Cornell University, 1982-83. Co-founder, Cinema 750 film society, Rennselaer, N.Y., 1968-70; organizing moderator for series of forums on the humanities, sponsored by the National Endowment for the Humanities, New York State Library, and Albany Public Library. Panelist, New York State Council on the Arts, 1980-83. *Military service:* U.S. Army, 1950-52.

MEMBER: Writers' Guild of America, PEN.

AWARDS, HONORS: Award for reporting, Puerto Rican Civic Association (Miami, Fla.), 1957; Page One Award, Newspaper Guild, 1965, for reporting; the *Times-Union* won the New York State Publishers Award for Community Service, 1965, on the basis of several of Kennedy's articles on Albany's slums; NAACP award, 1965, for reporting; Writer of the Year Award, Friends of the Albany Public Library, 1975; D.H.L., Russell Sage College, 1980; National Endowment for the Arts fellowship, 1981; MacArthur Foundation fellowship, 1983; National Book Critics Circle Award, 1983, and Pulitzer Prize for fiction, 1984, both for *Ironweed;* New York State Governor's Arts Award; honored by the citizens of Albany and the State University of New York at Albany with a "William Kennedy's Albany" celebration, September 6-9, 1984; Before Columbus Foundation American Book Award, 1985, for *O Albany!;* Brandeis University Creative Arts Award, 1986.

WRITINGS:

The Ink Truck (novel), Dial Press, 1969, Viking, 1984.
Legs (novel), Coward, 1975.
(Contributor) *Gabriel Garcia Marquez* (criticism), Taurus Ediciones, 1982.
Billy Phelan's Greatest Game (novel), Viking, 1978.
Getting It All, Saving It All: Some Notes By an Extremist, New York State Governor's Conference on Libraries, 1978.
Ironweed (novel), Viking, 1983.
O Albany!: An Urban Tapestry (nonfiction), Viking, 1983, published as *O Albany! Improbable City of Political Wizards, Fearless Ethnics, Spectacular Aristocrats, Splendid Nobodies, and Underrated Scoundrels,* Penguin, 1985.
(Contributor of essay) *The Capitol in Albany* (photographs), Aperture, 1986.
(With son, Brendan Kennedy) *Charley Malarkey and the Belly Button Machine* (juvenile), Atlantic Monthly Press, 1986.
(With Francis Coppola and Mario Puzo) *The Cotton Club,* St. Martin's Press, 1986.
(Author of introduction) *The Making of Ironweed,* Penguin, 1988.
Quinn's Book, Viking, 1988.

SCREENPLAYS

(With Francis Ford Coppola) "The Cotton Club," Orion Pictures Corporation, 1984.
"Ironweed," Tri-Star Pictures, 1987.

OTHER

Author of unpublished novel *The Angels and the Sparrows;* author of monographs and brochures for New York State Department of Education, New York State University System, New York Governor's Conference on Libraries, Empire State College, Schenectady Museum, and New York State Library. Contributor of short fiction to journals, including *Esquire, San Juan Review, Glen Falls Review, Epoch,* and *Harper's.* Contributor of articles, interviews, and reviews to periodicals, including *New York Times Magazine, New York Times Book Review, Washington Post Book World, New Republic,* and *Look.*

WORK IN PROGRESS: A novel about the Phelan family in the early and mid-20th century.

SIDELIGHTS: Novels by Irish-American writer William Kennedy did not receive much critical attention when they first appeared. He was known primarily as a respected and versatile journalist who had worked for Albany, New York's *Times-Union,* the Miami *Herald,* and Puerto Rico's San Juan *Star.* Columbia Journalism Review writer Michael Robertson cites former editor William J. Dorvillier's comment that Kennedy was "one of the best complete journalists—as reporter, editor, whatever—that I've known in sixty years in the business." But when Kennedy's 1983 novel *Ironweed* won the Pulitzer Prize, his fiction was given new life. Three early novels were reissued and became best sellers. Hollywood also took note. Francis Ford Coppola enlisted him to write the screenplay for *The Cotton Club,* and he wrote screen versions of his three other books.

Journalism plays an important role in most of Kennedy's books. Many of them present fictionalized newspapermen in narrating or supporting roles. The city of Albany, New York also figures prominently in the novels *Legs, Billy Phelan's Greatest Game, Ironweed,* and *Quinn's Book,* as well as his first novel, *The Ink Truck,* and his recent collection of essays, *O Albany!* "Albany is to this gifted writer what the city of Paterson [, New Jersey] was to William Carlos Williams, and like our great laureate of urban plenitude, he wrests from an unlikely source a special kind of lyricism," Joel Conarroe states in *New York Times Book Review.*

O Albany! was written before *Ironweed*'s spectacular reception secured so much long-overdue literary recognition for Kennedy. *O Albany!* is based in part upon a series of articles Kennedy wrote about city neighborhoods for the *Times-Union* in the mid-1960s. *Publishers Weekly* reviewer Joseph Barbato maintains that the essays in *O Albany!* provide readers with a "nonfiction delineation of Kennedy's imaginative source—an upstate city of politicians and hoodlums, of gambling dens and ethnic neighborhoods, which for all its isolation remains, he insists 'as various as the American psyche' and rich in stories and characters." Christopher Lehmann-Haupt agrees in the *New York Times* that "even more absorbing than the detail and the enthusiasm is the raw material of Mr. Kennedy's fiction, present on every page [of the essays]. Even if one doesn't give a damn for Albany, it is always interesting to watch the author's imagination at play in the city and its history, for one is witnessing the first steps in a novelist's creative process." As Kennedy explains in his introduction to *O Albany!,* "I write this book not as a booster of Albany, which I am, nor as an apologist for the city, which I sometimes am, but rather as a person whose imagination has become fused with a single place, and in that place finds all the elements that a man ever needs for the life of the soul."

Kennedy didn't always think of Albany as a rich fictional source. He grew up in Albany, "the only child of a working-class couple from the Irish neighborhood of North Albany," according to a Toronto *Globe and Mail* article, and after graduation from college worked at a small daily before spending two years as a sports writer for an Army weekly. After leaving the Army, he worked for the Albany *Times-Union,* but grew restless with the job. One day, he told *Washington Post* reviewer Curt Suplee, "I got a great interview with Satchmo [Louis Armstrong]. And the editor threw it away. The guy said, 'What the hell, he's just another band leader.'. . . I knew I had to break out." Albany seemed too provincial, Kennedy told Suplee: "I really didn't like Albany—I felt it was an old man's town, moribund, no action."

After moving to Puerto Rico in search of more exotic material, Kennedy found that his distance from Albany helped him to see its more interesting features. The author explained this process to Douglas Bauer of the *Washington Post Book World:* "[As a reporter in Albany] I wrote stories on my day off and they were set in Albany and they were lousy. Then I went away, and worked in Miami and Puerto Rico. In San Juan, I tried the same thing. I wrote stories about Puerto Rico, and I didn't like them, either. Finally, I said, the hell with it, I'm going to write about Albany and it was the first time a place truly engaged me. I think I needed to be in San Juan to sufficiently fictionalize Albany as a place. I started a novel, and every day I amazed myself at how much I knew about the people I was writing about. I had a concern for them. There was a substance to them that made some sense." As Kennedy told *New York Times* writer Susan Chira, "I felt I had probably outgrown Albany, the way you outgrow childhood.... But I hadn't. When I was writing about Puerto Rico, it was o.k., but then I began to write about Albany, and it seemed to come far more easily, with a richness that was absent in the other work. It proved to me I really didn't need to go off to these exotic places. I felt like I didn't have to go anywhere else. It was really a young writer's education in discovering his own turf."

Legs, Billy Phelan's Greatest Game, and *Ironweed* are all set in the Albany of the 1930s. Margaret Croyden states in *New York Times Magazine* that the books "are inexorably linked to [Kennedy's] native city . . . during the Depression years, when Albany was a wide-open city, run by Irish bosses and their corrupt political machine. This sense of place gives Kennedy's work a rich texture, a deep sense of authenticity." Chira adds that Albany, "often dismissed by outsiders as provincial and drab, lives in Mr. Kennedy's acclaimed fiction as a raucous town that symbolizes all that was glorious and corrupt, generous and sordid in the America of the 20's and 30's."

The distinguishing mark of Kennedy as a writer, says *People* contributor Michael Ryan, is that he is "absolutely unsentimental and unsparing." Ryan explains, "In his fictional world, good deeds are not automatically rewarded, love is not eternal, and death is frequent, offhand and cruel. He demurs at the suggestion that he is preternaturally unkind to the gangsters, hoboes, has-beens and almost-were athletes and would-be entertainers who populate his fiction: 'I don't see how you can say that I'm more cruel than God. God is the cruelest cat in town.' " Though Kennedy, who won his success as a novelist despite numerous setbacks and disappointments, has had his share of troubled times, he told Ryan, "my observations and my characters are not equatable with my own life. People keep asking me now, 'Are you going to write books with happy endings?' My answer to that is no."

Kennedy's transition from reporter to novelist began in the 1960s. When master novelist Saul Bellow came to San Juan as writer-in-residence in 1963, Kennedy enrolled in the class. Bellow's encouragement prompted Kennedy to change his position from managing editor of the *Star* to part-time editor so that he could devote his time to writing novels. Publishers rejected the early novels, and when Kennedy returned to Albany to care for his ailing father, he wrote controversial articles for the *Times-Union.* His statements on the poverty and other social problems of the city were seen as criticisms of the local power structure and were branded "un-American." News writing occupied only half of his time; the rest was given to the novels, and finally in

1969, his first official novel *The Ink Truck* was published. He started his next novel, centered on gangster Jack "Legs" Diamond. When a publisher bought the book based on a few chapters, Kennedy immersed himself in exhaustive research for two years, seeking to authenticate the gangster world of the 1920s.

The Ink Truck is a novel about an Albany newspaper strike featuring a main character described by *Time* reviewer R. Z. Sheppard as "a columnist named Bailey, a highly sexed free spirit with a loud checkered sports jacket, a long green scarf and a chip on his shoulder as big as the state capitol." "It is my hope," Kennedy told *Library Journal* in 1969, that *The Ink Truck* "will stand as an analgesic inspiration to all weird men of good will and rotten luck everywhere." The novel, Sheppard relates, culminates in "a poignant conclusion, yet it does not show Kennedy at his full spellbinding power. Much of the book is inspired blarney, fun to read and probably fun to write."

When first published, *The Ink Truck* was generally ignored, but, as Kennedy indicates in *O Albany!,* he began to view his hometown as "an inexhaustible context for the stories I planned to write, as abundant in mythic qualities as it was in political ambition, remarkably consequential greed and genuine fear of the Lord. I saw it as being as various as the American psyche itself, of which it was truly a crucible: It was always a melting pot for immigrants as was New York or Boston, and it epitomizes today the transfer of power from the Dutch, to the English to the ethnic coalitions." Writing in *Village Voice Literary Supplement,* Mark Caldwell summarizes, Albany's "been run by the Dutch, the English, and the Irish, inhabited by trappers, Indians, soldiers, burghers, farmers, canal-workers, and bureaucrats. It's known every form of government from virtual fiefdom under the Dutch patroons to an old-fashioned and still surviving ward-heeling Democratic machine."

This political landscape dominates Kennedy's novels. Kennedy wrote in *O Albany!* that "it was a common Albany syndrome for children to grow up obsessed with being a Democrat. Your identity was fixed by both religion and politics, but from the political hierarchy came the way of life: the job, the perpetuation of the job, the dole when there was no job, the loan when there was no dole, the security of the neighborhood, the new street-light, the new sidewalk, the right to run your bar after hours or to open a cardgame on the sneak. These things came to you not by right of citizenship. Republicans had no such rights. They came to you because you gave allegiance to Dan O'Connell and his party."

Kennedy's knowledge of Albany's political machinery is first-hand. A *Globe and Mail* reporter indicates that Kennedy's "father sold pies, cut hair, worked in a foundry, wrote illegal numbers, ran political errands for the Democratic ward heelers, and was rewarded by the Machine by being made a deputy sherriff." And, as Croyden explains, William Sr. "often took his son with him to political clubs and gambling joints where young Bill Kennedy, with his eye and ear for detail and for the tone and temper of Irish-Americans, listened and watched and remembered." Kennedy, writes Doris Grumbach in *Saturday Review,* "knows every bar, hotel, store, bowling alley, pool hall, and whorehouse that ever opened in North Albany. He knows where the Irish had their picnics and parties—and what went on at them; where their churches were; where they bet on horses, played the numbers, and bet on poker. He can re-create with absolute accuracy the city conversations."

One of the few Kennedy novels that does not rely heavily on firsthand experience is *Legs,* for which he did extensive research on the gangster era. *Legs,* according to Suplee, is a "fictional biography" of Jack 'Legs' Diamond, the "vicious" Irish-American ganster-bootlegger "who in 1931 was finally shot to death" at an Albany rooming house. Kennedy's novel chronicles "'Legs' attempts to smuggle heroin, his buying of politicians, judges and cops," and his womanizing, relates W. T. Lhamon in *New Republic.* A bully and a torturer who frequently betrayed associates, Diamond made many enemies. Several attemps were made on his life, and to many people, he seemed unkillable. Though vicious, Diamond was also a glamorous figure. Legs Diamond, points out Suplee, "evolved into a national obsession, a godsend for copy-short newsmen, a mesmerizing topic in tavern or tearoom. Yet profoundly evil."

While writing the novel, Kennedy told Suplee, he tried to analyze Diamond's appeal: "So why do we like him? *That's* the thing." Kennedy said to Croyden, "Legs is another version of the American Dream—that you can grow up and shoot your way to fame and fortune. On the other hand, the people that live this kind of life are human beings like you or me. People did love Legs Diamond." Suplee notes that "among the book's many answers is Diamond's odd integrity: 'It is one thing to be corrupt. It is another to behave in a psychologically responsible way toward your own evil.' Legs becomes a litmus, huge and hugely awful, at whom folks could gape 'with curiosity, ambivalent benevolence, and a sense of mystery at the meaning of their own response.' "

Kennedy's second novel in the Albany cycle, *Billy Phelan's Greatest Game,* explores the same territory. *Newsweek* reviewer Peter S. Prescott relates, "the year is 1938, the time is almost always after dark, and the characters . . . are constantly reminded of times further past, of the floods and strikes, the scandals and murders of a quarter century before." The plot of the novel is related by reporter Martin Daugherty. Through his eyes, writes Suplee, "we watch Billy—a pool shark, bowling ace and saloon-wise hustler with a pitilessly rigid code of ethics—prowl among Albany's night-town denizens. But when kidnappers abduct the sole child of an omnipotent clan (patterned on the family of the late Dan O'Connell, of Albany's Democratic machine), Billy is pushed to turn informer, and faces competing claims of conscience."

Billy Phelan's Greatest Game received mildly favorable critical attention, as did *Legs,* but didn't sell particularly well; all three of the author's earlier novels sold only a few thousand copies. The first one hundred pages of *Ironweed,* the story of Billy's father who left the family when Billy was nine, were originally accepted by Viking, but the book later lost the marketing backing it needed. In 1979, Kennedy agreed it would be best to submit the novel elsewhere. It was rejected twelve more times, and the author was disillusioned—past fifty and in debt—when Saul Bellow wrote Viking, admonishing them for slighting Kennedy's talent and asking them to reconsider their decision not to publish *Ironweed.* Viking heeded Bellow's letter, in which the Nobel Prize-winner referred to Kennedy's "Albany novels," calling them "a distinguished group of books," Kennedy told *CA.* His editor at the house fell upon the idea of reissuing *Billy Phelan's Greatest Game* and *Legs,* then out of print, for simultaneous publication with *Ironweed,* and he made the occasion a publishing event focusing on the author's long-standing plan to compose a "cycle" of novels.

By itself, *Ironweed* did not appear to be a good publishing risk. The subject matter is relentlessly downbeat. *Ironweed* portrays "the world of the down-and-outer, the man who drifts by the windows of boarding houses and diners with a slouch hat and a brain whose most vivid images are 20 years old," writes *Detroit News* critic James F. Veseley. Other editors had wanted Kennedy

to rewrite *Ironweed* because of the book's unconventional use of language. *New York Review of Books* critic Robert Towers writes that, in *Ironweed,* Kennedy "largely abandons the rather breezy, quasi-journalistic narrative voice of his previous fiction and resorts to a more poetically charged, often surrealistic use of language as he re-creates the experiences and mental states of an alcoholic bum." As Kennedy told a Toronto *Globe and Mail* reporter, "They . . . objected that the book was overwritten, they didn't understand what I was doing in terms of language, they felt that no bum would ever talk like Francis does, or think like he does, that they thought of him only as a bum. They didn't understand that what I was striving for was to talk about the central eloquence of every human being. We all have this unutterable eloquence, and the closest you can get to it is to make it utterable at some point, in some way that separates it from the conscious level of life."

The figures in *Ironweed* are drawn from portraits Kennedy gathered for a nonfiction study of the street people of Albany, called *Lemon Weed.* Rejected by publishers, *Lemon Weed,* a collection of interviews with 'winos,' Kennedy told CA, was set aside while he worked on *Billy Phelan's Greatest Game.* After concentrating on the character Francis Phelan, Billy Phelan's father, the author decided to reshape the *Lemon Weed* material using the fictional Francis's point of view. Thus, "the specifics in 'Ironweed'—the traction strike, professional baseball, Irish immigrant experiences, a vast Irish cemetery, an Irish neighborhood, the Erie Canal and so forth—are the elements of life in Albany," Kennedy told Croyden. "Some people say that 'Ironweed' might have had any setting, and perhaps this is true. But the values that emerged are peculiar to my own town and to my own time and would not be the same in a smaller city, or a metropolis, or a city that was not Irish, or wasn't large enough to support a skid row."

Ironweed, "which refers to a tough-stemmed member of the sunflower family," according to Lehmann-Haupt, "recounts a few days in the life of an Albany skid-row bum, a former major-league third-baseman with a talent for running, particularly running away, although his ambition now, at the height of the Depression, has been scaled down to the task of getting through the next 20 minutes or so." Once Phelan ran from Albany after he threw a rock at a scab and killed him during a trolley strike, setting off a riot, but he was later in the habit of leaving the town and his family to play in the leagues every baseball season. When he accidentally dropped his newborn son—breaking his neck and killing him—while attempting to change the child's diapers, Francis ran from town and abandoned his family for good.

Now Phelan is back in Albany after twenty-two years, reports Towers, "lurching around the missions and flophouses of the city's South End." On a cold Halloween night and the following All Saints' Day in 1938, the weekend of Orson Welles's "War of the Worlds" broadcast, Phelan "encounters the ghosts of his friends, relatives, and murder victims, who shout at him on buses, appear in saloons wearing lapel flowers, talk with him from their graves in St. Agnes's cemetery," relates Caldwell. Kennedy tells two stories in *Ironweed,* Webster Schott observes in the *Washington Post Book World;* the first, he says, "is the gloriously checkered history of Francis Phelan as young lover of the neighbor lady in silk, star of baseball diamonds in Toronto and Dayton, wrathful killer of at least three men, and joyous victim of sin forever on the run. The other is of a newer Francis Phelan emerging during the crucial present of the novel—three days during which Francis moves from shoveling graves to picking rags, loses his Vassar-educated hobo girlfriend and a faithful drinking partner to the ravages of bumming, and finds himself face-to-face in his old house with the wife and children he left.

The purpose of Kennedy's intertwining these narrative lines is to see whether he and we can locate a center around which order can be made of Francis' life. But none holds. What we see is the infinite complexity of personality, the effect of accident, and the awesome force of emotion on our lives."

Kennedy's next novel, *Quinn's Book,* set in pre-Civil War Albany, begins another cycle centered on residents of New York's capitol city. In the beginning, pre-teen narrator Daniel Quinn witnesses a spectacular drowning accident on the banks of the Hudson River followed by a deviant sexual act in which a whore, presumed drowned, miraculously revives. It is also his first meeting with "Maud the wondrous," a girl he saves from drowning who becomes the love of his life. "The end is a whirl of events that include sketches of high life in Saratoga and accounts of horse races, boxing matches and a draft riot," Richard Eder relates in the *Los Angeles Times Book Review.* He continues, "Daniel shocks a fashionable audience with a bitterly realistic account of his Civil War experiences. Hillegond is savagely murdered; her murderer is killed by two owls jointly and mysteriously controlled by Maud and a magical platter owned by Daniel. The two lovers are lushly and definitively reunited." With these events, says Eder, *Quinn's Book* "elevates portions or approximations of New York history—Dutch, English, Irish—into legend."

Most reviews of *Quinn's Book* were favorable. Although George Garrett, writing in Chicago's *Tribune Books* calls *Quinn's Book* "one of the most bloody and violent novels" he has read, the gore is necessary to tell the whole truth about life in Albany, he adds. In this regard, Garrett elaborates, the author's "integrity is unflinching. Yet this is, too, a profoundly funny and joyous story, as abundant with living energy as any novel you are likely to read this year or for a long time to come." Some readers feel that the idiomatic language Kennedy uses to evoke a past era sometimes misses the mark; however, counters T. Coraghessan Boyle in the *New York Times Book Review,* "the language of 'Quinn's Book' rises above occasional lapses, and Quinn, as the book progresses, becomes increasingly eloquent, dropping the convoluted syntax in favor of a cleaner, more contemporary line. And if the history sometimes overwhelms the story, it is always fascinating. . . . Mr. Kennedy does indeed have the power to peer into the past, to breathe life into it and make it indispensible, and Quinn's battle to control his destiny and win Maud is by turns grim, amusing and deeply moving. In an era when so much of our fiction is content to accomplish so little, 'Quinn's Book' is a revelation. Largeminded, ardent, alive on every page with its author's passion for his place and the events that made it, it is a novel to savor." Concludes Toronto *Globe and Mail* reviewer H. J. Kirchhoff, "This is historical fiction suffused with mysticism and myth. . . . *Quinn's Book* is superlative fiction."

Kennedy's work in the movies has also succeeded, by charming audiences and attracting the industry's top performers. In *The Cotton Club,* co-authored with Francis Ford Coppola of "Godfather" fame, characters from gangster-wars of the 1930s cross paths with the stars of the Harlem night club scene. Its main characters are two sets of brothers. Richard Gere, who plays cornet at the club, falls in love with the mistress of mobster boss Dutch Schultz. Like Gere, tap dancer Gregory Hines has to leave his brother-partner behind and go solo to fulfill his ambitions. Both Gere and Hines try to avoid getting caught up in the mob on their way to stardom. The $50 million dollar film, says Sheila Benson in the *Los Angeles Times,* is carried less by the story line than by its "outrageous, joyous musical numbers by the singers, tap dancers, barbecue shouters and showgirls of the Cotton Club. . . . These numbers are integral to the action and each one of them may be show stoppers, but this show never

stops." The film's remarkable scenes, of which there are many, include a state-of-the-art display of tap dancing performed by "a dozen emeritus tappers," love scenes that mix eroticism and the threat of violence, and a "dazzling" conclusion—"Hines' unaccompanied, bravura tap dance that becomes a montage of murder and farewell in which theatricality and reality are finally blurred," Benson notes. Toronto *Globe and Mail* contributor Jay Scott notes that this "mythic movie about movie myths" is as much about "the jazzy showmanship of movie-making" as it is about love and fame in the '30s. Scott explains that the film's effective use of cross-cutting, its "willingness to play with fantasy and reality, with movies and magic, results in one of the most technically exhilarating finales ever shot."

Since *The Cotton Club*'s success, Kennedy told *Esquire,* "I've been offered five or six other projects, but I'm not going to do them. I'd only go through all this for my own books." Argentinian film maker Hector Babenco took interest in Kennedy's Pulitzer winner and talked the author into making it his next feature film. Though generally opposed to foreign directors who try to make films having predominantly American themes, Kennedy was persuaded to work with Babenco because of the director's enthusiasm and complete understanding of the character Francis Phelan. Jack Nicholson plays Phelan opposite Meryl Streep in the film version of *Ironweed.* Haunted by the failures of his past into a life of dereliction, Phelan weaves in and out of the present, encountering ghosts from his past. Babenco excels at reproducing the "surreal dimension [that] is so important to the book and to the movie—the ghosts become materialized," Kennedy told Nina Darnton of the *New York Times.* Though not all reviewers agree with his assessment, the author is also pleased that the actors brought to the screen some of the "poetry" of the novel that was lost in the transition from print to film. He told Darnton, "Meryl and Jack had the ability to draw on elements of the book, to use throw-away lines from certain parts of the story, and with a look, a few words, a way of living in the past and present at the same time, which is what Helen does in the book, they were able to retain the interior life of the characters that might otherwise have been lost." The roles were challenging for the veteran stars, but "the risks paid off," Michael Ryan notes in a *People* article on the making of the film. Film critics in both New York and Los Angeles voted Nicholson Best Actor of 1988; Streep's performance was also highly acclaimed.

Explaining why characters like Francis Phelan interest him, Kennedy told Croyden, "When you take a character into his most extreme condition, you get extreme explanations, and you begin to discover what lurks in the far corners of the soul. I really do believe that that's the way a writer finds things out. I love the surrealistic, the mystical elements of life. There is so much mysteriousness going on in everybody's life." The author also admires the persistence that overcomes hopeless situations. In *Ironweed,* Phelan is the one derelict who is not overcome by the mean circumstances of street life. Kennedy told Suplee, "That's the kind of characters I've been writing about. The refusal to yield to what appears to be fate. If you don't die and you don't quit, then there's a chance."

MEDIA ADAPTATIONS: Ironweed became an Orion release in 1988.

BIOGRAPHICAL/CRITICAL SOURCES:

BOOKS

Contemporary Literary Criticism, Gale, Volume 6, 1976, Volume 28, 1984, Volume 34, 1985, Volume 53, 1989.
Dictionary of Literary Biography Yearbook 1985, Gale, 1986.

Kennedy, William, *Legs,* Coward, 1975.
Kennedy, William, *O Albany! An Urban Tapestry,* Viking, 1983.
McCaffery, Larry and Sinda Gregory, *Alive and Writing: Interviews with American Authors of the 1980s,* University of Illinois Press, 1987.

PERIODICALS

America, May 19, 1984.
Atlantic, June, 1978.
Best Sellers, October 15, 1969.
Book World, April 23, 1978.
Chicago Tribune, January 23, 1983.
Commonweal, October 13, 1978, September 9, 1983.
Detroit News, January 30, 1983, February 26, 1984.
Esquire, March, 1985.
Film Comment, April, 1985.
Globe and Mail (Toronto), September 1, 1984, December 15, 1984, May 21, 1988.
Hudson Review, summer, 1983.
Library Journal, October 1, 1969.
Listener, May 6, 1976.
Los Angeles Times, December 14, 1984.
Los Angeles Times Book Review, December 26, 1982, September 23, 1984, May 22, 1988.
Missouri Review, Volume 3, number 2, 1985.
New Republic, May 24, 1975, February 14, 1983.
Newsweek, June 23, 1975, May 8, 1978, January 31, 1983, February 6, 1984.
New Yorker, February 7, 1983.
New York Review of Books, March 31, 1983.
New York Times, January 10, 1983, September 17, 1983, December 23, 1983, September 22, 1984, March 12, 1987, July 19, 1987, September 18, 1987, December 13, 1987, May 16, 1988.
New York Times Book Review, January 23, 1983, November 13, 1983, January 1, 1984, September 30, 1984, October 2, 1986, May 22, 1988.
New York Times Magazine, August 26, 1984.
Observer, October 20, 1969.
Paris Review, winter, 1989.
People, December 24, 1984, January 18, 1988.
Publishers Weekly, December 9, 1983.
Recorder, winter, 1985.
Saturday Review, April 29, 1978.
Time, January 24, 1983, October 1, 1984, December 17, 1984.
Times Literary Supplement, October 5, 1984.
Tribune Books (Chicago), May 8, 1988.
Village Voice Literary Supplement, February, 1983, October, 1984.
Washington Post, October 5, 1969, May 18, 1975, December 28, 1983.
Washington Post Book World, January 16, 1983, January 29, 1984, October 14, 1984, May 8, 1988.

*   *   *

KENNY, Charles J.
See GARDNER, Erle Stanley

*   *   *

KENYATTA, Jomo   1891(?)-1978

PERSONAL: Name originally Kamau wa Ngengi; baptized as Johnstone Kamau, 1914; known subsequently as Johnstone Kenyatta and Jomo Kenyatta; born c. October 20, 1891 (some sources say 1889, 1890, 1893, 1897, or 1898), in Ichaweri (some sources say Ngenda), British East Africa Protectorate (now Kenya); died August 21 (some sources say August 22), 1978, in Mombasa, Kenya; son of Muigai (a small farmer and herdsman) and Wambui; married Grace Wahu, November 28, 1922; married Edna Grace Clarke (a schoolteacher and governess), May 11, 1942; married third wife, Grace; married fourth wife, Ngina; children: (first marriage) Peter Mugai, Margaret Wambui; (second marriage) Peter Magana; (third marriage) Jane Wambui; (fourth marriage) Uhuru, Muhoho, Nyokabi (some sources say a total of four sons and four daughters). *Education:* Attended Woodbroke College, 1931-32; studied in Moscow, U.S.S.R., c. 1932; attended London School of Economics and Political Science, c. 1936.

CAREER: Courier for sisal company in Nairobi, British East Africa Protectorate (now Kenya), c. 1915; interpreter for Supreme Court in Nairobi, 1919; stores clerk and water meter reader for city of Nairobi, 1922-28; Kikuyu Central Association, general secretary beginning in 1928, envoy in London, England, beginning in 1929; University of London, London, England, assistant in phonetics at School of Oriental and African Studies, beginning in 1933; farm worker in England and lecturer for British Army and Workers' Educational Association, c. 1939-45; Independent Teachers' College, Githunguri, Kenya, vice-principal, 1946-47, principal, beginning in 1947; president of Kenya African Union (political party), beginning in 1947; imprisoned at Lokitaung, Kenya, 1953-59; detained in Lodwar, Kenya, 1959-61, and Marlal, Kenya, 1961; president of Kenya African National Union (political party), beginning in 1961; Government of Kenya, Nairobi, member of Legislative Council representing Fort Hall, beginning in 1962, minister of state for constitutional affairs and economic planning, 1962-63, prime minister and minister for internal security and defense, 1963-64, president, 1964-78. Helped organize fifth Pan-African Congress in Manchester, England, 1945; co-founder of Organization of African Unity. Actor in film "Sanders of the River," 1935.

MEMBER: International African Friends of Abyssinia (co-founder and honorary secretary), International African Service Bureau.

AWARDS, HONORS: Knight of Grace in Order of St. John of Jerusalem, 1972; Order of Golden Ark from World Wildlife Fund, 1974; honorary fellow of London School of Economics and Political Science; honorary doctorates from Victoria University of Manchester and University of East Africa.

WRITINGS:

(Contributor) Nancy Cunard, editor, *Negro Anthology,* privately printed, 1934.
Facing Mount Kenya: The Tribal Life of the Gikuyu, introduction by Bronislaw Malinowski, Secker & Warburg, 1938, Vintage, 1962, AMS Press, 1978.
(With Lilias E. Armstrong) *The Phonetic and Tonal Structure of Kikuyu,* Oxford University Press, 1940.
My People of Kikuyu and the Life of Chief Wangombe, United Society for Christian Literature, 1942, Oxford University Press, 1966.
Kenya: The Land of Conflict, Panaf Service, 1945, International African Service Bureau, 1971.
Harambee! The Prime Minister of Kenya's Speeches, 1963-1964, From the Attainment of Internal Self-Government to the Threshold of the Kenya Republic, foreword by Malcolm MacDonald, edited by Anthony Cullen, Oxford University Press, 1964.

Suffering Without Bitterness: The Founding of the Kenya Nation, East African Publishing House, 1968.

The Challenge of Uhuru: The Progress of Kenya, 1968 to 1970; Selected and Prefaced Extracts From the Public Speeches of Jomo Kenyatta, President of the Republic of Kenya, East African Publishing House, 1971.

Founder and editor of *Muigwithania,* 1928-30. Contributor to periodicals, including *Daily Worker, Labour Monthly, Manchester Guardian, Negro Worker,* and *Sunday Worker.*

SIDELIGHTS: Jomo Kenyatta led the newly independent African nation of Kenya from 1964 until his death in 1978. He grew up in a traditional African culture as a member of Kenya's largest ethnic group, the Kikuyu. (His exact age is a matter of conjecture because the Kikuyu classified themselves by age-group, ignoring an individual's birthday.) Son of a small farmer and herdsman, Kenyatta saw firsthand how black Africans suffered when white settlers took over their land. As a young man Kenyatta moved to the capital city of Nairobi, where he held a succession of minor jobs. In 1928 he became general secretary of the Kikuyu Central Association (KCA), which sought to improve the living conditions of the Kikuyu under British rule, and as part of his job he traveled widely among his people. The periodical he edited for the association, *Muigwithania,* is believed to be the first black journal in Kenya. The next year Kenyatta went to England as a KCA representative, lobbying successfully for independent Kikuyu schools and unsuccessfully for land reform.

Kenyatta spent most of the next seventeen years in England, promoting the cause of black Kenyans in a wide variety of forums. He wrote letters to the Colonial Office and articles for British periodicals, joined Pan-African groups such as the International African Service Bureau, and lobbied influential guests at London cocktail parties. He commiserated with black activists such as Paul Robeson, famous American singer and actor; W. E. B. Du Bois, a leader of America's National Association for the Advancement of Colored People; and Kwame Nkrumah, future president of Ghana. Traveling widely in Europe, Kenyatta studied for several months at an institute in Moscow that hoped to inspire Communist revolutionaries. (When he later became president of Kenya, however, he declared his country unsuitable for communism.) Some of Kenyatta's political concerns are summarized in the short work *Kenya: Land of Conflict.*

Although Kenyatta never earned a bachelor's degree, he became a graduate student in anthropology at the London School of Economics and Political Science in the mid-1930s, turning a series of papers he wrote about Kikuyu culture into the book *Facing Mount Kenya.* The work uses the format and terminology of a Western scholarly study, devoting chapters to religion, education, sexual practices, and land ownership. But *Facing Mount Kenya* is also a defense of Kenyatta's African background, for it suggests that European influence had harmed the Kikuyu, whose culture at its most untouched was as worthy of respect as that of Europe. In the *New York Times Book Review,* John Barkham said that Kenyatta's eagerness to defend his people had compromised his work, but the *Times Literary Supplement* praised the book as "very readable and highly instructive," noting that Kenyatta had maintained professional standards and had stated his opinions with "due restraint." *Facing Mount Kenya* has been reprinted several times since it first appeared, and in 1953 *Christian Science Monitor* reviewer Marian Sorenson suggested that the book remained a useful background source for understanding black complaints against colonial rule.

Kenyatta returned to Kenya in 1946 and was elected president of a prominent political party, the Kenya African Union. He championed a reform program that included voting rights for blacks, an end to racial discrimination, and a more equitable distribution of land. At the same time, however, a black clandestine movement known as the Mau Mau began efforts to force the British from Kenya, murdering a small number of white settlers and many blacks suspected of collaborating with the white regime. British authorities, already concerned by Kenyatta's political prominence, became convinced that he was involved with the Mau Mau despite his public repudiation of its violence. Arrested in 1952, Kenyatta was tried and sentenced to prison as a Mau Mau organizer. Many sources cast doubt on the state's case against him.

As opposition to the colonial regime continued, the British resigned themselves to Kenya's eventual independence. Kenyatta, who remained highly popular while in prison and detention, was released from exile in a remote province in 1961. He was soon elected president of Kenya's largest political party, the African National Union, and led his country to independence in 1964. Kenyatta's national agenda, which included giving blacks a more balanced share of the Kenyan economy and creating a sense of social unity, is reflected in *Harambee,* a collection of his speeches. The book was named for Kenyatta's political rallying cry—Swahili for "let us all pull together!"

Although Kenyatta insisted that Kenya become a one-party state and suppressed rivals to his personal rule, his political philosophy was notably pragmatic. Certain speeches in *Suffering Without Bitterness* outline Kenyatta's doctrine of "African socialism"—an eclectic mixture of individual initiative and concern for the common good. Assessing Kenyatta's career in *New Times,* Charles Mohr wrote that the Kenyan leader's "admirers and critics alike had come to see him as perhaps the leading exponent in Africa of moderate politics [and] laissez-faire economics." Kenyatta allowed nonblacks to remain and contribute their skills to the new country. The economy prospered, and with government encouragement blacks increasingly entered the fields of business and large-scale farming, helping to create Africa's largest black middle class. The press was "nearly free," as Kenneth Labich and James Pringle wrote in *Newsweek.* Kenyatta remained interested in Pan-Africanism, helping to found the Organization of African Unity and a short-lived common market with the neighboring states of Uganda and Tanzania.

Although Kenyatta faced recurrent political discontent—including complaints that he countenanced nepotism and official corruption—when he died in 1978 commentators generally held that he was a great asset to his country and would be difficult to replace. "The Kenya he governed," Mohr asserted, "is today one of the most . . . free societies on the continent."

BIOGRAPHICAL/CRITICAL SOURCES:

BOOKS

Arnold, Guy, *Kenyatta and the Politics of Kenya,* Dent, 1974.
Murray-Brown, Jeremy, *Kenyatta,* Allen & Unwin, 1972, Dutton, 1973, 2nd edition, Allen & Unwin, 1979.

PERIODICALS

Christian Science Monitor, August 27, 1953.
New York Times, August 22, 1978.
New York Times Book Review, September 6, 1953.
Times Literary Supplement, March 11, 1939.

OBITUARIES:

PERIODICALS

Newsweek, September 4, 1978.

New Times, September 18, 1978.
New York Times, November 6, 1978.
Time, September 4, 1978.

* * *

KEROUAC, Jack
See KEROUAC, Jean-Louis Lebrid de

* * *

KEROUAC, Jean-Louis Lebrid de 1922-1969
(Jean-Louis Incogniteau, Jean-Louis, Jack Kerouac,
John Kerouac)

PERSONAL: Born March 12, 1922, in Lowell, Mass.; died October 21, 1969, of a stomach hemorrhage in St. Petersburg, Fla.; buried in Lowell, Mass.; son of Leo Alcide (a job printer) and Gabrielle-Ange (a shoe-factory worker; maiden name, Levesque) Kerouac; married Frankie Edith Parker, August 22, 1944 (marriage annulled, 1945); married Joan Haverty, November 17, 1950 (divorced); married Stella Sampas, November 18, 1966; children: (second marriage) Jan Michele Hackett. *Education:* Attended Horace Mann School for Boys, New York, N.Y.; attended Columbia College, 1940-42; attended New School for Social Research, 1948-49. *Religion:* Roman Catholic.

CAREER: Writer. Worked at odd jobs in garages and as a sports reporter for the Lowell (Mass.) *Sun,* 1942; was a railroad brakeman with the Southern Pacific Railroad, San Francisco, Calif., 1952-53; traveled around the United States and Mexico; was a fire lookout for the U.S. Agriculture Service in northwest Washington, 1956. *Military service:* U.S. Merchant Marine, 1942 and 1943. U.S. Navy, 1943.

MEMBER: Authors Guild, Authors League of America.

AWARDS, HONORS: American Academy of Arts and Sciences grant, 1955.

WRITINGS:

(Under name John Kerouac) *The Town and the City,* Harcourt, 1950, reprinted under name Jack Kerouac, Grosset, 1960, reprinted, Harcourt, 1978.
(Under name John Kerouac) *Visions of Gerard* (also see below), Farrar, Straus, 1963, reprinted under name Jack Kerouac, McGraw, 1976.

Contributor to *Columbia Review* (under pseudonym Jean-Louis Incogniteau) and to *New World Writing* (under pseudonym Jean-Louis).

NOVELS; UNDER NAME JACK KEROUAC

On the Road, Viking, 1957, reprinted, Penguin, 1987, critical edition with notes by Scott Donaldson published as *On the Road: Text and Criticism,* Penguin, 1979.
The Dharma Bums, Viking, 1958, reprinted, Buccaneer Books, 1976.
The Subterraneans (also see below), Grove, 1958, 2nd edition, 1981.
Doctor Sax: Faust Port Three, Grove, 1959, reprinted, 1988.
Maggie Cassidy: A Love Story, Avon, 1959, reprinted, McGraw, 1978.
Excerpts from Visions of Cody, New Directions, 1959, enlarged edition published as *Visions of Cody,* McGraw, 1972.
Tristessa, Avon, 1960 (published in England with *Visions of Gerard,* Deutsch, 1964), reprinted, McGraw, 1978.
Big Sur, Farrar, Straus, 1962, reprinted, McGraw, 1981.

Desolation Angels, Coward, 1965.
Satori in Paris (also see below), Grove, 1966, reprinted, 1988.
Vanity of Duluoz: An Adventurous Education, 1935-46, Coward, 1968.
Pic, Grove, 1971 (published in England with *The Subterraneans as Two Novels,* Deutsch, 1973; published with *Satori in Paris,* Grove, 1986).

Also author, with William S. Burroughs, of unpublished novel "And the Hippos Were Boiled in Their Tanks," and of unpublished novels "The Sea Is My Brother," "Buddha Tells Us," and "Secret Mullings about Bill."

POETRY; UNDER NAME JACK KEROUAC

Mexico City Blues: Two Hundred Forty-Two Choruses, Grove, 1959, reprinted, 1987.
Hugo Weber, Portents, 1967.
Someday You'll Be Lying, privately printed, 1968.
A Lost Haiku, privately printed, 1969.
Scattered Poems, City Lights, 1971.
(With Albert Saijo and Lew Welch) *Trip Trap: Haiku along the Road from San Francisco to New York, 1959,* Grey Fox, 1973.
Heaven and Other Poems, Grey Fox, 1977.
San Francisco Blues, Beat Books, 1983.
Hymn: God Pray for Me, Caliban, 1985.
American Haikus, Caliban, 1986.

SOUND RECORDINGS; UNDER NAME JACK KEROUAC

"Jack Kerouac Steve Allen Poetry for the Beat Generation," Hanover, 1959.
"Jack Kerouac Blues and Haikus," Hanover, 1959.
"Readings by Jack Kerouac on the Beat Generation," Verve, 1959.

OTHER; UNDER NAME JACK KEROUAC

(Contributor) *January 1st 1959: Fidel Castro,* Totem, 1959.
Rimbaud, City Lights, 1959.
The Scripture of the Golden Eternity (philosophy and religion), Corinth Books, 1960, new edition, 1970.
Book of Dreams, City Lights, 1961.
(Author of introduction) *The Americans,* photographs by Robert Frank, Grove, 1960, revised and enlarged edition, 1978.
Lonesome Traveler (autobiography), McGraw, 1960, reprinted, Grove, 1989.
(Ad lib narrator) *Pull My Daisy* (screenplay), Grove, 1961.
A Pun for Al Gelpi (broadside), [Cambridge], 1966.
A Memoir in Which Is Revealed Secret Lives and West Coast Whispers, Giligia, 1970.
Two Early Stories, Aloe Editions, 1973.
Home at Christmas, Oliphant, 1973.
Old Angel Midnight, Unicorn Bookshop, 1976.
(With Allen Ginsberg) *Take Care of My Ghost, Ghost* (letters), Ghost Press, 1977.
Une veille de Noel, Knight, 1980.
(With Carolyn Cassady) *Dear Carolyn: Letters to Carolyn Cassady,* Unspeakable Visions, 1983.

Also author of *Before the Road: Young Cody and the Birth of Hippie,* and of *Not Long Ago Joy Abounded at Christmas,* 1972. Author of pamphlet, "Nosferatu (Dracula)," New York Film Society, 1960. Contributor to periodicals, including *Ark-Moby, Paris Review, Evergreen Review, Big Table, Black Mountain Review,* and *Chicago Review.* Contributor of regular column, "The Last Word," to *Escapade,* 1959-61.

SIDELIGHTS: Jean-Louis Lebrid de Kerouac became famous as Jack Kerouac, author of *On the Road,* the novel that is considered the quintessential statement of the 1950s literary movement known as the Beat Generation. *On the Road* described the growing friendship of two men, Sal Paradise and Dean Moriarty, and their criss-crossing journeys over the American continent. On a deeper level, it was the story of the narrator's search for religious truth and for values more profound than those embraced by most of mid-twentieth-century America. In both form and subject *On the Road* was completely unlike the formal, elitist fiction that dominated the era, and it was ridiculed accordingly by Kerouac's contemporaries in the literary establishment, who viewed it as "an insane parody of the mobility of automotive America," wrote Dennis McNally in *Desolate Angel: Jack Kerouac, the Beat Generation, and America.* The book spoke to many readers, however, expressing their own unarticulated dissatisfaction with the repressive climate of the United States after World War II. "It is difficult, separated as we are by time and temper from that period, to convey the liberating effect that *On the Road* had on young people all over America," wrote Bruce Cook in *The Beat Generation.* "There was a sort of instantaneous flash of recognition that seemed to send thousands of them out into the streets, proclaiming that Kerouac had written their story, that *On the Road* was their book." More and more people took their cue from Kerouac's novel and adopted a lifestyle that emphasized personal freedom over social conformity, expanded consciousness over material wealth. The mass media jokingly referred to these modern Bohemians as "beatniks" and portrayed Kerouac as their leader. In this position he achieved a celebrity status uncommon for a novelist, but it was an uncomfortable role for Kerouac, a shy, insecure man ill-equipped to deal with fame. As the scattered beat scene evolved into the hippie counterculture of the 1960s, Kerouac continued to be named the progenitor of it all, but by that time he had withdrawn from public life, frustrated by critics' continuing attacks on his work. It was not until several years after his death that Kerouac began to be recognized as an important artist, one who, according to *Midwest Quarterly* contributor Carole Gottlieb Vopat, has "provided an enduring portrait of the national psyche; like Fitzgerald, he has defined America and delineated American life for his generation."

Kerouac was born to French-Canadian parents in the working-class "Little Canada" neighborhood of Lowell, Massachusetts, a mill town some thirty miles northwest of Boston. He spoke only French until the age of seven, and his French-Canadian heritage, along with the Roman Catholic faith in which he was raised, strongly influenced him throughout his life. He was a highly imaginative child who created a private world of racing stables and sports teams, then wrote his own newspapers to report their performances. Diaries, radio plays, and a novel entitled "Jack Kerouac Explores the Merrimack" were some of his other childhood writing projects. He was an excellent student, and by the time he entered Lowell High School, he was also developing into a gifted athlete. It was his performance on the high school football team that provided his ticket out of Lowell: he was offered a football scholarship to Columbia University. New York City was a world away from Lowell. Forty percent of Kerouac's home town received some form of public assistance, but at the Horace Mann School (where he spent a year preparing for Columbia's Ivy League standards) his classmates were the heirs to Manhattan's fortunes. Kerouac seemed amusingly rustic to them, but he was well-liked, and his new friends guided his explorations of the city. He found its vibrance and diversity inspirational.

He had a checkered career at Columbia. A broken leg kept him from playing much football in 1940, and his 1941 season was marked by disagreements with his coach. Furthermore, Kerouac was beginning to feel deeply troubled by the great shift in morals brought about by the Second World War. A whole way of life seemed to be vanishing, and as McNally observed, "Studying and practicing seemed trivial exercises in an apocalyptic world." Late in 1941 Kerouac left the university for a hitch in the Merchant Marine. In his off-duty hours he read the works of Thomas Wolfe and worked on a novel he called "The Sea Is My Brother." He returned briefly to Columbia in 1942, left to join the Navy, then found himself unable to submit to the military discipline of that service. This earned him some time in the psychiatric ward of Bethesda Naval Hospital, but he eventually received an honorable discharge for "indifferent character." Kerouac reentered the less-regimented Merchant Marine for some time before returning to New York City, although not to Columbia. It was at this time that he began to meet the people who would profoundly influence the rest of his life and his work—the people who would in fact be the core of the Beat Generation.

"Cutting away the amateurs, the opportunists, and the figures whose generational identification was fleeting or less than wholehearted on their own part, the Beat Generation—as a literary school—pretty much amounts to Kerouac and his friends William Burroughs and Allen Ginsberg," suggested Barry Gifford and Lawrence Lee in *Jack's Book: An Oral Biography of Jack Kerouac.* Allen Ginsberg was a seventeen-year-old Columbia freshman when he and Kerouac first met. Later he would write the most famous Beat poem, "Howl." The two became like brothers, excitedly discussing their literary and philosophical ideas. Several years older than Kerouac, William Burroughs was a shadowy figure who had worked as an adman, a detective, an exterminator, and a bartender. He would eventually publish the novels *Junky* and *Naked Lunch.* Now he served as Kerouac's tutor, introducing him to the works of Spengler, Nietzsche, and Celine. He also provided an intimate introduction to the underground society of Times Square, to morphine, and to amphetamines.

Though very different in temperament and experience, these three men were alike in their detachment from the values that characterized most of the United States in the 1940s. They regarded with suspicion the rapid growth of bureaucracy and technocracy, which most Americans considered proof of their country's global supremacy. McNally related that when Hiroshima and Nagasaki were destroyed by atomic bombs, "two million hysterical New Yorkers surged into Times Square drunk with joy," but Kerouac and his friends were less enthusiastic about the awesome new bomb. In fact, Burroughs symbolically dressed himself in a crimson devil's suit to join the celebrating crowd in Times Square. "Seen in the blinding glare of the mushroom cloud, this new nation was hell as far as [Kerouac] was concerned," wrote McNally. "The war had left the federal government tripled in size and corporate assets doubled, with an accompanying increase in 'efficiency' and a decrease in the visionary and human qualities that Jack prized." Rejecting the blind patriotism of the moment, the three men groped for what Ginsberg called the "New Vision," a set of values that would make sense to them in the post-atomic world. McNally stated that "their tutors [were] the renegades of high culture like Yeats, Rimbaud, and Baudelaire—[men who] had abandoned politics and religion for beauty."

In 1945 their intense talk, the mood of nihilistic despair, and Kerouac's heavy use of benzedrine took their toll. Thrombophlebitis made his legs swell painfully, and he was confined to a hospital bed. His father and mother had come to New York in search of factory work two years earlier; now Leo Kerouac began to die a painful death of stomach cancer. Released from the hospital, Jack returned not to his intellectual friends in the city, but to his parents' shabby home in Ozone Park. For many months he cared for his father, who berated his son for his aimless life, his worthless friends and his foolish artistic aspirations. On his deathbed Leo repeatedly made Jack swear to support his mother, and Jack promised that he would.

It was in the hope of fulfilling that promise that he returned to his mother's home after Leo's burial and began working on a new novel, an idealized autobiography that would be published in 1950 as *The Town and the City*. This book "reflected his return to family, replacing the New Vision aura of symbolic decadence with the style of his first love, Thomas Wolfe," remarked McNally. "The work was underlaid not only with his new insight into death but with the idealism of Goethe's autobiography *Dichtung und Wahrheit* (*Poetry and Truth*), Kerouac's main reading matter that summer and fall. . . . Goethe calmly rejected satire and preached an affirmative love of life, and more, told Jack that all of his work was merely 'fragments of a great confession'. . . . Jack worked at his own confession . . . for two years, grimly struggling from morning until late at night to recite the history of the Kerouacs and America."

Stretches of work on *The Town and the City* were broken by occasional visits to friends in New York, and on one such trip, Kerouac met the man who would inspire some of his best work. Neal Cassady was the motherless son of a derelict from Denver, Colorado. Cassady grew up in a series of skid row hotels, eating in missions, begging quarters for his father, and avoiding his brutal older brothers. He had been born in an automobile, and he was fourteen years old when he stole his first car. Cassady quickly became addicted to the feeling of freedom he experienced behind the wheel. By the time he was twenty-one, he'd stolen five hundred cars, been arrested ten times, convicted six times, and spent fifteen months in jail. Nightmares of his father's wasted life tormented Cassady in prison, but he found relief by reading philosophy. In 1947 he arrived in New York City, hungry for knowledge and hoping to enter Columbia. Cassady's nervous energy generated an almost constant stream of ideas, talk, and action. Kerouac admired him because he'd retained his tremendous enthusiasm for living in spite of his deprived childhood, and found his openness refreshing "after seven years of cynical East Coast sophistication," commented McNally. "Twenty-year-old Neal swept into [Kerouac's] life like a Wild West siren singing freedom, kicks, a 'wild yea-saying overburst of American joy,' as Jack characterized him, enthusiastically flying after food and sex like a holy primitive, a 'natural man'; he was the embodiment of Jack's American dream."

The two men quickly developed an intense friendship, but when Cassady's plan to enter Columbia collapsed, he returned to Denver. Four months later, Kerouac took a break from his work on *The Town and the City* to hitchhike west and join his friend. Once there, he found Cassady preoccupied by his love affairs with his mistress, his estranged fifteen-year-old wife, and Allen Ginsberg, so Kerouac continued on to San Francisco alone, then returned to New York by bus. This first of many restless journeys around the United States provided Kerouac with the ending he needed for *The Town and the City*. The finished book opened with a lyrical re-creation of a New England childhood, featuring a large, happy family with strong foundations. War scatters the family, however, and eventually even its anchor, the father, must tear up his roots and move to the city. His death there symbolized the final destruction of the idyllic way of life evoked in the novel's first half. In a final scene which prefigured the *On the Road* story, the most promising son turned his back on conventional success and took to the open road in search of a new way of life. *The Town and the City* was cordially reviewed upon its publication in 1950. Although there were objections to the message implied in the novel's closing scene, most critics noted the book's vitality and praised its style as powerful and evocative.

Kerouac was elated to be a published novelist, but by the time *The Town and the City* appeared he was struggling with his next book. Its subject was Neal Cassady. Kerouac wanted this new novel to reflect the fevered pace of modern life; the gracious prose he'd used in *The Town and the City* was inappropriate for that purpose. After several false starts, Kerouac found the inspiration for a new style in the letters he received from Cassady. Kerouac remembered them in a *Paris Review* interview with Ted Berrigan as "all first person, fast, mad, confessional, completely serious, all detailed." In one 40,000-word letter, Cassady described his seduction of a woman he met on a bus. It read "with spew and rush, without halt, all unified and molten flow; no boring moments, everything significant and interesting, sometimes breathtaking in speed and brilliance," as McNally quoted Ginsberg. Kerouac decided to model his book about Cassady on the style of these letters. Instead of revising, he would let the story assume its own shape, allowing details and impressions to accumulate as they do in life. Threading a long roll of paper through his typewriter so he would not have to pause at the end of each page, Kerouac sat down in April, 1951, to pour out the story of his friendship with Cassady. In twenty days he had completed a 175,000-word, single-spaced paragraph that was the first version of *On the Road*. McNally assessed the author's output: "The sentences were short and tight, clickety-pop word bursts that caught the rhythm of the high-speed road life as no author before him ever had. . . . [The book was] bursting with energy, with a feeling of life struggling inside a deathly society, energy burning bright before the laws of entropy and the nation caught up."

"Spontaneous prose" was Kerouac's name for the high-speed writing method he was developing. *Dictionary of Literary Biography* contributor George Dardess explained what this style symbolized to the author: " 'Spontaneous prose' was the way by which the inner mind, trapped as Kerouac finally felt it to be by social, psychological, and grammatical restrictions, could free itself from its muteness and take verbal shape in the outside world. The result of this liberation would not be chaotic, however, since the inner mind was innately shapely and would cause the words with which it expressed itself to be shapely. . . . Spontaneous prose became a metaphor for the paradoxes of the human condition as Kerouac, the Roman Catholic, conceived it: hopelessly corrupted and compromised, yet somehow, in ways only indirectly glimpsed and never fully understood, redeemable, even in the midst of its sin." Spontaneous prose had contemporary parallels in music and the visual arts, noted McNally: "At roughly the same time and place and in response to the same stimuli—a world at once accelerating and constricting—the painter Jackson Pollock and the musician Charlie Parker had accomplished similar revolutions in their own art forms. . . . All three men were working-class sons of matrifocal families who refused to 'adjust' to the conformist society of mid-century or the accepted styles of their disciplines, and for their efforts were labeled psychopaths and falsely associated with violence. Each ignored the critical authorities in their field and stood emotionally naked before their audiences, spewing words, notes, or paintdrops that were like the fiery rain of a volcano: The rain captured the passing moment in a luminous veil of particulars that depicted the universal as an expression of the artist's own self. . . . [Parker] played with the raw energy of a high-power line, and it was that stabbing electricity that Jack had attempted to put into *On the Road,* that mortal sense that the candle must burn furiously, else the times will surely snuff it out."

After retyping his giant roll of manuscript, Kerouac confidently submitted it to Robert Giroux, the editor who had handled *The Town and the City.* Giroux rejected it, becoming the first of many editors to do so. Part of the problem was the experimental prose, but even after Kerouac had reluctantly revised the manuscript to read in a more conventional style, he was unable to sell *On the Road.* The greatest barrier to its acceptance was the author's empathy with social outcasts. Kerouac wrote of the dignity and spirituality of blacks, Mexicans, hobos, and even drug addicts. His attitudes denied "complacency and middle-class notions of propriety and status"; they "seemed incomprehensible in 1957," wrote John Tytell in *Naked Angels: The Lives and Literature of the Beat Generation.* "One of the readers for Viking Press, for example, while appreciating Kerouac's lavish power, was dismayed by the raw sociology of the book, finding in it the quintessence of 'everything that is bad and horrible about this otherwise wonderful age we live in.' The characters were irredeemable psychopaths and hopeless neurotics who lived exclusively for sensation. This judgment, delivered prior to publication, can stand as a sign of how those born before the war would see the book."

On the Road was apparently unpublishable, but Kerouac remained passionately committed to his confessional style. In fact, the six years between *On the Road's* completion and its publication were the most productive of the author's life. He began a series of novels which he thought of as one vast story, in the tradition of Proust's *Remembrance of Things Past.* As he moved between New York, San Francisco, and Mexico City, Kerouac paused for intense writing sessions that yielded more than eight books, including *Tristessa, Doctor Sax: Faust Part Three,* and *Visions of Cody.* In them he told the stories of his family and friends, striving to do so with complete emotional honesty. His approach could be exhausting. For example, he wrote *The Subterraneans* in response to his breakup with a woman he called "Mardou Fox" in his book. On the day Kerouac realized their affair was over, he swallowed some benzedrine, inserted a roll of teletype paper in his typewriter, and in three days produced what is considered one of his best novels. Kerouac characterized that effort to Berrigan as "really a fantastic athletic feat as well as mental. . . . After I was done . . . I was pale as a sheet and had lost fifteen pounds and looked strange in the mirror." Kerouac was able to maintain unswerving faith in the value of his own writing, but he was tormented by the fact that no publisher would accept his work during those years. In 1954 he found a measure of relief from his frustration in his study of Buddhist texts. "It does not seem difficult to explain Kerouac's attraction to Buddhism," mused Dardess. "Torn as he often was by the paradox of God's seemingly simultaneous presence and absence in the world he saw, Kerouac could seize with relief on Buddhism's annihilation of the paradox." Through his later novels, the author was one of the first people to introduce the concepts of Buddhism to the American public.

While Kerouac remained largely anonymous, some of his friends were becoming well known. In 1952 John Clellon Holmes published an article entitled "This Is the Beat Generation," using a term Kerouac had offhandedly coined to compare modern feelings of disillusionment with those of the Lost Generation writers. In 1955 Allen Ginsberg and other poets gave an influential reading at the Six Gallery in San Francisco, and were subsequently featured in a widely-read issue of *Evergreen Review.* Ginsberg's "Howl" was the subject of a highly-publicized obscenity trial in

1956. By that year there was sufficient public awareness of the emerging Beat writers for Viking Press to risk purchasing *On the Road,* after Kerouac agreed to extensive cuts, revisions, and name changes (Kerouac is "Sal Paradise" in the novel and Neal Cassady is "Dean Moriarty"). Its 1957 publication was hailed as "a historic occasion" in the *New York Times* by Gilbert Millstein, the editor who had earlier commissioned Holmes's "This Is the Beat Generation" article. He wrote: " 'On the Road' is the most beautifully executed, the clearest and most important utterance yet made by the generation Kerouac himself named years ago as 'beat,' and whose principal avatar he is. Just as, more than any other novel of the Twenties, 'The Sun Also Rises' came to be regarded as the testament of the 'Lost Generation,' so it seems certain that 'On the Road' will come to be known as that of the 'Beat Generation'. . . . There are sections . . . in which the writing is of a beauty almost breathtaking. There is a description of a cross-country automobile ride fully the equal, for example, of the train ride told by Thomas Wolfe in 'Of Time and the River.' There are details of a trip to Mexico . . . that are, by turns, awesome, tender and funny. . . . 'On the Road' is a major novel."

Most critics perceived the book in a different light, however. McNally summarized: "The *Times Book Review* waffled, first praising the book as 'enormously readable and entertaining,' then dismissing it as 'a sideshow—the freaks are fascinating although they are hardly part of our lives'. . . . It was 'verbal goofballs' to *Saturday Review,* 'infantile, perversely negative' to the *Herald Tribune,* 'lack[ed] . . . seriousness' to *Commonweal,* 'like a slob running a temperature' to the *Hudson Review,* and a 'series of Neanderthal grunts' to *Encounter.* The *New Yorker* labeled Dean Moriarty 'a wild and incomprehensible ex-convict'; the *Atlantic* thought him 'more convincing as an eccentric than as a representative of any segment of humanity,' and *Time* diagnosed him as a victim of the Ganser Syndrome, whereby people weren't really mad—they only seemed to be." McNally concluded: "To understand *On the Road* one somehow needed an affinity for the intuitive and the sensual, for the romantic quest as opposed to the generally analytic realm of the critics. Since most critics had never experienced anything like the *Road,* they denied its existence as art and proclaimed it a 'Beat Generation' tract of rebellion, then pilloried it as immoral." "According to the critics who wrote these reviews, ecstasy, when it occurred in a noninstitutional setting like the backseat of a car, was indistinguishable from mental and physical illness, filth, incoherence, deceit, criminal violence, degeneracy, and mindless folly," concurred Dardess. "This assumption said much, for those who had ears to hear it, about the depth of those critics' fears of their emotions and of their pride in the narrow limits of their intellects. But it did not say much of anything about *On the Road.*"

Readers ignored the critics' negative appraisal of Kerouac and made *On the Road* a best seller for many weeks. The book came "at just the right time" to trigger a powerful response, William Burroughs told *Washington Post* interviewer Henry Allen. "The alienation, restlessness and dissatisfaction were already there," and *On the Road* offered a rallying point for the discontented; the book became a symbol for a rapidly evolving social movement. Kerouac was suddenly a celebrity, faced with many offers to explain the beat phenomenon in lecture halls, on radio, and on television. Public speaking was a nerve-wracking ordeal for him, but he did his best to publicize his novel. Unfortunately, these engagements often ended with Kerouac "uselessly trying to explain mystical poetry to pragmatic reporters who wanted nothing from him but hot copy," suggested McNally. The adulation of his fans proved even harder for him to cope with than the hostility of his critics. More than once, the writer was mobbed by crowds who came to hear him read. "Abuse he could comprehend, but not the blankness of an image-blinded fan," observed McNally. Kerouac began drinking heavily, and "the private person inside him began to crumble. . . . Even immersed in his booze, 'my liquid suit of armor, my shield which not even Flash Gordon's super ray gun could penetrate,' it was difficult for him to talk with people. Hungover and trembling, he groaned to John Holmes, 'I can't stand to meet anybody anymore. They talk to me like I wasn't me.' The fans wanted Jack to be Dean Moriarty, the free American cowboy, the limitless man who lived on life's mental frontiers. What no one beyond friends knew was that *On the Road* was six years old and superseded by a body of work Jack considered superior. Worse still, the Great God Public had condemned Jack to the easy-to-catalogue stereotype role of the bohemian novelist; evermore, he would be the King of the Beats."

Kerouac's stack of unpublished manuscripts ranged from the tender memories of a brother who died in childhood, simply expressed in *Visions of Gerard,* to the baroque surrealism of *Doctor Sax: Faust Part Three,* a novel of guilt and shadows. All of it was deemed unpublishable by *On the Road*'s editor. "Viking was not interested in bringing out a quirky legend, merely books," observed Gifford and Lee. Kerouac responded to the demand for a saleable manuscript with ten days of writing that produced *The Dharma Bums.* According to Gifford and Lee, *The Dharma Bums* was written "with an air of patient explanation, as though addressed to a book editor." Just as *On the Road* focused on Neal Cassady, *The Dharma Bums* provided a portrait of Gary Snyder, a poet and student of Oriental religions who had become Kerouac's friend in 1955. Viking again insisted that names be changed to avoid possible lawsuits, so Kerouac appeared as "Ray Smith," Snyder as "Japhy Ryder." *The Dharma Bums* characterized Ray and Japhy as modern religious wanderers in search of dharma, or truth. It is especially notable for Japhy Ryder's speech describing his vision of "a great rucksack revolution" of millions of young Americans, all becoming "Dharma Bums refusing to subscribe to the general demand that they consume . . . all that crap they didn't really want anyway such as refrigerators, TV sets, . . . certain hair oils and deodorants and general junk you finally always see a week later in the garbage anyway." It was an accurate prophecy of the hippies of the next decade.

The rest of Kerouac's work was published piecemeal, and never appeared as the interconnected series of novels he envisioned. *The Subterraneans, Doctor Sax: Faust Part Three, Maggie Cassidy: A Love Story, Mexico City Blues, Tristessa,* and *Lonesome Traveler* all came out within two years, most of them as inexpensive paperbacks. "Despite the fact that these titles included some of his strongest and most original spontaneous extended narrative, especially *Doctor Sax,* . . . the critics paid less and less attention to [Kerouac] as a serious writer in the furor over the emergence of the beat generation [as a social phenomenon]," wrote Ann Charters in the *Dictionary of Literary Biography.* Alfred Kazin's comments on *The Dharma Bums* typify most critics' dismissal of Kerouac as an artist. Kazin wrote in *Harper's:* "It is ridiculous that novels can now be sent off as quickly as they are written and published immediately afterwards in order to satisfy the hopped-up taste of people who, when they open a novel, want to feel that they are not missing a thing. The sluttishness of a society whose mass ideal seems to be unlimited consumption of all possible goods and services is the reason for the 'success' of writers [like Kerouac]."

Kerouac was unable to finish any writing projects for almost four years after completing *The Dharma Bums* late in 1958. He made several false starts, but even in his mother's house, his privacy was invaded by reporters and teenaged admirers who slipped through his bedroom window to steal his journals. By 1960, "the words had stopped," wrote Gifford and Lee. His subject had always been his own life, but "Jack found himself unable to translate what had happened to him since *On the Road* was published into a novel. . . . If he remained true to his aim of 'one vast book,' he would have to tell the story of a man incapable of dealing with his own success, unable to begin a family of his own, to find peace, to tend his art." Kerouac retreated to the tranquillity of a friend's cabin in California's remote Big Sur region, but once there he suffered a serious alcoholic breakdown, including a series of terrifying hallucinations of himself as a prize in a war between angels and devils. It took him a year to recuperate from the experience, but it provided him with the material for what Gifford and Lee referred to as "his capstone novel," *Big Sur,* "his single book dealing with the effects of the fame which had destroyed him." Ironically, when *Big Sur* was published in 1962 "it received excellent reviews, perhaps because it portrayed the 'King of the Beats' brought low, perhaps because of its frightening honesty."

But the joy had gone out of writing for Kerouac, as he told Ted Berrigan in a *Paris Review* interview: "I had a ritual once of lighting a candle and writing by its light and blowing it out when I was done for the night . . . also kneeling and praying before starting . . . but now I simply hate to write. . . . Frankly I do feel my mind is going. So another 'ritual' as you call it, is to pray to Jesus to preserve my sanity and my energy so I can help my family: That being my paralyzed mother, and my wife, and the ever-present kitties. . . . What I do now is write something like an average of 8,000 words a sitting, in the middle of the night, and another about a week later, resting and sighing in between. I really hate to write." Kerouac became increasingly reclusive throughout the 1960s, and in 1969, he died of a stomach hemorrhage caused by chronic alcoholism.

Several years after Kerouac's death, his book *Visions of Cody* was published. Like *On the Road, Visions of Cody* was a prolonged meditation on Neal Cassady. In fact, the opening section was one of the false starts Kerouac made on the story that eventually became *On the Road. Visions of Cody* covered the same events as Kerouac's most famous book, but it was written in a style so unusual that he'd only been able to publish excerpts of it during his lifetime. When printed in its entirety in 1973, the book prompted *New York Times* reviewer Anatole Broyard to "propose, once and for all, a pox on 'spontaneity' in fiction. Spontaneity is a psychological, not a literary, quality. . . . The notion that what comes naturally is naturally welcome is one of the great idiocies of our age. What is 'Visions of Cody' about? Well, I've read it and I'm damned if I know." But while reviews like Broyard's echoed the hostility of Kerouac's original critics, more of them reflected a growing respect for the author's work. Aaron Latham's *New York Times Book Review* assessment of *Visions of Cody* began by stating that " 'On the Road' was the 'Huckleberry Finn' of the mid-20th century," and went on to compare Kerouac to Thomas Wolfe, Louis-Ferdinand Celine, Mark Twain, and Jean Genet. "You will find some of Kerouac's very best writing in this book," summarized Latham. "It is funny. It is serious. It is eloquent. To read 'On the Road' but not 'Visions of Cody' is to take a nice sightseeing tour but to forgo the spectacular rapids of Jack Kerouac's wildest writing." Numerous biographies and scholarly works on Kerouac began appearing in the late 1970s, indicating that a complete reassessment of his literary output was taking place.

"Probably no famous American writer has been so mishandled by critics, who with few exceptions ignored the larger design in Kerouac's books, the integrity of his theme of individualism, his romantic optimism and his reverence for life, as well as the remarkable energy and humor of his novels, the originality of his prose method and the religious context of all his writing," declared Ann Charters in the *Dictionary of Literary Biography.* Kerouac's early detractors often referred to both his plots and his narrative voice as monotonous, but Charters challenged that judgement, calling his body of work "one of the most ambitious projects conceived by any modern writer in its scope, depth, and variety." Tytell commented similarly: "In so many ways there is something essentially American about Kerouac's writing; his restless energies could never settle for a final form, and each of his novels demonstrates an eager variety in their differences from each other, and from conventional expectations of what novels should be like."

Kerouac is now ranked among America's most important novelists by many commentators. Seymour Krim told the *National Observer,* "The only way you can understand Kerouac is as an American phenomenon. He is in the great American tradition of fiction from Thomas Wolfe right back through Mark Twain to Herman Melville. He did a lot to bring our fiction back home. His wild enthusiasm for all that is right and wrong with the country is really unique." Latham also emphasized Kerouac's role in revitalizing twentieth-century American prose: "When an effete literary language . . . threatened to silence all other voices, Kerouac . . . discovered the vernacular."

Kerouac's freedom with language is generally acknowledged as a liberating influence on many writers who came after him, including Ken Kesey, Charles Bukowski, Tom Robbins, and Richard Brautigan, as well as songwriter Bob Dylan. His nakedly confessional style led to the subjective reportage or "New Journalism" of Hunter S. Thompson and Tom Wolfe. Latham related that "when 'On the Road' made Jack Kerouac famous, [Truman] Capote delivered his famous one-liner: 'That's not writing, it's just typewriting.' But would he have written 'In Cold Blood' as a non-fiction novel if Jack Kerouac had not helped to make the form respectable?"

Finally, although Kerouac came to bitterly resent being cast as a social figurehead, his novels did make a significant impact on the lives of many who read them. According to Tytell, "On the Road still has a large and growing audience. For many, it was the book that most motivated dissatisfaction with the atmosphere of unquestioning acceptance that stifled the fifties; remarkably, despite the passage of time and its relative unpopularity among older university instructors, its audience grows, and young people especially gravitate to a force in it." Charters concluded: "What has been increasingly clear in the last twenty years is that the fabric of American culture has never been the same since 'Sal Paradise' and 'Dean Moriarty' went on the road. As Burroughs said, 'Kerouac opened a million coffee bars and sold a trillion Levis to both sexes. . . . Woodstock rises from his pages.' "

There is no major collection of Kerouac's papers in any university library. One notebook is at the University of Texas, Austin; five notebooks and a typescript are in the Berg Collection of the New York Public Library; some of his correspondence with Allen Ginsberg is at the Butler Library of Columbia University; other letters are in the Gary Snyder Archives at the library of the University of California, Davis. Ginsberg and other poets created the Jack Kerouac School of Disembodied Poetics at the Naropa Institute in Boulder, Colorado. *Moody Street Irregulars: A Jack Kerouac Newsletter,* edited by Joy Walsh and Michael Basinski, was established in 1978.

AVOCATIONAL INTERESTS: Reading, walking, late TV movies, and tape-recording FM musical programs.

MEDIA ADAPTATIONS: The Subterraneans was adapted as a film of the same title by Metro-Goldwyn-Mayer in 1960, starring George Peppard and Leslie Caron. A play based on Kerouac's life and works was produced in New York in 1976.

BIOGRAPHICAL/CRITICAL SOURCES:

BOOKS

Authors in the News, Volume 1, Gale, 1976.
Balakian, Nona, and Charles Simmons, *The Creative Present: Notes on Contemporary American Fiction,* Doubleday, 1963.
Cassady, Carolyn, *Heart Beat: My Life with Jack and Neal,* Creative Arts Book Co., 1977.
Challis, Chris, *Quest for Kerouac,* Faber, 1984.
Charters, Ann, *Kerouac: A Biography,* Straight Arrow, 1973.
Charters, Ann, *A Bibliography of Works by Jock Kerouac, 1939-1975,* Phoenix Book Shop, 1975.
Clark, Tom, *Jack Kerouac,* Harcourt, 1984.
Concise Dictionary of American Literary Biography, Volume 1: *The New Consciousness, 1941-1968,* Gale, 1987.
Contemporary Literary Criticism, Gale, Volume 1, 1973, Volume 2, 1974, Volume 3, 1975, Volume 5, 1976, Volume 14, 1980, Volume 29, 1984.
Cook, Bruce, *The Beat Generation,* Scribner, 1971.
Dictionary of Literary Biography, Gale, Volume 2: *American Novelists since World War II,* 1978, Volume 16: *The Beats: Literary Bohemians in Postwar America,* Gale, 1983.
Dictionary of Literary Biography Documentary Series, Volume 3, Gale, 1983.
Donaldson, Scott, editor, *On the Road: Text and Criticism,* Viking, 1979.
Feied, Frederick, *No Pie in the Sky: The Hobo as American Culture Hero in the Works of Jack London, John Dos Passos, and Jack Kerouac,* Citadel, 1964.
Fiedler, Leslie, *Waiting for the End,* Stein & Day, 1964.
French, Warren, editor, *The Fifties: Fiction, Poetry, Drama,* Everett/Edwards. 1970.
French, Warren, *Jack Kerouac,* Twayne, 1986.
Fuller, Edmund, *Man in Modern Fiction: Some Minority Opinions on Contemporary American Writings,* Random House, 1958.
Gaffie, Luc, *Jack Kerouac: The New Picaroon,* Postillion Press, 1977.
Gifford, Barry, *Kerouac's Town,* Capra, 1973, revised edition, Creative Arts Book Co., 1977.
Gifford, Barry, and Lawrence Lee, *Jack's Book: An Oral Biography of Jack Kerouac,* St. Martin's, 1978.
Ginsberg, Allen, *Allen Verbatim: Lectures on Poetry, Politics, Consciousness,* McGraw, 1974.
Hipkiss, Robert A., *Jack Kerouac: Prophet of the New Romanticism,* University of Kansas Press, 1977.
Holmes, John Clellon, *Nothing More to Declare,* Dutton, 1967.
Huebel, Harry Russell, *Jack Kerouac,* Boise State University, 1979.
Hunt, Tim, *Kerouac's Crooked Road: Development of a Fiction,* Archon Books, 1981.
Jarvis, Charles E., *Visions of Kerouac,* Ithaca Press, 1973.
Jones, Granville H., *Lectures on Modern Novelists,* Carnegie Institute, 1963.

Kerouac, Jack, *Lonesome Traveler,* McGraw, 1960.

Kerouac, Jack, and Allen Ginsberg, *Take Care of My Ghost, Ghost,* Ghost Press, 1977.

Kerouac, Jack, and Carolyn Cassady, *Dear Carolyn: Letters to Carolyn Cassady,* Unspeakable Visions, 1983.

Lindberg, Gary, *The Confidence Man in American Literature,* Oxford University Press, 1982.

McNally, Dennis, *Desolate Angel: Jack Kerouac, the Beat Generation, and America,* McGraw, 1979.

Milewski, Robert J., *Jack Kerouac: An Annotated Bibliography of Secondary Sources, 1944-1979,* Scarecrow, 1981.

Montgomery, John, *The Kerouac We Knew: Unposed Portraits: Action Shots,* Fels & Firn, 1982.

Moore, Harry T., editor, *Contemporary American Novelists,* Southern Illinois University Press, 1964.

Nicosia, Gerald, *Memory Babe: A Critical Biography of Jack Kerouac,* Grove, 1983.

Nisonger, T. E., *Jack Kerouac: A Bibliography of Biographical and Critical Material, 1950-1979,* Bull Bibliography, 1980.

Parkinson, Thomas, editor, *A Casebook on the Beat,* Crowell, 1961.

Podhoretz, Norman, *Doings and Undoings,* Farrar, Straus, 1964.

Tanner, Tony, *City of Words,* Harper, 1971.

Tytell, John, *Naked Angels: The Lives and Literature of the Beat Generation,* McGraw, 1976.

Waldmeir, Joseph J., editor, *Recent American Fiction,* Houghton, 1963.

PERIODICALS

American Literature, May, 1974.
Atlantic, July, 1965.
Best Sellers, February 15, 1968.
Books, December, 1966.
Books Abroad, summer, 1967.
Books and Bookmen, May, 1969.
Chicago Review, winter-spring, 1959.
Chicago Tribune, August 22, 1986.
Commonweal, February 2, 1959.
Contemporary Literature, summer, 1974.
Critique: Studies in Modern Fiction, Volume 14, number 3, 1973.
Detroit Free Press, November 13, 1986.
Evergreen Review, summer, 1958, spring, 1959.
Harper's, October, 1959.
Hudson Review, winter, 1959-60, spring, 1967.
Listener, June 27, 1968.
Los Angeles Times, September 19, 1986, September 20, 1986.
Midwest Quarterly, summer, 1973.
National Observer, February 5, 1968, December 9, 1968.
New Statesman, November 23, 1973.
Newsweek, December 19, 1960.
New York Post, March 10, 1959.
New York Review of Books, May 20, 1965, April 11, 1968.
New York Times, September 5, 1957, May 4, 1965, June 8, 1965, January 9, 1973, April 16, 1986.
New York Times Book Review, May 2, 1965, February 26, 1967, February 18, 1968, January 28, 1973.
Observer, November 19, 1967.
Observer Review, November 19, 1967.
Paris Review, summer, 1968.
Partisan Review, Volume 40, number 2, 1973.
Playboy, June, 1959.
Prairie Schooner, spring, 1974.
Reporter, April 3, 1958.
Review of Contemporary Fiction, Volume 3, number 2, 1983.

Saturday Review, January 11, 1958, May 2, 1959, June 12, 1965, December 2, 1972.
Small Press Review, March, 1983.
South Atlantic Quarterly, autumn, 1974.
Spectator, November 24, 1967, March 28, 1969, August 10, 1974, August 24, 1974.
Stand, Volume 16, number 2, 1975.
Tamarack Review, spring, 1959.
Time, February 23, 1968.
Times Literary Supplement, May 26, 1966, February 1, 1968, March 27, 1969, April 6, 1973, November 2, 1973, September 13, 1974, April 22, 1977.
Village Voice, September 18, 1957, November 12, 1958.
Virginia Quarterly Review, spring, 1973.
Washington Post, October 22, 1969, August 2, 1982.
Washington Post Book World, April 8, 1973.

OTHER

"What Happened to Kerouac?" (documentary film), produced by Richard Lerner, 1986.

OBITUARIES:

PERIODICALS

Detroit Free Press, October 22, 1969.
L'Express, October 27-November 2, 1969.
Newsweek, November 3, 1969.
New York Times, October 22, 1969.
Publishers Weekly, November 3, 1969.
Rolling Stone, November 29, 1969.
Time, October 31, 1969.
Variety, October 29, 1969.
Village Voice, October 30, 1969, November 28, 1969.
Washington Post, October 22, 1969.

*   *   *

KEROUAC, John
  See KEROUAC, Jean-Louis Lebrid de

*   *   *

KERR, M. E.
  See MEAKER, Marijane (Agnes)

*   *   *

KESEY, Ken (Elton) 1935-

PERSONAL: Born September 17, 1935, in La Junta, Colo.; of Fred A. and Geneva (Smith) Kesey; married Faye Haxby, May 20, 1956; children: Shannon, Zane, Jed. *Education:* University of Oregon, B.A., 1957; Stanford University, graduate study 1958-59.

ADDRESSES: Home—85829 Ridgeway Rd., Pleasant Hill, OR 97401. *Agent*—Sterling Lord Agency, Inc., 660 Madison Ave., York, NY 10021.

CAREER: Writer and farmer. Night attendant in psychiatric Veterans Administration Hospital, Menlo Park, Calif., 1961; president, Intrepid Trips, Inc. (motion picture company), 1964.

AWARDS, HONORS: Woodrow Wilson fellowship; Saxton Fund fellowship, 1959; Oregon, Distinguished Service, 1978.

WRITINGS:

One Flew Over the Cuckoo's Nest (novel), Viking, 1962, new edition with criticism, edited by John C. Pratt, 1973.

Sometimes a Great Notion (novel), Viking, 1964, reprinted, 1981.

(Contributor) *The Last Whole Earth Catalog: Access to Tools,* Portola Institute, 1971.

(Editor with Paul Krassner and contributor) *The Last Supplement to the Whole Earth Catalog,* Portola Institute, 1971.

(Contributor) *Kesey's Garage Sale* (collection; interviews, articles, and screenplay "Over the Border"), introduction by Arthur Miller, Viking, 1973.

(Author of introduction) Paul Krassner, editor, *Best of "The Realist": The Sixties' Most Outrageously Irreverent Magazine,* Running Press, 1984.

Demon Box (collection of essays, poetry, and stories, including "The Day Superman Died"), Viking, 1986.

The Little Trickler, The Squirrel (for children), Penguin, 1988.

(With others) *Caverns* (mystery novel), Penguin, 1989.

Also author of two unpublished novels, "End of Autumn" and "Zoo." Work included in anthologies, including *Stanford Short Stories 1962,* edited by Wallace Stegner and Richard Scowcroft, Stanford University Press, 1962. A collection of Kesey's manuscripts is housed at the University of Oregon.

WORK IN PROGRESS: The Further Inquiry, a biography of Neal Cassady, for Viking; *Sailor Song,* a novel about Alaska, also for Viking.

SIDELIGHTS: Ken Kesey's career as writer and cultural hero is best understood in relation to two geographical locations: western Oregon and the San Francisco Bay area, centers for the important shaping influences in his life. His travel back and forth between these places is paralleled by a corresponding fluctuation in interests and values. In his life as well as his fiction, there exist tensions between country and city; between family roots and individual discovery; between traditional Christian values and those of a new counterculture; between the straight and the drug cultures; and between respectability and outlawry.

Kesey's family, both the paternal and maternal lines, were farmers and ranchers. Like the Stampers of his second novel, *Sometimes a Great Notion,* they were "a stringy-muscled brood of restless and stubborn west-walkers." Not pioneers or visionaries doing the Lord's work or blazing trail for a growing nation, they were simply a restless clan looking for new opportunities, moving from Tennessee and Arkansas to Texas and New Mexico, then to Colorado, and finally to Oregon. From this family background, Kesey inherited frontier American attitudes and values that have determined the principal themes of his fiction. M. Gilbert Porter titled his study *The Art of Grit: Ken Kesey's Fiction,* a phrase suggestive of the values of strength, courage, and self-sufficiency that play a central role in the author's work.

Kesey's father, Fred, who embodied these qualities, was a sort of John Wayne hero in his son's eyes. Both Ken and Fred Kesey were strong-minded, which produced some friction between them, but the younger Kesey retained great admiration for his father. Father-son relationships are important in Kesey's unpublished and published novels, and his autobiographical short fiction of the 1970s and 1980s treats his father with tenderness and admiration.

Fred Kesey loved the outdoors. He took his sons on the rivers and in the woods with him from their early years, and they responded to the outdoor life with enthusiasm. Ken Kesey's experiences with trout and salmon fishing and duck and deer hunting were an important part of his early years; he naturally drew upon these experiences when he began writing fiction. Hunting and fishing serve strategic functions in both *One Flew over the Cuckoo's Nest* and *Sometimes a Great Notion.* The family also liked competition, such as wrestling, boxing, and racing. Sundays were often spent at Grandfather Kesey's farm, where young Ken tested his strength and abilities against those of his brother and cousins. Tests of physical strength play an important role in the novels.

At those gatherings, anecdotes and yarns were also exchanged, told in a colorful rural vernacular rich in homely similes. This talk, an outgrowth of a long tradition of frontier American oral storytelling, shaped Kesey's patterns of expression. His fiction is markedly vernacular and filled with anecdotes and tales, and even in conversation he has a habit of expressing himself in little anecdotes or parables with a downhome flavor. An important family source of stories was Kesey's Grandmother Smith, a woman remarkably spunky and self-sufficient into her nineties. She was the model for Grandma Whittier, the narrator of "Seven Prayers by Grandma Whittier," an unfinished novel serialized between 1974 and 1981 in *Spit in the Ocean,* a magazine Kesey published sporadically during the 1970s and 1980s.

Kesey told Linda Gaboriau in a 1972 interview for *Crawdaddy* that he was "a hard shell Baptist, born and raised." Although his parents were not regular churchgoers, their values and standards were Baptist; and Grandmother Smith, who did attend church, was an avid reader of the Bible. Perhaps through her influence, Kesey has retained a great fondness for the sacred scriptures. In his enumeration of tools (that is, books, people, and things of special significance to him) in *The Last Supplement to the Whole Earth Catalog,* the Bible heads the list.

From childhood Kesey has been fascinated with the possibilities of imagination and with a realm of experience beyond the ordinary. He has actively searched for ways to penetrate that realm. According to the *Crawdaddy* interview, as a boy he had sent for some decals of Batman comic-book characters, and when the package arrived it contained a bonus, a small book of magic. Kesey became interested in magic and later ordered a catalog of stage illusions: "I got into a lot of theatrical magic and did shows all through high school and in college. I went from this into ventriloquism (and even had a show on TV), and from ventriloquism into hypnotism. And from hypnotism into dope. But it's always been the same trip, the same kind of search." In this search lies the explanation of how a straight-living small-town boy of Baptist background, who was voted most likely to succeed by his high school class and was a successful athlete and student, became a style-setting leader of a psychedelic counterculture movement and a fugitive from justice.

After finishing high school in Springfield, Oregon, Kesey enrolled at the University of Oregon in nearby Eugene. In both high school and college he was active in athletics and drama. Giving up football after his freshman year to focus on wrestling, he eventually received a scholarship as the outstanding college wrestler in the Northwest. Like their creator, the main characters in Kesey's novels are physically strong and keenly competitive. Blending the western hero and the highly competitive athlete, they are self-reliant men out to prove something, unwilling to concede defeat even against overwhelming opposition. The two strains—of western hero and athlete—are clearly apparent in Hank Stamper, the main character in *Sometimes a Great Notion.*

Kesey's interest in drama led him to a speech and communications major, which involved him in acting and training for radio and television writing. After his senior year in high school and his freshman year in college, he spent the summers in Hollywood seeking parts in films. His love of costumes and performance and his practice in impersonation partly explain the remarkable clothing and antics of Kesey and the Merry Pranksters described by Tom Wolfe in *The Electric Kool-Aid Acid Test.* Kesey's interest in films and film writing is reflected in his fiction. His novels, particularly *Sometimes a Great Notion,* display such cinematic techniques as fade-ins, flashbacks, and simultaneous action in different locations. They also borrow from popular movie genres such as the western and the horror film. And the main item in *Kesey's Garage Sale* is a screenplay titled "Over the Border."

Even with active participation in athletics, theater, and fraternity life, and marriage to his high school sweetheart, Faye Haxby, a year before graduation, Kesey maintained high grades and received a Woodrow Wilson fellowship. Among his many activities, he had developed an interest in writing fiction and enrolled in the creative-writing program at Stanford University during the fall of 1958. It would be difficult to overestimate the significance of this decision. First of all, it brought him in contact with teachers who were writers and critics, such as Wallace Stegner, Richard Scowcroft, Malcolm Cowley, and Frank O'Connor as well as with fellow students such as Wendell Berry, Larry McMurtry, and Robert Stone, all of whom would become well-known writers. But even more important, Kesey's years at Stanford exposed him to a cultural radicalism that was to transform his life. Perry Lane, a small area of cottages near the Stanford golf course, was the focal point for this cultural experimentation. During the late 1950s and early 1960s it became a center for Bohemian life patterned after Beat living in San Francisco's North Beach, just forty miles away. Writing of Perry Lane in the periodical *Free You,* Vie Lovell, the friend to whom *One Flew over the Cuckoo's Nest* is dedicated, described what was going on there: "We pioneered what have since become the hall-marks of hippy culture: LSD and other psychedelics too numerous to mention, body painting, light shows and mixed media presentations, total aestheticism, be-ins, exotic costumes, strobe lights, sexual mayhem, freakouts and the deification of psychoticism, eastern mysticism, and the rebirth of hair." The pioneering claim in this list of questionable distinctions may be overblown, but the statement probably indicates fairly accurately the milieu of Perry Lane. On a tape in the Kesey archives at the University of Oregon, the writer said of his Perry Lane experience, "All that came before led up to it; all that comes after will be the result of it."

The most significant discovery for Kesey came when, at Vic Lovell's suggestion, he volunteered for drug experiments being conducted at the Veteran's Administration Hospital in Menlo Park. He was paid to take a number of hallucinatory drugs, one of which was LSD, and to report in detail their effects. Later, he became an aide at the hospital. The hospital work provided inspiration and material for *One Flew over the Cuckoo's Nest,* and the VA experiments set him on a course of personal experimentation with drugs through which he searched for ways to heighten consciousness.

An unpublished novel titled "Zoo," written during Kesey's first years at Stanford and treating his North Beach experience, manifests the transforming impact of the Perry Lane experience. It embodies the Oregon-California polarity that has determined his career as writer and public figure—the tension between down-home conventional values (family, farming, Christianity) and counterculture experiments in expanding consciousness through drugs, uninhibited indulgence, and self-expression. During this period Kesey also wrote eighty pages of story outline for a novel about Perry Lane. But these efforts merely served as apprentice work for the remarkable creative outpouring of *One Flew over the Cuckoo's Nest* and *Sometimes a Great Notion,* both products of the Perry Lane years.

One Flew over the Cuckoo's Nest was a critical success from its publication in 1962. Its popularity, especially among young people, grew steadily, and its sales surpassed one million by the beginning of the 1970s, when it became the contemporary novel most frequently used in college courses. It is one of the few modern American works to appear in three forms: novel, play, and film. The play, adapted by Dale Wasserman, appeared on Broadway with Kirk Douglas as McMurphy in 1963 and was revived in 1971. Although the Broadway productions were unsuccessful, the play has enjoyed continued popularity on college campuses. The film version in 1975, directed by Milos Forman and starring Jack Nicholson, was a box-office hit and won six Academy Awards.

The novel tells how Randle Patrick McMurphy, a cocky, fast-talking inmate of a prison farm who has had himself committed to a mental hospital to avoid work, creates upheaval in the ward that is so efficiently and repressively directed by Nurse Ratched. His self-confidence and irrepressible sense of humor inspire the passive, dehumanized patients to rebel against Big Nurse and the "Combine" of society she represents. McMurphy ultimately sacrifices himself in the process of teaching his fellow patients the saving lessons of laughter and self-reliance.

The work's remarkable success proves that its themes are engaging and congenial to contemporary audiences. Upon its first appearance, in the early 1960s, the novel supplied a critique of an American society that had been portrayed in the 1950s as a lonely crowd of organization men who could achieve affluence only through strict conformity. That critique continued to suit the mood of the 1970s and 1980s because larger themes were involved: the modern world as technologized and consequently divorced from nature; contemporary society as repressive; authority as mechanical and destructive; contemporary man as weak, frightened, and sexless, a victim of rational but loveless forces beyond his control. The novel's apparent message that people need to get back in touch with their world, to open doors of perception, to enjoy spontaneous sensuous experience, and to resist the manipulative forces of a technological society was particularly appealing to the young, but not just to them. An admiration for self-reliant action as its own source of authority runs deep in the American psyche.

Another reason for the novel's appeal is that it treats or touches upon a wide variety of subjects, issues, and disciplines. In a 1977 *Lex et Scientia,* the official organ of the International Academy of Law and Science, devoted an entire 100-page double issue to essays on *One Flew over the Cuckoo's Nest,* which the editor, Ralph Porzio, describes as "a cornucopia of source material from disciplines so numerous and varied as to challenge the mind and imagination." It reaches, he says, into such areas as psychology, psychiatry, medicine, literature, human relations, drama, art, cosmology, and law, and it carries overtones of religion, American culture, and folk culture. Furthermore, the novel explores these subjects through a mixture of tragedy, pathos, and humor. If this assessment is correct, it is not surprising that the novel has been used as a text for courses in a variety of disciplines.

The multitude of interests the book has attracted is of course paralleled by the large number of responses it has evoked. A partial list of topics that show up in treatments of *One Flew over the Cuckoo's Nest* includes the following diverse items: the patterns of romance, the patterns of comedy, the patterns of tragedy, black humor, the absurd, the hero in modern dress, the comic Christ, the folk and western heroes, the fool as mentor, the Grail Knight, attitudes toward sex, abdication of masculinity, the politics of laughter, mechanistic and totemistic symbolization, the comic strip, the ritualistic father-figure, and the psychopathic savior.

The novel has been treated most extensively as comedy by Ronald Wallace in *The Last Laugh: Form and Affirmation in the Contemporary American Comic Novel.* Its basic conflict, according to Wallace, is between two archetypal characters originating in ancient comedy: the aiazon, the boastful, self-deceived fool, and the eiron, the witty self-deprecator who pretends ignorance in order to defeat his opponent. In addition to acting as eiron, McMurphy functions as what Wallace calls "A Dionysian Lord of Misrule" who "presides over a comic fertility ritual and restores instinctual life to the patients." On the other hand, Michael M. Boardman, in the *Journal of Narrative Technique,* argues that the novel has tragic power and is related to the great tragedies of all ages because it portrays a conflict that is not merely between individuals but sets the protagonist against himself; as in William Shakespeare's tragedies, the struggle between Big Nurse and McMurphy becomes a fight between two opposed principles within McMurphy's being. Richard Blessing, in the *Journal of Popular Culture,* views *One Flew over the Cuckoo's Nest* as a western novel reflecting characters, language, and values associated with the American frontier: "Essentially, the McMurphy who enters the ward is a frontier hero, an anachronistic paragon of rugged individualism, relentless energy, capitalistic shrewdness, virile coarseness and productive strength. He is Huck Finn with muscles, Natty Bumppo with pubic hair. He is the descendant of the pioneer who continually fled civilization and its feminizing and gentling influence." Terry G. Sherwood suggests in *Critique* that the novel demonstrates a noteworthy use of comic strip conventions in a serious novel; as in comic strips, *One Flew over the Cuckoo's Nest* turns on the mythic confrontation of Good and Evil.

Some readers have misgivings about the kind of individualism and freedom advocated by the novel. Bruce E. Wallis in *Cithera,* for example, sees it as merely a matter of jokes, games, obscenity, and verbal disrespect and doubts that throwing butter at walls, breaking windows, stealing boats, and doing what comes naturally really provides the answer for achieving lasting sanity and self-esteem. For him, the novel's "yes" to life is anarchic and places too much emphasis on the sexual and scatological as weapons against the impersonal and repressive aspects of society.

Other readers are alarmed at the novel's portrayal of women. In a *Lex et Scientia* essay Leslie Horst says that not only is that portrayal demeaning, "but considerable hatred of women is justified in the logic of the novel. The plot demands that the dreadful women who break the rules men have made for them become the targets of the reader's wrath." Similarly, Elizabeth McMahon argues in *CEA Critic* that "the Big Nurse happens also to be the Big Victim when viewed with an awareness of the social and economic exploitation of women." In a particularly caustic attack on *One Flew over the Cuckoo's Nest,* Robert Forrey insists in *Modern Fiction Studies* that "the premise of the novel is that women ensnare, emasculate, and, in some cases, crucify men."

These charges of antifeminism have naturally generated counterarguments. Ronald Wallace argues that "to fault Kesey for his treatment of women and blacks is to miss the comedy of a device that has informed comic art from Aristophanes to Erica Jong, the reversal of traditional roles." Michael Boardman justifies the novel's portrayal of women as necessary to its tragic purpose; the drama of the story requires that Big Nurse be very nearly an incarnation of evil. Consequently, Boardman insists, to have made Big Nurse more "human," more understandable, as McMahon

suggests Kesey should have done, would have been to attenuate the force of the tragic action. Ronald Billingsley, in an unpublished dissertation, acknowledges that women serve as antagonists for the men in the novel but asserts that the real conflict is not between men and women: "It would be a serious mistake to read the novel as the work of a misogynist. Big Nurse and her emasculating ilk are no more truly feminine than the Acutes and Dr. Spivey are truly masculine. Like machines, these women are neuter, asexual devices that respond to *power*." Clearly, the amount and diversity of critical attention it has received, combined with its general popularity, have assured *One Flew over the Cuckoo's Nest* an enduring place in twentieth-century American fiction.

Kesey knew that his second novel would be measured by the first. Determined not to repeat what he had done in *One Flew over the Cuckoo's Nest,* he aimed at something different and more ambitious. He had experimented with narrative technique in the first novel by having one of the patients tell the story; he carried the experiments considerably further in the second. In many ways *Sometimes a Great Notion* is markedly different from *One Flew over the Cuckoo's Nest.* It is significantly larger in scope as well as in length, it is technically more complex, and it contains a greater range of prose styles. But in theme, situation, and characterization the second novel parallels the first in obvious ways. Kesey's friend since their Stanford days, Ken Babbs, once made a statement that so captured the writer's imagination that he quoted it a number of times and included it in *Sometimes a Great Notion:* "A man should have the right to be as big as he feels it's in him to be." This statement provides the essential theme for both novels.

That Kesey's rural background and athletic interests were balanced with keen intellectual and artistic concerns first became apparent during his college years. He felt comfortable both with friends engaged in writing and drama and with friends in athletics; each set of associates wondered what he saw in the other. It was probably inevitable that the two sides of his personality would find separate expression in his fiction, as they do in *Sometimes a Great Notion.* Gordon Lish, in a *Genesis West* interview, asked "Where are you going in *Great Notion?* What is it you're testing?" Kesey answered: "For one thing, I want to find out which side of me really is: the woodsy, logger side—complete with homespun homilies and crackerbarrel corniness, a valid side of me that I like—or its opposition. The two Stamper brothers in the novel are each one of the ways I think I am."

The Stamper brothers, Hank and Leland, are members of a family of wildcat loggers who refuse to go on strike and are thus in conflict with the striking loggers' union and their union-dominated community. Hank, the elder son and head of the family business, bears the brunt of this pressure. In addition, he must contend with his Ivy-League-educated half brother, Leland, who seeks revenge for Hank's sexual relationship with the younger man's mother by seducing Hank's wife. In the course of these conflicts, each brother learns significant lessons from the other.

Following the lead of William Faulkner, whose work he greatly admired, Kesey attempts in this novel to convey the complex subjective reality of a primary event through multiple perceptions, both objective and subjective, and through merging and telescoping time. Because the usual linear order of language is inadequate for Kesey's purpose, he tries such unconventional methods as multiple points of view, which sometimes shift several times in a single paragraph; cinematic techniques; fluidity in time and location; and conscious authorial intrusion. The result is a remarkably complex and ambitious achievement, something that cannot be fully understood and appreciated in a single reading.

Although it is a significant artistic achievement, *Sometimes a Great Notion* is not as widely known as *One Flew over the Cuckoo's Nest*. The extraordinary sales of the first novel were due largely to a young audience that the second novel did not reach, perhaps because of the book's size and technical complexity. Consequently there was no word-of-mouth praise, no underground rooting, as was the case with the first book. Reviews, although good in New York, were absent elsewhere. Likewise, the film version did not approach the success of the award-winning version of *One Flew over the Cuckoo's Nest*. The actors were famous (Paul Newman, Henry Fonda, Lee Remick) and appropriately cast, and the novel provided an interesting story line even when the elements not reproducible by the film medium were subtracted. But ineffective editing weakened the movie; gaps in continuity marred the effect and fragmented the experience of the film.

About the time Kesey was completing *Sometimes a Great Notion* in 1963, a developer bought Perry Lane, served notice to the residents, and bulldozed the cottages. With money earned form the first novel, the Keseys bought a place in nearby La Honda. In the spring of 1964, Kesey and a group that had gathered about him at La Honda and that called themselves the Merry Pranksters traveled across country and back in a 1939 International Harvester bus converted into a kind of camper and painted in a spontaneous and reckless array of vivid colors. The bus, later widely imitated by hippies the world over, had a sign in front saying "Further" and a sign on the back saying "Caution: Weird Load." The trip was a sort of communal psychedelic version of Kerouac's *On the Road*. The ostensible reason for the trip was to visit the World's Fair and to be in New York when *Sometimes a Great Notion* was published. More important reasons were to experiment as a group with drugs and to make a movie of the experience as it happened. Kesey invested a good deal of money in equipment for what became known as "The Movie," a fragmented documentary partially filmed under the influence of drugs and currently stored in Los Angeles. The bus trip and later escapades of the Pranksters are reported in *The Electric Kool-Aid Acid Test*, one of the best-known works of Tom Wolfe's New Journalism. According to the Keseys, the book contains factual errors and distortions but accurately captures the spirit and atmosphere of the events.

Kesey's experience as guinea pig at the VA hospital awakened in him a keen curiosity about the consciousness-altering effects of drugs, particularly LSD, which was not illegal at the time. At La Honda he began pursuing that curiosity with like-minded friends. They found that drug experiences could be supplemented or enhanced by various audiovisual aids, ranging from day-glo paint to sophisticated electronic equipment. Participants also created games and activities designed to produce new awareness and perceptions and to test drugs' effects upon interpersonal relations and communication. The group expanded, and the informal experiments, which were essentially parties, became more public. Eventually they became planned public events, the so-called "acid tests." From these developments came acid rock, light shows, psychedelic posters, mixed media entertainment, and many elements of the hippie culture. Kesey, with his charismatic personality, became a leader in the psychedelic movement and a counterculture hero.

Though playful, theatrical, and sometimes irresponsible, Kesey's escapades with the Pranksters had at their core a serious aesthetic and spiritual pursuit. After two successful novels, he turned away from writing, hoping to find new forms of perception and expression. "I'd rather be a lightning rod than a seismograph," he told Tom Wolfe in *The Electric Kool-Aid Acid Test*. The new forms of expression he aimed at "would be all one experience, with all the senses opened wide, words, music, lights, sounds, touch *lightning*."

As Wolfe makes clear, Kesey's experiments with drugs were also a kind of spiritual or religious search. Nineteenth-century American Transcendentalism, among the manifestations of the mystic impulse, provides interesting points of comparison. A number of parallels link Kesey with a tradition in American literature that found its most complete expression in Ralph Waldo Emerson, Henry David Thoreau, and Walt Whitman. Emerson defined Transcendentalism as Idealism in 1842; Kesey's search was Idealism in the 1960s. Scrape off the day-glo paint, unplug the amplifiers, stash the dope, and the similarities are more apparent. Kesey shared with the Transcendentalists such attitudes as these: (1) love of nature, with the expectation that nature teaches the most important truths; (2) an eclectic approach to finding knowledge, with conventions and institutions largely ignored or resisted; (3) an impatience with the limitations of language; (4) a confidence in intuitive knowledge and an obsession with a transcendental experience; (5) an attraction to the vernacular hero; (6) a feeling that reform must begin with the self; and (7) a predisposition toward mysticism.

Eventually, Kesey's drug activities got him in trouble with the law. Arrested twice for possession of marijuana and fearing a harsh sentence, he fled to Mexico in early 1966 with his friends in the famous bus, but returned after about six months and was arrested in San Francisco. Eventually he served sentences totaling about five months in the San Mateo County Jail and later at the San Mateo County Sheriff's Honor Camp. Upon release he moved to a farm in Pleasant Hill, near Eugene, Oregon, where he has remained. Wolfe's book perpetuated and expanded Kesey's reputation as a pioneer in the youth drug culture, and after its publication the Keseys were plagued by visitors to the farm, sometimes several hundred in a weekend. Some came expecting to live there; others, like pilgrims, wanted to get stoned at the feet of the master. Gradually the number of visitors decreased. Kesey has maintained contact with many of his friends from the 1960s, but has devoted himself primarily to farming, rearing his family, performing community service, and working sporadically at writing.

The development of Kesey's work is of interest to those who want to know if drugs enabled him to expand his consciousness or enlarge his imaginative powers. The relationship between chemical stimulants and creativity has perennial fascination, and Kesey is a particularly instructive case. His experiments, the efforts of an intelligent and accomplished literary artist who pursued them with faith and commitment, are bound to tell observers much about drugs and creativity. Yet from the standpoint of literary productivity, the drug and counterculture activities may have done more harm than good; after twenty-two years Kesey has not completed another novel.

In 1973, Kesey's *Garage Sale* was published. A group project deriving from the Prankster era (from the so-called "Prankster Archives"), it manifests the flavor and spirit of that period. After an introduction by Arthur Miller, the book is organized into "5 Hot Items." The first, "Who Flew over What?" is an essay by Kesey describing his introduction to drugs, his work as an aide at the VA hospital, and the writing of *One Flew over the Cuckoo's Nest*. The essay is illustrated with Kesey's sketches of the characters, done when he was writing the novel. The second item, comprising nearly half of the book, is "Over the Border," a fictionalized account of Kesey's flight to Mexico; the screenplay is profusely illustrated with drawings by Paul Foster. The third section "Tools from My Chest," is a collection that first appeared in *The Last Supplement to the Whole Earth Catalog,* which Kesey had edited with Paul Krassner. These are short comments on people, books, and things that Kesey considered significant. "Hot Item Number 4" is a miscellany consisting of some of Kesey's notes while in jail, a short essay on creativity, an interview, a letter from Neal Cassady, and poems by Hugh Romney and Allen Ginsberg. The fifth item is "An Impolite Interview with Ken Kesey" done by Paul Krassner. Added at the end is a "surprise bonus," an exchange of correspondence between Kesey and Laurence Gonzales of *Tri-Quarterly.*

Much of this material had appeared previously in underground magazines, and some reviewers saw the book as a thrown-together combination of recycled spare parts designed to make money. Those who knew little about Kesey's activities with the Pranksters were puzzled why anyone would be interested in the Prankster Archives anyway. Admittedly, the book is a kind of counterculture document directed to other members of the club, but it is also more than that. It reveals much about Kesey's interests and values, his relationship to the 1960s counterculture, and his quest for expanded consciousness. It provides some answers to such questions as these: Why did Kesey turn aside from writing novels? What was he seeking in drugs and counterculture activities? What are the results or consequences of that search? "Over the Border" is particularly relevant to such questions, because in it Kesey provides a penetrating evaluation of himself as leader and guru.

Kesey's next book, *Demon Box,* did not appear until 1986. Like Kesey's *Garage Sale,* it is a miscellaneous collection of items, most of which had appeared earlier in magazines. And like Kesey's *Garage Sale,* the focus is on the Prankster era and its resulting experiences or aftershocks. Most of the items are autobiographical sketches, essays, and travelogues, skillfully fictionalized to make them resonate with larger implications. One selection, "Good Friday," is the first installment of the unfinished novel, "Seven Prayers of Grandma Whittier," that Kesey had serialized in six issues of *Spit in the Ocean.* The projected seventh issue, intended to contain the conclusion of the novel, had not appeared as of late 1986. A number of the sketches or stories describe visits to his farm by friends from the psychedelic revolution or by rootless young people, including Hell's Angels, attracted by his connection with that revolution. The travelogues describe visits to Egypt and China. The account of the trip to Egypt, "The Search for the Secret Pyramid," first appeared in *Rolling Stone* and later in *Spit in the Ocean.* The trip to China to cover the Beijing marathon produced "Finding Doctor Fung," first published in *Rolling Stone,* and "Run into Great Wall," first appearing in *Running* magazine, which sponsored the trip.

The diverse pieces in *Demon Box* are unified by a narrative persona, Devlin Deboree. Kesey first used this version of himself in "Over the Border," along with fictional names for his family and friends. He has employed this cast of characters consistently ever since. The name Devlin Deboree (note the alliterating consonants and the end sounds similar to Ken Kesey) suggests "devil" and "debris," which could be taken to refer to bedeviling ruins and rubble or to one who bedevils ruins and rubble (that is, one who raises the devil with the debris in American culture). Or it may be an updated version of Thomas Carlyle's Teufelsdroeckh ("devil's dirt"), who in *Sartor Resartus* is an earlier seeker of higher consciousness. In any case, this persona allows Kesey fic-

tional latitude for shaping actual events into suggestive patterns of meaning.

Seeking or questing is another unifying element in *Demon Box,* and the book's epigraph focuses on the term "Tarnished Galahad," which the judge applied to Kesey at his trial. Central and persistent in all of Kesey's writing since the 1960s, the quest motif captures his enduring and eclectic search for heightened perception, for transcendent experience or wisdom. Kesey's hunger began when comic books, magic, and hypnotism triggered his imagination in childhood, and this hunger has led him through the gamut of mind-altering drugs, occult knowledge, esoteric philosophy, Eastern spiritual thought, and anything else that offered the least promise.

Kesey's fiction displays a distinctive blending of American traditions. It is obviously an extension of the Beat movement; it reflects the concerns and attitudes of American Transcendentalism; it has the vernacular flavor of frontier humor and the oral tale tradition; it manifests the themes and character types of the western; and it borrows from sources ranging from the works of Faulkner to comic books and cowboy movies.

Kesey's achievement can be summarized in the following way. First of all, his expression of cherished American traditions and values is original and engaging. Americans perhaps have never been as individualistic, self-reliant, and in tune with nature as their myths suggest, but they certainly praise those qualities and celebrate them in such figures as Randle McMurphy, Hank Stamper, and Grandma Whittier. Second, Kesey's humor is rarely contrived or strained but grows naturally out of the situations and idioms of his characters; it is seldom merely an end in itself. Third, the writer's intelligence is distinguished by a gift for perceiving lessons from experience, morals in simple events. This preacher's gift causes his narratives to reverberate with meaning. Fourth, his profound awareness of the distinction between the thoroughly rational and the complexly human allows for the mystery of human personality, the spiritual component from which real freedom, creativity, and moral character derive. Fifth, Kesey's technical inventiveness in manipulating point of view and experimenting with other narrative techniques has produced notable accomplishments. And sixth, his honesty and self-criticism allow for balance and complexity in creating characters. McMurphy is criminal and psychotic as well as heroic; Hank is coarse and bigoted as well as admirably strong; Grandma Whittier, with all her compassion and common sense, can still be foolish at times. And Devlin Deboree is a candidly self-critical version of Kesey himself.

Despite these achievements, some aspects of Kesey's career remain disturbing. Perhaps more was lost than gained by his California experience: At the height of his literary creation, the drug experiments and the attempt to go beyond writing distracted him and dissipated his creative energies; the legal entanglements were unsettling and created debilitating anger and bitterness. In view of the achievement of *One Flew over the Cuckoo's Nest* and *Sometimes a Great Notion* and the long novelistic quiet that followed them, many observers feel that Kesey took wrong turns in his career, that promise went unfulfilled and talent was diverted from its proper course. But judging the way a man makes use of his creative gifts is as hazardous as it is easy. Regardless of what Kesey writes or fails to write in the future, he merits respect and recognition for two remarkable novels; furthermore, the autobiographical mode he has adopted since those novels is not without distinction as narrative art and significance as cultural commentary.

MEDIA ADAPTATIONS: One Flew over the Cuckoo's Nest was adapted for the stage and produced on Broadway at the Cort Theatre on November 13, 1963, and adapted for film by United Artists in 1975; *Sometimes a Great Notion* was adapted for film by Universal in 1972.

BIOGRAPHICAL/CRITICAL SOURCES:

BOOKS

Acton, Jay, Alan Le Mond, and Parker Hodges, *Mug Shots: Who's Who in the New Earth,* World Publishing, 1972.

Allen, Mary, *The Necessary Blankness: Women in Major American Fiction of the Sixties,* University of Illinois Press, 1976.

Billingsley, Ronald G., *The Artistry of Ken Kesey,* University of Oregon, 1971.

Boyers, Robert, *Excursions: Selected Literary Essays,* Kennikat, 1977.

Carnes, Bruce, *Ken Kesey,* Boise State University, 1974.

Contemporary Literary Criticism, Gale, Volume 1, 1973, Volume 3, 1975, Volume 6, 1976, Volume 11, 1979.

Cook, Bruce, *The Beat Generation,* Scribner, 1971.

Dictionary of Literary Biography, Gale, Volume 2: *American Novelists since World War II,* 1978, Volume 16: *The Beats: Literary Bohemians in Postwar America,* 1983.

Feigelson, Naomi, *The Underground Revolution: Hippies, Yippies, and Others,* Funk, 1970.

Fiedler, Leslie A., *Love and Death in the American Novel,* Stein & Day, 1966.

Finholt, Richard, *American Visionary Fiction: Mad Metaphysics as Salvation Psychology,* Kennikat, 1978.

Harris, Charles B., *Contemporary American Novelists of the Absurd,* College & University Press, 1971.

Kesey, Ken, *One Flew over the Cuckoo's Nest* (novel), Viking, 1962, new edition with criticism, edited by John C. Pratt, 1973.

Kesey, *Sometimes a Great Notion* (novel), Viking, 1964.

Krassner, Paul, *How a Satirical Editor Became a Yippie Conspirator in Ten Easy Years,* Putnam, 1971.

Labin, Suzanne, *Hippies, Drugs, and Promiscuity,* Arlington House, 1972.

Leeds, Barry H., *Ken Kesey,* Ungar, 1981.

Olderman, Raymond M., *Beyond the Waste Land: A Study of the American Novel in the Nineteen-Sixties,* Yale University Press, 1972.

Porter, M. Gilbert, *The Art of Grit: Ken Kesey's Fiction,* University of Missouri Press, 1982.

Strelow, Michael, *Kesey,* Northwest Review Books, 1977.

Tanner, Tony, *City of Words: American Fiction, 1957-1970,* Harper, 1971.

Wallace, Ronald, *The Last Laugh: Form and Affirmation in the Contemporary American Comic Novel,* University of Missouri Press, 1971.

Wolfe, Tom, *The Electric Kool-Aid Acid Test,* Farrar, Straus, 1968.

PERIODICALS

Annals of the American Academy of Political and Social Science, Volume 376, 1968.

Ann Arbor Argus, Volume 2, number 4, 1970.

Atlantic, August, 1964.

Books Abroad, Volume 39, number 2, 1965.

Boundary, Volume 3, 1975.

Bulletin of the Rocky Mountain Modern Language Association, Volume 23, 1969.

CEA Critic, Volume 37, 1975.

Centennial Review, Volume 16, 1972, Volume 17, 1973.

Chicago Tribune, February 4, 1962.

Chicago Tribune Book World, July 27, 1986.

Cithara, Volume 12, 1972.

Commonweal, March 16, 1962.

Connecticut Review, April, 1974.

Crawdaddy, Volume 29, 1972.

Critique, Volume 5, 1962, Volume 13, 1971.

Explicator, Volume 31, 1973, Volume 32, 1973.

Free You, Volume 2, 1968.

Genesis West, Volume 2, fall, 1963.

Globe & Mail (Toronto), September 6, 1986.

Hudson Review, Volume 15, summer, 1962, Volume 17, winter, 1964-65.

Journal of American Studies, Volume 5, 1971.

Journal of Narrative Technique, Volume 9, 1979.

Journal of Popular Culture, Volume 4, winter, 1971.

Kenyon Review, Volume 27, winter, 1965.

Lex et Scientia, Volume 13, Issue 1-2, 1977.

Library Journal, June 1, 1964, November 1, 1973, January 15, 1974.

Literature and Psychology, Volume 25, number 1, 1975.

London Magazine, December, 1969.

Los Angeles Times, September 24, 1986.

Los Angeles Times Book Review, August 31, 1986.

Manchester Guardian Weekly, March 4, 1972.

Massachusetts Review, Volume 8, 1967.

Meanjin, Volume 35, 1976.

Midwest Quarterly, Volume 19, 1978.

Modern Fiction Studies, Volume 19, 1973, Volume 21, 1975.

Nation, February 23, 1974.

National Observer, October 20, 1973.

Newsweek, August 3, 1964.

New Times, Volume 2, number 12, 1974.

New Yorker, April 21, 1962, December 1, 1975.

New York Herald Tribune, February 25, 1962, July 27, 1964, August 2, 1964.

New York Review of Books, September 10, 1964.

New York Times, July 27, 1964, January 18, 1966, March 12, 1966, October 21, 1966, August 4, 1986.

New York Times Book Review, February 4, 1962, August 2, 1964, August 18, 1968, October 7, 1973, August 4, 1986, September 14, 1986.

Northwest Review, Volume 6, spring, 1963, Volume 16, number 1-2, spring, 1977.

People, March 22, 1976.

Playboy, October, 1967.

Prairie Schooner, Volume 39, spring, 1965.

Ramparts, November, 1967.

Realist, Number 90, 1971, Number 91, 1971, Number 94, 1972.

Rolling Stone, March 7, 1970, September 27, 1973, July 18, 1974.

Saturday Review, April 14, 1962, July 25, 1964, October 23, 1965.

Southern Humanities Review, Volume 6, 1972.

Southern Review, Volume 3, 1967.

Southwest Review, Volume 58, 1973.

Spectator, March 8, 1963.

Studies in American Fiction, Volume 3, number 1, 1975.

Time, February 16, 1962, July 24, 1964, February 12, 1965, September 8, 1986.

Times Literary Supplement, February 24, 1966, February 25, 1972.

Washington Post, June 9, 1974.

Washington Post Book World, August 10, 1986.

Western American Literature, Volume 9, 1974, Volume 10, 1975.

Wisconsin Studies in Contemporary Literature, Volume 5, 1964, Volume 7, 1966.

* * *

KIDDER, Tracy 1945-

PERSONAL: Born November 12, 1945, in New York, N.Y.; son of Henry Maynard (a lawyer) and Reine (a high school teacher; maiden name, Tracy) Kidder; married Frances T. Toland, January 2, 1971. *Education:* Harvard University, A.B., 1967; University of Iowa, M.F.A., 1974.

ADDRESSES: Agent—Georges Borchardt, Inc., 136 East 57th St., New York, N.Y. 10022.

CAREER: Writer, 1974—. *Military service:* U.S. Army, served in intelligence in Vietnam; became lieutenant.

AWARDS, HONORS: Atlantic First Award from *Atlantic Monthly* for short story, "The Death of Major Great"; Sidney Hillman Foundation Prize, 1978, for article, "Soldiers of Misfortune"; Pulitzer Prize and American Book Award, both 1982, for *The Soul of a New Machine;* National Book Critics Circle Award for nonfiction, 1986, for *House;* Christopher Award and National Book Critics Circle Award nomination for nonfiction, both 1989, for *Among Schoolchildren.*

WRITINGS:

NONFICTION

The Road to Yuba City: A Journey Into the Juan Corona Murders, Doubleday, 1974.
The Soul of a New Machine, Little, Brown, 1981.
House, Houghton, 1985.
Among Schoolchildren, Houghton, 1989.

Contributing editor, *Atlantic Monthly,* 1982—. Contributor to newspapers and magazines, including *New York Times Book Review, Science '83,* and *Country Journal.*

SIDELIGHTS: Tracy Kidder's *The Soul of a New Machine* garnered him two prestigious literary awards in 1982 and proved, by its critical reception, that technical subjects can be comprehensible and intriguing to laymen when they are skillfully presented.

The book details the eighteen-month-long struggle of engineers at Data General Corporation to create a competitive super-mini computer. Kidder, a newcomer to this highly technical world, spent months in a basement laboratory at the corporation's Massachusetts headquarters observing teams of young engineers at work: the hardware specialists, or "Hardy Boys," who put the computer's circuitry together, and the "Microkids," who developed the code that fused the hardware and software of the system. In the story of the assembly, the setbacks, and the perfection of the thirty-two "bit" prototype computer, the Eagle, Kidder exposes the inner workings of a highly competitive industry, illustrates both concentrated teamwork and moments of virtuosity on the part of the project's brilliant engineers, and produces what reviewer Edward R. Weidlein, in the *Washington Post Book World,* judged "a true-life adventure" and "compelling entertainment."

Critics agreed that Kidder's masterful handling of the complex subject matter in *The Soul of a New Machine* was one of the book's strongest features. "Even someone like this reviewer," wrote Christopher Lehmann-Haupt of the *New York Times,* "who barely understood the difference between computer hardware and software when he began 'The Soul of a New Machine,'

was able to follow every step of the debugging mystery, even though it involves binary arithmetic, Boolean algebra, and a grasp of the difference between a System Cache and an Instruction Processor." Weidlein concurred, observing that Kidder "offers a fast, painless, enjoyable means to an initial understanding of computers, allowing us to understand the complexity of machines we could only marvel at before."

Kidder's portraits of the Eagle's engineers were applauded by reviewers as well. Samuel C. Florman claimed that in Kidder's narrative, the young men "are portrayed as eccentric knights errant, clad in blue jeans and open collars, seeking with awesome intensity the grail of technological achievement." A *New Yorker* review echoed Florman, declaring that Kidder "gives a full sense of the mind and motivation, the creative genius of the computer engineer." The *Saturday Review* claimed that *The Soul of a New Machine* "tells a human story of tremendous effort."

Critics also lauded *The Soul of a New Machine* for its departure from the standard journalistic approach to nonfiction. Florman, for instance, found that "Kidder has endowed the tale with such pace, texture and poetic implication that he has elevated it to a high level of narrative art." Jeremy Bernstein, in the *New York Review of Books,* declared, "I strongly recommend Tracy Kidder's book. I do not know anything quite like it. It tells a story far removed from our daily experience, and while it may seem implausible, it has the ring of truth."

In his 1985 book, *House,* Kidder chronicles the building of a house in Massachusetts. Kidder focuses on the complex relationships among home buyer, architect, and builder that existed during the project. *New York Times* critic Paul Goldberger noted that *House* "is the story of the building of a house, and it is told with such clarity, intelligence and grace it makes you wonder why no one has written a book like it before." R. Z. Sheppard of *Time* had similar praise for the book and its author. "The author is a virtuoso of lucid and compelling narrative," commented Sheppard. "The result is . . . a subtle examination of cultural and class differences."

Critics also praised Kidder's next book, *Among Schoolchildren,* "a celebration of one good schoolteacher," writes Phillip Lopate in the *Washington Post Book World.* The teacher is Chris Zajac, an elementary-school teacher in Holyoke, Massachusetts. Kidder details one school year in Zajac's life, in which she must deal with students of different abilities and different ethnic and social backgrounds. Chicago *Tribune Books* contributor Gerald Grant states that "Kidder has written a wonderful, compassionate book about teaching. While we have some cause for despair about the operation of the system, we have grounds for hope if his book helps draw more Mrs. Zajacs into our classrooms."

BIOGRAPHICAL/CRITICAL SOURCES:

BOOKS

Bestsellers 90, Issue 1, Gale, 1990.

PERIODICALS

Chicago Tribune, September 29, 1985.
Globe and Mail (Toronto), December 14, 1985.
Los Angeles Times, November 12, 1985.
Newsweek, October 28, 1985.
New Yorker, October 19, 1981.
New York Review of Books, October 8, 1981.
New York Times, August 11, 1981, September 5, 1985, October 3, 1985, August 30, 1989.
New York Times Book Review, August 23, 1981, November 29, 1981, October 6, 1985, September 17, 1989.

Saturday Review, December, 1981.
Time, October 14, 1985.
Tribune Books (Chicago), August 13, 1989.
Washington Post Book World, September 9, 1981, October 6, 1985, September 3, 1989.

*   *   *

KIENZLE, William X(avier) 1928-
(Mark Boyle)

PERSONAL: Born September 11, 1928, in Detroit, Mich.; son of Alphonzo and Mary Louise (Boyle) Kienzle; married Javan Herman Andrews (an editor and researcher), 1974. *Education:* Sacred Heart Seminary College, B.A., 1950; also attended St. John's Seminary, 1950-54, and University of Detroit, 1968. *Politics:* Independent. *Religion:* Roman Catholic.

ADDRESSES: Home—2465 Middlebelt, West Bloomfield, Mich. 48033-1685.

CAREER: Ordained Roman Catholic priest, 1954; left priesthood, 1974; Roman Catholic Archdiocese of Detroit, Detroit, Mich., archdiocesan priest in five parishes, 1954-74, editor in chief of *Michigan Catholic,* 1962-74; *MPLS.* magazine, Minneapolis, Minn., editor in chief, 1974-77; Western Michigan University, Kalamazoo, associate director of Center for Contemplative Studies, 1977-78; University of Dallas, Irving, Tex., director of Center for Contemplative Studies, 1978-79; writer, 1979—.

MEMBER: Authors Guild, Authors League of America, Crime Writers Association, American Crime Writers League.

AWARDS, HONORS: Michigan Knights of Columbus journalism award, 1963, for general excellence; honorable mention from Catholic Press Association, 1974, for editorial writing.

WRITINGS:

MYSTERY NOVELS

The Rosary Murders, Andrews & McMeel, 1979.
Death Wears a Red Hat, Andrews & McMeel, 1980.
Mind over Murder, Andrews & McMeel, 1981.
Assault with Intent, Andrews & McMeel, 1982.
Shadow of Death, Andrews & McMeel, 1983.
Kill and Tell, Andrews & McMeel, 1984.
Sudden Death, Andrews, McMeel & Parker, 1985.
Deathbed, Andrews, McMeel & Parker, 1986.
Deadline for a Critic, Andrews, McMeel & Parker, 1987.
Marked for Murder, Andrews & McMeel, 1988.
Eminence, Andrews & McMeel, 1989.
Masquerade, Andrews & McMeel, 1990.

OTHER

Contributor under pseudonym Mark Boyle to *MPLS.* magazine.

WORK IN PROGRESS: A mystery novel for Andrews & McMeel.

SIDELIGHTS: Though he no longer delivers the sermons that captivated his parishioners, William X. Kienzle is still telling stories. After leaving the priesthood in 1974, he "exchanged his pulpit for a typewriter," as Bill Dunn describes in *Publishers Weekly,* and began writing the tales that have made him a bestselling mystery author. The twenty years he spent in the clergy now provide the raw material for his popular series involving Father Robert Koesler, an amateur sleuth and sharply defined priest who resembles Kienzle in several ways. "The fictitious Father Koesler divides his time between his pastoral duties within

the Detroit archdiocese and his journalistic duties as an editor of the area's Catholic newspaper, just as Kienzle spent his time during the 1960's," *Detroit News Magazine* writer Andrea Wojack observes.

Despite these similarities, Wojack does not envision Koesler as Kienzle in disguise. Rather, she sees him as a product of both Kienzle's background and "the tradition of clerical detectives in fiction, like Chesterton's Father Brown and Harry Kemelman's Rabbi Small." Andrew M. Greeley similarly observes in the *Los Angeles Times Book Review:* "William Kienzle is the Harry Kemelman of Catholicism, and his priest detective, Robert Koesler . . . is the Detroit response to Rabbi Small." The critic adds: "I am not suggesting that Kienzle is consciously imitating Kemelman—though there would be nothing wrong with such imitation. Rather I am arguing that religio-ethnic subcultures are fertile seedbeds for mystery stories. Kienzle's sensitivity to pathos and foolishness, shallow fads and rigid ideologies, mindless nonsense and deep faith of the contemporary Catholic scene compares favorably with Kemelman's vivid description of suburban Jewish life."

A native Detroiter, Kienzle also uses the city and its Catholic parishes as a backdrop for his fiction, reportedly drawing many of his characters from people he has known. "Kienzle's portrayal of various priests obviously [are] an insider's (or ex-insider's) work," a *Detroit News* contributor comments. "He seems accurate, yet relaxed, in his depictions of the clergy, and his genuine affection for many of them far outruns any tendency toward satiric thrust." In addition, Father Koesler's solutions rely on his knowledge of the Church and its workings; in the recent *Eminence,* for example, "Koesler's command of ecclesiastical detail is full and fascinating," *Los Angeles Times Book Review* critic Charles Champlin states, and "the uses of Latin and points of Canon law are significant clues."

Despite Kienzle's assertion that his novels are, as Dunn reports, "first of all thrillers," many critics find a deeper meaning in his work. In his review of *Mind over Murder,* for example, *Detroit Free Press* managing editor Neal Shine observes: "There has always been the sense that there's as much message as mystery in Kienzle's books. Kienzle is a former Detroit priest whose feelings about some of the ways in which the Catholic Church deports itself can hardly be called ambivalent. In *Mind over Murder* he goes to the heart of the matter for a lot of Catholics—marriage and the Church. The people with the clearest motives for rubbing out the monsignor are those who have run up against his incredibly inflexible rulings on marriage." *Chicago Tribune* writer Peter Gorner likewise remarks that in *Deadline for a Critic* "Kienzle addresses serious modern issues"; nevertheless, the author also "stops to digress and tell us his wonderful stories." The critic concludes that "Kienzle's books are more small morality plays than classic mysteries. He always is welcomed to my shelves."

Although Kienzle includes philosophical inquiries and religious asides in his books, his primary strength lies in the development of the mystery. In *Kill and Tell,* for example, "we're back to basics with a fascinating cast of three-dimensional characters who *act* like people caught up in a baffling case, a protagonist in Father Koesler who is both wry and intelligent, and an honest-to-badness murder at a tension-filled cocktail party that is truly puzzling," Don G. Campbell recounts in the *Los Angeles Times Book Review. Best Sellers* contributor Tony Bednarczyk likewise asserts that in *The Rosary Murders,* which he calls a "well paced, tightly written novel," the author, "more importantly, creates well defined characters that inhabit his story rather than decorate it.'' '' 'The Rosary Murders' quickly established Father Koesler as among the most likable and authentic of all recent sleuths and gave his wise and compassionate creator a midlife career and a new pulpit,'' Gorner concludes. ''Since then, few mystery series have been more cozy and persuasive.''

MEDIA ADAPTATIONS: The Rosary Murders was produced by Take One Productions in 1987.

BIOGRAPHICAL/CRITICAL SOURCES:

BOOKS

Contemporary Authors Autobiography Series, Volume 1, Gale, 1984.
Contemporary Literary Criticism, Volume 25, Gale, 1983.

PERIODICALS

Best Sellers, July, 1979.
Chicago Tribune, May 29, 1985, April 8, 1987, May 3, 1989.
Chicago Tribune Book World, July 11, 1982.
Detroit Free Press, February 22, 1980, April 26, 1981.
Detroit News, July 15, 1979, April 5, 1981.
Detroit News Magazine, March 16, 1980.
Los Angeles Times, April 24, 1981, May 7, 1987.
Los Angeles Times Book Review, June 22, 1980, May 23, 1982, August 5, 1984, May 7, 1987, April 9, 1989.
Michigan Magazine, August 11, 1985.
New York Times Book Review, June 15, 1980, June 21, 1981, May 23, 1982.
Publishers Weekly, April 18, 1980.

*   *   *

KIM
See SIMENON, Georges (Jacques Christian)

*   *   *

KING, Francis (Henry) 1923-
(Frank Cauldwell)

PERSONAL: Born March 4, 1923, in Adelboden, Switzerland; son of Eustace Arthur Cecil and Faith (Read) King. *Education:* Balliol College, Oxford, B.A., 1949, M.A., 1951.

ADDRESSES: Home—19 Gordon Place, London W8 4JE, England. *Agent*—A. M. Heath & Co., 40-42 William IV St., London WC2N 4DD, England.

CAREER: British Council lecturer in Florence, Italy, 1949-50, Salonica, Greece, 1950-52, and Athens, Greece, 1953-57, assistant representative in Helsinki, Finland, 1957-58, and regional director in Kyoto, Japan, 1959-63; *Sunday Telegraph,* London, England, literary critic, 1964—, drama critic, 1978—.

MEMBER: Royal Society of Literature (fellow), Society of Authors (England; chairman, 1975-77), PEN (president of English center, 1978—).

AWARDS, HONORS: Somerset Maugham Award, 1952, for *The Dividing Stream;* Katherine Mansfield Short Story Prize, 1965, for ''The Japanese Umbrella''; Order of the British Empire, 1979; Yorkshire Post Prize, 1983.

WRITINGS:

To the Dark Tower (novel), Home & Van Thal, 1946.
Never Again (novel), Home & Van Thal, 1947.
An Air That Kills (novel), Home & Van Thal, 1948.
The Dividing Stream (novel), Longmans, Green, 1951.

Rod of Incantation (poems), Longmans, Green, 1952.
The Dark Glasses, Longmans, Green, 1954.
(Under pseudonym Frank Cauldwell) *The Firewalkers: A Memoir,* John Murray, 1955, reprinted under name Francis King, GMP, 1985.
(Editor) *Introducing Greece,* Methuen, 1956, revised edition, 1968.
The Widow (novel), Longmans, Green, 1957.
The Man on the Rock (novel), Pantheon, 1957.
So Hurt and Humiliated (short stories), Longmans, Green, 1959.
The Custom House (novel), Longmans, Green, 1961, Doubleday, 1962.
The Japanese Umbrella, and Other Stories, Longmans, Green, 1964.
The Last of the Pleasure Gardens (novel), Longmans, Green, 1965.
The Waves behind the Boat (novel), Longmans, Green, 1967.
The Brighton Belle, and Other Stories, Longmans, 1968.
A Domestic Animal (novel), Longmans, 1970.
(With Martin Huerlimann) *Japan,* translated from the German by D. J. S. Thomson, Thames & Hudson, 1970.
Flights (two short novels; contains ''The Infection'' and ''The Cure''), Hutchinson, 1973.
A Game of Patience (novel), Hutchinson, 1974.
The Needle (novel), Hutchinson, 1975.
Hard Feelings, and Other Stories, Hutchinson, 1976.
Danny Hill: Memoirs of a Prominent Gentleman (farce), Hutchinson, 1977.
The Action (novel), Hutchinson, 1978.
E. M. Forster and His World, Scribner, 1978.
(Editor with Ronald Harwood) *New Stories,* Hutchinson, 1978.
Indirect Method, and Other Stories, Hutchinson, 1980.
(Editor and author of introduction) *My Sister and Myself: The Diaries of J. R. Ackerley,* Hutchinson, 1982.
Florence, Newsweek, 1982.
Act of Darkness (novel), Hutchinson, 1982, Little, Brown, 1983.
Voices in an Empty Room (novel), Little, Brown, 1984.
(Editor and author of introduction) Lafcadio Hearn, *Writings from Japan: An Anthology,* Penguin, 1984.
(Editor) *Twenty Stories: A South East Asia Collection,* Secker & Warburg, 1985.
One Is a Wanderer (selected stories), Little, Brown, 1985.
Frozen Music (novel), Hutchinson, 1987.
The Woman Who Was God (novel), Hutchinson, 1988.

Contributor to *Penguin Modern Stories, 12,* edited by Judith Burnley, Penguin, 1982.

SIDELIGHTS: A *New York Times* reviewer once referred to Francis King as a writer ''with intensity of purpose skillfully concealed behind a facile style, swift-paced dialogue and a spoofing surface-irony.'' Others have used words such as ''cold,'' ''comfortless,'' and even ''bloodless'' to describe King's fiction, in which he grimly explores the ''mad oddities of the human condition'' in a very carefully composed and rather detached, yet completely gripping style. As a *Spectator* critic observes: ''There has always been a dark side to Mr. King's novels, somewhat contradicting the conventional view of him as one of our more placid writers; although he is no Poe, and would not want to be, he is adept at casting various forms of terror and unease within his apparently calm, collected prose. . . . [He] never dabbles in overstatement. He is also too fastidious to bother with the throughly modern under-statement; he is, rather, a master of the precise statement—going very well with his constant effort to keep up appearances: the appearance of his characters, of his prose, and of the neatly but tightly formed shape of his narrative. But beneath this surface, some dark fantasies swoop and glitter. . . . [King's] darting imagination is only barely kept in check by the iron discipline he imposes upon his own writing."

A commentator in *Punch,* calling King "a master of the *frisson*" (literally, a shiver or shudder), notes that he has a "sure touch" in matters concerning "decadence and decay," or, as an *Observer Review* critic states, "murder, brutality and 'perversion' constantly appear in [King's stories in] the most surprising—and natural—way." A *Books and Bookmen* reviewer claims that readers "are at the mercy of whatever Mr. King chooses as his weapon: humour, wit, irony or compassion. His style is pared down to its lovely bones. His sentences lie in wait and blip you on the head, just as you were thinking how frank and nice they were. . . . His eye is wickedly sharp on detail, the eye of a painter, of a comedian. . . . [He] is fascinated by bizarre relationships. . . . [King writes] in gruesome but never tasteless detail. He is a fastidious, an elegant, a knowing writer."

King once told *CA:* "I see myself as being like a house-builder, patiently, persistently and laboriously placing brick on brick, to create the edifice that, however ramshackle, is my *oeuvre.* Some passers-by look up at that edifice and say 'That looks all right.' Others look up and say 'Shouldn't those windows be bigger? That roof looks as though it might leak.' I try not to be influenced by such comments, favourable or unfavourable. I merely want to carry out the invisible blue-print that is within me.

"When I once refused to accept the suggestions of an American editor as to how to improve one of my books, he wrote back resignedly: 'What a pity . . . We might have had a best-seller there.' Because of this mulishness (if that is how one must regard it), it is only in the last half-dozen years that my novels have started to make me an adequate income. In consequence I have always been obliged to do other jobs. . . . I do not regret the hours spent on these treadmills, since they have brought me into contact with people whom, otherwise, I might have never met. My years living abroad have been particularly valuable, freeing me from the English obsession with class. The profoundest experience of my life was my four-and-a-half years in Japan, where I developed self-discipline, a sense of duty and a love of hard work from the example of the Japanese.

"Critics often describe my view of the world as 'dark.' But it is a darkness illuminated (I hope) by acts of decency, generosity and valour. These acts are often performed in my novels (as in life) by seemingly insignificant people—the very old, the very young, the uneducated, the poor. Significantly, the woman whom I portray as a lay saint in *Act of Darkness* is, to most people in that novel, a figure of fun, to be mocked and patronised."

BIOGRAPHICAL/CRITICAL SOURCES:

BOOKS

Contemporary Literary Criticism, Gale, Volume 8, 1978, Volume 53, 1989.
Dictionary of Literary Biography, Volume 15: *British Novelists, 1930-1959,* Gale, 1983.

PERIODICALS

Books and Bookmen, June, 1968, December, 1975, November, 1978.
Book World, November 27, 1988.
Listener, April 27, 1967, September 12, 1974, October 2, 1975, December 16, 1976, October 19, 1978.
London Magazine, June, 1968.
Los Angeles Times, October 16, 1983.
New Statesman, June 23, 1967, September 5, 1975.

Newsweek, January 9, 1983.
New York Times, January 19, 1958, October 10, 1983, January 29, 1986.
New York Times Book Review, December 25, 1983, December 9, 1984, February 28, 1988, January 15, 1989.
Observer Review, April 28, 1968.
Punch, April 24, 1968.
Spectator, September 6, 1975, October 2, 1976, October 8, 1983.
Times (London), August 29, 1985, August 27, 1987, April 21, 1988.
Times Literary Supplement, May 11, 1967, September 13, 1974, April 29, 1978, November 14, 1980, April 30, 1982, October 23, 1983, September 13, 1985, April 29-May 5, 1988.
Washington Post Book World, December 7, 1984, March 27, 1988.

*   *   *

KING, Larry L. 1929-

PERSONAL: Born January 1, 1929, in Putnam, Tex.; son of Clyde Clayton (a farmer and blacksmith) and Cora Lee (Clark) King; married second wife, Rosemarie Coumarias (a photographer), February 20, 1965 (deceased, 1972); married Barbara S. Blaine (an attorney), May 6, 1979; children: (first marriage) Cheryl Ann, Kerri Lee, Bradley Clayton; (third marriage) Lindsay, Blaine. *Education:* Attended Texas Technological College (now Texas Tech University), 1949-50. *Politics:* Liberal-Internationalist-Democrat.

ADDRESSES: Agent—Barbara S. Blaine, Suite 1000, 1015 15th St., N.W., Washington, D.C. 20005.

CAREER: Oil field worker in Texas, 1944-46; newspaper reporter in Hobbs, N.M., 1949, Midland, Tex., 1950-51, and Odessa, Tex., 1952-54; radio station KCRS, Midland, Tex., news director, 1951-52; administrative assistant to U.S. Congressman J. T. Rutherford, Washington, D.C., 1955-62, and James C. Wright, Jr., 1962-64; *Capitol Hill* (magazine), Washington, D.C., editor, 1965; free-lance writer, 1964—. President, Texhouse Corp., 1979—. Member of Kennedy-Johnson campaign team, traveling in Southwest, 1960. Ferris Professor of Journalism, Princeton University, 1973-75. *Military Service:* U.S. Army, Signal Corps, writer, 1946-48; became staff sergeant.

MEMBER: PEN International, National Writers Union, National Academy of Television Arts and Sciences, Authors Guild, Authors League of America, Dramatists Guild, Screenwriters Guild East, Actors' Equity.

AWARDS, HONORS: Neiman fellow at Harvard University, 1969-70; National Book Award nomination, 1971, for *Confessions of a White Racist;* Stanley Walker Journalism Award, Texas Institute of Letters, 1973, for "The Lost Frontier"; Duke Fellow of Communications at Duke University, 1976; Tony Award nomination for best book of a musical, 1979, for "The Best Little Whorehouse in Texas"; Emmy award, 1981, for "CBS Reports" (documentary on statehouse politics); elected to Texas Institute of Letters, 1970, and Texas Walk of Stars, 1987.

WRITINGS:

The One-Eyed Man (novel; Literary Guild selection), New American Library, 1966.
. . . And Other Dirty Stories (collected articles), World, 1968.
Confessions of a White Racist (nonfiction), Viking, 1971.
The Old Man and Lesser Mortals (collected articles), Viking, 1974.
(With Peter Masterson) "The Best Little Whorehouse in Texas" (musical; also see below), first produced in New York at Ac-

tors Studio, October, 1977, produced on Broadway at 46th Street Theater, June 19, 1978.

(With Bobby Baker) *Wheeling and Dealing,* Norton, 1978.

(With Ben Z. Grant) "The Kingfish" (play), first produced in Washington, D.C. at New Playwrights' Theater, August 9, 1979.

Of Outlaws, Con Men, Whores, Politicians and Other Artists (collected articles), Viking, 1980.

That Terrible Night Santa Got Lost in the Woods (also see below), with drawings by Pat Oliphant, Encino Press, 1981.

(With Masterson and Colin Higgins) "The Best Little Whorehouse in Texas" (screenplay; based on his musical of the same title), Universal Pictures, 1982.

The Whorehouse Papers (nonfiction), Viking, 1982.

None but a Blockhead: On Being a Writer (nonfiction), Viking, 1986.

Warning: Writer at Work (nonfiction), Texas Christian University Press, 1986.

Christmas: 1933 (play based on the book *That Terrible Night Santa Got Lost in the Woods;* first produced in Memphis, Tenn., at Circuit Playhouse, 1986), Samuel French, 1987.

The History of Calhan and Vicinity, 1888-1988, Gaddy, 1987.

"The Golden Shadows Old West Museum" (play), first produced in Little Rock, Ark., at Arkansas Repertory Theater, c. 1988, produced in Washington, D.C., at American Playwrights Theater, 1989.

The Night Hank Williams Died (play; first produced at Memphis State University, 1985, new version produced in Washington, D.C., at New Playwrights' Theater, February 3, 1988), Southern Methodist University Press, 1989.

Because of Lozo Brown (children's book), illustrated by Amy Schwartz, Viking, 1989.

The Blue Chip Prospect, Penguin Books, 1989.

Contributing editor, *Texas Observer,* 1964-76, *Harper's,* 1967-71, *New Times,* 1974-77, *Texas Monthly,* beginning 1973, and *Parade* magazine, beginning 1983.

SIDELIGHTS: "Make no mistake about it—Larry L. King knows how to write," states Norman J. Ornstein in the *Washington Post Book World.* "Whether his subject is politics or country music, his locale New York, Texas, Washington or Las Vegas, King can weave together words, phrases and ideas to engross, touch, titillate or outrage the reader." King has applied his writing skills to diverse projects, from a serious look at racial prejudice in *Confessions of a White Racist* to his bawdy musical-comedy "The Best Little Whorehouse in Texas." Although the author has made his home in Washington, D.C., for many years, his Texan background influences all his writing; as *New York Times Book Review* contributor Richard Lingeman comments, King's work "is mostly about Texas, even when it is about such lesser places as Washington and New York City."

King had worked in the nation's capitol as an administrative assistant for several years when, in 1964, he impulsively left his position to return to Texas and write a novel. *The One-Eyed Man* examines the struggle for integration in a Southern university, a timely subject in the early 1960s. Critics dealt harshly with King's first novel, however. He turned his attention to magazine writing and soon found success in that field. In the *New Republic,* Foster Hirsch characterized King's magazine work as that of a man who "is flagrantly a new journalist" with a highly personal style. Several collections of his articles have been published, including . . . *And Other Dirty Stories, The Old Man and Lesser Mortals,* and *Of Outlaws, Con Men, Whores, Politicians and Other Artists;* all have been very favorably reviewed.

Despite *The One-Eyed Man*'s failure, reviewer Jonathan Yardley finds that King has many of the finer qualities of a novelist. Discussing *The Old Man and Lesser Mortals* in the *Washington Post Book World,* Yardley notes that most collections of a journalist's work only serve to point out the ephemeral nature of much magazine writing. He believes, however, "the pieces that Larry King has brought together in *The Old Man* do not merely weather the transition, they thrive on it. That is because King's work is notable for the persistence and consistency with which it explores certain themes. King is a novelist masquerading in journalist's clothing . . . and he has the novelist's sense of thematic unity. . . . He returns over and again to the same preoccupations. Chief among them, perhaps, are a reverence for the American past and a fierce dislike for the shabby commercialism with which it is being replaced. . . . King succeeds, however, in revering the past without sentimentalizing it."

Foster Hirsch also finds *The Old Man and Lesser Mortals* to be a remarkably unified collection. He suggests that the articles are bound together by King's "continuing wrestling match with his heritage. Small-town folksiness underlies the slick magazine writer's polish." Whether writing about a trip to the Alamo, a visit to a small-town diner, or a football game, "King 'works' his material for larger purposes than local color portraiture. His trips home afford glimpses of the national state of mind. . . . Skillfully King builds his miniature subjects into capacious essays on the American character. . . . With these circumscribed, personally accented pieces drawn from the American heartland, King is unfailingly vivid."

Confessions of a White Racist is as intensely personal as any of King's magazine pieces, and it is widely regarded as his most serious work. It begins with the author's youth in west Texas, where intolerance toward blacks was the unquestioned norm. King relates how he assimilated those local attitudes, then grew beyond them and left his homeland. He found, however, that prejudice was as deeply rooted, if better concealed, in Washington and Cambridge as it was in Texas. Eventually he began to question the authenticity of his own tolerance. Christopher Lehmann-Haupt writes in the *New York Times* that "King is saying that . . . since the end of World War II, when President Truman ordered the desegregation of America's armed forces, we have scarcely lifted a finger to remove the stain of racism from our national fabric—all Supreme Court decisions, court orders, and benign neglect to the contrary notwithstanding. . . . He has reached the conclusion that those of us who are not white racists are simply not white."

Geoffrey Wolff praises King's emotional honesty in his *Newsweek* review of *Confessions of a White Racist,* stating, "Its twisting, backtracking course through the author's racial prejudice bespeaks an authentic complication of values." Other critics feel that for all its honesty, *Confessions* has little new to say on its subject. Walker Percy comments in the *New York Times Book Review:* "One would have wanted from King, an astute and sensitive political observer, a book which started where this one ended." But Hodding Carter III, writing in *Book World,* calls *Confessions* "a gut-rending, excruciatingly honest account of one white man's attempt to confront and overcome within himself the sickness which afflicts us all. There is little that is loving or tender about *Confessions of a White Racist.* King hides nothing, obscures nothing, fuzzes nothing over—and thereby helps the more timid of us do the same for ourselves."

King's best-known project is far removed from the pessimistic tone of *Confessions.* "The Best Little Whorehouse in Texas" is a rowdy musical-comedy based loosely on an article King sold to *Playboy* magazine in 1974 concerning the closing of a famous country brothel in Texas. Judith Martin of the *Washington Post* calls the show, which pits hypocritical do-gooders against the essentially decent women of the "Chicken Ranch," "a spirited celebration of an old-fashioned concept of naughtiness." "The Best Little Whorehouse in Texas" became one of Broadway's longest-running plays; a film version was also produced, starring Dolly Parton and Burt Reynolds. The play took King from the uncertain life of a free-lance journalist to the 1979 Tony Awards ceremony.

But success was not without problems, as King "hilariously and venomously chronicles . . . with country-boy cunning" in what *Time* reviewer J. D. Reed considers his "best book," *The Whorehouse Papers.* Disagreements with collaborators, personality clashes, and a feeling of powerlessness as his original work was changed by others all contributed to King's worsening alcoholism as work on the musical progressed. Therefore, finds Reed, "beyond the ribaldry and self-promotion lies a melancholy, intriguing tale of a writer in trouble." King emerges from his first Broadway venture "brutalized, agonized and hospitalized, although 'about two-thirds rich.' " Robert M. Kaus also finds much to admire in *The Whorehouse Papers,* which he calls in the *New York Times Book Review* "a sharply written, funny, even moving book. . . . This is a book about making it, about how—for money, fame, or the sheer joy of it—people get things done. Such books are usually enlightening, often inspirational. This one is both. They could make a musical out of it."

AVOCATIONAL INTERESTS: Breeding show dogs, singing opera, ballet dancing.

BIOGRAPHICAL/CRITICAL SOURCES:

BOOKS

King, Larry L., *. . . And Other Dirty Stories,* World, 1968.
King, Larry L., *Confessions of a White Racist,* Viking, 1971.
King, Larry L., *The Old Man and Lesser Mortals,* Viking, 1974.
King, Larry L., *The Whorehouse Papers,* Viking, 1982.
King, Larry L., *None but a Blockhead: On Being a Writer,* Viking, 1986.

PERIODICALS

Book World, July 4, 1971.
Chicago Tribune, May 23, 1980, July 26, 1982.
Detroit News, May 16, 1982.
Life, June 11, 1971.
New Republic, March 16, 1974.
Newsweek, June 7, 1971.
New York Review of Books, September 2, 1971.
New York Times, August 27, 1968, May 24, 1971, January 31, 1974, July 21, 1982, February 6, 1986, April 10, 1988, January 22, 1989, January 25, 1989, July 2, 1989.
New York Times Book Review, November 3, 1968, June 27, 1971, April 29, 1980, April 25, 1982, February 23, 1986.
Time, May 24, 1982.
Washington Post, June 8, 1979, August 11, 1979, January 25, 1980, April 28, 1982.
Washington Post Book World, February 17, 1974, April 7, 1980, February 12, 1986.

* * *

KING, Martin Luther, Jr. 1929-1968

PERSONAL: Given name, Michael, changed to Martin; born January 15, 1929, in Atlanta, Ga.; assassinated April 4, 1968, in Memphis, Tenn.; originally buried in South View Cemetery, Atlanta; reinterred at Martin Luther King, Jr., Center for Nonviolent Social Change, Atlanta; son of Martin Luther (a minister) and Alberta Christine (a teacher; maiden name, Williams) King; married Coretta Scott (a concert singer), June 18, 1953; children: Yolanda Denise, Martin Luther III, Dexter Scott, Bernice Albertine. *Education:* Morehouse College, B.A., 1948; Crozer Theological Seminary, B.D., 1951; Boston University, Ph.D., 1955, D.D., 1959; Chicago Theological Seminary, D.D., 1957; attended classes at University of Pennsylvania and Harvard University.

CAREER: Ordained Baptist minister, 1948; Dexter Avenue Baptist Church, Montgomery, Ala., pastor, 1954-60; Southern Christian Leadership Conference (S.C.L.C.), Atlanta, founder, 1957, and president, 1957-68; Ebenezer Baptist Church, Atlanta, co-pastor with his father, 1960-68. Vice-president, National Sunday School and Baptist Teaching Union Congress of National Baptist Convention; president, Montgomery Improvement Association.

MEMBER: National Association for the Advancement of Colored People (NAACP), Alpha Phi Alpha, Sigma Pi Phi, Elks.

AWARDS, HONORS: Selected one of ten outstanding personalities of 1956 by *Time,* 1957; Spingarn Medal, National Association for the Advancement of Colored People, 1957; L.H.D., Morehouse College, 1957, and Central State College, 1958; L.L.D., Howard University, 1957, and Morgan State College, 1958; Anisfield-Wolf Award, 1958, *Stride Toward Freedom;* *Time* Man of the Year, 1963; Nobel Prize for Peace, 1964; Judaism and World Peace Award, Synagogue Council of America, 1965; Brotherhood Award, 1967, for *Where Do We Go from Here: Chaos or Community?;* Nehru Award for International Understanding, 1968; Presidential Medal of Freedom, 1977; received numerous awards for leadership of Montgomery Movement; two literary prizes were named in his honor by National Book Committee and Harper & Row.

WRITINGS:

Stride Toward Freedom: The Montgomery Story, Harper, 1958, reprinted, 1987.
The Measure of a Man, Christian Education Press (Philadelphia), 1959, memorial edition, Pilgrim Press, 1968, reprinted, Fortress, 1988.
Pilgrimage to Nonviolence (monograph; originally published in *Christian Century*), Fellowship of Reconciliation, 1960.
Letter From Birmingham City Jail, American Friends Service Committee, 1963, published as *Letter From Birmingham Jail* (also see below), Overbrook Press, 1968.
Why We Can't Wait (includes "Letter From Birmingham Jail"), Harper, 1964, reprinted, New American Library, 1987.
Where Do We Go From Here: Chaos or Community?, Harper, 1967, memorial edition with an introduction by wife, Coretta Scott King, Bantam, 1968 (published in England as *Chaos or Community?,* Hodder & Stoughton, 1968).
(Author of introduction) William Bradford Huie, *Three Lives for Mississippi,* New American Library, 1968.
(Contributor) John Henrik Clarke and others, editors, *Black Titan: W. E. B. Du Bois,* Beacon Press, 1970.

Works represented in anthologies. Contributor to periodicals, including *Harper's, Nation,* and *Christian Century.*

SPEECHES

The Montgomery Story, [San Francisco, Calif.], 1956.

I Have a Dream, John Henry and Mary Louise Dunn Bryant Foundation (Los Angeles), 1963.

Nobel Lecture, Harper, 1965.

Address at Valedictory Service, University of the West Indies (Mona, Jamaica), 1965.

The Ware Lecture, Unitarian Universalist Association (Boston), 1966.

Conscience for Change, Canadian Broadcasting Co., 1967.

Beyond Vietnam, Altoan Press, 1967.

Declaration of Independence From the War in Vietnam, [New York], 1967.

A Drum Major for Justice, Taurus Press, 1969.

A Testament of Hope (originally published in *Playboy,* January, 1969), Fellowship of Reconciliation, 1969.

OMNIBUS VOLUMES

"Unwise and Untimely?" (letters; originally appeared in *Liberation,* June, 1963), Fellowship of Reconciliation, 1963.

Strength to Love (sermons), Harper, 1963, reprinted, Walker, 1985.

A Martin Luther King Treasury, Educational Heritage (New York), 1964.

The Wisdom of Martin Luther King in His Own Words, edited by staff of Bill Alder Books, Lancer Books, 1968.

"I Have a Dream": The Quotations of Martin Luther King, Jr., edited and compiled by Lotte Hoskins, Grosset, 1968.

The Trumpet of Conscience (transcripts of radio broadcasts), introduction by C. S. King, Harper, 1968.

We Shall Live in Peace: The Teachings of Martin Luther King, Jr., edited by Deloris Harrison, Hawthorn, 1968.

Speeches about Vietnam, Clergy and Laymen Concerned About Vietnam (New York), 1969.

A Martin Luther King Reader, edited by Nissim Ezekiel, Popular Prakashan (Bombay), 1969.

Words and Wisdom of Martin Luther King, Taurus Press, 1970.

Speeches of Martin Luther King, Jr., commemorative edition, Martin Luther King, Jr., Memorial Center (Atlanta), 1972.

Loving Your Enemies, Letter From Birmingham Jail [and] *Declaration of Independence From the War in Vietnam* (also see below), A. J. Muste Memorial Institute, 1981.

The Words of Martin Luther King, Jr., edited and with an introduction by C. S. King, Newmarket Press, 1983.

A Testament of Hope: The Essential Writings of Martin Luther King, Jr., edited by James Melvin Washington, Harper, 1986.

WORK IN PROGRESS: King's papers are being edited by Clayborn Carson to be published in a twelve-volume set over a fifteen-year period.

SIDELIGHTS: "We've got some difficult days ahead," civil rights activist Martin Luther King, Jr., told a crowd gathered at Memphis's Clayborn Temple on April 3, 1968, in a speech now collected in *The Words of Martin Luther King, Jr.* "But it really doesn't matter to me now," he continued, "because I've been to the mountaintop. . . . And I've seen the promised land. I may not get there with you. But I want you to know tonight that we as a people will get to the promised land." Uttered the day before his assassination, King's words were prophetic of his death. They were also a challenge to those he left behind to see that his "promised land" of racial equality became a reality; a reality to which King devoted the last twelve years of his life.

Just as important as King's dream was the way he chose to achieve it: through nonviolent resistance. He embraced nonviolence as a method for social reform after being introduced to the nonviolent philosophy of Mahatma Gandhi while doing gradu-

ate work at Pennsylvania's Crozer Seminary. Gandhi had led a bloodless revolution against British colonial rule in India. According to Stephen B. Oates in *Let the Trumpet Sound: The Life of Martin Luther King, Jr.,* King became "convinced that Gandhi's was the only moral and practical way for oppressed people to struggle against social injustice."

What King achieved during the little over a decade that he worked in civil rights was remarkable. "Rarely has one individual," noted Flip Schulke and Penelope O. McPhee in *King Remembered,* "espousing so difficult a philosophy, served as a catalyst for so much significant social change. . . . There are few men of whom it can be said their lives changed the world. But at his death the American South hardly resembled the land where King was born. In the twelve years between the Montgomery bus boycott and King's assassination, Jim Crow was legally eradicated in the South."

The first public test of King's adherence to the nonviolent philosophy came in December, 1955, when he was elected president of the Montgomery [Alabama] Improvement Association (M.I.A.), a group formed to protest the arrest of Rosa Parks, a black woman who refused to give up her bus seat to a white. Planning to end the humiliating treatment of blacks on city bus lines, King organized a bus boycott that was to last more than a year. Despite receiving numerous threatening phone calls, being arrested, and having his home bombed, King and his boycott prevailed. Eventually, the U.S. Supreme Court declared Montgomery's bus segregation laws illegal and, in December, 1956, King rode on Montgomery's first integrated bus.

"Montgomery was the soil," wrote King's widow in her autobiography, *My Life With Martin Luther King, Jr.,* "in which the seed of a new theory of social action took root. Black people found in nonviolent, direct action a militant method that avoided violence but achieved dramatic confrontation which electrified and educated the whole nation."

King was soon selected president of an organization of much wider scope than the M.I.A., the Southern Christian Leadership Conference (S.C.L.C.). The members of this group were black leaders from throughout the South, many of them ministers like King. Their immediate goal was for increased black voter registration in the South with an eventual elimination of segregation.

Nineteen fifty-seven found King drawn more and more into the role of national and even international spokesman for civil rights. In February a *Time* cover story on King called him "a scholarly . . . Baptist minister . . . who in little more than a year has risen from nowhere to become one of the nation's remarkable leaders of men." In March, he was invited to speak at the ceremonies marking the independence from Great Britain of the new African republic of Ghana.

The following year, King's first book, *Stride Toward Freedom: The Montgomery Story,* which told the history of the boycott, was published. *New York Times* contributor Abel Plenn called the work "a document of far-reaching importance for present and future chroniclings of the struggle for civil rights in this country." A *Times Literary Supplement* writer quoted U.S. Episcopalian Bishop James Pike's reaction to the book: *Stride Toward Freedom* "may well become a Christian classic. It is a rare combination: sound theology and ethics, and the autobiography of one of the greatest men of our time."

In 1959, two important events happened. First, King and his wife were able to make their long-awaited trip to India where they visited the sites of Gandhi's struggle against the British and met with people who had been acquainted with the Indian leader. Second, King resigned as pastor of Dexter Avenue Baptist Church in Montgomery so he could be closer to S.C.L.C.'s headquarters in Atlanta and devote more of his time to the civil rights effort.

King's trip to India seemed to help make up his mind to move to Atlanta. The trip greatly inspired King, as Oates observed: "He came home with a deeper understanding of nonviolence and a deep commitment as well. For him, nonviolence was no longer just a philosophy and a technique of social change; it was now a whole way of life."

Despite his adherence to the nonviolent philosophy, King was unable to avoid the bloodshed that was to follow. Near the end of 1962, he decided to focus his energies on the desegregation of Birmingham, Alabama. Alabama's capital was at that time what King called in his book *Why We Can't Wait,* "the most segregated city in America," but that was precisely why he had chosen it as his target.

In *Why We Can't Wait* King detailed the advance planning that was the key to the success of the Birmingham campaign. Most important was the training in nonviolent techniques given by the S.C.L.C.'s Leadership Training Committee to those who volunteered to participate in the demonstrations. "The focus of these training sessions," King noted in his book, "was the socio-dramas designed to prepare the demonstrators for some of the challenges they could expect to face. The harsh language and physical abuse of the police and self-appointed guardians of the law were frankly presented, along with the non-violent creed in action: to resist without bitterness; to be cursed and not reply; to be beaten and not hit back."

One of the unusual aspects of the Birmingham campaign was King's decision to use children in the demonstrations. When the protests came to a head on May 3, 1963, it was after nearly one thousand young people had been arrested the previous day. As another wave of protestors, mostly children and teenagers, took to the streets, they were hit with jets of water from fire hoses. Police dogs were then released on the youngsters.

The photographs circulated by the media of children being beaten down by jets of water and bitten by dogs brought cries of outrage from throughout the country and the world. U.S. president John F. Kennedy sent a Justice Department representative to Birmingham to work for a peaceful solution to the problem. Within a week negotiators produced an agreement that met King's major demands, including desegregation of lunch counters, restrooms, fitting rooms, and drinking fountains in the city and the hiring of blacks in positions previously closed to them.

Although the Birmingham campaign ended in triumph for King, at the outset he was criticized for his efforts. Imprisoned at the beginning of the protest for disobeying a court injunction forbidding him from leading any demonstrations in Birmingham, King spent some of his time in jail composing an open letter answering his critics. This document, called "Letter From Birmingham Jail," appeared later in his book *Why We Can't Wait.* Oates viewed the letter as "a classic in protest literature, the most elegant and learned expression of the goals and philosophy of the nonviolent movement ever written."

In the letter King addressed those who said that as an outsider he had no business in Birmingham. King reasoned: "I am in Birmingham because injustice is here. . . . I cannot sit idly by in Atlanta and not be concerned about what happens in Birmingham. Injustice anywhere is a threat to justice everywhere. We are caught in an inescapable network of mutuality, tied in a single garment of destiny."

Another important event of 1963 was a massive march on Washington, D.C., which King planned together with leaders of other civil rights organizations. When the day of the march came, an estimated 250 thousand people were on hand to hear King and other dignitaries speak at the march's end point, the Lincoln Memorial.

While King's biographers noted that the young minister struggled all night writing words to inspire his people on this historic occasion, when his turn came to speak, he deviated from his prepared text and gave a speech that Schulke and McPhee called "the most eloquent of his career." In the speech, which contained the rhythmic repetition of the phrase "I have a dream," King painted a vision of the "promised land" of racial equality and justice for all, which he would return to often in speeches and sermons in the years to come, including his final speech in Memphis. Schulke and McPhee explained the impact of the day: "The orderly conduct of the massive march was an active tribute to [King's] philosophy of non-violence. Equally significant, his speech made his voice familiar to the world and lives today as one of the most moving orations of our time."

On January 3, 1964, King was proclaimed "Man of the Year" by *Time* magazine, the first black to be so honored. Later that same year, King's book, *Why We Can't Wait,* was published. In the book King gave his explanation of why 1963 was such a critical year for the civil rights movement. He believed that celebrations commemorating the one-hundredth anniversary of Lincoln's Emancipation Proclamation reminded American blacks of the irony that while Lincoln made the slaves free in the nineteenth century, their twentieth-century grandchildren still did not feel free.

Reviewers generally hailed the work as an important document in the history of the civil rights movement. In *Book Week,* J. B. Donovan called it "a basic handbook on non-violent direct action." *Critic* contributor C. S. Stone praised the book's "logic and eloquence" and observed that it aimed a death blow "at two American dogmas—racial discrimination, and the even more insidious doctrine that nourishes it, gradualism."

In December of 1964, King received the Nobel Peace Prize, becoming the twelfth American, the third black, and the youngest—he was thirty-five—person ever to receive the award. He donated the $54,600 prize to the S.C.L.C. and other civil rights groups. The Nobel Prize gave King even wider recognition as a world leader. "Overnight," commented Schulke and McPhee, "King became . . . a symbol of world peace. He knew that if the Nobel Prize was to mean anything, he must commit himself more than ever to attaining the goals of the black movement through peace."

The next two years were marked by both triumph and despair. First came King's campaign for voting rights, concentrating on a voters registration drive in Selma, Alabama. Selma would be, according to Oates, "King's finest hour."

Voting rights had been a major concern of King's since as early as 1957 but, unfortunately, little progress had been made. In the country surrounding Selma, for example, only 335 of 32,700 blacks were registered voters. Various impediments to black registration, including poll taxes and complicated literacy tests, were common throughout the South.

Demonstrations continued through February and on into early March, 1965, in Selma. One day nearly five hundred school children were arrested and charged with juvenile delinquency after they cut classes to show their support for King. In another incident, more than one hundred adults were arrested when they picketed the county courthouse. On March 7, state troopers beat nonviolent demonstrators who were trying to march from Selma to Montgomery to present their demands to Alabama governor George Wallace.

Angered by such confrontations, King sent telegrams to religious leaders throughout the nation calling for them to meet in Selma for a "ministers' march" to Montgomery. Although some fifteen hundred marchers assembled, they were again turned back by a line of state troopers, but this time violence was avoided.

King was elated by the show of support he received from the religious leaders from around the country who joined him in the march, but his joy soon turned to sorrow when he learned later that same day that several of the white ministers who had marched with him had been beaten by club-wielding whites. One of them died two days later.

The brutal murder of a clergyman seemed to focus the attention of the nation on Selma. Within a few days, President Lyndon B. Johnson made a televised appearance before a joint session of Congress in which he demanded passage of a voting rights bill. In the speech Johnson compared the sites of revolutionary war battles such as Concord and Lexington with their modern-day counterpart, Selma, Alabama.

Although Johnson had invited King to be his special guest in the Senate gallery during the address, King declined the honor, staying instead in Selma to complete plans to again march on Montgomery. A federal judge had given his approval to the proposed Selma-to-Montgomery march and had ordered Alabama officials not to interfere. The five-day march finally took place as hundreds of federal troops stood by overseeing the safety of the marchers.

Later that year, Johnson signed the 1965 Voting Rights Act into law, this time with King looking on. The act made literacy tests as a requirement for voting illegal, gave the Attorney General the power to supervise federal elections in seven southern states, and urged the Attorney General to challenge the legality of poll taxes in state and local elections in four Southern states. "Political analysts," Oates observed, "almost unanimously attributed the voting act to King's Selma campaign. . . . Now, thanks to his own political sagacity, his understanding of how nonviolent, direct-action protest could stimulate corrective federal legislation, King's long crusade to gain southern Negroes the right to vote . . . was about to be realized."

By this time, King was ready to embark on his next project, moving his nonviolent campaign to the black ghettoes of the North. Chicago was chosen as his first target, but the campaign did not go the way King had planned. Rioting broke out in the city just two days after King initiated his program. He did sign an open-housing agreement with Chicago mayor Richard Daley but, according to Oates, many blacks felt it accomplished little.

Discord was beginning to be felt within the civil rights movement. King was afraid that advocates of "black power" would doom his dream of a nonviolent black revolution. In his next book, *Where Do We Go From Here: Chaos or Community?*, published in 1967, he explored his differences with those using the "black power" slogan.

According to *New York Times Book Review* contributor Gene Roberts, while King admitted in the volume that black power leaders "foster[ed] racial pride and self-help programs," he also expressed regret that the slogan itself produced "fear among whites and [made] it more difficult to fashion a meaningful inter-

racial political coalition. But above all, he [deplored] . . . an acceptance of violence by many in the movement."

In *Saturday Review* Milton R. Knovitz noted other criticisms of the movement which King voiced in the book. King saw black power as "negative, even nihilistic in its direction," "rooted in hopelessness and pessimism," and "committed to racial—and ethical—separatism." In *America*, R. F. Drinan wrote, "Dr. King's analysis of the implications of the black power movement is possibly the most reasoned rejection of the concept by any major civil rights leader in the country."

Where Do We Go From Here touched on several issues that became King's major concerns during the last two years of his life. He expressed the desire to continue nonviolent demonstrations in the North, to stop the war in Vietnam, and to join underprivileged persons of all races in a coalition against poverty.

His first wish never materialized. Instead of nonviolent protest, riots broke out in Boston, Detroit, Milwaukee and more than thirty other U.S. cities between the time King finished the manuscript for the book and when it was published in late summer.

By that time, King had already spoken out several times on Vietnam. His first speech to be entirely devoted to the topic was given on April 15, 1967, at a huge antiwar rally held at the United Nations Building in New York City. Even though some of King's followers begged him not to participate in antiwar activities, fearful that King's actions would antagonize the Johnson administration which had been so supportive in civil rights matters, King could not be dissuaded.

In *The Trumpet of Conscience,* a collection of radio addresses published posthumously, King explained why speaking out on Vietnam was so important to him. He wrote: "I cannot forget that the Nobel Prize for Peace was also a commission—a commission to work harder than I ever worked before for the 'brotherhood of man.' This is a calling which takes me beyond national allegiances."

Commenting on King's opposition to the war, Coretta King observed that her husband's "peace activity marked incontestably a major turning point in the thinking of the nation. . . . I think history will mark his boldness in speaking out so early and eloquently—despite singularly virulent opposition—as one of his major contributions."

When King was assassinated in Memphis on April 4, 1968, he was in the midst of planning his Poor People's Campaign. Plans called for recruitment and training in nonviolent techniques of three thousand poor people from each of fifteen different parts of the country. The campaign would culminate when they were brought to Washington, D.C., to disrupt government operations until effective antipoverty legislation was enacted.

On hearing of King's death, angry blacks in 125 cities across the nation rioted. As a result, thirty people died, hundreds suffered injuries, and more than thirty million dollars worth of property damage was incurred. But, fortunately, rioting was not the only response to his death. Accolades came from around the world as one by one world leaders paid their respects to the martyred man of peace. Eventually, King's widow and other close associates saw to it that a permanent memorial—the establishment of Martin Luther King, Jr.'s birthday as a national holiday in the United States—would assure that his memory would live on forever.

In her introduction to *The Trumpet of Conscience,* Coretta King quoted from one of King's most famous speeches as she gave her thoughts on how she hoped future generations would remember her husband. "Remember him," she wrote, "as a man who tried to be 'a drum major for justice, a drum major for peace, a drum major for righteousness.' Remember him as a man who refused to lose faith in the ultimate redemption of mankind."

BIOGRAPHICAL/CRITICAL SOURCES:

BOOKS

Bennett, Lerone, Jr., *What Manner of Man,* Johnson Publishing (Chicago, Ill.), 1964.

Bishop, Jim, *The Days of Martin Luther King, Jr.,* Putnam, 1971.

Bleiweiss, Robert M., editor, *Marching to Freedom: The Life of Martin Luther King, Jr.,* New American Library, 1971.

Clayton, Edward T., *Martin Luther King, Jr.: The Peaceful Warrior,* Prentice-Hall, 1968.

Collins, David R., *Not Only Dreamers: The Story of Martin Luther King, Sr., and Martin Luther King, Jr.,* Brethren Press, 1986.

Davis, Lenwood G., *I Have a Dream: The Life and Times of Martin Luther King, Jr.,* Adams Book Co., 1969.

Frank, Gerold, *An American Death: The True Story of the Assassination of Dr. Martin Luther King, Jr., and the Greatest Manhunt of Our Time,* Doubleday, 1972.

Garrow, David J., *Bearing the Cross: Martin Luther King, Jr., and the Southern Christian Leadership Conference,* Morrow, 1986.

Harrison, Deloris, editor, *We Shall Live in Peace: The Teachings of Martin Luther King, Jr.,* Hawthorn, 1968.

King, Coretta Scott, *My Life with Martin Luther King, Jr.,* Holt, 1969.

King, Martin Luther, Jr., *The Trumpet of Conscience,* with an introduction by Coretta Scott King, Harper, 1968.

King, Martin Luther, Jr., *The Words of Martin Luther King, Jr.,* edited and with an introduction by Coretta Scott King, Newmarket Press, 1983.

Lewis, David, L., *King: A Critical Biography,* Praeger, 1970.

Lincoln, Eric C., editor, *Martin Luther King. Jr.: A Profile,* Hill & Wang, 1970, revised edition, 1984.

Lokos, Lionel, *House Divided: The Life and Legacy of Martin Luther King,* Arlington House, 1968.

Lomax, Louis E., *To Kill a Black Man,* Holloway, 1968.

Martin Luther King, Jr.: The Journey of a Martyr, Universal Publishing & Distributing, 1968.

Martin Luther King, Jr., 1929-1968, Johnson Publishing (Chicago, Ill.), 1968.

Martin Luther King, Jr., Norton, 1976.

Miller, William Robert, *Martin Luther King, Jr.: His Life, Martyrdom, and Meaning for the World,* Weybright, 1968.

Oates, Stephen B., *Let the Trumpet Sound: The Life of Martin Luther King, Jr.,* Harper, 1982.

Paulsen, Gary and Dan Theis, *The Man Who Climbed the Mountain: Martin Luther King,* Raintree, 1976.

Playboy Interviews, Playboy Press, 1967.

Schulke, Flip, editor, *Martin Luther King, Jr.: A Documentary . . . Montgomery to Memphis,* with an introduction by Coretta Scott King, Norton, 1976.

Schulke, Flip and Penelope O. McPhee, *King Remembered,* with a foreword by Jesse Jackson, Norton, 1986.

Small, Mary Luins, *Creative Encounters With "Dear Dr. King": A Handbook of Discussions, Activities, and Engagements on Racial Injustice, Poverty, and War,* edited by Saunders Redding, Buckingham Enterprises, 1969.

Smith, Kenneth L. and Ira G. Zepp, Jr., *Search for the Beloved Community: The Thinking of Martin Luther King, Jr.,* Judson, 1974.

Westin, Alan, and Barry Mahoney, *The Trial of Martin Luther King,* Crowell, 1975.

Witherspoon, William Roger, *Martin Luther King, Jr.: To the Mountaintop,* Doubleday, 1985.

PERIODICALS

AB Bookman's Weekly, April 22, 1968.

America, August 17, 1963, October 31, 1964, July 22, 1967, April 20, 1968.

American Vision, January/February, 1986.

Antioch Review, spring, 1968.

Books Abroad, autumn, 1970.

Book World, July 9, 1967, September 28, 1969.

Choice, February, 1968.

Christian Century, August 23, 1967, January 14, 1970, August 26, 1970.

Christian Science Monitor, July 6, 1967.

Commonweal, November 17, 1967, May 3, 1968.

Critic, August, 1964.

Ebony, April, 1961, May, 1968, July, 1968, April, 1984, January, 1986, January, 1987, April, 1988.

Economist, April 6, 1968.

Esquire, August, 1968.

Harper's, February, 1961.

Life, April 19, 1968, January 10, 1969, September 12, 1969, September 19, 1969.

Listener, April 11, 1968, April 25, 1968.

Los Angeles Times Book Review, December 11, 1983.

National Review, February 13, 1987, February 27, 1987.

Negro Digest, August, 1968.

Negro History Bulletin, October, 1956, November, 1956, May, 1968.

New Republic, February 3, 1986, January 5, 1987.

New Statesman, March 22, 1968.

Newsweek, January 27, 1986.

New Yorker, June 22, 1967, July 22, 1967, April 13, 1968, February 24, 1986, April 6, 1987.

New York Herald Tribune, October 16, 1964.

New York Post, October 15, 1964.

New York Review of Books, August 24, 1967, January 15, 1987.

New York Times, October 12, 1958, October 15, 1964, July 12, 1967, April 12, 1968, April 13, 1968.

New York Times Book Review, September 3, 1967, February 16, 1969, February 16, 1986, November 30, 1986.

Punch, April 3, 1968.

Ramparts, May, 1968.

Saturday Review, July 8, 1967, April 20, 1968.

Time, February 18, 1957, January 3, 1964, February 5, 1965, February 12, 1965, April 19, 1968, October 3, 1969, January 27, 1986, January 19, 1987.

Times (London), April 6, 1968.

Times Literary Supplement, April 18, 1968.

Virginia Quarterly Review, autumn, 1968.

Washington Post, January 14, 1970.

Washington Post Book World, January 19, 1986, January 18, 1987.

OBITUARIES:

PERIODICALS

New York Times, April 5, 1968.

Time, April 12, 1968.

Times (London), April 5, 1968.

KING, Stephen (Edwin) 1947-
(Steve King; pseudonyms: Richard Bachman, John Swithen)

PERSONAL: Born September 21, 1947, in Portland, Me.; son of Donald (a merchant sailor) and Nellie Ruth (Pillsbury) King; married Tabitha Jane Spruce (a novelist), January 2, 1971; children: Naomi Rachel, Joseph Hill, Owen Phillip. *Education:* University of Maine at Orono, B.Sc., 1970. *Politics:* Democrat.

ADDRESSES: Home—Bangor and Center Lovell, Me. *Office*—P.O. Box 1186, Bangor, Me. 04001. *Agent*—Arthur Greene, 101 Park Ave., New York, N.Y. 10178.

CAREER: Writer. Has worked as a janitor, a laborer in an industrial laundry, and in a knitting mill. Hampden Academy (high school), Hampden, Me., English teacher, 1971-73; University of Maine, Orono, writer in residence, 1978-79. Owner, Philtrum Press, a publishing house, and WZON-AM, a rock 'n' roll radio station, both in Bangor, Me. Has made cameo appearances in films "Knightriders," as Steven King, 1980, "Creepshow," 1982, "Maximum Overdrive," 1986, and "Pet Sematary," 1989; has also appeared in American Express credit card television commercial. Served as judge for 1977 World Fantasy Awards, 1978. Participated in radio honor panel with George A. Romero, Peter Straub, and Ira Levin, moderated by Dick Cavett on WNET in New York, October 30-31, 1980.

MEMBER: Authors Guild, Authors League of America.

AWARDS, HONORS: Carrie named to *School Library Journal's* Book List, 1975; World Fantasy Award nominations, 1976, for *'Salem's Lot,* 1979, for *The Stand* and *Night Shift,* 1980, for *The Dead Zone,* 1981, for "The Mist," and 1983, for "The Breathing Method: A Winter's Tale" in *Different Seasons;* Hugo Award nomination from World Science Fiction Society, and Nebula Award nomination from Science Fiction Writers of America, both 1978, both for *The Shining;* Balrog Awards, second place in best novel category for *The Stand,* and second place in best collection category for *Night Shift,* both 1979; *The Long Walk* was named to the American Library Association's list of best books for young adults, 1979; World Fantasy Award, 1980, for contributions to the field, and 1982, for story "Do the Dead Sing?"; Career Alumni Award, University of Maine at Orono, 1981; *Firestarter* was named to the American Library Association's list of best books for young adults, 1981; Nebula Award nomination, Science Fiction Writers of America, 1981, for story "The Way Station"; special British Fantasy Award for outstanding contribution to the genre, British Fantasy Society, 1982, for *Cujo;* Hugo Award, World Science Fiction Convention, 1982, for *Stephen King's Danse Macabre;* named Best Fiction Writer of the Year, *Us* Magazine, 1982; Locus Award for best collection, Locus Publications, 1986, for *Stephen King's Skeleton Crew.*

WRITINGS:

NOVELS

Carrie: A Novel of a Girl with a Frightening Power (also see below), Doubleday, 1974, movie edition published as *Carrie,* New American Library/Times Mirror, 1975.
'Salem's Lot (Literary Guild alternate selection; also see below), Doubleday, 1975, television edition, New American Library, 1979.
The Shining (Literary Guild main selection; also see below), Doubleday, 1977, movie edition, New American Library, 1980.

The Stand, Doubleday, 1978, revised edition with illustrations by Berni Wrightson, 1990 (also published in a limited edition, Doubleday, 1990).
The Dead Zone (Literary Guild dual main selection), Viking, 1979, movie edition published as *The Dead Zone: Movie Tie-In,* New American Library, 1980.
Firestarter (Literary Guild main selection), Viking, 1980, reprinted with afterword by King, 1981 (also published in a limited, aluminum-coated, asbestos-cloth edition, Phantasia Press [Huntington Woods, Mich.], 1980).
Cujo, Viking, 1981 (also published in a limited edition, Mysterious Press, 1981).
Pet Sematary (Literary Guild dual main selection), Doubleday, 1983.
Christine (Literary Guild dual main selection), Viking, 1983 (also published with illustrations by Stephen Gervais in a limited edition, Donald M. Grant [West Kingston, R.I.], 1983).
(With Peter Straub) *The Talisman,* Viking Press/Putnam, 1984 (also published in a limited two-volume edition, Donald M. Grant, 1984).
The Eyes of the Dragon (young adult; Book-of-the-Month Club alternate selection), limited edition with illustrations by Kenneth R. Linkhauser, Philtrum Press, 1984, new edition with illustrations by David Palladini, Viking, 1987.
It (Book-of-the-Month Club main selection), Viking, 1986 (first published in limited German edition as *Es,* Heyne [Munich, West Germany], 1986).
Misery (Book-of-the-Month Club main selection), Viking, 1987.
The Tommyknockers (Book-of-the-Month Club main selection), Putnam, 1987.
The Dark Half (Book-of-the-Month Club main selection), Viking, 1989.

NOVELS UNDER PSEUDONYM RICHARD BACHMAN

Rage (also see below), New American Library/Signet, 1977.
The Long Walk (also see below), New American Library/Signet, 1979.
Roadwork: A Novel of the First Energy Crisis (also see below) New American Library/Signet, 1981.
The Running Man (also see below), New American Library/Signet, 1982.
Thinner, New American Library, 1984.

SHORT FICTION

Night Shift (story collection; also see below), introduction by John D. MacDonald, Doubleday, 1978, published as *Night Shift: Excursions into Horror,* New American Library/Signet, 1979.
Different Seasons (novellas; Book-of-the-Month Club main selection; contains: "Rita Hayworth and Shawshank Redemption: Hope Springs Eternal," published in a large-type edition as *Rita Hayworth and Shawshank Redemption: A Story from "Different Seasons,"* Thorndike Press, 1983; "Apt Pupil: Summer of Corruption"; "The Body: Fall from Innocence"; and "The Breathing Method: A Winter's Tale," published in a large-type edition as *The Breathing Method,* Chivers Press, 1984), Viking, 1982.
Cycle of the Werewolf (novella; also see below), illustrations by Berni Wrightson, limited portfolio edition published with "Berni Wrightson: An Appreciation," Land of Enchantment (Westland, Mich.), 1983, new edition, New American Library, 1985.

Stephen King's Skeleton Crew (story collection), illustrations by J. K. Potter, Viking, 1985 (also published in a limited edition, Scream Press, 1985).

My Pretty Pony, illustrations by Barbara Kruger, Knopf, 1989 (also published in a limited edition, Library Fellows of New York's Whitney Museum of American Art, 1989).

Four Past Midnight (novellas), Penguin, 1990.

Also author of short story "Slade," a western, and, under pseudonym John Swithen, of short story "The Fifth Quarter."

"THE DARK TOWER" SERIES

The Dark Tower: The Gunslinger, illustrations by Michael Whelan, limited edition, Donald M. Grant, 1982, 2nd limited edition, 1984, published as *The Gunslinger,* New American Library, 1988.

The Drawing of Three, illustrations by Phil Hale, New American Library, 1989.

SCREENPLAYS

Stephen King's Creep Show: A George A. Romero Film (based upon King's stories: "Father's Day," "The Lonesome Death of Jordy Verrill," previously published as "Weeds," "The Crate," and "They're Creeping Up on You"; released by Warner Brothers as "Creepshow," 1982), illustrations by Berni Wrightson and Michele Wrightson, New American Library, 1982.

"Cat's Eye" (based upon King's stories: "Quitters, Inc.," "The Ledge," and "The General"), Metro Goldwyn Mayer/ United Artists, 1984.

Silver Bullet (based upon King's novella *Cycle of the Werewolf,* also included; released by Paramount Pictures/Dino de Laurentiis's North Carolina Film Corp., 1985), illustrations by Berni Wrightson, New American Library/Signet, 1985.

(And director) *Maximum Overdrive* (based upon King's stories "The Mangler," "Trucks," and "The Lawnmower Man"; released by Dino de Laurentiis' North Carolina Film Corp., 1986), New American Library, 1986.

"Pet Sematary" (based upon King's novel of same title), Laurel Production, 1989.

Also author of teleplay "Sorry, Right Number" for "Tales from the Dark Side" series, and of screenplay "The Stand," based upon his novel of same title. Author of unproduced versions of screenplays, including "Children of the Corn," "Cujo," "The Dead Zone," "The Shotgunners," "The Shining," "Something Wicked This Way Comes," and "Daylight Dead," based upon three stories from *Night Shift*—"Strawberry Spring," "I Know What You Need," and "Battleground."

OMNIBUS EDITIONS

Stephen King (contains *The Shining, 'Salem's Lot, Night Shift,* and *Carrie*), W. S. Heinemann/Octopus Books, 1981.

The Bachman Books: Four Early Novels (contains *Rage, The Long Walk, Roadwork,* and *The Running Man*), with introduction "Why I Was Richard Bachman," New American Library, 1985.

OTHER

(Under name Steve King) *The Star Invaders* (privately published stories), Triad, Inc., and Gaslight Books (Durham, Me.), 1964.

Another Quarter Mile: Poetry, Dorrance, 1979.

Stephen King's Danse Macabre (nonfiction), Everest House, 1981 (also published in limited edition).

The Plant (privately published episodes of a comic horror novel in progress), Philtrum Press (Bangor, Me.), Part I, 1982, Part II, 1983, Part III, 1985.

Black Magic and Music: A Novelist's Perspective on Bangor (pamphlet), Bangor Historical Society, 1983.

Stephen King's Year of Fear 1986 Calendar (color illustrations from novels and drawings from King's short stories published in horror magazines with accompanying text), New American Library, 1985.

Nightmares in the Sky: Gargoyles and Grotesques, photographs by f.Stop FitzGerald, Viking, 1988.

Contributor of stories to numerous anthologies. Also author of weekly column "King's Garbage Truck" for *Maine Campus,* February 20, 1969 through May 21, 1970, and of monthly book review column for *Adelina,* June through November, 1980. Contributor of short fiction and poetry to numerous magazines, including *Art, Cosmopolitan, Ellery Queen's Mystery Magazine, Fantasy and Science Fiction, Heavy Metal, Ladies' Home Journal, Magazine of Fantasy and Science Fiction, Maine Review, Omni, Playboy, Redbook, Rolling Stone, Science Fiction Digest, Twilight Zone Magazine, Whisper,* and *Yankee.*

WORK IN PROGRESS: A volume of four novellas entitled *Four after Midnight,* a horror novel entitled *Needful Things,* a psychological thriller entitled *Dolores Claiborne, The Cannibals: Livre Noir,* a detective story in French, and a sequel to *'Salem's Lot.*

SIDELIGHTS: "With Stephen King," muses Chelsea Quinn Yarbro in *Fear Itself: The Horror Fiction of Stephen King,* "you never have to ask 'Who's afraid of the big bad wolf?'—You are. And he knows it." Throughout a prolific array of novels, short stories, and screenwork in which elements of horror, fantasy, science fiction, and humor meld, King deftly arouses fear from dormancy. The breadth and durability of his popularity alone evince his mastery as a compelling storyteller. "Nothing is as unstoppable as one of King's furies, except perhaps King's word processor," remarks Gil Schwartz in *People* magazine, which selected King as one of twenty individuals who have defined the decade of the eighties. And although the critical reception of his work has not necessarily matched its sweeping success with readers, colleagues and several critics alike discern within it a substantial and enduring literary legitimacy. In *American Film,* for instance, Darrell Ewing and Dennis Meyers call him "the chronicler of contemporary America's dreams, desires, and fears." And fantasy writer Orson Scott Card, citing King's "brilliant" exploration of current American myths and legends, proclaims in a *Contemporary Authors* interview with Jean W. Ross: "If someone in the future wants to see what American life was like, what Americans cared about, what our stories were in the seventies and eighties, they'll read Stephen King." Moreover, says Card, in fifty years, King will be "regarded as the dominant literary figure of the time. A lot of us feel that way."

Credited with reviving the macabre in both fiction and film, "this maker of nightmares," says Andrew Klavan in the *Village Voice,* has finally become synonymous with the genre itself. A publishing marvel with nearly one hundred million copies of his work in print worldwide, not only is he the first writer to have had three, four, and finally five titles appear simultaneously on *New York Times'* bestseller lists, he remained on those lists continuously for more than a decade—frequently at the top for months at a stretch. Moreover, his recent *The Dark Half* commanded a record-shattering first printing for hardcover fiction of one and a half million copies. As David Streitfeld assesses it in the *Washington Post,* "King has passed beyond bestsellerdom into a special sort of nirvana reserved for him alone." Widely translated, King's work has also been regularly adapted for the screen and recorded on audio and video cassette, prompting Curt Suplee, in the *Washington Post Book World,* to call him "a one-man entertainment industry." While pointing out that King has not "single-handedly and overnight" transformed horror into the marketing sensation that it is, literary critic Leslie Fiedler concedes in *Kingdom of Fear: The World of Stephen King* that "no other writer in the genre [has] ever before produced so long a series of smash successes . . . so that he has indeed finally become—in his own words—a 'brand name.' " But as Paul Weingarten makes clear in the *Chicago Tribune Magazine,* "Stephen King, like any good brand name, delivers."

The genre of horror fiction, which boasts an avid and loyal readership, dates almost to the origins of the novel itself. Fiedler explains, for instance, that just as the portrayal of mundanity in Samuel Richardson's work represents a disavowal of the fantastic elements of Medieval and Renaissance Romance, "a kind of neo-fantastic fiction which abandoned the recognizable present in favor of an exotic past" emerged near the end of the eighteenth century as a partial reaction against the popular, sentimental, domestic novel. Consequently, in the aftermath of the French Revolution, continues Fiedler, "the fantastic was reborn in sinister form, as terrifying nightmare rather than idyllic dream," and was manifested in 1818 by the first and perhaps the best known of horror stories—Mary Wollstonecraft Shelley's *Frankenstein, Or the New Prometheus.* The novel was not critically well regarded during its time, though, and a similar reception awaited its progeny—Robert Louis Stevenson's *Dr. Jekyll and Mr. Hyde* and Bram Stoker's *Dracula.* Although the modern horror tale is founded in these three works, he notes in *Stephen King's Danse Macabre,* his study of the Gothic arts, especially literature, film, and television, "all three live a kind of half-life outside the bright circle of English literature's acknowledged classics."

While striking a deep and responsive chord within its readers, the genre of horror is frequently trivialized by critics who tend to regard it, when at all, less seriously than mainstream fiction. In an interview with Charles Platt in *Dream Makers: The Uncommon Men & Women Who Write Science Fiction,* King suspects that "most of the critics who review popular fiction have no understanding of it as a whole." Regarding the "propensity of a small but influential element of the literary establishment to ghettoize horror and fantasy and instantly relegate them beyond the pale of so-called serious literature," King tells Eric Norden in a *Playboy* interview, "I'm sure those critics' nineteenth-century precursors would have contemptuously dismissed [Edgar Allan] Poe as the great American hack." But as he contends in "The Horror Writer and the Ten Bears," his foreword to *Kingdom of Fear:* "Horror isn't a hack market now, and never was. The genre is one of the most delicate known to man, and it must be handled with great care and more than a little love." Furthermore, in a panel discussion at the 1984 World Fantasy Convention in Ottawa, reprinted in *Bare Bones: Conversations on Terror with Stephen King,* he predicts that horror writers "might actually have a serious place in American literature in a hundred years or so."

The genre survived on the fringe of respectability through movies and comic books, observes Fiedler, adding that during the repressive 1950s, "the far-from-innocent kids . . . fought back; surreptitiously indulging in the literature of horror, even as they listened to the rock music disapproved of by their fathers and mothers." Profoundly an offspring of the 1950s, King imparts the influence of its music and movies to the content and style of his fiction. In *Esquire,* Barney Cohen describes King's writing style as "American yahoo—big, brassy, and bodacious"; and ac-

cording to Gary Williams Crawford in *Discovering Stephen King,* it derives not only from the American literary tradition of Realism, but the horror and science fiction film, and the horror comic book as well. King grew up with rock 'n' roll, played rhythm guitar in a rock band, and still enjoys playing—even though the family feline invariably leaves the room, he told the audience in a talk presented at a public library in Billerica, Massachusetts, reprinted in *Bare Bones.* As owner of a local rock radio station, he often works to the blare of its music, and laces much of his fiction with its lyrics. And as a lifelong fan of film, he conveys a cinematic immediacy to his books: "I see them almost as movies in my head," he explains to Michael Kilgore in a *Tampa Tribune* interview.

The first motion picture King remembers seeing is "The Creature from the Black Lagoon," but another film proved more portentous. He relates to Norden that he still has difficulty expressing how "terribly frightened and alone and depressed" he felt when, in 1957, a theatre manager interrupted "Earth vs. the Flying Saucers" to announce to the audience that the Soviet Union had launched the satellite "Sputnik": "At that moment, the fears of my fictional horror vividly intersected with the reality of potential nuclear holocaust; a transition from fantasy to a real world suddenly became far more ominous and threatening." King believes that his entire generation is beset with terrifying itself because it is the first to mature under the threat of nuclear war; he adds in a *Penthouse* magazine interview with Bob Spitz that, consequently, it has been "forced to live almost entirely without romance and forced to find some kind of supernatural outlet for the romantic impulses that are in all of us." King suggests in *Danse Macabre* that "we make up horrors to help us cope with the real ones"; and, as he relates to Keith Bellows in a *Sourcebook* interview, "The more frightened people become about the real world, the easier they are to scare." Douglas E. Winter comments in the *Washington Post Book World* that "in a time of violence and confusion, it is little wonder then that so many readers have embraced the imaginative talents of Stephen King."

King's ability to comprehend "the attraction of fantastic horror to the denizen of the late 20th century" according to Deborah L. Notkin in *Fear Itself,* partially accounts for his unrivaled popularity in the genre. But what distinguishes him is the way in which he transforms the ordinary into the horrific. Pointing out in the *Atlantic* that horror frequently represents "the symbolic depiction of our common experience," Lloyd Rose observes that "King takes ordinary emotional situations—marital stress, infidelity, peer-group-acceptance worries—and translates them into violent tales of vampires and ghosts. He writes supernatural soap operas." But to Crawford, King is "a uniquely sensitive author" within the Gothic literary tradition, which he describes as "essentially a literature of nightmare, a conflict between waking life and the darkness within the human mind." Perpetuating the legacy of Edgar Allan Poe, Nathaniel Hawthorne, Herman Melville, Henry James, and H. P. Lovecraft, "King is heir to the American Gothic tradition in that he has placed his horrors in contemporary settings and has depicted the struggle of an American culture to face the horrors within it," explains Crawford, and because "he has shown the nightmare of our idealistic civilization."

Some critics, though, attribute King's extraordinary accomplishments simply to a deep and genuine enjoyment of, as well as respect for, the genre itself. According to Don Herron in *Discovering Stephen King,* for instance, "The fact that King *is* a horror fan is of more importance to his fiction than his past as a teacher, his aims as an artist, or even his ability as a craftsman." Herron suggests that although King's work may very well represent "a psychological mirror of our times," he doubts whether "the majority of fans or even his most intelligent critics read him for Deep Meaning." In Herron's estimation, most readers begin "a new Stephen King book with thrills of expectation, waiting for this guy who's *really* a horror *fan,* see, to jump out of the old closet and yell 'Boo!!!' "

"We value his unique ability to scare the living daylights out of us," says William F. Nolan in *Kingdom of Fear,* because "King, more than any other modern master of Dark Fantasy, knows how to activate our primal fears." Referring to himself as a "sort of Everyman" where fear is concerned, King admits to Kilgore that perhaps his books succeed because his own fears, some of which are the natural residue of childhood, are simply "very ordinary fears." Only through exercising his imagination, he adds, has he honed his "perceptions of them." Although he indicates to Norden that he never experienced anything paranormal as a child, he does recall being "terrified and fascinated by death—death in general and my own in particular—probably as a result of listening to all those radio shows as a kid and watching some pretty violent TV shows." Religion, too, provided its share of trepidations. "It scared me to death as a kid," he confesses to Spitz. "I was raised Methodist, and I was scared that I was going to hell. The horror stories that I grew up on were biblical stories . . . the best horror stories ever written." As an adult, though, he shares a widespread anxiety over society's propensity toward self-destruction, frets about his family's security, is resolutely superstitious, and is prey to such pedestrian terrors as bugs, airplanes, and getting stuck in crowded elevators. He also retains a vigorous fear of the dark. "The dark is a big one," he admits in the talk presented at the Billerica library. "I don't like the dark." Or as he elaborates to Norden: "There's a lot of mystery in the world, a lot of dark, shadowy corners we haven't explored yet. We shouldn't be too smug about dismissing out of hand everything we can't understand. The dark can have *teeth,* man!"

"The desire to be scared is a childish impulse, belonging to innocence rather than to experience," writes Barbara Tritel in the *New York Times Book Review.* "Frightening escapist literature lets us escape not to a realm of existential terror . . . but to the realm of childhood, when, within some cozy setting, we were able to titillate ourselves with fear." And in Tritel's opinion, "King has understood and answered a profound and popular need." While most of his fiction is aimed at an adult audience, young people are especially drawn to it, and children are vital to it. Unlike his portrayals of women, which he acknowledges are at times weak, some of his strongest characters are children; and his realistic depictions of them have earned much critical praise. Lauding King's "energetic and febrile imagination," Richard R. Lingeman adds in the *New York Times* that he has "a radar fix on young people."

Observing that children suspend their disbelief easily, King argues in *Danse Macabre* that, ironically, they are actually "better able to deal with fantasy and terror *on its own terms* than their elders are." In an interview for *High Times,* for instance, he marvels at the resilience of a child's mind and the inexplicable, yet seemingly harmless, attraction of children to nightmare-inducing stories: "We start kids off on things like 'Hansel and Gretel,' which features child abandonment, kidnapping, attempted murder, forcible detention, cannibalism, and finally murder by cremation. And the kids love it." Adults are capable of distinguishing between fantasy and reality, but in the process of growing up, laments King in *Danse Macabre,* they develop "a good case of mental tunnel vision and a gradual ossification of the imaginative faculty"; thus, he perceives the task of the fantasy or horror writer as enabling one to become "for a little

while, a child again." In *Time,* King discusses the prolonged obsession with childhood that his generation has had. "We went on playing for a long time, almost feverishly," he recalls. "I write for that buried child in us, but I'm writing for the grown-up too. I want grown-ups to look at the child long enough to be able to give him up."

Of his own childhood, King recounts to Norden that he was only two when his father (whose surname was originally Spansky, but was also known as Pollack before he legally changed his name to King) caroused his way out of the family one night, never to be heard from again. Several years thereafter, King discovered that his father had also had an affection for science fiction and horror stories, and had even submitted, albeit unsuccessfully, stories of his own to several men's magazines. With few resources after the departure of King's father, the family moved to the Midwest then back East to Connecticut before returning to Maine when King was about eleven to live with and help care for his ailing grandparents. Despite his mother's valiant efforts to provide for herself and two sons, King tells Norden that their's was a "pretty shirttail existence." Remembering being "prey to a lot of conflicting emotions as a child," King explains, "I had friends and all that, but I often felt unhappy and different, estranged from other kids my age." Not surprisingly, throughout most of King's adolescence, the written word afforded a powerful diversion.

"Writing has always been it for me," King indicates in a panel discussion at the 1984 World Fantasy Convention in Ottawa, reprinted in *Bare Bones.* Science fiction and adventure stories comprised his first literary efforts. Having written his first story at the age of seven, King began submitting short fiction to magazines at twelve, and published his first story at eighteen. In high school, he authored a small, satiric newspaper entitled "The Village Vomit"; and in college, he penned a popular and eclectic series of columns called "King's Garbage Truck." He also started writing the novels he eventually published under the short-lived pseudonymous ruse of Richard Bachman—novels that focus more on elements of human alienation and brutality than supernatural horror. After graduation, King supplemented his teaching salary through various odd jobs, and by submitting stories to men's magazines. Searching for a form of his own, and responding to a friend's challenge to break out of the machismo mold of his short fiction, King wrote what he describes to Peck as "a parable of women's consciousness." Retrieving the discarded manuscript from the trash, though, King's wife Tabitha, a writer herself, suggested that he ought to expand it. And because King completed the first draft of *Carrie* at the time William Peter Blatty's *The Exorcist* and Thomas Tryon's *The Other* were being published, the novel was marketed as horror fiction, and the genre had found its juggernaut. Or, as Herron puts it in *Fear Itself,* "Like a mountain, King is there."

"Stephen King has made a dent in the national consciousness in a way no other horror writer has, at least during his own lifetime," states Alan Warren in *Discovering Stephen King.* "He is a genuine phenomenon." A newsletter—"Castle Rock"—has been published since 1985 to keep his ever-increasing number of fans well-informed; and Book-of-the-Month Club is reissuing all of his bestsellers as the Stephen King Library collection. In his preface to *Fear Itself,* "On Becoming a Brand Name," King describes the process as a fissional one in that a "writer produces a series of books which ricochet back and forth between hardcover and softcover at an ever increasing speed." Resorting to a pseudonym to get even more work into print accelerated the process for King; but according to Stephen P. Brown in *Kingdom of Fear,* although the ploy was not entirely "a vehicle for

King to move his earliest work out of the trunk," it certainly triggered myriad speculations about, as well as hunts for, other possible pseudonyms he may also have used. In his essay "Why I Was Bachman" in *The Bachman Books: Four Early Novels by Stephen King*, King recalls that he simply considered it a good idea at the time, especially since he wanted to try to publish something without the attendant commotion that a Stephen King title would have unavoidably generated; also, his publisher believed that he had already saturated the market. King's prodigious literary output and multi-million-dollar contracts, though, have generated critical challenges to the inherent worth of his fiction; deducing that he has been somehow compromised by commercial success, some critics imply that he writes simply to fulfill contractual obligations. But as King tells Norden, "Money really has nothing to do with it one way or the other. I love writing the things I write, and I wouldn't and *couldn't* do anything else."

King writes daily, exempting only Christmas, the Fourth of July, and his birthday. He likes to work on two things simultaneously, beginning his day early with a two- or three-mile walk: "What I'm working on in the morning is what I'm *working* on," he says in a panel discussion at the 1980 World Fantasy Convention in Baltimore, reprinted in *Bare Bones*. He devotes his afternoon hours to rewriting. And according to his *Playboy* interview, while he is not particular about working conditions, he is about his output. Despite chronic headaches, occasional insomnia, and even a fear of writer's block, he produces six pages daily; "And that's like engraved in stone," he tells Moore.

Likening the physical act of writing to "autohypnosis, a series of mental passes you go through before you start," King explains to Peck that "if you've been doing it long enough, you immediately fall into a trance. I just write about what I feel I want to write about. I'm like a kid. . . . I like to make believe." King explains to Moore that although he begins with ideas and a sense of direction, he does not outline: "I'm never sure where the story's going or what's going to happen with it. It's a discovery." Neither does he prepare for his novels in any particularly conscious way: "Some of the books have germinated for a long time," he tells Christopher Evans in a *Minneapolis Star* interview. "That is to say, they are ideas that won't sink." Also, research follows the writing so as not to impede it: "Afterward," he comments to Moore, "I develop the soul of a true debater . . . and find out the things that support my side." Besieged by questions about where his ideas originate, King tells Norden, "Like most writers, I dredge my memory for material, but I'm seldom really explicitly autobiographical." And, while he indicates to Randi Henderson in a *Baltimore Sun* interview that his ideas often begin in a dreamlike fashion in which "disconnected elements . . . will kind of click together," he adds in his foreword to *Kingdom of Fear* that they can also come from his nightmares, "Not the nighttime variety, as a rule, but the ones that hide just beyond the doorway that separates the conscious from the unconscious."

King describes himself in *Waldenbooks Book Notes* as one of the eternal "Halloween people," replete with "vampire bat and a rattlesnake on my desk—both mercifully stuffed"; but a customary response when people first encounter him is that he does not seem weird enough. Noting that "they're usually disappointed," he tells Joyce Lynch Dewes Moore in *Mystery*: "They say, 'You're not a monster!' " And when he is asked, endlessly, "Why do you write that stuff?," he replies that aside from being "warped, of course," writing horror fiction serves as "a kind of psychological protection. It's like drawing a magic circle around myself and my family," he explains to the audience at the Biller-

ica library. But King also approximates the role of horror writer to that of an "old Welsh sin eater" called upon to consume the sins of the dying so their souls might hurry unblemished into heaven; "I and my fellow horror writers are absorbing and defusing all your fears and anxieties and insecurities and taking them upon ourselves," King tells Norden. "We're sitting in the darkness beyond the flickering warmth of your fire, cackling into our caldrons and spinning out our spider webs of words, all the time sucking the sickness from your minds and spinning it out into the night."

Aware that "people want to be scared," as he relates to Abe Peck in a *Rolling Stone College Papers* interview, and truly delighted to be able to accommodate them, King rejects the criticism that he preys on the fears of others. As he explains to Jack Matthews in a *Detroit Free Press* interview, such people simply avoid his books just as those who are afraid of speed and heights, especially in tandem, shun roller coasters. And that, he declares to Paul Janeczko in *English Journal*, is precisely what he believes he owes his readers—"a good ride on the roller coaster." Regarding what he finds to be an essential reassurance that underlies and impels the genre itself, King remarks in *Danse Macabre* that "beneath its fangs and fright wig," horror fiction is really quite conservative. The scare we experience from reading it is safe, he tells Henderson, because "there's a real element of, thank God it isn't me, in the situation." Comparing horror fiction with the morality plays of the late middle ages, for instance, he believes that its primary function is "to reaffirm the virtues of the norm by showing us what awful things happen to people who venture into taboo lands." Also, there is the solace in knowing that "when the lights go down in the theatre or when we open the book that the evildoers will almost certainly be punished, and measure will be returned for measure." But King admits to Norden that despite all the discussion by writers generally about "horror's providing a socially and psychologically useful catharsis for people's fears and aggressions, the brutal fact of the matter is that we're still in the business of public executions."

"Death is a significant element in nearly all horror fiction," writes Michael A. Morrison in *Fantasy Review*, "and it permeates King's novels and short stories." Noting in *Danse Macabre*, that a universal fear with which each of us must personally struggle is "the fear of dying," King explains to Spitz that "everybody goes out to horror movies, reads horror novels—and it's almost as though we're trying to preview the end." But he submits that "if the horror story is our rehearsal for death, then its strict moralities make it also a reaffirmation of life and good will and simple imagination—just one more pipeline to the infinite." While he believes that horror is "one of the ways we walk our imagination," as he tells Matthews, he does worry about the prospect of a mentally unstable reader patterning behavior after some fictional brutality. Remarking that "evil is basically stupid and unimaginative and doesn't need creative inspiration from me or anybody else," King tells Norden, for instance, that "despite knowing all that rationally, I have to admit that it is unsettling to feel that I could be linked in any way, however tenuous, to somebody else's murder."

King, who was absorbed as an adolescent by the capacity of evil to appear deceptively benign, separates the evil with which horror fiction is concerned into two types: that which resides within the human mind or heart and represents "an act of free and conscious will," and that which threatens from without and is "predestinate . . . like a stroke of lightning," he says in *Danse Macabre*. "He is obviously an intelligent, sensitive and voluptuously terrified man who writes horror stories as a way of worrying about life and death," observes Annie Gottlieb in the *New York*

Times Book Review. "He knows that we have been set down in a frightening universe, full of real demons like death and disease, and perhaps the most frightening thing in it is the human mind." King recognizes, as he says in *Time,* that "there is a part of us that needs to vicariously exorcise the darker side of our feelings," and much of his fiction probes mental perturbation. Relating to Norden that one of his darkest childhood fears was of going suddenly and completely insane, King explains that writing is a way of exorcising his own nightmares and destructiveness: "Writing is necessary for my sanity. I can externalize my fears and insecurities and night terrors on paper, which is what people pay shrinks a small fortune to do." While the process is therapeutic for the writer, it seems to extend its benefits to the reader, as well. Summarizing what he finds as one of King's most important qualities as a writer, Clive Barker states in *Kingdom of Fear:* "He shows us . . . that on the journey which he has so eloquently charted, where no terror shows its face but on a street that we have ourselves trodden, it is not, finally, the stale formulae and the trite metaphysics we're taught from birth that will get us to the end of the ride alive; it is our intimacy with our dark and dreaming selves."

Although King has frequently referred to his own work as "the literary equivalent of a Big Mac and a large fries from McDonalds," Winter cites the general hallmarks of King's fiction as "effortless, colloquial prose and an unerring instinct for the visceral." Yet, because King likes to work within traditional themes, myths, and forms, however, some critics find his work derivative and contend that he ought to be concentrating his considerable creative energy and talent in areas traditionally deemed more literary or serious. King indicates to Norden that while he has never considered himself "a blazingly original writer in the sense of conceiving totally new and fresh plot ideas," what he tries to do is "to pour new wine from old bottles." Acknowledging that he has always viewed his own work as "more humdrum or more mundane than the sort of thing the really great writers do," King tells Moore that "you take what talent you have, and you just try to do what you can with it. That's all you can do."

Careful to keep his own fame in perspective, King tells Mel Allen in *Yankee* magazine, "I'm very leery of thinking that I'm somebody. Because nobody really is. Everybody is able to do something well, but in this country there's a premium put on stardom." Describing what he calls the "occupational hazard of the successful writer in America," King tells Kilgore that "once you begin to be successful, then you have to avoid being gobbled up. America has developed this sort of cannibalistic cult of celebrity, where first you set the guy up, and then you eat him." Pertaining to such disparaging critiques as a *Time* condemnation of him as a master of "postliterate prose," and an uncomplimentary *Village Voice* profile, King tells Norden: "People like me really do irritate people like them, you know. In effect, they're saying, 'What right do you have to entertain people. This is a serious world with a lot of serious problems. Let's sit around and pick scabs; *that's* art.'" But as Cohen points out, "People consume horror in order to be scared, not *arted.*" King, however, suggests in *Danse Macabre* that horror actually "achieves the level of art simply because it is looking for something beyond art, something that predates art: it is looking for what I would call phobic pressure points. The good horror tale will dance its way to the center of your life and find the secret door to the room you believed no one but you knew of."

Although he does not necessarily feel that he has been treated unfairly by the critics, King expresses what it is like to witness the written word turned into filmed images that are less than generously received by critics. "Whenever I publish a book, I feel like a trapper caught by the Iroquois," he tells Peck. "They're all lined up with tomahawks, and the idea is to run through with your head down, and everybody gets to take a swing. . . . Finally, you get out the other side and you're bleeding and bruised, and *then* it gets turned into a movie, and you're there in front of the same line and everybody's got their tomahawks out again." Nevertheless, in his essay "Why I Was Bachman," he readily admits that he really has little to complain about: "I'm still married to the same woman, my kids are healthy and bright, and I'm being well paid for doing something I love." And despite the financial security and recognition, or perhaps because of its intrinsic responsibility, King strives to improve at his craft. "It's getting later and I want to get better, because you only get so many chances to do good work," he states in a panel discussion at the 1984 World Fantasy Convention in Ottawa. "There's no justification not to at least try to do good work when you make the money."

According to Warren in *Discovering Stephen King,* though, there is absolutely nothing to suggest that success has been detrimental to King; "As a novelist, King has been remarkably consistent." Noting, for instance, that "for generations it was given that brevity was the soul of horror, that the ideal format for the tale of terror was the short story," Warren points out that "King was among the first to challenge that concept, writing not just successful novels of horror, but long novels." Moreover, says Warren, "his novels have gotten longer." King quips in the *Chicago Tribune Magazine* that his "philosophy has always been take a good thing and beat it 'til it don't move no more"; and although some critics fault him for overwriting, Warren suggests that "the sheer scope and ambitious nature of his storytelling demands a broad canvas." Referring to this as "the very pushiness of his technique," the *New York Times'* Christopher Lehmann-Haupt similarly contends that "the more he exasperates us by overpreparing, the more effectively his preparations eventually pay off."

"I just want to scare people," King remarks to Kilgore. "I'm very humble about that." And in Yarbro's estimation, "King knows how to evoke those special images that hook into all the archetypal forms of horror that we have thrived on since earliest youth." Recognized for the varied and vivid descriptions he consistently renders of the emotion he so skillfully summons, King claims no other technique for inducing fear than lulling a reader into complacency and then "turn[ing] the monsters loose," as he relates in a *Shayol* interview. To create a comfortably familiar world for the reader so that the horrors experienced within it will seem more real, he imbues his fiction with touchstones of reality—recognizable brand names, products, people, and events. King does, however, delineate a certain hierarchy of fear that he tries to attain, telling Norden: "There's terror on top, the finest emotion any writer can induce; then horror; and, on the very lowest level of all, the gag instinct of revulsion. Naturally, I'll try to terrify you first, and if that doesn't work, I'll try to horrify you, and if I can't make it there, I'll try to gross you out. I'm not proud. . . . So if somebody wakes up screaming because of what I wrote, I'm delighted. If he merely tosses his cookies, it's still a victory but on a lesser scale. I suppose the ultimate triumph would be to have somebody drop dead of a heart attack, literally scared to death. I'd say, 'Gee, that's a shame,' and I'd mean it, but part of me would be thinking, Jesus, that really *worked!*"

Influenced by the naturalistic novels of writers such as Theodore Dreiser and Frank Norris, King confesses to Janeczko that his personal outlook for the world's future is somewhat bleak; on the other hand, one of the things he finds most comforting in his own work is an element of optimism. "In almost all cases, I've begun with a premise that was really black," he says in a panel discussion at the 1980 World Fantasy Convention in Baltimore, reprinted in *Bare Bones.* "And a more pleasant resolution has forced itself upon that structure." But as Andrew M. Greeley maintains in *Kingdom of Fear:* "Unlike some other horror writers who lack his talents and sensitivity, Stephen King never ends his stories with any cheap or easy hope. People are badly hurt, they suffer and some of them die, but others survive the struggle and manage to grow. The powers of evil have not yet done them in." According to Notkin, though, the reassurance King brings to his own readers derives from a basic esteem for humanity itself, "For whether he is writing about vampires, about the death of 99 percent of the population, or about innocent little girls with the power to break the earth in half, King never stops emphasizing his essential liking for people."

"You have got to love the people in the story, because there is no horror without love and without feeling," King explains to Platt. "Horror is the contrasting emotion to our understanding of all the things that are good and normal." While stressing the importance of characterization, he regards the story itself as the most integral part of crafting fiction. "If you can tell a story, everything else becomes possible," he explains to Mat Schaffer in the *Boston Sunday Review,* reprinted in *Bare Bones.* "But without story, nothing is possible, because nobody wants to hear about your sensitive characters if there's nothing happening in your story. And the same is true with mood. Story is the only thing that's important." Harris speaks for several critics when he observes that King is at his best when he "is simply himself, and when he loses consciousness of himself as a writer—the way the old tale-teller around the campfire occasionally will—he can be outstanding." Praising King's "page-flipping narrative drive, yanking the reader along with eye-straining velocity," Brown describes his prose as "invisible," and points to those moments of pure transport in which "the reader is caught in the rush of events and forgets that words are being read. It is a quality as rare as it is critically underappreciated."

"There's unmistakable genius in Stephen King," begrudges Walter Kendrick in the *Village Voice,* adding that he writes "with such fierce conviction, such blind and brutal power, that no matter how hard you fight—and needless to say, I fought—he's irresistible." The less reserved critical affirmations of King's work extend from expressions of pragmatism to those of metaphor. Lehmann-Haupt, for example, a self-professed King addict, offers his evaluation of King's potential versus his accomplishments as a writer of horror fiction: "Once again, as I edged myself nervously toward the climax of one of his thrillers, I found myself considering what wonders Stephen King could accomplish if he would only put his storytelling talents to serious use. And then I had to ask myself: if Mr. King's aim in writing . . . was not entirely serious by some standard that I was vaguely invoking, then why, somebody please tell me, was I holding on to his book so hard that my knuckles had begun to turn white?" Winter assesses King's contribution to the genre in his study *Stephen King: The Art of Darkness* this way: "Death, destruction, and destiny await us all at the end of the journey—in life as in horror fiction. And the writer of horror stories serves as the boatman who ferries people across that Reach known as the River Styx—offering us a full dress rehearsal of death, while returning us momentarily to our youth. In the horror fiction of Stephen King, we can embark upon the night journey, make the descent down the dark hole, cross that narrowing Reach, and return again in safety to the surface—to the near shore of the river of death. For our boatman has a master's hand."

AVOCATIONAL INTERESTS: Reading (mostly fiction), jigsaw puzzles, playing the guitar ("I'm terrible and so try to bore no one but myself"), movies, bowling.

MEDIA ADAPTATIONS: Several of King's novels have been adapted for the screen or stage, including *Carrie, 'Salem's Lot, The Shining, Cujo, The Dead Zone, Christine, Firestarter, The Running Man,* and *Misery.* "Stand by Me," based upon King's novella *The Body,* was filmed in 1986 by Columbia Pictures. *It* has been produced as a six-hour miniseries scheduled for telecast by ABC-TV in 1990. *Apt Pupil: Summer of Corruption* is being developed for production by Richard Kobritz; and *The Talisman* has been optioned for a television miniseries. Several of King's short stories have also been adapted for the screen.

BIOGRAPHICAL/CRITICAL SOURCES:

BOOKS

Authors and Artists for Young Adults, Volume 1, Gale, 1989.
Beahm, George, editor, *The Stephen King Companion,* Andrews and McMeel, 1989.
Collings, Michael R., *Stephen King as Richard Bachman,* Starmont House, 1985.
Collings, *The Many Facets of Stephen King,* Starmont House, 1985.
Collings, and David Engebretson, *The Shorter Works of Stephen King,* Starmont House, 1985.
Collings, *The Annotated Guide to Stephen King: A Primary and Secondary Bibliography of the Works of America's Premier Horror Writer,* Starmont House, 1986.
Collings, *The Films of Stephen King,* Starmont House, 1986.
Collings, *The Stephen King Phenomenon,* Starmont House, 1987.
Contemporary Authors, New Revision Series, Gale, Volume 29, 1989.
Contemporary Literary Criticism, Gale, Volume 12, 1980, Volume 26, 1983, Volume 37, 1985.
Dictionary of Literary Biography Yearbook: 1980, Gale, 1981.
Horsting, Jessie, *Stephen King: At the Movies,* Signet/Starlog, 1986.
Kimberling, C. Ronald, *Kenneth Burke's Dramatism and Popular Arts,* Bowling Green State University Popular Press, 1982.
King, Stephen, *Stephen King's Danse Macabre,* Everest House, 1981.
Platt, Charles, *Dream Makers: The Uncommon Men & Women Who Write Science Fiction,* Berkley, 1983.
Schweitzer, Darrell, editor, *Discovering Stephen King,* Starmont House, 1985.
Underwood, Tim, and Chuck Miller, editors, *Fear Itself: The Horror Fiction of Stephen King,* Underwood-Miller, 1982.
Underwood and Miller, editors, *Kingdom of Fear: The World of Stephen King,* Underwood-Miller, 1986.
Underwood and Miller, editors, *Bare Bones: Conversations on Terror with Stephen King,* McGraw-Hill, 1988.
Winter, Douglas E., editor, *Shadowings: The Reader's Guide to Horror Fiction, 1981-1982,* Starmont House, 1983.
Winter, *Stephen King: The Art of Darkness,* New American Library, 1984.

PERIODICALS

American Film, June, 1986.
Atlantic, September, 1986.
Boston Globe, October 10, 1980.
Boston Sunday Review, October 31, 1983.
Castle Rock: The Stephen King Newsletter, July, 1986.

Chernobog, Volume 18, 1980 (King issue).
Chicago Tribune Book World, June 8, 1980.
Chicago Tribune Magazine, October 27, 1985.
Cinefantastique, spring, 1981, Volume 12, numbers 2 and 3, 1982, Volume 15, number 2, 1985.
Detroit Free Press, November 12, 1982.
Detroit News, September 26, 1979.
English Journal, January, 1979, February, 1980, January, 1983, December, 1983, December, 1984.
Esquire, November, 1984.
Fantasy Review, January, 1984.
Film Comment, May/June, 1981, May/June, 1986.
Film Journal, April 12, 1982.
High Times, January, 1981, June, 1981.
Los Angeles Times, April 23, 1978, December 10, 1978, August 26, 1979, September 28, 1980, May 10, 1981, September 6, 1981, May 8, 1983, November 20, 1983, November 18, 1984, August 25, 1985.
Los Angeles Times Book Review, August 29, 1982.
Macleans, August 11, 1986.
Miami Herald, March 24, 1984.
Minneapolis Star, September 8, 1979.
Mystery, March, 1981.
New Republic, February 21, 1981.
Newsweek, August 31, 1981, May 2, 1983.
New Yorker, January 15, 1979.
New York Times, March 1, 1977, August 14, 1981, August 11, 1982, April 12, 1983, October 21, 1983, November 8, 1984, June 11, 1985, April 4, 1987, January 25, 1988.
New York Times Book Review, May 26, 1974, October 24, 1976, February 20, 1977, March 26, 1978, February 4, 1979, September 23, 1979, May 11, 1980, May 10, 1981, September 27, 1981, August 29, 1982, April 3, 1983, November 6, 1983, November 4, 1984, June 9, 1985, February 22, 1987, December 6, 1987.
New York Times Magazine, May 11, 1980.
Penthouse, April, 1982.
People, March 7, 1977, December 29, 1980-January 5, 1981, May 18, 1981, January 28, 1985, fall, 1989.
Playboy, June, 1983.
Prevue, May, 1982.
Psychology Today, September, 1975.
Publisher's Weekly, January 17, 1977, May 11, 1984.
Rolling Stone, April, 1982.
Rolling Stone College Papers, winter, 1980, winter, 1983.
San Francisco Chronicle, August 15, 1982.
Saturday Review, September, 1981, November, 1984.
Shayol, summer, 1979, winter, 1982.
Sourcebook, 1982.
Tampa Tribune, August 31, 1980.
Time, August 30, 1982, July 1, 1985, October 6, 1986.
Twilight Zone Magazine, April, 1981, June, 1981, May, 1982.
USA Today, October 14, 1982, May 10, 1985.
Village Voice, April 29, 1981, October 23, 1984, March 3, 1987.
Voice Literary Supplement, September, 1982, November, 1985.
Waldenbooks Book Notes August, 1983.
Washington Post, August 26, 1979, April 9, 1985, May 8, 1987.
Washington Post Book World, May 26, 1974, October 1, 1978, August 26, 1980, April 12, 1981, August 22, 1982, March 23, 1983, October 2, 1983, November 13, 1983, June 16, 1985.
Writer, July, 1986, July, 1988.
Writer's Digest, November, 1973, June, 1977, October, 1978.
Yankee, March, 1979.

—*Sketch by Sharon Malinowski*

KING, Steve
See KING, Stephen (Edwin)

* * *

KINGSTON, Maxine (Ting Ting) Hong 1940-

PERSONAL: Born October 27, 1940, in Stockton, Calif.; daughter of Tom (a scholar, a manager of a gambling house, a laundry worker) and Ying Lan (a practitioner of medicine and midwifery, a field hand, and a laundry worker; maiden name, Chew) Hong; married Earll Kingston (an actor), November 23, 1962; children: Joseph Lawrence Chung Mei. *Education:* University of California, Berkeley, A.B., 1962, teaching certificate, 1965.

ADDRESSES: Home—Oakland, Calif. *Agent*—John Schaffner Literary Agency, 114 East 28th St., New York, N.Y. 10016.

CAREER: Writer. Sunset High School, Hayward, Calif., teacher of English and mathematics, 1965-67; Kahuku High School, Kahuku, Hawaii, teacher of English, 1967; Kahaluu Drop-In School, Kahaluu, Hawaii, teacher, 1968; Honolulu Business College, Honolulu, Hawaii, teacher of English as a second language, 1969; Kailua High School, Kailua, Hawaii, teacher of language arts, 1969; Mid-Pacific Institute, Honolulu, teacher of language arts, 1970-77; University of Hawaii, Honolulu, visiting associate professor of English, beginning 1977.

AWARDS, HONORS: General nonfiction award from National Book Critics Circle, 1976, for *The Woman Warrior: Memoirs of a Girlhood Among Ghosts; Mademoiselle* Magazine Award, 1977; Anisfield-Wolf Race Relations Award, 1978; *The Woman Warrior* was named one of the top ten nonfiction works of the decade by *Time* magazine, 1979; National Education Association writing fellow, 1980; named Living Treasure of Hawaii, 1980; *China Men* was named to the American Library Association Notable Books List, 1980; American Book Award for general nonfiction, 1981, for *China Men;* Stockton (Calif.) Arts Commission Award, 1981; Hawaii Writers Award, 1983.

WRITINGS:

(Contributor) Jerry Walker, editor, *Your Reading,* National Council of Teachers of English, 1975.
The Woman Warrior: Memoirs of a Girlhood Among Ghosts, Knopf, 1976, Lane, 1977.
China Men (Book-of-the-Month Club selection), Knopf, 1980.
Hawaii One Summer, Meadow Press, 1987.
Tripmaster Monkey: His Fake Book, Knopf, 1988.

Contributor of stories and articles to periodicals, including *New York Times Magazine, Ms., New Yorker, New West, New Dawn, American Heritage,* and *Washington Post.*

SIDELIGHTS: Maxine Hong Kingston "blends myth, legend, history, and autobiography into a genre of her own invention," writes Susan Currier in the *Dictionary of Literary Biography Yearbook: 1980.* Her books *The Woman Warrior: Memoirs of a Girlhood Among Ghosts* and *China Men* are classified as nonfiction, but, according to Anne Tyler in *New Republic,* "in a deeper sense, they are fiction at its best—novels, fairytales, epic poems." Both books are based on the history and myth imparted to Kingston by members of her family and other Chinese-American "story-talkers" who lived in her childhood community in Stockton, California.

The Woman Warrior is described by Currier as "a personal work, an effort to reconcile American and Chinese female identities." *Washington Post Book World* reviewer William McPherson comments that it is "a strange, sometimes savagely terrifying and, in the literal sense, wonderful story of growing up caught between two highly sophisticated and utterly alien cultures, both vivid, often menacing and equally mysterious." Primarily a memoir of Kingston's childhood, *The Woman Warrior* also concerns itself with the lives of other women in her family, as embellished or imagined by the author. According to *Washington Post* critic Henry Allen, "in a wild mix of myth, memory, history and a lucidity which verges on the eerie," Kingston describes "their experiences as women, as Chinese coming to America and as Americans." "Its companion volume, *China Men . . .* attempts a broader synthesis," indicates Currier, "dealing with male Chinese 'sojourners' in North America and Hawaii, but it is inextricably tied to the autobiographical interests of *The Woman Warrior.*" Kingston's mother dominates *The Woman Warrior,* her father, *China Men,* writes Currier. "In both books," she comments, "additional characters flesh out the social, political, and cultural history Kingston introduces." *China Men* also includes the fictionalized histories of several members of Kingston's family and the community in which she grew up.

Harper's critic Frances Taliaferro remarks that the books' "titles plainly speak their ostensible subjects, female and male; just as plainly the books must be read together. Though I have no inherited command of the terms yin and yang, it seems to me that like those opposing principles the two books form one whole, for the shaping imagination is indivisible. Kingston told *New York Times Book Review* critic Timothy Pfaff that she considers the two works "one big book. I was writing them more or less simultaneously. The final chapter in 'China Men' began as a short story that I was working on before I even started 'The Woman Warrior.'"

Many of the stories included in *The Woman Warrior* are reconstructed from those Kingston's mother related to her as "lessons 'to grow up on,' " writes Currier. Kingston's mother, referred to as Brave Orchid in the book, married her father in China, before he immigrated to New York City. For fifteen years he worked in a laundry and sent part of the money he earned back to China, enabling Brave Orchid to study for certifications in medicine and midwifery, which eventually provided her with a good income and respect in what *Ms.* critic Sara Blackburn calls "a starving society where girl children were a despised and useless commodity." She came to the United States when her husband sent for her, having to give up her medical practice to work for the benefit of her family as a laundress and field hand. Her first two children had died in China while she was alone, but within her first year in the United States, at the age of forty-five, she gave birth to Maxine in Stockton, California, where the family later settled.

Maxine was named after a lucky blonde American gamester in a gambling parlor her father managed. The first of her mother's six American-born children, she grew up surrounded not only by the ghosts of the ancestors and characters who peopled her mother's tales, but also by Americans who, as "foreigners," were considered "ghosts" by her mother. And, according to *New York Times Book Review* critic Jane Kramer, the young Maxine, "in a country full of ghosts, is already a half-ghost to her mother." Kingston's memoir, described by *Time* critic Paul Gray as "drenched in alienation," is also characterized by ambiguity, since, as he points out, it "haunts a region somewhere between autobiography and fiction." It is difficult to distinguish whether the narrator of the book's stories "is literally Maxine Hong Kingston," Gray comments. "Art has intervened here. The stories may or may not be transcripts of actual experience."

The book is divided into five different sections; Kingston's character is central to the second and fifth sections, in each instance, identifying herself with a legendary warrior woman. The tales Kingston's mother told her about heroines and swordswomen were "especially appealing," writes Currier, since the actual status of females in Chinese culture was so low. Such myths had long coexisted with an ancient tradition of female oppression. As *New York Review of Books* critic Diane Johnson remarks, "messages which for Western girls have been confusingly obscured by the Victorian pretense of woman worship are in the Chinese tradition elevated to epigram: 'When fishing for treasures in the flood, be careful not to pull in girls.' " Furthermore, points out Johnson, Maxine "has been given hints of female power, and also explicit messages of female powerlessness from her mother, who in China had been a doctor and now toiled in the family laundry." Kingston dreamed of becoming an avenger, "like Fa Mu Lan," writes Kramer, "the girl of her mother's chants who fought gloriously in battle centuries ago and became a legend to the Chinese people . . . and then . . . took off her armor to be a perfect, obedient wife in her husband's house." The fantasy was impractical in Kingston's childhood community, but, as an adult, she eventually fights a more solitary, unconventional battle by coming to terms with her family through her writing.

For example, in *The Woman Warrior,* she tells the story of her father's sister whose name was never revealed to her American nephews and nieces. "No Name" aunt became pregnant with an illegitimate child while her husband was in America. Villagers raided and destroyed the family compound on the day she bore the child, and she committed "spite suicide with the baby in the family well. Since the aunt was regarded as a curse to the family, discussed only within the context of a homily, Kingston had to imagine the circumstances of her life, retelling the story in several possible variations. Sympathy for this relative was an act of rebellion: as Currier writes, "Deliberately forgotten by her family, 'No Name' aunt has an avenger in the niece, who, fifty years later, devotes 'pages of paper to her, though not origamied into houses and clothes.'" Kingston tells her mother's story in part three, concentrating on the fifteen-year interval between her husband's departure and her own arrival in the United States. Currier comments that "of the . . . women of her generation whose stories are told in this book, she is the most heroic."

Kingston turns to the men of her family in *China Men,* a book which also "span(s) two continents and several generations," according to Currier. *New York Times* reviewer John Leonard comments that it is "framed, on the one hand, by a wedding and a funeral, and, on the other, by the birth of boys. . . . In between is sheer magic: poetry, parable, nightmare, the terror and exhilaration of physical labor, the songs of survival, the voices of the dead, the feel of wood and blood, the smell of flowers and wounds. History meets sensuality." In *China Men,* writes Allen, Kingston "describes the men slaving for a dollar a week building sugar plantations; smuggling themselves into America in packing crates; building the railroads; adopting new names, such as Edison, Roosevelt and Worldster." Although women are not prominent as characters in *China Men,* Kingston told Pfaff, "There still are women who take the role of storyteller. The women are not centerstage, but without the female storyteller, I couldn't have gotten into some of the stories."

In order to "understand the men with whom she is connected," Kingston adopts many of the same techniques she used in *The Woman Warrior,* indicates *New York Times Book Review* critic Mary Gordon, "the blend of myth, legend and history, the fevered voice, relentless as a truth-seeking child's." She begins with the story of her father, who has trained as a scholar in

China, and, according to Gray, "is subject to black moods and bitterness over his low estate" during much of Maxine's childhood. Perhaps in reflection of his heritage, "his angriest curses vilify women's bodies," writes Gray. "The girl both understands and is bewildered." But, since her father was not a "story-talker" like Brave Orchid, and was silent about his past, Kingston must "piece together the few facts she has and invent the rest," Gordon writes. *Newsweek* critic Jean Strouse comments that "in a dreamlike mix of memory and desire, she tries out versions of her father's life, weaving them through her narrative." Not only does the author recreate his life in China and provide five different versions of how he entered the United States; she also widely separates the story of "the father from China" from that of the man she knew and refers to as "the American father."

In Kingston's tale, "the father from China" found his skills in calligraphy and poetry useless in the United States. After emigrating, he became part-owner of a laundry in New York City, writes Frederick Wakeman, Jr. in the *New York Review of Books,* "along with three other China Men who spend their salaries on $200 suits, dime-a-dance girls, motorcycles, and flying lessons." Kingston follows this account of idyllic bachelor existence with an ancient Chinese ghost story about a beautiful spirit woman who, writes Wakeman, "beguiles a handsome traveler until he loses nearly all memory of his family back home." Eventually, the man is "released from her spell" and returns to his wife. "In the same way," points out Wakeman, "the father from China turns away from the lure of his three high-living friends, and puts the temptations of bachelorhood behind him after his wife joins him in New York." But, according to Kingston, soon after Brave Orchid arrived in the United States and weaned her husband away from his companions—she cooked the men elaborate meals and insisted they keep the Chinese holidays—the partners cheated the father from China out of his share of the business. The couple then left for California where "the American father" had to struggle to support his family.

The book, comments Strouse, "is about a great deal more than sexual warfare, however. It tells of emigration, persecution, work, endurance, ritual, change, loss and the eternal invention of the new." In a later section of the book, Kingston presents the story of the father she knew in Stockton, and she ends *China Men* with characters of her own generation, relating the tale of a brother's tour of duty in Vietnam and his attempts to locate relatives in Hong Kong. Rounding out the book are the highly representative, embellished histories of earlier China Men who preceded her father to America. She tells of a greatgrandfather who traveled to Hawaii to clear the land and work on a sugar plantation. The overseers forbade talking, she relates, and Gordon maintains that "nowhere is Mrs. Kingston's technique—the close focus, the fascination with the details of survival strategies, the repetitive fixated tone—more successful than in her description of the plantation workers' talking into the earth in defiance of the silence imposed upon them by white bosses. The men dig holes and shout their longings, their frustrations, down the hole to China, frightening their overseers, who leave them alone." "The poignancy of that moment is the fruit of stunning historical reconstruction coupled with the imagination of a novelist," Gray indicates.

Another grandfather was hired by the Central Pacific Railroad in the 1860's to work in the Sierra Nevadas, helping to link the continent by rail, she writes. *Los Angeles Times Book Review* critic Phyllis Quan remarks that Kingston portrays this grandfather "as part of that band of migrant workers who fled the white demons' ceremonial photograph sessions held upon the completion of the tracks and were bound to other destinations, leaving a network of steel trails as the only evidence of their presence." In Taliaferro's words, he "comes closest of all these China Men to the strange essentials. Deep in the tunneled rock, he sees immovable time. Riding the wickerwork basket of the dynamiter's trade, he swings athwart cliffs and ravines, overcome by beauty and fear." Gordon indicates that Kingston's "success at depicting the world of men without women must be the envy of any woman writer who has tried to capture this foreign territory. Her understanding of the lacerations of crushing physical work and the consolations of community is expressed in nearly perfect prose." She adds: "In comparison with these tales of her ancestors, the story of the brother who goes to Vietnam is a disappointment. . . . Since Mrs. Kingston's particular genius is most suited to illuminating incomprehensible lives, the brother's life, being more understandable, does not call up her highest gifts."

Quan has similar criticisms, commenting that the second half of the book loses "the cohesion and vitality of myth of the first half," but she believes that this discontinuity is due to the fact that Kingston interrupts her narrative with a section called "The Laws," "a somewhat rude but informative overview of the immigration and naturalization policies affecting Chinese people." Kingston discussed this section with Pfaff, commenting that "the mainstream culture doesn't know the history of Chinese-Americans, which has been written and written well. That ignorance makes a tension for me. So all of a sudden, right in the middle of the stories, plunk—there is an eight-page section of pure history. It starts with the Gold Rush and then goes right through the various exclusion acts, year by year. . . . It really affects the shape of the book, and it might look quite clumsy. But on the other hand, maybe it will affect the shape of the novel in the future. Now maybe another Chinese-American writer won't have to write that history." And, as Kingston writes, "the reason the second half of the book has fewer myths is that our modern daily life has lost its myths. I am exploring how we live without nature, how we live with machines and battleships."

Throughout the rest of the work, Kingston often blends history with pure fantasy. "What makes the book more than nonfiction," writes Tyler, "are its subtle shifts between the concrete and the mythical." *Washington Post Book World* critic Edmund White comments that "by delving into her own girlhood memories, by listening to the tall tales her Chinese immigrant parents told her . . . by researching the past in books and by daydreaming her way into other lives, the author has stitched together a unique document so brightly colored that it seems to be embroidery sewn in brilliant silk threads, a picture of fabulous dragons sinuously coiling around real people, a mandarin square of triumph and privation, of memorable fact and still more vivid fancy." Kingston, he indicates, has "freely woven fairy tales into her recital of facts and rendered her account magical." As Tyler comments, "Edges blur; the dividing line passes unnoticed. We accept one fact and then the next, and then suddenly we find ourselves believing in the fantastic. Is it true that when one of the brothers was born, a white Christmas card flew into the room like a dove?"

In her imaginative fervor, Kingston often alters and even popularizes classical Chinese myths. Although, in general, Wakeman finds *China Men* praiseworthy, he writes that "as Kingston herself has admitted, many of the myths she describes are largely her own reconstructions. Often, they are only remotely connected with the original Chinese legends they invoke; and sometimes they are only spurious folklore, a kind of self-indulgent fantasy that blends extravagant personal imagery with appropriately *voelkisch* themes." He adds that "precisely because the myths are usually so consciously contrived, her pieces of distant

China lore often seem jejune and even inauthentic—especially to readers who know a little bit about the original high culture which Kingston claims as her birthright."

However, Kingston writes that, as a sinologist, Wakeman "is a scholar on what he calls the 'high tradition,' and so he sees me as one who doesn't get it right, and who takes liberties with it. In actuality, I am writing in the peasant talk-story Cantonese tradition ('low,' if you will), which is the heritage of Chinese Americans. Chinese Americans have changed the stories, but Mr. Wakeman compares our new stories to the ancient, scholarly ones from the old country, and finds them somehow inauthentic." Furthermore, claims Gordon, "the straight myth and the straight history are far less compelling than the mixture [Kingston] creates." As Kingston told Pfaff, "I have come to feel that the myths that have been handed down from the past are not something that we should be working toward, so I try to deal with them quickly—get them over with—and then return to a realistic kind of present. This time I'm leaving it to my readers to figure out how the myths and the modern stories connect. Like me, and I'm assuming like other people, the characters in the book have to figure out how what they've been told connects—or doesn't connect—with what they experience." "This sort of resurrection," concludes Wakeman, "is an important way for Kingston to establish a link between her present Americanness and the China of her ancestor's past. The myths—which by their very nature mediate the irreconcilable—initially make it possible for her to rediscover an otherwise lost China, and then summoning it, lay that spirit to rest."

BIOGRAPHICAL/CRITICAL SOURCES:

BOOKS

Contemporary Literary Criticism, Gale, Volume 12, 1980, Volume 19, 1981.
Dictionary of Literary Biography Yearbook: 1980, Gale, 1981.
Kingston, Maxine Hong, *The Woman Warrior: Memoirs of a Girlhood Among Ghosts,* Knopf, 1976.
Kingston, Maxine Hong, *China Men,* Knopf, 1980.

PERIODICALS

America, February 26, 1976.
Christian Science Monitor, August 11, 1980.
Harper's, October, 1976, August, 1980.
Horizon, July, 1980.
International Fiction Review, January, 1978.
Los Angeles Times Book Review, June 22, 1980, April 23, 1989.
Mademoiselle, March, 1977.
Ms., January, 1977, August, 1980.
New Republic, June 21, 1980.
Newsweek, October 11, 1976, June 16, 1980.
New Yorker, November 15, 1976.
New York Review of Books, February 3, 1977, August 14, 1980.
New York Times, September 17, 1976, June 3, 1980, April 14, 1989.
New York Times Book Review, November 7, 1976, June 15, 1980.
San Francisco Review of Books, September 2, 1980.
Saturday Review, July, 1980.
Southwest Review, spring, 1978.
Time, December 6, 1976, June 30, 1980.
Times Literary Supplement, January 27, 1978, September 15, 1989.
Tribune Books (Chicago), April 16, 1989.
Washington Post, June 26, 1980.
Washington Post Book World, October 10, 1976, June 22, 1980, April 16, 1989.

KINNELL, Galway 1927-

PERSONAL: Born February 1, 1927, in Providence, R.I.; son of James Scott and Elizabeth (Mills) Kinnell; married Ines Delgado de Torres; children: Maud Natasha, Fergus. *Education:* Princeton University, A.B. (summa cum laude), 1948; University of Rochester, M.A., 1949.

ADDRESSES: Home—Sheffield, Vt. 05866; and 432 Hudson St., New York, N.Y. 10014.

CAREER: Poet and translator. Alfred University, Alfred, N.Y., instructor in English, 1949-51; University of Chicago, Chicago, Ill., supervisor of liberal arts program at downtown campus, 1951-55; University of Grenoble, Grenoble, France, American lecturer, 1956-57; University of Nice, Nice, France, lecturer in summer session, 1957; University of Iran, Teheran, Fulbright lecturer, 1959-60; Columbia University, New York, N.Y., adjunct associate professor, 1972, adjunct professor, 1974, 1976; University of Hawaii at Manoa, Honolulu, Citizens' Professor, 1979-81; New York University, New York City, director of writing program, 1981-84, Samuel F. B. Morse Professor of Arts and Sciences, 1985—. Visiting professor, Queens College of the City University of New York, 1971, Pittsburgh Poetry Forum, 1971, Brandeis University, 1974, Skidmore College, 1975, and University of Delaware, 1978. Poet-in-residence, Juniata College, 1964, Reed College, 1966-67, Colorado State University, 1968, University of Washington, 1968, University of California, Irvine, 1968-69, University of Iowa, 1970, and Holy Cross College, 1977. Visiting poet, Sarah Lawrence College, 1972-78, Princeton University 1976, and University of Hawaii. Resident writer, Deya Institute (Mallorca, Spain), 1969-70; visiting writer, Macquarie University (Sydney, Australia), 1979. Director, Squaw Valley Community of Writers, 1979—. Field worker for Congress of Racial Equality (CORE), 1963. *Military service:* U.S. Navy, 1944-46.

MEMBER: PEN, National Academy and Institute of Arts and Letters, Corporation of Yaddo.

AWARDS, HONORS: Ford grant, 1955; Fulbright scholarship, 1955-56; Guggenheim fellowships, 1961-62, 1974-75; National Institute of Arts and Letters grant, 1962; Longview Foundation award, 1962; Rockefeller Foundation grants, 1962-63, 1968; Bess Hokin Prize, 1965, and Eunice Tietjens Prize, 1966, both from *Poetry* magazine; Cecil Hemley Poetry Prize, Ohio University Press, 1968, for translation of Yves Bonnefoy's work; special mention by judges of National Book Awards for Poetry, 1969, for *Body Rags;* Ingram Merrill Foundation award, 1969; Amy Lowell travelling fellowship, 1969-70; National Endowment for the Arts grant, 1969-70; Brandeis University Creative Arts Award, 1969; Shelley Prize, Poetry Society of America, 1974; Medal of Merit, National Institute of Arts and Letters, 1975; London Translation Prize, 1979; American Book Award for Poetry co-recipient and Pulitzer Prize for Poetry, both 1983, both for *Selected Poems;* MacArthur fellow, 1984; National Book Award for Poetry, 1984, for *Selected Poems;* National Book Critics Circle Award, 1986, for *The Past;* appointed Vermont State Poet, 1989-1993.

WRITINGS:

POETRY

What a Kingdom It Was, Houghton, 1960.
Flower Herding on Mount Monadnock, Houghton, 1964.
Body Rags, Houghton, 1968.
Poems of Night, Rapp & Carroll (London), 1968.
The Hen Flower, Sceptre Press, 1969.

First Poems: 1946-1954, Perishable Press, 1970.

The Shoes of Wandering, Perishable Press, 1971.

The Book of Nightmares, Houghton, 1971.

The Avenue Bearing the Initial of Christ into the New World: Poems 1946-1964, Houghton, 1974.

Mortal Acts, Mortal Words, Houghton, 1980.

Selected Poems, Houghton, 1982.

The Fundamental Project of Technology (single poem), Ewert, 1983.

The Past (includes *The Fundamental Project of Technology*) Houghton, 1985.

TRANSLATOR

Rene Hardy, *Bitter Victory,* Doubleday, 1956.

Henri Lehmann, *Pre-Columbian Ceramics,* Viking, 1962.

The Poems of Francois Villon, New American Library, 1965, new edition, University Press of New England, 1982.

Yves Bonnefoy, *On the Motion and Immobility of Douve,* Ohio University Press, 1968.

Yvan Goll, *Lackawanna Elegy,* Sumac Press, 1970.

OTHER

(Contributor) *Contemporary American Poetry* (anthology), edited by Donald Hall, Penguin, 1962.

Black Light (novel), Houghton, 1966, revised edition, North Point Press, 1980.

(Contributor) *Where Is Vietnam?: American Poets Respond* (anthology), edited by Walter Lowenfels, Doubleday, 1967.

The Poetics of the Physical World (annual writer lecture), Colorado State University, 1969.

Walking Down the Stairs: Selections from Interviews, University of Michigan Press, 1978.

How the Alligator Missed Breakfast (juvenile), Houghton, 1982.

Thoughts Occasioned by the Most Insignificant of All Human Events (essay on state of poetry in America; first published in *Pleasures of Learning,* 1958), Ewert, 1982.

Remarks on Accepting the American Book Award, Ewert, 1984.

(Author of postscript) Paul Zweig, *Eternity's Woods,* Wesleyan University, 1985.

(Contributor) Scott Walker, editor, *Buying Time* (anthology of poetry by recipients of National Endowment for the Arts grants), Graywolf Press, 1985.

(Editor and author of introduction) *The Essential Whitman,* Ecco Press, 1987.

Contributor to *Pocket Book of Modern Verse* and many other anthologies. Contributor of poetry to numerous journals and periodicals, including *New Yorker, Hudson Review, Poetry, Nation, Choice, Harper's,* and *New World Writing.*

SIDELIGHTS: Although also an author of prose and a translator, Galway Kinnell is best known for his poetry. Kinnell writes in lyric free verse and employs recurring imagery throughout the body of his work. His poetry "has been devoted to a remarkably consistent, though by no means limited, range of concerns," according to Charles Frazier of the *Dictionary of Literary Biography.* Vernon Young, in the *Hudson Review,* defines the scope of Kinnell's writing: "By turn and with level facility, Kinnell is a poet of the landscape, a poet of soliloquy, a poet of the city's underside and a poet who speaks for thieves, pushcart vendors and lumberjacks with an unforced simulation of the vernacular." The theme of death also permeates his poetry as he seeks to derive understanding of the total life experience. Alan Helms states in *Partisan Review,* "Kinnell's willed choice and his one necessity are to explore the confusion of a life beyond salvation, a death beyond redemption. The result is often compelling reading."

Kinnell frequently identifies with nonhuman elements in an effort to return to nature, where death is both necessary and cruel. A. Poulin, Jr., writing in *Contemporary American Poetry,* states, "For Kinnell, then, poetry is primal experience and myth, the most elemental kind of prayer." Frazier comments, "Most of Kinnell's best poetry is in this propitiatory mode, evoking natural objects, creatures, and landscapes to come to terms with and attempt to transcend temporality."

Kinnell's verse pays homage to numerous great poets, including Ezra Pound, Robert Frost, William Carlos Williams, T. S. Eliot, William Blake, E. E. Cummings, and Robert Lowell. Critics most often compare his work, however, to that of Walt Whitman because of its transcendental philosophy and personal intensity. Robert Langbaum observes in *American Poetry Review,* "Like the romantic poets to whose tradition he belongs, Kinnell tries to pull an immortality out of our mortality." Charles Molesworth, in *Western Humanities Review,* notes a poetic legacy in Kinnell's writing from Pound, Blake and Whitman. Yet Molesworth perceives an ultimate difference from these poets in terms of Kinnell's poetic direction, claiming "Kinnell became a shamanist, rather than a historicist, of the imagination." While Pound and Blake recorded their perceptions of spiritual realities, Kinnell's poetry conveys the authenticity and intensity of actual participation in them.

Like William Carlos Williams and Robert Frost, Kinnell records the actual speech of other voices in his narrative poems. However, his narrative structure is most like Whitman's, built from the natural rhythms of speech and the balanced rhetoric of Biblical poetry. Frazier notes an overall influence by Whitman on Kinnell's work: "In developing his sense of the potentiality of free verse to correspond not to some external pattern but to what he calls 'the rhythm of what's being said,' Kinnell points most often to Walt Whitman, rather than to Ezra Pound or William Carlos Williams, as the single greatest formal influence on his poetry. Whitmanesque roughness and colloquiality make themselves felt not only in the longer, looser poems . . ., but also in the shorter, more personal lyrics."

To illustrate his themes, Kinnell chooses earthy, natural elements: animals, blood, stars, skeletons, insects. These primitive images help him explore the subconscious archetypal experiences common to all humans. Another recurring image is the regenerative power of nature, sometimes seen in the least promising settings. Jerome McGann writes in the *Chicago Review* that "in [Galway Kinnell] we see that the idea of paradise gets reborn in the cultivation of waste places." Among his key images are fire and death, which take on a religious significance in his verse. Kinnell utilizes burning and death as cyclical phenomena: consumption by flame leads to death, which in turn allows rebirth. According to Richard Howard in his *Alone with America: Essays on the Art of Poetry in the United States since 1950:* "The poetry of Galway Kinnell is an Ordeal by Fire. . . . It is fire—in its constant transformations, its endless resurrection—which is reality, for Kinnell. . . . The agony of that knowledge—the knowledge or at least the conviction that all must be consumed in order to be reborn, must be reduced to ash in order to be redeemed—gives Galway Kinnell's poetry its astonishing resonance." Alan Williamson comments in *American Poetry* since 1960, "In poem after poem, Kinnell resuffers one identical ordeal, accepting death in order to be able to accept life, and concomitantly—like his Thoreau in 'The Last River'—accepting cruel appetites in order to accept his full animal being, and avoid a crueller sado-masochistic spirituality." McGann perceives a similar vision in Kinnell's work, stating: "Life is found in death, fountains in deserts, gain in loss, spring in winter, light in darkness. All these matters are the recurrent subjects of Kinnell's verse. He is a hero of the Absolute whose civilization exists in a burning mind which dreams forever upon itself, its first imagining."

Among those poems that capture the essence of Kinnell's primitive, animalistic vision are several selections from *Body Rags.* "Kinnell's animal poems are explorations of the poet's deepest self," explains Marjorie G. Perloff in *Contemporary Literature.* In perhaps the best known of these poems, "The Bear," Kinnell "seeks entrance into a primitive state of identification with the nonhuman," comments Frazier. The poem, based on an actual incident in which a hunter consumes a bear's excrement, was inspired by an E. E. Cummings poem. Writing in *Modern Poetry Studies,* John Hobbs relates how "The Bear" originated: "Speaking of the origins of 'The Bear' in an interview Kinnell said: 'I guess I had just read Cummings's poem on Olaf. . . . And then I remembered this bear story, how the bear's shit was infused with blood, so that the hunter by eating the bear's excrement was actually nourished by what the bear's wound infused into it.' " "The Bear" extrapolates the incident and follows the hunter as his identity merges with that of the bear he stalks. Hobbs adds, "To the question of a conflict between the sacredness of all life and killing the bear, we can see that the hunter slowly becomes the bear, even after its death. . . . In a sense, the hunter hunts and kills himself."

Writing in the *Washington Post Book World,* Robert Hass comments that in Kinnell's *Selected Poems,* "which samples almost 30 years of writing, it is increasingly clear that Kinnell's ambition all along has been to hold death up to life, as if he had it by the scruff of the neck, and to keep it there until he has extracted a blessing from it." "To have poetry that matters, you have to carry every experience through, take it to its ultimate point," Kinnell told *Los Angeles Times* contributor Berkley Hudson. Often in his poems, as in "The Bear," Kinnell observes his subject so closely that he merges with it and speaks from its perspective. For example, in "Testament of the Thief," the poet's study of various addicts leads to a comment on his own compulsion to write poetry—a process he has compared to extracting a tapeworm "whom you can drag forth / only by winding him up on a matchstick / a quarter turn a day for the rest of your days: / this map of my innards." And in "The Porcupine," he identifies with a torn animal that eviscerates itself in its flight from pain.

Kinnell weaves this kind of pointedly unlovely image into many of his poems in order to present a balanced and accurate depiction of life. Hudson cites Kinnell's explanation: "I've tried to carry my poetry as far as I could, to dwell on the ugly as fully, as far, and as long, as I could stomach it. Probably more than most poets I have included in my work the unpleasant because I think if you are ever going to find any kind of truth to poetry it has to be based on all of experience rather than on a narrow segment of cheerful events."

Kinnell achieved major recognition with two works, *The Avenue Bearing the Initial of Christ into the New World: Poems, 1946-1964*—a collection in which the title poem "is still arguably as good as anything he has written," asserts Williamson—and *The Book of Nightmares.* About the poem "Avenue," which explores life on Avenue C in New York's lower East Side, Williamson adds, "It reminds one of Crane and early Lowell in its sonority, but more of [T. S. Eliot's] 'The Waste Land'—if, indeed, of anything in literature in its ability to include a seething cauldron of urban sensations, of randomness and ugliness, yet hold its own poetic shape." James Atlas of *Poetry* concurs with Williamson's opinion of Eliot's influence on the work: "*The Avenue Bearing*

the Initial of Christ into the New World is one of the most vivid legacies of [*The Waste Land*] in English, building its immense rhetorical power from the materials of several dialects, litanies of place, and a profound sense of the spiritual disintegration that Eliot divined in modern urban life. And, like Eliot's, Kinnell's is a religious poem. . . . Since it is impossible to isolate any single passage from the magnificent sprawl of this poem, I can only suggest its importance by stressing that my comparison of it to [*The Waste Land*] was intended to be less an arbitrary reference than an effort to estimate the poem's durable achievement."

The Book of Nightmares "emerges as one of the best long poems of recent years," according to Langbaum. "[It] is, like so many poems, autobiographical and confessional. . . . Kinnell uses free verse; but he universalizes his experience through an imagery that connects it with cosmic process." Langbaum concludes that "even with its weak spots, its few lapses in intensity, *The Book of Nightmares* is major poetry." Fred Moramarco describes *The Book of Nightmares* in *Western Humanities Review* as "simply a stunning work, rich in its imagery, haunting in its rhythms, evocative and terrifyingly accurate in its insights."

Poems in the later volumes *Mortal Acts, Mortal Words* and *The Past* maintain the balance and intensity of *The Book of Nightmares,* but critics discern a change in Kinnell's orientation. Michiko Kakutani of the *New York Times* observes, "Human mortality, as ever, remain[s] Mr. Kinnell's great subject, but one sense[s] that his perspective has begun to shift. Whereas the earlier works focused on the skull beneath the skin," or the hidden horror of life, "the later ones dwell, however tentatively, on the undying spirit, on the possibility that death may mean not mere extinction, but a reconciliation with the universe's great ebb and flow." Furthermore, though they illustrate the inevitability of loss, they reaffirm that affection survives separations and betrayals; that poetry salvages some of what we must finally lose forever; and that life—even corrupt life—is worth living.

Selected Poems, for which Kinnell won the Pulitzer Prize and was co-winner of the American Book Award, is "more than a good introduction to Galway Kinnell's work," writes Morris Dickstein in the *New York Times Book Review.* "It is a full scale dossier for those who consider him, at 55, one of the true master poets of his generation and a writer whose career exemplifies some of what is best in contemporary poetry. . . . There are few others writing today in whose work we feel so strongly the full human presence." Hass adds, "Kinnell is widely read by the young who read poetry. If this were a different culture, he would simply be widely read. . . . The common reader—the one who reads at night or on the beach for pleasure and instruction and diversion—who wants to sample the poetry being written in [his] part of the 20th century could do very well beginning with Galway Kinnell's *Selected Poems.*"

BIOGRAPHICAL/CRITICAL SOURCES:

BOOKS

Cambon, Glauco, *Recent American Poetry,* University of Minnesota, 1962.
Contemporary Literary Criticism, Gale, Volume 1, 1973, Volume 2, 1974, Volume 3, 1975, Volume 5, 1976, Volume 13, 1980, Volume 29, 1984.
Dickey, James, *Babel to Byzantium,* Farrar, Straus, 1956, new edition, 1968.
Dictionary of Literary Biography, Gale, Volume 5: *American Poets since World War II,* 1980.
Dictionary of Literary Biography Yearbook, 1987, Gale, 1988.

Galway Kinnell: A Bibliography and Index of His Published Works and Criticism of Them, Frederick W. Crumb Memorial Library, State University College (Potsdam, N.Y.), 1968.

Guimond, James, *Seeing and Healing: The Poetry of Galway Kinnell,* Associated Faculty Press, 1988.

Howard, Richard, *Alone with America: Essays on the Art of Poetry in the United States since 1950,* Atheneum, 1965, new edition, 1969.

Kinnell, Galway, *Body Rags,* Houghton, 1968.

Kinnell, *Walking down the Stairs: Selections from Interviews,* University of Michigan Press, 1978.

Kinnell, *Mortal Acts, Mortal Words,* Houghton, 1980.

Mills, Ralph, *Cry of the Human,* University of Illinois Press, 1975.

Nelson, Howard, editor, *On the Poetry of Galway Kinnell: The Wages of Dying,* University of Michigan, 1987.

Poulin, Jr., A., editor, *Contemporary American Poetry,* Houghton, 1985.

Shaw, Robert B., editor, *American Poetry since 1960: Some Critical Perspectives,* Dufour, 1974.

Zimmerman, Lee, *Intricate and Simple Things: The Poetry of Galway Kinnell,* University of Illinois Press, 1987.

PERIODICALS

American Book Review, March, 1987.
American Poetry Review, March/April, 1979.
Atlantic Monthly, February, 1972.
Beloit Poetry Journal, spring, 1968, fall-winter, 1971-72.
Carleton Miscellany, spring-summer, 1972.
Chicago Review, Volume 25, number 1, 1973, Volume 27, number 1, 1975.
Chicago Tribune Book World, June 8, 1980, February 2, 1986.
Commonweal, November 4, 1960, December 24, 1971, August 15, 1986.
Contemporary Literature, winter, 1973, autumn, 1979.
Explicator, April, 1975.
Hudson Review, summer, 1968, autumn, 1971, winter, 1974-75, spring, 1986.
Kenyon Review, summer, 1986.
Los Angeles Times, June 16, 1983.
Massachusetts Review, summer, 1984.
Modern Poetry Studies, winter, 1974, number 11, 1982.
New Republic, July 27, 1974, August 3, 1974.
New York Times, September 1, 1971, November 2, 1985.
New York Times Book Review, July 5, 1964, February 18, 1968, November 21, 1971, January 12, 1975, June 22, 1980, September 19, 1982, March 2, 1986.
Parnassus, fall/winter, 1974, spring/summer/fall/winter, 1980.
Partisan Review, winter, 1967, Volume XLIV, number 2, 1977.
Perspective, spring, 1968.
Poetry, February, 1961, February, 1967, November, 1972, February, 1975.
Princeton University Library Chronicle, autumn, 1963.
Shenandoah, fall, 1973.
Times Literary Supplement, September 21, 1969, March 1, 1985, November 12, 1987.
Washington Post Book World, September 5, 1982, January 5, 1986.
Western Humanities Review, spring, 1972, summer, 1973.
Yale Review, autumn, 1968.

KINSELLA, Thomas 1928-

PERSONAL: Surname accented on first syllable; born May 4, 1928, in Dublin, Ireland; son of John Paul (a trade unionist and brewery worker) and Agnes (Casserly) Kinsella; married Eleanor Walsh, December 28, 1955; children: Sara, John, Mary. *Education:* University College, Dublin, diploma in public administration, 1949.

ADDRESSES: Home—47 Percy Ln., Dublin 4, Ireland. *Office*—English Department, Temple University, Philadelphia, Pa. 19103; and Peppercanister Press, 47 Percy Ln., Dublin 4, Ireland.

CAREER: Poet. Irish Civil Service, Dublin, Ireland, Land Commission, junior executive officer, 1946-50, Department of Finance, administrative officer, 1950-60, assistant principal officer, 1960-65; Southern Illinois University at Carbondale, poet-in-residence, 1965-67, professor of English, 1967-70; Temple University, Philadelphia, Pa., professor of English, 1970—, founding director, Temple-in-Dublin Irish Tradition program, 1976—. Founding director, Peppercanister Press, Dublin, 1972—; director, Dolmen Press Ltd. and Cuala Press Ltd., Dublin. Artistic director, Lyric Players Theatre, Belfast, Ireland.

MEMBER: Irish Academy of Letters.

AWARDS, HONORS: Guinness Poetry Award, 1958, for *Another September;* Irish Arts Council Triennial Book Award, 1961, for *Poems and Translations;* Denis Devlin Memorial Award, 1964-66, for *Wormwood,* and 1967-69, for *Nightwalker and Other Poems;* Guggenheim fellowship, 1968-69 and 1971-72.

WRITINGS:

POETRY

The Starlit Eye, Dolmen Press, 1952.
Three Legendary Sonnets, Dolmen Press, 1952.
Per Imaginem, Dolmen Press, 1953.
Death of a Queen, Dolmen Press, 1956.
Poems, Dolmen Press, 1956.
Another September (Poetry Book Society choice), Dolmen Press, 1958, revised edition, 1962.
Moralities, Dolmen Press, 1960.
(Contributor) Robin Skelton, editor, *Six Irish Poets,* Oxford University Press, 1962.
(With Douglas Livingstone and Anne Sexton) *Poems,* Oxford University Press, 1968.
Poems and Translations, Dolmen Press, Atheneum, 1961.
(With John Montague and Richard Murphy) *Three Irish Poets,* [Dublin], 1961.
Downstream (Poetry Book Society choice), Dolmen Press, 1962.
Wormwood, Dolmen Press, 1966.
Nightwalker, Dolmen Press, 1967.
Nightwalker and Other Poems, Dolmen Press, 1968, Knopf, 1969.
Tear, Pym-Randall, 1969.
Finistere, Dolmen Press, 1971.
Notes from the Land of the Dead: Poems, Cuala Press, 1972, published as *Notes from the Land of the Dead and Other Poems,* Knopf, 1973.
Butcher's Dozen: A Lesson for the Octave of Widgery, Peppercanister, 1972.
A Selected Life, Peppercanister, 1972.
Vertical Man, Peppercanister, 1973.
The Good Fight, Peppercanister, 1973.
New Poems, 1973, Dolmen Press, 1973.
Selected Poems, 1956-1968, Dolmen Press, 1973.

One, Peppercanister, 1974.

A Technical Supplement, Peppercanister, 1975.

Song of the Night and Other Poems, Peppercanister, 1978.

The Messenger, Peppercanister, 1978.

Poems, 1956-1973, Wake Forest University Press, 1979.

Peppercanister Poems, 1972-1978 (also see below), Wake Forest University Press, 1979.

Fifteen Dead (also see below), Dufour, 1979.

Peppercanister Poems, 1972-1978 [and] *Fifteen Dead,* Wake Forest University Press, 1979.

One and Other Poems, Dolmen Press, 1979.

Poems, 1956-76, Dolmen Press, 1980.

Songs of the Psyche, Peppercanister, 1985.

Her Vertical Smile, Peppercanister, 1985.

Blood and Family, Oxford University Press, 1989.

TRANSLATOR FROM THE GAELIC

The Breastplate of Saint Patrick, Dolmen Press, 1954, published as *Faeth Fiada: The Breastplate of Saint Patrick,* 1957.

Longes Mac n-Usnig, *The Exile and Death of the Sons of Usnech,* Dolmen Press, 1954.

Thirty Three Triads, Dolmen Press, 1955.

The Tain, Dolmen Press, 1969, Oxford University Press, 1970, reprinted, 1985.

Sean O'Tuama, editor, *An Duanaire—An Irish Anthology: Poems of the Dispossessed, 1600-1900,* Dolmen Press, 1980, University of Pennsylvania Press, 1981.

OTHER

(Contributing editor) *The Dolmen Miscellany of Irish Writing,* Dolmen Press, 1962.

(With W. B. Yeats) *Davis, Mangan, Ferguson?: Tradition and the Irish Writer* (essays), Dolmen Press, 1970.

(Editor) Austin Clarke, *Selected Poems of Austin Clarke,* Dolmen Press, 1980.

(Editor) Sean O'Riada, *Our Musical Heritage* (lectures on Irish traditional music), Gael-Linn, 1981.

(Editor and translator from the Gaelic) *The New Oxford Book of Irish Verse,* Oxford University Press, 1986.

WORK IN PROGRESS: Poetry.

SIDELIGHTS: Calvin Bedient maintains in the *New York Times Book Review* that Thomas Kinsella "can hardly write a worthless poem." He is "probably the most accomplished, fluent, and ambitious Irish poet of the younger generation," according to *New York Times Book Review* critic John Montague, while Thomas H. Jackson in *Dictionary of Literary Biography* judges that Kinsella's "technical virtuosity and the profound originality of his subject matter set him apart from his contemporaries." He "seems to me to have the most distinctive voice of his generation in Ireland, though it is also the most versatile and the most sensitive to 'outside' influences," M. L. Rosenthal indicates in *The New Poets: American and British Poetry since World War II.*

Kinsella has described himself as coming from "a typical Dublin family," Jackson reports. His father, a longtime socialist, was a member of the Labour Party and the Left Book Club, and by means of a series of grants and scholarships, Kinsella pursued a science degree at University College in Dublin, where he ultimately obtained a diploma in public administration. He entered the Irish civil service in 1946, but, with the encouragement of his wife in particular, also pursued his craft. During those early years, he met Liam Miller, founder of Dolmen Press, who published several of Kinsella's works; later Kinsella became a director of the press. He also established an important friendship at that time with Sean O'Riada, a musician described by a *Times*

Literary Supplement critic as "the most distinguished of modern Irish composers," who became, in Jackson's words, "a much-loved participant in [Kinsella's] growing intellectual life. O'Riada "expressed in his life as much as in his music what seems to be a current Irish ambition in the arts—namely, to contain the world in the capacious and elegant vessel of the Irish imagination and tradition," explains the *Times Literary Supplement* critic.

Kinsella, too, "has explored Irish themes more and more in his later verse," writes Jackson, "but only in terms of exploring his own consciousness and consciousness in general." His poems since 1956, Kinsella writes *CA,* have been "almost entirely lyrical—have dealt with love, death and the artistic act; with persons and relationships, places and objects, seen against the world's processes of growth, maturing and extinction." By the time he wrote *Nightwalker and Other Poems,* which was first published in 1968, he had become "more and more concerned—in longer poems—with questions of value and order, seeing the human function (in so far as it is not simply to survive the ignominies of existence) as the eliciting of order from experience—the detection of the significant substance of the individual and common past and its translation imaginatively, scientifically, bodily, into an increasingly coherent and capacious entity; or the attempt to do this, to the point of failure." A *Times Literary Supplement* reviewer characterizes Kinsella's earlier poems as "on the whole less distraughtly introspective than [his more] recent work" but indicates that "they display the same fine knack of delving deeply into self-communion while staying nervously responsive to an actual world."

"All Kinsella's finest [early] poems are written in partial forfeiture to the inevitable destruction of life and pleasure," Calvin Bedient maintains in *Eight Contemporary Poets.* The theme of his first major collection *Another September,* according to Jackson, "is order, the fruit of art, which in Kinsella's view is one major form of the mind's stance against mutability and corruption." Most of the poems in that volume, particularly "Baggot Street Deserta," confront "with stoic acceptance the grim fact of loss as a chief keynote of life," Jackson comments. In Kinsella's eyes "life is a tide of loss, disorder, and corruption, and the poetic impulse is an impulse to stem that tide, to place form where time leaves disorder and pain." Kinsella's collection *Downstream,* which includes five poems published earlier as *Moralities,* also conveys a "preoccupation with the passing of time—change as dying, change as birth—that has marked Kinsella's poetic mind from very early on," indicates Jackson.

In *Downstream,* Kinsella "turns more to the things people actually do in and with their lives. That many of the poems' titles refer to jobs, types of people, and life choices signals the linkage of the temporal and the abstract, the deeply buried and the visibly lived." This volume includes the "earliest of Kinsella's journey poems," points out Jackson, "A Country Walk" and "Downstream." And, in the opinion of John D. Engle in *Parnassus,* these are Kinsella's "most lasting early poems."

Beginning with *Downstream* and continuing with the short sequence *Wormwood* and the cumulative *Nightwalker and Other Poems,* "Kinsella emerged as a master not of slick verse but more saddened, more naked, more groping—of a poetry of subdued but unrelenting power," Bedient indicates. "Here surfaced a poetry that, if almost completely without a surprising use of words, all being toned to a grave consistency, has yet the eloquence of a restrained sorrow, a sorrow so lived-in that it seems inevitable. With its sensitive density of mood, its unself-conscious manner, there is nothing in this poetry for other poets to imitate. Its great quality is the modesty and precision of its seriousness."

The poem "Nightwalker" itself is "a long nocturnal meditation on Ireland past and present, on the poet's consciousness as a source of order amid decay and betrayal," Jackson relates. The culminating poem in *Nightwalker and Other Poems,* "Phoenix Park," is a journey poem described by Jackson as "an ambitious composition that shows how far the poet has come since his earliest work. The title is the name of Dublin's largest park, but it bears connotation of the phoenix itself, the bird that rises from the ashes of its own cremation to live another millennium." John Montague in *New York Times Book Review* refers to the poem as the poet's "farewell to Ireland, in the shape of a drive with his wife along the Liffey [River], as well as an extension of the theme of married love." The poet and his wife, who are about to leave Dublin, drive past "various places meaningful to them," according to Jackson, and "the poet recalls their significance or associations . . . ; he reviews symbolic moments of his life, where he partook of possibilities which his children came to pursue or re-enact."

Modern travel poems like these face "a solitary consciousness towards place and time yet do not, as it were, sit still, are not even ostensibly at rest, but move through the world, continually stimulated to new observations, reactions, associations," Bedient observes. "Cast through space, these poems bring a flutter to the tentativeness of consciousness, which they heighten. They ride on motion the way, and at the same time as, the mind floats on duration. . . . They say that life is only here and now, and fleeting, a thing that cannot stand still," Bedient explains, "and more, that space is as unfathomably deep as time, in time's body, but at least outside ourselves, both mercifully and cruelly outside. The poems increase the sense of exposure to existence as actual travel renews and magnifies the sensation of living."

As the couple in "Phoenix Park" pass by familiar landmarks, Jackson reports, "the lovers' marriage is seen as a powerful form which overcomes loss and the chaos of life. Their love is 'the one positive dream' to which the speaker of 'Phoenix Park' refers as the exception to the fact that 'There's a fever now that eats everything.'. . . He expatiates on the implications of their love as evincing the 'laws of order,' on their love as ordeal, a continual wounding and healing, and a continual growing, and arrives at a sense of existence as a necessary ordeal—when we think we have attained some abstract 'ultimate,' living must end."

After the publication of *Nightwalker and Other Poems,* Kinsella permanently left the civil service to enter academic life and become a full-time writer. He also set up Peppercanister Press at his home in Dublin, primarily to publish limited editions of his works in progress. *Butcher's Dozen: A Lesson for the Octave of Widgery,* the press's first publication, is described by M. L. Rosenthal in *New York Times Book Review* as a "rough-hewn, deliberately populist dream-visionary poem" on the 1972 shooting-down of thirteen demonstrators in Derry by British troopers and the investigation that followed. But, according to Edna Longley in *Times Literary Supplement,* "despite these latent social and political contours," Kinsella's writing "overwhelmingly takes the traditional form of self-searching. (It is a deeper question whether the extreme isolation of his poetic persona owes more to culture than to idiosyncrasy.)"

Kinsella indicates to *CA* that his poetry of this time begins to involve a turning "downward into the psyche toward origin and myth," and that it is "set toward some kind of individuation." The theme of his next major work *Notes from the Land of the Dead and Other Poems,* according to a *Times Literary Supple-*

ment critic, "is the spiritual journey from despair and desolation, 'nightnothing', to a painful self-renewal." The poems in this work abandon syntax, Jackson comments, "because they have left the world to which syntax is relevant and moved to the world of dream, phantasm, and myth, the world in short of psychic exploration."

The volume includes an untitled prologue that Jackson describes "as a mystical version of a Kinsellan wandering poem [which] recounts the speaker's descent into a psychic underworld, a reversion to the embryo stage." And "the low point of coherent consciousness in this exploration is [the poem] 'All Is Emptiness and Must Spin,'" relates Jackson. John D. Engle explains in *Parnassus* that in *Notes from the Land of the Dead and Other Poems,* "Kinsella heads down, a quest hero, into the past and subconscious; he would retrieve the scary flotsam of memory, a dying old harpy of a grandmother or, perhaps, obsessive shadow-plays drawn from a childhood reading of the *Book of Invasions,* Ireland's ancient and wild Genesis. After the confusing bobs and weaves of something like a plot, he bears back his prize: a new awareness, at once modest and enough to change one's life."

Discussing *Notes from the Land of the Dead and Other Poems* in the *New York Times Book Review,* Bedient finds Kinsella's style "an almost constant pleasure," but also complains that, here, "Ireland's best living poet has brooded himself to pieces." Vernon Young in *Parnassus* mentions the fact that, for many years, Kinsella translated "The Tain," an eighth-century Irish epic, "and in that translation you can find both the savage emblems and the bleak outlook of the independent poems [in *Notes from the Land of the Dead and Other Poems*]: as if the repetitive sanguinary deeds of the epic (to my mind a monotonously vindictive chronicle without a tremor of mercy or grace) had been used to compound the lethal evidence of mindless struggle forecast by the origin of the species."

However, Engle remarks that "the poetry of *Notes* is not as extravagantly disheveled as it occasionally seems, and what comes dressed as nihilism turns out to be something else." Kinsella was influenced by Jung, points out Jackson, and "where the earlier work was so concerned with the idea of suffering and pain as the motives of growth, the ordeal as a linear meeting of successive tests, these new poems take up the Jungian idea of a creative union of opposites. The ordeal of suffering and growth becomes the more comprehensive rhythm of destruction and creation, decay and regeneration, death and birth."

Kinsella continues in the same thematic direction with *Peppercanister Poems, 1972-1978,* which, along with the poem "Butcher's Dozen," includes meditations on the deaths of Kinsella's father and his friend, Sean O'Riada, and, according to Jackson, several poems "dealing with the poet's family history and himself as artist." And in an eight-poem sequence "One," Engle comments, Kinsella "plunges again through the crust of appearance into this region of process and origin. The eight poems send his thoughts again into a hoard of personal and common memory, back to his own childhood and further still to merge with those of Ireland's first wave of settlers. . . . This is Jung country."

"Jung and Kinsella's idea that creation and destruction, love and hate, life and death are interinvolved is an attempt to reclaim the wholeness of existence, not to deny its beauty," Jackson points out. "The poems here actually enact that stance: out of the death of a friend, of a father, or political matters comes poetry before our very eyes. Nor is being rooted in the prerational the same as being confined to it." Kinsella, Engle indicates, "is at home now in darkness, the secret shadows where we create and were created. If he invites us into a world that at times proves too elaborately personal, if he tries to do too much with his poems, these are generous blunders. They shouldn't obscure the fact that Kinsella is a serious poet of invention and honesty." Rosenthal concludes that "he is among the true poets, not only of Ireland but among all who write in English in our day."

BIOGRAPHICAL/CRITICAL SOURCES:

BOOKS

Bedient, Calvin, *Eight Contemporary Poets,* Oxford University Press, 1974.
Contemporary Literary Criticism, Gale, Volume 4, 1975, Volume 19, 1981.
Dictionary of Literary Biography, Volume 27: *Poets of Great Britain and Ireland, 1945-1960,* Gale, 1984.
Dunn, Douglas, editor, *Two Decades of Irish Writing,* Dufour, 1975.
Harmon, Maurice, *The Poetry of Thomas Kinsella: "With Darkness for a Nest,"* Wolfhound Press, 1974.
Kersnowski, Frank L., *The Outsiders: Poets of Contemporary Ireland,* Texas Christian University Press, 1975.
Kinsella, Thomas, *Nightwalker and Other Poems,* Dolmen Press, 1968, Knopf, 1969.
Kinsella, Thomas, *Notes from the Land of the Dead and Other Poems,* Knopf, 1973.
Orr, Peter, editor, *The Poet Speaks: Interviews with Contemporary Poets,* Routledge and Kegan Paul, 1966.
Rosenthal, M. L., *The New Poets: American and British Poetry since World War II,* Oxford University Press, 1967.
Rosenthal, M. L., *Poetry and the Common Life,* Oxford University Press, 1974. *Viewpoints: Poets in Conversation with John Haffenden,* Faber, 1981.

PERIODICALS

America, March 16, 1974.
Commonweal, June 6, 1980.
Eire-Ireland, number 2, 1967.
Genre, winter, 1979.
Hudson Review, winter, 1968-69.
Nation, June 5, 1972.
New Statesman, November 9, 1973.
New York Times Book Review, August 18, 1968, June 16, 1974, February 24, 1980.
Parnassus, spring-summer, 1975, spring, 1981.
Poetry, January, 1975.
Times Literary Supplement, October 5, 1967, December 18, 1969, December 8, 1972, August 17, 1973, November 23, 1973, December 19, 1980.
Village Voice, March 14, 1974.

*   *   *

KINSELLA, W(illiam) P(atrick) 1935-

PERSONAL: Born May 25, 1935, in Edmonton, Alberta, Canada; son of John Matthew (a contractor) and Olive (a printer; maiden name, Elliot) Kinsella; married Mildred Clay, September 10, 1965 (divorced, 1978); married Ann Knight (a writer), December 30, 1978; children: Shannon, Erin. *Education:* University of Victoria, B.A., 1974; University of Iowa, M.F.A., 1978. *Politics:* "Rhinoceros Party." *Religion:* Atheist.

ADDRESSES: Home and office—Box 400, White Rock, British Columbia, Canada V4B 5G3; Box 1615, Iowa City, Iowa 52244. *Agent*—Colbert Agency, 303 Davenport, Toronto, Ontario, Canada M5R 1K5.

CAREER: Government of Alberta, Edmonton, clerk, 1954-56; Retail Credit Co., Edmonton, Alberta, manager, 1956-61; City of Edmonton, Edmonton, account executive, 1961-67; Caesar's Italian Village (restaurant), Victoria, British Columbia, owner, 1967-72; student and taxicab driver in Victoria, 1974-76; University of Iowa, Iowa City, instructor, 1976-78; University of Calgary, Calgary, Alberta, assistant professor of English and creative writing, 1978-83; writer, 1983—.

MEMBER: Writers' Union of Canada, American Amateur Press Association, Society of American Baseball Researchers, American Atheists, Enoch Emery Society.

AWARDS, HONORS: Award from Canadian Fiction, 1976, for story, "Illianna Comes Home"; honorable mention in *Best American Short Stories 1980,* for "Fiona the First"; Houghton Mifflin Literary Fellowship, 1982, Books in Canada First Novel Award, 1983, and Canadian Authors Association prize, 1983, all for *Shoeless Joe;* Writers Guild of Alberta O'Hagan novel medal, 1984, for *The Moccasin Telegraph;* Alberta Achievement Award for Excellence in Literature; Leacock Medal for Humor, 1987, for *The Fencepost Chronicles;* Author of the Year Award, Canadian Booksellers Association, 1987.

WRITINGS:

Dance Me Outside (stories), Oberon Press, 1977, published as *Dance Me Outside: More Tales from the Ermineskin Reserve,* David Godine, 1986.
Scars (stories), Oberon Press, 1978.
Shoeless Joe Jackson Comes to Iowa (stories; also see below), Oberon Press, 1980.
Born Indian, Oberon Press, 1981.
Shoeless Joe (novel; based on title story in *Shoeless Joe Jackson Comes to Iowa*), Houghton, 1982.
The Ballad of the Public Trustee (chapbook), William Hoffer Standard Editions, 1982.
The Moccasin Telegraph (stories), Penguin Canada, 1983, published as *The Moccasin Telegraph and Other Tales,* David Godine, 1984, published as *The Moccasin Telegraph and Other Stories,* Penguin, 1985.
The Thrill of the Grass (chapbook; also see below), William Hoffer Standard Editions, 1984.
The Thrill of the Grass (story collection; contains "The Thrill of the Grass"), Penguin Books, 1984.
The Alligator Report (stories), Coffee House Press, 1985.
The Iowa Baseball Confederacy (novel), Houghton, 1986.
Five Stories (chapbook), William Hoffer Standard Editions, 1986.
The Fencepost Chronicles (stories), Collins, 1986, Houghton, 1987.
The Further Adventures of Slugger McBatt: Baseball Stories by W. P. Kinsella, Houghton, 1988.
The Miss Hobbema Pageant, Harper, 1990.

Also author of *Touching the Bases* and *Red Wolf, Red Wolf.* Contributor of the essay "Nuke the Whales and Piss in the Ocean" to *Visions of the Promised Land,* 1986. Contributor to numerous anthologies, including *Best Canadian Stories: 1977, 1981, 1985, Aurora: New Canadian Writing 1979, Best American Short Stories 1980, More Stories from Western Canada, Oxford Anthology of Canadian Literature, Pushcart Prize Anthology 5, The Spirit That Moves Us Reader, Introduction to Fiction, The Temple of Baseball, Penguin Book of Modern Canadian Short Stories, The Armchair Book of Baseball, Small Wonders, Illusion Two, West of Fiction, Anthology of Canadian Literature in English, Volume II, Contexts: Anthology 3, Aquarius, New Worlds, The Process of Writing, A Sense of Place, The Anthology Anthol-*

ogy, *New Voices 2, 3, Rainshadow,* and *Here's the Story.* Also contributor of more than two hundred stories to American and Canadian magazines, including *Sports Illustrated, Arete: Journal of Sports Literature, Story Quarterly, Matrix,* and *Canadian Fiction Magazine.*

WORK IN PROGRESS: A novel about baseball in the Dominican Republic, *Butterfly Winter;* a novel about an ex-baseball player, *If Wishes Were Horses;* two collections of stories, tentatively titled *The Sun Dog Society* and *Mother Tucker's Yellow Duck.*

SIDELIGHTS: W. P. Kinsella, a Canadian author of novels and stories, has attracted an international readership with his imaginative fictions. Many of Kinsella's short stories follow the daily escapades of characters living on a Cree Indian reservation, while his longer works, *Shoeless Joe* and *The Iowa Baseball Confederacy,* mix magic and the mundane in epic baseball encounters. A determined writer who published his first story collection at the age of forty-two, Kinsella has won numerous awards, among them the prestigious Houghton Mifflin Literary Fellowship. He told *CA:* "I am an old-fashioned storyteller. I try to make people laugh and cry. A fiction writer's duty is to entertain. If you can then sneak in something profound or symbolic, so much the better."

"Fiction writing," Kinsella told the *Toronto Globe and Mail,* ". . . consists of ability, imagination, passion and stamina." He suggested that stamina is the most important ingredient of success, and he defined the quality as "keeping your buns on the chair and writing even when you don't feel like it" and "getting up at 5 a.m., running water over your fingers so they will make the typewriter keys work for an hour or two before you go off to your hateful job." He admitted: "I did that for 20 years while I beat my head against the walls of North American literature." Indeed, Kinsella calculates that he wrote more than fifty unpublishable stories while perfecting his craft. He also worked at numerous jobs in Edmonton, Alberta and Victoria, British Columbia, including managing a credit company, running his own pizza restaurant, and driving a taxicab. "No matter what I did, I always thought of myself as a writer," he remembered in *Publishers Weekly.* "You're born with a compulsion to write." Kinsella was in his thirties when he began attending college at the University of Victoria and in his forties when his fiction began to sell regularly. Reflecting on his own experiences, he told the *Globe and Mail:* "I know it's a cliche, but though inspiration is nice, 98 per cent of writing is accomplished by perspiration."

A Cree Indian named Silas Ermineskin brought Kinsella literary recognition beginning in 1974. Kinsella experienced his first sustained success writing about a fictional cast of reservation-dwellers from Silas's point of view, and since then he has published nearly one hundred short stories about the Crees, many of which are collected in *Dance Me Outside, Scars, Born Indian* and *The Moccasin Telegraph.* Both Canadian and American critics express admiration for Kinsella's accomplishment. *Prairie Schooner* contributor Frances W. Kaye notes: "W. P. Kinsella is not an Indian, a fact that would not be extraordinary were it not for the stories Kinsella writes about . . . a Cree World. Kinsella's Indians are counterculture figures in the sense that their lives counter the predominant culture of North America, but there is none of the worshipfully inaccurate portrayal of 'the Indian' that has appeared from Fenimore Cooper through Gary Snyder." In *Wascana Review,* George Woodcock likewise cites Kinsella for an approach that "restores proportion and brings an artistic authenticity to the portrayal of contemporary Indian life which we have encountered rarely in recent years." Anthony

Brennan offers a similar assessment in *Fiddlehead,* writing that *Dance Me Outside* "is all the more refreshing because it quite consciously eschews ersatz heroics and any kind of nostalgic, mythopoeic reflections on a technicolor golden age."

Critics also praise Kinsella's Indian stories for their insight into human nature. *Village Voice* contributor Stanley Crouch commends Kinsella for his "ability to make what superficially seems only Indian problems come off as the universal struggle with insipid laws and bureaucrats." Kaye feels that what makes the stories work is Kinsella's "eye for detail and his sense of how a few remembered images come together to create a place and a people that compel belief." Brennan calls the fiction "low-key, deliberately unspectacular, full of rueful mirth and a carefully accumulated wisdom," concluding, "It is pleasant to find a man who can mock the pathetic attempts of the 'apples'—those with red skin desperate to be white inside—and who would surely be able to nail those white writers who desperately try to invent a new identity as red warriors."

In 1980 Kinsella published *Shoeless Joe Jackson Comes to Iowa,* a collection of short pieces set in Iowa, urban Canada and San Francisco. The title story also was selected to appear in an anthology entitled *Aurora: New Canadian Writers 1979.* An editor at Houghton Mifflin saw Kinsella's contribution to *Aurora* and contacted the author about expanding the story into a novel. "It was something that hadn't occurred to me at all," Kinsella recalled in *Publishers Weekly.* "I told [the editor], 'I've never written anything longer than 5 pages, but if you want to work with me, I'll try it.'" Much to Kinsella's surprise, the editor agreed. Kinsella set to work expanding "Shoeless Joe Jackson Comes to Iowa," but he decided instead to leave the story intact as the first chapter and build on the plot with a variety of other material. "I enjoyed doing it very much," he said. "They were such wonderful characters I'd created, and I liked being audacious in another way. I put in no sex, no violence, no obscenity, none of that stuff that sells. I wanted to write a book for imaginative readers, an affirmative statement about life."

Shoeless Joe, a novel-length baseball fable set on an Iowa farm, won Kinsella the Houghton Mifflin Literary Fellowship in 1982. The story follows a character named Ray Kinsella in his attempts to summon the spirits of the tarnished 1919 Chicago White Sox by building a ballpark in his cornfield. Among the ghostly players lured to Kinsella's perfectly mowed grass is Shoeless Joe Jackson, the White Sox star player who fell in scandal when it was revealed that his team threw the World Series. As the story progresses, the same mysterious loudspeaker voice that suggested construction of the ballpark says, "Ease his pain," and Ray Kinsella sets off to kidnap author J. D. Salinger for a visit to Fenway Park. The novel blends baseball lore with legend and historical figures with fictional characters. "I've mixed in so much, I'm not sure what's real and what's not," Kinsella told *Publishers Weekly,* "but as long as you can convince people you know what you're talking about, it doesn't matter. If you're convincing, they'll believe it."

Kinsella does seem to have convinced most critics with the novel *Shoeless Joe.* According to Alan Cheuse in the *Los Angeles Times,* the work "stands as fictional homage to our national pastime, with resonances so American that the book may be grounds for abolishing our northern border." *Detroit News* writer Ben Brown claims: "What we have here is a gentle, unselfconscious fantasy balanced perilously in the air above an Iowa cornfield. It's a balancing act sustained by the absolutely fearless, sentimentality-risking honesty of the author. And it doesn't hurt a bit that he's a master of the language. . . . This is an utterly beautiful piece of work." A dissenting opinion is offered by Jonathan Yardley in the *Washington Post,* who suggests that *Shoeless Joe* "is a book of quite unbelievable self-indulgence, a rambling exercise the only discernible point of which seems to be to demonstrate, ad infinitum and ad nauseum, what a wonderful fellow is its narrator/author." Conversely, *Christian Science Monitor* contributor Maggie Lewis praises the work, concluding: "The descriptions of landscape are poetic, and the baseball details will warm fans' hearts and not get in the way of mere fantasy lovers. This book would make great reading on a summer vacation. In fact, this book *is* a summer vacation." Cheuse concludes that *Shoeless Joe* "in its ritual celebration of the game of baseball proves its author to be a writer worth further conjuring. A baseball book for this season, and perhaps many more to come, it takes its time to create a world of compelling whimsy."

Kinsella continues his fascination with baseball in his 1986 novel *The Iowa Baseball Confederacy.* Jonathan Webb describes the work in *Quill and Quire:* "The Iowa Baseball Confederacy contains bigger magic, larger and more spectacular effects, than anything attempted in *Shoeless Joe.* Kinsella is striving for grander meaning: the reconciliation of immovable forces—love and darker emotions—on conflicting courses." Time travel and a ballgame that lasts in excess of 2,600 innings are two of the supernatural events in the story; characters as diverse as Teddy Roosevelt and Leonardo da Vinci make cameo appearances. *Chicago Tribune Book World* contributor Gerald Nemanic writes: "Freighted with mythical machinery, 'The Iowa Baseball Confederacy' requires the leavening of some sprightly prose. Kinsella is equal to it. His love for baseball is evident in the lyrical descriptions of the game."

In the *Globe and Mail,* William French suggests that Kinsella lifts baseball to a higher plane in his novels. The author, French notes, is "attracted as much to the metaphysical aspects as the physical, intrigued by how baseball transcends time and place and runs like a subterranean stream-of-consciousness through the past century or so of American history. . . . His baseball novels are animated by a light-hearted wit and bubbling imagination, a respect for mystery and magic." "To be obsessed with baseball is to be touched by grace in Kinsella's universe," writes Webb, "and a state of grace gives access to magic." Webb feels that in *The Iowa Baseball Confederacy,* Kinsella fails to persuade the reader to go along with his magic. French likewise states: "In the end [of the novel], Kinsella's various themes don't quite connect. But it hardly matters; we're able to admire the audacity of Kinsella's vision and the sheen of his prose without worrying too much about his ultimate meaning." *Los Angeles Times Book Review* contributor Roger Kahn calls *The Iowa Baseball Confederacy* "fun and lyric and poignant." Kahn adds: "We are reading a writer here, a real writer, Muses be praised. But we are also adrift in a delicate world of fantasy, weird deaths and, I suppose, symbolism. Sometimes the work is confusing, as Kinsella adds a fantasy on top of an illusion beyond a mirage. But I never lost my wonder at how the ballgame would turn out; any author who can hold you for 2,614 innings deserves considerable praise."

The success of his baseball books notwithstanding, Kinsella continues to produce short fiction on a variety of themes. *The Alligator Report,* also published in 1986, contains stories that pay homage to surrealist Richard Brautigan, one of Kinsella's favorite authors. In a *Village Voice* review, Jodi Daynard claims: "Kinsella's new stories replace humor with wit, regional dialect with high prose. . . . He uses surrealism most effectively to highlight the delicate balance between solitude and alienation, not to achieve a comic effect. . . . These are images that resonate—not comic ones, alas, but stirring, not woolly-wild, but urban

gothic." *New York Times Book Review* contributor Harry Marten contends that in *The Alligator Report* Kinsella continues "to define a world in which magic and reality combine to make us laugh and think about the perceptions we take for granted."

Kinsella received his Master's Degree from the University of Iowa in 1978 and subsequently taught English and creative writing at the University of Calgary until 1983. Since then he has supported himself by writing and has indulged a favorite whim by travelling across the United States and Canada to see major league baseball games. "I'm not a fanatic," he told *Publishers Weekly.* "It may appear so, but I'm not. My feeling for baseball is a little like Cordelia's statement to King Lear. She said she loved him as a daughter loves a father. No more and no less." He went on to admit that his enthusiasm for the game is purely that of a spectator. "I don't play baseball," he said. "I throw like a girl." Kinsella has expressed stronger opinions about what he feels are the necessary components of good fiction. "The secret of a fiction writer," he told the *Globe and Mail,* "is to make the dull interesting by imagination and embellishment, and to tone down the bizarre until it is believable. . . . Stories or novels are not about events, but about the people that events happen to. The fact that the Titanic is sinking or a skyscraper toppling—or even that the world is ending—is not important unless you have created an appealing character who is going to suffer if the dreaded event happens." The author who has been called "a fabulist of great skill" and "a gifted Canadian writer" once told *CA:* "There are no gods, there is no magic; I may be a wizard though, for it takes a wizard to know there are none. My favorite quotation is by Donald Barthelme: 'The aim of literature is to create a strange object covered with fur which breaks your heart.' "

MEDIA ADAPTATIONS: Shoeless Joe was adapted and produced as the motion picture "Field of Dreams," released in 1989 by Twentieth Century-Fox. *Dance Me Outside* has been optioned for a motion picture by Norman Jewlson.

BIOGRAPHICAL/CRITICAL SOURCES:

BOOKS

Contemporary Authors Autobiography Series, Volume 7, Gale, 1988.
Contemporary Literary Criticism, Gale, Volume 27, 1984, Volume 43, 1987.

PERIODICALS

Books in Canada, October, 1981, February, 1984, November, 1984.
Canadian Literature, summer, 1982.
Chicago Tribune Book World, April 25, 1982, March 30, 1986.
Christian Science Monitor, July 9, 1982.
Detroit Free Press, May 4, 1986.
Detroit News, May 2, 1982, May 16, 1982.
Fiddlehead, fall, 1977 spring, 1981.
Globe and Mail (Toronto), November 17, 1984, April 27, 1985, April 12, 1986.
Library Journal, February 1, 1982.
Los Angeles Times, August 26, 1982.
Los Angeles Times Book Review, May 23, 1982, July 6, 1986.
Maclean's, May 11, 1981, April 19, 1982, July 23, 1984.
Newsweek, August 23, 1982.
New York Times Book Review, July 25, 1982, September 2, 1984, January 5, 1986, April 20, 1986.
Prairie Schooner, spring 1979.
Publishers Weekly, April 16, 1982.
Quill and Quire, June, 1982, September, 1984, April, 1986.
Village Voice, December 4, 1984, April 1, 1986.

Wascana Review, fall, 1976
Washington Post, March 31, 1982.
Western American Literature, February, 1978.

*   *   *

KIPLING, (Joseph) Rudyard   1865-1936

PERSONAL: Born December 30, 1865, in Bombay, India; died of intestinal hemorrhage, January 8, 1936, in London, England; buried in the Poets' Corner of Westminster Abbey in London; son of John Lockwood (an architect, teacher, and minister) and Alice (MacDonald) Kipling; married Caroline Starr Balestier, January 18, 1892; children: Josephine (died, 1899), John (killed in action, World War I), Elsie Bambridge. *Education:* Attended schools in England through the secondary level.

ADDRESSES: Home—Bateman's, Burwash, Sussex, England.

CAREER: Poet, essayist, novelist, journalist, and writer of short stories. Worked as a journalist for *Civil and Military Gazette,* Lahore, India, 1882-89; assistant editor and overseas correspondent for the Allahabad *Pioneer,* Allahabad, India, 1887-89; associate editor and correspondent for *The Friend,* Bloemfontein, South Africa, 1900, covering the Boer War. Rector of University of St. Andrews, 1922-25.

MEMBER: Academie des Sciences et Politiques (France; foreign associate member), Magdalene College, Cambridge (honorary fellow, 1932-36), Athenaeum Club (literary), Carlton Club (political).

AWARDS, HONORS: Poet laureate, 1895, and Order of Merit award (both refused); Nobel Prize for Literature, 1907; Gold Medal of Royal Society of Literature, 1926; LL.D. from McGill University, 1899; D.Litt. from Durham and Oxford universities, 1907, Cambridge University, 1908, Edinburgh University, 1920, Paris and Strasbourg universities, 1921; honorary Ph.D., Athens University, 1924.

WRITINGS:

POETRY

Schoolboy Lyrics, privately printed, 1881.
(With sister, Beatrice Kipling) *Echoes: By Two Writers,* Civil and Military Gazette Press (Lahore), 1884.
Departmental Ditties and Other Verses, Civil and Military Gazette Press, 1886, 2nd edition, enlarged, Thacker, Spink (Calcutta), 1886, 3rd edition, further enlarged, 1888, 4th edition, still further enlarged, W. Thacker (London), 1890, deluxe edition, 1898.
Departmental Ditties, Barrack-Room Ballads and Other Verses (contains the fifty poems of the fourth edition of *Departmental Ditties and Other Verses* and seventeen new poems later published as *Ballads and Barrack-Room Ballads*), United States Book Co., 1890, revised edition published as *Departmental Ditties and Ballads and Barrack-Room Ballads,* Doubleday & McClure, 1899.
Ballads and Barrack-Room Ballads, Macmillan, 1892, new edition, with additional poems, 1893, published as *The Complete Barrack-Room Ballads of Rudyard Kipling,* edited by Charles Carrington, Methuen, 1973, reprint published as *Barrack Room Ballads and Other Verses,* White Rose Press, 1987.
The Rhyme of True Thomas, D. Appleton, 1894.
The Seven Seas, D. Appleton, 1896, reprinted, Longwood Publishing Group, 1978.
Recessional (Victorian ode in commemoration of queen's jubilee), M. F. Mansfield, 1897.

Mandalay, drawings by Blanche McManus, M. F. Mansfield, 1898, reprinted, Doubleday, Page, 1921.
The Betrothed, drawings by McManus, M. F. Mansfield and A. Wessells, 1899.
Poems, Ballads, and Other Verses, illustrations by V. Searles, H. M. Caldwell, 1899.
Belts, A. Grosset, 1899.
Cruisers, Doubleday & McClure, 1899.
The Reformer, Doubleday, Page, 1901.
The Lesson, Doubleday, Page, 1901.
The Five Nations, Doubleday, Page, 1903.
The Muse Among the Motors, Doubleday, Page, 1904.
The Sons of Martha, Doubleday, Page, 1907.
The City of Brass, Doubleday, Page, 1909.
Cuckoo Song, Doubleday, Page, 1909.
A Patrol Song, Doubleday, Page, 1909.
A Song of the English, illustrations by W. Heath Robinson, Doubleday, Page, 1909.
If, Doubleday, Page, 1910, reprinted, Doubleday, 1959.
The Declaration of London, Doubleday, Page, 1911.
The Spies' March, Doubleday, Page, 1911.
Three Poems (contains "The River's Tale," "The Roman Centurion Speaks," "The Pirates in England"), Doubleday, Page, 1911.
Songs From Books, Doubleday, Page, 1912.
An Unrecorded Trial, Doubleday, Page, 1913.
For All We Have and Are, Methuen, 1914.
The Children's Song, Macmillan, 1914.
A Nativity, Doubleday, Page, 1917.
A Pilgrim's Way, Doubleday, Page, 1918.
The Supports, Doubleday, Page, 1919.
The Years Between, Doubleday, Page, 1919.
The Gods of the Copybook Headings, Doubleday, Page, 1919, reprinted, 1921.
The Scholars, Doubleday, Page, 1919.
Great-Heart, Doubleday, Page, 1919.
Danny Deever, Doubleday, Page, 1921.
The King's Pilgrimage, Doubleday, Page, 1922.
Chartres Windows, Doubleday, Page, 1925.
A Choice of Songs, Doubleday, Page, 1925.
Sea and Sussex, with an introductory poem by the author and illustrations by Donald Maxwell, Doubleday, Page, 1926.
A Rector's Memory, Doubleday, Page, 1926.
Supplication of the Black Aberdeen, illustrations by G. L. Stampa, Doubleday, Doran, 1929.
The Church That Was at Antioch, Doubleday, Doran, 1929.
The Tender Achilles, Doubleday, Doran, 1929.
Unprofessional, Doubleday, Page, 1930.
The Day of the Dead, Doubleday, Doran, 1930.
Neighbours, Doubleday, Doran, 1932.
The Storm Cone, Doubleday, Doran, 1932.
His Apologies, illustrations by Cecil Aldin, Doubleday, Doran, 1932.
The Fox Meditates, Doubleday, Doran, 1933.
To the Companions, Doubleday, Doran, 1933.
Bonfires on the Ice, Doubleday, Doran, 1933.
Our Lady of the Sackcloth, Doubleday, Doran, 1935.
Hymn of the Breaking Strain, Doubleday, Doran, 1935.
Doctors, The Waster, The Flight, Cain and Abel, The Appeal, Doubleday, Doran, 1939.
B.E.L., Doubleday, Doran, 1944.

SHORT STORIES

In Black and White, A. H. Wheeler (Allahabad), 1888, 1st American edition, Lovell, 1890.

Plain Tales From the Hills, Thacker, Spink, 1888, 2nd edition, revised, 1889, lst English edition, revised, Macmillan, 1890, lst American edition, revised, Doubleday & McClure, 1899, reprint edited by H. R. Woudhuysen, Penguin, 1987.

The Phantom 'Rickshaw and Other Tales, A. H. Wheeler, 1888, revised edition, 1890, reprinted, Hurst, 1901.

The Story of the Gadsbys: A Tale With No Plot, A. H. Wheeler, 1888, 1st American edition, Lovell, 1890.

Soldiers Three: A Collection of Stories Setting Forth Certain Passages in the Lives and Adventures of Privates Terence Mulvaney, Stanley Ortheris, and John Learoyd, A. H. Wheeler, 1888, 1st American edition, revised, Lovell, 1890, reprinted, Belmont, 1962.

Under the Deodars, A. H. Wheeler, 1888, 1st American edition, enlarged, Lovell, 1890.

The Courting of Dinah Shadd and Other Stories, with a biographical and critical sketch by Andrew Lang, Harper, 1890, reprinted, Books for Libraries, 1971.

His Private Honour, Macmillan, 1891.

The Smith Administration, A. H. Wheeler, 1891.

Mine Own People, introduction by Henry James, United States Book Co., 1891.

Many Inventions, D. Appleton, 1893, reprinted, Macmillan, 1982.

Mulvaney Stories, 1897, reprinted, Books for Libraries, 1971.

The Day's Work, Doubleday & McClure, 1898, reprinted, Books for Libraries, 1971, reprinted with introduction by Constantine Phipps, Penguin, 1988.

The Drums of the Fore and Aft, illustrations by L. J. Bridgman, Brentano's, 1898.

The Man Who Would Be King, Brentano's, 1898.

Black Jack, F. T. Neely, 1899.

Without Benefit of Clergy, Doubleday & McClure, 1899.

The Brushwood Boy, illustrations by Orson Lowell, Doubleday & McClure, 1899, reprinted, with illustrations by F. H. Townsend, Doubleday, Page, 1907.

Railway Reform in Great Britain, Doubleday, Page, 1901.

Traffics and Discoveries, Doubleday, Page, 1904, reprinted, Penguin, 1987.

They, Scribner, 1904.

Abaft the Funnel, Doubleday, Page, 1909.

Actions and Reactions, Doubleday, Page, 1909.

Cold Iron, Macmillan, 1909.

A Doctor of Medicine, Macmillan, 1909.

The Wrong Thing, Macmillan, 1909.

Gloriana, Macmillan, 1909.

The Conversion of St. Wilfrid, Macmillan, 1909.

The Tree of Justice, Macmillan, 1909.

Brother Square-Toes, Macmillan, 1910.

Simple Simon, Macmillan, 1910.

A Priest in Spite of Himself, Macmillan, 1910.

A Diversity of Creatures, Doubleday, Page, 1917, reprinted, Macmillan, 1966.

"The Finest Story in the World" and Other Stories, Little Leather Library, 1918.

Debits and Credits, Doubleday, Page, 1926, reprinted, Macmillan, 1965.

Thy Servant a Dog, Told by Boots, illustrations by Marguerite Kirmse, Doubleday, Doran, 1930.

Beauty Spots, Doubleday, Doran, 1931.

Limits and Renewals, Doubleday, Doran, 1932.

The Pleasure Cruise, Doubleday, Doran, 1933.

Collected Dog Stories, illustrations by Kirmse, Doubleday, Doran, 1934.

Ham and the Porcupine, Doubleday, Doran, 1935.

Teem: A Treasure-Hunter, Doubleday, Doran, 1935.

The Maltese Cat: A Polo Game of the 'Nineties, illustrations by Lionel Edwards, Doubleday, Doran, 1936.

"Thy Servant a Dog" and Other Dog Stories, illustrations by G. L. Stampa, Macmillan, 1938, reprinted, 1982.

Their Lawful Occasions, White Rose Press, 1987.

NOVELS

The Light That Failed, J. B. Lippincott, 1891, revised edition, Macmillan, 1891, reprinted, Penguin, 1988.

(With Wolcott Balestier) *The Naulahka: A Story of West and East,* Macmillan, 1892, reprinted, Doubleday, Page, 1925.

Kim, illustrations by father, J. Lockwood Kipling, Doubleday, Page, 1901, new edition, with illustrations by Stuart Tresilian, Macmillan, 1958, reprinted, with introduction by Alan Sandison, Oxford University Press, 1987.

CHILDREN'S BOOKS

"Wee Willie Winkie" and Other Child Stories, A. H. Wheeler, 1888, 1st American edition, Lovell, 1890, reprinted, Penguin, 1988.

The Jungle Book (short stories and poems; also see below), illustrations by J. L. Kipling, W. H. Drake, and P. Frenzeny, Macmillan, 1894, adapted and abridged by Anne L. Nelan, with illustrations by Earl Thollander, Fearon, 1967, reprinted, with illustrations by J. L. Kipling and Drake, Macmillan, 1982.

The Second Jungle Book (short stories and poems), illustrations by J. L. Kipling, Century Co., 1895, reprinted, Macmillan, 1982.

"Captains Courageous": A Story of the Grand Banks, Century Co., 1897, abridged edition, illustrated by Rafaello Busoni, Hart Publishing, 1960, reprinted, with an afterword by C. A. Bodelsen, New American Library, 1981.

Stalky and Co. (short stories), Doubleday & McClure, 1899, reprinted, Bantam, 1985, new and abridged edition, Pendulum Press, 1977.

Just So Stories for Little Children (short stories and poems), illustrations by the author, Doubleday, Page, 1902, reprinted, Silver Burdett, 1986.

Rewards and Fairies (short stories and poems), illustrations by Frank Craig, Doubleday, Page, 1910, revised edition, with illustrations by Charles E. Brock, Macmillan, 1926, reprinted, Penguin, 1988.

Toomai of the Elephants, Macmillan, 1937.

How the Rhinoceros Got His Skin, illustrations by Feodor Rojankovsky, Garden City Publishing, 1942, reprinted, with illustrations by Leonard Weisgard, Walker, 1974, published as *How the Rhino Got His Skin,* Putnam, 1988, published with audiocassette, Picture Book Studio, 1988.

How the Leopard Got His Spots, illustrations by Rojankovsky, Garden City Publishing, 1942, reprinted, P. Bedrick, 1986, published with audiocassette, Picture Book Studio, 1989.

How the Camel Got His Hump, illustrations by Rojankovsky, Garden City Publishing, 1942, reprinted, with illustrations by Erica Weihs, Rand McNally, 1955, reprinted with new illustrations, Warne, 1988, published with audiocassette, Picture Book Studio, 1989.

The Elephant's Child, illustrations by Rojankovsky, Garden City Publishing, 1942, reprinted, with illustrations by Lorinda Bryan Cauley, Harcourt, 1988, published with audiocassette, Knopf, 1986.

Puck of Pook's Hill (short stories and poems), Doubleday, 1946, reprinted, New American Library, 1988.

The Cat That Walked by Himself, illustrations by Rojankovsky, Garden City Publishing, 1947, reprinted, with illustrations by William Stobbs, P. Bedrick, 1983.

Mowgli, the Jungle Boy, illustrations by William Bartlett, Grosset, 1951.

How the Whale Got His Throat, illustrations by Don Madden, Addison-Wesley, 1971, published as *How the Whale Got His Throat: Just So Stories,* Putnam, 1988.

Disney Read-Aloud Film Classics: The Jungle Book, Crown, 1981.

The Butterfly That Stamped: A Just So Story, illustrations by Alan Baker, P. Bedrick, 1982.

The Beginning of the Armadillos: A Just So Story, illustrations by Charles Keeping, P. Bedrick, 1983.

The Crab That Played With the Sea: A Just So Story, illustrations by Michael Freeman, P. Bedrick, 1983.

Cinderella and How the Elephant Got His Trunk, EDC, 1985.

Tales From the Jungle Book, adapted by Robin McKinley, Random House, 1985.

The Miracle of Purun Bhagat, Creative Education, 1985.

Rikki-Tikki-Tavi, Ideals, 1985.

The Sing-Song of Old Man Kangaroo, P. Bedrick, 1986.

Gunga Din, Harcourt, 1987.

How the Alphabet Was Made, P. Bedrick, 1987.

How the First Letter Was Written, P. Bedrick, 1987.

TRAVEL WRITINGS

Letters of Marque, A. H. Wheeler, 1891.

American Notes, M. J. Ivers, 1891, reprinted, Ayer Co., 1974, revised edition published as *American Notes: Rudyard Kipling's West,* University of Oklahoma Press, 1981.

From Sea to Sea and Other Sketches, two volumes, Doubleday & McClure, 1899, published as one volume, Doubleday, Page, 1909, reprinted, 1925.

Letters to the Family: Notes on a Recent Trip to Canada, Macmillan of Canada, 1908.

Letters of Travel, 1892-1913, Doubleday, Page, 1920.

Land and Sea Tales, Doubleday, Page, 1923.

Souvenirs of France, Macmillan, 1933.

Brazilian Sketches, Doubleday, Doran, 1940.

Letters From Japan, edited with an introduction and notes by Donald Richie and Yoshimori Harashima, Kenkyusha, 1962.

NAVAL AND MILITARY WRITINGS

A Fleet in Being: Notes of Two Trips With the Channel Squadron, Macmillan, 1899.

The Army of a Dream, Doubleday, Page, 1904, reprinted, White Rose Press, 1987.

The New Army, Doubleday, Page, 1914.

The Fringes of the Fleet, Doubleday, Page, 1915.

France at War: On the Frontier of Civilization, Doubleday, Page, 1915.

Sea Warfare, Macmillan, 1916, Doubleday, Page, 1917.

Tales of "The Trade," Doubleday, Page, 1916.

The Eyes of Asia, Doubleday, Page, 1918.

The Irish Guards, Doubleday, Page, 1918.

The Graves of the Fallen, Imperial War Graves Commission, 1919.

The Feet of the Young Men, photographs by Lewis R. Freeman, Doubleday, Page, 1920.

The Irish Guards in the Great War: Edited and Compiled From Their Diaries and Papers, two volumes, Doubleday, Page, 1923, Volume I: *The First Battalion,* Volume II: *The Second Battalion and Appendices.*

OTHER

The City of Dreadful Night and Other Places (articles), A. H. Wheeler, 1891.

(With Charles R. L. Fletcher) *A History of England,* Doubleday, Page, 1911, published as *Kipling's Pocket History of England,* with illustrations by Henry Ford, Greenwich, 1983.

"The Harbor Watch" (one-act play; unpublished), 1913.

"The Return of Imray" (play; unpublished), 1914.

How Shakespeare Came to Write "The Tempest," introduction by Ashley H. Thorndike, Dramatic Museum of Columbia University, 1916.

London Town: November 11, 1918-1923, Doubleday, Page, 1923.

The Art of Fiction, J. A. Allen, 1926.

Mary Kingsley, Doubleday, Doran, 1932.

Proofs of Holy Writ, Doubleday, Doran, 1934.

Something of Myself for My Friends Known and Unknown (autobiography), Doubleday, Doran, 1937, reprinted, Penguin Classics, 1989.

Rudyard Kipling to Rider Haggard: The Record of a Friendship, edited by Morton Cohen, Hutchinson, 1965.

"O Beloved Kids": Rudyard Kipling's Letters to His Children, selected and edited by Elliot L. Gilbert, Harcourt, 1984.

Many of Kipling's works first appeared in periodicals, including four Anglo-Indian newspapers, the *Civil and Military Gazette,* the *Pioneer, Pioneer News, Week's News;* the *Scots Observer* and its successor, the *National Observer; London Morning Post,* the London *Times,* the *English Illustrated Magazine, Macmillan's Magazine, McClure's Magazine, Pearson's Magazine, Spectator, Atlantic, Ladies' Home Journal,* and *Harper's Weekly.*

Works collected in more than one hundred omnibus volumes.

SIDELIGHTS: As quoted in Andrew Rutherford's *Kipling's Mind and Art,* the literary critic Edmund Wilson correctly observed in 1941, five years after Rudyard Kipling's death, that he had "in a sense been dropped out of modern literature." This fact of literary history is remarkable because during his lifetime Kipling published a vast amount of writing that was tremendously popular and critically acclaimed. Living in India, where he was born and raised—although he was educated in England—Kipling by age twenty-three had published a book of poems, *Departmental Ditties* (1886), a series of thirty-nine short stories collected under the title *Plain Tales From the Hills* (1888), and six briefer collections of short stories. Importantly, Kipling's work was read not only in colonial India; his fame quickly spread to the literary as well as commercial capital of the British empire, London.

During his life he was repeatedly offered—and repeatedly he refused—knighthood and membership in distinguished learned and political societies. Moreover, he was lionized by many of the most powerful contemporary men of letters, including Edmund Gosse, Thomas Hardy, Rider Haggard, W. E. Henley, Henry and William James, Andrew Lang, Charles Eliot Norton, and George Saintsbury. Kipling also shared the company of British royalty, ministers of states, and U.S. presidents Grover Cleveland, Theodore Roosevelt, and Woodrow Wilson. In 1907 Kipling was awarded the Nobel Prize for Literature, the first English writer to receive it. In 1927 a Kipling Society was formed in his honor, although he did not encourage it. In January, 1936, the daily changes in his declining health as he suffered from a fatal hemorrhage were reported by the major newspapers around the world. His ashes were set beside the memorial to Charles Dickens in England's most hallowed place for its great writers, Poets' Corner in Westminster Abbey. His collected stories—roughly 250 of them—had sold 15 million volumes, and he had published

5 novels, more than 500 poems, several books of history, speeches, travel writings, essays, and an autobiography. In his writing he may not have achieved the ideal he ascribes to St. Paul in a poem called "At His Execution"—to be "all things to all men." But through the quantity as well as the quality of his work and its popularity, Kipling seemed to come as close as a writer can to this criterion.

With such a record of achievement, why was Kipling "dropped out of modern literature"? The answer, in short, is that both the style and content of Kipling's work quickly went out of fashion when literary modernism gained acceptance. Kipling's writing was widely rejected as imperialist, paternalist, reactionary, jingoistic, simple-minded, militarist, and vulgar. Ironically, however, the great modernist poet T. S. Eliot was among the first to argue for Kipling's rehabilitation and revival. His not merely fashionable but timeless literary skill had already been recognized by another great modernist writer, James Joyce, who, as quoted in Norman Page's *Kipling Companion,* wrote to his brother in 1907 that "if I knew Ireland as well as R. K. seems to know India, I fancy I could write something good."

A subject of study by major writers and critics like T. S. Eliot and Edmund Wilson in 1941, George Orwell in 1942, and Lionel Trilling in 1943, Kipling's writings began in the 1940s to come out of the shadows of twentieth-century modernism. He was, and still is, as Shamsul Islam wrote in *Kipling's "Law,"* "perhaps the most controversial figure in English literature," yet his strengths as a writer remain. First, Kipling possessed strong ability as a storyteller. As Kingsley Amis noted in *Rudyard Kipling and His World,* Kipling's "range is wide: the tragic, the comic, the satiric, the macabre, anecdote, fantasy, history, science fiction, children's tales." As J. M. S. Tompkins suggested in *The Art of Rudyard Kipling,* the sheer "variety" and "the resource and depth of Kipling's art" are most impressive in both his prose and verse, for they are, as T. S. Eliot observed in his introduction to *A Choice of Kipling's Verse,* "inseparable." Storytelling was Kipling's strongest desire in prose and verse. Also, in the course of his work Kipling became the last great English writer to address frequently and directly issues of contemporary politics. He was, in addition, the last great English writer to make explicit and extensive allusions to Scripture. And, as Orwell noted, Kipling more than any "English writer of our times . . . added phrases to the language. He coined 'East is East, and West is West,' 'And what should they know of England who only England know,' 'the light that failed,' 'The female of the species is more deadly than the male,' and 'East of Suez.' "

As Eliot—like Kipling's earliest readers—recognized, Kipling demonstrated "perfect competence" in his writing. Wilson, as quoted in *Kipling's Mind and Art,* thought that Kipling owed "his superiority as a craftsman" to his knowledge of "the ablest writers" of nineteenth-century fiction. Confirming Wilson's view, Kipling himself recalled in his autobiography that when he first arrived in London from India to pursue his literary ambitions he "was struck by the slenderness of some of the writers' equipment." He "could not see how they got along with so casual a knowledge of French work, and, apparently of much English grounding that I had supposed indispensable." On another occasion Kipling in part specified what he meant by the "English grounding" that he thought aspiring writers should have. He recommended reading William Hazlitt and, before the nineteenth century, Richard Crashaw "for words and emotions" and Jonathan Swift "purely for style." Kipling's style might be aptly characterized as a strange hybrid of Crashaw's extreme emotionalism, Swift's insistent literalness and lucidity, and Hazlitt's unpretentious yet sharp journalistic elegance.

Whatever his models for style, Kipling early in his life realized his literary predilections. He was "The Man Who Could Write," as the title of a poem of 1886 suggested. Moreover, Kipling worked seven years for an Anglo-Indian newspaper, the *Civil and Military Gazette.* He may have known the English literary greats but he also had to produce copy, realizing that as a writer he was essentially "a hireling, paid to do what [he] was paid to do." However negligibly Kipling regarded his early journalistic work, it gave him what every young writer needs most: the opportunity to practice basic writing skills. In addition, when the paper was short on news or advertising, Kipling was able to supply his earliest ballads as filler.

Schooled in the English classics but also in the necessary practicalities of journalistic prose, Kipling's style seemed to aspire to the virtues of both kinds of writing. He cultivated clear, easily understood, matter-of-fact statements but also claimed in the 1886 poem "A General Summary," "The artless songs I sing / Do not deal with anything / New or never said before." Kipling's profound sense of the timeless truths of great literature as opposed to the merely timely notions of good journalism was apparent in his appreciating that "if you go no further back than the [Bible's] Book of Job you will find that letters . . . were born perfect." Kipling practiced journalism as well as literature yet he believed in neither social nor literary progress. Rather, he seemed intent on perfecting a style of writing that would communicate as much and as well as possible with as many as possible. In his time he was successful in achieving this literary ideal. Not only his wide audience but also his literary peers attested to his success in appealing to many different levels of readers.

Approval of Kipling was not unanimous; Robert Buchanan, in an article from *Kipling: The Critical Heritage,* pronounced Kipling's writing vulgar, brutal, inflammatory, illiberal, irreligious, and sexually indecent—abuse that, as Orwell noted, Kipling's work might still draw. His egalitarian aesthetic ideal was and is challengeable. However, most interesting is Kipling's articulation of this ideal throughout his writing. As Kipling wrote in "The Last Rhyme of True Thomas," he wanted "To sing wi' the priests at the market-cross, / Or run wi' the dogs in the naked street." He knew the dangers if a writer tried to appeal too broadly, advising "never play down to your public—not because some of them do not deserve it, but because it is bad for your hand."

Nevertheless, Kipling also knew first hand the danger of writing to appeal to no one except the dead classics. At the outset of his career many writers and critics proclaimed that art should be created solely for its own sake. It need not have a social function or any function at all. Kipling's aim in writing was different. His art appealed not only to art but to society as well; he counted himself part of society: "I have eaten your bread and salt. / I have drunk your water and wine. / The deaths ye have died I have watched beside, / And the lives ye led were mine." Thus, according to Bonamy Dobree in *Rudyard Kipling: Realist and Fabulist,* Kipling revivified "the poetic diction of his day . . . and [came] back to poetry written 'in a language such as men doe use' as Ben Jonson put it." Regarding his own place and time and role as a writer, in the "Prelude to 'Barrack Room Ballads,' " Kipling professed to "Thomas Atkins," a representative name for every British soldier, "I have made for you a song, / . . . have tried for to explain / Both your pleasure and your pain."

The study of the style of Kipling's prolific work leads, as Bernard Bergonzi wrote in an essay for *The Age of Kipling,* to a recognition of "the strange complexity of his art, and . . . how completely it resists any neat and limiting formula." To consider only the poetry, his body of work encompasses a wide variety of poetic kinds, tone, diction, imagery, and prosodic technique. He was, in Dobree's words, a "master of versification," thriving within the traditional boundaries of rhyme and meter in English. Consequently, he had no need for modernist free verse, which he compared to "fishing with barbless hooks."

C. H. Sisson, writing in *English Poetry: 1900-1950,* considered Kipling's "real contribution to the verse of the twentieth century" to be "his plainness." To make such a quality a virtue in writing was a main tenet of much modernist poetry, too. However, in the nineteenth century also there was a beautiful plainness to be found in the verse of Christina Rossetti and Thomas Hardy, both of whom Kipling knew. He frequently matched their bleak yet stirring notes in works such as "The Widower": "For a season there must be pain— / For a little, little space shall lose sight of her face, / Take back the old life again / While She is at rest in her place." Kipling's poetry is admirably plain also because, as G. K. Chesterton recorded in *Heretics,* "he . . . perceived the significance and philosophy of steam and of slang." Chesterton was alluding in particular to Kipling's "McAndrew's Hymn," in which a steamship engineer pits his Scots Calvinist code of life, which he finds symbolized in the powerful workings of his steam engines, against contemporary materialism. Although the verse was composed in highly musical fourteen-syllable couplets, Kipling managed a slangy tone throughout. Furthermore, like many of Kipling's poems, "McAndrew's Hymn" is replete with allusions to the Bible's Old and New Testaments. To his credit as a poetic craftsman, Kipling let neither prosodic formality nor an almost evangelistic fervor vitiate his conversational diction, as is seen, too, in his making the very artificial and difficult sestina form accommodate plain speech in the "Sestina of the Tramp-Royal." "McAndrew's Hymn" also exemplifies Kipling's expertise in the dramatic monologue. Many of his best poems—such as "The Explorer," "Mulholland's Contract," and "The Mary Gloster"—are in this form, and interestingly Kipling extended it to include inanimate things. Poems like "The Deep Sea-Cables," "The Bell-Buoy," and "Song of the Dynamo" portray these things speaking their own special wisdom. Yet they are also plain objects in which Kipling identified near vatic significance.

Masterfully practicing his plain style in a wide variety of poetic kinds and genres, Kipling nevertheless managed to avoid sending a merely plain or banal message through his writing. His plain writing was frequently in the service of an actively philosophical and didactic mind. In his writing he spoke plainly but what his language signified was not necessarily easy to understand or accept. The opening lines of "Cities and Thrones and Powers" are plainly lyrical but their message is impossibly difficult: "Cities and Thrones and Powers / Stand in Time's eye / Almost as long as flowers, / Which daily die." In comparing the life span of civilizations and humankind to "This season's Daffodil" that "never hears / What change, what chance, what chill, / Cut down last year's," Kipling's imagery, like the evocation of the seasons in the Old Testament book of Ecclesiastes or Christ's exhortation in the New Testament to "consider the lilies of the field," sweetens the most bitter of historical truths. The simple stanza's placement of the word *almost* is particularly cutting.

Chesterton observed of Kipling that "above all, he . . . had something to say, a definite view of things to utter." In his autobiography Kipling recalled that as a young journalist he had to learn "that . . . statements of . . . facts are not well seen by responsible official authorities." His sister remembered him once writing a poem and wondering aloud, "What am I trying to say?" In his verse as well as his fiction Kipling frequently had

a strong didactic purpose. English poet John Keats said, "We hate poetry that has a palpable design upon us," but Kipling had little sympathy with this sentiment. His verse especially had a "palpable design" on readers and consequently it often either enraged or pleased them immensely. Nevertheless, Kipling was fully aware of the dangers for a poet as well as for a young journalist with a "palpable design." Therefore, to mollify his strong views he frequently resorted to allegory. He admitted his predicament and stated its solution in a poem called "The Fabulists": "When all the world would keep a matter hid, / Since truth is seldom friend to any crowd, / Men write in fable, as old Aesop did, / Jest at that which none will name aloud. / And thus they needs must do, or it will fall / Unless they please they are not heard at all."

Notwithstanding Kipling's frequent and skillful use of allegory, his didacticism and its attendant clarity of verbal expression are among his writing's greatest strengths. As Eliot wrote, "We expect to have to defend a poet against the charge of obscurity; we have to defend Kipling against the charge of excessive lucidity." Each piece of his work can be considered as an illustration of a philosophical, ethical, or social dilemma, although it can be public or personal, grave or lighthearted. As quoted in *Aspects of Kipling's Art,* Graham Hough noted that Kipling "addresses his readers in confidence that he will be understood." For him this required more than verbal undertones and overtones, subtlety, implicitness, and suggestive evocation. His writing bears such qualities but in addition, in Sisson's words, "He seems to be after the irrefutable prose statement, whether the subject is important or not." For example his short stories, as in *Puck of Pook's Hill,* are laced with aphorisms, and his verse has been called poetry of statement or, in Robert Conquest's phrase from an essay in *The Age of Kipling,* "poetry of clarification." As C. S. Lewis said of Renaissance poet Philip Sidney's *Arcadia,* so can be said of Kipling's work in general: it is forensic on every page.

One more of the greatest strengths of Kipling's writing—and it is one through which he also hoped that "people would not only read but remember" him—is the oral quality of his work. It was written to be spoken. And it was spoken by him. As he recalled in his autobiography, "I made my own experiments in the weights, colours, perfumes, and attributes of words as read aloud so that they may hold the ear. . . . There is no line of my verse or prose which has not been mouthed till the tongue has made all smooth, and memory, after many recitals, has mechanically skipped the grosser superfluities." Attesting to Kipling's vocal enactment of his work in the midst of its composition, his cousin Florence Macdonald remembered how "when composing verse he would often set it to a tune, usually to a hymn tune, and I have heard him walking up and down the room singing a verse over and over again to get the lilt and swing of it." Another cousin, Angela Thirkell, reminisced how Kipling "used to try out" his work "on a nursery audience." If Kipling wrote some of the most notable children's stories in English then it is because he realized that children especially appreciate the greatness of literature by hearing it. According to Thirkell, *Kipling's Just So Stories* were "a poor thing in print compared with the fun of hearing them told in Cousin Ruddy's deep unhesitating voice. There was a ritual about them, each phrase having its special intonation which had to be exactly the same each time and without which the stories are dried husks. There was an inimitable cadence, an emphasis on certain words, an exaggeration of certain phrases, a kind of intoning here and there which made his telling unforgettable." Since Kipling devoted so much attention to the oral as well as aural quality of literature, particularly unfortunate and poignant is his being the last great English writer who was not recorded reading his own work.

Kipling's emphasis on "the weights, colours, perfumes . . . of words . . . mouthed till the tongue has made all smooth" in his "verse or prose" suggests, as James Harrison wrote in *Rudyard Kipling,* a kind of "love affair with the spoken word." Harrison further observes that "speech is Kipling's principal method of characterization . . . since [his] ear was attuned to a wide range of voices and accents, and he clearly enjoyed exercising his virtuoso skill at reproducing them on paper." He could give a text the tone of a music hall, as in "Tommy" or "The Widow at Windsor," or of a Westminster Abbey, as in the hymn of "Recessional." The American sailors of *Captains Courageous,* the lonely soldiers of *Barrack Room Ballads,* the British Viceroy of India ("One Viceroy Resigns"), the lowly Indian *bhisti* water carrier of the British Army during battle ("Gunga Din"), the animals of *The Jungle Book,* the incarnate Indian gods of "The Bridge Builders": Kipling gives these characters distinctive voices. Revealing his characters primarily through their manners of speaking, Kipling naturally was led to write many dramatic monologues and ballads, the two poetic forms that rely most on conversational tone. Moreover, throughout his works Kipling frequently imitated or parodied the ways that people actually speak—for instance, in his heavy use of dialect and slang—particularly revealing the influence of Dickens's writing.

Many themes recur in Kipling's work, among which are politics and the imperialism of the West in the East, soldiers and war, work and machines, art itself, and history. He spent most of his life until he was twenty-three in India. Predictably, therefore, it and the East in general were the setting and subject of much of his early writing. During Kipling's entire lifetime England ruled India. For that matter, British imperialism—or the British empire—also reached into South Africa, the Middle East, and Southeast Asia. As Eliot noted: "We must accustom ourselves to recognizing that for Kipling the Empire was not merely an idea, a good idea or a bad one; it was something the reality of which he felt. And in his expression of his feeling he was certainly not aiming at flattery of national, racial or imperial vanity, or attempting to propagate a political programme: he was aiming to communicate the awareness of something in existence of which he felt that most people were very imperfectly aware." In his belief that England had a right and responsibility to rule foreign lands, Kipling differed from no major English writer before him. He avidly supported British imperialism while he bitterly criticized its administration. Nevertheless, in Andrew Rutherford's words, Kipling's "pride in imperial achievement" went along with his "awareness of the human cost to the Empire builders." Eric Stokes observed in an essay from *The Age of Kipling* that "Kipling's most ardent literary admirers have found [his] overt imperialism an embarrassment and try to shuffle it off." While Kipling's imperialism cannot be ignored or justified, his viewpoint was unique and neither politic nor patronizing. He repeatedly emphasized that the "human cost" for the building and maintaining of an empire was hardly suffered or even realized by the English who enjoyed its fruits at home or administered it from Whitehall.

Kipling's strong yet unique brand of imperialism was not the only distinguishing feature of his politics as reflected in his writing. Generally he was, in Dobree's words, attracted to "public themes." Usually taking the form of verse, Kipling's political observations had a wide circulation. They were highly respected too; so much so that between 1890 and World War I he was dubbed the people's laureate, although his frequently controversial, original, inflammatory, and unpredictable political sympa-

thies probably prevented his appointment as the official poet laureate. He was the last in a tradition of great English poets—including Alfred Tennyson and William Wordsworth, Alexander Pope and Jonathan Swift, John Dryden, John Milton and Andrew Marvell—who directly, publicly, and polemically addressed the important political issues of their time. Orwell considered Kipling a "gutter patriot," and he earned this designation with ranting verses like "For All We Have and Are," written in 1914 to raise the British war fever by warning "The Hun is at the Gate." What George Shepperson in an essay for *The Age of Kipling* calls Kipling's "unadulterated patriotism," however, was not always positive. As Orwell also observed about Kipling's patriotic prose and poetry, "Few people who have criticized England from the inside have said bitterer things about her." For instance, his epitaph for "A Dead Statesman" could hardly comfort the political establishment: "I could not dig: I dared not rob: / Therefore I lied to please the mob. / Now all my lies are proved untrue / And I must face the men I slew. / What tale shall serve me here among / Mine angry and defrauded young?"

Such political writing is not merely timely. Like the great political yet literary English writers before him, Kipling in his best work can be appreciated without much knowledge of the detailed background of the issues and parties he was praising or blaming. The greatest political writing makes artful yet astute observations about the politics of all countries and all times, as does Kipling's "The Peace of Dives," which implies, in Ralph Durand's words, "that those who control the world's money decide between themselves how, and when, and for how long king should draw sword against king, and people rise up against people." Great political writing can also have a prophetic dimension—Orwell's *1984,* for instance. Kipling's poem "The Press," written in 1907, foretold how newspapers would achieve political power comparable to that of the biblical beast Leviathan: "That King over all the children of pride / Is the Press—the Press—the Press!"

Closely related to Kipling's imperialism and politics was his writing about soldiers and war. The lives of British soldiers in India, the far East, the Boer War, and World War I and the lives of veterans inspired many of his short stories and poems. C. E. Carrington claims that Kipling's literary "treatment of the British soldier" was the greatest since Shakespeare's in his history plays. Kipling portrayed soldiers at war and peace, in triumph and defeat, in hope and despair, ridiculous and serious, callous and sentimental, happy-go-lucky and self-determined, as heroes and cowards, saviors and murderers. According to Eliot, Kipling's "concern was to make the soldier known, not to idealize him." Furthermore, Kipling's writing about soldiers expressed anxiety and rage at civilian society's apathetic or mean and unjust treatment of them. Orwell contended "that Kipling's 'message' was one that the big public did not want, and, indeed has never accepted. The mass of the people, in the 'nineties as now, were anti-militarist, bored by the Empire, and only unconsciously patriotic." In his fiction Kipling tried to combat this tendency by writing detailed yet diverting accounts of the ups and downs of life in the military. In his poems he frequently adopted the persona or point of view of a British regular.

As a writer who had repeatedly portrayed military life Kipling was prepared to confront the unprecedented realities of World War I, although Paul Fussell has argued in *The Great War and Modern Memory* that no contemporary writer and not even the English language itself was able to adequately describe such horrors. Kipling wrote about the war in an impressive variety of ways. He edited a two-volume history entitled *The Irish Guards in the Great War,* about his son's battalion. He wrote poems about some of the new weaponry of "Mine Sweepers" and "Sea Warfare" and, in a poem called "Gethsemane," about a poison gas attack which he compares to a New Testament story about Christ's agony in the garden: "The men lay on the grass, . . . / I prayed my cup might pass. / It didn't pass—it didn't pass— / It didn't pass from me. / I drank it when we met the gas / Beyond Gethsemane." Kipling was also concerned with the plight of veterans after the war, writing poems about their prolonged battle fatigue such as "The Mother's Son," about their inability to control during peacetime their violent tendencies that the war encouraged as in "The Expert," about their transformation from experienced soldiers into scholars as portrayed in "The Scholars," and about their eventual recognition as possible heroes as related in "The Verdicts."

Kipling sought not to criticize or analyze the war but to memorialize its casualties. He did this most successfully in his "Epitaphs of the War." Appointed as the "Honorary Literary Advisor" for the Imperial War Graves Commission, he was the author of the general epitaph for all the veterans' cemeteries: "Their name liveth forevermore." However, Kipling's unofficial "Epitaphs of the War" were far more particular, emotional, and disturbing. Bergonzi judges them his "most moving and authentic poetry." They were about the fate of green recruits—and, critics say, Kipling's own son—as in "The Beginner": "On the first hour of my first day / In the front trench I fell / (Children in boxes at a play / Stand up to watch it well.)" They also treated the leveling ironies of social class on the battlefield, as in "A Servant": "We were together since the War began. / He was my servant—and the better man." They dealt with the inscrutable personal tragedy of "The Coward": "I could not look on Death, which being known, / Men led me to him, blindfolded and alone." And they portrayed the suffering and casualties among the parents who lost their children in war, as in "An Only Son": "I have slain my Mother. She / (Blessing her slayer) died of grief for me." Sharply reflecting the casualties of war among many different types of people both on the battlefield and at home, Kipling's "Epitaphs" are among the greatest poetic sequences of the twentieth century. They are the climax of his thirty years of writing on military topics.

Chesterton thought that Kipling's writing about soldiers and war was indicative of his interest in a larger topic: "He is a poet rather of all disciplines and skills." Moreover, C. S. Lewis in an essay from *The Age of Kipling* wrote that Kipling was "first and foremost the poet of work." Again Chesterton thought that "Kipling's subject is not that valour which properly belongs to war, but that interdependence of efficiency which belongs quite as much to engineers, or sailors, or mules, or railway engines. And thus it is that when he writes of engineers, or sailors, or mules, or steam engines, he writes at his best. The real poetry, the 'true romance'. . . is the romance of the divisions of labour and the discipline of all the trades. He sings the arts of peace much more accurately than the arts of war. . . . Everything is military in the sense that everything depends upon obedience. . . . Everywhere men have made the way for us with sweat and submission." There is plenty in Kipling's prose and verse to support Chesterton's point of view and "work" certainly is one of Kipling's major themes.

Kipling had a philosophy about work, and his writing manifested his work ethic. Often he would reduce or simplify a complex issue by determining the work it involved. For example, in "McAndrew's Hymn" the tough Calvinist McAndrew claims in his engine room that "From coupler-flange to spindle-guide I see Thy Hand, O God— / Predestination in the stride o' yon connectin'-rod. / John Calvin might ha' forged the same—

enormous, certain, slow— / Ay, wrought it in the furnace-flame—*my* 'Institutio.'" Theology and religious commitment are understood through the technical terms of "crosshead-gibs" and "follower-bolts." When "McAndrew's Hymn" was first published, Kipling prefaced it with his recommendation that "to appreciate the poem thoroughly, it should be read in a ship's engine room when the engines are doing their work." In "The Wage Slaves" Kipling suggested that while idealism, the sublime, truth, and beauty may be "glorious" in "the guarded heights / Where the guardian souls abide," he nevertheless must live on a lower, more worldly and practical plane with "the bondslaves of our day, / Whom dirt and danger press— / Co-heirs of insolence, delay, / And leagued unfaithfulness." Similarly in "The Sons of Martha," verses that Carrington thinks "best summarize [Kipling's] social philosophy," he defended Martha's working while Mary meditated, although in the New Testament story Christ tells Martha that she should not criticize Mary because she, in the words of Luke's Gospel, "hath chosen that good part." Kipling disagreed, and in a like vein he suggested in "Cain and Abel," about an Old Testament story of fratricide, that Cain was treated unjustly because he worked harder than Abel.

It should be recalled that in his poem about Shakespeare Kipling called him "The Craftsman," that is, not the artist or poet or writer. Moreover, as he was interested in many kinds of work and workers so did Kipling regard writing itself to be work or craft as opposed to something more special called "art." Looking at "work," poet W. H. Auden distinguished the word from "labor" and "play." According to Auden, to play was a pleasure and to labor was not. To work, however, was a human ideal, and Auden considered writing to be work. Kipling wrote that for him, "mercifully, the mere act of writing was a physical pleasure." Nonetheless, Kipling repeatedly in his writing elevated various kinds of work as pleasure, indeed "physical pleasure." Since his father was an architect, and his uncle was the Victorian painter and illustrator Edmund Burne-Jones, Kipling when young would have had much direct experience of artists at work and performing like craftsmen. Such contact might have initially caused him to reject what W. L. Renwick in *Kipling's Mind and Art* called "romantic aestheticism that fails—or refuses—to understand that the fine work of art is also a good job of work."

Another recurrent theme in Kipling's writings, and one that appeared most frequently in the latter half of his literary career, was history. However, it was a history for the most part apolitical and ancient. It was rooted in the land, particularly the English countryside of Sussex, where Kipling had bought a large seventeenth-century house called Bateman's. In his autobiography Kipling recalled about the move "how patiently the cards were stacked and dealt into my hands. . . . The Old Things of our Valley glided into every aspect of our outdoor works. Earth, Air, Water, and People had been—I saw it at last—in full conspiracy to give me ten times as much as I could compass, even if I wrote a complete history of England, as that might have touched or reached our Valley." Kipling's at times feverish commitment to British imperialism and politics was cooled and soothed by the local "clay," "wiseturf," "white cliff-edge," "sunlight," "sea fogs," "sheep bells . . . ship bells," "dewpond," "close-bit thyme," "rolled scarp," "deep ghylls," and "huge oaks" of Sussex. Their "Memory, Use, and Love" were "deeper than . . . speech and thought, / Beyond . . . reasons's sway."

Published in 1906, Kipling's *Puck of Pook's Hill*, and its 1910 sequel, *Rewards and Fairies*, grew out of his living among Sussex's "ferny ride," "dympled track," "secret Weald," "little mill," "stilly woods," "windy levels," and "pastures wide and lone," as "Puck's Song" records. *Puck of Pook's Hill* presents the fairy Puck who, upon meeting two children, tells them a series of stories about the successive generations—from Roman times to the French Revolution—that have inhabited the land where these children now blithely play. Actually, Kipling himself while living in Sussex discovered an ancestral vision of history that prevailed regardless of the gloominess of the political present, which he bleakly characterized, in "The Storm Cone," as nothing less than history's apocalyptic midnight with "dawn . . . very far" and "the tempest long foretold" slowly approaching "but sure to hold." As Norman Page remarks, "Kipling's imagination was powerfully stimulated by the sense of the past evoked by the Sussex countryside and by archaeological and historical sites in the immediate vicinity" of his home. His theme became "the presence of the past in English rural life."

In his autobiography Kipling jauntily recalled that as a young newspaperman in India, when he was sent out on an assignment, "the dead of all times were about [him] in the vast forgotten Moslem cemeteries round the Station, where one's hoof of a morning might break through to the corpse below; skulls and bones tumbled out of our mud garden walls, and were turned up among the flowers by the Rains; and at every point were tombs of the dead. Our chief picnic rendezvous and some of our public offices had been memorials to desired dead women; and Fort Lahore . . . was a mausoleum of ghosts." Living and writing in Sussex, Kipling found a more pastoral historical setting than India, but still he delighted in the realization that "the dead of all times were" around him. As an extraordinarily popular writer in his time, he also suffused his writing with images of the living, entertaining readers with a vast and varied literary output.

MEDIA ADAPTATIONS: Kipling's writings adapted for film, stage, radio, or television include *The Light That Failed, The Naulahka, The Vampire, The Jungle Books, Captains Courageous, Kim, The Just So Stories, Gunga Din, Without Benefit of Clergy, The Man Who Would Be King,* "Mowgli and Kaa," "Mowgli Among the Wolves," "Wee Willie Winkie," "Soldiers Three," and "How the Animals Came to Live With Man."

BIOGRAPHICAL/CRITICAL SOURCES:

BOOKS

Amis, Kingsley, *Rudyard Kipling and His World,* Thames & Hudson, 1975, Scribner, 1975.

Barkenhead, Lord, *Rudyard Kipling,* Weidenfeld & Nicolson, 1978, Random House, 1978.

Bodelsen, C. A., *Aspects of Kipling's Art,* Barnes & Noble, 1964.

Carrington, Charles Edmund, *The Life of Rudyard Kipling,* Doubleday, 1955, published as *Rudyard Kipling,* Penguin, 1989.

Chandler, Lloyd H., *A Summary of the Work of Rudyard Kipling,* Grolier Club, 1930.

Chesterton, G. K., *Heretics,* John Lane, 1905.

Cornell, Louis L., *Kipling in India,* St. Martin's, 1966.

Durand, Ralph, *A Handbook to the Poetry of Rudyard Kipling,* Hodder & Stoughton, 1914.

Dictionary of Literary Biography, Gale, Volume 19: *British Poets, 1840-1914,* 1983, Volume 34: *British Novelists, 1890-1929: Traditionalists,* 1985.

Dobree, Bonamy, *Rudyard Kipling: Realist and Fabulist,* Oxford University Press, 1967.

Faber, Richard, *The Vision and the Need,* Faber, 1966.

Fido, Martin, *Rudyard Kipling,* Viking, 1974.

Flint, R. W., *Marinetti: Selected Writings,* Farrar, Straus, 1971.

Fussell, Paul, *The Great War and Modern Memory,* Oxford University Press, 1975.

Gilbert, Elliot L., editor, *"O Beloved Kids": Rudyard Kipling's Letters to His Children,* Harcourt, 1984.

Gilbert, *The Good Kipling: Studies in the Short Story,* Ohio University Press, 1970.

Gilbert, editor, *Kipling and His Critics,* P. Owen, 1965.

Green, Roger Lancelyn, editor, *Kipling: The Critical Heritage,* Barnes & Noble, 1971.

Gross, John, editor, *The Age of Kipling,* Simon & Schuster, 1972.

Gross, editor, *Rudyard Kipling: The Man, His Work, and His World,* Weidenfeld & Nicolson, 1972.

Harrison, James, *Rudyard Kipling,* Twayne, 1982.

Henn, T. R., *Kipling,* Oliver & Boyd, 1967.

Howe, Irving, editor, *The Portable Kipling,* Viking, 1982.

Islam, Shamsul, *Kipling's "Law": A Study of His Philosophy of Life,* foreword by J. M. S. Tompkins, Macmillan (London), 1975.

Kamen, Gloria, *Kipling: Storyteller of East and West,* Atheneum, 1985.

Kipling, Rudyard, *A Book of Words: Selections From Speeches and Addresses Delivered Between 1906 and 1927,* Doubleday, Doran, 1928.

Kipling, *A Choice of Kipling's Verse,* selected and introduced by T. S. Eliot, Faber, 1941, Scribner, 1943.

Kipling, *Rudyard Kipling: Illustrated,* Avenel Books, 1982.

Kipling, *Rudyard Kipling's Verse: Definitive Edition,* Doubleday, Doran, 1940.

Kipling, *Something of Myself for My Friends Known and Unknown,* Doubleday, Doran, 1937.

Orel, Harold, editor, *Kipling: Interviews and Recollections,* two volumes, Barnes & Noble, 1983.

Orwell, George, *The Collected Essays, Journalism, and Letters of George Orwell,* Volume 2: *My Country Right or Left, 1940-1943,* edited by Sonia Orwell and Ian Angus, Harcourt, 1968.

Page, Norman, *A Kipling Companion,* Macmillan, (London), 1984.

Rutherford, Andrew, editor, *Kipling's Mind and Art: Selected Critical Essays,* Stanford University Press, 1964.

Stewart, J. I. M., *Rudyard Kipling,* Dodd, 1966.

Stewart, J. I. M., *Eight Modern Writers,* Oxford University Press, 1963.

Stewart, James McG., *Rudyard Kipling: A Bibliographical Catalogue,* edited by A. W. Yeats, Dalhousie University Press and University of Toronto Press, 1959.

Sisson, C. H., *English Poetry: 1900-1950,* St. Martin's, 1971.

Tompkins, Joyce Marjorie Sanxter, *The Art of Rudyard Kipling,* Methuen, 1959.

Trilling, Lionel, *The Selected Letters of John Keats,* Doubleday, 1951.

Twentieth-Century Literary Criticism, Gale, Volume 8, 1982, Volume 17, 1985.

Wilson, Angus, *The Strange Ride of Rudyard Kipling: His Life and Works,* Secker & Warburg, 1977, Viking, 1978.

PERIODICALS

Dalhousie Review, fall, 1960.

Detroit Free Press, July 7, 1986.

Los Angeles Times Book Review, August 5, 1984.

Modern Fiction Studies, summer, 1961, summer, 1984.

Proceedings of the British Academy, Volume 51, 1965.

Sewanee Review, winter, 1944.

Times (London), December 6, 1984.

Times Literary Supplement, January 15, 1960, September 2, 1960.

*   *   *

KIRK, Russell (Amos) 1918-

PERSONAL: Born October 19, 1918, in Plymouth, Mich.; son of Russell Andrew and Marjorie (Pierce) Kirk; married Annette Yvonne Cecile Courtemanche, September 19, 1964; children: Monica, Cecilia, Felicia, Andrea. *Education:* Michigan State College (now University), B.A., 1940; Duke University, M.A., 1941; St. Andrews University, D.Litt., 1952. *Politics:* Republican.

ADDRESSES: Home and office—Piety Hill, Mecosta, Mich. 49332.

CAREER: Michigan State College (now University), East Lansing, assistant professor of the history of civilization, 1946-53; writer, editor, and lecturer, 1953—. Distinguished visiting professor and visiting research professor at numerous colleges and universities, 1953—; Long Island University, research professor of politics at Merriweather Campus (now C. W. Post Center), 1957-61, university professor, 1958-61. President, Educational Reviewer (foundation), 1960—, and Marguerite Eyer Wilbur Foundation, 1979—. Director of social science program, Educational Research Council of America, 1979-84. Justice of the peace, Morton Township, Mecosta County, Mich., 1961-64. *Military service:* U.S. Army, Chemical Warfare Service, 1941-45; became staff sergeant.

AWARDS, HONORS: American Council of Learned Societies senior fellow, 1950-51; Guggenheim fellow, 1956; honorary degrees from Boston College, 1956, St. John's University, New York, N.Y., 1957, Park College, 1961, Le Moyne College, 1963, Loyola College, Baltimore, Md., Olivet College, Gannon College, Niagara University, Pepperdine University, Albion College, Central Michigan University, and Grand Valley State College; Ann Radcliffe Award for Gothic fiction, 1966, for *Old House of Fear* and *The Surly Sullen Bell;* Christopher Award, 1972, for *Eliot and His Age: T. S. Eliot's Moral Imagination in the Twentieth Century;* World Fantasy Award for short fiction, 1977, for "There's a Long, Long Trail a-Winding"; Weaver Award of Ingersoll Prizes for scholarly humane letters, 1984; constitutional fellowship, National Endowment for the Humanities, 1985; Freedom Leadership Award, Hillsdale College, 1985; Fulbright lecturer in Scotland, 1987; distinguished fellow, Heritage Foundation.

WRITINGS:

Randolph of Roanoke, University of Chicago Press, 1951, enlarged edition published as *John Randolph of Roanoke,* Henry Regnery, 1964, 3rd edition, Liberty Fund, 1978.
The Conservative Mind: From Burke to Santayana, Henry Regnery, 1953, 3rd revised edition published as *The Conservative Mind: From Burke to Eliot,* 1960, 7th revised edition, 1986.
St. Andrews, Batsford, 1954.
A Program for Conservatives, Henry Regnery, 1954, abridged edition published as *Prospects for Conservatives,* 1956, revised edition, Regnery Gateway, 1989.
Academic Freedom, Henry Regnery, 1955, reprinted, Greenwood Press, 1977.
Beyond the Dreams of Avarice, Henry Regnery, 1956.
The Intelligent Woman's Guide to Conservatism, Devin-Adair, 1957.
The American Cause, Henry Regnery, 1957, reprinted, Greenwood Press, 1975.

Old House of Fear (gothic novel), Fleet Press, 1961, 2nd edition, 1963.
The Surly Sullen Bell (collection of supernatural tales), Fleet Press, 1962.
Lost Lake: Confessions of a Bohemian Tory, Fleet Press, 1963.
The Intemperate Professor and Other Cultural Splenetics, Louisiana State University Press, 1965, recent edition, Sherwood Sugden, 1986.
A Creature of the Twilight (novel), Fleet Press, 1966.
Edmund Burke: A Genius Reconsidered, Arlington House, 1967, revised edition, Sherwood Sugden, 1985.
(With James McClellan) *The Political Principles of Robert A. Taft,* Fleet Press, 1967.
Enemies of the Permanent Things: Observations of Abnormality in Literature and Politics, Arlington House, 1969, revised edition, Sherwood Sugden, 1984.
Eliot and His Age: T. S. Eliot's Moral Imagination in the Twentieth Century, Random House, 1971, revised edition, Sherwood Sugden, 1984.
The Roots of American Order, Open Court, 1974, 2nd edition, Pepperdine University Press, 1980.
(With John Chamberlain) *Great Issues 73: A Forum on Important Questions Facing the American Public,* Volume 5, Troy State University Press, 1974.
Decadence and Renewal in the Higher Learning, Henry Regnery, 1978.
Lord of the Hollow Dark (gothic novel), St. Martin's, 1979.
The Princess of All Lands (collection of supernatural tales), Arkham, 1979.
(With others) *Objections to Conservatism,* Heritage Foundation, 1981.
(With others) *Government's Role in Solving Societal Problems,* edited by Clark Edwards, Associated Faculty Press, 1982.
(Editor) *The Portable Conservative Reader,* Viking, 1982.
Reclaiming a Patrimony, Heritage Foundation, 1982.
Watchers at the Strait Gate (collection of supernatural tales), Arkham, 1984.
(Editor) *The Assault on Religion: Commentaries on the Decline of Religious Liberty,* University Press of America, 1986.
(Editor) Irving Babbitt, *Literature and the American College,* National Humanities Institute, 1986.
(Editor) James Monroe, *The People, the Sovereigns,* James River Press, 1987.
The Wise Men Know What Wicked Things Are Written on the Sky, Regnery Gateway, 1987.
(Editor with Kenneth Shorey) *Collected Letters of John Randolph of Roanoke to Dr. John Brockenbrough, 1812-1833,* Transaction, 1988.
Work and Prosperity (high-school economics textbook), Beka Books, 1989.
(Editor) W. H. Mallock, *A Critical Examination of Socialism,* Transaction, 1989.

Also editor of additional books; contributor of introductions and articles to over forty-five books. Co-founder and educational columnist, *National Review,* 1956-83; author of newspaper column, "To the Point," Los Angeles Times Syndicate, 1962-75. Contributor to encyclopedias and dictionaries, including *Encyclopaedia Britannica, Collier's Encyclopedia, World Book Encyclopedia, Dictionary of Southern History,* and *Dictionary of Political Science.* Contributor of more than 500 articles, essays, and short stories to periodicals in the United States, Great Britain, Canada, Australia, Norway, Austria, Spain, Argentina, and Italy, including *Fortune, New York Times Magazine, Southern Partisan, Wall Street Journal, Yale Review, Sewanee Review, Journal of the History of Ideas, America, Modern Age, Commonweal,* and *Kenyon*

Review. Modern Age, founder and editor, 1957-59, currently member of editorial advisory board; editor, *University Bookman,* 1960—.

WORK IN PROGRESS: A memoir, tentatively titled *The Sword of Imagination;* a collection of his lectures on the U.S. Constitution.

SIDELIGHTS: Russell Kirk is "singularly responsible for the resurgence of conservatism in America," Victoria Kailas and Richard Harrold say in the *Grand Rapids Magazine.* The author, who founded the *National Review* with William F. Buckley, Jr., in 1956, "laid the cornerstone of modern conservative thought" with his 1953 book, *The Conservative Mind: From Burke to Santayana,* explains S. J. Masty in the *Washington Times.* Kailas and Harrold add that the book "is credited with sparking the political trend that is finding its fulfillment today in the presidency of Ronald Reagan."

The Conservative Mind examines the importance of eighteenth-century political theorist Edmund Burke, but as Donald Atwell Zoll points out in the *Political Science Reviewer,* "it is not merely an obvious affection for Edmund Burke that links Russell Kirk with the eighteenth century. His emergence in the arena of contemporary letters reveals the transmigration of an eighteenth century spirit, the revival of the literary grace and versatility of the century of high baroque. He personifies the still lively *arete* of a more leisurely age, the urbane versatility of the literati of the era of Addison and Steel, Swift, Pope, Chesterfield, Johnson and Burke."

Kirk is indeed versatile. He is the first American to have received an earned doctorate of letters from the senior Scottish university, St. Andrews, and according to Masty in another *Washington Times* article, the doctorate of letters is that country's highest academic degree, "far more demanding than a Ph.D." He is a vigorous critic of the American educational system, which he believes has lost touch with the country's religious and philosophical heritage.

Furthermore, as the author of *Eliot and His Age: T. S. Eliot's Moral Imagination in the Twentieth Century,* Kirk believes that the poet "was 'the principle champion of the moral imagination in the twentieth century,' " George Scott-Moncrieff relates in the *Sewanee Review.* In the words of Charles Lam Markmann in the *Nation,* Kirk is of the opinion that "it was Eliot's purpose—not that he was vain enough to suppose that he could achieve it—to redeem the time, in Kirk's phrase, from the moral and intellectual decay into which he considered that it had sunk; he was the poet and the philosopher of 'the horror, and the boredom, and the glory' of the first half of the 20th century."

Kirk is also the author of a few Gothic novels and ghost story collections. According to Masty, he is "credited with resurrecting the Gothic novel some 20 years ago," while Don Herron judges in an article in *Discovering Modern Horror Fiction* that Kirk "has emerged as the premier writer of classical ghost stories in America." Yet Herron adds that Kirk's "renown in the supernatural area is possibly the least of [his] fame." With the publication of *The Conservative Mind,* Herron reports, Kirk "was hailed as a major conservative political thinker and writer, and soon became a prominent figure among the New Conservatives."

Kailas and Harrold note that, as Rick Brookhiser, managing editor of the *National Review,* explains it, "Russell Kirk was really the first in the post-war conservative movement. After World War II, conservatism was fairly feeble politically and very anemic intellectually, and Kirk's *The Conservative Mind* was really the first book that believed the title existed. It defined its own

title. Before he came along, some people were for free-market, some people, anti-communism, and some had unfocused nostalgia for the past. Russell Kirk tried to draw the threads together. The contribution he made was asserting there was conservatism and conservatism in America." In *The Conservative Mind,* indicates Zoll, Kirk "reintroduced the broken web of historical social conservatism by the deceptively simple device of describing it and declaring it to be yet lively."

The Conservative Mind: From Burke to Santayana, which was revised in 1960 as *The Conservative Mind: From Burke to Eliot,* examines conservative thought within the American and British philosophical tradition. As Frederick D. Wilhelmsen reports in *Commonweal,* "working inductively from the thought of a host of varied and sometimes opposed thinkers, the author attempts to find a common conservative philosophy and attitude that runs through Burke, Adams, Coleridge, Randolph, and Calhoun, Tocqueville, Bronson, Disraeli, Newman, and others." Peter Viereck explains in *Saturday Review* that "it is Kirk's thesis that the traditionalist Burke and not the radical Paine represented the true spirit of the revolution made by George Washington." Furthermore, adds Masty, Kirk argues in the book that conservatism "was more than what was commonly assumed in this century. He contended that conservatism is, in fact, a coherent school of thought different from simple doctrines of anti-communism or Chamber of Commerce boosterism. . . . In Mr. Kirk's world, there is room for tradition, hierarchy, culture, and organic change."

The book was widely praised. According to John Chamberlain in the *Chicago Sunday Tribune, The Conservative Mind* "is in every respect a brilliant book. It is brilliant in its conception, brilliant in its avoidance of cliches, brilliant in its ability to relate a man to his landscape . . . and brilliant in its choice of significant figures in the history of intellectual conservatism." As a reviewer in the *New York Herald Tribune Book Review* points out, "to be a conservative in the United States has for so long been considered identical with being backward and even faintly alien, that Mr. Kirk's proud justification of the term is to be welcomed. His book is carefully wrought and honestly made. It embodies a point of view which deserves a hearing."

A few were more critical of the work. Wilhelmsen admits that Kirk "has marshalled an impressive list of American and British conservative thinkers" in support of his views, yet "the question I would ask him and all conservatives is this: what is the key to the spirit conservatism is fighting? Unless that spirit be understood in its very essence, the fight is in vain. Until Mr. Kirk leads his investigation into this ground I am afraid his restoration of the conservative heritage will remain incomplete." In the opinion of a *Times Literary Supplement* critic, *The Conservative Mind* should have actually been two books: one an evaluation of the history of modern conservative thought, and the other a prescriptive analysis of the "ills of modern English and American society." And Peter Gay of the *Political Science Quarterly* claims that in "attempting to prove the existence and moral and intellectual respectability of a conservative ideology, Mr. Kirk has only succeeded in doing the opposite."

In general, the response to *The Conservative Mind* was positive, though. Most agree that the book established Kirk in the publishing world, Masty points out. And critics of the era were receptive to the new viewpoints Kirk had to present. As Gordon Keith Chalmers writes in a 1953 *New York Times* review of the book, "in a time when the activities of Senator [Joseph R.] McCarthy have deluded many into thinking him a conservative, it is important to be exact about the nature of liberty and the conservative account of it." Kirk's "account of the ideas, decisions and beliefs that have produced [some of the highest American] virtues merits the responsible attention of all informed persons who are not rattled by unpopular labels," Chalmers concludes.

Kirk followed *The Conservative Mind* with several books that expanded upon similar themes. *A Program for Conservatives,* according to Francis G. Wilson in *Saturday Review,* "is a program for the reform of the individual spirit first of all, for a self-conscious organization and buttressing of conservative attitudes, and for the support of many legislative experiments tending toward the restoration of a conservative way of life." Raymond English of the *New York Times* calls *A Program for Conservatives* "necessary and most welcome," while Wilson judges that it is "a brilliant contribution to the defense of conservatives and to the rejection of liberalism."

Frederick D. Wilhelmsen reports in the *National Review* that in *Enemies of the Permanent Things: Observations of Abnormality in Literature and Politics,* Kirk "interprets American liberalism as largely imported from nineteenth-century English and German models. . . . Distinguishing territorial democracy from plebiscitary, Kirk argues that they are antithetical and that the drift towards the latter in our day portends an even further centralization of governmental power in Washington." Wilhelmsen indicates that "in all cases, Kirk is the friend of diversity in unity, of analogy, and the enemy of any rationalist structuring of society around the principle of mass production," and he believes that "all friends of civilization are in [Kirk's] debt for his having written a profoundly elegant critique of the enemies of the permanent things."

The Roots of American Order, says *National Review* critic M. Stanton Evans, spells out "with graceful erudition the philosophical and historical antecedents, not only of our political system, but of our culture, beliefs, and practices in general." Here, Kirk most forcefully concludes that "all aspects of any civilization arise out of a people's religion. . . . All order . . . [grows] out of general belief in truths that are perceived by the moral imagination," reports Chilton Williamson, Jr., in the *National Review.* "It is thus our religious heritage, bequeathed us in its primal form by the ancient Hebrews, that is the taproot of American order."

In an assessment of the author's theoretical work, Zoll criticizes Kirk for his "frequent hostility to science and empiricism" in general, which he feels "may be misplaced." In Zoll's opinion, the author "too easily assumes that science and its methods are identical to the parody of them presented by his positivistically-oriented foes. His social criticism and corresponding recommendations, resting as they do upon theological, historical and literary insights, would be more formidable if buttressed by the empirically-derived evidences of contemporary science. He is not fully aware, perhaps, to what extent such evidential reflection would be conducive to the defense of the 'permanent things' or the revival of the 'moral imagination.' "

The basis for Kirk's particular conservative outlook, which includes an antipathy to the mechanistic, may be found in his youth. According to Herron, the author's "biography indicates longstanding acquaintance with works of supernaturalism and Romance, with people and places spectral and romantic." He grew up in Plymouth, Michigan but spent many of his summers at Piety Hill, the family ancestral home in Mecosta, Michigan. There, Kirk, who is often called the Wizard of Mecosta, now lives with his wife and four daughters, with the family acting as host to a wide variety of people, including refugees, transients,

and graduate students who pursue independent studies under Kirk's tutelage and guidance.

His early traditional education influenced the development of his later political philosophy. Kirk "was reared on books and walks and good conversation," Herron reports, while Kailas and Harrold add that "the basis of Kirk's entire conservative philosophy is inspired by the classical Greek and Roman ways of thinking" with which the author began to acquaint himself while he was growing up. As Kirk told Kailas and Harrold, "I suppose I chiefly acquired from the ancient philosophers a sense of the vanity of human relations—as a consequence, [I came] not to expect too much of life, accept the universe as it is; to be content with the life and mind of the spirit." Furthermore, Kirk related, "I learned from Plato and Aristotle, human nature is not perfectable, nor is society. . . . The attempt of creating a heaven upon earth is doomed to failure. Our best efforts succeed only in making a temporarily tolerable society, not one that is perfect."

Kirk's affinity for the mysterious and religious, as well as his disaffection with the rational and scientific stem from childhood experiences at Piety Hill, which is widely thought to be haunted. Kirk's ancestors were members of a Spiritualist church that was built in the town. Seances were also held at Piety Hill in the 1880s and 1890s, and Masty reports that "the boy Russell was oft told how his great-grandmother, Stella Johnson, was levitated in her rocking chair, or how the mahogany Empire table, heavy and round, rose upwards as well." According to Masty, "the ghosts of Piety Hill, nearly all relatives of the good doctor, have been seen for decades by the obscure and famous alike, folk that a newspaper or a jury would rank as credible sources." This background provided Kirk with his interest in the supernatural, an aspect he explores in his gothic novels and ghost stories: "My interest in ghosts arises from my knowledge of my ancestors and the spirits here," he told Kailas and Harrold.

Herron reports, though, that it was not until Kirk was in the army, when he was stationed in the Great Salt Lake Desert and had time for a good deal of reading and thinking, that he truly "came to recognize the nature of his own mind." Herron quotes the author: "Mine was not an Enlightened mind. I now was aware: it was a Gothic mind, medieval in its temper and structure. I did not love cold harmony and perfect regularity of organization; what I sought was variety, mystery, tradition, the venerable, the awful. I despised sophisters and calculators; I was groping for faith, honor, and prescriptive loyalties. I would have given any number of neo-classical pediments for one poor battered gargoyle."

Kirk's brand of conservatism and his interest in the supernatural seem to complement each other. *New York Times Book Review* critic Jack Sullivan writes that Kirk "once called the supernatural tale an 'inherently conservative' form that demonstrates the truths of orthodox Christianity in the face of newfangled heresies." And as Herron points out, Kirk's originality in his supernatural fiction "is best seen in the philosophical background common to all his tales, no matter how apparently unrelated they may seem at first reading."

Modern Age critic Edward Wagenknecht notes that in Kirk's preface to his 1984 collection of short stories, *Watchers at the Strait Gate,* Kirk indicates that he most admires those in the field who, like C. S. Lewis, George MacDonald, and Charles Williams, wrote tales "with 'elements of parable and fable in them,' which made their work 'experiments in the moral imagination' and 'instruments for the recovery of moral order.' " Wagenknecht explains that, "since human beings understand life best in terms of parable or allegory, the kind of material employed by such writers seems to him better adapted to achieve these ends than those drawn from either the realm of 'twentieth-century naturalism' or 'the mechanized empire of science fiction' that is only an extension of it." Wagenknecht adds that, "rejecting materialism, Kirk not only boldly affirms 'the reality of a realm of spirit' but also believes that something may well exist 'above human nature, and something below it.' "

The author published his first work of supernatural fiction, *Old House of Fear,* in 1961. Herron reports that in this book, Kirk "transports the Gothic conventions into our century, rattling ghostly chains in a rousing yarn." The book most clearly illustrates how political theory and the supernatural can sometimes be inseparable for Kirk. A *Time* reviewer remarks that Kirk "has expertly stuffed his book with all the claptrappings of the Gothic romance, but what he has actually achieved is a political morality tale. For all the apparent ectoplasm floating about it, the Old House of Fear is haunted not by ghosts but by the shadow of the welfare state."

The novel relates the story of a lawyer dispatched by a wealthy Michigan industrialist, Duncan MacAskival, to secure the purchase of an island off Scotland that is the MacAskival clan's ancestral home. After a series of misfortunes, the lawyer finally makes his way to the island. He finds the only livable house on the island, which is referred to as "The Old House of Fear," although the name is actually Gaelic, with "fear" spelled "faer," "fir," or "fhir," and meaning "man." Two of the clan's remaining members, the island's aged owner and a beautiful young girl, still live there. The lawyer encounters a diabolical doctor, an IRA bombman, and a crew of communist spies, and is imprisoned in the old house. As Herron reports, though, the lawyer "escapes along waterclogged tunnels dug from the rock centuries before by burrowing Picts, and finally leads an armed remnant of the ancient MacAskival clan against the victims holed up in the Old House of Fear. Adventurous stuff!"

Besides his three volumes of short stories, Kirk has published two other novels, *A Creature of the Twilight* and *Lord of the Hollow Dark.* Herron reports that although *A Creature of the Twilight* has traces of supernaturalism, it is basically an "adventure, a tale of revolution in the Third World, with attendant battles and political machinations."

On the other hand, Herron considers *Lord of the Hollow Dark* both a Gothic novel and a mystical Romance, as well as "a dramatic synthesis of terror and spiritual transcendence." In this book, several characters with names taken from the work of T. S. Eliot gather at an ancient castle outside of Edinburgh for an Ash Wednesday rite. They hope the rite will provide them with a mystical experience Kirk calls the "timeless moment," but their host has only evil intentions. Sullivan explains that the horror in *Lord of the Hollow Dark* "is not so much modern fads as the entire modern world," while Thomas Howard comments in the *National Review* that the novel portrays "the frightening vision of evil, and the blissful vision of sanctity emerging from the conflict in which goodness withstands evil and in which transfiguration and redemption are at work." Herron describes the book as "a virtuoso literary performance."

Kirk's later works of supernatural fiction are thematically similar. After *Lord of the Hollow Dark,* Herron reports, Kirk's "scattered stories become . . . not merely separate fictions written to startle or entertain, but part of a Kirkian cosmology not greatly different from the myth cycle H. P. Lovecraft eventually built up in his tales." As Herron declares, "in Kirk's world Hell and its terrors are quite real. Ghosts wander the earth trapped in purgatory. And God can be as fearful a thing as man can imagine."

Several of Kirk's works have been translated into foreign languages.

MEDIA ADAPTATIONS: "Soworth Place," a short story from *The Surly Sullen Bell,* was televised by Rod Serling as an episode of "Night Gallery"; *Old House of Fear* was read aloud in a series of broadcasts over the BBC Home Service.

AVOCATIONAL INTERESTS: Telling ghost stories, "vigorous" walking, historic and architectural preservation.

BIOGRAPHICAL/CRITICAL SOURCES:

BOOKS

Authors in the News, Volume 1, Gale, 1976.
Bradford, M. E., *A Better Guide than Reason: Studies in the American Revolution,* Sherwood Sugden, 1979.
Brown, Charles, *Russell Kirk: A Bibliography,* Clarke Historical Library, Central Michigan University, 1981.
Contemporary Authors Autobiography Series, Volume 9, Gale, 1989.
Contemporary Issues Criticism, Volume 1, Gale, 1982.
Hart, Jeffrey, *The American Dissent,* Doubleday, 1966.
Kirk, Russell, *Eliot and His Age: T. S. Eliot's Moral Imagination in the Twentieth Century,* Random House, 1971, revised edition, Sherwood Sugden, 1984.
Kirk, R., *The Roots of American Order,* Open Court, 1974, 2nd edition, Pepperdine University Press, 1980.
Kirk, R., *Watchers at the Strait Gate,* Arkham, 1984.
Nash, George, *The Conservative Intellectual Movement in America since 1945,* Basic Books, 1976.
Regnery, Henry, *Memoirs of a Dissident Publisher,* Harcourt, 1979.
Rossiter, Clinton, *Conservatism in America,* Vintage Books, 1962.
Schweitzer, Darrell, editor, *Discovering Modern Horror Fiction,* Starmont House, 1985.
Smith, Canon Basil A., *The Scallion Stone,* Whispers Press, 1980.
Strange Powers of E.S.P., Belmont Books, 1969.

PERIODICALS

Alternative, fall, 1971.
America, May 17, 1969, March 25, 1972, October 27, 1979.
American Political Science Review, September, 1953, December, 1958, June, 1977.
Book World, March 12, 1972.
Center Journal, summer, 1985.
Chicago Sunday Tribune, May 17, 1953, October 24, 1954.
Christian Science Monitor, November 29, 1954.
Commonweal, June 19, 1953, May 20, 1955, July 13, 1956, May 12, 1972.
Detroit Free Press, January 11, 1987.
Detroit News, May 7, 1972.
Esquire, November, 1972, February, 1975.
Gothic, June, 1980.
Grand Rapids Magazine, May, 1986.
History Today, October, 1953.
Illini Review, November, 1985.
Journal of General Education, summer, 1980.
Michigan History, September/October, 1979, September/October, 1983.
Modern Age, fall, 1979, summer/fall, 1982, winter, 1983, winter, 1984, summer, 1985.
Nation, April 12, 1958, March 27, 1972.
National Review, February 12, 1963, February 8, 1966, September 19, 1967, April 9, 1968, August 26, 1969, March 3,

1972, January 17, 1975, April 27, 1979, May 30, 1980, April 16, 1982, May 27, 1983, December 31, 1985.

New Republic, August 24, 1953.

New York Herald Tribune Book Review, August 2, 1953.

New York Times, May 17, 1953, November 21, 1954.

New York Times Book Review, November 21, 1954, June 18, 1961, March 26, 1972, November 4, 1979.

Policy Review, fall, 1979.

Political Science Quarterly, December, 1953.

Political Science Reviewer, fall, 1972.

Publishers Weekly, December 20, 1971.

Romanticist, Number 3, 1979.

Saturday Review, October 3, 1953, November 6, 1954.

Sewanee Review, April, 1970, October, 1972.

Shenandoah, spring, 1956.

Southern Partisan, spring/summer, 1981.

Time, July 6, 1953, July 7, 1961.

Times Literary Supplement, July 3, 1953, February 22, 1968, October 8, 1982.

University Bookman, spring, 1968, summer, 1968, summer, 1979.

Virginia Quarterly Review, summer, 1975.

Wall Street Journal, July 23, 1979.

Washington Post Book World, April 4, 1982.

Washington Times, October 31, 1985, January 7, 1986.

Yale Review, September, 1954.

*   *   *

KIS, Danilo 1935-

PERSONAL: Surname is pronounced "kish"; born February 22, 1935, in Subotica, Yugoslavia; son of Eduard and Milica (Dragicevic) Kis. *Education:* University of Belgrade, B.A., 1958.

ADDRESSES: Home—3/5 rue Tesson, Paris 75010, France. *Agent*—Adam Bromberg, Tegnergatan 29, 11140 Stockholm, Sweden.

CAREER: Writer. Teacher of Serbo-Croation and Yugoslavian at University of Strasbourg, Strasbourg, France, 1961-63, and in Bordeaux, France, 1973-76, and Lille, France, 1979-83.

AWARDS, HONORS: Award from *NiN,* 1972, for *Pescanik;* Ivan Goran Kovacic Award from *Vjesnik* (Zagreb, Yugoslavia), 1977, for *Grobnica za Borisa Davidovica;* Grand Aigle d'Or from the City of Nice, 1980, for body of work; Award Ivo Andric, 1984, for *Enciklopedija mrtvih.*

WRITINGS:

IN ENGLISH

Basta, pepeo (novel), Prosveta, 1965, translation from the Serbo-Croatian by William J. Hannaher published as *Garden, Ashes,* Harcourt, 1978.

Grobnica za Borisa Davidovica (stories), Liber, 1976, translation by Duska Mikic-Mitchell published as *A Tomb for Boris Davidovich,* Harcourt, 1978.

Enciklopedija mrtvih (stories), Globus/Prosveta, 1983, translation by Michael Henry Heim published as *The Encyclopedia of the Dead,* Faber, 1989.

IN SERBO-CROATIAN

Mansarda (novel; title means "Attic"), Kosmos, 1962.

Psalam 44 (novel; title means "Psalm 44"), Kosmos, 1962.

Ranijadi (stories; title means "Youthful Grief"), Nolit, 1970.

Pescanik (novel; title means "Hourglass"), Prosveta, 1972.

Po-etika (essays), Volume 1, Nolit, 1972, Volume 2, Ideje, 1974.

Cas anatomije (essays; title means "The Anatomy Lesson"), Nolit, 1978.

Djela Danila Kisa (selected works), ten volumes, Globus/Prosveta, 1983.

Also author of plays, including "Elektra," "Noc i magla," "Papagaj," and "Drveni sanduk Tomasa Vulfa" (for television). Translator of poems from French, Hungarian, and Russian. Contributor to periodicals, including *Delo, Knizevnost, New York Times Book Review,* and *Vidici.*

SIDELIGHTS: Many critics consider Danilo Kis a major Yugoslavian writer. He first came to the attention of Western readers with *Garden, Ashes,* a short novel about an East European family during World War II. The story is narrated by the son, Andreas Scham, who relates how the war forced his family from their comfortable home on a tree-lined street to a hovel in an abandoned railyard. Young Scham also recounts bow the Holocaust claimed his father, a railroad official given to poetry and alcohol. Although much of *Garden, Ashes* is conveyed in a realistic manner, it ends rather mystically, with Scham's father, an apparent victim of Nazi terrorism, possibly surviving the war to live out his final years under various disguises and pseudonyms.

Ernst Pawel, reviewing *Garden, Ashes* in *Nation* after the novel was reprinted in 1978, described Kis's work as "a singularly moving evocation of being a child without childhood, and of a family trying to survive the end of the world." Pawel, who remarked that the novel is somewhat autobiographical—Kis's family fled Yugoslavia during the war, and his father presumably died in a concentration camp—praised Kis's ability to transform "childhood and exile into an original vision of exceptional force and beauty." Pawel was particularly impressed with Kis's style, which he described as a "potent blend of poignancy and sardonic irreverence," and he deemed the novel "superb."

Equally impressive to many reviewers was *A Tomb for Boris Davidovich,* Kis's cycle of short stories about anti-Semitism and the Stalin purges. Notable among the book's seven tales is the title work, in which Davidovich's defiance before his Commuunist interrogators leads to the systematic assassination of other prisoners and eventually compels him to a ghastly suicide. Another disturbing tale concerns one of Davidovich's fourteenth-century ancestors, a Jew whose refusal to recant his faith results in a grisly bloodbath. Kis's depiction of these and other horrifying events prompted many critical comments like those of Zora Devmja Zimmerman, who wrote in *World Literature Today* that *A Tomb for Boris Davidovich* was "a stunning statement on political persecution."

Some critics accorded special attention to Kis's technique of poetic journalism in *A Tomb for Boris Davidovich.* Zimmerman noted Kis's "gaunt, stark prose" and added that the "descriptions of interior worlds are given as though they were reports, as though Kis had transcribed secret confidences from informants." Joseph Brodsky, in his introduction to a later printing of *Boris Davidovich,* lauded Kis's unique method, in which "his emphasis on imagery and detail . . . puts his horrific subject matter into the most adequate perspective." Brodsky attributed the book's impact to its unusual form and contended, "It is not that the thought is felt but, rather, that the feeling is thought."

Although *A Tomb for Boris Davidovich* brought Kis acclaim in the West, its initial publication proved less rewarding in his native Yugoslavia, where the writers union, reacting to the book's anti-Stalinism, sought to besmirch Kis by accusing him of plagiarizing writers such as Alexander Solzhenitsyn and James Joyce. Kis responded by publishing *Cas anatomije,* which Ernst

Pawel described as "a 344-page polemic counterblast." Pawel added that *Cas anatomije* proved "quite successful" in Yugoslavia, but Kis eventually moved to France.

Aside from *Gardens, Ashes* and *A Tomb for Boris Davidovich,* Kis has produced such works as *Rani jadi,* a collection of stories concerning the family of *Garden, Ashes,* and *Pescanik,* a novel about the Holocaust. Kis told *CA* that Pescanik will be published in English as *Hourglass.*

BIOGRAPHICAL/CRITICAL SOURCES:

PERIODICALS

Christian Science Monitor, September 22, 1975.
Cross Currents 3, 1984.
Nation, September 16, 1978.
New Republic, January 6, 1979.
New Statesman, December 19, 1975.
World Literature Today, summer, 1977, winter, 1977, autumn, 1979.

*   *   *

KISSINGER, Henry A(lfred) 1923-

PERSONAL: Born May 27, 1923, in Fuerth, Germany; came to United States in 1938; naturalized in 1943; son of Louis and Paula (Stern) Kissinger; married Ann Fleischer, February 6, 1949 (divorced, July, 1964); married Nancy Sharon Maginnes, March 30, 1974; children: (first marriage) Elizabeth, David. *Education:* Harvard University, A.B. (summa cum laude), 1950, M.A., 1952, Ph.D., 1954.

ADDRESSES: Office—Suite 400, 1800 K Street N.W., Washington, D.C. 20006.

CAREER: Harvard University, Cambridge, Mass., instructor, 1954-55, lecturer, 1957-59, associate professor, 1959-62, professor of government, 1962-71, executive director of International Studies Seminar, 1951-71, member of faculty of Center for International Affairs, 1957-71, director of Defense Studies Program, 1958-71; United States Government, Washington, D.C., director of National Security Council and special assistant to President Nixon, 1969-74, secretary of state, 1973-77; Georgetown University, Washington, D.C., professor of diplomacy in School of Foreign Service and counselor to Center for Strategic and International Studies, 1977—; Kissinger Associates, Inc., Washington, D.C., chairman, 1977—.

Consultant, U.S. Operations Research Office, 1950-61, Psychological Strategy Board, 1952, Operations Coordinating Board, 1955, Weapons Systems Evaluation Group of Joint Chiefs of Staff, 1956-60, National Security Council, 1961-62, RAND Corporation, 1961—, Arms Control and Disarmament Agency, 1961-68, U.S. Department of State, 1965-69, and President's Foreign Intelligence Advisory Board, 1980—. Director of special studies project, Rockefeller Brothers Fund, Inc., 1956-58. Senior fellow, Aspen Institute, 1977—. Counselor to Chase Manhattan Bank, 1978—. Trustee of Rockefeller Brothers Fund, Inc., and Metropolitan Museum of Modern Art, 1978—. Lecturer at numerous universities in America and abroad. Contributing analyst, ABC News, 1980—. *Military service:* U.S. Army, Counter-Intelligence Corps, 1943-46, received Bronze Star; U.S. Army Reserve, 1946-59, became captain.

MEMBER: American Political Science Association, American Academy of Arts and Sciences (member of special committee on international relations, 1961-62), Council on Foreign Relations (director of study group on nuclear weapons and foreign policy,

1955-56), Phi Beta Kappa, Century Club, River Club (both New York), Federal City Club, Metropolitan Club (both Washington, D.C.).

AWARDS, HONORS: Harvard University national scholarship; Harvard non-stipendiary fellowship; Harvard Detur; Rockefeller Foundation fellowship; Woodrow Wilson Prize for best book in fields of government, politics, and international affairs and Overseas Press Club citation, both 1958, both for *Nuclear Weapons and Foreign Policy;* Guggenheim fellowship, 1965-66; honorary doctorate, Brown University, 1969; "Man of the Year" citation from *Time* magazine, 1972; American Institute for Public Service Award for distinguished public service, and Nobel Peace Prize, both 1973; American Legion Distinguished Service Medal and Wateler Peace Prize, both 1974; Presidential Medal of Freedom, 1977; American Book Award, 1980, for *White House Years;* Books-across-the-Sea Ambassador of Honor Award from English-Speaking Union, 1984, for *Years of Upheaval.*

WRITINGS:

A World Restored: Castlereagh, Metternich and the Restoration of Peace, 1812-1822, Houghton, 1957, reprinted, 1973.
Nuclear Weapons and Foreign Policy, Harper, 1957, abridged edition, Norton, 1969.
The Necessity for Choice: Prospects of American Foreign Policy, Harper, 1961, reprinted, Greenwood Press, 1984.
The Troubled Partnership: A Reappraisal of the Atlantic Alliance, McGraw, 1965, reprinted, Greenwood Press, 1982.
(Editor) *Problems of National Strategy: A Book of Readings,* Praeger, 1966.
American Foreign Policy: Three Essays, Norton, 1969, 3rd edition, 1977.
White House Years (memoirs; first published serially in *Time,* October 1, 1979-October 15, 1979), Little, Brown, 1979.
For the Record: Selected Statements 1977-1980, Little, Brown, 1981.
Years of Upheaval (memoirs), Little, Brown, 1982.
American Foreign Policy: A Global View, Gower, 1982.
Report of the National Bipartisan Commission on Central America, U.S. Government Printing Office, 1984.
Observations: Selected Speeches and Essays, 1982-1984, Little, Brown, 1985.
(With McGeorge Bundy) *The Dimensions of Diplomacy,* University Microfilms International, 1989.

SIDELIGHTS: As director of the National Security Council and then secretary of state during the Nixon presidency, Henry A. Kissinger wielded enormous diplomatic authority, especially in foreign relations. In fact, writes Max Frankel in the *New York Times Book Review,* between the summers of 1973 and 1974, "the refugee from Nazi Germany became the most glamorous and probably most powerful man in America." Kissinger won the Nobel Prize for his efforts toward ending the Vietnam War; he also dealt with tense situations in the Middle East and the always sensitive arena of U.S.-Soviet relations. In the *New Republic,* John Osborne called Kissinger "the one indispensable man on Nixon's staff," a Harvard-trained academic who never seemed to fit into easy political categories. *Washington Post Book World* contributor Townsend Hoopes has similarly stated that as Nixon's closest advisor, Kissinger "became the one oasis of distinction in the desert of that mediocre and squalid administration."

Since "retiring" from public service in 1977, Kissinger has devoted most of his time to writing and to serving as a political analyst on television. He remains the most readily recognizable ex-cabinet member of any modern administration, "one of our most enduring elder statesmen," to quote a *Parade* magazine correspondent. Kissinger's best-known books include two detailed chronicles of his years in the Nixon administration, *White House Years* and *Years of Upheaval*. A work well over one thousand pages long, *White House Years* won the American Book Award in 1980; Hoopes finds the work "a pleasure to read," with "clean, sure narrative reporting, . . . gemlike definitions of complicated diplomatic situations and philosophic observations that occasionally rise to the level of majesty."

Heinz Alfred Kissinger—who changed his name to Henry when he came to the United States—was born in Fuerth, Germany in 1923. Kissinger's father was a school teacher who lost his job due to discrimination against Jews. In 1938 the Kissinger family fled Germany, settling in New York City. Henry attended school at George Washington High, earning straight A grades; he later went to night school to study accounting while working days in a factory. A wartime stint in the army offered Kissinger his first opportunities for advancement. Drafted in 1943, he first served in the 84th Infantry Division, then transferred to the Counter-Intelligence Corps. While still in his early twenties, Kissinger was placed in charge of reorganizing municipal governments in occupied Germany; he remained with the Military Intelligence Reserve until 1959.

After the Second World War, Kissinger decided to return to college. He won a New York state scholarship to Harvard University, where he earned his bachelor's, master's, and doctorate degrees in government. He then remained at Harvard as an instructor, eventually working his way to full professor. Concurrently he began to serve as a consultant to several government bureaus, including the army's Operations Research Office and the Psychological Strategy Board of the Joint Chiefs of Staff. In one capacity or another, Kissinger served the Eisenhower, Kennedy, and Johnson administrations, all while he carried a heavy load of responsibility at Harvard. He also authored several books during the period, especially *Nuclear Weapons and Foreign Policy* (1957) and *The Troubled Partnership: A Reappraisal of the Atlantic Alliance* (1965). Hoopes observes that these and other Kissinger works offer "the premise that the key to global balance in the modern world is the U.S.-Soviet relationship; . . . that there are really no other relationships of consequence. In his view, U.S.-Soviet interactions pervade every issue on the globe; there are no local isolable crises; 'linkage' is universal, and 'credibility' the only goal." *Nuclear Weapons and Foreign Policy* won the Woodrow Wilson Prize in 1958 and established Kissinger's reputation as an expert on global diplomacy.

In 1968 Kissinger offered his services as advisor and speech-writer to presidential candidate Nelson Rockefeller. Rockefeller did not win the Republican nomination, but the candidate who did—Richard Nixon—invited Kissinger to become his principal foreign policy advisor. Kissinger accepted the position of director of the National Security Council, and he quickly became more influential than several of Nixon's cabinet members. On trips abroad as well as in the most significant policy planning meetings, Kissinger often dominated; he is credited with the initiation of the first Strategic Arms Limitation Talks with the Soviet Union, with initiation of normal relations with Communist China, and most importantly, with negotiations to end the Vietnam War. Hoopes writes: "Kissinger's rise to undoubted power and prominence . . . owed a great deal to Nixon's peculiar *modus operandi* in foreign and defense affairs. In a more open and discursive administration, he would have been only one of several competing advisers with his influence correspondingly diluted. Under Nixon, he became the principal keeper of the keys—*the* adviser, spokesman and negotiator on all major foreign policies."

As the Nixon administration became mired in the Watergate scandal, Kissinger was made Secretary of State. He served both Nixon and his successor Gerald Ford in this capacity until 1977. The last year of Nixon's presidency is chronicled in *Years of Upheaval*, a book that also explores Kissinger's role in the peace talks between Egypt and Israel. In the *Washington Post Book World*, McGeorge Bundy calls *Years of Upheaval* "a remarkable achievement," adding: "It has hundreds of pages that should be of deep interest to more general readers, and . . . it can be sampled to great advantage and indeed does not seem intended for complete study by every buyer." *New York Times* correspondent Christoper Lehmann-Haupt finds the work "brilliantly argued, skillfully paced, sensitively proportioned, consistently charming, altogether masterly and by far the most consequential memoir to come out of the Nixon administration." Frankel concludes: "[Kissinger] manages to present some ugly truths without burning too many bridges. That has been his craft, in life and in office, and so it is in print."

Kissinger has served more recent administrations as a member of the Foreign Intelligence Advisory Board. In that capacity he has made fact-finding missions to Latin America and elsewhere, strictly on a nonpartisan basis. Never one to avoid the limelight, Kissinger has also kept up a busy schedule of television appearances and public lectures—Hoopes notes that the statesman "understands better than most that this is the Age of Celebrity and that a popular image is an important reinforcement of power." Still, writes Hoopes, "the luster of Kissinger's image as statesman is more reliably maintained through his written works than through his television appearances." *Spectator* contributor Colin Welch claims that Kissinger's books offer "an insight into the workings of a mind at once fair and broad, lucid, powerful, benign and prodigiously well stocked. . . . This mind addresses itself successively to ever-changing circumstances and problems new or newly perceived, tirelessly exploring and reflecting, reaching conclusions *pro tem,* only to modify, reject or replace them later." Welch concludes: "We are confronted not with reasoning completed but with reasoning in progress, and, God willing, more to come."

WORK IN PROGRESS: A book "about the meaning of diplomacy," for Simon & Schuster.

BIOGRAPHICAL/CRITICAL SOURCES:

BOOKS

Allen, Gary, *Kissinger,* Devin-Adair, 1976.
Bell, Coral, *The Diplomacy of Detente: The Kissinger Era,* St. Martin's, 1977.
Blumenfeld, Ralph, and others, *Henry Kissinger: The Private and Public Story,* New American Library, 1974.
Brandon, Henry, *The Retreat of American Power: The Inside Story of How Nixon and Kissinger Changed American Policy for Years to Come,* Doubleday, 1973.
Brown, Seyom, *The Crises of Power: Foreign Policy in the Kissinger Years,* Columbia University Press, 1979.
Dickson, Peter, *Kissinger and the Meaning of History,* Cambridge University Press, 1978.
Kalb, Marvin and Bernard Kalb, *Kissinger,* Little, Brown, 1974.
Landau, David, *Kissinger: The Uses of Power,* Houghton, 1972.
Mazlish, Bruce, *Kissinger: The European Mind in American Policy,* Basic Books, 1976.
Morris, Roger, *Uncertain Greatness: Henry Kissinger and American Foreign Policy,* Harper, 1977.

Shawcross, William, *Sideshow: Kissinger, Nixon, and the Destruction of Cambodia,* Simon & Schuster, 1979.

Sobel, Lester A., editor, *Kissinger and Detente,* Facts on File, 1975.

Stoessinger, John G., *Henry Kissinger: The Anguish of Power,* Norton, 1976.

Szulc, Tad, *The Illusion of Peace: A Diplomatic History of the Nixon Years,* Viking, 1978.

PERIODICALS

Atlantic, December, 1969, May, 1979, February, 1980.
Books and Arts, December 21, 1979.
Chicago Tribune Book World, March 28, 1982.
Christian Century, September 3, 1969.
Detroit Free Press, January 12, 1979, November 14, 1979.
Detroit News, June 10, 1979.
Detroit News Magazine, November 11, 1979.
Harper's, January, 1971.
Los Angeles Times Book Review, February 1, 1981, April 18, 1982.
National Review, April 6, 1971.
New Republic, January 31, 1981.
Newsweek, December 16, 1968, October 26, 1970, November 2, 1970, September 3, 1973, March 1, 1976, April 30, 1979, October 29, 1979.
New Yorker, July 12, 1969, May 14, 1979.
New York Review of Books, June 28, 1979.
New York Times, December 3, 1968, February 19, 1970, October 17, 1973, October 16, 1979, October 23, 1979, March 24, 1982, April 13, 1987.
New York Times Book Review, June 29, 1969, April 22, 1979, November 11, 1979, February 1, 1981, April 4, 1982.
New York Times Magazine, June 1, 1969, November 14, 1971, October 28, 1973, December 16, 1979.
Parade, January 11, 1987.
Saturday Review, June 9, 1979.
Spectator, September 14, 1985.
Time, September 3, 1973, April 4, 1974, October 21, 1974, November 17, 1975, December 27, 1976, January 24, 1977, February 28, 1977, October 1, 1979, October 8, 1979, October 15, 1979.
Times (London), April 1, 1982.
Times Literary Supplement, October 15, 1982, December 13, 1985.
Village Voice, October 22, 1979.
Washington Post, October 14, 1979.
Washington Post Book World, April 27, 1969, April 29, 1979, November 25, 1979, March 28, 1982, August 11, 1985.

—*Sketch by Anne Janette Johnson*

*   *   *

KNOWLES, John 1926-

PERSONAL: Born September 16, 1926, in Fairmont, W.Va.; son of James Myron and Mary Beatrice (Shea) Knowles. *Education:* Graduate of Phillips Exeter Academy, 1945; Yale University, B.A., 1949.

ADDRESSES: *Home*—New York, N.Y.

CAREER: *Hartford Courant,* Hartford, Conn., reporter, 1950-52; free-lance writer, 1952-56; *Holiday,* associate editor, 1956-60; full-time writer, 1960—. Writer in residence at University of North Carolina at Chapel Hill, 1963-64, and Princeton University, 1968-69.

AWARDS, HONORS: Rosenthal award from National Institute of Arts and Letters, and William Faulkner Foundation award, both 1960, for *A Separate Peace.*

WRITINGS:

A Separate Peace (novel), Macmillan, 1960.
Morning in Antibes (novel), Macmillan, 1962.
Double Vision: American Thoughts Abroad (travel), Macmillan, 1964.
Indian Summer (novel), Random House, 1966.
Phineas (short stories), Random House, 1968.
The Paragon (novel), Random House, 1971.
Spreading Fires (novel), Random House, 1974.
A Vein of Riches (novel), Little, Brown, 1978.
Peace Breaks Out (novel), Holt, 1981.
A Stolen Past (novel), Holt, 1983.
The Private Life of Axie Reed (novel), Dutton, 1986.

A collection of Knowles's manuscripts is housed in Beinecke Library at Yale University, New Haven, Connecticut.

WORK IN PROGRESS: A memoir of the author's friend, writer Truman Capote.

SIDELIGHTS: John Knowles is an acclaimed American novelist whose first—and most famous—novel, *A Separate Peace,* received both the Faulkner Foundation Prize and the Rosenthal Award of the National Institute of Arts and Letters. *A Separate Peace* is Knowles's most lyrical work, describing in rich, evocative language the idyllic lives of school boys during the first years of American involvement in World War II. The plot is deceptively simple. The narrator, Gene Forrester, and his friend, Phineas (Finny), are both students at Devon, an Eastern seaboard private school much like Exeter, which Knowles attended. Gene is the more conscientious student of the two, and Phineas the more athletically and socially gifted. Though their bond is a strong one, it eventually suffers from competition. Gene, growing increasingly resentful of Phineas's popularity, finally causes him crippling injury by pushing him from a tree. A kangaroo court session ensues, with Gene accused of deliberately injuring Phineas, who leaves suddenly, again injures himself, and dies during surgery.

From this episode, Gene eventually accepts the necessity of exploring himself based upon his admission of guilt. Jay L. Halio, writing about *A Separate Peace* in *Studies in Short Fiction,* observes that "the prevailing attitude seems to be that before man can be redeemed back into social life, he must first come to terms with himself."

The setting and plot of *A Separate Peace* play upon a series of contrasts between negative and positive elements, the combination of which stresses the need to tolerate, understand, and integrate radically opposing perceptions and experiences. The school itself stands between two rivers, the Devon and the Naguamsett, one pure and fresh, the other ugly and dirty. As James Ellis concludes in the *English Journal,* the Devon symbolizes Eden, a place of joy and happiness, while the Naguamsett indicates a landscape destroyed by personal greed and callousness toward the environment. The winds of war, blowing just beyond the lives of the boys, and the battle between Gene and Phineas encapsulate Knowles's twin purposes—to both explore the competing sides of an individual's personality and to imply, as McDonald has noted, that the conflict of nations is an extension of self-conflict and the antipathy one person feels toward another.

These internal and external conflicts result from fear, whether based on hatred, inadequacy, exposure, or rejection. This view of life as a battle between two opposing selves, persons, or camps—the solution being acceptance and love of others—is the most dominant theme of Knowles's fiction. It first appears in *A Separate Peace,* but it is never far from the center of later works.

Published twenty-two years after *A Separate Peace, Peace Breaks Out* will "take its place alongside the earlier books as a fine novel," Dick Abrahamson argues in the *English Journal.* Knowles's second Devon School novel takes place in 1945, and its main character and center of consciousness is Pete Hallam, a young teacher of history and physical education who has from World War II. Hallam has not only been wounded, captured, and incarcerated in a prison camp, but has also been abandoned by his wife. Because of the traumas he has suffered, he is not always articulate and tends to be somewhat cynical in his attempt to retreat into the past. Although also essentially romantic in nature, he has lost the ability to love, and he returns to Devon to lay the past to rest and to regain some sense of love and compassion.

At Devon, the innocence Hallam remembers is missing. Schoolboys, too, have been affected by the war—or perhaps Pete has simply matured enough through his own suffering to recognize the flaws in human nature. The conflict that helps Pete to understand himself is between two bright, articulate, and bitter students, Hochschwender and Wexford, who "hated each other. But also and simultaneously they seemed to hate something about themselves. There was a curious, fundamental similarity between them which made their mutual aversion almost incendiary." Bright and insecure, Eric Hochschwender riles the other students with his outrageous statements about German superiority and his denial of the atrocities of World War II. Motivated in part by his insignificant Wisconsin background, his obviously Germanic name, and his fears of rejection, Eric primarily assumes this position to test the tolerance of others, believing that under the surface of American liberalism is a strong strain of intolerance and bigotry. He is correct, and he himself becomes the target of that bigotry.

Never called by his first name, Wexford is equally bright, but, as the scion of a wealthy Massachusetts family and as the editor of the student newspaper, he is given considerable respect. This respect is not well-deserved, for his collection of money for a memorial window in the chapel is designed only to enhance his own reputation. Dishonest, intolerant, and elitist, Wexford tries to convince others that Eric is a threat to the Devon spirit and the traditional New England, prep-school way of life. He incites the other boys into thinking that Hochschwender broke the memorial window and they attack Eric, causing him to have a fatal heart seizure.

The situation in *Peace Breaks Out* strongly resembles that of the earlier *A Separate Peace,* but Knowles's message is now more bleak. Whereas Gene's crime is discovered and he suffers personal guilt, thereby maturing in his understanding of himself and others, Wexford is not found out and gains no self-knowledge. Pete believes that Wexford himself has broken the window and sowed the seeds of hatred against Eric, but the teacher takes no measure to expose Wexford as a fraud and a cheat. The book suggests that Wexford will continue to go through life cheating. The plunge that Knowles's characters take into the maelstrom of desires and conflicts thus does not always result in illumination and insight.

A second group of novels—*Indian Summer, A Stolen Past,* and *The Paragon*—deals with Wexford-like figures who have power and authority generated by money, which becomes a substitute for human warmth and sexual expression. The forum for this exploration is no longer Devon but Yale and its immediate environs. All three novels depend upon the mutually reinforcing oppositions between the rich and the middle class, the quest for money and the desire for a good life, and excessive rationality and healthy sexuality.

Second only to *A Separate Peace* in critical acclaim, *Indian Summer* concerns Cleet Kinsolving and his gradual realization of the emptiness of wealth and position. The spontaneous, impulsive, and intuitive Cleet, grandson of an Indian woman, contrasts with the more controlled, rational, spoiled, and mercantile Neil Reardon. Unlike many of Knowles's characters, Cleet understands himself: to "roll out his life full force" meant "to be strong, to be happy, to be physically tired at night, to have love and sex at one and the same time, to be proud of himself." When Cleet follows his native instincts, he feels complete and satisfied; when he becomes trapped in the rationalist-mercantile pursuits of others, he nearly destroys himself. Related to this view of the self is the perception of place. The Midwest and West are equated with personal freedom and lack of social restraint; Connecticut and the East are equated with acquisitiveness, self-denial, and atrophying social conventions.

After his discharge from the Army Air Force in 1946, Cleet takes a job in Kansas, working for a small crop-dusting firm and living in a tiny motel cabin. This Thoreau-like existence under the "vaults and domes of sky" emphasizes a simple, natural life, undiminished by material possessions. Here, in the midwest, Cleet's feelings and senses—his sight, hearing, taste, and sexuality—are at their finest.

What Cleet fears most is the entrapment symbolized by the East. The appearance in Kansas of his childhood friend, Cornelius (Neil) Reardon, realizes those fears. Cleet, in accepting Neil's offer of a two-hundred-dollars weekly job in Cleet's home town of Wetherford, sells himself out to the Eastern establishment. Neil embodies the lust for acquisition, and he uses emotional attachments, generosity, loyalty, and philanthropy for his own ends so that they become deception, bribery, ambition, and willfulness. His marriage is empty, and his books and lectures merely hide his fear of failure. Even his desire to have a son is born of fear—to perpetuate himself and ensure material immortality against an uncertain future.

To be true to his vision of himself, Cleet is obliged to leave the Reardons and return to the Midwest, where he can put the dishonesty and stifling conventions of the East behind him. Before he returns to Kansas, he seduces Neil's wife, but since he means no ill toward her and is primarily responding to her own unrepressed sexual desires, he suffers no guilt about his conduct. His departure for Kansas reaffirms the fundamental nineteenth-century American romantic view: truth to oneself depends upon responding to spirituality rather than materialism.

Although the narrator of the 1983 novel *A Stolen Past* has also been born in the East (Maryland) and educated there (at Devon and Yale), he has been no more faithful to it than Cleet. As a mature adult recalling his college experiences, Allan Prieston is realistic, knowing that he can never totally recapture the past; but he is also philosophical, understanding that the past will take its toll unless fully recognized and incorporated. A writer, Allan attempts to find his own literary voice and separate himself from his formative influences, notably mentor Reeves Lockhart. Allan recalls Reeves as an exceptional teacher, but in dignifying Reeve's memory, Allan failed to understand the loneliness, alcoholism, and crippling perfectionism that also plagued this teacher. By coming to terms with Reeves's weaknesses, however, Allan is better able to deal with his own limitations and feelings of inadequacy so that he can finally affirm himself as a "mischievous, conniving rascal and a cheat: a writer."

Whereas Allan's friendship with Reeves represents the possibilities and limitations of the mentor-student relationship, Allan's friendship with Greg Trouvenskoy addresses peer admiration. Initially Allan idolizes Greg's maturity, good looks, popularity with men and women, and background. The son of noble Russians who escaped the Bolshevik revolution, Greg conveys a sense of wealth and prestige, punctuated by the family's possession of the wonderful Militsa Diamond, their sole remaining treasure from the grand days in St. Petersburg. Handsome and elegant, full of wonderful stories of the Romanoffs and other Russian figures, Greg's parents fulfill Allan's every exotic impulse. They also make him aware of the weaknesses of the aristocratic, feudal system, for they have been dispossessed and are now American citizens and New Deal Democrats. They have survived because they have the inner resources to make the transition from wealth and power to more average social positions.

Greg, however, is weaker than Allan imagined, proving secretly jealous, especially of Allan's relation with Reeves. In certain respects, Greg is adversely affected by his Russian roots—he has his parents' temper, passions, and recklessness without their versatility. He is also more affected by the loss of wealth than are his parents. His failure to come to terms with their past and his present forces him to steal their diamond, an act that eventually causes the death of his father.

In *The Paragon,* main character Louis Colfax learns that individual people and events together create history. Of a family that had been rich in the nineteenth century, Louis grows up with few material advantages and is surrounded by family members who are psychologically and socially damaged—passive, pious, repressive, oppressive, and alcoholic. Louis feels himself psychologically impaired by his environment. In his many despairing moments he withdraws and hopes to put an end to the cycle of biological and environmental determinism. In the end, he recognizes that his problems have been determined not only by his bizarre family but also by his own independent character and actions.

In *The Paragon* Knowles suggests that each person and culture has a repressed side referred to as "the animal inside the human." Indeed, in talking with his fiancee Charlotte Mills, Louis says, "I love you too much, like a man *and* like a woman. . . . I think I'm a lesbian." He believes that she has her masculine side, just as he has his feminine side, and that both must be recognized and embraced. Knowles implies that all human beings have these opposing characteristics, one often suppressing another and destroying the balanced personality, and he suggests that this is even true of institutions and nations. Juxtaposed against male institutional power in *The Paragon* is the power of nature. The image of an Hawaiian volcano represents for Lou all of nature's raw power: "This was the ultimate, uncontrollable force on earth. No fence could stop it, no wall, no channel. No will could stop it, no bomb." *The Paragon,* then, pits the masculine against the feminine, the rational against the emotional, and the institutional against the natural.

Despite *The Paragon's* complexity, critics have not been altogether appreciative of the book. Jonathan Yardley states in the *New Republic* that he likes the novel but finds it derivative of *A Separate Peace* and inherently false in tone. James Aronson in the *Antioch Review* agrees: "the dialogue is faked and stagey, the characters are stereotyped, the parallels between 1950 and 1970 are tritely obvious, and the shape of the novel is curiously disjointed." However, Webster Schott in the *New York Times Book Review,* finds much to admire, especially in the conception of the protagonist: "the title is important. It's not 'A Paragon.' It's '*The Paragon.*' And Knowles's model or pattern of perfection for youth and manhood is a seeking, nonconforming, erratically brilliant and socially maladjusted college student. For Knowles the perfect model must be less than perfect. Not an irony. A moral position."

In *A Vein of Riches* Knowles's presents his strongest indictment of the rich by sympathetically portraying West Virginia miners who struck against rapacious coal barons between 1918 and 1921 The Catherwood family—Clarkson, Minnie, and Lyle represent the attitudes of other mine-owner families towards the laboring classes and their own family affairs. The first part of the book primarily centers on the Catherwoods' views of the strikers, black servants, and the economy; the second, on the family's increasing financial difficulties and their problems in discovering personal fulfillment and meaning. In their personal roles and attitudes to others, the Catherwoods become a microcosm of the ownership class—what the strikers call "bloated capitalists" and "economic royalists." Shortsighted and greedy, they do not have the ability to manage the mines and guarantee prosperity and calm in both good times and bad.

In *A Vein of Riches,* then, Knowles discloses the viciousness that lies beneath the surface of American capitalism. The true vein of riches, he suggests, may be a vivid imagination, powerful emotions, and a sharp conscience.

Morning in Antibes, the first of Knowles's Mediterranean novels, treats class conflict, marital issues, and international relations. Here the setting is Juan-les-Pins on the Riviera, the playground of the rich from America (Nicholas and Liliane Bodine and Jimmy Smoot), France (Marc, Constance, and Titou de la Croie), and elsewhere. In contrast to the rich, those who work on the Riviera—the restaurateurs and servants, even the transvestites who participate in nightclub acts—are faced with hard daily schedules, little money, and the scorn of their patrons.

Also set in Southern France, *Spreading Fires* is a gothic tale of insanity and guilt, and in it Knowles explores deeply seated sexual attitudes. The book's protagonist is Brendan Lucas, a well-heeled American diplomat who rents a spacious villa overlooking the Mediterranean near Cannes. This area exudes sexuality in "the musky air, the sticky sea, the sensuous food, the sensual wine." Although Brendan does not overtly share in that pervasive sensuality, he has, as Christopher Lehmann-Haupt puts it in the *New York Times,* "unresolved Oedipal rage" and homosexual anxieties. The conflict between sexuality and repression serves as the central issue of the book. For Knowles, sexual emotion is a side of the self that must be recognized.

Though best known for his novels, Knowles also produced *Phineas,* a collection of stories about adolescent boys and young men reaching a greater understanding of life. James P. Degman of the *Kenyon Review* admires Knowles's dramatization of the torments of sensitive and intelligent adolescents, particularly in "Phineas," "A Turn with the Sun," and "Summer Street." An early version of the scene from *A Separate Peace* in which the narrator causes Finny to fall from a tree, "Phineas" focuses upon the narrator's attempts at confession and reconciliation. "A Turn with the Sun," set like "Phineas" at the Devon School, portrays an alienated young protagonist whose beautiful dive into a cold river ironically consolidates his relationship with his comrades and brings on his death. "Summer Street," in which a young boy copes with his anxieties about the birth of a sister, treats the development of imagination—both the quality of wonder and enchantment, as well as the fear of the unknown. Some people, the story implies, have little imagination and will be mired in their environment; others suppress their imagination and lose access to a rich world; still others have this talent but need to foster and channel it so that it does not prove an instrument of evasion.

Conflicting personality traits, genders, and ways of functioning infuse all of Knowles's work. These themes are reinforced in Knowles's nonfiction book, *Double Vision: American Thoughts Abroad*. In this travel account, Knowles regales the reader with his impressions of Arab spontaneity and Greek hospitality, but he also criticizes America's puritanical Protestant habits, repressed sexuality, tendency toward violence in its cities, and unfair distribution of jobs and wealth. Knowles's own personal apprehensions and fear about the strangeness of Arab culture, its "paralyzed battlefield," raises another concern, the American fear of other cultures. This fear of the unknown, the strangeness of other people, is, the author implies, deeply human, but especially characteristic of Americans. Yet Knowles is not altogether negative about America and its ideals. He likes American directness and honesty, the great energy of its people, and the feeling of governmental stability. He is hopeful that America will, with time, create a civilization in harmony with nature, one that stresses tolerance and equal rights for blacks and women, that erases oppositions.

Throughout his fiction, John Knowles shows a concern for middle- and upper-class Americans. He sees, and perhaps shares, their hunger for wealth, but he also knows their weaknesses and those of the American system. He exposes the effects of greed, obsessive social propriety, puritanical religion, and stifled emotions, qualities that lead to rivalry, suppression, and self-destruction. Yet these forces can be countered, Knowles suggests, by letting go—by abandoning urban competition, by restoring the primacy of emotions, by allowing love to flourish, and by returning to nature.

A film version of *A Separate Peace* was released by Paramount Pictures in 1972.

BIOGRAPHICAL/CRITICAL SOURCES:

BOOKS

Contemporary Literary Criticism, Gale, Volume I, 1973, Volume IV, 1975, Volume X, 1979.
Dictionary of Literary Biography, Volume VI: *American Novelists Since World War II*, Gale, 1980.

PERIODICALS

Book Week, July 24, 1966.
Chicago Tribune Book World, March 29, 1981.
Clearing House, September, 1973.
Commonweal, December 9, 1960.
English Journal, April, 1969, December, 1969.
Harper's, July, 1966.
Life, August 5, 1966.
Los Angeles Times, April 2, 1981, May 2, 1986, August 27, 1986.
Los Angeles Times Book Review, August 28, 1983.
Manchester Guardian, May 1, 1959.
Newsweek, April 20, 1981.
New York Times, February 3, 1978, April 16, 1986.
New York Times Book Review, February 7, 1960, August 14, 1966, June 4, 1978, March 22, 1981, October 17, 1982, October 30, 1983, May 11, 1986.
New Statesman, May 2, 1959.
Saturday Review, August 13, 1966.
Time, April 6, 1981.

Times Literary Supplement, May 1, 1959, August 31, 1984.
Washington Post Book World, March 15, 1981.

* * *

KNOX, Calvin M.
See SILVERBERG, Robert

* * *

KNYE, Cassandra
See DISCH, Thomas M(ichael)

* * *

KOESTLER, Arthur 1905-1983

PERSONAL: Born September 5, 1905, in Budapest, Hungary; committed suicide March 3, 1983, in London, England; became a British subject after World War II; son of Hendrik (a promoter) and Adela (Jeiteles) Koestler; married Dorothy Asher, 1935 (divorced, 1950); married Mamaine Paget, 1950 (divorced, 1952); married Cynthia Jefferies, 1965. *Education:* Attended University of Vienna, 1922-26.

CAREER: Writer. Worked as a farmer in Palestine, an assistant to an Arabian architect, and an editor of a Cairo weekly, 1926-29; became foreign correspondent for Ullstein Publications, Germany, serving as Middle East correspondent, 1927-29, and as Paris correspondent, 1929-30; became science editor of *Vossische Zeitung* and foreign editor of *B.Z.am Mittag*, 1930; became member of the Communist Party, 1931; was the only journalist taking part in the "Graf Zeppelin" Arctic expedition, 1931; in the thirties he traveled through Central Asia and spent one year in the U.S.S.R.; war correspondent in Spain for *News Chronicle*, 1936, captured by Fascists, 1937, sentenced to death, and released through the intervention of the British government; left Communist Party in 1938, at the time of the Moscow Trials; editor of *Zukunft*, 1938; in 1939, he was imprisoned in France after war was declared, released in 1940, and escaped to England; worked for the Ministry of Information, the British Broadcasting Corp., and as a night ambulance driver. *Military service:* French Foreign Legion, 1940; British Pioneer Corps, 1941-42.

AWARDS, HONORS: Chubb fellow, Yale University, 1950; Royal Society of Literature fellow, 1958, named Companion of Literature, 1974; fellow, Center for Advanced Study in the Behavioral Sciences, 1964-65; Sonning Prize, University of Copenhagen, 1968; LL.D., Queen's University, 1968; Commander of the Order of the British Empire, 1972; fellow, Royal Astronomical Society, 1976; D.Litt., Leeds University, 1977.

WRITINGS:

Von Weissen Naechten und Roten Tagen, Ukrainian State Publishers for National Minorities (Kharkov), 1933.
Menschenopfer Unerhoert, Carrefour (Paris), 1937.
Spanish Testament (autobiography), Gollancz, 1937, abridged edition published as *Dialogue with Death*, Macmillan, 1942, reprinted, Hutchinson, 1966.
Scum of the Earth (autobiography), Macmillan, 1941, reprinted, 1968.
The Yogi and the Commissar and Other Essays, Macmillan, 1945.
(Contributor) *The Challenge of Our Time*, P. Marshall, 1948.
Insight and Outlook: An Inquiry Into the Common Foundations of Science, Art, and Social Ethics, Macmillan, 1949.

Promise and Fulfillment: Palestine, 1917-1949 (history), Macmillan, 1949.

(Contributor) Richard Howard Stafford Crossman, editor, *The God That Failed: Six Studies in Communism,* Harper, 1950, reprinted, Arno, 1975.

Arrow in the Blue (first part of autobiography), Macmillan, 1952.

The Invisible Writing (second part of autobiography), Macmillan, 1954.

The Trail of the Dinosaur and Other Essays, Macmillan, 1955.

Reflections on Hanging, Gollancz, 1956, Macmillan, 1957.

The Sleepwalkers: A History of Man's Changing Vision of the Universe, Macmillan, 1959, excerpt published as *The Watershed: A Biography of Johannes Kepler,* Anchor Books, 1960.

The Lotus and the Robot (nonfiction), Hutchinson, 1960, Macmillan, 1961.

(With others) *Control of the Mind,* McGraw, 1961.

(With C. H. Rolph) *Hanged by the Neck: An Exposure of Capital Punishment in England,* Penguin, 1961.

(Editor) *Suicide of a Nation?: An Enquiry into the State of Britain Today,* Hutchinson, 1963, Macmillan, 1964.

The Act of Creation (nonfiction), Macmillan, 1964, new edition, Hutchinson, 1976.

(With others) *Studies in Psychology,* University of London Press, 1965.

(With others) *Celebration of the Bicentenary of John Smithson,* Smithsonian Institution Press, 1966.

The Ghost in the Machine (nonfiction), Hutchinson, 1967, Macmillan, 1968.

Drinkers of Infinity: Essays, 1955-1967, Hutchinson, 1968, Macmillan, 1969.

(Editor with J. R. Smythies) *Beyond Reductionism: New Perspectives in the Life Sciences,* Hutchinson, 1969, Macmillan, 1970, new edition, Hutchinson, 1972.

(Contributor) *The Ethics of Change,* Canadian Broadcasting Corp., 1969.

The Case of the Midwife Toad (nonfiction), Hutchinson, 1971, Random House, 1972.

The Roots of Coincidence (nonfiction), Random House, 1972.

The Lion and the Ostrich (lecture), Oxford University Press, 1973.

(With Alister Hardy and Robert Harvie) *The Challenge of Chance: Experiments and Speculations,* Hutchinson, 1973, published as *The Challenge of Chance: A Mass Experiment in Telepathy and Its Unexpected Outcome,* Random House, 1974.

The Heel of Achilles: Essays, 1968-1973, Hutchinson, 1974, Random House, 1975.

The Thirteenth Tribe: The Khazar Empire and Its Heritage, Random House, 1976.

(With Arnold Joseph Toynbee and others) *Life After Death,* McGraw, 1976.

Janus: A Summing Up, Random House, 1978.

Bricks to Babel: A Selection From 50 Years of His Writings, Chosen with New Commentary by the Author, Random House, 1981.

(With wife, Cynthia Koestler) *Stranger on the Square,* edited by Harold Harris, Random House, 1984.

NOVELS

The Gladiators, Macmillan, 1939, 2nd edition, Graphic Books, 1956.

Darkness at Noon (Book-of-the-Month Club selection), J. Cape, 1940, Macmillan, 1941, reprinted, Franklin Library, 1979.

Arrival and Departure, Macmillan, 1943, revised edition, Hutchinson, 1966, Macmillan, 1967.

Thieves in the Night: Chronicle of an Experiment, Macmillan, 1946, reprinted, 1967.

The Age of Longing, Macmillan, 1951, reprinted, Hutchinson, 1970.

The Call Girls, Hutchinson, 1972, Random House, 1973.

Also author of screenplay "Lift Your Head, Comrade," 1944. Contributor to *Encyclopaedia Britannica, Encyclopaedia of Philosophy,* and *Encyclopaedia of Sexual Knowledge.* Contributor to periodicals.

SIDELIGHTS: Arthur Koestler gained international recognition with the publication of his novel *Darkness at Noon,* a fictionalized account of the Moscow Trials of 1938 in which many Bolshevik revolutionaries were put to death by the Soviet Government. "Koestler's object," a reviewer for *Encounter* noted, "was to expose the reality which lay behind the facade of the great Russian state trials of the 1930s, and he did it so effectively that to thousands, even millions, of people, Communism and the Communist party . . . have never looked the same again." Peter Medawar observed that Koestler's novel "changed the direction of the flow of thought on political matters, and it is as such that he will live and continue to be read."

Darkness at Noon grew out of Koestler' own disillusionment with the Soviet Union and Communism after seven years of membership in the German Communist Party. He saw the Moscow Trials as both an abandonment of the Soviet Union's Communist ideals and as dangerously totalitarian in nature. "All the big shots, our heroes . . . were denounced, unmasked as British or American agents," Koestler said about the trials. "When most of my friends had been liquidated in the U.S.S.R., I sent my farewell letter to the German Communist Party." "I went to Communism as one goes to a spring of fresh water," Koestler once explained, "and I left Communism as one clambers out of a poisoned river strewn with the wreckage of flooded cities and the corpses of the drowned." As Jenni Calder observed, through his political writing Koestler presented "his life as an example that could teach and help the understanding of a certain period of history. He had made mistakes. These mistakes could be partially justified if they could be used to illustrate and interpret history."

Koestler's subsequent writings continued to examine the problems of political idealism and power. In such books as *The Yogi and the Commissar, Thieves in the Night,* and *Arrival and Departure,* he explored the problems involved in transforming one's ideals into political action. *The Yogi and the Commissar* contrasts the differences between religious and political ideals and methods of change. *Thieves in the Night* concerns the settlement of Israel by Jews who have long been victims and must now become rulers. *Arrival and Departure* is about a young revolutionary who suffers a nervous breakdown.

By the 1950s, Koestler concentrated less on his political writing and eventually gave it up entirely. "There was a danger," Philip Toynbee wrote, "that Koestler would remain in the constricting armour of his anti-Communism, but Koestler saw the danger clearly enough [and] shed that armour." Speaking of his abandonment of political writing, Koestler stated, "I have said all I have to say on these subjects which had occupied me for the best part of a quarter century; now the errors are atoned, the bitter passion has burnt itself out, Cassandra has gone hoarse—let others carry on."

Leaving politics behind him, Koestler devoted his energies to writing about scientific and philosophical matters. He became, as Robert Boyers wrote, "a learned and witty man who seems to enjoy writing about almost everything." Koestler examined such topics as evolution, psychology, the history of science, capital punishment, and the nature of artistic creation. "Koestler's ideas," Lothar Kahn stated, "probably range over a wider terrain than those of any other writer of our time. Few contemporaries have treated ideologies more analytically and in more original fashion." Medawar, admitting that Koestler "is not a scientist, though he has had some good ideas, . . . and he is not nearly critical or tough-minded enough to be a creative philosopher," believed that he is "an enormously intelligent man with a truly amazing power to apprehend knowledge and grasp the gist of quite difficult theories." P. Witonski disagreed. "Arthur Koestler's forays into the history of science," he wrote, "have done little to enhance his reputation, save among those uneducated in science."

Koestler's most widely-known non-political work was *The Act of Creation,* a study of the creative process in many aspects of human behavior. The book received a mixed critical reaction. E. R. Hilgard believed that "reading the book is a rich experience, for the author wanders widely through science, art, and literature, uses charming and varied analogies, and says countless quotable things. If his book is not the last word on creativity, that is not much of a weakness. It is a serious work, immensely learned, and thoughtful." Anthony Lejeune, however, calls *The Act of Creation* "an unsatisfactory book," claiming that "Mr. Koestler had a worthwhile idea" that "would have made an admirable short essay." Elizabeth Janeway notes that "though I can't help but point out [Koestler's] short-comings [in writing about] the field I know most about, there is something here." She praises Koestler as a "master of the very difficult trade of synthesizing a mass of material [and] of serving up to the general reader facts that he would otherwise never know, and—most important—of explaining why they matter and how they relate to each other."

Koestler holds a distinctive place in contemporary thought and letters. "Koestler," a writer for *Time* stated, "is a rare protean figure in modern intellectual life—a successful journalist, novelist, and popular philosopher. His concern for ultimate issues and his idealistic involvement lend weight to his fiction. His wit, clarity, and brilliance of exposition make his . . . volumes of political, scientific, and philosophical theory highly enjoyable as well as provocative." "To be the author," Alasdair MacIntyre stated, "of one great novel and several good ones, to have written imaginatively on the history of science and polemically on the nature of the human mind, to have involved oneself continually in argument on politics and religion—each of these alone would make up an exceptional intellectual life. But Koestler's life embraces them all."

MEDIA ADAPTATIONS: Darkness at Noon was made into a stage play by Sidney Kingsley and produced on Broadway in 1951. The book has also been translated into over thirty languages.

AVOCATIONAL INTERESTS: Chess, canoeing.

BIOGRAPHICAL/CRITICAL SOURCES:

BOOKS

Arthur Koestler, Cahiers de l'Herne (Paris), 1975.
Atkins, John, *Arthur Koestler,* Neville Spearman, 1956, reprinted, Norwood, 1977.
Baker, Denys Val, editor, *Writers of Today,* Sidgwick & Jackson, 1946.
Books in General, Chatto & Windus, 1953.

Breit, Harvey, *The Writer Observed,* World Publishing, 1956.
Burgess, Anthony, *The Novel Now: A Guide to Contemporary Fiction,* Norton, 1967.
Burgess, Anthony, *Urgent Copy: Literary Studies,* Norton, 1968.
Calder, Jenni, *Chronicles of Conscience: A Study of George Orwell and Arthur Koestler,* University of Pittsburgh Press, 1969.
Contemporary Literary Criticism, Gale, Volume 1, 1973, Volume 3, 1975, Volume 6, 1976, Volume 8, 1978, Volume 15, 1980, Volume 33, 1985.
The Crisis of the Human Person: Some Personalist Interpretations, Longmans, Green, 1949.
Harris, Harold, editor, *Astride the Two Cultures: Arthur Koestler at Seventy,* Random House, 1976.
Huber, Peter Alfred, *Arthur Koestler: Das Literarische Werk,* Fretz & Wasmuth Verlag, 1962.
Kahan, Lothar, *Mirrors of the Jewish Mind: A Gallery of Portraits of European Jewish Writers of Our Time,* A. S. Barnes, 1968.
Koestler, Arthur, *Spanish Testament,* Gollancz, 1937, abridged edition published as *Dialogue with Death,* Macmillan, 1942.
Koestler, Arthur, *Scum of the Earth,* Macmillan, 1941.
Koestler, Arthur, *Arrow in the Blue,* Macmillan, 1952.
Koestler, Arthur, *The Invisible Writing,* Macmillan, 1954.
Lewis, John and Reginald Bishop, *Philosophy of Betrayal,* Russia Today Society, 1945.
Mays, Wolfe, *Arthur Koestler,* Judson, 1973.
Merrill, Reed B. and Thomas Frazier, editors, *Arthur Koestler: An International Bibliography,* Ardis, 1978.
Mikes, George, *Arthur Koestler: The Story of a Friendship,* Deutsch, 1984.
Nevada, J., *Arthur Koestler,* Robert Anscombe & Co., 1948.
Orwell, George, *George Orwell: Critical Essays,* Secker & Warburg, 1954.
Pearson, Sidney A., Jr., *Arthur Koestler,* Twayne, 1978.
Sperber, Murray, *Arthur Koestler: A Collection of Critical Essays,* Prentice-Hall, 1978.
Woodcock, George, *The Writer and Politics,* Porcupine Press, 1948.

PERIODICALS

America, November 13, 1976.
Atlantic, December, 1968, May, 1973.
Books & Bookmen, December, 1972, May, 1976.
Book World, June 30, 1974.
Christian Century, February 26, 1975.
Christian Science Monitor, October 23, 1969, May 4, 1972.
Commentary, November, 1964.
Commonweal, March 4, 1977.
Contemporary Review, June, 1974.
Cornhill, autumn, 1946.
Critic, August, 1978.
Detroit News, April 2, 1972.
Economist, April 24, 1976.
Encounter, July, 1964, February, 1968, January, 1970.
Esquire, March, 1972.
Guardian Weekly, October 28, 1972.
Harper's, January, 1965.
Hudson Review, summer, 1968.
Life, December 29, 1972.
Listener, September 12, 1968, April 8, 1976.
Midstream, February, 1977.
Ms., October, 1975.
Nation, July 3, 1954, November 20, 1976.

National Review, November 17, 1964, June 30, 1970, November 12, 1976.
Natural History, June, 1972.
New Leader, May 14, 1973.
New Republic, February 1, 1975, May 13, 1978.
New Statesman, July 3, 1954, October 1, 1971.
Newsweek, August 30, 1976.
New Yorker, April 21, 1973.
New York Review of Books, December 17, 1964, October 28, 1976.
New York Times, June 23, 1970.
New York Times Magazine, August 30, 1970.
Observer, October 15, 1967, September 8, 1968, October 5, 1969.
Psychology Today, October, 1973, January, 1977.
Saturday Review, October 17, 1964, March 6, 1976.
Science, January 1, 1965, May 12, 1972.
Sewanee Review, autumn, 1965.
Spectator, October 1, 1965, April 27, 1974.
Time, March 1, 1968, August 23, 1976.
Times Literary Supplement, July 2, 1964, November 2, 1967, October 27, 1972, June 11, 1976.
Virginia Quarterly Review, autumn, 1978.
Wall Street Journal, July 26, 1973.
Washington Post, March 13, 1983.

OBITUARIES:

BOOKS

Dictionary of Literary Biography Yearbook: 1983, Gale, 1984.

PERIODICALS

Chicago Tribune, March 4, 1983.
Los Angeles Times, March 4, 1983.
Newsweek, March 14, 1983.
New York Times, March 4, 1983.
Publishers Weekly, March 18, 1983.
Time, March 14, 1983.
Times (London), March 4, 1983.
Washington Post, March 4, 1983.*

*　　*　　*

KONIGSBURG, E(laine) L(obl) 1930-

PERSONAL: Born February 10, 1930, in New York, N.Y.; daughter of Adolph (a businessman) and Beulah (Klein) Lobl; married David Konigsburg (a psychologist), July 6, 1952; children: Paul, Laurie, Ross. *Education:* Carnegie Institute of Technology (now Carnegie-Mellon University), B.S., 1952; graduate study, University of Pittsburgh, 1952-54. *Religion:* Jewish.

ADDRESSES: Office—c/o Atheneum Publishers, 15 Fifth Ave., New York, N.Y. 10003.

CAREER: Writer. Shenago Valley Provision Co., Sharon, Pa., bookkeeper, 1947-48; Bartram School, Jacksonville, Fla., science teacher, 1954-55, 1960-62.

AWARDS, HONORS: Jennifer, Hecate, Macbeth, William McKinley, and Me, Elizabeth was chosen as an honor book in *Book Week* Children's Spring Book Festival, 1967, and as a Newbery Honor Book, 1968; Newbery Medal, 1968, and William Allen White Award, 1970, both for *From the Mixed-Up Files of Mrs. Basil E. Frankweiler;* Carnegie-Mellon Merit Award, 1971; American Library Association notable children's book and National Book Award nomination, both 1974, both for *A Proud Taste for Scarlet and Miniver;* American Library Association best book for young adults, for *The Second Mrs. Giaconda,* and

Father's Arcane Daughter; American Library Association notable children's book and American Book Award nomination, 1980, both for *Throwing Shadows.*

WRITINGS:

SELF-ILLUSTRATED JUVENILES

Jennifer, Hecate, Macbeth, William McKinley, and Me, Elizabeth, Atheneum, 1967.
From the Mixed-Up Files of Mrs. Basil E. Frankweiler, Atheneum, 1967.
About the B'nai Bagels, Atheneum, 1969.
(George), Atheneum, 1970.
A Proud Taste for Scarlet and Miniver, Atheneum, 1973.
The Dragon in the Ghetto Caper, Atheneum, 1974."

JUVENILES

Altogether, One at a Time (short stories), illustrated by Gail E. Haley, Mercer Meyer, Gary Parker, and Laurel Schindelman, Atheneum, 1971.
The Second Mrs. Giaconda, illustrated with museum plates, Atheneum, 1975.
Father's Arcane Daughter, Atheneum, 1976.
Throwing Shadows (short stories), Atheneum, 1979.
Journey to an 800 Number, Atheneum, 1982 (published in England as *Journey by First Class Camel,* Hamish Hamilton, 1983).
Up from Jericho Tel, Atheneum, 1986.

OTHER

Also author of promotional pamphlets for Atheneum.

SIDELIGHTS: E. L. Konigsburg is best known as the author and illustrator of humorous juvenile books. Konigsburg's books are not simply amusing, however; almost every story contains an element of seriousness, usually in the form of a child's search for identity. "Questions of identity—'What kind of person can I become?'—are fundamentally serious ideas, even if the surface is comedy, and they are present in nearly all Elaine Konigsburg's stories," observes David Rees in *Horn Book.* Konigsburg's ability to incorporate humor into serious subject matter makes her "a lively, amusing and painlessly educational storyteller," writes Alice Fleming in the *New York Times Book Review.*

Konigsburg's original intention was to write books that reflected the middle-class background of her own children. Her Newbery Award-winning book, From the *Mixed-Up Files of Mrs. Basil E. Frankweiler,* for example, was directly influenced by her children's behavior on a family picnic. Konigsburg writes in *Forty Percent More than Everything You Want to Know about E. L. Konigsburg* that after listening to her children complain about ants, warm milk, and melted cupcake icing, I thought to myself that if my children ever left home, they would never become barbarians even if they were captured by pirates. Civilization was not a veneer to them; it was a crust. They would want at least all the comforts of home plus a few dashes of extra elegance. Where, I wondered, would they ever consider running to if they ever left home? They certainly would never consider any place less elegant than the Metropolitan Museum of Art."

From the Mixed-Up Files of Mrs. Basil E. Frankweiler tells the story of two children who do just that. Claudia, tired of being big sister to three siblings and bored with suburbia, decides to run away from home. She takes along Jamie, her thrifty brother, for financial assistance. Their temporary home is the New York Metropolitan Museum of Art, where they bathe in the fountain and sleep in a musty, nineteenth-century bed. While exploring the museum, they become intrigued by an angel reputed to have been sculpted by Michelangelo. Claudia, determined to establish her identity before she returns home, is convinced the discovering the origin of the statue will help her accomplish this goal. Their search leads them to Mrs. Frankweiler, the original owner of the statue, who teaches them "that true individuality is interior—and often secret at that," writes Elva Harmon in the *Library Journal.*

Claudia and Jamie "are wholly and refreshingly recognizable and real," comments a *Times Literary Supplement* reviewer, who later states that Mrs. Frankweiler, on the other hand, "one appreciates but does not wholly believe in. She is a little too fancy-baked, from smart New Yorker-land." Rees shares the same reservations about Frankweiler. He describes her as "a kind of fairy godmother and *deus ex machina,* who sorts out the problem and the children, whereas the children should have sorted out both the problem and themselves on their own."

The children's disregard for the museum rules and lack of concern for their family has caused some reviewers to question the book's appropriateness for children. A *Times Literary Supplement* critic, however, calls it a "particularly honest observation . . . that it never occurs to the children to worry about their parents, to imagine the agonies through which they must be going." A similar opinion is shared by Harmon who maintains that anyone rejecting the book on the basis of the children's misbehavior "would be denying their patrons the reading pleasure of an unusual book, extremely well written."

In *(George),* one of Konigsburg's later books, the protagonist's identity crisis is much more serious than that of the average child. Ben has had an alter ego, George, since he was a young boy. Until Ben's twelfth year, George had been known only to Ben and his immediate family. But when Ben, an exceptional student, is placed in a high school chemistry class, George begins to vocalize, thus disturbing the class. Consequently, Ben is sent to a psychiatrist who helps him merge the two personalities. George's presence has prompted some reviewers to label Ben as schizophrenic. Konigsburg told *CA,* however, that she prefers to think of George as Ben's "inner self." This "decision to treat the darker, more socially unacceptable side of [Ben] . . . as a real, separate person" greatly contributes to the success of *(George),* comments Rees, who also praises "the skill with which Mrs. Konigsburg turns this apparently formidable material into a light-hearted, genuinely comic novel."

Compared to Konigsburg's first three books, *(George)* is "far more complex, demanding more from the reader and giving away less," notes a *Times Literary Supplement* reviewer, who also observes that *(George)* is the first novel in which Konigsburg "writes as herself, and somehow her own voice is not as consistent or as beguiling as the voices of the personae she invented." The critic nevertheless concludes that "Konigsburg could not write a dull book if she tried, but it should be made clear that this . . . book . . . is strictly for older readers, who are prepared to accept a foreign idiom, who will be intrigued by the notion of symbiosis, and who like being made to think."

Konigsburg's books have been marketed by her publisher as being appropriate for the middle-aged child. Konigsburg at first found the terms "middle-aged" and "child" contradictory, but after researching the Middle Ages, she began to find parallels between the characteristics of that period and the preadolescent child. Konigsburg writes in *The Genesis of "A Proud Taste for Scarlet and Miniver":* "Examine the art of the Middle Ages, and you find literal interpretations of 'the light of God' and the 'mouth of Hell.' A middle-aged child listens literally and inter-

prets literally, too. Look at a painting or a piece of sculpture from the Middle Ages, and it is hard to find perspective. A middle-aged child lacks perspective in his philosophy as well as his art."

By the time she was convinced that the term middle-aged child was really quite apt, Konigsburg had developed a love for the Middle Ages. Wishing to express her interest in this period, she wrote *A Proud Taste for Scarlet and Miniver,* a portrait of Eleanor of Aquitaine, wife of Louis VII of France and Henry II of England. The story is told in flashbacks by Eleanor, Henry's mother Empress Matilda, Abbot Suger, and others as they sit in heaven awaiting the arrival of Henry, who has been temporarily detained in hell.

Konigsburg departs from her usual choice of a protagonist in this book but not without good reason as she explains in *The Genesis of "A Proud Taste for Scarlet and Miniver":* "I wanted to write about this queen, this woman's libber, for children. I wanted to do it accurately, but didn't want to invent a small child character and plop him into the twelfth century. I felt I didn't need to do that. Eleanor of Aquitaine already had an age in common with children: the Middle Ages." In addition, Eleanor has "a certain ruthlessness" that is common to Konigsburg's other protagonists as well, writes Penelope Farmer, who also remarks in the *Times Literary Supplement* that, consequently, "the gap between Eleanor and Mrs. Konigsburg's previous heroines is perhaps not after all so great. Eleanor as seen here is nothing if not the prototype of Claudia, Jennifer, et al." Konigsburg's portrayal of "Eleanor—ambitious, intelligent, energetic—will delight youngsters who crave an emancipated heroine," declares Jennifer Farley Smith in the *Christian Science Monitor.*

In addition to novels, Konigsburg has written two collections of short stories for juveniles. The stories in the second collection, *Throwing Shadows,* "with their high humor, easy pace and sharp social comment" are reminiscent of stories by William Saroyan and Langston Hughes, according to Cynthia King in the *New York Times Book Review.* In each of the four stories, "a child encounters an adult, and both are changed," writes King. In "At the Home," for example, young Philip's awareness of the horrors of war is heightened by the stories of a Hungarian refugee who was imprisoned at Auschwitz during World War II. When the refugee complains that the people in the nursing home are boring, Philip, in turn, instructs her by saying, "You have to overcome your prejudice about old people." Although the characters and settings are different, *Throwing Shadows* contains a familiar voice, observes King. "It is the voice of . . . a skeptic who . . . can make you laugh while illuminating the poignancies, inequities and paradoxes of contemporary life."

Many of Konigsburg's books have been published in England, including *From the Mixed-Up Files of Mrs. Basil E. Frankweiler, (George),* and *Journey to an 800 Number* (published in England as *Journey by First Class Camel*). Konigsburg's books are undeniably American, a fact that has not diminished her popularity with British readers. Rather, "her books which are more specifically American . . . have been the most successful in England," comments Rees, who also explains that Konigsburg's "value to British readers is that she can make something universal out of a setting that is specifically American; in other words, though her writing at its finest may use language and present material and viewpoints that seem thoroughly transatlantic, her children and teenagers could be found in any place; their problems in coming to terms with themselves and with an adult world that at best is messy and at worst corrupt are the problems of the young everywhere."

BIOGRAPHICAL/CRITICAL SOURCES:

BOOKS

Children's Literature Review, Volume 1, Gale, 1976.
Konigsburg, E. L., *The Genesis of "A Proud Taste for Scarlet and Miniver"* (pamphlet), Atheneum, 1973.
Konigsburg, *Forty Percent More Than Everything You Want to Know about E. L. Konigsburg* (pamphlet), Atheneum, 1974.
Konigsburg, *Throwing Shadows,* Atheneum, 1979.
Townsend, John Rowe, *A Sounding of Storytellers: Essays on Contemporary Writers for Children,* Penguin Books, 1979.

PERIODICALS

Chicago Tribune Book World, February 2, 1986.
Christian Science Monitor, May 1, 1974.
Horn Book, December, 1970, April, 1973, February, 1978, April, 1980.
Learning Today, fall, 1981.
Library Journal, October 15, 1967.
New York Times Book Review, November 5, 1967, March 30, 1969, November 8, 1970, May 30, 1971, October 14, 1973, November 4, 1973, October 5, 1975, November 7, 1976, December 9, 1979, May 30, 1982, May 25, 1986.
Saturday Review, November 14, 1970.
Times (London), June 16, 1983.
Times Literary Supplement, October 3, 1968, April 3, 1969, July 2, 1971, April 4, 1975, March 25, 1977, June 16, 1983.
Washington Post Book World, April 11, 1982, May 11, 1986.

*   *   *

KONWICKI, Tadeusz 1926-

PERSONAL: Born July 22, 1926, in Nowa Wilejka, Poland; son of Michal (a metal worker) and Jadwiga (Kiezun) Konwicki; married Danuta Lenica, April 25, 1949; children: Maria, Anna. *Education:* Attended University of Warsaw and Jagellonian University of Cracow, 1945-49.

ADDRESSES: Home—U1 Gorskiego, i m 68, 00-O33 Warsaw, Poland.

CAREER: Novelist, screenwriter, film director, and journalist. Director of films, including *Ostatni dzien lata,* 1960, *Zaduszki,* 1962, *Salto,* 1964, *Matura,* 1965, and *Jak daleko stad, jak blisko,* 1972. *Wartime service:* Member of Polish underground during World War II; awarded several medals for service.

MEMBER: Polish Writers' Union, Union of Polish Filmmakers.

AWARDS, HONORS: State Prize for Literature, 1950, for *Przy budowie,* and 1954, for *Wladza;* Venice Film Festival Grand Prix, 1958, for *Ostatni dzien lata;* special jury prize from Mannheim Film Festival, 1962, for *Zaduszki;* prize from San Remo Film Festival, 1972, for screenplay, *Jak daleko stad, jak blisko;* Mondello Prize for Literature, 1981.

WRITINGS:

NOVELS

Wladza (title means "The Power"), Czytelnik, 1954.
Godzina smutku (title means "The Hour of Sadness"), Czytelnik, 1954.
Klucz (title means "The Key"), Nasza Ksiegarnia (Warsaw), 1955.
Rojsty (title means "The Marshes"), Czytelnik, 1956.
Z oblezonego miasta (title means "From the Besieged Town"), Iskry, 1956.
Dziura w niebie (title means "A Hole in the Sky"), Iskry, 1959.

Sennik wspolczesny, Iskry (Warsaw), 1963, translation by David Welsh published as *A Dreambook for Our Time,* M.I.T. Press, 1969.
Wniebowstapienie (title means "Ascension"), Iskry, 1967.
Nic ablo Nic (title means "Nothing or Nothing"), Czytelnik, 1971.
Kronika wypadkow milosnych (title means "The Chronicle of Love Events"), Czytelnik, 1974.
Kalendarz i klepsydra (title means "A Calendar and an Hourglass"), Czytelnik, 1976.
Kompleks polski, Index on Censorship (London), 1977, translation by Richard Lourie published as *The Polish Complex,* Farrar, Straus, 1982.
Mala apokalipsa, Index on Censorship, 1979, translation by Lourie published as *A Minor Apocalypse,* Farrar, Straus, 1983.
Wschody i zachody kziezyca, Index on Censorship, 1982, translation by Lourie published as *Moonrise, Moonset,* Farrar, Straus, 1987.

SCREENPLAYS

Kariera (title means "The Career"), Film Polski, 1955.
Wajda's Kanal, Film Polski, 1957.
Ostatni dzien lata (title means "The Last Day of Summer"), Film Polski, 1958.
Matka Joanna od Aniolow (title means "Mother Joan of the Angels"), Film Polski, 1961.
Zaduszki (title means "Halloween"), Film Polski, 1962.
(With J. Kawalerowicz) *Faraon* (title means "Pharaoh"), Film Polski, 1965.
Salto, Film Polski, 1965.
Matura (title means "Entrance Examination"), 1965.
Zimowy zmlerzch (title means "Winter's Twilight"), 1956.
Jowita, Film Polski, 1967.
Ostatni dzien lata (screenplays; contains *Ostatni dzien lata, Zaduszki, Salto, Matura, Zimowy zmlerzch,* and *Jak daleko stad, jak blisko*), Iskry, 1966, revised edition, 1973.
Jak daleko stad, jak blisko (title means "So Far, So Near"), Film Polski, 1972.

OTHER

Przy budowie (short stories; title means "At the Building Site"), Czytelnik, 1950.
Zwierzoczlekoupior (juvenile), illustrations by wife, Danuta Konwicki, Czytelnik (Warsaw), 1969, translation by George Korwin-Rodziszewski and Audrey Korwin-Rodziszewski published as *The Anthropos-Specter-Beast,* S. G. Phillips, 1977.
Dlaczego kot jest kot (juvenile; title means "Why a Cat Is a Cat"), KAW (Warsaw), 1976.

SIDELIGHTS: It was not until the 1956 political and cultural "thaw" in Poland that Tadeusz Konwicki and his contemporaries were able to have their major works published. Prior to that time, Konwicki published minor works, including a collection of short stories and a novel, both of which won the State Prize for Literature and are, in the opinion of Jerzy Krzyzanowski of *Books Abroad,* "cliches of socialist-realist fiction . . . modeled on Soviet novels," the results of severe state-imposed censorship.

The publication of *Rojsty* in 1956 is considered a turning point in Konwicki's literary career. The author had waited eight years to publish the somber and satirical account of a young man's desperate attempts to become a hero. *Rojsty* is based on Konwicki's own bitter experiences as a guerrilla fighter with the Home Army of the Polish underground, when the guerrillas successfully liberated the city of Wilno from Nazi occupation and were punished with arrest, deportation, and imprisonment by the advancing Soviet troops. Konwicki managed to escape the concentration camp roundup and join another group in fighting the Soviet invaders. The unit disbanded when the men realized that the situation was indeed hopeless. As Krzyzanowski observed, "The psychological wounds inflicted by those tragic events were to remain in his memory during the years to come, affecting, and to a great extent shaping, his artistic vision."

A Dreambook for Our Time was Konwicki's first novel to appear in English translation and has been compared to the works of Albert Camus and Joseph Conrad. Writing in *World Literature Today,* Ruel K. Wilson theorized that the novel's great overnight success was due to its "brutal frankness of subject matter and imagery." With this book Konwicki began a painful exploration into a world of tormented survivors where, in the words of Wilson, "the past holds them all prisoner, for their attitudes toward the present have been conditioned by their experiences before and during the German occupation."

Dreambook's protagonist, Oldster, is a former partisan consumed with guilt and seeking retribution for his wartime actions. As the novel opens, he "awakens after a suicide attempt, surrounded by inquisitive faces in the remote village to which he has drifted," related Neal Ascherson in the *New York Review of Books.* "We understand," Ascherson continued, "that he is solitary, crushed and bewildered by memories of the war and the postwar years to which, although some fifteen years in the past, he can still give no meaning. But the other inhabitants are in the same pass. Nothing is happening in this somnolent place, malarial with sinister memories of violence and mystery." Oldster has returned to this valley and forest, the scene of his crime, to find forgiveness.

During the war he had been assigned to kill a fellow countryman who had betrayed partisans to the Germans. Carrying out the order, Oldster had fired his shot with his victim's young daughter as witness. But not having shot to kill, Oldster is convinced that the man has survived and is living in the valley. He also suspects that the partisan chief, who gave the execution order, is still hiding in the nearby forest. "Whether this is delusion, obsession, mania, is never made clear," stated critic Abraham Rothberg.

After experiencing much torment and loneliness, Oldster meets a man who can give him some perspective. "During the war too, I kept to the political average," the man tells him. "Most of the nation neither fought at the front, nor hid in the forests, nor suffered in concentration camps. The ordinary majority stayed in their badly heated houses, ate frozen potatoes and dealt a little in the black market. I did the same. Nobody gave me a medal for what I did during the occupation, but nobody reproved me either. I didn't gain anything, but I didn't lose anything." Oldster finally realizes, Rothberg observed, "that the present, however unheroic and boring, must be lived in and endured. After giving up the nightmare of the past, both its horror and heroism, half-willing, half-pushed, half-knowing, half-duped, he is constrained to leave the valley, saying in the very last lines of the book: '. . . I would scramble with the remains of my strength out of these seething depths to the edge of reality, and would get up to an ordinary, commonplace day, with its usual troubles, its everyday toil, its so well-known familiar drudgery.' "

In *Dreambook,* Konwicki achieves a surrealistic quality with what Mark Schechner in the *Nation* called "a blurring of perception." Schechner explained: "This is indeed a dreambook for not only does the past inhabit the present with inescapable recollections but present events themselves dissolve in a dreamlike haze of uncertainty. Here . . . the terrors of war lead to emotional anesthesia. . . . As in a play by Beckett, the simplest acts are performed with maddening difficulty, and the most routine thoughts and recollections are achieved only through a tedious grasping with the will to forget."

Wilson found *Dreambook*'s vision of humanity "gloomy and nihilistic." He elaborated: "Konwicki's grim caricatures perturb and sometimes amuse the reader, although they evoke little sympathy. . . . the novel's message is highly symbolic. The dream atmosphere, visual, pungent, yet impressionistic, inclines us to accept the work for what it is: a montage of apocalyptic events seen and relived by an obsessive and guilty imagination." V. D. Mihailovich in *Saturday Review* drew a comparison between Konwicki's writing style and film technique: "The author, who is also a movie director, mixes dramatic episodes, flashbacks, nightmarish reveries, and inner monologues with abandon." He praised Konwicki's "wide use of metaphors, symbols, and irony," which he felt "enlivens the style." Mihailovich further stated: "Though the characters are full-blooded eccentrics, their antics are in harmony with their inner mechanisms. A certain dreamlike quality, a gossamer of things long past yet somehow still clinging to life, pervades Konwicki's facile and poetic narration. As a result the reader is rewarded with illustrations of the consequences of indelible war experiences and with beautiful prose as well."

Delving further into the nightmarish world of the guilty survivor, Konwicki produced a subsequent novel, *Wniebowstapienie.* Here "the horrors of war memories give way to the torments of life in the corrupted post-war society," Krzyzanowski said. *Wniebowstapienie*'s characters are ghost-like, creatures for whom the city of Warsaw serves as a purgatory. "Building the plot around a bank robbery, Konwicki leads his characters through the streets, restaurants, parks and jails but most frequently gathers them together in the empty marble halls of the Palast [Warsaw's Palace of Culture], its basements and power stations, juxtaposing their enormous size and deserted spaces with the ugliness and pettiness of everyday life in contemporary Poland. Such an ironic twist," Krzyzanowski wrote, "adds a grotesque flavor to that somber and masterfully written novel, in which realistic presentation of characters and scenery achieves another dimension of supernatural and symbolic vision." Because of its pessimistic depiction of Polish society, *Wniebowstapienie* was banned in that country. David Welsh recalled: "Gomulka, then First Secretary to the Party, is believed personally to have ordered the withdrawal of all 30,000 copies some months later, and a wall of silence descended on Konwicki, although he since has been allowed to publish a couple of innocuous novels. His 'editor' is said to have been degraded to 'editing' labels for bottles of mineral water, no doubt with a cut in her wages."

Like many of his earlier writings, Konwicki's unconventional tale *The Anthropos-Specter-Beast* is woven with elements of the dreamworld. In a review of the original Polish edition Welsh called it "even more comic and weird than [Konwicki's] previous work." He continued: "Ostensibly written for children . . . it is not meant for 'good children,' as they will not benefit from it (says Konwicki). The book exists on at least three levels: the narrative itself which can be related to *Winnie-the-Pooh* and *Alice in Wonderland;* the 'real world,' bearing in mind always that reality is something peculiarly ambiguous in Konwicki's fiction; and the narrator's dream. Konwicki's handling of these three levels is masterly."

Nic ablo Nic is considered by some critics to be Konwicki's most ambitious novel. According to Krzyzanowski, it "explores all the passions, obsessions, fears and complexes he has inherited from the violent past and which he sees in the present." Konwicki came from that portion of Poland which was lost to the Soviet Union during World War II, and his feelings of sorrow and estrangement from the loss of his homeland are intensely expressed in *Nic ablo Nic.* Although Konwicki made a "sentimental journey" to the land of his childhood in one of his minor novels, noted Krzyzanowski, only in the author's major works "does he transform it into an everpresent image of major importance."

When the Polish motion picture industry became somewhat liberated from rigid ideological standards in the late 1950's, Konwicki discovered a new mode of expression. His subsequent films, with themes of self-destructive guilt and deep sexual frustration, are closely related to his novels. One such film is *Ostatni dzien lata,* a melancholy story of two young lovers who meet on the beach. Krzyzanowski described the film's poignant imagery: "In the fast-moving shadows of jet fighters screaming overhead like modern symbols of doom and destruction the lovers are able to enjoy just a brief moment of happiness, since neither their past experiences nor the uncertain future can provide them with any lasting relationship." The film ends as the young woman awakens to find only her lover's quickly disappearing footprints in the blowing sand. Krzyzanowski observed that "the image of water as a primordial source and a final grave for all things also appears in Konwicki's subsequent works." He also mentioned that "the motifs of impending doom, the impossibility of sharing one's own past, and the futility of seeking lasting happiness—enhanced with images and visual symbols" found in the film, are forbearers to the themes of *A Dreambook of Our Time.* Konwicki's next film, *Salto,* is considered to be "a visual postscript" to *Dreambook.*

Speaking of his life in an article for the *Contemporary Authors Autobiography Series,* Konwicki explains: "I often look back at myself. Each time I do, shivers run down my spine. I have made many mistakes and could have made many more. I have written quite a few dead pages. I don't have a clean, bright biography. There were tumbles into the gutter and arduous efforts to get out of there. . . . But the strangest thing is that if I could live it all over again, I would choose the same way. . . . I have lived as the times wished—or rather a particle of the times, a small whirlpool which sprang out of nowhere and will end in nothingness. Why should I be wiser than my times, I from whom you have taken away belief in human genius?"

BIOGRAPHICAL/CRITICAL SOURCES:

BOOKS

Contemporary Authors Autobiography Series, Volume 9, Gale, 1989.
Contemporary Literary Criticism, Gale, Volume 8, 1978, Volume 28, 1984, Volume 54, 1989.

PERIODICALS

Best Sellers, September, 1983.
Books Abroad, winter, 1971; summer, 1974.
Christian Science Monitor, October 13, 1983.
Modern Fiction Studies, spring, 1986.
Nation, June 19, 1976.
New Republic, April 10, 1976; November 21, 1983.
New Yorker, February 21, 1983; January 2, 1984.
New York Review of Books, May 27, 1976; March 4, 1982; October 13, 1983; December 17, 1987.
New York Times, August 13, 1987.
New York Times Book Review, May 17, 1970; January 10, 1982; October 23, 1983; August 30, 1987.

Polish Review, Volume 29, number 3, 1984.
Saturday Review, June 20, 1970.
Times Literary Supplement, July 22-28, 1988.
Village Voice, September 15, 1987.
World Literature Today, summer, 1977; spring, 1980.

*   *   *

KOONTZ, Dean R(ay) 1945-
(David Axton, Brian Coffey, Deanna Dwyer, K. R. Dwyer, John Hill, Leigh Nichols, Anthony North, Richard Paige, Owen West)

PERSONAL: Born July 9, 1945, in Everett, Penn.; son of Ray and Florence Koontz; married Gerda Ann Cerra, October 15, 1966.

ADDRESSES: Home—Orange, CA. *Agent*—Claire M. Smith, Harold Ober Associates, 40 East 49th St., New York, NY 10017.

CAREER: Writer. Teacher-counsellor with Appalachian Poverty Program, 1966-67; high school English teacher, 1967-69; writer, 1969—.

MEMBER: Mystery Writers of America, Horror Writers of America.

AWARDS, HONORS: Atlantic Monthly creative writing award, 1966, for story "The Kittens"; Hugo Award nomination, World Science Fiction Convention, 1971, for novella *Beastchild.*

WRITINGS:

NOVELS

Star Quest, Ace Books, 1968.
The Fall of the Dream Machine, Ace Books, 1969.
Fear That Man, Ace Books, 1969.
Anti-Man, Paperback Library, 1970.
Beastchild, Lancer Books, 1970.
Dark of the Woods, Ace Books, 1970.
The Dark Symphony, Lancer Books, 1970.
Hell's Gate, Lancer Books, 1970.
The Crimson Witch, Curtis Books, 1971.
A Darkness in My Soul, DAW Books, 1972.
The Flesh in the Furnace, Bantam, 1972.
Starblood, Lancer Books, 1972.
Time Thieves, Ace Books, 1972.
Warlock, Lancer Books, 1972.
A Werewolf among Us, Ballantine, 1973.
Hanging On, M. Evans, 1973.
The Haunted Earth, Lancer Books, 1973.
Demon Seed, Bantam, 1973.
(Under pseudonym Anthony North) *Strike Deep,* Dial, 1974.
After the Last Race, Atheneum, 1974.
Nightmare Journey, Putnam, 1975.
(Under pseudonym John Hill) *The Long Sleep,* Popular Library, 1975.
Night Chills, Atheneum, 1976.
(Under pseudonym David Axton) *Prison of Ice,* Lippincott, 1976.
The Vision, Putnam, 1977.
Whispers, Putnam, 1980.
Phantoms, Putnam, 1983.
Darkfall, Berkley, 1984 (published in England as *Darkness Comes,* W. H. Allen, 1984).
Twilight Eyes, Land of Enchantment, 1985.
(Under pseudonym Richard Paige) *The Door to December,* New American Library, 1985.
Strangers (Literary Guild selection), Putnam, 1986.

Watchers, Putnam, 1987.
Lightning, Putnam, 1988.
The Bad Place, Putnam, 1990.
Cold Fire, Putnam, 1991.

OTHER

(With wife, Gerda Koontz) *The Pig Society* (nonfiction), Aware
     Press, 1970.
(With G. Koontz) *The Underground Lifestyles Handbook,*
     Aware Press, 1970.
Soft Come the Dragons (story collection), Ace Books, 1970.
Writing Popular Fiction, Writer's Digest, 1973.
How to Write Best-Selling Fiction, Writer's Digest, 1981.

CONTRIBUTOR

Robert Haskins, editor, *Infinity 3,* Lancer Books, 1972.
Harlan Ellison, editor, *Again, Dangerous Visions,* Doubleday,
     1972.
Haskins, editor, *Infinity 4,* Lancer Books, 1972.
Haskins, editor, *Infinity 5,* Lancer Books, 1973.
Roger Elwood, editor, *Flame Tree Planet,* Concordia, 1973.
Elwood and Vic Ghidalia, editors, *Androids, Time Machines,
     and Blue Giraffes,* Follett, 1973.
Elwood, editor, *Future City,* Simon & Schuster, 1973.
Elwood, editor, *Children of Infinity,* Putnam, 1974.
Edward L. Ferman and Barry N. Malzberg, editors, *Final Stage,*
     Charterhouse, 1974.
Night Visions Four, Dark Harvest, 1987.
Night Visions Six, Dark Harvest, 1988.

UNDER PSEUDONYM BRIAN COFFEY

Blood Risk, Bobbs-Merrill, 1973.
Surrounded, Bobbs-Merrill, 1974.
The Wall of Masks, Bobbs-Merrill, 1975.
The Face of Fear, Bobbs-Merrill, 1977.
The Voice of the Night, Doubleday, 1981.

Also author, under pseudonym Brian Coffey, of script for
"CHIPs" television series, 1978.

UNDER PSEUDONYM DEANNA DWYER

The Demon Child, Lancer, 1971.
Legacy of Terror, Lancer, 1971.
Children of the Storm, Lancer, 1972.
The Dark of Summer, Lancer, 1972.
Dance with the Devil, Lancer, 1973.

UNDER PSEUDONYM K. R. DWYER

Chase, Random House, 1972.
Shattered, Random House, 1973.
Dragonfly, Random House, 1975.

UNDER PSEUDONYM LEIGH NICHOLS

The Key to Midnight, Pocket Books, 1979.
The Eyes of Darkness, Pocket Books, 1981.
The House of Thunder, Pocket Books, 1982.
Twilight, Pocket Books, 1984.
Shadowfires, Avon, 1987.

UNDER PSEUDONYM OWEN WEST

The Funhouse (novelization of screenplay), Jove, 1980.
The Mask, Jove, 1981.

SIDELIGHTS: Dean R. Koontz told *CA:* "I began writing when
I was a child, for both reading and writing provided much
needed escape from the poverty in which we lived and from my

father's frequent fits of alcohol-induced violence. I started selling
my work while I was still in college, and by the time I was twenty-five I had sold a dozen novels. This prolific production was
both a boon and a curse. Even the low advances from my early
science fiction novels were welcome, for my wife and I began
married life with much less than five hundred dollars to our
name. The curse lies in the fact that much of the early work is
of lower quality than what came after, both because I was so
young and unself-critical and because the low earnings of each
book forced me to write a lot of them in order to keep financially
afloat. Of all my science fiction, a genre I departed in 1972, I am
only well pleased with *The Flesh in the Furnace, Beastchild,* and
to a lesser extent, *Demon Seed.*

"I mark the beginning of my *real* career as a writer with the publication of *Chase* (a suspense novel that dealt with the effects of
Vietnam on a veteran, which must have been one of the first novels to do so), in 1972, and *Hanging On* (a comic novel) in 1973,
when I moved out of science fiction into the mainstream and suspense fields. Since then, I have attempted, book by book, to
speak to the reader's intellect and emotions as well as to his desire for a 'good read.' I believe the best fiction does three things
well: tells an involving story, makes the reader think, and makes
the reader feel. *Night Chills,* a story about mind-control and the
dangers to individual liberty in a high-technology world, received more critical notice than any of my books to that point.
The Vision, with a touch of the occult, was the first book of mine
to be selected by major book clubs and to receive a substantial
paperback advance, but my real breakthrough came in 1980,
with *Whispers,* a very long psychological suspense novel dealing
with the unknowable and often unrecognized effects that we
have on one another's lives. To date, *Whispers* has sold more
than three million copies worldwide. *Phantoms,* a long novel that
attempts to stretch the horror genre to encompass a rational
world view, and *Darkfall,* my only novel of the supernatural,
were sidesteps in my career, for I do not currently intend to write
any more straight horror novels, though much of what I write
will surely straddle that genre.

"*Strangers,* my latest book, is my most successful to date, not
merely financially but (I think) also in terms of craftsmanship
and art. It was chosen as a Literary Guild main selection. It and
Whispers are the exemplars to which I will refer while working
on future novels. Both of these books rely heavily on character
and background for their impact. Without doubt, both novels
have strong, suspenseful plots, as well, and I intend that all of
my future novels will be what are called 'page turners'; however,
the older I get the more I find that well-drawn characters and
vivid backgrounds are just as important as plot to the success of
a book.

"Recently, my paperback publisher has been reissuing books
that were originally published under pen names, and as I read
the galleys for the new editions, I am frequently surprised—and
pleased—to discover that even years ago, when I was starting
out, my fiction usually embodied the worldview that I now work
consciously to embed within my books. For all its faults, I find
the human species—and Western culture—to be primarily
noble, honorable, and admirable. In an age when doomsayers are
to be heard in every corner of the land, I find great hope in our
species and in the future we will surely make for ourselves. I have
no patience whatsoever for misanthropic fiction, of which there
is too much these days. In fact, that is one reason why I do not
wish to have the 'horror novel' label applied to my books even
when it is sometimes accurate; too many current horror novels
are misanthropic, senselessly bleak, and I do not wish to be
lumped with them. I am no pollyanna, by any means, but I think

we live in a time of marvels, not a time of disaster, and I believe we can solve every problem that confronts us if we keep our perspective and our freedom. Very little if any great and long-lasting fiction has been misanthropic. I strongly believe that, in addition to entertaining, it is the function of fiction to explore the way we live, reinforce our noble traits, and suggest ways to improve the world where we can. If a writer is misanthropic, if he believes we are doomed and that perhaps we even *deserve* to be doomed, then he has a one-book message, and he might as well quit writing after his first publication."

MEDIA ADAPTATIONS: Demon Seed was filmed by Metro-Goldwyn-Mayer/Warner Bros. in 1977; *Shattered* was filmed by Warner Bros. in 1977.

BIOGRAPHICAL/CRITICAL SOURCES:

BOOKS

Twentieth-Century Science-Fiction Writers, St. James, 1986.

PERIODICALS

Analog, January, 1984.
Chicago Tribune Book World, April 12, 1981.
New York Times Book Review, January 12, 1975, February 29, 1976, May 22, 1977, September 11, 1977, February 18, 1990.
Observer, January 1978.
Times Literary Supplement, September 11, 1981.

* * *

KOPIT, Arthur (Lee) 1937-

PERSONAL: Surname is pronounced "*cope*-it"; surname originally Koenig; born May 10, 1937, in New York, N.Y.; son of George (a sales manager) and Maxine (Dubin) Kopit; married Leslie Ann Garis, 1968; children: Alex, Ben, Kathleen. *Education:* Harvard University, B.A. (cum laude), 1959.

ADDRESSES: Home—Connecticut. *Agent*—Luis Sanjurjo, International Creative Management, 40 West 57th St., New York, N.Y. 10019.

CAREER: Free-lance playwright, writer, and director. Playwright in residence at Wesleyan University, 1975-76; adjunct professor of play writing at Yale University, 1977-80; instructor for play writing workshop at City College, 1982—.

MEMBER: Dramatists Guild, Phi Beta Kappa.

AWARDS, HONORS: Vernon Rice Award and Outer Circle Award, 1962, both for "Oh Dad, Poor Dad, Mama's Hung You in the Closet and I'm Feelin' So Sad"; Guggenheim fellowship, 1967; Rockefeller grants, 1968 and 1977; nomination for Antoinette Perry Award ("Tony"), c. 1969, for "Indians"; National Institute of Arts and Letters award, 1971; National Endowment for the Arts grant, 1974; Wesleyan University Center for the Humanities fellowship, 1974; CBS fellowship, 1977-80; Italia Prize for radio play, 1979; award from Fund for New American Plays, 1989, for "Discovery of America."

WRITINGS:

PLAYS

"The Questioning of Nick," first produced in Cambridge, Mass., 1957, produced in New York City, 1974 (also see below).
"Gemini," produced in Cambridge, 1957.
(With Wally Lawrence) "Don Juan in Texas," produced in Cambridge, 1957.

"On the Runway of Life, You Never Know What's Coming Off Next," produced in Cambridge, 1957.
"Across the River and Into the Jungle," produced in Cambridge, 1958.
"Aubade," produced in Cambridge, 1958.
"Sing to Me Through Open Windows," produced in Cambridge, 1959, revised version produced in New York City, 1965 (also see below).
Oh Dad, Poor Dad, Mama's Hung You in the Closet and I'm Feelin' So Sad: A Pseudoclassical Tragifarce in a Bastard French Tradition (first produced in Cambridge, Mass., 1960, produced in London, 1961, produced in New York City, 1962), Hill & Wang, 1960.
"And as for the Ladies," first produced in New York City, 1963, produced as "Chamber Music" in London, 1971 (also see below).
"Mhil'daim," produced in New York City, 1963.
"Asylum; or, What the Gentlemen Are up to, and as for the Ladies," produced in New York City, 1963.
"The Hero," produced in New York City, 1964 (also see below).
"The Conquest of Everest," produced in New York City, 1964 (also see below).
"The Day the Whores Came out to Play Tennis," produced in Cambridge, 1964, produced in New York City, 1965 (also see below).
"The Day the Whores Came Out to Play Tennis," and Other Plays (contains "The Questioning of Nick," "Sing to Me Through Open Windows," "Chamber Music," "The Hero," "The Conquest of Everest," and "The Day the Whores Came out to Play Tennis"), Hill & Wang, 1965, (published in England as *"Chamber Music" and Other Plays,* Methuen, 1969).
"An Incident in the Park," published in *Pardon Me, Sir, But Is My Eye Hurting Your Elbow?,* edited by Bob Booker and George Foster, Geis, 1968.
Indians (first produced in London, 1968, produced in New York City, 1969), Hill & Wang, 1969.
"What's Happened to the Thorne's House," produced in Peru, Vt., 1972.
"Louisiana Territory; or, Lewis and Clark—Lost and Found," produced in Middletown, Conn., 1975.
Secrets of the Rich (first produced in Waterford, Conn., 1976), Hill & Wang, 1978.
Wings (first broadcast on National Public Radio, 1978; produced in New York City at the New York Shakespeare Festival, 1978), Hill & Wang, 1978.
Good Help Is Hard to Find (first produced in New York City, 1981), French, 1982.
(Author of book) *Nine* (music and lyrics by Maury Yeston; based on Mario Fratti's adaptation of Federico Fellini's film "8 1/2"; first produced in Waterford, 1981, produced in New York City, 1982), French, 1983.
Ghosts (based on a play by Henrik Ibsen; first produced in New York City, 1982), French, 1984.
End of the World (first produced in New York City, 1984, produced as "The Assignment" in Southampton, England, 1985), Hill & Wang, 1984.
"Bone-the-Fish," produced in Louisville, Ky., 1989.
"Discovery of America," produced in Los Angeles, Calif., c. 1989.

OTHER

Also author of teleplay "The Questioning of Nick," 1959, and "Promontory Point Revisited," a segment of "Foul," on the New York Television Theatre, 1969. Contributor to *Harvard Advocate.*

SIDELIGHTS: After writing several successful plays while still a student at Harvard University, Kopit gained public attention and critical acclaim with "Oh Dad, Poor Dad, Mama's Hung You in the Closet and I'm Feelin' So Sad." Commenting on Kopit's view of life, George Wellwarth cited a passage of dialogue from the play: "Life is a lie, my sweet. Not words but Life itself. Life in all its ugliness. It builds green trees that tease your eyes and draw you under them. Then when you're there in the shade and you breathe in and say, 'Oh God, how beautiful,' that's when the bird on the branch lets go his droppings and hits you on the head. Life, my sweet, beware. It isn't what it seems. I've seen what it can do." Wellwarth continued: "Like most modern playwrights . . . Kopit has a distinct tendency to view the rotting underside of life from below. . . . There is nothing particularly new about this—Kopit's contribution lies in the wry imagination he brings to his description of life as he sees it."

Unlike many writers who apparently flourish in a cosmopolitan setting, Kopit prefers to write in isolation. "Vermont in the winter . . . any holiday resort in the off season . . . Majorca . . . [in] a huge hotel almost empty" have been among his choices. *Antiquarian Bookman* noted Kopit's response to a particularly productive weekend of writing: " 'The Conquest of Everest' and 'The Hero' were both written in 1964 on a pleasant March weekend. 'The Hero' has no dialogue because I was struck dumb by the prospect of writing two plays in a single day."

A few days after the New York opening of "Indians," Lewis Funke discussed the origin of the play with Kopit. Funke reported, "Such are the quirks of the creative process that if General Westmoreland had not made some remarks about the accidental tragedies of the war in Vietnam, which Arthur Kopit read as he listened to Charles Ives's 'Fourth Symphony,' he might never have written 'Indians.' " "For a long time I had wanted to do a play dealing with the subject. I knew it would have to be epical in scope. But I didn't know how to do it," recalled Kopit. After the experience of reading Westmoreland's remarks and hearing the music, Kopit remembered, "I knew almost instantly that I would write a play that would explore what happens when a social and political power imposes itself on a lesser power and creates a mythology to justify it, as we did with the Indians, as we have tried to do in Vietnam, what others have done elsewhere. And, in the manner of the symphony it would be a kind of mosaic, a counterpoint of memory and reality."

Credited by such critics as Clive Barnes with successfully avoiding the use of "those old linear guidelines of a beginning, a middle, and an end" in favor of a less structured style, Kopit openly appreciates the efforts of other playwrights who try bold, innovative methods. "There's a new vitality returning to [the theatre], which curiously enough hasn't much to do with the writers. I mean activities like Peter Brooke's experiments at the Round House, with a flexible audience. I think flexibility about what the theatre is, that's important," Kopit told Brendan Hennessy.

Kopit seems to be more comfortable writing when he is able to maintain a certain distance between himself and his characters. In his interview with Hennessy, he said he left a novel unfinished to do "Indians" because "the pose is so different. The playwright is at a distance from his characters. I find the narrator's role, getting inside his characters, intimidating." As for directing his own plays, Kopit told Hennessy he prefers to delay the decision and "after seeing one or two productions" perhaps take over the production as he did in Paris with "Oh Dad, Poor Dad."

In answer to Hennessy's questions about his hopes for the future and his ambitions, Kopit replied: "I'd like to write a play a year, I admire those who write a lot: Osborne, Albee, and others. You're less vulnerable to critics that way—no matter how one play is received, you've always got another on the way. In any case, the important plays come by accident. You can't sit down and write an important play."

Ranking among Kopit's most important works is "Wings," an acclaimed Broadway play about an aging former stunt flyer struggling to regain language after she suffers a stroke. In the *New York Times* Richard Eder deemed it "remarkable . . . an intensely moving vision, one of uncanny perception; a voyage of illumination into an area that seems totally dark at first, then begins to yield up patterns." Inspired by Kopit's initial observations of patients at a clinic where his father, also a stroke victim, was treated, the play reveals the woman's disjointed thoughts, dramatizes her inability to communicate with doctors who seem to be speaking gibberish, and rejoices in her words regained. In the *Chicago Tribune,* Linda Winer judged the play "more than a drama about disease. [It] explores the coming together of body-machine and body-spirit. It approaches the weird magic of language, the relationship between actions and what we call them." Calling the play "brilliant," Eder concluded that the character's "battle to speak is the image for what is tongue-tied in all of us."

BIOGRAPHICAL/CRITICAL SOURCES:

BOOKS

Contemporary Authors, Autobiography Series, Volume 3, Gale, 1986.
Contemporary Literary Criticism, Gale, Volume 1, 1973, Volume 18, 1981, Volume 33, 1985.
Dictionary of Literary Biography, Volume 7: *Twentieth-Century American Dramatists,* Gale, 1981.
Wellwarth, George, *Theatre of Protest and Paradox,* New York University Press, 1964.

PERIODICALS

Antiquarian Bookman, March 22, 1965.
Books, June, 1967.
Chicago Tribune, October 21, 1979.
Christian Science Monitor, May 23, 1969, March 16, 1970.
Commonweal, November 7, 1969.
Cue, October 25, 1969.
Detroit Free Press, April 29, 1986.
Evergreen Review, October, 1969.
London Magazine, October, 1968.
Los Angeles Times, May 26, 1984, June 24, 1985.
Nation, November 3, 1969.
National Observer, October 20, 1969.
New Leader, November 24, 1969.
New Republic, November 8, 1969.
Newsweek, November 27, 1969, December 22, 1969, May 28, 1984.
New York, October 27, 1969.
New Yorker, October 18, 1969.
New York Times, July 9, 1968, July 21, 1968, May 18, 1969, October 14, 1969, November 9, 1969, November 15, 1969, November 19, 1969, December 30, 1970, March 8, 1978, June 25, 1978, January 29, 1979, April 15, 1979, May 7, 1984, May 20, 1984.
New York Times Magazine, April 29, 1984.
Observer Review, July 7, 1968.
Prompt, Number 12, 1968.
Punch, July 17, 1968.
Saturday Review, June 7, 1969.
Spectator, July 12, 1968.

Time, March 3, 1967, April 5, 1968, June 6, 1969, October 24, 1969.

Times (London), October 1, 1985.

Transatlantic Review, April, 1968.

Variety, March 7, 1969, May 14, 1969, October 15, 1969, October 22, 1969, April 1, 1970.

Village Voice, March 9, 1967.

Vogue, November 15, 1969.

Washington Post, November 23, 1968, May 11, 1969, October 15, 1969, June 22, 1978, March 29, 1984, April 7, 1984, December 23, 1988.

* * *

KOSINSKI, Jerzy (Nikodem) 1933-
(Joseph Novak)

PERSONAL: Born June 14, 1933, in Lodz, Poland; came to United States in 1957, naturalized in 1965; son of Mieczyslaw (a classicist) and Elzbieta (a concert pianist; maiden name, Liniecka) Kosinski; married Mary Hayward Weir (an art collector), 1962 (died, 1968); married Katherina von Fraunhofer (an advertising executive), 1987. *Education:* University of Lodz, B.A., 1950, M.A. (history), 1953, M.A. (political science), 1955; Ph.D. candidate in sociology at Polish Academy of Sciences, 1955-57, and at Columbia University, 1958-63; graduate study at New School for Social Research, 1962-66.

ADDRESSES: Office—c/o Scientia-Factum, Inc., Hemisphere House, 60 West 57th St., New York, N.Y. 10019.

CAREER: Writer and photographer. Ski instructor in Zakopane, Poland, winters, 1950-56; assistant professor (aspirant) of sociology, Polish Academy of Sciences, Warsaw, 1955-57; researcher at Lomonosov University, Moscow, 1957; on first arriving in the United States, variously employed as a paint scraper on excursion-line boats, a truck driver, chauffeur, and cinema projectionist; resident fellow in English at Center for Advanced Studies, Wesleyan University, 1967-68; visiting lecturer in English and resident senior fellow of the Council of Humanities, Princeton University, 1969-70; professor of English and resident fellow of Davenport College and School of Drama, Yale University, 1970-73; fellow of Timothy Dwight College, Yale University, 1986—. Has also worked as a screen actor, portraying Grigory Zinoviev in "Reds," a Paramount Pictures film produced and directed by Warren Beatty, 1981. Has had one-man photographic exhibitions at the State's Crooked Circle Gallery in Warsaw, 1957, and has exhibited his photographs throughout the world.

MEMBER: P.E.N. (president, 1973-75), International League for Human Rights (director, 1973-79), American Foundation for Polish-Jewish Studies (president, 1987—), Authors League of America, American Federation of Television and Radio Artists, American Civil Liberties Union (chairman of artists and writers committee), Authors Guild, Screen Actors Guild, Century Association.

AWARDS, HONORS: Ford Foundation fellowship, 1958-60; Prix du Meilleur Livre Etranger (France), 1966, for *The Painted Bird;* Guggenheim fellowship in creative writing, 1967-68; National Book Award, 1969, for *Steps;* award in literature from National Institute of Arts and Letters and the American Academy of Arts and Letters, 1970; John Golden fellowship in playwriting from Yale University, 1970-72; Brith Sholom Humanitarian Freedom Award, 1974; First Amendment Award from American Civil Liberties Union, 1978; best screenplay of the

year award from Writers Guild of America, 1979, and from the British Academy of Film and Television Arts, 1981, both for *Being There;* Polonia Media National Achievement Perspectives Award, 1980; Spertus College of Judaica International Award, 1982; Ph.D. from Spertus College, 1982.

WRITINGS:

FICTION

The Painted Bird, abridged edition, Houghton, 1965, complete edition, Modern Library, 1970, complete and revised 10th anniversary edition, with an introduction by the author, Houghton, 1976.

Steps, Random House, 1968.

Being There (also see below), Harcourt, 1971.

The Devil Tree, Harcourt, 1973, revised and expanded edition, St. Martin's, 1981.

Cockpit, Houghton, 1975.

Blind Date, Houghton, 1977.

Passion Play (also see below) St. Martin's, 1979.

Pinball, Bantam, 1982.

The Hermit of Sixty-ninth Street, Henry Holt, 1988.

SCREENPLAYS

Being There (based on his novel of the same title; filmed by Lorimar; released by United Artists, 1979), Scientia-Factum, 1977.

Passion Play (based on his novel of the same title), Recorded Picture Co., 1987.

NONFICTION

(Under pseudonym Joseph Novak) *The Future Is Ours, Comrade: Conversations with the Russians,* Doubleday, 1960.

(Under pseudonym Joseph Novak) *No Third Path: A Study of Collective Behavior,* Doubleday, 1962.

(Editor) *Socjologia Amerykanska: Wybor Prac, 1950-1960* (title means "American Sociology: Translations of Selected Works, 1950-1960"), Polish Institute of Arts and Sciences (New York), 1962.

Notes of the Author on "The Painted Bird," Scientia-Factum, 1965.

The Art of the Self: Essays a propos "Steps," Scientia-Factum, 1968.

Also author of *Dokumenty walki o Czlowieka: Wspomnienia Proletariatczykow* (title means "Documents Concerning the Struggle of Man: The Reminiscences of the Members of 'Proletariat' ") and *Program Rewolucji Jakoba Jaworskiego* (title means "The Program of the People's Revolution of Jakob Jaworski").

Contributor of articles to periodicals, including *Dialectics and Humanism, Esquire, Life, New York,* and *Paris Review.*

WORK IN PROGRESS: Selected Essays, 1958-87; a play, titled *Bruno and I.*

SIDELIGHTS: A controversial novelist, Jerzy Kosinski first stunned the literary world in 1965 with *The Painted Bird*—a graphic account of an abandoned child's odyssey through war-torn Eastern Europe—which some critics consider the best piece of literature to emerge from World War II. Kosinski's second novel, *Steps,* was equally successful and won a National Book Award in 1969. Other novels, all part of an elaborate fictional cycle, followed; though Kosinski labels them fiction, his books parallel his real-life experiences, earning him the reputation of a writer who mingles art and life. In fact, the author termed his 1988 novel, *The Hermit of Sixty-ninth Street,* an "autofiction."

The only child of Jewish intellectuals, Kosinski enjoyed a sheltered childhood until he was six years old. Then Hitler invaded Poland, disrupting the young boy's family and irrevocably altering the shape of his life. As Jews, Kosinski's parents were forced into hiding, and eventually the child was entrusted to a stranger's care. Though he was soon placed with a foster mother, she died within two months of his arrival, and, until the end of the war when he was reunited with his parents, young Kosinski wandered from one remote peasant village to another, living by his wits. By the time he was nine, Kosinski had been so traumatized by his experience that he was struck mute. "Once I regained my speech after the war, the trauma began," he told Barbara Learning of *Penthouse.* "The Stalinist [system in Poland] went after me, asking questions I didn't want to hear, demanding answers I would not give."

When the State refused to grant him and his family permission to emigrate to the West, Kosinski used the deceptive techniques he had mastered as a runaway to plot his escape. He was twenty-four, a doctoral student at the Polish Academy of Sciences in Warsaw, when he undertook an elaborate and dangerous ruse. Inventing four academicians in four different branches of learning, Kosinski contrived to have them sponsor him for a research project in the United States. It took him more than two years to obtain the passport and the necessary travel documents, but by the winter of 1957, he was ready. He arrived in New York City a few days before Christmas—friendless, penniless, and with only a rudimentary knowledge of the spoken American idiom.

Since that time, Jerzy Kosinski has become an American success story. Quickly mastering the language, he enrolled in a Ph.D. program, launched a writing career, and married the rich widow of an American steel baron. A prize-winning photographer, Kosinski is also an amateur athlete and, according to the *New York Times Magazine,* "a polo-playing pet of the jet set." In 1981, he added a screen debut to his list of accomplishments, earning critical praise for his portrayal of the Soviet bureaucrat Grigory Zinoviev in Warren Beatty's film "Reds." Despite the tremendous variety that characterizes both his personal and professional life, Kosinski remains deeply committed to writing: "Fiction is the center of my life," he told Margaria Fichtner in a *Chicago Tribune* interview. "Anything I do revolves around what I write and what I write very often revolves around what I do."

To gather material Kosinski frequently prowls the streets of New York and other cities, sometimes traveling in disguise. "I like to go out at night," he told Ron Base in the *Washington Post.* "I like to see strange things, meet strange people, see people at their most abandoned. I like people who are driven. The sense of who they are is far greater."

Though Kosinski cloaks these experiences under a fictive mask, critics say the autobiographical elements of his writing are unmistakable. "Mostly, in his novels," writes Barbara Gelb in the *New York Times Magazine,* "he describes actual events as a newspaper reporter would, altering details only slightly to fictionalize them." *Detroit News* writer Ben Brown agrees, delineating the following similarities between Kosinski and his characters: "Like the boy wanderer in *The Painted Bird* (1965), Kosinski was an abandoned child, wandering alone through the rural villages of Eastern Europe during World War II. Like the emigrant photographer-social scientist in *Cockpit* (1975), Kosinski, also a photographer-social scientist, escaped from [Poland] by creating a hole in the post-Stalinist bureaucracy through which he could slide to freedom in the West. By view of his marriage . . . Kosinski was surrounded by the kind of vast inherited wealth he gave Jonathan Wahlen in *The Devil Tree* (1973). And

like Fabian in *Passion Play* [1979] . . . Kosinski is an expert horseman [and] an avid polo player." In fact, according to Ron Base, Kosinski "never strays far from his own life in order to discover his novels' protagonists, and given the life he leads, who can blame him? Everything including his past and present seems calculated to yield a novel every three years or so."

But Ross Wetzsteon believes it is not calculation but necessity which motivates Kosinski's pen: "He [was] fated to become a writer in order to survive. To admit his past is real would be to allow it to cripple him; to admit his fiction is autobiographical would be to allow himself to be devastated by the horror of its experiences. 'I am not the person who experienced those horrors,' Kosinski is saying, but rather, 'I am the one who conquered them.' " And Kosinski, writing in *Notes of the Author on "The Painted Bird,"* reinforces this point of view: "We fit experiences into molds which simplify, shape and give them an acceptable emotional clarity. *The remembered event becomes a fiction, a structure made to accomodate certain feelings.* If there were not these structures, art would be too personal for the artist to create, much less for the audience to grasp. *There is no art which is reality; rather, art is the using of symbols by which an otherwise unstateable subjective reality is made manifest.*"

The "subjective reality" that is "made manifest" in Kosinski's fiction is the ability of the individual to survive. "The whole didactic point of my novels is how you redeem yourself if you are pressed or threatened by the chances of daily life, how you see yourself as a romantic character when you are grotesque, a failure," Kosinski told Ben Brown in a *Detroit News* interview. Though the theme is recurrent, Kosinski approaches it differently in each book, as Lawrence Cunningham explains in *America:* "At times, as in *The Painted Bird,* the individual is the victim of society, while in *Cockpit,* a Kafkaesque secret agent named Tarden wages a one-man war against the whole of society and those members of it who epitomize the brutality of that society. In *Being There* . . . the hero of the novel betrays the whole of American society not because of his power or viciousness, but because of his simplicity, naivete and sheer ignorance of how the culture game is played." Notwithstanding these differences, Cunningham believes the novels share the same moral ambivalence: "In Kosinski's . . . universe there is, at the same time, grand moral testimony to the worth of the individual and a curious shrinking from the common bonds of trusting humanity. . . . Kosinski is a survivor. If his experience has not permitted him to teach us much about human relationships, it has been, nonetheless, a vade mecum [or manual] of making it in this very tough world."

And what makes this "alien world" of Kosinski's so frightening, according to Elizabeth Stone, is the sharp chill of recognition it causes the reader to feel. "In the lives of Kosinski's characters, there is something of ourselves," she writes in *Psychology Today.* "Kosinski's novels pierce the social skin and go deeper. They are all accounts of the self in extreme psychological peril, and they make sense the way dreams make sense. Whatever they say to the rational mind—about police states, political prisoners, and social evil—to the anarchic primitive troubled sleeper in all of us, the novels recreate the aura of nightmare paranoia, rouse fears of psychic petrification, depersonalization, engulfment. . . . His characters chronicle not only what, at its worst, the world is like, but also what, at *our* worst, it feels like. His thematic preoccupations are the dangerous deceitfulness of appearances: isolation, loneliness, anxiety, and violence in a Hobbesian world. . . . And what each novel probes is: given an infinitude of dangers—many of them dangers of our own perceptions—by what strategies can we survive?"

Not surprisingly, the survival techniques his characters employ are similar to tactics Kosinski himself has used. One, according to Stone, is giving voice to experience—as Kosinski does in his writing, and as the nameless protagonist of *The Painted Bird* does when he regains his speech. Another, Stone continues, is by cultivating invisibility and turning it into an advantage—which Kosinski does when he travels in disguise and which Levanter of *Blind Date* does when he rapes a girl from behind, thus preventing her from identifying him. Though Kosinski has said repeatedly that he has never seen himself as a victim, critics maintain that his characters—and even Kosinski himself—are obsessed with revenge. While he prefers to view revenge as a "defense rather than an obsession," Kosinski does not disagree. "My characters often defend themselves against entrapments by oppressive societies," he told Barbara Leaming. "I see revenge as the last vestige of the eminently threatened self. When I was a student at the Stalinist university and the party threatened me with prison unless I would reform or openly perform an act of self-criticism and repent, I warned them, 'Don't forget, if I go down, some of you will go with me.' Revenge can be a positive force—the victim's final dignity."

In Kosinski's case, retaliation for the injustices he had suffered under the Communist system came with the publication of his first book, a nonfiction collection of essays, written when he had been a student in the United States for about two years. Described by Barbara Gelb as "a strongly anti-communist tract," *The Future Is Ours, Comrade: Conversations with the Russians* became an instant best seller and was serialized by the *Saturday Evening Post* and *Reader's Digest.* It was the first of two books that Kosinski would write on communism and, like the subsequent *No Third Path: A Study of Collective Behavior,* it was published pseudonymously. Kosinski's reasons for taking a pen name remain unclear. Kosinski told Ron Base, "I didn't think my spoken English was good enough [to publicly defend my sociological methods, my ethics and philosophy, he added in a note to *CA*.] So I published it under the pen name Joseph Novak." But earlier Kosinski had offered *Washington Post Book World* interviewer Daniel J. Cahill a different explanation: "When you're a student you're supposed to read serious books—not publish them. The pen name allowed me to conduct my studies uninterrupted by the controversy that my books triggered among my fellow students and professors. A side benefit of a pen name is that it allows you to recommend your own books, to those who don't know you've written them, as the very best on the subject—without ever feeling immodest."

One of the people who read the first Novak book was Mary Weir, the thirty-one-year-old widow of steel magnate Ernest Weir. More than fifty years her senior, Ernest died leaving his wife a fortune. "In addition to a Park Avenue apartment, there were houses in Hobe Sound and Southampton, a permanently reserved floor at the Ritz in Paris and a large suite at the Connaught in London, as well as a villa in Florence," reports Barbara Gelb. Mary Weir read *The Future Is Ours, Comrade* shortly after a trip she had taken to Russia and agreed so wholeheartedly with Kosinski's observations that she wrote him a fan letter. Kosinski, in a characteristic blending of fact and fiction, recounts the event in his novel *Pinball.* "Long ago," says Domostroy, one of its protagonists and, Kosinski told *CA,* an obvious stand-in for the author, "when I had received enough fan letters to know how similar they all were, I received one unusual one. The writer, a woman, said she knew me only from my work, . . . but her analysis . . . was so acute, as were her perceptions of . . . the undercurrents of my life, that I was flat-out enthralled."

They arranged a meeting, but Mary, knowing that Kosinski had envisioned her as a frail, elderly widow, impersonated her own secretary to put him at ease. Himself a master of disguise, Kosinski was charmed when he discovered her trick, and the couple was married in 1962. In the Cahill interview, Kosinski described their life together and how it enhanced his art: "During my marriage, I had often thought that it was Stendhal or F. Scott Fitzgerald, both preoccupied with wealth they did not have, who deserved to have had my experience. I wanted to start writing fiction and, frankly, was tempted to begin with a novel that . . . would utilize my immediate experience, the dimension of wealth, power and high society that surrounded me, not the poverty I had seen and experienced so shortly before. But during my marriage I was too much a part of Mary's world to extract from it the nucleus of what I saw, of what I felt. And as a writer, I perceived fiction as the art of imaginative extraction. So instead, I decided to write my first novel *The Painted Bird* about a homeless boy in the war-torn Eastern Europe, an existence I've known but also one that was shared by millions of Europeans, yet was foreign to Mary and our American friends. The novel was my gift to Mary, and to her world."

Although the book initiated Kosinski's career as a novelist, it came at a time of personal tragedy. Mary died of an incurable illness in 1968. "In a curious way," writes Ron Base, "her death provided him with the ultimate freedom. Now he could draw on all the possibilities of his life without worrying about embarrassing wives and children." Though he did pursue these themes in a number of later books, his next novel is similar in setting and theme to *The Painted Bird.* "The protagonist-narrator of *Steps* is alternately the dark-complected boy of Kosinski's first novel . . . and that same boy as an adult," observes William Plummer in the *Village Voice.* A series of seemingly unconnected and often brutal episodes, the book, according to Stanley Kauffmann in the *New Republic,* "is a piercing view of [Kosinski's] past as part of the world's present. For me, the title does not signify progress from one place to another or from one state to another, but simply action about experience: steps taken to accommodate experience and continuing reality to the possibility of remaining alive. . . . The book says finally: 'Hell. Horror. Lust. Cruelty. Ego. Buy *my* hell and horror and lust and cruelty and ego. Life is—just possibly—worth living if we can imagine it better and imagine it worse.' "

Steps won a National Book Award in 1969; however, since that time Kosinski thinks the attitude of the publishing world toward literature has changed. "Today that book would not win," he told Carol Lawson in a 1979 interview for the *New York Times Book Review.* "There is a heavy sentimental climate in the book community in New York." His assessment appears to have been correct: When, as an experiment, a young reporter retyped *Steps* and submitted it under a different name, he found that it went unrecognized and rejected by every major publishing house—including the one that had originally printed it. Undaunted, Kosinski reworked the incident and included it in his 1982 novel, *Pinball.*

Even at the time it was published, *Steps* aroused controversy. While critics generally agree that the book is beautifully written, several, including Geoffrey Wolff writing in *New Leader,* question its morality: "Kosinski's power and talent are not in doubt. I can think of few writers who are able to so persuasively describe an event, set a scene, communicate an emotion. Nonetheless, the use he has set his power to is in doubt. His purpose is serious, I am sure, but he misreads our tolerance. He has created what never was on land or sea and arrogantly expects us to take his creations, his self-consuming octopus, his other monsters, as emblems." Echoing this sentiment, Robert Alter writes in the *New York Times Book Review* that *Steps* "is scarcely a novel at all but rather a series of discontinuous erotic jottings, sometimes brutal, generally deficient in feeling, and finally repetitious." According to *New York Times* reviewer Christopher Lehmann-Haupt, the problem is not just what Kosinski writes, but how he writes it: "Lacking a sense of the language, and thus lacking any style of his own, the author gropes for any passable cliche. It is just what happens in bad pornography."

Kosinski bridles at such comparisons. "Pornography views sex as physical, not spiritual," he told Barbara Leaming. "It does to sex what totalitarianism does to politics: it reduces it to a single dimension. But for me, as for all my fictional characters, sex is a spiritual force, a core of their being, indeed, the procreative basis for self-definition." Those critics who find his heavy doses of sex and violence gratuitous don't understand what he's trying to do, Kosinski maintains. "I am astonished again and again at how superficially people read books," he told Ben Brown of the *Detroit News.* "I know what I write. I know why I do it the way that I do it. There's no greater sense of responsibility than (my own). But I have a certain vision of literature I will not sacrifice for sentimental critics brought up on *Fiddler on the Roof.*"

Among those critics who do appreciate Kosinski's writing is Arnost Lustig, who writes in the *Washington Post Book World* that "Kosinski develops his own style and technique, trying to avoid the classical plot and trying not to get lost in a limitless and chaotic jungle without beginning, middle and end. His style is in harmony with his need to express new things about our life and the world we do live in, to express the inexpressible. Sometimes his way of writing and the structure of [*Blind Date*] reminds one of a steam engine where energy grows to the point where it either explodes or moves forward. Accumulating stories of different, sometimes ambiguous meaning, giving to himself as well as to the reader the same chance for interpretation, he traces the truth in the deepest corners of our outdoor and indoor lives, of our outer appearance and our inner reality."

A perfectionist about his work, Kosinski writes slowly and re-writes extensively, averaging three to four years per book. For example, he rewrote *Passion Play,* his 1979 novel, almost a dozen times and then further altered it in three different sets of galleys and two page-proofs, where he condensed the text by one-third. Above his ten percent publisher's allowance, Kosinski must bear the cost of such corrections. He does not, however, complain. "When I face the galley-proofs I feel as though my whole life was at stake on every page and that a messy paragraph could mess up my whole life from now on," he told Daniel J. Cahill. "As I have no children, no family, no relatives, no business or estate to speak of, my books are my only *spiritual* accomplishment, my life's most private frame of reference, and I would gladly pay all I earn to make it my best."

To that end Kosinski has regularly and, he told *CA,* "openly" employed free-lance editors to help him review his manuscripts. The types of alterations his assistants make (collating corrections, checking galleys against retyped manuscripts, and watching for the inadvertent repetition of an action or a word) are purely mechanical activities in Kosinski's opinion. But Geoffrey Stokes and Eliot Fremont-Smith of the *Village Voice* disagree, charging in the June 22, 1982 issue that "Kosinski's ethics and his very role as author have been seriously challenged." While the *Village Voice* allegations cover a broad spectrum, ranging from complaints that Kosinski lied about his past to charges that his first two books were actually written and financed by the Central Intelligence Agency, the most serious accusations con-

cern Kosinski's unacknowledged dependence on his assistants. Fremont-Smith and Stokes allege that Kosinski not only wrote *The Painted Bird* in Polish and had it secretly translated into English but, in his later novels, depended upon his free-lance editors for "the sort of *composition* that we usually call writing."

As proof, the reporters offer the testimony of several free lancers formerly in Kosinski's part-time employ, including John Hackett, now professor of English at the University of Texas, Barbara Mackey, now assistant director at the Denver Arts Center, and Richard Hayes, a former professor of drama at New York University and the University of California, Berkeley. While none of these people see themselves as Kosinski's "collaborators," both Hackett, who worked on *Cockpit,* and Hayes, who assisted with a draft of *Passion Play,* insist they were more than "mere" proofreaders, the former noting that he helped with the manuscript, the latter saying that he "invested [Kosinski's] language with a certain Latinate style." However, when Mackey, the assistant who worked on the 1973 edition of *The Devil Tree,* was contacted by the *Washington Post Book World* for a follow-up story, she insisted, "I did *nothing* but editing," and went on to criticize what she calls the *Village Voice*'s "shoddy journalism." Furthermore, she continued, Stokes asked her "leading questions" and assured her that their discussion was off the record and that he would get back to her about permission to use her name.

A number of Kosinski's publishing house editors have also come to his defense. In a *Publishers Weekly* article, Les Pockell, the editor of *Passion Play* and *The Devil Tree,* says that the charges are "totally ludicrous. It's clear no one in the article is asserting that he or she wrote the book." Because Kosinski is "obsessive" about his writing, Pockell continues, "he retained people to copy edit. It's always a situation of submitting recommendations to an author to approve or not approve, and the recommendations are always a reaction to the author's material." And Pockell told the *Los Angeles Times Calendar* that he felt Stokes and Fremont-Smith "played upon the ignorance of the general public about the conventions of publishing" and added that "to turn Kosinski's working methods into something sinister makes one wonder about their motives."

In a letter to the *Village Voice,* Austen Olney, editor in chief of Houghton Mifflin, says: "I have been marginally involved with the three Kosinski novels published by Houghton Mifflin and can attest to the fact that he is a difficult and demanding author who makes endless (and to my way of thinking often niggling) corrections in proof. I have been sometimes overwhelmed by his flamboyant conceits and his artful social manipulations, but I have never had any reason to believe that he has ever needed or used any but the most routine editorial assistance. The remarkable consistency of tone in all his novels seems to me sufficient evidence that they all come from his hands alone."

But perhaps the strongest reaction to the *Village Voice* charges comes from Kosinski himself. While affirming the reporters' first amendment right to print the piece, Kosinski told the *Washington Post Book World* that "there is not a single factual thing in that article." Furthermore, he informed the *Village Voice* reporters: "Not a single comma, not a single word is not mine—and not the mere presence of the word but the reasons why as well. This goes for manuscript, middle drafts, final draft, and every f——ing galley—first page proofs, second and third, hardcover editions and paperback editions." Nonetheless, the controversy has taken its toll. Comparing himself to an injured victim, Kosinski told the *Washington Post Book World,* "Like any other assassination, the damage has been done."

In the aftermath of the controversy the *New York Times* published a 6,000-word feature article by John Corry, examining the origin as well as the nature of the various charges made against the author. "Jerzy Kosinski," he writes, "has become a man defined by rumors. . . . His works are being discredited by rumors because his life is being discredited by rumors. That he is a writer is almost incidental. He is an intellectual, a creative person, under ideological attack. The ideology was born in Eastern Europe, and so were the most damaging rumors. They have been around for seventeen years, only now they have grown more insistent."

Despite the shadow that Stokes and Fremont-Smith have cast on his writing career, Kosinski's acting debut remains an unqualified success. Critics were delighted by Kosinski's portrayal of the Soviet bureaucrat Grigory Zinoviev in "Reds." Observes the *Time* magazine critic: "As [journalist John] Reed's Soviet nemesis, novelist Jerzy Kosinski acquits himself nicely—a tundra of ice against Reed's all-American fire." *Newsweek* compliments Kosinski's "delightfully abrasive" performance, comparing him to "an officious terrier gnawing on the bone of Marxist-Leninist dogma."

In a London *Times* interview, Kosinski explains how Warren Beatty, who not only directed but also starred in the film as John Reed, elicited the performance: "[Beatty] hired as extras for members of Zinoviev's committee recent Soviet emigres who had moved to Spain. They hadn't learnt foreign languages yet. They spoke only Russian. Being Soviet, they didn't like me because I was a Pole and I've lived in America for 25 years. They thought I was a very bad actor. And they regard Zinoviev in the blind way of Soviet propaganda as a Jewish cosmopolitan who, although he helped Lenin to power, was executed by Stalin in the 1930s purges, probably justly. [In such an atmosphere] I was thrown back on my Soviet past; I felt frightened and disillusioned. And Warren Beatty/John Reed would come in with his naivete and his sweet American smile telling me, as Reed, that he wanted to see his wife and, as Beatty, about the problems he was having with the film. And I, both as Zinoviev and as Kosinski, sat there saying: What do you know of the troubles of life? What do you know of authentic pain and grief and anguish. . . . The hostility transferred itself to my acting."

Ironically, Kosinski's initial reaction to Beatty's invitation was to turn the offer down. "But then," Kosinski told *CA,* "Barry Diller, the head of Paramount called me and asked me about my decision. He said, 'You used to be known to seek new exploits, and to go after a new experience so you'll have something to write about. You have never played in a movie. Why don't you want to do it?' I mumbled something about being uncertain about portraying someone else—without creative control, which as a novelist I retain in my own work. Then Barry said, 'Well, think again. As an actor you can certainly afford to turn such a chance down. But should you—as a novelist?' I reflected. 'Tell Warren I'll be on the set tomorrow,' I said, mentally already packing my bags."

MEDIA ADAPTATIONS: Kosinski recorded "Selected Readings from *The Painted Bird*" for CMS Records in 1967. Scenes from *Steps* were performed on the television show "Critique" in 1969.

AVOCATIONAL INTERESTS: Yoga, horseback riding (polo and jump), skiing, swimming, photography.

BIOGRAPHICAL/CRITICAL SOURCES:

BOOKS

Aldridge, John Watson, editor, *The Devil in the Fire: Retrospective Essays on American Literature and Culture, 1951-71,* Harper's Magazine Press, 1972.
Bellamy, Joe D., editor, *The New Fiction: Interviews with Innovative American Writers,* University of Illinois Press, 1974.
Cahill, Daniel, *The Fiction of Jerzy Kosinski,* Iowa State University Press, 1982.
Contemporary Literary Criticism, Gale, Volume I, 1973, Volume II, 1974, Volume III, 1975, Volume VI, 1976, Volume X, 1979, Volume XV, 1980, Volume LIII, 1989.
Dictionary of Literary Biography, Gale, Volume 2: *American Novelists since World War II,* 1978, Yearbook: 1982, 1983.
Haydn, Hiram, *Facts and Faces,* Harcourt, 1974.
Hicks, Jack, *In the Singer's Temple: The Romance of Terror and Jerzy Kosinski,* University of North Carolina Press, 1981.
Karl, Frederick R., *American Fictions, 1940-1980,* Harper, 1983.
Klinkowitz, Jerome, *Literary Disruptions: The Making of a Post-Contemporary American Fiction,* University of Illinois Press, 1975.
Kosinski, Jerzy, *Notes of the Author on "The Painted Bird,"* Scientia-Factum, 1965.
Langer, Lawrence L., *Holocaust and the Literary Imagination,* Yale University Press, 1975.
Lavers, Norman, *Jerry Kosinski,* G. K. Hall, 1982.
Plimpton, George, editor, *Writers at Work: The "Paris Review" Interviews,* Volume V, Penguin, 1981.
Sherwin, Byron L., *Jerzy Kosinski: Literary Alarmclock,* Cabala Press, 1982.
Tiefenthaler, Sepp, *Jerzy Kosinski,* Bouvier Publishers (Bonn), 1980.

PERIODICALS

America, November 11, 1978.
American Photographer, June, 1980, February, 1981.
Centennial Review, winter, 1972.
Chicago Review, summer, 1980.
Chicago Tribune, January 19, 1980.
Christian Science Monitor, March 1, 1979.
Commentary, June, 1966.
Commonweal, July 1, 1966.
Critique, Volume XXII, number 2, 1981.
Denver Post, February 11, 1973, September 7, 1979.
Denver Quarterly, autumn, 1969, spring, 1971, winter, 1973.
Detroit News, October 7, 1979.
Fiction International, fall, 1973.
Globe and Mail (Toronto), August 20, 1988.
Guardian, June 25, 1973.
Harper's, October, 1965, March, 1969.
Listener, May 8, 1969.
Los Angeles Times, November 14, 1984.
Los Angeles Times Calendar Magazine, April 22, 1973, August 1, 1982.
Manchester Guardian, October 21, 1960.
Media and Methods, April, 1975.
Nation, November 29, 1965.
National Review, February 8, 1966.
New Horizon, November 8, 1987.
New Leader, October 7, 1968.
New Republic, October 26, 1968, June 26, 1971.
New Statesman, October 22, 1960.
Newsweek, April 26, 1971, February 19, 1973, September 10, 1979, December 7, 1981.

New York Post, August 21, 1969, February 19, 1973.

New York Review of Books, February 27, 1969.

New York Times, December 12, 1966, September 13, 1979, December 23, 1979, February 25, 1982, November 7, 1982, November 18, 1982.

New York Times Book Review, May 22, 1960, October 31, 1965, October 20, 1968, February 11, 1973, August 10, 1975, October 21, 1979, July 3, 1988.

New York Times Magazine, February 21, 1982.

North American Review, spring, 1973, March, 1980.

Paris Review, summer, 1972.

Penthouse, July, 1982.

People, September 10, 1979.

Philadelphia Inquirer, February 18, 1973, February 21, 1982.

Polo, December, 1979, May, 1985.

Przeglad Polski (New York), June 18, 1987.

Psychology Today, December, 1977.

Publishers Weekly, April 26, 1971, July 9, 1982.

Rolling Stone, April, 1979.

San Francisco Review of Books, March, 1978.

Saturday Review, November 13, 1965, April 17, 1971, April 24, 1971, March 11, 1972.

Sun-Times (Chicago), July 25, 1982, August 15, 1982, November 28, 1982.

Third Press Review, September/October, 1975.

Time, October 18, 1968, April 26, 1971, October 31, 1977, June 26, 1978, February 19, 1979, September 17, 1979, December 7, 1981.

Times (London), March 10, 1982.

Times Literary Supplement, May 19, 1966.

U.S. News and World Report, January 8, 1979.

Village Voice, August 11, 1975, October 31, 1977, June 22, 1982, July 6, 1982, August 10, 1982.

Washington Post, August 30, 1971, March 25, 1973, November 27, 1977, September 16, 1979, February 4, 1980, February 21, 1982, April 5, 1989.

Washington Post Book World, November 27, 1977, September 16, 1979, February 21, 1982, July 11, 1982, July 10, 1988.

*   *   *

KRANTZ, Judith   1927-

PERSONAL: Born January 9, 1927, in New York, N.Y.; daughter of Jack D. (an advertising executive) and Mary (an attorney; maiden name, Braeger) Tarcher; married Stephen Krantz (an independent film producer and author); children: Nicholas, Anthony. *Education:* Wellesley College, B.A., 1948.

ADDRESSES: Home—Beverly Hills, Calif. *Agent*—Morton Janklow, 598 Madison Ave., New York, N.Y. 10022. *Office*—c/o Stephen Krantz Productions, Inc., 9601 Wilshire Blvd., Suite 343 Beverly Hills, Calif. 90210.

CAREER: Novelist. Fashion publicist in Paris, France, 1948-49; *Good Housekeeping,* New York City, fashion editor, 1949-56; contributing writer, *McCall's,* 1956-59, and *Ladies Home Journal,* 1959-71; contributing West Coast editor, *Cosmopolitan,* 1971-79.

WRITINGS:

NOVELS

Scruples, Crown, 1978.

Princess Daisy, Crown, 1980.

Mistral's Daughter (Doubleday Book Club selection; Literary Guild dual selection), Crown, 1982.

I'll Take Manhattan, Crown, 1986.

Till We Meet Again, Crown, 1988.

Dazzle, Crown, 1991.

SIDELIGHTS: "I'm living proof that you can never do anything until you try," Judith Krantz has maintained on numerous occasions since the publication of her first novel, *Scruples.* Before she achieved such phenomenal success as an author, Krantz worked as a fashion editor for *Good Housekeeping,* then became a freelance journalist after the birth of her eldest son. It wasn't until a number of years later, at the age of fifty-one, that she published *Scruples,* her first work of fiction since her college days. Cynthia Gorney notes in an interview with Krantz published in the *Washington Post:* "There had been one short-story writing class, in her sophomore year at Wellesley, but the professor gave her a B, so she dumped fiction writing." According to Gorney, Krantz "understood herself to be a journalist" during her years as a freelancer. "Journalists have notebooks," Krantz explains. "Journalists have tape recorders. I thought if I tried to do something from my imagination, there wasn't anything there. I didn't realize I had an imagination until I wrote *Scruples.*"

Krantz was encouraged to try writing fiction by her husband, independent film producer and author Stephen Krantz, who for years remarked that his wife had such an exceptional talent for description and a real eye for detail that she had to be a natural-born novelist. Krantz agrees with his assessment, stating in the *Washington Post:* "I'm a stickler for detail. I don't know if anybody doing the so-called commercial fiction researches as thoroughly as I do. I try to create characters who are a little bit larger than life."

After her youngest son graduated from high school, Krantz began working on a novel, writing six-and-a-half hours a day, five days a week. After nine months *Scruples* was completed. "I truly enjoy writing," the author revealed to Jill Gerston of the *Philadelphia Inquirer.* "If I didn't, I could never close myself in my room for almost a year." Krantz then asked family friend and lawyer Morton L. Janklow to read the manuscript. Janklow says he knew immediately that *Scruples* was destined to be a bestseller, and he agreed to serve as Krantz's literary agent. Although *Scruples* was at first rejected by an editor at Simon & Schuster, Crown Publishers eventually purchased the hardcover rights and released it in March of 1978. Four months later the novel became the number one bestseller, according to the *New York Times,* and remained on its bestseller list for almost one year.

Because *Scruples* sold more than 220,000 copies in hardcover and more than three million in paperback, there was much interest in Krantz's second novel, *Princess Daisy.* In September, 1979, six months before the hardcover edition was scheduled to appear in bookstores, Bantam Books purchased the paperback rights to *Princess Daisy* for an advance of $3,208,875, which was then the highest price ever paid for the reprint rights to a work of fiction. The sale ended what the *New York Times* describes as "a fourteen and a half hour auction that involved eight of the nine leading paperback [publishing] houses."

The purchase of reprint rights to *Princess Daisy* for such a huge sum triggered discussions concerning the high fees paid to successful authors for their work. According to Tony Chiu in the *New York Times,* "the sale [of Princess Daisy] renewed criticism among some publishing executives of the growing practice of investing in 'blockbuster' properties to the possible detriment of less commercial authors." Chiu goes on to state that one publishing executive "estimated the sum Bantam paid for the Krantz book could have obtained the reprint rights to sixty books not in the blockbuster category."

Replying to these objections, Marc Jaffe, then president and publisher of Bantam Books, stated according to *Publishers Weekly* that this point of view is "an accountant's, not an editor's way of looking at publishing. Bantam is in the business of publishing all across the spectrum of reader interest—books for young readers, reference works, translations, general nonfiction, novels of all kinds. We are also in the blockbuster business. We hope to continue to acquire blockbusters we're excited about at whatever the cost. We will also continue to acquire all the other kinds of books we publish."

Furthermore, Jaffe explains to Tom Zito of the *Washington Post, Princess Daisy* is the type of book that can really help publishing instead of injuring it: "This is a book that will pull people into the bookstores. There's nothing like a big best seller to pull the industry along." And Krantz's former editor at Crown, Larry Freundlich, states in the *New York Times* that "it's intellectual purblindness to think that if you give one author three million, you're taking it from someone else. That amount of money should not be considered anything other than investment capital—no publisher will pay it unless he is more than reasonably certain that it can be earned back. Judy Krantz writes subtly about love, and pointedly about merchandising. She's a remarkably good novelist speaking to the center of America's venal interest."

Krantz's ability to "pull people into the bookstores" amazes people in the publishing industry and disturbs many of her outspoken critics. Her "ability to tap a readership" (in the words of a *New York Times* writer) has led many to compare her to the late Jacqueline Susann, author of such books as *Valley of the Dolls, Once Is Not Enough,* and *The Love Machine.* Grace Glueck writes in the *New York Times Book Review* that "philosophically, Mrs. Krantz is an absolutist of the Susann persuasion. A painting is a masterpiece, or nothing; a woman is a beauty, or nobody; sex has to be the sun and the moon and the stars."

Krantz's interest in and talent for promoting her books has also been compared to Susann's. "She's very wise in the ways of publicity, just as Jacqueline Susann was," observes Kay Sexton, a vice-president of B. Dalton Bookseller, in *New York Times Magazine.* And in the same article, Howard Kaminsky, editor-in-chief of Warner Books (the paperback publisher of *Scruples*), remarks, "Both as promoters and novelists, Jackie and Judy are in the same tradition."

In order to publicize her first novel, Krantz spearheaded an extensive, $50,000 promotional campaign that included touring the country from coast-to-coast autographing copies of her novel at bookstores and appearing on television and radio talk shows. "It turned out that I was a natural on television," Krantz says in an interview with Claudia Dreyfus for *Newsday's LI* magazine. "I discovered that I had a quality that communicates itself on camera. Eventually, there came a time with *Scruples* when, instead of [our] running after publicity, it came to us." Krantz has given the promotion of her other novels the same dedication.

After the publication of *Mistral's Daughter,* Krantz told Penny Perrick of the *London Times* that she realizes her novels are not Pulitzer Prize material. "If [they] were, I'd think something terrible had happened. I know perfectly well that I'm not a literary writer, I just write the way it comes naturally. For lack of another word it is storytelling." On this same theme Krantz explains to Pat Nation of the *Los Angeles Times:* "I'm a storyteller. . . . If I can't be a Doris Lessing or Iris Murdoch, it doesn't depress me. What I do is entertainment and I do it as well as I can." Larry Freundlich, Krantz's former editor, remarks in the *New York Times Magazine:* "Judy's writing has the same at-

traction as *People* magazine. You learn about the lives of men and women. She answers all the burning questions you never dared ask. . . . It would make Judy's work grotesque to burden it with attempts at profundity and truth. She doesn't vulgarize her story by trying to make subtle points that don't exist." Krantz explains further in the *Chicago Tribune:* "If you deal in the world of glamour, and that's my turf . . . then you're not taken seriously as a writer, and everyone focuses on how much money you make. But I want to make something very plain—I'm not complaining. Because I chose my turf, and you can't complain when you get a little flack and you knew to expect it. It may hurt a little . . . but you can't complain. You can't have it both ways." As Helen Gurley Brown, a long-time friend of Krantz's and editor of *Cosmopolitan* magazine, observes in the *New York Times Magazine:* "So many people act as if it's easy to write like Judy; as if they could do it, too, if only they would denigrate themselves. They're insane with jealousy! The most difficult thing in the world is to make things simple enough, and enticing enough, to cause readers to turn the page."

MEDIA ADAPTATIONS: Scruples was produced as a three-part, six-hour television miniseries on CBS-TV in February, 1980; *Princess Daisy* was produced as a two-part, four-hour television miniseries on NBC-TV in November, 1983; *Mistral's Daughter* aired on CBS-TV in September, 1984.

BIOGRAPHICAL/CRITICAL SOURCES:

PERIODICALS

Booklist, April 1, 1980.
Chicago Sun Times, February 25, 1980.
Chicago Tribune, March 9, 1980.
Detroit Free Press, November 6, 1983.
Detroit News, September 30, 1979, February 10, 1980, November 6, 1983.
LI, July 6, 1980.
Library Journal, March 1, 1978, February 15, 1980, November 15, 1982.
London Times, May 13, 1983.
Los Angeles Times, May 19, 1978, September 25, 1979, November 26, 1982, July 13, 1988, August 11, 1988.
Newsweek, February 18, 1980.
New Yorker, October 13, 1980.
New York Post, March 3, 1978.
New York Times, September 14, 1979, January 30, 1980, March 2, 1980, December 8, 1982, September 24, 1984, May 1, 1986, May 2, 1986.
New York Times Book Review, March 19, 1978, March 2, 1980, January 2, 1983.
New York Times Magazine, March 2, 1980.
People, June 26, 1978, October 1, 1979, October 18, 1982, December 13, 1982.
Philadelphia Inquirer, May 19, 1980.
Publishers Weekly, January 16, 1978, September 24, 1979, January 11, 1980, July 17, 1981, October 15, 1982, May 16, 1986.
Time, February 18, 1980.
Village Voice, February 18, 1980.
Washington Post, March 3, 1978, September 14, 1979, February 26, 1980, August 3, 1988.
Washington Post Book World, January 27, 1980.

*   *   *

KROETSCH, Robert 1927-

PERSONAL: Born June 26, 1927, in Heisler, Alberta, Canada; son of Paul (a farmer) and Hilda (Weller) Kroetsch; married

Mary Jane Lewis, January 13, 1956; children: Laura Caroline, Margaret Ann. *Education:* University of Alberta, B A., 1948; McGill University, graduate study, 1954-55; Middlebury College, M.A., 1956; University of Iowa, Ph.D., 1961.

ADDRESSES: Home—5-634, Kenaston Blvd., Winnipeg, Manitoba, Canada. *Agent*— Raines & Raines, 475 Fifth Ave., New York, N.Y. 10017. *Office*—Department of English, University of Manitoba, Winnipeg, Manitoba, Canada R3T 2N2.

CAREER: Yellowknife Transportation Co. (riverboats), Northwest Tertitories, Canada, laborer and purser, 1948-50; U.S. Air Force, Goose Bay, Labrador, civilian information and education specialist, 1951-54; State University of New York at Binghamton, assistant professor, 1961-65, associate professor, 1965-68, professor of English, 1968-78; University of Manitoba, Winnipeg, professor of English, 1978—.

MEMBER: Modern Language Association of America, American Association of University Professors.

AWARDS, HONORS: Fellowship to Bread Loaf Writers' Conference, 1966; Governor General's Award for fiction, 1969.

WRITINGS:

NOVELS

But We Are Exiles, St. Martin's, 1966.
The Words of My Roaring, St. Martin's, 1966.
The Studhorse Man, Simon & Schuster, 1970.
Gone Indian, New Press, 1973.
Badlands, New Press, 1975.
What the Crow Said, General Publishing, 1978.
Alibi, Beaufort Books, 1983.

POEMS

The Stone Hammer Poems, 1960-1975, Oolichan Books, 1975.
Seed Catalogue: Poems, Turnstone Press, 1978.
The Ledger, Brick/Nairn, 1979.
The Sad Phoenician, Coach House Press, 1979.
The Criminal Intensities of Love as Paradise, Oolichan Books, 1981.
Field Notes, General Publishing, 1981.
Advice to My Friends: A Continuing Poem, Stoddart, 1985.
Excerpts from the Real World: A Prose Poem in Ten Parts, Oolichan Books, 1986.

OTHER

Alberta: Description and Travel, St. Martin's, 1959.
(With James Bacque and Pierre Gravel) *Creation,* New Press, 1970.
(Author of introduction) Glen Sorestad, *Prairie Pub Poems,* Thistledown, 1976.
(Editor) *Sundog: Stories From Saskatchewan,* Coteau Books, 1980.
The Crow Journals, NeWest Press, 1980.
(Author of preface) Eli Mandel, *Dreaming Backwards,* General Publishing, 1981.
(Editor) Daphne Marlatt, *How Hug a Stone,* Turnstone, 1983.
Letters to Salonika, Grand Union Press, 1983.
(Editor with Smaro Kamboureli) Douglas Barbour, *Visible Visions: The Selected Poetry of Douglas Barbour,* NeWest Press, 1984.
(Editor with Reingard M. Nischik) *Gaining Ground: European Critics on Canadian Literature,* NeWest Press, 1985.
The Lovely Treachery of Words: Essays Selected and New, Oxford University Press, 1989.

Contributor to *Montrealer, Maclean's, Globe and Mail, Books in Canada, Canadian Literature,* and other publications.

SIDELIGHTS: "I'm interested in sharing with the reader the fact that I'm making a fiction," Canadian novelist and poet Robert Kroetsch told Geoff Hancock in an interview for *Canadian Fiction Magazine.* Abandoning what he calls "the old style realism," Kroetsch has adopted an approach that pulls the reader into the fiction-making process. Connie Harvey writing in *Essays on Canadian Writing* explains, "Kroetsch wants to force the reader into a direct perceptual approach to the material so that he, as well as the narrator, creates the work."

According to Harvey, Kroetsch's use of language helps create a "voice" that allows for this direct perceptual experience. "With gerunds and participles, verbals that operate as nouns, and adjectives, Kroetsch is able to list the details of a scene without interrupting the flow of action, thereby creating an immediate experience for the reader's perception," Harvey says. In thus engaging the reader, notes Louis MacKendrick in *Essays on Canadian Writing,* Kroetsch hopes to overcome "the tyranny of language." He breaks free of "the word's received meaning and absolutes into a contemporary world of fresh usage" by "demythologizing, deconstructing, unnaming, uncreating, or uninventing," MacKendrick says.

In an *Essays on Canadian Writing* interview, Kroetsch justifies this novel approach by pointing out that "creation and destruction go hand in hand." But, he continues, "my destruction takes the form of trying to make an old story work, for instance having almost to destroy the old story to tell it anew." According to Kroetsch, the old stories, instead of illuminating the world, sometimes stop people from seeing it. "It's like a pair of glasses that don't quite fit anymore," he explains later in that interview. To improve vision, Kroetsch has said he wants to "uninvent" a mythology and to set another one in its place.

The theme of Kroetsch's first novel *But We Are Exiles* is drawn from the ancient myth of Narcissus. (Son of a river-god, Narcissus was a vain creature who loved only himself. When the wood-nymph Echo fell in love with him, he scorned her, and, as punishment for his vanity Nemesis, goddess of law and justice, caused him to fall in love with his own reflection seen in a pool. Narcissus gazed at his image until he wasted away.) In Kroetsch's story, protagonist Peter Guy pilots a work boat up Canada's MacKenzie River in search of the drowned body of the boat owner, Mike Hornyak. Accompanying him is Kettle Fraser, Hornyak's wife and Guy's former lover. Writing in *Canadian Literature,* Peter Thomas says that in loving both Hornyak and Guy, Fraser recognizes the two faces of Narcissus. The faceless condition in which Guy finds Hornyak's body is a revelation of his own emptiness, according to Thomas who writes that Guy "joins with the image he has tried to reject" when he climbs into the barge which holds the corpse. It is the myth of Narcissus, concludes Thomas now writing in *Essays on Canadian Writing,* which "provides the main structural symbolism in the relations of Peter Guy/Mike Hornyak, two faces of self-love embracing at the conclusion, and their Echo Kettle Fraser."

The Studhorse Man, described by Kroetsch as the *Odyssey* retold on dry land, is another example of an old tale that has been infused with new life. Narrated by Demeter Proudfoot, a lunatic who spends much of his time in an asylum bathtub, the story is an account of how the last of the studhorse men, Hazard Lepage, takes a perfect virgin stallion (named Poseidon) across Alberta in search of a perfect mare. Lepage's fiance, Martha Proudfoot, remains at home. By the book's end, the horse has trampled Lepage to death and Demeter has gone mad under the strain of knowing Lepage and trying to tell his story. Martha, however, survives. "The book's pattern is circular, as is Hazard's journey," observes *New York Times* book reviewer Paul West, "and the point—made in a manner that fuses prairie tall-tale with Odyssean myth—is that perfectionists procrastinate and thus waste their lives while life in general goes muddling on around them."

Despite the unhappy fate of its main character, *The Studhorse Man* is "flanked by bouts of farce," according to West. Writing in *Canadian Literature,* critic Peter Thomas describes the work as a "complex and essentially comic confabulation" and thinks this "tale told by an idiot" is an assault on realism: "The myths of Demeter and Poseidon . . . are fragmented and distorted schemes of reference in *The Studhorse Man.* Their order is mocked as it is realized." And yet, *Essays on Canadian Writing*'s MacKendrick observes, in this as in his other novels, "Kroetsch's unrestraint is more idea than performance, for he retains all the virtues of story and storytelling while imitating their conventions and parodying their devices. . . . In his hands, the possibilities and improbabilities of [this technique] have an exciting life."

MEDIA ADAPTATIONS: The Words of My Roaring was adapted for the stage and first produced in Calgary at Theatre Calgary in 1980; *The Studhorse Man* was adapted for the stage and first produced in Toronto at Theatre Passe Muraille in 1981.

BIOGRAPHICAL/CRITICAL SOURCES:

BOOKS

Contemporary Literary Criticism, Volume 5, Gale, 1976.
Dictionary of Literary Biography, Gale, Volume 53: *Canadian Writers Since 1960,* 1986.
Lecker, Robert, *Robert Kroetsch,* Twayne, 1986.
Neuman, Shirley and Robert R. Wilson, *Labyrinths of Voice: Conversations With Robert Kroetsch,* NeWest Press, 1982.
Thomas, Peter, *Robert Kroetsch,* Douglas & McIntyre, 1980.

PERIODICALS

Books in Canada, October, 1983.
Canadian Fiction Magazine, spring/summer, 1977.
Canadian Forum, October-November, 1978, June-July, 1981.
Canadian Literature, summer, 1974.
Essays on Canadian Writing, fall, 1977, summer, 1978, summer/fall, 1980.
Journal of Canadian Fiction, summer, 1972.
New York Times Book Review, April 26, 1970.
Open Letter, spring, 1983, summer/fall, 1984.
Red Cedar Review, spring, 1985.
University of Windsor Review, spring, 1972.

*   *   *

KRUTZCH, Gus
    See ELIOT, T(homas) S(tearns)

*   *   *

KUENG, Hans 1928-

PERSONAL: Born March 19, 1928, in Sursee, Lucerne, Switzerland; son of Hans (a merchant) and Emma (Gut) Kueng. *Education:* Pontifical Gregorian University, Rome, Licentiate in philosophy, 1951, Licentiate in theology, 1955; Institut Catholique, Sorbonne, University of Paris, Dr.theol., 1957; also studied in Berlin, London, Amsterdam, and Madrid.

ADDRESSES: Home—Waldhaeuserstrasse 23, D-74 Tuebingen, West Germany. *Office*—Institute for Ecumenical Research, University of Tuebingen, Tuebingen, West Germany.

CAREER: Ordained Roman Catholic priest, 1954; performed pastoral work at St. Leodegar, Lucerne, Switzerland, 1957-59; University of Muenster, Muenster, West Germany, assistant in dogmatic theology, 1959-60; University of Tuebingen, Tuebingen, West Germany, ordinary (full) professor of dogmatic theology, 1960-63, ordinary professor of dogmatic and ecumenical theology, 1963-80 (removed and censored by the Vatican), ordinary professor of ecumenical theology, 1980—, director of Institute for Ecumenical Research, 1963—. Peritus (official theological consultant) at Second Vatican Council, appointed by Pope John XXIII, 1962. Lecturer at numerous universities in Europe, America, Asia, and Australia; visiting professor at Union Theological Seminary, New York, 1968, University of Basel, 1969, University of Chicago Divinity School, 1981, and University of Michigan, 1983; Terry lecturer at Yale University, 1978.

MEMBER: Arbeitsgemeinschaft Deutschspachige Dogmatiker.

AWARDS, HONORS: LL.D., University of St. Louis, 1963; D.D., Pacific School of Religion, 1966, and University of Glasglow, 1971; HH.D., Loyola University of Chicago, 1970; Ludwig Thoma Medal, 1975.

WRITINGS:

Rechtfertigung: Die Lehre Karl Barths und eine katholische Besinnung (doctoral thesis; with letter by Karl Barth), Johannes Verlag, 1957, 4th enlarged edition, 1964, translation by Thomas Collins, Edmund E. Tolk, and David Granskou published as *Justification: The Doctrine of Karl Barth and a Catholic Reflection,* Thomas Nelson, 1964.

Konzil und Wiedervereinigung: Erneuerung als Ruf in die Einheit, Herder, 1960, translation by Cecily Hastings published as *The Council and Reunion,* Sheed (London), 1961, published as *The Council, Reform, and Reunion,* Sheed (New York), 1962, new edition, Doubleday, 1965.

Damit die Welt glaube: Briefe an junge Menschen, Pfeiffer, 1962, 5th edition, 1968, translation by Hastings published as *That the World May Believe,* Sheed (New York), 1963 (published in England as *That the World May Believe: Letters to Young People,* Sheed [London], 1963).

Strukturen der Kirche, Herder, 1962, translation by Salvator Attanasio published as *Structures of the Church,* preface by Cardinal Richard Cushing, Thomas Nelson, 1964.

Kirche im Konzil, Herder, 1963, 2nd edition, 1964, translation by Hastings published as *The Council in Action: Theological Reflections on the Second Vatican Council,* Sheed (New York), 1963 (translation by Hastings and N. D. Smith published in England as *The Living Church,* Sheed [London], 1963, translation by Hastings, William Glen-Doepel, and H. R. Bronk published in England as *The Changing Church,* 1965).

Freiheit in der Welt: Sir Thomas More, Benziger, 1964, translation by Hastings published as *Freedom in the World: Sir Thomas More,* Sheed, 1965 (also see below).

Theologe und Kirche, Benziger, 1964, translation by Hastings published as *The Theologian and the Church,* Sheed, 1965 (also see below).

Kirche in Freiheit, Benziger, 1964, translation by Hastings published as *The Church and Freedom,* Sheed, 1965 (also see below).

Christenheit als Minderheit: Die Kirche unter den Weltreligionen, Benziger, 1965 (also see below).

Freedom Today (includes *Freedom in the World: Sir Thomas More, The Theologian and the Church, The Church and Freedom,* and a translation of *Christenheit als Minderheit: Die Kirche unter den Weltreligionen*), translation by Hastings, Sheed, 1966, original German edition published as *Freiheit des Christen,* Buchclub Ex Libris (Zurich), 1971.

Gott und das Leid, Benziger, 1967.

Die Kirche, Herder, 1967, translation by Ray and Rosaleen Ockenden published as *The Church,* Sheed, 1967, abridged German edition published as *Was ist Kirche?,* Herder, 1970.

Wahrhaftigkeit: Zur Zukunft der Kirche, Herder, 1968, translation by Edward Quinn published as *Truthfulness: The Future of the Church,* Sheed, 1968.

Menschwerdung Gottes: Eine Einfuehrung in Hegels theologisches Denken als Prolegomena zu einer kuenftigen Christologie, Herder, 1970.

Unfehlbar? Eine Anfrage, Benziger, 1970, translation by Quinn published as *Infallible? An Inquiry,* Doubleday, 1971 (translation by Eric Mosbacher published in England as *Infallible? An Enquiry,* Collins, 1971).

Wozu Priester? Ein Hilfa, Benziger, 1971, translation by Robert C. Collins published as *Why Priests? A Proposal for a New Church Ministry,* Doubleday, 1972 (translation by John Cumming published in England as *Why Priests?,* Collins, 1972).

Fehlbar? Eine Bilanz, Benziger, 1973.

Was in der Kirche bleiben muss, Benziger, 1973, translation published as *What Must Remain in the Church,* Collins, 1977.

Christ sein?, Piper, 1974, published as *Die christliche Herausforderung,* 1980, translation by Quinn published as *On Being a Christian,* Doubleday, 1976, abridged translation published as *The Christian Challenge: A Shortened Version of "On Being a Christian,"* 1979.

Zwanzig Thesen zum Christsein, Piper, 1975 (also see below).

(With Pinchas Lapide) *Jesus im Widerstreit: Ein juedisch-christlicher Dialog,* Calwer Verlag (Stuttgart) and Koesel (Munich), 1976 (also see below), translation by Quinn published as *Brother or Lord? A Jew and a Christian Talk Together about Jesus,* Fount Paperbacks, 1977.

Was ist Firmung?, Benziger, 1976 (also see below).

Gottesdienst, warum?, Benziger, 1976.

Heute noch an Gott glauben?, Piper, 1977.

Existiert Gott? Antwort auf die Gottesfrage der Neuzeit, Piper, 1978, translation by Quinn published as *Does God Exist? An Answer for Today* (Book-of-the-Month Club alternate selection), Doubleday, 1980.

Signposts for the Future (collection of fourteen articles originally published separately in German; includes translations of *Zwanzig Thesen zum Christsein, Was ist Firmung?,* and *Jesus im Widerstreit: Ein juedisch-christlicher Dialog*), Doubleday, 1978.

Freud and the Problem of God (Terry lectures; originally published in *Existiert Gott?*), translation by Quinn, Yale University Press, 1979.

Kirche—gehalten in der Wahrheit?, Benziger, 1979, translation by Quinn published as *The Church—Maintained in Truth? A Theological Meditation,* Seabury, 1980.

Vierundzwanzigste Thesen zur Gottesfrage, Piper, 1979.

(With Edward Schillebeeckx, David Tracey, and others) *Consensus in Theology? A Dialogue with Hans Kueng, Edward Schillebeeckx,* edited by Leonard Swidler, Westminster Press, 1980.

Kunst und Sinnfrage, Benziger, 1980, translation by Quinn published as *Art and the Question of Meaning,* Crossroad, 1981.

Wegzeichen in die Zukunft: Programmatisches fuer eine christlichere Kirche, Rowohlt, 1980.

Ewiges Leben?, Piper, 1982, translation by Edward Quinn published as *Eternal Life? Life After Death as a Medical, Philosophical, and Theological Problem,* Doubleday, 1984.

(With others) *Christentum und Weltreligionen: Hinfuehrung zum Dialog mit Islam, Hinduismus und Buddhismus,* Piper, 1984, translation by Peter Heinegg published as *Christianity and the World Religions: Paths of Dialogue With Islam, Hinduism, and Buddhism,* Doubleday, 1986.

(With David Tracy) *Theologie, wohin? Auf dem Weg zu einem neuen Paradigma,* Benziger, 1984.

(With Walter Jens) *Dichtung und Religion: Pascal, Gryphius, Lessing, Hoelderlin, Novalis, Kierkegaard, Dostojewski, Kafka,* Kindler, 1985.

(With Norbert Greinacher) *Katholische kirche, wohin? Wider den Verrat am Konzil,* Piper, 1986.

(With others) *Theologie und Literatur: Zum Strand des Dialogs,* Kindler, 1986.

Church and Change: The Irish Experience, Macmillan, 1986.

Theologie im Aufbruch: Eine okumenische Grundlegung, Piper, 1987.

The Incarnation of God: An Introduction to Hegel's Theological Thought as a Prolegomena to a Future Christology, translation by J. R. Stephenson of original German manuscript *Menschwerdung Gottes,* Crossword, 1987.

Why I am Still a Christian, edited by E. C. Huges, translation by David Smith and others of original German manuscript *Woran man sich halten kann,* Abingdon Press, 1987.

EDITOR

(With Yves Congar and Daniel O'Hanlon) *Konzilsreden,* Benziger, 1964, translation published as *Council Speeches of Vatican II,* Paulist Press, 1964.

The Church and Ecumenism, Paulist Press, 1965.

Do We Know the Others?, Paulist Press, 1966.

The Sacraments: An Ecumenical Dilemma, Paulist Press, 1967.

(And author of introduction and contributor) *Apostolic Succession: Rethinking a Barrier to Unity,* Paulist Press, 1968.

The Future of Ecumenism, Paulist/Newman, 1969.

Post-Ecumenical Christianity, Herder, 1970.

Papal Ministry in the Church, Herder, 1971 (published in England as *The Petrine Ministry in the Church,* Burns & Oates, 1971).

The Plurality of Ministries, Herder, 1972.

(With Walter Kasper) *Polarization in the Church,* Seabury, 1973.

Fehlbar? Eine Bilanz, Benziger, 1973.

(With Kasper) *Christians and Jews,* Seabury, 1974.

(With David Tracy and Johann B. Metz) *Toward Vatican III: The Work That Needs to Be Done,* Seabury, 1978.

(With Moltmann) *Why Did God Make Me?,* Seabury, 1978.

(With Moltmann) *An Ecumenical Confession of Faith?,* Seabury, 1979.

(With Moltmann) *Conflicts about the Holy Spirit,* Seabury, 1979.

(With Moltmann) *Conflicting Ways of Interpreting the Bible,* Seabury, 1980.

(With Moltmann) *Who Has the Say in the Church?,* Seabury, 1981.

(With Moltmann) *The Right to Dissent,* Seabury, 1982.

(With Moltmann) *Mary in the Churches,* Seabury, 1983.

(With Moltmann) *Christianity Among World Religions,* T. & T. Clark, 1986.

(With Leonard Swidler) *The Church in Anguish: Has the Vatican Betrayed Vatican II?,* Harper, 1987.

Also editor of "Theological Meditations" and "Concilium" series; co-editor of "Oekumenische Forschungan" ("Ecumenical Investigations") series, Herder, 1967—.

EDITOR AND AUTHOR OF PREFACE

Karl Rahner, *Belief Today,* Sheed, 1967.
The Unknown God? (translation of volumes by Joseph Moeller, Herbert Haag, and Gotthold Hasenhuettl originally published separately in German), Sheed, 1967.
Life in the Spirit (translation of volumes by Karl H. Schelkle, Thomas A. Sartory, and Michael Pfliegler originally published separately in German), Sheed, 1968.

CONTRIBUTOR

Maxmilian Roesle and Oscar Cullman, editors, *Begegnung der Christen: Festschrift O. Karrer,* Evangelisches Verlagswerk (Stuttgart), 1959, translation edited by D. J. Callahan, Heiko A. Oberman, and O'Hanlon published as *Christianity Divided: Protestant and Catholic Theological Issues,* Sheed, 1961.
Joseph Ratzinger and Heinrich Fries, editors, *Einsicht und Glaube: Festschrift G. Soehngen,* Herder, 1962.
Looking Toward the Council: An Inquiry among Christians, Herder, 1962.
John Courtney Murray, editor, *Freedom and Man,* Kenedy, 1965.
Walter Scheel, *Mut zu kritischer Sympathie,* Piper, 1977.

Also contributor to *Lexikon fuer Theologie und Kirche II, Handbuch theologischer Grundbegriffe,* and *Theologisches Jahrbuch.*

OTHER

Contributor of more than four hundred articles to periodicals in Germany, Switzerland, the Netherlands, England, and the United States, including *Cross Currents, Sign, Catholic Digest, Sunday Visitor, New York Times, Commonweal, Christian Century,* and *Critic.* Co-editor of *Tuebingen Theologische Quartalschrift,* 1960-64, and *Revue Internationale de Theologie Concilium,* 1965—; associate editor of *Journal of Ecumenical Studies,* 1964—.

AVOCATIONAL INTERESTS: Classical music, water sports, skiing.

BIOGRAPHICAL/CRITICAL SOURCES:

BOOKS

Duggan, G. H., *Hans Kueng and Reunion,* Newman Press, 1964.
Eingel, U. and Walter Jens, *Um nichts als die Wahrheit,* Piper, 1978.
Greinacher, N. and H. Haag, *Der Fall Kueng,* Piper, 1980.
Haering, Hermann and J. Nolte, *Diskussion um Hans Kueng "Die Kirche,"* Freiburg-Basel-Wien, 1971.
Haering, Hermann and Karl-Joseph Kuschel, *Hans Kueng: His Work and His Way,* translation by Robert Nowell, Fount Paperbacks, 1979.
Nowell, Robert, *A Passion for Truth—Hans Kueng: A Biography,* Collins, 1981.
Robinson, Donald, *The One Hundred Most Important People in the World Today,* Putnam, 1970.
Swidler, Leonard, *Kueng in Conflict,* Doubleday, 1981.

PERIODICALS

America, October 19, 1963, May 22, 1965, April 20, 1968, November 20, 1976, September 22, 1979, July 19-26, 1980.
Best Sellers, April 15, 1971, July 1, 1972, April, 1977, July, 1978, September, 1979.

Christian Century, September 1, 1965, June 1, 1966, September 11, 1968, May 19, 1971, March 2, 1977, November 24, 1978, September 24, 1980.
Commonweal, July 5, 1963, August 7, 1964, February 5, 1965, May 6, 1966, February 28, 1969, April 9, 1971, August 25, 1972, May 23, 1975, December 3, 1976, March 4, 1977, June 24, 1977, March 3, 1978, February 29, 1980, May 9, 1980, November 7, 1980.
Critic, October, 1963, December, 1964-January, 1965, April, 1965, June, 1966, June, 1968, December, 1968, July, 1971, spring, 1977, October, 1979, October, 1980, November, 1980.
Detroit Free Press, September 25, 1983.
Economist, January 22, 1977.
Los Angeles Times, November 14, 1980.
Los Angeles Times Book Review, January 4, 1987, July 29, 1987.
National Review, May 3, 1966.
New Republic, May 15, 1971, July 21, 1979, July 28, 1979, November 8, 1980.
New Statesman, January 16, 1981.
Newsweek, January 25, 1971, July 16, 1973, December 6, 1976.
New Yorker, February 7, 1977.
New York Review of Books, August 22, 1968, February 7, 1980.
New York Times, June 11, 1967, February 8, 1980.
New York Times Book Review, October 27, 1963, March 7, 1965, May 5, 1968, April 4, 1971, September 17, 1972, December 19, 1976, July 22, 1979, January 11, 1981, April 19, 1981, May 6, 1984.
New York Times Magazine, October 12, 1975.
Observer, January 16, 1977.
Publishers Weekly, September 26, 1980.
Saturday Review, June 9, 1962, December 21, 1963, March 29, 1969, April 10, 1971.
Spectator, January 22, 1977.
Time, July 8, 1962, September 20, 1963, February 23, 1968, July 16, 1973, March 3, 1975, January 3, 1977.
Times (London), January 8, 1987.
Times Literary Supplement, October 21, 1965, August 1, 1968, November 21, 1980, September 25, 1987.
Washington Post Book World, November 28, 1976.

*   *   *

KUMIN, Maxine (Winokur) 1925-

PERSONAL: Born June 6, 1925, in Philadelphia, Pa.; daughter of Peter and Doll (Simon) Winokur; married Victor Montwid Kumin (an engineering consultant), June 29, 1946; children: Jane Simon, Judith Montwid, Daniel David. *Education:* Radcliffe College, A.B., 1946, A.M., 1948.

ADDRESSES: Home—Joppa Rd., Warner, N.H. O3278. *Agent*—Emilie Jacobson, Curtis Brown Ltd., 1O Astor Place, New York, N.Y. 10003.

CAREER: Poet, children's author, and fiction writer. Tufts University, Medford, Mass., instructor, 1958-61, lecturer in English, 1965-68; Radcliffe College, Cambridge, Mass., scholar of Radcliffe Institute for Independent Study, 1961-63; University of Massachusetts-Amherst, visiting lecturer in English, 1973; Columbia University, New York, N.Y., adjunct professor of writing, 1975; Brandeis University, Waltham, Mass., Fannie Hurst Professor of Literature, 1975; Princeton University, Princeton, N.J., visiting senior fellow and lecturer, 1977; Washington University, St. Louis, Mo., Fannie Hurst Professor of Literature, 1977; Randolph-Macon Woman's College, Lynchburg, Va., Carolyn Wilkerson Bell Visiting Scholar, 1978; Woodrow Wilson Visiting Fellow, 1979; Princeton University, visiting lecturer, 1979 and 1981-82; Bucknell University, Lewisburg, Pa., poet in residence, 1983; Massachusetts Institute of Technology, Cambridge, Mass., visiting professor, 1984; Atlantic Center for the Arts, New Smyrna Beach, Fla., master artist, 1984. Member of staff, Bread Loaf Writers' Conference, 1969-71, 1973, 1975, and 1977. Traveled with the U.S. Information Agency's Arts America Tour, 1983. Poetry consultant to Library of Congress, 1981-82.

MEMBER: Poetry Society of America, Radcliffe Alumnae Association.

AWARDS, HONORS: Lowell Mason Palmer Award, 1960; National Endowment for the Arts grant, 1966; National Council on the Arts and Humanities fellow, 1967-68; William Marion Reedy Award, 1968; Eunice Tietjens Memorial Prize, Poetry, 1972; Pulitzer Prize for poetry, 1973, for *Up Country: Poems of New England;* Borestone Mountain Award, 1976; Radcliffe College Alumnae Recognition Award, 1978; American Academy and Institute of Arts and Letters award, 1980, for excellence in literature; Academy of American Poets fellowship, 1986. D.Hum.Lett., Centre College, 1976, Davis and Elkins College, 1977, Regis College, 1979, New England College, 1982, Claremont Graduate School, 1983, and University of New Hampshire, 1984.

WRITINGS:

POETRY

Halfway, Holt, 1961.
The Privilege, Harper, 1965.
The Nightmare Factory, Harper, 1970.
Up Country: Poems of New England, with drawings by Barbara Swan, Harper, 1972.
House, Bridge, Fountain, Gate, Viking, 1975.
The Retrieval System, Viking, 1978.
Our Ground Time Here Will Be Brief: New and Selected Poems, Viking, 1982.
Closing the Ring: Selected Poems, The Press of Appletree Alley, Bucknell University, 1984.
The Long Approach, Viking, 1985.
Nurture, Penguin, 1989.

NOVELS

Through Dooms of Love, Harper, 1965 (published in England as *A Daughter and Her Loves,* Gollancz, 1965).
The Passions of Uxport, Harper, 1968.
The Abduction, Harper, 1971.
The Designated Heir, Viking, 1974.

JUVENILE

Sebastian and the Dragon, Putnam, 1960.
Spring Things, Putnam, 1961.
A Summer Story, Putnam, 1961.
Follow the Fall, Putnam, 1961.
A Winter Friend, Putnam, 1961.
Mittens in May, Putnam, 1962.
No One Writes a Letter to the Snail, Putnam, 1962.
(With Anne Sexton) *Eggs of Things,* Putnam, 1963.
Archibald the Traveling Poodle, Putnam, 1963.
(With Sexton) *More Eggs of Things,* Putnam, 1964.
Speedy Digs Downside Up, Putnam, 1964.
The Beach before Breakfast, Putnam, 1964.
Paul Bunyan, Putnam, 1966.
Faraway Farm, Norton, 1967.
The Wonderful Babies of 1809 and Other Years, Putnam, 1968.

When Grandmother Was Young, Putnam, 1969.
When Mother Was Young, Putnam, 1970.
When Great-Grandmother Was Young, illustrated by Don Almquist, Putnam, 1971.
(With Sexton) *Joey and the Birthday Present,* illustrated by Evaline Ness, McGraw, 1971.
(With Sexton) *The Wizard's Tears,* McGraw, 1975.
What Color Is Caesar?, illustrated by Ness, McGraw, 1978.
The Microscope, illustrated by Arnold Lobel, Harper, 1984.

SHORT STORIES

Why Can't We Live Together Like Civilized Human Beings?, Viking, 1982.

ESSAYS

To Make a Prairie: Essays on Poets, Poetry, and Country Living, University of Michigan Press, 1980.
In Deep: Country Essays, Viking, 1987.

OTHER

Contributor to *Anne Sexton: The Artist and Her Critics,* edited by J. D. McClatchy, Indiana University Press, 1987. Former columnist, *Writer.* Contributor of poetry to *New Yorker, Atlantic, Poetry, Saturday Review,* and other periodicals.

SIDELIGHTS: "Besides the poetry by which she is best known, [Maxine] Kumin writes charming children's books and good readable fiction," Alicia Ostriker reports in the *New York Times Book Review.* Kumin's novels have been widely praised, but her poetry has brought her many honors, including a 1973 Pulitzer Prize for *Up Country: Poems of New England.* A former poetry consultant for the Library of Congress, Kumin has also been a staff member of the Bread Loaf Writers' Conference. Tim Clark reports in *Yankee* magazine that when she's not giving readings, the popular guest lecturer "tends her horses, shovels manure, weeds her garden, and celebrate[s] small, ordinary things" on her farm in Warner, New Hampshire. In an interview with Joan Norris published in *Crazy Horse,* Kumin discloses, "Practically all of [my poems] have come out of this geography and this state of mind.

"I'm usually described as a pastoral, or a New England poet. I have been twitted with the epithet 'Roberta Frost,' which is not a bad thing to be," Kumin told interviewer Karla Hammond in the *Western Humanities Review.* Critics have also called Kumin a transcendentalist like Thoreau, and a confessional poet like her friend the late Anne Sexton. But *New York Times* reviewer Michiko Kakutani finds her most like Galway Kinnell, since both are "concerned with human mortality, with the love shared between parents and their children, with the seasonal patterns of nature and the possibility of retrieving and preserving the past." In many ways, critics also point out, Kumin is not like other poets. "In a period when most contemporary poetry reflects a chaotic and meaningless universe, Kumin is one of a handful of poets who insist upon order," Susan Ludvigson elaborates in the *Dictionary of Literary Biography.* Whatever her link to other poets may be, Philip Booth maintains that "what is remarkable . . . is the extent to which poets like Maxine Kumin can survive and outdistance both their peers and themselves by increasingly trusting those elements of their work which are most strongly individual." For Kumin, as he notes in the *American Poetry Review,* these elements include "the dailiness of farm life and farm death."

Because her "well-made poems and stories are two ways of coming at the same immemorial preoccupations: aging and mortality," a contributor to *Nation* deems Kumin's work "the fiction and poetry of maturity." The works are also mature in the sense that Kumin did not begin to write and publish until mid-life, though she had shown the inclination to write poetry much earlier. During high school, she wrote "very bad late adolescent romantic poetry," she told Clark. And later, as a freshman at Radcliffe, Kumin presented a sheaf of poems to the instructor for his comments. Kumin told Norris, "He had written on the front: 'Say it with flowers, but for God's sake don't try to write poems.' That just closed me off. I didn't try to write another poem for about six years." By that time she had become the wife of an engineer, the mother of three children, a resident of a Boston suburb, and, as she told Clark, "acutely miserable." When Kumin began writing again as a kind of therapy, she at last found encouragement in workshops at the Boston Center for Adult Education.

Poems she worked on during this time recollect her childhood in a home on a hill "between a convent and a madhouse." In these poems, writes Ludvigson, Kumin displays "an early mastery of technique" and "deals skillfully with subjects that she continues to explore throughout her career: religious and cultural identity, the fragility of human life, loss and the everpresent threat of loss, the relation of man to nature." Many of them are collected in Kumin's first book of poems, *Halfway,* which came out in 1961 when the poet was thirty-six.

Another outcome of the workshops was Kumin's friendship with Anne Sexton. Both homemakers with children when they began their literary careers, they wrote four children's books together, and in general contributed to each other's development. "Maxine, a Radcliffe graduate, possessed a technical expertise and an analytical detachment that balanced Anne's mercurial brilliance," explain Linda Gray Sexton and Lois Ames, the editors of *Anne Sexton: A Self-Portrait in Letters.* The two poets "often communicated daily, by letter if separated by oceans, otherwise by telephone. They supervised each other's poetry and prose, 'workshopping' line by line for hours." Consequently, critics have tried to trace a strong mutual influence, but both poets have denied one; Ludvigson notes, "In a 1974 interview in *Women's Studies,* each claimed she never tampered with the other's voice, and each offered, according to Sexton, 'to think how to shape, how to make better, but not, how to make like me.'" Nonetheless, there were some significant exchanges. As Kumin relates in her chapter of *Anne Sexton: The Artist and Her Critics,* Sexton had written several poems based on fairy tales which later became part of her Pulitzer Prize-winner, *Transformations.* Sexton "had no thought of a collection at first," says Kumin. "I urged and bullied her to go on after the first few poems to think in terms of a whole book of them." Kumin also suggested the title. "We had been talking about the way many contemporary poets translated from languages they did not themselves read, but used trots or had the poems filtered through an interpreter, and that these poems were adaptations. It struck me then that Anne's poems about the fairy tales went one step further and were transformations." Sexton had reciprocated by suggesting the title for the book that was to become Kumin's Pulitzer Prize winner. "In that same conversation Annie was urging me to collect the pastoral poems I'd written, and I said, 'but what would I call it?' and she said, '*Up Country,* of course.'"

"It is the tie between Kumin and Sexton that fascinates many readers," Ludvigson notes. The interest peaked when Sexton committed suicide in 1974. "There's a kind of sexual thrill that runs through the public every time a poet does himself in," Kumin told Clark, revealing her anger about the increased attention. "When a poet kills . . . herself, it confirms something very gratifying to the public view: that life is really tough, and these

sensitive flowers can't take it. And the rest of us who stay alive show that we're . . . strong enough to keep going." She also deprecates those who regard Sexton's suicide as the "culmination of her work. What people don't understand is that writing about the topic, when you're depressed, or suicidal, is what keeps you alive."

"Though she is often linked with her friend Anne Sexton, Kumin is not for the most part, a confessional poet," writes Ludvigson. Rather, observes Monroe K. Spears in a *Washington Post Book World Review,* "much of her poetry throughout is openly autobiographical, and the reader becomes acquainted with her family . . ., her Frostian New Hampshire neighbor Henry Manley, . . . and so on." Ostriker remarks that "children, especially daughters, keep cropping up, growing as they go, from Mrs. Kumin's earliest works to her most recent. No poet writes more richly and more subtly of mother-daughter relations." "Loss of the parent, relinquishment of the child" are two central themes Kumin identified in a lecture on her work given at Princeton in 1977, which is reprinted in *To Make a Prairie: Essays on Poets, Poetry and Country Living.* Booth explains the presence of these themes in Kumin's book, *The Retrieval System:* "[Kumin] is familiar (in every sense) with how one's parents depart toward death at nearly the same time one's children leave to find lives of their own. Inevitable as such desertions may be, their coincidence (multiplied by [Sexton's] close-in suicide) is the shock which these seismographic poems record and try to recover from." Booth believes Kumin's poems "amply show that suffering doesn't require confession to validate pain," and that her "mode is memorial rather than confessional."

"Transcendental" is another label sometimes applied to Kumin but often modified; while Kumin's poetry may call up images of Thoreau and "insist on man's affinity with the natural world," Ludvigson notes that it falls short of suggesting the "merging of the self with nature" that transcendentalism requires. Joyce Carol Oates writes in the *New York Times Book Review* that *Up Country* "acknowledges its debt to Thoreau" but provides "a sharp-edged, unflinching and occasionally nightmarish subjectivity exasperatingly absent in Thoreau." "Like Rilke, [Kumin] hates the approximate. A poet of nature, she insists on showing the natural world as it really is, and not as a benign fantasy," Clark maintains. Ludvigson suggests that "her unsentimental relationship with nature . . . allows Kumin to write poems . . . which are ostensibly 'about' the necessary killing of woodchucks and mysterious tracks in the snow, but which chill us with her portrayal of man's capacity for brutality." Brad Crenshaw considers it "a major plus" that Kumin "is not much addicted to transcendental escapes." Rather, as he elaborates in a *Parnassus* review of *Our Ground Time Here Will Be Brief,* "the voice of the poems is that of a strong woman. In an unforgiving environment, Kumin neither flinches at the strenuous physical labors that comprise her usual responsibilities, nor quails before her emotional disappointments. She's mentally tough. Her poetry records how she stands up to the disasters of weather, disease, difficult births and lamentable deaths, and how she's confident she'll remain standing until the very end."

Whereas critics debate Kumin's similarity to Thoreau, they unanimously recognize her similarity to Robert Frost. The works of both poets show a close attention to the details of New England rural life. Kumin told Hammond, "I particularly observe things in nature because they interest me, but don't think of it as observing. What I'm always after is to get the facts: to be true to the actuality." Attention to nature provides Kumin with images well-suited to her themes of loss and survival. Oates explains, "Any group of poems that deal with nature is more or less committed to the honoring of cycles, the birth/death/birth wheel, the phenomenon of creatures giving way to creatures." Booth concurs, "the distinctive nature of Maxine Kumin's present poems derives from the primary fact that she lives in, and writes from, a world where constant (if partial) recovery of what's 'lost' is as sure as the procession of the equinoxes, or as familiar as mucking-out the horses' daily dung."

Kumin's preference for traditional verse forms also likens her to Frost. Not only is there an order "to be discovered . . . in the natural world," she told Martha George Meek in a *Massachusetts Review* interview, "there is also an order that a human can impose on the chaos of his emotions and the chaos of events." Kumin achieves this order by structuring her poetry, controlling the most emotional subjects by fitting them to exacting patterns of syllable count and rhyme. As she told Hammond, "The harder—that is, the more psychically difficult—the poem is to write, the more likely I am to choose a difficult pattern to pound it into. This is true because, paradoxically, the difficulty frees me to be more honest and more direct."

When Kumin finds she has more to say than a poem's structure will accommodate, she approaches her subject again in fiction. "I tend to steal from myself," she said in an interview at Interlochen, Michigan, in 1977, printed in *To Make a Prairie*. "The compass of the poem is so small and so demanding, you have to be so selective, and there are so many things that get left out that you feel cheated. So you take all those things . . . and they get into fiction." Comparing Kumin's work in both genres, *Chicago Tribune Book World* contributor Catherine Petroski comments, "Kumin's practice of poetry buttresses her practice of short fiction: The turns of phrase and points of view come from a poet, not a recorder of events. Similarly, the concerns of fiction—the chains of cause and effect, the explorations of character, the sense of scene—have much to do with the power of Kumin's best poems." Spears sums up, "One of the pleasures of reading Kumin is to see the same experience appear differently in the different forms of poems, stories, and novels."

If there is one experience that Kumin confronts in all her works, it is loss. Kumin talks about her obsession with mortality in the conclusion of a *Country Journal* article in which she reflects on the death of a foal: "A horse-friend from New York state writes me her condolences. She too has lost not one foal, but twin Thoroughbreds. . . . According to some astrological prognosticatory chart, we are both sixes on the scale. Sixes, Mary Beth writes, practice all their lives to die well, 'act as Morticians of All Life and hold private burying rituals in their hearts.' " Accordingly, Kumin believes "very strongly that poetry is essentially elegiac in its nature, and that all poems are in one sense or another elegies"; as she explained to Hammond, "Love poems, particularly, are elegies because if we were not informed with a sense of dying we wouldn't be moved to write love poems."

"Kumin writes as well as ever in her customary modes," Robert B. Shaw says of *The Long Approach*, Kumin's eighth book of poems. Many critics concur with Shaw's assessment, yet they respond with negative criticism to the poems in it that look at world problems such as pollution, religious persecution, nuclear holocaust, and famine. These poems "are aimed resolutely outward," writes *Washington Post Book World* contributor Wendy Lesser, who believes that the "poems on 'issues'. . .founder on their opinion making." Holly Prado, writing in the *Los Angeles Times Book Review*, concurs that the poet "doesn't arrive at her best work until . . . she arrives at her farm in New Hampshire." In this part of the book, Kumin "reverts to what is close, ordinary, . . . [upon] which she can meditate with X-ray gaze,"

Harold Beaver explains in the *New York Times Book Review*. In his analysis of *The Long Approach* in *Poetry* magazine, Shaw suggests, "If Kumin wishes to venture into public terrain, perhaps her voice, which is essentially private, needs to adjust itself to the new and very different demands she is now placing on it. This will no doubt take some time. It can be assumed, at any rate, that a poet of her intelligence stands an even chance of solving the problems involved."

Looking back at Kumin's career so far, Booth comments that the poet "has simply gotten better and better at what she has always been good at: a resonant language, an autobiographical immediacy, unsystematized intelligence, and radical compassion. One does not learn compassion without having suffered." Crenshaw notes that "Americans traditionally have preferred their women poets to be depressed and victimized," but he claims that Kumin's "posture regarding despair" sets her apart from "the sweet innocents who have been driven to insane passions and flamboyant destructions." "In celebrating the past, and her own part in its passing, she celebrates in herself the very capacity to survive," writes Booth, whereas Crenshaw concludes, "It's the existential obligation of mortality that [Kumin] . . . must endure on its own terms. Her poetry is a record of her endurance."

BIOGRAPHICAL CRITICAL SOURCES:

BOOKS

Authors in the News, Volume 2, Gale, 1976.
Contemporary Literary Criticism, Gale, Volume 5, 1976, Volume 13, 1980, Volume 28, 1984.
Dictionary of Literary Biography, Volume 5: *American Poets since World War II,* Gale, 1980.
Kumin, Maxine, *Halfway,* Holt, 1961.
Kumin, Maxine, *To Make a Prairie: Essays on Poets, Poetry, and Country Living,* University of Michigan Press, 1980.
McClatchy, J. D., editor, *Anne Sexton: The Artist and Her Critics,* Indiana University Press, 1978.
Sexton, Linda Gray and Lois Ames, editors, *Anne Sexton: A Self-Portrait in Letters,* Houghton, 1977.

PERIODICALS

America, February 28, 1976.
American Poetry Review, March, 1976, November, 1978.
Atlantic, October, 1971.
Book World, May 5, 1968, October 10, 1971.
Chicago Tribune Book World, August 29, 1982, February 2, 1986.
Choice, January, 1966.
Christian Science Monitor, August 9, 1961, February 28, 1973.
Country Journal, spring, 1979.
Crazy Horse, summer, 1975.
Los Angeles Times Book Review, June 13, 1982, December 1, 1985.
Massachusetts Review, spring, 1975.
Nation, July 24, 1982.
New Leader, January 22, 1973.
New Republic, August 10, 1974.
New Yorker, December 4, 1971.
New York Times, June 26, 1974.
New York Times Book Review, March 28, 1965, May 5, 1968, November 19, 1972, June 23, 1974, September 7, 1975, April 23, 1978, August 8, 1982, March 2, 1986, August 30, 1987, November 5, 1989.
Parnassus, spring/summer, 1973, spring, 1985.
Poetry, January, 1979.
Prairie Schooner, spring, 1976.

Saturday Review, May 6, 1961, December 25, 1965, May 9, 1970, March 25, 1972.
Sewanee Review, spring, 1974.
Shenandoah, spring, 1976.
Times Literary Supplement, May 9, 1975.
Village Voice, September 5, 1974, July 20, 1982.
Virginia Quarterly Review, spring, 1971.
Washington Post, May 6, 1980.
Washington Post Book World, June 22, 1982, February 2, 1986, June 16, 1987.
Western Humanities Review, spring, 1979.
Yale Review, autumn, 1968.
Yankee, December, 1975.

*   *   *

KUNDERA, Milan   1929-

PERSONAL: Born April 1, 1929, in Brno, Czechoslovakia; immigrated to France, 1975, naturalized French citizen, 1981; son of Ludvik (a pianist and musicologist) and Milada (Janosikova) Kundera; married Vera Hrabankova, September 30, 1967. *Education:* Studied music under Paul Haas and Vaclav Kapral; attended Charles University, Prague, and Film Faculty, Academy of Music and Dramatic Arts, Prague, 1956.

ADDRESSES: Home—10 rue Littre, Paris 75006, France. *Office*—Ecole des hautes etudes en sciences sociales, 54 boulevard Raspail, Paris 75006, France.

CAREER: Writer. Worked as a laborer and jazz pianist in provincial Czechoslovakia; Film Faculty, Academy of Music and Dramatic Arts, Prague, Czechoslovakia, assistant professor, 1958-69; Universite de Rennes II, Rennes, France, invited professor of comparative literature, 1975-79; Ecole des hautes etudes en sciences sociales, Paris, France, professor, 1980—.

MEMBER: Czechoslovak Writers Union (member of central committee, 1963-69), American Academy of Arts and Letters.

AWARDS, HONORS: Klement Lukes Prize, 1963, for *Majitele klicu;* Czechoslovak Writers Union prize, 1968, for *Zert;* Czechoslovak Writers' Publishing House prize, 1969, for *Smesne lasky;* Prix Medicis, 1973, for *La Vie est ailleurs;* Premio Letterario Mondello, 1978, for *The Farewell Party;* Common Wealth Award for distinguished service in literature, 1981, for the body of his novelistic work; Prix Europa for literature, 1982, for the body of his novelistic work; honorary doctorate, University of Michigan, 1983; *Los Angeles Times* Book Prize for fiction, 1984, for *The Unbearable Lightness of Being;* Jerusalem Prize for Literature on the Freedom of Man in Society, 1985; finalist for Ritz Paris Hemingway Award, 1985; Prix de le Critique de l'Academie Francaise, Prix Nelly Sachs, and Ostereichischere Staatspreis fuer Europeische Litterateur, all 1987.

WRITINGS:

NOVELS

Zert (also see below), Ceskoslovensky Spisovatel (Czechoslovak Writers Union; Prague), 1967, translation by David Hamblyn and Oliver Stallybrass published as *The Joke,* Coward, 1969, new complete translation by Michael Henry Heim with author's preface published as *The Joke,* Harper, 1982.
Zivot je jinde, Sixty-Eight Publishers (Toronto), 1979, translation from the original Czech manuscript by Francois Kerel first published as *La Vie est ailleurs,* Gallimard (Paris), 1973, translation from the original Czech manuscript by Peter Kussi published as *Life Is Elsewhere,* Knopf, 1974.

Valcik na rozloucenou, Sixty-Eight Publishers, 1979, translation from the original Czech manuscript by Kussi published as *The Farewell Party,* Knopf, 1976.
Kniha smichu a zapomneni, Sixty-Eight Publishers, 1981, translation from the original Czech manuscript by Kerel first published as *Le Livre du rire et de l'oubli,* Gallimard, 1979, translation from the original Czech manuscript by Heim published as *The Book of Laughter and Forgetting,* Knopf, 1980, published with an interview with the author by Philip Roth, Penguin Books, 1981.
The Unbearable Lightness of Being, translation from the original Czech manuscript, *Nesnesitelna lehkost byti,* by Heim, Harper, 1984.

OTHER

Clovek zahrada sira (poetry; title means "Man: A Broad Garden"), Ceskoslovensky Spisovatel, 1953.
Posledni maj (poetry; title means "The Last May"), Ceskoslovensky Spisovatel, 1955, revised edition, 1963.
Monology (poetry; title means "Monologues"), Ceskoslovensky Spisovatel, 1957, revised edition, 1964.
Umeni rontanu (study of writer Vladislav Vancura), Ceskoslovensky Spisovatel, 1960, translation by Linda Asher published as *The Art of the Novel,* Grove, 1988.
Majitele klicu (play; title means "The Owners of the Keys"; first produced in Prague at National Theatre, April, 1962), Orbis, 1962.
Smesne lasky: Tri melancholicke anekdoty (short stories; title means "Laughable Loves: Three Melancholy Anecdotes"; also see below), Ceskoslovensky Spisovatel, 1963.
Druhy sesit smesnych lasek (short stories; title means "The Second Book of Laughable Loves"; also see below), Ceskoslovensky Spisovatel, 1965.
Dve usi dve svatby (play), Dilia (Prague), 1968.
Treti sesit smesnych lasek (short stories; title means "Book of Laughable Loves"; also see below), Ceskoslovensky Spisovatel, 1968.
(With Jaromil Jires) "The Joke" (screenplay; based on Kundera's novel *Zert*), direction by Jires, Smida-Fikar—Studio de Cinema de Barrandov, 1968.
"Ptakovina" (two-act play), first produced in Liberec, Czechoslovakia at Divadlo F. X. Saldy, January, 1969.
Smesne lasky (selection of seven of the short stories previously published in *Smesne tasky: Tri melancholicke anekdoty, Druhy sesit smesnych lasek,* and *Treti sesit smesnych lasek*), Ceskoslovensky Spisovatel, 1970, translation by Suzanne Rappaport with introduction by Roth published as *Laughable Loves,* Knopf, 1974.
Jacques et son maitre: Hommage a Denis Diderot (three-act play; first produced in Paris at Theatre des Maturins, 1981), published with an introduction by the author, Gallimard, 1981, translation by Heim published as *Jacques and His Master* (produced in Cambridge, Mass. at American Repertory Theatre, January, 1985), Harper, 1985, translation by Simon Callow produced as "Jacques and His Master" in Toronto at Free Theatre, May 14, 1986.

Milan Kundera's narrative works have also been translated into German, Dutch, Danish, Norwegian, Swedish, Finnish, Portuguese, Spanish, Italian, Serbian, Slovene, Greek, Turkish, Hebrew, and Japanese. Contributor of essays to *New York Times Book Review.* Member of editorial board of *Literarni noviny,* 1963-67 and 1968, and of *Literarni listy,* 1968-69.

SIDELIGHTS: Milan Kundera, a Czech novelist now living in France, "is one of the finest and most consistently interesting novelists in Europe and America," writes Richard Locke in the *Washington Post Book World.* Writing from experience, Kundera "has brought Eastern Europe to the attention of the Western reading public, and he has done so with insights that are universal in their appeal," notes Olga Carlisle in the *New York Times Magazine.* His novels, according to David Lodge in the *Times Literary Supplement,* "[investigate], with a bold combination of abstraction, sensuality and wit, the problematic interrelationship of sex, love, death and the ultimate mystery of being itself." "Playfully mixing history with philosophy and fantasy," adds Michiko Kakutani in the *New York Times,* "Mr. Kundera creates a world in which routine expectations are undercut, ideals and reason mocked." Kundera's blending of fact and fiction has earned for him international recognition and, for his novels, major awards from France, Italy, Israel, and the United States.

In June 1967, Kundera appeared before the Fourth Czechoslovak Writers Congress to introduce the policy statement of the Writers Union, a document prepared in advance, cleared by the Czechoslovak Communist Party Central Committee, and traditionally approved without significant discussion by the writers. It was a critical time for the Czechoslovak nation. A campaign by some of the writers to speed reform and liberalization of cultural policy together with their criticism of Czechoslovakia's role in the Arab-Israeli conflict had prompted the Party to increase censorship and other repressive tactics. The Union and the Party were heading for a confrontation, and the Congress provided an occasion. Rejecting convention, Kundera opened discussion of the draft statement with "a defence of open criticism and an attack on the repression of it," notes A. French in *Czech Writers and Politics, 1945-1969.* Many who followed spoke freely; immediately following the Congress, the government stepped up repressive measures against the outspoken writers.

By January 1968, however, the reform movement, which had spread into the political arena, emerged into the open. Alexander Dubcek replaced the dictatorial Antonin Novotny as First Secretary of the Party and steps were taken to humanize Czechoslovakia's socialism. Many credited the writers—especially visible were Ludvik Vaculik, Ivan Klima, Kundera, and the Slovak, Ladislav Mnacko—with initiating this progress, and as French points out, "political realists at the center of power recognised their influence and the moral authority they had acquired in the eyes of the public."

Kundera had begun writing his first novel, *Zert* (*The Joke*), in 1962 and had submitted it to a Prague publisher in December 1965. "Though they promised to do their best to bring it out," he writes in the preface to the 1982 edition of *The Joke,* "they never really believed they would succeed. The spirit of the work was diametrically opposed to the official ideology." But Kundera had held firm against the demands of government censors; finally in 1967, the novel was published, unchanged. "Three editions of *The Joke* appeared in quick succession and incredibly large printings, and each sold out in a matter of days," the author explains. During the enlightened Prague Spring of 1968, a time when Czechoslovakia was rediscovering its cultural freedom and writers were held in high esteem, Milan Kundera was one of the major literary figures of the day.

Within four months, however, Czechoslovakia would be invaded by troops from the U.S.S.R., Poland, East Germany, Hungary, and Bulgaria, and the occupation would bring the reform movement to an end. During the next few years, Kundera's books would be removed from libraries and bookstores, his plays banned; he would lose his job and his right to work and publish in Czechoslovakia. At first, he would be forbidden to travel in the West. Finally in 1975, he would be permitted to accept a teaching position in Rennes, France. Four years later, after the publication of *Le Livre du rire et de l'oubli* (*The Book of Laughter and Forgetting*), the Czechoslovak government would revoke his citizenship.

Silenced in Czechoslovakia immediately after the invasion, Kundera became a writer without an audience. He did write two novels that were published in translation abroad, but not until he had settled in France could he feel at home with this new audience. As an artist, Kundera had experimented with music, painting, cinema, and theater, but he found his home in the novel. Today, although he has become one of the West's most respected novelists, in essays and interviews he directs discussion away from himself toward literature; he is an outspoken proponent of the novel. "I often hear it said that the novel has exhausted all its possibilities," he writes in a 1985 essay in the *New York Times Book Review.* "I have the opposite impression: during its 400-year history, the novel has missed many of its possibilities; it has left many great opportunities unexplored, many paths forgotten, calls unheard."

To take advantage of the possibilities offered by the novel, Kundera combines autobiography and fiction, history and fantasy, satire and philosophical discourse. From his reading of Laurence Sterne, Denis Diderot, Franz Kafka, Hermann Broch, and others, the author has formulated his own aesthetic of the novel, an outline of the characteristics that define his work. He offers this outline in a 1982 essay in the *New York Times Book Review:* "The novel [is] an investigation into human existence. A novel makes sense only when it reveals an unknown side to human existence. The novel proclaims no truth, no morality. . . . The novel represents a great intellectual synthesis. . . . The novel is the only form of art capable of moving in time with complete ease."

Structure is another important element in the Kundera novel, and it is often one reviewers discuss. Some believe that because of structure, his novels should be placed in other categories—*The Book of Laughter and Forgetting* as a collection of short stories, for instance. Kundera has little regard for labels: "There is enormous freedom latent within the novelistic form," he tells Philip Roth in the *New York Times Book Review.* "It is a mistake to regard a certain stereotyped structure as the inviolable essence of the novel." He adds that in his view of the novel "the unity of a book need not stem from the plot, but can be provided by the theme."

For a number of practitioners of the novel, plot suggests causality, but for Kundera, as he explains in his aesthetic of the novel, "the novel is composed like a piece of music, . . . on the principle of a theme and variations, the elaboration of a theme. The unity of a novel comes from several basic words, which gradually take on the force of philosophical categories." In order to elaborate a theme, the author must "master the technique of ellipsis, the art of condensation. Otherwise, [he falls] into the trap of endless length," he explains to Christian Salmon in the *Paris Review.* In this way, following the example of modern composers, juxtaposing variations and emphasizing only the essential, Kundera hopes to renew the novel. He suggests in his interview with Salmon that too often the novel "is encumbered by 'technique,' by rules that do the author's work for him: present a character, describe a milieu, bring the action into its historical setting, fill up the lifetime of the characters with useless episodes. Every change of scene requires new expositions, descriptions, explanations. My purpose is to rid the novel of the automatism of novelistic technique, of novelistic word-spinning."

A final element of the novel in Kundera's aesthetic is its form. This varies from author to author, he believes, but each individual author has characteristic forms that recur in his writing. "The architectural blueprint of a work, [form] is something the writer bears within him as an obsession," Kundera writes in the *New York Times Book Review;* "it is an archetype, the irreducible pattern of his personality." Kundera's novels are dominated by a form based on the number seven. Except for *Valcik na rozloucenou (The Farewell Party),* each was written with seven sections. Even *Smesne lasky (Laughable Loves),* originally ten short stories published in Czechoslovakia in three books, became a single book of seven stories. The author tells Salmon that when in writing *The Unbearable Lightness of Being* he consciously tried to vary the pattern, it still emerged in the end. "I am not indulging in some superstitious affectation about magic numbers, nor making a rational calculation. Rather, I am driven by a deep, unconscious, incomprehensible need, a formal archetype from which I cannot escape."

While growing up in Czechoslovakia, Kundera had witnessed the dismemberment of a young republic by Nazis in search of *Lebensraum,* or living space. He had witnessed the postwar political purges. Then, in the rise of Communism, he had found the promise of better times; but the promise had been broken after the Communist coup of 1948. "I was 19," he writes in the *New York Times Book Review.* "I learned about fanaticism, dogmatism and political trials through bitter experience; I learned what it meant to be intoxicated by power, be repudiated by power, feel guilty in the face of power and revolt against it." Twenty years later, he saw another promise crushed, this time by invading Soviet tanks.

As a writer, Kundera is fascinated by man's struggle against power, and this conflict emerges as the central theme of his novels. Power—sterile, serious, focused on the future—dominates his public world and strives to rob the individual of authority, understanding, and history, absorbing him into "the people." Kundera believes that the small world of intimate life is the only refuge available. As he tells Philip Roth in the *Village Voice,* "Intimate life [is] understood as one's personal secret, as something valuable, inviolable, the basis of one's originality." Here, to a small degree, the individual can attempt to exercise his freedom and react against the state. Through eroticism, humor, and memory, Kundera's characters make their stand in the face of power. By setting in opposition eroticism and sterility, humor and seriousness, memory and forgetting, Kundera "discovers" the variations of his central theme.

"Sex, in Kundera, is a means of rebelling against authority," writes J. Hoberman in the *Voice Literary Supplement.* "Often, it's the only means." As Roth points out in *Reading Myself and Others,* "Erotic play and power are the subjects frequently at the center of the stories that Kundera calls, collectively, *Laughable Loves.*" In these stories, some characters use sexual encounters to exercise their personal power; others see them as a measure of self-worth. In "Symposium," for example, "Doctor Havel . . . refuses to go to bed with an importunate nurse because to refuse is an assertion of freedom," relates Gabriele Annan in the *Times Literary Supplement.* In another story, the same character explains to a young admirer of his exploits: "In life, my friend, it is not a question of winning the greatest number of women, because that is too external a success. Rather, it is a question of cultivating one's own demanding taste, because in it is mirrored the extent of one's personal worth."

In a review in the *Nation,* Elizabeth Pochoda discusses the role of sexuality in *Laughable Loves:* "For many of the young men

in Kundera's stories love comes primarily in the form of sexual conquest, and promises adventures outside of the life plan, a rare chance to experience the unexpected and to acquire a sense of power." She adds that "the would-be seducers attempt to circumvent the habitual oppression of their daily lives through love because love is voluntary, or so they think." In the end, according to Pochoda, "the characters who push hardest for certainty in love are the most laughable and the most disappointed. They take a holiday from one form of tyranny and unwittingly uncover another, their own."

"Sexuality as a weapon (in this case, the weapon of he who is otherwise wholly assailable) is to the point of *The Joke* as well," explains Roth. "To revenge himself upon the political friend who had turned upon him back in his remote student days, Ludvik Jahn . . . coldly conceives a plan to seduce the man's wife." In *The Farewell Party,* a young girl tries to seduce her guardian "simply so that she can feel, for once, the triumph of her will over circumstance," Elizabeth Pochoda observes in the *Nation.* Tamina of *The Book of Laughter and Forgetting* submits to Hugo, hoping that in return he will retrieve her precious diaries from Czechoslovakia. And, as Thomas DePietro relates in *Commonweal,* "Like so many of Kundera's Don Juans, Tomas [of *The Unbearable Lightness of Being*] finds in his private, erotic life the freedom and power he so lacks in the public sphere." In the end, however, Kundera's characters fail to achieve their aims. Their stories reveal Kundera's belief that as an escape, a weapon, or a tool, sex creates its own hazards. "Something must always go wrong when sex and love are made to bear the whole burden of personal freedom," suggests Pochoda, the reason being that "as individuals, [Kundera's characters] operate on too small a scale. Everyone has his plot, but there is always another and larger plot which gathers up and transforms the designs of individuals."

"Few contemporary writers have succeeded as Kundera has in combining a cool, elegant, formal objectivity with warm, intimate (almost embarrassingly intimate) pictures of the imperfect realities of adult love," maintains Edmund White in the *Nation.* But as an artist, Kundera finds in the sexual exchange more than examples of flawed love and failed rebellion. "I have the feeling that a scene of physical love generates an extremely sharp light which suddenly reveals the essence of characters and sums up their life situation," he explains to Roth in the *New York Times Book Review.* He continues, "The erotic scene is the focus where all the themes of the story converge and where its deepest secrets are located."

For Kundera, the seriousness of a world dominated by power fosters self-deception, evident in misunderstanding and extremism among individuals. In such a world, humor becomes an important characteristic. "I learned the value of humor during the time of Stalinist terror," Kundera tells Roth. "I could always recognize a person who was not a Stalinist, a person whom I needn't fear, by the way he smiled. A sense of humor was a trustworthy sign of recognition. Ever since, I have been terrified by a world that is losing its sense of humor." In his fiction, Kundera explores the nature of humor under totalitarian pressure, often focusing on the roles of the joke and laughter.

The dangers of a world lacking a sense of humor are evident in *The Joke.* Having missed an opportunity to cultivate his desire for Marketa because of her choice to attend a Party training session, Ludvik responds to her enthusiastic letters with a spiteful joke, written on a postcard: "Optimism is the opium of the people! A healthy atmosphere stinks of stupidity! Long live Trotsky!" But members of the power structure have no appreciation of jokes. His comrades learn of the card and expel him from the Party and the university. He is banished to work the provincial coal mines. Years later, his revenge, an "erotic power play, is thwarted, and turns into yet another joke at his expense," writes Roth in *Reading Myself and Others.*

The jokes that turn against Ludvik and other Kundera characters often seem cruel. Yet as Josephine Woll points out in the *New Republic,* the backfired joke serves to illuminate the character's self-deception: "With no illusions left to cover his nakedness, Ludvik comes to an acceptance—of himself, his past, those who wronged him and those whom he wronged. He accepts the possibility of innocence in the midst of devastation, and the need not only to hate that devastation, but to commiserate with the things thus devastated." Antonin J. Liehm adds in *The Politics of Culture:* "We are too grave about our lives; we moan and wring our hands and curse and explain and beg for understanding, and yet most likely what we need, above all, is the courage to laugh at our existence and through laughter to clear the way for understanding. And in this way, we earn the right to laugh at cowards, at those who refuse to understand."

In *The Book of Laughter and Forgetting,* Kundera constructs an inquiry into the meaning of laughter. "People nowadays do not even realize that one and the same external phenomenon embraces two completely contradictory internal attitudes," he writes in this novel. "There are two kinds of laughter, and we lack the words to distinguish them." Kundera explains that the first, the laughter of the devil, is not associated with evil, but rather with the belief that God's world is meaningless; the second, the laughter of angels, is not associated with good, but with the belief that in God's world, everything has meaning. "Both kinds of laughter belong among life's pleasures, but when it is carried to extremes it also denotes a dual apocalypse," he observes in the *New York Times Book Review* interview. In the extreme, the devil's laughter is absolute skepticism; the angel's laughter is fanaticism.

Kundera's writings illustrate how in a totalitarian state both fanaticism and skepticism can promote self-deception. "In fact," writes Peter Kussi in *World Literature Today,* "self-deception is such a striking element in Kundera's stories and novels that his protagonists could really be divided into two moral types: those who are satisfied to remain self-deluded and those struggling for a measure of self-awareness." The author believes that the happily self-deluded, whom he associates with the laughter of angels, and with immaturity and lyricism, have been the dominant group in recent Czech history and culture. In his second novel, *Zivot je jinde* (*Life Is Elsewhere*), Kundera focuses on this. "The novel is a sly and merciless lampoon of revolutionary romanticism," observes a *Time* reviewer, "and it deals with lyric poetry as a species of adolescent neurosis." The author tells Liehm that the lyrical age "is the period of youth when a person is a mystery to himself and therefore exhausts himself in endless self-contemplation. Other people are merely mirrors in which he searches for his own significance and worth." Jaromil, the young poet of *Life Is Elsewhere,* is of this age. Notes the *Time* reviewer: "He tries to spy on the maid as she takes her bath, and fails, but produces a vivid poem about his 'aquatic love.' The genius of lyric poetry, Kundera observes, 'is the genius of inexperience.' " Eventually, as Neal Ascherson points out in the *New York Review of Books,* Jaromil dies an "absurd death (from a chill caught deliberately on a balcony, after he has been insulted at a party)."

In *The Book of Laughter and Forgetting,* Kundera presents the image of poet Paul Eluard dancing in a circle lifted aloft by a girl laughing the laughter of angels. In 1950, Eluard was called upon by Andre Breton to help save their mutual friend Zavis Kalandra from hanging. (Kalandra, a Prague surrealist, had been accused by the Stalinists of betraying the people.) "But Eluard was too busy dancing in the gigantic ring encircling Paris, Moscow, Warsaw, Prague, Sofia, and Athens, encircling all the socialist countries and all the Communist parties of the world; too busy reciting his beautiful poems about joy and brotherhood," Kundera writes in his novel. As a poet himself during this period, Kundera tells Liehm, "I got a close look at poets who adorned things that weren't worth it, and am still able to remember vividly this state of passionate lyrical enthusiasm which, getting drunk on its frenzy, is unable to see the real world through its own grandiose haze." In Czechoslovakia, where poetry is the preferred literary form, he adds, "on the other side of the wall behind which people were jailed and tormented, Gullibility, Ignorance, Childishness, and Enthusiasm blithely promenaded in the sun." "Milan Kundera," notes Ascherson, "who made his own transition from poetry to novel-writing, is one of the deadliest exponents of the argument that there have been too many poets, too few novelists: too much romantic narcissism and too little sober illustration of what is within the capacity of the human animal and what is not."

"The struggle of man against power is the struggle of memory against forgetting," Kundera declares through Mirek, one of his characters in *The Book of Laughter and Forgetting.* In the *New York Times Book Review* interview, he elaborates: "[Forgetting] is the great private problem of man: death as the loss of the self. . . . [The self] is the sum of everything we remember. Thus, what terrifies us about death is not the loss of the future but the loss of the past. Forgetting is a form of death ever present within life." The loss of the past can make learning impossible and present actions meaningless. After completing the act that he hoped would bring him revenge, Ludvik of *The Joke* relates: "I contemplated how I too (at this very moment) was caught up in that vast and inevitable forgetting. . . . A wave of depression came over me, not so much because the day had been futile as because not even its futility would remain; it would be forgotten. . . . And the society itself would be forgotten and all the errors and injustices that obsessed me, consumed me, that I'd vainly attempted to fix, right, rectify."

For Kundera, memory is a means of self-preservation, but one with its own burdens. "Mirek . . . ultimately does himself in by trying to destroy memories that are embarrassing to his present self-esteem," observes Charles Michener in *Newsweek.* Those not buoyed up by blissful forgetting often drown in tragedy. "Ludvik's boyhood friend Jaroslav [is] a simple man who is capable of remembering and who suffers in his inability to forget," notes Hana Demetz in the *Washington Post Book World.* Tamina, the central character of *The Book of Laughter and Forgetting,* hopes that recovering the diaries she left in Czechoslovakia will enable her to revive the fading memory of her dead husband and the love they shared. Hers is a "personal struggle . . . to remember details that give life emotional continuity," John Updike indicates in the *New York Times Book Review.* Unable to give in to forgetting, Tamina is destroyed by the offspring of totalitarian power, Kundera's "nation of children." In *The Unbearable Lightness of Being,* "this sense of the past, of continuity—heaviness—is seen as a positive foil to the fleeting sensations and frivolity—lightness—which form contemporary existence," observes Christopher Hawtree in the *Spectator.* Even so, like Tamina, Tereza in *The Unbearable Lightness of Being* is burdened by her sense of the past and is often victimized by the lightness of others.

Charles Michener calls *The Book of Laughter and Forgetting* "an impassioned plea for the struggle of memory against the obliterating forces of modern life [and] an eloquent act of personal memory by a Czech writer living abroad who is forbidden to publish in his own country." In each of his novels, Kundera, aware of the terrible loss associated with forgetting, attempts to retain the past, especially his own. "He writes variations on that past," observes Joseph McLellan in the *Washington Post,* "but his purpose is not to alter or destroy it; rather, through these variations, he seeks to understand it, to penetrate its reality to the microscopic level, and to share with the rest of us what he has found."

Kundera's experience within the world of publishing, both in the East and West, has on occasion resembled the jokes turned against his characters. *The Joke* itself emerged from the Czechoslovak state censor unchanged. It rapidly became a best-seller in that Communist country, then was banned after the Soviet invasion. Louis Aragon hailed the French edition among the twentieth century's greatest novels. The publishers of the first English edition then issued the work in a greatly altered form. "Individual chapters have been shortened, rewritten, simplified, some of them omitted," Kundera protested in a letter to the *Times Literary Supplement.* Comparing these changes to those made to one of his plays before it was staged in the Soviet Union, he added, "the mentality of a London bookseller and that of a Moscow official responsible for art seem to have a mysterious kinship. The depth of their contempt for art is equally unfathomable."

In his preface to the novel's 1982 edition, Kundera proposes that "the ideologues in Prague took *The Joke* for a pamphlet against socialism and banned it; the foreign publisher took it for a political fantasy that became reality for a few weeks and rewrote it accordingly." Both turned *The Joke* into a joke at Kundera's expense. The "ideological dictatorship" of the East combined with the "journalistic oversimplification" of the West "to prevent a work of art from telling its own truth in its own words," he contends.

A critical debate to determine Kundera's significance has accompanied each of his books published in the West. Some reviewers emphasize the political nature of his work; others focus on the universal quality of his art. Viewed together, these critical variations suggest the complexity of Kundera's work. *National Review* contributor D. Keith Mano observes in his discussion of *The Joke:* "Eastern European novels are often exploited for their convenient psywar impact. And, of course, Czech or Russian art can never be wholly neutral or without accent. To some degree it must sound dissident." But he adds that Kundera's novel "sets out to transcend this inherent dissidence. For that reason it is a brilliant, an exquisite, and a very problematical book."

Josephine Woll praises the author's insight into the interplay between the individual and the difficult social situation in which he finds himself. "Kundera's brilliance resides in his ability to strip away the lies and disguises which Ludvik and the others need to survive, and which their society has institutionalized and sanctified," she writes. But Vivian Gomick, writing in the *Village Voice,* is critical of Kundera's technique. She maintains that "with all his great gifts for imaginative writing [the author] has essentially forsworn the novelist's obligation to make people out of his characters. He is content to let his characters serve as cartoon figures in a landscape of indictment that lacks sufficient dimension to declare itself a portrait of the human condition." In the judgment of *Saturday Review* contributor Vasa D. Mihailovich, however, what Kundera does is probe "his characters'

minds by constantly shifting the focus and by letting them tell of their own thoughts and feelings in a confessional style."

In Mihailovich's view, Kundera employs his novelistic skills to illuminate a political issue. "The author's fine instinct for the right detail, his knack for wry humor, biting satire, and even grotesque, and his subtle philosophizing underscore the tragedy of the Czech people." And as Michael Berman suggests, this tragedy has implications beyond its immediate context. He concludes in his *New York Times Book Review* article that *The Joke* does reveal "a great deal about the background to liberalization in Czechoslovakia, and—more important—it offers a genuinely humane look at inhumanity. [It] is a work of sharp psychological perception and great literary finesse."

With the publication of *The Book of Laughter and Forgetting* five years after Kundera's flight to France, some critics began to view his work in the context of exile literature. In Elaine Kendall's estimation, " 'The Book of Laughter and Forgetting' is a model of the exile's novel: bittersweet and sardonic but somehow neither corrosive nor sentimental." She adds in her *Los Angeles Times* review that "Kundera deals in the gradual erosions of totalitarianism: the petty indignities, the constant discomforts and the everyday disillusions."

The book "calls itself a novel," writes John Leonard in the *New York Times,* "although it is part fairy tale, part literary criticism, part political tract, part musicology and part autobiography. It can call itself whatever it wants to, because the whole is genius." Norman Podhoretz relates his response to the book in an open letter to Kundera printed in *Commentary:* "What compelled me most when I first opened [it] was not its form or its aesthetic character but its intellectual force, the astonishing intelligence controlling and suffusing every line." *New York Review of Books* contributor Robert M. Adams spotlights Kundera's control when he notes, "Again and again, in this artfully artless book an act or gesture turns imperceptibly into its exact opposite—a circle of unity into a circle of exclusion, playful children into cruel monsters, a funeral into a farce, freedom into lockstep, nudity into a disguise, laughter into sadism, poetry into political machinery, artificial innocence into cynical exploitation. These subtle transformations and unemphasized points of distant correspondence are the special privileges of a meticulously crafted fiction." Concludes Adams, "That a book which combines so delicately dry wit and a deep sense of humanity should cause the author to be deprived of his citizenship is one more of the acute ironies of our time."

In his review of *The Unbearable Lightness of Being* in the *Times Literary Supplement,* David Lodge describes the relationship between the intimate concerns of the individual and the larger concerns of politics in Kundera's world: "Although the characters' lives are shaped by political events, they are not determined by them. Tereza and Tomas return to Czechoslovakia for emotional, not ideological reasons. He refuses to retract his article not as a courageous act of political defiance, but more out of bloody-mindedness and complicated feelings about his son, who is involved in the dissident movement." As Richard Eder observes in the *Los Angeles Times,* "For the most part, 'The Unbearable Lightness [of Being]' succeeds remarkably in joining a series of provocative and troubling speculations about human existence to characters that charm and move us." He adds, "Kundera leads us captivatingly into the bleakness of our days." Thomas DePietro offers a similar view: "For all its burning compassion, extraordinary intelligence, and dazzling artistry, [this novel] leaves us with many questions, questions about love and death, about love and transcendence. These are our burdens, the existential questions that never change but need to be asked anew." "Often witty, sometimes terrifying and always profound, Kundera brings genuine wisdom to his novels at a time when many of his fellow practitioners of the craft aspire only to cleverness," concludes Ian Pearson in *Macleans.*

Since losing his Czech home, audience, and citizenship, Kundera has found each in France. He tells Roth in the *Village Voice* that "the years in France have been the best years of my life." Moreover, as Edmund White comments in the *Nation,* "Kundera—despite his irony, his abiding suspicion of any cant, any uniformity of opinion and especially of kitsch—is currently the favored spokesman for the uneasy conscience of the French intellectual." But Kundera understands the laughable nature of fame. He says in the *Village Voice* interview: "When was a little boy in short pants I dreamed about a miraculous ointment that would make me invisible. Then I became an adult, began to write, and wanted to be successful. Now I'm successful and would like to have the ointment that would make me invisible."

MEDIA ADAPTATIONS: The Unbearable Lightness of Being was adapted by Philip Kaufman for a film of the same title in 1988.

BIOGRAPHICAL/CRITICAL SOURCES:

BOOKS

Contemporary Literary Criticism, Gale, Volume IV, 1975, Volume IX, 1978, Volume XIX, 1981, Volume XXXII, 1985.
Dolezel, Lubomir, *Narrative Modes in Czech Literature,* University of Toronto Press, 1973.
French, A., *Czech Writers and Politics, 1945-1969,* East European Monographs, 1982.
Goetz-Stankiewicz, Marketa, *The Silenced Theatre: Czech Playwrights without a Stage,* University of Toronto Press, 1979.
Kundera, Milan, *Laughable Loves,* translation by Suzanne Rappaport with introduction by Philip Roth, Knopf, 1974.
Kundera, Milan, *The Book of Laughter and Forgetting,* translation by Michael Henry Heim published with an interview with the author by Philip Roth, Penguin Books, 1981.
Kundera, Milan, *The Joke,* translation by Heim with author's preface, Harper, 1982.
Liehm, Antonin J., *The Politics of Culture,* translation from the Czech by Peter Kussi, Grove, 1972.
Porter, Robert, *Milan Kundera: A Voice from Central Europe,* Arkona (Denmark), 1981.
Roth, Philip, *Reading Myself and Others,* Farrar, Straus, 1975.
Trensky, Paul I., *Czech Drama since World War II,* M. E. Sharpe, 1978.
Zeman, Z. A. B., *Prague Spring,* Hill & Wang, 1969.

PERIODICALS

Commentary, December, 1980, October, 1984.
Commonweal, May 18, 1984.
Critical Quarterly, spring/summer, 1984.
Dissent, winter, 1983.
Globe and Mail (Toronto), April 28, 1984.
Los Angeles Times, January 5, 1981, May 2, 1984.
Macleans, May 14, 1984.
Nation, August 28, 1967, November 6, 1967, August 26, 1968, September 18, 1976, October 2, 1976, May 12, 1984.
National Review, March 20, 1981, January 21, 1983.
New Republic, May 18, 1968, September 6, 1975, February 4, 1983.
Newsweek, July 29, 1974, November 24, 1980, November 8, 1982, April 30, 1984, February 4, 1985.

New York Review of Books, May 21, 1970, August 8, 1974, September 16, 1976, February 5, 1981, May 10, 1984.
New York Times, November 6, 1980, January 18, 1982, April 2, 1984.
New York Times Book Review, January 1970, July 28, 1974, September 5, 1976, November 30, 1980, October 24, 1982, April 29, 1984, January 6, 1985, April 10, 1988.
New York Times Magazine, May 19, 1985.
Paris Review, summer, 1984.
Partisan Review, Volume LI, 1985, Volume LII, 1985.
Saturday Review, December 20, 1969.
Spectator, June 10, 1978, February 13, 1982, June 23, 1984.
Time, August 5, 1974.
Times (London), February 17, 1983, May 24, 1984.
Times Literary Supplement, October 30, 1969, March 3, 1978, July 21, 1978, February 5, 1982, May 25, 1984, June 24, 1988.
Village Voice, December 24, 1980, November 23, 1982, June 26, 1984.
Voice Literary Supplement, November, 1983.
Washington Post, November 22, 1980.
Washington Post Book World, December 19, 1982, April 22, 1984, March 27, 1988.
World Literature Today, spring, 1983.

*   *   *

KUNG, Hans
 See KUENG, Hans

*   *   *

KUNITZ, Stanley (Jasspon) 1905-

PERSONAL: Born July 29, 1905, in Worcester, Mass.; son of Solomon Z. (a manufacturer) and Yetta Helen (Jasspon) Kunitz; married Helen Pearce, 1930 (divorced, 1937); married Eleanor Evans, November 21, 1939 (divorced, 1958); married Elise Asher (an artist), June 21, 1958; children: (second marriage) Gretchen. *Education:* Harvard University, A.B.(summa cum laude), 1926, A.M., 1927.

ADDRESSES: Home—37 West 12th St., New York, N.Y. 10011.

CAREER: Poet. *Wilson Library Bulletin,* New York City, editor, 1928-42; Bennington College, Bennington, Vt., professor of English, 1946-49; Potsdam State Teachers College (now State University of New York College at Potsdam), Potsdam, N.Y., professor of English, 1949-50; New School for Social Research, New York City, lecturer in English, 1950-58; Poetry Center of the Young Men's Hebrew Association, New York City, director of poetry workshop, 1958-62; Columbia University, New York City, lecturer, 1963-66, adjunct professor of writing in School of the Arts, 1967-85. Member of staff of writing division, Fine Arts Work Center in Provincetown, 1968—. Fellow, Yale University, 1969; visiting senior fellow, Council of the Humanities, and Old Dominion Fellow in creative writing, Princeton University, 1978-79. Director of seminar, Potsdam Summer Workshop in Creative Arts, 1949-53; poet in residence, University of Washington, 1955-56, Queens College (now Queens College of the City University of New York), 1956-57, Brandeis University, 1958-59, and Princeton University, 1979. Danforth Visiting Lecturer at colleges and universities in the United States, 1961-63; visiting professor, Yale University, 1972, and Rutgers University, 1974. Lectured and gave poetry readings under cultural exchange program in USSR and Poland, 1967, in Senegal and Ghana, 1976, and in Israel and Egypt, 1980. Library of Congress, Washington, D.C., consultant on poetry, 1974-76, honorary consultant in American letters, 1976-83. *Military service:* U.S. Army, Air Transport Command, 1943-45; became staff sergeant.

MEMBER: American Academy and Institute of Arts and Letters (secretary, 1985-88), Academy of American Poets (chancellor, 1970—), Phi Beta Kappa, Poets House (New York City; president, 1985—).

AWARDS, HONORS: Oscar Blumenthal Prize, 1941; John Simon Guggenheim Memorial fellowship, 1945-46; Amy Lowell travelling fellowship, 1953-54; Levinson Prize, *Poetry* magazine, 1956; *Saturday Review* award, 1957; Ford Foundation grant, 1958-59; Harriet Monroe Poetry Award, University of Chicago, 1958; National Institute of Arts and Letters award, 1959; Pulitzer Prize, 1959, for *Selected Poems, 1928-1958;* Litt.D., Clark University, 1961, Anna Maria College, 1977; Brandeis University creative arts award medal, 1965; Academy of American Poets fellowship, 1968; New England Poetry Club Golden Rose Trophy, 1970; American Library Association notable book citation, 1979, for *The Poems of Stanley Kunitz, 1928-1978;* L.H.D., Worcester State College, 1980, State University of New York at Brockport, 1987; Lenore Marshall Award for Poetry, 1980; National Endowment for the Arts senior fellowship, 1984; Bollingen Prize in Poetry, Yale University Library, 1987; Walt Whitman Award citation of merit, with designation as State Poet of New York, 1987; named Walt Whitman Birthplace Poet, 1989.

WRITINGS:

Intellectual Things (verse), Doubleday, Doran, 1930.
Passport to the Wolf: A Selection of Poems, Holt, 1944.
Selected Poems, 1928-1958, Atlantic-Little, Brown, 1958.
The Testing-Tree: Poems, Atlantic-Little, Brown, 1971.
(Translator with Max Hayward) *Poems of Anna Akhmatova,* Atlantic-Little, Brown, 1973.
The Terrible Threshold: Selected Poems, 1940-70, Secker & Warburg, 1974.
The Coat without a Seam: Sixty Poems, 1930-1972, Gehenna Press, 1974.
(Translator) Andrei Voznesensky, *Story under Full Sail,* Doubleday, 1974.
Robert Lowell: Poet of Terribilita, Pierpont Morgan Library, 1974.
A Kind of Order, a Kind of Folly: Essays and Conversations, Atlantic-Little, Brown, 1975.
(Editor and author of introduction) Ivan Drach, *Orchard Lamps,* Sheep Meadow Press, 1978.
The Lincoln Relics (verse), Graywolf Press, 1978.
Poems of Stanley Kunitz: 1928-1978, Atlantic-Little, Brown, 1979.
The Wellfleet Whale and Companion Poems, Sheep Meadow Press, 1983.
Next-to-Last Things: New Poems and Essays, Atlantic Monthly Press, 1985.

EDITOR

Living Authors: A Book of Biographies, H. W. Wilson, 1931.
(With Howard Haycraft) *Authors Today and Yesterday: A Companion Volume to "Living Authors,"* H. W. Wilson, 1933.
(With Haycraft) *The Junior Book of Authors: An Introduction to the Lives of Writers and Illustrators for Younger Readers,* H. W. Wilson, 1934, 2nd revised edition, 1951.

(With Haycraft) *British Authors of the Nineteenth Century,* H. W. Wilson, 1936.
(With Haycraft) *American Authors, 1600-1900: A Biographical Dictionary of American Literature,* H. W. Wilson, 1938, 8th edition, 1977.
(With Haycraft) *Twentieth Century Authors: A Biographical Dictionary of Modern Literature,* H. W. Wilson, 1942, first supplement, 1955.
(With Haycraft) *British Authors before 1800: A Biographical Dictionary,* H. W. Wilson, 1952.
Poems of John Keats, Crowell, 1964.
(With Vineta Colby) *European Authors, 1000-1900: A Biographical Dictionary of European Literature,* H. W. Wilson, 1967.
(Editor) *Selections: University and College Poetry Prizes, 1973-78,* Academy of American Poets, 1980.
(Editor with John Wakeman) *World Authors, 1970-1975: A Biographical Dictionary,* H. W. Wilson, 1980.
(And author of introduction) *The Essential Blake,* Ecco Press, 1987.

CONTRIBUTOR

John Fischer and Robert B. Silvers, editors, *Writing in America,* Rutgers University Press, 1960.
Anthony J. Ostroff, editor, *The Contemporary Poet as Artist and Critic,* Little, Brown, 1964.
Vineta Colby, editor, *American Culture in the Sixties,* H. W. Wilson, 1964.
(Of translations) Andrei Voznesensky, *Antiworlds,* Basic Books, 1966.
(Of translations) Voznesensky, *Antiworlds* [and] *The Fifth Ace,* Anchor Books, 1967.
Robert Lowell and others, editors, *Randall Jarrell, 1914-1965,* Farrar, Straus, 1967.
(Of translations) Yevgeny Yevtushenko, *Stolen Apples,* Doubleday, 1971.

CONTRIBUTOR TO POETRY ANTHOLOGIES

Oscar Williams, editor, *War Poets: An Anthology of the War Poetry of the 20th Century,* John Day, 1945.
W. H. Auden, editor, *The Criterion Book of Modern American Verse,* Criterion, 1956.
John Ciardi, editor, *How Does a Poem Mean?,* Houghton, 1959.
Louis Untermeyer, editor, *Modern American Poetry,* Harcourt, 1962.
Paul Engle and Joseph Langland, editors, *Poet's Choice,* Dial, 1962.
John Wain, editor, *Anthology of Modern Poetry,* Hutchinson, 1963.
John Malcolm Brinnin and Bill Read, *The Modern Poets,* McGraw, 1963.
Elder Olson, editor, *American Lyric Poems: From Colonial Times to the Present,* Appleton, 1964.
William J. Martz, editor, *The Distinctive Voice,* Scott, Foresman, 1966.
Walter Lowenfels, editor, *Where Is Vietnam?: American Poets Respond,* Doubleday-Anchor, 1967.
Richard Ellmann and Robert O'Clair, editors, *Norton Anthology of Modern Poetry,* Norton, 1973.
Daryl Hine and Joseph Parisi, editors, *Poetry Anthology 1912-1977: Sixty-five Years of America's Most Distinguished Verse Magazine,* Houghton, 1978.
Fifty Years of American Poetry: Anniversary Volume for the Academy of American Poets, Abrams, 1984.
A. Poulin, Jr., editor, *Contemporary American Poetry,* Houghton, 4th edition, 1985.

OTHER

General editor, "Yale Series of Younger Poets," Yale University Press, 1969-77. Contributor to many periodicals, including *Atlantic, New Republic, New Yorker, Antaeus, New York Review of Books, American Poetry Review,* and *Harper's.*

SIDELIGHTS: Poet Stanley Kunitz "has always been a fine and quiet singer," writes James Whitehead in *Saturday Review.* A published poet for nearly sixty years, Kunitz has exerted a subtle influence on such major poets as Theodore Roethke and Robert Lowell and has provided encouragement to hundreds of younger poets as well. His output has been modest but enduring: since 1930 he has published ten volumes of poetry. Conceding that he has never been a prolific poet, Kunitz comments in *Publishers Weekly:* "I think that explains why I am able to continue as a poet into my late years. If I hadn't had an urgent impulse, if the poem didn't seem to me terribly important, I never wanted to write it and didn't. And that persisted." While the highly-crafted nature of Kunitz's initial works delayed critical attention, in 1959 Kunitz was awarded the Pulitzer Prize in poetry for his *Selected Poems, 1928-1958.* Critical opinion suggests that in the years since, Kunitz's poetry has steadily increased in quality. *Virginia Quarterly Review* contributor Jay Parini, for instance, observes: "The restraints of [Kunitz's] art combine with a fierce dedication to clarity and intellectual grace to assure him of a place among the essential poets of his generation, which includes Roethke, Lowell, Auden, and Eberhart."

Kunitz's early poetry collections, *Intellectual Things* and *Passport to the War,* earned him a reputation as an intellectual poet. Reflecting Kunitz's admiration for the English metaphysical poets like John Donne and William Blake, these intricate poems, rich in metaphor and allusion, were recognized more for their craft than their substance. Thus, they were somewhat slow to garner widespread critical attention. As *New York Review of Books* contributor Vernon Young observes, Kunitz "is notable for his intelligence, and intelligence tends to wait a longer time for recognition or acquires it within a relatively limited circle." Kunitz insists, however, that his motive in writing those early poems was not "merely to be clever and to juggle ideas and ironies," he states in the *Washington Post.* "I was, even in those very earliest poems, really trying to find out who I am, where I am going, why I am here. I still ask the same questions."

Kunitz followed his Pulitzer Prize-winning work with *The Testing-Tree.* Published thirteen years after *Selected Poems, 1928-1958, The Testing-Tree* represents a significant stylistic departure, according to critics. Robert Lowell, for example, comments in the *New York Times Book Review* that the two volumes "are landmarks of the old and the new style. The smoke has blown off. The old Delphic voice has learned to speak 'words that cats and dogs can understand.'" *Dictionary of Literary Biography* contributor Marie Henault concurs: "*The Testing-Tree* [reveals] a new, freer poetry, looser forms, shorter lines, lowercase line beginnings. . . . Overall the Kunitz of this book is a 'new' Kunitz, one who has grown and changed in the thirteen years since *Selected Poems.*"

Kunitz comments on these two styles in *Publishers Weekly:* "My early poems were very intricate, dense and formal. . . . They were written in conventional metrics and had a very strong beat to the line. . . . In my late poems I've learned to depend on a simplicity that seems almost nonpoetic on the surface, but has reverberations within that keep it intense and alive. . . . I think that as a young poet I looked for what Keats called 'a fine excess,' but as an old poet I look for spareness and rigor and a world of compassion." Gregory Orr offers this view in *American*

Poetry Review: "There is a stylistic shift, but more deeply than that there is a fundamental shift in Kunitz's relation to the world and to his life. If the earlier poems were often structured as intense, lyricized metaphysical and intellectual allegories whose discoveries and dramas involved transcending the physical world, then the later work is marked by a deep shift toward acceptance of the physical world and the existence of others. The intensity of many early Kunitz poems is the intensity of passionate intellect, but later work opens itself to a new world of feeling."

While Kunitz's style may have changed over the years, his themes have not. One of his most common themes concerns the simultaneity of life and death. Kunitz comments in the *New York Times:* "The deepest thing I know is that I am living and dying at once, and my conviction is to report that dialogue. It is a rather terrifying thought that is at the root of much of my poetry." Other themes concern "rebirth, the quest, and the night journey (or descent into the underworld)," explains Kunitz in *Poetry.*

Kunitz's willingness to explore such grave themes has prompted critics to applaud his courage, and to describe him as a risk taker. Analyzing one of Kunitz's better known poems, "King of the River," a selection from *The Testing-Tree, New York Times Book Review* contributor Robert B. Shaw writes: "This poem is emblematic in more ways than one: Kunitz's willingness to risk bombast, platitude or bathos in his contemplation of what he calls 'mystery' is evident in it. Mystery—of the self, of time, of change and fate—is not facilely dispelled but approached with imaginative awe in his work; in our rationalistic century this is swimming against the stream. This is a form of artistic heroism; and when Kunitz's scorning of safety meshes firmly with his technical skills, the outcome is poetry of unusual power and depth." Mary Oliver similarly observes in *Kenyon Review* that "what is revealed, then, is courage. Not the courage of words only, but the intellectual courage that insists on the truth, which is never simple."

A *Poetry* critic believes that "the risks [Kunitz] has taken have ever sprung from inner necessity; they have the stamp of personal rightness upon them." Some critics speculate that Kunitz's thematic concerns stem from the trauma associated with the suicide of his father prior to Kunitz's birth. Orr writes: "To read Kunitz rightly we must accept that there is a hurt, a negation, at the beginning of Kunitz's life that resonates and persists through the whole life and that affects all the important aspects of his life. This negation is not only the primary negation of death (his father's suicide and the early death of a beloved stepfather telescoped together), but the secondary negation of the mother's unwillingness or inability to 'forgive.' "

In *The Testing-Tree* Kunitz "ruthlessly prods [these] wounds," writes Stanley Moss in the *Nation.* "His primordial curse is the suicide of his father before his birth. The poems take us into the sacred woods and houses of his 66 years, illuminate the images that have haunted him. . . . [Kunitz] searches for secret reality and the meaning of the unknown father. He moves from the known to the unknown to the unknowable not necessarily in that order." Lowell comments: "One reads [*The Testing-Tree*] from cover to cover with the ease of reading good prose fiction. . . . I don't know of another in prose or verse that gives in a few pages the impression of a large autobiography." Writes a *Yale Review* critic: "*The Testing-Tree,* Kunitz's first book in the thirteen years since the publication of . . . *Selected Poems,* resounds with the upheaval of a spiritual recluse coming back to the world, to voice, after a long self-banishment: the voice surprised at its own return from muteness with intense shocks of awakening like those of a body amazed to have exhumed itself from a premature burial." Concludes Moss: "At a time when literature seems to edge us toward suicide, or lead us into hell, Kunitz stands with Roethke on 'the terrible threshold' and says, 'I dance for the joy of surviving.' "

Kunitz's essential optimism is revealed further in his celebration of rural life, *Next-to-Last Things: New Poems and Essays,* published in 1985. *New York Times Book Review* contributor R. W. Flint observes: "The sharp and seasoned good humor Stanley Kunitz brings to the poems, essays, interviews and aphorisms in 'Next-to-Last Things' is a tonic in our literary life. . . . Paradox and complication entice him, and he now cheerfully discusses a body of poetry, his own, that he rightly finds to have been 'essentially dark and grieving—elegiac.' "

Kunitz reflects on similar themes in *Next-to-Last Things,* but critics note that both his perception of these themes and his style have undergone further transitions. Oliver writes: "Here Kunitz reveals himself personally and professionally in considerable detail. His early life—the fatherlessness which plays an important role in his work—is discussed with candor as though, after years of dealing physically with this fact, the potency and perhaps some of the sorrow too have been erased." *Chicago Tribune Book World* contributor James Idema notes that Kunitz's poetry has become yet more austere: "The poems that open the book are leaner than those from the early and middle years, narrower on their pages. . . . Some of them are serene and melancholy, as you might expect. Most reflect the sky-and-weather environment of his Provincetown summer home, where he is most comfortable confronting 'the great simplicities.' But the best ones are full of action and vivid imagery.' "

Parini concludes: "We may be grateful for this poet who has paid his dues. He has erred in the directions of intellect and heart, but he has learned from his errors and managed, poem by poem, to snatch from the ineluctable sea of experience a few prize words; his best work feels beyond language itself to the mysterious and 'delicate engine' of life which is, always, before mere words themselves."

BIOGRAPHICAL/CRITICAL SOURCES:

BOOKS

A Celebration for Stanley Kunitz on His 80th Birthday, Sheep Meadow Press, 1986.

Contemporary Literary Criticism, Gale, Volume 6, 1976, Volume 11, 1979, Volume 14, 1980.

Dictionary of Literary Biography, Volume 48: *American Poets: 1880-1945, Second Series,* Gale, 1986.

Henault, Marie, *Stanley Kunitz,* Twayne, 1980.

Hungerford, Edward, editor, *Poets in Progress,* Northwestern University Press, 1962, revised edition, 1967.

Mills, Ralph J., Jr., *Contemporary American Poetry,* Random House, 1965.

Orr, Gregory, *Stanley Kunitz: An Introduction to the Poetry,* Columbia University Press, 1985.

Ostroff, Anthony J., editor, *The Contemporary Poet as a Critic and Artist,* Little, Brown, 1964.

Rodman, Selden, *Tongues of Fallen Angels,* New Directions, 1974.

Rosenthal, M. L., *The Modern Poets: A Critical Introduction,* Oxford University Press, 1960.

PERIODICALS

American Poetry Review, March/April, 1976, July, 1980, September/October, 1985.

Chicago Tribune Book World, December 22, 1985.

Contemporary Literature, winter, 1974.

Harper's, February, 1986.

Iowa Review, spring, 1974.

Kenyon Review, summer, 1986.

Nation, September 20, 1971.

New York Quarterly, fall, 1970.

New York Review of Books, November 22, 1979.

New York Times, July 7, 1979, March 11, 1987.

New York Times Book Review, November 11, 1965, March 21, 1971, July 22, 1979.

Paris Review, spring, 1982.

Poetry, September, 1980.

Prairie Schooner, summer, 1980.

Publishers Weekly, December 20, 1985.

Saturday Review, September 27, 1958, December 18, 1971.

Times Literary Supplement, May 30, 1980.

Virginia Quarterly Review, spring, 1980.

Washington Post, May 12, 1987.

Washington Post Book World, September 30, 1979.

Yale Literary Magazine, May, 1968.

Yale Review, autumn, 1971.